BUTTERWORTHS INTERNATIONAL COMMERCIAL LITIGATION HANDBOOK

BUTTERWORTHS INTERNATIONAL COMMERCIAL LITIGATION HANDBOOK

Second edition

Consultant Editors

Andrew Dickinson, MA (Oxon), BCL

Solicitor Advocate and Consultant, Clifford Chance LLP

Graham S McBain, MA (Cantab), LLB (Cantab), LLM (Harv)

Solicitor

Roger Baggallay, MA (Oxon)

Partner, Clifford Chance LLP

Laurence Murphy, MA, LLB, QC

Advocate

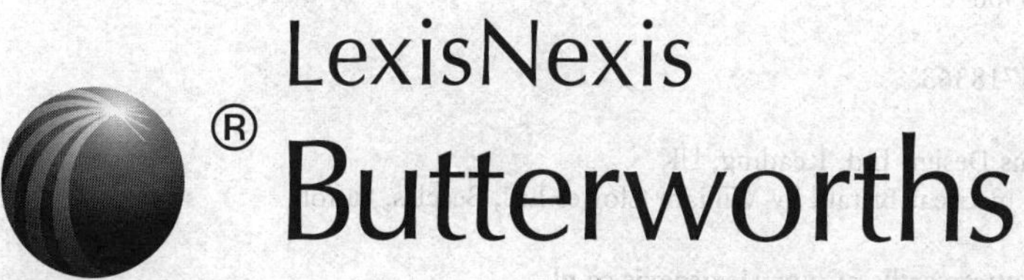

MEMBERS OF THE LEXISNEXIS GROUP WORLDWIDE

United Kingdom	LexisNexis Butterworths, a Division of Reed Elsevier (UK) Ltd, Halsbury House, 35 Chancery Lane, LONDON, WC2A 1EL, and RSH, 1–3 Baxter's Place, Leith Walk, EDINBURGH EH1 3AF
Argentina	LexisNexis Argentina, BUENOS AIRES
Australia	LexisNexis Butterworths, CHATSWOOD, New South Wales
Austria	LexisNexis Verlag ARD Orac GmbH & Co KG, VIENNA
Canada	LexisNexis Butterworths, MARKHAM, Ontario
Chile	LexisNexis Chile Ltda, SANTIAGO DE CHILE
Czech Republic	Nakladatelství Orac sro, PRAGUE
France	LexisNexis SA, PARIS
Germany	LexisNexis Deutschland GmbH, FRANKFURT and MUNSTER
Hong Kong	LexisNexis Butterworths, HONG KONG
Hungary	HVG-Orac, BUDAPEST
India	LexisNexis Butterworths, NEW DELHI
Italy	Giuffrè Editore, MILAN
Malaysia	Malayan Law Journal Sdn Bhd, KUALA LUMPUR
New Zealand	LexisNexis Butterworths, WELLINGTON
Poland	Wydawnictwo Prawnicze LexisNexis, WARSAW
Singapore	LexisNexis Butterworths, SINGAPORE
South Africa	LexisNexis Butterworths, DURBAN
Switzerland	Stämpfli Verlag AG, BERNE
USA	LexisNexis, DAYTON, Ohio

A CIP catalogue record for this book is available from the British Library.

ISBN 10: 1405718366

ISBN 13: 9781405718363

Typeset by Columns Design Ltd, Reading, UK
Printed and bound in Great Britain by William Clowes Ltd, Beccles, Suffolk

Visit LexisNexis Butterworths at www.lexisnexis.co.uk

PREFACE

Butterworths International Commercial Litigation Handbook collects together United Kingdom primary and secondary legislation, with key European Community and international materials, relating to international commercial disputes before courts and arbitral tribunals in England and Wales and in Scotland.

The materials are organised in five Parts, as follows:

Part I	Statutes
Part II	Civil Procedure Rules
Part III	Statutory Instruments
Part IV	EC materials
Part V	Other International Materials

For ease of reference, within each part except Part II, the materials are grouped under subject headings, including:

- Jurisdiction and Foreign Judgments
- Applicable Law
- International Commercial and Financial Law
- International Arbitration
- International Carriage: Air, Rail and Road
- International Carriage: Sea
- State Immunity and International Organisations
- Cross-Border Insolvency
- Evidence
- Service of Documents

The materials selected share the common characteristic that they relate to cross-border aspects of commercial litigation before UK courts. For reasons of space, materials (particularly civil procedure and insolvency rules) which may apply equally to domestic and international litigation have generally been omitted. Legislation which applies to Scotland has been included. Legislation relating to Northern Ireland only has been omitted.

The tables at the end of the Handbook summarise the current status of the European jurisdiction instruments (Regulation 44/2001/EC and the 1968 Brussels and 1988 Lugano Conventions), the New York Convention on the recognition and enforcement of arbitration agreements, the EC Service Regulation (Regulation 1348/2000/EC) and The Hague Service and Evidence Conventions.

We would like to express our gratitude to Butterworths' editorial staff, who undertook the considerable task of gathering together and revising these materials for publication. We would also like to thank the following for their input and support: Judith Prior, Joanna Jerrard-Dunne, Jo Delaney and Brian Cain (Clifford Chance), Oliver Parker and Eral Knight (Department for Constitutional Affairs), Ed Peel (Keble College, Oxford) and Dr Christine Boch.

The contents of the Handbook take into account materials available as at 1st June 2006.

Andrew Dickinson
Roger Baggallay
Graham McBain
Laurence Murphy QC

July 2006

CONTENTS

Materials which apply only to Scotland are marked with an asterisk.

Part I Statutes

A. Jurisdiction and Foreign Judgments

B. Applicable Law

C. International Commercial and Financial Law

D. International Arbitration

E. International Carriage: Air, Rail and Road

F. International Carriage: Sea

G. State Immunity and International Organisations

H. Cross-Border Insolvency

I. Evidence

J. Other

Part II Civil Procedure Rules

Part III Statutory Instruments

SECTION A

A. Jurisdiction and Foreign Judgments

I. Other

Part IV EC Materials

A. EC Treaties

B. Jurisdiction and Foreign Judgments

C. Applicable Law

D. International Commercial and Financial Law

E. International Carriage: Air

F. Cross-Border Insolvency

G. Service of documents

H. Evidence

I. Other

Part V Other International Materials

A. Jurisdiction and Foreign Judgments

B. Applicable Law

C. International Commercial and Financial Law

D. International Arbitration

E. International Carriage: Air, Rail and Road

F. International Carriage: Sea

G. State Immunity

H. Cross-Border Insolvency

I. Service and Evidence

J. Other

Tables

PART I
STATUTES

A. JURISDICTION AND FOREIGN JUDGMENTS

SHERIFF COURTS (SCOTLAND) ACT 1907

(7 Edw 7 c 51)

An Act to regulate and amend the Laws and practice relating to the civil procedure in Sheriff Courts in Scotland, and for other purposes

[28 August 1907]

PRELIMINARY

1 Short title

This Act may be cited for all purposes as the Sheriff Courts (Scotland) Act, 1907.

[1]

3 Interpretation

In construing this Act (unless where the context is repugnant to such construction)—

(a) "Sheriff" includes sheriff-substitute;

(b) "Tenant" includes sub-tenant;

(e) "Lease" includes sub-lease;

(d) "Action" includes every civil proceeding competent in the ordinary sheriff court;

(e) "Person" includes company, corporation, or association and firm of any description nominate or descriptive, or any Board corporate or unincorporate;

(f) "Sheriff clerk" includes sheriff-clerk depute;

(g) "Agent" means a law-agent enrolled in terms of the Law Agents (Scotland) Act, 1873;

(h) "Final judgment" means an interlocutor which, by itself, or taken along with previous interlocutors, disposes of the subject-matter of the cause, notwithstanding that judgment may not have been pronounced on every question raised, and that expenses found due may not have been modified, taxed or decerned for;

(i) …

(j) "Small Debt Acts" means and includes the Small Debt (Scotland) Acts, 1837 to 1889, and Acts explaining or amending the same;

(k) "Initial writ" means the statement of claim, petition, note of appeal, or other document by which the action is initiated;

(l) "Procurator-Fiscal" means procurator-fiscal in the sheriff-court;

(m) …

(n) "Pursuer" means and includes any person making a claim or demand, or seeking any warrant or order competent in the sheriff court;

(o) "Defender" means and includes any person who is required to be called in any action;

(p) "Summary application" means and includes all applications of a summary nature brought under the common law jurisdiction of the sheriff, and all applications, whether by appeal or otherwise, brought under any Act of Parliament which provides, or, according to any practice in the sheriff court, which allows that the same shall be disposed of in a summary manner, but which does not more particularly define in what form the same shall be heard, tried, and determined;

[(q) …].

[2]

NOTES

Para (i) repealed by the Sheriff Courts (Scotland) Act 1971, Sch 2, Pt II; para (m) repealed by the Statute Law (Repeals) Act 1989; para (q) repealed by the Law Reform (Miscellaneous Provisions) (Scotland) Act 1980, Sch 3.

JURISDICTION

4 Jurisdiction

The jurisdiction of the sheriffs, within their respective sheriffdoms shall extend to and include all navigable rivers, ports, harbours, creeks, shores, and anchoring grounds in or adjoining such sheriffdoms. And the powers and jurisdictions formerly competent to the High Court of Admiralty in Scotland in all maritime causes and proceedings, civil and criminal, including such as may apply to persons furth of Scotland, shall be competent to the sheriffs, provided the defender shall upon any legal ground of jurisdiction be amenable to the jurisdiction of the sheriff before whom such cause or proceeding may be raised, and provided also that it shall not be competent to the sheriff to try any crime committed on the seas which it would not be competent for him to try if the crime had been committed on land: Provided always that where sheriffdoms are separated by a river, firth, or estuary, the sheriffs on either side shall have concurrent jurisdictions over the intervening space occupied by water.

[3]

NOTES

Repealed in relation to criminal proceedings by the Criminal Procedure (Scotland) Act 1975, Sch 10, Pt I.

[5A Power of sheriff to order sheriff clerk to execute deeds relating to heritage

(1) This section applies where—

(a) an action relating to heritable property is before the sheriff; or

(b) it appears to the sheriff that an order under this section is necessary to implement a decree of a sheriff relating to heritable property.

(2) Where the grantor of any deed relating to the heritable property cannot be found or refuses or is unable or otherwise fails to execute the deed, the sheriff may—

(a) where subsection (1)(a) above applies, on application;

(b) where subsection (1)(b) above applies, on summary application,

by the grantee, make an order dispensing with the execution of the deed by the grantor and directing the sheriff clerk to execute the deed.

(3) Where in pursuance of an order under this section a deed is executed by the sheriff clerk, it shall have the like force and effect as if it had been executed by the grantor.

(4) In this sections—

"grantor" means a person who is under an obligation to execute the deed; and

"grantee" means the person to whom that obligation is owed.]

[4]

NOTES

Inserted by the Law Reform (Miscellaneous Provisions) (Scotland) Act 1985, s 17.

6 Action competent in sheriff court

[Subject to section 8 of the Domicile and Matrimonial Proceedings Act 1973] [and Chapter III of Part I of the Family Law Act 1986] any action competent in the sheriff court may be brought within the jurisdiction of the sheriff—

(a) Where the defender (or when there are several defenders where one of them) resides within the jurisdiction, or having resided there for at least forty days immediately prior to the raising of the action has ceased to reside there for less than forty days and whose present residence in Scotland is unknown:

(b) Where the defender carries on business, and has a place of business within the sheriffdom, and is cited either personally or at such place of business:

(c) Where the defender is a person not otherwise subject to the jurisdiction of the courts of Scotland, and a ship or vessel of which he is owner or part owner or master, or goods, debts, money, or other moveable property belonging to him, have been arrested within the jurisdiction:

(d) Where the defender is the owner or part owner or tenant or joint tenant, whether individually or as a trustee, of heritable property within the jurisdiction, and the action relates to such property or to his interest therein:

(e) Where the action is for interdict against an alleged wrong being committed or threatened to be committed within the jurisdiction:

(f) Where the action relates to a contract the place of execution or performance of which is within the jurisdiction, and the defender is personally cited there:

(g) Where in an action of furthcoming or multiplepoinding the fund or subject in medio is situated within the jurisdiction; or the arrestee or holder of the fund is subject to the jurisdiction of the court:

(h) Where the party sued is the pursuer in any action pending within the jurisdiction against the party suing:

[(i) Where the action is founded on delict, and the delict forming the cause of action was committed within the jurisdiction:]

(j) Where the defender prorogates the jurisdiction of the court.

[5]

NOTES

Words in first pair of square brackets inserted by the Domicile and Matrimonial Proceedings Act 1973, s 12, Sch 4, para 1; words in second pair of square brackets inserted by the Family Law Act 1986, s 68(1), Sch 1, para 3; para (i) substituted by the Law Reform (Jurisdiction in Delict) Act 1971 s 1(2).

This section is disapplied in relation to actions to which the Administration of Justice Act 1956, s 45 applies: see the Administration of Justice Act 1956, s 45(6).

This section is disapplied to the extent that it determines jurisdiction in relation to any matter to which the Civil Jurisdiction and Judments Act 1982, Sch 8 applies: see the Civil Jurisdiction and Judments Act 1982, s 20(3).

7 Private jurisdiction in causes under fifty pounds value

..., all causes not exceeding fifty pounds in value exclusive of interest and expenses competent in the sheriff court shall be brought and followed forth in the sheriff court only, and shall not be subject to review by the Court of Session: Provided that in actions ad factum praestandum, where the value of the cause is not disclosed, the same shall be deemed to exceed fifty pounds, unless in the course of the cause the sheriff shall determine, as after provided, that the value thereof is less than fifty pounds: Provided also that nothing herein contained shall affect any right of appeal competent under any Act of Parliament in force for the time being.

[6]

NOTES

Words omitted repealed by the Law Reform (Miscellaneous Provisions) (Scotland Act) 1980, Sch 3 and the Sheriff Courts (Scotland) Act 1971, Sch 2, Pt II.

8–38 (*In so far as unrepealed, outside the scope of this work.*)

PROCEDURE RULES

39 Procedure rules

Subject to the provisions of any Act of Parliament in force after the passing of this Act, the procedure in all civil causes shall be conform to the rules of procedure set forth in the First Schedule hereto annexed. Such rules shall be construed and have effect as part of this Act.

[7]

40–49 (*In so far as unrepealed, outside the scope of this work.*)

SUMMARY APPLICATIONS

50 Summary applications

In summary applications (where a hearing is necessary) the sheriff shall appoint the application to be heard at a diet to be fixed by him, and at that or any subsequent diet (without record of evidence unless the sheriff shall order a record) shall summarily dispose of the matter and give his judgment in writing: Provided that wherever in any Act of Parliament an application is directed to be heard, tried, and determined summarily or in the manner provided by section fifty-two of the Sheriff Courts (Scotland) Act, 1876, such direction shall be read and construed as if it referred to this section of this Act: Provided also that nothing contained in this Act shall affect any right of appeal provided by any Act of Parliament under which a summary application is brought.

[8]

51, 52 (*S 51 repealed by the Statute Law (Repeals) Act 1973; s 52 repealed by the Statute Law Revision Act 1927.*)

(*First Schedule sets out the Ordinary Cause Rules, of which certain relevant Chapters are printed in Pt II of this book at* **[1001]**; *Second Schedule contains repeals.*)

ADMINISTRATION OF JUSTICE ACT 1920

(10 & 11 Geo 5 c 81)

ARRANGEMENT OF SECTIONS

PART II
RECIPROCAL ENFORCEMENT OF JUDGMENTS IN THE UNITED KINGDOM AND IN OTHER PARTS OF HIS MAJESTY'S DOMINIONS

PART III
MISCELLANEOUS

An Act to amend the law with respect to the administration of justice, ... to facilitate the reciprocal enforcement of judgments and awards in the United Kingdom and other parts of His Majesty's Dominions or Territories under His Majesty's protection ...

[23 December 1920]

NOTES

Words omitted from long title repealed by the Statute Law Revision Act 1927.

1–8 (*Ss 1, 5–8 repealed by the Supreme Court of Judicature (Consolidation) Act 1925, s 226, Sch 6; ss 2, 3(1) repealed by the Administration of Justice Act 1925, s 29, Sch 5; s 3(2) repealed by the Courts Act 1971, s 56, Sch 11, Pt IV; s 3(3) repealed by the Statute Law Revision Act 1927; s 4 repealed by the Magistrates' Courts Act 1952, s 132, Sch 6.*)

PART II
RECIPROCAL ENFORCEMENT OF JUDGMENTS IN THE UNITED KINGDOM AND IN OTHER PARTS OF HIS MAJESTY'S DOMINIONS

NOTES

Application: this Part of this Act only applies to territories to which it applied at the date of the making of the Reciprocal Enforcement of Judgments (General Application to His Majesty's Dominions etc) Order 1933, SR & O 1933/1073 at **[2001]** (ie 10 November 1933); see s 7(1) of the 1933 Act at **[22]**.

Modification: by the Zimbabwe (Independence and Membership of the Commonwealth) (Consequential Provisions) Order 1980, SI 1980/701, art 7, Schedule, para 4(1), this Part of this Act has effect in relation to Zimbabwe as if the reference therein to a part of His Majesty's Dominions outside the

United Kingdom, or to persons or things related thereto, included a reference to a Commonwealth country and to persons or things related to a Commonwealth country.

9 Enforcement in the United Kingdom of judgments obtained in superior courts in other British dominions

(1) Where a judgment has been obtained in a superior court in any part of His Majesty's dominions outside the United Kingdom to which this Part of this Act extends, the judgment creditor may apply to the High Court in England or Ireland, or to the Court of Session in Scotland, at any time within twelve months after the date of the judgment, or such longer period as may be allowed by the court, to have the judgment registered in the court, and on any such application the court may, if in all the circumstances of the case they think it is just and convenient that the judgment should be enforced in the United Kingdom, and subject to the provisions of this section, order the judgment to be registered accordingly.

(2) No judgment shall be ordered to be registered under this section if—
- (a) the original court acted without jurisdiction; or
- (b) the judgment debtor, being a person who was neither carrying on business nor ordinarily resident within the jurisdiction of the original court, did not voluntarily appear or otherwise submit or agree to submit to the jurisdiction of that court; or
- (c) the judgment debtor, being the defendant in the proceedings, was not duly served with the process of the original court and did not appear, notwithstanding that he was ordinarily resident or was carrying on business within the jurisdiction of that court or agreed to submit to the jurisdiction of that court; or
- (d) the judgment was obtained by fraud; or
- (e) the judgment debtor satisfies the registering court either that an appeal is pending, or that he is entitled and intends to appeal, against the judgment; or
- (f) the judgment was in respect of a cause of action which for reasons of public policy or for some other similar reason could not have been entertained by the registering court.

(3) Where a judgment is registered under this section—
- (a) the judgment shall, as from the date of registration, be of the same force and effect, and proceedings may be taken thereon, as if it had been a judgment originally obtained or entered up on the date of registration in the registering court;
- (b) the registering court shall have the same control and jurisdiction over the judgment as it has over similar judgments given by itself, but in so far only as relates to execution under this section;
- (c) the reasonable costs of and incidental to the registration of the judgment (including the costs of obtaining a certified copy thereof from the original court and of the application for registration) shall be recoverable in like manner as if they were sums payable under the judgment.

(4) Rules of court shall provide—
- (a) for service on the judgment debtor of notice of the registration of a judgment under this section; and
- (b) for enabling the registering court on an application by the judgment debtor to set aside the registration of a judgment under this section on such terms as the court thinks fit; and
- (c) for suspending the execution of a judgment registered under this section until the expiration of the period during which the judgment debtor may apply to have the registration set aside.

(5) In any action brought in any court in the United Kingdom on any judgment which might be ordered to be registered under this section, the plaintiff shall not be entitled to recover any costs of the action unless an application to register the judgment under this section has previously been refused or unless the court otherwise orders.

[9]

[10 Issue of certificates of judgments obtained in the United Kingdom

(1) Where—
- (a) a judgment has been obtained in the High Court in England or Northern Ireland, or in the Court of Session in Scotland, against any person; and

(b) the judgment creditor wishes to secure the enforcement of the judgment in a part of Her Majesty's dominions outside the United Kingdom to which this Part of this Act extends,

the court shall, on an application made by the judgment creditor, issue to him a certified copy of the judgment.

(2) The reference in the preceding subsection to Her Majesty's dominions shall be construed as if that subsection had come into force in its present form at the commencement of this Act.]

[10]

NOTES

Substituted by the Civil Jurisdiction and Judgments Act 1982, s 35(2).

11 Power to make rules

Provision may be made by rules of court for regulating the practice and procedure (including scales of fees and evidence), in respect of proceedings of any kind under this Part of this Act.

[11]

NOTES

For applicable procedural rules, see Civil Procedure Rules 1998, SI 1998/3132, rr 74.2–74.11 at **[1518]–[1527]**; Act of Sederunt (Rules of the Court of Session 1994) 1994, SI 1994/1443, rr 62.4–62.11 at **[1133]–[1140]**.

12 Interpretation

(1) In this Part of this Act, unless the context otherwise requires—

The expression "judgment" means any judgment or order given or made by a court in any civil proceedings, whether before or after the passing of this Act, whereby any sum of money is made payable, and includes an award in proceedings on an arbitration if the award has, in pursuance of the law in force in the place where it was made, become enforceable in the same manner as a judgment given by a court in that place:

The expression "original court" in relation to any judgment means the court by which the judgment was given:

The expression "registering court" in relation to any judgment means the court by which the judgment was registered:

The expression "judgment creditor" means the person by whom the judgment was obtained, and includes the successors and assigns of that person:

The expression "judgment debtor" means the person against whom the judgment was given, and includes any person against whom the judgment is enforceable in the place where it was given.

(2) Subject to rules of court, any of the powers conferred by this Part of this Act on any court may be exercised by a judge of the court.

[12]

13 Power to apply Part II of Act to territories under His Majesty's protection

His Majesty may by Order in Council declare that this Part of this Act shall apply to any territory which is under His Majesty's protection, or in respect of which a mandate is being exercised by the Government of any part of His Majesty's dominions, as if that territory were part of His Majesty's dominions, and on the making of any such Order this Part of this Act shall, subject to the provisions of the Order, have effect accordingly.

[13]

NOTES

Orders in Council: see the note to s 14 of this Act at **[14]**.

14 Extent of Part II of Act

(1) Where His Majesty is satisfied that reciprocal provisions have been made by the legislature of any part of His Majesty's dominions outside the United Kingdom for the

enforcement within that part of His dominions of judgments obtained in the High Court in England, the Court of Session in Scotland, and the High Court in Ireland, His Majesty may by Order in Council declare that this Part of this Act shall extend to that part of His dominions, and on any such Order being made this Part of this Act shall extend accordingly.

(2) An Order in Council under this section may be varied or revoked by a subsequent Order.

[(3) Her Majesty may by Order in Council under this section consolidate any Orders in Council under this section which are in force when the consolidating Order is made.]

[14]

NOTES

Sub-s (3): added by the Civil Jurisdiction and Judgments Act 1982, s 35(3).

Orders in Council: the Reciprocal Enforcement of Judgments (Administration of Justice Act 1920, Part II) (Consolidation) Order 1984, SI 1984/129 at **[2104]**; the Reciprocal Enforcement of Judgments (Administration of Justice Act 1920, Part II) (Amendment) Order 1997, SI 1997/2601(providing that Pt II of this Act no longer extends to Gibraltar); the Reciprocal Enforcement of Foreign Judgments (Australia) Order 1994, SI 1994/1901, art 9 (providing that Pt II of this Act no longer extents to New South Wales, Northern Territory of Australia, Queensland, South Australia, Tasmania, Victoria and Western Australia). See further the note to the 1984 Order at **[2108]**.

Pt II (ss 15–20) (*S 15 relates to questions of foreign law to be decided by a judge; s 16 repealed by the Arbitration Act 1934, s 21(6), Sch 3; s 17 repealed by the Administration of Estates Act 1925, s 56, Sch 2, Pt II; s 18 repealed by the Administration of Justice Act 1925, s 29(4), Sch 5; ss 19, 20 repealed by the Supreme Court of Judicature* (*Consolidation*) *Act 1925, s 226, Sch 6.*)

21 Short title and application

(1) This Act may be cited as the Administration of Justice Act 1920.

(2) …

(3) This Act, except Part II thereof, applies only to England and Wales.

[15]

NOTES

Sub-s (2): repealed by the Statute Law Revision Act 1927.

(*Schedule repealed by the Statute Law Revision Act 1927.*)

FOREIGN JUDGMENTS (RECIPROCAL ENFORCEMENT) ACT 1933

(23 & 24 Geo c 13)

ARRANGEMENT OF SECTIONS

PART I
REGISTRATION OF FOREIGN JUDGMENTS

PART II
MISCELLANEOUS AND GENERAL

An Act to make provision for the enforcement in the United Kingdom of judgments given in foreign countries which accord reciprocal treatment to judgments given in the United Kingdom, for facilitating the enforcement in foreign countries of judgments given in the United Kingdom, and for other purposes in connection with the matters aforesaid

[13 April 1933]

PART I
REGISTRATION OF FOREIGN JUDGMENTS

1 Power to extend Part I of Act to foreign countries giving reciprocal treatment

[(1) If, in the case of any foreign country, Her Majesty is satisfied that, in the event of the benefits conferred by this Part of this Act being extended to, or to any particular class of, judgments given in the courts of that country or in any particular class of those courts, substantial reciprocity of treatment will be assured as regards the enforcement in that country of similar judgments given in similar courts of the United Kingdom, She may by Order in Council direct—

(a) that this Part of this Act shall extend to that country;

(b) that such courts of that country as are specified in the Order shall be recognised courts of that country for the purposes of this Part of this Act; and

(c) that judgments of any such recognised court, or such judgments of any class so specified, shall, if within subsection (2) of this section, be judgments to which this Part of this Act applies.

(2) Subject to subsection (2A) of this section, a judgment of a recognised court is within this subsection if it satisfies the following conditions, namely—

(a) it is either final and conclusive as between the judgment debtor and the judgment creditor or requires the former to make an interim payment to the latter; and

(b) there is payable under it a sum of money, not being a sum payable in respect of taxes or other charges of a like nature or in respect of a fine or other penalty; and

(c) it is given after the coming into force of the Order in Council which made that court a recognised court.

(2A) The following judgments of a recognised court are not within subsection (2) of this section—

(a) a judgment given by that court on appeal from a court which is not a recognised court;

(b) a judgment or other instrument which is regarded for the purposes of its enforcement as a judgment of that court but which was given or made in another country;

(c) a judgment given by that court in proceedings founded on a judgment of a court in another country and having as their object the enforcement of that judgment.]

(3) For the purposes of this section, a judgment shall be deemed to be final and conclusive notwithstanding that an appeal may be pending against it, or that it may still be subject to appeal, in the courts of the country of the original court.

(4) His Majesty may by a subsequent Order in Council vary or revoke any Order previously made under this section.

[(5) Any Order in Council made under this section before its amendment by the Civil Jurisdiction and Judgments Act 1982 which deems any court of a foreign country to be a superior court of that country for the purposes of this Part of this Act shall (without prejudice to subsection (4) of this section) have effect from the time of that amendment as if it provided for that court to be a recognised court of that country for those purposes, and for any final and conclusive judgment of that court, if within subsection (2) of this section, to be a judgment to which this Part of this Act applies.]

[16]

NOTES

Sub-ss (1), (2), (2A): substituted for original sub-ss (1), (2) by the Civil Jurisdiction and Judgments Act 1982, s 35(1), Sch 10, para 1(1), (2).

Sub-s (5): added by the Civil Jurisdiction and Judgments Act 1982, s 35(1), Sch 10, para 1(1), (3).

Extension of Part I: Pt I of this Act has been extended, with modifications, by the following Acts to include certain other foreign judgments, but only in relation to proceedings under those Acts—the Carriage of Goods by Road Act 1965, s 4, the Nuclear Installations Act 1965, s 17(3), (4), the International Transport Conventions Act 1983, s 6, the Merchant Shipping Act 1995, ss 166(4), 177(4). Regulations, in connection with the Convention on International Carriage by Rail, dealing with the enforcement of judgments, may, in particular, make provision about the application of Pt I of this Act; see the Railways and Transport Safety Act 2003, s 103, Sch 6, para 8.

Orders in Council: the Reciprocal Enforcement of Foreign Judgments (France) Order in Council 1936, SI 1936/609 at **[2003]**; the Reciprocal Enforcement of Foreign Judgments (Belgium) Order in Council 1936, SI 1936/1169 at **[2010]**; the Reciprocal Enforcement of Judgments (Pakistan) Order 1958, SI 1958/141 at **[2017]**; the Reciprocal Enforcement of Judgments (India) Order 1958, SI 1958/425 at **[2021]**; the Reciprocal Enforcement of Foreign Judgments (Germany) Order 1961, SI 1961/1199 at **[2026]**; the Reciprocal Enforcement of Foreign Judgments (Norway) Order 1962, SI 1962/636 at **[2035]**; the Reciprocal Enforcement of Foreign Judgments (Austria) Order 1962, SI 1962/1339 at **[2043]**; the Reciprocal Enforcement of Foreign Judgments (the Netherlands) Order 1969, SI 1969/1063 at **[2051]**; the Reciprocal Enforcement of Foreign Judgments (Israel) Order 1971, SI 1971/1039 at **[2059]**; the Reciprocal Enforcement of Foreign Judgments (Guernsey) Order 1973, SI 1973/610 at **[2073]**; the Reciprocal Enforcement of Foreign Judgments (Isle of Man) Order 1973, SI 1973/611 at **[2076]**; the Reciprocal Enforcement of Foreign Judgments (Jersey) Order 1973, SI 1973/612 at **[2079]**; the Reciprocal Enforcement of Foreign Judgments (Italy) Order 1973, SI 1973/1894 at **[2082]**; the Reciprocal Enforcement of Foreign Judgments (Tonga) Order 1980, SI 1980/1523 at **[2090]**; the Reciprocal Enforcement of Foreign Judgments (Suriname) Order 1981, SI 1981/735 at **[2097]**; the Reciprocal Enforcement of Foreign Judgments (Canada) Order 1987, SI 1987/468 at **[2108]**; the Reciprocal Enforcement of Foreign Judgments (Australia) Order 1994, SI 1994/1901 at **[2129]**.

It should, however, be noted that the statutory instruments giving effect to the conventions with France (SR&O 1933/1073) at **[2001]**, Belgium (SR&O 1936/1169) at **[2010]**, Germany (SI 1961/1199) at **[2026]**, Austria (SI 1962/1339) at **[2043]**, the Netherlands (SI 1969/1063) at **[2051]** and Italy (SI 1973/1894) at **[2082]** no longer apply to judgments falling within the scope of the 1968 Brussels Convention (see the Civil Jurisdiction and Judgments Act 1982, s 9(1) at **[58]** and the Brussels Convention, Arts 55, 56 at **[3029]**). Nor, it would seem, do they apply to judgments falling within the scope of Council Regulation 44/2001/EC on jurisdiction and the recognition and enforcement of judgments in civil and commercial matters, the successor to the 1968 Brussels Convention (see Council Regulation 44/2001/EC, Arts 69, 70 at **[3147]**, **[3148]**, but note that there is no equivalent of s 9(1) of the 1982 Act, which expressly applies those articles to legislation implementing the conventions). Further, the statutory instrument giving effect to the convention with Norway (SI 1962/636) at **[2035]** no longer applies to judgments falling within the scope of the 1988 Lugano Convention (see Civil Jurisdiction and Judgments Act 1982, s 9(1) at **[58]** and the Lugano Convention, Arts 55, 56 at **[3063]**). The SIs may continue to apply to judgments falling outside the scope of the Brussels and Lugano Conventions and Council Regulation 44/2001/EC and, in the case of the Netherlands, to judgments from the Netherlands Antilles to which the Conventions and Council Regulation 44/2001/EC do not extend.

2 Application for, and effect of, registration of foreign judgment

(1) A person, being a judgment creditor under a judgment to which this Part of this Act applies, may apply to the High Court at any time within six years after the date of the judgment, or, where there have been proceedings by way of appeal against the judgment, after the date of the last judgment given in those proceedings, to have the judgment registered in the High Court, and on any such application the court shall, subject to proof of the prescribed matters and to the other provisions of this Act, order the judgment to be registered:

Provided that a judgment shall not be registered if at the date of the application—

(a) it has been wholly satisfied; or

(b) it could not be enforced by execution in the country of the original court.

(2) Subject to the provisions of this Act with respect to the setting aside of registration—

(a) a registered judgment shall, for the purposes of execution, be of the same force and effect; and

(b) proceedings may be taken on a registered judgment; and

(c) the sum for which a judgment is registered shall carry interest; and

(d) the registering court shall have the same control over the execution of a registered judgment;

as if the judgment had been a judgment originally given in the registering court and entered on the date of registration:

Provided that execution shall not issue on the judgment so long as, under this Part of the Act and the Rules of Court made thereunder, it is competent for any party to make an application to have the registration of the judgment set aside, or, where such an application is made, until after the application has been finally determined.

(3) …

(4) If at the date of the application for registration the judgment of the original court has been partly satisfied, the judgment shall not be registered in respect of the whole sum payable under the judgment of the original court, but only in respect of the balance remaining payable at that date.

(5) If, on an application for the registration of a judgment, it appears to the registering court that the judgment is in respect of different matters and that some, but not all, of the provisions of the judgment are such that if those provisions had been contained in separate judgments those judgments could properly have been registered, the judgment may be registered in respect of the provisions aforesaid but not in respect of any other provisions contained therein.

(6) In addition to the sum of money payable under the judgment of the original court, including any interest which by the law of the country of the original court becomes due under the judgment up to the time of registration, the judgment shall be registered for the reasonable costs of and incidental to registration, including the costs of obtaining a certified copy of the judgment from the original court.

[17]

NOTES

Sub-s (3): repealed by the Administration of Justice Act 1977, ss 4, 32(4), Sch 5, Pt I.

3 Rules of court

(1) The power to make [Civil Procedure Rules], shall, subject to the provisions of this section, include power to make rules for the following purposes—

(a) For making provision with respect to the giving of security for costs by persons applying for the registration of judgments;

(b) For prescribing the matters to be proved on an application for the registration of a judgment and for regulating the mode of proving those matters;

(c) For providing for the service on the judgment debtor of notice of the registration of a judgment;

(d) For making provision with respect to the fixing of the period within which an application may be made to have the registration of the judgment set aside and with respect to the extension of the period so fixed;

(e) For prescribing the method by which any question arising under this Act whether a foreign judgment can be enforced by execution in the country of the original court, or what interest is payable under a foreign judgment under the law of the original court, is to be determined;

(f) For prescribing any matter which under this Part of this Act is to be prescribed.

(2) Rules made for the purposes of this Part of this Act shall be expressed to have, and shall have, effect subject to any such provisions contained in Order in Council made under section one of this Act as are declared by the said Orders to be necessary for giving effect to agreements made between His Majesty and foreign countries in relation to matters with respect to which there is power to make rules of court for the purposes of this Part of this Act.

[18]

NOTES

Sub-s (1): words in square brackets substituted for the words "rules of court under section 84 of the Supreme Court Act 1981", in relation to England and Wales, by the Courts Act 2003, s 109(1), Sch 8, para 78.

Orders in Council: the Reciprocal Enforcement of Foreign Judgments (Suriname) Order 1981, SI 1981/735 at **[2097]**.

For applicable procedural rules, see Civil Procedure Rules 1998, SI 1998/3132, rr 74.2–74.11 at **[1518]–[1527]**; Act of Sederunt (Rules of the Court of Session 1994) 1994, SI 1994/1443, rr 62.4–62.10 at **[1133]–[1139]**.

4 Cases in which registered judgments must, or may, be set aside

(1) On an application in that behalf duly made by any party against whom a registered judgment may be enforced, the registration of the judgment—

(a) shall be set aside if the registering court is satisfied—
  (i) that the judgment is not a judgment to which this Part of this Act applies or was registered in contravention of the foregoing provisions of this Act; or
  (ii) that the courts of the country of the original court had no jurisdiction in the circumstances of the case; or
  (iii) that the judgment debtor, being the defendant in the proceedings in the original court, did not (notwithstanding that process may have been duly served on him in accordance with the law of the country of the original court) receive notice of those proceedings in sufficient time to enable him to defend the proceedings and did not appear; or
  (iv) that the judgment was obtained by fraud; or
  (v) that the enforcement of the judgment would be contrary to public policy in the country of the registering court; or
  (vi) that the rights under the judgment are not vested in the person by whom the application for registration was made;

(b) may be set aside if the registering court is satisfied that the matter in dispute in the proceedings in the original court had previously to the date of the judgment in the original court been the subject of a final and conclusive judgment by a court having jurisdiction in the matter.

(2) For the purposes of this section the courts of the country of the original court shall, subject to the provisions of subsection (3) of this section, be deemed to have had jurisdiction—

(a) in the case of a judgment given in an action in personam—
  (i) if the judgment debtor, being a defendant in the original court, submitted to the jurisdiction of that court by voluntarily appearing in the proceedings …; or
  (ii) if the judgment debtor was plaintiff in, or counter-claimed in, the proceedings in the original court; or
  (iii) if the judgment debtor, being a defendant in the original court, had before the commencement of the proceedings agreed, in respect of the subject matter of the proceedings, to submit to the jurisdiction of that court or of the courts of the country of that court; or
  (iv) if the judgment debtor, being a defendant in the original court, was at the time when the proceedings were instituted resident in, or being a body corporate had its principal place of business in, the country of that court; or
  (v) if the judgment debtor, being a defendant in the original court, had an office or place of business in the country of that court and the proceedings in that court were in respect of a transaction effected through or at that office or place;

(b) in the case of a judgment given in an action of which the subject matter was immovable property or in an action in rem of which the subject matter was movable property, if the property in question was at the time of the proceedings in the original court situate in the country of that court;

(c) in the case of a judgment given in an action other than any such action as is mentioned in paragraph (a) or paragraph (b) of this subsection, if the jurisdiction of the original court is recognised by the law of the registering court.

(3) Notwithstanding anything in subsection (2) of this section, the courts of the country of the original court shall not be deemed to have had jurisdiction—

(a) if the subject matter of the proceedings was immovable property outside the country of the original court; or

(b) …

(c) if the judgment debtor, being a defendant in the original proceedings, was a person who under the rules of public international law was entitled to immunity from the jurisdiction of the courts of the country of the original court and did not submit to the jurisdiction of that court.

[19]

NOTES

Sub-s (2): words omitted repealed by the Civil Jurisdiction and Judgments Act 1982, s 54, Sch 14.

Sub-s (3): para (b) repealed by the Civil Jurisdiction and Judgments Act 1982, ss 53(2), 54, Sch 13, Pt II, paras 8(2), 9(2), Sch 14.

5 Powers of registering court on application to set aside registration

(1) If, on an application to set aside the registration of a judgment, the applicant satisfies the registering court either that an appeal is pending, or that he is entitled and intends to appeal, against the judgment, the court, if it thinks fit, may, on such terms as it may think just, either set aside the registration or adjourn the application to set aside the registration until after the expiration of such period as appears to the court to be reasonably sufficient to enable the applicant to take the necessary steps to have the appeal disposed of by the competent tribunal.

(2) Where the registration of a judgment is set aside under the last foregoing subsection, or solely for the reason that the judgment was not at the date of the application for registration enforceable by execution in the country of the original court, the setting aside of the registration shall not prejudice a further application to register the judgment when the appeal has been disposed of or if and when the judgment becomes enforceable by execution in that country, as the case may be.

(3) Where the registration of a judgment is set aside solely for the reason that the judgment, notwithstanding that it had at the date of the application for registration been partly satisfied, was registered for the whole sum payable thereunder, the registering court shall, on the application of the judgment creditor, order judgment to be registered for the balance remaining payable at that date.

[20]

6 Foreign judgments which can be registered not to be enforceable otherwise

No proceedings for the recovery of a sum payable under a foreign judgment, being a judgment to which this Part of this Act applies, other than proceedings by way of registration of the judgment, shall be entertained by any court in the United Kingdom.

[21]

7 Power to apply Part I of Act to British dominions, protectorates and mandated territories

(1) His Majesty may by Order in Council direct that this Part of this Act shall apply to His Majesty's dominions outside the United Kingdom and to judgments obtained in the courts of the said dominions as it applies to foreign countries and judgments obtained in the courts of foreign countries, and in the event of His Majesty so directing, this Act shall have effect accordingly and Part II of the Administration of Justice Act 1920, shall cease to have effect except in relation to those parts of the said dominions to which it extends at the date of the Order.

(2) If at any time after His Majesty has directed as aforesaid an Order in Council is made under section one of this Act extending Part I of this Act to any part of His Majesty's dominions to which the said Part II extends as aforesaid, the said Part II shall cease to have effect in relation to that part of His Majesty's dominions.

(3) References in this section to His Majesty's dominions outside the United Kingdom shall be construed as including references to any territories which are under His Majesty's protection and to any territories in respect of which a mandate under the League of Nations has been accepted by His Majesty.

[22]

NOTES

Modifications: by the Zimbabwe (Independence and Membership of the Commonwealth) (Consequential Provisions) Order 1980, SI 1980/701, art 7, Schedule, para 4(1), this section has effect in relation to Zimbabwe as if the reference therein to a part of His Majesty's Dominions outside the United Kingdom, or to persons or things related thereto, include a reference to a Commonwealth country and to persons or things related to a Commonwealth country; by the Pakistan Act 1990, Schedule, para 8, this section has effect as if references to Her Majesty's dominion's outside the United Kingdom include references to any Commonwealth country.

Orders in Council: the Reciprocal Enforcement of Judgments (General Application to His Majesty's Dominions etc) Order 1933, SR & O 1933/1073 at **[2001]**.

Mandate under the League of Nations: there are no longer any United Kingdom mandated or trust territories.

PART II
MISCELLANEOUS AND GENERAL

8 General effect of certain foreign judgments

(1) Subject to the provisions of this section, a judgment to which Part I of this Act applies or would have applied if a sum of money had been payable thereunder, whether it can be registered or not, and whether, if it can be registered, it is registered or not, shall be recognised in any court in the United Kingdom as conclusive between the parties thereto in all proceedings founded on the same cause of action and may be relied on by way of defence or counterclaim in any such proceedings.

(2) This section shall not apply in the case of any judgment—

(a) where the judgment has been registered and the registration thereof has been set aside on some ground other than—

(i) that a sum of money was not payable under the judgment; or

(ii) that the judgment had been wholly or partly satisfied; or

(iii) that at the date of the application the judgment could not be enforced by execution in the country of the original court; or

(b) where the judgment has not been registered, it is shown (whether it could have been registered or not) that if it had been registered the registration thereof would have been set aside on an application for that purpose on some ground other than one of the grounds specified in paragraph (a) of this subsection.

(3) Nothing in this section shall be taken to prevent any court in the United Kingdom recognising any judgment as conclusive of any matter of law or fact decided therein if that judgment would have been so recognised before the passing of this Act.

[23]

9 Power to make foreign judgments unenforceable in United Kingdom if no reciprocity

(1) If it appears to His Majesty that the treatment in respect of recognition and enforcement accorded by the courts of any foreign country to judgments given in the … courts of the United Kingdom is substantially less favourable than that accorded by the courts of the United Kingdom to judgments of the … courts of that country, His Majesty may by Order in Council apply this section to that country.

(2) Except in so far as His Majesty may by Order in Council under this section otherwise direct, no proceedings shall be entertained in any court in the United Kingdom for the recovery of any sum alleged to be payable under a judgment given in a court of a country to which this section applies.

(3) His Majesty may by a subsequent Order in Council vary or revoke any Order previously made under this section.

[24]

NOTES

Sub-s (1): words omitted repealed by the Civil Jurisdiction and Judgments Act 1982, ss 35(1), 54, Sch 10, para 2, Sch 14.

[10 Provision for issue of copies of, and certificates in connection with, UK judgments

(1) Rules may make provision for enabling any judgment creditor wishing to secure the enforcement in a foreign country to which Part I of this Act extends of a judgment to which this subsection applies, to obtain, subject to any conditions specified in the rules—

(a) a copy of the judgment; and

(b) a certificate giving particulars relating to the judgment and the proceedings in which it was given.

(2) Subsection (1) applies to any judgment given by a court or tribunal in the United Kingdom under which a sum of money is payable, not being a sum payable in respect of taxes or other charges of a like nature or in respect of a fine or other penalty.

(3) In this section "rules"—

(a) in relation to judgments given by a court, means rules of court;

(b) in relation to judgments given by any other tribunal, means rules or regulations made by the authority having power to make rules or regulations regulating the procedure of that tribunal.]

[25]

NOTES

Substituted by the Civil Jurisdiction and Judgments Act 1982, s 35(1), Sch 10, para 3.

For applicable procedural rules, see Civil Procedure Rules 1998, SI 1998/3132, rr 74.12 and 74.13 at **[1528]**, **[1529]**; Act of Sederunt (Rules of the Court of Session 1994) 1994, SI 1994/1443, r 62.11 at **[1140]**.

[10A Arbitration awards

The provisions of this Act, except sections 1(5) and 6, shall apply as they apply to a judgment, in relation to an award in proceedings on an arbitration which has, in pursuance of the law in force in the place where it was made, become enforceable in the same manner as a judgment given by a court in that place.]

[26]

NOTES

Inserted by the Civil Jurisdiction and Judgments Act 1982, s 35(1), Sch 10, para 4.

11 Interpretation

(1) In this Act, unless the context otherwise requires, the following expressions have the meanings hereby assigned to them respectively, that is to say—

"Appeal" includes any proceeding by way of discharging or setting aside a judgment or an application for a new trial or a stay of execution;

"Country of the original court" means the country in which the original court is situated;

["Court", except in section 10 of this Act, includes a tribunal;]

"Judgment" means a judgment or order given or made by a court in any civil proceedings, or a judgment or order given or made by a court in any criminal proceedings for the payment of a sum of money in respect of compensation or damages to an injured party;

"Judgment creditor" means the person in whose favour the judgment was given and includes any person in whom the rights under the judgment have become vested by succession or assignment or otherwise;

"Judgment debtor" means the person against whom the judgment was given, and includes any person against whom the judgment is enforceable under the law of the original court;

.....

"Original court" in relation to any judgment means the court by which the judgment was given;

"Prescribed" means prescribed by rules of court;

"Registration" means registration under Part I of this Act, and the expressions "register" and "registered" shall be construed accordingly;

"Registering court" in relation to any judgment means the court to which an application to register the judgment is made.

(2) For the purposes of this Act, the expression "action in personam" shall not be deemed to include any matrimonial cause or any proceedings in connection with any of the following matters, that is to say, matrimonial matters, administration of the estates of deceased persons, bankruptcy, winding up of companies, lunacy, or guardianship of infants.

[27]

NOTES

Sub-s (1): definition "Court" inserted, and definition omitted repealed, by the Civil Jurisdiction and Judgments Act 1982, ss 35(1), 54, Sch 10, para 5, Sch 14.

12 Application to Scotland This Act in its application to Scotland shall have effect subject to the following modifications—

(a) For any reference to the High Court … there shall be substituted a reference to the Court of Session;

(b) The Court of Session shall, subject to the provisions of subsection (2) of section three of this Act, have power by Act of Sederunt to make rules for the purposes specified in subsection (1) of the said section:

(c) Registration under Part I of this Act shall be effected by registering in the Books of Council and Session or in such manner as the Court of Session may by Act of Sederunt prescribe:

(d) …

(e) For any reference to the entering of a judgment there shall be substituted a reference to the signing of the interlocutor embodying the judgment.

[28]

NOTES

Words omitted from para (a) and the whole of para (d) repealed by the Civil Jurisdiction and Judgments Act 1982, s 54, Sch 14.

13 (*Applies to Northern Ireland only.*)

14 Short title

This Act may be cited as the Foreign Judgments (Reciprocal Enforcement) Act 1933.

[29]

ADMINISTRATION OF JUSTICE ACT 1956

(4 & 5 Eliz 2 c 46)

ARRANGEMENT OF SECTIONS

PART IV
GENERAL PROVISIONS AS TO ENFORCEMENT OF JUDGMENTS AND ORDERS

PART V
ADMIRALTY JURISDICTION AND ARRESTMENT OF SHIPS IN SCOTLAND

PART VI
MISCELLANEOUS AND SUPPLEMENTAL

An Act to amend the law relating to Admiralty jurisdiction, legal proceedings in connection with ships and aircraft and the arrest of ships and other property, to make further provision as to the appointment, tenure of office, powers and qualifications of certain judges and officers, to make certain other amendments of the law relating to the Supreme Court and the county courts and of the law relating to the enforcement of certain judgments, orders and decrees, to enable certain funds in court in the Lancashire Chancery Court to be transferred to the official trustees of charitable funds or the Church Commissioners, and for purposes connected with the matters aforesaid

[5 July 1956]

1–33 (*Ss 1–20 repealed by the Supreme Court Act 1981, s 152(4), Sch 7; ss 21–24, 26–30, 31(1), (3), (4), 32, 33(3) repealed by the County Courts Act 1959, s 204, Sch 3; s 25 repealed by the Judicial Pensions Act 1981, s 36(2), Sch 4; s 31(2) repealed by the Matrimonial Causes Act 1965, s 45, Sch 2; s 33(1), (2) spent.*)

PART IV
GENERAL PROVISIONS AS TO ENFORCEMENT OF JUDGMENTS AND ORDERS

34–39 (*Ss 34, 36, 38 repealed by the Supreme Court Act 1981, s 152(4), Sch 7; s 35 repealed by the Charging Orders Act 1979, s 7(2); s 37 repealed by the Courts and Legal Services Act 1990, s 125(7), Sch 20; s 39 repealed by the County Courts Act 1959, s 204, Sch 3.*)

40 Effect of registration of judgments of courts outside England and Wales

Section five of the Debtors Act 1869, as amended by any subsequent enactment, and …, as so amended, shall have effect as if—

(a) any judgment of the High Court of Northern Ireland or decreet of the Court of Session a certificate of which has been registered in the High Court under section one or section three of the Judgments Extension Act 1868; and

(b) any judgment, as defined in Part II of the Administration of Justice Act 1920, which has been registered in the High Court under the said Part II; and

(c) any judgment, as defined in the Inferior Courts Judgments Extension Act 1882, a certificate of which has been registered in the High Court or in a county court under that Act,

were a judgment of the High Court or, as the case may be, of that county court, and proceedings may be taken under [the said Act of 1869] accordingly.

[30]

NOTES

Words omitted repealed, and words in square brackets substituted, by the Insolvency Act 1985, s 235(1), (3), Sch 8, para 11, Sch 10, Pt III.

Judgments Extension Act 1868 and Inferior Courts Judgments Extension Act: both Acts repealed with savings by the Civil Jurisdiction and Judgments Act 1982, ss 53, 54, Sch 13, Pt II, para 2, Sch 14.

41–44 (*S 41 repealed by the County Courts Act 1959, s 204, Sch 3; ss 42–44 repealed by the Supreme Court Act 1981, s 152(4), Sch 7.*)

PART V
ADMIRALTY JURISDICTION AND ARRESTMENT OF SHIPS IN SCOTLAND

NOTES

In this Part of this Act, references to ships include, in certain cases, references to hovercraft; see the Hovercraft Act 1968, ss 2, 4(3).

45 Jurisdiction in relation to collisions, etc

(1) Subject to the provisions of this Part of this Act, any court having Admiralty jurisdiction shall have jurisdiction to entertain, as against any defender, an action to which this section applies, if, but only if,—

(a) the defender has his habitual residence or a place of business in the area for which the court acts, or

(b) the cause of action arose in the area for which the court acts and either within inland waters or within the limits of a port, or

(c) an action arising out of the same incident or series of incidents is proceeding in the court or has been heard and determined by the court, or

(d) the defender has prorogated the jurisdiction of the court, or

(e) a ship in which the defender owns one or more shares has been arrested (whether ad fundandam jurisdictionem or on the dependence of the action) within the area for which the court acts.

(2) Where an action to which this section applies is raised in a court having jurisdiction by virtue only of one or more of the provisions of the preceding subsection other than paragraph (d) thereof, and it appears to the court that cognate proceedings are depending in a competent court outside Scotland, the first mentioned court shall sist the action if so moved by any party thereto, and shall not recall the sist until satisfied that the cognate proceedings have been discontinued or have otherwise come to an end:

Provided that nothing in this subsection shall prevent the first mentioned court from entertaining any application as to diligence in the action.

In this subsection "cognate proceedings", in relation to any action, means proceedings instituted, before the granting of warrant for service in the action, by the pursuer in the action against any other party to the action, being proceedings in respect of the same incident or series of incidents as those with which the action is concerned.

(3) This section applies to actions for payment of reparation arising out of one or more of the following incidents, that is to say—

(a) any collision between ships, or

(b) the carrying out of, or the omission to carry out, a manoeuvre in the case of one or more of two or more ships, or

(c) the non-compliance, on the part of one or more of two or more ships, with the collision regulations.

(4) In this section—

"inland waters" includes any part of the sea adjacent to the coast of the United Kingdom certified by the Secretary of State to be waters falling by international law to be treated as within the territorial sovereignty of Her Majesty apart from the operation of that law in relation to territorial waters;

"port" means any port, harbour, river, estuary, haven, dock, canal or other place so long as a person or body of persons is empowered by or under an Act or charter to make charges in respect of ships entering it or using the facilities therein, and "limits of a port" means the limits thereof as fixed by or under the Act in question or, as the case may be, by the relevant charter or custom;

"charges" means any charges with the exception of light dues, local light dues and any other charges in respect of lighthouses, buoys or beacons and of charges in respect of pilotage.

(5) For the avoidance of doubt it is hereby declared that any reference in this section to an action for payment of reparation does not include a reference to an action to make good a lien.

(6) Section six of the Sheriff Courts (Scotland) Act, 1907 (as amended by any subsequent enactment), shall cease to have effect in relation to actions to which this section applies.

[31]

46 Exclusion of jurisdiction in cases falling within Rhine Convention

No court shall have jurisdiction to determine any claim or question certified by the Secretary of State to be a claim or question which, under the Rhine Navigation Convention, falls to be determined in accordance with the provisions thereof.

In this section "the Rhine Navigation Convention" means the Convention of the seventh of October, eighteen hundred and sixty-eight, as revised by any subsequent Convention.

[32]

47 Arrest of ships on the dependence of an action or in rem

(1) Subject to the provisions of this section and section fifty of this Act, no warrant issued after the commencement of this Part of this Act for the arrest of property on the dependence of an action or in rem shall have effect as authority for the detention of a ship unless the conclusion in respect of which it is issued is appropriate for the enforcement of a claim to which this section applies, and, in the case of a warrant to arrest on the dependence of an action, unless either—

(a) the ship is the ship with which the action is concerned, or

(b) all the shares in the ship are owned by the defender against whom that conclusion is directed.

(2) This section applies to any claim arising out of one or more of the following, that is to say—

(a) damage done or received by any ship;

(b) loss of life or personal injury sustained in consequence of any defect in a ship or in her apparel or equipment, or of the wrongful act, neglect or default of the owners, characters or persons in possession or control of a ship or of the master or crew thereof or of any other person for whose wrongful acts, neglects or defaults the owners, characters or persons in possession or control of a ship are responsible, being an act, neglect or default in the navigation or management of the ship, in the loading, unloading or discharge of goods on, in or from the ship or in the embarkation, carriage or disembarkation of persons on, in or from the ship;

[(c) the Salvage Convention, 1989;

(ca) any contract for or in relation to salvage services;]

(d) any agreement relating to the use or hire of any ship whether by charterparty or otherwise;

(e) any agreement relating to the carriage of goods in any ship whether by charterparty or otherwise;

(f) loss of, or damage to, goods carried in any ship;

(g) general average;

(h) any bottomry bond;

(i) towage;

(j) pilotage;

(k) the supply of goods or materials to a ship for her operation or maintenance;

(l) the construction, repair or equipment of any ship;

(m) liability for dock charges or dues;

(n) liability for payment of wages … of a master or member of the crew of a ship;

(o) master's disbursements, including disbursements made by shippers, charterers or agents on behalf of a ship or her owner;

(p) any dispute as to the ownership or right to possession of any ship or as to the ownership of any share in a ship;

(q) any dispute between co-owners of any ship as to the ownership, possession, employment or earnings of that ship;

(r) the mortgage or hypothecation of any ship or any share in a ship;

(s) any forfeiture or condemnation of any ship, or of goods which are being, or have been, carried, or have been attempted to be carried, in any ship, or for the restoration of a ship or any such goods after seizure.

(3) In any proceedings having a conclusion appropriate for the enforcement of any claim such as is mentioned in paragraphs (p) to (s) of the last preceding subsection a warrant may be issued—

(a) if the conclusion is a pecuniary conclusion, for the arrest of the ship on the dependence of the action; or

(b) in any other case (whether or not the claimant is entitled to a lien over the ship), for the arrest of the ship in rem;

but there shall not be issued in respect of any such conclusion as aforesaid (whether pecuniary or otherwise) a warrant to arrest, either in rem or on the dependence of the action, any ship other than the ship to which the conclusion relates.

(4) Subject to the preceding subsection, nothing in this section shall be taken to authorise—

(a) the use of an arrestment on the dependence of an action otherwise than in respect of a pecuniary conclusion, or

(b) the use of an arrestment in rem otherwise than in respect of a conclusion appropriate for the making good of a lien.

(5) A warrant for the arrest of a ship in rem issued by virtue of paragraph (b) of subsection (3) of this section in a case where the person in whose favour it is issued is not entitled to a lien over the ship shall have effect as authority for the detention of the ship as security for the implementation of the decree of the court so far as it affects that ship:

Provided that the court may, on the application of any person having an interest, recall the arrestment if satisfied that sufficient bail or other security for such implementation has been found.

(6) Nothing in this section shall authorise the arrest, whether on the dependence of an action or in rem, of a ship while it is on passage.

(7) Nothing in this section shall authorise the arrest, whether on the dependence of an action or in rem, of a ship in respect of any claim against the Crown, or the arrest, detention or sale of any of Her Majesty's ships or Her Majesty's aircraft.

In this subsection "Her Majesty's ships" and "Her Majesty's aircraft" have the meanings assigned to them by subsection (2) of section thirty-eight of the Crown Proceedings Act, 1947.

[(8) In—

(a) paragraph (c) of subsection (2) above, the "Salvage Convention, 1989" means the International Convention on Salvage 1989 as it has effect under [section 224 of the Merchant Shipping Act 1995];

(b) paragraph (ca) of that subsection, the reference to salvage services includes services rendered in saving life from a ship and the reference to any claim arising out of any contract for or in relation to salvage services includes any claim arising out of such a contract whether or not arising during the provision of such services,

and the claims mentioned in subsections (2)(c) and (ca) shall be construed as including claims available by virtue of section 87 of the Civil Aviation Act 1982.]

[33]

NOTES

Sub-s (2): paras (c), (ca) substituted for original para (c) by the Merchant Shipping (Salvage and Pollution) Act 1994, s 1(6), Sch 2, para 4(1), (2)(a); words omitted from para (n) repealed by the Merchant Shipping Act 1995, s 314(1), (2), Sch 12, Sch 13, para 29(1), (2)(a).

Sub-s (8): original sub-s (8) repealed by the Statute Law Revision Act 1963; new sub-s (8) added by the Merchant Shipping (Salvage and Pollution) Act 1994, s 1(6), Sch 2, para 4(1), (2)(b); words in square brackets substituted by the Merchant Shipping Act 1995, s 314(1), (2), Sch 12, Sch 13, para 29(1), (2)(b).

48 Interpretation of Part V

In this Part of this Act, unless the context otherwise requires,—

(a) references to an action, a pursuer and a defender include respectively references to a counter-claim, the person making a counter-claim and the person against whom a counter-claim is made;

(b) any reference to a conclusion includes a reference to a crave, and "pecuniary conclusion" does not include a conclusion for expenses;

(c) any reference to a warrant to arrest property includes a reference to letters of arrestment and to a precept of arrestment;

(d) any reference to a lien includes a reference to any hypothec or charge;

(e) . . .

(f) the following expressions have the meanings hereby assigned to them respectively, that is to say—

"collision regulations" means [safety regulations under section 85 of the Merchant Shipping Act 1995];

"goods" includes baggage;

"master" has the same meaning as in the [Merchant Shipping Act 1995], and accordingly includes every person (except a pilot) having command or charge of a ship;

"ship" includes any description of vessel used in navigation not propelled by oars;

"towage" and "pilotage" in relation to an aircraft, mean towage and pilotage while the aircraft is waterborne.

[34]

NOTES

Para (e) repealed by the Merchant Shipping (Salvage and Pollution) Act 1994, ss 1(6), 10, Sch 2, para 4(1), (3), Sch 4; words in square brackets in para (f) substituted by the Merchant Shipping Act 1995, s 314(2), Sch 13, para 29(1), (3).

49 (*Repealed in part by the Merchant Shipping Act 1995, s 314(1), Sch 12 and in part by the Animal Health Act 1981, s 96(2), Sch 6.*)

50 Application and commencement of Part V

(1) This Part of this Act shall apply to Scotland only.

(2) This Part of this Act shall come into operation on such day as the Secretary of State may appoint by order made by statutory instrument.

(3) Nothing in this Part of this Act shall affect any action in respect of which warrant for service has been granted before the commencement of this Part of this Act.

[35]

NOTES

Orders: the Administration of Justice Act, 1956, (Part V), Commencement Order 1956, SI 1956/2099.

PART VI
MISCELLANEOUS AND SUPPLEMENTAL

51 Modification of Foreign Judgments (Reciprocal Enforcement) Act 1933, in relation to certain parts of Her Majesty's dominions

Where an Order in Council is made extending Part I of the Foreign Judgments (Reciprocal Enforcement) Act 1933, to a part of Her Majesty's dominions or other territory to which Part II of the Administration of Justice Act 1920 extends, the said Part I shall, in relation to that part of Her Majesty's dominions or other territory, have effect as if—

(a) …

(b) the fact that a judgment was given before the coming into operation of the Order did not prevent it from being a judgment to which the said Part I applies, but the time limited for the registration of a judgment were, in the case of a judgment so given, twelve months from the date of the judgment or such longer period as may be allowed by the High Court in England and Wales, the Court of Session in Scotland, or the High Court in Northern Ireland;

(c) any judgment registered in any of the said courts under the said Part II before the coming into operation of the Order had been registered in that court under the said Part I and anything done in relation thereto under the said Part II or any rules of court or other provisions applicable to the said Part II had been done under the said Part I or the corresponding rules of court or other provisions applicable to the said Part I.

[36]

NOTES

Para (a): repealed by the Civil Jurisdiction and Judgments Act 1982, s 54, Sch 14.

52–56 *(S 52 repealed by the Courts Act 1971, s 56(4), Sch 11, Pts II, IV; s 53 repealed by the Courts and Legal Services Act 1990, s 125(2), (7), Sch 17, para 3, Sch 20; ss 54, 56 repealed by the Supreme Court Act 1981, ss 149(2)(a), 152(4), Sch 7; s 55(1)–(3), (5) relate to Northern Ireland; s 55(4) repealed by the Northern Ireland Constitution Act 1973, s 41(1), Sch 6, Pt I.)*

57 Short title, repeal, extent and commencement

(1) This Act may be cited as the Administration of Justice Act 1956.

(2) …

(3) This Act, except Part V and section fifty-one thereof, shall not extend to Scotland.

(4) The provisions of this Act, other than Part V thereof, section fifty-five thereof and the First Schedule thereto shall come into force on such day as the Lord Chancellor may appoint by order made by statutory instrument, and he may appoint different days for different purposes.

[37]

NOTES

Sub-s (2): repealed by the Statute Law (Repeals) Act 1974.
Orders: the Administration of Justice Act 1956 (Commencement) Order 1956, SI 1956/1065.

(Sch 1, Pts I, II apply to Northern Ireland only; Sch 1, Pt III, Sch 2 repealed by the Statute Law (Repeals) Act 1974.)

SHERIFF COURTS (SCOTLAND) ACT 1971

(1971 c 58)

NOTES

Only section 32 is reproduced here.

An Act to amend the law with respect to sheriff courts in Scotland, and for purposes connected therewith

[27 July 1971]

PART III
CIVIL JURISDICTION, PROCEDURE AND APPEALS

Regulation of procedure in civil proceedings

32 Power of Court of Session to regulate civil procedure in sheriff court

(1) Subject to the provisions of this section, the Court of Session may by act of sederunt regulate and prescribe the procedure and practice to be followed in any civil proceedings in the sheriff court (including any matters incidental or relating to any such procedure or practice), and, without prejudice to the generality of the foregoing words, the power conferred on the Court of Session by this section shall extend to—

(a) regulating the procedure to be followed in connection with execution or diligence following on any civil proceedings;

(b) prescribing the manner in which, the time within which, and the conditions on which, an appeal may be taken to the sheriff principal from an interlocutor of a sheriff, or to the Court of Session from an interlocutor of a sheriff principal or a sheriff (including an interlocutor applying the verdict of a jury), or any application may be made to the sheriff court, or anything required or authorised to be done in relation to any civil proceedings shall or may be done;

(c) prescribing the form of any document to be used in, or for the purposes of, any civil proceedings or any execution or diligence following thereon, and the person by whom, and the manner in which, any such document as aforesaid is to be authenticated;

(d) regulating the procedure to be followed in connection with the production and recovery of documents;

[(e) providing in respect of any category of civil proceedings for written statements (including affidavits) and reports, admissible under section 2(1)(b) of the Civil Evidence (Scotland) Act 1988, to be received in evidence, on such conditions as may be prescribed, without being spoken to by a witness;]

[(ea) regulating the procedure to be followed in connection with the making of orders under sections 12(1) and (6) and 13(2) of the Vulnerable Witnesses (Scotland) Act 2004 (asp 3) ("the 2004 Act");

(eb) regulating, so far as not regulated by the 2004 Act, the use of special measures authorised by virtue of that Act to be used;]

(f) making such provision as may appear to the Court of Session to be necessary or expedient with respect to the payment, investment or application of any sum of money awarded to or in respect of a person under legal disability in any action in the sheriff court;

(g) regulating the summoning, remuneration and duties of assessors;

(h) making such provision as may appear to the Court of Session to be necessary or expedient for carrying out the provisions of this Act or of any enactment conferring powers or imposing duties on sheriffs principal or sheriffs or relating to proceedings in the sheriff courts;

[(i) regulating the expenses which may be awarded by the sheriff to parties in proceedings before him:]

[(j) permitting a person who is not an advocate or solicitor and is not represented by an advocate or solicitor to transmit, whether orally or in writing, the views of a child to the sheriff for the purposes of any enactment which makes provision (however expressed) for the sheriff to have regard to those views]

[(k) prescribing the procedure to be followed in appointing a person under section 3(4) of the Adults with Incapacity (Scotland) Act 2000 (asp 4) and the functions of such a person]

[(l) permitting a party to proceedings which relate to an attachment to be represented, in such circumstances as may be specified in the act of sederunt, by a person who is neither an advocate nor a solicitor]

[(m) permitting the debtor or hirer in proceedings for—

(i) a time order under section 129 of the Consumer Credit Act 1974 (time orders), or

(ii) variation or revocation, under section 130(6) of that Act (variation and revocation of time orders), of a time order made under section 129,

to be represented by a person who is neither an advocate nor a solicitor]:

Provided that nothing contained in an act of sederunt made under this section shall derogate from—

(i) the provisions of sections 35 to 38 of this Act [(as amended by the Law Reform (Miscellaneous Provisions) (Scotland) Act 1985)] with respect to summary causes, or

(ii) the provisions of subsection (8) of section 20 of the Race Relations Act 1968 with respect to the remuneration to be paid to assessors appointed under subsection (7) of that section.

(2) An act of sederunt under this section may contain such incidental, supplemental or consequential provisions as appear to the Court of Session to be necessary or expedient for the purposes of that act, including, but without prejudice to the generality of the foregoing words, provisions amending, repealing or revoking any enactment (whether passed or made before or after the commencement of this Act) relating to matters with respect to which an act of sederunt may be made under this section.

(3) Before making an act of sederunt under this section with respect to any matter the Court of Session shall (unless that act embodies, with or without modifications, draft rules submitted to them by the Sheriff Court Rules Council under section 34 of this Act) consult the said Council, and shall take into consideration any views expressed by the Council with respect to that matter.

(4) Section 34 of the Administration of Justice (Scotland) Act 1933 (power of Court of Session to regulate civil procedure in sheriff court) shall cease to have effect, but any act of sederunt made under or having effect by virtue of that section shall, if and so far as it is in force immediately before the commencement of this Act, continue in force and shall have effect, and be treated, as if it had been made under this section.

[38]

NOTES

Sub-s (1): para (e) substituted by the Civil Evidence (Scotland) Act 1988, s 2(4); paras (ea), (eb) inserted for certain purposes and inserted as from a day to be appointed for remaining purposes by the Vulnerable Witnesses (Scotland) Act 2004, s 14(2); para (i) and words in final pair of square brackets inserted by the Law Reform (Miscellaneous Provisions) (Scotland) Act 1985, Sch 2, para 12; para (j) inserted by the Children (Scotland) Act 1995, s 105(4), Sch 4, para 18(1), (2); para (k) inserted by the Adults with Incapacity (Scotland) Act 2000, s 88(2), Sch 5, para 13; para (l) inserted by the Debt Arrangement and Attachment (Scotland) Act 2002, s 43; para (m) inserted by the Consumer Credit Act 2006, s 16(4), as from a day to be appointed.

SUPREME COURT ACT 1981

(1981 c 54)

NOTES

Title substituted by the title "Senior Courts Act 1981" by the Constitutional Reform Act 2005, s 59(5), Sch 11, Pt 1, para 1, as from a day to be appointed.

ARRANGEMENT OF SECTIONS

PART II
JURISDICTION

THE HIGH COURT

General jurisdiction

Admiralty jurisdiction

Other particular fields of jurisdiction

Powers

GENERAL PROVISIONS

Law and equity

PART VI
MISCELLANEOUS AND SUPPLEMENTARY

Supplementary

An Act to consolidate with amendments the Supreme Court of Judicature (Consolidation) Act 1925 and other enactments relating to the Supreme Court in England and Wales and the administration of justice therein; to repeal certain obsolete or unnecessary enactments so relating; to amend Part VIII of the Mental Health Act 1959, the Courts-Martial (Appeals) Act 1968, the Arbitration Act 1979 and the law relating to county courts; and for connected purposes

[28 July 1981]

1–14 ((*Pt I*) *relate to the constitution of the Supreme Court.*)

PART II
JURISDICTION

15–18 (*Relate to the jurisdiction of the Court of Appeal.*)

THE HIGH COURT

General jurisdiction

19 General jurisdiction

(1) The High Court shall be a superior court of record.

(2) Subject to the provisions of this Act, there shall be exercisable by the High Court—

(a) all such jurisdiction (whether civil or criminal) as is conferred on it by this or any other Act; and

(b) all such other jurisdiction (whether civil or criminal) as was exercisable by it immediately before the commencement of this Act (including jurisdiction conferred on a judge of the High Court by any statutory provision).

(3) Any jurisdiction of the High Court shall be exercised only by a single judge of that court, except in so far as it is—

(a) by or by virtue of rules of court or any other statutory provision required to be exercised by a divisional court; or

(b) by rules of court made exercisable by a master, registrar or other officer of the court, or by any other person.

(4) The specific mention elsewhere in this Act of any jurisdiction covered by subsection (2) shall not derogate from the generality of that subsection.

[39]

Admiralty jurisdiction

20 Admiralty jurisdiction of High Court

(1) The Admiralty jurisdiction of the High Court shall be as follows, that is to say—

(a) jurisdiction to hear and determine any of the questions and claims mentioned in subsection (2);

(b) jurisdiction in relation to any of the proceedings mentioned in subsection (3);

(c) any other Admiralty jurisdiction which it had immediately before the commencement of this Act; and

(d) any jurisdiction connected with ships or aircraft which is vested in the High Court apart from this section and is for the time being by rules of court made or coming into force after the commencement of this Act assigned to the Queen's Bench Division and directed by the rules to be exercised by the Admiralty Court.

(2) The questions and claims referred to in subsection (1)(a) are—

(a) any claim to the possession or ownership of a ship or to the ownership of any share therein;

(b) any question arising between the co-owners of a ship as to possession, employment or earnings of that ship;

(c) any claim in respect of a mortgage of or charge on a ship or any share therein;

(d) any claim for damage received by a ship;

(e) any claim for damage done by a ship;

(f) any claim for loss of life or personal injury sustained in consequence of any defect in a ship or in her apparel or equipment, or in consequence of the wrongful act, neglect or default of—

(i) the owners, charterers or persons in possession or control of a ship; or

(ii) the master or crew of a ship, or any other person for whose wrongful acts, neglects or defaults the owners, charterers or persons in possession or control of a ship are responsible,

being an act, neglect or default in the navigation or management of the ship, in the loading, carriage or discharge of goods on, in or from the ship, or in the embarkation, carriage or disembarkation of persons on, in or from the ship;

(g) any claim for loss of or damage to goods carried in a ship;

(h) any claim arising out of any agreement relating to the carriage of goods in a ship or to the use or hire of a ship;

[(j) any claim—

(i) under the Salvage Convention 1989;

(ii) under any contract for or in relation to salvage services; or

(iii) in the nature of salvage not falling within (i) or (ii) above;

or any corresponding claim in connection with an aircraft;]

(k) any claim in the nature of towage in respect of a ship or an aircraft;

(l) any claim in the nature of pilotage in respect of a ship or an aircraft;

(m) any claim in respect of goods or materials supplied to a ship for her operation or maintenance;

(n) any claim in respect of the construction, repair or equipment of a ship or in respect of dock charges or dues;

(o) any claim by a master or member of the crew of a ship for wages (including any sum allotted out of wages or adjudged by a superintendent to be due by way of wages);

(p) any claim by a master, shipper, charterer or agent in respect of disbursements made on account of a ship;

(q) any claim arising out of an act which is or is claimed to be a general average act;

(r) any claim arising out of bottomry;

(s) any claim for the forfeiture or condemnation of ship or of goods which are being or have been carried, or have been attempted to be carried, in a ship, or for the restoration of a ship or any such goods after seizure, or for droits of Admiralty.

(3) The proceedings referred to in subsection (1)(b) are—

(a) any application to the High Court under [the Merchant Shipping Act 1995];

(b) any action to enforce a claim for damage, loss of life or personal injury arising out of—

(i) a collision between ships; or

(ii) the carrying out of or omission to carry out a manoeuvre in the case of one or more of two or more ships; or

(iii) non-compliance, on the part of one or more of two or more ships, with the collision regulations;

(c) any action by shipowners or other persons under the [Merchant Shipping Act 1995] for the limitation of the amount of their liability in connection with a ship or other property.

(4) The jurisdiction of the High Court under subsection (2)(b) includes power to settle any account outstanding and unsettled between the parties in relation to the ship, and to direct that the ship, or any share thereof, shall be sold, and to make such other order as the court thinks fit.

(5) Subsection (2)(e) extends to—

(a) any claim in respect of a liability incurred under [Chapter III of Part VI of the Merchant Shipping Act 1995]; and

(b) any claim in respect of a liability falling on the [International Oil Pollution Compensation Fund, or on the [International Oil Pollution Compensation Fund 1992], under Chapter IV of Part VI of the Merchant Shipping Act 1995].

[(6) In subsection (2)(j)—

(a) the "Salvage Convention 1989" means the International Convention on Salvage, 1989 as it has effect under [section 224 of the Merchant Shipping Act 1995];

(b) the reference to salvage services includes services rendered in saving life from a ship and the reference to any claim under any contract for or in relation to salvage services includes any claim arising out of such a contract whether or not arising during the provision of the services;

(c) the reference to a corresponding claim in connection with an aircraft is a reference to any claim corresponding to any claim mentioned in subparagraph (i) or (ii) of paragraph (j) which is available under section 87 of the Civil Aviation Act 1982.]

(7) The preceding provisions of this section apply—

(a) in relation to all ships or aircraft, whether British or not and whether registered or not and wherever the residence or domicile of their owners may be;

(b) in relation to all claims, wherever arising (including, in the case of cargo or wreck salvage, claims in respect of cargo or wreck found on land); and

(c) so far as they relate to mortgages and charges, to all mortgages or charges, whether registered or not and whether legal or equitable, including mortgages and charges created under foreign law:

Provided that nothing in this subsection shall be construed as extending the cases in which money or property is recoverable under any of the provisions of the [Merchant Shipping Act 1995].

[40]

NOTES

Sub-s (2): para (j) substituted by the Merchant Shipping (Salvage and Pollution) Act 1994, s 1(6), Sch 2, para 6(1), (2).

Sub-ss (3), (7): words in square brackets substituted by the Merchant Shipping Act 1995, s 314(2), Sch 13, para 59(1), (2)(a), (d).

Sub-s (5): words in first and second (outer) pairs of square brackets substituted by the Merchant Shipping Act 1995, s 314(2), Sch 13, para 59(1), (2)(b); words in third (inner) pair of square brackets substituted by the Merchant Shipping and Maritime Security Act 1997, s 29(1), Sch 6, para 2.

Sub-s (6): substituted by the Merchant Shipping (Salvage and Pollution) Act 1994, s 1(6), Sch 2, para 6(1), (3); words in square brackets substituted by the Merchant Shipping Act 1995, s 314(2), Sch 13, para 59(1), (2)(c).

21 Mode of exercise of Admiralty jurisdiction

(1) Subject to section 22, an action in personam may be brought in the High Court in all cases within the Admiralty jurisdiction of that court.

(2) In the case of any such claim as is mentioned in section 20(2)(a), (c) or (s) or any such question as is mentioned in section 20(2)(b), an action in rem may be brought in the High Court against the ship or property in connection with which the claim or question arises.

(3) In any case in which there is a maritime lien or other charge on any ship, aircraft or other property for the amount claimed, an action in rem may be brought in the High Court against that ship, aircraft or property.

(4) In the case of any such claim as is mentioned in section 20(2)(e) to (r), where—

(a) the claim arises in connection with a ship; and

(b) the person who would be liable on the claim in an action in personam ("the relevant person") was, when the cause of action arose, the owner or charterer of, or in possession or in control of, the ship,

an action in rem may (whether or not the claim gives rise to a maritime lien on that ship) be brought in the High Court against—

(i) that ship, if at the time when the action is brought the relevant person is either the beneficial owner of that ship as respects all the shares in it or the charterer of it under a charter by demise; or

(ii) any other ship of which, at the time when the action is brought, the relevant person is the beneficial owner as respects all the shares in it.

(5) In the case of a claim in the nature of towage or pilotage in respect of an aircraft, an action in rem may be brought in the High Court against that aircraft if, at the time when the action is brought, it is beneficially owned by the person who would be liable on the claim in an action in personam.

(6) Where, in the exercise of its Admiralty jurisdiction, the High Court orders any ship, aircraft or other property to be sold, the court shall have jurisdiction to hear and determine any question arising as to the title to the proceeds of sale.

(7) In determining for the purposes of subsections (4) and (5) whether a person would be liable on a claim in an action in personam it shall be assumed that he has his habitual residence or a place of business within England or Wales.

(8) Where, as regards any such claim as is mentioned in section 20(2)(e) to (r), a ship has been served with a writ or arrested in an action in rem brought to enforce that claim, no other ship may be served with a writ or arrested in that or any other action in rem brought to enforce that claim; but this subsection does not prevent the issue, in respect of any one such claim, of a writ naming more than one ship or of two or more writs each naming a different ship.

[41]

22 Restrictions on entertainment of actions in personam in collision and other similar cases

(1) This section applies to any claim for damage, loss of life or personal injury arising out of—

(a) a collision between ships; or

(b) the carrying out of, or omission to carry out, a manoeuvre in the case of one or more of two or more ships; or

(c) non-compliance, on the part of one or more of two or more ships, with the collision regulations.

(2) The High Court shall not entertain any action in personam to enforce a claim to which this section applies unless—

(a) the defendant has his habitual residence or a place of business within England or Wales; or

(b) the cause of action arose within inland waters of England or Wales or within the limits of a port of England or Wales; or

(c) an action arising out of the same incident or series of incidents is proceeding in the court or has been heard and determined in the court.

In this subsection—

"inland waters" includes any part of the sea adjacent to the coast of the United Kingdom certified by the Secretary of State to be waters falling by international law to be treated as within the territorial sovereignty of Her Majesty apart from the operation of that law in relation to territorial waters;

"port" means any port, harbour, river, estuary, haven, dock, canal or other place so long as a person or body of persons is empowered by or under an Act to make charges in respect of ships entering it or using the facilities therein, and "limits of a port" means the limits thereof as fixed by or under the Act in question or, as the case may be, by the relevant charter or custom;

"charges" means any charges with the exception of light dues, local light dues and any other charges in respect of lighthouses, buoys or beacons and of charges in respect of pilotage.

(3) The High Court shall not entertain any action in personam to enforce a claim to which this section applies until any proceedings previously brought by the plaintiff in any court outside England and Wales against the same defendant in respect of the same incident or series of incidents have been discontinued or otherwise come to an end.

(4) Subsections (2) and (3) shall apply to counterclaims (except counterclaims in proceedings arising out of the same incident or series of incidents) as they apply to actions, the references to the plaintiff and the defendant being for this purpose read as references to the plaintiff on the counterclaim and the defendant to the counterclaim respectively.

(5) Subsections (2) and (3) shall not apply to any action or counterclaim if the defendant thereto submits or has agreed to submit to the jurisdiction of the court.

(6) Subject to the provisions of subsection (3), the High Court shall have jurisdiction to entertain an action in personam to enforce a claim to which this section applies whenever any of the conditions specified in subsection (2)(a) to (c) is satisfied, and the rules of court relating to the service of process outside the jurisdiction shall make such provision as may appear to the rule-making authority to be appropriate having regard to the provisions of this subsection.

(7) Nothing in this section shall prevent an action which is brought in accordance with the provisions of this section in the High Court being transferred, in accordance with the enactments in that behalf, to some other court.

(8) For the avoidance of doubt it is hereby declared that this section applies in relation to the jurisdiction of the High Court not being Admiralty jurisdiction, as well as in relation to its Admiralty jurisdiction.

[42]

23 High Court not to have jurisdiction in cases within Rhine Convention

The High Court shall not have jurisdiction to determine any claim or question certified by the Secretary of State to be a claim or question which, under the Rhine Navigation Convention, falls to be determined in accordance with the provisions of that Convention; and any proceedings to enforce such a claim which are commenced in the High Court shall be set aside.

[43]

24 Supplementary provisions as to Admiralty jurisdiction

(1) In sections 20 to 23 and this section, unless the context otherwise requires—

"collision regulations" means [safety regulations under section 85 of the Merchant Shipping Act 1995];

"goods" includes baggage;

"master" has the same meaning as in the [Merchant Shipping Act 1995], and accordingly includes every person (except a pilot) having command or charge of a ship;

"the Rhine Navigation Convention" means the Convention of the 7th October 1868 as revised by any subsequent Convention;

"ship" includes any description of vessel used in navigation and (except in the definition of "port" in section 22(2) and in subsection (2)(c) of this section) includes, subject to section 2(3) of the Hovercraft Act 1968, a hovercraft;

"towage" and "pilotage", in relation to an aircraft, mean towage and pilotage while the aircraft is waterborne.

(2) Nothing in sections 20 to 23 shall—

(a) be construed as limiting the jurisdiction of the High Court to refuse to entertain an action for wages by the master or a member of the crew of a ship, not being a British ship;

(b) affect the provisions of section [226 of the Merchant Shipping Act 1995] (power of a receiver of wreck to detain a ship in respect of a salvage claim); or

(c) authorise proceedings in rem in respect of any claim against the Crown, or the arrest, detention or sale of any of Her Majesty's ships or Her Majesty's aircraft, or, subject to section 2(3) of the Hovercraft Act 1968, Her Majesty's hovercraft, or of any cargo or other property belonging to the Crown.

(3) In this section—

"Her Majesty's ships" and "Her Majesty's aircraft" have the meanings given by section 38(2) of the Crown Proceedings Act 1947;

"Her Majesty's hovercraft" means hovercraft belonging to the Crown in right of Her Majesty's Government in the United Kingdom or Her Majesty's Government in Northern Ireland.

[44]

NOTES

Sub-ss (1), (2): words in square brackets substituted by the Merchant Shipping Act 1995, s 314(2), Sch 13, para 59(1), (3).

Other particular fields of jurisdiction

25, 26 (*Relate to probate jurisdiction and matrimonial jurisdiction of the High Court.*)

27 Prize jurisdiction of High Court

The High Court shall, in accordance with section 19(2), have as a prize court—

(a) all such jurisdiction as is conferred on it by the Prize Acts 1864 to 1944 (in which references to the High Court of Admiralty are by virtue of paragraph 1 of Schedule 4 to this Act to be construed as references to the High Court); and

(b) all such other jurisdiction on the high seas and elsewhere as it had as a prize court immediately before the commencement of this Act.

[45]

28, 28A, 29–31 (*Relate to other particular fields of jurisdiction.*)

Powers

32–36 (*Relate to the powers of the High Court.*)

37 Powers of High Court with respect to injunctions and receivers

(1) The High Court may by order (whether interlocutory or final) grant an injunction or appoint a receiver in all cases in which it appears to the court to be just and convenient to do so.

(2) Any such order may be made either unconditionally or on such terms and conditions as the court thinks just.

(3) The power of the High Court under subsection (1) to grant an interlocutory injunction restraining a party to any proceedings from removing from the jurisdiction of the High Court, or otherwise dealing with, assets located within that jurisdiction shall be exercisable in cases where that party is, as well as in cases where he is not, domiciled, resident or present within that jurisdiction.

(4) The power of the High Court to appoint a receiver by way of equitable execution shall operate in relation to all legal estates and interests in land; and that power—

(a) may be exercised in relation to an estate or interest in land whether or not a charge has been imposed on that land under section 1 of the Charging Orders Act 1979 for the purpose of enforcing the judgment, order or award in question; and

(b) shall be in addition to, and not in derogation of, any power of any court to appoint a receiver in proceedings for enforcing such a charge.

(5) Where an order under the said section 1 imposing a charge for the purpose of enforcing a judgment, order or award has been, or has effect as if, registered under section 6 of the Land Charges Act 1972, subsection (4) of the said section 6 (effect of non-registration of writs and orders registrable under that section) shall not apply to an order appointing a receiver made either—

(a) in proceedings for enforcing the charge; or

(b) by way of equitable execution of the judgment, order or award or, as the case may be, of so much of it as requires payment of moneys secured by the charge.

[46]

38–48 (*Relate to other powers, other provisions and to the Crown Court.*)

GENERAL PROVISIONS

Law and equity

49 Concurrent administration of law and equity

(1), (2) (*Relate to general principles of law and equity.*)

(3) Nothing in this Act shall affect the power of the Court of Appeal or the High Court to stay any proceedings before it, where it thinks fit to do so, either of its own motion or on the application of any person, whether or not a party to the proceedings.

[47]

50–128 (*Ss 50–52 relate to general provisions concerning remedies and costs; ss 53–83 relate to practice and procedure in the Court of Appeal, the High Court and the Crown Court; ss 84–87 relate to the power to make rules of court, the Supreme Court Rule Committee and the Crown Court Rule Committee; ss 88–104 relate to officers and offices; ss 105–128 relate to probate causes and matters.*)

PART VI
MISCELLANEOUS AND SUPPLEMENTARY

129–149 (*Ss 129–142 relate to miscellaneous provisions; s 143 repealed by the Administration of Justice Act 1982, s 75, Sch 9, Pt I; s 144 repealed by the Mental Health Act 1983, s 148(3), Sch 6; s 145 amends the Courts-Martial (Appeals) Act 1968; s 146 substitutes the Courts Act 1971, s 24; s 147 adds the Solicitors Act 1974, s 50(3); s 148 inserts the Arbitration Act 1979, ss 1(6A), 2(2A) and amends s 2(3) thereof in relation to decisions of the High Court pronounced on or after 1 January 1982; s 149 repealed by the County Courts Act 1984, s 148(3), Sch 4.*)

Supplementary

150 (*Relates to Admiralty jurisdiction.*)

151 Interpretation of this Act, and rules of construction for other Acts and documents

(1) In this Act, unless the context otherwise requires—

"action" means any civil proceedings commenced by writ or in any other manner prescribed by rules of court;

.....

"judgment" includes a decree;

"jurisdiction" includes powers;

.....

(2)–(4) (*Repealed in part; remainder relates to interpretation of provisions outside the scope of this work.*)

(5) The provisions of Schedule 4 (construction of references to superseded courts and officers) shall have effect.

[48]

NOTES

Sub-s (1): definitions omitted repealed in part; remainder outside the scope of this work.

152 (*Relates to amendments, transitional provisions, savings and repeals.*)

153 Citation, commencement and extent

(1) This Act may be cited as the *Supreme Court Act 1981*.

(2) This Act, except the provisions mentioned in subsection (3), shall come into force on 1st January 1982; and references to the commencement of this Act shall be construed as references to the beginning of that day.

(3) Sections 72, 143 and 152(2) and this section shall come into force on the passing of this Act.

(4), (5) (*Relate to the extent of the Act.*)

[49]

NOTES

Sub-s (1): words in italics substituted by the words "Senior Courts Act 1981" by the Constitutional Reform Act 2005, s 59(5), Sch 11, Pt 1, para 1(2), as from a day to be appointed.

(*Sch 1 relates to the distribution of business in High Court; Sch 2 relates to the offices in the Supreme Court; Sch 3 repealed by the County Courts Act 1984, s 148(3), Sch 4; Sch 4 relates to the construction of references to superseded courts and officers; Sch 5, in so far as unrepealed, contains consequential amendments; Sch 6 relates to transitional provisions and savings; Sch 7 contains repeals.*)

CIVIL JURISDICTION AND JUDGMENTS ACT 1982

(1982 c 27)

ARRANGEMENT OF SECTIONS

PART I
IMPLEMENTATION OF THE CONVENTIONS

Main implementing provisions

Supplementary provisions as to recognition and enforcement of judgments

Other supplementary provisions

PART II
JURISDICTION, AND RECOGNITION AND ENFORCEMENT OF JUDGMENTS, WITHIN UNITED KINGDOM

PART III
JURISDICTION IN SCOTLAND

PART IV
MISCELLANEOUS PROVISIONS

Provisions relating to jurisdiction

Provisions relating to recognition and enforcement of judgments

Jurisdiction, and recognition and enforcement of judgments, as between United Kingdom and certain territories

PART V
SUPPLEMENTARY AND GENERAL PROVISIONS

Domicile

PART I

An Act to make further provision about the jurisdiction of courts and tribunals in the United Kingdom and certain other territories and about the recognition and enforcement of judgments given in the United Kingdom or elsewhere; to provide for the modification of certain provisions relating to legal aid; and for connected purposes

[13 July 1982]

PART I
IMPLEMENTATION OF THE CONVENTIONS

Main implementing provisions

1 Interpretation of references to the Conventions and Contracting States

(1) In this Act—

"the 1968 Convention" means the Convention on jurisdiction and the enforcement of judgments in civil and commercial matters (including the Protocol annexed to that Convention), signed at Brussels on 27th September 1968;

"the 1971 Protocol" means the Protocol on the interpretation of the 1968 Convention by the European Court, signed at Luxembourg on 3rd June 1971;

"the Accession Convention" means the Convention on the accession to the 1968 Convention and the 1971 Protocol of Denmark, the Republic of Ireland and the United Kingdom, signed at Luxembourg on 9th October 1978;

["the 1982 Accession Convention" means the Convention on the accession of the Hellenic Republic to the 1968 Convention and the 1971 Protocol, with the adjustments made to them by the Accession Convention, signed at Luxembourg on 25th October 1982;]

["the 1989 Accession Convention" means the Convention on the accession of the Kingdom of Spain and the Portuguese Republic to the 1968 Convention and the 1971 Protocol, with the adjustments made to them by the Accession Convention and the 1982 Accession Convention, signed at Donostia—San Sebastián on 26th May 1989;]

["the 1996 Accession Convention" means the Convention on the accession of the Republic of Austria, the Republic of Finland and the Kingdom of Sweden to the 1968 Convention and the 1971 Protocol, with the adjustments made to them by the Accession Convention, the 1982 Accession Convention and the 1989 Accession Convention, signed at Brussels on 29th November 1996;]

[["the Brussels Conventions"] means the 1968 Convention, the 1971 Protocol, the Accession Convention, the 1982 Accession Convention[, the 1989 Accession Convention and the 1996 Accession Convention]]

["the Lugano Convention" means the Convention on jurisdiction and the enforcement of judgments in civil and commercial matters (including the Protocols annexed to that Convention) opened for signature at Lugano on 16th September 1988 and signed by the United Kingdom on 18th September 1989]

["the Regulation" means Council Regulation (EC) No 44/2001 of 22nd December 2000 on jurisdiction and the recognition and enforcement of judgments in civil and commercial matters].

(2) In this Act, unless the context otherwise requires—

[(a) references to, or to any provision of, the 1968 Convention or the 1971 Protocol are references to that Convention, Protocol or provision as amended by the Accession Convention, the 1982 Accession Convention[, the 1989 Accession Convention and the 1996 Accession Convention]; and]

[(aa) references to, or to any provision of, the Lugano Convention are references to that Convention as amended on the accession to it of Poland; and]

[(b) any reference in any provision to a numbered Article without more is a reference—

(i) to the Article so numbered of the 1968 Convention, in so far as the provision applies in relation to that Convention, and

(ii) to the Article so numbered of the Lugano Convention, in so far as the provision applies in relation to that Convention,

and any reference to a sub-division of a numbered Article shall be construed accordingly.]

[(3) [In this Act—

"Contracting State", without more, in any provision means—

(a) in the application of the provision in relation to the Brussels Conventions, a Brussels Contracting State; and

(b) in the application of the provision in relation to the Lugano Convention, a Lugano Contracting State;]

["Brussels Contracting State" means Denmark (which is not bound by the Regulation, but was one of the parties acceding to the 1968 Convention under the Accession Convention);]

["Lugano Contracting State" means—

(a) one of the original parties to the Lugano Convention, that is to say Austria, Belgium, Denmark, Finland, France, the Federal Republic of Germany, the Hellenic Republic, Iceland, the Republic of Ireland, Italy, Luxembourg, the Netherlands, Norway, Portugal, Spain, Sweden, Switzerland and the United Kingdom; or

(b) a party who has subsequently acceded to that Convention, that is to say, Poland]

being a State in relation to which that Convention has taken effect in accordance with paragraph 3 or 4 of Article 61.]

["Regulation State" in any provision, in the application of that provision in relation to the Regulation, has the same meaning as "Member State" in the Regulation, that is all Members States except Denmark].]

[(4) Any question arising as to whether it is the Regulation, any of the Brussels Conventions, or the Lugano Convention which applies in the circumstances of a particular case shall be determined as follows—

(a) in accordance with Article 54B of the Lugano Convention (which determines the relationship between the Brussels Conventions and the Lugano Convention); and

(b) in accordance with Article 68 of the Regulation (which determines the relationship between the Brussels Conventions and the Regulation).]

[50]

NOTES

Sub-s (1): definition "the 1982 Accession Convention" inserted by the Civil Jurisdiction and Judgments Act 1982 (Amendment) Order 1989, SI 1989/1346, art 3; definition "the 1989 Accession Convention" inserted by the Civil Jurisdiction and Judgments Act 1982 (Amendment) Order 1990, SI 1990/2591, art 3; definition "the 1996 Accession Convention" inserted by the Civil Jurisdiction and Judgments Act 1982 (Amendment) Order 2000, SI 2000/1824, art 3(a); definition "the Brussels Conventions" substituted for definition "the Conventions" by SI 1990/2591, art 4, words in first pair of square brackets therein substituted by the Civil Jurisdiction and Judgments Act 1991, s 2(1), (2), words in second pair of square brackets substituted by SI 2000/1824, art 3(b); definition "the Lugano Convention" added by the Civil Jurisdiction and Judgments Act 1991, s 2(1), (3); definition "the Regulation" added by the Civil Jurisdiction and Judgments Order 2001, SI 2001/3929, art 4, Sch 2, Pt I, para 1(a).

Sub-s (2): para (a) substituted by SI 1990/2591, art 5; words in square brackets in para (a) substituted, and para (aa) inserted, by SI 2000/1824, arts 4, 9; para (b) substituted by the Civil Jurisdiction and Judgments Act 1991, s 2(1), (4).

Sub-s (3): substituted by SI 1990/2591, art 6; words in first pair of square brackets substituted by the Civil Jurisdiction and Judgments Act 1991, s 2(1), (5); definition "Brussels Contracting State" substituted and definition "Regulation State" added by SI 2001/3929, art 4, Sch 2, Pt I, para 1(b); definition "Lugano Contracting State" inserted by the Civil Jurisdiction and Judgments Act 1991, s 2(1), (6), words in square brackets therein substituted by SI 2000/1824, art 10.

Sub-s (4): added by SI 2001/3929, art 4, Sch 2, Pt I, para 1(c).

2 The [Brussels Conventions] to have the force of law

(1) The [Brussels Conventions] shall have the force of law in the United Kingdom, and judicial notice shall be taken of them.

[(2) For convenience of reference there are set out in Schedules 1, 2, 3, 3A[, 3B and 3C] respectively the English texts of—

(a) the 1968 Convention as amended by Titles II and III of the Accession Convention, by Titles II and III of the 1982 Accession Convention … by Titles II and III of, and Annex I(d) to, the 1989 Accession Convention [and by Titles II and III of the 1996 Accession Convention];

(b) the 1971 Protocol as amended by Title IV of the Accession Convention, by Title IV of the 1982 Accession Convention … by Title IV of the 1989 Accession Convention [and by Title IV of the 1996 Accession Convention];

(c) Titles V and VI of the Accession Convention (transitional and final provisions) as amended by Title V of the 1989 Accession Convention;

(d) Titles V and VI of the 1982 Accession Convention (transitional and final provisions); and

(e) Titles VI and VII of the 1989 Accession Convention (transitional and final provisions),

[(f) Titles V and VI of the 1996 Accession Convention (transitional and final provisions),]

being texts prepared from the authentic English texts referred to in Articles 37 and 41 of the Accession Convention, in Article 17 of the 1982 Accession Convention[, in Article 34 of the 1989 Accession Convention and in Article 18 of the 1996 Accession Convention].]

[51]

NOTES

Section heading, sub-s (1): words in square brackets substituted by the Civil Jurisdiction and Judgments Act 1991, s 3, Sch 2, para 1.

Sub-s (2): substituted by the Civil Jurisdiction and Judgments Act 1982 (Amendment) Order 1990, SI 1990/2591, art 7; words in first and final pairs of square brackets substituted, words omitted repealed, words in square brackets in paras (a), (b) inserted and para (f) added by the Civil Jurisdiction and Judgments Act 1982 (Amendment) Order 2000, SI 2000/1824, art 6.

The 1968 Brussels Convention (as amended) has been largely superseded by Council Regulation 44/2001/EC – see Introductory Note at the beginning of Part IV(B) at para **[3029]**.

3 Interpretation of the [Brussels Conventions]

(1) Any question as to the meaning or effect of any provision of the [Brussels Conventions] shall, if not referred to the European Court in accordance with the 1971 Protocol, be determined in accordance with the principles laid down by and any relevant decision of the European Court.

(2) Judicial notice shall be taken of any decision of, or expression of opinion by, the European Court on any such question.

(3) Without prejudice to the generality of subsection (1), the following reports (which are reproduced in the Official Journal of the Communities), namely—

(a) the reports by Mr P Jenard on the 1968 Convention and the 1971 Protocol; and

(b) the report by Professor Peter Schlosser on the Accession Convention[; and

(c) the report by Professor Demetrios I Evrigenis and Professor K D Kerameus on the 1982 Accession Convention][; and

(d) the report by Mr Martinho de Almeida Cruz, Mr Manuel Desantes Real and Mr P Jenard on the 1989 Accession Convention,]

may be considered in ascertaining the meaning or effect of any provision of the [Brussels Conventions] and shall be given such weight as is appropriate in the circumstances.

[52]

NOTES

Section heading, sub-s (1): words in square brackets substituted by the Civil Jurisdiction and Judgments Act 1991, s 3, Sch 2, para 1.

Sub-s (3): words in first pair of square brackets inserted by the Civil Jurisdiction and Judgments Act 1982 (Amendment) Order 1989, SI 1989/1346, art 8; word in second pair of square brackets inserted by the Civil Jurisdiction and Judgments Act 1982 (Amendment) Order 1990, SI 1990/2591, art 8; words in third pair of square brackets substituted by the Civil Jurisdiction and Judgments Act 1991, s 3, Sch 2, para 1.

[3A The Lugano Convention to have the force of law

(1) The Lugano Convention shall have the force of law in the United Kingdom, and judicial notice shall be taken of it.

(2) For convenience of reference there is set out in Schedule 3C the English text of the Lugano Convention [as amended on the accession of Poland to that Convention].]

[53]

NOTES

Inserted, together with s 3B at **[54]**, by the Civil Jurisdiction and Judgments Act 1991, s 1(1).

Sub-s (2): words in square brackets added by the Civil Jurisdiction and Judgments Act 1982 (Amendment) Order 2000, SI 2000/1824, art 11.

See further the Introductory Note at the beginning of Part IV(B) at para **[3029]**.

[3B Interpretation of the Lugano Convention

(1) In determining any question as to the meaning or effect of a provision of the Lugano Convention, a court in the United Kingdom shall, in accordance with Protocol No 2 to that Convention, take account of any principles laid down in any relevant decision delivered by a court of any other Lugano Contracting State concerning provisions of the Convention.

(2) Without prejudice to any practice of the courts as to the matters which may be considered apart from this section, the report on the Lugano Convention by Mr P Jenard and Mr G Möller (which is reproduced in the Official Journal of the Communities of 28th July 1990) may be considered in ascertaining the meaning or effect of any provision of the Convention and shall be given such weight as is appropriate in the circumstances.]

[54]

NOTES

Inserted as noted to s 3A at **[53]**.

Supplementary provisions as to recognition and enforcement of judgments

4 Enforcement of judgments other than maintenance orders

(1) A judgment, other than a maintenance order, which is the subject of an application under Article 31 [of the 1968 Convention or of the Lugano Convention] for its enforcement in any part of the United Kingdom shall, to the extent that its enforcement is authorised by the appropriate court, be registered in the prescribed manner in that court.

In this subsection "the appropriate court" means the court to which the application is made in pursuance of Article 32 (that is to say, the High Court or the Court of Session).

(2) Where a judgment is registered under this section, the reasonable costs or expenses of and incidental to its registration shall be recoverable as if they were sums recoverable under the judgment.

(3) A judgment registered under this section shall, for the purposes of its enforcement, be of the same force and effect, the registering court shall have in relation to its enforcement the same powers, and proceedings for or with respect to its enforcement may be taken, as if the judgment had been originally given by the registering court and had (where relevant) been entered.

(4) Subsection (3) is subject to Article 39 (restriction on enforcement where appeal pending or time for appeal unexpired), to section 7 and to any provision made by rules of court as to the manner in which and conditions subject to which a judgment registered under this section may be enforced.

[55]

NOTES

Sub-s (1): words in square brackets inserted by the Civil Jurisdiction and Judgments Act 1991, s 3, Sch 2, para 2.

This section is modified, in relation to its application to authentic instruments and court settlements which are maintenance orders, by the Civil Jurisdiction and Judgments (Authentic Instruments and Court Settlements) Order 1993, SI 1993/604, art 2 at **[2121]**.

5 (*Relates to maintenance orders.*)

6 Appeals under Article 37, second paragraph and Article 41

(1) The single further appeal on a point of law referred to [in the 1968 Convention and the Lugano Convention] in Article 37, second paragraph and Article 41 in relation to the recognition or enforcement of a judgment other than a maintenance order lies—

(a) in England and Wales or Northern Ireland, to the Court of Appeal or to the *House of Lords* in accordance with Part II of the Administration of Justice Act 1969 (appeals direct from the High Court to the *House of Lords*);

(b) in Scotland, to the Inner House of the Court of Session.

(2) Paragraph (a) of subsection (1) has effect notwithstanding section 15(2) of the Administration of Justice Act 1969 (exclusion of direct appeal to *the House of Lords* in cases where no appeal to *that House* lies from a decision of the Court of Appeal).

(3) The single further appeal on a point of law referred to [in each of those Conventions] in Article 37, second paragraph and Article 41 in relation to the recognition or enforcement of a maintenance order lies—

(a) in England and Wales, to the High Court by way of case stated in accordance with section 111 of the Magistrates' Courts Act 1980;

(b) in Scotland, to the Inner House of the Court of Session;

(c) (*applies to Northern Ireland only*).

[56]

NOTES

Sub-s (1): words in square brackets inserted by the Civil Jurisdiction and Judgments Act 1991, s 3, Sch 2, para 3; words in italics substituted by the words "Supreme Court" by the Constitutional Reform Act 2005, s 40(4), Sch 9, Pt 1, para 39(a), as from a day to be appointed.

Sub-s (2): words in italics substituted by the words "the Supreme Court" by the Constitutional Reform Act 2005, s 40(4), Sch 9, Pt 1, para 39(b), as from a day to be appointed.

Sub-s (3): words in square brackets inserted by the Civil Jurisdiction and Judgments Act 1991, s 3, Sch 2, para 3.

This section is modified in relation to authentic instruments and court settlements which are not maintenance orders, and in relation to authentic instruments and court settlements which are maintenance orders, by the Civil Jurisdiction and Judgments (Authentic Instruments and Court Settlements) Order 1993, SI 1993/604, arts 2, 3 at **[2122]**, **[2123]**.

7 Interest on registered judgments

(1) Subject to subsection (4), where in connection with an application for registration of a judgment under section 4 or 5 the applicant shows—

(a) that the judgment provides for the payment of a sum of money; and

(b) that in accordance with the law of the Contracting State in which the judgment was given interest on that sum is recoverable under the judgment from a particular date or time,

the rate of interest and the date or time from which it is so recoverable shall be registered with the judgment and, subject to any provision made under subsection (2), the debt resulting, apart from section 4(2), from the registration of the judgment shall carry interest in accordance with the registered particulars.

(2) Provision may be made by rules of court as to the manner in which and the periods by reference to which any interest payable by virtue of subsection (1) is to be calculated and paid, including provision for such interest to cease to accrue as from a prescribed date.

(3) Costs or expenses recoverable by virtue of section 4(2) shall carry interest as if they were the subject of an order for the payment of costs or expenses made by the registering court on the date of registration.

(4) (*Relates to maintenance awards.*)

(5) Except as mentioned in subsection (4), debts under judgments registered under section 4 or 5 shall carry interest only as provided by this section.

[57]

NOTES

This section is modified in relation to authentic instruments and court settlements which are not maintenance orders, and in relation to authentic instruments and court settlements which are maintenance orders, by the Civil Jurisdiction and Judgments (Authentic Instruments and Court Settlements) Order 1993, SI 1993/604, arts 2, 3 at **[2122]**, **[2123]**.

8 (*Relates to maintenance awards.*)

Other supplementary provisions

9 Provisions supplementary to Title VII of 1968 Convention

(1) The provisions of Title VII of the 1968 Convention [and, apart from Article 54B, of Title VII of the Lugano Convention] (relationship between [the Convention in question] and other conventions to which Contracting States are or may become parties) shall have effect in relation to—

(a) any statutory provision, whenever passed or made, implementing any such other convention in the United Kingdom; and

(b) any rule of law so far as it has the effect of so implementing any such other convention,

as they have effect in relation to that other convention itself.

[(1A) …]

(2) Her Majesty may by Order in Council declare a provision of a convention entered into by the United Kingdom to be a provision whereby the United Kingdom assumed an obligation of a kind provided for in Article 59 (which allows a Contracting State to agree with a third State to withhold recognition in certain cases from a judgment given by a court in another Contracting State which took jurisdiction on one of the grounds mentioned in the second paragraph of Article 3).

[58]

NOTES

Sub-s (1): words in first pair of square brackets inserted, and words in second pair of square brackets substituted, by the Civil Jurisdiction and Judgments Act 1991, s 3, Sch 2, para 4.

"Any statutory provision" etc (in sub-s (1)(a)) – see final note to Foreign Judgments (Reciprocal Enforcement) Act 1933, s 1 at **[16]** above.

Sub-s (1A): inserted by the Civil Jurisdiction and Judgments Act 1991, s 1(2); repealed by the Civil Jurisdiction and Judgments Order 2001, SI 2001/3929, art 4, Sch 2, Pt I, para 2.

Orders in Council (sub-s (2)): the Reciprocal Enforcement of Foreign Judgments (Canada) Order 1987, SI 1987/468 at **[2108]**; the Reciprocal Enforcement of Foreign Judgments (Australia) Order 1994, SI 1994/1901 at **[2129]**.

In addition, by virtue of Art 57 of the 1968 Convention (set out in Pt IV(B) of this work at **[3029]**) and Art 57 of the Lugano Convention (set out in Pt IV(B) of this work at **[3069]**), other multilateral conventions which, in relation to particular matters, govern jurisdiction or the recognition or enforcement of judgments, are unaffected by those Conventions. The main conventions are listed in note 59 in Annex II to the report by Professor Peter Schlosser on the Accession Convention, set out in Pt IV(B) of this work at **[3047M]**.

10 Allocation within UK of jurisdiction with respect to trusts and consumer contracts

(1) The provisions of this section have effect for the purpose of allocating within the United Kingdom jurisdiction in certain proceedings in respect of which the 1968 Convention [or the Lugano Convention] confers jurisdiction on the courts of the United Kingdom generally and to which section 16 does not apply.

(2) Any proceedings which by virtue of Article 5(6) (trusts) are brought in the United Kingdom shall be brought in the courts of the part of the United Kingdom in which the trust is domiciled.

(3) Any proceedings which by virtue of the first paragraph of Article 14 (consumer contracts) are brought in the United Kingdom by a consumer on the ground that he is himself domiciled there shall be brought in the courts of the part of the United Kingdom in which he is domiciled.

[59]

NOTES

Sub-s (1): words in square brackets inserted by the Civil Jurisdiction and Judgments Act 1991, s 3, Sch 2, para 5.

11 Proof and admissibility of certain judgments and related documents

(1) For the purposes of the 1968 Convention [and the Lugano Convention]—

(a) a document, duly authenticated, which purports to be a copy of a judgment given by a court of a Contracting State other than the United Kingdom shall without further proof be deemed to be a true copy, unless the contrary is shown; and

(b) the original or a copy of any such document as is mentioned in Article 46(2) or 47 (supporting documents to be produced by a party seeking recognition or enforcement of a judgment) shall be evidence, and in Scotland sufficient evidence, of any matter to which it relates.

(2) A document purporting to be a copy of a judgment given by any such court as is mentioned in subsection (1)(a) is duly authenticated for the purposes of this section if it purports—

(a) to bear the seal of that court; or

(b) to be certified by any person in his capacity as a judge or officer of that court to be a true copy of a judgment given by that court.

(3) Nothing in this section shall prejudice the admission in evidence of any document which is admissible apart from this section.

[60]

NOTES

Sub-s (1): words in square brackets inserted by the Civil Jurisdiction and Judgments Act 1991, s 3, Sch 2, para 6.

This section is modified in relation to its application to authentic instruments and court settlements by the Civil Jurisdiction and Judgments (Authentic Instruments and Court Settlements) Order 1993, SI 1993/604, art 4 at **[2124]**.

12 Provision for issue of copies of, and certificates in connection with, UK judgments

Rules of court may make provision for enabling any interested party wishing to secure under the 1968 Convention [or the Lugano Convention] the recognition or enforcement in another Contracting State of a judgment given by a court in the United Kingdom to obtain, subject to any conditions specified in the rules—

(a) a copy of the judgment; and

(b) a certificate giving particulars relating to the judgment and the proceedings in which it was given.

[61]

NOTES

Words in square brackets inserted by the Civil Jurisdiction and Judgments Act 1991, s 3, Sch 2, para 7.

This section is modified in relation to its application to authentic instruments and court settlements by the Civil Jurisdiction and Judgments (Authentic Instruments and Court Settlements) Order 1993, SI 1993/604, art 5 at **[2125]**.

Rules of court: the Magistrates' Courts (Civil Jurisdiction and Judgments Act 1982) Rules 1986, SI 1986/1962. See also Civil Procedure Rules 1998, SI 1998/3132, rr 74.12 and 74.13 at **[1528], [1529]**; Act of Sederunt (Rules of the Court of Session 1994) 1994, SI 1994/1443, r 62.40 at **[1169]**.

13 Modifications to cover authentic instruments and court settlements

(1) Her Majesty may by Order in Council provide that—

(a) any provision of this Act relating to the recognition or enforcement in the United Kingdom or elsewhere of judgments to which the 1968 Convention [or the Lugano Convention] applies; and

(b) any other statutory provision, whenever passed or made, so relating,

shall apply, with such modifications as may be specified in the Order, in relation to documents and settlements within Title IV of the 1968 Convention [or, as the case may be, Title IV of the Lugano Convention] (authentic instruments and court settlements enforceable in the same manner as judgments) as if they were judgments to which [the Convention in question] applies.

(2) An Order in Council under this section may make different provision in relation to different descriptions of documents and settlements.

(3) Any Order in Council under this section shall be subject to annulment in pursuance of a resolution of either House of Parliament.

[62]

NOTES

Sub-s (1): words in first and second pairs of square brackets inserted, and words in third pair of square brackets substituted, by the Civil Jurisdiction and Judgments Act 1991, s 3, Sch 2, para 8.

Orders in Council: the Civil Jurisdiction and Judgments (Authentic Instruments and Court Settlements) Order 1993, SI 1993/604 at **[2121]**.

14 Modifications consequential on revision of the Conventions

(1) If at any time it appears to Her Majesty in Council that Her Majesty's Government in the United Kingdom have agreed to a revision of [the Lugano Convention or any of the Brussels Conventions], including in particular any revision connected with the accession to [the Lugano Convention or] the 1968 Convention of one or more further states, Her Majesty may by Order in Council make such modifications of this Act or any other statutory provision, whenever passed or made, as Her Majesty considers appropriate in consequence of the revision.

(2) An Order in Council under this section shall not be made unless a draft of the Order has been laid before Parliament and approved by a resolution of each House of Parliament.

(3) In this section "revision" means an omission from, addition to or alteration of [the Lugano Convention or any of the Brussels Conventions] and includes replacement of [the Lugano Convention or any of the Brussels Conventions] to any extent by another convention, protocol or other description of international agreement.

[63]

NOTES

Sub-s (1): words in first pair of square brackets substituted, and words in second pair of square brackets inserted, by the Civil Jurisdiction and Judgments Act 1991, s 3, Sch 2, para 9.

Sub-s (3): words in square brackets substituted by the Civil Jurisdiction and Judgments Act 1991, s 3, Sch 2, para 9.

15 Interpretation of Part I and consequential amendments

(1) In this Part, unless the context otherwise requires—

"judgment" has the meaning given by Article 25;

"maintenance order" means a maintenance judgment within the meaning of the 1968 Convention [or, as the case may be, the Lugano Convention];

"payer", in relation to a maintenance order, means the person liable to make the payments for which the order provides;

"prescribed" means prescribed by rules of court.

(2) References in this Part to a judgment registered under section 4 or 5 include, to the extent of its registration, references to a judgment so registered to a limited extent only.

(3) Anything authorised or required by the 1968 Convention [the Lugano Convention] or this Part to be done by, to or before a particular magistrates' court may be done by, to or before any magistrates' court acting [in the same local justice area (or, in Northern Ireland, for the same] petty sessions district) as that court.

(4) The enactments specified in Part I of Schedule 12 shall have effect with the amendments specified there, being amendments consequential on this Part.

[64]

NOTES

Sub-s (1): words in square brackets inserted by the Civil Jurisdiction and Judgments Act 1991, s 3, Sch 2, para 10.

Sub-s (3): words in first pair of square brackets inserted by the Civil Jurisdiction and Judgments Act 1991, s 3, Sch 2, para 10; words in second pair of square brackets substituted by the Courts Act 2003, s 109(1), Sch 8, para 269.

This section is modified in relation to its application to authentic instruments and court settlements by the Civil Jurisdiction and Judgments (Authentic Instruments and Court Settlements) Order 1993, SI 1993/604, art 6 at **[2121]**.

PART II
JURISDICTION, AND RECOGNITION AND ENFORCEMENT OF JUDGMENTS, WITHIN UNITED KINGDOM

16 Allocation within UK of jurisdiction in certain civil proceedings

(1) The provisions set out in Schedule 4 (which contains a modified version of [Chapter II of the Regulation]) shall have effect for determining, for each part of the United Kingdom, whether the courts of law of that part, or any particular court of law in that part, have or has jurisdiction in proceedings where—

[(a) the subject-matter of the proceedings is within the scope of the Regulation as determined by Article 1 of the Regulation (whether or not the Regulation has effect in relation to the proceedings); and]

(b) the defendant or defender is domiciled in the United Kingdom or the proceedings are of a kind mentioned in [Article 22 of the Regulation] (exclusive jurisdiction regardless of domicile).

(2) …

(3) In determining any question as to the meaning or effect of any provision contained in Schedule 4—

(a) regard shall be had to any relevant principles laid down by the European Court in connection with Title II of the 1968 Convention [or Chapter II of the Regulation] and to any relevant decision of that court as to the meaning or effect of any provision of that Title [or that Chapter]; and

(b) without prejudice to the generality of paragraph (a), the reports mentioned in section 3(3) may be considered and shall, so far as relevant, be given such weight as is appropriate in the circumstances.

(4) The provisions of this section and Schedule 4 shall have effect subject to [the Regulation,] the 1968 Convention [and the Lugano Convention] and to the provisions of section 17.

(5) …

[65]

NOTES

Sub-s (1): words in square brackets substituted by the Civil Jurisdiction and Judgments Order 2001, SI 2001/3929, art 4, Sch 2, Pt II, para 3(a).

Sub-s (2): repealed by SI 2001/3929, art 4, Sch 2, Pt II, para 3(b).

Sub-s (3): words in square brackets inserted by SI 2001/3929, art 4, Sch 2, Pt II, para 3(c).

Sub-s (4): words in first pair of square brackets inserted by SI 2001/3929, art 4, Sch 2, Pt II, para 3(d); words in second pair of square brackets inserted by the Civil Jurisdiction and Judgments Act 1991, s 3, Sch 2, para 11.

Sub-s (5): amends the Maintenance Orders Act 1950, s 15(1)(a).
Transitional provision: see s 53(2), Sch 13, Pt II, para 1 at **[97]**, **[111]**.

17 Exclusion of certain proceedings from Schedule 4

(1) Schedule 4 shall not apply to proceedings of any description listed in Schedule 5 or to proceedings in Scotland under any enactment which confers jurisdiction on a Scottish court in respect of a specific subject-matter on specific grounds.

(2) Her Majesty may by Order in Council—

(a) add to the list in Schedule 5 any description of proceedings in any part of the United Kingdom; and

(b) remove from that list any description of proceedings in any part of the United Kingdom (whether included in the list as originally enacted or added by virtue of this subsection).

(3) An Order in Council under subsection (2)—

(a) may make different provisions for different descriptions of proceedings, for the same description of proceedings in different courts or for different parts of the United Kingdom; and

(b) may contain such transitional and other incidental provisions as appear to Her Majesty to be appropriate.

(4) An Order in Council under subsection (2) shall not be made unless a draft of the Order has been laid before Parliament and approved by a resolution of each House of Parliament.

NOTES

Orders in Council: none have yet been made under sub-s (2).

[66]

18 Enforcement of UK judgments in other parts of UK

(1) In relation to any judgment to which this section applies—

(a) Schedule 6 shall have effect for the purpose of enabling any money provisions contained in the judgment to be enforced in a part of the United Kingdom other than the part in which the judgment was given; and

(b) Schedule 7 shall have effect for the purpose of enabling any non-money provisions so contained to be so enforced.

(2) In this section "judgment" means any of the following (references to the giving of a judgment being construed accordingly)—

(a) any judgment or order (by whatever name called) given or made by a court of law in the United Kingdom;

(b) any judgment or order not within paragraph (a) which has been entered in England and Wales or Northern Ireland in the High Court or a county court;

(c) any document which in Scotland has been registered for execution in the Books of Council and Session or in the sheriff court books kept for any sheriffdom;

(d) any award or order made by a tribunal in any part of the United Kingdom which is enforceable in that part without an order of a court of law;

(e) an arbitration award which has become enforceable in the part of the United Kingdom in which it was given in the same manner as a judgment given by a court of law in that part;

[(f) an order made, or a warrant issued, under Part 8 of the Proceeds of Crime Act 2002 for the purposes of a civil recovery investigation within the meaning given by section 341 of that Act;]

and, subject to the following provisions of this section, this section applies to all such judgments.

(3) Subject to subsection (4), this section does not apply to—

(a) a judgment given in proceedings in a magistrates' court in England and Wales or Northern Ireland;

(b) a judgment given in proceedings other than civil proceedings;

[(ba) a judgment given in the exercise of jurisdiction in relation to insolvency law, within the meaning of section [426 of the Insolvency Act 1986];]

(c) a judgment given in proceedings relating to—

(i), (ii) …
(iii) the obtaining of title to administer the estate of a deceased person.
[(d) an order made under Part 2, 3 or 4 of the Proceeds of Crime Act 2002 (confiscation).]

(4) This section applies, whatever the nature of the proceedings in which it is made, to—
(a) a decree issued under section 13 of the Court of Exchequer (Scotland) Act 1856 (recovery of certain rentcharges and penalties by process of the Court of Session);
(b) an order which is enforceable in the same manner as a judgment of the High Court in England and Wales by virtue of section 16 of the Contempt of Court Act 1981 or section 140 of the *Supreme Court Act 1981* (which relate to fines for contempt of court and forfeiture of recognisances).

[(4A) This section does not apply as respects—
(a) the enforcement in Scotland of orders made by the High Court or a county court in England and Wales under or for the purposes of Part VI of the Criminal Justice Act 1988 or the Drug Trafficking Act 1994 (confiscation of the proceeds of certain offences or of drug trafficking); or
(b) the enforcement in England and Wales of orders made by the Court of Session [or by the sheriff] under or for the purposes of [the Proceeds of Crime (Scotland) Act 1995].]

(5) This section does not apply to so much of any judgment as—
(a) is an order to which section 16 of the Maintenance Orders Act 1950 applies (and is therefore an order for whose enforcement in another part of the United Kingdom provision is made by Part II of that Act);
(b) concerns the status or legal capacity of an individual;
(c) relates to the management of the affairs of a person not capable of managing his own affairs;
(d) is a provisional (including protective) measure other than an order for the making of an interim payment;

and except where otherwise stated references to a judgment to which this section applies are to such a judgment exclusive of any such provisions.

(6) The following are within subsection (5)(b), but without prejudice to the generality of that provision—
(a) *a decree* of judicial separation or of separation;
[(b) any order which is a Part I order for the purposes of the Family Law Act 1986.]

(7) This section does not apply to a judgment of a court outside the United Kingdom which falls to be treated for the purposes of its enforcement as a judgment of a court of law in the United Kingdom by virtue of registration under Part II of the Administration of Justice Act 1920, Part I of the Foreign Judgments (Reciprocal Enforcement) Act 1933, Part I of the Maintenance Orders (Reciprocal Enforcement) Act 1972 or section 4 or 5 of this Act.

(8) A judgment to which this section applies, other than a judgment within paragraph (e) of subsection (2), shall not be enforced in another part of the United Kingdom except by way of registration under Schedule 6 or 7.

[67]

NOTES

Sub-s (2): para (f) added by the Proceeds of Crime Act 2002 (Investigations in different parts of the United Kingdom) Order 2003, SI 2003/425, art 34.

Sub-s (3): para (ba) inserted, and sub-paras (c)(i), (ii) repealed, by the Insolvency Act 1985, s 235(1), (3), Sch 8, para 36, Sch 10, Pt IV; words in square brackets in para (ba) substituted by the Insolvency Act 1986, s 439(2), Sch 14; para (d) added by the Proceeds of Crime Act 2002, s 456, Sch 11, paras 1, 11.

Sub-s (4): words in italics substituted by the words "Senior Courts Act 1981" by the Constitutional Reform Act 2005, s 59(5), Sch 11, Pt 1, para 1(2), as from a day to be appointed.

Sub-s (4A): inserted by the Drug Trafficking Offences Act 1986, s 39(4); substituted by the Drug Trafficking Act 1994, s 65(1), Sch 1, para 6; words in first pair of square brackets inserted by the Criminal Justice (Scotland) Act 1995, s 117, Sch 6, para 183; words in second pair of square brackets substituted by the Criminal Procedure (Consequential Provisions) (Scotland) Act 1995, ss 4, 5, Sch 3, Sch 4, para 42.

Sub-s (6): words in italics in para (a) substituted by the words "an order or decree" by the Family Law Act 1996, s 66(1), Sch 8, para 30, as from a day to be appointed, subject to savings in s 66(2), Sch 9, para 5 thereof; para (b) substituted by the Courts and Legal Services Act 1990, s 116, Sch 16, para 41.

This section is modified in relation to its application to authentic instruments and court settlements by the Civil Jurisdiction and Judgments (Authentic Instruments and Court Settlements) Order 1993, SI 1993/604, art 7 at **[2121]**.

In relation to the disapplication of this section as respects the enforcement in England and Wales of orders made by the High Court in Northern Ireland under the Criminal Justice (Confiscation) (Northern Ireland) Order 1990, on or after 1 September 1995, in relation to drug trafficking offences, see the Drug Trafficking Act 1994 (Enforcement of Northern Ireland Confiscation Orders) Order 1995, SI 1995/1967, art 2(2).

In relation to the disapplication of this section as respects the enforcement in England and Wales of orders made by the High Court in Northern Ireland under the Criminal Justice (Confiscation) (Northern Ireland) Order 1990, on or after 1 September 1995, in relation to offences other than drug trafficking offences, see the Criminal Justice Act 1988 (Enforcement of Northern Ireland Confiscation Orders) Order 1995, SI 1995/1968, art 2(2).

Transitional provision: see s 53(2), Sch 13, Pt II, paras 2, 3 at **[97]**, **[111]**.

Regulations: the Employment Tribunals (Enforcement of Orders in Other Jurisdictions) (Scotland) Regulations 2002, SI 2002/2972.

19 Recognition of UK judgments in other parts of UK

(1) A judgment to which this section applies given in one part of the United Kingdom shall not be refused recognition in another part of the United Kingdom solely on the ground that, in relation to that judgment, the court which gave it was not a court of competent jurisdiction according to the rules of private international law in force in that other part.

(2) Subject to subsection (3), this section applies to any judgment to which section 18 applies.

(3) This section does not apply to—

(a) the documents mentioned in paragraph (c) of the definition of "judgment" in section 18(2);

(b) the awards and orders mentioned in paragraphs (d) and (e) of that definition;

(c) the decrees and orders referred to in section 18(4).

[68]

NOTES

Transitional provision: see s 53(2), Sch 13, Pt II, para 4 at **[97]**, **[111]**.

PART III
JURISDICTION IN SCOTLAND

20 Rules as to jurisdiction in Scotland

(1) Subject to [the Regulation, to] Parts I and II and to the following provisions of this Part, Schedule 8 has effect to determine in what circumstances a person may be sued in civil proceedings in the Court of Session or in a sheriff court.

(2) Nothing in Schedule 8 affects the competence as respects subject-matter or value of the Court of Session or of the sheriff court.

(3) Section 6 of the Sheriff Courts (Scotland) Act 1907 shall cease to have effect to the extent that it determines jurisdiction in relation to any matter to which Schedule 8 applies.

(4) …

(5) In determining any question as to the meaning or effect of any provision contained in Schedule 8 …—

(a) regard shall be had to any relevant principles laid down by the European Court in connection with Title II of the 1968 Convention [or Chapter II of the Regulation] and to any relevant decision of that court as to the meaning or effect of any provision of that Title [or that Chapter]; and

(b) without prejudice to the generality of paragraph (a), the reports mentioned in section 3(3) may be considered and shall, so far as relevant, be given such weight as is appropriate in the circumstances.

[69]

NOTES

Sub-s (1): words in square brackets inserted by the Civil Jurisdiction and Judgments Order 2001, SI 2001/3929, art 4, Sch 2, Pt III, para 6(a).

Sub-s (4): repealed by SI 2001/3929, art 4, Sch 2, Pt III, para 6(b).

Sub-s (5): words omitted repealed and words in square brackets inserted by SI 2001/3929, art 4, Sch 2, Pt III, para 6(c).

Transitional provision: see s 53(2), Sch 13, Pt II, para 5 at **[97]**, **[111]**.

21 Continuance of certain existing jurisdictions

(1) Schedule 8 does not affect—

(a) the operation of any enactment which confers jurisdiction on a Scottish court in respect of a specific subject-matter on specific grounds;

(b) without prejudice to the foregoing generality, the jurisdiction of any court in respect of any matter mentioned in Schedule 9.

(2) Her Majesty may by Order in Council—

(a) add to the list in Schedule 9 any description of proceedings; and

(b) remove from that list any description of proceedings (whether included in the list as originally enacted or added by virtue of this subsection).

(3) An Order in Council under subsection (2) may—

(a) make different provision for different descriptions of proceedings or for the same description of proceedings in different courts; and

(b) contain such transitional and other incidental provisions as appear to Her Majesty to be appropriate.

(4) An Order in Council under subsection (2) shall not be made unless a draft of the Order has been laid before Parliament and approved by a resolution of each House of Parliament.

[70]

22 Supplementary provisions

(1) Nothing in Schedule 8 shall prevent a court from declining jurisdiction on the ground of *forum non conveniens*.

(2) Nothing in Schedule 8 affects the operation of any enactment or rule of law under which a court may decline to exercise jurisdiction because of the prorogation by parties of the jurisdiction of another court.

(3) For the avoidance of doubt, it is declared that nothing in Schedule 8 affects the *nobile officium* of the Court of Session.

(4) Where a court has jurisdiction in any proceedings by virtue of Schedule 8, that court shall also have jurisdiction to determine any matter which—

(a) is ancillary or incidental to the proceedings; or

(b) requires to be determined for the purposes of a decision in the proceedings.

[71]

23 Savings and consequential amendments

(1) Nothing in Schedule 8 shall affect—

(a) the power of any court to vary or recall a maintenance order granted by that court;

(b) the power of a sheriff court under section 22 of the Maintenance Orders Act 1950 (discharge and variation of maintenance orders registered in sheriff courts) to vary or discharge a maintenance order registered in that court under Part II of that Act; or

(c) the power of a sheriff court under section 9 of the Maintenance Orders (Reciprocal Enforcement) Act 1972 (variation and revocation of maintenance orders registered in United Kingdom courts) to vary or revoke a registered order within the meaning of Part I of that Act.

(2) The enactments specified in Part II of Schedule 12 shall have effect with the amendments specified there, being amendments consequential on Schedule 8.

[72]

PART IV
MISCELLANEOUS PROVISIONS

Provisions relating to jurisdiction

24 Interim relief and protective measures in cases of doubtful jurisdiction

(1) Any power of a court in England and Wales or Northern Ireland to grant interim relief pending trial or pending the determination of an appeal shall extend to a case where—

(a) the issue to be tried, or which is the subject of the appeal, relates to the jurisdiction of the court to entertain the proceedings; or

(b) the proceedings involve the reference of any matter to the European Court under the 1971 Protocol[; or

(c) the proceedings involve a reference of any matter relating to the Regulation to the European Court under Article 68 of the Treaty establishing the European Community].

(2) Any power of a court in Scotland to grant protective measures pending the decision of any hearing shall apply to a case where—

(a) the subject of the proceedings includes a question as to the jurisdiction of the court to entertain them; or

(b) the proceedings involve the reference of a matter to the European Court under the 1971 Protocol[; or

(c) the proceedings involve a reference of any matter relating to the Regulation to the European Court under Article 68 of the Treaty establishing the European Community].

(3) Subsections (1) and (2) shall not be construed as restricting any power to grant interim relief or protective measures which a court may have apart from this section.

[73]

NOTES

Sub-ss (1), (2): para (c) and word "or" immediately preceding it added by the Civil Jurisdiction and Judgments Order 2001, SI 2001/3929, art 4, Sch 2, Pt IV, para 9.

25 Interim relief in England and Wales and Northern Ireland in the absence of substantive proceedings

(1) The High Court in England and Wales or Northern Ireland shall have power to grant interim relief where—

(a) proceedings have been or are to be commenced in a [Brussels or Lugano Contracting State] [or a Regulation State] other than the United Kingdom or in a part of the United Kingdom other than that in which the High Court in question exercises jurisdiction; and

[(b) they are or will be proceedings whose subject-matter is within the scope of the Regulation as determined by Article 1 of the Regulation (whether or not the Regulation has effect in relation to the proceedings).]

(2) On an application for any interim relief under subsection (1) the court may refuse to grant that relief if, in the opinion of the court, the fact that the court has no jurisdiction apart from this section in relation to the subject-matter of the proceedings in question makes it inexpedient for the court to grant it.

(3) Her Majesty may by Order in Council extend the power to grant interim relief conferred by subsection (1) so as to make it exercisable in relation to proceedings of any of the following descriptions, namely—

(a) proceedings commenced or to be commenced otherwise than in a [Brussels or Lugano Contracting State] [or Regulation State];

[(b) proceedings whose subject-matter is not within the scope of the Regulation as determined by Article 1 of the Regulation;]

(c) …

(4) An Order in Council under subsection (3)—

(a) may confer power to grant only specified descriptions of interim relief;

(b) may make different provision for different classes of proceedings, for proceedings pending in different countries or courts outside the United Kingdom or in different parts of the United Kingdom, and for other different circumstances; and

(c) may impose conditions or restrictions on the exercise of any power conferred by the Order.

(5) …

(6) Any Order in Council under subsection (3) shall be subject to annulment in pursuance of a resolution of either House of Parliament.

(7) In this section "interim relief", in relation to the High Court in England and Wales or Northern Ireland, means interim relief of any kind which that court has power to grant in proceedings relating to matters within its jurisdiction, other than—

(a) a warrant for the arrest of property; or
(b) provision for obtaining evidence.

[74]

NOTES

Sub-s (1): words in first pair of square brackets substituted by the Civil Jurisdiction and Judgments Act 1991, s 3, Sch 2, para 12; words in second pair of square brackets inserted and para (b) substituted by the Civil Jurisdiction and Judgments Order 2001, SI 2001/3929, art 4, Sch 2, Pt IV, para 10(a).

Sub-s (3): words in first pair of square brackets substituted by the Civil Jurisdiction and Judgments Act 1991, s 3, Sch 2, para 12; words in second pair of square brackets inserted and para (b) substituted by SI 2001/3929, art 4, Sch 2, Pt IV, para 10(b); para (c) repealed by the Arbitration Act 1996, s 107(2), Sch 4.

Sub-s (5): repealed by the Arbitration Act 1996, s 107(2), Sch 4.

Orders in Council: the Civil Jurisdiction and Judgments Act 1982 (Interim Relief) Order 1997, SI 1997/302 at **[2138]**.

26 Security in Admiralty proceedings in England and Wales or Northern Ireland in case of stay, etc

(1) Where in England and Wales or Northern Ireland a court stays or dismisses Admiralty proceedings on the ground that the dispute in question should be submitted … to the determination of the courts of another part of the United Kingdom or of an overseas country, the court may, if in those proceedings property has been arrested or bail or other security has been given to prevent or obtain release from arrest—

(a) order that the property arrested be retained as security for the satisfaction of any award or judgment which—
  (i) is given in respect of the dispute in the … legal proceedings in favour of which those proceedings are stayed or dismissed; and
  (ii) is enforceable in England and Wales or, as the case may be, in Northern Ireland; or
(b) order that the stay or dismissal of those proceedings be conditional on the provision of equivalent security for the satisfaction of any such award or judgment.

(2) Where a court makes an order under subsection (1), it may attach such conditions to the order as it thinks fit, in particular conditions with respect to the institution or prosecution of the relevant … legal proceedings.

(3) Subject to any provision made by rules of court and to any necessary modifications, the same law and practice shall apply in relation to property retained in pursuance of an order made by a court under subsection (1) as would apply if it were held for the purposes of proceedings in that court.

[75]

NOTES

Sub-ss (1), (2): words omitted repealed by the Arbitration Act 1996, s 107(2), Sch 4.

Transitional provision: see s 53(2), Sch 13, Pt II, para 6 at **[97]**, **[111]**.

27 Provisional and protective measures in Scotland in the absence of substantive proceedings

(1) The Court of Session may, in any case to which this subsection applies—

(a) subject to subsection (2)(c), grant a warrant for the arrestment of any assets situated in Scotland;
(b) subject to subsection (2)(c), grant a warrant of inhibition over any property situated in Scotland; and
(c) grant interim interdict.

(2) Subsection (1) applies to any case in which—

(a) proceedings have been commenced but not concluded, or, in relation to paragraph (c) of that subsection, are to be commenced, in another [Brussels or Lugano Contracting State][, in another Regulation State] or in England and Wales or Northern Ireland;

[(b) the subject-matter of the proceedings is within the scope of the Regulation as determined by Article 1 of the Regulation; and]

(c) in relation to paragraphs (a) and (b) of subsection (1), such a warrant could competently have been granted in equivalent proceedings before a Scottish court;

but it shall not be necessary, in determining whether proceedings have been commenced for the purpose of paragraph (a) of this subsection, to show that any document has been served on or notice given to the defender.

(3) Her Majesty may by Order in Council confer on the Court of Session power to do anything mentioned in subsection (1) or in section 28 in relation to proceedings of any of the following descriptions, namely—

(a) proceedings commenced otherwise than in a [Brussels or Lugano Contracting State] [or Regulation State];

[(b) proceedings whose subject-matter is not within the scope of the Regulation as determined by Article 1 of the Regulation;]

(c) arbitration proceedings;

(d) in relation to subsection (1)(c) or section 28, proceedings which are to be commenced otherwise than in a [Brussels or Lugano Contracting State] [or Regulation State].

(4) An Order in Council under subsection (3)—

(a) may confer power to do only certain of the things mentioned in subsection (1) or in section 28;

(b) may make different provision for different classes of proceedings, for proceedings pending in different countries or courts outside the United Kingdom or in different parts of the United Kingdom, and for other different circumstances; and

(c) may impose conditions or restrictions on the exercise of any power conferred by the Order.

(5) Any Order in Council under subsection (3) shall be subject to annulment in pursuance of a resolution of either House of Parliament.

[76]

NOTES

Sub-s (2): words in first pair of square brackets substituted by the Civil Jurisdiction and Judgments Act 1991, s 3, Sch 2, para 12; words in second pair of square brackets inserted and para (b) substituted by the Civil Jurisdiction and Judgments Order 2001, SI 2001/3929, art 4, Sch 2, Pt IV, para 11(a), (b).

Sub-s (3): words in first and fourth pairs of square brackets substituted by the Civil Jurisdiction and Judgments Act 1991, s 3, Sch 2, para 12; words in second and fifth pairs of square brackets inserted and para (b) substituted by SI 2001/3929, art 4, Sch 2, Pt IV, para 11(c).

Orders in Council: the Civil Jurisdiction and Judgments Act 1982 (Provisional and Protective Measures) (Scotland) Order 1997, SI 1997/2780 at **[2146]**.

28 Application of s 1 of Administration of Justice (Scotland) Act 1972

When any proceedings have been brought, or are likely to be brought, in another [Brussels or Lugano Contracting State][, in a Regulation State] or in England and Wales or Northern Ireland in respect of any matter which is within the scope of the [Regulation] as determined in Article 1, the Court of Session shall have the like power to make an order under section 1 of the Administration of Justice (Scotland) Act 1972 [as amended by the Law Reform (Miscellaneous Provisions) (Scotland) Act 1985] as if the proceedings in question had been brought, or were likely to be brought, in that court.

[77]

NOTES

Words in first pair of square brackets substituted by the Civil Jurisdiction and Judgments Act 1991, s 3, Sch 2, para 12; words in second pair of square brackets inserted and words in third pair of square brackets substituted by the Civil Jurisdiction and Judgments Order 2001, SI 2001/3929, art 4, Sch 2, Pt IV, para 12; words in fourth pair of square brackets inserted by the Law Reform (Miscellaneous Provisions) (Scotland) Act 1985, s 59(1), Sch 2, para 24.

29 (*Amends the County Courts* (*Northern Ireland*) *Order 1980, SI 1980/397.*)

30 Proceedings in England and Wales or Northern Ireland for torts to immovable property

(1) The jurisdiction of any court in England and Wales or Northern Ireland to entertain proceedings for trespass to, or any other tort affecting, immovable property shall extend to cases in which the property in question is situated outside that part of the United Kingdom unless the proceedings are principally concerned with a question of the title to, or the right to possession of, that property.

(2) Subsection (1) has effect subject to the 1968 Convention [and the Lugano Convention] [and the Regulation] and to the provisions set out in Schedule 4.

[78]

NOTES

Sub-s (2): words in first pair of square brackets inserted by the Civil Jurisdiction and Judgments Act 1991, s 3, Sch 2, para 13; words in second pair of square brackets inserted by the Civil Jurisdiction and Judgments Order 2001, SI 2001/3929, art 4, Sch 2, Pt IV, para 13.

Provisions relating to recognition and enforcement of judgments

31 Overseas judgments given against states, etc

(1) A judgment given by a court of an overseas country against a state other than the United Kingdom or the state to which that court belongs shall be recognised and enforced in the United Kingdom if, and only if—

(a) it would be so recognised and enforced if it had not been given against a state; and

(b) that court would have had jurisdiction in the matter if it had applied rules corresponding to those applicable to such matters in the United Kingdom in accordance with sections 2 to 11 of the State Immunity Act 1978.

(2) References in subsection (1) to a judgment given against a state include references to judgments of any of the following descriptions given in relation to a state—

(a) judgments against the government, or a department of the government, of the state but not (except as mentioned in paragraph (c)) judgments against an entity which is distinct from the executive organs of government;

(b) judgments against the sovereign or head of state in his public capacity;

(c) judgments against any such separate entity as is mentioned in paragraph (a) given in proceedings relating to anything done by it in the exercise of the sovereign authority of the state.

(3) Nothing in subsection (1) shall affect the recognition or enforcement in the United Kingdom of a judgment to which Part I of the Foreign Judgments (Reciprocal Enforcement) Act 1933 applies by virtue of section 4 of the Carriage of Goods by Road Act 1965, section 17(4) of the Nuclear Installations Act 1965, section [166(4) of the Merchant Shipping Act 1995], [*section 6 of the International Transport Conventions Act 1983*] …

(4) Sections 12, 13 and 14(3) and (4) of the State Immunity Act 1978 (service of process and procedural privileges) shall apply to proceedings for the recognition or enforcement in the United Kingdom of a judgment given by a court of an overseas country (whether or not that judgment is within subsection (1) of this section) as they apply to other proceedings.

(5) In this section "state", in the case of a federal state, includes any of its constituent territories.

[79]

NOTES

Sub-s (3): words in first pair of square brackets substituted by the Merchant Shipping Act 1995, s 314(2), Sch 13, para 66(a); words in second pair of square brackets substituted by the International Transport Conventions Act 1983, s 11, further substituted by the words "regulation 8 of the Railways (Convention on International Carriage by Rail) Regulations 2005" by the Railways (Convention on International Carriage by Rail) Regulations 2005, SI 2005/2092, reg 9(2), Sch 3, para 2, as from a day to be specified in the London, Edinburgh and Belfast Gazettes; words omitted repealed by the Statute Law (Repeals) Act 2004.

Transitional provision: see s 53(2), Sch 13, Pt II, para 7 at **[97]**, **[111]**.

32 Overseas judgments given in proceedings brought in breach of agreement for settlement of disputes

(1) Subject to the following provisions of this section, a judgment given by a court of an overseas country in any proceedings shall not be recognised or enforced in the United Kingdom if—

(a) the bringing of those proceedings in that court was contrary to an agreement under which the dispute in question was to be settled otherwise than by proceedings in the courts of that country; and

(b) those proceedings were not brought in that court by, or with the agreement of, the person against whom the judgment was given; and

(c) that person did not counterclaim in the proceedings or otherwise submit to the jurisdiction of that court.

(2) Subsection (1) does not apply where the agreement referred to in paragraph (a) of that subsection was illegal, void or unenforceable or was incapable of being performed for reasons not attributable to the fault of the party bringing the proceedings in which the judgment was given.

(3) In determining whether a judgment given by a court of an overseas country should be recognised or enforced in the United Kingdom, a court in the United Kingdom shall not be bound by any decision of the overseas court relating to any of the matters mentioned in subsection (1) or (2).

(4) Nothing in subsection (1) shall affect the recognition or enforcement in the United Kingdom of—

(a) a judgment which is required to be recognised or enforced there under the 1968 Convention [or the Lugano Convention] [or the Regulation];

(b) a judgment to which Part I of the Foreign Judgments (Reciprocal Enforcement) Act 1933 applies by virtue of section 4 of the Carriage of Goods by Road Act 1965, section 17(4) of the Nuclear Installations Act 1965, … , [*section 6 of the International Transport Conventions Act 1983*] … or [section 34(1)(a) of the Merchant Shipping Act 1995].

[80]

NOTES

Sub-s (4): words in first pair of square brackets in para (a) inserted by the Civil Jurisdiction and Judgments Act 1991, s 3, Sch 2, para 14; words in second pair of square brackets in para (a) inserted by the Civil Jurisdiction and Judgments Order 2001, SI 2001/3929, art 4, Sch 2, Pt IV, para 14; in para (b) words omitted in the first place repealed and words in second pair of square brackets substituted by the Merchant Shipping Act 1995, s 314(1), (2), Sch 12, Sch 13, para 66(b); words in first pair of square brackets in para (b) substituted by the International Transport Conventions Act 1983, s 11, further substituted by the words "regulation 8 of the Railways (Convention on International Carriage by Rail) Regulations 2005" by the Railways (Convention on International Carriage by Rail) Regulations 2005, SI 2005/2092, reg 9(2), Sch 3, para 2, as from a day to be specified in the London, Edinburgh and Belfast Gazettes; words omitted from para (b) in the second place repealed by the Statute Law (Repeals) Act 2004.

Transitional provision: see s 53(2), Sch 13, Pt II, para 8 at **[97]**, **[111]**.

33 Certain steps not to amount to submission to jurisdiction of overseas court

(1) For the purposes of determining whether a judgment given by a court of an overseas country should be recognised or enforced in England and Wales or Northern Ireland, the person against whom the judgment was given shall not be regarded as having submitted to the jurisdiction of the court by reason only of the fact that he appeared (conditionally or otherwise) in the proceedings for all or any one or more of the following purposes, namely—

(a) to contest the jurisdiction of the court;

(b) to ask the court to dismiss or stay the proceedings on the ground that the dispute in question should be submitted to arbitration or to the determination of the courts of another country;

(c) to protect, or obtain the release of, property seized or threatened with seizure in the proceedings.

(2) Nothing in this section shall affect the recognition or enforcement in England and Wales or Northern Ireland of a judgment which is required to be recognised or enforced there under the 1968 Convention [or the Lugano Convention] [or the Regulation].

[81]

NOTES

Sub-s (2): words in first pair of square brackets inserted by the Civil Jurisdiction and Judgments Act 1991, s 3, Sch 2, para 15; words in second pair of square brackets inserted by the Civil Jurisdiction and Judgments Order 2001, SI 2001/3929, art 4, Sch 2, Pt IV, para 15.

Transitional provision: see s 53(2), Sch 13, Pt II, para 9 at **[97]**, **[111]**.

34 Certain judgments a bar to further proceedings on the same cause of action

No proceedings may be brought by a person in England and Wales or Northern Ireland on a cause of action in respect of which a judgment has been given in his favour in proceedings between the same parties, or their privies, in a court in another part of the United Kingdom or in a court of an overseas country, unless that judgment is not enforceable or entitled to recognition in England and Wales or, as the case may be, in Northern Ireland.

[82]

NOTES

Transitional provision: see 53(2), Sch 13, Pt II, para 10 at **[97]**, **[111]**.

35 Minor amendments relating to overseas judgments

(1) The Foreign Judgments (Reciprocal Enforcement) Act 1933 shall have effect with the amendments specified in Schedule 10, being amendments whose main purpose is to enable Part I of that Act to be applied to judgments of courts other than superior courts, to judgments providing for interim payments and to certain arbitration awards.

(2), (3) …

[83]

NOTES

Sub-s (2): substitutes the Administration of Justice Act 1920, s 10 at **[10]**.

Sub-s (3): adds the Administration of Justice Act 1920, s 14(3) at **[14]**.

36–38 (*S 36 applies to Northern Ireland only; s 37 in so far as unrepealed, relates to maintenance provisions; s 38 amends the Protection of Trading Interests Act 1980, s 7.*)

Jurisdiction, and recognition and enforcement of judgments, as between United Kingdom and certain territories

39 Application of provisions corresponding to 1968 Convention in relation to certain territories

(1) Her Majesty may by Order in Council make provision corresponding to the provision made by the 1968 Convention as between the Contracting States to that Convention, with such modifications as appear to Her Majesty to be appropriate, for regulating, as between the United Kingdom and any of the territories mentioned in subsection (2), the jurisdiction of courts and the recognition and enforcement of judgments.

(2) The territories referred to in subsection (1) are—

(a) the Isle of Man;
(b) any of the Channel Islands;
[(c) any colony].

(3) An Order in Council under this section may contain such supplementary and incidental provisions as appear to Her Majesty to be necessary or expedient, including in particular provisions corresponding to or applying any of the provisions of Part I with such modifications as may be specified in the Order.

(4) Any Order in Council under this section shall be subject to annulment in pursuance of a resolution of either House of Parliament.

[84]

NOTES

Sub-s (2): para (c) substituted for original paras (c), (d) by the Civil Jurisdiction and Judgments Act 1982 (Amendment) Order 1990, SI 1990/2591, art 10.

Orders in Council: the Civil Jurisdiction and Judgments Act 1982 (Gibraltar) Order 1997, SI 1997/2602 at **[2140]**.

40 (*Sub-s (1) repealed by the Legal Aid Act 1988, s 45(2), Sch 6; sub-s (2) repealed by the Legal Aid (Scotland) Act 1986, s 45(3), Sch 5; sub-s (3) amends the Legal Aid, Advice and Assistance (Northern Ireland) Order 1981, SI 1981/288, art 22.*)

PART V
SUPPLEMENTARY AND GENERAL PROVISIONS

Domicile

41 Domicile of individuals

(1) Subject to Article 52 (which contains provisions for determining whether a party is domiciled in a Contracting State), the following provisions of this section determine, for the purposes of the 1968 Convention [the Lugano Convention] and this Act, whether an individual is domiciled in the United Kingdom or in a particular part of, or place in, the United Kingdom or in a state other than a Contracting State.

(2) An individual is domiciled in the United Kingdom if and only if—

(a) he is resident in the United Kingdom; and

(b) the nature and circumstances of his residence indicate that he has a substantial connection with the United Kingdom.

(3) Subject to subsection (5), an individual is domiciled in a particular part of the United Kingdom if and only if—

(a) he is resident in that part; and

(b) the nature and circumstances of his residence indicate that he has a substantial connection with that part.

(4) An individual is domiciled in a particular place in the United Kingdom if and only if he—

(a) is domiciled in the part of the United Kingdom in which that place is situated; and

(b) is resident in that place.

(5) An individual who is domiciled in the United Kingdom but in whose case the requirements of subsection (3)(b) are not satisfied in relation to any particular part of the United Kingdom shall be treated as domiciled in the part of the United Kingdom in which he is resident.

(6) In the case of an individual who—

(a) is resident in the United Kingdom, or in a particular part of the United Kingdom; and

(b) has been so resident for the last three months or more,

the requirements of subsection (2)(b) or, as the case may be, subsection (3)(b) shall be presumed to be fulfilled unless the contrary is proved.

(7) An individual is domiciled in a state other than a Contracting State if and only if—

(a) he is resident in that state; and

(b) the nature and circumstances of his residence indicate that he has a substantial connection with that state.

[85]

NOTES

Sub-s (1): words in square brackets inserted by the Civil Jurisdiction and Judgments Act 1991, s 3, Sch 2, para 16.

42 Domicile and seat of corporation or association

(1) For the purposes of this Act the seat of a corporation or association (as determined by this section) shall be treated as its domicile.

(2) The following provisions of this section determine where a corporation or association has its seat—

(a) for the purpose of Article 53 (which for the purposes of the 1968 Convention [or, as the case may be, the Lugano Convention] equates the domicile of such a body with its seat); and

(b) for the purposes of this Act other than the provisions mentioned in section 43(1)(b) and (c).

(3) A corporation or association has its seat in the United Kingdom if and only if—

(a) it was incorporated or formed under the law of a part of the United Kingdom and has its registered office or some other official address in the United Kingdom; or

(b) its central management and control is exercised in the United Kingdom.

(4) A corporation or association has its seat in a particular part of the United Kingdom if and only if it has its seat in the United Kingdom and—

(a) it has its registered office or some other official address in that part; or

(b) its central management and control is exercised in that part; or

(c) it has a place of business in that part.

(5) A corporation or association has its seat in a particular place in the United Kingdom if and only if it has its seat in the part of the United Kingdom in which that place is situated and—

(a) it has its registered office or some other official address in that place; or

(b) its central management and control is exercised in that place; or

(c) it has a place of business in that place.

(6) Subject to subsection (7), a corporation or association has its seat in a state other than the United Kingdom if and only if—

(a) it was incorporated or formed under the law of that state and has its registered office or some other official address there; or

(b) its central management and control is exercised in that state.

(7) A corporation or association shall not be regarded as having its seat in a Contracting State other than the United Kingdom if it is shown that the courts of that state would not regard it as having its seat there.

(8) In this section—

"business" includes any activity carried on by a corporation or association, and "place of business" shall be construed accordingly;

"official address", in relation to a corporation or association, means an address which it is required by law to register, notify or maintain for the purpose of receiving notices or other communications.

[86]

NOTES

Sub-s (2): words in square brackets in para (a) inserted by the Civil Jurisdiction and Judgments Act 1991, s 3, Sch 2, para 17.

43 Seat of corporation or association for purposes of Article 16(2) and related provisions

(1) The following provisions of this section determine where a corporation or association has its seat for the purposes of—

(a) Article 16(2) [of the 1968 Convention or of the Lugano Convention] (which confers exclusive jurisdiction over proceedings relating to the formation or dissolution of such bodies, or to the decisions of their organs);

(b) [rules 4 and 11(b)] in Schedule 4; and

(c) [rules 2(l) and 5(1)(b)] in Schedule 8.

(2) A corporation or association has its seat in the United Kingdom if and only if—

(a) it was incorporated or formed under the law of a part of the United Kingdom; or

(b) its central management and control is exercised in the United Kingdom.

(3) A corporation or association has its seat in a particular part of the United Kingdom if and only if it has its seat in the United Kingdom and—

(a) subject to subsection (5), it was incorporated or formed under the law of that part; or

(b) being incorporated or formed under the law of a state other than the United Kingdom, its central management and control is exercised in that part.

(4) A corporation or association has its seat in a particular place in Scotland if and only if it has its seat in Scotland and—

(a) it has its registered office or some other official address in that place; or

(b) it has no registered office or other official address in Scotland, but its central management and control is exercised in that place.

(5) A corporation or association incorporated or formed under—

(a) an enactment forming part of the law of more than one part of the United Kingdom; or

(b) an instrument having effect in the domestic law of more than one part of the United Kingdom,

shall, if it has a registered office, be taken to have its seat in the part of the United Kingdom in which that office is situated, and not in any other part of the United Kingdom.

(6) Subject to subsection (7), a corporation or association has its seat in a Contracting State other than the United Kingdom if and only if—

(a) it was incorporated or formed under the law of that state; or

(b) its central management and control is exercised in that state.

(7) A corporation or association shall not be regarded as having its seat in a Contracting State other than the United Kingdom if—

(a) it has its seat in the United Kingdom by virtue of subsection (2)(a); or

(b) it is shown that the courts of that other state would not regard it for the purposes of Article 16(2) as having its seat there.

(8) In this section "official address" has the same meaning as in section 42.

[87]

NOTES

Sub-s (1): words in square brackets in para (a) inserted by the Civil Jurisdiction and Judgments Act 1991, s 3, Sch 2, para 18; words in square brackets in paras (b), (c) substituted by the Civil Jurisdiction and Judgments Order 2001, SI 2001/3929, art 4, Sch 2, Pt V, para 16.

44 Persons deemed to be domiciled in the United Kingdom for certain purposes

(1) This section applies to—

(a) proceedings within Section 3 of Title II of the 1968 Convention [or Section 3 of Title II of the Lugano Convention] (insurance contracts), and

(b) proceedings within Section 4 of [Title II of either of those Conventions] (consumer contracts).

(2) A person who, for the purposes of proceedings to which this section applies arising out of the operations of a branch, agency or other establishment in the United Kingdom, is deemed for the purposes of the 1968 Convention [or, as the case may be, of the Lugano Convention] to be domiciled in the United Kingdom by virtue of—

(a) Article 8, second paragraph (insurers); or

(b) Article 13, second paragraph (suppliers of goods, services or credit to consumers),

shall, for the purposes of those proceedings, be treated for the purposes of this Act as so domiciled and as domiciled in the part of the United Kingdom in which the branch, agency or establishment in question is situated.

[88]

NOTES

Sub-s (1): words in first pair of square brackets inserted, and words in second pair of square brackets substituted, by the Civil Jurisdiction and Judgments Act 1991, s 3, Sch 2, para 19(1).

Sub-s (2): words in square brackets inserted by the Civil Jurisdiction and Judgments Act 1991, s 3, Sch 2, para 19(2).

45 Domicile of trusts

(1) The following provisions of this section determine, for the purposes of the 1968 Convention [the Lugano Convention] and this Act, where a trust is domiciled.

(2) A trust is domiciled in the United Kingdom if and only if it is by virtue of subsection (3) domiciled in a part of the United Kingdom.

(3) A trust is domiciled in a part of the United Kingdom if and only if the system of law of that part is the system of law with which the trust has its closest and most real connection. **[89]**

NOTES

Sub-s (1): words in square brackets inserted by the Civil Jurisdiction and Judgments Act 1991, s 3, Sch 2, para 20.

46 Domicile and seat of the Crown

(1) For the purposes of this Act the seat of the Crown (as determined by this section) shall be treated as its domicile.

(2) The following provisions of this section determine where the Crown has its seat—
- (a) for the purposes of the 1968 Convention [and the Lugano Convention] [(in each of which] Article 53 equates the domicile of a legal person with its seat); and
- (b) for the purposes of this Act.

(3) Subject to the provisions of any Order in Council for the time being in force under subsection (4)—
- (a) the Crown in right of Her Majesty's government in the United Kingdom has its seat in every part of, and every place in, the United Kingdom; and
- [(aa) the Crown in right of the Scottish Administration has its seat in, and in every place in, Scotland,]
- (b) the Crown in right of Her Majesty's government in Northern Ireland has its seat in, and in every place in, Northern Ireland.

(4) Her Majesty may by Order in Council provide that, in the case of proceedings of any specified description against the Crown in right of Her Majesty's government in the United Kingdom, the Crown shall be treated for the purposes of the 1968 Convention [the Lugano Convention] and this Act as having its seat in, and in every place in, a specified part of the United Kingdom and not in any other part of the United Kingdom.

(5) An Order in Council under subsection (4) may frame a description of proceedings in any way, and in particular may do so by reference to the government department or officer of the Crown against which or against whom they fall to be instituted.

(6) Any Order in Council made under this section shall be subject to annulment in pursuance of a resolution of either House of Parliament.

(7) Nothing in this section applies to the Crown otherwise than in right of Her Majesty's government in the United Kingdom[, the Scottish Administration] or Her Majesty's government in Northern Ireland.

[90]

NOTES

Sub-s (2): words in first pair of square brackets inserted, and words in second pair of square brackets substituted, by the Civil Jurisdiction and Judgments Act 1991, s 3, Sch 2, para 21(1).

Sub-s (3): para (aa) inserted by the Scotland Act 1998, s 125, Sch 8, para 18(1), (2).

Sub-s (4): words in square brackets inserted by the Civil Jurisdiction and Judgments Act 1991, s 3, Sch 2, para 21(2).

Sub-s (7): words in square brackets inserted by the Scotland Act 1998, s 125, Sch 8, para 18(1), (3).

Other supplementary provisions

47 Modifications occasioned by decisions of European Court as to meaning or effect of [Brussels Conventions]

(1) Her Majesty may by Order in Council—
- (a) make such provision as Her Majesty considers appropriate for the purpose of bringing the law of any part of the United Kingdom into accord with the [Brussels Conventions] as affected by any principle laid down by the European Court in connection with the [Brussels Conventions] or by any decision of that court as to the meaning or effect of any provision of the [Brussels Conventions]; or
- (b) make such modifications of Schedule 4 or Schedule 8, or of any other statutory provision affected by any provision of either of those Schedules, as Her Majesty

considers appropriate in view of any principle laid down by the European Court in connection with Title II of the 1968 Convention or of any decision of that court as to the meaning or effect of any provision of that Title.

(2) The provision which may be made by virtue of paragraph (a) of subsection (1) includes such modifications of this Act or any other statutory provision, whenever passed or made, as Her Majesty considers appropriate for the purpose mentioned in that paragraph.

(3) The modifications which may be made by virtue of paragraph (b) of subsection (1) include modifications designed to produce divergence between any provision of Schedule 4 or Schedule 8 and a corresponding provision of Title II of the 1968 Convention as affected by any such principle or decision as is mentioned in that paragraph.

(4) An Order in Council under this section shall not be made unless a draft of the Order has been laid before Parliament and approved by a resolution of each House of Parliament. **[91]**

NOTES

Section heading, sub-s (1): words in square brackets substituted by the Civil Jurisdiction and Judgments Act 1991, s 3, Sch 2, para 22.

48 Matters for which rules of court may provide

(1) Rules of court may make provision for regulating the procedure to be followed in any court in connection with any provision of this Act [the Lugano Convention or the Brussels Conventions] [or the Regulation].

(2) Rules of court may make provision as to the manner in which and the conditions subject to which a certificate or judgment registered in any court under any provision of this Act [or the Regulation] may be enforced, including provision for enabling the court or, in Northern Ireland the Enforcement of Judgments Office, subject to any conditions specified in the rules, to give directions about such matters.

(3) Without prejudice to the generality of subsections (1) and (2), the power to make rules of court for magistrates' courts, and in Northern Ireland the power to make Judgment Enforcement Rules, shall include power to make such provision as the rule-making authority considers necessary or expedient for the purposes of the provisions of [the Lugano Convention, the Brussels Conventions][, the Regulation] and this Act relating to maintenance proceedings and the recognition and enforcement of maintenance orders, and shall in particular include power to make provision as to any of the following matters—

- (a) authorising the service in another Contracting State [or Regulation State] of process issued by or for the purposes of a magistrates' court and the service and execution in England and Wales or Northern Ireland of process issued in another Contracting State [or Regulation State];
- (b) requesting courts in other parts of the United Kingdom or in other Contracting States [or Regulation States] to take evidence there for the purposes of proceedings in England and Wales or Northern Ireland;
- (c) the taking of evidence in England and Wales or Northern Ireland in response to similar requests received from such courts;
- (d) the circumstances in which and the conditions subject to which any powers conferred under paragraphs (a) to (c) are to be exercised;
- (e) the admission in evidence, subject to such conditions as may be prescribed in the rules, of statements contained in documents purporting to be made or authenticated by a court in another part of the United Kingdom or in another Contracting State [or Regulation State], or by a judge or official of such a court, which purport—
  - (i) to set out or summarise evidence given in proceedings in that court or to be documents received in evidence in such proceedings or copies of such documents; or
  - (ii) to set out or summarise evidence taken for the purposes of proceedings in England and Wales or Northern Ireland, whether or not in response to any such request as is mentioned in paragraph (b); or
  - (iii) to record information relating to the payments made under an order of that court;
- (f) the circumstances and manner in which a magistrates' court may or must vary or

revoke a maintenance order registered in that court, cancel the registration of, or refrain from enforcing, such an order or transmit such an order for enforcement in another part of the United Kingdom;

(g) the cases and manner in which courts in other parts of the United Kingdom or in other Contracting States [or Regulation States] are to be informed of orders made, or other things done, by or for the purposes of a magistrates' court;

(h) the circumstances and manner in which a magistrates' court may communicate for other purposes with such courts;

(i) the giving of notice of such matters as may be prescribed in the rules to such persons as may be so prescribed and the manner in which such notice is to be given.

(4) Nothing in this section shall be taken as derogating from the generality of any power to make rules of court conferred by any other enactment.

[92]

NOTES

Sub-s (1): words in first pair of square brackets substituted by the Civil Jurisdiction and Judgments Act 1991, s 3, Sch 2, para 23; words in second pair of square brackets added by the Civil Jurisdiction and Judgments Order 2001, SI 2001/3929, art 4, Sch 2, Pt V, para 17(a).

Sub-s (2): words in square brackets inserted by SI 2001/3929, art 4, Sch 2, Pt V, para 17(b).

Sub-s (3): words in first pair of square brackets substituted by the Civil Jurisdiction and Judgments Act 1991, s 3, Sch 2, para 23; words in second pair of square brackets and words in square brackets in paras (a), (b), (e), (g) inserted by SI 2001/3929, art 4, Sch 2, Pt V, para 17(c).

This section is modified in relation to its application to authentic instruments and court settlements by the Civil Jurisdiction and Judgments (Authentic Instruments and Court Settlements) Order 1993, SI 1993/604, art 8 at **[2128]** and by the Civil Jurisdiction and Judgments (Authentic Instruments and Court Settlements) Order 2001, SI 2001/3928, art 4 at **[2156]**.

Rules of court: the Act of Sederunt (Civil Jurisdiction of the Sheriff Court) 1986, SI 1986/1946; the Act of Sederunt (Enforcement of Judgments under the Civil Jurisdiction and Judgments Act 1982) 1986, SI 1986/1947; the Magistrates' Courts (Civil Jurisdiction and Judgments Act 1982) Rules 1986, SI 1986/1962; the Act of Sederunt (Enforcement of Judgments under the Civil Jurisdiction and Judgments Act 1982) (Authentic Instruments and Court Settlements) 1993, SI 1993/2346. See also Civil Procedure Rules 1998, SI 1998/3132, rr 6.18 and 6.19 at **[1347]**, **[1348]**, r 12.1 at **[1394]** and Pt 74 at **[1517]**; Act of Sederunt (Rules of the Court of Session 1994) 1994, SI 1994/1443, rr 62.4–62.11 at **[1130]–[1140]**.

49 Saving for powers to stay, sist, strike out or dismiss proceedings

Nothing in this Act shall prevent any court in the United Kingdom from staying, sisting, striking out or dismissing any proceedings before it, on the ground of *forum non conveniens* or otherwise, where to do so is not inconsistent with the 1968 Convention [or, as the case may be, the Lugano Convention].

[93]

NOTES

Words in square brackets inserted by the Civil Jurisdiction and Judgments Act 1991, s 3, Sch 2, para 24.

General

50 Interpretation: general

In this Act, unless the context otherwise requires—

["the Accession Convention", ["the 1982 Accession Convention", "the 1989 Accession Convention" and "the 1996 Accession Convention"] have the meaning given by section 1(1);]

"Article" and references to sub-divisions of numbered Articles are to be construed in accordance with section 1(2)(b);

"association" means an unincorporated body of persons;

["Brussels Contracting State" has the meaning given by section 1(3);

"the Brussels Conventions" has the meaning given by section 1(1);]

"Contracting State" has the meaning given by section 1(3);

"the 1968 Convention" has the meaning given by section 1(1), and references to that Convention and to provisions of it are to be construed in accordance with section 1(2)(a);

.....

"corporation" means a body corporate, and includes a partnership subsisting under the law of Scotland;

"court", without more, includes a tribunal;

"court of law", in relation to the United Kingdom, means any of the following courts, namely—

(*a*) *the House of Lords,*

(b) in England and Wales or Northern Ireland, the Court of Appeal, the High Court, the Crown Court, a county court and a magistrates' court,

(c) in Scotland, the Court of Session and a sheriff court;

"the Crown" is to be construed in accordance with section 51(2);

"enactment" includes an enactment comprised in Northern Ireland legislation;

"judgment", subject to sections 15(1) and 18(2) and to paragraph 1 of Schedules 6 and 7, means any judgment or order (by whatever name called) given or made by a court in any civil proceedings;

["Lugano Contracting State" has the meaning given by section 1(3);

"the Lugano Convention" has the meaning given by section 1(1);]

"magistrates' court", in relation to Northern Ireland, means a court of summary jurisdiction;

"modifications" includes additions, omissions and alterations;

"overseas country" means any country or territory outside the United Kingdom;

"part of the United Kingdom" means England and Wales, Scotland or Northern Ireland;

"the 1971 Protocol" has the meaning given by section 1(1), and references to that Protocol and to provisions of it are to be construed in accordance with section 1(2)(a);

["the Regulation" has the meaning given by section 1(1);

"Regulation State" has the meaning given by section 1(3);]

"rules of court", in relation to any court, means rules, orders or regulations made by the authority having power to make rules, orders or regulations regulating the procedure of that court, and includes—

(a) in Scotland, Acts of Sederunt;

(b) (*applies to Northern Ireland only*);

"statutory provision" means any provision contained in an Act, or in any Northern Ireland legislation, or in—

(a) subordinate legislation (as defined in section 21(1) of the Interpretation Act 1978); or

(b) any instrument of a legislative character made under any Northern Ireland legislation;

"tribunal"—

(a) means a tribunal of any description other than a court of law;

(b) in relation to an overseas country, includes, as regards matters relating to maintenance within the meaning of the 1968 Convention, any authority having power to give, enforce, vary or revoke a maintenance order.

[94]

NOTES

Definition "the Accession Convention" substituted by the Civil Jurisdiction and Judgments Act 1982 (Amendment) Order 1990, SI 1990/2591, art 9, words in square brackets substituted by the Civil Jurisdiction and Judgments Act 1982 (Amendment) Order 2000, SI 2000/1824, art 7; definitions "Brussels Contracting State", "the Brussels Conventions", "Lugano Contracting State" and "the Lugano Convention" inserted, and definition "the Conventions" omitted repealed, by the Civil Jurisdiction and Judgments Act 1991, s 3, Sch 2, para 25; definitions "the Regulation" and "Regulation State" inserted by the Civil Jurisdiction and Judgments Order 2001, SI 2001/3929, art 4, Sch 2, Pt V, para 18; in definition "court of law", para (a) substituted by the Constitutional Reform Act 2005, s 145, Sch 17, Pt 2, para 23, as from a day to be appointed, as follows—

"(a) the Supreme Court,".

---

51 Application to Crown

(1) This Act binds the Crown.

(2) In this section and elsewhere in this Act references to the Crown do not include references to Her Majesty in Her private capacity or to Her Majesty in right of Her Duchy of Lancaster or to the Duke of Cornwall.

[95]

52 Extent

(1) This Act extends to Northern Ireland.

(2) Without prejudice to the power conferred by section 39, Her Majesty may by Order in Council direct that all or any of the provisions of this Act apart from that section shall extend, subject to such modifications as may be specified in the Order, to any of the following territories, that is to say—

(a) the Isle of Man;
(b) any of the Channel Islands;
[(c) any colony].

[96]

NOTES

Sub-s (2): para (c) substituted for original paras (c), (d) by the Civil Jurisdiction and Judgments Act 1982 (Amendment) Order 1990, SI 1990/2591, art 11.

Orders in Council: the Protection of Trading Interests Act 1980 (Jersey) Order 1983, SI 1983/607; the Protection of Trading Interests Act 1980 (Guernsey) Order 1983, SI 1983/1703; the Protection of Trading Interests Act 1980 (Isle of Man) Order 1983, SI 1983/1704.

53 Commencement, transitional provisions and savings

(1) This Act shall come into force in accordance with the provisions of Part I of Schedule 13.

(2) The transitional provisions and savings contained in Part II of that Schedule shall have effect in relation to the commencement of the provisions of this Act mentioned in that Part.

[97]

NOTES

Orders: the Civil Jurisdiction and Judgments Act 1982 (Commencement No 1) Order 1984, SI 1984/1553; the Civil Jurisdiction and Judgments Act 1982 (Commencement No 2) Order 1986, SI 1986/1781; the Civil Jurisdiction and Judgments Act 1982 (Commencement No 3) Order 1986, SI 1986/2044.

54 Repeals

The enactments mentioned in Schedule 14 are hereby repealed to the extent specified in the third column of that Schedule.

[98]

55 Short title

This Act may be cited as the Civil Jurisdiction and Judgments Act 1982.

[99]

SCHEDULES

(*Sch 1 contains the text of the 1968 Convention ("the Brussels Convention"), as amended, printed in Pt IV(B) of this work, at* **[3029]**; *Sch 2 contains the text of the 1971 Protocol, as amended, printed in Pt IV(B) of this work, at* **[3033]**.)

[SCHEDULE 3

TEXT OF TITLES V AND VI OF ACCESSION CONVENTION, AS AMENDED

Section 2(2)

TITLE V

TRANSITIONAL PROVISIONS

Article 34

1. The 1968 Convention and the 1971 Protocol, with the amendments made by this Convention, shall apply only to legal proceedings instituted and to authentic instruments formally drawn up or registered after the entry into force of this Convention in the State of origin and, where recognition or enforcement of a judgment or authentic instrument is sought, in the State addressed.

2. However, as between the six Contracting States to the 1968 Convention, judgments given after the date of entry into force of this Convention in proceedings instituted before that date shall be recognised and enforced in accordance with the provisions of Title III of the 1968 Convention as amended.

3. Moreover, as between the six Contracting States to the 1968 Convention and the three States mentioned in Article 1 of this Convention, and as between those three States, judgments given after the date of entry into force of this Convention between the State of origin and the State addressed in proceedings instituted before that date shall also be recognised and enforced in accordance with the provisions of Title III of the 1968 Convention as amended if jurisdiction was founded upon rules which accorded with the provisions of Title II, as amended, or with provisions of a convention concluded between the State of origin and the State addressed which was in force when the proceedings were instituted.

Articles 35, 36

[*Deleted.*]

TITLE VI
FINAL PROVISIONS

Article 37

The Secretary-General of the Council of the European Communities shall transmit a certified copy of the 1968 Convention and of the 1971 Protocol in the Dutch, French, German and Italian languages to the Governments of the Kingdom of Denmark, Ireland and the United Kingdom of Great Britain and Northern Ireland.

The texts of the 1968 Convention and the 1971 Protocol, drawn up in the Danish, English and Irish languages, shall be annexed to this Convention. The texts drawn up in the Danish, English and Irish languages shall be authentic under the same conditions as the original texts of the 1968 Convention and the 1971 Protocol.

Article 38

This Convention shall be ratified by the signatory States. The instruments of ratification shall be deposited with the Secretary-General of the Council of the European Communities.

Article 39

This Convention shall enter into force, as between the States which shall have ratified it, on the first day of the third month following the deposit of the last instrument of ratification by the original Member States of the Community and one new Member State.

It shall enter into force for each new Member State which subsequently ratifies it on the first day of the third month following the deposit of its instrument of ratification.

Article 40

The Secretary-General of the Council of the European Communities shall notify the signatory States of—

(a) the deposit of each instrument of ratification;
(b) the dates of entry into force of this Convention for the Contracting States.

Article 41

This Convention, drawn up in a single original in the Danish, Dutch, English, French, German, Irish and Italian languages, all seven texts being equally authentic, shall be deposited in the archives of the Secretariat of the Council of the European Communities. The Secretary-General shall transmit a certified copy to the Government of each signatory State.]

[100]

NOTES

Substituted by the Civil Jurisdiction and Judgments Act 1982 (Amendment) Order 1990, SI 1990/2591, art 12(3), Sch 3.

[SCHEDULE 3A
TEXT OF TITLES V AND VI OF 1982 ACCESSION CONVENTION
Section 2(2)

TITLE V
TRANSITIONAL PROVISIONS

Article 12

1. The 1968 Convention and the 1971 Protocol, as amended by the 1978 Convention and this Convention, shall apply only to legal proceedings instituted and to authentic instruments formally drawn up or registered after the entry into force of this Convention in the State of origin and, where recognition or enforcement of a judgment or authentic instrument is sought, in the State addressed.

2. However, judgments given after the date of entry into force of this Convention between the State of origin and the State addressed in proceedings instituted before that date shall be recognised and enforced in accordance with the provisions of Title III of the 1968 Convention as amended by the 1978 Convention and this Convention, if jurisdiction was founded upon rules which accorded with the provisions of Title II of the 1968 Convention, as amended, or with the provisions of a convention which was in force between the State of origin and the State addressed when the proceedings were instituted.

TITLE VI
FINAL PROVISIONS

Article 13

The Secretary-General of the Council of the European Communities shall transmit a certified copy of the 1968 Convention, of the 1971 Protocol and of the 1978 Convention in the Danish, Dutch, English, French, German, Irish and Italian languages to the Government of the Hellenic Republic.

The texts of the 1968 Convention, of the 1971 Protocol and of the 1978 Convention, drawn up in the Greek language, shall be annexed to this Convention. The texts drawn up in the Greek language shall be authentic under the same conditions as the other texts of the 1968 Convention, the 1971 Protocol and the 1978 Convention.

Article 14

This Convention shall be ratified by the signatory States. The instruments of ratification shall be deposited with the Secretary-General of the Council of the European Communities.

Article 15

This Convention shall enter into force, as between the States which have ratified it, on the first day of the third month following the deposit of the last instrument of ratification by the Hellenic Republic and those States which have put into force the 1978 Convention in accordance with Article 39 of that Convention.

It shall enter into force for each Member State which subsequently ratifies it on the first day of the third month following the deposit of its instrument of ratification.

Article 16

The Secretary-General of the Council of the European Communities shall notify the signatory States of—

(a) the deposit of each instrument of ratification;
(b) the dates of entry into force of this Convention for the Contracting States.

Article 17

This Convention, drawn up in a single original in the Danish, Dutch, English, French, German, Greek, Irish and Italian languages, all eight texts being equally authentic, shall be deposited in the archives of the General Secretariat of the Council of the European Communities. The Secretary-General shall transmit a certified copy to the Government of each signatory State.]

[101]

NOTES

Inserted by the Civil Jurisdiction and Judgments Act 1982 (Amendment) Order 1989, SI 1989/1346, art 9(3), Sch 3.

[SCHEDULE 3B

TEXT OF TITLES VI AND VII OF 1989 ACCESSION CONVENTION

Section 2(2)

TITLE VI

TRANSITIONAL PROVISIONS

Article 29

1. The 1968 Convention and the 1971 Protocol, as amended by the 1978 Convention, the 1982 Convention and this Convention, shall apply only to legal proceedings instituted and to authentic instruments formally drawn up or registered after the entry into force of this Convention in the State of origin and, where recognition or enforcement of a judgment or authentic instrument is sought, in the State addressed.

2. However, judgments given after the date of entry into force of this Convention between the State of origin and the State addressed in proceedings instituted before that date shall be recognised and enforced in accordance with the provisions of Title III of the 1968 Convention, as amended by the 1978 Convention, the 1982 Convention and this Convention, if jurisdiction was founded upon rules which accorded with the provisions of Title II of the 1968 Convention, as amended, or with the provisions of a Convention which was in force between the State of origin and the State addressed when the proceedings were instituted.

TITLE VII

FINAL PROVISIONS

Article 30

1. The Secretary-General of the Council of the European Communities shall transmit a certified copy of the 1968 Convention, of the 1971 Protocol, of the 1978 Convention and of the 1982 Convention in the Danish, Dutch, English, French, German, Greek, Irish and Italian languages to the Governments of the Kingdom of Spain and of the Portuguese Republic.

2. The texts of the 1968 Convention, of the 1971 Protocol, of the 1978 Convention and of the 1982 Convention, drawn up in the Portuguese and Spanish languages, are set out in Annexes II, III, IV and V to this Convention. The texts drawn up in the Portuguese and Spanish languages shall be authentic under the same conditions as the other texts of the 1968 Convention, the 1971 Protocol, the 1978 Convention and the 1982 Convention.

Article 31

This Convention shall be ratified by the signatory States. The instruments of ratification shall be deposited with the Secretary-General of the Council of the European Communities.

Article 32

1. This Convention shall enter into force on the first day of the third month following the date on which two signatory States, of which one is the Kingdom of Spain or the Portuguese Republic, deposit their instruments of ratification.

2. This Convention shall take effect in relation to any other signatory State on the first day of the third month following the deposit of its instrument of ratification.

Article 33

The Secretary-General of the Council of the European Communities shall notify the signatory States of—

(a) the deposit of each instrument of ratification;
(b) the dates of entry into force of this Convention for the Contracting States.

Article 34

This Convention, drawn up in a single original in the Danish, Dutch, English, French, German, Greek, Irish, Italian, Portuguese and Spanish languages, all 10 texts being equally authentic, shall be deposited in the archives of the General Secretariat of the Council of the European Communities. The Secretary-General shall transmit a certified copy to the Government of each signatory State.]

[102]

NOTES

Inserted by the Civil Jurisdiction and Judgments Act 1982 (Amendment) Order 1990, SI 1990/2591, art 12(4), Sch 4.

[SCHEDULE 3BB
TEXT OF TITLES V AND VI OF 1996 ACCESSION CONVENTION

Section 2(2)

TITLE V
TRANSITIONAL PROVISIONS

Article 13

1. The 1968 Convention and the 1971 Protocol, as amended by the 1978 Convention, the 1982 Convention, the 1989 Convention and by this Convention, shall apply only to legal proceedings instituted and to authentic instruments formally drawn up or registered after the entry into force of this Convention in the State of origin and, where recognition or enforcement of a judgment or authentic instrument is sought, in the State addressed.

2. However, judgments given after the date of entry into force of this Convention between the State of origin and the State addressed in proceedings instituted before that date shall be recognised and enforced in accordance with the provisions of Title III of the 1968 Convention, as amended by the 1978 Convention, the 1982 Convention, the 1989 Convention and this Convention, if jurisdiction was founded upon rules which accorded with the provisions of Title II, as amended, of the 1968 Convention, or with the provisions of a convention which was in force between the State of origin and the State addressed when the proceedings were instituted.

TITLE VI
FINAL PROVISIONS

Article 14

1. The Secretary-General of the Council of the European Union shall transmit a certified copy of the 1968 Convention, of the 1971 Protocol, of the 1978 Convention, of the 1982 Convention and of the 1989 Convention in the Danish, Dutch, English, German, Greek, Irish, Italian, Spanish and Portuguese languages to the Governments of the Republic of Austria, the Republic of Finland and the Kingdom of Sweden.

2. The texts of the 1968 Convention, of the 1971 Protocol, of the 1978 Convention, of the 1982 Convention and of the 1989 Convention, drawn up in the Finnish and Swedish languages, shall be authentic under the same conditions as the other texts of the 1968 Convention, the 1971 Protocol, and 1978 Convention, the 1982 Convention and the 1989 Convention.

Article 15

This Convention shall be ratified by the signatory States. The instruments of ratification shall be deposited with the Secretary-General of the Council of the European Union.

Article 16

1. This Convention shall enter into force on the first day of the third month following the date on which two signatory States, one of which is the Republic of Austria, the Republic of Finland or the Kingdom of Sweden, deposit their instruments of ratification.

2. This Convention shall produce its effects for any other signatory State on the first day of the third month following the deposit of its instrument of ratification.

Article 17

The Secretary-General of the Council of the European Union shall notify the signatory States of:

(a) the deposit of each instrument of ratification;

(b) the dates of entry into force of this Convention for the Contracting States.

Article 18

This Convention, drawn up in a single original in the Danish, Dutch, English, Finnish, French, German, Greek, Irish, Italian, Portuguese, Spanish and Swedish languages, all twelve texts being equally authentic, shall be deposited in the archives of the General Secretariat of the Council of the European Union. The Secretary-General shall transmit a certified copy to the Government of each signatory State.]

[103]

NOTES

Commencement: 1 January 2001.

Inserted by the Civil Jurisdiction and Judgments Act 1982 (Amendment) Order 2000, SI 2000/1824, art 8(3), Sch 3.

(*Sch 3C contains the text of the Lugano Convention, printed in Pt IV(B) of this work at* **[3063]**.)

[SCHEDULE 4

CHAPTER II OF THE REGULATION AS MODIFIED: RULES FOR ALLOCATION OF JURISDICTION WITHIN UK

General

1 Subject to the rules of this Schedule, persons domiciled in a part of the United Kingdom shall be sued in the courts of that part.

2 Persons domiciled in a part of the United Kingdom may be sued in the courts of another part of the United Kingdom only by virtue of rules 3 to 13 of this Schedule.

Special jurisdiction

3 A person domiciled in a part of the United Kingdom may, in another part of the United Kingdom, be sued—

(a) in matters relating to a contract, in the courts for the place of performance of the obligation in question;

(b) in matters relating to maintenance, in the courts for the place where the maintenance creditor is domiciled or habitually resident or, if the matter is ancillary to proceedings concerning the status of a person, in the court which, according to its own law, has jurisdiction to entertain those proceedings, unless that jurisdiction is based solely on the nationality of one of the parties;

(c) in matters relating to tort, delict or quasi-delict, in the courts for the place where the harmful event occurred or may occur;

(d) as regards a civil claim for damages or restitution which is based on an act giving rise to criminal proceedings, in the court seised of those proceedings, to the extent that that court has jurisdiction under its own law to entertain civil proceedings;

(e) as regards a dispute arising out of the operations of a branch, agency or other establishment, in the courts for the place in which the branch, agency or other establishment is situated;

(f) as settlor, trustee or beneficiary of a trust created by the operation of a statute, or by a written instrument, or created orally and evidenced in writing, in the courts of the part of the United Kingdom in which the trust is domiciled;

(g) as regards a dispute concerning the payment of remuneration claimed in respect of the salvage of a cargo or freight, in the court under the authority of which the cargo or freight in question—

(i) has been arrested to secure such payment; or

(ii) could have been so arrested, but bail or other security has been given;

provided that this provision shall apply only if it is claimed that the defendant has an interest in the cargo or freight or had such an interest at the time of salvage;

(h) in proceedings—

(i) concerning a debt secured on immovable property; or

(ii) which are brought to assert, declare or determine proprietary or possessory rights, or rights of security, in or over movable property, or to obtain authority to dispose of movable property,

in the courts of the part of the United Kingdom in which the property is situated.

4 Proceedings which have as their object a decision of an organ of a company or other legal person or of an association of natural or legal persons may, without prejudice to the other provisions of this Schedule, be brought in the courts of the part of the United Kingdom in which that company, legal person or association has its seat.

5 A person domiciled in a part of the United Kingdom may, in another part of the United Kingdom, also be sued—

(a) where he is one of a number of defendants, in the courts for the place where any one of them is domiciled, provided the claims are so closely connected that it is expedient to hear and determine them together to avoid the risk of irreconcilable judgments resulting from separate proceedings;

(b) as a third party in an action on a warranty or guarantee or in any other third party proceedings, in the court seised of the original proceedings, unless these were instituted solely with the object of removing him from the jurisdiction of the court which would be competent in his case;

(c) on a counter-claim arising from the same contract or facts on which the original claim was based, in the court in which the original claim is pending;

(d) in matters relating to a contract, if the action may be combined with an action against the same defendant in matters relating to rights in rem in immovable property, in the court of the part of the United Kingdom in which the property is situated.

6 Where by virtue of this Schedule a court of a part of the United Kingdom has jurisdiction in actions relating to liability arising from the use or operation of a ship, that court, or any other court substituted for this purpose by the internal law of that part, shall also have jurisdiction over claims for limitation of such liability.

Jurisdiction over consumer contracts

7(1) In matters relating to a contract concluded by a person, the consumer, for a purpose which can be regarded as being outside his trade or profession, jurisdiction shall be determined by this rule and rules 8 and 9, without prejudice to rule 3(e) and (h)(ii), if—

(a) it is a contract for the sale of goods on instalment credit terms; or

(b) it is a contract for a loan repayable by instalments, or for any other form of credit, made to finance the sale of goods; or

(c) in all other cases, the contract has been concluded with a person who pursues commercial or professional activities in the part of the United Kingdom in which the consumer is domiciled or, by any means, directs such activities to that part or to other parts of the United Kingdom including that part, and the contract falls within the scope of such activities.

(2) This rule shall not apply to a contract of transport other than a contract which, for an inclusive price, provides for a combination of travel and accommodation, or to a contract of insurance.

8(1) A consumer may bring proceedings against the other party to a contract either in the courts of the part of the United Kingdom in which that party is domiciled or in the courts of the part of the United Kingdom in which the consumer is domiciled.

(2) Proceedings may be brought against a consumer by the other party to the contract only in the courts of the part of the United Kingdom in which the consumer is domiciled.

(3) The provisions of this rule shall not affect the right to bring a counter-claim in the court in which, in accordance with this rule and rules 7 and 9, the original claim is pending.

9 The provisions of rules 7 and 8 may be departed from only by an agreement—
- (a) which is entered into after the dispute has arisen; or
- (b) which allows the consumer to bring proceedings in courts other than those indicated in those rules; or
- (c) which is entered into by the consumer and the other party to the contract, both of whom are at the time of conclusion of the contract domiciled or habitually resident in the same part of the United Kingdom, and which confers jurisdiction on the courts of that part, provided that such an agreement is not contrary to the law of that part.

Jurisdiction over individual contracts of employment

10(1) In matters relating to individual contracts of employment, jurisdiction shall be determined by this rule, without prejudice to rule 3(e).

(2) An employer may be sued—
- (a) in the courts of the part of the United Kingdom in which he is domiciled; or
- (b) in the courts of the part of the United Kingdom where the employee habitually carries out his work or in the courts of that part where he last did so; or
- (c) if the employee does not or did not habitually carry out his work in any one place, in the courts of the part of the United Kingdom where the business which engaged the employee is or was situated.

(3) An employer may bring proceedings only in the courts of the part of the United Kingdom in which the employee is domiciled.

(4) The provisions of this rule shall not affect the right to bring a counter-claim in the court in which, in accordance with this rule, the original claim is pending.

(5) The provisions of this rule may be departed from only by an agreement on jurisdiction—
- (a) which is entered into after the dispute has arisen; or
- (b) which allows the employee to bring proceedings in courts other than those indicated in this rule.

Exclusive jurisdiction

11 The following courts shall have exclusive jurisdiction, regardless of domicile:—
- (a)
  - (i) in proceedings which have as their object rights *in rem* in immovable property or tenancies of immovable property, the courts of the part of the United Kingdom in which the property is situated;
  - (ii) however, in proceedings which have as their object tenancies of immovable property concluded for temporary private use for a maximum period of six consecutive months, the courts of the part of the United Kingdom in which the defendant is domiciled shall also have jurisdiction, provided that the tenant is a natural person and that the landlord and the tenant are domiciled in the same part of the United Kingdom;
- (b) in proceedings which have as their object the validity of the constitution, the nullity or the dissolution of companies or other legal persons or associations of natural or legal persons, the courts of the part of the United Kingdom in which the company, legal person or association has its seat;
- (c) in proceedings which have as their object the validity of entries in public registers, the courts of the part of the United Kingdom in which the register is kept;
- (d) in proceedings concerned with the enforcement of judgments, the courts of the part of the United Kingdom in which the judgment has been or is to be enforced.

Prorogation of jurisdiction

12(1) If the parties have agreed that a court or the courts of a part of the United Kingdom are to have jurisdiction to settle any disputes which have arisen or which may arise in connection with a particular legal relationship, and, apart from this Schedule, the agreement would be effective to confer jurisdiction under the law of that part, that court or those courts shall have jurisdiction.

(2) The court or courts of a part of the United Kingdom on which a trust instrument has conferred jurisdiction shall have jurisdiction in any proceedings brought against a settlor, trustee or beneficiary, if relations between these persons or their rights or obligations under the trust are involved.

(3) Agreements or provisions of a trust instrument conferring jurisdiction shall have no legal force if they are contrary to the provisions of rule 9, or if the courts whose jurisdiction they purport to exclude have exclusive jurisdiction by virtue of rule 11.

13(1) Apart from jurisdiction derived from other provisions of this Schedule, a court of a part of the United Kingdom before which a defendant enters an appearance shall have jurisdiction.

(2) This rule shall not apply where appearance was entered to contest the jurisdiction, or where another court has exclusive jurisdiction by virtue of rule 11.

Examination as to jurisdiction and admissibility

14 Where a court of a part of the United Kingdom is seised of a claim which is principally concerned with a matter over which the courts of another part of the United Kingdom have exclusive jurisdiction by virtue of rule 11, it shall declare of its own motion that it has no jurisdiction.

15(1) Where a defendant domiciled in one part of the United Kingdom is sued in a court of another part of the United Kingdom and does not enter an appearance, the court shall declare of its own motion that it has no jurisdiction unless its jurisdiction is derived from the provisions of this Schedule.

(2) The court shall stay the proceedings so long as it is not shown that the defendant has been able to receive the document instituting the proceedings or an equivalent document in sufficient time to enable him to arrange for his defence, or that all necessary steps have been taken to this end.

Provisional, including protective, measures

16 Application may be made to the courts of a part of the United Kingdom for such provisional, including protective, measures as may be available under the law of that part, even if, under this Schedule, the courts of another part of the United Kingdom have jurisdiction as to the substance of the matter.]

[104]

NOTES

Commencement: 1 March 2002.

Substituted by the Civil Jurisdiction and Judgments Order 2001, SI 2001/3929, art 4, Sch 2, Pt II, para 4.

SCHEDULE 5
PROCEEDINGS EXCLUDED FROM SCHEDULE 4

Section 17

Proceedings under the Companies Acts

1. Proceedings for the winding up of a company under the [Insolvency Act 1986] or the [Insolvency (Northern Ireland) Order 1989], or proceedings relating to a company as respects which jurisdiction is conferred on the court having winding up jurisdiction under either of those Acts.

Patents, trade marks, designs and similar rights

2. Proceedings concerned with the registration or validity of patents, trade marks, designs or other similar rights required to be deposited or registered.

Protection of Trading Interests Act 1980

3. Proceedings under section 6 of the Protection of Trading Interests Act 1980 (recovery of sums paid or obtained pursuant to a judgment for multiple damages).

Appeals etc from tribunals

4. Proceedings on appeal from, or for review of, decisions of tribunals.

5. (*Relates to maintenance.*)

Proceedings under certain conventions, etc

6. Proceedings brought in any court in pursuance of—
   (a) any statutory provision which, in the case of any convention to which Article 57[, or Article 71 of the Regulation,] applies (conventions relating to specific matters which override the general rules …), implements the convention or makes provision with respect to jurisdiction in any field to which the convention relates; and
   (b) any rule of law so far as it has the effect of implementing any such convention.

Certain Admiralty proceedings in Scotland

7. Proceedings in Scotland in an Admiralty cause where the jurisdiction of the Court of Session or, as the case may be, of the sheriff is based on arrestment *in rem* or *ad fundandam jurisdictionem* of a ship, cargo or freight.

Register of aircraft mortgages

8. Proceedings for the rectification of the register of aircraft mortgages kept by the Civil Aviation Authority.

Continental Shelf Act 1964

9. Proceedings brought in any court in pursuance of an order under [section 11 of the Petroleum Act 1998].

[Financial Services Act 1986

10. Proceedings such as are mentioned in [section 415 of the Financial Services and Markets Act 2000].]

[105]

NOTES

Para 1: words in first pair of square brackets substituted by the Insolvency Act 1986, s 439(2), Sch 14; words in second pair of square brackets substituted by the Insolvency (Northern Ireland) Order 1989, SI 1989/2405, art 381(2), Sch 9, Pt II, para 32.

Para 2: by virtue of the Patents, Designs and Marks Act 1986, s 2(3), Sch 2, Pt I, para 1(2)(j) (repealed, as from a day to be appointed, by the Trade Marks Act 1994, s 106(2), Sch 5), any reference to a trade mark in this paragraph includes a reference to a service mark; and by virtue of the Trade Marks Act 1994, s 106(1), Sch 4, para 1, as from a day to be appointed, any such reference shall also be construed as a reference to a trade mark or registered trade mark within the meaning of the 1994 Act.

Para 6: words in square brackets inserted and words omitted repealed by the Civil Jurisdiction and Judgments Order 2001, SI 2001/3929, art 4, Sch 2, Pt II, para 5.

Para 9: words in square brackets substituted by the Petroleum Act 1998, s 50, Sch 4, para 17(a).

Para 10: added, together with the heading preceding it, by the Financial Services Act 1986, s 188(2); substituted by the Companies Act 1989, s 200(2); words in square brackets substituted by the Financial Services and Markets Act 2000, s 432(1), Sch 20, para 3.

SCHEDULE 6
ENFORCEMENT OF UK JUDGMENTS (MONEY PROVISIONS)

Section 18

Preliminary

1. In this Schedule—
"judgment" means any judgment to which section 18 applies and references to the giving of a judgment shall be construed accordingly;
"money provision" means a provision for the payment of one or more sums of money;
"prescribed" means prescribed by rules of court.

Certificates in respect of judgments

2.(1) Any interested party who wishes to secure the enforcement in another part of the United Kingdom of any money provisions contained in a judgment may apply for a certificate under this Schedule.

(2) The application shall be made in the prescribed manner to the proper officer of the original court, that is to say—
- (a) in relation to a judgment within paragraph (a) of the definition of "judgment" in section 18(2), the court by which the judgment or order was given or made;
- (b) in relation to a judgment within paragraph (b) of that definition, the court in which the judgment or order is entered;
- (c) in relation to a judgment within paragraph (c) of that definition, the court in whose books the document is registered;
- (d) in relation to a judgment within paragraph (d) of that definition, the tribunal by which the award or order was made;
- (e) in relation to a judgment within paragraph (e) of that definition, the court which gave the judgment or made the order by virtue of which the award has become enforceable as mentioned in that paragraph.

3. A certificate shall not be issued under this Schedule in respect of a judgment unless under the law of the part of the United Kingdom in which the judgment was given—
- (a) either—
  - (i) the time for bringing an appeal against the judgment has expired, no such appeal having been brought within that time; or
  - (ii) such an appeal having been brought within that time, that appeal has been finally disposed of; and
- (b) enforcement of the judgment is not for the time being stayed or suspended, and the time available for its enforcement has not expired.

4.(1) Subject to paragraph 3, on an application under paragraph 2 the proper officer shall issue to the applicant a certificate in the prescribed form—
- (a) stating the sum or aggregate of the sums (including any costs or expenses) payable under the money provisions contained in the judgment, the rate of interest, if any, payable thereon and the date or time from which any such interest began to accrue;
- (b) stating that the conditions specified in paragraph 3(a) and (b) are satisfied in relation to the judgment; and
- (c) containing such other particulars as may be prescribed.

(2) More than one certificate may be issued under this Schedule (simultaneously or at different times) in respect of the same judgment.

Registration of certificates

5.(1) Where a certificate has been issued under this Schedule in any part of the United Kingdom, any interested party may, within six months from the date of its issue, apply in the prescribed manner to the proper officer of the superior court in any other part of the United Kingdom for the certificate to be registered in that court.

(2) In this paragraph "superior court" means, in relation to England and Wales or Northern Ireland, the High Court and, in relation to Scotland, the Court of Session.

(3) Where an application is duly made under this paragraph to the proper officer of a superior court, he shall register the certificate in that court in the prescribed manner.

General effect of registration

6.(1) A certificate registered under this Schedule shall, for the purposes of its enforcement, be of the same force and effect, the registering court shall have in relation to its enforcement the same powers, and proceedings for or with respect to its enforcement may be taken, as if the certificate had been a judgment originally given in the registering court and had (where relevant) been entered.

(2) Sub-paragraph (1) is subject to the following provisions of this Schedule and to any provision made by rules of court as to the manner in which and the conditions subject to which a certificate registered under this Schedule may be enforced.

Costs or expenses

7. Where a certificate is registered under this Schedule, the reasonable costs or expenses of and incidental to the obtaining of the certificate and its registration shall be recoverable as if they were costs or expenses stated in the certificate to be payable under a money provision contained in the original judgment.

Interest

8.(1) Subject to any provision made under sub-paragraph (2), the debt resulting, apart from paragraph 7, from the registration of the certificate shall carry interest at the rate, if any, stated in the certificate from the date or time so stated.

(2) Provision may be made by rules of court as to the manner in which and the periods by reference to which any interest payable by virtue of sub-paragraph (1) is to be calculated and paid, including provision for such interest to cease to accrue as from a prescribed date.

(3) All such sums as are recoverable by virtue of paragraph 7 carry interest as if they were the subject of an order for costs or expenses made by the registering court on the date of registration of the certificate.

(4) Except as provided by this paragraph sums payable by virtue of the registration of a certificate under this Schedule shall not carry interest.

Stay or sisting of enforcement in certain cases

9. Where a certificate in respect of a judgment has been registered under this Schedule, the registering court may, if it is satisfied that any person against whom it is sought to enforce the certificate is entitled and intends to apply under the law of the part of the United Kingdom in which the judgment was given for any remedy which would result in the setting aside or quashing of the judgment, stay (or, in Scotland, sist) proceedings for the enforcement of the certificate, on such terms as it thinks fit, for such period as appears to the court to be reasonably sufficient to enable the application to be disposed of.

Cases in which registration of a certificate must or may be set aside

10. Where a certificate has been registered under this Schedule, the registering court—
- (a) shall set aside the registration if, on an application made by any interested party, it is satisfied that the registration was contrary to the provisions of this Schedule;
- (b) may set aside the registration if, on an application so made, it is satisfied that the matter in dispute in the proceedings in which the judgment in question was given had previously been the subject of a judgment by another court or tribunal having jurisdiction in the matter.

[106]

NOTES

Transitional provision: see s 53(2), Sch 13, Pt II, para 2 at **[97]**, **[111]**.

SCHEDULE 7
ENFORCEMENT OF UK JUDGMENTS (NON-MONEY PROVISIONS)

Section 18

Preliminary

1. In this Schedule—

"judgment" means any judgment to which section 18 applies and references to the giving of a judgment shall be construed accordingly;

"non-money provision" means a provision for any relief or remedy not requiring payment of a sum of money;

"prescribed" means prescribed by rules of court.

Certified copies of judgments

2.(1) Any interested party who wishes to secure the enforcement in another part of the United Kingdom of any non-money provisions contained in a judgment may apply for a certified copy of the judgment.

(2) The application shall be made in the prescribed manner to the proper officer of the original court, that is to say—

(a) in relation to a judgment within paragraph (a) of the definition of "judgment" in section 18(2), the court by which the judgment or order was given or made;

(b) in relation to a judgment within paragraph (b) of that definition, the court in which the judgment or order is entered;

(c) in relation to a judgment within paragraph (c) of that definition, the court in whose books the document is registered;

(d) in relation to a judgment within paragraph (d) of that definition, the tribunal by which the award or order was made;

(e) in relation to a judgment within paragraph (e) of that definition, the court which gave the judgment or made the order by virtue of which the award has become enforceable as mentioned in that paragraph.

3. A certified copy of a judgment shall not be issued under this Schedule unless under the law of the part of the United Kingdom in which the judgment was given—

(a) either—

(i) the time for bringing an appeal against the judgment has expired, no such appeal having been brought within that time; or

(ii) such an appeal having been brought within that time, that appeal has been finally disposed of; and

(b) enforcement of the judgment is not for the time being stayed or suspended, and the time available for its enforcement has not expired.

4.(1) Subject to paragraph 3, on an application under paragraph 2 the proper officer shall issue to the applicant—

(a) a certified copy of the judgment (including any money provisions or excepted provisions which it may contain); and

(b) a certificate stating that the conditions specified in paragraph 3(a) and (b) are satisfied in relation to the judgment.

(2) In sub-paragraph (1)(a) "excepted provision" means any provision of a judgment which is excepted from the application of section 18 by subsection (5) of that section.

(3) There may be issued under this Schedule (simultaneously or at different times)—

(a) more than one certified copy of the same judgment; and

(b) more than one certificate in respect of the same judgment.

Registration of judgments

5.(1) Where a certified copy of a judgment has been issued under this Schedule in any part of the United Kingdom, any interested party may apply in the prescribed manner to the superior court in any other part of the United Kingdom for the judgment to be registered in that court.

(2) In this paragraph "superior court" means, in relation to England and Wales or Northern Ireland, the High Court and, in relation to Scotland, the Court of Session.

(3) An application under this paragraph for the registration of a judgment must be accompanied by—

(a) a certified copy of the judgment issued under this Schedule; and

(b) a certificate issued under paragraph 4(1)(b) in respect of the judgment not more than six months before the date of the application.

(4) Subject to sub-paragraph (5), where an application under this paragraph is duly made to a superior court, the court shall order the whole of the judgment as set out in the certified copy to be registered in that court in the prescribed manner.

(5) A judgment shall not be registered under this Schedule by the superior court in any part of the United Kingdom if compliance with the non-money provisions contained in the judgment would involve a breach of the law of that part of the United Kingdom.

General effect of registration

6.(1) The non-money provisions contained in a judgment registered under this Schedule shall, for the purposes of their enforcement, be of the same force and effect, the registering court shall have in relation to their enforcement the same powers, and proceedings for or with respect to their enforcement may be taken, as if the judgment containing them had been originally given in the registering court and had (where relevant) been entered.

(2) Sub-paragraph (1) is subject to the following provisions of this Schedule and to any provision made by rules of court as to the manner in which and the conditions subject to which the non-money provisions contained in a judgment registered under this Schedule may be enforced.

Costs or expenses

7.(1) Where a judgment is registered under this Schedule, the reasonable costs or expenses of and incidental to—

(a) the obtaining of the certified copy of the judgment and of the necessary certificate under paragraph 4(1)(b) in respect of it; and

(b) the registration of the judgment,

shall be recoverable as if on the date of registration there had also been registered in the registering court a certificate under Schedule 6 in respect of the judgment and as if those costs or expenses were costs or expenses stated in that certificate to be payable under a money provision contained in the judgment.

(2) All such sums as are recoverable by virtue of sub-paragraph (1) shall carry interest as if they were the subject of an order for costs or expenses made by the registering court on the date of registration of the judgment.

Stay or sisting of enforcement in certain cases

8. Where a judgment has been registered under this Schedule, the registering court may, if it is satisfied that any person against whom it is sought to enforce the judgment is entitled and intends to apply under the law of the part of the United Kingdom in which the judgment was given for any remedy which would result in the setting aside or quashing of the judgment, stay (or, in Scotland, sist) proceedings for the enforcement of the judgment, on such terms as it thinks fit, for such period as appears to the court to be reasonably sufficient to enable the application to be disposed of.

Cases in which registered judgment must or may be set aside

9. Where a judgment has been registered under this Schedule, the registering court—

(a) shall set aside the registration if, on an application made by any interested party, it is satisfied that the registration was contrary to the provisions of this Schedule;

(b) may set aside the registration if, on an application so made, it is satisfied that the matter in dispute in the proceedings in which the judgment was given had previously been the subject of a judgment by another court or tribunal having jurisdiction in the matter.

[107]

NOTES

Transitional provision: see s 53(2), Sch 13, Pt II, para 3 at **[97]**, **[111]**.

[SCHEDULE 8
RULES AS TO JURISDICTION IN SCOTLAND

General

1. Subject to the following rules, persons shall be sued in the courts for the place where they are domiciled.

Special jurisdiction

2. Subject to rules 3 (jurisdiction over consumer contracts), 4 (jurisdiction over individual contracts of employment), 5 (exclusive jurisdiction) and 6 (prorogation), a person may also be sued—

(a) where he has no fixed residence, in a court within whose jurisdiction he is personally cited;

(b) in matters relating to a contract, in the courts for the place of performance of the obligation in question;

(c) in matters relating to delict or quasi-delict, in the courts for the place where the harmful event occurred or may occur;

(d) as regards a civil claim for damages or restitution which is based on an act giving rise to criminal proceedings, in the court seised of those proceedings to the extent that the court has jurisdiction to entertain civil proceedings;

(e) in matters relating to maintenance, in the courts for the place where the maintenance creditor is domiciled or habitually resident or, if the matter is ancillary to proceedings concerning the status of a person, in the court which has jurisdiction to entertain those proceedings, provided that an action for adherence and aliment or of affiliation and aliment shall be treated as a matter relating to maintenance which is not ancillary to proceedings concerning the status of a person;

(f) as regards a dispute arising out of the operations of a branch, agency or other establishment, in the courts for the place in which the branch, agency or other establishment is situated;

(g) in his capacity as settlor, trustee or beneficiary of a trust domiciled in Scotland created by the operation of a statute, or by a written instrument, or created orally and evidenced in writing, in the Court of Session, or the appropriate sheriff court within the meaning of section 24A of the Trusts (Scotland) Act 1921;

(h) where he is not domiciled in the United Kingdom, in the courts for any place where—

   (i) any movable property belonging to him has been arrested; or

   (ii) any immovable property in which he has any beneficial interest is situated;

(i) in proceedings which are brought to assert, declare or determine proprietary or possessory rights, or rights of security, in or over movable property, or to obtain authority to dispose of movable property, in the courts for the place where the property is situated;

(j) in proceedings for interdict, in the courts for the place where it is alleged that the wrong is likely to be committed;

(k) in proceedings concerning a debt secured over immovable property, in the courts for the place where the property is situated;

(l) in proceedings which have as their object a decision of an organ of a company or other legal person or of an association of natural or legal persons, in the courts for the place where that company, legal person or association has its seat;

(m) in proceedings concerning an arbitration which is conducted in Scotland or in which the procedure is governed by Scots law, in the Court of Session;

(n) in proceedings principally concerned with the registration in the United Kingdom or the validity in the United Kingdom of patents, trade marks, designs or other similar rights required to be deposited or registered, in the Court of Session;

(o)
  (i) where he is one of a number of defenders, in the courts for the place where any one of them is domiciled, provided the claims are so closely connected that it is expedient to hear and determine them together to avoid the risk of irreconcilable judgments resulting from separate proceedings;
  (ii) as a third party in an action on a warranty or guarantee or in any other third party proceedings, in the court seised of the original proceedings, unless these were instituted solely with the object of removing him from the jurisdiction of the court which would be competent in his case;
  (iii) on a counterclaim arising from the same contract or facts on which the original claim was based, in the court in which the original claim is pending;

(p) in matters relating to a contract, if the action may be combined with an action against the same defender in matters relating to rights in rem in immovable property, in the courts for the place where the property is situated;

(q) as regards a claim for limitation of liability arising from the use or operation of a ship, in the court having jurisdiction in the action relating to such liability.

Jurisdiction over consumer contracts

3.(1) In matters relating to a contract concluded by a person, the consumer, for a purpose which can be regarded as being outside his trade or profession, subject to rule 5, jurisdiction shall be determined by this rule if—

(a) it is a contract for the sale of goods on instalment credit terms; or
(b) it is a contract for a loan repayable by instalments, or for any other form of credit, made to finance the sale of goods; or
(c) in all other cases, the contract has been concluded with a person who pursues commercial or professional activities in Scotland or, by any means, directs such activities to Scotland or to several places including Scotland, and the contract falls within the scope of such activities.

(2) This rule shall not apply to a contract of transport other than a contract which, for an inclusive price, provides for a combination of travel and accommodation.

(3) A consumer may bring proceedings against the other party to a contract only in—

(a) the courts for the place in which that party is domiciled;
(b) the courts for the place in which he is himself domiciled; or
(c) any court having jurisdiction by virtue of rule 2(f) or (i).

(4) Proceedings may be brought against a consumer by the other party to the contract only in the courts for the place where the consumer is domiciled or any court having jurisdiction under rule 2(i).

(5) The provisions of this rule shall not affect the right to bring a counterclaim in the court in which, in accordance with this rule, the original claim is pending.

(6) The provisions of this rule may be departed from only by an agreement—

(a) which is entered into after the dispute has arisen; or
(b) which allows the consumer to bring proceedings in courts other than those indicated in this rule; or
(c) which is entered into by the consumer and the other party to the contract, both of whom are at the time of conclusion of the contract domiciled or habitually resident in the same Regulation State, and which confers jurisdiction on the courts of that Regulation State, provided that such an agreement is not contrary to the law of that Regulation State.

Jurisdiction over individual contracts of employment

4.(1) In matters relating to individual contracts of employment, jurisdiction shall be determined by this rule, without prejudice to rule 2(f).

(2) An employer may be sued—

(a) in the courts for the place where he is domiciled; or

(b) in the courts for the place where the employee habitually carries out his work or in the courts for the last place where he did so; or

(c) if the employee does not or did not habitually carry out his work in any one place, in the courts for the place where the business which engaged the employee is or was situated.

(3) An employer may bring proceedings only in the courts for the place in which the employee is domiciled.

(4) The provisions of this rule shall not affect the right to bring a counter-claim in the court in which, in accordance with this rule, the original claim is pending.

(5) The provisions of this rule may be departed from only by an agreement on jurisdiction—

(a) which is entered into after the dispute has arisen; or

(b) which allows the employee to bring proceedings in courts other than those indicated in this rule.

Exclusive jurisdiction

5.(1) Notwithstanding anything contained in any of rules 1 to 4 above or 6 to 9 below but subject to paragraph (3) below, the following courts shall have exclusive jurisdiction:—

(a) in proceedings which have as their object rights *in rem* in, or tenancies of, immovable property, the courts for the place where the property is situated;

(b) in proceedings which have as their object the validity of the constitution, the nullity or the dissolution of companies or other legal persons or associations of natural or legal persons, the courts for the place where the company, legal person or association has its seat;

(c) in proceedings which have as their object the validity of entries in public registers, the courts for the place where the register is kept;

(d) in proceedings concerned with the enforcement of judgments, the courts for the place where the judgment has been or is to be enforced.

(2) No court shall exercise jurisdiction in a case where immovable property, the seat of a body mentioned in paragraph (1)(b) above, a public register or the place where a judgment has been or is to be enforced is situated outside Scotland and where paragraph (1) would apply if the property, seat, register or, as the case may be, place of enforcement were situated in Scotland.

(3) In proceedings which have as their object tenancies of immovable property concluded for temporary private use for a maximum period of six consecutive months, the courts for the place in which the defender is domiciled shall also have jurisdiction, provided that the tenant is a natural person and that the landlord and tenant are domiciled in Scotland.

Prorogation of jurisdiction

6.(1) If the parties have agreed that a court is to have jurisdiction to settle any disputes which have arisen or which may arise in connection with a particular legal relationship, that court shall have jurisdiction.

(2) Such an agreement conferring jurisdiction shall be either—

(a) in writing or evidenced in writing; or

(b) in a form which accords with practices which the parties have established between themselves; or

(c) in international trade or commerce, in a form which accords with a usage of which the parties are or ought to have been aware and which in such trade or commerce is widely known to, and regularly observed by, parties to contracts of the type involved in the particular trade or commerce concerned.

(3) Any communication by electronic means which provides a durable record of the agreement shall be equivalent to "writing".

(4) The court on which a trust instrument has conferred jurisdiction shall have exclusive jurisdiction in any proceedings brought against a settlor, trustee or beneficiary, if relations between these persons or their rights or obligations under the trust are involved.

(5) Where an agreement or a trust instrument confers jurisdiction on the courts of the United Kingdom or of Scotland, proceedings to which paragraph (1) or, as the case may be, (4) above applies may be brought in any court in Scotland.

(6) Agreements or provisions of a trust instrument conferring jurisdiction shall have no legal force if the courts whose jurisdiction they purport to exclude have exclusive jurisdiction by virtue of rule 5 or where rule 5(2) applies.

7.(1) Apart from jurisdiction derived from other provisions of this Schedule, a court before whom a defender enters an appearance shall have jurisdiction.

(2) This rule shall not apply where appearance was entered to contest jurisdiction, or where another court has exclusive jurisdiction by virtue of rule 5 or where rule 5(2) applies.

Examination as to jurisdiction and admissibility

8. Where a court is seised of a claim which is principally concerned with a matter over which another court has exclusive jurisdiction by virtue of rule 5, or where it is precluded from exercising jurisdiction by rule 5(2), it shall declare of its own motion that it has no jurisdiction.

9. Where in any case a court has no jurisdiction which is compatible with this Schedule, and the defender does not enter an appearance, the court shall declare of its own motion that it has no jurisdiction.]

[108]

NOTES

Commencement: 1 March 2002.

Substituted by the Civil Jurisdiction and Judgments Order 2001, SI 2001/3929, art 4, Sch 2, Pt III, para 7.

SCHEDULE 9
PROCEEDINGS EXCLUDED FROM SCHEDULE 8

Section 21

1. Proceedings concerning the status or legal capacity of natural persons (including proceedings for separation) other than proceedings which consist solely of proceedings … of affiliation and aliment.

2. Proceedings for regulating the custody of children.

[2A. Proceedings relating to parental responsibilities within the meaning of section 1(3) of the Children (Scotland) Act 1995 or parental rights within the meaning of section 2(4) of that Act.]

3. Proceedings relating to [guardianship of children] and all proceedings relating to the management of the affairs of persons who are incapable of managing their own affairs.

4. Proceedings in respect of sequestration in bankruptcy; or the winding up of a company or other legal person; or proceedings in respect of a judicial arrangement or judicial composition with creditors.

5. Proceedings relating to a company where, by any enactment, jurisdiction in respect of those proceedings is conferred on the court having jurisdiction to wind it up.

6. Admiralty causes in so far as the jurisdiction is based on arresting *in rem* or *ad fundandam jurisdictionem* of a ship, cargo or freight.

7. Commissary proceedings.

8. Proceedings for the rectification of the register of aircraft mortgages kept by the Civil Aviation Authority.

9. Proceedings under section 7(3) of the Civil Aviation (Eurocontrol) Act 1962 (recovery of charges for air navigation services and proceedings for damages against Eurocontrol).

10. Proceedings brought in pursuance of an order under [section 11 of the Petroleum Act 1998].

11. Proceedings under section 6 of the Protection of Trading Interests Act 1980 (recovery of sums paid or obtained pursuant to a judgment for multiple damages).

12. Appeals from or review of decisions of tribunals.

13. Proceedings which are not in substance proceedings in which a decree against any person is sought.

14. Proceedings brought in any court in pursuance of—

(a) any statutory provision which, in the case of any convention to which Article 57[, or Article 71 of the Regulation,] applies (conventions relating to specific matters which override the general rules …), implements the convention; and

(b) any rule of law so far as it has the effect of implementing any such convention.

[109]

NOTES

Para 1: words omitted repealed by the Family Law (Scotland) Act 1985, s 28(2), Sch 2.

Para 2A: inserted by the Children (Scotland) Act 1995, s 105(4), Sch 4, para 31.

Para 3: words in square brackets substituted by the Age of Legal Capacity (Scotland) Act 1991, s 10(1), Sch 1, para 38.

Para 10: words in square brackets substituted by the Petroleum Act 1998, s 50, Sch 4, para 17(b).

Para 14: words in square brackets inserted and words omitted repealed by the Civil Jurisdiction and Judgments Order 2001, SI 2001/3929, art 4, Sch 2, Pt III, para 8.

(*Sch 10 amends the Foreign Judgments* (*Reciprocal Enforcement*) *Act 1933 at* **[16]**; *Sch 11 makes consequential amendments to provisions relating to maintenance; Sch 12 makes further consequential amendments to provisions outside the scope of this work.*)

SCHEDULE 13
COMMENCEMENT, TRANSITIONAL PROVISIONS AND SAVINGS

Section 53

PART I
COMMENCEMENT

Provisions coming into force on Royal Assent

1. The following provisions come into force on Royal Assent—

Provision	*Subject-matter*
section 53(1) and Part I of this Schedule	Commencement
section 55	Short title

Provisions coming into force six weeks after Royal Assent

2. The following provisions come into force at the end of the period of six weeks beginning with the day on which this Act is passed—

Provision	*Subject-matter*
Section 24(1)(a), (2)(a) and (3).	Interim relief and protective measures in cases of doubtful jurisdiction.
…	…
section 30	Proceedings in England and Wales or Northern Ireland for torts to immovable property.

Provision	*Subject-matter*
section 31	Overseas judgments given against states.
section 32	Overseas judgments given in breach of agreement for settlement of disputes.
section 33	Certain steps not to amount to submission to jurisdiction of overseas court.
section 34	Certain judgments a bar to further proceedings on the same cause of action.
section 35(3)	Consolidation of Orders in Council under section 14 of the Administration of Justice Act 1920.
section 38	Overseas judgments counteracting an award of multiple damages.
section 40	Power to modify enactments relating to legal aid, etc
section 49	Saving for powers to stay, sist, strike out or dismiss proceedings.
section 50	Interpretation: general.
section 51	Application to Crown.
section 52	Extent.
paragraphs 7 to 10 of Part II of this Schedule and section 53(2) so far as relates to those paragraphs	Transitional provisions and savings.
section 54 and Schedule 14 so far as relating to the repeal of provisions in section 4 of the Foreign Judgments (Reciprocal Enforcement) Act 1933	Repeals consequential on sections 32 and 33.

Provisions coming into force on a day to be appointed

3.(1) The other provisions of this Act come into force on such day as the Lord Chancellor and the Lord Advocate may appoint by order made by statutory instrument.

(2) Different days may be appointed under this paragraph for different purposes.

[110]

NOTES

Words omitted relate to provisions not printed in this work.

Orders: the Civil Jurisdiction and Judgments Act 1982 (Commencement No 1) Order 1984, SI 1984/1553; the Civil Jurisdiction and Judgments Act 1982 (Commencement No 2) Order 1986, SI 1986/1781; the Civil Jurisdiction and Judgments Act 1982 (Commencement No 3) Order 1986, SI 1986/2044.

PART II
TRANSITIONAL PROVISIONS AND SAVINGS

Section 16 and Schedule 4

1.(1) Section 16 and Schedule 4 shall not apply to any proceedings begun before the commencement of that section.

(2) Nothing in section 16 or Schedule 4 shall preclude the bringing of proceedings in any part of the United Kingdom in connection with a dispute concerning a contract if the parties to the dispute had agreed before the commencement of the section that the contract was to be governed by the law of that part of the United Kingdom.

Section 18 and Schedule 6 and associated repeals

2.(1) In relation to a judgment a certificate whereof has been registered under the 1868 Act or the 1882 Act before the repeal of that Act by this Act, the 1868 Act or, as the case may be, the 1882 Act shall continue to have effect notwithstanding its repeal.

(2) Where by virtue of sub-paragraph (1) the 1882 Act continues to have effect in relation to an order to which section 47 of the Fair Employment (Northern Ireland) Act 1976 (damages etc for unfair discrimination) applies, that section shall continue to have effect in relation to that order notwithstanding the repeal of that section by this Act.

(3) A certificate issued under Schedule 6 shall not be registered under that Schedule in a part of the United Kingdom if the judgment to which that certificate relates is the subject of a certificate registered in that part under the 1868 Act or the 1882 Act.

(4) In this paragraph—
"the 1868 Act" means the Judgments Extension Act 1868;
"the 1882 Act" means the Inferior Courts Judgments Extension Act 1882;
"judgment" has the same meaning as in section 18.

Section 18 and Schedule 7

3. Schedule 7 and, so far as it relates to that Schedule, section 18 shall not apply to judgments given before the coming into force of that section.

4. Section 19 shall not apply to judgments given before the commencement of that section.

Section 20 and Schedule 8

5. Section 20 and Schedule 8 shall not apply to any proceedings begun before the commencement of that section.

Section 26

6. The power conferred by section 26 shall not be exercisable in relation to property arrested before the commencement of that section or in relation to bail or other security given—

(a) before the commencement of that section to prevent the arrest of property; or
(b) to obtain the release of property arrested before the commencement of that section; or
(c) in substitution (whether directly or indirectly) for security given as mentioned in sub-paragraph (a) or (b).

Section 31

7. Section 31 shall not apply to any judgment—

(a) which has been registered under Part II of the Administration of Justice Act 1920 or Part I of the Foreign Judgments (Reciprocal Enforcement) Act 1933 before the time when that section comes into force; or
(b) in respect of which proceedings at common law for its enforcement have been finally determined before that time.

Section 32 and associated repeal

8.(1) Section 32 shall not apply to any judgment—

(a) which has been registered under Part II of the Administration of Justice Act 1920, Part I of the Foreign Judgments (Reciprocal Enforcement) Act 1933 or Part I of the Maintenance Orders (Reciprocal Enforcement) Act 1972 before the time when that section comes into force; or
(b) in respect of which proceedings at common law for its enforcement have been finally determined before that time.

(2) Section 4(3)(b) of the Foreign Judgments (Reciprocal Enforcement) Act 1933 shall continue to have effect, notwithstanding its repeal by this Act, in relation to a judgment registered under Part I of that Act before the commencement of section 32.

Section 33 and associated repeal

9.(1) Section 33 shall not apply to any judgment—
- (a) which has been registered under Part II of the Administration of Justice Act 1920 or Part I of the Foreign Judgments (Reciprocal Enforcement) Act 1933 before the time when that section comes into force; or
- (b) in respect of which proceedings at common law for its enforcement have been finally determined before that time.

(2) The repeal by this Act of words in section 4(2)(a)(i) of the Foreign Judgments (Reciprocal Enforcement) Act 1933 shall not affect the operation of that provision in relation to a judgment registered under Part I of that Act before the commencement of section 33.

Section 34

10. Section 34 shall not apply to judgments given before the commencement of that section. **[111]**

NOTES

Fair Employment (Northern Ireland) Act 1976, s 47: repealed by s 54 of, and Sch 14 to, this Act.

Judgments Extension Act 1868: Inferior Courts Extension Act 1882: repealed by s 54 of, and Sch 14 to, this Act.

(*Sch 14 contains repeals.*)

COMPANIES ACT 1985

(1985 c 6)

ARRANGEMENT OF SECTIONS

PART XXIII
OVERSEA COMPANIES

CHAPTER I
REGISTRATION, ETC

PART XXV
MISCELLANEOUS AND SUPPLEMENTARY PROVISIONS

PART XXVI
INTERPRETATION

PART XXVII
FINAL PROVISIONS

An Act to consolidate the greater part of the Companies Acts

[11 March 1985]

NOTES

The provisions of the Companies Act 1985 reproduced here (with the exception of s 747) will be repealed if the Company Law Reform Bill [HL] is enacted in its present form (see the draft Bill, cl 880, Sch 15 (25 April 2006)). For the proposed new rules concerning service on UK and overseas companies, see cls 678, 756 of the draft Bill.

1–690 *((Pts I–XXII) relate to the formation and administration, etc of companies within the UK. Ss 36 to 36C which apply to companies incorporated outside Great Britain by virtue of the Foreign Companies (Execution of Documents) Regulations 1994, SI 1994/950 at* **[2174]** *and ss 38 and 39 are reproduced in Part I(B) of this work at* **[173]**, **[174]**).)

PART XXIII
OVERSEA COMPANIES

CHAPTER I
REGISTRATION, ETC

[690A Branch registration under the Eleventh Company Law Directive (89/666/EEC)

(1) This section applies to any limited company which—

(a) is incorporated outside the United Kingdom and Gibraltar, and

(b) has a branch in Great Britain.

(2) Schedule 21A to this Act (Branch registration under the Eleventh Company Law Directive (89/666/EEC)) shall have effect in relation to any company to which this section applies.]

[112]

NOTES

Inserted, subject to transitional provisions, together with s 690B, by the Oversea Companies and Credit and Financial Institutions (Branch Disclosure) Regulations 1992, SI 1992/3179, reg 3, Sch 2, Pt I, paras 1, 2.

[690B Scope of sections 691 and 692

Sections 691 and 692 shall not apply to any limited company which—

(a) is incorporated outside the United Kingdom and Gibraltar, and

(b) has a branch in the United Kingdom.]

[113]

NOTES

Inserted as noted to s 690A at **[112]**.

691 Documents to be delivered to registrar

(1) When a company incorporated outside Great Britain establishes a place of business in Great Britain, it shall within one month of doing so deliver to the registrar of companies for registration—

(a) a certified copy of the charter, statutes or memorandum and articles of the company or other instrument constituting or defining the company's constitution, and, if the instrument is not written in the English language, a certified translation of it; and

(b) a return in the prescribed form containing—

(i) a list of the company's directors and secretary, containing [(subject to subsection (5))] the particulars specified in the next subsection,

(ii) a list of the names and addresses of some one or more persons resident in Great Britain authorised to accept on the company's behalf service of process and any notices required to be served on it,

(iii) a list of the documents delivered in compliance with paragraph (a) of this subsection, and

(iv) [subject to subsection (3A),] a statutory declaration (made by a director or secretary of the company or by any person whose name and address are given in the list required by sub-paragraph (ii)), stating the date on which the company's place of business in Great Britain was established.

[(2) The list referred to in subsection (1)(b)(i) shall contain the following particulars with respect to each director—

(a) in the case of an individual—

(i) his name,

(ii) any former name,

(iii) his usual residential address,

(iv) his nationality,

(v) his business occupation (if any),

(vi) if he has no business occupation but holds other directorships, particulars of them, and

(vii) his date of birth;

(b) in the case of a corporation or Scottish firm, its corporate or firm name and registered or principal office.

(3) The list referred to in subsection (1)(b)(i) shall contain the following particulars with respect to the secretary (or, where there are joint secretaries, with respect to each of them)—

(a) in the case of an individual, his name, any former name and his usual residential address;

(b) in the case of a corporation or Scottish firm, its corporate or firm name and registered or principal office.

Where all the partners in a firm are joint secretaries of the company, the name and principal office of the firm may be stated instead of the particulars required by paragraph (a).

[(3A) In place of the statutory declaration referred to in sub-paragraph (iv) of paragraph (b) of subsection (1), there may be delivered to the registrar of companies using electronic communications a statement made by any person by whom the declaration could have been made stating the date on which the company's place of business in Great Britain was established.]

(4) In subsections (2)(a) and (3)(a) above—

(a) "name" means a person's Christian name (or other forename) and surname, except that in the case of a peer, or an individual usually known by a title, the title may be stated instead of his Christian name (or other forename) and surname, or in addition to either or both of them; and

(b) the reference to a former name does not include—

(i) in the case of a peer, or an individual normally known by a British title, the name by which he was known previous to the adoption of or succession to the title, or

(ii) in the case of any person, a former name which was changed or disused before he attained the age of 18 years or which has been changed or disused for 20 years or more, or

(iii) in the case of a married woman, the name by which she was known previous to the marriage.]

[(4A) Any person who makes a false statement under subsection (3A) which he knows to be false or does not believe to be true is liable to imprisonment or a fine, or both.]

[(5) Where a confidentiality order made under section 723B is in force in respect of a director or secretary required to be specified in the list under subsection (1)(b)(i)—

(a) if the order is in respect of a director, subsection (2) has effect in respect of that director as if the reference in subsection (2)(a)(iii) to his usual residential address were a reference to the address for the time being notified by him to the company under regulations made under sections 723B to 723F;

(b) if the order is in respect of a secretary, subsection (3) has effect in respect of that secretary as if the reference in subsection (3)(a) to his usual residential address were a reference to the address for the time being notified by him to the company under such regulations; and

(c) in either case the company shall deliver to the registrar, in addition to the return required by subsection (1), a return in the prescribed form containing the usual residential address of the director or secretary to whom the confidentiality order relates, and any such return shall be delivered to the registrar within one month of the company establishing a place of business in Great Britain.]

[114]

NOTES

Sub-s (1): in para (b)(i) words in square brackets inserted by the Companies (Particulars of Usual Residential Address) (Confidentiality Orders) Regulations 2002, SI 2002/912, reg 16, Sch 2, para 5(1), (2); in para (b)(iv) words in square brackets inserted by the Companies Act 1985 (Electronic Communications) Order 2000, SI 2000/3373, art 26(1), (2).

Sub-ss (2)–(4): substituted for original sub-s (2) by the Companies Act 1989, s 145, Sch 19, para 6.

Sub-ss (3A), (4A): inserted by SI 2000/3373, art 26(1), (3), (4).

Sub-s (5): added by SI 2002/912, reg 16, Sch 2, para 5(1), (3).

692 Registration of altered particulars

(1) If any alteration is made in—

(a) the charter, statutes, or memorandum and articles of an oversea company or any such instrument as is mentioned above, or

(b) the directors or secretary of an oversea company or the particulars contained in the list of the directors and secretary, or

(c) the names or addresses of the persons authorised to accept service on behalf of an oversea company,

the company shall, within the time specified below, deliver to the registrar of companies for registration a return containing the prescribed particulars of the alteration.

[(1A) If an individual in respect of whom a confidentiality order under section 723B is in force becomes a director or secretary of an oversea company—

(a) the return required to be delivered to the registrar under subsection (1) shall contain the address for the time being notified by the director or secretary to the company under regulations made under sections 723B to 723F, but shall not contain his usual residential address; and

(b) with that return the company shall deliver to the registrar a return in the prescribed form containing the usual residential address of that director or secretary.

(1B) If a confidentiality order under section 723B is made in respect of an existing director or secretary of an oversea company, the company shall within the time specified below deliver to the registrar of companies for registration a return in the prescribed form containing the address for the time being notified to it by the director or secretary under regulations made under sections 723B to 723F.

(1C) If while a confidentiality order made under section 723B is in force in respect of a director or secretary of an oversea company there is an alteration in his usual residential address, the company shall within the time specified below deliver to the registrar of companies for registration a return in the prescribed form containing the new address.]

(2) If any change is made in the corporate name of an oversea company, the company shall, within the time specified below, deliver to the registrar of companies for registration a return containing the prescribed particulars of the change.

(3) The time for delivery of the returns required by subsections (1)[, (1B), (1C)] and (2) is—

(a) in the case of an alteration to which subsection (1)(c) applies, 21 days after the making of the alteration, and

(b) otherwise, 21 days after the date on which notice of the alteration or change in question could have been received in Great Britain in due course of post (if despatched with due diligence).

[115]

NOTES

Sub-ss (1A)–(1C): inserted by the Companies (Particulars of Usual Residential Address) (Confidentiality Orders) Regulations 2002, SI 2002/912, reg 16, Sch 2, para 6(1), (2).

Sub-s (3): words in square brackets inserted by SI 2002/912, reg 16, Sch 2, para 6(1), (3).

[692A Change in registration regime

(1) Where a company ceases to be a company to which section 690A applies and, immediately after ceasing to be such a company—

(a) continues to have in Great Britain a place of business which it had immediately before ceasing to be such a company, and

(b) does not have a branch in Northern Ireland,

it shall be treated for the purposes of section 691 as having established the place of business on the date when it ceased to be a company to which section 690A applies.

(2) Where a limited company incorporated outside the United Kingdom and Gibraltar—

(a) ceases to have a branch in Northern Ireland, and

(b) both immediately before and immediately after ceasing to do so, has a place of business, but not a branch, in Great Britain,

it shall be treated for the purposes of section 691 as having established the place of business on the date when it ceased to have a branch in Northern Ireland.

(3) Where a company—

(a) becomes a company to which section 690A applies,

(b) immediately after becoming such a company, has in a part of Great Britain an established place of business but no branch, and

(c) immediately before becoming such a company, had an established place of business in that part,

sections 691 and 692 shall, in relation to that part, continue to apply to the company (notwithstanding section 690B) until such time as it gives notice to the registrar for that part that it is a company to which that section applies.

(4) Schedule 21B to this Act (transitional provisions in relation to change in registration regime) shall have effect.]

[116]

NOTES

Inserted by the Oversea Companies and Credit and Financial Institutions (Branch Disclosure) Regulations 1992, SI 1992/3179, reg 3(1), Sch 2, Pt I, paras 1, 4.

693 Obligation to state name and other particulars

[(1)] Every oversea company shall—

(*a*) *in every prospectus inviting subscriptions for its shares or debentures in Great Britain, state the country in which the company is incorporated,*

(b) conspicuously exhibit on every place where it carries on business in Great Britain the company's name and the country in which it is incorporated,

(c) cause the company's name and the country in which it is incorporated to be stated in legible characters in all bill-heads and letter paper, and in all notices and other official publications of the company, and

(d) if the liability of the members of the company is limited, cause notice of that fact to be stated in legible characters *in every such prospectus as above mentioned and* in all bill-heads, letter paper, notices and other official publications of the company in Great Britain, and to be affixed on every place where it carries on its business.

[(2) Every company to which section 690A applies shall, in the case of each branch of the company registered under paragraph 1 of Schedule 21A, cause the following particulars to be stated in legible characters in all letter paper and order forms used in carrying on the business of the branch—

(a) the place of registration of the branch, and

(b) the registered number of the branch.

(3) Every company to which section 690A applies, which is not incorporated in a Member State and which is required by the law of the country in which it is incorporated to be

registered shall, in the case of each branch of the company registered under paragraph 1 of Schedule 21A, cause the following particulars to be stated in legible characters in all letter paper and order forms used in carrying on the business of the branch—

(a) the identity of the registry in which the company is registered in its country of incorporation, and

(b) the number with which it is registered.

(4) Every company to which section 690A applies and which is not incorporated in a Member State shall, in the case of each branch of the company registered under paragraph 1 of Schedule 21A, cause the following particulars to be stated in legible characters in all letter paper and order forms used in carrying on the business of the branch—

(a) the legal form of the company,

(b) the location of its head office, and

(c) if applicable, the fact that it is being wound up.]

[117]

NOTES

Sub-s (1): numbered as such by the Oversea Companies and Credit and Financial Institutions (Branch Disclosure) Regulations 1992, SI 1992/3179, reg 3(1), Sch 2, Pt I, paras 1, 6; para (a) and words in italics in para (d) repealed with savings, for certain purposes relating to financial services, by the Financial Services Act 1986, s 212(3), Sch 17, Pt I.

Sub-ss (2)–(4): added by SI 1992/3179, reg 3(1), Sch 2, Pt I, paras 1, 6.

[694 Regulation of oversea companies in respect of their names

(1) If it appears to the Secretary of State that the corporate name of an oversea company is a name by which the company, had it been formed under this Act, would on the relevant date [(determined in accordance with subsections (3A) and (3B))] have been precluded from being registered by section 26 either—

(a) because it falls within subsection (1) of that section, or

(b) if it falls within subsection (2) of that section, because the Secretary of State would not approve the company's being registered with that name,

the Secretary of State may serve a notice on the company, stating why the name would not have been registered.

(2) If the corporate name of an oversea company is in the Secretary of State's opinion too like a name appearing on the relevant date in the index of names kept by the registrar of companies under section 714 or which should have appeared in that index on that date, or is the same as a name which should have so appeared, the Secretary of State may serve a notice on the company specifying the name in the index which the company's name is too like or which is the same as the company's name.

(3) No notice shall be served on a company under subsection (1) or (2) later than 12 months after the relevant date, …

[(3A) For the purposes of subsections (1) to (3), the relevant date, in relation to a company, is the date on which it has complied with paragraph 1 of Schedule 21A or section 691(1) or, if there is more than one such date, the first date on which it has complied with that paragraph or that subsection since becoming an oversea company.

(3B) But where the company's corporate name has changed since the date ascertained in accordance with subsection (3A), the relevant date is the date on which the company has, in respect of the change or, if more than one, the latest change, complied with paragraph 7(1) of Schedule 21A or section 692(2), as the case may be.]

(4) An oversea company on which a notice is served under subsection (1) or (2)—

(a) may deliver to the registrar of companies for registration a statement in the prescribed form specifying a name approved by the Secretary of State other than its corporate name under which it proposes to carry on business in Great Britain, and

(b) may, after that name has been registered, at any time deliver to the registrar for registration a statement in the prescribed form specifying a name approved by the Secretary of State (other than its corporate name) in substitution for the name previously registered.

(5) The name by which an oversea company is for the time being registered under subsection (4) is, for all purposes of the law applying in Great Britain (including this Act and the Business Names Act 1985), deemed to be the company's corporate name; but—

(a) this does not affect references to the corporate name in this section, or any rights or obligations of the company, or render defective any legal proceedings by or against the company, and

(b) any legal proceedings that might have been continued or commenced against the company by its corporate name or its name previously registered under this section may be continued or commenced against it by its name for the time being so registered.

(6) An oversea company on which a notice is served under subsection (1) or (2) shall not at any time after the expiration of 2 months from the service of that notice (or such longer period as may be specified in that notice) carry on business in Great Britain under its corporate name.

Nothing in this subsection, or in section 697(2) (which imposes penalties for its contravention) invalidates any transaction entered into by the company.

(7) The Secretary of State may withdraw a notice served under subsection (1) or (2) at any time before the end of the period mentioned in subsection (6); and that subsection does not apply to a company served with a notice which has been withdrawn.

[118]

NOTES

Sub-s (1): words in square brackets substituted by the Oversea Companies and Credit and Financial Institutions (Branch Disclosure) Regulations 1992, SI 1992/3179, reg 3(1), Sch 2, Pt I, paras 1, 7(1), (2).
Sub-s (3): words omitted repealed by SI 1992/3179, reg 3(1), Sch 2, Pt I, paras 1, 7(1), (3).
Sub-ss (3A), (3B): inserted by SI 1992/3179, reg 3(1), Sch 2, Pt I, paras 1, 7(1), (4).

[694A Service of documents: companies to which section 690A applies

(1) This section applies to any company to which section 690A applies.

(2) Any process or notice required to be served on a company to which this section applies in respect of the carrying on of the business of a branch registered by it under paragraph 1 of Schedule 21A is sufficiently served if—

(a) addressed to any person whose name has, in respect of the branch, been delivered to the registrar as a person falling within paragraph 3(e) of that Schedule, and

(b) left at or sent by post to the address for that person which has been so delivered.

(3) Where—

(a) a company to which this section applies makes default, in respect of a branch, in delivering to the registrar the particulars mentioned in paragraph 3(e) of Schedule 21A, or

(b) all the persons whose names have, in respect of a branch, been delivered to the registrar as persons falling within paragraph 3(e) of that Schedule are dead or have ceased to reside in Great Britain, or refuse to accept service on the company's behalf, or for any reason cannot be served,

a document may be served on the company in respect of the carrying on of the business of the branch by leaving it at, or sending it by post to, any place of business established by the company in Great Britain.

(4) Where a company to which this section applies has more than one branch in Great Britain, any notice or process required to be served on the company which is not required to be served in respect of the carrying on of the business of one branch rather than another shall be treated for the purposes of this section as required to be served in respect of the carrying on of the business of each of its branches.]

[119]

NOTES

Inserted by the Oversea Companies and Credit and Financial Institutions (Branch Disclosure) Regulations 1992, SI 1992/3179, reg 3(1), Sch 2, Pt I, paras 1, 8.

695 Service of documents on oversea company

(1) Any process or notice required to be served on an oversea company [to which section 691 applies] is sufficiently served if addressed to any person whose name has been delivered to the registrar under preceding sections in this Part and left at or sent by post to the address which has been so delivered.

(2) However—

(a) where such a company makes default in delivering to the registrar the name and address of a person resident in Great Britain who is authorised to accept on behalf of the company service of process or notices, or

(b) if at any time all the persons whose names and addresses have been so delivered are dead or have ceased so to reside, or refuse to accept service on the company's behalf, or for any reason cannot be served,

a document may be served on the company by leaving it at, or sending it by post to, any place of business established by the company in Great Britain.

[120]

NOTES

Sub-s (1): words in square brackets inserted by the Oversea Companies and Credit and Financial Institutions (Branch Disclosure) Regulations 1992, SI 1992/3179, reg 3(1), Sch 2, Pt I, paras 1, 9.

[695A Registrar to whom documents to be delivered: companies to which section 690A applies

(1) References to the registrar, in relation to a company to which section 690A applies, (except references in Schedule 21C [or Chapter III of this Part]) shall be construed in accordance with the following provisions.

(2) The documents which a company is required to deliver to the registrar shall be delivered—

(a) to the registrar for England and Wales, if required to be delivered in respect of a branch in England and Wales; and

(b) to the registrar for Scotland, if required to be delivered in respect of a branch in Scotland.

(3) If a company closes a branch in a part of Great Britain, it shall forthwith give notice of that fact to the registrar for that part; and from the date on which notice is so given it is no longer obliged to deliver documents to that registrar in respect of that branch.

(4) In subsection (3) above, the reference to closing a branch in either part of Great Britain includes a reference to a branch ceasing to be situated in that part on becoming situated elsewhere.]

[121]

NOTES

Inserted by the Oversea Companies and Credit and Financial Institutions (Branch Disclosure) Regulations 1992, SI 1992/3179, reg 3(1), Sch 2, Pt I, paras 1, 10.

Sub-s (1): words in square brackets inserted by the Companies Act 1989, s 107, Sch 16, para 1A (as inserted by SI 1992/3179, reg 4, Sch 3, para 16) as from a day to be appointed.

696 Office where documents to be filed

(1) Any document which an oversea company [to which section 691 applies] is required to deliver to the registrar of companies shall be delivered to the registrar at the registration office in England and Wales or Scotland, according to where the company has established a place of business.

(2) If the company has established a place of business both in England and Wales and in Scotland, the document shall be delivered at the registration office both in England and Wales and in Scotland.

(3) References in this Part [(except references in Schedule 21C)] to the registrar of companies[, in relation to a company to which section 691 applies,] are to be construed in accordance with the above subsections.

(4) If an oversea company [to which section 691 applies] ceases to have a place of business in either part of Great Britain, it shall forthwith give notice of that fact to the registrar of companies for that part; and as from the date on which notice is so given the obligation of the company to deliver any document to the registrar ceases.

[122]

NOTES

Sub-s (1): words in square brackets inserted by the Oversea Companies and Credit and Financial Institutions (Branch Disclosure) Regulations 1992, SI 1992/3179, reg 3(1), Sch 2, Pt I, paras 1, 11(a).

Sub-s (3): words in square brackets inserted by SI 1992/3179, regs 3(1), 4, Sch 2, Pt I, para 11(b), Sch 3, paras 3, 4.
Sub-s (4): words in square brackets inserted by SI 1992/3179, reg 3(1), Sch 2, Pt I, paras 1, 11(c).
Substituted by the Companies Act 1989, s 145, Sch 19, para 13 (as amended by SI 1992/3179, reg 4, Sch 3, para 17), as from a day to be appointed, as follows—

"696 Registrar to whom documents to be delivered

(1) References to the registrar in relation to an oversea company [to which section 691 applies] (except references [in Schedule 21C or Chapter III of this Part)], shall be construed in accordance with the following provisions.

(2) The documents which an oversea company is required to deliver to the registrar shall be delivered—

(a) to the registrar for England and Wales if the company has established a place of business in England and Wales, and

(b) to the registrar for Scotland if the company has established a place of business in Scotland;

and if the company has an established place of business in both parts of Great Britain, the documents shall be delivered to both registrars.

(3) If a company ceases to have a place of business in either part of Great Britain, it shall forthwith give notice of that fact to the registrar for that part; and from the date on which notice is so given it is no longer obliged to deliver documents to that registrar."

697 Penalties for non-compliance

(1) If an oversea company fails to comply with any of sections 691 to 693 and 696, the company, and every officer or agent of the company who knowingly and wilfully authorises or permits the default, is liable to a fine and, in the case of a continuing offence, to a daily default fine for continued contravention.

(2) If an oversea company contravenes section 694(6), the company and every officer or agent of it who knowingly and wilfully authorises or permits the contravention is guilty of an offence and liable to a fine and, for continued contravention, to a daily default fine.

[(3) If an oversea company fails to comply with section 695A or Schedule 21A, the company, and every officer or agent of the company who knowingly and wilfully authorises or permits the default, is liable to a fine and, in the case of a continuing offence, to a daily default fine for continued contravention.]

[123]

NOTES

Sub-s (3): added by the Oversea Companies and Credit and Financial Institutions (Branch Disclosure) Regulations 1992, SI 1992/3179, reg 3(1), Sch 2, Pt I, paras 1, 12.

698 Definitions ...

[(1)] For purposes of this Chapter—

"certified" means certified in the prescribed manner to be a true copy or a correct translation;

"director", in relation to an oversea company, includes shadow director; and

"secretary" includes any person occupying the position of secretary by whatever name called.

[(2) For the purposes of this Part (except section 699A and Schedule 21C):

(a) where a branch comprises places of business in more than one part of the United Kingdom the branch shall be treated as being situated in that part of the United Kingdom where its principal place of business is situated; and

(b) "branch" means a branch within the meaning of the Council Directive concerning disclosure requirements in respect of branches opened in a Member State by certain types of company governed by the law of another State (the Eleventh Company Law Directive, 89/666/EEC).]

[124]

NOTES

Words omitted from section heading repealed by the Oversea Companies and Credit and Financial Institutions (Branch Disclosure) Regulations 1992, SI 1992/3179, reg 3(1), Sch 2, Pt I, paras 1, 13(1), (2).
Sub-s (1): numbered as such by SI 1992/3179, reg 3(1), Sch 2, Pt I, paras 1, 13(1), (2).
Sub-s (2): added by SI 1992/3179, reg 3(1), Sch 2, Pt I, paras 1, 13(1), (3).

699 Channel Islands and Isle of Man companies

(1) With the exceptions specified in subsection (3) below, the provisions of this Act requiring documents to be forwarded or delivered to or filed with the registrar of companies and applying to companies formed and registered under Part I apply also (if they would not otherwise) to an oversea company [to which section 691 applies] incorporated in the Channel Islands or the Isle of Man.

(2) Those provisions apply to such a company—

(a) if it has established a place of business in England and Wales, as if it were registered in England and Wales,

(b) if it has established a place of business in Scotland, as if it were registered in Scotland, and

(c) if it has established a place of business both in England and Wales and in Scotland, as if it were registered in both England and Wales and Scotland,

with such modifications as may be necessary and, in particular, apply in a similar way to documents relating to things done outside Great Britain as if they had been done in Great Britain.

(3) The exceptions are—

section 6(1) (resolution altering company's objects),

section 18 (alteration of memorandum or articles by statute or statutory instrument),

[section 242(1)] (directors' duty to file accounts),

section 288(2) (notice to registrar of change of directors or secretary), and

section 380 (copies of certain resolutions and agreements to be sent to registrar within 15 days), so far as applicable to a resolution altering a company's memorandum or articles.

[125]

NOTES

Sub-s (1): words in square brackets inserted by the Oversea Companies and Credit and Financial Institutions (Branch Disclosure) Regulations 1992, SI 1992/3179, reg 3(1), Sch 2, Pt I, paras 1, 14.

Sub-s (3): words in square brackets substituted by the Companies Act 1989, s 23, Sch 10, para 12.

699A–715A (*In so far as unrepealed, ss 699A–703* (*Ch II*) *relate to the delivery of accounts and reports; ss 703A–703N* (*Ch III*) *relate to the registration of charges; ss 703O–703R* (*Ch IV*) *relate to winding up etc; ss 704–715A* (*Pt XXIV*) *relate to the registrar of companies, his functions and offices.*)

PART XXV
MISCELLANEOUS AND SUPPLEMENTARY PROVISIONS

716–724 (*In so far as unrepealed, contain miscellaneous and supplementary provisions.*)

725 Service of documents

(1) A document may be served on a company by leaving it at, or sending it by post to, the company's registered office.

(2) Where a company registered in Scotland carries on business in England and Wales, the process of any court in England and Wales may be served on the company by leaving it at, or sending it by post to, the company's principal place of business in England and Wales, addressed to the manager or other head officer in England and Wales of the company.

(3) Where process is served on a company under subsection (2), the person issuing out the process shall send a copy of it by post to the company's registered office.

[126]

726–734 (*Contain miscellaneous and supplementary provisions.*)

PART XXVI
INTERPRETATION

735 "Company", etc

(1) In this Act—

(a) "company" means a company formed and registered under this Act, or an existing company;

(b) "existing company" means a company formed and registered under the former Companies Acts, but does not include a company registered under the Joint Stock Companies Acts, the Companies Act 1862 or the Companies (Consolidation) Act 1908 in what was then Ireland;

(c) "the former Companies Acts" means the Joint Stock Companies Acts, the Companies Act 1862, the Companies (Consolidation) Act 1908, the Companies Act 1929 and the Companies Acts 1948 to 1983.

(2) "Public company" and "private company" have the meanings given by section 1(3).

(3) "The Joint Stock Companies Acts" means the Joint Stock Companies Act 1856, the Joint Stock Companies Acts 1856, 1857, the Joint Stock Banking Companies Act 1857 and the Act to enable Joint Stock Banking Companies to be formed on the principle of limited liability, or any one or more of those Acts (as the case may require), but does not include the Joint Stock Companies Act 1844.

(4) The definitions in this section apply unless the contrary intention appears.

[127]

NOTES

In relation to the application of this section, with modifications, for the purposes of a converting Societas Europaea on and after registration, see the European Public Limited-Liability Company Regulations 2004, SI 2004/2326, reg 88, Sch 4, paras 5, 11.

735A–744A (*Contain further interpretative provision.*)

PART XXVII
FINAL PROVISIONS

745, 746 (*S 745 makes provision as to Northern Ireland; s 746 relates to commencement.*)

747 Citation

This Act may be cited as the Companies Act 1985.

[128]

SCHEDULES

(*Schs 1–21 outside the scope of this work.*)

[SCHEDULE 21A
BRANCH REGISTRATION UNDER THE ELEVENTH COMPANY LAW DIRECTIVE (89/666/EEC)

Section 690A

Duty to register

1.(1) A company shall, within one month of having opened a branch in a part of Great Britain, deliver to the registrar for registration a return in the prescribed form containing—

(a) such particulars about the company as are specified in paragraph 2,

(b) such particulars about the branch as are specified in paragraph 3, and

(c) if the company is one to which section 699AA applies, such particulars in relation to the registration of documents under Schedule 21D as are specified in paragraph 4.

(2) The return shall, except where sub-paragraph (3) below applies, be accompanied by the documents specified in paragraph 5 and, if the company is one to which Part I of Schedule 21D applies, the documents specified in paragraph 6.

(3) This sub-paragraph applies where—

(a) at the time the return is delivered, the company has another branch in the United Kingdom,

(b) the return contains a statement to the effect that the documents specified in paragraph 5, and, if the company is one to which Part I of Schedule 21D applies, paragraph 6, are included in the material registered in respect of the other branch, and

(c) the return states where the other branch is registered and what is its registered number.

(4) In sub-paragraph (1) above, the reference to having opened a branch in a part of Great Britain includes a reference to a branch having become situated there on ceasing to be situated elsewhere.

(5) If at the date on which the company opens the branch in Great Britain the company is subject to any proceedings referred to in section 703P(1) (winding up) or 703Q(1) (insolvency proceedings etc), the company shall deliver a return under section 703P(1) or (as the case may be) 703Q(1) within one month of that date.

If on or before that date a person has been appointed to be liquidator of the company and continues in that office at that date, section 703P(3) and (4) (liquidator to make return within 14 days of appointment) shall have effect as if it required a return to be made under that section within one month of the date of the branch being opened.

Particulars required

2.(1) The particulars referred to in paragraph 1(1)(a) are—

(a) the corporate name of the company,

(b) its legal form,

(c) if it is registered in the country of its incorporation, the identity of the register in which it is registered and the number with which it is so registered,

(d) a list of its directors and secretary, containing [(subject to paragraph 4A)]—

(i) with respect to each director, the particulars specified in sub-paragraph (3) below, and

(ii) with respect to the secretary (or where there are joint secretaries, with respect to each of them) the particulars specified in sub-paragraph (4) below,

(e) the extent of the powers of the directors to represent the company in dealings with third parties and in legal proceedings, together with a statement as to whether they may act alone or must act jointly and, if jointly, the name of any other person concerned, and

(f) whether the company is an institution to which section 699A (or the equivalent provision in Northern Ireland) applies.

(2) In the case of a company which is not incorporated in a Member State, those particulars also include—

(a) the law under which the company is incorporated,

(b) (in the case of a company to which either paragraphs 2 and 3 of Part I of Schedule 21C or Schedule 21D applies) the period for which the company is required by the law under which it is incorporated to prepare accounts, together with the period allowed for the preparation and public disclosure of accounts for such a period, and

(c) unless disclosed by the documents specified in paragraph 5—

(i) the address of its principal place of business in its country of incorporation,

(ii) its objects, and

(iii) the amount of its issued share capital.

(3) The particulars referred to in sub-paragraph (1)(d)(i) above are—

(a) in the case of an individual—

(i) his name,

(ii) any former name,

(iii) his usual residential address,

(iv) his nationality,

(v) his business occupation (if any),

(vi) particulars of any other directorships held by him, and

(vii) his date of birth;

(b) in the case of a corporation or Scottish firm, its corporate or firm name and registered or principal office.

(4) The particulars referred to in sub-paragraph (1)(d)(ii) above are—

(a) in the case of an individual, his name, any former name and his usual residential address;

(b) in the case of a corporation or Scottish firm, its corporate or firm name and registered or principal office.

Where all the partners in a firm are joint secretaries of the company, the name and principal office of the firm may be stated instead of the particulars required by paragraph (a) above.

(5) In sub-paragraphs (3)(a) and (4)(a) above—

(a) "name" means a person's forename and surname, except that in the case of a peer, or an individual usually known by a title, the title may be stated instead of his forename and surname, or in addition to either or both of them; and

(b) the reference to a former name does not include—

(i) in the case of a peer, or an individual normally known by a title, the name by which he was known previous to the adoption of or succession to the title;

(ii) in the case of any person, a former name which was changed or disused before he attained the age of 18 years or which has been changed or disused for 20 years or more;

(iii) in the case of a married woman, the name by which she was known previous to the marriage.

(6) Where—

(a) at the time a return is delivered under paragraph 1(1) the company has another branch in the same part of Great Britain as the branch covered by the return; and

(b) the company has delivered the particulars required by sub-paragraphs (1)(b) to (f) and (2) to (5) to the registrar with respect to that branch (or to the extent it is required to do so by virtue of Schedule 21B to this Act) and has no outstanding obligation to make a return to the registrar in respect of that branch under paragraph 7 in relation to any alteration to those particulars,

the company may adopt the particulars so delivered as particulars which the registrar is to treat as having been filed by the return by referring in the return to the fact that the particulars have been filed in respect of that other branch and giving the number with which the other branch is registered.

3. The particulars referred to in paragraph 1(1)(b) are—

(a) the address of the branch,

(b) the date on which it was opened,

(c) the business carried on at it,

(d) if different from the name of the company, the name in which that business is carried on,

(e) a list of the names and addresses of all persons resident in Great Britain authorised to accept on the company's behalf service of process in respect of the business of the branch and of any notices required to be served on the company in respect of the business of the branch,

(f) a list of the names and [(subject to paragraph 4A)] usual residential addresses of all persons authorised to represent the company as permanent representatives of the company for the business of the branch,

(g) the extent of the authority of any person falling within paragraph (f) above, including whether that person is authorised to act alone or jointly, and

(h) if a person falling within paragraph (f) above is not authorised to act alone, the name of any person with whom he is authorised to act.

4. The particulars referred to in paragraph 1(1)(c) are—

(a) whether it is intended to register documents under paragraph 2(2) or, as the case may be, 10(1) of Schedule 21D in respect of the branch or in respect of some other branch in the United Kingdom, and

(b) if it is, where that other branch is registered and what is its registered number.

[4A. Where a confidentiality order made under section 723B is in force in respect of a director or secretary required to be specified in the list under paragraph 2(1)(d) or a permanent representative required to be specified in the list under paragraph 3(f)—

(a) if the order is in respect of a director, paragraph 2(1)(d) has effect in respect of that director as if the reference in paragraph 2(3)(a)(iii) to his usual residential address were a reference to the address for the time being notified by him to the company under regulations made under sections 723B to 723F;

(b) if the order is in respect of a secretary, paragraph 2(1)(d) has effect in respect of that secretary as if the reference in paragraph 2(4)(a) to his usual residential address were a reference to the address for the time being notified by him to the company under such regulations;

(c) if the order is in respect of a permanent representative, paragraph 3(f) has effect in respect of that representative as if the reference to his usual residential address were a reference to the address for the time being notified by him to the company under such regulations; and

(d) in any case the company shall deliver to the registrar, in addition to the return required by paragraph 1(1) a return in the prescribed form containing particulars of the usual residential address of the director, secretary or permanent representative to whom the confidentiality order relates, and any such return shall be delivered to the registrar within one month of having opened a branch in a part of Great Britain.]

Documents required

5. The first documents referred to in paragraph 1(2) are—

(a) a certified copy of the charter, statutes or memorandum and articles of the company (or other instrument constituting or defining the company's constitution), and

(b) if any of the documents mentioned in paragraph (a) above is not written in the English language, a translation of it into English certified in the prescribed manner to be a correct translation.

6.(1) The second documents referred to in paragraph 1(2) are—

(a) copies of the latest accounting documents prepared in relation to a financial period of the company to have been publicly disclosed in accordance with the law of the country in which it is incorporated before the end of the period allowed for compliance with paragraph 1 in respect of the branch or, if earlier, the date on which the company complies with paragraph 1 in respect of the branch, and

(b) if any of the documents mentioned in paragraph (a) above is not written in the English language, a translation of it into English certified in the prescribed manner to be a correct translation.

(2) In sub-paragraph (1)(a) above, "financial period" and "accounting documents" shall be construed in accordance with paragraph 6 of Schedule 21D.

Alterations

7.(1) If, after a company has delivered a return under paragraph 1(1) above, any alteration is made in—

(a) its charter, statutes or memorandum and articles (or other instrument constituting or defining its constitution), or

(b) any of the particulars referred to in paragraph 1(1),

the company shall, within the time specified below, deliver to the registrar for registration a return in the prescribed form containing the prescribed particulars of the alteration.

In the case of an alteration in any of the documents referred to in paragraph (a), the return shall be accompanied by a certified copy of the document as altered, together with, if the document is not written in the English language, a translation of it into English certified in the prescribed manner to be a correct translation.

(2) The time for the delivery of the return required by sub-paragraph (1) above is—

(a) in the case of an alteration in any of the particulars specified in paragraph 3, 21 days after the alteration is made; or

(b) in the case of any other alteration, 21 days after the date on which notice of the alteration in question could have been received in Great Britain in due course of post (if despatched with due diligence).

(3) Where—

(a) a company has more than one branch in Great Britain, and

(b) an alteration relates to more than one of those branches,

sub-paragraph (1) above shall have effect to require the company to deliver a return in respect of each of the branches to which the alteration relates.

(4) For the purposes of sub-paragraph (3) above—

(a) an alteration in any of the particulars specified in paragraph 2 shall be treated as relating to every branch of the company (though where the company has more than one branch in a part of Great Britain a return in respect of an alteration in any of those particulars which gives the branch numbers of two or more such branches shall be treated as a return in respect of each branch whose number is given), but

(b) an alteration in the company's charter, statutes or memorandum and articles (or other instrument constituting or defining its constitution) shall only be treated as relating to a branch if the document altered is included in the material registered in respect of it.

8.(1) Sub-paragraph (2) below applies where—

(a) a company's return under paragraph 1(1) includes a statement to the effect mentioned in paragraph 1(3)(b), and

(b) the statement ceases to be true so far as concerns the documents specified in paragraph 5.

(2) The company shall, within the time specified below, deliver to the registrar of companies for registration in respect of the branch to which the return relates—

(a) the documents specified in paragraph 5, or

(b) a return in the prescribed form—

(i) containing a statement to the effect that those documents are included in the material which is registered in respect of another branch of the company in the United Kingdom, and

(ii) stating where the other branch is registered and what is its registered number.

(3) The time for complying with sub-paragraph (2) above is 21 days after the date on which notice of the fact that the statement in the earlier return has ceased to be true could have been received in Great Britain in due course of post (if despatched with due diligence).

(4) Sub-paragraph (2) above shall also apply where, after a company has made a return under sub-paragraph (2)(b) above, the statement to the effect mentioned in sub-paragraph (2)(b)(i) ceases to be true.

(5) For the purposes of sub-paragraph (2)(b), where the company has more than one branch in a part of Great Britain a return which gives the branch numbers of two or more such branches shall be treated as a return in respect of each branch whose number is given.]

[9.(1) If an individual in respect of whom a confidentiality order under section 723B is in force becomes a director, secretary or permanent representative of a company that has delivered a return under paragraph 1(1)—

(a) the return required to be delivered to the registrar under paragraph 7(1) shall contain the address for the time being notified to the company by the director, secretary or permanent representative under regulations made under sections 723B to 723F, but shall not contain his usual residential address; and

(b) with the return under paragraph 7(1) the company shall deliver to the registrar a return in the prescribed form containing the usual residential address of that director, secretary or permanent representative.

(2) If after a company has delivered a return under paragraph 1(1) a confidentiality order under section 723B is made in respect of an existing director, secretary or permanent representative of the company, the company shall within the time specified below deliver to the registrar of companies for registration a return in the prescribed form containing the address for the time being notified to it by the director, secretary or permanent representative under regulations made under sections 723B to 723F.

(3) Sub-paragraph (4) applies if, at any time after a company has delivered a return under paragraph 1(1), there is an alteration in the usual residential address of a director, secretary or permanent representative of the company in respect of whom a confidentiality order under section 723B is in force.

(4) The company shall within the time specified below deliver to the registrar of companies for registration a return in the prescribed form containing the new address.

(5) The time for the delivery of a return required by sub-paragraph (2) or (4) is 21 days after the date on which notice of the alteration in question could have been received in Great Britain in due course of post (if despatched with due diligence).

(6) Where a company has more than one branch in Great Britain and any provision of this paragraph requires a return to be made to the registrar, that provision requires the

company to deliver a return in respect of each of the branches; but a return which gives the branch numbers of two or more such branches shall be treated as a return in respect of each branch whose number is given.] **[129]**

NOTES

Inserted by the Oversea Companies and Credit and Financial Institutions (Branch Disclosure) Regulations 1992, SI 1992/3179, reg 3(1), Sch 2, Pt I, paras 1, 3.

Paras 2, 3: words in square brackets inserted by the Companies (Particulars of Usual Residential Address) (Confidentiality Orders) Regulations 2002, SI 2002/912, reg 16, Sch 2, para 8(1), (2).

Para 4A: inserted by SI 2002/912, reg 16, Sch 2, para 8(1), (3).

Para 9: added by SI 2002/912, reg 16, Sch 2, para 8(1), (4).

(Schs 21B–25 outside the scope of this work.)

COURT OF SESSION ACT 1988

(1988 c 36)

An Act to consolidate, with amendments to give effect to recommendations of the Scottish Law Commission, certain enactments relating to the constitution, administration and procedure of the Court of Session and procedure on appeal therefrom to the House of Lords; and to repeal, in accordance with recommendations of the Scottish Law Commission, certain enactments relating to the aforesaid matters which are no longer of practical utility

[29 July 1988]

1–4 *(Pt I relates to the constitution and administration of the Court.)*

PART II
GENERAL POWERS OF THE COURT IN RELATION TO PROCEDURE

5 Power to regulate procedure etc by act of sederunt

The Court shall have power by act of sederunt—

(a) to regulate and prescribe the procedure and practice to be followed in various categories of causes in the Court or in execution or diligence following on such causes, whether originating in the said Court or brought there by way of appeal, removal, remit, stated case, or other like process, and any matters incidental or relating to any such procedure or practice including (but without prejudice to the foregoing generality) the manner in which, the time within which, and the conditions on which any interlocutor of a Lord Ordinary may be submitted to the review of the Inner House, or any application to the Court, or any thing required or authorised to be done in relation to any such causes as aforesaid shall or may be made or done;

(b) to prescribe the form of any summons, defence, petition, answer, writ, pleading, extract of a decree or other document whatsoever to be used in, or for the purposes of, any such causes as aforesaid, or in, or for the purposes of, execution or diligence following on such causes and the manner in which, and the person by whom, any such summons, petition, writ, pleading, extract of a decree or document shall be signed or authenticated;

(c) to prescribe the manner in which, the time within which, and the conditions on which any verdict of a jury may be submitted to the review of the Inner House on any ground set out in section 29 of this Act;

(d) to regulate the production and recovery of documents;

[(da) to regulate the procedure to be followed in proceedings in the Court in connection with the making of orders under sections 12(1) and (6) and 13(2) of the Vulnerable Witnesses (Scotland) Act 2004 (asp 3) ("the 2004 Act");

(db) to regulate, so far as not regulated by the 2004 Act, the use in any proceedings in the Court of any special measures authorised by virtue of that Act to be used;]

(e) to provide in any category of causes before the Court, for [written statements (including affidavits) and reports, admissible under section 2(1)(b) of the Civil

Evidence (Scotland) Act 1988, to be received in evidence, on such conditions as may be prescribed, without being spoken to by a witness];

[(ee) to permit a person who is not an advocate or solicitor and is not represented by an advocate or solicitor to transmit, whether orally or in writing, the views of a child to the Court for the purposes of any enactment which makes provision (however expressed) for the Court to have regard to those views;]

(f) to provide for the payment into Court and the investment or application of sums of money awarded in any action of damages in the Court to a pupil or a minor;

(g) to regulate the fees of solicitors practising before the Court (other than such fees as the Secretary of State may regulate under or by virtue of section 33 of the Legal Aid (Scotland) Act 1986);

(h) to regulate the expenses which may be awarded to parties in causes before the Court;

(i) to regulate the summoning, remuneration, and duties of assessors;

(j) to fix the ordinary sessions of the Court and to regulate the days on which and times at which the Court shall sit;

(k) to prescribe the matters with which the vacation judge may deal;

(l) to make such regulations as may be necessary to carry out the provisions of this Act or of any Act conferring powers or imposing duties on the Court or relating to proceedings therein; and

(m) to modify, amend or repeal any provision of any enactment including this Act relating to matters with respect to which an act of sederunt may be made under this Act.

[130]

NOTES

Paras (da), (db) inserted for certain purposes and inserted as from a day to be appointed for remaining purposes by the Vulnerable Witnesses (Scotland) Act 2004, s 14(1); words in square brackets in para (e) substituted by the Civil Evidence (Scotland) Act 1988, s 2(3); para (ee) inserted by the Children (Scotland) Act 1995, s 105(4), Sch 4, para 45; para (g) repealed by the Law Reform (Miscellaneous Provisions) (Scotland) Act 1990, s 74, Sch 9, as from a day to be appointed.

6 Allocation of business etc by act of sederunt

With a view to securing that causes coming before the Court may be heard and determined with as little delay as is possible, and to the simplifying of procedure and the reduction of expense in causes before the Court, the Court shall, in the exercise of the powers conferred on it by section 5 of this Act, provide by act of sederunt—

(i) for the classification of the causes brought into the Court according to the manner in which they are initiated, and for the institution of (a) an Ordinary Roll; (b) an Admiralty and Commercial Roll; and (c) a Consistorial Roll; and the assignment to the Consistorial Roll of all consistorial causes and to the Ordinary Roll or to the Admiralty and Commercial Roll of all other causes initiated by summons, according to the subject matter of such causes;

(ii) for the allocation of the causes before the Inner House among the Divisions thereof and of the causes before the Outer House among the Lords Ordinary;

(iii) for enabling the enforcement of a maritime lien over a ship by an action *in rem* directed against the ship and all persons interested therein without naming them and concluding for the sale of the ship and the application of the proceeds in extinction *pro tanto* of the lien, and for enabling arrestment of the ship on the dependence of such an action, and for the regulation of the procedure in any such action;

(iv) for enabling the inclusion, in any such action as is mentioned in paragraph (iii) above, of conclusions *in personam* against the registered owners of the vessel, whether their names are or are not known to the pursuer, and the granting of decree in any such action containing such conclusions against any compearing defender;

(v) for the inclusion in defences to any action of any counter claim arising out of the matters on which the action is based, to the effect of enabling such counter claim to be enforced without a separate action being raised;

(vi) for enabling trustees under any trust deed to obtain the direction of the Court on questions relating to the investment, distribution, management or administration of the trust estate, or the exercise of any power vested in, or the performance of any duty imposed on, the trustees notwithstanding that such direction may affect contingent interests in the trust estate, whether of persons in existence at, or of persons who may be born after, the date of the direction;

(vii) for enabling arrestment *ad fundandam jurisdictionem* to proceed on a warrant contained in the summons in like manner as arrestment on the dependence of the action.

[131]

7 (*Relates to fees on remit to accountants.*)

8 Rules Council

(1) The Rules Council established under section 18 of the Administration of Justice (Scotland) Act 1933 shall continue and shall consist of the Lord President *ex officio*, two other judges of the Court to be appointed by the Lord President, five members of the Faculty of Advocates to be appointed by the Faculty, and five solicitors, of whom not less than two shall be solicitors practising before the Court, to be appointed by the Council of the Law Society of Scotland.

(2) The members of the Rules Council, other than the Lord President, shall, so long as they retain the respective qualifications set out in subsection (1) above, hold office for three years and be eligible for reappointment.

(3) Any vacancy in the membership of the Rules Council occurring by death, resignation, or other cause prior to the expiry of three years from the date of appointment of the member whose office is so vacated shall be filled by the appointment by the person or body by whom that member was appointed of another person possessing the same qualification:

Provided that any person appointed in pursuance of this subsection to fill a vacancy shall remain a member of the council only until the expiry of three years from the date of the appointment of the member whose office is so vacated.

(4) The Rules Council may from time to time frame rules regarding any of the matters relating to the Court, being matters which the court is empowered to regulate by act of sederunt, and shall submit any rules so framed to the Court, and the Court shall consider such rules and, if approved, embody them (with or without amendment) in an act of sederunt.

(5) At any meeting of the Rules Council seven members shall form a quorum.

[132]

9–50 (*Pts III–VI relate to ordinary actions, other causes, appeal and review, and miscellaneous provisions.*)

PART VII
SUPPLEMENTARY

51 Interpretation

In this Act unless the context otherwise requires—

"action" means a cause initiated by a summons;

"the Court" means the Court of Session and, in any provision conferring a power on the Court with regard to a cause before it, means, as the case may be, a Division of the Inner House, a Division sitting with an additional judge or judges or a Lord Ordinary;

"enactment" includes an act of sederunt;

"the Inner House" means, in any provision conferring power on it, a Division thereof;

"the Lord President" means the Lord President of the Court of Session;

"prescribed" means prescribed by act of sederunt;

"solicitor" has the same meaning as in section 65(1) of the Solicitors (Scotland) Act 1980.

[133]

52 (*Relates to consequential amendments, repeals and savings.*)

53 Short title, commencement and extent

(1) This Act may be cited as the Court of Session Act 1988.

(2) This Act shall come into force on the expiry of the period of 2 months beginning with the date on which it is passed.

(3) This Act extends to Scotland only.

[134]

CIVIL JURISDICTION AND JUDGMENTS ACT 1991

(1991 c 12)

An Act to give effect to the Convention on jurisdiction and the enforcement of judgments in civil and commercial matters, including the Protocols annexed thereto, opened for signature at Lugano on 16th September 1988; and for purposes connected therewith

[9 May 1991]

1, 2 (*Amend the Civil Jurisdiction and Judgments Act 1982, ss 1, 9 at* **[50]**, **[58]** *and insert ss 3A, 3B in that Act at* **[53]**, **[54]**.)

3 Other amendments of the 1982 Act

The 1982 Act shall have effect with the amendments specified in Schedule 2 to this Act, which are either consequential on the amendments made by sections 1 and 2 above or otherwise for the purpose of implementing the Lugano Convention.

[135]

4 Application to the Crown

The amendments of the 1982 Act made by this Act bind the Crown in accordance with the provisions of section 51 of that Act.

[136]

5 Short title, interpretation, commencement and extent

(1) This Act may be cited as the Civil Jurisdiction and Judgments Act 1991.

(2) In this Act—

"the 1982 Act" means the Civil Jurisdiction and Judgments Act 1982;

"the Lugano Convention" has the same meaning as it has in the 1982 Act by virtue of section 2(3) above.

(3) This Act shall come into force on such day as the Lord Chancellor and the Lord Advocate may appoint in an order made by statutory instrument.

(4) This Act extends to Northern Ireland.

[137]

NOTES

Orders: the Civil Jurisdiction and Judgments Act 1991 (Commencement) Order 1992, SI 1992/745.

(*Sch 1 inserts the Civil Jurisdiction and Judgments Act 1982, Sch 3C, set out at* **[3063]**; *Sch 2 makes further consequential amendments to the 1982 Act.*)

CIVIL PROCEDURE ACT 1997

(1997 c 12)

An Act to amend the law about civil procedure in England and Wales; and for connected purposes

[27 February 1997]

Rules and directions

1 Civil Procedure Rules

(1) There are to be rules of court (to be called "Civil Procedure Rules") governing the practice and procedure to be followed in—

(a) the civil division of the Court of Appeal,
(b) the High Court, and
(c) county courts.

(2) Schedule 1 (which makes further provision about the extent of the power to make Civil Procedure Rules) is to have effect.

(3) The power to make Civil Procedure Rules is to be exercised with a view to securing that the civil justice system is accessible, fair and efficient.

[138]

NOTES

Sub-s (3): substituted by the Courts Act 2003, s 82(1), as from a day to be appointed, as follows—

"(3) Any power to make … Civil Procedure Rules is to be exercised with a view to securing that—
(a) the system of civil justice is accessible, fair and efficient, and
(b) the rules are both simple and simply expressed.".

New sub-s (3): words omitted repealed by the Constitutional Reform Act 2005, ss 15(1), 146, Sch 4, Pt 1, paras 261, 262, Sch 18, Pt 2.

2–3A *(Relate to the process for making Civil Procedure Rules.)*

4 Power to make consequential amendments

(1) The Lord Chancellor may[, after consulting the Lord Chief Justice,] by order amend, repeal or revoke any enactment to the extent he considers necessary or desirable in consequence of—

(a) section 1 or 2, or
(b) Civil Procedure Rules.

(2) The Lord Chancellor may[, after consulting the Lord Chief Justice,] by order amend, repeal or revoke any enactment passed or made before the commencement of this section to the extent he considers necessary or desirable in order to facilitate the making of Civil Procedure Rules.

(3) Any power to make an order under this section is exercisable by statutory instrument.

(4) A statutory instrument containing an order under subsection (1) shall be subject to annulment in pursuance of a resolution of either House of Parliament.

(5) No order may be made under subsection (2) unless a draft of it has been laid before and approved by resolution of each House of Parliament.

[(6) The Lord Chief Justice may nominate a judicial office holder (as defined in section 109(4) of the Constitutional Reform Act 2005) to exercise his functions under subsection (1) or (2).]

[139]

NOTES

Sub-ss (1), (2): words in square brackets inserted by the Constitutional Reform Act 2005, s 15(1), Sch 4, Pt 1, paras 261, 267(1), (2).

Sub-s (6): added by the Constitutional Reform Act 2005, s 15(1), Sch 4, Pt 1, paras 261, 267(1), (3).

[5 Practice directions

(1) Practice directions may be given in accordance with Part 1 of Schedule 2 to the Constitutional Reform Act 2005.

(2) Practice directions given otherwise than under subsection (1) may not be given without the approval of—

(a) the Lord Chancellor, and
(b) the Lord Chief Justice.

(3) Practice directions (whether given under subsection (1) or otherwise) may provide for any matter which, by virtue of paragraph 3 of Schedule 1, may be provided for by Civil Procedure Rules.

(4) The power to give practice directions under subsection (1) includes power—

(a) to vary or revoke directions given by any person;

(b) to give directions containing different provision for different cases (including different areas);

(c) to give directions containing provision for a specific court, for specific proceedings or for a specific jurisdiction.

(5) Subsection (2)(a) does not apply to directions to the extent that they consist of guidance about any of the following—

(a) the application or interpretation of the law;

(b) the making of judicial decisions.

(6) Subsection (2)(a) does not apply to directions to the extent that they consist of criteria for determining which judges may be allocated to hear particular categories of case; but the directions may, to that extent, be given only—

(a) after consulting the Lord Chancellor, and

(b) with the approval of the Lord Chief Justice.]

[140]

NOTES

Commencement: 3 April 2006.

Substituted by the Constitutional Reform Act 2005, s 13(2), Sch 2, Pt 2, para 6.

6–8 (*Relate to the Civil Justice Council, court orders for preserving evidence* (*reproduced at* **[635]** *below*) *and disclosure.*)

General

9 Interpretation

(1) A court the practice and procedure of which is governed by Civil Procedure Rules is referred to in this Act as being "within the scope" of the rules; and references to a court outside the scope of the rules are to be read accordingly.

(2) In this Act—

"enactment" includes an enactment contained in subordinate legislation (within the meaning of the Interpretation Act 1978), and

"practice directions" means directions as to the practice and procedure of any court within the scope of Civil Procedure Rules.

[141]

10 (*Relates to minor and consequential amendments.*)

11 Short title, commencement and extent

(1) This Act may be cited as the Civil Procedure Act 1997.

(2) Sections 1 to 10 are to come into force on such day as the Lord Chancellor may by order made by statutory instrument appoint, and different days may be appointed for different purposes.

(3) This Act extends to England and Wales only.

[142]

NOTES

Orders: the Civil Procedure Act 1997 (Commencement No 1) Order 1997, SI 1997/841; the Civil Procedure Act 1997 (Commencement No 2) Order 1999, SI 1999/1009.

SCHEDULE 1
CIVIL PROCEDURE RULES

Section 1

Matters dealt with by the former rules

1. Among the matters which Civil Procedure Rules may be made about are any matters which were governed by the former Rules of the Supreme Court or the former county court rules (that is, the Rules of the Supreme Court (Revision) 1965 and the County Court Rules 1981).

Exercise of jurisdiction

2. Civil Procedure Rules may provide for the exercise of the jurisdiction of any court within the scope of the rules by officers or other staff of the court.

Removal of proceedings

3.(1) Civil Procedure Rules may provide for the removal of proceedings at any stage—
- (a) within the High Court (for example, between different divisions or different district registries), or
- (b) between county courts.

(2) In sub-paragraph (1)—
- (a) "provide for the removal of proceedings" means—
  - (i) provide for transfer of proceedings, or
  - (ii) provide for any jurisdiction in any proceedings to be exercised (whether concurrently or not) elsewhere within the High Court or, as the case may be, by another county court without the proceedings being transferred, and
- (b) "proceedings" includes any part of proceedings.

Evidence

4. Civil Procedure Rules may modify the rules of evidence as they apply to proceedings in any court within the scope of the rules.

Application of other rules

5.(1) Civil Procedure Rules may apply any rules of court which relate to a court which is outside the scope of Civil Procedure Rules.

(2) Any rules of court, not made by the Civil Procedure Rule Committee, which apply to proceedings of a particular kind in a court within the scope of Civil Procedure Rules may be applied by Civil Procedure Rules to other proceedings in such a court.

(3) In this paragraph "rules of court" includes any provision governing the practice and procedure of a court which is made by or under an enactment.

(4) Where Civil Procedure Rules may be made by applying other rules, the other rules may be applied—
- (a) to any extent,
- (b) with or without modification, and
- (c) as amended from time to time.

Practice directions

6. Civil Procedure Rules may, instead of providing for any matter, refer to provision made or to be made about that matter by directions.

Different provision for different cases etc

7. The power to make Civil Procedure Rules includes power to make different provision for different cases or different areas, including different provision—
  (a) for a specific court or specific division of a court, or
  (b) for specific proceedings, or a specific jurisdiction,

specified in the rules.

[143]

(*Sch 2 contains minor and consequential amendments.*)

PETROLEUM ACT 1998

(1998 c 17)

An Act to consolidate certain enactments about petroleum, offshore installations and submarine pipelines

[11 June 1998]

1–9 (*Pt I outside the scope of this work.*)

PART II
OFFSHORE ACTIVITIES

10 (*Outside the scope of this work.*)

11 Application of civil law

(1) Her Majesty may by Order in Council—
  (a) provide that, in such cases and subject to such exceptions as may be prescribed by the Order, questions arising out of acts or omissions taking place on, under or above waters to which this section applies in connection with any activity mentioned in subsection (2) shall be determined in accordance with the law in force in such part of the United Kingdom as may be specified in the Order; and
  (b) make provision for conferring jurisdiction with respect to such questions on courts in any part of the United Kingdom so specified.

(2) The activities referred to in subsection (1) are—
  (a) activities connected with the exploration of, or the exploitation of the natural resources of, the shore or bed of waters to which this section applies or the subsoil beneath it; and
  (b) without prejudice to the generality of paragraph (a), activities carried on from, by means of or on, or for purposes connected with, installations to which subsection (3) applies.

(3) This subsection applies to any installation which is or has been maintained, or is intended to be established, for the carrying on of any of the following activities, namely—
  (a) the exploitation or exploration of mineral resources in or under the shore or bed of waters to which this section applies;
  (b) the storage of gas in or under the shore or bed of such waters or the recovery of gas so stored;
  (c) the conveyance of things by means of a pipe, or system of pipes, constructed or placed on, in or under the shore or bed of such waters; and
  (d) the provision of accommodation for persons who work on or from an installation which is or has been maintained, or is intended to be established, for the carrying on of an activity within paragraph (a), (b) or (c) or this paragraph.

(4) The fact that an installation has been maintained for the carrying on of an activity within subsection (3) shall be disregarded for the purposes of that subsection if, since it was so maintained, it has been outside waters to which this section applies or has been maintained for the carrying on of an activity not falling within that subsection.

(5) Any jurisdiction conferred on a court under this section shall be without prejudice to any jurisdiction exercisable apart from this section by that or any other court.

(6) This section applies to installations notwithstanding that they are for the time being in transit.

(7) A statutory instrument containing an Order in Council under this section shall be subject to annulment in pursuance of a resolution of either House of Parliament.

(8) The waters to which this section applies are—

(a) tidal waters and parts of the sea in or adjacent to the United Kingdom up to the seaward limits of the territorial sea;

(b) waters in an area designated under section 1(7) of the Continental Shelf Act 1964;

(c) waters in an area specified under section 10(8); and

(d) in relation to installations which are or have been maintained, or are intended to be established, in waters within paragraph (a), (b) or (c), waters in a foreign sector of the continental shelf which are adjacent to such waters.

[144]

NOTES

Orders: by virtue of s 49 of, and Sch 3, Pt I, para 1(2) to, this Act, the Civil Jurisdiction (Offshore Activities) Order 1987, SI 1987/2197 at **[2116]** now has effect as if made under this section.

12 (*Outside the scope of this work.*)

13 Interpretation of Part II

In this Part of this Act—

"foreign sector of the continental shelf" has the meaning given by section 48(1); and

"installation" includes any floating structure or device maintained on a station by whatever means.

[145]

14–45 (*Pts III, IV outside the scope of this work.*)

PART V
MISCELLANEOUS AND GENERAL

46–51 (*Outside the scope of this work.*)

52 Commencement

(1) Section 5(1) to (4) and (11) and this section shall come into force on the passing of this Act.

(2) The provisions mentioned in subsection (3) shall come into force on such day as the Secretary of State may by order appoint, and different days may be appointed for different provisions or different purposes.

(3) The provisions referred to in subsection (2) are—

in Schedule 4, paragraphs 8, 10, 11, 13, 34 and 40; and

in Schedule 5, the repeals of—

the Employment (Continental Shelf) Act 1978;

section 287(5) of the Trade Union and Labour Relations (Consolidation) Act 1992; and

section 201(5) of the Employment Rights Act 1996.

(4) Subject to subsections (1) and (2), this Act shall come into force on such day as the Secretary of State may by order appoint.

(5) Orders under this section shall be made by statutory instrument.

[146]

NOTES

Orders: the Petroleum Act 1998 (Commencement No 1) Order 1999, SI 1999/161.

53 Short title and extent

(1) This Act may be cited as the Petroleum Act 1998.

(2) This Act, except for sections 7 and 8, extends to Northern Ireland.

[147]

(*Schs 1–5 outside the scope of this work.*)

B. APPLICABLE LAW

BILLS OF EXCHANGE ACT 1882

(45 & 46 Vict c 61)

ARRANGEMENT OF SECTIONS

PART I
PRELIMINARY

An Act to codify the law relating to Bills of Exchange, Cheques, and Promissory Notes
[18 August 1882]

NOTES
By the Bills of Exchange (Time of Noting) Act 1917, s 2, the Bills of Exchange Act 1882 and the 1917 Act may be cited by the collective title of the Bills of Exchange Acts 1882 to 1917.

PART I
PRELIMINARY

1 Short title

This Act may be cited as the Bills of Exchange Act, 1882.

[148]

2 Interpretation of terms

In this Act, unless the context otherwise requires,—
"Acceptance" means an acceptance completed by delivery or notification.

"Action" includes counter claim and set off.
"Banker" includes a body of persons whether incorporated or not who carry on the business of banking.
"Bankrupt" includes any person whose estate is vested in a trustee or assignee under the law for the time being in force relating to bankruptcy.
"Bearer" means the person in possession of a bill or note which is payable to bearer.
"Bill" means bill of exchange, and "note" means promissory note.
"Delivery" means transfer of possession, actual or constructive, from one person to another.
"Holder" means the payee or indorsee of a bill or note who is in possession of it, or the bearer thereof.
"Indorsement" means an indorsement completed by delivery.
"Issue" means the first delivery of a bill or note, complete in form to a person who takes it as a holder.
"Person" includes a body of persons whether incorporated or not.
["Postal operator" has the meaning given by section 125(1) of the Postal Services Act 2000.]
"Value" means valuable consideration.
"Written" includes printed, and "writing" includes print.

[149]

NOTES

Definition "Postal operator" inserted by the Postal Services Act 2000 (Consequential Modifications No 1) Order 2001, SI 2001/1149, art 3(1), Sch 1, para 4(1), (2).

PART II
BILLS OF EXCHANGE

Form and interpretation

3 Bill of exchange defined

(1) A bill of exchange is an unconditional order in writing, addressed by one person to another, signed by the person giving it, requiring the person to whom it is addressed to pay on demand or at a fixed or determinable future time a sum certain in money to or to the order of a specified person, or to bearer.

(2) An instrument which does not comply with these conditions, or which orders any act to be done in addition to the payment of money, is not a bill of exchange.

(3) An order to pay out of a particular fund is not unconditional within the meaning of this section; but an unqualified order to pay, coupled with (a) an indication of a particular fund out of which the drawee is to re-imburse himself or a particular account to be debited with the amount, or (b) a statement of the transaction which gives rise to the bill, is unconditional.

(4) A bill is not invalid by reason—
(a) That it is not dated;
(b) That it does not specify the value given, or that any value has been given therefor;
(c) That it does not specify the place where it is drawn or the place where it is payable.

[150]

NOTES

Bill of exchange: a bill of exchange drawn on or after 15 February 1971 is invalid if the sum payable is an amount of money wholly or partly in shillings or pence, see the Decimal Currency Act 1969, s 2(1).

4 Inland and foreign bills

(1) An inland bill is a bill which is or on the face of it purports to be (a) both drawn and payable within the British Islands, or (b) drawn within the British Islands upon some person resident therein. Any other bill is a foreign bill.

For the purposes of this Act "British Islands" mean any part of the United Kingdom of Great Britain and Ireland, the islands of Man, Guernsey, Jersey, Alderney, and Sark, and the islands adjacent to any of them being part of the dominions of Her Majesty.

(2) Unless the contrary appear on the face of the bill the holder may treat it as an inland bill.

[151]

5–38 (*Relate to bills of exchange in a domestic context.*)

General Duties of the Holder

39–43 (*Relate to bills of exchange in a domestic context.*)

44 Duties as to qualified acceptances

(1) The holder of a bill may refuse to take a qualified acceptance, and if he does not obtain an unqualified acceptance may treat the bill as dishonoured by non-acceptance.

(2) Where a qualified acceptance is taken, and the drawer or an indorser has not expressly or impliedly authorised the holder to take a qualified acceptance, or does not subsequently assent thereto, such drawer or indorser is discharged from his liability on the bill.

The provisions of this subsection do not apply to a partial acceptance, whereof due notice has been given. Where a foreign bill has been accepted as to part, it must be protested as to the balance.

(3) When the drawer or indorser of a bill receives notice of a qualified acceptance, and does not within a reasonable time express his dissent to the holder he shall be deemed to have assented thereto.

[152]

45–50 (*Relate to bills of exchange in a domestic context.*)

51 Noting or protest of bill

(1) Where an inland bill has been dishonoured it may, if the holder think fit, be noted for non-acceptance or non-payment, as the case may be; but it shall not be necessary to note or protest any such bill in order to preserve the recourse against the drawer or indorser.

(2) Where a foreign bill, appearing on the face of it to be such, has been dishonoured by non-acceptance it must be duly protested for non-acceptance, and where such a bill, which has not been previously dishonoured by non-acceptance, is dishonoured by non-payment it must be duly protested for non-payment. If it be not so protested the drawer and indorsers are discharged. Where a bill does not appear on the face of it to be a foreign bill, protest thereof in case of dishonour is unnecessary.

(3) A bill which has been protested for non-acceptance may be subsequently protested for non-payment.

(4) Subject to the provisions of this Act, when a bill is noted or protested, [it may be noted on the day of its dishonour and must be noted not later than the next succeeding business day]. When a bill has been duly noted, the protest may be subsequently extended as of the date of the noting.

(5) Where the acceptor of a bill becomes bankrupt or insolvent or suspends payment before it matures, the holder may cause the bill to be protested for better security against the drawer and indorsers.

(6) A bill must be protested at the place where it is dishonoured: Provided that—

(a) When a bill is presented through [a postal operator], and returned by post dishonoured, it may be protested at the place to which it is returned and on the day of its return if received during business hours, and if not received during business hours, then not later than the next business day:

(b) When a bill drawn payable at the place of business or residence of some person other than the drawee has been dishonoured by non-acceptance, it must be protested for non-payment at the place where it is expressed to be payable, and no further presentment for payment to, or demand on, the drawee is necessary.

(7) A protest must contain a copy of the bill, and must be signed by the notary making it, and must specify—

(a) The person at whose request the bill is protested:

(b) The place and date of protest, the cause or reason for protesting the bill, the demand made, and the answer given, if any, or the fact that the drawee or acceptor could not be found.

(8) Where a bill is lost or destroyed, or is wrongly detained from the person entitled to hold it, protest may be made on a copy or written particulars thereof.

(9) Protest is dispensed with by any circumstances which would dispense with notice of dishonour. Delay in noting or protesting is excused when the delay is caused by circumstances beyond the control of the holder, and not imputable to his default, misconduct, or negligence. When the cause of delay ceases to operate the bill must be noted or protested with reasonable diligence.

[153]

NOTES

Sub-s (4): words in square brackets substituted by the Bills of Exchange (Time of Noting) Act 1917, s 1.

Sub-s (6): in para (a) words in square brackets substituted by the Postal Services Act 2000 (Consequential Modifications No 1) Order 2001, SI 2001/1149, art 3(1), Sch 1, para 4(1), (6).

52–71 (*Relate to bills of exchange in a domestic context.*)

Conflict of laws

72 Rules where laws conflict

Where a bill drawn in one country is negotiated, accepted, or payable in another, the rights, duties, and liabilities of the parties thereto are determined as follows—

(1) The validity of a bill as regards requisites in form is determined by the law of the place of issue, and the validity as regards requisites in form of the supervening contracts, such as acceptance, or indorsement, or acceptance suprà protest, is determined by the law of the place where such contract was made.

Provided that—

(a) Where a bill is issued out of the United Kingdom it is not invalid by reason only that it is not stamped in accordance with the law of the place of issue;

(b) Where a bill, issued out of the United Kingdom, conforms, as regards requisites in form, to the law of the United Kingdom, it may, for the purpose of enforcing payment thereof, be treated as valid as between all persons who negotiate, hold, or become parties to it in the United Kingdom.

(2) Subject to the provisions of this Act, the interpretation of the drawing, indorsement, acceptance, or acceptance suprà protest of a bill, is determined by the law of the place where such contract is made.

Provided that where an inland bill is indorsed in a foreign country the indorsement shall as regards the payer be interpreted according to the law of the United Kingdom.

(3) The duties of the holder with respect to presentment for acceptance or payment and the necessity for or sufficiency of a protest or notice of dishonour, or otherwise, are determined by the law of the place where the act is done or the bill is dishonoured.

(4) …

(5) Where a bill is drawn in one country and is payable in another, the due date thereof is determined according to the law of the place where it is payable.

[154]

NOTES

Sub-s (4): repealed by the Administration of Justice Act 1977, ss 4, 32(4), Sch 5, Pt I, except in relation to bills drawn before 29 August 1977.

PART III
CHEQUES ON A BANKER

73 Cheque defined

A cheque is a bill of exchange drawn on a banker payable on demand.

Except as otherwise provided in this Part, the provisions of this Act applicable to a bill of exchange payable on demand apply to a cheque.

[155]

74–82 (*Ss 74–82 relate to bills of exchange and promissory notes in a domestic context.*)

PART IV
PROMISSORY NOTES

83 Promissory note defined

(1) A promissory note is an unconditional promise in writing made by one person to another signed by the maker, engaging to pay, on demand or at a fixed or determinable future time, a sum certain in money, to, or to the order of, a specified person or to bearer.

(2) An instrument in the form of a note payable to maker's order is not a note within the meaning of this section unless and until it is indorsed by the maker.

(3) A note is not invalid by reason only that it contains also a pledge of collateral security with authority to sell or dispose thereof.

(4) A note which is, or on the face of it purports to be, both made and payable within the British Islands is an inland note. Any other note is a foreign note.

[156]

84–88 (*Ss 84–88 relate to promissory notes in a domestic context.*)

89 Application of Part II to notes

(1) Subject to the provisions in this part, and except as by this section provided, the provisions of this Act relating to bills of exchange apply, with the necessary modifications, to promissory notes.

(2) In applying those provisions the maker of a note shall be deemed to correspond with the acceptor of a bill, and the first indorser of a note shall be deemed to correspond with the drawer of an accepted bill payable to drawer's order.

(3) The following provisions as to bills do not apply to notes; namely, provisions relating to—

(a) Presentment for acceptance;
(b) Acceptance;
(c) Acceptance *suprà protest*;
(d) Bills in a set.

(4) Where a foreign note is dishonoured, protest thereof is unnecessary.

[157]

PART V
SUPPLEMENTARY

90–97 (*Relate to bills of exchange and promissory notes in a domestic context.*)

98 Saving of summary diligence in Scotland

Nothing in this Act or in any repeal effected thereby shall extend or restrict, or in any way alter or affect the law and practice in Scotland in regard to summary diligence.

[158]

99 (*Relates to construction with other Acts.*)

100 Parole evidence allowed in certain judicial proceedings in Scotland

In any judicial proceeding in Scotland, any fact relating to a bill of exchange, bank cheque, or promissory note, which is relevant to any question of liability thereon, may be proved by parole evidence:

Provided that this enactment shall not in any way affect the existing law and practice whereby the party who is, according to the tenour of any bill of exchange, bank cheque, or promissory note, debtor to the holder in the amount thereof, may be required, as a condition of obtaining a sist of diligence, or suspension of a charge, or threatened charge, to make such consignation, or to find such caution as the court or judge before whom the cause is depending may require.

…

[159]

NOTES

Words omitted repealed by the Prescription and Limitation (Scotland) Act 1973, s 16(2), Sch 5, Pt I.

(*First Schedule relate to bills of exchange and promissory notes in a domestic context; Second Schedule repealed by the Statute Law Revision Act 1898.*)

PRESCRIPTION AND LIMITATION (SCOTLAND) ACT 1973

(1973 c 52)

An Act to replace the Prescription Acts of 1469, 1474 and 1617 and make new provision in the law of Scotland with respect to the establishment and definition by positive prescription of title to interests in land and of positive servitudes and public right of way, and with respect to the extinction of rights and obligations by negative prescription; to repeal certain enactments relating to limitation of proof; to re-enact with modifications certain enactments relating to the time-limits for bringing legal proceedings where damages are claimed which consist of or include damages or solatium in respect of personal injuries or in respect of a person's death and the time-limit for claiming contribution between wrongdoers; and for purposes connected with the matters aforesaid

[25 July 1973]

1–23 (*Ss 1–3 relate to interests in land generally, and in special cases, and positive servitudes and public rights of way; s 4 relates to judicial interruption of periods of possession; s 5 makes further provision supplementary to ss 1–3; ss 6–8A relate to the extinction of obligations by prescriptive periods of five and twenty years, the extinction of other rights relating to property by prescriptive periods of twenty years and the extinction of obligations to make contributions between wrongdoers; s 9 defines "relevant claim" for purposes of ss 6–8; ss 10–18, 20–23 relate to relevant acknowledgement for purposes of sections 6 and 7, the obligation to make reparation, savings, the prohibition of contracting out, the computation of prescriptive periods, interpretation, the limitation of actions, extensions of time-limits, transitional provisions and interpretation.*)

PART III
SUPPLEMENTAL

[23A Private international law application

(1) Where the substantive law of a country other than Scotland falls to be applied by a Scottish court as the law governing an obligation, the court shall apply any relevant rules of law of that country relating to the extinction of the obligation or the limitation of time within which proceedings may be brought to enforce the obligation to the exclusion of any corresponding rule of Scots law.

(2) This section shall not apply where it appears to the court that the application of the relevant foreign rule of law would be incompatible with the principles of public policy applied by the court.

(3) This section shall not apply in any case where the application of the corresponding rule of Scots law has extinguished the obligation, or barred the bringing of proceedings prior to the coming into force of the Prescription and Limitation (Scotland) Act 1984.]

[160]

NOTES

Inserted by the Prescription and Limitation (Scotland) Act 1984, s 4, in relation to proceedings commenced on or after 26 September 1984.

24 (*Relates to the Crown.*)

25 Short title, commencement and extent

(1) This Act may be cited as the Prescription and Limitation (Scotland) Act 1973.

(2) … this Act shall come into operation, as follows—

(a) Parts II and III of this Act, Part II of Schedule 4 to this Act and Part II of Schedule 5 to this Act shall come into operation on the date on which this Act is passed;

(b) except as aforesaid this Act shall come into operation on the expiration of three years from the said date.

(3) …

(4) This Act extends to Scotland only.

[161]

NOTES

Sub-s (2): words omitted repealed by the Prescription and Limitation (Scotland) Act 1984, s 6(2), Sch 2.

Sub-s (3): repealed by the Prescription and Limitation (Scotland) Act 1984, s 6(2), Sch 2.

(*Sch 1 relates to obligations affected by prescriptive periods of five years under s 6; Sch 2 relates to appropriate dates for certain obligations for purposes of s 6; Sch 3 relates to rights and obligations which are imprescriptible for the purposes of ss 7 and 8 and Sch 1; Schs 4 and 5 contain amendments and repeals.*)

FOREIGN LIMITATION PERIODS ACT 1984

(1984 c 16)

ARRANGEMENT OF SECTIONS

An Act to provide for any law relating to the limitation of actions to be treated, for the purposes of cases in which effect is given to foreign law or to determinations by foreign courts, as a matter of substance rather than as a matter of procedure

[24 May 1984]

NOTES

Application to arbitral proceedings: this Act applies to arbitral proceedings as it applies to legal proceedings, see the Arbitration Act 1996, s 13(1) at **[302]**.

1 Application of foreign limitation law

(1) Subject to the following provisions of this Act, where in any action or proceedings in a court in England and Wales the law of any other country falls (in accordance with rules of private international law applicable by any such court) to be taken into account in the determination of any matter—

(a) the law of that other country relating to limitation shall apply in respect of that matter for the purposes of the action or proceedings; and

(b) except where that matter falls within subsection (2) below, the law of England and Wales relating to limitation shall not so apply.

(2) A matter falls within this subsection if it is a matter in the determination of which both the law of England and Wales and the law of some other country fall to be taken into account.

(3) The law of England and Wales shall determine for the purposes of any law applicable by virtue of subsection (1)(a) above whether, and the time at which, proceedings have been commenced in respect of any matter; and, accordingly, section 35 of the Limitation Act 1980 (new claims in pending proceedings) shall apply in relation to time limits applicable by virtue of subsection (1)(a) above as it applies in relation to time limits under that Act.

(4) A court in England and Wales, in exercising in pursuance of subsection (1)(a) above any discretion conferred by the law of any other country, shall so far as practicable exercise that discretion in the manner in which it is exercised in comparable cases by the courts of that other country.

(5) In this section "law", in relation to any country, shall not include rules of private international law applicable by the courts of that country or, in the case of England and Wales, this Act.

[162]

2 Exceptions to s 1

(1) In any case in which the application of section 1 above would to any extent conflict (whether under subsection (2) below or otherwise) with public policy, that section shall not apply to the extent that its application would so conflict.

(2) The application of section 1 above in relation to any action or proceedings shall conflict with public policy to the extent that its application would cause undue hardship to a person who is, or might be made, a party to the action or proceedings.

(3) Where, under a law applicable by virtue of section 1(1)(a) above for the purposes of any action or proceedings, a limitation period is or may be extended or interrupted in respect of the absence of a party to the action or proceedings from any specified jurisdiction or country, so much of that law as provides for the extension or interruption shall be disregarded for those purposes.

(4) …

[163]

NOTES

Sub-s (4): amends the Limitation (Enemies and War Prisoners) Act 1945, s 2(1).

3 Foreign judgments on limitation points

Where a court in any country outside England and Wales has determined any matter wholly or partly by reference to the law of that or any other country (including England and Wales) relating to limitation, then, for the purposes of the law relating to the effect to be given in England and Wales to that determination, that court shall, to the extent that it has so determined the matter, be deemed to have determined it on its merits.

[164]

4 Meaning of law relating to limitation

(1) Subject to subsection (3) below, references in this Act to the law of any country (including England and Wales) relating to limitation shall, in relation to any matter, be construed as references to so much of the relevant law of that country as (in any manner) makes provision with respect to a limitation period applicable to the bringing of proceedings in respect of that matter in the courts of that country and shall include—

(a) references to so much of that law as relates to, and to the effect of, the application, extension, reduction or interruption of that period; and

(b) a reference, where under that law there is no limitation period which is so applicable, to the rule that such proceedings may be brought within an indefinite period.

(2) In subsection (1) above "relevant law", in relation to any country, means the procedural and substantive law applicable, apart from any rules of private international law, by the courts of that country.

(3) References in this Act to the law of England and Wales relating to limitation shall not include the rules by virtue of which a court may, in the exercise of any discretion, refuse equitable relief on the grounds of acquiescence or otherwise; but, in applying those rules to a case in relation to which the law of any country outside England and Wales is applicable by virtue of section 1(1)(a) above (not being a law that provides for a limitation period that has expired), a court in England and Wales shall have regard, in particular, to the provisions of the law that is so applicable.

[165]

5 (*Repealed by the Arbitration Act 1996, s 107(2), Sch 4.*)

6 Application to Crown

(1) This Act applies in relation to any action or proceedings by or against the Crown as it applies in relation to actions and proceedings to which the Crown is not a party.

(2) For the purposes of this section references to an action or proceedings by or against the Crown include references to—

(a) any action or proceedings by or against Her Majesty in right of the Duchy of Lancaster;

(b) any action or proceedings by or against any Government department or any officer of the Crown as such or any person acting on behalf of the Crown;

(c) any action or proceedings by or against the Duke of Cornwall.

[166]

7 Short title, commencement, transitional provision and extent

(1) This Act may be cited as the Foreign Limitation Periods Act 1984.

(2) This Act shall come into force on such day as the Lord Chancellor may by order made by statutory instrument appoint.

(3) Nothing in this Act shall—

(a) affect any action, proceedings or arbitration commenced in England and Wales before the day appointed under subsection (2) above; or

(b) apply in relation to any matter if the limitation period which, apart from this Act, would have been applied in respect of that matter in England and Wales expired before that day.

(4) This Act extends to England and Wales only.

[167]

NOTES

Orders: the Foreign Limitation Periods Act 1984 (Commencement) Order 1985, SI 1985/1276.

COMPANIES ACT 1985

(1985 c 6)

An Act to consolidate the greater part of the Companies Acts

[11 March 1985]

NOTES

Ss 690A–699, 725, 735, 747, Sch 21A are reproduced in Part I(A) at **[112]** et seq. See also introductory note regarding the Company Law Reform Bill at **[112]**.

PART I
FORMATION AND REGISTRATION OF COMPANIES; JURIDICAL STATUS AND MEMBERSHIP

1–34 (*Relate to the formation of companies and company names.*)

CHAPTER III
A COMPANY'S CAPACITY; FORMALITIES OF CARRYING ON BUSINESS

35–35B (*Relate to a company's capacity.*)

[36 Company contracts: England and Wales

Under the law of England and Wales a contract may be made—

(a) by a company, by writing under its common seal, or

(b) on behalf of a company, by any person acting under its authority, express or implied;

and any formalities required by law in the case of a contract made by an individual also apply, unless a contrary intention appears, to a contract made by or on behalf of a company.]

[168]

NOTES

Substituted by the Companies Act 1989, s 130(1).

The Limited Liability Partnerships Act 2000 provides for the creation of Limited Liability Partnerships (LLPs). The Limited Liability Partnerships Regulations 2001, SI 2001/1090 regulate LLPs by applying to them, with modifications, the appropriate provisions of this Act: see SI 2001/1090, reg 4, Sch 2, Pt I.

For application to companies incorporated outside Great Britain, see Foreign Companies (Execution of Documents) Regulations 1994, SI 1994/950 at **[2174]**.

[36A Execution of documents: England and Wales

(1) Under the law of England and Wales the following provisions have effect with respect to the execution of documents by a company.

(2) A document is executed by a company by the affixing of its common seal.

(3) A company need not have a common seal, however, and the following subsections apply whether it does or not.

(4) A document signed by a director and the secretary of a company, or by two directors of a company, and expressed (in whatever form of words) to be executed by the company has the same effect as if executed under the common seal of the company.

[(4A) Where a document is to be signed by a person as a director or the secretary of more than one company, it shall not be taken to be duly signed by that person for the purposes of subsection (4) unless the person signs it separately in each capacity.]

(5) …

(6) In favour of a purchaser a document shall be deemed to have been duly executed by a company if it purports to be signed by a director and the secretary of the company, or by two directors of the company, …

A "purchaser" means a purchaser in good faith for valuable consideration and includes a lessee, mortgagee or other person who for valuable consideration acquires an interest in property.

[(7) This section applies in the case of a document which is (or purports to be) executed by a company in the name or on behalf of another person whether or not that person is also a company.]

[(8) For the purposes of this section, a document is (or purports to be) signed, in the case of a director or the secretary of a company which is not an individual, if it is (or purports to be) signed by an individual authorised by the director or secretary to sign on its behalf.]]

[169]

NOTES

Inserted by the Companies Act 1989, s 130(2).

Sub-s (4A): inserted by the Regulatory Reform (Execution of Deeds and Documents) Order 2005, SI 2005/1906, art 10(1), Sch 1, paras 9, 10, except in relation to instruments executed before 15 September 2005.

Sub-s (5): repealed by SI 2005/1906, art 10(2), Sch 2, except in relation to instruments executed before 15 September 2005.

Sub-s (6): words omitted repealed by SI 2005/1906, arts 5, 10(2), Sch 2, except in relation to instruments executed before 15 September 2005.

Sub-ss (7), (8): added by SI 2005/1906, arts 7(2), 10(1), Sch 1, paras 9, 11, except in relation to instruments executed before 15 September 2005.

The Limited Liability Partnerships Act 2000 provides for the creation of Limited Liability Partnerships (LLPs). The Limited Liability Partnerships Regulations 2001, SI 2001/1090 regulate LLPs by applying to them, with modifications, the appropriate provisions of this Act: see SI 2001/1090, reg 4, Sch 2, Pt I.

For application to companies incorporated outside Great Britain, see Foreign Companies (Execution of Documents) Regulations 1994, SI 1994/950 at **[2174]**.

[36AA Execution of deeds: England and Wales

(1) A document is validly executed by a company as a deed for the purposes of section 1(2)(b) of the Law of Property (Miscellaneous Provisions) Act 1989, if and only if—

(a) it is duly executed by the company, and

(b) it is delivered as a deed.

(2) A document shall be presumed to be delivered for the purposes of subsection (1)(b) upon its being executed, unless a contrary intention is proved.]

[170]

NOTES

Commencement: 15 September 2005.

Inserted by the Regulatory Reform (Execution of Deeds and Documents) Order 2005, SI 2005/1906, art 6, except in relation to instruments executed before 15 September 2005.

For application to companies incorporated outside Great Britain, see Foreign Companies (Execution of Documents) Regulations 1994, SI 1994/950 at **[2174]**.

[36B Execution of documents by companies

(1) Notwithstanding the provisions of any enactment, a company need not have a company seal.

(2) For the purposes of any enactment—

(a) providing for a document to be executed by a company by affixing its common seal; or

(b) referring (in whatever terms) to a document so executed,

a document signed or subscribed by or on behalf of the company in accordance with the provisions of the Requirements of Writing (Scotland) Act 1995 shall have effect as if so executed.

(3) In this section "enactment" includes an enactment contained in a statutory instrument.]

[171]

NOTES

Inserted, in relation to Scotland only, by the Companies Act 1989, s 130(3).

Substituted by the Requirements of Writing (Scotland) Act 1995, s 14(1), Sch 4, para 51.

The Limited Liability Partnerships Act 2000 provides for the creation of Limited Liability Partnerships (LLPs). The Limited Liability Partnerships (Scotland) Regulations 2001, SSI 2001/128 regulate LLPs by applying to them, with modifications, the appropriate provisions of this Act: see SSI 2001/128, regs 3, Sch 1.

In relation to documents signed or subscribed between 31 July 1990 and 1 December 1990, see the Law Reform (Miscellaneous Provisions) (Scotland) Act 1990, s 72(2)–(5).

For application to companies incorporated outside Great Britain, see Foreign Companies (Execution of Documents) Regulations 1994, SI 1994/950 at **[2174]**.

[36C Pre-incorporation contracts, deeds and obligations

(1) A contract which purports to be made by or on behalf of a company at a time when the company has not been formed has effect, subject to any agreement to the contrary, as one made with the person purporting to act for the company or as agent for it, and he is personally liable on the contract accordingly.

(2) Subsection (1) applies—

(a) to the making of a deed under the law of England and Wales, and

(b) to the undertaking of an obligation under the law of Scotland,

as it applies to the making of a contract.]

[172]

NOTES

Inserted by the Companies Act 1989, s 130(4).

The Limited Liability Partnerships Act 2000 provides for the creation of Limited Liability Partnerships (LLPs). The Limited Liability Partnerships Regulations 2001, SI 2001/1090 regulate LLPs by applying to them, with modifications, the appropriate provisions of this Act: see SI 2001/1090, reg 4, Sch 2, Pt I.

For application to companies incorporated outside Great Britain, see Foreign Companies (Execution of Documents) Regulations 1994, SI 1994/950 at **[2174]**.

37 (*Relates to a company's endorsement of bills of exchange and promissory notes.*)

38 Execution of deeds abroad

(1) A company may, […] by writing under its common seal, empower any person, either generally or in respect of any specified matters, as its attorney, to execute deeds on its behalf in any place elsewhere than in the United Kingdom.

[(2) A deed executed by such an attorney on behalf of the company has the same effect as if it were executed under the company's common seal.]

[(3) This section does not extend to Scotland.]

[173]

NOTES

Sub-s (1): words omitted inserted by the Companies Act 1989, s 130(7), Sch 17, para 1(2), and repealed by the Law Reform (Miscellaneous Provisions) (Scotland) Act 1990, s 74, Sch 8, Part II, para 33, Sch 9.

Sub-s (2): substituted by the Companies Act 1989, s 130(7), Sch 17, para 1(3).

Sub-s (3): added by the Requirements of Writing (Scotland) Act 1995, s 14(1), Sch 4, para 52.

The Limited Liability Partnerships Act 2000 provides for the creation of Limited Liability Partnerships (LLPs). The Limited Liability Partnerships Regulations 2001, SI 2001/1090 regulate LLPs by applying to them, with modifications, the appropriate provisions of this Act: see SI 2001/1090, reg 4, Sch 2, Pt I.

39 Power of company to have official seal for use abroad

(1) A company [which has a common seal] whose objects require or comprise the transaction of business in foreign countries may, if authorised by its articles, have for use in any territory, district, or place elsewhere than in the United Kingdom, an official seal, which shall be a facsimile of [its common seal], with the addition on its face of the name of every territory, district or place where it is to be used.

[(2) The official seal when duly affixed to a document has the same effect as the company's common seal.]

[(2A) Subsection (2) does not extend to Scotland.]

(3) A company having an official seal for use in any such territory, district or place may, by writing under its common seal, [or as respects Scotland by writing in accordance with the Requirements of Writing (Scotland) Act 1995] […] authorise any person appointed for the purpose in that territory, district or place to affix the official seal to any deed or other document to which the company is party in that territory, district or place.

(4) As between the company and a person dealing with such an agent, the agent's authority continues during the period (if any) mentioned in the instrument conferring the authority, or if no period is there mentioned, then until notice of the revocation or determination of the agent's authority has been given to the person dealing with him.

(5) The person affixing the official seal shall certify in writing on the deed or other instrument to which the seal is affixed the date on which and the place at which it is affixed.

[174]

NOTES

Sub-s (1): words in first pair of square brackets inserted and words in second pair of square brackets substituted by the Companies Act 1989, s 130(7), Sch 17, para 2(2).

Sub-s (2): substituted by the Companies Act 1989, s 130(7), Sch 17, para 2(3).

Sub-s (2A): inserted, in relation to Scotland only, by the Requirements of Writing (Scotland) Act 1995, s 14(1), Sch 4, para 53(a).

Sub-s (3): words in square brackets inserted, in relation to Scotland only, by the Requirements of Writing (Scotland) Act 1995, s 14(1), Sch 4, para 53(b); words omitted inserted by the Companies Act 1989, s 130(7), Sch 17, para 2(4), repealed by the Law Reform (Miscellaneous Provisions) (Scotland) Act 1990, s 74, Sch 8, Part II, para 33, Sch 9.

The Limited Liability Partnerships Act 2000 provides for the creation of Limited Liability Partnerships (LLPs). The Limited Liability Partnerships Regulations 2001, SI 2001/1090 regulate LLPs by applying to them, with modifications, the appropriate provisions of this Act: see SI 2001/1090, reg 4, Sch 2, Pt I.

40–744 *(Ss 690A–699, 725, 735, 747 are reproduced in Part I(A) at* **[112]** *et seq. Remainder outside the scope of this work.)*

PART XXVII
FINAL PROVISIONS

745 *(Applies to Northern Ireland only.)*

746 Commencement

… this Act comes into force on 1st July 1985.

[175]

NOTES

Words omitted repealed by the Companies Act 1989, s 212, Sch 24.

747 Citation

This Act may be cited as the Companies Act 1985.

[176]

(Schs 1–25 outside the scope of this work. Sch 21A is reproduced at **[129]**.*)*

RECOGNITION OF TRUSTS ACT 1987

(1987 c 14)

An Act to enable the United Kingdom to ratify the Convention on the law applicable to trusts and on their recognition which was signed on behalf of the United Kingdom on 10th January 1986

[9 April 1987]

1 Applicable law and recognition of trusts

(1) The provisions of the Convention set out in the Schedule to this Act shall have the force of law in the United Kingdom.

(2) Those provisions shall, so far as applicable, have effect not only in relation to the trusts described in Articles 2 and 3 of the Convention but also in relation to any other trusts of property arising under the law of any part of the United Kingdom or by virtue of a judicial decision whether in the United Kingdom or elsewhere.

(3) In accordance with Articles 15 and 16 such provisions of the law as are there mentioned shall, to the extent there specified, apply to the exclusion of the other provisions of the Convention.

(4) In Article 17 the reference to a State includes a reference to any country or territory (whether or not a party to the Convention and whether or not forming part of the United Kingdom) which has its own system of law.

(5) Article 22 shall not be construed as affecting the law to be applied in relation to anything done or omitted before the coming into force of this Act.

[177]

2 Extent

(1) This Act extends to Northern Ireland.

(2) Her Majesty may by Order in Council direct that this Act shall also form part of the law of the Isle of Man, any of the Channel Islands or any colony.

(3) An Order in Council under subsection (2) above may modify this Act in its application to any of the territories there mentioned and may contain such supplementary provisions as Her Majesty considers appropriate.

(4) An Order in Council under subsection (2) above shall be subject to annulment in pursuance of a resolution of either House of Parliament.

[178]

NOTES

Orders in Council: the Recognition of Trusts Act 1987 (Overseas Territories) Order 1989, SI 1989/673, extending this Act to Bermuda, British Antarctic Territory, Falkland Islands, St Helena and Dependencies, South Georgia and the South Sandwich Islands, Sovereign Base Areas of Akrotiri and Dhekelia and the Virgin Islands.

3 Short title, commencement and application to the Crown

(1) This Act may be cited as the Recognition of Trusts Act 1987.

(2) This Act shall come into force on such date as the Lord Chancellor and the Lord Advocate may appoint by an order made by statutory instrument.

(3) This Act binds the Crown.

[179]

NOTES

By virtue of the Scotland Act 1998, s 44(1)(c), the Lord Advocate ceased, on 20 May 1999 (see SI 1998/3178), to be a Minister of the Crown and became a member of the Scottish Executive. Accordingly, certain functions of the Lord Advocate are transferred to the Secretary of State (or as the case may be the Secretary of State for Scotland), or the Advocate General for Scotland: see the Transfer of Functions (Lord Advocate and Secretary of State) Order 1999, SI 1999/678 and the Transfer of Functions (Lord Advocate and Advocate General for Scotland) Order 1999, SI 1999/679.

Orders: the Recognition of Trusts Act 1987 (Commencement) Order 1987, SI 1987/1177.

(*Schedule contains the text of the Convention on the Law applicable to trusts and on their recognition, printed in Part V(B) of this work at* **[4036]**.)

COMPANIES ACT 1989

(1989 c 40)

An Act to amend the law relating to company accounts; to make new provision with respect to the persons eligible for appointment as company auditors; to amend the Companies Act 1985 and certain other enactments with respect to investigations and powers to obtain information and to confer new powers exercisable to assist overseas regulatory authorities; to make new provision with respect to the registration of company charges and otherwise to amend the law relating to companies; to amend the Fair Trading Act 1973; to enable provision to be made for the payment of fees in connection with the exercise by the Secretary of State, the Director General of Fair Trading and the Monopolies and Mergers Commission of their functions under Part V of that Act; to make provision for safeguarding the operation of certain financial markets; to amend the Financial Services Act 1986; to enable provision to be made for the recording and transfer of title to securities without a written instrument; the Company Directors Disqualification Act 1986, the Company Securities (Insider Dealing) Act 1985, the Policyholders Protection Act 1975 and the law relating to building societies; and for connected purposes

[16 November 1989]

NOTES

This is a major Act, most parts of which are outside the scope of this work and are therefore omitted. Provisions omitted are not annotated.

PART V
OTHER AMENDMENTS OF COMPANY LAW

Miscellaneous

130 Company contracts and execution of documents by companies

(1)–(5) …

(6) The Secretary of State may make provision by regulations applying sections 36 to 36C of the Companies Act 1985 (company contracts; execution of documents; [execution of deeds;] pre-incorporation contracts, deeds and obligations) to companies incorporated outside Great Britain, subject to such exceptions, adaptations or modifications as may be specified in the regulations.

Regulations under this subsection shall be made by statutory instrument which shall be subject to annulment in pursuance of a resolution of either House of Parliament.

(7) Schedule 17 contains further minor and consequential amendments relating to company contracts, the execution of documents by companies and related matters.

[180]

NOTES

Sub-ss (1), (2), (4), (5): substitute the Companies Act 1985, s 36 at **[168]**, insert ss 36A, 36C in that Act at **[169]**, **[172]**, and amend Sch 22 to that Act.

Sub-s (3): repealed by the Law Reform (Miscellaneous Provisions) (Scotland) Act 1990, s 74, Sch 9.

Sub-s (6): words in square brackets inserted by the Regulatory Reform (Execution of Deeds and Documents) Order 2005, SI 2005/1906, art 10(1), Sch 1, para 16, except in relation to instruments executed before 15 September 2005.

Regulations: the Foreign Companies (Execution of Documents) Regulations 1994, SI 1994/950 at **[2174]**.

PART X
MISCELLANEOUS AND GENERAL PROVISIONS

General

215 Commencement and transitional provisions

(1) The following provisions of this Act come into force on Royal Assent—
- (a) in Part V (amendments of company law), section 141 (application to declare dissolution of company void);
- (b) in Part VI (mergers)—
  - (i) sections 147 to 150, and
  - (ii) paragraphs 2 to 12, 14 to 16, 18 to 20, 22 to 25 of Schedule 20, and section 153 so far as relating to those paragraphs;
- (c) in Part VIII (amendments of the Financial Services Act 1986), section 202 (offers of short-dated debentures);
- (d) in Part X (miscellaneous and general provisions), the repeals made by Schedule 24 in sections 71, 74, 88 and 89 of, and Schedule 9 to, the Fair Trading Act 1973, and section 212 so far as relating to those repeals.

(2) The other provisions of this Act come into force on such day as the Secretary of State may appoint by order made by statutory instrument; and different days may be appointed for different provisions and different purposes.

(3) An order bringing into force any provision may contain such transitional provisions and savings as appear to the Secretary of State to be necessary or expedient.

(4) The Secretary of State may also by order under this section amend any enactment which refers to the commencement of a provision brought into force by the order so as to substitute a reference to the actual date on which it comes into force.

[181]

NOTES

Functions of the Secretary of State exercised under sub-ss (2)–(4), partially transferred to the Treasury, by the Transfer of Functions (Financial Services) Order 1992, SI 1992/1315, art 2(2)(c).

Order (relating to s 130): the Companies Act 1989 (Commencement No 6 and Transitional and Saving Provisions) Order 1990, SI 1990/1392.

CONTRACTS (APPLICABLE LAW) ACT 1990

(1990 c 36)

ARRANGEMENT OF SECTIONS

An Act to make provision as to the law applicable to contractual obligations in the case of conflict of laws

[26 July 1990]

NOTES

The Commission of the European Communities has proposed that the Rome Convention on the law applicable to contractual obligations (1980) at **[3205]**, to which the Contracts (Applicable Law) Act 1990 gives effect, be replaced by a European Community Regulation on the law applicable to contractual obligations (see COM (2005) 650 final: http://europa.eu.int/eur-lex/lex/LexUriServ/site/en/com/2005/com2005_0650en01.pdf, the so-called "Rome I" Regulation). The United Kingdom, in accordance with Protocol No 4 to the EC Treaty at **[3013]**, has elected not to opt in to that proposal, with the result that the Regulation in its final form will not be binding on the UK, unless it elects (with the Commission's approval) to be bound following conclusion of the negotiations.

1 Meaning of "the Conventions"

In this Act—

(a) "the Rome Convention" means the Convention on the law applicable to contractual obligations opened for signature in Rome on 19th June 1980 and signed by the United Kingdom on 7th December 1981;

(b) "the Luxembourg Convention" means the Convention on the accession of the Hellenic Republic to the Rome Convention signed by the United Kingdom in Luxembourg on 10th April 1984; and

(c) "the Brussels Protocol" means the first Protocol on the interpretation of the Rome Convention by the European Court signed by the United Kingdom in Brussels on 19th December 1988;

[(d) "the Funchal Convention" means the Convention on the accession of the Kingdom of Spain and the Portuguese Republic to the Rome Convention and the Brussels Protocol, with adjustments made to the Rome Convention by the Luxembourg Convention, signed by the United Kingdom in Funchal on 18th May 1992;]

[(e) "the 1996 Accession Convention" means the Convention on the accession of the Republic of Austria, the Republic of Finland and the Kingdom of Sweden to the Rome Convention and the Brussels Protocol, with the adjustments made to the Rome Convention by the Luxembourg Convention and the Funchal Convention, signed by the United Kingdom in Brussels on 29th November 1996;]

and [these Conventions and this Protocol] are together referred to as "the Conventions".

[182]

NOTES

Para (d) inserted and words in final pair of square brackets substituted by the Contracts (Applicable Law) Act 1990 (Amendment) Order 1994, SI 1994/1900, arts 3, 4; para (e) inserted by the Contracts (Applicable Law) Act 1990 (Amendment) Order 2000, SI 2000/1825, art 3.

2 Conventions to have force of law

(1) Subject to subsections (2) and (3) below, the Conventions shall have the force of law in the United Kingdom.

[(1A) The internal law for the purposes of Article 1(3) of the Rome Convention is the provisions of the regulations for the time being in force under section 424(3) of the Financial Services and Markets Act 2000.]

(2) Articles 7(1) and 10(1)(e) of the Rome Convention shall not have the force of law in the United Kingdom.

(3) Notwithstanding Article 19(2) of the Rome Convention, the Conventions shall apply in the case of conflicts between the laws of different parts of the United Kingdom.

(4) For ease of reference there are set out in [Schedules 1, 2, 3[, 3A and 3B]] to this Act respectively the English texts of—

(a) the Rome Convention;
(b) the Luxembourg Convention; …
(c) the Brussels Protocol[, and
[(d) the Funchal Convention; and
(e) the 1996 Accession Convention].]

[183]

NOTES

Sub-s (1A): inserted by the Insurance Companies (Amendment) Regulations 1993, SI 1993/174 reg 9; substituted by the Financial Services and Markets Act 2000 (Consequential Amendments and Repeals) Order 2001, SI 2001/3649, art 320.

Sub-s (4): words in first (outer) pair of square brackets substituted, word omitted repealed and words in third (outer) pair of square brackets added by the Contracts (Applicable Law) Act 1990 (Amendment) Order 1994, SI 1994/1900, arts 5, 6; words in second (inner) pair of square brackets substituted and paras (d), (e) substituted for para (d) as originally enacted by the Contracts (Applicable Law) Act 1990 (Amendment) Order 2000, SI 2000/1825, art 4.

3 Interpretation of Conventions

(1) Any question as to the meaning or effect of any provision of the Conventions shall, if not referred to the European Court in accordance with the Brussels Protocol, be determined in accordance with the principles laid down by, and any relevant decision of, the European Court.

(2) Judicial notice shall be taken of any decision of, or expression of opinion by, the European Court on any such question.

(3) Without prejudice to any practice of the courts as to the matters which may be considered apart from this subsection—

(a) the report on the Rome Convention by Professor Mario Giuliano and Professor Paul Lagarde which is reproduced in the Official Journal of the Communities of 31st October 1980 may be considered in ascertaining the meaning or effect of any provision of that Convention; and
(b) any report on the Brussels Protocol which is reproduced in the Official Journal of the Communities may be considered in ascertaining the meaning or effect of any provision of that Protocol.

[184]

4 Revision of Conventions etc

(1) If at any time it appears to Her Majesty in Council that Her Majesty's Government in the United Kingdom—

(a) have agreed to a revision of any of the Conventions (including, in particular, any revision connected with the accession to the Rome Convention of any state); or

(b) have given notification in accordance with Article 22(3) of the Rome Convention that either or both of the provisions mentioned in section 2(2) above shall have the force of law in the United Kingdom,

Her Majesty may by Order in Council make such consequential modifications of this Act or any other statutory provision, whenever passed or made, as Her Majesty considers appropriate.

(2) An Order in Council under subsection (1) above shall not be made unless a draft of the Order has been laid before Parliament and approved by a resolution of each House.

(3) In subsection (1) above—

"modifications" includes additions, omissions and alterations;

"revision" means an omission from, addition to or alteration of any of the Conventions and includes replacement of any of the Conventions to any extent by another convention, protocol or other description of international agreement; and

"statutory provision" means any provision contained in an Act, or in any Northern Ireland legislation, or in—

(a) subordinate legislation (as defined in section 21(1) of the Interpretation Act 1978); or

(b) any instrument of a legislative character made under any Northern Ireland legislation.

[185]

NOTES

Orders in Council: Contracts (Applicable Law) Act 1990 (Amendment) Order 1994, SI 1994/1900.

5 (*Introduces Sch 4* (*consequential amendments*).)

6 Application to Crown

This Act binds the Crown.

[186]

7 Commencement

This Act shall come into force on such day as the Lord Chancellor and the Lord Advocate may by order made by statutory instrument appoint; and different days may be appointed for different provisions or different purposes.

[187]

NOTES

By virtue of the Scotland Act 1998, s 44(1)(c), the Lord Advocate ceased, on 20 May 1999, to be a Minister of the Crown and became a member of the Scottish Executive. Accordingly, certain functions of the Lord Advocate are transferred to the Secretary of State (or as the case may be the Secretary of State for Scotland), or the Advocate General for Scotland: see the Transfer of Functions (Lord Advocate and Secretary of State) Order 1999, SI 1999/678 and the Transfer of Functions (Lord Advocate and Advocate General for Scotland) Order 1999, SI 1999/679.

Orders: Contracts (Applicable Law) Act 1990 (Commencement No 1) Order 1991, SI 1991/707; the Contracts (Applicable Law) Act 1990 (Commencement No 2) Order 2004, SI 2004/3448.

8 Extent

(1) This Act extends to Northern Ireland.

(2) Her Majesty may by Order in Council direct that all or any of the provisions of this Act shall extend to any of the following territories, namely—

(a) the Isle of Man;

(b) any of the Channel Islands;

(c) Gibraltar;

(d) the Sovereign Base Areas of Akrotiri and Dhekelia (that is to say, the areas mentioned in section 2(1) of the Cyprus Act 1960).

(3) An Order in Council under subsection (2) above may modify this Act in its application to any of the territories mentioned in that subsection and may contain such supplementary provisions as Her Majesty considers appropriate; and in this subsection "modify" shall be construed in accordance with section 4 above.

[188]

9 Short title

This Act may be cited as the Contracts (Applicable Law) Act 1990.

[189]

(*Sch 1 contains the text of the Rome Convention, printed in Pt IV(C) of this work at* **[3205]**.)

SCHEDULE 2
THE LUXEMBOURG CONVENTION

Section 2

The High Contracting Parties to the Treaty establishing the European Economic Community,

Considering that the Hellenic Republic, in becoming a Member of the Community, undertook to accede to the Convention on the law applicable to contractual obligations, opened for signature in Rome on 19 June 1980,

Have decided to conclude this Convention, and to this end have designated as their plenipotentiaries—

(Designation of plenipotentiaries)

Who, meeting within the Council, having exchanged their full powers, found in good and due form,

HAVE AGREED AS FOLLOWS—

Article 1

The Hellenic Republic hereby accedes to the Convention on the law applicable to contractual obligations, opened for signature in Rome on 19 June 1980.

Article 2

The Secretary-General of the Council of the European Communities shall transmit a certified copy of the Convention on the law applicable to contractual obligations in the Danish, Dutch, English, French, German, Irish and Italian languages to the Government of the Hellenic Republic.

The text of the Convention on the law applicable to contractual obligations in the Greek language is annexed hereto. The text in the Greek language shall be authentic under the same conditions as the other texts of the Convention on the law applicable to contractual obligations.

Article 3

This Convention shall be ratified by the Signatory States. The instruments of ratification shall be deposited with the Secretary-General of the Council of the European Communities.

Article 4

This Convention shall enter into force, as between the States which have ratified it, on the first day of the third month following the deposit of the last instrument of ratification by the Hellenic Republic and seven States which have ratified the Convention on the law applicable to contractual obligations.

This Convention shall enter into force for each Contracting State which subsequently ratifies it on the first day of the third month following the deposit of its instrument of ratification.

Article 5

The Secretary-General of the Council of the European Communities shall notify the Signatory States of—

(a) the deposit of each instrument of ratification;
(b) the dates of entry into force of this Convention for the Contracting States.

Article 6

This Convention, drawn up in a single original in the Danish, Dutch, English, French, German, Greek, Irish and Italian languages, all eight texts being equally authentic, shall be deposited in the archives of the General Secretariat of the Council of the European Communities. The Secretary-General shall transmit a certified copy to the Government of each Signatory State.

[190]

(*Sch 3 contains the text of the Brussels Protocol, printed in Pt IV(C) of this work at* **[3208]**.)

[SCHEDULE 3A
THE FUNCHAL CONVENTION

Section 2

The High Contracting Parties to the Treaty establishing the European Economic Community.

Considering that the Kingdom of Spain and the Portuguese Republic, in becoming Members of the Community, undertook to accede to the Convention on the law applicable to contractual obligations, opened for signature in Rome on 19th June 1980.

Have decided to conclude this Convention, and to this end have designated as their plenipotentiaries—

(Designation of plenipotentiaries).

Who, meeting within the Council, having exchanged their full powers, found in good and due form.

HAVE AGREED AS FOLLOWS—

Article 1

The Kingdom of Spain and the Portuguese Republic hereby accede to the Convention on the law applicable to contractual obligations, opened for signature in Rome on 19th June 1980.

Article 2

The Convention on the law applicable to contractual obligations is hereby amended as follows—

(1) Article 22(2), Article 27 and the second sentence of Article 30(3) shall be deleted;
(2) The reference to Article 27 in Article 31(d) shall be deleted.

Article 3

The Secretary-General of the Council of the European Communities shall transmit a certified copy of the Convention on the law applicable to contractual obligations in the Danish, Dutch, English, French, German, Greek, Irish and Italian languages to the Governments of the Kingdom of Spain and the Portuguese Republic.

Article 4

This Convention shall be ratified by the Signatory States. The instruments of ratification shall be deposited with the Secretary-General of the Council of the European Communities.

Article 5

This Convention shall enter into force, as between the States which have ratified it, on the first day of the third month following deposit of the last instrument of ratification by the Kingdom of Spain or the Portuguese Republic and by one State which has ratified the Convention on the law applicable to contractual obligations.

This Convention shall enter into force for each Contracting State which subsequently ratifies it on the first day of the third month following that of deposit of its instrument of ratification.

Article 6

The Secretary-General of the Council of the European Communities shall notify the Signatory States of—

(a) the deposit of each instrument of ratification;

(b) the dates of entry into force of this Convention for the Contracting States.

Article 7

This Convention, drawn up in a single original in the Danish, Dutch, English, French, German, Greek, Irish, Italian, Portuguese and Spanish languages, all ten texts being equally authentic, shall be deposited in the archives of the General Secretariat of the Council of the European Communities. The Secretary-General shall transmit a certified copy to the Government of each Signatory State.]

[191]

NOTES

Inserted by the Contracts (Applicable Law) Act 1990 (Amendment) Order 1994, SI 1994/1900, art 9, Schedule.

[SCHEDULE 3B
THE 1996 ACCESSION CONVENTION

Section 2

The High Contracting Parties to the Treaty establishing the European Community.

Considering that the Republic of Austria, the Republic of Finland and the Kingdom of Sweden, in becoming Members of the European Union, undertook to accede to the Convention on the Law applicable to Contractual Obligations, opened for signature in Rome on 19th June 1980, and to the First and Second Protocols on its interpretation by the Court of Justice,

Have agreed as follows:

TITLE I
GENERAL PROVISIONS

Article 1

The Republic of Austria, the Republic of Finland and the Kingdom of Sweden hereby accede to:

(a) the Convention on the Law applicable to Contractual Obligations, opened for signature in Rome on 19th June 1980, hereinafter referred to as "the Convention of 1980", as it stands following incorporation of all the adjustments and amendments made thereto by:

— the Convention signed in Luxembourg on 10th April 1984, hereinafter referred to as "the Convention of 1984", on the accession of the Hellenic Republic to the Convention on the Law applicable to Contractual Obligations;

— the Convention signed in Funchal on 18th May 1992, hereinafter referred to as "the Convention of 1992", on the accession of the Kingdom of Spain and the Portuguese Republic to the Convention on the Law applicable to Contractual Obligations;

(b) the First Protocol, signed on 19th December 1988, hereinafter referred to as "the First Protocol of 1988", on the interpretation by the Court of Justice of the European Communities of the Convention on the Law applicable to Contractual Obligations;

(c) the Second Protocol, signed on 19th December 1988, hereinafter referred to as "the Second Protocol of 1988", conferring on the Court of Justice of the European Communities certain powers to interpret the Convention on the Law applicable to Contractual Obligations.

(*Titles II, III* (*Arts 2, 3*) *substitute the Protocol annexed to the Convention of 1980 and amend the First Protocol of 1988, Art 2*(*a*).)

TITLE IV
FINAL PROVISIONS

Article 4

1. The Secretary-General of the Council of the European Union shall transmit a certified copy of the Convention of 1980, the Convention of 1984, the First Protocol of 1988, the Second Protocol of 1988 and the Convention of 1992 in the Danish, Dutch, English, French, German, Greek, Irish, Italian, Spanish and Portuguese languages to the Governments of the Republic of Austria, the Republic of Finland and the Kingdom of Sweden.

2. The text of the Convention of 1980, the Convention of 1984, the First Protocol of 1988, the Second Protocol of 1988 and the Convention of 1992 in the Finnish and Swedish languages shall be authentic under the same conditions as the other texts of the Convention of 1980, the Convention of 1984, the First Protocol of 1988, the Second Protocol of 1988 and the Convention of 1992.

Article 5

This Convention shall be ratified by the Signatory States. The instruments of ratification shall be deposited with the Secretary-General of the Council of the European Union.

Article 6

1. This Convention shall enter into force, as between the States which have ratified it, on the first day of the third month following the deposit of the last instrument of ratification by the Republic of Austria, the Republic of Finland or the Kingdom of Sweden and by one Contracting State which has ratified the Convention on the Law applicable to Contractual Obligations.

2. This Convention shall enter into force for each Contracting State which subsequently ratifies it on the first day of the third month following the deposit of its instrument of ratification.

Article 7

The Secretary-General of the Council of the European Union shall notify the Signatory States of:

(a) the deposit of each instrument of ratification;
(b) the dates of entry into force of this Convention for the Contracting States.

Article 8

This Convention, drawn up in a single original in the Danish, Dutch, English, Finnish, French, German, Greek, Irish, Italian, Portuguese, Spanish and Swedish languages, all twelve texts being equally authentic, shall be deposited in the archives of the General Secretariat of the Council of the European Union. The Secretary-General shall transmit a certified copy to the Government of each Signatory State.]

[192]

NOTES

Inserted by the Contracts (Applicable Law) Act 1990 (Amendment) Order 2000, SI 2000/1825, art 7, Schedule.

(*Sch 4 contains consequential amendments.*)

FOREIGN CORPORATIONS ACT 1991

(1991 c 44)

An Act to make provision about the status in the United Kingdom of bodies incorporated or formerly incorporated under the laws of certain territories outside the United Kingdom

[25 July 1991]

1 Recognition of corporate status of certain foreign corporations

(1) If at any time—

(a) any question arises whether a body which purports to have or, as the case may be, which appears to have lost corporate status under the laws of a territory which is not at that time a recognised State should or should not be regarded as having legal personality as a body corporate under the law of any part of the United Kingdom, and

(b) it appears that the laws of that territory are at that time applied by a settled court system in that territory,

that question and any other material question relating to the body shall be determined (and account shall be taken of those laws) as if that territory were a recognised State.

(2) For the purposes of subsection (1) above—

(a) "a recognised State" is a territory which is recognised by Her Majesty's Government in the United Kingdom as a State;

(b) the laws of a territory which is so recognised shall be taken to include the laws of any part of the territory which are acknowledged by the federal or other central government of the territory as a whole; and

(c) a material question is a question (whether as to capacity, constitution or otherwise) which, in the case of a body corporate, falls to be determined by reference to the laws of the territory under which the body is incorporated.

(3) Any registration or other thing done at a time before the coming into force of this section shall be regarded as valid if it would have been valid at that time, had subsections (1) and (2) above then been in force.

[193]

2 Citation, extent and commencement

(1) This Act may be cited as the Foreign Corporations Act 1991.

(2) This Act extends to Northern Ireland.

(3) This Act shall come into force at the end of the period of two months beginning with the day on which it is passed.

[194]

PRIVATE INTERNATIONAL LAW (MISCELLANEOUS PROVISIONS) ACT 1995

(1995 c 42)

ARRANGEMENT OF SECTIONS

PART III
CHOICE OF LAW IN TORT AND DELICT

PART IV
SUPPLEMENTAL

An Act to make provision about interest on judgment debts and arbitral awards expressed in a currency other than sterling; to make further provision as to marriages entered into by unmarried persons under a law which permits polygamy; to make provision for choice of law rules in tort and delict; and for connected purposes

[8 November 1995]

NOTES

In 2003, the Commission of the European Communities proposed a Regulation on the law applicable to non-contractual obligations (the so-called "Rome II" Regulation) which, if adopted, will provide uniform rules of applicable law for torts and other non-contractual obligations, substantially replacing the existing Member State rules (including those contained in Part III of this Act). In January 2006, the Commission revised its proposal (see http://ec.europa.eu/justice_home/doc_centre/civil/doc/com_2006_83_en.pdf) and in April 2006 the EC Council reached political agreement on the "Rome II" proposal. Any Council common position would, however, be subject to approval by the European Parliament and the proposed Regulation appears unlikely to come into force before 2008.

1–8 *(Ss 1–4 (Pt I): s 1 inserts the Administration of Justice Act 1970, s 44A; s 2 inserts the County Courts Act 1984, s 74(5A); s 3 repealed by the Arbitration Act 1996, s 107(2), Sch 4; s 4 repealed in part by the Proceeds of Crime Act 2002, s 457, Sch 12, remainder amends the Crown Proceedings Act 1947, s 24(1) and the Agricultural Holdings Act 1986, Sch 11, para 22, and modifies the Agricultural Holdings Act 1948, Sch 6, para 20B; ss 5–8 (Pt II) relate to polygamy.)*

PART III
CHOICE OF LAW IN TORT AND DELICT

9 Purpose of Part III

(1) The rules in this Part apply for choosing the law (in this Part referred to as "the applicable law") to be used for determining issues relating to tort or (for the purposes of the law of Scotland) delict.

(2) The characterisation for the purposes of private international law of issues arising in a claim as issues relating to tort or delict is a matter for the courts of the forum.

(3) The rules in this Part do not apply in relation to issues arising in any claim excluded from the operation of this Part by section 13 below.

(4) The applicable law shall be used for determining the issues arising in a claim, including in particular the question whether an actionable tort or delict has occurred.

(5) The applicable law to be used for determining the issues arising in a claim shall exclude any choice of law rules forming part of the law of the country or countries concerned.

(6) For the avoidance of doubt (and without prejudice to the operation of section 14 below) this Part applies in relation to events occurring in the forum as it applies in relation to events occurring in any other country.

(7) In this Part as it extends to any country within the United Kingdom, "the forum" means England and Wales, Scotland or Northern Ireland, as the case may be.

(8) In this Part "delict" includes quasi-delict.

[195]

10 Abolition of certain common law rules

The rules of the common law, in so far as they—

(a) require actionability under both the law of the forum and the law of another country for the purpose of determining whether a tort or delict is actionable; or

(b) allow (as an exception from the rules falling within paragraph (a) above) for the law of a single country to be applied for the purpose of determining the issues, or any of the issues, arising in the case in question,

are hereby abolished so far as they apply to any claim in tort or delict which is not excluded from the operation of this Part by section 13 below.

[196]

11 Choice of applicable law: the general rule

(1) The general rule is that the applicable law is the law of the country in which the events constituting the tort or delict in question occur.

(2) Where elements of those events occur in different countries, the applicable law under the general rule is to be taken as being—

(a) for a cause of action in respect of personal injury caused to an individual or death resulting from personal injury, the law of the country where the individual was when he sustained the injury;

(b) for a cause of action in respect of damage to property, the law of the country where the property was when it was damaged; and

(c) in any other case, the law of the country in which the most significant element or elements of those events occurred.

(3) In this section "personal injury" includes disease or any impairment of physical or mental condition.

[197]

12 Choice of applicable law: displacement of general rule

(1) If it appears, in all the circumstances, from a comparison of—

(a) the significance of the factors which connect a tort or delict with the country whose law would be the applicable law under the general rule; and

(b) the significance of any factors connecting the tort or delict with another country,

that it is substantially more appropriate for the applicable law for determining the issues arising in the case, or any of those issues, to be the law of the other country, the general rule is displaced and the applicable law for determining those issues or that issue (as the case may be) is the law of that other country.

(2) The factors that may be taken into account as connecting a tort or delict with a country for the purposes of this section include, in particular, factors relating to the parties, to any of the events which constitute the tort or delict in question or to any of the circumstances or consequences of those events.

[198]

13 Exclusion of defamation claims from Part III

(1) Nothing in this Part applies to affect the determination of issues arising in any defamation claim.

(2) For the purposes of this section "defamation claim" means—

(a) any claim under the law of any part of the United Kingdom for libel or slander or for slander of title, slander of goods or other malicious falsehood and any claim under the law of Scotland for verbal injury; and

(b) any claim under the law of any other country corresponding to or otherwise in the nature of a claim mentioned in paragraph (a) above.

[199]

14 Transitional provision and savings

(1) Nothing in this Part applies to acts or omissions giving rise to a claim which occur before the commencement of this Part.

(2) Nothing in this Part affects any rules of law (including rules of private international law) except those abolished by section 10 above.

(3) Without prejudice to the generality of subsection (2) above, nothing in this Part—

(a) authorises the application of the law of a country outside the forum as the applicable law for determining issues arising in any claim in so far as to do so—

(i) would conflict with principles of public policy; or

(ii) would give effect to such a penal, revenue or other public law as would not otherwise be enforceable under the law of the forum; or

(b) affects any rules of evidence, pleading or practice or authorises questions of procedure in any proceedings to be determined otherwise than in accordance with the law of the forum.

(4) This Part has effect without prejudice to the operation of any rule of law which either has effect notwithstanding the rules of private international law applicable in the particular circumstances or modifies the rules of private international law that would otherwise be so applicable.

[200]

15 Crown application

(1) This Part applies in relation to claims by or against the Crown as it applies in relation to claims to which the Crown is not a party.

(2) In subsection (1) above a reference to the Crown does not include a reference to Her Majesty in Her private capacity or to Her Majesty in right of Her Duchy of Lancaster or to the Duke of Cornwall.

(3) Without prejudice to the generality of section 14(2) above, nothing in this section affects any rule of law as to whether proceedings of any description may be brought against the Crown.

[201]

PART IV
SUPPLEMENTAL

16 Commencement

(1), (2) (*Relate to the commencement of Pts I and II.*)

(3) Part III shall come into force on such day as the Lord Chancellor and the Lord Advocate may by order made by statutory instrument appoint; and different days may be appointed for the commencement of Part III as it extends to England and Wales, Scotland or Northern Ireland.

[202]

NOTES

By virtue of the Scotland Act 1998, s 44(1)(c), the Lord Advocate ceased, on 20 May 1999, to be a Minister of the Crown and became a member of the Scottish Executive. Accordingly, certain functions of the Lord Advocate are transferred to the Secretary of State (or as the case may be the Secretary of State for Scotland), or the Advocate General for Scotland: see the Transfer of Functions (Lord Advocate and Secretary of State) Order 1999, SI 1999/678 and the Transfer of Functions (Lord Advocate and Advocate General for Scotland) Order 1999, SI 1999/679.

Orders: the Private International Law (Miscellaneous Provisions) Act 1995 (Commencement) Order 1996, SI 1996/995; the Private International Law (Miscellaneous Provisions) Act 1995 (Commencement No 2) Order 1996.

17 (*Applies to Northern Ireland only.*)

18 Extent

(1) Any amendment made by this Act has the same extent as the enactment being amended.

(2) (*Relates to the extent of Pt II.*)

(3) Part III extends to England and Wales, Scotland and Northern Ireland.

[203]

19 Short title

This Act may be cited as the Private International Law (Miscellaneous Provisions) Act 1995.

[204]

(*Schedule: para 1 amends the Matrimonial Proceedings (Polygamous Marriages) Act 1972, s 2; para 2 amends the Matrimonial Causes Act 1973, ss 11, 47; para 3 substitutes the Matrimonial Homes Act 1983, s 10(2); para 4 amends the Social Security Contributions Act 1992, ss 121(1), 147(5).*)

C. INTERNATIONAL COMMERCIAL AND FINANCIAL LAW

UNIFORM LAWS ON INTERNATIONAL SALES ACT 1967

(1967 c 45)

An Act to give effect to two Conventions with respect to the international sale of goods; and for purposes connected therewith

[14 July 1967]

1 Application of Uniform Law on the International Sale of Goods

(1) In this Act "the Uniform Law on Sales" means the Uniform Law on the International Sale of Goods forming the Annex to the First Convention and set out, with the modification provided for by Article III of that Convention, in Schedule 1 to this Act; and "the First Convention" means the Convention relating to a Uniform Law on the International Sale of Goods done at The Hague on 1st July 1964.

(2) The Uniform Law on Sales shall, subject to the following provisions of this section, have the force of law in the United Kingdom.

(3) While an Order of Her Majesty in Council is in force declaring that a declaration by the United Kingdom under Article V of the First Convention (application only by choice of parties) has been made and not withdrawn the Uniform Law on Sales shall apply to a contract of sale only if it has been chosen by the parties to the contract as the law of the contract.

[(4) In determining the extent of the application of the Uniform Law on Sales by virtue of Article 4 thereof (choice of parties)—

(a) in relation to a contract made before 18th May 1973, no provision of the law of any part of the United Kingdom shall be regarded as a mandatory provision within the meaning of that Article;

(b) in relation to a contract made on or after 18th May 1973 and before 1st February 1978, no provision of that law shall be so regarded except sections 12 to 15, 55 and 56 of the Sale of Goods Act 1979;

(c) in relation to a contract made on or after 1st February 1978, no provision of that law shall be so regarded except sections [12 to 15B] of the Sale of Goods Act 1979.]

(5) If Her Majesty by Order in Council declares what States are Contracting States and in respect of what territories or what declarations under Article II of the First Convention are for the time being in force, the Order shall, while in force, be conclusive for the purposes of paragraph 1 or, as the case may be, paragraph 5 of Article 1 of the Uniform Law on Sales; but any Order in Council under this subsection may be varied or revoked by a subsequent Order in Council.

(6) The Uniform Law on Sales shall not apply to contracts concluded before such date as Her Majesty may by Order in Council declare to be the date on which the First Convention comes into force in respect of the United Kingdom.

(7) Any Order in Council under the preceding provisions of this section shall be laid before Parliament after being made.

(8) An Order in Council made under subsection (3) of this section may be revoked by a subsequent Order in Council; but no recommendation shall be made to Her Majesty in Council to make an Order under this subsection unless a draft thereof has been laid before and approved by each House of Parliament.

[205]

NOTES

Sub-s (4): substituted by the Sale of Goods Act 1979, s 63, Sch 2, para 15; words in square brackets substituted by the Sale and Supply of Goods Act 1994, s 7, Sch 2 para 3.

Orders: the Uniform Laws on International Sales Order 1972, SI 1972/973; the Uniform Laws on International Sales Order 1987, SI 1987/2061.

2 Application of Uniform Law on the Formation of Contracts for the International Sale of Goods

(1) In this Act "the Uniform Law on Formation" means the Law forming Annex I to the Second Convention as set out, with the modifications provided for by paragraph 3 of Article I of that Convention, in Schedule 2 to this Act; and "the Second Convention" means the Convention relating to a Uniform Law on the Formation of Contracts for the International Sale of Goods done at the Hague on 1st July 1964.

(2) Subject to subsection (3) of this section the Uniform Law on Formation shall have the force of law in the United Kingdom.

(3) The Uniform Law on Formation shall not apply to offers, replies and acceptances made before such date as Her Majesty may by Order in Council declare to be the date on which the Second Convention comes into force in respect of the United Kingdom.

(4) An Order in Council under this section shall be laid before Parliament after being made.

[206]

NOTES

Orders in Council: the Uniform Laws on International Sales Order 1972, SI 1972/973.

3 Revision of Uniform Laws

(1) If by any international Convention the Uniform Law on Sales or the Uniform Law on Formation is amended Her Majesty may by Order in Council modify the Schedules to this Act in such manner as appears to Her necessary for the purpose of giving effect to the Convention.

(2) No recommendation shall be made to Her Majesty in Council to make an Order under this section unless a draft thereof has been laid before and approved by each House of Parliament.

[207]

4 Application to Isle of Man and Channel Islands

Her Majesty may by Order in Council direct that the provisions of this Act shall extend, with such exceptions, adaptations and modifications as may be specified in the Order, to the Isle of Man or any of the Channel Islands; and an Order in Council under this section may be varied or revoked by a subsequent Order in Council.

[208]

5 Short title

This Act may be cited as the Uniform Laws on International Sales Act 1967.

[209]

(Sch 1 contains the text of the Uniform Law on the International Sale of Goods, printed in Pt V(C) at **[4064]***; Sch 2 contains the text of the Uniform Law on the Formation of Contracts for the International Sale of Goods, printed in Pt V(C) at* **[4070]**.)

UNFAIR CONTRACT TERMS ACT 1977

(1977 c 50)

ARRANGEMENT OF SECTIONS

PART I
AMENDMENT OF LAW FOR ENGLAND AND WALES AND NORTHERN IRELAND

Introductory

Avoidance of liability for negligence, breach of contract, etc

An Act to impose further limits on the extent to which under the law of England and Wales and

Northern Ireland civil liability for breach of contract, or for negligence or other breach of duty, can be avoided by means of contract terms and otherwise, and under the law of Scotland civil liability can be avoided by means of contract terms

[26 October 1977]

PART I
AMENDMENT OF LAW FOR ENGLAND AND WALES AND NORTHERN IRELAND

Introductory

1 Scope of Part I

(1) For the purposes of this Part of this Act, "negligence" means the breach—

(a) of any obligation, arising from the express or implied terms of a contract, to take reasonable care or exercise reasonable skill in the performance of the contract;

(b) of any common law duty to take reasonable care or exercise reasonable skill (but not any stricter duty);

(c) of the common duty of care imposed by the Occupiers' Liability Act 1957 or the Occupiers' Liability Act (Northern Ireland) 1957.

(2) This Part of this Act is subject to Part III; and in relation to contracts, the operation of sections 2 to 4 and 7 is subject to the exceptions made by Schedule 1.

(3) In the case of both contract and tort, sections 2 to 7 apply (except where the contrary is stated in section 6(4)) only to business liability, that is liability for breach of obligations or duties arising—

(a) from things done or to be done by a person in the course of a business (whether his own business or another's); or

(b) from the occupation of premises used for business purposes of the occupier;

and references to liability are to be read accordingly [but liability of an occupier of premises for breach of an obligation or duty towards a person obtaining access to the premises for recreational or educational purposes, being liability for loss or damage suffered by reason of the dangerous state of the premises, is not a business liability of the occupier unless granting that person such access for the purposes concerned falls within the business purposes of the occupier].

(4) In relation to any breach of duty or obligation, it is immaterial for any purpose of this Part of this Act whether the breach was inadvertent or intentional, or whether liability for it arises directly or vicariously.

[210]

NOTES

Sub-s (3): words in square brackets added in relation to England and Wales by the Occupiers' Liability Act 1984, s 2.

Avoidance of liability for negligence, breach of contract, etc

2 Negligence liability

(1) A person cannot by reference to any contract term or to a notice given to persons generally or to particular persons exclude or restrict his liability for death or personal injury resulting from negligence.

(2) In the case of other loss or damage, a person cannot so exclude or restrict his liability for negligence except in so far as the term or notice satisfies the requirement of reasonableness.

(3) Where a contract term or notice purports to exclude or restrict liability for negligence a person's agreement to or awareness of it is not of itself to be taken as indicating his voluntary acceptance of any risk.

[211]

3 Liability arising in contract

(1) This section applies as between contracting parties where one of them deals as consumer or on the other's written standard terms of business.

(2) As against that party, the other cannot by reference to any contract term—

(a) when himself in breach of contract, exclude or restrict any liability of his in respect of the breach; or

(b) claim to be entitled—

(i) to render a contractual performance substantially different from that which was reasonably expected of him, or

(ii) in respect of the whole or any part of his contractual obligation, to render no performance at all,

except in so far as (in any of the cases mentioned above in this subsection) the contract term satisfies the requirement of reasonableness.

[212]

4 Unreasonable indemnity clauses

(1) A person dealing as consumer cannot by reference to any contract term be made to indemnify another person (whether a party to the contract or not) in respect of liability that may be incurred by the other for negligence or breach of contract, except in so far as the contract term satisfies the requirement of reasonableness.

(2) This section applies whether the liability in question—

(a) is directly that of the person to be indemnified or is incurred by him vicariously;

(b) is to the person dealing as consumer or to someone else.

[213]

Liability arising from sale or supply of goods

5 "Guarantee" of consumer goods

(1) In the case of goods of a type ordinarily supplied for private use or consumption, where loss or damage—

(a) arises from the goods proving defective while in consumer use; and

(b) results from the negligence of a person concerned in the manufacture or distribution of the goods,

liability for the loss or damage cannot be excluded or restricted by reference to any contract term or notice contained in or operating by reference to a guarantee of the goods.

(2) For these purposes—

(a) goods are to be regarded as "in consumer use" when a person is using them, or has them in his possession for use, otherwise than exclusively for the purposes of a business; and

(b) anything in writing is a guarantee if it contains or purports to contain some promise or assurance (however worded or presented) that defects will be made good by complete or partial replacement, or by repair, monetary compensation or otherwise.

(3) This section does not apply as between the parties to a contract under or in pursuance of which possession or ownership of the goods passed.

[214]

6 Sale and hire-purchase

(1) Liability for breach of the obligations arising from—

(a) section 12 of the Sale of Goods Act 1979] (seller's implied under-takings as to title, etc);

(b) section 8 of the Supply of Goods (Implied Terms) Act 1973 (the corresponding thing in relation to hire-purchase),

cannot be excluded or restricted by reference to any contract term.

(2) As against a person dealing as consumer, liability for breach of the obligations arising from—

(a) [section 13, 14 or 15 of the 1979 Act] (seller's implied undertakings as to conformity of goods with description or sample, or as to their quality or fitness for a particular purpose);

(b) section 9, 10 or 11 of the 1973 Act (the corresponding things in relation to hire-purchase),

cannot be excluded or restricted by reference to any contract term.

(3) As against a person dealing otherwise than as consumer, the liability specified in subsection (2) above can be excluded or restricted by reference to a contract term, but only in so far as the term satisfies the requirement of reasonableness.

(4) The liabilities referred to in this section are not only the business liabilities defined by section 1(3), but include those arising under any contract of sale of goods or hire-purchase agreement.

[215]

NOTES

Sub-ss (1), (2): words in square brackets substituted by the Sale of Goods Act 1979, s 63, Sch 2, para 19.

7 Miscellaneous contracts under which goods pass

(1) Where the possession or ownership of goods passes under or in pursuance of a contract not governed by the law of sale of goods or hire-purchase, subsections (2) to (4) below apply as regards the effect (if any) to be given to contract terms excluding or restricting liability for breach of obligation arising by implication of law from the nature of the contract.

(2) As against a person dealing as consumer, liability in respect of the goods' correspondence with description or sample, or their quality or fitness for any particular purpose, cannot be excluded or restricted by reference to any such term.

(3) As against a person dealing otherwise than as consumer, that liability can be excluded or restricted by reference to such a term, but only in so far as the term satisfies the requirement of reasonableness.

[(3A) Liability for breach of the obligations arising under section 2 of the Supply of Goods and Services Act 1982 (implied terms about title etc in certain contracts for the transfer of the property in goods) cannot be excluded or restricted by references to any such term.]

(4) Liability in respect of—

(a) the right to transfer ownership of the goods, or give possession; or

(b) the assurance of quiet possession to a person taking goods in pursuance of the contract,

cannot [(in a case to which subsection (3A) above does not apply)] be excluded or restricted by reference to any such term except in so far as the term satisfies the requirement of reasonableness.

(5) …

[216]

NOTES

Sub-s (3A): inserted by the Supply of Goods and Services Act 1982, s 17(2).
Sub-s (4): words in square brackets inserted by the Supply of Goods and Services Act 1982, s 17(3).
Sub-s (5): repealed by the Regulatory Reform (Trading Stamps) Order 2005, SI 2005/871, art 6, Schedule.

Other provisions about contracts

8 (*Substitutes the Misrepresentation Act 1967, s 3, and the Misrepresentation Act (Northern Ireland) 1967, s 3.*)

9 Effect of breach

(1) Where for reliance upon it a contract term has to satisfy the requirement of reasonableness, it may be found to do so and be given effect accordingly notwithstanding that the contract has been terminated either by breach or by a party electing to treat it as repudiated.

(2) Where on a breach the contract is nevertheless affirmed by a party entitled to treat it as repudiated, this does not of itself exclude the requirement of reasonableness in relation to any contract term.

[217]

10 Evasion by means of secondary contract

A person is not bound by any contract term prejudicing or taking away rights of his which arise under, or in connection with the performance of, another contract, so far as those rights extend to the enforcement of another's liability which this Part of this Act prevents that other from excluding or restricting.

[218]

Explanatory provisions

11 The "reasonableness" test

(1) In relation to a contract term, the requirement of reasonableness for the purposes of this Part of this Act, section 3 of the Misrepresentation Act 1967 and section 3 of the Misrepresentation Act (Northern Ireland) 1967 is that the term shall have been a fair and reasonable one to be included having regard to the circumstances which were, or ought reasonably to have been, known to or in the contemplation of the parties when the contract was made.

(2) In determining for the purposes of section 6 or 7 above whether a contract term satisfies the requirement of reasonableness, regard shall be had in particular to the matters specified in Schedule 2 to this Act; but this subsection does not prevent the court or arbitrator from holding, in accordance with any rule of law, that a term which purports to exclude or restrict any relevant liability is not a term of the contract.

(3) In relation to a notice (not being a notice having contractual effect), the requirement of reasonableness under this Act is that it should be fair and reasonable to allow reliance on it, having regard to all the circumstances obtaining when the liability arose or (but for the notice) would have arisen.

(4) Where by reference to a contract term or notice a person seeks to restrict liability to a specified sum of money, and the question arises (under this or any other Act) whether the term or notice satisfies the requirement of reasonableness, regard shall be had in particular (but without prejudice to subsection (2) above in the case of contract terms) to—

- (a) the resources which he could expect to be available to him for the purpose of meeting the liability should it arise; and
- (b) how far it was open to him to cover himself by insurance.

(5) It is for those claiming that a contract term or notice satisfies the requirement of reasonableness to show that it does.

[219]

12 "Dealing as consumer"

(1) A party to a contract "deals as consumer" in relation to another party if—

- (a) he neither makes the contract in the course of a business nor holds himself out as doing so; and
- (b) the other party does make the contract in the course of a business; and
- (c) in the case of a contract governed by the law of sale of goods or hire-purchase, or by section 7 of this Act, the goods passing under or in pursuance of the contract are of a type ordinarily supplied for private use or consumption.

[(1A) But if the first party mentioned in subsection (1) is an individual paragraph (c) of that subsection must be ignored.]

[(2) But the buyer is not in any circumstances to be regarded as dealing as consumer—

- (a) if he is an individual and the goods are second hand goods sold at public auction at which individuals have the opportunity of attending the sale in person;
- (b) if he is not an individual and the goods are sold by auction or by competitive tender.]

(3) Subject to this, it is for those claiming that a party does not deal as consumer to show that he does not.

[220]

NOTES

Sub-s (1A): inserted by the Sale and Supply of Goods to Consumers Regulations 2002, SI 2002/3045, reg 14(1), (2).

Sub-s (2): substituted by SI 2002/3045, reg 14(1), (3).

13 Varieties of exemption clause

(1) To the extent that this Part of this Act prevents the exclusion or restriction of any liability it also prevents—

(a) making the liability or its enforcement subject to restrictive or onerous conditions;
(b) excluding or restricting any right or remedy in respect of the liability, or subjecting a person to any prejudice in consequence of his pursuing any such right or remedy;
(c) excluding or restricting rules of evidence or procedure;

and (to that extent) sections 2 and 5 to 7 also prevent excluding or restricting liability by reference to terms and notices which exclude or restrict the relevant obligation or duty.

(2) But an agreement in writing to submit present or future differences to arbitration is not to be treated under this Part of this Act as excluding or restricting any liability.

[221]

14 Interpretation of Part I

In this Part of this Act—

"business" includes a profession and the activities of any government department or local or public authority;
"goods" has the same meaning as in [the Sale of Goods Act 1979];
"hire-purchase agreement" has the same meaning as in the Consumer Credit Act 1974;
"negligence" has the meaning given by section 1(1);
"notice" includes an announcement, whether or not in writing, and any other communication or pretended communication; and
"personal injury" includes any disease and any impairment of physical or mental condition.

[222]

NOTES

Words in square brackets in definition "goods" substituted by the Sale of Goods Act 1979, s 63, Sch 2, para 20.

PART II
AMENDMENT OF LAW FOR SCOTLAND

15 Scope of Part II

(1) This Part of this Act … , is subject to Part III of this Act and does not affect the validity of any discharge or indemnity given by a person in consideration of the receipt by him of compensation in settlement of any claim which he has.

(2) Subject to subsection (3) below, sections 16 to 18 of this Act apply to any contract only to the extent that the contract—

(a) relates to the transfer of the ownership or possession of goods from one person to another (with or without work having been done on them);
(b) constitutes a contract of service or apprenticeship;
(c) relates to services of whatever kind, including (without prejudice to the foregoing generality) carriage, deposit and pledge, care and custody, mandate, agency, loan and services relating to the use of land;
(d) relates to the liability of an occupier of land to persons entering upon or using that land;
(e) relates to a grant of any right or permission to enter upon or use land not amounting to an estate or interest in the land.

(3) Notwithstanding anything in subsection (2) above, sections 16 to 18—

(a) do not apply to any contract to the extent that the contract—
  (i) is a contract of insurance (including a contract to pay an annuity on human life);
  (ii) relates to the formation, constitution or dissolution of any body corporate or unincorporated association or partnership;

(b) apply to—
a contract of marine salvage or towage;
a charter party of a ship or hovercraft;
a contract for the carriage of goods by ship or hovercraft; or,
a contract to which subsection (4) below relates,
only to the extent that—
(i) both parties deal or hold themselves out as dealing in the course of a business (and then only in so far as the contract purports to exclude or restrict liability for breach of duty in respect of death or personal injury); or
(ii) the contract is a consumer contract (and then only in favour of the consumer).

(4) This subsection relates to a contract in pursuance of which goods are carried by ship or hovercraft and which either—
(a) specifies ship or hovercraft as the means of carriage over part of the journey to be covered; or
(b) makes no provision as to the means of carriage and does not exclude ship or hovercraft as that means,
in so far as the contract operates for and in relation to the carriage of the goods by that means. **[223]**

NOTES

Sub-s (1): words omitted repealed by the Law Reform (Miscellaneous Provisions) (Scotland) Act 1990, ss 68(1), (2), 74, Sch 9.

16 Liability for breach of duty

(1) [Subject to subsection (1A) below,] where a term of a contract[, or a provision of a notice given to persons generally or to particular persons,] purports to exclude or restrict liability for breach of duty arising in the course of any business or from the occupation of any premises used for business purposes of the occupier, that term [or provision]—
(a) shall be void in any case where such exclusion or restriction is in respect of death or personal injury;
(b) shall, in any other case, have no effect if it was not fair and reasonable to incorporate the term in the contract [or, as the case may be, if it is not fair and reasonable to allow reliance on the provision].

[(1A) Nothing in paragraph (b) of subsection (1) above shall be taken as implying that a provision of a notice has effect in circumstances where, apart from that paragraph, it would not have effect.]

(2) Subsection (1)(a) above does not affect the validity of any discharge and indemnity given by a person, on or in connection with an award to him of compensation for pneumoconiosis attributable to employment in the coal industry, in respect of any further claim arising from his contracting that disease.

(3) Where under subsection (1) above a term of a contract [or a provision of a notice] is void or has no effect, the fact that a person agreed to, or was aware of, the term [or provision] shall not of itself be sufficient evidence that he knowingly and voluntarily assumed any risk. **[224]**

NOTES

Sub-ss (1), (3): words in square brackets inserted by the Law Reform (Miscellaneous Provision) (Scotland) Act 1990, s 68(1), (3)(a), (c).

Sub-s (1A): inserted by the Law Reform (Miscellaneous Provision) (Scotland) Act 1990, s 68(1), (3)(b).

17 Control of unreasonable exemptions in consumer or standard form contracts

(1) Any term of a contract which is a consumer contract or a standard form contract shall have no effect for the purpose of enabling a party to the contract—
(a) who is in breach of a contractual obligation, to exclude or restrict any liability of his to the consumer or customer in respect of the breach;
(b) in respect of a contractual obligation, to render no performance, or to render a performance substantially different from that which the consumer or customer reasonably expected from the contract;

if it was not fair and reasonable to incorporate the term in the contract.

(2) In this section "customer" means a party to a standard form contract who deals on the basis of written standard terms of business of the other party to the contract who himself deals in the course of a business.

[225]

18 Unreasonable indemnity clauses in consumer contracts

(1) Any term of a contract which is a consumer contract shall have no effect for the purpose of making the consumer indemnify another person (whether a party to the contract or not) in respect of liability which that other person may incur as a result of breach of duty or breach of contract, if it was not fair and reasonable to incorporate the term in the contract.

(2) In this section "liability" means liability arising in the course of any business or from the occupation of any premises used for business purposes of the occupier.

[226]

19 "Guarantee" of consumer goods

(1) This section applies to a guarantee—

- (a) in relation to goods which are of a type ordinarily supplied for private use or consumption; and
- (b) which is not a guarantee given by one party to the other party to a contract under or in pursuance of which the ownership or possession of the goods to which the guarantee relates is transferred.

(2) A term of a guarantee to which this section applies shall be void in so far as it purports to exclude or restrict liability for loss or damage (including death or personal injury)—

- (a) arising from the goods proving defective while—
  - (i) in use otherwise than exclusively for the purposes of a business; or
  - (ii) in the possession of a person for such use; and
- (b) resulting from the breach of duty of a person concerned in the manufacture or distribution of the goods.

(3) For the purposes of this section, any document is a guarantee if it contains or purports to contain some promise or assurance (however worded or presented) that defects will be made good by complete or partial replacement, or by repair, monetary compensation or otherwise.

[227]

20 Obligations implied by law in sale and hire-purchase contracts

(1) Any term of a contract which purports to exclude or restrict liability for breach of the obligations arising from—

- (a) section 12 of the Sale of Goods Act [1979] (seller's implied undertakings as to title etc);
- (b) section 8 of the Supply of Goods (Implied Terms) Act 1973 (implied terms as to title in hire-purchase agreements),

shall be void.

(2) Any term of a contract which purports to exclude or restrict liability for breach of the obligations arising from—

- (a) section 13, 14 or 15 of the said Act of [1979] (seller's implied undertakings as to conformity of goods with description or sample, or as to their quality or fitness for a particular purpose);
- (b) section 9, 10 or 11 of the said Act of 1973 (the corresponding provisions in relation to hire-purchase), shall—
  - (i) in the case of a consumer contract, be void against the consumer;
  - (ii) in any other case, have no effect if it was not fair and reasonable to incorporate the term in the contract.

[228]

NOTES

Sub-ss (1), (2): numbers in square brackets substituted by the Sale of Goods Act 1979, ss 62, 63, Sch 2, para 21.

21 Obligations implied by law in other contracts for the supply of goods

(1) Any term of a contract to which this section applies purporting to exclude or restrict liability for breach of an obligation—

(a) such as is referred to in subsection (3)(a) below—

(i) in the case of a consumer contract, shall be void against the consumer, and

(ii) in any other case, shall have no effect if it was not fair and reasonable to incorporate the term in the contract;

(b) such as is referred to in subsection (3)(b) below, shall have no effect if it was not fair and reasonable to incorporate the term in the contract.

(2) This section applies to any contract to the extent that it relates to any such matter as is referred to in section 15(2)(a) of this Act, but does not apply to—

(a) a contract of sale of goods or a hire-purchase agreement; or

(b) a charterparty of a ship or hovercraft unless it is a consumer contract (and then only in favour of the consumer).

(3) An obligation referred to in this subsection is an obligation incurred under a contract in the course of a business and arising by implication of law from the nature of the contract which relates—

(a) to the correspondence of goods with description or sample, or to the quality or fitness of goods for any particular purpose; or

(b) to any right to transfer ownership or possession of goods, or to the enjoyment of quiet possession of goods.

(4) …

[229]

NOTES

Sub-s (2A): inserted by the Law Reform (Miscellaneous Provision) (Scotland) Act 1990, s 68(1), (4)(a).

Sub-s (3): words in square brackets inserted by the Law Reform (Miscellaneous Provision) (Scotland) Act 1990, s 68(1), (4)(b).

Sub-s (4): repealed by the Regulatory Reform (Trading Stamps) Order 2005, SI 2005/871, art 6, Schedule.

22 Consequence of breach

For the avoidance of doubt, where any provision of this Part of this Act requires that the incorporation of a term in a contract must be fair and reasonable for that term to have effect—

(a) if that requirement is satisfied, the term may be given effect to notwithstanding that the contract has been terminated in consequence of breach of that contract;

(b) for the term to be given effect to, that requirement must be satisfied even where a party who is entitled to rescind the contract elects not to rescind it.

[230]

23 Evasion by means of secondary contract

Any term of any contract shall be void which purports to exclude or restrict, or has the effect of excluding or restricting—

(a) the exercise, by a party to any other contract, of any right or remedy which arises in respect of that other contract in consequence of breach of duty, or of obligation, liability for which could not by virtue of the provisions of this Part of this Act be excluded or restricted by a term of that other contract;

(b) the application of the provisions of this Part of this Act in respect of that or any other contract.

[231]

24 The "reasonableness" test

(1) In determining for the purposes of this Part of this Act whether it was fair and reasonable to incorporate a term in a contract, regard shall be had only to the circumstances which were, or ought reasonably to have been, known to or in the contemplation of the parties to the contract at the time the contract was made.

(2) In determining for the purposes of section 20 or 21 of this Act whether it was fair and reasonable to incorporate a term in a contract, regard shall be had in particular to the matters specified in Schedule 2 to this Act; but this subsection shall not prevent a court or arbiter from

holding, in accordance with any rule of law, that a term which purports to exclude or restrict any relevant liability is not a term of the contract.

[(2A) In determining for the purposes of this Part of this Act whether it is fair and reasonable to allow reliance on a provision of a notice (not being a notice having contractual effect), regard shall be had to all the circumstances obtaining when the liability arose or (but for the provision) would have arisen.]

(3) Where a term in a contract [or a provision of a notice] purports to restrict liability to a specified sum of money, and the question arises for the purposes of this Part of this Act whether it was fair and reasonable to incorporate the term in the contract [or whether it is fair and reasonable to allow reliance on the provision], then, without prejudice to subsection (2) above [in the case of a term in a contract], regard shall be had in particular to—

(a) the resources which the party seeking to rely on that term [or provision] could expect to be available to him for the purpose of meeting the liability should it arise;

(b) how far it was open to that party to cover himself by insurance.

(4) The onus of proving that it was fair and reasonable to incorporate a term in a contract [or that it is fair and reasonable to allow reliance on a provision of a notice] shall lie on the party so contending.

[232]

NOTES

Sub-s (2A): inserted by the Law Reform (Miscellaneous Provision) (Scotland) Act 1990, s 68(1), (4)(a).

Sub-ss (3), (4): words in square brackets inserted by the Law Reform (Miscellaneous Provision) (Scotland) Act 1990, s 68(1), (4)(b), (c).

25 Interpretation of Part II

(1) In this Part of this Act—

"breach of duty" means the breach—

(a) of any obligation, arising from the express or implied terms of a contract, to take reasonable care or exercise reasonable skill in the performance of the contract;

(b) of any common law duty to take reasonable care or exercise reasonable skill;

(c) of the duty of reasonable care imposed by section 2(1) of the Occupiers' Liability (Scotland) Act 1960;

"business" includes a profession and the activities of any government department or local or public authority;

"consumer" has the meaning assigned to that expression in the definition in this section of "consumer contract";

"consumer contract" means [subject to subsections (1A) and (1B) below] a contract … in which—

(a) one party to the contract deals, and the other party to the contract ("the consumer") does not deal or hold himself out as dealing, in the course of a business, and

(b) in the case of a contract such as is mentioned in section 15(2)(a) of this Act, the goods are of a type ordinarily supplied for private use or consumption;

and for the purposes of this Part of this Act the onus of proving that a contract is not to be regarded as a consumer contract shall lie on the party so contending;

"goods" has the same meaning as in [the Sale of Goods Act 1979];

"hire-purchase agreement" has the same meaning as in section 189(1) of the Consumer Credit Act 1974;

["notice" includes an announcement, whether or not in writing, and any other communication or pretended communication;]

"personal injury" includes any disease and any impairment of physical or mental condition.

[(1A) Where the consumer is an individual, paragraph (b) in the definition of "consumer contract" in subsection (1) must be disregarded.

(1B) The expression of "consumer contract" does not include a contract in which—

(a) the buyer is an individual and the goods are second hand goods sold by public auction at which individuals have the opportunity of attending in person; or

(b) the buyer is not an individual and the goods are sold by auction or competitive tender.]

(2) In relation to any breach of duty or obligation, it is immaterial for any purpose of this Part of this Act whether the act or omission giving rise to that breach was inadvertent or intentional, or whether liability for it arises directly or vicariously.

(3) In this Part of this Act, any reference to excluding or restricting any liability includes—

(a) making the liability or its enforcement subject to any restrictive or onerous conditions;
(b) excluding or restricting any right or remedy in respect of the liability, or subjecting a person to any prejudice in consequence of his pursuing any such right or remedy;
(c) excluding or restricting any rule of evidence or procedure;
(d) …

but does not include an agreement to submit any question to arbitration.

(4) …

(5) In sections 15 and 16 and 19 to 21 of this Act, any reference to excluding or restricting liability for breach of an obligation or duty shall include a reference to excluding or restricting the obligation or duty itself.

[233]

NOTES

Sub-s (1): in definition "consumer contract" words in square brackets inserted and words omitted repealed by the Sale and Supply of Goods to Consumers Regulations 2002, SI 2002/3045, reg 14(1), (4)(a); words in square brackets in definition "goods" substituted by the Sale of Goods Act 1979, ss 62, 63, Sch 2, para 22; definition "notice" inserted by the Law Reform (Miscellaneous Provision) (Scotland) Act 1990, s 68(1), (5)(a).

Sub-ss (1A), (1B): inserted by SI 2002/3045, reg 14(1), (4)(b).

Sub-s (3): para (d) repealed by the Law Reform (Miscellaneous Provision) (Scotland) Act 1990, ss 68(1), (5)(b), 74, Sch 9.

Sub-s (4): repealed by the Law Reform (Miscellaneous Provision) (Scotland) Act 1990, ss 68(1), (5)(b), 74, Sch 9.

PART III
PROVISIONS APPLYING TO WHOLE OF UNITED KINGDOM

Miscellaneous

26 International supply contracts

(1) The limits imposed by this Act on the extent to which a person may exclude or restrict liability by reference to a contract term do not apply to liability arising under such a contract as is described in subsection (3) below.

(2) The terms of such a contract are not subject to any requirement of reasonableness under section 3 or 4: and nothing in Part II of this Act shall require the incorporation of the terms of such a contract to be fair and reasonable for them to have effect.

(3) Subject to subsection (4), that description of contract is one whose characteristics are the following—

(a) either it is a contract of sale of goods or it is one under or in pursuance of which the possession or ownership of goods passes; and
(b) it is made by parties whose places of business (or, if they have none, habitual residences) are in the territories of different States (the Channel Islands and the Isle of Man being treated for this purpose as different States from the United Kingdom).

(4) A contract falls within subsection (3) above only if either—

(a) the goods in question are, at the time of the conclusion of the contract, in the course of carriage, or will be carried, from the territory of one State to the territory of another; or
(b) the acts constituting the offer and acceptance have been done in the territories of different States; or

(c) the contract provides for the goods to be delivered to the territory of a State other than that within whose territory those acts were done.

[234]

27 Choice of law clauses

(1) Where the [law applicable to] a contract is the law of any part of the United Kingdom only by choice of the parties (and apart from that choice would be the law of some country outside the United Kingdom) sections 2 to 7 and 16 to 21 of this Act do not operate as part [of the law applicable to the contract].

(2) This Act has effect notwithstanding any contract term which applies or purports to apply the law of some country outside the United Kingdom, where (either or both)—

(a) the term appears to the court, or arbitrator or arbiter to have been imposed wholly or mainly for the purpose of enabling the party imposing it to evade the operation of this Act; or

(b) in the making of the contract one of the parties dealt as consumer, and he was then habitually resident in the United Kingdom, and the essential steps necessary for the making of the contract were taken there, whether by him or by others on his behalf.

(3) In the application of subsection (2) above to Scotland, for paragraph (b) there shall be substituted—

"(b) the contract is a consumer contract as defined in Part II of this Act, and the consumer at the date when the contract was made was habitually resident in the United Kingdom, and the essential steps necessary for the making of the contract were taken there, whether by him or by others on his behalf."

[235]

NOTES

Sub-s (1): words in square brackets substituted by the Contracts (Applicable Law) Act 1990, s 5, Sch 4, para 4.

28 Temporary provision for sea carriage of passengers

(1) This section applies to a contract for carriage by sea of a passenger or of a passenger and his luggage where the provisions of the Athens Convention (with or without modification) do not have, in relation to the contract, the force of law in the United Kingdom.

(2) In a case where—

(a) the contract is not made in the United Kingdom, and

(b) neither the place of departure nor the place of destination under it is in the United Kingdom,

a person is not precluded by this Act from excluding or restricting liability for loss or damage, being loss or damage for which the provisions of the Convention would, if they had the force of law in relation to the contract, impose liability on him.

(3) In any other case, a person is not precluded by this Act from excluding or restricting liability for that loss or damage—

(a) in so far as the exclusion or restriction would have been effective in that case had the provisions of the Convention had the force of law in relation to the contract; or

(b) in such circumstances and to such extent as may be prescribed, by reference to a prescribed term of the contract.

(4) For the purposes of subsection (3)(a), the values which shall be taken to be the official values in the United Kingdom of the amounts (expressed in gold francs) by reference to which liability under the provisions of the Convention is limited shall be such amounts in sterling as the Secretary of State may from time to time by order made by statutory instrument specify.

(5) In this section,—

(a) the references to excluding or restricting liability include doing any of those things in relation to the liability which are mentioned in section 13 or section 25(3) and (5); and

(b) "the Athens Convention" means the Athens Convention relating to the Carriage of Passengers and their Luggage by Sea, 1974; and

(c) "prescribed" means prescribed by the Secretary of State by regulations made by statutory instrument;

and a statutory instrument containing the regulations shall be subject to annulment in pursuance of a resolution of either House of Parliament.

[236]

NOTES

The Athens Convention: Cmnd 6326; set out in the Merchant Shipping Act 1979, Sch 3 and given the force of law by s 14 of that Act (as from 1 January 1996, replaced by the Merchant Shipping Act 1995, Sch 6 and s 183 respectively); brought fully into force on 30 April 1987 by the Merchant Shipping Act 1979 (Commencement No 11) Order 1987, SI 1987/635.

Modifications: the Merchant Shipping Act 1995, s 184(2), provides that Orders in Council made under s 184(1) of the Act may modify this section as the Secretary of State considers appropriate. By the Carriage of Passengers and their Luggage by Sea (Interim Provisions) Order 1980, SI 1980/1092 (made under s 16(1), (2) of the 1979 Act and now having effect under s 184 of the 1995 Act), this section ceased to apply to any contract to which that Order applies on 1 January 1981, but continues to apply to any contract made before that date. Contracts made after 30 April 1987 are governed by the Athens Convention, subject, in the case of contracts for domestic carriage, to modifications contained in the Carriage of Passengers and their Luggage by Sea (Domestic Carriage) Order 1987, SI 1987/670.

Orders: as a result of the coming into force of the 1976 Protocol to the Athens Convention which replaced the references to gold francs in the Convention with references to special drawing rights, no equivalents for gold francs are now provided for by order under this section.

29 Saving for other relevant legislation

(1) Nothing in this Act removes or restricts the effect of, or prevents reliance upon, any contractual provision which—

(a) is authorised or required by the express terms or necessary implication of an enactment; or

(b) being made with a view to compliance with an international agreement to which the United Kingdom is a party, does not operate more restrictively than is contemplated by the agreement.

(2) A contract term is to be taken—

(a) for the purposes of Part I of this Act, as satisfying the requirement of reasonableness; and

(b) for those of Part II, to have been fair and reasonable to incorporate,

if it is incorporated or approved by, or incorporated pursuant to a decision or ruling of, a competent authority acting in the exercise of any statutory jurisdiction or function and is not a term in a contract to which the competent authority is itself a party.

(3) In this section—

"competent authority" means any court, arbitrator or arbiter, government department or public authority;

"enactment" means any legislation (including subordinate legislation) of the United Kingdom or Northern Ireland and any instrument having effect by virtue of such legislation; and

"statutory" means conferred by an enactment.

[237]

30 (*Repealed by the Consumer Safety Act 1978, s 10(1), Sch 3.*)

General

31 Commencement; amendments; repeals

(1) This Act comes into force on 1st February 1978.

(2) Nothing in this Act applies to contracts made before the date on which it comes into force, but subject to this, it applies to liability for any loss or damage which is suffered on or after that date.

(3) The enactments specified in Schedule 3 to this Act are amended as there shown.

(4) The enactments specified in Schedule 4 to this Act are repealed to the extent specified in column 3 of that Schedule.

[238]

32 Citation and extent

(1) This Act may be cited as the Unfair Contract Terms Act 1977.

(2) Part I of this Act extends to England and Wales and to Northern Ireland; but it does not extend to Scotland.

(3) Part II of this Act extends to Scotland only.

(4) This Part of this Act extends to the whole of the United Kingdom.

[239]

SCHEDULES

SCHEDULE 1
SCOPE OF SECTIONS 2 TO 4 AND 7

Section 1(2)

1. Sections 2 to 4 of this Act do not extend to—
   (a) any contract of insurance (including a contract to pay an annuity on human life);
   (b) any contract so far as it relates to the creation or transfer of an interest in land, or to the termination of such an interest, whether by extinction, merger, surrender, forfeiture or otherwise;
   (c) any contract so far as it relates to the creation or transfer of a right or interest in any patent, trade mark, copyright [or design right], registered design, technical or commercial information or other intellectual property, or relates to the termination of any such right or interest;
   (d) any contract so far as it relates—
      (i) to the formation or dissolution of a company (which means any body corporate or unincorporated association and includes a partnership), or
      (ii) to its constitution or the rights or obligations of its corporators or members;
   (e) any contract so far as it relates to the creation or transfer of securities or of any right or interest in securities.

2. Section 2(1) extends to—
   (a) any contract of marine salvage or towage;
   (b) any charterparty of a ship or hovercraft; and
   (c) any contract for the carriage of goods by ship or hovercraft;

but subject to this sections 2 to 4 and 7 do not extend to any such contract except in favour of a person dealing as consumer.

3. Where goods are carried by ship or hovercraft in pursuance of a contract which either—
   (a) specifies that as the means of carriage over part of the journey to be covered, or
   (b) makes no provision as to the means of carriage and does not exclude that means,

then sections 2(2), 3 and 4 do not, except in favour of a person dealing as consumer, extend to the contract as it operates for and in relation to the carriage of the goods by that means.

4. Section 2(1) and (2) do not extend to a contract of employment, except in favour of the employee.

5. Section 2(1) does not affect the validity of any discharge and indemnity given by a person, on or in connection with an award to him of compensation for pneumoconiosis attributable to employment in the coal industry, in respect of any further claim arising from his contracting that disease.

[240]

NOTES

Para 1: words in square brackets in sub-para (c) inserted by the Copyright, Designs and Patents Act 1988, s 303(1), Sch 7, para 24.

By the Trade Marks Act 1994, s 106(1), Sch 4, para 1, the reference in para 1(c) to a trade mark is to be construed as a reference to a trade mark within the meaning of that Act.

SCHEDULE 2
"GUIDELINES" FOR APPLICATION OF REASONABLENESS TEST

Sections 11(2), 24(2)

The matters to which regard is to be had in particular for the purposes of sections 6(3), 7(3) and (4), 20 and 21 are any of the following which appear to be relevant—

(a) the strength of the bargaining positions of the parties relative to each other, taking into account (among other things) alternative means by which the customer's requirements could have been met;
(b) whether the customer received an inducement to agree to the term, or in accepting it had an opportunity of entering into a similar contract with other persons, but without having to accept a similar term;
(c) whether the customer knew or ought reasonably to have known of the existence and extent of the term (having regard, among other things, to any custom of the trade and any previous course of dealing between the parties);
(d) where the term excludes or restricts any relevant liability if some condition is not complied with, whether it was reasonable at the time of the contract to expect that compliance with that condition would be practicable;
(e) whether the goods were manufactured, processed or adapted to the special order of the customer.

[241]

(Sch 3, in so far as unrepealed, specifies amendments of the Supply of Goods (Implied Terms) Act 1973, ss 14, 15 (as originally enacted and as substituted by the Consumer Credit Act 1974); Sch 4 contains repeals.)

LATE PAYMENT OF COMMERCIAL DEBTS (INTEREST) ACT 1998

(1998 c 20)

ARRANGEMENT OF SECTIONS

PART I
STATUTORY INTEREST ON QUALIFYING DEBTS

PART II
CONTRACT TERMS RELATING TO LATE PAYMENT OF QUALIFYING DEBTS

PART III
GENERAL AND SUPPLEMENTARY

An Act to make provision with respect to interest on the late payment of certain debts arising under commercial contracts for the supply of goods or services; and for connected purposes.

[11 June 1998]

PART I
STATUTORY INTEREST ON QUALIFYING DEBTS

1 Statutory interest

(1) It is an implied term in a contract to which this Act applies that any qualifying debt created by the contract carries simple interest subject to and in accordance with this Part.

(2) Interest carried under that implied term (in this Act referred to as "statutory interest") shall be treated, for the purposes of any rule of law or enactment (other than this Act) relating to interest on debts, in the same way as interest carried under an express contract term.

(3) This Part has effect subject to Part II (which in certain circumstances permits contract terms to oust or vary the right to statutory interest that would otherwise be conferred by virtue of the term implied by subsection (1)).

[242]

NOTES

Commencement: 1 November 1998–7 August 2002 (for details, see commencement note under s 17 at **[260]**).

2 Contracts to which Act applies

(1) This Act applies to a contract for the supply of goods or services where the purchaser and the supplier are each acting in the course of a business, other than an excepted contract.

(2) In this Act "contract for the supply of goods or services" means—
- (a) a contract of sale of goods; or
- (b) a contract (other than a contract of sale of goods) by which a person does any, or any combination, of the things mentioned in subsection (3) for a consideration that is (or includes) a money consideration.

(3) Those things are—
- (a) transferring or agreeing to transfer to another the property in goods;
- (b) bailing or agreeing to bail goods to another by way of hire or, in Scotland, hiring or agreeing to hire goods to another; and
- (c) agreeing to carry out a service.

(4) For the avoidance of doubt a contract of service or apprenticeship is not a contract for the supply of goods or services.

(5) The following are excepted contracts—
- (a) a consumer credit agreement;
- (b) a contract intended to operate by way of mortgage, pledge, charge or other security; and
- (c) …

(6) …

(7) In this section—

"business" includes a profession and the activities of any government department or local or public authority;

"consumer credit agreement" has the same meaning as in the Consumer Credit Act 1974;

"contract of sale of goods" and "goods" have the same meaning as in the Sale of Goods Act 1979;

["government department" includes any part of the Scottish Administration;]

"property in goods" means the general property in them and not merely a special property.

[243]

NOTES

Commencement: 1 November 1998–7 August 2002 (for details, see commencement note under s 17 at **[260]**).

Sub-s (5): para (c) repealed in relation to England, Wales and Northern Ireland by the Late Payment of Commercial Debts Regulations 2002, SI 2002/1674, reg 2(1), (2), and in relation to Scotland by the Late Payment of Commercial Debts (Scotland) Regulations 2002, SSI 2002/335, reg 2(1), (2).

Sub-s (6): repealed in relation to England, Wales and Northern Ireland by SI 2002/1674, reg 2(1), (2), and in relation to Scotland by SSI 2002/335, reg 2(1), (2).

Sub-s (7): definition "government department" inserted by the Scotland Act 1998 (Consequential Modifications) (No 2) Order 1999, SI 1999/1820, art 4, Sch 2, Pt I, para 132.

[2A Application of the Act to Advocates

The provisions of this Act apply to a transaction in respect of which fees are paid for professional services to a member of the Faculty of Advocates as they apply to a contract for the supply of services for the purpose of this Act.]

[244]

NOTES

Commencement: 7 August 2002.

Inserted, in relation to Scotland, by the Late Payment of Commercial Debts (Scotland) Regulations 2002, SSI 2002/335, reg 2(1), (3).

3 Qualifying debts

(1) A debt created by virtue of an obligation under a contract to which this Act applies to pay the whole or any part of the contract price is a "qualifying debt" for the purposes of this Act, unless (when created) the whole of the debt is prevented from carrying statutory interest by this section.

(2) A debt does not carry statutory interest if or to the extent that it consists of a sum to which a right to interest or to charge interest applies by virtue of any enactment (other than section 1 of this Act).

This subsection does not prevent a sum from carrying statutory interest by reason of the fact that a court, arbitrator or arbiter would, apart from this Act, have power to award interest on it.

(3) A debt does not carry (and shall be treated as never having carried) statutory interest if or to the extent that a right to demand interest on it, which exists by virtue of any rule of law, is exercised.

(4), (5) …

[245]

NOTES

Commencement: 1 November 1998–7 August 2002 (for details, see commencement note under s 17 at **[260]**).

Sub-ss (4), (5): repealed in relation to England, Wales and Northern Ireland by the Late Payment of Commercial Debts Regulations 2002, SI 2002/1674, reg 2(1), (3), and in relation to Scotland by the Late Payment of Commercial Debts (Scotland) Regulations 2002, SSI 2002/335, reg 2(1), (4).

4 Period for which statutory interest runs

(1) Statutory interest runs in relation to a qualifying debt in accordance with this section (unless section 5 applies).

(2) Statutory interest starts to run on the day after the relevant day for the debt, at the rate prevailing under section 6 at the end of the relevant day.

(3) Where the supplier and the purchaser agree a date for payment of the debt (that is, the day on which the debt is to be created by the contract), that is the relevant day unless the debt relates to an obligation to make an advance payment.

A date so agreed may be a fixed one or may depend on the happening of an event or the failure of an event to happen.

(4) Where the debt relates to an obligation to make an advance payment, the relevant day is the day on which the debt is treated by section 11 as having been created.

(5) In any other case, the relevant day is the last day of the period of 30 days beginning with—

(a) the day on which the obligation of the supplier to which the debt relates is performed; or

(b) the day on which the purchaser has notice of the amount of the debt or (where that amount is unascertained) the sum which the supplier claims is the amount of the debt,

whichever is the later.

(6) Where the debt is created by virtue of an obligation to pay a sum due in respect of a period of hire of goods, subsection (5)(a) has effect as if it referred to the last day of that period.

(7) Statutory interest ceases to run when the interest would cease to run if it were carried under an express contract term.

(8) In this section "advance payment" has the same meaning as in section 11.

[246]

NOTES

Commencement: 1 November 1998–7 August 2002 (for details, see commencement note under s 17 at **[260]**).

5 Remission of statutory interest

(1) This section applies where, by reason of any conduct of the supplier, the interests of justice require that statutory interest should be remitted in whole or part in respect of a period for which it would otherwise run in relation to a qualifying debt.

(2) If the interests of justice require that the supplier should receive no statutory interest for a period, statutory interest shall not run for that period.

(3) If the interests of justice require that the supplier should receive statutory interest at a reduced rate for a period, statutory interest shall run at such rate as meets the justice of the case for that period.

(4) Remission of statutory interest under this section may be required—

(a) by reason of conduct at any time (whether before or after the time at which the debt is created); and

(b) for the whole period for which statutory interest would otherwise run or for one or more parts of that period.

(5) In this section "conduct" includes any act or omission.

[247]

NOTES

Commencement: 1 November 1998–7 August 2002 (for details, see commencement note under s 17 at **[260]**).

[5A Compensation arising out of late payment

(1) Once statutory interest begins to run in relation to a qualifying debt, the supplier shall be entitled to a fixed sum (in addition to the statutory interest on the debt).

(2) That sum shall be—

(a) for a debt less than £1,000, the sum of £40;

(b) for a debt of £1,000 or more, but less than £10,000, the sum of £70;

(c) for a debt of £10,000 or more, the sum of £100.

(3) The obligation to pay an additional fixed sum under this section in respect of a qualifying debt shall be treated as part of the term implied by section 1(1) in the contract creating the debt.]

[248]

NOTES

Commencement: 7 August 2002.

Inserted in relation to England, Wales and Northern Ireland by the Late Payment of Commercial Debts Regulations 2002, SI 2002/1674, reg 2(1), (4), and in relation to Scotland by the Late Payment of Commercial Debts (Scotland) Regulations 2002, SSI 2002/335, reg 2(1), (5).

6 Rate of statutory interest

(1) The Secretary of State shall by order made with the consent of the Treasury set the rate of statutory interest by prescribing—

(a) a formula for calculating the rate of statutory interest; or

(b) the rate of statutory interest.

(2) Before making such an order the Secretary of State shall, among other things, consider the extent to which it may be desirable to set the rate so as to—

(a) protect suppliers whose financial position makes them particularly vulnerable if their qualifying debts are paid late; and

(b) deter generally the late payment of qualifying debts.

[249]

NOTES

Commencement: 1 November 1998–7 August 2002 (for details, see commencement note under s 17 at **[260]**).

Orders: the Late Payment of Commercial Debts (Rate of Interest) (No 3) Order 2002, SI 2002/1675; the Late Payment of Commercial Debts (Rate of Interest) (Scotland) Order 2002, SSI 2002/336.

PART II
CONTRACT TERMS RELATING TO LATE PAYMENT OF QUALIFYING DEBTS

7 Purpose of Part II

(1) This Part deals with the extent to which the parties to a contract to which this Act applies may by reference to contract terms oust or vary the right to statutory interest that would otherwise apply when a qualifying debt created by the contract (in this Part referred to as "the debt") is not paid.

(2) This Part applies to contract terms agreed before the debt is created; after that time the parties are free to agree terms dealing with the debt.

(3) This Part has effect without prejudice to any other ground which may affect the validity of a contract term.

[250]

NOTES

Commencement: 1 November 1998–7 August 2002 (for details, see commencement note under s 17 at **[260]**).

8 Circumstances where statutory interest may be ousted or varied

(1) Any contract terms are void to the extent that they purport to exclude the right to statutory interest in relation to the debt, unless there is a substantial contractual remedy for late payment of the debt.

(2) Where the parties agree a contractual remedy for late payment of the debt that is a substantial remedy, statutory interest is not carried by the debt (unless they agree otherwise).

(3) The parties may not agree to vary the right to statutory interest in relation to the debt unless either the right to statutory interest as varied or the overall remedy for late payment of the debt is a substantial remedy.

(4) Any contract terms are void to the extent that they purport to—

(a) confer a contractual right to interest that is not a substantial remedy for late payment of the debt, or

(b) vary the right to statutory interest so as to provide for a right to statutory interest that is not a substantial remedy for late payment of the debt,

unless the overall remedy for late payment of the debt is a substantial remedy.

(5) Subject to this section, the parties are free to agree contract terms which deal with the consequences of late payment of the debt.

[251]

NOTES

Commencement: 1 November 1998–7 August 2002 (for details, see commencement note under s 17 at **[260]**).

9 Meaning of "substantial remedy"

(1) A remedy for the late payment of the debt shall be regarded as a substantial remedy unless—

(a) the remedy is insufficient either for the purpose of compensating the supplier for late payment or for deterring late payment; and

(b) it would not be fair or reasonable to allow the remedy to be relied on to oust or (as the case may be) to vary the right to statutory interest that would otherwise apply in relation to the debt.

(2) In determining whether a remedy is not a substantial remedy, regard shall be had to all the relevant circumstances at the time the terms in question are agreed.

(3) In determining whether subsection (1)(b) applies, regard shall be had (without prejudice to the generality of subsection (2)) to the following matters—

(a) the benefits of commercial certainty;

(b) the strength of the bargaining positions of the parties relative to each other;

(c) whether the term was imposed by one party to the detriment of the other (whether by the use of standard terms or otherwise); and

(d) whether the supplier received an inducement to agree to the term.

[252]

NOTES

Commencement: 1 November 1998–7 August 2002 (for details, see commencement note under s 17 at **[260]**).

10 Interpretation of Part II

(1) In this Part—

"contract term" means a term of the contract creating the debt or any other contract term binding the parties (or either of them);

"contractual remedy" means a contractual right to interest or any contractual remedy other than interest;

"contractual right to interest" includes a reference to a contractual right to charge interest;

"overall remedy", in relation to the late payment of the debt, means any combination of a contractual right to interest, a varied right to statutory interest or a contractual remedy other than interest;

"substantial remedy" shall be construed in accordance with section 9.

(2) In this Part a reference (however worded) to contract terms which vary the right to statutory interest is a reference to terms altering in any way the effect of Part I in relation to the debt (for example by postponing the time at which interest starts to run or by imposing conditions on the right to interest).

(3) In this Part a reference to late payment of the debt is a reference to late payment of the sum due when the debt is created (excluding any part of that sum which is prevented from carrying statutory interest by section 3).

[253]

NOTES

Commencement: 1 November 1998–7 August 2002 (for details, see commencement note under s 17 at **[260]**).

PART III
GENERAL AND SUPPLEMENTARY

11 Treatment of advance payments of the contract price

(1) A qualifying debt created by virtue of an obligation to make an advance payment shall be treated for the purposes of this Act as if it was created on the day mentioned in subsection (3), (4) or (5) (as the case may be).

(2) In this section "advance payment" means a payment falling due before the obligation of the supplier to which the whole contract price relates ("the supplier's obligation") is performed, other than a payment of a part of the contract price that is due in respect of any part performance of that obligation and payable on or after the day on which that part performance is completed.

(3) Where the advance payment is the whole contract price, the debt shall be treated as created on the day on which the supplier's obligation is performed.

(4) Where the advance payment is a part of the contract price, but the sum is not due in respect of any part performance of the supplier's obligation, the debt shall be treated as created on the day on which the supplier's obligation is performed.

(5) Where the advance payment is a part of the contract price due in respect of any part performance of the supplier's obligation, but is payable before that part performance is completed, the debt shall be treated as created on the day on which the relevant part performance is completed.

(6) Where the debt is created by virtue of an obligation to pay a sum due in respect of a period of hire of goods, this section has effect as if—

(a) references to the day on which the supplier's obligation is performed were references to the last day of that period; and

(b) references to part performance of that obligation were references to part of that period.

(7) For the purposes of this section an obligation to pay the whole outstanding balance of the contract price shall be regarded as an obligation to pay the whole contract price and not as an obligation to pay a part of the contract price.

[254]

NOTES

Commencement: 1 November 1998–7 August 2002 (for details, see commencement note under s 17 at **[260]**).

12 Conflict of laws

(1) This Act does not have effect in relation to a contract governed by the law of a part of the United Kingdom by choice of the parties if—

(a) there is no significant connection between the contract and that part of the United Kingdom; and

(b) but for that choice, the applicable law would be a foreign law.

(2) This Act has effect in relation to a contract governed by a foreign law by choice of the parties if—

(a) but for that choice, the applicable law would be the law of a part of the United Kingdom; and

(b) there is no significant connection between the contract and any country other than that part of the United Kingdom.

(3) In this section—

"contract" means a contract falling within section 2(1); and

"foreign law" means the law of a country outside the United Kingdom.

[255]

NOTES

Commencement: 1 November 1998–7 August 2002 (for details, see commencement note under s 17 at **[260]**).

13 Assignments, etc

(1) The operation of this Act in relation to a qualifying debt is not affected by—

(a) any change in the identity of the parties to the contract creating the debt; or

(b) the passing of the right to be paid the debt, or the duty to pay it (in whole or in part) to a person other than the person who is the original creditor or the original debtor when the debt is created.

(2) Any reference in this Act to the supplier or the purchaser is a reference to the person who is for the time being the supplier or the purchaser or, in relation to a time after the debt in question has been created, the person who is for the time being the creditor or the debtor, as the case may be.

(3) Where the right to be paid part of a debt passes to a person other than the person who is the original creditor when the debt is created, any reference in this Act to a debt shall be construed as (or, if the context so requires, as including) a reference to part of a debt.

(4) A reference in this section to the identity of the parties to a contract changing, or to a right or duty passing, is a reference to it changing or passing by assignment or assignation, by operation of law or otherwise.

[256]

NOTES

Commencement: 1 November 1998–7 August 2002 (for details, see commencement note under s 17 at **[260]**).

14 Contract terms relating to the date for payment of the contract price

(1) This section applies to any contract term which purports to have the effect of postponing the time at which a qualifying debt would otherwise be created by a contract to which this Act applies.

(2) Sections 3(2)(b) and 17(1)(b) of the Unfair Contract Terms Act 1977 (no reliance to be placed on certain contract terms) shall apply in cases where such a contract term is not contained in written standard terms of the purchaser as well as in cases where the term is contained in such standard terms.

(3) In this section "contract term" has the same meaning as in section 10(1).

[257]

NOTES

Commencement: 1 November 1998–7 August 2002 (for details, see commencement note under s 17 at **[260]**).

15 Orders and regulations

(1) Any power to make an order or regulations under this Act is exercisable by statutory instrument.

(2) Any statutory instrument containing an order or regulations under this Act, other than an order under section 17(2), shall be subject to annulment in pursuance of a resolution of either House of Parliament.

[258]

NOTES

Commencement: 1 November 1998–7 August 2002 (for details, see commencement note under s 17 at **[260]**).

16 Interpretation

(1) In this Act—

"contract for the supply of goods or services" has the meaning given in section 2(2);

"contract price" means the price in a contract of sale of goods or the money consideration referred to in section 2(2)(b) in any other contract for the supply of goods or services;

"purchaser" means (subject to section 13(2)) the buyer in a contract of sale or the person who contracts with the supplier in any other contract for the supply of goods or services;

"qualifying debt" means a debt falling within section 3(1);
"statutory interest" means interest carried by virtue of the term implied by section 1(1); and
"supplier" means (subject to section 13(2)) the seller in a contract of sale of goods or the person who does one or more of the things mentioned in section 2(3) in any other contract for the supply of goods or services.

(2) In this Act any reference (however worded) to an agreement or to contract terms includes a reference to both express and implied terms (including terms established by a course of dealing or by such usage as binds the parties).

[259]

NOTES

Commencement: 1 November 1998–7 August 2002 (for details, see commencement note under s 17 at **[260]**).

17 Short title, commencement and extent

(1) This Act may be cited as the Late Payment of Commercial Debts (Interest) Act 1998.

(2) This Act (apart from this section) shall come into force on such day as the Secretary of State may by order appoint; and different days may be appointed for different descriptions of contract or for other different purposes.

An order under this subsection may specify a description of contract by reference to any feature of the contract (including the parties).

(3) The Secretary of State may by regulations make such transitional, supplemental or incidental provision (including provision modifying any provision of this Act) as the Secretary of State may consider necessary or expedient in connection with the operation of this Act while it is not fully in force.

(4) This Act does not affect contracts of any description made before this Act comes into force for contracts of that description.

(5) This Act extends to Northern Ireland.

[260]

NOTES

Commencement: 1 November 1998 (in relation to contracts for the supply of goods or services made on or after that date between a small business supplier and a purchaser who is a specified UK public authority, and in relation to contracts for the supply of goods or services made on or after that date between a small business supplier and a large business purchaser); 1 July 1999 (in relation to contracts for the supply of goods or services made on or after that date between a small business supplier and any purchaser who is a specified UK public authority); 1 September 2000 (in relation to contracts for the supply of goods or services made on or after that date between a small business supplier and any purchaser falling within the Schedule to SI 2000/2225); 1 November 2000 (in relation to contracts for the supply of goods or services made on or after that date between a small business supplier and a small business purchaser); 7 August 2002 (otherwise).

Orders: the Late Payment of Commercial Debts (Interest) Act 1998 (Commencement No 1) Order 1998, SI 1998/2479; the Late Payment of Commercial Debts (Interest) Act 1998 (Transitional Provisions) Regulations 1998, SI 1998/2481; the Late Payment of Commercial Debts (Interest) Act 1998 (Commencement No 2) Order 1999, SI 1999/1816; the Late Payment of Commercial Debts (Interest) Act 1998 (Commencement No 3) Order 2000, SI 2000/2225; the Late Payment of Commercial Debts (Interest) Act 1998 (Commencement No 4) Order 2000, SI 2000/2740; the Late Payment of Commercial Debts (Interest) Act 1998 (Commencement No 5) Order 2002, SI 2002/1673; the Late Payment of Commercial Debts (Interest) Act 1998 (Commencement No 6) (Scotland) Order 2002, SSI 2002/337.

D. INTERNATIONAL ARBITRATION

ARTICLES OF REGULATION CONCERNING THE SESSION 1695

NOTES

Authority: Judicatories Act 1693 (repealed).

25TH ACT

That, for the cutting off of groundless and expensive pleas and processes in time coming, the Lords of Session sustain no reduction of any decreet-arbitral that shall be pronounced hereafter upon a subscribed submission at the instance of either of the parties-submitters, upon any cause or reason whatsoever, unless that of corruption, bribery, or falsehood, to be alleged against the judges-arbitrators who pronounced the same.

[261]

ARBITRATION ACT 1950

(14 Geo 6 c 27)

ARRANGEMENT OF SECTIONS

PART II
ENFORCEMENT OF CERTAIN FOREIGN AWARDS

PART III
GENERAL

An Act to consolidate the Arbitration Acts 1889 to 1934

[28 July 1950]

1–34 *((Pt I): ss 1–20, 22–34 repealed by the Arbitration Act 1996, s 107(2), Sch 4; s 21 repealed by the Arbitration Act 1979, ss 1(1), 8(3).)*

PART II
ENFORCEMENT OF CERTAIN FOREIGN AWARDS

35 Awards to which Part II applies

(1) This Part of this Act applies to any award made after the twenty-eighth day of July, nineteen hundred and twenty-four—

(a) in pursuance of an agreement for arbitration to which the protocol set out in the First Schedule to this Act applies; and

(b) between persons of whom one is subject to the jurisdiction of some one of such Powers as His Majesty, being satisfied that reciprocal provisions have been made, may by Order in Council declare to be parties to the convention set out in the Second Schedule to this Act, and of whom the other is subject to the jurisdiction of some other of the Powers aforesaid; and

(c) in one of such territories as His Majesty, being satisfied that reciprocal provisions have been made, may by Order in Council declare to be territories to which the said convention applies;

and an award to which this Part of this Act applies is in this Part of this Act referred to as "a foreign award".

(2) His Majesty may by a subsequent Order in Council vary or revoke any Order previously made under this section.

(3) Any Order in Council under section one of the Arbitration (Foreign Awards) Act 1930, which is in force at the commencement of this Act shall have effect as if it had been made under this section.

[262]

NOTES

Orders in Council: the Arbitration (Foreign Awards) Order 1984, SI 1984/1168 at **[2274]**.

36 Effect of foreign awards

(1) A foreign award shall, subject to the provisions of this Part of this Act, be enforceable in England either by action or in the same manner as the award of an arbitrator is enforceable by virtue of [section 66 of the Arbitration Act 1996].

(2) Any foreign award which would be enforceable under this Part of this Act shall be treated as binding for all purposes on the persons as between whom it was made, and may accordingly be relied on by any of those persons by way of defence, set off or otherwise in any legal proceedings in England, and any references in this Part of this Act to enforcing a foreign award shall be construed as including references to relying on an award.

[263]

NOTES

Sub-s (1): substituted, in relation to Scotland, by s 41(3) of this Act at **[268]**; words in square brackets substituted by the Arbitration Act 1996, s 107(1), Sch 3, para 10.

37 Conditions for enforcement of foreign awards

(1) In order that a foreign award may be enforceable under this Part of this Act it must have—

(a) been made in pursuance of an agreement for arbitration which was valid under the law by which it is governed;

(b) been made by the tribunal provided for in the agreement or constituted in manner agreed upon by the parties;

(c) been made in conformity with the law governing the arbitration procedure;

(d) become final in the country in which it was made;

(e) been in respect of a matter which may lawfully be referred to arbitration under the law of England;

and the enforcement thereof must not be contrary to the public policy or the law of England.

(2) Subject to the provisions of this subsection, a foreign award shall not be enforceable under this Part of this Act if the court dealing with the case is satisfied that—

(a) the award has been annulled in the country in which it was made; or

(b) the party against whom it is sought to enforce the award was not given notice of the arbitration proceedings in sufficient time to enable him to present his case, or was under some legal incapacity and was not properly represented; or

(c) the award does not deal with all the questions referred or contains decisions on matters beyond the scope of the agreement for arbitration:

Provided that, if the award does not deal with all the questions referred, the court may, if it thinks fit, either postpone the enforcement of the award or order its enforcement subject to the giving of such security by the person seeking to enforce it as the court may think fit.

(3) If a party seeking to resist the enforcement of a foreign award proves that there is any ground other than the non-existence of the conditions specified in paragraphs (a), (b) and (c) of subsection (1) of this section, or the existence of the conditions specified in paragraphs (b) and (c) of subsection (2) of this section, entitling him to contest the validity of the award, the court may, if it thinks fit, either refuse to enforce the award or adjourn the hearing until after the expiration of such period as appears to the court to be reasonably sufficient to enable that party to take the necessary steps to have the award annulled by the competent tribunal.

[264]

38 Evidence

(1) The party seeking to enforce a foreign award must produce—

(a) the original award or a copy thereof duly authenticated in manner required by the law of the country in which it was made; and

(b) evidence proving that the award has become final; and

(c) such evidence as may be necessary to prove that the award is a foreign award and that the conditions mentioned in paragraphs (a), (b) and (c) of subsection (1) of the last foregoing section are satisfied.

(2) In any case where any document required to be produced under subsection (1) of this section is in a foreign language, it shall be the duty of the party seeking to enforce the award to produce a translation certified as correct by a diplomatic or consular agent of the country to which that party belongs, or certified as correct in such other manner as may be sufficient according to the law of England.

(3) Subject to the provisions of this section, rules of court may be made under section [84 of the *Supreme Court Act 1981*] with respect to the evidence which must be furnished by a party seeking to enforce an award under this Part of this Act.

[265]

NOTES

Sub-s (3): words in square brackets substituted by the Supreme Court Act 1981, s 152(1), Sch 5; whole sub-section substituted, in relation to Scotland, by s 41(4) of this Act at **[268]**; words in italics substituted by the words "Senior Courts Act 1981" by the Constitutional Reform Act 2005, s 59(5), Sch 11, Pt 1, para 1(2), as from a day to be appointed.

39 Meaning of "final award"

For the purposes of this Part of this Act, an award shall not be deemed final if any proceedings for the purpose of contesting the validity of the award are pending in the country in which it was made.

[266]

40 Saving for other rights, etc

Nothing in this Part of this Act shall—

(a) prejudice any rights which any person would have had of enforcing in England any award or of availing himself in England of any award if neither this Part of this Act nor Part I of the Arbitration (Foreign Awards) Act 1930, had been enacted; or

(b) apply to any award made on an arbitration agreement governed by the law of England.

[267]

41 Application of Part II to Scotland

(1) The following provisions of this section shall have effect for the purpose of the application of this Part of this Act to Scotland.

(2) For the references to England there shall be substituted references to Scotland.

(3) For subsection (1) of section thirty-six there shall be substituted the following subsection—

"(1) A foreign award shall, subject to the provisions of this Part of this Act, be enforceable by action, or, if the agreement for arbitration contains consent to the registration of the award in the Books of Council and Session for execution and the award is so registered, it shall, subject as aforesaid, be enforceable by summary diligence".

(4) For subsection (3) of section thirty-eight there shall be substituted the following subsection—

"(3) The Court of Session shall, subject to the provisions of this section, have power, … , to make provision by Act of Sederunt with respect to the evidence which must be furnished by a party seeking to enforce in Scotland an award under this Part of this Act, …".

[268]

NOTES

Sub-s (4): words omitted repealed by the Law Reform (Miscellaneous Provisions) (Scotland) Act 1966, s 10, Schedule, Pt I.

42, 43 *(S 42(1)–(3) applies to Northern Ireland only; s 42(4) repealed by the Judicature (Northern Ireland) Act 1978, s 122(2), Sch 7, Pt I; s 43 repealed by the Statute Law (Repeals) Act 1978.)*

PART III
GENERAL

44 Short title, commencement and repeal

(1) This Act may be cited as the Arbitration Act 1950.

(2) This Act shall come into operation on the first day of September, nineteen hundred and fifty.

(3) The Arbitration Act 1889, the Arbitration Clauses (Protocol) Act 1924, and the Arbitration Act 1934 are hereby repealed except in relation to arbitrations commenced (within the meaning of subsection (2) of section twenty-nine of this Act) before the commencement of this Act, and the Arbitration (Foreign Awards) Act 1930 is hereby repealed; and any reference in any Act or other document to any enactment hereby repealed shall be construed as including a reference to the corresponding provision of this Act.

[269]

SCHEDULE 1
PROTOCOL ON ARBITRATION CLAUSES SIGNED ON BEHALF OF HIS MAJESTY AT A MEETING OF THE ASSEMBLY OF THE LEAGUE OF NATIONS HELD ON THE TWENTY-FOURTH DAY OF SEPTEMBER, NINETEEN HUNDRED AND TWENTY-THREE

Section 35

The undersigned, being duly authorised, declare that they accept, on behalf of the countries which they represent, the following provisions—

1. Each of the Contracting States recognises the validity of an agreement whether relating to existing or future differences between parties, subject respectively to the jurisdiction of different Contracting States by which the parties to a contract agree to submit to arbitration all or any differences that may arise in connection with such contract relating to commercial matters or to any other matter capable of settlement by arbitration, whether or not the arbitration is to take place in a country to whose jurisdiction none of the parties is subject.

Each Contracting State reserves the right to limit the obligation mentioned above to contracts which are considered as commercial under its national law. Any Contracting State which avails itself of this right will notify the Secretary-General of the League of Nations, in order that the other Contracting States may be so informed.

2. The arbitral procedure, including the constitution of the arbitral tribunal, shall be governed by the will of the parties and by the law of the country in whose territory the arbitration takes place.

The Contracting States agree to facilitate all steps in the procedure which require to be taken in their own territories, in accordance with the provisions of their law governing arbitral procedure applicable to existing differences.

3. Each Contracting State undertakes to ensure the execution by its authorities and in accordance with the provisions of its national laws of arbitral awards made in its own territory under the preceding articles.

4. The tribunals of the Contracting Parties, on being seized of a dispute regarding a contract made between persons to whom Article 1 applies and including an arbitration agreement whether referring to present or future differences which is valid in virtue of the said article and capable of being carried into effect, shall refer the parties on the application of either of them to the decision of the arbitrators.

Such reference shall not prejudice the competence of the judicial tribunals in case the agreement or the arbitration cannot proceed or become inoperative.

5. The present Protocol, which shall remain open for signature by all States, shall be ratified. The ratifications shall be deposited as soon as possible with the Secretary-General of the League of Nations, who shall notify such deposit to all the signatory States.

6. The present Protocol shall come into force as soon as two ratifications have been deposited. Thereafter it will take effect, in the case of each Contracting State, one month after the notification by the Secretary-General of the deposit of its ratification.

7. The present Protocol may be denounced by any Contracting State on giving one year's notice. Denunciation shall be effected by a notification addressed to the Secretary-General of the League, who will immediately transmit copies of such notification to all the other signatory States and inform them of the date of which it was received. The denunciation shall take effect one year after the date on which it was notified to the Secretary-General, and shall operate only in respect of the notifying State.

8. The Contracting States may declare that their acceptance of the present Protocol does not include any or all of the under-mentioned territories: that is to say, their colonies, overseas possessions or territories, protectorates or the territories over which they exercise a mandate.

The said States may subsequently adhere separately on behalf of any territory thus excluded. The Secretary-General of the League of Nations shall be informed as soon as possible of such adhesions. He shall notify such adhesions to all signatory States. They will take effect one month after the notification by the Secretary-General to all signatory States.

The Contracting States may also denounce the Protocol separately on behalf of any of the territories referred to above. Article 7 applies to such denunciation.

[270]

(*Sch 2 contains the text of the 1927 Geneva Convention on Arbitral awards, printed in Pt V(D) of this work, at* **[4220]**.)

ARBITRATION (INTERNATIONAL INVESTMENT DISPUTES) ACT 1966

(1966 c 41)

ARRANGEMENT OF SECTIONS

ENFORCEMENT OF CONVENTION AWARDS

PROCEDURAL PROVISIONS

IMMUNITIES AND PRIVILEGES

SUPPLEMENTAL

An Act to implement an international Convention on the settlement of investment disputes between States and nationals of other States

[13 December 1966]

ENFORCEMENT OF CONVENTION AWARDS

1 Registration of Convention awards

(1) This section has effect as respects awards rendered pursuant to the Convention on the settlement of investment disputes between States and nationals of other States which was opened for signature in Washington on 18th March 1965.

That Convention is in this Act called "the Convention", and its text is set out in the Schedule to this Act.

(2) A person seeking recognition or enforcement of such an award shall be entitled to have the award registered in the High Court subject to proof of the prescribed matters and to the other provisions of this Act.

(3) …

(4) In addition to the pecuniary obligations imposed by the award, the award shall be registered for the reasonable costs of and incidental to registration.

(5) If at the date of the application for registration the pecuniary obligations imposed by the award have been partly satisfied, the award shall be registered only in respect of the balance, and accordingly if those obligations have then been wholly satisfied, the award shall not be registered.

(6) The power to make rules of court under section [84 of the *Supreme Court Act 1981*] shall include power—

(a) to prescribe the procedure for applying for registration under this section, and to require an applicant to give prior notice of his intention to other parties,

(b) to prescribe the matters to be proved on the application and the manner of proof, and in particular to require the applicant to furnish a copy of the award certified pursuant to the Convention,

(c) to provide for the service of notice of registration of the award by the applicant on other parties,

and in this and the next following section "prescribed" means prescribed by rules of court.

(7) For the purposes of this and the next following section—

(a) "award" shall include any decision interpreting, revising or annulling an award, being a decision pursuant to the Convention, and any decision as to costs which under the Convention is to form part of the award,

(b) an award shall be deemed to have been rendered pursuant to the Convention on the date on which certified copies of the award were pursuant to the Convention dispatched to the parties.

(8) This and the next following section shall bind the Crown (but not so as to make an award enforceable against the Crown in a manner in which a judgment would not be enforceable against the Crown).

[271]

NOTES

Sub-s (3): repealed by the Administration of Justice Act 1977, ss 4(1), (2), (4), 32(4), Sch 5, Pt I, except in relation to awards registered before 29 August 1992.

Sub-s (6): words in square brackets substituted by the Supreme Court Act 1981, s 152(1), Sch 5; words in italics substituted by the words "Senior Courts Act 1981" by the Constitutional Reform Act 2005, s 59(5), Sch 11, Pt 1, para 1(2), as from a day to be appointed.

2 Effect of registration

(1) Subject to the provisions of this Act, an award registered under section 1 above shall, as respects the pecuniary obligations which it imposes, be of the same force and effect for the purposes of execution as if it had been a judgment of the High Court given when the award was rendered pursuant to the Convention and entered on the date of registration under this Act, and, so far as relates to such pecuniary obligations—

(a) proceedings may be taken on the award,

(b) the sum for which the award is registered shall carry interest,

(c) the High Court shall have the same control over the execution of the award,

as if the award had been such a judgment of the High Court.

(2) Rules of court under section [84 of the *Supreme Court Act 1981*] may contain provisions requiring the court on proof of the prescribed matters to stay execution of any award registered under this Act so as to take account of cases where enforcement of the award has been stayed (whether provisionally or otherwise) pursuant to the Convention, and may provide for the provisional stay of execution of the award where an application is made pursuant to the Convention which, if granted, might result in a stay of enforcement of the award.

[272]

NOTES

Sub-s (2): words in square brackets substituted by the Supreme Court Act 1981, s 152(1), Sch 5; words in italics substituted by the words "Senior Courts Act 1981" by the Constitutional Reform Act 2005, s 59(5), Sch 11, Pt 1, para 1(2), as from a day to be appointed.

PROCEDURAL PROVISIONS

[3 Application of provisions of Arbitration Act 1996

(1) The Lord Chancellor may by order direct that any of the provisions contained in sections 36 and 38 to 44 of the Arbitration Act 1996 (provisions concerning the conduct of arbitral proceedings, &c) shall apply to such proceedings pursuant to the Convention as are specified in the order with or without any modifications or exceptions specified in the order.

(2) Subject to subsection (1), the Arbitration Act 1996 shall not apply to proceedings pursuant to the Convention, but this subsection shall not be taken as affecting section 9 of that Act (stay of legal proceedings in respect of matter subject to arbitration).

(3) An order made under this section—

(a) may be varied or revoked by a subsequent order so made, and

(b) shall be contained in a statutory instrument.]

[273]

NOTES

Substituted by the Arbitration Act 1996, s 107(1), Sch 3, para 24.

IMMUNITIES AND PRIVILEGES

4 Status, immunities and privileges conferred by the Convention

(1) In Section 6 of Chapter I of the Convention (which governs the status, immunities and privileges of the International Centre for Settlements of Investment Disputes established by the Convention, of members of its Council and Secretariat and of persons concerned with

conciliation or arbitration under the Convention) Articles 18 to 20, Article 21(a) (with Article 22 as it applies Article 21(a)), Article 23(1) and Article 24 shall have the force of law.

(2) Nothing in Article 24(1) of the Convention as given the force of law by this section shall be construed as—

(a) entitling the said Centre to import goods free of customs duty without any restriction on their subsequent sale in the country to which they were imported, or
(b) conferring on that Centre any exemption from duties or taxes which form part of the price of goods sold, or
(c) conferring on that Centre any exemption from duties or taxes which are no more than charges for services rendered.

(3) For the purposes of Article 20 and Article 21(a) of the Convention as given the force of law by this section, a statement to the effect that the said Centre has waived an immunity in the circumstances specified in the statement, being a statement certified by the Secretary-General of the said Centre (or by the person acting as Secretary-General), shall be conclusive evidence.

[274]

SUPPLEMENTAL

5 Government contribution to expenses under the Convention

The Treasury may discharge any obligations of Her Majesty's Government in the United Kingdom arising under Article 17 of the Convention (which obliges the Contracting States to meet any deficit of the International Centre for Settlement of Investment Disputes established under the Convention), and any sums required for that purpose shall be met out of money provided by Parliament.

[275]

6 Application to British possessions, etc

(1) Her Majesty may by Order in Council direct that the provisions of this Act shall extend, with such exceptions, adaptations and modifications as may be specified in the Order, to—

(a) the Isle of Man,
(b) any of the Channel Islands,
(c) any colony, or any country or place outside Her Majesty's dominions in which for the time being Her Majesty has jurisdiction, or any territory consisting partly of one or more colonies and partly of one or more such countries or places.

(2) An Order in Council under this section—

(a) may contain such transitional and other supplemental provisions as appear to Her Majesty to be expedient;
(b) may be varied or revoked by a subsequent Order in Council under this section.

[276]

NOTES

Orders in Council: the Arbitration (International Investment Disputes) Act 1966 (Application to Colonies etc) Order 1967, SI 1967/159, as amended by SI 1967/249 (extending this Act, with certain exceptions, adaptations and modifications, to the following territories (many of which have subsequently become independent Commonwealth countries): Antigua, Bahamas, Bermuda, British Honduras, British Solomon Islands Protectorate, Cayman Islands, Dominica, Falkland Islands, Fiji, Gibraltar, Gilbert and Ellice Islands Colony, Grenada, Hong Kong, Mauritius, Montserrat, St Christopher, Nevis and Anguilla, St Helena, St Lucia, St Vincent, Seychelles, Swaziland, Turks and Caicos Islands and Virgin Islands); the Arbitration (International Investment Disputes) Act 1966 (Application to Tonga) Order 1967, SI 1967/585 (extending this Act to Tonga); the Arbitration (International Investment Disputes) (Guernsey) Order 1968, SI 1968/1199 (extending this Act to Guernsey); the Arbitration (International Investment Disputes) (Jersey) Order 1979, SI 1979/572 (extending this Act to Jersey).

7 Application to Scotland

In the application of this Act to Scotland—

(a) for any reference to the High Court there shall be substituted a reference to the Court of Session;
(b) the Court of Session shall have power by Act of Sederunt to make rules for the purposes specified in section 1(6) and section 2(2) of this Act;

(c) registration under section 1 of this Act shall be effected by registering in the Books of Council and Session, or in such manner as the Court of Session may by Act of Sederunt prescribe;

(d) for any reference to the entering of a judgment there shall be substituted a reference to the signing of the interlocutor embodying the judgment;

(e) for section 3 of this Act there shall be substituted the following section—

"3 Proceedings in Scotland

(1) The Secretary of State may by order make provision, in relation to such proceedings pursuant to the Convention as are specified in the order, being proceedings taking place in Scotland, for the attendance of witnesses, the taking of evidence and the production of documents.

(2) …

(3) An order made under this section—

(a) may be varied or revoked by a subsequent order so made, and

(b) shall be contained in a statutory instrument."

and in any reference in this Act, or in the Convention as given the force of law in Scotland by this Act, to the staying of execution or enforcement of an award registered under this Act the expression "stay" shall be construed as meaning sist.

[277]

NOTES

Subsection (2) of section 3 as set out repealed by the Evidence (Proceedings in other Jurisdictions) Act 1975, s 8(2), Sch 2.

8 (*Applies to Northern Ireland only.*)

9 Short title and commencement

(1) This Act may be cited as the Arbitration (International Investment Disputes) Act 1966.

(2) This Act shall come into force on such day as Her Majesty may by Order in Council certify to be the day on which the Convention comes into force as regards the United Kingdom.

[278]

NOTES

Orders in Council: the Arbitration (International Investment Disputes) Act 1966 (Commencement) Order 1966, SI 1966/1597 (certifying that the Convention came into force as regards the United Kingdom on 18 January 1967).

(*The Schedule contains the text of the Convention on the Settlement of Investment Disputes Between States and Nationals of Other States, printed in Pt V(D) of this work at* **[4223]**.)

ADMINISTRATION OF JUSTICE (SCOTLAND) ACT 1972

(1972 c 59)

NOTES

Only section 3 is reproduced here.

An Act to confer extended powers on the courts in Scotland to order the inspection of documents and other property, and related matters; to enable an appeal to be taken to the House of Lords from an interlocutor of the Court of Session on a motion for a new trial; to enable a case to be stated on a question of law to the Court of Session in an arbitration; and to enable alterations to be made by act of sederunt in the rate of interest to be included in sheriff court decrees or extracts

[9 August 1972]

3 Power of arbiter to state case to Court of Session

(1) Subject to express provision to the contrary in an agreement to refer to arbitration, the arbiter or oversman may, on the application of a party to the arbitration, and shall, if the Court of Session on such an application so directs, at any stage in the arbitration state a case for the opinion of that Court on any question of law arising in the arbitration.

(2) This section shall not apply to an arbitration under any enactment which confers a power to appeal to or state a case for the opinion of a court or tribunal in relation to that arbitration.

(3) …

(4) This section shall not apply in relation to an agreement to refer to arbitration made before the commencement of this Act.

[279]

NOTES

Sub-s (3): repealed by the Trade Union and Labour Relations (Consolidation) Act 1992, s 300(1), Sch 1.

This section is disapplied in relation to an arbitration under the Law Reform (Miscellaneous Provisions) (Scotland) Act 1980, s 25: see the Law Reform (Miscellaneous Provisions) (Scotland) Act 1980, s 25(3).

This section is disapplied in relation to any determination made by an arbiter under the Electricity Act 1989, Pt I: see the Electricity Act 1989, s 64(2).

This section is disapplied in relation to any determination made by an arbiter under the Railways Act 1993: see the Railways Act 1993, s 151(9).

ARBITRATION ACT 1975

(1975 c 3)

ARRANGEMENT OF SECTIONS

EFFECT OF ARBITRATION AGREEMENT ON COURT PROCEEDINGS

ENFORCEMENT OF CONVENTION AWARDS

GENERAL

An Act to give effect to the New York Convention on the Recognition and Enforcement of Foreign Arbitral Awards

[25 February 1975]

Effect of arbitration agreement on court proceedings

1 Staying court proceedings where party proves arbitration agreement

(1) If any party to an arbitration agreement to which this section applies, or any person claiming through or under him, commences any legal proceedings in any court against any other party to the agreement, or any person claiming through or under him, in respect of any

matter agreed to be referred, any party to the proceedings may at any time after appearance, and before delivering any pleadings or taking any other steps in the proceedings, apply to the court to stay the proceedings; and the court, unless satisfied that the arbitration agreement is null and void, inoperative or incapable of being performed or that there is not in fact any dispute between the parties with regard to the matter agreed to be referred, shall make an order staying the proceedings.

(2) This section applies to any arbitration agreement which is not a domestic arbitration agreement; and neither section 4(1) of the Arbitration Act 1950 nor section 4 of the Arbitration Act (Northern Ireland) 1937 shall apply to an arbitration agreement to which this section applies.

(3) In the application of this section to Scotland, for the references to staying proceedings there shall be substituted references to sisting proceedings.

(4) In this section "domestic arbitration agreement" means an arbitration agreement which does not provide, expressly or by implication, for arbitration in a State other than the United Kingdom and to which neither—

- *(a) an individual who is a national of, or habitually resident in, any State other than the United Kingdom; nor*
- *(b) a body corporate which is incorporated in, or whose central management and control is exercised in, any State other than the United Kingdom;*

is a party at the time the proceedings are commenced.

[280]

NOTES

Repealed, except in relation to Scotland, by the Arbitration Act 1996, s 107(2), Sch 4.

Enforcement of Convention awards

2 Replacement of former provisions

Sections 3 to 6 of this Act shall have effect with respect to the enforcement of Convention awards; and where a Convention award would, but for this section, be also a foreign award within the meaning of Part II of the Arbitration Act 1950, that Part shall not apply to it.

[281]

NOTES

Repealed, except in relation to Scotland, by the Arbitration Act 1996, s 107(2), Sch 4.

3 Effect of Convention awards

(1) A Convention award shall, subject to the following provisions of this Act, be enforceable—

- *(a) in England and Wales, either by action or in the same manner as the award of an arbitrator is enforceable by virtue of section 26 of the Arbitration Act 1950;*
- *(b) in Scotland, either by action or, in a case where the arbitration agreement contains consent to the registration of the award in the Books of Council and Session for execution and the award is so registered, by summary diligence;*
- *(c) in Northern Ireland, either by action or in the same manner as the award of an arbitrator is enforceable by virtue of section 16 of the Arbitration Act (Northern Ireland) 1937.*

(2) Any Convention award which would be enforceable under this Act shall be treated as binding for all purposes on the persons as between whom it was made, and may accordingly be relied on by any of those persons by way of defence, set off or otherwise in any legal proceedings in the United Kingdom; and any reference in this Act to enforcing a Convention award shall be construed as including references to relying on such an award.

[282]

NOTES

Repealed, except in relation to Scotland, by the Arbitration Act 1996, s 107(2), Sch 4.

4 Evidence

The party seeking to enforce a Convention award must produce—

(*a*) *the duly authenticated original award or a duly certified copy of it; and*

(*b*) *the original arbitration agreement or a duly certified copy of it; and*

(*c*) *where the award or agreement is in a foreign language, a translation of it certified by an official or sworn translator or by a diplomatic or consular agent.*

[283]

NOTES

Repealed, except in relation to Scotland, by the Arbitration Act 1996, s 107(2), Sch 4.

5 Refusal of enforcement

(*1*) *Enforcement of a Convention award shall not be refused except in the cases mentioned in this section.*

(*2*) *Enforcement of a Convention award may be refused if the person against whom it is invoked proves—*

(*a*) *that a party to the arbitration agreement was (under the law applicable to him) under some incapacity; or*

(*b*) *that the arbitration agreement was not valid under the law to which the parties subjected it or, failing any indication thereon, under the law of the country where the award was made; or*

(*c*) *that he was not given proper notice of the appointment of the arbitrator or of the arbitration proceedings or was otherwise unable to present his case; or*

(*d*) (*subject to subsection* (4) *of this section*) *that the award deals with a difference not contemplated by or not falling within the terms of the submission to arbitration or contains decisions on matters beyond the scope of the submission to arbitration; or*

(*e*) *that the composition of the arbitral authority or the arbitral procedure was not in accordance with the agreement of the parties or, failing such agreement, with the law of the country where the arbitration took place; or*

(*f*) *that the award has not yet become binding on the parties, or has been set aside or suspended by a competent authority of the country in which, or under the law of which, it was made.*

(*3*) *Enforcement of a Convention award may also be refused if the award is in respect of a matter which is not capable of settlement by arbitration, or if it would be contrary to public policy to enforce the award.*

(*4*) *A Convention award which contains decisions on matters not submitted to arbitration may be enforced to the extent that it contains decisions on matters submitted to arbitration which can be separated from those on matters not so submitted.*

(*5*) *Where an application for the setting aside or suspension of a Convention award has been made to such a competent authority as is mentioned in subsection* (2) (*f*) *of this section, the court before which enforcement of the award is sought may, if it thinks fit, adjourn the proceedings and may, on the application of the party seeking to enforce the award, order the other party to give security.*

[284]

NOTES

Repealed, except in relation to Scotland, by the Arbitration Act 1996, s 107(2), Sch 4.

6 Saving

Nothing in this Act shall prejudice any right to enforce or rely on an award otherwise than under this Act or Part II of the Arbitration Act 1950.

[285]

NOTES

Repealed, except in relation to Scotland, by the Arbitration Act 1996, s 107(2), Sch 4.

General

7 Interpretation

(1) In this Act—

"arbitration agreement" means an agreement in writing (including an agreement contained in an exchange of letters or telegrams) to submit to arbitration present or future differences capable of settlement by arbitration;

"Convention award" means an award made in pursuance of an arbitration agreement in the territory of a State, other than the United Kingdom, which is a party to the New York Convention; and

"the New York Convention" means the Convention on the Recognition and Enforcement of Foreign Arbitral Awards adopted by the United Nations Conference on International Commercial Arbitration on 10th June 1958.

(2) If Her Majesty by Order in Council declares that any State specified in the Order is a party to the New York Convention the Order shall, while in force, be conclusive evidence that that State is a party to that Convention.

(3) An Order in Council under this section may be varied or revoked by a subsequent Order in Council.

[286]

NOTES

Repealed, except in relation to Scotland, by the Arbitration Act 1996, s 107(2), Sch 4.

Orders: the Arbitration (Foreign Awards) Order 1984, SI 1984/1168 at **[2274]**; the Arbitration (Foreign Awards) Order 1989, SI 1989/1348 at **[2279]**.

8 Short title, repeals, commencement and extent

(1) This Act may be cited as the Arbitration Act 1975.

(2) ...

(3) This Act shall come into operation on such date as the Secretary of State may by order made by statutory instrument appoint.

(4) This Act extends to Northern Ireland.

[287]

NOTES

Repealed, except in relation to Scotland, by the Arbitration Act 1996, s 107(2), Sch 4.

Orders: the Arbitration Act 1975 (Commencement) Order 1975, SI 1975/1662.

LAW REFORM (MISCELLANEOUS PROVISIONS) (SCOTLAND) ACT 1990

(1990 c 40)

An Act, as respects Scotland, to make new provision for the regulation of charities; to provide for the establishment of a board having functions in connection with the provision of conveyancing and executry services by persons other than solicitors, advocates and incorporated practices; to provide as to rights of audience in courts of law, legal services and judicial appointments, and for the establishment and functions of an ombudsman in relation to legal services; to amend the law relating to liquor licensing; to make special provision in relation to the giving of evidence by children in criminal trials; to empower a sheriff court to try offences committed in the district of a different sheriff court in the same sheriffdom; to provide as to probation and community service orders and the supervision and care of persons on probation and on release from prison and for supervised attendance as an alternative to imprisonment on default in paying a fine; to amend Part I of the Criminal Justice (Scotland) Act 1987 with respect to the registration and enforcement of confiscation orders in relation to the proceeds of drug trafficking; to amend section 24 of the Housing (Scotland) Act 1987; to provide a system for the settlement by arbitration of international commercial disputes; to amend Part II of the Unfair Contract Terms

Act 1977; and to make certain other miscellaneous reforms of the law

[1 November 1990]

1–55 (*In so far as unrepealed, relate to charities, legal services and make amendments to the Licensing (Scotland) Act 1976.*)

PART IV
MISCELLANEOUS REFORMS

56–65 (*In so far as unrepealed, relate to criminal and family matters.*)

Arbitration

66 UNCITRAL Model Law on International Commercial Arbitration

(1) In this section, "the Model Law" means the UNCITRAL Model Law on International Commercial Arbitration as adopted by the United Nations Commission on International Trade Law on 21st June 1985.

(2) The Model Law shall have the force of law in Scotland in the form set out in Schedule 7 to this Act (which contains the Model Law with certain modifications to adapt it for application in Scotland).

(3) The documents of the United Nations Commission on International Trade Law and its working group relating to the preparation of the Model Law may be considered in ascertaining the meaning or effect of any provision of the Model Law as set out in Schedule 7 to this Act.

(4) The parties to an arbitration agreement may, notwithstanding that the arbitration would not be an international commercial arbitration within the meaning of article 1 of the Model Law as set out in Schedule 7 to this Act, agree that the Model Law as set out in that Schedule shall apply, and in such a case the Model Law as so set out shall apply to that arbitration.

(5) Subsection (4) above is without prejudice to any other enactment or rule of law relating to arbitration.

(6) Subject to subsections (7) and (8) below, this section shall apply in relation to an arbitration agreement whether entered into before or after the date when this section comes into force.

(7) Notwithstanding subsection (6) above, this section shall not apply with respect to any arbitration which has commenced but has not been concluded on the date when this section comes into force.

(8) The parties to an arbitration agreement entered into before the date when this section comes into force may agree that the foregoing provisions of this section shall not apply to that arbitration agreement.

[288]

67–72 (*Relate to matters of civil procedure.*)

PART V
GENERAL

73, 74 (*Relate to finance and amendments and repeals.*)

75 Citation, commencement and extent

(1) This Act may be cited as the Law Reform (Miscellaneous Provisions) (Scotland) Act 1990.

(2) Subject to subsections (3) and (4) below, this Act shall come into force on such day as the Secretary of State may appoint by order made by statutory instrument and different days may be appointed for different provisions and for different purposes.

(3) The provisions of—

(a) Part III and section 66 of this Act and so much of section 74 as relates to those provisions; and

(b) (*relates to the commencement of provisions outside the scope of this work*)

shall come into force at the end of the period of two months beginning with the day on which this Act is passed.

(4) (*Relates to the commencement of provisions outside the scope of this work.*)

(5) Subject to subsections (6) and (7) below, this Act extends to Scotland only.

(6), (7) (*In so far as unrepealed, relate to the extent of provisions outside the scope of this work.*)

[289]

(*Schs 1–6 relate to Scottish Conveyancing and Executry Services Board, publication of applications made under s 25 of this Act, Scottish Legal Services Ombudsman, judicial appointments, applications for children's certificates and further provisions relating to supervised attendance orders; Sch 7 contains the text of the UNCITRAL Model Law on International Commercial Arbitration, printed in Pt V(D) of this work, at* **[4233]**; *Sch 8 contains amendments; Sch 9 contains repeals.*)

ARBITRATION ACT 1996

(1996 c 23)

ARRANGEMENT OF SECTIONS

PART I
ARBITRATION PURSUANT TO AN ARBITRATION AGREEMENT

Introductory

The arbitration agreement

Stay of legal proceedings

Commencement of arbitral proceedings

The arbitral tribunal

Powers of the court in relation to award

Miscellaneous

Supplementary

PART II
OTHER PROVISIONS RELATING TO ARBITRATION

Domestic arbitration agreements

Consumer arbitration agreements

Small claims arbitration in the county court

Appointment of judges as arbitrators

Statutory arbitrations

An Act to restate and improve the law relating to arbitration pursuant to an arbitration agreement; to make other provision relating to arbitration and arbitration awards; and for connected purposes

[17 June 1996]

PART I
ARBITRATION PURSUANT TO AN ARBITRATION AGREEMENT

Introductory

1 General principles

The provisions of this Part are founded on the following principles, and shall be construed accordingly—

(a) the object of arbitration is to obtain the fair resolution of disputes by an impartial tribunal without unnecessary delay or expense;

(b) the parties should be free to agree how their disputes are resolved, subject only to such safeguards as are necessary in the public interest;

(c) in matters governed by this Part the court should not intervene except as provided by this Part.

[290]

2 Scope of application of provisions

(1) The provisions of this Part apply where the seat of the arbitration is in England and Wales or Northern Ireland.

(2) The following sections apply even if the seat of the arbitration is outside England and Wales or Northern Ireland or no seat has been designated or determined—

(a) sections 9 to 11 (stay of legal proceedings, &c), and
(b) section 66 (enforcement of arbitral awards).

(3) The powers conferred by the following sections apply even if the seat of the arbitration is outside England and Wales or Northern Ireland or no seat has been designated or determined—
(a) section 43 (securing the attendance of witnesses), and
(b) section 44 (court powers exercisable in support of arbitral proceedings);
but the court may refuse to exercise any such power if, in the opinion of the court, the fact that the seat of the arbitration is outside England and Wales or Northern Ireland, or that when designated or determined the seat is likely to be outside England and Wales or Northern Ireland, makes it inappropriate to do so.

(4) The court may exercise a power conferred by any provision of this Part not mentioned in subsection (2) or (3) for the purpose of supporting the arbitral process where—
(a) no seat of the arbitration has been designated or determined, and
(b) by reason of a connection with England and Wales or Northern Ireland the court is satisfied that it is appropriate to do so.

(5) Section 7 (separability of arbitration agreement) and section 8 (death of a party) apply where the law applicable to the arbitration agreement is the law of England and Wales or Northern Ireland even if the seat of the arbitration is outside England and Wales or Northern Ireland or has not been designated or determined.

[291]

3 The seat of the arbitration

In this Part "the seat of the arbitration" means the juridical seat of the arbitration designated—
(a) by the parties to the arbitration agreement, or
(b) by any arbitral or other institution or person vested by the parties with powers in that regard, or
(c) by the arbitral tribunal if so authorised by the parties,
or determined, in the absence of any such designation, having regard to the parties' agreement and all the relevant circumstances.

[292]

4 Mandatory and non-mandatory provisions

(1) The mandatory provisions of this Part are listed in Schedule 1 and have effect notwithstanding any agreement to the contrary.

(2) The other provisions of this Part (the "non-mandatory provisions") allow the parties to make their own arrangements by agreement but provide rules which apply in the absence of such agreement.

(3) The parties may make such arrangements by agreeing to the application of institutional rules or providing any other means by which a matter may be decided.

(4) It is immaterial whether or not the law applicable to the parties' agreement is the law of England and Wales or, as the case may be, Northern Ireland.

(5) The choice of a law other than the law of England and Wales or Northern Ireland as the applicable law in respect of a matter provided for by a non-mandatory provision of this Part is equivalent to an agreement making provision about that matter.

For this purpose an applicable law determined in accordance with the parties' agreement, or which is objectively determined in the absence of any express or implied choice, shall be treated as chosen by the parties.

[293]

5 Agreements to be in writing

(1) The provisions of this Part apply only where the arbitration agreement is in writing, and any other agreement between the parties as to any matter is effective for the purposes of this Part only if in writing.

The expressions "agreement", "agree" and "agreed" shall be construed accordingly.

(2) There is an agreement in writing—
(a) if the agreement is made in writing (whether or not it is signed by the parties),

(b) if the agreement is made by exchange of communications in writing, or
(c) if the agreement is evidenced in writing.

(3) Where parties agree otherwise than in writing by reference to terms which are in writing, they make an agreement in writing.

(4) An agreement is evidenced in writing if an agreement made otherwise than in writing is recorded by one of the parties, or by a third party, with the authority of the parties to the agreement.

(5) An exchange of written submissions in arbitral or legal proceedings in which the existence of an agreement otherwise than in writing is alleged by one party against another party and not denied by the other party in his response constitutes as between those parties an agreement in writing to the effect alleged.

(6) References in this Part to anything being written or in writing include its being recorded by any means.

[294]

The arbitration agreement

6 Definition of arbitration agreement

(1) In this Part an "arbitration agreement" means an agreement to submit to arbitration present or future disputes (whether they are contractual or not).

(2) The reference in an agreement to a written form of arbitration clause or to a document containing an arbitration clause constitutes an arbitration agreement if the reference is such as to make that clause part of the agreement.

[295]

7 Separability of arbitration agreement

Unless otherwise agreed by the parties, an arbitration agreement which forms or was intended to form part of another agreement (whether or not in writing) shall not be regarded as invalid, non-existent or ineffective because that other agreement is invalid, or did not come into existence or has become ineffective, and it shall for that purpose be treated as a distinct agreement.

[296]

8 Whether agreement discharged by death of a party

(1) Unless otherwise agreed by the parties, an arbitration agreement is not discharged by the death of a party and may be enforced by or against the personal representatives of that party.

(2) Subsection (1) does not affect the operation of any enactment or rule of law by virtue of which a substantive right or obligation is extinguished by death.

[297]

Stay of legal proceedings

9 Stay of legal proceedings

(1) A party to an arbitration agreement against whom legal proceedings are brought (whether by way of claim or counterclaim) in respect of a matter which under the agreement is to be referred to arbitration may (upon notice to the other parties to the proceedings) apply to the court in which the proceedings have been brought to stay the proceedings so far as they concern that matter.

(2) An application may be made notwithstanding that the matter is to be referred to arbitration only after the exhaustion of other dispute resolution procedures.

(3) An application may not be made by a person before taking the appropriate procedural step (if any) to acknowledge the legal proceedings against him or after he has taken any step in those proceedings to answer the substantive claim.

(4) On an application under this section the court shall grant a stay unless satisfied that the arbitration agreement is null and void, inoperative, or incapable of being performed.

(5) If the court refuses to stay the legal proceedings, any provision that an award is a condition precedent to the bringing of legal proceedings in respect of any matter is of no effect in relation to those proceedings.

[298]

10 Reference of interpleader issue to arbitration

(1) Where in legal proceedings relief by way of interpleader is granted and any issue between the claimants is one in respect of which there is an arbitration agreement between them, the court granting the relief shall direct that the issue be determined in accordance with the agreement unless the circumstances are such that proceedings brought by a claimant in respect of the matter would not be stayed.

(2) Where subsection (1) applies but the court does not direct that the issue be determined in accordance with the arbitration agreement, any provision that an award is a condition precedent to the bringing of legal proceedings in respect of any matter shall not affect the determination of that issue by the court.

[299]

11 Retention of security where Admiralty proceedings stayed

(1) Where Admiralty proceedings are stayed on the ground that the dispute in question should be submitted to arbitration, the court granting the stay may, if in those proceedings property has been arrested or bail or other security has been given to prevent or obtain release from arrest—

(a) order that the property arrested be retained as security for the satisfaction of any award given in the arbitration in respect of that dispute, or

(b) order that the stay of those proceedings be conditional on the provision of equivalent security for the satisfaction of any such award.

(2) Subject to any provision made by rules of court and to any necessary modifications, the same law and practice shall apply in relation to property retained in pursuance of an order as would apply if it were held for the purposes of proceedings in the court making the order.

[300]

Commencement of arbitral proceedings

12 Power of court to extend time for beginning arbitral proceedings, &c

(1) Where an arbitration agreement to refer future disputes to arbitration provides that a claim shall be barred, or the claimant's right extinguished, unless the claimant takes within a time fixed by the agreement some step—

(a) to begin arbitral proceedings, or

(b) to begin other dispute resolution procedures which must be exhausted before arbitral proceedings can be begun,

the court may by order extend the time for taking that step.

(2) Any party to the arbitration agreement may apply for such an order (upon notice to the other parties), but only after a claim has arisen and after exhausting any available arbitral process for obtaining an extension of time.

(3) The court shall make an order only if satisfied—

(a) that the circumstances are such as were outside the reasonable contemplation of the parties when they agreed the provision in question, and that it would be just to extend the time, or

(b) that the conduct of one party makes it unjust to hold the other party to the strict terms of the provision in question.

(4) The court may extend the time for such period and on such terms as it thinks fit, and may do so whether or not the time previously fixed (by agreement or by a previous order) has expired.

(5) An order under this section does not affect the operation of the Limitation Acts (see section 13).

(6) The leave of the court is required for any appeal from a decision of the court under this section.

[301]

13 Application of Limitation Acts

(1) The Limitation Acts apply to arbitral proceedings as they apply to legal proceedings.

(2) The court may order that in computing the time prescribed by the Limitation Acts for the commencement of proceedings (including arbitral proceedings) in respect of a dispute which was the subject matter—

(a) of an award which the court orders to be set aside or declares to be of no effect, or

(b) of the affected part of an award which the court orders to be set aside in part, or declares to be in part of no effect,

the period between the commencement of the arbitration and the date of the order referred to in paragraph (a) or (b) shall be excluded.

(3) In determining for the purposes of the Limitation Acts when a cause of action accrued, any provision that an award is a condition precedent to the bringing of legal proceedings in respect of a matter to which an arbitration agreement applies shall be disregarded.

(4) In this Part "the Limitation Acts" means—

(a) in England and Wales, the Limitation Act 1980, the Foreign Limitation Periods Act 1984 and any other enactment (whenever passed) relating to the limitation of actions;

(b) in Northern Ireland, the Limitation (Northern Ireland) Order 1989, the Foreign Limitation Periods (Northern Ireland) Order 1985 and any other enactment (whenever passed) relating to the limitation of actions.

[302]

14 Commencement of arbitral proceedings

(1) The parties are free to agree when arbitral proceedings are to be regarded as commenced for the purposes of this Part and for the purposes of the Limitation Acts.

(2) If there is no such agreement the following provisions apply.

(3) Where the arbitrator is named or designated in the arbitration agreement, arbitral proceedings are commenced in respect of a matter when one party serves on the other party or parties a notice in writing requiring him or them to submit that matter to the person so named or designated.

(4) Where the arbitrator or arbitrators are to be appointed by the parties, arbitral proceedings are commenced in respect of a matter when one party serves on the other party or parties notice in writing requiring him or them to appoint an arbitrator or to agree to the appointment of an arbitrator in respect of that matter.

(5) Where the arbitrator or arbitrators are to be appointed by a person other than a party to the proceedings, arbitral proceedings are commenced in respect of a matter when one party gives notice in writing to that person requesting him to make the appointment in respect of that matter.

[303]

The arbitral tribunal

15 The arbitral tribunal

(1) The parties are free to agree on the number of arbitrators to form the tribunal and whether there is to be a chairman or umpire.

(2) Unless otherwise agreed by the parties, an agreement that the number of arbitrators shall be two or any other even number shall be understood as requiring the appointment of an additional arbitrator as chairman of the tribunal.

(3) If there is no agreement as to the number of arbitrators, the tribunal shall consist of a sole arbitrator.

[304]

16 Procedure for appointment of arbitrators

(1) The parties are free to agree on the procedure for appointing the arbitrator or arbitrators, including the procedure for appointing any chairman or umpire.

(2) If or to the extent that there is no such agreement, the following provisions apply.

(3) If the tribunal is to consist of a sole arbitrator, the parties shall jointly appoint the arbitrator not later than 28 days after service of a request in writing by either party to do so.

(4) If the tribunal is to consist of two arbitrators, each party shall appoint one arbitrator not later than 14 days after service of a request in writing by either party to do so.

(5) If the tribunal is to consist of three arbitrators—
- (a) each party shall appoint one arbitrator not later than 14 days after service of a request in writing by either party to do so, and
- (b) the two so appointed shall forthwith appoint a third arbitrator as the chairman of the tribunal.

(6) If the tribunal is to consist of two arbitrators and an umpire—
- (a) each party shall appoint one arbitrator not later than 14 days after service of a request in writing by either party to do so, and
- (b) the two so appointed may appoint an umpire at any time after they themselves are appointed and shall do so before any substantive hearing or forthwith if they cannot agree on a matter relating to the arbitration.

(7) In any other case (in particular, if there are more than two parties) section 18 applies as in the case of a failure of the agreed appointment procedure.

[305]

17 Power in case of default to appoint sole arbitrator

(1) Unless the parties otherwise agree, where each of two parties to an arbitration agreement is to appoint an arbitrator and one party ("the party in default") refuses to do so, or fails to do so within the time specified, the other party, having duly appointed his arbitrator, may give notice in writing to the party in default that he proposes to appoint his arbitrator to act as sole arbitrator.

(2) If the party in default does not within 7 clear days of that notice being given—
- (a) make the required appointment, and
- (b) notify the other party that he has done so,

the other party may appoint his arbitrator as sole arbitrator whose award shall be binding on both parties as if he had been so appointed by agreement.

(3) Where a sole arbitrator has been appointed under subsection (2), the party in default may (upon notice to the appointing party) apply to the court which may set aside the appointment.

(4) The leave of the court is required for any appeal from a decision of the court under this section.

[306]

18 Failure of appointment procedure

(1) The parties are free to agree what is to happen in the event of a failure of the procedure for the appointment of the arbitral tribunal.

There is no failure if an appointment is duly made under section 17 (power in case of default to appoint sole arbitrator), unless that appointment is set aside.

(2) If or to the extent that there is no such agreement any party to the arbitration agreement may (upon notice to the other parties) apply to the court to exercise its powers under this section.

(3) Those powers are—
- (a) to give directions as to the making of any necessary appointments;
- (b) to direct that the tribunal shall be constituted by such appointments (or any one or more of them) as have been made;
- (c) to revoke any appointments already made;
- (d) to make any necessary appointments itself.

(4) An appointment made by the court under this section has effect as if made with the agreement of the parties.

(5) The leave of the court is required for any appeal from a decision of the court under this section.

[307]

19 Court to have regard to agreed qualifications

In deciding whether to exercise, and in considering how to exercise, any of its powers under section 16 (procedure for appointment of arbitrators) or section 18 (failure of appointment procedure), the court shall have due regard to any agreement of the parties as to the qualifications required of the arbitrators.

[308]

20 Chairman

(1) Where the parties have agreed that there is to be a chairman, they are free to agree what the functions of the chairman are to be in relation to the making of decisions, orders and awards.

(2) If or to the extent that there is no such agreement, the following provisions apply.

(3) Decisions, orders and awards shall be made by all or a majority of the arbitrators (including the chairman).

(4) The view of the chairman shall prevail in relation to a decision, order or award in respect of which there is neither unanimity nor a majority under subsection (3).

[309]

21 Umpire

(1) Where the parties have agreed that there is to be an umpire, they are free to agree what the functions of the umpire are to be, and in particular—

(a) whether he is to attend the proceedings, and

(b) when he is to replace the other arbitrators as the tribunal with power to make decisions, orders and awards.

(2) If or to the extent that there is no such agreement, the following provisions apply.

(3) The umpire shall attend the proceedings and be supplied with the same documents and other materials as are supplied to the other arbitrators.

(4) Decisions, orders and awards shall be made by the other arbitrators unless and until they cannot agree on a matter relating to the arbitration.

In that event they shall forthwith give notice in writing to the parties and the umpire, whereupon the umpire shall replace them as the tribunal with power to make decisions, orders and awards as if he were sole arbitrator.

(5) If the arbitrators cannot agree but fail to give notice of that fact, or if any of them fails to join in the giving of notice, any party to the arbitral proceedings may (upon notice to the other parties and to the tribunal) apply to the court which may order that the umpire shall replace the other arbitrators as the tribunal with power to make decisions, orders and awards as if he were sole arbitrator.

(6) The leave of the court is required for any appeal from a decision of the court under this section.

[310]

22 Decision-making where no chairman or umpire

(1) Where the parties agree that there shall be two or more arbitrators with no chairman or umpire, the parties are free to agree how the tribunal is to make decisions, orders and awards.

(2) If there is no such agreement, decisions, orders and awards shall be made by all or a majority of the arbitrators.

[311]

23 Revocation of arbitrator's authority

(1) The parties are free to agree in what circumstances the authority of an arbitrator may be revoked.

(2) If or to the extent that there is no such agreement the following provisions apply.

(3) The authority of an arbitrator may not be revoked except—

(a) by the parties acting jointly, or

(b) by an arbitral or other institution or person vested by the parties with powers in that regard.

(4) Revocation of the authority of an arbitrator by the parties acting jointly must be agreed in writing unless the parties also agree (whether or not in writing) to terminate the arbitration agreement.

(5) Nothing in this section affects the power of the court—

(a) to revoke an appointment under section 18 (powers exercisable in case of failure of appointment procedure), or

(b) to remove an arbitrator on the grounds specified in section 24.

[312]

24 Power of court to remove arbitrator

(1) A party to arbitral proceedings may (upon notice to the other parties, to the arbitrator concerned and to any other arbitrator) apply to the court to remove an arbitrator on any of the following grounds—

(a) that circumstances exist that give rise to justifiable doubts as to his impartiality;

(b) that he does not possess the qualifications required by the arbitration agreement;

(c) that he is physically or mentally incapable of conducting the proceedings or there are justifiable doubts as to his capacity to do so;

(d) that he has refused or failed—

(i) properly to conduct the proceedings, or

(ii) to use all reasonable despatch in conducting the proceedings or making an award,

and that substantial injustice has been or will be caused to the applicant.

(2) If there is an arbitral or other institution or person vested by the parties with power to remove an arbitrator, the court shall not exercise its power of removal unless satisfied that the applicant has first exhausted any available recourse to that institution or person.

(3) The arbitral tribunal may continue the arbitral proceedings and make an award while an application to the court under this section is pending.

(4) Where the court removes an arbitrator, it may make such order as it thinks fit with respect to his entitlement (if any) to fees or expenses, or the repayment of any fees or expenses already paid.

(5) The arbitrator concerned is entitled to appear and be heard by the court before it makes any order under this section.

(6) The leave of the court is required for any appeal from a decision of the court under this section.

[313]

NOTES

See further, in relation to the application of this section, with modifications, for the purposes of arbitrations conducted in accordance with the Scheme: the ACAS Arbitration Scheme (Great Britain) Order 2004, SI 2004/753, art 4, Schedule, para 52EW.

25 Resignation of arbitrator

(1) The parties are free to agree with an arbitrator as to the consequences of his resignation as regards—

(a) his entitlement (if any) to fees or expenses, and

(b) any liability thereby incurred by him.

(2) If or to the extent that there is no such agreement the following provisions apply.

(3) An arbitrator who resigns his appointment may (upon notice to the parties) apply to the court—

(a) to grant him relief from any liability thereby incurred by him, and

(b) to make such order as it thinks fit with respect to his entitlement (if any) to fees or expenses or the repayment of any fees or expenses already paid.

(4) If the court is satisfied that in all the circumstances it was reasonable for the arbitrator to resign, it may grant such relief as is mentioned in subsection (3)(a) on such terms as it thinks fit.

(5) The leave of the court is required for any appeal from a decision of the court under this section.

[314]

26 Death of arbitrator or person appointing him

(1) The authority of an arbitrator is personal and ceases on his death.

(2) Unless otherwise agreed by the parties, the death of the person by whom an arbitrator was appointed does not revoke the arbitrator's authority.

[315]

27 Filling of vacancy, &c

(1) Where an arbitrator ceases to hold office, the parties are free to agree—

(a) whether and if so how the vacancy is to be filled,
(b) whether and if so to what extent the previous proceedings should stand, and
(c) what effect (if any) his ceasing to hold office has on any appointment made by him (alone or jointly).

(2) If or to the extent that there is no such agreement, the following provisions apply.

(3) The provisions of sections 16 (procedure for appointment of arbitrators) and 18 (failure of appointment procedure) apply in relation to the filling of the vacancy as in relation to an original appointment.

(4) The tribunal (when reconstituted) shall determine whether and if so to what extent the previous proceedings should stand.

This does not affect any right of a party to challenge those proceedings on any ground which had arisen before the arbitrator ceased to hold office.

(5) His ceasing to hold office does not affect any appointment by him (alone or jointly) of another arbitrator, in particular any appointment of a chairman or umpire.

[316]

28 Joint and several liability of parties to arbitrators for fees and expenses

(1) The parties are jointly and severally liable to pay to the arbitrators such reasonable fees and expenses (if any) as are appropriate in the circumstances.

(2) Any party may apply to the court (upon notice to the other parties and to the arbitrators) which may order that the amount of the arbitrators' fees and expenses shall be considered and adjusted by such means and upon such terms as it may direct.

(3) If the application is made after any amount has been paid to the arbitrators by way of fees or expenses, the court may order the repayment of such amount (if any) as is shown to be excessive, but shall not do so unless it is shown that it is reasonable in the circumstances to order repayment.

(4) The above provisions have effect subject to any order of the court under section 24(4) or 25(3)(b) (order as to entitlement to fees or expenses in case of removal or resignation of arbitrator).

(5) Nothing in this section affects any liability of a party to any other party to pay all or any of the costs of the arbitration (see sections 59 to 65) or any contractual right of an arbitrator to payment of his fees and expenses.

(6) In this section references to arbitrators include an arbitrator who has ceased to act and an umpire who has not replaced the other arbitrators.

[317]

29 Immunity of arbitrator

(1) An arbitrator is not liable for anything done or omitted in the discharge or purported discharge of his functions as arbitrator unless the act or omission is shown to have been in bad faith.

(2) Subsection (1) applies to an employee or agent of an arbitrator as it applies to the arbitrator himself.

(3) This section does not affect any liability incurred by an arbitrator by reason of his resigning (but see section 25).

[318]

Jurisdiction of the arbitral tribunal

30 Competence of tribunal to rule on its own jurisdiction

(1) Unless otherwise agreed by the parties, the arbitral tribunal may rule on its own substantive jurisdiction, that is, as to—

(a) whether there is a valid arbitration agreement,

(b) whether the tribunal is properly constituted, and

(c) what matters have been submitted to arbitration in accordance with the arbitration agreement.

(2) Any such ruling may be challenged by any available arbitral process of appeal or review or in accordance with the provisions of this Part.

[319]

31 Objection to substantive jurisdiction of tribunal

(1) An objection that the arbitral tribunal lacks substantive jurisdiction at the outset of the proceedings must be raised by a party not later than the time he takes the first step in the proceedings to contest the merits of any matter in relation to which he challenges the tribunal's jurisdiction.

A party is not precluded from raising such an objection by the fact that he has appointed or participated in the appointment of an arbitrator.

(2) Any objection during the course of the arbitral proceedings that the arbitral tribunal is exceeding its substantive jurisdiction must be made as soon as possible after the matter alleged to be beyond its jurisdiction is raised.

(3) The arbitral tribunal may admit an objection later than the time specified in subsection (1) or (2) if it considers the delay justified.

(4) Where an objection is duly taken to the tribunal's substantive jurisdiction and the tribunal has power to rule on its own jurisdiction, it may—

(a) rule on the matter in an award as to jurisdiction, or

(b) deal with the objection in its award on the merits.

If the parties agree which of these courses the tribunal should take, the tribunal shall proceed accordingly.

(5) The tribunal may in any case, and shall if the parties so agree, stay proceedings whilst an application is made to the court under section 32 (determination of preliminary point of jurisdiction).

[320]

32 Determination of preliminary point of jurisdiction

(1) The court may, on the application of a party to arbitral proceedings (upon notice to the other parties), determine any question as to the substantive jurisdiction of the tribunal.

A party may lose the right to object (see section 73).

(2) An application under this section shall not be considered unless—

(a) it is made with the agreement in writing of all the other parties to the proceedings, or

(b) it is made with the permission of the tribunal and the court is satisfied—

(i) that the determination of the question is likely to produce substantial savings in costs,

(ii) that the application was made without delay, and

(iii) that there is good reason why the matter should be decided by the court.

(3) An application under this section, unless made with the agreement of all the other parties to the proceedings, shall state the grounds on which it is said that the matter should be decided by the court.

(4) Unless otherwise agreed by the parties, the arbitral tribunal may continue the arbitral proceedings and make an award while an application to the court under this section is pending.

(5) Unless the court gives leave, no appeal lies from a decision of the court whether the conditions specified in subsection (2) are met.

(6) The decision of the court on the question of jurisdiction shall be treated as a judgment of the court for the purposes of an appeal.

But no appeal lies without the leave of the court which shall not be given unless the court considers that the question involves a point of law which is one of general importance or is one which for some other special reason should be considered by the Court of Appeal.

[321]

The arbitral proceedings

33 General duty of the tribunal

(1) The tribunal shall—

(a) act fairly and impartially as between the parties, giving each party a reasonable opportunity of putting his case and dealing with that of his opponent, and

(b) adopt procedures suitable to the circumstances of the particular case, avoiding unnecessary delay or expense, so as to provide a fair means for the resolution of the matters falling to be determined.

(2) The tribunal shall comply with that general duty in conducting the arbitral proceedings, in its decisions on matters of procedure and evidence and in the exercise of all other powers conferred on it.

[322]

34 Procedural and evidential matters

(1) It shall be for the tribunal to decide all procedural and evidential matters, subject to the right of the parties to agree any matter.

(2) Procedural and evidential matters include—

(a) when and where any part of the proceedings is to be held;

(b) the language or languages to be used in the proceedings and whether translations of any relevant documents are to be supplied;

(c) whether any and if so what form of written statements of claim and defence are to be used, when these should be supplied and the extent to which such statements can be later amended;

(d) whether any and if so which documents or classes of documents should be disclosed between and produced by the parties and at what stage;

(e) whether any and if so what questions should be put to and answered by the respective parties and when and in what form this should be done;

(f) whether to apply strict rules of evidence (or any other rules) as to the admissibility, relevance or weight of any material (oral, written or other) sought to be tendered on any matters of fact or opinion, and the time, manner and form in which such material should be exchanged and presented;

(g) whether and to what extent the tribunal should itself take the initiative in ascertaining the facts and the law;

(h) whether and to what extent there should be oral or written evidence or submissions.

(3) The tribunal may fix the time within which any directions given by it are to be complied with, and may if it thinks fit extend the time so fixed (whether or not it has expired).

[323]

35 Consolidation of proceedings and concurrent hearings

(1) The parties are free to agree—

(a) that the arbitral proceedings shall be consolidated with other arbitral proceedings, or

(b) that concurrent hearings shall be held,

on such terms as may be agreed.

(2) Unless the parties agree to confer such power on the tribunal, the tribunal has no power to order consolidation of proceedings or concurrent hearings.

[324]

36 Legal or other representation

Unless otherwise agreed by the parties, a party to arbitral proceedings may be represented in the proceedings by a lawyer or other person chosen by him.

[325]

37 Power to appoint experts, legal advisers or assessors

(1) Unless otherwise agreed by the parties—

(a) the tribunal may—

(i) appoint experts or legal advisers to report to it and the parties, or

(ii) appoint assessors to assist it on technical matters,

and may allow any such expert, legal adviser or assessor to attend the proceedings; and

(b) the parties shall be given a reasonable opportunity to comment on any information, opinion or advice offered by any such person.

(2) The fees and expenses of an expert, legal adviser or assessor appointed by the tribunal for which the arbitrators are liable are expenses of the arbitrators for the purposes of this Part.

[326]

38 General powers exercisable by the tribunal

(1) The parties are free to agree on the powers exercisable by the arbitral tribunal for the purposes of and in relation to the proceedings.

(2) Unless otherwise agreed by the parties the tribunal has the following powers.

(3) The tribunal may order a claimant to provide security for the costs of the arbitration.

This power shall not be exercised on the ground that the claimant is—

(a) an individual ordinarily resident outside the United Kingdom, or

(b) a corporation or association incorporated or formed under the law of a country outside the United Kingdom, or whose central management and control is exercised outside the United Kingdom.

(4) The tribunal may give directions in relation to any property which is the subject of the proceedings or as to which any question arises in the proceedings, and which is owned by or is in the possession of a party to the proceedings—

(a) for the inspection, photographing, preservation, custody or detention of the property by the tribunal, an expert or a party, or

(b) ordering that samples be taken from, or any observation be made of or experiment conducted upon, the property.

(5) The tribunal may direct that a party or witness shall be examined on oath or affirmation, and may for that purpose administer any necessary oath or take any necessary affirmation.

(6) The tribunal may give directions to a party for the preservation for the purposes of the proceedings of any evidence in his custody or control.

[327]

39 Power to make provisional awards

(1) The parties are free to agree that the tribunal shall have power to order on a provisional basis any relief which it would have power to grant in a final award.

(2) This includes, for instance, making—

(a) a provisional order for the payment of money or the disposition of property as between the parties, or

(b) an order to make an interim payment on account of the costs of the arbitration.

(3) Any such order shall be subject to the tribunal's final adjudication; and the tribunal's final award, on the merits or as to costs, shall take account of any such order.

(4) Unless the parties agree to confer such power on the tribunal, the tribunal has no such power.

This does not affect its powers under section 47 (awards on different issues, &c).

[328]

40 General duty of parties

(1) The parties shall do all things necessary for the proper and expeditious conduct of the arbitral proceedings.

(2) This includes—

(a) complying without delay with any determination of the tribunal as to procedural or evidential matters, or with any order or directions of the tribunal, and

(b) where appropriate, taking without delay any necessary steps to obtain a decision of the court on a preliminary question of jurisdiction or law (see sections 32 and 45).

[329]

41 Powers of tribunal in case of party's default

(1) The parties are free to agree on the powers of the tribunal in case of a party's failure to do something necessary for the proper and expeditious conduct of the arbitration.

(2) Unless otherwise agreed by the parties, the following provisions apply.

(3) If the tribunal is satisfied that there has been inordinate and inexcusable delay on the part of the claimant in pursuing his claim and that the delay—

(a) gives rise, or is likely to give rise, to a substantial risk that it is not possible to have a fair resolution of the issues in that claim, or

(b) has caused, or is likely to cause, serious prejudice to the respondent,

the tribunal may make an award dismissing the claim.

(4) If without showing sufficient cause a party—

(a) fails to attend or be represented at an oral hearing of which due notice was given, or

(b) where matters are to be dealt with in writing, fails after due notice to submit written evidence or make written submissions,

the tribunal may continue the proceedings in the absence of that party or, as the case may be, without any written evidence or submissions on his behalf, and may make an award on the basis of the evidence before it.

(5) If without showing sufficient cause a party fails to comply with any order or directions of the tribunal, the tribunal may make a peremptory order to the same effect, prescribing such time for compliance with it as the tribunal considers appropriate.

(6) If a claimant fails to comply with a peremptory order of the tribunal to provide security for costs, the tribunal may make an award dismissing his claim.

(7) If a party fails to comply with any other kind of peremptory order, then, without prejudice to section 42 (enforcement by court of tribunal's peremptory orders), the tribunal may do any of the following—

(a) direct that the party in default shall not be entitled to rely upon any allegation or material which was the subject matter of the order;

(b) draw such adverse inferences from the act of non-compliance as the circumstances justify;

(c) proceed to an award on the basis of such materials as have been properly provided to it;

(d) make such order as it thinks fit as to the payment of costs of the arbitration incurred in consequence of the non-compliance.

[330]

Powers of court in relation to arbitral proceedings

42 Enforcement of peremptory orders of tribunal

(1) Unless otherwise agreed by the parties, the court may make an order requiring a party to comply with a peremptory order made by the tribunal.

(2) An application for an order under this section may be made—

(a) by the tribunal (upon notice to the parties),

(b) by a party to the arbitral proceedings with the permission of the tribunal (and upon notice to the other parties), or

(c) where the parties have agreed that the powers of the court under this section shall be available.

(3) The court shall not act unless it is satisfied that the applicant has exhausted any available arbitral process in respect of failure to comply with the tribunal's order.

(4) No order shall be made under this section unless the court is satisfied that the person to whom the tribunal's order was directed has failed to comply with it within the time prescribed in the order or, if no time was prescribed, within a reasonable time.

(5) The leave of the court is required for any appeal from a decision of the court under this section.

[331]

43 Securing the attendance of witnesses

(1) A party to arbitral proceedings may use the same court procedures as are available in relation to legal proceedings to secure the attendance before the tribunal of a witness in order to give oral testimony or to produce documents or other material evidence.

(2) This may only be done with the permission of the tribunal or the agreement of the other parties.

(3) The court procedures may only be used if—
(a) the witness is in the United Kingdom, and
(b) the arbitral proceedings are being conducted in England and Wales or, as the case may be, Northern Ireland.

(4) A person shall not be compelled by virtue of this section to produce any document or other material evidence which he could not be compelled to produce in legal proceedings.

[332]

44 Court powers exercisable in support of arbitral proceedings

(1) Unless otherwise agreed by the parties, the court has for the purposes of and in relation to arbitral proceedings the same power of making orders about the matters listed below as it has for the purposes of and in relation to legal proceedings.

(2) Those matters are—
(a) the taking of the evidence of witnesses;
(b) the preservation of evidence;
(c) making orders relating to property which is the subject of the proceedings or as to which any question arises in the proceedings—
(i) for the inspection, photographing, preservation, custody or detention of the property, or
(ii) ordering that samples be taken from, or any observation be made of or experiment conducted upon, the property;
and for that purpose authorising any person to enter any premises in the possession or control of a party to the arbitration;
(d) the sale of any goods the subject of the proceedings;
(e) the granting of an interim injunction or the appointment of a receiver.

(3) If the case is one of urgency, the court may, on the application of a party or proposed party to the arbitral proceedings, make such orders as it thinks necessary for the purpose of preserving evidence or assets.

(4) If the case is not one of urgency, the court shall act only on the application of a party to the arbitral proceedings (upon notice to the other parties and to the tribunal) made with the permission of the tribunal or the agreement in writing of the other parties.

(5) In any case the court shall act only if or to the extent that the arbitral tribunal, and any arbitral or other institution or person vested by the parties with power in that regard, has no power or is unable for the time being to act effectively.

(6) If the court so orders, an order made by it under this section shall cease to have effect in whole or in part on the order of the tribunal or of any such arbitral or other institution or person having power to act in relation to the subject-matter of the order.

(7) The leave of the court is required for any appeal from a decision of the court under this section.

[333]

45 Determination of preliminary point of law

(1) Unless otherwise agreed by the parties, the court may on the application of a party to arbitral proceedings (upon notice to the other parties) determine any question of law arising in the course of the proceedings which the court is satisfied substantially affects the rights of one or more of the parties.

An agreement to dispense with reasons for the tribunal's award shall be considered an agreement to exclude the court's jurisdiction under this section.

(2) An application under this section shall not be considered unless—

(a) it is made with the agreement of all the other parties to the proceedings, or

(b) it is made with the permission of the tribunal and the court is satisfied—

(i) that the determination of the question is likely to produce substantial savings in costs, and

(ii) that the application was made without delay.

(3) The application shall identify the question of law to be determined and, unless made with the agreement of all the other parties to the proceedings, shall state the grounds on which it is said that the question should be decided by the court.

(4) Unless otherwise agreed by the parties, the arbitral tribunal may continue the arbitral proceedings and make an award while an application to the court under this section is pending.

(5) Unless the court gives leave, no appeal lies from a decision of the court whether the conditions specified in subsection (2) are met.

(6) The decision of the court on the question of law shall be treated as a judgment of the court for the purposes of an appeal.

But no appeal lies without the leave of the court which shall not be given unless the court considers that the question is one of general importance, or is one which for some other special reason should be considered by the Court of Appeal.

[334]

NOTES

See further, in relation to the application of this section, with modifications, for the purposes of arbitrations conducted in accordance with the Scheme: the ACAS Arbitration Scheme (Great Britain) Order 2004, SI 2004/753, art 4, Schedule, para 110EW.

The award

46 Rules applicable to substance of dispute

(1) The arbitral tribunal shall decide the dispute—

(a) in accordance with the law chosen by the parties as applicable to the substance of the dispute, or

(b) if the parties so agree, in accordance with such other considerations as are agreed by them or determined by the tribunal.

(2) For this purpose the choice of the laws of a country shall be understood to refer to the substantive laws of that country and not its conflict of laws rules.

(3) If or to the extent that there is no such choice or agreement, the tribunal shall apply the law determined by the conflict of laws rules which it considers applicable.

[335]

NOTES

Sub-s (1)(b): see further, in relation to the application of this sub-s, with modifications, for the purposes of arbitrations conducted in accordance with the Scheme: the ACAS Arbitration Scheme (Great Britain) Order 2004, SI 2004/753, art 5.

47 Awards on different issues, &c

(1) Unless otherwise agreed by the parties, the tribunal may make more than one award at different times on different aspects of the matters to be determined.

(2) The tribunal may, in particular, make an award relating—
(a) to an issue affecting the whole claim, or
(b) to a part only of the claims or cross-claims submitted to it for decision.

(3) If the tribunal does so, it shall specify in its award the issue, or the claim or part of a claim, which is the subject matter of the award.

[336]

48 Remedies

(1) The parties are free to agree on the powers exercisable by the arbitral tribunal as regards remedies.

(2) Unless otherwise agreed by the parties, the tribunal has the following powers.

(3) The tribunal may make a declaration as to any matter to be determined in the proceedings.

(4) The tribunal may order the payment of a sum of money, in any currency.

(5) The tribunal has the same powers as the court—
(a) to order a party to do or refrain from doing anything;
(b) to order specific performance of a contract (other than a contract relating to land);
(c) to order the rectification, setting aside or cancellation of a deed or other document.

[337]

49 Interest

(1) The parties are free to agree on the powers of the tribunal as regards the award of interest.

(2) Unless otherwise agreed by the parties the following provisions apply.

(3) The tribunal may award simple or compound interest from such dates, at such rates and with such rests as it considers meets the justice of the case—
(a) on the whole or part of any amount awarded by the tribunal, in respect of any period up to the date of the award;
(b) on the whole or part of any amount claimed in the arbitration and outstanding at the commencement of the arbitral proceedings but paid before the award was made, in respect of any period up to the date of payment.

(4) The tribunal may award simple or compound interest from the date of the award (or any later date) until payment, at such rates and with such rests as it considers meets the justice of the case, on the outstanding amount of any award (including any award of interest under subsection (3) and any award as to costs).

(5) References in this section to an amount awarded by the tribunal include an amount payable in consequence of a declaratory award by the tribunal.

(6) The above provisions do not affect any other power of the tribunal to award interest.

[338]

50 Extension of time for making award

(1) Where the time for making an award is limited by or in pursuance of the arbitration agreement, then, unless otherwise agreed by the parties, the court may in accordance with the following provisions by order extend that time.

(2) An application for an order under this section may be made—
(a) by the tribunal (upon notice to the parties), or
(b) by any party to the proceedings (upon notice to the tribunal and the other parties),
but only after exhausting any available arbitral process for obtaining an extension of time.

(3) The court shall only make an order if satisfied that a substantial injustice would otherwise be done.

(4) The court may extend the time for such period and on such terms as it thinks fit, and may do so whether or not the time previously fixed (by or under the agreement or by a previous order) has expired.

(5) The leave of the court is required for any appeal from a decision of the court under this section.

[339]

51 Settlement

(1) If during arbitral proceedings the parties settle the dispute, the following provisions apply unless otherwise agreed by the parties.

(2) The tribunal shall terminate the substantive proceedings and, if so requested by the parties and not objected to by the tribunal, shall record the settlement in the form of an agreed award.

(3) An agreed award shall state that it is an award of the tribunal and shall have the same status and effect as any other award on the merits of the case.

(4) The following provisions of this Part relating to awards (sections 52 to 58) apply to an agreed award.

(5) Unless the parties have also settled the matter of the payment of the costs of the arbitration, the provisions of this Part relating to costs (sections 59 to 65) continue to apply.
[340]

52 Form of award

(1) The parties are free to agree on the form of an award.

(2) If or to the extent that there is no such agreement, the following provisions apply.

(3) The award shall be in writing signed by all the arbitrators or all those assenting to the award.

(4) The award shall contain the reasons for the award unless it is an agreed award or the parties have agreed to dispense with reasons.

(5) The award shall state the seat of the arbitration and the date when the award is made.
[341]

53 Place where award treated as made

Unless otherwise agreed by the parties, where the seat of the arbitration is in England and Wales or Northern Ireland, any award in the proceedings shall be treated as made there, regardless of where it was signed, despatched or delivered to any of the parties.
[342]

54 Date of award

(1) Unless otherwise agreed by the parties, the tribunal may decide what is to be taken to be the date on which the award was made.

(2) In the absence of any such decision, the date of the award shall be taken to be the date on which it is signed by the arbitrator or, where more than one arbitrator signs the award, by the last of them.
[343]

55 Notification of award

(1) The parties are free to agree on the requirements as to notification of the award to the parties.

(2) If there is no such agreement, the award shall be notified to the parties by service on them of copies of the award, which shall be done without delay after the award is made.

(3) Nothing in this section affects section 56 (power to withhold award in case of non-payment).
[344]

56 Power to withhold award in case of non-payment

(1) The tribunal may refuse to deliver an award to the parties except upon full payment of the fees and expenses of the arbitrators.

(2) If the tribunal refuses on that ground to deliver an award, a party to the arbitral proceedings may (upon notice to the other parties and the tribunal) apply to the court, which may order that—

(a) the tribunal shall deliver the award on the payment into court by the applicant of the fees and expenses demanded, or such lesser amount as the court may specify,

(b) the amount of the fees and expenses properly payable shall be determined by such means and upon such terms as the court may direct, and

(c) out of the money paid into court there shall be paid out such fees and expenses as may be found to be properly payable and the balance of the money (if any) shall be paid out to the applicant.

(3) For this purpose the amount of fees and expenses properly payable is the amount the applicant is liable to pay under section 28 or any agreement relating to the payment of the arbitrators.

(4) No application to the court may be made where there is any available arbitral process for appeal or review of the amount of the fees or expenses demanded.

(5) References in this section to arbitrators include an arbitrator who has ceased to act and an umpire who has not replaced the other arbitrators.

(6) The above provisions of this section also apply in relation to any arbitral or other institution or person vested by the parties with powers in relation to the delivery of the tribunal's award.

As they so apply, the references to the fees and expenses of the arbitrators shall be construed as including the fees and expenses of that institution or person.

(7) The leave of the court is required for any appeal from a decision of the court under this section.

(8) Nothing in this section shall be construed as excluding an application under section 28 where payment has been made to the arbitrators in order to obtain the award.

[345]

57 Correction of award or additional award

(1) The parties are free to agree on the powers of the tribunal to correct an award or make an additional award.

(2) If or to the extent there is no such agreement, the following provisions apply.

(3) The tribunal may on its own initiative or on the application of a party—

(a) correct an award so as to remove any clerical mistake or error arising from an accidental slip or omission or clarify or remove any ambiguity in the award, or

(b) make an additional award in respect of any claim (including a claim for interest or costs) which was presented to the tribunal but was not dealt with in the award.

These powers shall not be exercised without first affording the other parties a reasonable opportunity to make representations to the tribunal.

(4) Any application for the exercise of those powers must be made within 28 days of the date of the award or such longer period as the parties may agree.

(5) Any correction of an award shall be made within 28 days of the date the application was received by the tribunal or, where the correction is made by the tribunal on its own initiative, within 28 days of the date of the award or, in either case, such longer period as the parties may agree.

(6) Any additional award shall be made within 56 days of the date of the original award or such longer period as the parties may agree.

(7) Any correction of an award shall form part of the award.

[346]

58 Effect of award

(1) Unless otherwise agreed by the parties, an award made by the tribunal pursuant to an arbitration agreement is final and binding both on the parties and on any persons claiming through or under them.

(2) This does not affect the right of a person to challenge the award by any available arbitral process of appeal or review or in accordance with the provisions of this Part.

[347]

Costs of the arbitration

59 Costs of the arbitration

(1) References in this Part to the costs of the arbitration are to—

(a) the arbitrators' fees and expenses,

(b) the fees and expenses of any arbitral institution concerned, and

(c) the legal or other costs of the parties.

(2) Any such reference includes the costs of or incidental to any proceedings to determine the amount of the recoverable costs of the arbitration (see section 63).

[348]

60 Agreement to pay costs in any event

An agreement which has the effect that a party is to pay the whole or part of the costs of the arbitration in any event is only valid if made after the dispute in question has arisen.

[349]

61 Award of costs

(1) The tribunal may make an award allocating the costs of the arbitration as between the parties, subject to any agreement of the parties.

(2) Unless the parties otherwise agree, the tribunal shall award costs on the general principle that costs should follow the event except where it appears to the tribunal that in the circumstances this is not appropriate in relation to the whole or part of the costs.

[350]

62 Effect of agreement or award about costs

Unless the parties otherwise agree, any obligation under an agreement between them as to how the costs of the arbitration are to be borne, or under an award allocating the costs of the arbitration, extends only to such costs as are recoverable.

[351]

63 The recoverable costs of the arbitration

(1) The parties are free to agree what costs of the arbitration are recoverable.

(2) If or to the extent there is no such agreement, the following provisions apply.

(3) The tribunal may determine by award the recoverable costs of the arbitration on such basis as it thinks fit.

If it does so, it shall specify—

(a) the basis on which it has acted, and

(b) the items of recoverable costs and the amount referable to each.

(4) If the tribunal does not determine the recoverable costs of the arbitration, any party to the arbitral proceedings may apply to the court (upon notice to the other parties) which may—

(a) determine the recoverable costs of the arbitration on such basis as it thinks fit, or

(b) order that they shall be determined by such means and upon such terms as it may specify.

(5) Unless the tribunal or the court determines otherwise—

(a) the recoverable costs of the arbitration shall be determined on the basis that there shall be allowed a reasonable amount in respect of all costs reasonably incurred, and

(b) any doubt as to whether costs were reasonably incurred or were reasonable in amount shall be resolved in favour of the paying party.

(6) The above provisions have effect subject to section 64 (recoverable fees and expenses of arbitrators).

(7) Nothing in this section affects any right of the arbitrators, any expert, legal adviser or assessor appointed by the tribunal, or any arbitral institution, to payment of their fees and expenses.

[352]

64 Recoverable fees and expenses of arbitrators

(1) Unless otherwise agreed by the parties, the recoverable costs of the arbitration shall include in respect of the fees and expenses of the arbitrators only such reasonable fees and expenses as are appropriate in the circumstances.

(2) If there is any question as to what reasonable fees and expenses are appropriate in the circumstances, and the matter is not already before the court on an application under section 63(4), the court may on the application of any party (upon notice to the other parties)—

(a) determine the matter, or
(b) order that it be determined by such means and upon such terms as the court may specify.

(3) Subsection (1) has effect subject to any order of the court under section 24(4) or 25(3)(b) (order as to entitlement to fees or expenses in case of removal or resignation of arbitrator).

(4) Nothing in this section affects any right of the arbitrator to payment of his fees and expenses.

[353]

65 Power to limit recoverable costs

(1) Unless otherwise agreed by the parties, the tribunal may direct that the recoverable costs of the arbitration, or of any part of the arbitral proceedings, shall be limited to a specified amount.

(2) Any direction may be made or varied at any stage, but this must be done sufficiently in advance of the incurring of costs to which it relates, or the taking of any steps in the proceedings which may be affected by it, for the limit to be taken into account.

[354]

Powers of the court in relation to award

66 Enforcement of the award

(1) An award made by the tribunal pursuant to an arbitration agreement may, by leave of the court, be enforced in the same manner as a judgment or order of the court to the same effect.

(2) Where leave is so given, judgment may be entered in terms of the award.

(3) Leave to enforce an award shall not be given where, or to the extent that, the person against whom it is sought to be enforced shows that the tribunal lacked substantive jurisdiction to make the award.

The right to raise such an objection may have been lost (see section 73).

(4) Nothing in this section affects the recognition or enforcement of an award under any other enactment or rule of law, in particular under Part II of the Arbitration Act 1950 (enforcement of awards under Geneva Convention) or the provisions of Part III of this Act relating to the recognition and enforcement of awards under the New York Convention or by an action on the award.

[355]

NOTES

See further, in relation to the application of this section, with modifications, for the purposes of arbitrations conducted in accordance with the Scheme: the ACAS Arbitration Scheme (Great Britain) Order 2004, SI 2004/753, art 4, Schedule, para 183EW.

67 Challenging the award: substantive jurisdiction

(1) A party to arbitral proceedings may (upon notice to the other parties and to the tribunal) apply to the court—

(a) challenging any award of the arbitral tribunal as to its substantive jurisdiction; or
(b) for an order declaring an award made by the tribunal on the merits to be of no effect, in whole or in part, because the tribunal did not have substantive jurisdiction.

A party may lose the right to object (see section 73) and the right to apply is subject to the restrictions in section 70(2) and (3).

(2) The arbitral tribunal may continue the arbitral proceedings and make a further award while an application to the court under this section is pending in relation to an award as to jurisdiction.

(3) On an application under this section challenging an award of the arbitral tribunal as to its substantive jurisdiction, the court may by order—

(a) confirm the award,
(b) vary the award, or
(c) set aside the award in whole or in part.

(4) The leave of the court is required for any appeal from a decision of the court under this section.

[356]

NOTES

See further, in relation to the application of this section, with modifications, for the purposes of arbitrations conducted in accordance with the Scheme: the ACAS Arbitration Scheme (Great Britain) Order 2004, SI 2004/753, art 4, Schedule, para 187EW.

68 Challenging the award: serious irregularity

(1) A party to arbitral proceedings may (upon notice to the other parties and to the tribunal) apply to the court challenging an award in the proceedings on the ground of serious irregularity affecting the tribunal, the proceedings or the award.

A party may lose the right to object (see section 73) and the right to apply is subject to the restrictions in section 70(2) and (3).

(2) Serious irregularity means an irregularity of one or more of the following kinds which the court considers has caused or will cause substantial injustice to the applicant—

(a) failure by the tribunal to comply with section 33 (general duty of tribunal);
(b) the tribunal exceeding its powers (otherwise than by exceeding its substantive jurisdiction: see section 67);
(c) failure by the tribunal to conduct the proceedings in accordance with the procedure agreed by the parties;
(d) failure by the tribunal to deal with all the issues that were put to it;
(e) any arbitral or other institution or person vested by the parties with powers in relation to the proceedings or the award exceeding its powers;
(f) uncertainty or ambiguity as to the effect of the award;
(g) the award being obtained by fraud or the award or the way in which it was procured being contrary to public policy;
(h) failure to comply with the requirements as to the form of the award; or
(i) any irregularity in the conduct of the proceedings or in the award which is admitted by the tribunal or by any arbitral or other institution or person vested by the parties with powers in relation to the proceedings or the award.

(3) If there is shown to be serious irregularity affecting the tribunal, the proceedings or the award, the court may—

(a) remit the award to the tribunal, in whole or in part, for reconsideration,
(b) set the award aside in whole or in part, or
(c) declare the award to be of no effect, in whole or in part.

The court shall not exercise its power to set aside or to declare an award to be of no effect, in whole or in part, unless it is satisfied that it would be inappropriate to remit the matters in question to the tribunal for reconsideration.

(4) The leave of the court is required for any appeal from a decision of the court under this section.

[357]

NOTES

See further, in relation to the application of this section, with modifications, for the purposes of arbitrations conducted in accordance with the Scheme: the ACAS Arbitration Scheme (Great Britain) Order 2004, SI 2004/753, art 4, Schedule, para 194EW.

69 Appeal on point of law

(1) Unless otherwise agreed by the parties, a party to arbitral proceedings may (upon notice to the other parties and to the tribunal) appeal to the court on a question of law arising out of an award made in the proceedings.

An agreement to dispense with reasons for the tribunal's award shall be considered an agreement to exclude the court's jurisdiction under this section.

(2) An appeal shall not be brought under this section except—

- (a) with the agreement of all the other parties to the proceedings, or
- (b) with the leave of the court.

The right to appeal is also subject to the restrictions in section 70(2) and (3).

(3) Leave to appeal shall be given only if the court is satisfied—

- (a) that the determination of the question will substantially affect the rights of one or more of the parties,
- (b) that the question is one which the tribunal was asked to determine,
- (c) that, on the basis of the findings of fact in the award—
  - (i) the decision of the tribunal on the question is obviously wrong, or
  - (ii) the question is one of general public importance and the decision of the tribunal is at least open to serious doubt, and
- (d) that, despite the agreement of the parties to resolve the matter by arbitration, it is just and proper in all the circumstances for the court to determine the question.

(4) An application for leave to appeal under this section shall identify the question of law to be determined and state the grounds on which it is alleged that leave to appeal should be granted.

(5) The court shall determine an application for leave to appeal under this section without a hearing unless it appears to the court that a hearing is required.

(6) The leave of the court is required for any appeal from a decision of the court under this section to grant or refuse leave to appeal.

(7) On an appeal under this section the court may by order—

- (a) confirm the award,
- (b) vary the award,
- (c) remit the award to the tribunal, in whole or in part, for reconsideration in the light of the court's determination, or
- (d) set aside the award in whole or in part.

The court shall not exercise its power to set aside an award, in whole or in part, unless it is satisfied that it would be inappropriate to remit the matters in question to the tribunal for reconsideration.

(8) The decision of the court on an appeal under this section shall be treated as a judgment of the court for the purposes of a further appeal.

But no such appeal lies without the leave of the court which shall not be given unless the court considers that the question is one of general importance or is one which for some other special reason should be considered by the Court of Appeal.

[358]

NOTES

See further, in relation to the application of this section, with modifications, for the purposes of arbitrations conducted in accordance with the Scheme: the ACAS Arbitration Scheme (Great Britain) Order 2004, SI 2004/753, art 4, Schedule, para 200EW.

70 Challenge or appeal: supplementary provisions

(1) The following provisions apply to an application or appeal under section 67, 68 or 69.

(2) An application or appeal may not be brought if the applicant or appellant has not first exhausted—

- (a) any available arbitral process of appeal or review, and
- (b) any available recourse under section 57 (correction of award or additional award).

(3) Any application or appeal must be brought within 28 days of the date of the award or, if there has been any arbitral process of appeal or review, of the date when the applicant or appellant was notified of the result of that process.

(4) If on an application or appeal it appears to the court that the award—

(a) does not contain the tribunal's reasons, or
(b) does not set out the tribunal's reasons in sufficient detail to enable the court properly to consider the application or appeal,

the court may order the tribunal to state the reasons for its award in sufficient detail for that purpose.

(5) Where the court makes an order under subsection (4), it may make such further order as it thinks fit with respect to any additional costs of the arbitration resulting from its order.

(6) The court may order the applicant or appellant to provide security for the costs of the application or appeal, and may direct that the application or appeal be dismissed if the order is not complied with.

The power to order security for costs shall not be exercised on the ground that the applicant or appellant is—

(a) an individual ordinarily resident outside the United Kingdom, or
(b) a corporation or association incorporated or formed under the law of a country outside the United Kingdom, or whose central management and control is exercised outside the United Kingdom.

(7) The court may order that any money payable under the award shall be brought into court or otherwise secured pending the determination of the application or appeal, and may direct that the application or appeal be dismissed if the order is not complied with.

(8) The court may grant leave to appeal subject to conditions to the same or similar effect as an order under subsection (6) or (7).

This does not affect the general discretion of the court to grant leave subject to conditions.

[359]

NOTES

See further, in relation to the application of this section, with modifications, for the purposes of arbitrations conducted in accordance with the Scheme: the ACAS Arbitration Scheme (Great Britain) Order 2004, SI 2004/753, art 4, Schedule, para 205EW.

71 Challenge or appeal: effect of order of court

(1) The following provisions have effect where the court makes an order under section 67, 68 or 69 with respect to an award.

(2) Where the award is varied, the variation has effect as part of the tribunal's award.

(3) Where the award is remitted to the tribunal, in whole or in part, for reconsideration, the tribunal shall make a fresh award in respect of the matters remitted within three months of the date of the order for remission or such longer or shorter period as the court may direct.

(4) Where the award is set aside or declared to be of no effect, in whole or in part, the court may also order that any provision that an award is a condition precedent to the bringing of legal proceedings in respect of a matter to which the arbitration agreement applies, is of no effect as regards the subject matter of the award or, as the case may be, the relevant part of the award.

[360]

NOTES

See further, in relation to the application of this section, with modifications, for the purposes of arbitrations conducted in accordance with the Scheme: the ACAS Arbitration Scheme (Great Britain) Order 2004, SI 2004/753, art 4, Schedule, para 212EW.

Miscellaneous

72 Saving for rights of person who takes no part in proceedings

(1) A person alleged to be a party to arbitral proceedings but who takes no part in the proceedings may question—

(a) whether there is a valid arbitration agreement,

(b) whether the tribunal is properly constituted, or

(c) what matters have been submitted to arbitration in accordance with the arbitration agreement,

by proceedings in the court for a declaration or injunction or other appropriate relief.

(2) He also has the same right as a party to the arbitral proceedings to challenge an award—

(a) by an application under section 67 on the ground of lack of substantive jurisdiction in relation to him, or

(b) by an application under section 68 on the ground of serious irregularity (within the meaning of that section) affecting him;

and section 70(2) (duty to exhaust arbitral procedures) does not apply in his case.

[361]

73 Loss of right to object

(1) If a party to arbitral proceedings takes part, or continues to take part, in the proceedings without making, either forthwith or within such time as is allowed by the arbitration agreement or the tribunal or by any provision of this Part, any objection—

(a) that the tribunal lacks substantive jurisdiction,

(b) that the proceedings have been improperly conducted,

(c) that there has been a failure to comply with the arbitration agreement or with any provision of this Part, or

(d) that there has been any other irregularity affecting the tribunal or the proceedings,

he may not raise that objection later, before the tribunal or the court, unless he shows that, at the time he took part or continued to take part in the proceedings, he did not know and could not with reasonable diligence have discovered the grounds for the objection.

(2) Where the arbitral tribunal rules that it has substantive jurisdiction and a party to arbitral proceedings who could have questioned that ruling—

(a) by any available arbitral process of appeal or review, or

(b) by challenging the award,

does not do so, or does not do so within the time allowed by the arbitration agreement or any provision of this Part, he may not object later to the tribunal's substantive jurisdiction on any ground which was the subject of that ruling.

[362]

74 Immunity of arbitral institutions, &c

(1) An arbitral or other institution or person designated or requested by the parties to appoint or nominate an arbitrator is not liable for anything done or omitted in the discharge or purported discharge of that function unless the act or omission is shown to have been in bad faith.

(2) An arbitral or other institution or person by whom an arbitrator is appointed or nominated is not liable, by reason of having appointed or nominated him, for anything done or omitted by the arbitrator (or his employees or agents) in the discharge or purported discharge of his functions as arbitrator.

(3) The above provisions apply to an employee or agent of an arbitral or other institution or person as they apply to the institution or person himself.

[363]

75 Charge to secure payment of solicitors' costs

The powers of the court to make declarations and orders under section 73 of the Solicitors Act 1974 or Article 71H of the Solicitors (Northern Ireland) Order 1976 (power to charge property recovered in the proceedings with the payment of solicitors' costs) may be exercised in relation to arbitral proceedings as if those proceedings were proceedings in the court.

[364]

Supplementary

76 Service of notices, &c

(1) The parties are free to agree on the manner of service of any notice or other document required or authorised to be given or served in pursuance of the arbitration agreement or for the purposes of the arbitral proceedings.

(2) If or to the extent that there is no such agreement the following provisions apply.

(3) A notice or other document may be served on a person by any effective means.

(4) If a notice or other document is addressed, pre-paid and delivered by post—

(a) to the addressee's last known principal residence or, if he is or has been carrying on a trade, profession or business, his last known principal business address, or

(b) where the addressee is a body corporate, to the body's registered or principal office,

it shall be treated as effectively served.

(5) This section does not apply to the service of documents for the purposes of legal proceedings, for which provision is made by rules of court.

(6) References in this Part to a notice or other document include any form of communication in writing and references to giving or serving a notice or other document shall be construed accordingly.

[365]

77 Powers of court in relation to service of documents

(1) This section applies where service of a document on a person in the manner agreed by the parties, or in accordance with provisions of section 76 having effect in default of agreement, is not reasonably practicable.

(2) Unless otherwise agreed by the parties, the court may make such order as it thinks fit—

(a) for service in such manner as the court may direct, or

(b) dispensing with service of the document.

(3) Any party to the arbitration agreement may apply for an order, but only after exhausting any available arbitral process for resolving the matter.

(4) The leave of the court is required for any appeal from a decision of the court under this section.

[366]

NOTES

See further, in relation to the application of this section, with modifications, for the purposes of arbitrations conducted in accordance with the Scheme: the ACAS Arbitration Scheme (Great Britain) Order 2004, SI 2004/753, art 4, Schedule, para 223EW.

78 Reckoning periods of time

(1) The parties are free to agree on the method of reckoning periods of time for the purposes of any provision agreed by them or any provision of this Part having effect in default of such agreement.

(2) If or to the extent there is no such agreement, periods of time shall be reckoned in accordance with the following provisions.

(3) Where the act is required to be done within a specified period after or from a specified date, the period begins immediately after that date.

(4) Where the act is required to be done a specified number of clear days after a specified date, at least that number of days must intervene between the day on which the act is done and that date.

(5) Where the period is a period of seven days or less which would include a Saturday, Sunday or a public holiday in the place where anything which has to be done within the period falls to be done, that day shall be excluded.

In relation to England and Wales or Northern Ireland, a "public holiday" means Christmas Day, Good Friday or a day which under the Banking and Financial Dealings Act 1971 is a bank holiday.

[367]

NOTES

See further, in relation to the application of this section, with modifications, for the purposes of arbitrations conducted in accordance with the Scheme: the ACAS Arbitration Scheme (Great Britain) Order 2004, SI 2004/753, art 4, Schedule, para 224EW.

79 Power of court to extend time limits relating to arbitral proceedings

(1) Unless the parties otherwise agree, the court may by order extend any time limit agreed by them in relation to any matter relating to the arbitral proceedings or specified in any provision of this Part having effect in default of such agreement.

This section does not apply to a time limit to which section 12 applies (power of court to extend time for beginning arbitral proceedings, &c).

(2) An application for an order may be made—

(a) by any party to the arbitral proceedings (upon notice to the other parties and to the tribunal), or

(b) by the arbitral tribunal (upon notice to the parties).

(3) The court shall not exercise its power to extend a time limit unless it is satisfied—

(a) that any available recourse to the tribunal, or to any arbitral or other institution or person vested by the parties with power in that regard, has first been exhausted, and

(b) that a substantial injustice would otherwise be done.

(4) The court's power under this section may be exercised whether or not the time has already expired.

(5) An order under this section may be made on such terms as the court thinks fit.

(6) The leave of the court is required for any appeal from a decision of the court under this section.

[368]

80 Notice and other requirements in connection with legal proceedings

(1) References in this Part to an application, appeal or other step in relation to legal proceedings being taken "upon notice" to the other parties to the arbitral proceedings, or to the tribunal, are to such notice of the originating process as is required by rules of court and do not impose any separate requirement.

(2) Rules of court shall be made—

(a) requiring such notice to be given as indicated by any provision of this Part, and

(b) as to the manner, form and content of any such notice.

(3) Subject to any provision made by rules of court, a requirement to give notice to the tribunal of legal proceedings shall be construed—

(a) if there is more than one arbitrator, as a requirement to give notice to each of them; and

(b) if the tribunal is not fully constituted, as a requirement to give notice to any arbitrator who has been appointed.

(4) References in this Part to making an application or appeal to the court within a specified period are to the issue within that period of the appropriate originating process in accordance with rules of court.

(5) Where any provision of this Part requires an application or appeal to be made to the court within a specified time, the rules of court relating to the reckoning of periods, the extending or abridging of periods, and the consequences of not taking a step within the period prescribed by the rules, apply in relation to that requirement.

(6) Provision may be made by rules of court amending the provisions of this Part—

(a) with respect to the time within which any application or appeal to the court must be made,

(b) so as to keep any provision made by this Part in relation to arbitral proceedings in step with the corresponding provision of rules of court applying in relation to proceedings in the court, or

(c) so as to keep any provision made by this Part in relation to legal proceedings in step with the corresponding provision of rules of court applying generally in relation to proceedings in the court.

(7) Nothing in this section affects the generality of the power to make rules of court.

[369]

NOTES

See further, in relation to the application of this section, with modifications, for the purposes of arbitrations conducted in accordance with the Scheme: the ACAS Arbitration Scheme (Great Britain) Order 2004, SI 2004/753, art 4, Schedule, para 217EW.

81 Saving for certain matters governed by common law

(1) Nothing in this Part shall be construed as excluding the operation of any rule of law consistent with the provisions of this Part, in particular, any rule of law as to—

(a) matters which are not capable of settlement by arbitration;

(b) the effect of an oral arbitration agreement; or

(c) the refusal of recognition or enforcement of an arbitral award on grounds of public policy.

(2) Nothing in this Act shall be construed as reviving any jurisdiction of the court to set aside or remit an award on the ground of errors of fact or law on the face of the award.

[370]

NOTES

See further, in relation to the application of this section, with modifications, for the purposes of arbitrations conducted in accordance with the Scheme: the ACAS Arbitration Scheme (Great Britain) Order 2004, SI 2004/753, art 4, Schedule, para 209EW.

82 Minor definitions

(1) In this Part—

"arbitrator", unless the context otherwise requires, includes an umpire;

"available arbitral process", in relation to any matter, includes any process of appeal to or review by an arbitral or other institution or person vested by the parties with powers in relation to that matter;

"claimant", unless the context otherwise requires, includes a counterclaimant, and related expressions shall be construed accordingly;

"dispute" includes any difference;

"enactment" includes an enactment contained in Northern Ireland legislation;

"legal proceedings" means civil proceedings in the High Court or a county court;

"peremptory order" means an order made under section 41(5) or made in exercise of any corresponding power conferred by the parties;

"premises" includes land, buildings, moveable structures, vehicles, vessels, aircraft and hovercraft;

"question of law" means—

(a) for a court in England and Wales, a question of the law of England and Wales, and

(b) for a court in Northern Ireland, a question of the law of Northern Ireland;

"substantive jurisdiction", in relation to an arbitral tribunal, refers to the matters specified in section 30(1)(a) to (c), and references to the tribunal exceeding its substantive jurisdiction shall be construed accordingly.

(2) References in this Part to a party to an arbitration agreement include any person claiming under or through a party to the agreement.

[371]

NOTES

The Northern Ireland Act 1998 makes new provision for the government of Northern Ireland for the purpose of implementing the Belfast Agreement (the agreement reached at multi-party talks on Northern Ireland and set out in Command Paper 3883). As a consequence of that Act, any reference in this section to the Parliament of Northern Ireland or the Assembly established under the Northern Ireland Assembly

Act 1973, s 1, certain office-holders and Ministers, and any legislative act and certain financial dealings thereof, shall, for the period specified, be construed in accordance with Sch 12, paras 1–11 to the 1998 Act.

83 Index of defined expressions: Part I

In this Part the expressions listed below are defined or otherwise explained by the provisions indicated—

agreement, agree and agreed	section 5(1)
agreement in writing	section 5(2) to (5)
arbitration agreement	sections 6 and 5(1)
arbitrator	section 82(1)
available arbitral process	section 82(1)
claimant	section 82(1)
commencement (in relation to arbitral proceedings)	section 14
costs of the arbitration	section 59
the court	section 105
dispute	section 82(1)
enactment	section 82(1)
legal proceedings	section 82(1)
Limitation Acts	section 13(4)
notice (or other document)	section 76(6)
party—	
—in relation to an arbitration agreement	section 82(2)
—where section 106(2) or (3) applies	section 106(4)
peremptory order	section 82(1) (and see section 41(5))
premises	section 82(1)
question of law	section 82(1)
recoverable costs	sections 63 and 64
seat of the arbitration	section 3
serve and service (of notice or other document)	section 76(6)
substantive jurisdiction (in relation to an arbitral tribunal)	section 82(1) (and see section 30(1)(a) to (c))
upon notice (to the parties or the tribunal)	section 80
written and in writing	section 5(6)

[372]

84 Transitional provisions

(1) The provisions of this Part do not apply to arbitral proceedings commenced before the date on which this Part comes into force.

(2) They apply to arbitral proceedings commenced on or after that date under an arbitration agreement whenever made.

(3) The above provisions have effect subject to any transitional provision made by an order under section 109(2) (power to include transitional provisions in commencement order).

[373]

PART II
OTHER PROVISIONS RELATING TO ARBITRATION

Domestic arbitration agreements

85 Modification of Part I in relation to domestic arbitration agreement

(1) In the case of a domestic arbitration agreement the provisions of Part I are modified in accordance with the following sections.

(2) For this purpose a "domestic arbitration agreement" means an arbitration agreement to which none of the parties is—

(a) an individual who is a national of, or habitually resident in, a state other than the United Kingdom, or

(b) a body corporate which is incorporated in, or whose central control and management is exercised in, a state other than the United Kingdom,

and under which the seat of the arbitration (if the seat has been designated or determined) is in the United Kingdom.

(3) In subsection (2) "arbitration agreement" and "seat of the arbitration" have the same meaning as in Part I (see sections 3, 5(1) and 6).

[374]

NOTES

Commencement: to be appointed.

86 Staying of legal proceedings

(1) In section 9 (stay of legal proceedings), subsection (4) (stay unless the arbitration agreement is null and void, inoperative, or incapable of being performed) does not apply to a domestic arbitration agreement.

(2) On an application under that section in relation to a domestic arbitration agreement the court shall grant a stay unless satisfied—

(a) that the arbitration agreement is null and void, inoperative, or incapable of being performed, or

(b) that there are other sufficient grounds for not requiring the parties to abide by the arbitration agreement.

(3) The court may treat as a sufficient ground under subsection (2)(b) the fact that the applicant is or was at any material time not ready and willing to do all things necessary for the proper conduct of the arbitration or of any other dispute resolution procedures required to be exhausted before resorting to arbitration.

(4) For the purposes of this section the question whether an arbitration agreement is a domestic arbitration agreement shall be determined by reference to the facts at the time the legal proceedings are commenced.

[375]

NOTES

Commencement: to be appointed.

87 Effectiveness of agreement to exclude court's jurisdiction

(1) In the case of a domestic arbitration agreement any agreement to exclude the jurisdiction of the court under—

(a) section 45 (determination of preliminary point of law), or

(b) section 69 (challenging the award: appeal on point of law),

is not effective unless entered into after the commencement of the arbitral proceedings in which the question arises or the award is made.

(2) For this purpose the commencement of the arbitral proceedings has the same meaning as in Part I (see section 14).

(3) For the purposes of this section the question whether an arbitration agreement is a domestic arbitration agreement shall be determined by reference to the facts at the time the agreement is entered into.

[376]

NOTES

Commencement: to be appointed.

88 Power to repeal or amend sections 85 to 87

(1) The Secretary of State may by order repeal or amend the provisions of sections 85 to 87.

(2) An order under this section may contain such supplementary, incidental and transitional provisions as appear to the Secretary of State to be appropriate.

(3) An order under this section shall be made by statutory instrument and no such order shall be made unless a draft of it has been laid before and approved by a resolution of each House of Parliament.

[377]

Consumer arbitration agreements

89 Application of unfair terms regulations to consumer arbitration agreements

(1) The following sections extend the application of the Unfair Terms in Consumer Contracts Regulations 1994 in relation to a term which constitutes an arbitration agreement.

For this purpose "arbitration agreement" means an agreement to submit to arbitration present or future disputes or differences (whether or not contractual).

(2) In those sections "the Regulations" means those regulations and includes any regulations amending or replacing those regulations.

(3) Those sections apply whatever the law applicable to the arbitration agreement.

[378]

90 Regulations apply where consumer is a legal person

The Regulations apply where the consumer is a legal person as they apply where the consumer is a natural person.

[379]

91 Arbitration agreement unfair where modest amount sought

(1) A term which constitutes an arbitration agreement is unfair for the purposes of the Regulations so far as it relates to a claim for a pecuniary remedy which does not exceed the amount specified by order for the purposes of this section.

(2) Orders under this section may make different provision for different cases and for different purposes.

(3) The power to make orders under this section is exercisable—

- (a) for England and Wales, by the Secretary of State with the concurrence of the Lord Chancellor,
- (b) for Scotland, by the Secretary of State . . . , and
- (c) for Northern Ireland, by the Department of Economic Development for Northern Ireland with the concurrence of the Lord Chancellor.

(4) Any such order for England and Wales or Scotland shall be made by statutory instrument which shall be subject to annulment in pursuance of a resolution of either House of Parliament.

(5) Any such order for Northern Ireland shall be a statutory rule for the purposes of the Statutory Rules (Northern Ireland) Order 1979 and shall be subject to negative resolution, within the meaning of section 41(6) of the Interpretation Act (Northern Ireland) 1954.

[380]

NOTES

Sub-s (3): words omitted from para (b) repealed by the Transfer of Functions (Lord Advocate and Secretary of State) Order 1999, SI 1999/678, art 6.

Transfer of functions: functions of the Lord Advocate transferred with savings to the Secretary of State for Scotland by virtue of SI 1999/678, art 2, Schedule.

Orders: the Unfair Arbitration Agreements (Specified Amount) Order 1999, SI 1999/2167.

Small claims arbitration in the county court

92 Exclusion of Part I in relation to small claims arbitration in the county court

Nothing in Part I of this Act applies to arbitration under section 64 of the County Courts Act 1984.

[381]

Appointment of judges as arbitrators

93 Appointment of judges as arbitrators

(1) A judge of the Commercial Court or an official referee may, if in all the circumstances he thinks fit, accept appointment as a sole arbitrator or as umpire by or by virtue of an arbitration agreement.

(2) A judge of the Commercial Court shall not do so unless the Lord Chief Justice has informed him that, having regard to the state of business in the High Court and the Crown Court, he can be made available.

(3) An official referee shall not do so unless the Lord Chief Justice has informed him that, having regard to the state of official referees' business, he can be made available.

(4) The fees payable for the services of a judge of the Commercial Court or official referee as arbitrator or umpire shall be taken in the High Court.

(5) In this section—

"arbitration agreement" has the same meaning as in Part I; and

"official referee" means a person nominated under section 68(1)(a) of the *Supreme Court Act 1981* to deal with official referees' business.

(6) The provisions of Part I of this Act apply to arbitration before a person appointed under this section with the modifications specified in Schedule 2.

[382]

NOTES

Sub-s (5): in definition "official referee" words in italics substituted by the words "Senior Courts Act 1981" by the Constitutional Reform Act 2005, s 59(5), Sch 11, Pt 1, para 1(2), as from a day to be appointed.

Statutory arbitrations

94 Application of Part I to statutory arbitrations

(1) The provisions of Part I apply to every arbitration under an enactment (a "statutory arbitration"), whether the enactment was passed or made before or after the commencement of this Act, subject to the adaptations and exclusions specified in sections 95 to 98.

(2) The provisions of Part I do not apply to a statutory arbitration if or to the extent that their application—

(a) is inconsistent with the provisions of the enactment concerned, with any rules or procedure authorised or recognised by it, or

(b) is excluded by any other enactment.

(3) In this section and the following provisions of this Part "enactment"—

(a) in England and Wales, includes an enactment contained in subordinate legislation within the meaning of the Interpretation Act 1978;

(b) in Northern Ireland, means a statutory provision within the meaning of section 1(f) of the Interpretation Act (Northern Ireland) 1954.

[383]

95 General adaptation of provisions in relation to statutory arbitrations

(1) The provisions of Part I apply to a statutory arbitration—

(a) as if the arbitration were pursuant to an arbitration agreement and as if the enactment were that agreement, and

(b) as if the persons by and against whom a claim subject to arbitration in pursuance of the enactment may be or has been made were parties to that agreement.

(2) Every statutory arbitration shall be taken to have its seat in England and Wales or, as the case may be, in Northern Ireland.

[384]

96 Specific adaptations of provisions in relation to statutory arbitrations

(1) The following provisions of Part I apply to a statutory arbitration with the following adaptations.

(2) In section 30(1) (competence of tribunal to rule on its own jurisdiction), the reference in paragraph (a) to whether there is a valid arbitration agreement shall be construed as a reference to whether the enactment applies to the dispute or difference in question.

(3) Section 35 (consolidation of proceedings and concurrent hearings) applies only so as to authorise the consolidation of proceedings, or concurrent hearings in proceedings, under the same enactment.

(4) Section 46 (rules applicable to substance of dispute) applies with the omission of subsection (1)(b) (determination in accordance with considerations agreed by parties).

[385]

97 Provisions excluded from applying to statutory arbitrations

The following provisions of Part I do not apply in relation to a statutory arbitration—

(a) section 8 (whether agreement discharged by death of a party);

(b) section 12 (power of court to extend agreed time limits);

(c) sections 9(5), 10(2) and 71(4) (restrictions on effect of provision that award condition precedent to right to bring legal proceedings).

[386]

98 Power to make further provision by regulations

(1) The Secretary of State may make provision by regulations for adapting or excluding any provision of Part I in relation to statutory arbitrations in general or statutory arbitrations of any particular description.

(2) The power is exercisable whether the enactment concerned is passed or made before or after the commencement of this Act.

(3) Regulations under this section shall be made by statutory instrument which shall be subject to annulment in pursuance of a resolution of either House of Parliament.

[387]

PART III
RECOGNITION AND ENFORCEMENT OF CERTAIN FOREIGN AWARDS

Enforcement of Geneva Convention awards

99 Continuation of Part II of the Arbitration Act 1950

Part II of the Arbitration Act 1950 (enforcement of certain foreign awards) continues to apply in relation to foreign awards within the meaning of that Part which are not also New York Convention awards.

Recognition and enforcement of New York Convention awards

100 New York Convention awards

(1) In this Part a "New York Convention award" means an award made, in pursuance of an arbitration agreement, in the territory of a state (other than the United Kingdom) which is a party to the New York Convention.

(2) For the purposes of subsection (1) and of the provisions of this Part relating to such awards—

(a) "arbitration agreement" means an arbitration agreement in writing, and

(b) an award shall be treated as made at the seat of the arbitration, regardless of where it was signed, despatched or delivered to any of the parties.

In this subsection "agreement in writing" and "seat of the arbitration" have the same meaning as in Part I.

(3) If Her Majesty by Order in Council declares that a state specified in the Order is a party to the New York Convention, or is a party in respect of any territory so specified, the Order shall, while in force, be conclusive evidence of that fact.

(4) In this section "the New York Convention" means the Convention on the Recognition and Enforcement of Foreign Arbitral Awards adopted by the United Nations Conference on International Commercial Arbitration on 10th June 1958.

[388]

NOTES

"Party to the New York Convention": see Table 2 at **[4677]** below.

Orders in Council: by virtue of the Interpretation Act 1978, s 17(2)(b), the Arbitration (Foreign Awards) Order 1984, SI 1984/1168 at **[2274]**, the Arbitration (Foreign Awards) Order 1989, SI 1989/1348 at **[2279]** and the Arbitration (Foreign Awards) Order 1993, SI 1993/1256 at **[2282]** have effect as if made under this section.

101 Recognition and enforcement of awards

(1) A New York Convention award shall be recognised as binding on the persons as between whom it was made, and may accordingly be relied on by those persons by way of defence, set-off or otherwise in any legal proceedings in England and Wales or Northern Ireland.

(2) A New York Convention award may, by leave of the court, be enforced in the same manner as a judgment or order of the court to the same effect.

As to the meaning of "the court" see section 105.

(3) Where leave is so given, judgment may be entered in terms of the award.

[389]

102 Evidence to be produced by party seeking recognition or enforcement

(1) A party seeking the recognition or enforcement of a New York Convention award must produce—

(a) the duly authenticated original award or a duly certified copy of it, and

(b) the original arbitration agreement or a duly certified copy of it.

(2) If the award or agreement is in a foreign language, the party must also produce a translation of it certified by an official or sworn translator or by a diplomatic or consular agent.

[390]

103 Refusal of recognition or enforcement

(1) Recognition or enforcement of a New York Convention award shall not be refused except in the following cases.

(2) Recognition or enforcement of the award may be refused if the person against whom it is invoked proves—

(a) that a party to the arbitration agreement was (under the law applicable to him) under some incapacity;

(b) that the arbitration agreement was not valid under the law to which the parties subjected it or, failing any indication thereon, under the law of the country where the award was made;

(c) that he was not given proper notice of the appointment of the arbitrator or of the arbitration proceedings or was otherwise unable to present his case;

(d) that the award deals with a difference not contemplated by or not falling within the terms of the submission to arbitration or contains decisions on matters beyond the scope of the submission to arbitration (but see subsection (4));

(e) that the composition of the arbitral tribunal or the arbitral procedure was not in accordance with the agreement of the parties or, failing such agreement, with the law of the country in which the arbitration took place;

(f) that the award has not yet become binding on the parties, or has been set aside or suspended by a competent authority of the country in which, or under the law of which, it was made.

(3) Recognition or enforcement of the award may also be refused if the award is in respect of a matter which is not capable of settlement by arbitration, or if it would be contrary to public policy to recognise or enforce the award.

(4) An award which contains decisions on matters not submitted to arbitration may be recognised or enforced to the extent that it contains decisions on matters submitted to arbitration which can be separated from those on matters not so submitted.

(5) Where an application for the setting aside or suspension of the award has been made to such a competent authority as is mentioned in subsection (2)(f), the court before which the award is sought to be relied upon may, if it considers it proper, adjourn the decision on the recognition or enforcement of the award.

It may also on the application of the party claiming recognition or enforcement of the award order the other party to give suitable security.

[391]

104 Saving for other bases of recognition or enforcement

Nothing in the preceding provisions of this Part affects any right to rely upon or enforce a New York Convention award at common law or under section 66.

[392]

PART IV
GENERAL PROVISIONS

105 Meaning of "the court": jurisdiction of High Court and county court

(1) In this Act "the court" means the High Court or a county court, subject to the following provisions.

(2) The Lord Chancellor may by order make provision—

(a) allocating proceedings under this Act to the High Court or to county courts; or

(b) specifying proceedings under this Act which may be commenced or taken only in the High Court or in a county court.

(3) The Lord Chancellor may by order make provision requiring proceedings of any specified description under this Act in relation to which a county court has jurisdiction to be commenced or taken in one or more specified county courts.

Any jurisdiction so exercisable by a specified county court is exercisable throughout England and Wales or, as the case may be, Northern Ireland.

[(3A) The Lord Chancellor must consult the Lord Chief Justice of England and Wales or the Lord Chief Justice of Northern Ireland (as the case may be) before making an order under this section.

(3B) The Lord Chief Justice of England and Wales may nominate a judicial office holder (as defined in section 109(4) of the Constitutional Reform Act 2005) to exercise his functions under this section.

(3C) The Lord Chief Justice of Northern Ireland may nominate any of the following to exercise his functions under this section—

(a) the holder of one of the offices listed in Schedule 1 to the Justice (Northern Ireland) Act 2002;

(b) a Lord Justice of Appeal (as defined in section 88 of that Act).]

(4) An order under this section—

(a) may differentiate between categories of proceedings by reference to such criteria as the Lord Chancellor sees fit to specify, and

(b) may make such incidental or transitional provision as the Lord Chancellor considers necessary or expedient.

(5) An order under this section for England and Wales shall be made by statutory instrument which shall be subject to annulment in pursuance of a resolution of either House of Parliament.

(6) An order under this section for Northern Ireland shall be a statutory rule for the purposes of the Statutory Rules (Northern Ireland) Order 1979 which shall be subject to annulment in pursuance of a resolution of either House of Parliament in like manner as a statutory instrument and section 5 of the Statutory Instruments Act 1946 shall apply accordingly.

[393]

NOTES

Sub-ss (3A)–(3C): inserted by the Constitutional Reform Act 2005, s 15(1), Sch 4, Pt 1, para 250.

Orders: the High Court and County Courts (Allocation of Arbitration Proceedings) Order 1996, SI 1996/3215 at **[2284]**.

106 Crown application

(1) Part I of this Act applies to any arbitration agreement to which Her Majesty, either in right of the Crown or of the Duchy of Lancaster or otherwise, or the Duke of Cornwall, is a party.

(2) Where Her Majesty is party to an arbitration agreement otherwise than in right of the Crown, Her Majesty shall be represented for the purposes of any arbitral proceedings—

(a) where the agreement was entered into by Her Majesty in right of the Duchy of Lancaster, by the Chancellor of the Duchy or such person as he may appoint, and

(b) in any other case, by such person as Her Majesty may appoint in writing under the Royal Sign Manual.

(3) Where the Duke of Cornwall is party to an arbitration agreement, he shall be represented for the purposes of any arbitral proceedings by such person as he may appoint.

(4) References in Part I to a party or the parties to the arbitration agreement or to arbitral proceedings shall be construed, where subsection (2) or (3) applies, as references to the person representing Her Majesty or the Duke of Cornwall.

[394]

107 Consequential amendments and repeals

(1) The enactments specified in Schedule 3 are amended in accordance with that Schedule, the amendments being consequential on the provisions of this Act.

(2) The enactments specified in Schedule 4 are repealed to the extent specified.

[395]

108 Extent

(1) The provisions of this Act extend to England and Wales and, except as mentioned below, to Northern Ireland.

(2) The following provisions of Part II do not extend to Northern Ireland—

section 92 (exclusion of Part I in relation to small claims arbitration in the county court), and

section 93 and Schedule 2 (appointment of judges as arbitrators).

(3) Sections 89, 90 and 91 (consumer arbitration agreements) extend to Scotland and the provisions of Schedules 3 and 4 (consequential amendments and repeals) extend to Scotland so far as they relate to enactments which so extend, subject as follows.

(4) The repeal of the Arbitration Act 1975 extends only to England and Wales and Northern Ireland.

[396]

109 Commencement

(1) The provisions of this Act come into force on such day as the Secretary of State may appoint by order made by statutory instrument, and different days may be appointed for different purposes.

(2) An order under subsection (1) may contain such transitional provisions as appear to the Secretary of State to be appropriate.

[397]

NOTES

Orders: the Arbitration Act 1996 (Commencement No 1) Order 1996, SI 1996/3146.

110 Short title

This Act may be cited as the Arbitration Act 1996.

[398]

SCHEDULES

SCHEDULE 1
MANDATORY PROVISIONS OF PART I

Section 4(1)

sections 9 to 11 (stay of legal proceedings);

section 12 (power of court to extend agreed time limits);

section 13 (application of Limitation Acts);

section 24 (power of court to remove arbitrator);

section 26(1) (effect of death of arbitrator);

section 28 (liability of parties for fees and expenses of arbitrators);

section 29 (immunity of arbitrator);

section 31 (objection to substantive jurisdiction of tribunal);

section 32 (determination of preliminary point of jurisdiction);

section 33 (general duty of tribunal);

section 37(2) (items to be treated as expenses of arbitrators);

section 40 (general duty of parties);

section 43 (securing the attendance of witnesses);

section 56 (power to withhold award in case of non-payment);

section 60 (effectiveness of agreement for payment of costs in any event);

section 66 (enforcement of award);

sections 67 and 68 (challenging the award: substantive jurisdiction and serious irregularity), and sections 70 and 71 (supplementary provisions; effect of order of court) so far as relating to those sections;

section 72 (saving for rights of person who takes no part in proceedings);

section 73 (loss of right to object);

section 74 (immunity of arbitral institutions, &c);

section 75 (charge to secure payment of solicitors' costs).

[399]

SCHEDULE 2
MODIFICATIONS OF PART I IN RELATION TO JUDGE-ARBITRATORS

Section 93(6)

Introductory

1. In this Schedule "judge-arbitrator" means a judge of the Commercial Court or official referee appointed as arbitrator or umpire under section 93.

General

2.(1) Subject to the following provisions of this Schedule, references in Part I to the court shall be construed in relation to a judge-arbitrator, or in relation to the appointment of a judge-arbitrator, as references to the Court of Appeal.

(2) The references in sections 32(6), 45(6) and 69(8) to the Court of Appeal shall in such a case be construed as references to the *House of Lords*.

Arbitrator's fees

3.(1) The power of the court in section 28(2) to order consideration and adjustment of the liability of a party for the fees of an arbitrator may be exercised by a judge-arbitrator.

(2) Any such exercise of the power is subject to the powers of the Court of Appeal under sections 24(4) and 25(3)(b) (directions as to entitlement to fees or expenses in case of removal or resignation).

Exercise of court powers in support of arbitration

4.(1) Where the arbitral tribunal consists of or includes a judge-arbitrator the powers of the court under sections 42 to 44 (enforcement of peremptory orders, summoning witnesses, and other court powers) are exercisable by the High Court and also by the judge-arbitrator himself.

(2) Anything done by a judge-arbitrator in the exercise of those powers shall be regarded as done by him in his capacity as judge of the High Court and have effect as if done by that court.

Nothing in this sub-paragraph prejudices any power vested in him as arbitrator or umpire.

Extension of time for making award

5.(1) The power conferred by section 50 (extension of time for making award) is exercisable by the judge-arbitrator himself.

(2) Any appeal from a decision of a judge-arbitrator under that section lies to the Court of Appeal with the leave of that court.

Withholding award in case of non-payment

6.(1) The provisions of paragraph 7 apply in place of the provisions of section 56 (power to withhold award in the case of non-payment) in relation to the withholding of an award for non-payment of the fees and expenses of a judge-arbitrator.

(2) This does not affect the application of section 56 in relation to the delivery of such an award by an arbitral or other institution or person vested by the parties with powers in relation to the delivery of the award.

7.(1) A judge-arbitrator may refuse to deliver an award except upon payment of the fees and expenses mentioned in section 56(1).

(2) The judge-arbitrator may, on an application by a party to the arbitral proceedings, order that if he pays into the High Court the fees and expenses demanded, or such lesser amount as the judge-arbitrator may specify—

(a) the award shall be delivered,

(b) the amount of the fees and expenses properly payable shall be determined by such means and upon such terms as he may direct, and

(c) out of the money paid into court there shall be paid out such fees and expenses as may be found to be properly payable and the balance of the money (if any) shall be paid out to the applicant.

(3) For this purpose the amount of fees and expenses properly payable is the amount the applicant is liable to pay under section 28 or any agreement relating to the payment of the arbitrator.

(4) No application to the judge-arbitrator under this paragraph may be made where there is any available arbitral process for appeal or review of the amount of the fees or expenses demanded.

(5) Any appeal from a decision of a judge-arbitrator under this paragraph lies to the Court of Appeal with the leave of that court.

(6) Where a party to arbitral proceedings appeals under sub-paragraph (5), an arbitrator is entitled to appear and be heard.

Correction of award or additional award

8. Subsections (4) to (6) of section 57 (correction of award or additional award: time limit for application or exercise of power) do not apply to a judge-arbitrator.

Costs

9. Where the arbitral tribunal consists of or includes a judge-arbitrator the powers of the court under section 63(4) (determination of recoverable costs) shall be exercised by the High Court.

10.(1) The power of the court under section 64 to determine an arbitrator's reasonable fees and expenses may be exercised by a judge-arbitrator.

(2) Any such exercise of the power is subject to the powers of the Court of Appeal under sections 24(4) and 25(3)(b) (directions as to entitlement to fees or expenses in case of removal or resignation).

Enforcement of award

11. The leave of the court required by section 66 (enforcement of award) may in the case of an award of a judge-arbitrator be given by the judge-arbitrator himself.

Solicitors' costs

12. The powers of the court to make declarations and orders under the provisions applied by section 75 (power to charge property recovered in arbitral proceedings with the payment of solicitors' costs) may be exercised by the judge-arbitrator.

Powers of court in relation to service of documents

13.(1) The power of the court under section 77(2) (powers of court in relation to service of documents) is exercisable by the judge-arbitrator.

(2) Any appeal from a decision of a judge-arbitrator under that section lies to the Court of Appeal with the leave of that court.

Powers of court to extend time limits relating to arbitral proceedings

14.(1) The power conferred by section 79 (power of court to extend time limits relating to arbitral proceedings) is exercisable by the judge-arbitrator himself.

(2) Any appeal from a decision of a judge-arbitrator under that section lies to the Court of Appeal with the leave of that court.

[400]

NOTES

Para 2: in sub-para (2), words in italics substituted by the words "Supreme Court" by the Constitutional Reform Act 2005, s 40(4), Sch 9, Pt 1, para 60, as from a day to be appointed.

(*Sch 3, in so far as unrepealed, contains amendments; Sch 4 contains repeals.*)

E. INTERNATIONAL CARRIAGE: AIR, RAIL AND ROAD

CARRIAGE BY AIR ACT 1961

(9 & 10 Eliz 2 c 27)

ARRANGEMENT OF SECTIONS

An Act to give effect to the Convention concerning international carriage by air known as "the Warsaw Convention as amended at The Hague, 1955", to enable the rules contained in that Convention to be applied, with or without modification, in other cases and, in particular, to non-international carriage by air; and for connected purposes

[22 June 1961]

NOTES

This Act has been amended by the Carriage by Air and Road Act 1979 to take account of the Warsaw Convention (as amended by the 1955 Hague Protocol) by certain Protocols signed in Montreal on 25 September 1975. As noted in the footnotes to this Act some of these amendments are not yet in force.

[1 Convention to have the force of law

(1) The applicable provisions of the Carriage by Air Conventions have the force of law in the United Kingdom in relation to any carriage by air to which they apply, irrespective of the nationality of the aircraft performing that carriage.

(2) Subsection (1) does not apply in relation to Community air carriers to the extent that the provisions of the Council Regulation have the force of law in the United Kingdom.

(3) Subsection (1) is subject to the other provisions of this Act.

(4) If more than one of the Carriage by Air Conventions applies to a carriage by air, the applicable provisions that have the force of law in the United Kingdom are those of whichever is the most recent applicable Convention in force.

(5) The Carriage by Air Conventions are—
(a) the Convention known as "the Warsaw Convention as amended at The Hague, 1955" ("the Convention");
(b) that Convention as further amended by Protocol No 4 of Montreal, 1975 ("the Convention as amended"); and
(c) the Convention known as "the Montreal Convention 1999" ("the Montreal Convention").

(6) "The applicable provisions" means—
(a) the provisions of the Convention set out in Schedule 1,
(b) the provisions of the Convention as amended set out in Schedule 1A, and
(c) the provisions of the Montreal Convention set out in Schedule 1B,

so far as they relate to the rights and liabilities of carriers, carriers' servants and agents, passengers, consignors, consignees and other persons.

(7) In this Act a reference to an Article of, or Protocol to, any of the Carriage by Air Conventions is a reference to that Article or Protocol as it appears in the Schedule in which it is set out.

(8) If there is any inconsistency between the text in English in Part I of Schedule 1 or 1A and the text in French in Part II of that Schedule, the French text shall prevail.]

[401]

NOTES

Commencement: 28 June 2004.

Substituted by the Carriage by Air Acts (Implementation of the Montreal Convention 1999) Order 2002, SI 2002/263, art 2(1), (2).

2 Designation of High Contracting Parties

(1) Her Majesty may by Order in Council from time to time certify who are[, either generally or in respect of specified matters,] the High Contracting Parties to [any of the Carriage by Air Conventions], in respect of what territories they are respectively parties and to what extent they have availed themselves of the provisions of[—

(a) the Additional Protocol at the end of the Convention;

(b) the Additional Protocol at the end of the Convention as amended; or

(c) Article 57(a) of the Montreal Convention.]

[(1A) Her Majesty may by Order in Council certify any revision of the limits of liability established under the Montreal Convention.]

[(2) The provisions of the Carriage by Air Conventions mentioned in subsection (2A) shall not be read as extending references in the applicable provisions to the territory of a High Contracting Party (except such as are references to the territory of any State, whether a High Contracting Party or not) to include any territory in respect of which that High Contracting Party is not a party.

(2A) The provisions are—

(a) Article 40A(2) of the Convention;

(b) Article 40A(2) of the Convention as amended; and

(c) paragraph 1 of Article 56 of the Montreal Convention.]

(3) An Order in Council under this section shall, except so far as it has been superseded by a subsequent Order, be conclusive evidence of the matters so certified.

(4) An Order in Council under this section may contain such transitional and other consequential provisions as appear to Her Majesty to be expedient.

[402]

NOTES

Sub-s (1): words in first pair of square brackets inserted by the Carriage by Air and Road Act 1979, s 1(2), Sch 2, para 2, as from a day to be appointed; words in second and third pairs of square brackets substituted by the Carriage by Air Acts (Implementation of the Montreal Convention 1999) Order 2002, SI 2002/263, art 2(1), (3).

Sub-s (1A): inserted by SI 2002/263, art 2(1), (4).

Sub-ss (2), (2A): substituted for sub-s (2), as originally enacted, by SI 2002/263, art 2(1), (5).

Orders in Council: the Carriage by Air (Parties to Convention) Order 1999, SI 1999/1313 at **[2292]**; the Carriage by Air (Parties to Protocol No 4 of Montreal, 1975) Order 2000, SI 2000/3061 at **[2298]**.

3 Fatal accidents

References in section one of the Fatal Accidents Act 1846, as it applies in England and Wales, and [in Article 3(1) of the Fatal Accidents (Northern Ireland) Order 1977] to a wrongful act, neglect or default shall include references to any occurrence which gives rise to a liability under[—

(a) Article 17 of the Convention;

(b) Article 17 of the Convention as amended; or

(c) Article 17.1 of the Montreal Convention.]

[403]

NOTES

Words in first pair of square brackets substituted by the Fatal Accidents (Northern Ireland) Order 1977, SI 1977/1251; words in second pair of square brackets substituted by the Carriage by Air Acts (Implementation of the Montreal Convention 1999) Order 2002, SI 2002/263, art 2(1), (6).

Fatal Accidents Act 1846: repealed and replaced by the Fatal Accidents Act 1976.

4 Limitation of liability

[(1) It is hereby declared that the limitations on liability in the applicable provisions mentioned in subsection (1A) apply whatever the nature of the proceedings by which liability may be enforced.

(1A) The provisions are—

(a) Article 22 of the Convention;

(b) Article 22 of the Convention as amended; and

(c) Articles 21 and 22 of the Montreal Convention.

(1B) The limitation for each passenger in—

(a) paragraph (1) of Article 22 of the Convention or of the Convention as amended, and

(b) Article 21 and paragraph (1) of Article 22 of the Montreal Convention,

applies to the aggregate liability of the carrier in all proceedings which may be brought against him under the law of any part of the United Kingdom, together with any proceedings brought against him outside the United Kingdom.]

(2) A court before which proceedings are brought to enforce a liability which is limited by [a provision mentioned in subsection (3A)] [or Article 22A] may at any stage of the proceedings make any such order as appears to the court to be just and equitable in view of [that provision] [or Article 22A] and of any other proceedings which have been, or are likely to be, commenced in the United Kingdom or elsewhere to enforce the liability in whole or in part.

(3) Without prejudice to the last foregoing subsection, a court before which proceedings are brought to enforce a liability which is limited by [a provision mentioned in subsection (3A)] [or Article 22A] shall, where the liability is, or may be, partly enforceable in other proceedings in the United Kingdom or elsewhere, have jurisdiction to award an amount less than the court would have awarded if the limitation applied solely to the proceedings before the court, or to make any part of its award conditional on the result of any other proceedings.

[(3A) The provisions are—

(a) Article 22 of the Convention;

(b) Article 22 of the Convention as amended; and

(c) Articles 21, 22 and 44 of the Montreal Convention.]

(4) *The Minister of Aviation may from time to time by order made by statutory instrument specify the respective amounts which for the purposes of the said Article 22, and in particular of paragraph (5) of that Article, are to be taken as equivalent to the sums expressed in francs which are mentioned in that Article.*

(5) References in this section to the said Article 22 [of the Convention or of the Convention as amended] [and Article 22A] include, subject to any necessary modifications, references to that Article as applied by Article 25A [of that Convention].

[404]

NOTES

Sub-ss (1)–(1B): substituted for sub-s (1), as originally enacted, by the Carriage by Air Acts (Implementation of the Montreal Convention 1999) Order 2002, SI 2002/263, art 2(1), (7).

Sub-s (2): words in first and third pairs of square brackets substituted by SI 2002/263, art 2(1), (8); words in second and fourth pairs of square brackets inserted by the Carriage by Air and Road Act 1979, s 1(2), Sch 2, para 4(a), as from a day to be appointed.

Sub-s (3): words in first pair of square brackets substituted by SI 2002/263, art 2(1), (9); words in second pair of square brackets inserted by the Carriage by Air and Road Act 1979, s 1(2), Sch 2, para 4(a), as from a day to be appointed.

Sub-s (3A): inserted by SI 2002/263, art 2(1), (10).

Sub-s (4): repealed by the Carriage by Air and Road Act 1979, ss 1(2), 6(4)(a), Sch 2, para 4(c), as from a day to be appointed.

Sub-s (5): words in first and third pairs of square brackets inserted by SI 2002/263, art 2(1), (11); words in second pair of square brackets inserted by the Carriage by Air and Road Act 1979, s 1(2), Sch 2, para 4(a), as from a day to be appointed.

Minister of Aviation: the Ministry of Aviation was dissolved by the Transfer of Functions (Civil Aviation) Order 1966, SI 1966/741, and the functions of the Minister were initially divided between the Board of Trade and the Minister of Technology. Following many subsequent reorganisations, the functions of the Minister are now exercisable by the Secretary of State for the Environment, Transport and the Regions: see the Secretary of State for the Environment, Transport and the Regions Order 1997, SI 1997/2971, art 3.

Orders: the Carriage by Air (Sterling Equivalents) Order 1999, SI 1999/2811.

[4A Notice of partial loss

(1) [References to damage in the provisions mentioned in subsection (2)] shall be construed as including loss of part of the baggage or cargo in question and the reference to the receipt of baggage or cargo shall, in relation to loss of part of it, be construed as receipt of the remainder of it.

[(2) The provisions are—

(a) Article 26(2) of the Convention;

(b) Article 26(2) of the Convention as amended; and

(c) Article 31(2) of the Montreal Convention.]]

[405]

NOTES

Inserted by the Carriage by Air Act 1979, s 2(1), (2).

Sub-s (1): words in square brackets substituted by the Carriage by Air Acts (Implementation of the Montreal Convention 1999) Order 2002, SI 2002/263, art 2(1), (12).

Sub-s (2): substituted by SI 2002/263, art 2(1), (13).

5 Time for bringing proceedings

(1) No action against a carrier's servant or agent which arises out of damage to which [any of the Carriage by Air Conventions applies] shall, if he was acting within the scope of his employment, be brought after more than two years, reckoned from the date of arrival at the destination or from the date on which the aircraft ought to have arrived, or from the date on which the carriage stopped.

(2) [The provisions mentioned in subsection (4)] shall not be read as applying to any proceedings for contribution between [persons liable for any damage to which [any of the Carriage by Air Conventions] relates], …

(3) [Subsections (1) and (2) and the provisions mentioned in subsection (4)] shall have effect as if references in those provisions to an action included references to [arbitral proceedings]; [and the provisions of section 14 of the Arbitration Act 1996 apply to determine when such proceedings are commenced].

[(4) The provisions are—

(a) Article 29 of the Convention;

(b) Article 29 of the Convention as amended; and

(c) Article 35 of the Montreal Convention.

(5) If the Montreal Convention applies, "carrier" in this section includes an actual carrier as defined by Article 39 of that Convention.]

[406]

NOTES

Sub-s (1): words in square brackets substituted by the Carriage by Air Acts (Implementation of the Montreal Convention 1999) Order 2002, SI 2002/263, art 2(1), (14).

Sub-s (2): words in first and third (inner) pairs of square brackets substituted by SI 2002/263, art 2(1), (15); words in second (outer) pair of square brackets substituted by the Civil Liability (Contribution) Act 1978, s 9(1), Sch 1, para 5(2); words omitted repealed by the Limitation Act 1963, s 4(4).

Sub-s (3): words in first pair of square brackets substituted by SI 2002/263, art 2(1), (16); words in second and third pairs of square brackets substituted by the Arbitration Act 1996, s 107(1), Sch 3, para 13.

Sub-ss (4), (5): added by SI 2002/263, art 2(1), (17).

6 Contributory negligence

[(1)] It is hereby declared that for the purposes of [the provisions mentioned in subsection (2)] the Law Reform (Contributory Negligence) Act 1945 (including that Act as applied to Scotland), and section two of the Law Reform (Miscellaneous Provisions) Act (Northern Ireland) 1948, are provisions of the law of the United Kingdom under which a court may exonerate the carrier wholly or partly from his liability.

[(2) The provisions are—

(a) Article 21 of the Convention;

(b) Article 21 of the Convention as amended; and

(c) Article 20 of the Montreal Convention.]

[407]

NOTES

Sub-s (1): numbered as such and words in square brackets substituted by the Carriage by Air Acts (Implementation of the Montreal Convention 1999) Order 2002, SI 2002/263, art 2(1), (18).

Sub-s (2): added by SI 2002/263, art 2(1), (19).

7 Power to exclude aircraft in use for military purposes

(1) Her Majesty may from time to time by Order in Council direct that this section shall apply, or shall cease to apply, to the United Kingdom or any other State specified in the Order.

(2) The [applicable provisions] to this Act shall not apply to the carriage of persons, cargo and baggage for the military authorities of a State to which this section applies in aircraft registered in that State if the whole capacity of the aircraft has been reserved by or on behalf of those authorities.

[408]

NOTES

Sub-s (2): words in square brackets substituted by the Carriage by Air Acts (Implementation of the Montreal Convention 1999) Order 2002, SI 2002/263, art 2(1), (20).

[8 Actions against parties to Conventions

(1) Each party to a Carriage by Air Convention, for the purposes of any action brought in a court in the United Kingdom in accordance with a provision mentioned in subsection (5) to enforce a claim in respect of carriage undertaken by him, is deemed to have submitted to the jurisdiction of that court.

(2) Accordingly, rules of court may provide for the manner in which any such action is to be commenced and carried on.

(3) But nothing in this section shall authorise the issue of execution against the property of any party to a Carriage by Air Convention.

(4) Subsections (1) and (2) do not apply to a party to a Carriage by Air Convention who has availed himself, in relation to a provision mentioned in subsection (5), of—

(a) the Additional Protocol at the end of the Convention,

(b) the Additional Protocol at the end of the Convention as amended; or

(c) Article 57(a) of the Montreal Convention.

(5) The provisions are—

(a) Article 28 of the Convention;

(b) Article 28 of the Convention as amended;

(c) Articles 33 and 46 of the Montreal Convention.

(6) "Party" means—

(a) in relation to the Convention and the Convention as amended, a High Contracting Party; and

(b) in relation to the Montreal Convention, a State Party.]

[409]

NOTES

Commencement: 28 June 2004.

Substituted by the Carriage by Air Acts (Implementation of the Montreal Convention 1999) Order 2002, SI 2002/263, art 2(1), (21).

[8A Amendments consequential on revision of Convention

(1) If at any time it appears to Her Majesty in Council that Her Majesty's Government in the United Kingdom have agreed to a revision of the Convention, Her Majesty may by Order in Council [make such amendments of this Act, the Carriage by Air (Supplementary

Provisions) Act 1962 and section 5(1) of the Carriage by Air and Road Act 1979] as Her Majesty considers appropriate in consequence of the revision.

(2) In the preceding subsection "revision" means an omission from, addition to or alteration of the Convention and includes replacement of the Convention or part of it by another convention.

(3) An Order in Council under this section shall not be made unless a draft of the Order has been laid before Parliament and approved by a resolution of each House of Parliament.]

[410]

NOTES

Inserted by the Carriage by Air and Road Act 1979, s 3(1).

Sub-s (1): words in square brackets substituted by the International Transport Conventions Act 1983, s 9, Sch 2, para 1.

Orders in Council: the Carriage by Air Acts (Implementation of Protocol No 4 of Montreal, 1975) Order 1999, SI 1999/1312; the Carriage by Air Acts (Implementation of the Montreal Convention 1999) Order 2002, SI 2002/263.

9 Application to British possessions, etc

(1) Her Majesty may by Order in Council direct that this Act shall extend, subject to such exceptions, adaptations and modifications as may be specified in the Order, to—

(a) the Isle of Man;
(b) any of the Channel Islands;
(c) any colony or protectorate, protected state or United Kingdom trust territory.

The references in this subsection to a protectorate, to a protected state and to a United Kingdom trust territory shall be construed as if they were references contained in the British Nationality Act 1948.

(2) An Order in Council under this section may contain such transitional and other consequential provisions as appear to Her Majesty to be expedient, and may be varied or revoked by a subsequent Order in Council.

[411]

NOTES

Orders in Council: the Carriage by Air (Jersey) Order 1967, SI 1967/803; the Carriage by Air (Guernsey) Order 1967, SI 1967/804; the Carriage by Air (Overseas Territories) Order 1967, SI 1967/809; the Carriage by Air (Application of Provisions) (Overseas Territories) Order 1967, SI 1967/810; the Civil Aviation (Isle of Man) (Revocation) Order 1995, SI 1995/1297.

10 Application to carriage by air not governed by Convention

(1) Her Majesty may by Order in Council apply [the applicable provisions of any of the Carriage by Air Conventions], together with any other provisions of this Act, to carriage by air, not being carriage by air to which the [Convention in question] applies, of such descriptions as may be specified in the Order, subject to such exceptions, adaptations and modifications, if any, as may be so specified.

(2) An Order in Council under this section may be made to apply to any of the countries or places mentioned in paragraphs (a), (b) and (c) of subsection (1) of the last foregoing section.

(3) An Order in Council under this section may contain such transitional and other consequential provisions as appear to Her Majesty to be expedient, and may confer any functions under the Order on a Minister of the Crown in the United Kingdom or on any Governor or other authority in any of the countries or places mentioned in paragraphs (a), (b) and (c) of subsection (1) of the last foregoing section, including a power to grant exemptions from any requirements imposed by such an Order.

(4) An Order in Council under this section may be varied or revoked by a subsequent Order in Council.

(5) An Order in Council under this section shall not be made unless a draft of the Order has been laid before Parliament and approved by a resolution of each House of Parliament:

Provided that this subsection shall not apply to an Order which applies only to the Isle of Man or all or any of the Channel Islands.

[412]

NOTES

Sub-s (1): words in square brackets substituted by the Carriage by Air Acts (Implementation of the Montreal Convention 1999) Order 2002, SI 2002/263, art 2(1), (22).

Orders in Council: the Carriage by Air Acts (Application of Provisions) (Jersey) Order 1967, SI 1967/806; the Carriage by Air Acts (Application of Provisions) (Guernsey) Order 1967, SI 1967/807; the Carriage by Air Acts (Application of Provisions) (Overseas Territories) Order 1967, SI 1967/810; the Carriage by Air Acts (Application of Provisions) Order 2004, SI 2004/1899.

11 Application to Scotland

In the application of this Act to Scotland—

(a) there shall be substituted—

(i), (ii) …

(iii) for any reference to the obtaining of judgment, a reference to the pronouncing of decree;

(iv) for any reference to the issuing of execution, a reference to the execution of diligence;

(v) for any reference to an arbitrator, a reference to an arbiter; and

(vi) for any reference to a plaintiff, a reference to a pursuer;

(b) for section three there shall be substituted the following section—

"3 Fatal accidents

The reference in[—

(a) Article 17 of the Convention,

(b) Article 17 of the Convention as amended, and

(c) Article 17.1 of the Montreal Convention,]

to the liability of a carrier for damage sustained in the event of the death of a passenger shall be construed as including liability to such persons as are entitled, apart from this Act, to sue the carrier (whether for patrimonial damage or solatium or both) in respect of the death.";

(c) in section five, subsection (1) shall have effect notwithstanding anything in [section 17 of the Prescription and Limitation (Scotland) Act 1973]; and in subsection (3), for the words from "and [the provisions of section 14 of the Arbitration Act 1996"] to the end of the subsection there shall be substituted the words "and for the purpose of this subsection [arbitral proceedings] shall be deemed to be commenced when one party to the arbitration serves on the other party or parties a notice requiring him or them to appoint an arbiter or to agree to the appointment of an arbiter, or, where the arbitration agreement provided that the reference shall be to a person named or designated in the agreement, requiring him or them to submit the dispute to the person so named or designated."

[413]

NOTES

Paras (a)(i), (ii) repealed by the Limitation Act 1963, s 10(5); in para (b), in s 3 as set out, words in square brackets substituted by the Carriage by Air Acts (Implementation of the Montreal Convention 1999) Order 2002, SI 2002/263, art 2(1), (23); in para (c) words in first pair of square brackets substituted by the Prescriptions and Limitation (Scotland) Act 1973, s 23(1), Sch 4, Pt II, words in second and third pairs of square brackets substituted by the Arbitration Act 1996, s 107(1), Sch 3, para 13(3).

12 (*Applies to Northern Ireland only.*)

13 Application to Crown

This Act shall bind the Crown.

[414]

14 Short title, interpretation and repeals

(1) This Act may be cited as the Carriage by Air Act 1961.

[(2) In this Act—

"the applicable provisions" has the meaning, given in section 1(6);

"the Carriage by Air Conventions" has the meaning given in section 1(5);

"the Convention", "the Convention as amended" and "the Montreal Convention" have the meaning given in section 1(5);

["the Council Regulation" means Council Regulation (EC) No 2027/97 as amended by Regulation (EC) No 889/2002 of the European Parliament and of the Council as it has effect in accordance with the Agreement on the European Economic Area signed at Oporto on 2nd May 1992 as adjusted by the Protocol signed at Brussels on 17th March 1993 as amended by the Decisions of the EEA Joint Committee No 34/98 of 30th April 1998 and No 142/2002 of 8th November 2002;]

"Community air carrier" has the meaning given by Article 2 of the Council Regulation; and

"court" includes (in an arbitration allowed by the Convention) an arbitrator.]

(3) ...

[415]

NOTES

Sub-s (2): substituted by the Carriage by Air Acts (Implementation of the Montreal Convention 1999) Order 2002, SI 2002/263, art 2(1), (24); definition "the Council Regulation" substituted by the Air Carrier Liability Regulations 2004, SI 2004/1418, reg 5.

Sub-s (3): repealed by the Statute Law (Repeals) Act 2004.

(Sch 1 contains the text of the Warsaw Convention with the amendments made in it by the Hague Protocol, printed in Pt V(E) of this work at **[4311]***; Sch 1A, as inserted by the Carriage by Air Acts (Implementation of Protocol No 4 of Montreal, 1975) Order 1999, SI 1999/1312, art 2(1), (6), Schedule, contains the text of the Warsaw Convention with the Amendments made in it by The Hague Protocol and Protocol No 4 of Montreal, 1975, printed in Pt V(E) of this work at* **[4315]***; Sch 1B, as inserted by the Carriage by Air Acts (Implementation of the Montreal Convention 1999) Order 2002, SI 2002/263, art 2(1), (25), Sch 1, contains the text of the Convention for the Unification of Certain Rules for International Carriage by Air, printed in Pt V(E) of this work at* **[4381]***; Sch 2 repealed by the Statute Law (Repeals) Act 1974.)*

CARRIAGE BY AIR (SUPPLEMENTARY PROVISIONS) ACT 1962

(10 & 11 Eliz 2 c 43)

ARRANGEMENT OF SECTIONS

An Act to give effect to the Convention, supplementary to the Warsaw Convention, for the unification of certain rules relating to international carriage by air performed by a person other than the contracting carrier; and for connected purposes

[19 July 1962]

NOTES

This Act has been amended by the Carriage by Air and Road Act 1979 to take account of the Warsaw Convention (as amended by the 1955 Hague Protocol) by certain Protocols signed in Montreal on 25 September 1975. As noted in the footnotes to this Act some of these amendments are not yet in force.

1 Supplementary Convention to have force of law

(1) The provisions of the Convention, supplementary to the Warsaw Convention, for the unification of certain rules relating to international carriage by air performed by a person

other than the contracting carrier, as set out in the Schedule to this Act, shall, so far as they relate to the rights and liabilities of carriers, carriers' servants and agents, passengers, consignors, consignees, and other persons, and subject to the provisions of this Act, have the force of law in the United Kingdom in relation to any carriage by air to which the Convention applies, irrespective of the nationality of the aircraft performing that carriage.

(2) If there is any inconsistency between the text in English in Part I of the Schedule to this Act and the text in French in Part II of that Schedule, the text in French shall prevail.

[416]

2 Interpretation of Supplementary Convention

(1) In the Schedule to this Act "the Warsaw Convention" means—

(a) before the day on which section one of the Carriage by Air Act 1961, comes into force, the Convention set out in the First Schedule to the Carriage by Air Act 1932, and

(b) on and after that day, [whichever is applicable to the carriage in question of the Conventions set out in Schedules 1 and 1A] to the said Act of 1961,

...

(2) In Articles VII and VIII in the Schedule to this Act "court" includes (in an arbitration allowed by the Conventions referred to in the foregoing subsection or by Article IX, 3 in the Schedule to this Act) an arbitrator.

(3) In the application to Scotland of the Schedule to this Act and of the foregoing provisions of this section, for references to an arbitrator and a plaintiff there shall be substituted respectively references to an arbiter and a pursuer.

[417]

NOTES

Sub-s (1): words in square brackets in para (b) substituted by the Carriage by Air Acts (Implementation of Protocol No 4 of Montreal, 1975) Order 1999, SI 1999/1312, art 3(1), (2); words omitted repealed by the Statute Law (Repeals) Act 2004.

Carriage by Air Act 1932: repealed by the Carriage by Air Act 1961, ss 1(1), (3), 14(3), Sch 2.

3 Application of provisions of Acts of 1961 and 1932

(1) In ... [subsection (3A)(a) and (b)] of section four of the said Act of 1961 (which explain the limitations on liability in Article 22 in [Schedule 1 or 1A] to that Act and enable a court to make appropriate orders and awards to give effect to those limitations) references to the said Article 22 shall include, subject to any necessary modifications, references to Article VI in the Schedule to this Act.

(2) In section five of the said Act of 1961 (which limits the time for bringing proceedings against a carrier's servant or agent and to obtain contribution from a carrier) references to a carrier [in a case where the Convention or the Convention as amended, as defined in section 1(5) of that Act, applies] include references to an actual carrier as defined in paragraph (c) of Article I in the Schedule to this Act as well as to a contracting carrier as defined in paragraph (b) of that Article.

(3) In section eight of the said Act of 1961 (which relates to actions against States brought in the United Kingdom in accordance with Article 28 in [Schedule 1 or 1A] to that Act) ... the reference to Article 28 shall include a reference to Article VIII in the Schedule to this Act.

[418]

NOTES

Sub-s (1): words omitted repealed by the Civil Liability (Contribution) Act 1978, s 9(2), Sch 2; words in first pair of square brackets substituted by the Carriage by Air Acts (Implementation of the Montreal Convention 1999) Order 2002, SI 2002/263, art 3(1), (2); words in second pair of square brackets substituted by the Carriage by Air Acts (Implementation of Protocol No 4 of Montreal, 1975) Order 1999, SI 1999/1312, art 3(1), (3).

Sub-s (2): words in square brackets inserted by SI 2002/263, art 3(1), (3).

Sub-s (3): words in square brackets substituted by SI 1999/1312, art 3(1), (3); words omitted repealed by the Statute Law (Repeals) Act 2004.

4 (*Repealed by the Statute Law (Repeals) Act 2004.*)

[4A Amendments consequential on revision of Supplementary Convention

(1) Section 8A of the said Act of 1961 (which among other things enables Her Majesty in Council to alter that Act and this Act in consequence of any revision of the convention to which that Act relates) shall have effect in relation to a revision of the Convention in the Schedule to this Act as it has effect in relation to a revision of the Convention mentioned in that section but as if the reference in that section to the said Act of 1961 were omitted.

(2) An order under the said section 8A may relate both to that Act and this Act; and in the preceding subsection "revision", in relation to the Convention in the Schedule to this Act, means an omission from, addition to or alteration of that Convention and includes replacement of that Convention or part of it by another convention.]

[419]

NOTES

Inserted by the Carriage by Air and Road Act 1979, s 3(2).

Orders in Council: the Carriage by Air Acts (Implementation of the Montreal Convention 1999) Order 2002, SI 2002/263.

5 Application to British possessions, etc, and to carriage by air not governed by Supplementary Convention

(1) Section nine of the said Act of 1961 (which enables Her Majesty to extend that Act to British possessions and other territories) shall (except so far as it relates to United Kingdom trust territories) apply to this Act as it applies to that Act, and an order under that section may relate to both that Act and this Act.

(2) Section ten of the said Act of 1961 (which enables Her Majesty to apply [Schedules 1 and 1A] and other provisions of that Act to carriage by air which is not governed by [the Conventions set out in those Schedules]) shall apply to the Schedule and other provisions of this Act as it applies to that Act, and an order under that section may relate to both that Act and this Act.

(3), (4) ...

[420]

NOTES

Sub-s (2): words in square brackets substituted by the Carriage by Air Acts (Implementation of Protocol No 4 of Montreal, 1975) Order 1999, SI 1999/1312, art 3(1), (4).

Sub-ss (3), (4): repealed by the Statute Law (Repeals) Act 2004.

Orders in Council: the Carriage by Air (Jersey) Order 1967, SI 1967/803; the Carriage by Air (Guernsey) Order 1967, SI 1967/804; the Carriage by Air (Overseas Territories) Order 1967, SI 1967/809; the Carriage by Air Acts (Application of Provisions) (Overseas Territories) Order 1967, SI 1967/810.

6 Application to Crown

(1) This Act shall bind the Crown.

(2) ...

[421]

NOTES

Sub-s (2): repealed by the Statute Law (Repeals) Act 2004.

7 Short title, commencement and saving

(1) This Act may be cited as the Carriage by Air (Supplementary Provisions) Act 1962.

(2), (3) ...

[422]

NOTES

Sub-ss (2), (3): repealed by the Statute Law (Repeals) Act 2004.

Orders in Council: the Carriage by Air (Supplementary Provisions) Act 1962 (Commencement) Order 1964, SI 1964/486.

(Schedule contains the text of the Convention, supplementary to the Warsaw Convention, for the unification of certain rules relating to International Carriage by Air performed by a person other than the contracting carrier, printed in Pt V(E) of this work at **[4313]***.)*

CARRIAGE OF GOODS BY ROAD ACT 1965

(1965 c 37)

ARRANGEMENT OF SECTIONS

An Act to give effect to the Convention on the Contract for the International Carriage of Goods by Road signed at Geneva on 19th May 1956; and for purposes connected therewith

[5 August 1965]

1 Convention to have force of law

Subject to the following provisions of this Act, the provisions of the Convention on the Contract for the International Carriage of Goods by Road (in this Act referred to as "the Convention"), as set out in the Schedule to this Act, shall have the force of law in the United Kingdom so far as they relate to the rights and liabilities of persons concerned in the carriage of goods by road under a contract to which the Convention applies.

[423]

2 Designation of High Contracting Parties

(1) Her Majesty may by Order in Council from time to time certify who are the High Contracting Parties to the Convention and in respect of what territories they are respectively parties.

(2) An Order in Council under this section shall, except so far as it has been superseded by a subsequent Order, be conclusive evidence of the matters so certified.

[424]

NOTES

Orders in Council: the Carriage of Goods by Road (Parties to Convention) Order 1967, SI 1967/1683.

3 Power of court to take account of other proceedings

(1) A court before which proceedings are brought to enforce a liability which is limited by article 23 in the Schedule to this Act may at any stage of the proceedings make any such order as appears to the court to be just and equitable in view of the provisions of the said article 23 and of any other proceedings which have been, or are likely to be, commenced in the United Kingdom or elsewhere to enforce the liability in whole or in part.

(2) Without prejudice to the preceding subsection, a court before which proceedings are brought to enforce a liability which is limited by the said article 23 shall, where the liability is, or may be, partly enforceable in other proceedings in the United Kingdom or elsewhere,

have jurisdiction to award an amount less than the court would have awarded if the limitation applied solely to the proceedings before the court, or to make any part of its award conditional on the result of any other proceedings.

[425]

4 Registration of foreign judgments

(1) Subject to the next following subsection, Part I of the Foreign Judgments (Reciprocal Enforcement) Act 1933 (in this section referred to as "the Act of 1933") shall apply, whether or not it would otherwise have so applied, to any judgment which—

(a) has been given in any such action as is referred to in paragraph 1 of article 31 in the Schedule to this Act, and

(b) has been so given by any court or tribunal of a territory in respect of which one of the High Contracting Parties, other than the United Kingdom, is a party to the Convention, and

(c) has become enforceable in that territory.

(2) In the application of Part I of the Act of 1933 in relation to any such judgment as is referred to in the preceding subsection, section 4 of that Act shall have effect with the omission of subsections (2) and (3).

(3) The registration, in accordance with Part I of the Act of 1933, of any such judgment as is referred to in subsection (1) of this section shall constitute, in relation to that judgment, compliance with the formalities for the purposes of paragraph 3 of article 31 in the Schedule to this Act.

[426]

5 Contribution between carriers

(1) Where a carrier under a contract to which the Convention applies is liable in respect of any loss or damage for which compensation is payable under the Convention, nothing in [section 1 of the Civil Liability (Contribution) Act 1978], or section 3(2) of the Law Reform (Miscellaneous Provisions) (Scotland) Act 1940 shall confer on him any right to recover contribution in respect of that loss or damage from any other carrier who, in accordance with article 34 in the Schedule to this Act, is a party to the contract of carriage.

(2) The preceding subsection shall be without prejudice to the operation of article 37 in the Schedule to this Act.

[427]

NOTES

Sub-s (1): words in square brackets substituted by the Civil Liability (Contribution) Act 1978, s 9(1), Sch 1, para 7.

6 Actions against High Contracting Parties

Every High Contracting Party to the Convention shall, for the purposes of any proceedings brought in a court in the United Kingdom in accordance with the provisions of article 31 in the Schedule to this Act to enforce a claim in respect of carriage undertaken by that Party, be deemed to have submitted to the jurisdiction of that court, and accordingly rules of court may provide for the manner in which any such action is to be commenced and carried on; but nothing in this section shall authorise the issue of execution, or in Scotland the execution of diligence, against the property of any High Contracting Party.

[428]

7 Arbitrations

(1) Any reference in the preceding provisions of this Act to a court includes a reference to an arbitration tribunal acting by virtue of article 33 in the Schedule to this Act.

(2) For the purposes of article 32 in the Schedule to this Act, as it has effect (by virtue of the said article 33) in relation to arbitrations,—

[(a) as respects England and Wales and Northern Ireland, the provisions of section 14(3) to (5) of the Arbitration Act 1996 (which determine the time at which an arbitration is commenced) apply;]

(b) …

(c) as respects Scotland, an arbitration shall be deemed to be commenced when one party to the arbitration serves on the other party or parties a notice requiring him or them to appoint an arbiter or to agree to the appointment of an arbiter or, where the arbitration agreement provides that the reference shall be to a person named or designated in the agreement, requiring him or them to submit the dispute to the person so named or designated.

[429]

NOTES

Sub-s (2): para (a) substituted for original paras (a), (b), and para (b) repealed, by the Arbitration Act 1996, s 107, Sch 3, para 21, Sch 4.

8 Resolution of conflicts between Conventions on carriage of goods

(1) If it appears to Her Majesty in Council that there is any conflict between the provisions of this Act (including the provisions of the Convention as set out in the Schedule to this Act) and any provisions relating to the carriage of goods for reward by land, sea or air contained in—

(a) any other Convention which has been signed or ratified by or on behalf of Her Majesty's Government in the United Kingdom before the passing of this Act, or

(b) any enactment of the Parliament of the United Kingdom giving effect to such a Convention,

Her Majesty may by Order in Council make such provision as may seem to Her to be appropriate for resolving that conflict by amending or modifying this Act or any such enactment.

(2) Any statutory instrument made by virtue of this section shall be subject to annulment in pursuance of a resolution of either House of Parliament.

[430]

[8A Amendments consequential on revision of Convention

(1) If at any time it appears to Her Majesty in Council that Her Majesty's Government in the United Kingdom have agreed to any revision of the Convention, Her Majesty may by Order in Council make such amendment of—

[(a) this Act; and]

(c) section 5(1) of the Carriage by Air and Road Act 1979,

as appear to Her to be appropriate in consequence of the revision.

(2) In the preceding subsection "revision" means an omission from, addition to or alteration of the Convention and includes replacement of the Convention or part of it by another convention.

(3) An Order in Council under this section shall not be made unless a draft of the Order has been laid before Parliament and approved by a resolution of each House of Parliament.]

[431]

NOTES

Inserted by the Carriage by Air and Road Act 1979, s 3(3).

Sub-s (1): para (a) substituted for original paras (a), (b) by the International Transport Conventions Act 1983, s 9, Sch 2, para 2.

9 Application to British possessions, etc

Her Majesty may by Order in Council direct that this Act shall extend, subject to such exceptions, adaptations and modifications as may be specified in the Order, to—

(a) the Isle of Man;

(b) any of the Channel Islands;

(c) any colony;

(d) …

[432]

NOTES

Para (d): repealed by the Statute Law (Repeals) Act 1993.

Orders in Council: the Carriage of Goods by Road (Gibraltar) Order 1967, SI 1967/820; the Carriage of Goods by Road (Isle of Man) Order 1981, SI 1981/1543; the Carriage of Goods by Road (Guernsey) Order 1986, SI 1986/1882.

10 Application to Scotland

In its application to Scotland, the Schedule to this Act shall have effect as if—

(a) any reference therein to a plaintiff included a reference to a pursuer;
(b) any reference therein to a defendant included a reference to a defender; and
(c) any reference to security for costs included a reference to caution for expenses.

[433]

11 (*S 11(1), (2) applies to Northern Ireland only; s 11(3) repealed by the Northern Ireland Constitution Act 1973, s 41(1), Sch 6, Pt I.*)

12 Orders in Council

An Order in Council made under any of the preceding provisions of this Act may contain such transitional and supplementary provisions as appear to Her Majesty to be expedient and may be varied or revoked by a subsequent Order in Council made under that provision.

[434]

13 Application to Crown

This Act shall bind the Crown.

[435]

14 Short title, interpretation and commencement

(1) This Act may be cited as the Carriage of Goods by Road Act 1965.

(2) The persons who, for the purposes of this Act, are persons concerned in the carriage of goods by road under a contract to which the Convention applies are—

(a) the sender,
(b) the consignee,
(c) any carrier who, in accordance with article 34 in the Schedule to this Act or otherwise, is a party to the contract of carriage,
(d) any person for whom such a carrier is responsible by virtue of article 3 in the Schedule to this Act,
(e) any person to whom the rights and liabilities of any of the persons referred to in paragraphs (a) to (d) to this subsection have passed (whether by assignment or assignation or by operation of law).

(3) Except in so far as the context otherwise requires, any reference in this Act to an enactment shall be construed as a reference to that enactment as amended or extended by or under any other enactment.

(4) This Act shall come into operation on such day as Her Majesty may by Order in Council appoint; but nothing in this Act shall apply in relation to any contract or the carriage of goods by road made before the day so appointed.

[436]

NOTES

Orders in Council: the Carriage of Goods by Road Act 1965 (Commencement) Order 1967, SI 1967/819.

(*Schedule contains the text of the Convention on the Contract for the International Carriage of Goods by Road, printed in Pt V(E) of this work at* **[4319]**.)

CARRIAGE BY AIR AND ROAD ACT 1979

(1979 c 28)

An Act to enable effect to be given to provisions of certain protocols signed at Montreal on 25th September 1975 which further amend the convention relating to carriage by air known as the Warsaw Convention as amended at The Hague 1955; to modify article 26(2) of the said convention both as in force apart from those protocols and as in force by virtue of them; to provide for the amendment of certain Acts relating to carriage by air or road in consequence of the revision of relevant conventions; and to replace references to gold francs in the Carriage of Goods by Road Act 1965 and the Carriage of Passengers by Road Act 1974 by references to special drawing rights

[4 April 1979]

1 Alterations of texts of carriage by air convention

(1) For Schedule 1 to the Carriage by Air Act 1961 (which contains the English and French texts of the Warsaw Convention mentioned in the title to this Act as it has the force of law in the United Kingdom by virtue of section 1 of that Act) there shall be substituted Schedule 1 to this Act (which contains the English and French texts of that Convention as amended by provisions of protocols No 3 and No 4 which were signed at Montreal on 25th September 1975).

(2) The said Act of 1961 and the Carriage by Air (Supplementary Provisions) Act 1962 shall have effect with the amendments set out in Schedule 2 to this Act (which are consequential upon the changes of texts made by the preceding subsection or are connected with the coming into force of those texts).

(3) Neither of the preceding subsections shall affect rights and liabilities arising out of an occurrence which took place before the coming into force of that subsection or, if the subsection comes into force in pursuance of section 7(2) of this Act for some purposes only, arising out of an occurrence which took place before it comes into force for those purposes. **[437]**

NOTES

Commencement: to be appointed.

2, 3 (*S 2 inserts the Carriage by Air Act 1961, s 4A at* **[405]**; *s 3(1) inserts s 8A in the 1961 Act at* **[410]**; *s 3(2) inserts the Carriage by Air (Supplementary Provisions) Act 1962, s 4A at* **[419]**; *s 3(3) inserts the Carriage of Goods by Road Act 1965, s 8A at* **[431]**; *s 3(4) repealed by the Statute Law (Repeals) Act 2004*.)

4 Replacement of gold francs by special drawing rights for the purposes of certain enactments relating to carriage by air or road

(1)–(3) …

(4) If judgment in respect of a liability limited by the said Article 22, 23 … is given—

(a) in the case of a liability by the said Article 22, at a time when the amendments made by this section to that Article are in force for the purposes of the liability; or

(b) in any other case, at a time when the amendments made by this section to the other Article in question are in force,

then notwithstanding that the liability arose before the amendments in question came into force, the judgment shall be in accordance with that Article as amended by this section and, in a case falling within the said Article 13 or 16, in accordance with the said Article 19 as so amended.

[438]

NOTES

Commencement: 1 December 1997 (sub-s (1), sub-s (4) in so far as relates to the amendment of the Carriage by Air Act 1961); 28 December 1980 (sub-s (2) sub-s (4), in so far as relates to the amendment of the Carriage of Goods by Road Act 1965); to be appointed (sub-s (4), otherwise).

Sub-s (1): amends the Carriage by Air Act 1961, Sch 1, Pts I, II, as set out at **[4311]**.

Sub-s (2): substitutes the Carriage of Goods by Road Act 1965, Schedule, Article 23, as set out at **[4319]**.

Sub-s (3): repealed by the Statute Law (Repeals) Act 2004.

Sub-s (4): words omitted repealed by the Statute Law (Repeals) Act 2004.

5 Conversion of special drawing rights into sterling

(1) For the purposes of Articles 22 and 22A of Schedule 1 to this Act and the Articles 22, 23 … mentioned in the preceding section as amended by that section, the value on a particular day of one special drawing right shall be treated as equal to such a sum in sterling as the International Monetary Fund have fixed as being the equivalent of one special drawing right—

(a) for that day; or

(b) if no sum has been so fixed for that day, for the last day before that day for which a sum has been so fixed.

(2) A certificate given by or on behalf of the Treasury stating—

(a) that a particular sum in sterling has been fixed as aforesaid for a particular day; or

(b) that no sum has been so fixed for a particular day and that a particular sum in sterling has been so fixed for a day which is the last day for which a sum has been so fixed before that particular day,

shall be conclusive evidence of those matters for the purposes of the preceding subsection; and a document purporting to be such a certificate shall in any proceedings be received in evidence and, unless the contrary is proved, be deemed to be such a certificate.

(3) The Treasury may charge a reasonable fee for any certificate given by or on behalf of the Treasury in pursuance of the preceding subsection, and any fee received by the Treasury by virtue of this subsection shall be paid into the Consolidated Fund.

[439]

NOTES

Commencement: 1 December 1997 (in so far as relates to the amendment of the Carriage by Air Act 1961); 28 December 1980 (in so far as relates to the amendment of the Carriage of Goods by Road Act 1965); to be appointed (otherwise).

Sub-s (1): words omitted repealed by the Statute Law (Repeals) Act 2004.

6 Supplemental

(1) It is hereby declared that the powers to make Orders in Council conferred by—

(a) sections 8A, 9 and 10 of the Carriage by Air Act 1961 (which provide for the amendment of that Act and other Acts in consequence of a revision of the relevant convention and for the application of that Act to the countries mentioned in section 9 and to such carriage by air as is mentioned in section 10); and

(b) sections 8, 8A and 9 of the Carriage of Goods by Road Act 1965 (which provide for the resolution of conflicts between provisions of that Act and certain other provisions relating to carriage by road, for the amendment of that Act in consequence of a revision of the relevant convention and for the application of that Act to the countries mentioned in section 9) …

(c) …

include power to make Orders in Council in respect of the Act in question as amended by this Act.

(2) It is hereby declared that Schedule 1 to the said Act of 1961 as originally enacted or, if subsection (1) of section 4 of this Act has come into force, as amended by that subsection, remains in force in relation to any matter in relation to which Schedule 1 to this Act is not for the time being in force and that the reference to Schedule 1 to that Act in section 2(1)(b) of the Carriage by Air (Supplementary Provisions) Act 1962 is to be construed as a reference to both the Schedules 1 aforesaid so far as each is for the time being in force.

(3) This Act binds the Crown.

(4) …

[440]

NOTES

Commencement: 28 December 1980 (sub-s (1)(b)); 1 December 1997 (sub-s (1)(a), in so far as relates to the Carriage by Air Act 1961, ss 9, 10; sub-s (3), certain purposes); 12 October 2000 (sub-s (1)(a), remaining purposes; sub-s (3), certain purposes); to be appointed (otherwise).

Sub-s (1): words omitted repealed by the Statute Law (Repeals) Act 2004.

Sub-s (4): repeals the Carriage by Air Act 1961, s 4(4) at **[404]**; repealed in part by the Statute Law (Repeals) Act 2004.

7 Short title and commencement

(1) This Act may be cited as the Carriage by Air and Road Act 1979.

(2) This Act, except section 2, shall come into force on such days as Her Majesty may by Order in Council appoint, and—

(a) different days may be appointed in pursuance of this subsection for different provisions of this Act or for different purposes of the same provision;

(b) it is hereby declared that a day or days may be appointed in pursuance of this subsection in respect of subsection (1) of section 1 of this Act and Schedule 1 to this Act notwithstanding that the protocols mentioned in that subsection are not in force in accordance with the provisions in that behalf of those protocols.

[441]

NOTES

Orders in Council: the Carriage by Air and Road Act 1979 (Commencement No 1) Order 1980, SI 1980/1966; the Carriage by Air and Road Act 1979 (Commencement No 2) Order 1997, SI 1997/2565; the Carriage by Air and Road Act 1979 (Commencement No 3) Order 1998, SI 1998/2562; the Carriage by Air and Road Act 1979 (Commencement No 4) Order 2000, SI 2000/2768.

(Sch 1 contains the text of the Warsaw Convention as amended at the Hague in 1955 and by Protocols No 3 and No 4 signed at Montreal in 1975, printed in Pt V(E) of this work, at **[4315]***; Sch 2 amends the Carriage by Air Act 1961, ss 2, 4 at* **[402]**, **[404]** *and the Carriage by Air (Supplementary Provisions) Act 1962, Schedule (as set out at* **[4313]***) and is repealed in part by the Statute Law (Repeals) Act 2004.)*

INTERNATIONAL TRANSPORT CONVENTIONS ACT 1983

(1983 c 14)

ARRANGEMENT OF SECTIONS

The Railway Convention

Other international transport conventions

Supplementary

An Act to give effect to the Convention concerning International Carriage by Rail signed on behalf of the United Kingdom on 9th May 1980; and to make further provision for the amendment of Acts giving effect to other international transport conventions so as to take account of revisions of the conventions to which they give effect

[11 April 1983]

The Railway Convention

1 Convention to have the force of law

(1) The Convention concerning International Carriage by Rail signed on behalf of the United Kingdom on 9th May 1980 shall have the force of law in the United Kingdom.

(2) In this Act "the Convention" means the Convention referred to in subsection (1) above including, except where the context otherwise requires—

(a) the protocol on the privileges and immunities of the intergovernmental organisation set up by the Convention; and

(b) the uniform rules in Appendix A and Appendix B to the Convention together with the Annexes to Appendix B.

(3) The provisions having the force of law by virtue of this section are—

(a) the provisions of the Convention as presented to Parliament in April 1982 and set out in Command Paper 8535 [as amended by—

(i) Part I of the Protocol of Decisions adopted by the Revision Committee constituted by the Convention in the course of its first session held at Berne from 14th to 21st December 1989, presented to Parliament in 1991 and set out in Command Paper 1690, and

(ii) Part I of the Protocol of Decisions adopted by that Committee in the course of its second session held at Berne from 28th to 31st May 1990 as so presented and set out in Command Paper 1689][, and

(iii) the Protocol amending the Convention adopted by the 2nd General Assembly of the Intergovernmental Organisation for International Carriage by Rail (OTIF) constituted by the Convention held at Berne from 17th to 20th December 1990 as presented to Parliament in 1993 and set out in Command Paper 2232]; and

(b) as respects Annexes I, II and III to Appendix B to the Convention, the provisions referred to in that Command Paper;

and judicial notice shall be taken of those provisions as if they were contained in this Act.

(4) If after the coming into force of this section the provisions referred to in paragraph (a) of subsection (3) above are republished in one or more Command Papers in the Treaty Series that subsection shall have effect as if it referred to that or those Command Papers instead of to the Command Paper there mentioned.

[442]

NOTES

Repealed by the Railways (Convention on International Carriage by Rail) Regulations 2005, SI 2005/2092, reg 9(1), Sch 2, para 1, as from the day specified in the London, Edinburgh and Belfast Gazettes on which the Protocol signed at Vilnius on 3 June 1999 to modify the "Convention concerning International Carriage by Rail (COTIF) of 9th May 1980" enters into force in respect of the United Kingdom: see SI 2005/2092, reg 1.

Sub-s (3): words in first pair of square brackets inserted by the International Transport Conventions Act 1983 (Amendment) Order 1992, SI 1992/237, art 2; words in second pair of square brackets inserted by the International Transport Conventions Act 1983 (Amendment) Order 1994, SI 1994/1907, art 2.

2 Designation of Member States etc

(1) Her Majesty may by Order in Council from time to time certify who are the Member States for the purposes of the Convention.

(2) An Order in Council under subsection (1) above may also certify whether the United Kingdom or any other Member State has made a reservation under—

(a) paragraph 3 of Article 12 of the Convention (arbitration); or

(b) paragraph 1 of Article 3 in Appendix A to the Convention (exclusion of own nationals etc).

(3) Her Majesty may by Order in Council from time to time certify whether the uniform rules referred to in section 1(2)(b) above are suspended by virtue of paragraph 3 of Article 20 of the Convention (suspension pending agreement to amendments) in respect of traffic with or between any Member States.

(4) An Order in Council under this section shall, except so far as it has been superseded by a subsequent Order, be conclusive evidence of the matters so certified.

[443]

NOTES

Repealed by the Railways (Convention on International Carriage by Rail) Regulations 2005, SI 2005/2092, reg 9(1), Sch 2, para 1, as from the day specified in the London, Edinburgh and Belfast

Gazettes on which the Protocol signed at Vilnius on 3 June 1999 to modify the "Convention concerning International Carriage by Rail (COTIF) of 9th May 1980" enters into force in respect of the United Kingdom: see SI 2005/2092, reg 1.

3 Fatal accidents

(1) Where by virtue of the Convention any person has a right of action in respect of the death of a passenger by reason of his being a person whom the passenger was under a legal duty to maintain—

(a) subject to subsection (2) below, no action in respect of the passenger's death shall be brought for the benefit of that person under the Fatal Accidents Act 1976; but

(b) nothing in section 2(3) of that Act (not more than one action in respect of the same subject-matter of complaint) shall prevent an action being brought under that Act for the benefit of any other person.

(2) Nothing in subsection (1)(a) above affects the right of any person to claim damages for bereavement under section 1A of the said Act of 1976.

(3) Section 4 of the said Act of 1976 (exclusion of certain benefits in assessment of damages) shall apply in relation to an action brought by any person under the Convention as it applies in relation to an action under that Act.

(4) Where separate proceedings are brought under the Convention and under the said Act of 1976 in respect of the death of a passenger, a court, in awarding damages under that Act, shall take into account any damages awarded in the proceedings brought under the Convention and shall have jurisdiction to make any part of its award conditional on the result of those proceedings.

(5) In the application of this section to Northern Ireland references to the said Act of 1976 and to sections 1A, 2(3) and 4 of that Act shall be construed as references to the Fatal Accidents (Northern Ireland) Order 1977 and Articles 3A, 4(3) and 6 of that Order.

(6) The provisions of Schedule 1 to this Act shall, as respects Scotland, have effect in lieu of the foregoing provisions of this section.

[444]

NOTES

Repealed by the Railways (Convention on International Carriage by Rail) Regulations 2005, SI 2005/2092, reg 9(1), Sch 2, para 1, as from the day specified in the London, Edinburgh and Belfast Gazettes on which the Protocol signed at Vilnius on 3 June 1999 to modify the "Convention concerning International Carriage by Rail (COTIF) of 9th May 1980" enters into force in respect of the United Kingdom: see SI 2005/2092, reg 1.

4 Power of court of take account of other proceedings

(1) A court before which proceedings are brought to enforce a liability which is limited by any of the provisions of the Convention may at any stage of the proceedings make any such order as appears to the court to be just and equitable in view of those provisions and of any other proceedings which have been, or are likely to be, commenced in the United Kingdom or elsewhere to enforce the liability in whole or in part.

(2) Without prejudice to subsection (1) above, a court before which proceedings are brought to enforce a liability which is limited as aforesaid shall, where the liability is or may be partly enforceable in other proceedings in the United Kingdom or elsewhere, have jurisdiction to award an amount less than the court would have awarded if the limitation applied solely to the proceedings before the court, or to make any part of its award conditional on the result of any other proceedings.

[445]

NOTES

Repealed by the Railways (Convention on International Carriage by Rail) Regulations 2005, SI 2005/2092, reg 9(1), Sch 2, para 1, as from the day specified in the London, Edinburgh and Belfast Gazettes on which the Protocol signed at Vilnius on 3 June 1999 to modify the "Convention concerning International Carriage by Rail (COTIF) of 9th May 1980" enters into force in respect of the United Kingdom: see SI 2005/2092, reg 1.

5 Conversion of special drawing rights into sterling

(1) The special drawing rights by reference to which any liability is limited by the Convention shall, in the case of judicial proceedings or an arbitration in the United Kingdom, be converted into their sterling equivalent on the day of the judgment or award.

(2) For the purposes of this section the value on a particular day of a special drawing right shall be treated as equal to such a sum in sterling as the International Monetary Fund have fixed as being the equivalent of one special drawing right—

- *(a) for that day; or*
- *(b) if no sum has been so fixed for that day, for the last day before that day for which a sum has been so fixed.*

(3) A certificate given by or on behalf of the Treasury stating—

- *(a) that a particular sum in sterling has been fixed as aforesaid for a particular day; or*
- *(b) that no sum has been so fixed for a particular day and that a particular sum in sterling has been so fixed for a day which is the last day for which a sum has been so fixed before the particular day,*

shall be conclusive evidence of those matters for the purposes of subsection (2) above; and a document purporting to be such a certificate shall in any proceedings be received in evidence and, unless the contrary is proved, be deemed to be such a certificate.

(4) The Treasury may charge a reasonable fee for any certificate given under this section; and any fee received by the Treasury by virtue of this subsection shall be paid into the Consolidated Fund.

[446]

NOTES

Repealed by the Railways (Convention on International Carriage by Rail) Regulations 2005, SI 2005/2092, reg 9(1), Sch 2, para 1, as from the day specified in the London, Edinburgh and Belfast Gazettes on which the Protocol signed at Vilnius on 3 June 1999 to modify the "Convention concerning International Carriage by Rail (COTIF) of 9th May 1980" enters into force in respect of the United Kingdom: see SI 2005/2092, reg 1.

6 Enforcement of judgments

(1) Subject to subsection (2) below, Part I of the Foreign Judgments (Reciprocal Enforcement) Act 1933 shall apply, whether or not it would otherwise have applied, to any judgment which—

- *(a) has been pronounced as mentioned in paragraph 1 of Article 18 of the Convention by a court in a Member State other than the United Kingdom; and*
- *(b) has become enforceable under the law applied by that court.*

(2) In the application of Part I of the said Act of 1933 in relation to any such judgment section 4 of that Act shall have effect with the omission of subsections (2) and (3).

(3) The registration, in accordance with Part I of the said Act of 1933, of any such judgment shall constitute compliance with the required formalities referred to in paragraph 1 of Article 18 of the Convention.

[447]

NOTES

Repealed by the Railways (Convention on International Carriage by Rail) Regulations 2005, SI 2005/2092, reg 9(1), Sch 2, para 1, as from the day specified in the London, Edinburgh and Belfast Gazettes on which the Protocol signed at Vilnius on 3 June 1999 to modify the "Convention concerning International Carriage by Rail (COTIF) of 9th May 1980" enters into force in respect of the United Kingdom: see SI 2005/2092, reg 1.

7 Examination of luggage

Paragraph 4 of Article 15 and paragraph 2 of Article 22 in Appendix A to the Convention (examination of luggage) shall not in the United Kingdom authorise the opening of any piece of luggage except in the presence of a constable.

[448]

NOTES

Repealed by the Railways (Convention on International Carriage by Rail) Regulations 2005, SI 2005/2092, reg 9(1), Sch 2, para 1, as from the day specified in the London, Edinburgh and Belfast Gazettes on which the Protocol signed at Vilnius on 3 June 1999 to modify the "Convention concerning International Carriage by Rail (COTIF) of 9th May 1980" enters into force in respect of the United Kingdom: see SI 2005/2092, reg 1.

8 Amendments consequential on revision of Convention

(1) If at any time it appears to Her Majesty in Council that Her Majesty's Government in the United Kingdom have agreed to a revision of the Convention, Her Majesty may by Order in Council make such amendments of this Act as Her Majesty considers appropriate in consequence of the revision.

(2) In subsection (1) above "revision" means an omission from, addition to or alteration of the Convention and includes replacement of the Convention or part of it by another convention.

(3) No recommendation shall be made to Her Majesty to make an Order under this section unless a draft of it has been laid before Parliament and approved by a resolution of each House of Parliament.

(4) An Order under this section may contain such transitional and supplementary provisions as appear to Her Majesty to be expedient.

[449]

NOTES

Repealed by the Railways (Convention on International Carriage by Rail) Regulations 2005, SI 2005/2092, reg 9(1), Sch 2, para 1, as from the day specified in the London, Edinburgh and Belfast Gazettes on which the Protocol signed at Vilnius on 3 June 1999 to modify the "Convention concerning International Carriage by Rail (COTIF) of 9th May 1980" enters into force in respect of the United Kingdom: see SI 2005/2092, reg 1.

Other international transport conventions

9 Power to make amendments consequential on revision of other international transport conventions

The Acts mentioned in Schedule 2 to this Act (which give effect to other international transport conventions) shall have effect with the amendments there specified, being amendments making further provision for enabling those Acts to be modified so as to take account of revisions of the conventions to which they give effect.

[450]

Supplementary

10 Application to Crown

This Act binds the Crown.

[451]

11 Short title, repeals and commencement

(1) This Act may be cited as the International Transport Conventions Act 1983.

(2) The enactments mentioned in Schedule 3 to this Act are hereby repealed to the extent specified in the third column of that Schedule; …

(3) Section 1 above shall come into force on such day as Her Majesty may by Order in Council certify to be the day on which the Convention comes into force as regards the United Kingdom; and subsection (2) above shall have effect from that day.

(4) The provisions having the force of law by virtue of section 1 above do not affect any rights or liabilities arising out of an occurrence before the coming into force of those provisions; and subsection (2) above does not affect any enactment in its application to any such rights or liabilities.

[452]

NOTES

Sub-s (2): words omitted amend the Civil Jurisdiction and Judgments Act 1982, ss 31(3), 32(4).

Sub-ss (3), (4): repealed by the Railways (Convention on International Carriage by Rail) Regulations 2005, SI 2005/2092, reg 9(1), Sch 2, para 1, as from the day specified in the London, Edinburgh and Belfast Gazettes on which the Protocol signed at Vilnius on 3 June 1999 to modify the "Convention concerning International Carriage by Rail (COTIF) of 9th May 1980" enters into force in respect of the United Kingdom: see SI 2005/2092, reg 1.

Orders in Council: the International Transport Conventions Act 1983 (Certification of Commencement of Convention) Order 1985, SI 1985/612, revoked by SI 2005/2092, reg 9(1), Sch 2, para 3(a), as from the day specified in the London, Edinburgh and Belfast Gazettes on which the Protocol signed at Vilnius on 3 June 1999 to modify the "Convention concerning International Carriage by Rail (COTIF) of 9th May 1980" enters into force in respect of the United Kingdom: see SI 2005/2092, reg 1.

(Sch 1 amends the Damages (Scotland) Act 1976, repealed by the Railways (Convention on International Carriage by Rail) Regulations 2005, SI 2005/2092, reg 9(1), Sch 2, para 1, as from the day specified in the London, Edinburgh and Belfast Gazettes on which the Protocol signed at Vilnius on 3rd June 1999 to modify the "Convention concerning International Carriage by Rail (COTIF) of 9th May 1980" enters into force in respect of the United Kingdom; Sch 2: para 1 amends the Carriage by Air Act 1961, s 8A(1) at **[410]***; para 2 amends the Carriage of Goods by Road Act 1965, s 8A(1) at* **[431]***; para 3 repealed by the Statute Law (Repeals) Act 2004; para 4 substitutes the International Carriage of Perishable Foodstuffs Act 1976, s 16(1); Sch 3 contains repeals.)*

F. INTERNATIONAL CARRIAGE: SEA

CARRIAGE OF GOODS BY SEA ACT 1971

(1971 c 19)

ARRANGEMENT OF SECTIONS

An Act to amend the law with respect to the carriage of goods by sea

[8 April 1971]

NOTES

By the Hovercraft (Civil Liability) Order 1986, SI 1986/1305, art 4, Sch 2, this Act applies, with modifications, in relation to the carriage of goods by hovercraft (other than passengers' baggage) as it applies in relation to goods on board or carried by ship. See also the Hovercraft Act 1968, ss 1(1)(i), (ii), and 6(3).

---

1 Application of Hague Rules as amended

(1) In this Act, "the Rules" means the International Convention for the unification of certain rules of law relating to bills of lading signed at Brussels on 25th August 1924, as amended by the Protocol signed at Brussels on 23rd February 1968 [and by the Protocol signed at Brussels on 21st December 1979].

(2) The provisions of the Rules, as set out in the Schedule to this Act, shall have the force of law.

(3) Without prejudice to subsection (2) above, the said provisions shall have effect (and have the force of law) in relation to and in connection with the carriage of goods by sea in ships where the port of shipment is a port in the United Kingdom, whether or not the carriage is between ports in two different States within the meaning of Article X of the Rules.

(4) Subject to subsection (6) below, nothing in this section shall be taken as applying anything in the Rules to any contract for the carriage of goods by sea, unless the contract expressly or by implication provides for the issue of a bill of lading or any similar document of title.

(5) …

(6) Without prejudice to Article X(c) of the Rules, the Rules shall have the force of law in relation to—

(a) any bill of lading if the contract contained in or evidenced by it expressly provides that the Rules shall govern the contract, and

(b) any receipt which is a non-negotiable document marked as such if the contract contained in or evidenced by it is a contract for the carriage of goods by sea which expressly provides that the Rules are to govern the contract as if the receipt were a bill of lading,

but subject, where paragraph (b) applies, to any necessary modifications and in particular with the omission in Article III of the Rules of the second sentence of paragraph 4 and of paragraph 7.

(7) If and so far as the contract contained in or evidenced by a bill of lading or receipt within paragraph (a) or (b) of subsection (6) above applies to deck cargo or live animals, the Rules as given the force of law by that subsection shall have effect as if Article I (c) did not exclude deck cargo and live animals.

In this subsection "deck cargo" means cargo which by the contract of carriage is stated as being carried on deck and is so carried.

[453]

NOTES

Sub-s (1): words in square brackets inserted by the Merchant Shipping Act 1981, s 2(1) (this amendment continues to have effect by virtue of the Merchant Shipping Act 1995, s 314(2), Sch 13, para 45(1), (2)).

Sub-s (5): repealed by the Merchant Shipping Act 1981, s 5(3), Schedule.

[1A Conversion of special drawing rights into sterling

(1) For the purposes of Article IV of the Rules the value on a particular day of one special drawing right shall be treated as equal to such a sum in sterling as the International Monetary Fund have fixed as being the equivalent of one special drawing right—

(a) for that day; or

(b) if no sum has been so fixed for that say, for the last day before that day for which a sum has been so fixed.

(2) A certificate given by or on behalf of the Treasury stating—

(a) that a particular sum in sterling has been fixed as aforesaid for a particular day; or

(b) that no sum has been so fixed for a particular day and that a particular sum in sterling has been so fixed for a day which is the last day for which a sum has been so fixed before the particular day,

shall be conclusive evidence of those matters for the purposes of subsection (1) above; and a document purporting to be such a certificate shall in any proceedings be received in evidence and, unless the contrary is proved, be deemed to be such a certificate.

(3) The Treasury may charge a reasonable fee for any certificate given in pursuance of subsection (2) above, and any fee received by the Treasury by virtue of this subsection shall be paid into the Consolidated Fund.]

[454]

NOTES

Inserted by the Merchant Shipping Act 1995, s 314(2), Sch 13, para 45(1), (3).

2 Contracting States, etc

(1) If Her Majesty by Order in Council certifies to the following effect, that is to say, that for the purposes of the Rules—

(a) a State specified in the Order is a contracting State, or is a contracting State in respect of any place or territory so specified; or

(b) any place or territory specified in the Order forms part of a State so specified (whether a contracting State or not),

the Order shall, except so far as it has been superseded by a subsequent Order, be conclusive evidence of the matters so certified.

(2) An Order in Council under this section may be varied or revoked by a subsequent Order in Council.

[455]

NOTES

Orders in Council: the Carriage of Goods by Sea (Parties to Convention) Order 1985, SI 1985/443 at **[2338]**.

3 Absolute warranty of seaworthiness not to be implied in contracts to which Rules apply

There shall not be implied in any contract for the carriage of goods by sea to which the Rules apply by virtue of this Act any absolute undertaking by the carrier of the goods to provide a seaworthy ship.

[456]

4 Application of Act to British possessions, etc

(1) Her Majesty may by Order in Council direct that this Act shall extend, subject to such exceptions, adaptations and modifications as may be specified in the Order, to all or any of the following territories, that is—

(a) any colony (not being a colony for whose external relations a country other than the United Kingdom is responsible),

(b) any country outside Her Majesty's dominions in which Her Majesty has jurisdiction in right of Her Majesty's Government of the United Kingdom.

(2) An Order in Council under this section may contain such transitional and other consequential and incidental provisions as appear to Her Majesty to be expedient, including provisions amending or repealing any legislation about the carriage of goods by sea forming part of the law of any of the territories mentioned in paragraphs (a) and (b) above.

(3) An Order in Council under this section may be varied or revoked by a subsequent Order in Council.

[457]

NOTES

Orders in Council: the Carriage of Goods by Sea (Bermuda) Order 1980, SI 1980/1507; the Carriage of Goods by Sea (Bermuda) Order 1982, SI 1982/1662; the Carriage of Goods by Sea (Overseas Territories) Order 1982, SI 1982/1664; the Merchant Shipping (Revocation) (Bermuda) Order 2002, SI 2002/3147.

5 Extension of application of Rules to carriage from ports in British possessions, etc

(1) Her Majesty may by Order in Council provide that section 1(3) of this Act shall have effect as if the reference therein to the United Kingdom included a reference to all or any of the following territories, that is—

(a) the Isle of Man;

(b) any of the Channel Islands specified in the Order;

(c) any colony specified in the Order (not being a colony for whose external relations a country other than the United Kingdom is responsible);

(d) …

(e) any country specified in the Order, being a country outside Her Majesty's dominions in which Her Majesty has jurisdiction in right of Her Majesty's Government of the United Kingdom.

(2) An Order in Council under this section may be varied or revoked by a subsequent Order in Council.

[458]

NOTES

Sub-s (1): para (d) repealed by the Statute Law (Repeals) Act 1989.

6 Supplemental

(1) This Act may be cited as the Carriage of Goods by Sea Act 1971.

(2) It is hereby declared that this Act extends to Northern Ireland.

(3) The following enactments shall be repealed, that is—

(a) the Carriage of Goods by Sea Act 1924,

(b) section 12(4)(a) of the Nuclear Installations Act 1965,

and without prejudice to section 38(1) of the Interpretation Act 1889, the reference to the said Act of 1924 in section 1(1)(i)(ii) of the Hovercraft Act 1968 shall include a reference to this Act.

[(4) It is hereby declared that for the purposes of Article VIII of the Rules section 186 of the Merchant Shipping Act 1995 (which entirely exempts shipowners and others in certain circumstances or loss of, or damage to, goods) is a provision relating to limitation of liability.]

(5) This Act shall come into force on such day as Her Majesty may by Order in Council appoint, and, for the purposes of the transition from the law in force immediately before the day appointed under this subsection to the provisions of this Act, the Order appointing the day may provide that those provisions shall have effect subject to such transitional provisions as may be contained in the Order.

[459]

NOTES

Sub-s (4): substituted by the Merchant Shipping Act 1995, s 314(3), Sch 13, para 45(1), (4).

Interpretation Act 1889, s 38(1): repealed by the Interpretation Act 1978, s 25, Sch 3 and replaced by s 17(2)(a) of, and Sch 2, para 3 to, that Act.

Orders in Council: the Carriage of Goods by Sea Act 1971 (Commencement) Order 1977, SI 1977/981.

(*Schedule contains the text of the Hague Rules as amended by the Brussels Protocol, printed in Pt V(F) of this work at* **[4406]**.)

CARRIAGE OF GOODS BY SEA ACT 1992

(1992 c 50)

ARRANGEMENT OF SECTIONS

An Act to replace the Bills of Lading Act 1855 with new provision with respect to bills of lading and certain other shipping documents

[16 July 1992]

NOTES

This Act repeals the Bills of Lading Act 1855 and enacts new provisions relating not only to bills of lading but also to sea waybills and ship's delivery orders. The Act reforms and updates the law in respect of rights of suit relating to contracts for the carriage of goods by sea in accordance with the recommendations made by the Law Commission and the Scottish Law Commission in their report 'Rights of Suit in respect of Carriage of Goods by Sea' (Law Com No 196, Scot Law Com No 130, HC 250), published in March 1991.

1 Shipping documents etc to which Act applies

(1) This Act applies to the following documents, that is to say—

(a) any bill of lading;

(b) any sea waybill; and

(c) any ship's delivery order.

(2) References in this Act to a bill of lading—

(a) do not include references to a document which is incapable of transfer either by indorsement or, as a bearer bill, by delivery without indorsement; but

(b) subject to that, do include references to a received for shipment bill of lading.

(3) References in this Act to a sea waybill are references to any document which is not a bill of lading but—

(a) is such a receipt for goods as contains or evidences a contract for the carriage of goods by sea; and

(b) identifies the person to whom delivery of the goods is to be made by the carrier in accordance with that contract.

(4) References in this Act to a ship's delivery order are references to any document which is neither a bill of lading nor a sea waybill but contains an undertaking which—

(a) is given under or for the purposes of a contract for the carriage by sea of the goods to which the document relates, or of goods which include those goods; and

(b) is an undertaking by the carrier to a person identified in the document to deliver the goods to which the document relates to that person.

(5) The Secretary of State may by regulations make provision for the application of this Act to cases where [an electronic communications network] or any other information technology is used for effecting transactions corresponding to—

(a) the issue of a document to which this Act applies;
(b) the indorsement, delivery or other transfer of such a document; or
(c) the doing of anything else in relation to such a document.

(6) Regulations under subsection (5) above may—
(a) make such modifications of the following provisions of this Act as the Secretary of State considers appropriate in connection with the application of this Act to any case mentioned in that subsection; and
(b) contain supplemental, incidental, consequential and transitional provision;

and the power to make regulations under that subsection shall be exercisable by statutory instrument subject to annulment in pursuance of a resolution of either House of Parliament.

[460]

NOTES

Sub-s (5): words in square brackets substituted by the Communications Act 2003, s 406(1), Sch 17, para 119.

2 Rights under shipping documents

(1) Subject to the following provisions of this section, a person who becomes—
(a) the lawful holder of a bill of lading;
(b) the person who (without being an original party to the contract of carriage) is the person to whom delivery of the goods to which a sea waybill relates is to be made by the carrier in accordance with that contract; or
(c) the person to whom delivery of the goods to which a ship's delivery order relates is to be made in accordance with the undertaking contained in the order,

shall (by virtue of becoming the holder of the bill or, as the case may be, the person to whom delivery is to be made) have transferred to and vested in him all rights of suit under the contract of carriage as if he had been a party to that contract.

(2) Where, when a person becomes the lawful holder of a bill of lading, possession of the bill no longer gives a right (as against the carrier) to possession of the goods to which the bill relates, that person shall not have any rights transferred to him by virtue of subsection (1) above unless he becomes the holder of the bill—
(a) by virtue of a transaction effected in pursuance of any contractual or other arrangements made before the time when such a right to possession ceased to attach to possession of the bill; or
(b) as a result of the rejection to that person by another person of goods or documents delivered to the other person in pursuance of any such arrangements.

(3) The rights vested in any person by virtue of the operation of subsection (1) above in relation to a ship's delivery order—
(a) shall be so vested subject to the terms of the order; and
(b) where the goods to which the order relates form a part only of the goods to which the contract of carriage relates, shall be confined to rights in respect of the goods to which the order relates.

(4) Where, in the case of any document to which this Act applies—
(a) a person with any interest or right in or in relation to goods to which the document relates sustains loss or damage in consequence of a breach of the contract of carriage; but
(b) subsection (1) above operates in relation to that document so that rights of suit in respect of that breach are vested in another person,

the other person shall be entitled to exercise those rights for the benefit of the person who sustained the loss or damage to the same extent as they could have been exercised if they had been vested in the person for whose benefit they are exercised.

(5) Where rights are transferred by virtue of the operation of subsection (1) above in relation to any document, the transfer for which that subsection provides shall extinguish any entitlement to those rights which derives—
(a) where that document is a bill of lading, from a person's having been an original party to the contract of carriage; or
(b) in the case of any document to which this Act applies, from the previous operation of that subsection in relation to that document;

but the operation of that subsection shall be without prejudice to any rights which derive from a person's having been an original party to the contract contained in, or evidenced by, a sea waybill and, in relation to a ship's delivery order, shall be without prejudice to any rights deriving otherwise than from the previous operation of that subsection in relation to that order.

[461]

3 Liabilities under shipping documents

(1) Where subsection (1) of section 2 of this Act operates in relation to any document to which this Act applies and the person in whom rights are vested by virtue of that subsection—

(a) takes or demands delivery from the carrier of any of the goods to which the document relates;

(b) makes a claim under the contract of carriage against the carrier in respect of any of those goods; or

(c) is a person who, at a time before those rights were vested in him, took or demanded delivery from the carrier of any of those goods,

that person shall (by virtue of taking or demanding delivery or making the claim or, in a case falling within paragraph (c) above, of having the rights vested in him) become subject to the same liabilities under that contract as if he had been a party to that contract.

(2) Where the goods to which a ship's delivery order relates form a part only of the goods to which the contract of carriage relates, the liabilities to which any person is subject by virtue of the operation of this section in relation to that order shall exclude liabilities in respect of any goods to which the order does not relate.

(3) This section, so far as it imposes liabilities under any contract on any person, shall be without prejudice to the liabilities under the contract of any person as an original party to the contract.

[462]

4 Representations in bills of lading

A bill of lading which—

(a) represents goods to have been shipped on board a vessel or to have been received for shipment on board a vessel; and

(b) has been signed by the master of the vessel or by a person who was not the master but had the express, implied or apparent authority of the carrier to sign bills of lading,

shall, in favour of a person who has become the lawful holder of the bill, be conclusive evidence against the carrier of the shipment of the goods or, as the case may be, of their receipt for shipment.

[463]

5 Interpretation

(1) In this Act—

"bill of lading", "sea waybill" and "ship's delivery order" shall be construed in accordance with section 1 above;

"the contract of carriage"—

(a) in relation to a bill of lading or sea waybill, means the contract contained in or evidenced by that bill or waybill; and

(b) in relation to a ship's delivery order, means the contract under or for the purposes of which the undertaking contained in the order is given;

"holder", in relation to a bill of lading, shall be construed in accordance with subsection (2) below;

"information technology" includes any computer or other technology by means of which information or other matter may be recorded or communicated without being reduced to documentary form; . . .

. . .

(2) References in this Act to the holder of a bill of lading are references to any of the following persons, that is to say—

(a) a person with possession of the bill who, by virtue of being the person identified in the bill, is the consignee of the goods to which the bill relates;

(b) a person with possession of the bill as a result of the completion, by delivery of the bill, of any indorsement of the bill or, in the case of a bearer bill, of any other transfer of the bill;

(c) a person with possession of the bill as a result of any transaction by virtue of which he would have become a holder falling within paragraph (a) or (b) above had not the transaction been effected at a time when possession of the bill no longer gave a right (as against the carrier) to possession of the goods to which the bill relates;

and a person shall be regarded for the purposes of this Act as having become the lawful holder of a bill of lading wherever he has become the holder of the bill in good faith.

(3) References in this Act to a person's being identified in a document include references to his being identified by a description which allows for the identity of the person in question to be varied, in accordance with the terms of the document, after its issue; and the reference in section 1(3)(b) of this Act to a document's identifying a person shall be construed accordingly.

(4) Without prejudice to sections 2(2) and 4 above, nothing in this Act shall preclude its operation in relation to a case where the goods to which a document relates—

(a) cease to exist after the issue of the document; or

(b) cannot be identified (whether because they are mixed with other goods or for any other reason);

and references in this Act to the goods to which a document relates shall be construed accordingly.

(5) The preceding provisions of this Act shall have effect without prejudice to the application, in relation to any case, of the rules (the Hague-Visby Rules) which for the time being have the force of law by virtue of section 1 of the Carriage of Goods by Sea Act 1971. **[464]**

NOTES

Sub-s (1): words omitted repealed by the Communications Act 2003, s 406(7), Sch 19(1).

6 Short title, repeal, commencement and extent

(1) This Act may be cited as the Carriage of Goods by Sea Act 1992.

(2) The Bills of Lading Act 1855 is hereby repealed.

(3) This Act shall come into force at the end of the period of two months beginning with the day on which it is passed; but nothing in this Act shall have effect in relation to any document issued before the coming into force of this Act.

(4) This Act extends to Northern Ireland.

[465]

MERCHANT SHIPPING ACT 1995

(1995 c 21)

ARRANGEMENT OF SECTIONS

PART VII
LIABILITY OF SHIPOWNERS AND OTHERS

Carriage of passengers and luggage by sea

Limitation of liability of shipowners, etc and salvors for maritime claims

An Act to consolidate the Merchant Shipping Acts 1894 to 1994 and other enactments relating to merchant shipping

[19 July 1995]

1–182 ((*Pts I–VI) relate to British ships and their registration, masters and seamen, safety, fishing vessels and the prevention of pollution.*)

PART VII
LIABILITY OF SHIPOWNERS AND OTHERS

Carriage of passengers and luggage by sea

183 Scheduled convention to have force of law

(1) The provisions of the Convention relating to the Carriage of Passengers and their Luggage by Sea as set out in Part I of Schedule 6 (hereafter in this section and in Part II of that Schedule referred to as "the Convention") shall have the force of law in the United Kingdom.

(2) The provisions of Part II of that Schedule shall have effect in connection with the Convention and subsection (1) above shall have effect subject to the provisions of that Part.

(3) If it appears to Her Majesty in Council that there is a conflict between the provisions of this section or of Part I or II of Schedule 6 and any provisions relating to the carriage of passengers or luggage for reward by land, sea or air in—

(a) any convention which has been signed or ratified by or on behalf of the government of the United Kingdom before 4th April 1979 (excluding the Convention); or

(b) any enactment of the Parliament of the United Kingdom giving effect to such a convention,

She may by Order in Council make such modifications of this section or that Schedule or any such enactment as She considers appropriate for resolving the conflict.

(4) If it appears to Her Majesty in Council that the government of the United Kingdom has agreed to any revision of the Convention She may by Order in Council make such modification of Parts I and II of Schedule 6 as She considers appropriate in consequence of the revision.

(5) Nothing in subsection (1) or (2) above or in any modification made by virtue of subsection (3) or (4) above shall affect any rights or liabilities arising out of an occurrence which took place before the day on which the said subsection (1) or (2) above, or as the case may be, the modification, comes into force.

(6) This section shall bind the Crown, and any Order in Council made by virtue of this section may provide that the Order or specified provisions of it shall bind the Crown.

(7) A draft of an Order in Council proposed to be made under subsection (3) or (4) above shall not be submitted to Her Majesty in Council unless the draft has been approved by a resolution of each House of Parliament.

[466]

184 Application of Schedule 6 to carriage within British Islands

(1) Her Majesty may by Order in Council provide that Part I of Schedule 6—

(a) shall have the force of law in the United Kingdom, with such modifications as are specified in the Order, in relation to, and to matters connected with, a contract of carriage where the places of departure and destination under the contract are within the British Islands and under the contract there is no intermediate port of call outside those Islands; and

(b) shall, as modified in pursuance of paragraph (a) above, have effect in relation to, and to matters connected with, any such contract subject to the provisions of Part II of that Schedule or to those provisions with such modifications as are specified in the Order.

(2) An Order in Council made by virtue of subsection (1) above may contain such provisions, including provisions modifying section 28 of the Unfair Contract Terms Act 1977 (which relates to certain contracts as respects which the Convention mentioned in section 183(1) does not have the force of law in the United Kingdom), as the Secretary of State considers appropriate for the purpose of dealing with matters arising in connection with any contract to which the said section 28 applies before the Order is made.

(3) An Order in Council made by virtue of subsection (1) above may provide that the Order or specified provisions of it shall bind the Crown.

(4) A draft of an Order in Council proposed to be made by virtue of subsection (1) above shall not be submitted to Her Majesty in Council unless the draft of the Order in Council has been approved by a resolution of each House of Parliament.

(5) In subsection (1) above expressions to which meanings are assigned by article 1 of the Convention set out in Part I of Schedule 6 have those meanings but any reference to a contract of carriage excludes such a contract which is not for reward.

[467]

NOTES

Orders in Council: by virtue of the Interpretation Act 1978, s 17(2)(b), the Carriage of Passengers and their Luggage by Sea (Interim Provisions) Order 1980, SI 1980/1092 at **[2330]** and the Carriage of Passengers and their Luggage by Sea (Domestic Carriage) Order 1987, SI 1987/670 at **[2345]**, have effect as if made under this section.

Limitation of liability of shipowners, etc and salvors for maritime claims

185 Limitation of liability for maritime claims

(1) The provisions of the Convention on Limitation of Liability for Maritime Claims 1976 as set out in Part I of Schedule 7 (in this section and Part II of that Schedule referred to as "the Convention") shall have the force of law in the United Kingdom.

(2) The provisions of Part II of that Schedule shall have effect in connection with the Convention, and subsection (1) above shall have effect subject to the provisions of that Part.

[(2A) Her Majesty may by Order in Council make such modifications of Parts I and II of Schedule 7 as She considers appropriate in consequence of the revision of the Convention by the Protocol of 1996 amending the Convention (in this section referred to as "the 1996 Protocol").

(2B) If it appears to Her Majesty in Council that the Government of the United Kingdom has agreed to any further revision of the Convention or to any revision of article 8 of the 1996 Protocol, She may by Order in Council make such modifications of Parts I and II of Schedule 7 and subsections (2C) and (2D) below as She considers appropriate in consequence of the revision.

(2C) The Secretary of State may by order make such amendments of Parts I and II of Schedule 7 as appear to him to be appropriate for the purpose of giving effect to any amendment of a relevant limit which is adopted in accordance with article 8 of the 1996 Protocol.

(2D) In subsection (2C) above "a relevant limit" means any of the limits for the time being specified in either of the following provisions of the Convention—

(a) article 6, paragraph 1, and

(b) article 7, paragraph 1.

(2E) No modification made by virtue of subsection (2A), (2B) or (2C) above shall affect any rights or liabilities arising out of an occurrence which took place before the day on which the modification comes into force.]

(3) The provisions having the force of law under this section shall apply in relation to Her Majesty's ships as they apply in relation to other ships.

(4) The provisions having the force of law under this section shall not apply to any liability in respect of loss of life or personal injury caused to, or loss of or damage to any property of, a person who is on board the ship in question or employed in connection with that ship or with the salvage operations in question if—

(a) he is so on board or employed under a contract of service governed by the law of any part of the United Kingdom; and

(b) the liability arises from an occurrence which took place after the commencement of this Act.

In this subsection, "ship" and "salvage operations" have the same meaning as in the Convention.

[(5) A draft of an Order in Council proposed to be made by virtue of subsection (2A) or (2B) above shall not be submitted to Her Majesty in Council unless it has been approved by a resolution of each House of Parliament.]

[468]

NOTES

Sub-ss (2A)–(2E): inserted by the Merchant Shipping and Maritime Security Act 1997, s 15(1).
Sub-s (5): added by the Merchant Shipping and Maritime Security Act 1997, s 15(2).

186 Exclusion of liability

(1) Subject to subsection (3) below, the owner of a United Kingdom ship shall not be liable for any loss or damage in the following cases, namely—

(a) where any property on board the ship is lost or damaged by reason of fire on board the ship; or

(b) where any gold, silver, watches, jewels or precious stones on board the ship are lost or damaged by reason of theft, robbery or other dishonest conduct and their nature and value were not at the time of shipment declared by their owner or shipper to the owner or master of the ship in the bill of lading or otherwise in writing.

(2) Subject to subsection (3) below, where the loss or damage arises from anything done or omitted by any person in his capacity of master or member of the crew or (otherwise than in that capacity) in the course of his employment as a servant of the owner of the ship, subsection (1) above shall also exclude the liability of—

(a) the master, member of the crew or servant; and

(b) in a case where the master or member of the crew is the servant of a person whose liability would not be excluded by that subsection apart from this paragraph, the person whose servant he is.

(3) This section does not exclude the liability of any person for any loss or damage resulting from any such personal act or omission of his as is mentioned in Article 4 of the Convention set out in Part I of Schedule 7.

(4) This section shall apply in relation to Her Majesty's ships as it applies in relation to other ships.

(5) In this section "owner", in relation to a ship, includes any part owner and any charterer, manager or operator of the ship.

[469]

Multiple fault; apportionment, liability and contribution

187 Damage or loss: apportionment of liability

(1) Where, by the fault of two or more ships, damage or loss is caused to one or more of those ships, to their cargoes or freight, or to any property on board, the liability to make good the damage or loss shall be in proportion to the degree in which each ship was in fault.

(2) If, in any such case, having regard to all the circumstances, it is not possible to establish different degrees of fault, the liability shall be apportioned equally.

(3) This section applies to persons other than the owners of a ship who are responsible for the fault of the ships, as well as to the owners of a ship and where, by virtue of any charter or demise, or for any other reason, the owners are not responsible for the navigation and management of the ship, this section applies to the charterers or other persons for the time being so responsible instead of the owners.

(4) Nothing in this section shall operate so as to render any ship liable for any loss or damage to which the fault of the ship has not contributed.

(5) Nothing in this section shall affect the liability of any person under a contract of carriage or any contract, or shall be construed as imposing any liability upon any person from which he is exempted by any contract or by any provision of law, or as affecting the right of any person to limit his liability in the manner provided by law.

(6) In this section "freight" includes passage money and hire.

(7) In this section references to damage or loss caused by the fault of a ship include references to any salvage or other expenses, consequent upon that fault, recoverable at law by way of damages.

[470]

188 Loss of life or personal injuries: joint and several liability

(1) Where loss of life or personal injuries are suffered by any person on board a ship owing to the fault of that ship and of any other ship or ships, the liability of the owners of the ships shall be joint and several.

(2) Subsection (3) of section 187 applies also to this section.

(3) Nothing in this section shall be construed as depriving any person of any right of defence on which, apart from this section, he might have relied in an action brought against him by the person injured, or any person or persons entitled to sue in respect of such loss of life, or shall affect the right of any person to limit his liability in the manner provided by law.

(4) Subsection (7) of section 187 applies also for the interpretation of this section.

[471]

189 Loss of life or personal injuries: right of contribution

(1) Where loss of life or personal injuries are suffered by any person on board a ship owing to the fault of that ship and any other ship or ships, and a proportion of the damages is recovered against the owners of one of the ships which exceeds the proportion in which the ship was in fault, they may recover by way of contribution the amount of the excess from the owners of the other ship or ships to the extent to which those ships were respectively in fault.

(2) Subsection (3) of section 187 applies also to this section.

(3) Nothing in this section authorises the recovery of any amount which could not, by reason of any statutory or contractual limitation of, or exemption from, liability, or which could not for any other reason, have been recovered in the first instance as damages by the persons entitled to sue therefor.

(4) In addition to any other remedy provided by law, the persons entitled to any contribution recoverable under this section shall, for the purposes of recovering it, have the same rights and powers as the persons entitled to sue for damages in the first instance.

[472]

Time limit for proceedings against owners or ship

190 Time limit for proceedings against owners or ship

(1) This section applies to any proceedings to enforce any claim or lien against a ship or her owners—

(a) in respect of damage or loss caused by the fault of that ship to another ship, its cargo or freight or any property on board it; or

(b) for damages for loss of life or personal injury caused by the fault of that ship to any person on board another ship.

(2) The extent of the fault is immaterial for the purposes of this section.

(3) Subject to subsections (5) and (6) below, no proceedings to which this section applies shall be brought after the period of two years from the date when—

(a) the damage or loss was caused; or

(b) the loss of life or injury was suffered.

(4) Subject to subsections (5) and (6) below, no proceedings under any of sections 187 to 189 to enforce any contribution in respect of any overpaid proportion of any damages for loss of life or personal injury shall be brought after the period of one year from the date of payment.

(5) Any court having jurisdiction in such proceedings may, in accordance with rules of court, extend the period allowed for bringing proceedings to such extent and on such conditions as it thinks fit.

(6) Any such court, if satisfied that there has not been during any period allowed for bringing proceedings any reasonable opportunity of arresting the defendant ship within—

(a) the jurisdiction of the court, or

(b) the territorial sea of the country to which the plaintiff's ship belongs or in which the plaintiff resides or has his principal place of business,

shall extend the period allowed for bringing proceedings to an extent sufficient to give a reasonable opportunity of so arresting the ship.

[473]

Limitation of liability of harbour, conservancy, dock and canal authorities

191 Limitation of liability

(1) This section applies in relation to the following authorities and persons, that is to say, a harbour authority, a conservancy authority and the owners of any dock or canal.

(2) The liability of any authority or person to which this section applies for any loss or damage caused to any ship, or to any goods, merchandise or other things whatsoever on board any ship shall be limited in accordance with subsection (5) below by reference to the tonnage of the largest United Kingdom ship which, at the time of the loss or damage is, or within the preceding five years has been, within the area over which the authority or person discharges any functions.

(3) The limitation of liability under this section relates to the whole of any losses and damages which may arise on any one distinct occasion, although such losses and damages may be sustained by more than one person, and shall apply whether the liability arises at common law or under any general or local or private Act, and notwithstanding anything contained in such an Act.

(4) This section does not exclude the liability of an authority or person to which it applies for any loss or damage resulting from any such personal act or omission of the authority or person as is mentioned in Article 4 of the Convention set out in Part I of Schedule 7.

(5) The limit of liability shall be ascertained by applying to the ship by reference to which the liability is to be determined the method of calculation specified in paragraph 1(b) of Article 6 of the Convention set out in Part I of Schedule 7 read with paragraph 5(1) and (2) of Part II of that Schedule.

(6) Articles 11 and 12 of that Convention and paragraphs 8 and 9 of Part II of that Schedule shall apply for the purposes of this section.

(7) For the purposes of subsection (2) above a ship shall not be treated as having been within the area over which a harbour authority or conservancy authority discharges any functions by reason only that it has been built or fitted out within the area, or that it has taken shelter within or passed through the area on a voyage between two places both situated outside that area, or that it has loaded or unloaded mails or passengers within the area.

(8) Nothing in this section imposes any liability for any loss or damage where no liability exists apart from this section.

(9) In this section—

"dock" includes wet docks and basins, tidal docks and basins, locks, cuts, entrances, dry docks, graving docks, gridirons, slips, quays, wharves, piers, stages, landing places and jetties; and

"owners of any dock or canal" includes any authority or person having the control and management of any dock or canal, as the case may be.

[474]

Application to Crown and its ships

192 Application to Crown and its ships

(1) Sections 185, 186, 187, 188, 189 and 190 (except subsection (6)) apply in the case of Her Majesty's ships as they apply in relation to other ships and section 191 applies to the Crown in its capacity as an authority or person specified in subsection (1).

(2) In this section "Her Majesty's ships" means—

(a) ships of which the beneficial interest is vested in Her Majesty;

(b) ships which are registered as Government ships;

(c) ships which are for the time being demised or sub-demised to or in the exclusive possession of the Crown;

except that it does not include any ship in which Her Majesty is interested otherwise than in right of Her Government in the United Kingdom unless that ship is for the time being demised or sub-demised to Her Majesty in right of Her Government in the United Kingdom or in the exclusive possession of Her Majesty in that right.

(3) In the application of subsection (2) above to Northern Ireland, any reference to Her Majesty's Government in the United Kingdom includes a reference to Her Government in Northern Ireland.

[475]

[Regulations requiring insurance or security

192A Compulsory insurance or security

(1) Subject to subsections (2) and (3) below, the Secretary of State may make regulations requiring that, in such cases as may be prescribed by the regulations, while a ship is in United Kingdom waters, there must be in force in respect of the ship—

(a) a contract of insurance insuring such person or persons as may be specified by the regulations against such liabilities as may be so specified and satisfying such other requirements as may be so specified, or

(b) such other security relating to those liabilities as satisfies requirements specified by or under the regulations.

(2) Regulations under this section shall not apply in relation to—

(a) a qualifying foreign ship while it is exercising—

(i) the right of innocent passage, or

(ii) the right of transit passage through straits used for international navigation,

(b) any warship, or

(c) any ship for the time being used by the government of any State for other than commercial purposes.

(3) Regulations under this section may not require insurance or security to be maintained in respect of a ship in relation to any liability in any case where an obligation to maintain insurance or security in respect of that ship in relation to that liability is imposed by section 163 or by or under an Order in Council under section 182B.

(4) Regulations under this section may require that, where a person is obliged to have in force in respect of a ship a contract of insurance or other security, such documentary evidence as may be specified by or under the regulations of the existence of the contract of insurance or other security must be carried in the ship and produced on demand, by such persons as may be specified in the regulations, to such persons as may be so specified.

(5) Regulations under this section may provide—

(a) that in such cases as are prescribed a ship which contravenes the regulations shall be liable to be detained and that section 284 shall have effect, with such modifications (if any) as are prescribed by the regulations, in relation to the ship,

(b) that a contravention of the regulations shall be an offence punishable on summary conviction by a fine of an amount not exceeding £50,000, or such less amount as is prescribed by the regulations, and on conviction on indictment by a fine, and

(c) that any such contravention shall be an offence punishable only on summary conviction by a fine of an amount not exceeding £50,000, or such less amount as is prescribed by the regulations.

(6) Regulations under this section may—

(a) make different provision for different cases,

(b) make provision in terms of any document which the Secretary of State or any person considers relevant from time to time, and

(c) include such incidental, supplemental and transitional provision as appears to the Secretary of State to be expedient for the purposes of the regulations.]

[476]

NOTES

Inserted, together with preceding cross-heading, by the Merchant Shipping and Maritime Security Act 1997, s 16.

Regulations: the Merchant Shipping (Compulsory Insurance: Ships Receiving Trans-shipped Fish) Regulations 1998, SI 1998/209.

193–291 ((*Pts VIII–XII*) *relate to lighthouses, salvage and wreck, enforcement officers and powers, and legal proceedings.*)

PART XIII
SUPPLEMENTAL

292–312 (*Relate to general administrative and financial provisions, subordinate legislation, the application of the Act to certain classes of ships, and special provision for Scots law.*)

Final provisions

313–315 (*Relate to interpretation, repeals, consequential amendments and transitional provisions.*)

316 Short title and commencement

(1) This Act may be cited as the Merchant Shipping Act 1995.

(2) This Act shall come into force on 1st January 1996.

[477]

(Schs 1, 2, 4, 5, 5A relate to private law provisions for registered ships, regulations for submersible and supporting apparatus, transitional provision in connection with the prevention of pollution and the liability of the International Oil Pollution Compensation Fund; Sch 3 repealed by the Merchant Shipping (Load Line) Regulations 1998, SI 1998/2241, reg 3(1)(d).)

SCHEDULE 6
CONVENTION RELATING TO THE CARRIAGE OF PASSENGERS AND THEIR LUGGAGE BY SEA

Section 183

PART I
TEXT OF CONVENTION

Article 1
Definitions

In this Convention the following expressions have the meaning here assigned to them:

1.—(a) "carrier" means a person by or on behalf of whom a contract carriage has been concluded, whether the carriage is actual performed by him or by a performing carrier;

(b) "performing carrier" means a person other than the carrier, being the owner, charterer or operator of a ship, who actually performs the who or a part of the carriage;

2. "contract of carriage" means a contract made by or on behalf of a carrier the carriage by sea of a passenger or of a passenger and his luggage, as the may be;

3. "ship" means only a seagoing vessel, excluding an air-cushion vehicle;

4. "passenger" means any person carried in a ship,

(a) under a contract of carriage, or

(b) who, with the consent of the carrier, is accompanying a vehicle or live animals which are covered by a contract for the carriage of goods not governed by this Convention;

5. "luggage" means any article or vehicle carried by the carrier under a contract of carriage, excluding:

(a) articles and vehicles carried under a charter party, bill of lading or other contract primarily concerned with the carriage of goods, and

(b) live animals;

6. "cabin luggage" means luggage which the passenger has in his cabin or is otherwise in his possession, custody or control. Except for the application of paragraph 8 of this Article and Article 8, cabin luggage includes luggage which passenger has in or on his vehicle;

7. "loss of or damage to luggage" includes pecuniary loss resulting from the luggage not having been re-delivered to the passenger within a reasonable time after the arrival of the ship on which the luggage has been or should have been carried, but does not include delays resulting from labour disputes;

8. "carriage" covers the following periods:

(a) with regard to the passenger and his cabin luggage, the period during which the passenger and/or his cabin luggage are on board the ship or in the course of embarkation or disembarkation, and the period during which the passenger and his cabin luggage are transported by water from land to the ship or vice versa, if the cost of such transport is included in the fare or if the vessel used for the purpose of auxiliary transport has been put at the disposal of the passenger by the carrier. However, with regard to the passenger, carriage does not include the period during which he is in a marine terminal or station or on a quay or in or on any other port installation;

(b) with regard to cabin luggage, also the period during which the passenger is in a marine terminal or station or on a quay or in or on any other port installation if that luggage has been taken over by the carrier or his servant or agent and has not been re-delivered to the passenger;

(c) with regard to other luggage which is not cabin luggage, the period from the time of its taking over by the carrier or his servant or agent onshore or on board until the time of its re-delivery by the carrier or his servant or agent;

9. "international carriage" means any carriage in which, according to the contract of carriage, the place of departure and the place of destination are situated in two different States, or in a single State if, according to the contract carriage or the scheduled itinerary, there is an intermediate port of call in another State.

Article 2
Application

1. This Convention shall apply to any international carriage if:
   (a) the ship is flying the flag of or is registered in a State Party to the Convention, or
   (b) the contract of carriage has been made in a State Party to the Convention, or
   (c) the place of departure or destination, according to the contract carriage, is in a State Party to this Convention.

2. Notwithstanding paragraph 1 of this Article, this Convention shall apply when the carriage is subject, under any other international convention concerning the carriage of passengers or luggage by another mode of transport to a civil liability regime under the provisions of such convention, in so far those provisions have mandatory application to carriage by sea.

Article 3
Liability of the carrier

1. The carrier shall be liable for the damage suffered as a result of the death or personal injury to a passenger and the loss of or damage to luggage if the incident which caused the damage so suffered occurred in the course of the carriage and was due to the fault or neglect of the carrier or of his servants agents acting within the scope of their employment.

2. The burden of proving that the incident which caused the loss or damage occurred in the course of the carriage, and the extent of the loss or damage, shall lie with the claimant.

3. Fault or neglect of the carrier or of his servants or agents acting within the scope of their employment shall be presumed, unless the contrary is proved, if the death of or personal injury to the passenger or the loss of or damage to cabin luggage arose from or in connection with the shipwreck, collision, stranding explosion or fire, or defect in the ship. In respect of loss of or damage to other luggage, such fault or neglect shall be presumed, unless the contrary is proved irrespective of the nature of the incident which caused the loss or damage. In all other cases the burden of proving fault or neglect shall lie with the claimant.

Article 4
Performing carrier

1. If the performance of the carriage or part thereof has been entrusted to a performing carrier, the carrier shall nevertheless remain liable for the entitled carriage according to the provisions of this Convention. In addition, the performing carrier shall be subject and entitled to the provisions of the Convention for the part of the carriage performed by him.

2. The carrier shall, in relation to the carriage performed by the performing carrier, be liable for the acts and omissions of the performing carrier and of his servants and agents acting within the scope of their employment.

3. Any special agreement under which the carrier assumes obligations not imposed by this Convention or any waiver of rights conferred by this Convention shall affect the performing carrier only if agreed by him expressly and in writing.

4. Where and to the extent that both the carrier and the performing carrier are liable, their liability shall be joint and several.

5. Nothing in this Article shall prejudice any right of recourse as between the carrier and the performing carrier.

Article 5
Valuables

The carrier shall not be liable for the loss of or damage to monies, negotiable securities, gold, silverware, jewellery, ornaments, works of art, or other valuables, except where such valuables have been deposited with the carrier for the agreed purpose of safe-keeping in which case the carrier shall be liable up to the limit provided for in paragraph 3 of Article 8 unless a higher limit is agreed on in accordance with paragraph 1 of Article 10.

Article 6
Contributory fault

If the carrier proves that the death of or personal injury to a passenger or the loss of or damage to his luggage was caused or contributed to by the fault or neglect of the passenger, the court seized of the case may exonerate the carrier wholly or partly from his liability in accordance with the provisions of the law of at court.

Article 7
Limit of liability personal injury

1. The liability of the carrier for the death of or personal injury to a passenger shall in no case exceed 46,666 units of account per carriage. Where in accordance with the law of the court seized of the case damages are awarded in the form of periodical income payments, the equivalent capital value of those payments shall not exceed the said limit.

2. Notwithstanding paragraph 1 of this Article, the national law of any State Party to this Convention may fix, as far as carriers who are nationals of such State are concerned, a higher per capita limit of liability.

Article 8
Limit of liability for loss of or damage to luggage

1. The liability of the carrier for the loss of or damage to cabin luggage shall no case exceed 833 units of account per passenger, per carriage.

2. The liability of the carrier for the loss of or damage to vehicles including all luggage carried in or on the vehicle shall in no case exceed 3,333 units of account vehicle per carriage.

3. The liability of the carrier for the loss of or damage to luggage other than that mentioned in paragraphs 1 and 2 of this Article shall in no case exceed 1,200 bits of account per passenger, per carriage.

4. The carrier and the passenger may agree that the liability of the carrier shall be subject to a deduction not exceeding 117 units of account in the case of damage to a vehicle and not exceeding 13 units of account per passenger in the case of loss of or damage to other luggage, such sum to be deducted from the loss or damage.

Article 9
Unit of account and conversion

The Unit of Account mentioned in this Convention is the special drawing right as defined by the International Monetary Fund. The amounts mentioned Articles 7 and 8 shall be converted into the national currency of the State of the court seized of the case on the basis of the value of that currency on the date the judgment or the date agreed upon by the Parties.

Article 10
Supplementary provisions on limits of liability

1. The carrier and the passenger may agree, expressly and in writing, to higher limits of liability than those prescribed in Articles 7 and 8.

2. Interest on damages and legal costs shall not be included in the limits of liability prescribed in Articles 7 and 8.

Article 11
Defences and limits for carriers' servants

If an action is brought against a servant or agent of the carrier or of the performing carrier arising out of damage covered by this Convention, such servant or agent, if he proves that he acted within the scope of his employment, shall be entitled to avail himself of the defences and limits of liability which the carrier or the performing carrier is entitled to invoke under this Convention.

Article 12
Aggregation of claims

1. Where the limits of liability prescribed in Articles 7 and 8 take effect, they shall apply to the aggregate of the amounts recoverable in all claims arising out of the death of or personal injury to any one passenger or the loss of or damage to his luggage.

2. In relation to the carriage performed by a performing carrier, the aggregate of the amounts recoverable from the carrier and the performing carrier and from their servants and agents acting within the scope of their employment shall not exceed the highest amount which could be awarded against either the carrier or the performing carrier under this Convention, but none of the persons mentioned shall be liable for a sum in excess of the limit applicable to him.

3. In any case where a servant or agent of the carrier or of the performing carrier is entitled under Article 11 of this Convention to avail himself of the limit of liability prescribed in Articles 7 and 8, the aggregate of the amount recoverable from the carrier, or the performing carrier as the case may be, an from that servant or agent, shall not exceed those limits.

Article 13
Loss of right to limit liability

1. The carrier shall not be entitled to the benefit of the limits of liability prescribed in Articles 7 and 8 and paragraph 1 of Article 10, if it is proved that the damage resulted from an act or omission of the carrier done with the intent to cause such damage, or recklessly and with knowledge that such damage would probably result.

2. The servant or agent of the carrier or of the performing carrier shall not be entitled to the benefit of those limits if it is proved that the damage resulted from an act or omission of that servant or agent done with the intent to cause such damage, or recklessly and with knowledge that such damage would probably result.

Article 14
Basis for claims

No action for damages for the death of or personal injury to a passenger, or for the loss of or damage to luggage, shall be brought against a carrier or performing carrier otherwise than in accordance with this Convention.

Article 15
Notice of loss or damage to luggage

1. The passenger shall give written notice to the carrier or his agent:

(a) in the case of apparent damage to luggage:
(i) for cabin luggage, before or at the time of disembarkation of the passenger;
(ii) for all other luggage, before or at the time of its re-delivery;
(b) in the case of damage to luggage which is not apparent, or loss of luggage, within 15 days from the date of disembarkation or re-delivery or from the time when such re-delivery should have taken place.

2. If the passenger fails to comply with this Article, he shall be presumed, unless the contrary is proved, to have received the luggage undamaged.

3. The notice in writing need not be given if the condition of the luggage has the time of its receipt been the subject of joint survey or inspection.

Article 16
Time-bar for actions

1. Any action for damages arising out of the death of or personal injury to a passenger or for the loss of or damage to luggage shall be time-barred after a period of two years.

2. The limitation period shall be calculated as follows:

(a) in the case of personal injury, from the date of disembarkation of the passenger:
(b) in the case of death occurring during carriage, from the date when the passenger should have disembarked, and in the case of personal injury occurring during carriage and resulting in the death of the passenger after disembarkation, from the date of death, provided that this period shall not exceed three years from the date of disembarkation;
(c) in the case of loss of or damage to luggage, from the date of disembarkation or from the date when disembarkation should have taken place, whichever is later.

3. The law of the court seized of the case shall govern the grounds of suspension and interruption of limitation periods, but in no case shall an action under this Convention be brought after the expiration of a period of three years from the date of disembarkation of the passenger or from the date when disembarkation should have taken place, whichever is later.

4. Notwithstanding paragraphs 1, 2 and 3 of this Article, the period of limitation may be extended by a declaration of the carrier or by agreement of the parties after the cause of action has arisen. The declaration or agreement shall be in writing.

Article 17
Competent jurisdiction

1. An action arising under this Convention shall, at the option of the claimant, be brought before one of the courts listed below, provided that the court located in a State Party to this Convention:

(a) the court of the place of permanent residence or principal place of business of the defendant, or
(b) the court of the place of departure or that of the destination according to the contract of carriage, or
(c) a court of the State of the domicile or permanent residence of the claimant, if the defendant has a place of business and is subject to jurisdiction in that State, or
(d) a court of the State where the contract of carriage was made, if the defendant has a place of business and is subject to jurisdiction in the State.

2. After the occurrence of the incident which has caused the damage, the parties may agree that the claim for damages shall be submitted to any jurisdiction or to arbitration.

Article 18
Invalidity of contractual provisions

Any contractual provision concluded before the occurrence of the incident which has caused the death of or personal injury to a passenger or the loss of or damage to his luggage, purporting to relieve the carrier of his liability toward the passenger or to prescribe a lower limit of liability than that fixed in this Convention except as provided in paragraph 4 of Article 8, and any such provision purporting to shift the burden of proof which rests on the carrier, or having the effect of restricting the option specified in paragraph 1 of Article 17 shall be null and void, but the nullity of that provision shall not render void the contract of carriage which shall remain subject to the provisions of this Convention.

Article 19
Other conventions on limitation of liability

This Convention shall not modify the rights or duties of the carrier, the performing carrier, and their servants or agents provided for in international conventions relating to the limitation of liability of owners of seagoing ships.

Article 20
Nuclear damage

No liability shall arise under this Convention for damage caused by a nuclear incident:

(a) if the operator of a nuclear installation is liable to such damage under either the Paris Convention of 29 July 1960 on Third Party Liability in the Field of Nuclear Energy as amended by its Additional Protocol of 28 January 1964, or the Vienna Convention of 21 May 1963 on Civil Liability for Nuclear Damage, or

(b) if the operator of a nuclear installation is liable for such damage by virtue of a national law governing the liability for such damage, provided that such law is in all respects as favourable to persons who may suffer damage as either the Paris or the Vienna Conventions.

Article 21
Commercial carriage by public authorities

This Convention shall apply to commercial carriage undertaken by States or Public Authorities under contracts of carriage within the meaning of Article 1.

[478]

NOTES

Modification: in Article 7, para 1 the limit of liability of carriers is modified, in relation to any carrier whose principal place of business is in the United Kingdom, by the Carriage of Passengers and their Luggage by Sea (United Kingdom Carriers) Order 1998, SI 1998/2917, art 3.

PART II
PROVISIONS HAVING EFFECT IN CONNECTION WITH CONVENTION

Interpretation

1. In this Part of this Schedule any reference to a numbered article is a reference to the article of the Convention which is so numbered and any expression to which a meaning is assigned by article 1 of the Convention has that meaning.

Provisions adapting or supplementing specified articles of the Convention

2. For the purposes of paragraph 2 of article 2, provisions of such an international convention as is mentioned in that paragraph which apart from this paragraph do not have mandatory application to carriage by sea shall be treated as having mandatory application to carriage by sea if it is stated in the contract of carriage for the carriage in question that those provisions are to apply in connection with the carriage.

3. The reference to the law of the court in article 6 shall be construed as a reference to the Law Reform (Contributory Negligence) Act 1945 except that in relation to Northern Ireland it shall be construed as a reference to section 2 of the Law Reform (Miscellaneous Provisions) Act (Northern Ireland) 1948.

4. The Secretary of State may by order provide that, in relation to a carrier whose principal place of business is in the United Kingdom, paragraph 1 of article 7 shall have effect with the substitution for the limit for the time being specified in that paragraph of a different limit specified in the order (which shall not be lower than 46,666 units of account).

5.(1) For the purpose of converting from special drawing rights into sterling the amounts mentioned in articles 7 and 8 of the Convention in respect of which a judgment is given, one special drawing right shall be treated as equal to such a sum in sterling as the International Monetary Fund have fixed as being the equivalent of one special drawing right for—

(a) the day on which the judgment is given; or

(b) if no sum has been so fixed for that day, the last day before that day for which a sum has been so fixed.

(2) A certificate given by or on behalf of the Treasury stating—

(a) that a particular sum in sterling has been fixed as mentioned in sub-paragraph (1) above for a particular day; or

(b) that no sum has been so fixed for that day and a particular sum in sterling has been so fixed for a day which is the last day for which a sum has been so fixed before the particular day,

shall be conclusive evidence of those matters for the purposes of articles 7 to 9 of the Convention; and a document purporting to be such a certificate shall, in any proceedings, be received in evidence and, unless the contrary is proved, be deemed to be such a certificate.

6. It is hereby declared that by virtue of article 12 the limitations on liability there mentioned in respect of a passenger or his luggage apply to the aggregate liabilities of the persons in question in all proceedings for enforcing the liabilities or any of them which may be brought whether in the United Kingdom or elsewhere.

[7. Article 16 shall apply to arbitral proceedings as it applies to an action; and, as respects England and Wales and Northern Ireland, the provisions of section 14 of the Arbitration Act 1996 apply to determine for the purposes of that Article when an arbitration is commenced.]

8. The court before which proceedings are brought in pursuance of article 17 to enforce a liability which is limited by virtue of article 12 may at any stage of the proceedings make such orders as appear to the court to be just and equitable in view of the provisions of article 12 and of any other proceedings which have been or are likely to be begun in the United Kingdom or elsewhere to enforce the liability in whole or in part; and without prejudice to the generality of the preceding provisions of this paragraph such a court shall, where the liability is or may be partly enforceable in other proceedings in the United Kingdom or elsewhere, have jurisdiction to award an amount less than the court would have awarded if the limitation applied solely to the proceedings before the court or to make any part of its award conditional on the results of any other proceeding.

Other provisions adapting or supplementing the Convention

9. Any reference in the Convention to a contract of carriage excludes contract of carriage which is not for reward.

10. If Her Majesty by Order in Council declares that any State specified in the Order is a party to the Convention in respect of a particular country the Order shall, subject to the provisions of any subsequent Order made by virtue of this paragraph, be conclusive evidence that the State is a party to the Convention in respect of that country.

11. The Secretary of State may by order make provision—

(a) for requiring a person who is the carrier in relation to a passenger to give to the passenger, in a manner specified in the order, notice of such of the provisions of Part I of this Schedule as are so specified;

(b) for a person who fails to comply with a requirement imposed on him by the order to be guilty of an offence and liable on summary convection to a fine of an amount not exceeding level 4 on the standard scale or not exceeding a lesser amount.

Application of ss 185 and 186 of this Act

12. It is hereby declared that nothing in the Convention affects the operation of section 185 of this Act (which limits a shipowner's liability in certain cases of loss of life, injury or damage).

13. Nothing in section 186 of this Act (which among other things limits a shipowner's liability for the loss or damage of goods in certain cases) shall relieve a person of any liability imposed on him by the Convention.

[479]

NOTES

Para 7: substituted by the Arbitration Act 1996, s 107(1), Sch 3, para 61.

Orders in Council: the Carriage of Passengers and their Luggage by Sea (United Kingdom Carriers) Order 1998, SI 1998/2917 at **[2357]**; and by virtue of the Interpretation Act 1978, s 17(2)(b), the Carriage of Passengers and their Luggage by Sea (Interim Provisions) (Notice) Order 1980, SI 1980/1125 at **[2334]**, the Carriage of Passengers and their Luggage by Sea (Notice) Order 1987, SI 1987/703 at **[2349]** and the Carriage of Passengers and their Luggage by Sea (Parties to Convention) Order 1987, SI 1987/931 at **[2353]** have effect as if made under this Part.

SCHEDULE 7
CONVENTION ON LIMITATION OF LIABILITY FOR MARITIME CLAIMS 1976

Section 185

PART I
TEXT OF CONVENTION

CHAPTER I
THE RIGHT OF LIMITATION

Article 1
Persons entitled to limit liability

1. Shipowners and salvors, as hereinafter defined, may limit their liability in accordance with the rules of this Convention for claims set out in Article 2.

2. The term "shipowner" shall mean the owner, charterer, manager or operator of a seagoing ship.

3. Salvor shall mean any person rendering services in direct connection with salvage operations. Salvage operations shall also include operations referred to in Article 2, paragraph 1(d), (e) and (f).

4. If any claims set out in Article 2 are made against any person for whose act, neglect or default the shipowner or salvor is responsible, such person shall be entitled to avail himself of the limitation of liability provided for in this convention.

5. In this Convention the liability of a shipowner shall include liability in an action brought against the vessel herself.

6. An insurer of liability for claims subject to limitation in accordance with the rules of this Convention shall be entitled to the benefits of this Convention to the same extent as the assured himself.

7. The act of invoking limitation of liability shall not constitute an admission of liability.

Article 2
Claims subject to limitation

1. Subject to Articles 3 and 4 the following claims, whatever the basis of liability may be, shall be subject to limitation of liability:

(a) claims in respect of loss of life or personal injury or loss of or damage to property (including damage to harbour works, basins and waterways and aids to navigation), occurring on board or in direct connection with the operation of the ship or with salvage operations, and consequential loss resulting therefrom;

(b) claims in respect of loss resulting from delay in the carriage by sea of cargo, passengers or their luggage;

(c) claims in respect of other loss resulting from infringement of rights other than contractual rights, occurring in direct connection with the operation of the ship or salvage operations;

(d) claims in respect of the raising, removal, destruction or the rendering harmless of a ship which is sunk, wrecked, stranded or abandoned, including anything that is or has been on board such ship;

(e) claims in respect of the removal, destruction or the rendering harmless of the cargo of the ship;

(f) claims of a person other than the person liable in respect of measure taken in order to avert or minimise loss for which the person liable ma limit his liability in accordance with this Convention, and further loss caused by such measures.

2. Claims set out in paragraph 1 shall be subject to limitation of liability even if brought by way of recourse or for indemnity under a contract or otherwise. However, claims set out under paragraph 1(d), (e) and (f) shall not be subject to limitation of liability to the extent that they relate to remuneration under a contract with the person liable.

Article 3
Claims excepted from limitation

The rules of this Convention shall not apply to:

[(a) claims for salvage, including, if applicable, any claim for special compensation under Article 14 of the International Convention on Salvage 1989, as amended, or contribution in general average;]

(b) claims for oil pollution damage within the meaning of the International Convention on Civil Liability for Oil Pollution Damage dated 29th November 1969 or of any amendment or Protocol thereto which is in force;

(c) claims subject to any international convention or national legislation governing or prohibiting limitation of liability for nuclear damage;

(d) claims against the shipowner of a nuclear ship for nuclear damage;

(e) claims by servants of the shipowner or salvor whose duties are connected with the ship or the salvage operations, including claims of their heirs, dependants or other persons entitled to make such claims, if under the law governing the contract of service between the shipowner or salvor and such servants the shipowner or salvor is not entitled to limit his liability in respect of such claims, or if he is by such law only permitted to limit his liability to an amount greater than that provided for in Article 6.

Article 4
Conduct barring limitation

A person liable shall not be entitled to limit his liability if it is proved that the loss resulted from his personal act or omission, committed with the intent to cause such loss, or recklessly and with knowledge that such loss would probably result.

Article 5
Counterclaims

Where a person entitled to limitation of liability under the rules of this Convention has a claim against the claimant arising out of the same occurrence, their respective claims shall be set off against each other and the provisions of this Convention shall only apply to the balance, if any.

CHAPTER II
LIMITS OF LIABILITY

Article 6
The general limits

[1. The limits of liability for claims other than those mentioned in Article 7, arising on any distinct occasion, shall be calculated as follows:

(a) in respect of claims for loss of life or personal injury,
   (i) 2 million Units of Account for a ship with a tonnage not exceeding 2,000 tons,
   (ii) for a ship with a tonnage in excess thereof, the following amount in addition to that mentioned in (i):
   for each ton from 2,001 to 30,000 tons, 800 Units of Account;
   for each ton from 30,001 to 70,000 tons, 600 Units of Account; and
   for each ton in excess of 70,000 tons, 400 Units of Account,

(b) in respect of any other claims,
   (i) 1 million Units of Account for a ship with a tonnage not exceeding 2,000 tons,
   (ii) for a ship with a tonnage in excess thereof the following amount in addition to that mentioned in (i):
   for each ton from 2,001 to 30,000 tons, 400 Units of Account;
   for each ton from 30,001 to 70,000 tons, 300 Units of Account; and
   for each ton in excess of 70,000 tons, 200 Units of Account.]

2. Where the amount calculated in accordance with paragraph 1(a) is insufficient to pay the claims mentioned therein in full, the amount calculated in accordance with paragraph 1(b) shall be available for payment of the unpaid balance of claims under paragraph 1(a) and such unpaid balance shall rank rateably with claims mentioned under paragraph 1(b).

4. The limits of liability for any salvor not operating from any ship or for any salvor operating solely on the ship to, or in respect of which he is rendering salvage services, shall be calculated according to a tonnage of 1,500 tons.

Article 7
The limit for passenger claims

[1. In respect of claims arising on any distinct occasion for loss of life or personal injury to passengers of ship, the limit of liability of the shipowner thereof shall be an amount of 175,000 Units of Account multiplied by the number of passengers which the ship is authorised to carry according to the ship's certificate.]

2. For the purpose of this Article "claims for loss of life or personal injury to passengers of a ship" shall mean any such claims brought by or on behalf of any person carried in that ship:

(a) under a contract of passenger carriage, or
(b) who, with the consent of the carrier, is accompanying a vehicle or live animals which are covered by a contract for the carriage of goods.

Article 8
Unit of Account

The Unit of Account referred to in Articles 6 and 7 is the special drawing right as defined by the International Monetary Fund. The amounts mentioned in articles 6 and 7 shall be converted into the national currency of the State in which limitation is sought, according to the value of that currency at the date the limitation fund shall have been constituted, payment is made, or security is given which under the law of that State is equivalent to such payment.

Article 9
Aggregation of claims

1. The limits of liability determined in accordance with Article 6 shall apply to the aggregate of all claims which arise on any distinct occasion:

(a) against the person or persons mentioned in paragraph 2 of Article 1 and any person for whose act, neglect or default he or they are responsible; or
(b) against the shipowner of a ship rendering salvage services from that ship and the salvor or salvors operating from such ship and any person for whose act, neglect or default he or they are responsible; or
(c) against the salvor or salvors who are not operating from a ship or who are operating solely on the ship to, or in respect of which, the salvage services are rendered and any person for whose act, neglect or default he or they are responsible.

PART I STATUTES

2. The limits of liability determined in accordance with Article 7 shall apply to the aggregate of all claims subject thereto which may arise on any distinct occasion against the person or persons mentioned in paragraph 2 of Article 1 in respect of the ship referred to in Article 7 and any person for whose act, neglect or default he or they are responsible.

Article 10
Limitation of liability without constitution of a limitation fund

1. Limitation of liability may be invoked notwithstanding that a limitation fund as mentioned in Article 11 has not been constituted.

2. If limitation of liability is invoked without the constitution of a limitation fund, the provisions of Article 12 shall apply correspondingly.

3. Questions of procedure arising under the rules of this Article shall be decided in accordance with the national law of the State Party in which action is brought.

CHAPTER III
THE LIMITATION FUND

Article 11
Constitution of the Fund

1. Any person alleged to be liable may constitute a fund with the Court or other competent authority in any State Party in which legal proceedings are instituted in respect of claims subject to limitation. The fund shall be constituted in the sum of such of the amounts set out in Articles 6 and 7 as are applicable to claims for which that person may be liable, together with interest thereon from the date of the occurrence giving rise to the liability until the date of the constitution of the fund. Any fund thus constituted shall be available only for the payment of claims in respect of which limitation of liability can be invoked.

2. A fund may be constituted, either by depositing the sum, or by producing a guarantee acceptable under the legislation of the State Party where the fund is constituted and considered to be adequate by the Court or other competent authority.

3. A fund constituted by one of the persons mentioned in paragraph 1(a), (b) or (c) or paragraph 2 of Article 9 or his insurer shall be deemed constituted all persons mentioned in paragraph 1(a), (b) or (c) or paragraph 2, respectively.

Article 12
Distribution of the fund

1. Subject to the provisions of paragraphs 1 and 2 of Article 6 and of Article 7, the fund shall be distributed among the claimants in proportion to their established claims against the fund.

2. If, before the fund is distributed, the person liable, or his insurer, has settled a claim against the fund such person shall, up to the amount he has paid, acquire by subrogation the rights which the person so compensated would have enjoyed under this Convention.

3. The right of subrogation provided for in paragraph 2 may also be exercised by persons other than those therein mentioned in respect of any amount of compensation which they may have paid, but only to the extent that such subrogation is permitted under the applicable national law.

4. Where the person liable or any other person establishes that he may be compelled to pay, at a later date, in whole or in part any such amount of compensation with regard to which such person would have enjoyed a right of subrogation pursuant to paragraphs 2 and 3 had the compensation been paid before the fund was distributed, the Court or other competent authority of the State where the fund has been constituted may order that a sufficient sum shall be provisionally set aside to enable such person at such later date to enforce his claim against the fund.

Article 13
Bar to other actions

1. Where a limitation fund has been constituted in accordance with Article 11, any person having made a claim against the fund shall be barred from exercising any right in respect of such a claim against any other assets of a person by or on behalf of whom the fund has been constituted.

2. After a limitation fund has been constituted in accordance with Article 11, any ship or other property, belonging to a person on behalf of whom the fund has been constituted, which has been arrested or attached within the jurisdiction of a State Party for a claim which may be raised against the fund, or any security given, may be released by order of the Court or other competent authority of such State. However, such release shall always be ordered if the limitation fund has been constituted:
   (a) at the port where the occurrence took place, or, if it took place out of port, at the first port of call thereafter; or
   (b) at the port of disembarkation in respect of claims for loss of life or personal injury; or
   (c) at the port of discharge in respect of damage to cargo; or
   (d) in the State where the arrest is made.

3. The rules of paragraphs 1 and 2 shall apply only if the claimant may bring a claim against the limitation fund before the Court administering that fund and the fund is actually available and freely transferable in respect of that claim.

Article 14
Governing law

Subject to the provisions of this Chapter the rules relating to the constitution and distribution of a limitation fund, and all rules of procedure in connection therewith, shall be governed by the law of the State Party in which the fund constituted.

CHAPTER IV
SCOPE OF APPLICATION

Article 15

[1.] This Convention shall apply whenever any person referred to in Article 1 seeks to limit his liability before the Court of a State Party or seeks to procure the release of a ship or other property or the discharge of any security given within the jurisdiction of any such State.

[2. A State Party may regulate by specific provisions of national law the system of limitation of liability to be applied to vessels which are:
   (a) according to the law of that State, ships intended for navigation on inland waterways;
   (b) ships of less than 300 tons.

A State Party which makes use of the option provided for in this paragraph shall inform the depositary of the limits of liability adopted in its national legislation or of the fact that there are none.

3bis. Notwithstanding the limit of liability prescribed in paragraph 1 of article 7, a State Party may regulate by specific provisions of national law the system of liability to be applied to claims for loss of life or personal injury to passengers of a ship, provided that the limit of liability is not lower than that prescribed in paragraph 1 of article 7. A State Party which makes use of the option provided for in this paragraph shall inform the Secretary-General of the limits of liability adopted or of the fact that there are none.]

[Article 18
Reservations

1. Any State may, at the time of signature, ratification, acceptance, approval or accession, or at any time thereafter, reserve the right:
   (a) to exclude the application of article 2, paragraphs 1(d) and (e);
   (b) to exclude claims for damage within the meaning of the International Convention

on Liability and Compensation for Damage in Connection with the Carriage of Hazardous and Noxious Substances by Sea, 1996 or of any amendment or Protocol thereto.

No other reservations shall be admissible to the substantive provisions of this Convention.] **[480]**

NOTES

Art 3: para (a) substituted by the Merchant Shipping (Convention on Limitation of Liability for Maritime Claims) (Amendment) Order 1998, SI 1998/1258, art 3.
Art 6: para 1 substituted by SI 1998/1258, art 4(a).
Art 7: para 1 substituted by SI 1998/1258, art 4(b).
Art 15: text numbered as para 1 and paras 2, 3*bis* added by SI 1998/1258, art 5.
Art 18: added by SI 1998/1258, art 6.
Note: in Article 6 there is no paragraph 3 in the Queen's Printer's copy.

PART II
PROVISIONS HAVING EFFECT IN CONNECTION WITH CONVENTION

Interpretation

1. In this Part of this Schedule any reference to a numbered article is a reference to the article of the Convention which is so numbered.

Right to limit liability

2. [Subject to paragraph 6 below,] the right to limit liability under the Convention shall apply in relation to any ship whether seagoing or not, and the definition of "shipowner" in paragraph 2 of article 1 shall be construed accordingly.

Claims subject to limitation

[2A. …

3.(1) Paragraph 1(d) of article 2 shall not apply unless provision has been made by an order of the Secretary of State for the setting up and management of a fund to be used for the making to harbour or conservancy authorities of payments needed to compensate them for the reduction, in consequence of the said paragraph 1(d), of amounts recoverable by them in claims of the kind there mentioned, and to be maintained by contributions from such authorities raised and collected by them in respect of vessels in like manner as other sums so raised by them.

(2) Any order under sub-paragraph (1) above may contain such incidental and supplemental provisions as appear to the Secretary of State to be necessary or expedient.

Claims excluded from limitation

[4.(1) Claims for damage within the meaning of the International Convention on Liability and Compensation for Damage in Connection with the Carriage of Hazardous and Noxious Substances by Sea 1996, or any amendment of or Protocol to that Convention, which arise from occurrences which take place after the coming into force of the first Order in Council made by Her Majesty under section 182B of this Act shall be excluded from the Convention.]

(2) The claims excluded from the Convention by paragraph (b) of article 3 are claims in respect of any liability incurred under section 153 of this Act.

(3) The claims excluded from the Convention by paragraph (c) of article 3 are claims made by virtue of any of sections 7 to 11 of the Nuclear Installations Act 1965.

The general limits

5.(1) In the application of article 6 to a ship with a tonnage less than 300 tons that article shall have effect as if—

(a) paragraph 1(a)(i) referred to [1,000,000] Units of Account; and
(b) paragraph 1(b)(i) referred to [500,000] Units of Account.

(2) For the purposes of article 6 and this paragraph a ship's tonnage shall be its gross tonnage calculated in such manner as may be prescribed by an order made by the Secretary of State.

(3) Any order under this paragraph shall, so far as appears to the Secretary of State to be practicable, give effect to the regulations in Annex 1 of the International Convention on Tonnage Measurement of Ships 1969.

Limit for passenger claims

[6.(1) Article 7 shall not apply in respect of any seagoing ship; and shall have effect in respect of any ship which is not seagoing as if, in paragraph 1 of that article—

(a) after "thereof" there were inserted "in respect of each passenger,".
(b) the words from "multiplied" onwards were omitted.]

(2) In paragraph 2 of article 7 the reference to claims brought on behalf of a person includes a reference to any claim in respect of the death of a person under the Fatal Accidents Act 1976, the Fatal Accidents (Northern Ireland) Order 1977 or the Damages (Scotland) Act 1976.

Units of Account

7.(1) For the purpose of converting the amounts mentioned in articles 6 and 7 from special drawing rights into sterling one special drawing right shall be treated as equal to such a sum in sterling as the International Monetary Fund have fixed as being the equivalent of one special drawing right for—

(a) the relevant date under paragraph 1 of article 8; or
(b) if no sum has been so fixed for that date, the last preceding date for which a sum has been so fixed.

(2) A certificate given by or on behalf of the Treasury stating—

(a) that a particular sum in sterling has been fixed as mentioned in sub-paragraph (1) above for a particular date; or
(b) that no sum has been so fixed for that date and that a particular sum in sterling has been so fixed for a date which is the last preceding date for which a sum has been so fixed,

shall be conclusive evidence of those matters for the purposes of those articles; and a document purporting to be such a certificate shall, in any proceedings, be received in evidence and, unless the contrary is proved, be deemed to be such a certificate.

Constitution of fund

8.(1) The Secretary of State may, with the concurrence of the Treasury, by order prescribe the rate of interest to be applied for the purposes of paragraph 1 of article 11.

(2) Any statutory instrument containing an order under sub-paragraph (1) above shall be laid before Parliament after being made.

(3) Where a fund is constituted with the court in accordance with article 11 for the payment of claims arising out of any occurrence, the court may stay any proceedings relating to any claim arising out of that occurrence which are pending against the person by whom the fund has been constituted.

Distribution of fund

9. No lien or other right in respect of any ship or property shall affect the proportions in which under article 12 the fund is distributed among several claimants.

Bar to other actions

10. Where the release of a ship or other property is ordered under paragraph 2 of article 13 the person on whose application it is ordered to be released shall be deemed to have submitted to (or, in Scotland, prorogated) the jurisdiction of the court to adjudicate on the claim for which the ship or property was arrested or attached.

Meaning of "court"

11. References in the Convention and the preceding provisions of this Part of this Schedule to the court are references to the High Court or, in relation to Scotland, the Court of Session.

Meaning of "ship"

12. References in the Convention and in the preceding provisions of this Part of this Schedule to a ship include references to any structure (whether completed or in course of completion) launched and intended for use in navigation as a ship or part of a ship.

Meaning of "State Party"

[13. An Order in Council made for the purposes of this paragraph and declaring that any State specified in the Order is a party to the Convention as amended by the 1996 Protocol shall, subject to the provisions of any subsequent Order made for those purposes, be conclusive evidence that the State is a party to the Convention as amended by the 1996 Protocol.]

[481]

NOTES

Para 2: words in square brackets inserted by the Merchant Shipping (Convention on Limitation of Liability for Maritime Claims) (Amendment) Order 1998, SI 1998/1258, art 7(a).

Para 2A: inserted by SI 1998/1258, art 7(b); repealed by the Merchant Shipping (Convention on Limitation of Liability for Maritime Claims) (Amendment) Order 2004, SI 2004/1273, art 2.

Para 4: sub-para (1) substituted by SI 1998/1258, art 7(c).

Para 5: figures in square brackets substituted by SI 1998/1258, art 7(d).

Para 6: sub-para (1) substituted by SI 1998/1258, art 7(e).

Para 13: substituted by SI 1998/1258, art 7(f).

Orders: the Merchant Shipping (Liability of Shipowners and Others) (Rate of Interest) Order 1998, SI 1998/1795; and by virtue of the Interpretation Act 1978, s 17(2)(b), the Merchant Shipping (Liability of Shipowners and Others) (Calculation of Tonnage) Order 1986, SI 1986/1040, has effect as if made under this Part.

Order in Council: by virtue of the Interpretation Act 1978, s 17(2)(b), the Limitation of Liability for Maritime Claims (Parties to Convention) Order 1986, SI 1986/2224 at **[2341]**, has effect as if made under this Part.

(Schs 8, 10–14 relate to lighthouses, the International Convention on Salvage 1989, the funding of maritime services, and contain consequential amendments, repeals and transitional provisions; Sch 9 repealed by the Merchant Shipping and Maritime Security Act 1997, s 29(1), (2), Sch 6, para 9, Sch 7, Pt I.)

G. STATE IMMUNITY AND INTERNATIONAL ORGANISATIONS

INTERNATIONAL ORGANISATIONS ACT 1968

(1968 c 48)

ARRANGEMENT OF SECTIONS

An Act to make new provision (in substitution for the International Organisations (Immunities and Privileges) Act 1950 and the European Coal and Steel Community Act 1955) as to privileges, immunities and facilities to be accorded in respect of certain international organisations and in respect of persons connected with such organisations and other persons; and for purposes connected with the matters aforesaid

[26 July 1968]

NOTES

By the International Organisations Act 1981, s 6(1), this Act and the 1981 Act may be cited together by the collective title of the International Organisations Acts 1968 and 1981.

1 Organisations of which United Kingdom is a member

(1) This section shall apply to any organisation declared by Order in Council to be an organisation of which—

(a) the United Kingdom, or Her Majesty's Government in the United Kingdom, and

[(b) any other sovereign Power or the Government of any other sovereign Power,]

are members.

(2) Subject to subsection (6) of this section, Her Majesty may by Order in Council made under this subsection specify an organisation to which this section applies and make any one or more of the following provisions in respect of the organisation so specified (in the following provisions of this section referred to as "the organisation"), that is to say—

(a) confer on the organisation the legal capacities of a body corporate;

(b) provide that the organisation shall, to such extent as may be specified in the Order, have the privileges and immunities set out in Part I of Schedule 1 to this Act;

(c) confer the privileges and immunities set out in Part II of Schedule 1 to this Act, to such extent as may be specified in the Order, on persons of any such class as is mentioned in the next following subsection;

(d) confer the privileges and immunities set out in Part III of Schedule 1 to this Act, to such extent as may be specified in the Order, on such classes of officers and servants of the organisation (not being classes mentioned in the next following subsection) as may be so specified.

(3) The classes of persons referred to in subsection (2)(c) of this section are—

(a) persons who (whether they represent Governments or not) are representatives to the organisation or representatives on, or members of, any organ, committee or other subordinate body of the organisation (including any sub-committee or other subordinate body of a subordinate body of the organisation);

(b) such number of officers of the organisation as may be specified in the Order, being the holders (whether permanent, temporary or acting) of such high offices in the organisation as may be so specified; and

(c) persons employed by or serving under the organisation as experts or as persons engaged on missions for the organisation.

(4) Where an Order in Council is made under subsection (2) of this section, the provisions of Part IV of Schedule 1 to this Act shall have effect by virtue of that Order (in those provisions, as they so have effect, referred to as "the relevant Order"), except in so far as that Order otherwise provides.

(5) Where an Order in Council is made under subsection (2) of this section, then for the purpose of giving effect to any agreement made in that behalf between the United Kingdom or Her Majesty's Government in the United Kingdom and the organisation Her Majesty may by the same or any subsequent Order in Council make either or both of the following provisions, that is to say—

(a) confer the exemptions set out in paragraph 13 of Schedule 1 of this Act, to such extent as may be specified in the Order, in respect of officers and servants of the organisation of any class specified in the Order in accordance with subsection (2)(d) of this section and in respect of members of the family of any such officer or servant who form part of his household;

(b) confer the exemptions set out in Part V of that Schedule in respect of—

(i) members of the staff of the organisation recognised by Her Majesty's Government in the United Kingdom as holding a rank equivalent to that of a diplomatic agent, and

(ii) members of the family of any such member of the staff of the organisation who form part of his household.

(6) Any Order in Council made under subsection (2) or subsection (5) of this section shall be so framed as to secure—

(a) that the privileges and immunities conferred by the Order are not greater in extent than those which, at the time when the Order takes effect, are required to be conferred in accordance with any agreement to which the United Kingdom or Her Majesty's Government in the United Kingdom is then a party (whether made with [any other sovereign Power or Government or made with one or more organisations such as are mentioned in subsection (1) of this section), and

(b) that no privilege or immunity is conferred on any person as the representative of the United Kingdom, or of Her Majesty's Government in the United Kingdom, or as a member of the staff of such a representative.

[(7) Notwithstanding subsection (6)(a) of this section, where any agreement to which the United Kingdom or Her Majesty's Government in the United Kingdom is a party requires the conferral of any privileges and immunities on the spouse of any individual, Her Majesty may by Order in Council confer the same privileges and immunities on the civil partner of that individual.]

[482]

NOTES

Sub-ss (1), (6): words in square brackets substituted by the International Organisations Act 1981, s 1(1).

Sub-s (7): added by the Civil Partnership Act 2004 (International Immunities and Privileges, Companies and Adoption) Order 2005, SI 2005/3542, art 2(1).

Orders in Council: the table below lists the organisations in respect of which Privileges and Immunities Orders have been made under this section. Selected Orders in Council are reproduced in Part III G.

Organisation	Order in Council
Advisory Centre on WTO Law	2001/1868
Agency for International Trade Information and Co-operation (Legal Capacities)	2004/3332
African Development Bank	1983/142
African Development Fund	1973/958
Asian Development Bank	1974/1251
Caribbean Development Bank	1972/113
Central Treaty Organisation	1974/1252
Commission for the Conservation of Antarctic Marine Living Resources*	1981/1108
Common Fund for Commodities	1981/1802
Commonwealth Agricultural Bureaux*	1982/1071
Commonwealth Foundation*	1983/143
Commonwealth Telecommunications Organisation	1983/144
Customs Co-operation Council	1974/1253
European Bank for Reconstruction and Development	1991/757
European Centre for Medium-range Weather Forecasts	1975/158
European Communities (Immunities and Privileges of the European Police Force)*	1997/2973
European Forest Institute (Legal Capacities)*	2005/3426
European Molecular Biology Laboratory	1994/1890
European Organisation for the Exploitation of Meteorological Satellites (EUMETSAT)	1988/1298
European Organisation for Nuclear Research	1972/115
European Organisation for the Safety of Air Navigation (Eurocontrol)*	1970/1940
European Patent Organisation	1978/179
European Police College*	2004/3334
European Police Office (Legal Capacities)*	1996/3157, revoked by SI 1997/2973, art 2, as from a day to be appointed and published in the London Gazette
European Space Agency	1978/1105
European Telecommunications Satellite Organisation (EUTELSAT)	1988/1299
Financial Support Fund of the OECD	1976/224
Food and Agriculture Organisation	1974/1260
Inter-American Development Bank	1976/222
Inter-Governmental Maritime Consultative Organisation	1986/1862
Interim Commission for the International Trade Organisation	1972/699
International Atomic Energy Agency	1974/1256
International Civil Aviation Organisation	1974/1260
International Cocoa Organisation	1975/411
International Coffee Organisation	1969/733
International Copper Study Group (Legal Capacities)	1999/2033
International Court of Justice	1974/1261
International Fund for Agricultural Development	1977/824
International Fund for Ireland	1986/2017
International Hydrographic Organisation	1972/119

Organisation	Order in Council
International Institute for the Management of Technology	1972/670
International Jute Organisation	1983/1111
International Labour Organisation	1974/1260
International Lead and Zinc Study Group	1978/1893
International Maritime Organisation	2002/1826
International Mobile Satellite Organisation	1999/1125
International Monetary Fund	1977/825
International Natural Rubber Organisation*	1981/1804
International Oil Pollution Compensation Fund	1979/912
International Oil Pollution Compensation Fund	1996/1295
International Rubber Study Group	1978/181
International Sea-Bed Authority	1996/270
International Sea-bed Authority	2000/1815
International Sugar Organisation	1969/734
International Telecommunications Satellite Organisation (INTELSAT)	1979/911
International Telecommunication Union	1974/1260
International Tin Council	1972/120
International Tribunal for the Law of the Sea*	2005/2047
International Tropical Timber Organisation (Legal Capacities)*	1984/1152
International Trust Fund for Tuvalu*	1988/245
International Union for the Protection of New Varieties of Plants (Legal Capacities)	1985/446
International Whaling Commission	1975/1210
International Wheat Council (and Food Aid Committee)	1968/1863
North Atlantic Treaty Organisation	1974/1257
OSPAR Commission*	1997/2975
Organisation for Economic Co-operation and Development	1974/1258
Organisation for Joint Armament Cooperation	2000/1105
Organisation for the Prohibition of Chemical Weapons	2001/3921
Oslo and Paris Commissions	1979/914
Preparatory Commission for the Comprehensive Nuclear-Test-Ban Treaty Organization*	2004/1282
South East Asia Treaty Organisation	1974/1259
Specialized Agencies of the United Nations (Immunities and Privileges of UNESCO)	2001/2560
United Nations and International Court of Justice	1974/1261
United Nations Educational, Scientific and Cultural Organisation	1974/1260
United Nations Industrial Development Organisation*	1982/1074
Universal Postal Union	1974/1260
World Health Organisation	1974/1260
World Intellectual Property Organisation	1974/1260
World Meteorological Organisation	1974/1260
World Trade Organisation	1995/266

The Orders indicated by asterisks will come into force on a day to be notified in the London Gazette.

An Order in Council under this section may confer immunities on representatives of the United Kingdom to the Assembly of Western European Union or the Consultative Assembly of the Council of Europe, notwithstanding the provisions of sub-s (6) above (see the International Organisations Act 1981, s 4 at **[532]**) or on representatives to any conference convened in the United Kingdom (see s 5A of this Act at **[488]**).

For further provisions as to Orders in Council, see s 10 at **[493]**. For similar Orders in Council made under the Foreign Organisations (Immunities and Privileges) Act 1950 which remain in force by virtue of s 12(5) of this Act, see s 12 at **[495]**.

2 Specialised agencies of United Nations

(1) Where an Order in Council under section 1(2) of this Act is made in respect of an organisation which is a specialised agency of the United Nations having its headquarters or principal office in the United Kingdom, then for the purpose of giving effect to any agreement between the United Kingdom or Her Majesty's Government in the United Kingdom and that organisation Her Majesty may by the same or any other Order in Council confer the exemptions, privileges and reliefs specified in the next following subsection, to such extent as may be specified in the Order, on officers of the organisation who are recognised by Her Majesty's Government in the United Kingdom as holding a rank equivalent to that of a diplomatic agent.

(2) The exemptions, privileges and reliefs referred to in the preceding subsection are—

(a) the like exemption or relief from income tax, capital gains tax and rates as, in accordance with Article 34 of the 1961 Convention Articles, is accorded to a diplomatic agent, and

[(aa) the like exemption or relief from being [liable to pay anything in respect of council tax], as in accordance with that Article is accorded to a diplomatic agent, and]

(b) the exemptions, privileges and reliefs specified in paragraphs 10 to 12 of Schedule 1 to this Act [and the exemption comprised in paragraph 9 of that Schedule from vehicle excise duty …].

(3) Where by virtue of subsection (1) of this section any of the exemptions, privileges and reliefs referred to in subsection (2)(b) of this section are conferred on persons as being officers of the organisation, Her Majesty may by the same or any other Order in Council confer the like exemptions, privileges and reliefs on persons who are members of the families of those persons and form part of their households.

(4) The powers conferred by the preceding provisions of this section shall be exercisable in addition to any power exercisable by virtue of subsection (2) or subsection (5) of section 1 of this Act; and any exercise of the powers conferred by those provisions shall have effect without prejudice to the operation of subsection (4) of that section.

(5) [Subsections (6) and (7)] of section 1 of this Act shall have effect in relation to the preceding provisions of this section as [those subsections have] effect in relation to subsections (2) and (5) of that section.

(6) In this section "specialised agency" has the meaning assigned to it by Article 57 of the Charter of the United Nations.

[483]

NOTES

Sub-s (2): para (aa) inserted by the Local Government Finance Act 1988, s 137, Sch 12, Pt III, para 40, words in square brackets in para (aa) substituted by the Local Government Finance Act 1992, s 117(1), Sch 13, para 27; words in square brackets in para (b) added by the Diplomatic and other Privileges Act 1971, s 3 and words omitted therefrom repealed by the Vehicle Excise and Registration Act 1994, s 65, Sch 5, Pt I.

Sub-s (5): words in square brackets substituted by the Civil Partnership Act 2004 (International Immunities and Privileges, Companies and Adoption) Order 2005, SI 2005/3542, art 2(2).

Orders in Council: the International Maritime Organisation (Immunities and Privileges) Order 2002, SI 2002/1826.

See also notes to s 1 at **[482]**.

3 (*Repealed by the European Communities Act 1972, s 4, Sch 3, Pt IV.*)

4 Other organisations of which United Kingdom is not a member

Where an organisation … of which two or more … sovereign Powers, or the Governments of two or more such Powers, are members but of which neither the United Kingdom nor Her Majesty's Government in the United Kingdom is a member, maintains or proposes to maintain an establishment in the United Kingdom, then for the purpose of giving effect to any agreement made in that behalf between the United Kingdom or Her Majesty's Government in the United Kingdom and that organisation, Her Majesty may by Order in Council specifying the organisation make either or both of the following provisions in respect of the organisation, that is to say—

(a) confer on the organisation the legal capacities of a body corporate, and

(b) provide that the organisation shall, to such extent as may be specified in the Order, be entitled to the like exemption or relief from taxes on income and capital gains as is accorded to a foreign sovereign Power. **[484]**

NOTES

Words omitted in the first place repealed by the European Communities Act 1972, s 4, Sch 3, Pt IV; words omitted in the second place repealed by the International Organisations Act 1981, ss 1(2), 6(4), Schedule.

Orders in Council: the African Development Bank (Privileges) Order 1983, SI 1983/142.

See also notes to s 1 at **[482]**.

[4A International commodity organisations

(1) In this section, "international commodity organisation" means any such organisation as is mentioned in section 4 of this Act (international organisations of which the United Kingdom is not a member) which appears to Her Majesty to satisfy each of the following conditions—

(a) that the members of the organisation are States or the Governments of States in which a particular commodity is produced or consumed;

(b) that the exports or imports of that commodity from or to those States account (when taken together) for a significant volume of the total exports or imports of that commodity throughout the world; and

(c) that the purpose or principal purpose of the organisation is—

(i) to regulate trade in that commodity (whether as an import or an export or both) or to promote or study that trade; or

(ii) to promote research into that commodity or its uses or further development.

(2) Subject to the following provisions of this section, an Order made under section 4 of this Act with respect to an international commodity organisation may, for the purpose there mentioned and to such extent as may be specified in the Order—

(a) provide that the organisation shall have the privileges and immunities set out in paragraphs 2, 3, 4, 6 and 7 of Schedule 1 to this Act;

(b) confer on persons of any such class as is mentioned in subsection (3) of this section the privileges and immunities set out in paragraphs 11 and 14 of that Schedule;

(c) provide that the official papers of such persons shall be inviolable; and

(d) confer on officers and servants of the organisation of any such class as may be specified in the Order the privileges and immunities set out in paragraphs 13, 15 and 16 of that Schedule.

(3) The classes of persons referred to in subsection (2)(b) of this section are—

(a) persons who (whether they represent Governments or not) are representatives to the organisation or representatives on, or members of, any organ, committee or other subordinate body of the organisation (including any sub-committee or other subordinate body of a subordinate body of the organisation);

(b) persons who are members of the staff of any such representative and who are recognised by Her Majesty's Government in the United Kingdom as holding a rank equivalent to that of a diplomatic agent.

(4) An Order in Council made under section 4 of this Act shall not confer on any person of such class as is mentioned in subsection (3) of this section any immunity in respect of a civil action arising out of an accident caused by a motor vehicle or other means of transport belonging to or driven by such a person, or in respect of a traffic offence involving such a vehicle and committed by such a person.

(5) In this section "commodity" means any produce of agriculture, forestry or fisheries or any mineral, either in its natural state or having undergone only such processes as are necessary or customary to prepare the produce or mineral for the international market.]

[485]

NOTES

Inserted by the International Organisations Act 1981, s 2.
Orders in Council: see the notes to s 1 at **[482]**.

[4B Bodies established under Treaty on European Union

(1) This section applies to any body—

(a) established under Title V (provisions on a common foreign and security policy) or Title VI (provisions on police and judicial cooperation in criminal matters) of the Treaty on European Union signed at Maastricht on 7th February 1992 as amended from time to time; and

(b) in relation to which the United Kingdom, or Her Majesty's Government in the United Kingdom, has obligations by virtue of any instrument under that Treaty or by virtue of any agreement to which the United Kingdom, or Her Majesty's Government in the United Kingdom, is a party (whether made with another sovereign Power or the Government of such a Power or not).

(2) Her Majesty may by Order in Council make any one or more of the following provisions in respect of a specified body to which this section applies—

(a) confer on the body the legal capacities of a body corporate;

(b) provide that the body shall, to such extent as is specified, have such specified privileges and immunities as (having regard to the obligations referred to in subsection (1)(b)) it is in the opinion of Her Majesty in Council appropriate for the body to have;

(c) confer on such specified classes of persons mentioned in subsection (3), to such extent as is specified, such specified privileges and immunities as (having regard to those obligations) it is in the opinion of Her Majesty in Council appropriate to confer on them.

(3) The persons mentioned in subsection (2)(c) are—

(a) the body's officers or staff;

(b) other persons connected with the body,

and members of their families who form part of their households.

(4) In this section, "specified" means specified in the Order in Council.]

[486]

NOTES

Commencement: 7 June 2005.
Inserted by the International Organisations Act 2005, s 5.

5 International judicial and other proceedings

(1) Her Majesty may by Order in Council confer on any class of persons to whom this section applies such privileges, immunities and facilities as in the opinion of Her Majesty in Council are or will be required for giving effect—

(a) to any agreement to which, at the time when the Order takes effect, the United Kingdom or Her Majesty's Government in the United Kingdom is or will be a party, or

(b) to any resolution of the General Assembly of the United Nations.

(2) This section applies to any persons who are for the time being—

(a) judges or members of any international tribunal, or persons exercising or performing, or appointed (whether permanently or temporarily) to exercise or perform, any jurisdiction or functions of such a tribunal;

(b) registrars or other officers of any international tribunal;

(c) parties to any proceedings before any international tribunal;

(d) agents, advisers or advocates (by whatever name called) for any such parties;

(e) witnesses in, or assessors for the purposes of, any proceedings before any international tribunal.

(3) For the purposes of this section any petition, complaint or other communication which, with a view to action to be taken by or before an international tribunal,—

(a) is made to the tribunal, or

(b) is made to a person through whom, in accordance with the constitution, rules or practice of the tribunal, such a communication can be received by the tribunal,

shall be deemed to be proceedings before the tribunal, and the person making any such communication shall be deemed to be a party to such proceedings.

(4) Without prejudice to subsection (3) of this section, any reference in this section to a party to proceedings before an international tribunal shall be construed as including a reference to—

(a) any person who, for the purposes of any such proceedings, acts as next friend, guardian or other representative (by whatever name called) of a party to the proceedings, and

(b) any person who (not being a person to whom this section applies apart from this paragraph) is entitled or permitted, in accordance with the constitution, rules or practice of an international tribunal, to participate in proceedings before the tribunal by way of advising or assisting the tribunal in the proceedings.

(5) In this section "international tribunal" means any court (including the International Court of Justice), tribunal, commission or other body which, in pursuance of any such agreement or resolution as is mentioned in subsection (1) of this section,—

(a) exercises, or is appointed (whether permanently or temporarily) for the purpose of exercising, any jurisdiction, or

(b) performs, or is appointed (whether permanently or temporarily) for the purpose of performing, any functions of a judicial nature or by way of arbitration, conciliation or inquiry,

and includes any individual who, in pursuance of any such agreement or resolution, exercises or performs, or is appointed (whether permanently or temporarily) for the purpose of exercising or performing, any jurisdiction or any such functions.

[487]

NOTES

For the application of this section to members of the family of a judge of the European Court of Human Rights as it applies to a judge of that court, see the International Organisations Act 2005, s 7 at **[554]**.

Orders in Council: the European Commission and the Court of Human Rights (Immunities and Privileges) Order 1970, SI 1970/1941 at **[2389]**; the Organisation for Economic Co-operation and Development (Immunities and Privileges) Order 1974, SI 1974/1258 at **[2395]**; the United Nations and International Court of Justice (Immunities and Privileges) Order 1974, SI 1974/1261 at **[2433]**; the INTELSAT (Immunities and Privileges) Order 1979, SI 1979/911; the European Committee for the Prevention of Torture and Inhuman or Degrading Treatment or Punishment (Immunities and Privileges) Order 1988, SI 1988/926; the International Tribunal for the Law of the Sea (Immunities and Privileges) Order 1996, SI 1996/272; the European Court of Human Rights (Immunities and Privileges) Order 2000, SI 2000/1817 at **[2496]**; the International Tribunal for the Law of the Sea (Immunities and Privileges) Order 2005, SI 2005/2047.

See also notes to s 1 at **[482]**.

[5A Orders under ss 1 and 4 extending to UK conferences

(1) An Order in Council made under section 1 of this Act in respect of any organisation, or section 4 of this Act in respect of an international commodity organisation, may to such extent as may be specified in the Order, and subject to the following provisions of this section,—

(a) confer on persons of any such class as may be specified in the Order, being persons who are or are to be representatives (whether of Governments or not) at any conference which the organisation may convene in the United Kingdom—

(i) in the case of an Order under section 1, the privileges and immunities set out in Part II of Schedule 1 to this Act;

(ii) in the case of an Order under section 4, the privileges and immunities set out in paragraphs 11 and 14 of that Schedule; and

(b) in the case of an Order under section 4, provide that the official papers of such persons shall be inviolable.

(2) Where in the exercise of the power conferred by subsection (1)(a) of this section an Order confers privileges and immunities on persons of any such class as is mentioned in that paragraph, the provisions of paragraphs 19 to 22 of Schedule 1 to this Act shall have effect in

relation to the members of the official staffs of such persons as if in paragraph 19 of that Schedule "representative" were defined as a person of such a class.

(3) The powers exercisable by virtue of this section may be exercised notwithstanding the provisions of any such agreement as is mentioned in section 1(6)(a) of this Act, but no privilege or immunity may thereby be conferred on any such representative, or member of his staff, as is mentioned in section 1(6)(b) of this Act.

(4) In this section "international commodity organisation" has the meaning given by section 4A(1) of this Act.

(5) This section is without prejudice to section 6 of this Act.]

[488]

NOTES

Inserted by the International Organisations Act 1981, s 3.

6 Representatives at international conferences in United Kingdom

(1) This section applies to any conference which is, or is to be, held in the United Kingdom and is, or is to be, attended by representatives—

(a) of the United Kingdom, or of Her Majesty's Government in the United Kingdom, and

[(b) of any other sovereign Power or the Government of any other sovereign Power.]

(2) Her Majesty may by Order in Council specify one or more classes of persons who are, or are to be, representatives of [a sovereign power (other than the United Kingdom)], or of the Government of such a Power, at a conference to which this section applies, and confer on persons of the class or classes in question, to such extent as may be specified in the Order, the privileges and immunities set out in Part II of Schedule 1 to this Act.

(3) Where an Order in Council is made under subsection (2) of this section in relation to a particular conference, then, except in so far as that Order otherwise provides, the provisions of paragraphs 19 to 22 of Schedule 1 to this Act shall have effect in relation to members of the official staffs of persons of a class specified in the Order in accordance with that subsection as if in paragraph 19 of that Schedule "representative" were defined as a person of a class so specified in the Order.

[489]

NOTES

Sub-ss (1), (2): words in square brackets substituted by the International Organisations Act 1981, s 1(3).

Orders in Council: the CSCE Information Forum (Immunities and Privileges) Order 1989, SI 1989/480; the G8 Gleneagles (Immunities and Privileges) Order 2005, SI 2005/1456.

See also notes to s 1 at **[482]**.

7 Priority of telecommunications

So far as may be necessary for the purpose of giving effect to the International Telecommunication Convention done at Montreux on 12th November 1965 or any subsequent treaty or agreement whereby that Convention is amended or superseded, priority shall, wherever practicable, be given to messages from, and to replies to messages from, any of the following, that is to say—

(a) the Secretary General of the United Nations;

(b) the heads of principal organs of the United Nations; and

(c) the International Court of Justice.

[490]

NOTES

International Telecommunication Convention: Cmnd 3054.

8 Evidence

If in any proceedings a question arises whether a person is or is not entitled to any privilege or immunity by virtue of this Act or any Order in Council made thereunder, a certificate issued by or under the authority of the Secretary of State stating any fact relating to that question shall be conclusive evidence of that fact.

[491]

9 Financial provisions

Any amount refunded under any arrangements made in accordance with any provisions of Schedule 1 to this Act relating to refund of [duty] [value added tax or car tax]—

(a) if the arrangements were made by the Secretary of State, shall be paid out of moneys provided by Parliament, or

(b) if the arrangements were made by the Commissioners of Customs and Excise, shall be paid out of the moneys standing to the credit of the General Account of those Commissioners.

[492]

NOTES

Word in first pair of square brackets substituted by the Customs and Excise Management Act 1979, s 177(1), Sch 4, para 12, Table, Pt I; words in second pair of square brackets substituted by the Finance Act 1972, ss 55(5), (7).

10 Orders in Council

(1) No recommendation shall be made to Her Majesty in Council to make an Order under any provision (other than section 6) of this Act unless a draft of the Order has been laid before Parliament and approved by a resolution of each House of Parliament.

(2) Any Order in Council made under section 6 of this Act shall be subject to annulment in pursuance of a resolution of either House of Parliament.

(3) Any power conferred by any provision of this Act to make an Order in Council shall include power to revoke or vary the Order by a subsequent Order in Council made under that provision.

[493]

11 Interpretation

(1) In this Act "the 1961 Convention Articles" means the Articles (being certain Articles of the Vienna Convention on Diplomatic Relations signed in 1961) which are set out in Schedule 1 to the Diplomatic Privileges Act 1964, and "the International Court of Justice" means the court set up by that name under the Charter of the United Nations.

(2) Expressions used in this Act to which a meaning is assigned by Article 1 of the 1961 Convention Articles, and other expressions which are used both in this Act and in those Articles, shall, except in so far as the context otherwise requires, be construed as having the same meanings in this Act as in those Articles.

(3) For the purpose of giving effect to any arrangements made in that behalf between Her Majesty's Government in the United Kingdom and any organisation, premises which are not premises of the organisation but are recognised by that Government as being temporarily occupied by the organisation for its official purposes shall, in respect of such period as may be determined in accordance with the arrangements, be treated for the purposes of this Act as if they were premises of the organisation.

(4) Except in so far as the context otherwise requires, any reference in this Act to an enactment is a reference to that enactment as amended or extended by or under any other enactment.

[494]

12 Consequential amendments, repeals and transitional provisions

(1), (2) …

(3) References in any enactment to the powers conferred by the International Organisations (Immunities and Privileges) Act 1950 shall be construed as including references to the powers conferred by this Act.

(4) Subject to the following provisions of this section, the enactments specified in Schedule 2 to this Act are hereby repealed to the extent specified in the third column of that Schedule.

(5) Any Order in Council which has been made, or has effect as if made, under an enactment repealed by subsection (4) of this section and is in force immediately before the passing of this Act shall continue to have effect notwithstanding the repeal of that enactment and, while any such Order in Council continues to have effect in relation to an organisation,—

(a) the enactment in question shall continue to have effect in relation to that organisation as if that enactment had not been repealed, and

(b) section 8 of this Act shall have effect as if in that section any reference to this Act or an Order in Council made thereunder included a reference to that enactment or that Order in Council.

(6) Any such Order in Council as is mentioned in subsection (5) of this section—

(a) if made, or having effect as if made, under section 1 of the International Organisations (Immunities and Privileges) Act 1950, may be revoked or varied as if it had been made under section 1 of this Act;

(b) if made, or having effect as if made, under section 3 of that Act, may be revoked or varied as if it had been made under section 5 of this Act.

(7) ...

[495]

NOTES

Sub-s (1): repealed by the Civil Aviation Act 1982, s 109, Sch 16; see now Sch 4, para 1(2) to that Act.
Sub-s (2): amends the Consular Relations Act 1968, s 1(3).
Sub-s (7): repealed by the Statute Law (Repeals) Act 1993.
Orders in Council: the following Orders in Council are saved by sub-s (5): the International Organisations (Immunities and Privileges of the Commission for Technical Co-operation in Africa South of the Sahara) Order 1955, SI 1955/1208; the International Organisations (Immunities and Privileges of Western European Union) Order 1955, SI 1955/1209; the Council of Europe (Immunities and Privileges) Order 1960, SI 1960/442; the Western European Union (Immunities and Privileges) Order 1960, SI 1960/444.
International Organisations (Immunities and Privileges) Act 1950: repealed by sub-s (4) above and Sch 2 to this Act.

13 Short title

This Act may be cited as the International Organisations Act 1968.

[496]

SCHEDULES

SCHEDULE 1
PRIVILEGES AND IMMUNITIES

Sections 1, 2, 3, 6

PART I
PRIVILEGES AND IMMUNITIES OF THE ORGANISATION

1. Immunity from suit and legal process.

2. The like inviolability of official archives and premises of the organisation as, in accordance with the 1961 Convention Articles, is accorded in respect of the official archives and premises of a diplomatic mission.

3.(1) Exemption or relief from taxes, other than [duties (whether of customs or excise)] and taxes on the importation of goods.

(2) The like relief from rates as in accordance with Article 23 of the 1961 Convention Articles is accorded in respect of the premises of a diplomatic mission.

4. Exemption from [duties (whether of customs or excise)] and taxes on the importation of goods imported by or on behalf of the organisation for its official use in the United Kingdom, or on the importation of any publications of the organisation imported by it or on its behalf,

such exemption to be subject to compliance with such conditions as the Commissioners of Customs and Excise may prescribe for the protection of the Revenue.

5. Exemption from prohibitions and restrictions on importation or exportation in the case of goods imported or exported by the organisation for its official use and in the case of any publications of the organisation imported or exported by it.

6. Relief, under arrangements made either by the Secretary of State or by the Commissioners of Customs and Excise, by way of refund of [duty (whether of customs or excise) paid on imported hydrocarbon oil (within the meaning of the Hydrocarbon Oil Duties Act 1979) or value added tax paid on the importation of such oil which is] bought in the United Kingdom and used for the official purposes of the organisation, such relief to be subject to compliance with such conditions as may be imposed in accordance with the arrangements.

7. Relief, under arrangements made by the Secretary of State, by way of refund of [car tax paid on any vehicles and value added tax paid on the supply of any goods or services] which are used for the official purposes of the organisation, such relief to be subject to compliance with such conditions as may be imposed in accordance with the arrangements.

[497]

NOTES

Paras 3, 4, 6: words in square brackets substituted by the Customs and Excise Management Act 1979, s 177(1), Sch 4, para 12, Table, Pt I.

Para 7: words in square brackets substituted by the Finance Act 1972, s 55(5), (7).

PART II
PRIVILEGES AND IMMUNITIES OF REPRESENTATIVES, MEMBERS OF SUBORDINATE BODIES, HIGH OFFICERS, EXPERTS, AND PERSONS ON MISSIONS

8. For the purpose of conferring on any person any such exemption, privilege or relief as is mentioned in any of the following paragraphs of this Part of this Schedule, any reference in that paragraph to the representative or officer shall be construed as a reference to that person.

9. The like immunity from suit and legal process, the like inviolability of residence, and the like exemption or relief from taxes and rates, other than [duties (whether of customs or excise)] and taxes on the importation of goods, as are accorded to or in respect of the head of a diplomatic mission.

[9A. The like inviolability of official premises as is accorded in respect of the premises of a diplomatic mission.]

[9B. The like exemption or relief from being [liable to pay anything in respect of council tax], as is accorded to or in respect of the head of a diplomatic mission.]

10. The like exemption from [duties (whether of customs or excise)] and taxes on the importation of articles imported for the personal use of the representative or officer or of members of his family forming part of his household, including articles intended for his establishment [and the like privilege as to the importation of such articles], as in accordance with paragraph 1 of Article 36 of the 1961 Convention Articles is accorded to a diplomatic agent.

11. The like exemption and privileges in respect of the personal baggage of the representative or officer as in accordance with paragraph 2 of Article 36 of those Articles are accorded to a diplomatic agent, as if in that paragraph the reference to paragraph 1 of that Article were a reference to paragraph 10 of this Schedule.

12. Relief, under arrangements made either by the Secretary of State or by the Commissioners of Customs and Excise, by way of refund of [duty (whether of customs or excise) paid on imported hydrocarbon oil (within the meaning of Hydrocarbon Oil Duties Act 1979) or value added tax paid on the importation of such oil which is] bought in the

United Kingdom by or on behalf of the representative or officer, such relief to be subject to compliance with such conditions as may be imposed in accordance with the arrangements.

13. Exemptions whereby, [for the purposes of the enactments relating to ... social security, including enactments in force in Northern Ireland—

(a) services rendered for the organisation by the representative or officer shall be deemed to be excepted from any class of employment in respect of which contributions *or premiums* under those enactments are payable, but]

(b) no person shall be rendered liable to pay any contribution [or premium] which he would not be required to pay if those services were not deemed to be so excepted.

[498]

NOTES

Para 9: words in square brackets substituted by the Customs and Excise Management Act 1979, s 177(1), Sch 4, para 12, Table, Pt I.

Para 9A: inserted by the International Organisations Act 1981, s 5(1).

Para 9B: inserted by the Local Government and Housing Act 1989, s 194(1), Sch 11, para 14; words in square brackets substituted by the Local Government Finance Act 1992, s 117(1), Sch 13, para 28.

Para 10: words in first pair of square brackets substituted by the Customs and Excise Management Act 1979, s 177(1), Sch 4, para 12, Table, Pt I; words in second pair of square brackets inserted by the International Organisations Act 1981, s 5(2).

Para 12: words in square brackets substituted by the Customs and Excise Management Act 1979, s 177(1), Sch 4, para 12, Table, Pt I.

Para 13: words in first pair of square brackets substituted by the Social Security Act 1973, ss 100, 101, Sch 27, para 80(a) except that the words "or premiums" in italics are not in force; words omitted repealed by the Social Security (Consequential Provisions) Act 1975, ss 1(2), 5, Sch 1, Pt I; words in square brackets in sub-para (b) inserted by the Social Security Act 1973, ss 100, 101, Sch 27, para 80(b), as from a day to be appointed.

PART III
PRIVILEGES AND IMMUNITIES OF OTHER OFFICERS OR SERVANTS

14. Immunity from suit and legal process in respect of things done or omitted to be done in the course of the performance of official duties.

15. Exemption from income tax in respect of emoluments received as an officer or servant of the organisation.

16. The like exemption from [duties (whether of customs or excise)] and taxes on the importation of articles which—

(a) at or about the time when an officer or servant of the organisation first enters the United Kingdom as such an officer or servant are imported for his personal use or that of members of his family forming part of his household, including articles intended for his establishment, and

(b) are articles which were in his ownership or possession or that of such a member of his family, or which he or such a member of his family was under contract to purchase, immediately before he so entered the United Kingdom,

[and the like privilege as to the importation of such articles] as in accordance with paragraph 1 of Article 36 of the 1961 Convention Articles is accorded to a diplomatic agent.

17. Exemption from [duties (whether of customs or excise)] and taxes on the importation of any motor vehicle imported by way of replacement of a motor vehicle in respect of which the conditions specified in sub-paragraphs (a) and (b) of paragraph 16 of this Schedule were fulfilled, such exemption to be subject to compliance with such conditions as the Commissioners of Customs and Excise may prescribe for the protection of the Revenue.

18. The like exemption and privileges in respect of the personal baggage of an officer or servant of the organisation as in accordance with paragraph 2 of Article 36 of the 1961 Convention Articles are accorded to a diplomatic agent, as if in that paragraph the reference to paragraph 1 of that Article were a reference to paragraph 16 of this Schedule.

[499]

NOTES

Para 16: words in first pair of square brackets substituted by the Customs and Excise Management Act 1979, s 177(1), Sch 4, para 12, Table, Pt I; words in second pair of square brackets inserted by the International Organisations Act 1981, s 5(3).

Para 17: words in square brackets substituted by the Customs and Excise Management Act 1979, s 177(1), Sch 4, para 12, Table, Pt I.

PART IV
PRIVILEGES AND IMMUNITIES OF OFFICIAL STAFFS AND OF FAMILIES OF REPRESENTATIVES, HIGH OFFICERS AND OFFICIAL STAFFS

19. In this Part of this Schedule—

(a) "representative" means a person who is such a representative to the organisation specified in the relevant Order or such a representative on, or member of, an organ, committee or other subordinate body of that organisation as is mentioned in section 1(3)(a) of this Act;

(b) "member of the official staff" means a person who accompanies a representative as part of his official staff in his capacity as a representative;

[(c) references to importation, in relation to value added tax, shall include references to anything charged with tax in accordance with section [10 or 15 of the Value Added Tax Act 1994] (acquisitions from other member States and importations from outside the European Community), and "imported" shall be construed accordingly.]

20. A member of the official staff who is recognised by Her Majesty's Government in the United Kingdom as holding a rank equivalent to that of a diplomatic agent shall be entitled to the privileges and immunities set out in Part II of this Schedule to the like extent as, by virtue of the relevant Order, the representative whom he accompanies is entitled to them.

21.(1) Subject to sub-paragraph (2) of this paragraph, a member of the official staff who is not so recognised, and who is employed in the administrative or technical service of the representative whom he accompanies, shall be entitled to the privileges and immunities set out in paragraphs 9 and 13 of this Schedule to the like extent as, by virtue of the relevant Order, that representative is entitled to them.

(2) Such a member of the official staff shall not by virtue of the preceding sub-paragraph be entitled to immunity from any civil proceedings in respect of any cause of action arising otherwise than in the course of his official duties.

(3) Such a member of the official staff shall also be entitled to the exemption set out in paragraph 16 of this Schedule as if he were an officer of the organisation specified in the relevant Order.

22. A member of the official staff who is employed in the domestic service of the representative whom he accompanies shall be entitled to the following privileges and immunities, that is to say—

(a) immunity from suit and legal process in respect of things done or omitted to be done in the course of the performance of official duties, and

(b) the exemptions set out in paragraph 13 of this Schedule,

to the like extent as, by virtue of the relevant Order, that representative is entitled to them, and shall be entitled to exemption from taxes on his emoluments in respect of that employment to the like extent as, by virtue of the relevant Order, that representative is entitled to exemption from taxes on his emoluments as a representative.

23.(1) Persons who are members of the family of a representative and form part of his household shall be entitled to the privileges and immunities set out in Part II of this Schedule to the like extent as, by virtue of the relevant Order, that representative is entitled to them.

(2) Persons who are members of the family and form part of the household of an officer of the organisation specified in the relevant Order, where that officer is the holder (whether permanent, temporary or acting) of an office specified in that Order in accordance with section 1(3)(b) of this Act, shall be entitled to the privileges and immunities set out in Part II of this Schedule to the like extent as, by virtue of the relevant Order, that officer is entitled to them.

(3) Persons who are members of the family and form part of the household of such a member of the official staff as is mentioned in paragraph 20 of this Schedule shall be entitled to the privileges and immunities set out in Part II of this Schedule to the like extent as, by virtue of that paragraph, that member of the official staff is entitled to them.

(4) Persons who are members of the family and form part of the household of such a member of the official staff as is mentioned in paragraph 21 of this Schedule shall be entitled to the privileges and immunities set out in paragraphs 9 and 13 of this Schedule to the like extent as, by virtue of paragraph 21 of this Schedule, that member of the official staff is entitled to them.

[500]

NOTES

Para 19: sub-para (c) added by the Finance (No 2) Act 1992, s 14, Sch 3, Pt III, para 90, words in square brackets in sub-para (c) substituted by the Value Added Tax Act 1994, s 100(1), Sch 14, para 4.

PART V
ESTATE DUTY AND CAPITAL GAINS TAX ON DEATH

24. In the event of the death of the person in respect of whom the exemptions under this paragraph are conferred, exemptions from—

(a) estate duty leviable on his death under the law of any part of the United Kingdom in respect of movable property which is in the United Kingdom immediately before his death and whose presence in the United Kingdom at that time is due solely to his presence there in the capacity by reference to which the exemptions are conferred, and

(b) …

[501]

NOTES

Sub-para (b) repealed by the Taxation of Chargeable Gains Act 1992, s 290(3), Sch 12.

(*Sch 2 contains repeals.*)

STATE IMMUNITY ACT 1978

(1978 c 33)

ARRANGEMENT OF SECTIONS

PART I
PROCEEDINGS IN UNITED KINGDOM BY OR AGAINST OTHER STATES

Immunity from jurisdiction

Exceptions from immunity

Procedure

Supplementary provisions

PART II
JUDGMENTS AGAINST UNITED KINGDOM IN CONVENTION STATES

PART III
MISCELLANEOUS AND SUPPLEMENTARY

An Act to make new provision with respect to proceedings in the United Kingdom by or against other States; to provide for the effect of judgments given against the United Kingdom in the courts of States parties to the European Convention on State Immunity, to make new provision with respect to the immunities and privileges of heads of State; and for connected purposes

[20 July 1978]

NOTES

The United Kingdom has signed but not yet ratified the 2004 UN Convention on State Immunity, reproduced at **[4414]**.

PART I
PROCEEDINGS IN UNITED KINGDOM BY OR AGAINST OTHER STATES

Immunity from jurisdiction

1 General immunity from jurisdiction

(1) A State is immune from the jurisdiction of the courts of the United Kingdom except as provided in the following provisions of this Part of this Act.

(2) A court shall give effect to the immunity conferred by this section even though the State does not appear in the proceedings in question.

[502]

Exceptions from immunity

2 Submission to jurisdiction

(1) A State is not immune as respects proceedings in respect of which it has submitted to the jurisdiction of the courts of the United Kingdom.

(2) A State may submit after the dispute giving rise to the proceedings has arisen or by a prior written agreement; but a provision in any agreement that it is to be governed by the law of the United Kingdom is not to be regarded as a submission.

(3) A State is deemed to have submitted—
(a) if it has instituted the proceedings; or
(b) subject to subsections (4) and (5) below, if it has intervened or taken any step in the proceedings.

(4) Subsection (3)(b) above does not apply to intervention or any step taken for the purpose only of—
(a) claiming immunity; or
(b) asserting an interest in property in circumstances such that the State would have been entitled to immunity if the proceedings had been brought against it.

(5) Subsection (3)(b) above does not apply to any step taken by the State in ignorance of facts entitling it to immunity if those facts could not reasonably have been ascertained and immunity is claimed as soon as reasonably practicable.

(6) A submission in respect of any proceedings extends to any appeal but not to any counter-claim unless it arises out of the same legal relationship or facts as the claim.

(7) The head of a State's diplomatic mission in the United Kingdom, or the person for the time being performing his functions, shall be deemed to have authority to submit on behalf of the State in respect of any proceedings; and any person who has entered into a contract on behalf of and with the authority of a State shall be deemed to have authority to submit on its behalf in respect of proceedings arising out of the contract.

[503]

3 Commercial transactions and contracts to be performed in United Kingdom

(1) A State is not immune as respects proceedings relating to—
(a) a commercial transaction entered into by the State; or
(b) an obligation of the State which by virtue of a contract (whether a commercial transaction or not) falls to be performed wholly or partly in the United Kingdom.

(2) This section does not apply if the parties to the dispute are States or have otherwise agreed in writing; and subsection (1)(b) above does not apply if the contract (not being a commercial transaction) was made in the territory of the State concerned and the obligation in question is governed by its administrative law.

(3) In this section "commercial transaction" means—
(a) any contract for the supply of goods or services;
(b) any loan or other transaction for the provision of finance and any guarantee or indemnity in respect of any such transaction or of any other financial obligation, and
(c) any other transaction or activity (whether of a commercial, industrial, financial, professional or other similar character) into which a State enters or in which it engages otherwise than in the exercise of sovereign authority;

but neither paragraph of subsection (1) above applies to a contract of employment between a State and an individual.

[504]

4 Contracts of employment

(1) A State is not immune as respects proceedings relating to a contract of employment between the State and an individual where the contract was made in the United Kingdom or the work is to be wholly or partly performed there.

(2) Subject to subsections (3) and (4) below, this section does not apply if—
(a) at the time when the proceedings are brought the individual is a national of the State concerned; or
(b) at the time when the contract was made the individual was neither a national of the United Kingdom nor habitually resident there; or
(c) the parties to the contract have otherwise agreed in writing.

(3) Where the work is for an office, agency or establishment maintained by the State in the United Kingdom for commercial purposes, subsection (2)(a) and (b) above do not exclude the application of this section unless the individual was, at the time when the contract was made, habitually resident in that State.

(4) Subsection (2)(c) above does not exclude the application of this section where the law of the United Kingdom requires the proceedings to be brought before a court of the United Kingdom.

(5) In subsection (2)(b) above "national of the United Kingdom" [means—

(a) a British citizen, a [British overseas territories citizen][, a British National (Overseas)] or a British Overseas citizen; or

(b) a person who under the British Nationality Act 1981 is a British subject, or

(c) a British protected person (within the meaning of that Act)].

(6) In this section "proceedings relating to a contract of employment" includes proceedings between the parties to such a contract in respect of any statutory rights or duties to which they are entitled or subject as employer or employee.

[505]

NOTES

Sub-s (5): words in first (outer) pair of square brackets substituted by the British Nationality Act 1981, s 52(6) Sch 7; words in second (inner) pair of square brackets substituted by virtue of the British Overseas Territories Act 2002, s 2(3); words in third (inner) pair of square brackets inserted by the Hong Kong (British Nationality) Order 1986, SI 1986/948, art 8, Schedule.

5 Personal injuries and damage to property

A State is not immune as respects proceedings in respect of—

(a) death or personal injury; or

(b) damage to or loss of tangible property,

caused by an act or omission in the United Kingdom.

[506]

6 Ownership, possession and use of property

(1) A State is not immune as respects proceedings relating to—

(a) any interest of the State in, or its possession or use of, immovable property in the United Kingdom; or

(b) any obligation of the State arising out of its interest in, or its possession or use of, any such property.

(2) A State is not immune as respects proceedings relating to any interest of the State in movable or immovable property, being an interest arising by way of succession, gift or bona vacantia.

(3) The fact that a State has or claims an interest in any property shall not preclude any court from exercising in respect of it any jurisdiction relating to the estates of deceased persons or persons of unsound mind or to insolvency, the winding up of companies or the administration of trusts.

(4) A court may entertain proceedings against a person other than a State notwithstanding that the proceedings relate to property—

(a) which is in the possession or control of a State; or

(b) in which a State claims an interest,

if the State would not have been immune had the proceedings been brought against it or, in a case within paragraph (b) above, if the claim is neither admitted nor supported by prima facie evidence.

[507]

7 Patents, trade-marks etc

A State is not immune as respects proceedings relating to—

(a) any patent, trade-mark, design or plant breeders' rights belonging to the State and registered or protected in the United Kingdom or for which the State has applied in the United Kingdom;

(b) an alleged infringement by the State in the United Kingdom of any patent, trade-mark, design, plant breeders' rights or copyright; or

(c) the right to use a trade or business name in the United Kingdom.

[508]

NOTES

Trade-mark: the references to a trade mark in paras (a), (b) are to be construed as references to a trade mark within the meaning of the Trade Marks Act 1994, by virtue of s 106(1) of, and Sch 4, para 1 to that Act.

8 Membership of bodies corporate etc

(1) A State is not immune as respects proceedings relating to its membership of a body corporate, an unincorporated body or a partnership which—

(a) has members other than States; and

(b) is incorporated or constituted under the law of the United Kingdom or is controlled from or has its principal place of business in the United Kingdom,

being proceedings arising between the State and the body or its other members or, as the case may be, between the State and the other partners.

(2) This section does not apply if provision to the contrary has been made by an agreement in writing between the parties to the dispute or by the constitution or other instrument establishing or regulating the body or partnership in question.

[509]

9 Arbitrations

(1) Where a State has agreed in writing to submit a dispute which has arisen, or may arise, to arbitration, the State is not immune as respects proceedings in the courts of the United Kingdom which relate to the arbitration.

(2) This section has effect subject to any contrary provision in the arbitration agreement and does not apply to any arbitration agreement between States.

[510]

10 Ships used for commercial purposes

(1) This section applies to—

(a) Admiralty proceedings; and

(b) proceedings on any claim which could be made the subject of Admiralty proceedings.

(2) A State is not immune as respects—

(a) an action in rem against a ship belonging to that State; or

(b) an action in personam for enforcing a claim in connection with such a ship,

if, at the time when the cause of action arose, the ship was in use or intended for use for commercial purposes.

(3) Where an action in rem is brought against a ship belonging to a State for enforcing a claim in connection with another ship belonging to that State, subsection (2)(a) above does not apply as respects the first-mentioned ship unless, at the time when the cause of action relating to the other ship arose, both ships were in use or intended for use for commercial purposes.

(4) A State is not immune as respects—

(a) an action in rem against a cargo belonging to that State if both the cargo and the ship carrying it were, at the time when the cause of action arose, in use or intended for use for commercial purposes; or

(b) an action in personam for enforcing a claim in connection with such a cargo if the ship carrying it was then in use or intended for use as aforesaid.

(5) In the foregoing provisions references to a ship or cargo belonging to a State include references to a ship or cargo in its possession or control or in which it claims an interest; and, subject to subsection (4) above, subsection (2) above applies to property other than a ship as it applies to a ship.

(6) Sections 3 to 5 above do not apply to proceedings of the kind described in subsection (1) above if the State in question is a party to the Brussels Convention and the claim relates to the operation of a ship owned or operated by that State, the carriage of cargo or passengers on any such ship or the carriage of cargo owned by that State on any other ship.

[511]

11 Value added tax, customs duties etc

A State is not immune as respects proceedings relating to its liability for—

(a) value added tax, any duty of customs or excise or any agricultural levy; or

(b) rates in respect of premises occupied by it for commercial purposes.

[512]

Procedure

12 Service of process and judgments in default of appearance

(1) Any writ or other document required to be served for instituting proceedings against a State shall be served by being transmitted through the Foreign and Commonwealth Office to the Ministry of Foreign Affairs of the State and service shall be deemed to have been effected when the writ or document is received at the Ministry.

(2) Any time for entering an appearance (whether prescribed by rules of court or otherwise) shall begin to run two months after the date on which the writ or document is received as aforesaid.

(3) A State which appears in proceedings cannot thereafter object that subsection (1) above has not been complied with in the case of those proceedings.

(4) No judgment in default of appearance shall be given against a State except on proof that subsection (1) above has been complied with and that the time for entering an appearance as extended by subsection (2) above has expired.

(5) A copy of any judgment given against a State in default of appearance shall be transmitted through the Foreign and Commonwealth Office to the Ministry of Foreign Affairs of that State and any time for applying to have the judgment set aside (whether prescribed by rules of court or otherwise) shall begin to run two months after the date on which the copy of the judgment is received at the Ministry.

(6) Subsection (1) above does not prevent the service of a writ or other document in any manner to which the State has agreed and subsections (2) and (4) above do not apply where service is effected in any such manner.

(7) This section shall not be construed as applying to proceedings against a State by way of counter-claim or to an action in rem; and subsection (1) above shall not be construed as affecting any rules of court whereby leave is required for the service of process outside the jurisdiction.

[513]

13 Other procedural privileges

(1) No penalty by way of committal or fine shall be imposed in respect of any failure or refusal by or on behalf of a State to disclose or produce any document or other information for the purposes of proceedings to which it is a party.

(2) Subject to subsections (3) and (4) below—

(a) relief shall not be given against a State by way of injunction or order for specific performance or for the recovery of land or other property; and

(b) the property of a State shall not be subject to any process for the enforcement of a judgment or arbitration award or, in an action in rem, for its arrest, detention or sale.

(3) Subsection (2) above does not prevent the giving of any relief or the issue of any process with the written consent of the State concerned; and any such consent (which may be contained in a prior agreement) may be expressed so as to apply to a limited extent or generally; but a provision merely submitting to the jurisdiction of the courts is not to be regarded as a consent for the purposes of this subsection.

(4) Subsection (2)(b) above does not prevent the issue of any process in respect of property which is for the time being in use or intended for use for commercial purposes; but, in a case not falling within section 10 above, this subsection applies to property of a State party to the European Convention on State Immunity only if—

(a) the process is for enforcing a judgment which is final within the meaning of section 18(1)(b) below and the State has made a declaration under Article 24 of the Convention; or

(b) the process is for enforcing an arbitration award.

(5) The head of a State's diplomatic mission in the United Kingdom, or the person for the time being performing his functions, shall be deemed to have authority to give on behalf of the State any such consent as is mentioned in subsection (3) above and, for the purposes of subsection (4) above, his certificate to the effect that any property is not in use or intended for use by or on behalf of the State for commercial purposes shall be accepted as sufficient evidence of that fact unless the contrary is proved.

(6) In the application of this section to Scotland—
(a) the reference to "injunction" shall be construed as a reference to "interdict";
(b) for paragraph (b) of subsection (2) above there shall be substituted the following paragraph—
"(b) the property of a State shall not be subject to any diligence for enforcing a judgment or order of a court or a decree arbitral or, in an action in rem, to arrestment of sale."; and
(c) any reference to "process" shall be construed as a reference to "diligence", any reference to "the issue of any process" as a reference to "the doing of diligence" and the reference in subsection (4)(b) above to "an arbitration award" as a reference to "a decree arbitral".

[514]

Supplementary provisions

14 States entitled to immunities and privileges

(1) The immunities and privileges conferred by this Part of this Act apply to any foreign or commonwealth State other than the United Kingdom; and references to a State include references to—
(a) the sovereign or other head of that State in his public capacity;
(b) the government of that State; and
(c) any department of that government,

but not to any entity (hereafter referred to as a "separate entity") which is distinct from the executive organs of the government of the State and capable of suing or being sued.

(2) A separate entity is immune from the jurisdiction of the courts of the United Kingdom if, and only if—
(a) the proceedings relate to anything done by it in the exercise of sovereign authority; and
(b) the circumstances are such that a State (or, in the case of proceedings to which section 10 above applies, a State which is not a party to the Brussels Convention) would have been so immune.

(3) If a separate entity (not being a State's central bank or other monetary authority) submits to the jurisdiction in respect of proceedings in the case of which it is entitled to immunity by virtue of subsection (2) above, subsections (1) to (4) of section 13 above shall apply to it in respect of those proceedings as if references to a State were references to that entity.

(4) Property of a State's central bank or other monetary authority shall not be regarded for the purposes of subsection (4) of section 13 above as in use or intended for use for commercial purposes; and where any such bank or authority is a separate entity subsections (1) to (3) of that section shall apply to it as if references to a State were references to the bank or authority.

(5) Section 12 above applies to proceedings against the constituent territories of a federal State; and Her Majesty may by Order in Council provide for the other provisions of this Part of this Act to apply to any such constituent territory specified in the Order as they apply to a State.

(6) Where the provisions of this Part of this Act do not apply to a constituent territory by virtue of any such Order subsections (2) and (3) above shall apply to it as if it were a separate entity.

[515]

NOTES

Orders in Council: the State Immunity (Federal States) Order 1979, SI 1979/457 at **[2461]**; the State Immunity (Federal States) Order 1993, SI 1993/2809 at **[2479]**.

15 Restriction and extension of immunities and privileges

(1) If it appears to Her Majesty that the immunities and privileges conferred by this Part of this Act in relation to any State—
(a) exceed those accorded by the law of that State in relation to the United Kingdom; or

(b) are less than those required by any treaty, convention or other international agreement to which that State and the United Kingdom are parties,

Her Majesty may by Order in Council provide for restricting or, as the case may be, extending those immunities and privileges to such extent as appears to Her Majesty to be appropriate.

(2) Any statutory instrument containing an Order under this section shall be subject to annulment in pursuance of a resolution of either House of Parliament.

[516]

NOTES

Orders in Council: the State Immunity (Merchant Shipping) (Revocation) Order 1999, SI 1999/668.

16 Excluded matters

(1) This Part of this Act does not affect any immunity or privilege conferred by the Diplomatic Privileges Act 1964 or the Consular Relations Act 1968; and—

(a) section 4 above does not apply to proceedings concerning the employment of the members of a mission within the meaning of the Convention scheduled to the said Act of 1964 or of the members of a consular post within the meaning of the Convention scheduled to the said Act of 1968;

(b) section 6(1) above does not apply to proceedings concerning a State's title to or its possession of property used for the purposes of a diplomatic mission.

(2) This Part of this Act does not apply to proceedings relating to anything done by or in relation to the armed forces of a State while present in the United Kingdom and, in particular, has effect subject to the Visiting Forces Act 1952.

(3) This Part of this Act does not apply to proceedings to which section 17(6) of the Nuclear Installations Act 1965 applies.

(4) This Part of this Act does not apply to criminal proceedings.

(5) This Part of this Act does not apply to any proceedings relating to taxation other than those mentioned in section 11 above.

[517]

17 Interpretation of Part I

(1) In this Part of this Act—

"the Brussels Convention" means the International Convention for the Unification of Certain Rules Concerning the Immunity of State-owned Ships signed in Brussels on 10th April 1926;

"commercial purposes" means purposes of such transactions or activities as are mentioned in section 3(3) above;

"ship" includes hovercraft.

(2) In sections 2(2) and 13(3) above references to an agreement include references to a treaty, convention or other international agreement.

(3) For the purposes of sections 3 to 8 above the territory of the United Kingdom shall be deemed to include any [British overseas territory] in respect of which the United Kingdom is a party to the European Convention on State Immunity.

(4) In sections 3(1), 4(1), 5 and 16(2) above references to the United Kingdom include references to its territorial waters and any area designated under section 1(7) of the Continental Shelf Act 1964.

(5) In relation to Scotland in this Part of this Act "action in rem" means such an action only in relation to Admiralty proceedings.

[518]

NOTES

Sub-s (3): words in square brackets substituted by virtue of the British Overseas Territories Act 2002, s 1(2).

Brussels Convention: the text of the Brussels Convention is set out in Cmd 5672.

PART II
JUDGMENTS AGAINST UNITED KINGDOM IN CONVENTION STATES

18 Recognition of judgments against United Kingdom

(1) This section applies to any judgment given against the United Kingdom by a court in another State party to the European Convention on State Immunity, being a judgment—

(a) given in proceedings in which the United Kingdom was not entitled to immunity by virtue of provisions corresponding to those of sections 2 to 11 above, and

(b) which is final, that is to say, which is not or is no longer subject to appeal or, if given in default of appearance, liable to be set aside.

(2) Subject to section 19 below, a judgment to which this section applies shall be recognised in any court in the United Kingdom as conclusive between the parties thereto in all proceedings founded on the same cause of action and may be relied on by way of defence or counter-claim in such proceedings.

(3) Subsection (2) above (but not section 19 below) shall have effect also in relation to any settlement entered into by the United Kingdom before a court in another State party to the Convention which under the law of that State is treated as equivalent to a judgment.

(4) In this section references to a court in a State party to the Convention include references to a court in any territory in respect of which it is a party.

[519]

19 Exceptions to recognition

(1) A court need not give effect to section 18 above in the case of a judgment—

(a) if to do so would be manifestly contrary to public policy or if any party to the proceedings in which the judgment was given had no adequate opportunity to present his case; or

(b) if the judgment was given without provisions corresponding to those of section 12 above having been complied with and the United Kingdom has not entered an appearance or applied to have the judgment set aside.

(2) A court need not give effect to section 18 above in the case of a judgment—

(a) if proceedings between the same parties, based on the same facts and having the same purpose—

(i) are pending before a court in the United Kingdom and were the first to be instituted; or

(ii) are pending before a court in another State party to the Convention, were the first to be instituted and may result in a judgment to which that section will apply; or

(b) if the result of the judgment is inconsistent with the result of another judgment given in proceedings between the same parties and—

(i) the other judgment is by a court in the United Kingdom and either those proceedings were the first to be instituted or the judgment of that court was given before the first-mentioned judgment became final within the meaning of subsection (1)(b) of section 18 above; or

(ii) the other judgment is by a court in another State party to the Convention and that section has already become applicable to it.

(3) Where the judgment was given against the United Kingdom in proceedings in respect of which the United Kingdom was not entitled to immunity by virtue of a provision corresponding to section 6(2) above, a court need not give effect to section 18 above in respect of the judgment if the court that gave the judgment—

(a) would not have had jurisdiction in the matter if it had applied rules of jurisdiction corresponding to those applicable to such matters in the United Kingdom; or

(b) applied a law other than that indicated by the United Kingdom rules of private international law and would have reached a different conclusion if it had applied the law so indicated.

(4) In subsection (2) above references to a court in the United Kingdom include references to a court in any [British overseas territory] in respect of which the United Kingdom is a party to the Convention, and references to a court in another State party to the Convention include references to a court in any territory in respect of which it is a party.

[520]

NOTES

Sub-s (4): words in square brackets substituted by virtue of the British Overseas Territories Act 2002, s 1(2).

PART III
MISCELLANEOUS AND SUPPLEMENTARY

20 Heads of State

(1) Subject to the provisions of this section and to any necessary modifications, the Diplomatic Privileges Act 1964 shall apply to—

(a) a sovereign or other head of State;

(b) members of his family forming part of his household; and

(c) his private servants,

as it applies to the head of a diplomatic mission, to members of his family forming part of his household and to his private servants.

(2) The immunities and privileges conferred by virtue of subsection (1)(a) and (b) above shall not be subject to the restrictions by reference to nationality or residence mentioned in Article 37(1) or 38 in Schedule 1 to the said Act of 1964.

(3) Subject to any direction to the contrary by the Secretary of State, a person on whom immunities and privileges are conferred by virtue of subsection (1) above shall be entitled to the exemption conferred by section 8(3) of the Immigration Act 1971.

(4) Except as respects value added tax and duties of customs or excise, this section does not affect any question whether a person is exempt from, or immune as respects proceedings relating to, taxation.

(5) This section applies to the sovereign or other head of any State on which immunities and privileges are conferred by Part I of this Act and is without prejudice to the application of that Part to any such sovereign or head of State in his public capacity.

[521]

21 Evidence by certificate

A certificate by or on behalf of the Secretary of State shall be conclusive evidence on any question—

(a) whether any country is a State for the purposes of Part I of this Act, whether any territory is a constituent territory of a federal State for those purposes or as to the person or persons to be regarded for those purposes as the head or government of a State;

(b) whether a State is a party to the Brussels Convention mentioned in Part I of this Act;

(c) whether a State is a party to the European Convention on State Immunity, whether it has made a declaration under Article 24 of that Convention or as to the territories in respect of which the United Kingdom or any other State is a party;

(d) whether, and if so when, a document has been served or received as mentioned in section 12(1) or (5) above.

[522]

NOTES

Brussels Convention: see the note to s 17 at **[518]**.

22 General interpretation

(1) In this Act "court" includes any tribunal or body exercising judicial functions; and references to the courts or law of the United Kingdom include references to the courts or law of any part of the United Kingdom.

(2) In this Act references to entry of appearance and judgments in default of appearance include references to any corresponding procedures.

(3) In this Act "the European Convention on State Immunity" means the Convention of that name signed in Basle on 16th May 1972.

(4) In this Act "[British overseas territory]" means—
(a) any of the Channel Islands;
(b) the Isle of Man;
(c) any colony other than one for whose external relations a country other than the United Kingdom is responsible; or
(d) any country or territory outside Her Majesty's dominions in which Her Majesty has jurisdiction in right of the government of the United Kingdom.

(5) Any power conferred by this Act to make an Order in Council includes power to vary or revoke a previous Order.

[523]

NOTES

Sub-s (4): words in square brackets substituted by virtue of the British Overseas Territories Act 2002, s 1(2).

European Convention on State Immunity: the text of this Convention is set out in Cmnd 5081.

23 Short title, repeals, commencement and extent

(1) This Act may be cited as the State Immunity Act 1978.

(2) …

(3) Subject to subsection (4) below, Parts I and II of this Act do not apply to proceedings in respect of matters that occurred before the date of the coming into force of this Act and, in particular—
(a) sections 2(2) and 13(3) do not apply to any prior agreement, and
(b) sections 3, 4 and 9 do not apply to any transaction, contract or arbitration agreement,
entered into before that date.

(4) Section 12 above applies to any proceedings instituted after the coming into force of this Act.

(5) This Act shall come into force on such date as may be specified by an order made by the Lord Chancellor by statutory instrument.

(6) This Act extends to Northern Ireland.

(7) Her Majesty may by Order in Council extend any of the provisions of this Act, with or without modification, to any [British overseas territory].

[524]

NOTES

Sub-s (2): repeals the Administration of Justice (Miscellaneous Provisions) Act 1938, s 13, and the Law Reform (Miscellaneous Provisions) (Scotland) Act 1940, s 7.

Sub-s (7): words in square brackets substituted by virtue of the British Overseas Territories Act 2002, s 1(2).

Orders: the State Immunity Act 1978 (Commencement) Order 1978, SI 1978/1572.

Orders in Council: the State Immunity (Overseas Territories) Order 1979, SI 1979/458, extending the provisions of this Act, with modifications, to the following dependent territories: Belize, British Antarctic Territory, British Virgin Islands, Cayman Islands, Falkland Islands and Dependencies, Gilbert Islands, Hong Kong, Montserrat, Pitcairn, Henderson, Ducie and Oeno Islands, Sovereign Base Areas of Akrotiri and Dhekelia, Turks and Caicos Islands; the State Immunity (Guernsey) Order 1980, SI 1980/871, extending the provisions of this Act, with exceptions, adaptations and modifications, to the Bailiwick of Guernsey; the State Immunity (Isle of Man) Order 1981, SI 1981/1112, extending the provisions of this Act, with modifications, to the Isle of Man; the State Immunity (Jersey) Order 1985, SI 1985/1642, extending the provisions of this Act, with modifications, to the Bailiwick of Jersey.

INTERNATIONAL MONETARY FUND ACT 1979

(1979 c 29)

ARRANGEMENT OF SECTIONS

An Act to consolidate the enactments relating to the International Monetary Fund and to repeal, as obsolete, the European Monetary Agreement Act 1959 and the entries relating to it in Schedule 2 to the National Loans Act 1968

[4 April 1979]

1 Payments to International Monetary Fund

(1) All sums which the Government of the United Kingdom requires for the purpose of paying to the International Monetary Fund in accordance with the Fund's Articles of Agreement—

(a) subscriptions of such amounts as may from time to time be authorised by order of the Treasury in the event of proposals being made for increases in the United Kingdom's quota under section 3(a) of Article III;

(b) any sums payable under section 11 of Article V (maintenance of value of assets);

(c) any sums required for implementing the guarantee required by section 3 of Article XIII (guarantee against loss resulting from failure or default of designated depository); and

(d) any compensation required to be paid to the Fund or any member of it under Schedule J or K (withdrawal of members and liquidation),

shall be paid out of the National Loans Fund.

(2) The power of the Treasury to make orders under subsection (1)(a) above shall be exercisable by statutory instrument; and no such order shall be made until a draft of it has been laid before and approved by a resolution of the House of Commons.

(3) All sums which the Government of the United Kingdom requires for the purpose of paying any charges payable to the International Monetary Fund under section 8 of Article V of the Fund's Articles of Agreement shall be paid out of the Exchange Equalisation Account.

[525]

NOTES

International Monetary Fund; Articles of Agreement: the International Monetary Fund was established by an Agreement drawn up at the United Nations Monetary and Financial Conference held at Bretton Woods, New Hampshire, USA, in July 1944. The original Articles of Agreement were published as Treaty Series No 21 (1946), Cmd 6885; the first Amendment was published as Treaty Series No 44 (1978), Cmnd 7205; and the second Amendment was published as Treaty Series No 83 (1978), Cmnd 7331. The second Amendment contains the full text of the Articles of Agreement as amended; it does not set out the actual amendments made at that time.

Orders: the International Monetary Fund (Increase in Subscription) Order 1980, SI 1980/1131; the International Monetary Fund (Increase in Subscription) Order 1983, SI 1983/998; the International Monetary Fund (Increase in Subscription) Order 1990, SI 1990/2352; the International Monetary Fund (Increase in Subscription) Order 1998, SI 1998/1854.

2 Loans to Fund

[(1) The Treasury may make loans to the International Monetary Fund in accordance with the Fund's borrowing arrangements; but the aggregate amount outstanding in respect of the principal of loans under this section shall not exceed [2,577] million special drawing rights.

(1A) For the purposes of subsection (1) above, a loan under this section, or repayment of such a loan, in any currency shall be treated as a loan or, as the case may be, repayment of the amount of special drawing rights which for the purposes of those arrangements is the value of the loan or repayment.]

(2) The Treasury may by order raise or further raise the limit on lending imposed by subsection (1) above.

(3) The power of the Treasury to make orders under subsection (2) above shall be exercisable by statutory instrument; and no such order shall be made until a draft of it has been laid before and approved by a resolution of the House of Commons.

(4) Sums to be lent under this section shall be issued out of the National Loans Fund.

(5) In this section "the Fund's borrowing arrangements" means arrangements made by the International Monetary Fund for enabling it to borrow the currency of any member of the Fund taking part in the arrangements.

[526]

NOTES

Sub-s (1): substituted, together with sub-s (1A), for original sub-s (1), by the International Monetary Arrangements Act 1983, s 1; figure in square brackets substituted by the International Monetary Fund (Limit on Lending) Order 1997, SI 1997/1611, art 2.

Sub-s (1A): substituted, together with sub-s (1), for original sub-s (1) by the International Monetary Arrangements Act 1983, s 1.

Orders: the International Monetary Fund (Limit on Lending) Order 1997, SI 1997/1611.

3 Receipts from Fund

Sums received by the Government of the United Kingdom from the International Monetary Fund (other than sums received by reason of the operation of the Exchange Equalisation Account) shall be paid into the National Loans Fund.

[527]

4 Power of Treasury to create and issue notes and other obligations to Fund

(1) The Treasury may, if they think fit so to do, create and issue to the International Monetary Fund, in such form as they think fit, any such non-interest-bearing and non-negotiable notes or other obligations as are provided for by section 4 of Article III of the Fund's Articles of Agreement.

(2) The sums payable under any such notes or other obligations shall be charged on the National Loans Fund with recourse to the Consolidated Fund.

[528]

5 Immunities and privileges etc

(1) Without prejudice to the powers conferred by the International Organisations Act 1968 or any other Act, Her Majesty may by Order in Council make such provision as She may consider reasonably necessary for carrying into effect any of the provisions of the Articles of Agreement of the International Monetary Fund relating to the status, immunities and privileges of the Fund and its governors, executive directors, alternates, officers and employees, or as to the unenforceability of exchange contracts.

(2) Subject to subsection (3) below, Orders in Council made under this section may be so made as to extend to any of the Channel Islands, the Isle of Man, any colony and, to the extent that Her Majesty has jurisdiction there, to any country outside Her Majesty's dominions in which Her Majesty has jurisdiction in right of the Government of the United Kingdom.

(3) If, whether before or after the coming into force of this Act, effect is given by or under the law of any part of Her Majesty's dominions or other territory to the provisions of the Articles of Agreement of the International Monetary Fund specified in subsection (1) above, no Order in Council made under this section shall extend to that part of Her Majesty's dominions or other territory as respects any period as respects which effect is so given to those provisions.

[529]

NOTES

Orders in Council: by virtue of s 6(2), the Bretton Woods Agreements Order in Council 1946, SR & O 1946/36 at **[2362]**, and the International Monetary Fund (Immunities and Privileges) Order 1977, SI 1977/825 at **[2455]**, have effect as if made under this section.

6 Repeals and saving

(1) The enactments specified in Part I of the Schedule to this Act (consequential repeals) and Part II of that Schedule (obsolete enactments) are hereby repealed to the extent specified in the third column of that Schedule.

(2) Without prejudice to sections 14 and 17(2) of the Interpretation Act 1978 (implied powers to revoke, amend and re-enact subordinate legislation and savings for such legislation

where enactments are repealed and re-enacted), any Order in Council made under section 3 of the Bretton Woods Agreements Act 1945 and in force immediately before this Act comes into force shall have effect, so far as it applies to the International Monetary Fund, as if made under section 5 above and may accordingly, so far as it so applies, be amended or revoked by an Order in Council under that section.

[530]

NOTES

Bretton Woods Agreement Act 1945, s 3: s 3 of the 1945 Act was repealed in part by s 6(1) of and the Schedule to this Act. The whole of the 1945 Act was repealed by the Overseas Development and Co-operation Act 1980, s 18(1), Sch 2, Pt 1.

7 Short title and commencement

(1) This Act may be cited as the International Monetary Fund Act 1979.

(2) This Act shall come into force on the expiration of the period of one month from the date on which it is passed.

[531]

(*Schedule contains repeals.*)

INTERNATIONAL ORGANISATIONS ACT 1981

(1981 c 9)

An Act to make further provision as to the privileges and immunities to be accorded in respect of certain international organisations and in respect of persons connected with such organisations and other persons, and for the purposes connected therewith

[15 April 1981]

1–3 (*S 1 amends the International Organisations Act 1968, ss 1, 4, 6 at* **[482]**, **[484]**, **[489]**; *ss 2, 3 insert ss 4A, 5A in the 1968 Act at* **[485]**, **[488]**.)

4 Immunities for UK representatives to certain Assemblies

Notwithstanding section 1(6)(b) of the 1968 Act (Orders under section 1 not to confer privileges or immunities on representatives of the United Kingdom, etc), an Order in Council made under section 1 of that Act may confer immunities on representatives of the United Kingdom to the Assembly of Western European Union or to the Consultative Assembly of the Council of Europe.

[532]

NOTES

Western European Union: the Western European Union was created in 1954 by the Protocols signed at Paris on 23 October 1954 (Treaty Series No 39 (1955), Cmd 9498) to the Treaty of Economic Social and Cultural Collaboration and Collective Self-Defence, signed at Brussels on 17 March 1948 (Treaty Series No 1 (1949), Cmd 7599). These were supplemented by the Agreement signed at Paris on 14 December 1958 (Treaty Series No 37 (1962), Cmnd 1712) in implementation of Art V of Protocol No 11 of the Brussels Treaty of 17 March 1948 as modified by the Protocols signed at Paris on 23 October 1954.

Council of Europe: the Council of Europe was created in 1949 by the Statute of the Council of Europe signed at London on 5 May 1949 (Treaty Series No 51 (1949), Cmd 7778). The Consultative Assembly is one of the main organs of the Council and, by virtue of art 40 of the Statute of the Council of Europe, all representatives are to have immunity from arrest and all legal proceedings in the territories of all member States in respect of words spoken and votes cast in debates of the Assembly or its committees or commissions.

Orders in Council: up to the date of publication no Order in Council had been made under the International Organisations Act 1968, s 1 by virtue of this section. The existing Orders in Council under that section relating to the organisations mentioned in this section are the Council of Europe (Immunities and Privileges) Order 1960, SI 1960/442, and the International Organisations (Immunities and Privileges of Western European Union) Order 1955, SI 1955/1209, and the Western European Union (Immunities and Privileges) Order 1960, SI 1960/444, which revokes and replaces SI 1955/1209, but had not been brought into force up to the date of publication.

5 (*Inserts Sch 1, para 9A in the International Organisations Act 1968 at* **[498]** *and amends paras 10, 16 of that Schedule at* **[498]**, **[499]**.)

6 Citation, interpretation, extent and repeals

(1) This Act may be cited as the International Organisations Act 1981; and this Act and the 1968 Act may be cited together as the International Organisations Acts 1968 and 1980.

(2) In this Act "the 1968 Act" means the International Organisations Act 1968.

(3) It is hereby declared that this Act extends to Northern Ireland.

(4) The enactments mentioned in the Schedule to this Act are hereby repealed to the extent specified in the third column of that Schedule.

[533]

(*Schedule contains repeals.*)

MULTILATERAL INVESTMENT GUARANTEE AGENCY ACT 1988

(1988 c 8)

ARRANGEMENT OF SECTIONS

An Act to enable the United Kingdom to give effect to the Convention establishing the Multilateral Investment Guarantee Agency

[24 March 1988]

Preliminary

1 The Convention establishing the Agency

(1) In this Act "the Convention" means the Convention establishing the Multilateral Investment Guarantee Agency which was signed on behalf of the United Kingdom on 9th April 1986 and presented to Parliament as Command Paper No Cm 150 on 25th June 1987.

(2) The provisions of the Convention referred to in sections 2 to 7 below together with certain related provisions, are set out in the Schedule to this Act.

[534]

Payments to and from the Agency

2 Payments to and from the Agency

(1) The Secretary of State may with the consent of the Treasury make out of money provided by Parliament—

(a) any payment in cash required to be made by the United Kingdom under Article 7(i) of the Convention;

(b) any payment required to be made by the United Kingdom for redeeming such notes or obligations as are there mentioned; and

(c) any payment required to be made by the United Kingdom under Article 7(ii) of the Convention.

(2) The Secretary of State may with the consent of the Treasury by order make provision—

(a) for the payment out of money provided by Parliament of any sums required by the Secretary of State for making any other payments by the United Kingdom under the Convention; and

(b) for the payment into the Consolidated Fund of any sums received by the United Kingdom in pursuance of the Convention.

(3) The power to make an order under subsection (2) above shall be exercisable by statutory instrument; and no such order shall be made unless a draft of it has been laid before and approved by the House of Commons.

[535]

NOTES

Orders: the Multilateral Investment Guarantee Agency (Further Subscription to Capital Stock) Order 2000, SI 2000/1406.

Status, privileges and immunities of the Agency

3 Status, privileges and immunities of the Agency

(1) The Articles of the Convention specified in subsection (2) below shall have the force of law in the United Kingdom.

(2) The Articles referred to in subsection (1) above are Articles 1(b), 44, 45, 46(a), 47, 48(i) and 50.

(3) Nothing in Article 47(a) shall be construed—

(a) as entitling the Agency to import goods free of duty or tax without restriction on their subsequent sale in the country to which they were imported;

(b) except as provided in subsection (4) below, as conferring on the Agency any exemption from duties or taxes which form part of the price of goods sold, or

(c) as conferring on the Agency any exemption from duties or taxes which are no more than charges for services rendered.

(4) The Secretary of State shall make arrangements for refunding to the Agency, subject to compliance with such conditions as may be imposed in accordance with the arrangements, car tax paid on new vehicles, and value added tax paid on the supply of goods or services, which are necessary for the exercise of the official activities of the Agency.

(5) If in any proceedings any question arises whether a person is or is not entitled to any privilege or immunity by virtue of this section, a certificate issued by or under the authority of the Secretary of State stating any fact relevant to that question shall be conclusive evidence of that fact.

[536]

Arbitration proceedings under the Convention

4 Registration and enforcement of arbitration awards

(1) A party to a dispute which is the subject of an award rendered pursuant to Article 4 of Annex II to the Convention shall be entitled to have the award registered in the High Court subject to proof of such matters as are prescribed by rules of court and to the other provisions of this section.

(2) In addition to any sum payable under the award, the award shall be registered for the reasonable costs of and incidental to registration.

(3) If at the date of the application for registration any sum payable under the award has been partly paid, the award shall be registered only in respect of the balance and accordingly if that sum has then been wholly paid the award shall not be registered.

(4) An award registered under this section shall be of the same force and effect for the purpose of execution as if it had been a judgment of the High Court given when the award was rendered as mentioned in subsection (1) above and entered on the date of registration under this section and—

(a) proceedings may be taken on the award;
(b) any sum for which the award is registered shall carry interest; and
(c) the High Court shall have the same control over the execution of the award,

as if the award has been such a judgment of the High Court.

(5) This section shall bind the Crown but not so as to make an award enforceable against the Crown in a manner in which a judgment would not be enforceable against the Crown; and an award shall not be enforceable against a State to which the provisions of Part I of the State Immunity Act 1978 apply except in accordance with those provisions.

(6) In this section "award" includes any decision interpreting an award; and for the purposes of this section an award shall be deemed to have been rendered pursuant to Article 4 of Annex II when a copy of it is transmitted to each party as provided in paragraph (h) of that Article.

[537]

5 Rules of court

The power to make rules under section 84 of the Supreme Court Act 1981 shall include the power—

(a) to prescribe the procedure for applying for registration under section 4 above and to require an applicant to give prior notice of his intention to other parties;
(b) to prescribe the matters to be proved on the application and the manner of proof;
(c) to provide for the service of notice of registration of the award by the applicant on other parties; and
(d) to make provision requiring the court on proof of such matters as may be prescribed by the rules to stay execution of an award registered under section 4 above in cases where enforcement of the award has been stayed pursuant to Article 4 of Annex II to the Convention.

[538]

[6 Application of Arbitration Act

(1) The Lord Chancellor may by order made by statutory instrument direct that any of the provisions of sections 36 and 38 to 44 of the Arbitration Act 1996 (provisions in relation to the conduct of the arbitral proceedings, &c) apply, with such modifications or exceptions as are specified in the order, to such arbitration proceedings pursuant to Annex II to the Convention as are specified in the order.

(2) Except as provided by an order under subsection (1) above, no provision of Part I of the Arbitration Act 1996 other than section 9 (stay of legal proceedings) applies to any such proceedings.]

[539]

NOTES

Substituted by the Arbitration Act 1996, s 107(1), Sch 3, para 49.

Functions under this section: functions under this section are transferred, in so far as they are exercisable in or as regards Scotland, to the Scottish Ministers, by the Scotland Act 1998 (Transfer of Functions to the Scottish Ministers etc) Order 1999, SI 1999/1750, art 2, Sch 1.

7 Scotland

In the application of this Act to Scotland—

(a) for any reference in section 4 to the High Court there shall be substituted a reference to the Court of Session;

(b) registration under that section shall be effected by registering in the Books of Council and Session, or in such manner as the Court of Session may by Act of Sederunt prescribe;

(c) for the reference in that section to costs there shall be substituted a reference to expenses;

(d) for the reference in that section to the entering of a judgment there shall be substituted a reference to the signing of the interlocutor embodying the judgment;

(e) the Court of Session shall have power by Act of Sederunt to make rules for the purposes specified in section 5;

(f) for the references in that section and Article 4 of Annex II to the Convention to the staying of proceedings and execution or enforcement of an award there shall be substituted references to the sist of such proceedings, execution or enforcement; and

(g) for section 6 above there shall be substituted the following section—

"6 Proceedings in Scotland

The [Secretary of State] may by order made by statutory instrument make provision, in relation to such arbitration proceedings pursuant to Annex II to the Convention as are specified in the order, being proceedings taking place in Scotland, for the attendance of witnesses, the taking of evidence and the production of documents."

[540]

NOTES

Para (g): in section 6 as it applies to Scotland, words in square brackets substituted by virtue of the Transfer of Functions (Lord Advocate and Secretary of State) Order 1999, SI 1999/678, art 2(1), Schedule.

8 (*Applies to Northern Ireland only.*)

Supplemental

9 Short title, commencement and extent

(1) This Act may be cited as the Multilateral Investment Guarantee Agency Act 1988.

(2) This Act shall come into force on such date as the Secretary of State may appoint by an order made by statutory instrument.

(3) This Act extends to Northern Ireland.

(4) Her Majesty may by Order in Council make provision for extending the provisions of sections 3, 4, 5 and 6 above, with such modifications and exceptions as may be specified in the Order, to any of the Channel Islands, the Isle of Man or any colony.

[541]

NOTES

Orders under sub-s (2): the Multilateral Investment Guarantee Agency Act 1988 (Commencement) Order 1988, SI 1988/715.

Orders in Council under sub-s (4): the Multilateral Investment Guarantee Agency (Overseas Territories) Order 1988, SI 1988/791.

SCHEDULE
PROVISIONS OF THE CONVENTION ESTABLISHING THE MULTILATERAL INVESTMENT GUARANTEE AGENCY

Section 1(2)

CHAPTER I

Article 1

Establishment and Status of the Agency

(a) There is hereby established the Multilateral Investment Guarantee Agency (hereinafter called the Agency).

(b) The Agency shall possess full juridical personality and, in particular, the capacity to:

(i) contract;
(ii) acquire and dispose of movable and immovable property; and
(iii) institute legal proceedings.

CHAPTER II

Article 7

Division and Calls of Subscribed Capital

The initial subscription of each member shall be paid as follows—

(i) Within ninety days from the date on which this Convention enters into force with respect to such member, ten per cent. of the price of each share shall be paid in cash as stipulated in Section (a) of Article 8 and an additional ten per cent. in the form of nonnegotiable, non-interest-bearing promissory notes or similar obligations to be encashed pursuant to a decision of the Board in order to meet the Agency's obligations.
(ii) The remainder shall be subject to call by the Agency when required to meet its obligations.

Article 8

Payment of Subscription of Shares

(a) Payments of subscriptions shall be made in freely usable currencies except that payments by developing member countries may be made in their own currencies up to twenty-five per cent. of the paid-in cash portion of their subscriptions payable under Article 7(i).

(b) Calls on any portion of unpaid subscriptions shall be uniform on all shares.

(c) If the amount received by the Agency on a call shall be insufficient to meet the obligations which have necessitated the call, the Agency may make further successive calls on unpaid subscriptions until the aggregate amount received by it shall be sufficient to meet such obligations.

(d) Liability on shares shall be limited to the unpaid portion of the issue price.

CHAPTER V

Article 30

Structure of the Agency

The Agency shall have a Council of Governors, a Board of Directors, a President and staff to perform such duties as the Agency may determine.

Article 31

The Council

(b) The Council shall be composed of one Governor and one Alternate appointed by each member in such manner as it may determine. The Council shall select one of the Governors as Chairman.

Article 32

The Board

(b) Each Director may appoint an Alternate with full power to act for him in case of the Director's absence or inability to act.

CHAPTER VII

Article 44

Legal Process

Actions other than those within the scope of Articles 57 and 58 may be brought against the Agency only in a court of competent jurisdiction in the territories of a member in which the Agency has an office or has appointed an agent for the purpose of accepting service or notice of process. No such action against the Agency shall be brought (i) by members or persons acting for or deriving claims from members or (ii) in respect of personnel matters. The property and assets of the Agency shall, wherever located and by whomsoever held, be immune from all forms of seizure, attachment or execution before the delivery of the final judgment or award against the Agency.

Article 45

Assets

(a) The property and assets of the Agency, wherever located and by whomsoever held, shall be immune from search, requisition, confiscation. expropriation or any other form of seizure by executive or legislative action.

(b) To the extent necessary to carry out its operations under this Convention, all property and assets of the Agency shall be free from restrictions, regulations, controls and moratoria of any nature; provided that property and assets acquired by the Agency as successor to or subrogee of a holder of a guarantee, a reinsured entity or an investor insured by a reinsured entity shall be free from applicable foreign exchange restrictions, regulations and controls in force in the territories of the member concerned to the extent that the holder, entity or investor to whom the Agency was subrogated was entitled to such treatment.

(c) For purposes of this Chapter, the term "assets" shall include the assets of the Sponsorship Trust Fund referred to in Annex I to this Convention and other assets administered by the Agency in furtherance of its objective.

Article 46

Archives and Communications

(a) The archives of the Agency shall be inviolable, wherever they may be.

Article 47

Taxes

(a) The Agency, its assets, property and income, and its operations and transactions authorised by this Convention, shall be immune from all taxes and customs duties. The Agency shall also be immune from liability for the collection or payment of any tax or duty.

(b) Except in the case of local nationals, no tax shall be levied on or in respect of expense allowances paid by the Agency to Governors and their Alternates or on or in respect of salaries, expense allowances or other emoluments paid by the Agency to the Chairman of the Board, Directors, their Alternates, the President or staff of the Agency.

(c) No taxation of any kind shall be levied on any investment guaranteed or reinsured by the Agency (including any earnings therefrom) or any insurance policies reinsured by the Agency (including any premiums and other revenues therefrom) by whomsoever held: (i) which discriminates against such investment or insurance policy solely because it is guaranteed or reinsured by the Agency; or (ii) if the sole jurisdictional basis for such taxation is the location of any office or place of business maintained by the Agency.

Article 48

Officials of the Agency

All Governors, Directors, Alternates, the President and staff of the Agency:

(i) shall be immune from legal process with respect to acts performed by them in their official capacity;

Article 50

Waiver

The immunities, exemptions and privileges provided in this Chapter are granted in the interests of the Agency and may be waived, to such extent and upon such conditions as the Agency may determine, in cases where such a waiver would not prejudice its interests. The Agency shall waive the immunity of any of its staff in cases where, in its opinion, the immunity would impede the course of justice and can be waived without prejudice to the interests of the Agency.

CHAPTER IX

Article 56

Interpretation and Application of the Convention

(a) Any question of interpretation or application of the provisions of this Convention arising between any member of the Agency and the Agency or among members of the Agency shall be submitted to the Board for its decision. Any member which is particularly affected by the question and which is not otherwise represented by a national in the Board may send a representative to attend any meeting of the Board at which such question is considered.

(b) In any case where the Board has given a decision under Section (a) above, any member may require that the question be referred to the Council, whose decision shall be final. Pending the result of the referral to the Council, the Agency may, so far as it deems necessary, act on the basis of the decision of the Board.

Article 57

Disputes between the Agency and Members

(a) Without prejudice to the provisions of Article 56 and of Section (b) of this Article, any dispute between the Agency and a member or an agency thereof and any dispute between the Agency and a country (or agency thereof) which has ceased to be a member, shall be settled in accordance with the procedure set out in Annex II to this Convention.

(b) Disputes concerning claims of the Agency acting as subrogee of an investor shall be settled in accordance with either (i) the procedure set out in Annex II to this Convention, or (ii) an agreement to be entered into between the Agency and the member concerned on an alternative method or methods for the settlement of such disputes. In the latter case, Annex II to this Convention shall serve as a basis for such an agreement which shall, in each case, be approved by the Board by special majority prior to the undertaking by the Agency of operations in the territories of the member concerned.

Article 58

Disputes Involving Holders of a Guarantee or Reinsurance

Any dispute arising under a contract of guarantee or reinsurance between the parties thereto shall be submitted to arbitration for final determination in accordance with such rules as shall be provided for or referred to in the contract of guarantee or reinsurance.

ANNEX I

Article 2

Sponsorship Trust Fund

(a) Premiums and other revenues attributable to guarantees of sponsored investments, including returns on the investment of such premiums and revenues, shall be held in a separate account which shall be called the Sponsorship Trust Fund.

(b) All administrative expenses and payments on claims attributable to guarantees issued under this Annex shall be paid out of the Sponsorship Trust Fund.

(c) The assets of the Sponsorship Trust Fund shall be held and administered for the joint account of sponsoring members and shall be kept separate and apart from the assets of the Agency.

ANNEX II

Article 1

Application of the Annex

All disputes within the scope of Article 57 of this Convention shall be settled in accordance with the procedure set out in this Annex, except in the cases where the Agency has entered into an agreement with a member pursuant to Section (b)(ii) of Article 57.

Article 4

Arbitration

(a) Arbitration proceedings shall be instituted by means of a notice by the party seeking arbitration (the claimant) addressed to the other party or parties to the dispute (the respondent). The notice shall specify the nature of the dispute, the relief sought and the name of the arbitrator appointed by the claimant. The respondent shall, within thirty days after the date of receipt of the notice, notify the claimant of the name of the arbitrator appointed by it. The two parties shall, within a period of thirty days from the date of appointment of the second arbitrator, select a third arbitrator, who shall act as President of the Arbitral Tribunal (the Tribunal).

(b) If the Tribunal shall not have been constituted within sixty days from the date of the notice, the arbitrator not yet appointed or the President not yet selected shall be appointed, at the joint request of the parties, by the Secretary-General of ICSID (the International Centre for Settlement of Investment Disputes). If there is no such joint request, or if the Secretary-General shall fail to make the appointment within thirty days of the request, either party may request the President of the International Court of Justice to make the appointment.

(c) No party shall have the right to change the arbitrator appointed by it once the hearing of the dispute has commenced. In case any arbitrator (including the President of the Tribunal) shall resign, die, or become incapacitated, a successor shall be appointed in the manner followed in the appointment of his predecessor and such successor shall have the same powers and duties of the arbitrator he succeeds.

(d) The Tribunal shall convene first at such time and place as shall be determined by the President. Thereafter, the Tribunal shall determine the place and dates of its meetings.

(e) Unless otherwise provided in this Annex or agreed upon by the parties, the Tribunal shall determine its procedure and shall be guided in this regard by the arbitration rules adopted pursuant to the Convention on the Settlement of Investment Disputes between States and Nationals of Other States.

(f) The Tribunal shall be the judge of its own competence except that, if an objection is raised before the Tribunal to the effect that the dispute falls within the jurisdiction of the Board or the Council under Article 56 or within the jurisdiction of a judicial or arbitral body designated in an agreement under Article 1 of this Annex and the Tribunal is satisfied that the objection is genuine, the objection shall be referred by the Tribunal to the Board or the Council or the designated body, as the case may be, and the arbitration proceedings shall be stayed until a decision has been reached on the matter, which shall be binding upon the Tribunal.

(g) The Tribunal shall, in any dispute within the scope of this Annex, apply the provisions of this Convention, any relevant agreement between the parties to the dispute, the Agency's by-laws and regulations, the applicable rules of international law, the domestic law of the member concerned as well as the applicable provisions of the investment contract, if any. Without prejudice to the provisions of this Convention, the Tribunal may decide a dispute *ex aequo et bono* if the Agency and the member concerned so agree. The Tribunal may not bring a finding of *non liquet* on the ground of silence or obscurity of the law.

(h) The Tribunal shall afford a fair hearing to all the parties. All decisions of the Tribunal shall be taken by a majority vote and shall state the reasons on which they are based. The award of the Tribunal shall be in writing, and shall be signed by at least two arbitrators and a copy thereof shall be transmitted to each party. The award shall be final and binding upon the parties and shall not be subject to appeal, annulment or revision.

(i) If any dispute shall arise between the parties as to the meaning or scope of an award, either party may, within sixty days after the award was rendered, request interpretation of the award by an application in writing to the President of the Tribunal which rendered the award. The President shall, if possible, submit the request to the Tribunal which rendered the award and shall convene such Tribunal within sixty days after receipt of the application. If this shall not be possible, a new Tribunal shall be constituted in accordance with the provisions of Sections (a) to (d) above. The Tribunal may stay enforcement of the award pending its decision on the requested interpretation.

(j) Each member shall recognize an award rendered pursuant to this Article as binding and enforceable within its territories as if it were a final judgment of a court in that member. Execution of the award shall be governed by the laws concerning the execution of judgments in force in the State in whose territories such execution is sought and shall not derogate from the law in force relating to immunity from execution.

(k) Unless the parties shall agree otherwise, the fees and remuneration payable to the arbitrators shall be determined on the basis of the rates applicable to ICSID arbitration. Each party shall defray its own costs associated with the arbitration proceedings. The costs of the Tribunal shall be borne by the parties in equal proportion unless the Tribunal decides otherwise. Any question concerning the division of the costs of the Tribunal or the procedure for payment of such costs shall be decided by the Tribunal.

[542]

INTERNATIONAL DEVELOPMENT ACT 2002

(2002 c 1)

An Act to make provision relating to the provision of assistance for countries outside the United Kingdom; to make provision with respect to certain international financial institutions and the Commonwealth Scholarship Commission; and for connected purposes

[26 February 2002]

1–10 (*Pt 1 relates to development assistance.*)

PART 2
MISCELLANEOUS AND GENERAL

International financial institutions

11 Multilateral development banks

(1) This section applies where the Government of the United Kingdom is at the time this section comes into force, or at a later time becomes, bound to make a relevant payment to a multilateral development bank.

(2) For the purposes of this section—

"multilateral development bank" means an international financial institution having as one of its objects economic development, either generally or in any region of the world; and

"relevant payment", in relation to such a bank, means—

(a) an initial subscription, or other initial contribution to the capital stock of the bank, that the international agreement for the establishment and operation of the bank requires the members of the bank to make, or

(b) a further payment to the bank required to be made by the members under any arrangements.

(3) The Secretary of State may—

(a) on behalf of the Government of the United Kingdom, make—

(i) the relevant payment, or

(ii) where it has been paid, any payment required to maintain its value; or

(b) make a payment to redeem any non-interest-bearing and non-negotiable notes, or other obligations, issued or created by him, that are accepted by the bank in accordance with the agreement or arrangements under which the relevant payment is required to be made.

(4) Subsection (3) applies to a payment only if it is approved for the purposes of this section by an order made by the Secretary of State with the approval of the Treasury.

(5) No order shall be made under subsection (4) unless a draft of it has been laid before and approved by the House of Commons.

[543]

NOTES

Commencement: 17 June 2002.

Orders: the African Development Fund (Additional Subscriptions) Order 2002, SI 2002/2404; the Caribbean Development Bank (Further Payments) Order 2002, SI 2002/2405; the International Development Association (Thirteenth Replenishment) Order 2002, SI 2003/700; the African Development Fund (Ninth Replenishment) Order 2003, SI 2003/1739; the International Fund for Agricultural Development (Fifth Replenishment) Order 2003, SI 2003/2157; the International Fund for Agricultural Development (Sixth Replenishment) Order 2004, SI 2004/3170; the International Development Association (Fourteenth Replenishment) Order 2006, SI 2006/1071.

In addition, by virtue of Sch 5, para 1 to this Act, the following orders have effect as if made under this section: the International Development Association (Sixth Replenishment: Interim Payments) Order 1981, SI 1981/517; the International Development Association (Sixth Replenishment) Order 1981, SI 1981/1504; the International Development Association (Special Contributions) Order 1983, SI 1983/1299; the International Development Association (Seventh Replenishment) Order 1985, SI 1985/80; the International Development Association (Eighth Replenishment) Order 1988, SI 1988/750; the International Development Association (Ninth Replenishment) Order 1991, SI 1991/462; the International Development Association (Tenth Replenishment) Order 1993, SI 1993/2046; the International Development Association (Interim Trust Fund) Order 1997, SI 1997/840; the International Development Association (Eleventh Replenishment) Order 1998, SI 1998/1149; the International Development Association (Twelfth Replenishment) Order 2000, SI 2000/1399.

In addition, by virtue of the Interpretation Act 1978, s 17(2)(b), the following orders have effect as if made under this section: the International Development Association (Additional Payments) Order 1969, SI 1969/429; the International Development Association (Third Replenishment: Interim Payments) Order 1971, SI 1971/1773; the International Development Association (Third Replenishment) Order 1972, SI 1972/1576; the International Development Association (Fourth Replenishment: Interim Payments) Order 1974, SI 1974/1881; the International Development Association (Fourth Replenishment) Order 1975, SI 1975/1088; the International Development Association (Fifth Replenishment: Interim Payments) Order 1977, SI 1977/1839; the International Development Association (Fifth Replenishment) Order 1978, SI 1978/472.

---

12 Immunities and privileges of international financial institutions

(1) Her Majesty may by Order in Council make such provision as She considers reasonably necessary for giving effect to any relevant provision of the agreement establishing an international financial institution.

(2) For this purpose a provision is "relevant" if it relates to the status, immunities or privileges of—

(a) the international financial institution,

(b) its governors, directors or executive-directors or alternates, or

(c) its officers or employees.

(3) For the purposes of this section the following are "international financial institutions"—

(a) the International Bank for Reconstruction and Development;

(b) the International Finance Corporation;

(c) the International Development Association.

(4) No recommendation may be made to Her Majesty in Council to make an Order under this section unless a draft of the Order has been laid before Parliament and approved by resolution of each House of Parliament.

(5) The Secretary of State may by order amend subsection (3) by making additions to or deletions from the institutions that are for the time being listed there.

(6) This section is without prejudice to the powers conferred by the International Organisations Act 1968 (c 48) or any other Act.

[544]

NOTES
Commencement: 17 June 2002.
By virtue of the Interpretation Act 1978, s 17(2)(b), the following orders have effect as if made under this Act: the Bretton Woods Agreements Order in Council 1946, SR & O 1946/36; the International Finance Corporation Order 1955, SI 1955/1954; the International Development Association Order 1960, SI 1960/1383.

13, 14 (*Relate to the Commonwealth Scholarship Commission.*)

Miscellaneous repeals

15 Repeals in the Overseas Development and Co-operation Act 1980

The following provisions of the Overseas Development and Co-operation Act 1980 (c 63) shall cease to have effect—

(a) section 3 (abortive exploratory expenditure connected with overseas enterprises);
(b) section 7 (the Asian Development Bank);
(c) section 8 (guarantees of International Bank's loans to colonial territories).

[545]

NOTES
Commencement: 17 June 2002.

General

16 Financial provision

(1) There shall be paid out of money provided by Parliament—

(a) any expenses incurred by the Secretary of State by virtue of this Act;
(b) any sums required by him for fulfilling any guarantee given under this Act;
(c) any increase attributable to this Act in the sums payable out of money so provided by virtue of any other Act.

(2) There shall be paid into the Consolidated Fund any sums received by the Secretary of State—

(a) by way of interest on, or repayment of, a loan made under this Act,
(b) as a result of the disposal of any securities acquired under this Act, or by way of a dividend or other payment in respect of such securities, or
(c) by way of payment under section 7 for any assistance under this Act, other than financial assistance.

(3) In this section "securities" has the same meaning as in section 6.

[546]

NOTES
Commencement: 17 June 2002.

17 Interpretation

(1) In this Act—

"assistance" has the meaning given in section 5;
"country" includes any territory or region;
"development assistance" has the meaning given in section 1.

(2) For the purposes of this Act references to the population of a country include references to any future population of the country and to any part of the population (present or future).

[547]

NOTES
Commencement: 17 June 2002.

18 Orders

(1) Any power conferred by this Act to make an order is exercisable by statutory instrument.

(2) A statutory instrument made by the Secretary of State under any power conferred by this Act to make an order, except an order under section 11(4) or 20(2), is subject to annulment in pursuance of a resolution of either House of Parliament.

(3) A statutory instrument made by the Scottish Ministers under the power conferred by section 9(5) is subject to annulment in pursuance of a resolution of the Scottish Parliament.
[548]

NOTES
Commencement: 17 June 2002.

19 Consequential amendments and repeals

(1) Schedule 3 (consequential amendments) has effect.

(2) The enactments specified in Schedule 4 are repealed to the extent specified.
[549]

NOTES
Commencement: 17 June 2002.

20 Short title, commencement and extent

(1) This Act may be cited as the International Development Act 2002.

(2) This Act shall come into force on such day as the Secretary of State may by order appoint.

(3) Schedule 5 (which makes transitional provisions and savings in connection with the commencement of this Act) has effect.

(4) Any amendment contained in Schedule 3 or repeal contained in Schedule 4 has the same extent as the enactment to which it relates.

(5) Subject to that, this Act extends to Northern Ireland.
[550]

NOTES
Commencement: 17 June 2002.
Orders: the International Development Act 2002 (Commencement) Order 2002, SI 2002/1408.

(Sch 1 relates to statutory bodies; Sch 2 relates to the Commonwealth Scholarship Commission; Sch 3 contains consequential amendments; Sch 4 contains repeals; Sch 5 contains transitional provisions.)

INTERNATIONAL ORGANISATIONS ACT 2005

(2005 c 20)

An Act to make provision about privileges, immunities and facilities in connection with certain international organisations

[7 April 2005]

1 Commonwealth Secretariat

(1), (2) …

(3) This section does not have effect in relation to any written contract entered into by or on behalf of the Commonwealth Secretariat before this section comes into force.

(4) "The Commonwealth Secretariat" has the same meaning as in the Commonwealth Secretariat Act 1966.

[551]

NOTES

Commencement: 11 July 2005.
Sub-s (1): amends the Commonwealth Secretariat Act 1966, s 1, Schedule.
Sub-s (2): repeals the Arbitration Act 1996, Sch 3, para 23.

2 Commonwealth Secretariat Arbitral Tribunal

(1)–(3) …

(4) If the Commonwealth Secretariat Arbitral Tribunal is replaced by a successor, the Secretary of State may by order made by statutory instrument amend the Commonwealth Secretariat Act 1966 (c 10) in whatever way he considers appropriate for the purpose of conferring, in relation to the successor, immunities and privileges equivalent to those conferred by virtue of subsections (2) and (3).

(5) No order under subsection (4) may be made unless a draft of the statutory instrument containing the order has been laid before, and approved by resolution of, each House of Parliament.

[552]

NOTES

Commencement: 11 July 2005.
Sub-ss (1)–(3): amend the Commonwealth Secretariat Act 1966, s 1(2), Schedule.

3 (*Amends the Commonwealth Secretariat Act 1966, Schedule.*)

4 Organisation for Security and Co-operation in Europe

(1) If at any time the Organisation for Security and Co-operation in Europe ("the OSCE") is not for the purposes of section 1 of the International Organisations Act 1968 (c 48) ("the 1968 Act") an organisation of which—

(a) the United Kingdom, or Her Majesty's Government in the United Kingdom, and

(b) at least one other sovereign Power, or the Government of such a Power,

are members, it is to be treated for those purposes as such an organisation.

(2) Any agreement or formal understanding between the United Kingdom or Her Majesty's Government in the United Kingdom and any other sovereign Power or the Government of such a Power and relating to the OSCE is to be treated for the purposes of section 1(5) and (6)(a) of the 1968 Act as an agreement between the United Kingdom and the OSCE.

[553]

NOTES

Commencement: 7 June 2005.

5, 6 (*S 5 inserts the International Organisations Act 1968, s 4B at* **[486]**; *s 6 amends the International Criminal Court Act 2001, Sch 1, para 1.*)

7 European Court of Human Rights

Section 5 of the 1968 Act (privileges relating to international judicial proceedings) applies to members of the family of a judge of the European Court of Human Rights as it applies to a judge of that court.

[554]

NOTES

Commencement: 7 June 2005.

8 International Tribunal for the Law of the Sea

The International Tribunal for the Law of the Sea is to be treated for the purposes of section 1 of the 1968 Act (organisations of which the United Kingdom is a member) as an organisation of which—

(a) the United Kingdom, or Her Majesty's Government in the United Kingdom, and

(b) at least one other sovereign Power, or the Government of such a Power,

are members.

[555]

NOTES

Commencement: 7 June 2005.

Orders: the International Tribunal for the Law of the Sea (Immunities and Privileges) Order 2005, SI 2005/2047

9 Repeals

The Schedule contains a list of enactments repealed by this Act.

[556]

NOTES

Commencement: 7 June 2005.

10 Devolution

For the purposes of the Scotland Act 1998 (c 46), sections 4, 5, 7 and 8 of this Act are to be taken to be pre-commencement enactments within the meaning of that Act.

[557]

NOTES

Commencement: 7 June 2005.

11 Short title, interpretation, commencement and extent

(1) This Act may be cited as the International Organisations Act 2005.

(2) In this Act "the 1968 Act" means the International Organisations Act 1968 (c 48).

(3) Except for sections 1 to 3, this Act comes into force at the end of the period of two months beginning with the day on which it is passed.

(4) Sections 1 to 3 come into force on such day as the Secretary of State by order made by statutory instrument appoints, and he may appoint different days for different purposes.

(5) This Act extends to Northern Ireland.

[558]

NOTES

Commencement: 7 June 2005.

Orders: the International Organisations Act 2005 (Commencement) Order 2005, SI 2005/1870.

(*Schedule contains repeals.*)

H. CROSS-BORDER INSOLVENCY

BANKRUPTCY (SCOTLAND) ACT 1985

(1985 c 66)

An Act to reform the law of Scotland relating to sequestration and personal insolvency; and for connected purposes

[30 October 1985]

NOTES

This is a major Act, most parts of which are outside the scope of this work and are therefore omitted. Provisions omitted are not annotated.

Miscellaneous and supplementary

63 Power to cure defects in procedure

(1) The sheriff may, on the application of any person having an interest—

(a) if there has been a failure to comply with any requirement of this Act or any regulations made under it, make an order waiving any such failure and, so far as practicable, restoring any person prejudiced by the failure to the position he would have been in but for the failure;

(b) if for any reason anything required or authorised to be done in, or in connection with, the sequestration process cannot be done, make such order as may be necessary to enable that thing to be done.

(2) The sheriff, in an order under subsection (1) above, may impose such conditions, including conditions as to expenses, as he thinks fit and may—

(a) authorise or dispense with the performance of any act in the sequestration process;

(b) appoint as permanent trustee on the debtor's estate a person who would be eligible to be elected under section 24 of this Act, whether or not in place of an existing trustee;

(c) extend or waive any time limit specified in or under this Act.

(3) An application under subsection (1) above—

(a) may at any time be remitted by the sheriff to the Court of Session, of his own accord or on an application by any person having an interest;

(b) shall be so remitted, if the Court of Session so directs on an application by any such person,

if the sheriff or the Court of Session, as the case may be, considers that the remit is desirable because of the importance or complexity of the matters raised by the application.

(4) The permanent trustee shall record in the sederunt book the decision of the sheriff or the Court of Session under this section.

[559]

78 Short title, commencement and extent

(1) This Act may be cited as the Bankruptcy (Scotland) Act 1985.

(2) This Act, except this section, shall come into force on such day as the Secretary of State may by order made by statutory instrument appoint; and different days may be so appointed for different purposes and for different provisions.

(3) An order under subsection (2) above may contain such transitional provisions and savings as appear to the Secretary of State necessary or expedient in connection with the provisions brought into force (whether wholly or partly) by the order.

(4) Without prejudice to section 75(3) to (5) of this Act, this Act applies to sequestrations as regards which the petition—

(a) is presented on or after the date of coming into force of section 5 of this Act; or

(b) was presented before, but in respect of which no award of sequestration has been made by, that date.

(5) This Act, except the provisions mentioned in subsection (6) below, extends to Scotland only.

(6) The provisions referred to in subsection (5) above are sections 8(5), 22(8) (including that subsection as applied by section 48(7)), 46, 55 and 73(5), paragraph 16(b) of Schedule 4 and paragraph 3 of Schedule 5.

[560]

INSOLVENCY ACT 1986

(1986 c 45)

ARRANGEMENT OF SECTIONS

THE FIRST GROUP OF PARTS
COMPANY INSOLVENCY; COMPANIES WINDING UP

PART II
ADMINISTRATION

PART III
RECEIVERSHIP

CHAPTER III
RECEIVERS' POWERS IN GREAT BRITAIN AS A WHOLE

PART IV
WINDING UP OF COMPANIES REGISTERED
UNDER THE COMPANIES ACTS

CHAPTER VI
WINDING UP BY THE COURT

Jurisdiction (England and Wales)

Jurisdiction (Scotland)

Grounds and effect of winding-up petition

PART V
WINDING UP OF UNREGISTERED COMPANIES

An Act to consolidate the enactments relating to company insolvency and winding up (including the winding up of companies that are not insolvent, and of unregistered companies); enactments relating to the insolvency and bankruptcy of individuals; and other enactments bearing on those two subject matters, including the functions and qualification of insolvency practitioners, the public administration of insolvency, the penalisation and redress of malpractice and wrongdoing, and the avoidance of certain transactions at an undervalue

[25 July 1986]

NOTES

Commencement: this Act came into force on 29 December 1986 by virtue of s 443 and the Insolvency Act 1985 (Commencement No 5) Order 1986, SI 1986/1924, art 3.

Modification in relation to solicitors: the provisions of this Act, except s 413 and Sch 7, are applied, with modifications, in relation to a "recognised body" under the Administration of Justice Act 1985, s 9, by the Solicitors' Incorporated Practices Order 1991, SI 1991/2684, arts 2–5, Sch 1, as amended by SI 2001/645.

Modification in relation to Scotland: by virtue of the Scotland Act 1998, s 125, Sch 8, para 23, (i) anything directed to be done, or which may be done, to or by the registrar of companies in Scotland by virtue of ss 53(1), 54(3), 61(6), 62(5) (so far as relating to the giving of notice), 67(1), 69(2), 84(3), 94(3), 106(3) and (5), 112(3), 130(1), 147(3), 170(2) and 172(8), or the Financial Services Authority by virtue of any of those provisions as applied (with or without modifications) in relation to friendly societies, industrial and provident societies or building societies, shall, or (as the case may be) may, also be done to or by the Accountant in Bankruptcy, and (ii) anything directed to be done, or which may be done, to or by the registrar of companies in Scotland by virtue of ss 89(3), 109(1), 171(5) and (6), 173(2)(a) and 192(1), or the Financial Services Authority by virtue of any of those provisions as applied (with or without modification) in relation to friendly societies, industrial and provident societies or building societies, shall instead be done to or by the Accountant in Bankruptcy.

Modification in relation to insolvent partnerships: this Act is extensively applied and modified in relation to insolvent partnerships; see the Insolvent Partnerships Order 1994, SI 1994/2421.

Modification in relation to limited liability partnerships: the provisions of this Act relating to companies and partnerships are applied with modifications to limited liability partnerships; see the Limited Liability Partnerships (Scotland) Regulations 2001, SSI 2001/128 and the Limited Liability Partnerships Regulations 2001, SI 2001/1090.

Modification in relation to open-ended investment companies: where an open-ended investment company is wound up as an unregistered company under Pt V, the provisions of this Act apply for the purposes of the winding up subject to certain modifications; see the Open-Ended Investment Companies Regulations 2001, SI 2001/1228.

Application to foreign companies: the Secretary of State may by order provide for this Act to apply, with or without modification, in relation to a company incorporated outside Great Britain; see the Enterprise Act 2002, s 254.

Application to UK insurers: as to the application of this Act to UK insurers, see the Insurers (Reorganisation and Winding Up) Regulations 2004, SI 2004/353 at **[2596]**.

Companies Act: references in this Act to the Companies Act are to the Companies Act 1985.

This is a major Act, most parts of which are outside the scope of this work and are therefore omitted. Provisions omitted are not annotated.

THE FIRST GROUP OF PARTS
COMPANY INSOLVENCY; COMPANIES WINDING UP

NOTES

Application to limited liability partnerships: Pts I–IV, VI, VII of this Group of Parts are applied, with modifications, to limited liability partnerships, by the Limited Liability Partnerships Regulations 2001, SI 2001/1090, reg 5, Sch 4.

[PART II
ADMINISTRATION

NOTES

Application to industrial and provident societies and friendly societies: this Part may be applied, with or without modification, in relation to industrial and provident societies and friendly societies by order of the Treasury, with the concurrence of the Secretary of State; see the Enterprise Act 2002, s 255.

8 Administration

Schedule B1 to this Act (which makes provision about the administration of companies) shall have effect.]

[561]

NOTES

This Part (Pt II (s 8)) substituted for existing Pt II (ss 8–27) by the Enterprise Act 2002, s 248(1), except in relation to special administration regimes.

PART III
RECEIVERSHIP

NOTES

European Economic Interest Groupings: as to the application of this Part of this Act to European Economic Interest Groupings, see the European Economic Interest Grouping Regulations 1989, SI 1989/638, reg 19(1).

CHAPTER III
RECEIVERS' POWERS IN GREAT BRITAIN AS A WHOLE

72 Cross-border operation of receivership provisions

(1) A receiver appointed under the law of either part of Great Britain in respect of the whole or any part of any property or undertaking of a company and in consequence of the company having created a charge which, as created, was a floating charge may exercise his powers in the other part of Great Britain so far as their exercise is not inconsistent with the law applicable there.

(2) In subsection (1) "receiver" includes a manager and a person who is appointed both receiver and manager.

[562]

PART IV
WINDING UP OF COMPANIES REGISTERED UNDER THE COMPANIES ACTS

NOTES

Modification of this Part in relation to building societies: this Part is applied with modifications in relation to the winding up of building societies; see the Building Societies Act 1986, s 90, Sch 15.

Application of this Part in relation to financial markets: this Part is applied with modifications in relation to certain proceedings begun before the commencement of the Companies Act 1989, s 182, in respect of insolvency proceedings regarding members of recognised investment exchanges and clearing houses and persons to whom market charges have been granted; see s 182 of the 1989 Act.

Modification of this Part in relation to friendly societies: as to the application, with modifications, of this Part to the winding up of incorporated friendly societies under the Friendly Societies Act 1992, s 21(1) or 22(2), see s 23 of, and Sch 10 to, that Act.

Modification of this Part in relation to industrial and provident societies: this Part is applied with modifications to an order or resolution to wind up a society registered under the Industrial and Provident Societies Act 1965; see s 55 of that Act.

CHAPTER VI
WINDING UP BY THE COURT

Jurisdiction (England and Wales)

117 High Court and county court jurisdiction

(1) The High Court has jurisdiction to wind up any company registered in England and Wales.

(2) Where the amount of a company's share capital paid up or credited as paid up does not exceed £120,000, then (subject to this section) the county court of the district in which the company's registered office is situated has concurrent jurisdiction with the High Court to wind up the company.

(3) The money sum for the time being specified in subsection (2) is subject to increase or reduction by order under section 416 in Part XV.

(4) The Lord Chancellor [may, with the concurrence of the Lord Chief Justice, by order] in a statutory instrument exclude a county court from having winding-up jurisdiction, and for the purposes of that jurisdiction may attach its district, or any part thereof, to any other county court, and may by statutory instrument revoke or vary any such order.

In exercising the powers of this section, the Lord Chancellor shall provide that a county court is not to have winding-up jurisdiction unless it has for the time being jurisdiction for the purposes of Parts VIII to XI of this Act (individual insolvency).

(5) Every court in England and Wales having winding-up jurisdiction has for the purposes of that jurisdiction all the powers of the High Court; and every prescribed officer of the court shall perform any duties which an officer of the High Court may discharge by order of a judge of that court or otherwise in relation to winding up.

(6) For the purposes of this section, a company's "registered office" is the place which has longest been its registered office during the 6 months immediately preceding the presentation of the petition for winding up.

[(7) This section is subject to Article 3 of the EC Regulation (jurisdiction under EC Regulation).]

[(8) The Lord Chief Justice may nominate a judicial office holder (as defined in section 109(4) of the Constitutional Reform Act 2005) to exercise his functions under this section.]

[563]

NOTES

Sub-s (4): words in square brackets substituted by the Constitutional Reform Act 2005, s 15(1), Sch 4, Pt 1, paras 185, 186(1), (2).

Sub-s (7): added by the Insolvency Act 1986 (Amendment) (No 2) Regulations 2002, SI 2002/1240, regs 3, 6.

Sub-s (8): added by the Constitutional Reform Act 2005, s 15(1), Sch 4, Pt 1, paras 185, 186(1), (3).

Presentation of the petition for winding up: as to the modification of references to "the presentation of the petition for winding up" in this section and s 120 at **[564]** for the purposes of the Company Directors Disqualification Act 1986, s 6(3), see s 6(3A) of that Act.

Orders: the Civil Courts Order 1983, SI 1983/713.

Jurisdiction (Scotland)

120 Court of Session and sheriff court jurisdiction

(1) The Court of Session has jurisdiction to wind up any company registered in Scotland.

(2) When the Court of Session is in vacation, the jurisdiction conferred on that court by this section may (subject to the provisions of this Part) be exercised by the judge acting as vacation judge …

(3) Where the amount of a company's share capital paid up or credited as paid up does not exceed £120,000, the sheriff court of the sheriffdom in which the company's registered office is situated has concurrent jurisdiction with the Court of Session to wind up the company; but—

- (a) the Court of Session may, if it thinks expedient having regard to the amount of the company's assets to do so—
  - (i) remit to a sheriff court any petition presented to the Court of Session for winding up such a company, or
  - (ii) require such a petition presented to a sheriff court to be remitted to the Court of Session; and
- (b) the Court of Session may require any such petition as above-mentioned presented to one sheriff court to be remitted to another sheriff court; and
- (c) in a winding up in the sheriff court the sheriff may submit a stated case for the opinion of the Court of Session on any question of law arising in that winding up.

(4) For purposes of this section, the expression "registered office" means the place which has longest been the company's registered office during the 6 months immediately preceding the presentation of the petition for winding up.

(5) The money sum for the time being specified in subsection (3) is subject to increase or reduction by order under section 416 in Part XV.

[(6) This section is subject to Article 3 of the EC Regulation (jurisdiction under EC Regulation).]

[564]

NOTES

Sub-s (2): words omitted repealed by the Court of Session Act 1988, s 52(2), Sch 2, Pt III.

Sub-s (6): added by the Insolvency Act 1986 (Amendment) (No 2) Regulations 2002, SI 2002/1240, regs 3, 7.

Presentation of the petition for winding up: see the note to s 117 at **[563]**.

Modification: as to the application, with modifications, of this section, to European Economic Interest Groupings, see the European Economic Interest Grouping Regulations 1989, SI 1989/638, reg 19(2).

121 Power to remit winding up to Lord Ordinary

(1) The Court of Session may, by Act of Sederunt, make provision for the taking of proceedings in a winding up before one of the Lords Ordinary; and, where provision is so made, the Lord Ordinary has, for the purposes of the winding up, all the powers and jurisdiction of the court.

(2) However, the Lord Ordinary may report to the Inner House any matter which may arise in the course of a winding up.

[565]

Grounds and effect of winding-up petition

124 Application for winding up

(1) Subject to the provisions of this section, an application to the court for the winding up of a company shall be by petition presented either by the company, or the directors, or by any creditor or creditors (including any contingent or prospective creditor or creditors), contributory or contributories[, or by a liquidator (within the meaning of Article 2(b) of the EC Regulation) appointed in proceedings by virtue of Article 3(1) of the EC Regulation or a temporary administrator (within the meaning of Article 38 of the EC Regulation)] [or by [the designated officer for a magistrates' court] in the exercise of the power conferred by section 87A of the Magistrates' Courts Act 1980 (enforcement of fines imposed on companies)], or by all or any of those parties, together or separately.

(2) Except as mentioned below, a contributory is not entitled to present a winding-up petition unless either—

(a) the number of members is reduced below 2, or

(b) the shares in respect of which he is a contributory, or some of them, either were originally allotted to him, or have been held by him, and registered in his name, for at least 6 months during the 18 months before the commencement of the winding up, or have devolved on him through the death of a former holder.

(3) A person who is liable under section 76 to contribute to a company's assets in the event of its being wound up may petition on either of the grounds set out in section 122(1)(f) and (g), and subsection (2) above does not then apply; but unless the person is a contributory otherwise than under section 76, he may not in his character as contributory petition on any other ground.

This subsection is deemed included in Chapter VII of Part V of the Companies Act (redeemable shares; purchase by a company of its own shares) for the purposes of the Secretary of State's power to make regulations under section 179 of that Act.

[(3A) A winding-up petition on the ground set out in section 122(1)(fa) may only be presented by one or more creditors.]

(4) A winding-up petition may be presented by the Secretary of State—

(a) if the ground of the petition is that in section 122(1)(b) or (c), or

[(b) in a case falling within section 124A [or 124B] below.]

[(4A) A winding-up petition may be presented by the Regulator of Community Interest Companies in a case falling within section 50 of the Companies (Audit, Investigations and Community Enterprise) Act 2004.]

(5) Where a company is being wound up voluntarily in England and Wales, a winding-up petition may be presented by the official receiver attached to the court as well as by any other person authorised in that behalf under the other provisions of this section; but the court shall not make a winding-up order on the petition unless it is satisfied that the voluntary winding up cannot be continued with due regard to the interests of the creditors or contributories.

[566]

NOTES

Sub-s (1): words in first pair of square brackets inserted by the Insolvency Act 1986 (Amendment) (No 2) Regulations 2002, SI 2002/1240, regs 3, 8; words in second (outer) pair of square brackets inserted by the Criminal Justice Act 1988, s 62(2)(b); words in third (inner) pair of square brackets substituted by the Courts Act 2003, s 109(1), Sch 8, para 294.

Sub-s (3A): inserted by the Insolvency Act 2000, s 1, Sch 1, paras 1, 7.

Sub-s (4): para (b) substituted by the Companies Act 1989, s 60(2), words in square brackets inserted by the European Public Limited-Liability Company Regulations 2004, SI 2004/2326, reg 73(4)(a).

Sub-s (4A): inserted by the Companies (Audit, Investigations and Community Enterprise) Act 2004, s 50(3).

Petitions for winding up: for the circumstances in which the Financial Services Authority may present a petition for the winding up of a registered friendly society, see the Friendly Societies Act 1974, s 87; see also the Agricultural Marketing Act 1958, s 3(2), Sch 2, para 4(5) as to the presentation, by the appropriate Minister, of a petition for the winding up of an agricultural marketing board; see also the Charities Act 1993, s 63(1) for the circumstances in which the Attorney General, in addition to any person authorised by this Act, may present a petition for a charity to be wound up.

[124A Petition for winding-up on grounds of public interest

(1) Where it appears to the Secretary of State from—

(a) any report made or information obtained under Part XIV [(except section 448A)] of the Companies Act 1985 (company investigations, &c),

[(b) any report made by inspectors under—

(i) section 167, 168, 169 or 284 of the Financial Services and Markets Act 2000, or

(ii) where the company is an open-ended investment company (within the meaning of that Act), regulations made as a result of section 262(2)(k) of that Act;

(bb) any information or documents obtained under section 165, 171, 172, 173 or 175 of that Act,]

(c) any information obtained under section 2 of the Criminal Justice Act 1987 or section 52 of the Criminal Justice (Scotland) Act 1987 (fraud investigations), or

(d) any information obtained under section 83 of the Companies Act 1989 (powers exercisable for purpose of assisting overseas regulatory authorities),

that it is expedient in the public interest that a company should be wound up, he may present a petition for it to be wound up if the court thinks it just and equitable for it to be so.

(2) This section does not apply if the company is already being wound up by the court.]

[567]

NOTES

Inserted by the Companies Act 1989, s 60(3).

Sub-s (1): words in square brackets in para (a) inserted by the Companies (Audit, Investigations and Community Enterprise) Act 2004, s 25(1), Sch 2, Pt 3, para 27; paras (b), (bb) substituted for original para (b) by the Financial Services and Markets Act 2000 (Consequential Amendments and Repeals) Order 2001, SI 2001/3649, art 305.

Criminal Justice (Scotland) Act 1987, s 52: repealed by the Criminal Procedure (Consequential Provisions) (Scotland) Act 1995, s 6(1), Sch 5; see now the Criminal Law (Consolidation) (Scotland) Act 1995, s 28.

[124B Petition for winding up of SE

(1) Where—

(a) an SE whose registered office is in Great Britain is not in compliance with Article 7 of Council Regulation (EC) No 2157/2001 on the Statute for a European company (the "EC Regulation") (location of head office and registered office), and

(b) it appears to the Secretary of State that the SE should be wound up, he may present a petition for it to be wound up if the court thinks it is just and equitable for it to be so.

(2) This section does not apply if the SE is already being wound up by the court.

(3) In this section "SE" has the same meaning as in the EC Regulation.]

[568]

NOTES

Commencement: 8 October 2004.

Inserted by the European Public Limited-Liability Company Regulations 2004, SI 2004/2326, reg 73(3).

PART V
WINDING UP OF UNREGISTERED COMPANIES

NOTES

Application of this Part in relation to agricultural marketing boards: an agricultural marketing scheme may provide for the winding up of the board and, for that purpose, may apply this Part of the Act with certain modifications; see the Agricultural Marketing Act 1958, s 3(3), Sch 2, para 4.

Application of this Part in relation to friendly societies: for the purposes of the Friendly Societies Act 1992, s 52 (application to court in relation to regulation of friendly societies' business), this Part is applied in relation to the winding up of registered friendly societies; see s 52(9) of the 1992 Act.

Application of this Part in relation to financial markets: this Part is applied with modifications in relation to certain proceedings begun before the commencement of the Companies Act 1989, s 182, in respect of insolvency proceedings regarding members of recognised investment exchanges and clearing houses and persons to whom market charges have been granted; see s 182 of the 1989 Act.

Application of this Part in relation to the winding up of an open-ended investment company: see the Open-Ended Investment Companies Regulations 2001, SI 2001/1228, reg 31.

220 Meaning of "unregistered company"

(1) For the purposes of this Part, the expression "unregistered company" includes *any trustee savings bank certified under the enactments relating to such banks*, any association and any company, with the following exceptions—

(a) … ,

(b) a company registered in any part of the United Kingdom under the Joint Stock Companies Acts or under the legislation (past or present) relating to companies in Great Britain.

(2) On such day as the Treasury appoints by order under section 4(3) of the Trustee Savings Banks Act 1985, the words in subsection (1) from "any trustee" to "banks" cease to have effect and are hereby repealed.

[569]

NOTES

Sub-s (1): words in italics formerly in the Companies Act 1985, s 665(1), and an additional word "and" following the word "banks" which is not reproduced, were repealed by the Trustee Savings Banks Act 1985, ss 4(3), 7(3), Sch 4. The repeal of those words was brought into force on 21 July 1986 by virtue of the Trustee Savings Banks Act 1985 (Appointed Day) (No 4) Order 1986, SI 1986/1223 (made under s 4(3) of that Act). It is thought, therefore, that, as construed in accordance with s 437, Sch 11, para 27 post, the words specified in sub-s (1) above, by virtue of sub-s (2) above, have ceased to have effect and are thus repealed; para (a) repealed by the Transport and Works Act 1992, ss 65(1)(f), 68(1), Sch 4, Pt I.

221 Winding up of unregistered companies

(1) Subject to the provisions of this Part, any unregistered company may be wound up under this Act; and all the provisions of this Act and the Companies Act about winding up apply to an unregistered company with the exceptions and additions mentioned in the following subsections.

(2) If an unregistered company has a principal place of business situated in Northern Ireland, it shall not be wound up under this Part unless it has a principal place of business situated in England and Wales or Scotland, or in both England and Wales and Scotland.

(3) For the purpose of determining a court's winding-up jurisdiction, an unregistered company is deemed—

(a) to be registered in England and Wales or Scotland, according as its principal place of business is situated in England and Wales or Scotland, or

(b) if it has a principal place of business situated in both countries, to be registered in both countries;

and the principal place of business situated in that part of Great Britain in which proceedings are being instituted is, for all purposes of the winding up, deemed to be the registered office of the company.

(4) No unregistered company shall be wound up under this Act voluntarily[, except in accordance with the EC Regulation].

(5) The circumstances in which an unregistered company may be wound up are as follows—

(a) if the company is dissolved, or has ceased to carry on business, or is carrying on business only for the purpose of winding up its affairs;
(b) if the company is unable to pay its debts;
(c) if the court is of opinion that it is just and equitable that the company should be wound up.

(6) A petition for winding up a trustee savings bank may be presented by the Trustee Savings Banks Central Board or by a commissioner appointed under section 35 of the Trustee Savings Banks Act 1981 as well as by any person authorised under Part IV of this Act to present a petition for the winding up of a company.

On such day as the Treasury appoints by order under section 4(3) of the Trustee Savings Banks Act 1985, this subsection ceases to have effect and is hereby repealed.

(7) In Scotland, an unregistered company which the Court of Session has jurisdiction to wind up may be wound up by the court if there is subsisting a floating charge over property comprised in the company's property and undertaking, and the court is satisfied that the security of the creditor entitled to the benefit of the floating charge is in jeopardy. For this purpose a creditor's security is deemed to be in jeopardy if the court is satisfied that events have occurred or are about to occur which render it unreasonable in the creditor's interests that the company should retain power to dispose of the property which is subject to the floating charge.

[570]

NOTES

Sub-s (4): words in square brackets added by the Insolvency Act 1986 (Amendment) (No 2) Regulations 2002, SI 2002/1240, regs 3, 9.

Sub-s (6): the Companies Act 1985, s 666(6), from which sub-s (6) above was principally derived, was repealed by the Trustee Savings Banks Act 1985, ss 4(3), 7(3), Sch 4, as from 21 July 1986 by virtue of the Trustee Savings Banks Act 1985 (Appointed Day) (No 4) Order 1986, SI 1986/1223 (made under s 4(3) of that Act). It is thought, therefore, that, as construed in accordance with s 437, Sch 11, para 27, sub-s (6) above has ceased to have effect and is thus repealed.

In relation to the application of sub-ss (1), (5) above, in respect of the Lloyd's of London insurance market, see the Insurers (Reorganisation and Winding Up) (Lloyd's) Regulations 2005, SI 2005/1998, reg 29 at **[2685]**.

222 Inability to pay debts: unpaid creditor for £750 or more

(1) An unregistered company is deemed (for the purposes of section 221) unable to pay its debts if there is a creditor, by assignment or otherwise, to whom the company is indebted in a sum exceeding £750 then due and—

(a) the creditor has served on the company, by leaving at its principal place of business, or by delivering to the secretary or some director, manager or principal officer of the company, or by otherwise serving in such manner as the court may approve or direct, a written demand in the prescribed form requiring the company to pay the sum due, and
(b) the company has for 3 weeks after the service of the demand neglected to pay the sum or to secure or compound for it to the creditor's satisfaction.

(2) The money sum for the time being specified in subsection (1) is subject to increase or reduction by regulations under section 417 in Part XV; but no increase in the sum so specified affects any case in which the winding-up petition was presented before the coming into force of the increase.

[571]

223 Inability to pay debts: debt remaining unsatisfied after action brought

An unregistered company is deemed (for the purposes of section 221) unable to pay its debts if an action or other proceeding has been instituted against any member for any debt or demand due, or claimed to be due, from the company, or from him in his character of member, and—

(a) notice in writing of the institution of the action or proceeding has been served on the company by leaving it at the company's principal place of business (or by delivering it to the secretary, or some director, manager or principal officer of the company, or by otherwise serving it in such manner as the court may approve or direct), and

(b) the company has not within 3 weeks after service of the notice paid, secured or compounded for the debt or demand, or procured the action or proceeding to be stayed or sisted, or indemnified the defendant or defender to his reasonable satisfaction against the action or proceeding, and against all costs, damages and expenses to be incurred by him because of it.

[572]

224 Inability to pay debts: other cases

(1) An unregistered company is deemed (for purposes of section 221) unable to pay its debts—

(a) if in England and Wales execution or other process issued on a judgment, decree or order obtained in any court in favour of a creditor against the company, or any member of it as such, or any person authorised to be sued as nominal defendant on behalf of the company, is returned unsatisfied;

(b) if in Scotland the induciae of a charge for payment on an extract decree, or an extract registered bond, or an extract registered protest, have expired without payment being made;

(c) if in Northern Ireland a certificate of unenforceability has been granted in respect of any judgment, decree or order obtained as mentioned in paragraph (a);

(d) it is otherwise proved to the satisfaction of the court that the company is unable to pay its debts as they fall due.

(2) An unregistered company is also deemed unable to pay its debts if it is proved to the satisfaction of the court that the value of the company's assets is less than the amount of its liabilities, taking into account its contingent and prospective liabilities.

[573]

225 Oversea company may be wound up though dissolved

[(1)] Where a company incorporated outside Great Britain which has been carrying on business in Great Britain ceases to carry on business in Great Britain, it may be wound up as an unregistered company under this Act, notwithstanding that it has been dissolved or otherwise ceased to exist as a company under or by virtue of the laws of the country under which it was incorporated.

[(2) This section is subject to the EC Regulation.]

[574]

NOTES

Sub-s (1): numbered as such by the Insolvency Act 1986 (Amendment) (No 2) Regulations 2002, SI 2002/1240, regs 3, 10.

Sub-s (2): added by SI 2002/1240, regs 3, 10.

226 Contributories in winding up of unregistered company

(1) In the event of an unregistered company being wound up, every person is deemed a contributory who is liable to pay or contribute to the payment of any debt or liability of the company, or to pay or contribute to the payment of any sum for the adjustment of the rights of members among themselves, or to pay or contribute to the payment of the expenses of winding up the company.

(2) Every contributory is liable to contribute to the company's assets all sums due from him in respect of any such liability as is mentioned above.

(3) In the case of an unregistered company engaged in or formed for working mines within the stannaries, a past member is not liable to contribute to the assets if he has ceased to be a member for 2 years or more either before the mine ceased to be worked or before the date of the winding-up order.

(4) In the event of the death, bankruptcy or insolvency of any contributory, the provisions of this Act with respect to the personal representatives, to the heirs and legatees of heritage of the heritable estate in Scotland of deceased contributories, and to the trustees of bankrupt or insolvent contributories, respectively apply.

[575]

227 Power of court to stay, sist or restrain proceedings

The provisions of this Part with respect to staying, sisting or restraining actions and proceedings against a company at any time after the presentation of a petition for winding up and before the making of a winding-up order extend, in the case of an unregistered company, where the application to stay, sist or restrain is presented by a creditor, to actions and proceedings against any contributory of the company.

[576]

228 Actions stayed on winding-up order

Where an order has been made for winding up an unregistered company, no action or proceeding shall be proceeded with or commenced against any contributory of the company in respect of any debt of the company, except by leave of the court, and subject to such terms as the court may impose.

[577]

229 Provisions of this Part to be cumulative

(1) The provisions of this Part with respect to unregistered companies are in addition to and not in restriction of any provisions in Part IV with respect to winding up companies by the court; and the court or liquidator may exercise any powers or do any act in the case of unregistered companies which might be exercised or done by it or him in winding up companies formed and registered under the Companies Act.

(2) However, an unregistered company is not, except in the event of its being wound up, deemed to be a company under the Companies Act, and then only to the extent provided by this Part of this Act.

[578]

PART VII
INTERPRETATION FOR FIRST GROUP OF PARTS

NOTES

Modification of this Part in relation to building societies: this Part is applied with modifications in relation to the winding up, etc, of building societies; see the Building Societies Act 1986, ss 90, 90A, Schs 15, 15A.

Modification of this Part in relation to friendly societies: as to the application, with modifications, of this Part to the winding up of incorporated friendly societies by virtue of the Friendly Societies Act 1992, s 21(1) or 22(2), see s 23 of, and Sch 10 to, the 1992 Act.

247 "Insolvency" and "go into liquidation"

(1) In this Group of Parts, except in so far as the context otherwise requires, "insolvency", in relation to a company, includes the approval of a voluntary arrangement under Part I, [or the appointment of an administrator or an administrative receiver].

(2) For the purposes of any provision in this Group of Parts, a company goes into liquidation if it passes a resolution for voluntary winding up or an order for its winding up is made by the court at a time when it has not already gone into liquidation by passing such a resolution.

[(3) The reference to a resolution for voluntary winding up in subsection (2) includes a reference to a resolution which is deemed to occur by virtue of—

(a) paragraph 83(6)(b) of Schedule B1, or

(b) an order made following conversion of administration or a voluntary arrangement into winding up by virtue of Article 37 of the EC Regulation.]

[579]

NOTES

Sub-s (1): words in square brackets substituted by the Enterprise Act 2002, s 248(3), Sch 17, paras 9, 33(1), (2), except in relation to special administration regimes.

Sub-s (3): added by the Insolvency Act 1986 (Amendment) (No 2) Regulations 2002, SI 2002/1240, regs 3, 12; substituted by the Enterprise Act 2002, s 248(3), Sch 17, paras 9, 33(1), (3), except in relation to special administration regimes.

PART XV
SUBORDINATE LEGISLATION

General insolvency rules

411 Company insolvency rules

(1) Rules may be made—

(a) in relation to England and Wales, by the Lord Chancellor with the concurrence of the Secretary of State [and, in the case of rules that affect court procedure, with the concurrence of the Lord Chief Justice], or

(b) in relation to Scotland, by the Secretary of State,

for the purpose of giving effect to Parts I to VII of this Act [or the EC Regulation].

(2) Without prejudice to the generality of subsection (1), or to any provision of those Parts by virtue of which rules under this section may be made with respect to any matter, rules under this section may contain—

(a) any such provision as is specified in Schedule 8 to this Act or corresponds to provision contained immediately before the coming into force of section 106 of the Insolvency Act 1985 in rules made, or having effect as if made, under section 663(1) or (2) of the Companies Act (old winding-up rules), and

(b) such incidental, supplemental and transitional provisions as may appear to the Lord Chancellor or, as the case may be, the Secretary of State necessary or expedient.

[(2A) For the purposes of subsection (2), a reference in Schedule 8 to this Act to doing anything under or for the purposes of a provision of this Act includes a reference to doing anything under or for the purposes of the EC Regulation (in so far as the provision of this Act relates to a matter to which the EC Regulation applies).

(2B) Rules under this section for the purpose of giving effect to the EC Regulation may not create an offence of a kind referred to in paragraph 1(1)(d) of Schedule 2 to the European Communities Act 1972.]

(3) In Schedule 8 to this Act "liquidator" includes a provisional liquidator; and references above in this section to Parts I to VII of this Act are to be read as including the Companies Act so far as relating to, and to matters connected with or arising out of, the insolvency or winding up of companies.

(4) Rules under this section shall be made by statutory instrument subject to annulment in pursuance of a resolution of either House of Parliament.

(5) Regulations made by the Secretary of State under a power conferred by rules under this section shall be made by statutory instrument and, after being made, shall be laid before each House of Parliament.

(6) Nothing in this section prejudices any power to make rules of court.

[(7) The Lord Chief Justice may nominate a judicial office holder (as defined in section 109(4) of the Constitutional Reform Act 2005) to exercise his functions under this section.]

[580]

NOTES

Sub-s (1): words in first pair of square brackets inserted by the Constitutional Reform Act 2005, s 15(1), Sch 4, Pt 1, paras 185, 188(1), (2); words in second pair of square brackets inserted by the Insolvency Act 1986 (Amendment) Regulations 2002, SI 2002/1037, regs 2, 3(1).

Sub-ss (2A), (2B): inserted by SI 2002/1037, regs 2, 3(2).

Sub-s (7): added by the Constitutional Reform Act 2005, s 15(1), Sch 4, Pt 1, paras 185, 188(1), (3).

Extension of the application of the rules: rules may be made under this section for the purposes of the Building Societies Act 1986, with respect to the winding up, etc, of building societies; see s 90A of, and Sch 15A, Pt I, para 4(1) to, the 1986 Act.

Rules made under this section apply for the purposes of a petition for a special administration order under the Water Industry Act 1991; see ss 23(3), 24(3) of, and Sch 3, Pt II, para 11(4) to, the 1991 Act.

Rules may be made under this section for the purposes of the Friendly Societies Act 1992, with respect to the winding up of incorporated friendly societies; see s 23 of, and Sch 10, Pt IV, para 69(1)(a) to, the 1992 Act.

Rules may be made under this section for the purposes of the Railways Act 1993, with respect to giving effect to the railway administration order provisions of the 1993 Act (ie ss 59–65 of, and Schs 6, 7 to, that Act); see s 59(5) thereof.

Company directors disqualification: this section and ss 414, 420, 422 and 434 are applied by the Company Directors Disqualification Act 1986, s 21(2), (3) for the purposes of certain provisions of that Act.

Rules: the Insolvency (Scotland) Rules 1986, SI 1986/1915 at **[2502]**; the Insurance Companies (Winding-up) (Scotland) Rules 1986, SI 1986/1918; the Insolvency Rules 1986, SI 1986/1925 at **[2520]**; the Companies (Unfair Prejudice Applications) Proceedings Rules 1986, SI 1986/2000; the Insolvent Companies (Disqualification of Unfit Directors) Proceedings Rules 1987, SI 1987/2023; the Insolvent Companies (Reports on Conduct of Directors) Rules 1996, SI 1996/1909; the Insolvent Companies (Reports on Conduct of Directors) (Scotland) Rules 1996, SI 1996/1910; the Railway Administration Order Rules 2001, SI 2001/3352; the Insurers (Winding up) Rules 2001, SI 2001/3635; the Insurers (Winding up) (Scotland) Rules 2001, SI 2001/4040.

Regulations: the Insolvency Regulations 1994, SI 1994/2507.

412 Individual insolvency rules (England and Wales)

(1) The Lord Chancellor may, with the concurrence of the Secretary of State [and, in the case of rules that affect court procedure, with the concurrence of the Lord Chief Justice], make rules for the purpose of giving effect to Parts VIII to XI of this Act [or the EC Regulation].

(2) Without prejudice to the generality of subsection (1), or to any provision of those Parts by virtue of which rules under this section may be made with respect to any matter, rules under this section may contain—

- (a) any such provision as is specified in Schedule 9 to this Act or corresponds to provision contained immediately before the appointed day in rules made under section 132 of the Bankruptcy Act 1914; and
- (b) such incidental, supplemental and transitional provisions as may appear to the Lord Chancellor necessary or expedient.

[(2A) For the purposes of subsection (2), a reference in Schedule 9 to this Act to doing anything under or for the purposes of a provision of this Act includes a reference to doing anything under or for the purposes of the EC Regulation (in so far as the provision of this Act relates to a matter to which the EC Regulation applies).

(2B) Rules under this section for the purpose of giving effect to the EC Regulation may not create an offence of a kind referred to in paragraph 1(1)(d) of Schedule 2 to the European Communities Act 1972.]

(3) Rules under this section shall be made by statutory instrument subject to annulment in pursuance of a resolution of either House of Parliament.

(4) Regulations made by the Secretary of State under a power conferred by rules under this section shall be made by statutory instrument and, after being made, shall be laid before each House of Parliament.

(5) Nothing in this section prejudices any power to make rules of court.

[(6) The Lord Chief Justice may nominate a judicial office holder (as defined in section 109(4) of the Constitutional Reform Act 2005) to exercise his functions under this section.]

[581]

NOTES

Sub-s (1): words in first pair of square brackets inserted by the Constitutional Reform Act 2005, s 15(1), Sch 4, Pt 1, paras 185, 189(1), (2); words in second pair of square brackets inserted by the Insolvency Act 1986 (Amendment) Regulations 2002, SI 2002/1037, regs 2, 3(3).

Sub-ss (2A), (2B): inserted by SI 2002/1037, regs 2, 3(4).

Sub-s (6): added by the Constitutional Reform Act 2005, s 15(1), Sch 4, Pt 1, paras 185, 189(1), (3).

Extension of the application of the rules: by the Land Charges Act 1972, s 16(2), the power to make rules under this section includes power to make rules as respects the registration and re-registration of a bankruptcy petition under s 5 of that Act, and a bankruptcy order under s 6 of that Act, as if the registration and re-registration were required by Pts VIII–XI of this Act.

Rules made under this section relating to the audit of the accounts of a trustee in bankruptcy (see Sch 9, para 27(c)) are applied to the audit of the accounts of the trustee under a deed of arrangement by the Deeds of Arrangement Act 1914, s 15(1).

Rules: the Insolvency Rules 1986, SI 1986/1925 at **[2520]**; the Bankruptcy (Financial Services and Markets Act 2000) Rules 2001, SI 2001/3634.

Regulations: the Insolvency Regulations 1994, SI 1994/2507.

Bankruptcy Act 1914, s 132: repealed by the Insolvency Act 1985, s 235(3), Sch 10, Pt III.

413 Insolvency Rules Committee

(1) The committee established under section 10 of the Insolvency Act 1976 (advisory committee on bankruptcy and winding-up rules) continues to exist for the purpose of being consulted under this section.

(2) The Lord Chancellor shall consult the committee before making any rules under section 411 or 412 [other than rules which contain a statement that the only provision made by the rules is provision applying rules made under section 411, with or without modifications, for the purposes of provision made by [any of sections 23 to 26 of the Water Industry Act 1991 or Schedule 3 to that Act]] [or by any of sections 59 to 65 of, or Schedule 6 or 7 to, the Railways Act 1993].

(3) Subject to the next subsection, the committee shall consist of—

(a) a judge of the High Court attached to the Chancery Division;
(b) a circuit judge;
(c) a registrar in bankruptcy of the High Court;
(d) the registrar of a county court;
(e) a practising barrister;
(f) a practising solicitor; and
(g) a practising accountant;

and the appointment of any person as a member of the committee shall be made [in accordance with subsection (3A) or (3B)].

[(3A) The Lord Chief Justice must appoint the persons referred to in paragraphs (a) to (d) of subsection (3), after consulting the Lord Chancellor.

(3B) The Lord Chancellor must appoint the persons referred to in paragraphs (e) to (g) of subsection (3), after consulting the Lord Chief Justice.]

(4) The Lord Chancellor may appoint as additional members of the committee any persons appearing to him to have qualifications or experience that would be of value to the committee in considering any matter with which it is concerned.

[(5) The Lord Chief Justice may nominate a judicial office holder (as defined in section 109(4) of the Constitutional Reform Act 2005) to exercise his functions under this section.]

[582]

NOTES

Sub-s (2): words in first (outer) pair of square brackets substituted by the Water Act 1989, s 190(1), Sch 25, para 78(2); words in second (inner) pair of square brackets substituted by the Water Consolidation (Consequential Provisions) Act 1991, s 2(1), Sch 1, para 46; words in third pair of square brackets added by the Railways Act 1993, s 152, Sch 12, para 25.

Sub-s (3): words in square brackets substituted by the Constitutional Reform Act 2005, s 15(1), Sch 4, Pt 1, paras 185, 190(1), (2).

Sub-ss (3A), (3B): inserted by the Constitutional Reform Act 2005, s 15(1), Sch 4, Pt 1, paras 185, 190(1), (3).

Sub-s (5): added by the Constitutional Reform Act 2005, s 15(1), Sch 4, Pt 1, paras 185, 190(1), (4).

PART XVII
MISCELLANEOUS AND GENERAL

426 Co-operation between courts exercising jurisdiction in relation to insolvency

(1) An order made by a court in any part of the United Kingdom in the exercise of jurisdiction in relation to insolvency law shall be enforced in any other part of the United Kingdom as if it were made by a court exercising the corresponding jurisdiction in that other part.

(2) However, without prejudice to the following provisions of this section, nothing in subsection (1) requires a court in any part of the United Kingdom to enforce, in relation to property situated in that part, any order made by a court in any other part of the United Kingdom.

(3) The Secretary of State, with the concurrence in relation to property situated in England and Wales of the Lord Chancellor, may by order make provision for securing that a trustee or assignee under the insolvency law of any part of the United Kingdom has, with such modifications as may be specified in the order, the same rights in relation to any property

situated in another part of the United Kingdom as he would have in the corresponding circumstances if he were a trustee or assignee under the insolvency law of that other part.

(4) The courts having jurisdiction in relation to insolvency law in any part of the United Kingdom shall assist the courts having the corresponding jurisdiction in any other part of the United Kingdom or any relevant country or territory.

(5) For the purposes of subsection (4) a request made to a court in any part of the United Kingdom by a court in any other part of the United Kingdom or in a relevant country or territory is authority for the court to which the request is made to apply, in relation to any matters specified in the request, the insolvency law which is applicable by either court in relation to comparable matters falling within its jurisdiction.

In exercising its discretion under this subsection, a court shall have regard in particular to the rules of private international law.

(6) Where a person who is a trustee or assignee under the insolvency law of any part of the United Kingdom claims property situated in any other part of the United Kingdom (whether by virtue of an order under subsection (3) or otherwise), the submission of that claim to the court exercising jurisdiction in relation to insolvency law in that other part shall be treated in the same manner as a request made by a court for the purpose of subsection (4).

(7) Section 38 of the Criminal Law Act 1977 (execution of warrant of arrest throughout the United Kingdom) applies to a warrant which, in exercise of any jurisdiction in relation to insolvency law, is issued in any part of the United Kingdom for the arrest of a person as it applies to a warrant issued in that part of the United Kingdom for the arrest of a person charged with an offence.

(8) Without prejudice to any power to make rules of court, any power to make provision by subordinate legislation for the purpose of giving effect in relation to companies or individuals to the insolvency law of any part of the United Kingdom includes power to make provisions for the purpose of giving effect in that part to any provision made by or under the preceding provisions of this section.

(9) An order under subsection (3) shall be made by statutory instrument subject to annulment in pursuance of a resolution of either House of Parliament.

(10) In this section "insolvency law" means—

(a) in relation to England and Wales, provision [extending to England and Wales and] made by or under this Act or sections [1A,] 6 to 10, [12 to 15], 19(c) and 20 (with Schedule 1) of the Company Directors Disqualification Act 1986 [and sections 1 to 17 of that Act as they apply for the purposes of those provisions of that Act];

(b) in relation to Scotland, provision extending to Scotland and made by or under this Act, sections [1A,] 6 to 10, [12 to 15], 19(c) and 20 (with Schedule 1) of the Company Directors Disqualification Act 1986 [and sections 1 to 17 of that Act as they apply for the purposes of those provisions of that Act], Part XVIII of the Companies Act or the Bankruptcy (Scotland) Act 1985;

(c) in relation to Northern Ireland, provision made by or under [the Insolvency (Northern Ireland) Order 1989] [*or Part II of the Companies* (*Northern Ireland*) *Order 1989*];

(d) in relation to any relevant country or territory, so much of the law of that country or territory as corresponds to provisions falling within any of the foregoing paragraphs;

and references in this subsection to any enactment include, in relation to any time before the coming into force of that enactment the corresponding enactment in force at that time.

(11) In this section "relevant country or territory" means—

(a) any of the Channel Islands or the Isle of Man, or

(b) any country or territory designated for the purposes of this section by the Secretary of State by order made by statutory instrument.

[(12) In the application of this section to Northern Ireland—

(a) for any reference to the Secretary of State there is substituted a reference to the Department of Economic Development in Northern Ireland;

(b) in subsection (3) for the words "another part of the United Kingdom" and the words "that other part" there are substituted the words "Northern Ireland";

(c) for subsection (9) there is substituted the following subsection—

"(9) An order made under subsection (3) by the Department of Economic Development in Northern Ireland shall be a statutory rule for the purposes of the

Statutory Rules (Northern Ireland) Order 1979 and shall be subject to negative resolution within the meaning of section 41(6) of the Interpretation Act (Northern Ireland) 1954.".]

[583]

NOTES

Sub-s (10): words in first and second pairs of square brackets in para (a) and words in first and third pairs of square brackets in para (b) inserted, and words in third and fourth pairs of square brackets in para (a) and words in second pair of square brackets in para (b) substituted, by the Insolvency Act 2000, s 8, Sch 4, Pt II, para 16(1), (3); words in first pair of square brackets in para (c) substituted by the Insolvency (Northern Ireland) Order 1989, SI 1989/2405 (NI 19), art 381(2), Sch 9, Pt II, para 41(a); words in second pair of square brackets in para (c) added by the Companies (Northern Ireland) Order 1989, SI 1989/2404, arts 25(2), 36, Sch 4, Pt I, para 1, and substituted by the words "or the Company Directors Disqualification (Northern Ireland) Order 2002" by the Company Directors Disqualification (Northern Ireland) Order 2002, SI 2002/3150 (NI 4), art 26(2), Sch 3, para 2, as from a day to be appointed.

Sub-s (12): added by SI 1989/2405, art 381(2), Sch 9, Pt II, para 41(b), but not yet in operation so far as amends sub-s (11)(b) to give the Department of Economic Development in Northern Ireland power to make an order designating relevant countries for the purposes of this section as it applies to Northern Ireland.

Insolvency law: references to insolvency law in this section include, in relation to a part of the UK, provisions made by or under the Companies Act 1989, Pt VII, and, in relation to a relevant country or territory, so much of the law of that country or territory as corresponds to any such provisions; see the Companies Act 1989, s 183(1). See also, as to insolvency proceedings in other jurisdictions, s 183(2), (3) thereof.

See further, the Insolvency Act 2000, s 14 at **[592]**, which enables the Secretary of State to give effect to the United Nations Commission on International Trade Law model law on cross-border insolvency by secondary legislation and provides that any such secondary legislation may include amendments to this section.

Criminal Law Act 1977, s 38: repealed by the Criminal Justice and Public Order Act 1994, s 168(3), Sch 11.

Orders: the Co-operation of Insolvency Courts (Designation of Relevant Countries and Territories) Order 1986, SI 1986/2123 at **[2564]**; the Co-operation of Insolvency Courts (Designation of Relevant Countries) Order 1996, SI 1996/253 at **[2591]**; the Co-operation of Insolvency Courts (Designation of Relevant Country) Order 1998, SI 1998/2766 at **[2594]**.

PART XVIII
INTERPRETATION

NOTES

Modification of this Part in relation to building societies: this Part is applied, with modifications, in relation to the winding up, etc, of building societies; see the Building Societies Act 1986, s 90A, Sch 15.

436 Expressions used generally

In this Act, except in so far as the context otherwise requires (and subject to Parts VII and XI)—

"the appointed day" means the day on which this Act comes into force under section 443;

"associate" has the meaning given by section 435;

"business" includes a trade or profession;

"the Companies Act" means the Companies Act 1985;

"conditional sale agreement" and "hire-purchase agreement" have the same meanings as in the Consumer Credit Act 1974;

["the EC Regulation" means Council Regulation (EC) No 1346/2000;]

["EEA State" means a state that is a Contracting Party to the Agreement on the European Economic Area signed at Oporto on 2nd May 1992 as adjusted by the Protocol signed at Brussels on 17th March 1993;]

"modifications" includes additions, alterations and omissions and cognate expressions shall be construed accordingly;

"property" includes money, goods, things in action, land and every description of property wherever situated and also obligations and every description of interest, whether present or future or vested or contingent, arising out of, or incidental to, property;

"records" includes computer records and other non-documentary records;

"subordinate legislation" has the same meaning as in the Interpretation Act 1978; and "transaction" includes a gift, agreement or arrangement, and references to entering into a transaction shall be construed accordingly.

[584]

NOTES

Definition "the EC Regulation" inserted by the Insolvency Act 1986 (Amendment) Regulations 2002, SI 2002/1037, regs 2, 4; definition "EEA State" inserted by the Insolvency Act 1986 (Amendment) Regulations 2005, SI 2005/879, regs 2(1), (3), 3, except in relation to a voluntary arrangement under Pt I of this Act or the appointment of an administrator under Pt II of this Act that took effect before 13 April 2005.

[436A Proceedings under EC Regulation: modified definition of property

In the application of this Act to proceedings by virtue of Article 3 of the EC Regulation, a reference to property is a reference to property which may be dealt with in the proceedings.]

[585]

NOTES

Commencement: 31 May 2002.
Inserted by the Insolvency Act 1986 (Amendment) (No 2) Regulations 2002, SI 2002/1240, regs 3, 18.

PART XIX
FINAL PROVISIONS

437 Transitional provisions, and savings

The transitional provisions and savings set out in Schedule 11 to this Act shall have effect, the Schedule comprising the following Parts—

Part I: company insolvency and winding up (matters arising before appointed day, and continuance of proceedings in certain cases as before that day);
Part II: individual insolvency (matters so arising, and continuance of bankruptcy proceedings in certain cases as before that day);
Part III: transactions entered into before the appointed day and capable of being affected by orders of the court under Part XVI of this Act;
Part IV: insolvency practitioners acting as such before the appointed day; and
Part V: general transitional provisions and savings required consequentially on, and in connection with, the repeal and replacement by this Act and the Company Directors Disqualification Act 1986 of provisions of the Companies Act, the greater part of the Insolvency Act 1985 and other enactments.

[586]

NOTES

Insolvency Act 1985: that Act was mostly repealed by the combined effect of s 438 of, and Sch 12 to, this Act and the Company Directors Disqualification Act 1986, s 23(2), Sch 4.

440 Extent (Scotland)

(1) Subject to the next subsection, provisions of this Act contained in the first Group of Parts extend to Scotland except where otherwise stated.

(2) The following provisions of this Act do not extend to Scotland—

(a) In the first Group of Parts—
section 43;
sections 238 to 241; and
section 246;

(b) the second Group of Parts;

(c) in the third Group of Parts—
sections 399 to 402,
sections 412, 413, 415, [415A(3),] 418, 420 and 421,
sections 423 to 425, and
section 429(1) and (2); and

(d) in the Schedules—
Parts II and III of Schedule 11; and

Schedules 12 and 14 so far as they repeal or amend enactments which extend to England and Wales only.

[587]

NOTES

Sub-s (2): section reference in square brackets inserted by the Enterprise Act 2002, s 270(4).

442 Extent (other territories)

Her Majesty may, by Order in Council, direct that such of the provisions of this Act as are specified in the Order, being provisions formerly contained in the Insolvency Act 1985, shall extend to any of the Channel Islands or any colony with such modifications as may be so specified.

[588]

NOTES

Orders: the Insolvency Act 1986 (Guernsey) Order 1989, SI 1989/2409.

443 Commencement

This Act comes into force on the day appointed under section 236(2) of the Insolvency Act 1985 for the coming into force of Part III of that Act (individual insolvency and bankruptcy), immediately after that Part of that Act comes into force for England and Wales.

[589]

NOTES

See the note "Commencement" at the beginning of this Act.

444 Citation

This Act may be cited as the Insolvency Act 1986.

[590]

SCHEDULES

[SCHEDULE B1
ADMINISTRATION

Section 8

ARRANGEMENT OF SCHEDULE

NATURE OF ADMINISTRATION

Administration

1.—(1) For the purposes of this Act "administrator" of a company means a person appointed under this Schedule to manage the company's affairs, business and property.

(2) For the purposes of this Act—

(a) a company is "in administration" while the appointment of an administrator of the company has effect,

(b) a company "enters administration" when the appointment of an administrator takes effect,

(c) a company ceases to be in administration when the appointment of an administrator of the company ceases to have effect in accordance with this Schedule, and

(d) a company does not cease to be in administration merely because an administrator vacates office (by reason of resignation, death or otherwise) or is removed from office.

2. A person may be appointed as administrator of a company—
(a) by administration order of the court under paragraph 10,
(b) by the holder of a floating charge under paragraph 14, or
(c) by the company or its directors under paragraph 22.

Purpose of administration

3.—(1) The administrator of a company must perform his functions with the objective of—
(a) rescuing the company as a going concern, or
(b) achieving a better result for the company's creditors as a whole than would be likely if the company were wound up (without first being in administration), or
(c) realising property in order to make a distribution to one or more secured or preferential creditors.

(2) Subject to sub-paragraph (4), the administrator of a company must perform his functions in the interests of the company's creditors as a whole.

(3) The administrator must perform his functions with the objective specified in sub-paragraph (1)(a) unless he thinks either—
(a) that it is not reasonably practicable to achieve that objective, or
(b) that the objective specified in sub-paragraph (1)(b) would achieve a better result for the company's creditors as a whole.

(4) The administrator may perform his functions with the objective specified in sub-paragraph (1)(c) only if—
(a) he thinks that it is not reasonably practicable to achieve either of the objectives specified in sub-paragraph (1)(a) and (b), and
(b) he does not unnecessarily harm the interests of the creditors of the company as a whole.

GENERAL

Interpretation

111.—(1) In this Schedule—
"administrative receiver" has the meaning given by section 251,
"administrator" has the meaning given by paragraph 1 and, where the context requires, includes a reference to a former administrator,

.....

"correspondence" includes correspondence by telephonic or other electronic means,
"creditors' meeting" has the meaning given by paragraph 50,
"enters administration" has the meaning given by paragraph 1,
"floating charge" means a charge which is a floating charge on its creation,
"in administration" has the meaning given by paragraph 1,
"hire-purchase agreement" includes a conditional sale agreement, a chattel leasing agreement and a retention of title agreement,
"holder of a qualifying floating charge" in respect of a company's property has the meaning given by paragraph 14,
"market value" means the amount which would be realised on a sale of property in the open market by a willing vendor,
"the purpose of administration" means an objective specified in paragraph 3, and
"unable to pay its debts" has the meaning given by section 123.

[(1A) In this Schedule, "company" means—
(a) a company within the meaning of section 735(1) of the Companies Act 1985,
(b) a company incorporated in an EEA State other than the United Kingdom, or
(c) a company not incorporated in an EEA State but having its centre of main interests in a member State other than Denmark.

(1B) In sub-paragraph (1A), in relation to a company, "centre of main interests" has the same meaning as in the EC Regulation and, in the absence of proof to the contrary, is presumed to be the place of its registered office (within the meaning of that Regulation).]

(2) A reference in this Schedule to a thing in writing includes a reference to a thing in electronic form.

(3) In this Schedule a reference to action includes a reference to inaction.

[Non-UK companies

111A. A company incorporated outside the United Kingdom that has a principal place of business in Northern Ireland may not enter administration under this Schedule unless it also has a principal place of business in England and Wales or Scotland (or both in England and Wales and in Scotland).]

[591]

NOTES

Commencement: 15 September 2003.

Inserted by the Enterprise Act 2002, s 248(2), Sch 16, except in relation to special administration regimes.

Para 111: in sub-para (1) definition "company" repealed, and sub-paras (1A), (1B) inserted by the Insolvency Act 1986 (Amendment) Regulations 2005, SI 2005/879, regs 2(1), (4)(a), (b), 3, except in relation to a voluntary arrangement under Pt I of this Act or the appointment of an administrator under Pt II of this Act that took effect before 13 April 2005. The definition "company" previously read as follows:

""company" includes a company which may enter administration by virtue of Article 3 of the EC Regulation,".

Para 111A: inserted by SI 2005/879, regs 2(1), (4)(c), 3, except in relation to a voluntary arrangement under Pt I of this Act or the appointment of an administrator under Pt II of this Act that took effect before 13 April 2005.

Application: paras 1, 111 are applied, with modifications in relation to the conduct of energy administration, by the Energy Act 2004, s 159(1), Sch 20, Pts 1–3.

INSOLVENCY ACT 2000

(2000 c 39)

An Act to amend the law about insolvency; to amend the Company Directors Disqualification Act 1986; and for connected purposes

[30 November 2000]

1–13 (*Relate to voluntary arrangements and the disqualification of company directors.*)

14 Model law on cross-border insolvency

(1) The Secretary of State may by regulations make any provision which he considers necessary or expedient for the purpose of giving effect, with or without modifications, to the model law on cross-border insolvency.

(2) In particular, the regulations may—
- (a) apply any provision of insolvency law in relation to foreign proceedings (whether begun before or after the regulations come into force),
- (b) modify the application of insolvency law (whether in relation to foreign proceedings or otherwise),
- (c) amend any provision of section 426 of the Insolvency Act 1986 (co-operation between courts),

and may apply or, as the case may be, modify the application of insolvency law in relation to the Crown.

(3) The regulations may make different provision for different purposes and may make—
- (a) any supplementary, incidental or consequential provision, or
- (b) any transitory, transitional or saving provision,

which the Secretary of State considers necessary or expedient.

(4) In this section—

"foreign proceedings" has the same meaning as in the model law on cross-border insolvency,

"insolvency law" has the same meaning as in section 426(10)(a) and (b) of the Insolvency Act 1986,

"the model law on cross-border insolvency" means the model law contained in Annex I of the report of the 30th session of UNCITRAL.

(5) Regulations under this section are to be made by statutory instrument and may only be made if a draft has been laid before and approved by resolution of each House of Parliament.

(6) Making regulations under this section requires the agreement—

(a) if they extend to England and Wales, of the Lord Chancellor,

(b) if they extend to Scotland, of the Scottish Ministers.

[592]

NOTES

Regulations: the Cross-Border Insolvency Regulations 2006, SI 2006/1030 at **[2733]**.

General

15 (*Amends the Financial Services and Markets Act 2000, s 356 and introduces Sch 5 to that Act.*)

16 Commencement

(1) The preceding provisions of this Act (including the Schedules) are to come into force on such day as the Secretary of State may by order made by statutory instrument appoint.

(2) Subsection (1) does not apply to section 14 (which accordingly comes into force on the day on which this Act is passed).

(3) An order under this section may make different provision for different purposes and may make—

(a) any supplementary, incidental or consequential provision, and

(b) any transitory, transitional or saving provision,

which the Secretary of State considers necessary or expedient.

[593]

NOTES

Orders: the Insolvency Act 2000 (Commencement No 1 and Transitional Provisions) Order 2001, SI 2001/766; the Insolvency Act 2000 (Commencement No 2) Order 2001, SI 2001/1751; the Insolvency Act 2000 (Commencement No 3 and Transitional Provisions) Order 2002, SI 2002/2711.

17 (*Applies to Northern Ireland only.*)

18 Short title

This Act may be cited as the Insolvency Act 2000.

[594]

(*Sch 1 contains amendments to the Insolvency Act 1986 regarding a moratorium where directors propose a voluntary arrangement; Sch 2 contains amendments to the Insolvency Act 1986 and the Building Societies Act 1986 regarding company voluntary arrangements; Sch 3 contains amendments to the Insolvency Act 1986 regarding individual voluntary arrangements; Sch 4 contains consequential amendments; Sch 5 contains repeals.*)

I. EVIDENCE

EVIDENCE ACT 1851

(1851 c 99)

An Act to amend the Law of Evidence

[7 August 1851]

NOTES

Short title: given to this Act by the Short Titles Act 1896.

(*Preamble repealed by the Statute Law Revision Act 1892.*)

1–6 (*S 1 repealed by the Statute Law Revision Act 1875; ss 2, 3, 5 relate to evidence of parties to proceedings, and evidence in criminal proceedings and in relation to wills; s 4 repealed by the Evidence Further Amendment Act 1869, s 1; s 6 repealed by the Supreme Court Act 1981, s 152(4), Sch 7, and the Judicature (Northern Ireland) Act 1978, s 122(2), Sch 7, Pt I.*)

7 Proof of foreign and colonial acts of state, judgments, etc

All proclamations, treaties, and other acts of state of any foreign state or of any British colony, and all judgments, decrees, orders, and other judicial proceedings of any court of justice in any foreign state or in any British colony, and all affidavits, pleadings, and other legal documents filed or deposited in any such court, may be proved in any court of justice, or before any person having by law or by consent of parties authority to hear, receive, and examine evidence, either by examined copies or by copies authenticated as herein-after mentioned; that is to say, if the document sought to be proved be a proclamation, treaty, or other act of state, the authenticated copy to be admissible in evidence must purport to be sealed with the seal of the foreign state or British colony to which the original document belongs; and if the document sought to be proved be a judgment, decree, order, or other judicial proceeding of any foreign or colonial court, or an affidavit, pleading, or other legal document filed or deposited in any such court, the authenticated copy to be admissible in evidence must purport either to be sealed with the seal of the foreign or colonial court to which the original document belongs, or, in the event of such court having no seal, to be signed by the judge, or, if there be more than one judge, by any one of the judges of the said court; and such judge shall attach to his signature a statement in writing on the said copy that the court whereof he is a judge has no seal; but if any of the aforesaid authenticated copies shall purport to be sealed or signed as herein-before respectively directed, the same shall respectively be admitted in evidence in every case in which the original document could have been received in evidence, without any proof of the seal where a seal is necessary, or of the signature, or of the truth of the statement attached thereto, where such signature and statement are necessary, or of the judicial character of the person appearing to have made such signature and statement.

[595]

NOTES

By virtue of the Foreign Jurisdiction Act 1890, s 5, Sch 1, this section and s 11 at **[597]** may be applied by Order in Council to any foreign country in which Her Majesty has jurisdiction as if that country were a British possession. No such Order in Council has yet been made.

8, 9 (*S 8 repealed by the Statute Law (Repeals) Act 1989; s 9 applies to Northern Ireland only.*)

10 Proof of documents in England and Wales

Every document which by any law now in force or hereafter to be in force is or shall be admissible in evidence of any particular in any court of justice in Ireland, without proof of the seal or stamp or signature authenticating the same, or of the judicial or official character of the person appearing to have signed the same, shall be admitted in evidence to the same extent and for the same purposes in any court of justice in England or Wales, or before any person having in England or Wales by law or by consent of parties authority to hear, receive, and examine evidence, without proof of the seal or stamp or signature authenticating the same, or of the judicial or official character of the person appearing to have signed the same.

[596]

11 Proof of documents in the colonies

Every document which by any law now in force or hereafter to be in force is or shall be admissible in evidence of any particular in any court of justice in England or Wales or Ireland without proof of the seal or stamp or signature authenticating the same, or of the judicial or official character of the person appearing to have signed the same, shall be admitted in evidence to the same extent and for the same purposes in any court of justice of any of the British colonies, or before any person having in any of such colonies by law or by consent of parties authority to hear, receive, and examine evidence, without proof of the seal or stamp or signature authenticating the same, or of the judicial or official character of the person appearing to have signed the same.

[597]

NOTES

Repealed in relation to British India by the Statute Law Revision Act 1875.

12–17 (*S 12 repealed by the Statute Law Revision Act 1875; ss 13–16 relate to evidence of previous convictions, public documents and penalties for falsely certifying documents; s 17 repealed by the Forgery Act 1913, s 20, Schedule, Pt I.*)

18 Extent of Act

This Act shall not extend to Scotland.

[598]

19, 20 (*S 19 relates to interpretation; s 20 repealed by the Statute Law Revision Act 1875.*)

BRITISH LAW ASCERTAINMENT ACT 1859

(1859 c 63)

An Act to afford Facilities for the more certain Ascertainment of the Law administered in one Part of Her Majesty's Dominions when pleaded in the Courts of another Part thereof

[13 August 1859]

NOTES

Short title: given to this Act by the Short Titles Act 1896.

(*Preamble repealed by the Statute Law Revision Act 1892.*)

1 Courts in one part of Her Majesty's dominions may remit a case for the opinion in law of a court in any other part thereof

If in any action depending in any court within Her Majesty's dominions, it shall be the opinion of such court, that it is necessary or expedient for the proper disposal of such action to ascertain the law applicable to the facts of the case as administered in any other part of Her Majesty's dominions on any point on which the law of such other part of Her Majesty's dominions is different from that in which the court is situate, it shall be competent to the court in which such action may depend to direct a case to be prepared setting forth the facts, as these may be ascertained by verdict of a jury or other mode competent, or may be agreed upon by the parties, or settled by such person or persons as may have been appointed by the court for that purpose in the event of the parties not agreeing; and upon such case being approved of by such court or a judge thereof, they shall settle the questions of law arising out of the same on which they desire to have the opinion of another court, and shall pronounce an order remitting the same, together with the case, to the court in such other part of Her Majesty's dominions, being one of the superior courts thereof, whose opinion is desired upon the law administered by them as applicable to the facts set forth in such case, and desiring them to pronounce their opinion on the questions submitted to them in the terms of the Act; and it shall be competent to any of the parties to the action to present a petition to the court whose opinion is to be obtained, praying such last-mentioned court to hear parties or their counsel, and to pronounce their opinion thereon in terms of this Act, or to pronounce their opinion without hearing parties or counsel; and the court to which such petition shall be presented shall, if they think fit, appoint an early day for hearing parties or their counsel on such case, and shall thereafter pronounce their opinion upon the questions of law as administered by them which are submitted to them by the court; and in order to their pronouncing such opinion they shall be entitled to take such further procedure thereupon as to them shall seem proper.

[599]

2 Certified copies of opinion to be given

Upon such opinion being pronounced, a copy thereof, certified by an officer of such court, shall be given to each of the parties to the action by whom the same shall be required, and shall be deemed and held to contain a correct record of such opinion.

[600]

3 Opinion to be applied by the court making the remit, etc

It shall be competent to any of the parties to the action, after having obtained such certified copy of such opinion, to lodge the same with an officer of the court in which the action may be depending, who may have the official charge thereof, together with a notice of motion, setting forth that the party will, on a certain day named in such notice, move the court to apply the opinion contained in such certified copy thereof to the facts set forth in the case herein-before specified; and the said court shall thereupon apply such opinion to such facts, in the same manner as if the same had been pronounced by such court itself upon a case reserved for opinion of the court, or upon special verdict of a jury; or the said last-mentioned court shall, if it think fit, when the said opinion has been obtained before trial, order such opinion to be submitted to the jury with the other facts of the case as evidence, or conclusive evidence, as the court may think fit, of the foreign law therein stated; and the said opinion shall be so submitted to the jury.

[601]

4 Her Majesty in Council or *House of Lords* on appeal may adopt or reject opinion

In the event of an appeal to Her Majesty in Council or to *the House of Lords* in any such action, it shall be competent to bring under the review of Her Majesty in Council or of *the House of Lords* the opinion pronounced as aforesaid by any court whose judgments are reviewable by Her Majesty in Council or by *the House of Lords*; and Her Majesty in Council or *that House* may respectively adopt or reject such opinion of any court whose judgments are respectively reviewable by them, as the same shall appear to them to be well founded or not in law.

[602]

NOTES

Section heading: words in italics substituted by the words "Supreme Court" by the Constitutional Reform Act 2005, s 40(4), Sch 9, Pt 1, para 1(a), as from a day to be appointed.

Words in italics substituted by the words "the Supreme Court" by the Constitutional Reform Act 2005, s 40(4), Sch 9, Pt 1, para 1(b), as from a day to be appointed.

5 Interpretation of terms

In the construction of this Act, the word "action" shall include every judicial proceeding instituted in any court, civil, criminal, or ecclesiastical; and the words "Superior Courts" shall include, in England, the Superior Courts of Law at Westminster, …, the Lords Justices, the Master of the Rolls or any Vice Chancellor, the Judge of the Court of Admiralty, the Judge Ordinary of the Court for Divorce and Matrimonial Causes, and the Judge of the Court of Probate; in Scotland, the High Court of Justiciary, and the Court of Session acting by either of its divisions; in Ireland, the Superior Courts of Law at Dublin, the Master of the Rolls, and the Judge of the Admiralty Court; and in any other part of Her Majesty's dominions, the Superior Courts of Law or Equity therein.

[603]

NOTES

Words omitted repealed by the Constitutional Reform Act 2005, ss 15(1), 146, Sch 4, Pt 1, para 15, Sch 18, Pt 2.

COLONIAL LAWS VALIDITY ACT 1865

(1865 c 63)

An Act to remove Doubts as to the Validity of Colonial Laws

[29 June 1865]

NOTES

Short title: given to this Act by the Short Titles Act 1896.

See further, as to the disapplication of this Act for certain purposes: the Australia Act 1985, s 3.

1 Interpretation

The term "colony" shall in this Act include all of Her Majesty's possessions abroad in which there shall exist a legislature, as herein-after defined, except the Channel Islands, the Isle of Man …

The terms "legislature" and "colonial legislature" shall severally signify the authority, other than the Imperial Parliament or Her Majesty in Council, competent to make laws for any colony:

The term "representative legislature" shall signify any colonial legislature which shall comprise a legislative body of which one half are elected by inhabitants of the colony:

The term "colonial law" shall include laws made for any colony either by such legislature as aforesaid or by Her Majesty in Council:

An Act of Parliament, or any provision thereof, shall, in construing this Act, be said to extend to any colony when it is made applicable to such colony by the express words or necessary intendment of any Act of Parliament:

The term "governor" shall mean the officer lawfully administering the government of any colony:

The term "letters patent" shall mean letters patent under the Great Seal of the United Kingdom of Great Britain and Ireland.

[604]

NOTES

Words omitted repealed by the Burma Independence Act 1947, s 5, Sch 2, and the Statute Law (Repeals) Act 1976.

2–5 (*Relate to colonial laws and their repugnancy or inconsistency, and to the ability of colonial legislatures to alter their constitutions.*)

6 Evidence of passing, disallowance, and assent

The certificate of the clerk or other proper officer of a legislative body in any colony to the effect that the document to which it is attached is a true copy of any colonial law assented to by the governor of such colony, or of any Bill reserved for the signification of Her Majesty's pleasure by the said governor, shall be prima facie evidence that the document so certified is a true copy of such law or Bill, and, as the case may be, that such law has been duly and properly passed and assented to, or that such Bill has been duly and properly passed and presented to the governor; and any proclamation purporting to be published by authority of the governor in any newspaper in the colony to which such law or Bill shall relate, and signifying Her Majesty's disallowance of any such colonial law, or Her Majesty's assent to any such reserved Bill as aforesaid, shall be primâ facie evidence of such disallowance or assent.

[605]

7 (*Repealed by the Statute Law Revision Act 1989.*)

DOCUMENTARY EVIDENCE ACT 1868

(1868 c 37)

ARRANGEMENT OF SECTIONS

An Act to amend the Law relating to Documentary Evidence in certain Cases

[25 June 1868]

NOTES

For the modification of this Act in relation to the Secretary of State for Transport, Local Government and the Regions, the Secretary of State for Environment, Food and Rural Affairs, see the Secretaries of State for Transport, Local Government and the Regions and for Environment, Food and Rural Affairs Order 2001, SI 2001/2568, arts 3(5), 4(5), Schedule (made under the Ministers of the Crown Act 1975, ss 1, 2).

For the modification of this Act in relation to the Chief Land Registrar, see the Land Registration Act 2002, s 99, Sch 7, para 6.

For the modification of this Act in relation to the First Secretary of State and the Secretary of State for Transport, see the Transfer of Functions (Transport, Local Government and the Regions) Order 2002, SI 2002/2626, art 19 (made under the Ministers of the Crown Act 1975, ss 1, 2).

For the modification of this Act in relation to the Secretary of State for Constitutional Affairs, see the Secretary of State for Constitutional Affairs Order 2003, SI 2003/1887, art 3(5) (made under the Ministers of the Crown Act 1975, ss 1, 2).

(*Preamble repealed by the Statute Law Revision Act 1893.*)

1 Short title

This Act may be cited for all purposes as "The Documentary Evidence Act 1868."

[606]

2 Mode of proving certain documents

Prima facie evidence of any proclamation, order, or regulation issued before or after the passing of this Act by Her Majesty, or by the Privy Council, also of any proclamation, order, or regulation issued before or after the passing of this Act by or under the authority of any such department of the Government or officer [or office-holder in the Scottish Administration] as is mentioned in the first column of the schedule hereto, may be given in all courts of justice, and in all legal proceedings whatsoever, in all or any of modes herein-after mentioned; that is to say:

(1) By the production of a copy of the Gazette purporting to contain such proclamation, order, or regulation.

(2) By the production of a copy of such proclamation, order, or regulation, purporting to be printed by the Government printer, or, where the question arises in a court in any British colony or possession, of a copy purporting to be printed under the authority of the legislature of such British colony or possession.

(3) By the production, in the case of any proclamation, order, or regulation issued by Her Majesty or by the Privy Council, of a copy or extract purporting to be certified to be true by the clerk of the Privy Council, or by any one of the lords or others of the Privy Council, and, in the case of any proclamation, order, or regulation issued by or under the authority of any of the said departments or officers [or office-holders], by the production of a copy or extract purporting to be certified to be true by the person or persons specified in the second column of the said schedule in connexion with such department or officer [or office-holder].

Any copy or extract made in pursuance of this Act may be in print or in writing, or partly in print and partly in writing.

No proof shall be required of the handwriting or official position of any person certifying, in pursuance of this Act, to the truth of any copy of or extract from any proclamation, order, or regulation.

[607]

NOTES

Words in square brackets inserted by the Scotland Act 1998 (Consequential Modifications) (No 1) Order 1999, SI 1999/1042, art 3, Sch 1, Pt I, para 1(1), (2).

By the Military Lands Act 1892, s 17(3), a byelaw under that Act is deemed to be a regulation within the meaning of this Act, and may be proved accordingly.

By the Documentary Evidence Act 1895, s 1, regulations referred to in this Act include any document issued by the Board of Agriculture.

By the Forestry Act 1967, s 2(4), Sch 1, Pt 1, para 5(2), regulations referred to in this Act include any document issued by the Forestry Commissioners.

By the Ministers of the Crown Act 1975, s 6, Sch 1, para 8, regulations referred to in this Act include any document issued by the Minister for Civil Service and any Minister eligible for a salary under the Ministerial and other Salaries Act 1975, Sch 1, Pt II, head 2.

By the Public Lending Right Act 1979, s 1(3), Schedule, para 6, regulations referred to in this Act include any documents issued by the Registrar of Public Lending Right.

By the Telecommunications Act 1984, s 1(7), Sch 1, para 7, (repealed by the Communications Act 2003, s 406(7), Sch 19(1), as from a day to be appointed), regulations referred to in this Act include any document issued by the Director General of Telecommunications.

By the Transfer of Functions (Arts, Libraries and National Heritage) Order 1986, SI 1986/600, art 4, references to orders and regulations include references to any document issued by the Lord President.

By the Transfer of Functions (Health and Social Security) Order 1988, SI 1988/1843, art 5(1)(a), in the application of this section to the Secretary of State for Health and the Secretary of State for Social Security, references in this section to orders and regulations include references to any document.

By the Transfer of Functions (Economic Statistics) Order 1989, SI 1989/992, art 6(1), regulations referred to in this Act include any document issued by the Central Statistical Office.

By the Water Resources Act 1991, s 193(3)(b), a main river map is deemed to be a document within the meaning of this Act.

By the Transfer of Functions (Education and Employment) Order 1995, SI 1995/2986, art 10(5), in the application of this Act to the Secretary of State for Education and Employment, references to orders and regulations include references to any document.

By the Northern Ireland Arms Decommissioning Act 1997, s 1(2), this section applies to a decommissioning scheme under that Act.

By the Northern Ireland Act 1998, s 88, regulations referred to in this Act include any document issued by the Social Security, Child Support and Pensions Joint Authority and by s 95A(11) of the 1998 Act, this Act applies to a direction given by the Secretary of State under ss 30A, 47B, 51B of that Act.

By the Terrorism Act 2000, s 120(4), this Act applies to an authorisation given in writing by the Secretary of State for the purposes of the 2000 Act as it applies to an order made by him.

By the Transfer of Functions (Transport, Local Government and the Regions) Order 2002, SI 2002/2626, art 19, in the application of this section in relation to the First Secretary of State and the Secretary of State for Transport, references to orders and regulations include references to any document.

By the Commissioners for Revenue and Customs Act 2005, s 24(5), this section applies to a Revenue and Customs document as it applies to documents mentioned in this section.

By the Education Act 2005, ss 1(6), 19(3), Sch 1, para 6, Sch 2, para 6, regulations referred to in this Act include any document issued by Her Majesty's Chief Inspector of Schools in England or by Her Majesty's Chief Inspector of Education and Training in Wales.

3 Act to be in force in colonies

Subject to any law that may be from time to time made by the legislature of any British colony or possession, this Act shall be in force in every such colony and possession.

[608]

4 (*Repealed, except in relation to Scotland, by the Statute Law* (*Repeals*) *Act 1993.*)

5 Interpretation

[(1)] The following words shall in this Act have the meaning herein-after assigned to them, unless there is something in the context repugnant to such construction; (that is to say),

"British colony and possession" shall for the purposes of this Act include the Channel Islands, the Isle of Man … , and all other Her Majesty's dominions.

"Legislature" shall signify any authority, other than the Imperial Parliament or Her Majesty in Council, competent to make laws for any colony or possession.

["office-holder in the Scottish Administration" has the same meaning as in the Scotland Act 1998.]

"Privy Council" shall include Her Majesty in Council and the lords and others of Her Majesty's Privy Council, or any of them, and any committee of the Privy Council that is not specially named in the schedule hereto.

"Government printer" shall mean and include the printer to Her Majesty, [the Queen's Printer for Scotland,] and any printer purporting to be the printer authorized to print the statutes, ordnances, acts of state, or other public acts of the legislature of any British colony or possession, or otherwise to be the Government printer of such colony or possession.

"Gazette" shall include the London Gazette, the Edinburgh Gazette, and the [Belfast] Gazette, or any of such Gazettes.

[(2) . . .]

[609]

NOTES

Sub-s (1): numbered as such by virtue of, and words omitted from "British colony and possession" repealed by, the Government of India (Adaptation of Acts of Parliament) Order 1937, SR & O 1937/230; definition "office-holder in the Scottish Administration" inserted and in definition "Government printer" words in square brackets inserted by the Scotland Act 1998 (Consequential Modifications) (No 1) Order 1999, SI 1999/1042, art 3, Sch 1, Pt I, para 1(1), (3); in definition "Gazette" word in square brackets substituted by virtue of the General Adaptation of Enactments (Northern Ireland) Order 1921, SR & O 1921/1804, art 7.

Sub-s (2): added by SR & O 1937/230; repealed by the Statute Law (Repeals) Act 1976.

6 (*Relates to application of Act in proving documents.*)

SCHEDULE

Column 1 Name of Department or Officer	Column 2 Names of Certifying Officers
The ... Treasury	Any Commissioner, Secretary, or Assistant Secretary of the Treasury.
The Commissioners for executing the office of Lord High Admiral	Any of the Commissioners for executing the office of Lord High Admiral, or either of the Secretaries to the said Commissioners.
Secretaries of State	Any Secretary or Under-Secretary of State.
[Any office-holder in the Scottish Administration]	[A member of the staff of the Scottish Administration]
Committee of Privy Council for Trade	Any member of the Committee of Privy Council for Trade, or any Secretary or Assistant Secretary of the said Committee.
...	...

[610]

NOTES

Words omitted in the first place repealed by the Statute Law Revision Act 1893; words in square brackets inserted by the Scotland Act 1998 (Consequential Modifications) (No 1) Order 1999, SI 1999/1042, art 3, Sch 1, Pt I, para 1(1), (4); final entry omitted repealed by the Statute Law (Repeals) Act 1989.

This Schedule is extended in relation to various authorities as follows—

Central Statistical Office	Transfer of Functions (Economic Statistics) Order 1989, SI 1989/992, art 6(1)
Charity Commissioners for England and Wales	Charities Act 1993, s 1, Sch 1, para 3(2),
Chief Inspector of Schools in England	Education Act 2005, s 1, Sch 1, para 6
Chief Inspector of Education and Training in Wales	Education Act 2005, s 19, Sch 2, para 6, (as from 1 September 2006)

Chief Land Registrar	Land Registration Act 2002, s 99(4), Sch 7, para 6
Commissioners of Inland Revenue and Commissioners of Customs and Excise	Commissioners for Revenue and Customs Act 2005, s 24(5)–(7)
Crown Estate Commissioners	Crown Estate Act 1961, s 1, Sch 1, para 6
Defence Council	Defence (Transfer of Functions) (No 1) Order 1964, SI 1964/488, art 2(1), Sch 1, Pt I
Director General of Telecommunications	Telecommunications Act 1984, s 1, Sch 1, para 7 (repealed by the Communications Act 2003, s 406(7), Sch 19(1), as from a day to be appointed)
First Minister and deputy First Minister of Northern Ireland acting jointly	Northern Ireland (Modification of Enactments—No 1) Order 1999, SI 1999/663, art 4
First Secretary of State and the Secretary of State for Transport	Transfer of Functions (Transport, Local Government and the Regions) Order 2002, SI 2002/2626, art 19
Forestry Commissioners	Forestry Act 1967, s 2, Sch 1, Pt I, para 5(2)
Lord President of Council	Transfer of Functions (Arts, Libraries and National Heritage) Order 1986, SI 1986/600, art 4
Minister of Agriculture, Fisheries and Food	Documentary Evidence Act 1895, s 1
Minister for the Civil Service and any Minister eligible for a salary under the Ministerial and other Salaries Act 1975, Sch 1, Pt II, head 2	Ministers of the Crown Act 1975, s 6, Sch 1
OFCOM	Communications Act 2003, s 403(8)
Registrar of Public Lending Right	Public Lending Right Act 1979, s 1(3), Schedule, para 6
Secretary of State for Education and Employment	Transfer of Functions (Education and Employment) Order 1995, SI 1995/2986, art 10(5)
Secretary of State for Health and Secretary of State for Social Security	Transfer of Functions (Health and Social Security) Order 1988, SI 1988/1843, art 5(1)(b)
Social Security, Child Support and Pensions Joint Authority	Northern Ireland Act 1998, s 88(6)
Strategic Rail Authority	Transport Act 2000, s 204, Sch 14, Pt V, para 25

COMMISSIONERS FOR OATHS ACT 1889

(1889 c 10)

An Act for amending and consolidating enactments relating to the administration of Oaths
[31 May 1889]

1, 2 (*Relate to the appointment and powers of commissioners for oaths and to the powers of certain officers to administer oaths.*)

3 Taking of oaths out of England

(1) Any oath or affidavit required for the purpose of any court or matter in England, or for the purpose of the registration of any instrument in any part of the United Kingdom, may be taken or made in any place out of England before any person having authority to administer an oath in that place.

(2) In the case of a person having such authority otherwise than by the law of a foreign country, judicial and official notice shall be taken of his seal or signature affixed, impressed, or subscribed to or on any such oath or affidavit.

[611]

4–14 (*Ss 4–6 relate to the appointment of persons to administer oaths for prize proceedings, details to be included when oath is taken and powers as to oaths and notarial* *acts abroad; s 7 repealed by the Perjury Act 1911, s 17, Schedule, and the Statute Law Revision Act (Northern Ireland) 1954; ss 8–10 repealed by the Forgery Act 1913, s 20, Schedule, Pt I; s 11 contains definitions; ss 12, 14 repealed by the Statute Law Revision Act 1908; s 13 repealed by the Statute Law (Repeals) Act 1977.)*

15 Short title

This Act may be cited as the Commissioners for Oaths Act 1889.

[612]

EVIDENCE (COLONIAL STATUTES) ACT 1907

(1907 c 16)

An Act to facilitate the admission in evidence of statutes passed by the Legislatures of British possessions and protectorates, including Cyprus

[21 August 1907]

1 Proof of statutes of British possessions

(1) Copies of Acts, ordinances, and statutes passed (whether before or after the passing of this Act) by the Legislature of any British possession, and of orders, regulations, and other instruments issued or made, whether before or after the passing of this Act, under the authority of any such Act, ordinance, or statute, if purporting to be printed by the Government printer, shall be received in evidence by all courts of justice in the United Kingdom without any proof being given that the copies were so printed.

(2) *If any person prints any copy or pretended copy of any such Act, ordinance, statute, order, regulation, or instrument which falsely purports to have been printed by the Government printer, or tenders in evidence any such copy or pretended copy which falsely purports to have been so printed, knowing that it was not so printed, he shall on conviction be liable to be sentenced to imprisonment with or without hard labour for a period not exceeding twelve months.*

(3) In this Act—

The expression "Government printer" means, as respects any British possession, the printer purporting to be the printer authorised to print the Acts, ordinances, or statutes of the Legislature of that possession, or otherwise to be the Government printer of that possession:

The expression "British possession" means any part of His Majesty's dominions exclusive of the United Kingdom, and, where parts of those dominions are under both a central and a local Legislature, shall include both all parts under the central Legislature and each part under a local Legislature.

(4) Nothing in this Act shall affect the Colonial Laws Validity Act 1865.

(5) His Majesty may by Order in Council extend this Act to Cyprus and any British protectorate, and where so extended this Act shall apply as if Cyprus or the protectorate were a British possession, and with such other necessary adaptations as may be made by the Order.

[613]

NOTES

Sub-s (2): repealed, except in relation to Scotland, by the Statute Law (Repeals) Act 1993.

Orders in Council: the Evidence (Colonial Statutes) Act 1907 extension to Cyprus and certain British Protectorates Order in Council 1909, SR & O 1909/1230.

Note: the protectorates to which this Act was extended are no longer protectorates, and Cyprus is now an independent republic; however, the Order in Council may still be relevant to the Sovereign Base Areas of Akrotiri and Dhekelia, which were retained when Cyprus became independent.

2 Short title

This Act may be cited as the Evidence (Colonial Statutes) Act 1907.

[614]

EVIDENCE (FOREIGN, DOMINION AND COLONIAL DOCUMENTS) ACT 1933

(1933 c 4)

An Act to make further and better provision with respect to the admissibility in evidence in the United Kingdom of entries contained in the public registers of other countries and with respect to the proof by means of duly authenticated official certificates of entries in such registers and in consular registers and of other matters

[29 March 1933]

1 Proof and effect of foreign, dominion and colonial registers and certain official certificates

(1) …

(2) An Order in Council made under [section 5 of the Oaths and Evidence (Overseas Authorities and Countries) Act 1963] may provide that in all parts of the United Kingdom—

(a) a register of the country to which the Order relates, being such a register as is specified in the Order, shall be deemed to be a public register kept under the authority of the law of that country and recognised by the courts thereof as an authentic record, and to be a document of such a public nature as to be admissible as evidence of the matters regularly recorded therein;

(b) such matters as may be specified in the Order shall, if recorded in such a register, be deemed, until the contrary is proved, to be regularly recorded therein;

(c) subject to any conditions specified in the Order and to any requirements of rules of court a document purporting to be issued in the country to which the Order relates as an official copy of an entry in such a register as is so specified, and purporting to be authenticated as such in the manner specified in the Order as appropriate in the case of such a register, shall, without evidence as to the custody of the register or of inability to produce it and without any further or other proof, be received as evidence that the register contains such an entry;

(d) subject as aforesaid a certificate purporting to be given in the country to which the Order relates as an official certificate of any such class as is specified in the Order, and purporting to be signed by the officer, and to be authenticated in the manner specified in the Order as appropriate in the case of a certificate of that class, shall be received as evidence of the facts stated in the certificate;

(e) no official document issued in the country to which the Order relates as proof of any matters for the proof of which provision is made by the Order shall, if otherwise admissible in evidence, be inadmissible by reason only that it is not authenticated by the process known as legalisation.

(3) Official books of record preserved in a central registry and containing entries copied from original registers may, if those entries were copied by officials in the course of their duty, themselves be treated for the purposes of this section as registers.

(4) In this section the expression "country" means a Dominion, the Isle of Man, any of the Channel Islands, a British colony or protectorate, a foreign country, a colony or protectorate of a foreign country, or any mandated territory:

Provided that where a part of a country is under both a local and a central legislature, an Order under this section may be made as well with respect to that part, as with respect to all the parts under that central legislature.

(5) …

[615]

NOTES

Sub-ss (1), (5): repealed by the Oaths and Evidence (Overseas Authorities and Countries) Act 1963, s 5(2).

Sub-s (2): words in square brackets substituted by the Oaths and Evidence (Overseas Authorities and Countries) Act 1963, s 5(2).

The relevant power to make orders under this section is now contained in the Oaths and Evidence (Overseas Authorities and Countries) Act 1963, s 5(1) at **[620]**. For a saving for Orders in Council under this section as originally enacted, see s 5(2) of the 1963 Act at **[620]**.

2 (*Repealed by the British Nationality Act 1948, s 34, Sch 4, Pt II.*)

3 Short title

This Act may be cited as the Evidence (Foreign, Dominion and Colonial Documents) Act 1933.

[616]

OATHS AND EVIDENCE (OVERSEAS AUTHORITIES AND COUNTRIES) ACT 1963

(1963 c 27)

ARRANGEMENT OF SECTIONS

An Act to authorise the administration of oaths and the performance of notarial acts by representatives of, and other persons empowered by the authorities of, countries overseas, and by representatives of Her Majesty in post overseas; and to amend the Foreign Tribunals Evidence Act 1856 and the Evidence (Foreign, Dominion and Colonial Documents) Act 1933

[31 July 1963]

1 Taking of evidence for foreign civil proceedings

Any person appointed by a court or other judicial authority of any foreign country shall have power in the United Kingdom to administer oaths for the purpose of taking evidence for use in proceedings, not being criminal proceedings carried on under the law of that country.

[617]

2 Administration of oaths etc by representatives of protecting Power

(1) Where in any country or area Her Majesty has for the time being no diplomatic or consular representatives appointed on the advice of Her Government in the United Kingdom, and arrangements made on such advice are in force for the representation of interests of Her Majesty in the country or area through diplomatic or consular representatives of any other country, Her Majesty may by Order in Council provide for empowering such representatives to administer oaths and do notarial acts.

(2) An Order under this section may prescribe the facts to be stated in the jurat by any person by whom an oath is administered by virtue of the Order; and any document purporting to have subscribed thereto the signature of any person in testimony of any oath being administered before him, and containing in the jurat a statement of the facts required to be stated therein by the Order, shall be received in evidence without proof of the signature being the signature of that person or of the facts so stated.

[618]

3 Amendment of 52 & 53 Vict c 10, s 6

Section 6 of the Commissioners for Oaths Act 1889 (powers of British ambassadors, ministers etc to administer oaths) shall have effect as if the diplomatic ranks specified therein included the rank of counsellor.

[619]

4 (*Repealed by the Evidence (Proceedings in Other Jurisdictions) Act 1975, s 8(2), Sch 2.*)

5 Amendment of 23 & 24 Geo 5 c 4

(1) If Her Majesty in Council is satisfied as respects any country that—

(a) there exist in that country public registers kept under the authority of the law of that country and recognised by the courts of that country as authentic records, and
(b) that the registers are regularly and properly kept,

Her Majesty may by Order in Council make in respect of that country and all or any of those registers such provision as is specified in subsection (2) of section 1 of the Evidence (Foreign, Dominion and Colonial Documents) Act 1933.

(2) The foregoing subsection shall have effect in substitution for subsection (1) of the said section 1, and accordingly subsections (1) and (5) of the said section 1 are hereby repealed, in subsection (2) of that section for the words "this section" there shall be substituted "section 5 of the Oaths and Evidence (Overseas Authorities and Countries) Act 1963", and subsection (4) of that section (interpretation of "country") shall apply for the interpretation of the foregoing subsection as it applies for the interpretation of the said section 1; but any Order in Council made under the said section 1 and in force at the commencement of this Act shall continue in force until revoked, or as varied, by an Order in Council under this section.

[620]

NOTES

Orders in Council: the Evidence (Antigua) Order 1965, SI 1965/312; the Evidence (Cayman Islands) Order 1965, SI 1965/313; the Evidence (Aden) Order 1965, SI 1965/1527; the Evidence (Kenya) Order 1965, SI 1965/1712; the Evidence (Basutoland) Order 1965, SI 1965/1719; the Evidence (Bechuanaland Protectorate) Order 1965, SI 1965/1720; the Evidence (Saint Lucia) Order 1965, SI 1965/1721; the Evidence (Swaziland) Order 1965, SI 1965/1865; the Evidence (Grenada) Order 1966, SI 1966/82; the Evidence (Turks and Caicos Islands) Order 1966, SI 1966/83; the Evidence (Denmark) Order 1969, SI 1969/144; the Evidence (Italy) Order 1969, SI 1969/145; the Evidence (United States of America) Order 1969, SI 1969/146; the Evidence (Republic of Ireland) Order 1969, SI 1969/1059; the Evidence (the Netherlands) Order 1970, SI 1970/284; the Evidence (Federal Republic of Germany) Order 1970, SI 1970/819; the Evidence (Luxembourg) Order 1972, SI 1972/116; the Evidence (British Indian Ocean Territory) Order 1984, SI 1984/857.

In addition, by virtue of sub-s (2) above, the following Orders in Council, originally made under the Evidence (Foreign, Dominion and Colonial Documents) Act 1933, s 1(1), continue in force: the Evidence (Belgium) Order 1933, SR & O 1933/383; the Evidence (France) Order in Council 1937, SR & O 1937/515; the Evidence (Commonwealth of Australia) Order 1938, SR & O 1938/739; the Evidence (New Zealand) Order 1959, SI 1959/1306; the Evidence (Bahamas) Order 1961, SI 1961/2041; the Evidence (Barbados) Order 1962, SI 1962/641; the Evidence (Bermuda) Order 1961, SI 1961/2042; the Evidence (British Guiana) Order 1961, SI 1961/2043; the Evidence (British Honduras) Order 1961, SI 1961/2044; the Evidence (Dominica) Order 1961, SI 1961/2045; the Evidence (Fiji) Order 1961, SI 1961/2046; the Evidence (Gibraltar) Order 1961, SI 1961/2047; the Evidence (Mauritius) Order 1961, SI 1961/2048; the Evidence (St Helena) Order 1961, SI 1961/2049; the Evidence (Sarawak) Order 1961, SI 1961/2050; the Evidence (Tanganyika) Order 1961, SI 1961/2051; the Evidence (Uganda) Order 1961, SI 1961/2052; the Evidence (Zanzibar) Order 1961, SI 1961/2053; the Evidence (Hong Kong) Order 1962, SI 1962/642; the Evidence (Jamaica) Order 1962, SI 1962/643; the Evidence (Montserrat) Order 1962, SI 1962/644; the Evidence (British Antarctic Territory) Order 1962, SI 1962/2605; the Evidence (Certain Provinces of Canada) Order 1962, SI 1962/2606; the Evidence (Falkland Islands) Order 1962, SI 1962/2607; the Evidence (Seychelles) Order 1962, SI 1962/2608; the Evidence (Sierra Leone) Order 1962, SI 1962/2609.

6 Interpretation

(1) In this Act "diplomatic or consular representative" means a member of the diplomatic, consular or other foreign service of any country, and includes a person for the time being exercising diplomatic or consular functions.

(2) References in this Act to the administration of an oath shall include references to the taking of an affidavit, and references in section 2(2) of this Act shall be construed accordingly.

(3) Any power conferred by this Act to make an Order shall include power to vary or revoke the Order.

[621]

7 Short title and extent

(1) This Act may be cited as the Oaths and Evidence (Overseas Authorities and Countries) Act 1963.

(2) It is hereby declared that this Act extends to Northern Ireland.

(3) Her Majesty may by Order in Council direct that any provisions of this Act shall extend to the Isle of Man or any of the Channel Islands, with such adaptations or

modifications as may be specified in the Order; and where any provision is so extended any Order made thereunder shall have the like extent notwithstanding that it was made before the coming into operation of the Order under this subsection, but as so extended shall have effect subject to any adaptations or modifications specified in the last-mentioned Order.

[622]

NOTES

Orders in Council: the Oaths and Evidence (Isle of Man) Order 1965, SI 1965/1129; the Oaths and Evidence (Guernsey) Order 1966, SI 1966/1019.

ADMINISTRATION OF JUSTICE (SCOTLAND) ACT 1972

(1972 c 59)

NOTES

Only section 1 is reproduced here.

An Act to confer extended powers on the courts in Scotland to order the inspection of documents and other property, and related matters; to enable an appeal to be taken to the House of Lords from an interlocutor of the Court of Session on a motion for a new trial; to enable a case to be stated on a question of law to the Court of Session in an arbitration; and to enable alterations to be made by act of sederunt in the rate of interest to be included in sheriff court decrees or extracts

[9 August 1972]

1 Extended powers of courts to order inspection of documents and other property, etc

(1) Without prejudice to the existing powers of the Court of Session and of the sheriff court, those courts shall have power, subject to the provisions of subsection (4) of this section, to order the inspection, photographing, preservation, custody and detention of documents and other property (including, where appropriate, land) which appear to the court to be property as to which any question may relevantly arise in any existing civil proceedings before that court or in civil proceedings which are likely to be brought, and to order the production and recovery of any such property, the taking of samples thereof and the carrying out of any experiment thereon or therewith.

(2) Notwithstanding any rule of law or practice to the contrary, the court may exercise the powers mentioned in subsection (1) of this section—

(a) where proceedings have been commenced, on the application, at any time after such commencement, of a party to or minuter in the proceedings, or any other person who appears to the court to have an interest to be joined as such party or minuter;

(b) where proceedings have not been commenced, on the application at any time of a person who appears to the court to be likely to be a party to or minuter in proceedings which are likely to be brought;

unless there is special reason why the application should not be granted.

(3) The powers conferred on the Court of Session by section 16 of the Administration of Justice (Scotland) Act 1933 to regulate its own procedure and the powers conferred on that Court by section 32 of the Sheriff Courts (Scotland) Act 1971 to regulate the procedure of the sheriff court shall include power to regulate and prescribe the procedure to be followed, and the form of any document to be used, in any application under the foregoing provisions of this section in a case where the application is in respect of proceedings which have not been commenced, and such incidental, supplementary and consequential provisions as appear appropriate; and without prejudice to the said generality, the said powers shall include power to provide in such a case for the application to be granted *ex parte*, for the intimation of the application to such persons (if any) as the court thinks fit, and for the finding of caution where appropriate for any loss, damage or expenses which may be incurred as a result of the application.

(4) Nothing in this section shall affect any rule of law or practice relating to the privilege of witnesses and havers, confidentiality of communications and withholding or non-disclosure

of information on the grounds of public interest; and section 47 of the Crown Proceedings Act 1947 (recovery of documents in possession of Crown) shall apply in relation to any application under this section in respect of a document or other property as it applied before the commencement of this section to an application for commission and diligence for the recovery of a document.

[623]

CIVIL EVIDENCE ACT 1972

(1972 c 30)

An Act to make, for civil proceedings in England and Wales, provision as to the admissibility in evidence of statements of opinion and the reception of expert evidence; and to facilitate proof in such proceedings of any law other than that of England and Wales

[12 June 1972]

1–3 (*S 1 repealed by the Civil Evidence Act 1995, s 15(2), Sch 2; ss 2, 3 relate to expert witnesses.*)

4 Evidence of foreign law

(1) It is hereby declared that in civil proceedings a person who is suitably qualified to do so on account of his knowledge or experience is competent to give expert evidence as to the law of any country or territory outside the United Kingdom, or of any part of the United Kingdom other than England and Wales, irrespective of whether he has acted or is entitled to act as a legal practitioner there.

(2) Where any question as to the law of any country or territory outside the United Kingdom, or of any part of the United Kingdom other than England and Wales, with respect to any matter has been determined (whether before or after the passing of this Act) in any such proceedings as are mentioned in subsection (4) below, then in any civil proceedings (not being proceedings before a court which can take judicial notice of the law of that country, territory or part with respect to that matter)—

(a) any finding made or decision given on that question in the first-mentioned proceedings shall, if reported or recorded in citable form, be admissible in evidence for the purpose of proving the law of that country, territory or part with respect to that matter; and

(b) if that finding or decision, as so reported or recorded, is adduced for that purpose, the law of that country, territory or part with respect to that matter shall be taken to be in accordance with that finding or decision unless the contrary is proved:

Provided that paragraph (b) above shall not apply in the case of a finding or decision which conflicts with another finding or decision on the same question adduced by virtue of this subsection in the same proceedings.

(3) Except with the leave of the court, a party to any civil proceedings shall not be permitted to adduce any such finding or decision as is mentioned in subsection (2) above by virtue of that subsection unless he has in accordance with rules of court given to every other party to the proceedings notice that he intends to do so.

(4) The proceedings referred to in subsection (2) above are the following, whether civil or criminal, namely—

(a) proceedings at first instance in any of the following courts, namely the High Court, the Crown Court, a court of quarter sessions, the Court of Chancery of the county palatine of Lancaster and the Court of Chancery of the county palatine of Durham;

(b) appeals arising out of any such proceedings as are mentioned in paragraph (a) above;

(c) proceedings before the Judicial Committee of the Privy Council on appeal (whether to Her Majesty in Council or to the Judicial Committee as such) from any decision of any court outside the United Kingdom.

(5) For the purposes of this section a finding or decision on any such question as is mentioned in subsection (2) above shall be taken to be reported or recorded in citable form, if, but only if, it is reported or recorded in writing in a report, transcript or other document

which, if that question had been a question as to the law of England and Wales, could be cited as an authority in legal proceedings in England and Wales.

[624]

5 (*Relates to interpretation, the application to arbitrations and contains savings.*)

6 Short title, extent and commencement

(1) This Act may be cited as the Civil Evidence Act 1972.

(2) This Act shall not extend to Scotland or Northern Ireland.

(3) This Act, except sections … 4(2) to (5), shall come into force on 1st January 1973, and sections … 4(2) to (5) shall come into force on such day as the Lord Chancellor may by order made by statutory instrument appoint; and different days may be so appointed for different purposes or for the same purposes in relation to different courts or proceedings or otherwise in relation to different circumstances.

[625]

NOTES

Sub-s (3): words omitted repealed by the Civil Evidence Act 1995, s 15(2), Sch 2.

Orders: the Civil Evidence Act 1972 (Commencement No 1) Order 1974, SI 1974/280; the Civil Evidence Act 1972 (Commencement No 2) Order 1974, SI 1974/1137.

EVIDENCE (PROCEEDINGS IN OTHER JURISDICTIONS) ACT 1975

(1975 c 34)

ARRANGEMENT OF SECTIONS

Evidence for civil proceedings

Evidence for international proceedings

Supplementary

An Act to make new provision for enabling the High Court, the Court of Session and the High Court of Justice in Northern Ireland to assist in obtaining evidence required for the purposes of proceedings in other jurisdictions; to extend the powers of those courts to issue process effective throughout the United Kingdom for securing the attendance of witnesses; and for purposes connected with those matters

[22 May 1975]

Evidence for civil proceedings

1 Application to United Kingdom court for assistance in obtaining evidence for civil proceedings in other court

Where an application is made to the High Court, the Court of Session or the High Court of Justice in Northern Ireland for an order for evidence to be obtained in the part of the United Kingdom in which it exercises jurisdiction, and the court is satisfied—

(a) that the application is made in pursuance of a request issued by or on behalf of a court or tribunal ("the requesting court") exercising jurisdiction in any other part of the United Kingdom or in a country or territory outside the United Kingdom; and

(b) that the evidence to which the application relates is to be obtained for the purposes of civil proceedings which either have been instituted before the requesting court or whose institution before that court is contemplated,

the High Court, Court of Session or High Court of Justice in Northern Ireland, as the case may be, shall have the powers conferred on it by the following provisions of this Act.

[626]

2 Power of United Kingdom court to give effect to application for assistance

(1) Subject to the provisions of this section, the High Court, the Court of Session and the High Court of Justice in Northern Ireland shall each have power, on any such application as is mentioned in section 1 above, by order to make such provision for obtaining evidence in the part of the United Kingdom in which it exercises jurisdiction as may appear to the court to be appropriate for the purpose of giving effect to the request in pursuance of which the application is made; and any such order may require a person specified therein to take such steps as the court may consider appropriate for that purpose.

(2) Without prejudice to the generality of subsection (1) above but subject to the provisions of this section, an order under this section, in particular, make provision—

(a) for the examination of witnesses, either orally or in writing;

(b) for the production of documents;

(c) for the inspection, photographing, preservation, custody or detention of any property;

(d) for the taking of samples of any property and the carrying out of any experiments on or with any property;

(e) for the medical examination of any person;

(f) without prejudice to paragraph (e) above, for the taking and testing of samples of blood from any person.

(3) An order under this section shall not require any particular steps to be taken unless they are steps which can be required to be taken by way of obtaining evidence for the purposes of civil proceedings in the court making the order (whether or not proceedings of the same description as those to which the application for the order relates); but this subsection shall not preclude the making of an order requiring a person to give testimony (either orally or in writing) otherwise than on oath where this is asked for by the requesting court.

(4) An order under this section shall not require a person—

(a) to state what documents relevant to the proceedings to which the application for the order relates are or have been in his possession, custody or power; or

(b) to produce any documents other than particular documents specified in the order as being documents appearing to the court making the order to be, or to be likely to be, in his possession, custody or power.

(5) A person who, by virtue of an order under this section, is required to attend at any place shall be entitled to the like conduct money and payment for expenses and loss of time as on attendance as a witness in civil proceedings before the court making the order.

[627]

3 Privilege of witnesses

(1) A person shall not be compelled by virtue of an order under section 2 above to give any evidence which he could not be compelled to give—

(a) in civil proceedings in the part of the United Kingdom in which the court that made the order exercises jurisdiction; or

(b) subject to subsection (2) below, in civil proceedings in the country or territory in which the requesting court exercises jurisdiction.

(2) Subsection (1)(b) above shall not apply unless the claim of the person in question to be exempt from giving the evidence is either—

(a) supported by a statement contained in the request (whether it is so supported unconditionally or subject to conditions that are fulfilled); or

(b) conceded by the applicant for the order;

and where such a claim made by any person is not supported or conceded as aforesaid he may (subject to the other provisions of this section) be required to give the evidence to which the claim relates but that evidence shall not be transmitted to the requesting court if that court, on the matter being referred to it, upholds the claim.

(3) Without prejudice to subsection (1) above, a person shall not be compelled by virtue of an order under section 2 above to give any evidence if his doing so would be prejudicial to the security of the United Kingdom; and a certificate signed by or on behalf of the Secretary of State to the effect that it would be so prejudicial for that person to do so shall be conclusive evidence of that fact.

(4) In this section references to giving evidence include references to answering any question and to producing any document and the reference in subsection (2) above to the transmission of evidence given by a person shall be construed accordingly.

[628]

4 Extension of powers of High Court etc in relation to obtaining evidence for proceedings in that court

[The Attendance of Witnesses Act 1854 (which enables the Court of Session to order the issue of a warrant of citation in special form, enforceable throughout the United Kingdom, for the attendance of a witness at a trial) shall] have effect as if references to attendance at a trial included references to attendance before an examiner or commissioner appointed by the court or a judge thereof in any cause or matter in that court, including an examiner or commissioner appointed to take evidence outside the jurisdiction of the court.

[629]

NOTES

Words in square brackets substituted by the Supreme Court Act 1981, s 152(1), Sch 5.

5 (*Repealed by the Criminal Justice* (*International Co-operation*) *Act 1990, s 31*(*3*)*, Sch 5.*)

Evidence for international proceedings

6 Power of United Kingdom court to assist in obtaining evidence for international proceedings

(1) Her Majesty may by Order in Council direct that, subject to such exceptions, adaptations or modifications as may be specified in the Order, the provisions of sections 1 to 3 above shall have effect in relation to international proceedings of any description specified in the order.

(2) An Order in Council under this section may direct that section 1(4) of the Perjury Act 1911 or [article 3(4) of the Perjury (Northern Ireland) Order 1979] shall have effect in relation to international proceedings to which the Order applies as it has effect in relation to a judicial proceeding in a tribunal of a foreign state.

(3) In this section "international proceedings" means proceedings before the International Court of Justice or any other court, tribunal, commission, body or authority (whether consisting of one or more persons) which, in pursuance of any international agreement or any resolution of the General Assembly of the United Nations, exercises any jurisdiction or performs any functions of a judicial nature or by way of arbitration, conciliation or inquiry or is appointed (whether permanently or temporarily) for the purpose of exercising any jurisdiction or performing any such functions.

[630]

NOTES

Sub-s (2): words in square brackets substituted by the Perjury (Northern Ireland) Order 1979, SI 1979/1714, art 19(1), Sch 1, para 26.

Orders in Council: the Evidence (European Court) Order 1976, SI 1976/428; the Evidence (Proceedings in Other Jurisdictions) (Isle of Man) Order 1979, SI 1979/1711, extending this Act and the

1976 Order, subject to modifications, to the Isle of Man; the Evidence (Proceedings in Other Jurisdictions) (Guernsey) Order 1980, SI 1980/1956, extending this Act and the 1976 Order, subject to modifications, to the Bailiwick of Guernsey.

Supplementary

7 Rules of court

[Civil Procedure Rules or rules of court under] section 7 of the Northern Ireland Act 1962 [may make provision]—

(a) as to the manner in which any such application as is mentioned in section 1 above is to be made;

(b) subject to the provisions of this Act, as to the circumstances in which an order can be made under section 2 above; and

(c) as to the manner in which any such reference as is mentioned in section 3(2) above is to be made;

and any such rules may include such incidental, supplementary and consequential provision as the authority making the rules, may consider necessary or expedient.

[631]

NOTES

Words in square brackets substituted by the Courts Act 2003, s 109(1), Sch 8, para 177.

8 Consequential amendments and repeals

(1) The enactments mentioned in Schedule 1 to this Act shall have effect subject to the amendments there specified, being amendments consequential on the provisions of this Act.

(2) The enactments mentioned in Schedule 2 to this Act are hereby repealed to the extent specified in the third column of that Schedule.

(3) Nothing in this section shall affect—

(a) any application to any court or judge which is pending at the commencement of this Act;

(b) any certificate given for the purposes of any such application;

(c) any power to make an order on such an application; or

(d) the operation or enforcement of any order made on such an application.

(4) Subsection (3) above is without prejudice to section 38(2) of the Interpretation Act 1889 (effect of repeals).

[632]

NOTES

Interpretation Act 1889: see now the Interpretation Act 1978.

9 Interpretation

(1) In this Act—

"civil proceedings", in relation to the requesting court, means proceedings in any civil or commercial matter;

"requesting court" has the meaning given in section 1 above;

"property" includes any land, chattel or other corporeal property of any description;

"request" includes any commission, order or other process issued by or on behalf of the requesting court.

(2) In relation to any application made in pursuance of a request issued by the High Court under [section 56 of the County Courts Act 1984] or the High Court of Justice in Northern Ireland under [Article 43 of the County Courts (Northern Ireland) Order 1980] the reference in section 1(b) above to proceedings instituted before the requesting court shall be construed as a reference to the relevant proceedings in the county court.

(3) Any power conferred by this Act to make an Order in Council includes power to revoke or vary any such Order by a subsequent Order in Council.

(4) Nothing in this Act shall be construed as enabling any court to make an order that is binding on the Crown or on any person in his capacity as an officer or servant of the Crown.

(5) Except so far as the context otherwise requires, any reference in this Act to any enactment is a reference to that enactment as amended or extended by or under any other enactment.

[633]

NOTES

Sub-s (2): words in first pair of square brackets substituted by the County Courts Act 1984, s 148(1), Sch 2, para 53; words in second pair of square brackets substituted by the County Courts (Northern Ireland) Order 1980, SI 1980/397, art 68(2), Sch 1, Pt II.

10 Short title, commencement and extent

(1) This Act may be cited as the Evidence (Proceedings in Other Jurisdictions) Act 1975.

(2) This Act shall come into operation of such day as Her Majesty may by Order in Council appoint.

(3) Her Majesty may by Order in Council make provision for extending any of the provisions of this Act (including section 6 or any Order in Council made thereunder), with such exceptions, adaptations or modifications as may be specified, in the Order, to any of the Channel Islands, the Isle of Man, any colony (other than a colony for whose external relations a country other than the United Kingdom is responsible) or any country or territory outside Her Majesty's dominions in which Her Majesty has jurisdiction in right of Her Majesty's Government in the United Kingdom.

[634]

NOTES

Orders in Council: the Evidence (Proceedings in Other Jurisdictions) Act 1975 (Commencement) Order 1976, SI 1976/429; the Evidence (Proceedings in Other Jurisdictions) (Cayman Islands) Order 1978, SI 1978/1890; the Evidence (Proceedings in Other Jurisdictions) (Falkland Islands and Dependencies) Order 1978, SI 1978/1891; the Evidence (Proceedings in Other Jurisdictions) (Gibraltar) Order 1978, SI 1978/1892; the Evidence (Proceedings in Other Jurisdictions) (Sovereign Base Areas of Akrotiri and Dhekelia) Order 1978, SI 1978/1920; the Evidence (Proceedings in Other Jurisdictions) (Isle of Man) Order 1979, SI 1979/1711; the Evidence (Proceedings in Other Jurisdictions) (Guernsey) Order 1980, SI 1980/1956; the Evidence (Proceedings in Other Jurisdictions) (Jersey) Order 1983, SI 1983/1700; the Evidence (Proceedings in Other Jurisdictions) (Anguilla) Order 1986, SI 1986/218; the Bermuda (Evidence) Order 1987, SI 1987/662; the Evidence (Proceedings in Other Jurisdictions) (Turks and Caicos Islands) Order 1987, SI 1987/1266.

(*Sch 1 in so far as unrepealed, contains amendments; Sch 2 contains repeals.*)

CIVIL PROCEDURE ACT 1997

(1997 c 12)

An Act to amend the law about civil procedure in England and Wales; and for connected purposes

[27 February 1997]

1–6 (*Relate to civil procedure rules and directions* (*ss 1, 4 and 5 reproduced at* **[138]**–**[140]**), *and the Civil Justice Council.*)

Court orders

7 Power of courts to make orders for preserving evidence, etc

(1) The court may make an order under this section for the purpose of securing, in the case of any existing or proposed proceedings in the court—

(a) the preservation of evidence which is or may be relevant, or

(b) the preservation of property which is or may be the subject-matter of the proceedings or as to which any question arises or may arise in the proceedings.

(2) A person who is, or appears to the court likely to be, a party to proceedings in the court may make an application for such an order.

(3) Such an order may direct any person to permit any person described in the order, or secure that any person so described is permitted—

(a) to enter premises in England and Wales, and
(b) while on the premises, to take in accordance with the terms of the order any of the following steps.

(4) Those steps are—

(a) to carry out a search for or inspection of anything described in the order, and
(b) to make or obtain a copy, photograph, sample or other record of anything so described.

(5) The order may also direct the person concerned—

(a) to provide any person described in the order, or secure that any person so described is provided, with any information or article described in the order, and
(b) to allow any person described in the order, or secure that any person so described is allowed, to retain for safe keeping anything described in the order.

(6) An order under this section is to have effect subject to such conditions as are specified in the order.

(7) This section does not affect any right of a person to refuse to do anything on the ground that to do so might tend to expose him or his spouse [or civil partner] to proceedings for an offence or for the recovery of a penalty.

(8) In this section—

"court" means the High Court, and
"premises" includes any vehicle;

and an order under this section may describe anything generally, whether by reference to a class or otherwise.

[635]

NOTES

Sub-s (7): words in square brackets inserted by the Civil Partnership Act 2004, s 261(1), Sch 27, para 154.

8–10 (*Relate to disclosure interpretation* (*reproduced at* **[141]**)*, and minor and consequential amendments.*)

11 Short title, commencement and extent

(1) This Act may be cited as the Civil Procedure Act 1997.

(2) Sections 1 to 10 are to come into force on such day as the Lord Chancellor may by order made by statutory instrument appoint, and different days may be appointed for different purposes.

(3) This Act extends to England and Wales only.

[636]

NOTES

Orders: the Civil Procedure Act 1997 (Commencement No 1) Order 1997, SI 1997/841; the Civil Procedure Act 1997 (Commencement No 2) Order 1999, SI 1999/1009.

(*Sch 1 relates to civil procedure rules* (*reproduced at* **[143]**)*; Sch 2 contains minor and consequential amendments.*)

J. OTHER

EUROPEAN COMMUNITIES ACT 1972

(1972 c 68)

An Act to make provision in connection with the enlargement of the European Communities to include the United Kingdom, together with (for certain purposes) the Channel Islands, the Isle of Man and Gibraltar

[17 October 1972]

PART I
GENERAL PROVISIONS

1 Short title and interpretation

(1) This Act may be cited as the European Communities Act 1972.

(2) In this Act ...—

"the Communities" means the European Economic Community, the European Coal and Steel Community and the European Atomic Energy Community;

"the Treaties" or "the Community Treaties" means, subject to subsection (3) below, the pre-accession treaties, that is to say, those described in Part I of Schedule 1 to this Act, taken with—

(a) the treaty relating to the accession of the United Kingdom to the European Economic Community and to the European Atomic Energy Community, signed at Brussels on the 22nd January 1972; and

(b) the decision, of the same date, of the Council of the European Communities relating to the accession of the United Kingdom to the European Coal and Steel Community; [and

(c) the treaty relating to the accession of the Hellenic Republic to the European Economic Community and to the European Atomic Energy Community, signed at Athens on 28th May 1979; and

(d) the decision, of 24th May 1979, of the Council relating to the accession of the Hellenic Republic to the European Coal and Steel Community;] [and

(e) the decisions of the Council of 7th May 1985, 24th June 1988, 31st October 1994 and 29th September 2000, on the Communities' system of own resources; and]

[(g) the treaty relating to the accession of the Kingdom of Spain and the Portuguese Republic to the European Economic Community and to the European Atomic Energy Community, signed at Lisbon and Madrid on 12th June 1985; and

(h) the decision, of 11th June 1985, of the Council relating to the accession of the Kingdom of Spain and the Portuguese Republic to the European Coal and Steel Community;] [and

(j) the following provisions of the Single European Act signed at Luxembourg and The Hague on 17th and 28th February 1986, namely Title II (amendment of the treaties establishing the Communities) and, so far as they relate to any of the Communities or any Community institution, the preamble and Titles I (common provisions) and IV (general and final provisions);] [and

(k) Titles II, III and IV of the Treaty on European Union signed at Maastricht on 7th February 1992, together with the other provisions of the Treaty so far as they relate to those Titles, and the Protocols adopted at Maastricht on that date and annexed to the Treaty establishing the European Community with the exception of the Protocol on Social Policy on page 117 of Cm 1934] [and

(l) the decision, of 1st February 1993, of the Council amending the Act concerning the election of the representatives of the European Parliament by direct universal suffrage annexed to Council Decision 76/787/ECSC, EEC, Euratom of 20th September 1976] [and

(m) the Agreement on the European Economic Area signed at Oporto on 2nd May 1992 together with the Protocol adjusting that Agreement signed at Brussels on 17th March 1993] [and

(n) the treaty concerning the accession of the Kingdom of Norway, the Republic of Austria, the Republic of Finland and the Kingdom of Sweden to the European Union, signed at Corfu on 24th June 1994;] [and

(o) the following provisions of the Treaty signed at Amsterdam on 2nd October 1997 amending the Treaty on European Union, the Treaties establishing the European Communities and certain related Acts—

(i) Articles 2 to 9,

(ii) Article 12, and

(iii) the other provisions of the Treaty so far as they relate to those Articles,

and the Protocols adopted on that occasion other than the Protocol on Article J.7 of the Treaty on European Union] [and

(p) the following provisions of the Treaty signed at Nice on 26th February 2001 amending the Treaty on European Union, the Treaties establishing the European Communities and certain related Acts—

(i) Articles 2 to 10, and

(ii) the other provisions of the Treaty so far as they relate to those Articles,

and the Protocols adopted on that occasion;]

and any other treaty entered into by any of the Communities, with or without any of the member States, or entered into, as a treaty ancillary to any of the Treaties, by the United Kingdom; [and

(q) the treaty concerning the accession of the Czech Republic, the Republic of Estonia, the Republic of Cyprus, the Republic of Latvia, the Republic of Lithuania, the Republic of Hungary, the Republic of Malta, the Republic of Poland, the Republic of Slovenia and the Slovak Republic to the European Union, signed at Athens on 16th April 2003;] [and

(r) the treaty concerning the accession of the Republic of Bulgaria and Romania to the European Union, signed at Luxembourg on 25th April 2005;]

and any expression defined in Schedule 1 to this Act has the meaning there given to it.

(3) If Her Majesty by Order in Council declares that a treaty specified in the Order is to be regarded as one of the Community Treaties as herein defined, the Order shall be conclusive that it is to be so regarded; but a treaty entered into by the United Kingdom after the 22nd January 1972, other than a pre-accession treaty to which the United Kingdom accedes on terms settled on or before that date, shall not be so regarded unless it is so specified, nor be so specified unless a draft of the Order in Council has been approved by resolution of each House of Parliament.

(4) For purposes of subsections (2) and (3) above, "treaty" includes any international agreement, and any protocol or annex to a treaty or international agreement.

[637]

NOTES

Sub-s (2): words omitted repealed by the Interpretation Act 1978, s 25(1), Sch 3; in definition ""the Treaties" or "the Community Treaties"" paras (c), (d) inserted by the European Communities (Greek Accession) Act 1979, s 1, para (e) substituted for existing paras (e), (f) (as inserted by the European Communities (Finance) Act 1985, s 1), by the European Communities (Finance) Act 1995, s 1, para (e) and word "and" immediately preceding it substituted by the European Communities (Finance) Act 2001, s 1, paras (g), (h) and word "and" immediately preceding them inserted by the European Communities (Spanish and Portuguese Accession) Act 1985, s 1, para (j) and word "and" immediately preceding it inserted by the European Communities (Amendment) Act 1986, s 1, para (k) and word "and" immediately preceding it inserted by the European Communities (Amendment) Act 1993, s 1(1), para (l) and word "and" immediately preceding it inserted by the European Parliamentary Elections Act 1993, s 3(2) and amendment continued by the European Parliamentary Elections Act 2002, s 15, Sch 3, para 1, para (m) and word "and" immediately preceding it inserted by the European Economic Area Act 1993, s 1, para (n) and word "and" immediately preceding it inserted by the European Union (Accessions) Act 1994, s 1, para (o) and word "and" immediately preceding it inserted by the European Communities (Amendment) Act 1998, s 1, para (p) and word "and" immediately preceding it inserted by the European Communities (Amendment) Act 2002, s 1(1), para (q) and word "and" immediately preceding it inserted by the European Union (Accessions) Act 2003, s 1(1), para (r) and word "and" immediately preceding it inserted by the European Union (Accessions) Act 2006, s 1(1).

Orders in Council: the Orders in Council which have been made under this section and declare that a treaty is to be regarded as a Community Treaty, as defined in this Act, are not listed in this work.

2 General implementation of Treaties

(1) All such rights, powers, liabilities, obligations and restrictions from time to time created or arising by or under the Treaties, and all such remedies and procedures from time to time provided for by or under the Treaties, as in accordance with the Treaties are without further enactment to be given legal effect or used in the United Kingdom shall be recognised and available in law, and be enforced, allowed and followed accordingly; and the expression "enforceable Community right" and similar expressions shall be read as referring to one to which this subsection applies.

(2) Subject to Schedule 2 to this Act, at any time after its passing Her Majesty may by Order in Council, and any designated Minister or department may by regulations, make provision—

(a) for the purpose of implementing any Community obligation of the United Kingdom, or enabling any such obligation to be implemented, or of enabling any rights enjoyed or to be enjoyed by the United Kingdom under or by virtue of the Treaties to be exercised; or

(b) for the purpose of dealing with matters arising out of or related to any such obligation or rights or the coming into force, or the operation from time to time, of subsection (1) above;

and in the exercise of any statutory power or duty, including any power to give directions or to legislate by means of orders, rules, regulations or other subordinate instrument, the person entrusted with the power or duty may have regard to the objects of the Communities and to any such obligation or rights as aforesaid.

In this subsection "designated Minister or department" means such Minister of the Crown or government department as may from time to time be designated by Order in Council in relation to any matter or for any purpose, but subject to such restrictions or conditions (if any) as may be specified by the Order in Council.

(3) There shall be charged on and issued out of the Consolidated Fund or, if so determined by the Treasury, the National Loans Fund the amounts required to meet any Community obligation to make payments to any of the Communities or member States, or any Community obligation in respect of contributions to the capital or reserves of the European Investment Bank or in respect of loans to the Bank, or to redeem any notes or obligations issued or created in respect of any such Community obligation; and, except as otherwise provided by or under any enactment,—

(a) any other expenses incurred under or by virtue of the Treaties or this Act by any Minister of the Crown or government department may be paid out of moneys provided by Parliament; and

(b) any sums received under or by virtue of the Treaties or this Act by any Minister of the Crown or government department, save for such sums as may be required for disbursements permitted by any other enactment, shall be paid into the Consolidated Fund or, if so determined by the Treasury, the National Loans Fund.

(4) The provision that may be made under subsection (2) above includes, subject to Schedule 2 to this Act, any such provision (of any such extent) as might be made by Act of Parliament, and any enactment passed or to be passed, other than one contained in this Part of this Act, shall be construed and have effect subject to the foregoing provisions of this section; but, except as may be provided by any Act passed after this Act, Schedule 2 shall have effect in connection with the powers conferred by this and the following sections of this Act to make Orders in Council and regulations.

(5) … and the references in that subsection to a Minister of the Crown or government department and to a statutory power or duty shall include a Minister or department of the Government of Northern Ireland and a power or duty arising under or by virtue of an Act of the Parliament of Northern Ireland.

(6) A law passed by the legislature of any of the Channel Islands or of the Isle of Man, or a colonial law (within the meaning of the Colonial Laws Validity Act 1865) passed or made for Gibraltar, if expressed to be passed or made in the implementation of the Treaties and of the obligations of the United Kingdom thereunder, shall not be void or inoperative by reason of any inconsistency with or repugnancy to an Act of Parliament, passed or to be passed, that extends to the Island or Gibraltar or any provision having the force and effect of an Act there

(but not including this section), nor by reason of its having some operation outside the Island or Gibraltar; and any such Act or provision that extends to the Island or Gibraltar shall be construed and have effect subject to the provisions of any such law.

[638]

NOTES

Sub-s (5): words omitted repealed by the Northern Ireland Constitution Act 1973, s 41(1), Sch 6, Part I. Modified by the Scotland Act 1998, s 125, Sch 8, para 15.

Functions under this section: by the Scotland Act 1998 (Transfer of Functions to the Scottish Ministers etc) Order 1999, SI 1999/1750, art 3, Sch 2, certain functions under sub-s (2) which were exercisable by a Minister of the Crown are, in so far as they are exercisable in or as regards Scotland, exercisable by the Scottish Ministers acting concurrently with the Minister of the Crown concerned. See also art 7(4) of the 1999 Order.

Functions under this section: certain functions under this section are transferred, in so far as they are exercisable in or as regards Scotland, to the Scottish Ministers, by the Scotland Act 1998 (Transfer of Functions to the Scottish Ministers etc) Order 2005, SI 2005/849, arts 2, 6, Schedule.

Certain functions under this section, so far as they are exercisable in or as regards Scotland, are exercisable by the Scottish Ministers concurrently with the Minister of the Crown: see the Scotland Act 1998 (Transfer of Functions to the Scottish Ministers etc) Order 2006, SI 2006/304, arts 3(1)(a), (2), 5.

Orders in Council (only the Orders reproduced in this work are listed here): the European Communities (Enforcement of Community Judgments) Order 1972, SI 1972/1590 at **[2067]**; the Extraterritorial US Legislation (Sanctions against Cuba, Iran and Libya) (Protection of Trading Interests) Order 1996, SI 1996/3171 at **[2777]**; the Unfair Terms in Consumer Contracts Regulations 1999, SI 1999/2083 at **[2191]**; the Financial Markets and Insolvency (Settlement Finality) Regulations 1999, SI 1999/2979 at **[2179]**; the European Communities (Service of Judicial and Extrajudicial Documents) (Scotland) Regulations 2001, SSI 2001/172 at **[2149]**; the Civil Jurisdiction and Judgments (Authentic Instruments and Court Settlements) Order 2001, SI 2001/3928 at **[2153]**; the Civil Jurisdiction and Judgments Order 2001, SI 2001/3929 at **[2157]**; the Electronic Commerce (EC Directive) Regulations SI 2002/2013 at **[2235]**; the Financial Collateral Arrangements (No 2) Regulations 2003, SI 2003/3226 at **[2258]**; the Insurers (Reorganisation and Winding Up) Regulations SI 2004/353 at **[2596]**; the Credit Institutions (Reorganisation and Winding Up) Regulations SI 2004/1045 at **[2647]**; the Air Carrier Liability Regulations 2004, SI 2004/1418 at **[2301]**; the Insurers (Reorganisation and Winding Up) (Lloyd's) Regulations 2005, SI 2005/1998 at **[2685]**.

3 Decisions on, and proof of, Treaties and Community instruments, etc

(1) For the purposes of all legal proceedings any question as to the meaning or effect of any of the Treaties, or as to the validity, meaning or effect of any Community instrument, shall be treated as a question of law (and, if not referred to the European Court, be for determination as such in accordance with the principles laid down by and any relevant [decision of the European Court or any court attached thereto)].

(2) Judicial notice shall be taken of the Treaties, of the Official Journal of the Communities and of any decision of, or expression of opinion by, the European Court [or any court attached thereto] on any such question as aforesaid; and the Official Journal shall be admissible as evidence of any instrument or other act thereby communicated of any of the Communities or of any Community institution.

(3) Evidence of any instrument issued by a Community institution, including any judgment or order of the European Court [or any court attached thereto], or of any document in the custody of a Community institution, or any entry in or extract from such a document, may be given in any legal proceedings by production of a copy certified as a true copy by an official of that institution; and any document purporting to be such a copy shall be received in evidence without proof of the official position or handwriting of the person signing the certificate.

(4) Evidence of any Community instrument may also be given in any legal proceedings—

(a) by production of a copy purporting to be printed by the Queen's Printer;

(b) where the instrument is in the custody of a government department (including a department of the Government of Northern Ireland), by production of a copy certified on behalf of the department to be a true copy by an officer of the department generally or specially authorised so to do;

and any document purporting to be such a copy as is mentioned in paragraph (b) above of an instrument in the custody of a department shall be received in evidence without proof of the official position or handwriting of the person signing the certificate, or of his authority to do so, or of the document being in the custody of the department.

(5) In any legal proceedings in Scotland evidence of any matter given in a manner authorised by this section shall be sufficient evidence of it.

[639]

NOTES

Sub-s (1): words in square brackets substituted by the European Communities (Amendment) Act 1986, s 2.

Sub-ss (2), (3): words in square brackets inserted by the European Communities (Amendment) Act 1986, s 2.

Modified, so as to have effect as if references to a government department include any part of the Scottish Administration, by the Scotland Act 1998, s 125, Sch 8, para 15(4).

In relation to the application of sub–ss (2)–(5) to the EFTA Court and the EFTA Surveillance Authority, see the European Economic Area Act 1993, s 4.

4–12 *(Pt II outside the scope of this work.)*

(Sch 1 contains definitions relating to Communities.)

SCHEDULE 2
PROVISIONS AS TO SUBORDINATE LEGISLATION

Section 2

1(1) The powers conferred by section 2(2) of this Act to make provision for the purposes mentioned in section 2(2)(a) and (b) shall not include power—

(a) to make any provision imposing or increasing taxation; or

(b) to make any provision taking effect from a date earlier than that of the making of the instrument containing the provision; or

(c) to confer any power to legislate by means of orders, rules, regulations or other subordinate instrument, other than rules of procedure for any court or tribunal; or

(d) to create any new criminal offence punishable with imprisonment for more than two years or punishable on summary conviction with imprisonment for more than *three months* or with a fine of more than [level 5 on the standard scale] (if not calculated on a daily basis) or with a fine of more than [£100 a day].

(2) Sub-paragraph (1)(c) above shall not be taken to preclude the modification of a power to legislate conferred otherwise than under section 2(2), or the extension of any such power to purposes of the like nature as those for which it was conferred; and a power to give directions as to matters of administration is not to be regarded as a power to legislate within the meaning of sub-paragraph (1)(c).

[(3) In sub-paragraph (1)(d), "the prescribed term" means—

(a) in relation to England and Wales, where the offence is a summary offence, 51 weeks;

(b) in relation to England and Wales, where the offence is triable either way, twelve months;

(c) in relation to Scotland and Northern Ireland, three months.]

2(1) Subject to paragraph 3 below, where a provision contained in any section of this Act confers power to make regulations (otherwise than by modification or extension of an existing power), the power shall be exercisable by statutory instrument.

(2) Any statutory instrument containing an Order in Council or regulations made in the exercise of a power so conferred, if made without a draft having been approved by resolution of each House of Parliament, shall be subject to annulment in pursuance of a resolution of either House.

3 Nothing in paragraph 2 above shall apply to any Order in Council made by the Governor of Northern Ireland or to any regulations made by a Minister or department of the Government of Northern Ireland; but where a provision contained in any section of this Act confers power to make such an Order in Council or regulations, then any Order in Council or regulations made in the exercise of that power, if made without a draft having been approved by resolution of each House of the Parliament of Northern Ireland, shall be subject to negative resolution within the meaning of section 41(6) of the Interpretation Act (Northern Ireland) 1954 as if the Order or regulations were a statutory instrument within the meaning of that Act.

[4(1) The power to make orders under section 5(1) or (2) of this Act shall be exercisable in accordance with the following provisions of this paragraph.

(2) The power to make such orders shall be exercisable by statutory instrument and includes power to amend or revoke any such order made in the exercise of that power.

(3) Any statutory instrument containing any such order shall be subject to annulment in pursuance of a resolution of the House of Commons except in a case falling within sub-paragraph (4) below.

(4) Subject to sub-paragraph (6) below, where an order imposes or increases any customs duty, or restricts any relief from customs duty under the said section 5, the statutory instrument containing the order shall be laid before the House of Commons after being made and, unless the order is approved by that House before the end of the period of 28 days beginning with the day on which it was made, it shall cease to have effect at the end of that period, but without prejudice to anything previously done under the order or to the making of a new order.

In reckoning the said period of 28 days no account shall be taken of any time during which Parliament is dissolved or prorogued or during which the House of Commons is adjourned for more than 4 days.

(5) Where an order has the effect of altering the rate of duty on any goods in such a way that the new rate is not directly comparable with the old, it shall not be treated for the purposes of sub-paragraph (4) above as increasing the duty on those goods if it declares the opinion of the Treasury to be that, in the circumstances existing at the date of the order, the alteration is not calculated to raise the general level of duty on the goods.

(6) Sub-paragraph (4) above does not apply in the case of an instrument containing an order which states that it does not impose or increase any customs duty or restrict any relief from customs duty otherwise than in pursuance of a Community obligation.

5 As soon as may be after the end of each financial year the Secretary of State shall lay before each House of Parliament a report on the exercise during that year of the powers conferred by section 5(1) and (2) of this Act with respect to the imposition of customs duties and the allowance of exemptions and reliefs from duties so imposed (including the power to amend or revoke orders imposing customs duties or providing for any exemption or relief from duties so imposed).]

[640]

NOTES

Para 1: words in italics in sub-para (1)(d) substituted by the words "the prescribed term" and sub-para (3) inserted by the Criminal Justice Act 2003, s 283, Sch 27, para 3(1)–(3), as from a day to be appointed; in sub-para (1)(d) first-mentioned maximum fine increased and converted to a level on the standard scale by the Criminal Justice Act 1982, ss 37, 40, 46, words in second pair of square brackets substituted by the Criminal Law Act 1977, ss 32(3), 65(10).

Paras 4, 5: inserted by the Customs and Excise Duties (General Reliefs) Act 1979, s 19(1), Sch 2, para 5.

The Northern Ireland Act 1998 makes new provision for the government of Northern Ireland for the purpose of implementing the Belfast Agreement (the agreement reached at multi-party talks on Northern Ireland and set out in Command Paper 3883). As a consequence of that Act, any reference in this Schedule to the Parliament of Northern Ireland or the Assembly established under the Northern Ireland Assembly Act 1973, s 1, certain office-holders and Ministers, and any legislative act and certain financial dealings thereof, shall, for the period specified, be construed in accordance with Sch 12, paras 1–11 to the 1998 Act.

(Sch 3 contains repeals; Sch 4 contains amendments.)

PROTECTION OF TRADING INTERESTS ACT 1980

(1980 c 11)

ARRANGEMENT OF SECTIONS

An Act to provide protection from requirements, prohibitions and judgments imposed or given under the laws of countries outside the United Kingdom and affecting the trading or other interests of persons in the United Kingdom

[20 March 1980]

1 Overseas measures affecting United Kingdom trading interests

(1) If it appears to the Secretary of State—

(a) that measures have been or are proposed to be taken by or under the law of any overseas country for regulating or controlling international trade; and

(b) that those measures, in so far as they apply or would apply to things done or to be done outside the territorial jurisdiction of that country by persons carrying on business in the United Kingdom, are damaging or threaten to damage the trading interests of the United Kingdom,

the Secretary of State may by order direct that this section shall apply to those measures either generally or in their application to such cases as may be specified in the order.

(2) The Secretary of State may by order make provision for requiring, or enabling the Secretary of State to require, a person in the United Kingdom who carries on business there to give notice to the Secretary of State of any requirement or prohibition imposed or threatened to be imposed on that person pursuant to any measures in so far as this section applies to them by virtue of an order under subsection (1) above.

(3) The Secretary of State may give to any person in the United Kingdom who carries on business there such directions for prohibiting compliance with any such requirement or prohibition as aforesaid as he considers appropriate for avoiding damage to the trading interests of the United Kingdom.

(4) The power of the Secretary of State to make orders under subsection (1) or (2) above shall be exercisable by statutory instrument subject to annulment in pursuance of a resolution of either House of Parliament.

(5) Directions under subsection (3) above may be either general or special and may prohibit compliance with any requirement or prohibition either absolutely or in such cases or subject to such conditions as to consent or otherwise as may be specified in the directions; and general directions under that subsection shall be published in such manner as appears to the Secretary of State to be appropriate.

(6) In this section "trade" includes any activity carried on in the course of a business of any description and "trading interests" shall be construed accordingly.

[641]

NOTES

Orders: the Protection of Trading Interests (US Re-export Control) Order 1982, SI 1982/885 at **[2766]**; the Protection of Trading Interests (US Antitrust Measures) Order 1983, SI 1983/900 at **[2769]**; the Protection of Trading Interests (US Cuban Assets Control Regulations) Order 1992, SI 1992/2449 at **[2773]**.

2 Documents and information required by overseas courts and authorities

(1) If it appears to the Secretary of State—

(a) that a requirement has been or may be imposed on a person or persons in the United Kingdom to produce to any court, tribunal or authority of an overseas country any commercial document which is not within the territorial jurisdiction of that country or to furnish any commercial information to any such court, tribunal or authority; or

(b) that any such authority has imposed or may impose a requirement on a person or persons in the United Kingdom to publish any such document or information,

the Secretary of State may, if it appears to him that the requirement is inadmissible by virtue of subsection (2) or (3) below, give directions for prohibiting compliance with the requirement.

(2) A requirement such as is mentioned in subsection (1)(a) or (b) above is inadmissible—

(a) if it infringes the jurisdiction of the United Kingdom or is otherwise prejudicial to the sovereignty of the United Kingdom; or

(b) if compliance with the requirement would be prejudicial to the security of the United Kingdom or to the relations of the government of the United Kingdom with the government of any other country.

(3) A requirement such as is mentioned in subsection (1)(a) above is also inadmissible—

(a) it is made otherwise than for the purposes of civil or criminal proceedings which have been instituted in the overseas country; or

(b) if it requires a person to state what documents relevant to any such proceedings are or have been in his possession, custody or power or to produce for the purposes of any such proceedings any documents other than particular documents specified in the requirement.

(4) Directions under subsection (1) above may be either general or special and may prohibit compliance with any requirement either absolutely or in such cases or subject to such conditions as to consent or otherwise as may be specified in the directions; and general directions under that subsection shall be published in such manner as appears to the Secretary of State to be appropriate.

(5) For the purposes of this section the making of a request or demand shall be treated as the imposition of a requirement if it is made in circumstances in which a requirement to the same effect could be or could have been imposed; and

(a) any request or demand for the supply of a document or information which, pursuant to the requirement of any court, tribunal or authority of an overseas country, is addressed to a person in the United Kingdom, or

(b) any requirement imposed by such a court, tribunal or authority to produce or furnish any document or information to a person specified in the requirement,

shall be treated as a requirement to produce or furnish that document or information to that court, tribunal or authority.

(6) In this section "commercial document" and "commercial information" mean respectively a document or information relating to a business of any description and "document" includes any record or device by means of which material is recorded or stored. **[642]**

3 Offences under ss 1 and 2

(1) Subject to subsection (2) below, any person who without reasonable excuse fails to comply with any requirement imposed under subsection (2) of section 1 above or knowingly contravenes any directions given under subsection (3) of that section or section 2(1) above shall be guilty of an offence and liable—

(a) on conviction on indictment, to a fine;

(b) on summary conviction, to a fine not exceeding the statutory maximum.

(2) A person who is neither a citizen of the United Kingdom and Colonies nor a body corporate incorporated in the United Kingdom shall not be guilty of an offence under subsection (1) above by reason of anything done or omitted outside the United Kingdom in contravention of directions under section 1(3) or 2(1) above.

(3) No proceedings for an offence under subsection (1) above shall be instituted in England, Wales or Northern Ireland except by the Secretary of State or with the consent of the Attorney General or, as the case may be, the Attorney General for Northern Ireland.

(4) Proceedings against any person for an offence under this section may be taken before the appropriate court in the United Kingdom having jurisdiction in the place where that person is for the time being.

(5) …

[643]

NOTES

Sub-s (5): repealed by the Statute Law (Repeals) Act 1993.

4 Restriction of Evidence (Proceedings in Other Jurisdictions) Act 1975

A court in the United Kingdom shall not make an order under section 2 of the Evidence (Proceedings in Other Jurisdictions) Act 1975 for giving effect to a request issued by or on behalf of a court or tribunal of an overseas country if it is shown that the request infringes the jurisdiction of the United Kingdom or is otherwise prejudicial to the sovereignty of the United Kingdom, and a certificate signed by or on behalf of the Secretary of State to the effect that it infringes that jurisdiction or is so prejudicial shall be conclusive evidence of that fact.

[644]

5 Restriction on enforcement of certain overseas judgments

(1) A judgment to which this section applies shall not be registered under Part II of the Administration of Justice Act 1920 or Part I of the Foreign Judgments (Reciprocal Enforcement) Act 1933 and no court in the United Kingdom shall entertain proceedings at common law for the recovery of any sum payable under such a judgment.

(2) This section applies to any judgment given by a court of an overseas country, being—
- (a) a judgment for multiple damages within the meaning of subsection (3) below;
- (b) a judgment based on a provision or rule of law specified or described in an order under subsection (4) below and given after the coming into force of the order; or
- (c) a judgment on a claim for contribution in respect of damages awarded by a judgment falling within paragraph (a) or (b) above.

(3) In subsection (2)(a) above a judgment for multiple damages means a judgment for an amount arrived at by doubling, trebling or otherwise multiplying a sum assessed as compensation for the loss or damage sustained by the person in whose favour the judgment is given.

(4) The Secretary of State may for the purposes of subsection (2)(b) above make an order in respect of any provision or rule of law which appears to him to be concerned with the prohibition or regulation of agreements, arrangements or practices designed to restrain, distort or restrict competition in the carrying on of business of any description or to be otherwise concerned with the promotion of such competition as aforesaid.

(5) The power of the Secretary of State to make orders under subsection (4) above shall be exercisable by statutory instrument subject to annulment in pursuance of a resolution of either House of Parliament.

(6) Subsection (2)(a) above applies to a judgment given before the date of the passing of this Act as well as to a judgment given on or after that date but this section does not affect any judgment which has been registered before that date under the provisions mentioned in subsection (1) above or in respect of which such proceedings as are there mentioned have been finally determined before that date.

[645]

NOTES

Orders: the Protection of Trading Interests (Australian Trade Practices) Order 1988, SI 1988/569 at **[2771]**.

6 Recovery of awards of multiple damages

(1) This section applies where a court of an overseas country has given a judgment for multiple damages with the meaning of section 5(3) above against—
- (a) a citizen of the United Kingdom and Colonies; or
- (b) a body corporate incorporated in the United Kingdom or in a territory outside the United Kingdom for whose international relations Her Majesty's Government in the United Kingdom are responsible; or
- (c) a person carrying on business in the United Kingdom,

(in this section referred to as a "qualifying defendant") and an amount on account of the damages has been paid by the qualifying defendant either to the party in whose favour the judgment was given or to another party who is entitled as against the qualifying defendant to contribution in respect of the damages.

(2) Subject to subsections (3) and (4) below, the qualifying defendant shall be entitled to recover from the party in whose favour the judgment was given so much of the amount referred to in subsection (1) above as exceeds the part attributable to compensation; and that part shall be taken to be such part of the amount as bears to the whole of it the same

proportion as the sum assessed by the court that gave the judgment as compensation for the loss or damage sustained by that party bears to the whole of the damages awarded to that party.

(3) Subsection (2) above does not apply where the qualifying defendant is an individual who was ordinarily resident in the overseas country at the time when the proceedings in which the judgment was given were instituted or a body corporate which had its principal place of business there at that time.

(4) Subsection (2) above does not apply where the qualifying defendant carried on business in the overseas country and the proceedings in which the judgment was given were concerned with activities exclusively carried on in that country.

(5) A court in the United Kingdom may entertain proceedings on a claim under this section notwithstanding that the person against whom the proceedings are brought is not within the jurisdiction of the court.

(6) The reference in subsection (1) above to an amount paid by the qualifying defendant includes a reference to an amount obtained by execution against his property or against the property of a company which (directly or indirectly) is wholly owned by him; and references in that subsection and subsection (2) above to the party in whose favour the judgment was given or to a party entitled to contribution include references to any person in whom the rights of any such party have become vested by succession or assignment or otherwise.

(7) This section shall, with the necessary modifications, apply also in relation to any order which is made by a tribunal or authority of an overseas country and would, if that tribunal or authority were a court, be a judgment for multiple damages within the meaning of section 5(3) above.

(8) This section does not apply to any judgment given or order made before the passing of this Act.

[646]

7 Enforcement of overseas judgment under provision corresponding to s 6

(1) If it appears to Her Majesty that the law of an overseas country provides or will provide for the enforcement in that country of judgments given under section 6 above, Her Majesty may by Order in Council provide for the enforcement in the United Kingdom of [judgments of any description specified in the Order which are given under any provision of the law of that country relating to the recovery of sums paid or obtained pursuant to a judgment for multiple damages within the meaning of section 5(3) above, whether or not that provision corresponds to section 6 above].

[(1A) Such an Order in Council may, as respects judgments to which it relates—

(a) make different provisions for different descriptions of judgment; and

(b) impose conditions or restrictions on the enforcement of judgments of any description.]

(2) An Order under this section may apply, with or without modification, any of the provisions of the Foreign Judgments (Reciprocal Enforcement) Act 1933.

[647]

NOTES

Sub-s (1): words in square brackets substituted by the Civil Jurisdiction and Judgments Act 1982, s 38(1), (2).

Sub-s (1A): inserted by the Civil Jurisdiction and Judgments Act 1982, s 38(1), (3).

Orders in Council: the Reciprocal Enforcement of Foreign Judgments (Australia) Order 1994, SI 1994/1901 at **[2129]**.

8 Short title, interpretation, repeals and extent

(1) This Act may be cited as the Protection of Trading Interests Act 1980.

(2) In this Act "overseas country" means any country or territory outside the United Kingdom other than one for whose international relations Her Majesty's Government in the United Kingdom are responsible.

(3) References in this Act to the law or a court, tribunal or authority of an overseas country include, in the case of a federal state, references to the law or a court, tribunal or authority of any constituent part of that country.

(4) References in this Act to a claim for, or to entitlement to, contribution are references to a claim or entitlement based on an enactment or rule of law.

(5), (6) …

(7) This Act extends to Northern Ireland.

(8) Her Majesty may by Order in Council direct that this Act shall extend with such exceptions, adaptations and modifications, if any, as may be specified in the Order to any territory outside the United Kingdom, being a territory for the international relations of which Her Majesty's Government in the United Kingdom are responsible.

[648]

NOTES

Sub-s (5): repealed in part by the Magistrates' Courts Act 1980, s 154(3), Sch 9; remainder repeals the Shipping Contracts and Commercial Documents Act 1964.

Sub-s (6): repeals the Shipping Contracts and Commercial Documents Act 1964.

Orders in Council: the Protection of Trading Interests Act 1980 (Jersey) Order 1983, SI 1983/607, extending this Act, with exceptions, adaptations and modifications, to the Bailiwick of Jersey; the Evidence (Proceedings in Other Jurisdictions) (Jersey) Order 1983, SI 1983/1700; the Protection of Trading Interests Act 1980 (Guernsey) Order 1983, SI 1983/1703, extending this Act, with exceptions, adaptations and modifications, to the Bailiwick of Guernsey; the Protection of Trading Interests Act 1980 (Isle of Man) Order 1983, SI 1983/1704, extending this Act, with exceptions, adaptations and modifications, to the Isle of Man.

HUMAN RIGHTS ACT 1998

(1998 c 42)

ARRANGEMENT OF SECTIONS

Introduction

Legislation

Public authorities

Remedial action

Other rights and proceedings

Derogations and reservations

An Act to give further effect to rights and freedoms guaranteed under the European Convention on Human Rights; to make provision with respect to holders of certain judicial offices who become judges of the European Court of Human Rights; and for connected purposes

[9 November 1998]

NOTES

The functions of the Lord Chancellor under this Act (except ss 5, 10, 18, 19, Sch 4) are transferred to the Secretary of State by the Secretary of State for Constitutional Affairs Order 2003, SI 2003/1887, arts 4–6, Sch 1 (made under the Ministers of the Crown Act 1975, ss 1, 2).

Introduction

1 The Convention Rights

(1) In this Act "the Convention rights" means the rights and fundamental freedoms set out in—

(a) Articles 2 to 12 and 14 of the Convention,
(b) Articles 1 to 3 of the First Protocol, and
(c) [Article 1 of the Thirteenth Protocol],

as read with Articles 16 to 18 of the Convention.

(2) Those Articles are to have effect for the purposes of this Act subject to any designated derogation or reservation (as to which see sections 14 and 15).

(3) The Articles are set out in Schedule 1.

(4) The [Secretary of State] may by order make such amendments to this Act as he considers appropriate to reflect the effect, in relation to the United Kingdom, of a protocol.

(5) In subsection (4) "protocol" means a protocol to the Convention—

(a) which the United Kingdom has ratified; or
(b) which the United Kingdom has signed with a view to ratification.

(6) No amendment may be made by an order under subsection (4) so as to come into force before the protocol concerned is in force in relation to the United Kingdom.

[649]

NOTES

Sub-s (1): words in square brackets in para (c) substituted by the Human Rights Act 1998 (Amendment) Order 2004, SI 2004/1574, art 2(1).

Sub-s (4): words in square brackets substituted by the Secretary of State for Constitutional Affairs Order 2003, SI 2003/1887, art 9, Sch 2, para 10(1).

2 Interpretation of Convention rights

(1) A court or tribunal determining a question which has arisen in connection with a Convention right must take into account any—

(a) judgment, decision, declaration or advisory opinion of the European Court of Human Rights,

(b) opinion of the Commission given in a report adopted under Article 31 of the Convention,

(c) decision of the Commission in connection with Article 26 or 27(2) of the Convention, or

(d) decision of the Committee of Ministers taken under Article 46 of the Convention,

whenever made or given, so far as, in the opinion of the court or tribunal, it is relevant to the proceedings in which that question has arisen.

(2) Evidence of any judgment, decision, declaration or opinion of which account may have to be taken under this section is to be given in proceedings before any court or tribunal in such manner as may be provided by rules.

(3) In this section "rules" means rules of court or, in the case of proceedings before a tribunal, rules made for the purposes of this section—

(a) by … [the Lord Chancellor or] the Secretary of State, in relation to any proceedings outside Scotland;

(b) by the Secretary of State, in relation to proceedings in Scotland; or

(c) by a Northern Ireland department, in relation to proceedings before a tribunal in Northern Ireland—

(i) which deals with transferred matters; and

(ii) for which no rules made under paragraph (a) are in force.

[650]

NOTES

Sub-s (3): words omitted from para (a) repealed by the Secretary of State for Constitutional Affairs Order 2003, SI 2003/1887, art 9, Sch 2, para 10(2); words in square brackets in para (a) inserted by the Transfer of Functions (Lord Chancellor and Secretary of State) Order 2005, SI 2005/3429, art 8, Schedule, para 3.

By the Transfer of Functions (Lord Chancellor and Secretary of State) Order 2005, SI 2005/3429, art 3(2), the functions of the Secretary of State under sub-s (3)(a) are to be exercisable concurrently with the Lord Chancellor.

Legislation

3 Interpretation of legislation

(1) So far as it is possible to do so, primary legislation and subordinate legislation must be read and given effect in a way which is compatible with the Convention rights.

(2) This section—

(a) applies to primary legislation and subordinate legislation whenever enacted;

(b) does not affect the validity, continuing operation or enforcement of any incompatible primary legislation; and

(c) does not affect the validity, continuing operation or enforcement of any incompatible subordinate legislation if (disregarding any possibility of revocation) primary legislation prevents removal of the incompatibility.

[651]

4 Declaration of incompatibility

(1) Subsection (2) applies in any proceedings in which a court determines whether a provision of primary legislation is compatible with a Convention right.

(2) If the court is satisfied that the provision is incompatible with a Convention right, it may make a declaration of that incompatibility.

(3) Subsection (4) applies in any proceedings in which a court determines whether a provision of subordinate legislation, made in the exercise of a power conferred by primary legislation, is compatible with a Convention right.

(4) If the court is satisfied—
- (a) that the provision is incompatible with a Convention right, and
- (b) that (disregarding any possibility of revocation) the primary legislation concerned prevents removal of the incompatibility,

it may make a declaration of that incompatibility.

(5) In this section "court" means—
- *(a)* *the House of Lords;*
- (b) the Judicial Committee of the Privy Council;
- (c) the Courts-Martial Appeal Court;
- (d) in Scotland, the High Court of Justiciary sitting otherwise than as a trial court or the Court of Session;
- (e) in England and Wales or Northern Ireland, the High Court or the Court of Appeal;
- [(f) the Court of Protection, in any matter being dealt with by the President of the Family Division, the Vice-Chancellor or a puisne judge of the High Court.]

(6) A declaration under this section ("a declaration of incompatibility")—
- (a) does not affect the validity, continuing operation or enforcement of the provision in respect of which it is given; and
- (b) is not binding on the parties to the proceedings in which it is made.

[652]

NOTES

Sub-s (5): para (f) added by the Mental Capacity Act 2005, s 67(1), Sch 6, para 43, as from a day to be appointed; para (a) substituted by the Constitutional Reform Act 2005, s 40(4), Sch 9, Pt 1, para 66(1), (2), as from a day to be appointed as follows—

"(a) the Supreme Court;".

5 Right of Crown to intervene

(1) Where a court is considering whether to make a declaration of incompatibility, the Crown is entitled to notice in accordance with rules of court.

(2) In any case to which subsection (1) applies—
- (a) a Minister of the Crown (or a person nominated by him),
- (b) a member of the Scottish Executive,
- (c) a Northern Ireland Minister,
- (d) a Northern Ireland department,

is entitled, on giving notice in accordance with rules of court, to be joined as a party to the proceedings.

(3) Notice under subsection (2) may be given at any time during the proceedings.

(4) A person who has been made a party to criminal proceedings (other than in Scotland) as the result of a notice under subsection (2) may, with leave, appeal to the *House of Lords* against any declaration of incompatibility made in the proceedings.

(5) In subsection (4)—

"criminal proceedings" includes all proceedings before the Courts-Martial Appeal Court; and

"leave" means leave granted by the court making the declaration of incompatibility or by the *House of Lords*.

[653]

NOTES

Sub-ss (4), (5): words in italics substituted by the words "Supreme Court" by the Constitutional Reform Act 2005, s 40(4), Sch 9, Pt 1, para 66(1), (3), as from a day to be appointed.

Transfer of functions: the function under sub-s (2) shall be exercisable by the National Assembly for Wales concurrently with any Minister of the Crown by whom it is exercisable, in so far as it relates to any proceedings in which a court is considering whether to make a declaration of incompatibility within the meaning of s 4 of this Act, in respect of subordinate legislation made by the National Assembly, and subordinate legislation made, in relation to Wales, by a Minister of the Crown in the exercise of a function which is exercisable by the National Assembly: see the National Assembly for Wales (Transfer of Functions) (No 2) Order 2000, SI 2000/1830, art 2.

Public authorities

6 Acts of public authorities

(1) It is unlawful for a public authority to act in a way which is incompatible with a Convention right.

(2) Subsection (1) does not apply to an act if—

(a) as the result of one or more provisions of primary legislation, the authority could not have acted differently; or

(b) in the case of one or more provisions of, or made under, primary legislation which cannot be read or given effect in a way which is compatible with the Convention rights, the authority was acting so as to give effect to or enforce those provisions.

(3) In this section "public authority" includes—

(a) a court or tribunal, and

(b) any person certain of whose functions are functions of a public nature,

but does not include either House of Parliament or a person exercising functions in connection with proceedings in Parliament.

(4) In subsection (3) "Parliament" does not include the House of Lords in its judicial capacity.

(5) In relation to a particular act, a person is not a public authority by virtue only of subsection (3)(b) if the nature of the act is private.

(6) "An act" includes a failure to act but does not include a failure to—

(a) introduce in, or lay before, Parliament a proposal for legislation; or

(b) make any primary legislation or remedial order.

[654]

NOTES

Sub-s (4): repealed by the Constitutional Reform Act 2005, ss 40(4), 146, Sch 9, Pt 1, para 66(1), (4), Sch 18, Pt 5, as from a day to be appointed.

7 Proceedings

(1) A person who claims that a public authority has acted (or proposes to act) in a way which is made unlawful by section 6(1) may—

(a) bring proceedings against the authority under this Act in the appropriate court or tribunal, or

(b) rely on the Convention right or rights concerned in any legal proceedings, but only if he is (or would be) a victim of the unlawful act.

(2) In subsection (1)(a) "appropriate court or tribunal" means such court or tribunal as may be determined in accordance with rules; and proceedings against an authority include a counterclaim or similar proceeding.

(3) If the proceedings are brought on an application for judicial review, the applicant is to be taken to have a sufficient interest in relation to the unlawful act only if he is, or would be, a victim of that act.

(4) If the proceedings are made by way of a petition for judicial review in Scotland, the applicant shall be taken to have title and interest to sue in relation to the unlawful act only if he is, or would be, a victim of that act.

(5) Proceedings under subsection (1)(a) must be brought before the end of—

(a) the period of one year beginning with the date on which the act complained of took place; or

(b) such longer period as the court or tribunal considers equitable having regard to all the circumstances,

but that is subject to any rule imposing a stricter time limit in relation to the procedure in question.

(6) In subsection (1)(b) "legal proceedings" includes—
(a) proceedings brought by or at the instigation of a public authority; and
(b) an appeal against the decision of a court or tribunal.

(7) For the purposes of this section, a person is a victim of an unlawful act only if he would be a victim for the purposes of Article 34 of the Convention if proceedings were brought in the European Court of Human Rights in respect of that act.

(8) Nothing in this Act creates a criminal offence.

(9) In this section "rules" means—
(a) in relation to proceedings before a court or tribunal outside Scotland, rules made by … [the Lord Chancellor or] the Secretary of State for the purposes of this section or rules of court,
(b) in relation to proceedings before a court or tribunal in Scotland, rules made by the Secretary of State for those purposes,
(c) in relation to proceedings before a tribunal in Northern Ireland—
(i) which deals with transferred matters; and
(ii) for which no rules made under paragraph (a) are in force,
rules made by a Northern Ireland department for those purposes,

and includes provision made by order under section 1 of the Courts and Legal Services Act 1990.

(10) In making rules, regard must be had to section 9.

(11) The Minister who has power to make rules in relation to a particular tribunal may, to the extent he considers it necessary to ensure that the tribunal can provide an appropriate remedy in relation to an act (or proposed act) of a public authority which is (or would be) unlawful as a result of section 6(1), by order add to—
(a) the relief or remedies which the tribunal may grant; or
(b) the grounds on which it may grant any of them.

(12) An order made under subsection (11) may contain such incidental, supplemental, consequential or transitional provision as the Minister making it considers appropriate.

(13) "The Minister" includes the Northern Ireland department concerned.

[655]

NOTES

Sub-s (9): words omitted from para (a) repealed by the Secretary of State for Constitutional Affairs Order 2003, SI 2003/1887, art 9, Sch 2, para 10(2); words in square brackets inserted by the Transfer of Functions (Lord Chancellor and Secretary of State) Order 2005, SI 2005/3429, art 8, Schedule, para 3.

By the Transfer of Functions (Lord Chancellor and Secretary of State) Order 2005, SI 2005/3429, art 3(2), the functions of the Secretary of State under sub-s (9)(a), and under sub-s (11) by virtue thereof, are to be exercisable concurrently with the Lord Chancellor.

Rules: the Human Rights Act 1998 (Jurisdiction) (Scotland) Rules 2000, SSI 2000/301; the Proscribed Organisations Appeal Commission (Human Rights Act Proceedings) Rules 2001, SI 2001/127.

8 Judicial remedies

(1) In relation to any act (or proposed act) of a public authority which the court finds is (or would be) unlawful, it may grant such relief or remedy, or make such order, within its powers as it considers just and appropriate.

(2) But damages may be awarded only by a court which has power to award damages, or to order the payment of compensation, in civil proceedings.

(3) No award of damages is to be made unless, taking account of all the circumstances of the case, including—
(a) any other relief or remedy granted, or order made, in relation to the act in question (by that or any other court), and
(b) the consequences of any decision (of that or any other court) in respect of that act,

the court is satisfied that the award is necessary to afford just satisfaction to the person in whose favour it is made.

(4) In determining—
(a) whether to award damages, or
(b) the amount of an award,

the court must take into account the principles applied by the European Court of Human Rights in relation to the award of compensation under Article 41 of the Convention.

(5) A public authority against which damages are awarded is to be treated—
 (a) in Scotland, for the purposes of section 3 of the Law Reform (Miscellaneous Provisions) (Scotland) Act 1940 as if the award were made in an action of damages in which the authority has been found liable in respect of loss or damage to the person to whom the award is made;
 (b) for the purposes of the Civil Liability (Contribution) Act 1978 as liable in respect of damage suffered by the person to whom the award is made.

(6) In this section—
"court" includes a tribunal;
"damages" means damages for an unlawful act of a public authority; and
"unlawful" means unlawful under section 6(1).

[656]

9 Judicial acts

(1) Proceedings under section 7(1)(a) in respect of a judicial act may be brought only—
 (a) by exercising a right of appeal;
 (b) on an application (in Scotland a petition) for judicial review; or
 (c) in such other forum as may be prescribed by rules.

(2) That does not affect any rule of law which prevents a court from being the subject of judicial review.

(3) In proceedings under this Act in respect of a judicial act done in good faith, damages may not be awarded otherwise than to compensate a person to the extent required by Article 5(5) of the Convention.

(4) An award of damages permitted by subsection (3) is to be made against the Crown; but no award may be made unless the appropriate person, if not a party to the proceedings, is joined.

(5) In this section—
"appropriate person" means the Minister responsible for the court concerned, or a person or government department nominated by him;
"court" includes a tribunal;
"judge" includes a member of a tribunal, a justice of the peace [(or, in Northern Ireland, a lay magistrate)] and a clerk or other officer entitled to exercise the jurisdiction of a court;
"judicial act" means a judicial act of a court and includes an act done on the instructions, or on behalf, of a judge; and
"rules" has the same meaning as in section 7(9).

[657]

NOTES

Sub-s (5): in definition "judge" words in square brackets inserted by the Justice (Northern Ireland) Act 2002, s 10(6), Sch 4, para 39.

Rules: the Human Rights Act 1998 (Jurisdiction) (Scotland) Rules 2000, SSI 2000/301.

Remedial action

10 Power to take remedial action

(1) This section applies if—
 (a) a provision of legislation has been declared under section 4 to be incompatible with a Convention right and, if an appeal lies—
  (i) all persons who may appeal have stated in writing that they do not intend to do so;
  (ii) the time for bringing an appeal has expired and no appeal has been brought within that time; or
  (iii) an appeal brought within that time has been determined or abandoned; or
 (b) it appears to a Minister of the Crown or Her Majesty in Council that, having regard to a finding of the European Court of Human Rights made after the coming into force of this section in proceedings against the United Kingdom, a provision of legislation is incompatible with an obligation of the United Kingdom arising from the Convention.

(2) If a Minister of the Crown considers that there are compelling reasons for proceeding under this section, he may by order make such amendments to the legislation as he considers necessary to remove the incompatibility.

(3) If, in the case of subordinate legislation, a Minister of the Crown considers—

(a) that it is necessary to amend the primary legislation under which the subordinate legislation in question was made, in order to enable the incompatibility to be removed, and

(b) that there are compelling reasons for proceeding under this section,

he may by order make such amendments to the primary legislation as he considers necessary.

(4) This section also applies where the provision in question is in subordinate legislation and has been quashed, or declared invalid, by reason of incompatibility with a Convention right and the Minister proposes to proceed under paragraph 2(b) of Schedule 2.

(5) If the legislation is an Order in Council, the power conferred by subsection (2) or (3) is exercisable by Her Majesty in Council.

(6) In this section "legislation" does not include a Measure of the Church Assembly or of the General Synod of the Church of England.

(7) Schedule 2 makes further provision about remedial orders.

[658]

NOTES

Orders: the Mental Health Act 1983 (Remedial) Order 2001, SI 2001/3712; the Naval Discipline Act 1957 (Remedial) Order 2004, SI 2004/66.

Other rights and proceedings

11 Safeguard for existing human rights

A person's reliance on a Convention right does not restrict—

(a) any other right or freedom conferred on him by or under any law having effect in any part of the United Kingdom; or

(b) his right to make any claim or bring any proceedings which he could make or bring apart from sections 7 to 9.

[659]

12 Freedom of expression

(1) This section applies if a court is considering whether to grant any relief which, if granted, might affect the exercise of the Convention right to freedom of expression.

(2) If the person against whom the application for relief is made ("the respondent") is neither present nor represented, no such relief is to be granted unless the court is satisfied—

(a) that the applicant has taken all practicable steps to notify the respondent; or

(b) that there are compelling reasons why the respondent should not be notified.

(3) No such relief is to be granted so as to restrain publication before trial unless the court is satisfied that the applicant is likely to establish that publication should not be allowed.

(4) The court must have particular regard to the importance of the Convention right to freedom of expression and, where the proceedings relate to material which the respondent claims, or which appears to the court, to be journalistic, literary or artistic material (or to conduct connected with such material), to—

(a) the extent to which—

(i) the material has, or is about to, become available to the public; or

(ii) it is, or would be, in the public interest for the material to be published;

(b) any relevant privacy code.

(5) In this section—

"court" includes a tribunal; and

"relief" includes any remedy or order (other than in criminal proceedings).

[660]

13 Freedom of thought, conscience and religion

(1) If a court's determination of any question arising under this Act might affect the exercise by a religious organisation (itself or its members collectively) of the Convention right to freedom of thought, conscience and religion, it must have particular regard to the importance of that right.

(2) In this section "court" includes a tribunal.

[661]

Derogations and reservations

14 Derogations

(1) In this Act "designated derogation" means—

(a) …

(b) any derogation by the United Kingdom from an Article of the Convention, or of any protocol to the Convention, which is designated for the purposes of this Act in an order made by the [Secretary of State].

(2) …

(3) If a designated derogation is amended or replaced it ceases to be a designated derogation.

(4) But subsection (3) does not prevent the [Secretary of State] from exercising his power under subsection (1) … to make a fresh designation order in respect of the Article concerned.

(5) The [Secretary of State] must by order make such amendments to Schedule 3 as he considers appropriate to reflect—

(a) any designation order; or

(b) the effect of subsection (3).

(6) A designation order may be made in anticipation of the making by the United Kingdom of a proposed derogation.

[662]

NOTES

Sub-s (1): words omitted repealed by the Human Rights (Amendment) Order 2001, SI 2001/1216, art 2(a); words in square brackets substituted by the Secretary of State for Constitutional Affairs Order 2003, SI 2003/1887, art 9, Sch 2, para 10(1).

Sub-s (2): repealed by SI 2001/1216, art 2(b).

Sub-s (4): words in square brackets substituted by SI 2003/1887, art 9, Sch 2, para 10(1); reference omitted repealed by SI 2001/1216, art 2(c).

Sub-s (5): words in square brackets substituted by SI 2003/1887, art 9, Sch 2, para 10(1).

Orders: the Human Rights Act 1998 (Designated Derogation) Order 2001, SI 2001/3644.

15 Reservations

(1) In this Act "designated reservation" means—

(a) the United Kingdom's reservation to Article 2 of the First Protocol to the Convention; and

(b) any other reservation by the United Kingdom to an Article of the Convention, or of any protocol to the Convention, which is designated for the purposes of this Act in an order made by the [Secretary of State].

(2) The text of the reservation referred to in subsection (1)(a) is set out in Part II of Schedule 3.

(3) If a designated reservation is withdrawn wholly or in part it ceases to be a designated reservation.

(4) But subsection (3) does not prevent the [Secretary of State] from exercising his power under subsection (1)(b) to make a fresh designation order in respect of the Article concerned.

(5) The [Secretary of State] must by order make such amendments to this Act as he considers appropriate to reflect—

(a) any designation order; or

(b) the effect of subsection (3).

[663]

NOTES

Sub-ss (1), (4), (5): words in square brackets substituted by the Secretary of State for Constitutional Affairs Order 2003, SI 2003/1887, art 9, Sch 2, para 10(1).

16 Period for which designated derogations have effect

(1) If it has not already been withdrawn by the United Kingdom, a designated derogation ceases to have effect for the purposes of this Act … at the end of the period of five years beginning with the date on which the order designating it was made.

(2) At any time before the period—

(a) fixed by subsection (1) … , or

(b) extended by an order under this subsection,

comes to an end, the [Secretary of State] may by order extend it by a further period of five years.

(3) An order under section 14(1) … ceases to have effect at the end of the period for consideration, unless a resolution has been passed by each House approving the order.

(4) Subsection (3) does not affect—

(a) anything done in reliance on the order; or

(b) the power to make a fresh order under section 14(1)…

(5) In subsection (3) "period for consideration" means the period of forty days beginning with the day on which the order was made.

(6) In calculating the period for consideration, no account is to be taken of any time during which—

(a) Parliament is dissolved or prorogued; or

(b) both Houses are adjourned for more than four days.

(7) If a designated derogation is withdrawn by the United Kingdom, the [Secretary of State] must by order make such amendments to this Act as he considers are required to reflect that withdrawal.

[664]

NOTES

Sub-ss (1), (3), (4): words omitted repealed by the Human Rights Act (Amendment) Order 2001, SI 2001/1216, art 3(a), (c), (d).

Sub-s (2): words omitted repealed by SI 2001/1216, art 3(b); words in square brackets substituted by the Secretary of State for Constitutional Affairs Order 2003, SI 2003/1887, art 9, Sch 2, para 10(1).

Sub-s (7): words in square brackets substituted by SI 2003/1887, art 9, Sch 2, para 10(1).

17 Periodic review of designated reservations

(1) The appropriate Minister must review the designated reservation referred to in section 15(1)(a)—

(a) before the end of the period of five years beginning with the date on which section 1(2) came into force; and

(b) if that designation is still in force, before the end of the period of five years beginning with the date on which the last report relating to it was laid under subsection (3).

(2) The appropriate Minister must review each of the other designated reservations (if any)—

(a) before the end of the period of five years beginning with the date on which the order designating the reservation first came into force; and

(b) if the designation is still in force, before the end of the period of five years beginning with the date on which the last report relating to it was laid under subsection (3).

(3) The Minister conducting a review under this section must prepare a report on the result of the review and lay a copy of it before each House of Parliament.

[665]

Judges of the European Court of Human Rights

18 Appointment to European Court of Human Rights

(1) In this section "judicial office" means the office of—

(a) Lord Justice of Appeal, Justice of the High Court or Circuit judge, in England and Wales;

(b) judge of the Court of Session or sheriff, in Scotland;

(c) Lord Justice of Appeal, judge of the High Court or county court judge, in Northern Ireland.

(2) The holder of a judicial office may become a judge of the European Court of Human Rights ("the Court") without being required to relinquish his office.

(3) But he is not required to perform the duties of his judicial office while he is a judge of the Court.

(4) In respect of any period during which he is a judge of the Court—

(a) a Lord Justice of Appeal or Justice of the High Court is not to count as a judge of the relevant court for the purposes of section 2(1) or 4(1) of the *Supreme Court Act 1981* (maximum number of judges) nor as a judge of the *Supreme Court* for the purposes of section 12(1) to (6) of that Act (salaries etc);

(b) a judge of the Court of Session is not to count as a judge of that court for the purposes of section 1(1) of the Court of Session Act 1988 (maximum number of judges) or of section 9(1)(c) of the Administration of Justice Act 1973 ("the 1973 Act") (salaries etc);

(c) a Lord Justice of Appeal or judge of the High Court in Northern Ireland is not to count as a judge of the relevant court for the purposes of section 2(1) or 3(1) of the Judicature (Northern Ireland) Act 1978 (maximum number of judges) nor as a judge of the *Supreme Court* of Northern Ireland for the purposes of section 9(1)(d) of the 1973 Act (salaries etc);

(d) a Circuit judge is not to count as such for the purposes of section 18 of the Courts Act 1971 (salaries etc);

(e) a sheriff is not to count as such for the purposes of section 14 of the Sheriff Courts (Scotland) Act 1907 (salaries etc);

(f) a county court judge of Northern Ireland is not to count as such for the purposes of section 106 of the County Courts Act (Northern Ireland) 1959 (salaries etc).

(5) If a sheriff principal is appointed a judge of the Court, section 11(1) of the Sheriff Courts (Scotland) Act 1971 (temporary appointment of sheriff principal) applies, while he holds that appointment, as if his office is vacant.

(6) Schedule 4 makes provision about judicial pensions in relation to the holder of a judicial office who serves as a judge of the Court.

(7) The Lord Chancellor or the Secretary of State may by order make such transitional provision (including, in particular, provision for a temporary increase in the maximum number of judges) as he considers appropriate in relation to any holder of a judicial office who has completed his service as a judge of the Court.

[(7A) The following paragraphs apply to the making of an order under subsection (7) in relation to any holder of a judicial office listed in subsection (1)(a)—

(a) before deciding what transitional provision it is appropriate to make, the person making the order must consult the Lord Chief Justice of England and Wales;

(b) before making the order, that person must consult the Lord Chief Justice of England and Wales.

(7B) The following paragraphs apply to the making of an order under subsection (7) in relation to any holder of a judicial office listed in subsection (1)(c)—

(a) before deciding what transitional provision it is appropriate to make, the person making the order must consult the Lord Chief Justice of Northern Ireland;

(b) before making the order, that person must consult the Lord Chief Justice of Northern Ireland.

(7C) The Lord Chief Justice of England and Wales may nominate a judicial office holder (within the meaning of section 109(4) of the Constitutional Reform Act 2005) to exercise his functions under this section.

(7D) The Lord Chief Justice of Northern Ireland may nominate any of the following to exercise his functions under this section—

(a) the holder of one of the offices listed in Schedule 1 to the Justice (Northern Ireland) Act 2002;

(b) a Lord Justice of Appeal (as defined in section 88 of that Act).]

[666]

NOTES

Sub-s (4): in para (a) words in italics in the first place where they occur substituted by the words "Senior Courts Act 1981", words in italics in the second place where they occur substituted by the words "Senior Courts" and words in italics in para (c) substituted by the words "Court of Judicature" by the Constitutional Reform Act 2005, s 59(5), Sch 11, Pt 1, para 1(2), Pt 2, para 4(1), (3), Pt 3, para 6(1), (3), as from a day to be appointed.

Sub-ss (7A)–(7D): added by the Constitutional Reform Act 2005, s 15(1), Sch 4, Pt 1, para 278.

Orders: the Judicial Pensions (European Court of Human Rights) Order 1998, SI 1998/2768.

Parliamentary procedure

19 Statements of compatibility

(1) A Minister of the Crown in charge of a Bill in either House of Parliament must, before Second Reading of the Bill—

(a) make a statement to the effect that in his view the provisions of the Bill are compatible with the Convention rights ("a statement of compatibility"); or

(b) make a statement to the effect that although he is unable to make a statement of compatibility the government nevertheless wishes the House to proceed with the Bill.

(2) The statement must be in writing and be published in such manner as the Minister making it considers appropriate.

[667]

Supplemental

20 Orders etc under this Act

(1) Any power of a Minister of the Crown to make an order under this Act is exercisable by statutory instrument.

(2) The power of … [the Lord Chancellor or] the Secretary of State to make rules (other than rules of court) under section 2(3) or 7(9) is exercisable by statutory instrument.

(3) Any statutory instrument made under section 14, 15 or 16(7) must be laid before Parliament.

(4) No order may be made by … [the Lord Chancellor or] the Secretary of State under section 1(4), 7(11) or 16(2) unless a draft of the order has been laid before, and approved by, each House of Parliament.

(5) Any statutory instrument made under section 18(7) or Schedule 4, or to which subsection (2) applies, shall be subject to annulment in pursuance of a resolution of either House of Parliament.

(6) The power of a Northern Ireland department to make—

(a) rules under section 2(3)(c) or 7(9)(c), or

(b) an order under section 7(11),

is exercisable by statutory rule for the purposes of the Statutory Rules (Northern Ireland) Order 1979.

(7) Any rules made under section 2(3)(c) or 7(9)(c) shall be subject to negative resolution; and section 41(6) of the Interpretation Act (Northern Ireland) 1954 (meaning of "subject to negative resolution") shall apply as if the power to make the rules were conferred by an Act of the Northern Ireland Assembly.

(8) No order may be made by a Northern Ireland department under section 7(11) unless a draft of the order has been laid before, and approved by, the Northern Ireland Assembly.

[668]

NOTES

Sub-ss (2), (4): words omitted repealed by the Secretary of State for Constitutional Affairs Order 2003, SI 2003/1887, art 9, Sch 2, para 10(2); words in square brackets inserted by the Transfer of Functions (Lord Chancellor and Secretary of State) Order 2005, SI 2005/3429, art 8, Schedule, para 3.

21 Interpretation, etc

(1) In this Act—

"amend" includes repeal and apply (with or without modifications);

"the appropriate Minister" means the Minister of the Crown having charge of the appropriate authorised government department (within the meaning of the Crown Proceedings Act 1947);

"the Commission" means the European Commission of Human Rights;

"the Convention" means the Convention for the Protection of Human Rights and Fundamental Freedoms, agreed by the Council of Europe at Rome on 4th November 1950 as it has effect for the time being in relation to the United Kingdom;

"declaration of incompatibility" means a declaration under section 4;

"Minister of the Crown" has the same meaning as in the Ministers of the Crown Act 1975;

"Northern Ireland Minister" includes the First Minister and the deputy First Minister in Northern Ireland;

"primary legislation" means any—

(a) public general Act;
(b) local and personal Act;
(c) private Act;
(d) Measure of the Church Assembly;
(e) Measure of the General Synod of the Church of England;
(f) Order in Council—
  (i) made in exercise of Her Majesty's Royal Prerogative;
  (ii) made under section 38(1)(a) of the Northern Ireland Constitution Act 1973 or the corresponding provision of the Northern Ireland Act 1998; or
  (iii) amending an Act of a kind mentioned in paragraph (a), (b) or (c);

and includes an order or other instrument made under primary legislation (otherwise than by the National Assembly for Wales, a member of the Scottish Executive, a Northern Ireland Minister or a Northern Ireland department) to the extent to which it operates to bring one or more provisions of that legislation into force or amends any primary legislation;

"the First Protocol" means the protocol to the Convention agreed at Paris on 20th March 1952;

.....

"the Eleventh Protocol" means the protocol to the Convention (restructuring the control machinery established by the Convention) agreed at Strasbourg on 11th May 1994;

["the Thirteenth Protocol" means the protocol to the Convention (concerning the abolition of the death penalty in all circumstances) agreed at Vilnius on 3rd May 2002;]

"remedial order" means an order under section 10;

"subordinate legislation" means any—

(a) Order in Council other than one—
  (i) made in exercise of Her Majesty's Royal Prerogative;
  (ii) made under section 38(1)(a) of the Northern Ireland Constitution Act 1973 or the corresponding provision of the Northern Ireland Act 1998; or
  (iii) amending an Act of a kind mentioned in the definition of primary legislation;
(b) Act of the Scottish Parliament;
(c) Act of the Parliament of Northern Ireland;
(d) Measure of the Assembly established under section 1 of the Northern Ireland Assembly Act 1973;
(e) Act of the Northern Ireland Assembly;
(f) order, rules, regulations, scheme, warrant, byelaw or other instrument made

under primary legislation (except to the extent to which it operates to bring one or more provisions of that legislation into force or amends any primary legislation);

(g) order, rules, regulations, scheme, warrant, byelaw or other instrument made under legislation mentioned in paragraph (b), (c), (d) or (e) or made under an Order in Council applying only to Northern Ireland;

(h) order, rules, regulations, scheme, warrant, byelaw or other instrument made by a member of the Scottish Executive, a Northern Ireland Minister or a Northern Ireland department in exercise of prerogative or other executive functions of Her Majesty which are exercisable by such a person on behalf of Her Majesty;

"transferred matters" has the same meaning as in the Northern Ireland Act 1998; and "tribunal" means any tribunal in which legal proceedings may be brought.

(2) The references in paragraphs (b) and (c) of section 2(1) to Articles are to Articles of the Convention as they had effect immediately before the coming into force of the Eleventh Protocol.

(3) The reference in paragraph (d) of section 2(1) to Article 46 includes a reference to Articles 32 and 54 of the Convention as they had effect immediately before the coming into force of the Eleventh Protocol.

(4) The references in section 2(1) to a report or decision of the Commission or a decision of the Committee of Ministers include references to a report or decision made as provided by paragraphs 3, 4 and 6 of Article 5 of the Eleventh Protocol (transitional provisions).

(5) Any liability under the Army Act 1955, the Air Force Act 1955 or the Naval Discipline Act 1957 to suffer death for an offence is replaced by a liability to imprisonment for life or any less punishment authorised by those Acts; and those Acts shall accordingly have effect with the necessary modifications.

[669]

NOTES

Sub-s (1): definition "the Sixth Protocol" omitted repealed and definition "the Thirteenth Protocol" inserted by the Human Rights Act 1998 (Amendment) Order 2004, SI 2004/1574, art 2(2).

Emergency regulations made under the Civil Contingencies Act 2004, s 20 are to be treated as subordinate legislation and not primary legislation for the purposes of this Act: see s 30(2) of the 2004 Act.

22 Short title, commencement, application and extent

(1) This Act may be cited as the Human Rights Act 1998.

(2) Sections 18, 20 and 21(5) and this section come into force on the passing of this Act.

(3) The other provisions of this Act come into force on such day as the Secretary of State may by order appoint; and different days may be appointed for different purposes.

(4) Paragraph (b) of subsection (1) of section 7 applies to proceedings brought by or at the instigation of a public authority whenever the act in question took place; but otherwise that subsection does not apply to an act taking place before the coming into force of that section.

(5) This Act binds the Crown.

(6) This Act extends to Northern Ireland.

(7) Section 21(5), so far as it relates to any provision contained in the Army Act 1955, the Air Force Act 1955 or the Naval Discipline Act 1957, extends to any place to which that provision extends.

[670]

NOTES

Orders: the Human Rights Act 1998 (Commencement) Order 1998, SI 1998/2882; the Human Rights Act 1998 (Commencement No 2) Order 2000, SI 2000/1851.

(Sch 1 contains the text of certain Articles of the European Convention for the Protection of Human Rights and Fundamental Freedoms and related Protocols, reproduced in Pt V(J) of this work, at **[4457]**.*)*

SCHEDULE 2
REMEDIAL ORDERS

Section 10

Orders

1.(1) A remedial order may—
(a) contain such incidental, supplemental, consequential or transitional provision as the person making it considers appropriate;
(b) be made so as to have effect from a date earlier than that on which it is made;
(c) make provision for the delegation of specific functions;
(d) make different provision for different cases.

(2) The power conferred by sub-paragraph (1)(a) includes—
(a) power to amend primary legislation (including primary legislation other than that which contains the incompatible provision); and
(b) power to amend or revoke subordinate legislation (including subordinate legislation other than that which contains the incompatible provision).

(3) A remedial order may be made so as to have the same extent as the legislation which it affects.

(4) No person is to be guilty of an offence solely as a result of the retrospective effect of a remedial order.

Procedure

2. No remedial order may be made unless—
(a) a draft of the order has been approved by a resolution of each House of Parliament made after the end of the period of 60 days beginning with the day on which the draft was laid; or
(b) it is declared in the order that it appears to the person making it that, because of the urgency of the matter, it is necessary to make the order without a draft being so approved.

Orders laid in draft

3.(1) No draft may be laid under paragraph 2(a) unless—
(a) the person proposing to make the order has laid before Parliament a document which contains a draft of the proposed order and the required information; and
(b) the period of 60 days, beginning with the day on which the document required by this sub-paragraph was laid, has ended.

(2) If representations have been made during that period, the draft laid under paragraph 2(a) must be accompanied by a statement containing—
(a) a summary of the representations; and
(b) if, as a result of the representations, the proposed order has been changed, details of the changes.

Urgent cases

4.(1) If a remedial order ("the original order") is made without being approved in draft, the person making it must lay it before Parliament, accompanied by the required information, after it is made.

(2) If representations have been made during the period of 60 days beginning with the day on which the original order was made, the person making it must (after the end of that period) lay before Parliament a statement containing—
(a) a summary of the representations; and
(b) if, as a result of the representations, he considers it appropriate to make changes to the original order, details of the changes.

(3) If sub-paragraph (2)(b) applies, the person making the statement must—
(a) make a further remedial order replacing the original order; and

(b) lay the replacement order before Parliament.

(4) If, at the end of the period of 120 days beginning with the day on which the original order was made, a resolution has not been passed by each House approving the original or replacement order, the order ceases to have effect (but without that affecting anything previously done under either order or the power to make a fresh remedial order).

Definitions

5. In this Schedule—

"representations" means representations about a remedial order (or proposed remedial order) made to the person making (or proposing to make) it and includes any relevant Parliamentary report or resolution; and

"required information" means—

(a) an explanation of the incompatibility which the order (or proposed order) seeks to remove, including particulars of the relevant declaration, finding or order; and

(b) a statement of the reasons for proceeding under section 10 and for making an order in those terms.

Calculating periods

6. In calculating any period for the purposes of this Schedule, no account is to be taken of any time during which—

(a) Parliament is dissolved or prorogued; or

(b) both Houses are adjourned for more than four days.

[7.(1) This paragraph applies in relation to—

(a) any remedial order made, and any draft of such under an order proposed to be made,—

(i) by the Scottish Ministers; or

(ii) within devolved competence (within the meaning of the Scotland Act 1998) by Her Majesty in Council; and

(b) any document or statement to be laid in connection with such an order (or proposed order).

(2) This Schedule has effect in relation to any such order (or proposed order), document or statement subject to the following modifications.

(3) Any reference to Parliament, each House of Parliament or both Houses of Parliament shall be construed as a reference to the Scottish Parliament.

(4) Paragraph 6 does not apply and instead, in calculating the period for the purposes of this Schedule, no account is to be taken of any time during which the Scottish Parliament is dissolved or is in recess for more than four days.]

[671]

NOTES

Para 7: added by the Scotland Act 1998 (Consequential Modifications) Order 2000, SI 2000/2040, art 2(1), Schedule, Pt I, para 21;

Orders: the Mental Health Act 1983 (Remedial) Order 2001, SI 2001/3712; the Naval Discipline Act 1957 (Remedial) Order 2004, SI 2004/66.

SCHEDULE 3
DEROGATION AND RESERVATION

Sections 14 and 15

(Original Sch 3, Pt I repealed by the Human Rights Act (Amendment) Order 2001, SI 2001/1216; new Sch 3, Pt I inserted by the Human Rights Act (Amendment No 2) Order 2001, SI 2001/4032, art 2, Schedule and repealed by the Human Rights Act 1998 (Amendment) Order 2005, SI 2005/1071, art 2.)

PART II
RESERVATION

At the time of signing the present (First) Protocol, I declare that, in view of certain provisions of the Education Acts in the United Kingdom, the principle affirmed in the second sentence of Article 2 is accepted by the United Kingdom only so far as it is compatible with the provision of efficient instruction and training, and the avoidance of unreasonable public expenditure.

Dated 20 March 1952. Made by the United Kingdom Permanent Representative to the Council of Europe.

[672]

SCHEDULE 4
JUDICIAL PENSIONS

Section 18(6)

Duty to make orders about pensions

1.(1) The appropriate Minister must by order make provision with respect to pensions payable to or in respect of any holder of a judicial office who serves as an ECHR judge.

(2) A pensions order must include such provision as the Minister making it considers is necessary to secure that—

- (a) an ECHR judge who was, immediately before his appointment as an ECHR judge, a member of a judicial pension scheme is entitled to remain as a member of that scheme;
- (b) the terms on which he remains a member of the scheme are those which would have been applicable had he not been appointed as an ECHR judge; and
- (c) entitlement to benefits payable in accordance with the scheme continues to be determined as if, while serving as an ECHR judge, his salary was that which would (but for section 18(4)) have been payable to him in respect of his continuing service as the holder of his judicial office.

Contributions

2. A pensions order may, in particular, make provision—

- (a) for any contributions which are payable by a person who remains a member of a scheme as a result of the order, and which would otherwise be payable by deduction from his salary, to be made otherwise than by deduction from his salary as an ECHR judge; and
- (b) for such contributions to be collected in such manner as may be determined by the administrators of the scheme.

Amendments of other enactments

3. A pensions order may amend any provision of, or made under, a pensions Act in such manner and to such extent as the Minister making the order considers necessary or expedient to ensure the proper administration of any scheme to which it relates.

Definitions

4. In this Schedule—

"appropriate Minister" means—

- (a) in relation to any judicial office whose jurisdiction is exercisable exclusively in relation to Scotland, the Secretary of State; and
- (b) otherwise, the Lord Chancellor;

"ECHR judge" means the holder of a judicial office who is serving as a judge of the Court;

"judicial pension scheme" means a scheme established by and in accordance with a pensions Act;

"pensions Act" means—

- (a) the County Courts Act (Northern Ireland) 1959;
- (b) the Sheriffs' Pensions (Scotland) Act 1961;

(c) the Judicial Pensions Act 1981; or
(d) the Judicial Pensions and Retirement Act 1993; and

"pensions order" means an order made under paragraph 1.

[673]–[1000]

NOTES

Orders: the Judicial Pensions (European Court of Human Rights) Order 1998, SI 1998/2768.

PART II
CIVIL PROCEDURE RULES

ACT OF SEDERUNT (SHERIFF COURT ORDINARY CAUSE RULES) 1993

(SI 1993/1956 (S 223))

NOTES

Made: 29 July 1993.

Authority: the Sheriff Courts (Scotland) Extracts Act 1892, s 13; the Sheriff Courts (Scotland) Act 1971, s 32; the Administration of Justice (Scotland) Act 1972, s 1(3); the Domicile and Matrimonial Proceedings Act 1973, Sch 3, para 5; the Sex Discrimination Act 1975, s 66(7); the Divorce (Scotland) Act 1976, s 11; the Presumption of Death (Scotland) Act 1977, s 15; the Adoption (Scotland) Act 1978, s 59(1); the Debtors (Scotland) Act 1987, ss 97, 102.

Commencement: 1 January 1994.

Only the rules relevant to this work are reproduced here. They are set out as they appear in the Sheriff Court (Scotland) Act 1907, First Schedule, as substituted by the Act of Sederunt (Sheriff Court Ordinary Cause Rules) 1993, SI 1993/1956, s 2, Schedule, in respect of causes commenced on or after 1 January 1994, and as further amended as noted.

ARRANGEMENT OF THE RULES

CHAPTER 1
CITATION, INTERPRETATION, REPRESENTATION AND FORMS

CHAPTER 2
RELIEF FROM COMPLIANCE WITH RULES

CHAPTER 3
COMMENCEMENT OF CAUSES

CHAPTER 5
CITATION, SERVICE AND INTIMATION

CHAPTER 7
UNDEFENDED CAUSES

CHAPTER 8
REPONING

CHAPTER 28
RECOVERY OF EVIDENCE

CHAPTER 30
DECREES, EXTRACTS AND EXECUTION

CHAPTER 40
COMMERCIAL ACTIONS

APPENDIX 1
FORMS

CHAPTER 1
CITATION, INTERPRETATION, REPRESENTATION AND FORMS

1.1 Citation

These Rules may be cited as the Ordinary Cause Rules 1993.

[1001]

CHAPTER 2
RELIEF FROM COMPLIANCE WITH RULES

2.1 Relief from failure to comply with rules

(1) The sheriff may relieve a party from the consequences of failure to comply with a provision in these Rules which is shown to be due to mistake, oversight or other excusable cause, on such conditions as he thinks fit.

(2) Where the sheriff relieves a party from the consequences of a failure to comply with a provision in these Rules under paragraph (1), he may make such order as he thinks fit to enable the cause to proceed as if the failure to comply with the provision had not occurred.

[1002]

CHAPTER 3
COMMENCEMENT OF CAUSES

3.1 Form of initial writ

[(1) A cause shall be commenced—

(a) in the case of an ordinary cause, by initial writ in Form G1; or

(b) in the case of a commercial action within the meaning of Chapter 40, by initial writ in Form G1A.]

(2) The initial writ shall be written, typed or printed on A4 size paper of durable quality and shall not be backed or folded.

(3) Where the pursuer has reason to believe that an [agreement] exists prorogating jurisdiction over the subject-matter of the cause to another court, the [initial] writ shall contain details of that agreement.

(4) Where the pursuer has reason to believe that proceedings are pending before another court involving the same cause of action and between the same parties as those named in the instance of the [initial] writ, the initial writ shall contain details of those proceedings.

(5) An article of condescendence shall be included in the [initial] writ averring—

(a) the ground of jurisdiction; and

(b) the facts upon which the ground of jurisdiction is based.

(6) Where the residence, registered office or place of business, as the case may be, of the defender is not known and cannot reasonably be ascertained, the pursuer shall set out in the instance that the whereabouts of the defender are not known and aver in the condescendence what steps have been taken to ascertain his present whereabouts.

(7) The initial writ shall be signed by the pursuer or his solicitor (if any) and the name and address of that solicitor shall be stated on the back of every service copy of that writ.

[1003]

NOTES

Para (1): substituted by the Act of Sederunt (Ordinary Cause Rules) Amendment (Commercial Actions) 2001, SSI 2001/8, r 2(1), (2).

Paras (3)–(5): words in square brackets substituted by the Act of Sederunt (Sheriff Court Ordinary Cause Rules Amendment) (Miscellaneous) 1996, SI 1996/2445, r 3(1), (2).

3.2 Actions relating to heritable property

(1) In an action relating to heritable property, it shall not be necessary to call as a defender any person by reason only of any interest he may have as the holder of a heritable security over the heritable property.

(2) Intimation of such an action shall be made to the holder of the heritable security referred to in paragraph (1)

(a) where the action relates to any heritable right or title; and

(b) in any other case, where the sheriff so orders.

[(3) In an action falling within section 1(1)(b) or (c) of the Mortgage Rights (Scotland) Act 2001, the initial writ shall include averments about those persons who appear to the pursuer to be entitled to apply for an order under section 2 of that Act and such persons shall, so far as known to the pursuer, be called as defenders for their interest.]

[1004]

NOTES

Para (3): added by the Act of Sederunt (Amendment of Ordinary Cause Rules and Summary Applications, Statutory Applications and Appeals etc Rules) (Applications under the Mortgage Rights (Scotland) Act 2001) 2002, SSI 2002/7, r 2(1), (2).

3.3 Warrants of citation

(1) The warrant of citation in any cause other than—

- (a) a family action within the meaning of rule 33.1(1),
- (b) an action of multiplepoinding,
- (c) an action in which a time to pay direction under the Debtors (Scotland) Act 1987 may be applied for by the defender,
- [(d) an action to which rule 3.2(3) applies,]
- [(e) a civil partnership action within the meaning of rule 33A.1(1)(c).]

shall be in [Form O1].

(2) In a cause in which a time to pay direction under the Debtors (Scotland) Act 1987 may be applied for the defender, the warrant of citation shall be in [Form O2].

(3) In a cause in which a warrant of citation in accordance with [Form O2] is appropriate, there shall be served on the defender (with the initial writ and warrant) a notice in [Form O3].

[(4) In an action to which rule 3.2(3) applies, the warrant of citation shall be in Form O2A.]

[1005]

NOTES

Para (1): sub-para (d) added by the Act of Sederunt (Amendment of Ordinary Cause Rules and Summary Applications, Statutory Applications and Appeals etc Rules) (Applications under the Mortgage Rights (Scotland) Act 2001) 2002, SSI 2002/7, r 2(1), (3)(a); para (e) added by the Act of Sederunt (Ordinary Cause Rules) Amendment (Family Law (Scotland) Act 2006 etc) 2006, SSI 2006/207, r 2(1), (2); words in third pair of square brackets substituted by the Act of Sederunt (Sheriff Court Ordinary Cause Rules Amendment) (Miscellaneous) 1996, SI 1996/2445, r 3(1), (3).

Paras (2), (3): words in square brackets substituted by SI 1996/2445, r 3(1), (3).

Para (4): added by SSI 2002/7, r 2(1), (3)(b).

3.4 Warrants for arrestment to found jurisdiction

(1) Where an application for a warrant for arrestment to found jurisdiction may be made, it shall be made in the crave of the [initial] writ.

(2) Averments to justify the granting of such a warrant shall be included in the condescendence.

[1006]

NOTES

Para (1): word in square brackets substituted by the Act of Sederunt (Sheriff Court Ordinary Cause Rules Amendment) (Miscellaneous) 1996, SI 1996/2445, r 3(1), (4).

3.5 Warrants and precepts for arrestment on dependence

(1) A copy of—

- (a) an initial writ with warrant to cite which includes a warrant to arrest on the dependence,
- (b) defences which include, or a minute of amendment which includes, a counterclaim with warrant granted to arrest on the dependence endorsed on that writ,

certified as a true copy by the pursuer or defender, as the case may be, or his solicitor, shall be sufficient warrant to arrest on the dependence if it is otherwise competent to do so.

(2) A precept of arrestment may be issued by the sheriff on production to him of—

- (a) an initial writ containing a crave for payment of money on which a warrant of citation has been issued;

(b) defences which include, or a minute of amendment which includes, a counterclaim containing a crave for payment of money; or

(c) a document of liquid debt.

[(3) Averments to justify the granting of a warrant to arrest on the dependence, or a precept of arrestment, shall be included in the condescendence of an initial writ or the statement of claim in a counterclaim.]

[1007]

NOTES

Para (3): added by the Act of Sederunt (Ordinary Cause, Summary Application, Summary Cause and Small Claim Rules) Amendment (Miscellaneous) 2004, SSI 2004/197, r 2(1), (2)(b).

3.6 Period of notice after citation

(1) Subject to rule 5.6(1) (service where address of person is not known) and to paragraph (2) of this rule, a cause shall proceed after one of the following periods of notice has been given to the defender—

(a) where the defender is resident or has a place of business within Europe, 21 days after the date of execution of service; or

(b) where the defender is resident or has a place of business outside Europe, 42 days after the date of execution of service.

(2) Subject to paragraph (3), the sheriff may, on cause shown, shorten or extend the period of notice on such conditions as to the method or manner of service as he thinks fit.

(3) A period of notice may not be reduced to a period of less than 2 days.

(4) Where a period of notice expires on a Saturday, Sunday, or public or court holiday, the period of notice shall be deemed to expire on the next day on which the sheriff clerk's office is open for civil court business.

[1008]

CHAPTER 5
CITATION, SERVICE AND INTIMATION

5.1 Signature of warrants

(1) Subject to paragraph (2), a warrant for citation, or [intimation] may be signed by the sheriff or sheriff clerk.

(2) The following warrants shall be signed by the sheriff:—

(a) a warrant containing an order shortening or extending the period of notice or any other order other than a warrant which the sheriff clerk may sign;

[(b) a warrant for arrestment to found jurisdiction;

(ba) a warrant for arrestment on the dependence; and]

(c) a warrant for intimation ordered under rule 33.8 (intimation where [alleged] association)

[(d) a warrant for intimation ordered under rule 33A.8 (intimation where alleged association).]

(3) Where the sheriff clerk refuses to sign a warrant which he may sign, the party presenting the initial writ may apply to the sheriff for the warrant.

[1009]

NOTES

Para (1): word in square brackets substituted by the Act of Sederunt (Ordinary Cause, Summary Application, Summary Cause and Small Claim Rules) Amendment (Miscellaneous) 2004, SSI 2004/197, r 2(1), (3)(a).

Para (2): sub-paras (b), (ba) substituted for sub-para (b) as originally enacted by SSI 2004/197, r 2(1), (3)(b); word in square brackets in sub-para (c) substituted and sub-para (d) added by the Act of Sederunt (Ordinary Cause Rules) Amendment (Family Law (Scotland) Act 2006 etc) 2006, SSI 2006/207, r 2(1), (3).

5.2 Form of citation and certificate

(1) Subject to rule 5.6 (service where address of person is not known), in any cause other than—

PART II CIVIL PROCEDURE RULES

(a) a family action within the meaning of rule 33.1(1),
[(aa) a civil partnership action within the meaning of rule 33A.1(1);]
(b) an action of multiplepoinding, ...
(c) an action in which a time to pay direction under the Debtors (Scotland) Act 1987 may be applied for by the defender, [or]
[(d) an action to which rule 3.2(3) applies,]

[citation of] any person shall be in Form O4 which shall be attached to a copy of the [initial] writ and warrant of citation and shall have appended to it a notice of intention to defend in Form O7.

(2) In a cause in which a time to pay direction under the Debtors (Scotland) Act 1987 may be applied for by the defender, citation shall be in Form O5 which shall be attached to a copy of the initial writ and warrant of citation and shall have appended to it a notice of intention to defend in Form O7.

[(2A) In an action to which rule 3.2(3) applies, citation shall be in Form O5A which shall be attached to a copy of the initial writ and warrant of citation and shall have appended to it a notice of intention to defend in Form O7.]

(3) The certificate of citation in any cause other than a family action within the meaning of rule 33.1(1) or an action of multiplepoinding shall be in Form O6 which shall be attached to the initial writ.

(4) Where citation is by a sheriff officer, one witness shall be sufficient for the execution of citation.

(5) Where citation is by a sheriff officer, the certificate of citation shall be signed by the sheriff officer and the witness and shall state—
(a) the method of citation; and
(b) where the method of citation was other than personal or postal citation, the full name and designation of any person to whom the citation was delivered.

(6) Where citation is executed under paragraph 3 of rule 5.4 (depositing or affixing by sheriff officer), the certificate shall include a statement—
(a) of the method of service previously attempted;
(b) of the circumstances which prevented such service being executed; and
(c) that a copy was sent in accordance with the provisions of paragraph (4) of that rule.

[1010]

NOTES

Para (1): sub-para (aa) inserted by the Act of Sederunt (Ordinary Cause Rules) Amendment (Family Law (Scotland) Act 2006 etc) 2006, SSI 2006/207, r 2(1), (4); words omitted revoked, and words in second and third pairs of square brackets inserted by the Act of Sederunt (Amendment of Ordinary Cause Rules and Summary Applications, Statutory Applications and Appeals etc Rules) (Applications under the Mortgage Rights (Scotland) Act 2001) 2002, SSI 2002/7, r 2(1), (4)(a)–(c); words in third and fourth pairs of square brackets substituted by the Act of Sederunt (Sheriff Court Ordinary Cause Rules Amendment) (Miscellaneous) 1996, SI 1996/2445, r 3(1), (5).

Para (2A): inserted by SSI 2002/7, r 2(1), (4)(d).

5.3 Postal service or intimation

(1) In any cause in which service or intimation of any document or citation of any person may be by recorded delivery, such service, intimation or citation shall be by the first class recorded delivery service.

(2) Notwithstanding the terms of section 4(2) of the Citation Amendment (Scotland) Act 1882 (time from which period of notice reckoned), where service or intimation is by post, the period of notice shall run from the beginning of the day after the date of posting.

(3) On the face of the envelope used for postal service or intimation under this rule there shall be written or printed the following notice—

"This envelope contains a citation to or intimation from (specify the court). If delivery cannot be made at the address shown it is to be returned immediately to: The Sheriff Clerk (insert address of sheriff clerk's office).".

(4) The certificate of citation or intimation in the case of postal service shall have attached to it any relevant postal receipts.

[1011]

5.4 Service within Scotland by sheriff officer

(1) An initial writ, decree, charge, warrant or any other order or writ following upon such initial writ or decree served by a sheriff officer on any person shall be served—

(a) personally; or

(b) by being left in the hands of a resident at the person's dwelling place or an employee at his place of business.

(2) Where service is executed under paragraph (1)(b), the certificate of citation or service shall contain the full name and designation of any person in whose hands the intial writ, decree, charge, warrant or other order or writ, as the case may be, was left.

(3) Where a sheriff officer has been unsuccessful in executing service in accordance with paragraph (1), he may, after making diligent enquiries, serve the document in question—

(a) by depositing it in that person's dwelling place or place of business; or

(b) by affixing it to the door of that person's dwelling place or place of business.

(4) Subject to rule 6.1 (service of schedule of arrestment), where service is executed under paragraph (3), the sheriff officer shall, as soon as possible after such service, send a letter containing a copy of the document by ordinary first class post to the address at which he thinks it most likely that the person on whom service has been executed may be found.

[(5) Where the firm which employs the sheriff officer has in its possession—

(a) the document or a copy of it certified as correct by the pursuer's solicitor, the sheriff officer may serve the document upon the defender without having the document or certified copy in his possession, in which case he shall if required to do so by the person on whom service is executed and within a reasonable time of being so required, show the document or certified copy to the person; or

(b) a certified copy of the interlocutor pronounced allowing service of the document, the sheriff officer may serve the document without having in his possession the certified copy interlocutor if he has in his possession a facsimile copy of the certified copy interlocutor (which he shall show, if required, to the person on whom service is executed).]

[1012]

PART II CIVIL PROCEDURE RULES

NOTES

Para (5): added by the Act of Sederunt (Ordinary Cause, Summary Application, Summary Cause and Small Claim Rules) Amendment (Miscellaneous) 2003, SSI 2003/26, r 2(1), (3).

5.5 Service on persons furth of Scotland

(1) Subject to the following provisions of this rule, an initial writ, decree, charge, warrant or any other order or writ following upon such initial writ or decree served on a person furth of Scotland shall be served—

(a) at a known residence or place of business in England, Wales, Northern Ireland, the Isle of Man, the Channel Islands or any country with which the United Kingdom does not have a convention providing for service of writs in that country—

  (i) in accordance with the rules for personal service under the domestic law of the place in which service is to be executed; or

  (ii) by posting in Scotland a copy of the document in question in a registered letter addressed to the person at his residence or place of business;

(b) in a country which is a party to the Hague Convention on the Service Abroad of Judicial and Extra-Judicial Documents in Civil or Commercial Matters dated 15th November 1965 or the Convention in Schedule 1 or 3C to the Civil Jurisdiction and Judgments Act 1982—

  (i) by a method prescribed by the internal law of the country where service is to be executed for the service of documents in domestic actions upon persons who are within its territory;

  (ii) by or through the central, or other appropriate, authority in the country where service is to be executed at the request of the [Secretary of State for Foreign and Commonwealth Affairs];

  (iii) by or through a British Consular Office in the country where service is to be executed at the request of the [Secretary of State for Foreign and Commonwealth Affairs];

  (iv) where the law of the country in which the person resides permits, by posting in Scotland a copy of the document in a registered letter addressed to the person at his residence; or

(v) where the law of the country in which service is to be executed permits, service by an huissier, other judicial officer or competent official of the country where service is to be executed; … [or]

(c) in a country with which the United Kingdom has a convention on the service of writs in that country other than the conventions mentioned in sub-paragraph (b), by one of the methods approved in the relevant convention[; …

(d) …].

[(1A) In a country to which the Council Regulation applies, service—

(a) may be effected by the methods prescribed in paragraph (1)(b)(ii) and (iii) only in exceptional circumstances; and

(b) is effected only if the receiving agency has informed the person that acceptance of service may be refused on the ground that the document has not been translated in accordance with paragraph (6).]

(2) Any document which requires to be posted in Scotland for the purposes of this rule shall be posted by a solicitor or a sheriff officer; and on the face of the envelope there shall be written or printed the notice set out in rule 5.3(3).

(3) In the case of service by a method referred to in paragraph (1)(b)(ii) and (iii), the pursuer shall—

(a) send a copy of the writ and warrant of service with citation attached, or other document, as the case may be, with a request for service by the method indicated in the request to the [Secretary of State for Foreign and Commonwealth Affairs]; and

(b) lodge in process a certificate signed by the authority which executed service stating that it has been, and the manner in which it was, served.

(4) In the case of service by a method referred to in paragraph (1)(b)(v), the pursuer or the sheriff officer, shall—

(a) send a copy of the writ and warrant for service with citation attached, or other document, as the case may be, with a request for service by the method indicated in the request to the official in the country in which service is to be executed; and

(b) lodge in process a certificate of the official who executed service stating that it has been, and the manner in which is was, served.

(5) Where service is executed in accordance with paragraph (1)(a)(i) or (1)(b)(i) other than on another party in the United Kingdom, the Isle of Man or the Channel Islands, the party executing service shall lodge a certificate by a person who is conversant with the law of the country concerned and who practises or has practised law in that country or is a duly accredited representative of the Government of that country, stating that the method of service employed is in accordance with the law of the place where service was executed.

(6) Every writ, document, citation or notice on the face of the envelope mentioned in rule 5.3(3) shall be accompanied by a translation in …—

[(a) an official language of the country in which service is to be executed; or

(b) in a country to which the Council Regulation applies, a language of the member state of transmission that is understood by the person on whom service is being executed.]

(7) A translation referred to in paragraph (6) shall be certified as correct by the person making it; and the certificate shall—

(a) include his full name, address and qualifications; and

(b) be lodged with the execution of citation or service.

[(8) In this rule "the Council Regulation" means Council Regulation (EC) No 1348/2000 on the service in the Member States of judicial and extrajudicial documents in civil or commercial matters.]

[1013]

NOTES

Para (1): words in square brackets in sub-para (b)(ii), (iii) substituted by the Act of Sederunt (Sheriff Court Ordinary Cause Rules Amendment) (Miscellaneous) 1996, SI 1996/2445, r 3(1), (6); word omitted from sub-para (b)(v) revoked and sub-para (d) and word "or" immediately preceding it inserted by the Act of Sederunt (Ordinary Cause, Summary Application, Summary Cause and Small Claim Rules) Amendment (Miscellaneous) 2003, SSI 2003/26, r 2(1), (4); word "or" in square brackets inserted and para (d) and word immediately preceding it revoked by the Act of Sederunt (Ordinary Cause, Summary Application, Summary Cause and Small Claim Rules) Amendment (Miscellaneous) 2004, SSI 2004/197, r 2(1), (4)(a).

Para (1A): inserted by SSI 2004/197, r 2(1), (4)(b).
Para (3): words in square brackets substituted by SI 1996/2445, r 3(1), (6).
Para (6): words omitted revoked and sub-paras (a), (b) added by SSI 2004/197, r 2(1), (4)(c).
Para (8): added by SSI 2004/197, r 2(1), (4)(d).

5.6 Service where address of person is not known

(1) Where the address of a person to be cited or served with a document is not known and cannot reasonably be ascertained, the sheriff shall grant warrant for citation or service upon that person—

(a) by the publication of an advertisement in Form G3 in a specified newspaper circulating in the area of the last known address of that person, or

(b) by displaying on the walls of court a copy of the instance and crave of the initial writ, the warrant of citation and a notice in Form G4;

and the period of notice fixed by the sheriff shall run from the date of publication of the advertisement or display on the walls of court, as the case may be.

(2) Where service requires to be executed under paragraph (1), the pursuer shall lodge a service copy of the initial writ and a copy of any warrant of citation with the sheriff clerk from whom they may be uplifted by the person for whom they are intended.

(3) Where a person has been cited or served in accordance with paragraph (1) and, after the cause has commenced, his address becomes known, the sheriff may allow the initial writ to be amended subject to such conditions as to re-service, intimation, expenses or transfer of the cause as he thinks fit.

(4) Where advertisement in a newspaper is required for the purpose of citation or service under this rule, a copy of the newspaper containing the advertisement shall be lodged with the sheriff clerk by the pursuer.

(5) Where display on the walls of court is required under paragraph (1)(b), the pursuer shall supply to the sheriff clerk for that purpose a certified copy of the instance and crave of the initial writ and any warrant of citation.

[1014]

5.7 Persons carrying on business under trading or descriptive name

(1) A person carrying on a business under a trading or descriptive name may sue or be sued in such trading or descriptive name alone; and an extract—

(a) of a decree pronounced in the sheriff court, or

(b) of a decree proceeding upon any deed, decree arbitral, bond, protest of a bill, promissory note or banker's note or upon any other obligation or document on which execution may proceed, recorded in the sheriff court books, …

[against such person under such trading or descriptive name shall be a valid] warrant for diligence against such person.

(2) An initial writ, decree, charge, warrant or any other order or writ following upon such initial writ or decree in a cause in which a person carrying on business under a trading or descriptive name sues or is sued in that name shall be served—

(a) at any place of business or office at which such business is carried on within the sheriffdom of the sheriff court in which the cause is brought; or

(b) where there is no place of business within that sheriffdom, at any place where such business is carried on (including the place of business or office of the clerk or secretary of any company, corporation or association or firm).

[1015]

NOTES

Para (1): words omitted revoked and words in square brackets substituted by the Act of Sederunt (Sheriff Court Ordinary Cause Rules Amendment) (Miscellaneous) 1996, SI 1996/2445, r 3(1), (7).

5.8 Endorsation unnecessary

An initial writ, decree, charge, warrant or any other order or writ following upon such initial writ or decree may be served, enforced or otherwise lawfully executed anywhere in Scotland without endorsation by a sheriff clerk; and, if executed by a sheriff officer, may be so executed by a sheriff officer of the court which granted it or by a sheriff officer of the sheriff court district in which it is to be executed.

[1016]

5.9 Re-service

Where it appears to the sheriff that there has been any failure or irregularity in citation or service on a person, he may order the pursuer to re-serve the initial writ on such conditions as he thinks fit.

[1017]

5.10 No objection to regularity of citation, service or intimation

(1) A person who appears in a cause shall not be entitled to state any objection to the regularity of the execution of citation, service or intimation on him; and his appearance shall remedy any defect in such citation, service or intimation.

(2) Nothing in paragraph (1) shall preclude a party from pleading that the court has no jurisdiction.

[1018]

CHAPTER 7
UNDEFENDED CAUSES

7.2 Minute for granting of decree without attendance

(1) Subject to the following paragraphs, where the defender—

(a) does not lodge a notice of intention to defend,

(b) does not lodge an application for a time to pay direction under the Debtors (Scotland) Act 1987,

(c) has lodged such an application for a time to pay direction and the pursuer does not object to the application or to any recall or restriction of an arrestment sought in the application,

the sheriff may, on the pursuer endorsing a minute for decree on the initial writ, at any time after the expiry of the period for lodging that notice or application, grant decree in absence or other order in terms of the minute so endorsed without requiring the attendance of the pursuer in court.

(2) The sheriff shall not grant decree under paragraph (1)

(a) unless it appears ex facie of the initial writ that a ground of jurisdiction exists under the Civil Jurisdiction and Judgments Act 1982 where that Act applies; and

(b) the cause is not a cause—

(i) in which decree may not be granted without evidence;

(ii) to which paragraph (4) applies; or

(iii) to which rule 33.31 (procedure in undefended family action for a section 11 order) applies.

(3) Where a defender is domiciled in another part of the United Kingdom or in another Contracting State, the sheriff shall not grant decree in absence until it has been shown that the defender has been able to receive the initial writ in sufficient time to arrange for his defence or that all necessary steps have been taken to that end; and for the purposes of this paragraph—

(a) the question whether a person is domiciled in another part of the United Kingdom shall be determined in accordance with sections 41 and 42 of the Civil Jurisdiction and Judgments Act 1982;

(b) the question whether a person is domiciled in another Contracting State shall be determined in accordance with Article 52 of [the Convention in] Schedule 1 or 3C to that Act; and

(c) the term "Contracting State" has the meaning assigned in section 1 of that Act.

(4) Where an initial writ has been served in a country to which the Hague Convention on the Service Abroad of Judicial and Extra-Judicial Documents in [Civil or Commercial] Matters dated 15th November 1965 applies, decree shall not be granted until it is established to the satisfaction of the sheriff that the requirements of Article 15 of that Convention have been complied with.

[1019]

NOTES

Para (3): words in square brackets in sub-para (b) inserted by the Act of Sederunt (Sheriff Court Ordinary Cause Rules Amendment) (Miscellaneous) 1996, SI 1996/2445, r 3(1), (8)(a).

Para (4): words in square brackets substituted by SI 1996/2445, r 3(1), (8)(b).

CHAPTER 8
REPONING

8.1 Reponing

(1) In any cause other than—

(a) a cause mentioned in rule 33.1(1)(a) to (h) [(n) or (o)] (certain family actions), or

[(aa) a cause mentioned in rule 33A.1(a), (b) or (f) (certain civil partnership actions)]

(b) a cause to which Chapter 37 (causes under the Presumption of death (Scotland) Act 1977) applies,

the defender [or any party with a statutory title or interest] may apply to be reponed by lodging with the sheriff clerk, before implement in full of a decree in absence, a reponing note setting out his proposed defence [or the proposed order or direction,] and explaining his failure to appear.

(2) A copy of the note lodged under paragraph (1) shall be served on the pursuer [and any other party].

(3) The sheriff may, on considering the reponing note, recall the decree so far as not implemented subject to such order as to expenses as he thinks fit; and the cause shall thereafter proceed as if[—

(a)] the defender had lodged a notice of intention to defend and the period of notice had expired on the date on which the decree in absence was recalled[; or

(b) the party seeking the order or direction had lodged the appropriate application on the date when the decree was recalled]

(4) A reponing note, when duly lodged with the sheriff clerk and served upon the pursuer [and any other party], shall have effect to sist diligence.

[(4A) Where an initial writ has been served on a defender furth of the United Kingdom under rule 5.5(1)(b) (service on persons furth of Scotland) and decree in absence has been pronounced against him as a result of his failure to enter appearance, the court may, on the defender applying to be reponed in accordance with paragraph (1) above, recall the decree and allow defences to be received if—

(a) without fault on his part, he did not have knowledge of the initial writ in sufficient time to defend;

(b) he has disclosed a prima facie defence to the action on the merits; and

(c) the reponing note is lodged within a reasonable time after he had knowledge of the decree or in any event before the expiry of one year from the date of decree.]

(5) Any interlocutor or order recalling, or incidental to the recall of, a decree in absence shall be final and not subject to appeal.

[1020]

NOTES

Para (1): in sub-para (a) words in square brackets inserted and sub-para (aa) inserted by the Act of Sederunt (Ordinary Cause Rules) Amendment (Family Law (Scotland) Act 2006 etc) 2006, SSI 2006/207, r 2(1), (5); words in second and third pairs of square brackets inserted by the Act of Sederunt (Ordinary Cause, Summary Application, Summary Cause and Small Claim Rules) Amendment (Miscellaneous) 2004, SSI 2004/197, r 2(1), (5)(a).

Paras (2)–(4): words in square brackets inserted by SSI 2004/197, r 2(1), (5)(b)–(d).

Para (4A): inserted by the Act of Sederunt (Sheriff Court Ordinary Cause Rules Amendment) (Miscellaneous) 2000, SSI 2000/239, r 3(1), (2).

CHAPTER 28
RECOVERY OF EVIDENCE

28.1 Application and interpretation of this Chapter

(1) This Chapter applies to the recovery of any evidence in a cause depending before the sheriff.

(2) In this Chapter, "the Act of 1972" means the Administration of Justice (Scotland) Act 1972.

[1021]

28.2 Application for commission and diligence for recovery of documents or for orders under section 1 of the Act of 1972

(1) An application by a party for—

PART II CIVIL PROCEDURE RULES

(a) a commission and diligence for the recovery of a document, or
(b) an order under section 1 of the Act of 1972

shall be made by motion.

(2) At the time of lodging a motion under paragraph (1), a specification of—

(a) the document or other property sought to be inspected, photographed, preserved, taken into custody, detained, produced, recovered, sampled or experimented on or with, as the case may be, or
(b) the matter in respect of which information is sought as to the identity of a person who might be a witness or a defender,

shall be lodged in process.

[(3) A copy of the specification lodged under paragraph (2) and the motion made under paragraph (1) shall be intimated by the applicant to –

(a) every other party;
(b) in respect of an application under section 1(1) of the Act of 1972, any third party haver; and
(c) where necessary, the Lord Advocate.]

(4) Where the sheriff grants a motion made under paragraph (1) in whole or in part, he may order the applicant to find caution or give such other security as he thinks fit.

(5) The Lord Advocate may appear at the hearing of any motion under paragraph (1). **[1022]**

NOTES

Para (3): substituted by the Act of Sederunt (Sheriff Court Ordinary Cause Rules Amendment) (Miscellaneous) 1996, SI 1996/2445, r 3(1), (32).

28.3 Optional procedure before executing commission and diligence

(1) The party who has obtained a commission and diligence for the recovery of a document on an application made under rule 28.2(1)(a), may at any time before executing it against a haver, serve on the haver an order in Form G11 (in this rule referred to as "the order"); and if so, the provisions of this rule shall apply.

(2) The order [and a copy of the specification referred to in rule 28.2(2) as approved by the court] shall be served on the haver or his known solicitor and shall be complied with by the haver in the manner and within the period specified in the order.

(3) Not later than the day after the date on which the order, [the certificate appended to Form G11] and any document is received by the sheriff clerk from a haver, he shall intimate that fact to each party.

(4) No party, other than the party who served the order, may uplift such a document until after the expiry of 7 days after the date of intimation under paragraph (3).

(5) Where the party who served the order fails to uplift such a document within 7 days after the date of intimation under paragraph (3), the sheriff clerk shall intimate that failure to every other party.

(6) Where no party has uplifted such a document within 14 days after the date of intimation under paragraph (5), the sheriff clerk shall return it to the haver who delivered it to him.

(7) Where a party who has uplifted such a document does not wish to lodge it, he shall return it to the sheriff clerk who shall—

(a) intimate the return of the document to every other party; and
(b) if no other party uplifts the document within 14 days after the date of intimation, return it to the haver.

(8) If the party who served the order is not satisfied—

(a) that full compliance has been made with the order, or
(b) that adequate reasons for non-compliance have been given,

he may execute the commission and diligence under rule 28.4.

(9) Where an extract from a book of any description (whether the extract is certified or not) is produced under the order, the sheriff may, on the motion of the party who served the order, direct that that party shall be allowed to inspect the book and take copies of any entries falling within the specification.

(10) Where any question of confidentiality arises in relation to a book directed to be inspected under paragraph (9), the inspection shall be made, and any copies shall be taken, at the sight of the commissioner appointed in the interlocutor granting the commission and diligence.

(11) The sheriff may, on cause shown, order the production of any book (not being a banker's book or book of public record) containing entries falling under a specification, notwithstanding the production of a certified extract [from that book].

[1023]

NOTES

Paras (2), (11): words in square brackets inserted by the Act of Sederunt (Sheriff Court Ordinary Cause Rules Amendment) (Miscellaneous) 1996, SI 1996/2445, r 3(1), (33)(a), (c).

Para (3): words in square brackets substituted by SI 1996/2445, r 3(1), (33)(b).

28.4 Execution of commission and diligence for recovery of documents

(1) The party who seeks to execute a commission and diligence for recovery of a document obtained on an application made under rule 28.2(1)(a) shall—

(a) provide the commissioner with a copy of the specification, a copy of the pleadings (including any adjustments and amendments) and a certified copy of the interlocutor of his appointment; and

(b) instruct the clerk and any shorthand writer considered necessary by the commissioner or any party; and

(c) be responsible for the fees of the commissioner and his clerk, and of any shorthand writer.

(2) The commissioner shall, in consultation with the parties, fix a diet for the execution of the commission.

(3) The interlocutor granting such a commission and diligence shall be sufficient authority for citing a haver to appear before the commissioner.

(4) A citation in Form G13 shall be served on the haver with a copy of the specification and, where necessary for a proper understanding of the specification, a copy of the pleadings (including any adjustments and amendments)[; and the party citing the haver shall lodge a certificate of citation in Form G12].

(5) The parties and the haver shall be entitled to be represented by a solicitor or person having a right of audience before the sheriff at the execution of the commission.

(6) At the commission, the commissioner shall—

(a) administer the oath de fideli administratione to any [clerk and any] shorthand writer appointed for the commission; and

(b) administer to the haver the oath in Form G14, or, where the haver elects to affirm, the affirmation in Form G15.

(7) The report of the execution of the commission and diligence, any document recovered and an inventory of that document, shall be sent by the commissioner to the sheriff clerk.

(8) Not later than the day after the date on which such a report, document and inventory, if any, are received by the sheriff clerk, he shall intimate to the parties that he has received them.

(9) No party, other than the party who served the order, may uplift such a document until after the expiry of 7 days after the date of intimation under paragraph (8).

(10) Where the party who served the order fails to uplift such a document within 7 days after the date of intimation under paragraph (8), the sheriff clerk shall intimate that failure to every other party.

(11) Where no party has uplifted such a document within 14 days after the date of intimation under paragraph (10), the sheriff clerk shall return it to the haver.

(12) Where a party who has uplifted such a document does not wish to lodge it, he shall return it to the sheriff clerk who shall—

(a) intimate the return of the document to every other party; and

(b) if no other party uplifts the document within 14 days of the date of intimation, return it to the haver.

[1024]

NOTES

Paras (4), (6): words in square brackets inserted by the Act of Sederunt (Sheriff Court Ordinary Cause Rules Amendment) (Miscellaneous) 1996, SI 1996/2445, r 3(1), (34).

28.5 Execution of orders for production or recovery of documents or other property under section 1(1) of the Act of 1972

(1) An order under section 1(1) of the Act of 1972 for the production or recovery of a document or other property shall grant a commission and diligence for the production or recovery of that document or other property.

(2) Rules 28.3 (optional procedure before executing commission and diligence) and 28.4 (execution of commission and diligence for recovery of documents) shall apply to an order to which paragraph (1) applies as they apply to a commission and diligence for the recovery of a document.

[1025]

28.6 Execution of orders for inspection etc of documents or other property under section 1(1) of the Act of 1972

(1) An order under section 1(1) of the Act of 1972 for the inspection or photographing of a document or other property, the taking of samples or the carrying out of any experiment thereon or therewith, shall authorise and appoint a specified person to photograph, inspect, take samples of, or carry out any experiment on or with any such document or other property, as the case may be, subject to such conditions, if any, as the sheriff thinks fit.

(2) A certified copy of the interlocutor granting such an order shall be sufficient authority for the person specified to execute the order.

(3) When such an order is executed, the party who obtained the order shall serve on the haver a copy of the interlocutor granting it, a copy of the specification and, where necessary for a proper understanding of the specification, a copy of the pleadings (including any adjustments and amendments).

[1026]

28.7 Execution of orders for preservation etc of documents or other property under section 1(1) of the Act of 1972

(1) An order under section 1(1) of the Act of 1972 for the preservation, custody and detention of a document or other property shall grant a commission and diligence for the detention and custody of that document or other property.

(2) The party who has obtained an order under paragraph (1) shall—

- (a) provide the commissioner with a copy of the specification, a copy of the pleadings (including any adjustments and amendments) and a certified copy of the interlocutor of his appointment;
- (b) be responsible for the fees of the commissioner and his clerk; and
- (c) serve a copy of the order on the haver.

(3) The report of the execution of the commission and diligence, any document or other property taken by the commissioner and an inventory of such property, shall be sent by the commissioner to the sheriff clerk for the further order of the sheriff.

[1027]

28.8 Confidentiality

(1) Where confidentiality is claimed for any evidence sought to be recovered under any of the following rules, such evidence shall[, where practicable,] be enclosed in a sealed packet:—

28.3 (optional procedure before executing commission and diligence),
28.4 (execution of commission and diligence for recovery of documents),
28.5 (execution of orders for production or recovery of documents or other property under section 1(1) of the Act of 1972),
28.7

(2) A motion to have such a sealed packet opened up [or such recovery allowed] may be lodged by—

(a) the party who obtained the commission and diligence; or
(b) any other party after the date of intimation by the sheriff clerk under rule 28.3(5) or 28.4(10) (intimation of failure to uplift documents).

(3) In addition to complying with rule 15.2 (intimation of motions), the party lodging such a motion shall intimate the terms of the motion to the haver by post by the first class recorded delivery service.

(4) The person claiming confidentiality may oppose a motion made under paragraph (2).

[1028]

NOTES

Paras (1), (2): words in square brackets inserted by the Act of Sederunt (Sheriff Court Ordinary Cause Rules Amendment) (Miscellaneous) 1996, SI 1996/2445, r 3(1), (36).

28.9 Warrants for production of original documents from public records

(1) Where a party seeks to obtain from the keeper of any public record production of the original of any register or deed in his custody for the purposes of a cause, he shall apply to the sheriff by motion.

(2) Intimation of a motion under paragraph (1) shall be given to the keeper of the public record concerned at least 7 days before the motion is lodged.

(3) In relation to a public record kept by the Keeper of the Registers of Scotland or the Keeper of the Records of Scotland, where it appears to the sheriff that it is necessary for the ends of justice that a motion under this rule should be granted, he shall pronounce an interlocutor containing a certificate to that effect; and the party applying for production may apply by letter (enclosing a copy of the interlocutor duly certified by the sheriff clerk), addressed to the Deputy Principal Clerk of Session, for an order from the Court of Session authorising the Keeper of the Registers or the Keeper of the Records, as the case may be, to exhibit the original of any register or deed to the sheriff.

(4) The Deputy Principal Clerk of Session shall submit the application sent to him under paragraph (3) to the Lord Ordinary in chambers who, if satisfied, shall grant a warrant for production or exhibition of the original register or deed sought.

(5) A certified copy of the warrant granted under paragraph (4) shall be served on the keeper of the public record concerned.

(6) The expense of the production or exhibition of such an original register or deed shall be met, in the first instance, by the party who applied by motion under paragraph (1).

[1029]

28.10 Commissions for examination of witnesses

(1) This rule applies to a commission—

(a) to take the evidence of a witness who—
  (i) is resident beyond the jurisdiction of the court;
  (ii) although resident within the jurisdiction of the court, resides at some place remote from that court;
  (iii) by reason of age, infirmity or sickness, is unable to attend the diet of proof;
  …
(b) in respect of the evidence of a witness which is in danger of being lost, to take the evidence to lie in retentis[; or]
[(c) on special cause shown, to take evidence of a witness on a ground other than one mentioned in sub-paragraph (a) or (b).]

(2) An application by a party for a commission to examine a witness shall be made by motion; and that party shall specify in the motion the name and address of at least one proposed commissioner for approval and appointment by the sheriff.

(3) The interlocutor granting such a commission shall be sufficient authority for citing the witness to appear before the commissioner.

(4) At the commission, the commissioner shall—

(a) administer the oath de fideli administratione to any [clerk and any] shorthand writer appointed for the commission; and

(b) administer to the witness the oath in Form G14, or where the witness elects to affirm; the affirmation in Form G15.

(5) Where a commission is granted for the examination of a witness, the commission shall proceed without interrogatories unless, on cause shown, the sheriff otherwise directs.

[1030]

NOTES

Para (1): words omitted revoked, words in first pair of square brackets substituted and sub-para (c) added by the Act of Sederunt (Sheriff Court Ordinary Cause Rules Amendment) (Miscellaneous) 1996, SI 1996/2445, r 3(1), (37)(a).

Para (4): words in square brackets inserted by SI 1996/2445, r 3(1), (37)(b).

28.11 Commissions on interrogatories

(1) Where interrogatories have not been dispensed with, the party who obtained the commission to examine a witness under rule 28.10 shall lodge draft interrogatories in process.

(2) Any other party may lodge cross-interrogatories.

(3) The interrogatories and any cross-interrogatories, when adjusted, shall be extended and returned to the sheriff clerk for approval and the settlement of any dispute as to their contents by the sheriff.

(4) The party who has obtained the commission shall—

(a) provide the commissioner with a copy of the pleadings (including any adjustments and amendments), the approved interrogatories and any cross-interrogatories and a certified copy of the interlocutor of his appointment;

(b) instruct the clerk; and

(c) be responsible, in the first instance, for the fee of the commissioner and his clerk.

(5) The commissioner shall, in consultation with the parties, fix a diet for the execution of the commission to examine the witness.

(6) The executed interrogatories, any document produced by the witness and an inventory of that document, shall be sent by the commissioner to the sheriff clerk.

(7) Not later than the day after the date on which the executed interrogatories, any document and an inventory of that document, are received by the sheriff clerk, he shall intimate to each party that he has received them.

(8) The party who obtained the commission to examine the witness shall lodge in process—

(a) the report of the commission; and

(b) the executed interrogatories and any cross-interrogatories.

[1031]

28.12 Commissions without interrogatories

(1) Where interrogatories have been dispensed with, the party who has obtained a commission to examine a witness under rule 28.10 shall—

(a) provide the commissioner with a copy of the pleadings (including any adjustments and amendments) and a certified copy of the interlocutor of his appointment;

(b) fix a diet for the execution of the commission in consultation with the commissioner and every other party;

(c) instruct the clerk and any shorthand writer; and

(d) be responsible for the fees of the commissioner, his clerk and any shorthand writer.

(2) All parties shall be entitled to be present and represented at the execution of the commission.

(3) The report of the execution of the commission, any document produced by the witness and an inventory of that document, shall be sent by the commissioner to the sheriff clerk.

(4) Not later than the day after the date on which such a report, any document and an inventory of that document are received by the sheriff clerk, he shall intimate to each party that he has received them.

(5) The party who obtained the commission to examine the witness shall lodge the report in process.

[1032]

28.13 Evidence taken on commission

(1) Subject to the following paragraphs of this rule and to all questions of relevancy and admissibility, evidence taken on commission under rule 28.11 or 28.12 may be used as evidence at any proof of the cause.

(2) Any party may object to the use of such evidence at a proof; and the objection shall be determined by the sheriff.

(3) Such evidence shall not be used at a proof if the witness becomes available to attend the diet of proof.

(4) A party may use such evidence in accordance with the preceding paragraphs of this rule not-withstanding that it was obtained at the instance of another party.

[1033]

28.14 Letters of request

(1) [Subject to paragraph (7), this] rule applies to an application for a letter of request to a court or tribunal outside Scotland to obtain evidence of the kind specified in paragraph (2), being evidence obtainable within the jurisdiction of that court or tribunal, for the purposes of a cause depending before the sheriff.

(2) An application to which paragraph (1) applies may be made in relation to a request—

(a) for the examination of a witness[,]

(b) for the inspection, photographing, preservation, custody, detention, production or recovery of, or the taking of samples of, or the carrying out of any experiment on or with, a document or other property, as the case may be[,]

[(c) for the medical examination of any person,

(d) for the taking and testing of samples of blood from any person, or

(e) for any other order for obtaining evidence,

for which an order could be obtained from the sheriff.]

(3) Such an application shall be made by minute in Form G16 together with a proposed letter of request in Form G17.

(4) It shall be a condition of granting a letter of request that any solicitor for the applicant[, or a party litigant, as the case may be, shall be personally liable, in the first instance,] for the whole expenses which may become due and payable in respect of the letter of request to the court or tribunal obtaining the evidence and to any witness who may be examined for the purpose; and he shall consign into court such sum in respect of such expenses as the sheriff thinks fit.

(5) Unless the court or tribunal to which a letter of request is addressed is a court or tribunal in a country or territory—

(a) where English is an official language, or

(b) in relation to which the sheriff clerk certifies that no translation is required,

then the applicant shall, before the issue of the letter of request, lodge in process a translation of that letter and any interrogatories and cross-interrogatories into the official language of that court or tribunal.

(6) The letter of request when issued, any interrogatories and cross-interrogatories adjusted as required by rule 28.11 and the translations (if any), shall be forwarded by the sheriff clerk to the Foreign and Commonwealth Office or to such person and in such manner as the sheriff may direct.

[(7) This rule does not apply to any request for the taking of evidence under Council Regulation (EC) No 1206/2001 of 28th May 2001 on cooperation between the courts of the Member States in the taking of evidence in civil or commercial matters.]

[1034]

NOTES

Para (1): words in square brackets substituted by the Act of Sederunt (Taking of Evidence in the European Community) 2003, SSI 2003/601, r 4(1), (2)(a).

Para (2): commas in square brackets substituted and words in third pair of square brackets added by the Act of Sederunt (Sheriff Court Ordinary Cause Rules Amendment) (Miscellaneous) 1996, SI 1996/2445, r 3(1), (38)(a).

Para (4): words in square brackets inserted by SI 1996/2445, r 3(1), (38)(b).

Para (7): added by SSI 2003/601, r 4(1), (2)(b).

[28.14A Taking of evidence in the European Community

(1) This rule applies to any request—

(a) for the competent court of another Member State to take evidence under Article 1.1(a) of the Council Regulation; or

(b) that the court shall take evidence directly in another Member State under Article 1.1(b) of the Council Regulation.

(2) An application for a request under paragraph (1) shall be made by minute in Form G16, together with the proposed request in form A or I (as the case may be) in the Annex to the Council Regulation.

(3) In this rule, "the Council Regulation" means Council Regulation (EC) No 1206/2001 of 28th May 2001 on cooperation between the courts of the Member States in the taking of evidence in civil or commercial matters.]

[1035]

NOTES

Commencement: 1 January 2004.

Inserted by the Act of Sederunt (Taking of Evidence in the European Community) 2003, SSI 2003/601, r 4(1), (3).

28.15 Citation of witnesses and havers

The following rules shall apply to the citation of a witness or haver to a commission under this Chapter as they apply to the citation of a witness for a proof:—

rule 29.7 (citation of witnesses), except paragraph (4),
rule 29.9 (second diligence against a witness),
rule 29.10 (failure of witness to attend).

[1036]

CHAPTER 30
DECREES, EXTRACTS AND EXECUTION

30. 3 Decrees for payment in foreign currency

(1) Where decree has been granted for payment of a sum of money in a foreign currency or the sterling equivalent, a party requesting extract of the decree shall do so by minute endorsed on or annexed to the initial writ stating the rate of exchange prevailing on the date of the decree sought to be extracted or the date, or within 3 days before the date, on which the extract is ordered, and the sterling equivalent at that rate for the principal sum and interest decerned for.

(2) A certificate in Form G18, from the Bank of England or a bank which is an institution authorised under the Banking Act 1987 certifying the rate of exchange and the sterling equivalent shall be lodged with the minute requesting extract of the decree.

(3) The extract decree issued by the sheriff clerk shall mention any certificate referred to in paragraph (2).

[1037]

[CHAPTER 40
COMMERCIAL ACTIONS

40.1 Application and interpretation of this Chapter

(1) This Chapter applies to a commercial action.

(2) In this Chapter—

(a) "commercial action" means-an action arising out of, or concerned with, any transaction or dispute of a commercial or business nature including, but not limited to, actions relating to—

(i) the construction of a commercial document;
(ii) the sale or hire purchase of goods;
(iii) the export or import of merchandise;
(iv) the carriage of goods by land, air or sea;
(v) insurance;
(vi) banking;
(vii) the provision of services;
(viii) a building, engineering or construction contract; or
(ix) a commercial lease; and

(b) "commercial action" does not include an action in relation to consumer credit transactions.

(3) A commercial action may be raised only in a sheriff court where the Sheriff Principal for the sheriffdom has directed that the procedure should be available.]

[1038]

NOTES

Commencement: 1 March 2001.
Chapter 40 (rr 40.1–17) added by the Act of Sederunt (Ordinary Cause Rules) Amendment (Commercial Actions) 2001, SSI 2001/8, para 2(1), (5).

[40.2 Proceedings before a nominated sheriff

All proceedings in a commercial action shall be brought before—

(a) a sheriff of the sheriffdom nominated by the Sheriff Principal; or
(b) where a nominated sheriff is not available, any other sheriff of the sheriffdom.]

[1039]

NOTES

Commencement: 1 March 2001.
Added as noted to r 40.1 at **[1038]**.

[40.3 Procedure in commercial actions

(1) In a commercial action the sheriff may make such order as he thinks fit for the progress of the case in so far as not inconsistent with the provisions in this Chapter.

(2) Where any hearing is continued, the reason for such continuation shall be recorded in the interlocutor.]

[1040]

NOTES

Commencement: 1 March 2001.
Added as noted to r 40.1 at **[1038]**.

[40.4 Election of procedure for commercial actions

The pursuer may elect to adopt the procedure in this Chapter by bringing an action in Form G1A.]

[1041]

NOTES

Commencement: 1 March 2001.
Added as noted to r 40.1 at **[1038]**.

[40.5 Transfer of action to be a commercial action

(1) In an action within the meaning of rule 40.1(2) in which the pursuer has not made an election under rule 40.4, any party may apply by motion at any time to have the action appointed to be a commercial action.

(2) An interlocutor granted under paragraph (1) shall include a direction as to further procedure.]

[1042]

PART II CIVIL PROCEDURE RULES

NOTES

Commencement: 1 March 2001.
Added as noted to r 40.1 at **[1038]**.

[40.6 Appointment of a commercial action as an ordinary cause

(1) At any time before, or at the Case Management Conference, the sheriff shall appoint a commercial action to proceed as an ordinary cause—

(a) on the motion of a party where—

(i) detailed pleadings are required to enable justice to be done between the parties; or

(ii) any other circumstances warrant such an order being made; or

(b) on the joint motion of parties.

(2) If a motion to appoint a commercial action to proceed as an ordinary action is refused, no subsequent motion to appoint the action to proceed as an ordinary cause shall be considered except on a material change of circumstances.

(3) Where the sheriff orders that a commercial action shall proceed as an ordinary cause the interlocutor granting such shall prescribe—

(a) a period of adjustment, if appropriate; and

(b) the date, time and place for any options hearing fixed.

(4) In determining what order to make in deciding that a commercial action proceed as an ordinary cause the sheriff shall have regard to the periods prescribed in rule 9.2.]

[1043]

NOTES

Commencement: 1 March 2001.
Added as noted to r 40.1 at **[1038]**.

[40.7 Special requirements for initial writ in a commercial action

(1) Where the construction of a document is the only matter in dispute no pleadings or pleas-in-law require to be included in the initial writ.

(2) There shall be appended to an initial writ in Form G1A a list of the documents founded on or adopted as incorporated in the initial writ.]

[1044]

NOTES

Commencement: 1 March 2001.
Added as noted to r 40.1 at **[1038]**.

[40.8 Notice of Intention to Defend

(1) Where the defender intends to—

(a) challenge the jurisdiction of the court;

(b) state a defence; or

(c) make a counterclaim,

he shall, before the expiry of the period of notice lodge with the sheriff clerk a notice of intention to defend in Form O7 and shall, at the same time, send a copy to the pursuer.

(2) The lodging of a notice of intention to defend shall not imply acceptance of the jurisdiction of the court.]

[1045]

NOTES

Commencement: 1 March 2001.
Added as noted to r 40.1 at **[1038]**.

[40.9 Defences

(1) Where a notice of intention to defend has been lodged, the defender shall lodge defences within 7 days after the expiry of the period of notice.

(2) There shall be appended to the defences a list of the documents founded on or adopted as incorporated in the defences.

(3) Subject to the requirement that each article of condescendence in the initial writ need not be admitted or denied, defences shall be in the form of answers that allow the extent of the dispute to be identified and shall have appended a note of the pleas in law of the defender.]

[1046]

NOTES

Commencement: 1 March 2001.
Added as noted to r 40.1 at **[1038]**.

[40.10 Fixing date for Case Management Conference

(1) On the lodging of defences, the sheriff clerk shall fix a date and time for a Case Management Conference, which date shall be on the first suitable courtday occurring not sooner than 14 days, nor later than 28 days after the date of expiry of the period of notice.

(2) On fixing the date for the Case Management Conference, the sheriff clerk shall—

(a) forthwith intimate to the parties the date and time of the Case Management Conference; and

(b) prepare and sign an interlocutor recording that information.

(3) The fixing of the date of the Case Management Conference shall not affect the right of a party to make application by motion, to the court.]

[1047]

NOTES

Commencement: 1 March 2001.
Added as noted to r 40.1 at **[1038]**.

[40.11 Applications for summary decree in a commercial action

Where a pursuer, in terms of rule 17.2(1) (applications for summary decree), or a defender in terms of rule 17.3(1) (application of summary decree to counterclaims), applies for summary decree in a commercial action, the period of notice mentioned in rule 17.2(3) shall be 48 hours.]

[1048]

NOTES

Commencement: 1 March 2001.
Added as noted to r 40.1 at **[1038]**.

[40.12 Case Management Conference

(1) At the Case Management Conference in a commercial action the sheriff shall seek to secure the expeditious resolution of the action.

(2) Parties shall be prepared to provide such information as the sheriff may require to determine—

(a) whether, and to what extent, further specification of the claim and defences is required; and

(b) the orders to make to ensure the expeditious resolution of the action.

(3) The orders the sheriff may make in terms of paragraph 2(b) may include but shall not be limited to—

(a) the lodging of written pleadings by any party to the action which may be restricted to particular issues;

(b) the lodging of a statement of facts by any party which may be restricted to particular issues;

(c) allowing an amendment by a party to his pleadings;

(d) disclosure of the identity of witnesses and the existence and nature of documents relating to the action or authority to recover documents either generally or specifically;

(e) the lodging of documents constituting, evidencing or relating to the subject matter of the action or any invoices, correspondence or similar documents;

PART II CIVIL PROCEDURE RULES

(f) the exchanging of lists of witnesses;
(g) the lodging of reports of skilled persons or witness statements;
(h) the lodging of affidavits concerned with any of the issues in the action;
(i) the lodging of notes of arguments setting out the basis of any preliminary plea;
(j) fixing a debate or proof, with or without any further preliminary procedure, to determine the action or any particular aspect thereof;
(k) the lodging of joint minutes of admission or agreement;
(l) recording admissions made on the basis of information produced; or
(m) any order which the sheriff thinks will result in the speedy resolution of the action (including the use of alternative dispute resolution), or requiring the attendance of parties in person at any subsequent hearing.

(4) In making any order in terms of paragraph (3) the sheriff may fix a period within which such order shall be complied with.

(5) The sheriff may continue the Case Management Conference to a specified date where he considers it necessary to do so—
(a) to allow any order made in terms of paragraph (3) to be complied with; or
(b) to advance the possibility of resolution of the action.

(6) Where the sheriff makes an order in terms of paragraph (3) he may ordain the pursuer to—
(a) make up a record; and
(b) lodge that record in process,
within such period as he thinks fit.]

[1049]

NOTES

Commencement: 1 March 2001.
Added as noted to r 40.1 at **[1038]**.

[40.13 Lodging of productions

Prior to any proof or other hearing at which the documents listed in terms of rules 40.7(2) and 40.9(2) are to be referred to parties shall, in addition to lodging the productions in terms of rule 21.1, prepare, for the use of the sheriff, a working bundle in which the documents are arranged chronologically or in another appropriate order.]

[1050]

NOTES

Commencement: 1 March 2001.
Added as noted to r 40.1 at **[1038]**.

[40.14 Hearing for further procedure

At any time before final judgement, the sheriff may—
(a) of his own motion or on the motion of any party, fix a hearing for further procedure; and
(b) make such other order as he thinks fit.]

[1051]

NOTES

Commencement: 1 March 2001.
Added as noted to r 40.1 at **[1038]**.

[40.15 Failure to comply with rule or order of sheriff

Any failure by a party to comply timeously with a provision in this Chapter or any order made by the sheriff in a commercial action shall entitle the sheriff, of his own motion—
(a) to refuse to extend any period for compliance with a provision in these Rules or an order of the court;
(b) to dismiss the action or counterclaim, as the case may be, in whole or in part;
(c) to grant decree in respect of all or any of the craves of the initial writ or counterclaim, as the case may be; or
(d) to make an award of expenses,

as he thinks fit.]

[1052]

NOTES

Commencement: 1 March 2001.
Added as noted to r 40.1 at **[1038]**.

[40.16 Determination of action

It shall be open to the sheriff, at the end of any hearing, to restrict any interlocutor to a finding.]

[1053]

NOTES

Commencement: 1 March 2001.
Added as noted to r 40.1 at **[1038]**.

[40.17 Parts of Process

All parts of process lodged in a commercial action shall be clearly marked "Commercial Action".]

[1054]

NOTES

Commencement: 1 March 2001.
Added as noted to r 40.1 at **[1038]**.

APPENDIX 1
FORMS

[FORM G16
FORM OF MINUTE FOR LETTER OF REQUEST

Rules 28.14(3), 28.14A(2)

Form of minute for [letter of request] [taking of evidence in the European Community]*

SHERIFFDOM OF (*insert name of sheriffdom*)

AT (*insert place of sheriff court*)

MINUTE FOR PURSUER [DEFENDER]*

in the cause

[AB] (*insert designation and address*)

Pursuer

against

[CD] (*insert designation and address*)

Defender

Court ref no

The Minuter states that the evidence specified in the attached [letter of request] [Form A] [Form I]* is required for the purpose of these proceedings and craves the court to issue [a letter of request] [that Form]* to (*specify in the case of a letter of request the central or other appropriate authority of the country or territory in which the evidence is to be obtained, and in the case of Form A or I the applicable court, tribunal, central body or competent authority*) to obtain the evidence specified.

Date (*insert date*) Signed (*insert designation and address*)

* *delete as applicable]*

[1055]

NOTES
Commencement: 1 January 2004.
Substituted by the Act of Sederunt (Taking of Evidence in the European Community) 2003, SSI 2003/601, para 4(1), (4), Sch 1.

ACT OF SEDERUNT (RULES OF THE COURT OF SESSION 1994) 1994

(SI 1994/1443)

NOTES
Made: 31 May 1994.
Authority: Court of Session Act 1988, s 5.
Commencement: 5 September 1994.
Only the rules relevant to this work are reproduced here.

1 Citation and commencement

(1) This Act of Sederunt may be cited as the Act of Sederunt (Rules of the Court of Session 1994) 1994 and shall come into force on 5th September 1994.

(2) This Act of Sederunt shall be inserted in the Books of Sederunt.

[1056]

2 Rules of the Court of Session

The provisions of Schedule 2 to this Act of Sederunt shall have effect for the purpose of providing new rules for the Court of Session.

[1057]

3 (*Relates to amendments, repeals, revocations and savings.*)

SCHEDULE 2
THE RULES OF THE COURT OF SESSION 1994

Paragraph 2

ARRANGEMENT OF THE RULES

CHAPTER 1
CITATION, APPLICATION, ETC

CHAPTER 2
RELIEF FROM COMPLIANCE WITH RULES

CHAPTER 13
SUMMONSES, NOTICE, WARRANTS AND CALLING

CHAPTER 16
SERVICE, INTIMATION AND DILIGENCE

PART ONE
SERVICE AND INTIMATION

PART TWO
DILIGENCE

CHAPTER 19
DECREES IN ABSENCE

CHAPTER 35
RECOVERY OF EVIDENCE

PART II

CHAPTER 47
COMMERCIAL ACTIONS

CHAPTER 59
APPLICATIONS FOR LETTERS

CHAPTER 62
RECOGNITION, REGISTRATION AND ENFORCEMENT OF FOREIGN JUDGMENTS, ETC

PART I
GENERAL PROVISIONS

PART II
REGISTRATION AND ENFORCEMENT UNDER THE ADMINISTRATION OF JUSTICE ACT 1920 AND THE FOREIGN JUDGMENTS (RECIPROCAL ENFORCEMENT) ACT 1933

PART III
REGISTRATION OF AWARDS UNDER THE ARBITRATION (INTERNATIONAL INVESTMENT DISPUTES) ACT 1966

PART IV
EUROPEAN COMMUNITY JUDGMENTS

PART V
RECOGNITION AND ENFORCEMENT OF JUDGMENTS UNDER THE CIVIL JURISDICTION AND JUDGMENTS ACT 1982 OR UNDER COUNCIL REGULATION (EC) NO 44/2001 OF 22ND DECEMBER 2001

PART VI
REGISTRATION UNDER THE MERCHANT SHIPPING (LINER CONFERENCES) ACT 1982

PART VII
RECIPROCAL ENFORCEMENT OF ORDERS IN RELATION TO CONFISCATION OF PROCEEDS OF CRIME AND TO FORFEITURE OF PROPERTY USED IN CRIME

PART II

PART VIII
REGISTRATION OF AWARDS UNDER THE MULTILATERAL INVESTMENT GUARANTEE AGENCY ACT 1988

PART IX
RECOGNITION AND ENFORCEMENT OF ARBITRAL AWARDS UNDER THE MODEL LAW ON INTERNATIONAL COMMERCIAL ARBITRATION

PART X
RECOGNITION, REGISTRATION AND ENFORCEMENT OF MISCELLANEOUS DECISIONS

PART XI
REGISTRATION AND ENFORCEMENT OF JUDGMENTS UNDER COUNCIL REGULATION (EC) NO 2201/2003 OF 27 NOVEMBER 2003

PART XII
EUROPEAN ENFORCEMENT ORDERS

PART XIII
UNCITRAL MODEL LAW ON CROSS-BORDER INSOLVENCY

CHAPTER 64
APPLICATIONS UNDER SECTION 1 OF THE ADMINISTRATION OF JUSTICE (SCOTLAND) ACT 1972

CHAPTER 65
REFERENCES TO THE EUROPEAN COURT OF JUSTICE

CHAPTER 66
APPLICATIONS UNDER THE EVIDENCE (PROCEEDINGS IN OTHER JURISDICTIONS) ACT 1975

PART II

Preliminary

CHAPTER 1
CITATION, APPLICATION, [ETC]

NOTES

Chapter heading: word in square brackets substituted by the Act of Sederunt (Rules of the Court of Session Amendment No 5) (Miscellaneous) 1999, SI 1999/1386, r 2(1), (2)(a).

1.1 Citation

These Rules may be cited as the Rules of the Court of Session 1994.

[1058]

1.2 Application

These Rules apply to any cause whether initiated before or after the coming into force of these Rules.

[1059]

1.3 Interpretation etc

(1) In these Rules, unless the context otherwise requires—

"the Act of 1988" means the Court of Session Act 1988;

"act" means an order of the court which is extractable, other than a decree;

"agent", except in rule 16.2(2)(e) (service furth of United Kingdom by party's authorised agent) and rule 16.14(1) (arrestment of cargo), means a solicitor or person having a right to conduct the litigation;

"the Auditor" means the Auditor of the Court of Session;

"cause" means any proceedings;

"clerk of court" means the clerk of session acting as such;

"clerk of session" means a depute clerk of session or an assistant clerk of session, as the case may be;

"counsel" means a practising member of the Faculty of Advocates;

"depute clerk of session" means a depute clerk of session and justiciary;

"Deputy Principal Clerk" means the Deputy Principal Clerk of Session;

"document" has the meaning assigned to it in section 9 of the Civil Evidence (Scotland) Act 1988;

"the Extractor" means the Extractor of the Court of Session or the Extractor of the acts and decrees of the Teind Court, as the case may be;

"Keeper of the Records" means the Keeper of the Records of Scotland;

"Keeper of the Registers" means the Keeper of the Registers of Scotland;

"other person having a right of audience" means a person having a right of audience before the court by virtue of Part II of the Law Reform (Miscellaneous Provisions) (Scotland) Act 1990 (legal services) in respect of the category and nature of the cause in question;

"party" means a person who has entered appearance in an action or lodged a writ in the process of a cause (other than a minuter seeking leave to be sisted to a cause); and "parties" shall be construed accordingly;

"period of notice" means—

(a) in relation to service, or intimation on a warrant for intimation before calling, of a summons, the period determined in accordance with rule 13.4 (period of notice in summonses); and

(b) in relation to service of any other writ, intimation of a writ other than intimation referred to in sub-paragraph (a), or the period for lodging answers to a writ, the period determined in accordance with rule 14.6 (period of notice for lodging answers);

"person having a right to conduct the litigation" means a person having a right to conduct litigation by virtue of Part II of the Law Reform (Miscellaneous Provisions) (Scotland) Act 1990 in respect of the category and nature of the cause in question;

"Principal Clerk" means the Principal Clerk of Session and Justiciary;

"principal writ" means the writ by which a cause is initiated before the court;

"proof" includes proof before answer;

"rolls" means the lists of the business of the court issued from time to time by the Keeper of the Rolls;

"send" includes deliver; and "sent" shall be construed accordingly;

"step of process" means a document lodged in process other than a production;

"summons" includes the condescendence and pleas-in-law annexed to it;

"vacation judge" means a judge of the court sitting as such in vacation;

"writ" means summons, petition, note, application, appeal, minute, defences, answers, counter-claim, issue or counter-issue, as the case may be.

(2) For the purpose of these Rules—

(a) "affidavit" includes an affirmation and a statutory or other declaration; and

(b) an affidavit shall be sworn or affirmed before a notary public or any other competent authority.

(3) Where a power is conferred in these Rules on the Lord President to make directions, the power may be exercised in his absence by the Lord Justice-Clerk.

(4) Where a provision in these Rules imposes an obligation on a principal officer, the obligation may be performed by a clerk of session authorised by him or by another principal officer; and in this paragraph "principal officer" means the Principal Clerk, Deputy Principal Clerk, Deputy Principal Clerk (Administration), Keeper of the Rolls or Principal Extractor.

(5) Unless the context otherwise requires, where a provision in these Rules requires a party to intimate, give written intimation, or send a document, to another party, it shall be sufficient compliance with that provision if intimation is given or the document is sent, as the case may be, to the agent acting in the cause for that party.

(6) Unless the context otherwise requires, anything done or required to be done by a party under a provision in these Rules may be done by the agent for that party acting on his behalf.

(7) Where a provision in these Rules requires a document to be lodged in an office or department of the Office of Court within [or not later than] a specified period and the last day of that period is a day on which that office or department is closed, the period shall be extended to include the next day on which that office or department, as the case may be, is open or on such other day as may be specified in a notice published in the rolls.

(8) Unless the context otherwise requires, a reference to a specified Chapter, Part, rule or form is a reference to the Chapter, Part, rule, or the form in the appendix, so specified in these Rules; and a reference to a specified paragraph, sub-paragraph or head is a reference to that paragraph of the rule or form, that sub-paragraph of the paragraph or that head of the sub-paragraph, in which the reference occurs.

[1060]

NOTES

Para (7): words in square brackets inserted by the Act of Sederunt (Rules of the Court of Session Amendment No 5) (Family Actions and Miscellaneous) 1996, SI 1996/2587, r 2(1), (2).

1.4, 1.5 (*Relate to forms and the Advocate General.*)

CHAPTER 2
RELIEF FROM COMPLIANCE WITH RULES

2.1 Relief for failure to comply with rules

(1) The court may relieve a party from the consequences of a failure to comply with a provision in these Rules shown to be due to mistake, oversight or other excusable cause on such conditions, if any, as the court thinks fit.

(2) Where the court relieves a party from the consequences of a failure to comply with a provision in these Rules under paragraph (1), the court may pronounce such interlocutor as it thinks fit to enable the cause to proceed as if the failure to comply with the provision had not occurred.

[1061]

Initiation and progress of proceedings

CHAPTER 13
SUMMONSES, NOTICE, WARRANTS AND CALLING

13.1 Initiation of causes by summons

Subject to any other provision in these Rules, all causes originating in the court shall be commenced in the Outer House by summons.

[1062]

13.2 Form of summonses

(1) Subject to any other provision in these Rules, a summons shall be in Form 13.2-A.

(2) A conclusion in a summons shall be stated in accordance with the appropriate style, if any, in Form 13.2-B.

(3) Subject to rule 46.6(3) (no condescendence or pleas-in-law in ship collision actions), there shall be annexed to a summons—

(a) a statement, in the form of numbered articles of the condescendence, of the averments of fact which form the grounds of the claim; and

(b) appropriate pleas-in law.

(4) A condescendence shall include averments stating—

(a) in an action to which the Civil Jurisdiction and Judgments Act 1982 applies, the domicile of the defender (to be determined in accordance with the provisions of that Act) so far as known to the pursuer;

(b) the ground of jurisdiction of the court, unless jurisdiction would arise only if the defender prorogated the jurisdiction of the court without contesting jurisdiction;

(c) unless the court has exclusive jurisdiction, whether or not there is an agreement prorogating the jurisdiction of a court in another country; and

(d) whether or not there are proceedings involving the same cause of action in subsistence between the parties in a country to which the convention in Schedule 1 or 3C to the Civil Jurisdiction and Judgments Act 1982 applies and the date any such proceedings commenced.

(5) A summons may include warrants for diligence and intimation in so far as permitted under these Rules.

[1063]

13.3 Address of defender

In a summons, the pursuer shall—

(a) set out in the instance the known residence, registered office, other official address or place of business of the defender where he is to be served; or

(b) where that residence, office, address or place, as the case may be, is not known and cannot reasonably be ascertained, set out in the instance that the whereabouts of the defender are not known and aver in the condescendence what steps have been taken to ascertain his present whereabouts.

[1064]

13.4 Period of notice in summonses

(1) Subject to any other provision in these Rules, the period of notice in a summons shall be—

(a) in the case of service within Europe, 21 days from whichever is the later of the date of execution of service or the giving of intimation before calling on a warrant for intimation;

(b) in the case of service furth of Europe under rule 16.2(2) (d) or (e) (service by an huissier etcor personally), 21 days from whichever is the later of the date of execution of service or the giving of intimation before calling on a warrant for intimation;

(c) in the case of service furth of Europe other than under sub-paragraph (b), 42 days from whichever is the later of the date of execution of service or the giving of intimation before calling on a warrant for intimation; and

(d) in the case of service by advertisement under rule 16.5 (service where address of person is not known), other than in an action to which rule 49.12 (notice of family actions by advertisement) applies, 6 months from the date of publication of the advertisement.

(2) An application may be made by motion to shorten or extend the period of notice in a summons.

(3) Where a motion under paragraph (2) is made after signeting of the summons but before service—

(a) the summons shall be produced to the court; and

(b) the decision of the Lord Ordinary on the motion shall be final and not subject to review.

[1065]

13.5 Signeting

(1) A summons shall pass the signet.

(2) No summons shall bear any date but the date of signeting, which date shall be treated as the date of the summons.

(3) A summons shall be signeted and registered by a clerk of session acting under authority from the Principal Clerk (by virtue of a commission granted to him by the Keeper of the Signet).

(4) Subject to paragraph (5), a summons shall be presented to the General Department during its normal office hours for signeting and registration.

(5) In an emergency, a summons may be signeted and registered outwith the normal office hours.

[1066]

[13.6 Authority for service and intimation on signeting

When signeted, a summons shall be authority for—

(a) service on the defender designed in the instance;

(b) intimation of the summons on any person on whom intimation is required in these Rules where a warrant for that purpose has been inserted in the summons.]

[1067]

NOTES

Commencement: 10 November 2003.

Substituted, together with r 13.6A, for r 13.6 as originally enacted, by the Act of Sederunt (Rules of the Court of Session Amendment No 6) (Diligence on the Dependence) 2003, SSI 2003/537, r 2(1), (2).

[13.6A Authority for diligence etc before calling

(1) Before the calling of a summons, the pursuer may apply by motion for authority for—

(a) arrestment to found jurisdiction; or

(b) diligence by—

(i) inhibition on the dependence of the action;

(ii) arrestment on the dependence of the action where there is a conclusion for the payment of money;

(iii) arrestment in rem; or

(iv) dismantling a ship,

where a warrant in the appropriate form in Form 13.2-A has been inserted in the summons.

(2) Where a Lord Ordinary pronounces an interlocutor granting a motion under paragraph (1)—

(a) he shall record his interlocutor by signing the warrant in the summons; and

(b) the signed warrant shall be sufficient authority for execution of the arrestment to found jurisdiction or, as the case may be, the diligence.]

[1068]

NOTES

Commencement: 10 November 2003.

Substituted, together with r 13.6, as noted to r 13.6 at **[1067]**.

PART II

13.7 Service and intimation of summonses

(1) Where a summons is to be executed, a copy of the summons which has passed the signet shall be—

(a) served on the defender with a citation in Form 13.7 attached to it; and
(b) intimated to any person named in a warrant for intimation.

(2) Where service of a summons is not executed within a year and a day after the date of signeting, the instance shall fall.

[1069]

[13.8 Authority for intimation after signeting

Where a warrant for intimation referred to in rule 13.6(b) is not obtained when the summons is signeted, the pursuer may apply by motion for authority for intimation of the summons on any person on whom intimation is required in these Rules.]

[1070]

NOTES

Commencement: 10 November 2003.
Substituted, together with r 13.8A, for r 13.8 as originally enacted, by the Act of Sederunt (Rules of the Court of Session Amendment No 6) (Diligence on the Dependence) 2003, SSI 2003/537, r 2(1), (3).

[13.8A Authority for diligence etc after calling

(1) After the calling of a summons, a pursuer may apply by motion for authority for—

(a) arrestment to found jurisdiction; or
(b) diligence by—
  (i) inhibition on the dependence of the action;
  (ii) arrestment on the dependence of the action where there is a conclusion for the payment of money;
  (iii) arrestment in rem; or
  (iv) dismantling a ship,

(2) A certified copy of an interlocutor granting a motion under paragraph (1) shall be sufficient authority for execution of the arrestment to found jurisdiction or, as the case may be, the diligence.]

[1071]

NOTES

Commencement: 10 November 2003.
Substituted, together with r 13.8, as noted to r 13.8 at **[1070]**.

[13.9 Effect of authority for inhibition on the dependence

(1) Where a pursuer has been granted authority for inhibition on the dependence of an action, the signed warrant or, as the case may be, a certified copy of the interlocutor granting the motion under rule 13.8A—

(a) shall have the same effect as letters of inhibition;
(b) may be executed at the same time as the summons is served or at any time thereafter; and
(c) may be registered with a certificate of execution in the Register of Inhibitions and Adjudications.

(2) A notice of a certified copy of an interlocutor granting authority for inhibition under rule 13.8A may be registered under section 155 of the Titles to Land Consolidation (Scotland) Act 1868(a); and such registration shall have the same effect as registration of a notice under that section.]

[1072]

NOTES

Commencement: 10 November 2003.
Substituted by the Act of Sederunt (Rules of the Court of Session Amendment No 6) (Diligence on the Dependence) 2003, SSI 2003/537, r 2(1), (4).

[13.10 Recall etc of arrestment or inhibition

(1) An application by any person having an interest—

(a) to loose, restrict or recall an arrestment; or
(b) to recall, in whole or in part, an inhibition,

shall be made by motion.]

(2) Where the court grants a motion under paragraph (1), it may do so, on such conditions, if any, as to caution or other security and expenses it thinks fit.

(3) Where a motion under paragraph (1) is enrolled before calling of the summons, the pursuer shall produce the principal summons or a copy of it, with the certificate of execution of service of the arrest or inhibition, as the case may be.

[1073]

NOTES

Heading, para (1): substituted by the Act of Sederunt (Rules of the Court of Session Amendment No 6) (Diligence on the Dependence) 2003, SSI 2003/537, r 2(1), (5).

13.11 Movement of arrested property

(1) Any person having an interest may apply by motion for a warrant authorising the movement of a vessel or cargo which is the subject of an arrestment mentioned in [rule 13.6A].

(2) Where the court grants a warrant sought under paragraph (1), it may make such further order as it thinks fit to give effect to that warrant.

(3) A warrant granted on a motion under paragraph (1) shall be without prejudice to the validity and subsistence of the arrestment.

[1074]

NOTES

Para (1): words in square brackets substituted by the Act of Sederunt (Rules of the Court of Session Amendment No 6) (Diligence on the Dependence) 2003, SSI 2003/537, r 2(1), (6).

13.12 Intimation of actions relating to heritable property

(1) In an action relating to heritable property, it shall not be necessary to call a person as a defender by reason only of any interest he may have as the holder of a heritable security over the heritable property; but intimation of the summons shall be given to that person by notice of intimation in Form 13.12 attached to a copy of the summons.

(2) A warrant for intimation under paragraph (1) shall be inserted in the summons by the pursuer in the following terms:- "Warrant to intimate to (name and address) as a person who is believed to be a heritable creditor of the defender.".

(3) A person on whom intimation has been made under this rule may apply by motion for leave to be sisted as a party and to lodge defences.

[1075]

13.13 Calling

(1) A summons shall not be called earlier than the day on which the period of notice expires.

(2) A summons shall be lodged for calling not later than 12.30 pm on the second day before that on which it is to be called.

(3) A summons may be called—

(a) during session, on a sederunt day; or
(b) in vacation, on a calling day of which notice has been given in the rolls.

(4) A summons lodged for calling shall be accompanied by a typewritten slip containing the instance, subject to the following provisions:—

(a) where there is more than one pursuer or defender, the slip shall contain only the name and designation of the first pursuer or defender, as the case may be, followed by the words "and Another [or Others, as the case may be]"; and
(b) in naming and designing a pursuer or defender who is a body of persons (such as a trust or a partnership), whether individual members are also parties or not, it shall be sufficient to use the collective name of that body.

(5) The calling of a summons shall be published in the rolls on the date on which the summons calls.

(6) Where a summons has not called within a year and a day after the expiry of the period of notice, the instance shall fall.

[1076]

13.14 Protestation for not calling summons

(1) Where the pursuer does not lodge the summons for calling within 7 days after the date on which the period of notice expires, the defender, on production of the service copy summons, may apply by motion for an order ordaining the pursuer to lodge the summons for calling within 7 days, or such other period as the court thinks fit, after the date of the order.

(2) Where the court pronounces an interlocutor under paragraph (1), the defender shall serve a certified copy of that interlocutor on the pursuer.

(3) Where the pursuer fails to lodge the summons within the period ordered by the court under paragraph (1), the defender may apply by motion—

(a) for declarator that the instance has fallen;
(b) for recall of any diligence mentioned in rule 13.6(c) which has been executed; and
(c) for payment to the defender of his expenses of process under this rule.

(4) An interlocutor granting a motion under paragraph (3) shall be final and not subject to review.

[1077]

CHAPTER 16
SERVICE, INTIMATION AND DILIGENCE

PART ONE
SERVICE AND INTIMATION

16.1 Service and Intimation

(1) Subject to any other provision in these Rules or any other enactment, service of a document required under these Rules on a person shall be executed—

(a) in the case of an individual—
  (i) personally, by tendering the document and any citation or notice, as the case may be, to that individual;
  (ii) by leaving the document and any citation or notice, as the case may be, in the hands of a person, or failing which, depositing it, in a dwelling place where the person executing service, after due enquiry, has reasonable grounds for believing that that individual resides but is not available;
  (iii) by leaving the document and any citation or notice, as the case may be, in the hands of a person at, or depositing it in, a place of business where the person executing service, after due enquiry, has reasonable grounds for believing that that individual carries on business; or
  (iv) by posting the document and any citation or notice, as the case may be, to the known dwelling place of that individual;
(b) in the case of any other person—
  (i) by leaving the document and any citation or notice, as the case may be, in the hands of an individual at, or depositing it in, the registered office, other official address or a place of business, of that other person, in such a way that it is likely to come to the attention of that other person; or
  (ii) by posting the document and any citation or notice, as the case may be, to the registered office, other official address or a place of business, of that other person.

(2) Service of a principal writ on a person whose known residence is the same as that of the party on whose behalf service is to be executed shall be executed personally.

(3) Subject to paragraph (4), where service has been executed, the party on whose behalf service has been executed shall attach to the document served and lodge in process—

(a) a certificate of service as required by these Rules;
(b) a copy of any notice or advertisement ordered to be published; and
(c) a copy of any interlocutor ordering service of that document.

(4) In relation to a petition or note, where service has been executed by a petitioner or noter, he shall attach the documents required by paragraph (3)(a) and (b) to a copy of the petition or note, as the case may be, marked "Execution Copy" and certified a true copy.

[1078]

16.2 Service furth of United Kingdom

(1) Subject to any other enactment, this rule applies to service of a document on a person on whom service is to be executed in a country furth of the United Kingdom.

(2) Service under this rule may be executed by any of the following methods of service, if, and in a manner, permitted under a convention providing for service in that country or by the laws of that country:—

(a) by post to the known residence, registered office or place of business, as the case may be, of the person on whom service is to be executed;

(b) through the central, or other appropriate, authority of that country, at the request of the Secretary of State for Foreign and Commonwealth Affairs;

(c) through a British consular office in that country, at the request of the Secretary of State for Foreign and Commonwealth Affairs;

(d) by an huissier, other judicial officer or competent official of that country, at the request of a messenger-at-arms, a party or his agent; or

(e) personally by the party executing service or his authorised agent tendering the document and the citation (if any) to the person on whom service is to be executed.

(3) Where service is to be executed through a central, or other appropriate, authority, or through a British consular officer, at the request of the Secretary of State for Foreign and Commonwealth Affairs, the party executing service shall—

(a) send a copy of the document, with a request for service by the method indicated in the request, to the Secretary of State for Foreign and Commonwealth Affairs; and

(b) lodge in process a certificate signed by the authority which executed service stating that it has been, and the manner in which it was, served.

(4) Where service is to be executed by an huissier, other judicial officer or competent official at the request of a messenger-at-arms—

(a) the messenger-at-arms shall send a copy of the document with a request for service by the method indicated in the request to the official in the country in which service is to be executed; and

(b) the party on whose behalf service has been executed shall lodge in process a certificate of the official who executed service stating that it has been, and the manner in which it was, served.

(5) Where service has been executed personally by the party executing service or his authorised agent—

(a) the execution of service shall be witnessed by one witness who shall sign the certificate of service (which shall state his name, occupation and address); and

(b) the person who executed service shall complete a certificate of service in Form 16.2.

(6) Where service is executed by a method mentioned in paragraph (2)(a) or (e), the party executing service shall lodge in process a certificate by a person qualified in the law of the country, or a duly accredited representative of the country, in which service was executed stating that the method of service used is permitted by the law of that country.

[1079]

[16.2A Service under the Council Regulation

(1) In this rule—

"competent receiving agency" and "Member State" have the same meaning as in the Council Regulation; and

"Council Regulation" means Council Regulation (EC) No 1348/2000 on the service in the Member States of judicial and extrajudicial documents in civil or commercial matters.

(2) This rule applies to service of a document under the Council Regulation on a person on whom service is to be executed in a Member State other than the United Kingdom.

(3) Where a document is being served by a competent receiving authority under Article 7 of the Council Regulation, rule 16.6(1) (translations of documents) shall not apply.

(4) Where a document has been served by a competent receiving authority under Article 7 of the Council Regulation, the party executing service shall lodge the certificate of service mentioned in Article 10 of the Council Regulation.]

[1080]

NOTES

Commencement: 1 March 2004.

Inserted by the Act of Sederunt (Rules of the Court of Session Amendment) (Miscellaneous) 2004, SSI 2004/52, r 2(1), (3).

16.3 Service by messenger-at-arms

(1) Service by a method mentioned in rule 16.1(1)(a)(i), (ii) or (iii), or (b)(i), shall be executed by a messenger-at-arms who shall—

(a) explain the purpose of service to any person on whom he executes service;

(b) complete a citation or notice, as the case may be, and a certificate of service in Form 16.3; and

(c) send the certificate of service to the pursuer.

(2) Such service shall be witnessed by one witness who shall sign the certificate of service (which shall state his name, occupation and address).

(3) Where service is executed by a method mentioned in rule 16.1(1)(a)(ii) or (iii), or (b)(i), and the document served is left in the hands of a person other than the person on whom service is to be executed, that document and the citation or notice of intimation, as the case may be, shall be placed in an envelope (bearing the notice specified in rule 16.4(2)) and sealed by the messenger-at-arms.

(4) [Subject to paragraph (4A)], a messenger-at-arms shall, when he executes service of a document, have in his possession—

(a) in the case of service of a copy of a principal writ, the principal writ or a copy of it certified as correct by the agent for the party whose writ it is, and

(b) where an interlocutor has been pronounced allowing service of the document, a certified copy of that interlocutor, which he shall show, if required, to the person on whom he executes service.

[(4A) Where the firm which employs the messenger-at-arms has in its possession—

(a) the principal writ or a certified copy of it, it shall be competent for the messenger-at-arms to execute service of the document without having that writ or certified copy in his possession, in which case he shall, if required to do so by the person on whom service is executed and within a reasonable time of being so required, show the principal writ or certified copy to the person;

(b) a certified copy of the interlocutor, it shall be competent for the messenger-at-arms to execute service of the document if he has in his possession a facsimile copy of the certified copy interlocutor which he shall show, if required, to the person on whom he executes service.]

(5) The certificate of service required under paragraph (1) shall include the full name and designation of any person in whose hands any document and the citation or notice, as the case may be, were left.

(6) In the application of this rule to service in a part of the United Kingdom furth of Scotland, reference to a messenger-at-arms shall be construed as a reference to a person entitled to serve Supreme Court writs in that part.

[1081]

NOTES

Para (4): words in square brackets inserted by the Act of Sederunt (Rules of the Court of Session Amendment No 4) (Miscellaneous) 2001, SSI 2001/305, r 2(1).

Para (4A): inserted by SSI 2001/305, r 2(2).

16.4 Service by post

(1) This rule applies to service of a document by post but is subject to rule 61.2(3) and (4) (order as respects intimation of petition for appointment of judicial factor) [but is subject to rule 61.2(3) and (4) (order as respects intimation of petition for appointment of judicial factor)].

(2) Service by post shall be executed by—
(a) a messenger-at-arms, or
(b) an agent,

posting a copy of the document to be served with any citation or notice, as the case may be, by registered post or first class recorded delivery service addressed to the person on whom service is to be executed and having on the face of the envelope a notice in the following terms:- "This envelope contains a citation to, or intimation from, the Court of Session. If delivery of the letter cannot be made it must be returned immediately to the Deputy Principal Clerk of Session, Court of Session, 2 Parliament Square, Edinburgh EH1 1RQ.".

(3) Where English is not an official language of the country in which service is to be executed, a translation in an official language of that country of the notice required under paragraph (2) shall appear on the face of the envelope.

(4) The person executing service of a document shall complete—
(a) a citation or notice, as the case may be; and
(b) a certificate of service in Form 16.4.

(5) A Post Office receipt of posting by registered post or a certificate of posting by the first class recorded delivery service, as the case may be, issued and stamped by the Post Office shall be attached to the certificate of service.

(6) The date of execution of service shall be deemed to be the day after the date of posting.

(7) Subject to rule 16.11 (no objection to regularity of service or intimation), the execution of service by post shall be valid unless the person on whom service was sought to have been made proves that the envelope and its contents were not tendered or left at his address.

[1082]

NOTES

Para (1): words in square brackets added by the Act of Sederunt (Rules of the Court of Session Amendment No 7) (Judicial Factors) 1997, SI 1997/1720, r 4.

16.5 Service where address of person is not known

(1) Where the residence of the person to be served with a document is not known and cannot reasonably be ascertained or service on that person cannot be executed under rule 16.1 (methods and manner of service) or 16.2 (service furth of United Kingdom), the party who wishes to execute service may apply by motion—
(a) for an order for service by the publication of an advertisement in a specified newspaper circulating in the area of the last known residence of that person or elsewhere; or
(b) on special cause shown, for an order to dispense with service; and
(c) stating the last known residence of that person and what steps have been taken to ascertain his present whereabouts.

(2) On enrolling such a motion, a copy of the document to be served shall be lodged with the Deputy Principal Clerk who shall retain it for a period of three years and from whom it may be uplifted by the person for whom it is intended.

(3) Where an intelocutor has been pronounced ordering publication of an advertisement under this rule—
(a) the advertisement shall be in Form 16.5; and
(b) publication of the advertisement shall have effect as if service of the document had been executed on the date of publication.

(4) Where an interlocutor has been pronounced dispensing with service under this rule—
(a) service of the document shall be deemed to have been executed on the date of the interlocutor; and
(b) the period of notice shall be dispensed with.

(5) A motion under paragraph (1) made before calling shall be heard in chambers.

(6) Where publication of an advertisement has been made under this rule, there shall be lodged in process—
(a) a copy of the newspaper containing the advertisement; or

PART II

(b) a certificate of publication by the publisher stating the date of publication and the text of the advertisement. **[1083]**

16.6 Translations of documents served or advertised abroad

(1) [Subject to rule 16.2A] where English is not an official language of the country in which a document is to be served, the document shall be accompanied by a translation in an official language of that country.

(2) An advertisement authorised under rule 16.5 (service where address of person is not known) to be published in a newspaper in a country in which English is not an official language of that country shall be in an official language of that country.

(3) With any certificate of service, or advertisement under rule 16.5, in a language other than English there shall be lodged a translation in English.

(4) A translation under this rule shall be certified as correct by the translator; and the certificate shall include his full name, address and qualifications. **[1084]**

NOTES

Para (1): words in square brackets inserted by the Act of Sederunt (Rules of the Court of Session Amendment) (Miscellaneous) 2004, SSI 2004/52, r 2(1), (4).

16.7 Intimation of documents

(1) Subject to rule 16.8 (intimation on a warrant to intimate), rule 16.9 (written intimation) and any other provision in these Rules, where intimation of a document is to be given under these Rules to any person, the intimation shall be given—

(a) personally, by tendering the document and the notice of intimation (if any) to that person; or

(b) by registered post or the first class recorded delivery service—

(i) in the case of an individual, addressed to the known, or last known, dwelling place or a place of business of that individual; or

(ii) in the case of any other person, addressed to the registered office, other official address or a place of business of that person.

(2) Where intimation has been given in accordance with paragraph (1), the party on whose behalf intimation has been given shall attach to the principal writ or lodge in process, as the case may be—

(a) certificate of intimation in Form 16.7;

(b) a copy of any notice of intimation which was intimated; and

(c) a copy of any interlocutor ordering the intimation. **[1085]**

16.8 Intimation on a warrant to intimate

(1) Where intimation of a document is to be given to a person for whom a warrant to intimate has been obtained, the intimation shall be made in the same manner as service of a document; and the following rules shall, with the necessary modifications, apply to that intimation as they apply to service of a document:- rule 16.1 (methods and manner of service),

rule 16.2 (service furth of United Kingdom),
[rule 16.2A (service under the Council Regulation),]
rule 16.3 (service by messenger-at-arms),
rule 16.4 (service by post),
rule 16.5 (service where address of person is not known),
rule 16.6 (translations of documents served or advertised abroad).

(2) Where intimation has been given in accordance with paragraph (1), the party on whose behalf intimation has been given shall attach a copy of any notice of intimation to the certificate of intimation. **[1086]**

NOTES

Para (1): words in square brackets inserted by the Act of Sederunt (Rules of the Court of Session Amendment) (Miscellaneous) 2004, SSI 2004/52, r 2(1), (5).

16.9 Written intimation

Where a provision in these Rules requires written intimation to be given to a person, that intimation may be made by first class post or other means of delivery to that person.

[1087]

16.10 Acceptance of service or intimation and dispensing with period of notice

(1) An agent may accept service or intimation of a document on behalf of the person on whom service is to be executed or to whom intimation is to be given and may dispense with any period of notice.

(2) A person on whom service of a document is executed or to whom intimation of a document is given may dispense with any period of notice as respects him in relation to that document.

(3) Where a period of notice is dispensed with under paragraph (1) or (2), it shall be deemed to expire on the day on which the party on whose behalf service is executed or intimation is given receives written intimation that the period of notice has been dispensed with.

[1088]

16.11 No objection to regularity of service or intimation

(1) A person who enters the process of a cause shall not be entitled to state any objection to the regularity of the execution of service or intimation of a document on him; and his appearance shall be deemed to remedy any defect in such service or intimation.

(2) Nothing in paragraph (1) shall preclude a person from pleading that the court has no jurisdiction.

[1089]

PART TWO
DILIGENCE

16.12 [Execution] of diligence

(1) This rule applies to—

(a) the execution of any diligence on a warrant, act or decree of the court other than—

(i) an arrestment to which rule 16.13 (arrestment of ships and arrestment in rem of cargo on board ship) applies; or

(ii) an arrestment to which rule 16.14(1) (arrestment in rem of cargo landed or transhipped) applies; and

(b) diligence in execution of a writ registered for execution in the Books of Council and Session.

(2) Subject to the following paragraphs of this rule, the execution of any diligence by virtue of these Rules on a person shall be executed by a messenger-at-arms in the same manner as service of a document is permitted under rule 16.1(1)(a)(i), (ii) or (iii) or (b)(i) (methods and manner of service); and, where appropriate, the following provisions of Part I (service and intimation) shall, with the necessary modifications, apply to the execution of diligence as they apply to service of a document:—

rule 16.3(1) to (4) (service by messenger-at-arms),

rule 16.4(2)(a), (3), (6) and (7) (service by post).

(3) In the application under this rule, by virtue of paragraph (2), of—

(a) sub-paragraph (b) of paragraph (1) of rule 16.3 (completion of citation or notice and certificate of service) for the reference to Form 16.3 in that sub-paragraph there shall be substituted a reference to the appropriate form of certificate of execution in rule 16.15 (forms for diligence); and

(b) sub-paragraph (b) of paragraph (4) of rule 16.4 (completion of citation or notice and certificate of service), for the reference to Form 16.4 in that sub-paragraph, there shall be substituted a reference to the appropriate form of certificate of execution in rule 16.15.

(4) The execution of such diligence on—

(a) an individual who is resident furth of Scotland,

(b) a person who has no registered office, other official address or a place of business in Scotland,

(c) a person whose residence is not known and cannot reasonably be ascertained, or
(d) a person on whom service cannot be executed in a manner permitted

under paragraph (2), shall be executed edictally by a messenger-at-arms leaving or depositing the appropriate schedule mentioned in rule 16.15 at the office of the Extractor.

(5) Where the execution of diligence is made edictally under paragraph (4), a copy of the schedule left at the office of the Extractor shall be sent by a messenger-at-arms by registered post or the first class recorded delivery service to the place furth of Scotland where the person on whom diligence is executed edictally resides, has his registered office, official address or place of business, as the case may be, or such last known place.

(6) A messenger-at-arms executing diligence shall have in his possession—

(a) in the case of diligence on a warrant in a principal writ, the principal writ or a copy of it certified as correct by the agent for the party whose writ it is,
(b) in the case of diligence on a warrant in an interlocutor, a certified copy of that interlocutor, or
(c) in the case of diligence on an extract of an act or a decree, or a document registered in the Books of Council and Session, the extract, which he shall show, if required, to any person on whom he executes diligence.

(7) The party on whose behalf diligence has been executed in a cause depending before the court shall attach the certificate of execution to the document containing the warrant for diligence.

[1090]

NOTES

Section heading: word in square brackets substituted by the Act of Sederunt (Rules of the Court of Session 1994 Amendment No 3) (Miscellaneous) 1994, SI 1994/2901, r 2(1), (4).

16.13 Arrestment of ships and arrestment in rem of cargo on board ship

(1) An arrestment of a ship in rem or on the dependence, or an arrestment in rem of cargo on board ship, may be executed on any day by a messenger-at-arms who shall affix the schedule of arrestment—

(a) to the mainmast of the ship;
(b) to the single mast of the ship; or
(c) where there is no mast, to some prominent part of the ship.

(2) In the execution of an arrestment of a ship on the dependence, the messenger-at-arms shall, in addition to complying with paragraph (1), mark the initials "ER" above the place where the schedule of arrestment is fixed.

(3) On executing an arrestment under paragraph (1), the messenger-at-arms shall deliver a copy of the schedule of arrestment and a copy of the certificate of execution of it to the master of the ship, or other person on board in charge of the ship or cargo, as the case may be, as representing the owners of, or parties interested in, the ship or cargo, as the case may be.

(4) Where the schedule of arrestment and the copy of the certificate of execution of it cannot be delivered as required under paragraph (3)—

(a) the certificate of execution shall state that fact; and
(b) either- (i) the arrestment shall be executed by serving it on the harbour master of the port where the ship lies; or

(ii) where there is no harbour master, or the ship is not in a harbour, the pursuer shall enrol a motion for such further order as to intimation and advertisement, if any, as may be necessary.

(5) A copy of the schedule of arrestment and a copy of the certificate of excution of it shall be delivered by the messenger-at-arms to the harbour master, if any, of any port where the ship lies.

(6) In this rule, "ship" has the meaning assigned in section 48(f) of the Administration of Justice Act 1956.

[1091]

16.14 Arrestment of cargo

(1) Where cargo has been, or is in the course of being, landed or transhipped, whether or not it has been delivered to its owner or his agent, any arrestment in rem of the cargo shall be executed by a messenger-at-arms who shall serve the schedule of arrestment—

(a) on the custodian for the time being of such cargo; or
(b) where the cargo has been landed on the quay or into a shed of any port or harbour authority, to the harbour master.

(2) An arrestment, other than an arrestment to which paraghraph (1) applies, of cargo on board ship may be executed on any day by a messenger-at-arms who shall serve the schedule of arrestment on the owner of the cargo or other proper arrestee.

[1092]

16.15 Forms for diligence

(1) In the execution of diligence, the following forms shall be used:—
(a) in the case of—
(i) an arrestment to found jurisdiction (other than the arrestment of a ship), a schedule in Form 16.15-A and a certificate of execution in Form 16.15-H;
(ii) an arrestment of a ship to found jurisdiction, a schedule in Form 16.15-AA and a certificate of execution in Form 16.15-HH;
(b) subject to sub-paragraph (e), in the case of an arrestment on the dependence, a schedule in Form 16.15-B and a certificate of execution in Form 16.15-H;
(c) in the case of an arrestment in rem of a ship, cargo or other maritime res to enforce a maritime hypothec or lien, a schedule in Form 16.15-C and a certificate of execution in Form 16.15-I;
(d) in the case of an arrestment in rem of a ship to enforce a non-pecuniary claim, a schedule in Form 16.15-D and a certificate of execution in Form 16.15-I.
(e) in the case of an arrestment on the dependence of—
(i) a cargo on board a ship, a schedule in Form 16.15-B;
(ii) a ship, a schedule in Form 16.15-BB,
and a certificate of execution in Form 16.15-J;
(f) subject to paragraph (g), in the case of an arrestment in execution, a schedule in Form 16.15-E and a certificate of execution in Form 16.15-H;
(g) in the case of an earnings arrestment, or a current maintenance arrestment, within the meaning of Part III of the Debtors (Scotland) Act 1987 a schedule in Form 30 (in respect of an earnings arrestment), or Form 34 (in respect of a current maintenance arrestment), and a certificate of execution in Form 60, in the Schedule to the Act of Sederunt (Proceedings in the Sheriff Court under the Debtors (Scotland) Act 1987) 1988;
(h) in the case of an inhibition, a schedule in Form 16.15-F and a certificate of execution in Form 16.15-H;
(i) in the case of the execution of a charge for payment of money, a charge in Form 16.15-G and a certificate of execution in Form 16.15-K; and
[(j) in the case of an attachment, a schedule in form 3, and a report of attachment in form 8, in Appendix 1 of Schedule 1 to the Act of Sederunt (Debt Arrangement and Attachment (Scotland) Act 2002) 2002.]

(2) Where two or more of the arrestments mentioned in paragraph (1)(a), (b), (c) and (d) are to be executed, they may be combined in one schedule of arrestment.

[1093]

NOTES

Para (1): sub-para (j) substituted by the Act of Sederunt (Debt Arrangement and Attachment (Scotland) Act 2002) 2002, SSI 2002/560, r 4, Sch 3, para 5.

CHAPTER 19
DECREES IN ABSENCE

19. 1 Decrees in absence

(1) This rule applies to any action other than an action in which the court may not grant decree without evidence.

(2) Where a defender—
(a) fails to enter appearance in accordance with rule 17.1(1), or
(b) having entered appearance, fails to lodge defences in accordance with rule 18.1(2), the pursuer may apply by motion for decree in absence against him.

(3) A motion enrolled under paragraph (2) shall specify—

PART II CIVIL PROCEDURE RULES

(a) the decree sought; and
(b) where appropriate, whether expenses are sought—
(i) as taxed by the Auditor; or
(ii) as elected by the pursuer under Part I of Chapter III of the Table of Fees in rule 42.16.

(4) Where a motion has been enrolled under paragraph (2), the court shall grant decree in absence in terms of all or any of the conclusions of the summons—
(a) subject to such restrictions, if any, as may be set out in a minute appended to the summons and signed by the pursuer;
(b) if satisfied that it has jurisdiction;
(c) if satisfied that the rules of service have been complied with; and
(d) where the summons was served on the defender furth of Scotland, if satisfied about service on the defender—
(i) in a case to which the Civil Jurisdiction and Judgments Act 1982 applies, as required by Article 20(2) or (3) of the convention in Schedule 1, or 3C, or Article 20(2) of Schedule 4, to that Act as the case may be;
(ii) in a case in which service has been executed on the defender under the Hague Convention on the Service Abroad of Judicial and Extrajudicial Documents in Civil or Commercial Matters dated 15th November 1965, as required by Article 15 of that convention; or
(iii) in a case in which service has been executed on the defender under a convention between the United Kingdom and the country in which service was executed, as required by the provisions of that convention.

(5) In an undefended action in which a defender is designed as resident or carrying on business furth of the United Kingdom and has no known solicitor in Scotland, the court shall, in the interlocutor granting decree in absence against him, supersede extract of that decree for such period beyond 7 days as it thinks fit to allow for the number of days required in the ordinary course of post for the transmission of a letter from Edinburgh to the residence, registered office, other official address or place of business, as the case may be, of that defender and the transmission of an answer from there to Edinburgh.

(6) Where a copy of the summons has been served on the defender furth of the United Kingdom under rule 16.2 and decree in absence is pronounced against him as a result of his failure to enter appearance, a certified copy of the interlocutor granting decree shall be served on him forthwith by the pursuer.

(7) Where a decree in absence on which a charge may be made has been granted after personal service of a summons on the defender or after the defender has entered appearance, and—
(a) the decree has not been recalled,
(b) the decree has been extracted,
(c) a charge on the decree has not been brought under review by suspension, and
(d) 60 days have elapsed since the expiry of the charge,

that decree shall have effect as a decree *in foro contentioso*.

[1094]

19.2. Recall of decrees in absence

(1) A decree in absence may not be reclaimed against.

(2) A defender may, not later than—
(a) 7 days after the date of a decree in absence against him, or
(b) the last day of the period for which extract of the decree has been superseded,

apply by motion for recall of the decree and to allow defences to be received.

(3) Where a defender enrols a motion under paragraph (2), he shall—
(a) at the same time lodge defences in process;
(b) have paid the sum of £25 to the pursuer; and
(c) lodge the receipt for that sum in process.

(4) On compliance by the defender with paragraphs (2) and (3), the court shall recall the decree against him and allow the defences to be received; and the action shall proceed as if the defences had been lodged timeously.

(5) Where a summons has been served on a defender furth of the United Kingdom under rule 16.2 and decree in absence has been pronounced against him as a result of his failure to enter appearance, the court may, on the motion of that defender, recall the decree and allow defences to be received if—

(a) without fault on his part, he did not have knowledge of the summons in sufficient time to defend;

(b) he has disclosed a *prima facie* defence to the action on the merits; and

(c) the motion is enrolled within a reasonable time after he had knowledge of the decree or in any event before the expiry of one year from the date of the decree;

and, where that decree is recalled, the action shall proceed as if the defences had been lodged timeously.

(6) On enrolling a motion under paragraph (5), the defender shall lodge defences in process.

(7) The recall of a decree under this rule shall be without prejudice to the validity of anything already done or transacted, of any contract made or obligation incurred, or of any appointment made or power granted, in or by virtue of that decree.

[1095]

CHAPTER 35
RECOVERY OF EVIDENCE

35.1 Application and interpretation of this Chapter

(1) This Chapter applies to the recovery of any evidence in a cause depending before the court.

(2) In this Chapter, "the Act of 1972" means the Administration of Justice (Scotland) Act 1972.

[1096]

35.2 Applications for commission and diligence for recovery of documents or for orders under section 1 of the Act of 1972

(1) An application by a party for—

(a) a commission and diligence for the recovery of a document, or

(b) an order under section 1 of the Act of 1972,

shall be made by motion.

(2) At the time of enrolling a motion under paragraph (1), a specification of—

(a) the document or other property sought to be inspected, photographed, preserved, taken into custody, detained, produced, recovered, sampled or experimented on or with, as the case may be, or

(b) the matter in respect of which information is sought as to the identity of a person who might be a witness or a defender,

shall be lodged in process.

(3) A copy of the specification lodged under paragraph (2) and the motion made under paragraph (1) shall be intimated by the applicant to—

(a) every other party;

(b) in respect of an application for an order under section 1(1) of the Act of 1972, any third party haver; and

[(c) where necessary—

(i) the Advocate General for Scotland (in a case where the document or other property sought is in the possession of either a public authority exercising functions in relation to reserved matters within the meaning of Schedule 5 to the Scotland Act 1998, or a cross-border public authority within the meaning of section 88(5) of that Act); or

(ii) the Lord Advocate (in any other case),

and if there is any doubt, both.]

(4) Where the Lord Ordinary grants a motion made under paragraph (1), in whole or in part, in an action before calling of the summons, he may order the applicant to find such caution or give such other security as he thinks fit.

(5) The decision of the Lord Ordinary on a motion under paragraph (1) in an action before calling of the summons shall be final and not subject to review.

(6) The Lord Advocate may appear at the hearing of any motion under paragraph (1).

[1097]

PART II

NOTES

Para (3): sub-para (c) substituted by the Act of Sederunt (Rules of the Court of Session Amendment No 4) (Miscellaneous) 2001, SSI 2001/305, r 6.

[35.3 Optional procedure before executing commission and diligence

(1) Subject to rule 35.3A (optional procedure where there is a party litigant or confidentiality is claimed), this rule applies where a party has obtained a commission and diligence for the recovery of a document on an application made under rule 35.2(1)(a).

(2) Such a party may, at any time before executing the commission and diligence against a haver, serve on the haver an order in Form 35.3-A (in this rule referred to as "the order").

(3) The order and a copy of the specification referred to in rule 35.2(2), as approved by the court, shall be served on the haver or his known agent and shall be complied with by the haver in the manner and within the period specified in the order.

(4) Not later than the day after the date on which the order, and any document recovered, is received from a haver by the party who obtained the order, that party—

- (a) shall given written intimation of that fact in Form 35.3-B to the Deputy Principal Clerk and every other party; and
- (b) shall—
  - (i) if the document has been sent by post, send a written receipt for the document in Form 35.3-C to the haver; or
  - (ii) if the document has been delivered by hand, give a written receipt in Form 35.3-C to the person delivering the document.

(5) Where the party who has recovered any such document does not lodge it in process within 14 days of receipt of it, he shall—

- (a) forthwith give written intimation to every other party that that party may borrow, inspect or copy the document within 14 days after the date of that intimation; and
- (b) in so doing, identify the document.

(6) Where any party, who has obtained any such document under paragraph (5), wishes to lodge the document in process, he shall—

- (a) lodge the document within 14 days after receipt of it; and
- (b) at the same time, send a written receipt for the document in Form 35.3.-D to the party who obtained the order.

(7) Where—

- (a) no party wishes to lodge or borrow any such document under paragraph (5), the document shall be returned to the haver by the party who obtained the order within 14 days after the expiry of the period specified in sub-paragraph (a) of that paragraph; or
- (b) any such document has been uplifted by another party under paragraph (5) and that party does not wish to lodge it in process, the document shall be returned to the haver by that party within 21 days after the date of receipt of it by him.

(8) Any such document lodged in process shall be returned to the haver by the party lodging it within 14 days after the expiry of any period allowed for appeal or reclaiming or, where an appeal or reclaiming motion has been marked, from the disposal of any such appeal or reclaiming motion.

(9) If any party fails to return any such document as provided for in paragraph (7) or (8), the haver shall be entitled to apply by motion (whether or not the cause is in dependence) for an order that the document be returned to him and for the expenses occasioned by that motion.

(10) The party holding any such document (being the party who last issued a receipt for it) shall be responsible for its safekeeping during the period that the document is in his custody or control.

(11) If the party who served the order is not satisfied that—

- (a) full compliance has been made with the order, or
- (b) adequate reasons for non-compliance have been given,

he may execute the commission and diligence under rule 35.4.

(12) Where an extract from a book of any description (whether the extract is certified or not) is produced under the order, the court may, on the motion of the party who served the order, direct that that party shall be allowed to inspect the book and take copies of any entries falling within the specification.

(13) Where any question of confidentiality arises in relation to a book directed to be inspected under paragraph (12), the inspection shall be made, and any copies shall be taken, at the sight of the commissioner appointed in the interlocutor granting the commission and diligence.

(14) The court may, on cause shown, order the production of any book (not being a banker's book or book of public record) containing entries falling under a specification, notwithstanding the production of a certified extract from that book.]

[1098]

NOTES

Substituted by the Act of Sederunt (Rules of the Court of Session Amendment No 4) (Miscellaneous) 1996, SI 1996/2168, r 2(1), (6).

[35.3A Optional procedure where there is a party litigant or confidentiality is claimed

(1) This rule shall apply where—
 (a) any of the parties to the action is a party litigant; or
 (b) confidentiality is claimed for any document in the possession of a haver.

(2) Rule 35.3 (optional procedure before executing commission and diligence) shall not apply where paragraph (1) of this rule applies.

(3) The party who has obtained a commission and diligence for the recovery of a document on an application made under rule 35.2(1)(a) may, at any time before executing it against a haver, serve on the haver an order in Form 35.3A-A (in this rule referred to as "the order").

(4) The order and a copy of the specification referred to in rule 35.2(2), as approved by the court, shall be served on the haver or his known agent and shall be complied with by the haver in the manner and within the period specified in the order.

(5) Not later than the day after the date on which the order, and any document recovered, is received from a haver by the Deputy Principal Clerk, he shall given written intimation of that fact to each party.

(6) No party, other than the party who served the order, may uplift any such document until after the expiry of 7 days after the date of intimation under paragraph (5).

(7) Where the party who served the order fails to uplift any such document within 7 days after the date of intimation under paragraph (5), the Deputy Principal Clerk shall give written intimation of that failure to every other party.

(8) Where no party has uplifted any such document within 14 days after the date of intimation under paragraph (7), the Deputy Principal Clerk shall return it to the haver who delivered it to him.

(9) Where a party who has uplifted any such document does not wish to lodge it, he shall return it to the Deputy Principal Clerk who shall—
 (a) give written intimation of the return of the document to every other party; and
 (b) if no other party uplifts the document within 14 days after the date of intimation, return it to the haver.

(10) Any such document lodged in process shall be returned to the haver by the party lodging it within 14 days after the expiry of any period allowed for appeal or reclaiming or, where an appeal or reclaiming motion has been marked, from the disposal of any such appeal or reclaiming motion.

(11) If any party fails to return any such document as provided for in paragraph (9) or (10), the haver shall be entitled to apply by motion (whether or not the cause is in dependence) for an order that the document be returned to him and for the expenses occasioned by that motion.

(12) The party holding any such document (being the party who last issued a receipt for it) shall be responsible for its safekeeping during the period that the document is in his custody or control.

(13) If the party who served the order is not satisfied that—
(a) full compliance has been made with the order, or
(b) adequate reasons for non-compliance have been given,

he may execute the commission and diligence under rule 35.4.

(14) Where an extract from a book of any description (whether the extract is certified or not) is produced under the order, the court may, on the motion of the party who served the order, direct that that party shall be allowed to inspect the book and take copies of any entries falling within the specification.

(15) Where any question of confidentiality arises in relation to a book directed to be inspected under paragraph (14), the inspection shall be made, and any copies shall be taken, at the sight of the commissioner appointed in the interlocutor granting the commission and diligence.

(16) The court may, on cause shown, order the production of any book (not being a banker's book or book of public record) containing entries falling under a specification, notwithstanding the production of a certified extract from that book.]

[1099]

NOTES

Inserted by the Act of Sederunt (Rules of the Court of Session Amendment No 4) (Miscellaneous) 1996, SI 1996/2168, r 2(1), (7).

35.4 Execution of commission and diligence for recovery of documents

(1) The party who seeks to execute a commission and diligence for recovery of a document obtained on an application under rule 35.2(1)(a) shall—
(a) provide the commissioner with a copy of the specification, a copy of the pleadings (including any adjustments and amendments) and a certified copy of the interlocutor of his appointment;
(b) fix a diet for the execution of the commission in consultation with every other party;
(c) instruct the clerk and any shorthand writer; and
(d) be responsible, in the first instance, for the fees of the commissioner, his clerk and any shorthand writer.

(2) The interlocutor granting such a commission and diligence shall be sufficient authority for citing a haver to appear before the commissioner.

(3) A haver shall be cited to appear at a commission for the recovery of documents by service on him of a citation in Form 35.4-A
(a) by registered post or the first class recorded delivery service; or
(b) personally, by messenger-at-arms.

(4) A certificate of citation of a haver—
(a) under paragraph (3)(a) shall be in Form 35.4-B; and
(b) under paragraph (3)(b) shall be in Form 35.4-C.

(5) There shall be served on the haver with the citation a copy of the specification and, where necessary for a proper understanding of the specification, a copy of the pleadings (including any adjustments and amendments).

(6) The agent for a party, or a party litigant, as the case may be, shall be personally liable, in the first instance, for the fees and expenses of a haver cited to appear at a commission for that party.

(7) The parties and the haver shall be entitled to be represented by counsel or other person having a right of audience, or an agent, at the execution of the commission.

(8) At the commission, the commissioner shall—
(a) administer the oath de fideli administratione to the clerk and shorthand writer appointed for the commission; and
(b) administer to the haver the oath in Form 35.4-D, or, where the haver elects to affirm, the affirmation in Form 35.4-E.

(9) The report of the execution of the commission and diligence, any document recovered and an inventory of that document, shall be sent by the commissioner to the Deputy Principal Clerk.

(10) Not later than the day after the date on which such a report, any document recovered and an inventory of that document are received by the Deputy Principal Clerk, he shall give written intimation to the parties that he has received them.

(11) No party, other than the party who served the order, may uplift such a document until after the expiry of 7 days after the date of intimation under paragraph (10).

(12) Where the party who served the order fails to uplift such a document within 7 days after the date of intimation under paragraph [(10)], the Deputy Principal Clerk shall give written intimation of that failure to every other party.

(13) Where no party has uplifted such a document within 14 days after the date of intimation under paragraph (12), the Deputy Principal Clerk shall return it to the haver.

(14) Where a party who has uplifted such a document does not wish to lodge it, he shall return it to the Deputy Principal Clerk who shall—

(a) give written intimation of the return of the document to every other party; and
(b) if no other party uplifts the document within 14 days of the date of intimation, return it to the haver.

[1100]

NOTES

Para (12): number in square brackets substituted by the Act of Sederunt (Rules of the Court of Session 1994 Amendment No 3) (Miscellaneous) 1994, SI 1994/2901, r 2(1), (7).

35.5 Execution of orders for production or recovery of documents or other property under section 1(1) of the Act of 1972

(1) An order under section 1(1) of the Act of 1972 for the production or recovery of a document or other property shall grant a commission and diligence for the production or recovery of that document or other property.

(2) Rule 35.3 (optional procedure before executing commission and diligence) and rule 35.4 (execution of commission and diligence for recovery of documents) shall apply to an order to which paragraph (1) applies as they apply to a commission and diligence for the recovery of a document.

[1101]

35.6 Execution of orders for inspection etc of documents or other property under section 1(1) of the Act of 1972

(1) An order under section 1(1) of the Act of 1972 for the inspection or photographing of a document or other property, the taking of samples or the carrying out of any experiment thereon or therewith, shall authorise and appoint a specified person to photograph, inspect, take samples of, or carry out any experiment with or on, any such document or other property, as the case may be, subject to such conditions, if any, as the court thinks fit.

(2) A certified copy of the interlocutor granting such an order shall be sufficient authority for the person specified to execute the order.

(3) When such an order is executed, the party who obtained the order shall serve on the haver a certified copy of the interlocutor granting it, a copy of the specification and, where necessary for a proper understanding of the specification, a copy of the pleadings (including any adjustments and amendments).

[1102]

35.7 Execution of orders for preservation etc of documents or other property under section 1(1) of the Act of 1972

(1) An order under section 1(1) of the Act of 1972 for the preservation, custody and detention of a document or other property shall grant a commission and diligence for the detention and custody of that document or other property.

(2) The party who has obtained an order under paragraph (1) shall—

(a) provide the commissioner with a copy of the specification, a copy of the pleadings (including any adjustments and amendments) and a certified copy of the interlocutor of his appointment;
(b) be responsible for the fees of the commissioner and his clerk; and
(c) serve a copy of the order on the haver.

(3) The report of the execution of the commission and diligence, any document or other property taken by the commissioner and an inventory of such property, shall be sent by the commissioner to the Deputy Principal Clerk for the further order of the court.

[1103]

35.8 Confidentiality

(1) Where confidentiality is claimed for any document or other property sought to be recovered under any of the following rules, such document or other property shall, where practicable, be enclosed in a sealed packet:—

rule 35.3 (optional procedure before executing commission and diligence),
rule 35.4 (execution of commission and diligence for recovery of documents),
rule 35.5 (execution of orders for production or recovery of documents or other property under section 1(1) of the Act of 1972),
rule 35.7 (execution of orders for preservation etc of documents or other property under section 1(1) of the Act of 1972)

(2) A motion to have such a sealed packet opened up or such recovery allowed may be made by—

(a) the party who obtained the commission and diligence; or
(b) any other party after the date of intimation by the Deputy Principal Clerk under rule 35.3(5) or 35.4(12) (intimation of failure to uplift documents).

(3) In addition to complying with rule 23.3 (intimation of motions), the party enrolling such a motion shall intimate the terms of the motion to the person claiming confidentiality by registered post or the first class recorded delivery service.

(4) The person claiming confidentiality may oppose a motion made under paragraph (2).

[1104]

35.9 Warrants for production of original documents from public records

(1) Where a party seeks to obtain from the keeper of any public record production of the original of any register or deed in his custody for the purposes of a cause, he shall apply to the court by motion.

(2) Written intimation of a motion under paragraph (1) shall be given to the keeper of the public record concerned at least 2 days before the motion is enrolled.

(3) Where it appears to the court that it is necessary for the ends of justice that a motion under this rule should be granted, authority shall be given to such keeper, on production of a certified copy of the interlocutor granting the motion, to produce or exhibit, as the case may be, the original register or deed to the court.

(4) The expense of the production or exhibition of such an original register or deed shall be met, in the first instance, by the party who applied by motion under paragraph (1).

[1105]

35.10 Warrants for transmission of processes

(1) A party who seeks to lodge in process any process in the custody of the Keeper of the Records, or any process depending or which depended in any inferior court in Scotland, may apply by motion to the court for a warrant to authorise and direct the Keeper of the Records or the clerk of the inferior court, as the case may be, on production of a certified copy of the interlocutor granting the motion, to transmit that process to the Deputy Principal Clerk.

(2) A party who enrols a motion under paragraph (1) shall give written intimation of the motion to the Keeper of the Records or the clerk of the inferior court, as the case may be, at least 2 days before the motion is enrolled.

(3) The Deputy Principal Clerk shall grant a receipt for any process transmitted to him under an order made under paragraph (1) and lodge it in the process of the cause.

(4) No process transmitted under paragraph (1) may be borrowed.

(5) After a process transmitted under paragraph (1) ceases to be required, the Deputy Principal Clerk shall return it to the Keeper of the Records or the clerk of the inferior court, as the case may be.

[1106]

35.11 Commissions for examination of witnesses

(1) This rule applies to a commission—

(a) to take the evidence of a witness on a ground mentioned in section 10(b) of the Act of 1988;

(b) in respect of the evidence of a witness which is in danger of being lost, to take the evidence to lie in retentis; or

(c) on special cause shown, to take the evidence of a witness on a ground other than one mentioned in sub-paragraph (a) or (b).

(2) An application by a party for a commission to examine a witness shall be made by motion; and that party shall specify in the motion the name and address of at least one proposed commissioner for approval and appointment by the court.

(3) Where a motion under paragraph (2) is made in an action before calling of the summons—

(a) the applicant shall give written intimation of the motion to every other person named in the instance; and

(b) the decision of the Lord Ordinary shall be final and not subject to review.

(4) The interlocutor granting such a commission shall be sufficient authority for citing the witness to appear before the commissioner.

(5) A witness shall be cited to give evidence at a commission by service on him of a citation in Form 35.11-A.

(a) by registered post or the first class recorded delivery service; or

(b) personally, by a messenger-at-arms.

(6) The certificate of citation of a witness—

(a) under paragraph (5)(a) shall be in Form 35.11-B; and

(b) under paragraph (5)(b) shall be in Form 35.11-C.

(7) The agent for a party, or a party litigant, as the case may be, shall be personally liable, in the first instance, for the fees and expenses of a witness cited to appear at a commission for that party.

(8) At the commission, the commissioner shall—

(a) administer the oath de fideli administratione to the clerk and any shorthand writer appointed for the commission; and

(b) administer to the witness the oath in Form 35.4-D, or, where the witness elects to affirm, the affirmation in Form 35.4-E.

(9) In a cause involving the collision of ships, such an application shall be granted on condition, where necessary, that the applicant shall, at least 24 hours before the evidence is taken, lodge in process a preliminary act which the commissioner shall be entitled to open before the witness is examined.

(10) Where a commission is granted for the examination of a witness, the court may, on the motion of any party and on cause shown, dispense with interrogatories.

[1107]

35.12 Commissions on interrogatories

(1) Where interrogatories have not been dispensed with, the party who obtained the commission to examine a witness under rule 35.11 shall lodge draft interrogatories to be adjusted at the sight of the clerk of court.

(2) Any other party may lodge cross-interrogatories to be adjusted at the sight of the clerk of court.

(3) The interrogatories and any cross-interrogatories, when adjusted, shall be extended and returned to the clerk of court for approval.

(4) The party who has obtained the commission shall—

(a) provide the commissioner with a copy of the pleadings (including any adjustments and amendments), the approved interrogatories and any cross-interrogatories and a certified copy of the interlocutor of his appointment;

(b) instruct the clerk; and

(c) be responsible, in the first instance, for the fee of the commissioner and his clerk.

(5) The commissioner shall, in consultation with the parties, fix a diet for the execution of the commission to examine the witness.

(6) The executed interrogatories, any document produced by the witness and an inventory of that document, shall be sent by the commissioner to the Deputy Principal Clerk.

(7) Not later than the day after the date on which the executed interrogatories, any document and an inventory of that document, are received by the Deputy Principal Clerk, he shall give written intimation to each party that he has received them.

(8) The party who obtained the commission to examine the witness shall lodge in process—

(a) the report of the commission; and
(b) the executed interrogatories and any cross-interrogatories.

[1108]

35.13 Commissions without interrogatories

(1) Where interrogatories have been dispensed with, the party who has obtained a commission to examine a witness under rule 35.11 shall—

(a) provide the commissioner with a copy of the pleadings (including any adjustments and amendments) and a certified copy of the interlocutor of his appointment;
(b) fix a diet for the execution of the commission in consultation with the commissioner and every other party;
(c) instruct the clerk and any shorthand writer; and
(d) be responsible, in the first instance, for the fees of the commissioner, his clerk and any shorthand writer.

(2) All parties shall be entitled to be present and represented by counsel or other person having a right of audience, or agent, at the execution of the commission.

(3) The report of the execution of the commission, any document produced by the witness and an inventory of that document, shall be sent by the commissioner to the Deputy Principal Clerk.

(4) Not later than the day after the date on which such a report, any document and an inventory of that document are received by the Deputy Principal Clerk, he shall give written intimation to each party that he has received them.

(5) The party who obtained the commission to examine the witness shall lodge the report in process.

[1109]

35.14 Evidence taken on commission

(1) Subject to the following paragraphs of this rule and to all questions of relevancy and admissibility, evidence taken on commission under rule 35.12 or 35.13 may be used as evidence at any proof or jury trial of the cause.

(2) Any party may object to the use of such evidence at a proof or jury trial; and the objection shall be determined by the court.

(3) Such evidence shall not be used at a proof or jury trial if the witness becomes available to attend the diet of proof or jury trial, as the case may be.

(4) A party may use such evidence in accordance with the preceding paragraphs of this rule notwithstanding that it was obtained at the instance of another party.

[1110]

35.15 Letters of request

(1) This rule applies to an application for a letter of request to a court or tribunal outside Scotland to obtain evidence of the kind specified in paragraph (2), being evidence obtainable within the jurisdiction of that court or tribunal, for the purposes of a cause depending before the Court of Session.

(2) An application to which paragraph (1) applies may be made in relation to a request—

(a) for the examination of a witness,
(b) for the inspection, photographing, preservation, custody, detention, production or recovery of, or the taking of samples of, or the carrying out of any experiment on or with, a document or other property, as the case may be,
(c) for the medical examination of any person,
(d) for the taking and testing of samples of blood from any person, or

(e) for any other order for obtaining evidence, for which an order could be obtained in the Court of Session.

(3) Such an application shall be made by minute in Form 35.15-A with a proposed letter of request in Form 35.15-B.

(4) It shall be a condition of granting a letter of request that the agent for the applicant, or a party litigant, as the case may be, shall be personally liable, in the first instance, for the whole expenses which may become due and payable in respect of the letter of request to the court or tribunal obtaining the evidence and to any witness or haver who may be examined for the purpose; and he shall consign into court such sum in respect of such expenses as the court thinks fit.

(5) Unless the court or tribunal to which a letter of request is addressed is a court or tribunal in a country or territory—

(a) where English is an official language, or

(b) in relation to which the Deputy Principal Clerk certifies that no translation is required, then the applicant shall, before the issue of the letter of request, lodge in process a translation of that letter and any interrogatories and cross-interrogatories into the official language of that court or tribunal.

(6) The letter of request when issued, any interrogatories and cross-interrogatories adjusted as required by rule 35.12 and the translations (if any), shall be forwarded by the Deputy Principal Clerk to such person and in such manner as the Lord President may direct. **[1111]**

[35.16 Applications for requests that evidence be taken under the Council Regulation

(1) In this rule—

"the Council Regulation" means the Council Regulation (EC) No 1206/2001 of 28 May 2001 on co-operation between the courts of the Member States in the taking of evidence in civil or commercial matters;

"Member State" has the same meaning as in Article 1(3) of the Council Regulation;

"request" means a request to which Article 1(1)(a) of the Council Regulation applies; and

"requested court" has the same meaning as in Article 2(1) of the Council Regulation.

(2) This rule applies to an application under the Council Regulation for a request to a requested court in a Member State other than the United Kingdom for the purposes of a cause depending before the Court of Session.

(3) An application to which paragraph (2) applies shall be made by minute in Form 35.16-A with a proposed request in form A (request for the taking of evidence) or form I (request for direct taking of evidence) set out in the Annex to the Council Regulation.

(4) It shall be a condition of granting an application for a request that the agent for the applicant, or a party litigant, as the case may be, shall be personally liable, in the first instance, for any reimbursement required by the requested court in respect of any fees paid to experts and interpreters and the costs occasioned by the use of any requested special procedure in executing the request for evidence, or the use of requested communications technology at the performance of the taking of evidence; and that he shall consign into court any such sum as is required by the requested court as deposit or advance towards the costs of executing the request.

(5) Unless the requested court is in a country or territory—

(a) where English is an official language, or

(b) in relation to which the Deputy Principal Clerk certifies that no translation is required,

then the applicant shall, before the issue of the request, lodge in process a translation of the request and any interrogatories and cross-interrogatories into the official language of that country or territory.

(6) Where an application under this rule has been granted, the request shall be forwarded by the Deputy Principal Clerk to—

(a) the requested court; or

(b) the central body or competent authority designated by the other Member State to be responsible for taking decisions on requests to take evidence directly.

(7) The Deputy Principal Clerk shall, as soon as reasonably practicable after receipt of any communication from the requested court, send written intimation of that communication to the parties.

PART II CIVIL PROCEDURE RULES

(8) If a request is made to take the evidence of a witness directly in another Member State, the Deputy Principal Clerk shall intimate to the witness who is to give evidence, a notice in Form 35.16-B and the witness shall return Form 35.16-C to the Deputy Principal Clerk, within 14 days after the date of intimation of the notice.]

[1112]

NOTES

Commencement: 30 November 2004.

Added by the Act of Sederunt (Rules of the Court of Session Amendment No 6) (Miscellaneous) 2004, SSI 2004, SSI 2004/514, r 2(1), (3).

Special provisions in relation to particular proceedings

[CHAPTER 47
COMMERCIAL ACTIONS

47.1 Application and interpretation of this Chapter

(1) This Chapter applies to a commercial action.

(2) In this Chapter—

"commercial action" means an action arising out of, or concerned with, any transaction or dispute of a commercial or business nature in which an election has been made under rule 47.3(1) or which has been transferred under rule 47.10;

"preliminary hearing" means a hearing under rule 47.11;

"procedural hearing" means a hearing under rule 47.12.

[1113]

NOTES

Ch 47 (rr 47.1–47.16) substituted by the Act of Sederunt (Rules of the Court of Session 1994 Amendment No 1) (Commercial Actions) 1994, SI 1994/2310, r 3(4).

[47.2 Proceedings before commercial judge

All proceedings in the Outer House in a commercial action shall be brought before a judge of the court nominated by the Lord President as a commercial judge or, where a commercial judge is not available, any other judge of the court (including the vacation judge); and "commercial judge" shall be construed accordingly.]

[1114]

NOTES

Substituted as noted to r 47.1 at **[1113]**.

[47.3 Election of procedure for commercial actions and form of summons

(1) The pursuer may elect to adopt the procedure in this Chapter by bringing an action in which there are inserted the words "Commercial Action" immediately below the words "IN THE COURT OF SESSION" where they occur above the instance, and on the backing, of the summons and any copy of it.

(2) A summons in a commercial action shall—

(a) specify, in the form of conclusions, the orders sought;

(b) identify the parties to the action and the transaction or dispute from which the action arises;

(c) summarise the circumstances out of which the action arises; and

(d) set out the grounds on which the action proceeds.

(3) There shall be appended to a summons in a commercial action a schedule listing the documents founded on or adopted as incorporated in the summons.]

[1115]

NOTES

Substituted as noted to r 47.1 at **[1113]**.

[47.4 Disapplication of certain rules

(1) The requirement in rule 4.1(4) for a step of process to be folded lengthwise shall not apply in a commercial action.

(2) An open record shall not be made up in, and Chapter 22 (making up and closing records) shall not apply to, a commercial action unless otherwise ordered by the court.

(3) The following rules shall not apply to a commercial action:—
rule 6.2 (fixing and allocation of diets in Outer House),
rule 25.1(3) (form of counterclaim),
rule 25.2(2) (applications for warrants for diligence in counterclaims),
rule 36.3 (lodging productions).]

[1116]

NOTES

Substituted as noted to r 47.1 at **[1113]**.

[47.5 Procedure in commercial actions

Subject to the provisions of this Chapter, the procedure in a commercial action shall be such as the commercial judge shall order or direct.]

[1117]

NOTES

Substituted as noted to r 47.1 at **[1113]**.

[47.6 Defences

(1) Defences in a commercial action shall be in the form of answers to the summons with any additional statement of facts or legal grounds on which it is intended to rely.

(2) There shall be appended to the defences in a commercial action a schedule listing the documents founded on or adopted as incorporated in the defences.]

[1118]

NOTES

Substituted as noted to r 47.1 at **[1113]**.

[47.7 Counterclaims and third party notices

(1) A party seeking to lodge a counterclaim or to serve a third party notice shall apply by motion to do so.

(2) The commercial judge shall, on a motion to lodge a counterclaim or to serve a third party notice, make such order and give such directions as he thinks fit with regard to—

(a) the time within which a counterclaim may be lodged or a third party notice served and any answers lodged;

(b) where the motion is made before the preliminary hearing, a date for the preliminary hearing if it is to be a date other than the date referred to in rule 47.8(2); and

(c) any application for a warrant to use any form of diligence which would have been permitted under rule 13.6(c) (warrants for diligence in summons) had the warrant been sought in a summons in a separate action.

(3) Paragraphs (2) and (3) of rule 47.3 shall apply to the form of a counterclaim as they apply to the form of a summons.]

[1119]

NOTES

Substituted as noted to r 47.1 at **[1113]**.

[47.8 Commercial Roll

(1) All proceedings in an action in which an election has been made under rule 47.3(1) or which has been transferred under rule 47.10 shall, in the Outer House, be heard and determined on the Commercial Roll on such dates and at such times as shall be fixed by the commercial judge.

(2) A commercial action shall call on the Commercial Roll for a preliminary hearing within 14 days after defences have been lodged.

(3) The appearance of a commercial action on the Commercial Roll for a hearing on a specified date shall not affect the right of any party to apply by motion at any time under these Rules.]

[1120]

NOTES

Substituted as noted to r 47.1 at **[1113]**.

[47.9 Withdrawal of action from Commercial Roll

(1) At any time before or at the preliminary hearing, the commercial judge shall—

(a) on the motion of a party, withdraw a commercial action from the procedure in this Chapter and appoint it to proceed as an ordinary action where, having regard to—

(i) the likely need for detailed pleadings to enable justice to be done between the parties,

(ii) the length of time required for preparation of the action, or

(iii) any other relevant circumstances,

he is satisfied that the speedy and efficient determination of the action would not be served by the cause being dealt with as a commercial action; and

(b) on the motion of a party with the consent of all other parties, withdraw a commercial action from the Commercial Roll and appoint it to proceed as an ordinary action.

[(1A) At any time before or at the preliminary hearing, the commercial judge may—

(a) on the motion of a party; or

(b) *ex proprio motu*, after hearing the parties to the action,

if he is satisfied that the action is not a commercial action, withdraw it from the procedure in this Chapter and appoint it to proceed as an ordinary action.]

(2) If a motion to withdraw a commercial action from the Commercial Roll made before or renewed at a preliminary hearing is refused, no subsequent motion to withdraw the action from the Commercial Roll shall be considered except on special cause shown.]

[1121]

NOTES

Substituted as noted to r 47.1 at **[1113]**.

Para (1A): inserted by the Act of Sederunt (Rules of the Court of Session Amendment) (Miscellaneous) 2000, SSI 2000/66, r 2(1), (7).

[47.10 Transfer of action to Commercial Roll

(1) In an action within the meaning of rule 47.1(2) (definition of commercial action) in which the pursuer has not made an election under rule 47.3(1), any party may apply by motion at any time to have the action appointed to be a commercial action on the Commercial Roll.

(2) A motion enrolled under paragraph (1) shall be heard by the commercial judge on such a date and at such a time as the Keeper of the Rolls shall fix in consultation with the commercial judge.

(3) Where an interlocutor is pronounced under paragraph (1) appointing an action to be a commercial action on the Commercial Roll, the action shall be put out by order for a preliminary hearing within 14 days—

(a) if defences have been lodged, after the date of that interlocutor; or

(b) if defences have not been lodged, after defences have been lodged.]

[1122]

NOTES

Substituted as noted to r 47.1 at **[1113]**.

[47.11 Preliminary hearing

(1) Unless a commercial action is withdrawn under rule 47.9 from the Commercial Roll then, at the preliminary hearing of a commercial action in which an election has been made under rule 47.3(1), the commercial judge—

(a) shall determine whether and to what extent and in what manner further specification of the claim and defences should be provided;

(b) may make an order in respect of any of the following matters:—

(i) detailed written pleadings to be made by a party either generally or restricted to particular issues;

(ii) a statement of facts to be made by one or more parties either generally or restricted to particular issues;

(iii) the allowing of an amendment by a party to his pleadings;

(iv) disclosure of the identity of witnesses and the existence and nature of documents relating to the action or authority to recover documents either generally or specifically;

(v) documents constituting, evidencing or relating to the subject-matter of the action or any invoices, correspondence or similar documents relating to it to be lodged in process within a specified period;

(vi) each party to lodge in process, and sent to every other party, a list of witnesses;

(vii) reports of skilled persons or witness statements to be lodged in process;

(viii) affidavits concerned with any of the issues in the action to be lodged in process; and

(ix) the action to proceed to a hearing without any further preliminary procedure either in relation to the whole or any particular aspect of the action;

(c) may fix the period within which any such order shall be complied with;

(d) may continue the preliminary hearing to a date to be appointed by him; and

(e) may make such other order as he thinks fit for the speedy determination of the action.

(2) Where the commercial judge makes an order under paragraph (1)(b)(i) or (ii) or (c), he may ordain the pursuer to—

(a) make up a record; and

(b) lodge that record in process within such period as the commercial judge thinks fit.

(3) At the conclusion of the preliminary hearing, the court shall, unless it has made an order under paragraph (1)(b)(ix) (order to proceed without a further hearing), fix a date for a procedural hearing to determine further procedure.

(4) The date fixed under paragraph (3) for a procedural hearing shall not be extended except on special cause shown on a motion enrolled not less than 7 days before the date fixed for the procedural hearing.]

[1123]

NOTES

Substituted as noted to r 47.1 at **[1113]**.

47.12 Procedural hearing

(1) Not less than 3 days before the date fixed under rule 47.11(3) for the procedural hearing, each party shall—

(a) lodge a written statement of his proposals for further procedure which shall, inter alia, state—

(i) whether he seeks to have the commercial action appointed to debate or to have the action sent to proof on the whole or any part of it; and

(ii) what the issues are which he considers should be sent to debate or proof;

(b) lodge a list of the witnesses he proposes to cite or call to give evidence, identifying the matters to which each witness will speak;

(c) lodge the reports of any skilled persons;

(d) where it is sought to have the action appointed to debate, lodge a note of argument consisting of concise numbered paragraphs stating the legal propositions on which it is proposed to submit that any preliminary plea should be sustained or repelled with reference to the principal authorities and statutory provisions to be founded on; and

(e) send a copy of any such written statement, lists, reports or note of argument, as the case may be, to every other party.

(2) At the procedural hearing, the commercial judge—

(a) shall determine whether the commercial action should be appointed to debate or sent to proof on the whole or any part of the action;

(b) where the action is appointed to debate or sent to proof, may order that written arguments on any question of law should be submitted;

(c) where the action is sent to proof, may determine whether evidence at the proof should be by oral evidence, the production of documents or affidavits on any issue;

(d) may determine, in the light of any witness statements, affidavits or reports produced, that proof is unnecessary on any issue;

(e) may direct that there should be consultation between skilled persons with a view to reaching agreement about any points held in common;

(f) without prejudice to Chapter 12 (assessors), may appoint an expert to examine, on behalf of the court, any reports of skilled persons or other evidence submitted and to report to the court within such period as the commercial judge may specify;

(g) may remit an issue to a person of skill;

(h) may direct that proof of the authenticity of a document or other formal matters may be dispensed with;

(i) if invited to do so by all parties, direct the action to be determined on the basis of written submissions, or such other material, without any oral hearing; and

(j) may continue the procedural hearing to a date to be appointed by him.

[1124]

NOTES

Substituted as noted to r 47.1 at **[1113]**.

47.13 Debates

Chapter 28 (procedure roll) shall apply to a debate ordered in a commercial action under rule 47.12(2)(a) as it applies to a cause appointed to the Procedure Roll.

[1125]

NOTES

Substituted as noted to r 47.1 at **[1113]**.

47.14 Lodging of productions for proof

(1) Any document not previously lodged required for any proof in a commercial action shall be lodged as a production not less than 7 days before the date fixed for the proof.

(2) No document may be lodged as a production after the date referred to in paragraph (1), even by agreement of all parties, unless the court is satisfied that any document sought to be lodged could not with reasonable diligence have been lodged in time.

[1126]

NOTES

Substituted as noted to r 47.1 at **[1113]**.

47.15 Hearings for further procedure

At any time before final judgment, the commercial judge may, at his own instance or on the motion of any party, have a commercial action put out for hearing for further procedure; and the commercial judge may make such order as he thinks fit.

[1127]

NOTES

Substituted as noted to r 47.1 at **[1113]**.

47.16 Failure to comply with rule or order of commercial judge

Any failure by a party to comply timeously with a provision in these Rules or any order made by the commercial judge in a commercial action shall entitle the judge, at his own instance—

(a) to refuse to extend any period for compliance with a provision in these Rules or an order of the court,

(b) to dismiss the action or counterclaim, as the case may be; in whole or in part,

(c) to grant decree in respect of all or any of the conclusions of the summons or counterclaim, as the case may be, or (d) to make an award of expenses,

as he thinks fit.]

[1128]

NOTES

Substituted as noted to r 47.1 at **[1113]**.

CHAPTER 59
APPLICATIONS FOR LETTERS

59.1 Applications for letters of arrestment or inhibition

(1) An application for letters of arrestment or inhibition may be made, as the case may be, in—

(a) Form 59.1-A (arrestment);

(b) Form 59.1-B (inhibition where decree granted, foreign judgment registered for execution or other document having the same force and effect as an extract of a decree of the Court of Session);

(c) Form 59.1-C (inhibition on deed registered for execution); …

(d) Form 59.1-D (inhibition on dependence of action in sheriff court)[; …

(e) Form 59.1-E (inhibition in respect of future or contingent debt)][; or

(f) Form 59.1-F (inhibition on contract for transfer of heritable property)]

(2) An application under paragraph (1) shall be presented [to the Deputy Principal Clerk] together with any relevant supporting documents.

(3) [Except where the application is in Form [59.1-D or] 59.1-E], if the Deputy Principal Clerk is satisfied that the applicant for such letters is entitled to a warrant for arrestment or inhibition—

(a) he shall sign and date the warrant in such an application; and

(b) the application shall be signeted;

and such signeted application and warrant shall constitute letters of arrestment or inhibition, as the case may be.

(4) [Where the application is in any of Forms 59.1-A to [59.1-C]] [or is in Form 59.1-F], if the Deputy Principal Clerk refuses to sign and date such warrant, the application shall, on request, be placed before the Lord Ordinary; and the decision of the Lord Ordinary shall be final and not subject to review.

[(4A) Where the application is in Form [59.1-D or] 59.1-E, it shall be placed before the Lord Ordinary together with any such documents as are mentioned in paragraph (2); and if the Lord Ordinary is satisfied as is mentioned in paragraph (3)—

(a) he shall sign and date the warrant in the application; and

(b) the application shall be signeted

and such signeted application and warrant shall constitute letters of inhibition.

(4B) The decision of the Lord Ordinary as respects an application in Form [59.1-D or] 59.1-E shall be final and not subject to review.]

(5) An application for letters of arrestment or inhibition on the dependence of an action to which a claim under section 19 of the Family Law (Scotland) Act 1985 applies shall be placed before the Lord Ordinary; and the decision of the Lord Ordinary shall be final and not subject to review.

[1129]

NOTES

Para (1): word omitted from sub-para (c) revoked, and sub-para (e) and preceding word added, by the Act of Sederunt (Rules of the Court of Session Amendment) (Miscellaneous) 1998, SI 1998/890, r 2(1), 13(a); word omitted from sub-para (d) revoked, and sub-para (f) and preceding word added, by the Act of Sederunt (Rules of the Court of Session Amendment No 7) (Miscellaneous) 1999, SSI 1999/109, r 2(1), (5)(a).

Para (2): words in square brackets substituted by the Act of Sederunt (Rules of the Court of Session Amendment No 4) (Miscellaneous) 1997, SI 1997/1050, r 2(1), (8).

Para (3): words in first (outer) pair of square brackets inserted by SI 1998/890, r 2(1), (13)(b); words in second (inner) pair of square brackets substituted by the Act of Sederunt (Rules of the Court of Session Amendment No 6) (Diligence on the Dependence) 2003, SSI 2003/537, r 2(1), (9)(a).

Para (4): words in first (outer) pair of square brackets inserted by SI 1998/890, r 2(1), (13)(c); words in second (inner) pair of square brackets substituted by SSI 2003/537, r 2(1), (9)(b); words in third pair of square brackets inserted by SSI 1999/109, r 2(1), (5)(b).

Paras (4A), (4B): inserted by SI 1998/890, r 2(1), (13)(d); words in square brackets substituted by SSI 2003/537, r 2(1), (9)(a).

Other proceedings in relation to statutory applications

CHAPTER 62
RECOGNITION, REGISTRATION AND ENFORCEMENT OF FOREIGN JUDGMENTS, ETC

PART I
GENERAL PROVISIONS

62.1 Disapplication of certain rules to this Chapter

[Subject to Part XIII] the following rules shall not apply to a petition or application under this Chapter:—

14.5 (first order in petitions),
14.6 (period of notice for lodging answers).
14.7 (intimation and service of petitions),
14.9 (unopposed petitions).

[1130]

NOTES

Words in square brackets inserted by the Act of Sederunt (Rules of the Court of Session Amendment No 2) (UNCITRAL Model Law on Cross-Border Insolvency) 2006, SSI 2006/199, r 2(1), (2).

62.2 Certificate of currency conversion

(1) Where the sum payable under a judgment, award, recommendation or determination to be registered in accordance with a provision of this Chapter is expressed in a currency other than sterling, the petitioner or applicant, as the case may be, before applying to the Keeper of the Registers for registration of such a document, shall lodge in the Petition Department—

(a) a certified statement of the rate of exchange prevailing at—
  (i) the date of the judgment, award, recommendation or determination,
  (ii) the date on which the certified statement is lodged, or
  (iii) a date within three days before the date on which the certified statement is lodged,

and of the sterling equivalent, at that rate, of the principal sum, interest and expenses contained in the judgment, award, recommendation or determination, as the case may be; and

(b) a certificate of currency conversion in Form 62.2.

(2) The certified statement required under paragraph (1) shall be by an official in the Bank of England or an institution authorised under the Banking Act 1987.

(3) On receipt of the documents specified in paragraph (1), the clerk of session shall, if satisfied with the terms of those documents, sign and date the certificate of currency conversion.

[1131]

62.3 Translation of document lodged

Where a judgment, award, or other document lodged with a petition or application to which this Chapter applies is in a language other than English, there shall be produced with the petition a translation into English certified as correct by the translator; and the certificate shall include his full name, address and qualification.

[1132]

PART II
REGISTRATION AND ENFORCEMENT UNDER THE ADMINISTRATION OF JUSTICE ACT 1920 AND THE FOREIGN JUDGMENTS (RECIPROCAL ENFORCEMENT) ACT 1933

62.4 Application and interpretation of this Part

(1) This Part applies to an application to the court under the Administration of Justice Act 1920 or the Foreign Judgments (Reciprocal Enforcement) Act 1933.

(2) In this Part—

"the Act of 1920" means the Administration of Justice Act 1920;

"the Act of 1933" means the Foreign Judgments (Reciprocal Enforcement) Act 1933.

[1133]

62.5 Applications for registration under the Act of 1920 or 1933

(1) An application under section 9 of the Act of 1920 (enforcement in United Kingdom of judgments obtained in superior courts in other British Dominions etc) shall be made by petition.

(2) An application under section 2 of the Act of 1933 (application for registration of a foreign judgment) shall be made by petition.

[1134]

62.6 Supporting documents

(1) There shall be produced with the petition for registration referred to in rule 62.5 an affidavit—

(a) referring to the judgment or a certified copy of the judgment issued by the original court and authenticated by its seal; and

(b) stating—

(i) the full name, title, trade or business and the usual or last known place of residence or business of the judgment creditor and the judgment debtor respectively;

(ii) that the petitioner is entitled to have the judgment registered under the Act of 1920 or the Act of 1933, as the case may be;

(iii) where the judgment is in respect of several matters, only some of which may be registered, those in respect of which the petitioner seeks registration;

(iv) the amount of the interest, if any, which under the law of the country of the original court has become due under the judgment up to the date of the affidavit;

(v) the amount of the judgment which is unsatisfied;

(vi) that at the date of presentation of the petition the judgment may be enforced by execution in the country of the original court;

(vii) that if the judgment were registered, the registration would not be, or be liable to be, set aside under section 4 of the Act of 1933; and

(viii) that the judgment is not a judgment to which section 5 of the Protection of Trading Interests Act 1980 (restriction on enforcement of certain overseas judgments) applies.

(2) There shall be produced with a petition referred to in rule 62.5 such other evidence with respect to the matters referred to in sub-paragraphs (b)(iv) and (b)(vi) of paragraph (1) as may be required having regard to the provisions of an order in Council made under section 1 of the Act of 1933 (power to extend the Act of 1933 to the country of the original court).

[1135]

62.7 Warrant for registration under the Act of 1920 or 1933

(1) The court shall, on being satisfied that the petition complies with the requirements of the Act of 1920 or the Act of 1933, as the case may be, pronounce an interlocutor granting warrant for the registration of the judgment.

(2) The interlocutor under paragraph (1) shall specify a date by which the judgment debtor may apply to the court to set aside the registration; and in fixing such date, regard shall be had to the place of residence of the judgment debtor.

(3) In fixing the date under paragraph (2), the court shall have regard, in the case of a judgment debtor furth of Scotland, to the periods for superseding extract of a decree in absence in rule 19.1(5). **[1136]**

62.8 Registration of judgments under the Act of 1920 or 1933

(1) Where the court pronounces an interlocutor under rule 62.7(1) granting warrant for registration, the Deputy Principal Clerk shall enter details of the judgment in a register of judgments under the Act of 1920 or the Act of 1933, as the case may be, kept in the Petition Department.

(2) On presentation by the petitioner to the Keeper of the Registers of—
(a) a certified copy of the interlocutor under rule 62.7(1) granting warrant for registration,
(b) the judgment or a certified copy of the judgment and any translation of it, and
(c) any certificate of currency conversion under [rule 62.2(1)(b)],

they shall be registered in the register of judgments of the Books of Council and Session.

(3) An extract of a registered judgment with a warrant for execution shall not be issued by the Keeper of the Registers until the certificate mentioned in rule 62.10(3) is produced to him. **[1137]**

NOTES

Para (2): words in square brackets substituted by the Act of Sederunt (Rules of the Court of Session Amendment No 4) (Miscellaneous) 1996, SI 1996/2168, r 2(1), (13).

62.9 Service on judgment debtor

On registration of a judgment under rule 62.8(2), the petitioner shall serve a notice of the registration on the judgment debtor in Form 62.9. **[1138]**

62.10 Application to set aside registration under the Act of 1920 or 1933

(1) An application by a judgment debtor to set aside the registration of a judgment shall be made by note and supported by affidavit and any documentary evidence.

(2) In relation to such an application, the court may order such inquiry as it thinks fit.

(3) Where no such application is made by the date specified in the interlocutor pronounced under rule 62.7(2) or where the application has been made and refused, the Deputy Principal Clerk shall, at the request of the petitioner, issue a certificate to that effect.

(4) Subject to paragraph (5), where such an application is granted, a certificate to that effect issued by the Deputy Principal Clerk shall be sufficient warrant to the Keeper of the Registers to cancel the registration and return the judgment to the petitioner.

(5) Where the court makes an order under section 5(3) of the Act of 1933 (judgment ordered to be registered for balance payable), it shall pronounce an interlocutor—
(a) recalling the warrant for registration granted under rule 62.7; and
(b) granting warrant for registration of the judgment in respect of the balance remaining payable at the date of the original petition for registration. **[1139]**

62.11 Application for enforcement abroad under the Act of 1920 or 1933

(1) An application under section 10 of the Act of 1920 or the Act of 1933, as the case may be, for a certified copy of a judgment pronounced by the court shall be made by letter to the Deputy Principal Clerk.

(2) On receipt of such an application, the Deputy Principal Clerk shall issue under the seal of the court a copy of the judgment certified by him in Form 62.11.

(3) Where such an application is made under section 10 of the Act of 1933, the Deputy Principal Clerk shall issue with the certified copy of the judgment a further certificate under the seal of the court signed by him containing the details, and having appended the documents, mentioned in paragraph (4).

(4) A certificate under paragraph (3) shall—
- (a) state—
  - (i) the manner in which the principal writ or counterclaim was served on the judgment debtor;
  - (ii) whether or not the judgment debtor entered appearance or lodged answers in the process of the cause;
  - (iii) any objections made to the jurisdiction:
  - (iv) that the time limit for appeal has expired and that no appeal has been taken, or that an appeal was taken but was refused; and
  - (v) such other particulars as may be required by the foreign court which may enable execution of the judgment; and
- (b) number, identify and have appended to it a copy of—
  - (i) the principal writ or counterclaim showing the manner in which such writ was served on the judgment debtor;
  - (ii) the pleadings, if any, in the cause resulting in the judgment; and
  - (iii) a copy of the opinion, if any, of the judge or judges who issued the judgment.

(5) Where necessary, the applicant shall provide the copies of the documents mentioned in paragraph (4).

[1140]

PART III
REGISTRATION OF AWARDS UNDER THE ARBITRATION (INTERNATIONAL INVESTMENT DISPUTES) ACT 1966

62.12 Application and interpretation of this Part

(1) This Part applies to the registration of awards under the Arbitration (International Investment Disputes) Act 1966.

(2) In this Part—

"the Act of 1966" means the Arbitration (International Investment Disputes) Act 1966;

"award" has the meaning assigned to it in section 1(7) of the Act of 1966;

"the Convention" means the convention mentioned in section 1(1) of the Act of 1966.

[1141]

62.13 Applications for registration under the Act of 1966

(1) An application for recognition or enforcement of an award under Article 54 of the Convention shall be made by petition.

(2) There shall be produced with such a petition an affidavit—
- (a) exhibiting a copy of the award certified under the Convention; and
- (b) stating—
  - (i) the full name, title, trade or business and the usual or the last known place of residence or, where appropriate, of the business of the petitioner and of the party against whom the award was made;
  - (ii) that the petitioner is entitled to have the award registered under the Act of 1966;
  - (iii) the amount of the award which is unsatisfied;
  - (iv) whether the enforcement of the award has been sisted (provisionally or otherwise) under the Convention and whether any, and if so what, application has been made under the Convention which, if granted, might result in a sist of enforcement of the award.

[1142]

62.14 Warrant for registration under the Act of 1966

The court shall, subject to rule 62.17 (sist of enforcement), on being satisfied that the petition complies with the requirements of the Act of 1966, pronounce an interlocutor granting warrant for the registration of the award.

[1143]

62.15 Registration under the Act of 1966

(1) Where the court pronounces an interlocutor under rule 62.14 granting warrant for registration, the Deputy Principal Clerk shall enter details of the interlocutor and the award in a register of awards under the Act of 1966.

(2) On presentation by the petitioner to the Keeper of the Registers of—
(a) a certified copy of the interlocutor under rule 62.14,
(b) a certified copy of the award and any translation of it, and
(c) any certificate of currency conversion under [rule 62.2(1)(b)],
they shall be registered in the register of judgments of the Books of Council and Session.

(3) An extract of the registered award with warrant for execution shall not be issued by the Keeper of the Registers until a certificate of service under rule 62.16 is produced to him.
[1144]

NOTES

Para (2): words in square brackets substituted by the Act of Sederunt (Rules of the Court of Session Amendment No 4) (Miscellaneous) 1996, SI 1996/2168, r 2(1), (13).

62.16 Service on party against whom award made

On registration under rule 62.15, the petitioner shall forthwith serve a notice of the registration on the party against whom the award was made in Form 62.16.
[1145]

62.17 Sist of enforcement under the Act of 1966

(1) Where it appears to the court that—
(a) the enforcement of the award has been sisted (whether provisionally or otherwise) under the Convention, or
(b) any application has been made under the Convention which, if granted, might result in a sist of the enforcement of the award,
the court shall, or in the case referred to in sub-paragraph (b) may, sist the petition for such time as it thinks fit.

(2) Where the court has granted a warrant for registration under rule 62.14, the party against whom the award was made may apply to the court for suspension or interdict of execution of the award.

(3) An application under paragraph (2) shall—
(a) be made on ground (a) or (b) of paragraph (1);
(b) notwithstanding rule 60.2 (form of applications for suspension), be made by note in the process of the petition under rule 62.13; and
(c) be accompanied by an affidavit stating the relevant facts.
[1146]

PART IV
EUROPEAN COMMUNITY JUDGMENTS

62.18 Interpretation of this Part

(1) In this Part—
"Community judgment" means any decision, judgment or order which is enforceable under or in accordance with—
(a) Article [244 or 256] of the EEC Treaty,
(b) Article 18, 159 or 164 of the Euratom Treaty, or
(c) Article 44 or 92 of the ECSC Treaty;
"Euratom inspection order" means an order made by or in the exercise of the functions of the President of the European Court or by the Commission of the European Communities under Article 81 of the Eurotom Treaty;
"European Court" means the Court of Justice of the European Communities;
"order for enforcement" means an order by or under the authority of the Secretary of State that the Community judgment to which it is appended is to be registered for enforcement in the United Kingdom.

(2) In paragraph (1), the expressions "EEC Treaty", "Euratom Treaty" and "ECSC Treaty" have the meanings assigned respectively in Schedule 1 to the European Communities Act 1972.
[1147]

NOTES

Para (1): words in square brackets in sub-para (a) substituted by the Act of Sederunt (Rules of the Court of Session Amendment No 4) (References to the Court of Justice of the European Communities) 1999, SI 1999/1281, r 2(1), (2).

62.19 Register of European Community judgments

A register shall be kept by the Deputy Principal Clerk for the purpose of registering—

(a) any Community judgment to which the Secretary of State has attached an order for enforcement;

(b) any Euratom inspection order; or

(c) any order of the European Court that enforcement of a registered Community judgment shall be suspended.

[1148]

62.20 Applications for registration of European Community judgments

(1) An application for registration of a Community judgment or Euratom inspection order shall be made by petition.

(2) Where the application is for registration of a Community judgment under which a sum of money is payable, the petition shall set out—

(a) the name, trade or business and the usual or last known place of residence or business of the judgment debtor, so far as known to the petitioner; and

(b) the amount of the judgment which remains unsatisfied.

(3) There shall be produced with a petition referred to in paragraph (1) the Community judgment and the order for its enforcement or the Euratom inspection order, as the case may be, or a copy of it.

[1149]

62.21 Warrant for registration of European Community judgments

(1) On an application being made under rule 62.20, the court shall direct that any Euratom inspection order or any Community judgment which has appended to it an order for enforcement shall be entered in the register kept under rule 62.19 and—

(a) in respect of a Community judgment, subject to paragraph (2), pronounce an interlocutor granting warrant for registration of the judgment in the Books of Council and Session; or

(b) in respect of a Euratom inspection order, pronounce such interlocutor as is necessary for the purpose of ensuring that effect is given to that order.

(2) Where it appears that a Community judgment under which a sum of money is payable has been partly satisfied at the date of the application under rule 62.20, warrant for registration in the Books of Council and Session shall be granted only in respect of the balance remaining payable at that date.

[1150]

62.22 Registration of European Community judgments

(1) On presentation by the petitioner to the Keeper of the Registers of—

(a) a certified copy of an interlocutor pronounced under rule 62.21(1)(a),

(b) the Community judgment or a certified copy of it and any translation of it, and

(c) any certificate of currency conversion under [rule 62.2(1)(b)],

they shall immediately be registered in the register of judgments of the Books of Council and Session.

On registration under paragraph (1), the Keeper of the Registers shall issue an extract of the registered Community judgment with a warrant for execution.

[1151]

NOTES

Para (1): words in square brackets substituted by the Act of Sederunt (Rules of the Court of Session Amendment No 4) (Miscellaneous) 1996, SI 1996/2168, r 2(1), (13).

62.23 Service on judgment debtor of European Community judgment

On an interlocutor being pronounced under rule 62.21(1)(a), the petitioner shall forthwith serve a copy of it on the person against whom the Community judgment was given or the Euratom inspection order was made, as the case may be.

[1152]

62.24 Variation or cancellation of registration

(1) An application for the variation or cancellation of any registration shall be made by note in the process of the petition under rule 62.20(1).

(2) Where the court grants an application under paragraph (1), it may direct that the entry in the register kept under rule 62.19, and, in the case of variation of a Community judgment, the entry in the Books of Council and Session, shall be varied as sought by the noter.

[1153]

62.25 Suspension of enforcement of Community judgments

(1) An order of the European Court that enforcement of a registered Community judgment be suspended—

(a) shall—

(i) on production of the order to the Court of Session, and

(ii) on application made by note,

be registered forthwith, and

(b) shall be of the same effect as if the order had been an order made by the Court of Session on the date of its registration suspending the execution of the judgment for the same period and on the same conditions as are stated in the order of the European Court.

(2) No steps to enforce the judgment mentioned in paragraph (1) shall be taken while such an order of the European Court remains in force.

[1154]

[PART V
RECOGNITION AND ENFORCEMENT OF JUDGMENTS UNDER THE CIVIL JURISDICTION AND JUDGMENTS ACT 1982 OR UNDER COUNCIL REGULATION (EC) NO 44/2001 OF 22ND DECEMBER 2001

62.26 Application and interpretation of this Part

(1) This Part applies to the recognition and enforcement of a judgment under the Civil Jurisdiction and Judgments Act 1982 or under the Council Regulation.

(2) Unless the context otherwise requires, in this Part—

"the Act of 1982" means the Civil Jurisdiction and Judgments Act 1982;

"Contracting State" has the meaning assigned in section 1(3) of the Act of 1982;

"judgment" includes an authentic instrument or court settlement;

"the Council Regulation" means Council Regulation (EC) No 44/2001 of 22nd December 2000 on jurisdiction and the recognition and enforcement of judgments in civil and commercial matters;

"Member State" has the same meaning as Member State in the Council Regulation.]

[1155]

NOTES

Commencement: 1 March 2004.

Pt V (rr 62.26–62.42) substituted by the Act of Sederunt (Rules of the Court of Session Amendment) (Miscellaneous) 2004, SSI 2004/52, r 2(1), (14).

[62.27 Disapplication of certain rules to this Part

The following provisions shall not apply to an application under this Part in addition to those rules mentioned in rule 62.1:—

rule 4.1(1) (printed form for petition),

rule 14.4 (form of petitions).]

[1156]

NOTES

Commencement: 1 March 2004.

Substituted as noted to r 62.26 at **[1155]**.

[62.28 Enforcement of judgments, authentic instruments or court settlements from another Contracting State or Member State

(1) An application under—

(a) section 4 of, and Article 31 (enforcement of judgment from another Contracting State) or Article 50 (enforcement of authentic instrument or court settlement from another Contracting State) of the Convention in Schedule 1 or 3C to, the Act of 1982; or

(b) Article 38 (enforcement of judgment from Member State), Article 57 (enforcement of authentic instrument from another Member State) or Article 58 (enforcement of court settlement from another Member State) of the Council Regulation,

shall be made by petition in Form 62.28.

(2) Subject to paragraph (3), there shall be produced with the petition—

(a) an authentic copy of the judgment to be registered;

(b) a document which establishes that, according to the law of the country in which the judgment has been given, the judgment is enforceable and has been served;

(c) where judgment has been given in absence (that is to say, in default of appearance), the original or a certified copy of the document which establishes that the party against whom judgment was given in absence was served with the document initiating the proceedings or with an equivalent document;

(d) where applicable, a document showing that the applicant is in receipt of legal aid in the country in which the judgment was given;

(e) an affidavit stating—

(i) whether the judgment provides for the payment of a sum of money;

(ii) whether interest is recoverable on the judgment under the law of the country in which judgment was given and, if so, the rate of interest, the date from which interest is due and the date on which interest ceases to accrue;

(iii) an address within the jurisdiction of the court for service on or intimation to the petitioner;

(iv) the usual or last known place of residence or business of the person against whom the judgment was given;

(v) the grounds on which the petitioner is entitled to enforce the judgment; and

(vi) the part of the judgment which is unsatisfied.

(3) Paragraph (2)(b) and (d) shall not apply to a petition under Article 38 (enforcement of judgment from another Member State), Article 57 (enforcement of authentic instrument from another Member State) or Article 58 (enforcement of settlement from another Member State) of the Council Regulation but there shall be produced with such a petition a certificate under Article 54 (standard form of certificate of judgment), Article 57 (standard form of certificate of authentic instrument) or Article 58 (standard form of certificate of court settlement) of the Council Regulation.

(4) Where the petitioner does not produce a document required under paragraph (2)(a) to (d) or (3), the court may—

(a) fix a period within which that document is to be lodged;

(b) accept an equivalent document; or

(c) dispense with the requirement to produce the document.]

[1157]

NOTES

Commencement: 1 March 2004.
Substituted as noted to r 62.26 at **[1155]**.

[62.29 Protective measures and interim interdict

(1) On lodging a petition, the petitioner may, at any time until the expiry of the period for lodging an appeal referred to in rule 62.34 or its disposal, apply by motion for a warrant for the execution of protective measures.

(2) On lodging such a petition, the petitioner may, at any time until the expiry of the period for lodging an appeal mentioned in rule 62.34 or its disposal, apply by motion for an interim interdict.]

[1158]

NOTES

Commencement: 1 March 2004.
Substituted as noted to r 62.26 at **[1155]**.

[62.30 Warrant for registration under the Act of 1982 or the Council Regulation

(1) The court shall, on being satisfied that the petition complies with the requirements of the Act of 1982 or, as the case may be, the Council Regulation, pronounce an interlocutor—

(a) granting warrant for the registration of the judgment;
(b) granting warrant for the execution of protective measures; and
(c) where necessary, granting decree in accordance with Scots law.

(2) The interlocutor pronounced under paragraph (1) shall specify—

(a) the period within which an appeal mentioned in rule 62.34 against the interlocutor may be made; and
(b) that the petitioner—
  (i) may register the judgment under rule 62.32; and
  (ii) may not proceed to execution until the expiry of the period for lodging such an appeal or its disposal.]

[1159]

NOTES

Commencement: 1 March 2004.
Substituted as noted to r 62.26 at **[1155]**.

[62.31 Intimation to petitioner

Where the court pronounces an interlocutor under rule 62.30(1) granting warrant for registration, the Deputy Principal Clerk shall intimate such interlocutor to the petitioner by sending to his address for service in Scotland a certified copy of the interlocutor by registered post or the first class recorded delivery service.]

[1160]

NOTES

Commencement: 1 March 2004.
Substituted as noted to r 62.26 at **[1155]**.

[62.32 Registration under the Act of 1982 or the Council Regulation

(1) Where the court pronounces an interlocutor under rule 62.30(1) granting warrant for registration, the Deputy Principal Clerk shall enter the judgment in a register of judgments, authentic instruments and court settlements under the Act of 1982 and the Council Regulation kept in the Petition Department.

(2) On presentation by the petitioner to the Keeper of the Registers of—

(a) a certified copy of the interlocutor under rule 62.30(1) granting warrant for registration;
(b) an authentic copy of the judgment and any translation of it; and
(c) any certificate of currency conversion under rule 62.2(1)(b),

they shall be registered in the register of judgments of the Books of Council and Session.

(3) On registration under paragraph (2), the Keeper of the Registers shall issue an extract of the registered judgment with a warrant for execution.]

[1161]

NOTES

Commencement: 1 March 2004.
Substituted as noted to r 62.26 at **[1155]**.

[62.33 Service of warrant for registration under the Act of 1982 or the Council Regulation

The petitioner shall serve a copy of the interlocutor granting warrant for registration of a judgment and a notice in Form 62.33 on the person liable under the judgment.]

[1162]

NOTES

Commencement: 1 March 2004.
Substituted as noted to r 62.26 at **[1155]**.

[62.34 Appeals under the Act of 1982 or the Council Regulation

(1) An appeal under Article 37 of the convention in Schedule 1 or 3C to the Act of 1982 (appeal against granting of warrant for registration) or an appeal under Article 43 (appeals by either party) of the Council Regulation against the granting of a warrant for registration shall be made by motion—

(a) to the Lord Ordinary; and

(b) within one month of service under rule 62.33 (service of warrant for registration under the Act of 1982 or the Council Regulation) or within two months of such service where service was executed on a person domiciled in another Contracting State or, as the case may be, Member State.

(2) An appeal under Article 40 of the convention in Schedule 1 or 3C to the Act of 1982 (appeal against refusal to grant warrant for registration) or an appeal under Article 43 (appeals by either party) of the Council Regulation against a refusal to grant warrant for registration shall be made by motion—

(a) to the Lord Ordinary; and

(b) within one month of the interlocutor pronounced under rule 62.30(1) (warrant for registration under the Act of 1982 or the Council Regulation).

(3) Where the respondent in any such appeal is domiciled furth of the United Kingdom—

(a) in relation to an appeal under paragraph (1), intimation of the motion shall be made to the address for service of the respondent in Scotland; and

(b) in relation to an appeal under paragraph (2), intimation of the motion shall be made in accordance with rule 16.2 (service furth of United Kingdom) or rule 16.5 (service where address of person is not known), as the case may be.

(4) Where an appeal under paragraph (1) is successful, the court shall, on the motion of the appellant, pronounce an interlocutor recalling any protective measure or interim interdict.]

[1163]

NOTES

Commencement: 1 March 2004.

Substituted as noted to r 62.26 at **[1155]**.

[62.35 Reclaiming under the Act of 1982 or the Council Regulation

(1) Any party dissatisfied with the interlocutor of the Lord Ordinary in any appeal mentioned in rule 62.34 (appeals under the Act of 1982 or the Council Regulation) may reclaim on a point of law against that interlocutor.

(2) Where a reclaiming motion under paragraph (1) against the registration of a judgment is successful, the court shall, on the motion of the appellant, pronounce an interlocutor recalling any protective measure or interim interdict.]

[1164]

NOTES

Commencement: 1 March 2004.

Substituted as noted to r 62.26 at **[1155]**.

[62.36 Recognition of judgments from another Contracting State or Member State

(1) For the purposes of Article 26 of the convention in Schedule 1 or 3C to the Act of 1982 and Article 33 of the Council Regulation, an interlocutor pronounced under rule 62.30(1) (warrant for registration under the Act of 1982 or the Council Regulation) shall imply recognition of the judgment so dealt with.

(2) In an application under Article 26(2) of the convention in Schedule 1 or 3C to the Act of 1982 (application for recognition of a judgment) or Article 33(2) of the Council Regulation (application for recognition of a judgment), rules 62.26 to 62.35 shall apply to such an application as they apply to an application under Article 31 of that convention, subject to the following provisions:—

(a) it shall not be necessary to produce any documents required by rule 62.28(2)(b) and (d); and

(b) rule 62.32 shall not apply.]

[1165]

NOTES

Commencement: 1 March 2004.
Substituted as noted to r 62.26 at **[1155]**.

[62.37 Enforcement of judgments from another part of the United Kingdom in Scotland (money provisions)

(1) An application under paragraph 5 of Schedule 6 to the Act of 1982 (application for registration in the Court of Session of a certificate in relation to a money provision in a judgment from another part of the United Kingdom) shall be made by presenting to the Keeper of the Registers—

(a) a certificate under paragraph 4(1) of Schedule 6 to the Act of 1982; and
(b) any certificate of currency conversion under rule 62.2(1)(b).

(2) On presentation of the certificate mentioned in paragraph (1)(a), the Keeper of the Registers shall—

(a) register the certificate in the register of judgments of the Books of Council and Session; and
(b) issue an extract of the certificate with a warrant for execution.

(3) An application under—

(a) paragraph 9 of Schedule 6 to the Act of 1982 (application to sist proceedings for enforcement of a certificate registered under paragraph (2) of this rule); or
(b) paragraph 10 of Schedule 6 to the Act of 1982 (application for reduction of registration),

shall be made by petition.]

[1166]

NOTES

Commencement: 1 March 2004.
Substituted as noted to r 62.26 at **[1155]**.

[62.38 Enforcement of judgments from another part of the United Kingdom in Scotland (non-money provisions)

(1) An application under paragraph 5 of Schedule 7 to the Act of 1982 (application for registration in the Court of Session of a non-money provision in a judgment from another part of the United Kingdom) shall be made by petition in Form 62.38.

(2) There shall be produced with the petition under paragraph (1)—

(a) a certified copy of the judgment of the original court; and
(b) a certificate under paragraph 4(1)(b) of Schedule 7 to the Act of 1982.

(3) The petition under paragraph (1) shall be heard by the Lord Ordinary in chambers and shall not require any appearance for the applicant unless the court so requires.

(4) The court shall, on being satisfied that the petition complies with the requirements of section 18 of, and Schedule 7 to, the Act of 1982, pronounce an interlocutor—

(a) granting warrant for the registration of the judgment; and
(b) where necessary, granting decree in accordance with Scots law.

(5) Where the court pronounces an interlocutor under paragraph (4), rule 62.32 shall apply to the registration of a judgment under this rule as it applies to the registration of a judgment under that rule.

(6) An application under—

(a) paragraph 8 of Schedule 7 to the Act of 1982 (application to sist proceedings for enforcement of a judgment registered under paragraph (5) of this rule); or
(b) paragraph 9 of Schedule 7 to the Act of 1982 (application to reduce the registration under paragraph (5) of this rule),

shall be made by petition.]

[1167]

NOTES

Commencement: 1 March 2004.
Substituted as noted to r 62.26 at **[1155]**.

[62.39 Cancellation of registration under the Act of 1982 or the Council Regulation

Where—

(a) an interlocutor under rule 62.30(1) (warrant for registration under the Act of 1982 or the Council Regulation) is recalled and registration under rule 62.32 (registration under the Act of 1982 or the Council Regulation) is ordered to be cancelled after an appeal under Article 37 of the convention in Schedule 1 or 3C to the Act of 1982 or an appeal under Article 43 of the Council Regulation; or

(b) registration under rule 62.37(2) (registration of judgments from another part of the United Kingdom in Scotland (money provisions)) or rule 62.38(5) (registration of judgments from another part of the United Kingdom in Scotland (non-money provisions)) is reduced,

a certificate to that effect by the Deputy Principal Clerk shall be sufficient warrant to the Keeper of the Registers to cancel the registration and return the judgment, certificate or other documents to the person who applied for registration.]

[1168]

NOTES

Commencement: 1 March 2004.
Substituted as noted to r 62.26 at **[1155]**.

[62.40 Enforcement in another Contracting State or Member State of Court of Session judgments etc

(1) Where a person seeks to apply under section 12 of the Act of 1982 for recognition or enforcement in another Contracting State of a judgment given by the court or a court settlement in the court, he shall apply by letter to the Deputy Principal Clerk for—

(a) a certificate in Form 62.40-A;

(b) a certified copy of the judgment; and

(c) if required, a certified copy of the opinion of the court.

(2) Where a person seeks to apply under Chapter III of the Council Regulation for recognition or enforcement in another Member State of a judgment given by the court, he shall apply by letter to the Deputy Principal Clerk for—

(a) a certificate under Article 54 of the Judgments Regulation;

(b) a certified copy of the judgment; and

(c) if required, a certified copy of the opinion of the court.

(3) The Deputy Principal Clerk shall not issue a certificate under paragraph (1)(a) or 2(a) unless there is produced to him an execution of service of the judgment on the person on whom it is sought to be enforced.

(4) Where a person seeks to apply under Article 50 of the convention in Schedule 1 or 3C to the Act of 1982 for enforcement of an authentic instrument or court settlement registered for execution in the Books of Council and Session, he shall apply by letter to the Keeper of the Registers for—

(a) a certificate in Form 62.40-B or; and

(b) an extract of the authentic instrument or court settlement.

(5) Where a person seeks to apply under Article 57 or 58 of the Council Regulation for enforcement in another Member State of an authentic instrument or court settlement registered for execution in the Books of Council and Session, he shall apply by letter to the Keeper of the Registers for—

(a) a certificate under Article 57 or 58 of the Council Regulation; and

(b) an extract of the authentic instrument or court settlement.

(6) The Keeper of the Registers shall not issue a certificate under paragraph (4) or (5) unless there is produced to him an affidavit verifying that enforcement has not been suspended and that the time available for enforcement has not expired.]

[1169]

NOTES

Commencement: 1 March 2004.
Substituted as noted to r 62.26 at **[1155]**.

[62.41 Enforcement in another part of the United Kingdom of Court of Session judgments or documents registered for execution (money provisions)

(1) Where a person seeks to apply under Schedule 6 to the Act of 1982 for enforcement in another part of the United Kingdom of a money provision in a judgment given by the court, he shall apply by letter to the Deputy Principal Clerk for a certificate in Form 62.41 A.

(2) The Deputy Principal Clerk shall not issue a certificate under paragraph (1) unless there is produced to him an affidavit stating—

(a) the sum or aggregate of sums including interest and expenses payable and unsatisfied;
(b) that the time for making an appeal against such judgment has expired or such appeal has been finally determined;
(c) that enforcement of the judgment has not been suspended and the time available for its enforcement has not expired; and
(d) the address of the party entitled to enforce, and the usual or last known address of the party liable to execution on, the judgment.

(3) Where a person seeks to apply under Schedule 6 to the Act of 1982 for enforcement in another part of the United Kingdom of a document registered for execution in the Books of Council and Session, he shall apply by letter to the Keeper of the Registers for—

(a) a certificate in Form 62.41 B; and
(b) an extract of the document.

(4) The Keeper of the Registers shall not issue a certificate under paragraph (3) unless there is produced to him an affidavit which includes the statements required under paragraph (2)(a), (c) and (d).]

[1170]

NOTES

Commencement: 1 March 2004.
Substituted as noted to r 62.26 at **[1155]**.

[62.42 Enforcement in another part of the United Kingdom of Court of Session judgments or documents registered for execution (non-money provisions)

(1) Where a person seeks to apply under Schedule 7 to the Act of 1982 for enforcement in another part of the United Kingdom of a non-money provision in a judgment of the court, he shall apply by letter to the Deputy Principal Clerk for—

(a) a certificate in Form 62.42 A; and
(b) a certified copy of such judgment.

(2) The Deputy Principal Clerk shall not issue a certificate under paragraph (1) unless there is produced to him an affidavit stating—

(a) that the time for making an appeal against such judgment has expired or such appeal has been finally determined; and
(b) the address of the party entitled to enforce, and the usual or last known address of the party liable to execution on, the judgment or registered document.

(3) Where the Deputy Principal Clerk issues a certificate in Form 62.42-A, he shall attach it to the certified copy judgment.

(4) Where a person seeks to apply under Schedule 7 to the Act of 1982 for enforcement in another part of the United Kingdom of a non-money provision in a document registered for execution in the Books of Council and Session, he shall apply by letter to the Keeper of the Registers for—

(a) a certificate in Form 62.42; and
(b) an extract of the document.

(4) The Keeper of the Registers shall not issue a certificate under paragraph (4) unless there is produced to him an affidavit referred to in paragraph (2).

(5) Where the Keeper of the Registers issues a certificate in Form 62.42-B, he shall attach it to the extract of the document.]

[1171]

NOTES

Commencement: 1 March 2004.
Substituted as noted to r 62.26 at **[1155]**.

PART VI
REGISTRATION UNDER THE MERCHANT SHIPPING (LINER CONFERENCES) ACT 1982

62.43 Application and interpretation of this Part

(1) This part applies to an application under section 9 of the Merchant Shipping (Liner Conferences) Act 1982 (recognition and enforcement of recommendations, etc, of conciliators).

(2) In this Part, "the Liner Conferences Act" means the Merchant Shipping (Liner Conferences) Act 1982.

[1172]

NOTES

Commencement: 5 September 1994.

62.44 Applications for registration under the Liner Conferences Act

(1) An application under—

(a) section 9(1)(b) of the Liner Conferences Act (application for registration for enforcement of a recommendation, determination or award), or

(b) section 9(3) of that Act (application for registration for enforcement of a determination of costs),

shall be made by petition.

(2) A petition under section 9(1)(b) of the Liner Conferences Act shall include averments in relation to—

(a) the reasons for the petition; and

(b) where appropriate, the limited extent to which the recommendation is enforceable under section 9(2) of that Act.

(3) There shall be produced with the petition—

(a) a certified copy of the recommendation, the reasons for the recommendation and the record of settlement;

(b) a copy of the acceptance of the recommendation by the parties on whom it is binding.

(4) There shall be produced with a petition under section 9(3) of the Liner Conferences Act a certified copy of the determination of costs.

[1173]

NOTES

Commencement: 5 September 1994.

62.45 Warrant for registration under the Liner Conferences Act

The court, on being satisfied that the recommendation, determination or award may be registered, shall pronounce an interlocutor granting warrant for registration of the recommendation, determination or award, as the case may be.

[1174]

NOTES

Commencement: 5 September 1994.

62.46 Registration under the Liner Conferences Act

(1) Where the court pronounces an interlocutor under rule 62.45 granting warrant for registration—

(a) the Deputy Principal Clerk shall enter the warrant in the register of recommendations, determinations and awards to be registered under section 9 of the Liner Conferences Act: and

(b) the petitioner shall serve a copy of the interlocutor containing such warrant on the party against whom the recommendation, determination or award may be enforced.

(2) On presentation by the petitioner to the Keeper of the Registers of—

(a) a certified copy of the interlocutor under rule 62.45 granting warrant for registration,

(b) a certified copy of the recommendation, determination or award to be registered and any translation of it, and

(c) where necessary, a certificate of currency conversion under [rule 62.2(1)(b)],

they shall be registered in the register of judgments of the Books of Council and Session.

(3) On registration under paragraph (2), the Keeper of the Registers shall issue an extract of the registered recommendation, determination or award, as the case may be, with a warrant for execution.

[1175]

NOTES

Para (2): words in square brackets substituted by the Act of Sederunt (Rules of the Court of Session Amendment No 4) (Miscellaneous) 1996, SI 1996/2168, r 2(1), (13).

PART VII
[RECIPROCAL ENFORCEMENT OF ORDERS IN RELATION TO CONFISCATION OF PROCEEDS OF CRIME AND TO FORFEITURE OF PROPERTY USED IN CRIME]

NOTES

Heading substituted by the Act of Sederunt (Rules of the Court of Session Amendment No 3) (External Orders Affecting Proceeds of Crime) 1999, SI 1999/1220, r 2(1), (2).

62.47 Interpretation of this Part

In this Part—

.....

.....

"the Act of 1989" means the Prevention of Terrorism (Temporary Provisions) Act 1989;

["the Act of 1995" means the Proceeds of Crime (Scotland) Act 1995;]

["the Act of 2000" means the Terrorism Act 2000;]

"money order" means an order for the payment of money;

"non-money order" means an order which is not a money order[;]

["the Order of 1995" means the Prevention of Terrorism (Temporary Provisions) Act 1989 (Enforcement of External Orders) Order 1995;

["the Order of 1999" means the Criminal Justice (International Co-operation) Act 1990 (Enforcement of Overseas Forfeiture Orders) (Scotland) Order 1999;];

["the Overseas Forfeiture Order of 2005" means the Criminal Justice (International Co-operation) Act 1990 (Enforcement of Overseas Forfeiture Orders) (Scotland) Order 2005;

"the POCA Order of 2005" means the Proceeds of Crime Act 2002 (External Requests and Orders) Order 2005]

"relevant enactment" means … the Act of 1989, the Act of 1995[, [the Act of 2000] the Order of 1995[, the Order of 1999, the Overseas Forfeiture Order of 2005 or the POCA Order of 2005],] as the case may be.]

[1176]

NOTES

First definition omitted, definition "the Act of 1995" inserted, semi-colon in square brackets substituted, and definitions "the Order of 1995" and "relevant enactment" added, by the Act of Sederunt (Rules of the Court of Session Amendment No 3) (Miscellaneous) 1996, SI 1996/1756, r 2(1), (26); second definition omitted, and words omitted from definition "relevant enactment" revoked by the Act of Sederunt (Rules of the Court of Session Amendment No 4) (Miscellaneous) 1996, SI 1996/2168, r 2(1), (15); definition "the Act of 2000" inserted and words in second (inner) pair of square brackets in definition "relevant enactment" inserted by the Act of Sederunt (Rules of the Court of Session Amendment No 6) (Terrorism Act 2000) 2001, SSI 2001/494, r 2; definition "the Order of 1999" inserted, and words in first (outer) pair of square brackets in definition "relevant enactment" substituted, by the Act of Sederunt (Rules of the Court of Session Amendment No 3) (External Orders Affecting Proceeds of Crime) 1999, SI 1999/1220, r 2(1), (3); definitions "the Overseas Forfeiture Order of 2005", "the POCA Order of 2005" inserted and words in third (inner) pair of square brackets in definition "relevant enactment" substituted by the Act of Sederunt (Rules of the Court of Session Amendment No 10) (Proceeds of Crime: External Requests and Orders etc) 2005, SSI 2005/663, r 2(1), (2)(a).

62.48 Applications for registration under the [relevant enactment]

(1) An application to which this rule applies shall be made by petition.

(2) This rule applies to an application under any of the following provisions:—

[(a)] paragraph 19(2) of Schedule 4 to the Act of 1989 (application for registration of an England and Wales order, Northern Ireland order or Islands order)[;]

[[(b]) section 36(1) of the Act of 1995 (application for registration of an order to which section 35 of the Act of 1995 applies);

[(c)] section 41(1) of the Act of 1995 (application for registration of external confiscation order);

[(d)] article 15(1) of the Order of 1995 (application for registration of external forfeiture order [in relation to terrorism]);

[(e)] article 16(1) of the Order of 1995 (application for registration of external restraint order);]

[(f) article 5(1) of the Order of 1999 (application for registration of external forfeiture order other than in relation to terrorism).]

[(g) paragraph 27(3) of Schedule 4 to the Act of 2000 (application for registration of an England and Wales order, Northern Ireland order or Islands order;]

[(h) article 13(1) of the Overseas Forfeiture Order of 2005 (applications to give effect to external forfeiture orders);

(i) article 66(1) of the POCA Order of 2005 (applications to give effect to external orders).]

(3) There shall be produced with a petition under paragraph (1) a certified copy of the order which is sought to be registered.

[1177]

NOTES

Heading: words in square brackets substituted by the Act of Sederunt (Rules of the Court of Session Amendment No 3) (Miscellaneous) 1996, SI 1996/1756, r 2(1), (27)(a).

Para (2): original sub-paras (a), (b) omitted, original sub-paras (c), (d) renamed as sub-paras (a), (b), semicolon in square brackets substituted, and sub-paras (c)–(f) added, by SI 1996/1756, r 2(1), (27)(b); sub-para (a) (as renamed) omitted and sub-paras (b)–(f) renamed as sub-paras (a)–(e) by the Act of Sederunt (Rules of the Court of Session Amendment No 4) (Miscellaneous) 1996, SI 1996/2168, r 2(1), (16); words in square brackets in sub-para (d) inserted and whole of sub-para (f) added by the Act of Sederunt (Rules of the Court of Session Amendment No 3) (External Orders Affecting Proceeds of Crime) 1999, SI 1999/1220, r 2(1), (4); sub-para (g) added by the Act of Sederunt (Rules of the Court of Session Amendment No 6) (Terrorism Act 2000) 2001, SSI 2001/494, r 3; sub-paras (h), (i) added by the Act of Sederunt (Rules of the Court of Session Amendment No 10) (Proceeds of Crime: External Requests and Orders etc) 2005, SSI 2005/663, r 2(1), (2)(b).

62.49 Warrant for registration under the [relevant enactment]

The court shall, on being satisfied that the application complies with the requirements of the [relevant enactment], as the case may be—

(a) pronounce an interlocutor granting warrant for execution of a non-money order; or

(b) pronounce an interlocutor granting warrant for the registration of a money order.

[1178]

NOTES

Words in square brackets substituted by the Act of Sederunt (Rules of the Court of Session Amendment No 3) (Miscellaneous) 1996, SI 1996/1756, r 2(1), (28).

62.50 Registration under the [relevant enactment]

(1) Where the court pronounces an interlocutor under rule 62.49, the Deputy Principal Clerk shall enter the order in the register for the registration of orders under the [relevant enactment].

(2) On presentation by the petitioner to the Keeper of the Registers of—

(a) a certified copy of the interlocutor pronounced under rule 62.49(b), and

(b) a certified copy of the order to be registered,

they shall be registered in the register of judgments of the Books of Council and Session.

(3) On registration under paragraph (2), the Keeper of the Registers shall issue an extract of the registered order with a warrant for execution.

[1179]

NOTES

Words in square brackets substituted by the Act of Sederunt (Rules of the Court of Session Amendment No 3) (Miscellaneous) 1996, SI 1996/1756, r 2(1), (29).

62.51 Service of warrant for registration under the [relevant enactment]

The petitioner shall serve a copy of the interlocutor, pronounced under rule 62.49 granting warrant for registration, and a notice in Form 62.51 on the person against whom the order may be enforced.

[1180]

NOTES

Heading: words in square brackets substituted by the Act of Sederunt (Rules of the Court of Session Amendment No 3) (Miscellaneous) 1996, SI 1996/1756, r 2(1), (30).

[62.51A Further provision as respects warrant for registration

Where an interlocutor granting warrant for the registration of an external confiscation order is pronounced and the order falls to be remitted for enforcement to the Sheriff of Lothian and Borders at Edinburgh, the Deputy Principal Clerk shall send a certified copy of the interlocutor, within four days after it is pronounced, to the sheriff clerk at Edinburgh.]

[1181]

NOTES

Inserted by the Act of Sederunt (Rules of the Court of Session Amendment No 3) (External Orders Affecting Proceeds of Crime) 1999, SI 1999/1220, r 2(1), (5).

62.52 Suspension of enforcement under the Act of [… 1995]

(1) Where an order [under … or section 36(1) of the Act of 1995] has been registered under rule 62.50, the court may, on the application of the person against whom the order may be enforced, if satisfied that an application has been made to the court which made the order to have it set aside or quashed—

(a) suspend enforcement of the order; and
(b) sist any proceedings for enforcement of the order.

(2) Notwithstanding rule 60.2 (form of applications for suspension), an application under paragraph (1) shall be made by note in the process in the petition under rule 62.48(1).

[1182]

NOTES

Heading: words in square brackets substituted by the Act of Sederunt (Rules of the Court of Session Amendment No 3) (Miscellaneous) 1996, SI 1996/1756, r 2(1), (31)(a); words omitted revoked by the Act of Sederunt (Rules of the Court of Session Amendment No 4) (Miscellaneous) 1996, SI 1996/2168, r 2(1), (17)(a).

Para (1): words in square brackets inserted by SI 1996/1756, r 2(1), (31)(b); words omitted revoked by SI 1996/2168, r 2(1), (17)(b).

62.53 Modification and cancellation of registration [under the Act of … 1989 or 1995] [or 2000]

(1) An application to modify or cancel the registration of an order [under the Act of … 1989 or 1995] [or 2000] registered under rule 62.50 shall be made—

(a) by the petitioner, by motion; or
(b) by any other interested party, by note.

(2) There shall be produced with the application under paragraph (1) a certified copy of any order which modifies or revokes the registered order or which causes the order to cease to have effect.

(3) The court shall, on being satisfied—

(a) that the registered order has been modified, revoked or has ceased to have effect, or
(b) that the registration of an external confiscation order should be cancelled in terms of section [41(3) of the Act of 1995],

pronounce an interlocutor so modifying or cancelling the registration, as the case may be, and grant warrant for the registration of a certified copy of the interlocutor in the [register of judgments of the] Books of Council and Session.

(4) Where the court pronounces an interlocutor under paragraph (3), the Deputy Principal Clerk shall modify or cancel the registration in the register kept under rule 62.50(1) in accordance with that interlocutor.

[1183]

NOTES

Heading: words in first pair of square brackets added by the Act of Sederunt (Rules of the Court of Session Amendment No 3) (Miscellaneous) 1996, SI 1996/1756, r 2(1), (32)(a); number omitted revoked by the Act of Sederunt (Rules of the Court of Session Amendment No 4) (Miscellaneous) 1996, SI 1996/2168, r 2(1), (18)(a); words in second pair of square brackets added by the Act of Sederunt (Rules of the Court of Session Amendment No 6) (Terrorism Act 2000) 2001, SSI 2001/494, r 4(a).

Para (1): words in first pair of square brackets inserted by SI 1996/1756, r 2(1), (32)(b); number omitted revoked by SI 1996/2168, r 2(1), (18)(b); words in second pair of square brackets inserted by SSI 2001/494, r 4(b).

Para (3): words in first pair of square brackets substituted, and words in second pair of square brackets inserted, by SI 1996/1756, r 2(1), (32)(c).

[62.54 Incidental applications

(1) Any of the following applications shall be made in the prayer of the petition under rule 62.48(1) to which it relates or, if the prayer of that petition has been granted, by motion in the process of that petition:—

(a) an application under section 32(1) of the Act of 1995 for a warrant for inhibition;
(b) an application under section 33(1) of the Act of 1995 (warrant for arrestment);
(c) an application under paragraph 16(1) (warrant for inhibition), or paragraph 16A(1) (warrant for arrestment), of Schedule 4 to the Act of 1989 as applied by paragraph 19(5) of that Schedule or by article 18 of the Order of 1995, as the case may be.

(2) Either of the following applications shall be made in the prayer of the petition under rule 62.48(1) to which it relates or, if the prayer of the petition has been granted, by note in the process of that petition:—

(a) an application under sub-paragraph (4) of paragraph 19 of Schedule 4 to the Act of 1989 for an order in implementation of an England and Wales, Northern Ireland or Islands forfeiture order registered in the Court of Session under that paragraph;
(b) an application under article 17 of the Order of 1995 for an order in implementation of an external forfeiture order registered in the Court of Session under article 15(1) of that Order.

(3) Where the court makes an order by virtue of paragraph 19(4) of Schedule 4 to the Act of 1989 or article 17 of the Order of 1995 appointing an administrator, rules 76.24 to 76.26 (which relate to the duties of an administrator) shall apply to an administrator appointed by virtue of that paragraph or article as they apply to an order in implementation of a forfeiture order.]

[1184]

NOTES

Substituted by the Act of Sederunt (Rules of the Court of Session Amendment No 4) (Miscellaneous) 1996, SI 1996/2168, r 2(1), (19).

[62.54A Cancellation of registration or variation of property under the Overseas Forfeiture Order of 2005 or the POCA Order of 2005

(1) An application under article 16(3) of the Overseas Forfeiture Order of 2005 (application for cancellation of registration or variation of property) or article 69(3) of the POCA Order of 2005 (application for cancellation of registration or variation of property) shall be made—

(a) by the Lord Advocate, by motion; or
(b) by any other interested party, by note.

(2) There shall be produced with an application under paragraph (1), a certified copy of any order which modifies or revokes the registered order or which causes the registered order to cease to have effect.

(3) The court shall, on pronouncing an interlocutor granting an application under paragraph (1), grant warrant for the registration of a certified copy of the interlocutor in the register of judgments of the Books of Council and Session.

(4) Where the court pronounces an interlocutor granting an application under paragraph (1), the Deputy Principal Clerk shall cancel or, as the case may be, vary the registration in the register kept under rule 62.50(1) in accordance with that interlocutor.]

[1185]

NOTES

Commencement: 31 December 2005.

Inserted, together with r 62.54B by the Act of Sederunt (Rules of the Court of Session Amendment No 10) (Proceeds of Crime: External Requests and Orders etc) 2005, SSI 2005/663, r 2(1), (2)(c).

[62.54B Registration under the POCA Order in Council of 2005: further provision

(1) Rule 62.2 (certificate of currency conversion) shall not apply to an application under article 66(1) of the POCA Order of 2005 (application to give effect to external orders).

(2) An application under article 72(4) (payment within a specified period) or article 72(6) (extension of specified period) of the POCA Order of 2005 shall be made by motion in the process relating to the granting of the application under article 66(1) of the POCA Order of 2005.

(3) The Deputy Principal Clerk shall send to the sheriff clerk appointed under article 69(1)(c) of the POCA Order of 2005 a certified copy of the interlocutor granting warrant for registration under rule 62.49 and of any subsequent interlocutor granting an application under–

- (a) rule 62.54A(1) (application for cancellation of registration or variation of property);
- (b) paragraph (3) of this rule (payment within specified period and extension of specified period);
- (c) rule 76.28(1)(i) (enforcement administrators); or
- (d) rule 76.28(3)(i) (recall and variation of order appointing administrator),

in respect of the registered order.]

[1186]

NOTES

Commencement: 31 December 2005.

Inserted as noted to r 62.54A at **[1185]**.

PART VIII
REGISTRATION OF AWARDS UNDER THE MULTILATERAL INVESTMENT GUARANTEE AGENCY ACT 1988

62.55 Registration of awards under the Multilateral Investment Guarantee Agency Act 1988

Part III shall, with the necessary modifications, apply to an award under Article 4 of Annex II to the convention referred to in section 1(1) of the Multilateral Investment Guarantee Agency Act 1988 as it applies to an award under the convention mentioned in section 1(1) of the Arbitration (International Investment Disputes) Act 1966.

[1187]

PART IX
RECOGNITION AND ENFORCEMENT OF ARBITRAL AWARDS UNDER THE MODEL LAW ON INTERNATIONAL COMMERCIAL ARBITRATION

62.56 Application and interpretation of this Part

(1) This Part applies to an application under article 35 of the Model Law in Schedule 7 to the Law Reform (Miscellaneous Provisions) (Scotland) Act 1990 (applications for enforcement of arbitral award).

(2) In this Part—

"the Act of 1990" means the Law Reform (Miscellaneous Provisions) (Scotland) Act 1990;

"arbitral award" means an award to which the Model Law, as applied by section 86 of the Act of 1990, applies;

"the Model Law" means the Model Law on International Commercial Arbitration as set out in Schedule 7 to the Act of 1990.

[1188]

62.57 Applications for registration under the Act of 1990

(1) An application for enforcement of an arbitral award under article 35 of the Model Law shall be made by petition.

(2) There shall be produced with such a petition—

(a) the authenticated original arbitral award or a certified copy of it;

(b) the original arbitration agreement referred to in article 7 of the Model Law or a certified copy of it;

(c) an affidavit stating—

(i) the full name, title, trade or business and the usual or last known place of residence or, where appropriate, of the business of the petitioner and the party against whom the arbitral award was made;

(ii) the amount of the arbitral award which is unsatisfied;

(iii) that the arbitral award has become binding on the parties and has not been set aside or suspended by a court of the country in which, or under the law of which, that award was made; and

(iv) whether any application has been made under the Model Law which, if granted, might result in the setting aside of the award.

[1189]

62.58 Registration under the Act of 1990

(1) The court, on being satisfied that the arbitral award may be registered, shall grant warrant for registration.

(2) Where the court pronounces an interlocutor under paragraph (1), the Deputy Principal Clerk shall enter the arbitral award in a register of arbitral awards under article 35 of the Model Law.

(3) On presentation by the petitioner to the Keeper of the Registers of—

(a) a certified copy of the interlocutor of the warrant for registration,

(b) a certified copy of the arbitral award to be registered and any translation of it, and

(c) any certificate of currency conversion under rule [62.2(1)(b)],

they shall be registered in the register of judgments of the Books of Council and Session.

(4) An extract of a registered arbitral award with warrant for execution shall not be issued by the Keeper of the Registers until a certificate of service under rule 62.59 (service on party against whom arbitral award made) is produced to him.

[1190]

NOTES

Para (3): words in square brackets substituted by the Act of Sederunt (Rules of the Court of Session Amendment No 4) (Miscellaneous) 1996, SI 1996/2168, r 2(1), (13).

62.59 Service on party against whom arbitral award made

On registration under rule 62.58, the petitioner shall forthwith serve a notice of the registration on the party against whom the arbitral award was made in Form 62.16.

[1191]

62.60 Application for refusal of recognition or enforcement under the Act of 1990

(1) An application under article 36(1)(a) of the Model Law (request by party against whom arbitral award made for refusal of recognition or enforcement) shall be made by note.

(2) A note referred to in paragraph (1)—

(a) may crave—

(i) suspension or interdict of any past or future steps in the execution of the arbitral award, including registration or enforcement of the award; and

(ii) recall of any interlocutor pronounced under rule 62.58(1) (registration under the Act of 1990); and

(b) shall be supported by affidavit and any documentary evidence.

(3) Where any interlocutor pronounced under rule 62.58(1) is recalled, a certificate to that effect issued by the Deputy Principal Clerk shall be sufficient warrant to the Keeper of the Registers to cancel the registration and return the documents registered to the petitioner on whose application the interlocutor under the rule was pronounced.

[1192]

[PART X
RECOGNITION, REGISTRATION AND ENFORCEMENT OF MISCELLANEOUS DECISIONS

62.61 Application and interpretation of this Part

(1) This Part applies to the recognition, registration or enforcement, as the case may be, of an award, decision, judgment or order under any of the following instruments:—

(a) Article 34.1 (enforcement of arbitral award) of the procedural rules on conciliation and arbitration of contracts financed by the European Development Fund;

(b) Article 20 of the United Nations (International Tribunal) (Former Yugoslavia) Order 1996 (enforcement of orders for the preservation or restitution of property);

[(c) Article 20 of the United Nations (International Tribunal) (Rwanda) Order 1996 (enforcement of orders for the preservation or restitution of property).]

(2) In this Part—

"decision" includes award, judgment or order;

"relevant instrument" means an instrument mentioned in paragraph (1).]

[1193]

NOTES

Pt X (rr 62.61–66) inserted by the Act of Sederunt (Rules of the Court of Session Amendment No 4) (Miscellaneous) 1996, SI 1996/2168, r 2(1), (19).

Para (1): sub-para (c) added by the Act of Sederunt (Rules of the Court of Session Amendment No 4) (Miscellaneous) 2001, SSI 2001/305, r 14.

[62.62 Applications under this Part

(1) An application for recognition, registration or enforcement, as the case may be, of a decision under a relevant instrument shall be made by petition.

(2) There shall be produced with such a petition an affidavit—

(a) exhibiting a copy of the decision certified under the relevant instrument; and

(b) stating—

(i) the full name, title, trade or business and the usual or the last known place of residence or, where appropriate, of business of the petitioner and of the party against whom the decision was made;

(ii) that the petitioner is entitled to have the decision recognised, registered or enforced, as the case may be, under the relevant instrument;

(iii) the extent to which the decision is unsatisfied; and

(iv) whether the enforcement of the decision has been sisted (provisionally or otherwise) under the relevant instrument and whether any, and if so what, application has been made under the relevant instrument which, if granted, might result in a sist of enforcement of the decision.]

[1194]

NOTES

Inserted as noted to r 62.61 at **[1193]**.

[62.63 Recognition, or warrant for registration or for enforcement under this Part

The court shall, on being satisfied that the petition complies with the requirements of the relevant instrument, pronounce an interlocutor recognising or granting warrant for the registration or enforcement of the decision, as the case may be.]

[1195]

NOTES

Inserted as noted to r 62.61 at **[1193]**.

[62.64 Registration for enforcement under this Part

(1) Where the court pronounces an interlocutor under rule 62.63 granting warrant for registration or enforcement, as the case may be, the Deputy Principal Clerk shall enter details of the interlocutor and the decision in a register of decisions under this Part.

(2) On presentation by the petitioner to the Keeper of the Registers of—
(a) a certified copy of the interlocutor under rule 62.63,
(b) a certified copy of the decision and any translation of it, and
(c) any certificate of currency conversion under rule 62.2(1)(b),
they shall be registered in the register of judgments of the Books of Council and Session.

(3) An extract of a registered decision with warrant for execution shall not be issued by the Keeper of the Registers until a certificate of service under rule 62.65 is produced to him.]

[1196]

NOTES

Inserted as noted to r 62.61 at **[1193]**.

[62.65 Service on party against whom award made

On registration under rule 62.64, the petitioner shall forthwith serve a notice of the registration on the party against whom the decision was made in Form 62.65.]

[1197]

NOTES

Inserted as noted to r 62.61 at **[1193]**.

[62.66 Sist of enforcement under this Part

(1) Where it appears to the court that—
(a) the enforcement of the decision has been sisted (whether provisionally or otherwise) under the relevant instrument, or
(b) any application has been made under the relevant instrument which, if granted, might result in a sist of the enforcement of the award,
the court shall, or in the case referred to in sub-paragraph (b) may, sist the petition for such period as it thinks fit.

(2) Where the court has granted a warrant for registration under rule 62.63, the party against whom the decision was made may apply to the court for suspension or interdict of execution of the award.

(3) An application under paragraph (2) shall—
(a) be made on ground (a) or (b) of paragraph (1);
(b) notwithstanding rule 60.2 (form of applications for suspension), be made by note in the process of the petition under rule 62.62; and
(c) be accompanied by an affidavit stating the relevant facts.]

[1198]

NOTES

Inserted as noted to r 62.61 at **[1193]**.

[PART XI
REGISTRATION AND ENFORCEMENT OF JUDGMENTS UNDER COUNCIL REGULATION (EC) NO 2201/2003 OF 27 NOVEMBER 2003

62.67 Application and interpretation of this Part

(1) This Part applies to the registration and enforcement of a judgment under the Council Regulation.

(2) In this Part, unless the context otherwise requires—
"the Council Regulation" means Council Regulation (EC) No 2201/2003 of 27th November 2003 on jurisdiction and the recognition and enforcement of judgments in matrimonial matters and matters of parental responsibility;
"judgment" includes an authentic instrument or enforceable agreement; and

"Member State" has the same meaning as in Article 2(3) of the Council Regulation.]
[1199]

NOTES

Commencement: 2 March 2005.
Pt XI (rr 62.67–62.80) inserted by the Act of Sederunt (Rules of the Court of Session Amendment) (Jurisdiction, Recognition and Enforcement of Judgments) 2005, SSI 2005/135, r 2(1), (2).

[62.68 Disapplication of certain rules to this Part

The following rules shall not apply to an application under this Part:—

4.1(1)(printed form for petition),
14.4 (form of petitions),
14.5 (first order in petitions),
14.6 (period of notice for lodging answers),
14.7 (intimation and service of petitions),
14.9 (unopposed petitions).]

[1200]

NOTES

Commencement: 2 March 2005.
Inserted as noted to r 62.67 at **[1199]**.

[62.69 Enforcement of judgments from another Member State

(1) An application under Article 28 of the Council Regulation (enforceable judgments) shall be made by petition in Form 62.69.

(2) There shall be produced with the petition—

(a) an authentic copy of the judgment to be registered;
(b) a certificate under Article 39 of the Council Regulation (standard forms of certificate);
(c) where judgment has been given in absence (that is to say, in default of appearance)—
 (i) the original or a certified copy of the document which establishes that the party against whom judgment was given in absence was served with the document initiating proceedings or with an equivalent; or
 (ii) a document indicating that the party against whom the judgment was given in absence has accepted the judgment unequivocally;
(d) where applicable, a document showing that the applicant is in receipt of legal aid in the country in which the judgment was given;
(e) an affidavit stating—
 (i) an address within the jurisdiction of the court for service on or intimation to the petitioner;
 (ii) the name and address of the petitioner and his interest in the judgment;
 (iii) the name and date of birth of each child in respect of whom the judgment was made, the present whereabouts or suspected whereabouts of that child and the name of any person with whom he is alleged to be;
 (iv) the name and address of any other person with an interest in the judgment;
 (v) whether the judgment is already registered and, if so, where it is registered;
 (vi) details of any order known to the petitioner which affects a child in respect of whom the judgment was made and fulfils the conditions necessary for its recognition in Scotland.

(3) Where the petitioner does not produce a document required by paragraph (2)(b) to (e), the court may—

(a) fix a period within which that document is to be lodged;
(b) accept an equivalent document; or
(c) dispense with the requirement to produce the document.]

[1201]

NOTES

Commencement: 2 March 2005.
Inserted as noted to r 62.67 at **[1199]**.

[62.70 Warrant for registration under the Council Regulation

(1) The court shall, on being satisfied that the petition complies with the requirements of the Council Regulation, pronounce an interlocutor—
- (a) granting warrant for the registration of the judgment; and
- (b) where necessary, granting decree in accordance with Scots law.

(2) The interlocutor pronounced under paragraph (1) shall specify—
- (a) the period within which an appeal mentioned in rule 62.74 (appeals under the Council Regulation) against the interlocutor may be made; and
- (b) that the petitioner—
  - (i) may register the judgment under rule 62.72 (registration under the Council Regulation); and
  - (ii) may not proceed to execution until the expiry of the period for lodging such appeal or its disposal.]

[1202]

NOTES

Commencement: 2 March 2005.
Inserted as noted to r 62.67 at **[1199]**.

[62.71 Intimation to the petitioner

Where the court pronounces an interlocutor under rule 62.70(1) the Deputy Principal Clerk shall intimate such interlocutor to the petitioner by sending to his address for service in Scotland a certified copy of the interlocutor by registered post or the first class recorded delivery service.]

[1203]

NOTES

Commencement: 2 March 2005.
Inserted as noted to r 62.67 at **[1199]**.

[62.72 Registration under the Council Regulation

(1) Where the court pronounces an interlocutor under rule 62.70(1) granting warrant for registration, the Deputy Principal Clerk shall enter the judgment in the register of judgments, authentic instruments and court settlements kept in the Petition Department.

(2) On presentation by the petitioner to the Keeper of the Registers of—
- (a) a certified copy of the interlocutor under rule 62.70(1) granting warrant for registration,
- (b) an authentic copy of the judgment and any translation of it, and
- (c) any certificate of currency conversion under rule 62.2(1)(b) for any order concerning costs and expenses of proceedings under the Council Regulation;

they shall be registered in the register of judgments of the Books of Council and Session.

(3) On registration under paragraph (2), the Keeper of the Registers of Scotland shall issue an extract of the registered document with a warrant for execution.]

[1204]

NOTES

Commencement: 2 March 2005.
Inserted as noted to r 62.67 at **[1199]**.

[62.73 Service of warrant for registration under the Council Regulation

The petitioner shall serve a copy of the interlocutor under rule 62.70(1) granting warrant for registration of a judgment and notice in Form 62.73 on the person against whom enforcement is sought.]

[1205]

NOTES

Commencement: 2 March 2005.
Inserted as noted to r 62.67 at **[1199]**.

PART II
CIVIL PROCEDURE RULES

[62.74 Appeals under the Council Regulation

(1) An appeal under Article 33 (appeals against the enforcement decision) of the Council Regulation shall be made by motion—

(a) to the Lord Ordinary; and

(b) where the appeal is against the granting of warrant for registration under rule 62.70(1) within one month of service under rule 62.73 (service of warrant for registration under the Council Regulation) or within two months of such service where service was executed on a person domiciled in another Member State.

(2) Where the respondent in any such appeal is domiciled furth of the United Kingdom—

(a) in relation to an appeal against the granting of warrant for registration under rule 62.70(1), intimation of the motion shall be made to the address for service of the respondent in Scotland;

(b) in relation to an appeal against a refusal to grant warrant for registration under rule 62.70(1), intimation of the motion shall be made in accordance with rule 16.2 (service furth of United Kingdom) or rule 16.5 (service where address of the person is not known), as the case may be.]

[1206]

NOTES

Commencement: 2 March 2005.
Inserted as noted to r 62.67 at **[1199]**.

[62.75 Reclaiming under the Council Regulation

Any party dissatisfied with the interlocutor of the Lord Ordinary in any appeal mentioned in rule 62.74 (appeals under the Council Regulation) may reclaim on a point of law against that interlocutor.]

[1207]

NOTES

Commencement: 2 March 2005.
Inserted as noted to r 62.67 at **[1199]**.

[62.76 Recognition of judgments from another Member State

(1) For the purpose of Article 21 of the Council Regulation (recognition of a judgment), an interlocutor pronounced under rule 62.70(1) (warrant for registration under the Council Regulation) shall imply recognition of the judgment so dealt with.

(2) In an application under Article 21(3) of the Council Regulation for recognition of a judgment, rules 62.67 to 62.75 shall apply to such an application as they apply to an application under Article 28 of the Council Regulation (declarator of enforceability).

(3) In an application under Article 21(3) of the Council Regulation for non-recognition of a judgment, the rules under this part shall apply to such an application as they apply to an application under Article 28 of the Council Regulation (declarator of enforceability) subject to the following provisions—

(a) where the application relies on grounds under Article 22(b) or 23(c) of the Council Regulation (judgment given in default of appearance) for the judgment not to be recognised, it shall not be necessary to produce documents required by rule 62.69(2)(c)(document establishing service or acceptance of judgment); and

(b) rule 62.69(2)(b)(certificate under Article 39 of the Council Regulation); rule 62.70(warrant for registration under the Council Regulation); and rule 62.72(registration under the Council Regulation); shall not apply.]

[1208]

NOTES

Commencement: 2 March 2005.
Inserted as noted to r 62.67 at **[1199]**.

[62.77 Cancellation of registration under the Council Regulation

Where an interlocutor under rule 62.70(1) (warrant for registration under the Council Regulation) is recalled and registration under rule 62.72(2) (registration under the Council

Regulation) is ordered to be cancelled after an appeal under Article 33 of the Council Regulation (appeal against decision on enforceability) a certificate to that effect by the Deputy Principal Clerk shall be sufficient warrant to the Keeper of the Registers to cancel the registration and return the judgment, certificate or other documents to the person who applied for registration.]

[1209]

NOTES

Commencement: 2 March 2005.
Inserted as noted to r 62.67 at **[1199]**.

[62.78 Enforcement in another Member State of Court of Session judgments etc

(1) Where a person seeks to apply under the Council Regulation for recognition or enforcement in another Member State of a judgment given by the court, he shall apply by letter to the Deputy Principal Clerk for—

(a) a certificate under Article 39 of the Council Regulation (certificates concerning judgments in matrimonial matters or on matters of parental responsibility);
(b) a certified copy of the judgment; and
(c) if required, a certified copy of the opinion of the court.

(2) The Deputy Principal Clerk shall not issue a certificate under paragraph (1)(a) above unless there is produced to him an execution of service of the judgment on the person against whom it is sought to be enforced.

(3) Where a judgment granting rights of access delivered by the Court of Session acquires a cross-border character after the judgment has been delivered and a party seeks to enforce the judgment in another Member State, he shall apply by letter to the Deputy Principal Clerk for—

(a) a certificate under Article 41 of the Council Regulation (certificate concerning rights of access); and
(b) a certified copy of the judgment.]

[1210]

NOTES

Commencement: 2 March 2005.
Inserted as noted to r 62.67 at **[1199]**.

[62.79 Rectification of certificates under Articles 41 and 42 of the Council Regulation

Where a party seeks rectification of a certificate issued under Article 41 or 42 of the Council Regulation (certificate concerning rights of access or return of a child) he shall apply by letter to the Deputy Principal Clerk stating the details of the certificate that are to be rectified.]

[1211]

NOTES

Commencement: 2 March 2005.
Inserted as noted to r 62.67 at **[1199]**.

[62.80 Practical arrangements for the exercise of rights of access

(1) An application by a party having an enforceable judgment granting a right of access, that has been certified under Article 41 of the Council Regulation or registered for enforcement, seeking an order making practical arrangements for organising the exercise of rights of access under Article 48 of the Council Regulation, shall be made by petition.

(2) There shall be produced with the petition—

(a) an authentic copy of the judgment;
(b) any certificate under Article 41 of the Council Regulation;
(c) any extract of the registered judgment with a warrant for execution; and
(d) where applicable, a document showing that the applicant is in receipt of legal aid in the country where the judgment was given.]

[1212]

NOTES

Commencement: 2 March 2005.
Inserted as noted to r 62.67 at **[1199]**.

[PART XII
EUROPEAN ENFORCEMENT ORDERS

62.81 Interpretation and application of this Part

(1) In this Part—

"the Regulation" means Regulation (EC) No 805/2004 of the European Parliament and of the Council of 21 April 2004 creating a European Enforcement Order for uncontested claims;

"Council Regulation (EC) No 44/2001" means Council Regulation (EC) No 44/2001 of 22 December 2000 on jurisdiction and the recognition and enforcement of judgments in civil and commercial matters;

"authentic instrument" has the same meaning as in Article 4(3) of the Regulation;

"court settlement" means a settlement where the debtor has expressly agreed to a claim within the meaning of Article 4(2) of the Regulation by admission or by means of a settlement which has been approved by a court or concluded before a court in the course of proceedings; and

"judgment" has the same meaning as in Article 4(1) of the Regulation.

(3) This Part applies to judgments, court settlements and authentic instruments on uncontested claims certified as European Enforcement Orders under the Regulation.

(4) Subject to rule 62.84 (certification of authentic instrument), rule 62.87 (rectification or withdrawal of certificate), rule 62.88(1) (application for registration), and rule 62.88(3) (application for refusal, stay or limitation of enforcement), an application shall be made to the Deputy Principal Clerk by letter.

(5) Rule 62.1 shall not apply to a petition under rule 62.88(3) of this Part (application for refusal, stay or limitation of enforcement).]

[1213]

NOTES

Commencement: 21 October 2005.
Pt XII (rr 62.81–62.89) inserted by the Act of Sederunt (Rules of the Court of Session Amendment No 8) (Miscellaneous) 2005, SSI 2005/521, r 2(1), (2).

[62.82 Certification of decree in absence or decree by default

(1) An application for certification under Article 6(1) (judgment on uncontested claim) or Article 8 (partial European Enforcement Order) of the Regulation shall be accompanied by an affidavit—

(a) verifying that the judgment was of an uncontested claim within the meaning of Article 3(1)(b) or (c) of the Regulation and that the court proceedings met the requirements set out in Chapter III of the Regulation (minimum standards for uncontested claims procedures);

(b) providing the information required by the form of certificate in Annex I to the Regulation (European Enforcement Order – judgment);

(c) verifying that the judgment is enforceable in Scotland, and does not conflict with the rules of jurisdiction laid down in Articles 3 and 6 of Chapter II of Council Regulation (EC) No 44/2001; and

(d) stating that where the debtor was a consumer and the judgment related to a contract concluded by the debtor for a purpose outside his trade or profession the judgment was given in the Member State of the debtors domicile within the meaning of Article 59 of Council Regulation (EC) No 44/2001.

(2) The Deputy Principal Clerk shall not issue a certificate under paragraph (1) unless there is produced to him an execution of service of the judgment on the person against whom it is sought to be enforced.]

[1214]

NOTES

Commencement: 21 October 2005.
Inserted as noted to r 62.81 at **[1213]**.

[62.83 Certification of court settlement

An application for certification under Article 24 of the Regulation (court settlement) shall be accompanied by an affidavit—

(a) verifying that the debtor admitted the claim or entered into a settlement that was approved by the court or concluded before the court in the course of proceedings and is enforceable in Scotland;
(b) verifying that the settlement concerned a claim within the meaning of Article 4(2) of the Regulation (payment of money); and
(c) providing the information required by the form of certificate in Annex II to the Regulation (European Enforcement Order – court settlement).]

[1215]

NOTES

Commencement: 21 October 2005.
Inserted as noted to r 62.81 at **[1213]**.

[62.84 Certification of authentic instrument

An application for certification under Article 25(1) of the Regulation (authentic instrument) shall be by letter to the Keeper of the Registers and shall be accompanied by an affidavit—

(a) verifying that the authentic instrument concerns a claim within the meaning of Article 4(2) of the Regulation (payment of money);
(b) verifying that the authentic instrument is enforceable in Scotland; and
(c) providing the information required by the form of certificate in Annex III to the Regulation (European Enforcement Order – authentic instrument).]

[1216]

NOTES

Commencement: 21 October 2005.
Inserted as noted to r 62.81 at **[1213]**.

[62.85 Certificate of lack or limitation of enforceability

An application for certification under Article 6(2) of the Regulation (lack or limitation of enforceability) shall be accompanied by an affidavit—

(a) stating the date on which the judgment, court settlement or authentic instrument was certified as a European Enforcement Order; and
(b) providing the information required by the form of certificate in Annex IV to the Regulation (certificate of lack or limitation of enforceability).]

[1217]

NOTES

Commencement: 21 October 2005.
Inserted as noted to r 62.81 at **[1213]**.

[62.86 Replacement certificate

An application under Article 6(3) of the Regulation (replacement certificate) shall be accompanied by an affidavit providing the information required by the form of certificate in Annex V to the Regulation (European Enforcement Order – replacement certificate following a challenge).]

[1218]

NOTES

Commencement: 21 October 2005.
Inserted as noted to r 62.81 at **[1213]**.

[62.87 Rectification or withdrawal of certificate

An application under Article 10(1) of the Regulation (rectification or withdrawal of European Enforcement Order certificate) shall be made in the form set out in Annex VI to the Regulation and, subject to rule 62.1 (disapplication of certain rules in Chapter 14 to this Chapter), shall be treated as a petition.]

[1219]

NOTES

Commencement: 21 October 2005.
Inserted as noted to r 62.81 at **[1213]**.

[62.88 Registration for enforcement

(1) An application for registration for enforcement of a judgment, court settlement or authentic instrument certified as a European Enforcement Order shall be made by presenting to the Keeper of the Registers—

(a) a certificate under Article 20(2)(b) of the Regulation (European Enforcement Order certificate);
(b) a copy of the judgment, court settlement, or authentic instrument in accordance with Article 20(2)(a) of the Regulation (enforcement procedure);
(c) where the certificate under Article 20(2)(b) is in a language other than English, a translation of the certificate into English certified as correct by the translator and stating the full name, address and qualification of the translator; and
(d) any certificate of currency conversion under rule 62.2(1)(b).

(2) On presentation of the documents mentioned in sub-paragraphs (a) to (d) of paragraph (1) the Keeper of the Registers shall—

(a) register the certificate in the register of judgments of the Books of Council and Session; and
(b) issue an extract of the certificate with a warrant for execution.

(3) An application under—

(a) Article 21 of the Regulation (refusal of enforcement); or
(b) Article 23 of the Regulation (stay or limitation of enforcement),

shall be made by petition.]

[1220]

NOTES

Commencement: 21 October 2005.
Inserted as noted to r 62.81 at **[1213]**.

[62.89 Refusal, stay or limitation of enforcement

An interlocutor certified by the Deputy Principal Clerk shall be sufficient warrant to the Keeper of the Registers—

(a) where enforcement is refused under rule 62.88(3)(a), to cancel the registration of the certificate of the European Enforcement Order and return the judgment, certificate or other documents to the person who sought registration; or
(b) where enforcement is stayed or limited under rule 62.88(3)(b), to—
    (i) register the interlocutor in the register of judgements of the Books of Council and Session; and
    (ii) issue an extract of the interlocutor.]

[1221]

NOTES

Commencement: 21 October 2005.
Inserted as noted to r 62.81 at **[1213]**.

[PART XIII
UNCITRAL MODEL LAW ON CROSS-BORDER INSOLVENCY

62.90 Application and interpretation of this Part

(1) This Part applies to applications under the Model Law and applications under the Scottish Provisions.

(2) In this Part—

"application for an interim remedy" means an application under article 19 of the Model Law for an interim remedy by a foreign representative;

"former representative" means a foreign representative who has died or who for any other reason has ceased to be the foreign representative in the foreign proceeding in relation to the debtor;

"main proceeding" means proceedings opened in accordance with Article 3(1) of the EC Insolvency Regulation and falling within the definition of insolvency proceedings in Article 2(a) of the EC Insolvency Regulation;

"the Model Law" means the UNCITRAL Model Law on Cross-Border Insolvency as set out in Schedule 1 to the Cross-Border Insolvency Regulations 2006;

"modification or termination order" means an order by the court pursuant to its powers under the Model Law modifying or terminating recognition of a foreign proceeding, the restraint, sist and suspension referred to in article 20(1) of the Model Law or any part of it or any remedy granted under article 19 or 21 of the Model Law;

"recognition application" means an application by a foreign representative in accordance with article 15 of the Model Law for an order recognising the foreign proceeding in which he has been appointed;

"recognition order" means an order by the court recognising a proceeding as a foreign main proceeding or a foreign non-main proceeding, as appropriate;

"review application" means an application to the court for a modification or termination order;

"the Scottish Provisions" are the provisions of Schedule 3 to the Cross-Border Insolvency Regulations 2006; and

words and phrases defined in the Model Law have the same meaning when used in this Part.

(3) References in this Part to a debtor who is of interest to the Financial Services Authority are references to a debtor who—

- (a) is, or has been, an authorised person within the meaning of section 31 of the Financial Services and Markets Act 2000 (authorised persons);
- (b) is, or has been, an appointed representative within the meaning of section 39 (exemption of appointed representatives) of that Act; or
- (c) is carrying on, or has carried on, a regulated activity in contravention of the general prohibition.

(4) In paragraph (3) "the general prohibition" has the meaning given by section 19 of the Financial Services and Markets Act 2000 and the reference to "regulated activity" shall be construed in accordance with—

- (a) section 22 of that Act (classes of regulated activity and categories of investment);
- (b) any relevant order under that section; and
- (c) Schedule 2 to that Act (regulated activities).]

[1222]

NOTES

Commencement: 6 April 2006.

Pt XIII (rr 62.90–62.96) inserted by the Act of Sederunt (Rules of the Court of Session Amendment No 2) (UNCITRAL Model Law on Cross-Border Insolvency) 2006, SSI 2006/199, r 2(1), (3).

[62.91 General

(1) Rule 62.1 (disapplication of certain rules to Chapter 62) shall not apply to an application to which this Part relates.

(2) Unless otherwise specified in this Part, an application under the Model Law or the Scottish Provisions shall be made by petition.

(3) For the purposes of the application of rule 14.5(1) (first order for intimation, service and advertisement) to a petition under this Part, where necessary, the petitioner shall seek an order for service of the petition on:—

- (a) the foreign representative;
- (b) the debtor;
- (c) any British insolvency officeholder acting in relation to the debtor;
- (d) any person appointed an administrative receiver of the debtor or as a receiver or manager of the property of the debtor in Scotland;
- (e) any member State liquidator who has been appointed in main proceedings in relation to the debtor;
- (f) any foreign representative who has been appointed in any other foreign proceeding regarding the debtor;

PART II

(g) if there is pending in Scotland a petition for the winding up or sequestration of the debtor, the petitioner in those proceedings;

(h) any person who is or may be entitled to appoint an administrator of the debtor under paragraph 14 of Schedule B1 to the Insolvency Act 1986 (appointment of administrator by holder of qualifying floating charge); and

(i) the Financial Services Authority if the debtor is a debtor who is of interest to that Authority.

(4) On the making of—

(a) a recognition order;

(b) an order granting an interim remedy under article 19 of the Model Law;

(c) an order granting a remedy under article 21 of the Model Law;

(d) an order confirming the status of a replacement foreign representative; or

(e) a modification or termination order,

the Deputy Principal Clerk shall send a certified copy of the interlocutor to the foreign representative.]

[1223]

NOTES

Commencement: 6 April 2006.
Inserted as noted to r 62.90 at **[1222]**.

[62.92 Recognition application

(1) A petition containing a recognition application shall include averments as to—

(a) the name of the applicant and his address for service in Scotland;

(b) the name of the debtor in respect of which the foreign proceeding is taking place;

(c) the name or names in which the debtor carries on business in the country where the foreign proceeding is taking place and in this country, if other than the name given under sub-paragraph (b);

(d) the principal or last known place of business of the debtor in Great Britain (if any) and, in the case of an individual, his last known place of residence in Great Britain, (if any);

(e) any registered number allocated to the debtor under the Companies Act 1985;

(f) the foreign proceeding in respect of which recognition is applied for, including the country in which it is taking place and the nature of the proceeding;

(g) whether the foreign proceeding is a proceeding within the meaning of article 2(i) of the Model Law;

(h) whether the applicant is a foreign representative within the meaning of article 2(j) of the Model Law;

(i) the address of the debtor's centre of main interests and, if different, the address of its registered office or habitual residence as appropriate;

(j) if the debtor does not have its centre of main interests in the country where the foreign proceeding is taking place, whether the debtor has an establishment within the meaning of article 2(e) of the Model Law in that country, and if so, its address.

(3) There shall be lodged with the petition—

(a) an affidavit sworn by the foreign representative as to the matters averred under paragraph (2);

(b) the evidence and statement required under article 15(2) and (3) respectively of the Model Law;

(c) any other evidence which in the opinion of the applicant will assist the court in deciding whether the proceeding in respect of which the application is made is a foreign proceeding within the meaning of article 2(i) of the Model Law and whether the applicant is a foreign representative within the meaning of article 2(j) of the Model Law; and

(d) evidence that the debtor has its centre of main interests or an establishment, as the case may be, within the country where the foreign proceeding is taking place.

(4) The affidavit to be lodged under paragraph (3)(a) shall state whether, in the opinion of the applicant, the EC Insolvency Regulation applies to any of the proceedings identified in accordance with article 15(3) of the Model Law and, if so, whether those proceedings are main proceedings, secondary proceedings or territorial proceedings.

(5) Any subsequent information required to be given to the court by the foreign representative under article 18 of the Model Law shall be given by amendment of the petition.]

[1224]

NOTES

Commencement: 6 April 2006.
Inserted as noted to r 62.90 at **[1222]**.

[62.93 Application for interim remedy

(1) An application for an interim remedy shall be made by note in process.

(2) There shall be lodged with the note an affidavit sworn by the foreign representative stating—

(a) the grounds on which it is proposed that the interim remedy applied for should be granted;
(b) the details of any proceeding under British insolvency law taking place in relation to the debtor;
(c) whether to the foreign representative's knowledge, an administrative receiver or receiver or manager of the debtor's property is acting in relation to the debtor;
(d) an estimate of the assets of the debtor in Scotland in respect of which the remedy is applied for;
(e) all other matters that would in the opinion of the foreign representative assist the court in deciding whether or not to grant the remedy applied for, including whether, to the best of the knowledge and belief of the foreign representative, the interests of the debtor's creditors (including any secured creditors or parties to hire-purchase agreements) and any other interested parties, including if appropriate the debtor, are adequately protected; and
(f) whether to the best of the foreign representative's knowledge and belief, the grant of any of the remedy applied for would interfere with the administration of the foreign main proceeding.]

[1225]

NOTES

Commencement: 6 April 2006.
Inserted as noted to r 62.90 at **[1222]**.

[62.94 Application for remedy

(1) An application under article 21 of the Model Law for a remedy shall be made by note in process.

(2) There shall be lodged with the note an affidavit sworn by the foreign representative stating—

(a) the grounds on which it is proposed that the remedy applied for should be granted;
(b) an estimate of the value of the assets of the debtor in Scotland in respect of which the remedy is requested;
(c) in the case of an application by a foreign representative who is or believes that he is a representative of a foreign non-main proceeding, the reasons why the applicant believes that the remedy relates to assets that, under the law of Great Britain, should be administered in the foreign non-main proceeding or concerns information required in that proceeding; and
(d) all other matters that would in the opinion of the foreign representative assist the court in deciding whether or not it is appropriate to grant the remedy requested, including whether, to the best of the knowledge and belief of the foreign representative, the interests of the debtor's creditors (including any secured creditors or parties to hire-purchase agreements) and any other interested parties, including if appropriate the debtor, are adequately protected.]

[1226]

NOTES

Commencement: 6 April 2006.
Inserted as noted to r 62.90 at **[1222]**.

[62.95 Application for confirmation of status of replacement foreign representative

(1) An application under paragraph 2(3) of the Scottish Provisions for an order confirming the status of a replacement foreign representative shall be made by note in process.

(2) The note shall include averments as to—

(a) the name of the replacement foreign representative and his address for service within Scotland;

(b) the circumstances in which the former foreign representative ceased to be foreign representative in the foreign proceeding in relation to the debtor (including the date on which he ceased to be the foreign representative);

(c) his own appointment as replacement foreign representative in the foreign proceeding (including the date of that appointment).

(3) There shall be lodged with the note—

(a) an affidavit sworn by the foreign representative as to the matters averred under paragraph (2);

(b) a certificate from the foreign court affirming—

(i) the cessation of the appointment of the former foreign representative as foreign representative, and

(ii) the appointment of the applicant as the foreign representative in the foreign proceeding, or

(c) in the absence of such a certificate, any other evidence acceptable to the court of the matters referred to in sub-paragraph (a).]

[1227]

NOTES

Commencement: 6 April 2006.
Inserted as noted to r 62.90 at **[1222]**.

[62.96 Review application

(1) A review application shall be made by note in process.

(2) There shall be lodged with the note an affidavit sworn by the applicant as to—

(a) the grounds on which it is proposed that the remedy applied for should be granted; and

(b) all other matters that would in the opinion of the applicant assist the court in deciding whether or not it is appropriate to grant the remedy requested, including whether, to the best of the knowledge and belief of the applicant, the interests of the debtor's creditors (including any secured creditors or parties to hire-purchase agreements) and any other interested parties, including if appropriate the debtor, are adequately protected.]

[1228]

NOTES

Commencement: 6 April 2006.
Inserted as noted to r 62.90 at **[1222]**.

[CHAPTER 64
APPLICATIONS UNDER SECTION 1 OF THE ADMINISTRATION OF JUSTICE (SCOTLAND) ACT 1972

64.1 Application of this Chapter

This Chapter applies to an application for an order under section 1 of the Administration of Justice (Scotland) Act 1972 made where a cause is not depending before the court in which the application may be made.]

[1229]

NOTES

Chapter 64 (rr 64.1–64.13) substituted by the Act of Sederunt (Rules of the Court of Session Amendment No 4) (Applications under s 1 of the Administration of Justice (Scotland) Act 1972) 2000, SSI 2000/319, r 2(1), Sch 1.

[64.2 Form and content of application

(1) An application to which this Chapter applies shall be made by petition.

(2) The statement of facts shall set out—

(a) a list of documents and other property (in this Chapter and in [Form 64.6] referred to as the "listed items") which the petitioner wishes to be made the subject of the order;

(b) the address of the premises within which the petitioner believes the listed items are to be found;

(c) the facts which give rise to the petitioner's belief that were the order not to be granted the listed items or any of them would cease to be available for the purposes of the said section 1.]

[1230]

NOTES

Substituted as noted to r 64.1 at **[1229]**.

Para (2): words in square brackets in sub-para (a) substituted by the Act of Sederunt (Rules of the Court of Session Amendment) (Miscellaneous) 2004, SSI 2004/52, r 2(1), (15).

[64.3 Accompanying documents

The petitioner shall lodge with the application—

(a) an affidavit supporting the averments in the petition;

(b) an undertaking by the petitioner that he—

(i) will comply with any order of the court as to payment of compensation if it is subsequently discovered that the order, or the implementation of the order, has caused loss to the respondent or, where the haver is not the respondent, to the haver; and

(ii) will bring within a reasonable time of the execution of the order any proceedings which he decides to bring; and

(iii) will not, without leave of the court, use any information, documents or other property obtained as a result of the order, except for the purpose of any proceedings which he decides to bring and to which the order relates.]

[1231]

NOTES

Substituted as noted to r 64.1 at **[1229]**.

[64.4 Modification of undertakings

The court may, on cause shown, modify, by addition, deletion or substitution, the undertaking mentioned in rule 64.3(b).]

[1232]

NOTES

Substituted as noted to r 64.1 at **[1229]**.

[64.5 Intimation and service of application

(1) Before granting the application, the court may order such intimation and service of the petition to be given or executed, as the case may be, as it thinks fit.

(2) Any person receiving intimation or service of the petition by virtue of an order under paragraph (1) may appear and oppose the application.]

[1233]

NOTES

Substituted as noted to r 64.1 at **[1229]**.

[64.6 Form of order

An order made under this Chapter shall be in [Form 64.6].]

[1234]

NOTES

Substituted as noted to r 64.1 at **[1229]**.

Words in square brackets in sub-para (a) substituted by the Act of Sederunt (Rules of the Court of Session Amendment) (Miscellaneous) 2004, SSI 2004/52, r 2(1), (15).

[64.7 Caution and other security

On granting, in whole or in part, the application the court may order the petitioner to find such caution or other security as it thinks fit.]

[1235]

NOTES

Substituted as noted to r 64.1 at **[1229]**.

[64.8 Execution of order

The order of the court shall be served by the Commissioner in person and it shall be accompanied by the affidavit referred to in rule 64.3(a).]

[1236]

NOTES

Substituted as noted to r 64.1 at **[1229]**.

[64.9 Duties of commissioner

The Commissioner appointed by the court shall, on executing the order—

- (a) give to the haver a copy of the notice in [Form 64.6];
- (b) explain to the haver—
  - (i) the meaning and effect of the order;
  - (ii) that he may be entitled to claim that some or all of the listed items are confidential or privileged;
- (c) inform the haver of his right to seek legal advice;
- (d) enter the premises and take all reasonable steps to fulfil the terms of the order;
- (e) where the order has authorised the recovery of any of the listed items, prepare an inventory of all the listed items to be recovered before recovering them;
- (f) send any recovered listed items to the Deputy Principal Clerk of Session to await the further order of the court.]

[1237]

NOTES

Substituted as noted to r 64.1 at **[1229]**.

Words in square brackets in sub-para (a) substituted by the Act of Sederunt (Rules of the Court of Session Amendment) (Miscellaneous) 2004, SSI 2004/52, r 2(1), (16).

[64.10 Confidentiality

(1) Where confidentiality is claimed for any listed item, that listed item shall, where practicable, be enclosed in a sealed envelope.

(2) A motion to have such a sealed envelope opened may be made by the party who obtained the order and he shall intimate the terms of the motion, by registered post or first class delivery, to the person claiming confidentiality.

(3) A person claiming confidentiality may oppose a motion made under paragraph (2).]

[1238]

NOTES

Substituted as noted to r 64.1 at **[1229]**.

[64.11 Restrictions on service

(1) Except on cause shown, the order may be served on Monday to Friday only, between the hours of 9am and 5pm only.

(2) The order shall not be served at the same time as a search warrant granted in the course of a criminal investigation.

(3) The Commissioner may be accompanied only by—

(a) any person whom he considers necessary to assist him to execute the order;

(b) such representatives of the petitioner as are named in the order and if it is likely that the premises will be occupied by an unaccompanied female and the Commissioner is not herself female, one of the people accompanying the Commissioner shall be female.

(4) If it appears to the Commissioner when he comes to serve the order that the premises are occupied by an unaccompanied female and the Commissioner is neither female nor accompanied by a female, the Commissioner shall not enter the premises.]

[1239]

NOTES

Substituted as noted to r 64.1 at **[1229]**.

[64.12 Right of haver to consult

The haver may seek legal or other professional advice of his choice and where the purpose of seeking this advice is to help him to decide whether to ask the court to vary the order the Commissioner shall not commence to search for or to take any other steps to take possession of or preserve the listed items.]

[1240]

NOTES

Substituted as noted to r 64.1 at **[1229]**.

[64.13 Return of documents etc to haver

The Deputy Principal Clerk of Session shall return the recovered listed items to the haver if the petitioner has taken no further action within 8 weeks of the date on which they are sent to him under rule 64.9(f).]

[1241]

NOTES

Substituted as noted to r 64.1 at **[1229]**.

CHAPTER 65
REFERENCES TO THE EUROPEAN COURT OF JUSTICE

65.1 Interpretation of this Chapter

(1) In this Chapter—

"appeal" includes an application for leave to appeal;

"the European Court" means the Court of Justice of the European Communities;

"reference" means a reference to the European Court for—

(a) a preliminary ruling under Article [234] of the EEC Treaty, Article 150 of the Euratom Treaty, or Article 41 of the ECSC Treaty;

(b) a preliminary ruling on the interpretation of the Conventions, mentioned in Article 1 of Schedule 2 to the Civil Jurisdiction and Judgments Act 1982, under Article 3 of that Schedule; or

(c) a preliminary ruling on the interpretation of the instruments, mentioned in Article 1 of Schedule 3 to the Contracts (Applicable Law) Act 1990, under Article 2 of that Schedule.

(2) The expressions "EEC Treaty", "Euratom Treaty" and "ECSC Treaty" have the meanings assigned respectively in Schedule 1 to the European Communities Act 1972.

[1242]

NOTES

Para (1): number in square brackets in sub-para (a) substituted by the Act of Sederunt (Rules of the Court of Session Amendment No 4) (References to the Court of Justice of the European Communities) 1999, SI 1999/1281, r 2(1), (3).

65.2 Applications for reference

A reference may be made by the court at its own instance or on the motion of a party …

[1243]

NOTES

Words omitted revoked by the Act of Sederunt (Rules of the Court of Session Amendment No 4) (References to the Court of Justice of the European Communities) 1999, SI 1999/1281, r 2(1), (4).

65.3 Preparation of case for reference

(1) Where the court decides that a reference shall be made, it shall pronounce an interlocutor giving directions to the parties about the manner and time in which the reference is to be drafted and adjusted.

[(1A) Except in so far as the court may otherwise direct, a reference shall be prepared in accordance with Form 65.3.

(1B) In preparing a reference, the parties shall have regard to the guidance set out in the annex to these Rules.]

(2) When the reference has been drafted [and any adjustments required by the court have been made], the court shall make and sign the reference.

(3) A certified copy of the interlocutor making the reference shall be annexed to the reference.

[1244]

NOTES

Paras (1A), (1B): inserted by the Act of Sederunt (Rules of the Court of Session Amendment No 4) (References to the Court of Justice of the European Communities) 1999, SI 1999/1281, r 2(1), (5)(a).

Para (2): words in square brackets substituted by SI 1999/1281, r 2(1), (5)(b).

65.4 Sist of cause

(1) Subject to paragraph (2), on a reference being made. the cause shall, unless the court when making such a reference otherwise orders, be sisted until the European Court has given a preliminary ruling on the question referred to it.

(2) The court may recall a sist made under paragraph (1) for the purpose of making an interim order which a due regard to the interests of the parties may require.

[1245]

65.5 Transmission of reference

(1) Subject to paragraph (2), a copy of the reference, certified by the Deputy Principal Clerk, shall be transmitted by him to the Registrar of the European Court.

(2) Unless the court otherwise directs, a copy of the reference shall not be sent to the Registrar of the European Court where a reclaiming motion or appeal against the making of the reference is pending.

(3) For the purpose of paragraph (2), a reclaiming motion or an appeal shall be treated as pending—

(a) until the expiry of the time for marking that reclaiming motion or appeal; or

(b) where a reclaiming motion or an appeal has been made, until it has been determined.

[1246]

CHAPTER 66
APPLICATIONS UNDER THE EVIDENCE (PROCEEDINGS IN OTHER JURISDICTIONS) ACT 1975

66.1 Interpretation of this Chapter

In this Chapter—

"the Act of 1975" means the Evidence (Proceedings in Other Jurisdictions) Act 1975;

"civil proceedings" has the meaning assigned in section 9(1) of the Act of 1975;

"requesting court" has the meaning assigned in section 9(1) of the Act of 1975.

[1247]

66.2 Disapplication of certain rules to this Chapter

The following rules shall not apply to an application to which this Chapter applies:—
rule 14.5 (first order in petitions),
rule 14.6 (period of notice for lodging answers),
rule 14.7 (intimation and service of petitions),
rule 14.9 (unopposed petitions).

[1248]

66.3 Form of applications under the Act of 1975

(1) An application under section 1 of the Act of 1975 (application for assistance in obtaining evidence for foreign civil proceedings) shall be made by petition.

(2) …

(3) Where the letter of request is in a language other than English, there shall be produced with the petition a translation into English certified as correct by the translator; and the certificate shall include his full name, address and qualifications.

[1249]

NOTES

Para (2): revoked by the Act of Sederunt (Rules of the Court of Session Amendment No 2) (Miscellaneous) 1998, SI 1998/2637, r 2(6).

66.4 Intimation of order and citation

(1) Where the court pronounces an interlocutor making an order under section 2(1) of the Act of 1975, the petitioner shall—

(a) intimate a certified copy of that interlocutor to any witness or haver named in the interlocutor; and

(b) cite such witness or haver to give evidence.

(2) Rule 35.4(3) and (4) (citation of haver to commission) and rule 35.11(5) and (6) (citation of witness to commission) shall, with the necessary modifications, apply to the citation of a haver or witness, as the case may be, under this rule.

[1250]

66.5 Variation or recall of orders

A witness or haver who has received intimation and citation under rule 66.4 may apply to the court by motion to have the order under section 2(1) of the Act of 1975 varied or recalled.

[1251]

66.6 Procedure where witness claims he is not compellable

(1) Where a witness or haver who has received intimation and citation under rule 66.4—

(a) claims that he is not a compellable witness or haver by virtue of section 3(1)(b) of the Act of 1975, and

(b) is required to give evidence,

the court or any commissioner appointed by the court shall take the evidence and record it in a document separate from the record of any other evidence; and that document shall be kept by the Deputy Principal Clerk.

(2) Where evidence is taken under paragraph (1) of this rule, the court or the commissioner, as the case may be, shall certify the grounds of the claim made under section 3(1)(b) of the Act of 1975.

(3) On certification under paragraph (2), the deputy Principal Clerk shall send the certificate to the requesting court with a request to it to determine the claim.

(4) On receipt of the determination from the requesting court, the Deputy Principal Clerk shall—

(a) give written intimation of the determination to the witness or haver who made the claim; and

(b) in accordance with the determination, send the document in which the evidence is recorded to, as the case may be—
   (i) the requesting court, or
   (ii) where the claim is upheld, the witness or haver.

[1252]

66.7 Applications for evidence for proceedings under the European Patent Convention

Where the court makes an order under section 1 of the Act of 1975 as applied by section 92(1) of the Patents Act 1977, an officer of the European Patent Office may apply by motion—

(a) to examine any witness; or
(b) to request the court or commissioner, as the case may be, to put specified questions to any witness.

[1253]

(*Chapters 67–80 outside the scope of this work.*)

APPENDIX 1
FORMS

NOTES

Only the forms relevant to this work are reproduced here. They can be viewed at http://www.scotcourts.gov.uk/session/rules/forms/index.asp.

RULES OF THE COURT OF SESSION
FORMS

RECOGNITION, REGISTRATION AND ENFORCEMENT OF FOREIGN JUDGMENTS, ETC

FORM 62.2

Rule 62.2(1)(b)

Form of certificate of currency conversion

IN THE COURT OF SESSION

in the

Application of

(*name, designation and address of applicant*(*s*))

under the Civil Jurisdiction and Judgments Act 1982 for registration of a judgment [*or other document*] of the (*name of court*) of (*date of judgment*) in the cause (*name of pursuer*) against (*name of defender*).

In a terms of a certificate dated at (*place*) on (*date*) the sterling equivalent of (*a*) the principal sum is (£ . p); (*b*) the interest thereon is (£ . p); and (*c*) the expenses is (£ . p) at the rate of exchange prevailing at that date.

Date:

(*Signed*)

Depute [*or* Assistant] Clerk of Session

FORM 62.9

Rule 62.9

Form of notice to judgment debtor of registration of judgment under the Administration of Justice Act 1920 or the Foreign Judgments (Reciprocal Enforcement) Act 1933

IN THE COURT OF SESSION

in the PETITION of

[AB] (*designation and address*)

Petitioner
for
Registration of a judgment of (*name of court*)
dated (*date*)
under
section 9 of the Administration of Justice Act 1920
[*or* section 2 of the Foreign Judgments (Reciprocal Enforcement) Act 1933]

Date: (*date of posting or other method of service*)

To: (*name of judgment debtor*)

TAKE NOTICE

That a judgment (*give details*) has been registered in the register of judgments of the Books of Council and Session on (*date*) on the application of the petitioner in the above petition.

If you intend to apply to the court to have the judgment set aside you must do so by note on or before (*insert date court has fixed under RCS 1994, r 62.7(2)*). You must lodge the note in the process of the above petition in the Petition Department, Court of Session, 2 Parliament Square, Edinburgh EH1 1RQ.

IF YOU ARE UNCERTAIN ABOUT THE EFFECT OF THIS NOTICE, you should consult a solicitor, Citizens Advice Bureau or other local advice agency or adviser immediately.

(*Signed*)

Messenger-at-Arms

[*or* Solicitor [*or* Agent] for pursuer]

(*Address*)

FORM 62.11

Rule 62.11

Form of certificate to be appended to copy of judgment certified under section 10 of the Administration of Justice Act 1920 or the Foreign Judgments (Reciprocal Enforcement) Act 1933

I, Deputy Principal Clerk of Session, certify that the foregoing extract decree is a true copy of a judgment obtained in the Court of Session. This certificate is issued in accordance with section 10 of the Administration of Justice Act 1920 [*or* Foreign Judgments (Reciprocal Enforcement) Act 1933] and in obedience to an interlocutor of Lord (*name*) dated (*date*).

Date:

(*Signed*)

Deputy Principal Clerk of Session
(*Stamp*)

FORM 62.16

Rule 62.16

Form of notice of registration of award under the Arbitration (International Investments Disputes) Act 1966

REGISTRATION OF AWARD UNDER THE ARBITRATION (INTERNATIONAL INVESTMENTS DISPUTES) ACT 1966

Date: (*date of posting or other method of service*)

To: (*name and address of person on whom service executed*)

TAKE NOTICE

That on (*date*) [Lord (*name*) in] the Court of Session, Edinburgh granted warrant for the registration of (*identify award to be registered*) on the application of (*name and address of petitioner*).

The above award was registered in the Books of Council and Session on (*date*) for execution (enforcement). An application will be made to the Keeper of the Registers of Scotland for an extract of the registered award with warrant for execution.

(*Signed*)

Messenger-at-Arms

[*or* Solicitor [*or* Agent] for petitioner]

(*Address*)

[FORM 62.28

Rule 62.28

Form of petition for registration of a judgment under section 4 of the Civil Jurisdiction and Judgments Act 1982 or under Article 38, Article 57 or Article 58 of the Council Regulation

UNTO THE RIGHT HONOURABLE THE LORDS OF COUNCIL AND SESSION

PETITION

of

[AB] (*designation and address*)

under the Civil Jurisdiction and Judgments Act 1982 [*or* under Council Regulation (EC) No 44/2001 of 22nd December 2000 on jurisdiction and the recognition and enforcement of judgments in civil and commercial matters]

for registration of

a judgment [*or* authentic instrument *or* court settlement] [of the (name of court)]

dated the day of

HUMBLY SHEWETH:—

1. That this petition is presented by (*name*) to register a judgment [*or authentic instrument or court settlement*] [of the (*name of court*) of (*date of judgment*)].

2. That in the cause in which the judgment [*or* as the case may be] was pronounced, [AB] was pursuer [*or* defender *or* (*as the case may be*)] and CD was defender [*or* pursuer *or as the case may be*].

3. That the petitioner is a party having an interest to enforce the judgment [*or as the case may be*] because (*state reasons*).

4. That this petition is supported by the affidavit of (*name of deponent*) and the documents produced with it.

5. That the petitioner seeks warrant to register the judgment [*or as the case may be*] [and for decree in terms thereof] [and for decree to be pronounced in the following or such other terms as to the court may seem proper:— (*state terms in which decree is to be pronounced in accordance with Scots law*)].

6. That the petitioner seeks the authority of the court to execute the protective measure[s] of (*state measures*), for the following reasons (*state reasons*).

7. That this petition is made under section 4 of, and under Article 31 [*or* 50] of the Convention in Schedule 1 [*or* 3C] to, the Civil Jurisdiction and Judgments Act 1982 [*or* under Article 38 [*or* 57 *or* 58] of the Council Regulation (EC) No 44/2001 of 22 December 2000 on jurisdiction and the recognition and enforcement of judgments in civil and commercial matters] and rule 62.28 of the Rules of the Court of Session 1994.

According to Justice etc

(*Signed*)

Petitioner

[*or* Solicitor [*or* Agent] for the petitioner]

(*Address of solicitor or agent*)

[*or counsel or other person having a right of audience*]]

[FORM 62.33

Rule 62.33

Form of notice of decree and warrant for registration of a judgment under section 4 of the Civil Jurisdiction and Judgments Act 1982 or under Article 38, Article 57 or Article 58 of the Council Regulation

IN THE COURT OF SESSION

in the

PETITION

of

[AB] (*designation and address*)

under section 4 of the Civil Jurisdiction and Judgments Act 1982 [or under Article 38 [*or* 57 *or* 58] of Council Regulation (EC) No 22/2002 of 22nd December 2000 on jurisdiction and the recognition and enforcement of judgments in civil and commercial matters]

Date: (*date of posting or other method of service*)

To: (*name of person against whom judgment was given and decree and warrant granted*).

TAKE NOTICE

That an interlocutor dated the day of , a certified copy of which is attached, was pronounced in the Court of Session granting decree and warrant for registration of the judgment [*or as the case may be*] [of the (*name of court*)] dated the day of , for (*state briefly the terms of the judgment*).

You have the right to appeal to a Lord Ordinary in the Outer House of the Court of Session, Parliament Square, Edinburgh EH1 1RQ against the interlocutor granting decree and warrant for registration within one month [*or* two months *as the case may be*] after the date of service of this notice upon you. The date of service is the date stated at the top of this notice unless service has been executed by post in which case the notice of service is the day after that date.

An appeal must be by motion enrolled in the process of the petition.

The registered judgment and decree of the Court of Session may not be enforced in Scotland until the expiry of the period within which you may appeal and any appeal has been disposed of.

Intimation of an appeal should be made to the petitioner, [AB], at the following address for service in Scotland:— (*address*)

(*Signed*)

Messenger-at-Arms

[*or* Petitioner [*or* Solicitor [*or* Agent] for petitioner]]

(*Address*)]

FORM 62.38

Rule 62.38(1)

Form of petition for registration of a judgment under paragraph 5 of Schedule 7 to the Civil Jurisdiction and Judgments Act 1982

UNTO THE RIGHT HONOURABLE THE LORDS OF COUNCIL AND SESSION

PETITION

of

[AB] (*designation and address*)

under the Civil Jurisdiction and Judgments Act 1982

PART II

for registration of

a judgment of the (*name of court*)

dated the day of

HUMBLY SHEWETH:—

1. That this petition is presented by (*name*) to register a judgment [*or decision or other order*] of the (*name of court*) of (*date of judgment*).

2. That in the cause in which the judgment [*or decision or other order*] was pronounced [AB] was plaintiff [*or* defendant *or as the case may be*] and [CD] was defendant [*or* plaintiff *or as the case may be*].

3. That the petitioner is a party having an interest to enforce the judgment [*or decision or other order*] because (*state reasons*).

4. That the petitioner believes and avers that the usual [*or* last known] address of the (*state party liable in execution*) is (*state address*).

5. That the petitioner seeks warrant to register the judgment [and for decree in terms thereof] [and for decree to be pronounced in the following or such other terms as to the court may seem proper:— (*state terms in which decree is to be pronounced in accordance with Scots law*)].

6. That this petition is made under paragraph 5(1) of Schedule 7 to the Civil Jurisdiction and Judgments Act 1982 and rule 62.38 of the Rules of the Court of Session 1994.

According to Justice etc

(*Signed*)

Petitioner

[*or* Solicitor [*or* Agent] for petitioner]

(*Address of solicitor or agent*)

[*or counsel or other person having a right of audience*]

FORM 62.40-A

Rule 62.40(1)(a)

Form of certificate under section 12 of the Civil Jurisdiction and Judgments Act 1982 of a judgment given by the court or a court settlement

IN THE COURT OF SESSION

CERTIFICATE

under the Civil Jurisdiction and Judgments Act 1982

in the cause

[*or* in the petition of]

[AB] (*designation and address*)

Pursuer [*or* Petitioner]

against

[CD] (*designation and address*)

Defender [*or* Respondent]

I, , a Deputy Principal Clerk of the Court of Session, do hereby certify—

1. That the summons [*or* petition], brought [*or* presented] by the pursuer [*or* petitioner] [AB] was executed by citation of the defender [CD] served on him [*or* was served on the respondent [CD]] on the day of by (*state method of service*).

2. That in the summons [*or* petition] the pursuer, sought [payment of the sum of £ in respect of (*state briefly the nature of the claim*)] [and (*state other conclusions of the summons or orders sought in the prayer of petition*)].

3. [That the defender [CD] entered appearance on the day of] [and lodged defences on the day of [*or* That the defender [CD] did not enter appearance].

4. That the pursuer [*or* petitioner] obtained decree [*or other order*] against the defender [*or* respondent] in the Court of Session for [payment of the sum of £] [or *state briefly the terms of the interlocutor or opinion of the court*] [and *state briefly other conclusions of the summons or orders sought in the prayer of the petition granted*] with the expenses of the cause in the sum of £ , all in terms of the certified copy of the interlocutor [and joint minute] attached.

5. That [no] objection to the jurisdiction of the court has been made [on the grounds that].

6. That the decree [in terms of the joint minute] includes interest at the rate of per cent a year on the total of the sum of £ and expenses of £ from the day of until payment.

7. That the interlocutor containing the decree [*or other order or settlement*] has been served on the defender.

8. That the time for reclaiming (appealing) against the interlocutor has expired [and no reclaiming motion (appeal) has been enrolled within that time] [*or* and a reclaiming motion (appeal) having been enrolled within that time, has [not] been finally disposed of].

9. That enforcement of the decree has not for the time being been suspended and the time available for its enforcement has not expired.

10. That the whole pleadings of the parties are contained in the Closed Record [*or* summons *or* petition], a copy of which is attached.

11. That this certificate is issued under section 12 of the Civil Jurisdiction and Judgments Act 1982 and rule 62.40(1) of the Rules of the Court of Session 1994.

Dated the day of .

(*Signed*)

Deputy Principal Clerk of Session

FORM 62.40-B

Rule 62.40(3

Form of certificate by Keeper of the Registers of writ registered for execution in the Books of Council and Session for registration under Article 50 of Schedule 1 or 3C to the Civil Jurisdiction and Judgments Act 1982

REGISTERS OF SCOTLAND

CERTIFICATE

under the Civil Jurisdiction and Judgments Act 1982

of

Deed [*or other writ*]

Between

[AB] (*address*)

and

[CD] (*address*)

registered for execution in the Books of Council and Session

I, , the Keeper of the Registers of Scotland, and as such, Keeper of the Register of Deeds, Bonds, Protests, Judgments and other writs registered for execution in the Books of Council and Session, do hereby certify—

1. That [AB] registered in the Books of Council and Session on the day of for execution against [CD] a (*describe writ and state terms of writ for which enforcement is to be sought*).

2. That the extract of the deed [*or other writ*] attached hereto is a true copy of the deed [*or other writ*] registered for execution AB].

[3. That the deed [*or other writ*] carries interest at the rate of per cent a year from the day of until payment].

[4. That enforcement of the deed] [*or other writ*] has not for the time being been suspended and that the time available for its enforcement has not expired.

5. That this certificate is issued under Article 50 of Schedule 1 [*or* 3C] to the Civil Jurisdiction and Judgments Act 1982 and rule 62.40(3) of the Rules of the Court of Session 1994.

Dated the day of .

(*Signed*)

Keeper of Registers of Scotland

FORM 62.41-A

Rule 62.41(1)

Form of certificate of money provisions in an interlocutor for registration under Schedule 6 to the Civil Jurisdiction and Judgments Act 1982

IN THE COURT OF SESSION

CERTIFICATE

under the Civil Jurisdictions and Judgments Act 1982

in the cause

[*or* in the petition of]

[AB] (*designation and address*)

Pursuer [*or* Petitioner]

Against

[CD] (*designation and address*)

Defender [*or* Respondent]

I, a Deputy Principal Clerk of the Court of Session, do hereby certify—

1. That the pursuer AB obtained decree [*or other order*] against the defender [CD] on the day of in the Court of Session for payment of the sum of £ in respect of (*state briefly the nature of the claim and terms of the interlocutor*) with the sum of £ as expenses.

2. That the interlocutor granting decree [*or other order*] was obtained on the grounds (*state grounds briefly*).

3. That the decree [*or other order*] carries interest at the rate of per cent a year on the total of the sum of £ and expenses of £ from the day of until payment.

4. That the time for reclaiming (appealing) against the interlocutor has expired [and no reclaiming motion (appeal) has been enrolled within that time] [and a reclaiming motion (appeal) having been enrolled within that time, has been finally disposed of].

5. That enforcement of the decree [*or other order*] has not for the time being been suspended and the time available for its enforcement has not expired.

Dated the day of

(*Signed*)

Deputy Principal Clerk of Session

FORM 62.41-B

Rule 62.41(3)

Form of certificate by the Keeper of the Registers of money provisions in a writ registered for execution in the Books of Council and Session for registration under Schedule 6 to the Civil Jurisdiction and Judgments Act 1982

REGISTERS OF SCOTLAND

CERTIFICATE

under the Civil Jurisdiction and Judgments Act 1982

of

Deed [*or other writ*]

between

[AB] (*address*)

and

[CD] (*address*)

registered for execution in the Books of Council and Session

I, , Keeper of the Registers of Scotland, and as such, Keeper of the Register of Deeds, Bonds, Protests, Judgments and other writs registered for execution in the Books of Council and Session, do hereby certify—

1. That [AB] registered in the Books of Council and Session on the day of for execution against [CD] a (*describe writ and state terms of money provision in writ for which enforcement is to be sought*).

2. That the money provision in the deed [*or other writ*] carries interest at the rate of per cent a year from the day of until payment.

3. That enforcement of the deed [*or other writ*] has not for the time being been suspended and that the time available for its enforcement has not expired.

4. That this certificate is issued under paragraph 4(1) of Schedule 6 to the Civil Jurisdiction and Judgments Act 1982 and rule 62.41(3) of the Rules of the Court of Session 1994.

Dated the day of .

(*Signed*)

Keeper of the Registers of Scotland

FORM 62.42-A

Rule 62.42(1)

Form of certificate of non-money provisions in an interlocutor for registration under Schedule 7 to the Civil Jurisdiction and Judgments Act 1982

IN THE COURT OF SESSION

CERTIFICATE

under the Civil Jurisdiction and Judgments Act 1982

in the cause

[*or* in the PETITION of]

[AB] (*designation and address*)

Pursuer [*or* Petitioner]

against

[CD] (*designation and address*)

Defender [*or* Respondent]

I, , a Deputy Principal Clerk of the Court of Session, do hereby certify—

1. That the copy of the interlocutor attached hereto is a true copy of the decree [*or other order*] obtained in the Court of Session [and that the copy of the opinion of the court attached hereto is a true copy thereof] and is issued in accordance with section 18 of the Civil Jurisdiction and Judgments Act 1982.

2. That the time for reclaiming (appealing) against the interlocutor has expired [and no reclaiming motion (appeal) has been enrolled within that time] [and a reclaiming motion (appeal) having been enrolled within that time has been finally disposed of].

3. That enforcement of the decree [*or other order*] has not for the time being been suspended and the time available for its enforcement has not expired.

4. That this certificate is issued under paragraph 4(1)(b) of Schedule 7 to the Civil Jurisdiction and Judgments Act 1982 and rule 62.42(1) of the Rules of the Court of Session 1994.

Dated the day of .

(*Signed*)

Deputy Principal Clerk of Session

FORM 62.42-B

Rule 62.42(4), (5)

Form of certificate by Keeper of the Registers of non-money provisions in a writ registered for execution in the Books of Council and Session for registration under Schedule 7 to the Civil Jurisdiction and Judgments Act 1982

REGISTERS OF SCOTLAND

CERTIFICATE

under the Civil Jurisdiction and Judgments Act 1982

of

Deed [*or other writ*]

between

[AB] (*address*)

and

[CD] (*address*)

registered for execution in the Books of Council and Session

I, , the Keeper of the Registers of Scotland, and as such, Keeper of the Register of Deeds, Bonds, Protests, Judgments and other writs registered for execution in the Books of Council and Session, do hereby certify—

1. That the extract of the deed [*or other writ*] attached hereto is a true copy of the deed [*or other writ*] registered for execution by [AB] and is issued in accordance with section 18 of the Civil Jurisdiction and Judgments Act 1982.

2. That enforcement of the deed [*or other writ*] has not for the time being suspended and that the time available for its enforcement has not expired.

3. That this certificate is issued under paragraph 4(1)(b) of Schedule 7 to the Civil Jurisdiction and Judgments Act 1982 and rule 62.42(4) of the Rules of the Court of Session 1994.

Dated the day of .

(*Signed*)

Keeper of the Registers of Scotland

FORM 62.51

Rule 62.51

Form of notice of decree and warrant for registration of an order under the Criminal Justice (Scotland) Act 1987, the Criminal Justice Act 1988 or the Prevention of Terrorism (Temporary Provisions) Act 1989

IN THE COURT OF SESSION

in the

PETITION of

[AB] (*designation and address*)

under section 28 [or 30A] of the Criminal

Justice (Scotland) Act 1987

[*or* section 90 of the Criminal Justice Act 1988]

[*or* paragraph 19(2) of Schedule 4 to the Prevention of Terrorism (Temporary Provisions) Act 1989]

for

registration of an order of

(*name of court*)

Dated the day of

To: (*name of person against whom the order was made and decree and warrant for registration granted*)

TAKE NOTICE

An interlocutor dated the day of , a certified copy of which is attached, was pronounced in the Court of Session granting decree and warrant for registration in the Court of Session [and for registration in the Register of Judgments of the Books of Council and Session] of the order of the (*name of court*) dated the day of that (*briefly describe order*).

The order was registered in the Court of Session on (*date*).

[The order was registered in the Register of Judgments of the Books of Council and Session on (*date*) and an extract of the registered order and decree with warrant for execution has been issued by the Keeper of the Registers. Diligence in execution of the order may now be taken against you to enforce the order.]

Dated this day of .

(*Signed*)

Messenger-at-Arms

[*or* Petitioner[[*or* Solicitor [*or* Agent] for petitioner]

(*Address*)

[FORM 62.65

Form of notice of registration of decision under a relevant instrument

REGISTRATION OF A DECISION (*or as the case may be*) UNDER THE (*specify the relevant instrument*)

Date: (*date of posting or other method of service*)

To: (*name and address of person on whom service executed*)

TAKE NOTICE

That on (*date*) [Lord (*name*) in] the Court of Session, Edinburgh granted warrant for the registration of (*identify decision to be registered*) on the application of (*name and address of petitioner*).

The above award was registered in the Books of Council and Session on (*date*) for execution (ie enforcement). An application will be made to the Keeper of the Registers of Scotland for an extract of the registered award with warrant for execution.

(*Signed*)

Solicitor [*or* Agent] for petitioner

(*Address*)]

[FORM 62.69

Form of petition for enforcement of a judgment under Article 28 of the Council Regulation

UNTO THE RIGHT HONOURABLE THE LORDS OF COUNCIL AND SESSION

PETITION

of

[AB] (*designation and address*)

under Council Regulation (EC) No 2201/2003 of 27th November 2003 on jurisdiction and the recognition and enforcement of judgments in matrimonial matters and matters of parental responsibility

for registration of

a judgment [*or* authentic instrument *or* enforceable agreement][of the (*name of court*)]

dated the day of

HUMBLY SHEWETH:—

1. That this petition is presented by [AB] to register a judgment [*or* (*as the case may be*)][of the (*name of court*)] of (*date of judgment or as the case may be*).

2. That in the cause in which the judgment [*or* (*as the case may be*)] was pronounced, [AB] was pursuer [*or* defender *or* (*as the case may be*)] and [CD] was defender [*or* pursuer *or* (*as the case may be*)].

3. That the petitioner is a party having an interest to enforce the judgment [*or* (*as the case may be*)] because (*state reasons*).

4. That this petition is supported by the affidavit of (*name of deponent*) and the documents produced with it.

5. That the petitioner seeks warrants to register the judgment [*or* (*as the case may be*)] [and for decree in terms thereof] [*or* and for decree to be pronounced in the following or such other terms as to the court seem proper:—(*state terms in which decree is to be pronounced in accordance with Scots law*)].

6. That the petition is made under Article 28 of the Council Regulation (EC) No 2201/2003 of 27th November 2003 on jurisdiction and the recognition and enforcement of judgments in matrimonial matters and matters of parental responsibility and rule 62.69 of the Rules of the Court of Session 1994 [*or* (*as the case may be*)].

According to Justice etc

(*Signed*)

Petitioner

[*or* Solicitor [*or* Agent] for petitioner]

[*Address of solicitor or agent*]

[*or counsel or other person having a right of audience*].]

[FORM 62.73

Form of notice of decree and warrant for registration of a judgment under Article 28 of the Council Regulation

IN THE COURT OF SESSION

in the

PETITION of

[AB] (*designation and address*)

under Council Regulation (EC) No 2201/2003 of 27th November 2003 on jurisdiction and the recognition and enforcement of judgments in matrimonial matters and matters of parental responsibility

for registration of

a judgment [*or* authentic instrument *or* enforceable agreement][of the (*name of court*)]

dated the day of

Date: (*date of posting or other method of service*)

To: (*name of person against whom judgment was given and decree and warrant granted*)

TAKE NOTICE

That an interlocutor dated the day of , a certified copy of which is attached, was pronounced at the Court of Session granting decree and warrant for registration of the judgment [*or* (*as the case may be*)][of the (*name of court*) dated the day of , for (*state briefly the terms of the judgment*).

You have the right to appeal to a Lord Ordinary in the Outer House of the Court of Session, Parliament Square, Edinburgh, EH1 1RQ against the interlocutor granting decree and warrant for registration within one month [*or* two months (*as the case may be*)] after the date of service of this notice upon you. The date of service is the date stated at the top of this notice unless service has been executed by post in which case the date of service is the day after that date.

An appeal must be by motion enrolled in the process of the petition.

The registered judgment and decree of the Court of Session may not be enforced in Scotland until the expiry of the period within which you may appeal and any appeal has been disposed of.

Intimation of an appeal should be made to the petitioner, [AB], at the following address for service in Scotland:— (*specify address*)

(*Signed*)

Messenger-at-Arms

[*or* Petitioner [*or* Solicitor [*or* Agent] for Petitioner]] (*Address*)]

[FORM 64.6]

Form of order of court in procedure for recovery of documents under Chapter 64

ORDER BY THE COURT OF SESSION

In the Petition

[AB] (*designation and address*)

Petitioner

against

[CD] (*designation and address*)

Respondent

Date: (*date of interlocutor*)

To: (*name and address of party or parties or named third party haver, from whom the documents and other property are sought to be recovered*)

THE COURT having heard Counsel and being satisfied that it is appropriate to make an order under section 1 of the Administration of Justice (Scotland) Act 1972:

APPOINTS the Petition to be intimated on the walls of the court in common form and to be served upon the person(s) named and designed in the Petition;

APPOINTS (*name and designation of Commissioner*) to be Commissioner of the court;

GRANTS commission and diligence;

ORDERS the Commissioner to explain to the haver on executing the order—

(1) the meaning and effect of the order;

(2) that the haver may be entitled to claim that certain of the documents and other property are confidential or privileged;

(3) that the haver has a right to seek legal or other professional advice of his choice;

and to give the haver a copy of the Notice in Form 64-B of the Rules of Court.

GRANTS warrant to and authorises the said Commissioner, whether the haver has allowed entry or not—

(1) to enter, between the hours of 9am and 5pm on Monday to Friday, (*or, where the court has found cause shown under rule 64.11(1), otherwise specify the time*) the premises at (*address of premises*) and any other place in Scotland owned or occupied by the haver at which it appears to the Commissioner that any of the items set out in the statement of facts in the application to the court (the "listed items") may be located;

(2) unless the haver is taking legal or other professional advice on the question of having the order varied—

(a) to search for and take all other steps which he considers necessary to take possession of or preserve (*specify the listed items*); and

(b) to take possession of and to preserve all or any of the listed items and to consign them with the Deputy Principal Clerk of Session to be held by him pending the further orders of the court; and for that purpose.

ORDERS the haver or his servants or agents to allow the Commissioner, any person whom the Commissioner considers necessary to assist him, and the Petitioner's representatives to enter the premises named in the order and, unless the haver has sought legal or other professional advice on the question of having the order varied, to allow them—

(1) to search for the listed items and take such other steps as the Commissioner considers it is reasonable to take to execute the order;

(2) to provide access to information stored on any computer owned or used by him by supplying or providing the means to overcome any and all security mechanisms inhibiting access thereto;

(3) to allow the Commissioner, any person whom the Commissioner considers necessary to assist him, and the Petitioner's representatives to remain in the premises until such time as the search is complete, including allowing them to continue the search on subsequent days if necessary;

(4) to inform the Commissioner immediately of the whereabouts of the listed items;

(5) to provide the Commissioner with a list of the names and addresses of everyone who has supplied him with any of the listed items and of the names and addresses of everyone to whom he has given any of the listed items;

and not to destroy, conceal or tamper with any of the listed items except in accordance with the terms of this order;

FURTHER AUTHORISES (*specify the representatives*) to be the sole representatives of the Petitioner to accompany the Commissioner for the purpose of identification of the said documents and other property.

SCHEDULE TO THE ORDER OF THE COURT

Undertakings given by Petitioner

The Petitioner has given the following undertakings—

1. That he will comply with any order of the court as to payment of compensation if it is subsequently discovered that the order, or the implementation of the order, has caused loss to the respondent or, where the respondent is not the haver, to the haver.

2. That he will bring within a reasonable time of the execution of the order any proceedings which he decides to bring.

3. That he will not, without leave of the court, use any information, documents or other property obtained as a result of the order, except for the purpose of any proceedings which he decides to bring and to which the order relates.

(*or as modified under rule 64.4*)

[FORM 64.9]

Notice to accompany order of the court when served by Commissioner

IMPORTANT

NOTICE TO PERSON ON WHOM THIS ORDER IS SERVED

1. This order orders you to allow the person appointed and named in the order as Commissioner to enter your premises to search for, examine and remove or copy the items mentioned in the order.

2. It also allows entry to the premises to any person appointed and named in the order as a representative of the person who has been granted the order and to any person accompanying the Commissioner to assist him.

3. No-one else is given authority to enter the premises.

4. You should read the order immediately.

5. You have the right to seek legal or other professional advice of your choice and you are advised to do so as soon as possible.

6. Consultation under paragraph 5 will not prevent the Commissioner from entering your premises for the purposes mentioned in paragraph 1 but if the purpose of your seeking advice is to help you to decide if you should ask the court to vary the order he will not be able to search the premises.

7. The Commissioner is obliged to explain the meaning and effect of the order to you.

8. He is also obliged to explain to you that you are entitled to claim that the items, or some of them, are protected as confidential or privileged.

9. You are entitled to ask the court to vary the order provided that—

you take steps to do so at once; and

you allow the Commissioner, any person appointed as a representative of the person who has been granted the order and any person accompanying the Commissioner to assist him, to enter the premises—but not to start the search—meantime.

10. The Commissioner and the people mentioned as representatives or assistants have a right to enter the premises even if you refuse to allow them to do so, unless—

you are female and alone in the premises and there is no female with the Commissioner (where the Commissioner is not herself female), in which case they have no right to enter the premises; the Commissioner serves the order before 9am or after 5pm on a weekday or at any time on a Saturday or Sunday (except where the court has specifically allowed this, which will be stated in the order);

in which cases you should refuse to allow entry.

11. You are entitled to insist that there is no-one (or no-one other than X) present who could gain commercially from anything which might be read or seen on your premises.

12. You are required to hand over the Commissioner any of the items mentioned in the order which are in your possession.

13. You may be found liable for contempt of court if you refuse to comply with the order.

[1254]

NOTES

Forms 62.28, 62.33: substituted by the Act of Sederunt (Rules of the Court of Session Amendment) (Miscellaneous) 2004, SSI 2004/52, r 2(1), (18)(c), Schedule, Pt 2.

Form 62.65: inserted by the Act of Sederunt (Rules of the Court of Session Amendment No 4) (Miscellaneous) 1996, SI 1996/2168, r 2(1), (38)(f), Schedule.

Forms 62.69, 62.73: inserted by the Act of Sederunt (Rules of the Court of Session Amendment) (Jurisdiction, Recognition and Enforcement of Judgments) 2005, SSI 2005/135, r 2(1), (8)(b), Schedule, Pt 2.

Forms 64.6, 64.9: inserted by the Act of Sederunt (Rules of the Court of Session Amendment No 4) (Applications under s 1 of the Administration of Justice (Scotland) Act 1972) 2000, SSI 2000/319, r 2(2), Sch 2; Form numbers substituted by SSI 2004/52, r 2(1), (18)(d), (e).

PRACTICE NOTE 6—COMMERCIAL ACTIONS

NOTES

This Practice Note supplements RCS, Pt 47 at **[1113]**.

Application and interpretation of Chapter 47: RCS 1994, r 47.1

1. The actions to which the rules apply are intended to comprise all actions arising out of or concerned with any relationship of a commercial or business nature, whether contractual or not, and to include, but not to be limited to—

- the construction of a commercial or mercantile document,
- the sale or hire purchase of goods,
- the export or import of merchandise,
- the carriage of goods by land, air or sea,
- insurance,
- banking,
- the provision of financial services,
- mercantile agency,
- mercantile usage or a custom of trade,
- a building, engineering or construction contract,
- a commercial lease.

Some Admiralty actions *in personam*, such as actions relating to or arising out of bills of lading, may also be suitable for treatment of commercial actions if they do not require the special facilities of Admiralty procedure in relation to defenders whose names are not known.

Commercial judge: RCS 1994, r 47.2

2. The commercial judge may hear and determine a commercial action when the court is in session or in vacation: rule 10.7.

Election of procedure: RCS 1994, r 47.3

3.—(1) The initial pleadings in a commercial action are expected to be in an abbreviated form: the purpose of the pleadings is to give notice of the essential elements of the case to the court and the other parties to the action. Compliance with the requirements of paragraph 11 of the practice note will enable the essential elements of the case to be presented in the pleadings in succinct form. Where damages are sought, a summary statement of the claim or a statement in the form of an account will normally be sufficient. Where it is sought to obtain from the court a decision only on the construction of a document, it is permissible for the summons to contain an appropriate conclusion without a condescendence or pleas-in-law. The conclusion in such a case should specify the document, the construction of which is in dispute and conclude for the construction contended for.

(2) Rule 47.3(3) is intended to require a party to produce with its summons the "core" or essential documents to establish the contract or transaction with which the cause is concerned. Under rule 27.1(1)(a) documents founded on or adopted as incorporated in a summons must be lodged at the time the summons is lodged for calling.

(3) When the summons is lodged for signetting, a commercial action registration form (Form CA 1), copies of which are available from the General Department, must be completed, lodged in process and a copy served with the summons.

Disapplication of certain rules: RCS 1994, r 47.4

4. The ordinary rules of the Rules of the Court of Session 1994 apply to a commercial action to which Chapter 47 applies except insofar as specifically excluded under rule 47.4 or which are excluded by implication because of a provision in Chapter 47.

Procedure in commercial actions: RCS 1994 r 47.5

5. The procedure in, and progress of, a commercial action is under the direct control of the commercial judge. He will take a proactive approach.

Defences: RCS 1994 r 47.6

6.—(1) In the first instance detailed averments are not required in the defences any more than in the summons and it is not necessary that each allegation should be admitted or denied provided that the extent of the dispute is reasonably well identified. One of the objectives of the procedure is to make the extent of written pleadings subject to the control of the court. Compliance with the requirements of paragraph 11 of this practice note will enable the essential elements of the defence to be presented in the defences in succinct form.

(2) Under rule 27(1)(1)(b), documents founded on or adopted as incorporated in defence must be lodged at the time the defences are lodged.

(3) Defences must be lodged within 7 days after the summons is lodged for calling: rule 18.1(1).

(4) The defenders must complete a commercial action registration form (Form CA 1) and lodge it in process, or complete the process copy, with the information required.

Counterclaims and Third Party Notices: RCS 1994, r 47.7.

7. No counterclaim or the bringing in of a third party may be pursued without an order from the commercial judge.

Commercial Roll: RCS 1994, r 47.8

8. In the Outer House, an action, and all proceedings in it, in which an election has been made to adopt the procedure in Chapter 47 for commercial actions or which has been transferred under rule 47.10 to be dealt with as a commercial action, shall be heard and determined on the Commercial Roll.

Withdrawal of action from Commercial Roll: RCS 1994, r 47.9

9. The object of rule 47.9 is to enable cases which are unsuitable for the commercial procedure to be removed from the Commercial Roll, but it should be understood that the commercial procedure is not to be regarded as limited to cases which are straightforward or simple or as excluding cases which involve the investigation of difficult and complicated facts.

Transfer of actions to Commercial Roll: RCS 1994, r 47.10

10.—(1) An ordinary action which has not been brought as a commercial action under rule 47.3(1) may be transferred to the Commercial Roll as a commercial action on application by motion by any party (including the pursuer) to the commercial judge if it is an action within the meaning of a commercial action in rule 47.1(2).

(2) An interlocutor granting or refusing a motion to transfer an action to the Commercial Roll may be reclaimed against only with leave of the commercial judge within 14 days after the date of the interlocutor: rule 38.4(6).

Pre-action communication

11.—(1) Before a commercial action is commenced it is important that, save in exceptional cases, the matters in dispute should have been discussed and focused in pre-litigation communications between the prospective parties' legal advisers. This is because the commercial action procedure is intended for cases in which there is a real dispute between the parties which requires to be resolved by judicial decision, rather than other means; and because the procedure functions best if issues have been investigated and ventilated prior to the raising of the action.

(2) It is therefore expected that, before a commercial action has begun, the solicitors acting for the pursuers will have:

(i) fully set out in correspondence to the intended defender the nature of the claim and the factual and legal grounds on which it proceeds;
(ii) supplied to the intended defender copies of any documents relied upon; and
(iii) where the issue sought to be litigated is one for which expert evidence is necessary, obtained and disclosed, to the intended defender, the expert's report.

For their part, solicitors acting for the defender are expected to respond to such pre-litigation communications by setting out the defender's position in substantial terms; and by disclosing any document or expert's report upon which the defender relies. To that response the solicitors for the pursuers are expected to give a considered and reasoned reply. Both parties may wish to consider whether all or some of the dispute may be amenable to some form of alternative dispute resolution.

(3) Saving cases involving an element of urgency, actions should not be raised using the commercial procedure, until the nature and extent of the dispute between the parties has been the subject of careful discussion between the parties and/or their representatives and the action can be said to be truly necessary.

Preliminary hearing on Commercial Roll: RCS 1994 r 47.11

12.—(1) The preliminary hearing will normally be conducted on the basis that the provisions of paragraph 11 in relation to pre-action communication have been complied with. The preliminary hearing, and any continuations thereof, are not designed to give parties the opportunity to formulate their claim and response thereto.

(2) Parties should lodge, prior to the preliminary hearing, and for consideration at the preliminary hearing all correspondence and other documents which set out their respective

material contentions of fact and law which show their compliance with the provisions of paragraph 11. These provisions are supplementary to the provisions of rule 47.3(3).

(3) Where it appears to the court that the need to grant any request for a continuation of a preliminary hearing is brought about by a failure to comply with the provisions of paragraph 11, this may result in the party responsible for any such failure having the expenses of the continued hearing awarded against him on an agent/client basis. Apart from that possible disposal, motions for continuations of the preliminary hearings which are sought simply to enable information to be obtained, which could and should have been obtained, prior to the preliminary hearing, may be refused.

(4) At the preliminary hearing the parties should be in a position to lodge a document setting out in concise form the issues which they contend require judicial determination. The statement of issues should, where possible, be set out in an agreed document.

(5) In applying rule 47.11(3), the court will expect to set realistic time limits; but once established those time limits will be expected to be achieved and extension will only be granted in certain circumstances. This emphasises the importance of ensuring that parties at the preliminary hearing are in a position to explain fully what will be required. Since it is part of the administration of commercial causes that wherever possible a commercial action should at all stages be heard before the same judge, it is important to avoid repeated appearances of the action on the commercial roll. For that reason it is necessary to try to give the court accurate information in order to enable the appropriate time limits for a particular case to be established in the manner which is both realistic and does not prejudice the overall requirement that commercial actions should be dealt with expeditiously.

Procedural Hearing on Commercial Roll: RCS 1994, r 47.12

13.—(1) The procedural hearing is also an important hearing at which parties will be expected to be in a position to discuss realistically the issues involved in the action and the method of disposing of them. It should normally be expected that by the time of the procedural hearing the parties' positions will have been ascertained and identified and that all prospects for settlement have been fully discussed. In consequence it is expected that, once a case has passed beyond the stage of a procedural hearing, it will not settle.

(2) This is one of the ways in which it is sought to meet the problem of ensuring that the judge is in the position to deal realistically with the procedure which he cannot do unless he is given information on which to proceed.

(3) Rule 47.12(2) is the kernel of the procedures and it is intended to enable the court to direct what is really to happen.

Debates: RCS 1994, r 47.13

14. A debate in a commercial action is not heard on the Procedure Roll but on the Commercial Roll. The provisions of Chapter 28 of the RCS 1994 (Procedure Roll), however, do apply to a debate in a commercial action.

Pre-Proof By Order Hearing

15. When a proof, or proof before answer, has been allowed, the court will normally also fix a pre-proof by order hearing to take place in advance of the proof diet. The general purpose of such a hearing is to ascertain the parties' state of preparation for the proof hearing and to review the estimated duration of that hearing.

Without prejudice to the foregoing generality, the following matters will be dealt with at the pre-proof by order hearing:

(1) Consideration of any joint minute of admissions, agreed by the parties, which should be lodged no later than two days prior to the pre-proof by order hearing.

(2) A review of the documents, or other productions which the parties at the time of the pre-proof by order hearing consider will be relied upon at the proof hearing. Any such document should be lodged no later than two days prior to the pre-proof by order hearing.

(3) The up-to-date position with regard to any expert reports which are to be relied upon by the parties will be reviewed. The parties should be in a position to advise the court of what consultation, if any, has taken place between their respective experts with a view to reaching agreement about any points held in common and what matters remain truly in dispute between them.

(4) Where a proof before answer has been allowed, parties should produce, for consideration, at the pre-proof by order hearing, a statement of legal arguments and lists of authorities which they may seek to rely on at the diet of proof before answer, insofar as these have not already been lodged.

Lodging of productions: RCS 1994, r 47.14

16. Before any proof or other hearing at which reference is to be made to documents, parties shall, as well as lodging their productions, prepare for the use of the court a working bundle in which the documents are arranged chronologically or in another appropriate order without multiple copies of the same document.

Hearings for further procedure: RCS 1994, r 47.15

17. The commercial judge or a party may have a commercial action put out for a hearing other than a preliminary or procedural hearing to deal with a procedural or other matter which has arisen for which provision has not been made.

Failure to comply with rule or order of commercial judge: RCS 1994, r 47.16

18. The purpose of this rule is to provide for discipline to ensure effective supervision of case management.

General

19—(1) Arrangements will be made to ensure that (save in exceptional circumstances) at all appearances of an action in the commercial roll the same judge shall preside. Parties are expected to arrange that counsel, or solicitors having rights of audience responsible for the conduct of the case, and authorised to take any necessary decision on questions both of substance and procedure, are available and appear at any calling in the commercial roll.

(2) Where any pleadings or other documents are to be adjusted, the party proposing adjustment shall do so by preparing a new copy of the document as adjusted in which the new material is indicated by underlining, side-lining, a difference in typeface, or other means.

(3) An interlocutor pronounced on the commercial roll, other than a final interlocutor, may be reclaimed against only with leave of the commercial judge within 14 days after the date of the interlocutor: rule 38.4(7).

Revocation of previous practice note

20.1. The Practice Note No 12 of 1994 (commercial actions) is hereby revoked.

[1255]–[1300]

CIVIL PROCEDURE RULES 1998

(SI 1998/3132)

NOTES

Made: 10 December 1998.

Authority: Civil Procedure Act 1997, s 2.

Commencement: 26 April 1999.

The Civil Procedure Rules 1998, which came into force on 26 April 1999 replacing both the Rules of the Supreme Court (Revision) 1965 and the County Court Rules 1984, introduce a radically modified regime for the conduct of litigation in England and Wales. The new Rules (the relevant parts of which are reproduced below) must be read together with any Practice Direction supplementing them, and in the case of specialist proceedings (see Part 49), subject to the relevant Practice Direction which applies to those proceedings. For example, the procedures for commencing and managing litigation are substantially different in the Commercial Court.

Certain provisions of the former Rules of the Supreme Court have been retained (in amended form) by Part 50 of the new Rules. Those provisions, including those for service out of the jurisdiction, are contained in Schedule 1 to the Rules. Arrangements for proceedings commenced before 26 April 1999 are contained in a Practice Direction issued under Part 51 of the new Rules.

Importantly, the new Rules and Practice Directions (including the provisions of Schedule 1) must be applied in the light of the overriding objective set out in Part 1. The overriding objective, the cornerstone of the new regime, provides that "these Rules are a new procedural code with the overriding objective of enabling the court to deal with cases justly" (Rule 1.1). As appears below, Rule 1.2 contains guidelines as to the concept of "dealing with cases justly".

Guidance as to the meaning of terms marked 'GL' is to be found in the Glossary at para **[1550]**.

ARRANGEMENT OF RULES

PART I
OVERRIDING OBJECTIVE

PART 2
APPLICATION AND INTERPRETATION OF THE RULES

PART 3
THE COURT'S CASE MANAGEMENT POWERS

PART 6
SERVICE OF DOCUMENTS

I GENERAL RULES ABOUT SERVICE

II SPECIAL PROVISIONS ABOUT SERVICE OF THE CLAIM FORM

III SPECIAL PROVISIONS ABOUT SERVICE OUT OF THE JURISDICTION

IV SERVICE OF FOREIGN PROCESS

PART 7
HOW TO START PROCEEDINGS—THE CLAIM FORM

PART 8
ALTERNATIVE PROCEDURE FOR CLAIMS

PART 9
RESPONDING TO PARTICULARS OF CLAIM—GENERAL

PART 10
ACKNOWLEDGMENT OF SERVICE

PART 11
DISPUTING THE COURT'S JURISDICTION

PART 12
DEFAULT JUDGMENT

PART 13
SETTING ASIDE OR VARYING DEFAULT JUDGMENT

PART 23
GENERAL RULES ABOUT APPLICATIONS FOR COURT ORDERS

PART 25
INTERIM REMEDIES AND SECURITY FOR COSTS

I INTERIM REMEDIES

II SECURITY FOR COSTS

PART 32
EVIDENCE

PART 33
MISCELLANEOUS RULES ABOUT EVIDENCE

PART 34
DEPOSITIONS AND COURT ATTENDANCES BY WITNESSES

II EVIDENCE FOR FOREIGN COURTS

III TAKING OF EVIDENCE—MEMBER STATES OF THE EUROPEAN UNION

PART 40
JUDGMENTS AND ORDERS

I JUDGMENTS, ORDERS, SALE OF LAND ETC

III DECLARATORY JUDGMENTS

PART 58
COMMERCIAL COURT

PART 59
MERCANTILE COURTS

PART 61
ADMIRALTY CLAIMS

PART 62
ARBITRATION CLAIMS

I CLAIMS UNDER THE 1996 ACT

II OTHER ARBITRATION CLAIMS

III ENFORCEMENT

PART 68
REFERENCES TO THE EUROPEAN COURT

PART 74
ENFORCEMENT OF JUDGMENTS IN DIFFERENT JURISDICTIONS

I ENFORCEMENT IN ENGLAND AND WALES OF JUDGMENTS OF FOREIGN COURTS

II ENFORCEMENT IN FOREIGN COUNTRIES OF JUDGMENTS OF THE HIGH COURT AND COUNTY COURTS

III ENFORCEMENT OF UNITED KINGDOM JUDGMENTS IN OTHER PARTS OF THE UNITED KINGDOM

IV ENFORCEMENT IN ENGLAND AND WALES OF EUROPEAN COMMUNITY JUDGMENTS

V EUROPEAN ENFORCEMENT ORDERS

PART 1
OVERRIDING OBJECTIVE

1.1 The overriding objective

(1) These Rules are a new procedural code with the overriding objective of enabling the court to deal with cases justly.

(2) Dealing with a case justly includes, so far as is practicable—

- (a) ensuring that the parties are on an equal footing;
- (b) saving expense;
- (c) dealing with the case in ways which are proportionate—
  - (i) to the amount of money involved;
  - (ii) to the importance of the case;
  - (iii) to the complexity of the issues; and
  - (iv) to the financial position of each party;
- (d) ensuring that it is dealt with expeditiously and fairly; and allotting to it an appropriate share of the court's resources, while taking into account the need to allot resources to other cases.

[1301]

1.2 Application by the court of the overriding objective

The court must seek to give effect to the overriding objective when it—

(a) exercises any power given to it by the Rules; or
(b) interprets any rule[, subject to rule 76.2].

[1302]

NOTES

Words in square brackets inserted by the Civil Procedure (Amendment No 2) Rules 2005, SI 2005/656, r 3.

1.3 Duty of the parties

The parties are required to help the court to further the overriding objective.

[1303]

1.4 Court's duty to manage cases

(1) The court must further the overriding objective by actively managing cases.

(2) Active case management includes—

(a) encouraging the parties to co-operate with each other in the conduct of the proceedings;
(b) identifying the issues at an early stage;
(c) deciding promptly which issues need full investigation and trial and accordingly disposing summarily of the others;
(d) deciding the order in which issues are to be resolved;
(e) encouraging the parties to use an alternative dispute resolution[(GL)] procedure if the court considers that appropriate and facilitating the use of such procedure;
(f) helping the parties to settle the whole or part of the case;
(g) fixing timetables or otherwise controlling the progress of the case;
(h) considering whether the likely benefits of taking a particular step justify the cost of taking it;
(i) dealing with as many aspects of the case as it can on the same occasion;
(j) dealing with the case without the parties needing to attend at court;
(k) making use of technology; and
(l) giving directions to ensure that the trial of a case proceeds quickly and efficiently.

[1304]

PART 2
APPLICATION AND INTERPRETATION OF THE RULES

NOTES

Practice Direction—Court Offices.

2.1 Application of the Rules

(1) Subject to paragraph (2), these Rules apply to all proceedings in—

(a) county courts;
(b) the High Court; and
(c) the Civil Division of the Court of Appeal.

(2) These Rules do not apply to proceedings of the kinds specified in the first column of the following Table (proceedings for which rules may be made under the enactments specified in the second column) except to the extent that they are applied to those proceedings by another enactment—

	Proceedings	Enactments
1	Insolvency proceedings	Insolvency Act 1986, ss 411 and 412
2	Non-contentious or common form probate proceedings	*Supreme Court Act 1981*, s 127

	Proceedings	Enactments
3	Proceedings in the High Court when acting as a Prize Court	Prize Courts Act 1894, s 3
4	Proceedings before the judge within the meaning of Part VII of the Mental Health Act 1983	Mental Health Act 1983, s 106
5	Family proceedings	Matrimonial and Family Proceedings Act 1981, s 40
[6	Adoption proceedings	Adoption Act 1976, s 66 [or Adoption and Children Act 2002, s 141]]
[7	Election petitions in the High Court	Representation of the People Act 1983, s.182]

[1305]

NOTES

Para (2): in the Table, words in italics substituted by the words "Senior Courts Act 1981" by the Constitutional Reform Act 2005, s 59(5), Sch 11, Pt 1, para 1(2), as from a day to be appointed; in the Table, entry 6 added by the Civil Procedure (Amendment) Rules 1999, SI 1999/1008, r 3, words in square brackets added by the Civil Procedure (Amendment No 4) Rules 2005, SI 2005/3515, r 3; in the Table entry 7 added by the Civil Procedure (Amendment No 2) Rules 2003, SI 2003/1242, r 3.

2.2 The glossary

(1) The glossary at the end of these Rules is a guide to the meaning of certain legal expressions used in the Rules, but is not to be taken as giving those expressions any meaning in the Rules which they do not have in the law generally.

(2) Subject to paragraph (3), words in these Rules which are included in the glossary are followed by "(GL)".

(3) The words "counterclaim", "damages", "practice form" and "service", which appear frequently in the Rules, are included in the glossary but are not followed by "(GL)".

[1306]

2.3 Interpretation

(1) In these Rules—

"child" has the meaning given by rule 21.1(2);

["civil restraint order" means an order restraining a party—

(a) from making any further applications in current proceedings (a limited civil restraint order);

(b) from issuing certain claims or making certain applications in specified courts (an extended civil restraint order); or

(c) from issuing any claim or making any application in specified courts (a general civil restraint order).]

"claim for personal injuries" means proceedings in which there is a claim for damages in respect of personal injuries to the claimant or any other person or in respect of a person's death, and "personal injuries" includes any disease and any impairment of a person's physical or mental condition;

"claimant" means a person who makes a claim;

"CCR" is to be interpreted in accordance with Part 50;

"court officer" means a member of the court staff;

"defendant" means a person against whom a claim is made;

["defendant's home court" means—

(a) if the claim is proceeding in a county court, the county court for the district in which the defendant resides or carries on business; and

(b) if the claim is proceeding in the High Court, the district registry for the district in which the defendant resides or carries on business or, where there is no such district registry, the Royal Courts of Justice;]

(Rule 6.5 provides for a party to give an address for service.)

"filing", in relation to a document, means delivering it, by post or otherwise, to the court office;
"judge" means, unless the context otherwise requires, a judge, Master or district judge or a person authorised to act as such;
"jurisdiction" means, unless the context otherwise requires, England and Wales and any part of the territorial waters of the United Kingdom adjoining England and Wales;
"legal representative" means a barrister or a solicitor, solicitor's employee or other authorised litigator (as defined in the Courts and Legal Services Act 1990) who has been instructed to act for a party in relation to a claim;
"litigation friend" has the meaning given by Part 21;
"patient" has the meaning given by rule 2 1.1(2);
"RSC" is to be interpreted in accordance with Part 50;
"statement of case"—
(a) means a claim form, particulars of claim where these are not included in a claim form, defence, Part 20 claim, or reply to defence; and
(b) includes any further information given in relation to them voluntarily or by court order under rule 18.1;
"statement of value" is to be interpreted in accordance with rule 16.3;
"summary judgment" is to be interpreted in accordance with Part 24.

(2) A reference to a "specialist list" is a reference to a list(GL) that has been designated as such by a [rule or] practice direction.

(3) Where the context requires, a reference to "the court" means a reference to a particular county court, a district registry, or the Royal Courts of Justice.

[1307]

NOTES

Para (1): definition "civil restraint order" inserted by the Civil Procedure (Amendment No 2) Rules 2004, SI 2004/2072, r 3; definition "defendant's home court" substituted by the Civil Procedure (Amendment No 4) Rules 2000, SI 2000/2092, r 3.

Para (2): words in square brackets substituted by the Civil Procedure (Amendment No 5) Rules 2001, SI 2001/4015, r 3.

2.4 Power of judge, Master or district judge to perform functions of the court

Where these Rules provide for the court to perform any act then, except where an enactment, rule or practice direction provides otherwise, that act may be performed—
(a) in relation to proceedings in the High Court, by any judge, Master or district judge of that Court; and
(b) in relation to proceedings in a county court, by any judge or district judge.

[1308]

2.5 Court staff

(1) Where these Rules require or permit the court to perform an act of a formal or administrative character, that act may be performed by a court officer.

(2) A requirement that a court officer carry out any act at the request of a party is subject to the payment of any fee required by a Fees Order for the carrying out of that act.

(Rule 3.2 allows a court officer to refer to a judge before taking any step)

[1309]

2.6 Court documents to be sealed

(1) The court must seal(GL) the following documents on issue—
(a) the claim form; and
(b) any other document which a rule or practice direction requires it to seal.

(2) The court may place the seal(GL) on the document—
(a) by hand; or
(b) by printing a facsimile of the seal on the document whether electronically or otherwise.

(3) A document purporting to bear the court's seal(GL) shall be admissible in evidence without further proof.

[1310]

2.7 Court's discretion as to where it deals with cases

The court may deal with a case at any place that it considers appropriate.

[1311]

2.8 Time

(1) This rule shows how to calculate any period of time for doing any act which is specified—

(a) by these Rules;
(b) by a practice direction; or
(c) by a judgment or order of the court.

(2) A period of time expressed as a number of days shall be computed as clear days.

(3) In this rule "clear days" means that in computing the number of days—

(a) the day on which the period begins; and
(b) if the end of the period is defined by reference to an event, the day on which that event occurs,

are not included.

Examples

(i) Notice of an application must be served at least 3 days before the hearing.
An application is to be heard on Friday 20 October.
The last date for service is Monday 16 October.

(ii) The court is to fix a date for a hearing.
The hearing must be at least 28 days after the date of notice.
If the court gives notice of the date of the hearing on 1 October, the earliest date for the hearing is 30 October.

(iii) Particulars of claim must be served within 14 days of service of the claim form.
The claim form is served on 2 October.

The last day for service of the particulars of claim is 16 October.

(4) Where the specified period—

(a) is 5 days or less; and
(b) includes—
  (i) a Saturday or Sunday; or
  (ii) a Bank Holiday, Christmas Day or Good Friday,

that day does not count.

Example

Notice of an application must be served at least 3 days before the hearing.
An application is to be heard on Monday 20 October.
The last date for service is Tuesday 14 October.

(5) When the period specified—

(a) by these Rules or a practice direction; or
(b) by any judgment or court order,

for doing any act at the court office ends on a day on which the office is closed, that act shall be in time if done on the next day on which the court office is open.

[1312]

2.9 Dates for compliance to be calendar dates and to include time of day

(1) Where the court gives a judgment, order or direction which imposes a time limit for doing any act, the last date for compliance must, wherever practicable

(a) be expressed as a calendar date; and
(b) include the time of day by which the act must be done.

(2) Where the date by which an act must be done is inserted in any document, the date must, wherever practicable, be expressed as a calendar date.

[1313]

2.10 Meaning of "month" in judgments, etc

Where "month" occurs in any judgment, order, direction or other document, it means a calendar month.

[1314]

2.11 Time limits may be varied by parties

Unless these Rules or a practice direction provide otherwise or the court orders otherwise, the time specified by a rule or by the court for a person to do any act may be varied by the written agreement of the parties.

(Rules 3.8 (sanctions have effect unless defaulting party obtains relief), 28.4 (variation of case management timetable—fast track) and 29.5 (variation of case management timetable—multi-track) provide for time limits that cannot be varied by agreement between the parties)

[1315]

PART 3
THE COURT'S CASE MANAGEMENT POWERS

3.1 The court's general powers of management

(1) The list of powers in this rule is in addition to any powers given to the court by any other rule or practice direction or by any other enactment or any powers it may otherwise have.

(2) Except where these Rules provide otherwise, the court may—

(a) extend or shorten the time for compliance with any rule, practice direction or court order (even if an application for extension is made after the time for compliance has expired);
(b) adjourn or bring forward a hearing;
(c) require a party or a party's legal representative to attend the court;
(d) hold a hearing and receive evidence by telephone or by using any other method of direct oral communication;
(e) direct that part of any proceedings (such as a counterclaim) be dealt with as separate proceedings;
(f) stay(GL) the whole or part of any proceedings or judgment either generally or until a specified date or event;
(g) consolidate proceedings;
(h) try two or more claims on the same occasion;
(i) direct a separate trial of any issue;
(j) decide the order in which issues are to be tried;
(k) exclude an issue from consideration;
(l) dismiss or give judgment on a claim after a decision on a preliminary issue;
[(ll) order any party to file and serve an estimate of costs;]
(m) take any other step or make any other order for the purpose of managing the case and furthering the overriding objective.

(3) When the court makes an order, it may—

(a) make it subject to conditions, including a condition to pay a sum of money into court; and
(b) specify the consequence of failure to comply with the order or a condition.

(4) Where the court gives directions it may take into account whether or not a party has complied with any relevant pre-action protocol(GL).

(5) The court may order a party to pay a sum of money into court if that party has, without good reason, failed to comply with a rule, practice direction or a relevant pre-action protocol.

(6) When exercising its power under paragraph (5) the court must have regard to—

(a) the amount in dispute; and
(b) the costs which the parties have incurred or which they may incur.

[(6A) Where a party pays money into court following an order under paragraph (3) or (5), the money shall be security for any sum payable by that party to any other party in the proceedings, subject to the right of a defendant under rule 37.2 to treat all or part of any money paid into court as a Part 36 payment.

(Rule 36.2 explains what is meant by a Part 36 payment)]

(7) A power of the court under these Rules to make an order includes a power to vary or revoke the order.

[1316]

NOTES

Para (2): sub-para (ll) inserted by the Civil Procedure (Amendment No 3) Rules 2005, SI 2005/2292, r 3.

Para (6A): inserted by the Civil Procedure (Amendment) Rules 1999, SI 1999/1008, r 4.

3.2 Court officer's power to refer to a judge

Where a step is to be taken by a court officer—

(a) the court officer may consult a judge before taking that step;
(b) the step may be taken by a judge instead of the court officer.

[1317]

3.3 Court's power to make order of its own initiative

(1) Except where a rule or some other enactment provides otherwise, the court may exercise its powers on an application or of its own initiative.

(Part 23 sets out the procedure for making an application)

(2) Where the court proposes to make an order of its own initiative—

(a) it may give any person likely to be affected by the order an opportunity to make representations; and
(b) where it does so it must specify the time by and the manner in which the representations must be made.

(3) Where the court proposes—

(a) to make an order of its own initiative; and
(b) to hold a hearing to decide whether to make the order,

it must give each party likely to be affected by the order at least 3 days' notice of the hearing.

(4) The court may make an order of its own initiative without hearing the parties or giving them an opportunity to make representations.

(5) Where the court has made an order under paragraph (4)—

(a) a party affected by the order may apply to have it set aside(GL), varied or stayed(GL);and
(b) the order must contain a statement of the right to make such an application.

(6) An application under paragraph (5)(a) must be made—

(a) within such period as may be specified by the court; or
(b) if the court does not specify a period, not more than 7 days after the date on which the order was served on the party making the application.

[(7) If the court of its own initiative strikes out a statement of case or dismisses an application [(including an application for permission to appeal or for permission to apply for judicial review)], and it considers that the claim or application is totally without merit—

(a) the court's order must record that fact; and
(b) the court must at the same time consider whether it is appropriate to make a civil restraint order.]

[1318]

NOTES

Para (7): inserted by the Civil Procedure (Amendment No 2) Rules 2004, SI 2004/2072, r 4; words in square brackets inserted by the Civil Procedure (Amendment No 3) Rules 2005, SI 2005/2292, r 4.

3.4 Power to strike out a statement of case

(1) In this rule and rule 3.5, reference to a statement of case includes reference to part of a statement of case.

(2) The court may strike out(GL) a statement of case if it appears to the court—

(a) that the statement of case discloses no reasonable grounds for bringing or defending the claim;
(b) that the statement of case is an abuse of the court's process or is otherwise likely to obstruct the just disposal of the proceedings; or
(c) that there has been a failure to comply with a rule, practice direction or court order.

(3) When the court strikes out a statement of case it may make any consequential order it considers appropriate.

(4) Where—

(a) the court has struck out a claimant's statement of case;
(b) the claimant has been ordered to pay costs to the defendant; and
(c) before the claimant pays those costs, he starts another claim against the same defendant, arising out of facts which are the same or substantially the same as those relating to the claim in which the statement of case was struck out,

the court may, on the application of the defendant, stay(GL) that other claim until the costs of the first claim have been paid.

(5) Paragraph (2) does not limit any other power of the court to strike out(GL) a statement of case.

[(6) If the court strikes out a claimant's statement of case and it considers that the claim is totally without merit—

(a) the court's order must record that fact; and
(b) the court must at the same time consider whether it is appropriate to make a civil restraint order.]

[1319]

NOTES

Para (6): added by the Civil Procedure (Amendment No 2) Rules 2004, SI 2004/2072, r 5.
Practice Direction—Striking out a Statement of Case.

3.5 Judgment without trial after striking out

(1) This rule applies where—

(a) the court makes an order which includes a term that the statement of case of a party shall be struck out if the party does not comply with the order; and
(b) the party against whom the order was made does not comply with it.

(2) A party may obtain judgment with costs by filing a request for judgment if—

(a) the order referred to in paragraph (1)(a) relates to the whole of a statement of case; and
(b) where the party wishing to obtain judgment is the claimant, the claim is for—
  (i) a specified amount of money;
  (ii) an amount of money to be decided by the court;
  (iii) delivery of goods where the claim form gives the defendant the alternative of paying their value; or
  (iv) any combination of these remedies.

[(3) Where judgment is obtained under this rule in a case to which paragraph (2)(b)(iii) applies, it will be judgment requiring the defendant to deliver the goods, or (if he does not do so) pay the value of the goods as decided by the court (less any payments made).]

[(4)] The request must state that the right to enter judgment has arisen because the court's order has not been complied with.

[(5)] A party must make an application in accordance with Part 23 if he wishes to obtain judgment under this rule in a case to which paragraph (2) does not apply.

[1320]

NOTES

Para (3): inserted by the Civil Procedure (Amendment) Rules 2000, SI 2000/221, r 3(c).
Paras (4), (5): numbered as such by SI 2000/221, r 3(a), (b).

3.6 Setting aside judgment entered after striking out

(1) A party against whom the court has entered judgment under rule 3.5 may apply to the court to set the judgment aside.

(2) An application under paragraph (1) must be made not more than 14 days after the judgment has been served on the party making the application.

(3) If the right to enter judgment had not arisen at the time when judgment was entered, the court must set aside(GL) the judgment.

(4) If the application to set aside(GL) is made for any other reason, rule 3.9 (relief from sanctions) shall apply.

[1321]

3.7 Sanctions for non-payment of certain fees

[(1) This rule applies where—

(a) an allocation questionnaire or a [pre-trial check list (listing questionnaire)] is filed without payment of the fee specified by the relevant Fees Order;

(b) the court dispenses with the need for an allocation questionnaire or a [pre-trial check list] or both;

(c) these Rules do not require an allocation questionnaire or a [pre-trial check list] to be filed in relation to the claim in question; or

(d) the court has made an order giving permission to proceed with a claim for judicial review.

(Rule 26.3 provides for the court to dispense with the need for an allocation questionnaire and rules 28.5 and 29.6 provide for the court to dispense with the need for a [pre-trial check list])

(Rule 54.12 provides for the service of the order giving permission to proceed with a claim for judicial review)

(2) The court will serve a notice on the claimant requiring payment of the fee specified in the relevant Fees Order if, at the time the fee is due, the claimant has not paid it or made an application for exemption or remission.]

(3) The notice will specify the date by which the claimant must pay the fee.

(4) If the claimant does not—

(a) pay the fee; or

(b) make an application for an exemption from or remission of the fee, by the date specified in the notice—

(i) [the claim will automatically be struck out without further order of the court]; and

(ii) the claimant shall be liable for the costs which the defendant has incurred unless the court orders otherwise.

(Rule 44.12 provides for the basis of assessment where a right to costs arises under this rule)

(5) Where an application for exemption from or remission of a fee is refused, the court will serve notice on the claimant requiring payment of the fee by the date specified in the notice.

(6) If the claimant does not pay the fee by the date specified in the notice—

(a) [the claim will automatically be struck out without further order of the court]; and

(b) the claimant shall be liable for the costs which the defendant has incurred unless the court orders otherwise.

[(7) If—

(a) a claimant applies to have the claim reinstated; and

(b) the court grants relief,

the relief shall be conditional on the claimant either paying the fee or filing evidence of exemption from payment or remission of the fee within the period specified in paragraph (8).

(8) The period referred to in paragraph (7) is—

(a) if the order granting relief is made at a hearing at which a claimant is present or represented, 2 days from the date of the order;

(b) in any other case, 7 days from the date of service of the order on the claimant.]

[1322]

NOTES

Para (1): substituted together with para (2) by the Civil Procedure (Amendment No 4) Rules 2000, SI 2000/2092, r 4; words in square brackets substituted by the Civil Procedure (Amendment) Rules 2002, SI 2002/2058, r 3.

Para (2): substituted together with para (1) by SI 2000/2092, r 4.

Paras (4), (6): words in square brackets substituted by the Civil Procedure (Amendment No 3) Rules 2005, SI 2005/2292, r 5.

Paras (7), (8): substituted for para (7) as originally enacted by the Civil Procedure (Amendment No 2) Rules 2003, SI 2003/1242, r 4.
Practice Direction—Sanctions for Non-Payment of Fees.

[3.7A

(1) This rule applies where a defendant files a counterclaim without—
(a) payment of the fee specified by the relevant Fees Order; or
(b) making an application for an exemption from or remission of the fee.

(2) The court will serve a notice on the defendant requiring payment of the fee specified in the relevant Fees Order if, at the time the fee is due, the defendant has not paid it or made an application for exemption or remission.

(3) The notice will specify the date by which the defendant must pay the fee.

(4) If the defendant does not—
(a) pay the fee; or
(b) make an application for an exemption from or remission of the fee,

by the date specified in the notice, the counterclaim will automatically be struck out without further order of the court.

(5) Where an application for exemption from or remission of a fee is refused, the court will serve notice on the defendant requiring payment of the fee by the date specified in the notice.

(6) If the defendant does not pay the fee by the date specified in the notice, the counterclaim will automatically be struck out without further order of the court.

(7) If—
(a) the defendant applies to have the counterclaim reinstated; and
(b) the court grants relief,

the relief will be conditional on the defendant either paying the fee or filing evidence of exemption from payment or remission of the fee within the period specified in paragraph (8).

(8) The period referred to in paragraph (7) is—
(a) if the order granting relief is made at a hearing at which the defendant is present or represented, 2 days from the date of the order;
(b) in any other case, 7 days from the date of service of the order on the defendant.]

[1323]

NOTES

Commencement: 1 October 2005.
Inserted by the Civil Procedure (Amendment No 3) Rules 2005, SI 2005/2292, r 6.

[3.7B Sanctions for dishonouring cheque

(1) This rule applies where any fee is paid by cheque and that cheque is subsequently dishonoured.

(2) The court will serve a notice on the paying party requiring payment of the fee which will specify the date by which the fee must be paid.

(3) If the fee is not paid by the date specified in the notice—
(a) where the fee is payable by the claimant, the claim will automatically be struck out without further order of the court;
(b) where the fee is payable by the defendant, the defence will automatically be struck out without further order of the court,

and the paying party shall be liable for the costs which any other party has incurred unless the court orders otherwise.

(Rule 44.12 provides for the basis of assessment where a right to costs arises under this rule)

(4) If—
(a) the paying party applies to have the claim or defence reinstated; and
(b) the court grants relief,

the relief shall be conditional on that party paying the fee within the period specified in paragraph (5).

(5) The period referred to in paragraph (4) is—
- (a) if the order granting relief is made at a hearing at which the paying party is present or represented, 2 days from the date of the order;
- (b) in any other case, 7 days from the date of service of the order on the paying party.

(6) For the purposes of this rule, "claimant" includes a Part 20 claimant and "claim form" includes a Part 20 claim.]

[1324]

NOTES

Commencement: 1 October 2005.
Inserted by the Civil Procedure (Amendment No 3) Rules 2005, SI 2005/2292, r 7.

3.8 Sanctions have effect unless defaulting party obtains relief

(1) Where a party has failed to comply with a rule, practice direction or court order, any sanction for failure to comply imposed by the rule, practice direction or court order has effect unless the party in default applies for and obtains relief from the sanction.

(Rule 3.9 sets out the circumstances which the court may consider on an application to grant relief from a sanction)

(2) Where the sanction is the payment of costs, the party in default may only obtain relief by appealing against the order for costs.

(3) Where a rule, practice direction or court order—
- (a) requires a party to do something within a specified time, and
- (b) specifies the consequence of failure to comply,

the time for doing the act in question may not be extended by agreement between the parties.

[1325]

3.9 Relief from sanctions

(1) On an application for relief from any sanction imposed for a failure to comply with any rule, practice direction or court order the court will consider all the circumstances including—
- (a) the interests of the administration of justice;
- (b) whether the application for relief has been made promptly;
- (c) whether the failure to comply was intentional;
- (d) whether there is a good explanation for the failure;
- (e) the extent to which the party in default has complied with other rules, practice directions, court orders and any relevant pre-action protocol[GL];
- (f) whether the failure to comply was caused by the party or his legal representative;
- (g) whether the trial date or the likely trial date can still be met if relief is granted;
- (h) the effect which the failure to comply had on each party; and
- (i) the effect which the granting of relief would have on each party.

(2) An application for relief must be supported by evidence.

[1326]

3.10 General power of the court to rectify matters where there has been an error of procedure

Where there has been an error of procedure such as a failure to comply with a rule or practice direction—
- (a) the error does not invalidate any step taken in the proceedings unless the court so orders; and
- (b) the court may make an order to remedy the error.

[1327]

[3.11 Power of the court to make civil restraint orders

A practice direction may set out—
- (a) the circumstances in which the court has the power to make a civil restraint order against a party to proceedings;
- (b) the procedure where a party applies for a civil restraint order against another party; and

(c) the consequences of the court making a civil restraint order.]

[1328]

NOTES

Commencement: 1 October 2004.
Added by the Civil Procedure (Amendment No 2) Rules 2004, SI 2004/2072, r 6.
Practice Direction—Civil Restraint Orders.

Parts 4, 5 (*Pt 4 relates to forms; Pt 5 to court documents.*)

PART 6
SERVICE OF DOCUMENTS

NOTES

Practice Direction—Service; see para **[1552]**.

I GENERAL RULES ABOUT SERVICE

6.1 Part 6 rules about service apply generally

The rules in this Part apply to the service of documents, except where—

(a) any other enactment, a rule in another Part, or a practice direction makes a different provision; or
(b) the court orders otherwise.

[(For service in possession claims, see Part 55).]

[1329]

NOTES

Cross-reference substituted by the Civil Procedure (Amendment No 3) Rules 2005, SI 2005/2292, r 9.

6.2 Methods of service—general

(1) A document may be served by any of the following methods—

(a) personal service, in accordance with rule 6.4;
(b) first class post [(or an alternative service which provides for delivery on the next working day)];
(c) leaving the document at a place specified in rule 6.5;
(d) through a document exchange in accordance with the relevant practice direction; or
(e) by fax or other means of electronic communication in accordance with the relevant practice direction.

(Rule 6.8 provides for the court to permit service by an alternative method)

(2) A company may be served by any method permitted under this Part as an alternative to the methods of service set out in—

(a) section 725 of the Companies Act 1985 (service by leaving a document at or posting it to an authorised place);
(b) section 695 of that Act (service on overseas companies); and
(c) section 694A of that Act (service of documents on companies incorporated outside the UK and Gibraltar and having a branch in Great Britain).

[1330]

NOTES

Para (1): words in square brackets in sub-para (b) inserted by the Civil Procedure (Amendment No 4) Rules 2005, SI 2005/3515, r 4(a).

6.3 Who is to serve

(1) The court will serve a document which it has issued or prepared except where—

(a) a rule provides that a party must serve the document in question;

(b) the party on whose behalf the document is to be served notifies the court that he wishes to serve it himself;
(c) a practice direction provides otherwise;
(d) the court orders otherwise; or
(e) the court has failed to serve and has sent a notice of non-service to the party on whose behalf the document is to be served in accordance with rule 6.11.

(2) Where the court is to serve a document, it is for the court to decide which of the methods of service specified in rule 6.2 is to be used.

(3) Where a party prepares a document which is to be served by the court, that party must file a copy for the court, and for each party to be served.

[1331]

6.4 Personal service

(1) A document to be served may be served personally, except as provided in [paragraphs (2) and (2A)].

(2) Where a solicitor—
(a) is authorised to accept service on behalf of a party; and
(b) has notified the party serving the document in writing that he is so authorised,

a document must be served on the solicitor, unless personal service is required by an enactment, rule, practice direction or court order.

[(2A) In civil proceedings by or against the Crown, as defined in rule 66.1(2), documents required to be served on the Crown may not be served personally.]

(3) A document is served personally on an individual by leaving it with that individual.

(4) A document is served personally on a company or other corporation by leaving it with a person holding a senior position within the company or corporation.

(The service practice direction sets out the meaning of "senior position")

(5) A document is served personally on a partnership where partners are being sued in the name of their firm by leaving it with—
(a) a partner; or
(b) a person who, at the time of service, has the control or management of the partnership business at its principal place of business.

[1332]

NOTES

Para (1): words in square brackets substituted by the Civil Procedure (Amendment No 3) Rules 2005, SI 2005/2292, r 10(a).
Para (2A): inserted by SI 2005/2292, r 10(b).

6.5 Address for service

(1) Except as provided by [Section III of this Part] (service out of the jurisdiction) a document must be served within the jurisdiction.
("Jurisdiction" is defined in rule 2.3)

(2) A party must give an address for service within the jurisdiction.

[Such address must include a full postcode, unless the court orders otherwise.

(Paragraph 2.4 of the Practice Direction to Part 16 contains provision about the content of an address for service).]

(3) Where a party—
(a) does not give the business address of his solicitor as his address for service; and
(b) resides or carries on business within the jurisdiction,

he must give his residence or place of business as his address for service.

(4) Any document to be served—
(a) by first class post [(or an alternative service which provides for delivery on the next working day)];
(b) by leaving it at the place of service;
(c) through a document exchange; or

(d) by fax or by other means of electronic communication,

must be sent or transmitted to, or left at, the address for service given by the party to be served.

(5) Where—

(a) a solicitor is acting for the party to be served; and

(b) the document to be served is not the claim form;

the party's address for service is the business address of his solicitor.

(Rule 6.13 specifies when the business address of a defendant's solicitor may be the defendant's address for service in relation to the claim form)

[(Rule 42.1 provides that if the business address of his solicitor is given that solicitor will be treated as acting for that party)]

(6) Where—

(a) no solicitor is acting for the party to be served; and,

(b) the party has not given an address for service,

the document must be sent or transmitted to, or left at, the place shown in the following table.

(Rule 6.2(2) sets out the statutory methods of service on a company)

Nature of party to be served	*Place of service*
Individual	Usual or last known residence.
Proprietor of a business	Usual or last known residence; or Place of business or last known place of business.
Individual who is suing or being sued in the name of a firm	Usual or last known residence; or Principal or last known place of business of the firm.
Nature of party to be served	Place of service
Corporation incorporated in England and Wales other than a company	Principal office of the corporation; or Any place within the jurisdiction where the corporation carries on its activities and which has a real connection with the claim.
Company registered in England and Wales	Principal office of the company; or Any place of business of the company within the jurisdiction which has a real connection with the claim.
Any other company or corporation	Any place within the jurisdiction where the corporation carries on its activities; or Any place of business of the company within the jurisdiction.

(7) This rule does not apply where an order made by the court under rule 6.8 (service by an alternative method) specifies where the document in question may be served.

[(8) In civil proceedings by or against the Crown, as defined in rule 66.1(2)—

(a) service on the Attorney General must be effected on the Treasury Solicitor;

(b) service on a government department must be effected on the solicitor acting for that department as required by section 18 of the Crown Proceedings Act 1947.

(The practice direction to Part 66 gives the list published under section 17 of that Act of the solicitors acting for the different government departments on whom service is to be effected, and of their addresses).]

[1333]

NOTES

Para (1): words in square brackets substituted by the Civil Procedure (Amendment) Rules 2000, SI 2000/221, r 4(3).

Para (2): words in square brackets added by the Civil Procedure (Amendment No 3) Rules 2005, SI 2005/2292, r 11(a).

Para (4): words in square brackets in sub-para (a) inserted by the Civil Procedure (Amendment No 4) Rules 2005, SI 2005/3515, r 4(b).

Para (5): words in square brackets added by the Civil Procedure (Amendment No 4) Rules 2000, SI 2000/2092, r 5.

Para (8): added by SI 2005/2292, r 11(b).

6.6 Service of documents on children and patients

(1) The following table shows the person on whom a document must be served if it is a document which would otherwise be served on a child or a patient—

Type of document	*Nature of party*	*Person to be served*
Claim form	Child who is not also a patient	One of the child's parents or guardians; or if there is no parent or guardian, the person with whom the child resides or in whose care the child is.
Claim form	Patient	The person authorised under Part VII of the Mental Health Act 1983 to conduct the proceedings in the name of the patient or on his behalf; or if there is no person so authorised, the person with whom the patient resides or in whose care the patient is.
Application for an order appointing a litigation friend, where a child or patient has no litigation friend	Child or patient	See rule 21.8.
Any other document	Child or patient	The litigation friend who is conducting proceedings on behalf of the child or patient.

(2) The court may make an order permitting a document to be served on the child or patient, or on some person other than the person specified in the table in this rule.

(3) An application for an order under paragraph (2) may be made without notice.

(4) The court may order that, although a document has been served on someone other than the person specified in the table, the document is to be treated as if it had been properly served.

(5) This rule does not apply where the court has made an order under rule 21.2(3) allowing a child to conduct proceedings without a litigation friend.

(Part 21 contains rules about the appointment of a litigation friend)

[1334]

6.7 Deemed service

(1) A document which is served in accordance with these rules or any relevant practice direction shall he deemed to be served on the day shown in the following table—

Method of service	*Deemed day of service*
First class post [or an alternative service which provides for delivery on the next working day)]	The second day after it was posted.
Document exchange	The second day after it was left at the document exchange.
Delivering the document to or	The day after it was delivered to or left at the permitted address.
Fax	—If it is transmitted on a business day before 4 pm, on that day; or —in any other case, on the business day after the day on which it is transmitted.
Other electronic method	The second day after the day on which it is transmitted.

[…]

[(2) If a document is served personally—
(a) after 5 p.m., on a business day; or
(b) at any time on a Saturday, Sunday or a Bank Holiday,
it will be treated as being served on the next business day.]

(3) In this rule—
"business day" means any day except Saturday, Sunday or a bank holiday; and
"bank holiday" includes Christmas Day and Good Friday.

[1335]

NOTES

Para (1): words in square brackets in Table entry relating to first class post inserted by the Civil Procedure (Amendment No 4) Rules 2005, SI 2005/3515, r 4(c); words omitted in square brackets added by the Civil Procedure (Amendment) Rules 2000, SI 2000/221, r 4(4)(a), revoked by the Civil Procedure (Amendment No 3) Rules 2005, SI 2005/2292, r 12.

Para (2): substituted by SI 2000/221, r 4(4)(b).

6.8 Service by an alternative method

(1) Where it appears to the court that there is a good reason to authorise service by a method not permitted by these Rules, the court may make an order permitting service by an alternative method.

(2) An application for an order permitting service by an alternative method—
(a) must be supported by evidence; and
(b) may be made without notice.

(3) An order permitting service by an alternative method must specify—
(a) the method of service; and
(b) the date when the document will be deemed to be served.

[1336]

6.9 Power of court to dispense with service

(1) The court may dispense with service of a document.

(2) An application for an order to dispense with service may be made without notice.

[1337]

6.10 Certificate of service

Where a rule, practice direction or court order requires a certificate of service, the certificate must [state the details set out in the following table]—

Method of service	*Details to be certified*
Post	Date of posting
Personal	Date of personal service
Document exchange	Date of delivery to the document exchange
Delivery of document to or leaving it at a permitted place	Date when the document was delivered to or left at the permitted place
Fax	Date and time of transmission
Other electronic means	Date of transmission and the means used
Alternative method permitted by the court	As required by the court

[1338]

NOTES

Words in square brackets substituted by the Civil Procedure (Amendment No 4) Rules 2004, SI 2004/1306, r 4.

Para (2): substituted by SI 2000/221, r 4(4)(b).

[6.11 Notification of outcome of postal service by the court

Where—

(a) a document to be served by the court is served by post; and

(b) such document is returned to the court,

the court must send notification to the party who requested service stating that the document has been returned.]

[1339]

NOTES

Commencement: 1 October 2005.

Substituted, together with r 6.11A, by the Civil Procedure (Amendment No 3) Rules 2005, SI 2005/2292, r 13.

[6.11A Notice of non-service by bailiff

Where—

(a) the court bailiff is to serve a document; and

(b) the bailiff is unable to serve it,

the court must send notification to the party who requested service.]

[1340]

NOTES

Commencement: 1 October 2005.

Substituted as noted to r 6.11 at **[1339]**.

II SPECIAL PROVISIONS ABOUT SERVICE OF THE CLAIM FORM

6.12 General rules about service subject to special rules about service of claim form

The general rules about service are subject to the special rules about service contained in rules 6.13 to 6.16.

[1341]

6.13 Service of claim form by the court—defendant's address for service

(1) Where a claim form is to be served by the court, the claim form must include the defendant's address for service.

(2) For the purposes of paragraph (1), the defendant's address for service may be the business address of the defendant's solicitor if he is authorised to accept service on the defendant's behalf but not otherwise.

(Rule 6.5 contains general provisions about the address for service)

[(Paragraph 2.4 of the Practice Direction to Part 16 contains provision about the content of an address for service).]

[1342]

NOTES

Cross-reference in square brackets added by the Civil Procedure (Amendment No 3) Rules 2005, SI 2005/2292, r 14.

6.14 Certificate of service relating to the claim form

(1) Where a claim form is served by the court, the court must send the claimant a notice which will include the date when the claim form is deemed to be served under rule 6.7.

(2) Where the claim form is served by the claimant—

(a) he must file a certificate of service within 7 days of service of the claim form; and

(b) he may not obtain judgment in default under Part 12 unless he has filed the certificate of service.

(Rule 6.10 specifies what a certificate of service must show)

[1343]

6.15 Service of the claim form by contractually agreed method

(1) Where—

(a) a contract contains a term providing that, in the event of a claim being issued in relation to the contract, the claim form may be served by a method specified in the contract; and

(b) a claim form containing only a claim in respect of that contract is issued,

the claim form shall, subject to paragraph (2), be deemed to be served on the defendant if it is served by a method specified in the contract.

(2) Where the claim form is served out of the jurisdiction in accordance with the contract, it shall not be deemed to be served on the defendant unless—

(a) permission to serve it out of the jurisdiction has been granted under [rule 6.20]; or

(b) it may be served without permission under [rule 6.19].

[1344]

NOTES

Para (2): words in square brackets substituted by the Civil Procedure (Amendment No 2) Rules 2000, SI 2000/940, r 4.

6.16 Service of claim form on agent of principal who is overseas

(1) Where—

(a) the defendant is overseas; and

(b) the conditions specified in paragraph (2) are satisfied,

the court may, on an application only, permit a claim form relating to a contract to be served on a defendant's agent.

(2) The court may not make an order under this rule unless it is satisfied that—

(a) the contract to which the claim relates was entered into within the jurisdiction with or through the defendant's agent; and

(b) at the time of the application either the agent's authority has not been terminated or he is still in business relations with his principal.

(3) An application under this rule—

(a) must be supported by evidence; and

(b) may be made without notice.

(4) An order under this rule must state a period within which the defendant must respond to the particulars of claim.

(Rule 9.2 sets out how a defendant may respond to particulars of claim)

(5) The power conferred by this rule is additional to the power conferred by rule 6.8 (service by an alternative method).

(6) Where the court makes an order under this rule, the claimant must send to the defendant copies of—

(a) the order; and

(b) the claim form.

[1345]

[III SPECIAL PROVISIONS ABOUT SERVICE OUT OF THE JURISDICTION

NOTES

Practice Direction—Service out of the Jurisdiction; see para **[1553]**.

6.17 Scope of this Section

This Section contains rules about—

(a) service out of the jurisdiction;

(b) how to obtain the permission of the court to serve out of the jurisdiction; and

(c) the procedure for serving out of the jurisdiction.

(Rule 2.3 defines "jurisdiction")]

[1346]

NOTES

Section III (rr 6.17–6.31) added by the Civil Procedure (Amendment) Rules 2000, SI 2000/221, r 4(5), Sch 1, Pt II.

[6.18 Definitions

For the purposes of this Part—

(a) "the 1982 Act" means the Civil Jurisdiction and Judgments Act 1982;

(b) "the Hague Convention" means the Convention on the service abroad of judicial and extra-judicial documents in civil or commercial matters signed at the Hague on November 15, 1965;

(c) "Contracting State" has the meaning given by section 1(3) of the 1982 Act;

(d) "Convention territory" means the territory or territories of any Contracting State to which the Brussels or Lugano Conventions (as defined in section 1(1) of the 1982 Act) apply;

(e) "Civil Procedure Convention" means the Brussels and Lugano Conventions and any other Convention entered into by the United Kingdom regarding service outside the jurisdiction;

[(ea) "the Service Regulation" means Council Regulation (EC) No 1348/2000 of 29 May 2000 on the service in the Member States of judicial and extrajudicial documents in civil or commercial matters;]

(f) "United Kingdom Overseas Territory" means those territories as set out in the relevant practice direction.

[(g) "domicile" is to be determined—

(i) in relation to a Convention territory, in accordance with sections 41 to 46 of the 1982 Act;

(ii) in relation to a Regulation State, in accordance with the Judgments Regulation and paragraphs 9 to 12 of Schedule 1 to the Civil Jurisdiction and Judgments Order 2001;]

(h) "claim form" includes petition and application notice; …

(i) "claim" includes petition and application[; and

(j) "the Judgments Regulation" means Council Regulation (EC) No 44/2001 of 22nd December 2000 on jurisdiction and the recognition and enforcement of judgments in civil and commercial matters; and

(k) "Regulation State" in any provision, in the application of that provision in relation to the Regulation, has the same meaning as "Member State" in the Judgments Regulation, that is all Member States except Denmark.]

(Rule 6.30 provides that where an application notice is to be served out of the jurisdiction under this Part, rules 6.21(4), 6.22 and 6.23 do not apply)]

[1347]

NOTES

Added as noted to r 6.17 at **[1346]**.

Para (ea) inserted by the Civil Procedure (Amendment No 2) Rules 2001, SI 2001/1388, r 3; para (g) substituted, word omitted from para (h) revoked, and paras (j), (k) added together with preceding word "and" by the Civil Procedure (Amendment No 5) Rules 2001, SI 2001/4015, r 4.

[6.19 Service out of the jurisdiction where the permission of the court is not required

(1) A claim form may be served on a defendant out of the jurisdiction where each claim included in the claim form made against the defendant to be served is a claim which the court has power to determine under the 1982 Act and—

(a) no proceedings between the parties concerning the same claim are pending in the courts of [any other part of the United Kingdom] or any other Convention territory; and

(b)

(i) the defendant is domiciled in the United Kingdom or in any Convention territory;

[(ii) Article 16 of Schedule 1 or 3C to the 1982 Act, or paragraph 11 of Schedule 4 to that Act, refers to the proceedings; or

(iii) the defendant is a party to an agreement conferring jurisdiction to which Article 17 of Schedule 1 or 3C to the 1982 Act, or paragraph 12 of Schedule 4 to that Act, refers.]

[(1A) A claim form may be served on a defendant out of the jurisdiction where each claim included in the claim form made against the defendant to be served is a claim which the court has power to determine under the Judgments Regulation and—

(a) no proceedings between the parties concerning the same claim are pending in the courts of any other part of the United Kingdom or any other Regulation State; and

(b)

(i) the defendant is domiciled in the United Kingdom or in any Regulation State;

(ii) Article 22 of the Judgments Regulation refers to the proceedings; or

(iii) the defendant is a party to an agreement conferring jurisdiction to which Article 23 of the Judgments Regulation refers.]

(2) A claim form may be served on a defendant out of the jurisdiction where each claim included in the claim form made against the defendant to be served is a claim which, under any other enactment, the court has power to determine, although—

(a) the person against whom the claim is made is not within the jurisdiction; or

(b) the facts giving rise to the claim did not occur within the jurisdiction.

(3) Where a claim form is to be served out of the jurisdiction under this rule, it must contain a statement of the grounds on which the claimant is entitled to serve it out of the jurisdiction.]

[1348]

NOTES

Added as noted to r 6.17 at **[1346]**.

Para (1): words in square brackets in sub-para (a) substituted by the Civil Procedure (Amendment No 5) Rules 2001, SI 2001/4015, r 5; sub-paras (b)(ii), (iii) substituted by the Civil Procedure (Amendment) Rules 2002, SI 2002/2058, r 5(c).

Para (1A): inserted by SI 2001/4015, r 6.

[6.20 Service out of the jurisdiction where the permission of the court is required

In any proceedings to which rule 6.19 does not apply, a claim form may be served out of the jurisdiction with the permission of the court if—

General grounds

(1) a claim is made for a remedy against a person domiciled within the jurisdiction;

(2) a claim is made for an injunction(GL) ordering the defendant to do or refrain from doing an act within the jurisdiction;

(3) a claim is made against someone on whom the claim form has been or will be served and—

(a) there is between the claimant and that person a real issue which it is reasonable for the court to try; and

(b) the claimant wishes to serve the claim form on another person who is a necessary or proper party to that claim;

[(3A) a claim is a Part 20 claim and the person to be served is a necessary or proper party to the claim against the Part 20 claimant.]

Claims for interim remedies

(4) a claim is made for an interim remedy under section 25(1) of the 1982 Act;

Claims in relation to contracts

(5) a claim is made in respect of a contract where the contract—

(a) was made within the jurisdiction;
(b) was made by or through an agent trading or residing within the jurisdiction;
(c) is governed by English law; or
(d) contains a term to the effect that the court shall have jurisdiction to determine any claim in respect of the contract;

(6) a claim is made in respect of a breach of contract committed within the jurisdiction;

(7) a claim is made for a declaration that no contract exists where, if the contract was found to exist, it would comply with the conditions set out in paragraph (5);

Claims in tort

(8) a claim is made in tort where—

(a) damage was sustained within the jurisdiction; or
(b) the damage sustained resulted from an act committed within the jurisdiction;

Enforcement

(9) a claim is made to enforce any judgment or arbitral award;

Claims about property within the jurisdiction

(10) the whole subject matter of a claim relates to property located within the jurisdiction;

Claims about trusts etc

(11) a claim is made for any remedy which might be obtained in proceedings to execute the trusts of a written instrument where—

(a) the trusts ought to be executed according to English law; and
(b) the person on whom the claim form is to be served is a trustee of the trusts;

(12) a claim is made for any remedy which might be obtained in proceedings for the administration of the estate of a person who died domiciled within the jurisdiction;

(13) a claim is made in probate proceedings which includes a claim for the rectification of a will;

(14) a claim is made for a remedy against the defendant as constructive trustee where the defendant's alleged liability arises out of acts committed within the jurisdiction;

(15) a claim is made for restitution where the defendant's alleged liability arises out of acts committed within the jurisdiction;

…

Claims by the Inland Revenue

(16) a claim is made by the Commissioners of the Inland Revenue relating to duties or taxes against a defendant not domiciled in Scotland or Northern Ireland;

Claim for costs order in favour of or against third parties

(17) a claim is made by a party to proceedings for an order that the court exercise its power under section 51 of the *Supreme Court Act 1981* to make a costs order in favour of or against a person who is not a party to those proceedings;

(Rule 48.2 sets out the procedure where the court is considering whether to exercise its discretion to make a costs order in favour of or against a non-party)

[Admiralty claims

(17A) a claim is—

(a) in the nature of salvage and any part of the services took place within the jurisdiction; or

(b) to enforce a claim under section 153, 154 or 175 of the Merchant Shipping Act 1995.]

Claims under various enactments

(18) a claim [is] made under an enactment specified in the relevant practice direction.]

[1349]

NOTES

Added as noted to r 6.17 at **[1346]**.

Para (3A): added by the Civil Procedure (Amendment No 3) Rules 2000, SI 2000/1317, r 3.

Para (15): words omitted revoked by the Civil Procedure (Amendment No 5) Rules 2001, SI 2001/4015, r 7(a).

Para (17): words in italics substituted by the words "Senior Courts Act 1981" by the Constitutional Reform Act 2005, s 59(5), Sch 11, Pt 1, para 1(2), as from a day to be appointed.

Para (17A): inserted together with preceding cross-heading, by SI 2001/4015, r 7(b).

Para (18): word in square brackets inserted by the Civil Procedure (Amendment No 2) Rules 2001, SI 2001/1388, r 4.

[6.21 Application for permission to serve claim form out of jurisdiction

(1) An application for permission under rule 6.20 must be supported by written evidence stating—

(a) the grounds on which the application is made and the paragraph or paragraphs of rule 6.20 relied on;

(b) that the claimant believes that his claim has a reasonable prospect of success; and

(c) the defendant's address or, if not known, in what place or country the defendant is, or is likely, to be found.

(2) Where the application is made in respect of a claim referred to in rule 6.20(3), the written evidence must also state the grounds on which the witness believes that there is between the claimant and the person on whom the claim form has been, or will be served, a real issue which it is reasonable for the court to try.

[(2A) The court will not give permission unless satisfied that England and Wales is the proper place in which to bring the claim.]

(3) Where—

(a) the application is for permission to serve a claim form in Scotland or Northern Ireland; and

(b) it appears to the court that the claimant may also be entitled to a remedy there, the court, in deciding whether to give permission, shall—

(i) compare the cost and convenience of proceeding there or in the jurisdiction; and

(ii) (where relevant) have regard to the powers and jurisdiction of the Sheriff court in Scotland or the county courts or courts of summary jurisdiction in Northern Ireland.

(4) An order giving permission to serve a claim form out of the jurisdiction must specify the periods within which the defendant may—

(a) file an acknowledgment of service;

(b) file or serve an admission; and

(c) file a defence.

(Part 11 sets out the procedure by which a defendant may dispute the court's jurisdiction)

[(The second practice direction to this Part sets out how the periods referred to in paragraphs (a), (b) and (c) are calculated.)]]

[1350]

NOTES

Added as noted to r 6.17 at **[1346]**.

Para (2A): inserted by the Civil Procedure (Amendment No 2) Rules 2000, SI 2000/940, r 5.

Para (4): words in square brackets added by the Civil Procedure (Amendment No 5) Rules 2001, SI 2001/4015, r 8.

[6.22 Period for acknowledging service or admitting the claim where the claim form is served out of the jurisdiction under rule 6.19

(1) This rule sets out the period for filing an acknowledgment of service or filing or serving an admission where a claim form has been served out of the jurisdiction under rule 6.19.

(Part 10 contains rules about the acknowledgment of service and Part 14 contains rules about admissions)

(2) If the claim form is to be served under rule 6.19(1) [or (1A)] in Scotland, Northern Ireland or in the European territory of another Contracting State [or Regulation State] the period is—

(a) where the defendant is served with a claim form which states that particulars of claim are to follow, 21 days after the service of the particulars of claim; and

(b) in any other case, 21 days after service of the claim form.

(3) If the claim form is to be served under rule 6.19(1) in any other territory of a Contracting State the period is—

(a) where the defendant is served with a claim form which states that particulars of claim are to follow, 31 days after the service of the particulars of claim; and

(b) in any other case, 31 days after service of the claim form.

(4) If the claim form is to be served under—

(a) rule 6.19(1) [or (1A)] in a country not referred to in paragraphs (2) or (3); or

(b) rule 6.19(2),

the period is set out in the relevant practice direction.]

[1351]

NOTES

Added as noted to r 6.17 at **[1346]**.

Paras (2), (4): words in square brackets inserted by the Civil Procedure (Amendment No 5) Rules 2001, SI 2001/4015, r 9.

[6.23 Period for filing a defence where the claim form is served out of the jurisdiction under rule 6.19

(1) This rule sets out the period for filing a defence where a claim form has been served out of the jurisdiction under rule 6.19.

(Part 15 contains rules about the defence)

(2) If the claim form is to be served under rule 6.19(1) [or (1A)] in Scotland, Northern Ireland or in the European territory of another Contracting State [or Regulation State] the period is—

(a) 21 days after service of the particulars of claim; or

(b) if the defendant files an acknowledgment of service, 35 days after service of the particulars of claim.

(3) If the claim form is to be served under rule 6.19(1) in any other territory of a Contracting State the period is—

(a) 31 days after service of the particulars of claim; or

(b) if the defendant files an acknowledgment of service, 45 days after service of the particulars of claim.

(4) If the claim form is to be served under—

(a) rule 6.19(1) [or (1A)] in a country not referred to in paragraphs (2) or (3); or

(b) rule 6.19(2),

the period is set out in the relevant practice direction.]

[1352]

NOTES

Added as noted to r 6.17 at **[1346]**.

Paras (2), (4): words in square brackets inserted by the Civil Procedure (Amendment No 5) Rules 2001, SI 2001/4015, r 10.

[6.24 Method of service—general provisions

(1) Where a claim form is to be served out of the jurisdiction, it may be served by any method—

(a) permitted by the law of the country in which it is to be served;

(b) provided for by—

(i) rule 6.25 (service through foreign governments, judicial authorities and British Consular authorities); …

[(ii) rule 6.26A (service in accordance with the Service Regulation); or]

[(iii)] [rule 6.27] (service on a State); or

(c) permitted by a Civil Procedure Convention.

(2) Nothing in this rule or in any court order shall authorise or require any person to do anything in the country where the claim form is to be served which is against the law of that country.]

[1353]

NOTES

Added as noted to r 6.17 at **[1346]**.

Para (1): word omitted revoked, sub-para (b)(ii) inserted and sub-para (b)(iii) numbered as such by the Civil Procedure (Amendment No 2) Rules 2001, SI 2001/1388, r 5; words in square brackets in sub-para (b)(iii) substituted by the Civil Procedure (Amendment) Rules 2001, SI 2001/256, r 4.

[6.25 Service through foreign governments, judicial authorities and British Consular authorities

(1) Where a claim form is to be served on a defendant in any country which is a party to the Hague Convention, the claim form may be served—

(a) through the authority designated under the Hague Convention in respect of that country; or

(b) if the law of that country permits—

(i) through the judicial authorities of that country, or

(ii) through a British Consular authority in that country.

(2) Where—

(a) paragraph (4) (service in Scotland etc, other than under the Hague Convention) does not apply; and

(b) a claim form is to be served on a defendant in any country which is a party to a Civil Procedure Convention (other than the Hague Convention) providing for service in that country,

the claim form may be served, if the law of that country permits—

(i) through the judicial authorities of that country; or

(ii) through a British Consular authority in that country (subject to any provisions of the applicable convention about the nationality of persons who may be served by such a method).

(3) Where—

(a) paragraph (4) (service in Scotland etc, other than under the Hague Convention) does not apply; and

(b) a claim form is to be served on a defendant in any country with respect to which there is no Civil Procedure Convention providing for service in that country,

the claim form may be served, if the law of that country so permits—

(i) through the government of that country, where that government is willing to serve it; or

(ii) through a British Consular authority in that country.

(4) Except where a claim form is to be served in accordance with paragraph (1) (service under the Hague Convention), the methods of service permitted by this rule are not available where the claim form is to be served in—

(a) Scotland, Northern Ireland, the Isle of Man or the Channel Islands;

(b) any Commonwealth State; [or]

(c) any United Kingdom Overseas Territory[.]

(d) …

[(5) This rule does not apply where service is to be effected in accordance with the Service Regulation.]]

[1354]

NOTES

Added as noted to r 6.17 at **[1346]**.

Para (4): word and punctuation mark in square brackets substituted and sub-para (d) revoked by the Civil Procedure (Amendment No 2) Rules 2001, SI 2001/1388, r 6(a).

Para (5): added by SI 2001/1388, r 6(b).

[6.26 Procedure where service is to be through foreign governments, judicial authorities and British Consular authorities

(1) This rule applies where the claimant wishes to serve the claim form through—

(a) the judicial authorities of the country where the claim form is to be served;

(b) a British Consular authority in that country;

(c) the authority designated under the Hague Convention in respect of that country; or

(d) the government of that country.

(2) Where this rule applies, the claimant must file—

(a) a request for service of the claim form by the method in paragraph (1) that he has chosen;

(b) a copy of the claim form;

(c) any translation required under rule 6.28; and

(d) any other documents, copies of documents or translations required by the relevant practice direction.

(3) When the claimant files the documents specified in paragraph (2), the court officer will—

(a) seal(GL) the copy of the claim form; and

(b) forward the documents to the Senior Master.

(4) The Senior Master will send documents forwarded under this rule—

(a) where the claim form is being served through the authority designated under the Hague Convention, to that authority; or

(b) in any other case, to the Foreign and Commonwealth Office with a request that it arranges for the claim to be served by the method indicated in the request for service filed under paragraph (2) or, where that request indicates alternative methods, by the most convenient method.

(5) An official certificate which—

(a) states that the claim form has been served in accordance with this rule either personally, or in accordance with the law of the country in which service was effected;

(b) specifies the date on which the claim form was served; and

(c) is made by—

(i) a British Consular authority in the country where the claim form was served;

(ii) the government or judicial authorities in that country; or

(iii) any other authority designated in respect of that country under the Hague Convention,

shall be evidence of the facts stated in the certificate.

(6) A document purporting to be an official certificate under paragraph (5) shall be treated as such a certificate, unless it is proved not to be.

[(7) This rule does not apply where service is to be effected in accordance with the Service Regulation.]]

[1355]

NOTES

Added as noted to r 6.17 at **[1346]**.

Para (7): added by the Civil Procedure (Amendment No 2) Rules 2001, SI 2001/1388, r 7

[6.26A Service in accordance with the Service Regulation

(1) This rule applies where a claim form is to be served in accordance with the Service Regulation.

(2) The claimant must file the claim form and any translations or other documents required by the Service Regulation.

(3) When the claimant files the documents referred to in paragraph (2), the court officer will—

(a) seal[(GL)] the copy of the claim form; and
(b) forward the documents to the Senior Master.

(4) Rule 6.31 does not apply.

(The Service Regulation is annexed to the relevant practice direction)]

[1356]

NOTES

Commencement: 31 May 2001.
Inserted by the Civil Procedure (Amendment No 2) Rules 2001, SI 2001/1388, r 8.

[6.27 Service of claim form on State where court permits service out of the jurisdiction

(1) This rule applies where a claimant wishes to serve the claim form on a State.

(2) The claimant must file in the Central Office of the Royal Courts of Justice—

(a) a request for service to be arranged by the Foreign and Commonwealth Office;
(b) a copy of the claim form; and
(c) any translation required under rule 6.28.

(3) The Senior Master will send documents filed under this rule to the Foreign and Commonwealth Office with a request that it arranges for the claim form to be served.

(4) An official certificate by the Foreign and Commonwealth Office stating that a claim form has been duly served on a specified date in accordance with a request made under this rule shall be evidence of that fact.

(5) A document purporting to be such a certificate shall be treated as such a certificate, unless it is proved not to be.

(6) Where—

(a) section 12(6) of the State Immunity Act 1978 applies; and
(b) the State has agreed to a method of service other than through the Foreign and Commonwealth Office,

the claim may be served either by the method agreed or in accordance with this rule.

(Section 12(6) of the State Immunity Act 1978 provides that section 12(1) of that Act, which prescribes a method for serving documents on a State, does not prevent the service of a claim form or other document in a manner to which the State has agreed)

(7) In this rule "State" has the meaning given by section 14 of the State Immunity Act 1978.]

[1357]

NOTES

Added as noted to r 6.17 at **[1346]**.

[6.28 Translation of claim form

(1) Except where paragraph (4) or (5) applies, every copy of the claim form filed under rule 6.26 (service through judicial authorities, foreign governments etc) or 6.27 (service on State) must be accompanied by a translation of the claim form.

(2) The translation must be—

(a) in the official language of the country in which it is to be served; or
(b) if there is more than one official language of that country, in any official language which is appropriate to the place in the country where the claim form is to be served.

(3) Every translation filed under this rule must be accompanied by a statement by the person making it that it is a correct translation, and the statement must include—

(a) the name of the person making the translation;
(b) his address; and

(c) his qualifications for making a translation.

(4) The claimant is not required to file a translation of a claim form filed under rule 6.26 (service through judicial authorities, foreign governments etc) where the claim form is to be served—

(a) in a country of which English is an official language; or
(b) on a British subject,

unless a Civil Procedure Convention expressly requires a translation.

(5) The claimant is not required to file a translation of a claim form filed under rule 6.27 (service on State) where English is an official language of the State where the claim form is to be served.]

[1358]

NOTES

Added as noted to r 6.17 at **[1346]**.

[6.29 Undertaking to be responsible for expenses of the Foreign and Commonwealth Office

Every request for service filed under rule 6.26 (service through judicial authorities, foreign governments etc) or rule 6.27 (service on State) must contain an undertaking by the person making the request—

(a) to be responsible for all expenses incurred by the Foreign and Commonwealth Office or foreign judicial authority; and
(b) to pay those expenses to the Foreign and Commonwealth Office or foreign judicial authority on being informed of the amount.]

[1359]

NOTES

Added as noted to r 6.17 at **[1346]**.

[6.30 Service of documents other than the claim form

(1) Where an application notice is to be served out of the jurisdiction under this Section of this Part—

(a) rules 6.21(4), 6.22 and 6.23 do not apply; and
(b) where the person on whom the application notice has been served is not a party to proceedings in the jurisdiction in which the application is made, that person may make an application to the court under rule 11(1) as if he were a defendant and rule 11(2) does not apply.

(Rule 6.21(4) provides that an order giving permission to serve a claim form out of the jurisdiction must specify the periods within which the defendant may (a) file an acknowledgment of service, (b) file or serve an admission, and (c) file a defence)

(Rule 6.22 provides rules for the period for acknowledging service or admitting the claim where the claim form is served out of the jurisdiction under rule 6.19)

(Rule 6.23 provides rules for the period for filing a defence where the claim form is served out of the jurisdiction under rule 6.19)

(The practice direction supplementing this Section of this Part provides that where an application notice is to be served out of the jurisdiction in accordance with this Section of this Part, the court must have regard to the country in which the application notice is to be served in setting the date for the hearing of the application and giving any direction about service of the respondent's evidence)

(Rule 11(1) provides that a defendant may make an application to the court to dispute the court's jurisdiction to try the claim or argue that the court should not exercise its jurisdiction. Rule 11(2) provides that a defendant who wishes to make such an application must first file an acknowledgment of service in accordance with Part 10)

(2) Unless paragraph (3) applies, where the permission of the court is required for a claim form to be served out of the jurisdiction the permission of the court must also be obtained for service out of the jurisdiction of any other document to be served in the proceedings.

(3) Where—

(a) the court gives permission for a claim form to be served out of the jurisdiction; and

(b) the claim form states that particulars of claim are to follow, the permission of the court is not required to serve the particulars of claim out of the jurisdiction.]

[1360]

NOTES

Added as noted to r 6.17 at **[1346]**.

[6.31 Proof of service

Where—

(a) a hearing is fixed when the claim is issued;

(b) the claim form is served on a defendant out of the jurisdiction; and

(c) that defendant does not appear at the hearing,

the claimant may take no further steps against that defendant until the claimant files written evidence showing that the claim form has been duly served.]

[1361]

NOTES

Added as noted to r 6.17 at **[1346]**.

[IV SERVICE OF FOREIGN PROCESS

6.32 Scope and definitions

(1) This Section of this Part—

(a) applies to the service in England or Wales of any court process in connection with civil or commercial proceedings in a foreign court or tribunal; but

(b) does not apply where the Service Regulation applies.

(The Service Regulation is annexed to the relevant practice direction)

(2) In this Section—

(a) "convention country"—

(i) means a foreign country in relation to which there is a civil procedure convention providing for service in that country of process of the High Court; and

(ii) includes a country which is a party to the Convention on the Service Abroad of Judicial and Extra-Judicial Documents in Civil or Commercial Matters signed at the Hague on 15 November 1965; and

(b) "process server" means—

(i) a process server appointed by the Lord Chancellor to serve documents to which this Section applies, or

(ii) his authorised agent.]

[1362]

NOTES

Commencement: 2 December 2002.

Section IV (rr 6.32–6.35) added by the Civil Procedure (Amendment) Rules 2002, SI 2002/2058, r 5(d), Sch 1, Pt II.

[6.33 Request for service

Process will be served where the Senior Master receives—

(a) a written request for service—

(i) where the foreign court or tribunal is in a convention country, from a consular or other authority of that country; or

(ii) from the Secretary of State for Foreign and Commonwealth Affairs, with a recommendation that service should be effected;

(b) a translation of that request into English;

(c) two copies of the process to be served; and

(d) unless the foreign court or tribunal certifies that the person to be served understands the language of the process, two copies of a translation of it into English.]

[1363]

NOTES

Commencement: 2 December 2002.
Added as noted to r 6.32 at **[1362]**.

[6.34 Method of service

The process must be served as directed by the Senior Master.]

[1364]

NOTES

Commencement: 2 December 2002.
Added as noted to r 6.32 at **[1362]**.

[6.35 After service

(1) The process server must—

(a) send the Senior Master a copy of the process, and

(i) proof of service; or

(ii) a statement why the process could not be served; and

(b) if the Senior Master directs, specify the costs incurred in serving or attempting to serve the process.

(2) The Senior Master will send the following documents to the person who requested service—

(a) a certificate, sealed with the seal of the Supreme Court for use out of the jurisdiction, stating—

(i) when and how the process was served or the reason why it has not been served; and

(ii) where appropriate, an amount certified by a costs judge to be the costs of serving or attempting to serve the process; and

(b) a copy of the process.]

[1365]

NOTES

Commencement: 2 December 2002.
Added as noted to r 6.32 at **[1362]**.

PART 7
HOW TO START PROCEEDINGS—THE CLAIM FORM

NOTES

Practice Direction—How to start proceeding; the claim form.

7.1 Where to start proceedings

Restrictions on where proceedings may be started are set out in the relevant practice direction.

[1366]

7.2 How to start proceedings

(1) Proceedings are started when the court issues a claim form at the request of the claimant.

(2) A claim form is issued on the date entered on the form by the court.

(A person who seeks a remedy from the court before proceedings are started or in relation to proceedings which are taking place, or will take place, in another jurisdiction must make an application under Part 23)

(Part 16 sets out what the claim form must include)

[(The costs practice direction sets out the information about a funding arrangement to be provided with the claim form where the claimant intends to seek to recover an additional liability)

("Funding arrangements" and "additional liability" are defined in rule 43.2).]

[1367]

NOTES

Para (2): words in square brackets added by the Civil Procedure (Amendment No 3) Rules 2000, SI 2000/1317, r 4.

7.3 Right to use one claim form to start two or more claims

A claimant may use a single claim form to start all claims which can be conveniently disposed of in the same proceedings.

[1368]

7.4 Particulars of claim

(1) Particulars of claim must—
- (a) be contained in or served with the claim form; or
- (b) subject to paragraph (2) be served on the defendant by the claimant within 14 days after service of the claim form.

(2) Particulars of claim must be served on the defendant no later than the latest time for serving a claim form.

(Rule 7.5 sets out the latest time for serving a claim form)

(3) Where the claimant serves particulars of claim separately from the claim form in accordance with paragraph (1)(b), he must, within 7 days of service on the defendant, file a copy of the particulars together with a certificate of service.

(Part 16 sets out what the particulars of claim must include)

(Part 22 requires particulars of claim to be verified by a statement of truth)

(Rule 6.10 makes provision for a certificate of service)

[1369]

7.5 Service of a claim form

(1) After a claim form has been issued, it must be served on the defendant.

(2) The general rule is that a claim form must be served within 4 months after the date of issue.

(3) The period for service is 6 months where the claim form is to be served out of the jurisdiction.

[1370]

7.6 Extension of time for serving a claim form

(1) The claimant may apply for an order extending the period within which the claim form may be served.

(2) The general rule is that an application to extend the time for service must be made—
- (a) within the period for serving the claim form specified by rule 7.5; or
- (b) where an order has been made under this rule, within the period for service specified by that order.

(3) If the claimant applies for an order to extend the time for service of the claim form after the end of the period specified by rule 7.5 or by an order made under this rule, the court may make such an order only if—
- (a) the court has been unable to serve the claim form; or
- (b) the claimant has taken all reasonable steps to serve the claim form but has been unable to do so; and
- (c) in either case, the claimant has acted promptly in making the application.

(4) An application for an order extending the time for service—

(a) must be supplied by evidence; and
(b) may be made without notice.

[1371]

7.7 Application by defendant for service of claim form

(1) Where a claim form has been issued against a defendant, but has not yet been served on him, the defendant may serve a notice on the claimant requiring him to serve the claim form or discontinue the claim within a period specified in the notice.

(2) The period specified in a notice served under paragraph (1) must be at least 14 days after service of the notice.

(3) If the claimant fails to comply with the notice, the court may, on the application of the defendant—
(a) dismiss the claim; or
(b) make any other order it thinks just.

[1372]

7.8 Form for defence etc must be served with particulars of claim

(1) When particulars of claim are served on a defendant, whether they are contained in the claim form, served with it or served subsequently, they must be accompanied by—
(a) a form for defending the claim;
(b) a form for admitting the claim; and
(c) a form for acknowledging service.

(2) Where the claimant is using the procedure set out in Part 8 (alternative procedure for claims)—
(a) paragraph (1) does not apply; and
(b) a form for acknowledging service must accompany the claim form.

[1373]

7.9 Fixed date and other claims

A practice direction—
(a) may set out the circumstances in which the court may give a fixed date for a hearing when it issues a claim;
(b) may list claims in respect of which there is a specific claim form for use and set out the claim form in question; and
(c) may disapply or modify these Rules as appropriate in relation to the claims referred to paragraphs (a) and (b).

[1374]

NOTES

Practice Direction—Consumer Credit Act Claim.
Practice Direction—Claims for the Recovery of Taxes.

7.10, 7.11 (*Relate to the Production Centre for the issue of claim forms and to human rights.*)

[7.12 Electronic issue of claims

(1) A practice direction may make provision for a claimant to start a claim by requesting the issue of a claim form electronically.

(2) The practice direction may, in particular—
(a) specify—
(i) the types of claim which may be issued electronically; and
(ii) the conditions which a claim must meet before it may be issued electronically;
(b) specify—
(i) the court where the claim will be issued; and
(ii) the circumstances in which the claim will be transferred to another court;
(c) provide for the filing of other documents electronically where a claim has been started electronically;

(d) specify the requirements that must be fulfilled for any document filed electronically; and

(e) provide how a fee payable on the filing of any document is to be paid where that document is filed electronically.

(3) The practice direction may disapply or modify these Rules as appropriate in relation to claims started electronically.]

[1375]

NOTES

Commencement: 1 February 2004.

Added by the Civil Procedure (Amendment No 5) Rules 2003, SI 2003/3361, r 3.

PART 8
ALTERNATIVE PROCEDURE FOR CLAIMS

NOTES

Practice Direction—Alternative Procedure for Claims.

8.1 Types of claim in which Part 8 procedure may be followed

(1) The Part 8 procedure is the procedure set out in this Part.

(2) A claimant may use the Part 8 procedure where—

(a) he seeks the court's decision on a question which is unlikely to involve a substantial dispute of fact; or

(b) paragraph (6) applies.

(3) The court may at any stage order the claim to continue as if the claimant had not used the Part 8 procedure and, if it does so, the court may give any directions it considers appropriate.

(4) Paragraph (2) does not apply if a practice direction provides that the Part 8 procedure may not be used in relation to the type of claim in question.

(5) Where the claimant uses the Part 8 procedure he may not obtain default judgment under Part 12.

(6) A rule or practice direction may, in relation to a specified type of proceedings—

(a) require or permit the use of the Part 8 procedure; and

(b) disapply or modify any of the rules set out in this Part as they apply to those proceedings.

(Rule 8.9 provides for other modifications to the general rules where the Part 8 procedure is being used)

[1376]

8.2 Contents of the claim form

Where the claimant uses the Part 8 procedure the claim form must state—

(a) that this Part applies;

(b)

(i) the question which the claimant wants the court to decide; or

(ii) the remedy which the claimant is seeking and the legal basis for the claim to that remedy;

(c) if the claim is being made under an enactment, what that enactment is;

(d) if the claimant is claiming in a representative capacity, what that capacity is; and

(e) if the defendant is sued in a representative capacity, what that capacity is.

(Part 22 provides for the claim form to be verified by a statement of truth)

(Rule 7.5 provides for service of the claim form)

[(The costs practice direction sets out the information about a funding arrangement to be provided with the claim form where the claimant intends to seek to recover an additional liability)

("Funding arrangement" and "additional liability" are defined in rule 43.2)]

[1377]

NOTES

Cross-references in square brackets added by the Civil Procedure (Amendment No 3) Rules 2000, SI 2000/1317, r 5.

[8.2A Issue of claim form without naming defendants

[(1) A practice direction may set out the circumstances in which a claim form may be issued under this Part without naming a defendant.

(2) The practice direction may set out those cases in which an application for permission must be made by application notice before the claim form is issued.]

(3) The application notice for permission—
- (a) need not be served on any other person; and
- (b) must be accompanied by a copy of the claim form that the applicant proposes to issue.

(4) Where the court gives permission it will give directions about the future management of the claim.]

[1378]

NOTES

Inserted by the Civil Procedure (Amendment) Rules 2000, SI 2000/221, r 5.
Paras (1), (2): substituted by the Civil Procedure (Amendment) Rules 2001, SI 2001/256, r 5.

8.3 Acknowledgment of service

(1) The defendant must—
- (a) file an acknowledgment of service in the relevant practice form not more than 14 days after service of the claim form; and
- (b) serve the acknowledgment of service on the claimant and any other party.

(2) The acknowledgment of service must state—
- (a) whether the defendant contests the claim; and
- (b) if the defendant seeks a different remedy from that set out in the claim form, what that remedy is.

(3) The following rules of Part 10 (acknowledgment of service) apply—
- (a) rule 10.3(2) (exceptions to the period for filing an acknowledgment of service); and
- (b) rule 10.5 (contents of acknowledgment of service).

(4) …

[(The costs practice direction sets out the information about a funding arrangement to be provided with the acknowledgment of service where the defendant intends to seek to recover an additional liability)

("Funding arrangement" and "additional liability" are defined in rule 43.2)]

[1379]

NOTES

Para (4): revoked by the Civil Procedure (Amendment No 5) Rules 2001, SI 2001/4015, r 8.
Cross-references in square brackets added by the Civil Procedure (Amendment No 3) Rules 2000, SI 2000/1317, r 6.

8.4 Consequence of not filing an acknowledgment of service

(1) This rule applies where—
- (a) the defendant has failed to file an acknowledgment of service; and
- (b) the time period for doing so has expired.

(2) The defendant may attend the hearing of the claim but may not take part in the hearing unless the court gives permission.

[1380]

8.5 Filing and serving written evidence

(1) The claimant must file any written evidence on which he intends to rely when he files his claim form.

(2) The claimant's evidence must be served on the defendant with the claim form.

(3) A defendant who wishes to rely on written evidence must file it when he files his acknowledgment of service.

(4) If he does so, he must also, at the same time, serve a copy of his evidence on the other parties.

(5) The claimant may, within 14 days of service of the defendant's evidence on him, file further written evidence in reply.

(6) If he does so, he must also, within the same time limit, serve a copy of his evidence on the other parties.

(7) The claimant may rely on the matters set out in his claim form as evidence under this rule if the claim form is verified by a statement of truth.

[1381]

8.6 Evidence—general

(1) No written evidence may be relied on at the hearing of the claim unless—
- (a) it has been served in accordance with rule 8.5; or
- (b) the court gives permission.

(2) The court may require or permit a party to give oral evidence at the hearing.

(3) The court may give directions requiring the attendance for cross-examination[GL] of a witness who has given written evidence.

(Rule 32.1 contains a general power for the court to control evidence)

[1382]

8.7 Part 20 claims

Where the Part 8 procedure is used, Part 20 (counterclaims and other additional claims) applies except that a party may not make a Part 20 claim (as defined by rule 20.2) without the court's permission.

[1383]

8.8 Procedure where defendant objects to use of the Part 8 procedure

(1) Where the defendant contends that the Part 8 procedure should not be used because—
- (a) there is a substantial dispute of fact; and
- (b) the use of the Part 8 procedure is not required or permitted by a rule or practice direction, he must state his reasons when he files his acknowledgment of service.

(Rule 8.5 requires a defendant who wishes to rely on written evidence to file it when he files his acknowledgment of service)

(2) When the court receives the acknowledgment of service and any written evidence it will give directions as to the future management of the case.

(Rule 8.1(3) allows the court to make an order that the claim continue as if the claimant had not used the Part 8 procedure)

[1384]

8.9 Modifications to the general rules

Where the Part 8 procedure is followed—
- (a) provision is made in this Part for the matters which must be stated in the claim form and the defendant is not required to file a defence and therefore—
  - (i) Part 16 (statements of case) does not apply;
  - (ii) Part 15 (defence and reply) does not apply;
  - (iii) any time limit in these Rules which prevents the parties from taking a step before a defence is filed does not apply; and
  - (iv) the requirement under rule 7.8 to serve on the defendant a form for defending the claim does not apply;

(b) the claimant may not obtain judgment by request on an admission and therefore—
(i) rules 14.4 to 14.7 do not apply; and
(ii) the requirement under rule 7.8 to serve on the defendant a form for admitting the claim does not apply; and

the claim shall be treated as allocated to the multi-track and therefore Part 26 does not apply.

[1385]

PART 9
RESPONDING TO PARTICULARS OF CLAIM—GENERAL

9.1 Scope of this Part

(1) This Part sets out how a defendant may respond to particulars of claim.

(2) Where the defendant receives a claim form which states that particulars of claim are to follow, he need not respond to the claim until the particulars of claim have been served on him.

[1386]

9.2 Defence, admission or acknowledgment of service

When particulars of claim are served on a defendant, the defendant may—
(a) file or serve an admission in accordance with Part 14;
(b) file a defence in accordance with Part 15,

(or do both, if he admits only part of the claim); or
(c) file an acknowledgment of service in accordance with Part 10.

[(Paragraph 10.6 of the Practice Direction to Part 16 contains provision about the content of the admission, defence or acknowledgment of service).]

[1387]

NOTES

Cross-reference in square brackets added by the Civil Procedure (Amendment No 3) Rules 2005, SI 2005/2292, r 16.

PART 10
ACKNOWLEDGMENT OF SERVICE

NOTES

Practice Direction—Acknowledgment of Service.

10.1 Acknowledgment of service

(1) This Part deals with the procedure for filing an acknowledgment of service.

(2) Where the claimant uses the procedure set out in Part 8 (alternative procedure for claims) this Part applies subject to the modifications set out in rule 8.3.

(3) A defendant may file an acknowledgment of service if—
(a) he is unable to file a defence within the period specified in rule 15.4; or
(b) he wishes to dispute the court's jurisdiction.

(Part 11 sets out the procedure for disputing the court's jurisdiction)

[1388]

10.2 Consequence of not filing an acknowledgment of service

If—
(a) a defendant fails to file an acknowledgment of service within the period specified in rule 10.3; and
(b) does not within that period file a defence in accordance with Part 15 or serve or file an admission in accordance with Part 14,

the claimant may obtain default judgment if Part 12 allows it.

[1389]

10.3 The period for filing an acknowledgment of service

(1) The general rule is that the period for filing an acknowledgment of service is—
(a) where the defendant is served with a claim form which states that particulars of claim are to follow, 14 days after service of the particulars of claim; and
(b) in any other case, 14 days after service of the claim form.

(2) The general rule is subject to the following rules—
(a) [rule 6.22] (which specifies how the period for filing an acknowledgment of service is calculated where the claim form is served out of the jurisdiction); …
(b) rule 6.16(4) (which requires the court to specify the period for responding to the particulars of claim when it makes an order under that rule)[; and
(c) rule 6.21(4) (which requires the court to specify the period within which the defendant may file an acknowledgment of service calculated by reference to Practice Direction 6B when it makes an order giving permission to serve a claim form out of the jurisdiction).]

[1390]

NOTES

Para (2): words in square brackets in sub-para (a) substituted by the Civil Procedure (Amendment No 2) Rules 2000, SI 2000/940, r 6; word omitted revoked, and para (c) and word "and" immediately preceding it added, by the Civil Procedure (Amendment No 3) Rules 2005, SI 2005/2292, r 17.

10.4 Notice to claimant that defendant has filed an acknowledgment of service

On receipt of an acknowledgment of service, the court must notify the claimant in writing.

[1391]

10.5 Contents of acknowledgment of service

An acknowledgment of service must—
(a) be signed by the defendant or his legal representative; and
(b) include the defendant's address for service.

(Rule 6.5 provides that an address for service must he within the jurisdiction)

[(Rule 19.8A modifies this Part where a notice of claim is served under that rule to bind a person not a party to the claim)]

[1392]

NOTES

Words in square brackets added by the Civil Procedure (Amendment) Rules 2001, SI 2001/256, r 6.

PART 11
DISPUTING THE COURT'S JURISDICTION

11 Procedure for disputing the court's jurisdiction

(1) A defendant who wishes to—
(a) dispute the court's jurisdiction to try the claim; or
(b) argue that the court should not exercise its jurisdiction,

may apply to the court for an order declaring that it has no such jurisdiction or should not exercise any jurisdiction which it may have.

(2) A defendant who wishes to make such an application must first file an acknowledgment of service in accordance with Part 10.

(3) A defendant who files an acknowledgment of service does not, by doing so, lose any right that he may have to dispute the court's jurisdiction.

(4) An application under this rule must—
[(a) be made within 14 days after filing an acknowledgment of service; and]
(b) be supported by evidence.

…

(5) If the defendant—

(a) files an acknowledgment of service; and

(b) does not make such an application within the period [specified in paragraph (4)],

he is to be treated as having accepted that the court has jurisdiction to try the claim.

(6) An order containing a declaration that the court has no jurisdiction or will not exercise its jurisdiction may also make further provision including—

(a) setting aside the claim form;

(b) setting aside service of the claim form;

(c) discharging any order made before the claim was commenced or before the claim form was served; and

(d) staying(GL) the proceedings.

(7) If on an application under this rule the court does not make a declaration—

(a) the acknowledgment of service shall cease to have effect; …

(b) the defendant may file a further acknowledgment of service within 14 days or such other period as the court may direct[; and

(c) the court shall give directions as to the filing and service of the defence in a claim under Part 7 or the filing of evidence in a claim under Part 8 in the event that a further acknowledgment of service is filed.]

(8) If the defendant files a further acknowledgment of service in accordance with paragraph (7)(b) he shall be treated as having accepted that the court has jurisdiction to try the claim.

[(9) If a defendant makes an application under this rule, he must file and serve his written evidence in support with the application notice, but he need not before the hearing of the application file—

(a) in a Part 7 claim, a defence; or

(b) in a Part 8 claim, any other written evidence.]

(10) …

[1393]

NOTES

Para (4): sub-para (a) substituted and words omitted revoked by the Civil Procedure (Amendment No 5) Rules 2001, SI 2001/4015, r 12(a), (b).

Para (5): words in square brackets substituted by SI 2001/4015, r 12(c).

Para (7): word omitted revoked, and para (c) and word "and" immediately preceding it added, by the Civil Procedure (Amendment No 3) Rules 2005, SI 2005/2292, r 18.

Para (9): substituted by SI 2001/4015, r 12(d).

Para (10): revoked by SI 2001/4015, r 12(e).

PART 12
DEFAULT JUDGMENT

NOTES

Practice Direction—Default Judgment; see para **[1554]**.

12.1 Meaning of "default judgment"

In these Rules, "default judgment" means judgment without trial where a defendant—

(a) has failed to file an acknowledgment of service; or

(b) has failed to file a defence.

(Part 10 contains provisions about filing an acknowledgment of service and Part 15 contains provisions about filing a defence)

[1394]

12.2 Claims in which default judgment may not be obtained

A claimant may not obtain a default judgment—

(a) on a claim for delivery of goods subject to an agreement regulated by the Consumer Credit Act 1974;

(b) where he uses the procedure set out in Part 8 (alternative procedure for claims); or

(c) in any other case where a practice direction provides that the claimant may not obtain default judgment.

[1395]

12.3 Conditions to be satisfied

(1) The claimant may obtain judgment in default of an acknowledgment of service only if—

(a) the defendant has not filed an acknowledgment of service or a defence to the claim (or any part of the claim); and

(b) the relevant time for doing so has expired.

[(2) Judgment in default of defence may be obtained only—

(a) where an acknowledgment of service has been filed but a defence has not been filed;

(b) in a counterclaim made under rule 20.4, where a defence has not been filed,

and, in either case, the relevant time limit for doing so has expired.]

(Rules 10.3 and 15.4 deal respectively with the period for filing an acknowledgment of service and the period for filing a defence)

[(Rule 20.4 makes general provision for a defendant's counterclaim against a claimant, and rule 20.4(3) provides that Part 10 (acknowledgment of service) does not apply to a counterclaim made under that rule)]

(3) The claimant may not obtain a default judgment if—

[(a) the defendant has applied—

(i) to have the claimant's statement of case struck out under rule 3.4; or

(ii) for summary judgment under Part 24,

and, in either case, that application has not been disposed of;]

(b) the defendant has satisfied the whole claim (including any claim for costs) on which the claimant is seeking judgment; or

(c)

(i) the claimant is seeking judgment on a claim for money; and

(ii) the defendant has filed or served on the claimant an admission under rule 14.4 or 14.7 (admission of liability to pay all of the money claimed) together with a request for time to pay.

(Part 14 sets out the procedure where a defendant admits a money claim and asks for time to pay)

(Rule 6.14 provides that, where the claim form is served by the claimant, he may not obtain default judgment unless he has filed a certificate of service)

[(Article 19(1) of Council Regulation (EC) No 1348/2000 of 29 May 2000 on the service in the Member States of judicial and extrajudicial documents in civil or commercial matters applies in relation to judgment in default where the claim form is served in accordance with that Regulation)]

[1396]

NOTES

Para (2): substituted, and cross-reference in square brackets added, by the Civil Procedure (Amendment) Rules 2000, SI 2000/221, r 6(a), (b).

Para (3): sub-para (a) substituted by SI 2000/221, r 6(c).

Cross-reference in square brackets added by the Civil Procedure (Amendment No 2) Rules 2001, SI 2001/1388, r 9.

12.4 Procedure for obtaining default judgment

(1) Subject to paragraph (2), a claimant may obtain a default judgment by filing a request in the relevant practice form where the claim is for—

(a) a specified amount of money;

(b) an amount of money to be decided by the court;

(c) delivery of goods where the claim form gives the defendant the alternative of paying their value; or

(d) any combination of these remedies.

(2) The claimant must make an application in accordance with Part 23 if he wishes to obtain a default judgment—

(a) on a claim which consists of or includes a claim for any other remedy; or
(b) where rule 12.9 or rule 12.10 so provides[,

and where the defendant is an individual, the claimant must provide the defendant's date of birth (if known) in Part C of the application notice.]

(3) Where a claimant—
(a) claims any other remedy in his claim form in addition to those specified in paragraph (1); but
(b) abandons that claim in his request for judgment,

he may still obtain a default judgment by filing a request under paragraph (1).

[(4) In civil proceedings against the Crown, as defined in rule 66.1(2), a request for a default judgment must be considered by a Master or district judge, who must in particular be satisfied that the claim form and particulars of claim have been properly served on the Crown in accordance with section 18 of the Crown Proceedings Act 1947 and rule 6.5(8).]

[1397]

NOTES

Para (2): words in square brackets substituted by the Civil Procedure (Amendment No 3) Rules 2005, SI 2005/2292, r 19(a).
Para (4): added by SI 2005/2292, r 19(b).

12.5 Nature of judgment where default judgment obtained by filing a request

(1) Where the claim is for a specified sum of money, the claimant may specify in a request filed under rule 12.4(1)—
(a) the date by which the whole of the judgment debt is to be paid; or
(b) the times and rate at which it is to be paid by instalments.

(2) Except where paragraph (4) applies, a default judgment on a claim for a specified amount of money obtained on the filing of a request, will be judgment for the amount of the claim (less any payments made) and costs—
(a) to be paid by the date or at the rate specified in the request for judgment; or
(b) if none is specified, immediately.

(Interest may be included in a default judgment obtained by filing a request if the conditions set out in Rule 12.6 are satisfied)

(Rule 45.4 provides for fixed costs on the entry of a default judgment)

(3) Where the claim is for an unspecified amount of money, a default judgment obtained on the filing of a request will be for an amount to be decided by the court and costs.

(4) Where the claim is for delivery of goods and the claim form gives the defendant the alternative of paying their value, a default judgment obtained on the filing of a request will be judgment requiring the defendant to—
(a) deliver the goods or (if he does not do so) pay the value of the goods as decided by the court (less any payments made); and
(b) pay costs.

(Rule 12.7 sets out the procedure for deciding the amount of a judgment or the value of the goods)

(5) The claimant's right to enter judgment requiring the defendant to deliver goods is subject to rule 40.14 (judgment in favour of certain part owners relating to the detention of goods).

[1398]

12.6 Interest

(1) A default judgment on a claim for a specified amount of money obtained on the filing of a request may include the amount of interest claimed to the date of judgment if—
(a) the particulars of claim include the details required by rule 16.4;
(b) where interest is claimed under section 35A of the *Supreme Court Act 1981* or section 69 of the County Courts Act 1984, the rate is no higher than the rate of interest payable on judgment debts at the date when the claim form was issued; and
(c) the claimant's request for judgment includes a calculation of the interest claimed

for the period from the date up to which interest was stated to be calculated in the claim form to the date of the request for judgment.

(2) In any case where paragraph (1) does not apply, judgment will be for an amount of interest to be decided by the court.

(Rule 12.7 sets out the procedure for deciding the amount of interest)

[1399]

NOTES

Para (1): words in italics in sub-para (b) substituted by the words "Senior Courts Act 1981" by the Constitutional Reform Act 2005, s 59(5), Sch 11, Pt 1, para 1(2), as from a day to be appointed.

12.7 Procedure for deciding an amount or value

(1) This rule applies where the claimant obtains a default judgment on the filing of a request under rule 12.4(1) and judgment is for—

(a) an amount of money to be decided by the court;
(b) the value of goods to be decided by the court; or
(c) an amount of interest to be decided by the court.

(2) Where the court enters judgment it will—

(a) give any directions it considers appropriate; and
(b) if it considers it appropriate, allocate the case.

[1400]

12.8 Claim against more than one defendant

(1) A claimant may obtain a default judgment on request under this Part on a claim for money or a claim for delivery of goods against one of two or more defendants, and proceed with his claim against the other defendants.

(2) Where a claimant applies for a default judgment against one of two or more defendants—

(a) if the claim can be dealt with separately from the claim against the other defendants—
  (i) the court may enter a default judgment against that defendant; and
  (ii) the claimant may continue the proceedings against the other defendants;
(b) if the claim cannot be dealt with separately from the claim against the other defendants—
  (i) the court will not enter default judgment against that defendant; and
  (ii) the court must deal with the application at the same time as it disposes of the claim against the other defendants.

(3) A claimant may not enforce against one of two or more defendants any judgment obtained under this Part for possession of land or for delivery of goods unless—

(a) he has obtained a judgment for possession or delivery (whether or not obtained under this Part) against all the defendants to the claim; or
(b) the court gives permission.

[1401]

12.9 Procedure for obtaining a default judgment for costs only

(1) Where a claimant wishes to obtain a default judgment for costs only—

(a) if the claim is for fixed costs, he may obtain it by filing a request in the relevant practice form;
(b) if the claim is for any other type of costs, he must make an application in accordance with Part 23.

(2) Where an application is made under this rule for costs only, judgment shall be for an amount to be decided by the court.

(Part 45 sets out when a claimant is entitled to fixed costs)

[1402]

12.10 Default judgment obtained by making an application

The claimant must make an application in accordance with Part 23 where—

[(a) the claim is—
   (i) a claim against a child or patient;
   (ii) a claim in tort by one spouse or civil partner against the other.]
(b) he wishes to obtain a default judgment where the defendant has failed to file an acknowledgment of service—
   (i) against a defendant who has been served with the claim out of the jurisdiction under [rule 6.19(1)] [or (1A)] (service without leave …);
   (ii) against a defendant domiciled in Scotland or Northern Ireland or in any other Convention territory [or Regulation State];
   (iii) against a State;
   (iv) against a diplomatic agent who enjoys immunity from civil jurisdiction by virtue of the Diplomatic Privileges Act 1964; or
   (v) against persons or organisations who enjoy immunity from civil jurisdiction pursuant to the provisions of the International Organisations Acts 1968 and 1981.

[1403]

NOTES

Para (a) substituted by the Civil Procedure (Amendment No 3) Rules 2005, SI 2005/2292, r 20; in para (b) words in first pair of square brackets substituted by the Civil Procedure (Amendment No 2) Rules 2000, SI 2000/940, r 7, words in second and third pairs of square brackets inserted and words omitted revoked by the Civil Procedure (Amendment No 5) Rules 2001, SI 2001/4015, r 13.

12.11 Supplementary provisions where applications for default judgment are made

(1) Where the claimant makes an application for a default judgment, judgment shall be such judgment as it appears to the court that the claimant is entitled to on his statement of case.

(2) Any evidence relied on by the claimant in support of his application need not be served on a party who has failed to file an acknowledgment of service.

(3) An application for a default judgment on a claim against a child or patient or a claim in tort between spouses [or civil partners] must be supported by evidence.

(4) An application for a default judgment may be made without notice if—
[(a) the claim under the Civil Jurisdiction and Judgments Act 1982 or the Judgments Regulation, was served in accordance with rules 6.19(1) or 6.19(1A) as appropriate;]
(b) the defendant has failed to file an acknowledgment of service; and
(c) notice does not need to be given under any other provision of these Rules.

(5) Where an application is made against a State for a default judgment where the defendant has failed to file an acknowledgment of service—
(a) the application may be made without notice, but the court hearing the application may direct that a copy of the application notice be served on the State;
(b) if the court—
   (i) grants the application; or
   (ii) directs that a copy of the application notice be served on the State,

the judgment or application notice (and the evidence in support) may be served out of the jurisdiction without any further order;
(c) where paragraph (5)(b) permits a judgment or an application notice to be served out of the jurisdiction, the procedure for serving the judgment or the application notice is the same as for serving a claim form under [Section III of Part 6] except where an alternative method of service has been agreed under section 12(6) of the State Immunity Act 1978.

(Rule 23.1 defines "application notice")

(6) For the purposes of this rule and rule 12.10—
[(a) "domicile" is to be determined—
   (i) in relation to a Convention territory, in accordance with sections 41 to 46 of the Civil Jurisdiction and Judgments Act 1982;
   (ii) in relation to a Regulation State, in accordance with the Judgments Regulation and paragraphs 9 to 12 of Schedule 1 to the Civil Jurisdiction and Judgments Order 2001;]
(b) "Convention territory" means the territory or territories of any Contracting State,

as defined by section 1(3) of the Civil Jurisdiction and Judgments Act 1982, to which the Brussels Conventions or Lugano Convention apply;

(c) "State" has the meaning given by section 14 of the State Immunity Act 1978; …

(d) "Diplomatic agent" has the meaning given by Article 1 (e) of Schedule 1 to the Diplomatic Privileges Act 1964;

[(e) "the Judgments Regulation" means Council Regulation (EC) No 44/2001 of 22nd December 2000 on jurisdiction and the recognition and enforcement of judgments in civil and commercial matters; and

(f) "Regulation State" has the same meaning as "Member State" in the Judgments Regulation, that is all Member States except Denmark.]

[1404]

NOTES

Para (3): words in square brackets inserted by the Civil Procedure (Amendment No 3) Rules 2005, SI 2005/2292, r 21.

Para (4): sub-para (a) substituted by the Civil Procedure (Amendment No 5) Rules 2001, SI 2001/4015, r 14(a).

Para (5): words in square brackets in para (c) substituted by the Civil Procedure (Amendment No 2) Rules 2000, SI 2000/940, r 8.

Para (6): sub-para (a) substituted, word omitted from sub-para (c) revoked and sub-paras (e), (f) added by SI 2001/4015, r 14(b).

PART 13
SETTING ASIDE OR VARYING DEFAULT JUDGMENT

13.1 Scope of this Part

The rules in this Part set out the procedure for setting aside or varying judgment entered under Part 12 (default judgment).

(CCR Order 22 r.10 sets out the procedure for varying the rate at which a judgment debt must be paid)

[1405]

13.2 Cases where the court must set aside judgment entered under Part 12

The court must set aside(GL) a judgment entered under Part 12 if judgment was wrongly entered because—

(a) in the case of a judgment in default of an acknowledgment of service, any of the conditions in rule 12.3(1) and 12.3(3) was not satisfied;

(b) in the case of a judgment in default of a defence, any of the conditions in rule 12.3(2) and 12.3(3) was not satisfied; or

(c) the whole of the claim was satisfied before judgment was entered.

[1406]

13.3 Cases where the court may set aside or vary judgment entered under Part 12

(1) In any other case, the court may set aside(GL) or vary a judgment entered under Part 12 if—

(a) the defendant has a real prospect of successfully defending the claim; or

(b) it appears to the court that there is some other good reason why—

(i) the judgment should be set aside or varied; or

(ii) the defendant should be allowed to defend the claim.

(2) In considering whether to set aside(GL) or vary a judgment entered under Part 12, the matters to which the court must have regard include whether the person seeking to set aside the judgment made an application to do so promptly.

(Rule 3.1(3) provides that the court may attach conditions when it makes an order)

[(Article 19(4) of Council Regulation (EC) No 1348/2000 of 29 May 2000 on the service in the Member States of judicial and extrajudicial documents in civil or commercial matters applies to applications to appeal a judgment in default when the time limit for appealing has expired)]

[1407]

NOTES

Cross-reference in square brackets added by the Civil Procedure (Amendment No 2) Rules 2001, SI 2001/1388, r 10.

13.4 Application to set aside or vary judgment—procedure

(1) Where—

(a) the claim is for a specified amount of money;

(b) the judgment was obtained in a court which is not the defendant's home court;

(c) the claim has not been transferred to another defendant's home court under rule 14.12 (admission—determination of rate of payment by judge) or rule 26.2 (automatic transfer); and

(d) the defendant is an individual,

the court will transfer an application by a defendant under this Part to set aside[(GL)] or vary judgment to the defendant's home court.

…

[(1A) …]

(2) Paragraph (1) does not apply where the claim was commenced in a specialist list.

(3) An application under rule 13.3 (cases where the court may set aside[(GL)] or vary judgment) must be supported by evidence.

[1408]

NOTES

Para (1): words omitted revoked by the Civil Procedure (Amendment) Rules 1999, SI 1999/1008, r 5.

Para (1A): inserted by SI 1999/1008, r 5; revoked by the Civil Procedure (Amendment No 4) Rules 2000, SI 2000/2092, r 7.

13.5 *(Revoked by the Civil Procedure (Amendment) Rules 2004, SI 2004/1306, r 21(a).)*

13.6 Abandoned claim restored where default judgment set aside

Where—

(a) the claimant claimed a remedy in addition to one specified in rule 12.4(1) (claims in respect of which the claimant may obtain default judgment by filing a request);

(b) the claimant abandoned his claim for that remedy in order to obtain default judgment on request in accordance with rule 12.4(3); and

(c) that default judgment is set aside[(GL)] under this Part,

the abandoned claim is restored when the default judgment is set aside.

[1409]

Parts 14–22 *(Pt 14 relates to admissions; Pt 15 to defence and reply; Pt 16 to statements of case; Pt 17 to amendments to statements of case; Pt 18 to further information; Pt 19 to addition and substitution of parties; Pt 20 to counterclaims and other additional claims; Pt 21 to children and patients; Pt 22 to statements of truth.)*

PART 23
GENERAL RULES ABOUT APPLICATIONS FOR COURT ORDERS

NOTES

Practice Direction—Applications; see para **[1555]**.

Practice Direction—Pilot Scheme for Telephone Hearings.

23.1 Meaning of "application notice" and "respondent"

In this Part—

"application notice" means a document in which the applicant states his intention to seek a court order; and

"respondent" means—

(a) the person against whom the order is sought; and

(b) such other person as the court may direct.

[1410]

23.2 Where to make an application

(1) The general rule is that an application must be made to the court where the claim was started.

(2) If a claim has been transferred to another court since it was started, an application must be made to the court to which the claim has been transferred.

(3) If the parties have been notified of a fixed date for the trial, an application must be made to the court where the trial is to take place.

(4) If an application is made before a claim has been started, it must be made to the court where it is likely that the claim to which the application relates will be started unless there is good reason to make the application to a different court.

(5) If an application is made after proceedings to enforce judgment have begun, it must be made to any court which is dealing with the enforcement of the judgment unless any rule or practice direction provides otherwise.

[1411]

23.3 Application notice to be filed

(1) The general rule is that an applicant must file an application notice.

(2) An applicant may make an application without filing an application notice if—
- (a) this is permitted by a rule or practice direction; or
- (b) the court dispenses with the requirement for an application notice.

[1412]

23.4 Notice of an application

(1) The general rule is that a copy of the application notice must be served on each respondent.

(2) An application may be made without serving a copy of the application notice if this is permitted by—
- (a) a rule;
- (b) a practice direction; or
- (c) a court order.

(Rule 23.7 deals with service of a copy of the application notice)

[1413]

23.5 Time when an application is made

Where an application must be made within a specified time, it is so made if the application notice is received by the court within that time.

[1414]

23.6 What an application notice must include

An application notice must state—
- (a) what order the applicant is seeking; and
- (b) briefly, why the applicant is seeking the order.

(Part 22 requires an application notice to be verified by a statement of truth if the applicant wishes to rely on matters set out in his application notice as evidence)

[1415]

23.7 Service of a copy of an application notice

(1) A copy of the application notice—
- (a) must be served as soon as practicable after it is filed; and
- (b) except where another time limit is specified in these Rules or a practice direction, must in any event be served at least 3 days before the court is to deal with the application.

(2) If a copy of the application notice is to be served by the court, the applicant must, when he files the application notice, file a copy of any written evidence in support.

PART II

(3) When a copy of an application notice is served it must be accompanied by—

(a) a copy of any written evidence in support; and

(b) a copy of any draft order which the applicant has attached to his application.

(4) If—

(a) an application notice is served; but

(b) the period of notice is shorter than the period required by these Rules or a practice direction,

the court may direct that, in the circumstances of the case, sufficient notice has been given and hear the application.

(5) This rule does not require written evidence—

(a) to be filed if it has already been filed; or

(b) to be served on a party on whom it has already been served.

(Part 6 contains the general rules about service of documents including who must serve a copy of the application notice).

[1416]

23.8 Applications which may be dealt with without a hearing

The court may deal with an application without a hearing if—

(a) the parties agree as to the terms of the order sought;

(b) the parties agree that the court should dispose of the application without a hearing, or

(c) the court does not consider that a hearing would be appropriate.

[1417]

23.9 Service of application where application made without notice

(1) This rule applies where the court has disposed of an application which it permitted to be made without service of a copy of the application notice.

(2) Where the court makes an order, whether granting or dismissing the application, a copy of the application notice and any evidence in support must, unless the court orders otherwise, be served with the order on any party or other person—

(a) against whom the order was made; and

(b) against whom the order was sought.

(3) The order must contain a statement of the right to make an application to set aside(GL) or vary the order under rule 23.10.

[1418]

23.10 Application to set aside or vary order made without notice

[(1) A person who was not served with a copy of the application notice before an order was made under rule 23.9 may apply to have the order set aside(GL) or varied.]

(2) An application under this rule must be made within 7 days after the date on which the order was served on the person making the application.

[1419]

NOTES

Para (1): substituted by the Civil Procedure (Amendment) Rules 2000, SI 2000/221, r 11.

23.11 Power of the court to proceed in the absence of a party

(1) Where the applicant or any respondent fails to attend the hearing of an application, the court may proceed in his absence.

(2) Where—

(a) the applicant or any respondent fails to attend the hearing of an application; and

(b) the court makes an order at the hearing,

the court may, on application or of its own initiative, re-list the application.

(Part 40 deals with service of orders).

[1420]

[23.12 Dismissal of totally without merit applications

If the court dismisses an application [(including an application for permission to appeal or for permission to apply for judicial review)] and it considers that the application is totally without merit—

(a) the court's order must record that fact; and

(b) the court must at the same time consider whether it is appropriate to make a civil restraint order.]

[1421]

NOTES

Commencement: 1 October 2004.

Added by the Civil Procedure (Amendment No 2) Rules 2004, SI 2004/2072, r 9.

Words in square brackets inserted by the Civil Procedure (Amendment No 3) Rules 2005, SI 2005/2292, r 26.

Part 24 (*Relates to summary judgment.*)

PART 25
[INTERIM REMEDIES AND SECURITY FOR COSTS]

NOTES

Title: substituted by the Civil Procedure (Amendment) Rules 2000, SI 2000/221, r 13(1).

Practice Directions—Interim Injunctions; see para **[1557]**.

Practice Directions—Interim Payments.

[I INTERIM REMEDIES]

NOTES

Section heading: inserted by the Civil Procedure (Amendment) Rules 2000, SI 2000/221, r 13(2), Sch 3, Pt I.

25.1 Orders for interim remedies

(1) The court may grant the following interim remedies—

(a) an interim injunction(GL);

(b) an interim declaration;

(c) an order—

(i) for the detention, custody or preservation of relevant property;

(ii) for the inspection of relevant property;

(iii) for the taking of a sample of relevant property;

(iv) for the carrying out of an experiment on or with relevant property;

(v) for the sale of relevant property which is of a perishable nature or which for any other good reason it is desirable to sell quickly; and

(vi) for the payment of income from relevant property until a claim is decided;

(d) an order authorising a person to enter any land or building in the possession of a party to the proceedings for the purposes of carrying out an order under sub-paragraph (c);

(e) an order under section 4 of the Torts (Interference with Goods) Act 1977 to deliver up goods;

(f) an order (referred to as a "freezing injunction(GL)")—

(i) restraining a party from removing from the jurisdiction assets located there; or

(ii) restraining a party from dealing with any assets whether located within the jurisdiction or not;

(g) an order directing a party to provide information about the location of relevant property or assets or to provide information about relevant property or assets which are or may be the subject of an application for a freezing injunction(GL);

(h) an order (referred to as a "search order") under section 7 of the Civil Procedure Act 1997 (order requiring a party to admit another party to premises for the purpose of preserving evidence etc);

(i) an order under section 33 of the *Supreme Court Act 1981* or section 52 of the County Courts Act 1984 (order for disclosure of documents or inspection of property before a claim has been made);
(j) an order under section 34 of the *Supreme Court Act 1981* or section 53 of the County Courts Act 1984 (order in certain proceedings for disclosure of documents or inspection of property against a non-party);
(k) an order (referred to as an order for interim payment) under rule 25.6 for payment by a defendant on account of any damages, debt or other sum (except costs) which the court may hold the defendant liable to pay;
(l) an order for a specified fund to be paid into court or otherwise secured, where there is a dispute over a party's right to the fund;
(m) an order permitting a party seeking to recover personal property to pay money into court pending the outcome of the proceedings and directing that, if he does so, the property shall be given up to him; …
(n) an order directing a party to prepare and file accounts relating to the dispute[; …
(o) an order directing any account to be taken or inquiry to be made by the court][; and
(p) an order under Article 9 of Council Directive (EC) 2004/48 on the enforcement of intellectual property rights (order in intellectual property proceedings making the continuation of an alleged infringement subject to the lodging of guarantees).]

(Rule 34.2 provides for the court to issue a witness summons requiring a witness to produce documents to the court at the hearing or on such date as the court may direct)

(2) In paragraph (1)(c) and (g), "relevant property" means property (including land) which is the subject of a claim or as to which any question may arise on a claim.

(3) The fact that a particular kind of interim remedy is not listed in paragraph (1) does not affect any power that the court may have to grant that remedy.

(4) The court may grant an interim remedy whether or not there has been a claim for a final remedy of that kind.

[1422]

NOTES

Para (1): words in italics in sub-paras (i), (j) substituted by the words "Senior Courts Act 1981" by the Constitutional Reform Act 2005, s 59(5), Sch 11, Pt 1, para 1(2), as from a day to be appointed; word omitted from sub-para (m) revoked and sub-para (o) and word immediately preceding it added by the Civil Procedure (Amendment) Rules 2002, SI 2002/2058, r 7; word omitted from sub-para (n) revoked and sub-para (p) and word immediately preceding it added by the Civil Procedure (Amendment No 2) Rules 2005, SI 2005/656, r 7(a).

25.2 Time when an order for an interim remedy may be made

(1) An order for an interim remedy may be made at any time, including—
(a) before proceedings are started; and
(b) after judgment has been given.

(Rule 7.2 provides that proceedings are started when the court issues a claim form)

(2) However—
(a) paragraph (1) is subject to any rule, practice direction or other enactment which provides otherwise;
(b) the court may grant an interim remedy before a claim has been made only if—
(i) the matter is urgent; or
(ii) it is otherwise desirable to do so in the interests of justice; and
(c) unless the court otherwise orders, a defendant may not apply for any of the orders listed in rule 25.1(1) before he has filed either an acknowledgement of service or a defence.

(Part 10 provides for filing an acknowledgment of service and Part 15 for filing a defence)

[(3) Where it grants an interim remedy before a claim has been commenced, the court should give directions requiring a claim to be commenced.]

(4) In particular, the court need not direct that a claim be commenced where the application is made under section 33 of the *Supreme Court Act 1981* or section 52 of the County Courts Act 1984 (order for disclosure, inspection etc before commencement of a claim).

[1423]

NOTES

Para (3): substituted by the Civil Procedure (Amendment No 4) Rules 2005, SI 2005/3515, r 7(b).

Para (4): words in italics substituted by the words "Senior Courts Act 1981" by the Constitutional Reform Act 2005, s 59(5), Sch 11, Pt 1, para 1(2), as from a day to be appointed.

25.3 How to apply for an interim remedy

(1) The court may grant an interim remedy on an application made without notice if it appears to the court that there are good reasons for not giving notice.

(2) An application for an interim remedy must be supported by evidence, unless the court orders otherwise.

(3) If the applicant makes an application without giving notice, the evidence in support of the application must state the reasons why notice has not been given.

(Part 3 lists general powers of the court).

(Part 23 contains general rules about making an application).

[1424]

25.4 Application for an interim remedy where there is no related claim

(1) This rule applies where a party wishes to apply for an interim remedy but—

(a) the remedy is sought in relation to proceedings which are taking place, or will take place, outside the jurisdiction; or

(b) the application is made under section 33 of the *Supreme Court Act 1981* or section 52 of the County Courts Act 1984 (order for disclosure, inspection etc before commencement) before a claim has been commenced.

(2) An application under this rule must be made in accordance with the general rules about applications contained in Part 23.

(The following provisions are also relevant—

— Rule 25.5 (inspection of property before commencement or against a non-party)

— Rule 31.16 (orders for disclosure of documents before proceedings start)

— Rule 31.17 (orders for disclosure of documents against a person not a party)).

[1425]

NOTES

Para (1): words in italics substituted by the words "Senior Courts Act 1981" by the Constitutional Reform Act 2005, s 59(5), Sch 11, Pt 1, para 1(2), as from a day to be appointed.

25.5 Inspection of property before commencement or against a non-party

(1) This rule applies where a person makes an application under—

(a) section 33(1) of the *Supreme Court Act 1981* or section 52(1) of the County Courts Act 1984 (inspection etc of property before commencement);

(b) section 34(3) of the *Supreme Court Act 1981* or section 53(3) of the County Courts Act 1984 (inspection etc of property against a non-party).

(2) The evidence in support of such an application must show, if practicable by reference to any statement of case prepared in relation to the proceedings or anticipated proceedings, that the property—

(a) is or may become the subject matter of such proceedings; or

(b) is relevant to the issues that will arise in relation to such proceedings.

(3) A copy of the application notice and a copy of the evidence in support must be served on—

(a) the person against whom the order is sought; and

(b) in relation to an application under section 34(3) of the *Supreme Court Act 1981* or section 53(3) of the County Courts Act 1984, every party to the proceedings other than the applicant.

[1426]

NOTES

Paras (1), (3): words in italics substituted by the words "Senior Courts Act 1981" by the Constitutional Reform Act 2005, s 59(5), Sch 11, Pt 1, para 1(2), as from a day to be appointed.

25.6 Interim payments—general procedure

(1) The claimant may not apply for an order for an interim payment before the end of the period for filing an acknowledgement of service applicable to the defendant against whom the application is made.

(Rule 10.3 sets out the period for filing an acknowledgement of service)

(Rule 25.1(1)(k) defines an interim payment)

(2) The claimant may make more than one application for an order for an interim payment.

(3) A copy of an application notice for an order for an interim payment must—
- (a) be served at least 14 days before the hearing of the application; and
- (b) be supported by evidence.

(4) If the respondent to an application for an order for an interim payment wishes to rely on written evidence at the hearing, he must—
- (a) file the written evidence; and
- (b) serve copies on every other party to the application,

at least 7 days before the hearing of the application.

(5) If the applicant wishes to rely on written evidence in reply, he must—
- (a) file the written evidence; and
- (b) serve a copy on the respondent,

at least 3 days before the hearing of the application.

(6) This rule does not require written evidence—
- (a) to be filed if it has already been filed; or
- (b) to be served on a party on whom it has already been served.

(7) The court may order an interim payment in one sum or in instalments.

(Part 23 contains general rules about applications).

[1427]

25.7 Interim payments—conditions to be satisfied and matters to be taken into account

[(1) The court may only make an order for an interim payment where any of the following conditions are satisfied—
- (a) the defendant against whom the order is sought has admitted liability to pay damages or some other sum of money to the claimant;
- (b) the claimant has obtained judgment against that defendant for damages to be assessed or for a sum of money (other than costs) to be assessed;
- (c) it is satisfied that, if the claim went to trial, the claimant would obtain judgment for a substantial amount of money (other than costs) against the defendant from whom he is seeking an order for an interim payment whether or not that defendant is the only defendant or one of a number of defendants to the claim;
- (d) the following conditions are satisfied—
  - (i) the claimant is seeking an order for possession of land (whether or not any other order is also sought); and
  - (ii) the court is satisfied that, if the case went to trial, the defendant would be held liable (even if the claim for possession fails) to pay the claimant a sum of money for the defendant's occupation and use of the land while the claim for possession was pending; or
- (e) in a claim in which there are two or more defendants and the order is sought against any one or more of those defendants, the following conditions are satisfied—
  - (i) the court is satisfied that, if the claim went to trial, the claimant would obtain judgment for a substantial amount of money (other than costs) against at least one of the defendants (but the court cannot determine which); and
  - (ii) all the defendants are either—
    - (a) a defendant that is insured in respect of the claim;
    - (b) a defendant whose liability will be met by an insurer under section 151 of the Road Traffic Act 1988 or an insurer acting under the Motor Insurers Bureau Agreement, or the Motor Insurers Bureau where it is acting itself; or

(c) a defendant that is a public body.]

(2), (3) …

(4) The court must not order an interim payment of more than a reasonable proportion of the likely amount of the final judgment.

(5) The court must take into account—

(a) contributory negligence; and

(b) any relevant set-off or counterclaim.

[1428]

NOTES

Para (1): substituted by the Civil Procedure (Amendment No 4) Rules 2004, SI 2004/3419, r 5(a).
Paras (2), (3): revoked by SI 2004/3419, r 5(b).

25.8 Powers of court where it has made an order for interim payment

(1) Where a defendant has been ordered to make an interim payment, or has in fact made an interim payment (whether voluntarily or under an order), the court may make an order to adjust the interim payment.

(2) The court may in particular—

(a) order all or part of the interim payment to be repaid;

(b) vary or discharge the order for the interim payment;

(c) order a defendant to reimburse, either wholly or partly, another defendant who has made an interim payment.

(3) The court may make an order under paragraph (2)(c) only if—

(a) the defendant to be reimbursed made the interim payment in relation to a claim in respect of which he has made a claim against the other defendant for a contribution(GL), indemnity(GL) or other remedy; and

(b) where the claim or part to which the interim payment relates has not been discontinued or disposed of, the circumstances are such that the court could make an order for interim payment under rule 25.7.

(4) The court may make an order under this rule without an application by any party if it makes the order when it disposes of the claim or any part of it.

(5) Where—

(a) a defendant has made an interim payment; and

(b) the amount of the payment is more than his total liability under the final judgment or order,

the court may award him interest on the overpaid amount from the date when he made the interim payment.

[1429]

25.9 Restriction on disclosure of an interim payment

The fact that a defendant has made an interim payment, whether voluntarily or by court order, shall not be disclosed to the trial judge until all questions of liability and the amount of money to be awarded have been decided unless the defendant agrees.

[1430]

25.10 Interim injunction to cease if claim is stayed

If—

(a) the court has granted an interim injunction(GL) [other than a freezing injunction]; and

(b) the claim is stayed(GL) other than by agreement between the parties, the interim injunction(GL) shall be set aside(GL) unless the court orders that it should continue to have effect even though the claim is stayed.

[1431]

NOTES

Words in square brackets inserted by the Civil Procedure (Amendment No 5) Rules 2001, SI 2001/4015, r 17.

[25.11 Interim injunction to cease after 14 days if claim struck out

(1) If—

(a) the court has granted an interim injunction(GL); and

(b) the claim is struck out under rule 3.7 (sanction for non-payment of certain fees),

the interim injunction shall cease to have effect 14 days after the date that the claim is struck out unless paragraph (2) applies.

(2) If the claimant applies to reinstate the claim before the interim injunction ceases to have effect under paragraph (1), the injunction shall continue until the hearing of the application unless the court orders otherwise.]

[1432]

NOTES

Added by the Civil Procedure (Amendment) Rules 1999, SI 1999/1008, r 8(b).

[II SECURITY FOR COSTS

25.12(1) A defendant to any claim may apply under this Section of this Part for security for his costs of the proceedings.

(Part 3 provides for the court to order payment of sums into court in other circumstances. Rule 20.3 provides for this Section of this Part to apply to Part 20 claims)

(2) An application for security for costs must be supported by written evidence.

(3) Where the court makes an order for security for costs, it will—

(a) determine the amount of security; and

(b) direct—

(i) the manner in which; and

(ii) the time within which

the security must be given.]

[1433]

NOTES

Section II (rr 25.12–25.15) added by the Civil Procedure (Amendment) Rules 2000, SI 2000/221, r 13(3), Sch 3, Pt II.

[25.13 Conditions to be satisfied

(1) The court may make an order for security for costs under rule 25.12 if—

(a) it is satisfied, having regard to all the circumstances of the case, that it is just to make such an order; and

(b)

(i) one or more of the conditions in paragraph (2) applies, or

(ii) an enactment permits the court to require security for costs.

(2) The conditions are—

[(a) the claimant is—

(i) resident out of the jurisdiction; but

(ii) not resident in a Brussels Contracting State, a Lugano Contracting State or a Regulation State, as defined in section 1(3) of the Civil Jurisdiction and Judgments Act 1982;]

(b) ...

(c) the claimant is a company or other body (whether incorporated inside or outside Great Britain) and there is reason to believe that it will be unable to pay the defendant's costs if ordered to do so;

(d) the claimant has changed his address since the claim was commenced with a view to evading the consequences of the litigation;

(e) the claimant failed to give his address in the claim form, or gave an incorrect address in that form;

(f) the claimant is acting as a nominal claimant, other than as a representative claimant under Part 19, and there is reason to believe that he will be unable to pay the defendant's costs if ordered to do so;

(g) the claimant has taken steps in relation to his assets that would make it difficult to enforce an order for costs against him.

(Rule 3.4 allows the court to strike out a statement of case and Part 24 for it to give summary judgment)]

[1434]

NOTES

Added as noted to r 25.12 at **[1433]**.

Para (2): sub-para (a) substituted and sub-para (b) revoked by the Civil Procedure (Amendment No 2) Rules 2002, SI 2002/3219, r 3.

[25.14 Security for costs other than from the claimant

(1) The defendant may seek an order against someone other than the claimant, and the court may make an order for security for costs against that person if—

(a) it is satisfied, having regard to all the circumstances of the case, that it is just to make such an order; and

(b) one or more of the conditions in paragraph (2) applies.

(2) The conditions are that the person—

(a) has assigned the right to the claim to the claimant with a view to avoiding the possibility of a costs order being made against him; or

(b) has contributed or agreed to contribute to the claimant's costs in return for a share of any money or property which the claimant may recover in the proceedings; and

is a person against whom a costs order may be made.

(Rule 48.2 makes provision for costs orders against non-parties)]

[1435]

NOTES

Added as noted to r 25.12 at **[1433]**.

[25.15 Security for costs of an appeal

(1) The court may order security for costs of an appeal against—

(a) an appellant;

(b) a respondent who also appeals,

on the same grounds as it may order security for costs against a claimant under this Part.

(2) The court may also make an order under paragraph (1) where the appellant, or the respondent who also appeals, is a limited company and there is reason to believe it will be unable to pay the costs of the other parties to the appeal should its appeal be unsuccessful.]

[1436]

NOTES

Added as noted to r 25.12 at **[1433]**.

Parts 26–31 (*Pt 26 relates to case management—preliminary stage; Pt 27 to the small claims track; Pt 28 to the fast track; Pt 29 to the multi-track; Pt 30 to transfer; Pt 31 to disclosure and inspection of documents.*)

PART 32
EVIDENCE

Rules 32.1–32.16 (*Relate to specific aspects of evidence in civil proceedings.*)

32.17 Affidavit made outside the jurisdiction

A person may make an affidavit(GL) outside the jurisdiction in accordance with—

(a) this Part; or

(b) the law of the place where he makes the affidavit(GL).

[1437]

Rules 32.18–32.20 (*Relate to notices and notarial acts and instruments.*)

PART 33
MISCELLANEOUS RULES ABOUT EVIDENCE

33.1–33.6 (*Contain miscellaneous rules about evidence.*)

33.7 Evidence of finding on question of foreign law

(1) This rule sets out the procedure which must be followed by a party who intends to put in evidence a finding on a question of foreign law by virtue of section 4(2) of the Civil Evidence Act 1972.

(2) He must give any other party notice of his intention.

(3) He must give the notice—
- (a) if there are to be witness statements, not later than the latest date for serving them; or
- (b) otherwise, not less than 21 days before the hearing at which he proposes to put the finding in evidence.

(4) The notice must—
- (a) specify the question on which the finding was made; and
- (b) enclose a copy of a document where it is reported or recorded.

[1438]

Rules 33.8, 33.9 (*Contain miscellaneous rules about evidence.*)

PART 34
[WITNESSES, DEPOSITIONS AND EVIDENCE FOR FOREIGN COURTS]

NOTES

Heading: substituted by the Civil Procedure (Amendment) Rules 2002, SI 2002/2058, r 12(a).
Practice Direction—Depositions and Court Attendance by Witnesses; see para **[1558]**.
Practice Direction—Fees for Examiners of the Court.

[I WITNESSES AND DEPOSITIONS]

NOTES

Section heading: inserted by the Civil Procedure (Amendment) Rules 2002, SI 2002/2058, r 12(c).

Rules 34.1–34.12 (*Relate to witness summonses and evidence by deposition.*)

34.13 Where a person to be examined is out of the jurisdiction—letter of request

[(1) This rule applies where a party wishes to take a deposition from a person who is—
- (a) out of the jurisdiction; and
- (b) not in a Regulation State within the meaning of Section III of this Part.

(1A) The High Court may order the issue of a letter of request to the judicial authorities of the country in which the proposed deponent is.]

(2) A letter of request is a request to a judicial authority to take the evidence of that person, or arrange for it to be taken.

(3) The High Court may make an order under this rule in relation to county court proceedings.

(4) If the government of [a] country … allows a person appointed by the High Court to examine a person in that country, the High Court may make an order appointing a special examiner for that purpose.

(5) A person may be examined under this rule on oath or affirmation or in accordance with any procedure permitted in the country in which the examination is to take place.

(6) If the High Court makes an order for the issue of a letter of request, the party who sought the order must file—
- (a) the following documents and, except where paragraph (7) applies, a translation of them—

(i) a draft letter of request;
(ii) a statement of the issues relevant to the proceedings;
(iii) a list of questions or the subject matter of questions to be put to the person to be examined; and

(b) an undertaking to be responsible for the Secretary of State's expenses.

(7) There is no need to file a translation if—

(a) English is one of the official languages of the country where the examination is to take place; or

(b) a practice direction has specified that country as a country where no translation is necessary.

[1439]

NOTES

Paras (1), (1A): substituted for para (1) as originally enacted by the Civil Procedure (Amendment No 4) Rules 2003, SI 2003/2113, r 7.

Para (4): word in square brackets substituted and word omitted repealed by the Civil Procedure (Amendment) Rules 1999, SI 1999/1008, r 11(a).

[34.13A Letter of request—Proceeds of Crime Act 2002

(1) This rule applies where a party to existing or contemplated proceedings in—

(a) the High Court; or

(b) a magistrates' court,

under Part 5 of the Proceeds of Crime Act 2002 (civil recovery of the proceeds etc of unlawful conduct) wishes to take a deposition from a person who is out of the jurisdiction.

(2) The High Court may, on the application of such a party, order the issue of a letter of request to the judicial authorities of the country in which the proposed deponent is.

(3) Paragraphs (4) to (7) of rule 34.13 shall apply irrespective of where the proposed deponent is, and rule 34.23 shall not apply in cases where the proposed deponent is in a Regulation State within the meaning of Section III of this Part.]

[1440]

NOTES

Commencement: 1 February 2004.

Inserted by the Civil Procedure (Amendment No 5) Rules 2003, SI 2003/3361, r 6.

Rules 34.14, 34.15 (*Relate to examiners of the court.*)

[II EVIDENCE FOR FOREIGN COURTS

[34.16 Scope and interpretation

(1) This Section applies to an application for an order under the 1975 Act for evidence to be obtained, other than an application made as a result of a request by a court in [another Regulation State].

(2) In this Section—

(a) "the 1975 Act" means the Evidence (Proceedings in Other Jurisdictions) Act 1975; and

(b) "Regulation State" has the same meaning as in Section III of this Part.]

[1441]

NOTES

Commencement: 1 January 2004.

Section II (rr 34.16–34.21) added by the Civil Procedure (Amendment) Rules 2002, SI 2002/2058, r 12(d)(ii), Sch 2, Pt II.

Substituted by the Civil Procedure (Amendment No 4) Rules 2003, SI 2003/2113, r 8.

Para (1): words in square brackets substituted by the Civil Procedure (Amendment) Rules 2004, SI 2004/1306, r 6.

[34.17 Application for order

An application for an order under the 1975 Act for evidence to be obtained—

(a) must be—
  (i) made to the High Court;
  (ii) supported by written evidence; and
  (iii) accompanied by the request as a result of which the application is made, and where appropriate, a translation of the request into English; and
(b) may be made without notice.]

[1442]

NOTES

Commencement: 2 December 2002.
Added as noted to r 34.16 at **[1441]**.

[34.18 Examination

(1) The court may order an examination to be taken before—
  (a) any fit and proper person nominated by the person applying for the order;
  (b) an examiner of the court; or
  (c) any other person whom the court considers suitable.

(2) Unless the court orders otherwise—
  (a) the examination will be taken as provided by rule 34.9; and
  (b) rule 34.10 applies.

(3) The court may make an order under rule 34.14 for payment of the fees and expenses of the examination.]

[1443]

NOTES

Commencement: 2 December 2002.
Added as noted to r 34.16 at **[1441]**.

[34.19 Dealing with deposition

(1) The examiner must send the deposition of the witness to the Senior Master unless the court orders otherwise.

(2) The Senior Master will—
  (a) give a certificate sealed with the seal of the Supreme Court for use out of the jurisdiction identifying the following documents—
    (i) the request;
    (ii) the order of the court for examination; and
    (iii) the deposition of the witness; and
  (b) send the certificate and the documents referred to in paragraph (a) to—
    (i) the Secretary of State; or
    (ii) where the request was sent to the Senior Master by another person in accordance with a Civil Procedure Convention, to that other person,

for transmission to the court or tribunal requesting the examination.]

[1444]

NOTES

Commencement: 2 December 2002.
Added as noted to r 34.16 at **[1441]**.

[34.20 Claim to privilege

(1) This rule applies where—
  (a) a witness claims to be exempt from giving evidence on the ground specified in section 3(1)(b) of the 1975 Act; and
  (b) that claim is not supported or conceded as referred to in section 3(2) of that Act.

(2) The examiner may require the witness to give the evidence which he claims to be exempt from giving.

(3) Where the examiner does not require the witness to give that evidence, the court may order the witness to do so.

(4) An application for an order under paragraph (3) may be made by the person who obtained the order under section 2 of the 1975 Act.

(5) Where such evidence is taken—
- (a) it must be contained in a document separate from the remainder of the deposition;
- (b) the examiner will send to the Senior Master—
  - (i) the deposition; and
  - (ii) a signed statement setting out the claim to be exempt and the ground on which it was made.

(6) On receipt of the statement referred to in paragraph (5)(b)(ii), the Senior Master will—
- (a) retain the document containing the part of the witness's evidence to which the claim to be exempt relates; and
- (b) send the statement and a request to determine that claim to the foreign court or tribunal together with the documents referred to in rule 34.17.

(7) The Senior Master will—
- (a) if the claim to be exempt is rejected by the foreign court or tribunal, send the document referred to in paragraph (5)(a) to that court or tribunal;
- (b) if the claim is upheld, send the document to the witness; and
- (c) in either case, notify the witness and person who obtained the order under section 2 of the foreign court or tribunal's decision.]

[1445]

NOTES

Commencement: 2 December 2002.
Added as noted to r 34.16 at **[1441]**.

[34.21 Order under 1975 Act as applied by Patents Act 1977

Where an order is made for the examination of witnesses under section 1 of the 1975 Act as applied by section 92 of the Patents Act 1977 the court may permit an officer of the European Patent Office to—
- (a) attend the examination and examine the witnesses; or
- (b) request the court or the examiner before whom the examination takes place to put specified questions to them.]

[1446]

NOTES

Commencement: 2 December 2002.
Added as noted to r 34.16 at **[1441]**.

[III TAKING OF EVIDENCE—MEMBER STATES OF THE EUROPEAN UNION

34.22 Interpretation

In this Section—
- (a) "designated court" has the meaning given in the relevant practice direction;
- (b) "Regulation State" has the same meaning as "Member State" in the Taking of Evidence Regulation, that is all Member States except Denmark;
- (c) "the Taking of Evidence Regulation" means Council Regulation (EC) No 1206/2001 of 28 May 2001 on co-operation between the courts of the Member States in the taking of evidence in civil and commercial matters.

(The Taking of Evidence Regulation is annexed to the relevant practice direction)]

[1447]

NOTES

Commencement: 1 January 2004.
Section III (rr 34.22–34.24) added by the Civil Procedure (Amendment No 4) Rules 2003, SI 2003/2113, r 9, Sch 1, Pt II.

[34.23 Where a person to be examined is in another Regulation State

(1) [Subject to rule 34.13A, this] rule applies where a party wishes to take a deposition from a person [who is in another Regulation State].

(2) The court may order the issue of a request to a designated court ("the requested court") in the Regulation State in which the proposed deponent is.

(3) If the court makes an order for the issue of a request, the party who sought the order must file—

(a) a draft Form A as set out in the annex to the Taking of Evidence Regulation (request for the taking of evidence);

(b) except where paragraph (4) applies, a translation of the form;

(c) an undertaking to be responsible for costs sought by the requested court in relation to—

(i) fees paid to experts and interpreters; and

(ii) where requested by that party, the use of special procedures or communications technology; and

(d) an undertaking to be responsible for the court's expenses.

(4) There is no need to file a translation if—

(a) English is one of the official languages of the Regulation State where the examination is to take place; or

(b) the Regulation State has indicated, in accordance with the Taking of Evidence Regulation, that English is a language which it will accept.

(5) Where article 17 of the Taking of Evidence Regulation (direct taking of evidence by the requested court) allows evidence to be taken directly in another Regulation State, the court may make an order for the submission of a request in accordance with that article.

(6) If the court makes an order for the submission of a request under paragraph (5), the party who sought the order must file—

(a) a draft Form I as set out in the annex to the Taking of Evidence Regulation (request for direct taking of evidence);

(b) except where paragraph (4) applies, a translation of the form; and

(c) an undertaking to be responsible for the court's expenses.]

[1448]

NOTES

Commencement: 1 January 2004.

Added as noted to r 34.22 at **[1447]**.

Para (1): words in first pair of square brackets substituted by the Civil Procedure (Amendment No 5) Rules 2003, SI 2003/3361, r 7; words in second pair of square brackets substituted by the Civil Procedure (Amendment) Rules 2004, SI 2004/1306, r 7.

[34.24 Evidence for courts of other Regulation States

(1) This rule applies where a court in another Regulation State ("the requesting court") issues a request for evidence to be taken from a person who is in the jurisdiction.

(2) An application for an order for evidence to be taken—

(a) must be made to a designated court;

(b) must be accompanied by—

(i) the form of request for the taking of evidence as a result of which the application is made; and

(ii) where appropriate, a translation of the form of request; and

(c) may be made without notice.

(3) Rule 34.18(1) and (2) apply.

(4) The examiner must send—

(a) the deposition to the court for transmission to the requesting court; and

(b) a copy of the deposition to the person who obtained the order for evidence to be taken.]

[1449]

NOTES

Commencement: 1 January 2004.

Added as noted to r 34.22 at **[1447]**.

Parts 35–39 (*Pt 35 relates to experts and assessors; Pt 36 to offers to settle and payments into court; Pt 37 to miscellaneous provisions about payments into court; Pt 38 to discontinuance; Pt 39 to miscellaneous provisions relating to hearings.*)

PART 40
[JUDGMENTS, ORDERS, SALE OF LAND, ETC]

NOTES

Title: substituted by the Civil Procedure (Amendment) Rules 2000, SI 2000/221, r 18(1).

[I JUDGMENT AND ORDERS]

NOTES

Section heading: inserted by the Civil Procedure (Amendment) Rules 2000, SI 2000/221, r 18(2).

40.1–40.9 (*Relate to miscellaneous matters regarding judgment and Orders.*)

40.10 Judgment against a State in default of acknowledgment of service

(1) Where the claimant obtains default judgment under Part 12 on a claim against a State where the defendant has failed to file an acknowledgment of service, the judgment does not take effect until 2 months after service on the State of—

(a) a copy of the judgment; and

(b) a copy of the evidence in support of the application for permission to enter default judgment (unless the evidence has already been served on the State in accordance with an order made under Part 12).

(2) In this rule, "State" has the meaning given by section 14 of the State Immunity Act 1978.

[1450]

40.11–40.19 (*Rr 40.11–40.14 relate to miscellaneous matters regarding judgment and orders; Section II (rr 40.15–40.19) relate to miscellaneous matters regarding sale of land and conveyancing counsel.*)

[III DECLARATORY JUDGMENTS

40.20 The court may make binding declarations whether or not any other remedy is claimed.]

[1451]

NOTES

Commencement: 26 March 2001.
Section III (r 40.20) added by the Civil Procedure (Amendment) Rules 2001, SI 2001/256, r 13.

Parts 41–57 (*Pt 41 relates to provisional damages; Pt 42 to change of solicitor; Pt 43 to the scope of costs rules and definitions; Pt 44 to general rules about costs; Pt 45 to fixed costs; Pt 46 to fast track trials costs; Pt 47 to the procedure for detailed assessment of costs and default provisions; Pt 48 to costs—special cases; Pt 49 to specialist proceedings; Pt 50 to application of the schedules; Pt 51 to transitional arrangements; Pt 52 to appeals; Pt 53 to defamation claims; Pt 54 to judicial review; Pt 55 to possession claims; Pt 56 to landlord and tenant claims and miscellaneous provisions about land; Pt 57 to probate and inheritance.*)

PART 58
COMMERCIAL COURT

NOTES

Practice Direction—Commercial Court; see para **[1561]**.

[58.1 Scope of this Part and interpretation

(1) This Part applies to claims in the Commercial Court of the Queen's Bench Division.

(2) In this Part and its practice direction, "commercial claim" means any claim arising out of the transaction of trade and commerce and includes any claim relating to—

(a) a business document or contract;
(b) the export or import of goods;
(c) the carriage of goods by land, sea, air or pipeline;
(d) the exploitation of oil and gas reserves or other natural resources;
(e) insurance and re-insurance;
(f) banking and financial services;
(g) the operation of markets and exchanges;
(h) the purchase and sale of commodities;
(i) the construction of ships;
(j) business agency; and
(k) arbitration.]

[1452]

NOTES

Commencement: 25 March 2002.

Part 58 (rr 58.1–58.15) added by the Civil Procedure (Amendment No 5) Rules 2001, SI 2001/4015, r 29(a), Sch 2.

[58.2 Specialist list

(1) The commercial list is a specialist list for claims proceeding in the Commercial Court.

(2) One of the judges of the Commercial Court shall be in charge of the commercial list.]

[1453]

NOTES

Commencement: 25 March 2002.

Added as noted to r 58.1 at **[1452]**.

[58.3 Application of the Civil Procedure Rules

These Rules and their practice directions apply to claims in the commercial list unless this Part or a practice direction provides otherwise.]

[1454]

NOTES

Commencement: 25 March 2002.

Added as noted to r 58.1 at **[1452]**.

[58.4 Proceedings in the commercial list

(1) A commercial claim may be started in the commercial list.

(2) [Rule 30.5 applies] to claims in the commercial list, except that a Commercial Court judge may order a claim to be transferred to any other specialist list.

(Rule 30.5(3) provides that an application for the transfer of proceedings to or from a specialist list must be made to a judge dealing with claims in that list)]

[1455]

NOTES

Commencement: 25 March 2002.

Added as noted to r 58.1 at **[1452]**.

Para (2): words in square brackets substituted by the Civil Procedure (Amendment No 4) Rules 2005, SI 2005/3515, r 14.

[58.5 Claim form and particulars of claim

(1) If, in a Part 7 claim, particulars of claim are not contained in or served with the claim form—

(a) the claim form must state that, if an acknowledgment of service is filed which indicates an intention to defend the claim, particulars of claim will follow;
(b) when the claim form is served, it must be accompanied by the documents specified in rule 7.8(1);

(c) the claimant must serve particulars of claim within 28 days of the filing of an acknowledgment of service which indicates an intention to defend; and

(d) rule 7.4(2) does not apply.

(2) A statement of value is not required to be included in the claim form.

(3) If the claimant is claiming interest, he must—

(a) include a statement to that effect; and

(b) give the details set out in rule 16.4(2),

in both the claim form and the particulars of claim.]

[1456]

NOTES

Commencement: 25 March 2002.
Added as noted to r 58.1 at **[1452]**.

[58.6 Acknowledgment of service

(1) A defendant must file an acknowledgment of service in every case.

(2) Unless paragraph (3) applies, the period for filing an acknowledgment of service is 14 days after service of the claim form.

(3) Where the claim form is served out of the jurisdiction, or on the agent of a defendant who is overseas, the time periods provided by rules 6.16(4), 6.21(4) and 6.22 apply after service of the claim form.]

[1457]

NOTES

Commencement: 25 March 2002.
Added as noted to r 58.1 at **[1452]**.

[58.7 Disputing the court's jurisdiction

(1) Part 11 applies to claims in the commercial list with the modifications set out in this rule.

(2) An application under rule 11(1) must be made within 28 days after filing an acknowledgment of service.

(3) If the defendant files an acknowledgment of service indicating an intention to dispute the court's jurisdiction, the claimant need not serve particulars of claim before the hearing of the application.]

[1458]

NOTES

Commencement: 25 March 2002.
Added as noted to r 58.1 at **[1452]**.

[58.8 Default judgment

(1) If, in a Part 7 claim in the commercial list, a defendant fails to file an acknowledgment of service, the claimant need not serve particulars of claim before he may obtain or apply for default judgment in accordance with Part 12.

(2) Rule 12.6(1) applies with the modification that paragraph (a) shall be read as if it referred to the claim form instead of the particulars of claim.]

[1459]

NOTES

Commencement: 25 March 2002.
Added as noted to r 58.1 at **[1452]**.

[58.9 Admissions

(1) Rule 14.5 does not apply to claims in the commercial list.

(2) If the defendant admits part of a claim for a specified amount of money, the claimant may apply under rule 14.3 for judgment on the admission.

(3) Rule 14.14(1) applies with the modification that paragraph (a) shall be read as if it referred to the claim form instead of the particulars of claim.]

[1460]

NOTES

Commencement: 25 March 2002.
Added as noted to r 58.1 at **[1452]**.

[58.10 Defence and Reply

(1) Part 15 (defence and reply) applies to claims in the commercial list with the modification to rule 15.8 that the claimant must—

(a) file any reply to a defence; and
(b) serve it on all other parties,

within 21 days after service of the defence.

(2) Rule 6.23 (period for filing a defence where the claim form is served out of the jurisdiction) applies to claims in the commercial list, except that if the particulars of claim are served after the defendant has filed an acknowledgment of service the period for filing a defence is 28 days from service of the particulars of claim.]

[1461]

NOTES

Commencement: 25 March 2002.
Added as noted to r 58.1 at **[1452]**.

[58.11 Statements of case

The court may at any time before or after the issue of the claim form order a claim in the commercial list to proceed without the filing or service of statements of case.]

[1462]

NOTES

Commencement: 25 March 2002.
Added as noted to r 58.1 at **[1452]**.

[58.12 Part 8 claims

Part 8 applies to claims in the commercial list, with the modification that a defendant to a Part 8 claim who wishes to rely on written evidence must file and serve it within 28 days after filing an acknowledgment of service.]

[1463]

NOTES

Commencement: 25 March 2002.
Added as noted to r 58.1 at **[1452]**.

[58.13 Case management

(1) All proceedings in the commercial list are treated as being allocated to the multi-track and Part 26 does not apply.

(2) The following parts only of Part 29 apply—

(a) rule 29.3(2) (legal representative to attend case management conferences and pre-trial reviews);
(b) rule 29.5 (variation of case management timetable) with the exception of rule 29.5(1)(c).

(3) As soon as practicable the court will hold a case management conference which must be fixed in accordance with the practice direction.

(4) At the case management conference or at any hearing at which the parties are represented the court may give such directions for the management of the case as it considers appropriate.]

[1464]

NOTES

Commencement: 25 March 2002.
Added as noted to r 58.1 at **[1452]**.

[58.14 Disclosure—ships papers

(1) If, in proceedings relating to a marine insurance policy, the underwriters apply for specific disclosure under rule 31.12, the court may—

(a) order a party to produce all the ships papers; and
(b) require that party to use his best endeavours to obtain and disclose documents which are not or have not been in his control.

(2) An order under this rule may be made at any stage of the proceedings and on such terms, if any, as to staying the proceedings or otherwise, as the court thinks fit.]

[1465]

NOTES

Commencement: 25 March 2002.
Added as noted to r 58.1 at **[1452]**.

[58.15 Judgments and orders

(1) Except for orders made by the court on its own initiative and unless the court orders otherwise, every judgment or order will be drawn up by the parties, and rule 40.3 is modified accordingly.

(2) An application for a consent order must include a draft of the proposed order signed on behalf of all the parties to whom it relates.

(3) Rule 40.6 (consent judgments and orders) does not apply.]

[1466]

NOTES

Commencement: 25 March 2002.
Added as noted to r 58.1 at **[1452]**.

[PART 59
MERCANTILE COURTS

NOTES

Practice Direction—Mercantile Courts; see para **[1562]**.

59.1 Scope of this Part and interpretation

(1) This Part applies to claims in Mercantile Courts.

(2) A claim may only be started in a Mercantile Court if it—

(a) relates to a commercial or business matter in a broad sense; and
(b) is not required to proceed in the Chancery Division or in another specialist list.

(3) In this Part and its practice direction—

(a) "Mercantile Court" means a specialist list established within—
  (i) the district registries listed in the practice direction; and
  (ii) the Central London County Court,

to hear mercantile claims;

(b) "mercantile claim" means a claim proceeding in a Mercantile Court; and
(c) "Mercantile judge" means a judge authorised to sit in a Mercantile Court.]

[1467]

NOTES

Commencement: 25 March 2002.

Part 59 (rr 59.1–59.12) added by the Civil Procedure (Amendment No 5) Rules 2001, SI 2001/4015, r 29(b), Sch 3.

[59.2 Application of the Civil Procedure Rules

These Rules and their practice directions apply to mercantile claims unless this Part or a practice direction provides otherwise.]

[1468]

NOTES

Commencement: 25 March 2002.

Added as noted to r 59.1 at **[1467]**.

[59.3 Transfer of proceedings

[Rule 30.5 applies] with the modifications that—

(a) a Mercantile judge may transfer a mercantile claim to another Mercantile Court; and

(b) a Commercial Court judge may transfer a claim from the Commercial Court to a Mercantile Court.

(Rule 30.5(3) provides that an application for the transfer of proceedings to or from a specialist list must be made to a judge dealing with claims in that list)]

[1469]

NOTES

Commencement: 25 March 2002.

Added as noted to r 59.1 at **[1467]**.

Words in square brackets substituted by the Civil Procedure (Amendment No 4) Rules 2005, SI 2005/3515, r 15.

[59.4 Claim form and particulars of claim

(1) If particulars of claim are not contained in or served with the claim form—

(a) the claim form must state that, if an acknowledgment of service is filed which indicates an intention to defend the claim, particulars of claim will follow;

(b) when the claim form is served, it must be accompanied by the documents specified in rule 7.8(1);

(c) the claimant must serve particulars of claim within 28 days of the filing of an acknowledgment of service which indicates an intention to defend; and

(d) rule 7.4(2) does not apply.

(2) If the claimant is claiming interest, he must—

(a) include a statement to that effect; and

(b) give the details set out in rule 16.4(2),

in both the claim form and the particulars of claim.

(3) Rules 12.6(1)(a) and 14.14(1)(a) apply with the modification that references to the particulars of claim shall be read as if they referred to the claim form.]

[1470]

NOTES

Commencement: 25 March 2002.

Added as noted to r 59.1 at **[1467]**.

[59.5 Acknowledgment of service

(1) A defendant must file an acknowledgment of service in every case.

(2) Unless paragraph (3) applies, the period for filing an acknowledgment of service is 14 days after service of the claim form.

(3) Where the claim form is served out of the jurisdiction, or on the agent of a defendant who is overseas, the time periods provided by rules 6.16(4), 6.21(4) and 6.22 apply after service of the claim form.]

[1471]

NOTES

Commencement: 25 March 2002.
Added as noted to r 59.1 at **[1467]**.

[59.6 Disputing the court's jurisdiction

(1) Part 11 applies to mercantile claims with the modifications set out in this rule.

(2) An application under rule 11(1) must be made within 28 days after filing an acknowledgment of service.

(3) If the defendant files an acknowledgment of service indicating an intention to dispute the court's jurisdiction, the claimant need not serve particulars of claim before the hearing of the application.]

[1472]

NOTES

Commencement: 25 March 2002.
Added as noted to r 59.1 at **[1467]**.

[59.7 Default judgment

(1) Part 12 applies to mercantile claims, except that rules 12.10 and 12.11 apply as modified by paragraphs (2) and (3) of this rule.

(2) If, in a Part 7 claim—

(a) the claim form has been served but no particulars of claim have been served; and
(b) the defendant has failed to file an acknowledgment of service,

the claimant must make an application if he wishes to obtain a default judgment.

(3) The application may be made without notice, but the court may direct it to be served on the defendant.]

[1473]

NOTES

Commencement: 25 March 2002.
Added as noted to r 59.1 at **[1467]**.

[59.8 Admissions

(1) Rule 14.5 does not apply to mercantile claims.

(2) If the defendant admits part of a claim for a specified amount of money, the claimant may apply under rule 14.3 for judgment on the admission.]

[1474]

NOTES

Commencement: 25 March 2002.
Added as noted to r 59.1 at **[1467]**.

[59.9 Defence and Reply

(1) Part 15 (Defence and Reply) applies to mercantile claims with the modification to rule 15.8 that the claimant must—

(a) file any reply to a defence; and
(b) serve it on all other parties,

within 21 days after service of the defence.

(2) Rule 6.23 (period for filing a defence where the claim form is served out of the jurisdiction) applies to mercantile claims, except that if the particulars of claim are served

after the defendant has filed an acknowledgment of service the period for filing a defence is 28 days from service of the particulars of claim.]

[1475]

NOTES

Commencement: 25 March 2002.
Added as noted to r 59.1 at **[1467]**.

[59.10 Statements of case

The court may at any time before or after issue of the claim form order a mercantile claim to proceed without the filing or service of statements of case.]

[1476]

NOTES

Commencement: 25 March 2002.
Added as noted to r 59.1 at **[1467]**.

[59.11 Case management

(1) All mercantile claims are treated as being allocated to the multi-track, and Part 26 does not apply.

(2) The following parts only of Part 29 apply—

(a) rule 29.3(2) (appropriate legal representative to attend case management conferences and pre-trial reviews); and

(b) rule 29.5 (variation of case management timetable) with the exception of rule 29.5(1)(c).

(3) As soon as practicable the court will hold a case management conference which must be fixed in accordance with the practice direction.

(4) At the case management conference or at any hearing at which the parties are represented the court may give such directions for the management of the case as it considers appropriate.]

[1477]

NOTES

Commencement: 25 March 2002.
Added as noted to r 59.1 at **[1467]**.

[59.12 Judgments and orders

(1) Except for orders made by the court of its own initiative and unless the court otherwise orders every judgment or order will be drawn up by the parties, and rule 40.3 is modified accordingly.

(2) An application for a consent order must include a draft of the proposed order signed on behalf of all the parties to whom it relates.

(3) Rule 40.6 (consent judgments and orders) does not apply.]

[1478]

NOTES

Commencement: 25 March 2002.
Added as noted to r 59.1 at **[1467]**.

Part 60 (*Relates to Technology and Construction Court claims.*)

[PART 61
ADMIRALTY CLAIMS

NOTES

Practice Direction—Admiralty Claims.

61.1 Scope and interpretation

(1) This Part applies to admiralty claims.

(2) In this Part—
- (a) "admiralty claim" means a claim within the Admiralty jurisdiction of the High Court as set out in section 20 of the *Supreme Court Act 1981*;
- (b) "the Admiralty Court" means the Admiralty Court of the Queen's Bench Division of the High Court of Justice;
- (c) "claim in rem" means a claim in an admiralty action in rem;
- (d) "collision claim" means a claim within section 20(3)(b) of the *Supreme Court Act 1981*;
- (e) "limitation claim" means a claim under the Merchant Shipping Act 1995 for the limitation of liability in connection with a ship or other property;
- (f) "salvage claim" means a claim—
  - (i) for or in the nature of salvage;
  - (ii) for special compensation under Article 14 of Schedule 11 to the Merchant Shipping Act 1995;
  - (iii) for the apportionment of salvage; and
  - (iv) arising out of or connected with any contract for salvage services;
- (g) "caution against arrest" means a caution entered in the Register under rule 61.7;
- (h) "caution against release" means a caution entered in the Register under rule 61.8;
- (i) "the Register" means the Register of cautions against arrest and release which is open to inspection as provided by the practice direction;
- (j) "the Marshal" means the Admiralty Marshal;
- (k) "ship" includes any vessel used in navigation; and
- (l) "the Registrar" means the Queen's Bench Master with responsibility for Admiralty claims.

(3) Part 58 (Commercial Court) applies to claims in the Admiralty Court except where this Part provides otherwise.

(4) The Registrar has all the powers of the Admiralty judge except where a rule or practice direction provides otherwise.]

[1479]

NOTES

Commencement: 25 March 2002.

Part 61 (rr 61.1–61.13) added by the Civil Procedure (Amendment No 5) Rules 2001, SI 2001/4015, r 29(c), Sch 4.

Para (2): words in italics in sub-paras (a), (d) substituted by the words "Senior Courts Act 1981" by the Constitutional Reform Act 2005, s 59(5), Sch 11, Pt 1, para 1(2), as from a day to be appointed.

[61.2 Admiralty claims

(1) The following claims must be started in the Admiralty Court—
- (a) a claim—
  - (i) in rem;
  - (ii) for damage done by a ship;
  - (iii) concerning the ownership of a ship;
  - (iv) under the Merchant Shipping Act 1995;
  - (v) for loss of life or personal injury specified in section 20(2)(f) of the *Supreme Court Act 1981*;
  - (vi) by a master or member of a crew for wages;
  - (vii) in the nature of towage; or
  - (viii) in the nature of pilotage;
- (b) a collision claim;
- (c) a limitation claim; or
- (d) a salvage claim.

(2) Any other admiralty claim may be started in the Admiralty Court.

(3) Rule [30.5] applies to claims in the Admiralty Court except that the Admiralty Court may order the transfer of a claim to—
- (a) the Commercial list;
- (b) a Mercantile Court;
- (c) the Mercantile list at the Central London County Court; or

(d) any other appropriate court.]

[1480]

NOTES

Commencement: 25 March 2002.

Added as noted to r 61.1 at **[1479]**.

Para (1): words in italics in sub-para (a)(v) substituted by the words "Senior Courts Act 1981" by the Constitutional Reform Act 2005, s 59(5), Sch 11, Pt 1, para 1(2), as from a day to be appointed.

Para (3): number in square brackets substituted by the Civil Procedure (Amendment No 4) Rules 2005, SI 2005/3515, r 16.

[61.3 Claims in rem

(1) This rule applies to claims in rem.

(2) A claim in rem is started by the issue of an in rem claim form as set out in the practice direction.

(3) Subject to rule 61.4, the particulars of claim must—

(a) be contained in or served with the claim form; or

(b) be served on the defendant by the claimant within 75 days after service of the claim form.

(4) An acknowledgment of service must be filed within 14 days after service of the claim form.

(5) The claim form must be served—

(a) in accordance with the practice direction; and

(b) within 12 months after the date of issue and rules 7.5 and 7.6 are modified accordingly.

(6) If a claim form has been issued (whether served or not), any person who wishes to defend the claim may file an acknowledgment of service.]

[1481]

NOTES

Commencement: 25 March 2002.

Added as noted to r 61.1 at **[1479]**.

[61.4 Special provisions relating to collision claims

(1) This rule applies to collision claims.

(2) A claim form need not contain or be followed by particulars of claim and rule 7.4 does not apply.

(3) An acknowledgment of service must be filed.

(4) A party who wishes to dispute the court's jurisdiction must make an application under Part 11 within 2 months after filing his acknowledgment of service.

(5) Every party must—

(a) within 2 months after the defendant files the acknowledgment of service; or

(b) where the defendant applies under Part 11, within 2 months after the defendant files the further acknowledgment of service,

file at the court a completed collision statement of case in the form specified in the practice direction.

(6) A collision statement of case must be—

(a) in the form set out in the practice direction; and

(b) verified by a statement of truth.

(7) A claim form in a collision claim may not be served out of the jurisdiction unless—

(a) the case falls within section 22(2)(a), (b) or (c) of the *Supreme Court Act 1981*; or

(b) the defendant has submitted to or agreed to submit to the jurisdiction; and the court gives permission in accordance with Section III of Part 6.

(8) Where permission to serve a claim form out of the jurisdiction is given, the court will specify the period within which the defendant may file an acknowledgment of service and, where appropriate, a collision statement of case.

(9) Where, in a collision claim in rem ("the original claim")—

(a)

(i) a Part 20 claim; or

(ii) a cross claim in rem

arising out of the same collision or occurrence is made; and

(b)

(i) the party bringing the original claim has caused the arrest of a ship or has obtained security in order to prevent such arrest; and

(ii) the party bringing the Part 20 claim or cross claim is unable to arrest a ship or otherwise obtain security,

the party bringing the Part 20 claim or cross claim may apply to the court to stay the original claim until sufficient security is given to satisfy any judgment that may be given in favour of that party.

(10) The consequences set out in paragraph (11) apply where a party to a claim to establish liability for a collision claim (other than a claim for loss of life or personal injury)—

(a) makes an offer to settle in the form set out in paragraph (12) not less than 21 days before the start of the trial;

(b) that offer is not accepted; and

(c) the maker of the offer obtains at trial an apportionment equal to or more favourable than his offer.

(11) Where paragraph (10) applies the parties will, unless the court considers it unjust, be entitled to the following costs—

(a) the maker of the offer will be entitled to—

(i) all his costs from 21 days after the offer was made; and

(ii) his costs before then in the percentage to which he would have been entitled had the offer been accepted; and

(b) all other parties to whom the offer was made—

(i) will be entitled to their costs up to 21 days after the offer was made in the percentage to which they would have been entitled had the offer been accepted; but

(ii) will not be entitled to their costs thereafter.

(12) An offer under paragraph (10) must be in writing and must contain—

(a) an offer to settle liability at stated percentages;

(b) an offer to pay costs in accordance with the same percentages;

(c) a term that the offer remain open for 21 days after the date it is made; and

(d) a term that, unless the court orders otherwise, on expiry of that period the offer remains open on the same terms except that the offeree should pay all the costs from that date until acceptance.]

[1482]

NOTES

Commencement: 25 March 2002.

Added as noted to r 61.1 at **[1479]**.

Para (7): words in italics in sub-para (a) substituted by the words "Senior Courts Act 1981" by the Constitutional Reform Act 2005, s 59(5), Sch 11, Pt 1, para 1(2), as from a day to be appointed.

[61.5 Arrest

(1) In a claim in rem—

(a) a claimant; and

(b) a judgment creditor

may apply to have the property proceeded against arrested.

(2) The practice direction sets out the procedure for applying for arrest.

(3) A party making an application for arrest must—

(a) request a search to be made in the Register before the warrant is issued to determine whether there is a caution against arrest in force with respect to that property; and

(b) file a declaration in the form set out in the practice direction.

PART II CIVIL PROCEDURE RULES

(4) A warrant of arrest may not be issued as of right in the case of property in respect of which the beneficial ownership, as a result of a sale or disposal by any court in any jurisdiction exercising admiralty jurisdiction in rem, has changed since the claim form was issued.

(5) A warrant of arrest may not be issued against a ship owned by a State where by any convention or treaty, the United Kingdom has undertaken to minimise the possibility of arrest of ships of that State until—

(a) notice in the form set out in the practice direction has been served on a consular officer at the consular office of that State in London or the port at which it is intended to arrest the ship; and

(b) a copy of that notice is attached to any declaration under paragraph (3)(b).

(6) Except—

(a) with the permission of the court; or

(b) where notice has been given under paragraph (5),

a warrant of arrest may not be issued in a claim in rem against a foreign ship belonging to a port of a State in respect of which an order in council has been made under section 4 of the Consular Relations Act 1968, until the expiration of 2 weeks from appropriate notice to the consul.

(7) A warrant of arrest is valid for 12 months but may only be executed if the claim form—

(a) has been served; or

(b) remains valid for service at the date of execution.

(8) Property may only be arrested by the Marshal or his substitute.

(9) Property under arrest—

(a) may not be moved unless the court orders otherwise; and

(b) may be immobilised or prevented from sailing in such manner as the Marshal may consider appropriate.

(10) Where an in rem claim form has been issued and security sought, any person who has filed an acknowledgment of service may apply for an order specifying the amount and form of security to be provided.]

[1483]

NOTES

Commencement: 25 March 2002.
Added as noted to r 61.1 at **[1479]**.

[61.6 Security in claim in rem

(1) This rule applies if, in a claim in rem, security has been given to—

(a) obtain the release of property under arrest; or

(b) prevent the arrest of property.

(2) The court may order that the—

(a) amount of security be reduced and may stay the claim until the order is complied with; or

(b) claimant may arrest or re-arrest the property proceeded against to obtain further security.

(3) The court may not make an order under paragraph (2)(b) if the total security to be provided would exceed the value of the property at the time—

(a) of the original arrest; or

(b) security was first given (if the property was not arrested).]

[1484]

NOTES

Commencement: 25 March 2002.
Added as noted to r 61.1 at **[1479]**.

[61.7 Cautions against arrest

(1) Any person may file a request for a caution against arrest.

(2) When a request under paragraph (1) is filed the court will enter the caution in the Register if the request is in the form set out in the practice direction and—

(a) the person filing the request undertakes—

(i) to file an acknowledgment of service; and

(ii) to give sufficient security to satisfy the claim with interest and costs; or

(b) where the person filing the request has constituted a limitation fund in accordance with Article 11 of the Convention on Limitation of Liability for Maritime Claims 1976 he—

(i) states that such a fund has been constituted; and

(ii) undertakes that the claimant will acknowledge service of the claim form by which any claim may be begun against the property described in the request.

(3) A caution against arrest—

(a) is valid for 12 months after the date it is entered in the Register; but

(b) may be renewed for a further 12 months by filing a further request.

(4) Paragraphs (1) and (2) apply to a further request under paragraph (3)(b).

(5) Property may be arrested if a caution against arrest has been entered in the Register but the court may order that—

(a) the arrest be discharged; and

(b) the party procuring the arrest pays compensation to the owner of or other persons interested in the arrested property.]

[1485]

NOTES

Commencement: 25 March 2002.
Added as noted to r 61.1 at **[1479]**.

[61.8 Release and cautions against release

(1) Where property is under arrest—

(a) an in rem claim form may be served upon it; and

(b) it may be arrested by any other person claiming to have an in rem claim against it.

(2) Any person who—

(a) claims to have an in rem right against any property under arrest; and

(b) wishes to be given notice of any application in respect of that property or its proceeds of sale,

may file a request for a caution against release in the form set out in the practice direction.

(3) When a request under paragraph (2) is filed, a caution against release will be entered in the Register.

(4) Property will be released from arrest if—

(a) it is sold by the court;

(b) the court orders release on an application made by any party;

(c)

(i) the arresting party; and

(ii) all persons who have entered cautions against release

file a request for release in the form set out in the practice direction; or

(d) any party files—

(i) a request for release in the form set out in the practice direction (containing an undertaking); and

(ii) consents to the release of the arresting party and all persons who have entered cautions against release.

(5) Where the release of any property is delayed by the entry of a caution against release under this rule any person who has an interest in the property may apply for an order that the person who entered the caution pay damages for losses suffered by the applicant because of the delay.

(6) The court may not make an order under paragraph (5) if satisfied that there was good reason to—

(a) request the entry of; and

(b) maintain

PART II CIVIL PROCEDURE RULES

the caution.

(7) Any person—

(a) interested in property under arrest or in the proceeds of sale of such property; or

(b) whose interests are affected by any order sought or made,

may be made a party to any claim in rem against the property or proceeds of sale.

(8) Where—

(a)

(i) a ship is not under arrest but cargo on board her is; or

(ii) a ship is under arrest but cargo on board her is not; and

(b) persons interested in the ship or cargo wish to discharge the cargo,

they may, without being made parties, request the Marshal to authorise steps to discharge the cargo.

(9) If—

(a) the Marshal considers a request under paragraph (8) reasonable; and

(b) the applicant gives an undertaking in writing acceptable to the Marshal to pay—

(i) his fees; and

(ii) all expenses to be incurred by him or on his behalf

on demand,

the Marshal will apply to the court for an order to permit the discharge of the cargo.

(10) Where persons interested in the ship or cargo are unable or unwilling to give an undertaking as referred to in paragraph (9)(b), they may—

(a) be made parties to the claim; and

(b) apply to the court for an order for—

(i) discharge of the cargo; and

(ii) directions as to the fees and expenses of the Marshal with regard to the discharge and storage of the cargo.]

[1486]

NOTES

Commencement: 25 March 2002.

Added as noted to r 61.1 at **[1479]**.

[61.9 Judgment in default

(1) In a claim in rem (other than a collision claim) the claimant may obtain judgment in default of—

(a) an acknowledgment of service only if—

(i) the defendant has not filed an acknowledgment of service; and

(ii) the time for doing so set out in rule 61.3(4) has expired; and

(b) defence only if—

(i) a defence has not been filed; and

(ii) the relevant time limit for doing so has expired.

(2) In a collision claim, a party who has filed a collision statement of case within the time specified by rule 61.4(5) may obtain judgment in default of a collision statement of case only if—

(a) the party against whom judgment is sought has not filed a collision statement of case; and

(b) the time for doing so set out in rule 61.4(5) has expired.

(3) An application for judgment in default—

(a) under paragraph (1) or paragraph (2) in an in rem claim must be made by filing—

(i) an application notice as set out in the practice direction;

(ii) a certificate proving service of the claim form; and

(iii) evidence proving the claim to the satisfaction of the court; and

(b) under paragraph (2) in any other claim must be made in accordance with Part 12 with any necessary modifications.

(4) An application notice seeking judgment in default and, unless the court orders otherwise, all evidence in support, must be served on all persons who have entered cautions against release on the Register.

(5) The court may set aside or vary any judgment in default entered under this rule.

(6) The claimant may apply to the court for judgment against a party at whose instance a notice against arrest was entered where—
- (a) the claim form has been served on that party;
- (b) the sum claimed in the claim form does not exceed the amount specified in the undertaking given by that party in accordance with rule 61.7(2)(a)(ii); and
- (c) that party has not fulfilled that undertaking within 14 days after service on him of the claim form.]

[1487]

NOTES

Commencement: 25 March 2002.
Added as noted to r 61.1 at **[1479]**.

[61.10 Sale by the court, priorities and payment out

(1) An application for an order for the survey, appraisement or sale of a ship may be made in a claim in rem at any stage by any party.

(2) If the court makes an order for sale, it may—
- (a) set a time within which notice of claims against the proceeds of sale must be filed; and
- (b) the time and manner in which such notice must be advertised.

(3) Any party with a judgment against the property or proceeds of sale may at any time after the time referred to in paragraph (2) apply to the court for the determination of priorities.

(4) An application notice under paragraph (3) must be served on all persons who have filed a claim against the property.

(5) Payment out of the proceeds of sale will be made only to judgment creditors and—
- (a) in accordance with the determination of priorities; or
- (b) as the court orders.]

[1488]

NOTES

Commencement: 25 March 2002.
Added as noted to r 61.1 at **[1479]**.

[61.11 Limitation claims

(1) This rule applies to limitation claims.

(2) A claim is started by the issue of a limitation claim form as set out in the practice direction.

(3) The—
- (a) claimant; and
- (b) at least one defendant

must be named in the claim form, but all other defendants may be described.

(4) The claim form—
- (a) must be served on all named defendants and any other defendant who requests service upon him; and
- (b) may be served on any other defendant.

(5) The claim form may not be served out of the jurisdiction unless—
- (a) the claim falls within section 22(2)(a), (b) or (c) of the *Supreme Court Act 1981*;
- (b) the defendant has submitted to or agreed to submit to the jurisdiction of the court; or
- (c) the Admiralty Court has jurisdiction over the claim under any applicable Convention; and

the court grants permission in accordance with Section III of Part 6.

(6) An acknowledgment of service is not required.

(7) Every defendant upon whom a claim form is served must—
- (a) within 28 days of service file—
  - (i) a defence; or

(ii) a notice that he admits the right of the claimant to limit liability; or

(b) if he wishes to—

(i) dispute the jurisdiction of the court; or

(ii) argue that the court should not exercise its jurisdiction,

file within 14 days of service (or where the claim form is served out of the jurisdiction, within the time specified in rule 6.22) an acknowledgment of service as set out in the practice direction.

(8) If a defendant files an acknowledgment of service under paragraph (7)(b) he will be treated as having accepted that the court has jurisdiction to hear the claim unless he applies under Part 11 within 14 days after filing the acknowledgment of service.

(9) Where one or more named defendants admits the right to limit—

(a) the claimant may apply for a restricted limitation decree in the form set out in the practice direction; and

(b) the court will issue a decree in the form set out in the practice direction limiting liability only against those named defendants who have admitted the claimant's right to limit liability.

(10) A restricted limitation decree—

(a) may be obtained against any named defendant who fails to file a defence within the time specified for doing so; and

(b) need not be advertised, but a copy must be served on the defendants to whom it applies.

(11) Where all the defendants upon whom the claim form has been served admit the claimant's right to limit liability—

(a) the claimant may apply to the Admiralty Registrar for a general limitation decree in the form set out in the practice direction; and

(b) the court will issue a limitation decree.

(12) Where one or more of the defendants upon whom the claim form has been served do not admit the claimant's right to limit, the claimant may apply for a general limitation decree in the form set out in the practice direction.

(13) When a limitation decree is granted the court—

(a) may—

(i) order that any proceedings relating to any claim arising out of the occurrence be stayed;

(ii) order the claimant to establish a limitation fund if one has not been established or make such other arrangements for payment of claims against which liability is limited; or

(iii) if the decree is a restricted limitation decree, distribute the limitation fund; and

(b) will, if the decree is a general limitation decree, give directions as to advertisement of the decree and set a time within which notice of claims against the fund must be filed or an application made to set aside the decree.

(14) When the court grants a general limitation decree the claimant must—

(a) advertise it in such manner and within such time as the court directs; and

(b) file—

(i) a declaration that the decree has been advertised in accordance with paragraph (a); and

(ii) copies of the advertisements.

(15) No later than the time set in the decree for filing claims, each of the defendants who wishes to assert a claim must file and serve his statement of case on—

(a) the limiting party; and

(b) all other defendants except where the court orders otherwise.

(16) Any person other than a defendant upon whom the claim form has been served may apply to the court within the time fixed in the decree to have a general limitation decree set aside.

(17) An application under paragraph (16) must be supported by a declaration—

(a) stating that the applicant has a claim against the claimant arising out of the occurrence; and

(b) setting out grounds for contending that the claimant is not entitled to the decree, either in the amount of limitation or at all.

(18) The claimant may constitute a limitation fund by making a payment into court.

(19) A limitation fund may be established before or after a limitation claim has been started.

(20) If a limitation claim is not commenced within 75 days after the date the fund was established—
- (a) the fund will lapse; and
- (b) all money in court (including interest) will be repaid to the person who made the payment into court.

(21) Money paid into court under paragraph (18) will not be paid out except under an order of the court.

(22) A limitation claim for—
- (a) a restricted decree may be brought by counterclaim; and
- (b) a general decree may only be brought by counterclaim with the permission of the court.]

[1489]

NOTES

Commencement: 25 March 2002.
Added as noted to r 61.1 at **[1479]**.
Para (5): words in italics in sub-para (a) substituted by the words "Senior Courts Act 1981" by the Constitutional Reform Act 2005, s 59(5), Sch 11, Pt 1, para 1(2), as from a day to be appointed.

[61.12 Stay of proceedings

Where the court orders a stay of any claim in rem—
- (a) any property under arrest in the claim remains under arrest; and
- (b) any security representing the property remains in force,

unless the court orders otherwise.]

[1490]

NOTES

Commencement: 25 March 2002.
Added as noted to r 61.1 at **[1479]**.

[61.13 Assessors

The court may sit with assessors when hearing—
- (a) collision claims; or
- (b) other claims involving issues of navigation or seamanship, and

the parties will not be permitted to call expert witnesses unless the court orders otherwise.]

[1491]

NOTES

Commencement: 25 March 2002.
Added as noted to r 61.1 at **[1479]**.

[PART 62
ARBITRATION CLAIMS

NOTES

Practice Direction—Arbitration; see para **[1566]**.

62.1 Scope of this Part and interpretation

(1) This Part contains rules about arbitration claims.

(2) In this Part—
- (a) "the 1950 Act" means the Arbitration Act 1950;
- (b) "the 1975 Act" means the Arbitration Act 1975;
- (c) "the 1979 Act" means the Arbitration Act 1979;

PART II CIVIL PROCEDURE RULES

(d) "the 1996 Act" means the Arbitration Act 1996;
(e) references to—
  (i) the 1996 Act; or
  (ii) any particular section of that Act
include references to that Act or to the particular section of that Act as applied with modifications by the ACAS Arbitration Scheme (England and Wales) Order 2001; and
(f) "arbitration claim form" means a claim form in the form set out in the practice direction.

(3) Part 58 (Commercial Court) applies to arbitration claims in the Commercial Court, Part 59 (Mercantile Court) applies to arbitration claims in the Mercantile Court and Part 60 (Technology and Construction Court claims) applies to arbitration claims in the Technology and Construction Court, except where this Part provides otherwise.]

[1492]

NOTES

Commencement: 25 March 2002.
Part 62 (rr 62.1–62.21) added by the Civil Procedure (Amendment No 5) Rules 2001, SI 2001/4015, r 29(e), Sch 6.

[I CLAIMS UNDER THE 1996 ACT

62.2 Interpretation

(1) In this Section of this Part "arbitration claim" means—
(a) any application to the court under the 1996 Act;
(b) a claim to determine—
  (i) whether there is a valid arbitration agreement;
  (ii) whether an arbitration tribunal is properly constituted; or
what matters have been submitted to arbitration in accordance with an arbitration agreement;
(c) a claim to declare that an award by an arbitral tribunal is not binding on a party; and
(d) any other application affecting—
  (i) arbitration proceedings (whether started or not); or
  (ii) an arbitration agreement.

(2) This Section of this Part does not apply to an arbitration claim to which Sections II or III of this Part apply.]

[1493]

NOTES

Commencement: 25 March 2002.
Added as noted to r 62.1 at **[1492]**.

[62.3 Starting the claim

(1) Except where paragraph (2) applies an arbitration claim must be started by the issue of an arbitration claim form in accordance with the Part 8 procedure.

(2) An application under section 9 of the 1996 Act to stay legal proceedings must be made by application notice to the court dealing with those proceedings.

(3) The courts in which an arbitration claim may be started are set out in the practice direction.

(4) Rule [30.5] applies with the modification that a judge of the Technology and Construction Court may transfer the claim to any other court or specialist list.]

[1494]

NOTES

Commencement: 25 March 2002.
Added as noted to r 62.1 at **[1492]**.
Para (4): number in square brackets substituted by the Civil Procedure (Amendment No 4) Rules 2005, SI 2005/3515, r 17.

[62.4 Arbitration claim form

(1) An arbitration claim form must—

(a) include a concise statement of—

(i) the remedy claimed; and

(ii) any questions on which the claimant seeks the decision of the court;

(b) give details of any arbitration award challenged by the claimant, identifying which part or parts of the award are challenged and specifying the grounds for the challenge;

(c) show that any statutory requirements have been met;

(d) specify under which section of the 1996 Act the claim is made;

(e) identify against which (if any) defendants a costs order is sought; and

(f) specify either—

(i) the persons on whom the arbitration claim form is to be served, stating their role in the arbitration and whether they are defendants; or

(ii) that the claim is made without notice under section 44(3) of the 1996 Act and the grounds relied on.

(2) Unless the court orders otherwise an arbitration claim form must be served on the defendant within 1 month from the date of issue and rules 7.5 and 7.6 are modified accordingly.

(3) Where the claimant applies for an order under section 12 of the 1996 Act (extension of time for beginning arbitral proceedings or other dispute resolution procedures), he may include in his arbitration claim form an alternative application for a declaration that such an order is not needed.]

[1495]

NOTES

Commencement: 25 March 2002.
Added as noted to r 62.1 at **[1492]**.

[62.5 Service out of the jurisdiction

(1) The court may give permission to serve an arbitration claim form out of the jurisdiction if—

(a) the claimant seeks to—

(i) challenge; or

(ii) appeal on a question of law arising out of,

an arbitration award made within the jurisdiction;

(The place where an award is treated as made is determined by section 53 of the 1996 Act.)

(b) the claim is for an order under section 44 of the 1996 Act; or

(c) the claimant—

(i) seeks some other remedy or requires a question to be decided by the court affecting an arbitration (whether started or not), an arbitration agreement or an arbitration award; and

(ii) the seat of the arbitration is or will be within the jurisdiction or the conditions in section 2(4) of the 1996 Act are satisfied.

(2) An application for permission under paragraph (1) must be supported by written evidence—

(a) stating the grounds on which the application is made; and

(b) showing in what place or country the person to be served is, or probably may be found.

(3) Rules 6.24 to 6.29 apply to the service of an arbitration claim form under paragraph (1).

(4) An order giving permission to serve an arbitration claim form out of the jurisdiction must specify the period within which the defendant may file an acknowledgment of service.]

[1496]

NOTES

Commencement: 25 March 2002.
Added as noted to r 62.1 at **[1492]**.

[62.6 Notice

(1) Where an arbitration claim is made under section 24, 28 or 56 of the 1996 Act, each arbitrator must be a defendant.

(2) Where notice must be given to an arbitrator or any other person it may be given by sending him a copy of—

(a) the arbitration claim form; and
(b) any written evidence in support.

(3) Where the 1996 Act requires an application to the court to be made on notice to any other party to the arbitration, that notice must be given by making that party a defendant.]

[1497]

NOTES

Commencement: 25 March 2002.
Added as noted to r 62.1 at **[1492]**.

[62.7 Case management

(1) Part 26 and any other rule that requires a party to file an allocation questionnaire does not apply.

(2) Arbitration claims are allocated to the multi-track.

(3) Part 29 does not apply.

(4) The automatic directions set out in the practice direction apply unless the court orders otherwise.]

[1498]

NOTES

Commencement: 25 March 2002.
Added as noted to r 62.1 at **[1492]**.

[62.8 Stay of legal proceedings

(1) An application notice seeking a stay of legal proceedings under section 9 of the 1996 Act must be served on all parties to those proceedings who have given an address for service.

(2) A copy of an application notice under paragraph (1) must be served on any other party to the legal proceedings (whether or not he is within the jurisdiction) who has not given an address for service, at—

(a) his last known address; or
(b) a place where it is likely to come to his attention.

(3) Where a question arises as to whether—

(a) an arbitration agreement has been concluded; or
(b) the dispute which is the subject-matter of the proceedings falls within the terms of such an agreement,

the court may decide that question or give directions to enable it to be decided and may order the proceedings to be stayed pending its decision.]

[1499]

NOTES

Commencement: 25 March 2002.
Added as noted to r 62.1 at **[1492]**.

[62.9 Variation of time

(1) The court may vary the period of 28 days fixed by section 70(3) of the 1996 Act for—

(a) challenging the award under section 67 or 68 of the Act; and
(b) appealing against an award under section 69 of the Act.

(2) An application for an order under paragraph (1) may be made without notice being served on any other party before the period of 28 days expires.

(3) After the period of 28 days has expired—

(a) an application for an order extending time under paragraph (1) must—

(i) be made in the arbitration claim form; and

(ii) state the grounds on which the application is made;

(b) any defendant may file written evidence opposing the extension of time within 7 days after service of the arbitration claim form; and

(c) if the court extends the period of 28 days, each defendant's time for acknowledging service and serving evidence shall start to run as if the arbitration claim form had been served on the date when the court's order is served on that defendant.]

[1500]

NOTES

Commencement: 25 March 2002.
Added as noted to r 62.1 at **[1492]**.

[62.10 Hearings

(1) The court may order that an arbitration claim be heard either in public or in private.

(2) Rule 39.2 does not apply.

(3) Subject to any order made under paragraph (1)—

(a) the determination of—

(i) a preliminary point of law under section 45 of the 1996 Act; or

(ii) an appeal under section 69 of the 1996 Act on a question of law arising out of an award,

will be heard in public; and

(b) all other arbitration claims will be heard in private.

(4) Paragraph (3)(a) does not apply to—

(a) the preliminary question of whether the court is satisfied of the matters set out in section 45(2)(b); or

(b) an application for permission to appeal under section 69(2)(b).]

[1501]

NOTES

Commencement: 25 March 2002.
Added as noted to r 62.1 at **[1492]**.

[II OTHER ARBITRATION CLAIMS

62.11 Scope of this Section

(1) This Section of this Part contains rules about arbitration claims to which the old law applies.

(2) In this Section—

(a) "the old law" means the enactments specified in Schedules 3 and 4 of the 1996 Act as they were in force before their amendment or repeal by that Act; and

(b) "arbitration claim" means any application to the court under the old law and includes an appeal (or application for permission to appeal) to the High Court under section 1(2) of the 1979 Act.

(3) This Section does not apply to—

(a) a claim to which Section III of this Part applies; or

(b) a claim on the award.]

[1502]

NOTES

Commencement: 25 March 2002.
Added as noted to r 62.1 at **[1492]**.

[62.12 Applications to Judge

A claim—

PART II CIVIL PROCEDURE RULES

(a) seeking permission to appeal under section 1(2) of the 1979 Act;
(b) under section 1(5) of that Act (including any claim seeking permission); or
(c) under section 5 of that Act,

must be made in the High Court and will be heard by a judge of the Commercial Court unless any such judge directs otherwise.]

[1503]

NOTES

Commencement: 25 March 2002.
Added as noted to r 62.1 at **[1492]**.

[62.13 Starting the claim

(1) Except where paragraph (2) applies an arbitration claim must be started by the issue of an arbitration claim form in accordance with the Part 8 procedure.

(2) Where an arbitration claim is to be made in existing proceedings—
(a) it must be made by way of application notice; and
(b) any reference in this Section of this Part to an arbitration claim form includes a reference to an application notice.

(3) The arbitration claim form in an arbitration claim under section 1(5) of the 1979 Act (including any claim seeking permission) must be served on—
(a) the arbitrator or umpire; and
(b) any other party to the reference.]

[1504]

NOTES

Commencement: 25 March 2002.
Added as noted to r 62.1 at **[1492]**.

[62.14 Claims in District Registries

If—
(a) a claim is to be made under section 12(4) of the 1950 Act for an order for the issue of a witness summons to compel the attendance of the witness before an arbitrator or umpire; and
(b) the attendance of the witness is required within the district of a District Registry,

the claim may be started in that Registry.]

[1505]

NOTES

Commencement: 25 March 2002.
Added as noted to r 62.1 at **[1492]**.

[62.15 Time limits and other special provisions about arbitration claims

(1) An arbitration claim to—
(a) remit an award under section 22 of the 1950 Act;
(b) set aside an award under section 23(2) of that Act or otherwise; or
(c) direct an arbitrator or umpire to state the reasons for an award under section 1(5) of the 1979 Act,

must be made, and the arbitration claim form served, within 21 days after the award has been made and published to the parties.

(2) An arbitration claim to determine any question of law arising in the course of a reference under section 2(1) of the Arbitration Act 1979 must be made, and the arbitration claim form served, within 14 days after—
(a) the arbitrator or umpire gave his consent in writing to the claim being made; or
(b) the other parties so consented.

(3) An appeal under section 1(2) of the 1979 Act must be filed, and the arbitration claim form served, within 21 days after the award has been made and published to the parties.

(4) Where reasons material to an appeal under section 1(2) of the 1979 Act are given on a date subsequent to the publication of the award, the period of 21 days referred to in paragraph (3) will run from the date on which reasons are given.

(5) In every arbitration claim to which this rule applies—
(a) the arbitration claim form must state the grounds of the claim or appeal;
(b) where the claim or appeal is based on written evidence, a copy of that evidence must be served with the arbitration claim form; and
(c) where the claim or appeal is made with the consent of the arbitrator, the umpire or the other parties, a copy of every written consent must be served with the arbitration claim form.

(6) In an appeal under section 1(2) of the 1979 Act—
(a) a statement of the grounds for the appeal specifying the relevant parts of the award and reasons; and
(b) where permission is required, any written evidence in support of the contention that the question of law concerns—
(i) a term of a contract; or
(ii) an event,
which is not a "one-off" term or event,
must be filed and served with the arbitration claim form.

(7) Any written evidence in reply to written evidence under paragraph (6)(b) must be filed and served on the claimant not less than 2 days before the hearing.

(8) A party to a claim seeking permission to appeal under section 1(2) of the 1979 Act who wishes to contend that the award should be upheld for reasons not expressed or fully expressed in the award and reasons must file and serve on the claimant, a notice specifying the grounds of his contention not less than 2 days before the hearing.]

[1506]

NOTES

Commencement: 25 March 2002.
Added as noted to r 62.1 at **[1492]**.

[62.16 Service out of the jurisdiction

(1) Subject to paragraph (2)—
(a) any arbitration claim form in an arbitration claim under the 1950 Act or the 1979 Act; or
(b) any order made in such a claim,
may be served out of the jurisdiction with the permission of the court if the arbitration to which the claim relates—
(i) is governed by the law of England and Wales; or
(ii) has been, is being, or will be, held within the jurisdiction.

(2) An arbitration claim form seeking permission to enforce an award may be served out of the jurisdiction with the permission of the court whether or not the arbitration is governed by the law of England and Wales.

(3) An application for permission to serve an arbitration claim form out of the jurisdiction must be supported by written evidence—
(a) stating the grounds on which the application is made; and
(b) showing in what place or country the person to be served is, or probably may be found.

(4) Rules 6.24 to 6.29 apply to the service of an arbitration claim form under paragraph (1).

(5) An order giving permission to serve an arbitration claim form out of the jurisdiction must specify the period within which the defendant may file an acknowledgment of service.]

[1507]

NOTES

Commencement: 25 March 2002.
Added as noted to r 62.1 at **[1492]**.

PART II CIVIL PROCEDURE RULES

[III ENFORCEMENT

62.17 Scope of this Section

This Section of this Part applies to all arbitration enforcement proceedings other than by a claim on the award.]

[1508]

NOTES

Commencement: 25 March 2002.
Added as noted to r 62.1 at **[1492]**.

[62.18 Enforcement of awards

(1) An application for permission under—

(a) section 66 of the 1996 Act;
(b) section 101 of the 1996 Act;
(c) section 26 of the 1950 Act; or
(d) section 3(1)(a) of the 1975 Act,

to enforce an award in the same manner as a judgment or order may be made without notice in an arbitration claim form.

(2) The court may specify parties to the arbitration on whom the arbitration claim form must be served.

(3) The parties on whom the arbitration claim form is served must acknowledge service and the enforcement proceedings will continue as if they were an arbitration claim under Section I of this Part.

(4) With the permission of the court the arbitration claim form may be served out of the jurisdiction irrespective of where the award is, or is treated as, made.

(5) Where the applicant applies to enforce an agreed award within the meaning of section 51(2) of the 1996 Act—

(a) the arbitration claim form must state that the award is an agreed award; and
(b) any order made by the court must also contain such a statement.

(6) An application for permission must be supported by written evidence—

(a) exhibiting—
  (i) where the application is made under section 66 of the 1996 Act or under section 26 of the 1950 Act, the arbitration agreement and the original award (or copies);
  (ii) where the application is under section 101 of the 1996 Act, the documents required to be produced by section 102 of that Act; or
  (iii) where the application is under section 3(1)(a) of the 1975 Act, the documents required to be produced by section 4 of that Act;
(b) stating the name and the usual or last known place of residence or business of the claimant and of the person against whom it is sought to enforce the award; and
(c) stating either—
  (i) that the award has not been complied with; or
  (ii) the extent to which it has not been complied with at the date of the application.

(7) An order giving permission must—

(a) be drawn up by the claimant; and
(b) be served on the defendant by—
  (i) delivering a copy to him personally; or
  (ii) sending a copy to him at his usual or last known place of residence or business.

(8) An order giving permission may be served out of the jurisdiction—

(a) without permission; and
(b) in accordance with rules 6.24 to 6.29 as if the order were an arbitration claim form.

(9) Within 14 days after service of the order or, if the order is to be served out of the jurisdiction, within such other period as the court may set—

(a) the defendant may apply to set aside the order; and

(b) the award must not be enforced until after—
(i) the end of that period; or
(ii) any application made by the defendant within that period has been finally disposed of.

(10) The order must contain a statement of—
(a) the right to make an application to set the order aside; and
(b) the restrictions on enforcement under rule 62.18(9)(b).

(11) Where a body corporate is a party any reference in this rule to place of residence or business shall have effect as if the reference were to the registered or principal address of the body corporate.]

[1509]

NOTES
Commencement: 25 March 2002.
Added as noted to r 62.1 at **[1492]**.

[62.19 Interest on awards

(1) Where an applicant seeks to enforce an award of interest the whole or any part of which relates to a period after the date of the award, he must file a statement giving the following particulars—
(a) whether simple or compound interest was awarded;
(b) the date from which interest was awarded;
(c) where rests were provided for, specifying them;
(d) the rate of interest awarded; and
(e) a calculation showing—
(i) the total amount claimed up to the date of the statement; and
(ii) any sum which will become due on a daily basis.

(2) A statement under paragraph (1) must be filed whenever the amount of interest has to be quantified for the purpose of—
(a) obtaining a judgment or order under section 66 of the 1996 Act (enforcement of the award); or
(b) enforcing such a judgment or order.]

[1510]

NOTES
Commencement: 25 March 2002.
Added as noted to r 62.1 at **[1492]**.

[62.20 Registration in High Court of foreign awards

(1) Where—
(a) an award is made in proceedings on an arbitration in any part of a United Kingdom Overseas Territory (within the meaning of rule 6.18(f)) or other territory to which Part I of the Foreign Judgments (Reciprocal Enforcement) Act 1933 ("the 1933 Act") extends;
(b) Part II of the Administration of Justice Act 1920 extended to that part immediately before Part I of the 1933 Act was extended to that part; and
(c) an award has, under the law in force in the place where it was made, become enforceable in the same manner as a judgment given by a court in that place,

[rules 74.1 to 74.7 and 74.9 apply in relation to the award as they apply] in relation to a judgment given by the court subject to the modifications in paragraph (2).

(2) The modifications referred to in paragraph (1) are as follows—
(a) for references to the [State of origin] are substituted references to the place where the award was made; and
(b) the written evidence required by [rule 74.4] must state (in addition to the matters required by that rule) that to the best of the information or belief of the maker of the statement the award has, under the law in force in the place where it was made, become enforceable in the same manner as a judgment given by a court in that place.]

[1511]

NOTES

Commencement: 25 March 2002.

Added as noted to r 62.1 at **[1492]**.

Paras (1), (2): words in square brackets substituted by the Civil Procedure (Amendment) Rules 2002, SI 2002/2058, r 24.

[62.21 Registration of awards under the Arbitration (International Investment Disputes) Act 1966

(1) In this rule—

(a) "the 1966 Act" means the Arbitration (International Investment Disputes) Act 1966;

(b) "award" means an award under the Convention;

(c) "the Convention" means the Convention on the settlement of investment disputes between States and nationals of other States which was opened for signature in Washington on 18th March 1965;

(d) "judgment creditor" means the person seeking recognition or enforcement of an award; and

(e) "judgment debtor" means the other party to the award.

[(2) Subject to the provisions of this rule, the following provisions of Part 74 apply with such modifications as may be necessary in relation to an award as they apply in relation to a judgment to which Part I of the Foreign Judgments (Reciprocal Enforcement) Act 1933 applies—

(a) rule 74.1;

(b) rule 74.3;

(c) rule 74.4(1), (2)(a) to (d), and (4);

(d) rule 74.6 (except paragraph (3)(c) to (e)); and

(e) rule 74.9(2).]

(3) An application to have an award registered in the High Court under section 1 of the 1966 Act must be made in accordance with the Part 8 procedure.

(4) The written evidence required by [rule 74.4] in support of an application for registration must—

(a) exhibit the award certified under the Convention instead of the judgment (or a copy of it); and

(b) in addition to stating the matters referred to in [rule 74.4(2)(a) to (d)], state whether—

(i) at the date of the application the enforcement of the award has been stayed (provisionally or otherwise) under the Convention; and

(ii) any, and if so what, application has been made under the Convention, which, if granted, might result in a stay of the enforcement of the award.

(5) Where, on granting permission to register an award or an application made by the judgment debtor after an award has been registered, the court considers—

(a) that the enforcement of the award has been stayed (whether provisionally or otherwise) under the Convention; or

(b) that an application has been made under the Convention which, if granted, might result in a stay of the enforcement of the award,

the court may stay the enforcement of the award for such time as it considers appropriate.]

[1512]

NOTES

Commencement: 25 March 2002.

Added as noted to r 62.1 at **[1492]**.

Para (2): substituted by the Civil Procedure (Amendment) Rules 2002, SI 2002/2058, r 25(a).

Para (4): words in square brackets substituted by SI 2002/2058, r 25(b), (c).

Parts 63–67 (*Pt 63 relates to patents and other intellectual property claims; Pt 64 to estates, trusts and charities; Pt 65 to proceedings relating to anti-social behaviour and harassment; Pt 66 to Crown proceedings; Pt 67 to proceedings relating to solicitors.*)

[PART 68
REFERENCES TO THE EUROPEAN COURT

NOTES

Practice Direction—References to the European Court.

68.1 Interpretation

In this Part—

(a) "the court" means the court making the order;
(b) "the European Court" means the Court of Justice of the European Communities;
(c) "order" means an order referring a question to the European Court for a preliminary ruling under—
  (i) article 234 of the Treaty establishing the European Community;
  (ii) article 150 of the Euratom Treaty;
  (iii) article 41 of the ECSC Treaty;
  (iv) the Protocol of 3 June 1971 on the interpretation by the European Court of the Convention of 27 September 1968 on Jurisdiction and the Enforcement of Judgments in Civil and Commercial Matters; or
  (v) the Protocol of 19 December 1988 on the interpretation by the European Court of the Convention of 19 June 1980 on the Law applicable to Contractual Obligations.]

[1513]

NOTES

Commencement: 2 December 2002.
Part 68 (rr 68.1–68.4) added by the Civil Procedure (Amendment) Rules 2002, SI 2002/2058, r 26(b), Sch 6.

[68.2 Making of order of reference

(1) An order may be made at any stage of the proceedings—
  (a) by the court of its own initiative; or
  (b) on an application by a party in accordance with Part 23.

(2) An order may not be made—
  (a) in the High Court, by a Master or district judge;
  (b) in a county court, by a district judge.

(3) The request to the European Court for a preliminary ruling must be set out in a schedule to the order, and the court may give directions on the preparation of the schedule.]

[1514]

NOTES

Commencement: 2 December 2002.
Added as noted to r 68.1 at **[1513]**.

[68.3 Transmission to the European Court

(1) The Senior Master will send a copy of the order to the Registrar of the European Court.

(2) Where an order is made by a county court, the proper officer will send a copy of it to the Senior Master for onward transmission to the European Court.

(3) Unless the court orders otherwise, the Senior Master will not send a copy of the order to the European Court until—
  (a) the time for appealing against the order has expired; or
  (b) any application for permission to appeal has been refused, or any appeal has been determined.]

[1515]

NOTES

Commencement: 2 December 2002.
Added as noted to r 68.1 at **[1513]**.

[68.4 Stay of proceedings

Where an order is made, unless the court orders otherwise the proceedings will be stayed until the European Court has given a preliminary ruling on the question referred to it.]

[1516]

NOTES

Commencement: 2 December 2002.
Added as noted to r 68.1 at **[1513]**.

Parts 69–73 *(Pt 69 relates to the Court's power to appoint a receiver; Pt 70 to general rules about enforcement; Pt 71 to orders to obtain information from judgment debtors; Pt 72 to third party debt orders; Pt 73 to charging orders, stop orders and stop notices.)*

[PART 74
ENFORCEMENT OF JUDGMENTS IN DIFFERENT JURISDICTIONS

NOTES

Practice Direction—Enforcement of Judgments in Different Jurisdictions; see para **[1567]**.

74.1 Scope of this Part and interpretation

(1) Section I of this Part applies to the enforcement in England and Wales of judgments of foreign courts.

(2) Section II applies to the enforcement in foreign countries of judgments of the High Court and of county courts.

(3) Section III applies to the enforcement of United Kingdom judgments in other parts of the United Kingdom.

(4) Section IV applies to the enforcement in England and Wales of European Community judgments and Euratom inspection orders.

[(4A) Section V applies to—

(a) the certification of judgments and court settlements in England and Wales as European Enforcement Orders; and

(b) the enforcement in England and Wales of judgments, court settlements and authentic instruments certified as European Enforcement Orders by other Member States.]

(5) In this Part—

(a) "the 1920 Act" means the Administration of Justice Act 1920;

(b) "the 1933 Act" means the Foreign Judgments (Reciprocal Enforcement) Act 1933;

(c) "the 1982 Act" means the Civil Jurisdiction and Judgments Act 1982;

(d) "the Judgments Regulation" means Council Regulation (EC) No 44/2001 of 22nd December 2000 on jurisdiction and the recognition and enforcement of judgments in civil and commercial matters[;

(e) "the EEO Regulation" means Council Regulation (EC) No 805/2004 creating a European Enforcement Order for uncontested claims.]]

[(A copy of the EEO Regulation is annexed to Practice Direction 74B European Enforcement Orders and can be found at http://europa.eu.int/eur-lex/pri/en/oj/dat/2004/l_143/l_14320040430en00150039.pdf)]

[1517]

NOTES

Commencement: 2 December 2002.
Part 74 (rr 74.1–74.26) added by the Civil Procedure (Amendment) Rules 2002, SI 2002/2058, r 29(a), Sch 8.
Para (4A): inserted by the Civil Procedure (Amendment No 3) Rules 2005, SI 2005/2292, r 50(a).
Para (5): sub-para (e) added by SI 2005/2292, r 50(b).
Signpost added by SI 2005/2292, r 51.

[I ENFORCEMENT IN ENGLAND AND WALES OF JUDGMENTS OF FOREIGN COURTS

74.2 Interpretation

(1) In this Section—

(a) "Contracting State" has the meaning given in section 1(3) of the 1982 Act;

(b) "Regulation State" has the same meaning as "Member State" in the Judgments Regulation, that is all Member States except Denmark;

(c) "judgment" means, subject to any other enactment, any judgment given by a foreign court or tribunal, whatever the judgment may be called, and includes—

(i) a decree;

(ii) an order;

(iii) a decision;

(iv) a writ of execution; and

(v) the determination of costs by an officer of the court;

(d) "State of origin", in relation to any judgment, means the State in which that judgment was given.

(2) For the purposes of this Section, "domicile" is to be determined—

(a) in an application under the 1982 Act, in accordance with sections 41 to 46 that Act;

(b) in an application under the Judgments Regulation, in accordance with paragraphs 9 to 12 of Schedule 1 to the Civil Jurisdiction and Judgments Order 2001.]

[1518]

NOTES

Commencement: 2 December 2002.
Added as noted to r 74.1 at **[1517]**.

[74.3 Applications for registration

(1) This Section provides rules about applications under—

(a) section 9 of the 1920 Act, in respect of judgments to which Part II of that Act applies;

(b) section 2 of the 1933 Act, in respect of judgments to which Part I of that Act applies;

(c) section 4 of the 1982 Act; and

(d) the Judgments Regulation,

for the registration of foreign judgments for enforcement in England and Wales.

(2) Applications—

(a) must be made to the High Court; and

(b) may be made without notice.]

[1519]

NOTES

Commencement: 2 December 2002.
Added as noted to r 74.1 at **[1517]**.

[74.4 Evidence in support

(1) An application for registration of a judgment under the 1920, 1933 or 1982 Act must be supported by written evidence exhibiting—

(a) the judgment or a verified or certified or otherwise authenticated copy of it; and

(b) where the judgment is not in English, a translation of it into English—

(i) certified by a notary public or other qualified person; or

(ii) accompanied by written evidence confirming that the translation is accurate.

(2) The written evidence in support of the application must state—

(a) the name of the judgment creditor and his address for service within the jurisdiction;

(b) the name of the judgment debtor and his address or place of business, if known;

PART II
CIVIL PROCEDURE RULES

(c) the grounds on which the judgment creditor is entitled to enforce the judgment;
(d) in the case of a money judgment, the amount in respect of which it remains unsatisfied; and
(e) where interest is recoverable on the judgment under the law of the State of origin—
 (i) the amount of interest which has accrued up to the date of the application, or
 (ii) the rate of interest, the date from which it is recoverable, and the date on which it ceases to accrue.

(3) Written evidence in support of an application under the 1920 Act must also state that the judgment is not a judgment—
(a) which under section 9 of that Act may not be ordered to be registered; or
(b) to which section 5 of the Protection of Trading Interests Act 1980 applies.

(4) Written evidence in support of an application under the 1933 Act must also—
(a) state that the judgment is a money judgment;
(b) confirm that it can be enforced by execution in the State of origin;
(c) confirm that the registration could not be set aside under section 4 of that Act;
(d) confirm that the judgment is not a judgment to which section 5 of the Protection of Trading Interests Act 1980 applies;
(e) where the judgment contains different provisions, some but not all of which can be registered for enforcement, set out those provisions in respect of which it is sought to register the judgment; and
(f) be accompanied by any further evidence as to—
 (i) the enforceability of the judgment in the State of origin, and
 (ii) the law of that State under which any interest has become due under the judgment,

which may be required under the relevant Order in Council extending Part I of the 1933 Act to that State.

(5) Written evidence in support of an application under the 1982 Act must also exhibit—
(a) documents which show that, under the law of the State of origin, the judgment is enforceable on the judgment debtor and has been served;
(b) in the case of a judgment in default, a document which establishes that the party in default was served with the document instituting the proceedings or with an equivalent document; and
(c) where appropriate, a document showing that the judgment creditor is in receipt of legal aid in the State of origin.

(6) An application for registration under the Judgments Regulation must, in addition to the evidence required by that Regulation, be supported by the evidence required by paragraphs (1)(b) and (2)(e) of this rule.]

[1520]

NOTES

Commencement: 2 December 2002.
Added as noted to r 74.1 at **[1517]**.

[74.5 Security for costs

(1) Subject to paragraphs (2) and (3), section II of Part 25 applies to an application for security for the costs of—
(a) the application for registration;
(b) any proceedings brought to set aside the registration; and
(c) any appeal against the granting of the registration,

as if the judgment creditor were a claimant.

(2) A judgment creditor making an application under the 1982 Act or the Judgments Regulation may not be required to give security solely on the ground that he is resident out of the jurisdiction.

(3) Paragraph (1) does not apply to an application under the 1933 Act where the relevant Order in Council otherwise provides.]

[1521]

NOTES

Commencement: 2 December 2002.
Added as noted to r 74.1 at **[1517]**.

[74.6 Registration orders

(1) An order granting permission to register a judgment ("registration order") must be drawn up by the judgment creditor and served on the judgment debtor—

(a) by delivering it to him personally;
(b) as provided by section 725 of the Companies Act 1985; or
(c) in such other manner as the court may direct.

(2) Permission is not required to serve a registration order out of the jurisdiction, and rules 6.24, 6.25, 6.26 and 6.29 apply to such an order as they apply to a claim form.

(3) A registration order must state—

(a) full particulars of the judgment registered;
(b) the name of the judgment creditor and his address for service within the jurisdiction;
(c) the right of the judgment debtor—
  (i) in the case of registration following an application under the 1920 or the 1933 Act, to apply to have the registration set aside;
  (ii) in the case of registration following an application under the 1982 Act or under the Judgments Regulation, to appeal against the registration order;
(d) the period within which such an application or appeal may be made; and
(e) that no measures of enforcement will be taken before the end of that period, other than measures ordered by the court to preserve the property of the judgment debtor.]

[1522]

NOTES

Commencement: 2 December 2002.
Added as noted to r 74.1 at **[1517]**.

[74.7 Applications to set aside registration

(1) An application to set aside registration under the 1920 or the 1933 Act must be made within the period set out in the registration order.

(2) The court may extend that period; but an application for such an extension must be made before the end of the period as originally fixed or as subsequently extended.

(3) The court hearing the application may order any issue between the judgment creditor and the judgment debtor to be tried.]

[1523]

NOTES

Commencement: 2 December 2002.
Added as noted to r 74.1 at **[1517]**.

[74.8 Appeals

(1) An appeal against the granting or the refusal of registration under the 1982 Act or the Judgments Regulation must be made in accordance with Part 52, subject to the following provisions of this rule.

(2) Permission is not required—

(a) to appeal; or
(b) to put in evidence.

(3) If—

(a) the judgment debtor is not domiciled within a Contracting State or a Regulation State, as the case may be, and
(b) an application to extend the time for appealing is made within two months of service of the registration order,

the court may extend the period for filing an appellant's notice against the order granting registration, but not on grounds of distance.

(4) The appellant's notice must be served—

(a) where the appeal is against the granting of registration, within—

(i) one month; or

(ii) where service is to be effected on a party not domiciled within the jurisdiction, two months, of service of the registration order;

(b) where the appeal is against the refusal of registration, within one month of the decision on the application for registration.]

[1524]

NOTES

Commencement: 2 December 2002.
Added as noted to r 74.1 at **[1517]**.

[74.9 Enforcement

(1) No steps may be taken to enforce a judgment—

(a) before the end of the period specified in accordance with rule 74.6(3)(d), or that period as extended by the court; or

(b) where there is an application under rule 74.7 or an appeal under rule 74.8, until the application or appeal has been determined.

(2) Any party wishing to enforce a judgment must file evidence of the service on the judgment debtor of—

(a) the registration order; and

(b) any other relevant order of the court.

(3) Nothing in this rule prevents the court from making orders to preserve the property of the judgment debtor pending final determination of any issue relating to the enforcement of the judgment.]

[1525]

NOTES

Commencement: 2 December 2002.
Added as noted to r 74.1 at **[1517]**.

[74.10 Recognition

(1) Registration of a judgment serves as a decision that the judgment is recognised for the purposes of the 1982 Act and the Judgments Regulation.

(2) An application for recognition of a judgment is governed by the same rules as an application for registration of a judgment under the 1982 Act or under the Judgments Regulation, except that rule 74.4(5)(a) and (c) does not apply.]

[1526]

NOTES

Commencement: 2 December 2002.
Added as noted to r 74.1 at **[1517]**.

[74.11 Authentic instruments and court settlements

The rules governing the registration of judgments under the 1982 Act or under the Judgments Regulation apply as appropriate and with any necessary modifications for the enforcement of—

(a) authentic instruments which are subject to—

(i) article 50 of Schedule 1 to the 1982 Act;

(ii) article 50 of Schedule 3C to the 1982 Act; and

(iii) article 57 of the Judgments Regulation; and

(b) court settlements which are subject to—

(i) article 51 of Schedule 1 to the 1982 Act;

(ii) article 51 of Schedule 3C to the 1982 Act; and

(iii) article 58 of the Judgments Regulation.]

[1527]

NOTES

Commencement: 2 December 2002.
Added as noted to r 74.1 at **[1517]**.

[II ENFORCEMENT IN FOREIGN COUNTRIES OF JUDGMENTS OF THE HIGH COURT AND COUNTY COURTS

74.12 Application for a certified copy of a judgment

(1) This Section applies to applications—
- (a) to the High Court under section 10 of the 1920 Act;
- (b) to the High Court or to a county court under section 10 of the 1933 Act;
- (c) to the High Court or to a county court under section 12 of the 1982 Act; or
- (d) to the High Court or to a county court under article 54 of the Judgments Regulation.

(2) A judgment creditor who wishes to enforce in a foreign country a judgment obtained in the High Court or in a county court must apply for a certified copy of the judgment.

(3) The application may be made without notice.]

[1528]

NOTES

Commencement: 2 December 2002.
Added as noted to r 74.1 at **[1517]**.

[74.13 Evidence in support

(1) The application must be supported by written evidence exhibiting copies of—
- (a) the claim form in the proceedings in which judgment was given;
- (b) evidence that it was served on the defendant;
- (c) the statements of case; and
- (d) where relevant, a document showing that for those proceedings the applicant was an assisted person or an LSC funded client, as defined in rule 43.2(1)(h) and (i).

(2) The written evidence must—
- (a) identify the grounds on which the judgment was obtained;
- (b) state whether the defendant objected to the jurisdiction and, if he did, the grounds of his objection;
- (c) show that the judgment—
  - (i) has been served in accordance with Part 6 and rule 40.4, and
  - (ii) is not subject to a stay of execution;
- (d) state—
  - (i) the date on which the time for appealing expired or will expire;
  - (ii) whether an appeal notice has been filed;
  - (iii) the status of any application for permission to appeal; and
  - (iv) whether an appeal is pending;
- (e) state whether the judgment provides for the payment of a sum of money, and if so, the amount in respect of which it remains unsatisfied;
- (f) state whether interest is recoverable on the judgment, and if so, either—
  - (i) the amount of interest which has accrued up to the date of the application, or
  - (ii) the rate of interest, the date from which it is recoverable, and the date on which it ceases to accrue.]

[1529]

NOTES

Commencement: 2 December 2002.
Added as noted to r 74.1 at **[1517]**.

[III ENFORCEMENT OF UNITED KINGDOM JUDGMENTS IN OTHER PARTS OF THE UNITED KINGDOM

74.14 Interpretation

In this Section—

(a) "money provision" means a provision for the payment of one or more sums of money in a judgment whose enforcement is governed by section 18 of, and Schedule 6 to, the 1982 Act; and

(b) "non-money provision" means a provision for any relief or remedy not requiring payment of a sum of money in a judgment whose enforcement is governed by section 18 of, and Schedule 7 to, the 1982 Act.]

[1530]

NOTES

Commencement: 2 December 2002.
Added as noted to r 74.1 at **[1517]**.

[74.15 Registration of money judgments in the High Court

(1) This rule applies to applications to the High Court under paragraph 5 of Schedule 6 to the 1982 Act for the registration of a certificate for the enforcement of the money provisions of a judgment—

(a) which has been given by a court in another part of the United Kingdom, and

(b) to which section 18 of that Act applies.

(2) The certificate must within six months of the date of its issue be filed in the Central Office of the Supreme Court, together with a copy certified by written evidence to be a true copy.]

[1531]

NOTES

Commencement: 2 December 2002.
Added as noted to r 74.1 at **[1517]**.

[74.16 Registration of non-money judgments in the High Court

(1) This rule applies to applications to the High Court under paragraph 5 of Schedule 7 to the 1982 Act for the registration for enforcement of the non-money provisions of a judgment—

(a) which has been given by a court in another part of the United Kingdom, and

(b) to which section 18 of that Act applies.

(2) An application under paragraph (1) may be made without notice.

(3) An application under paragraph (1) must be accompanied—

(a) by a certified copy of the judgment issued under Schedule 7 to the 1982 Act; and

(b) by a certificate, issued not more than six months before the date of the application, stating that the conditions set out in paragraph 3 of Schedule 7 are satisfied in relation to the judgment.

(4) Rule 74.6 applies to judgments registered under Schedule 7 to the 1982 Act as it applies to judgments registered under section 4 of that Act.

(5) Rule 74.7 applies to applications to set aside the registration of a judgment under paragraph 9 of Schedule 7 to the 1982 Act as it applies to applications to set aside registrations under the 1920 and 1933 Acts.]

[1532]

NOTES

Commencement: 2 December 2002.
Added as noted to r 74.1 at **[1517]**.

[74.17 Certificates of High Court and county court money judgments

(1) This rule applies to applications under paragraph 2 of Schedule 6 to the 1982 Act for a certificate to enable the money provisions of a judgment of the High Court or of a county court to be enforced in another part of the United Kingdom.

(2) The judgment creditor may apply for a certificate by filing at the court where the judgment was given or has been entered written evidence stating—

(a) the name and address of the judgment creditor and, if known, of the judgment debtor;
(b) the sums payable and unsatisfied under the money provisions of the judgment;
(c) where interest is recoverable on the judgment, either—
  (i) the amount of interest which has accrued up to the date of the application, or
  (ii) the rate of interest, the date from which it is recoverable, and the date on which it ceases to accrue;
(d) that the judgment is not stayed;
(e) the date on which the time for appealing expired or will expire;
(f) whether an appeal notice has been filed;
(g) the status of any application for permission to appeal; and
(h) whether an appeal is pending.]

[1533]

NOTES

Commencement: 2 December 2002.
Added as noted to r 74.1 at **[1517]**.

[74.18 Certified copies of High Court and county court non-money judgments

(1) This rule applies to applications under paragraph 2 of Schedule 7 to the 1982 Act for a certified copy of a judgment of the High Court or of a county court to which section 18 of the Act applies and which contains non-money provisions for enforcement in another part of the United Kingdom.

(2) An application under paragraph (1) may be made without notice.

(3) The applicant may apply for a certified copy of a judgment by filing at the court where the judgment was given or has been entered written evidence stating—
(a) full particulars of the judgment;
(b) the name and address of the judgment creditor and, if known, of the judgment debtor;
(c) that the judgment is not stayed;
(d) the date on which the time for appealing expired or will expire;
(e) whether an appeal notice has been filed;
(f) the status of any application for permission to appeal; and
(g) whether an appeal is pending.]

[1534]

NOTES

Commencement: 2 December 2002.
Added as noted to r 74.1 at **[1517]**.

[IV ENFORCEMENT IN ENGLAND AND WALES OF EUROPEAN COMMUNITY JUDGMENTS

74.19 Interpretation

In this Section—
(a) "Community judgment" means any judgment, decision or order which is enforceable under—
  (i) article 244 or 256 of the Treaty establishing the European Community;
  (ii) article 18, 159 or 164 of the Euratom Treaty;
  (iii) article 44 or 92 of the ECSC Treaty; …
  (iv) article 82 of Council Regulation (EC) 40/94 of 20 December 1993 on the Community trade mark; [or
  (v) article 71 of Council Regulation (EC) 6/2002 of 12 December 2001 on Community designs;]
(b) "Euratom inspection order" means an order made by the President of the European Court, or a decision of the Commission of the European Communities, under article 81 of the Euratom Treaty;
(c) "European Court" means the Court of Justice of the European Communities;

(d) "order for enforcement" means an order under the authority of the Secretary of State that the Community judgment to which it is appended is to be registered for enforcement in the United Kingdom.]

[1535]

NOTES

Commencement: 2 December 2002.
Added as noted to r 74.1 at **[1517]**.
Word omitted from para (a)(iii) revoked and para (a)(v) and immediately preceding word added by the Civil Procedure (Amendment No 5) Rules 2003, SI 2003/3361, r 18.

[74.20 Application for registration of a Community judgment

An application to the High Court for the registration of a Community judgment may be made without notice.]

[1536]

NOTES

Commencement: 2 December 2002.
Added as noted to r 74.1 at **[1517]**.

[74.21 Evidence in support

(1) An application for registration must be supported by written evidence exhibiting—

- (a) the Community judgment and the order for its enforcement, or an authenticated copy; and
- (b) where the judgment is not in English, a translation of it into English—
  - (i) certified by a notary public or other qualified person; or
  - (ii) accompanied by written evidence confirming that the translation is accurate.

(2) Where the application is for registration of a Community judgment which is a money judgment, the evidence must state—

- (a) the name of the judgment creditor and his address for service within the jurisdiction;
- (b) the name of the judgment debtor and his address or place of business, if known;
- (c) the amount in respect of which the judgment is unsatisfied; and
- (d) that the European Court has not suspended enforcement of the judgment.]

[1537]

NOTES

Commencement: 2 December 2002.
Added as noted to r 74.1 at **[1517]**.

[74.22 Registration orders

(1) A copy of the order granting permission to register a Community judgment ("the registration order") must be served on every person against whom the judgment was given.

(2) The registration order must state the name and address for service of the person who applied for registration, and must exhibit—

- (a) a copy of the registered Community judgment; and
- (b) a copy of the order for its enforcement.

(3) In the case of a Community judgment which is a money judgment, the registration order must also state the right of the judgment debtor to apply within 28 days for the variation or cancellation of the registration under rule 74.23.]

[1538]

NOTES

Commencement: 2 December 2002.
Added as noted to r 74.1 at **[1517]**.

[74.23 Application to vary or cancel registration

(1) An application to vary or cancel the registration of a Community judgment which is a money judgment on the ground that at the date of registration the judgment had been partly or wholly satisfied must be made within 28 days of the date on which the registration order was served on the judgment debtor.

(2) The application must be supported by written evidence.]

[1539]

NOTES

Commencement: 2 December 2002.
Added as noted to r 74.1 at **[1517]**.

[74.24 Enforcement

No steps may be taken to enforce a Community judgment which is a money judgment—

(a) before the end of the period specified in accordance with rule 74.23(1); or
(b) where an application is made under that rule, until it has been determined.]

[1540]

NOTES

Commencement: 2 December 2002.
Added as noted to r 74.1 at **[1517]**.

[74.25 Application for registration of suspension order

(1) Where the European Court has made an order that the enforcement of a registered Community judgment should be suspended, an application for the registration of that order in the High Court is made by filing a copy of the order in the Central Office of the Supreme Court.

(2) The application may be made without notice.]

[1541]

NOTES

Commencement: 2 December 2002.
Added as noted to r 74.1 at **[1517]**.

[74.26 Registration and enforcement of a Euratom inspection order

(1) Rules 74.20, 74.21(1), and 74.22(1) and (2), which apply to the registration of a Community judgment, also apply to the registration of a Euratom inspection order but with the necessary modifications.

(2) An application under article 6 of the European Communities (Enforcement of Community Judgments) Order 1972 to give effect to a Euratom inspection order may be made on written evidence, and—

(a) where the matter is urgent, without notice;
(b) otherwise, by claim form.]

[1542]

NOTES

Commencement: 2 December 2002.
Added as noted to r 74.1 at **[1517]**.

[V EUROPEAN ENFORCEMENT ORDERS

NOTES

Practice Direction—European Enforcement Orders; see para **[1569]**.

74.27 Interpretation

In this Section—

(a) "European Enforcement Order" has the meaning given in the EEO Regulation;
(b) "EEO" means European Enforcement Order;
(c) "judgment", "authentic instrument", "member state of origin", "member state of enforcement", and "court of origin" have the meanings given by Article 4 of the EEO Regulation; and
(d) "Regulation State" has the same meaning as "Member State" in the EEO Regulation, that is all Member States except Denmark.]

[1543]

NOTES

Commencement: 21 October 2005.
Section V (rr 74.27–74.33) added by Civil Procedure (Amendment No 3) Rules 2005, SI 2005/2292, r 52, Sch 3.

[74.28 Certification of Judgments of the Courts of England and Wales

An application for an EEO certificate must be made by filing the relevant practice form in accordance with Article 6 of the EEO Regulation.]

[1544]

NOTES

Commencement: 21 October 2005.
Added as noted to r 74.27 at **[1543]**.

[74.29 Applications for a certificate of lack or limitation of enforceability

An application under Article 6(2) of the EEO Regulation for a certificate indicating the lack or limitation of enforceability of an EEO certificate must be made to the court of origin by application in accordance with Part 23.]

[1545]

NOTES

Commencement: 21 October 2005.
Added as noted to r 74.27 at **[1543]**.

[74.30 Applications for rectification or withdrawal

An application under Article 10 of the EEO Regulation for rectification or withdrawal of an EEO certificate must be made to the court of origin and may be made by application in accordance with Part 23.]

[1546]

NOTES

Commencement: 21 October 2005.
Added as noted to r 74.27 at **[1543]**.

[74.31 Enforcement of European Enforcement Orders in England and Wales

(1) A person seeking to enforce an EEO in England and Wales must lodge at the court in which enforcement proceedings are to be brought the documents required by Article 20 of the EEO Regulation.

(2) Where a person applies—

(a) to the High Court for a charging order, a writ of fieri facias or an attachment of earnings order; or
(b) to the county court for a warrant of execution or an attachment of earnings order,

to enforce an EEO expressed in a foreign currency, the application must contain a certificate of the sterling equivalent of the judgment sum at the close of business on the date nearest preceding the date of issue of the application.

(Section 1 of the Charging Orders Act 1979 provides that the High Court only has jurisdiction to make a charging order where the amount of the original judgment exceeds the county court limit.)

(Article 8 of the High Court and County Courts Jurisdiction Order 1991 provides that (1) judgments in excess of £5,000 shall only be enforced by execution against goods in the High Court (2) those in excess of £600 may be enforced in the High Court and (3) those for less than £600 shall only be enforced in the county court.).]

[1547]

NOTES

Commencement: 21 October 2005.
Added as noted to r 74.27 at **[1543]**.

[74.32 Refusal of Enforcement

(1) An application under Article 21 of the EEO Regulation that the court should refuse to enforce an EEO must be made by application in accordance with Part 23 to the court in which the EEO is being enforced.

(2) The judgment debtor must, as soon as practicable, serve copies of any order made under Article 21(1) on—

(a) all other parties to the proceedings and any other person affected by the order; and
(b) any court in which enforcement proceedings are pending in England and Wales.

(3) Upon service of the order on those persons all enforcement proceedings in England and Wales under the EEO, in respect of those persons upon whom, and those courts at which, the order has been served in accordance with paragraph (2), will cease.]

[1548]

NOTES

Commencement: 21 October 2005.
Added as noted to r 74.27 at **[1543]**.

[74.33 Stay or limitation of enforcement

(1) Where an EEO certificate has been lodged and the judgment debtor applies to stay or limit the enforcement proceedings under Article 23 of the EEO Regulation, such application must be made by application in accordance with Part 23 to the court in which the EEO is being enforced.

(2) The judgment debtor shall, as soon as practicable, serve a copy of any order made under the Article on—

(a) all other parties to the proceedings and any other person affected by the order; and
(b) any court in which enforcement proceedings are pending in England and Wales;

and the order will not have effect on any person until it has been served in accordance with this rule and they have received it.]

[1549]

NOTES

Commencement: 21 October 2005.
Added as noted to r 74.27 at **[1543]**.

Part 75 (*Relates to traffic enforcement.*)

GLOSSARY

SCOPE

This glossary is a guide to the meaning of certain legal expressions as used in these Rules, but it does not give the expressions any meaning in the Rules which they do not otherwise have in the law.

Expression	*Meaning*
Affidavit	A written, sworn statement of evidence.

Expression	*Meaning*
Alternative dispute resolution	Collective description of methods of resolving disputes otherwise than through the normal trial process.
Base rate	The interest rate set by the Bank of England which is used as the basis for other banks' rates.
Contribution	A right of someone to recover from a third person all or part of the amount which he himself is liable to pay.
Counterclaim	A claim brought by a defendant in response to the claimant's claim, which is included in the same proceedings as the claimant's claim.
Cross-examination (and see "evidence in chief")	Questioning of a witness by a party other than the party who called the witness.
Damages	A sum of money awarded by the court as compensation to the claimant.
— aggravated damages	Additional damages which the court may award as compensation for the defendant's objectionable behaviour
— exemplary damages	Damages which go beyond compensating for actual loss and are awarded to show the court's disapproval of the defendant's behaviour
Defence of tender before claim	A defence that, before the claimant started proceedings, the defendant unconditionally offered to the claimant the amount due or, if no specified amount is claimed, an amount sufficient to satisfy the claim.
Evidence in chief (and see "cross-examination")	The evidence given by a witness for the party who called him.
Indemnity	A right of someone to recover from a third party the whole amount which he himself is liable to pay.
Injunction	A court order prohibiting a person from doing something or requiring a person to do something.
Joint liability (and see "several liability")	Parties who are jointly liable share a single liability and each party can be held liable for the whole of it.
Limitation period	The period within which a person who has a right to claim against another person must start court proceedings to establish that right. The expiry of the period may be a defence to the claim.
List	Cases are allocated to different lists depending on the subject matter of the case. The lists are used for administrative purposes and may also have their own procedures and judges.
Official copy	A copy of an official document, supplied and marked as such by the office which issued the original.
Practice form	Form to be used for a particular purpose in proceedings, the form and purpose being specified by a practice direction.
Pre-action protocol	Statements of understanding between legal practitioners and others about pre-action practice and which are approved by a relevant practice direction.
Privilege	The right of a party to refuse to disclose a document or to refuse to answer questions on the ground of some special interest recognised by law.
Seal	A seal is a mark which the court puts on a document to indicate that the document has been issued by the court.

Expression	*Meaning*
Service	Steps required by rules of court to bring documents used in court proceedings to a person's attention.
Set aside	Cancelling a judgment or order or a step taken by a party in the proceedings.
Several liability (and see "joint liability")	A person who is severally liable with others may remain liable for the whole claim even where judgment has been obtained against the others.
Stay	A stay imposes a halt on proceedings, apart from taking any steps allowed by the Rules or the terms of the stay. Proceedings can be continued if a stay is lifted.
Strike out	Striking out means the court ordering written material to be deleted so that it may no longer be relied upon.
Without prejudice	Negotiations with a view to a settlement are usually conducted "without prejudice" which means that the circumstances in which the content of those negotiations may be revealed to the court are very restricted.

[1550]

(Sch 1 sets out selected Rules of the Supreme Court; Sch 2 sets out selected County Court Rules.)

PRACTICE DIRECTION 6—SERVICE

NOTES

This Practice Direction supplements CPR, Pt 6 at **[1329]**.

METHODS OF SERVICE

1.1 The various methods of service are set out in rule 6.2.

1.2 The following provisions apply to the specific methods of service referred to.

SERVICE BY NON-ELECTRONIC MEANS

Service by document exchange

2.1 Service by document exchange (DX) may take place only where:

(1) the party's address for service[1] includes a numbered box at a DX, or

(2) the writing paper of the party who is to be served or of his legal representative[2] sets out the DX box number, and

(3) the party or his legal representative has not indicated in writing that they are unwilling to accept service by DX.

2.2 Service by DX is effected by leaving the document addressed to the numbered box:

(1) at the DX of the party who is to be served, or

(2) at a DX which sends documents to that party's DX every business day.

SERVICE BY ELECTRONIC MEANS

Service by facsimile

3.1 Subject to the provisions of paragraph 3.3 below, where a document is to be served by electronic means—

(1) the party who is to be served or his legal representative must previously have expressly indicated in writing to the party serving—

(a) that he is willing to accept service by electronic means; and
(b) the fax number, e-mail address or electronic identification to which it should be sent; and

(2) the following shall be taken as sufficient written indication for the purposes of paragraph 3.1(1)—
(a) a fax number set out on the writing paper of the legal representative of the party who is to be served; or
(b) a fax number, e-mail address or electronic identification set out on a statement of case or a response to a claim filed with the court.

3.2 Where a party seeks to serve a document by electronic means he should first seek to clarify with the party who is to be served whether there are any limitations to the recipient's agreement to accept service by such means including the format in which documents are to be sent and the maximum size of attachments that may be received.

3.3 An address for service given by a party must be within the jurisdiction and any fax number must be at the address for service. Where an e-mail address or electronic identification is given in conjunction with an address for service, the e-mail address or electronic identification will be deemed to be at the address for service.

3.4 Where a document is served by electronic means, the party serving the document need not in addition send a hard copy by post or document exchange.

SERVICE ON CERTAIN INDIVIDUALS

Personal service on partners

4.1 Where partners are sued in the name of a partnership, service should be in accordance with rule 6.4(5) and the table set out in rule 6.5(5) where it refers to an "individual who is suing or being sued in the name of a firm".

4.2 A claim form or particulars of claim which are served by leaving them with a person at the principal or last known place of business of the partnership, must at the same time have served with them a notice as to whether that person is being served:
(1) as a partner,
(2) as a person having control or management of the partnership business, or
(3) as both.

Service on members of HM Forces and United States Air Force

5 The Lord Chancellor's Office issued a memorandum on 26 July 1979 as to service on members of HM Forces and guidance notes as to service on members of the United States Air Force. The provisions annexed to this practice direction are derived from that memorandum and guidance notes.

SERVICE GENERALLY

Personal service on a company or other corporation

6.1 Personal service on a registered company or corporation in accordance with rule 6.4(4) service is effected by leaving a document with "a person holding a senior position".

6.2 Each of the following persons is a person holding a senior position:
(1) in respect of a registered company or corporation, a director, the treasurer, secretary, chief executive, manager or other officer of the company or corporation, and
(2) in respect of a corporation which is not a registered company, in addition to those persons set out in (1), the mayor, chairman, president, town clerk or similar officer of the corporation.

CHANGE OF ADDRESS

7 A party or his legal representative who changes his address for service shall give notice in writing of the change as soon as it has taken place to the court and every other party.

Service by the court

8.1 Where the court effects service of a document in accordance with rule 6.3(1) and (2), the method will normally be by first class post.

8.2 Omitted.

8.3 Where the court effects service of a claim form, delivers a defence to a claimant or notifies a claimant that the defendant has filed an acknowledgment of service, the court will also serve or deliver a copy of any notice of funding that has been filed provided -

(a) it was filed at the same time as the claim form, defence or acknowledgment of service, and

(b) copies were provided for service.

CONTENT OF EVIDENCE

The following applications relating to service require evidence in support

9.1 An application for an order for service by an alternative method[3] should be supported by evidence stating:

(1) the reason an order for an alternative method of service is sought, and

(2) what steps have been taken to serve by other permitted means.

9.2 An application for service of a claim form relating to a contract on the agent of a principal who is overseas should be supported by evidence setting out:

(1) full details of the contract and that it was entered into within the jurisdiction with or through an agent who is either an individual residing or carrying on business within the jurisdiction, or a registered company or corporation having a registered office or a place of business within the jurisdiction,

(2) that the principal for whom the agent is acting was, at the time the contract was entered into and is at the time of making the application, neither an individual, registered company or corporation as described in (1) above, and

(3) why service out of the jurisdiction cannot be effected.

[1551]

1 See rule 6.5.
2 See rule 2.3 for the definition of legal representative.
3 See rule 6.8.

ANNEX

SERVICE ON MEMBERS OF HM FORCES

1. The following information is for litigants and legal representatives who wish to serve legal documents in civil proceedings in the courts of England and Wales on parties to the proceedings who are (or who, at the material time, were) regular members of Her Majesty's Forces.

2. The proceedings may take place in the county court or the High Court, and the documents to be served may be both originating claims, interim applications and pre-action applications. Proceedings for divorce or maintenance and proceedings in the Family Courts generally are subject to special rules as to service which are explained in a practice direction issued by the Senior District Judge of the Principal Registry on 26 June 1979.

3. In these instructions, the person wishing to effect service is referred to as the "claimant" and the person to be served is referred to as the "serviceman"; the expression "overseas" means outside the United Kingdom.

Enquiries as to address

4. As a first step, the claimant's legal representative will need to find out where the serviceman is serving, if he does not already know. For this purpose he should write to the appropriate officer of the Ministry of Defence as specified in paragraph 10, below.

5. The letter of enquiry should in every case show that the writer is a legal representative and that the enquiry is made solely with a view to the service of legal documents in civil proceedings.

6. In all cases the letter should give the full name, service number, rank or rating, and Ship, Arm or Trade, Regiment or Corps and Unit or as much of this information as is available. Failure to quote the service number and the rank or rating may result either in failure to identify the serviceman or in considerable delay.

7. The letter should contain an undertaking by the legal representative that, if the address is given, it will be used solely for the purpose of issuing and serving documents in the

proceedings and that so far as is possible the legal representative will disclose the address only to the court and not to his client or to any other person or body. A legal representative in the service of a public authority or private company should undertake that the address will be used solely for the purpose of issuing and serving documents in the proceedings and that the address will not be disclosed so far as is possible to any other part of his employing organisation or to any other person but only to the court. Normally on receipt of the required information and undertaking the appropriate office will give the service address.

8. If the legal representative does not give the undertaking, the only information he will receive will be whether the serviceman is at that time serving in England or Wales, Scotland, Northern Ireland or overseas.

9. It should be noted that a serviceman's address which ends with a British Forces Post Office address and reference (BFPO) will nearly always indicate that he is serving overseas.

10. The letter of enquiry should be addressed as follows:

(a) **Royal Navy Officers**

The Naval Secretary
Room 161
Victory Building
HM Naval Base
Portsmouth
Hants PO1 3LS

RN Ratings Commodore
Commodore Naval Drafting
Centurion Building
Grange Road
Gosport
Hants PO13 9XA

RN Medical and Dental Officers
The Medical Director General
(Naval)
Room 114
Victory Building
HM Naval Base
Portsmouth
Hants PO1 3LS

Officers of Queen Alexandra's Royal Naval Nursing Service
The Matron-in-Chief
QARNNS
Room 139
Victory Building
HM Naval Base
Portsmouth
Hants PO1 3LS

Naval Chaplains
Director General Naval
Chaplaincy Service

Room 201
Victory Building
HM Naval Base
Portsmouth
Hants PO1 3LS

(b) **Royal Marine Officers and Ranks**

Personnel Section
West Battery
Whale Island
Portsmouth
Hants PO2 8DX

RM Ranks HQRM

(DRORM)
West Battery
Whale Island
Portsmouth
Hants PO2 8DX

(c) **Army Officers and other Ranks**

Ministry of Defence

Army Personnel Centre
Secretariat, Public Enquiries
RM CD424
Kentigern House
65 Brown Street
Glasgow G2 8EH

(d) **Royal Air Force and Officers and Other Ranks**

Personnel Management Centre (RAF)
Building 248
RAF Innsworth
Gloucester GL3 1EZ

Assistance in serving documents on servicemen

11. Once the claimant's legal representative has learnt the serviceman's address, he may use that address as the address for service by post, in cases where this method of service is allowed by the Civil Procedure Rules. There are, however, some situations in which service of the proceedings, whether in the High Court or in the county court, has to be effected personally; in these cases an appointment will have to be sought, through the Commanding Officer of the Unit, Establishment or Ship concerned, for the purpose of effecting service. The procedure for obtaining an appointment is described below, and it applies whether personal service is to be effected by the claimant's legal representative or his agent or by a court bailiff, or, in the case of proceedings served overseas (with the leave of the court) through the British Consul or the foreign judicial authority.

12. The procedure for obtaining an appointment to effect personal service is by application to the Commanding Officer of the Unit, Establishment or Ship in which the serviceman is serving. The Commanding Officer may grant permission for the document server to enter the Unit, Establishment or Ship but if this is not appropriate he may offer arrangements for the serviceman to attend at a place in the vicinity of the Unit, Establishment

or Ship in order that he may be served. If suitable arrangements cannot be made the legal representative will have evidence that personal service is impracticable, which may be useful in an application for service by an alternative method.

General

13. Subject to the procedure outlined in paragraphs 11 and 12, there are no special arrangements to assist in the service of process when a serviceman is outside the United Kingdom. The appropriate office will however give an approximate date when the serviceman is likely to return to the United Kingdom.

14. It sometimes happens that a serviceman has left the service by the time that the enquiry is made. If the claimant's legal representative confirms that the proceedings result from an occurrence when the serviceman was in the Forces and he gives the undertaking referred to in paragraph 7, the last known private address after discharge will normally be provided. In no other case however will the Department disclose the private address of a member of HM Forces.

SERVICE ON MEMBERS OF UNITED STATES AIR FORCE

15. In addition to the information contained in the memorandum of 26 July 1979, the Lord Chancellor's Office, some doubts having been expressed as to the correct procedure to be followed by persons having civil claims against members of the United States Air Force in this country, issued the following notes for guidance with the approval of the appropriate United States authorities:

16. Instructions have been issued by the US authorities to the commanding officers of all their units in this country that every facility is to be given for the service of documents in civil proceedings on members of the US Air Force. The proper course to be followed by a creditor or other person having a claim against a member of the US Air Force is for him to communicate with the commanding officer or, where the unit concerned has a legal officer, with the legal officer of the defendant's unit requesting him to provide facilities for the service of documents on the defendant. It is not possible for the US authorities to act as arbitrators when a civil claim is made against a member of their forces. It is, therefore, essential that the claim should either be admitted by the defendant or judgment should be obtained on it, whether in the High Court or a county court. If a claim has been admitted or judgment has been obtained and the claimant has failed to obtain satisfaction within a reasonable period, his proper course is then to write to: Office of the Staff Judge Advocate, Headquarters, Third Air Force, RAF. Mildenhall, Suffolk, enclosing a copy of the defendant's written admission of the claim or, as the case may be, a copy of the judgment. Steps will then be taken by the Staff Judge Advocate to ensure that the matter is brought to the defendant's attention with a view to prompt satisfaction of the claim.

[1552]

PRACTICE DIRECTION 6B—SERVICE OUT OF THE JURISDICTION

NOTES

This Practice Direction supplements CPR, Pt 6, Section III at **[1346]**.

SERVICE IN OTHER MEMBER STATES OF THE EUROPEAN UNION

A1.1 Where service is to be effected in another Member of State of the European Union, Council Regulation (EC) No 1348/2000 of 29 May 2000 on the service in the Member States of judicial and extrajudicial documents in civil or commercial matters ("the Service Regulation") applies.

A1.2 The Service Regulation is annexed to this practice direction.

(Article 20(1) of the Service Regulation provides that the Regulation prevails over other provisions contained in bilateral or multilateral agreements or arrangements concluded by the Member of States and in particular Article IV of the Protocol to the Brussels Convention of 1968 and the Hague Convention of 15 November 1965)

Originally published in the official languages of the European Community in the *Official Journal of the European Communities* by the Office for Official Publications of the European Communities.

SERVICE OUT OF THE JURISDICTION WHERE PERMISSION OF THE COURT IS NOT REQUIRED

1.1 The usual form of words of the statement required by Rule 6.19(3) where the court has power to determine the claim under the 1982 Act should be:—

"I state that the High Court of England and Wales has power under the Civil Jurisdiction and Judgments Act 1982 to hear this claim and that no proceedings are pending between the parties in Scotland, Northern Ireland or another Convention territory of any Contracting State as defined by section 1(3) of the Act".

1.2 However, in proceedings to which Rule 6.19(1)(b)(ii) applies, the statement should be:—

"I state that the High Court of England and Wales has power under the Civil Jurisdiction and Judgments Act 1982, the claim having as its object rights in rem in immovable property or tenancies in immovable property (or otherwise in accordance with the provisions of Article 16 of Schedule 1 or 3C to that Act, or paragraph 11 of Schedule 4 to that Act) to which any of those provisions applies, to hear the claim and that no proceedings are pending between the parties in Scotland, Northern Ireland or another Convention territory of any Contracting State as defined by Section 1(3) of the Act".

1.3 And in proceedings to which Rule 6.19(1)(b)(iii) applies, the statement should be:—

"I state that the High Court of England and Wales has power under the Civil Jurisdiction and Judgments Act 1982, the defendant being a party to an agreement conferring jurisdiction to which Article 17 of Schedule 1 or 3C to that Act or paragraph 12 of Schedule 4 to that Act applies, to hear the claim and that no proceedings are pending between the parties in Scotland, Northern Ireland or another Convention territory of any Contracting State as defined by Section 1(3) of the Act".

1.3A The usual form of words of the statement required by Rule 6.19(3) where the Judgments Regulation applies should be:—

"I state that the High Court of England and Wales has power under Council Regulation (EC) No 44/2001 of 22nd December 2000 (on jurisdiction and the recognition and enforcement of judgments in civil and commercial matters) to hear this claim and that no proceedings are pending between the parties in Scotland, Northern Ireland or any other Regulation State as defined by section 1(3) of the Civil Jurisdiction and Judgments Act 1982."

1.3B However, in proceedings to which Rule 6.19(1A)(b)(ii) applies, the statement should be:—

"I state that the High Court of England and Wales has power under Council Regulation (EC) No 44/2001 of 22nd December 2000 (on jurisdiction and the recognition and enforcement of judgments in civil and commercial matters), the claim having as its object rights in rem in immovable property or tenancies in immovable property (or otherwise in accordance with the provisions of Article 22 of that Regulation) to which Article 22 of that Regulation applies, to hear this claim and that no proceedings are pending between the parties in Scotland, Northern Ireland or any other Regulation State as defined by section 1(3) of the Civil Jurisdiction and Judgments Act 1982."

1.3C And in proceedings to which Rule 6.19(1A)(b)(iii) applies, the statement should be:—

"I state that the High Court of England and Wales has power under Council Regulation (EC) No 44/2001 of 22nd December 2000 (on jurisdiction and the recognition and enforcement of judgments in civil and commercial matters), the defendant being a party to an agreement conferring jurisdiction to which Article 23 of that Regulation applies, to hear this claim and that no proceedings are pending between the parties in Scotland, Northern Ireland or any other Regulation State as defined by section 1(3) of the Civil Jurisdiction and Judgments Act 1982."

1.3D In proceedings to which Rule 6.19(2) applies, the statement should be:

"I state that the High Court of England and Wales has power to hear this claim under [state the provisions of the relevant enactment] which satisfies the requirements of rule 6.19(2), and that no proceedings are pending between the parties in Scotland or Northern Ireland, or in another Contracting State or Regulation State as defined by section 1(3) of the Civil Jurisdiction and Judgments Act 1982."

1.4 A claim form appearing to be for service on a defendant under the provisions of Rule 6.19 which does not include a statement in the form of 1.1, 1.2, 1.3, 1.3A, 1.3B, 1.3C or 1.3D above will be marked on issue "Not for service out of the jurisdiction".

1.5 Where a claim form is served without particulars of claim, it must be accompanied by a copy of Form N1C (notes for defendants).

SERVICE OUT OF THE JURISDICTION WHERE PERMISSION IS REQUIRED

Documents to be filed under Rule 6.26(2)(d)

2.1 A complete set of the following documents must be provided for each party to be served out of the jurisdiction:

(1) A copy of particulars of claim if not already incorporated in or attached to the claim.
(2) A duplicate of the claim form of the particulars of claim and of any documents accompanying the claim and of any translation required by Rule 6.28.
(3) Forms for responding to the claim.
(4) Any translation required under Rule 6.28 and paragraphs 4.1 and 4.2, in duplicate.

2.2 The documents to be served in certain countries require legalisation and the Foreign Process Section (Room E02), Royal Courts of Justice will advise on request. Some countries require legislation and some require a formal letter of request, see Form No 34 to Table 2 of Practice Direction to Part 4 which must be signed by the Senior Master of the Queen's Bench Division irrespective of the Division of the High Court or any county court in which the order was made.

SERVICE IN SCOTLAND, NORTHERN IRELAND, THE CHANNEL ISLANDS, THE ISLE OF MAN, COMMONWEALTH COUNTRIES AND UNITED KINGDOM OVERSEAS TERRITORIES

3.1 Where Rule 6.25(4) applies, service should be effected by the claimant or his agent direct except in the case of a Commonwealth State where the judicial authorities have required service to be in accordance with Rule 6.24(1)(b)(i). These are presently Malta and Singapore.

3.2 For the purposes of Rule 6.25(4)(c), the following countries are United Kingdom Overseas Territories:—

(a) Anguilla;
(b) Bermuda;
(c) British Antarctic Territory
(d) British Indian Ocean Territory
(e) Cayman Islands;
(f) Falklands Islands;
(g) Gibraltar;
(h) Monserrat;
(i) Pitcairn, Henderson, Ducie and Oeno;
(j) St Helena and Dependencies;
(k) South Georgia and South Sandwich Islands;
(l) Sovereign Base Areas of Akrotiri and Dhekalia;
(m) Turks and Caicos Islands; and
(n) Virgin Islands.

TRANSLATIONS

4.1 Rule 6.28 applies to particulars of claim not included in a claim form as well as to claim forms.

4.2 Where a translation of a claim form is required under Rule 6.28, the claimant must also file a translation of all the forms that will accompany the claim form.

(It should be noted that English is not an official language in the Province of Quebec).

SERVICE WITH THE PERMISSION OF THE COURT UNDER CERTAIN ACTS

5.1 Rule 6.20(18) provides that a claim form may be served out of the jurisdiction with the Court's permission if the claim is made under an enactment specified in the relevant Practice Direction.

5.2 These enactments are:
(1) The Nuclear Installations Act 1965,
(2) The Social Security Contributions and Benefits Act 1992,
(3) The Directive of the Council of the European Communities dated 15 March 1976 No 76/308/EEC, where service is to be effected in a member state of the European Union,
(4) The Drug Trafficking Offences Act 1994,
(7) Part VI of the Criminal Justice Act 1988,
(8) The Inheritance (Provision for Family and Dependants) Act 1975,
(9) Part II of the Immigration and Asylum Act 1999,
(10) Schedule 2 to the Immigration Act 1971,
(11) The Financial Services and Markets Act 2000,
(12) The Pensions Act 1995,
(13) The Pensions Act 2004.

5.3 Under the State Immunity Act 1978, the foreign state being served is allowed an additional two months over the normal period for filing an acknowledgment of service or defence or for filing or serving an admission allowed under paragraphs 7.3 and 7.4.

SERVICE OF PETITIONS, APPLICATION NOTICES AND ORDERS

6.1 The provisions of Section III of Part 6 (special provisions about service out of the jurisdiction) apply to service out of the jurisdiction of a petition, application notice or order.

(Rule 6.30(1) contains special provisions relating to application notices).

6.2 Where an application notice is to be served out of the jurisdiction in accordance with Section III of Part 6 the Court must have regard to the country in which the application notice is to be served in setting the date for the hearing of the application and giving any direction about service of the respondent's evidence.

6.3 Where the permission of the Court is required for a claim form to be served out of the jurisdiction the permission of the Court, unless rule 6.30(3) applies, must also be obtained for service out of the jurisdiction of any other document to be served in the proceedings and the provisions of this Practice Direction will, so far as applicable to that other document, apply.

6.4 When particulars of claim are served out of the jurisdiction any statement as to the period for responding to the claim contained in any of the forms required by Rule 7.8 to accompany the particulars of claim must specify the period prescribed under Rule 6.22 or 6.23 or (as the case may be) by the order permitting service out of the jurisdiction (see Rule 6.21(4)).

PERIOD FOR RESPONDING TO A CLAIM FORM

7.1 Where a claim form has been served out of the jurisdiction without permission under Rule 6.19—
(1) Rule 6.22 sets out the period for filing an acknowledgement of service or filing or serving an admission and where Rule 6.22(4) applies, the period will be calculated in accordance with paragraph 7.3 having regard to the Table below;
(2) Rule 6.23 sets out the period for filing a defence and where Rule 6.23(4) applies, the period will be calculated in accordance with paragraph 7.4 having regard to the Table below.

7.2 Where an order grants permission to serve a claim form out of the jurisdiction, the periods within which the defendant may—
(1) file an acknowledgment of service
(2) file or serve an admission;
(3) file a defence

will be calculated in accordance with paragraphs 7.3 and 7.4 having regard to the Table below.

(Rule 6.21(4) requires an order giving permission for a claim form to be served out of the jurisdiction to specify the period within which the defendant may respond to the claim form).

7.3 The period for filing an acknowledgment of service under Part 10 or filing or serving an admission under Part 14 is—
(1) where the defendant is served with a claim form which states that particulars of claim are to follow, the number of days listed in the Table after service of the particulars of claim; and
(2) in any other case, the number of days listed in the Table after service of the claim form.

For example: where a defendant has been served with a claim form (accompanied by particulars of claim) in the Bahamas, the period for acknowledging service or admitting the claim is 22 days after service.

7.4 The period for filing a defence under Part 15 is—

(1) the number of days listed in the Table after service of the particulars of claim, or

(2) where the defendant has filed an acknowledgment of service, the number of days listed in the Table plus an additional 14 days after the service of the particulars of claim.

For example, where a defendant has been served with particulars of claim in Gibraltar and has acknowledged service, the period for filing a defence is 45 days after service of the particulars of claim.

PERIOD FOR RESPONDING TO AN APPLICATION NOTICE

8.1 Where an application notice or order needs to be served out of the jurisdiction, the period for responding to service is 7 days less than the number of days listed in the Table.

ADDRESS FOR SERVICE & FURTHER INFORMATION

10.1 A defendant is required by Rule 6.5(2) to give an address for service within the jurisdiction.

10.2 Further information concerning service out of the jurisdiction can be obtained from the Foreign Process Section, Room E02 [E10], Royal Courts of Justice, Strand, London WC2A 2LL (telephone 020 7947 6691).

TABLE

Place or country	*Number of days*
Abu Dhabi	22
Afghanistan	23
Albania	25
Algeria	22
Angola	22
Anguilla	31
Antigua	23
Antilles (Netherlands)	31
Argentina	22
Armenia	21
Ascension	31
Australia	25
Austria	21
Azores	23
Bahamas	22
Bahrain	22
Balearic Islands	21
Bangladesh	23
Barbados	23
Belarus	21
Belgium	21
Belize	23
Benin	25
Bermuda	31

Place or country	*Number of days*
Bhutan	28
Bolivia	23
Bosnia-Hercegovina	21
Botswana	23
Brazil	22
Brunei	25
Bulgaria	23
Burkina Faso	23
Burma	23
Burundi	22
Cameroon	22
Canada	22
Canary Islands	22
Cape Verde Islands	25
Caroline Islands	31
Cayman Islands	31
Central African Republic	25
Chad	25
Chile	22
China	24
Christmas Island	27
Cocos (Keeling) Islands	41
Colombia	22
Comoros	23
Congo (People's Republic)	25
Corsica	21
Costa Rica	23
Croatia	21
Cuba	24
Cyprus	31
Cyrenaica (see Libya)	21
Czech Republic	21
Denmark	21
Djibouti	22
Dominica	23
Dominican Republic	23
Dubai	22
Ecuador	22
Egypt (Arab Rebublic)	22
El Salvador (Republic of)	25
Equatorial Guinea	23
Estonia	21
Ethiopia	22

Place or country	*Number of days*
Falkland Islands and Dependencies	31
Faroe Islands	31
Fiji	23
Finland	24
France	21
French Guiana	31
French Polynesia	31
French West Indies	31
Gabon	25
Gambia	22
Georgia	21
Germany	21
Ghana	22
Gibraltar	31
Greece	21
Greenland	31
Grenada	24
Guatemala	24
Guernsey	18
Guyana	22
Haiti	23
Holland (Netherlands)	21
Honduras	24
Hong Kong	31
Hungary	22
Iceland	22
India	23
Indonesia	22
Iran	22
Iraq	22
Ireland (Republic of)	21
Ireland (Northern)	21
Isle of Man	18
Israel	22
Italy	21
Ivory Coast	22
Jamaica	22
Japan	23
Jersey	18
Jordan	23
Kampuchea	38
Kazakhstan	21
Kenya	22

Place or country	*Number of days*
Kirgizstan	21
Korea (North)	28
Korea (South)	24
Kuwait	22
Laos	30
Latvia	21
Lebanon	22
Lesotho	23
Liberia	22
Libya	21
Liechtenstein	21
Lithuania	21
Luxembourg	21
Macau	31
Macedonia	21
Madagascar	23
Madeira	31
Malawi	23
Malaya	24
Maldive Islands	26
Mali	25
Malta	21
Mariana Islands	26
Marshall Islands	32
Mauritania	23
Mauritius	22
Mexico	23
Moldova	21
Monaco	21
Montserrat	31
Morocco	22
Mozambique	23
Nauru Island	36
Nepal	23
Netherlands	21
Nevis	24
New Caledonia	31
New Hebrides (now Vanuatu)	29
New Zealand	26
New Zealand Island Territories	50
Nicaragua	24
Niger (Republic of)	25
Nigeria	22

Place or country	Number of days
Norfolk Island	31
Norway	21
Oman (Sultanate of)	22
Pakistan	23
Panama (Republic of)	26
Papua New Guinea	26
Paraguay	22
Peru	22
Philippines	23
Pitcairn Island	31
Poland	21
Portugal	21
Portuguese Timor	31
Puerto Rico	23
Qatar	23
Reunion	31
Romania	22
Russia	21
Rwanda	23
Sabah	23
St Helena	31
St Kitts—Nevis	24
St Lucia	24
St Pierre and Miquelon	31
St Vincent and the Grenadines	24
Samoa (USA Territory) (See also Western Samoa)	30
Sarawak	28
Saudi Arabia	24
Scotland	21
Senegal	22
Seychelles	22
Sharjah	24
Sierra Leone	22
Singapore	22
Slovakia	21
Slovenia	21
Society Islands (French Polynesia)	31
Solomon Islands	29
Somali Democratic Republic	22
South Africa (Republic of)	22
South Georgia (Falkland Island Dependencies)	31

Place or country	*Number of days*
South Orkneys	21
South Shetlands	21
Spain	21
Spanish Territories of	31
Sri Lanka	23
Sudan	22
Suriname	22
Swaziland	22
Sweden	21
Switzerland	21
Syria	23
Taiwan	23
Tajikistan	21
Tanzania	22
Thailand	23
Tibet	34
Tobago	23
Togo	22
Tonga	30
Tortola	31
Trinidad & Tobago	23
Tristan Da Cunha	31
Tunisia	22
Turkey	21
Turkmenistan	21
Turks & Caicos Islands	31
Uganda	22
Ukraine	21
United States of America	22
Uruguay	22
Uzbekistan	21
Vanuatu	29
Vatican City State	21
Venezuela	22
Vietnam	28
Virgin Islands—British (Tortola)	31
Virgin Islands—USA	24
Wake Island	25
Western Samoa	34
Yemen (Republic of)	30
Yugoslavia (except for Bosnia-Herzegovina Croatia Macedonia and Slovenia)	21
Zaire	25

PART II CIVIL PROCEDURE RULES

Place or country	*Number of days*
Zambia	23
Zimbabwe	22

[1553]

(*The Appendix contains the original text of Council Regulation (EC) No 1348/2000 of 29 May 2000 on the service in the Member States of judicial and extrajudicial documents in civil or commercial matters; that Regulation, as amended, is reproduced in Pt IV(G) of this work at* **[3528]**.)

PRACTICE DIRECTION 12—DEFAULT JUDGMENT

NOTES
This Practice Direction supplements CPR, Pt 12 at **[1394]**.

DEFAULT JUDGMENT

1.1 A default judgment is judgment without a trial where a defendant has failed to file either:
  (1) an acknowledgment of service, or
  (2) a defence.

For this purpose a defence includes any document purporting to be a defence.

(See Part 10 and the practice direction which supplements it for information about the acknowledgment of service, and Parts 15 and 16 and the practice directions which supplement them for information about the defence and what it should contain.)

1.2 A claimant may not obtain a default judgment under Part 12 (notwithstanding that no acknowledgment of service or defence has been filed) if:
  (1) the procedure set out in Part 8 (Alternative Procedure for Claims) is being used, or
  (2) the claim is for delivery of goods subject to an agreement regulated by the Consumer Credit Act 1974, or

1.3 Other rules and practice directions provide that default judgment under Part 12 cannot be obtained in particular types of proceedings. Examples are:
  (1) admiralty proceedings;
  (2) arbitration proceedings;
  (3) contentious probate proceedings;
  (4) claims for provisional damages;
  (5) possession claims.

OBTAINING DEFAULT JUDGMENT

2.1 Rules 12.4(1) and 12.9(1) describe the claims in respect of which a default judgment may be obtained by filing a request in the appropriate practice form.

2.2 A default judgment on:
  (1) the claims referred to in rules 12.9(1)(b) and 12.10, and
  (2) claims other than those described in rule 12.4(1),

can only be obtained if an application for default judgment is made and cannot be obtained by filing a request.

2.3 The following are some of the types of claim which require an application for a default judgment:
  (1) against children and patients,[1]
  (2) for costs (other than fixed costs) only,[2]
  (3) by one spouse or civil partner against the other[3] on a claim in tort,[4]
  (4) for delivery up of goods where the defendant will not be allowed the alternative of paying their value, and
  (5) Omitted.

(6) against persons or organisations who enjoy immunity from civil jurisdiction under the provisions of the International Organisations Acts 1968 and 1981.

Default judgment by request

3.1 Requests for default judgment:

(1) in respect of a claim for a specified amount of money or for the delivery of goods where the defendant will be given the alternative of paying a specified sum representing their value, or for fixed costs only, must be in Form N205A or N225, and

(2) in respect of a claim where an amount of money (including an amount representing the value of goods) is to be decided by the court, must be in Form N205B or N227.

3.2 The forms require the claimant to provide the date of birth (if known) of the defendant where the defendant is an individual.

Evidence

4.1 Both on a request and on an application for default judgment the court must be satisfied that:

(1) the particulars of claim have been served on the defendant (a certificate of service on the court file will be sufficient evidence),

(2) either the defendant has not filed an acknowledgment of service or has not filed a defence and that in either case the relevant period for doing so has expired,

(3) the defendant has not satisfied the claim, and

(4) the defendant has not returned an admission to the claimant under rule 14.4 or filed an admission with the court under rule 14.6.

4.2 On an application against a child or patient:[5]

(1) a litigation friend[6] to act on behalf of the child or patient must be appointed by the court before judgment can be obtained, and

(2) the claimant must satisfy the court by evidence that he is entitled to the judgment claimed.

4.3 On an application where the defendant was served with the claim either:

(1) outside the jurisdiction[7] without leave under the Civil Jurisdiction and Judgments Act 1982, or the Judgments Regulation, or

(2) within the jurisdiction but when domiciled[8] in Scotland or Northern Ireland or in any other Convention territory[9] or Regulation State,

and the defendant has not acknowledged service, the evidence must establish that:

(a) the claim is one that the court has power to hear and decide,

(b) no other court has exclusive jurisdiction under the Act or Judgments Regulation to hear and decide the claim, and

(c) the claim has been properly served in accordance with Article 20 of Schedule 1 or 3C to the Act, paragraph 15 of Schedule 4 to the Act, or Article 26 of the Judgments Regulation.

4.4 On an application against a State[10] the evidence must:

(1) set out the grounds of the application,

(2) establish the facts proving that the State is excepted from the immunity conferred by section 1 of the State Immunity Act 1978,

(3) establish that the claim was sent through the Foreign and Commonwealth Office to the Ministry of Foreign Affairs of the State or, where the State has agreed to another form of service, that the claim was served in the manner agreed; and

(4) establish that the time for acknowledging service, (which is extended to two months by section 12(2) of the Act when the claim is sent through the Foreign and Commonwealth Office to the Ministry of Foreign Affairs of the State) has expired.

(See rule 40.8 for when default judgment against a State takes effect.)

4.5 Evidence in support of an application referred to in paragraphs 4.3 and 4.4 above must be by affidavit.

4.6 On an application for judgment for delivery up of goods where the defendant will not be given the alternative of paying their value, the evidence must identify the goods and state where the claimant believes the goods to be situated and why their specific delivery up is sought.

General

5.1 On all applications to which this practice direction applies, other than those referred to in paragraphs 4.3 and 4.4 above,[11] notice should be given in accordance with Part 23.

5.2 Where default judgment is given on a claim for a sum of money expressed in a foreign currency, the judgment should be for the amount of the foreign currency with the addition of "or the Sterling equivalent at the time of payment".

[1554]

---

1 See rule 12.10(a)(i).
2 See rule 12.9(b).
3 See rule 12.10(a)(ii).
4 Tort may be defined as an act or a failure to do an act which causes harm or damage to another person and which gives the other person a right to claim compensation without having to rely on a contract with the person who caused the harm or damage.
5 As defined in rule 21.1(2).
6 As defined in the practice direction which supplements Part 21.
7 As defined in rule 2.3.
8 As determined in accordance with the provisions of ss 41–46 of the Civil Jurisdictions and Judgments Act 1982.
9 Means the territory of a Contracting State as defined in s 1(3) of the Civil Jurisdiction and Judgments Act 1982.
10 As defined in s 14 of the State Immunity Act 1976.
11 See rule 12.11(4) and (5).

PRACTICE DIRECTION 23—APPLICATIONS

NOTES

This Practice Direction supplements CPR, Pt 23 at **[1410]**.

REFERENCE TO A JUDGE

1 A Master or district judge may refer to a judge any matter which he thinks should properly be decided by a judge, and the judge may either dispose of the matter or refer it back to the Master or district judge.

APPLICATION NOTICES

2.1 An application notice must, in addition to the matters set out in rule 23.6, be signed and include:

(1) the title of the claim,
(2) the reference number of the claim,
(3) the full name of the applicant,
(4) where the applicant is not already a party, his address for service, including a postcode. Postcode information may be obtained from www.royalmail.com or the Royal Mail Address Management Guide, and
(5) either a request for a hearing or a request that the application be dealt with without a hearing.

(Practice Form N244 may be used.)

2.2 On receipt of an application notice containing a request for a hearing the court will notify the applicant of the time and date for the hearing of the application.

2.3 On receipt of an application notice containing a request that the application be dealt with without a hearing, the application notice will be sent to a Master or district judge so that he may decide whether the application is suitable for consideration without a hearing.

2.4 Where the Master or district judge agrees that the application is suitable for consideration without a hearing, the court will so inform the applicant and the respondent and may give directions for the filing of evidence. (Rules 23.9 and 23.10 enable a party to apply for an order made without a hearing to be set aside or varied.)

2.5 Where the Master or district judge does not agree that the application is suitable for consideration without a hearing, the court will notify the applicant and the respondent of the time, date and place for the hearing of the application and may at the same time give directions as to the filing of evidence.

2.6 If the application is intended to be made to a judge, the application notice should so state. In that case, paragraphs 2.3, 2.4 and 2.5 will apply as though references to the Master or district judge were references to a judge.

2.7 Every application should be made as soon as it becomes apparent that it is necessary or desirable to make it.

2.8 Applications should wherever possible be made so that they can be considered at any other hearing for which a date has already been fixed or for which a date is about to be fixed. This is particularly so in relation to case management conferences, allocation and listing hearings and pre-trial reviews fixed by the court.

2.9 The parties must anticipate that at any hearing the court may wish to review the conduct of the case as a whole and give any necessary case management directions. They should be ready to assist the court in doing so and to answer questions the court may ask for this purpose.

2.10 Where a date for a hearing has been fixed and a party wishes to make an application at that hearing but he does not have sufficient time to serve an application notice he should inform the other party and the court (if possible in writing) as soon as he can of the nature of the application and the reason for it. He should then make the application orally at the hearing.

APPLICATIONS WITHOUT SERVICE OF APPLICATION NOTICE

3 An application may be made without serving an application notice only:

(1) where there is exceptional urgency,
(2) where the overriding objective is best furthered by doing so,
(3) by consent of all parties,
(4) with the permission of the court,
(5) where paragraph 2.10 above applies, or
(6) where a court order, rule or practice direction permits.

GIVING NOTICE OF AN APPLICATION

4.1 Unless the court otherwise directs or paragraph 3 of this practice direction applies the application notice must be served as soon as practicable after it has been issued and, if there is to be a hearing, at least 3 clear days before the hearing date (rule 23.7(1)(b)).

4.2 Where an application notice should be served but there is not sufficient time to do so, informal notification of the application should be given unless the circumstances of the application require secrecy.

PRE-ACTION APPLICATIONS

5 All applications made before a claim is commenced should be made under Part 23 of the Civil Procedure Rules. Attention is drawn in particular to rule 23.2(4).

TELEPHONE HEARINGS

6.1 The court may order than an application be dealt with by a telephone hearing.

6.1A The applicant should indicate on his application notice if he seeks a court order under paragraph 6.1. Where he has not done so but nevertheless wishes to seek an order the request should be made as early as possible.

6.2 An order under 6.1 will not normally be made unless every party entitled to be given notice of the application and to be heard at the hearing has consented to the order.

6.3

(1) Where a party entitled to be heard at the hearing of the application is acting in person, the court—
  (a) may not make an order under 6.1 except on condition that arrangements will be made for the party acting in person to be attended at the telephone hearing by a responsible person to whom the party acting in person is known and who can confirm to the court the identity of the party; and
  (b) may not give effect to an order under 6.1 unless the party acting in person is accompanied by a responsible person who at the commencement of the hearing confirms to the court the identity of the party.
(2) The "responsible person" may be a barrister, solicitor, legal executive, doctor, clergyman, police officer, prison officer or other person of comparable status.
(3) If the court makes an order under 6.1 it will give any directions necessary for the telephone hearing.

6.4 No representative of a party to an application being heard by telephone may attend the judge in person while the application is being heard unless the other party to the application has agreed that he may do so.

6.5 If an application is to be heard by telephone the following directions will apply, subject to any direction to the contrary:

(1) The applicant's legal representative must arrange the telephone conference for precisely the time fixed by the court. The telecommunications provider must be capable of connecting the parties and the court.

(2) He must tell the operator the telephone numbers of all those participating in the conference call and the sequence in which they are to be called.

(3) It is the responsibility of the applicant's legal representative to ascertain from all the other parties whether they have instructed counsel and, if so the identity of counsel, and whether the legal representative and counsel will be on the same or different telephone numbers.

(4) The sequence in which they are to be called will be:
  (a) the applicant's legal representative and (if on a different number) his counsel,
  (b) the legal representative (and counsel) for all other parties, and
  (c) the judge.

(5) The applicant's legal representative must arrange for the conference to be recorded on tape by the telecommunications provider whose system is being used and must send the tape to the court.

(6) Each speaker is to remain on the line after being called by the operator setting up the conference call. The call may be 2 or 3 minutes before the time fixed for the application.

(7) When the judge has been connected the applicant's legal representative (or his counsel) will introduce the parties in the usual way.

(8) If the use of a "speakerphone" by any party causes the judge or any other party any difficulty in hearing what is said the judge may require that party to use a hand held telephone.

(9) The telephone charges debited to the account of the party initiating the conference call will be treated as part of the costs of the application.

VIDEO CONFERENCING

7 Where the parties to a matter wish to use video conferencing facilities, and those facilities are available in the relevant court, they should apply to the Master or district judge for directions.

(Paragraph 29 and Annex 3 of Practice Direction 32 provide guidance on the use of video conferencing in the civil courts)

NOTE OF PROCEEDINGS

8 The procedural judge should keep, either by way of a note or a tape recording, brief details of all proceedings before him, including the dates of the proceedings and a short statement of the decision taken at each hearing.

EVIDENCE

9.1 The requirement for evidence in certain types of applications is set out in some of the rules and practice directions. Where there is no specific requirement to provide evidence it should be borne in mind that, as a practical matter, the court will often need to be satisfied by evidence of the facts that are relied on in support of or for opposing the application.

9.2 The court may give directions for the filing of evidence in support of or opposing a particular application. The court may also give directions for the filing of evidence in relation to any hearing that it fixes on its own initiative. The directions may specify the form that evidence is to take and when it is to be served.

9.3 Where it is intended to rely on evidence which is not contained in the application itself, the evidence, if it has not already been served, should be served with the application.

9.4 Where a respondent to an application wishes to rely on evidence which has not yet been served he should serve it as soon as possible and in any event in accordance with any directions the court may have given.

9.5 If it is necessary for the applicant to serve any evidence in reply it should be served as soon as possible and in any event in accordance with any directions the court may have given.

9.6 Evidence must be filed with the court as well as served on the parties. Exhibits should not be filed unless the court otherwise directs.

9.7 The contents of an application notice may be used as evidence (otherwise than at trial) provided the contents have been verified by a statement of truth.[1]

CONSENT ORDERS

10.1 Rule 40.6 sets out the circumstances where an agreed judgment or order may be entered and sealed.

10.2 Where all parties affected by an order have written to the court consenting to the making of the order a draft of which has been filed with the court, the court will treat the draft as having been signed in accordance with rule 40.6(7).

10.3 Where a consent order must be made by a judge (ie rule 40.6(2) does not apply) the order must be drawn so that the judge's name and judicial title can be inserted.

10.4 The parties to an application for a consent order must ensure that they provide the court with any material it needs to be satisfied that it is appropriate to make the order. Subject to any rule or practice direction a letter will generally be acceptable for this purpose.

10.5 Where a judgment or order has been agreed in respect of an application or claim where a hearing date has been fixed, the parties must inform the court immediately. (note that parties are reminded that under rules 28.4 and 29.5 the case management timetable cannot be varied by written agreement of the parties.)

OTHER APPLICATIONS CONSIDERED WITHOUT A HEARING

11.1 Where rule 23.8(b) applies the parties should so inform the court in writing and each should confirm that all evidence and other material on which he relies has been disclosed to the other parties to the application.

11.2 Where rule 23.8(c) applies the court will treat the application as if it were proposing to make an order on its own initiative.

Applications to stay claim where related criminal proceedings

11A.1 An application for the stay of civil proceedings pending the determination of related criminal proceedings may be made by any party to the civil proceedings or by the prosecutor or any defendant in the criminal proceedings.

11A.2 Every party to the civil proceedings must, unless he is the applicant, be made a respondent to the application.

11A.3 The evidence in support of the application must contain an estimate of the expected duration of the stay and must identify the respects in which the continuance of the civil proceedings may prejudice the criminal trial.

11A.4 In order to make an application under paragraph 11A.1, it is not necessary for the prosecutor or defendant in the criminal proceedings to be joined as a party to the civil proceedings.

MISCELLANEOUS

12.1 Except in the most simple application the applicant should bring to any hearing a draft of the order sought. If the case is proceeding in the Royal Courts of Justice and the order is unusually long or complex it should also be supplied on disk for use by the court office.

12.2 Where rule 23.11 applies, the power to re-list the application in rule 23.11(2) is in addition to any other powers of the court with regard to the order (for example to set aside, vary, discharge or suspend the order).

COSTS

13.1 Attention is drawn to the costs practice direction and, in particular, to the court's power to make a summary assessment of costs.

13.2 Attention is also drawn to rule 44.13(i) which provides that if an order makes no mention of costs, none are payable in respect of the proceedings to which it relates. **[1555]**

1 See Part 22.

PRACTICE DIRECTION 25—INTERIM INJUNCTIONS

NOTES
This Practice Direction supplements CPR, Pt 25 at **[1422]**.

JURISDICTION

1.1 High Court Judges and any other Judge duly authorised may grant "search orders"[1] and "freezing injunctions".[2]

1.2 In a case in the High Court, Masters and district judges have the power to grant injunctions:
(1) by consent,
(2) in connection with charging orders and appointments of receivers,
(3) in aid of execution of judgments.

1.3 In any other case any judge who has jurisdiction to conduct the trial of the action has the power to grant an injunction in that action.

1.4 A Master or district judge has the power to vary or discharge an injunction granted by any Judge with the consent of all the parties.

MAKING AN APPLICATION

2.1 The application notice must state:
(1) the order sought, and
(2) the date, time and place of the hearing.

2.2 The application notice and evidence in support must be served as soon as practicable after issue and in any event not less than 3 days before the court is due to hear the application.[3]

2.3 Where the court is to serve, sufficient copies of the application notice and evidence in support for the court and for each respondent should be filed for issue and service.

2.4 Whenever possible a draft of the order sought should be filed with the application notice and a disk containing the draft should also be available to the court in a format compatible with the word processing software used by the court. This will enable the court officer to arrange for any amendments to be incorporated and for the speedy preparation and sealing of the order.

EVIDENCE

3.1 Applications for search orders and freezing injunctions must be supported by affidavit evidence.

3.2 Applications for other interim injunctions must be supported by evidence set out in either:
(1) a witness statement, or
(2) a statement of case provided that it is verified by a statement of truth,[4] or
(3) the application provided that it is verified by a statement of truth,

unless the court, an Act, a rule or a practice direction requires evidence by affidavit.

3.3 The evidence must set out the facts on which the applicant relies for the claim being made against the respondent, including all material facts of which the court should be made aware.

3.4 Where an application is made without notice to the respondent, the evidence must also set out why notice was not given.

(See Part 32 and the practice direction that supplements it for information about evidence.)

URGENT APPLICATIONS AND APPLICATIONS WITHOUT NOTICE

4.1 These fall into two categories:
(1) applications where a claim form has already been issued, and

(2) applications where a claim form has not yet been issued,

and, in both cases, where notice of the application has not been given to the respondent.

4.2 These applications are normally dealt with at a court hearing but cases of extreme urgency may be dealt with by telephone.

4.3 Applications dealt with at a court hearing after issue of a claim form:

(1) the application notice, evidence in support and a draft order (as in 2.4 above) should be filed with the court two hours before the hearing wherever possible,

(2) if an application is made before the application notice has been issued, a draft order (as in 2.4 above) should be provided at the hearing, and the application notice and evidence in support must be filed with the court on the same or next working day or as ordered by the court, and

(3) except in cases where secrecy is essential, the applicant should take steps to notify the respondent informally of the application.

4.4 Applications made before the issue of a claim form:

(1) in addition to the provisions set out at 4.3 above, unless the court orders otherwise, either the applicant must undertake to the court to issue a claim form immediately or the court will give directions for the commencement of the claim,[5]

(2) where possible the claim form should be served with the order for the injunction,

(3) an order made before the issue of a claim form should state in the title after the names of the applicant and respondent "the Claimant and Defendant in an Intended Action".

4.5 Applications made by telephone:

(1) where it is not possible to arrange a hearing, application can be made between 10.00 am and 5.00 pm weekdays by telephoning the Royal Courts of Justice on 020 7947 6000 and asking to be put in contact with a High Court Judge of the appropriate Division available to deal with an emergency application in a High Court matter. The appropriate district registry may also be contacted by telephone. In county court proceedings, the appropriate county court should be contacted,

(2) where an application is made outside those hours the applicant should either

(a) telephone the Royal Courts of Justice on 020 7947 6000 where he will be put in contact with the clerk to the appropriate duty judge in the High Court (or the appropriate area Circuit Judge where known), or

(b) the Urgent Court Business Officer of the appropriate Circuit who will contact the local duty judge,

(3) where the facility is available it is likely that the judge will require a draft order to be faxed to him,

(4) the application notice and evidence in support must be filed with the court on the same or next working day or as ordered, together with two copies of the order for sealing,

(5) injunctions will be heard by telephone only where the applicant is acting by counsel or solicitors.

ORDERS FOR INJUNCTIONS

5.1 Any order for an injunction, unless the court orders otherwise, must contain:

(1) an undertaking by the applicant to the court to pay any damages which the respondent(s) (or any other party served with or notified of the order) sustain which the court considers the applicant should pay,

(2) if made without notice to any other party, an undertaking by the applicant to the court to serve on the respondent the application notice, evidence in support and any order made as soon as practicable,

(3) if made without notice to any other party, a return date for a further hearing at which the other party can be present,

(4) if made before filing the application notice, an undertaking to file and pay the appropriate fee on the same or next working day, and

(5) if made before issue of a claim form—

(a) an undertaking to issue and pay the appropriate fee on the same or next working day, or

(b) directions for the commencement of the claim.

5.2 An order for an injunction made in the presence of all parties to be bound by it or made at a hearing of which they have had notice, may state that it is effective until trial or further order.

5.3 Any order for an injunction must set out clearly what the respondent must do or not do.

FREEZING INJUNCTIONS

Orders to restrain disposal of assets worldwide and within England and Wales

6.1 An example of a Freezing Injunction is annexed to this practice direction.

6.2 This example may be modified as appropriate in any particular case. In particular, the court may, if it considers it appropriate, require the applicant's solicitors, as well as the applicant, to give undertakings.

SEARCH ORDERS

7.1 The following provisions apply to search orders in addition to those listed above.

7.2 **The Supervising Solicitor**

The Supervising Solicitor must be experienced in the operation of search orders. A Supervising Solicitor may be contacted either through the Law Society or, for the London area, through the London Solicitors Litigation Association.

7.3 **Evidence**:

(1) the affidavit must state the name, firm and its address, and experience of the Supervising Solicitor, also the address of the premises and whether it is a private or business address, and

(2) the affidavit must disclose very fully the reason the order is sought, including the probability that relevant material would disappear if the order were not made.

7.4 **Service**:

(1) the order must be served personally by the Supervising Solicitor, unless the court otherwise orders, and must be accompanied by the evidence in support and any documents capable of being copied,

(2) confidential exhibits need not be served but they must be made available for inspection by the respondent in the presence of the applicant's solicitors while the order is carried out and afterwards be retained by the respondent's solicitors on their undertaking not to permit the respondent—

(a) to see them or copies of them except in their presence, and

(b) to make or take away any note or record of them,

(3) the Supervising Solicitor may be accompanied only by the persons mentioned in the order,

(4) the Supervising Solicitor must explain the terms and effect of the order to the respondent in every day language and advise him—

(a) of his right to take legal advice and to apply to vary or discharge the order; and

(b) that he may be entitled to avail himself of—

(i) legal professional privilege; and

(ii) the privilege against self-incrimination,

(5) where the Supervising Solicitor is a man and the respondent is likely to be an unaccompanied woman, at least one other person named in the order must be a woman and must accompany the Supervising Solicitor, and

(6) the order may only be served between 9.30 am and 5.30 pm Monday to Friday unless the court otherwise orders.

7.5 **Search and custody of materials**:

(1) no material shall be removed unless clearly covered by the terms of the order,

(2) the premises must not be searched and no items shall be removed from them except in the presence of the respondent or a person who appears to be a responsible employee of the respondent,

(3) where copies of documents are sought, the documents should be retained for no more than 2 days before return to the owner,

(4) where material in dispute is removed pending trial, the applicant's solicitors should place it in the custody of the respondent's solicitors on their undertaking to retain it in safekeeping and to produce it to the court when required,

(5) in appropriate cases the applicant should insure the material retained in the respondent's solicitors' custody,

(6) the Supervising Solicitor must make a list of all material removed from the premises and supply a copy of the list to the respondent,

(7) no material shall be removed from the premises until the respondent has had reasonable time to check the list,

(8) if any of the listed items exists only in computer readable form, the respondent must

immediately give the applicant's solicitors effective access to the computers, with all necessary passwords, to enable them to be searched, and cause the listed items to be printed out,

(9) the applicant must take all reasonable steps to ensure that no damage is done to any computer or data,

(10) the applicant and his representatives may not themselves search the respondent's computers unless they have sufficient expertise to do so without damaging the respondent's system,

(11) the Supervising Solicitor shall provide a report on the carrying out of the order to the applicant's solicitors,

(12) as soon as the report is received the applicant's solicitors shall
  (a) serve a copy of it on the respondent, and
  (b) file a copy of it with the court, and

(13) where the Supervising Solicitor is satisfied that full compliance with paragraph 7.5(7) and (8) above is impracticable, he may permit the search to proceed and items to be removed without compliance with the impracticable requirements.

7.6 **General**

The Supervising Solicitor must not be an employee or member of the applicant's firm of solicitors.

7.7 If the court orders that the order need not be served by the Supervising Solicitor, the reason for so ordering must be set out in the order.

7.8 The search order must not be carried out at the same time as a police search warrant.

7.9 There is no privilege against self incrimination in:

(1) Intellectual Property cases in respect of a "related offence" or for the recovery of a "related penalty" as defined in section 72 Supreme Court Act 1981;

(2) proceedings for the recovery or administration of any property, for the execution of any trust or for an account of any property or dealings with property in relation to offences under the Theft Act 1968 (see section 31 Theft Act 1968); or

(3) proceedings in which a court is hearing an application for an order under Part IV or Part V of the Children Act 1989 (see section 98 Children Act 1989).

However, the privilege may still be claimed in relation to material or information required to be disclosed by an order, as regards potential criminal proceedings outside those statutory provisions.

7.10 Applications in intellectual property cases should be made in the Chancery Division.

7.11 An example of a Search Order is annexed to this Practice Direction. This example may be modified as appropriate in any particular case.

DELIVERY-UP ORDERS

8.1 The following provisions apply to orders, other than search orders, for delivery up or preservation of evidence or property where it is likely that such an order will be executed at the premises of the respondent or a third party.

8.2 In such cases the court shall consider whether to include in the order for the benefit or protection of the parties similar provisions to those specified above in relation to injunctions and search orders.

INJUNCTIONS AGAINST THIRD PARTIES

9.1 The following provisions apply to orders which will affect a person other than the applicant or respondent, who:

(1) did not attend the hearing at which the order was made; and

(2) is served with the order.

9.2 Where such a person served with the order requests—

(1) a copy of any materials read by the judge, including material prepared after the hearing at the direction of the judge or in compliance with the order; or

(2) a note of the hearing,

the applicant, or his legal representative, must comply promptly with the request, unless the court orders otherwise.

[1556]

ANNEX

FREEZING INJUNCTION

IN THE HIGH COURT OF JUSTICE

[ ] DIVISION

Before The Honourable Mr Justice

[ ]

Claim No

Dated

Applicant

Seal

Respondent

Name, address and reference of Respondent

PENAL NOTICE

IF YOU [ ]* DISOBEY THIS ORDER YOU MAY BE HELD TO BE IN CONTEMPT OF COURT AND MAY BE IMPRISONED, FINED OR HAVE YOUR ASSETS SEIZED.

ANY OTHER PERSON WHO KNOWS OF THIS ORDER AND DOES ANYTHING WHICH HELPS OR PERMITS THE RESPONDENT TO BREACH THE TERMS OF THIS ORDER MAY ALSO BE HELD TO BE IN CONTEMPT OF COURT AND MAY BE IMPRISONED, FINED OR HAVE THEIR ASSETS SEIZED.

*** Insert name of Respondent.**

This Order

1. This is a Freezing Injunction made against [ ] ("the Respondent") on [ ] by Mr Justice [ ] on the application of [ ] ("the Applicant"). The Judge read the Affidavits listed in Schedule A and accepted the undertakings set out in Schedule B at the end of this Order.
2. This order was made at a hearing without notice to the Respondent. The Respondent has a right to apply to the court to vary or discharge the order—see paragraph 13 below.
3. There will be a further hearing in respect of this order on [ ] ("the return date").
4. If there is more than one Respondent—
   (a) unless otherwise stated, references in this order to "the Respondent" mean both or all of them; and
   (b) this order is effective against any Respondent on whom it is served or who is given notice of it.

Freezing Injunction

[For injunction limited to assets in England and Wales]

5. Until the return date or further order of the court, the Respondent must not remove from England and Wales or in any way dispose of, deal with or diminish the value of any of his assets which are in England and Wales up to the value of £ .

[For worldwide injunction]

5. Until the return date or further order of the court, the Respondent must not—
   (1) remove from England and Wales any of his assets which are in England and Wales up to the value of £ ; or
   (2) in any way dispose of, deal with or diminish the value of any of his assets whether they are in or outside England and Wales up to the same value.

[For either form of injunction]

6. Paragraph 5 applies to all the Respondent's assets whether or not they are in his own name and whether they are solely or jointly owned. For the purpose of this order the

Respondent's assets include any asset which he has the power, directly or indirectly, to dispose of or deal with as if it were his own. The Respondent is to be regarded as having such power if a third party holds or controls the asset in accordance with his direct or indirect instructions.

7. This prohibition includes the following assets in particular—
   (a) the property known as [*title/address*] or the net sale money after payment of any mortgages if it has been sold;
   (b) the property and assets of the Respondent's business [known as [*name*]] [carried on at [*address*]] or the sale money if any of them have been sold; and
   (c) any money standing to the credit of any bank account including the amount of any cheque drawn on such account which has not been cleared.

[For injunction limited to assets in England and Wales]

8. If the total value free of charges or other securities ("unencumbered value") of the Respondent's assets in England and Wales exceeds £ , the Respondent may remove any of those assets from England and Wales or may dispose of or deal with them so long as the total unencumbered value of his assets still in England and Wales remains above £ .

[For worldwide injunction]

8.
   (1) If the total value free of charges or other securities ("unencumbered value") of the Respondent's assets in England and Wales exceeds £ , the Respondent may remove any of those assets from England and Wales or may dispose of or deal with them so long as the total unencumbered value of the Respondent's assets still in England and Wales remains above £ .
   (2) If the total unencumbered value of the Respondent's assets in England and Wales does not exceed £ , the Respondent must not remove any of those assets from England and Wales and must not dispose of or deal with any of them. If the Respondent has other assets outside England and Wales, he may dispose of or deal with those assets outside England and Wales so long as the total unencumbered value of all his assets whether in or outside England and Wales remains above £ .

Provision of Information

9.
   (1) Unless paragraph (2) applies, the Respondent must [immediately] [within hours of service of this order] and to the best of his ability inform the Applicant's solicitors of all his assets [in England and Wales] [worldwide] [exceeding £ in value] whether in his own name or not and whether solely or jointly owned, giving the value, location and details of all such assets.
   (2) If the provision of any of this information is likely to incriminate the Respondent, he may be entitled to refuse to provide it, but is recommended to take legal advice before refusing to provide the information. Wrongful refusal to provide the information is contempt of court and may render the Respondent liable to be imprisoned, fined or have his assets seized.

10. Within [ ] working days after being served with this order, the Respondent must swear and serve on the Applicant's solicitors an affidavit setting out the above information.

Exceptions to this Order

11.
   (1) This order does not prohibit the Respondent from spending £ a week towards his ordinary living expenses and also £ [*or* a reasonable sum] on legal advice and representation. [But before spending any money the Respondent must tell the Applicant's legal representatives where the money is to come from.]
   [(2) This order does not prohibit the Respondent from dealing with or disposing of any of his assets in the ordinary and proper course of business.]
   (3) The Respondent may agree with the Applicant's legal representatives that the above spending limits should be increased or that this order should be varied in any other respect, but any agreement must be in writing.
   (4) The order will cease to have effect if the Respondent—
      (a) provides security by paying the sum of £ into court, to be held to the order of the court; or
      (b) makes provision for security in that sum by another method agreed with the Applicant's legal representatives.

Costs

12. The costs of this application are reserved to the judge hearing the application on the return date.

Variation or Discharge of this Order

13. Anyone served with or notified of this order may apply to the court at any time to vary or discharge this order (or so much of it as affects that person), but they must first inform the Applicant's solicitors. If any evidence is to be relied upon in support of the application, the substance of it must be communicated in writing to the Applicant's solicitors in advance.

Interpretation of this Order

14. A Respondent who is an individual who is ordered not to do something must not do it himself or in any other way. He must not do it through others acting on his behalf or on his instructions or with his encouragement.
15. A Respondent which is not an individual which is ordered not to do something must not do it itself or by its directors, officers, partners, employees or agents or in any other way.

Parties other than the Applicant and Respondent

16. **Effect of this order**
It is a contempt of court for any person notified of this order knowingly to assist in or permit a breach of this order. Any person doing so may be imprisoned, fined or have their assets seized.
17. **Set off by banks**
This injunction does not prevent any bank from exercising any right of set off it may have in respect of any facility which it gave to the respondent before it was notified of this order.
18. **Withdrawals by the Respondent**
No bank need enquire as to the application or proposed application of any money withdrawn by the Respondent if the withdrawal appears to be permitted by this order.
[For worldwide injunction]
19. **Persons outside England and Wales**
(1) Except as provided in paragraph (2) below, the terms of this order do not affect or concern anyone outside the jurisdiction of this court.
(2) The terms of this order will affect the following persons in a country or state outside the jurisdiction of this court—
(a) the Respondent or his officer or agent appointed by power of attorney;
(b) any person who—
(i) is subject to the jurisdiction of this court;
(ii) has been given written notice of this order at his residence or place of business within the jurisdiction of this court; and
(iii) is able to prevent acts or omissions outside the jurisdiction of this court which constitute or assist in a breach of the terms of this order; and
(c) any other person, only to the extent that this order is declared enforceable by or is enforced by a court in that country or state.
[For worldwide injunction]
20. **Assets located outside England and Wales**
Nothing in this order shall, in respect of assets located outside England and Wales, prevent any third party from complying with—
(1) what it reasonably believes to be its obligations, contractual or otherwise, under the laws and obligations of the country or state in which those assets are situated or under the proper law of any contract between itself and the Respondent; and
(2) any orders of the courts of that country or state, provided that reasonable notice of any application for such an order is given to the Applicant's solicitors.

Communications with the Court

All communications to the court about this order should be sent to—
[Insert the address and telephone number of the appropriate Court Office]
If the order is made at the Royal Courts of Justice, communications should be addressed as follows—
Where the order is made in the Chancery Division
Room TM 505, Royal Courts of Justice, Strand, London WC2A 2LL quoting the case number. The telephone number is 0207 947 6754.
Where the order is made in the Queen's Bench Division
Room WG034, Royal Courts of Justice, Strand, London WC2A 2LL quoting the case number. The telephone number is 0207 947 6009.
Where the order is made in the Commercial Court
Room E201, Royal Courts of Justice, Strand, London WC2A 2LL quoting the case number. The telephone number is 0207 947 6826.
The offices are open between 10 am and 4.30 pm Monday to Friday.

Schedule A
Affidavits

The Applicant relied on the following affidavits—

[name]	[number of affidavit]	[date sworn]	[filed on behalf of]
(1)			
(2)			

Schedule B
Undertakings given to the court by the applicant

(1) If the court later finds that this order has caused loss to the Respondent, and decides that the Respondent should be compensated for that loss, the Applicant will comply with any order the court may make.

[(2) The Applicant will—

(a) on or before [*date*] cause a written guarantee in the sum of £ to be issued from a bank with a place of business within England or Wales, in respect of any order the court may make pursuant to paragraph (1) above; and

(b) immediately upon issue of the guarantee, cause a copy of it to be served on the Respondent.]

(3) As soon as practicable the Applicant will issue and serve a claim form [in the form of the draft produced to the court] [claiming the appropriate relief].

(4) The Applicant will [swear and file an affidavit] [cause an affidavit to be sworn and filed] [substantially in the terms of the draft affidavit produced to the court] [confirming the substance of what was said to the court by the Applicant's counsel/solicitors].

(5) The Applicant will serve upon the Respondent [together with this order] [as soon as practicable]—

(i) copies of the affidavits and exhibits containing the evidence relied upon by the Applicant, and any other documents provided to the court on the making of the application;

(ii) the claim form; and

(iii) an application notice for continuation of the order.

[(6) Anyone notified of this order will be given a copy of it by the Applicant's legal representatives.]

(7) The Applicant will pay the reasonable costs of anyone other than the Respondent which have been incurred as a result of this order including the costs of finding out whether that person holds any of the Respondent's assets and if the court later finds that this order has caused such person loss, and decides that such person should be compensated for that loss, the Applicant will comply with any order the court may make.

(8) If this order ceases to have effect (for example, if the Respondent provides security or the Applicant does not provide a bank guarantee as provided for above) the Applicant will immediately take all reasonable steps to inform in writing anyone to whom he has given notice of this order, or who he has reasonable grounds for supposing may act upon this order, that it has ceased to have effect.

[(9) The Applicant will not without the permission of the court use any information obtained as a result of this order for the purpose of any civil or criminal proceedings, either in England and Wales or in any other jurisdiction, other than this claim.]

[(10) The Applicant will not without the permission of the court seek to enforce this order in any country outside England and Wales [or seek an order of a similar nature including orders conferring a charge or other security against the Respondent or the Respondent's assets].]

Name and address of applicant's legal representatives

The Applicant's legal representatives are—

[Name, address, reference, fax and telephone numbers both in and out of office hours and e-mail.]

SEARCH ORDER	**IN THE HIGH COURT OF JUSTICE**
	[ ] DIVISION
Before The Honourable Mr Justice	**[ ]**

Claim No

Dated

Applicant

Seal

Respondent

Name, address and reference of Respondent

PENAL NOTICE

IF YOU [ ]* DISOBEY THIS ORDER YOU MAY BE HELD TO BE IN CONTEMPT OF COURT AND MAY BE IMPRISONED, FINED OR HAVE YOUR ASSETS SEIZED.

ANY OTHER PERSON WHO KNOWS OF THIS ORDER AND DOES ANYTHING WHICH HELPS OR PERMITS THE RESPONDENT TO BREACH THE TERMS OF THIS ORDER MAY ALSO BE HELD TO BE IN CONTEMPT OF COURT AND MAY BE IMPRISONED, FINED OR HAVE THEIR ASSETS SEIZED.

*** Insert name of Respondent.**

This Order

1. This is a Search Order made against [ ] ("the Respondent") on [ ] by Mr Justice [ ] on the application of [ ] ("the Applicant"). The Judge read the Affidavits listed in Schedule F and accepted the undertakings set out in Schedules C, D and E at the end of this order.
2. This order was made at a hearing without notice to the Respondent. The Respondent has a right to apply to the court to vary or discharge the order—see paragraph 27 below.
3. There will be a further hearing in respect of this order on [ ] ("the return date").
4. If there is more than one Respondent—
   (a) unless otherwise stated, references in this order to "the Respondent" mean both or all of them; and
   (b) this order is effective against any Respondent on whom it is served or who is given notice of it.
5. This order must be complied with by—
   (a) the Respondent;
   (b) any director, officer, partner or responsible employee of the Respondent; and
   (c) if the Respondent is an individual, any other person having responsible control of the premises to be searched.

The Search

6. The Respondent must permit the following persons[6]—
   (a) [ ] ("the Supervising Solicitor");
   (b) [ ], a solicitor in the firm of [ ], the Applicant's solicitors; and
   (c) up to [ ] other persons[7] being [*their identity or capacity*] accompanying them,

(together "the search party"), to enter the premises mentioned in Schedule A to this order and any other premises of the Respondent disclosed under paragraph 18 below and any vehicles under the Respondent's control on or around the premises ("the premises") so that they can search for, inspect, photograph or photocopy, and deliver into the safekeeping of the Applicant's solicitors all the documents and articles which are listed in Schedule B to this order ("the listed items").

7. Having permitted the search party to enter the premises, the Respondent must allow the search party to remain on the premises until the search is complete. In the event that it becomes necessary for any of those persons to leave the premises before the search is complete, the Respondent must allow them to re-enter the premises immediately upon their seeking re-entry on the same or the following day in order to complete the search.

Restrictions on Search

8. This order may not be carried out at the same time as a police search warrant.

9. Before the Respondent allows anybody onto the premises to carry out this order, he is entitled to have the Supervising Solicitor explain to him what it means in everyday language.

10. The Respondent is entitled to seek legal advice and to ask the court to vary or discharge this order. Whilst doing so, he may ask the Supervising Solicitor to delay starting the search for up to 2 hours or such other longer period as the Supervising Solicitor may permit. However, the Respondent must—

(a) comply with the terms of paragraph 27 below;
(b) not disturb or remove any listed items; and
(c) permit the Supervising Solicitor to enter, but not start to search.

11.

(1) Before permitting entry to the premises by any person other than the Supervising Solicitor, the Respondent may, for a short time (not to exceed two hours, unless the Supervising Solicitor agrees to a longer period)—

(a) gather together any documents he believes may be incriminating or privileged; and
(b) hand them to the Supervising Solicitor for him to assess whether they are incriminating or privileged as claimed.

(2) If the Supervising Solicitor decides that the Respondent is entitled to withhold production of any of the documents on the ground that they are privileged or incriminating, he will exclude them from the search, record them in a list for inclusion in his report and return them to the Respondent.

(3) If the Supervising Solicitor believes that the Respondent may be entitled to withhold production of the whole or any part of a document on the ground that it or part of it may be privileged or incriminating, or if the Respondent claims to be entitled to withhold production on those grounds, the Supervising Solicitor will exclude it from the search and retain it in his possession pending further order of the court.

12. If the Respondent wishes to take legal advice and gather documents as permitted, he must first inform the Supervising Solicitor and keep him informed of the steps being taken.

13. No item may be removed from the premises until a list of the items to be removed has been prepared, and a copy of the list has been supplied to the Respondent, and he has been given a reasonable opportunity to check the list.

14. The premises must not be searched, and items must not be removed from them, except in the presence of the Respondent.

15. If the Supervising Solicitor is satisfied that full compliance with paragraphs 13 or 14 is not practicable, he may permit the search to proceed and items to be removed without fully complying with them.

Delivery up of Articles/Documents

16. The Respondent must immediately hand over to the Applicant's solicitors any of the listed items, which are in his possession or under his control, save for any computer or hard disk integral to any computer. Any items the subject of a dispute as to whether they are listed items must immediately be handed over to the Supervising Solicitor for safe keeping pending resolution of the dispute or further order of the court.

17. The Respondent must immediately give the search party effective access to the computers on the premises, with all necessary passwords, to enable the computers to be searched. If they contain any listed items the Respondent must cause the listed items to be displayed so that they can be read and copied.[8] The Respondent must provide the Applicant's Solicitors with copies of all listed items contained in the computers. All reasonable steps shall be taken by the Applicant and the Applicant's solicitors to ensure that no damage is done to any computer or data. The Applicant and his representatives may not themselves search the Respondent's computers unless they have sufficient expertise to do so without damaging the Respondent's system.

Provision of Information

18. The Respondent must immediately inform the Applicant's Solicitors (in the presence of the Supervising Solicitor) so far as he is aware—

(a) where all the listed items are;
(b) the name and address of everyone who has supplied him, or offered to supply him, with listed items;
(c) the name and address of everyone to whom he has supplied, or offered to supply, listed items; and
(d) full details of the dates and quantities of every such supply and offer.

19. Within [ ] working days after being served with this order the Respondent must swear and serve an affidavit setting out the above information.[9]

Prohibited Acts

20. Except for the purpose of obtaining legal advice, the Respondent must not directly or indirectly inform anyone of these proceedings or of the contents of this order, or warn anyone that proceedings have been or may be brought against him by the Applicant until 4.30 pm on the return date or further order of the court.
21. Until 4.30 pm on the return date the Respondent must not destroy, tamper with, cancel or part with possession, power, custody or control of the listed items otherwise than in accordance with the terms of this order.
22. [Insert any negative injunctions.]
23. [Insert any further order]

Costs

24. The costs of this application are reserved to the judge hearing the application on the return date.

Restrictions on Service

25. This order may only be served between [ ] am/pm and [ ] am/pm [and on a weekday].[10]
26. This order must be served by the Supervising Solicitor, and paragraph 6 of the order must be carried out in his presence and under his supervision.

Variation and Discharge of this Order

27. Anyone served with or notified of this order may apply to the court at any time to vary or discharge this order (or so much of it as affects that person), but they must first inform the Applicant's solicitors. If any evidence is to be relied upon in support of the application, the substance of it must be communicated in writing to the Applicant's solicitors in advance.

Interpretation of this Order

28. Any requirement that something shall be done to or in the presence of the Respondent means—
(a) if there is more than one Respondent, to or in the presence of any one of them; and
(b) if a Respondent is not an individual, to or in the presence of a director, officer, partner or responsible employee.
29. A Respondent who is an individual who is ordered not to do something must not do it himself or in any other way. He must not do it through others acting on his behalf or on his instructions or with his encouragement.
30. A Respondent which is not an individual which is ordered not to do something must not do it itself or by its directors, officers, partners, employees or agents or in any other way.

Communications with the Court

All communications to the court about this order should be sent to—
[Insert the address and telephone number of the appropriate Court Office]
If the order is made at the Royal Courts of Justice, communications should be addressed as follows—
Where the order is made in the Chancery Division
Room TM 505, Royal Courts of Justice, Strand, London WC2A 2LL quoting the case number. The telephone number is 0207 947 6754.
Where the order is made in the Queen's Bench Division
Room WG034, Royal Courts of Justice, Strand, London WC2A 2LL quoting the case number. The telephone number is 0207 947 6009.
Where the order is made in the Commercial Court
Room E201, Royal Courts of Justice, Strand, London WC2A 2LL quoting the case number. The telephone number is 0207 947 6826.
The offices are open between 10 am and 4.30 pm Monday to Friday.

Schedule A

THE PREMISES

Schedule B

THE LISTED ITEMS

Schedule C

Undertakings given to the court by the applicant

(1) If the court later finds that this order or carrying it out has caused loss to the Respondent, and decides that the Respondent should be compensated for that loss, the Applicant will

comply with any order the court may make. Further if the carrying out of this order has been in breach of the terms of this order or otherwise in a manner inconsistent with the Applicant's solicitors' duties as officers of the court, the Applicant will comply with any order for damages the court may make.

[(2) As soon as practicable the Applicant will issue a claim form [in the form of the draft produced to the court] [claiming the appropriate relief].]

(3) The Applicant will [swear and file an affidavit] [cause an affidavit to be sworn and filed] [substantially in the terms of the draft affidavit produced to the court] [confirming the substance of what was said to the court by the Applicant's counsel/solicitors].

(4) The Applicant will not, without the permission of the court, use any information or documents obtained as a result of carrying out this order nor inform anyone else of these proceedings except for the purposes of these proceedings (including adding further Respondents) or commencing civil proceedings in relation to the same or related subject matter to these proceedings until after the return date.

[(5) The Applicant will maintain pending further order the sum of £ [ ] in an account controlled by the Applicant's solicitors.]

[(6) The Applicant will insure the items removed from the premises.]

Schedule D
Undertakings given by the applicant's solicitors

(1) The Applicant's solicitors will provide to the Supervising Solicitor for service on the Respondent—

(i) a service copy of this order;

(ii) the claim form (with defendant's response pack) or, if not issued, the draft produced to the court;

(iii) an application for hearing on the return date;

(iv) copies of the affidavits [*or draft affidavits*] and exhibits capable of being copied containing the evidence relied upon by the applicant;

(v) a note of any allegation of fact made orally to the court where such allegation is not contained in the affidavits or draft affidavits read by the judge; and

(vi) a copy of the skeleton argument produced to the court by the Applicant's [counsel/ solicitors].

(2) The Applicants' solicitors will answer at once to the best of their ability any question whether a particular item is a listed item.

(3) Subject as provided below the Applicant's solicitors will retain in their own safe keeping all items obtained as a result of this order until the court directs otherwise.

(4) The Applicant's solicitors will return the originals of all documents obtained as a result of this order (except original documents which belong to the Applicant) as soon as possible and in any event within [two] working days of their removal.

Schedule E
Undertakings given by the supervising solicitor

(1) The Supervising Solicitor will use his best endeavours to serve this order upon the Respondent and at the same time to serve upon the Respondent the other documents required to be served and referred to in paragraph (1) of Schedule D.

(2) The Supervising Solicitor will offer to explain to the person served with the order its meaning and effect fairly and in everyday language, and to inform him of his right to take legal advice (including an explanation that the Respondent may be entitled to avail himself of the privilege against self-incrimination and legal professional privilege) and to apply to vary or discharge this order as mentioned in paragraph 27 above.

(3) The Supervising Solicitor will retain in the safe keeping of his firm all items retained by him as a result of this order until the court directs otherwise.

(4) Unless and until the court otherwise orders, or unless otherwise necessary to comply with any duty to the court pursuant to this order, the Supervising Solicitor shall not disclose to any person any information relating to those items, and shall keep the existence of such items confidential.

(5) Within [48] hours of completion of the search the Supervising Solicitor will make and provide to the Applicant's solicitors, the Respondent or his solicitors and to the judge who made this order (for the purposes of the court file) a written report on the carrying out of the order.

Schedule F
Affidavits

The Applicant relied on the following affidavits—

[name] [number of affidavit] [date sworn] [filed on behalf of]

(1)

(2)

Name and address of applicant's solicitors

The Applicant's solicitors are—

[Name, address, reference, fax and telephone numbers both in and out of office hours.]

[1557]

1 Rule 25.1(1)(h).
2 Rule 25.1(1)(f).
3 Rule 23.7(1) and (2) and see rule 23.7(4) (short service).
4 See Part 22
5 Rule 25.2(3)
6 Where the premises are likely to be occupied by an unaccompanied woman and the Supervising Solicitor is a man, at least one of the persons accompanying him should be a woman.
7 None of these persons should be people who could gain personally or commercially from anything they might read or see on the premises, unless their presence is essential.
8 If it is envisaged that the Respondent's computers are to be imaged (i.e. the hard drives are to be copied wholesale, thereby reproducing listed items and other items indiscriminately), special provision needs to be made and independent computer specialists need to be appointed, who should be required to give undertakings to the court.
9 The period should ordinarily be longer than the period in paragraph (2) of Schedule D, if any of the information is likely to be included in listed items taken away of which the Respondent does not have copies.
10 Normally, the order should be served in the morning (not before 9.30 am) and on a weekday to enable the Respondent more readily to obtain legal advice.

PRACTICE DIRECTION 34—DEPOSITIONS AND COURT ATTENDANCE BY WITNESSES

NOTES

This Practice Direction supplements CPR, Pt 34 at **[1439]**. Only paras 4–11, and the Annexes, are reproduced here.

DEPOSITIONS

To be taken in England and Wales for use as evidence in proceedings in courts in England and Wales

4.1 A party may apply for an order for a person to be examined on oath before:

(1) a judge,
(2) an examiner of the court, or
(3) such other person as the court may appoint.[1]

4.2 The party who obtains an order for the examination of a deponent[2] before an examiner of the court[3] must:

(1) apply to the Foreign Process Section of the Masters' Secretary's Department at the Royal Courts of Justice for the allocation of an examiner,
(2) when allocated, provide the examiner with copies of all documents in the proceedings necessary to inform the examiner of the issues, and
(3) pay the deponent a sum to cover his travelling expenses to and from the examination and compensation for his loss of time.[4]

4.3 In ensuring that the deponent's evidence is recorded in full, the court or the examiner may permit it to be recorded on audiotape or videotape, but the deposition[5] must always be recorded in writing by him or by a competent shorthand writer or stenographer.

4.4 If the deposition is not recorded word for word, it must contain, as nearly as may be, the statement of the deponent; the examiner may record word for word any particular questions and answers which appear to him to have special importance.

4.5 If a deponent objects to answering any question or where any objection is taken to any question, the examiner must:
(1) record in the deposition or a document attached to it—
(a) the question,
(b) the nature of and grounds for the objection, and
(c) any answer given, and
(2) give his opinion as to the validity of the objection and must record it in the deposition or a document attached to it.

The court will decide as to the validity of the objection and any question of costs arising from it.

4.6 Documents and exhibits must:
(1) have an identifying number or letter marked on them by the examiner, and
(2) be preserved by the party or his legal representative[6] who obtained the order for the examination, or as the court or the examiner may direct.

4.7 The examiner may put any question to the deponent as to:
(1) the meaning of any of his answers, or
(2) any matter arising in the course of the examination.

4.8 Where a deponent:
(1) fails to attend the examination, or
(2) refuses to:
(a) be sworn, or
(b) answer any lawful question, or
(c) produce any document,

the examiner will sign a certificate[7] of such failure or refusal and may include in his certificate any comment as to the conduct of the deponent or of any person attending the examination.

4.9 The party who obtained the order for the examination must file the certificate with the court and may apply for an order that the deponent attend for examination or as may be.[8] The application may be made without notice.[9]

4.10 The court will make such order on the application as it thinks fit including an order for the deponent to pay any costs resulting from his failure or refusal.[10]

4.11 A deponent who wilfully refuses to obey an order made against him under Part 34 may be proceeded against for contempt of court.

4.12 A deposition must:
(1) be signed by the examiner,
(2) have any amendments to it initialled by the examiner and the deponent,
(3) be endorsed by the examiner with—
(a) a statement of the time occupied by the examination, and
(b) a record of any refusal by the deponent to sign the deposition and of his reasons for not doing so, and
(4) be sent by the examiner to the court where the proceedings are taking place for filing on the court file.

4.13 Rule 34.14 deals with the fees and expenses of an examiner.

Depositions to be taken abroad for use as evidence in proceedings before courts in England and Wales (where the Taking of Evidence Regulation does not apply)

5.1 Where a party wishes to take a deposition from a person outside the jurisdiction, the High Court may order the issue of a letter of request to the judicial authorities of the country in which the proposed deponent is.[11]

5.2 An application for an order referred to in paragraph 5.1 should be made by application notice in accordance with Part 23.

5.3 The documents which a party applying for an order for the issue of a letter of request must file with his application notice are set out in rule 34.13(6). They are as follows:
(1) a draft letter of request is set out in Annex A to this practice direction,
(2) a statement of the issues relevant to the proceedings,
(3) a list of questions or the subject matter of questions to be put to the proposed deponent,
(4) a translation of the documents in (1), (2) and 93) above, unless the proposed deponent is in a country of which English is an official language, and
(5) an undertaking to be responsible for the expenses of the Secretary of State.

In addition to the documents listed above the party applying for the order must file a draft order.

5.4 The above documents should be filed with the Masters' Secretary in Room E214, Royal Courts of Justice, Strand, London WC2A 2LL.

5.5 The application will be dealt with by the Senior Master of the Queen's Bench Division of the High Court who will, if appropriate, sign the letter of request.

5.6 Attention is drawn to the provisions of rule 23.10 (application to vary or discharge an order made without notice).

5.7 If parties are in doubt as to whether a translation under paragraph 5.3(4) above is required, they should seek guidance from the Foreign Process Section of the Masters' Secretary's Department.

5.8 A special examiner appointed under rule 34.13(4) may be the British Consul or the Consul-General or his deputy in the country where the evidence is to be taken if:

(1) there is in respect of that country a Civil Procedure Convention providing for the taking of evidence in that country for the assistance of proceedings in the High Court or other court in this country, or

(2) with the consent of the Secretary of State.

5.9 The provisions of paragraphs 4.1 to 4.12 above apply to the depositions referred to in this paragraph.

Depositions to be taken in England and Wales for use as evidence in proceedings before courts abroad pursuant to letters of request (where the Taking of Evidence Regulation does not apply)

6.1 Section II of Part 34 relating to obtaining evidence for foreign courts applies to letters of request and should be read in conjunction with this part of the practice direction.

6.2 The Evidence (Proceedings in Other Jurisdictions) Act 1975 applies to these depositions.

6.3 The written evidence supporting an application under rule 34.17 (which should be made by application notice—see Part 23) must include or exhibit—

(1) a statement of the issues relevant to the proceedings;

(2) a list of questions or the subject matter of questions to be put to the proposed deponent;

(3) a draft order; and

(4) a translation of the documents in (1) and (2) into English, if necessary.

6.4

(1) The Senior Master will send to the Treasury Solicitor any request—

(a) forwarded by the Secretary of State with a recommendation that effect should be given to the request without requiring an application to be made; or

(b) received by him in pursuance of a Civil Procedure Convention providing for the taking of evidence of any person in England and Wales to assist a court or tribunal in a foreign country where no person is named in the document as the applicant.

(2) In relation to such a request, the Treasury Solicitor may, with the consent of the Treasury—

(a) apply for an order under the 1975 Act; and

(b) take such other steps as are necessary to give effect to the request.

6.5 The order for the deponent to attend and be examined together with the evidence upon which the order was made must be served on the deponent.

6.6 Attention is drawn to the provisions of rule 23.10 (application to vary or discharge an order made without notice).

6.7 Arrangements for the examination to take place at a specified time and place before an examiner of the court or such other person as the court may appoint shall be made by the applicant for the order and approved by the Senior Master.

6.8 The provisions of paragraph 4.2 to 4.12 apply to the depositions referred to in this paragraph, except that the examiner must send the deposition to the Senior Master.

(For further information about evidence see Part 32 and the practice direction which supplements it.)

TAKING OF EVIDENCE BETWEEN EU MEMBER STATES

Taking of Evidence Regulation

7.1 Where evidence is to be taken—

(a) from a person in another Member State of the European Union for use as evidence in proceedings before courts in England and Wales; or

(b) from a person in England and Wales for use as evidence in proceedings before a court in another Member State,

Council Regulation (EC) No 1206/2001 of 28 May 2001 on co-operation between the courts of the Member States in the taking of evidence in civil or commercial matters ("the Taking of Evidence Regulation") applies.

7.2 The Taking of Evidence Regulation is annexed to this practice direction as Annex B.

7.3 The Taking of Evidence Regulation does not apply to Denmark. In relation to Denmark, therefore, rule 34.13 and Section II of Part 34 will continue to apply.

(Article 21(1) of the Taking of Evidence Regulation provides that the Regulation prevails over other provisions contained in bilateral or multilateral agreements or arrangements concluded by the Member States and in particular the Hague Convention of 1 March 1954 on Civil Procedure and the Hague Convention of 18 March 1970 on the Taking of Evidence Abroad in Civil or Commercial Matters.)

Originally published in the official languages of the European Community in the *Official Journal of the European Communities* by the Office for Official Publications of the European Communities.

Meaning of "designated court"

8.1 In accordance with the Taking of Evidence Regulation, each Regulation State has prepared a list of courts competent to take evidence in accordance with the Regulation indicating the territorial and, where appropriate, special jurisdiction of those courts.

8.2 Where Part 34, Section III refers to a "designated court" in relation to another Regulation State, the reference is to the court, referred to in the list of competent courts of that State, which is appropriate to the application in hand.

8.3 Where the reference is to the "designated court" in England and Wales, the reference is to the appropriate competent court in the jurisdiction. The designated courts for England and Wales are listed in Annex C to this practice direction.

Central Body

9.1 The Taking of Evidence Regulation stipulates that each Regulation State must nominate a Central Body responsible for—

(a) supplying information to courts;

(b) seeking solutions to any difficulties which may arise in respect of a request; and

(c) forwarding, in exceptional cases, at the request of a requesting court, a request to the competent court.

9.2 The United Kingdom has nominated the Senior Master, Queen's Bench Division, to be the Central Body for England and Wales.

9.3 The Senior Master, as Central Body, has been designated responsible for taking decisions on requests pursuant to Article 17 of the Regulation. Article 17 allows a court to submit a request to the Central Body or a designated competent authority in another Regulation State to take evidence directly in that State.

Evidence to be taken in another Regulation State for use in England and Wales

10.1 Where a person wishes to take a deposition from a person in another Regulation State, the court where the proceedings are taking place may order the issue of a request to the designated court in the Regulation State (Rule 34.23(2)). The form of request is prescribed as Form A in the Taking of Evidence Regulation.

10.2 An application to the court for an order under rule 34.23(2) should be made by application notice in accordance with Part 23.

10.3 Rule 34.23(3) provides that the party applying for the order must file a draft form of request in the prescribed form. Where completion of the form requires attachments or documents to accompany the form, these must also be filed.

PART II CIVIL PROCEDURE RULES

10.4 If the court grants an order under rule 34.23(2), it will send the form of request directly to the designated court.

10.5 Where the taking of evidence requires the use of an expert, the designated court may require a deposit in advance towards the costs of that expert. The party who obtained the order is responsible for the payment of any such deposit which should be deposited with the court for onward transmission. Under the provisions of the Taking of Evidence Regulation, the designated court is not required to execute the request until such payment is received.

10.6 Article 17 permits the court where proceedings are taking place to take evidence directly from a deponent in another Regulation State if the conditions of the article are satisfied. Direct taking of evidence can only take place if evidence is given voluntarily without the need for coercive measures. Rule 34.23(5) provides for the court to make an order for the submission of a request to take evidence directly. The form of request is Form I annexed to the Taking of Evidence Regulation and rule 34.23(6) makes provision for a draft of this form to be filed by the party seeking the order. An application for an order under rule 34.23(5) should be by application notice in accordance with Part 23.

10.7 Attention is drawn to the provisions of rule 23.10 (application to vary or discharge an order made without notice).

Evidence to be taken in England and Wales for use in another Regulation State

11.1 Where a designated court in England and Wales receives a request to take evidence from a court in a Regulation State, the court will send the request to the Treasury Solicitor.

11.2 On receipt of the request, the Treasury Solicitor may, with the consent of the Treasury, apply for an order under rule 34.24.

11.3 An application to the court for an order must be accompanied by the Form of request to take evidence and any accompanying documents, translated if required under paragraph 11.4.

11.4 The United Kingdom has indicated that, in addition to English, it will accept French as a language in which documents may be submitted. Where the form of request and any accompanying documents are received in French they will be translated into English by the Treasury Solicitor.

11.5 The order for the deponent to attend and be examined together with the evidence on which the order was made must be served on the deponent.

11.6 Arrangements for the examination to take place at a specified time and place shall be made by the Treasury Solicitor and approved by the court.

11.7 The court shall send details of the arrangements for the examination to such of

(a) the parties and, if any, their representatives; or
(b) the representatives of the foreign court,

who have indicated, in accordance with the Taking of Evidence Regulation, that they wish to be present at the examination.

11.8 The provisions of paragraph 4.3 to 4.12 apply to the depositions referred to in this paragraph.

[1558]

---

1 Rule 34.8(3).
2 See rule 34.8(2) for explanation of "deponent" and "deposition".
3 For the appointment of examiners of the court see rule 34.15.
4 Rule 34.8(6).
5 See rule 34.8(2) for explanation of "deponent" and "deposition".
6 For the definition of legal representative see rule 2.3.
7 Rule 34.10.
8 Rule 34.10(2) and (3).
9 Rule 34.10(3).
10 Rule 34.10(4).
11 Rule 34.13(1).

ANNEX A

Draft letter of request (where the Taking of Evidence Regulation does not apply)

To the Competent Judicial Authority of in the of

I [*name*] Senior Master of the Queen's Bench Division of the Supreme Court of England and Wales respectfully request the assistance of your court with regard to the following matters.

1. A claim is now pending in the Division of the High Court of Justice in England and Wales entitled as follows [*set out full title and claim number*] in which [*name*] of [*address*] is the claimant and [*name*) of [*address*] is the defendant.
2. The names and addresses of the representatives or agents of [*set out names and addresses of representatives of the parties*].
3. The claim by the claimant is for:—
   (a) [*set out the nature of the claim*]
   (b) [*the relief sought, and*]
   (c) [*a summary of the facts.*]
4. It is necessary for the purposes of justice and for the due determination of the matters in dispute between the parties that you cause the following witnesses, who are resident within your jurisdiction, to be examined. The names and addresses of the witnesses are as follows:
5. The witnesses should be examined on oath or if that is not possible within your laws or is impossible of performance by reason of the internal practice and procedure of your court or by reason of practical difficulties, they should be examined in accordance with whatever procedure your laws provide for in these matters.
6. Either/

The witnesses should be examined in accordance with the list of questions annexed hereto.

Or/

The witnesses should be examined regarding [*set out full details of evidence sought.*]

NB Where the witness is required to produce documents, these should be clearly identified.

7. I would ask that you cause me, or the agents of the parties (if appointed), to be informed of the date and place where the examination is to take place.
8. Finally, I request that you will cause the evidence of the said witnesses to be reduced into writing and all documents produced on such examinations to be duly marked for identification and that you will further be pleased to authenticate such examinations by the seal of your court or in such other way as is in accordance with your procedure and return the written evidence and documents produced to me addressed as follows:

Senior Master of the Queen's Bench Division
Royal Courts of Justice
Strand
London WC2A 2LL
England

[1559]

(*Annex B contains the original text of Council Regulation* (*EC*) *No 1206/2001 of 28 May 2001 on cooperation between the courts of the Member States in the taking of evidence in civil or commercial matters; that Regulation, as amended, is reproduced in Pt IV*(*H*) *of this work at* **[3598]**.)

ANNEX C

Designated courts in England and Wales under the Taking of Evidence Regulation (*see paragraph 8 above*)

Area	*Designated court*
London and South Eastern Circuit	Royal Courts of Justice (Queen's Bench Division)
Midland Circuit	Birmingham Civil Justice Centre
Western Circuit	Bristol County Court
Wales and Chester Circuit	Cardiff Civil Justice Centre
Northern Circuit	Manchester County Court
North Eastern Circuit	Leeds County Court

[1560]

PRACTICE DIRECTION 58—COMMERCIAL COURT

NOTES

This Practice Direction supplements CPR, Pt 58 at **[1452]**.

GENERAL

1.1 This practice direction applies to commercial claims proceeding in the commercial list of the Queen's Bench Division. It supersedes all previous practice directions and practice statements in the Commercial Court.

1.2 All proceedings in the commercial list, including any appeal from a judgment, order or decision of a master or district judge before the proceedings were transferred to the Commercial Court, will be heard or determined by a Commercial Court judge, except that—

(1) another judge of the Queen's Bench Division or Chancery Division may hear urgent applications if no Commercial Court judge is available; and
(2) unless the court otherwise orders, any application relating to the enforcement of a Commercial Court judgment or order for the payment of money will be dealt with by a master of the Queen's Bench Division or a district judge.

1.3 Provisions in other practice directions which refer to a master or district judge are to be read, in relation to claims in the commercial list, as if they referred to a Commercial Court judge.

1.4 The Admiralty and Commercial Registry in the Royal Courts of Justice is the administrative office of the court for all proceedings in the commercial list.

STARTING PROCEEDINGS IN THE COMMERCIAL COURT

2.1 Claims in the Commercial Court must be issued in the Admiralty and Commercial Registry.

2.2 When the Registry is closed, a request to issue a claim form may be made by fax, using the procedure set out in Appendix A to this practice direction. If a request is made which complies with that procedure, the claim form is issued when the fax is received by the Registry.

2.3 The claim form must be marked in the top right hand corner "Queen's Bench Division, Commercial Court".

2.4 A claimant starting proceedings in the commercial list, other than an arbitration claim, must use practice form N1(CC) for Part 7 claims or practice form N208(CC) for Part 8 claims.

APPLICATIONS BEFORE PROCEEDINGS ARE ISSUED

3.1 A party who intends to bring a claim in the commercial list must make any application before the claim form is issued to a Commercial Court judge.

3.2 The written evidence in support of such an application must state that the claimant intends to bring proceedings in the commercial list.

3.3 If the Commercial Court judge hearing the application considers that the proceedings should not be brought in the commercial list, he may adjourn the application to be heard by a master or by a judge who is not a Commercial Court judge.

TRANSFERRING PROCEEDINGS TO OR FROM THE COMMERCIAL COURT

4.1 If an application is made to a court other than the Commercial Court to transfer proceedings to the commercial list, the other court may—

(1) adjourn the application to be heard by a Commercial Court judge; or
(2) dismiss the application.

4.2 If the Commercial Court orders proceedings to be transferred to the commercial list—

(1) it will order them to be transferred to the Royal Courts of Justice; and
(2) it may give case management directions.

4.3 An application by a defendant, including a Part 20 defendant, for an order transferring proceedings from the commercial list should be made promptly and normally not later than the first case management conference.

4.4 A party applying to the Commercial Court to transfer a claim to the commercial list must give notice of the application to the court in which the claim is proceeding, and the Commercial Court will not make an order for transfer until it is satisfied that such notice has been given.

ACKNOWLEDGEMENT OF SERVICE

5.1 For Part 7 claims, a defendant must file an acknowledgment of service using practice form N9 (CC).

5.2 For Part 8 claims, a defendant must file an acknowledgment of service using practice form N210 (CC).

DEFAULT JUDGMENT AND ADMISSIONS

6. The practice directions supplementing Parts 12 and 14 apply with the following modifications—

(1) paragraph 4.1(1) of the practice direction supplementing Part 12 is to be read as referring to the service of the claim form; and

(2) the references to "particulars of claim" in paragraphs 2.1, 3.1 and 3.2 of the practice direction supplementing Part 14 are to be read as referring to the claim form.

VARIATION OF TIME LIMITS

7.1 If the parties, in accordance with rule 2.11, agree in writing to vary a time limit, the claimant must notify the court in writing, giving brief written reasons for the agreed variation.

7.2 The court may make an order overriding an agreement by the parties varying a time limit.

AMENDMENTS

8. Paragraph 2.2 of the practice direction supplementing Part 17 is modified so that amendments to a statement of case must show the original text, unless the court orders otherwise.

SERVICE OF DOCUMENTS

9. Unless the court orders otherwise, the Commercial Court will not serve documents or orders and service must be effected by the parties.

CASE MANAGEMENT

10.1 The following parts only of the practice direction supplementing Part 29 apply—

(1) paragraph 5 (case management conferences), excluding paragraph 5.9 and modified so far as is made necessary by other specific provisions of this practice direction; and

(2) paragraph 7 (failure to comply with case management directions).

10.2 If the proceedings are started in the commercial list, the claimant must apply for a case management conference—

(a) for a Part 7 claim, within 14 days of the date when all defendants who intend to file and serve a defence have done so; and

(b) for a Part 8 claim, within 14 days of the date when all defendants who intend to serve evidence have done so.

10.3 If the proceedings are transferred to the commercial list, the claimant must apply for a case management conference within 14 days of the date of the order transferring them, unless the judge held, or gave directions for, a case management conference when he made the order transferring the proceedings.

10.4 Any party may, at a time earlier than that provided in paragraphs 10.2 or 10.3, apply in writing to the court to fix a case management conference.

10.5 If the claimant does not make an application in accordance with paragraphs 10.2 or 10.3, any other party may apply for a case management conference.

10. 6 The court may fix a case management conference at any time on its own initiative. If it does so, the court will give at least 7 days notice to the parties, unless there are compelling reasons for a shorter period of notice.

10.7 Not less than 7 days before a case management conference, each party must file and serve—

(1) a completed case management information sheet; and
(2) an application notice for any order which that party intends to seek at the case management conference, other than directions referred to in the case management information sheet.

10.8 Unless the court orders otherwise, the claimant, in consultation with the other parties, must prepare—
(1) a case memorandum, containing a short and uncontroversial summary of what the case is about and of its material case history;
(2) a list of issues, with a section listing important matters which are not in dispute; and
(3) a case management bundle containing—
(a) the claim form;
(b) all statements of case (excluding schedules), except that, if a summary of a statement of case has been filed, the bundle should contain the summary, and not the full statement of case;
(c) the case memorandum;
(d) the list of issues;
(e) the case management information sheets and, if a pre-trial timetable has been agreed or ordered, that timetable;
(f) the principal orders of the court; and
(g) any agreement in writing made by the parties as to disclosure,

and provide copies of the case management bundle for the court and the other parties at least 7 days before the first case management conference or any earlier hearing at which the court may give case management directions.

10.9 The claimant, in consultation with the other parties, must revise and update the documents referred to in paragraph 10.8 appropriately as the case proceeds. This must include making all necessary revisions and additions at least 7 days before any subsequent hearing at which the court may give case management directions.

PRE-TRIAL REVIEW

11.1 At any pre-trial review or case management hearing, the court will ensure that case management directions have been complied with and give any further directions for the trial that are necessary.

11.2 Advocates who are to represent the parties at the trial should represent them at the pre-trial review and any case management hearing at which arrangements for the trial are to be discussed.

11.3 Before the pre-trial review, the parties must discuss and, if possible, agree a draft written timetable for the trial.

11.4 The claimant must file a copy of the draft timetable for the trial at least two days before the hearing of the pre-trial review. Any parts of the timetable which are not agreed must be identified and short explanations of the disagreement must be given.

11.5 At the pre-trial review, the court will set a timetable for the trial, unless a timetable has already been fixed or the court considers that it would be inappropriate to do so or appropriate to do so at a later time.

CASE MANAGEMENT WHERE THERE IS A PART 20 CLAIM

12. Paragraph 5 of the practice direction supplementing Part 20 applies, except that, unless the court otherwise orders, the court will give case management directions for Part 20 claims at the same case management conferences as it gives directions for the main claim.

EVIDENCE FOR APPLICATIONS

13.1 The general requirement is that, unless the court orders otherwise—
(1) evidence in support of an application must be filed and served with the application (see rule 23.7(3));
(2) evidence in answer must be filed and served within 14 days after the application is served; and
(3) evidence in reply must be filed and served within 7 days of the service of evidence in answer.

13.2 In any case in which the application is likely to require an oral hearing of more than half a day the periods set out in paragraphs 13.1(2) and (3) will be 28 days and 14 days respectively.

13.3 If the date fixed for the hearing of an application means that the times in paragraphs 13.1(2) and (3) cannot both be achieved, the evidence must be filed and served—
(1) as soon as possible; and
(2) in sufficient time to ensure that the application may fairly proceed on the date fixed.

13.4 The parties may, in accordance with rule 2.11, agree different periods from those in paragraphs 13.1(2) and (3) provided that the agreement does not affect the date fixed for the hearing of the application.

JUDGMENTS AND ORDERS

14.1 An application for a consent order must include a draft of the proposed order signed on behalf of all parties to whom it relates (see paragraph 10.4 of the practice direction supplementing Part 23).

14.2 Judgments and orders are generally drawn up by the parties (see rule 58.15). The parties are not therefore required to supply draft orders on disk (see paragraph 12.1 of the practice direction supplementing Part 23).

APPENDIX A
PROCEDURE FOR ISSUE OF CLAIM FORM WHEN REGISTRY IS CLOSED—PARAGRAPH 2.2

1. A request to issue a claim form may be made by fax when the Registry is closed, provided that—
(a) the claim form is signed by a solicitor acting on behalf of the claimant; and
(b) it does not require the permission of the court for its issue (unless such permission has already been given).

2. The solicitor requesting the issue of the claim form ("the issuing solicitor") must—
(a) endorse on the claim form and sign the endorsement set out below;
(b) send a copy of the claim form so endorsed to the Registry by fax for issue under paragraph 2.2 of this practice direction; and
(c) complete and sign a certificate in the form set out below, certifying that he has received a transmission report confirming that the fax has been transmitted in full, and stating the time and date of transmission.

3. When the Registry is next open to the public after the issue of a claim form in accordance with this procedure, the issuing solicitor or his agent must attend and deliver to the Registry—
(a) the original of the claim form which was sent by fax (including the endorsement and the certificate) or, if the claim form has been served, a true and certified copy of it;
(b) as many copies of the claim form as the Registry requires; and
(c) the transmission report.

4. When a court officer at the Registry has checked that—
(a) the claim form delivered under paragraph 3 matches the claim form received by fax; and
(b) the correct issue fee has been paid,

he will allocate a number to the case, and seal, mark as "original" and date the claim form with the date of issue (being the date when the fax is recorded at the Registry as having been received).

5. If the issuing solicitor has served the unsealed claim form on any person, he must as soon as practicable—
(a) inform that person of the case number; and
(b) if requested, serve him with a copy of the sealed and dated claim form at any address in England and Wales.

6. Any person served with a claim form issued under this procedure may, without paying a fee, inspect and take copies of the documents lodged at the Registry under paragraphs 2 and 3 above.

7. The issue of a claim form in accordance with this procedure takes place when the fax is recorded at the Registry as having been received, and the claim form has the same effect for all purposes as a claim form issued under Part 7 or 8. Unless the court otherwise orders, the sealed version of the claim form retained by the Registry is conclusive proof that the claim form was issued at the time and on the date stated.

8. If the procedure set out in this Appendix is not complied with, the court may declare that a claim form shall be treated as not having been issued.

ENDORSEMENT

A claim form issued pursuant to a request by fax must be endorsed as follows:

(1) This claim form is issued under paragraph 2.2 of the Commercial Court practice direction and may be served notwithstanding that it does not bear the seal of the Court.

(2) A true copy of this claim form and endorsement has been sent to the Admiralty and Commercial Registry, Royal Courts of Justice, Strand, London WC2A 2LL, at the time and date certified below by the solicitor whose name appears below ("the issuing solicitor").

(3) It is the duty of the issuing solicitor or his agent to attend at the Registry when it is next open to the public for the claim form to be sealed.

(4) Any person served with this unsealed claim form—

(a) will be notified by the issuing solicitor of the case number;

(b) may require the issuing solicitor to serve him with a copy of the sealed claim form at an address in England and Wales; and

(c) may inspect without charge the documents lodged at the Registry by the issuing solicitor.

(5) I, the issuing solicitor, undertake [to the Court, to the defendants named in this claim form, and to any other person served with this claim form]—

(a) that the statement in paragraph 2 above is correct;

(b) that the time and date given in the certificate with this endorsement are correct;

(c) that this claim form is a claim form which may be issued under paragraph 2.2 and Appendix A of the Commercial Court practice direction;

(d) that I will comply in all respects with the requirements of Appendix A of the Commercial Court practice direction; and

(e) that I will indemnify any person served with the claim form before it is sealed against any loss suffered as a result of the claim form being or becoming invalid as a result of any failure to comply with Appendix A of the Commercial Court practice direction.

(*Signed*)

Solicitor for the claimant

[**Note:** the endorsement may be signed in the name of the firm of solicitors rather than an individual solicitor, or by solicitors' agents in their capacity as agents acting on behalf of their professional clients.]

CERTIFICATE

The issuing solicitor must sign a certificate in the following form—

I certify that I have received a transmission report confirming that the transmission of a copy of this claim form to the Registry by fax was fully completed and that the time and date of transmission to the Registry were *[enter the time and date shown on the transmission report]*.

Dated

(*Signed*)

Solicitor for the claimant

[**Note:** the certificate must be signed in the name of the firm of solicitors rather than an individual solicitor, or by solicitors' agents in their capacity as agents acting on behalf of their professional clients.]

[1561]

NOTES

The following forms are the forms present at this position in the Civil Procedure Rules and can be found at http://www.dca.gov.uk/civil/procrules_fin/menus/forms.htm—

N1(CC) Claim Form
N1C(CC) Notes for defendant
N9(CC) Acknowledgement of service
N208(CC) Claim form (Part 8)
N208C(CC) Notes for defendant (Part 8)
N210(CC) Acknowledgement of service (Part 8)
N211(CC) Claim form (Part 20)
N211C(CC) Notes for Part 20 defendant
N213(CC) Acknowledgement of service (Part 20)

PRACTICE DIRECTION 59—MERCANTILE COURTS

NOTES

This Practice Direction supplements CPR, Pt 59 at **[1467]**.

GENERAL

1.1 This practice direction applies to mercantile claims.

1.2 Mercantile Courts are established in—

(1) the following district registries of the High Court—Birmingham, Bristol, Cardiff, Chester, Leeds, Liverpool, Manchester and Newcastle; and

(2) the Central London County Court (previously called the Business List and now called the Mercantile List).

1.3 All mercantile claims will be heard or determined by a Mercantile judge, except that—

(1) an application may be heard and determined by any other judge who, if the claim were not a mercantile claim, would have jurisdiction to determine it, if—

(a) the application is urgent and no Mercantile judge is available to hear it; or

(b) a Mercantile judge directs it to be heard by another judge; and

(2) unless the court otherwise orders, all proceedings for the enforcement of a Mercantile Court judgment or order for the payment of money will be dealt with by a district judge.

1.4 Provisions in other practice directions which refer to a master or district judge are to be read, in relation to mercantile claims, as if they referred to a Mercantile judge.

STARTING PROCEEDINGS IN A MERCANTILE COURT

2.1 A claim should only be started in a Mercantile Court if it will benefit from the expertise of a Mercantile judge.

2.2 The claim form must be marked in the top right hand corner "Queen's Bench Division, __________ District Registry, Mercantile Court" or "Central London County Court, Mercantile List" as appropriate.

2.3 A claim having a value less than £15,000 may not be issued in the Mercantile List at the Central London County Court without permission of the court.

2.4 A claim may be issued in the Mercantile List at the Central London County Court provided it has some connection with the South Eastern Circuit, for example, because—

(1) it is convenient for the claim to be dealt with in that court;

(2) the claim arises out of a transaction which took place within that circuit; or

(3) one of the parties resides or carries on business within that circuit.

APPLICATIONS BEFORE PROCEEDINGS ARE ISSUED

3.1 A party who intends to bring a claim in a Mercantile Court must make any application before the claim form is issued to a judge of that court.

3.2 The written evidence in support of such an application should show why the claim is suitable to proceed as a mercantile claim.

TRANSFER OF PROCEEDINGS TO OR FROM A MERCANTILE COURT

4.1 If a claim which has not been issued in a Mercantile Court is suitable to continue as a mercantile claim—

(1) any party wishing the claim to be transferred to a Mercantile Court may make an application for transfer to the court to which transfer is sought;

(2) if all parties consent to the transfer, the application may be made by letter to the mercantile listing officer of the court to which transfer is sought, stating why the case is suitable to be transferred to that court and enclosing the written consents of the parties, the claim form and statements of case.

4.2 If an application for transfer is made to a court which does not have power to make the order, that court may—

(1) adjourn the application to be heard by a Mercantile judge; or

(2) dismiss the application.

4.3 A Mercantile judge may make an order under rule 59.3 of his own initiative.

DEFAULT JUDGMENT AND ADMISSIONS

5. The practice directions supplementing Parts 12 and 14 apply with the following modifications—

(1) paragraph 4.1(1) of the practice direction supplementing Part 12 is to be read as referring to the service of the claim form; and

(2) the references to "particulars of claim" in paragraphs 2.1, 3.1 and 3.2 of the practice direction supplementing Part 14 are to be read as referring to the claim form.

VARIATION OF TIME LIMITS BY AGREEMENT

6.1 If the parties, in accordance with rule 2.11, agree in writing to vary a time limit, the claimant must notify the court in writing, giving brief written reasons for the agreed variation.

6.2 The court may make an order overriding an agreement by the parties varying a time limit.

CASE MANAGEMENT

7.1 The following parts only of the practice direction supplementing Part 29 apply—

(1) paragraph 5 (case management conferences), excluding paragraph 5.9 and modified so far as is made necessary by other specific provisions of this practice direction; and

(2) paragraph 7 (failure to comply with case management directions).

7.2 If proceedings are started in a Mercantile Court, the claimant must apply for a case management conference—

(1) for a Part 7 claim, within 14 days of the date when all defendants who intend to file and serve a defence have done so; and

(2) for a Part 8 claim, within 14 days of the date when all defendants who intend to serve evidence have done so.

7.3 If proceedings are transferred to a Mercantile Court, the claimant must apply for a case management conference within 14 days of receiving an acknowledgment of the transfer from the receiving court, unless the judge held, or gave directions for, a case management conference when he made the order transferring the proceedings.

7.4 Any party may, at a time earlier than that provided in paragraphs 7.2 or 7.3, apply in writing to the court to fix a case management conference.

7.5 If the claimant does not make an application in accordance with paragraphs 7.2 or 7.3, any other party may apply for a case management conference.

7.6 The court may fix a case management conference at any time on its own initiative. If it does so, the court will give at least 7 days notice to the parties, unless there are compelling reasons for a shorter period of notice.

7.7 Not less than 7 days before a case management conference—

(1) each party shall file and serve—

(a) a case management information sheet substantially in the form set out at Appendix A to this practice direction; and

(b) an application notice for any order which that party intends to seek at the case management conference, other than directions referred to in the case management information sheet; and

(2) the claimant (or other party applying for the conference) shall in addition file and serve—

(a) a case management file containing—

— the claim form;

— the statements of case (excluding schedules of more than 15 pages);

— any orders already made;

— the case management information sheets; and

— a short list of the principal issues to be prepared by the claimant; and

(b) a draft order substantially in the form set out at Appendix B to this practice direction, setting out the directions which that party thinks appropriate.

7.8 In appropriate cases—

(1) the parties may, not less than 7 days before the date fixed for the case management conference, submit agreed directions for the approval of the judge;

(2) the judge will then either—

(a) make the directions proposed; or

(b) make them with alterations; or
(c) require the case management conference to proceed; but

(3) the parties must assume that the conference will proceed until informed to the contrary.

7.9 If the parties submit agreed directions and the judge makes them with alterations, any party objecting to the alterations may, within 7 days of receiving the order containing the directions, apply to the court for the directions to be varied.

7.10 The directions given at the case management conference—

(1) will normally cover all steps in the case through to trial, including the fixing of a trial date or window, or directions for the taking of steps to fix the trial date or window; and

(2) may include the fixing of a progress monitoring date or dates, and make provision for the court to be informed as to the progress of the case at the date or dates fixed.

7.11 If the court fixes a progress monitoring date, it may after that date fix a further case management conference or a pre-trial review on its own initiative if—

(1) no or insufficient information is provided by the parties; or

(2) it is appropriate in view of the information provided.

PRE-TRIAL REVIEW AND QUESTIONNAIRE

8.1 The court may order a pre-trial review at any time.

8.2 Each party must file and serve a completed pre-trial check list substantially in the form set out in Appendix C to this practice direction—

(1) if a pre-trial review has been ordered, not less than 7 days before the date of the review; or

(2) if no pre-trial review has been ordered, not less than 6 weeks before the trial date.

8.3 When pre-trial check lists are filed under paragraph 8.2(2)—

(1) the judge will consider them and decide whether to order a pre-trial review; and

(2) if he does not order a pre-trial review, he may on his own initiative give directions for the further preparation of the case or as to the conduct of the trial.

8.4 At a pre-trial review—

(1) the parties should if possible be represented by the advocates who will be appearing at the trial;

(2) any representatives appearing must be fully informed and authorised for the purposes of the review; and

(3) the court will give such directions for the conduct of the trial as it sees fit.

EVIDENCE FOR APPLICATIONS

9.1 The general requirement is that, unless the court orders otherwise—

(1) evidence in support of an application must be filed and served with the application: see rule 23.7(3);

(2) evidence in answer must be filed and served within 14 days after the application is served;

(3) evidence in reply must be filed and served within 7 days of the service of the evidence in answer.

9.2 In any case in which the application is likely to require an oral hearing of more than half a day the periods set out in paragraphs 9.1(2) and (3) will be 28 days and 14 days respectively.

9.3 If the date fixed for the hearing of the application means that the times in paragraphs 9.1(2) and (3) cannot both be achieved, the evidence must be filed and served—

(1) as soon as possible; and

(2) in sufficient time to ensure that the application may fairly proceed on the date fixed.

9.4 The parties may, in accordance with rule 2.11, agree different periods from those provided above, provided that the agreement does not affect the ability to proceed on the date fixed for the hearing of the application.

FILES FOR APPLICATIONS

10. Before the hearing of any application, the applicant must—

(1) provide to the court and each other party an appropriate indexed file for the application with consecutively numbered pages; and

(2) attach to the file an estimate of the reading time required by the judge.

JUDGMENTS AND ORDERS

11.1 After any hearing the claimant must draw up a draft order, unless the decision was made on the application of another party in which case that party must do so.

11.2 A draft order must be submitted by the party responsible for drawing it up within 3 clear days of the decision, with sufficient copies for each party and for one to be retained by the court.

11.3 The sealed orders will be returned to the party submitting them, who will be responsible for serving the order on the other parties.

11.4 Orders must be dated with the date of the decision, except for consent orders submitted for approval, which must be left undated.

[1562]

ANNEX A

Case management information sheet—Mercantile Courts

[Title of Case]

This information sheet must be filed with Mercantile Listing at least 7 days before the Case Management Conference, and copies served on all other parties: see paragraph 7.7 of the Mercantile Courts Practice Direction.

Party filing:
Solicitors:
Advocate(s) for trial:
Date:

Substance of case

1. What in about 20 words maximum is the case about?
Please provide a separate concise list of issues in a complex case.

Parties

2. Are all parties still effective?
3. Do you intend to add any further party?

Statements of case

4. Do you intend to amend your statement of case?
5. Do you require any "further information"—see CPR 18?

Disclosure

6. By what date can you give standard disclosure?
7. Do you contend that to search for any type of document falling within CPR 31.6(b) would be unreasonable within CPR 31.7(2); if so, what type and on what grounds?
8. Is any specific disclosure required—CPR 31.12?
9. Is a full disclosure order appropriate?
10. By what dates could you give:
    (i) any specific disclosure referred to at 8; and
    (ii) full disclosure?

Admissions

11. Can you make any additional admissions?

Preliminary issues

12. Are any issues suitable for trial as preliminary issues? If yes, which?

Witnesses of fact

13. On how many witnesses of fact do you intend to rely at the trial (subject to the court's direction)?
14. Please name them, or explain why you do not.
15. Which of them will be called to give oral evidence?
16. When can you serve their witness statements?
17. Will any require an interpreter?

Expert evidence

18. Are there issues requiring expert evidence?
19. If yes, what issues?
20. Might a single joint expert be suitable on any issues (see CPR 35.7)?
21. What experts do you intend (subject to the court's direction) to call? Please give the number, their names and expertise.
22. By what date can you serve signed expert reports?
23. Should there be meetings of experts of like disciplines, of all disciplines? By when?
24. Which experts, if any, do you intend not to call at the trial?

25. Will any require an interpreter?

Trial

26. What are the advocates' present estimates of the length of the trial?
27. What is the earliest date that you think the case can be ready for trial?
28. Where should the trial be held?
29. Is a Pre-Trial Review advisable?

ADR

30. Might some form of Alternative Dispute Resolution assist to resolve the dispute or some part of it?
31. Has this been considered with the client?
32. Has this been considered with the other parties?
33. Do you want the case to be stayed pending ADR or other means of settlement—CPR 26.4; or any other directions relating to ADR?

Other applications

34. What applications, if any, not covered above, will you be making at the conference?

Costs

35. What, do you estimate, are your costs to date?
36. What, do you estimate, will be your costs to end of trial?

[Signature of party/solicitor]

[1563]

ANNEX B

Standard Directions in Mercantile Courts

[Title of case with Judge's name]

Order for Directions

made on [ ]

1. Standard disclosure is to be made by [ ].
Inspection on 48 hours notice to be completed by [ ].
2. Signed statements of witnesses of fact, and hearsay notices when required by CPR 33.2, are to be exchanged not later than [ ].
Unless otherwise ordered, the witness statements are to stand as the evidence in chief of the witnesses at trial.
3. Each party has permission to call at the trial expert witnesses as follows:

Number	Expertise	Issue(s) to be covered

whose reports are to be exchanged by [ ].

4. Experts of like disciplines are to:
 (i) meet without prejudice by [ ] to identify the issues between them and to attempt to reach agreement on such issues, and
 (ii) prepare a joint statement pursuant to CPR 35.12(3), by [ ].

or

3. Expert evidence in the following field(s) of expertise is limited to a written report by a single expert jointly instructed by the parties:

Expertise	Issue(s) to be covered

4.
 (i) The report of the single joint expert is to be produced by [ ].
 (ii) Any questions to the expert are to be presented to him by [ ] and answered by [ ].

(iii) Any party may apply not later than [ ] for an order that the expert witness shall give oral evidence at the trial.

5. The case will be tried in [ ] by judge alone, estimated length of trial [ ] days, [commencing on] [not before].

[The claimant is to apply to the mercantile listing officer to fix a date for the trial, not later than [ ], specifying dates which any party wishes to avoid.]

[6. The progress monitoring date is [ ]. Each party is to notify the court in writing by that date (with a copy to all other parties) of the progress of the case, including—

(i) whether the directions have been complied with in all respects;

(ii) if any directions are outstanding, which of them and why; and

(iii) whether a further case management conference or a pre-trial review is required.]

7. There will be a pre-trial review on [ ].

[In the event of both parties notifying the court in writing not less than [ ] days before the pre-trial review that it is not required, then it will be vacated.]

8. Signed pre-trial check lists are to be filed and served by [ ] [not less than 7 days before the pre-trial review] [not less than 6 weeks before the trial date].

9. Trial bundles must be agreed, prepared and delivered to counsel not less than [ ] days before the trial date, and to the court not less than [ ] days before the trial date.

10. Costs in the case.

DATED

[1564]

ANNEX C

Pre-trial check list—Mercantile Courts

[Title of Case]

Where a Pre-trial Review has been ordered, this check list must be filed with Mercantile Listing not less than 7 days before the Pre-trial Review, and copies served on all other parties.

Where a Pre-trial Review has not been ordered, it must be filed and served not less than 6 weeks before the trial date.

See paragraph 8.2 of the Mercantile Courts Practice Direction.

a. Trial Date:
b. Whether Pre-trial Review ordered:
c. Date of Review:
d. Party lodging:
e. Solicitors:
f. Advocate(s) for trial:
g. Date lodged:

[Note: this checklist should normally be completed with the involvement of the advocate(s) instructed for trial.]

1. Have all the directions made to date been carried out?
2. If not, what remains to be carried out? When will it be carried out?
3. Do you intend to take any further steps regarding:
   (i) statements of case?
   (ii) disclosure?
   (iii) witnesses and witness statements?
   (iv) experts and expert reports?

If yes in any case, what and by when?

4. Will the preparation of trial bundles be completed not later than 3 weeks before the date fixed for trial? If not, what is the position?
5. What witnesses of fact do you intend to call?
6. (Where directions for expert evidence have been given) what experts do you intend to call?
7. Is any interpreter needed: for whom?
8. If a Pre-trial Review has not been ordered, do you think one would be useful?
9. What are the advocate(s)' confirmed estimates of the minimum and maximum lengths of the trial? A confirmed estimate signed by the advocate(s) and dated must be attached.
10.
   (i) Might some form of alternative dispute resolution now assist?
   (ii) Has the question been considered with the client?
   (iii) Has the question been explored with the other parties to the case?

[Signature of party/solicitor]

[1565]

PRACTICE DIRECTION 62—ARBITRATION

NOTES
This Practice Direction supplements CPR, Pt 62 at **[1492]**.

SECTION I

1.1 This Section of this Practice Direction applies to arbitration claims to which Section I of Part 62 applies.

1.2 In this Section "the 1996 Act" means the Arbitration Act 1996.

1.3 Where a rule provides for a document to be sent, it may be sent—
(1) by first class post;
(2) through a document exchange; or
(3) by fax, electronic mail or other means of electronic communication.

62.3—Starting the claim

2.1 An arbitration claim under the 1996 Act (other than under section 9) must be started in accordance with the High Court and County Courts (Allocation of Arbitration Proceedings) Order 1996 by the issue of an arbitration claim form.

2.2 An arbitration claim form must be substantially in the form set out in Appendix A to this practice direction.

2.3 Subject to paragraph 2.1, an arbitration claim form—
(1) may be issued at the courts set out in column 1 of the table below and will be entered in the list set out against that court in column 2;
(2) relating to a landlord and tenant or partnership dispute must be issued in the Chancery Division of the High Court.

Court	*List*
Admiralty and Commercial Registry at the Royal Courts of Justice, London	Commercial list
Technology and Construction Court Registry, St. Dunstan's House, London	TCC list
District Registry of the High Court (where mercantile court established)	Mercantile list
District Registry of the High Court (where arbitration claim form marked "Technology and Construction Court" in top right hand corner)	TCC list
Central London County Court	Mercantile list

2.3A An arbitration claim form must, in the case of an appeal, or application for permission to appeal, from a judge-arbitrator, be issued in the Civil Division of the Court of Appeal. The judge hearing the application may adjourn the matter for oral argument before two judges of that court.

62.4—Arbitration claim form

Service

3.1 The court may exercise its powers under rule 6.8 to permit service of an arbitration claim form at the address of a party's solicitor or representative acting for him in the arbitration.

3.2 Where the arbitration claim form is served by the claimant he must file a certificate of service within 7 days of service of the arbitration claim form.

(Rule 6.10 specifies what a certificate of service must show).

Acknowledgment of service or making representations by arbitrator or ACAS

4.1 Where—

(1) an arbitrator; or
(2) ACAS (in a claim under the 1996 Act as applied with modifications by the ACAS Arbitration Scheme (England and Wales) Order 2001)

is sent a copy of an arbitration claim form (including an arbitration claim form sent under rule 62.6(2)), that arbitrator or ACAS (as the case may be) may—
(a) apply to be made a defendant; or
(b) make representations to the court under paragraph 4.3.

4.2 An application under paragraph 4.1(2)(a) to be made a defendant—
(1) must be served on the claimant; but
(2) need not be served on any other party.

4.3 An arbitrator or ACAS may make representations by filing written evidence or in writing to the court.

Supply of documents from court records

5.1 An arbitration claim form may only be inspected with the permission of the court.

62.7—Case management

6.1 The following directions apply unless the court orders otherwise.

6.2 A defendant who wishes to rely on evidence before the court must file and serve his written evidence—
(1) within 21 days after the date by which he was required to acknowledge service; or,
(2) where a defendant is not required to file an acknowledgement of service, within 21 days after service of the arbitration claim form.

6.3 A claimant who wishes to rely on evidence in reply to written evidence filed under paragraph 6.2 must file and serve his written evidence within 7 days after service of the defendant's evidence.

6.4 Agreed indexed and paginated bundles of all the evidence and other documents to be used at the hearing must be prepared by the claimant.

6.5 Not later than 5 days before the hearing date estimates for the length of the hearing must be filed together with a complete set of the documents to be used.

6.6 Not later than 2 days before the hearing date the claimant must file and serve—
(1) a chronology of the relevant events cross-referenced to the bundle of documents;
(2) (where necessary) a list of the persons involved; and
(3) a skeleton argument which lists succinctly—
(a) the issues which arise for decision;
(b) the grounds of relief (or opposing relief) to be relied upon;
(c) the submissions of fact to be made with the references to the evidence; and
(d) the submissions of law with references to the relevant authorities.

6.7 Not later than the day before the hearing date the defendant must file and serve a skeleton argument which lists succinctly—
(1) the issues which arise for decision;
(2) the grounds of relief (or opposing relief) to be relied upon;
(3) the submissions of fact to be made with the references to the evidence; and
(4) the submissions of law with references to the relevant authorities.

Securing the attendance of witnesses

7.1 A party to arbitral proceedings being conducted in England or Wales who wishes to rely on section 43 of the 1996 Act to secure the attendance of a witness must apply for a witness summons in accordance with Part 34.

7.2 If the attendance of the witness is required within the district of a district registry, the application may be made at that registry.

7.3 A witness summons will not be issued until the applicant files written evidence showing that the application is made with—
(1) the permission of the tribunal; or
(2) the agreement of the other parties.

Interim remedies

8.1 An application for an interim remedy under section 44 of the 1996 Act must be made in an arbitration claim form.

Applications under Sections 32 and 45 of the 1996 Act

9.1 This paragraph applies to arbitration claims for the determination of—

(1) a question as to the substantive jurisdiction of the arbitral tribunal under section 32 of the 1996 Act; and

(2) a preliminary point of law under section 45 of the 1996 Act.

9.2 Where an arbitration claim is made without the agreement in writing of all the other parties to the arbitral proceedings but with the permission of the arbitral tribunal, the written evidence or witness statements filed by the parties must set out any evidence relied on by the parties in support of their contention that the court should, or should not, consider the claim.

9.3 As soon as practicable after the written evidence is filed, the court will decide whether or not it should consider the claim and, unless the court otherwise directs, will so decide without a hearing.

Decisions without a hearing

10.1 Having regard to the overriding objective the court may decide particular issues without a hearing. For example, as set out in paragraph 9.3, the question whether the court is satisfied as to the matters set out in section 32(2)(b) or section 45(2)(b) of the 1996 Act.

10.2 The court will generally decide whether to extend the time limit under section 70(3) of the 1996 Act without a hearing. Where the court makes an order extending the time limit, the defendant must file his written evidence within 21 days from service of the order.

62.9—Variation of time

11.1 An application for an order under rule 62.9(1)—

(1) before the period of 28 days has expired, must be made in a Part 23 application notice; and

(2) after the period of 28 days has expired, must be set out in a separately identified part in the arbitration claim form.

Applications for permission to appeal

12.1 Where a party seeks permission to appeal to the court on a question of law arising out of an arbitration award, the arbitration claim form must—

(1) identify the question of law; and

(2) state the grounds

on which the party alleges that permission should be given.

12.2 The written evidence in support of the application must set out any evidence relied on by the party for the purpose of satisfying the court—

(1) of the matters referred to in section 69(3) of the 1996 Act; and

(2) that permission should be given.

12.3 The written evidence filed by the respondent to the application must—

(1) state the grounds on which the respondent opposes the grant of permission;

(2) set out any evidence relied on by him relating to the matters mentioned in section 69(3) of the 1996 Act; and

(3) specify whether the respondent wishes to contend that the award should be upheld for reasons not expressed (or not fully expressed) in the award and, if so, state those reasons.

12.4 The court will normally determine applications for permission to appeal without an oral hearing.

12.5 Where the court refuses an application for permission to appeal without an oral hearing, it must provide brief reasons.

12.6 Where the court considers that an oral hearing is required, it may give such further directions as are necessary.

SECTION II

13.1 This Section of this Practice Direction applies to arbitration claims to which Section II of Part 62 applies.

62.13—Starting the claim

14.1 An arbitration claim must be started in the Commercial Court and, where required to be heard by a judge, be heard by a judge of that court unless he otherwise directs.

SECTION III

15.1 This Section of this Practice Direction applies to enforcement proceedings to which Section III of Part 62 applies.

62.21—Registration of awards under the Arbitration (International Investment Disputes) Act 1966

16.1 Awards ordered to be registered under the 1966 Act and particulars will be entered in the Register kept for that purpose at the Admiralty and Commercial Registry.

[1566]

NOTES

The following forms are the forms present at this position in the Civil Procedure Rules and can be found at http://www.dca.gov.uk/civil/procrules_fin/menus/forms.htm—

N8 Claim form (arbitration)
N8A Notes for claimant
N8B Notes for defendant
N15 Acknowledgement of service (arbitration claim)

PRACTICE DIRECTION 74—ENFORCEMENT OF JUDGMENTS IN DIFFERENT JURISDICTIONS

NOTES

This Practice Direction supplements CPR, Pt 74 at **[1517]**.

1. This practice direction is divided into two sections—
   (1) Section I—Provisions about the enforcement of judgments
   (2) Section II—The Merchant Shipping (Liner Conferences) Act 1982

SECTION I
ENFORCEMENT OF JUDGMENTS

Meaning of "judgment"

2. In rule 74.2(1)(c), the definition of "judgment" is "subject to any other enactment". Such provisions include—
   (1) section 9(1) of the 1920 Act, which limits enforcement under that Act to judgments of superior courts;
   (2) section 1(1) of the 1933 Act, which limits enforcement under that Act to judgments of those courts specified in the relevant Order in Council;
   (3) section 1(2) of the 1933 Act, which limits enforcement under that Act to money judgments.

Registers

3. There will be kept in the Central Office of the Supreme Court at the Royal Courts of Justice, under the direction of the Senior Master—
   (1) registers of foreign judgments ordered by the High Court to be enforced following applications under—
      (a) section 9 of the 1920 Act;
      (b) section 2 of the 1933 Act;
      (c) section 4 of the 1982 Act; or
      (d) the Judgments Regulation;
   (2) registers of certificates issued for the enforcement in foreign countries of High Court judgments under the 1920, 1933 and 1982 Acts, and under article 54 of the Judgments Regulation;
   (3) a register of certificates filed in the Central Office of the High Court under rule 74.15(2) for the enforcement of money judgments given by the courts of Scotland or Northern Ireland;
   (4) a register of certificates issued under rule 74.16(3) for the enforcement of non-money judgments given by the courts of Scotland or Northern Ireland;

(5) registers of certificates issued under rules 74.17 and 74.18 for the enforcement of High Court judgments in Scotland or Northern Ireland under Schedule 6 or Schedule 7 to the 1982 Act; and

(6) a register of Community judgments and Euratom inspection orders ordered to be registered under article 3 of the European Communities (Enforcement of Community Judgments) Order 1972.

Making an application

4.1 Applications for the registration for enforcement in England and Wales of—

(1) foreign judgments under rule 74.3;

(2) judgments of courts in Scotland or Northern Ireland under rule 74.15 or 74.16; and

(3) European Community judgments under rule 74.20,

are assigned to the Queen's Bench Division and may be heard by a Master.

4.2 An application under rule 74.12 for a certified copy of a High Court or county court judgment for enforcement abroad must be made—

(1) in the case of a judgment given in the Chancery Division or the Queen's Bench Division of the High Court, to a Master or district judge;

(2) in the case of a judgment given in the Family Division of the High Court, to a district judge of that Division;

(3) in the case of a county court judgment, to a district judge.

4.3 An application under rule 74.17 or 74.18 for a certificate or a certified copy of a High Court or county court judgment for enforcement in Scotland or Northern Ireland must be made—

(1) in the case of a judgment given in the Chancery Division or the Queen's Bench Division of the High Court, to a Master or district judge;

(2) in the case of a judgment given in the Family Division of the High Court, to a district judge of that Division;

(3) in the case of a county court judgment, to a district judge.

4.4 The following applications must be made under Part 23—

(1) applications under rule 74.3 for the registration of a judgment;

(2) applications under rule 74.7 to set aside the registration of a judgment;

(3) applications under rule 74.12 for a certified copy of a judgment;

(4) applications under section III for a certificate for enforcement of a judgment;

(5) applications under rule 74.20 for the registration of a Community judgment;

(6) applications under rule 74.23 to vary or cancel the registration of a Community judgment; and

(7) applications under rule 74.25 for the registration of an order of the European Court that the enforcement of a registered Community judgment should be suspended.

Applications under the 1933 Act

5. Foreign judgments are enforceable in England and Wales under the 1933 Act where there is an agreement on the reciprocal enforcement of judgments between the United Kingdom and the country in which the judgment was given. Such an agreement may contain particular provisions governing the enforcement of judgments (for example limiting the categories of judgments which are enforceable, or the courts whose judgments are enforceable). Any such specific limitations will be listed in the Order in Council giving effect in the United Kingdom to the agreement in question, and the rules in Section I of Part 74 will take effect subject to such limitations.

Evidence in support of an application under the judgments regulation: rule 74.4(6)

6.1 Where a judgment is to be recognised or enforced in a Regulation State, Council Regulation (EC) No 44/2001 of 22nd December 2000 on jurisdiction and the recognition and enforcement of judgments in civil and commercial matters applies.

6.2 As a consequence of article 38(2) of the Judgments Regulation, the provisions in Chapter III of that Regulation relating to declaring judgments enforceable are the equivalent, in the United Kingdom, of provisions relating to registering judgments for enforcement.

6.3 Chapter III of, and Annex V to, the Judgments Regulation are annexed to this practice direction. They were originally published in the official languages of the European Community in the *Official Journal of the European Communities* by the Office for Official Publications of the European Communities.

6.4 Sections 2 and 3 of Chapter III of the Judgments Regulation (in particular articles 40, 53, 54 and 55, and Annex V) set out the evidence needed in support of an application.

6.5 The Judgments Regulation is supplemented by the Civil Jurisdiction and Judgments Order 2001, SI 2001 No 3929. The Order also makes amendments, in respect of that Regulation, to the Civil Jurisdiction and Judgments Act 1982.

Certified copies of judgments issued under rule 74.12

7.1 In an application by a judgment creditor under rule 74.12 for the enforcement abroad of a High Court judgment, the certified copy of the judgment will be an office copy, and will be accompanied by a certificate signed by a judge. The judgment and certificate will be sealed with the Seal of the Supreme Court.

7.2 In an application by a judgment creditor under rule 74.12 for the enforcement abroad of a county court judgment, the certified copy will be a sealed copy, and will be accompanied by a certificate signed by a judge.

7.3 In applications under the 1920, 1933 or 1982 Acts, the certificate will be in Form 110, and will have annexed to it a copy of the claim form by which the proceedings were begun.

7.4 In an application under the Judgments Regulation, the certificate will be in the form of Annex V to the Regulation.

Certificates under Section III of Part 74

8.1 A certificate of a money judgment of a court in Scotland or Northern Ireland must be filed for enforcement under rule 74.15(2) in the Action Department of the Central Office of the Supreme Court, Royal Courts of Justice, Strand, London WC2A 2LL. The copy will be sealed by a court officer before being returned to the applicant.

8.2 A certificate issued under rule 74.17 for the enforcement in Scotland or Northern Ireland of a money judgment of the High Court or of a county court will be in Form 111.

8.3 In an application by a judgment creditor under rule 74.18 for the enforcement in Scotland or Northern Ireland of a non-money judgment of the High Court or of a county court, the certified copy of the judgment will be a sealed copy to which will be annexed a certificate in Form 112.

Material additional to Section IV of Part 74

9.1 Enforcement of Community judgments and of Euratom inspection orders is governed by the European Communities (Enforcement of Community Judgments) Order 1972, SI 1972 No 1590.

9.2 The Treaty establishing the European Community is the Treaty establishing the European Economic Community (Rome, 1957); relevant amendments are made by the Treaty of Amsterdam (1997, Cm 3780).

9.3 The text of the Protocol of 3 June 1971 on the interpretation by the European Court of the Convention of 27 September 1968 on Jurisdiction and the Enforcement of Judgments in Civil and Commercial Matters is set out in Schedule 2 to the Civil Jurisdiction and Judgments Act 1982.

9.4 The text of the Protocol of 19 December 1988 on the interpretation by the European Court of the Convention of 19 June 1980 on the Law applicable to Contractual Obligations is set out in Schedule 3 to the Contracts (Applicable Law) Act 1990.

(*Section II not reproduced in this work.*)

[1567]

APPENDIX
PAGES FROM THE JUDGMENT REGULATION

SECTION 10

PROVISIONAL, INCLUDING PROTECTIVE, MEASURES

Article 31

Application may be made to the courts of a Member State for such provisional, including protective, measures as may be available under the law of that State, even if, under this Regulation, the courts of another Member State have jurisdiction as to the substance of the matter.

CHAPTER III
RECOGNITION AND ENFORCEMENT

Article 32

For the purposes of this Regulation, "judgment" means any judgment given by a court or tribunal of a Member State, whatever the judgment may be called, including a decree, order, decision or writ of execution, as well as the determination of costs or expenses by an officer of the court.

SECTION 1
RECOGNITION

Article 33

1. A judgment given in a Member State shall be recognised in the other Member States without any special procedure being required.

2. Any interested party who raises the recognition of a judgment as the principal issue in a dispute may, in accordance with the procedures provided for in Sections 2 and 3 of this Chapter, apply for a decision that the judgment be recognised.

3. If the outcome of proceedings in a court of a Member State depends on the determination of an incidental question of recognition that court shall have jurisdiction over that question.

Article 34

A judgment shall not be recognised:

1. if such recognition is manifestly contrary to public policy in the Member State in which recognition is sought;
2. where it was given in default of appearance, if the defendant was not served with the document which instituted the proceedings or with an equivalent document in sufficient time and in such a way as to enable him to arrange for his defence, unless the defendant failed to commence proceedings to challenge the judgment when it was possible for him to do so;
3. if it is irreconcilable with a judgment given in a dispute between the same parties in the Member State in which recognition is sought;
4. if it is irreconcilable with an earlier judgment given in another Member State or in a third State involving the same cause of action and between the same parties, provided that the earlier judgment fulfils the conditions necessary for its recognition in the Member State addressed.

Article 35

1. Moreover, a judgment shall not be recognised if it conflicts with Sections 3, 4 or 6 of Chapter II, or in a case provided for in Article 72.

2. In its examination of the grounds of jurisdiction referred to in the foregoing paragraph, the court or authority applied to shall be bound by the findings of fact on which the court of the Member State of origin based its jurisdiction.

3. Subject to the paragraph 1, the jurisdiction of the court of the Member State of origin may not be reviewed. The test of public policy referred to in point 1 of Article 34 may not be applied to the rules relating to jurisdiction.

Article 36

Under no circumstances may a foreign judgment be reviewed as to its substance.

Article 37

1. A court of a Member State in which recognition is sought of a judgment given in another Member State may stay the proceedings if an ordinary appeal against the judgment has been lodged.

2. A court of a Member State in which recognition is sought of a judgment given in Ireland or the United Kingdom may stay the proceedings if enforcement is suspended in the State of origin, by reason of an appeal.

SECTION 2
ENFORCEMENT

Article 38

1. A judgment given in a Member State and enforceable in that State shall be enforced in another Member State when, on the application of any interested party, it has been declared enforceable there.

2. However, in the United Kingdom, such a judgment shall be enforced in England and Wales, in Scotland, or in Northern Ireland when, on the application of any interested party, it has been registered for enforcement in that part of the United Kingdom.

Article 39

1. The application shall be submitted to the court or competent authority indicated in the list in Annex II.

2. The local jurisdiction shall be determined by reference to the place of domicile of the party against whom enforcement is sought, or to the place of enforcement.

Article 40

1. The procedure for making the application shall be governed by the law of the Member State in which enforcement is sought.

2. The applicant must give an address for service of process within the area of jurisdiction of the court applied to. However, if the law of the Member State in which enforcement is sought does not provide for the furnishing of such an address, the applicant shall appoint a representative ad litem.

3. The documents referred to in Article 53 shall be attached to the application.

Article 41

The judgment shall be declared enforceable immediately on completion of the formalities in Article 53 without any review under Articles 34 and 35. The party against whom enforcement is sought shall not at this stage of the proceedings be entitled to make any submissions on the application.

Article 42

1. The decision on the application for a declaration of enforceability shall forthwith be brought to the notice of the applicant in accordance with the procedure laid down by the law of the Member State in which enforcement is sought.

2. The declaration of enforceability shall be served on the party against whom enforcement is sought, accompanied by the judgment, if not already served on that party.

Article 43

1. The decision on the application for a declaration of enforceability may be appealed against by either party.

2. The appeal is to be lodged with the court indicated in the list in Annex III.

3. The appeal shall be dealt with in accordance with the rules governing procedure in contradictory matters.

4. If the party against whom enforcement is sought fails to appear before the appellate court in proceedings concerning an appeal brought by the applicant, Article 26(2) to (4) shall apply even where the party against whom enforcement is sought is not domiciled in any of the Member States.

5. An appeal against the declaration of enforceability is to be lodged within one month of service thereof. If the party against whom enforcement is sought is domiciled in a Member State other than that in which the declaration of enforceability was given, the time for appealing shall be two months and shall run from the date of service, either on him in person or at his residence. No extension of time may be granted on account of distance.

Article 44

The judgment given on the appeal may be contested only by the appeal referred to in Annex IV.

Article 45

1. The court with which an appeal is lodged under Article 43 or Article 44 shall refuse or revoke a declaration of enforceability only on one of the grounds specified in Articles 34 and 35. It shall give its decision without delay.

2. Under no circumstances may the foreign judgment be reviewed as to its substance.

Article 46

1. The court with which an appeal is lodged under Article 43 or Article 44 may, on the application of the party against whom enforcement is sought, stay the proceedings if an ordinary appeal has been lodged against the judgment in the Member State of origin or if the time for such an appeal has not yet expired; in the latter case, the court may specify the time within which such an appeal is to be lodged.

2. Where the judgment was given in Ireland or the United Kingdom, any form of appeal available in the Member State of origin shall be treated as an ordinary appeal for the purposes of paragraph 1.

3. The court may also make enforcement conditional on the provision of such security as it shall determine.

Article 47

1. When a judgment must be recognised in accordance with this Regulation, nothing shall prevent the applicant from availing himself of provisional, including protective, measures in accordance with the law of the Member State requested without a declaration of enforceability under Article 41 being required.

2. The declaration of enforceability shall carry with it the power to proceed to any protective measures.

3. During the time specified for an appeal pursuant to Article 43(5) against the declaration of enforceability and until any such appeal has been determined, no measures of enforcement may be taken other than protective measures against the property of the party against whom enforcement is sought.

Article 48

1. Where a foreign judgment has been given in respect of several matters and the declaration of enforceability cannot be given for all of them, the court or competent authority shall give it for one or more of them.

2. An applicant may request a declaration of enforceability limited to parts of a judgment.

Article 49

A foreign judgment which orders a periodic payment by way of a penalty shall be enforceable in the Member State in which enforcement is sought only if the amount of the payment has been finally determined by the courts of the Member State of origin.

Article 50

An applicant who, in the Member State of origin has benefited from complete or partial legal aid or exemption from costs or expenses, shall be entitled, in the procedure provided for in this Section, to benefit from the most favourable legal aid or the most extensive exemption from costs or expenses provided for by the law of the Member State addressed.

Article 51

No security, bond or deposit, however described, shall be required of a party who in one Member State applies for enforcement of a judgment given in another Member State on the ground that he is a foreign national or that he is not domiciled or resident in the State in which enforcement is sought.

Article 52

In proceedings for the issue of a declaration of enforceability, no charge, duty or fee calculated by reference to the value of the matter at issue may be levied in the Member State in which enforcement is sought.

SECTION 3
COMMON PROVISIONS

Article 53

1. A party seeking recognition or applying for a declaration of enforceability shall produce a copy of the judgment which satisfies the conditions necessary to establish its authenticity.

2. A party applying for a declaration of enforceability shall also produce the certificate referred to in Article 54, without prejudice to Article 55.

Article 54

The court or competent authority of a Member State where a judgment was given shall issue, at the request of any interested party, a certificate using the standard form in Annex V to this Regulation.

Article 55

1. If the certificate referred to in Article 54 is not produced, the court or competent authority may specify a time for its production or accept an equivalent document or, if it considers that it has sufficient information before it, dispense with its production.

2. If the court or competent authority so requires, a translation of the documents shall be produced. The translation shall be certified by a person qualified to do so in one of the Member States.

Article 56

No legalisation or other similar formality shall be required in respect of the documents referred to in Article 53 or Article 55(2), or in respect of a document appointing a representative ad litem.

ANNEX V
CERTIFICATE REFERRED TO IN ARTICLES 54 AND 58 OF THE REGULATION ON JUDGMENTS AND COURT SETTLEMENTS

(English, inglés, anglais, inglese, …)

1. Member State of origin
2. Court or competent authority issuing the certificate
    - 2.1. Name
    - 2.2. Address
    - 2.3. Tel/fax/e-mail
3. Court which delivered the judgment/approved the court settlement(*)
    - 3.1. Type of court
    - 3.2. Place of court
4. Judgment/court settlement(*)
    - 4.1. Date
    - 4.2. Reference number
    - 4.3. The parties to the judgment/court settlement(*)
        - 4.3.1. Name(s) of plaintiff(s)
        - 4.3.2. Name(s) of defendant(s)
        - 4.3.3. Name(s) of other party(ies), if any
    - 4.4. Date of service of the document instituting the proceedings where judgment was given in default of appearance
    - 4.5. Text of the judgment/court settlement(*) as annexed to this certificate
5. Names of parties to whom legal aid has been granted.

The judgment/court settlement(*) is enforceable in the Member State of origin (Articles 38 and 58 of the Regulation) against:

Name:

Done at .... , date ....

Signature and/or stamp ....

(*) Delete as appropriate.

[1568]

PRACTICE DIRECTION 74B—EUROPEAN ENFORCEMENT ORDERS

NOTES

This Practice Direction supplements CPR, Pt 74, Section V at **[1543]**.

COUNCIL REGULATION

1.1 Certification and enforcement of European Enforcement Orders is governed by Council Regulation (EC) No 805/2004 creating a European Enforcement Order for uncontested claims.

1.2 The EEO Regulation is annexed to this practice direction and can be found at http://europa.eu.int/eur-lex/pri/en/oj/dat/2004/l_143/l_14320040430en00150039.pdf. It was originally published in the official languages of the European Community in the *Official Journal of the European Communities* by the Office for Official Publications of the European Communities.

1.3 Section V of Part 74 sets out the procedure for enforcement under the EEO Regulation. A claim that does not meet the requirements of the EEO Regulation, or which the judgment creditor does not wish to enforce using the EEO Regulation, may be enforceable using another method of enforcement.

74.28—Certification of Judgments of the Courts of England and Wales

2.1 An application under rule 74.28 for a certificate of a High Court or county court judgment for enforcement in another Regulation State must be made using Form N219 or Form N219A—

(1) in the case of a judgment given in the Chancery or Queen's Bench Division of the High Court, or in a district registry, to a Master or district judge; or

(2) in the case of a county court judgment, to a district judge.

2.2 Where the application is granted, the court will send the EEO certificate and a sealed copy of the judgment to the person making the application. Where the court refuses the application, the court will give reasons for the refusal and may give further directions.

74.29—Applications for a certificate of lack of enforceability

3.1 An application must be supported by written evidence in support of the grounds on which the judgment has ceased to be enforceable or its enforceability has been suspended or limited.

74.30—Application for rectification or withdrawal

4.1 An application must be supported by written evidence in support of the grounds on which it is contended that the EEO should be rectified or withdrawn.

74.31—Enforcement of European Enforcement Orders in England and Wales

5.1 When an EEO is lodged at the court in which enforcement proceedings are to be brought, it will be assigned a case number.

5.2 A copy of a document will satisfy the conditions necessary to establish its authenticity if it is an official copy of the courts of the member state of origin.

PART II CIVIL PROCEDURE RULES

5.3 The judgment creditor must notify all courts in which enforcement proceedings are pending in England and Wales under the EEO if judgment is set aside in the court of origin, as soon as reasonably practicable after the order is served on the judgment creditor. Notification may be by any means available including fax, e-mail, post or telephone.

74.32—Refusal of Enforcement

6.1 An application must be accompanied by an official copy of the earlier judgment, any other documents relied upon and any translations required by the EEO Regulation and supported by written evidence stating—

(1) why the earlier judgment is irreconcilable; and

(2) why the irreconcilability was not, and could not have been, raised as an objection in the proceedings in the court of origin.

74.33—Stay or limitation of enforcement

7.1 An application must, unless the court orders otherwise, be accompanied by evidence of the application in the court of origin, including—

- (1) the application (or equivalent foreign process) or a copy of the application (or equivalent foreign process) certified by an appropriate officer of the court of origin; and
- (2) where that document is not in English, a translation of it into English—
  - (a) certified by a notary public or person qualified to certify a translation in the Member State of the court of origin under Article 20(2)(c) of the EEO Regulation; or
  - (b) accompanied by written evidence confirming that the translation is accurate.

7.2 The written evidence in support of the application must state—

- (1) that an application has been brought in the member state of origin;
- (2) the nature of that application, including the grounds on which the application is made and the order sought; and
- (3) the date on which the application was filed, the state of the proceedings and the date by which it is believed that the application will be determined.

If on the application of a debtor under rule 74.32 the court makes a conditional order under Article 23(b), the order shall be effective to bar enforcement until the creditor has lodged evidence at court that he has complied with such conditions. In cases other than where the order is conditional upon the creditor making a payment into court, the evidence lodged should be referred to the Master or district judge.

(*The Annex contains the original text of Regulation (EC) No 805/2004 of 21 April 2004 creating a European Enforcement Order for uncontested claims; that Regulation, as amended, is printed in Pt IV(B) of this work at* **[3161]**.)

[1569]

PRACTICE DIRECTION—INSOLVENCY PROCEEDINGS

PART ONE

1. GENERAL

1.1 In this Practice Direction:

- (1) "The Act" means the Insolvency Act 1986 and includes the Act as applied to limited liability partnerships by the Limited Liability Partnerships Regulations 2001;
- (2) "The Insolvency Rules" means the rules for the time being in force and made under s 411 and s 412 of the Act in relation to insolvency proceedings;
- (3) "CPR" means the Civil Procedure Rules and "CPR" followed by a Part or rule by number means the Part or rule with that number in those Rules;
- (4) "RSC" followed by an Order by number means the Order with that number set out in Schedule 1 to the CPR;
- (5) "Insolvency proceedings" means any proceedings under the Act, the Insolvency Rules, the Administration of Insolvent Estates of Deceased Persons Order 1986 (SI 1986/1999), the Insolvent Partnerships Order 1986 (SI 1986/2124) or the Insolvent Partnerships Order 1994 (SI 1994/2421).

(6) References to a "company" shall include a limited liability partnership and references to a "contributory" shall include a member of a limited liability partnership.

1.2 This Practice Direction shall come into effect on 26th April 1999 and shall replace all previous Practice Notes and Practice Directions relating to insolvency proceedings.

1.3 Except where the Insolvency Rules otherwise provide, service of documents in insolvency proceedings in the High Court will be the responsibility of the parties and will not be undertaken by the court.

1.4 Where CPR Part 2.4 provides for the court to perform any act, that act may be performed by a Registrar in Bankruptcy for the purpose of insolvency proceedings in the High Court.

1.5 A writ of execution to enforce any order made in insolvency proceedings in the High Court may be issued on the authority of a Registrar.

1.6

(1) This paragraph applies where an insolvency practitioner ("the outgoing office holder") holds office as a liquidator, administrator, trustee or supervisor in more than one case and dies, retires from practice as an insolvency practitioner or is otherwise unable or unwilling to continue in office.

(2) A single application may be made to a Judge of the Chancery Division of the High Court by way of ordinary application in Form 7.2 for the appointment of a substitute office holder or office holders in all cases in which the outgoing office holder holds office, and for the transfer of each such case to the High Court for the purpose only of making such an order.

(3) The application may be made by any of the following:

(i) the outgoing office holder (if he is able and willing to do so);

(ii) any person who holds office jointly with the outgoing office holder;

(iii) any person who is proposed to be appointed as a substitute for the outgoing office holder; or

(iv) any creditor in the cases where the substitution is proposed to be made.

(4) The outgoing office holder (if he is not the applicant) and every person who holds office jointly with the office holder must be made a respondent to the application, but it is not necessary to join any other person as a respondent or to serve the application upon any other person unless the Judge or Registrar in the High Court so directs.

(5) The application should contain schedules setting out the nature of the office held, the identity of the Court currently having jurisdiction over each case and its name and number.

(6) The application must be supported by evidence setting out the circumstances which have given rise to the need to make a substitution and exhibiting the written consent to act of each person who is proposed to be appointed in place of the outgoing office holder.

(7) The Judge will in the first instance consider the application on paper and make such order as he thinks fit. In particular he may do any of the following:

(i) make an order directing the transfer to the High Court of those cases not already within its jurisdiction for the purpose only of the substantive application;

(ii) if he considers that the papers are in order and that the matter is straightforward, make an order on the substantive application;

(iii) give any directions which he considers to be necessary including (if appropriate) directions for the joinder of any additional respondents or requiring the service of the application on any person or requiring additional evidence to be provided;

(iv) if he does not himself make an order on the substantive application when the matter is first before him, give directions for the further consideration of the substantive application by himself or another Judge of the Chancery Division or adjourn the substantive application to the Registrar for him to make such order upon it as is appropriate.

(8) An order of the kind referred to in sub-paragraph (6)(i) shall follow the draft order in Form PDIP 3 set out in the Schedule hereto and an order granting the substantive application shall follow the draft order in Form PDIP 4 set out in the schedule hereto (subject in each case to such modifications as may be necessary or appropriate).

(9) It is the duty of the applicant to ensure that a sealed copy of every order transferring any case to the High Court and of every order which is made on a substantive application is lodged with the court having jurisdiction over each case affected by such order for filing on the court file relating to that case.

(10) It will not be necessary for the file relating to any case which is transferred to the High Court in accordance with this paragraph to be sent to the High Court unless a Judge or Registrar so directs.

PART TWO
COMPANIES

2. ADVERTISEMENT OF WINDING UP PETITION

2.1 Insolvency Rule 4.11(2)(b) is mandatory, and designed to ensure that the class remedy of winding up by the court is made available to all creditors, and is not used as a means of putting pressure on the company to pay the petitioner's debt. Failure to comply with the rule, without good reason accepted by the court, may lead to the summary dismissal of the petition on the return date (Insolvency Rule 4.11(5)). If the court, in its discretion, grants an adjournment, this will be on condition that the petition is advertised in due time for the adjourned hearing. No further adjournment for the purpose of advertisement will normally be granted.

2.2 Copies of every advertisement published in connection with a winding up petition must be lodged with the Court as soon as possible after publication and in any event not later than the day specified in Insolvency Rule 4.14 of the Insolvency Rules 1986. This direction applies even if the advertisement is defective in any way (e g is published at a date not in accordance with the Insolvency Rules, or omits or misprints some important words) or if the petitioner decides not to pursue the petition (e g on receiving payment).

3. CERTIFICATE OF COMPLIANCE–TIME FOR FILING

3.1 In the High Court in order to assist practitioners and the Court the time laid down by Insolvency Rule 4.14 of the Insolvency Rules 1986, for filing a certificate of compliance and a copy of the advertisement, is hereby extended to not later than 4.30 pm on the Friday preceding the day on which the petition is to be heard. Applications to file the certificate and the copy advertisement after 4.30 pm on the Friday will only be allowed if some good reason is shown for the delay.

4. ERRORS IN PETITIONS

4.1 Applications for leave to amend errors in petitions which are discovered subsequent to a winding up order being made should be made to the Court Manager in the High Court and to the District Judge in the county court.

4.2 Where the error is an error in the name of the company, the Court Manager in the High Court and the District Judge in the county court may make any necessary amendments to ensure that the winding up order is drawn with the correct name of the company inserted. If there is any doubt, e g where there might be another company in existence which could be confused with the company to be wound up, the Court Manager will refer the application to the Registrar and the District Judge may refer it to the Judge.

4.3 Where an error is an error in the registered office of the company and any director or member of the company claims that the company was unaware of the petition by reason of it having been served at the wrong registered office it will be open to them to apply to rescind the winding up order in the usual way.

4.4 Where it is discovered that the company had been struck off the Register of Companies prior to the winding up order being made, the matter must be restored to the list before the order is entered to enable an order for the restoration of the name to be made as well as the order to wind up.

5. DISTRIBUTION OF BUSINESS

5.1 The following applications shall be made direct to the Judge and, unless otherwise ordered, shall be heard in public:—

(1) Applications to commit any person to prison for contempt;
(2) Applications for urgent interim relief (e g applications pursuant to s 127 of the Act prior to any winding up order being made);
(3) Applications to restrain the presentation or advertisement of a petition to wind up; or
(4) Applications for the appointment of a provisional liquidator;
(5) Petitions for administration orders or an interim order upon such a Petition;
(6) Applications after an administration order has been made pursuant to s 14(3) of the Act (for directions) or s 18(3) of the Act (to vary or discharge the order);

(7) Petitions to discharge administration orders and to wind up;
(8) Applications pursuant to s 5(3) of the Act (to stay a winding up or discharge an administration order or for directions) where a voluntary arrangement has been approved;
(9) Appeals from a decision made by a County Court or by a Registrar of the High Court.

5.2 Subject to paragraph 5.4 below all other applications shall be made to the Registrar or the District Judge in the first instance who may give any necessary directions and may, in the exercise of his discretion, either hear and determine it himself or refer it to the Judge.

5.3 The following matters will also be heard in public:
(1) Petitions to wind up;
(2) Public examinations;
(3) All matters and applications heard by the Judge, except those referred by the Registrar or the District Judge to be heard in private or so directed by the Judge to be heard.

5.4 In accordance with directions given by the Lord Chancellor the Registrar has authorised certain applications in the High Court to be dealt with by the Court Manager of the Companies Court, pursuant to Insolvency Rule 13.2(2). The applications are:
(1) To extend or abridge time prescribed by the Insolvency Rules in connection with winding up (Insolvency Rules 4.3 and 12.9);
(2) For substituted service of winding up petitions (Insolvency Rule 4.8(6));
(3) To withdraw petitions (Insolvency Rule 4.15);
(4) For the substitution of a petitioner (Insolvency Rule 4.19);
(5) By the Official Receiver for limited disclosure of a statement of affairs (Insolvency Rule 4.35);
(6) By the Official Receiver for relief from duties imposed upon him by the rules (Insolvency Rule 4.47);
(7) By the Official Receiver for permission to give notice of a meeting by advertisement only (Insolvency Rule 4.59);
(8) To transfer proceedings from the High Court to a County Court (Insolvency Rule 7.11);
(9) For permission to amend any originating application.

[NB In District Registries all such applications must be made to the District Judge.]

6. DRAWING UP OF ORDERS

6.1 The Court will draw up all orders except orders on the application of the Official Receiver or for which the Treasury Solicitor is responsible under the existing practice.

7. RESCISSION OF A WINDING UP ORDER

7.1 Any application for the rescission of a winding up order shall be made within seven days after the date on which the order was made (Insolvency Rule 7.47(4)). Notice of any such application must be given to the Official Receiver.

7.2 Applications will only be entertained if made (a) by a creditor, or (b) by a contributory, or (c) by the company jointly with a creditor or with a contributory. The application must be supported by written evidence of assets and liabilities.

7.3 In the case of an unsuccessful application the costs of the petitioning creditor, the supporting creditors and of the Official Receiver will normally be ordered to be paid by the creditor or the contributory making or joining in the application. The reason for this is that if the costs of an unsuccessful application are made payable by the company, they fall unfairly on the general body of creditors.

7.4 Cases in which the making of the winding up order has not been opposed may, if the application is made promptly, be dealt with on a statement by the applicant's legal representative of the circumstances; but apart from such cases, the court will normally require any application to be supported by written evidence.

7.5 There is no need to issue a form of application (Form 7.2) as the petition is restored before the Court.

8. RESTRAINT OF PRESENTATION OF A WINDING UP PETITION

8.1 An application to restrain presentation of a Winding up petition must be made to the Judge by the issue of an Originating Application (Form 7.1).

PART II
CIVIL PROCEDURE RULES

PART THREE
PERSONAL INSOLVENCY—BANKRUPTCY

9. DISTRIBUTION OF BUSINESS

9.1 The following applications shall be made direct to the Judge and unless otherwise ordered shall be heard in public:

(1) Applications for the committal of any person to prison for contempt;
(2) Application for injunctions or for the modification or discharge of injunctions;
(3) Applications for interlocutory relief or directions after the matter has been referred to the Judge.

9.2 All other applications shall be made to the Registrar or the District Judge in the first instance. He shall give any necessary directions and may, if the application is within his jurisdiction to determine, in his discretion either hear and determine it himself or refer it to the Judge.

9.3 The following matters shall be heard in public:

(1) The public examination of debtors;
(2) Opposed applications for discharge or for the suspension or lifting of the suspension of discharge;
(3) Opposed applications for permission to be a director;
(4) In any case where the petition was presented or the receiving order or order for adjudication was made before the appointed day, those matters and applications specified in Rule 8 of the Bankruptcy Rules 1952;
(5) All matters and applications heard by the Judge, except matters and applications referred by the Registrar or the District Judge to be heard by the Judge in private or directed by the Judge to be so heard.

9.4 All petitions presented will be listed under the name of the debtor.

9.5 In accordance with Directions given by the Lord Chancellor the Registrar has authorised certain applications in the High Court to be dealt with by the Court Manager of the Bankruptcy Court pursuant to Insolvency Rule 13.2(2). The applications are:

(1) by petitioning creditors: to extend time for hearing petitions (s 376 of the Act).
(2) by the Official Receiver:
    (a) To transfer proceedings from the High Court to a County Court (Insolvency Rule 7.13);
    (b) to amend the full title of the proceedings (Insolvency Rules 6.35 and 6.47).

[NB In District Registries all such applications must be made to the District Judge]

10. SERVICE ABROAD OF STATUTORY DEMAND

10.1 A statutory demand is not a document issued by the Court. Leave to serve out of the jurisdiction is not, therefore, required.

10.2 Insolvency Rule 6.3(2) ("Requirements as to service") applies to service of the statutory demand whether outside or within the jurisdiction.

10.3 A creditor wishing to serve a statutory demand outside the jurisdiction in a foreign country with which a civil procedure convention has been made (including the Hague Convention) may and, if the assistance of a British Consul is desired, must adopt the procedure prescribed by rule 6.25. In the case of any doubt whether the country is a "convention country", enquiries should be made of the Queen's Bench Masters' Secretary Department, Room E216, Royal Courts of Justice.

10.4 In all other cases, service of the demand must be effected by private arrangement in accordance with Insolvency Rule 6.3(2) and local foreign law.

10.5 When a statutory demand is to be served out of the jurisdiction, the time limits of 21 days and 18 days respectively referred to in the demand must be amended. For this purpose reference should be made to the table set out in the practice direction supplementing Section III of Part 6.

10.6 A creditor should amend the statutory demand as follows:

(1) For any reference to 18 days there must be substituted the appropriate number of days set out in the table plus 4 days, and
(2) for any reference to 21 days must be substituted the appropriate number of days in the table plus 7 days.

Attention is drawn to the fact that in all forms of the statutory demand the figure 18 and the figure 21 occurs in more than one place.

11. SUBSTITUTED SERVICE

Statutory demands:

11.1 The creditor is under an obligation to do all that is reasonable to bring the statutory demand to the debtor's attention and, if practicable, to cause personal service to be effected. Where it is not possible to effect prompt personal service, service may be effected by other means such as first class post or by insertion through a letter box.

11.2 Advertisement can only be used as a means of substituted service where:

(1) The demand is based on a judgment or order of any Court;

(2) The debtor has absconded or is keeping out of the way with a view to avoiding service; and,

(3) There is no real prospect of the sum due being recovered by execution or other process.

As there is no statutory form of advertisement, the Court will accept an advertisement in the following form:

STATUTORY DEMAND

(Debt for liquidated sum payable immediately following a judgment or order of the Court)

To (Block letters)
of

TAKE NOTICE that a statutory demand has been issued by:

Name of Creditor:
Address:

The creditor demands payment of £ the amount now due on a judgment or order of the (High Court of Justice Division) (....................... County Court) dated the day of 199 .

The statutory demand is an important document and it is deemed to have been served on you on the date of the first appearance of this advertisement. You must deal with this demand within 21 days of the service upon you or you could be made bankrupt and your property and goods taken away from you. If you are in any doubt as to your position, you should seek advice immediately from a solicitor or your nearest Citizens' Advice Bureau. The statutory demand can be obtained or is available for inspection and collection from:

Name:

Address:

(Solicitor for) the Creditor

Tel No Reference:

You have only 21 days from the date of the first appearance of this advertisement before the creditor may present a Bankruptcy Petition. You have only 18 days from that date within which to apply to the Court to set aside the demand.

11.3 In all cases where substituted service is effected, the creditor must have taken all those steps which would justify the Court making an order for substituted service of a petition. The steps to be taken to obtain an order for substituted service of a petition are set out below. Failure to comply with these requirements may result in the Court declining to file the petition: Insolvency Rule 6.11(9).

Petitions

11.4 In most cases, evidence of the following steps will suffice to justify an order for substituted service:

(1) One personal call at the residence and place of business of the debtor where both are known or at either of such places as is known. Where it is known that the debtor has more than one residential or business address, personal calls should be made at all the addresses.

(2) Should the creditor fail to effect service, a first class prepaid letter should be written

to the debtor referring to the call(s), the purpose of the same and the failure to meet with the debtor, adding that a further call will be made for the same purpose on the day of 19 at hours at (place). At least two business days notice should be given of the appointment and copies of the letter sent to all known addresses of the debtor. The appointment letter should also state that:

(a) in the event of the time and place not being convenient, the debtor is to name some other time and place reasonably convenient for the purpose;

(b) (Statutory Demands) if the debtor fails to keep the appointment the creditor proposes to serve the debtor by [advertisement] [post] [insertion through a letter box] or as the case may be, and that, in the event of a bankruptcy petition being presented, the Court will be asked to treat such service as service of the demand on the debtor;

(c) (Petitions) if the debtor fails to keep the appointment, application will be made to the Court for an order for substituted service either by advertisement, or in such other manner as the Court may think fit.

(3) In attending any appointment made by letter, inquiry should be made as to whether the debtor has received all letters left for him. If the debtor is away, inquiry should also be made as to whether or not letters are being forwarded to an address within the jurisdiction (England and Wales) or elsewhere.

(4) If the debtor is represented by a Solicitor, an attempt should be made to arrange an appointment for personal service through such Solicitor. The Insolvency Rules enable a Solicitor to accept service of a statutory demand on behalf of his client but there is no similar provision in respect of service of a bankruptcy petition.

(5) The written evidence filed pursuant to Insolvency Rule 6.11 should deal with all the above matters including all relevant facts as to the debtor's whereabouts and whether the appointment letter(s) have been returned.

11.5 Where the Court makes an order for service by first class ordinary post, the order will normally provide that service be deemed to be effected on the seventh day after posting. The same method of calculating service may be applied to calculating the date of service of a statutory demand.

12. SETTING ASIDE A STATUTORY DEMAND

12.1 The application (Form 6.4) and written evidence in support (Form 6.5) exhibiting a copy of the statutory demand must be filed in Court within 18 days of service of the statutory demand on the debtor. Where service is effected by advertisement in a newspaper the period of 18 days is calculated from the date of the first appearance of the advertisement. Three copies of each document must be lodged with the application to enable the Court to serve notice of the hearing date on the applicant, the creditor and the person named in Part B of the statutory demand.

12.2 Where, to avoid expense, copies of the documents are not lodged with the application in the High Court, any order of the Registrar fixing a venue is conditional upon copies of the documents being lodged on the next business day after the Registrar's order otherwise the application will be deemed to have been dismissed.

12.3 Where the statutory demand is based on a judgment or order, the Court will not at this stage go behind the judgment or order and inquire into the validity of the debt nor, as a general rule, will it adjourn the application to await the result of an application to set aside the judgment or order.

12.4 Where the debtor (a) claims to have a counterclaim, set off or cross demand (whether or not he could have raised it in the action in which the judgment or order was obtained) which equals or exceeds the amount of the debt or debts specified in the statutory demand, or (b) disputes the debt (not being a debt subject to a judgment or order) the Court will normally set aside the statutory demand if, in its opinion, on the evidence there is a genuine triable issue.

12.5 A debtor who wishes to apply to set aside a statutory demand after the expiration of 18 days from the date of service of the statutory demand must apply for an extension of time within which to apply. If the applicant wishes to apply for an injunction to restrain presentation of a petition the application must be made to the Judge. Paragraphs 1 and 2 of Form 6.5 (Affidavit in Support of Application to set Aside Statutory Demand) should be used in support of the application for an extension of time with the following additional paragraphs:

"(3) That to the best of my knowledge and belief the creditor(s) named in the demand has/have not presented a petition against me.

(4) That the reasons for my failure to apply to set aside the demand within 18 days after service are as follows: …"

If application is made to restrain presentation of a bankruptcy petition the following additional paragraph should be added:

"(5) Unless restrained by injunction the creditor(s) may present a bankruptcy petition against me."

13. PROOF OF SERVICE OF A STATUTORY DEMAND

13.1 Insolvency Rule 6.11(3) provides that, if the Statutory Demand has been served personally, the written evidence must be provided by the person who effected that service. Insolvency Rule 6.11(4) provides that, if service of the demand (however effected) has been acknowledged in writing, the evidence of service must be provided by the creditor or by a person acting on his behalf. Insolvency Rule 6.11(5) provides that, if neither paragraphs (3) or (4) apply, the written evidence must be provided by a person having direct knowledge of the means adopted for serving the demand.

13.2 Form 6.11 (Evidence of personal service of the statutory demand): this form should only be used where the demand has been served personally and acknowledged in writing (see Insolvency Rule 6.11(4)). If the demand has not been acknowledged in writing, the written evidence should be provided by the Process Server and Paragraphs 2 and 3 (part of Form 6.11) should be omitted (See Insolvency Rule 6.11(3)).

13.3 Form 6.12 (Evidence of Substituted Service of the Statutory Demand): this form can be used whether or not service of the demand has been acknowledged in writing. Paragraphs 4 and 5 (part) provide for the alternatives. Practitioners are reminded, however, that the appropriate person to provide the written evidence may not be the same in both cases. If the demand has been acknowledged in writing, the appropriate person is the creditor or a person acting on his behalf. If the demand has not been acknowledged, that person must be someone having direct knowledge of the means adopted for serving the demand.

Practitioners may find it more convenient to allow process servers to carry out the necessary investigation whilst reserving to themselves the service of the demand. In these circumstances Paragraph 1 should be deleted and the following paragraph substituted:

"1. Attempts have been made to serve the demand, full details of which are set out in the accompanying affidavit of …".

13.4 "Written evidence" means an affidavit or a witness statement.

14. EXTENSION OF HEARING DATE OF PETITION

14.1 Late applications for extension of hearing dates under Insolvency Rule 6.28, and failure to attend on the listed hearing of a petition, will be dealt with as follows:

(1) If an application is submitted less than two clear working days before the hearing date (for example, later than Monday for Thursday, or Wednesday for Monday) the costs of the application will not be allowed under Insolvency Rule 6.28(3).

(2) If the petition has not been served and no extension has been granted by the time fixed for the hearing of the petition, and if no one attends for the hearing, the petition will be re-listed for hearing about 21 days later. The Court will notify the petitioning creditor's solicitors (or the petitioning creditor in person), and any known supporting or opposing creditors or their solicitors, of the new date and times. Written evidence should then be filed on behalf of the petitioning creditor explaining fully the reasons for the failure to apply for an extension or to appear at the hearing, and (if appropriate) giving reasons why the petition should not be dismissed.

(3) On the re-listed hearing the Court may dismiss the petition if not satisfied it should be adjourned or a further extension granted.

14.2 All applications for extension should include a statement of the date fixed for the hearing of the petition.

14.3 The petitioning creditor should attend (by solicitors or in person) on or before the hearing date to ascertain whether the application has reached the file and been dealt with. It should not be assumed that an extension will be granted.

15. BANKRUPTCY PETITION

To help in the completion of the form of a creditor's bankruptcy petition, attention is drawn to the following points:

15.1 The petition does not require dating, signing or witnessing.

PART II CIVIL PROCEDURE RULES

15.2 In the title it is only necessary to recite the debtor's name e g Re John William Smith or Re J W Smith (Male). Any alias or trading name will appear in the body of the petition. This also applies to all other statutory forms other than those which require the "full title".

15.3 Where the petition is based on a statutory demand, only the debt claimed in the demand may be included in the petition.

15.4 In completing Paragraph 2 of the petition, attention is drawn to Insolvency Rule 6.8(1)(a) to (c), particularly where the "aggregate sum" is made up of a number of debts.

15.5 Date of service of the statutory demand (paragraph 4 of the petition):

(1) In the case of personal service, the date of service as set out in the affidavit of service should be recited and whether service is effected *before/after* 1700 hours on Monday to Friday or at any time on a Saturday or a Sunday: see CPR Part 6.7(2) and (3).

(2) In the case of substituted service (otherwise than by advertisement), the date alleged in the affidavit of service should be recited: see "11. Substituted Service" above.

(3) In the strictly limited case of service by advertisement under Insolvency Rule 6.3, the date to be alleged is the date of the advertisement's appearance or, as the case may be, its first appearance: see Insolvency Rules 6.3(3) and 6.11(8).

15.6 There is no need to include in the petition details of the person authorised to present it.

15.7 Certificates at the end of the petition:

(1) The period of search for prior petitions has been reduced to eighteen months.

(2) Where a statutory demand is based wholly or in part on a County Court judgment, the following certificate is to be added:

"I/We certify that on the of 19 I/We attended on the County Court and was/were informed by an officer of the Court that no money had been paid into Court in the action or matter v Claim No pursuant to the statutory demand."

This certificate will not be required when the demand also requires payment of a separate debt, not based on a County Court judgement, the amount of which exceeds the bankruptcy level (at present £750).

15.8 Deposit on petition: the deposit will be taken by the Court and forwarded to the Official Receiver. In the High Court, the petition fee and deposit should be handed to the Supreme Court Accounts Office, Fee Stamping Room, who will record the receipt and will impress two entries on the original petition, one in respect of the Court fee and the other in respect of the deposit. In the County Court, the petition fee and deposit should be handed to the duly authorised officer of the Court's staff who will record its receipt.

In all cases cheque(s) for the whole amount should be made payable to "HM Paymaster General".

15.9 On the hearing of a petition for a bankruptcy order, in order to satisfy the Court that the debt on which the petition is founded has not been paid or secured or compounded the Court will normally accept as sufficient a certificate signed by the person representing the petitioning creditor in the following form:

"I certify that I have/my firm has made enquiries of the petitioning creditor(s) within the last business day prior to the hearing/adjourned hearing and to the best of my knowledge and belief the debt on which the petition is founded is still due and owing and has not been paid or secured or compounded save as to ....

Signed .... Dated ...."

For convenience in the High Court this certificate will be incorporated in the attendance slip, which will be filed after the hearing. A fresh certificate will be required on each adjourned hearing.

15.10 On the occasion of the adjourned hearing of a petition for a bankruptcy order, in order to satisfy the Court that the petitioner has complied with Insolvency Rule 6.29, the petitioner will be required to file written evidence of the manner in which notice of the making of the order of adjournment and of the venue for the adjourned hearing has been sent to:

(i) the debtor, and

(ii) any creditor who has given notice under Insolvency Rule 6.23 but was not present at the hearing when the order for adjournment was made.

16. ORDERS WITHOUT ATTENDANCE

16.1 In suitable cases the High Court will normally be prepared to make orders under Part VIII of the Act (Individual Voluntary Arrangements), without the attendance of either party, provided there is no bankruptcy order in existence and (so far as is known) no pending petition. The orders are:

(1) A fourteen day interim order with the application adjourned 14 days for consideration of the nominee's report, where the papers are in order, and the nominee's signed consent to act includes a waiver of notice of the application or a consent by the nominee to the making of an interim order without attendance.

(2) A standard order on consideration of the nominee's report, extending the interim order to a date 7 weeks after the date of the proposed meeting, directing the meeting to be summoned and adjourning to a date about 3 weeks after the meeting. Such an Order may be made without attendance if the nominee's report has been delivered to the Court and complies with Section 256(1) of the Act and Insolvency Rule 5.10(2) and (3) and proposes a date for the meeting not less than 14 days from that on which the nominee's report is filed in Court under Insolvency Rule 5.10 nor more than 28 days from that on which that report is considered by the Court under Insolvency Rule 5.12.

(3) A "concertina" Order, combining orders as under (1) and (2) above. Such an order may be made without attendance if the initial application for an interim order is accompanied by a report of the nominee and the conditions set out in (1) and (2) above are satisfied.

(4) A final order on consideration of the Chairman's report. Such an order may be made without attendance if the Chairman's report has been filed and complies with Insolvency Rule 5.22(1). The order will record the effect of the Chairman's report and may discharge the interim order.

16.2 Provided that the conditions as under 16.1(2) and (4) above are satisfied and that the appropriate report has been lodged with the Court in due time the parties need not attend or be represented on the adjourned hearing for consideration of the Nominee's report or of the Chairman's report (as the case may be) unless they are notified by the Court that attendance is required. Sealed copies of the order made (in all four cases as above) will be posted by the Court to the applicant or his Solicitor and to the Nominee.

16.3 In suitable cases the Court may also make consent orders without attendance by the parties. The written consent of the parties will be required. Examples of such orders are as follows:

(1) <u>On applications to set aside a statutory demand</u>, orders:
   (a) dismissing the application, with or without an order for costs as may be agreed (permission will be given to present a petition on or after the seventh day after the date of the order, unless a different date is agreed);
   (b) setting aside the demand, with or without an order for costs as may be agreed; or
   (c) giving permission to withdraw the application with or without an order for costs as may be agreed.

(2) <u>On petitions</u>: where there is a list of supporting or opposing creditors in Form 6.21, or a statement signed by or on behalf of the petitioning creditor that no notices have been received from supporting or opposing creditors, orders:
   (a) dismissing the petition, with or without an order for costs as may be agreed, or
   (b) if the petition has not been served, giving permission to withdraw the petition (with no order for costs).

(3) <u>On other applications</u>, orders:
   (a) for sale of property, possession of property, disposal of proceeds of sale;
   (b) giving interim directions;
   (c) dismissing the application, with or without an order for costs as may be agreed;
   (d) giving permission to withdraw the application, with or without an order for costs as may be agreed.

If, (as may often be the case with orders under subparagraphs (3)(a) or (b) above) an adjournment is required, whether generally with liberty to restore or to a fixed date, the order by consent may include an order for the adjournment. If adjournment to a date is requested, a time estimate should be given and the Court will fix the first available date and time on or after the date requested.

16.4 The above lists should not be regarded as exhaustive, nor should it be assumed that an order will be made without attendance as requested.

16.5 The procedure outlined above is designed to save time and costs but is not intended to discourage attendance.

16.6 Applications for consent orders without attendance should be lodged at least two clear working days (and preferably longer) before any fixed hearing date.

16.7 Whenever a document is lodged or a letter sent, the correct case number, code (if any) and year (for example 123/SD/99 or 234/99) should be quoted. A note should also be given of the date and time of the next hearing (if any).

16.8 Attention is drawn to Paragraph 4.4(4) of the Practice Direction relating to CPR Part 44.

16A. BANKRUPTCY RESTRICTION ORDERS

Making the application

16A.1 An application for a bankruptcy restrictions order is made as an ordinary application in the bankruptcy.

16A.2 The application must be made within one year beginning with the date of the bankruptcy order unless the court gives permission for the application to be made after that period. The one year period does not run while the bankrupt's discharge has been suspended under section 279(3) of the Insolvency Act 1986.

16A.3 An application for a bankruptcy restrictions order may be made by the Secretary of State or the Official Receiver ("the Applicant"). The application must be supported by a report which must include:

(a) a statement of the conduct by reference to which it is alleged that it is appropriate for a bankruptcy restrictions order to be made; and

(b) the evidence relied on in support of the application (r 6.241 Insolvency Rules 1986).

16A.4 The report is treated as if it were an affidavit (r 7.9(2) Insolvency Rules 1986) and is prima facie evidence of any matter contained in it (r 7.9(3)).

16A.5 The application may be supported by evidence from other witnesses which may be given by affidavit or (by reason of r 7.57(5) Insolvency Rules 1986) by witness statement verified by a statement of truth.

16A.6 The court will fix a first hearing which must be not less than 8 weeks from the date when the hearing is fixed (r 6.241(4) Insolvency Rules 1986).

16A.7 Notice of the application and the venue fixed by the court must be served by the Applicant on the bankrupt not more than 14 days after the application is made. Service of notice must be accompanied by a copy of the application together with the evidence in support and a form of acknowledgment of service.

16A.8 The bankrupt must file in court an acknowledgment of service not more than 14 days after service of the application on him, indicating whether or not he contests the application. If he fails to do so he may attend the hearing of the application but may not take part in the hearing unless the court gives permission.

Opposing the application

16A.9 If the bankrupt wishes to oppose the application, he must within 28 days of service on him of the application and the evidence in support (or such longer period as the court may allow) file in court and (within three days thereof) serve on the Applicant any evidence which he wishes the court to take into consideration. Such evidence should normally be in the form of an affidavit or a witness statement verified by a statement of truth.

16A.10 The Applicant must file any evidence in reply within 14 days of receiving the evidence of the bankrupt (or such longer period as the court may allow) and must serve it on the bankrupt as soon as reasonably practicable.

Hearings

16A.11 Any hearing of an application for a bankruptcy restrictions order must be in public (r 6.241(5) Insolvency Rules 1986). The hearing will generally be before the registrar or district judge in the first instance who may:

(1) adjourn the application and give directions;

(2) make a bankruptcy restrictions order; or

(3) adjourn the application to the judge.

Making a bankruptcy restrictions order

16A.12 When the court is considering whether to make a bankruptcy restrictions order, it must not take into account any conduct of the bankrupt prior to 1 April 2004 (art. 7 Enterprise Act (Commencement No 4 and Transitional Provisions and Savings) Order 2003).

16A.13 The court may make a bankruptcy restrictions order in the absence of the bankrupt and whether or not he has filed evidence (r 6.244 Insolvency Rules 1986).

16A.14 When a bankruptcy restrictions order is made the court must send two sealed copies of the order to the Applicant (r 6.244(2) Insolvency Rules 1986), and as soon as reasonably practicable after receipt, the Applicant must send one sealed copy to the bankrupt (r 6.244(3)).

16A.15 A bankruptcy restrictions order comes into force when it is made and must specify the date on which it will cease to have effect, which must be between two and 15 years from the date on which it is made.

Interim bankruptcy restriction orders

16A.16 An application for an interim bankruptcy restrictions order may be made any time between the institution of an application for a bankruptcy restrictions order and the determination of that application (Sch 4A para. 5 Insolvency Act 1986). The application is made as an ordinary application in the bankruptcy.

16A.17 The application must be supported by a report as evidence in support of the application (r 6.246(1) Insolvency Rules 1986) which must include evidence of the bankrupt's conduct which is alleged to constitute the grounds for making an interim bankruptcy restrictions order and evidence of matters relating to the public interest in making the order.

16A.18 Notice of the application must be given to the bankrupt at least two business days before the date fixed for the hearing unless the court directs otherwise (r 6.245).

16A.19 Any hearing of the application must be in public (r 6.245).

16A.20 The court may make an interim bankruptcy restrictions order in the absence of the bankrupt and whether or not he has filed evidence (r 6.247).

16A.21 The bankrupt may apply to the court to set aside an interim bankruptcy restrictions order. The application is made by ordinary application in the bankruptcy and must be supported by an affidavit or witness statement verified by a statement of truth stating the grounds on which the application is made (r 6.248(2)).

16A.22 The bankrupt must send the Secretary of State, not less than 7 days before the hearing, notice of his application, notice of the venue, a copy of his application and a copy of the supporting affidavit. The Secretary of State may attend the hearing and call the attention of the court to any matters which seem to him to be relevant, and may himself give evidence or call witnesses.

16A.23 Where the court sets aside an interim bankruptcy restrictions order, two sealed copies of the order must be sent by the court, as soon as reasonably practicable, to the Secretary of State.

16A.24 As soon as reasonably practicable after receipt of sealed copies of the order, the Secretary of State must send a sealed copy to the bankrupt.

Bankruptcy restrictions undertakings

16A.25 Where a bankrupt has given a bankruptcy restrictions undertaking, the Secretary of State must file a copy in court and send a copy to the bankrupt as soon as reasonably practicable (r 6.250).

16A.26 The bankrupt may apply to annul a bankruptcy restrictions undertaking. The application is made as an ordinary application in the bankruptcy and must be supported by an affidavit or witness statement verified by a statement of truth stating the grounds on which it is made.

16A.27 The bankrupt must give notice of his application and the venue together with a copy of his affidavit in support to the Secretary of State at least 28 days before the date fixed for the hearing.

16A.28 The Secretary of State may attend the hearing and call the attention of the court to any matters which seem to him to be relevant and may himself give evidence or call witnesses.

16A.29 The court must send a sealed copy of any order annulling or varying the bankruptcy restrictions undertaking to the Secretary of State and the bankrupt.

PART FOUR
APPEALS

17. APPEALS IN INSOLVENCY PROCEEDINGS

17.1 This Part shall come into effect on 2nd May 2000 and shall replace and revoke Paragraph 17 of, and be read in conjunction with the Practice Direction—Insolvency Proceedings which came into effect on 26th April 1999 as amended.

17.2

(1) An appeal from a decision of a County Court (whether made by a District Judge or a Circuit Judge) or of a Registrar of the High Court in insolvency proceedings ("a first appeal") lies to a Judge of the High Court pursuant to s. 375(2) of the Act and Insolvency Rules 7.47(2) and 7.48(2) (as amended by s. 55 of the Access to Justice Act 1999).

(2) The procedure and practice for a first appeal are governed by Insolvency Rule 7.49 which imports the procedure and practice of the Court of Appeal. The procedure and practice of the Court of Appeal is governed by CPR Part 52 and its Practice Direction, which are subject to the provisions of the Act, the Insolvency Rules and this Practice Direction: see CPR Part 52 rule 1(4).

(3) A first appeal (as defined above) does not include an appeal from a decision of a Judge of the High Court.

17.3

(1) Section 55 of the Access to Justice Act 1999 has amended s. 375(2) of the Act and Insolvency Rules 7.47(2) and 7.48(2) so that an appeal from a decision of a Judge of the High Court made on a first appeal lies, with the permission of the Court of Appeal, to the Court of Appeal.

(2) An appeal from a Judge of the High Court in insolvency proceedings which is not a decision on a first appeal lies, with the permission of the Judge or of the Court of Appeal, to the Court of Appeal (see CPR Part 52 rule 3);

(3) The procedure and practice for appeals from a decision of a Judge of the High Court in insolvency proceedings (whether made on a first appeal or not) are also governed by Insolvency Rule 7.49 which imports the procedure and practice of the Court of Appeal as stated at Paragraph 17.2(2) above.

17.4 CPR Part 52 and its Practice Direction and Forms apply to appeals from a decision of a Judge of the High Court in insolvency proceedings.

17.5 An appeal from a decision of a Judge of the High Court in insolvency proceedings requires permission as set out in Paragraph 17.3(1) and (2) above.

17.6 A first appeal does not require the permission of any court.

17.7 Save as set out herein CPR Part 52 and its Practice Direction and Forms shall not apply to first appeals, but Paragraphs 17.8 to 17.23 inclusive of this Part of this Practice Direction shall apply to first appeals and only to first appeals.

17.8 Interpretation:

(a) the expressions "appeal court", "lower court", "appellant", "respondent" and "appeal notice" have the meanings given in CPR Part 52.1(3);

(b) "Registrar of Appeals" means in relation to an appeal filed at the Royal Courts of Justice in London a Bankruptcy Registrar, and in relation to an appeal filed in a District Registry in accordance with Paragraph 17.10(2) and (3) below a District Judge of the relevant District Registry.

(c) "appeal date" means the date fixed by the appeal court for the hearing of the appeal or the date fixed by the appeal court upon which the period within which the appeal will be heard commences.

17.9 An appellant's notice and a respondent's notice shall be in Form PDIP 1 and PDIP 2 set out in the Schedule hereto.

17.10

(1) An appeal from a decision of a Registrar in Bankruptcy shall, or from any decision made in any County Court may, be filed at the Royal Courts of Justice in London.

(2) An appeal from a decision made in the County Court exercising jurisdiction over an area within the Birmingham, Bristol, Cardiff, Leeds, Liverpool, Manchester, Newcastle Upon Tyne or Preston Chancery District Registries may be filed in the Chancery District Registry of the High Court appropriate to the area in which the decision was made.

17.11

(1) Where a party seeks an extension of time in which to file an appeal notice it must be requested in the appeal notice and the appeal notice should state the reason for the delay and the steps taken prior to the application being made; the court will fix a date for the hearing of the application and notify the parties of the date and place of hearing;

(2) The appellant must file the appellant's notice at the appeal court within—

(a) such period as may be directed by the lower court; or

(b) where the court makes no such direction, 14 days after the date of the decision of the lower court which the appellant wishes to appeal.

(3) Unless the appeal court orders otherwise, an appeal notice must be served by the appellant on each respondent—

(a) as soon as practicable; and

(b) in any event not later than 7 days, after it is filed.

17.12

(1) A respondent may file and serve a respondent's notice.

(2) A respondent who wishes to ask the appeal court to uphold the order of the lower court for reasons different from or additional to those given by the lower court must file a respondent's notice.

(3) A respondent's notice must be filed within—

(a) such period as may be directed by the lower court; or

(b) where the court makes no such direction, 14 days after the date on which the respondent is served with the appellant's notice.

(4) Unless the appeal court orders otherwise a respondent's notice must be served by the respondent on the appellant and any other respondent—

(a) as soon as practicable; and

(b) in any event not later than 7 days, after it is filed.

17.13

(1) An application to vary the time limit for filing an appeal notice must be made to the appeal court.

(2) The parties may not agree to extend any date or time limit set by—

(a) this Practice Direction; or

(b) an order of the appeal court or the lower court.

17.14 Unless the appeal court or the lower court orders otherwise an appeal shall not operate as a stay of any order or decision of the lower court.

17.15 An appeal notice may not be amended without the permission of the appeal court.

17.16 A Judge of the appeal court may strike out the whole or part of an appeal notice where there is compelling reason for doing so.

17.17

(1) In relation to an appeal the appeal court has all the powers of the lower court.

(2) The appeal court has power to—

(a) affirm, set aside or vary any order or judgment made or given by the lower court;

(b) refer any claim or issue for determination by the lower court;

(c) order a new trial or hearing;

(d) make a costs order.

(3) The appeal court may exercise its powers in relation to the whole or part of an order of the lower court.

17.18

(1) Every appeal shall be limited to a review of the decision of the lower court.

(2) Unless it orders otherwise, the appeal court will not receive—

(a) oral evidence; or

(b) evidence which was not before the lower court.

(3) The appeal court will allow an appeal where the decision of the lower court was—

(a) wrong; or

(b) unjust because of a serious procedural or other irregularity in the proceedings in the lower court.

(4) The appeal court may draw any inference of fact which it considers justified on the evidence.

(5) At the hearing of the appeal a party may not rely on a matter not contained in his appeal notice unless the appeal court gives permission.

17.19 The following applications shall be made to a Judge of the appeal court:

(1) for injunctions pending a substantive hearing of the appeal;

(2) for expedition or vacation of the hearing date of an appeal;

(3) for an order striking out the whole or part of an appeal notice pursuant to Paragraph 17.16 above;

(4) for a final order on paper pursuant to Paragraph 17.22(8) below.

17.20

(1) All other interim applications shall be made to the Registrar of Appeals in the first instance who may in his discretion either hear and determine it himself or refer it to the Judge.

(2) An appeal from a decision of a Registrar of Appeals lies to a Judge of the appeal court and does not require the permission of either the Registrar or Appeals of the Judge.

17.21 The procedure for interim applications is by way of ordinary application (see Insolvency Rule 12.7 and Sch 4, Form 7.2).

17.22 The following practice applies to all first appeals to a Judge of the High Court whether filed at the Royal Courts of Justice in London, or filed at one of the other venues referred to in Paragraph 17.10 above:

(1) on filing an appellant's notice in accordance with Paragraph 17.11(2) above, the appellant must file:
 (a) two copies of the appeal notice for the use of the court, one of which must be stamped with the appropriate fee, and a number of additional copies equal to the number of persons who are to be served with it pursuant to Paragraph 17.22(4) below;
 (b) a copy of the order under appeal; and
 (c) an estimate of time for the hearing.

(2) the above documents may be lodged personally or by post and shall be lodged at the address of the appropriate venue listed below:
 (a) if the appeal is to be heard at the Royal Courts of Justice in London the documents must be lodged at Room 110, Thomas More Building, The Royal Courts of Justice, Strand, London WC2A 2LL;
 (b) if the appeal is to be heard in Birmingham, the documents must be lodged at the District Registry of the Chancery Division of the High Court, 33 Bull Street, Birmingham B4 6DS;
 (c) if the appeal is to be heard in Bristol the documents must be lodged at the District Registry of the Chancery Division of the High Court, Third Floor, Greyfriars, Lewins Mead, Bristol, BS1 2NR;
 (d) if the appeal is to be heard in Cardiff the documents must be lodged at the District Registry in the Chancery Division of the High Court, First Floor, 2 Park Street, Cardiff, CF10 1ET;
 (e) if the appeal is to be heard in Leeds the documents must be lodged at the District Registry of the Chancery Division of the High Court, The Court House, 1 Oxford Row, Leeds LS1 3BG;
 (f) if the appeal is to be heard in Liverpool the documents must be lodged at the District Registry of the Chancery Division of the High Court, Liverpool Combined Court Centre, Derby Square, Liverpool L2 1XA;
 (g) if the appeal is to be heard in Manchester the documents must be lodged at the District Registry of the Chancery Division of the High Court, Courts of Justice, Crown Square, Manchester, M60 9DJ;
 (h) if the appeal is to be heard at Newcastle Upon Tyne the documents must be lodged at the District Registry of the Chancery Division of the High Court, The Law Courts, Quayside, Newcastle Upon Tyne NE1 3LA;
 (i) if the appeal is to be heard in Preston the documents must be lodged at the District Registry of the Chancery Division of the High Court, The Combined Court Centre, Ringway, Preston PR1 2LL.

(3) if the documents are correct and in order the court at which the documents are filed will fix the appeal date and will also fix the place of hearing. That court will send letters to all the parties to the appeal informing them of the appeal date and of the place of hearing and indicating the time estimate given by the appellant. The parties will be invited to notify the court of any alternative or revised time estimates. In the absence of any such notification the estimate of the appellant will be taken as agreed. The court will also send to the appellant a document setting out the court's requirement concerning the form and content of the bundle of documents for the use of the single judge. Not later than 7 days before the appeal date the bundle of documents must be filed by the appellant at the address of the relevant venue as set out in sub-paragraph 17.22(2) above and a copy of it must be served by the appellant on each respondent. The bundle should include an approved transcript of the judgment of the lower court or, where there is no officially recorded judgment, the document(s) referred to in paragraph 5.12 of the Practice Direction to CPR Part 52.

(4) the appeal notice must be served on all parties to the proceedings in the lower court who are directly affected by the appeal. This may include the Official Receiver, liquidator or trustee in bankruptcy.

(5) the appeal notice must be served by the appellant or by the legal representative of the appellant and may be effected by:

(a) any of the methods referred to in CPR Part 6 rule 2; or
(b) with permission of the court, an alternative method pursuant to CPR Part 6 rule 8.

(6) service of an appeal notice shall be proved by a Certificate of Service in accordance with CPR Part 6 rule 10 (CPR Form N215) which must be filed at the relevant venue referred to at Paragraph 17.22(2) above immediately after service.

(7) skeleton arguments, accompanied by a written chronology of events relevant to the appeal, should be filed at the address of the appropriate venue as set out in sub-paragraph 17.22(2) above, at least two clear days before the date fixed for the hearing. Failure to lodge may result in an adverse costs order being made by the single judge on the hearing of the appeal.

(8) where an appeal has been settled or where an appellant does not wish to continue with the appeal, the appeal may be disposed of on paper without a hearing. It may be dismissed by consent but the appeal court will not make an order allowing an appeal unless it is satisfied that the decision of the lower court was wrong. Any consent order signed by each party or letters of consent from each party must be lodged not later than 24 hours before the date fixed for the hearing of the appeal at the address of the appropriate venue as set out in sub-paragraph 17.22(2) above and will be dealt with by the Judge of the appeal court. Attention is drawn to paragraph 4.4(4) of the Practice Direction to CPR Part 44 regarding costs where an order is made by consent without attendance.

17.23 Only the following paragraphs of the Practice Direction to CPR Part 52, with any necessary modifications, shall apply to first appeals: 5.12 and 5.14 to 5.20 inclusive.

17.24

(1) Where, under the procedure relating to appeals in insolvency proceedings prior to the coming into effect of this Part of this Practice Direction, an appeal has been set down in the High Court or permission to appeal to the Court of Appeal has been granted before 2nd May 2000, the procedure and practice set out in this Part of this Practice Direction shall apply to such an appeal after that date.

(2) Where, under the procedure relating to appeals in insolvency proceedings prior to the coming into effect of this Part of this Practice Direction, any person has failed before 2nd May 2000 either:
(a) in the case of a first appeal, to set down in the High Court an appeal which relates to an order made (County Court) or sealed (High Court) after 27th March 2000 and before 2nd May 2000, or
(b) in the case of an appeal from a decision of a Judge of the High Court, to obtain any requisite permission to appeal to the Court of Appeal which relates to an order sealed in the same period,

the time for filing an appeal notice is extended to 16th May 2000 and application for any such permission should be made in the appeal notice.

17.25 This paragraph applies where a judge of the High Court has made a Bankruptcy order or a winding up order or dismissed an appeal against such an order and an application is made for a stay of proceedings pending appeal.

(1) the judge will not normally grant a stay of all proceedings but will confine himself to a stay of advertisement of the proceedings.

(2) where the judge has granted permission to appeal any stay of advertisement will normally be until the hearing of the appeal but on terms that the stay will determine without further order if an appellant's notice is not filed within the period prescribed by the rules.

(3) where the judge has refused permission to appeal any stay of advertisement will normally be for a period not exceeding 28 days. Application for any further stay of advertisement should be made to the Court of Appeal.

The Schedule

NOTES

This Schedule contains the following forms, which can be found at http://www.dca.gov.uk/civil/procrules_fin/menus/forms.htm#insolv

PDIP1 Appellant's Notice—Insolvency Proceedings
PDIP2 Respondent's Notice—Insolvency Proceedings
PDIP3 Draft Order—Multiple Transfer of Proceedings
PDIP4 Draft Order—Multiple Appointments of Office Holder

[1570]

PRACTICE DIRECTION: COMPETITION LAW—CLAIMS RELATING TO THE APPLICATION OF ARTICLES 81 AND 82 OF THE EC TREATY

Scope and Interpretation

1.1 This practice direction applies to any claim relating to the application of—

(a) Article 81 or Article 82 of the Treaty establishing the European Community; or

(b) Chapter I or Chapter II of Part I of the Competition Act 1998.

1.2 In this practice direction—

(a) "the Act" means the Competition Act 1998;

(b) "the Commission" means the European Commission;

(c) "the Competition Regulation" means Council Regulation (EC) No 1/2003 of 16 December 2002 on the implementation of the rules on competition laid down in Articles 81 and 82 of the Treaty;

(d) "national competition authority" means—

(i) the Office of Fair Trading; and

(ii) any other person or body designated pursuant to Article 35 of the Competition Regulation as a national competition authority of the United Kingdom;

(e) "the Treaty" means the Treaty establishing the European Community.

Venue

2.1 A claim to which this Practice Direction applies—

(a) must be commenced in the High Court at the Royal Courts of Justice; and

(b) will be assigned to the Chancery Division unless it comes within the scope of rule 58.1(2), in which case it will be assigned to the Commercial Court of the Queen's Bench Division.

2.2 Any party whose statement of case raises an issue relating to the application of Article 81 or 82 of the Treaty, or Chapter I or II of Part I of the Act, must—

(a) state that fact in his statement of case; and

(b) apply for the proceedings to be transferred to the Chancery Division at the Royal Courts of Justice, if they have not been commenced there, or in the Commercial or Admiralty Courts; or

(c) apply for the transfer of the proceedings to the Commercial Court, in accordance with rules 58.4(2) and 30.5(3). If such application is refused, the proceedings must be transferred to the Chancery Division of the High Court at the Royal Courts of Justice.

2.3 Rule 30.8 provides that where proceedings are taking place in the Queen's Bench Division (other than proceedings in the Commercial or Admiralty Courts), a district registry of the High Court or a county court, the court must transfer the proceedings to the Chancery Division at the Royal Courts of Justice if the statement of case raises an issue relating to the application of Article 81 or 82, or Chapter I or II. However, if any such proceedings which have been commenced in the Queen's Bench Division or a Mercantile Court fall within the scope of rule 58.1(2), any party to those proceedings may apply for the transfer of the proceedings to the Commercial Court, in accordance with rules 58.4(2) and 30.5(3). If the application is refused, the proceedings must be transferred to the Chancery Division of the High Court at the Royal Courts of Justice.

2.4 Where proceedings are commenced in or transferred to the Chancery Division at the Royal Courts of Justice in accordance with this paragraph, that court may transfer the proceedings or any part of the proceedings to another court if—

(a) the issue relating to the application of Article 81 or 82, or Chapter I or II, has been resolved; or

(b) the judge considers that the proceedings or part of the proceedings to be transferred does not involve any issue relating to the application of Article 81 or 82, or Chapter I or II.

(Rule 30.3 sets out the matters to which the court must have regard when considering whether to make a transfer order.)

Notice of proceedings

3. Any party whose statement of case raises or deals with an issue relating to the application of Article 81 or 82, or Chapter I or II, must serve a copy of the statement of case on the Office of Fair Trading at the same time as it is served on the other parties to the claim

(addressed to the Director of Competition Policy Co-ordination, Office of Fair Trading, Fleetbank House, 2–6 Salisbury Square, London EC4Y 8JX).

Case management

4.1 Attention is drawn to the provisions of article 15.3 of the Competition Regulation (co-operation with national courts), which entitles competition authorities and the Commission to submit written observations to national courts on issues relating to the application of Article 81 or 82 and, with the permission of the court in question, to submit oral observations to the court.

4.1A A national competition authority may also make written observations to the court, or apply for permission to make oral observations, on issues relating to the application of Chapter I or II.

4.2 If a national competition authority or the Commission intends to make written observations to the court, it must give notice of its intention to do so by letter to Chancery Chambers at the Royal Courts of Justice (including the claim number and addressed to the Court Manager, Room TM 6.06, Royal Courts of Justice, Strand, London WC2A 2LL) at the earliest reasonable opportunity.

4.3 An application by a national competition authority or the Commission for permission to make oral representations at the hearing of a claim must be made by letter to Chancery Chambers (including the claim number and addressed to the Court Manager, Room TM 6.06, Royal Courts of Justice, Strand, London WC2A 2LL) at the earliest reasonable opportunity, identifying the claim and indicating why the applicant wishes to make oral representations.

4.4 If a national competition authority or the Commission files a notice under paragraph 4.2 or an application under paragraph 4.3, it must at the same time serve a copy of the notice or application on every party to the claim.

4.5 Any request by a national competition authority or the Commission for the court to send it any documents relating to a claim should be made at the same time as filing a notice under paragraph 4.2 or an application under paragraph 4.3.

4.6 Where the court receives a notice under paragraph 4.2 it may give case management directions to the national competition authority or the Commission, including directions about the date by which any written observations are to be filed.

4.7 The court will serve on every party to the claim a copy of any directions given or order made—

(a) on an application under paragraph 4.3; or
(b) under paragraph 4.6.

4.8 In any claim to which this practice direction applies, the court shall direct a pre-trial review to take place shortly before the trial, if possible before the judge who will be conducting the trial.

Avoidance of conflict with Commission decisions

5.1 In relation to claims which raise an issue relating to the application of Article 81 or 82 of the Treaty, attention is drawn to the provisions of article 16 of the Competition Regulation (uniform application of Community competition law).

5.2 Every party to such a claim, and any national competition authority which has been served with a copy of a party's statement of case, is under a duty to notify the court at any stage of the proceedings if they are aware that—

(a) the Commission has adopted, or is contemplating adopting, a decision in relation to proceedings which it has initiated; and
(b) the decision referred to in (a) above has or would have legal effects in relation to the particular agreement, decision or practice in issue before the court.

5.3 Where the court is aware that the Commission is contemplating adopting a decision as mentioned in paragraph 5.2(a), it shall consider whether to stay the claim pending the Commission's decision.

Judgments

6. Where any judgment is given which decides on the application of Article 81 or Article 82 of the Treaty, the judge shall direct that a copy of the transcript of the judgment shall be sent to the Commission.

Judgments may be sent to the Commission electronically to comp-amicus@cec.eu.int or by post to the European Commission—DG Competition, B–1049, Brussels.

[1571]

THE ADMIRALTY & COMMERCIAL COURTS GUIDE

(February 2002)

Only Sections B, F and O, and Appendices 5 and 15, are reproduced here.

B. COMMENCEMENT, TRANSFER AND REMOVAL

B1 Commercial cases

B1.1 Rule 58.1(2) describes a "commercial claim" as follows:

"any claim arising out of the transaction of trade and commerce and includes any claim relating to—

(a) a business document or contract;
(b) the export or import of goods;
(c) the carriage of goods by land, sea, air or pipeline;
(d) the exploitation of oil and gas reserves or other natural resources;
(e) insurance and re-insurance;
(f) banking and financial services;
(g) the operation of markets and exchanges;
(h) the purchase and sale of commodities;
(i) the construction of ships;
(j) business agency; and
(k) arbitration."

B2 Starting a case in the Commercial Court

B2.1 Except for arbitration applications which are governed by the provisions of CPR Part 62 and section O of the Guide , the case will be begun by a claim form under Part 7 or Part 8.

B2.2 Save where otherwise specified, references in this Guide to a claim form are to a Part 7 claim form.

B2.3 The Commercial Court may give a fixed date for trial (see section D16), but it does not give a fixed date for a hearing when it issues a claim. Rules 7.9 and 7.10 and their associated practice directions do not apply to the Commercial Court.

B3 Part 7 claims

The form

B3.1 A claimant starting proceedings in the Commercial Court must use practice form N1(CC) for Part 7 claims: **PD58 §2.4**. A copy of this practice form is included at the end of the Guide.

Marking

B3.2 In accordance with PD58 §2.3 the claim form should be marked in the top right hand corner with the words "Queen's Bench Division, Commercial Court", and on the issue of the claim form out of the Registry the case will be entered in the Commercial List. Marking the claim form in this way complies sufficiently with PD7 §3.6(3).

Statement of value

B3.3 Rule 16.3, which provides for a statement of value to be included in the claim form, does not apply in the Commercial Court: **rule 58.5(2).**

Particulars of claim and the claim form

B3.4 Although particulars of claim may be served with the claim form, this is not a requirement in the Commercial Court. However, if the particulars of claim are not contained in or served with the claim form, the claim form must contain a statement that if an acknowledgment of service is filed indicating an intention to defend the claim, particulars of claim will follow: **rule 58.5(1)(a).**

B3.5 If particulars of claim do not accompany the claim form they must be served within 28 days after the defendant has filed an acknowledgment of service indicating an intention to defend the claim: **rule 58.5(1)(c).**

B3.6 The three forms specified in rule 7.8(1) must be served with the claim form. One of these is a form for acknowledging service: **rule 58.5(1)(b).**

Statement of truth

B3.7

(a) A claim form must be verified by a statement of truth: **rule 22.1.** Unless the court otherwise orders, any amendment to a claim form must also be verified: **rule 22.1(2).**

(b) The required form of statement of truth is set out at **PD7 §7.2.**

(c) A claim form will remain effective even where not verified by a statement of truth, unless it is struck out: **PD22 §4.1.**

(d) In certain cases the statement of truth may be signed by a person other than the party on whose behalf it is served or its legal representative: **section C1.8–1.9.**

Trial without service of particulars of claim or a defence

B3.8 The attention of the parties and their legal representatives is drawn to rule 58.11 which allows the court to order (before or after the issue of a claim form) that the case shall proceed without the filing or service of particulars of claim or defence or of any other statement of case.

Interest

B3.9 The claim form (and not only the particulars of claim) must comply with the requirements of rules 16.4(1)(b) and 16.4(2) concerning interest: **rule 58.5(3).**

B3.10 References to particulars of claim in rule 12.6(1)(a) (referring to claims for interest where there is a default judgment) and rule 14.14(1)(a) (referring to claims for interest where there is a judgment on admissions) may be treated as references to the claim form: **rules 58.8(2) and 58.9(3).**

Issue of a claim form when the Registry is closed

B3.11 A request for the issue of a Part 7 claim form may be made by fax at certain times when the Registry is closed to the public: **PD58 §2.2.** The procedure is set out in Appendix 3. Any further details may be obtained from the Registry. The fax number is 020 7947 6667.

B4 Part 8 claims

Form

B4.1 A claimant who wishes to commence a claim under CPR Part 8 must use practice form N208(CC): **PD58 §2.4**. A copy of this practice form is included at the end of this Guide.

B4.2 Attention is drawn to the requirement in rule 8.2(a) that where a claimant uses the Part 8 procedure his claim form must state that Part 8 applies. Similarly, PD7 §3.3 requires that the claim form state (if it be the case) that the claimant wishes his claim to proceed under Part 8 or that the claim is required to proceed under Part 8.

Marking and statement of truth

B4.3 Sections B3.2 (marking) and B3.7 (statement of truth) also apply to a claim form issued under Part 8.

Issue of a claim form when the Registry is closed

B4.4 A request for the issue of a Part 8 claim form may be made by fax at certain times when the Registry is closed to the public: **PD58 §2.2.** The procedure is set out in Appendix 3.

Time for filing evidence in opposition to a Part 8 claim

B4.5 A defendant to a Part 8 claim who wishes to rely on written evidence must file and serve it within 28 days after filing an acknowledgment of service: **rule 58.12.**

B5 Part 20 claims

Form

B5.1 Adapted versions of the Part 20 claim form and acknowledgment of service (Practice Forms no N211 and N213) and of the related Notes to Part 20 claimant and Part 20 defendant have been approved for use in the Commercial Court. Copies of the practice forms are included at the end of the Guide.

B6 Service of the claim form

Service by the parties

B6.1 Claim forms issued in the Commercial List are to be served by the parties, not by the Registry: **PD58 §9.**

Methods of service

B6.2 Methods of service are set out in CPR Part 6, which is supplemented by a Practice Direction.

B6.3 PD6 §§2.1 and 3.1 concern service by document exchange and by fax. Service of the claim form on the legal representative of the defendant by document exchange or fax will not be effective unless that legal representative has authority to accept service. It is desirable to obtain confirmation from the legal representative in writing that he has instructions to accept service of a claim form on behalf of the defendant.

Applications for extension of time

B6.4 Applications for an extension of time in which to serve a claim form are governed by rule 7.6. Rule 7.6(3)(a), which refers to service of the claim form by the court, does not apply in the Commercial Court.

B6.5 The evidence required on an application for an extension of time is set out in PD7 §8.2.

Certificate of service

B6.6 When the claimant has served the claim form he must file a certificate of service: **rule 6.14(2).** Satisfaction of this requirement is relevant, in particular, to the claimant's ability to obtain judgment in default (see Part 12) and to the right of a non-party to search for, inspect and take a copy of the claim form under rule 5.4(2)(a).

B7 Service of the claim form out of the jurisdiction

B7.1 Applications for permission to serve a claim form out of the jurisdiction are governed by rules 6.19 to 6.31. A guide to the appropriate practice is set out in Appendix 15.

B7.2 Service of process in some foreign countries may take a long time to complete; it is therefore important that solicitors take prompt steps to effect service.

B8 Acknowledgment of service

Part 7 claims

B8.1

(a) A defendant must file an acknowledgment of service in every case: **rule 58.6(1)**. An adapted version of practice form N9 (which includes the acknowledgment of service) has been approved for use in the Commercial Court. A copy of this practice form (Form N9(CC)) is included at the end of the Guide, together with adapted versions of the notes for claimants and defendants on completing and replying to a Part 7 claim form.

(b) The period for filing an acknowledgment of service is calculated from the service of the claim form, whether or not particulars of claim are contained in or accompany the claim form or are to follow service of the claim form. Rule 9.1(2), which provides that in certain circumstances the defendant need not respond to the claim until particulars of claim have been served on him, does not apply: rule 58.6(1).

Part 8 claims

B8.2

(a) A defendant must file an acknowledgment of service in every case: **rule 58.6(1)**. An adapted version of practice form N210 (acknowledgment of service of a Part 8 claim form) has been approved for use in the Commercial Court. A copy of this practice form (Form N210(CC)) is included at the end of the Guide, together with adapted versions of the notes for claimants and defendants on completing and replying to a Part 8 claim form.

(b) The time for filing an acknowledgment of service is calculated from the service of the claim form.

Acknowledgment of service in a claim against a firm

B8.3

(a) PD10 §4.4 allows an acknowledgment of service to be signed on behalf of a partnership by any of the partners or a person having the control or management of the partnership business, whether he be a partner or not.

(b) However, attention is drawn to Schedule 1 to the CPR which includes, with modifications, provisions previously contained in RSC Order 81 concerning acknowledgment of service by a person served as a partner who denies his liability as such. (see also the note at the end of CPR Part 10).

Time for filing acknowledgment of service

B8.4

(a) Except in the circumstances described in section B8.4(b) and B8.4(c), or is otherwise ordered by the court, the period for filing an acknowledgment of service is 14 days after service of the claim form.

(b) If the claim form has been served out of the jurisdiction without the permission of the court under rule 6.19, the time for filing an acknowledgment of service is governed by rule 6.22, save that in all cases time runs from the service of the claim form: **rule 58.6(3).**

(c) If the claim form has been served out of the jurisdiction with the permission of the court under rule 6.20 the time for filing an acknowledgment of service is governed by rule 6.21(4)(a), the second practice direction supplementing rule 6 and the table to which it refers, save that in all cases time runs from the service of the claim form: **rule 58.6(3).**

B9 Disputing the court's jurisdiction

Part 7 claims

B9.1

(a) If the defendant intends to dispute the court's jurisdiction or contend that the court should not exercise its jurisdiction he must

(i) file an acknowledgment of service—**rule 11(2)**; and

(ii) issue an application notice seeking the appropriate relief.

(b) An application to dispute the court's jurisdiction must be made within 28 days of filing an acknowledgment of service: **rule 58.7(2).**

(c) If the defendant wishes to rely on written evidence in support of that application, he must file and serve that evidence when he issues the application.

(d) If the defendant makes an application under rule 11(1), the claimant is not bound to serve particulars of claim until that application has been disposed of: **rule 58.7(3).**

Part 8 claims

B9.2

(a) The provisions of section B9.1(a)–(c) also apply in the case of Part 8 claims.

(b) If the defendant makes an application under rule 11(1), he is not bound to serve any written evidence on which he wishes to rely in opposition to the substantive claim until that application has been disposed of: **rule 11.9.**

Effect of an application challenging the jurisdiction

B9.3 An acknowledgment of service of a Part 7 or Part 8 claim form which is followed by an application challenging the jurisdiction under Part 11 does not constitute a submission by the defendant to the jurisdiction: **rules 11(3)** and **11(7).**

B9.4 If an application under Part 11 is unsuccessful, and the court then considers giving directions for filing and serving statements of case (in the case of a Part 7 claim) or evidence (in the case of a Part 8 claim), a defendant does not submit to the jurisdiction merely by asking for time to serve and file his statement of case or evidence, as the case may be.

B10 Default judgment

B10 Default judgment is governed by Part 12 and PD12. However, because in the Commercial Court the period for filing the acknowledgment of service is calculated from service of the claim form, the reference to "particulars of claim" in PD12 §4.1(1) should be read as referring to the claim form: **PD58 §6(1).**

B11 Admissions

B11

(a) Admissions are governed by CPR Part 14, and PD14, except that the references to "particulars of claim" in PD14 §§2.1, 3.1 and 3.2 should be read as referring to the claim form: **PD58 §6(2).**

(b) Adapted versions of the practice forms of admission (practice forms no N9A and no

N9C) have been approved for use in the Commercial Court. Copies of these practice forms (Forms N9A(CC) and N9C(CC)) are included at the end of the Guide.

B12 Transfer of cases into and out of the Commercial List

B12.1 The procedure for transfer and removal is set out in **PD58 §4**. All such applications must be made to the Commercial Court: **rule 30.5(3)**.

B12.2 Although an order to transfer a case to the Commercial List may be made at any stage, any application for such an order should normally be made at an early stage in the proceedings.

B12.3 Transfer to the Commercial List may be ordered for limited purposes only, but a transferred case will normally remain in the Commercial List until its conclusion.

B12.4 An order transferring a case out of the Commercial List may be made at any stage, but will not usually be made after a pre-trial timetable has been fixed at the case management conference (see section D8).

B12.5 Some commercial cases may more suitably, or as suitably, be dealt with in one of the Mercantile Courts. Parties should consider whether it would be more appropriate to begin proceedings in one of those courts and the Commercial Judge may on his own initiative order the case to be transferred there.

[1572]

F. APPLICATIONS

F1 Generally

F1.1

(a) Applications are governed by CPR Part 23 and PD23 as modified by rule 58 and PD58. As a result
  - (i) PD23 §§1 and 2.3–2.6 do not apply;
  - (ii) PD23 §§2.8 and 2.10 apply only if the proposed (additional) application will not increase the time estimate already given for the hearing for which a date has been fixed; and
  - (iii) PD23 §3 is subject in all cases to the judge's agreeing that the application may proceed without an application notice being served.

(b) An adapted version of practice form N244 (application notice) has been approved for use in the Commercial Court. A copy of this practice form (Form N244(CC)) is included at the end of the Guide.

F1.2 An application for a consent order must include a draft of the proposed order signed on behalf of all parties to whom it relates: **PD58 §14.1**.

F1.3 The requirement in PD23 §12.1 that a draft order be supplied on disk does not apply in the Commercial Court since orders are generally drawn up by the parties: **PD58 §14.2**.

Service

F1.4 Application notices are served by the parties, not by the court: **PD58 §9**.

Evidence

F1.5

(a) Particular attention is drawn to PD23 §9.1 which points out that even where no specific requirement for evidence is set out in the Rules or Practice Directions the court will in practice often need to be satisfied by evidence of the facts that are relied on in support of, or in opposition to, the application.

(b) Where convenient the written evidence relied on in support of an application may be included in the application notice, which may be lengthened for this purpose.

Time for service of evidence

F1.6 The time allowed for the service of evidence in relation to applications is governed by PD58 §13.

Hearings

F1.7

(a) Applications (other than arbitration applications) will be heard in public in accordance with rule 39.2, save where otherwise ordered.

(b) With certain exceptions, arbitration applications will normally be heard in private: **rule 62.10(3)**. See section O.

(c) An application without notice for a freezing injunction or a search order will normally be heard in private.

F1.8 Parties should pay particular attention to PD23 §2.9 which warns of the need to anticipate the court's wish to review the conduct of the case and give further management directions. The parties should be ready to give the court their assistance and should be able to answer any questions that the court may ask for this purpose.

F1.9 PD23 §§6.1–6.5 and §7 deal with the hearing of applications by telephone (other than an urgent application out of court hours) and the hearing of applications using video-conferencing facilities. These methods may be considered when an application needs to be made before a particular Commercial Judge who is currently on circuit. In most other cases applications are more conveniently dealt with in person.

F2 Applications without notice

F2.1 All applications should be made on notice, even if that notice has to be short, unless

(i) any rule or Practice Direction provides that the application may be made without notice; or

(ii) there are good reasons for making the application without notice, for example, because notice would or might defeat the object of the application.

F2.2 Where an application without notice does not involve the giving of undertakings to the court, it will normally be made and dealt with on paper, as, for example, applications for permission to serve a claim form out of the jurisdiction, and applications for an extension of time in which to serve a claim form.

F2.3 Any application for an interim injunction or similar remedy will require an oral hearing.

F2.4

(a) A party wishing to make an application without notice which requires an oral hearing before a judge should contact the Clerk to the Commercial Court at the earliest opportunity.

(b) If a party wishes to make an application without notice at a time when no commercial judge is available he should apply to the Queen's Bench Judge in Chambers (see section P1.1).

F2.5 On all applications without notice it is the duty of the applicant and those representing him to make full and frank disclosure of all matters relevant to the application.

F2.6 The papers lodged for the application should include two copies of a draft of the order sought. Save in exceptional circumstances where time does not permit, all the evidence relied upon in support of the application and any other relevant documents must be lodged in advance with the Clerk to the Commercial Court. If the application is urgent, the Clerk to the Commercial Court should be informed of the fact and of the reasons for the urgency.

F3 Expedited applications

F3.1 The Court will expedite the hearing of an application on notice in cases of sufficient urgency and importance.

F3.2 Where a party wishes to make an expedited application a request should be made to the Clerk to the Commercial Court on notice to all other parties.

F4 Paper applications

F4.1

(a) Although contested applications are usually best determined at an oral hearing, some applications may be suitable for determination on paper.

(b) Attention is drawn to the provisions of rule 23.8 and PD23 §11. If the applicant considers that the application is suitable for determination on paper, he should ensure before lodging the papers with the court

(i) that the application notice together with any supporting evidence has been served on the respondent;

(ii) that the respondent has been allowed the appropriate period of time in which to serve evidence in opposition;

(iii) that any evidence in reply has been served on the respondent; and

(iv) that there is included in the papers

(A) the written consent of the respondent to the disposal of the application without a hearing; or

(B) a statement by the applicant of the grounds on which he seeks to have the application disposed of without a hearing, together with confirmation that a copy has been served on the respondent.

(c) Only in exceptional cases will the court dispose of an application without a hearing in the absence of the respondent's consent.

F4.2

(a) Certain applications relating to the management of proceedings may conveniently be made in correspondence without issuing an application notice.

(b) It must be clearly understood that such applications are not applications without notice and the applicant must therefore ensure that a copy of the letter making the application is sent to all other parties to the proceedings.

(c) Accordingly, the following procedure should be followed when making an application of this kind:

(i) the applicant should first ascertain whether the application is opposed by the other parties;

(ii) if it is, the applicant should apply to the court by letter stating the nature of the order which it seeks and the grounds on which the application is made;

(iii) a copy the letter should be sent (by fax, where possible) to all other parties at the same time as it is sent to the court;

(iv) any other party wishing to make representations should do so by letter within two days (ie two clear days) of the date of the applicant's letter of application. The representations should be sent (by fax, where possible) to the applicant and all other parties at the same time as they are sent to the court;

(v) the court will advise its decision by letter to the applicant. The applicant must forthwith copy the court's letter to all other parties, by fax where possible.

F5 Ordinary applications

F5.1 Applications likely to require an oral hearing lasting half a day or less are regarded as "ordinary" applications.

F5.2 Ordinary applications will generally be heard on Fridays, but may be heard on other days. Where possible, the Listing Office will have regard to the availability of advocates when fixing hearing dates.

F5.3 Many ordinary applications, especially those in the non-Counsel list on Fridays, are very short indeed (eg applications to extend time). As in the past, it is likely that many, if not most, of such applications can be heard without evidence and on short (ie a few days) notice. The parties should however have in mind what is said in section F1.5(a) above.

F5.4

(a) The timetable for ordinary applications is set out in PD58 §13.1 and is as follows:

(i) evidence in support must be filed and served with the application;

(ii) evidence in answer must be filed and served within 14 days thereafter;

(iii) evidence in reply (if any) must be filed and served within 7 days thereafter.

(b) This timetable may be abridged or extended by agreement between the parties provided that any date fixed for the hearing of the application is not affected: **PD58 §13.4**. In appropriate cases, this timetable may be abridged by the Court.

F5.5 An application bundle (see section F11) must be lodged with the Listing Office by 1 pm one clear day before the date fixed for the hearing. The case management bundle will also be required on the hearing; this file will be passed by the Listing Office to the judge. Only where it is essential for the court on the hearing of the ordinary application to see the full version of a statement of case that has been summarised in accordance with section C1.4 above should a copy of that statement of case be lodged for the ordinary application.

F5.6 Save in very short and simple cases, skeleton arguments must be provided by all parties. These must be lodged with the Listing Office and served on the advocates for all other parties to the application by 1 pm on the day before the date fixed for the hearing (ie the immediately preceding day). Guidelines on the preparation of skeleton arguments are set out in Part 1 of Appendix 9.

F5.7 Thus, for an application estimated for a half day or less and due to be heard on a Friday:

(i) the application bundle must be lodged by 1 pm on Wednesday; and

(ii) skeleton arguments must be lodged by 1 pm on Thursday.

F5.8 The applicant should, as a matter of course, provide all other parties to the application with a copy of the application bundle at the cost of the receiving party. Further copies should be supplied on request, again at the cost of the receiving party.

F5.9 Problems with the lodging of bundles or skeleton arguments should be notified to the Clerk to the Commercial Court as far in advance as possible. **If the application bundle or skeleton argument is not lodged by the time specified, the application may be stood out of the list without further warning.**

F6 Heavy applications

F6.1 Applications likely to require an oral hearing lasting more than half a day are regarded as "heavy" applications.

F6.2 Heavy applications normally involve a greater volume of evidence and other documents and more extensive issues. They accordingly require a longer lead-time for preparation and exchange of evidence. Where possible the Listing Office will have regard to the availability of advocates when fixing hearing dates.

F6.3 The timetable for heavy applications is set out in PD58 §13.2 and is as follows:
- (i) evidence in support must be filed and served with the application;
- (ii) evidence in answer must be filed and served within 28 days thereafter;
- (iii) evidence in reply (if any) must be filed and served as soon as possible, and in any event within 14 days of service of the evidence in answer.

F6.4
- **(a)** An application bundle (see section F11) must be lodged with the Listing Office by 4 pm two days (ie two clear days) before the date fixed for the hearing. The case management bundle will also be required on the hearing; this file will be passed by the Listing Office to the judge.
- **(b)** Only where it is essential for the court on the hearing of the application to see the full version of a statement of case that has been summarised in accordance with section C1.4 above should a copy of that statement of case be lodged for the application.

F6.5 Skeleton arguments must be lodged with the Listing Office and served on the advocates for all other parties to the application as follows:
- (i) applicant's skeleton argument (with chronology unless one is unnecessary, and with a dramatis personae if one is warranted), by 4 pm two days (ie two clear days) before the hearing;
- (ii) respondent's skeleton argument, by 4 pm one day (ie one clear day) before the hearing.

Guidelines on the preparation of skeleton arguments are set out in Part 1 of Appendix 9.

F6.6 Thus, for an application estimated for more than half a day and due to be heard on a Thursday:
- (i) the application bundle and the applicant's skeleton argument must be lodged by 4 pm on Monday;
- (ii) the respondent's skeleton argument must be lodged by 4 pm on Tuesday.

F6.7 The applicant must, as a matter of course, provide all other parties to the application with a copy of the application bundle at the cost of the receiving party. Further copies must be supplied on request, again at the cost of the receiving party.

F6.8 Problems with the lodging of bundles or skeleton arguments should be notified to the Clerk to the Commercial Court as far in advance as possible. **If the application bundle or skeleton argument is not lodged by the time specified, the application may be stood out of the list without further warning**.

F7 Evidence

F7.1 Although evidence may be given by affidavit, it should generally be given by witness statement, except where PD32 requires evidence to be given on affidavit (as, for example, in the case of an application for a freezing injunction or a search order: **PD32 §1.4**). In other cases the Court may order that evidence be given by affidavit: **PD32 §1.4(1) and 1.6**.

F7.2 Witness statements and affidavits must comply with the requirements of PD32, save that photocopy documents should be used unless the court orders otherwise.

F7.3
- **(a)** Witness statements must be verified by a statement of truth signed by the maker of the statement: **rule 22.1**.
- **(b)** At hearings other than trial an applicant may rely on the application notice itself, and a party may rely on his statement of case, if the application notice or statement of case (as the case may be) is verified by a statement of truth: **rule 32.6(2)**.
- **(c)** A statement of truth in an application notice may also be signed as indicated in sections C1.8 and C1.9 above.

F7.4 Proceedings for contempt of court may be brought against a person who makes, or causes to be made, a false statement in a witness statement (or any other document verified by a statement of truth) without an honest belief in its truth: **rule 32.14(1)**.

F8 Reading time

F8

(a) It is essential for the efficient conduct of the court's business that the parties inform the court of the reading required in order to enable the judge to dispose of the application within the time allowed for the hearing and of the time likely to be required for that purpose. Accordingly

(i) each party must lodge with the Listing Office by 1 pm on the day before the date fixed for the hearing of an application (i e the immediately preceding day) a reading list with an estimate of the time required to complete the reading;

(ii) each party's reading list should identify the material **on both sides** which the court needs to read; and

(iii) if any advocate considers that the time required for reading is likely to exceed 2½ hours, the Listing Office must be warned of that fact **not later than 4.00 pm one clear day before the hearing of the application**.

(b) **Failure to comply with these requirements may result in the adjournment of the hearing.**

F9 Applications disposed of by consent

F9.1

(a) Consent orders may be submitted to the court in draft for approval and initialling without the need for attendance.

(b) Two copies of the draft, one of which (or a counterpart) must be signed on behalf of all parties to whom it relates, should be lodged at the Registry. The copies should be undated. The order will be dated with the date on which the judge initials it, but that does not prevent the parties acting on their agreement immediately if they wish.

(c) The parties should act promptly in lodging the copies at the Registry. If it is important that the orders are made by a particular date, that fact (and the reasons for it) should be notified in writing to the Registry.

F9.2 For the avoidance of doubt, this procedure is not normally available in relation to a case management conference or a pre-trial review. Whether or not the parties are agreed as between themselves on the directions that the court should be asked to consider giving at a case management conference or a pre-trial review, attendance will normally be required. See section D8.3.

F9.3 Where an order provides a time by which something is to be done the order should wherever possible state the particular date by which the thing is to be done rather than specify a period of time from a particular date or event: **rule 2.9**.

F10 Hearing dates, time estimates and time limits

F10.1 Dates for the hearing of applications to be attended by advocates are normally fixed after discussion with the counsel's clerks or with the solicitor concerned.

F10.2 The efficient working of the court depends on accurate estimates of the time needed for the oral hearing of an application. Over-estimating can be as wasteful as under-estimating.

F10.3 Subject to section F10.4, the Clerk to the Commercial Court will not accept or act on time estimates for the oral hearing of applications where those estimates exceed the following maxima:

Application to set aside service:	4 hours
Application for summary judgment:	4 hours
Application to set aside or vary interim remedy:	4 hours
Application to set aside or vary default judgment:	2 hours
Application to amend statement of case:	1 hour
Application for specific disclosure:	1 hour
Application for security for costs:	1 hour

F10.4 A longer listing time will only be granted upon application in writing specifying the additional time required and giving reasons why it is required. A copy of the written application should be sent to the advocates for all other parties in the case at the same time as it is sent to the Listing Office.

F10.5

(a) Not later than five days before the date fixed for the hearing the applicant must provide the Listing Office with his current estimate of the time required to dispose of the application.

(b) If at any time either party considers that there is a material risk that the hearing of the application will exceed the time currently allowed it must inform the Listing Office immediately.

F10.6

(a) All time estimates should be given on the assumption that the judge will have read in advance the skeleton arguments and the documents identified in the reading list. In this connection attention is drawn to section F8.

(b) A time estimate for an ordinary application should allow time for judgment and consequential matters; a time estimate for a heavy application should not.

F10.7 Save in the situation referred to at section F10.8, a separate estimate must be given for each application, including any application issued after, but to be heard at the same time as, another application.

F10.8 A separate estimate need not be given for any application issued after, but to be heard at the same time as, another application where the advocate in the case certifies in writing that

(i) the determination of the application first issued will necessarily determine the application issued subsequently; or

(ii) the matters raised in the application issued subsequently are not contested.

F10.9 If it is found at the hearing that the time required for the hearing has been significantly underestimated, the judge hearing the application may adjourn the matter and may make any special costs orders (including orders for the immediate payment of costs and wasted costs orders) as may be appropriate.

F10.10 Failure to comply with the requirements for lodging bundles for the application will normally result in the application not being heard on the date fixed at the expense of the party in default (see further sections F5.9 and F6.8 above). An order for immediate payment of costs may be made.

F11 Application bundles

F11.1

(a) Bundles for use on applications may be compiled in any convenient manner but must contain the following documents (preferably in separate sections in the following order):

(i) a copy of the application notice;

(ii) a draft of the order which the applicant seeks;

(iii) a copy of the statements of case;

(iv) copies of any previous orders which are relevant to the application;

(v) copies of the witness statements and affidavits filed in support of, or in opposition to, the application, together with any exhibits.

(b) Copies of the statements of case and of previous orders in the action should be provided in a separate section of the bundle. They should not be exhibited to witness statements.

(c) Witness statements and affidavits previously filed in the same proceedings should be included in the bundle at a convenient location. They should not be exhibited to witness statements.

F12 Chronologies, indices and dramatis personae

F12.1 For most applications it is of assistance for the applicant to provide a chronology. Dramatis personae are often useful as well.

F12.2 Guidelines on the preparation of chronologies and indices are set out in Part 2 of Appendix 9.

F13 Authorities

F13.1 On some applications there will be key authorities that it would be useful for the judge to read before the oral hearing of the application. Copies of these authorities should be provided with the skeleton arguments.

F13.2 It is also desirable for bundles of the authorities on which the parties wish to rely to be provided to the judge hearing the application as soon as possible after skeleton arguments have been exchanged.

F13.3 Unreported cases should only be cited where the advocate is ready to give an assurance that the transcript contains a statement of some principle of law, relevant to an issue on the application, of which the substance, as distinct from some mere choice of phraseology, is not to be found in any judgment that has appeared in one of the recognised series of law reports.

F14 Costs

F14.1 Costs are dealt with generally at section J13.

F14.2 Reference should be also be made to the rules governing the summary assessment of costs for shorter hearings contained in Parts 43 and 44.

F14.3 In carrying out a summary assessment of costs, the court may have regard amongst other matters to:

(i) advice from a Commercial Costs Judge or from the Chief Costs Judge on costs of specialist solicitors and counsel;

(ii) any survey published by the London Solicitors Litigation Association showing the average hourly expense rate for solicitors in London;

(iii) any information provided to the court at its request by one or more of the specialist associations (referred to at section A4.2) on average charges by specialist solicitors and counsel.

F15 Interim injunctions

Generally

F15.1

(a) Applications for interim injunctions are governed by CPR Part 25.

(b) Applications must be made on notice in accordance with the procedure set out in CPR Part 23 unless there are good reasons for proceeding without notice.

F15.2 A party who wishes to make an application for an interim injunction must give the Clerk to the Commercial Court as much notice as possible.

F15.3

(a) Except when the application is so urgent that there has not been any opportunity to do so, the applicant must issue his claim form and obtain the evidence on which he wishes to rely in support of the application before making the application.

(b) On applications of any weight, and unless the urgency means that this is not possible, the applicant should provide the court at the earliest opportunity with a skeleton argument.

(c) An affidavit, and not a witness statement, is required on an application for a freezing injunction or a search order: **PD25 §3.1**.

Fortification of undertakings

F15.4

(a) Where the applicant for an interim remedy is not able to show sufficient assets within the jurisdiction of the Court to provide substance to the undertakings given, particularly the undertaking in damages, he may be required to reinforce his undertakings by providing security.

(b) Security will be ordered in such form as the judge decides is appropriate but may, for example, take the form of a payment into court, a bond issued by an insurance company or a first demand guarantee or standby credit issued by a first-class bank.

(c) In an appropriate case the judge may order a payment to be made to the applicant's solicitors to be held by them as officers of the court pending further order. Sometimes the undertaking of a parent company may be acceptable.

Form of order

F15.5 Standard forms of wording for freezing injunctions and search orders are set out in Appendix 5. The forms have been adapted for use in the Commercial Court and should be followed unless the judge hearing a particular application considers there is good reason for adopting a different form.

F15.6 A phrase indicating that an interim remedy is to remain in force until judgment or further order means that it remains in force until the delivery of a final judgment. If an interim remedy continuing after judgment is required, say until judgment has been satisfied, an application to that effect must be made (see further section K1).

F15.7 It is good practice to draft an order for an interim remedy so that it includes a proviso which permits acts which would otherwise be a breach of the order to be done with the written consent of the claimant's solicitors. This enables the parties to agree in effect to variations (or the discharge) of the order without the necessity of coming back to the court.

Freezing injunctions

F15.8

(a) Freezing injunctions made on an application without notice will provide for a return date, unless the judge otherwise orders: **PD25 §5.1(3)**. In the usual course, the return date given will be a Friday (unless a date for a case management conference has already been fixed, in which event the return date given will in the usual course be that date).

(b) If, after service or notification of the injunction, one or more of the parties considers that more than 15 minutes will be required to deal with the matter on the return date the Listing Office should be informed forthwith and in any event no later than 4 pm on the Wednesday before the Friday fixed as the return date.

(c) If the parties agree, the return date may be postponed to a later date on which all parties will be ready to deal with any substantive issues. In this event, an agreed form of order continuing the injunction to the postponed return date should be submitted for consideration by a judge and if the order is made in the terms submitted there will be no need for the parties to attend on the day originally fixed as the return date.

(d) In such a case the defendant and any other interested party will continue to have liberty to apply to vary or set aside the order.

F15.9 A provision for the defendant to give notice of any application to discharge or vary the order is usually included as a matter of convenience but it is not proper to attempt to fetter the right of the defendant to apply without notice or on short notice if need be.

F15.10 As regards freezing injunctions in respect of assets outside the jurisdiction, the standard wording in relation to effects on third parties should normally incorporate wording to enable overseas branches of banks or similar institutions which have offices within the jurisdiction to comply with what they reasonably believe to be their obligations under the laws of the country where the assets are located or under the proper law of the relevant banking or other contract relating to such assets.

F15.11 Any bank or third party served with, notified of or affected by a freezing injunction may apply to the court without notice to any party for directions, or notify the court in writing without notice to any party, in the event that the order affects or may affect the position of the bank or third party under legislation, regulations or procedures aimed to prevent money laundering.

Search orders

F15.12 Attention is drawn to the detailed requirements in respect of search orders set out in PD25 §§7.1–8.3. The applicant for the search order will normally be required to undertake not to inform any third party of the search order or of the case until after a specified date.

Applications to discharge or vary freezing injunctions and search orders

F15.13 Applications to discharge or vary freezing injunctions and search orders are treated as matters of urgency for listing purposes. Those representing applicants for discharge or variation should ascertain before a date is fixed for the hearing whether, having regard to the evidence which they wish to adduce, the claimant would wish to adduce further evidence in opposition. If so, all reasonable steps must be taken by all parties to agree upon the earliest practicable date at which they can be ready for the hearing, so as to avoid the last minute need to vacate a fixed date. In cases of difficulty the matter should be referred to a judge who may be able to suggest temporary solutions pending the hearing.

F15.14 If a freezing injunction or search order is discharged on an application to discharge or vary, or on the return date, the judge will consider whether it is appropriate that he should assess damages at once and direct immediate payment by the applicant.

Applications under section 25 of the Civil Jurisdiction and Judgments Act 1982

F15.15 A Part 8 claim form (rather than an application notice: cf. rule 25.4(2)) must be used for an application under section 25 of the Civil Jurisdiction and Judgments Act 1982 ("Interim relief in England and Wales and Northern Ireland in the absence of substantive proceedings"). The modified Part 8 procedure used in the Commercial Court is referred to at section B4 above.

F16 Security for costs

F16.1 Applications for security for costs are governed by rules 25.12–14.

F16.2 The applicable practice is set out in Appendix 16.

[1573]

O. ARBITRATION

O1 Arbitration claims

O1.1

(a) Applications to the court under the Arbitration Acts 1950–1996 and other applications relating to arbitrations are known as "arbitration claims".

(b) The procedure applicable to arbitration claims is to be found in Part 62 and its associated practice direction. Separate provision is made

(i) by Section I for claims relating to arbitrations to which the Arbitration Act 1996 applies;

(ii) by Section II for claims relating to arbitrations to which the Arbitration Acts 1950–1979 ("the old law") apply; and

(iii) by Section III for enforcement proceedings.

(c) For a full definition of the expression "arbitration claim" see rule 62.2(1) (claims under the 1996 Act) and rule 62.11(2) (claims under the old law).

(d) Part 58 applies to arbitration claims in the Commercial Court insofar as no specific provision is made by Part 62: **rule 62.1(3)**.

Claims under the Arbitration Act 1996

O2 Starting an arbitration claim

O2.1 Subject to section O2.3 an arbitration claim must be started by the issue of an arbitration claim form in accordance with the Part 8 procedure: **rule 62.3(1)**.

O2.2 The claim form must be substantially in the form set out in Appendix A to practice direction 62: **PD62 §2.2**.

O2.3 An application to stay proceedings under section 9 of the Arbitration Act 1996 must be made by application notice in the proceedings: **rule 62.3(2)**.

O3 The arbitration claim form

O3.1 The arbitration claim form must contain, among other things, a concise statement of the remedy claimed and, if an award is challenged, the grounds for that challenge: **rule 62.4(1)**.

O3.2 Reference in the arbitration claim form to a witness statement or affidavit filed in support of the claim is not sufficient to comply with the requirements of rule 62.4(1).

O4 Service of the arbitration claim form

O4.1 An arbitration claim form issued in the Admiralty & Commercial Registry must be served by the claimant.

O4.2

(a) The rules governing service of the claim form are set out in Part 6 of the Civil Procedure Rules.

(b) Unless the court orders otherwise an arbitration claim form must be served on the defendant within 1 month from the date of issue: **rule 62.4(2)**.

O4.3

(a) An arbitration claim form may be served out of the jurisdiction with the permission of the court: **rule 62.5(1)**.

(b) Rules 6.24–6.29 apply to the service of an arbitration claim form out of the jurisdiction: rule **62.5(3)**.

O4.4 The court may exercise its powers under rule 6.8 to permit service of an arbitration claim form on a party at the address of the solicitor or other representative acting for him in the arbitration: **PD62 §3.1**.

O4.5 The claimant must file a certificate of service within 7 days of serving the arbitration claim form: **PD62 §3.2**.

O5 Acknowledgment of service

O5.1

(a) A defendant must file an acknowledgment of service of the arbitration claim form in every case: **rule 58.6(1)**.

(b) An adapted version of practice form N210 (acknowledgment of service of a Part 8 claim form) has been approved for use in the Commercial Court. A copy of this practice form (Form N210(CC)) is included at the end of the Guide, together with adapted versions of the notes for claimants and defendants on completing and replying to an arbitration claim form.

O5.2 The time for filing an acknowledgment of service is calculated from the service of the arbitration claim form.

O6 Standard directions

O6.1 The directions set out in **PD62 §6.2–6.7** apply unless the court orders otherwise.

O6.2 The claimant should apply for a hearing date as soon as possible after issuing an arbitration claim form or (in the case of an appeal) obtaining permission to appeal.

O6.3 A defendant who wishes to rely on evidence in opposition to the claim must file and serve his evidence within 21 days after the date by which he was required to acknowledge service: **PD62 §6.2**.

O6.4 A claimant who wishes to rely on evidence in response to evidence served by the defendant must file and serve his evidence within 7 days after the service of the defendant's evidence: **PD62 §6.3**.

O6.5 An application for directions in a pending arbitration claim should be made by application notice under Part 23.

O7 Interim remedies

O7.1 An application for an interim remedy under section 44 of the Arbitration Act 1996 must be made in an arbitration claim form: **PD62 §8.1**.

O8 Challenging the award

Challenge by way of appeal

O8.1 A party wishing to appeal against the award of an arbitrator or umpire must set out in the arbitration claim form

(i) the question of law on which the appeal is based; and
(ii) a succinct statement of the grounds of appeal,

identifying the relevant part(s) of the award and reasons.

O8.2 If the appeal is brought with the agreement of the other parties to the proceedings, a copy of their agreement in writing must be filed with the arbitration claim form.

O8.3 A party seeking permission to appeal must

(i) state in his arbitration claim form the grounds on which he contends that permission to appeal should be given **PD62 §12.1**; and
(ii) file and serve with the arbitration claim form any written evidence on which he wishes to rely for the purposes of satisfying the court of the matters referred to in section 69(3) of the 1996 Act: **PD62 §12.2**.

O8.4

(a) If the defendant wishes to oppose the claimant's application for permission to appeal he must file a witness statement setting out
 (i) the grounds on which he opposes the grant of permission; and
 (ii) any evidence on which he relies in relation to the matters mentioned in section 69(3) of the 1996 Act: **PD62 §§12.3(1) & (2)**.

(b) If the defendant wishes to contend that that the award should be upheld for reasons other than those expressed in the award, he must set out those reasons in his witness statement: **PD62 §12.3(3)**.

O8.5 The court will normally determine applications for permission to appeal without an oral hearing. If the court considers that an oral hearing is required, it will give further directions as appropriate.

Challenging an award for serious irregularity

O8.6

(a) An arbitration claim challenging an award on the ground of serious irregularity under section 68 of the 1996 Act is appropriate only in cases where there are grounds for thinking
 (i) that an irregularity has occurred which
 (ii) has caused or will cause **substantial** injustice to the party making the challenge.

(b) An application challenging an award on the ground of serious irregularity should therefore not be regarded as an alternative to, or a means of supporting, an application for permission to appeal.

O8.7 The challenge to the award must be supported by evidence of the circumstances on which the claimant relies as giving rise to the irregularity complained of and the nature of the injustice which has been or will be caused to him.

O8.8 If the nature of the challenge itself or the evidence filed in support of it leads the court to consider that the claim has no real prospect of success, the court may exercise its powers under rule 3.3(4) to dismiss the application summarily. In such cases the applicant will have the right to apply to the court to set aside the order and to seek directions for the hearing of the application.

Multiple claims

O8.9 If the arbitration claim form includes both a challenge to an award by way of appeal and a challenge on the ground of serious irregularity, the applications should be set out in separate sections of the arbitration claim form and the grounds on which they are made separately identified.

O8.10 In such cases the papers will be placed before a judge to consider how the applications may most appropriately be disposed of. It is usually more appropriate to dispose of the application to set aside or remit the award before considering the application for permission to appeal.

O9 Time limits

O9.1 An application to challenge an award under sections 67 or 68 of the 1996 Act or to appeal under section 69 of the Act must be brought within 28 days of the date of the award: **see section 70(3)**.

O9.2 The court has power to vary the period of 28 days fixed by section 70(3) of the 1996 Act: **rule 62.9(1)**. However, it is important that any challenge to an award be pursued without delay and the court will require cogent reasons for extending time.

O9.3 An application to extend time made **before** the expiry of the period of 28 days must be made in a Part 23 application notice, but the application notice need not be served on any other party: **rule 62.9(2)** and **PD62 §11.1(1)**.

O9.4 An application to extend time made **after** the expiry of the period of 28 days must be made in the arbitration claim form in which the applicant is seeking substantive relief: **rule 62.9(3)(a)**.

O9.5 An application to vary the period of 28 days will normally be determined without a hearing and prior to the consideration of the substantive application: **PD62 §10.2**.

Claims under the Arbitration Acts 1950–1979

O10 Starting an arbitration claim

O10.1 Subject to section O10.2 an arbitration claim must be started by the issue of an arbitration claim form in accordance with the Part 8 procedure: **rule 62.13(1)**.

O10.2 The claim form must be substantially in the form set out in Appendix A to PD62 §2.2.

O10.3 An application to stay proceedings on the grounds of an arbitration agreement must be made by application notice in the proceedings: **rule 62.13(2)**.

O11 The arbitration claim form

O11.1 An arbitration claim form must state the grounds of the claim or appeal: **rule 62.15(5)(a)**.

O11.2 Reference in the arbitration claim form to the witness statement or affidavit filed in support of the claim is not sufficient to comply with the requirements of rule 62.15(5)(a).

O12 Service of the arbitration claim form

O12.1 An arbitration claim form issued in the Admiralty & Commercial Registry must be served by the claimant.

O12.2 The rules governing service of the claim form are set out in Part 6 of the Civil Procedure Rules.

O12.3

(a) An arbitration claim form may be served out of the jurisdiction with the permission of the court: **rule 62.16(1)**.

(b) Rules 6.24–6.29 apply to the service of an arbitration claim form out of the jurisdiction: rule **62.16(4)**.

O12.4 Although not expressly covered by PD62, the court may in an appropriate case exercise its powers under rule 6.8 to permit service of an arbitration claim form on a party at the address of the solicitor or other representative acting for him in the arbitration.

O12.5 The claimant must file a certificate of service within 7 days of serving the claim form.

Acknowledgment of service

O13.1

(a) A defendant must file an acknowledgment of service in every case: **rule 58.6(1)**.

(b) An adapted version of practice form N210 (acknowledgment of service of a Part 8 claim form) has been approved for use in the Commercial Court. A copy of this practice form (Form N210(CC)) is included at the end of the Guide, together with adapted versions of the notes for claimants and defendants on completing and replying to an arbitration claim form.

O13.2 The time for filing an acknowledgment of service is calculated from the service of the arbitration claim form.

O14 Standard directions

O14.1 Where the claim or appeal is based on written evidence, a copy of that evidence must be served with the arbitration claim form: **rule 62.15(5)(b)**.

O14.2 Where the claim or appeal is made with the consent of the arbitrator or umpire or other parties, a copy of every written consent must be served with the arbitration claim form: **rule 62.15(5)(c)**.

O14.3 An application for directions in a pending arbitration claim should be made by application notice under Part 23.

O15 Interim remedies

O15.1 An application for an interim remedy under section 12(6) of the 1950 Act must be made in accordance with Part 25.

O15.2 The application must be made by arbitration claim form.

O15.3 A claim under section 12(4) of the 1950 Act for an order for the issue of a witness summons to compel the attendance of a witness before an arbitrator or umpire where the attendance of the witness is required within the district of a District Registry may be started in that Registry: **rule 62.14**.

O16 Challenging the award

Challenge by way of appeal

O16.1 A party wishing to appeal against the award of an arbitrator or umpire must file and serve with the arbitration claim form a statement of the grounds for the appeal, specifying the relevant part(s) of the award and reasons: **rule 62.15(6)**.

O16.2 A party seeking permission to appeal must also file and serve with the arbitration claim form any written evidence in support of the contention that the question of law concerns a term of the contract or an event which is not "one off": **rule 62.15(6)**.

O16.3 Any written evidence in reply must be filed and served not less than 2 days before the hearing of the application for permission to appeal: **rule 62.15(7)**.

O16.4 A party who wishes to contend that the award should be upheld for reasons other than those set out in the award and reasons must file and serve on the claimant a notice specifying the grounds of his contention not less than 2 days before the hearing of the application for permission to appeal: **rule 62.15(8)**.

O16.5 Applications for permission to appeal will be heard orally, but will not normally be listed for longer than half an hour. Skeleton arguments should be lodged.

Claims to set aside or remit the award

O16.6 A claim to set aside or remit an award on the grounds of misconduct should not be regarded as an alternative to, or a means of supporting, an application for permission to appeal.

O16.7 The directions set out in PD62 §§6.2–6.7 should be followed unless the court orders otherwise.

Multiple claims

O16.8 If the arbitration claim form includes both an appeal and an application to set aside or remit the award, the applications should be set out in separate sections of the arbitration claim form and the grounds on which they are made separately identified.

O16.9 The court may direct that one application be heard before the other or may direct that they be heard together, as may be appropriate. It is usually more appropriate to dispose of the application to set aside or remit the award before considering the application for permission to appeal.

O17 Time limits

O17.1

(a) Time limits governing claims under the 1950 and 1979 Acts are set out in rule 62.15.

(b) Different time limits apply to different claims. **It is important to consult rule 62.15 to ensure that applications are made within the time prescribed.**

(c) The court has power under rule 3.1(2) to vary the time limits prescribed by rule 62.15, but will require cogent reasons for doing so.

Provisions applicable to all arbitrations

Enforcement of awards

O18.1 All applications for permission to enforce awards are governed by Section III of Part 62: **rule 62.17.**

O18.2 An application for permission to enforce an award in the same manner as a judgment may be made without notice, but the court may direct that the arbitration claim form be served, in which case the application will continue as an arbitration claim in accordance with the procedure set out in Section I: **rule 62.18(1)–(3)**.

O18.3 An application for permission to enforce an award in the same manner as a judgment must be supported written evidence in accordance with **rule 62.18(6)**.

O18.4

(a) Two copies of the draft order must accompany the application.

(b) If the claimant wishes to enter judgment, the form of the judgment must correspond to the terms of the award.

(c) The defendant has the right to apply to the court to set aside an order made without notice giving permission to enforce the award and the order itself must state in terms

  (i) that the defendant may apply to set it aside within 14 days after service of the order or, if the order is to be served out of the jurisdiction, within such other period as the court may set; and

  (ii) that it may not be enforced until after the end of that period or any application by the defendant to set it aside has been finally disposed of: **rule 62.18(9) & (10)**.

Matters of general application

O19 Transfer of arbitration claims

O19.1 An arbitration claim which raises no significant point of arbitration law or practice will normally be transferred

(i) if a rent-review arbitration, to the Chancery Division;

(ii) if a construction or engineering arbitration, to the Technology and Construction Court;

(iii) if an employment arbitration, to the Central London County Court Mercantile List.

O19.2 Salvage arbitrations will normally be transferred to the Admiralty Court.

O20 Appointment of a Commercial Judge as sole arbitrator or umpire

O20.1 Section 93 of the Arbitration Act 1996 provides for the appointment of a Commercial Judge as sole arbitrator or umpire. The Act limits the circumstances in which a Judge may accept such an appointment.

O20.2 Enquiries should be directed to the Judge in charge of the Commercial List or the Clerk to the Commercial Court.

[1574]

APPENDIX 5
FORMS OF FREEZING INJUNCTION AND SEARCH ORDER

SEARCH ORDER

IN THE HIGH COURT OF JUSTICE
QUEEN'S BENCH DIVISION

COMMERCIAL COURT

Before The Honourable Mr Justice [ ]

Claim No

BETWEEN

Claimant(s)

- and -

Defendant(s)

Applicant(s)

Respondent(s)

PENAL NOTICE

If you [ ][1] disobey this order you may be held to be in contempt of court and may be imprisoned, fined or have your assets seized.

Any other person who knows of this Order and does anything which helps or permits the Respondent to breach the terms of this Order may also be held to be in contempt of court and may be imprisoned, fined or have their assets seized.

THIS ORDER

1. This is a Search Order made against [ ] ("the Respondent") on [ ] by Mr Justice [ ] on the application of [ ] ("the Applicant"). The Judge read the Affidavits listed in Schedule F and accepted the undertakings set out in Schedules C, D and E at the end of this order.

2. This order was made at a hearing without notice to the Respondent. The Respondent has a right to apply to the court to vary or discharge the order—see paragraph 27 below.

3 There will be a further hearing in respect of this order on [ ] ("the return date").

4. If there is more than one Respondent—
   (a) unless otherwise stated, references in this order to "the Respondent" mean both or all of them; and
   (b) this order is effective against any Respondent on whom it is served or who is given notice of it.

5. This order must be complied with by—
   (a) the Respondent;
   (b) any director, officer, partner or responsible employee of the Respondent; and
   (c) if the Respondent is an individual, any other person having responsible control of the premises to be searched.

THE SEARCH

6. The Respondent must permit the following persons[2]—

(a) [ ] ("the Supervising Solicitor");

(b) [ ], a solicitor in the firm of [ ], the Applicant's solicitors; and

(c) up to [ ] other persons[3] being [*their identity or capacity*] accompanying them,

(together "the search party"), to enter the premises mentioned in Schedule A to this order and any other premises of the Respondent disclosed under paragraph 18 below and any vehicles under the Respondent's control on or around the premises ("the premises") so that they can search for, inspect, photograph or photocopy, and deliver into the safekeeping of the Applicant's solicitors all the documents and articles which are listed in Schedule B to this order ("the listed items").

7. Having permitted the search party to enter the premises, the Respondent must allow the search party to remain on the premises until the search is complete. In the event that it becomes necessary for any of those persons to leave the premises before the search is complete, the Respondent must allow them to re-enter the premises immediately upon their seeking re-entry on the same or the following day in order to complete the search.

RESTRICTIONS ON SEARCH

8. This order may not be carried out at the same time as a police search warrant.

9. Before the Respondent allows anybody onto the premises to carry out this order, he is entitled to have the Supervising Solicitor explain to him what it means in everyday language.

10. The Respondent is entitled to seek legal advice and to ask the court to vary or discharge this order. Whilst doing so, he may ask the Supervising Solicitor to delay starting the search for up to 2 hours or such other longer period as the Supervising Solicitor may permit. However, the Respondent must-

(a) comply with the terms of paragraph 27 below;
(b) not disturb or remove any listed items; and
(c) permit the Supervising Solicitor to enter, but not start to search.

11. Before permitting entry to the premises by any person other than the Supervising Solicitor, the Respondent may, for a short time (not to exceed two hours, unless the Supervising Solicitor agrees to a longer period), gather together any documents he believes may be [incriminating or][4] privileged and hand them to the Supervising Solicitor for him to assess whether they are [incriminating or] privileged as claimed. If the Supervising Solicitor decides that any of the documents may be [incriminating or] privileged or is in any doubt as to their status, he will exclude them from the search and retain them in his possession pending further order of the court.

12. If the Respondent wishes to take legal advice and gather documents as permitted, he must first inform the Supervising Solicitor and keep him informed of the steps being taken.

13. No item may be removed from the premises until a list of the items to be removed has been prepared, and a copy of the list has been supplied to the Respondent, and he has been given a reasonable opportunity to check the list.

14. The premises must not be searched, and items must not be removed from them, except in the presence of the Respondent.

15. If the Supervising Solicitor is satisfied that full compliance with paragraphs 13 or 14 is not practicable, he may permit the search to proceed and items to be removed without fully complying with them.

DELIVERY UP OF ARTICLES/DOCUMENTS

16. The Respondent must immediately hand over to the Applicant's solicitors any of the listed items, which are in his possession or under his control, save for any computer or hard disk integral to any computer. Any items the subject of a dispute as to whether they are listed items must immediately be handed over to the Supervising Solicitor for safe keeping pending resolution of the dispute or further order of the court.

17. The Respondent must immediately give the search party effective access to the computers on the premises, with all necessary passwords, to enable the computers to be searched. If they contain any listed items the Respondent must cause the listed items to be displayed so that they can be read and copied.[5] The Respondent must provide the Applicant's Solicitors with copies of all listed items contained in the computers. All reasonable steps shall be taken by the Applicant and the Applicant's solicitors to ensure that no damage is done to any computer or data. The Applicant and his representatives may not themselves search the Respondent's computers unless they have sufficient expertise to do so without damaging the Respondent's system.

PROVISION OF INFORMATION

18. The Respondent must immediately inform the Applicant's Solicitors (in the presence of the Supervising Solicitor) so far as he is aware—

(a) where all the listed items are;

(b) the name and address of everyone who has supplied him, or offered to supply him, with listed items;

(c) the name and address of everyone to whom he has supplied, or offered to supply, listed items; and

(d) full details of the dates and quantities of every such supply and offer.

19. Within [ ] working days after being served with this order the Respondent must swear and serve an affidavit setting out the above information.[6]

PROHIBITED ACTS

20. Except for the purpose of obtaining legal advice, the Respondent must not directly or indirectly inform anyone of these proceedings or of the contents of this order, or warn anyone that proceedings have been or may be brought against him by the Applicant until 4.30 pm on the return date or further order of the court.

21. Until 4.30 pm on the return date the Respondent must not destroy, tamper with, cancel or part with possession, power, custody or control of the listed items otherwise than in accordance with the terms of this order.

22. [Insert any negative injunctions.]

23. [Insert any further order]

COSTS

24. The costs of this application are reserved to the judge hearing the application on the return date.

RESTRICTIONS ON SERVICE

25. This order may only be served between [ ] am/pm and [ ] am/pm [and on a weekday].[7]

26. This order must be served by the Supervising Solicitor, and paragraph 6 of the order must be carried out in his presence and under his supervision.

VARIATION AND DISCHARGE OF THIS ORDER

27. Anyone served with or notified of this order may apply to the court at any time to vary or discharge this order (or so much of it as affects that person), but they must first inform the Applicant's solicitors. If any evidence is to be relied upon in support of the application, the substance of it must be communicated in writing to the Applicant's solicitors in advance.

INTERPRETATION OF THIS ORDER

28. Any requirement that something shall be done to or in the presence of the Respondent means—

(a) if there is more than one Respondent, to or in the presence of any one of them; and

(b) if a Respondent is not an individual, to or in the presence of a director, officer, partner or responsible employee.

29. A Respondent who is an individual who is ordered not to do something must not do it himself or in any other way. He must not do it through others acting on his behalf or on his instructions or with his encouragement.

30. A Respondent which is not an individual which is ordered not to do something must not do it itself or by its directors, officers, partners, employees or agents or in any other way.

COMMUNICATIONS WITH THE COURT

All communications to the court about this order should be sent to Room E201, Royal Courts of Justice, Strand, London WC2A 2LL quoting the case number. The telephone number is 020 7947 6826.

The offices are open between 10 am and 4.30 pm Monday to Friday.

SCHEDULE A
THE PREMISES

SCHEDULE B
THE LISTED ITEMS

SCHEDULE C
UNDERTAKINGS GIVEN TO THE COURT BY THE APPLICANT

(1) If the court later finds that this order or carrying it out has caused loss to the Respondent, and decides that the Respondent should be compensated for that loss, the Applicant will comply with any order the court may make. Further if the carrying out of this order has been in breach of the terms of this order or otherwise in a manner inconsistent with the Applicant's solicitors' duties as officers of the court, the Applicant will comply with any order for damages the court may make.

[(2) As soon as practicable the Applicant will issue a claim form [in the form of the draft produced to the court] [claiming the appropriate relief].]

(3) The Applicant will [swear and file an affidavit] [cause an affidavit to be sworn and filed] [substantially in the terms of the draft affidavit produced to the court] [confirming the substance of what was said to the court by the Applicant's counsel/solicitors].

(4) The Applicant will not, without the permission of the court use any information or documents obtained as a result of carrying out this order nor inform anyone else of these proceedings except for the purposes of these proceedings (including adding further Respondents) or commencing civil proceedings in relation to the same or related subject matter to these proceedings until after the return date.

[(5) The Applicant will maintain pending further order the sum of £ [ ] in an account controlled by the Applicant's solicitors.]

[(6) The Applicant will insure the items removed from the premises.]

SCHEDULE D
UNDERTAKINGS GIVEN BY THE APPLICANT'S SOLICITORS

(1) The Applicant's solicitors will provide to the Supervising Solicitor for service on the Respondent—

(i) a service copy of this order;
(ii) the claim form (with defendant's response pack) or, if not issued, the draft produced to the court;
(iii) an application for hearing on the return date;
(iv) copies of the affidavits *[or draft affidavits]* and exhibits capable of being copied containing the evidence relied upon by the applicant;
(v) a note of any allegation of fact made orally to the court where such allegation is not contained in the affidavits or draft affidavits read by the judge; and
(vi) a copy of the skeleton argument produced to the court by the Applicant's [counsel/solicitors].

(2) The Applicants' solicitors will answer at once to the best of their ability any question whether a particular item is a listed item.

(3) Subject as provided below the Applicant's solicitors will retain in their own safe keeping all items obtained as a result of this order until the court directs otherwise.

(4) The Applicant's solicitors will return the originals of all documents obtained as a result of this order (except original documents which belong to the Applicant) as soon as possible and in any event within [two] working days of their removal.

SCHEDULE E
UNDERTAKINGS GIVEN BY THE SUPERVISING SOLICITOR

(1) The Supervising Solicitor will use his best endeavours to serve this order upon the Respondent and at the same time to serve upon the Respondent the other documents required to be served and referred to in paragraph (1) of Schedule D.

(2) The Supervising Solicitor will offer to explain to the person served with the order its meaning and effect fairly and in everyday language, and to inform him of his right to take legal advice (such advice to include an explanation that the Respondent may be entitled to avail himself of [the privilege against self-incrimination or] [legal professional privilege]) and to apply to vary or discharge this order as mentioned in paragraph 27 above.

(3) The Supervising Solicitor will retain in the safe keeping of his firm all items retained by him as a result of this order until the court directs otherwise.

(4) Within [48] hours of completion of the search the Supervising Solicitor will make and provide to the Applicant's solicitors, the Respondent or his solicitors and to the judge who made this order (for the purposes of the court file) a written report on the carrying out of the order.

SCHEDULE F
AFFIDAVITS

The Applicant relied on the following affidavits—

[name]	[number of affidavit]	[date sworn]	[filed on behalf of]
(1)			
(2)			

NAME AND ADDRESS OF APPLICANT'S SOLICITORS

The Applicant's solicitors are—

[Name, address, reference, fax and telephone numbers both in and out of office hours.]

**** FREEZING INJUNCTION ****

COMMERCIAL COURT

Before The Honourable Mr Justice [ ]

Claim No

BETWEEN

Claimant(s)

- and -

Defendant(s)

Applicant(s)

Respondent(s)

PENAL NOTICE

If you [ ][8] disobey this order you may be held to be in contempt of court and may be imprisoned, fined or have your assets seized.

Any other person who knows of this order and does anything which helps or permits the Respondent to breach the terms of this order may also be held to be in contempt of court and may be imprisoned, fined or have their assets seized.

THIS ORDER

1. This is a Freezing Injunction made against [ ] ("the Respondent") on [ ] by Mr Justice [ ] on the application of [ ] ("the Applicant"). The Judge read the Affidavits listed in Schedule A and accepted the undertakings set out in Schedule B at the end of this Order.

2. This order was made at a hearing without notice to the Respondent. The Respondent has a right to apply to the court to vary or discharge the order—see paragraph 13 below.

3. There will be a further hearing in respect of this order on [ ] ("the return date").

4. If there is more than one Respondent—
(a) unless otherwise stated, references in this order to "the Respondent" mean both or all of them; and
(b) this order is effective against any Respondent on whom it is served or who is given notice of it.

FREEZING INJUNCTION

[For injunction limited to assets in England and Wales]

5. Until the return date or further order of the court, the Respondent must not remove from England and Wales or in any way dispose of, deal with or diminish the value of any of his assets which are in England and Wales up to the value of £ .

[For worldwide injunction]

5. Until the return date or further order of the court, the Respondent must not—
(1) remove from England and Wales any of his assets which are in England and Wales up to the value of £
(2) in any way dispose of, deal with or diminish the value of any of his assets whether they are in or outside England and Wales up to the same value.

[For either form of injunction]

6. Paragraph 5 applies to all the Respondent's assets whether or not they are in his own name and whether they are solely or jointly owned. For the purpose of this order the Respondent's assets include any asset which he has the power, directly or indirectly, to dispose of or deal with as if it were his own. The Respondent is to be regarded as having such power if a third party holds or controls the asset in accordance with his direct or indirect instructions.

7. This prohibition includes the following assets in particular—
(a) the property known as *[title/address]* or the net sale money after payment of any mortgages if it has been sold;
(b) the property and assets of the Respondent's business [known as *[name]*] [carried on at *[address]*] or the sale money if any of them have been sold; and
(c) any money in the account numbered *[account number]* at *[title/address]*.

[For injunction limited to assets in England and Wales]

8. If the total value free of charges or other securities ("unencumbered value") of the Respondent's assets in England and Wales exceeds £ , the Respondent may remove any of those assets from England and Wales or may dispose of or deal with them so long as the total unencumbered value of his assets still in England and Wales remains above £ .

[For worldwide injunction]

8.
(1) If the total value free of charges or other securities ("unencumbered value") of the Respondent's assets in England and Wales exceeds £ , the Respondent may remove any of those assets from England and Wales or may dispose of or deal with them so long as the total unencumbered value of the Respondent's assets still in England and Wales remains above £
(2) If the total unencumbered value of the Respondent's assets in England and Wales does not exceed £ , the Respondent must not remove any of those assets from England and Wales and must not dispose of or deal with any of them. If the Respondent has other assets outside England and Wales, he may dispose of or deal with those assets outside England and Wales so long as the total unencumbered value of all his assets whether in or outside England and Wales remains above £

PROVISION OF INFORMATION

9.
(1) Unless paragraph (2) applies, the Respondent must [immediately] [within hours of service of this order] and to the best of his ability inform the Applicant's solicitors of all his assets [in England and Wales] [worldwide] [exceeding £ in value] whether in his own name or not and whether solely or jointly owned, giving the value, location and details of all such assets.
(2) If the provision of any of this information is likely to incriminate the Respondent, he may be entitled to refuse to provide it, but is recommended to take legal advice before

refusing to provide the information. Wrongful refusal to provide the information is contempt of court and may render the Respondent liable to be imprisoned, fined or have his assets seized.

10. Within [ ] working days after being served with this order, the Respondent must swear and serve on the Applicant's solicitors an affidavit setting out the above information.

EXCEPTIONS TO THIS ORDER

11.

(1) This order does not prohibit the Respondent from spending £ a week towards his ordinary living expenses and also £ [*or* a reasonable sum] on legal advice and representation. [But before spending any money the Respondent must tell the Applicant's legal representatives where the money is to come from.]

[(2) This order does not prohibit the Respondent from dealing with or disposing of any of his assets in the ordinary and proper course of business.]

(3) The Respondent may agree with the Applicant's legal representatives that the above spending limits should be increased or that this order should be varied in any other respect, but any agreement must be in writing.

(4) The order will cease to have effect if the Respondent—
(a) provides security by paying the sum of £ into court, to be held to the order of the court; or
(b) makes provision for security in that sum by another method agreed with the Applicant's legal representatives.

COSTS

12. The costs of this application are reserved to the judge hearing the application on the return date.

VARIATION OR DISCHARGE OF THIS ORDER

13. Anyone served with or notified of this order may apply to the court at any time to vary or discharge this order (or so much of it as affects that person), but they must first inform the Applicant's solicitors. If any evidence is to be relied upon in support of the application, the substance of it must be communicated in writing to the Applicant's solicitors in advance.

INTERPRETATION OF THIS ORDER

14. A Respondent who is an individual who is ordered not to do something must not do it himself or in any other way. He must not do it through others acting on his behalf or on his instructions or with his encouragement.

15. A Respondent which is not an individual which is ordered not to do something must not do it itself or by its directors, officers, partners, employees or agents or in any other way.

PARTIES OTHER THAN THE APPLICANT AND RESPONDENT

16. **Effect of this order**

It is a contempt of court for any person notified of this order knowingly to assist in or permit a breach of this order. Any person doing so may be imprisoned, fined or have their assets seized.

17. **Set off by banks**

This injunction does not prevent any bank from exercising any right of set off it may have in respect of any facility which it gave to the respondent before it was notified of this order.

18. **Withdrawals by the Respondent**

No bank need enquire as to the application or proposed application of any money withdrawn by the Respondent if the withdrawal appears to be permitted by this order.

[For worldwide injunction]

19. **Persons outside England and Wales**

(1) Except as provided in paragraph (2) below, the terms of this order do not affect or concern anyone outside the jurisdiction of this court.

(2) The terms of this order will affect the following persons in a country or state outside the jurisdiction of this court—

(a) the Respondent or his officer or agent appointed by power of attorney;

(b) any person who—
  (i) is subject to the jurisdiction of this court;
  (ii) has been given written notice of this order at his residence or place of business within the jurisdiction of this court; and
  (iii) is able to prevent acts or omissions outside the jurisdiction of this court which constitute or assist in a breach of the terms of this order; and
(c) any other person, only to the extent that this order is declared enforceable by or is enforced by a court in that country or state.

[For worldwide injunction]

20. **Assets located outside England and Wales**

Nothing in this order shall, in respect of assets located outside England and Wales, prevent any third party from complying with—

(1) what it reasonably believes to be its obligations, contractual or otherwise, under the laws and obligations of the country or state in which those assets are situated or under the proper law of any contract between itself and the Respondent; and

(2) any orders of the courts of that country or state, provided that reasonable notice of any application for such an order is given to the Applicant's solicitors.

COMMUNICATIONS WITH THE COURT

All communications to the court about this order should be sent to Room E201, Royal Courts of Justice, Strand, London WC2A 2LL quoting the case number. The telephone number is 020 7947 6826.

The offices are open between 10 am and 4.30 pm Monday to Friday.

SCHEDULE A
AFFIDAVITS

The Applicant relied on the following affidavits—

[name]	[number of affidavit]	[date sworn]	[filed on behalf of]
(1)			
(2)			

SCHEDULE B
UNDERTAKINGS GIVEN TO THE COURT BY THE APPLICANT

(1) If the court later finds that this order has caused loss to the Respondent, and decides that the Respondent should be compensated for that loss, the Applicant will comply with any order the court may make.

[(2) The Applicant will—
  (a) on or before *[date]* cause a written guarantee in the sum of £ to be issued from a bank with a place of business within England or Wales, in respect of any order the court may make pursuant to paragraph (1) above; and
  (b) immediately upon issue of the guarantee, cause a copy of it to be served on the Respondent.]

(3) As soon as practicable the Applicant will issue and serve a claim form [in the form of the draft produced to the court] [claiming the appropriate relief].

(4) The Applicant will [swear and file an affidavit] [cause an affidavit to be sworn and filed] [substantially in the terms of the draft affidavit produced to the court] [confirming the substance of what was said to the court by the Applicant's counsel/solicitors].

(5) The Applicant will serve upon the Respondent [together with this order] [as soon as practicable]—
  (i) copies of the affidavits and exhibits containing the evidence relied upon by the Applicant, and any other documents provided to the court on the making of the application;
  (ii) the claim form; and
  (iii) an application notice for continuation of the order.

[(6) Anyone notified of this order will be given a copy of it by the Applicant's legal representatives.]

(7) The Applicant will pay the reasonable costs of anyone other than the Respondent which have been incurred as a result of this order including the costs of finding out whether that person holds any of the Respondent's assets and if the court later finds that this order has caused such person loss, and decides that such person should be compensated for that loss, the Applicant will comply with any order the court may make.

(8) If this order ceases to have effect (for example, if the Respondent provides security or the Applicant does not provide a bank guarantee as provided for above) the Applicant will immediately take all reasonable steps to inform in writing anyone to whom he has given notice of this order, or who he has reasonable grounds for supposing may act upon this order, that it has ceased to have effect.

[(9) The Applicant will not without the permission of the court use any information obtained as a result of this order for the purpose of any civil or criminal proceedings, either in England and Wales or in any other jurisdiction, other than this claim.]

[(10) The Applicant will not without the permission of the court seek to enforce this order in any country outside England and Wales [or seek an order of a similar nature including orders conferring a charge or other security against the Respondent or the Respondent's assets].]

NAME AND ADDRESS OF APPLICANT'S LEGAL REPRESENTATIVES

The Applicant's legal representatives are—

[Name, address, reference, fax and telephone numbers both in and out of office hours and e-mail]

---

1 Insert name of Respondent.

2 Where the premises are likely to be occupied by an unaccompanied woman and the Supervising Solicitor is a man, at least one of the persons accompanying him should be a woman.

3 None of these persons should be people who could gain personally or commercially from anything they might read or see on the premises, unless their presence is essential.

4 References to incriminating documents should be omitted from orders made in intellectual property proceedings, where the privilege against self-incrimination does not apply—see paragraph 8.4 of the practice direction.

5 If it is envisaged that the Respondent's computers are to be imaged (i.e. the hard drives are to be copied wholesale, thereby reproducing listed items and other items indiscriminately), special provision needs to be made and independent computer specialists need to be appointed, who should be required to give undertakings to the court.

6 The period should ordinarily be longer than the period in paragraph (2) of Schedule D, if any of the information is likely to be included in listed items taken away of which the Respondent does not have copies.

7 Normally, the order should be served in the morning (not before 9.30 am) and on a weekday to enable the Respondent more readily to obtain legal advice.

8 Insert name of Respondent(s).

[1575]

APPENDIX 15
SERVICE OUT OF THE JURISDICTION: RELATED PRACTICE

Service out of the jurisdiction without permission

1. Before issuing a claim form or seeking permission to serve out of the jurisdiction, it is necessary to consider whether the jurisdiction of the English courts is affected by the Civil Jurisdiction and Judgments Act 1982. Where each claim in the claim form is a claim which the Court has by virtue of the Civil Jurisdiction and Judgments Act 1982 power to hear and determine, service of the claim form out of the jurisdiction may be effected without permission provided that the requirements of rule 6.19 are satisfied and the claim form is endorsed before issue with a statement that the court has power under the Act to hear and determine the claim against the defendant, and that no proceedings involving the same claim are pending between the parties in Scotland, Northern Ireland or another convention country. Care must be taken to see that the endorsement is not made unless the statement is accurate.

Application for permission: affidavit or witness statement

2.

(a) On applications for permission under rule 6.20 the written evidence must, amongst other things:

(i) identify the paragraph or paragraphs of rule 6.20 relied on as giving the court jurisdiction to order service out, together with a summary of the facts relied on as bringing the case within each such paragraph;

(ii) state the belief of the deponent that there is a good claim and state in what place or country the defendant is or probably may be found;

(iii) summarise the considerations relied upon as showing that the case is a proper one in which to subject a party outside the jurisdiction to proceedings within it;

(iv) draw attention to any features which might reasonably be thought to weigh against the making of the order sought;

(v) state the deponent's grounds of belief and sources of information;

(vi) exhibit copies of the documents referred to and any other significant documents.

(b) Where convenient the written evidence should be included in the form of application notice, rather than in a separate witness statement. The form of application notice may be extended for this purpose.

Application for permission: copies of draft order

3. The documents submitted with the application must include two copies of a draft of the order sought which must state the time allowed for acknowledgment of service in accordance with any applicable practice direction and paragraphs 6 and 7 below.

Application for permission: copy or draft of claim form

4. A copy or draft of the claim form which the applicant intends to issue and serve must be provided for the judge to initial. If the endorsement to the claim form includes causes of action or claims not covered by the grounds on which permission to serve out of the jurisdiction can properly be granted, permission will be refused unless the draft is amended to restrict it to proper claims. Where the application is for the issue of a concurrent claim form, the documents submitted must also include a copy of the original claim form.

Arbitration matters

5. Service out of the jurisdiction in arbitration matters is governed by Part 62. As to the 1968 Convention on Jurisdiction in the context of arbitration, see Article 1(4).

Practice under rules 6.19 and 6.20

6.

(a) Although a Part 7 claim form may contain or be accompanied by particulars of claim, there is no need for it to do so and in many cases particulars of claim will be served after the claim form: **rule 58.5**.

(b) A defendant should acknowledge service in every case: **rule 58.6(1)**.

(c) The period for filing acknowledgment of service will be calculated from the service of the claim form, whether or not particulars of claim are to follow: **rule 58.6**.

(d) The period for serving, and filing, particulars of claim (where they were not contained in the claim form and did not accompany the claim form) will be calculated from acknowledgment of service: **rule 58.5(1)(c)**.

(e) The period for serving and filing the defence will be calculated from service of the particulars of claim: **rule 58.10(2)**.

7. Time for serving and filing a defence is calculated as follows:

(i) where particulars of claim were included in or accompanied the claim form the period for serving and filing a defence is 21 or 31 days as prescribed by rule 6.23, or the number of days shown in the table in practice direction 6BPD, in either case plus an additional 14 days;

(ii) where particulars of claim were not included in and did not accompany the claim form, the period for serving and filing a defence is 28 days from the service of the particulars of claim.

[1576]

ACT OF SEDERUNT (SUMMARY CAUSE RULES) 2002

(SSI 2002/132)

NOTES

Made: 1 March 2002.
Authority: Sheriff Courts (Scotland) Act 1971, s 32.

Commencement: 10 June 2002.

1 Citation and commencement

(1) This Act of Sederunt may be cited as the Act of Sederunt (Summary Cause Rules) 2002 and shall come into force on 10th June 2002.

(2) This Act of Sederunt shall be inserted in the Books of Sederunt.

[1577]

NOTES

Commencement: 10 June 2002.

2 Summary Cause Rules

The provisions of Schedule 1 to this Act of Sederunt shall have effect for the purpose of providing rules for a summary cause other than a small claim.

[1578]

NOTES

Commencement: 10 June 2002.

3 Transitional provision

Nothing in Schedule 1 to this Act of Sederunt shall apply to a summary cause commenced before 10th June 2002 and any such action shall proceed according to the law and practice in force immediately before that date.

[1579]

NOTES

Commencement: 10 June 2002.

4 Revocation

The Acts of Sederunt mentioned in column (1) of Schedule 2 to this Act of Sederunt are revoked to the extent specified in column (3) of that Schedule except—

(a) in relation to any summary cause commenced before 10th June 2002; and

(b) for the purposes of the Act of Sederunt (Small Claim Rules) 1988.

[1580]

NOTES

Commencement: 10 June 2002.

SCHEDULE 1
SUMMARY CAUSE RULES 2002

Paragraph 2

NOTES

Only the rules relevant to this work are reproduced here. The relevant forms, in Appendix 1 of these Rules, are not reproduced, but can be found at http://www.scotcourts.gov.uk/sheriff/summary_cause/forms.asp.

CHAPTER 1
CITATION, INTERPRETATION AND APPLICATION

1.1 Citation, interpretation and application

(1) These Rules may be cited as the Summary Cause Rules 2002.

(2) In these Rules—

"the 1907 Act" means the Sheriff Courts (Scotland) Act 1907;

"the 1971 Act" means the Sheriff Courts (Scotland) Act 1971;

"the 1975 Act" means the Litigants in Person (Costs and Expenses) Act 1975;
"authorised lay representative" means a person to whom section 32(1) of the Solicitors (Scotland) Act 1980 (offence to prepare writs) does not apply by virtue of section 32(2)(a) of that Act;
"small claim" has the meaning assigned to it by section 35(2) of the 1971 Act;
"summary cause" has the meaning assigned to it by section 35(1) of the 1971 Act.

(3) Any reference to a specified Chapter or rule shall be construed as a reference to the Chapter or rule bearing that number in these Rules, and a reference to a specified paragraph, sub-paragraph or head shall be construed as a reference to the paragraph, sub-paragraph or head so numbered or lettered in the provision in which that reference occurs.

(4) A form referred to by number means the form so numbered in Appendix 1 to these Rules or a form substantially of the same effect with such variation as circumstances may require.

(5) The glossary in Appendix 2 to these Rules is a guide to the meaning of certain legal expressions used in these Rules, but is not to be taken as giving those expressions any meaning which they do not have in law generally.

(6) These Rules shall apply to a summary cause other than a small claim.

[1581]

NOTES
Commencement: 10 June 2002.

CHAPTER 4
COMMENCEMENT OF ACTION

4.1 Form of summons

(1) A summary cause action shall be commenced by summons, which shall be in Form 1.

(2) The form of claim in a summons may be in one of Forms 2, 3, 4, 5, 6, 7, 8 or 9.

[1582]

NOTES
Commencement: 10 June 2002.

4.2 Statement of claim

The pursuer must insert a statement of his claim in the summons to give the defender fair notice of the claim; and the statement must include—

(a) details of the basis of the claim including relevant dates; and
(b) if the claim arises from the supply of goods or services, a description of the goods or services and the date or dates on or between which they were supplied and, where relevant, ordered.

[1583]

NOTES
Commencement: 10 June 2002.

4.3 Defender's copy summons

A copy summons shall be served on the defender—

(a) where the action is for, or includes a claim for, payment of money—
  (i) in Form 1a where an application for a time to pay direction under the Debtors (Scotland) Act 1987 or time order under the Consumer Credit Act 1974 may be applied for; or
  (ii) in Form 1b in every other case;
(b) where the action is not for, and does not include a claim for, payment of money, in Form 1c; or
(c) in an action of multiplepoinding, in Form 1d.

[1584]

NOTES

Commencement: 10 June 2002.

4.4 Authentication and effect of summons

(1) A summons shall be authenticated by the sheriff clerk in some appropriate manner except where—

(a) he refuses to do so for any reason;

(b) the defender's address is unknown; or

(c) a party seeks to alter the normal period of notice specified in rule 4.5(2)[; or

(d) a warrant for arrestment on the dependence, or to found jurisdiction, is sought].

(2) If any of paragraphs (1)(a) [to (d)] applies, the summons shall be authenticated by the sheriff, if he thinks it appropriate.

(3) The authenticated summons shall be warrant for—

(a) service on the defender; and

(b) where the appropriate warrant has been sought in the summons—

(i) arrestment on the dependence; or

(ii) arrestment to found jurisdiction,

as the case may be.

[(4) Where a warrant for arrestment on the dependence, or to found jurisdiction, is sought, averments to justify that warrant must be included in the statement of claim.]

[1585]

NOTES

Commencement: 10 June 2002.

Para (1): sub-para (d) and word "; or" immediately preceding it, and para (4), inserted and words in square brackets in para (2) substituted by the Act of Sederunt (Ordinary Cause, Summary Application, Summary Cause and Small Claim Rules) Amendment (Miscellaneous) 2004, SSI 2004/197, r 4(1), (2).

4.5 Period of notice

(1) An action shall proceed after the appropriate period of notice of the summons has been given to the defender prior to the return day.

(2) The appropriate period of notice shall be—

(a) 21 days where the defender is resident or has a place of business within Europe; or

(b) 42 days where the defender is resident or has a place of business outwith Europe.

(3) The sheriff may, on cause shown, shorten or extend the period of notice on such conditions as to the form of service as he may direct, but in any case where the period of notice is reduced at least two days' notice must be given.

(4) If a period of notice expires on a Saturday, Sunday, public or court holiday, the period of notice shall be deemed to expire on the next day on which the sheriff clerk's office is open for civil court business.

(5) Notwithstanding the terms of section 4(2) of the Citation Amendment (Scotland) Act 1882, where service is by post the period of notice shall run from the beginning of the day next following the date of posting.

(6) The sheriff clerk shall insert in the summons—

(a) the return day, which is the last day on which the defender may return a form of response to the sheriff clerk; and

(b) the calling date, which is the date set for the action to call in court.

(7) The calling date shall be seven days after the return day.

[1586]

NOTES

Commencement: 10 June 2002.

4.6 Intimation

Any provision in these Rules requiring papers to be sent to or any intimation to be made to any party, applicant or claimant shall be construed as if the reference to the party, applicant or claimant included a reference to the solicitor representing that party, applicant or claimant.

[1587]

NOTES

Commencement: 10 June 2002.

CHAPTER 5
REGISTER OF SUMMARY CAUSES, SERVICE AND RETURN OF THE SUMMONS

5.1 Register of Summary Causes

(1) The sheriff clerk shall keep a register of summary cause actions and incidental applications made in such actions, which shall be known as the Register of Summary Causes.

(2) There shall be entered in the Register of Summary Causes a note of all actions, together with a note of all minutes under rule 24.1(1) (recall of decree) and the entry for each action or minute must contain the following particulars where appropriate:—

- (a) the names, designations and addresses of the parties;
- (b) whether the parties were present or absent at any hearing, including an inspection, and the names of their representatives;
- (c) the nature of the action;
- (d) the amount of any claim;
- (e) the date of issue of the summons;
- (f) the method of service;
- (g) the return day;
- (h) the calling date;
- (i) whether a form of response was lodged and details of it;
- (j) the period of notice if shortened or extended in accordance with rule 4.5(3);
- (k) details of any minute by the pursuer regarding an application for a time to pay direction or time order, or minute by the pursuer requesting decree or other order;
- (l) details of any interlocutors issued;
- (m) details of the final decree and the date of it; and
- (n) details of any variation or recall of a decree.

(3) There shall be entered in the Register of Summary Causes in the entry for the action to which they relate details of incidental applications including, where appropriate—

- (a) whether parties are present or absent at the hearing of the application, and the names of their representatives;
- (b) the nature of the application; and
- (c) the interlocutor issued or order made.

(4) The Register of Summary Causes must be—

- (a) authenticated in some appropriate manner by the sheriff in respect of each day any order is made or application determined in an action; and
- (b) open for inspection during normal business hours to all concerned without fee.

(5) The Register of Summary Causes may be kept in electronic or documentary form.

[1588]

NOTES

Commencement: 10 June 2002.

5.2 Persons carrying on business under trading or descriptive name

(1) A person carrying on a business under a trading or descriptive name may sue or be sued in such trading or descriptive name alone.

(2) An extract of—

- (a) a decree pronounced in an action; or
- (b) a decree proceeding upon any deed, decree arbitral, bond, protest of a bill, promissory note or banker's note or upon any other obligation or document on which execution may proceed, recorded in the sheriff court books,

against such person under such trading or descriptive name shall be a valid warrant for diligence against such person.

(3) A summons, decree, charge or other document following upon such summons or decree in an action in which a person carrying on business under a trading or descriptive name sues or is sued in that name may be served—

(a) at any place of business or office at which such business is carried on within the sheriffdom of the sheriff court in which the action is brought; or

(b) if there is no place of business within that sheriffdom, at any place where such business is carried on (including the place of business or office of the clerk or secretary of any company, corporation or association or firm).

[1589]

NOTES

Commencement: 10 June 2002.

5.3 Form of service and certificate thereof

(1) Subject to rule 5.5 (service where address of defender is unknown), a form of service in Form 11 must be enclosed with the defender's copy summons.

(2) After service has been effected a certificate of execution of service in Form 12 must be prepared and signed by the person effecting service.

(3) When service is by a sheriff officer, the certificate of execution of service must—

(a) be signed by him; and

(b) specify whether the service was personal or, if otherwise, the mode of service and the name of any person to whom the defender's copy summons was delivered.

(4) If service is effected in accordance with rule 5.4(2), the certificate must also contain a statement of—

(a) the mode of service previously attempted; and

(b) the circumstances which prevented such service from being effected.

[1590]

NOTES

Commencement: 10 June 2002.

5.4 Service within Scotland by sheriff officer

(1) A sheriff officer may validly serve any summons, decree, charge or other document following upon such summons or decree issued in an action by—

(a) personal service; or

(b) leaving it in the hands of—

(i) an inmate at the person's dwelling place; or

(ii) an employee at the person's place of business.

(2) If a sheriff officer has been unsuccessful in effecting service in accordance with paragraph (1), he may, after making diligent inquiries, serve the document—

(a) by depositing it in the person's dwelling place or place of business by means of a letter box or by other lawful means; or

(b) by affixing it to the door of the person's dwelling place or place of business.

(3) Subject to the requirements of rule 6.1 (service of schedule of arrestment), if service is effected in accordance with paragraph (2), the sheriff officer must thereafter send by ordinary post to the address at which he thinks it most likely that the person may be found a letter containing a copy of the document.

(4) In proceedings in or following on an action, it shall be necessary for any sheriff officer to be accompanied by a witness except where service, citation or intimation is to be made by post.

(5) Where the firm which employs the sheriff officer has in its possession—

(a) the document or a copy of it certified as correct by the pursuer's solicitor, the sheriff officer may serve the document upon the defender without having the document or certified copy in his possession (in which case he shall if required to do so by the person on whom service is executed and within a reasonable time of being so required, show the document or certified copy to the person); or

(b) a certified copy of the interlocutor pronounced allowing service of the document, the sheriff officer may serve the document without having in his possession the certified copy interlocutor if he has in his possession a facsimile copy of the certified copy interlocutor (which he shall show, if required, to the person on whom service is executed).

[1591]

NOTES

Commencement: 10 June 2002.

5.5 Service on persons whose address is unknown

(1) If the defender's address is unknown to the pursuer and cannot reasonably be ascertained by him, the sheriff may grant warrant to serve the summons—

(a) by the publication of an advertisement in Form 13 in a newspaper circulating in the area of the defender's last known address; or

(b) by displaying on the walls of court a notice in Form 14.

(2) Where a summons is served in accordance with paragraph (1), the period of notice, which must be fixed by the sheriff, shall run from the date of publication of the advertisement or display on the walls of court, as the case may be.

(3) If service is to be effected under paragraph (1), the pursuer must lodge a service copy of the summons with the sheriff clerk.

(4) The defender may uplift from the sheriff clerk the service copy of the summons lodged in accordance with paragraph (3).

(5) If display on the walls of court is required under paragraph (1)(b), the pursuer must supply to the sheriff clerk for that purpose a completed copy of Form 14.

(6) In every case where advertisement in a newspaper is required for the purpose of service, a copy of the newspaper containing said advertisement must be lodged with the sheriff clerk.

(7) If service has been made under this rule and thereafter the defender's address becomes known, the sheriff may allow the summons to be amended and, if appropriate, grant warrant for re-service subject to such conditions as he thinks fit.

[1592]

NOTES

Commencement: 10 June 2002.

5.6 Service by post

(1) If it is competent to serve or intimate any document or to cite any person by recorded delivery, such service, intimation or citation, must be made by the first class recorded delivery service.

(2) On the face of the envelope used for postal service under this rule, there must be written or printed a notice in Form 15.

(3) The certificate of execution of postal service must have annexed to it any relevant postal receipt.

[1593]

NOTES

Commencement: 10 June 2002.

5.7 Service on persons outwith Scotland

(1) If any summons, decree, charge or other document following upon such summons or decree, or any charge or warrant, requires to be served outwith Scotland on any person, it must be served in accordance with this rule.

(2) If the person has a known home or place of business in—

(a) England and Wales, Northern Ireland, the Isle of Man or the Channel Islands; or

(b) any country with which the United Kingdom does not have a convention providing for service of writs in that country,

the document must be served either—

(i) by posting in Scotland a copy of the document in question in a registered letter addressed to the person at his residence or place of business; or

(ii) in accordance with the rules for personal service under the domestic law of the place in which the document is to be served.

(3) Subject to paragraph (4), if the document requires to be served in a country which is a party to the Hague Convention on the Service Abroad of Judicial and Extra-Judicial Documents in Civil or Commercial Matters dated 15th November 1965 or the European Convention on Jurisdiction and Enforcement of Judgments in Civil and Commercial Matters as set out in Schedule 1 or 3C to the Civil Jurisdiction and Judgments Act 1982, it must be served—

(a) by a method prescribed by the internal law of the country where service is to be effected for the service of documents in domestic actions upon persons who are within its territory;

(b) by or through a British consular authority at the request of the Secretary of State for Foreign and Commonwealth Affairs;

(c) by or through a central authority in the country where service is to be effected at the request of the Secretary of State for Foreign and Commonwealth Affairs;

(d) where the law of the country in which the person resides permits, by posting in Scotland a copy of the document in a registered letter addressed to the person at his residence; or

(e) where the law of the country in which service is to be effected permits, service by an *huissier*, other judicial officer or competent official of the country where service is to be made.

[(4) If the document requires to be served in a country to which the Council Regulation applies, service—

(a) may be effected by the methods prescribed in paragraph (3)(b) or (c) only in exceptional circumstances; and

(b) is effected only if the receiving agency has informed the person that acceptance of service may be refused on the ground that the document has not been translated in accordance with paragraph (12).]

(5) If the document requires to be served in a country with which the United Kingdom has a convention on the service of writs in that country other than the conventions specified in paragraph (3) or the regulation specified in paragraph (4), it must be served by one of the methods approved in the relevant convention.

(6) Subject to paragraph (9), a document which requires to be posted in Scotland for the purposes of this rule must be posted by a solicitor or a sheriff officer, and the form of service and certificate of execution of service must be in Forms 11 and 12 respectively.

(7) On the face of the envelope used for postal service under this rule there must be written or printed a notice in Form 15.

(8) Where service is effected by a method specified in paragraph (3)(b) or (c), the pursuer must—

(a) send a copy of the summons and warrant for service with form of service attached, or other document, with a request for service to be effected by the method indicated in the request to the Secretary of State for Foreign and Commonwealth Affairs; and

(b) lodge in process a certificate of execution of service signed by the authority which has effected service.

(9) If service is effected by the method specified in paragraph (3)(e), the pursuer must—

(a) send to the official in the country in which service is to be effected a copy of the summons and warrant for service, with citation attached, or other document, with a request for service to be effected by delivery to the defender or his residence; and

(b) lodge in process a certificate of execution of service by the official who has effected service.

(10) Where service is executed in accordance with paragraph (2)(b)(ii) or (3)(a) other than on another party in—

(a) the United Kingdom;

(b) the Isle of Man; or

(c) the Channel Islands,

the party executing service must lodge a certificate stating that the form of service employed is in accordance with the law of the place where the service was executed.

(11) A certificate lodged in accordance with paragraph (10) shall be given by a person who is conversant with the law of the country concerned and who—

(a) practises or has practised law in that country; or
(b) is a duly accredited representative of the government of that country.

(12) Every summons or document and every citation and notice on the face of the envelope referred to in paragraph (7) must be accompanied by a translation in—

[(a) an official language of the country in which service is to be executed; or
(b) in a country to which the Council Regulation applies, a language of the member state of transmission that is understood by the person on whom service is being executed].

(13) A translation referred to in paragraph (12) must be certified as a correct translation by the person making it and the certificate must contain the full name, address and qualifications of the translator and be lodged along with the execution of such service.

[(14) In this rule "the Council Regulation" means Council Regulation (EC) No 1348/2000 on the service in the Member States of judicial and extrajudicial documents in civil or commercial matters.]

[1594]

NOTES

Commencement: 10 June 2002.

Para (4): substituted by the Act of Sederunt (Ordinary Cause, Summary Application, Summary Cause and Small Claim Rules) Amendment (Miscellaneous) 2004, SSI 2004/197, r 4(1), (3)(a).

Para (12): sub-paras (a), (b) substituted by SSI 2004/197, r 4(1), (3)(b).

Para (14): added by SSI 2004/197, r 4(1), (3)(c).

5.8 Endorsation by sheriff clerk of defender's residence not necessary

Any summons, decree, charge or other document following upon a summons or decree may be served, enforced or otherwise lawfully executed in Scotland without endorsation by a sheriff clerk and, if executed by a sheriff officer, may be so executed by a sheriff officer of the court which granted the summons, or by a sheriff officer of the sheriff court district in which it is to be executed.

[1595]

NOTES

Commencement: 10 June 2002.

5.9 Contents of envelope containing defender's copy summons

Nothing must be included in the envelope containing a defender's copy summons except—

(a) the copy summons;
(b) a response or other notice in accordance with these Rules; and
(c) any other document approved by the sheriff principal.

[1596]

NOTES

Commencement: 10 June 2002.

5.10 Re-service

(1) If it appears to the sheriff that there has been any failure or irregularity in service upon a defender, the sheriff may order the pursuer to re-serve the summons on such conditions as he thinks fit.

(2) If re-service has been ordered in accordance with paragraph (1) or rule 5.5(7) the action shall proceed thereafter as if it were a new action.

[1597]

NOTES

Commencement: 10 June 2002.

5.11 Defender appearing barred from objecting to service

(1) A person who appears in an action shall not be entitled to state any objection to the regularity of the execution of service or intimation on him and his appearance shall remedy any defect in such service or intimation.

(2) Nothing in paragraph (1) shall preclude a party pleading that the court has no jurisdiction.

[1598]

NOTES

Commencement: 10 June 2002.

5.12 Return of summons

(1) If any appearance in court is required on the calling date in respect of any party—

(a) the summons; and

(b) the relevant certificate of execution of service,

shall be returned to the sheriff clerk not later than two days before the calling date.

(2) If no appearance by any party is required on the calling date, only the certificate of execution of service need be returned to the sheriff clerk, not later than two days before the calling date.

(3) If the pursuer fails to proceed in accordance with paragraph (1) or (2) as appropriate, the sheriff may dismiss the action.

[1599]

NOTES

Commencement: 10 June 2002.

CHAPTER 6
ARRESTMENT

6.1 Service of schedule of arrestment

If a schedule of arrestment has not been personally served on an arrestee, the arrestment shall have effect only if a copy of the schedule is also sent by registered post or the first class recorded delivery service to—

(a) the last known place of residence of the arrestee; or

(b) if such place of residence is not known, or if the arrestee is a firm or corporation, to the arrestee's principal place of business if known, or, if not known, to any known place of business of the arrestee,

and the sheriff officer must, on the certificate of execution, certify that this has been done and specify the address to which the copy of the schedule was sent.

[1600]

NOTES

Commencement: 10 June 2002.

6.2 Arrestment before service

(1) An arrestment to found jurisdiction or an arrestment on the dependence of an action used prior to service shall cease to have effect, unless the summons is served within 21 days from the date of execution of the arrestment.

(2) When such an arrestment as is referred to in paragraph (1) has been executed, the party using it must forthwith report the execution to the sheriff clerk.

[1601]

NOTES

Commencement: 10 June 2002.

6.3 Recall and restriction of arrestment

(1) The sheriff may order that an arrestment on the dependence of an action or counterclaim shall cease to have effect if the party whose funds or property are arrested—

(a) pays into court; or

(b) finds caution to the satisfaction of the sheriff clerk in respect of,

the sum claimed together with the sum of £50 in respect of expenses.

(2) Without prejudice to paragraph (1), a party whose funds or property are arrested may at any time apply to the sheriff to exercise his powers to recall or restrict an arrestment on the dependence of an action or counterclaim, with or without consignation or caution.

(3) An application made under paragraph (2) must be intimated by the applicant to the party who instructed the arrestment.

(4) On payment into court in accordance with paragraph (1), or if the sheriff recalls or restricts an arrestment on the dependence of an action in accordance with paragraph (2) and any condition imposed by the sheriff has been complied with, the sheriff clerk must—

(a) issue to the party whose funds or property are arrested a certificate in Form 16 authorising the release of any sum or property arrested to the extent ordered by the sheriff; and

(b) send a copy of the certificate to—

(i) the party who instructed the arrestment; and

(ii) the party who has possession of the funds or property that are arrested.

[1602]

NOTES

Commencement: 10 June 2002.

CHAPTER 7
UNDEFENDED ACTION

7.1 Undefended action

(1) Subject to paragraphs (4), (5) and (6), where the defender has not lodged a form of response on or before the return day—

(a) the action shall not require to call in court on the calling date; and

(b) the pursuer must lodge a minute in Form 17 before the sheriff clerk's office closes for business on the second day before the calling date.

(2) If the pursuer does not lodge a minute in terms of paragraph (1), the sheriff must dismiss the action.

(3) If the sheriff is not prepared to grant the order requested in Form 17, the sheriff clerk must—

(a) fix a date, time and place for the pursuer to be heard; and

(b) inform the pursuer of—

(i) that date, time and place; and

(ii) the reasons for the sheriff wishing to hear him.

(4) Where no form of response has been lodged in an action—

(a) for recovery of possession of heritable property; or

(b) of sequestration for rent,

the action shall call in court on the calling date and the sheriff shall determine the action as he thinks fit.

(5) Where no form of response has been lodged in an action of multiplepoinding the action shall proceed in accordance with rule 27.9(1)(a).

(6) Where no form of response has been lodged in an action of count, reckoning and payment the action shall proceed in accordance with rule 29.2.

(7) If the defender does not lodge a form of response in time or if the sheriff is satisfied that he does not intend to defend the action on the merits or on the amount of the sum due, the sheriff may grant decree with expenses against him.

[1603]

NOTES

Commencement: 10 June 2002.

7.2 Application for time to pay direction or time order

(1) If the defender admits the claim, he may, where competent—

(a) make an application for a time to pay direction (including, where appropriate, an application for recall or restriction of an arrestment) or a time order by completing the appropriate part of the form of response contained in the defender's copy summons and lodging it with the sheriff clerk on or before the return day; or

(b) lodge a form of response indicating that he admits the claim and intends to apply orally for a time to pay direction (including, where appropriate, an application for recall or restriction of an arrestment) or time order.

(2) Where the defender has lodged an application in terms of paragraph (1)(a), the pursuer may intimate that he does not object to the application by lodging a minute in Form 18 before the time the sheriff clerk's office closes for business on the day occurring two days before the calling date stating that he does not object to the defender's application and seeking decree.

(3) If the pursuer intimates in accordance with paragraph (2) that he does not object to the application—

(a) the sheriff may grant decree on the calling date;
(b) the parties need not attend; and
(c) the action will not call in court.

(4) If the pursuer wishes to oppose the application for a time to pay direction or time order made in accordance with paragraph (1)(a), he must lodge a minute in Form 19 before the time the sheriff clerk's office closes for business on the day occurring two days before the calling date.

(5) Where the pursuer objects to an application in terms of paragraph (1)(a) or the defender has lodged a form of response in accordance with paragraph (1)(b), the action shall call on the calling date when the parties may appear and the sheriff must decide the application and grant decree accordingly.

(6) The sheriff shall decide an application in accordance with paragraph (5) whether or not any of the parties appear.

(7) Where the defender has lodged an application in terms of paragraph (1)(a) and the pursuer fails to proceed in accordance with either of paragraphs (2) or (4) the sheriff may dismiss the claim.

[1604]

NOTES

Commencement: 10 June 2002.

7.3 Decree in actions to which the Hague Convention or Civil Jurisdiction and Judgments Act 1982 apply

(1) If the summons has been served in a country to which the Hague Convention on the Service Abroad of Judicial and Extra-Judicial Documents in Civil or Commercial Matters dated 15th November 1965 applies, decree must not be granted until it is established to the satisfaction of the sheriff that the requirements of Article 15 of that Convention have been complied with.

(2) Where a defender is domiciled in another part of the United Kingdom or in another Contracting State, the sheriff shall not grant decree until it has been shown that the defender has been able to receive the summons in sufficient time to arrange his defence or that all necessary steps have been taken to that end.

(3) For the purposes of paragraph (2)—

(a) the question whether a person is domiciled in another part of the United Kingdom shall be determined in accordance with sections 41 and 42 of the Civil Jurisdiction and Judgments Act 1982;

(b) the question whether a person is domiciled in another Contracting State shall be determined in accordance with Article 52 of the Convention in Schedule 1 or 3C to that Act; and

(c) the term "Contracting State" has the meaning assigned in section 1 of that Act. **[1605]**

NOTES

Commencement: 10 June 2002.

CHAPTER 18
RECOVERY OF EVIDENCE AND ATTENDANCE OF WITNESSES

18.1 Diligence for recovery of documents

(1) At any time after a summons has been served, a party may make an incidental application in writing to the sheriff to grant commission and diligence to recover documents.

(2) A party who makes an application in accordance with paragraph (1) must list in the application the documents which he wishes to recover.

(3) A copy of the incidental application made under paragraph (1) must be intimated by the applicant to—

(a) every other party; and

(b) where necessary, the Advocate General for Scotland or the Lord Advocate (and if there is any doubt, both).

(4) The Advocate General for Scotland and the Lord Advocate may appear at the hearing of any incidental application under paragraph (1).

(5) The sheriff may grant commission and diligence to recover those documents in the list mentioned in paragraph (2) which he considers relevant to the action. **[1606]**

NOTES

Commencement: 10 June 2002.

18.2 Optional procedure before executing commission and diligence

(1) Any party who has obtained a commission and diligence for the recovery of documents may, at any time before executing it, serve by first class recorded delivery post on the person from whom the documents are sought to be recovered (or on his known solicitor or solicitors) an order with certificate attached in Form 24.

(2) Documents recovered in response to an order under paragraph (1) must be sent to, and retained by, the sheriff clerk who shall, on receiving them, advise the parties that the documents are in his possession and may be examined within his office during normal business hours.

(3) If the party who served the order is not satisfied that full production has been made under the specification, or that adequate reasons for non-production have been given, he may execute the commission and diligence in normal form, notwithstanding his adoption in the first instance of the foregoing procedure by order.

(4) At the commission, the commissioner shall—

(a) administer the appropriate oath or affirmation to any clerk and any shorthand writer appointed for the commission; and

(b) administer to the haver the oath in Form 20, or where the haver elects to affirm, the affirmation in Form 21.

(5) Documents recovered under this rule may be tendered as evidence at any hearing or proof without further formality, and rules 18.4(2), (3) and (4) shall apply to such documents. **[1607]**

18.3 Applications for orders under section 1 of the Administration of Justice (Scotland) Act 1972

(1) An application by a party for an order under section 1 of the Administration of Justice (Scotland) Act 1972, must be made by incidental application in writing.

(2) At the time of lodging an incidental application under paragraph (1), a specification of—

(a) the document or other property sought to be inspected, photographed, preserved, taken into custody, detained, produced, recovered, sampled or experimented with or upon, as the case may be; or
(b) the matter in respect of which information is sought as to the identity of a person who might be a witness or a defender,

must be lodged in process.

(3) A copy of the specification lodged under paragraph (2) and the incidental application made under paragraph (1) must be intimated by the applicant to—
(a) every other party;
(b) any third party haver; and
(c) where necessary, the Advocate General for Scotland or the Lord Advocate (and if there is any doubt, both).

(4) If the sheriff grants an incidental application under paragraph (1) in whole or in part, he may order the applicant to find such caution or give such other security as he thinks fit.

(5) The Advocate General for Scotland and the Lord Advocate may appear at the hearing of any incidental application under paragraph (1).

[1608]

NOTES

Commencement: 10 June 2002.

18.4 Confidentiality

(1) Confidentiality may be claimed for any evidence sought to be recovered under rule 18.2 or 18.3.

(2) Where confidentiality is claimed under paragraph (1), the documents or property in respect of which confidentiality is claimed shall be enclosed in a separate, sealed packet.

(3) A sealed packet referred to in paragraph (2) shall not be opened except by authority of the sheriff obtained on the incidental application of the party who sought the commission and diligence or order.

(4) The incidental application made under paragraph (3) must be intimated by the applicant to the party or parties from whose possession the documents specified in the commission and diligence or order were obtained.

(5) Any party received intimation under paragraph (4) may appear at the hearing of the application.

[1609]

NOTES

Commencement: 10 June 2002.

18.5 Preservation and obtaining of evidence

(1) Evidence in danger of being lost may be taken to be retained until required and, if satisfied that it is desirable so to do, the sheriff may, upon the application of any party at any time, either take it himself or grant authority to a commissioner to take it.

(2) The interlocutor granting such a commission shall be sufficient authority for citing the witness to appear before the commission.

(3) The evidence of any witness who—
(a) is resident beyond the sheriffdom;
(b) although resident within the sheriffdom, resides at some place remote from the court in which the proof is to be held; or
(c) is by reason of illness, age, infirmity or other sufficient cause unable to attend the proof,

may be taken in the same manner as is provided in paragraph (1).

(4) On special cause shown, evidence may be taken from any witness or haver on a ground other than one mentioned in paragraph (1) or (3).

(5) Evidence taken under paragraph (1), (3) or (4) may be taken down by—
(a) the sheriff;

(b) the commissioner; or
(c) a clerk or shorthand writer nominated by the sheriff or commissioner,

and such evidence may be recorded in narrative form or by question and answer as the sheriff or commissioner shall direct and the extended notes of such evidence certified by such clerk or shorthand writer shall be the notes of such oral evidence.

(6) At the commission, the commissioner shall or where the sheriff takes evidence himself, the sheriff shall—

(a) administer the appropriate oath or affirmation to any clerk and any shorthand writer appointed for the commission; and
(b) administer to the witness the oath in Form 20, or where the witness elects to affirm, the affirmation in Form 21.

[1610]

NOTES

Commencement: 10 June 2002.

18.6 Warrants for production of original documents from public records

(1) If a party seeks to obtain from the keeper of any public record production of the original of any register or deed in his custody for the purposes of an action, he must apply to the sheriff by incidental application.

(2) Intimation of an incidental application under paragraph (1) must be given to the keeper of the public record concerned at least seven days before the incidental application is lodged.

(3) In relation to a public record kept by the Keeper of the Registers of Scotland or the Keeper of the Records of Scotland—

(a) where it appears to the sheriff that it is necessary for the ends of justice that an incidental application under this rule should be granted, he must pronounce an interlocutor containing a certificate to that effect; and
(b) the party applying for production may apply by letter (enclosing a copy of the interlocutor duly certified by the sheriff clerk), addressed to the Deputy Principal Clerk of Session, for an order from the Court of Session authorising the Keeper of the Registers or the Keeper of the Records, as the case may be, to exhibit the original of any register or deed to the sheriff.

(4) The Deputy Principal Clerk of Session must submit the application sent to him under paragraph (3) to the Lord Ordinary in chambers who, if satisfied, shall grant a warrant for production or exhibition of the original register or deed sought.

(5) A certified copy of the warrant granted under paragraph (4) must be served on the keeper of the public record concerned.

(6) The expense of the production or exhibition of such an original register or deed must be met, in the first instance, by the party who applied by incidental application under paragraph (1).

[1611]

NOTES

Commencement: 10 June 2002.

18.7 Letter of request

(1) [Subject to paragraph (7), this] rule applies to an application for a letter of request to a court or tribunal outside Scotland to obtain evidence of the kind specified in paragraph (2), being evidence obtainable within the jurisdiction of that court or tribunal, for the purpose of an action depending before the sheriff.

(2) An application to which paragraph (1) applies may be made in relation to a request—

(a) for the examination of a witness;
(b) for the inspection, photographing, preservation, custody, detention, production or recovery of, or the taking of samples of, or the carrying out of any experiment on or with, a document or other property, as the case may be;
(c) for the medical examination of any person;
(d) for the taking and testing of samples of blood from any person; or

(e) for any other order for obtaining evidence,

for which an order could be obtained from the sheriff.

(3) Such an application must be made by minute in Form 25 together with a proposed letter of request in Form 25a.

(4) It shall be a condition of granting a letter of request that any solicitor for the applicant, or a party litigant, as the case may be, is to be personally liable, in the first instance, for the whole expenses which may become due and payable in respect of the letter of request to the court or tribunal obtaining the evidence and to any witness who may be examined for the purpose; and he must consign into court such sum in respect of such expenses as the sheriff thinks fit.

(5) Unless the court or tribunal to which a letter of request is addressed is a court or tribunal in a country or territory—

(a) where English is an official language; or

(b) in relation to which the sheriff clerk certifies that no translation is required,

then the applicant must, before the issue of the letter of request, lodge in process a translation of that letter and any interrogatories and cross-interrogatories into the official language of that court or tribunal.

(6) The letter of request when issued, any interrogatories and cross-interrogatories and the translations (if any) must be forwarded by the sheriff clerk to the Foreign and Commonwealth Office or to such person and in such manner as the sheriff may direct.

[(7) This rule does not apply to any request for the taking of evidence under Council Regulation (EC) No 1206/2001 of 28th May 2001 on cooperation between the courts of the Member States in the taking of evidence in civil or commercial matters.]

[1612]

NOTES

Commencement: 10 June 2002.

Para (1): words in square brackets substituted by the Act of Sederunt (Taking of Evidence in the European Community) 2003, SSI 2003/601, art 5(1), (2)(a).

Para (7): added by SSI 2003/601, art 5(1), (2)(b)

[18.7A Taking of evidence in the European Community

(1) This rule applies to any request—

(a) for the competent court of another Member State to take evidence under Article 1.1(a) of the Council Regulation; or

(b) that the court shall take evidence directly in another Member State under Article 1.1(b) of the Council Regulation.

(2) An application for a request under paragraph (1) shall be made by minute in Form 25B, together with the proposed request in form A or I (as the case may be) in the Annex to the Council Regulation.

(3) In this rule, "the Council Regulation" means Council Regulation (EC) No 1206/2001 of 28th May 2001 on cooperation between the courts of the Member States in the taking of evidence in civil or commercial matters.]

[1613]

NOTES

Commencement: 1 January 2004.

Inserted by the Act of Sederunt (Taking of Evidence in the European Community) 2003, SSI 2003/601, art 5(1), (3).

18.8 Citation of witnesses

(1) The citation of a witness or haver must be in Form 26 and the certificate of it must be in Form 26a.

(2) A party shall be responsible for securing the attendance of his witnesses or havers at a hearing and shall be personally liable for their expenses.

(3) The summons or the copy served on the defender shall be sufficient warrant for the citation of witnesses and havers.

(4) The period of notice given to witnesses or havers cited in terms of paragraph (3) must be not less than seven days.

(5) A witness or haver shall be cited—
- (a) by registered post or the first class recorded delivery service by the solicitor for the party on whose behalf he is cited; or
- (b) by a sheriff officer—
  - (i) personally;
  - (ii) by a citation being left with a resident at the person's dwelling place or an employee at his place of business;
  - (iii) by depositing it in that person's dwelling place or place of business;
  - (iv) by affixing it to the door of that person's dwelling place or place of business; or
  - (v) by registered post or the first class recorded delivery service.

(6) Where service is effected under paragraph (5) (b) (iii) or (iv), the sheriff officer shall, as soon as possible after such service, send by ordinary post to the address at which he thinks it most likely that the person may be found, a letter containing a copy of the citation.

[1614]

NOTES

Commencement: 10 June 2002.

18.9 Citation of witnesses by party litigants

(1) Where a party to an action is a party litigant he shall—
- (a) not later than 28 days before the diet of proof apply to the sheriff by incidental application to fix caution for expenses in such sum as the sheriff considers reasonable having regard to the number of witnesses he proposes to cite and the period for which they may be required to attend court; and
- (b) before instructing a solicitor or a sheriff officer to cite a witness, find caution in the sum fixed in accordance with paragraph (1).

(2) A party litigant who does not intend to cite all the witnesses referred to in his application under paragraph 1(a), may apply by incidental application for variation of the amount of caution.

[1615]

NOTES

Commencement: 10 June 2002.

18.10 Witnesses failing to attend

(1) A hearing must not be adjourned solely on account of the failure of a witness to appear unless the sheriff, on cause shown, so directs.

(2) A witness or haver who fails without reasonable excuse to answer a citation after having been properly cited and offered his travelling expenses if he has asked for them may be ordered by the sheriff to pay a penalty not exceeding £250.

(3) The sheriff may grant decree for payment of a penalty imposed under paragraph (2) above in favour of the party on whose behalf the witness or haver was cited.

(4) The sheriff may grant warrant for the apprehension of the witness or haver and for bringing him to court.

(5) A warrant mentioned in paragraph (4) shall be effective in any sheriffdom without endorsation and the expenses of it may be awarded against the witness or haver.

[1616]

NOTES

Commencement: 10 June 2002.

CHAPTER 23
DECREES, EXTRACTS, EXECUTION AND VARIATION

23.1 Decree

The sheriff must not grant decree against—
(a) a defender or a third party in respect of a claim; or
(b) a pursuer in respect of a counterclaim,

under any provision of these Rules unless satisfied that a ground of jurisdiction exists.

[1617]

NOTES

Commencement: 10 June 2002.

23.2 Final decree

The final decree of the sheriff principal or the sheriff shall be granted, where expenses are awarded, only after expenses have been dealt with in accordance with [rules 23.3, 23.3A and 23.3B].

[1618]

NOTES

Commencement: 10 June 2002.

Words in square brackets substituted by the Act of Sederunt (Summary Cause Rules) (Amendment) 2002, SSI 2002/516, r 2(1), (2).

23.3 Expenses

(1) Subject to [rule 23.3A and] paragraphs (2) to (4), the sheriff clerk must, with the approval of the sheriff, assess the amount of expenses including the fees and outlays of witnesses awarded in any cause, in accordance with the statutory table of fees of solicitors appropriate to the action.

(2) A party litigant, who is not represented by a solicitor or advocate and who would have been entitled to expenses if he had been so represented, may be awarded any outlays or expenses to which he might be found entitled by virtue of the 1975 Act or any enactment under that Act.

(3) A party who is or has been represented by an authorised lay representative and who would have been found entitled to expenses if he had been represented by a solicitor or an advocate may be awarded any outlays or expenses to which a party litigant might be found entitled in accordance with paragraph (2).

(4) A party who is not an individual, and—
(i) is or has been represented by an authorised lay representative;
(ii) if unrepresented, could not represent itself; and
(iii) would have been found entitled to expenses if it had been represented by a solicitor or an advocate,

may be awarded any outlays to which a party litigant might be found entitled under the 1975 Act or any enactment made under that Act.

(5) [Except where an account of expenses is allowed to be taxed under rule 23.3A, in] every case including an appeal where expenses are awarded, the sheriff clerk shall hear the parties or their solicitors on the claims for expenses including fees, if any, and outlays.

(6) Except where the sheriff principal or the sheriff has reserved judgment or where he orders otherwise, the hearing on the claim for expenses must take place immediately upon the decision being pronounced.

(7) When that hearing is not held immediately, the sheriff clerk must—
(a) fix the date, time and place when he shall hear the parties or their solicitors; and
(b) give all parties at least 14 days' notice in writing of the hearing so fixed.

(8) The party awarded expenses must—
(a) lodge his account of expenses in court at least seven days prior to the date of any hearing fixed under paragraph (7); and
(b) at the same time forward a copy of that account to every other party.

PART II
CIVIL PROCEDURE RULES

(9) The sheriff clerk must—
(a) fix the amount of the expenses; and
(b) report his decision to the sheriff principal or the sheriff in open court for his approval at a diet which the sheriff clerk has intimated to the parties.

(10) The sheriff principal or the sheriff, after hearing parties or their solicitors if objections are stated, must pronounce final decree including decree for payment of expenses as approved by him.

(11) In an appeal, the sheriff may pronounce decree under paragraph (10) on behalf of the sheriff principal.

(12) Failure by—
(a) any party to comply with any of the foregoing provisions of this rule; or
(b) the successful party or parties to appear at the hearing on expenses,

must be reported by the sheriff clerk to the sheriff principal or the sheriff at a diet which the sheriff clerk has intimated to the parties.

(13) In either of the circumstances mentioned in paragraphs (12)(a) or (b), the sheriff principal or sheriff must, unless sufficient cause be shown, pronounce decree on the merits of the action and find no expenses due to or by any party.

(14) A decree pronounced under paragraph (13) shall be held to be the final decree for the purposes of these Rules.

(15) The sheriff principal or sheriff may, if he thinks fit, on the application of the solicitor of any party to whom expenses may be awarded, made at or before the time of the final decree being pronounced, grant decree in favour of that solicitor for the expenses of the action.

[1619]

NOTES

Commencement: 10 June 2002.

Para (1): words in square brackets inserted by the Act of Sederunt (Summary Cause Rules) (Amendment) 2002, SSI 2002/516, r 2(1), (3)(a).

Para (5): words in square brackets substituted by SSI 2002/516, r 2(1), (3)(b).

[23.3A Taxation

(1) Either—

(a) the sheriff, on his own motion or on the motion of any party; or

(b) the sheriff clerk on cause shown,

may allow an account of expenses to be taxed by the auditor of court instead of being assessed by the sheriff clerk under rule 23.3.

(2) Where an account of expenses is lodged for taxation, the account and process shall be transmitted by the sheriff clerk to the auditor of court.

(3) The auditor of court shall—

(a) assign a diet of taxation not earlier than 7 days from the date he receives the account from the sheriff clerk; and

(b) intimate that diet forthwith from to the party who lodged the account.

(4) The party who lodged the account of expenses shall, on receiving intimation from the auditor of court under paragraph (3)—

(a) send a copy of the account; and

(b) intimate the date, time and place of the diet of taxation,

to every other party.

(5) After the account has been taxed, the auditor of court shall transmit the process with the account and his report to the sheriff clerk.

(6) Where the auditor of court has reserved consideration of the account at the date of the taxation, he shall intimate his decision to the parties who attended the taxation.

(7) Where no objections are lodged under rule 23.3B (objections to auditor's report), the sheriff may grant decree for the expenses as taxed.]

[1620]

NOTES

Commencement: 1 January 2003.

Inserted, together with r 23.3B, by the Act of Sederunt (Summary Cause Rules) (Amendment) 2002, SSI 2002/516, r 2(1), (4).

[23.3B Objections to auditor's report

(1) A party may lodge a note of objections to an account as taxed only where he attended the diet of taxation.

(2) Such a note shall be lodged within 7 days after—

(a) the diet of taxation; or

(b) where the auditor of court reserved consideration of the account under paragraph (6) of rule 23.3A, the date on which the auditor of court intimates his decision under that paragraph.

(3) The sheriff shall dispose of the objection in a summary manner, with or without answers.]

[1621]

NOTES

Commencement: 1 January 2003.

Inserted as noted to r 23.3A at **[1620]**.

23.4 Correction of interlocutor or note

At any time before extract, the sheriff may correct any clerical or incidental error in an interlocutor or note attached to it.

[1622]

NOTES

Commencement: 10 June 2002.

23.5 Taxes on funds under control of the court

(1) Subject to paragraph (2), in an action in which money has been consigned into court under the Sheriff Court Consignations (Scotland) Act 1893, no decree, warrant or order for payment to any person shall be granted until there has been lodged with the sheriff clerk a certificate by an authorised officer of the Inland Revenue stating that all taxes or duties payable to the Commissioners of Inland Revenue have been paid or satisfied.

(2) In an action of multiplepoinding, it shall not be necessary for the grant of a decree, warrant or order for payment under paragraph (1) that all of the taxes or duties payable on the estate of a deceased claimant have been paid or satisfied.

[1623]

NOTES

Commencement: 10 June 2002.

23.6 Extract of decree

(1) Extract of a decree signed by the sheriff clerk may be issued only after the lapse of 14 days from the granting of the decree unless the sheriff on application orders earlier extract.

(2) In an action (other than an action to which rule 30.2 applies) where an appeal has been lodged, the extract may not be issued until the appeal has been disposed of.

(3) The extract decree—

(a) may be written on the summons or on a separate paper;

(b) may be in one of Forms 28 to 28k; and

(c) shall be warrant for all lawful execution.

[1624]

NOTES

Commencement: 10 June 2002.

23.7 Charge

(1) The period for payment specified in any charge following on a decree for payment granted in an action shall be—

(a) 14 days if the person on whom it is served is within the United Kingdom; and
(b) 28 days if he is outside the United Kingdom or his whereabouts are unknown.

(2) The period in respect of any other form of charge on a decree in an action shall be 14 days.

[1625]

NOTES
Commencement: 10 June 2002.

23.8 Service of charge where address of defender is unknown

(1) If the address of a defender is not known to the pursuer, a charge shall be deemed to have been served on the defender if it is—

(a) served on the sheriff clerk of the sheriff court district where the defender's last known address is located; and
(b) displayed by the sheriff clerk on the walls of court for the period of the charge.

(2) On receipt of such a charge, the sheriff clerk must display it on the walls of court and it must remain displayed for the period of the charge.

(3) The period specified in the charge shall run from the first date on which it was displayed on the walls of court.

(4) On the expiry of the period of charge, the sheriff clerk must endorse a certificate in Form 29 on the charge certifying that it has been displayed in accordance with this rule and must then return it to the sheriff officer by whom service was executed.

[1626]

NOTES
Commencement: 10 June 2002.

23.9 Diligence on decree in actions for delivery

(1) In an action for delivery, the court may, when granting decree, grant warrant to search for and take possession of goods and to open shut and lockfast places.

(2) A warrant granted under paragraph (1) shall only apply to premises occupied by the defender.

[1627]

NOTES
Commencement: 10 June 2002.

23.10 Applications in same action for variation, etc of decree

(1) If by virtue of any enactment the sheriff, without a new action being initiated, may order that—

(a) a decree granted be varied, discharged or rescinded; or
(b) the execution of that decree in so far as it has not already been executed be sisted or suspended,

the party requesting the sheriff to make such an order must do so by lodging a minute to that effect, setting out briefly the reasons for the application.

(2) On the lodging of such a minute by the pursuer, the sheriff clerk must grant warrant for service upon the defender (provided that the pursuer has returned the extract decree).

(3) On the lodging of such a minute by the defender, the sheriff clerk must grant warrant for service upon the pursuer ordaining him to return the extract decree and may, where appropriate, grant interim sist of execution of the decree.

(4) Subject to paragraph (5), the minute shall not be heard in court unless seven days' notice of the minute and warrant has been given to the other parties by the party lodging the minute.

(5) The sheriff may, on cause shown, alter the period of seven days referred to in paragraph (4) but may not reduce it to less than two days.

(6) This rule shall not apply to any proceedings under the Debtors (Scotland) Act 1987 or to proceedings which may be subject to the provisions of that Act.

[1628]

NOTES

Commencement: 10 June 2002.

CHAPTER 35
ELECTRONIC TRANSMISSION OF DOCUMENTS

35.1 Extent of provision

(1) Any document referred to in these rules which requires to be—

(a) lodged with the sheriff clerk;
(b) intimated to a party; or
(c) sent by the sheriff clerk,

may be in electronic or documentary form, and if in electronic form may be lodged, intimated or sent by e-mail or similar means.

(2) Paragraph (1) does not apply to any certificate of execution of service, citation or arrestment, or to a decree or extract decree of the court.

(3) Where any document is lodged by e-mail or similar means the sheriff may require any principal document to be lodged.

[1629]

NOTES

Commencement: 10 June 2002.

35.2 Time of lodgement

The time of lodgement, intimation or sending shall be the time when the document was sent or transmitted.

[1630]

NOTES

Commencement: 10 June 2002.

(*Appendix 1 contains Forms.*)

APPENDIX 2
GLOSSARY

Rule 1.1(5)

Absolve

To find in favour of and exonerate the defender.

Absolvitor

An order of the court granted in favour of and exonerating the defender which means that the pursuer is not allowed to bring the same matter to court again.

Action of count, reckoning and payment

A legal procedure for requiring someone to account for their dealings with assets under their stewardship. For example, a trustee might be subject to such an action.

Action of furthcoming

A final stage of diligence or enforcement. It results in whatever has been subject to arrestment being made over to the person who is suing. For example, where a bank account has been arrested this results in the appropriate amount being transferred to the pursuer.

Appellant

A person making an appeal against the sheriff's decision. This might be the pursuer or the defender.

Arrestee

A person subject to an arrestment.

Arrestment on the dependence

A court order to freeze the goods or bank account of the defender until the court has heard the case.

Arrestment to found jurisdiction

A court order used against a person who has goods or other assets in Scotland to give the court jurisdiction to hear a case. This is achieved by preventing anything being done with the goods or assets until the case has been disposed of.

Authorised lay representative

A person other than a lawyer who represents a party to a summary cause.

Calling date

The date on which the case will first be heard in court.

Cause

Another word for case or claim.

Caution (pronounced kay-shun)

A security, usually a sum of money, given to ensure that some obligation will be carried out.

Certificate of execution of service

The document recording that an application to, or order or decree of, the court for service of documents has been effected.

Charge

An order to obey a decree of a court. A common type is one served on the defender by a sheriff officer on behalf of the pursuer who has won a case demanding payment of a sum of money.

Claim

The part of the summons which sets out the legal remedy which the pursuer is seeking.

Commission and diligence

Authorisation by the court for someone to take the evidence of a witness who cannot attend court or to obtain the production of documentary evidence. It is combined with a diligence authorising the person appointed to require the attendance of the witness and the disclosure of documents.

Consignation

The deposit in court, or with a third party, of money or an article in dispute.

Continuation

An order made by the sheriff postponing the completion of a hearing until a later date or dates.

Contribution, Right of

The right of one person who is legally liable to pay money to someone to claim a proportionate share from others who are also liable.

Counterclaim

A claim made by a defender in response to the pursuer's case and which is not necessarily a defence to that case. It is a separate but related case against the pursuer which is dealt with at the same time as the pursuer's case.

Damages

Money compensation payable for a breach of contract or some other legal duty.

Declarator of irritancy of a lease

A decision of a court finding that a tenant has failed to observe a term of a lease which may lead to the termination of the lease.

Decree

An order of the court containing the decision of the case in favour of one of the parties and granting the remedy sought or disposing of the case.

Decree of ejection

A decree ordering someone to leave land or property which they are occupying. For example, it is used to remove tenants in arrears with their rent.

Decree of removing

A court order entitling someone to recover possession of heritable property and ordering a person to leave land which he is occupying. For example, it is used to remove tenants in arrears with their rent.

Defender

Person against whom a summary cause is started.

Deliverance

A decision or order of a court.

Diet

Date for a court hearing.

Diligence

The collective term for the procedures used to enforce a decree of a court. These include arrestment of wages, goods or a bank account.

Dismissal

An order bringing to an end the proceedings in a summary cause. It is usually possible for a new summary cause to be brought if not time barred.

Domicile

The place where a person is normally resident or where, in the case of a company, it has its place of business or registered office.

Execution of service

See Certificate of execution of service.

Execution of a charge

The intimation of the requirement to obey a decree or order of a court.

Execution of an arrestment

The carrying out of an order of arrestment.

Expenses

The costs of a court case.

Extract decree

The document containing the order of the court made at the end of the summary cause. For example, it can be used to enforce payment of a sum awarded.

Fund in medio

See Multiplepoinding.

Haver

A person who holds documents which are required as evidence in a case.

Heritable property

Land and buildings as opposed to moveable property.

Huissier

An official in France and some other European countries who serves court documents.

Incidental application

An application that can be made during the course of a summary cause for certain orders. Examples are applications for the recovery of documents or to amend the statement of claim.

Interlocutor

The official record of the order or judgment of a court.

Interrogatories

Written questions put to someone in the course of a court case and which must be answered on oath.

Intimation

Giving notice to another party of some step in a summary cause.

Jurisdiction

The authority of a court to hear particular cases.

Ish

The date on which a lease terminates.

Letter of request

A document issued by the sheriff court requesting a foreign court to take evidence from a specified person within its jurisdiction or to serve Scottish court documents on that person.

Messenger at arms

Officers of court who serve documents issued by the Court of Session.

Minute

A document produced in the course of a case in which a party makes an application or sets out his position on some matter.

Minute for recall

A form lodged with the court by one party asking the court to recall a decree.

Multiplepoinding (pronounced "multiple pinding")

A special type of summary cause in which the holder of property, etc (referred to as the fund *in medio*) requires claimants upon it to appear and settle claims in court. For example, where the police come into possession of a stolen car of which two or more people claim to be owner this procedure could be used.

Options Hearing

A preliminary stage in an ordinary cause action.

Ordinary cause

Another legal procedure for higher value cases available in the sheriff court.

Party litigant

A person who conducts his own case.

Process

The court file containing the collection of documents relating to a case.

Productions

Documents or articles which are used in evidence.

Pursuer

The person who starts a summary cause.

Recall of an arrestment

A court order withdrawing an arrestment.

Restriction of an arrestment

An order releasing part of the money or property arrested.

Recall of a decree

An order revoking a decree which has been granted.

Recovery of documents

The process of obtaining documentary evidence which is not in the possession of the person seeking it (e g hospital records necessary to establish the extent of injuries received in a road accident).

Remit between procedures

A decision of the sheriff to transfer the summary cause to another court procedure e g small claim or ordinary cause procedure.

Respondent

When a decision of the sheriff is appealed against, the person making the appeal is called the appellant. The other side in the appeal is called the respondent.

Return day

The date by which the defender must send a written reply to the court and, where appropriate, the pursuer must return the summons to court.

Schedule of arrestment

The list of items which may be arrested.

Serve / service

Sending a copy of the summons or other court document to the defender or another party.

Sheriff clerk

The court official responsible for the administration of the sheriff court.

Sheriff officer

A person who serves court documents and enforces court orders.

Sist of action

The temporary suspension of a court case by court order.

Sist as a party

To add another person as a litigant in a case.

Small claim

Another legal procedure in the sheriff court for claims having a lower value than summary cause.

Specification of documents

A list lodged in court of documents for the recovery of which a party seeks a court order.

Stated case

An appeal procedure where the sheriff sets out his findings and the reasons for his decision and states the issues on which the decision of the sheriff principal is requested.

Statement of claim

The part of the summons in which pursuers set out details of their cases against defenders.

Summons

The form which must be filled in to begin a summary cause.

Time to pay direction

A court order for which a defender who is an individual may apply permitting a sum owed to be paid by instalments or by a single payment at a later date.

Time order

A court order which assists debtors who have defaulted on an agreement regulated by the Consumer Credit Act 1974 (c 39) and which may be applied for during a court action.

Warrant for diligence

Authority to carry out one of the diligence procedures.

Writ

A legally significant writing.

[1631]

(*Sch 2 contains revocations.*)

ACT OF SEDERUNT (TAKING OF EVIDENCE IN THE EUROPEAN COMMUNITY) 2003

(SSI 2003/601)

NOTES

Made: 11 December 2003.
Authority: Sheriff Courts (Scotland) Act 1971, s 32.
Commencement: 1 January 2004.

1 Citation, commencement and interpretation

(1) This Act of Sederunt may be cited as the Act of Sederunt (Taking of Evidence in the European Community) 2003, and shall come into force on 1st January 2004.

(2) This Act of Sederunt shall be inserted in the Books of Sederunt.

(3) In this Act of Sederunt—

"Council Regulation" means the Council Regulation (EC) No 1206/2001 of 28th May 2001 on cooperation between the courts of the Member States in the taking of evidence in civil or commercial matters;

"Ordinary Cause Rules" means Schedule 1 to the Sheriff Courts (Scotland) Act 1907; and

"Summary Cause Rules" means the Act of Sederunt (Summary Cause Rules) 2002.

[1632]

NOTES

Commencement: 1 January 2004.

2 Directions by the sheriff principal

(1) The sheriff principal of any sheriffdom on receipt of a request referred to in paragraph (2), may make a direction specifying—

(a) the sheriff responsible for execution of that request;
(b) the manner in which that request is to be executed; and
(c) the manner in which any representative of a requesting court may participate under Article 12 of the Council Regulation in the performance of the taking of evidence.

(2) A request is—

(a) under Article 1 of the Council Regulation by a court of a Member State that a sheriff court shall take evidence; or
(b) under Article 17 of the Council Regulation by the Scottish central body that a sheriff court shall take part in the performance of the taking of evidence by a court of a Member State.

[1633]

NOTES

Commencement: 1 January 2004.

3 Hearing on a request

(1) The sheriff responsible for executing a request under rule 2(1) shall, where appropriate, fix a diet for a hearing on that request.

(2) The sheriff shall grant a warrant for intimation of a hearing under paragraph (1) to such persons as the sheriff shall consider appropriate.

(3) The sheriff clerk shall, on a hearing being fixed under paragraph (1), intimate that hearing to the persons specified in paragraph (2) in any of the manners prescribed by rules 5.3 to 5.6 of the Ordinary Cause Rules.

[1634]

NOTES

Commencement: 1 January 2004.

4, 5 *(R 4 amends the Ordinary Cause Rules, r 28 at* **[1021]***; r 5 amends the Summary Cause Rules, r 18 at* **[1606]***.)*

(The Schedule sets out the Ordinary Cause Rules, Form G16 at **[1055]***.)*

PRACTICE NOTE 6
COMMERCIAL ACTIONS

Application and interpretation of Chapter 47: RCS 1994, r 47.1

1. The actions to which the rules apply are intended to comprise all actions arising out of or concerned with any relationship of a commercial or business nature, whether contractual or not, and to include, but not to be limited to—

the construction of a commercial or mercantile document,
the sale or hire purchase of goods,
the export or import of merchandise,
the carriage of goods by land, air or sea,
insurance,
banking,
the provision of financial services,
mercantile agency,
mercantile usage or a custom of trade,
a building, engineering or construction contract,
a commercial lease.

Some Admiralty actions *in personam*, such as actions relating to or arising out of bills of lading, may also be suitable for treatment of commercial actions if they do not require the special facilities of Admiralty procedure in relation to defenders whose names are not known.

Commercial judge: RCS 1994, r 47.2

2. The commercial judge may hear and determine a commercial action when the court is in session or in vacation: rule 10.7.

Election of procedure: RCS 1994, r 47.3

3.—(1) The initial pleadings in a commercial action are expected to be in an abbreviated form: the purpose of the pleadings is to give notice of the essential elements of the case to the court and the other parties to the action. Compliance with the requirements of paragraph 11 of the practice note will enable the essential elements of the case to be presented in the pleadings in succinct form. Where damages are sought, a summary statement of the claim or a statement in the form of an account will normally be sufficient. Where it is sought to obtain from the court a decision only on the construction of a document, it is permissible for the summons to contain an appropriate conclusion without a condescendence or pleas-in-law. The conclusion in such a case should specify the document, the construction of which is in dispute and conclude for the construction contended for.

(2) Rule 47.3(3) is intended to require a party to produce with its summons the "core" or essential documents to establish the contract or transaction with which the cause is concerned. Under rule 27.1(1)(a) documents founded on or adopted as incorporated in a summons must be lodged at the time the summons is lodged for calling.

(3) When the summons is lodged for signetting, a commercial action registration form (Form CA 1), copies of which are available from the General Department, must be completed, lodged in process and a copy served with the summons.

Disapplication of certain rules: RCS 1994, r 47.4

4. The ordinary rules of the Rules of the Court of Session 1994 apply to a commercial action to which Chapter 47 applies except insofar as specifically excluded under rule 47.4 or which are excluded by implication because of a provision in Chapter 47.

Procedure in commercial actions: RCS 1994 r 47.5

5. The procedure in, and progress of, a commercial action is under the direct control of the commercial judge. He will take a proactive approach.

Defences: RCS 1994 r 47.6

6.—(1) In the first instance detailed averments are not required in the defences any more than in the summons and it is not necessary that each allegation should be admitted or denied provided that the extent of the dispute is reasonably well identified. One of the objectives of the procedure is to make the extent of written pleadings subject to the control of the court. Compliance with the requirements of paragraph 11 of this practice note will enable the essential elements of the defence to be presented in the defences in succinct form.

(2) Under rule 27(1)(1)(b), documents founded on or adopted as incorporated in defence must be lodged at the time the defences are lodged.

(3) Defences must be lodged within 7 days after the summons is lodged for calling: rule 18.1(1).

(4) The defenders must complete a commercial action registration form (Form CA 1) and lodge it in process, or complete the process copy, with the information required.

Counterclaims and Third Party Notices: RCS 1994, r 47.7.

7. No counterclaim or the bringing in of a third party may be pursued without an order from the commercial judge.

Commercial Roll: RCS 1994, r 47.8

8. In the Outer House, an action, and all proceedings in it, in which an election has been made to adopt the procedure in Chapter 47 for commercial actions or which has been transferred under rule 47.10 to be dealt with as a commercial action, shall be heard and determined the Commercial Roll.

Withdrawal of action from Commercial Roll: RCS 1994, r 47.9

9. The object of rule 47.9 is to enable cases which are unsuitable for the commercial procedure to be removed from the Commercial Roll, but it should be understood that the commercial procedure is not to be regarded as limited to cases which are straightforward or simple or as excluding cases which involve the investigation of difficult and complicated facts.

Transfer of actions to Commercial Roll: RCS 1994, r 47.10

10.—(1) An ordinary action which has not been brought as a commercial action under rule 47.3(1) may be transferred to the Commercial Roll as a commercial action on application by motion by any party (including the pursuer) to the commercial judge if it is an action within the meaning of a commercial action in rule 47.1(2).

(2) An interlocutor granting or refusing a motion to transfer an action to the Commercial Roll may be reclaimed against only with leave of the commercial judge within 14 days after the date of the interlocutor: rule 38.4(6).

Pre-action communication

11.—(1) Before a commercial action is commenced it is important that, save in exceptional cases, the matters in dispute should have been discussed and focused in pre-litigation communications between the prospective parties' legal advisers. This is because the commercial action procedure is intended for cases in which there is a real dispute between the parties which requires to be resolved by judicial decision, rather than other means; and because the procedure functions best if issues have been investigated and ventilated prior to the raising of the action.

(2) It is therefore expected that, before a commercial action has begun, the solicitors acting for the pursuers will have:

(i) fully set out in correspondence to the intended defender the nature of the claim and the factual and legal grounds on which it proceeds;

(ii) supplied to the intended defender copies of any documents relied upon; and

(iii) where the issue sought to be litigated is one for which expert evidence is necessary, obtained and disclosed, to the intended defender, the expert's report.

For their part, solicitors acting for the defender are expected to respond to such pre-litigation communications by setting out the defender's position in substantial terms; and by disclosing any document or expert's report upon which the defender relies. To that response the solicitors for the pursuers are expected to give a considered and reasoned reply. Both parties may wish to consider whether all or some of the dispute may be amenable to some form of alternative dispute resolution.

(3) Saving cases involving an element of urgency, actions should not be raised using the commercial procedure, until the nature and extent of the dispute between the parties has been the subject of careful discussion between the parties and/or their representatives and the action can be said to be truly necessary.

Preliminary hearing on Commercial Roll: RCS 1994 r 47.11

12.—(1) The preliminary hearing will normally be conducted on the basis that the provisions of paragraph 11 in relation to pre-action communication have been complied with. The preliminary hearing, and any continuations thereof, are not designed to give parties the opportunity to formulate their claim and response thereto.

(2) Parties should lodge, prior to the preliminary hearing, and for consideration at the preliminary hearing all correspondence and other documents which set out their respective material contentions of fact and law which show their compliance with the provisions of paragraph 11. These provisions are supplementary to the provisions of rule 47.3(3).

(3) Where it appears to the court that the need to grant any request for a continuation of a preliminary hearing is brought about by a failure to comply with the provisions of paragraph 11, this may result in the party responsible for any such failure having the expenses of the continued hearing awarded against him on an agent/client basis. Apart from that possible disposal, motions for continuations of the preliminary hearings which are sought simply to enable information to be obtained, which could and should have been obtained, prior to the preliminary hearing, may be refused.

(4) At the preliminary hearing the parties should be in a position to lodge a document setting out in concise form the issues which they contend require judicial determination. The statement of issues should, where possible, be set out in an agreed document.

(5) In applying rule 47.11(3), the court will expect to set realistic time limits; but once established those time limits will be expected to be achieved and extension will only be granted in certain circumstances. This emphasises the importance of ensuring that parties at the preliminary hearing are in a position to explain fully what will be required. Since it is part of the administration of commercial causes that wherever possible a commercial action should at all stages be heard before the same judge, it is important to avoid repeated appearances of the action on the commercial roll. For that reason it is necessary to try to give the court accurate information in order to enable the appropriate time limits for a particular case to be established in the manner which is both realistic and does not prejudice the overall requirement that commercial actions should be dealt with expeditiously.

Procedural Hearing on Commercial Roll: RCS 1994, r 47.12

13.—(1) The procedural hearing is also an important hearing at which parties will be expected to be in a position to discuss realistically the issues involved in the action and the method of disposing of them. It should normally be expected that by the time of the procedural hearing the parties' positions will have been ascertained and identified and that all prospects for settlement have been fully discussed. In consequence it is expected that, once a case has passed beyond the stage of a procedural hearing, it will not settle.

(2) This is one of the ways in which it is sought to meet the problem of ensuring that the judge is in the position to deal realistically with the procedure which he cannot do unless he is given information on which to proceed.

(3) Rule 47.12(2) is the kernel of the procedures and it is intended to enable the court to direct what is really to happen.

Debates: RCS 1994, r 47.13

14. A debate in a commercial action is not heard on the Procedure Roll but on the Commercial Roll. The provisions of Chapter 28 of the RCS 1994 (Procedure Roll), however, do apply to a debate in a commercial action.

Pre-Proof By Order Hearing

15. When a proof, or proof before answer, has been allowed, the court will normally also fix a pre-proof by order hearing to take place in advance of the proof diet. The general purpose of such a hearing is to ascertain the parties' state of preparation for the proof hearing and to review the estimated duration of that hearing.

Without prejudice to the foregoing generality, the following matters will be dealt with at the pre-proof by order hearing:

(1) Consideration of any joint minute of admissions, agreed by the parties, which should be lodged no later than two days prior to the pre-proof by order hearing.

(2) A review of the documents, or other productions which the parties at the time of the pre-proof by order hearing consider will be relied upon at the proof hearing. Any such document should be lodged no later than two days prior to the pre-proof by order hearing.

(3) The up-to-date position with regard to any expert reports which are to be relied upon by the parties will be reviewed. The parties should be in a position to advise the court of what consultation, if any, has taken place between their respective experts with a view to reaching agreement about any points held in common and what matters remain truly in dispute between them.

(4) Where a proof before answer has been allowed, parties should produce, for consideration, at the pre-proof by order hearing, a statement of legal arguments and lists of authorities which they may seek to rely on at the diet of proof before answer, insofar as these have not already been lodged.

Lodging of productions: RCS 1994, r 47.14

16. Before any proof or other hearing at which reference is to be made to documents, parties shall, as well as lodging their productions, prepare for the use of the court a working bundle in which the documents are arranged chronologically or in another appropriate order without multiple copies of the same document.

Hearings for further procedure: RCS 1994, r 47.15

17. The commercial judge or a party may have a commercial action put out for a hearing other than a preliminary or procedural hearing to deal with a procedural or other matter which has arisen for which provision has not been made.

Failure to comply with rule or order of commercial judge: RCS 1994, r 47.16

18. The purpose of this rule is to provide for discipline to ensure effective supervision of case management.

General

19—(1) Arrangements will be made to ensure that (save in exceptional circumstances) at all appearances of an action in the commercial roll the same judge shall preside. Parties are expected to arrange that counsel, or solicitors having rights of audience responsible for the conduct of the case, and authorised to take any necessary decision on questions both of substance and procedure, are available and appear at any calling in the commercial roll.

(2) Where any pleadings or other documents are to be adjusted, the party proposing adjustment shall do so by preparing a new copy of the document as adjusted in which the new material is indicated by underlining, side-lining, a difference in typeface, or other means.

(3) An interlocutor pronounced on the commercial roll, other than a final interlocutor, may be reclaimed against only with leave of the commercial judge within 14 days after the date of the interlocutor: rule 38.4(7).

Revocation of previous practice note

20.1. The Practice Note No 12 of 1994 (commercial actions) is hereby revoked.

[1635]–[2000]

PART III
STATUTORY INSTRUMENTS

A. JURISDICTION AND FOREIGN JUDGMENTS

NOTES

The following section includes, among other materials, statutory instruments made under the Foreign Judgments (Reciprocal Enforcement) Act 1933, s 1 at **[16]** concerning the recognition and enforcement of judgments from designated foreign states, many of which give effect to conventions with those states. It should, however, be noted that the statutory instruments giving effect to the conventions with France (SR&O 1933/1073) at **[2001]**, Belgium (SR&O 1936/1169) at **[2010]**, Germany (SI 1961/1199) at **[2026]**, Austria (SI 1962/1339) at **[2043]**, the Netherlands (SI 1969/1063) at **[2051]** and Italy (SI 1973/1894) at **[2082]** no longer apply to judgments falling within the scope of the 1968 Brussels Convention (see the Civil Jurisdiction and Judgments Act 1982, s 9(1) at **[58]** and the Brussels Convention, Arts 55, 56 at **[3029]**). Nor, it would seem, do they apply to judgments falling within the scope of Council Regulation 44/2001/EC on jurisdiction and the recognition and enforcement of judgments in civil and commercial matters, the successor to the 1968 Brussels Convention (see Council Regulation 44/2001/EC, Arts 69, 70 at **[3147]**, **[3148]**, but note that there is no equivalent of s 9(1) of the 1982 Act, which expressly applies those provisions to legislation implementing the conventions). Further, the statutory instrument giving effect to the convention with Norway (SI 1962/636) no longer applies to judgments falling within the scope of the 1988 Lugano Convention (see the Civil Jurisdiction and Judgments Act 1982, s 9(1) at **[58]** and the Lugano Convention, Arts 55, 56 at **[3063]**). The SIs may continue to apply to judgments falling outside the scope of the Brussels and Lugano Conventions and Council Regulation 44/2001/EC and, in the case of the Netherlands, to judgments from the Netherlands Antilles to which the Conventions and Council Regulation 44/2001/EC do not extend.

RECIPROCAL ENFORCEMENT OF JUDGMENTS (GENERAL APPLICATION TO HIS MAJESTY'S DOMINIONS, ETC) ORDER 1933

(SR & O 1933/1073)

NOTES

Made: 10 November 1933.
Authority: Foreign Judgments (Reciprocal Enforcement) Act 1933, s 7(1).
Commencement: 10 November 1933.
Modification: by virtue of the Zimbabwe (Independence and Membership of the Commonwealth) (Consequential Provisions) Order 1980, SI 1980/701, this Order in Council has effect in relation to Zimbabwe as if references to a part of His Majesty's Dominions outside the United Kingdom, or to persons or things related thereto, included a reference to a Commonwealth country and to persons or things related to a Commonwealth country; by virtue of the Pakistan Act 1990, Schedule, para 8, for the purposes of any order in relation to Pakistan under Pt I of the 1933 Act, further to the Reciprocal Enforcement of Judgments (Pakistan) Order 1958, SI 1958/141 at **[2017]**, this Order in Council has effect as if references to Her Majesty's Dominions outside the United Kingdom included references to any Commonwealth Country.

It should be noted that there are no trust territories (formerly known as mandated territories) nor protectorates remaining for which the UK has responsibility.

1 Part I of the Foreign Judgments (Reciprocal Enforcement) Act 1933 shall apply to His Majesty's dominions outside the United Kingdom and to judgments obtained in the courts of the said dominions and to territories which are under His Majesty's protection or in respect of which a mandate has been accepted by His Majesty and to judgments obtained in the courts of the said territories.

[2001]

2 This Order may be cited as "The Reciprocal Enforcement of Judgments (General Application to His Majesty's Dominions, etc) Order 1933".

[2002]

RECIPROCAL ENFORCEMENT OF FOREIGN JUDGMENTS (FRANCE) ORDER IN COUNCIL 1936

(SI 1936/609)

NOTES

Made: 28 May 1936.
Authority: Foreign Judgments (Reciprocal Enforcement) Act 1933, s 1.

Commencement: 16 June 1936.

This order has been largely superseded by the 1968 Brussels Convention and Council Regulation 44/2001/EC. See Introductory Note at the beginning of this section.

1 This Order may be cited as "The Reciprocal Enforcement of Foreign Judgments (France) Order in Council, 1936", and shall come into operation on the 16th day of June, 1936.

[2003]

2 Part I of the Foreign Judgments (Reciprocal Enforcement) Act 1933 shall extend to France.

[2004]

3 The following courts of France shall be deemed superior courts of France for the purposes of Part I of the Foreign Judgments (Reciprocal Enforcement) Act 1933, that is to say:—

The Court of Cassation;
All Courts of Appeal;
All Tribunals of First Instance;
All Tribunals of Commerce.

[2005]

4 No security for costs shall be required to be given by any person making application for the registration of a judgment of a superior court in France.

[2006]

5 All French judgments which bear the executory formula prescribed by French law shall, in the absence of proof to the contrary, be deemed to be capable of execution in France. The executory formula at present prescribed by French law is that appended to the Convention signed between His Majesty and the President of the French Republic and annexed to this Order.

[2007]

6 If upon an application to register a judgment of a superior court in France, the interest due up to the date of judgment on the claim in respect of which the judgment is given has been determined in the said judgment, or if a certificate given by the original court is produced specifying the rate of interest due under French law upon the sum for which the judgment is given, the said judgment and the said certificate (as the case may be) shall be accepted as conclusive evidence as to the interest due up to the date of the said judgment and as to the rate of interest due under French law upon the sum for which the judgment is given. If the interest due up to the date of judgment on the claim in respect of which the judgment is given has not been determined in the judgment, or if no such certificate is produced, the party applying for registration may prove what is the interest due under the judgment by French law up to the time of registration or what is the rate of interest due under French law upon the sum for which the judgment is given.

[2008]

SCHEDULE
CONVENTION BETWEEN HIS MAJESTY IN RESPECT OF THE UNITED KINGDOM AND THE PRESIDENT OF THE FRENCH REPUBLIC PROVIDING FOR THE RECIPROCAL ENFORCEMENT OF JUDGMENTS IN CIVIL AND COMMERCIAL MATTERS, WITH PROTOCOL

CHAPTER I—GENERAL

Article 1

In This Convention—

1 The words "His Majesty" shall mean His Majesty the King of Great Britain, Ireland, and the British Dominions beyond the Seas, Emperor of India.

2 The words "territory of one (or of the other) High Contracting Party" mean—

(a) On the part of His Majesty, the United Kingdom (England and Wales, Scotland

and Northern Ireland), and any territories to which the Convention may be applicable by reason of extensions under Article 11 or accessions under Article 13, and

(b) On the part of the President of the French Republic, the metropolitan territory of France (including the adjacent islands and Corsica), and any territories to which the Convention may be applicable by reason of extensions under Article 12.

3 The words "superior court" mean—

(a) In the case of the United Kingdom, the House of Lords and for England and Wales the Supreme Court of Judicature (Court of Appeal and High Court of Justice) and the Courts of Chancery of the Counties Palatine of Lancaster and Durham; for Scotland the Court of Session; and for Northern Ireland, the Supreme Court of Judicature; and

(b) In the case of France, la Cour de Cassation, les Cours d'Appel, Les Tribunaux de première instance et les Tribunaux de commerce, and in the case of judgments for the payment of compensation to a "partie civile" in criminal proceedings, les Tribunaux correctionnels and les Cours d'Assises. All other Courts in these territories shall be deemed to be "inferior courts" for the purpose of this Convention.

4 The word "judgment" means any decision of a court however described (judgment order and the like) by which the rights of the parties are finally determined; and does not include (in particular) provisional, interlocutory or preparatory judgments.

5 The words "original court" mean in relation to any judgment the court by which such judgment was given; and the words "court applied to" the court in which it is sought to obtain recognition of a judgment or to which an application for the registration of a judgment or for the grant of an exequatur is made.

6 The words "judgment debtor" mean the person against whom the judgment was given in the original court and include, where necessary, any person against whom such judgment is enforceable: and the words "judgment creditor" mean the person in whose favour the judgment was given and include, where necessary, any other person entitled to avail himself of the judgment.

Article 2

1 The High Contracting Parties agree that judgments pronounced after the date of the entry into force of the present Convention by a Superior Court in the territory of one High Contracting Party shall, whatever the nationality of the judgment creditor or debtor, be recognised and enforced in the territory of the other in the cases and upon the conditions laid down in Articles 3–8 of the present Convention.

2 The provisions of the present Convention only apply to judgments in civil and commercial matters, including judgments for the payment of a sum of money as compensation upon the claim of an injured party appearing as "partie civile" in criminal proceedings.

3 Nevertheless the provisions of the present Convention do not apply—

(a) To judgments given on appeal from inferior courts;

(b) To judgments given in matters of status or family law (including judgments in matrimonial causes or concerning the pecuniary relations between the spouses as such); to judgments in matters of succession or administration of estates of deceased persons; or judgments in bankruptcy proceedings or proceedings relating to the winding up of companies or other bodies corporate.

4 It is understood that nothing in the present Convention shall be deemed to preclude the recognition and enforcement in the territory of one High Contracting Party, in accordance with the municipal law for the time being in force in the country concerned, of judgments pronounced by any court in the territory of the other High Contracting Party, being judgments to which the present Convention does not apply, or judgments given in circumstances where the provisions of the present Convention do not require such recognition or enforcement.

CHAPTER II—RECOGNITION

Article 3

1 The judgments referred to in Article 2 pronounced by a court in the territory of one High Contracting Party, shall be recognised in the courts of the territory of the other in all cases where no objection to the judgment can be established on any of the grounds hereinafter enumerated; that is to say, unless—

(a) The jurisdiction of the original court is not recognised under the rules of Private International Law with regard to jurisdiction observed by the court applied to;

(b) The judgment was given by default and the judgment debtor satisfies the court applied to that the defendant in the proceedings before the original court did not actually acquire knowledge of the proceedings in sufficient time to act upon it, whether or not such notice was served in accordance with the law of the country of the original court;

(c) The judgment is one which, for reasons of public policy, cannot be recognised by the court applied to, including cases where the judgment—

  (i) Is in respect of a cause of action which had already, as between the same parties, formed the subject of another judgment which is recognised under the law of the court applied to as final and conclusive;

  (ii) Has, in the opinion of the court applied to, been obtained by the fraud of any of the parties;

  (iii) Was given against a person, defendant in the proceedings before the original court who, in the opinion of the court applied to, under the rules of public international law was entitled to immunity from the jurisdiction of the original court;

  (iv) Is sought to be enforced against a person who is entitled to immunity from the jurisdiction of the court applied to under the rules of public international law;

(d) The judgment debtor satisfies the court applied to that proceedings by way of appeal, opposition or setting aside have been instituted against the judgment in the country of the original court. It is understood that, if such proceedings have not been actually instituted, but the time for lodging an appeal, opposition or application to set aside has not expired under the law of the country of the original court, the court applied to may, if it thinks fit, adjourn its decision on the recognition of the judgment so as to allow the judgment debtor a reasonable opportunity of instituting such proceedings.

2 It is understood that recognition shall not be refused merely on the ground that the original court has applied, in the choice of the system of law applicable to the case, rules of Private International Law different from those observed by the court applied to.

3 For the purposes of the present convention, the recognition of a judgment means that such judgment shall be treated as conclusive as to the matter thereby adjudicated upon in any further action as between the parties (judgment creditor and judgment debtor) and as to such matter shall constitute a defence in a further action between them in respect of the same cause of action.

Article 4

1 Notwithstanding the provisions of Article 3, para 1(a), and without prejudice to the provisions of paragraphs 2 and 3 of this article, the original court shall be recognised as possessing jurisdiction in all cases—

(a) Where the judgment debtor was in respect of the matter which is the subject of the judgment a plaintiff (including a plaintiff by intervention) or counter-claimant in the proceedings in the original court;

(b) Where the judgment debtor, being a defendant in the proceedings in the original court, submitted to the jurisdiction by voluntarily appearing in the proceedings. It is understood that the expression "voluntarily appearing in the proceedings" does not include an appearance merely for the purpose of protecting property situated within the jurisdiction of the original court from seizure, or of obtaining the release of property seized or for the purpose of contesting the jurisdiction of the original court;

(c) Where the judgment debtor, being a defendant in the proceedings in the original

court, had before the commencement of the proceedings concluded a valid agreement to submit to the jurisdiction of the courts of the country of the original court or of the original court in respect of the subject matter of the proceedings;
(d) Where the judgment debtor, being a defendant in the original court, was, at the time when the proceedings were instituted, resident in the country of the original court, or, being a company or other body corporate, had its head office in the country of the original court;
(e) Where the judgment debtor, being a defendant in the original court, had, within the country of the original court, either a business or commercial establishment or a branch office, and the proceedings were in respect of a transaction effected through, or at, such establishment or branch office.

Nevertheless the jurisdiction of the original court need not be recognised in the cases referred to in sub-paragraphs (d) and (e) above, if the judgment debtor satisfies the court applied to that the bringing of the proceedings in the original court was contrary to a valid agreement between the parties under which the dispute in question was to be settled otherwise than by proceedings in the original court.

2 The provisions of paragraph 1 of this article do not apply to judgments where the subject matter of the proceedings is immovable property, nor to judgments *in rem* in respect of movable property. Nevertheless in these cases the jurisdiction of the original court shall be recognised if such property was situated in the country of the original court at the time of the commencement of the proceedings in the original court.

3 Recognition of the jurisdiction of the original court shall not be refused on the ground that the original court had no jurisdiction under the law of its own country, if, under the law of the country of the original court, the judgment is conclusive until set aside.

CHAPTER III—EXECUTION OF JUDGMENTS

Article 5

1 The judgments referred to in Article 2 of the courts in the territory of one High Contracting Party shall be enforced in the territory of the other in the manner provided in Articles 6–8 of this chapter of the present Convention provided that the following conditions are fulfilled:—
(a) They are capable of being executed in the country of the original court;
(b) A definite sum of money is made payable thereby, other than a sum of money payable for any form of taxation, State or Municipal, or for any form of penalty;
(c) None of the objections set out in the preceding chapter to the recognition of the judgment can be established.

2 Where a judgment is rendered enforceable the costs recoverable under the judgment shall also be enforceable. Nevertheless the court applied to may on the application of judgment debtor limit the amount of the costs to a sum equal to 10 per cent of the sum for which the judgment is rendered enforceable.

Article 6

1 In order that any judgment of a superior court in the territory of the French Republic should be enforced in the United Kingdom, an application for its registration, accompanied by a certified copy of the judgment issued by the original court, including the reasons therefor and full particulars as regards the proceedings, should be made—
(a) In England and Wales, to the High Court of Justice;
(b) In Scotland to the Court of Session, and
(c) In Northern Ireland to the Supreme Court of Judicature, in accordance with the procedure of the court applied to.

2 A judgment bearing the executory formula prescribed by French law shall, in the absence of proof to the contrary, be deemed to the capable of execution in France within the meaning of Article 5, para 1(a). The formula at present in use is that set out in the annex to the present Convention.

3 If such application is made in respect of a judgment fulfilling the conditions laid down in Article 5, registration shall be granted, unless—

(a) The judgment debt has been wholly satisfied, or

(b) The right to enforce judgment is not vested in the person by whom the application is made.

Article 7

1 In order that any judgment of a court in the territory of His Majesty should be enforced in France it is necessary that an application for the grant of an exequatur accompanied by a certified copy of the judgment issued by the original court, including full particulars as regards the proceedings and the causes of action in respect of which it was given, should, in accordance with the procedure of the court applied to be duly made in France to the Tribunal of First Instance in whose jurisdiction the judgment debtor has his principal establishment (*domicile*) or any other tribunal competent by French law.

2 Any judgment in respect of which a certified copy has been issued by the original court shall be deemed to have been a judgment which was capable of execution in the country of the original court at the time the certificate was issued.

3 If such application is made in respect of a judgment fulfilling the conditions laid down in Article 5, an exequatur shall be granted unless—

(a) The judgment debt has been wholly satisfied;

(b) The right to enforce the judgment is not vested in the person by whom the application is made.

Article 8

1 Where any judgment has been registered under Article 6, or where an exequatur has been granted in respect of a judgment under Article 7, such judgments shall, as from the date of registration, or grant of exequatur be as regards all questions relating to its execution in the country of the court applied to of the same effect as if it had been a judgment originally given by the court applied to at the date of the registration or of the grant of the exequatur; and the court applied to shall have the same control and jurisdiction over the execution of the judgment as it has over the execution of similar judgments given by itself.

2 Any copy of any judgment certified by the original court and attested with its seal, shall be accepted without the necessity of further legalisation but translations of the documents may be required certified in the manner required by the procedure of the court applied to.

3 While the procedure for the registration of a judgment under Article 6 and the procedure for the grant of an exequatur to a judgment under Article 7 is regulated by the procedure of the country of the court applied to, it is the common intention of the High Contracting Parties that such procedure should be made as simple and rapid as possible. No deposit by way of security for costs or *cautio judicatum solvi* shall be required of any person making application for such registration, or for the grant of an exequatur.

4 A period of not less than six years, unless the law of the court applied to allows a longer period, running from the date of the judgment of the original court, if no proceedings have been taken against the judgment in the country of the original court or from the date of the judgment given in last instance if such proceedings have been taken, shall be allowed by the court applied to for the purpose of making any application for registration or the grant of exequatur.

5 It is understood—

(i) That, if it is found by the court applied to that the judgment whose enforcement is sought by registration under Article 6 or by the grant of an exequatur under Article 7, has been partly but not wholly satisfied by payment, registration or exequatur shall be granted in respect of the unpaid balance provided that the judgment is otherwise one which would be enforceable under the provisions of this Convention;

(ii) That if it is found by the court applied to that a judgment, whose enforcement is sought by registration under Article 6 or by grant of exequatur under Article 7, is one under which sums of money are payable in respect of different heads of claim and that reasons for the refusal of the registration or exequatur exist in respect of some but not of all, the grounds of claim, registration or exequatur shall be granted in respect of the sums of money due under those portions of the judgment to the enforcement of which no objection under the provisions of this Convention is established;

(iii) That, if under a judgment a sum of money is payable, which is expressed in a currency other than that of the country of the court applied to, the law of the country of the court applied to shall determine if, and if so in what manner and in what circumstances, the amount payable under the judgment may or shall be converted into the currency of the country of the court applied to for the purposes of the satisfaction or enforcement of the judgment debt.

6 When granting registration or exequatur the court applied to shall, if so requested by the proper party, include the amount due by way of interest up to the date of the grant of registration or exequatur. If the interest due on the claim up to the date of the judgment has been determined in the judgment of the original court, and a certificate emanating from the original court is produced, specifying the rate of interest due in accordance with the law of the country of the original court, upon the sum for which the judgment is given, the court applied to shall follow the indications so given in determining the amount of the interest. If this is not the case, the party claiming interest may prove what is the sum due under the law of the original court by way of interest on the claim which forms the subject of the judgment. As from the date of registration or exequatur, interest shall be allowed at 4 per cent on the total sum (principal and interest) in respect of which registration or exequatur is granted.

CHAPTER IV—FINAL PROVISIONS

Article 9

The High Contracting Parties agree that any difficulties which may arise in connexion with the interpretation or application of this Convention shall be settled through the diplomatic channel. It is, however, understood that the decisions of their respective courts cannot be reopened.

Article 10

The present Convention, of which the English and French texts are equally authentic, shall be subject to ratification. Ratifications shall be exchanged in Paris. The Convention shall come into force one month after the date on which ratifications are exchanged, and shall remain in force for three years after the date of its coming into force. If neither of the High Contracting Parties shall have given notice through the diplomatic channel to the other, not less than six months before the expiration of the said period of three years, of his intention to terminate the Convention, it shall remain in force until the expiration of six months from the day on which either of the High Contracting Parties shall have given notice to terminate it.

Article 11

1 His Majesty may, by a notification given through His Ambassador at Paris, at any time while the Convention is in force under Article 10, and provided that an agreement has been concluded by an exchange of notes of the points mentioned in paragraph 2 of this article, extend the operation of this Convention to the Channel Islands, the Isle of Man, any of his colonies, overseas territories or protectorates, or any territories under his suzerainty, or any mandated territories in respect of which the mandate is exercised by his Government in the United Kingdom.

2 Prior to any notification of extension in respect of any territory under the preceding paragraph, an agreement shall be concluded between the High Contracting Parties by an exchange of notes as to the courts of the territory concerned, which shall be deemed to be "superior courts" for the purposes of this Convention, and the courts to which application for registration of any judgment shall be made.

3 The date of the coming into force of any extension under this article shall be three months from the date of the notification given under the first paragraph of this article.

4 Either of the High Contracting Parties may, at any time after the expiry of three years from the coming into force of an extension of this Convention to any of the territories referred to in paragraph 1 of this article, terminate such extension on giving six months' notice of termination through the diplomatic channel.

5 The termination of the Convention under Article 10 shall, unless otherwise expressly agreed to by both High Contracting Parties, *ipso facto* terminate it in respect of any territories to which it has been extended under paragraph 1 of this article.

Article 12

1 The French Government may, by a notification given through the Ambassador of the French Republic in London at any time while the Convention is in force under Article 10, and provided that an agreement has been concluded by an exchange of notes on the points mentioned in paragraph 2 of this article, extend the operation of this Convention to Algeria, any colonies or protectorates of the French Republic or any mandated territories administered by the French Government.

2 Prior to any notification of extension in respect of any territory under the preceding paragraph, an agreement shall be concluded between the High Contracting Parties by an exchange of notes as to the courts of the territory concerned, which shall be deemed to be "superior courts" for the purposes of this Convention, and the courts to which application for the grant of exequatur in respect of any judgment or order shall be made.

3 The provisions of paragraphs 3, 4 and 5 of the preceding article shall apply to any territories to which this Convention has been extended under paragraph 1 of this article.

Article 13

1 The High Contracting Parties agree that His Majesty may at any time while the present Convention is in force, either under Article 10 or by virtue of any accession under this article, and provided that an agreement has been first concluded by an exchange of notes on the points mentioned in paragraph 2 of this article, by a notification given through the diplomatic channel accede to the present Convention in respect of any Member of the British Commonwealth of Nations whose Government may desire that such accession should be effected, provided that no notification of accession may be given at any time, when the President of the French Republic has given notice of termination in respect of all the territories of His Majesty to which the Convention applies.

2 Prior to any notification of accession under the preceding paragraph, an agreement shall be concluded between the High Contracting Parties by an exchange of notes as to courts of the country concerned which shall be deemed to be "superior courts" for the purposes of this Convention, and the courts to which an application for the registration of a judgment shall be made.

3 Any such accession shall take effect three months after the date of its notification.

4 After the expiry of three years from the date of the coming into force of any accession under paragraph 1 of this article, either of the High Contracting Parties may, by giving six months' notice of termination through the diplomatic channel, terminate the application of the Convention to any country in respect of which a notification of accession has been given. The termination of the Convention under Article 10 shall not affect its application to any such country.

5 Any notification of accession under paragraph 1 of this article may include any dependency or mandated territory administered by the Government of the country in respect of which such notification of accession is given; and any notice of termination in respect of any such country under paragraph 4 shall apply to any dependency or mandated territory which was included in the notification of accession in respect of that country.

ANNEX
(SEE ARTICLE 6, PARAGRAPH 2)

THE EXECUTORY FORMULA PRESCRIBED BY FRENCH LAW

The text of the executory formula at present in force is laid down by a decree of the 2nd September, 1871, which reads as follows: "Article 2. Les expéditions des jugements, arrêts, mandats de justice, ainsi que les grosses et expéditions des contrats et de tous autres actes susceptibles d'exécution forcée, seront intitulées ainsi qu'il suit:

"République française. Au nom du peuple français," et termineés par la formule suivante:

"En conséquence, le Président de la République française mande et ordonne à tous huissiers sur ce requis de mettre ledit arrêt ou ledit jugement, &c) à exécution, aux procureurs généraux et aux procureurs de la République près les tribunaux de première instance d'y tenir la main, à tous commandants et officiers de la force publique de prêter main-forte lorsqu'ils en seront légalement requis.

"En foi de quoi le présent arrêt (ou jugement, &c) a été signé par ."

PROTOCOL

The undersigned plenipotentiaries, at the moment of signing the Convention between His Majesty the King of Great Britain, Ireland and the British Dominions beyond the Seas, Emperor of India, and the President of the French Republic relating to the Reciprocal Enforcement of Judgments, declare that it is understood that nothing in Article 4 of the said Convention shall be deemed to oblige the French courts to recognise the jurisdiction of a court in the territory of His Majesty in cases relating to contracts of assurance in the cases covered by:—

1. The law of the 2nd January, 1902, relating to jurisdiction in the matter of assurance.
2. Articles 3 and 84 of the law of the 13th July, 1930, relating to contracts of assurance.

This protocol forms an integral part of the Convention to which it refers.

[2009]

RECIPROCAL ENFORCEMENT OF FOREIGN JUDGMENTS (BELGIUM) ORDER IN COUNCIL 1936

(SI 1936/1169)

NOTES

Made: 27 October 1936.
Authority: Foreign Judgments (Reciprocal Enforcement) Act 1933, s 1.
Commencement: 26 November 1936.
This order has been largely superseded by the 1968 Brussels Convention and Council Regulation 44/2001/EC. See Introductory Note at the beginning of this section.

1 This Order may be cited as "The Reciprocal Enforcement of Foreign Judgments (Belgium) Order in Council 1936", and shall come into operation on the 26th November, 1936.

[2010]

2 Part I of the Foreign Judgments (Reciprocal Enforcement) Act 1933 shall extend to Belgium.

[2011]

3 The following courts of Belgium shall be deemed superior courts of Belgium for the purposes of Part I of the Foreign Judgments (Reciprocal Enforcement) Act 1933, that is to say:—

The Court of Cassation;
All Courts of Appeal;
All Tribunals of First Instance;
All Tribunals of Commerce.

[2012]

4 No security for costs shall be required to be given by any person making application for the registration of a judgment of a superior court of Belgium.

[2013]

5 All Belgian judgments which bear the executory formula prescribed by Belgian law shall be deemed to be capable of execution in Belgium at the date when the executory formula was issued. The executory formula at present in force in Belgium is that appended to the Convention signed between His Majesty and His Majesty the King of the Belgians and annexed to this Order.

[2014]

6 If upon an application to register a judgment of a superior court in Belgium, the interest due up to the date of judgment on the claim in respect of which the judgment is given has been determined in the said judgment, or if a certificate given by the original court is produced specifying the rate of interest due under Belgian law upon the sum for which the judgment is given, the said judgment and the said certificate (as the case may be) shall be accepted as conclusive evidence as to the interest due up to the date of the said judgment and as to the rate of interest due under Belgian law upon the sum for which the judgment is given. If the interest due up to the date of judgment on the claim in respect of which the judgment is given has not been determined in the judgment, or if no such certificate is produced, the party applying for registration may prove what is the interest due under the judgment by Belgian law up to the time of registration or what is the rate of interest due under Belgian law upon the sum for which the judgment is given.

[2015]

SCHEDULE

CONVENTION BETWEEN HIS MAJESTY IN RESPECT OF THE UNITED KINGDOM AND HIS MAJESTY THE KING OF THE BELGIANS PROVIDING FOR THE RECIPROCAL ENFORCEMENT OF JUDGMENTS IN CIVIL AND COMMERCIAL MATTERS, WITH PROTOCOL

Article 1

In this Convention:

1 the words "His Majesty the King and Emperor" shall mean His Majesty the King of Great Britain, Ireland and the British Dominions beyond the Seas, Emperor of India;

2 the words "territory of one (or of the other) High Contracting Party" shall be interpreted as meaning:

(a) on the part of His Majesty the King and Emperor, the United Kingdom (England and Wales, Scotland and Northern Ireland), and any territories to which the Convention applies by reason of extensions under Article 11, of accessions under Article 13; and

(b) on the part of His Majesty the King of the Belgians, Belgium and any territories to which the Convention applies by reason of extension under Article 12;

3 the words "superior court" shall be deemed to mean:

(a) in the case of the United Kingdom, the House of Lords, and for England and Wales, the Supreme Court of Judicature (Court of Appeal and High Court of Justice) and the Courts of Chancery of the Counties Palatine of Lancaster and Durham; for Scotland, the Court of Session; and for Northern Ireland, the Supreme Court of Judicature;

(b) and in the case of Belgium, the Court of Cassation, all Courts of Appeal, Tribunals of First Instance and Tribunals of Commerce.

All other Courts in these territories shall be deemed to be "inferior courts" for the purpose of this Convention;

4 the word "judgment" means any decision of a court, however described (judgment, order and the like), by which the rights of the parties are finally determined;

5(a) the words "original court" shall be deemed to mean, in relation to any judgment, the court by which such judgment was given; and the words "court applied to," the court in which it is sought to obtain recognition of a judgment, or to which an application for registration or grant of exequatur is made;

(b) the words "judgment debtor" mean the person against whom the judgment was given in the original court, and include any person against whom such judgment is enforceable in the country of the original court; and the words "judgment creditor" mean the person in whose favour the judgment was given, and include his successor and assigns.

Article 2

1 Judgments pronounced after the date of the entry into force of the present Convention by a superior court in the territory of one High Contracting Party, other than judgments rendered on appeal from inferior courts, shall, whatever the nationality of the judgment creditor or debtor, be recognised and enforced in the territory of the other in the cases and upon the conditions laid down in Articles 3 to 8 inclusive of the present Convention.

2 Nothing in the present Convention shall be deemed to preclude the recognition and enforcement in the territory of one High Contracting Party, in accordance with the municipal law for the time being in force in the country concerned, of judgments pronounced by a court in the territory of the other High Contracting Party, being judgments to which the present Convention does not apply, or judgments given in circumstances where the provisions of the present Convention do not require such recognition or enforcement.

Article 3

1 Judgments in civil and commercial matters, given by any superior court in the territory of one High Contracting Party, and executory in the country of the original court, although still open to proceedings by way of opposition, appeal or setting aside shall, in the courts of the territory of the other, be recognised in all cases where no objection to the judgment can be established on any of the grounds hereinafter enumerated, that is to say, unless:

(a) In the case in question the jurisdiction of the original court is not recognised under the rules of Private International Law with regard to jurisdiction observed by the court applied to;

(b) The judgment was given in default, and the judgment debtor did not appear in the proceedings and satisfies the court applied to that he did not actually acquire knowledge of the proceedings in reasonably sufficient time to act upon it. It is understood that in all cases where it is proved that notice of the proceedings has been duly served on the defendant in conformity with the provisions of Article 3 or 4 of the Convention signed between the High Contracting Parties on the 21st June, 1922, it shall be deemed to be conclusive evidence that the defendant actually acquired knowledge of the proceedings;

(c) The judgment is one which is contrary to the public policy of the country of the court applied to;

(d) The judgment is in respect of a cause of action which had already at the date when it was given, as between the same parties, formed the subject of another judgment which is recognised under the law of the court applied to as final and conclusive;

(e) The judgment has, in the opinion of the court applied to, been obtained by fraud;

(f) In the opinion of the court applied to, the judgment was given against a person, defendant in the proceedings, who under the rules of public international law was entitled to immunity from the jurisdiction of the original court, and did not submit to the jurisdiction of the original court; or is sought to be enforced against a person who is entitled under the rules of public international law to immunity from the jurisdiction of the court applied to;

(g) The judgment debtor satisfies the court applied to that proceedings by way of appeal, opposition or setting aside have been instituted against the judgment in the country of the original court.

It is understood that if such proceedings have not been actually instituted, but the time for lodging an appeal, opposition or application to set aside has not expired under the law of the country of the original court, the court applied to may, if it thinks fit, adjourn its decision on the recognition of the judgment so as to allow the judgment debtor a reasonable opportunity of instituting such proceedings.

2 Recognition of a judgment shall not be refused merely on the ground that the original court has applied, in the choice of the system of law applicable to the case, rules of Private International Law different from those observed by the court applied to.

3 The recognition of a judgment under paragraph 1 of this article means that such judgment shall be treated as conclusive as to the matter thereby adjudicated upon in any further action as between the parties (judgment creditor and judgment debtor), and as to such matter shall constitute a defence against further action between them in respect of the same cause of action.

Article 4

1 Notwithstanding the provisions of Article 3, 1(a) and without prejudice to the provisions of paragraphs 2 and 3 of the present article, the original court shall be recognised as possessing jurisdiction in all cases:

(a) where the judgment debtor was in respect of the matter, which is the subject of the judgment, a plaintiff or counter-claimant in the proceedings in the original court;

(b) where the judgment debtor, being a defendant in the proceedings in the original court, submitted to the jurisdiction by voluntarily appearing in the proceedings. It is understood that the expression "voluntarily appearing in the proceedings" does not include an appearance merely for the purpose of protecting property situated within the jurisdiction of the original court from seizure, or of obtaining the release of property seized, or for the purpose of contesting the jurisdiction of the original court;

(c) where the judgment debtor, being a defendant in the proceedings in the original court, had before the commencement of the proceedings agreed, in respect of the subject matter of the proceedings, to submit to the jurisdiction of the original court or of the courts of the country of the original court;

(d) where, at the time when the proceedings were instituted, the judgment debtor, being a defendant in the original court, was resident in the country of the original court, or, being a company or other body corporate, had its head office in the country of the original court;

(e) where the judgment debtor, being a defendant in the original court, had, within the country of the original court, either a commercial establishment or a branch office, and the proceedings were in respect of a transaction effected through, or at, such establishment or branch office.

Nevertheless, the jurisdiction of the original court shall not be recognised in the cases referred to in sub-paragraphs (d) and (e) above if the judgment debtor satisfies the court applied to that the bringing of the proceedings in the original court was contrary to an agreement between the parties under which the dispute in question was to be settled otherwise than by proceedings in the courts of the country of the original court.

2 The provisions of paragraph 1 of this article do not apply to judgments where the subject matter of the proceedings is immovable property, nor to judgments *in rem* in respect of movable property. Nevertheless, in these cases the jurisdiction of the original court shall be recognised if such property was situated within the country of the original court.

3 The provisions of paragraph 1 of this article do not apply:

(a) to judgments in matters of family law or status (including divorces or other judgments in matrimonial causes);

(b) to judgments in matters of succession, or the administration of the estates of deceased persons;

(c) to judgments in bankruptcy proceedings, or proceedings for the winding up of companies or other bodies corporate.

In the case of judgments given in proceedings of the kind referred to in the present paragraph, the jurisdiction of the original court shall be recognised in all cases where such recognition is in accordance with the rules of Private International Law observed by the court applied to.

4 Recognition of the jurisdiction of the original court shall not be refused on the ground that the original court had no jurisdiction under the law of its own country, if the judgment is executory in the country of the original court.

Article 5

1 Judgments, to which the present article applies, given by a superior court in the territory of one High Contracting Party shall be enforced by the courts of the territory of the other High Contracting Party in the manner and upon the conditions set out in Articles 6 to 8 inclusive.

2 The judgments to which the present article applies are judgments in civil or commercial matters, including judgments for the payment of a sum of money as compensation upon the claim of an injured party appearing as "partie civile" in criminal proceedings,

(a) which are capable of being executed in the country of the original court although still open to proceedings by way of opposition, appeal or setting aside;
(b) whereby a definite sum of money is made payable, including judgments for the payment of costs in civil or commercial matters;
(c) to the recognition of which none of the objections set out in Article 3 can be established.

3 The provisions of this article do not apply to judgments for the payment of a sum of money for any form of taxation, State or Municipal, or for the payment of penalties.

Article 6

1 In order that any judgment of a superior court in the territory of His Majesty the King and Emperor should be enforced in Belgium, it is necessary that an application for the grant of an exequatur accompanied by a certified copy of the judgment issued by the original court, including full particulars as regards the proceedings and the causes of action in respect of which it was given, should be made in Belgium, in accordance with the procedure of the court applied to, to the Tribunal of First Instance of the district where the execution is sought.

2 Any judgment in respect of which a certified copy has been issued by the original court shall be deemed to have been a judgment which was capable of execution in the country of the original court at the time the certified copy was issued.

3 If such application is made, exequatur shall be granted unless the judgment debtor satisfies the court applied to:

(a) that the judgment debt has been wholly satisfied, or
(b) that the right to enforce the judgment debt is not vested in the person by whom the application is made.

Article 7

1 In order that any judgment of a superior court in the territory of His Majesty the King of the Belgians should be enforced in the United Kingdom, it is necessary that an application for its registration accompanied by a certified copy of the judgment issued by the original court, including the reasons therefor, should be duly made:

(a) in England and Wales to the High Court of Justice;
(b) in Scotland to the Court of Session;
(c) in Northern Ireland to the Supreme Court of Judicature, in accordance with the procedure of the Court applied to.

2 All Belgian judgments which bear the executory formula prescribed by Belgian law shall be deemed to be capable of execution in Belgium within the meaning of Article 5, 2(a). The formula at present in force is that set out in the Annex to the present Convention.

3 If such application is made, registration shall be granted unless the judgment debtor satisfies the court applied to:

(a) that the judgment debt has been wholly satisfied, or
(b) that the right to enforce the judgment debt is not vested in the person by whom the application is made.

Article 8

1 Where an exequatur has been granted in respect of any judgment under Article 6, or where any judgment has been registered under Article 7, such judgment shall, as from the date of registration or grant of exequatur, be as regards all questions relating to its execution in the country of the court applied to in the same position as a judgment originally given by the court applied to at the date of registration or grant of exequatur, and the court applied to shall have the same control and jurisdiction over the judgment, in so far as related to its execution, as it has over similar judgments given by itself.

2 A copy of any judgment, certified by the original court, and attested with its seal, shall be accepted without the necessity of further legalisation.

3 The procedure for the registration of a judgment under Article 7, and the procedure for the grant of an exequatur to a judgment under Article 6 shall be simple and summary, and no deposit by way of security for costs or *cautio judicatum solvi* shall be required of any person making application for such registration, or for the grant of an exequatur.

4 A period of not less than six years, running from the date of the judgment of the original court, if no proceedings have been taken against the judgment in the country of the original court, or from the date of the judgment given in the last instance if such proceedings have been taken, shall be allowed for the purpose of making an application for registration under Article 7 or for the grant of an exequatur under Article 6.

5 It is understood—

(1) that, if it is found by the court applied to that the judgment debt, whose enforcement is sought by registration under Article 7 or by exequatur under Article 6 has been partly but not wholly satisfied, registration or exequatur shall be granted so as to permit of its execution in respect of the unpaid balance provided that the judgment is otherwise one which satisfies the conditions laid down in the present Convention;

(2) that, if it is found by the court applied to that a judgment, whose enforcement is sought by registration under Article 7 or by exequatur under Article 6, is one under which sums of money are payable in respect of different heads of claim, and that reasons for the refusal of the registration or executory declaration exist in respect of some, but not of all, the grounds of claim, registration or exequatur shall be granted in respect of the sums of money due under those portions of the judgment to the enforcement of which on objection under the provisions of this Convention is established;

(3) that, if under a judgment a sum of money is payable, which is expressed in a currency other than that of the country of the court applied to, the law of the country of the court applied to shall determine if, and if so in what manner, the amount payable under the judgment may or shall be converted into the currency of the court applied to for the purposes of the satisfaction or enforcement of the judgment debt.

6 When granting registration or exequatur, the court applied to shall, if so requested by the proper party, include the amount due by way of interest up to the date of the grant of registration or exequatur. If the interest due on the claim up to the date of the judgment has been determined in the judgment of the original court, and a certificate is produced emanating from the original court, specifying the rate at which, in accordance with the law of the country of the original court, interest should be allowed as from that date upon the sum for which the judgment is given, the court applied to shall follow the indications so given in determining the amount of the interest. If this is not the case, the party claiming interest may prove what is the sum due under the law of the original court by way of interest on the claim which forms the subject of the judgment.

As from the date of registration or exequatur, interest shall be allowed at 4 per cent on the total sum (principal and interest) in respect of which registration or exequatur is granted.

Article 9

Any difficulties which may arise in connexion with the interpretation of this Convention shall be settled through the diplomatic channel.

It is, however, understood that the decisions of the respective courts of the territories of the High Contracting Parties cannot be reopened.

Article 10

The present Convention, of which the English and French texts are equally authentic, shall be subject to ratification. Ratifications shall be exchanged in London.

The Convention shall come into force one month after the date on which ratifications are exchanged, and shall remain in force for three years after the date of its coming into force. If neither of the High Contracting Parties shall have given notice through the diplomatic channel to the other not less than six months before the expiration of the said period of three years of his intention to terminate the Convention, it shall remain in force until the expiration of six months from the day on which either of the High Contracting Parties shall have given notice to terminate it.

Article 11

1 His Majesty the King and Emperor may at any time, while the Convention is in force under Article 10, and provided that an agreement has been first concluded by an exchange of notes on the points mentioned in paragraph 2 of this article, by a notification given through His Ambassador at Brussels, extend the operation of this Convention to the Channel Islands, the Isle of Man, any of His Colonies, overseas territories or Protectorates, or to any territories under His suzerainty, or to any mandated territories in respect of which the mandate is exercised by His Government in the United Kingdom.

2 Prior to any notification of extension in respect of any territory under the preceding paragraph, an agreement shall be concluded between the High Contracting Parties by exchange of notes as to the courts of the territory concerned which shall be deemed to be "superior courts" for the purpose of the Convention, and the courts to which application for registration of any judgment shall be made.

3 The date of the coming into force of any such extension shall be one month from the date of such notification.

4 Either of the High Contracting Parties may, at any time after the expiry of three years from the coming into force of an extension of this Convention to any of the territories referred to in paragraph 1 of this article, terminate such extension on giving six months' notice of termination through the diplomatic channel.

5 The termination of the Convention under Article 10 shall, unless otherwise expressly agreed to by both High Contracting Parties, *ipso facto* terminate it in respect of any territories to which it has been extended under paragraph 1 of this article.

Article 12

1 His Majesty the King of the Belgians may at any time, while the Convention is in force under Article 10, and provided that an agreement has been first concluded by an exchange of notes on the points mentioned in paragraph 2 of this article, extend this Convention to the Belgian Congo or to the mandated territories administered by Belgium by a notification given through His Ambassador in London.

2 Prior to any notification of extension in respect of any territory under the preceding paragraph, an agreement shall be concluded between the High Contracting Parties by exchange of notes as to the courts of the territory concerned which shall be deemed to be "superior courts" for the purposes of the present Convention, and the Courts to which application for the grant of an exequatur in respect of any judgment shall be made.

3 The provisions of paragraphs 3, 4 and 5 of Article 11 shall apply to any of the territories above mentioned to which this Convention has been extended.

Article 13

1 The High Contracting Parties agree that His Majesty the King and Emperor may, at any time, while the present Convention is in force, either under Article 10 or by virtue of any accession under this article, and provided that an agreement has been concluded by an exchange of notes on the points mentioned in paragraph 2 of this article, by a notification given through the diplomatic channel, accede to the present Convention in respect of any other member of the British Commonwealth of Nations whose Government may desire that such accession should be effected, provided that no notification of accession may be given at any time when His Majesty the King of the Belgians has given notice of termination in respect of all the territories of His Majesty the King and Emperor to which the Convention applies.

2 Prior to any notification of accession under the preceding paragraph an agreement shall be concluded between the High Contracting Parties by an exchange of notes as to the courts in the country concerned which shall be deemed to be "superior courts" for the purposes of the present Convention, and the courts to which application for registration of any judgments shall be made.

3 Any such accession shall take effect one month after the date of the notification.

4 After the expiry of three years from the date of the coming into force of any accession under paragraph 1 of this article, either of the High Contracting Parties may, by giving a six months' notice of termination through the diplomatic channel, terminate the application of the Convention to any country in respect of which a notification of accession has been given. The termination of the Convention under Article 10 shall not affect its application to any such country.

5 Any notification of accession under paragraph 1 of this article may include any dependency or mandated territory administered by the Government of the country in respect of which such notification of accession is given; and any notice of termination in respect of any such country under paragraph 4 shall apply to any dependency or mandated territory which was included in the notification of accession in respect of that country.

The undersigned Plenipotentiaries at the moment of signing the Convention between His Majesty the King of Great Britain, Ireland and the British Dominions beyond the Seas, Emperor of India, and His Majesty the King of the Belgians, relating to the Reciprocal Enforcement of Judgments, declare that it is understood that nothing in Article 4 of the said Convention shall be deemed to oblige the Belgian courts to recognise the jurisdiction of a court in the territory of His Majesty the King and Emperor in cases relating to contracts of assurance where the assured are persons of Belgian nationality and exclusive jurisdiction is conferred on the Belgian courts by Article 1 of the Belgian law of the 20th April, 1920 (which article is incorporated as Article 43 *bis* in the Belgian law of the 25th March, 1876, relating to the jurisdiction of the Belgian courts).

This Protocol shall be deemed to be an integral part of the Convention to which it relates.
[2016]

RECIPROCAL ENFORCEMENT OF JUDGMENTS (PAKISTAN) ORDER 1958

(SI 1958/141)

NOTES

Made: 28 January 1958.
Authority: Foreign Judgments (Reciprocal Enforcement) Act 1933, s 1.
Commencement: 28 January 1958.
By virtue of the Pakistan Act 1990, Schedule, para 8, the operation of this Order is not affected by any change in the status of Pakistan since the making of this Order; see further the introductory note "Modification" to the Reciprocal Enforcement of Judgments (General Application to His Majesty's Dominions, etc) Order 1933, SI 1933/1073, at **[2001]**.

1 This Order may be cited as the Reciprocal Enforcement of Judgments (Pakistan) Order, 1958.

[2017]

2 The Reciprocal Enforcement of Judgments (Pakistan) Order 1953, is hereby revoked provided that in relation to judgments given before the date of this Order the High Courts of Dacca and Lahore, the Chief Court at Karachi and the Judicial Commissioners' Courts at Peshawar and Quetta shall continue to be deemed to be Superior Courts for the purposes of Part I of the Act.

[2018]

3 Part I of the Act shall extend to all the territories of Pakistan.

[2019]

4 The following Courts of Pakistan shall be deemed Superior Courts for the purposes of Part I of the Act, that is to say—

(a) The Supreme Court of Pakistan and all High Courts.

(b) All District Courts.

(c) All other Courts whose civil jurisdiction is subject to no pecuniary limit provided that the Judgment sought to be registered under the Act is sealed with a seal showing that the jurisdiction of the Court is subject to no pecuniary limit.

[2020]

RECIPROCAL ENFORCEMENT OF JUDGMENTS (INDIA) ORDER 1958

(SI 1958/425)

NOTES

Made: 14 March 1958.
Authority: Foreign Judgments (Reciprocal Enforcement) Act 1933, s 1.
Commencement: 1 April 1958.

1 This Order may be cited as the Reciprocal Enforcement of Judgments (India) Order, 1958, and shall come into operation on the first day of April, 1958.

[2021]

2 The Reciprocal Enforcement of Judgments (India) Order, 1953, is hereby revoked provided that it shall continue to have effect in relation to judgments given before the coming into operation of this Order.

[2022]

3 Part I of the Act shall extend to the territories of India named in the Schedule hereto.

[2023]

4 The following Courts of the said territories shall be deemed Superior Courts of the said territories for the purposes of Part I of the said Act, that is to say—

(a) The Supreme Court.

(b) All High Courts and Judicial Commissioners' Courts.

(c) All District Courts.

(d) All other Courts whose civil jurisdiction is subject to no pecuniary limit provided that the Judgment sought to be registered under the said Act is sealed with a seal showing that the jurisdiction of the Courts is subject to no pecuniary limit.

[2024]

THE SCHEDULE

(1) The States of Andhra Pradesh (excepting the Scheduled Areas), Assam (except the Tribal Areas), Bihar, Bombay, Kerala, Madhya Pradesh, Madras, Mysore, Orissa, Punjab, Rajasthan, Uttar Pradesh and West Bengal.

(2) The Union Territories of Delhi, Himachal Pradesh, Tripura, Manipur and Andaman and Nicobar Islands.

[2025]

RECIPROCAL ENFORCEMENT OF FOREIGN JUDGMENTS (GERMANY) ORDER 1961

(SI 1961/1199)

NOTES

Made: 26 June 1961.
Authority: Foreign Judgments (Reciprocal Enforcement) Act 1933, s 1.
Commencement: 15 July 1961.
This order has been largely superseded by the 1968 Brussels Convention and Council Regulation 44/2001/EC. See Introductory Note at the beginning of this section.

1 Part I of the Foreign Judgments (Reciprocal Enforcement) Act, 1933, shall extend to the Federal Republic of Germany and to Land Berlin (West Berlin). References in this Order to the Federal Republic of Germany shall be deemed to include references to Land Berlin (West Berlin).

[2026]

2 The following courts of the Federal Republic of Germany shall be deemed superior courts of the Federal Republic of Germany for the purposes of Part I of the Foreign Judgments (Reciprocal Enforcement) Act, 1933, that is to say:—

The Landgerichte;
The Oberlandesgerichte (including the Kammergericht);
The Bayerische Oberste Landesgericht;
The Bundesgerichtshof.

[2027]

3 No security for costs shall be required to be given by any person making application for the registration of a judgment of a superior court of the Federal Republic of Germany.

[2028]

4 A judgment of a superior court in the Federal Republic of Germany shall be deemed to be capable of execution in the Federal Republic of Germany if a certificate issued by an officer of the original court is produced to that effect, but not otherwise.

[2029]

5 The rate of interest due under the law of the Federal Republic of Germany upon the sum in respect of which a judgment of a superior court of the Federal Republic of Germany is given shall be deemed to be that specified in the judgment or any certificate of the original court accompanying the judgment and, if no rate is so specified, no interest shall be deemed to be due thereon under the law of the Federal Republic of Germany.

[2030]

6 A translation of the judgment of a superior court of the Federal Republic of Germany or of any other document accompanying an application for registration of such a judgment may, if certified by a sworn translator or by a diplomatic or consular officer of either the United Kingdom or the Federal Republic of Germany, be accepted without further authentication.

[2031]

7 If before October 15, 1961, the Government of the Federal Republic of Germany shall have delivered a declaration to the Government of the United Kingdom of Great Britain and Northern Ireland that the said Convention shall not apply to Land Berlin (West Berlin), Part I of the Foreign Judgments (Reciprocal Enforcement) Act, 1933, shall not extend to Land Berlin (West Berlin).

[2032]

8 This Order may be cited as the Reciprocal Enforcement of Foreign Judgments (Germany) Order, 1961, and shall come into operation on the 15th day of July, 1961.

[2033]

SCHEDULE

CONVENTION BETWEEN THE UNITED KINGDOM OF GREAT BRITAIN AND NORTHERN IRELAND AND THE FEDERAL REPUBLIC OF GERMANY FOR THE RECIPROCAL RECOGNITION AND ENFORCEMENT OF JUDGMENTS IN CIVIL AND COMMERCIAL MATTERS

Her Majesty the Queen of the United Kingdom of Great Britain and Northern Ireland and of Her Other Realms and Territories, Head of the Commonwealth and the President of the Federal Republic of Germany,

Desiring to provide on the basis of reciprocity for the recognition and enforcement of judgements in civil and commercial matters;

Have resolved to conclude a Convention for this purpose and to that end have appointed as their Plenipotentiaries:

Her Majesty The Queen of the United Kingdom of Great Britain and Northern Ireland and of Her Other Realms and Territories, Head of the Commonwealth, (hereinafter referred to as Her Majesty The Queen):

For the United Kingdom of Great Britain and Northern Ireland:

His Excellency Sir Christopher Eden Steel, GCMG, MVO, Her Majesty's Ambassador Extraordinary and Plenipotentiary at Bonn,

The President of the Federal Republic of Germany:

Dr Albert Hilger van Scherpenberg, State-Secretary of the Federal Foreign Office, and Professor Dr Arthur Bulow, Ministerialdirigent in the Federal Ministry of Justice;

who, having communicated to each other their respective full powers found in good and due form, have agreed as follows:

Article I

For the purposes of the present Convention:

(1) The words "territory of one (or of the other) High Contracting Party" shall mean:

(a) in relation to Her Majesty The Queen, the United Kingdom (England and Wales, Scotland and Northern Ireland) and any territories to which the Convention may have been extended under Article XII, and

(b) in relation to the President of the Federal Republic of Germany, the territory of the Federal Republic of Germany.

(2) The words "superior court" shall mean:

(a) in the case of the United Kingdom, the House of Lords; and for England and Wales, the Supreme Court of Judicature (Court of Appeal and High Court of Justice) and the courts of Chancery of the Counties Palatine of Lancaster and Durham; for Scotland, the Court of Session and the Sheriff Courts; and for Northern Ireland, the Supreme Court of Judicature; and

(b) in the case of the Federal Republic of Germany, the Landgerichte, the Oberlandesgerichte, the Bayerische Oberste Landesgericht and the Bundesgerichtshof.

All other courts in these territories shall be "inferior courts" for the purposes of this Convention.

(3) The word "judgments" shall mean all decisions of a court, however described (ie, judgments, orders and the like), by which the rights of the parties are finally decided, and shall include gerichtliche Vergleiche, but shall not include orders for anticipatory seizure (Arrestbefehle), or other decisions by which only a provisional security is obtained for a claim or other interlocutory orders. The rights of the parties shall be deemed to be finally decided, notwithstanding that an appeal may be pending against the judgment or that it may still be subject to appeal in the courts of the country of the original court.

(4) The words "original court" shall mean, in relation to any judgment, the court by which such judgment was given; and the words "court or authority applied to", the court or authority in which it is sought to obtain recognition of a judgment or to which an application for the enforcement of a judgment is made.

PART III
STATUTORY INSTRUMENTS

(5) The words "judgment debtor" shall mean the person against whom the judgment was given in the original court and include any person who has succeeded to the liability under the judgment by the law of the country of the original court; and the words "judgment creditor", the person in whose favour the judgment was given and include his successors and assigns.

(6) The words "judgments in civil and commercial matters" shall not be deemed to include judgments given in proceedings for the recovery of any form of taxation (state or municipal) or for the recovery of penalties, but shall be deemed to include judgments given or made by a court in any criminal proceedings for the payment of a sum of money in respect of compensation or damages to an injured party.

(7) The word "appeal" shall include any proceedings by way of discharging or setting aside a judgment or an application for a new trial or a stay of execution.

(8) The words "action in personam" shall not be deemed to include any action in matters of family law or status (including divorces or other proceedings in matrimonial causes) or any proceedings in matters of succession or the administration of the estates of deceased persons.

Article II

(1) Judgments pronounced by a superior court in the territory of one High Contracting Party, other than judgments given on appeal from inferior courts, shall, whatever the nationality of the judgment creditor or debtor, be recognised and enforced in the territory of the other in the cases and upon the conditions laid down in Articles III to IX inclusive of the present Convention.

(2) Nevertheless the provisions of the present Convention shall not apply to judgments in bankruptcy proceedings or proceedings for the winding up of companies or other bodies corporate.

(3) Nothing in the present Convention shall be deemed to preclude the recognition and enforcement in the territory of one High Contracting Party, in accordance with the municipal law for the time being in force in the country concerned, of judgments pronounced by any court in the territory of the other High Contracting Party being judgments to which the present Convention does not apply, or judgments given in circumstances where the provisions of the present Convention do not require such recognition or enforcement.

Article III

(1) Judgments in civil and commercial matters, given after the date of the entry into force of the present Convention by any superior court in the territory of one High Contracting Party, shall be recognised in the territory of the other in all cases where there is no adjournment of the decision on the recognition of the judgment under paragraph (2) of this Article and where no objection to the judgment can be established on any of the grounds hereinafter enumerated: that is to say, unless:

(a) in the case in question, the jurisdiction of the original court is not recognised under the provisions of Article IV;

(b) the judgment was given by default, and the judgment debtor did not appear in the proceedings and satisfies the court or authority applied to that he did not actually acquire knowledge of the proceedings in reasonably sufficient time to act upon it. It is understood that in all cases where it is proved that notice of the proceedings has been duly served on the defendant in conformity with the provisions of Article 3 or 5 of the Convention signed between the United Kingdom and Germany on March 20, 1928, it shall be deemed to be conclusive evidence that the defendant actually acquired knowledge of the proceedings;

(c) the judgment is one which, for reasons of public policy, cannot be recognised by the court or authority applied to, including cases where the judgment:

(i) is in respect of a cause of action which had already, at the date of the judgment of the original court, as between the same parties, formed the subject of another judgment which is recognised under the law of the country of the court or authority applied to as final and conclusive;

(ii) has, in the opinion of the court or authority applied to, been obtained by fraud;

(iii) was given against a person, defendant in the proceedings before the original court who, in the opinion of the court or authority applied to, under the rules of public international law was entitled to immunity from the jurisdiction of the original court and did not submit to the jurisdiction of the original court;

(iv) is sought to be enforced against a person who is entitled to immunity from the jurisdiction of the court or authority applied to under the rules of public international law.

(2) Where the judgment debtor satisfies the court or authority applied to that proceedings by way of appeal have been instituted against the judgment in the country of the original court, or that such proceedings have not been actually instituted, but the time for appeal has not elapsed under the law of the country of the original court, the court or authority applied to may nevertheless recognise the judgment or may, if the judgment debtor makes an application to this effect, refuse to recognise the judgment or adjourn its decision on the recognition of the judgment so as to allow the judgment debtor a reasonable opportunity of completing or of instituting such proceedings.

(3) The recognition of a judgment shall not be refused merely on the ground that the original court has applied, in the choice of the system of law applicable to the case, rules of private international law different from those observed by the court or authority applied to.

(4) The recognition of a judgment means that such judgment shall be treated as conclusive as to the matter thereby adjudicated upon in any further action between the parties (judgment creditor and judgment debtor) and as to such matter shall constitute a defence in any further action between them in respect of the same cause of action.

Article IV

(1) For the purposes of sub-paragraph (a) of paragraph (1) of Article III the courts of the country of the original court shall be recognised as possessing jurisdiction:

(a) in the case of a judgment given in an action in personam:

(i) where the judgment debtor was a plaintiff or counter-claimant in the proceedings in the original court;

(ii) where the judgment debtor, being a defendant in the proceedings in the original court, submitted to the jurisdiction by voluntarily appearing in the proceedings. It is understood that the expression "voluntarily appearing in the proceedings" does not include an appearance merely for the purpose of protecting property situated in the country of the original court from seizure, or of obtaining the release of property seized, or for the purpose of contesting the jurisdiction of the original court;

(iii) where before the commencement of the proceedings the judgment debtor, being a defendant in the proceedings in the original court, had agreed, in respect of the subject matter of the proceedings, to submit to the jurisdiction of the courts of the country of the original court, or of the original court;

(iv) where the judgment debtor, being a defendant in the original court, was, at the time when the proceedings were instituted, resident in the country of the original court or, being a company or other body corporate, had its principal place of business in the country of the original court;

(v) where the judgment debtor, being a defendant in the original court, had either a commercial establishment or a branch office within the country of the original court, and the proceedings were in respect of a transaction effected through, or at, such establishment or branch office;

(b) in the case of a judgment given in an action of which the subject matter was immovable property or in an action in rem of which the subject matter was movable property, if such property at the time of the commencement of the proceedings in the original court was situated within the country of the original court;

(c) in the case of a judgment given in an action other than any such action as is mentioned in sub-paragraphs (a) and (b) of this paragraph (such as judgments in matters of family law or status, including divorces or other judgments in matrimonial causes, judgments in matters of succession or the administration of the estates of deceased persons), if the jurisdiction of the original court is recognised by the law observed by the court or authority applied to.

(2) The jurisdiction of the original court need not be recognised if the subject matter of the proceedings was immovable property outside the country of the original court.

(3) The jurisdiction of the original court need not be recognised in the cases specified in sub-paragraphs (a)(iv), (a)(v) and (b) of paragraph (1) of this Article, if the judgment debtor satisfies the court or authority applied to that the bringing of the proceedings in the original court was contrary to an agreement between the parties under which the dispute in question was to be settled otherwise than by proceedings in the courts of the country of the original court.

(4) Recognition of the jurisdiction of the original court shall not be refused on the ground that the original court had no jurisdiction under the law of its own country, if under the law of the country of the original court the judgment is conclusive unless and until the proper proceedings are taken to set it aside.

Article V

(1) Judgments, to which the present Article applies, given by a superior court in the territory of one High Contracting Party shall be enforced by the courts in the territory of the other High Contracting Party in the manner and upon the conditions set out in Articles VI to IX inclusive:

provided that, where the judgment debtor satisfies the court applied to that proceedings by way of appeal have been instituted against the judgment in the country of the original court, or that such proceedings have not been actually instituted, but the time for appeal has not elapsed under the law of the country of the original court, such judgments need not be enforced and the court applied to may take such measures with regard thereto as are permitted by its own law.

(2) The judgments to which the present Article applies are judgments:

(a) given in civil or commercial matters after the date of the coming into force of the present Convention;
(b) which are capable of being executed in the country of the original court;
(c) whereby a definite sum of money is made payable, including judgments for the payment of costs in civil or commercial matters;
(d) to the recognition of which none of the objections set out in Article III (read in conjunction with Article IV) can be established.

(3) If the amount of the costs to be paid under a judgment is not fixed by the judgment itself but by a separate order, such order shall be deemed to be part of the judgment for the purposes of this Convention.

Article VI

(1) In order that any judgment of a court in the territory of the Federal Republic of Germany should be enforced in the United Kingdom, an application by a judgment creditor for its registration should be made:

(a) in England and Wales to the High Court of Justice,
(b) in Scotland to the Court of Session,
(c) in Northern Ireland to the Supreme Court of Judicature,

in accordance with the procedure of the court applied to.

(2) The application for registration should be accompanied by:

(a) a certified copy of the judgment issued by the original court including the reasons therefor, or, where such reasons are not available, being accompanied by a document issued by the original court containing full particulars as regards the proceedings and the causes of action in respect of which the judgment was given, and
(b) a certificate issued by an officer of the original court that it is capable of execution in the country of the original court.

(3) The certified copy and certificate referred to in paragraph (2) of this Article shall be accepted by the court applied to without requiring further legalisation, but translations of such documents certified by a sworn translator or by a diplomatic or consular officer of either High Contracting Party shall be provided.

Article VII

(1) In order that any judgment of a court in the territory of Her Majesty The Queen should be enforced in the territory of the Federal Republic of Germany, an application for an executory declaration should be duly made in the Federal Republic of Germany to the Landgericht in whose jurisdiction the judgment debtor resides or possesses property, in accordance with the procedure of the court applied to.

(2) The application for the grant of an executory declaration should be accompanied by:
- (a) a certified copy of the judgment issued by the original court, and
- (b) a document issued by the original court containing full particulars as regards the proceedings and the causes of action in respect of which the judgment was given.

(3) Any judgment in respect of which a certified copy has been issued by the original court shall be deemed to have been a judgment which was capable of execution in the country of the original court at the time the certificate was issued.

(4) The certified copy and document, referred to in paragraph (2) of this Article, shall be accepted by the court applied to without requiring further legalisation, but translations thereof certified by a sworn translator or by a diplomatic or consular officer of either High Contracting Party shall be provided.

Article VIII

(1) The registration of a judgment under Article VI, or the grant of an executory declaration under Article VII, shall be refused, or if granted shall be set aside, if the judgment debtor satisfies the court applied to:
- (a) that, after the original court had given its judgment, the debt due under the judgment whose enforcement is sought had been satisfied by payment or otherwise, or
- (b) that the right to enforce the judgment is not vested in the person by whom the application is made.

(2) If upon such application being made, it is found by the court applied to:
- (a) that the debt due under the judgment whose enforcement is sought has become partly satisfied by payment or otherwise, or
- (b) that the judgment whose enforcement is sought is one under which sums of money are payable in respect of different heads of claim and that reasons for the refusal of the registration or executory declaration exist in respect of some, but not of all, the heads of claim,

registration or executory declaration shall be granted, as the case may be:
- (i) in respect of the unsatisfied balance, or
- (ii) in respect of the sums of money due under those portions of the judgment to the enforcement of which no objection based on the provisions of Article V (read in conjunction with Articles III and IV) is established.

Article IX

(1) Where an application is duly made for the registration of a judgment under Article VI or for a grant of an executory declaration under Article VII, the court applied to shall not entertain any objections to the grant of the application other than objections based on the provisions of Article V (read in conjunction with Articles III and IV) or an objection based on the grounds specified in Article VIII, and shall grant the application provided that none of the said objections have been shown to exist.

(2) The procedure for the registration of a judgment under Article VI and the procedure for the grant of an executory declaration under Article VII, shall be simple and summary. No security for costs shall be required of any person making application for such registration, or for the grant of an executory declaration. A period of not less than six years running from the date of the judgment of the original court, if no appeal has been brought to a higher court, or from the date of the judgment of the highest court appealed to, if an appeal has been brought, shall be allowed for the purpose of making any application for the registration or the grant of an executory declaration.

(3) Where a judgment is registered under Article VI or where an executory declaration is granted in respect of a judgment under Article VII, such judgment shall carry in respect of the interval between the date of the judgment of the original court and the date of the registration

or executory declaration, interest at the rate (if any) specified in the judgment or in any certificate of the original court accompanying the judgment. As from the date of the registration or of the executory declaration, interest shall be allowed at 4% per annum on the total sum (principle and interest) in respect of which the registration or executory declaration is granted.

(4) Where any judgment is registered under Article VI by a court in the territory of Her Majesty The Queen, or where an executory declaration is granted under Article VII, such judgment shall, as from the date of registration or executory declaration, be, as regards all questions relating to its execution in the country of the court applied to, in the same position as a judgment originally given by the court applied to.

(5) Where under a judgment a sum of money is payable, which is expressed in a currency other than that of the country of the court applied to, the law of the country of the court applied to shall determine if, and if so in what manner and in what circumstances, the amount payable under the judgment may or shall be converted into the currency of the country of the court applied to for the purposes of the satisfaction or enforcement of the judgment.

Article X

The High Contracting Parties agree that any difficulties which may arise in connexion with the interpretation or application of this Convention shall be settled through the diplomatic channel. It is, however, understood that the decisions of their respective courts cannot be re-opened.

Article XI

(1) The present Convention shall also apply to Land Berlin provided that the Government of the Federal Republic of Germany has not delivered a contrary declaration to the Government of the United Kingdom of Great Britain and Northern Ireland within three months from the date of entry into force of the Convention.

(2) Upon the application of this Convention to Land Berlin, references in the Convention to the Federal Republic of Germany or to the territory thereof shall be deemed also to be references to Land Berlin.

Article XII

(1) Her Majesty The Queen may, by a notification given through Her Ambassador at the seat of the Government of the Federal Republic of Germany, at any time while the present Convention is in force under Article XIII, and provided that an agreement has been concluded by an exchange of notes on the points mentioned in paragraph (2) of this Article, extend the operation of this Convention to any of the territories for the international relations of which Her Majesty's Government in the United Kingdom of Great Britain and Northern Ireland are responsible.

(2) Prior to any notification of extension in respect of any territory under the preceding paragraph, an agreement shall be concluded between the High Contracting Parties by an exchange of notes as to the courts of the territory concerned which shall be deemed to be "superior courts" for the purposes of this Convention, and the courts to which application for registration of any judgment shall be made.

(3) The date of the coming into force of any extension under this Article shall be three months from the date of the notification given under the first paragraph of this Article.

(4) Either of the High Contracting Parties may, at any time after the expiry of three years from the coming into force of an extension of this Convention to any of the territories referred to in paragraph (1) of this Article, terminate such extension on giving six months' notice of termination through the diplomatic channel.

(5) The termination of the Convention under Article XIII shall, unless otherwise expressly agreed to by both High Contracting Parties, ipso facto terminate it in respect of any territories to which it has been extended under paragraph (1) of this Article.

Article XIII

The present Convention shall be subject to ratification. Instruments of Ratification shall be exchanged in London. The Convention shall come into force one month after the date on which Instruments of Ratification are exchanged, and shall remain in force for three years after the date of its coming into force. If neither of the High Contracting Parties shall have given notice through the diplomatic channel to the other not less than six months before the expiration of the said period of three years of an intention to terminate the Convention, it shall remain in force until the expiration of six months from the day on which either of the High Contracting Parties shall have given notice to terminate it.

PROTOCOL OF SIGNATURE

At the same time of signing the Convention of this day's date between Her Majesty The Queen of the United Kingdom of Great Britain and Northern Ireland and of Her Other Realms and Territories, Head of the Commonwealth and the President of the Federal Republic of Germany relating to the reciprocal recognition and enforcement of judgments in civil and commercial matters, the undersigned Plenipotentiaries, being duly authorized thereto, declare that they have agreed that nothing in this Convention shall prevent a court or authority in the territory of the Federal Republic of Germany, in the special cases of Section 328 Paragraph 1 No 3 of the German Code of Civil Procedure, from declining to recognise or enforce any judgment against a German national, if, to the prejudice of the German national, it is not based on the laws which would have been applicable in accordance with German private international law, in respect of:

(a) the contracting of a marriage, if one of the betrothed persons is a German national (Article 13 Paragraph 1 of the Introductory Law to the Civil Code) or if the national law (Heimatrecht) of one of the betrothed persons refers to German law (Article 27 of the Introductory Law to the Civil Code);

(b) the form of a marriage celebrated in the Federal Republic of Germany (Article 13 Paragraph 3 of the Introductory Law to the Civil Code);

(c) divorce (Article 17 of the Introductory Law to the Civil Code);

(d) the legitimacy of a child (Article 18 of the Introductory Law to the Civil Code);

(e) the legitimisation of an illegitimate child (Article 22 of the Introductory Law to the Civil Code);

(f) the adoption of a child (Article 22 of the Introductory Law to the Civil Code).

The same shall apply for the recognition or enforcement of a judgment, if, by such judgment, the remarriage of the German or former German wife of a foreigner who has been declared dead, is not regarded as valid because the declaration of presumption of death effected in the Federal Republic of Germany is not recognised (Section 12 Paragraph 3 of the Missing Persons Law of January 15, 1951, in conjunction with Article 13 Paragraph 2 of the Introductory Law to the Civil Code).

[2034]

RECIPROCAL ENFORCEMENT OF FOREIGN JUDGMENTS (NORWAY) ORDER 1962

(SI 1962/636)

NOTES

Made: 28 March 1962.

Authority: Foreign Judgments (Reciprocal Enforcement) Act 1933, s 1.

Commencement: 6 April 1962.

This Order has been largely superseded by the 1988 Lugano Convention. See the Introductory Note at the beginning of this section.

1 Part I of the Foreign Judgments (Reciprocal Enforcement) Act, 1933, shall extend to the Kingdom of Norway.

[2035]

2 The following courts of the Kingdom of Norway shall be deemed superior courts of the Kingdom of Norway for the purposes of Part I of the Foreign Judgments (Reciprocal Enforcement) Act, 1933, that is to say:—

The Supreme Court;

The Courts of Appeal;
The County Courts;
The City Courts.

[2036]

3 No security for costs shall be required to be given by any person making application for the registration of a judgment of a superior court of the Kingdom of Norway.

[2037]

4 The applicant for the registration of a judgment of a superior court of the Kingdom of Norway shall in the affidavit of facts required by rules of court to support the application for the registration state whether the judgment is capable of execution by provisional execution (avsetning) or by ordinary execution.

[2038]

5 The rate of interest due under the law of the Kingdom of Norway upon the sum in respect of which a judgment of a superior court of the Kingdom of Norway is given shall be deemed to be that specified in the judgment or any certificate of the original court accompanying the judgment and, if no rate is so specified, no interest shall be deemed to be due thereon under the law of the Kingdom of Norway.

[2039]

6 A translation of the judgment of a superior court of the Kingdom of Norway or of any other document accompanying an application for registration of such a judgment shall, if certified by a sworn translator or by a diplomatic or consular officer of either the United Kingdom or the Kingdom of Norway, be accepted without further authentication.

[2040]

7 This Order may be cited as the Reciprocal Enforcement of Foreign Judgments (Norway) Order, 1962, and shall come into operation on the 6th day of April, 1962.

[2041]

SCHEDULE

CONVENTION BETWEEN THE GOVERNMENT OF THE UNITED KINGDOM OF GREAT BRITAIN AND NORTHERN IRELAND AND THE GOVERNMENT OF THE KINGDOM OF NORWAY PROVIDING FOR THE RECIPROCAL RECOGNITION AND ENFORCEMENT OF JUDGMENTS IN CIVIL MATTERS

GENERAL

Article I

For the purposes of the present Convention:

(1) The words "territory of one (or of the other) Contracting Party" mean:

(a) in relation to the United Kingdom of Great Britain and Northern Ireland (hereinafter referred to as "the United Kingdom"), England and Wales, Scotland, and Northern Ireland and any territories to which the Convention shall have been extended under Article X; and

(b) in relation to the Kingdom of Norway, Norway.

(2) The word "judgment" means any decision of a court, however described (judgment, order and the like), by which the rights of the parties are determined and which cannot be altered by that court. It includes judgments against which an appeal may be pending or which may still be subject to appeal in the courts of the country of the original court. If the amount of the costs or interest to be paid under a judgment is not fixed by the judgment itself but by a separate court order, such order shall be deemed to be part of the judgment for the purposes of this Convention.

(3) The words "original court" mean in relation to any judgment the court by which such judgment was given; and the words "court applied to", the court in which it is sought to obtain recognition of a judgment or to which an application for the registration of a judgment or for the acceptance of a judgment as enforceable is made.

(4) The words "judgment debtor" mean the person against whom the judgment was given in the original court and include, where necessary, any person against whom such judgment is enforceable under the law of the country of the original court; and the words "judgment creditor", the person in whose favour the judgment was given, and include, where necessary, any other person in whom the rights under the judgment have become vested.

(5) The word "appeal" includes any proceeding by way of discharging or setting aside a judgment or an application for a new trial or a stay of execution.

Article II

(1) Subject to the provision of paragraph (2) of this Article, the present Convention shall apply to judgments in civil matters and to judgments given or made by a court in any criminal proceedings for the payment of a sum of money in respect of compensation or damages to an injured party, pronounced after the date of the entry into force of the present Convention by the following courts:

(a) in the case of the United Kingdom, the House of Lords; for England and Wales, the Supreme Court of Judicature (Court of Appeal and High Court of Justice) and the Courts of Chancery of the Counties Palatine of Lancaster and Durham; for Scotland, the Court of Session and the Sheriff Court; and for Northern Ireland, the Supreme Court of Judicature; and

(b) in the case of the Kingdom of Norway, the Supreme Court, the Courts of Appeal, the County Courts and City Courts.

(2) The present Convention shall not apply to:

(a) judgments given on appeal from courts not referred to in paragraph (1) of this Article;

(b) judgments in matters of family law or status (including judgments in matrimonial causes or concerning the pecuniary relations between the spouses as such);

(c) judgments given in proceedings for the recovery of taxes or other charges of a like nature or for the recovery of a fine or other penalty.

RECOGNITION OF JUDGMENTS

(3) The present Convention shall not preclude the recognition and enforcement in the territory of one Contracting Party, in accordance with the municipal law for the time being in force in the country concerned, of judgments pronounced by any court in the territory of the other Contracting Party, being judgments to which the present Convention does not apply or judgments given in circumstances where the provisions of the present Convention do not require such recognition or enforcement.

Article III

(1) For the purposes of the present Convention, the recognition of a judgment means that such judgment shall be treated as conclusive as to the matter thereby adjudicated upon in any further action as between the same parties (judgment creditor and judgment debtor).

(2) Judgments pronounced in the territory of one Contracting Party shall be recognised in the territory of the other subject to the provisions of paragraphs (3) and (4) of this Article and where no objection to the judgment can be established on any of the following grounds:

(a) in the case in question, the jurisdiction of the original court is not recognised under the provisions of Article IV;

(b) the judgment debtor, being the defendant in the proceedings in the original court, did not (notwithstanding that process may have been duly served on him in accordance with the law of the country of the original court) receive notice of those proceedings in sufficient time to enable him to defend the proceedings and did not appear. It is understood that in all cases where it is proved that notice of the proceedings has been duly served on the defendant in conformity with the provisions of Article 3 or sub-paragraph (1) or (2) of paragraph (a) of Article 4 of the Convention on Legal Proceedings in Civil and Commercial Matters signed between the United Kingdom and Norway on January 30, 1931, it shall be deemed to be conclusive evidence that the defendant actually received notice of the proceedings;

(c) the judgment was, in the opinion of the court applied to, obtained by fraud;

(d) the recognition of the judgment would be contrary to public policy in the country of the court applied to;

(e) the judgment debtor, being a defendant in the original proceedings, was a person who, under the rules of public international law, was entitled to immunity from the jurisdiction of the courts of the country of the original court and did not submit to the jurisdiction of that court; or the judgment is sought to be enforced against a person who, under the rules of public international law, is entitled to immunity from the jurisdiction of the court applied to.

(3) Where the court applied to is satisfied that proceedings by way of appeal have been instituted against the judgment in the country of the original court, or that such proceedings have not been actually instituted, but the time for appeal has not elapsed under the law of the country of the original court, the court applied to may, in so far as the law of its country permits, recognise the judgment or may refuse to recognise the judgment or adjourn its decision on the recognition of the judgment so as to allow the judgment debtor an opportunity of completing or of instituting such proceedings.

(4) Where the court applied to is satisfied that the matter in dispute in the proceedings in the original court had previously to the date of the judgment in the original court been the subject of a judgment by a court having jurisdiction in the matter, the court applied to may refuse to recognise the judgment of the original court.

Article IV

(1) For the purposes of sub-paragraph (a) of paragraph (2) of Article III, the courts of the country of the original court shall, subject to the provisions of paragraphs (2), (3) and (4) of this Article, be recognised as possessing jurisdiction in all cases:

(a) if the judgment debtor, being a defendant in the proceedings in the original court, submitted to the jurisdiction of that court by voluntarily appearing in the proceedings otherwise than for the purpose of protecting, or obtaining the release of, property seized, or threatened with seizure, in the proceedings or of contesting the jurisdiction of that court; or

(b) if the judgment debtor was plaintiff in, or counter-claimed in, the proceedings in the original court; or

(c) if the judgment debtor, being a defendant in the proceedings in the original court, had before the commencement of the proceedings agreed, in respect of the subject matter of the proceedings, to submit to the jurisdiction of that court or of the courts of the country of that court; or

(d) if the judgment debtor, being a defendant in the original court, was, at the time when the proceedings were instituted, resident in, or being a body corporate had its principal place of business in, the country of that court; or

(e) if the judgment debtor, being a defendant in the original court, had an office or place of business in the country of that court and the proceedings in that court were in respect of a transaction effected through or at that office or place.

(2) The provisions of paragraph (1) of this Article shall not apply to judgments where the subject matter of the proceedings is immovable property, or to judgments in respect of movable property if they are conclusive, not only against the parties to the proceedings, but also against any other person claiming an interest in that property which is inconsistent with the judgment in question. Nevertheless the jurisdiction of the original court shall be recognised if such property was situated in the country of the original court at the time of the commencement of the proceedings in the original court.

(3) The provisions of paragraph (1) of this Article shall not apply to:

(a) judgments in matters of succession, or the administration of the estates of deceased persons;

(b) judgments in bankruptcy proceedings, or proceedings for the winding up of companies or other bodies corporate.

In the case of judgments given in proceedings of the kind referred to in the present paragraph, the jurisdiction of the original court shall be recognised in all cases where such recognition is in accordance with the law of the country of the court applied to.

(4) The jurisdiction of the original court need not be recognised in the cases specified in sub-paragraphs (d) and (e) of paragraph (1), and in paragraph (2) of this Article if the bringing of the proceedings in the original court was contrary to an agreement under which the dispute in question was to be settled otherwise than by proceedings in the courts of the country of that court.

ENFORCEMENT OF JUDGMENTS

(5) Recognition of the jurisdiction of the original court shall not be refused on the ground that the original court had no jurisdiction under the law of its own country if under the law of the country of the original court the judgment is conclusive unless and until the proper proceedings are taken to set it aside.

Article V

Judgments pronounced in the territory of one Contracting Party shall be enforced by execution in the territory of the other in the manner provided in Articles VI–VIII of the present Convention provided that the following conditions are fulfilled:

(a) that they are enforceable by execution (including Avsetning) in the country of the original court;

(b) there is payable thereunder a sum of money whether by way of costs or otherwise;

(c) the judgment debt has not been wholly satisfied;

(d) none of the objections set out in paragraphs (2) and (4) of Article III to the recognition of the judgment can be established;

and provided that, where the court applied to is satisfied that proceedings by way of appeal have been instituted against the judgment in the country of the original court or that such proceedings have not been instituted, but the time for appeal, if any, has not elapsed under the law of the country of the original court, such judgments need not be enforced but the court applied to shall, if so requested and unless the judgment debtor gives security, take such temporary measures in regard thereto as are prescribed by its own law in regard to judgments of the courts of its own country.

Article VI

(1) In order that any judgment pronounced in the Kingdom of Norway should be enforced in the United Kingdom, an application by a judgment creditor for its registration should, in accordance with the procedure of the court applied to, be made:

(a) in England and Wales, to the High Court of Justice;

(b) in Scotland, to the Court of Session; and

(c) in Northern Ireland, to the Supreme Court of Judicature.

(2) The application for registration should be accompanied by:

(a) a certified copy of the complete judgment authenticated by the court seal;

(b) an affidavit of the facts required by the rules of the court applied to including a statement as to whether at the date of the application the judgment can be enforced in Norway by Avsetning or ordinary execution;

(c) a translation of any document required by this paragraph (except any affidavit in English) certified by a sworn translator or by a diplomatic or consular officer of either Contracting Party.

(3) The documents enumerated in paragraph (2) shall require no further authentication.

(4) If an application is made in accordance with paragraphs (1) and (2) of this Article in respect of a judgment fulfilling the conditions laid down in Article V, registration shall be granted.

Article VII

(1) In order that any judgment pronounced in the United Kingdom should be enforced in the Kingdom of Norway, an application by a judgment creditor for its acceptance as enforceable should, in accordance with the procedure of the court applied to, be duly made in Norway to the court of execution in whose jurisdiction the judgment debtor has his principal establishment (bopel) or to any other court competent by Norwegian Law.

(2) The application should be accompanied by:

(a) a certified copy of the judgment authenticated by the court seal, or in the case of judgments of the sheriff court, authenticated by the signature of the sheriff clerk;

(b) a document issued by the original court giving full particulars as regards the proceedings and the causes of action in respect of which it was given and specifying whether at the date of the application the time for appeal has elapsed without any proceedings by way of appeal having been instituted against the judgment in the United Kingdom;

PART III STATUTORY INSTRUMENTS

(c) a translation of any document required by this paragraph certified by a sworn translator or by a diplomatic or consular officer of either Contracting Party.

(3) The documents enumerated in paragraph (2) shall require no further authentication.

(4) If an application is made in accordance with paragraphs (1) and (2) of this Article in respect of a judgment fulfilling the conditions laid down in Article V, it shall be accepted as enforceable.

Article VIII

(1) Where any judgment has been registered under Article VI, or where any judgment has been accepted as enforceable under Article VII, such judgment shall, as from the date of registration or acceptance as enforceable, and as regards all questions relating to its execution in the country of the court applied to be of the same effect as if it had been a judgment originally given in the country of the court applied to and the court applied to shall have the same control and jurisdiction over the execution of the judgment as it has over the execution of similar judgments given in its own country.

(2) The procedure for the registration of a judgment under Article VI and the procedure for the acceptance of a judgment as enforceable under Article VII shall be made as simple and rapid as possible, and no deposit by way of security for costs shall be required of any person making application for such registration, or for the acceptance of a judgment as enforceable.

(3) After a period of six years, running from the date of the judgment of the original court, if no proceedings have been taken against the judgment in the country of the original court, or from the date of the judgment given in the last instance if such proceedings have been taken, there shall be no obligation under the present Convention to enforce that judgment.

(4) If it is found by the court applied to that the judgment, in respect of which an application is made for registration under Article VI or for its acceptance as enforceable under Article VII, has been, at the date of such application, partly but not wholly satisfied by payment, the judgment shall be registered or accepted as enforceable in respect of the balance remaining payable at that date, provided that the judgment is otherwise one which would be enforceable under the provisions of the present Convention.

(5) If it is found by the court applied to that the judgment, in respect of which an application is made for registration under Article VI or for its acceptance as enforceable under Article VII, is in respect of different matters and that some, but not all, of the provisions of the judgment are such that if those provisions had been contained in separate judgments those judgments could properly have been registered or could have been accepted as enforceable, the judgment may be registered or accepted as enforceable in respect of the provisions aforesaid but not in respect of any other provisions contained therein.

(6) If under a judgment a sum of money is payable, which is expressed in a currency other than that of the country of the court applied to, the law of the country of the court applied to shall determine if, and if so, in what manner and in what circumstances, the amount payable under the judgment may or shall be converted into the currency of the country of the court applied to for the purpose of the satisfaction or enforcement of the judgment debt.

FINAL PROVISIONS

(7) When a judgment is registered or accepted as enforceable, there shall, if so requested by the judgment creditor, be included the costs of and incidental to registration or to the application for its acceptance as enforceable and the amount due by way of interest determined in accordance with the law of the country of the court applied to.

Article IX

Any difficulties which may arise in connexion with the interpretation or application of this Convention shall be settled through the diplomatic channel.

Article X

(1) The Government of the United Kingdom may, by a notification given through the diplomatic channel, at any time while the Convention is in force under Article XI, and

provided that an agreement has been concluded by an Exchange of Notes on the points mentioned in paragraph (2) of this Article, extend the operation of this Convention to any territory for whose international relations the Government of the United Kingdom are responsible.

(2) Prior to any notification of extension in respect of any territory under the preceding paragraph, an agreement shall be concluded between the Contracting Parties by an Exchange of Notes as to the courts of the territory concerned, which shall be courts to whose judgment the present shall apply and the courts to which application for registration of any judgment shall be made.

(3) The date of the coming into force of any extension under this Article shall be three months from the date of the notification given under paragraph (1) of this Article.

(4) Either of the Contracting Parties may, at any time after the expiry of three years from the coming into force of an extension of this Convention to any of the territories referred to in paragraph (1) of this Article, terminate such extension on giving six months' notice of termination through the diplomatic channel.

(5) The termination of the Convention under Article XI shall, unless otherwise expressly agreed by both Contracting Parties, *ipso facto* terminate it in respect of any territory to which it has been extended under paragraph (1) of this Article.

Article XI

The present Convention shall be subject to ratification. Instruments of ratification shall be exchanged at Oslo. The Convention shall come into force one month after the date on which the instruments of ratification are exchanged, and shall remain in force for three years after the date of its coming into force. If neither of the Contracting Parties shall have given notice through the diplomatic channel to the other, not less than six months before the expiration of the said period of three years, of intention to terminate the Convention, it shall remain in force until the expiration of six months from the date on which either of the Contracting Parties shall have given notice to terminate it.

[2042]

RECIPROCAL ENFORCEMENT OF FOREIGN JUDGMENTS (AUSTRIA) ORDER 1962

(SI 1962/1339)

NOTES

Made: 27 June 1962.
Authority: Foreign Judgments (Reciprocal Enforcement) Act 1933, s 1.
Commencement: 14 July 1962.
This order has been largely superseded by the 1968 Brussels Convention and Council Regulation 44/2001/EC. See Introductory Note at the beginning of this section.

1 Part I of the Foreign Judgments (Reciprocal Enforcement) Act 1933 shall extend to the Republic of Austria.

[2043]

2 The following courts of the Republic of Austria shall be deemed superior courts of the Republic of Austria for the purposes of Part I of the Foreign Judgments (Reciprocal Enforcement) Act 1933 that is to say:—

The Landesgerichte;
The Kreisgerichte;
The Handelsgerichte;
The Oberlandesgerichte;
The Oberste Gerichtshof.

[2044]

3 No security for costs shall be required to be given by any person making application for the registration of a judgment of a superior court of the Republic of Austria.

[2045]

4 A judgment of a superior court in the Republic of Austria shall be deemed to be capable of execution in the Republic of Austria if a certificate issued by an officer of the original court and endorsed on a certified copy of the judgment is produced to that effect, but not otherwise.

[2046]

5 The rate of interest due under the law of the Republic of Austria upon the sum in respect of which a judgment of a superior court of the Republic of Austria is given shall be deemed to be that specified in the judgment or any certificate of the original court accompanying the judgment and, if no rate is so specified, no interest shall be deemed to be due thereon under the law of the Republic of Austria.

[2047]

6 A translation of the judgment of a superior court of the Republic of Austria or of any other document accompanying an application for registration of such a judgment shall, if certified by a sworn translator or by a diplomatic or consular officer of either the United Kingdom or the Republic of Austria, be accepted without further authentication.

[2048]

7 This Order may be cited as the Reciprocal Enforcement of Foreign Judgments (Austria) Order 1962 and shall come into operation on 14th July 1962.

[2049]

SCHEDULE
CONVENTION BETWEEN THE UNITED KINGDOM OF GREAT BRITAIN AND NORTHERN IRELAND AND THE REPUBLIC OF AUSTRIA PROVIDING FOR THE RECIPROCAL RECOGNITION AND ENFORCEMENT OF JUDGMENTS IN CIVIL AND COMMERCIAL MATTERS

Her Majesty The Queen of the United Kingdom of Great Britain and Northern Ireland and of Her other Realms and Territories, Head of the Commonwealth (hereinafter referred to as "Her Britannic Majesty") and the Federal President of the Republic of Austria;

Desiring to provide on the basis of reciprocity for the recognition and enforcement of judgements in civil and commercial matters;

Having appointed for that purpose as their Plenipotentiaries:

Her Britannic Majesty
For the United Kingdom of Great Britain and Northern Ireland:
The Right Honourable Edward Richard George Heath, MBE, MP, Lord Privy Seal,

The Federal President of the Republic of Austria
For the Republic of Austria:
Herrn Dr Bruno Kreisky,
Federal Minister for Foreign Affairs;
Herrn Dr Christian Broda,
Federal Minister for Justice,

Who, having communicated to each other their Full Powers, found in good and due form, have agreed as follows:

GENERAL

Article I

For the purposes of the present Convention:

(1) The words "territory of one High Contracting Party" and the words "territory of the other High Contracting Party" shall mean either:

(a) the United Kingdom (England and Wales, Scotland and Northern Ireland) and any territories to which the Convention shall have been extended under Article XIII or,

(b) the Republic of Austria.

(2) The words "superior court" mean:

(a) in the case of the United Kingdom, the House of Lords; for England and Wales, the Supreme Court of Judicature (Court of Appeal and High Court of Justice) and the Courts of Chancery of the Counties Palatine of Lancaster and of Durham; for Scotland, the Court of Session and the Sheriff Court; and for Northern Ireland, the Supreme Court of Judicature; and

(b) in the case of the Republic of Austria, the Landesgerichte, the Kreisgerichte, the Handelsgerichte, the Oberlandesgerichte and the Oberste Gerichtshof.

All other courts in these territories shall be deemed to be "inferior courts" for the purposes of the present Convention.

(3) The words "original court" mean in relation to any judgment the court by which the judgment was given; and the words "court applied to", the court in which it is sought to obtain recognition of a judgment or to which an application for the registration of a judgment or for the grant of execution (Bewilligung der Exekution) is made.

(4) The word "judgment" means any decision of a court, however described (judgment, order and the like) by which the rights of the parties are finally determined, and shall include gerichtliche Vergleiche, but shall not include orders by which only a provisional security is granted (einstweilige Verfugungen). The rights of the parties shall be deemed to be finally determined notwithstanding that an appeal may be pending against the judgment or that it may still be subject to appeal in the courts of the country of the original court.

(5) The words "judgments in civil and commercial matters" shall not be deemed to include judgments given in proceedings for the recovery of any form of taxation or under which a fine or other penalty is payable, but shall be deemed to include judgments given by a court in any criminal proceedings for the payment of a sum of money in respect of damages to an injured party.

(6) The words "judgment debtor" mean the person against whom the judgment was given in the original court and include any person against whom the judgment is enforceable under the law of the country of the original court; and the words "judgment creditor", the person in whose favour the judgment was given, and include any person entitled to avail himself of the judgment.

(7) The word "appeal" includes any proceeding by way of discharging or setting aside a judgment or an application for a new trial or, in the case of a judgment given in the territory of Her Britannic Majesty, a stay of execution.

Article II

(1) Judgments in civil and commercial matters given by a superior court in the territory of one High Contracting Party, other than judgments given on appeal in proceedings in which an inferior court gave judgment at first instance, shall be recognised and enforced in the territory of the other High Contracting Party in accordance with the provisions of Articles III to X of the present Convention.

(2) Nothing in the present Convention shall be deemed to preclude the recognition and enforcement in the territory of one High Contracting Party, in accordance with the law for the time being in force in the country concerned, of judgments pronounced by any court in the territory of the other High Contracting Party, being judgments to which the present Convention does not apply.

RECOGNITION OF JUDGMENTS

Article III

(1) The judgments referred to in paragraph (1) of Article II of the present Convention given in the territory of one High Contracting Party shall, subject to the provisions of paragraphs (2) and (3) of this Article, be recognised in the territory of the other High Contracting Party, unless either:

(a) the court applied to is satisfied of the existence of any of the following objections to the judgment:

1. in the case in question, the jurisdiction of the original court is not recognised under the provisions of Article IV;
2. the judgment was obtained by fraud;

3. the recognition of the judgment would be contrary to public policy in the country of the court applied to;
4. the judgment debtor, being a defendant in the proceedings in the original court, was a person who, under public international law, was entitled to immunity from the jurisdiction of the courts of the country of the original court and did not submit to the jurisdiction of that court;
5. the judgment is sought to be enforced against a person who, under public international law, is entitled to immunity from the jurisdiction of the court applied to; or

(b) the judgment debtor satisfies the court applied to:

1. of the existence of any of the objections mentioned in the foregoing sub-paragraph; or
2. that the judgment was given by default and the judgment debtor, being the defendant in the proceedings in the original court, did not actually acquire knowledge of those proceedings at all, or did not acquire it in reasonably sufficient time to enable him to defend. In all cases where it is proved that notice of the proceedings has been duly served on the defendant in conformity with the provisions of Article 3 or sub-paragraph (1) or (2) of paragraph (a) of Article 4 of the Convention between the United Kingdom and Austria regarding legal proceedings in civil and commercial matters signed on March 31, 1931, the court applied to shall accept such service as conclusive evidence that the defendant actually acquired knowledge of the proceedings.

(2) Where the judgment debtor satisfies the court applied to that proceedings by way of appeal have been instituted against the judgment in the country of the original court, or that such proceedings have not been actually instituted, but that he is entitled and intends to appeal, the court applied to shall grant or withhold recognition of the judgment in accordance with the law of its country.

(3) Where the law of the country of the court applied to requires recognition to be withheld from a judgment on the ground that a previous judgment has been given in respect of the same cause of action as between the same parties by a court of competent jurisdiction, recognition shall be withheld.

(4) Recognition shall not be refused merely on the ground that the original court has applied, in the choice of the system of law applicable to the case, rules of private international law different from those observed by the court applied to.

Article IV

(1) For the purposes of sub-paragraph (a)1 of paragraph (1) of Article III the courts of the country of the original court shall, subject to the provisions of paragraphs (2) to (5) of this Article, be recognised as possessing jurisdiction in all cases:

(a) if the judgment debtor, being a defendant in the proceedings in the original court, was, at the time when the proceedings were instituted, resident in, or being a company or other body corporate had its registered or head office in, the country of that court; or

(b) if the judgment debtor, being a defendant in the proceedings in the original court, had a branch office or a commercial establishment in the country of that court and the proceedings in that court were in respect of a transaction effected through that branch office or establishment; or

(c) if the judgment debtor, being a defendant in the proceedings in the original court, had before the commencement of the proceedings agreed, in respect of the subject matter of the proceedings, to submit to the jurisdiction of that court or of the courts of the country of that court; or

(d) if the judgment debtor, being a defendant in the proceedings in the original court, submitted to the jurisdiction by voluntarily appearing in the proceedings. The expression "voluntarily appearing in the proceedings" does not include an appearance merely for the purpose of protecting property situated in the country of the original court from seizure, or of obtaining the release of property seized, or for the purpose of contesting the jurisdiction of the original court; or

(e) if the judgment debtor was plaintiff or counter-claimant in the proceedings in the original court.

(2) The provisions of paragraph (1) of this Article shall not apply to judgments where the subject matter of the proceedings was immovable property, but the jurisdiction of the original court shall be recognised if such property was situated in the country of the original court.

(3) The provisions of paragraph (1) of this Article shall not apply to judgments given in an action of which the subject matter was ships, aircraft or their cargo, if, according to the law of either High Contracting Party, they are conclusive not only against the parties to the proceedings but also against any other person claiming an interest in such ships, aircraft or their cargo inconsistent with the judgment. The jurisdiction of the original court shall, however, be recognised if such ships, aircraft or their cargo were situated in the country of the original court at the time of the commencement of the proceedings in the original court.

(4) The jurisdiction of the original court shall not be recognised in the cases specified in sub-paragraphs (a) and (b) of paragraph (1) and in paragraphs (2) and (3) of this Article, if the bringing of the proceedings in the original court was contrary to an agreement under which the dispute in question was to be settled otherwise than by proceedings in the courts of the country of the original court.

(5) The provisions of paragraph (1) of this Article shall not apply to judgments concerning:

(a) family law or personal status (including divorces or other judgments in matrimonial causes);

(b) succession or the administration of estates of deceased persons;

(c) bankruptcy proceedings, or proceedings for the winding up of companies or other bodies corporate;

however, in the case of such judgments, the jurisdiction of the courts of the country of the original court shall be recognised where such recognition is in accordance with the law of the country of the court applied to.

Article V

(1) The effect of the recognition of a judgment shall be that the judgment shall be treated as conclusive of any matter of law or fact decided therein in any further proceedings between the same parties founded on the same cause of action.

(2) No proceedings for the recovery of a sum of money payable under a judgment to which the present Convention applies shall be entertained by the courts of either High Contracting Party, other than proceedings for enforcement in accordance with Articles VI to X of the present Convention.

ENFORCEMENT OF JUDGMENTS

Article VI

(1) The judgments referred to in paragraph (1) of Article II of the present Convention given in the territory of one High Contracting Party shall, subject to the provisions of paragraphs (2) and (3) of this Article, be enforced in the territory of the other High Contracting Party in the manner provided in Articles VII to X of the present Convention provided that the following conditions are satisfied:

(a) none of the objections set out in Article III (read in conjunction with Article IV) to the recognition of the judgment exists;

(b) there is payable thereunder a sum of money;

(c) it can be established under the provisions of paragraph (5) of this Article that they could be enforced by execution in the country of the original court:

(2) Where the judgment debtor satisfies the Austrian court applied to that proceedings by way of appeal have been instituted against the judgment in the territory of Her Britannic Majesty, the Austrian court shall adopt the same procedure as on an application for a new trial (Wiederaufnahmsklage).

(3) Where the judgment debtor satisfies the court applied to in the territory of Her Britannic Majesty that proceedings by way of application for a new trial (Wiederaufnahmsklage) or to set aside the judgment (Nichtigkeitsklage) have been instituted against the judgment in Austria or that such proceedings have not been actually instituted but that he is entitled and intends to bring them, the court, if it thinks fit, may take such measures in regard thereto as are permitted by its own law.

(4) If the amount of the costs to be paid under a judgment is not fixed by the judgment itself but by a separate order, such order shall be deemed to be part of the judgment.

(5) A judgment in respect of which a certified copy has been issued by the original court shall, in the absence of proof to the contrary, be deemed to be capable of being enforced by execution in the country of the original court within the meaning of sub-paragraph (*c*) of paragraph (1) of this Article. A certified copy of a judgment issued by an Austrian court shall bear a certificate to the effect that it is capable of being enforced by execution (vollstreckbar).

Article VII

(1) In order that any judgment given in the territory of the Republic of Austria should be enforced in the territory of the United Kingdom, an application by a judgment creditor for its registration should, in accordance with the procedure of the court applied to, be made:

(a) in England and Wales, to the High Court of Justice;
(b) in Scotland, to the Court of Session; and
(c) in Northern Ireland, to the Supreme Court of Judicature.

(2) The application for registration should be accompanied by:

(a) a certified copy of the complete judgment authenticated by the court seal and bearing the certificate referred to in paragraph (5) of Article VI;
(b) an affidavit of the facts required by the rules of the court applied to;
(c) a translation of any document required by this paragraph (except any affidavit in English) certified by a sworn translator or by a diplomatic or consular officer of either High Contracting Party.

(3) The documents enumerated in paragraph (2) shall require no further authentication.

(4) If an application is made in accordance with paragraphs (1) and (2) of this Article in respect of a judgment fulfilling the conditions laid down in Article VI, registration shall be granted.

Article VIII

(1) In order that any judgment given in the territory of Her Britannic Majesty should be enforced in the territory of the Republic of Austria, an application by a judgment creditor for the grant of execution should, in accordance with the procedure of the court applied to, be made to the Landesgericht or Kreisgericht in whose jurisdiction the judgment debtor has his residence or, in the absence of such residence, where he possesses property.

(2) The application for the grant of execution should be accompanied by:

(a) a certified copy of the judgment authenticated by the court seal, or in the case of judgments of the Sheriff Court, authenticated by the signature of the Sheriff Clerk;
(b) a document issued by the original court giving particulars of the proceedings and a statement of the grounds on which the judgment was based;
(c) a translation of any document required by this paragraph certified by a sworn translator or by a diplomatic or consular officer of either High Contracting Party.

(3) The documents enumerated in paragraph (2) shall require no further authentication.

(4) If an application is made in accordance with paragraphs (1) and (2) of this Article in respect of a judgment fulfilling the conditions laid down in Article VI, execution shall be granted.

Article IX

From the date on which it is granted registration under Article VII or execution under Article VIII, a judgment shall, for the purpose of its execution by virtue of that grant, have effect in the country of the court applied to as if it were a judgment originally given in that country on that date.

Article X

(1) The procedure for the registration of a judgment under Article VII and the procedure for the grant of execution of a judgment under Article VIII shall be as simple and rapid as possible, and no security for costs shall be required of any person making application for such registration or for the grant of execution.

(2) A period of six years, running from the date of the judgment of the original court, if no appeal has been brought to a higher court in the country of the original court, or from the date of the judgment given in the last instance if such an appeal has been brought, shall be allowed by the court applied to for the purpose of making any application for registration or the first application for a grant of execution.

(3) If it is found by the court applied to that the judgment of the original court is in respect of different matters and that one or more, but not all, of the provisions of the judgment are such that, if those provisions had been contained in separate judgments, those judgments could properly have been registered or could have been granted execution, the judgment may be registered or granted execution in respect only of the provisions aforesaid.

(4) If under a judgment a sum of money is payable, which is expressed in a currency other than that of the country of the court applied to, the law of the country of the court applied to shall determine if, and if so, in what manner and in what conditions, the amount payable under the judgment may or shall be converted into the currency of the country of the court applied to for the purposes of the satisfaction or enforcement of the judgment debt.

(5) When granting registration or execution, the court applied to shall, if so requested by the judgment creditor, include the costs of and incidental to registration or the grant of execution.

(6) Where a judgment is granted registration under Article VII or execution under Article VIII such judgment shall carry, in respect of the period up to the date of the grant, interest at the rate (if any) specified in the judgment or in any certificate of the original court accompanying the judgment. As from the date of the grant, interest shall be allowed at 4 per cent. per annum on the total sum (principal and interest) in respect of which the registration or execution is granted.

FINAL PROVISIONS

Article XI

The present Convention shall apply only to judgments which are given after the date of its entry into force.

Article XII

Any difficulties which may arise in connexion with the interpretation or application of the present Convention shall be settled through the diplomatic channel. It is, however, understood that the judgments of courts in the territories of the High Contracting Parties cannot thereby be reopened or altered.

Article XIII

(1) Her Britannic Majesty may, by a notification given through the diplomatic channel, at any time while the Convention is in force under Article XIV, and provided that an agreement has been concluded by an Exchange of Notes on the points mentioned in paragraph (2) of this Article, extend the operation of the present Convention to any territory for whose international relations Her Britannic Majesty's Government in the United Kingdom of Great Britain and Northern Ireland are responsible.

(2) Prior to any notification of extension in respect of any territory under the preceding paragraph, an agreement shall be concluded between the High Contracting Parties by an Exchange of Notes as to the courts of the territory concerned, which shall be deemed to be "superior courts" for the purposes of the present Convention, and the Courts to which application for registration of any judgment shall be made.

(3) The date of the coming into force of any extension under this Article shall be three months from the date of the notification given under paragraph (1) of this Article.

(4) Either of the High Contracting Parties may, at any time after the expiry of three years from the coming into force of an extension of the present Convention, to any of the territories referred to in paragraph (1) of this Article, terminate such extension on giving six months' notice of termination through the diplomatic channel.

(5) The termination of the Convention under Article XIV shall, unless otherwise expressly agreed by both High Contracting Parties, also terminate it in respect of any territory to which it has been extended under paragraph (1) of this Article.

Article XIV

The present Convention shall be subject to ratification. Instruments of Ratification shall be exchanged at London. The Convention shall come into force one month after the date on which the Instruments of Ratification are exchanged, and shall remain in force for three years after the date of its coming into force. If neither of the High Contracting Parties shall have given notice through the diplomatic channel to the other, not less than six months before the expiration of the said period of three years, of intention to terminate the Convention, it shall remain in force until the expiration of six months from the date on which either of the High Contracting Parties shall have given notice to terminate it.

[2050]

RECIPROCAL ENFORCEMENT OF FOREIGN JUDGMENTS (THE NETHERLANDS) ORDER 1969

(SI 1969/1063)

NOTES

Made: 31 July 1969.
Authority: Foreign Judgments (Reciprocal Enforcement) Act 1933, s 1.
Commencement: 21 September 1969.
This order has been largely superseded by the 1968 Brussels Convention and Council Regulation 44/2001/EC. See Introductory Note at the beginning of this section.

1 This Order may be cited as the Reciprocal Enforcement of Foreign Judgments (the Netherlands) Order 1969 and shall come into operation on 21st September 1969.

[2051]

2 Part I of the Foreign Judgments (Reciprocal Enforcement) Act 1933 shall extend to the Kingdom of the Netherlands.

[2052]

3 The following courts of the Kingdom of the Netherlands shall be deemed superior courts of the Kingdom of the Netherlands for the purposes of Part I of the Foreign Judgments (Reciprocal Enforcement) Act 1933, that is to say:—

The Hoge Raad der Nederlanden;
The gerechtshoven;
The arrondissementsrechtbanken.

[In the case of the Netherlands Antilles:
The Hoge Raad der Nederlanden;
The Hof van Justitie der Nederlandse Antillen;
The Gerecht in Eerste Aanleg.]

[2053]

NOTES

Words in square brackets inserted by the Reciprocal Enforcement of Foreign Judgments (the Netherlands) (Amendment) Order 1977, SI 1977/2149.

4 No security for costs shall be required to be given by any person making application for the registration of a judgment of a superior court of the Kingdom of the Netherlands.

[2054]

5 A judgment of a superior court of the Kingdom of the Netherlands shall, in the absence of proof to the contrary, be deemed to be capable of execution in the Kingdom of the

Netherlands if a certified copy of the judgment is produced bearing the seal of the court and the executory formula "in naam der Koningin".

[2055]

6 The rate of interest due under the law of the Kingdom of the Netherlands upon the sum in respect of which a judgment of a superior court of the Kingdom of the Netherlands is given shall be deemed to be that specified in the judgment or any certificate of the original court accompanying the judgment and, if no rate is so specified, no interest shall be deemed to be due thereon under the law of the Kingdom of the Netherlands.

[2056]

7 A translation of the judgment of a superior court of the Kingdom of the Netherlands or of any other document accompanying an application for registration of such a judgment shall, if certified by a sworn translator or by a diplomatic or consular officer of either the United Kingdom or the Kingdom of the Netherlands, be accepted without further authentication.

[2057]

SCHEDULE

CONVENTION BETWEEN THE UNITED KINGDOM OF GREAT BRITAIN AND NORTHERN IRELAND AND THE KINGDOM OF THE NETHERLANDS PROVIDING FOR THE RECIPROCAL RECOGNITION AND ENFORCEMENT OF JUDGMENTS IN CIVIL MATTERS

Her Majesty the Queen of the United Kingdom of Great Britain and Northern Ireland and of Her other Realms and Territories, Head of the Commonwealth (hereinafter referred to as "Her Brittanic Majesty") and

Her Majesty the Queen of the Netherlands;

Desiring to provide on the basis of reciprocity for the recognition and enforcement of judgements in civil matters;

Have resolved to conclude a Convention to that end and have appointed as their Plenipotentiaries:

Her Brittanic Majesty:

For the United Kingdom of Great Britain and Northern Ireland:

His Excellency Sir Isham Peter Garran, KCMG, Her Brittanic Majesty's Ambassador Extraordinary and Plenipotentiary at The Hague and

The Right Honourable Lord Gardiner, Lord High Chancellor of Great Britain;

Her Majesty the Queen of the Netherlands:

His Excellency Mr H J de Koster, State Secretary for Foreign affairs;

Who, having communicated to each other their respective full powers, found in good and due form, have agreed as follows:

GENERAL

Article I

For the purposes of this Convention:

(1) The word "territory" means:

(a) in relation to the United Kingdom of Great Britain and Northern Ireland (hereinafter referred to as "the United Kingdom"), England and Wales, Scotland, and Northern Ireland and any territories in respect of which this Convention is in force by reason of an extension under paragraph 1(a) of Article X; and

(b) in relation to the Kingdom of the Netherlands, the European part of the Kingdom and any other part of the Kingdom in respect of which this Convention is in force by reason of an extension under paragraph 1(b) of Article X.

(2) The word "judgment" means any decision of a court, however described (judgment, order and the like), by which the rights of the parties are finally determined, notwithstanding that an appeal may be pending against the judgment or that it may be subject to appeal in the courts of the country of the original court. A "gerechtelijke minnelijke schikking" shall also

PART III STATUTORY INSTRUMENTS

be deemed to be a judgment for the purposes of this Convention. If the amount of the costs or interest to be paid under a judgment is not fixed by the judgment itself but by a separate court order, such order shall be deemed to be part of the judgment for the purposes of this Convention.

(3) The words "action in rem" mean an action which seeks to obtain a judgment which is conclusive not only against the parties to the proceedings but also against any other person claiming an interest in the subject matter of the action.

(4) The words "original court" mean in relation to any judgment the court by which such judgment was given; and the words "court applied to", the court in which it is sought to obtain recognition of a judgment or to which an application for the registration of a judgment or for the grant of execution is made.

(5) The words "judgment debtor" mean the person against whom the judgment was given in the original court and include, where necessary, any person against whom such judgment is enforceable under the law of the country of the original court; and the words "judgment creditor", the person in whose favour the judgment was given, and include, where necessary, any other person in whom the rights under the judgment have become vested.

(6) The word "appeal" includes any proceeding by way of discharging or setting aside a judgment or an application for a new trial or a stay of execution.

Article II

(1) Subject to the provisions of paragraphs (2) and (4) of this Article, this Convention shall apply to judgments in any civil proceedings given after the date of the entry into force of this Convention by the following courts:

(a) in the case of the United Kingdom, the House of Lords; for England and Wales, the Supreme Court of Judicature (Court of Appeal and High Court of Justice) and the Courts of Chancery of the Counties Palatine of Lancaster and Durham; for Scotland, the Court of Session and the Sheriff Court; and for Northern Ireland the Supreme Court of Judicature; and

(b) in the case of the Kingdom of the Netherlands, the Hoge Raad der Nederlanden, the gerechtshoven and the arrondissementsrechtbanken.

(2) This Convention shall not apply to:

(a) judgments given on appeal from courts not referred to in paragraph (1) of this Article;

(b) judgments given in proceedings for the recovery of taxes or other charges of a like nature or for the recovery of a fine or other penalty;

(c) judgments in matters of family law or status, including orders for maintenance;

(d) judgments in matters of succession or the administration of the estates of deceased persons;

(e) judgments in matters of bankruptcy or suspension of payments (surseance van betaling) or the winding up of companies.

(3) This Convention shall not preclude the recognition and enforcement in the territory of one High Contracting Party, in accordance with the municipal law for the time being in force in the country concerned, of judgments given by any court in the territory of the other High Contracting Party, being judgments to which this Convention does not apply or judgments given in circumstances where the provisions of this Convention do not require such recognition or enforcement.

(4) A High Contracting Party shall not be obliged to apply this Convention to any judgment given in respect to injury or damage of a description which is the subject of a Convention with respect to third party liability in the field of nuclear energy to which that High Contracting Party is also a Contracting Party.

RECOGNITION OF JUDGEMENTS

Article III

(1) For the purposes of this Convention, the effect of the recognition of a judgment shall be that it shall be treated as conclusive between the parties thereto in all proceedings founded on the same cause of action and it may be relied on by way of defence or counter-claim in any such proceedings.

(2) Subject to the provisions of paragraphs (3) to (5) of this Article judgments given in the territory of one High Contracting Party shall be recognised in the territory of the other except where the court applied to is satisfied of the existence of any of the following objections to the judgment:

(a) in the case in question, the jurisdiction of the original court is not recognised under the provisions of Article IV;

(b) the judgment debtor, being the defendant in the proceedings in the original court, did not (notwithstanding that process may have been duly served on him in accordance with the law of the country of the original court) receive notice of those proceedings in sufficient time to enable him to defend the proceedings and did not appear;

(c) the judgment was obtained by fraud;

(d) the recognition of the judgment would be contrary to public policy in the country of the court applied to;

(e) the judgment debtor, being a defendant in the original proceedings, was a person who, under the rules of public international law, was entitled to immunity from the jurisdiction of the courts of the country of the original court and did not submit to the jurisdiction of that court;

(f) the judgment is sought to be enforced against a person who, under the rules of public international law, is entitled to immunity from the jurisdiction of the court applied to.

(3) Where the judgment debtor satisfies the court applied to that an appeal is pending, or that he is entitled and intends to appeal against the judgment in the country of the original court, the court applied to may recognise the judgment or may, if the judgment debtor makes an application to this effect, either refuse to recognise the judgment or adjourn its decision on the recognition of the judgment so as to allow the judgment debtor a reasonable opportunity of completing or of instituting such appeal.

(4) Where the court applied to is satisfied that the matter in dispute in the proceedings in the original court had, previously to the date of the judgment in the original court, been the subject of a judgment by a court having jurisdiction in the matter, the court applied to may refuse to recognise the judgment of the original court.

(5) Recognition shall not be refused merely on the ground that the original court has applied, in the choice of the system of law applicable to the case, rules of private international law different from those observed by the court applied to.

Article IV

(1) For the purposes of sub-paragraph (a) of paragraph (2) of Article III, the courts of the country of the original court shall, subject to the provisions of paragraphs (2) to (4) of this Article, be recognised as possessing jurisdiction:

(a) if the judgment debtor, being a defendant in the proceedings in the original court, submitted to the jurisdiction of that court by voluntarily appearing in the proceedings otherwise than for the purpose of protecting, or obtaining the release of, property seized, or threatened with seizure, in the proceedings or of contesting the jurisdiction of that court; or

(b) if the judgment debtor was plaintiff or counterclaimant in the proceedings in the original court; or

(c) if the judgment debtor, being a defendant in the proceedings in the original court, had before the commencement of the proceedings agreed, in respect of the subject matter of the proceedings, to submit to the jurisdiction of that court or of the courts of the country of that court; or

(d) if the judgment debtor, being a defendant in the original court, was at the time when the proceedings were instituted, resident in, or being a body corporate, had its principal place of business in, the country of that court; or

(e) if the judgment debtor, being a defendant in the original court, had an office or place of business in the country of that court and the proceedings in that court were in respect of a transaction effected through or at that office or place.

(2) The provisions of paragraph (1) of this Article shall not apply to judgments where the subject matter of the proceedings was immovable property, but the jurisdiction of the original court shall be recognised if such property were situated in the country of the original court.

(3) The provisions of paragraph (1) of this Article shall not apply to judgments given in an action in rem concerning ships, aircraft or their cargo. The jurisdiction of the original court

shall, however, be recognised if such ships, aircraft or their cargo were situated in the country of the original court at the time of the commencement of the proceedings in the original court.

(4) The jurisdiction of the original court shall not be recognised in the cases specified in sub-paragraphs (d) and (e) of paragraph (1) and in paragraphs (2) and (3) of this Article, if the bringing of the proceedings in the original court was contrary to an agreement under which the dispute in question was to be settled otherwise than by proceedings in the courts of the country of the original court.

ENFORCEMENT OF JUDGEMENTS

Article V

(1) Subject to the provisions of paragraph (2) of this Article any judgment given in the territory of one High Contracting Party under which a sum of money is payable shall be enforced by execution in the territory of the other in the manner provided in Articles VI to VIII of this Convention:

Provided that the judgment shall not be enforced if:
- (a) the judgment debt has been wholly satisfied, or
- (b) the judgment could not be enforced by execution in the country of the original court, or
- (c) any of the objections to the recognition of the judgment set out in Article III exists.

(2) Where the judgment debtor satisfies the court applied to that an appeal is pending or that he is entitled and intends to appeal against the judgment in the country of the original court, the judgment need not be enforced, and the court applied to may take such measures in regard thereto as are permitted by the law of its country.

Article VI

(1) In order that any judgment given in the territory of the Kingdom of the Netherlands may be enforced in the United Kingdom, an application by a judgment creditor for its registration should, in accordance with the procedure of the court applied to, be made:
- (a) in England and Wales, to the High Court of Justice;
- (b) in Scotland, to the Court of Session; and
- (c) in Northern Ireland, to the Supreme Court of Judicature.

(2) The application for registration should be accompanied by:
- (a) a certified copy of the complete judgment authenticated by the court seal and bearing the formula "In naam der Koningin";
- (b) an affidavit of the facts required by the rules of the court applied to;
- (c) a translation into English of any document required by this paragraph certified by a sworn translator or by a diplomatic or consular officer of either High Contracting Party.

(3) The documents enumerated in paragraph (2) shall require no further authentication.

(4) If an application is made in accordance with paragraphs (1) and (2) of this Article in respect of a judgment fulfilling the conditions laid down in Article V, registration shall be granted.

Article VII

(1) In order that any judgment given in the territory of the United Kingdom may be enforced in the Kingdom of the Netherlands, an application by a judgment creditor for the grant of execution should, in accordance with the procedure of the court applied to, be made to the "arrondissementsrechtbank" in whose jurisdiction the judgment debtor is resident or owns property.

(2) The application for the grant of execution should be accompanied by:
- (a) a certified copy of the judgment authenticated by the court seal, or in the case of judgments of the Sheriff Court, authenticated by the signature of the Sheriff Clerk;
- (b) a document issued by the original court giving particulars of the proceedings and a statement of the grounds on which the judgment was based;
- (c) a translation into Dutch of any document required by this paragraph certified by a

sworn translator or by diplomatic or consular officer of either High Contracting Party, if such a translation is requested by the Court applied to.

(3) The documents enumerated in paragraph (2) shall require no further authentication.

(4) If an application is made in accordance with paragraphs (1) and (2) of this Article in respect of a judgment fulfilling the conditions laid down in Article V, execution shall be granted.

Article VIII

(1) From the date on which it is granted registration under Article VI or execution under Article VII a judgment shall, for the purposes of its execution by virtue of that grant, have effect in the country of the court applied to as if it were a judgment originally given in that country on that date.

(2) The procedure for the registration of a judgment under Article VI and the procedure for the grant of execution of a judgment under Article VII shall be as simple and rapid as possible, and no security for costs shall be required of any person making application for such registration or for the grant of execution.

(3) A period of not less than six years, running from the date of the judgment of the original court, if no appeal has been brought to a higher court in the country of the original court, or from the date of the judgment given in last instance if such an appeal has been brought, shall be allowed by the court applied to for the purpose of making any application for registration or for a grant of execution.

(4) If it is found by the court applied to that the judgment of the original court is in respect of different matters and that one or more, but not all, of the provisions of the judgment are such that, if those provisions had been contained in separate judgments, those judgments could properly have been registered or could have been granted execution, the judgment may be registered or granted execution in respect only of the provisions aforesaid.

(5) If it is found by the court applied to that the judgment has been at the date of the application partly but not wholly satisfied by payment, the judgment shall be registered or execution shall be granted in respect of the balance remaining payable at that date provided that the judgment is otherwise one which would be enforceable under the provisions of this Convention.

(6) If under a judgment a sum of money is payable, which is expressed in a currency other than that of the country of the court applied to, the law of that country shall determine if, and if so, in what manner and on what conditions, the amount payable under the judgment may or shall be converted into the currency of that country for the purposes of the satisfaction or enforcement of the judgment debt.

(7) When granting registration or execution, the court applied to shall, if so requested by the judgment creditor, include the reasonable costs of and incidental to the grant of registration or of execution.

(8) Where a judgment is granted registered or execution it shall carry, in respect of the period up to the date of the grant, interest at the rate specified in the judgment or in any certificate of the original court accompanying the judgment. As from the date of the grant, interest shall be allowed at 4 per cent per annum on the total sum (principal and interest) in respect of which the registration or execution is granted.

FINAL PROVISIONS

Article IX

Any difficulties which may arise in connection with the interpretation or application of this Convention shall be settled through the diplomatic channel.

Article X

(1) The Governments of the High Contracting Parties may at any time, by mutual agreement expressed in an Exchange of Notes, extend the operation of this Convention to:

(a) any territory for the international relations of which Her Britannic Majesty's Government in the United Kingdom are responsible;

(b) any part of the Kingdom of the Netherlands outside Europe.

(2) It shall also be specified in the Exchange of Notes referred to in the preceding paragraph which courts of the territory concerned or the part of the Kingdom concerned are to be named as the courts to whose judgments this Convention shall apply, and to which courts application for registration or grant of execution of any judgment shall be made.

(3) As regards judgments given in a territory after the extension to that territory has come into force, the courts specified in the relevant Exchange of Notes as the courts to whose judgments this Convention shall apply, shall be deemed to have been named in paragraph (1) of Article II.

(4) Any such extension shall come into force one month after the date of the Exchange of Notes.

(5) Either of the High Contracting Parties may, at any time after the expiry of three years from the coming into force of an extension of this Convention to any of the territories referred to in paragraph (1) of this Article, terminate such extension on giving six months' notice of termination through the diplomatic channel.

(6) The termination of this Convention under Article XI shall, unless otherwise expressly agreed by the High Contracting Parties, also terminate it in respect of any territory to which it has been extended under paragraph (1) of this Article.

Article XI

This Convention shall be subject to ratification. Instruments of ratification shall be exchanged at London. The Convention shall come into force three months after the date on which the Instruments of ratification are exchanged, and shall remain in force for three years after the date of its coming into force. If neither of the High Contracting Parties shall have given notice through the diplomatic channel to the other, not less than six months before the expiration of the said period of three years, of intention to terminate the Convention, it shall remain in force until the expiration of six months from the date on which either of the High Contracting Parties shall have given notice to terminate it.

[2058]

RECIPROCAL ENFORCEMENT OF FOREIGN JUDGMENTS (ISRAEL) ORDER 1971

(SI 1971/1039)

NOTES

Made: 23 June 1971.
Authority: Foreign Judgments (Reciprocal Enforcement) Act 1933, ss 1, 3.
Commencement: 26 July 1971.

1 This Order may be cited as the Reciprocal Enforcement of Foreign Judgments (Israel) Order 1971 and shall come into operation on 26th July 1971.

[2059]

2 Part I of the Foreign Judgments (Reciprocal Enforcement) Act 1933 shall extend to Israel.

[2060]

3 The following courts of Israel shall be deemed [recognised courts] of Israel for the purposes of Part I of the Foreign Judgments (Reciprocal Enforcement) Act 1933, that is to say—

The Supreme Court;
The District Courts;
[The Magistrates' Courts;]
Rabbinical Courts;
Moslem Religious Courts;

Christian Religious Courts;
Druze Religious Courts.

[2061]

NOTES

Words in first pair of square brackets substituted and words in second pair of square brackets inserted by the Reciprocal Enforcement of Foreign Judgments (Israel) (Amendment) Order 2003, SI 2003/2618, art 3.

4 No security for costs shall be required to be given by any person making application for the registration of a judgment of a [recognised court] of Israel.

[2062]

NOTES

Words in square brackets substituted by the Reciprocal Enforcement of Foreign Judgments (Israel) (Amendment) Order 2003, SI 2003/2618, art 4.

5 A judgment of a [recognised court] of Israel shall, in the absence of proof to the contrary, be deemed to be capable of execution in Israel if a certified copy of the judgment is produced authenticated by the court stamp and accompanied by a certificate issued by an officer of the original court that it is capable of execution in Israel.

[2063]

NOTES

Words in square brackets substituted by the Reciprocal Enforcement of Foreign Judgments (Israel) (Amendment) Order 2003, SI 2003/2618, art 4.

6 The rate of interest due under the law of Israel upon the sum in respect of which a judgment of a [recognised court] of Israel is given shall be deemed to be that specified in the judgment or any certificate of the original court accompanying the judgment and, if no rate is so specified, no interest shall be deemed to be due thereon under the law of Israel.

[2064]

NOTES

Words in square brackets substituted by the Reciprocal Enforcement of Foreign Judgments (Israel) (Amendment) Order 2003, SI 2003/2618, art 4.

7 A translation of the judgment of a [recognised court] of Israel or of any other document accompanying an application for registration of such a judgment shall, if certified by a notary or by a diplomatic or consular officer of either the United Kingdom or Israel, be accepted without further authentication.

[2065]

NOTES

Words in square brackets substituted by the Reciprocal Enforcement of Foreign Judgments (Israel) (Amendment) Order 2003, SI 2003/2618, art 4.

SCHEDULE
CONVENTION BETWEEN THE GOVERNMENT OF THE UNITED KINGDOM OF GREAT BRITAIN AND NORTHERN IRELAND AND THE GOVERNMENT OF ISRAEL PROVIDING FOR THE RECIPROCAL RECOGNITION AND ENFORCEMENT OF JUDGMENTS IN CIVIL MATTERS

GENERAL

ARTICLE 1

For the purposes of this Convention—

(a) "territory" shall be interpreted in accordance with the provisions of Article 10;

(b) "judgment" means any decision of a court, however described (judgment, order or the like), by which the rights of the parties are determined and which cannot be altered by that court. It includes judgments against which an appeal may be pending or which may still be subject to appeal in the courts of the country of the original court. If the amount of the costs or interest to be paid under a judgment is not fixed by the judgment itself but by a separate court order, such order shall be deemed to be part of the judgment for the purposes of this Convention;

(c) "original court" means in relation to any judgment the court by which such judgment was given; and "court applied to" the court in which it is sought to obtain recognition of a judgment or to which an application for the registration of a judgment or for the grant of an enforcement declaration is made;

(d) "judgment debtor" means the person against whom the judgment was given in the original court and includes, where necessary, any person against whom such judgment is enforceable under the law of the country of the original court;

(e) "judgment creditor" means the person in whose favour the judgment was given and includes, where necessary, any other person in whom the rights under the judgment have become vested under the law of the country of the original court;

(f) "appeal" includes any proceeding by way of discharging or setting aside a judgment or an application for a new trial or a stay of execution.

ARTICLE 2

(1) Subject to the provisions of paragraph (2) of this Article, this Convention shall apply to judgments in any civil proceedings, and to judgments in any criminal proceedings for the payment of a sum of money in respect of compensation or damages to an injured party, given after the date of the entry into force of this Convention by the following courts—

(a) in the case of the United Kingdom, the House of Lords; for England and Wales, the Supreme Court of Judicature (Court of Appeal and High Court of Justice) and the Courts of Chancery of the Counties Palatine of Lancaster and Durham; for Scotland, the Court of Session and the Sheriff Court; and for Northern Ireland, the Supreme Court of Judicature; and

(b) in the case of Israel, the Supreme Court, the District Courts, Rabbinical Courts, Moslem Religious Courts, Christian Religious Courts and Druze Religious Courts.

(2) This Convention shall not apply to—

(a) judgments given on appeal from courts not referred to in paragraph (1) of this Article;

(b) judgments given in proceedings for the recovery of taxes or other charges of a like nature or for the recovery of a fine or other penalty;

(c) judgments given in proceedings arising out of injury or damage falling within the definition of "nuclear damage" in the Vienna Convention of the 21st of May, 1963 on Civil Liability for Nuclear Damage.

(3) This Convention shall not preclude the recognition and enforcement in the territory of one Contracting Party, in accordance with the municipal law for the time being in force in the country concerned, of judgments given by any court in the territory of the other Contracting Party, being judgments to which this Convention does not apply or judgments given in circumstances where the provisions of this Convention do not require such recognition or enforcement.

RECOGNITION OF JUDGMENTS

ARTICLE 3

(1) For the purposes of this Convention, the recognition of a judgment means that the judgment shall be treated as conclusive as to the matter thereby adjudicated upon in any further action as between the same parties (judgment creditor and judgment debtor).

(2) Judgments given in the territory of one Contracting Party shall be recognised in the territory of the other subject to the provisions of paragraphs (3), (4) and (5) of this Article and where no objection to the judgment can be established on any of the following grounds—

(a) in the case in question, the jurisdiction of the original court is not recognised under the provisions of Article 4;

(b) the judgment debtor, being the defendant in the proceedings in the original court, did not, notwithstanding that process may have been duly served on him in accordance with the law of the country of the original court, receive notice of those proceedings in sufficient time to enable him to defend the proceedings and did not appear, or if it is proved to the court applied to that he was not afforded a reasonable opportunity to present his arguments and to produce his evidence;

(c) the judgment was, in the opinion of the court applied to, obtained by fraud;

(d) the recognition of the judgment is likely to prejudice the sovereignty or safety of the State or would be contrary to public policy;

(e) the judgment debtor, being a defendant in the original proceedings, was a person who, under the rules of public international law, was entitled to immunity from the jurisdiction of the courts of the country of the original court and did not submit to the jurisdiction of that court;

(f) the judgment is sought to be enforced against a person who, under the rules of public international law, is entitled to immunity from the jurisdiction of the court applied to.

(3) Where the court applied to is satisfied that proceedings by way of appeal have been instituted against the judgment in the country of the original court, or that such proceedings have not been actually instituted, but the time for appeal has not elapsed under the law of that country, the court applied to may, in so far as the law of its country permits, recognise the judgment, refuse to recognise the judgment or adjourn its decision on the recognition of the judgment so as to allow the judgment debtor an opportunity of completing or of instituting such proceedings.

(4) Where the court applied to is satisfied that the matter in dispute in the proceedings in the original court had, previously to the date of the judgment in the original court, been the subject of a judgment by a court having jurisdiction in the matter, the court applied to may refuse to recognise the judgment of the original court.

(5) Where the court applied to is satisfied that, at the time when proceedings were instituted in the original court in the matter in dispute, proceedings as to the same matter between the same parties were pending before any court or tribunal of the country of the court applied to, the latter may refuse to recognise the judgment of the original court.

ARTICLE 4

(1) For the purposes of sub-paragraph (a) of paragraph (2) of Article 3, the courts of the country of the original court shall, subject to the provisions of paragraphs (2) to (5) of this Article, be recognised as possessing jurisdiction in all cases—

(a) if the judgment debtor, being a defendant in the proceedings in the original court, submitted to the jurisdiction of that court by voluntarily appearing in the proceedings otherwise than for the purpose of protecting, or obtaining the release of, property seized, or threatened with seizure, in the proceedings or of contesting the jurisdiction of that court; or

(b) if the judgment debtor was plaintiff or counter-claimant in the proceedings in the original court; or

(c) if the judgment debtor, being a defendant in the proceedings in the original court, had before the commencement of the proceedings agreed, in respect of the subject matter of the proceedings, to submit to the jurisdiction of that court or of the courts of the country of that court; or

(d) if the judgment debtor, being a defendant in the original court, was, at the time when the proceedings were instituted, resident, or being a body corporate had its principal place of business, in the country of that court; or

(e) if the judgment debtor, being a defendant in the original court, had an office or place of business in the country of that court and the proceedings in that court were in respect of a transaction effected through or at that office or place.

(2) The provisions of paragraph (1) of this Article shall not apply to judgments where the subject matter of the proceedings was immovable property, unless such property was situated in the country of the original court.

(3) The provisions of paragraph (1) of this Article shall not apply to judgments given in actions of which the subject matter was ships, aircraft or their cargo, if, according to the law of either Contracting Party, they are conclusive not only against the parties to the proceedings but also against any other person claiming an interest in such ships, aircraft or their cargo inconsistent with the judgment. The jurisdiction of the original court shall, however, be recognised if such ships, aircraft or their cargo were situated in the country of the original court at the time of the commencement of the proceedings in that court.

(4) The jurisdiction of the original court need not be recognised in the cases specified in sub-paragraphs (d) and (e) of paragraph (1) and in paragraphs (2) and (3) of this Article, if the bringing of the proceedings in the original court was contrary to an agreement under which the dispute in question was to be settled otherwise than by proceedings in the courts of the country of the original court.

(5) The provisions of paragraph (1) of this Article shall not apply to judgments in any proceedings concerning matrimonial matters, administration of the estates of deceased persons, bankruptcy, winding up of companies, lunacy, guardianship of infants or paternity. However, in the case of such judgments, the jurisdiction of the courts of the country of the original court shall be recognised where such recognition is in accordance with the law of the country of the court applied to.

ENFORCEMENT OF JUDGMENTS

ARTICLE 5

(1) Subject to the provisions of paragraph (2) of this Article, judgments given in the territory of one Contracting Party shall be enforced by execution in the territory of the other in the manner provided in Articles 6 to 8 of this Convention, provided that the following conditions are fulfilled—

- (a) they are enforceable by execution in the country of the original court;
- (b) there is payable thereunder a sum of money;
- (c) the judgment debt has not been wholly satisfied;
- (d) they are recognised by the court applied to under the provisions of Article 3.

(2) Where the court applied to is satisfied that proceedings by way of appeal have been instituted against the judgment in the country of the original court, or that such proceedings have not been actually instituted, but the time for appeal has not elapsed under the law of that country, the court applied to may, in so far as the law of its country permits, enforce the judgment, refuse to enforce the judgment or adjourn its decision on the enforcement of the judgment so as to allow the judgment debtor an opportunity of completing or of instituting such proceedings.

ARTICLE 6

(1) In order that a judgment given in the courts of Israel may be enforced in the territory within the jurisdiction of the courts of the United Kingdom, an application by a judgment creditor for its registration should, in accordance with the procedure of the court applied to, be made—

- (a) in England and Wales, to the High Court of Justice;
- (b) in Scotland, to the Court of Session; and
- (c) in Northern Ireland, to the Supreme Court of Judicature.

(2) The application for registration should be accompanied by—

- (a) a certified copy of the complete judgment authenticated by the court stamp and accompanied by a certificate issued by an officer of the original court that it is capable of execution in the country of that court;
- (b) an affidavit of the facts required by the rules of the court applied to;
- (c) a translation into English of any document required by this paragraph certified by a notary or by a diplomatic or consular officer of either Contracting Party.

(3) The documents enumerated in paragraph (2) shall require no further authentication.

(4) If an application is made in accordance with paragraphs (1) and (2) of this Article in respect of a judgment fulfilling the conditions laid down in Article 5, registration shall be granted.

ARTICLE 7

(1) In order that a judgment given in the courts of the United Kingdom may be enforced in the territory within the jurisdiction of the courts of Israel, an application by a judgment creditor for the grant of an enforcement declaration should, in accordance with the procedure of the court applied to, be made to the District Court of Jerusalem.

(2) The application for the grant of an enforcement declaration should be accompanied by—

(a) a certified copy of the judgment authenticated by the court seal, or in the case of judgments of the Sheriff Court, authenticated by the signature of the Sheriff Clerk;
(b) an affidavit of the facts required by the rules of the court applied to;
(c) a certificate issued by the original court giving particulars of the proceedings and a statement of the grounds on which the judgment was based, and specifying whether at the date of the issue of the certificate the time for appeal has elapsed without any proceedings by way of appeal having been instituted against the judgment in the United Kingdom;
(d) a translation into Hebrew of any document required by this paragraph certified by a sworn translator or by a diplomatic or consular officer of either Contracting Party.

(3) The documents enumerated in paragraph (2) shall require no further authentication.

(4) If an application is made in accordance with paragraphs (1) and (2) of this Article in respect of a judgment fulfilling the conditions laid down in Article 5, an enforcement declaration shall be granted.

ARTICLE 8

(1) From the date on which it is granted registration under Article 6 or an enforcement declaration under Article 7 a judgment shall, for the purpose of its execution by virtue of that grant, have effect in the country of the court applied to as if it were a judgment originally given in that country on that date.

(2) The procedure for the registration of a judgment under Article 6 and the procedure for the grant of an enforcement declaration of a judgment under Article 7 shall be as simple and rapid as possible, and no security for costs shall be required of any person making application for such registration or for the grant of an enforcement declaration.

(3) A period of not less than six years, running from the date of the judgment of the original court if no appeal has been brought to a higher court in the country of the original court or from the date of the judgment given in the last instance if such an appeal has been brought, shall be allowed by the court applied to for the purpose of making any application for registration or for a grant of an enforcement declaration.

(4) If it is found by the court applied to that the judgment of the original court is in respect of different matters and that one or more, but not all, of the provisions of the judgment are such that, if those provisions had been contained in separate judgments, those judgments could properly have been registered or could have been granted an enforcement declaration, the judgment may be registered or granted an enforcement declaration in respect only of the provisions aforesaid.

(5) If it is found by the court applied to that the judgment has been, at the date of the application, partly but not wholly satisfied by payment, the judgment shall be registered or an enforcement declaration shall be granted in respect of the balance remaining payable at that date, provided that the judgment is otherwise one which would be enforceable under the provisions of this Convention.

(6) If under a judgment a sum of money is payable which is expressed in a currency other than that of the country of the court applied to, the law of the country of the court applied to shall determine if, and if so in what manner and in what conditions, the amount payable under the judgment may or shall be converted into the currency of the country of the court applied to for the purposes of the satisfaction or enforcement of the judgment debt.

(7) When granting registration or an enforcement declaration, the court applied to shall, if so requested by the judgment creditor, include the costs of an incidental to registration or the grant of an enforcement declaration.

(8) Where a judgment is granted registration or an enforcement declaration it shall carry, in respect of the period up to the date of the grant, interest at the rate, if any, specified in the judgment or in any certificate of the original court accompanying the judgment. As from the date of the grant, interest shall be allowed at 4 per cent per annum on the total sum (principal and interest) in respect of which the registration or the enforcement declaration is granted.

FINAL PROVISIONS

ARTICLE 9

Any difficulties which may arise in connexion with the interpretation or application of this Convention shall be settled through the diplomatic channel.

ARTICLE 10

(1) This Convention shall apply in the case of the Government of the United Kingdom of Great Britain and Northern Ireland to the territory within the jurisdiction of the courts of England and Wales, Scotland and Northern Ireland, and in the case of the Government of Israel, to the territory within the jurisdiction of the courts of Israel.

(2) The Government of the United Kingdom may, by a notification given through the diplomatic channel, at any time while this Convention is in force, and provided that an agreement has been concluded by an Exchange of Notes on the points mentioned in paragraph (3) of this Article, extend the operation of this Convention to any territory for whose international relations the Government of the United Kingdom are responsible.

(3) Prior to any notification of extension in respect of any territory under the preceding paragraph, an agreement shall be concluded between the Contracting Parties by an Exchange of Notes as to the courts of the territory concerned which shall be courts to whose judgments this Convention shall apply, and the courts to which application for the registration of any judgment shall be made.

(4) The date of the coming into force of any extension under this Article shall be three months from the date of the notification given under paragraph (2) of this Article.

(5) Either of the Contracting Parties may, at any time after the expiry of three years from the coming into force of an extension of this Convention to any of the territories referred to in paragraph (2) of this Article, terminate such extension on giving six months' notice of termination through the diplomatic channel.

(6) The termination of this Convention under Article 11 shall, unless otherwise expressly agreed by both Contracting Parties, also terminate it in respect of any territory to which it has been extended under paragraph (2) of this Article.

ARTICLE 11

This Convention shall be subject to ratification. Instruments of ratification shall be exchanged as soon as possible. The Convention shall come into force three months after the date on which the instruments of ratification are exchanged and shall remain in force for three years after the date of its coming into force. If neither of the Contracting Parties shall have given notice through the diplomatic channel to the other, not less than six months before the expiration of the said period of three years, of intention to terminate the Convention, it shall remain in force until the expiration of six months from the date on which either of the Contracting Parties shall have given notice to terminate it.

[2066]

EUROPEAN COMMUNITIES (ENFORCEMENT OF COMMUNITY JUDGMENTS) ORDER 1972

(SI 1972/1590)

NOTES

Made: 23 October 1972.
Authority: European Communities Act 1972, s 2(2).
Commencement: 1 January 1973; see art 1.

1 Citation and commencement

This Order may be cited as the European Communities (Enforcement of Community Judgments) Order 1972 and shall come into operation on the date on which the United Kingdom becomes a member of the European Communities.

[2067]

2 Interpretation

(1) In this Order—

"Community judgment" means any decision, judgment or order which is enforceable under or in accordance with Article 187 or 192 of the EEC Treaty, Article 18, 159 or 164 of the Euratom Treaty or Article 44 or 92 of the ECSC Treaty [or Article 82 of Regulation 40/94 of 20 December 1993 on the community trade mark] [or Article 71 of Regulation 6/2002 of 12 December 2001 on Community designs];

"Euratom inspection order" means an order made by or in the exercise of the functions of the President of the European Court or by the Commission of the European Communities under Article 81 of the Euratom Treaty;

"order for enforcement" means an order by or under the authority of the Secretary of State that the Community judgment to which it is appended is to be registered for enforcement in the United Kingdom; and

"the High Court" means in England and in Northern Ireland the High Court and in Scotland the Court of Session.

(2) The Interpretation Act 1889 shall apply to the interpretation of this Order as it applies to the interpretation of an Act of Parliament.

[2068]

NOTES

Para (1): in definition "Community judgment" words in first pair of square brackets inserted by the European Communities (Enforcement of Community Judgments) (Amendment) Order 1998, SI 1998/1259, art 2, words in second pair of square brackets inserted by the European Communities (Enforcement of Community Judgments) (Amendment) Order 2003, SI 2003/3204, art 2.

Interpretation Act 1889: see now the Interpretation Act 1978.

3 Registration of Community judgments and orders

(1) The High Court shall, upon application duly made for the purpose by the person entitled to enforce it, forthwith register any Community judgment to which the Secretary of State has appended an order for enforcement or any Euratom inspection order.

(2) . . .

(3) Rules of court shall be made requiring notice to be given of the registration of a Community judgment or Euratom inspection order to the persons against whom the judgment was given or the order was made.

(4) Where it appears that a Community judgment under which a sum of money is payable has been partly satisfied at the date of the application for its registration, the judgment shall be registered only in respect of the balance remaining payable at that date.

(5) Where, after the date of registration of a Community judgment under which a sum of money is payable, it is shown that at that date the judgment had been partly or wholly satisfied, the registration shall be varied or cancelled accordingly with effect from that date.

[2069]

NOTES

Para (2): revoked by the Administration of Justice Act 1977, ss 4, 32(4), Sch 5, Pt I.

4 Effect of registration of Community judgment

A Community judgment registered in accordance with Article 3 shall, for all purposes of execution, be of the same force and effect, and proceedings may be taken on the judgment, and any sum payable under the judgment shall carry interest, as if the judgment had been a judgment or order given or made by the High Court on the date of registration.

[2070]

5 Suspension of enforcement of Community judgments

An order of the European Court that enforcement of a registered Community judgment be suspended shall, on production to the High Court, be registered forthwith and shall be of the same effect as if the order had been an order made by the High Court on the date of its registration staying or sisting the execution of the judgment for the same period and on the same conditions as are stated in the order of the European Court; and no steps to enforce the judgment shall thereafter be taken while such an order remains in force.

[2071]

6 Effect of registration of Euratom inspection order

Upon registration of a Euratom inspection order in accordance with Article 3, the High Court may make such order as it thinks fit against any person for the purpose of ensuring that effect is given to the Euratom inspection order.

[2072]

RECIPROCAL ENFORCEMENT OF FOREIGN JUDGMENTS (GUERNSEY) ORDER 1973

(SI 1973/610)

NOTES

Made: 29 March 1973.

Authority: Foreign Judgments (Reciprocal Enforcement) Act 1933, s 1, as extended by the Reciprocal Enforcement of Judgments (General Application to His Majesty's Dominions, etc) Order 1933, SR & O 1933/1073 at **[2001]**.

Commencement: 1 May 1973.

1 This Order may be cited as the Reciprocal Enforcement of Foreign Judgments (Guernsey) Order 1973 and shall come into operation on 1st May 1973.

[2073]

2 Part I of the Foreign Judgments (Reciprocal Enforcement) Act 1933 shall extend to the Island of Guernsey.

[2074]

3 The following courts shall be deemed superior courts of Guernsey for the purposes of the said Part I, namely the Court of Appeal of Guernsey and the Royal Court sitting as an Ordinary Court or as a Full Court.

[2075]

RECIPROCAL ENFORCEMENT OF FOREIGN JUDGMENTS (ISLE OF MAN) ORDER 1973

(SI 1973/611)

NOTES

Made: 29 March 1973.

Authority: Foreign Judgments (Reciprocal Enforcement) Act 1933, s 1, as extended by the Reciprocal Enforcement of Judgments (General Application to His Majesty's Dominions, etc) Order 1933, SR & O 1933/1073 at **[2001]**.

Commencement: 1 May 1973.

1 This Order may be cited as the Reciprocal Enforcement of Foreign Judgments (Isle of Man) Order 1973 and shall come into operation on 1st May 1973.

[2076]

2 Part I of the Foreign Judgments (Reciprocal Enforcement) Act 1933 shall extend to the Isle of Man.

[2077]

3 Her Majesty's High Court of Justice of the Isle of Man (including the Staff of Government Division) shall be deemed the superior court of the Isle of Man for the purposes of the said Part I.

[2078]

RECIPROCAL ENFORCEMENT OF FOREIGN JUDGMENTS (JERSEY) ORDER 1973

(SI 1973/612)

NOTES

Made: 29 March 1973.

Authority: Foreign Judgments (Reciprocal Enforcement) Act 1933, s 1, as extended by the Reciprocal Enforcement of Judgments (General Application to His Majesty's Dominions, etc) Order 1933, SR & O 1933/1073 at **[2001]**.

Commencement: 1 May 1973.

1 This Order may be cited as the Reciprocal Enforcement of Foreign Judgments (Jersey) Order 1973 and shall come into operation on 1st May 1973.

[2079]

2 Part I of the Foreign Judgments (Reciprocal Enforcement) Act 1933 shall extend to the Bailiwick of Jersey.

[2080]

3 The Royal Court of Jersey and the Court of Appeal of Jersey shall be deemed superior courts of Jersey for the purposes of the said Part I.

[2081]

RECIPROCAL ENFORCEMENT OF FOREIGN JUDGMENTS (ITALY) ORDER 1973

(SI 1973/1894)

NOTES

Made: 13 November 1973.

Authority: Foreign Judgments (Reciprocal Enforcement) Act 1933, s 1.

Commencement: 16 January 1974.

This order has been largely superseded by the 1968 Brussels Convention and Council Regulation 44/2001/EC. See Introductory Note at the beginning of this section.

1—(1) This Order shall come into operation on 16th January 1974 and may be cited as the Reciprocal Enforcement of Foreign Judgments (Italy) Order 1973.

(2) The Interpretation Act 1889 shall apply for the interpretation of this Order as it applies for the interpretation of an Act of Parliament.

[2082]

2 Part I of the Foreign Judgments (Reciprocal Enforcement) Act 1933 shall extend to the Republic of Italy.

[2083]

3 The following courts of the Republic of Italy shall be deemed superior courts of the Republic of Italy for the purposes of Part I of the Foreign Judgments (Reciprocal Enforcement) Act 1933, that is to say:—

The Corte d'Appello
The Tribunale

[2084]

4 No security for costs shall be required to be given by any person making application for the registration of a judgment of a superior court of the Republic of Italy.

[2085]

5 A judgment of a superior court of the Republic of Italy shall, in the absence of proof to the contrary, be deemed to be capable of execution in the Republic of Italy if there is produced a certified copy of the judgment issued by the court and bearing the following executory formula:

"Comandiamo a tutti gli ufficiali giudiziari che ne siano richiesti e a chiunque spetti, di mettere a esecuzione il presente titolo, al pubblico ministero di darvi assistenza, e a tutti gli ufficiali della forza pubblica di concorrervi, quando ne siano legalmente richiesti."

[2086]

6

The rate of interest due under the law of the Republic of Italy upon the sum in respect of which a judgment of a superior court of the Republic of Italy is given shall be deemed to be that ordered in the judgment and, if no rate is so ordered, no interest shall be deemed to be due thereon under the law of the Republic of Italy unless the contrary is shown.

[2087]

SCHEDULE 1
CONVENTION BETWEEN THE UNITED KINGDOM OF GREAT BRITAIN AND NORTHERN IRELAND AND THE REPUBLIC OF ITALY FOR THE RECIPROCAL RECOGNITION AND ENFORCEMENT OF JUDGMENTS IN CIVIL AND COMMERCIAL MATTERS

Her Majesty the Queen of the United Kingdom of Great Britain and Northern Ireland and of Her other Realms and Territories, Head of the Commonwealth, and the President of the Republic of Italy,

Desiring to provide on the basis of reciprocity of the recognition and enforcement of judgements in civil and commercial matters;

Have resolved to conclude a Convention for this purpose and to that end have appointed as their Plenipotentiaries:

Her Majesty the Queen of the United Kingdom of Great Britain and Northern Ireland and of Her other Realms and Territories, Head of the Commonwealth (hereinafter referred to as Her Majesty):

For the United Kingdom of Great Britain and Northern Ireland:
H E Sir John Guthrie Ward, Her Majesty's Ambassador Extraordinary and Plenipotentiary at Rome,

The President of the Republic of Italy:
H E the Hon Giuseppe Lupis, Under-Secretary for Foreign Affairs,

who, having communicated to each other their respective Full Powers found in good and due form, have agreed as follows:

GENERAL

Article I

For the purposes of the present Convention:

(1) The territory of one (or of the other) High Contracting Party means
(a) in relation to the United Kingdom, England and Wales, Scotland, Northern Ireland, and any territories to which the Convention shall have been extended under Article X; and
(b) in relation to the Republic of Italy, Italy.

(2) The word "judgment" means any decision of a court, however described (judgment, order and the like), which is final and conclusive as between the parties thereto notwithstanding that it may still be subject to appeal.

(3) The words "original court" mean in relation to any judgment the court by which the judgment was given; and the words "court applied to", the court in which it is sought to obtain recognition of a judgment or to which an application for the registration of a judgment or for the grant of a *dichiarazione di efficacia* is made.

(4) The words "judgment debtor" mean the person against whom the judgment was given in the original court and include, where necessary, any person against whom such judgment is enforceable under the law of the country of the original court; and the words "judgment creditor", the person in whose favour the judgment was given, and include, where necessary, any other person in whom the rights under the judgment have become vested.

(5) The word "appeal" includes any proceeding by way of discharging or setting aside a judgment or an application for a new trial or a stay of execution.

Article II

(1) Subject to the provisions of paragraph (2) the present Convention shall apply to judgments in civil and commercial matters, pronounced after the date of the entry into force of the present Convention, by the following courts:

(a) In the case of the United Kingdom, the House of Lords; for England and Wales, the Supreme Court of Judicature (Court of Appeal and High Court of Justice) and the Courts of Chancery of the Counties Palatine of Lancaster and Durham; for Scotland, the Court of Session and the Sheriff Court; and for Northern Ireland, the Supreme Court of Judicature; and

(b) in the case of Italy, the Corte d'Appello and the Tribunale.

(2) The present Convention shall not apply to:

(a) judgments given on appeal from courts not referred to in paragraph (1) of this Article;

(b) judgments given in proceedings for the recovery of any form of taxation (state or municipal);

(c) judgments given in proceedings for the recovery of fines or penalties due to public authorities.

(3) The present Convention shall not preclude the recognition and enforcement of judgments given in circumstances where the present Convention does not contemplate recognition or enforcement.

RECOGNITION OF JUDGMENTS

Article III

(1) Judgments in civil and commercial matters, pronounced in the territory of one High Contracting Party, shall, whatever the nationality of the judgment creditor or debtor, be recognised in the courts of the territory of the other High Contracting Party, except where it can be established that:

(a) in the case in question, the jurisdiction of the original court is not recognised under the provisions of Article IV;

(b) the judgment was given by default and the judgment debtor, being the defendant in the proceedings in the original court, did not (notwithstanding that process may have been duly served on him in accordance with the law of the country of the original court) receive notice of those proceedings in sufficient time to enable him to defend the proceedings;

(c) the judgment was obtained by fraud;

(d) the recognition of the judgment would be contrary to public policy in the country of the court applied to;

(e) the judgment debtor, being a defendant in the original proceedings, was a person who, in the opinion of the court applied to, was entitled under the rules of public international law to immunity from the jurisdiction of the original court and did not submit to the jurisdiction of that court; or the judgment debtor, in the opinion of the court applied to, is entitled under the rules of public international law to immunity from the jurisdiction of that court at the time of application for registration or for a *dichiarazione di efficacia;*

(f) the judgment debtor satisfies the court applied to that proceedings by way of appeal have been instituted against the judgment in the country of the original court. It is understood that if such proceedings have not been actually instituted but it appears that the judgment debtor is entitled and intends to appeal, the court applied to may adjourn its decision on the recognition of the judgment, so as to allow the judgment debtor a reasonable opportunity of instituting such proceedings, or may accord it recognition on such terms as it may think fit including the imposition of a payment into court.

(2) Where the court applied to is satisfied that the matter in dispute in the proceedings in the original court

(a) had before the date of the judgment in the original court been the subject of a final and conclusive judgment between the same parties by a court having jurisdiction in the matter, or

(b) is the subject of proceedings between the same parties in the country of the court applied to which were commenced before the date of the judgment in the original court,

the court applied to may refuse to recognise the judgment of the original court.

(3) For the purposes of the present Convention, the effect of the recognition of a judgment shall be that such judgment shall be treated as conclusive as to the matter thereby adjudicated upon in any further action as between the same parties, and shall constitute a defence in any further action between them in respect of the same cause of action.

Article IV

(1) For the purposes of sub-paragraph (a) of paragraph (1) of Article III, the original court shall be recognised as possessing jurisdiction in all cases:

(a) where the judgment debtor, being a defendant in the proceedings in the original court, submitted to the jurisdiction of that court by voluntarily appearing in the proceedings upon the merits and not only for the purpose of protecting, or obtaining the release of, property seized, or threatened with seizure, in the proceedings, or of contesting the jurisdiction of that court; or

(b) where the judgment debtor was plaintiff in, or counterclaimed in, the proceedings in the original court; or

(c) where in a matter relating to contract the judgment debtor, being a defendant in the proceedings in the original court, had before the commencement of the proceedings agreed in the form required by the law of the country of the original court to submit himself in respect of the subject matter of the proceedings to the jurisdiction of the courts of the country of the original court; or

(d) where the judgment debtor, being a defendant in the original court, was, at the time when the proceedings were instituted, resident in, or being a body corporate had its registered or head office in, the country of that court; or

(e) where the judgment debtor, being a defendant in the original court, had an office or place of business in the country of that court and the proceedings in that court were in respect of a transaction effected through or at that office or place.

(2) The provisions of paragraph (1) of this Article shall not apply to judgments where the subject matter of proceedings is immovable property, or to judgments in actions *in rem* in respect of movable property. Nevertheless the jurisdiction of the original court shall be recognised if the immovable property was situated in the country of the original court or if the movable property was so situated at the time of the commencement of the proceedings in the original court.

(3) The provisions of paragraph (1) of this Article shall not apply:

(a) to judgments in matters of family law or status (including divorce decrees or other judgments in matrimonial causes);

(b) to judgments in matters of succession, or the administration of the estates of deceased persons;

(c) to judgments in bankruptcy proceedings;

(d) to judgments in proceedings for the winding up of companies or other bodies corporate.

In the case of judgments given in proceedings of the kind referred to in the present paragraph, the jurisdiction of the original court shall be recognised in all cases where such recognition is in accordance with the law of the country of the court applied to.

(4) In the cases specified in sub-paragraphs (d) and (e) of paragraph (1) and in paragraph (2) of this Article the jurisdiction of the original court need not be recognised, if recognition is contrary to the laws of the country of the court applied to, where the bringing of

the proceedings in the original court was contrary to a compromise or other agreement under which the dispute in question was to be settled otherwise than by proceedings in the courts of the country of that court.

ENFORCEMENT OF JUDGMENTS

Article V

(1) Judgments in civil and commercial matters, pronounced in the territory of one High Contracting Party, shall, whatever the nationality of the judgment creditor or debtor, be enforced in the territory of the other High Contracting Party in the manner provided in Articles VI, VII and VIII of the present Convention provided that the following conditions are fulfilled:

- (a) none of the objections set out in Article III (read in conjunction with Article IV) to the recognition of the judgment can be established;
- (b) it can be established under the provisions of paragraph (3) of this Article that they could be enforced by execution in the country of the original court;
- (c) there is payable thereunder a sum of money;
- (d) the judgment debt has not been wholly satisfied; and provided that, where the judgment debtor satisfies the court applied to that proceedings by way of appeal have been instituted against the judgment in the country of the original court or, if such proceedings have not been instituted, that he is entitled and intends to appeal, such a judgment need not be enforced and the court applied to may take such measures in regard thereto as are permitted by its own law. However, such a judgment may be enforced on such terms as the court applied to thinks fit including the imposition of a payment into court.

(2) If the amount of the costs to be paid under a judgment is not fixed by the judgment itself but by a separate order, such order shall be deemed to be part of the judgment for the purposes of the present Convention.

(3) A judgment in respect of which a certified copy has been issued by the original court shall, in the absence of proof to the contrary, be deemed to be capable of being enforced by execution in the country of the original court within the meaning of sub-paragraph (b) of paragraph (1) of this Article. A certified copy of a judgment issued by an Italian court shall bear the executory formula set out in the Annex to the present Convention.

Article VI

(1) In order that any judgment of a court of the Republic of Italy should be enforced in the United Kingdom, an application by a judgment creditor for its registration, accompanied by a certified copy of the judgment by the original court, should be made:

- (a) In England and Wales, to the High Court of Justice;
- (b) In Scotland, to the Court of Session; and
- (c) In Northern Ireland, to the Supreme Court of Judicature;

in accordance with the procedure of the court applied to.

(2) If such application is made in respect of a judgment fulfilling the conditions laid down in Article V, registration shall be granted.

Article VII

(1) In order that any judgment of a court in a territory of the United Kingdom should be enforced in Italy, an application by a judgment creditor for the grant of a *dichiarazione di efficacia* should, in accordance with the procedure of the court applied to, be made to the Corte d'Appello in whose jurisdiction the judgment is to be enforced. Such application should be accompanied by a certified copy of the judgment issued by the original court.

(2) If such application is made in respect of a judgment fulfilling the conditions laid in Article V, a *dichiarazione di efficacia* shall be granted.

Article VIII

(1) Where any judgment has been registered under Article VI, or where a *dichiarazione di efficacia* has been granted in respect of a judgment under Article VII, such judgment shall,

as from the date of registration or grant of a *dichiarazione di efficacia*, and as regards all questions relating to its execution in the country of the court applied to, be of the same effect as if it had been a judgment originally given by the court applied to at the date of the registration or of the grant of the *dichiarazione di efficacia*; and the court applied to shall have the same jurisdiction over the execution of the judgment as it has over the execution of judgments given by itself.

(2) A copy of any judgment certified by the original court shall be accepted without legislation, but certified translations of the judgment and other documents shall be required in accordance with the procedure of the court applied to.

(3) The procedure for the registration of a judgment under Article VI and the procedure for the grant of a *dichiarazione di efficacia* under Article VII shall be made as simple and rapid as possible, and no deposit by way of security for costs shall be required of any person making application for such registration, or for the grant of a *dichiarazione di efficacia.*

(4) A period of six years, unless the law of the court applied to allows a longer period, running from the date of the judgment of the original court or, where there have been proceedings by way of appeal against the judgment, from the date of the last judgment given in the appeal proceedings, shall be allowed by the court applied to for the purpose of making any application for registration or the grant of a *dichiarazione di efficacia.*

(5) If it is found by the court applied to that the judgment in respect of which an application is made for registration or for the grant of a *dichiarazione di efficacia* has been, at the date of such application partly but not wholly satisfied by payment, registration or a *dichiarazione di efficacia* shall be granted in respect of the balance remaining payable at that date provided that the judgment is one which would be enforceable under the provisions of the present Convention.

(6) If it is found by the court applied to that the judgment in respect of which an application is made for registration or for the grant of a *dichiarazione di efficacia* contains more than one provision and that some, but not all, of the provisions of the judgment are such that if those provisions had been contained in separate judgments those judgments could properly have been registered or could have been granted a *dichiarazione di efficacia*, the judgment may be registered or granted a *dichiarazione di efficacia* in respect of those provisions of which enforcement is permitted by the present Convention.

(7) If under a judgment a sum of money is payable which is expressed in a currency other than that of the country of the court applied to, the law of the country of the court applied to shall determine if, and if so, how, the amount payable under the judgment may or shall be converted into the currency of the country of the court applied to for the purposes of the satisfaction or enforcement of the judgment debt.

(8) When granting registration or a *dichiarazione di efficacia*, the court applied to shall, if so requested by the judgment creditor, include the costs of and incidental to registration or the grant of a *dichiarazione di efficacia* and the amount due by way of interest up to the date of the grant of registration or a *dichiarazione di efficacia.*

FINAL PROVISIONS

Article IX

Any difficulties which may arise in connexion with the interpretation or application of the present Convention shall be settled through the diplomatic channel, or through any other means agreed upon by the High Contracting Parties.

Article X

(1) Her Majesty may, by a notification given through the diplomatic channel, at any time while the present Convention is in force, and provided that an agreement has been concluded by an Exchange of Notes on the points mentioned in paragraph (2) of this Article, extend the operation of the present Convention to any territory for whose international relations Her Majesty's Government in the United Kingdom of Great Britain and Northern Ireland are responsible.

(2) Prior to any notification of extension in respect of any territory under paragraph (1) of this Article, an agreement shall be concluded between the High Contracting Parties by an

Exchange of Notes as to the judgments of the courts of the territory concerned to which the present Convention shall apply and the courts to which application for registration of any judgment shall be made.

(3) Any extension of the present Convention under this Article shall come into force three months from the date of the notification given under paragraph (1) of this Article.

(4) At any time after the expiry of three years from the coming into force of an extension of the present Convention to any of the territories referred to in paragraph (1) of this Article, either of the High Contracting Parties may terminate such extension on giving six months' notice of termination through the diplomatic channel.

(5) The termination of the present Convention under Article XI shall, unless otherwise expressly agreed by both High Contracting Parties, terminate it in respect of any territory to which it has been extended under paragraph (1) of this Article.

Article XI

The present Convention shall be subject to ratification. Instruments of Ratification shall be exchanged at London. The Convention shall come into force three months after the date on which the Instruments of Ratification are exchanged, and shall remain in force for three years. If neither of the High Contracting Parties shall have given notice through the diplomatic channel to the other, not less than six months before the expiration of the said period of three years, of intention to terminate the present Convention, it shall remain in force until the expiration of six months from the date on which either of the High Contracting Parties shall have given notice to terminate it.

ANNEX

The Executory Formula referred to in paragraph (3) of Article V is as follows:

"Comandiamo a tutti gli ufficiali giudiziari che ne siano richiesti e a chiunque spetti, di mettere a esecuzione il presente titolo, al pubblico ministero di darvi assistenza, e a tutti gli ufficiali della forza pubblica di concorrervi, quando ne siano legalmente richiesti."

[2088]

SCHEDULE 2

PROTOCOL AMENDING THE CONVENTION BETWEEN THE UNITED KINGDOM OF GREAT BRITAIN AND NORTHERN IRELAND AND THE ITALIAN REPUBLIC FOR THE RECIPROCAL RECOGNITION AND ENFORCEMENT OF JUDGMENTS IN CIVIL AND COMMERCIAL MATTERS, SIGNED AT ROME ON THE 7TH FEBRUARY, 1964

Her Majesty the Queen of the United Kingdom of Great Britain and Northern Ireland and of Her other Realms and Territories, Head of the Commonwealth (hereinafter referred to as "Her Britannic Majesty" and the President of the Italian Republic;

Desiring to amend the Convention between the United Kingdom of Great Britain and Northern Ireland and the Italian Republic for the reciprocal Recognition and Enforcement of Judgments in Civil and Commercial Matters, signed at Rome on the 7th February, 1964 (hereinafter referred to as "The Convention");

Have resolved to conclude a Protocol for that Purpose, and to that end have appointed as their Plenipotentiaries:

Her Britannic Majesty:

H E Sir Patrick Hancock, Her Majesty's Ambassador Extraordinary and Plenipotentiary at Rome

The President of the Italian Republic:

H E the Hon Angelo Salizzoni, Under-Secretary of State for Foreign Affairs

who, having communicated to each other their respective Full Powers, found in good and due form, have agreed as follows:

Article 1

A new paragraph shall be inserted at the end of Article II of the Convention, to read as follows:

"(4) A High Contracting Party shall not be obliged to apply the present Convention to any judgment given in respect of injury or damage of a description which is the subject of a convention with respect to third party liability in the field of nuclear energy to which that Party is also a Party."

Article 2

At the beginning of paragraph (1) of Article II of the Convention, the words:

"Subject to the provisions of paragraph (2)" shall be replaced by the words "Subject to the provisions of paragraphs (2) and (4) of this Article".

Article 3

The present Protocol shall enter into force on the same date as the Convention and shall have the same duration as the Convention.

[2089]

RECIPROCAL ENFORCEMENT OF FOREIGN JUDGMENTS (TONGA) ORDER 1980

(SI 1980/1523)

NOTES

Made: 13 October 1980.
Authority: Foreign Judgments (Reciprocal Enforcement) Act 1933, ss 1, 3.
Commencement: 18 December 1980.

1 This Order may be cited as the Reciprocal Enforcement of Foreign Judgments (Tonga) Order 1980 and shall come into operation on 18th December 1980.

[2090]

2 Part I of the Foreign Judgments (Reciprocal Enforcement) Act 1933 shall extend to Tonga.

[2091]

3 The Supreme Court of Tonga shall be deemed a superior court of Tonga for the purposes of Part I of the Foreign Judgments (Reciprocal Enforcement) Act 1933.

[2092]

4 A judgment of a superior court of Tonga shall, in the absence of proof to the contrary, be deemed to be capable of execution in Tonga if a certified copy of the judgment is produced authenticated by the court seal and bearing or accompanied by a certificate issued by an officer of the court that it is capable of execution in Tonga.

[2093]

5 The rate of interest due under the law of Tonga upon the sum in respect of which a judgment of a superior court of Tonga is given shall be deemed to be that specified in the judgment or any certificate of the original court accompanying the judgment and, if no rate is so specified, no interest shall be deemed to be due thereon under the law of Tonga.

[2094]

6 A translation of the judgment of a superior court of Tonga or of any other document accompanying an application for registration of such a judgment shall, if certified by a sworn translator, or by a diplomatic or consular officer of either the United Kingdom or Tonga, be accepted without further authentication.

[2095]

SCHEDULE

PART I
DEFINITIONS

ARTICLE 1

In this Convention, the following words and expressions shall, unless the context otherwise requires, have the meanings assigned to them in this Article.

(a) "Action in personam" shall not be deemed to include any matrimonial cause or any proceeding in connection with matrimonial matters, administration of estates of deceased persons, bankruptcy, winding up of companies, guardianship of infants, or judicial supervision of the administration of the property or affairs of a person who is incompetent or incapable of managing and administering his property and affairs.

(b) "Appeal" includes any proceeding by way of discharging or setting aside a judgment or an application for a new trial or a stay of execution.

(c) "Judgment" means any decision of a court, however described (judgment, order and the like), by which the rights of the parties are finally determined. It includes a judgment or order given or made by a court in any criminal proceedings for the payment of a sum of money in respect of compensation or damages to an injured party. It also includes judgments and orders against which an appeal may be pending or which may still be subject to appeal in the courts of the country of the original court. If the amount of the costs or interest to be paid under a judgment is not fixed by the judgment itself but by a separate court order, such order shall be deemed to be part of the judgment for the purposes of this Convention.

(d) "Judgment creditor" means the person in whose favour the judgment was given, and includes any person in whom the rights under the judgment have become vested by succession or assignment or otherwise.

(e) "Judgment debtor" means the person against whom the judgment was given in the original court and includes any person against whom the judgment is enforceable under the law of the country of the original court.

(f) "Original court" in relation to any judgment means the court by which the judgment was given; and "Court applied to" means the court to which an application for the registration of a judgment is made.

(g) "Superior court" means—
   (i) in the case of the United Kingdom of Great Britain and Northern Ireland (hereinafter referred to as "the United Kingdom"), the House of Lords; for England and Wales, the Supreme Court of Judicature (Court of Appeal, High Court of Justice and Crown Court); for Scotland, the Court of Session and the Sheriff Court; and for Northern Ireland, the Supreme Court of Judicature; and
   (ii) in the case of Tonga, the Supreme Court of Tonga.

(h) "Territory" means—
   (i) in relation to the United Kingdom, England and Wales, Scotland, Northern Ireland and any territories to which the Convention may have been extended under Article 11; and
   (ii) in relation to Tonga, the Kingdom of Tonga.

PART II
ENFORCEMENT OF JUDGMENTS

ARTICLE 2

(1) Any judgment of a superior court other than a judgment of such a court given on appeal from a court which is not a superior court, shall be a judgment to which this Part of this Convention applies, if—

(a) it is final and conclusive as between the parties thereto; and
(b) there is payable thereunder a sum of money, not being a sum payable in respect of taxes or other charges of a like nature or in respect of a fine or other penalty; and
(c) it is given after the date of the entry into force of this Convention.

(2) For the purposes of this Article, a judgment shall be deemed to be final and conclusive notwithstanding that an appeal may be pending against it, or that it may still be subject to appeal, in the courts of the country of the original court.

ARTICLE 3

(1) A person, being a judgment creditor under a judgment to which this Part of this Convention applies, may apply to the competent superior court at any time within a period of six years after the date of the judgment or, where there have been proceedings by way of appeal against the judgment, after the date of the last judgment given in those proceedings, to have the judgment registered, and on any such application the competent superior court shall, subject to such simple and rapid procedures as each Contracting Party may prescribe and to the other provisions of this Convention, order the judgment to be registered—

Provided that a judgment shall not be registered if at the date of the application—

(a) it has been wholly satisfied; or
(b) it could not be enforced by execution in the country of the original court; or
(c) the court is satisfied that the judgment debtor, being a defendant in the original proceedings, was a person who, in the opinion of the court applied to, was entitled under the rules of public international law to immunity from the jurisdiction of the courts of the country of the original court and did not submit to the jurisdiction of that court; or
(d) the court is satisfied that the judgment is sought to be enforced against a person who, in the opinion of the court applied to, is entitled under the rules of public international law to immunity from the jurisdiction of the court applied to.

(2) Subject to the provisions of this Convention with respect to the setting aside of registration—

(a) a registered judgment shall, for the purposes of execution, be of the same force and effect; and
(b) proceedings may be taken on it; and
(c) the sum for which it is registered shall, as from the date of the order giving leave to register the judgment, carry interest on the total sum (principal and interest, if any) in respect of which an order is made for leave to register the judgment, at a rate to be determined by the court applied to; and
(d) the court applied to shall have the same control over the execution of it;

as if it had been a judgment originally given in the court applied to and entered on the date of registration—

Provided that a judgment shall not be executed so long as, in accordance with the provisions of this Convention and the law of the court applied to, it is competent for any party to make an application to have the registration of the judgment set aside, or, where such an application is made, until the application has been finally determined.

(3) Where the sum payable under a judgment which is to be registered is expressed in a currency other than the currency of the country of the court applied to, the law of the country of the court applied to shall determine if, and if so in what manner and at what stage, the amount payable under the judgment may or shall be converted into the currency of the court applied to for the purposes of the satisfaction or enforcement of the judgment debt.

(4) If at the date of the application for registration the judgment of the original court has been partly satisfied, the judgment shall not be registered in respect of the whole sum payable under the judgment of the original court, but only in respect of the balance remaining payable at that date.

(5) If, on an application for the registration of a judgment, it appears to the court applied to that the judgment is in respect of different matters and that some, but not all, of the provisions of the judgment are such that if those provisions had been contained in separate judgments those judgments could properly have been registered, the judgment may be registered in respect of the provisions aforesaid but not in respect of any other provisions contained therein.

(6) In addition to the sum of money payable under the judgment of the original court, including any interest which by the law of the country of the original court becomes due under the judgment up to the time of registration, the judgment shall be registered for the reasonable costs of and incidental to registration, including the costs of obtaining a certified copy of the judgment from the original court.

ARTICLE 4

(1) In order that any judgment given in Tonga may be enforced in the United Kingdom, an application by a judgment creditor for its registration should, in accordance with the procedure of the court applied to, be made—

(a) in England and Wales, to the High Court of Justice;
(b) in Scotland, to the Court of Session; and
(c) in Northern Ireland, to the Supreme Court of Judicature.

(2) The application for registration should be accompanied by—

(a) a certified copy of the judgment authenticated by the court seal and bearing or accompanied by a certificate issued by an officer of the court that it is capable of execution in the country of that court;
(b) an affidavit of the facts required by the rules of the court applied to;
(c) a translation into English of any document which is in some other language and which is required by this paragraph, certified by a sworn translator or by a diplomatic or consular officer of either Contracting Party.

(3) The documents enumerated in paragraph (2) shall require no further authentication.

(4) If an application is made in accordance with paragraphs (1) and (2) of this Article in respect of a judgment fulfilling the conditions laid down in Article 3, registration shall be granted.

ARTICLE 5

(1) In order that any judgment given in the territory of the United Kingdom may be enforced in Tonga, an application by a judgment creditor for its registration should, in accordance with the procedure of the court applied to, be made to the Supreme Court of Tonga.

(2) The application for registration should be accompanied by—

(a) a certified copy of the judgment authenticated by the court seal (or in the case of judgments of the Sheriff Court, authenticated by the signature of the Sheriff Clerk) and bearing or accompanied by a certificate issued by an officer of the court that it is capable of execution in the country of that court;
(b) an affidavit of the facts required by the rules of the court applied to;
(c) a translation into English of any document which is in some other language and which is required by this paragraph, certified by a sworn translator or by a diplomatic or consular officer of either Contracting Party.

(3) The documents enumerated in paragraph (2) shall require no further authentication.

(4) If an application is made in accordance with paragraphs (1) and (2) of this Article in respect of a judgment fulfilling the conditions laid down in Article 3, registration shall be granted.

ARTICLE 6

(1) On an application in that behalf duly made by any party against whom a registered judgment may be enforced—

(a) the registration of the judgment shall be set aside if the court applied to is satisfied—
  (i) that the judgment is not a judgment to which this Part of this Convention applies, or the judgment was registered in contravention of the provisions of this Convention; or
  (ii) that the courts of the country of the original court had no jurisdiction in the circumstances of the case; or
  (iii) that the judgment debtor, being the defendant in the proceedings in the original court, did not (notwithstanding that process may have been duly served on him in accordance with the law of the country of the original court) receive notice of those proceedings in sufficient time to enable him to defend the proceedings and did not appear; or
  (iv) that the judgment was obtained by fraud; or
  (v) that the enforcement of the judgment would be contrary to public policy in the country of the court applied to; or
  (vi) that the rights under the judgment are not vested in the person by whom the application for registration was made;
(b) the registration of the judgment may be set aside if the court applied to is satisfied that the matter in dispute in the proceedings in the original court had previously to the date of the judgment in the original court been the subject of a final and conclusive judgment by a court having jurisdiction in the matter.

(2) For the purposes of this Article the courts of the country of the original court shall, subject to the provisions of paragraph (3) of this Article, be deemed to have had jurisdiction—

(a) in the case of a judgment given in an action in personam—

(i) if the judgment debtor, being a defendant in the original court, submitted to the jurisdiction of that court by voluntarily appearing in the proceedings otherwise than for the purpose of protecting, or obtaining the release of, property seized, or threatened with seizure, in the proceedings or of contesting the jurisdiction of that court; or

(ii) if the judgment debtor was plaintiff in, or counter-claimed in, the proceedings in the original court; or

(iii) if the judgment debtor, being a defendant in the original court, had before the commencement of the proceedings agreed, in respect of the subject matter of the proceedings, to submit to the jurisdiction of that court or of the courts of the country of that court; or

(iv) if the judgment debtor, being a defendant in the original court, was at the time when the proceedings were instituted resident in, or being a body corporate had its principal place of business in, the country of that court; or

(v) if the judgment debtor, being a defendant in the original court, had an office or place of business in the country of that court and the proceedings in that court were in respect of a transaction effected through or at that office or place;

(b) in the case of a judgment given in an action of which the subject matter was immovable property or in an action in rem of which the subject matter was movable property, if the property in question was at the time of the proceedings in the original court situated in the country of that court;

(c) in the case of a judgment given in an action other than any such action as is mentioned in sub-paragraph (a) or sub-paragraph (b) of this paragraph, if the jurisdiction of the original court is recognised by the law of the registering court.

(3) Notwithstanding anything in paragraph (2) of this Article, the courts of the country of the original court shall not be deemed to have had jurisdiction—

(a) if the subject matter of the proceedings was immovable property outside the country of the original court; or

(b) except in the cases mentioned in sub-sub-paragraphs (i), (ii), and (iii) of sub-paragraph (a) and in sub-paragraph (b) of paragraph (2) of this Article, if the bringing of the proceedings in the original court was contrary to an agreement under which the dispute in question was to be settled otherwise than by proceedings in the courts of the country of that court.

Where the judgment debtor satisfies the court applied to that an appeal is pending or that he is entitled and intends to appeal against the judgment in the country of the original court, the judgment need not be enforced, and the court applied to may take such measures in regard thereto as are permitted by the law of its country.

PART III
RECOGNITION OF JUDGMENTS

ARTICLE 8

(1) Subject to the provisions of this Article, a judgment given in the territory of one Contracting Party and to which Part II of this Convention applies or would have applied if a sum of money had been payable thereunder, whether it can be enforced or not, and whether, if it can be enforced, it is enforced or not, shall be recognised in the territory of the other as conclusive between the parties thereto in all proceedings founded on the same cause of action and shall be capable of being relied on by way of defence or counter-claim in any such proceedings.

(2) The provisions of paragraph (1) of this Article shall not apply in the case of any judgment—

(a) where the judgment has been registered and the registration thereof has been set aside on some ground other than—

(i) that a sum of money was not payable under the judgment; or

(ii) that the judgment had been wholly or partly satisfied; or

(iii) that at the date of the application for registration the judgment could not be enforced by execution in the country of the original court; or

(b) where the judgment has not been registered, it is shown (whether it could have been registered or not) that if it had been registered, the registration thereof would have been set aside on an application for that purpose on some ground other than one of the grounds specified in sub-paragraph (a) of this paragraph.

PART IV
GENERAL

ARTICLE 9

(1) Enforcement or recognition of a judgment shall not be refused merely on the ground that the original court has applied, in the choice of the system of law applicable to the case, rules of private international law different from those observed by the court applied to.

(2) Nothing in this Convention shall preclude the enforcement or recognition in the territory of one Contracting Party, in accordance with the municipal law for the time being in force in the country concerned, of judgments given in the territory of the other Contracting Party, being judgments to which this Convention does not apply or judgments given in circumstances where the provisions of this Convention do not require such enforcement or recognition.

PART V
FINAL PROVISIONS

ARTICLE 10

Any difficulties which may arise in connexion with the interpretation or application of this Convention shall be settled through the diplomatic channel.

ARTICLE 11

(1) Subject to paragraph (2) of this Article, the Government of the United Kingdom may, by notification given through the diplomatic channel at any time while this Convention is in force, extend its operation to any territory for the international relations of which they are responsible.

(2) Prior to any notification of extension in respect of any territory under the preceding paragraph, an agreement shall be concluded between the Contracting Parties by an Exchange of Notes as to the courts of the territory concerned which shall be courts to whose judgments this Convention shall apply, and the courts to which application for registration of any judgment shall be made.

(3) Any such extension shall come into force one month after the date of its notification.

(4) Either of the Contracting Parties may, at any time after the expiry of three years from the coming into force of an extension of this Convention to any of the territories referred to in paragraph (1) of this Article, terminate such extension on giving six months' notice of termination through the diplomatic channel.

(5) The termination of this Convention under Article 12 shall, unless otherwise expressly agreed by both Contracting Parties, also terminate it in respect of any territory to which it has been extended under paragraph (1) of this Article.

ARTICLE 12

This Convention shall be subject to ratification. Instruments of Ratification shall be exchanged at Nuku'alofa. The Convention shall enter into force three months after the date on which the Instruments of Ratification are exchanged, and shall remain in force for three years from the date of its entry into force. If neither of the Contracting Parties shall have given notice through the diplomatic channel to the other, not less than six months before the expiration of the said period of three years, of intention to terminate the Convention, it shall remain in force until the expiration of six months from the date on which either of the Contracting Parties shall have given notice to terminate it.

[2096]

RECIPROCAL ENFORCEMENT OF FOREIGN JUDGMENTS (SURINAME) ORDER 1981

(SI 1981/735)

NOTES

Made: 13 May 1981.
Authority: Foreign Judgments (Reciprocal Enforcement) Act 1933, ss 1, 3.
Commencement: 13 May 1981.

1 This Order may be cited as the Reciprocal Enforcement of Foreign Judgments (Suriname) Order 1981 and shall come into operation on 13th May 1981.

[2097]

2 Part I of the Foreign Judgments (Reciprocal Enforcement) Act 1933 shall extend to the Republic of Suriname.

[2098]

3 The following courts of the Republic of Suriname shall be deemed superior courts of the Republic of Suriname for the purposes of Part I of the Foreign Judgments (Reciprocal Enforcement) Act 1933, that is to say—

The Hof van Justitie van Suriname;
The Kantongerecht in het Eerste Kanton;
The Kantongerecht in het Derde Kanton.

[2099]

4 No security for costs shall be required to be given by any person making application for the registration of a judgment of a superior court of the Republic of Suriname.

[2100]

5 A judgment of a superior court of the Republic of Suriname shall, in the absence of proof to the contrary, be deemed to be capable of execution in the Republic of Suriname if a certified copy of the judgment is produced bearing the seal of the court and the executory formula "In naam van de Republiek".

[2101]

6 The rate of interest due under the law of the Republic of Suriname upon the sum in respect of which a judgment of a superior court of the Republic of Suriname is given shall be deemed to be that specified in the judgment or any certificate of the original court accompanying the judgment and, if no rate is so specified, no interest shall be deemed to be due thereon under the law of the Republic of Suriname.

[2102]

7 A translation of the judgment of a superior court of the Republic of Suriname or of any other document accompanying an application for registration of such a judgment shall, if certified by a sworn translator or by a diplomatic or consular officer of either the United Kingdom or the Republic of Suriname, be accepted without further authentication.

[2103]

(*Sch 1 contains the text of the Exchange of Notes, dated 2 September 1970, between the United Kingdom and the Netherlands, extending to Suriname and the Netherlands Antilles the convention of 17 November 1967 providing for the reciprocal recognition and enforcement of judgments in civil matters* (*which is set out in the Schedule to SI 1969/1063 at* **[2058]**)*; Sch 2, Pt I sets out the declaration of 29 November 1975 whereby the Government of the Republic of Suriname declared to the Secretary-General of the United Nations that, the territory of Suriname having become the sovereign state of the Republic of Suriname, it would be presumed that the Republic of Suriname had succeeded to the rights and obligations of the Kingdom of the Netherlands in respect of the Convention of 17 November 1967; Sch 2, Pt II sets out the Note of 17 May 1980 whereby the Government of the Republic of Suriname informed the Government of the United Kingdom that, in the event of a decision by the former to make a declaration of non-succession in respect of that Convention, it would take into account a six months' period of notice.*)

RECIPROCAL ENFORCEMENT OF JUDGMENTS (ADMINISTRATION OF JUSTICE ACT 1920, PART II) (CONSOLIDATION) ORDER 1984

(SI 1984/129)

NOTES

Made: 8 February 1984.
Authority: Administration of Justice Act 1920, s 14.
Commencement: 8 February 1984.

1 This Order may be cited as the Reciprocal Enforcement of Judgments (Administration of Justice Act 1920, Part II) (Consolidation) Order 1984 and shall come into operation on 8th February 1984.

[2104]

2 Part II of the Administration of Justice Act 1920 shall extend to the countries and territories specified in Schedule 1 to this Order.

[2105]

3 The Orders specified in Schedule 2 to this Order are hereby revoked.

[2106]

SCHEDULE 1

Article 2

[Anguilla
Antigua and Barbuda
Bahamas
Barbados
Belize
Bermuda
Botswana
British Indian Ocean Territory
British Virgin Islands
Cayman Islands
Christmas Island
Cocos (Keeling) Islands
Republic of Cyprus
Dominica
Falkland Islands
Fiji
The Gambia
Ghana
…
Grenada
Guyana
Hong Kong
Jamaica
Newfoundland
…
…
Nigeria
Territory of Norfolk Island
…
Papua New Guinea
…
St Christopher and Nevis
St Helena
St Lucia
St Vincent and the Grenadines
Saskatchewan
Seychelles
Sierra Leone
Singapore
Solomon Islands
…
Sovereign Base Areas of Akrotiri and Dhekelia in Cyprus
Sri Lanka
Swaziland
Tanzania
…

Kenya	Trinidad and Tobago
Kiribati	Turks and Caicos Islands
Lesotho	Tuvalu
Malawi	Uganda
Malaysia	…
Malta	…
Mauritius	Zambia
Montserrat	Zimbabwe]

[2107]

NOTES

Words in square brackets substituted by the Reciprocal Enforcement of Judgments (Administration of Justice Act 1920, Part II) (Amendment) Order 1985, SI 1985/1994, art 2, Schedule; first entry omitted revoked by the Reciprocal Enforcement of Judgments (Administration of Justice Act 1920, Part II) (Amendment) Order 1997, SI 1997/2601, art 2; remaining entries omitted revoked by the Reciprocal Enforcement of Foreign Judgments (Australia) Order 1994, SI 1994/1901, art 9(2); entry relating to Hong Kong is thought to be spent following the termination of British sovereignty and jurisdiction over Hong Kong as from 1 July 1997 under the Hong Kong Act 1985, s 1; judgments from Newfoundland and Saskatchewan are now enforceable under the Foreign Judgments (Reciprocal Enforcement) Act 1933 by virtue of the Reciprocal Enforcement of Foreign Judgments (Canada) Order 1987, SI 1987/468 at **[2108]**; since 1 May 2004, the Republic of Cyprus and Malta are Member States of the European Community and judgments from these States in civil and commercial matters are enforceable under Council Regulation 44/2001/EC on jurisdiction and the recognition and enforcement of judgments in civil and commercial matters at **[3080]**.

(*Sch 2 revokes various Orders.*)

RECIPROCAL ENFORCEMENT OF FOREIGN JUDGMENTS (CANADA) ORDER 1987

(SI 1987/468)

NOTES

Made: 18 March 1987.

Authority: Foreign Judgments (Reciprocal Enforcement) Act 1933, ss 1, 3; the Civil Jurisdiction and Judgments Act 1982, s 9(2).

Commencement: 18 March 1987.

It should be noted that the French translation of the Schedule contained in this Order in Council is not reproduced here.

1 This Order shall come into force on 18th March 1987 and may be cited as the Reciprocal Enforcement of Foreign Judgments (Canada) Order 1987.

[2108]

2 Part 1 of the Foreign Judgments (Reciprocal Enforcement) Act 1933 shall extend to Canada.

[2109]

3 The following courts of Canada shall be recognised courts of Canada for the purposes of Part I of the Foreign Judgments (Reciprocal Enforcement) Act 1933, that is to say the Federal Court of Canada and any court of the Province of [Alberta], British Columbia, Manitoba, New Brunswick [Newfoundland][, the Northwest Territories], Nova Scotia or Ontario[, Prince Edward Island][, Saskatchewan] [or the Yukon Territory].

[2110]

NOTES

Word in first pair of square brackets inserted by the Reciprocal Enforcement of Foreign Judgments (Canada) (Amendment) Order 1992, SI 1992/1731, art 2; word in second pair of square brackets inserted by the Reciprocal Enforcement of Foreign Judgments (Canada) (Amendment) Order 1991, SI 1991/1724, art 2; words in third pair of square brackets inserted by the Reciprocal Enforcement of Foreign Judgments (Canada) (Amendment) Order 1989, SI 1989/987, art 2; words in fourth pair of square brackets added by the Reciprocal Enforcement of Foreign Judgments (Canada) (Amendment) Order 1988, SI 1988/1304, reg 2; word in fifth pair of square brackets added by the Reciprocal Enforcement of Foreign Judgments (Canada) (Amendment) Order 1988, SI 1988/1853, art 2; words in final pair of square brackets added by the Reciprocal Enforcement of Foreign Judgments (Canada) (Amendment) Order 1987, SI 1987/2211, art 2.

4 The following judgments shall be judgments to which Part I of the Foreign Judgments (Reciprocal Enforcement) Act 1933 applies, that is to say any decision, however described (judgment, order and the like), given by a recognised court of Canada in a civil or commercial matter and including an award in proceedings on an arbitration which has become enforceable in the same manner as a judgment given by one of the said courts.

[2111]

5 A judgment given in one of the said courts of Canada shall, in the absence of proof to the contrary, be deemed to be capable of execution in Canada if a certified copy of the judgment and, if appropriate, a translation thereof into English, certified by a sworn translator, is produced.

[2112]

6 The rate of interest due under the law of Canada upon the sum in respect of which a judgment of one of the said courts of Canada is given shall be deemed to be that specified in the judgment or any certificate of the original court accompanying the judgment and, if no rate is so specified, no interest shall be deemed to be due thereon under the law of Canada unless the contrary is shown.

[2113]

7 It is hereby declared that—

(a) the provisions contained in articles 5 and 6 of this Order are necessary for giving effect to the Convention scheduled hereto in relation to matters with respect to which there is power to make rules of court for the purposes of Part I of the Foreign Judgments (Reciprocal Enforcement) Act 1933; and

(b) Article IX of the Convention scheduled hereto is a provision of a Convention whereby the United Kingdom assumes an obligation of the kind provided for in Article 59 of the Convention on jurisdiction and the enforcement of judgments in civil and commercial matters, signed at Brussels on 27th September 1968.

[2114]

8 (*Revokes the Reciprocal Enforcement of Foreign Judgments (Canada) Order 1986, SI 1986/2027.*)

SCHEDULE
CONVENTION BETWEEN THE UNITED KINGDOM OF GREAT BRITAIN AND NORTHERN IRELAND AND CANADA PROVIDING FOR THE RECIPROCAL RECOGNITION AND ENFORCEMENT OF JUDGMENTS IN CIVIL AND COMMERCIAL MATTERS

The Government of Great Britain and Northern Ireland and the Government of Canada,

Desiring to provide on the basis of reciprocity for the recognition and enforcement of judgments in civil and commercial matters,

Have agreed as follows—

PART I
DEFINITIONS

Article I

In this Convention

(a) "appeal" includes any proceeding by way of discharging or setting aside a judgment or an application for a new trial or a stay of execution;

(b) "the 1968 Convention" means the Convention of 27th September 1968 on Jurisdiction and the Enforcement of Judgments in Civil and Commercial Matters as amended;

(c) "court of a Contracting State" means
   (i) in relation to the United Kingdom, any court of the United Kingdom or of any territory to which this Convention extends pursuant to Article XIII;
   (ii) in relation to Canada, the Federal Court of Canada or any court of a province or territory to which this Convention extends pursuant to Article XII

and the expressions "court of the United Kingdom" and "court of Canada" shall be construed accordingly;

(d) "judgment" means any decision, however described (judgment, order and the like), given by a court in a civil or commercial matter, and includes an award in proceedings on an arbitration if the award has become enforceable in the territory of origin in the same manner as a judgment given by a court in that territory;

(e) "judgment creditor" means the person in whose favour the judgment was given, and includes his executors, administrators, successors and assigns;

(f) "judgment debtor" means the person against whom the judgment was given and includes any person against whom the judgment is enforceable under the law of the territory of origin;

(g) "original court" in relation to any judgment means the court by which the judgment was given;

(h) "registering court" means a court to which an application for the registration of a judgment is made;

(i) "territory of origin" means the territory for which the original court was exercising jurisdiction;

[(j) "the 1988 Convention" means the Convention of 16th September 1988 on Jurisdiction and the Enforcement of Judgments in Civil and Commercial Matters, signed at Lugano.]

PART II
SCOPE OF THE CONVENTION

Article II

1. Subject to the provisions of this Article, this Convention shall apply to any judgment given by a court of a Contracting State after the Convention enters into force and, for the purposes of Article IX, to any judgment given by a court of a third State which is party to the 1968 Convention [or to the 1988 Convention].

2. This Convention shall not apply to

(a) orders for the periodic payment of maintenance;

(b) the recovery of taxes, duties or charges of a like nature or the recovery of a fine or penalty;

(c) judgments given on appeal from decisions of tribunals other than courts;

(d) judgments which determine
   (i) the status or legal capacity of natural persons;
   (ii) custody or guardianship of infants;
   (iii) matrimonial matters;
   (iv) succession to or the administration of the estates of deceased persons;
   (v) bankruptcy, insolvency or the winding up of companies or other legal persons;
   (vi) the management of the affairs of a person not capable of managing his own affairs.

3. Part III of this Convention shall apply only to a judgment whereby a sum of money is made payable.

4. This Convention is without prejudice to any other remedy available to a judgment creditor for the recognition and enforcement in one Contracting State of a judgment given by a court of the other Contracting State.

PART III
ENFORCEMENT OF JUDGMENTS

Article III

1. Where a judgment has been given by a court of one Contracting State, the judgment creditor may apply in accordance with Article VI to a court of the other Contracting State at

any time within a period of six years after the date of the judgment (or, where there have been proceedings by way of appeal against the judgment, after the date of the last judgment given in those proceedings) to have the judgment registered, and on any such application the registering court shall, subject to such simple and rapid procedures as each Contracting State may prescribe and to the other provisions of this Convention, order the judgment to be registered.

2. In addition to the sum of money payable under the judgment of the original court including interest accrued to the date of registration, the judgment shall be registered for the reasonable costs of and incidental to registration, if any, including the costs of obtaining a certified copy of the judgment from the original court.

3. If, on an application for the registration of a judgment, it appears to the registering court that the judgment is in respect of different matters and that some, but not all, of the provisions of the judgment are such that if those provisions had been contained in separate judgments those judgments could properly have been registered, the judgment may be registered in respect of the provisions in respect of the provisions aforesaid but not in respect of any other provisions contained therein.

4. Subject to the other provisions of this Convention

(a) a registered judgment shall, for the purposes of enforcement, be of the same force and effect,

(b) proceedings may be taken on it, and

(c) the registering court shall have the same control over its enforcement,

as if it had been a judgment originally given in the registering court with effect from the date of registration.

Article IV

1. Registration of a judgment shall be refused or set aside if

(a) the judgment has been satisfied;

(b) the judgment is not enforceable in the territory of origin;

(c) the original court is not regarded by the registering court as having jurisdiction;

(d) the judgment was obtained by fraud;

(e) enforcement of the judgment would be contrary to public policy in the territory of the registering court;

(f) the judgment is a judgment of a country or territory other than the territory of origin which has been registered in the original court or has become enforceable in the territory of origin in the same manner as a judgment of that court; or

(g) in the view of the registering court the judgment debtor either is entitled to immunity from the jurisdiction of that court or was entitled to immunity in the original court and did not submit to its jurisdiction.

2. The law of the registering court may provide that registration of a judgment may or shall be set aside if

(a) the judgment debtor, being the defendant in the original proceedings, either was not served with the process of the original court or did not receive notice of those proceedings in sufficient time to enable him to defend the proceedings and, in either case, did not appear;

(b) another judgment has been given by a court having jurisdiction in the matter in dispute prior to the date of judgment in the original court; or

(c) the judgment is not final or an appeal is pending or the judgment debtor is entitled to appeal or to apply for leave to appeal against the judgment in the territory of origin.

3. If at the date of the application for registration the judgment of the original court has been partly satisfied, the judgment shall be registered only in respect of the balance remaining payable at that date.

4. A judgment shall not be enforced so long as, in accordance with the provisions of this Convention and the law of the registering court, it is competent for any party to make an application to have the registration of the judgment set aside or, where such an application is made, until the application has been finally determined.

Article V

1. For the purposes of Article IV(1)(c) the original court shall be regarded as having jurisdiction if

(a) the judgment debtor, being a defendant in the original court, submitted to the jurisdiction of that court by voluntarily appearing in the proceedings;
(b) the judgment debtor was plaintiff in, or counterclaimed in, the proceedings in the original court;
(c) the judgment debtor, being a defendant in the original court, had before the commencement of the proceedings agreed, in respect of the subject matter of the proceedings, to submit to the jurisdiction of that court or of the courts of the territory of origin;
(d) the judgment debtor, being a defendant in the original court, was at the time when the proceedings were instituted habitually resident in, or being a body corporate had its principal place of business in, the territory of origin;
(e) the judgment debtor, being a defendant in the original court, had an office or place of business in the territory of origin and the proceedings were in respect of a transaction effected through or at that office or place; or
(f) the jurisdiction of the original court is otherwise recognised by the registering court.

2. Notwithstanding anything in sub-paragraphs (d), (e) and (f) of paragraph (1), the original court shall not be regarded as having jurisdiction if
(a) the subject matter of the proceedings was immovable outside the territory of origin; or
(b) the bringing of the proceedings in the original court was contrary to an agreement under which the dispute in question was to be settled otherwise than by proceedings in the courts of the territory of origin.

PART IV
PROCEDURES

Article VI

1. Any application for the registration in the United Kingdom of a judgment of a court of Canada shall be made
(a) in England and Wales, to the High Court of Justice;
(b) in Scotland, to the Court of Session;
(c) in Northern Ireland, to the High Court of Justice.

2. Any application for the registration in Canada of a judgment of a court of the United Kingdom shall be made
(a) in the case of a judgment relating to a matter within the competence of the Federal Court of Canada, to the Federal Court of Canada;
(b) in the case of any other judgment, to a court of a province or territory designated by Canada pursuant to Article XII.

3. The practice and procedure governing registration (including notice to the judgment debtor and applications to set registration aside) shall, except as otherwise provided in this Convention, be governed by the law of the registering court.

4. The registering court may require that an application for registration be accompanied by
(a) the judgment of the original court or a certified copy thereof;
(b) a certified translation of the judgment, if given in a language other than the language of the territory of the registering court;
(c) proof of the notice given to the defendant in the original proceedings, unless this appears from the judgment; and
(d) particulars of such other matters as may be required by the rules of the registering court.

Article VII

All matters concerning
(a) the conversion of the sum payable under a registered judgment into the currency of the territory of the registering court, and
(b) the interest payable on the judgment with respect to the period following its registration,
shall be determined by the law of the registering court.

PART V
RECOGNITION OF JUDGMENTS

Article VIII

Any judgment given by a court of one Contracting State for the payment of a sum of money which could be registered under this Convention, whether or not the judgment has been registered, and any other judgment given by such a court, which if it were a judgment for the payment of a sum of money could be registered under this Convention, shall, unless registration has been or would be refused or set aside on any ground other than that the judgment has been satisfied or could not be enforced in the territory of origin, be recognised in a court of the other Contracting State as conclusive between the parties thereto in all proceedings founded on the same cause of action.

PART VI
RECOGNITION AND ENFORCEMENT OF THIRD STATE JUDGMENTS

Article IX

[1. The United Kingdom undertakes, in the circumstances permitted by Article 59 of the 1968 Convention and by Article 59 of the 1988 Convention, not to recognise or enforce under either of those Conventions any judgment given in a third State against a person domiciled or habitually resident in Canada.]

2. For the purposes of paragraph (1)
   (a) an individual shall be treated as domiciled in Canada if and only if he is resident in Canada and the nature and circumstances of his residence indicate that he has a substantial connection with Canada; and
   (b) a corporation or association shall be treated as domiciled in Canada if and only if it is incorporated or formed under a law in force in Canada and has a registered office there, or its central management and control is exercised in Canada.

PART VII
FINAL PROVISIONS

Article X

This Convention shall not affect any conventions, international instruments or reciprocal arrangements to which both Contracting States are or will be parties and which, in relation to particular matters, govern the recognition or enforcement of judgments.

Article XI

Either Contracting State may, on the exchange of instruments of ratification or at any time thereafter, declare that it will not apply the Convention to a judgment that imposes a liability which that State is under a treaty obligation toward any other State not to recognise or enforce. Any such declaration shall specify the treaty containing the obligation.

Article XII

1. On the exchange of instruments of ratification, Canada shall designate the provinces or territories to which this Convention shall extend and the courts of the provinces and territories concerned to which application for the registration of a judgment given by a court of the United Kingdom may be made.

2. The designation by Canada may be modified by a further designation given at any time thereafter.

3. Any designation shall take effect three months after the date on which it is given.

Article XIII

1. The United Kingdom may at any time while this Convention is in force declare that this Convention shall extend to the Isle of Man, any of the Channel Islands, Gibraltar or the

Sovereign Base Areas of Akrotiri and Dhekelia (being territories to which the 1968 Convention may be applied pursuant to Article 60 of that Convention).

2. Any declaration pursuant to paragraph (1) shall specify the courts of the territories to which application for the registration of a judgment given by a court of Canada shall be made.

3. Any declaration made by the United Kingdom pursuant to this Article may be modified by a further declaration given at any time thereafter.

4. Any declaration pursuant to this Article shall take effect three months after the date on which it is given.

Article XIV

1. This Convention shall be ratified; instruments of ratification shall be exchanged at London.

2. This Convention shall enter into force three months after the date on which instruments of ratification are exchanged.

3. This Convention may be terminated by notice in writing by either Contracting State and it shall terminate three months after the date of such notice.

[2115]

NOTES

Article I: para (j) added by the Reciprocal Enforcement of Foreign Judgments (Canada) (Amendment) Order 1995, SI 1995/2708, art 2(a).

Article II: words in square brackets in para 1 added by SI 1995/2708, art 2(b).

Article IX: para 1 substituted by SI 1995/2708, art 2(c).

CIVIL JURISDICTION (OFFSHORE ACTIVITIES) ORDER 1987

(SI 1987/2197)

NOTES

Made: 18 December 1987.

Authority: Oil and Gas (Enterprise) Act 1982, s 23, Continental Shelf Act 1964, ss 6, 7; to the extent this Order took effect under the Oil and Gas (Enterprise) Act 1982, s 23, it now has effect as if made under the Petroleum Act 1998, s 11, by virtue of s 49 of, and Sch 3, Pt I, para 1(2) to, that Act.

Commencement: 1 February 1988.

1 Citation and interpretation

(1) This Order may be cited as the Civil Jurisdiction (Offshore Activities) Order 1987.

(2) In this Order—

"the Act" means the Oil and Gas (Enterprise) Act 1982;

"co-ordinate" means a co-ordinate on European datum (1st Adjustment 1950);

"Dividing Line" means the dividing line as defined in Article 1 of the Agreement between the United Kingdom and the Federal Republic of Germany relating to the Delimitation of the Continental Shelf under the North Sea between the two countries, signed in London on 25 November 1971;

"installation" includes an installation in transit;

"line", in relation to any list of co-ordinates in this Order, unless it is otherwise provided, means a loxodromic line;

"relevant act" means an act or omission taking place on, under or above the offshore area in connection with any activity mentioned in section 23(2) of the Act;

"offshore area" means—

(a) tidal waters and parts of the sea adjacent to the United Kingdom up to the seaward limits of territorial waters;

(b) waters in any area for the time being designated under section 1(7) of the Continental Shelf Act 1964; and

(c) in relation to installations which are maintained in waters falling within paragraph (a) or (b) above, waters in a foreign sector of the continental shelf which are adjacent to such waters;

"the Scottish border" means—

(a) in the North Sea, a line—

(i) joining the following co-ordinates—

(1) 55 degrees 48’ 45”N; 2 degrees 01’ 54”W
(2) 55 degrees 49’ 50”N; 1 degrees 59’ 58”W
(3) 55 degrees 50’ 43”N; 1 degrees 58’ 09”W
(4) 55 degrees 50’ 47”N; 1 degrees 57’ 55”W
(5) 55 degrees 53’ 20”N; 1 degrees 48’ 28”W
(6) 55 degrees 53’ 29”N; 1 degrees 47’ 54”W
(7) 55 degrees 55’ 04”N; 1 degrees 43’ 32”W,

(ii) then following, in a south easterly direction, the seaward limits of United Kingdom territorial waters until the position 55 degrees 50’ 00”N; 1 degrees 27’ 31”W, and

(iii) then following, in an easterly direction, the parallel of latitude 55 degrees 50’ 00”N until its intersection with the Dividing Line;

(b) in the Irish Sea, a line joining the following co-ordinates—

(1) 54 degrees 37’ 54”N; 3 degrees 50’ 46”W
(2) 54 degrees 37’ 37”N; 3 degrees 51’ 04”W
(3) 54 degrees 37’ 00”N; 3 degrees 52’ 04”W
(4) 54 degrees 36’ 11”N; 3 degrees 53’ 51”W
(5) 54 degrees 33’ 17”N; 4 degrees 00’ 10”W
(6) 54 degrees 32’ 51”N; 4 degrees 01’ 06”W
(7) 54 degrees 31’ 55”N; 4 degrees 03’ 08”W
(8) 54 degrees 30’ 03”N’ 4 degrees 04’ 24”W,

then following the seaward limit of United Kingdom territorial waters to

(9) 54 degrees 30’ 22”N; 4 degrees 04’ 50”W
(10) 54 degrees 30’ 00”N; 4 degrees 05’ 29”W
(11) 54 degrees 30’ 00”N; 5 degrees 00’ 00”W;

"the Northern Irish border" means a line joining the following co-ordinates—

(1) 55 degrees 26’ 40”N; 6 degrees 34’ 37”W
(2) 55 degrees 23’ 36”N; 6 degrees 04’ 16”W
(3) 55 degrees 20’ 00”N; 6 degrees 00’ 00”W
(4) 55 degrees 10’ 00”N; 5 degrees 48’ 00”W
(5) 55 degrees 00’ 00”N; 5 degrees 36’ 00”W
(6) 54 degrees 50’ 00”N; 5 degrees 24’ 00”W
(7) 54 degrees 40’ 00”N; 5 degrees 12’ 00”W
(8) 54 degrees 30’ 00”N; 5 degrees 00’ 00”W
(9) 54 degrees 26’ 54”N; 5 degrees 00’ 00”W
(10) 54 degrees 20’ 00”N; 5 degrees 00’ 00”W
(11) 54 degrees 10’ 00”N; 5 degrees 12’ 00”W
(12) 54 degrees 00’ 00”N; 5 degrees 24’ 00”W;

"the English area" means such of the offshore area adjacent to England and Wales which lies to the south of the Scottish border and east of the Northern Irish border together with the internal waters of England and Wales in so far as they are tidal or constitute parts of the sea;

"the Scottish area" means such of the offshore area adjacent to Scotland which lies to the north of the Scottish border and east of the Northern Irish border together with the internal waters of Scotland in so far as they are tidal or constitute parts of the sea;

"the Northern Irish area" means such of the offshore area adjacent to Northern Ireland which lies to the west of the Northern Irish border together with the internal waters of Northern Ireland in so far as they are tidal or constitute parts of the sea.

[2116]

2 Application of English, Scottish and Northern Irish law

Subject to the provisions of any Order made under section 22(1) of the Act with respect to the application of criminal law—

(a) the law in force in England and Wales shall apply for the determination of questions arising out of relevant acts taking place in the English area;

(b) the law in force in Scotland shall apply for the determination of questions arising out of relevant acts taking place in the Scottish area; and

(c) the law in force in Northern Ireland shall apply for the determination of questions arising out of relevant acts taking place in the Northern Irish area.

[2117]

3 Jurisdiction

(1) The High Court shall have such jurisdiction for the determination of any questions arising out of a relevant act which, under Article 2(a) above, fall to be determined in accordance with the law in force in England and Wales as it would have if the relevant act had taken place in England or Wales.

(2) The Court of Session shall have such jurisdiction for the determination of any questions arising out of a relevant act which, under Article 2(b) above, fall to be determined in accordance with the law in force in Scotland as it would have if the relevant act had taken place in Scotland.

(3) The High Court in Northern Ireland shall have such jurisdiction for the determination of any questions arising out of a relevant act which, under Article 2(c) above, fall to be determined in accordance with the law in force in Northern Ireland as it would have if the relevant act had taken place in Northern Ireland.

[2118]

4 Application of Wireless Telegraphy Act 1949 and the Radioactive Substances Act 1960

For the purposes of the Wireless Telegraphy Act 1949, the Radioactive Substances Act 1960 and any regulations or orders under either of those Acts (subject, however, in the case of such regulations or orders made hereafter, to any contrary intention appearing therein) any installation in the English area and any waters in the offshore area within 500 metres of such an installation (not being waters lying in the Scottish or Northern Irish area and within 500 metres of an installation in either of those areas) shall be deemed to be situated in England and Wales; any installation in the Scottish area and any such waters within 500 metres of such an installation (not being waters lying in the English or Northern Irish area and within 500 metres of an installation in either of those areas) shall be deemed to be situated in Scotland; and any installation in the Northern Irish area and any such waters lying within 500 metres of such an installation (not being waters lying within the English or Scottish area and within 500 metres of an installation in either of those areas) shall be deemed to be situated in Northern Ireland.

[2119]

5 Commencement

This Order shall come into force on 1st February 1988.

[2120]

CIVIL JURISDICTION AND JUDGMENTS (AUTHENTIC INSTRUMENTS AND COURT SETTLEMENTS) ORDER 1993

(SI 1993/604)

NOTES

Made: 10 March 1993.
Authority: Civil Jurisdiction and Judgments Act 1982, s 13(1).
Commencement: 1 April 1993.

1—(1) This Order may be cited as the Civil Jurisdiction and Judgments (Authentic Instruments and Court Settlements) Order 1993 and shall come into force on 1st April 1993.

(2) In this Order—

(a) "the Act" means the Civil Jurisdiction and Judgments Act 1982,
(b) "the Convention" means a Convention mentioned in section 13 of the Act,
(c) "a Contracting State" means a Contracting State as defined in section 1 of the Act, and
(d) references to authentic instruments and court settlements are references to those instruments and settlements referred to in Articles 50 and 51 of Title IV of the Convention.

[2121]

2—(1) Subject to the modification specified in paragraph (2), the following provisions of the Act shall apply to authentic instruments and court settlements which are not maintenance orders as if they were judgments, other than maintenance orders, to which the Convention applies—

section 4 (enforcement of judgments other than maintenance orders),
section 6(1) and (2) (appeals under Article 37 second paragraph and Article 41),
section 7(1), (2), (3) and (5) (interest on registered judgments).

(2) In the application of section 4(3) of the Act to authentic instruments and court settlements, other than maintenance orders, for the words "as if the judgment had been originally given" there shall be substituted the words "as if it was a judgment which had been originally given".

[2122]

3—(1) Subject to the modification specified in paragraph (2), the following provisions of the Act shall apply to authentic instruments and court settlements which are maintenance orders as if they were maintenance orders to which the Convention applies—

section 5 (recognition and enforcement of maintenance orders),
section 6(3),
section 7(1), (2), (4) and (5),
section 8 (currency of payment under registered maintenance orders).

(2) In the application of section 5(4) of the Act to authentic instruments and court settlements which are maintenance orders, for the words "as if the order had been originally made" there shall be substituted the words "as if it was an order which had been originally made".

[2123]

4—(1) Subject to the modification specified in paragraph (2), section 11 of the Act (proof and admissibility of certain judgments and related documents) shall apply to authentic instruments and court settlements as if they were judgments which had been given by courts of Contracting States other than the United Kingdom and to which the Convention applies.

(2) In the application of section 11 to authentic instruments, for subsection (2) there shall be substituted the following—

"(2) A document purporting to be a copy of an authentic instrument drawn up or registered, and enforceable, in a Contracting State other than the United Kingdom is duly authenticated for the purposes of this section if it purports to be certified to be a true copy of such an instrument by a person duly authorised in that Contracting State to do so".

[2124]

5—(1) Subject to the modifications specified in paragraph (2), section 12 of the Act (provision for issue of copies of, and certificates in connection with, United Kingdom judgments) shall apply to authentic instruments as it applies to judgments.

(2) In the application of section 12 to authentic instruments—

(a) for the words "Rules of court may" there shall be substituted the words "The Court of Session may by Act of Sederunt";
(b) for the words "judgment given by a court in the United Kingdom" there shall be substituted the words "a judgment within section 18(2)(c)"; and
(c) the words "and the proceedings in which it was given" shall be omitted.

[2125]

6 Section 15(2) and (3) of the Act (interpretation of Part I of the Act and consequential amendments) shall apply to authentic instruments and court settlements as if they were judgments to which the Convention applies.

[2126]

7 The disapplication of section 18 of the Act (enforcement of United Kingdom judgments in other parts of United Kingdom) by subsection (7) thereof shall extend to authentic instruments and court settlements enforceable in a Contracting State outside the United Kingdom which fall to be treated for the purposes of their enforcement as judgments of a court of law in the United Kingdom by virtue of registration under section 4 or 5 of the Act, as applied by this Order.

[2127]

8 Section 48 of the Act (matters for which rules of court may provide) shall apply to authentic instruments and court settlements as if they were judgments to which the Convention applies.

[2128]

RECIPROCAL ENFORCEMENT OF FOREIGN JUDGMENTS (AUSTRALIA) ORDER 1994

(SI 1994/1901)

NOTES

Made: 19 July 1994.

Authority: Administration of Justice Act 1920, s 14(2); the Foreign Judgments (Reciprocal Enforcement) Act 1933, ss 1, 3; the Protection of Trading Interests Act 1980, s 7; the Civil Jurisdiction and Judgments Act 1982, s 9(2).

Commencement: see art 1.

1 This Order may be cited as the Reciprocal Enforcement of Foreign Judgments (Australia) Order 1994. It shall come into force on the date on which the Agreement between the Government of the United Kingdom of Great Britain and Northern Ireland and the Government of Australia, signed at Canberra on 23rd August 1990, providing for the reciprocal recognition and enforcement of judgments in civil and commercial matters shall enter into force, which date shall be notified in the London, Edinburgh and Belfast Gazettes.

[2129]

2 Part I of the Foreign Judgments (Reciprocal Enforcement) Act 1933 shall extend to Australia.

[2130]

3 The following courts of Australia (hereinafter referred to as "recognised courts") shall be recognised for the purposes of Part I of the Foreign Judgments (Reciprocal Enforcement) Act 1933, that is to say—

the High Court of Australia;
the Federal Court of Australia;
the Industrial Relations Court of Australia;
the Family Court of Australia;
the Family Court of Western Australia;
the Supreme Court exercising jurisdiction in respect of each Australian State or Territory;
the District Court of New South Wales;
the County Court of Victoria;
the District Courts in Queensland;
the District Court of Western Australia;
the Local Courts in, and the District Court and the Magistrates' Court of, South Australia;
the Courts of Requests in Tasmania; and
the Magistrates' Court of the Australian Capital Territory.

[2131]

4 The following judgments shall be judgments to which Part I of the Foreign Judgments (Reciprocal Enforcement) Act 1933 applies, that is to say—

(a) any judgment, decree, rule, order or other final decree for the payment of money (other than in respect of taxes or other charges of a like nature or an order requiring the payment of maintenance) given by a recognised court in respect of a civil or commercial matter;

(b) an award in proceedings on an arbitration conducted in Australia under the law applying there if the award has become enforceable in the same manner as a judgment in that country;

(c) a judgment or order given or made by a recognised court in criminal proceedings for the payment of money in respect of compensation or damages to an injured person.

[2132]

5 A judgment given in a recognised court shall, in the absence of proof to the contrary, be deemed to be capable of execution in Australia on production of a certified copy of the judgment.

[2133]

6 A judgment of a recognised court obtained under section 10 of the Foreign Proceedings (Excess of Jurisdiction) Act 1984 of Australia shall be enforceable in the same manner and circumstances as an award to which section 6(2) of the Protection of Trading Interests Act 1980 applies, where the judgment—

(a) was obtained after the coming into force of this Order; and

(b) relates to the recovery of sums paid or obtained pursuant to a judgment for multiple damages within the meaning of section 5(3) of the said Act of 1980; and

(c) is founded on an instrument made under section 9(1) of the said Act of 1984 which includes a statement that the Attorney-General is satisfied in accordance with either—

  (i) paragraph 9(1)(b)(ii) of that Act; or

  (ii) paragraph 9(1)(b)(i) and paragraph 9(1)(b)(ii) of that Act.

[2134]

7 The rate of interest due under the law in Australia upon the sum in respect of which a judgment of a recognised court is given shall be deemed to be that specified in the judgment or any certificate of the original court accompanying the judgment and, if no rate is so specified, no interest shall be deemed to be due thereon under the law in Australia unless the contrary is shown.

[2135]

8 It is hereby declared that—

(a) the provisions contained in articles 5 and 7 of this Order are necessary for giving effect to the Agreement scheduled hereto in relation to matters with respect to which there is power to make rules of court for the purposes of Part I of the Foreign Judgments (Reciprocal Enforcement) Act 1933; and

(b) Article 3 of the Agreement scheduled hereto is a provision of a convention whereby the United Kingdom assumes an obligation of the kind provided for in article 59 of the Convention on jurisdiction and the enforcement of judgments in civil and commercial matters, signed at Brussels on 27th September 1968.

[2136]

9 (*Revokes the Reciprocal Enforcement of Judgments (Australian Capital Territory) Order 1955, SI 1955/559 and amends the Reciprocal Enforcement of Judgments (Administration of Justice Act 1920, Part II) (Consolidation) Order 1984, SI 1984/129, Sch 1 at* **[2107]**.)

SCHEDULE

AGREEMENT BETWEEN THE GOVERNMENT OF THE UNITED KINGDOM OF GREAT BRITAIN AND NORTHERN IRELAND AND THE GOVERNMENT OF AUSTRALIA PROVIDING FOR THE RECIPROCAL RECOGNITION AND ENFORCEMENT OF JUDGMENTS IN CIVIL AND COMMERCIAL MATTERS

The Government of the United Kingdom of Great Britain and Northern Ireland and the Government of Australia,

Desiring to provide, on the basis of reciprocity, for the recognition and enforcement of judgments in civil and commercial matters;

Have agreed as follows—

ARTICLE 1

In this Agreement—

(a) "the 1968 Convention" means the Convention on Jurisdiction and the Enforcement of Judgments in Civil and Commercial Matters done at Brussels on 27th September 1968, as amended from time to time;

(b) "court of a Party" means one of the following courts—

  (i) in relation to Australia—

    (aa) the High Court of Australia;

(bb) the Federal Court of Australia;
(cc) the Family Court of Australia;
(dd) the Family Court of Western Australia;
(ee) the Supreme Court exercising jurisdiction in respect of each Australian State or Territory;
(ff) the District Court of New South Wales;
(gg) the County Court of Victoria;
(hh) the District Courts in Queensland;
(ii) the District Court of Western Australia;
(jj) the Local Courts in South Australia;
(kk) the Courts of Requests in Tasmania; or
(ll) the Magistrates' Court of the Australian Capital Territory;

(ii) in relation to the United Kingdom—
(aa) any superior court of the United Kingdom;
(bb) for England and Wales and Northern Ireland, any county court;
(cc) for Scotland, any sheriff court,

and such superior courts as may be specified by the United Kingdom in a declaration pursuant to Article 7 of this Agreement;

(iii) such other courts as may be agreed between the Parties;

(c) "judgment" means—
(i) any judgment, decree, rule, order or other final decree for the payment of money (other than in respect of taxes or other charges of like nature or an order requiring the payment of maintenance) given in the territory of a Party in respect of a civil or commercial matter;
(ii) an award in proceedings on an arbitration conducted in the territory of a Party under the law applying in that territory if the award has become enforceable in the same manner as a judgment in the territory of that Party; or
(iii) a judgment or order given or made by a court of a Party in criminal proceedings for the payment of money in respect of compensation or damages to an injured person;

(d) "registering court" means a court of a Party to which an application for the registration of a judgment is made.

ARTICLE 2

(1) Subject to paragraph (2) and to paragraph (3) of this Article, a judgment of a court of a Party, whether given before or after the entry into force of this Agreement, shall be recognised and enforced in the territory of the other Party on terms no less favourable than those—

(a) applicable to the recognition and enforcement of such judgments at the date of this Agreement, including the terms contained in the following provisions—
(i) in Australia—
(aa) the Foreign Proceedings (Excess of Jurisdiction) Act 1984 (Australia);
(bb) the Foreign Judgments Act 1973 of New South Wales;
(cc) the Foreign Judgments Act 1962 of Victoria;
(dd) the Reciprocal Enforcement of Judgments Act 1959 of Queensland;
(ee) the Foreign Judgments Act 1963 of Western Australia;
(ff) the Foreign Judgments Act 1971 of South Australia;
(gg) Part X of the Supreme Court Civil Procedure Act 1932 of Tasmania;
(hh) the Foreign Judgments (Reciprocal Enforcement) Ordinance 1954 of the Australian Capital Territory;
(ii) the Foreign Judgments (Reciprocal Enforcement) Act of the Northern Territory of Australia;
(jj) the Foreign Judgments (Reciprocal Enforcement) Ordinance 1978 of the Territory of Norfolk Island;
(kk) the Foreign Judgments (Reciprocal Enforcement) Ordinance 1977 of the Territory of Christmas Island;
(ll) the Reciprocal Enforcement of Judgments Ordinance as amended by the Reciprocal Enforcement of Judgments (Amendment) Ordinance 1963 of the Territory of Cocos (Keeling) Islands;

(ii) in the United Kingdom—
(aa) Part II of the Administration of Justice Act 1920, in respect of the Territory of Christmas Island, the Territory of Cocos (Keeling) Islands, New South Wales, the Territory of Norfolk Island, the

Northern Territory of Australia, Queensland, South Australia, Tasmania, Victoria and Western Australia;

(bb) the Foreign Judgments (Reciprocal Enforcement) Act 1933;

(cc) the Protection of Trading Interests Act 1980;

(b) provided by the law generally applicable in the registering court to the recognition and enforcement of foreign judgments at the date when application for recognition or enforcement is made.

(2) A judgment of a court of a Party, obtained under—

(a) section 10 of the Foreign Proceedings (Excess of Jurisdiction) Act 1984 of Australia, in a case where the judgment is founded on an instrument made under section 9(1) of that Act which includes a statement that the Attorney-General is satisfied in accordance with paragraph 9(1)(b)(ii) of that Act; or

(b) section 6 of the Protection of Trading Interests Act 1980 of the United Kingdom,

shall be entitled to be recognised and enforced in the territory of the other Party, in accordance with the provisions in the United Kingdom of section 7 of the Protection of Trading Interests Act 1980 and in Australia of section 12 of the Foreign Proceedings (Excess of Jurisdiction) Act 1984.

(3) Notice of any amendment to or repeal of any provision listed in sub-paragraph (1)(a) of this Article dealing with the terms of recognition and enforcement of foreign judgments shall be given to the other Party through the diplomatic channel at least three months, or such other time as may be mutually arranged between the Parties, before the amendment or repeal takes effect.

ARTICLE 3

(1) The United Kingdom undertakes, in the circumstances permitted by Article 59 of the 1968 Convention, not to recognise or enforce under that Convention any judgment within the meaning of that Convention given in a third State which is a Party to that Convention against a person domiciled or habitually resident in Australia.

(2) For the purposes of paragraph (1) of this Article—

(a) an individual shall be treated as domiciled in Australia if and only if he is resident in Australia and the nature and circumstances of his residence indicate that he has a substantial connection with Australia;

(b) a corporation or association shall be treated as domiciled in Australia if and only if it is incorporated or formed under a law in force in Australia and has a registered office there, or its central management and control is exercised in Australia; and

(c) in the case of an individual who—

(i) is resident in Australia; and

(ii) has been so resident for the last three months or more,

the requirements of Article 3(2)(a) shall be presumed to be fulfilled unless the contrary is proved.

ARTICLE 4

This Agreement shall not affect any treaties or arrangements to which both Parties are from time to time parties and which, in relation to particular matters, govern the recognition or enforcement of judgments.

ARTICLE 5

This Agreement shall not apply to any judgment that imposes a liability which a Party is obliged not to recognise or enforce by virtue of a treaty with a third State. That Party shall give notice of any such treaty to the other Party through the diplomatic channel.

ARTICLE 6

Either Party may, at the time of its notification under Article 9 or at any time thereafter, modify by declaration the list of its courts where a court replaces a court specified in Article 1(b)(i) or (ii) or agreed under Article 1(b)(iii) or specified in a declaration under this Article. Such a declaration shall be given through the diplomatic channel and shall take effect three months, or such other time as may be mutually arranged between the Parties, after the date on which it is given.

ARTICLE 7

(1) The United Kingdom may, at any time while this Agreement is in force, declare that this Agreement shall extend to any territory for whose international relations it is responsible.

(2) Any declaration made pursuant to paragraph (1) of this Article shall specify the superior courts of the territory to which application for the registration of a judgment given by a court of Australia shall be made.

(3) Any declaration made by the United Kingdom pursuant to this Article may be modified by a further declaration given at any time thereafter.

(4) Any declaration made pursuant to this Article shall be given through the diplomatic channel and shall take effect three months, or such other time as may be mutually arranged between the Parties, after the date on which it is given.

ARTICLE 8

The Parties shall consult at the request of either concerning the operation of this Agreement.

ARTICLE 9

(1) Each Party shall give notice to the other through the diplomatic channel of the completion of the procedures required by its law for the bringing into force of this Agreement. The Agreement shall enter into force on the date of the later of these notifications.

(2) This Agreement may be terminated by notice in writing by either Party through the diplomatic channel and it shall terminate three months after the date of such notice.

[2137]

CIVIL JURISDICTION AND JUDGMENTS ACT 1982 (INTERIM RELIEF) ORDER 1997

(SI 1997/302)

NOTES

Made: 12 February 1997.
Authority: Civil Jurisdiction and Judgments Act 1982, s 25(3).
Commencement: 1 April 1997.

1 This Order may be cited as the Civil Jurisdiction and Judgments Act 1982 (Interim Relief) Order 1997 and shall come into force on 1st April 1997.

[2138]

2 The High Court in England and Wales or Northern Ireland shall have power to grant interim relief under section 25(1) of the Civil Jurisdiction and Judgments Act 1982 in relation to proceedings of the following descriptions, namely—

(a) proceedings commenced or to be commenced otherwise than in a Brussels or Lugano Contracting State [or Regulation State];

[(b) proceedings whose subject-matter is not within the scope of the Regulation as determined by Article 1 of the Regulation.]

[2139]

NOTES

Words in square brackets in para (a) inserted, and para (b) substituted, by the Civil Jurisdiction and Judgments Order 2001, SI 2001/3929, art 5, Sch 3, para 26.

CIVIL JURISDICTION AND JUDGMENTS ACT 1982 (GIBRALTAR) ORDER 1997

(SI 1997/2602) (S 174)

NOTES

Made: 30 October 1997.
Authority: Civil Jurisdiction and Judgments Act 1982, s 39.
Commencement: 1 February 1998.

1 This Order may be cited as the Civil Jurisdiction and Judgments Act 1982 (Gibraltar) Order 1997 and shall come into force on 1st February 1998.

[2140]

2—(a) Provision corresponding to that made by the provisions of the 1968 Convention specified in paragraph (b) shall apply, so far as relevant, for the purpose of regulating, as between the United Kingdom and Gibraltar, the jurisdiction of courts and the recognition and enforcement of judgments.

(b) Those provisions are—
  (i) Titles I–V;
  (ii) Articles 54 and 57; and
  (iii) Article 65 and the Protocol referred to therein.

[2141]

3 For the purpose stated in Article 2 above the United Kingdom and Gibraltar shall be treated as if each were a separate Contracting State and the relevant provisions of the 1968 Convention and the 1982 Act shall be construed accordingly.

[2142]

4 In determining any question as to the meaning or effect of the provision (or any part of the provision) made by Article 2 above—
  (a) regard shall be had to any relevant principles laid down by the European Court in connection with Title II of the 1968 Convention and to any relevant decision of that court as to the meaning or effect of any provision of that Title; and
  (b) without prejudice to the generality of paragraph (a), the reports mentioned in section 3(3) of the 1982 Act may be considered and shall, so far as relevant, be given such weight as is appropriate in the circumstances.

[2143]

5 A judgment shall not be recognised under this Order if, had it been given in another Contracting State, recognition would be refused by virtue of an agreement to which Article 59 of the 1968 Convention applies.

[2144]

6 This Order extends to Northern Ireland.

[2145]

CIVIL JURISDICTION AND JUDGMENTS ACT 1982 (PROVISIONAL AND PROTECTIVE MEASURES) (SCOTLAND) ORDER 1997

(SI 1997/2780) (S 174)

NOTES

Made: 26 November 1997.
Authority: Civil Jurisdiction and Judgments Act 1982, s 27(3), (4).
Commencement: 1 January 1998.

1 This Order may be cited as the Civil Jurisdiction and Judgments Act 1982 (Provisional and Protective Measures) Order 1997 and shall come into force on 1st January 1998.

[2146]

2 The Court of Session shall have power to do anything mentioned in section 27(1) or 28 of the Civil Jurisdiction and Judgments Act 1982 in relation to proceedings of the following descriptions, namely—

(a) proceedings commenced otherwise than in a Brussels or Lugano Contracting State;

(b) proceedings whose subject-matter is not within the scope of the 1968 Convention as determined by Article 1 thereof.

[2147]

3 The Court of Session shall have power—

(a) to grant interim interdict under subsection (1)(c) of section 27 of the Civil Jurisdiction and Judgments Act 1982;

(b) to act as described in section 28 of that Act,

in relation to proceedings which are to be commenced otherwise than in a Brussels or Lugano Contracting State.

[2148]

EUROPEAN COMMUNITIES (SERVICE OF JUDICIAL AND EXTRA-JUDICIAL DOCUMENTS) (SCOTLAND) REGULATIONS 2001

(SSI 2001/172)

NOTES

Made: 8 May 2001.
Authority: European Communities Act 1972, s 2(2).
Commencement: 31 May 2001.

1 Citation, commencement and extent

(1) These Regulations may be cited as the European Communities (Service of Judicial and Extrajudicial Documents) (Scotland) Regulations 2001 and shall come into force on 31st May 2001.

(2) These Regulations extend to Scotland only.

[2149]

2 Interpretation

In these Regulations—

"the Council Regulation" means Council Regulation (EC) No 1348/2000 of 29th May 2000 on the service in the Member States of judicial and extrajudicial documents in civil or commercial matters;

"solicitor" shall have the same meaning as in section 4 of the Solicitors (Scotland) Act 1980.

[2150]

3 Designation of transmitting agencies and receiving agencies

For the purpose of Article 2 of the Council Regulation the following are hereby designated as transmitting agencies and as receiving agencies:—

(a) solicitors approved for that purpose by the Law Society of Scotland; and

(b) messengers-at-arms who are members of the Society of Messengers-at-Arms and Sheriff Officers.

[2151]

4 Designation of central body

For the purpose of Article 3 of the Council Regulation the Scottish Ministers are hereby designated as a central body.

[2152]

CIVIL JURISDICTION AND JUDGMENTS (AUTHENTIC INSTRUMENTS AND COURT SETTLEMENTS) ORDER 2001

(SI 2001/3928)

NOTES

Made: 11 December 2001.
Authority: European Communities Act 1972, s 2(2).
Commencement: 1 March 2002.

1—(1) This Order may be cited as the Civil Jurisdiction and Judgments (Authentic Instruments and Court Settlements) Order 2001 and shall come into force on 1st March 2002.

(2) In this Order—

"the Act" means the Civil Jurisdiction and Judgments Act 1982;

"the Regulation" means Council Regulation (EC) No 44/2001 of 22nd December 2000 on jurisdiction and the recognition and enforcement of judgments in civil and commercial matters;

"Regulation State" in any provision, in the application of that provision in relation to the Regulation, has the same meaning as "Member State" in the Regulation, that is all Member States except Denmark;

"the 2001 Order" means the Civil Jurisdiction and Judgments Order 2001.

(3) In this Order—

(a) references to authentic instruments and court settlements are references to those instruments and settlements referred to in Chapter IV of the Regulation; and

(b) references to judgments and maintenance orders are references to judgments and maintenance orders to which the Regulation applies.

[2153]

NOTES

Commencement: 1 March 2002.

2—(1) Subject to the modifications specified in paragraphs (2) and (3), paragraphs 1 to 6 of Schedule 1 to the 2001 Order shall apply, as appropriate, to authentic instruments and court settlements which—

(a) do not concern maintenance as if they were judgments,

(b) concern maintenance as if they were maintenance orders.

(2) In the application of paragraph 2(2) of Schedule 1 to the 2001 Order to authentic instruments and court settlements, for the words "as if the judgment had been originally given" there shall be substituted "as if it was a judgment which had been originally given".

(3) In the application of paragraph 3(3) of Schedule 1 to the 2001 Order to authentic instruments and court settlements, for the words "as if the order had been originally made" there shall be substituted the words "as if it was an order which had been originally made".

(4) Paragraph 8 of Schedule 1 to the 2001 Order shall apply to authentic instruments as if they were judgments and in its application—

(a) for sub-paragraph (1)(b) there shall be substituted the following—

"(b) a certificate obtained in accordance with Article 57 and Annex VI shall be evidence, and in Scotland sufficient evidence, that the authentic instrument is enforceable in the Regulation State of origin."; and

(b) for sub-paragraph (2) there shall be substituted the following—

"(2) A document purporting to be a copy of an authentic instrument drawn up or registered, and enforceable, in a Regulation State other than the United Kingdom is duly

PART III STATUTORY INSTRUMENTS

authenticated for the purposes of this paragraph if it purports to be certified to be a true copy of such an instrument by a person duly authorised in that Regulation State to do so.".

(5) Paragraph 8 of Schedule 1 to the 2001 Order shall apply to court settlements as if they were judgments and in its application for "Article 54" there shall be substituted "Article 58".

[2154]

NOTES

Commencement: 1 March 2002.

3 The disapplication of section 18 of the Act (enforcement of United Kingdom judgments in other parts of the United Kingdom) by section 18(7) will extend to authentic instruments and court settlements enforceable in a Regulation State outside the United Kingdom which will fall to be treated for the purposes of their enforcement as judgments of a court of law in the United Kingdom by virtue of registration under the Regulation.

[2155]

NOTES

Commencement: 1 March 2002.

4 Section 48 of the Act (matters for which rules of court may provide) will apply to authentic instruments and court settlements as if they were judgments or maintenance orders, as appropriate, to which the Regulation applies.

[2156]

NOTES

Commencement: 1 March 2002.

CIVIL JURISDICTION AND JUDGMENTS ORDER 2001

(SI 2001/3929)

NOTES

Made: 11 December 2001.
Authority: European Communities Act 1972, s 2(2).
Commencement: see art 1.

ARRANGEMENT OF ARTICLES

1 Citation and commencement

This Order may be cited as the Civil Jurisdiction and Judgments Order 2001 and shall come into force—

(a) as to articles 1 and 2, paragraphs 1(a), 1(b)(ii) and 17 of Schedule 2 and, so far as it relates to those paragraphs, article 4, on 25th January 2002; and
(b) as to the remainder of this Order, on 1st March 2002.

[2157]

NOTES

Commencement: 25 January 2002.

2 Interpretation

(1) In this Order—

"the Act" means the Civil Jurisdiction and Judgments Act 1982;

"the Regulation" means Council Regulation (EC) No 44/2001 of 22nd December 2000 on jurisdiction and the recognition and enforcement of judgments in civil and commercial matters;

"Regulation State" in any provision, in the application of that provision in relation to the Regulation, has the same meaning as "Member State" in the Regulation, that is all Member States except Denmark.

(2) In Schedule 2 to this Order, a section, Part, Schedule or paragraph referred to by number alone is a reference to the section, Part, Schedule or paragraph so numbered in the Act.

[2158]

NOTES

Commencement: 25 January 2002.

3 The Regulation

Schedule 1 to this Order (which applies certain provisions of the Act with modifications for the purposes of the Regulation) shall have effect.

[2159]

NOTES

Commencement: 1 March 2002.

4 Amendments to the Civil Jurisdiction and Judgments Act 1982

Schedule 2 to this Order (which makes amendments to the Act) shall have effect.

[2160]

NOTES

Commencement: 25 January 2002 (certain purposes); 1 March 2002 (remaining purposes).

5 Consequential amendments

Schedule 3 to this Order (which makes consequential amendments) shall have effect.

[2161]

NOTES

Commencement: 1 March 2002.

6 Transitional provisions

(1) Where proceedings are begun before 1st March 2002 in any part of the United Kingdom on the basis of jurisdiction determined in accordance with section 16 of, and Schedule 4 to, the Act, the proceedings may be continued as if the amendments made by paragraphs 3 and 4 of Schedule 2 to this Order had not been made and those amendments shall not apply in respect of any proceedings begun before that date.

(2) Where proceedings are begun before 1st March 2002 in any court in Scotland on the basis of jurisdiction determined in accordance with section 20 of, and Schedule 8 to, the Act, the proceedings may be continued as if the amendments made by paragraphs 6 and 7 of Schedule 2 to this Order had not been made and those amendments shall not apply in respect of any proceedings begun before that date.

[2162]

NOTES

Commencement: 1 March 2002.

SCHEDULE 1
THE REGULATION

Article 3

Interpretation

1(1) In this Schedule—

"court", without more, includes a tribunal;

"judgment" has the meaning given by Article 32 of the Regulation;

"magistrates' court", in relation to Northern Ireland, means a court of summary jurisdiction;

"maintenance order" means a maintenance judgment within the meaning of the Regulation;

"part of the United Kingdom" means England and Wales, Scotland or Northern Ireland;

"payer", in relation to a maintenance order, means the person liable to make the payments for which the order provides;

"prescribed" means prescribed by rules of court.

(2) In this Schedule, any reference to a numbered Article or Annex is a reference to the Article or Annex so numbered in the Regulation, and any reference to a sub-division of a numbered Article shall be construed accordingly.

(3) References in paragraphs 2 to 8 to a judgment registered under the Regulation include, to the extent of its registration, references to a judgment so registered to a limited extent only.

(4) Anything authorised or required by the Regulation or paragraphs 2 to 8 to be done by, to or before a particular magistrates' court may be done by, to or before any magistrates' court [acting in the same local justice area] (or, in Northern Ireland, [acting for the same] petty sessions district) as that court.

Enforcement of judgments other than maintenance orders (section 4)

2(1) Where a judgment is registered under the Regulation, the reasonable costs or expenses of and incidental to its registration shall be recoverable as if they were sums recoverable under the judgment.

(2) A judgment registered under the Regulation shall, for the purposes of its enforcement, be of the same force and effect, the registering court shall have in relation to its enforcement the same powers, and proceedings for or with respect to its enforcement may be taken, as if the judgment had been originally given by the registering court and had (where relevant) been entered.

(3) Sub-paragraph (2) is subject to Article 47 (restriction on enforcement where appeal pending or time for appeal unexpired), to paragraph 5 and to any provision made by rules of court as to the manner in which and conditions subject to which a judgment registered under the Regulation may be enforced.

Recognition and enforcement of maintenance orders (section 5)

3(1) The Secretary of State's function (under Article 39 and Annex II) of transmitting an application for the recognition or enforcement in the United Kingdom of a maintenance order (made under Article 38) to a magistrates' court shall be discharged—

(a) as respects England and Wales and Northern Ireland, by the Lord Chancellor;

(b) as respects Scotland, by the Scottish Ministers.

(2) Such an application shall be determined in the first instance by the prescribed officer of the court having jurisdiction in the matter.

(3) A maintenance order registered under the Regulation shall, for the purposes of its enforcement, be of the same force and effect, the registering court shall have in relation to its enforcement the same powers, and proceedings for or with respect to its enforcement may be taken, as if the order had been originally made by the registering court.

(4) Sub-paragraph (3) is subject to Article 47 (restriction on enforcement where appeal pending or time for appeal unexpired), to paragraph 5 and to any provision made by rules of court as to the manner in which and conditions subject to which an order registered under the Regulation may be enforced.

(5) A maintenance order which by virtue of the Regulation is enforceable by a magistrates' court in England and Wales shall, subject to the modifications of sections 76 and 93 of the Magistrates' Courts Act 1980 specified in sections 5(5B) and 5(5C) of the Act, be enforceable in the same manner as a magistrates' court maintenance order made by that court.

In this sub-paragraph "magistrates' court maintenance order" has the same meaning as in section 150(1) of the Magistrates' Courts Act 1980.

(6) A maintenance order which by virtue of the Regulation is enforceable by a magistrates' court in Northern Ireland shall, subject to the modifications of Article 98 of the Magistrates' Courts (Northern Ireland) Order 1981 specified in section 5(6A) of the Act, be enforceable as an order made by that court to which that Article applies.

(7) The payer under a maintenance order registered under the Regulation in a magistrates' court in England and Wales or Northern Ireland shall give notice of any changes of address to the proper officer of that court.

A person who without reasonable excuse fails to comply with this sub-paragraph shall be guilty of an offence and liable on summary conviction to a fine not exceeding level 2 on the standard scale.

(8) In sub-paragraph (7) "proper officer" means—
- (a) in relation to a magistrates' court in England and Wales, the [designated officer] for the court; and
- (b) in relation to a magistrates' court in Northern Ireland, the clerk of the court.

Appeals under Article 44 and Annex IV (section 6)

4(1) The single further appeal on a point of law referred to under Article 44 and Annex IV in relation to the recognition or enforcement of a judgment other than a maintenance order lies—
- (a) in England and Wales or Northern Ireland, to the Court of Appeal or to the House of Lords in accordance with Part II of the Administration of Justice Act 1969 (appeals direct from the High Court to the House of Lords);
- (b) in Scotland, to the Inner House of the Court of Session.

(2) Paragraph (a) of sub-paragraph (1) has effect notwithstanding section 15(2) of the Administration of Justice Act 1969 (exclusion of direct appeal to the House of Lords in cases where no appeal to that House lies from a decision of the Court of Appeal).

(3) The single further appeal on a point of law referred to in Article 44 and Annex IV in relation to the recognition or enforcement of a maintenance order lies—
- (a) in England and Wales, to the High Court by way of case stated in accordance with section 111 of the Magistrates' Courts Act 1980;
- (b) in Scotland, to the Inner House of the Court of Session;
- (c) in Northern Ireland, to the Court of Appeal.

Interest on registered judgments (section 7)

5(1) Subject to sub-paragraph (3), where in connection with an application for registration of a judgment under the Regulation the applicant shows—
- (a) that the judgment provides for the payment of a sum of money; and
- (b) that in accordance with the law of the Regulation State in which the judgment was given interest on that sum is recoverable under the judgment from a particular date or time,

the rate of interest and the date or time from which it is so recoverable shall be registered with the judgment and, subject to rules of court, the debt resulting, apart from paragraph 2(1), from the registration of the judgment shall carry interest in accordance with the registered particulars.

(2) Costs or expenses recoverable by virtue of paragraph 2(1) shall carry interest as if they were the subject of an order for the payment of costs or expenses made by the registering court on the date of registration.

(3) Interest on arrears of sums payable under a maintenance order registered under the Regulation in a magistrates' court in England and Wales or Northern Ireland shall not be recoverable in that court, but without prejudice to the operation in relation to any such order of section 2A of the Maintenance Orders Act 1958 or section 11A of the Maintenance and

Affiliation Orders Act (Northern Ireland) 1966 (which enable interest to be recovered if the order is re-registered for enforcement in the High Court).

(4) Except as mentioned in sub-paragraph (3), debts under judgments registered under the Regulation shall carry interest only as provided by this paragraph.

Currency of payment under registered maintenance orders (section 8)

6(1) Sums payable in the United Kingdom under a maintenance order by virtue of its registration under the Regulation, including any arrears so payable, shall be paid in the currency of the United Kingdom.

(2) Where the order is expressed in any other currency, the amounts shall be converted on the basis of the exchange rate prevailing on the date of registration of the order.

(3) For the purposes of this paragraph, a written certificate purporting to be signed by an officer of any bank in the United Kingdom and stating the exchange rate prevailing on a specified date shall be evidence, and in Scotland sufficient evidence, of the facts stated.

Allocation within United Kingdom of jurisdiction with respect to trusts and consumer contracts (section 10)

7(1) The provisions of this paragraph have effect for the purpose of allocating within the United Kingdom jurisdiction in certain proceedings in respect of which the Regulation confers jurisdiction on the courts of the United Kingdom generally and to which section 16 of the Act does not apply.

(2) Any proceedings which by virtue of Article 5(6) (trusts) are brought in the United Kingdom shall be brought in the courts of the part of the United Kingdom in which the trust is domiciled.

(3) Any proceedings which by virtue of the Article 16(1) (consumer contracts) are brought in the United Kingdom by a consumer on the ground that he is himself domiciled there shall be brought in the courts of the part of the United Kingdom in which he is domiciled.

Proof and admissibility of certain judgments and related documents (section 11)

8(1) For the purposes of the Regulation—

(a) a document, duly authenticated, which purports to be a copy of a judgment given by a court of a Regulation State other than the United Kingdom shall without further proof be deemed to be a true copy, unless the contrary is shown; and

(b) a certificate obtained in accordance with Article 54 and Annex V shall be evidence, and in Scotland sufficient evidence, that the judgment is enforceable in the Regulation State of origin.

(2) A document purporting to be a copy of a judgment given by any such court as is mentioned in sub-paragraph (1)(a) is duly authenticated for the purposes of this paragraph if it purports—

(a) to bear the seal of that court; or

(b) to be certified by any person in his capacity as a judge or officer of that court to be a true copy of a judgment given by that court.

(3) Nothing in this paragraph shall prejudice the admission in evidence of any document which is admissible apart from this paragraph.

Domicile of individuals (section 41)

9(1) Subject to Article 59 (which contains provisions for determining whether a party is domiciled in a Regulation State), the following provisions of this paragraph determine, for the purposes of the Regulation, whether an individual is domiciled in the United Kingdom or in a particular part of, or place in, the United Kingdom or in a state other than a Regulation State.

(2) An individual is domiciled in the United Kingdom if and only if—

(a) he is resident in the United Kingdom; and

(b) the nature and circumstances of his residence indicate that he has a substantial connection with the United Kingdom.

(3) Subject to sub-paragraph (5), an individual is domiciled in a particular part of the United Kingdom if and only if—
- (a) he is resident in that part; and
- (b) the nature and circumstances of his residence indicate that he has a substantial connection with that part.

(4) An individual is domiciled in a particular place in the United Kingdom if and only if he—
- (a) is domiciled in the part of the United Kingdom in which that place is situated; and
- (b) is resident in that place.

(5) An individual who is domiciled in the United Kingdom but in whose case the requirements of sub-paragraph (3)(b) are not satisfied in relation to any particular part of the United Kingdom shall be treated as domiciled in the part of the United Kingdom in which he is resident.

(6) In the case of an individual who—
- (a) is resident in the United Kingdom, or in a particular part of the United Kingdom; and
- (b) has been so resident for the last three months or more,

the requirements of sub-paragraph (2)(b) or, as the case may be, sub-paragraph (3)(b) shall be presumed to be fulfilled unless the contrary is proved.

(7) An individual is domiciled in a state other than a Regulation State if and only if—
- (a) he is resident in that state; and
- (b) the nature and circumstances of his residence indicate that he has a substantial connection with that state.

Seat of company, or other legal person or association for purposes of Article 22(2) (section 43)

10(1) The following provisions of this paragraph determine where a company, legal person or association has its seat for the purposes of Article 22(2) (which confers exclusive jurisdiction over proceedings relating to the formation or dissolution of such bodies, or to the decisions of their organs).

(2) A company, legal person or association has its seat in the United Kingdom if and only if—
- (a) it was incorporated or formed under the law of a part of the United Kingdom; or
- (b) its central management and control is exercised in the United Kingdom.

(3) Subject to sub-paragraph (4), a company, legal person or association has its seat in a Regulation State other than the United Kingdom if and only if—
- (a) it was incorporated or formed under the law of that state; or
- (b) its central management and control is exercised in that state.

(4) A company, legal person or association shall not be regarded as having its seat in a Regulation State other than the United Kingdom if—
- (a) it has its seat in the United Kingdom by virtue of sub-paragraph (2)(a); or
- (b) it is shown that the courts of that other state would not regard it for the purposes of Article 22(2) as having its seat there.

PART III STATUTORY INSTRUMENTS

Persons deemed to be domiciled in the United Kingdom for certain purposes (section 44)

11(1) This paragraph applies to
- (a) proceedings within Section 3 of Chapter II of the Regulation (insurance contracts),
- (b) proceedings within Section 4 of Chapter II of the Regulation (consumer contracts), and
- (c) proceedings within Section 5 of Chapter II of the Regulation (employment contracts).

(2) A person who, for the purposes of proceedings to which this paragraph applies arising out of the operations of a branch, agency or other establishment in the United Kingdom, is deemed for the purposes of the Regulation to be domiciled in the United Kingdom by virtue of—
- (a) Article 9(2) (insurers); or
- (b) Article 15(2) (suppliers of goods, services or credit to consumers), or

(c) Article 18(2) (employers),

shall, for the purposes of those proceedings, be treated as so domiciled and as domiciled in the part of the United Kingdom in which the branch, agency or establishment in question is situated.

Domicile of trusts (section 45)

12(1) The following provisions of this paragraph determine for the purposes of the Regulation where a trust is domiciled.

(2) A trust is domiciled in the United Kingdom if and only if it is by virtue of sub-paragraph (3) domiciled in a part of the United Kingdom.

(3) A trust is domiciled in a part of the United Kingdom if and only if the system of law of that part is the system of law with which the trust has its closest and most real connection. **[2163]**

NOTES

Commencement: 1 March 2002.

Para 1: in sub-para (4) words in first pair of square brackets substituted and words in second pair of square brackets inserted by the Courts Act 2003 (Consequential Provisions) (No 2) Order 2005, SI 2005/617, art 2, Schedule, para 194(a).

Para 3: in sub-para (8)(a) words in square brackets substituted by SI 2005/617, art 2, Schedule, para 194(b).

Modified, in relation to the application of this Schedule to authentic instruments and court settlements, by the Civil Jurisdiction and Judgments (Authentic Instruments and Court Settlements) Order 2001, SI 2001/3928, art 2.

(*Sch 2: Pt I (paras 1, 2) amends the Civil Jurisdiction and Judgments Act 1982, ss 1, 9 at* **[50]**, **[58]**; *Pt II (paras 3–5) amends s 16 of and Sch 5 to that Act at* **[65]**, **[105]**, *and substitutes Sch 4 to that Act at* **[104]**; *Pt III (paras 6–8) amends s 20 of and Sch 9 to that Act at* **[69]**, **[109]** *and substitutes Sch 8 to that Act at* **[108]**;*Pt IV (paras 9–15) amends ss 24, 25, 27, 28, 30, 32, 33 of that Act at* **[73]**, **[74]**, **[76]**, **[77]**, **[78]**, **[80]**, **[81]**; *Pt V (paras 16–18) amends ss 43, 48, 50 of that Act at* **[87]**, **[92]**, **[94]**; *Sch 3 contains consequential amendments.*)

ACT OF SEDERUNT (SHERIFF COURT EUROPEAN ENFORCEMENT ORDER RULES) 2005

(SSI 2005/523)

NOTES

Made: 18 October 2005.

Authority: Sheriff Courts (Scotland) Act 1971, s 32.

Commencement: 21 October 2005.

1 Citation, commencement and interpretation

(1) This Act of Sederunt may be cited as the Act of Sederunt (Sheriff Court European Enforcement Order Rules) 2005 and shall come into force on 21st October 2005.

(2) This Act of Sederunt shall be inserted in the Books of Sederunt.

(3) In this Act of Sederunt—

"authentic instrument" has the meaning assigned in Article 4(3) of the Regulation;

"Council Regulation (EC) No 44/2001" means Council Regulation (EC) No 44/2001 of 22 December 2000 on jurisdiction and the recognition and enforcement of judgments in civil and commercial matters;

"court of origin" has the meaning assigned in Article 4(6) of the Regulation;

"court settlement" means a settlement where the debtor has expressly agreed to a claim within the meaning of Article 4(2) of the Regulation by admission or by means of a settlement which has been approved by a court or concluded before a court in the course of proceedings; and

"judgment" has the meaning assigned by Article 4(1) of the Regulation; and "the Regulation" means Regulation (EC) No 805/2004 of the European Parliament and of the Council of 21 April 2004 creating a European Enforcement Order for uncontested claims.

(4) Any reference in this Act of Sederunt to a numbered form shall, unless the context otherwise requires, be construed as a reference to the form so numbered in the Schedule to this Act of Sederunt and includes a form substantially to the same effect with such variation as circumstances may require.

[2164]

NOTES

Commencement: 21 October 2005.

2 Application etc

(1) These Rules shall apply to applications under the Regulation where the sheriff court is the court of origin.

(2) An application shall—

(a) be made in writing to the sheriff clerk of the sheriff court in which the judgment was delivered or authentic instrument was registered; and

(b) subject to rule 8(1) (rectification or withdrawal of European Enforcement Order certificate) be made by letter.

[2165]

NOTES

Commencement: 21 October 2005.

3 Certification of decree in absence or decree by default

(1) An application for certification under Article 6(1) (judgment on uncontested claim) or Article 8 (partial European Enforcement Order) of the Regulation shall be accompanied by an affidavit—

(a) verifying that the judgment was of an uncontested claim within the meaning of Article 3(1)(b) or (c) of the Regulation and the court proceedings met the requirements set out in Chapter III of the Regulation;

(b) providing the information required by the form of certificate in Annex I to the Regulation (European Enforcement Order—judgment);

(c) verifying that the judgment is enforceable in Scotland and does not conflict with the rules of jurisdiction laid down in sections 3 and 6 of Chapter II of Council Regulation (EC) No 44/2001; and

(d) stating that where the debtor was a consumer and the judgment related to a contract concluded by the debtor for a purpose outside his trade or profession the judgment was given in the Member State of the debtor's domicile within the meaning of Article 59 of Council Regulation (EC) No 44/2001,

and an execution of service of the judgment under sub-paragraph (3).

(2) Before an application is made under Article 6(1) (application for certificate as European Enforcement Order) or Article 8 (partial European Enforcement Order certificate) of the Regulation, the party wishing to enforce the judgment shall serve the judgment on all parties against whom the judgment has been given in accordance with the requirements of Article 13 (service with proof of receipt by the debtor) or Article 14 (service without proof of receipt by the debtor) of the Regulation accompanied by a notice in Form 1.

(3) An execution of service of the judgment shall be in Form 2 unless a form of execution of service is provided by a person effecting service in another Member State.

(4) A certificate under Article 9(1) of the Regulation (European Enforcement Order certificate) shall be signed by the sheriff clerk.

[2166]

NOTES

Commencement: 21 October 2005.

4 Certification of court settlement

(1) An application for certification under Article 24 of the Regulation (court settlement) shall be accompanied by an affidavit—

(a) verifying that the debtor admitted the claim or entered into a court settlement that was approved by the court or concluded before the court in the course of proceedings and is enforceable in Scotland;

(b) verifying that the settlement concerned a claim within the meaning of Article 4(2) of the Regulation (payment of money); and

(c) providing the information required by the form of certificate in Annex II to the Regulation (European Enforcement Order—court settlement).

(2) A certificate under Article 24 of the Regulation (court settlement) shall be signed by the sheriff clerk.

[2167]

NOTES

Commencement: 21 October 2005.

5 Certificate of authentic instrument

(1) An application for certification under Article 25(1) of the Regulation (authentic instrument) shall be accompanied by an affidavit—

(a) verifying that the authentic instrument concerns a claim within the meaning of Article 4(2) of the Regulation (payment of money);

(b) verifying that the authentic instrument is enforceable in Scotland; and

(c) providing the information required by the form of certificate in Annex III to the Regulation (European Enforcement Order—authentic instrument).

(2) A certificate under Article 25(1) of the Regulation (authentic instrument) shall be signed by the sheriff clerk.

[2168]

NOTES

Commencement: 21 October 2005.

6 Certificate of lack or limitation of enforceability

(1) An application for certification under Article 6(2) of the Regulation (lack or limitation of enforceability) shall be accompanied by an affidavit—

(a) stating the date on which the judgment, court settlement or authentic instrument was certified as a European Enforcement Order; and

(b) providing the information required by the form of certificate in Annex IV to the Regulation (certificate of lack or limitation of enforceability).

(2) A certificate under Article 6(2) of the Regulation (lack or limitation of enforceability) shall be signed by the sheriff clerk.

[2169]

NOTES

Commencement: 21 October 2005.

7 Replacement certificate

(1) An application under Article 6(3) of the Regulation (replacement certificate) shall be accompanied by an affidavit providing the information required by the form of certificate in Annex V to the Regulation (European Enforcement Order—replacement certificate following a challenge).

(2) A certificate under Article 6(3) of the Regulation (replacement certificate) shall be signed by the sheriff clerk.

[2170]

NOTES

Commencement: 21 October 2005.

8 Rectification or withdrawal of European Enforcement Order certificate

(1) An application under Article 10(1) of the Regulation (rectification or withdrawal of European Enforcement Order certificate) shall be in the form set out in Annex VI to the Regulation and shall be lodged with the sheriff clerk.

(2) An application under paragraph (1) shall be determined by the sheriff in chambers and shall not require any appearance for the applicant unless the sheriff otherwise directs.

(3) Where the sheriff requires to hear parties on an application the sheriff clerk shall—
- (a) fix a date, time and place for the parties to be heard, and
- (b) inform the parties—
  - (i) of that date, time and place; and
  - (ii) of the reasons for the sheriff wishing to hear parties.

[2171]

NOTES

Commencement: 21 October 2005.

SCHEDULE

Rule 3(2)

FORM 1

FORM OF NOTICE TO ACCOMPANY SERVICE COPY OF JUDGMENT

To [AB] (*address*)

You are hereby served with a copy of the interlocutor of the Sheriff of at given on the day of 20 . [In terms of this interlocutor you are required to (*state requirements of interlocutor*). Your failure to do so may result in further steps being taken to enforce the interlocutor.]

(*Signed*)

(*Address*)

Solicitor [*or* Sheriff Officer]

(*Place and date*)

[2172]

FORM 2

EXECUTION OF SERVICE OF JUDGMENT WHERE SERVICE EFFECTED BY OFFICER OF COURT OR SOLICITOR IN SCOTLAND

Rule 3(3)

(*place and date*)

I, [AB] (*address*), hereby certify that upon the day of 20 , I duly served a copy of this judgment together with a notice under rule 3(2) of the Act of Sederunt (Sheriff Court European Enforcement Order Rules) 2005 upon [CD], defender. This I did by posting (*set forth mode of service; if by officer and not by post, add* in presence of [EF] (*address*) witness, hereto with me subscribing).

(*Signed*)

(*Address*)

Solicitor for Pursuer

[*or* Defender]

[*or*

(*Signed*)

Sheriff Officer

(*Signed*)

Witness]

[2173]

NOTES

Commencement: 21 October 2005.

B. APPLICABLE LAW

FOREIGN COMPANIES (EXECUTION OF DOCUMENTS) REGULATIONS 1994

(SI 1994/950)

NOTES

Made: 24 March 1994.
Authority: Companies Act 1989, s 130(6).
Commencement: 16 May 1994.

1 Citation and commencement

These Regulations may be cited as the Foreign Companies (Execution of Documents) Regulations 1994 and shall come into force on 16th May 1994.

[2174]

2 Application of sections 36 to 36C Companies Act 1985

[Sections 36, 36A, 36B and 36C] of the Companies Act 1985 shall apply to companies incorporated outside Great Britain with the adaptations and modifications set out in [regulations 3 to 5 below].

[2175]

NOTES

Words in square brackets substituted by the Foreign Companies (Execution of Documents) (Amendment) Regulations 1995, SI 1995/1729, reg 3.

3 References in the said [sections 36, 36A, 36B and 36C] to a company shall be construed as references to a company incorporated outside Great Britain.

[2176]

NOTES

Words in square brackets substituted by the Foreign Companies (Execution of Documents) (Amendment) Regulations 1995, SI 1995/1729, reg 4.

4 Adaptation of section 36

(1) Section 36 shall apply as if—

(a) after the words "common seal," in paragraph (a) there were inserted "or in any manner permitted by the laws of the territory in which the company is incorporated for the execution of documents by such a company,", and

(b) for paragraph (b) there were substituted—

"(b) on behalf of a company, by any person who, in accordance with the laws of the territory in which the company is incorporated, is acting under the authority (express or implied) of that company;".

[2177]

5 Adaptation of section 36A

Section 36A shall apply as if—

(a) at the end of subsection (2) there were inserted—

", or if it is executed in any manner permitted by the laws of the territory in which the company is incorporated for the execution of documents by such a company.",

(b) for subsection (4) there were substituted—

"(4) A document which—

(a) is signed by a person or persons who, in accordance with the laws of the territory in which the company is incorporated, is or are acting under the authority (express or implied) of that company, and

PART III STATUTORY INSTRUMENTS

(b) is expressed (in whatever form of words) to be executed by the company,

has the same effect in relation to that company as it would have in relation to a company incorporated in England and Wales if executed under the common seal of a company so incorporated.", and

(c) in subsection (6) for the words from "a director" to "directors of the company" there were substituted "a person or persons who, in accordance with the laws of the territory in which the company is incorporated, is or are acting under the authority (express or implied) of that company".

[2178]

6 *(Revoked by the Foreign Companies (Execution of Documents) (Amendment) Regulations 1995, SI 1995/1729, reg 5.)*

FINANCIAL MARKETS AND INSOLVENCY (SETTLEMENT FINALITY) REGULATIONS 1999

(SI 1999/2979)

NOTES

Made: 2 November 1999.
Authority: European Communities Act 1972, s 2(2).
Commencement: 11 December 1999.

(Regs 1–22 reproduced in Pt III(C) at **[2209]–[2230]***.)*

PART III
TRANSFER ORDERS EFFECTED THROUGH A DESIGNATED SYSTEM AND COLLATERAL SECURITY

General

23 Applicable law relating to securities held as collateral security

Where—

(a) securities (including rights in securities) are provided as collateral security to a participant or a central bank (including any nominee, agent or third party acting on behalf of the participant or the central bank), and

(b) a register, account or centralised deposit system located in an EEA State legally records the entitlement of that person to the collateral security,

the rights of that person as a holder of collateral security in relation to those securities shall be governed by the law of the EEA State or, where appropriate, the law of the part of the EEA State, where the register, account, or centralised deposit system is located.

[2179]

(Regs 24–26, and Schedule, reproduced in Pt III(C) at **[2231]–[2233]***.)*

FINANCIAL SERVICES AND MARKETS ACT 2000 (LAW APPLICABLE TO CONTRACTS OF INSURANCE) REGULATIONS 2001

(SI 2001/2635)

NOTES

Made: 19 July 2001.
Authority: Financial Services and Markets Act 2000, ss 424(3), 417(1), 428(3).
Commencement: 1 December 2001.

ARRANGEMENT OF REGULATIONS

PART I
GENERAL

PART II
CONTRACTS OF GENERAL INSURANCE

PART III
CONTRACTS OF LONG-TERM INSURANCE

PART I
GENERAL

1 Citation and commencement

These Regulations may be cited as the Financial Services and Markets Act 2000 (Law Applicable to Contracts of Insurance) Regulations 2001 and come into force on the day on which section 19 of the Act comes into force.

[2180]

NOTES

Commencement: 1 December 2001.

2 Interpretation

(1) In these Regulations—

"the Act" means the Financial Services and Markets Act 2000;

"the 1990 Act" means the Contracts (Applicable Law) Act 1990;

"applicable law", in relation to a contract of insurance, means the law that is applicable to that contract;

"contract of general insurance" and "contract of long-term insurance" have the meanings given by the Regulated Activities Order;

"EEA State of the commitment" means, in relation to a contract of long-term insurance entered into on a date—

(a) if the policyholder is an individual, the EEA State in which he resides on that date; or

(b) otherwise, the EEA State in which the establishment of the policyholder to which the contract relates is situated on that date;

"establishment", in relation to a person ("A"), means—

(a) A's head office;

(b) any of A's agencies;

(c) any of A's branches; or

(d) any permanent presence of A in an EEA State, which need not take the form of a branch or agency and which may consist of an office managed by A's staff or by a person who is independent of A but has permanent authority to act for A as if he were an agency;

PART III STATUTORY INSTRUMENTS

"large risk" has the meaning given by Article 5(d) of the first non-life insurance directive and includes risks specified by paragraph (iii) of that definition insured by professional associations, joint ventures or temporary groups;

"mandatory rules" means the rules from which the law allows no derogation by way of contract;

"the Regulated Activities Order" means the Financial Services and Markets Act 2000 (Regulated Activities) Order 2001.

(2) References to the EEA State where the risk covered by a contract of insurance is situated are to—

(a) if the contract relates to buildings or to buildings and their contents (in so far as the contents are covered by the same contract of insurance), the EEA State in which the property is situated;

(b) if the contract relates to vehicles of any type, the EEA State of registration;

(c) if the contract covers travel or holidays risks and has a duration of four months or less, the EEA State in which the policyholder entered into the contract;

(d) in any other case—

(i) if the policyholder is an individual, the EEA State in which he resides on the date the contract is entered into;

(ii) otherwise, the EEA State in which the establishment of the policyholder to which the contract relates is situated on that date.

(3) References to the country in which a person resides are to—

(a) if he is an individual, the country in which he has his habitual residence;

(b) in any other case, the country in which he has his central administration.

(4) Where an EEA State (including the United Kingdom) includes several territorial units, each of which has its own laws concerning contractual obligations, each unit is to be considered as a separate state for the purposes of identifying the applicable law under these Regulations.

[2181]

NOTES

Commencement: 1 December 2001.

3 Scope of these Regulations

(1) These Regulations do not apply to contracts of reinsurance.

(2) These Regulations apply to contracts of insurance which are entered into by friendly societies as follows—

(a) Part II applies to a contract of insurance entered into by a friendly society to which section 37(3) of the Friendly Societies Act 1992 applies;

(b) Part III applies to a contract of insurance entered into by a friendly society to which section 37(2) of that Act applies; and

(c) Part II applies to any other contract of insurance entered into by a friendly society which covers a risk situated in an EEA State with the following modifications—

(i) paragraph (1) of regulation 4 does not apply;

(ii) regulation 4 applies only where the policyholder is an individual; …

[(iii) regulation 7(1) applies as if for the words "the 1990 Act is to be treated as applying", there were substituted "a court in any part of the United Kingdom must apply the general rules of private international law of that part of the United Kingdom concerning contractual obligations"; and

(iv) regulation 7(2) and (3) apply as if for the words "the 1990 Act is to be treated as applying" in each case, there were substituted the words "the general rules of private international law of that part of the United Kingdom concerning contractual obligations apply"].

[2182]

NOTES

Commencement: 1 December 2001.

Para (2): word omitted from sub-para (c)(ii) revoked, and sub-para (c)(iii), (iv) substituted, for sub-para (c)(iii) as originally enacted, by the Financial Services and Markets Act 2000 (Law Applicable to Contracts of Insurance) (Amendment) Regulations 2001, SI 2001/3542, reg 2.

PART II
CONTRACTS OF GENERAL INSURANCE

4 Applicable law

(1) This Part applies to a contract of general insurance which covers risks situated in an EEA State.

(2) If the policyholder resides in the EEA State in which the risk is situated, the applicable law is the law of that EEA State unless, if such a choice is permitted under the law of that EEA State, the parties to the contract choose the law of another country.

(3) If the policyholder does not reside in the EEA State in which the risk is situated, the parties to the contract may choose as the applicable law either—

(a) the law of the EEA State in which the risk is situated; or
(b) the law of the country in which the policyholder resides.

(4) If the policyholder carries on a business (including a trade or profession) and the contract covers two or more risks relating to that business which are situated in different EEA States, the freedom of the parties to choose the applicable law conferred by this regulation extends to the law of any of those EEA States and of the country in which the policyholder resides.

(5) If any of the EEA States referred to in paragraph (3) or (4) grant greater freedom of choice of the applicable law, the parties to the contract may take advantage of that freedom.

(6) Notwithstanding paragraphs (2) to (4), if the risks covered by the contract are limited to events occurring in one EEA State other than the EEA State in which the risk is situated, the parties may choose the law of the former EEA State as the applicable law.

(7) Notwithstanding paragraphs (2) to (4), if the risk covered by the contract is a large risk the parties may choose any law as the applicable law.

(8) Where the foregoing provisions of this regulation allow the parties to the contract to choose the applicable law and if no choice has been made, or no choice has been made which satisfies the requirement set out in regulation 6(1), the applicable law is the law of the country, from amongst those considered in the relevant paragraph ("the relevant countries"), which is most closely connected with the contract; however, where a severable part of the contract has a closer connection with another relevant country, the law applicable to that part is, by way of exception, the law of that relevant country.

(9) For the purposes of paragraph (8), the contract is rebuttably presumed to be most closely connected with the EEA State in which the risk is situated.

[2183]

NOTES

Commencement: 1 December 2001.

5 Mandatory rules

(1) Nothing in regulation 4 restricts the application of the mandatory rules of any part of the United Kingdom, irrespective of the applicable law of the contract.

(2) If the parties to the contract choose the applicable law under regulation 4 and if all the other elements relevant to the situation at the time when the parties make their choice are connected with one EEA State only, the application of the mandatory rules of that EEA State is not prejudiced.

[2184]

NOTES

Commencement: 1 December 2001.

6 Choice of law

(1) Any choice made by the parties under regulation 4 must be expressed or demonstrated with reasonable certainty by the terms of the contract or the circumstances of the case.

(2) Where the parties to the contract may choose the applicable law under regulation 4, and where the risk to which the contract relates is covered by Community co-insurance

(within the meaning of Council Directive 78/473/EEC on the coordination of laws, regulations and administrative provisions relating to Community co-insurance), co-insurers other than the leading insurer (within the meaning of that Directive) are not to be treated as parties to the contract.

[2185]

NOTES

Commencement: 1 December 2001.

7 The 1990 Act

(1) Subject to the preceding provisions of this Part, the 1990 Act is to be treated as applying to the contract for the purposes of determining the applicable law.

(2) In determining whether the mandatory rules of another EEA State should be applied in accordance with regulation 5(2) where the parties have chosen the law of a part of the United Kingdom as the applicable law, the 1990 Act is to be treated as applying to the contract.

(3) In determining what freedom of choice the parties have under the law of a part of the United Kingdom, the 1990 Act is to be treated as applying to the contract.

[2186]

NOTES

Commencement: 1 December 2001.

PART III
CONTRACTS OF LONG-TERM INSURANCE

8 Applicable law

(1) This Part applies to a contract of long-term insurance if—

(a) where the policyholder is an individual, he resides in an EEA State;

(b) otherwise, the establishment of the policyholder to which the contract relates is situated in an EEA State.

(2) The applicable law is the law of the EEA State of the commitment unless, if such a choice is permitted under the law of that EEA State, the parties choose the law of another country.

(3) If the policyholder is an individual and resides in one EEA State but is a national or citizen of another, the parties to the contract may choose the law of the EEA State of which he is a national or citizen as the applicable law.

[2187]

NOTES

Commencement: 1 December 2001.

9 Mandatory rules

Nothing in regulation 8 affects the application of the mandatory rules of any part of the United Kingdom, irrespective of the applicable law of the contract.

[2188]

NOTES

Commencement: 1 December 2001.

10 The 1990 Act

(1) Subject to the preceding provisions of this Part, the 1990 Act is to be treated as applying to the contract for the purposes of determining the applicable law.

(2) In determining what freedom of choice the parties have under the law of a part of the United Kingdom, the 1990 Act is to be treated as applying to the contract.

[2189]

NOTES
Commencement: 1 December 2001.

FINANCIAL COLLATERAL ARRANGEMENTS (NO 2) REGULATIONS 2003

(SI 2003/3226)

NOTES
Made: 10 December 2003.
Authority: European Communities Act 1972, s 2(2).
Commencement: 11 December 2003 (reg 2); 26 December 2003 (otherwise).

(*Pts 1–4* (*regs 1–18*) *reproduced in Pt III*(*C*) *at* **[2258]–[2273]**.)

PART 5
CONFLICT OF LAWS

19 Standard test regarding the applicable law to book entry securities financial collateral arrangements

(1) This regulation applies to financial collateral arrangements where book entry securities collateral is used as collateral under the arrangement and are held through one or more intermediaries.

(2) Any question relating to the matters specified in paragraph (4) of this regulation which arises in relation to book entry securities collateral which is provided under a financial collateral arrangement shall be governed by the domestic law of the country in which the relevant account is maintained.

(3) For the purposes of paragraph (2) "domestic law" excludes any rule under which, in deciding the relevant question, reference should be made to the law of another country.

(4) The matters referred to in paragraph (2) are—
- (a) the legal nature and proprietary effects of book entry securities collateral;
- (b) the requirements for perfecting a financial collateral arrangement relating to book entry securities collateral and the transfer or passing of control or possession of book entry securities collateral under such an arrangement;
- (c) the requirements for rendering a financial collateral arrangement which relates to book entry securities collateral effective against third parties;
- (d) whether a person's title to or interest in such book entry securities collateral is overridden by or subordinated to a competing title or interest; and
- (e) the steps required for the realisation of book entry securities collateral following the occurrence of any enforcement event.

[2190]

NOTES
Commencement: 26 December 2003.

C. INTERNATIONAL COMMERCIAL AND FINANCIAL LAW

UNFAIR TERMS IN CONSUMER CONTRACTS REGULATIONS 1999

(SI 1999/2083)

NOTES

Made: 22 July 1999.
Authority: European Communities Act 1972, s 2(2).
Commencement: 1 October 1999.

ARRANGEMENT OF REGULATIONS

1 Citation and commencement

These Regulations may be cited as the Unfair Terms in Consumer Contracts Regulations 1999 and shall come into force on 1st October 1999.

[2191]

2 (*Revokes the Unfair Terms in Consumer Contracts Regulations 1994, SI 2004/3159.*)

3 Interpretation

(1) In these Regulations—

"the Community" means the European Community;

"consumer" means any natural person who, in contracts covered by these Regulations, is acting for purposes which are outside his trade, business or profession;

"court" in relation to England and Wales and Northern Ireland means a county court or the High Court, and in relation to Scotland, the Sheriff or the Court of Session;

"[OFT]" means [the Office of Fair Trading];

"EEA Agreement" means the Agreement on the European Economic Area signed at Oporto on 2nd May 1992 as adjusted by the protocol signed at Brussels on 17th March 1993;

"Member State" means a State which is a contracting party to the EEA Agreement;

"notified" means notified in writing;

"qualifying body" means a person specified in Schedule 1;

"seller or supplier" means any natural or legal person who, in contracts covered by these Regulations, is acting for purposes relating to his trade, business or profession, whether publicly owned or privately owned;

"unfair terms" means the contractual terms referred to in regulation 5.

[(1A) The references—

(a) in regulation 4(1) to a seller or a supplier, and

(b) in regulation 8(1) to a seller or supplier,

include references to a distance supplier and to an intermediary.

(1B) In paragraph (1A) and regulation 5(6)—

"distance supplier" means—

(a) a supplier under a distance contract within the meaning of the Financial Services (Distance Marketing) Regulations 2004, or

(b) a supplier of unsolicited financial services within regulation 15 of those Regulations; and

"intermediary" has the same meaning as in those Regulations.]

(2) In the application of these Regulations to Scotland for references to an "injunction" or an "interim injunction" there shall be substituted references to an "interdict" or "interim interdict" respectively.

[2192]

NOTES

Para (1): in definition "OFT" (definition "Director" as originally enacted) words in square brackets substituted by virtue of the Enterprise Act 2002, s 2.

Paras (1A), (1B): inserted by the Financial Services (Distance Marketing) Regulations 2004, SI 2004/2095, reg 24(1), (2).

4 Terms to which these Regulations apply

(1) These Regulations apply in relation to unfair terms in contracts concluded between a seller or a supplier and a consumer.

(2) These Regulations do not apply to contractual terms which reflect—

(a) mandatory statutory or regulatory provisions (including such provisions under the law of any Member State or in Community legislation having effect in the United Kingdom without further enactment);

(b) the provisions or principles of international conventions to which the Member States or the Community are party.

[2193]

5 Unfair terms

(1) A contractual term which has not been individually negotiated shall be regarded as unfair if, contrary to the requirement of good faith, it causes a significant imbalance in the parties' rights and obligations arising under the contract, to the detriment of the consumer.

(2) A term shall always be regarded as not having been individually negotiated where it has been drafted in advance and the consumer has therefore not been able to influence the substance of the term.

(3) Notwithstanding that a specific term or certain aspects of it in a contract has been individually negotiated, these Regulations shall apply to the rest of a contract if an overall assessment of it indicates that it is a pre-formulated standard contract.

(4) It shall be for any seller or supplier who claims that a term was individually negotiated to show that it was.

(5) Schedule 2 to these Regulations contains an indicative and non-exhaustive list of the terms which may be regarded as unfair.

[(6) Any contractual term providing that a consumer bears the burden of proof in respect of showing whether a distance supplier or an intermediary complied with any or all of the obligations placed upon him resulting from the Directive and any rule or enactment implementing it shall always be regarded as unfair.

(7) In paragraph (6)—

"the Directive" means Directive 2002/65/EC of the European Parliament and of the Council of 23 September 2002 concerning the distance marketing of consumer financial services and amending Council Directive 90/619/EEC and Directives 97/7/EC and 98/27/EC; and "rule" means a rule made by the Financial Services Authority under the Financial Services and Markets Act 2000 or by a designated professional body within the meaning of section 326(2) of that Act.]

[2194]

NOTES

Paras (6), (7): added by the Financial Services (Distance Marketing) Regulations 2004, SI 2004/2095, reg 24(1), (3).

6 Assessment of unfair terms

(1) Without prejudice to regulation 12, the unfairness of a contractual term shall be assessed, taking into account the nature of the goods or services for which the contract was concluded and by referring, at the time of conclusion of the contract, to all the circumstances attending the conclusion of the contract and to all the other terms of the contract or of another contract on which it is dependent.

(2) In so far as it is in plain intelligible language, the assessment of fairness of a term shall not relate—

(a) to the definition of the main subject matter of the contract, or

(b) to the adequacy of the price or remuneration, as against the goods or services supplied in exchange.

[2195]

7 Written contracts

(1) A seller or supplier shall ensure that any written term of a contract is expressed in plain, intelligible language.

(2) If there is doubt about the meaning of a written term, the interpretation which is most favourable to the consumer shall prevail but this rule shall not apply in proceedings brought under regulation 12.

[2196]

8 Effect of unfair term

(1) An unfair term in a contract concluded with a consumer by a seller or supplier shall not be binding on the consumer.

(2) The contract shall continue to bind the parties if it is capable of continuing in existence without the unfair term.

[2197]

9 Choice of law clauses

These Regulations shall apply notwithstanding any contract term which applies or purports to apply the law of a non-Member State, if the contract has a close connection with the territory of the Member States.

[2198]

10 Complaints—consideration by [OFT]

(1) It shall be the duty of the [OFT] to consider any complaint made to [it] that any contract term drawn up for general use is unfair, unless—

(a) the complaint appears to the [OFT] to be frivolous or vexatious; or

(b) a qualifying body has notified the [OFT] that it agrees to consider the complaint.

(2) The [OFT] shall give reasons for [its] decision to apply or not to apply, as the case may be, for an injunction under regulation 12 in relation to any complaint which these Regulations require [it] to consider.

(3) In deciding whether or not to apply for an injunction in respect of a term which the [OFT] considers to be unfair, [it] may, if [it] considers it appropriate to do so, have regard to any undertakings given to [it] by or on behalf of any person as to the continued use of such a term in contracts concluded with consumers.

[2199]

NOTES

Provision heading: reference to "OFT" in square brackets substituted by virtue of the Enterprise Act 2002, s 2(3).

Paras (1)–(3): words in square brackets substituted by virtue of the Enterprise Act 2002, s 2(3).

11 Complaints—consideration by qualifying bodies

(1) If a qualifying body specified in Part One of Schedule 1 notifies the [OFT] that it agrees to consider a complaint that any contract term drawn up for general use is unfair, it shall be under a duty to consider that complaint.

(2) Regulation 10(2) and (3) shall apply to a qualifying body which is under a duty to consider a complaint as they apply to the [OFT].

[2200]

NOTES

Paras (1), (2): references to "OFT" in square brackets substituted by virtue of the Enterprise Act 2002, s(3).

12 Injunctions to prevent continued use of unfair terms

(1) The [OFT] or, subject to paragraph (2), any qualifying body may apply for an injunction (including an interim injunction) against any person appearing to the [OFT] or that body to be using, or recommending use of, an unfair term drawn up for general use in contracts concluded with consumers.

(2) A qualifying body may apply for an injunction only where—

- (a) it has notified the [OFT] of its intention to apply at least fourteen days before the date on which the application is made, beginning with the date on which the notification was given; or
- (b) the [OFT] consents to the application being made within a shorter period.

(3) The court on an application under this regulation may grant an injunction on such terms as it thinks fit.

(4) An injunction may relate not only to use of a particular contract term drawn up for general use but to any similar term, or a term having like effect, used or recommended for use by any person.

[2201]

NOTES

Paras (1), (2): references to "OFT" in square brackets substituted by virtue of the Enterprise Act 2002, s 2(3).

13 Powers of the [OFT] and qualifying bodies to obtain documents and information

(1) The [OFT] may exercise the power conferred by this regulation for the purpose of—

- (a) facilitating [its] consideration of a complaint that a contract term drawn up for general use is unfair; or
- (b) ascertaining whether a person has complied with an undertaking or court order as to the continued use, or recommendation for use, of a term in contracts concluded with consumers.

(2) A qualifying body specified in Part One of Schedule 1 may exercise the power conferred by this regulation for the purpose of—

- (a) facilitating its consideration of a complaint that a contract term drawn up for general use is unfair; or
- (b) ascertaining whether a person has complied with—
  - (i) an undertaking given to it or to the court following an application by that body, or
  - (ii) a court order made on an application by that body,

as to the continued use, or recommendation for use, of a term in contracts concluded with consumers.

(3) The [OFT] may require any person to supply to [it], and a qualifying body specified in Part One of Schedule 1 may require any person to supply to it—

- (a) a copy of any document which that person has used or recommended for use, at the time the notice referred to in paragraph (4) below is given, as a pre-formulated standard contract in dealings with consumers;

PART III STATUTORY INSTRUMENTS

(b) information about the use, or recommendation for use, by that person of that document or any other such document in dealings with consumers.

(4) The power conferred by this regulation is to be exercised by a notice in writing which may—

(a) specify the way in which and the time within which it is to be complied with; and
(b) be varied or revoked by a subsequent notice.

(5) Nothing in this regulation compels a person to supply any document or information which he would be entitled to refuse to produce or give in civil proceedings before the court.

(6) If a person makes default in complying with a notice under this regulation, the court may, on the application of the [OFT] or of the qualifying body, make such order as the court thinks fit for requiring the default to be made good, and any such order may provide that all the costs or expenses of and incidental to the application shall be borne by the person in default or by any officers of a company or other association who are responsible for its default.

[2202]

NOTES

Provision heading: reference to "OFT" in square brackets substituted by virtue of the Enterprise Act 2002, s 2(3).

Paras (1), (3), (6): words in square brackets substituted by virtue of the Enterprise Act 2002, s 2(3).

14 Notification of undertakings and orders to [OFT]

A qualifying body shall notify the [OFT]—

(a) of any undertaking given to it by or on behalf of any person as to the continued use of a term which that body considers to be unfair in contracts concluded with consumers;
(b) of the outcome of any application made by it under regulation 12, and of the terms of any undertaking given to, or order made by, the court;
(c) of the outcome of any application made by it to enforce a previous order of the court.

[2203]

NOTES

References to "OFT" in square brackets substituted by virtue of the Enterprise Act 2002, s 2(3).

15 Publication, information and advice

(1) The [OFT] shall arrange for the publication in such form and manner as [it] considers appropriate, of—

(a) details of any undertaking or order notified to [it] under regulation 14;
(b) details of any undertaking given to [it] by or on behalf of any person as to the continued use of a term which the [OFT] considers to be unfair in contracts concluded with consumers;
(c) details of any application made by [it] under regulation 12, and of the terms of any undertaking given to, or order made by, the court;
(d) details of any application made by the [OFT] to enforce a previous order of the court.

(2) The [OFT] shall inform any person on request whether a particular term to which these Regulations apply has been—

(a) the subject of an undertaking given to the [OFT] or notified to [it] by a qualifying body; or
(b) the subject of an order of the court made upon application by [it] or notified to [it] by a qualifying body;

and shall give that person details of the undertaking or a copy of the order, as the case may be, together with a copy of any amendments which the person giving the undertaking has agreed to make to the term in question.

(3) The [OFT] may arrange for the dissemination in such form and manner as [it] considers appropriate of such information and advice concerning the operation of these Regulations as may appear to [it] to be expedient to give to the public and to all persons likely to be affected by these Regulations.

[2204]

NOTES

Paras (1)–(3): words in square brackets substituted by virtue of the Enterprise Act 2002, s 2(3).

[16 The functions of the Financial Services Authority

The functions of the Financial Services Authority under these Regulations shall be treated as functions of the Financial Services Authority under the [Financial Services and Markets Act 2000].]

[2205]

NOTES

Commencement: 1 May 2001.

Inserted by the Unfair Terms in Consumer Contracts (Amendment) Regulations 2001, SI 2001/1186, reg 2(a).

Words in square brackets substituted by the Financial Services and Markets Act 2000 (Consequential Amendments and Repeals) Order 2001, SI 2001/3649, art 583.

SCHEDULE 1
QUALIFYING BODIES

Regulation 3

PART ONE

[1 The Information Commissioner.

2 The Gas and Electricity Markets Authority.

3 The Director General of Electricity Supply for Northern Ireland.

4 The Director General of Gas for Northern Ireland.

5 [The Office of Communications].

6 [The Water Services Regulation Authority].

7 [The Office of Rail Regulation].

8 Every weights and measures authority in Great Britain.

9 The Department of Enterprise, Trade and Investment in Northern Ireland.

10 The Financial Services Authority.]

[2206]

NOTES

Commencement: 1 May 2001.

List substituted by the Unfair Terms in Consumer Contracts (Amendment) Regulations 2001, SI 2001/1186, reg 2(b).

Entry 5: words in square brackets substituted by the Communications Act 2003 (Consequential Amendments No 2) Order 2003, SI 2003/3182, art 2.

Entry 6: words in square brackets substituted by the Unfair Terms in Consumer Contracts (Amendment) and Water Act 2003 (Transitional Provision) Regulations 2006, SI 2006/523, reg 2.

Entry 7: words in square brackets substituted by virtue of the Railways and Transport Safety Act 2003, s 16(4), (5), Sch 3, para 4; for savings see s 16 of, and Sch 3 to, that Act.

PART TWO

11 Consumers' Association

[2207]

SCHEDULE 2
INDICATIVE AND NON-EXHAUSTIVE LIST OF TERMS WHICH MAY BE REGARDED AS UNFAIR

Regulation 5(5)

1 Terms which have the object or effect of—

PART III STATUTORY INSTRUMENTS

(a) excluding or limiting the legal liability of a seller or supplier in the event of the death of a consumer or personal injury to the latter resulting from an act or omission of that seller or supplier;
(b) inappropriately excluding or limiting the legal rights of the consumer vis-à-vis the seller or supplier or another party in the event of total or partial non-performance or inadequate performance by the seller or supplier of any of the contractual obligations, including the option of offsetting a debt owed to the seller or supplier against any claim which the consumer may have against him;
(c) making an agreement binding on the consumer whereas provision of services by the seller or supplier is subject to a condition whose realisation depends on his own will alone;
(d) permitting the seller or supplier to retain sums paid by the consumer where the latter decides not to conclude or perform the contract, without providing for the consumer to receive compensation of an equivalent amount from the seller or supplier where the latter is the party cancelling the contract;
(e) requiring any consumer who fails to fulfil his obligation to pay a disproportionately high sum in compensation;
(f) authorising the seller or supplier to dissolve the contract on a discretionary basis where the same facility is not granted to the consumer, or permitting the seller or supplier to retain the sums paid for services not yet supplied by him where it is the seller or supplier himself who dissolves the contract;
(g) enabling the seller or supplier to terminate a contract of indeterminate duration without reasonable notice except where there are serious grounds for doing so;
(h) automatically extending a contract of fixed duration where the consumer does not indicate otherwise, when the deadline fixed for the consumer to express his desire not to extend the contract is unreasonably early;
(i) irrevocably binding the consumer to terms with which he had no real opportunity of becoming acquainted before the conclusion of the contract;
(j) enabling the seller or supplier to alter the terms of the contract unilaterally without a valid reason which is specified in the contract;
(k) enabling the seller or supplier to alter unilaterally without a valid reason any characteristics of the product or service to be provided;
(l) providing for the price of goods to be determined at the time of delivery or allowing a seller of goods or supplier of services to increase their price without in both cases giving the consumer the corresponding right to cancel the contract if the final price is too high in relation to the price agreed when the contract was concluded;
(m) giving the seller or supplier the right to determine whether the goods or services supplied are in conformity with the contract, or giving him the exclusive right to interpret any term of the contract;
(n) limiting the seller's or supplier's obligation to respect commitments undertaken by his agents or making his commitments subject to compliance with a particular formality;
(o) obliging the consumer to fulfil all his obligations where the seller or supplier does not perform his;
(p) giving the seller or supplier the possibility of transferring his rights and obligations under the contract, where this may serve to reduce the guarantees for the consumer, without the latter's agreement;
(q) excluding or hindering the consumer's right to take legal action or exercise any other legal remedy, particularly by requiring the consumer to take disputes exclusively to arbitration not covered by legal provisions, unduly restricting the evidence available to him or imposing on him a burden of proof which, according to the applicable law, should lie with another party to the contract.

2 Scope of paragraphs 1(g), (j) and (l)

(a) Paragraph 1(g) is without hindrance to terms by which a supplier of financial services reserves the right to terminate unilaterally a contract of indeterminate duration without notice where there is a valid reason, provided that the supplier is required to inform the other contracting party or parties thereof immediately.
(b) Paragraph 1(j) is without hindrance to terms under which a supplier of financial services reserves the right to alter the rate of interest payable by the consumer or due to the latter, or the amount of other charges for financial services without notice where there is a valid reason, provided that the supplier is required to inform the other contracting party or parties thereof at the earliest opportunity and that the latter are free to dissolve the contract immediately.

Paragraph 1(j) is also without hindrance to terms under which a seller or supplier reserves the right to alter unilaterally the conditions of a contract of indeterminate duration, provided that he is required to inform the consumer with reasonable notice and that the consumer is free to dissolve the contract.

(c) Paragraphs 1(g), (j) and (l) do not apply to:
—transactions in transferable securities, financial instruments and other products or services where the price is linked to fluctuations in a stock exchange quotation or index or a financial market rate that the seller or supplier does not control;
—contracts for the purchase or sale of foreign currency, traveller's cheques or international money orders denominated in foreign currency.

(d) Paragraph 1(1) is without hindrance to price indexation clauses, where lawful, provided that the method by which prices vary is explicitly described.

[2208]

FINANCIAL MARKETS AND INSOLVENCY (SETTLEMENT FINALITY) REGULATIONS 1999

(SI 1999/2979)

NOTES

Made: 2 November 1999.
Authority: European Communities Act 1972, s 2(2).
Commencement: 11 December 1999.

ARRANGEMENT OF REGULATIONS

PART I
GENERAL

PART II
DESIGNATED SYSTEMS

PART III
TRANSFER ORDERS EFFECTED THROUGH A DESIGNATED SYSTEM AND COLLATERAL SECURITY

Collateral security charges

PART III
STATUTORY INSTRUMENTS

PART I
GENERAL

1 Citation, commencement and extent

(1) These Regulations may be cited as the Financial Markets and Insolvency (Settlement Finality) Regulations 1999 and shall come into force on 11th December 1999.

(2) …

[2209]

NOTES

Para (2): revoked by the Financial Markets and Insolvency (Settlement Finality) (Amendment) Regulations 2006, SI 2006/50, reg 2(1), (2).

---

2 Interpretation

(1) In these Regulations—

["the 2000 Act" means the Financial Services and Markets Act 2000;]

"central bank" means a central bank of an EEA State or the European Central Bank;

"central counterparty" means a body corporate or unincorporated association interposed between the institutions in a designated system and which acts as the exclusive counterparty of those institutions with regard to transfer orders;

"charge" means any form of security, including a mortgage and, in Scotland, a heritable security;

"clearing house" means a body corporate or unincorporated association which is responsible for the calculation of the net positions of institutions and any central counterparty or settlement agent in a designated system;

"collateral security" means any realisable assets provided under a charge or a repurchase or similar agreement, or otherwise (including money provided under a charge)—

(a) for the purpose of securing rights and obligations potentially arising in connection with a designated system ("collateral security in connection with participation in a designated system"); or

(b) to a central bank for the purpose of securing rights and obligations in connection with its operations in carrying out its functions as a central bank ("collateral security in connection with the functions of a central bank");

"collateral security charge" means, where collateral security consists of realisable assets (including money) provided under a charge, that charge;

["credit institution" means a credit institution as defined in [Article 1(1)(a)] of Directive 2000/12/EC of the European Parliament and of the Council, including the bodies set out in the list in Article 2(3);]

"creditors' voluntary winding-up resolution" means a resolution for voluntary winding up (within the meaning of the Insolvency Act 1986 [or the Insolvency (Northern Ireland) Order 1989]) where the winding up is a creditors' winding up (within the meaning of that Act [or that Order]);

"default arrangements" means the arrangements put in place by a designated system to limit systemic and other types of risk which arise in the event of a participant appearing to be unable, or likely to become unable, to meet its obligations in respect of a transfer order, including, for example, any default rules within the meaning of Part VII [or Part V] or any other arrangements for—

(a) netting,
(b) the closing out of open positions, or
(c) the application or transfer of collateral security;

"defaulter" means a person in respect of whom action has been taken by a designated system under its default arrangements;

"designated system" means a system which is declared by a designation order for the time being in force to be a designated system for the purposes of these Regulations;

"designating authority" means—

(a) in the case of a system—
 (i) which is, or the operator of which is, a recognised investment exchange or a recognised clearing house for the purposes of [the 2000 Act],
 (ii) which is, or the operator of which is, a listed person within the meaning of the Financial Markets and Insolvency (Money Market) Regulations 1995, or
 (iii) through which securities transfer orders are effected (whether or not payment transfer orders are also effected through that system),

 the Financial Services Authority;

(b) in any other case, the Bank of England;

"designation order" has the meaning given by regulation 4;

"EEA State" means a State which is a Contracting Party to the Agreement on the European Economic Area signed at Oporto on 2nd May 1992 as adjusted by the Protocol signed at Brussels on 17th March 1993;

"guidance", in relation to a designated system, means guidance issued or any recommendation made by it which is intended to have continuing effect and is issued in writing or other legible form to all or any class of its participants or users or persons seeking to participate in the system or to use its facilities and which would, if it were a rule, come within the definition of a rule;

"indirect participant" means a credit institution for which payment transfer orders are capable of being effected through a designated system pursuant to its contractual relationship with an institution;

"institution" means—

(a) a credit institution;
(b) an investment firm as defined in point 2 of Article 1 of Council Directive 93/22/EEC excluding the bodies set out in the list in Article 2(2)(a) to (k);
(c) a public authority or publicly guaranteed undertaking;
(d) any undertaking whose head office is outside the European Community and whose functions correspond to those of a credit institution or investment firm as defined in (a) and (b) above; or
(e) any undertaking which is treated by the designating authority as an institution in accordance with regulation 8(1),

which participates in a designated system and which is responsible for discharging the financial obligations arising from transfer orders which are effected through the system;

"netting" means the conversion into one net claim or obligation of different claims or obligations between participants resulting from the issue and receipt of transfer orders between them, whether on a bilateral or multilateral basis and whether through the interposition of a clearing house, central counterparty or settlement agent or otherwise;

["Part V" means Part V of the Companies (No 2) (Northern Ireland) Order 1990;]

"Part VII" means Part VII of the Companies Act 1989;

"participant" means—

(a) an institution,
(b) a body corporate or unincorporated association which carries out any combination of the functions of a central counterparty, a settlement agent or a clearing house, with respect to a system, or
(c) an indirect participant which is treated as a participant, or is a member of a class of indirect participants which are treated as participants, in accordance with regulation 9;

"protected trust deed" and "trust deed" shall be construed in accordance with section 73(1) of the Bankruptcy (Scotland) Act 1985 (interpretation);

"relevant office-holder" means—

(a) the official receiver;
(b) any person acting in relation to a company as its liquidator, provisional liquidator, or administrator;
(c) any person acting in relation to an individual (or, in Scotland, any debtor

within the meaning of the Bankruptcy (Scotland) Act 1985) as his trustee in bankruptcy or interim receiver of his property or as permanent or interim trustee in the sequestration of his estate or as his trustee under a protected trust deed; or

(d) any person acting as administrator of an insolvent estate of a deceased person;

and in sub-paragraph (b), "company" means any company, society, association, partnership or other body which may be wound up under the Insolvency Act 1986 [or the Insolvency (Northern Ireland) Order 1989];

"rules", in relation to a designated system, means rules or conditions governing the system with respect to the matters dealt with in these Regulations;

"securities" means (except for the purposes of the definition of "charge") any instruments referred to in section B of the Annex to Council Directive 93/22/EEC;

"settlement account" means an account at a central bank, a settlement agent or a central counterparty used to hold funds or securities (or both) and to settle transactions between participants in a designated system;

"settlement agent" means a body corporate or unincorporated association providing settlement accounts to the institutions and any central counterparty in a designated system for the settlement of transfer orders within the system and, as the case may be, for extending credit to such institutions and any such central counterparty for settlement purposes;

"the Settlement Finality Directive" means Directive 98/26/EC of the European Parliament and of the Council of 19th May 1998 on settlement finality in payment and securities settlement systems;

"transfer order" means—

(a) an instruction by a participant to place at the disposal of a recipient an amount of money by means of a book entry on the accounts of a credit institution, a central bank or a settlement agent, or an instruction which results in the assumption or discharge of a payment obligation as defined by the rules of a designated system ("a payment transfer order"); or

(b) an instruction by a participant to transfer the title to, or interest in, securities by means of a book entry on a register, or otherwise ("a securities transfer order");

"winding up" means—

(a) winding up by the court, or

(b) creditors' voluntary winding up,

within the meaning of the Insolvency Act 1986 [or the Insolvency (Northern Ireland) Order 1989] (but does not include members' voluntary winding up within the meaning of that Act [or that Order]).

(2) In these Regulations—

(a) references to the law of insolvency include references to every provision made by or under the Insolvency Act 1986[, the Insolvency (Northern Ireland) Order 1989] or the Bankruptcy (Scotland) Act 1985; and in relation to a building society references to insolvency law or to any provision of the Insolvency Act 1986 [or the Insolvency (Northern Ireland) Order 1989] are to that law or provision as modified by the Building Societies Act 1986;

(b) in relation to Scotland, references to—

(i) sequestration include references to the administration by a judicial factor of the insolvent estate of a deceased person,

(ii) an interim or permanent trustee include references to a judicial factor on the insolvent estate of a deceased person, and

(iii) "set off" include compensation.

(3) Subject to paragraph (1), expressions used in these Regulations which are also used in the Settlement Finality Directive have the same meaning in these Regulations as they have in the Settlement Finality Directive.

(4) References in these Regulations to things done, or required to be done, by or in relation to a designated system shall, in the case of a designated system which is neither a body corporate nor an unincorporated association, be treated as references to things done, or required to be done, by or in relation to the operator of that system.

[2210]

NOTES

Para (1): definition "the 2000 Act" substituted, for definition "the 1986 Act" as originally enacted, and in definition "designating authority" words in square brackets in para (a)(i) substituted, by the Financial Services and Markets Act 2000 (Consequential Amendments) Order 2002, SI 2002/1555, art 39(1), (2)(a), (b); definition "credit institution" substituted by the Banking Consolidation Directive (Consequential Amendments) Regulations 2000, SI 2000/2952, reg 17, Schedule, words in square brackets substituted by the Electronic Money (Miscellaneous Amendments) Regulations 2002, SI 2002/765, reg 7; in definitions "creditors' voluntary winding up resolution", "default arrangements", "relevant office-holder", "winding up", words in square brackets inserted, and definition "Part V" inserted, by the Financial Markets and Insolvency (Settlement Finality) (Amendment) Regulations 2006, SI 2006/50, reg 2(1), (3).

Para (2): in sub para (a) words in square brackets inserted by SI 2006/50, reg 2(1), (4).

PART II
DESIGNATED SYSTEMS

3 Application for designation

(1) Any body corporate or unincorporated association may apply to the designating authority for an order declaring it, or any system of which it is the operator, to be a designated system for the purposes of these Regulations.

(2) Any such application—

(a) shall be made in such manner as the designating authority may direct; and

(b) shall be accompanied by such information as the designating authority may reasonably require for the purpose of determining the application.

(3) At any time after receiving an application and before determining it, the designating authority may require the applicant to furnish additional information.

(4) The directions and requirements given or imposed under paragraphs (2) and (3) may differ as between different applications.

(5) Any information to be furnished to the designating authority under this regulation shall be in such form or verified in such manner as it may specify.

(6) Every application shall be accompanied by copies of the rules of the system to which the application relates and any guidance relating to that system.

[2211]

4 Grant and refusal of designation

(1) Where—

(a) an application has been duly made under regulation 3;

(b) the applicant has paid any fee charged by virtue of regulation 5(1); and

(c) the designating authority is satisfied that the requirements of the Schedule are satisfied with respect to the system to which the application relates;

the designating authority may make an order (a "designation order") declaring the system to be a designated system for the purposes of these Regulations.

(2) In determining whether to make a designation order, the designating authority shall have regard to systemic risks.

(3) Where an application has been made to the Financial Services Authority under regulation 3 in relation to a system through which both securities transfer orders and payment transfer orders are effected, the Authority shall consult the Bank of England before deciding whether to make a designation order.

(4) A designation order shall state the date on which it takes effect.

(5) Where the designating authority refuses an application for a designation order it shall give the applicant a written notice to that effect stating the reasons for the refusal.

[2212]

5 Fees

(1) The designating authority may charge a fee to an applicant for a designation order.

(2) The designating authority may charge a designated system a periodical fee.

(3) Fees chargeable by the designating authority under this regulation shall not exceed an amount which reasonably represents the amount of costs incurred or likely to be incurred—

(a) in the case of a fee charged to an applicant for a designation order, in determining whether the designation order should be made; and

(b) in the case of a periodical fee, in satisfying itself that the designated system continues to meet the requirements of the Schedule and is complying with any obligations to which it is subject by virtue of these Regulations.

[2213]

6 Certain bodies deemed to satisfy requirements for designation

(1) Subject to paragraph (2), an investment exchange or clearing house declared by an order for the time being in force to be a recognised investment exchange or recognised clearing house for the purposes of [the 2000 Act], whether that order was made before or is made after the coming into force of these Regulations, shall be deemed to satisfy the requirements in paragraphs 2 and 3 of the Schedule.

(2) Paragraph (1) does not apply to overseas investment exchanges or overseas clearing houses within the meaning of the 1986 Act.

[2214]

NOTES

Para (1): words in square brackets substituted by the Financial Services and Markets Act 2000 (Consequential Amendments) Order 2002, SI 2002/1555, art 39(1), (3).

7 Revocation of designation

(1) A designation order may be revoked by a further order made by the designating authority if at any time it appears to the designating authority—

(a) that any requirement of the Schedule is not satisfied in the case of the system to which the designation order relates; or

(b) that the system has failed to comply with any obligation to which it is subject by virtue of these Regulations.

(2) [Subsections (1) to (7) of section 298 of the 2000 Act] shall apply in relation to the revocation of a designation order under paragraph (1) as they apply in relation to the revocation of a recognition order under [section 297(2) of that Act]; and in those subsections as they so apply—

[(a) any reference to a recognised body shall be taken to be a reference to a designated system;

(b) any reference to members of a recognised body shall be taken to be a reference to participants in a designated system;

(c) references to the Authority shall, in cases where the Bank of England is the designating authority, be taken to be a reference to the Bank of England; and

(d) subsection (4)(a) shall have effect as if for "two months" there were substituted "three months"].

[(3) An order revoking a designation order—

(a) shall state the date on which it takes effect, being no earlier than three months after the day on which the revocation order is made; and

(b) may contain such transitional provisions as the designating authority thinks necessary or expedient.

(4) A designation order may be revoked at the request or with the consent of the designated system, and any such revocation shall not be subject to the restriction imposed by paragraph (3)(a), or to the requirements imposed by subsections (1) to (6) of section 298 of the 2000 Act.]

[2215]

NOTES

Para (2): words in first and second pairs of square brackets substituted and sub-paras (a)–(d) substituted, for sub-paras (a), (b) as originally enacted, by the Financial Services and Markets Act 2000 (Consequential Amendments) Order 2002, SI 2002/1555, art 39(1), (4).

Paras (3), (4): added by SI 2002/1555, art 39(1), (5).

8 Undertakings treated as institutions

(1) A designating authority may treat as an institution any undertaking which participates in a designated system and which is responsible for discharging financial obligations arising from transfer orders effected through that system, provided that—

(a) the designating authority considers such treatment to be required on grounds of systemic risk, and

(b) the designated system is one in which at least three institutions (other than any undertaking treated as an institution by virtue of this paragraph) participate and through which securities transfer orders are effected.

(2) Where a designating authority decides to treat an undertaking as an institution in accordance with paragraph (1), it shall give written notice of that decision to the designated system in which the undertaking is to be treated as a participant.

[2216]

9 Indirect participants treated as participants

(1) A designating authority may treat—

(a) an indirect participant as a participant in a designated system, or

(b) a class of indirect participants as participants in a designated system,

where it considers this to be required on grounds of systemic risk, and shall give written notice of any decision to that effect to the designated system.

[2217]

10 Provision of information by designated systems

(1) A designated system shall, on being declared to be a designated system, provide to the designating authority in writing a list of its participants and shall give written notice to the designating authority of any amendment to the list within seven days of such amendment.

(2) The designating authority may, in writing, require a designated system to furnish to it such other information relating to that designated system as it reasonably requires for the exercise of its functions under these Regulations, within such time, in such form, at such intervals and verified in such manner as the designating authority may specify.

(3) When a designated system amends, revokes or adds to its rules or its guidance, it shall within fourteen days give written notice to the designating authority of the amendment, revocation or addition.

(4) A designated system shall give the designating authority at least fourteen days' written notice of any proposal to amend, revoke or add to its default arrangements.

(5) Nothing in this regulation shall require a designated system to give any notice or furnish any information to the Financial Services Authority which it has given or furnished to the Authority pursuant to any requirement imposed by or under [section 293 of the 2000 Act] (notification requirements) or any other enactment.

[2218]

NOTES

Para (5): words in square brackets substituted by the Financial Services and Markets Act 2000 (Consequential Amendments) Order 2002, SI 2002/1555, art 39(1), (6).

11 Exemption from liability in damages

(1) Neither the designating authority nor any person who is, or is acting as, a member, officer or member of staff of the designating authority shall be liable in damages for anything done or omitted in the discharge, or purported discharge, of the designating authority's functions under these Regulations.

(2) Paragraph (1) does not apply—

(a) if the act or omission is shown to have been in bad faith; or

(b) so as to prevent an award of damages made in respect of an act or omission on the ground that the act or omission was unlawful as a result of section 6(1) of the Human Rights Act 1998 (acts of public authorities).

[2219]

12 Publication of information and advice

A designating authority may publish information or give advice, or arrange for the publication of information or the giving of advice, in such form and manner as it considers appropriate with respect to any matter dealt with in these Regulations.

[2220]

PART III
TRANSFER ORDERS EFFECTED THROUGH A DESIGNATED SYSTEM AND COLLATERAL SECURITY

13 Modifications of the law of insolvency

(1) The general law of insolvency has effect in relation to—

(a) transfer orders effected through a designated system and action taken under the rules of a designated system with respect to such orders; and

(b) collateral security,

subject to the provisions of this Part.

(2) Those provisions apply in relation to—

(a) insolvency proceedings in respect of a participant in a designated system; and

(b) insolvency proceedings in respect of a provider of collateral security in connection with the functions of a central bank, in so far as the proceedings affect the rights of the central bank to the collateral security;

but not in relation to any other insolvency proceedings, notwithstanding that rights or liabilities arising from transfer orders or collateral security fall to be dealt with in the proceedings.

(3) Subject to regulation 21, nothing in this Part shall have the effect of disapplying Part VII [or Part V].

[2221]

NOTES

Para (3): words in square brackets inserted by the Financial Markets and Insolvency (Settlement Finality) (Amendment) Regulations 2006, SI 2006/50, reg 2(1), (5).

14 Proceedings of designated system take precedence over insolvency proceedings

(1) None of the following shall be regarded as to any extent invalid at law on the ground of inconsistency with the law relating to the distribution of the assets of a person on bankruptcy, winding up, sequestration or under a protected trust deed, or in the administration of an insolvent estate—

(a) a transfer order;

(b) the default arrangements of a designated system;

(c) the rules of a designated system as to the settlement of transfer orders not dealt with under its default arrangements;

(d) a contract for the purpose of realising collateral security in connection with participation in a designated system otherwise than pursuant to its default arrangements; or

(e) a contract for the purpose of realising collateral security in connection with the functions of a central bank.

(2) The powers of a relevant office-holder in his capacity as such, and the powers of the court under the Insolvency Act 1986[, the Insolvency (Northern Ireland) Order 1989] or the Bankruptcy (Scotland) Act 1985, shall not be exercised in such a way as to prevent or interfere with—

(a) the settlement in accordance with the rules of a designated system of a transfer order not dealt with under its default arrangements;

(b) any action taken under its default arrangements;

(c) any action taken to realise collateral security in connection with participation in a designated system otherwise than pursuant to its default arrangements; or

(d) any action taken to realise collateral security in connection with the functions of a central bank.

This does not prevent the court from afterwards making any such order or decree as is mentioned in regulation 17(1) or (2).

(3) Nothing in the following provisions of this Part shall be construed as affecting the generality of the above provisions.

(4) A debt or other liability arising out of a transfer order which is the subject of action taken under default arrangements may not be proved in a winding up or bankruptcy, or in Scotland claimed in a winding up, sequestration or under a protected trust deed, until the completion of the action taken under default arrangements.

A debt or other liability which by virtue of this paragraph may not be proved or claimed shall not be taken into account for the purposes of any set-off until the completion of the action taken under default arrangements.

(5) Paragraph (1) has the effect that the following provisions (which relate to preferential debts and the payment of expenses etc) apply subject to paragraph (6), namely—

- (a) in the case of collateral security provided by a company (within the meaning of section 735 of the Companies Act 1985 [or Article 3 of the Companies (Northern Ireland) Order 1986])—
  - (i) section 175 of the Insolvency Act 1986 [or Article 149 of the Insolvency (Northern Ireland) Order 1989], and
  - (ii) where the company is [in administration], [section 40 (or, in Scotland, section 59 and 60(1)(e) of the Insolvency Act 1986, paragraph 99(3) of Schedule B1 to that Act] [or Articles 31(4) and 50 of the Insolvency (Northern Ireland) Order 1989], and section 196 of the Companies Act 1985; and
- (b) in the case of collateral security provided by an individual, section 328(1) and (2) of the Insolvency Act 1986 [or, in Northern Ireland, Article 300(1) and (2) of the Insolvency (Northern Ireland) Order 1989] or, in Scotland, in the case of collateral security provided by an individual or a partnership, section 51 of the Bankruptcy (Scotland) Act 1985 and any like provision or rule of law affecting a protected trust deed.

(6) The claim of a participant or central bank to collateral security shall be paid in priority to—

- (a) the expenses of the winding up mentioned in sections 115 and 156 of the Insolvency Act 1986 [or Articles 100 and 134 of the Insolvency (Northern Ireland) Order 1989], the expenses of the bankruptcy within the meaning of that Act [or that Order] or, as the case may be, the remuneration and expenses of the administrator mentioned in [paragraph 99(3) of Schedule B1 to that Act] [or in Article 31(4) of that Order], and
- (b) the preferential debts of the company or the individual (as the case may be) within the meaning given by section 386 of that Act [or Article 346 of that Order],

unless the terms on which the collateral security was provided expressly provide that such expenses, remuneration or preferential debts are to have priority.

(7) As respects Scotland—

- (a) the reference in paragraph (6)(a) to the expenses of bankruptcy shall be taken to be a reference to the matters mentioned in paragraphs (a) to (d) of section 51(1) of the Bankruptcy (Scotland) Act 1985, or any like provision or rule of law affecting a protected trust deed; and
- (b) the reference in paragraph (6)(b) to the preferential debts of the individual shall be taken to be a reference to the preferred debts of the debtor within the meaning of the Bankruptcy (Scotland) Act 1985, or any like definition applying with respect to a protected trust deed by virtue of any provision or rule of law affecting it.

[2222]

NOTES

Para (2): words in square brackets inserted by the Financial Markets and Insolvency (Settlement Finality) (Amendment) Regulations 2006, SI 2006/50, reg 2(1), (6)(a).

Para (5): words in first and second pairs of square brackets in sub-para (a), words in third pair of square brackets in sub-para (a)(ii), and words in square brackets in sub-para (b) inserted by SI 2006/50, reg 2(1), (6)(b)–(e); words in first and second pairs of square brackets in sub-para (a)(ii) substituted by the Enterprise Act 2002 (Insolvency) Order 2003, SI 2003/2096, art 5, Schedule, Pt 2, paras 74, 75(a).

Para (6): words in first, second and fourth pairs of square brackets in sub-para (a) and words in square brackets in sub-para (b) inserted by SI 2006/50, reg 2(1), (6)(f), (g); words in third pair of square brackets in sub-para (a) substituted by SI 2003/2096, art 5, Schedule, Pt 2, paras 74, 75(b).

15 Net sum payable on completion of action taken under default arrangements

(1) The following provisions apply with respect to any sum which is owed on completion of action taken under default arrangements by or to a defaulter but do not apply to any sum which (or to the extent that it) arises from a transfer order which is also a market contract within the meaning of Part VII [or Part V], in which case sections 162 and 163 of the Companies Act 1989 [or Articles 85 and 86 of the Companies (No 2) (Northern Ireland) Order 1990] apply subject to the modification made by regulation 21.

(2) If, in England and Wales [or Northern Ireland], a bankruptcy or winding-up order has been made or a creditors' voluntary winding-up resolution has been passed, the debt—

(a) is provable in the bankruptcy or winding up or, as the case may be, is payable to the relevant office-holder; and

(b) shall be taken into account, where appropriate, under section 323 of the Insolvency Act 1986 [or Article 296 of the Insolvency (Northern Ireland) Order 1989] (mutual dealings and set-off) or the corresponding provision applicable in the case of winding up;

in the same way as a debt due before the commencement of bankruptcy, the date on which the body corporate goes into liquidation (within the meaning of section 247 of the Insolvency Act 1986 [or Article 6 of the Insolvency (Northern Ireland) Order 1989]) or, in the case of a partnership, the date of the winding-up order.

(3) If, in Scotland, an award of sequestration or a winding-up order has been made, or a creditors' voluntary winding-up resolution has been passed, or a trust deed has been granted and it has become a protected trust deed, the debt—

(a) may be claimed in the sequestration or winding up or under the protected trust deed or, as the case may be, is payable to the relevant office-holder; and

(b) shall be taken into account for the purposes of any rule of law relating to set-off applicable in sequestration, winding up or in respect of a protected trust deed;

in the same way as a debt due before the date of sequestration (within the meaning of section 73(1) of the Bankruptcy (Scotland) Act 1985) or the commencement of the winding up (within the meaning of section 129 of the Insolvency Act 1986) or the grant of the trust deed.

[2223]

NOTES

Paras (1), (2): words in square brackets inserted by the Financial Markets and Insolvency (Settlement Finality) (Amendment) Regulations 2006, SI 2006/50, reg 2(1), (7).

16 Disclaimer of property, rescission of contracts, &c

(1) Sections 178, 186, 315 and 345 of the Insolvency Act 1986 [or Articles 152, 157, 288 and 318 of the Insolvency (Northern Ireland) Order 1989] (power to disclaim onerous property and court's power to order rescission of contracts, &c) do not apply in relation to—

(a) a transfer order; or

(b) a contract for the purpose of realising collateral security.

In the application of this paragraph in Scotland, the reference to sections 178, 315 and 345 shall be construed as a reference to any rule of law having the like effect as those sections.

(2) In Scotland, a permanent trustee on the sequestrated estate of a defaulter or a liquidator or a trustee under a protected trust deed granted by a defaulter is bound by any transfer order given by that defaulter and by any such contract as is mentioned in paragraph (1)(b) notwithstanding section 42 of the Bankruptcy (Scotland) Act 1985 or any rule of law having the like effect applying in liquidations or any like provision or rule of law affecting the protected trust deed.

(3) Sections 127 and 284 of the Insolvency Act 1986 [or Articles 107 and 257 of the Insolvency (Northern Ireland) Order 1989] (avoidance of property dispositions effected after commencement of winding up or presentation of bankruptcy petition), section 32(8) of the Bankruptcy (Scotland) Act 1985 (effect of dealing with debtor relating to estate vested in permanent trustee) and any like provision or rule of law affecting a protected trust deed, do not apply to—

(a) a transfer order, or any disposition of property in pursuance of such an order;

(b) the provision of collateral security;

(c) a contract for the purpose of realising collateral security or any disposition of property in pursuance of such a contract; or

(d) any disposition of property in accordance with the rules of a designated system as to the application of collateral security.

[2224]

NOTES

Paras (1), (3): words in square brackets inserted by the Financial Markets and Insolvency (Settlement Finality) (Amendment) Regulations 2006, SI 2006/50, reg 2(1), (8).

17 Adjustment of prior transactions

(1) No order shall be made in relation to a transaction to which this regulation applies under—

(a) section 238 or 339 of the Insolvency Act 1986 [or Article 202 or 312 of the Insolvency (Northern Ireland) Order 1989] (transactions at an undervalue);
(b) section 239 or 340 of that Act [or Article 203 or 313 of that Order] (preferences); or
(c) section 423 of that Act [or Article 367 of that Order] (transactions defrauding creditors).

(2) As respects Scotland, no decree shall be granted in relation to any such transaction—

(a) under section 34 or 36 of the Bankruptcy (Scotland) Act 1985 or section 242 or 243 of the Insolvency Act 1986 (gratuitous alienations and unfair preferences); or
(b) at common law on grounds of gratuitous alienations or fraudulent preferences.

(3) This regulation applies to—

(a) a transfer order, or any disposition of property in pursuance of such an order;
(b) the provision of collateral security;
(c) a contract for the purpose of realising collateral security or any disposition of property in pursuance of such a contract; or
(d) any disposition of property in accordance with the rules of a designated system as to the application of collateral security.

[2225]

NOTES

Para (1): words in square brackets inserted by the Financial Markets and Insolvency (Settlement Finality) (Amendment) Regulations 2006, SI 2006/50, reg 2(1), (9).

Collateral security charges

18 Modifications of the law of insolvency

The general law of insolvency has effect in relation to a collateral security charge and the action taken to enforce such a charge, subject to the provisions of regulation 19.

[2226]

19 Administration orders, &c

(1) The following provisions of [Schedule B1 to] the Insolvency Act 1986 (which relate to administration orders and administrators) do not apply in relation to a collateral security charge—

[(a) paragraph 43(2) including that provision as applied by paragraph 44; and
(b) paragraphs 70, 71 and 72 of that Schedule;]

and [paragraph 41(2) of that Schedule] (receiver to vacate office when so required by administrator) does not apply to a receiver appointed under such a charge.

[(1A) The following provisions of the Insolvency (Northern Ireland) Order 1989 (which relate to administration orders and administrators) do not apply in relation to a collateral security charge—

(a) Articles 23(1)(b) and 24(3)(c) (restrictions on enforcement of security while petition for administration order pending or order in force); and
(b) Article 28(1) and (2) (power of administrator to deal with charged property);

and Article 24(2) of that Order (receiver to vacate office when so required by administrator) does not apply to a receiver appointed under such a charge.]

(2) However, where a collateral security charge falls to be enforced after an administration order has been made or a petition for an administration order has been

presented, and there exists another charge over some or all of the same property ranking in priority to or *pari passu* with the collateral security charge, on the application of any person interested, the court may order that there shall be taken after enforcement of the collateral security charge such steps as the court may direct for the purpose of ensuring that the chargee under the other charge is not prejudiced by the enforcement of the collateral security charge.

[(2A) A reference in paragraph (2) to "an administration order" shall include the appointment of an administrator under paragraph 14 or 22 of Schedule B1 to the Insolvency Act 1986.]

(3) Sections 127 and 284 of the Insolvency Act 1986 [or Articles 107 and 257 of the Insolvency (Northern Ireland) Order 1989] (avoidance of property dispositions effected after commencement of winding up or presentation of bankruptcy petition), section 32(8) of the Bankruptcy (Scotland) Act 1985 (effect of dealing with debtor relating to estate vested in permanent trustee) and any like provision or rule of law affecting a protected trust deed, do not apply to a disposition of property as a result of which the property becomes subject to a collateral security charge or any transactions pursuant to which that disposition is made.

[2227]

NOTES

Para (1): words in first pair of square brackets inserted, sub-paras (a), (b) substituted, and words in third pair of square brackets substituted, by the Enterprise Act 2002 (Insolvency) Order 2003, SI 2003/2096, art 5, Schedule, Pt 2, paras 74, 76(a).

Para (1A): inserted by the Financial Markets and Insolvency (Settlement Finality) (Amendment) Regulations 2006, SI 2006/50, reg 2(1), (10)(a).

Para (2A): inserted by SI 2003/2096, art 5, Schedule, Pt 2, paras 74, 76(b).

Para (3): words in square brackets inserted by SI 2006/50, reg 2(1), (10)(b).

General

20 Transfer order entered into designated system following insolvency

(1) This Part does not apply in relation to any transfer order given by a participant which is entered into a designated system after—

(a) a court has made an order of a type referred to in regulation 22 in respect of that participant, or

(b) that participant has passed a creditors' voluntary winding-up resolution, or

(c) a trust deed granted by that participant has become a protected trust deed,

unless the conditions mentioned in paragraph (2) are satisfied.

(2) The conditions referred to in paragraph (1) are that—

(a) the transfer order is carried out on the same day that the event specified in paragraph (1)(a), (b) or (c) occurs, and

(b) the settlement agent, the central counterparty or the clearing house can show that it did not have notice of that event at the time of settlement of the transfer order.

(3) For the purposes of paragraph (2)(b), the relevant settlement agent, central counterparty or clearing house shall be taken to have notice of an event specified in paragraph (1)(a), (b) or (c) if it deliberately failed to make enquiries as to that matter in circumstances in which a reasonable and honest person would have done so.

[2228]

21 Disapplication of certain provisions of Part VII [and Part V]

(1) The provisions of the Companies Act 1989 [or the Companies (No 2) (Northern Ireland) Order 1990] mentioned in paragraph (2) do not apply in relation to—

(a) a market contract which is also a transfer order effected through a designated system; or

(b) a market charge which is also a collateral security charge.

(2) The provisions referred to in paragraph (1) are as follows—

(a) section 163(4) to (6) [and Article 86(3) to (5)] (net sum payable on completion of default proceedings);

(b) section 164(4) to (6) [and Article 87(3) to (5)] (disclaimer of property, rescission of contracts, &c); and

(c) section 175(5) and (6) [and Article 97(5) and (6)] (administration orders, &c).

[2229]

NOTES

Provision heading: words in square brackets inserted by the Financial Markets and Insolvency (Settlement Finality) (Amendment) Regulations 2006, SI 2006/50, reg 2(1), (11)(a).

Paras (1), (2): words in square brackets inserted by SI 2006/50, reg 2(1), (11)(b)–(e).

22 Notification of insolvency order or passing of resolution for creditors' voluntary winding up

(1) Upon the making of an order for bankruptcy, sequestration, administration or winding up in respect of a participant in a designated system, the court shall forthwith notify both the system and the designating authority that such an order has been made.

(2) Following receipt of—

(a) such notification from the court, or

(b) notification from a participant of the passing of a creditors' voluntary winding-up resolution or of a trust deed becoming a protected trust deed, pursuant to paragraph 5(4) of the Schedule,

the designating authority shall forthwith inform the Treasury of the notification.

[2230]

23 (*Relates to the applicable law relating to securities held as collateral security, reproduced at* **[2179]**.)

24 Applicable law where insolvency proceedings are brought

Where insolvency proceedings are brought in any jurisdiction against a person who participates, or has participated, in a system designated for the purposes of the Settlement Finality Directive, any question relating to the rights and obligations arising from, or in connection with, that participation and falling to be determined by a court in England and Wales[, the High Court in Northern Ireland] or in Scotland shall (subject to regulation 23) be determined in accordance with the law governing that system.

[2231]

NOTES

Words in square brackets inserted by the Financial Markets and Insolvency (Settlement Finality) (Amendment) Regulations 2006, SI 2006/50, reg 2(1), (12).

25 Insolvency proceedings in other jurisdictions

(1) The references to insolvency law in section 426 of the Insolvency Act 1986 (co-operation between courts exercising jurisdiction in relation to insolvency) include, in relation to a part of the United Kingdom, this Part and, in relation to a relevant country or territory within the meaning of that section, so much of the law of that country or territory as corresponds to this Part.

(2) A court shall not, in pursuance of that section or any other enactment or rule of law, recognise or give effect to—

(a) any order of a court exercising jurisdiction in relation to insolvency law in a country or territory outside the United Kingdom, or

(b) any act of a person appointed in such a country or territory to discharge any functions under insolvency law,

in so far as the making of the order or the doing of the act would be prohibited in the case of a court in England and Wales or Scotland[, the High Court in Northern Ireland] or a relevant office-holder by this Part.

(3) Paragraph (2) does not affect the recognition or enforcement of a judgment required to be recognised or enforced under or by virtue of the Civil Jurisdiction and Judgments Act 1982 [or Council Regulation (EC) No 44/2001 of 22nd December 2000 on jurisdiction and the recognition and enforcement of judgments in civil and commercial matters].

[2232]

NOTES

Para (2): words in square brackets inserted by the Financial Markets and Insolvency (Settlement Finality) (Amendment) Regulations 2006, SI 2006/50, reg 2(1), (13).

PART III STATUTORY INSTRUMENTS

Para (3): words in square brackets inserted by the Civil Jurisdiction and Judgments Order 2001, SI 2001/3929, art 5, Sch 3, para 27.

26 Systems designated in other EEA States … and Gibraltar

(1) Where an equivalent overseas order or equivalent overseas security is subject to the insolvency law of England and Wales or Scotland [or Northern Ireland], this Part shall apply—

(a) in relation to the equivalent overseas order as it applies in relation to a transfer order; and

(b) in relation to the equivalent overseas security as it applies in relation to collateral security in connection with a designated system.

(2) In paragraph (1)—

(a) "equivalent overseas order" means an order having the like effect as a transfer order which is effected through a system designated for the purposes of the Settlement Finality Directive in another EEA State … or Gibraltar; and

(b) "equivalent overseas security" means any realisable assets provided under a charge or a repurchase or similar agreement, or otherwise (including money provided under a charge) for the purpose of securing rights and obligations potentially arising in connection with such a system.

[2233]

NOTES

Provision heading: words omitted revoked by the Financial Markets and Insolvency (Settlement Finality) (Amendment) Regulations 2006, SI 2006/50, reg 2(1), (14)(a).

Para (1): words in square brackets inserted by SI 2006/50, reg 2(1), (14)(b).

Para (2): words omitted revoked by SI 2006/50, reg 2(1), (14)(c).

SCHEDULE
REQUIREMENTS FOR DESIGNATION OF SYSTEM

Regulation 4(1)

Establishment, participation and governing law

1(1) The head office of at least one of the participants in the system must be in … [the United Kingdom] and the law of England and Wales[, Northern Ireland] or Scotland must be the governing law of the system.

(2) There must be not less than three institutions participating in the system, unless otherwise determined by the designating authority in any case where—

(a) there are two institutions participating in a system; and

(b) the designating authority considers that designation is required on the grounds of systemic risk.

(3) The system must be a system through which transfer orders are effected.

(4) Where orders relating to financial instruments other than securities are effected through the system—

(a) the system must primarily be a system through which securities transfer orders are effected; and

(b) the designating authority must consider that designation is required on grounds of systemic risk.

Arrangements and resources

2 The system must have adequate arrangements and resources for the effective monitoring and enforcement of compliance with its rules or, as respects monitoring, arrangements providing for that function to be performed on its behalf (and without affecting its responsibility) by another body or person who is able and willing to perform it.

Financial resources

3 The system must have financial resources sufficient for the proper performance of its functions as a system.

Co-operation with other authorities

4 The system must be able and willing to co-operate, by the sharing of information and otherwise, with—

(a) the Financial Services Authority,

(b) the Bank of England,

(c) any relevant office-holder, and

(d) any authority, body or person having responsibility for any matter arising out of, or connected with, the default of a participant.

Specific provision in the rules

5(1) The rules of the system must—

(a) specify the point at which a transfer order takes effect as having been entered into the system,

(b) specify the point after which a transfer order may not be revoked by a participant or any other party, and

(c) prohibit the revocation by a participant or any other party of a transfer order from the point specified in accordance with paragraph (b).

(2) The rules of the system must require each institution which participates in the system to provide upon payment of a reasonable charge the information mentioned in sub-paragraph (3) to any person who requests it, save where the request is frivolous or vexatious. The rules must require the information to be provided within fourteen days of the request being made.

(3) The information referred to in sub-paragraph (2) is as follows—

(a) details of the systems which are designated for the purposes of the Settlement Finality Directive in which the institution participates, and

(b) information about the main rules governing the functioning of those systems.

(4) The rules of the system must require each participant upon—

(a) the passing of a creditors' voluntary winding up resolution, or

(b) a trust deed granted by him becoming a protected trust deed,

to notify forthwith both the system and the designating authority that such a resolution has been passed, or, as the case may be, that such a trust deed has become a protected trust deed.

Default arrangements

6 The system must have default arrangements which are appropriate for that system in all the circumstances.

[2234]

NOTES

Para 1: in sub-para (1) words omitted revoked and words in square brackets inserted by the Financial Markets and Insolvency (Settlement Finality) (Amendment) Regulations 2006, SI 2006/50, reg 2(1), (15).

ELECTRONIC COMMERCE (EC DIRECTIVE) REGULATIONS 2002

(SI 2002/2013)

NOTES

Made: 30 July 2002.
Authority: European Communities Act 1972, s 2(2).
Commencement: see reg 1.

ARRANGEMENT OF REGULATIONS

1 Citation and commencement

(1) These Regulations may be cited as the Electronic Commerce (EC Directive) Regulations 2002 and except for regulation 16 shall come into force on 21st August 2002.

(2) Regulation 16 shall come into force on 23rd October 2002.

[2235]

NOTES

Commencement: 21 August 2002.

2 Interpretation

(1) In these Regulations and in the Schedule—

"commercial communication" means a communication, in any form, designed to promote, directly or indirectly, the goods, services or image of any person pursuing a commercial, industrial or craft activity or exercising a regulated profession, other than a communication—

(a) consisting only of information allowing direct access to the activity of that person including a geographic address, a domain name or an electronic mail address; or

(b) relating to the goods, services or image of that person provided that the communication has been prepared independently of the person making it (and for this purpose, a communication prepared without financial consideration is to be taken to have been prepared independently unless the contrary is shown);

"the Commission" means the Commission of the European Communities;

"consumer" means any natural person who is acting for purposes other than those of his trade, business or profession;

"coordinated field" means requirements applicable to information society service providers or information society services, regardless of whether they are of a general nature or specifically designed for them, and covers requirements with which the service provider has to comply in respect of—

(a) the taking up of the activity of an information society service, such as requirements concerning qualifications, authorisation or notification, and

(b) the pursuit of the activity of an information society service, such as requirements concerning the behaviour of the service provider, requirements regarding the quality or content of the service including those applicable to advertising and contracts, or requirements concerning the liability of the service provider,

but does not cover requirements such as those applicable to goods as such, to the delivery of goods or to services not provided by electronic means;

"the Directive" means Directive 2000/31/EC of the European Parliament and of the Council of 8 June 2000 on certain legal aspects of information society services, in particular electronic commerce, in the Internal Market (Directive on electronic commerce);

"EEA Agreement" means the Agreement on the European Economic Area signed at Oporto on 2 May 1992 as adjusted by the Protocol signed at Brussels on 17 March 1993;

"enactment" includes an enactment comprised in Northern Ireland legislation and comprised in, or an instrument made under, an Act of the Scottish Parliament;

"enforcement action" means any form of enforcement action including, in particular—

(a) in relation to any legal requirement imposed by or under any enactment, any action taken with a view to or in connection with imposing any sanction (whether criminal or otherwise) for failure to observe or comply with it; and

(b) in relation to a permission or authorisation, anything done with a view to removing or restricting that permission or authorisation;

"enforcement authority" does not include courts but, subject to that, means any person who is authorised, whether by or under an enactment or otherwise, to take enforcement action;

"established service provider" means a service provider who is a national of a member State or a company or firm as mentioned in Article 48 of the Treaty and who effectively pursues an economic activity by virtue of which he is a service provider using a fixed establishment in a member State for an indefinite period, but the presence and use of the technical means and technologies required to provide the information society service do not, in themselves, constitute an establishment of the provider; in cases where it cannot be determined from which of a number of places of establishment a given service is provided, that service is to be regarded as provided from the place of establishment where the provider has the centre of his activities relating to that service; references to a service provider being established or to the establishment of a service provider shall be construed accordingly;

"information society services" (which is summarised in recital 17 of the Directive as covering "any service normally provided for remuneration, at a distance, by means of electronic equipment for the processing (including digital compression) and storage of data, and at the individual request of a recipient of a service") has the meaning set out in Article 2(a) of the Directive, (which refers to Article 1(2) of Directive 98/34/EC of the European Parliament and of the Council of 22 June 1998 laying down a procedure for the provision of information in the field of technical standards and regulations, as amended by Directive 98/48/EC of 20 July 1998);

"member State" includes a State which is a contracting party to the EEA Agreement;

"recipient of the service" means any person who, for professional ends or otherwise, uses an information society service, in particular for the purposes of seeking information or making it accessible;

"regulated profession" means any profession within the meaning of either Article 1(d) of Council Directive 89/48/EEC of 21 December 1988 on a general system for the recognition of higher-education diplomas awarded on completion of professional education and training of at least three years' duration or of Article 1(f) of Council Directive 92/51/EEC of 18 June 1992 on a second general system for the recognition of professional education and training to supplement Directive 89/48/EEC;

"service provider" means any person providing an information society service;

"the Treaty" means the treaty establishing the European Community.

(2) In regulation 4 and 5, "requirement" means any legal requirement under the law of the United Kingdom, or any part of it, imposed by or under any enactment or otherwise.

(3) Terms used in the Directive other than those in paragraph (1) above shall have the same meaning as in the Directive.

[2236]

NOTES

Commencement: 21 August 2002.

3 Exclusions

(1) Nothing in these Regulations shall apply in respect of—

(a) the field of taxation;

(b) questions relating to information society services covered by the Data Protection Directive and the Telecommunications Data Protection Directive and Directive 2002/58/EC of the European Parliament and of the Council of 12th July 2002 concerning the processing of personal data and the protection of privacy in the electronic communications sector (Directive on privacy and electronic communications);
(c) questions relating to agreements or practices governed by cartel law; and
(d) the following activities of information society services—
   (i) the activities of a public notary or equivalent professions to the extent that they involve a direct and specific connection with the exercise of public authority,
   (ii) the representation of a client and defence of his interests before the courts, and
   (iii) betting, gaming or lotteries which involve wagering a stake with monetary value.

[(2) These Regulations shall not apply in relation to any Act passed on or after the date these Regulations are made or in relation to the exercise of a power to legislate after that date.]

(3) In this regulation—

"cartel law" means so much of the law relating to agreements between undertakings, decisions by associations of undertakings or concerted practices as relates to agreements to divide the market or fix prices;

"Data Protection Directive" means Directive 95/46/EC of the European Parliament and of the Council of 24 October 1995 on the protection of individuals with regard to the processing of personal data and on the free movement of such data; and

"Telecommunications Data Protection Directive" means Directive 97/66/EC of the European Parliament and of the Council of 15 December 1997 concerning the processing of personal data and the protection of privacy in the telecommunications sector.

[2237]

NOTES

Commencement: 21 August 2002.

Para (2): substituted by the Electronic Commerce (EC Directive) (Extension) Regulations 2004, SI 2004/1178, reg 3.

See further, the Electronic Commerce (EC Directive) (Extension) Regulations 2003, SI 2003/115, reg 2, Schedule and the Electronic Commerce (EC Directive) (Extension) (No 2) Regulations 2003, SI 2003/2500, reg 2, Schedule, which provide for the extended application of these regulations, notwithstanding para (2) above.

See further, the Price Marking Order 2004, SI 2004/102, art 3(2), which provides for the extended application of these regulations, notwithstanding para (2) above.

See further, the Electronic Commerce (EC Directive) (Extension) Regulations 2004, SI 2004/1178, reg 2, which provide for the extended application of these regulations, notwithstanding para (2) above.

4 Internal market

(1) Subject to paragraph (4) below, any requirement which falls within the coordinated field shall apply to the provision of an information society service by a service provider established in the United Kingdom irrespective of whether that information society service is provided in the United Kingdom or another member State.

(2) Subject to paragraph (4) below, an enforcement authority with responsibility in relation to any requirement in paragraph (1) shall ensure that the provision of an information society service by a service provider established in the United Kingdom complies with that requirement irrespective of whether that service is provided in the United Kingdom or another member State and any power, remedy or procedure for taking enforcement action shall be available to secure compliance.

(3) Subject to paragraphs (4), (5) and (6) below, any requirement shall not be applied to the provision of an information society service by a service provider established in a member State other than the United Kingdom for reasons which fall within the coordinated field where its application would restrict the freedom to provide information society services to a person in the United Kingdom from that member State.

(4) Paragraphs (1), (2) and (3) shall not apply to those fields in the annex to the Directive set out in the Schedule.

(5) The reference to any requirements the application of which would restrict the freedom to provide information society services from another member State in paragraph (3) above does not include any requirement maintaining the level of protection for public health and consumer interests established by Community acts.

(6) To the extent that anything in these Regulations creates any new criminal offence, it shall not be punishable with imprisonment for more than two years or punishable on summary conviction with imprisonment for more than three months or with a fine of more than level 5 on the standard scale (if not calculated on a daily basis) or with a fine of more than £100 a day.

[2238]

NOTES

Commencement: 21 August 2002.

5 Derogations from Regulation 4

(1) Notwithstanding regulation 4(3), an enforcement authority may take measures, including applying any requirement which would otherwise not apply by virtue of regulation 4(3) in respect of a given information society service, where those measures are necessary for reasons of—

(a) public policy, in particular the prevention, investigation, detection and prosecution of criminal offences, including the protection of minors and the fight against any incitement to hatred on grounds of race, sex, religion or nationality, and violations of human dignity concerning individual persons;

(b) the protection of public health;

(c) public security, including the safeguarding of national security and defence, or

(d) the protection of consumers, including investors,

and proportionate to those objectives.

(2) Notwithstanding regulation 4(3), in any case where an enforcement authority with responsibility in relation to the requirement in question is not party to the proceedings, a court may, on the application of any person or of its own motion, apply any requirement which would otherwise not apply by virtue of regulation 4(3) in respect of a given information society service, if the application of that enactment or requirement is necessary for and proportionate to any of the objectives set out in paragraph (1) above.

(3) Paragraphs (1) and (2) shall only apply where the information society service prejudices or presents a serious and grave risk of prejudice to an objective in paragraph (1)(a) to (d).

(4) Subject to paragraphs (5) and (6), an enforcement authority shall not take the measures in paragraph (1) above, unless it—

(a) asks the member State in which the service provider is established to take measures and the member State does not take such measures or they are inadequate; and

(b) notifies the Commission and the member State in which the service provider is established of its intention to take such measures.

(5) Paragraph (4) shall not apply to court proceedings, including preliminary proceedings and acts carried out in the course of a criminal investigation.

(6) If it appears to the enforcement authority that the matter is one of urgency, it may take the measures under paragraph (1) without first asking the member State in which the service provider is established to take measures and notifying the Commission and the member State in derogation from paragraph (4).

(7) In a case where a measure is taken pursuant to paragraph (6) above, the enforcement authority shall notify the measures taken to the Commission and to the member State concerned in the shortest possible time thereafter and indicate the reasons for urgency.

(8) In paragraph (2), "court" means any court or tribunal.

[2239]

NOTES

Commencement: 21 August 2002.

6 General information to be provided by a person providing an information society service

(1) A person providing an information society service shall make available to the recipient of the service and any relevant enforcement authority, in a form and manner which is easily, directly and permanently accessible, the following information—

(a) the name of the service provider;
(b) the geographic address at which the service provider is established;
(c) the details of the service provider, including his electronic mail address, which make it possible to contact him rapidly and communicate with him in a direct and effective manner;
(d) where the service provider is registered in a trade or similar register available to the public, details of the register in which the service provider is entered and his registration number, or equivalent means of identification in that register;
(e) where the provision of the service is subject to an authorisation scheme, the particulars of the relevant supervisory authority;
(f) where the service provider exercises a regulated profession—
 (i) the details of any professional body or similar institution with which the service provider is registered;
 (ii) his professional title and the member State where that title has been granted;
 (iii) a reference to the professional rules applicable to the service provider in the member State of establishment and the means to access them; and
(g) where the service provider undertakes an activity that is subject to value added tax, the identification number referred to in Article 22(1) of the sixth Council Directive 77/388/EEC of 17 May 1977 on the harmonisation of the laws of the member States relating to turnover taxes—Common system of value added tax: uniform basis of assessment.

(2) Where a person providing an information society service refers to prices, these shall be indicated clearly and unambiguously and, in particular, shall indicate whether they are inclusive of tax and delivery costs.

[2240]

NOTES

Commencement: 21 August 2002.

7 Commercial communications

A service provider shall ensure that any commercial communication provided by him and which constitutes or forms part of an information society service shall—

(a) be clearly identifiable as a commercial communication;
(b) clearly identify the person on whose behalf the commercial communication is made;
(c) clearly identify as such any promotional offer (including any discount, premium or gift) and ensure that any conditions which must be met to qualify for it are easily accessible, and presented clearly and unambiguously; and
(d) clearly identify as such any promotional competition or game and ensure that any conditions for participation are easily accessible and presented clearly and unambiguously.

[2241]

NOTES

Commencement: 21 August 2002.

8 Unsolicited commercial communications

A service provider shall ensure that any unsolicited commercial communication sent by him by electronic mail is clearly and unambiguously identifiable as such as soon as it is received.

[2242]

NOTES

Commencement: 21 August 2002.

9 Information to be provided where contracts are concluded by electronic means

(1) Unless parties who are not consumers have agreed otherwise, where a contract is to be concluded by electronic means a service provider shall, prior to an order being placed by the recipient of a service, provide to that recipient in a clear, comprehensible and unambiguous manner the information set out in (a) to (d) below—

(a) the different technical steps to follow to conclude the contract;
(b) whether or not the concluded contract will be filed by the service provider and whether it will be accessible;
(c) the technical means for identifying and correcting input errors prior to the placing of the order; and
(d) the languages offered for the conclusion of the contract.

(2) Unless parties who are not consumers have agreed otherwise, a service provider shall indicate which relevant codes of conduct he subscribes to and give information on how those codes can be consulted electronically.

(3) Where the service provider provides terms and conditions applicable to the contract to the recipient, the service provider shall make them available to him in a way that allows him to store and reproduce them.

(4) The requirements of paragraphs (1) and (2) above shall not apply to contracts concluded exclusively by exchange of electronic mail or by equivalent individual communications.

[2243]

NOTES

Commencement: 21 August 2002.

10 Other information requirements

Regulations 6, 7, 8 and 9(1) have effect in addition to any other information requirements in legislation giving effect to Community law.

[2244]

NOTES

Commencement: 21 August 2002.

11 Placing of the order

(1) Unless parties who are not consumers have agreed otherwise, where the recipient of the service places his order through technological means, a service provider shall–

(a) acknowledge receipt of the order to the recipient of the service without undue delay and by electronic means; and
(b) make available to the recipient of the service appropriate, effective and accessible technical means allowing him to identify and correct input errors prior to the placing of the order.

(2) For the purposes of paragraph (1)(a) above—

(a) the order and the acknowledgement of receipt will be deemed to be received when the parties to whom they are addressed are able to access them; and
(b) the acknowledgement of receipt may take the form of the provision of the service paid for where that service is an information society service.

(3) The requirements of paragraph (1) above shall not apply to contracts concluded exclusively by exchange of electronic mail or by equivalent individual communications.

[2245]

NOTES

Commencement: 21 August 2002.

12 Meaning of the term "order"

Except in relation to regulation 9(1)(c) and regulation 11(1)(b) where "order" shall be the contractual offer, "order" may be but need not be the contractual offer for the purposes of regulations 9 and 11.

[2246]

NOTES
Commencement: 21 August 2002.

13 Liability of the service provider

The duties imposed by regulations 6, 7, 8, 9(1) and 11(1)(a) shall be enforceable, at the suit of any recipient of a service, by an action against the service provider for damages for breach of statutory duty.

[2247]

NOTES
Commencement: 21 August 2002.

14 Compliance with Regulation 9(3)

Where on request a service provider has failed to comply with the requirement in regulation 9(3), the recipient may seek an order from any court having jurisdiction in relation to the contract requiring that service provider to comply with that requirement.

[2248]

NOTES
Commencement: 21 August 2002.

15 Right to rescind contract

Where a person—

(a) has entered into a contract to which these Regulations apply, and

(b) the service provider has not made available means of allowing him to identify and correct input errors in compliance with regulation 11(1)(b),

he shall be entitled to rescind the contract unless any court having jurisdiction in relation to the contract in question orders otherwise on the application of the service provider.

[2249]

NOTES
Commencement: 21 August 2002.

16 Amendments to the Stop Now Orders (EC Directive) Regulations 2001

(1) The Stop Now Orders (EC Directive) Regulations 2001 are amended as follows.

(2) In regulation 2(3), at the end there shall be added—

"(k) regulations 6, 7, 8, 9, and 11 of the Electronic Commerce (EC Directive) Regulations 2002.".

(3) In Schedule 1, at the end there shall be added—

"**11** Directive 2000/31/EC of the European Parliament and of the Council of 8th June 2000 on certain legal aspects of information society services, in particular electronic commerce, in the Internal Market (Directive on Electronic Commerce).".

[2250]

NOTES
Commencement: 23 October 2002.

17 Mere conduit

(1) Where an information society service is provided which consists of the transmission in a communication network of information provided by a recipient of the service or the provision of access to a communication network, the service provider (if he otherwise would) shall not be liable for damages or for any other pecuniary remedy or for any criminal sanction as a result of that transmission where the service provider—

(a) did not initiate the transmission;

(b) did not select the receiver of the transmission; and
(c) did not select or modify the information contained in the transmission.

(2) The acts of transmission and of provision of access referred to in paragraph (1) include the automatic, intermediate and transient storage of the information transmitted where:

(a) this takes place for the sole purpose of carrying out the transmission in the communication network, and
(b) the information is not stored for any period longer than is reasonably necessary for the transmission.

[2251]

NOTES

Commencement: 21 August 2002.

18 Caching

Where an information society service is provided which consists of the transmission in a communication network of information provided by a recipient of the service, the service provider (if he otherwise would) shall not be liable for damages or for any other pecuniary remedy or for any criminal sanction as a result of that transmission where—

(a) the information is the subject of automatic, intermediate and temporary storage where that storage is for the sole purpose of making more efficient onward transmission of the information to other recipients of the service upon their request, and
(b) the service provider—
  (i) does not modify the information;
  (ii) complies with conditions on access to the information;
  (iii) complies with any rules regarding the updating of the information, specified in a manner widely recognised and used by industry;
  (iv) does not interfere with the lawful use of technology, widely recognised and used by industry, to obtain data on the use of the information; and
  (v) acts expeditiously to remove or to disable access to the information he has stored upon obtaining actual knowledge of the fact that the information at the initial source of the transmission has been removed from the network, or access to it has been disabled, or that a court or an administrative authority has ordered such removal or disablement.

[2252]

NOTES

Commencement: 21 August 2002.

19 Hosting

Where an information society service is provided which consists of the storage of information provided by a recipient of the service, the service provider (if he otherwise would) shall not be liable for damages or for any other pecuniary remedy or for any criminal sanction as a result of that storage where—

(a) the service provider—
  (i) does not have actual knowledge of unlawful activity or information and, where a claim for damages is made, is not aware of facts or circumstances from which it would have been apparent to the service provider that the activity or information was unlawful; or
  (ii) upon obtaining such knowledge or awareness, acts expeditiously to remove or to disable access to the information, and
(b) the recipient of the service was not acting under the authority or the control of the service provider.

[2253]

NOTES

Commencement: 21 August 2002.

20 Protection of rights

(1) Nothing in regulations 17, 18 and 19 shall—

(a) prevent a person agreeing different contractual terms; or

(b) affect the rights of any party to apply to a court for relief to prevent or stop infringement of any rights.

(2) Any power of an administrative authority to prevent or stop infringement of any rights shall continue to apply notwithstanding regulations 17, 18 and 19.

[2254]

NOTES

Commencement: 21 August 2002.

21 Defence in Criminal Proceedings: burden of proof

(1) This regulation applies where a service provider charged with an offence in criminal proceedings arising out of any transmission, provision of access or storage falling within regulation 17, 18 or 19 relies on a defence under any of regulations 17, 18 and 19.

(2) Where evidence is adduced which is sufficient to raise an issue with respect to that defence, the court or jury shall assume that the defence is satisfied unless the prosecution proves beyond reasonable doubt that it is not.

[2255]

NOTES

Commencement: 21 August 2002.

22 Notice for the purposes of actual knowledge

In determining whether a service provider has actual knowledge for the purposes of regulations 18(b)(v) and 19(a)(i), a court shall take into account all matters which appear to it in the particular circumstances to be relevant and, among other things, shall have regard to—

(a) whether a service provider has received a notice through a means of contact made available in accordance with regulation 6(1)(c), and

(b) the extent to which any notice includes—

(i) the full name and address of the sender of the notice;

(ii) details of the location of the information in question; and

(iii) details of the unlawful nature of the activity or information in question.

[2256]

NOTES

Commencement: 21 August 2002.

SCHEDULE

Regulation 4(4)

1 Copyright, neighbouring rights, rights referred to in Directive 87/54/EEC and Directive 96/9/EC and industrial property rights.

2 The freedom of the parties to a contract to choose the applicable law.

3 Contractual obligations concerning consumer contracts.

4 Formal validity of contracts creating or transferring rights in real estate where such contracts are subject to mandatory formal requirements of the law of the member State where the real estate is situated.

5 The permissibility of unsolicited commercial communications by electronic mail.

[2257]

NOTES

Commencement: 21 August 2002.

FINANCIAL COLLATERAL ARRANGEMENTS (NO 2) REGULATIONS 2003

(SI 2003/3226)

NOTES

Made: 10 December 2003.
Authority: European Communities Act 1972, s 2(2).
Commencement: see reg 1.

ARRANGEMENT OF REGULATIONS

PART 1
GENERAL

PART 2
MODIFICATION OF LAW REQUIRING FORMALITIES

PART 3
MODIFICATION OF INSOLVENCY LAW

PART 4
RIGHT OF USE AND APPROPRIATION

PART 1
GENERAL

1 Citation and commencement

(1) These Regulations may be cited as the Financial Collateral Arrangements (No 2) Regulations 2003.

PART III STATUTORY INSTRUMENTS

(2) Regulation 2 shall come into force on 11th December 2003 and all other Regulations thereof shall come into force on 26th December 2003.

[2258]

NOTES

Commencement: 11 December 2003 (certain purposes); 26 December 2003 (remaining purposes).

2 (*Revokes the Financial Collateral Arrangements Regulations 2003, SI 2003/3112.*)

3 Interpretation

In these Regulations—

"book entry securities collateral" means financial collateral subject to a financial collateral arrangement which consists of financial instruments, title to which is evidenced by entries in a register or account maintained by or on behalf of an intermediary;

"cash" means money in any currency, credited to an account, or a similar claim for repayment of money and includes money market deposits and sums due or payable to, or received between the parties in connection with the operation of a financial collateral arrangement or a close-out netting provision;

"close-out netting provision" means a term of a financial collateral arrangement, or of an arrangement of which a financial collateral arrangement forms part, or any legislative provision under which on the occurrence of an enforcement event, whether through the operation of netting or set-off or otherwise—

(a) the obligations of the parties are accelerated to become immediately due and expressed as an obligation to pay an amount representing the original obligation's estimated current value or replacement cost, or are terminated and replaced by an obligation to pay such an amount; or

(b) an account is taken of what is due from each party to the other in respect of such obligations and a net sum equal to the balance of the account is payable by the party from whom the larger amount is due to the other party;

"enforcement event" means an event of default, or any similar event as agreed between the parties, on the occurrence of which, under the terms of a financial collateral arrangement or by operation of law, the collateral-taker is entitled to realise or appropriate financial collateral or a close-out netting provision comes into effect;

"equivalent financial collateral" means—

(a) in relation to cash, a payment of the same amount and in the same currency;

(b) in relation to financial instruments, financial instruments of the same issuer or debtor, forming part of the same issue or class and of the same nominal amount, currency and description or, where the financial collateral arrangement provides for the transfer of other assets following the occurrence of any event relating to or affecting any financial instruments provided as financial collateral, those other assets;

and includes the original financial collateral provided under the arrangement;

"financial collateral arrangement" means a title transfer financial collateral arrangement or a security financial collateral arrangement, whether or not these are covered by a master agreement or general terms and conditions;

"financial collateral" means either cash or financial instruments;

"financial instruments" means—

(a) shares in companies and other securities equivalent to shares in companies;

(b) bonds and other forms of instruments giving rise to or acknowledging indebtedness if these are tradeable on the capital market; and

(c) any other securities which are normally dealt in and which give the right to acquire any such shares, bonds, instruments or other securities by subscription, purchase or exchange or which give rise to a cash settlement (excluding instruments of payment);

and includes units of a collective investment scheme within the meaning of the Financial Services and Markets Act 2000, eligible debt securities within the meaning of the Uncertificated Securities Regulations 2001, money market instruments, claims relating to or rights in or in respect of any of the financial instruments included in this definition and any rights, privileges or benefits attached to or arising from any such financial instruments;

"intermediary" means a person that maintains registers or accounts to which financial instruments may be credited or debited, for others or both for others and for its own account but does not include—

(a) a person who acts as a registrar or transfer agent for the issuer of financial instruments; or
(b) a person who maintains registers or accounts in the capacity of operator of a system for the holding and transfer of financial instruments on records of the issuer or other records which constitute the primary record of entitlement to financial instruments as against the issuer;

"non-natural person" means any corporate body, unincorporated firm, partnership or body with legal personality except an individual, including any such entity constituted under the law of a country or territory outside the United Kingdom or any such entity constituted under international law;

"relevant account" means, in relation to book entry securities collateral which is subject to a financial collateral arrangement, the register or account, which may be maintained by the collateral-taker, in which entries are made, by which that book entry securities collateral is transferred or designated so as to be in the possession or under the control of the collateral-taker or a person acting on its behalf;

"relevant financial obligations" means the obligations which are secured or otherwise covered by a financial collateral arrangement, and such obligations may consist of or include—
(a) present or future, actual or contingent or prospective obligations (including such obligations arising under a master agreement or similar arrangement);
(b) obligations owed to the collateral-taker by a person other than the collateral-provider;
(c) obligations of a specified class or kind arising from time to time;

"reorganisation measures" means—
(a) administration within the meaning of the Insolvency Act 1986 or the Insolvency (Northern Ireland) Order 1989;
(b) a company voluntary arrangement within the meaning of that Act or that Order;
(c) administration of a partnership within the meaning of that Act or that Order or, in the case of a Scottish partnership, the Bankruptcy (Scotland) Act 1985;
(d) a partnership voluntary arrangement within the meaning of the Insolvency Act 1986 or the Insolvency (Northern Ireland) Order 1989 or, in the case of a Scottish partnership, the Bankruptcy (Scotland) Act 1985; and
(e) the making of an interim order on an administration application;

"security financial collateral arrangement" means an agreement or arrangement, evidenced in writing, where—
(a) the purpose of the agreement or arrangement is to secure the relevant financial obligations owed to the collateral-taker;
(b) the collateral-provider creates or there arises a security interest in financial collateral to secure those obligations;
(c) the financial collateral is delivered, transferred, held, registered or otherwise designated so as to be in the possession or under the control of the collateral-taker or a person acting on its behalf; any right of the collateral-provider to substitute equivalent financial collateral or withdraw excess financial collateral shall not prevent the financial collateral being in the possession or under the control of the collateral-taker; and
(d) the collateral-provider and the collateral-taker are both non-natural persons;

"security interest" means any legal or equitable interest or any right in security, other than a title transfer financial collateral arrangement, created or otherwise arising by way of security including—
(a) a pledge;
(b) a mortgage;
(c) a fixed charge;
(d) a charge created as a floating charge where the financial collateral charged is delivered, transferred, held, registered or otherwise designated so as to be in the possession or under the control of the collateral-taker or a person acting on its behalf; any right of the collateral-provider to substitute equivalent financial collateral or withdraw excess financial collateral shall not prevent the financial collateral being in the possession or under the control of the collateral-taker; or
(e) a lien;

"title transfer financial collateral arrangement" means an agreement or arrangement, including a repurchase agreement, evidenced in writing, where—

(a) the purpose of the agreement or arrangement is to secure or otherwise cover the relevant financial obligations owed to the collateral-taker;

(b) the collateral-provider transfers legal and beneficial ownership in financial collateral to a collateral-taker on terms that when the relevant financial obligations are discharged the collateral-taker must transfer legal and beneficial ownership of equivalent financial collateral to the collateral-provider; and

(c) the collateral-provider and the collateral-taker are both non-natural persons;

"winding-up proceedings" means—

(a) winding up by the court; or

(b) voluntary winding up;

within the meaning of the Insolvency Act 1986 or the Insolvency (Northern Ireland) Order 1989 or, in the case of Scottish partnerships, the Bankruptcy (Scotland) Act 1985.

[2259]

NOTES

Commencement: 26 December 2003.

PART 2
MODIFICATION OF LAW REQUIRING FORMALITIES

4 Certain legislation requiring formalities not to apply to financial collateral arrangements

(1) Section 4 of the Statute of Frauds 1677 (no action on a third party's promise unless in writing and signed) shall not apply (if it would otherwise do so) in relation to a financial collateral arrangement.

(2) Section 53(1)(c) of the Law of Property Act 1925 (disposition of equitable interest to be in writing and signed) shall not apply (if it would otherwise do so) in relation to a financial collateral arrangement.

(3) Section 136 of the Law of Property Act 1925 (legal assignments of things in action) shall not apply (if it would otherwise do so) in relation to a financial collateral arrangement, to the extent that the section requires an assignment to be signed by the assignor or a person authorised on its behalf, in order to be effectual in law.

(4) Section 395 of the Companies Act 1985 (certain charges void if not registered) shall not apply (if it would otherwise do so) in relation to a security financial collateral arrangement or any charge created or otherwise arising under a security financial collateral arrangement

(5) Section 4 of the Industrial and Provident Societies Act 1967 (filing of information relating to charges) shall not apply (if it would otherwise do so) in relation to a security financial collateral arrangement or any charge created or otherwise arising under a security financial collateral arrangement.

[2260]

NOTES

Commencement: 26 December 2003.

5 Certain legislation affecting Scottish companies not to apply to financial collateral arrangements

Section 410 of the Companies Act 1985 (certain charges void if not registered (Scotland)) shall not apply (if it would otherwise do so) in relation to a security financial collateral arrangement or any charge created or otherwise arising under a security financial collateral arrangement.

[2261]

NOTES

Commencement: 26 December 2003.

6 No additional formalities required for creation of a right in security over book entry securities collateral in Scotland

(1) Where under the law of Scotland an act is required as a condition for transferring, creating or enforcing a right in security over any book entry securities collateral, that requirement shall not apply (if it would otherwise do so).

(2) For the purposes of paragraph (1) an "act"—

(a) is any act other than an entry on a register or account maintained by or on behalf of an intermediary which evidences title to the book entry securities collateral;

(b) includes the entering of the collateral-taker's name in a company's register of members.

[2262]

NOTES

Commencement: 26 December 2003.

7 Certain legislation affecting Northern Ireland companies and requiring formalities not to apply to financial collateral arrangements

Article 402 of the Companies (Northern Ireland) Order 1986 (certain charges void if not registered) shall not apply (if it would otherwise do so) in relation to a security financial collateral arrangement or any charge created or otherwise arising under a security financial collateral arrangement.

[2263]

NOTES

Commencement: 26 December 2003.

PART 3
MODIFICATION OF INSOLVENCY LAW

8 Certain legislation restricting enforcement of security not to apply to financial collateral arrangements

(1) The following provisions of Schedule B1 to the Insolvency Act 1986 (administration) shall not apply to any security interest created or otherwise arising under a financial collateral arrangement—

(a) paragraph 43(2) (restriction on enforcement of security or repossession of goods) including that provision as applied by paragraph 44 (interim moratorium); and

(b) paragraphs 70 and 71 (power of administrator to deal with charged property).

(2) Paragraph 41(2) of Schedule B1 to the Insolvency Act 1986 (receiver to vacate office when so required by administrator) shall not apply to a receiver appointed under a charge created or otherwise arising under a financial collateral arrangement.

(3) The following provisions of the Insolvency Act 1986 (administration) shall not apply in relation to any security interest created or otherwise arising under a financial collateral arrangement—

(a) sections 10(1)(b) and 11(3)(c) (restriction on enforcement of security while petition for administration order pending or order in force); and

(b) section 15(1) and 15(2) (power of administrator to deal with charged property).

(4) Section 11(2) of the Insolvency Act 1986 (receiver to vacate office when so required by administrator) shall not apply to a receiver appointed under a charge created or otherwise arising under a financial collateral arrangement.

(5) Paragraph 20 and sub-paragraph 12(1)(g) of Schedule A1 to the Insolvency Act 1986 (Effect of moratorium on creditors) shall not apply (if it would otherwise do so) to any security interest created or otherwise arising under a financial collateral arrangement.

[2264]

NOTES

Commencement: 26 December 2003.

9 (*Applies to Northern Ireland only.*))

10 Certain insolvency legislation on avoidance of contracts and floating charges not to apply to financial collateral arrangements

(1) In relation to winding-up proceedings of a collateral-taker or collateral-provider, section 127 of the Insolvency Act 1986 (avoidance of property dispositions, etc) shall not apply (if it would otherwise do so)—

(a) to any property or security interest subject to a disposition or created or otherwise arising under a financial collateral arrangement; or

(b) to prevent a close-out netting provision taking effect in accordance with its terms.

(2) Section 88 of the Insolvency Act 1986 (avoidance of share transfers, etc after winding-up resolution) shall not apply (if it would otherwise do so) to any transfer of shares under a financial collateral arrangement.

(3) Section 176A of the Insolvency Act 1986 (share of assets for unsecured creditors) shall not apply (if it would otherwise do so) to any charge created or otherwise arising under a financial collateral arrangement.

(4) Section 178 of the Insolvency Act 1986 (power to disclaim onerous property) or, in Scotland, any rule of law having the same effect as that section, shall not apply where the collateral-provider or collateral-taker under the arrangement is being wound up, to any financial collateral arrangement.

(5) Section 245 of the Insolvency Act 1986 (avoidance of certain floating charges) shall not apply (if it would otherwise do so) to any charge created or otherwise arising under a security financial collateral arrangement.

(6) Section 196 of the Companies Act 1985 (payment of debts out of assets subject to a floating charge (England and Wales) shall not apply (if it would otherwise do so) to any charge created or otherwise arising under a financial collateral arrangement.

[2265]

NOTES

Commencement: 26 December 2003.

11 Certain Northern Ireland insolvency legislation on avoidance of contracts and floating charges not to apply to financial collateral arrangements

(1) In relation to winding-up proceedings of a collateral-provider or collateral-taker, Article 107 of the Insolvency (Northern Ireland) Order 1989 (avoidance of property dispositions effected after commencement of winding up) shall not apply (if it would otherwise do so)—

(a) to any property or security interest subject to a disposition or created or otherwise arising under a financial collateral arrangement; or

(b) to prevent a close-out netting provision taking effect in accordance with its terms.

(2) Article 74 of that Order (avoidance of share transfers, etc after winding-up resolution) shall not apply (if it would otherwise do so) to any transfer of shares under a financial collateral arrangement.

(3) Article 152 of that Order (power to disclaim onerous property) shall not apply where the collateral-provider or collateral-taker under the arrangement is being wound-up, to any financial collateral arrangement.

(4) Article 207 of that Order (avoidance of certain floating charges) shall not apply (if it would otherwise do so) to any charge created or otherwise arising under a security financial collateral arrangement.

(5) Article 205 of the Companies (Northern Ireland) Order 1986 (payment of debts out of assets subject to a floating charge) shall not apply (if it would otherwise do so) to any charge created or otherwise arising under a financial collateral arrangement.

[2266]

NOTES

Commencement: 26 December 2003.

12 Close-out netting provisions to take effect in accordance with their terms

(1) A close-out netting provision shall, subject to paragraph (2), take effect in accordance with its terms notwithstanding that the collateral-provider or collateral-taker under the arrangement is subject to winding-up proceedings or reorganisation measures.

(2) Paragraph (1) shall not apply if at the time that a party to a financial collateral arrangement entered into such an arrangement or that the relevant financial obligations came into existence—

(a) that party was aware or should have been aware that winding up proceedings or re-organisation measures had commenced in relation to the other party;

(b) that party had notice that a meeting of creditors of the other party had been summoned under section 98 of the Insolvency Act 1986, or Article 84 of the Companies (Northern Ireland) Order 1989 or that a petition for the winding-up of the other party was pending;

(c) that party had notice that an application for an administration order was pending or that any person had given notice of an intention to appoint an administrator; or

(d) that party had notice that an application for an administration order was pending or that any person had given notice of an intention to appoint an administrator and liquidation of the other party to the financial collateral arrangement was immediately preceded by an administration of that party.

(3) For the purposes of paragraph (2)—

(a) winding-up proceedings commence on the making of a winding-up order by the court; and

(b) reorganisation measures commence on the appointment of an administrator, whether by a court or otherwise.

(4) Rules 2.85 (4)(a) and (c) and 4.90 (3)(b) of the Insolvency Rules 1986 (mutual credit and set-off) shall not apply to a close-out netting provision unless sub-paragraph (2)(a) applies.

[2267]

NOTES

Commencement: 26 December 2003.

13 Financial collateral arrangements to be enforceable where collateral-taker not aware of commencement of winding-up proceedings or reorganisation measures

(1) Where any of the events specified in paragraph (2) occur on the day of, but after the moment of commencement of, winding-up proceedings or reorganisation measures those events, arrangements and obligations shall be legally enforceable and binding on third parties if the collateral-taker can show that he was not aware, nor should have been aware, of the commencement of such proceedings or measures.

(2) The events referred to in paragraph (1) are—

(a) a financial collateral arrangement coming into existence;

(b) a relevant financial obligation secured by a financial collateral arrangement coming into existence; or

(c) the delivery, transfer, holding, registering or other designation of financial collateral so as to be in the possession or under the control of the collateral-taker.

(3) For the purposes of paragraph (1)—

(a) the commencement of winding-up proceedings means the making of a winding-up order by the court; and

(b) commencement of reorganisation measures means the appointment of an administrator, whether by a court or otherwise.

[2268]

NOTES

Commencement: 26 December 2003.

14 Modification of the Insolvency Rules 1986 and the Insolvency Rules (Northern Ireland) 1991

Where the collateral-provider or the collateral-taker under a financial collateral arrangement goes into liquidation or administration and the arrangement or a close out netting provision provides for, or the mechanism provided under the arrangement permits, either—

(a) the debt owed by the party in liquidation or administration under the arrangement, to be assessed or paid in a currency other than sterling; or

(b) the debt to be converted into sterling at a rate other than the official exchange rate prevailing on the date when that party went into liquidation or administration;

then rule 4.91 (liquidation), or rule 2.86 (administration) of the Insolvency Rules 1986 (debt in foreign currency), or rule 4.097 of the Insolvency Rules (Northern Ireland) 1991 (liquidation, debt in foreign currency), as appropriate, shall not apply unless the arrangement provides for an unreasonable exchange rate or the collateral-taker uses the mechanism provided under the arrangement to impose an unreasonable exchange rate in which case the appropriate rule shall apply.

[2269]

NOTES

Commencement: 26 December 2003.

15 Modification of the Insolvency (Scotland) Rules 1986

Where the collateral-provider or the collateral-taker under a financial collateral arrangement goes into liquidation or, in the case of a partnership, sequestration and the arrangement provides for, or the mechanism provided under the arrangement permits, either—

(a) the debt owed by the party in liquidation or sequestration under the arrangement, to be assessed or paid in a currency other than sterling; or

(b) the debt to be converted into sterling at a rate other than the official exchange rate prevailing on the date when that party went into liquidation or sequestration;

then rules 4.16 and 4.17 of the Insolvency (Scotland) Rules 1986 and section 49(3) of the Bankruptcy (Scotland) Act 1985 as applied by rule 4.16 (1)(c) of those rules (claims in foreign currency), as appropriate, shall not apply unless the arrangement provides for an unreasonable exchange rate or the collateral-taker uses the mechanism provided under the arrangement to impose an unreasonable exchange rate in which case the appropriate rule shall apply.

[2270]

NOTES

Commencement: 26 December 2003.

PART 4
RIGHT OF USE AND APPROPRIATION

16 Right of use under a security financial collateral arrangement

(1) If a security financial collateral arrangement provides for the collateral-taker to use and dispose of any financial collateral provided under the arrangement, as if it were the owner of it, the collateral-taker may do so in accordance with the terms of the arrangement.

(2) If a collateral-taker exercises such a right of use, it is obliged to replace the original financial collateral by transferring equivalent financial collateral on or before the due date for the performance of the relevant financial obligations covered by the arrangement or, if the arrangement so provides, it may set off the value of the equivalent financial collateral against or apply it in discharge of the relevant financial obligations in accordance with the terms of the arrangement.

(3) The equivalent financial collateral which is transferred in discharge of an obligation as described in paragraph (2), shall be subject to the same terms of the security financial collateral arrangement as the original financial collateral was subject to and shall be treated as having been provided under the security financial collateral arrangement at the same time as the original financial collateral was first provided.

(4) If a collateral-taker has an outstanding obligation to replace the original financial collateral with equivalent financial collateral when an enforcement event occurs, that obligation may be the subject of a close-out netting provision.

[2271]

NOTES

Commencement: 26 December 2003.

17 No requirement to apply to court to appropriate financial collateral under a security financial collateral arrangement

Where a legal or equitable mortgage is the security interest created or arising under a security financial collateral arrangement on terms that include a power for the collateral-taker to appropriate the collateral, the collateral-taker may exercise that power in accordance with the terms of the security financial collateral arrangement, without any order for foreclosure from the courts.

[2272]

NOTES

Commencement: 26 December 2003.

18 Duty to value collateral and account for any difference in value on appropriation

(1) Where a collateral-taker exercises a power contained in a security financial collateral arrangement to appropriate the financial collateral the collateral-taker must value the financial collateral in accordance with the terms of the arrangement and in any event in a commercially reasonable manner.

(2) Where a collateral-taker exercises such a power and the value of the financial collateral appropriated differs from the amount of the relevant financial obligations, then as the case may be, either—

(a) the collateral-taker must account to the collateral-provider for the amount by which the value of the financial collateral exceeds the relevant financial obligations; or

(b) the collateral-provider will remain liable to the collateral-taker for any amount whereby the value of the financial collateral is less than the relevant financial obligations.

[2273]

NOTES

Commencement: 26 December 2003.

(*Pt 5* (*reg 19*) *reproduced in Pt III*(*B*) *at* **[2190]**.))

D. INTERNATIONAL ARBITRATION

ARBITRATION (FOREIGN AWARDS) ORDER 1984

(SI 1984/1168)

NOTES

Made: 31 July 1984.

Authority: Arbitration Act 1950, s 35(1), (2), the Arbitration Act 1975, s 7(2), (3); to the extent this Order had effect under the Arbitration Act 1975, s 7(2), (3), it now has effect as if made under the Arbitration Act 1996, s 100(3), by virtue of the Interpretation Act 1978, s 17(2)(b).

Commencement: 1 August 1984.

For status of 1958 New York Convention, see Table 2 at **[4677]**.

1 Citation and commencement

This Order may be cited as the Arbitration (Foreign Awards) Order 1984 and shall come into operation on 1st August 1984.

[2274]

2 Geneva Convention States

(1) The Powers listed in Column 1 of Schedule 1 to this Order are parties to the Geneva Convention.

(2) The territories specified in Column 2 of the said Schedule are territories to which the Geneva Convention applies.

[2275]

3 New York Convention States

The States listed in Schedule 2 to this Order are parties to the New York Convention.

[2276]

4 (*Revokes the Arbitration* (*Foreign Awards*) *Order 1978, SI 1978/186, and the Arbitration* (*Foreign Awards*) *Order 1979, SI 1979/304.*)

SCHEDULE 1
GENEVA CONVENTION STATES

Column 1	Column 2
Powers party to the Geneva Convention	Territories to which the Geneva Convention applies
The United Kingdom of Great Britain and Northern Ireland	The United Kingdom of Great Britain and Northern Ireland
	Anguilla
	British Virgin Islands
	Cayman Islands
	Falkland Islands
	Falkland Islands Dependencies
	Gibraltar
	Hong Kong
	Montserrat
	Turks and Caicos Islands
Antigua and Barbuda	Antigua and Barbuda

Column 1	Column 2
Powers party to the Geneva Convention	Territories to which the Geneva Convention applies
Austria	Austria
Bahamas	Bahamas
Bangladesh	Bangladesh
Belgium	Belgium
Belize	Belize
Czechoslovakia	Czechoslovakia
Denmark	Denmark
Dominica	Dominica
Finland	Finland
France	France
Federal Republic of Germany	Federal Republic of Germany
German Democratic Republic	German Democratic Republic
Greece	Greece
Grenada	Grenada
Guyana	Guyana
India	India
Republic of Ireland	Republic of Ireland
Israel	Israel
Italy	Italy
Japan	Japan
Kenya	Kenya
Luxembourg	Luxembourg
Malta	Malta
Mauritius	Mauritius
Netherlands	Netherlands (including Curacao)
New Zealand	New Zealand
Pakistan	Pakistan
Portugal	Portugal
Romania	Romania
Saint Christopher and Nevis	Saint Christopher and Nevis
St Lucia	St Lucia
Spain	Spain
Sweden	Sweden
Switzerland	Switzerland
Tanzania	Tanzania
Thailand	Thailand
Western Samoa	Western Samoa
Yugoslavia	Yugoslavia
Zambia	Zambia

[2277]

SCHEDULE 2
NEW YORK CONVENTION STATES

Australia (including all the external territories for the international relations of which Australia is responsible)

Austria

Belgium

Belize

Benin

Botswana

Bulgaria

Byelorussian Soviet Socialist Republic

Cambodia

Central African Republic

Chile

Colombia

Cuba

Cyprus

Czechoslovakia

Denmark (including Greenland and the Faroe Islands)

Dijbouti

Ecuador

Egypt

Finland

France (including all the territories of the French Republic)

Federal Republic of Germany

German Democratic Republic

Ghana

Greece

Guatemala

Haiti

Holy See

Hungary

India

Republic of Ireland

Israel

Italy

Japan

Jordan

Korea

Kuwait

Luxembourg

Madagascar

[…]

Mexico

Monaco

Morocco

Netherlands (including the Netherlands Antilles)

New Zealand

Niger

Nigeria

Norway

[…]

Philippines

Poland

Romania

San Marino

South Africa

Spain

Sri Lanka

Sweden

Switzerland

Syria

Tanzania

Thailand

Trinidad and Tobago

Tunisia

Ukranian Soviet Socialist Republic

Union of Soviet Socialist Republics

United States of America (including all the territories for the international relations of which the United States of America is responsible)

Uruguay

Yugoslavia

[2278]

NOTES

Entries in square brackets inserted by SI 1985/455 and SI 1986/949; those instruments were revoked and replaced by the Arbitration (Foreign Awards) Order 1989, SI 1989/1348 at **[2279]**.

ARBITRATION (FOREIGN AWARDS) ORDER 1989

(SI 1989/1348)

NOTES

Made: 2 August 1989.

Authority: Arbitration Act 1975, s 7(2), (3); following the repeal of the Arbitration Act 1975, s 7(2), (3), this Order has effect as if made under the Arbitration Act 1996, s 100(3), by virtue of the Interpretation Act 1978, s 17(2)(b).

Commencement: 1 September 1989.

For status of 1958 New York Convention, see Table 2 at **[4677]**.

1 This Order may be cited as the Arbitration (Foreign Awards) Order 1989 and shall come into force on 1st September 1989.

[2279]

2 The States listed in the Schedule to this Order are parties to the New York Convention on the Recognition and Enforcement of Foreign Arbitral Awards which was adopted on 10th June 1958 and came into force in the United Kingdom of Great Britain and Northern Ireland on 23rd December 1975.

[2280]

3 (*Revokes the Arbitration* (*Foreign Awards*) (*Amendment*) *Order 1985, SI 1985/ 455, and the Arbitration* (*Foreign Awards*) *Order 1986, SI 1986/949.*)

THE SCHEDULE
NEW YORK CONVENTION STATES

Algeria

[Antigua and Barbuda]

Argentina

Bahrain

Burkina Faso

Cameroon

Canada

China

Costa Rica

Dominica

Kenya

Malaysia

Panama

Peru

Singapore

[2281]

NOTES

Words in square brackets substituted by the Arbitration (Foreign Awards) Order 1993, SI 1993/1256.

ARBITRATION (FOREIGN AWARDS) ORDER 1993

(SI 1993/1256)

NOTES

Made: 12 May 1993.

Authority: Arbitration Act 1975, s 7(2), (3); following the repeal of the Arbitration Act 1975, s 7(2), (3), this Order has effect as if made under the Arbitration Act 1996, s 100(3), by virtue of the Interpretation Act 1978, s 17(2)(b).

Commencement: 3 June 1993.

For status of 1958 New York Convention, see Table 2 at **[4677]**.

1 This Order may be cited as the Arbitration (Foreign Awards) Order 1993 and shall come into force on 3rd June 1993.

[2282]

2 Antigua and Barbuda is a party to the New York Convention on the Recognition and Enforcement of Foreign Arbitral Awards which was adopted on 10th June 1958 and came into force in the United Kingdom of Great Britain and Northern Ireland on 23rd December 1975.

[2283]

3 (*Amends the Arbitration (Foreign Awards) Order 1989, SI 1989/1348, Schedule at* **[2279]**.)

HIGH COURT AND COUNTY COURTS (ALLOCATION OF ARBITRATION PROCEEDINGS) ORDER 1996

(SI 1996/3215 (L 16))

NOTES

Made: 19 December 1996.

Authority: Arbitration Act 1996, s 105.

Commencement: 31 January 1997.

1—(1) This Order may be cited as the High Court and County Courts (Allocation of Arbitration Proceedings) Order 1996 and shall come into force on 31st January 1997.

(2) In this Order, "the Act" means the Arbitration Act 1996.

[2284]

2 Subject to articles 3 to 5, proceedings under the Act shall be commenced and taken in the High Court.

[2285]

3 Proceedings under section 9 of the Act (stay of legal proceedings) shall be commenced in the court in which the legal proceedings are pending.

[2286]

4 Proceedings under sections 66 and 101(2) (enforcement of awards) of the Act may be commenced in any county court.

[2287]

5—(1) Proceedings under the Act may be commenced and taken in [the Central London County Court Mercantile List].

(2) Where, in exercise of the powers conferred by sections 41 and 42 of the County Courts Act 1984 the High Court or the judge in charge of [the Central London County Court Mercantile List] orders the transfer of proceedings under the Act which were commenced in [the Central London County Court Mercantile List] to the High Court, those proceedings shall be taken in the High Court.

(3) Where, in exercise of its powers under section 40(2) of the County Courts Act 1984 the High Court orders the transfer of proceedings under the Act which were commenced in the High Court to [the Central London County Court Mercantile List], those proceedings shall be taken in [the Central London County Court Mercantile List].

(4) In exercising the powers referred to in paragraphs (2) and (3) regard shall be had to the following criteria—

(a) the financial substance of the dispute referred to arbitration, including the value of any claim or counterclaim;

(b) the nature of the dispute referred to arbitration (for example, whether it arises out of a commercial or business transaction or relates to engineering, building or other construction work);

(c) whether the proceedings are otherwise important and, in particular, whether they raise questions of importance to persons who are not parties, and

(d) the balance of convenience points to having the proceedings taken in [the Central London County Court Mercantile List],

and, where the financial substance of the dispute exceeds £200,000, the proceedings shall be taken in the High Court unless the proceedings do not raise questions of general importance to persons who are not parties.

[(5) The value of any claim or counterclaim shall be calculated in accordance with rule 16.3(6) of the Civil Procedure Rules 1998.]

[(6) In this article "the Central London County Court Mercantile List" means the Mercantile Court established at the Central London County Court pursuant to Part 59 of the Civil Procedure Rules 1998.]

[2288]

NOTES

Paras (1)–(4): words in square brackets substituted by the Civil Procedure (Modification of Enactments) Order 2002, SI 2002/439, arts 2, 11(a).

Para (5): substituted by the High Court and County Courts (Allocation of Arbitration Proceedings) (Amendment) Order 1999, SI 1999/1010, art 2.

Para (6): added by SI 2002/439, arts 2, 11(b).

6 Nothing in this Order shall prevent the judge in charge of the commercial list (within the meaning of section 62(3) of the *Supreme Court Act 1981*) from transferring proceedings under the Act to another list, court or Division of the High Court to which he has power to transfer proceedings and, where such an order is made, the proceedings may be taken in that list, court or Division as the case may be.

[2289]

NOTES

Words in italics substituted by the words "Senior Courts Act 1981" by the Constitutional Reform Act 2005, s 59(5), Sch 11, Pt 1, para 1(2), as from a day to be appointed.

UNFAIR ARBITRATION AGREEMENTS (SPECIFIED AMOUNT) ORDER 1999

(SI 1999/2167)

NOTES

Made: 28 July 1999.

Authority: Arbitration Act 1996, s 91(1), (3)(a), (b).

Commencement: 1 January 2000.

1 This Order may be cited as the Unfair Arbitration Agreements (Specified Amount) Order 1999 and shall come into force on 1st January 2000.

[2290]

2 (*Revokes the Unfair Arbitration Agreements (Specified Amount) Order 1996, SI 1996/3211.*)

3 The amount of £5,000 is hereby specified for the purposes of section 91 of the Arbitration Act 1996 (arbitration agreement unfair where modest amount sought).

[2291]

E. INTERNATIONAL CARRIAGE: AIR, RAIL AND ROAD

CARRIAGE BY AIR (PARTIES TO CONVENTION) ORDER 1999

(SI 1999/1313)

NOTES

Made: 11 May 1999.
Authority: Carriage by Air Act 1961, s 2(1).
Commencement: 11 May 1999.

1 This Order may be cited as the Carriage by Air (Parties to Convention) Order 1999.

[2292]

2 It is hereby certified that the High Contracting Parties to the Warsaw Convention,1929, to the Warsaw Convention as amended at The Hague, 1955, and to the Warsaw Convention as amended by Additional Protocol No 1 of Montreal, 1975, and the territories in respect of which they are respectively parties are as specified in Schedule 1 to this Order.

[2293]

3 In the said Schedule 1 an asterisk means that this Order does not certify that a State is a party, in respect of that territory, to the Convention named at the head of the column.

[2294]

4 It is hereby certified that the High Contracting Parties specified in Schedule 2 to this Order have availed themselves of the provisions of the Additional Protocol to the Convention to which they are hereby certified as Parties, by declaring that the first paragraph of article 2 of the Convention shall not apply to international carriage by air performed directly by the State or any territory or possession under its jurisdiction.

[2295]

5 (*Revokes the Carriage by Air (Parties to Convention) Order 1988, SI 1988/243.*)

SCHEDULES

SCHEDULE 1
HIGH CONTRACTING PARTIES TO THE WARSAW CONVENTION, 1929, TO THE WARSAW CONVENTION AS AMENDED AT THE HAGUE, 1955 AND TO THE WARSAW CONVENTION AS AMENDED BY ADDITIONAL PROTOCOL NO 1 OF MONTREAL, 1975

Articles 2, 3

High Contracting Parties	*Territories in respect of which they are respectively parties*	*Dates on which the Warsaw Convention, 1929 came into force*	*Dates on which the Warsaw Convention as amended at The Hague, 1955 came into force*	*Dates on which the Warsaw Convention as amended by Additional Protocol No 1 of Montreal, 1975 came into force*
The United Kingdom of Great Britain and Northern Ireland	Great Britain and Northern Ireland	15th May 1933	1st June 1967	15th February 1996
	The Channel Islands	15th May 1933	1st June 1967	15th February 1996
	The Isle of Man	15th May 1933	1st June 1967	15th February 1996
	Anguilla	3rd March 1935	*	15th February 1996
	Bermuda	3rd March 1935	1st June 1967	15th February 1996
	British Antarctic Territory	3rd March 1935	1st June 1967	15th February 1996
	British Indian Ocean Territory	3rd March 1935	1st June 1967	15th February 1996
	British Virgin Islands	3rd March 1935	1st June 1967	15th February 1996
	Cayman Islands	3rd March 1935	1st June 1967	15th February 1996
	Falkland Islands	3rd March 1935	1st June 1967	15th February 1996
	Gibraltar	3rd March 1935	1st June 1967	15th February 1996
	Montserrat	3rd March 1935	1st June 1967	15th February 1996
	Pitcairn, Henderson, Ducie and Oeno Islands	*	*	15th February 1996
	St Helena	3rd March 1935	1st June 1967	15th February 1996
	St Helena Dependencies	3rd March 1935	1st June 1967	15th February 1996
	South Georgia and the South Sandwich Islands	3rd March 1935	1st June 1967	15th February 1996
	The Sovereign Base Areas of Akrotiri and Dhekelia	3rd March 1935	1st June 1967	15th February 1996

High Contracting Parties	*Territories in respect of which they are respectively parties*	*Dates on which the Warsaw Convention, 1929 came into force*	*Dates on which the Warsaw Convention as amended at The Hague, 1955 came into force*	*Dates on which the Warsaw Convention as amended by Additional Protocol No 1 of Montreal, 1975 came into force*
	Turks and Caicos Islands	3rd March 1935	1st June 1967	15th February 1996
The Islamic State of Afghanistan	Afghanistan	21st May 1969	21st May 1969	*
The Democratic and Popular Republic of Algeria	Algeria	31st August	31st August 1964	*
The Republic of Angola	Angola	8th June 1998	8th June 1998	*
Antigua and Barbuda	Antigua and Barbuda	3rd March 1935	*	*
The Argentine Republic	Argentina	19th June 1952	10th September 1969	15th February 1996
The Commonwealth of Australia	Australia and all external territories for whose international affairs of which Australia is responsible	30th October 1935	1st August 1963	*
The Republic of Austria	Austria	27th December 1961	24th June 1971	*
The Commonwealth of the Bahamas	Bahamas	3rd March 1935	1st June 1967	*
The State of Bahrain	Bahrain	10th June 1998	10th June 1998	10th June 1998
The People's Republic of Bangladesh	Bangladesh	18th February 1935	1st August 1963	*
Barbados	Barbados	3rd March 1935	*	*
The Republic of Belarus	Belarus	25th December 1959	1st August 1963	*
The Kingdom of Belgium	Belgium	11th October 1936	25th November 1963	*
Belize	Belize	3rd March 1935	1st June 1967	*
The Republic of Benin	Benin	13th February 1933	1st August 1963	*

High Contracting Parties	*Territories in respect of which they are respectively parties*	*Dates on which the Warsaw Convention, 1929 came into force*	*Dates on which the Warsaw Convention as amended at The Hague, 1955 came into force*	*Dates on which the Warsaw Convention as amended by Additional Protocol No 1 of Montreal, 1975 came into force*
Bosnia and Herzegovina	Bosnia and Herzegovina	13th February 1933	1 August 1963	15th February 1996
The Republic of Botswana	Botswana	1st December 1952	*	*
The Federal Republic of Brazil	Brazil	13th February 1933	14th September 1964	15th February 1996
Brunei Darussalam	Brunei	2nd October 1936	*	*
The Republic of Bulgaria	Bulgaria	23rd September 1949	13th March 1964	*
The Republic of Burkina	Burkina Faso	9th March 1962	*	*
The Kingdom of Cambodia	Cambodia	13th February 1933	12th March 1997	*
The Republic of Cameroon	Cameroon	13th February 1933	1st August 1963	*
Canada	Canada	8th September 1947 (except for the Province of Newfoundland) 5th July 1939 (for Newfoundland)	17th July 1964	15th February 1996
The Republic of Chad	Chad	13th February 1933	11th September 1964	*
The Republic of Chile	Chile	31st May 1979	31st May 1979	15th February 1996
The People's Republic of China[1]	China	18th October 1958	18th November 1975	*
The Republic of Colombia	Colombia	13th November 1966	13th November 1966	15th February 1996
The Federal Islamic Republic of the Comoros	The Comoros	9th September 1991	*	*
The Republic of the Congo	Congo (Brazzaville)	13th February 1933	1st August 1963	*

High Contracting Parties	*Territories in respect of which they are respectively parties*	*Dates on which the Warsaw Convention, 1929 came into force*	*Dates on which the Warsaw Convention as amended at The Hague, 1955 came into force*	*Dates on which the Warsaw Convention as amended by Additional Protocol No 1 of Montreal, 1975 came into force*
The Democratic Republic of Congo	Congo (Democratic Republic)	11th October 1936	*	*
The Republic of Costa Rica	Costa Rica	8th August 1984	8th August 1984	*
The Republic of Côte d'Ivoire	Ivory Coast	13th February 1933	1st August 1963	*
The Republic of Croatia	Croatia	13th February 1933	1st August 1963	15th February 1996
The Republic of Cuba	Cuba	19th October 1964	28th November 1965	20th July 1998
The Republic of Cyprus	The territory of the Republic of Cyprus	3rd March 1935	21st October 1970	15th February 1996
The Czech Republic	The Czech Republic	15th February 1935	1st August 1963	*
The Kingdom of Denmark	Denmark, Greenland and the Faroe Islands	1st October 1937	1st August 1963	15th February 1996 (for Denmark only)
The Commonwealth of Dominica	Dominica	3rd March 1935	*	*
The Dominican Republic	Dominican Republic	25th May 1972	25th May 1972	*
The Republic of Ecuador	Ecuador	1st March 1970	1st March 1970	*
The Arab Republic of Egypt	Egypt	5th December 1955	1st August 1963	15th February 1996
The Republic of El Salvador	El Salvador	*	1st August 1963	*
The Republic of Equatorial Guinea	Equatorial Guinea	19th March 1989	*	*
The Republic of Estonia	Estonia	14th June 1998	14th June 1998	14th June 1998
The Federal Democratic Republic of Ethiopia	Ethiopia	12th November 1950	*	15th February 1996

High Contracting Parties	*Territories in respect of which they are respectively parties*	*Dates on which the Warsaw Convention, 1929 came into force*	*Dates on which the Warsaw Convention as amended at The Hague, 1955 came into force*	*Dates on which the Warsaw Convention as amended by Additional Protocol No 1 of Montreal, 1975 came into force*
The Republic of Fiji	Fiji	3rd March 1935	1st June 1967	*
The Republic of Finland	Finland	1st October 1937	23rd August 1977	15th February 1996
The French Republic	France and all Overseas Departments and territories subject to the sovereignty or authority of the French Republic	13th February 1933	1st August 1963	15th February 1996
The Gabonese Republic	Gabon	16th May 1969	16th May 1969	*
The Republic of The Gambia	The Gambia	3rd March 1935	*	*
The Federal Republic of Germany	Germany	29th December 1933	1st August 1963	*
The Republic of Ghana	Ghana	3rd March 1935	9th November 1997	9th November 1997
Grenada	Grenada	3rd March 1935	13th November 1985	*
The Republic of Guatemala	Guatemala	4th May 1997	26th October 1971	4th May 1997
The Republic of Guinea	Guinea	10th December 1961	7th January 1991	*
The Co-operative Republic of Guyana	Guyana	3rd March 1935	*	*
The Hellenic Republic	Greece	11th April 1938	21st September 1965	15th February 1996
The Republic of Honduras	Honduras	25th September 1994	*	15th May 1996
The Republic of Hungary	Hungary	27th August 1936	1st August 1963	*
The Republic of Iceland	Iceland	19th November 1948	1st August 1963	*
The Republic of India	India	18th February 1935	15th May 1973	*
The Republic of Indonesia	Indonesia	29th September 1933	*	*

High Contracting Parties	*Territories in respect of which they are respectively parties*	*Dates on which the Warsaw Convention, 1929 came into force*	*Dates on which the Warsaw Convention as amended at The Hague, 1955 came into force*	*Dates on which the Warsaw Convention as amended by Additional Protocol No 1 of Montreal, 1975 came into force*
The Islamic Republic of Iran	Iran	6th October 1975	6th October 1975	*
The Republic of Iraq	Iraq	26th September 1972	26th September 1972	*
The Republic of Ireland	The territory of the Republic of Ireland	19th December 1935	1st August 1963	15th February 1996
The State of Israel	Israel	6th January 1950	3rd November 1964	15th February 1996
The Italian Republic	Italy	15th May 1933	2nd August 1963	15th February 1996
Jamaica	Jamaica	3rd March 1935	*	*
Japan	Japan	18th August 1953	8th November 1967	*
The Hashemite Kingdom of Jordan	Jordan	17th March 1938	13th February 1974	*
The Republic of Kenya	Kenya	3rd March 1935	*	*
The Republic of Kiribati	Kiribati	3rd March 1935	1st June 1967	*
The Republic of Korea	South Korea	*	11th October 1967	*
The State of Kuwait	Kuwait	9th November 1975	9th November 1975	6th February 1997
The Laos People's Democratic Republic	Laos	13th February 1933	1st August 1963	*
The Republic of Latvia	Latvia	13th February 193	*	*
The Republic of Lebanon	Lebanon	24th January 1934	8th August 1978	*
The Kingdom of Lesotho	Lesotho	1st December 1952	15th January 1976	*
The Republic of Liberia	Liberia	31st July 1942	*	*
The Great Socialist People's Libyan Arab Jamahiriya	Libya	14th August 1969	14th August 1969	*

High Contracting Parties	*Territories in respect of which they are respectively parties*	*Dates on which the Warsaw Convention, 1929 came into force*	*Dates on which the Warsaw Convention as amended at The Hague, 1955 came into force*	*Dates on which the Warsaw Convention as amended by Additional Protocol No 1 of Montreal, 1975 came into force*
The Principality of Liechtenstein	Liechtenstein	7th August 1934	3rd April 1966	*
The Republic of Lithuania	Lithuania	*	19th February 1997	*
The Grand Duchy of Luxembourg	Luxembourg	5th January 1950	1st August 1963	*
The Democratic Republic of Madagascar	Madagascar	13th February 1933	1st August 1963	*
The Republic of Malawi	Malawi	25th January 1978	7th September 1971	*
Malaysia	Malaysia	2nd October 1936 (except for Malacca and Penang) 3rd March 1935 (for Malacca and Penang)	19th December 1974	*
The Republic of the Maldives	Maldives	11th November 1996	11th November 1996	*
The Republic of Mali	Mali	13th February 1933	29th March 1964	*
The Republic of Malta	Malta	3rd March 1935	*	*
The Islamic Republic of Mauritania	Mauritania	13th February 1933	*	*
Mauritius	Mauritius	3rd March 1935	1st June 1967	*
The United Mexican States	Mexico	15th May 1933	1st August 1963	15th February 1996
The Republic of Moldova	Moldova	19th June 1997	19th June 1997	*
The Principality of Monaco	Monaco	*	8th July 1979	*
Mongolia	Mongolia	29th July 1962	*	*

High Contracting Parties	*Territories in respect of which they are respectively parties*	*Dates on which the Warsaw Convention, 1929 came into force*	*Dates on which the Warsaw Convention as amended at The Hague, 1955 came into force*	*Dates on which the Warsaw Convention as amended by Additional Protocol No 1 of Montreal, 1975 came into force*
The Kingdom of Morocco	Morocco	5th April 1958	15th February 1976	*
The Union of Myanamar	Burma	18th February 1935	*	*
The Republic of Namibia	Namibia	22th March 1955	17th December 1967	*
The Republic of Nauru	Nauru	30th October 1935	1st August 1963	*
The Kingdom of Nepal	Nepal	13th May 1966	13th May 1966	*
The Kingdom of the Netherlands	The Netherlands and all territories subject to the sovereignty or authority of the Kingdom of the Netherlands	29th September 1933	1st August 1963	15th February 1996 (except for Aruba)
New Zealand	New Zealand (including the Cook Islands and the Tokelau Islands)	5th July 1937	14th June 1967	*
The Republic of Niger	Niger	13th February 1933	1st August 1963	*
The Federal Republic of Nigeria	Nigeria	3rd March 1935	29th September 1969	*
The Kingdom of Norway	Norway and all territories subject to the sovereignty or authority of the Kingdom of Norway	1st October 1937	1st August 1963	15th February 1996 (for Norway only)
The Sultanate of Oman	Oman	4th November 1976	2nd November 1987	*
The Islamic Republic of Pakistan	Pakistan	18th February 1935	1st August 1963	*
The Republic of Panama	Panama	10th January 1997	10th January 1997	*
The Independent State of Papua New Guinea	Papua New Guinea	30th October 1935	1st August 1963	*
The Republic of Paraguay	Paraguay	26th November 1969	26th November 1969	*

High Contracting Parties	*Territories in respect of which they are respectively parties*	*Dates on which the Warsaw Convention, 1929 came into force*	*Dates on which the Warsaw Convention as amended at The Hague, 1955 came into force*	*Dates on which the Warsaw Convention as amended by Additional Protocol No 1 of Montreal, 1975 came into force*
The Republic of Peru	Peru	3rd October 1988	3rd October 1988	2nd October 1997
The Republic of Philippines	The Philippines	7th February 1951	28th February 1967	*
The Republic of Poland	Poland	13th February 1933	1st August 1963	*
The Portuguese Republic	Portugal and all territories subject to the sovereignty or authority of the Portuguese Republic	18th June 1947	15th December 1963	15th February 1996
The State of Qatar	Qatar	21st March 1987	21st March 1987	*
Romania	Romania	13th February 1933	1st August 1963	*
The Russian Federation	Russia	18th November 1934	1st August 1963	*
The Rwandese Republic	Rwanda	11th October 1936	27th March 1991	*
The Federation of Saint Christopher and Nevis	Saint Christopher and Nevis	3rd March 1935	*	*
Saint Lucia	Saint Lucia	3rd March 1935	*	*
Saint Vincent and the Grenadines	Saint Vincent and the Grenadines	3rd March 1935	*	*
The Kingdom of Saudi Arabia	Saudi Arabia	27th April 1969	27th April 1969	*
The Republic of Senegal	Senegal	13th February 1933	17th September 1964	*
The Republic of Seychelles	Seychelles	22nd September 1980	22nd September 1980	*
The Republic of Sierra Leone	Sierra Leone	3rd March 1935	(see art 3 ante)	*
The Republic of Singapore	Singapore	3rd December 1971	4th February 1968	*
The Slovak Republic	Slovakia	13th February 1935	1st August 1963	*

High Contracting Parties	*Territories in respect of which they are respectively parties*	*Dates on which the Warsaw Convention, 1929 came into force*	*Dates on which the Warsaw Convention as amended at The Hague, 1955 came into force*	*Dates on which the Warsaw Convention as amended by Additional Protocol No 1 of Montreal, 1975 came into force*
Solomon Islands	Solomon Islands	3rd March 1935	1st June 1967	*
The Republic of South Africa	The Republic of South Africa	22nd March 1955	17th December 1967	*
	Namibia	22nd March 1955	17th December 1967	*
The Kingdom of Spain	Spain and all territories subject to the sovereignty or authority of the Kingdom of Spain	13th February 1933	6th March 1966	15th February 1996
The Democratic Socialist Republic of Sri Lanka	Sri Lanka	3rd March 1935	22nd March 1997	*
The Republic of Sudan	Sudan	12th May 1975	12th May 1975	*
The Republic of Suriname	Surinam	29th September 1933	1st August 1963	*
The Kingdom of Swaziland	Swaziland	1st December 1952	18th October 1971	*
The Kingdom of Sweden	Sweden	1st October 1937	1st August 1963	15th February 1996
The Swiss Confederation	Switzerland	7th August 1934	1st August 1963	15th February 1996
The Syrian Arab Republic	Syria	2nd March 1959	1st August 1963	*
The Republic of Tajikistan	Tajikistan	4th May 1994	*	*
The United Republic of Tanzania	Tanzania	3rd March 1935	*	*
The Former Yugoslav Republic of Macedonia	Macedonia	13th February 1933	1st August 1963	15th February 1996
The Republic of Togo	Togo	30th September 1980	30th September 1980	15th February 1996
The Kingdom of Tonga	Tonga	2nd October 1936	22nd May 1977	*

High Contracting Parties	*Territories in respect of which they are respectively parties*	*Dates on which the Warsaw Convention, 1929 came into force*	*Dates on which the Warsaw Convention as amended at The Hague, 1955 came into force*	*Dates on which the Warsaw Convention as amended by Additional Protocol No 1 of Montreal, 1975 came into force*
The Republic of Trinidad and Tobago	Trinidad and Tobago	3rd March 1935	8th August 1983	*
The Tunisian Republic	Tunisia	13th February 1933	13th February 1964	15th February 1996
The Republic of Turkey	Turkey	23rd June 1978	23rd June 1978	15th February 1996
Turkmenistan	Turkmenistan	20th March 1995	*	*
Tuvalu	Tuvalu	3rd March 1935	1st June 1967	*
The Republic of Uganda	Uganda	3rd March 1935	*	*
Ukraine	Ukraine	12th November 1959	1st August 1963	*
United Arab Emirates	United Arab Emirates	3rd July 1986	16th January 1994	*
The United States of America	The United States of America and all territories subject to the sovereignty or authority of the United States of America	29th October 1934	*	*
The Oriental Republic of Uruguay	Uruguay	2nd October 1979	*	*
The Republic of Uzbekistan	Uzbekistan	28th May 1997	*	28th May 1997
The Republic of Vanuatu	Vanuatu	24th January 1982	24th January 1982	*
The Republic of Venezuela	Venezuela	13th September 1955	1st August 1963	15th February 1996
The Socialist Republic of Vietnam	Vietnam	13th February 1933	9th January 1983	*
The Republic of Yemen	Yemen	4th August 1982	4th August 1982	*
The Federal Republic of Yugoslavia	Yugoslavia	13th February 1933	1st August 1963	15th February 1996

High Contracting Parties	*Territories in respect of which they are respectively parties*	*Dates on which the Warsaw Convention, 1929 came into force*	*Dates on which the Warsaw Convention as amended at The Hague, 1955 came into force*	*Dates on which the Warsaw Convention as amended by Additional Protocol No 1 of Montreal, 1975 came into force*
The Republic of Zambia	Zambia	3rd March 1935	23rd June 1970	*
The Republic of Zimbabwe	Zimbabwe	3rd April 1935	25th January 1981	*

[2296]

NOTES

1 The People's Republic of China assumed responsibility for the rights and obligations arising from the application of the Warsaw Convention, 1929 and the Warsaw Convention as amended at The Hague, 1955 to the Hong Kong Special Administrative Region (HKSAR) with effect from 1st July 1997.

SCHEDULE 2
HIGH CONTRACTING PARTIES WHICH HAVE AVAILED THEMSELVES OF THE PROVISIONS OF THE ADDITIONAL PROTOCOL TO THE CONVENTION TO WHICH THEY ARE CERTIFIED AS PARTIES IN SCHEDULE 1

Article 4

Canada

The Republic of Chile

The Republic of the Congo

The Republic of Cuba

The Federal Democratic Republic of Ethiopia

The Republic of the Philippines

The United States of America

[2297]

CARRIAGE BY AIR (PARTIES TO PROTOCOL NO 4 OF MONTREAL, 1975) ORDER 2000

(SI 2000/3061)

NOTES

Made: 15 November 2000.
Authority: Carriage by Air Act 1961, s 2(1), (4).
Commencement: 15 November 2000.

1 This Order may be cited as the Carriage by Air (Parties to Protocol No 4 of Montreal, 1975) Order 2000.

[2298]

2 It is hereby certified that the High Contracting Parties to the Warsaw Convention as amended at The Hague, 1955, as further amended by Protocol No 4 of Montreal, 1975, and the territories in respect of which they are respectively parties, are as specified in the Schedule to this Order.

[2299]

SCHEDULE
HIGH CONTRACTING PARTIES TO THE WARSAW CONVENTION AS AMENDED AT THE HAGUE, 1955, AS FURTHER AMENDED BY PROTOCOL NO 4 OF MONTREAL 1975

High Contracting Parties	Territories in respect of which they are respectively parties	Dates on which the Warsaw Convention as amended at The Hague, 1955, as further amended by Protocol No. 4 of Montreal, 1975, came into force
The United Kingdom of Great Britain and Northern Ireland	Great Britain and Northern Ireland	14 June 1998
The Argentine Republic	Argentina	14 June 1998
The Commonwealth of Australia	Australia and all external territories for whose international affairs Australia is responsible	14 June 1998

The Azerbaijani Republic	Azerbaijan	22 April 2000
The State of Bahrain	Bahrain	21 April 1999
Bosnia and Herzegovina	Bosnia and Herzegovina	14 June 1998
The Federal Republic of Brazil	Brazil	14 June 1998
Canada	Canada	25 November 1999
The Republic of Colombia	Colombia	14 June 1998
The Republic of Croatia	Croatia	14 June 1998
The Kingdom of Denmark	Denmark, and the Faeroe Islands	14 June 1998
The Republic of Ecuador	Ecuador	12 May 1999
The Arab Republic of Egypt	Egypt	14 June 1998
The Republic of Estonia	Estonia	14 June 1998
The Federal Democratic Republic of Ethiopia	Ethiopia	14 June 1998
The Republic of Finland	Finland	14 June 1998
The Republic of Ghana	Ghana	14 June 1998
The Hellenic Republic	Greece	14 June 1998
The Republic of Guatemala	Guatemala	14 June 1998
The Republic of Guinea	Guinea	12 May 1999
The Republic of Honduras	Honduras	12 September 1998
The Republic of Hungary	Hungary	14 June 1998
The Republic of Ireland	The territory of the Republic of Ireland	14 June 1998
The State of Israel	Israel	14 June 1998
The Italian Republic	Italy	14 June 1998
Japan	Japan	18 September 2000
The Hashemite Kingdom of Jordan	Jordan	20th October 1999
The Republic of Kenya	Kenya	4 October 1999
The State of Kuwait	Kuwait	14 June 1998
The Republic of Macedonia	Macedonia	14 June 1998
The Republic of Mauritius	Mauritius	12 September 1998
The Republic of Nauru	Nauru	12 September 1998
The Kingdom of the Netherlands	The Kingdom of the Netherlands in Europe	14 June 1998
	The Kingdom of the Netherlands in Europe	14 June 1998
The Republic of Niger	Niger	12 September 1998
The Kingdom of Norway	Norway and all territories subject to the sovereignty or authority of the Kingdom of Norway	14 June 1998
The Sultanate of Oman	Oman	12 September 1998
The Portuguese Republic	Portugal and all territories subject to the sovereignty or authority of the Portuguese Republic	14 June 1998

The Republic of Singapore	Singapore	12 September 1998
The Republic of Slovenia	Slovenia	14 June 1998
The Kingdom of Spain	Spain and all territories subject to the sovereignty or authority of the Kingdom of Spain	14 June 1998
The Kingdom of Sweden	Sweden	14 June 1998
The Swiss Confederation	Switzerland	14 June 1998
The Republic of Togo	Togo	14 June 1998
United Arab Emirates	United Arab Emirates	18 June 2000
The Republic of Turkey	Turkey	12 September 1998
The United States of America	The United States of America and all territories subject to the sovereignty or authority of the United States of America	4 March 1999
The Republic of Uzbekistan	Uzbekistan	12 September 1998
The Federal Republic of Yugoslavia	Yugoslavia	14 June 1998

[2300]

AIR CARRIER LIABILITY REGULATIONS 2004

(SI 2004/1418)

NOTES

Made: 24 May 2004.
Authority: European Communities Act 1972, s 2(2).
Commencement: 28 June 2004.

1 Citation and commencement

These Regulations may be cited as the Air Carrier Liability Regulations 2004 and shall come into force on 28th June 2004.

[2301]

NOTES

Commencement: 28 June 2004.

2 Interpretation

In these Regulations "the Council Regulation" means Council Regulation (EC) No 2027/97 as amended by Regulation (EC) No 889/2002 of the European Parliament and of the Council.

[2302]

NOTES

Commencement: 28 June 2004.

3 Enforcement of Articles 3a and 6 of the Council Regulation

(1) A Community air carrier that fails to make available the tariff required by Article 3a of the Council Regulation shall be guilty of an offence unless it proves that the failure to do so occurred without its consent or connivance and that it exercised all due diligence to prevent the failure.

(2) An air carrier that fails to comply with the requirements imposed on it by paragraphs 1 or 2 of Article 6 of the Council Regulation shall be guilty of an offence unless it proves that the failure to do so occurred without its consent or connivance and that it exercised all due diligence to prevent the failure.

[2303]

NOTES

Commencement: 28 June 2004.

4 Penalties

(1) A person guilty of an offence under these Regulations shall be liable—

(a) on summary conviction, to a fine not exceeding [the statutory maximum], and

(b) on conviction on indictment, to a fine.

(2) Where an offence under these Regulations has been committed by a body corporate and is proved to have been committed with the consent or connivance of or to be attributable to any neglect on the part of any director, manager, secretary or other similar officer of the body corporate or any such person who was purporting to act in such capacity, he, as well as the body corporate, shall be guilty of an offence and be liable to be proceeded against and punished accordingly.

(3) Where the affairs of a body corporate are managed by its members, paragraph (2) shall apply in relation to the acts and defaults of a member in connection with his functions of management as if he were a director of the body corporate.

(4) Where a Scottish partnership is guilty of an offence under these Regulations in Scotland and that offence is proved to have been committed with the consent or connivance of or to be attributable to any neglect on the part of a partner, he, as well as the partnership, shall be guilty of that offence and shall be liable to be proceeded against and punished accordingly.

[2304]

NOTES

Commencement: 28 June 2004.

Para (1): in sub-para (a) words in square brackets substituted by the Air Carrier Liability (No 2) Regulations 2004, SI 2004/1974, reg 3.

5, 6 (*Art 5 amends the Carriage by Air Act 1961, s 14 at* **[415]**; *art 6 revokes the Air Carrier Liability Order 1998, SI 1998/1751.*)

CARRIAGE BY AIR ACTS (APPLICATION OF PROVISIONS) ORDER 2004

(SI 2004/1899)

NOTES

Made: 27 July 2004.

Authority: Carriage by Air Act 1961, s 10.

Commencement: 6 August 2004.

ARRANGEMENT OF REGULATIONS

PART III STATUTORY INSTRUMENTS

1 Citation, commencement and effect

(1) This Order may be cited as the Carriage by Air Acts (Application of Provisions) Order 2004.

(2) This Order shall come into force on the tenth day after the day on which it is made.

(3) Nothing in this Order shall affect rights and liabilities arising out of an occurrence which took place before the coming into force of this Order.

[2305]

NOTES

Commencement: 6 August 2004.

2 Interpretation

In this Order—

"the Act of 1961" means the Carriage by Air Act 1961;

"the Act of 1962" means the Carriage by Air (Supplementary Provisions) Act 1962;

"the 1955 amended Convention" means the English text of the Warsaw Convention with the amendments made in it by the Hague Protocol as set out in Schedule 1 to the Act of 1961, and includes the Additional Protocol to the Warsaw Convention as set out at the end of that Schedule;

"Community air carrier" has the meaning given by Article 2 of the Council Regulation;

["the Council Regulation" means Council Regulation (EC) No 2027/97 as amended by Regulation (EC) No 889/2002 of the European Parliament and of the Council as it has effect in accordance with the Agreement on the European Economic Area signed at Oporto on 2nd May 1992 as adjusted by the Protocol signed at Brussels on 17th March 1993 as amended by the Decisions of the EEA Joint Committee No 34/98 of 30th April 1998 and No 142/2002 of 8th November 2002;]

"the Guadalajara Convention" means the English text of the Convention, supplementary to the Warsaw Convention, for the Unification of Certain Rules relating to International Carriage by Air performed by a Person other than the Contracting Carrier, as set out in the Schedule to the Act of 1962;

"the MP4 Convention" means the English text of the Warsaw Convention with the amendments made in it by the Hague Protocol and as further amended by Protocol No 4 of Montreal, 1975 as set out in Schedule 1A to the Act of 1961; and

"the Montreal Convention" means the Convention for the Unification of Certain Rules for International Carriage by Air done at Montreal on 28 May 1999.

[2306]

NOTES

Commencement: 6 August 2004.

Definition "the Council Regulation" substituted by the Air Carrier Liability (No 2) Regulations 2004, SI 2004/1974, reg 2.

3 Application

(1) This Order shall apply to all carriage by air, not being carriage to which the 1955 amended Convention, the MP4 amended Convention or the Montreal Convention applies.

(2) This Order shall not apply in relation to Community air carriers to the extent that the provisions of the Council Regulation have the force of law in the United Kingdom.

[2307]

NOTES
Commencement: 6 August 2004.

4 Non-international carriage

Schedule 1 to this Order shall have effect in respect of carriage to which this Order applies being carriage which is not international carriage as defined in Schedule 2 or Schedule 3.
[2308]

NOTES
Commencement: 6 August 2004.

5 International carriage under the unamended Warsaw Convention

(1) Schedule 2 to this Order shall have effect in respect of carriage to which this Order applies, being carriage which is international carriage as defined in that Schedule and not international carriage as defined in Schedule 3.

(2) Section 2 of the Act of 1961 shall apply to such carriage as aforesaid with the following exceptions, adaptations and modifications:
- (a) for "any of the Carriage by Air Conventions" there shall be substituted "the Warsaw Convention";
- (b) subsection (1)(b) and (c) shall be omitted;
- (c) subsection (1A) shall be omitted;
- (d) subsection (2A)(b) and (c) shall be omitted.

(3) Section 5 of the Act of 1961 shall apply to such carriage as aforesaid with the following exceptions, adaptations and modifications:
- (a) for "any of the Carriage by Air Conventions" there shall be substituted "the Warsaw Convention";
- (b) subsections (4)(b) and (c) and (5) shall be omitted.

(4) Section 8 of the Act of 1961 shall apply to such carriage as aforesaid with the following exceptions, adaptations and modifications:
- (a) for "a Carriage by Air Convention" there shall be substituted "the Warsaw Convention";
- (b) subsections (4)(b) and (c), (5)(b) and (c) and (6)(b) shall be omitted;
- (c) in subsection (6) "and the Convention as amended" shall be omitted.

[2309]

NOTES
Commencement: 6 August 2004.

6 International carriage under the unamended Warsaw Convention as amended by Additional Protocol No 1 of Montreal, 1975

(1) Schedule 3 to this Order shall have effect in respect of carriage to which this Order applies, being carriage which is international carriage as defined in that Schedule.

(2) Section 2 of the 1961 Act shall apply to such carriage as aforesaid with the following exceptions, adaptations and modifications:
- (a) for "a Carriage by Air Convention" there shall be substituted "the Warsaw Convention as amended by Additional Protocol No 1 of Montreal 1975";
- (b) subsection (1)(b) and (c) shall be omitted;
- (c) subsection (1A) shall be omitted;
- (d) subsection (2A)(b) and (c) shall be omitted.

(3) Section 5 of the Act of 1961 shall apply to such carriage as aforesaid with the following exceptions, adaptations and modifications:
- (a) for "any of the Carriage by Air Conventions" there shall be substituted "the Warsaw Convention as amended by Additional Protocol No 1 of Montreal 1975";
- (b) subsections (4)(b) and (c) and (5) shall be omitted.

(4) Section 8 to the Act of 1961 shall apply to such carriage as aforesaid, with the following exceptions, adaptations and modifications:

(a) for "a Carriage by Air Convention" there shall be substituted "the Warsaw Convention as amended by Additional Protocol No 1 of Montreal 1975";
(b) subsections (4)(b) and (c), (5)(b) and (c) and (6)(b) shall be omitted;
(c) in subsection (6) "and the Convention as amended" shall be omitted.

[2310]

NOTES

Commencement: 6 August 2004.

7 Application of certain provisions of the Acts

(1) Sections 3, 4, 4A, 6, 11 and 12 of the Act of 1961 shall apply to carriage to which Schedule 1 to this Order applies as if the references therein to the Convention and the Convention as amended and articles thereof were omitted and the reference to the Montreal Convention and articles thereof were references to the Montreal Convention and articles thereof as applied by this Order.

(2) Sections 3, 4, 4A, 6, 11 and 12 of the Act of 1961 shall apply to carriage to which Schedules 2 and 3 to this Order apply as if the references therein to the Convention as amended and the Montreal Convention and articles thereof were omitted and the reference to the Convention and articles thereof were references to the 1955 amended Convention and articles thereof as applied by this Order.

(3) Section 3(1) of the Act of 1962 shall apply to carriage to which Schedules 2 and 3 to this Order apply as if the reference therein to article VI in the Schedule to that Act was a reference to that article as applied by this Order.

[2311]

NOTES

Commencement: 6 August 2004.

8 Gratuitous carriage by the Crown

(1) Subject to paragraph 2, the Acts of 1961 and 1962, and this Order, shall apply to gratuitous carriage by the Crown as they apply to carriage by the Crown for reward.

(2) The Acts of 1961 and 1962, and this Order, shall not apply to gratuitous carriage by the Crown where that carriage is carriage of members of Her Majesty's naval, military or air forces undertaken during a time of actual or imminent hostilities or of severe international tension or of great national emergency.

[2312]

NOTES

Commencement: 6 August 2004.

9 Revocation

The Orders specified in Schedule 4 are hereby revoked.

[2313]

NOTES

Commencement: 6 August 2004.

SCHEDULE 1
NON-INTERNATIONAL CARRIAGE

Article 4

PART I
APPLICATION OF THE MONTREAL CONVENTION

The Montreal Convention as set out in Schedule 1B to the 1961 Act shall apply in respect of carriage described in article 4 of this Order subject to the following exceptions, adaptations and modifications—

(1) For "Convention" wherever it appears, there shall be substituted "Schedule".

(2) In Article 1.1 the word "international" shall be omitted.

(3) Article 1.2 and 1.3 shall not apply.

(4) Save for article 3.3 and 3.5 Chapter II shall not apply.

(5) In Article 22.4 for "or, if they were not issued, by the same record preserved by the other means referred to in paragraph 2 of Article 4," substitute "or any alternative record,".

(6) In Article 23.1 the second and third sentences shall be omitted.

(7) For Article 23.2 the following shall be substituted—

"The value on a particular day of one Special Drawing Right shall be treated as equal to such a sum in sterling as the International Monetary Fund has fixed as being the equivalent of one Special Drawing Right—

(a) for that day; or

(b) if no sum has been fixed for that day, for the last day before that day for which a sum has been so fixed.".

(8) For Article 23.3 the following shall be substituted—

"A certificate given by or on behalf of the Treasury stating—

(a) that a particular sum in sterling has been fixed by the International Monetary Fund as referred to in paragraph 2 for a particular day; or

(b) that no sum has been so fixed for a particular day and that a particular sum in sterling has been so fixed for a day which is the last day for which a sum has been so fixed before the particular day,

shall be conclusive evidence of those matters for the purposes of this article; and a document purporting to be such a certificate shall in any proceedings be received in evidence and, unless the contrary is proved, be deemed to be such a certificate.".

(9) Article 24 shall be omitted.

(10) In Article 31.1 the words from "and" to the end shall be omitted.

(11) Article 33 shall not apply.

(12) Article 34.2 shall not apply.

(13) In Article 36.1 the words from "and" where it first occurs to "Article 1" shall be omitted.

(14) In Article 42 the second sentence shall not apply.

(15) In Article 45 the second sentence shall not apply.

(16) Article 46 shall not apply.

(17) In Article 49 the words from "whether" to "jurisdiction" shall be omitted.

(18) Articles 50 and 51 shall not apply.

(19) Articles 53 to 57 shall not apply.

[2314]

NOTES

Commencement: 6 August 2004.

PART II

For convenience of reference the Montreal Convention, with the exceptions, adaptations and modifications made by this Schedule is here set out:

Non-international Carriage

CHAPTER I
GENERAL PROVISIONS

Article 1—Scope of Application

1 This Schedule applies to all carriage of persons, baggage or cargo performed by aircraft for reward. It applies equally to gratuitous carriage by aircraft performed by an air transport undertaking.

4 This Schedule applies also to carriage as set out in Chapter V, subject to the terms contained therein.

Article 2—Carriage Performed by State and Carriage of Postal Items

1 This Schedule applies to carriage performed by the State or by legally constituted public bodies provided it falls within the conditions laid down in Article 1.

2 In the carriage of postal items, the carrier shall be liable only to the relevant postal administration in accordance with the rules applicable to the relationship between the carriers and the postal administrations.

3 Except as provided in paragraph 2 of this Article, the provisions of this Schedule shall not apply to the carriage of postal items.

CHAPTER II
DOCUMENTATION AND DUTIES OF THE PARTIES RELATING TO THE CARRIAGE OF PASSENGERS, BAGGAGE AND CARGO

Article 3—Passengers and Baggage

3 The carrier shall deliver to the passenger a baggage identification tag for each piece of checked baggage.

5 Non-compliance with the provisions of the foregoing paragraphs shall not affect the existence or the validity of the contract of carriage, which shall, nonetheless be subject to the rules of this Schedule including those relating to limitation of liability.

CHAPTER III
LIABILITY OF THE CARRIER AND EXTENT OF COMPENSATION FOR DAMAGE

Article 17—Death and Injury of Passengers—Damage to Baggage

1 The carrier is liable for damage sustained in case of death or bodily injury of a passenger upon condition only that the accident which caused the death or injury took place on board the aircraft or in the course of any of the operations of embarking or disembarking.

2 The carrier is liable for damage sustained in case of destruction or loss of, or of damage to, checked baggage upon condition only that the event which caused the destruction, loss or damage took place on board the aircraft or during any period within which the checked baggage was in the charge of the carrier. However, the carrier is not liable if and to the extent that the damage resulted from the inherent defect, quality or vice of the baggage. In the case of unchecked baggage, including personal items, the carrier is liable if the damage resulted from its fault or that of its servants or agents.

3 If the carrier admits the loss of the checked baggage, or if the checked baggage has not arrived at the expiration of twenty-one days after the date on which it ought to have arrived, the passenger is entitled to enforce against the carrier the rights which flow from the contract of carriage.

4 Unless otherwise specified, in this Schedule the term "baggage" means both checked baggage and unchecked baggage.

Article 18—Damage to Cargo

1 The carrier is liable for damage sustained in the event of the destruction or loss of, or damage to, cargo upon condition only that the event which caused the damage so sustained took place during the carriage by air.

2 However, the carrier is not liable if and to the extent it proves that the destruction, or loss of, or damage to, the cargo resulted from one or more of the following:

(a) inherent defect, quality or vice of that cargo;
(b) defective packing of that cargo performed by a person other than the carrier or its servants or agents;
(c) an act of war or an armed conflict;
(d) an act of public authority carried out in connection with the entry, exit or transit of the cargo.

3 The carriage by air within the meaning of paragraph 1 of this Article comprises the period during which the cargo is in the charge of the carrier.

4 The period of the carriage by air does not extend to any carriage by land, by sea or by inland waterway performed outside an airport. If, however, such carriage takes place in the performance of a contract for carriage by air, for the purpose of loading, delivery or transhipment, any damage is presumed, subject to proof to the contrary, to have been the result of an event which took place during the carriage by air. If a carrier, without the consent of the consignor, substitutes carriage by another mode of transport for the whole or part of a carriage intended by the agreement between the parties to be carriage by air, such carriage by another mode of transport is deemed to be within the period of carriage by air.

Article 19—Delay

The carrier is liable for damage occasioned by delay in the carriage by air of passengers, baggage or cargo. Nevertheless, the carrier shall not be liable for damage occasioned by delay if it proves that it and its servants and agents took all measures that could reasonably be required to avoid the damage or that it was impossible for it or them to take such measures.

Article 20—Exoneration

If the carrier proves that the damage was caused or contributed to by the negligence or other wrongful act or omission of the person claiming compensation, or the person from whom he or she derives his or her rights, the carrier shall be wholly or partly exonerated from its liability to the claimant to the extent that such negligence or wrongful act or omission caused or contributed to the damage. When by reason of death or injury of a passenger compensation is claimed by a person other than the passenger, the carrier shall likewise be wholly or partly exonerated from its liability to the extent that it proves that the damage was caused or contributed to by the negligence or other wrongful act or omission of that passenger. This Article applies to all the liability provisions in this Schedule, including paragraph 1 of Article 21.

Article 21—Compensation in Case of Death or Injury of Passengers

1 For damages arising under paragraph 1 of Article 17 not exceeding 100,000 Special Drawing Rights for each passenger, the carrier shall not be able to exclude or limit its liability.

2 The carrier shall not be liable for damages arising under paragraph 1 of Article 17 to the extent that they exceed for each passenger 100,000 Special Drawing Rights if the carrier proves that:

(a) such damage was not due to the negligence or other wrongful act or omission of the carrier or its servants or agents; or
(b) such damage was solely due to the negligence or other wrongful act or ommission of a third party.

Article 22—Limits of Liability in Relation to Delay, Baggage and Cargo

1 In the case of damage caused by delay as specified in Article 19 in the carriage of persons, the liability of the carrier for each passenger is limited to 4,150 Special Drawing Rights.

2 In the carriage of baggage, the liability of the carrier in the case of destruction, loss, damage or delay is limited to 1,000 Special Drawing Rights for each passenger unless the passenger has made, at the time when the checked baggage was handed over to the carrier, a special declaration of interest in delivery at destination and has paid a supplementary sum if the case so requires. In that case the carrier will be liable to pay a sum not exceeding the declared sum, unless it proves that the sum is greater than the passenger's actual interest in delivery at destination.

3 In the carriage of cargo, the liability of the carrier in the case of destruction, loss, damage or delay is limited to a sum of 17 Special Drawing Rights per kilogramme, unless the

consignor has made, at the time when the package was handed over to the carrier, a special declaration of interest in delivery at destination and has paid a supplementary sum if the case so requires. In that case the carrier will be liable to pay a sum not exceeding the declared sum, unless it proves that the sum is greater than the consignor's actual interest in delivery at destination.

4 In the case of destruction, loss, damage or delay of part of the cargo, or of any object contained therein, the weight to be taken into consideration in determining the amount to which the carrier's liability is limited shall be only the total weight of the package or packages concerned. Nevertheless, when the destruction, loss, damage or delay of a part of the cargo, or of an object contained therein, affects the value of other packages covered by the same air waybill, or the same receipt or, if they were not issued, by the same record preserved by the other means referred to in paragraph 2 of Article 4, the total weight of such package or packages shall also be taken into consideration in determining the limit of liability.

5 The foregoing provisions of paragraphs 1 and 2 of this Article shall not apply if it is proved that the damage resulted from an act or omission of the carrier, its servants or agents, done with intent to cause damage or recklessly and with knowledge that damage would probably result; provided that, in the case of such act or omission of a servant or agent, it is also proved that such servant or agent was acting within the scope of its employment.

6 The limits prescribed in Article 21 and in this Article shall not prevent the court from awarding, in accordance with its own law, in addition, the whole or part of the court costs and of the other expenses of the litigation incurred by the plaintiff, including interest. The foregoing provision shall not apply if the amount of the damages awarded, excluding court costs and other expenses of the litigation, does not exceed the sum which the carrier has offered in writing to the plaintiff within a period of six months from the date of the occurrence causing the damage, or before the commencement of the action, if that is later.

Article 23—Conversion of Monetary Units

1 The sums mentioned in terms of Special Drawing Right in this Schedule shall be deemed to refer to the Special Drawing Right as defined by the International Monetary Fund. Conversion of the sums into national currencies shall, in case of judicial proceedings, be made according to the value of such currencies in terms of the Special Drawing Right at the date of the judgement.

2 The value on a particular day of one Special Drawing Right shall be treated as equal to such a sum in sterling as the International Monetary Fund have fixed as being the equivalent of one Special Drawing Right—

(a) for that day; or

(b) if no sum has been fixed for that day, for the last day before that day for which a sum has been so fixed.

3 A certificate given by or on behalf of the Treasury stating—

(a) that a particular sum in sterling has been fixed by the International Monetary Fund as referred to in paragraph 2 for a particular day; or

(b) that no sum has been so fixed for a particular day and that a particular sum in sterling has been so fixed for a day which is the last day for which a sum has been so fixed before the particular day,

shall be conclusive evidence of those matters for the purposes of this article; and a document purporting to be such a certificate shall in any proceedings be received in evidence and, unless the contrary is proved, be deemed to be such a certificate.

Article 25—Stipulation on Limits

A carrier may stipulate that the contract of carriage shall be subject to higher limits of liability than those provided for in this Schedule or to no limits of liability whatsoever.

Article 26—Invalidity of Contractual Provisions

Any provision tending to relieve the carrier of liability or to fix a lower limit than that which is laid down in this Schedule shall be null and void, but the nullity of any such provision does not involve the nullity of the whole contract, which shall remain subject to the provisions of this Schedule.

Article 27—Freedom to Contract

Nothing contained in this Schedule shall prevent the carrier from refusing to enter into any contract of carriage, from waiving any defences available under the Schedule, or from laying down conditions which do not conflict with the provisions of this Schedule.

Article 28—Advance Payments

In the case of aircraft accidents resulting in death or injury of passengers, the carrier shall, if required by its national law, make advance payments without delay to a natural person or persons who are entitled to claim compensation in order to meet the immediate economic needs of such persons. Such advance payments shall not constitute a recognition of liability and may be offset against any amounts subsequently paid as damages by the carrier.

Article 29—Basis of Claims

In the carriage of passengers, baggage and cargo, any action for damages, however founded, whether under this Schedule or in contract or in tort or otherwise, can only be brought subject to the conditions and such limits of liability as are set out in this Schedule without prejudice to the question as to who are the persons who have the right to bring suit and what are their respective rights. In any such action, punitive, exemplary or any other non-compensatory damages shall not be recoverable.

Article 30—Servants, Agents—Aggregation of Claims

1 If an action is brought against a servant or agent of the carrier arising out of damage to which the Schedule relates, such servant or agent, if they prove that they acted within the scope of their employment, shall be entitled to avail themselves of the conditions and limits of liability which the carrier itself is entitled to invoke under this Schedule.

2 The aggregate of the amounts recoverable from the carrier, its servants and agents, in that case, shall not exceed the said limits.

3 Save in respect of the carriage of cargo, the provisions of paragraphs 1 and 2 of this Article shall not apply if it is proved that the damage resulted from an act or omission of the servant or agent done with intent to cause damage or recklessly and with knowledge that damage would probably result.

Article 31—Timely Notice of Complaints

1 Receipt by the person entitled to delivery of checked baggage or cargo without complaint is *prima facie* evidence that the same has been delivered in good condition.

2 In the case of damage, the person entitled to delivery must complain to the carrier forthwith after the discovery of the damage, and, at the latest, within seven days from the date of receipt in the case of checked baggage and fourteen days from the date of receipt in the case of cargo. In the case of delay, the complaint must be made at the latest within twenty-one days from the date on which the baggage or cargo have been placed at his or her disposal.

3 Every complaint must be made in writing and given or dispatched within the times aforesaid.

4 If no complaint is made within the times aforesaid, no action shall lie against the carrier, save in the case of fraud on its part.

Article 32—Death of Person Liable

In the case of the death of the person liable, an action for damages lies in accordance with the terms of this Schedule against those legally representing his or her estate.

Article 34—Arbitration

1 Subject to the provisions of this Article, the parties to the contract of carriage for cargo may stipulate that any dispute relating to the liability of the carrier under this Schedule shall be settled by arbitration. Such agreement shall be in writing.

3 The arbitrator or arbitration tribunal shall apply the provisions of this Schedule.

4 The provisions of paragraphs 2 and 3 of this Article shall be deemed to be part of every arbitration clause or agreement, and any term of such clause or agreement which is inconsistent therewith shall be null and void.

Article 35—Limitation of Actions

1 The right to damages shall be extinguished if an action is not brought within a period of two years, reckoned from the date of arrival at the destination, or from the date on which the aircraft ought to have arrived, or from the date on which the carriage stopped.

2 The method of calculating that period shall be determined by the law of the court seised of the case.

Article 36—Successive Carriage

1 In the case of carriage to be performed by various successive carriers, each carrier which accepts passengers, baggage or cargo is subject to the rules set out in this Schedule and is deemed to be one of the parties to the contract of carriage in so far as the contract deals with that part of the carriage which is performed under its supervision.

2 In the case of carriage of this nature, the passenger or any person entitled to compensation in respect of him or her can take action only against the carrier which performed the carriage during which the accident or the delay occurred, save in the case where, by express agreement, the first carrier has assumed liability for the whole journey.

3 As regards baggage or cargo, the passenger or consignor will have a right of action against the first carrier, and the passenger or consignee who is entitled to delivery will have a right of action against the last carrier, and further, each may take action against the carrier which performed the carriage during which the destruction, loss, damage or delay took place. These carriers will be jointly and severally liable to the passenger or to the consignor or consignee.

Article 37—Right of Recourse against Third Parties

Nothing in this Schedule shall prejudice the question whether a person liable for damage in accordance with its provisions has a right of recourse against any other person.

CHAPTER IV
COMBINED CARRIAGE

Article 38—Combined Carriage

1 In the case of combined carriage performed partly by air and partly by any other mode of carriage, the provisions of this Schedule shall, subject to paragraph 4 of Article 18, apply only to the carriage by air, provided that the carriage by air falls within the terms of Article 1.

2 Nothing in this Schedule shall prevent the parties in the case of combined carriage from inserting in the document of air carriage conditions relating to other modes of carriage, provided that the provisions of this Schedule are observed as regards the carriage by air.

CHAPTER V
CARRIAGE BY AIR PERFORMED BY A PERSON OTHER THAN THE CONTRACTING CARRIER

Article 39—Contracting Carrier—Actual Carrier

The provisions of this Chapter apply when a person (hereinafter referred to as "the contracting carrier") as a principal makes a contract of carriage governed by this Schedule with a passenger or consignor or with a person acting on behalf of the passenger or consignor, and another person (hereinafter referred to as "the actual carrier") performs, by virtue of authority from the contracting carrier, the whole or part of the carriage, but is not with respect to such part a successive carrier within the meaning of this Schedule. Such authority shall be presumed in the absence of proof to the contrary.

Article 40—Respective Liability of Contracting and Actual Carriers

If an actual carrier performs the whole or part of carriage which, according to the contract referred to in Article 39, is governed by this Schedule, both the contracting carrier and the actual carrier shall, except as otherwise provided in this Chapter, be subject to the rules of this Schedule, the former for the whole of the carriage contemplated in the contract, the latter solely for the carriage which it performs.

Article 41—Mutual Liability

1 The acts and omissions of the actual carrier and of its servants and agents acting within the scope of their employment shall, in relation to the carriage performed by the actual carrier, be deemed to be also those of the contracting carrier.

2 The acts and omissions of the contracting carrier and of its servants and agents acting within the scope of their employment shall, in relation to the carriage performed by the actual carrier, be deemed to be also those of the actual carrier. Nevertheless, no such act or omission shall subject the actual carrier to liability exceeding the amounts referred to in Articles 21, 22, 23 and 24. Any special agreement under which the contracting carrier assumes obligations not imposed by this Schedule or any waiver of rights or defences conferred by this Schedule or any special declaration of interest in delivery at destination contemplated in Article 22 shall not affect the actual carrier unless agreed to by it.

Article 42—Addressee of Complaints and Instructions

Any complaint to be made or instruction to be given under this Schedule to the carrier shall have the same effect whether addressed to the contracting carrier or to the actual carrier.

Article 43—Servants and Agents

In relation to the carriage performed by the actual carrier, any servant or agent of that carrier or of the contracting carrier shall, if they prove that they acted within the scope of their employment, be entitled to avail themselves of the conditions and limits of liability which are applicable under this Schedule to the carrier whose servant or agent they are, unless it is proved that they acted in a manner that prevents the limits of liability from being invoked in accordance with this Schedule.

Article 44—Aggregation of Damages

In relation to the carriage performed by the actual carrier, the aggregate of the amounts recoverable from that carrier and the contracting carrier, and from their servants and agents acting within the scope of their employment, shall not exceed the highest amount which could be awarded against either the contracting carrier or the actual carrier under this Schedule, but none of the persons mentioned shall be liable for a sum in excess of the limit applicable to that person.

Article 45—Addressee of Claims

In relation to the carriage performed by the actual carrier, an action for damages may be brought, at the option of the plaintiff, against that carrier or the contracting carrier, or against both together or separately.

Article 47—Invalidity of Contractual Provisions

Any contractual provision tending to relieve the contracting carrier or the actual carrier of liability under this Chapter or to fix a lower limit than that which is applicable according to this Chapter shall be null and void, but the nullity of any such provision does not involve the nullity of the whole contract, which shall remain subject to the provisions of this Chapter.

Article 48—Mutual Relations of Contracting and Actual Carriers

Except as provided in Article 45, nothing in this Chapter shall affect the rights and obligations of the carriers between themselves, including any right of recourse or indemnification.

CHAPTER VI
OTHER PROVISIONS

Article 49—Mandatory Application

Any clause contained in the contract of carriage and all special agreements entered into before the damage occurred by which the parties purport to infringe the rules laid down by this Schedule, whether by deciding the law to be applied, or by altering the rules as to jurisdiction, shall be null and void.

Article 52—Definition of Days

The expression "days" when used in this Schedule means calendar days, not working days.

[2315]

NOTES

Commencement: 6 August 2004.

SCHEDULE 2

INTERNATIONAL CARRIAGE UNDER THE UNAMENDED WARSAW CONVENTION

Article 5

PART I

1 The 1955 amended Convention and the Guadalajara Convention shall apply in respect of carriage which is "international carriage" as defined in paragraph 2 of this part of this Schedule, with the exceptions, adaptations and modifications set forth in paragraphs 3 and 4.

2 For the purposes of Article 5 of this Order and of this Schedule "international carriage" shall have the meaning assigned to it by paragraph 3(2) of this part of this Schedule.

3 The 1955 amended Convention shall apply to international carriage as aforesaid, with the following exceptions, adaptations and modifications—

(1) For "Convention", wherever it appears, there shall be substituted "Schedule".

(2) For Article 1(2) there shall be substituted the following—

""International carriage" means any carriage in which, according to the contract made by the parties, the place of departure and the place of destination, whether or not there be a break in the carriage or a transhipment, are situated either within the territories of two States Parties to the Convention for the Unification of Certain Rules relating to International Carriage by Air signed at Warsaw on behalf of His Majesty on 12th October 1929, or within the territory of a single such State, if there is an agreed stopping place within the territory subject to the sovereignty, suzerainty, mandate or authority of another State, even though that State is not a party to the said Convention of 1929.".

(3) The following shall be substituted for Article 1(3)—

"(3) A carriage to be performed by several successive air carriers is deemed for the purposes of this schedule, to be one undivided carriage, if it has been regarded by the parties as a single operation, whether it had been agreed upon under the form of a single contract or of a series of contracts, and it does not lose its international character merely because one contract or a series of contracts is to be performed entirely within a territory subject to the sovereignty, suzerainty, mandate or authority of the same High Contracting Party."

(4) The following shall be substituted for Article 2—

"(1) This Schedule applies to carriage performed by the State, not being a State which has availed itself of the Additional Protocol to the Warsaw Convention, or by legally constituted public bodies, provided it falls within the conditions laid down in Article 1.

(2) This Schedule does not apply to carriage performed under the terms of any international postal Convention.".

(5) The following shall be substituted for Article 3—

"(1) For the carriage of passengers the carrier must deliver a passenger ticket which shall contain the following particulars—

(a) the place and date of issue;

(b) the place of departure and of destination;

(c) the agreed stopping places, provided that the carrier may reserve the right to alter the stopping places in case of necessity, and that if he exercises that right, the alteration shall not have the effect of depriving the carriage of its international character;

(d) the name and address of the carrier or carriers;
(e) a statement that the carriage is subject to the rules relating to liability established by the Warsaw Convention.

(2) The absence, irregularity or loss of the passenger ticket does not affect the existence or the validity of the contract of carriage, which shall none the less be subject to the rules of this Schedule. Nevertheless, if the carrier accepts a passenger without a passenger ticket having been delivered he shall not be entitled to avail himself of those provisions of this Schedule which exclude or limit his liability.".

(6) The following shall be substituted for Article 4—

"(1) For the carriage of baggage, other than small personal objects of which the passenger takes charge himself, the carrier must deliver a baggage check.

(2) The baggage check shall be made out in duplicate, one part for the passenger and the other part for the carrier.

(3) The baggage check shall contain the following particulars—
(a) the place and date of issue;
(b) the place of departure and of destination;
(c) the name and address of the carrier or carriers;
(d) the number of the passenger ticket;
(e) a statement that delivery of the baggage will be made to the bearer of the baggage check;
(f) the number and weight of the packages;
(g) the amount of the value declared in accordance with Article 22(2);
(h) a statement that the carriage is subject to the rules relating to liability established by the Warsaw Convention.

(4) The absence, irregularity or loss of the baggage check does not affect the existence or the validity of the contract of carriage, which shall none the less be subject to the rules of this Schedule. Nevertheless, if the carrier accepts baggage without a baggage check having been delivered, or if the baggage check does not contain the particulars set out at (d), (f) and (h) above, the carrier shall not be entitled to avail himself of those provisions of this Schedule which exclude or limit his liability".

(7) The following shall be substituted for Article 6(3)—

"(3) The carrier shall sign on acceptance of the cargo.".

(8) The following shall be substituted for Article 8—

"The air waybill shall contain the following particulars—
(a) the place and date of its execution;
(b) the place of departure and of destination;
(c) the agreed stopping places, provided that the carrier may reserve the right to alter the stopping places in case of necessity, and that if he exercises that right the alteration shall not have the effect of depriving the carriage of its international character;
(d) the name and address of the consignor;
(e) the name and address of the first carrier;
(f) the name and address of the consignee, if the case so requires;
(g) the nature of the cargo;
(h) the number of the packages, the method of packing and the particular marks or numbers upon them;
(i) the weight, the quantity and the volume or dimensions of the cargo;
(j) the apparent condition of the cargo and of the packing;
(k) the freight, if it has been agreed upon, the date and place of payment, and the person who is to pay it;
(l) if the cargo is sent for payment of delivery, the price of the cargo, and, if the case so requires, the amount of the expenses incurred;
(m) the amount of the value declared in accordance with Article 22 (2);
(n) the number of parts of the air waybill;
(o) the documents handed to the carrier to accompany the air waybill;
(p) the time fixed for the completion of the carriage and a brief note of the route to be followed, if these matters have been agreed upon;
(q) a statement that the carriage is subject to the rules relating to liability established by the Warsaw Convention.".

(9) The following shall be substituted for Article 9—

"If the carrier accepts cargo without an air waybill having been made out or if the air waybill does not contain all the particulars set out in Article 8 (a) to (i) inclusive and (q), the carrier shall not be entitled to avail himself of the provisions of this Schedule which exclude or limit his liability.".

(10) The following shall be substituted for Article 10(2)—

"(2) The consignor will be liable for all damage suffered by the carrier or any other person by reason of the irregularity, incorrectness or incompleteness of the said particulars and statements.".

(11) Article 15 (3) shall not apply.

(12) The following shall be inserted as Article 20(2):

"(2) In the carriage of cargo and baggage the carrier is not liable if he proves that the damage was occasioned by negligent pilotage or negligence in the handling of the aircraft or in navigation and that, in all other respects, he and his servants or agents have taken all necessary measures to avoid the damage."

(13) The following shall be substituted for Article 22—

"(1) In the carriage of passengers the liability of the carrier for each passenger is limited to the sum of 125,000 francs. Where, in accordance with the law of the Court seised of the case, damages may be awarded in the form of periodical payments, the equivalent capital value of the said payments shall not exceed 125,000 francs. Nevertheless, by special contract, the carrier and the passenger may agree to a higher limit of liability.

(2) In the carriage of registered baggage and of cargo, the liability of the carrier is limited to a sum of 250 francs per kilogramme, unless the consignor has made, at the time when the package was handed over to the carrier, a special declaration of the value at delivery and has paid a supplementary sum if the case so requires. In that case the carrier will be liable to pay a sum not exceeding the declared sum, unless he proves that that sum is greater than the actual value to the consignor at delivery.

(3) As regards objects of which the passenger takes charge himself the liability of the carrier is limited to 5,000 francs per passenger.

(4) The sums mentioned above shall be deemed to refer to the French franc consisting of 65 milligrammes gold of millesimal fineness 900. These sums may be converted into any national currency in round figures.".

(14) Article 23 (2) shall not apply.

(15) The following shall be substituted for Article 25—

"(1) The carrier shall not be entitled to avail himself of the provisions of this Schedule which exclude or limit his liability, if the damage is caused by his wilful misconduct or by such default on his part as, in accordance with the law of the court seised of the case, is considered to be equivalent to wilful misconduct.

(2) Similarly the carrier shall not be entitled to avail himself of the said provisions, if the damage is caused as aforesaid by any servant or agent of the carrier acting within the scope of his employment.".

(16) Article 25A shall not apply.

(17) The following shall be substituted for Article 26(2)—

"(2) In the case of damage, the person entitled to delivery must complain to the carrier forthwith after the discovery of the damage, and, at the latest, within three days from the date of receipt in the case of baggage and seven days from the date of receipt in the case of cargo. In the case of delay the complaint must be made at the latest within fourteen days from the date on which the baggage or cargo has been placed at his disposal.".

(18) In Article 28 (1), after "High Contracting Parties" there shall be added "to the Warsaw Convention".

(19) The following shall be substituted for Article 34—

"This Schedule does not apply to international carriage by air performed by way of experimental trial by air navigation undertakings with the view to the establishment of a regular line of air navigation, nor does it apply to carriage performed in extraordinary circumstances outside the normal scope of an air carrier's business.".

(20) Articles 36 and 40A shall not apply.

4 The Guadalajara Convention shall apply to international carriage within the meaning of this Schedule, with the following exceptions, adaptations and modifications.

(1) For "this Convention" wherever it appears there shall be substituted "the Guadalajara Convention as applied by this Schedule".

(2) In Article 1, the following shall be added as paragraph (a)—

""the Warsaw Convention" means the 1955 amended Convention as applied by this Schedule.".

[2316]

NOTES

Commencement: 6 August 2004.

PART II

For convenience of reference the 1955 amended Convention and the Guadalajara Convention, with the exceptions, adaptations and modifications by this Schedule, are here set out:

A *The 1955 amended Warsaw Convention, as applied by Schedule 2*

INTERNATIONAL CARRIAGE UNDER THE UNAMENDED WARSAW CONVENTION

CHAPTER I
SCOPE—DEFINITIONS

Article 1

(1) This Schedule applies to all international carriage of persons, baggage or cargo performed by aircraft for reward. It applies equally to gratuitous carriage by aircraft performed by an air transport undertaking.

(2) "International carriage" means any carriage in which, according to the contract made by the parties, the place of departure and the place of destination, whether or not there be a break in the carriage or a transhipment, are situated either within the territories of two States Parties to the Convention for the Unification of Certain Rules relating to the International Carriage by Air signed at Warsaw on behalf of His Majesty on 12th October 1929, or within the territory of a single such State, if there is an agreed stopping place within the territory subject to the sovereignty, suzerainty, mandate or authority of another State, even though that State is not a party to the said Convention of 1929.

(3) A carriage to be performed by several successive air carriers is deemed, for the purposes of this Schedule, to be one undivided carriage, if it has been regarded by the parties as a single operation, whether it had been agreed upon under the form of a single contract or of a series of contracts, and it does not lose its international character merely because one contract or a series of contracts is to be performed entirely within a territory subject to the sovereignty, suzerainty, mandate or authority of the same High Contracting Party.

Article 2

(1) This Schedule applies to carriage performed by the State, not being a State which has availed itself of the Additional Protocol to the Warsaw Convention, or by legally constituted public bodies, provided it falls within the conditions laid down in Article 1.

(2) This Schedule does not apply to carriage performed under the terms of any international postal Convention.

CHAPTER II
DOCUMENTS OF CARRIAGE

SECTION I—PASSENGER, TICKET

Article 3

(1) For the carriage of passengers the carrier must deliver a passenger ticket which shall contain the following particulars—

(a) the place and date of issue;
(b) the place of departure and of destination;
(c) the agreed stopping places, provided that the carrier may reserve the right to alter the stopping places in case of necessity, and that if he exercises that right, the alteration shall not have the effect of depriving the carriage of its international character;
(d) the name and address of the carrier or carriers;
(e) a statement that the carriage is subject to the rules relating to liability established by the Warsaw Convention.

(2) The absence, irregularity or loss of the passenger ticket does not affect the existence or the validity of the contract of carriage, which shall none the less be subject to the rules of this Schedule. Nevertheless, if the carrier accepts a passenger without a passenger ticket having been delivered he shall not be entitled to avail himself of those provisions of this Schedule which exclude or limit his liability.

SECTION 2—BAGGAGE CHECK

Article 4

(1) For the carriage of baggage, other than small personal objects of which the passenger takes charge himself, the carrier must deliver a baggage check.

(2) The baggage check shall be made out in duplicate, one part for the passenger and the other part for the carrier.

(3) The baggage check shall contain the following particulars—

(a) the place and date of issue;
(b) the place of departure and of destination;
(c) the name and address of the carrier or carriers;
(d) the number of the passenger ticket;
(e) a statement that delivery of the baggage will be made to the bearer of the baggage check;
(f) the number and weight of the packages;
(g) the amount of the value declared in accordance with Article 22(2);
(h) a statement that the carriage is subject to the rules relating to liability established by the Warsaw Convention.

(4) The absence, irregularity or loss of the baggage check does not affect the existence or the validity of the contract of carriage, which shall none the less be subject to the rules of this Schedule. Nevertheless, if the carrier accepts baggage without a baggage check having been delivered, or if the baggage check does not contain the particulars set out at (d), (f) and (h) above, the carrier shall not be entitled to avail himself of those provisions of this Schedule which exclude or limit his liability.

SECTION 3—AIR WAYBILL

Article 5

(1) Every carrier of cargo has the right to require the consignor to make out and hand over to him a document called an "air waybill"; every consignor has the right to require the carrier to accept this document.

(2) The absence, irregularity or loss of this document does not affect the existence or the validity of the contract of carriage which shall, subject to the provisions of Article 9, be none the less governed by the rules of this Schedule.

Article 6

(1) The air waybill shall be made out by the consignor in three original parts and be handed over with the cargo.

(2) The first part shall be marked "for the carrier", and shall be signed by the consignor. The second part shall be marked "for the consignee"; it shall be signed by the consignor and by the carrier and shall accompany the cargo. The third part shall be signed by the carrier and handed by him to the consignor after the cargo has been accepted.

(3) The carrier shall sign on acceptance of the cargo.

(4) The signature of the carrier may be stamped; that of the consignor may be printed or stamped.

(5) If, at the request of the consignor, the carrier makes out the air waybill, he shall be deemed, subject to proof to the contrary, to have done so on behalf of the consignor.

Article 7

The carrier of cargo has the right to require the consignor to make out separate waybills when there is more than one package.

Article 8

The air waybill shall contain the following particulars—

(a) the place and date of its execution;
(b) the place of departure and of destination;
(c) the agreed stopping places, provided that the carrier may reserve the right to alter the stopping places in case of necessity, and that if he exercises that right the alteration shall not have the effect of depriving the carriage of its international character;
(d) the name and address of the consignor;
(e) the name and address of the first carrier;
(f) the name and address of the consignee, if the case so requires;
(g) the nature of the cargo;
(h) the number of the packages, the method of packing and the particular marks or numbers upon them;
(i) the weight, the quantity and the volume or dimensions of the cargo;
(j) the apparent condition of the cargo and of the packing;
(k) the freight, if it has been agreed upon, the date and place of payment, and the person who is to pay it;
(l) if the cargo is sent for payment on delivery, the price of the cargo, and, if the case so requires, the amount of the expenses incurred;
(m) the amount of the value declared in accordance with Article 22(2);
(n) the number of parts of the air waybill;
(o) the documents handed to the carrier to accompany the air waybill;
(p) the time fixed for the completion of the carriage and a brief note of the route to be followed, if these matters have been agreed upon;
(q) a statement that the carriage is subject to the rules relating to liability established by the Warsaw Convention.

Article 9

If the carrier accepts cargo without an air waybill having been made out, or if the air waybill does not contain all the particulars set out in Article 8 (a) to (i) inclusive and (q), the carrier shall not be entitled to avail himself of the provisions of this Schedule which exclude or limit his liability.

Article 10

(1) The consignor is responsible for the correctness of the particulars and statements relating to the cargo which he inserts in the air waybill.

(2) The consignor will be liable for all damage suffered by the carrier or any other person by reason of the irregularity incorrectness or incompleteness of the said particulars and statements.

Article 11

(1) The air waybill is *prima facie* evidence of the conclusion of the contract, of the receipt of the cargo and of the conditions of carriage.

(2) The statements in the air waybill relating to the weight, dimensions and packing of the cargo, as well as those relating to the number of packages, are *prima facie* evidence of the facts stated; those relating to the quantity, volume and condition of the cargo do not constitute

evidence against the carrier except so far as they both have been, and are stated in the air waybill to have been, checked by him in the presence of the consignor, or relate to the apparent condition of the cargo.

Article 12

(1) Subject to his liability to carry out all his obligations under the contract of carriage, the consignor has the right to dispose of the cargo by withdrawing it at the aerodrome of departure or destination, or by stopping it in the course of the journey on any landing, or by calling for it to be delivered at the place of destination or in the course of the journey to a person other than the consignee named in the air waybill, or by requiring it to be returned to the aerodrome of departure. He must not exercise this right of disposition in such a way as to prejudice the carrier or other consignors and he must repay any expenses occasioned by the exercise of this right.

(2) If it is impossible to carry out the orders of the consignor the carrier must so inform him forthwith.

(3) If the carrier obeys the orders of the consignor for the disposition of the cargo without requiring the production of the part of the air waybill delivered to the latter, he will be liable, without prejudice to his right of recovery from the consignor, for any damage which may be caused thereby to any person who is lawfully in possession of that part of the air waybill.

(4) The right conferred on the consignor ceases at the moment when that of the consignee begins in accordance with Article 13. Nevertheless, if the consignee declines to accept the waybill or the cargo, or if he cannot be communicated with, the consignor resumes his right of disposition.

Article 13

(1) Except in the circumstances set out in the preceding Article, the consignee is entitled, on arrival of the cargo at the place of destination, to require the carrier to hand over to him the air waybill and to deliver the cargo to him, on payment of the charges due and on complying with the conditions of carriage set out in the air waybill.

(2) Unless it is otherwise agreed, it is the duty of the carrier to give notice to the consignee as soon as the cargo arrives.

(3) If the carrier admits the loss of the cargo, or if the cargo has not arrived at the expiration of seven days after the date on which it ought to have arrived, the consignee is entitled to put into force against the carrier the rights which flow from the contract of carriage.

Article 14

The consignor and the consignee can respectively enforce all the rights given them by Articles 12 and 13, each in his own name, whether he is acting in his own interest or in the interest of another, provided that he carries out the obligations imposed by the contract.

Article 15

(1) Articles 12, 13 and 14 do not affect either the relations of the consignor or the consignee with each other or the mutual relations of third parties whose rights are derived either from the consignor or from the consignee.

(2) The provisions of Articles 12, 13 and 14 can only be varied by express provision in the air waybill.

Article 16

(1) The consignor must furnish such information and attach to the air waybill such documents as are necessary to meet the formalities of customs, octroi or police before the cargo can be delivered to the consignee. The consignor is liable to the carrier for any damage occasioned by the absence, insufficiency or irregularity of any such information or documents, unless the damage is due to the fault of the carrier or his servants or agents.

(2) The carrier is under no obligation to enquire into the correctness or sufficiency of such information or documents.

CHAPTER III
LIABILITY OF THE CARRIER

Article 17

The carrier is liable for damage sustained in the event of the death or wounding of a passenger or any other bodily injury suffered by a passenger, if the accident which caused the damage so sustained took place on board the aircraft or in the course of any of the operations of embarking or disembarking.

Article 18

(1) The carrier is liable for damage sustained in the event of the destruction or loss of, or of damage to, any registered baggage or any cargo, if the occurrence which caused the damage so sustained took place during the carriage by air.

(2) The carriage by air within the meaning of the preceding paragraph comprises the period during which the baggage or cargo is in charge of the carrier, whether in an aerodrome or on board an aircraft, or, in the case of a landing outside an aerodrome in any place whatsoever.

(3) The period of carriage by air does not extend to any carriage by land, by sea or by river performed outside an aerodrome. If, however, such a carriage takes place in the performance of a contract for carriage by air, for the purpose of loading, delivery or transhipment, any damage is presumed, subject to proof to the contrary, to have been the result of an event which took place during the carriage by air.

Article 19

The carrier is liable for damage occasioned by delay in the carriage by air of passengers, baggage or cargo.

Article 20

(1) The carrier is not liable if he proves that he and his servants or agents have taken all necessary measures to avoid the damage or that it was impossible for him or them to take such measures.

(2) In the carriage of cargo and baggage the carrier is not liable if he proves that the damage was occasioned by negligent pilotage or negligence in the handling of the aircraft or in navigation and that, in all other respects, he and his servants or agents have taken all necessary measures to avoid the damage.

Article 21

If the carrier proves that the damage was caused by or contributed to by the negligence of the injured person the court may, in accordance with the provisions of its own law, exonerate the carrier wholly or partly from his liability.

Article 22

(1) In the carriage of passengers the liability of the carrier for each passenger is limited to the sum of 125,000 francs. Where, in accordance with the law of the court seised of the case, damages may be awarded in the form of periodical payments, the equivalent capital value of the said payments shall not exceed 125,000 francs. Nevertheless, by special contract, the carrier and the passenger may agree to a higher limit of liability.

(2) In the carriage of registered baggage and of cargo, the liability of the carrier is limited to a sum of 250 francs per kilogramme, unless the consignor has made, at the time when the package was handed over to the carrier, a special declaration of the value at delivery and has paid a supplementary sum if the case so requires. In that case the carrier will be liable to pay a sum not exceeding the declared sum, unless he proves that the sum is greater than the actual value to the consignor at delivery.

(3) As regards objects of which the passenger takes charge himself the liability of the carrier is limited to 5,000 francs per passenger.

(4) The sums mentioned above shall be deemed to refer to the French franc consisting of 65 milligrammes gold of millesimal fineness 900. These sums may he converted into any national currency in round figures.

Article 23

Any provision tending to relieve the carrier of liability or to fix a lower limit than that which is laid down in this Schedule shall be null and void, but the nullity of any such provision does not involve the nullity of the whole contract, which shall remain subject to the provisions of this Schedule.

Article 24

(1) In the cases covered by Articles 18 and 19 any action for damages, however founded, can only be brought subject to the conditions and limits set out in this Schedule.

(2) In the cases covered by Article 17 the provisions of the preceding paragraph also apply without prejudice to the questions as to who are the persons who have the right to bring suit and what are their respective rights.

Article 25

(1) The carrier shall not be entitled to avail himself of the provisions of this Schedule which exclude or limit his liability, if the damage is caused by his wilful misconduct, or by such default on his part as, in accordance with the law of the court seised of the case, is considered to be equivalent to wilful misconduct.

(2) Similarly the carrier shall not be entitled to avail himself of the said provisions if the damage is caused as aforesaid by any servant or agent of the carrier acting within the scope of his employment.

Article 26

(1) Receipt by the person entitled to delivery of baggage or cargo without complaint is prima facie evidence that the same has been delivered in good condition and in accordance with the document of carriage.

(2) In the case of damage, the person entitled to delivery must complain to the carrier forthwith after the discovery of the damage, and, at the latest, within three days from the date of receipt in the case of baggage and seven days from the date of receipt in the case of cargo. In the case of delay the complaint must be made at the latest within fourteen days from the date on which the baggage or cargo has been placed at his disposal.

(3) Every complaint must be made in writing upon the document of carriage or by separate notice in writing despatched within the times aforesaid.

(4) Failing complaint within the times aforesaid, no action shall lie against the carrier, save in the case of fraud on his part.

Article 27

In the case of the death of the person liable, an action for damages lies in accordance with the terms of this Schedule against those legally representing his estate.

Article 28

(1) An action for damages must be brought, at the option of the plaintiff, in the territory of one of the High Contracting Parties to the Warsaw Convention, either before the court having jurisdiction where the carrier is ordinarily resident, or has his principal place of business, or has an establishment by which the contract has been made or before the court having jurisdiction at the place of destination.

(2) Questions of procedure shall be governed by the law of the court seised of the case.

Article 29

(1) The right to damages shall be extinguished if an action is not brought within two years, reckoned from the date of arrival at the destination, or from the date on which the aircraft ought to have arrived, or from the date on which the carriage stopped.

(2) The method of calculating the period of limitation shall be determined by the law of the Court seised of the case.

Article 30

(1) In the case of carriage to be performed by various successive carriers and falling within the definition set out in the third paragraph of Article 1, each carrier who accepts passengers, baggage or cargo is subjected to the rules set out in this Schedule, and is deemed

to be one of the contracting parties to the contract of carriage in so far as the contract deals with that part of the carriage which is performed under his supervision.

(2) In the case of carriage of this nature, the passenger or his representative can take action only against the carrier who performed the carriage during which the accident or the delay occurred, save in the case where, by express agreement, the first carrier has assumed liability for the whole journey.

(3) As regards baggage or cargo, the passenger or consignor will have a right of action against the first carrier, and the passenger or consignee who is entitled to delivery will have a right of action against the last carrier, and further, each may take action against the carrier who performed the carriage during which the destruction, loss, damage or delay took place. These carriers will be jointly and severally liable to the passenger or to the consignor or consignee.

CHAPTER IV
PROVISIONS RELATING TO COMBINED CARRIAGE

Article 31

(1) In the case of combined carriage performed partly by air and partly by any other mode of carriage, the provisions of this Schedule apply to the carriage by air, provided that the carriage by air falls within the terms of Article 1.

(2) Nothing in this Schedule shall prevent the parties in the case of combined carriage from inserting in the document of air carriage conditions relating to other modes of carriage, provided that the provisions of this Schedule are observed as regards the carriage by air.

CHAPTER V
GENERAL AND FINAL PROVISIONS

Article 32

Any clause contained in the contract and all special agreements entered into before the damage occurred by which the parties purport to infringe the rules laid down by this Schedule, whether by deciding the law to be applied, or by altering the rules as to jurisdiction, shall be null and void. Nevertheless, for the carriage of cargo arbitration clauses are allowed, subject to this Schedule, if the arbitration is to take place within one of the jurisdictions referred to in the first paragraph of Article 28.

Article 33

Nothing contained in this Schedule shall prevent the carrier either from refusing to enter into any contract of carriage, or from making regulations which do not conflict with the provisions of this Schedule.

Article 34

This Schedule does not apply to international carriage by air performed by way of experimental trial by air navigation undertakings with the view to the establishment of a regular line of air navigation, nor does it apply to carriage performed in extraordinary circumstances outside the normal scope of an air carrier's business.

Article 35

The expression "days" when used in this Schedule means current days not working days.

ADDITIONAL PROTOCOL TO THE WARSAW CONVENTION

The High Contracting Parties reserve to themselves the right to declare at the time of ratification or of accession that the first paragraph of Article 2 of this Convention shall not apply to international carriage by air performed directly by the State, its colonies, protectorates or mandated territories or by any other territory under its sovereignty, suzerainty or authority.

B The Guadalajara Convention as applied by Schedule 2

INTERNATIONAL CARRIAGE UNDER THE UNAMENDED WARSAW CONVENTION

Article I

In the Guadalajara Convention as applied by this Schedule:

(a) "The Warsaw Convention" means the 1955 amended Convention as applied by this Schedule;

(b) "contracting carrier" means a person who as a principal makes an agreement for carriage governed by the Warsaw Convention with a passenger or consignor or with a person acting on behalf of the passenger or consignor;

(c) "actual carrier" means a person, other than the contracting carrier, who, by virtue of authority from the contracting carrier, performs the whole or part of the carriage contemplated in paragraph (b) but who is not with respect to such part a successive carrier within the meaning of the Warsaw Convention. Such authority is presumed in the absence of proof to the contrary.

Article II

If an actual carrier performs the whole or part of carriage which, according to the agreement referred to in Article 1, paragraph (b), is governed by the Warsaw Convention, both the contracting carrier and the actual carrier shall, except as otherwise provided in the Guadalajara Convention as applied by this Schedule, be subject to the rules of the Warsaw Convention, the former for the whole of the carriage contemplated in the agreement, the latter solely for the carriage which he performs.

Article III

1 The acts and omissions of the actual carrier and of his servants and agents acting within the scope of their employment shall, in relation to the carriage performed by the actual carrier, be deemed to be also those of the contracting carrier.

2 The acts and omissions of the contracting carrier and of his servants and agents acting within the scope of their employment shall, in relation to the carriage performed by the actual carrier, be deemed to be also those of the actual carrier. Nevertheless, no such act or omission shall subject the actual carrier to liability exceeding the limits specified in Article 22 of the Warsaw Convention. Any special agreement under which the contracting carrier assumes obligations not imposed by the Warsaw Convention or any waiver of rights conferred by that Convention or any special declaration of interest in delivery at destination contemplated in Article 22 of the said Convention, shall not affect the actual carrier unless agreed to by him.

Article IV

Any complaint to be made or order to be given under the Warsaw Convention to the carrier shall have the same effect whether addressed to the contracting carrier or to the actual carrier. Nevertheless, orders referred to in Article 12 of the Warsaw Convention shall only be effective if addressed to the contracting carrier.

Article V

In relation to the carriage performed by the actual carrier, any servant or agent of that carrier or of the contracting carrier shall, if he proves that he acted within the scope of his employment be entitled to avail himself of the limits of liability which are applicable under the Guadalajara Convention as applied by this Schedule to the carrier whose servant or agent he is unless it is proved that he acted in a manner which, under the Warsaw Convention, prevents the limits of liability from being invoked.

Article VI

In relation to the carriage performed by the actual carrier, the aggregate of the amounts recoverable from that carrier and the contracting carrier, and from their servants and agents acting within the scope of their employment, shall not exceed the highest amount which could be awarded against either the contracting carrier or the actual carrier under the Guadalajara Convention as applied by this Schedule, but none of the persons mentioned shall be liable for a sum in excess of the limit applicable to him

Article VII

In relation to the carriage performed by the actual carrier, an action for damages may be brought, at the option of the plaintiff, against that carrier or the contracting carrier, or against both together or separately. If the action is brought against only one of those carriers, that carrier shall have the right to require the other carrier to be joined in the proceedings, the procedure and effects being governed by the law of the Court seised of the case.

Article VIII

Any action for damages contemplated in Article VII of the Guadalajara Convention as applied by this Schedule must be brought, at the option of the plaintiff, either before a Court in which an action may be brought against the contracting carrier, as provided in Article 28 of the Warsaw Convention, or before the Court having jurisdiction at the place where the actual carrier is ordinarily resident or has his principal place of business.

Article IX

1 Any contractual provision tending to relieve the contracting carrier or the actual carrier of liability under the Guadalajara Convention as applied by this Schedule or to fix a lower limit than that which is applicable according to the Guadalajara Convention as applied by this Schedule shall be null and void, but the nullity of any such provision does not involve the nullity of the whole agreement, which shall remain subject to the provisions of the Guadalajara Convention as applied by this Schedule.

2 In respect of the carriage performed by the actual carrier, the preceding paragraph shall not apply to contractual provisions governing loss or damage resulting from the inherent defect, quality or vice of the cargo carried.

3 Any clause contained in an agreement for carriage and all special agreements entered into before the damage occurred by which the parties purport to infringe the rules laid down by the Guadalajara Convention as applied by this Schedule, whether by deciding the law to be applied, or by altering the rules as to jurisdiction, shall be null and void. Nevertheless, for the carriage of cargo arbitration clauses are allowed, subject to the Guadalajara Convention as applied by this Schedule, if the arbitration is to take place in one of the jurisdictions referred to in Article VIII.

Article X

Except as provided in Article VII, nothing in the Guadalajara Convention as applied by this Schedule shall affect the rights and obligations of the two carriers between themselves.

[2317]

NOTES

Commencement: 6 August 2004.

SCHEDULE 3

INTERNATIONAL CARRIAGE UNDER THE WARSAW CONVENTION AS AMENDED BY ADDITIONAL PROTOCOL NO 1 OF MONTREAL 1975

Article 6

PART I

1 The 1955 amended Convention and the Guadalajara Convention shall apply in respect of carriage which is "international carriage" as defined in paragraph 2 of this part of this Schedule, with the exceptions, adaptations and modifications set forth in paragraphs 3 and 4.

2 For the purposes of Article 6 of this Order and of this Schedule "international carriage" shall have the meaning assigned to it by paragraph 3(2) of this part of this Schedule.

3 The 1955 amended Convention shall apply to international carriage as aforesaid, with the following exceptions, adaptations and modifications—

(1) For "Convention", wherever it appears, there shall be substituted "Schedule".

(2) The following shall be substituted for Article 1(2)—

"(2) "International carriage" means any carriage in which, according to the contract made by the parties, the place of departure and the place of destination, whether or not there be a break in the carriage or a transhipment, are situated either within the territories of two States Parties to the Convention for the Unification of Certain Rules relating to International Carriage by Air signed at Warsaw on behalf of His Majesty on 12th October 1929 as amended by Additional Protocol No 1 of Montreal 1975, or within the territory of a single such State, if there is an agreed stopping place within the territory subject to the sovereignty, suzerainty, mandate or authority of another State, even though that State is not a party to the said Convention of 1929 as so amended.".

(3) The following shall be substituted for Article 1(3)—

"(3) A carriage to be performed by several successive air carriers is deemed for the purposes of this Schedule, to be one undivided carriage, if it has been regarded by the parties as a single operation, whether it had been agreed upon under the form of a single contract or of a series of contracts, and it does not lose its international character merely because one contract or a series of contracts is to be performed entirely within a territory subject to the sovereignty, suzerainty, mandate or authority of the same High Contracting Party.".

(4) The following shall be substituted for Article 2—

"Article 2

(1) This Schedule applies to carriage performed by the State, not being a State which has availed itself of the Additional Protocol to the Warsaw Convention, or by legally constituted public bodies, provided it falls within the conditions laid down in Article 1.

(2) This Schedule does not apply to carriage performed under the terms of any international postal Convention.".

(5) The following shall be substituted for Article 3—

"Article 3

(1) For the carriage of passengers the carrier must deliver a passenger ticket which shall contain the following particulars—

(a) the place and date of issue;
(b) the place of departure and of destination;
(c) the agreed stopping places, provided that the carrier may reserve the right to alter the stopping places in case of necessity, and that if he exercises that right, the alteration shall not have the effect of depriving the carriage of its international character;
(d) the name and address of the carrier or carriers;
(e) a statement that the carriage is subject to the rules relating to liability established by the Warsaw Convention.

(2) The absence, irregularity or loss of the passenger ticket does not affect the existence or the validity of the contract of carriage, which shall none the less be subject to the rules of this Schedule. Nevertheless, if the carrier accepts a passenger without a passenger ticket having been delivered he shall not be entitled to avail himself of those provisions of this Schedule which exclude or limit his liability.".

(6) The following shall be substituted for Article 4—

"Article 4

(1) For the carriage of baggage, other than small personal objects of which the passenger takes charge himself, the carrier must deliver a baggage check.

(2) The baggage check shall be made out in duplicate, one part for the passenger and the other part for the carrier.

(3) The baggage check shall contain the following particulars—

(a) the place and date of issue;
(b) the place of departure and of destination;
(c) the name and address of the carrier or carriers;
(d) the number of the passenger ticket;
(e) a statement that delivery of the baggage will be made to the bearer of the baggage check;
(f) the number and weight of the packages;
(g) the amount of the value declared in accordance with Article 22(2);
(h) a statement that the carriage is subject to the rules relating to liability established by the Warsaw Convention.

(4) The absence, irregularity or loss of the baggage check does not affect the existence or the validity of the contract of carriage, which shall none the less be subject to the rules of this Schedule. Nevertheless, if the carrier accepts baggage without a

baggage check having been delivered, or if the baggage check does not contain the particulars set out at (d), (f) and (h) above, the carrier shall not be entitled to avail himself of those provisions of this Schedule which exclude or limit his liability.".

(7) The following shall be substituted for Article 6(3)—

"(3) The carrier shall sign on acceptance of the cargo.".

(8) The following shall be substituted for Article 8—

"Article 8

The air waybill shall contain the following particulars—

(a) the place and date of its execution;
(b) the place of departure and of destination;
(c) the agreed stopping places, provided that the carrier may reserve the right to alter the stopping places in case of necessity, and that if he exercises that right the alteration shall not have the effect of depriving the carriage of its international character;
(d) the name and address of the consignor;
(e) the name and address of the first carrier;
(f) the name and address of the consignee, if the case so requires;
(g) the nature of the cargo;
(h) the number of the packages, the method of packing and the particular marks or numbers upon them;
(i) the weight, the quantity and the volume or dimensions of the cargo;
(j) the apparent condition of the cargo and of the packing;
(k) the freight, if it has been agreed upon, the date and place of payment, and the person who is to pay it;
(l) if the cargo is sent for payment on delivery, the price of the cargo, and, if the case so requires, the amount of the expenses incurred;
(m) the amount of the value declared in accordance with Article 22(2);
(n) the number of parts of the air waybill;
(o) the documents handed to the carrier to accompany the air waybill;
(p) the time fixed for the completion of the carriage and a brief note of the route to be followed, if these matters have been agreed upon;
(q) a statement that the carriage is subject to the rules relating to liability established by the Warsaw Convention.".

(9) The following shall be substituted for Article 9—

"Article 9

If the carrier accepts cargo without an air waybill having been made out, or if the air waybill does not contain all the particulars set out in Article 8 (a) to (i) inclusive and (q), the carrier shall not be entitled to avail himself of the provisions of this Schedule which exclude or limit his liability.".

(10) The following shall be substituted for Article 10(2)—

"(2) The consignor will be liable for all damage suffered by the carrier or any other person by reason of the irregularity, incorrectness or incompleteness of the said particulars and statements.".

(11) Article 15(3) shall not apply.

(12) The following shall be substituted for Article 20(2)—

"(2) In the carriage of cargo and baggage the carrier is not liable if he proves that the damage was occasioned by negligent pilotage or negligence in the handling of the aircraft or in navigation and that, in all other respects, he and his servants or agents have taken all necessary measures to avoid the damage.".

(13) The following shall be substituted for Article 22—

"Article 22

(1) In the carriage of passengers the liability of the carrier for each passenger is limited to the sum of 8,300 Special Drawing Rights. Where, in accordance with the law of the court seised of the case, damages may be awarded in the form of periodic payments, the equivalent capital value of the said payments shall not exceed this limit. Nevertheless, by special contract, the carrier and the passenger may agree to a high limit of liability.

PART III STATUTORY INSTRUMENTS

(2) In the carriage of registered baggage and of cargo, the liability of the carrier is limited to a sum of 17 Special Drawing Rights per kilogramme, unless the consignor has made, at the time when the package was handed over to the carrier, a special declaration of interest in delivery at destination and has paid a supplementary sum if the case so requires. In that case the carrier will be liable to pay a sum not exceeding the declared sum, unless he proves that the sum is greater than the consignor's actual interest in delivery at destination.

(3) As regards objects of which the passenger takes charge himself the liability of the carrier is limited to 332 Special Drawing Rights per passenger.

(4) The sums mentioned in terms of the Special Drawing Right in this Article shall be deemed to refer to the Special Drawing Right as defined by the International Monetary Fund. Conversion of the sums into national currencies shall, in case of judicial proceedings, be made according to the value of such currencies in terms of the Special Drawing Right at the date of the judgement. The value of a national currency, in terms of the Special Drawing Right, of a High Contracting Party which is a Member of the International Monetary Fund, shall be calculated in accordance with the method of valuation applied by the International Monetary Fund, in effect at the date of the judgement, for its operations and transactions. The value of a national currency, in terms of the Special Drawing Right, of a High Contracting Party which is not a Member of the International Monetary Fund, shall be calculated in a manner determined by that High Contracting Party.

Nevertheless, those States which are not Members of the International Monetary Fund and whose law does not permit the application of the provisions of paragraphs 1, 2 and 3 of Article 22 may at the time of ratification or accession or at any time thereafter declare that the limit of liability of the carrier in judicial proceedings in their territories is fixed at a sum of 125,000 monetary units per passenger with respect to paragraph 1 of Article 22; 250 monetary units per kilogramme with respect to paragraph 2 of Article 22; and 5,000 monetary units per passenger with respect to paragraph 3 of Article 22. This monetary unit corresponds to sixty-five and a half milligrammes of gold of millesimal fineness nine hundred. These sums may be converted into the national currency concerned in round figures. The conversion of these sums into national currency shall be made according to the law of the State concerned.".

(14) Article 23(2) shall not apply.

(15) The following shall be substituted for Article 25—

"Article 25

(1) The carrier shall not be entitled to avail himself of the provisions of this Schedule which exclude or limit his liability, if the damage is caused by his wilful misconduct or by such default on his part as, in accordance with the law of the court seised of the case, is considered to be equivalent to wilful misconduct.

(2) Similarly the carrier shall not be entitled to avail himself of the said provisions, if the damage is caused as aforesaid by any servant or agent of the carrier acting within the scope of his employment.".

(16) Article 25A shall not apply.

(17) The following shall be substituted for Article 26(2)—

"(2) In the case of damage, the person entitled to delivery must complain to the carrier forthwith after the discovery of the damage, and, at the latest, within three days from the date of receipt in the case of baggage and seven days from the date of receipt in the case of cargo. In the case of delay the complaint must be made at the latest within fourteen days from the date on which the baggage or cargo has been placed at his disposal.".

(18) In Article 28(1), after "High Contracting Parties" there shall be added "to the Warsaw Convention as amended by Additional Protocol No 1 of Montreal 1975".

(19) The following shall be substituted for Article 34—

"Article 34

This Schedule does not apply to international carriage by air performed by way of experimental trial by air navigation undertakings with the view to the establishment of a regular line of air navigation, nor does it apply to carriage performed in extraordinary circumstances outside the normal scope of an air carrier's business.".

(20) Articles 36 and 40A shall not apply.

4 The Guadalajara Convention shall apply to international carriage within the meaning of this Schedule, with the following exceptions, adaptations and modifications—

(1) For "this Convention" wherever it appears there shall be substituted "the Guadalajara Convention as applied by this Schedule".

(2) In Article 1, the following shall be added as paragraph (a)—

""the Warsaw Convention" means the 1955 amended Convention as applied by this Schedule.".

[2318]

NOTES

Commencement: 6 August 2004.

PART II

For convenience of reference the 1955 amended Convention and the Guadalajara Convention, with the exceptions, adaptations and modifications by this Schedule, are here set out—

A The 1955 amended Warsaw Convention, as applied by Schedule 3

INTERNATIONAL CARRIAGE UNDER THE UNAMENDED, WARSAW CONVENTION AS AMENDED BY ADDITIONAL PROTOCOL NO I OF MONTREAL 1975

CHAPTER 1
SCOPE—DEFINITIONS

Article 1

(1) This Schedule applies to all international carriage of persons, baggage or cargo performed by aircraft for reward. It applies equally to gratuitous carriage by aircraft performed by an air transport undertaking.

(2) "International carriage" means any carriage in which, according to the contract made by the parties, the place of departure and the place of destination, whether or not there be a break in the carriage or a transhipment, are situated either within the territories of two States Parties to the Convention for the Unification of Certain Rules relating to International Carriage by Air signed at Warsaw on behalf of His Majesty on 12th October 1929 as amended by Additional Protocol No 1 of Montreal 1975, or within the territory of a single such State, if there is an agreed stopping place within the territory subject to the sovereignty, suzerainty, mandate or authority of another State, even though that State is not a party to the said Convention of 1929 as so amended.

(3) A carriage to be performed by several successive air carriers is deemed, for the purposes of this Schedule, to be one undivided carriage, if it has been regarded by the parties as a single operation, whether it had been agreed upon under the form of a single contract or of a series of contracts, and it does not lose its international character merely because one contract or a series of contracts is to be performed entirely within a territory subject to the sovereignty, suzerainty, mandate or authority of the same High Contracting Party.

Article 2

(1) This Schedule applies to carriage performed by the State, not being a State which has availed itself of the Additional Protocol to the Warsaw Convention, or by legally constituted public bodies, provided it falls within the conditions laid down in Article 1.

(2) This Schedule does not apply to carriage performed under the terms of any international postal Convention.

CHAPTER II
DOCUMENTS OF CARRIAGE

SECTION 1
PASSENGER TICKET

Article 3

(1) For the carriage of passengers the carrier must deliver a passenger ticket which shall contain the following particulars—

(a) the place and date of issue;
(b) the place of departure and of destination;
(c) the agreed stopping places, provided that the carrier may reserve the right to alter the stopping places in case of necessity, and that if he exercises that right, the alteration shall not have the effect of depriving the carriage of its international character;
(d) the name and address of the carrier or carriers;
(e) a statement that the carriage is subject to the rules relating to liability established by the Warsaw Convention.

(2) The absence, irregularity or loss of the passenger ticket does not affect the existence or the validity of the contract of carriage, which shall none the less be subject to the rules of this Schedule. Nevertheless, if the carrier accepts a passenger without a passenger ticket having been delivered he shall not be entitled to avail himself of those provisions of this Schedule which exclude or limit his liability.

SECTION 2
BAGGAGE CHECK

Article 4

(1) For the carriage of baggage, other than small personal objects of which the passenger takes charge himself, the carrier must deliver a baggage check.

(2) The baggage check shall be made out in duplicate, one part for the passenger and the other part for the carrier.

(3) The baggage check shall contain the following particulars—

(a) the place and date of issue;
(b) the place of departure and of destination;
(c) the name and address of the carrier or carriers;
(d) the number of the passenger ticket;
(e) a statement that delivery of the baggage will be made to the bearer of the baggage check;
(f) the number and weight of the packages;
(g) the amount of the value declared in accordance with Article 22(2);
(h) a statement that the carriage is subject to the rules relating to liability established by the Warsaw Convention.

(4) The absence, irregularity or loss of the baggage check does not affect the existence or the validity of the contract of carriage, which shall none the less be subject to the rules of this Schedule. Nevertheless, if the carrier accepts baggage without a baggage check having been delivered, or if the baggage check does not contain the particulars set out at (d), (f) and (h) above, the carrier shall not be entitled to avail himself of those provisions of this Schedule which exclude or limit his liability.

SECTION 3
AIR WAYBILL

Article 5

(1) Every carrier of cargo has the right to require the consignor to make out and hand over to him a document called an "air waybill"; every consignor has the right to require the carrier to accept this document.

(2) The absence, irregularity or loss of this document does not affect the existence or the validity of the contract of carriage which shall, subject to the provisions of Article 9, be none the less governed by the rules of this Schedule.

Article 6

(1) The air waybill shall be made out by the consignor in three original parts and be handed over with the cargo.

(2) The first part shall be marked "for the carrier", and shall be signed by the consignor. The second part shall be marked "for the consignee"; it shall be signed by the consignor and by the carrier and shall accompany the cargo. The third part shall be signed by the carrier and handed by him to the consignor after the cargo has been accepted.

(3) The carrier shall sign on acceptance of the cargo.

(4) The signature of the carrier may be stamped; that of the consignor may be printed or stamped.

(5) If, at the request of the consignor, the carrier makes out the air waybill, he shall be deemed, subject to proof to the contrary, to have done so on behalf of the consignor.

Article 7

The carrier of cargo has the right to require the consignor to make out separate waybills when there is more than one package.

Article 8

The air waybill shall contain the following particulars—

(a) the place and date of its execution;
(b) the place of departure and of destination;
(c) the agreed stopping places, provided that the carrier may reserve the right to alter the stopping places in case of necessity, and that if he exercises that right the alteration shall not have the effect of depriving the carriage of its international character;
(d) the name and address of the consignor;
(e) the name and address of the first carrier;
(f) the name and address of the consignee, if the case so requires;
(g) the nature of the cargo;
(h) the number of the packages, the method of packing and the particular marks or numbers upon them;
(i) the weight, the quantity and the volume or dimensions of the cargo;
(j) the apparent condition of the cargo and of the packing;
(k) the freight, if it has been agreed upon, the date and place of payment, and the person who is to pay it;
(l) if the cargo is sent for payment on delivery, the price of the cargo, and, if the case so requires, the amount of the expenses incurred;
(m) the amount of the value declared in accordance with Article 22(2);
(n) the number of parts of the air waybill;
(o) the documents handed to the carrier to accompany the air waybill;
(p) the time fixed for the completion of the carriage and a brief note of the route to be followed, if these matters have been agreed upon;
(q) a statement that the carriage is subject to the rules relating to liability established by the Warsaw Convention.

Article 9

If the carrier accepts cargo without an air waybill having been made out, or if the air waybill does not contain all the particulars set out in Article 8(a) to (i) inclusive and (q), the carrier shall not be entitled to avail himself of the provisions of this Schedule which exclude or limit his liability.

Article 10

(1) The consignor is responsible for the correctness of the particulars and statements relating to the cargo which he inserts in the air waybill.

(2) The consignor will be liable for all damage suffered by the carrier or any other person by reason of the irregularity, incorrectness or incompleteness of the said particulars and statements.

Article 11

(1) The air waybill is prima facie evidence of the conclusion of the contract, of the receipt of the cargo and of the conditions of carriage.

(2) The statements in the air waybill relating to the weight, dimensions and packing of the cargo, as well as those relating to the number of packages, are prima facie evidence of the facts stated; those relating to the quantity, volume and condition of the cargo do not constitute evidence against the carrier except so far as they both have been, and are stated in the air waybill to have been, checked by him in the presence of the consignor, or relate to the apparent condition of the cargo.

Article 12

(1) Subject to his liability to carry out all his obligations under the contract of carriage, the consignor has the right to dispose of the cargo by withdrawing it at the aerodrome of departure or destination, or by stopping it in the course of the journey on any landing, or by calling for it to be delivered at the place of destination or in the course of the journey to a person other than the consignee named in the air waybill, or by requiring it to be returned to the aerodrome of departure. He must not exercise this right of disposition in such a way as to prejudice the carrier or other consignors and he must repay any expenses occasioned by the exercise of this right.

(2) If it is impossible to carry out the orders of the consignor the carrier must so inform him forthwith.

(3) If the carrier obeys the orders of the consignor for the disposition of the cargo without requiring the production of the part of the air waybill delivered to the latter, he will be liable, without prejudice to his right of recovery from the consignor, for any damage which may be caused thereby to any person who is lawfully in possession of that part of the air waybill.

(4) The right conferred on the consignor ceases at the moment when that of the consignee begins in accordance with Article 13. Nevertheless, if the consignee declines to accept the waybill or the cargo, or if he cannot be communicated with, the consignor resumes his right of disposition.

Article 13

(1) Except in the circumstances set out in the preceding Article, the consignee is entitled, on arrival of the cargo at the place of destination, to require the carrier to hand over to him the air waybill and to deliver the cargo to him, on payment of the charges due and on complying with the conditions of carriage set out in the air waybill.

(2) Unless it is otherwise agreed, it is the duty of the carrier to give notice to the consignee as soon as the cargo arrives.

(3) If the carrier admits the loss of the cargo, or if the cargo has not arrived at the expiration of seven days after the date on which it ought to have arrived, the consignee is entitled to put into force against the carrier the rights which flow from the contract of carriage.

Article 14

The consignor and the consignee can respectively enforce all the rights given them by Articles 12 and 13, each in his own name, whether he is acting in his own interest or in the interest of another, provided that he carries out the obligations imposed by the contract.

Article 15

(1) Articles 12, 13 and 14 do not affect either the relations of the consignor or the consignee with each other or the mutual relations of third parties whose rights are derived either from the consignor or from the consignee.

(2) The provisions of Articles 12, 13 and 14 can only be varied by express provision in the air waybill.

Article 16

(1) The consignor must furnish such information and attach to the air waybill such documents as are necessary to meet the formalities of customs, octroi or police before the cargo can be delivered to the consignee. The consignor is liable to the carrier for any damage occasioned by the absence, insufficiency or irregularity of any such information or documents, unless the damage is due to the fault of the carrier or his servants or agents.

(2) The carrier is under no obligation to enquire into the correctness or sufficiency of such information or documents.

CHAPTER III
LIABILITY OF THE CARRIER

Article 17

The carrier is liable for damage sustained in the event of the death or wounding of a passenger or any other bodily injury suffered by a passenger, if the accident which caused the damage so sustained took place on board the aircraft or in the course of any of the operations of embarking or disembarking.

Article 18

(1) The carrier is liable for damage sustained in the event of the destruction or loss of, or of damage to, any registered baggage or any cargo, if the occurrence which caused the damage so sustained took place during the carriage by air.

(2) The carriage by air within the meaning of the preceding paragraph comprises the period during which the baggage or cargo is in charge of the carrier, whether in an aerodrome or on board an aircraft, or, in the case of a landing outside an aerodrome in any place whatsoever.

(3) The period of the carriage by air does not extend to any carriage by land, by sea or by river performed outside an aerodrome. If, however, such a carriage takes place in the performance of a contract for carriage by air, for the purpose of loading, delivery or transhipment, any damage is presumed, subject to proof to the contrary, to have been the result of an event which took place during the carriage by air.

Article 19

The carrier is liable for damage occasioned by delay in the carriage by air of passengers, baggage or cargo.

Article 20

(1) The carrier is not liable if he proves that he and his servants or agents have taken all necessary measures to avoid the damage or that it was impossible for him or them to take such measures.

(2) In the carriage of cargo and baggage the carrier is not liable if he proves that the damage was occasioned by negligent pilotage or negligence in the handling of the aircraft or in navigation and that, in all other respects, he and his servants or agents have taken all necessary measures to avoid the damage.

Article 21

If the carrier proves that the damage was caused by or contributed to by the negligence of the injured person the court may, in accordance with the provisions of its own law, exonerate the carrier wholly or partly from his liability.

Article 22

(1) In the carriage of passengers the liability of the carrier for each passenger is limited to the sum of 8,300 Special Drawing Rights. Where, in accordance with the law of the court seised of the case, damages may be awarded in the form of periodic payments, the equivalent capital value of the said payments shall not exceed this limit. Nevertheless, by special contract, the carrier and the passenger may agree to a higher limit of liability.

(2) In the carriage of registered baggage and of cargo, the liability of the carrier is limited to a sum of 17 Special Drawing Rights per kilogramme, unless the consignor has made, at the time when the package was handed over to the carrier, a special declaration of interest in delivery at destination and has paid a supplementary sum if the case so requires. In that case the carrier will be liable to pay a sum not exceeding the declared sum, unless he proves that that sum is greater than the consignor's actual interest in delivery at destination.

(3) As regards objects of which the passenger takes charge himself the liability of the carrier is limited to 332 Special Drawing Rights per passenger.

(4) The sums mentioned in terms of the Special Drawing Right in this Article shall be deemed to refer to the Special Drawing Right as defined by the International Monetary Fund. Conversion of the sums into national currencies shall, in case of judicial proceedings, be made according to the value of such currencies in terms of the Special Drawing Right at the date of the judgement. The value of a national currency, in terms of the Special Drawing Right, of a High Contracting Party which is a Member of the Monetary Fund, shall be calculated in

accordance with the method of valuation applied by the International Monetary Fund, in effect at the date of the judgement, for its operations and transactions. The value of national currency, in terms of the Special Drawing Right, of a High Contracting Party which is not a Member of the International Monetary Fund, shall be calculated in a manner determined by that High Contracting Party.

Nevertheless, those States which are not Members of the International Monetary Fund and whose law does not permit the application of the provisions of paragraphs 1, 2 and 3 of Article 22 may at the time of ratification or accession or at any time thereafter declare that the limit of liability of the carrier in judicial proceedings in their territories is fixed at a sum of 125,000 monetary units per passenger with respect to paragraph 1 of Article 22; 250 monetary units per kilogramme with respect to paragraph 2 of Article 22; and 5,000 monetary units per passenger with respect to paragraph 3 of Article 22. This monetary unit corresponds to sixty-five and a half milligrammes of gold of millesimal fineness nine hundred. These sums may be converted into the national currency concerned in round figures. The conversion of these sums into national currency shall be made according to the law of the State concerned.

Article 23

Any provision tending to relieve the carrier of liability or to fix a lower limit than that which is laid down in this Schedule shall be null and void, but the nullity of any such provision does not involve the nullity of the whole contract, which shall remain subject to the provisions of this Schedule.

Article 24

(1) In the cases covered by Articles 18 and 19 any action for damages, however founded, can only be brought subject to the conditions and limits set out in this Schedule.

(2) In the cases covered by Article 17 the provisions of the preceding paragraph also apply, without prejudice to the questions as to who are the persons who have the right to bring suit and what are their respective rights.

Article 25

(1) The carrier shall not be entitled to avail himself of the provisions of this Schedule which exclude or limit his liability, if the damage is caused by his misconduct, or by such default on his part as, in accordance with the law of the court seised of the case, is considered to be equivalent to wilful misconduct.

(2) Similarly the carrier shall not be entitled to avail himself of the said provisions, if the damage is caused as aforesaid by any servant or agent of the carrier acting within the scope of his employment.

Article 26

(1) Receipt by the person entitled to delivery of baggage or cargo without complaint is prima facie evidence that the same has been delivered in good condition and in accordance with the document of carriage.

(2) In the case of damage, the person entitled to delivery must complain to the carrier forthwith after the discovery of the damage, and, at the latest, within three days from the date of receipt in the case of baggage and seven days from the date of receipt in the case of cargo. In the case of delay the complaint must be made at the latest within fourteen days from the date on which the baggage or cargo has been placed at his disposal.

(3) Every complaint must be made in writing upon the document of carriage or by separate notice in writing despatched within the times aforesaid.

(4) Failing complaint within the times aforesaid, no action shall lie against the carrier, save in the case of fraud on his part.

Article 27

In the case of the death of the person liable, an action for damages lies in accordance with the terms of this Schedule against those legally representing his estate.

Article 28

(1) An action for damages must be brought, at the option of the plaintiff in the territory of one of the High Contracting Parties to the Warsaw Convention as amended by Additional Protocol No 1 of Montreal 1975, either before the court having jurisdiction where the carrier

is ordinarily resident, or has his principal place of business, or has an establishment by which the contract has been made or before the Court having jurisdiction at the place of destination.

(2) Questions of procedure shall be governed by the law of the court seised of the case.

Article 29

(1) The right to damages shall be extinguished if an action is not brought within two years, reckoned from the date of arrival at did destination, or from the date on which the aircraft ought to have arrived, or from the date on which the carriage stopped.

(2) The method of calculating the period of limitation shall be determined by the law of the court seised of the case.

Article 30

(1) In the case of carriage to be performed by various successive carriers and falling within the definition set out in the third paragraph of Article 1, each carrier who accepts passengers, baggage or cargo is subjected to the rules set out in this Schedule, and is deemed to be one of the contracting parties to the contract of carriage in so far as the contract deals with that part of the carriage which is performed under his supervision.

(2) In the case of carriage of this nature, the passenger or his representative can take action only against the carrier who performed the carriage during which the accident or the delay occurred, save in the case where, by express agreement, the first carrier has assumed liability for the whole journey.

(3) As regards baggage or cargo, the passenger or consignor will have a right of action against the first carrier, and the passenger or consignee who is entitled to delivery will have a right of action against the last carrier, and further, each may take action against the carrier who performed the carriage during which the destruction, loss, damage or delay took place. These carriers will be jointly and severally liable to the passenger or to the consignor or consignee.

CHAPTER IV
PROVISIONS RELATING TO COMBINED CARRIAGE

Article 31

(1) In the case of combined carriage performed partly by air and partly by any other mode of carriage, the provisions of this Schedule apply only to the carriage by air, provided that the carriage by air falls within the terms of Article 1.

(2) Nothing in this Schedule shall prevent the parties in the case of combined carriage from inserting in the document of air carriage conditions relating to other modes of carriage, provided that the provisions of this Schedule are observed as regards the carriage by air.

CHAPTER V
GENERAL AND FINAL PROVISIONS

Article 32

Any clause contained in the contract and all special agreements entered into before the damage occurred by which the parties purport to infringe the rules laid down by this Schedule, whether by deciding the law to be applied, or by altering the rules as to jurisdiction, shall be null and void. Nevertheless, for the carriage of cargo arbitration clauses are allowed, subject to this Schedule, if the arbitration is to take place within one of the jurisdictions referred to in the first paragraph of Article 28.

Article 33

Nothing contained in this Schedule shall prevent the carrier either from refusing to enter into any contract of carriage, or from making regulations which do not conflict with the provisions of this Schedule.

Article 34

This Schedule does not apply to international carriage by air performed by way of experimental trial by air navigation undertakings with the view to the establishment of a regular line of air navigation, nor does it apply to carriage performed in extraordinary circumstances outside the normal scope of an air carrier's business.

Article 35

The expression "days" when used in this Schedule means current days not working days.

ADDITIONAL PROTOCOL TO THE WARSAW CONVENTION

The High Contracting Parties reserve to themselves the right to declare at the time of ratification or of accession that the first paragraph of Article 2 of this Convention shall not apply to international carriage by air performed directly by the State, its colonies, protectorates or mandated territories or by any other territory under its sovereignty, suzerainty or authority.

B The Guadalajara Convention as applied by Schedule 3

INTERNATIONAL CARRIAGE UNDER THE UNAMENDED WARSAW CONVENTION AS AMENDED BY ADDITIONAL PROTOCOL NO 1 OF MONTREAL 1975

Article I

In the Guadalajara Convention as applied by this Schedule:

(a) "The Warsaw Convention" means the 1955 amended Convention as applied by this Schedule;

(b) "contracting carrier" means a person who as a principal makes an agreement for carriage governed by the Warsaw Convention with a passenger or consignor or with a person acting on behalf of the passenger or consignor;

(c) "actual carrier" means a person, other than the contracting Carrier, who, by virtue of authority from the contracting carrier, performs the whole or part of the carriage contemplated in paragraph (b) but who is not with respect to such part a successive carrier within the meaning of the Warsaw Convention. Such authority is presumed in the absence of proof to the contrary.

Article II

If an actual carrier performs the whole or part of carriage which, according to the agreement referred to in Article 1, paragraph (b), is governed by the Warsaw Convention, both the contracting carrier and the actual carrier shall, except as otherwise provided in the Guadalajara, Convention as applied by this Schedule, be subject to the rules of the Warsaw Convention, the former for the whole of the carriage contemplated in the agreement, the latter solely for the carriage which he performs.

Article III

1 The acts and omissions of the actual carrier and of his servants and agents acting within the scope of their employment shall, in relation to the carriage performed by the actual carrier, be deemed to be also those of the contracting carrier.

2 The acts and omissions of the contracting carrier and of his servants and agents acting within the scope of their employment shall, in relation to the carriage performed by the actual carrier, be deemed to be also those of the actual carrier. Nevertheless, no such act or omission shall subject the actual carrier to liability exceeding the limits specified in Article 22 of the Warsaw Convention. Any special agreement under which the contracting carrier assumes obligations not imposed by the Warsaw Convention or any waiver of rights conferred by that Convention or any special declaration of interest in delivery at destination contemplated in Article 22 of the said Convention, shall not affect the actual carrier unless agreed to by him.

Article IV

Any complaint to be made or order to be given under the Warsaw Convention to the carrier shall have the same effect whether addressed to the contracting carrier or to the actual carrier. Nevertheless, orders referred to in Article 12 of the Warsaw Convention shall only be effective if addressed to the contracting carrier.

Article V

In relation to the carriage performed by the actual carrier, any servant or agent of that carrier or of the contracting carrier shall, if he proves that he acted within the scope of his employment be entitled to avail himself of the limits of liability which are applicable under the Guadalajara Convention as applied by this Schedule to the carrier whose servant or agent he is unless it is proved that he acted in a manner which, under the Warsaw Convention, prevents the limits of liability from being invoked.

Article VI

In relation to the carriage performed by the actual carrier, the aggregate of the amounts recoverable from that carrier and the contracting carrier, and from their servants and agents acting within the scope of their employment, shall not exceed the highest amount which could be awarded against either the contracting carrier or the actual carrier under the Guadalajara Convention as applied by this Schedule, but none of the persons mentioned shall be liable for a sum in excess of the limit applicable to him.

Article VII

In relation to the carriage performed by the actual carrier, an action for damages may be brought at the option of the plaintiff against that carrier or the contracting carrier, or against both together or separately. If the action is brought against only one of those carriers, that carrier shall have the right to require the other carrier to be joined in the proceedings, the procedure and effects being governed by the law of the court seised of the case.

Article VIII

Any action for damages contemplated in Article VII of the Guadalajara Convention as applied by this Schedule must be brought, at the option of the plaintiff either before a court in which an action may be brought against the contracting carrier, as provided in Article 28 of the Warsaw Convention, or before the court having jurisdiction at the place where the actual carrier is ordinarily resident or has his principal place of business.

Article IX

1 Any contractual provision tending to relieve the contracting carrier or the actual carrier of liability under the Guadalajara Convention as applied by this Schedule or to fix a lower limit than that which is applicable according to the Guadalajara Convention as applied by this Schedule shall be null and void, but the nullity of any such provision does not involve the nullity of the whole agreement, which shall remain subject to the provisions of the Guadalajara Convention as applied by this Schedule.

2 In respect of the carriage performed by the actual carrier, the preceding paragraph shall not apply to contractual provisions governing loss or damage resulting from the inherent defect, quality or vice of the cargo carried.

3 Any clause contained in an agreement for carriage and all special agreements entered into before the damage occurred by which the parties purport to infringe the rules laid down by the Guadalajara Convention as applied by this Schedule, whether by deciding the law to be applied or by altering the rules as to jurisdiction, shall be null and void. Nevertheless, for the carriage of cargo arbitration clauses are allowed, subject to the Guadalajara Convention as applied by this Schedule, if the arbitration is to take place in one of the jurisdictions referred to in Article VIII.

Article X

Except as provided in Article VII, nothing in the Guadalajara Convention as applied by this Schedule shall affect the rights and obligations of the two carriers between themselves.

[2319]

NOTES

Commencement: 6 August 2004.

(*Sch 4 contains revocations.*)

RAILWAYS (CONVENTION ON INTERNATIONAL CARRIAGE BY RAIL) REGULATIONS 2005

(SI 2005/2092)

NOTES

Made: 26 July 2005.

Authority: Railways and Transport Safety Act 2003, s 103, Sch 6, paras 2(a)–(f), (o), (p), 3(1), (2)(a), (b), 4(a)–(d), 7(1), (2)(a), (b), 8(1), (2), 9(1), (2)(a).
Commencement: see reg 1.

ARRANGEMENT OF REGULATIONS

1 Citation and commencement

These Regulations may be cited as the Railways (Convention on International Carriage by Rail) Regulations 2005 and shall come into force on the date, specified in the London, Edinburgh and Belfast Gazettes, on which the Protocol enters into force in respect of the United Kingdom.

[2320]

NOTES
Commencement: to be appointed.

2 Interpretation

(1) In these Regulations—

(a) except where the context otherwise requires a reference to an Article is a reference to the Article so numbered in the Convention and a reference to a paragraph of an Article shall be construed accordingly; and

(b) an expression used in these Regulations and in the Convention has the same meaning as in the Convention.

(2) In these Regulations—

"the 1933 Act" means the Foreign Judgments (Reciprocal Enforcement) Act 1933;

"the 1976 Act" means the Fatal Accidents Act 1976;

"the committees" means any of the following—

(a) the Revision Committee as described in Article 17;
(b) the RID Expert Committee as described in Article 18; and
(c) the Committee of Technical Experts as described in Article 20;

"the Convention" means the version of the "Convention concerning International Carriage by Rail (COTIF) of 9th May 1980" as set out after Article 7 of the Protocol and forming an integral part of the Protocol and comprising—

(a) the Convention itself;
(b) the Protocol on the Privileges and Immunities of the Intergovernmental Organisation for International Carriage by Rail referred to in paragraph 4 of Article 1; and
(c) Appendices A to G to the Convention, including the Annexes to Appendices C and F;

as modified in accordance with its provisions from time to time by a decision of one of the committees under paragraph 4, 5 or 6 of Article 33, as the case may be, whether such modification occurs before or after the coming into force of these Regulations; and

"the Protocol" means the Protocol signed at Vilnius on 3rd June 1999 to modify the "Convention concerning International Carriage by Rail (COTIF) of 9th May 1980".

[2321]

NOTES
Commencement: to be appointed.

3 Convention to have the force of law

(1) The Convention shall have the force of law in the United Kingdom, and judicial notice shall be taken of it.

(2) For the avoidance of doubt any question arising as to whether the Convention applies in the circumstances of a particular case falls to be determined in accordance with the provisions of paragraph 2 of Article 3.

[2322]

NOTES

Commencement: to be appointed.

4 Publication of information concerning the Convention

The Secretary of State shall publish in such manner as he thinks fit information concerning—

(a) any change to the list of parties to the Convention;
(b) any declaration, objection or reservation by a party to the Convention;
(c) the suspension of part of the Convention in relation to a party; and
(d) any modification to the Convention.

[2323]

NOTES

Commencement: to be appointed.

5 Fatal accidents

(1) Where by virtue of the Convention any person has a right of action in respect of the death of a passenger by reason of his being a person whom the passenger was under a legal duty to maintain—

(a) subject to paragraph (2), no action in respect of the passenger's death shall be brought for the benefit of that person under the 1976 Act, but
(b) nothing in section 2(3) of that Act (not more than one action in respect of the same subject matter of complaint) shall prevent an action being brought under that Act for the benefit of any other person.

(2) Nothing in paragraph (1)(a) affects the right of any person to claim damages for bereavement under section 1A of the 1976 Act.

(3) Section 4 of the 1976 Act (exclusion of certain benefits in assessment of damages) shall apply in relation to an action brought by any person under the Convention as it applies in relation to an action under that Act.

(4) Where separate proceedings are brought under the Convention and under the 1976 Act in respect of the death of a passenger, a court, in awarding damages under that Act, shall take into account any damages awarded in the proceedings brought under the Convention and shall have jurisdiction to make any part of its award conditional on the result of those proceedings.

(5) In the application of this regulation to Northern Ireland references to the 1976 Act and to sections 1A, 2(3) and 4 of that Act shall be construed as references to the Fatal Accidents (Northern Ireland) Order 1977 and Articles 3A, 4(3) and 6 of that Order.

(6) The provisions of Schedule 1 to these Regulations shall, as respects Scotland, have effect in lieu of paragraphs (1) to (5).

[2324]

NOTES

Commencement: to be appointed.

6 Power of court to take account of other proceedings

(1) A court before which proceedings are brought to enforce a liability which is limited by any of the provisions of the Convention may at any stage of the proceedings make any such order as appears to the court to be just and equitable in view of those provisions and of any other proceedings which have been, or are likely to be, commenced in the United Kingdom or elsewhere to enforce the liability in whole or in part.

(2) Without prejudice to paragraph (1), a court before which proceedings are brought to enforce a liability which is so limited shall, where the liability is or may be partly enforceable in other proceedings in the United Kingdom or elsewhere, have jurisdiction to award an amount less than the court would have awarded if the limitation applied solely to the proceedings before the court, or to make any part of its award conditional on the result of any other proceedings.

[2325]

NOTES

Commencement: to be appointed.

7 Conversion of special drawing rights into sterling

(1) The special drawing rights by reference to which any liability is limited by the Convention shall, in the case of judicial proceedings or an arbitration in the United Kingdom, be converted into their sterling equivalent on the day of the judgment or award or on such day as may be agreed between the parties to the judicial proceedings or arbitration.

(2) For the purposes of this regulation the value on a particular day of a special drawing right shall be treated as equal to such sum in sterling as the International Monetary Fund have fixed as being the equivalent of one special drawing right—

(a) for that day; or

(b) if no sum has been fixed for that day, for the last day before that day for which a sum has been so fixed.

[2326]

NOTES

Commencement: to be appointed.

8 Enforcement of judgments

(1) Subject to paragraph (2), Part I of the 1933 Act shall apply, whether or not it would otherwise have applied, to any judgment which—

(a) has been pronounced as mentioned in paragraph 1 of Article 12 by a court or tribunal in a State which is a party to the Convention for the time being, other than the United Kingdom; and

(b) has become enforceable under the law applied by that court or tribunal.

(2) In the application of Part I of the 1933 Act in relation to any such judgment section 4 of that Act shall have effect with the omission of subsections (2) and (3).

(3) The registration, in accordance with Part I of the 1933 Act, of any such judgment shall constitute compliance with the required formalities referred to in paragraph 1 of Article 12.

[2327]

NOTES

Commencement: to be appointed.

9 Repeals and revocations and consequential amendments

(1) Schedule 2 (repeals and revocations) shall have effect.

(2) Schedule 3 (consequential amendments) shall have effect.

(3) Nothing in regulation 3 affects any rights or liabilities arising out of an occurrence before its coming into force and paragraphs (1) and (2) above do not affect any enactment in its application to any such rights or liabilities.

[2328]

NOTES

Commencement: to be appointed.

SCHEDULE 1
FATAL ACCIDENTS: SCOTLAND

Regulation 5(6)

1(1) Subject to sub-paragraph (2), no enactment or rule of law shall have effect so as to permit a person who has a right of action under the Convention in respect of the death of a passenger by virtue of his being a person whom the passenger was under a legal duty to maintain to raise any other action in that respect for any loss of support suffered by him.

(2) Sub-paragraph (1) shall not apply in so far as the other action concludes for an award under section 1(4) of the Damages (Scotland) Act 1976.

2 Section 1(5) of the said Act of 1976 (exclusion of certain items in assessment of damages) shall apply to an action brought under the Convention as it applies to an action brought under that Act, but section 6 of that Act shall not apply to such an action under the Convention.

3 Where separate proceedings in respect of the death of a passenger are brought under the Convention and under any other enactment or rule of law the court, in awarding damages in such other proceedings, shall take into account any damages awarded in the proceedings brought under the Convention and may make any part of its award conditional on the result of those proceedings.

[2329]

NOTES

Commencement: to be appointed.

(*Sch 2 contains repeals and revocations; Sch 3 contains consequential amendments.*)

F. INTERNATIONAL CARRIAGE: SEA

CARRIAGE OF PASSENGERS AND THEIR LUGGAGE BY SEA (INTERIM PROVISIONS) ORDER 1980

(SI 1980/1092)

NOTES

Made: 28 July 1980.
Authority: Merchant Shipping Act 1995, s 184.
Commencement: 1 January 1981.

1 Citation, commencement and interpretation

(1) This Order may be cited as the Carriage of Passengers and their Luggage by Sea (Interim Provisions) Order 1980 and shall come into operation on 1st January 1981.

(2) In this Order "international carriage" has the same meaning as in Article 1.9 of the Convention relating to the Carriage of Passengers and their Luggage by Sea 1974 (hereinafter referred to as "the Athens Convention"), as set out in Part I of Schedule 3 to the 1979 Act.

[2330]

2 Application

This Order applies to the following contracts for the carriage of passengers or of passengers and their luggage by sea (being contracts for reward) made on or after 1st January 1981, that is to say:—

(a) any contract for international carriage which is made in the United Kingdom;
(b) any contract for international carriage under which a place in the United Kingdom is the place of departure or destination;
(c) any contract under which the places of departure and destination are in the area consisting of the United Kingdom, the Channel Islands and the Isle of Man and under which there is no intermediate port of call outside that area.

[2331]

3 Application and modification of the Athens Convention

(1) [Except in relation to contracts mentioned in paragraph (c) of Article 2 above made before 30th April 1987] paragraph (2) of this Article shall have effect only until such time as subsections (1) and (2) of section 14 of the 1979 Act (which provide for the Athens Convention to have the force of law in the United Kingdom and for certain related provisions to have effect) come into force.

(2) Part I of Schedule 3 to the 1979 Act (which sets out the text of the Athens Convention) shall have the force of law in the United Kingdom in relation to, and to matters connected with, contracts to which this Order applies, subject to the modifications specified in the Schedule hereto and (as so modified) shall so have effect subject to the provisions of Part II of the said Schedule 3 as modified by the Schedule hereto.

(3) This Order shall bind the Crown.

[2332]

NOTES

Para (1): words in square brackets inserted by the Carriage of Passengers and their Luggage by Sea (Domestic Carriage) Order 1987, SI 1987/670, art 4.

SCHEDULE

Article 3

Modifications to Part I of Schedule 3 of the 1979 Act

1. In Article 2, for paragraph 1 there shall be substituted—

"1. This Convention shall apply to any carriage if—

(a) it is international carriage and the contract of carriage is made in the United Kingdom; or

(b) it is international carriage and, under the contract of carriage, a place in the United Kingdom is the place of departure or destination; or

(c) under the contract of carriage, the places of departure and destination are in the area consisting of the United Kingdom, the Channel Islands and the Isle of Man and there is no intermediate port of call outside that area".

2. In Article 7, paragraph 2 shall be omitted.

3. In Article 17.1, the words "provided that the Court is located in a State Party to this Convention" shall be omitted.

Modification to Part II of Schedule 3 to the 1979 Act

4. Paragraph 10 of Part II of Schedule 3 to the 1979 Act shall be omitted.

[2333]

CARRIAGE OF PASSENGERS AND THEIR LUGGAGE BY SEA (INTERIM PROVISIONS) (NOTICE) ORDER 1980

(SI 1980/1125)

NOTES

Made: 30 July 1980.

Authority: Merchant Shipping Act 1979, Sch 3, Pt II, para 11; following the consolidation of the Merchant Shipping Act 1979, Sch 3, Pt II, para 11, this Order now has effect as if made under the Merchant Shipping Act 1995, Sch 6, Pt II, para 11, by virtue of the Interpretation Act 1978, s 17(2)(b).

Commencement: 1 January 1981.

1—(1) This Order may be cited as the Carriage of Passengers and their Luggage by Sea (Interim Provisions) (Notice) Order 1980 and shall come into operation on 1st January 1981.

(2) In this Order—

"carrier" "luggage" and "passenger" have the same meanings as in Article 1 of the Convention relating to the Carriage of Passengers and their Luggage by Sea 1974 (hereinafter referred to as "the Athens Convention"), as set out in Part I of Schedule 3 to the 1979 Act;

"the principal Order" means the Carriage of Passengers and their Luggage by Sea (Interim Provisions) Order 1980.

[2334]

2—(1) In relation to any contract of carriage to which the principal Order applies, the carrier shall give to the passenger notice of those provisions of the Athens Convention specified in the Schedule hereto.

(2) Such notice shall be given before departure and it shall be sufficient compliance with paragraph (1) if the notice contains a statement that—

(a) the provisions of the Athens Convention may be applicable; and

(b) the Athens Convention in most cases limits the carrier's liability for death or personal injury or loss of or damage to luggage (including a vehicle) and makes special provision for valuables; and

(c) the Athens Convention presumes that luggage has been delivered undamaged unless written notice is given to the carrier—

(i) in the case of apparent damage, before or at the time of disembarkation or re-delivery, or

(ii) in the case of damage which is not apparent or of loss, within 15 days from the date of disembarkation or re-delivery or from the time when such re-delivery should have taken place—

Provided that where a ticket is issued, and it is practicable to do so, the ticket itself shall contain a statement specifying the matters set out in subparagraphs (a) to (c).

[2335]

3 Any carrier who fails to comply with Article 2 above shall be guilty of an offence and liable on summary conviction to a fine of an amount not exceeding £500.

[2336]

SCHEDULE
PROVISIONS OF THE ATHENS CONVENTION OF WHICH NOTICE MUST BE GIVEN TO PASSENGERS

Article 2(1)

Article 5—Valuables;

Article 7—Limit of liability for personal injury;

Article 8—Limit of liability for loss of, or damage to, luggage;

Article 15—Notice of loss or damage to luggage.

[2337]

CARRIAGE OF GOODS BY SEA (PARTIES TO CONVENTION) ORDER 1985

(SI 1985/443)

NOTES

Made: 20 March 1985.
Authority: Carriage of Goods by Sea Act 1971, s 2.
Commencement: 10 April 1985.

1 This Order may be cited as the Carriage of Goods by Sea (Parties to Convention) Order 1985 and shall come into operation on 10th April 1985.

[2338]

2 It is hereby certified that the contracting States to the International Convention for the Unification of Certain Rules of Law relating to Bills of Lading signed at Brussels on 25th August 1924, as amended by the Protocol signed at Brussels on 23rd February 1968, and the territories in respect of which they are respectively contracting States are as listed in the Schedule to this Order.

[2339]

3 (*Revokes the Carriage of Goods by Sea* (*Parties to Convention*) *Order 1982, SI 1982/1665.*)

SCHEDULE

Article 2

Contracting States	*Territories in respect of which they are respectively parties*	*Dates on which the Convention as amended came into force*
The United Kingdom of Great Britain and Northern Ireland	Great Britain and Northern Ireland	23rd June 1977
	The Isle of Man	23rd June 1977
	Bermuda	1st February 1981
	British Antarctic Territory	20th January 1984
	British Virgin Islands	20th January 1984
	Cayman Islands	20th January 1984
	Falkland Islands	20th January 1984

	Falkland Islands Dependencies	20th January 1984
	Gibraltar	22nd December 1977
	Hong Kong	1st February 1981
	Montserrat	20th January 1984
	Turks and Caicos Islands	20th January 1984
The Kingdom of Belgium	Belgium	6th December 1978
[The Republic of Croatia	Croatia	28 January 1999]
The Kingdom of Denmark	Denmark	23rd June 1977
The Republic of Ecuador	Ecuador	23rd June 1977
The Arab Republic of Egypt	Egypt	30th April 1983
The Republic of Finland	Finland	1st March 1985
The French Republic	France	23rd June 1977
[Georgia	Georgia	20 May 1996]
The German Democratic Republic	German Democratic Republic	14th May 1979
[Italy	Italy	22 November 1985]
The Lebanese Republic	Lebanon	23rd June 1977
The Kingdom of the Netherlands	The Kingdom of the Netherlands in Europe	26th July 1982
The Kingdom of Norway	Norway	23rd June 1977
The Polish People's Republic	Poland	12th May 1980
The Republic of Singapore	Singapore	23rd June 1977
Spain	Spain	14th February 1984
The Democratic Socialist Republic of Sri Lanka	Sri Lanka	21st January 1982
The Kingdom of Sweden	Sweden	23rd June 1977
The Swiss Confederation	Switzerland	23rd June 1977
The Syrian Arab Republic	Syria	23rd June 1977
The Kingdom of Tonga	Tonga	13th September 1978

[2340]

NOTES

Entries relating to "The Republic of Croatia", "Georgia" and "Italy" inserted by the Carriage of Goods by Sea (Parties to Convention) (Amendment) Order 2000, SI 2000/1103, art 2.

LIMITATION OF LIABILITY FOR MARITIME CLAIMS (PARTIES TO CONVENTION) ORDER 1986

(SI 1986/2224)

NOTES

Made: 16 December 1986.

Authority: Merchant Shipping Act 1979, Sch 4, Pt II, para 13; following the consolidation of the Merchant Shipping Act 1979, Sch 4, Pt II, para 13, this Order now has effect as if made under the Merchant Shipping Act 1995, Sch 7, Pt II, para 13, by virtue of the Interpretation Act 1978, s 17(2)(b).

Commencement: 6 January 1987.

1 This Order may be cited as the Limitation of Liability for Maritime Claims (Parties to Convention) Order 1986 and shall come into operation on 6th January 1987.

[2341]

2 In this Order, "the Convention" means the Convention on Limitation of Liability for Maritime Claims 1976 as set out in Part I of Schedule 4 to the Merchant Shipping Act 1979.

[2342]

3 It is hereby declared that the States specified in the first column of the Schedule to this Order are parties to the Convention, and that each of those States is a party to the Convention in respect of the territories specified opposite thereto in the second column of the Schedule and with effect from the date of entry into force of the Convention for that State as specified in the third column of the Schedule.

[2343]

SCHEDULE

STATES WHICH ARE PARTIES TO THE CONVENTION

Article 3

States	Territories	Date of Entry into Force of the Convention
The United Kingdom of Great Britain and Northern Ireland	Great Britain and Northern Ireland	1st December 1986
	The Bailiwick of Guernsey	1st December 1986
	The Bailiwick of Jersey	1st December 1986
	Isle of Man	1st December 1986
	Bermuda	1st December 1986
	British Virgin Islands	1st December 1986
	Cayman Islands	1st December 1986
	Falkland Islands	1st December 1986
	Gibraltar	1st December 1986
	Hong Kong	1st December 1986
	Montserrat	1st December 1986
	Pitcairn, Henderson, Ducie and Oeno Islands	1st December 1986
	Saint Helena and Dependencies	1st December 1986
	Sovereign Base Areas of Akrotiri and Dhekelia	1st December 1986
	Turks and Caicos Islands	1st December 1986
The Commonwealth of the Bahamas	The Bahamas	1st December 1986
Belize	Belize	1st December 1986
The People's Republic of Benin	Benin	1st December 1986
The Kingdom of Denmark	Denmark	1st December 1986
The Republic of Finland	Finland	1st December 1986
The French Republic	France	1st December 1986
Japan	Japan	1st December 1986
The Republic of Liberia	Liberia	1st December 1986

States	Territories	Date of Entry into Force of the Convention
The Kingdom of Norway	Norway	1st December 1986
The People's Republic of Poland	Poland	1st December 1986
The Kingdom of Spain	Spain	1st December 1986
The Kingdom of Sweden	Sweden	1st December 1986
The Yemen Arab Republic	Yemen Arab Republic	1st December 1986

[2344]

CARRIAGE OF PASSENGERS AND THEIR LUGGAGE BY SEA (DOMESTIC CARRIAGE) ORDER 1987

(SI 1987/670)

NOTES

Made: 7 April 1987.

Authority: Merchant Shipping Act 1979, s 16(2), (5); following the consolidation of the Merchant Shipping Act 1979, s 16(2), (5), this Order now has effect as if made under the Merchant Shipping Act 1995, s 184, by virtue of the Interpretation Act 1978, s 17(2)(b).

Commencement: 30 April 1987.

1 This Order may be cited as the Carriage of Passengers and their Luggage by Sea (Domestic Carriage) Order 1987 and shall come into force on 30th April 1987.

[2345]

2 This Order applies to the following contracts for the carriage of passengers or of passengers and their luggage by sea (being contracts for reward) made on or after 30th April 1987, that is to say any contract under which the places of departure and destination are in the area consisting of the United Kingdom, the Channel Islands and the Isle of Man and under which there is no intermediate port of call outside that area.

[2346]

3—(1) Part I of Schedule 3 to the 1979 Act (which sets out the text of the Athens Convention) shall have the force of law in the United Kingdom in relation to, and to matters connected with, contracts to which this Order applies, subject to the modifications specified in the Schedule hereto and (as so modified) shall so have effect subject to the provisions of Part II of the said Schedule 3 as modified by the Schedule hereto.

(2) This Order shall bind the Crown.

[2347]

4 (*Amends the Carriage of Passengers and their Luggage by Sea (Interim Provisions) Order 1980, SI 1980/1092, art 3(1) at* **[2332]**.)

SCHEDULE

Article 3

MODIFICATIONS TO PART I OF SCHEDULE 3 TO THE 1979 ACT

1. In Article 2, for paragraph 1 there shall be substituted:—

"1. This Convention shall apply to any carriage if under the contract of carriage the places of departure and destination are in the area consisting of the United Kingdom, the Channel Islands and the Isle of Man and there is no intermediate port of call outside that area".

2. In Article 7, paragraph 2 shall be omitted.

3. In Article 17.1, the words "provided that the Court is located in a State Party to this Convention" shall be omitted.

MODIFICATIONS TO PART II OF SCHEDULE 3 TO THE 1979 ACT

4. Paragraph 10 of Part II of Schedule 3 to the 1979 Act shall be omitted.

[2348]

CARRIAGE OF PASSENGERS AND THEIR LUGGAGE BY SEA (NOTICE) ORDER 1987

(SI 1987/703)

NOTES

Made: 9 April 1987.

Authority: Carriage of Passengers and their Luggage by Sea (Domestic Carriage) Order 1987, SI 1987/670, art 3(1), Merchant Shipping Act 1979, Sch 3, Pt II, para 11; following the consolidation of the Merchant Shipping Act 1979, Sch 3, Pt II, para 11, to the extent that it is made under that Act, this Order now has effect as if made under the Merchant Shipping Act 1995, Sch 6, Pt II, by virtue of the Interpretation Act 1978, s 17(2)(b).

Commencement: 30 April 1987.

1—(1) This Order may be cited as the Carriage of Passengers and their Luggage by Sea (Notice) Order 1987 and shall come into force on 30th April 1987.

(2) In this Order—

"carrier", "luggage" and "passenger" have the same meanings as in article 1 of the Convention relating to the Carriage of Passengers and their Luggage by Sea 1974 (hereinafter referred to as "the Athens Convention"), as set out in Part I of Schedule 3 to the 1979 Act;

"the Domestic Carriage Order" means the Carriage of Passengers and their Luggage by Sea (Domestic Carriage) Order 1987.

[2349]

2—(1) In relation to any contract of carriage to which

(a) article 2 in Part I of Schedule 3 of the 1979 Act applies, where the contract for carriage is made in the United Kingdom, or where a place in the United Kingdom is the place of departure; or

(b) the Domestic Carriage Order applies

the carrier shall give to the passenger notice of those provisions of the Athens Convention specified in the Schedule hereto.

(2) Such notice shall be given before departure and it shall be sufficient compliance with paragraph (1) if the notice contains a statement that—

(a) the provisions of the Athens Convention may be applicable; and

(b) the Athens Convention in most cases limits the carrier's liability for death or personal injury or loss of or damage to luggage (including a vehicle) and makes special provision for valuables; and

(c) the Athens Convention presumes that luggage has been delivered undamaged unless written notice is given to the carrier—

(i) in the case of apparent damage, before or at the time of disembarkation or re-delivery, or

(ii) in the case of damage which is not apparent or of loss, within 15 days from the date of disembarkation or re-delivery or from the time when such re-delivery should have taken place;

Provided that where a ticket is issued, and it is practicable to do so, the ticket itself shall contain a statement specifying the matters set out in subparagraphs (a) to (c).

[2350]

3 Any carrier who fails to comply with article 2 above shall be guilty of an offence and liable on summary conviction to a fine of an amount not exceeding [level 4 on the standard scale].

[2351]

NOTES

Maximum fine converted to a level on the standard scale by virtue of the Criminal Justice Act 1988, s 52.

SCHEDULE

PROVISIONS OF THE ATHENS CONVENTION OF WHICH NOTICE MUST BE GIVEN TO PASSENGERS

Article 2(1)

Article 5—Valuables;

Article 7—Limit of liability for personal injury;

Article 8—Limit of liability for loss of, or damage to, luggage;

Article 15—Notice of loss or damage to luggage.

[2352]

CARRIAGE OF PASSENGERS AND THEIR LUGGAGE BY SEA (PARTIES TO CONVENTION) ORDER 1987

(SI 1987/931)

NOTES

Made: 18 May 1987.

Authority: Merchant Shipping Act 1979, Sch 3, Pt II, para 10; following the consolidation of the Merchant Shipping Act 1979, Sch 3, Part II, para 10, this Order now has effect as if made under the Merchant Shipping Act 1995, Sch 6, Pt II, by virtue of the Interpretation Act 1978, s 17(2)(b).

Commencement: 17 June 1987.

1 This Order may be cited as the Carriage of Passengers and their Luggage by Sea (Parties to Convention) Order 1987 and shall come into force on 17th June 1987.

[2353]

2 In this Order, "the Convention" means the Convention relating to the Carriage of Passengers and their Luggage by Sea as set out in Part I of Schedule 3 to the Merchant Shipping Act 1979.

[2354]

3 It is hereby declared that, in relation to a State specified in the first column of the Schedule to this Order, the State is a party to the Convention in respect of the country specified opposite thereto in the second column of the Schedule with effect from the date of entry into force of the Convention for that State as specified in the third column of the Schedule.

[2355]

SCHEDULE

STATES WHICH ARE PARTIES TO THE CONVENTION AND COUNTRIES IN RESPECT OF WHICH THE CONVENTION IS IN FORCE

Article 3

State	*Country*	*Date of Entry into Force of Convention*
The United Kingdom of Great Britain and Northern Ireland	Great Britain and Northern Ireland	30th April 1987
	The Bailiwick of Guernsey	
	The Bailiwick of Jersey	

State	Country	Date of Entry into Force of Convention
	The Isle of Man	
	Bermuda	
	British Virgin Islands	
	Cayman Islands	
	Falkland Islands	
	Gibraltar	
	Hong Kong	
	Montserrat	
	Pitcairn	
	Saint Helena and Dependencies	
The Argentine Republic	Argentina	28th April 1987
The Commonwealth of the Bahamas	The Bahamas	28th April 1987
The German Democratic Republic	German Democratic Republic	28th April 1987
The Republic of Liberia	Liberia	28th April 1987
The Polish People's Republic	Poland	28th April 1987
The Kingdom of Spain	Spain	28th April 1987
The Kingdom of Tonga	Tonga	28th April 1987
The Union of Soviet Socialist Republics	All territories comprised within the Soviet Socialist Republics	28th April 1987
The Yemen Arab Republic	Yemen Arab Republic	28th April 1987

[2356]

CARRIAGE OF PASSENGERS AND THEIR LUGGAGE BY SEA (UNITED KINGDOM CARRIERS) ORDER 1998

(SI 1998/2917)

NOTES

Made: 25 November 1998.
Authority: Merchant Shipping Act 1995, Sch 6, Pt II, para 4.
Commencement: 1 January 1999.

1 This Order may be cited as the Carriage of Passengers and their Luggage by Sea (United Kingdom Carriers) Order 1998 and shall come into force on 1st January 1999.

[2357]

2 (*Revokes the Carriage of Passengers and their Luggage by Sea (United Kingdom Carriers) Order 1987, SI 1987/855 and the Carriage of Passengers and their Luggage by Sea (United Kingdom Carriers) (Amendment) Order 1989, SI 1989/1880.*)

3 In relation to any carrier whose principal place of business is in the United Kingdom, paragraph 1 of Article 7 to the Convention Relating to the Carriage of Passengers and their Luggage by Sea, set out in Part I of Schedule 6 to the Merchant Shipping Act 1995, (including that paragraph as applied to domestic carriage by the Carriage of Passengers and their

Luggage by Sea (Domestic Carriage) Order 1987) shall have effect as if for the limit of 46,666 units of account there specified there were substituted a limit of 300,000 units of account.

[2358]

4 This Order does not apply in relation to any liability arising out of an occurrence which took place before the coming into force of the Order.

[2359]

MERCHANT SHIPPING (LIABILITY OF SHIPOWNERS AND OTHERS) (RATE OF INTEREST) ORDER 1999

(SI 1999/1922)

NOTES

Made: 6 July 1999.
Authority: Merchant Shipping Act 1995, Sch 7, Pt II, para 8(1).
Commencement: 1 September 1999.

1 Citation, commencement and interpretation

(1) This Order may be cited as the Merchant Shipping (Liability of Shipowners and Others) (Rate of Interest) Order 1999 and shall come into force on 1st September 1999.

(2) In this Order "the prescribed rate" means one per cent more than the base rate quoted from time to time by the Committee of London Clearing Bankers or, where there is for the time being more than one such rate, the lowest of them.

[2360]

2 (*Revokes the Merchant Shipping* (*Liability of Shipowners and Others*) (*Rate of Interest*) *Order 1998, SI 1998/1795.*)

3 Rate of Interest

The rate of interest for the purposes of article 11(1) of the Convention of Limitation of Liability for Maritime Claims 1976 shall be:—

(a) where the occurrence takes place before 1st September 1999 but the fund is constituted on or after that date:
  (i) 12 per cent from the date of the occurrence until 31st December 1994,
  (ii) 6.75 per cent on and after 1st January 1995 until 31st August 1998,
  (iii) 8.5 per cent on and after 1st September 1998 until 31st August 1999, and
  (iv) the prescribed rate on and after 1st September 1999 [until 30th December 2003], or

(b) where the occurrence takes place on or after 1st September 1999 [but before 31st December 2003], the prescribed rate [until 30th December 2003].

[2361]

NOTES

Words in square brackets in para (a)(iv) and words in first pair of square brackets in para (b) inserted by the Merchant Shipping (Liability of Shipowners and Others) (Rate of Interest) (Amendment) Order 2003, SI 2003/3136, art 2; words in second pair of square brackets in para (b) inserted by the Merchant Shipping (Liability of Shipowners and Others) (New Rate of Interest) Order 2004, SI 2004/931, art 3(2).

G. STATE IMMUNITY AND INTERNATIONAL ORGANISATIONS

BRETTON WOODS AGREEMENTS ORDER IN COUNCIL 1946

(SR & O 1946/36)

NOTES

Made: 10 January 1946.

Authority: Bretton Woods Agreements Act 1945, s 3 (now repealed); this Order now takes effect, so far as it applies to the International Monetary Fund, under the International Monetary Fund Act 1979, s 5 and, so far as it applies to the International Bank, under the Overseas Development and Cooperation Act 1980, s 9.

Commencement: 10 January 1946.

1 This Order may be cited as "The Bretton Woods Agreements Order in Council 1946".
[2362]

2(1) In this Order, the expressions "the Fund Agreement" and "the Bank Agreement" mean, respectively, the Agreement for the establishment and operation of an international body to be called the International Monetary Fund and the Agreement for the establishment and operation of an international body to be called the International Bank for Reconstruction and Development, which were signed on behalf of His Majesty's Government in the United Kingdom on the twenty-seventh day of December, nineteen hundred and forty-five, and the expressions "the Fund" and "the Bank" mean the bodies established under these Agreements respectively.

(2) The Interpretation Act 1889, shall apply to the interpretation of this Order as it applies to the interpretation of an Act of Parliament.
[2363]

3 To enable the Fund and the Bank to fulfil the functions with which they are respectively entrusted, the provisions of the Fund Agreement and the Bank Agreement set out in the Schedule to this Order shall have the force of law:

Provided that nothing in Section 9 of Article IX of the Fund Agreement or in Section 9 of Article VII of the Bank Agreement shall be construed as—

(a) entitling the Fund or the Bank to import goods free of customs duty without any restriction on their subsequent sale in the country to which they were imported; or

(b) conferring on the Fund or the Bank any exemption from duties or taxes which form part of the price of goods sold[, except that the Fund and the Bank shall have relief, under arrangements made by the Secretary of State, by way of refund of car tax paid on any vehicles and value added tax paid on the supply of any goods and services which are necessary for the exercise of the official activities of the Fund or the Bank, such relief to be subject to compliance with such conditions as may be imposed in accordance with the arrangements]; or

(c) conferring on the Fund or the Bank any exemption from taxes or duties which are in fact no more than charges for services rendered.
[2364]

NOTES

Words in square brackets inserted by the International Organisations (Immunities and Privileges) Miscellaneous Provisions Order 1976, SI 1976/221, art 3.

4 This Order shall extend to all parts of His Majesty's dominions (other than Dominions within the meaning of the Statute of Westminster 1931, territories administered by the Government of any such Dominion and British India) and, to the extent that His Majesty has jurisdiction therein, to all other territories in which His Majesty has from time to time jurisdiction (other than territories in respect of which a mandate from the League of Nations is being exercised by, or which are being administered by, the Government of such a Dominion as aforesaid and territories in India):

Provided that, if, whether before or after the passing of the Bretton Woods Agreements Act 1945, or the making of this Order, effect is given by or under the law of any part of His Majesty's dominions or other territory to any provisions of the said Agreements set out in the Schedule to this Order, this Order, so far as it gives effect to that provision, shall not extend to that part of His Majesty's dominions or other territory as respects any period as respects which effect is given as aforesaid to that provision.

[2365]

SCHEDULE
PROVISIONS OF AGREEMENT WHICH ARE TO HAVE FORCE OF LAW

PART I
FUND AGREEMENT

Article VIII, Section 2(b)

Exchange contracts which involve the currency of any Member and which are contrary to the exchange control regulations of that member maintained or imposed consistently with this Agreement shall be unenforceable in the territories of any member …

ARTICLE IX
STATUS, IMMUNITIES AND PRIVILEGES

....

Section 2. Status of the Fund.

The Fund shall possess full juridical personality, and, in particular, the capacity:

(i) to contract;
(ii) to acquire and dispose of immovable and movable property;
(iii) to institute legal proceedings.

Section 3. Immunity from judicial process.

The Fund, its property and its assets, wherever located and by whomsoever held, shall enjoy immunity from every form of judicial process except to the extent that it expressly waives its immunity for the purpose of any proceedings or by the terms of any contract.

Section 4. Immunity from other action.

Property and assets of the Fund, wherever located and by whomsoever held, shall be immune from search, requisition, confiscation, expropriation or any other form of seizure by executive or legislative action.

Section 5. Immunity of archives.

The archives of the Fund shall be inviolable.

Section 6. Freedom of assets from restrictions.

To the extent necessary to carry out the operations provided for in this Agreement, all property and assets of the Fund shall be free from restrictions, regulations, controls and moratoria of any nature.

....

(Section 8 revoked by the International Monetary Fund (Immunities and Privileges) Order 1977, SI 1977/825, art 3.)

Section 9. Immunities from taxation.

(a) The Fund, its assets, property, income and its operations and transactions authorised by this Agreement, shall be immune from all taxation and from all customs duties. The Fund shall also be immune from liability for the collection or payment of any tax or duty.

PART III
STATUTORY INSTRUMENTS

(b) No tax shall be levied on or in respect of salaries and emoluments paid by the Fund to executive directors, alternates, officers or employees of the Fund who are not local citizens, local subjects, or other local nationals.

(c) No taxation of any kind shall be levied on any obligation or security issued by the Fund, including any dividend or interest thereon, by whomsoever held:

(i) which discriminates against such obligation or security solely because of its origin; or

(ii) if the sole jurisdictional basis for such taxation is the place of currency in which it is issued, made payable or paid, or the location of any office or place of business maintained by the Fund.

[2366]

PART II
BANK AGREEMENT

ARTICLE VII
STATUS, IMMUNITIES AND PRIVILEGES

....

Section 2. Status of the Bank.

The Bank shall possess full juridical personality, and, in particular, the capacity:

(i) to contract;

(ii) to acquire and dispose of immovable and movable property;

(iii) to institute legal proceedings.

Section 3. Position of the Bank with regard to judicial process.

Actions may be brought against the Bank only in a court of competent jurisdiction in the territories of a member in which the Bank has an office, has appointed an agent for the purpose of accepting service or notice of process, or has issued or guaranteed securities. No actions shall, however, be brought by members or persons acting for or deriving claims from members. The property and assets of the Bank shall, wheresoever located and by whomsoever held, be immune from all forms of seizure, attachment or execution before the delivery of final judgment against the Bank.

Section 4. Immunity of assets from seizure.

Property and assets of the Bank, wherever located and by whomsoever held, shall be immune from search, requisition, confiscation, expropriation or any other form of seizure by executive or legislative action.

Section 5. Immunity of archives.

The archives of the Bank shall be inviolable.

Section 6. Freedom of assets from restrictions.

To the extent necessary to carry out the operations provided for in this Agreement and subject to the provisions of this Agreement, all property and assets of the Bank shall be free from restrictions, regulations, controls and moratoria of any nature.

....

Section 8. Immunities and privileges of officers and employees.

All governors, executive directors, alternates, officers and employees of the Bank

(i) shall be immune from legal process with respect to acts performed by them in their official capacity except when the Bank waives this immunity.

Section 9. Immunities from taxation.

(a) The Bank, its assets, property, income and its operations and transactions authorised by this Agreement, shall be immune from all taxation and from all customs duties. The Bank shall also be immune from liability for the collection or payment of any tax or duty.

(b) No tax shall be levied on or in respect of salaries and emoluments paid by the Bank to executive directors, alternates, officials or employees of the Bank who are not local citizens, local subjects, or other local nationals.

(c) No taxation of any kind shall be levied on any obligation or security issued by the Bank (including any dividend or interest thereon) by whomsoever held—

(i) which discriminates against such obligation or security solely because it is issued by the Bank; or

(ii) if the sole jurisdictional basis for such taxation is the place or currency in which it is issued, made payable or paid, or the location of any office or place of business maintained by the Bank.

(d) No taxation of any kind shall be levied on any obligation or security guaranteed by the Bank (including any dividend or interest thereon) by whomsoever held—

(i) which discriminates against such obligation or security solely because it is guaranteed by the Bank; or

(ii) if the sole jurisdictional basis for such taxation is the location of any office or place of business maintained by the Bank.

[2367]

INTERNATIONAL FINANCE CORPORATION ORDER 1955

(SI 1955/1954)

NOTES

Made: 22 December 1955.

Authority: International Finance Corporation Act 1955, s 3 (now repealed), then took effect under the Overseas Development and Co-operation Act 1980, s 9; following the repeal of that section, this Order now has effect as if made under the International Development Act 2002, s 12, by virtue of the Interpretation Act 1978, s 17(2)(b).

Commencement: 20 July 1956.

1(1) This Order may be cited as the International Finance Corporation Order 1955.

(2) This Order shall come into operation on the date on which her Majesty's Government in the United Kingdom becomes a member of the Corporation, which date shall be notified in the London Gazette.

[2368]

2(1) In this Order, "the Agreement" means the Agreement for the establishment and operation of an International Finance Corporation signed on behalf of her Majesty's Government in the United Kingdom on the twenty-fifth day of October, 1955, in pursuance of the Articles referred to in section one of the said Act; and "the Corporation" means the body established under the Agreement.

(2) The Interpretation Act 1889 shall apply to the interpretation of this Order as it applies to the interpretation of an Act of Parliament.

[2369]

3 The provisions of the Agreement set out in the Schedule to this Order shall have the force of law:

Provided that nothing in Section 9 of Article VI of the Agreement shall be construed as—

(a) entitling the Corporation to import goods free of customs duty without any restriction on their subsequent sale in the country to which they were imported; or

(b) conferring on the Corporation any exemption from duties or taxes which form part of the price of goods sold [,except that it shall have relief, under arrangements made by the Secretary of State, by way of refund of car tax paid on any vehicles and value added tax paid on the supply of any goods and services which are necessary for the exercise of its official activities, such relief to be subject to compliance with such conditions as may be imposed in accordance with the arrangements]; or

(c) conferring on the Corporation any exemption from duties or taxes which are in fact no more than charges for services rendered. **[2370]**

NOTES

Para (b): words in square brackets substituted by the International Organisations (Immunities and Privileges) Miscellaneous Provisions Order 1976, SI 1976/221, art 4.

4 This Order shall extend to all parts of Her Majesty's dominions (other than Canada, Australia, New Zealand, the Union of South Africa, Pakistan and Ceylon, and any territory administered by the Government of any of those countries) and, to the extent that Her Majesty has jurisdiction therein, to all other territories for whose foreign relations Her Majesty's Government in the United Kingdom is responsible:

Provided that if, whether before or after the passing of the International Finance Corporation Act 1955, and whether before or after the coming into force of this Order, effect is given by or under the law of any such part of Her Majesty's dominions or other territory to any provision of the Agreement set out in the Schedule to this Order, this Order, so far as it gives effect to that provision, shall not extend to that part of Her Majesty's dominions or other territory in respect of any period for which effect is so given to that provision.

[2371]

SCHEDULE
PROVISIONS OF THE AGREEMENT AS TO STATUS, IMMUNITIES AND PRIVILEGES

ARTICLE III
OPERATIONS

....

Section 5. Applicability of certain foreign exchange restrictions

Funds received by or payable to the Corporation in respect of an investment of the Corporation made in any member's territories pursuant to Section 1 of this Article shall not be free, solely by reason of any provision of this Agreement, from generally applicable foreign exchange restrictions, regulations and controls in force in the territories of that member.

ARTICLE VI
STATUS, IMMUNITIES AND PRIVILEGES

....

Section 2. Status of the Corporation

The Corporation shall possess full juridical personality and, in particular, the capacity:

(i) to contract;

(ii) to acquire and dispose of immovable and movable property;

(iii) to institute legal proceedings.

Section 3. Position of the Corporation with regard to judicial process

Actions may be brought against the Corporation only in a court of competent jurisdiction in the territories of a member in which the Corporation has an office, has appointed an agent for the purpose of accepting service or notice of process, or has issued or guaranteed securities. No actions shall, however, be brought by members of persons acting for or deriving claims from members. The property and assets of the Corporation shall, wheresoever located and by whomsoever held, be immune from all forms of seizure, attachment or execution before the delivery of final judgment against the Corporation.

Section 4. Immunity of assets from seizure

Property and assets of the Corporation, wherever located and by whomsoever held, shall be immune from search, requisition, confiscation, expropriation or any other form of seizure by executive or legislative action.

Section 5. Immunity of archives

The archives of the Corporation shall be inviolable.

Section 6. Freedom of assets from restrictions

To the extent necessary to carry out the operations provided for in this Agreement and subject to the provisions of Article III, Section 5, and the other provisions of this Agreement, all property and assets of the Corporation shall be free from restrictions, regulations, controls and moratoria of any nature.

....

Section 8. Immunities and privileges of officers and employees

All Governors, Directors, Alternates, officers and employees of the Corporation:

(i) shall be immune from legal process with respect to acts performed by them in their official capacity …

Section 9. Immunities from taxation

(a) The Corporation, its assets, property, income and its operations and transactions authorised by this Agreement, shall be immune from all taxation and from all customs duties. The Corporation shall also be immune from liability for the collection or payment of any tax or duty.

(b) No tax shall be levied on or in respect of salaries and emoluments paid by the Corporation to Directors, Alternates, officials or employees of the Corporation who are not local citizens, local subjects, or other local nationals.

(c) No taxation of any kind shall be levied on any obligation or security issued by the Corporation (including any dividend or interest thereon) by whomsoever held:

(i) which discriminates against such obligation or security solely because it is issued by the Corporation; or

(ii) if the sole jurisdictional basis for such taxation is the place or currency in which it is issued, made payable or paid, or the location of any office or place of business maintained by the Corporation.

(d) No taxation of any kind shall be levied on any obligation or security guaranteed by the Corporation (including any dividend or interest thereon) by whomsoever held

(i) which discriminates against such obligation or security solely because it is guaranteed by the Corporation; or

(ii) if the sole jurisdictional basis for such taxation is the location of any office or place of business maintained by the Corporation.

....

Section 11. Waiver

The Corporation in its discretion may waive any of the privileges and immunities conferred under this Article to such extent and upon such conditions as it may determine.

[2372]

INTERNATIONAL DEVELOPMENT ASSOCIATION ORDER 1960

(SI 1960/1383)

NOTES

Made: 3 August 1960.

PART III STATUTORY INSTRUMENTS

Authority: International Development Association Act 1960, s 3 (now repealed); then took effect under the Overseas Development and Co-operation Act 1980, s 9; following the repeal of that section, this Order now has effect as if made under the International Development Act 2002, s 12, by virtue of the Interpretation Act 1978, s 17(2)(b).
Commencement: 24 September 1960.

1(1) This Order may be cited as the International Development Association Order 1960.

(2) This Order shall come into operation on the date on which Her Majesty's Government in the United Kingdom becomes a member of the Association, which date shall be notified in the London Gazette.

[2373]

2(1) In this Order "the Agreement" and "the Association" have the same meanings respectively as in the International Development Association Act 1960.

(2) The Interpretation Act 1889 shall apply to the interpretation of this Order as it applies to the interpretation of an Act of Parliament.

[2374]

3 The provisions of the Agreement set out in the Schedule to this Order shall have the force of law:

Provided that nothing in Section 9 of Article VIII of the Agreement shall be construed as—

(a) entitling the Association to import goods free of customs duty without any restriction on their subsequent sale in the country to which they were imported; or

(b) conferring on the Association any exemption from duties or taxes which form part of the price of goods sold[, except that it shall have relief, under arrangements made by the Secretary of State, by way of refund of car tax paid on any vehicles and value added tax paid on the supply of any goods and services which are necessary for the exercise of its official activities, such relief to be subject to compliance with such conditions as may be imposed in accordance with the arrangements]; or

(c) conferring on the Association any exemption from duties or taxes which are in fact no more than charges for services rendered.

[2375]

NOTES

Para (b): words in square brackets inserted by the International Organisations (Immunities and Privileges) Miscellaneous Provisions Order 1976, SI 1976/221, art 4.

4 This Order shall extend to all parts of Her Majesty's dominions (other than Canada, Australia, New Zealand, the Union of South Africa and Ceylon, and any territory administered by the Government of any of those countries) and, to the extent that Her Majesty has jurisdiction therein, to all other territories for whose foreign relations Her Majesty's Government in the United Kingdom is responsible:

Provided that if, whether before or after the passing of the International Development Association Act 1960, and whether before or after the coming into operation of this Order, effect is given by or under the law of any such part of Her Majesty's dominions or other territory to any provision of the Agreement set out in the Schedule to this Order, this Order, so far as it gives effect to that provision, shall not extend to that part of Her Majesty's dominions or other territory in respect of any period for which effect is so given to that provision.

[2376]

SCHEDULE
PROVISIONS OF THE AGREEMENT AS TO STATUS, IMMUNITIES AND PRIVILEGES

ARTICLE VIII
STATUS, IMMUNITIES AND PRIVILEGES

....

Section 2. Status of the Association

The Association shall possess full judicial personality and, in particular, the capacity:

(i) to contract;

(ii) to acquire and dispose of immovable and movable property;

(iii) to institute legal proceedings.

Section 3. Position of the Association with Regard to Judicial Process

Actions may be brought against the Association only in a court of competent jurisdiction in the territories of a member in which the Association has an office, has appointed an agent for the purpose of accepting service or notice of process, or has issued or guaranteed securities. No actions shall, however, be brought by members or persons acting for or deriving claims from members. The property and assets of the Association shall, wheresoever located and by whomsoever held, be immune from all forms of seizure, attachment or execution before the delivery of final judgment against the Association.

Section 4. Immunity of Assets from Seizure

Property and assets of the Association, wherever located and by whomsoever held, shall be immune from search, requisition, confiscation, expropriation or any other form of seizure by executive or legislative action.

Section 5. Immunity of Archives

The archives of the Association shall be inviolable.

Section 6. Freedom of Assets from Restrictions

To the extent necessary to carry out the operations provided for in this Agreement and subject to the provisions of this Agreement, all property and assets of the Association shall be free from restrictions, regulations, controls and moratoria of any nature.

....

Section 8. Immunities and Privileges of Officers and Employees

All Governors, Executive Directors, Alternates, officers and employees of the Association:

(i) shall be immune from legal process with respect to acts performed by them in their official capacity except when the Association waives this immunity ...

Section 9. Immunities from Taxation

(a) The Association, its assets, property, income and its operations and transactions authorized by this Agreement, shall be immune from all taxation and from all customs duties. The Association shall also be immune from liability for the collection or payment of any tax or duty.

(b) No tax shall be levied on or in respect of salaries and emoluments paid by the Association to Executive Directors, Alternates officials or employees of the Association who are not local citizens, local subjects, or other local nationals.

(c) No taxation of any kind shall be levied on any obligation or security issued by the Association (including any dividend or interest thereon) by whomsoever held

(i) which discriminates against such obligation or security solely because it is issued by the Association; or

(ii) if the sole jurisdictional basis for such taxation is the place or currency in which it is issued, made payable or paid, or the location of any office or place of business maintained by the Association.

(d) No taxation of any kind shall be levied on any obligation or security guaranteed by the Association (including any dividend or interest thereon) by whomsoever held

(i) which discriminates against such obligation or security solely because it is guaranteed by the Association; or

(ii) if the sole jurisdictional basis for such taxation is the location of any office or place of business maintained by the Association.

[2377]

EUROCONTROL (IMMUNITIES AND PRIVILEGES) ORDER 1970

(SI 1970/1940)

NOTES

Made: 17 December 1970.
Authority: International Organisations Act 1968, s 1.
Commencement: see art 1(2).

1(1) This Order may be cited as the Eurocontrol (Immunities and Privileges) Order 1970.

(2) This Order shall come into operation on the day on which the Additional Protocol to the "Eurocontrol" International Convention relating to Co-operation for the Safety of Air Navigation signed in Brussels on 6th July 1970 enters into force. This date shall be notified in the London, Edinburgh and Belfast Gazettes.

[2378]

2(1) In this Order "the 1961 Convention Articles" means the Articles (being certain Articles of the Vienna Convention on Diplomatic Relations signed in 1961) which are set out in Schedule 1 to the Diplomatic Privileges Act 1964.

(2) The Interpretation Act 1889 shall apply for the interpretation of this Order as it applies for the interpretation of an Act of Parliament.

[2379]

3 The European Organisation for the Safety of Air Navigation (Eurocontrol) (hereinafter referred to as the Organisation) is an Organisation of which Her Majesty's Government in the United Kingdom and the governments of foreign sovereign Powers are members.

[2380]

4 The Organisation shall have relief, under arrangements made either by the Secretary of State or by the Commissioners of Customs and Excise, by way of refund of [customs duty paid on or value added tax paid on the importation of any hydrocarbon oils (within the meaning of the Hydrocarbon Oil (Customs and Excise) Act 1971)] which are bought in the United Kingdom and used for the official purposes of the Organisation, such relief to be subject to compliance with such conditions as may be imposed in accordance with the arrangements.

[2381]

NOTES

Words in square brackets inserted by the International Organisations (Immunities and Privileges) Miscellaneous Provisions Order 1975, SI 1975/1209, art 3, Schedule.

5 The Organisation shall have relief, under arrangements made by the Secretary of State, by way of refund of [car tax paid on any vehicles and value added tax paid on the supply of any goods or services] which are used for the official purposes of the Organisation, such relief to be subject to compliance with such conditions as may be imposed in accordance with the arrangements.

[2382]

NOTES

Words in square brackets inserted by the International Organisations (Immunities and Privileges) Miscellaneous Provisions Order 1975, SI 1975/1209, art 3, Schedule.

[5A The Organisation shall have relief, under arrangements made by the Secretary of State, by way of refund of Insurance Premium Tax and Air Passenger Duty paid by the organisation in the exercise of its official activities.]

[2383]

NOTES

Inserted by the International Organisations (Immunities and Privileges) Miscellaneous Provisions Order 1999, SI 1999/2034, art 2, Schedule.

6(1) Subject to the provisions of paragraph (2) of this Article, all officers and servants of the Organisation shall enjoy the like exemption from customs duties and taxes on the importation of articles which—

(i) at or about the time when the officer or servant first enters the United Kingdom as an officer or servant of the Organisation are imported for his personal use or that of members of his family forming part of his household, including articles intended for his establishment, and

(ii) are articles which were in his ownership or possession or that of such a member of his family immediately before he so entered the United Kingdom.

as in accordance with paragraph 1 of Article 36 of the 1961 Convention Articles is accorded to a diplomatic agent.

(2) The provisions of paragraph (1) of this Article shall not apply to any person who is a citizen of the United Kingdom and Colonies, a British subject by virtue of section 2, 13 or 16 of the British Nationality Act 1948 or the British Nationality Act 1965, or a British protected person within the meaning of the said Act of 1948.

[2384]

[7(1) The officers and servants of the Organisation shall, as from the date on which the salaries and emoluments received by them as officers and servants of the Organisation become subject to taxation by the Organisation for its benefit, enjoy exemption from income tax in respect of such salaries and emoluments.

(2) Nothing in this Article shall be interpreted as precluding such salaries and emoluments from being taken into account for the purpose of assessing the amount of taxation to be applied to income from other sources.]

[2385]

NOTES

Added by the Eurocontrol (Immunities and Privileges) (Amendment) Order 1980, SI 1980/1076, art 2.

[8 The Director General of the Organisation's Agency for the safety of air navigation shall enjoy immunity from suit and legal process in respect of acts, including words written or spoken, done by him in the exercise of his functions, except in the case of a motor traffic offence or in the case of damage caused by a motor vehicle belonging to or driven by him.]

[2386]

NOTES

Added, together with arts 9, 10, by the Eurocontrol (Immunities and Privileges) (Amendment) Order 1984, SI 1984/127, art 2.

[9 The officers and servants of the Organisation, provided that they are not British citizens and not permanently resident in the United Kingdom, and provided that the Organisation has established or jointed a social security scheme, shall enjoy exemptions whereby for the purpose of the enactments relating to social security, including enactments in force in Northern Ireland—

(i) services rendered for the Organisation by them shall be deemed to be excepted from any class of employment in respect of which contributions or premiums under those enactments are payable, but

(ii) no person shall be rendered liable to pay any contribution or premium which he would not be required to pay if those services were not deemed to be so excepted.]

[2387]

NOTES

Added as noted to art 8 at **[2386]**.

[10(1) Representatives of members of the Organisation shall enjoy, while exercising their functions and in the course of their journeys to and from the place of meeting, the like inviolability for all their official papers and documents as is accorded to diplomatic agents.

(2) Part IV of Schedule 1 to the Act shall not operate so as to confer such inviolability on any member of the family or on any member of the official staff of a representative.]

[2388]

NOTES

Added as noted to art 8 at **[2386]**.

EUROPEAN COMMISSION AND COURT OF HUMAN RIGHTS (IMMUNITIES AND PRIVILEGES) ORDER 1970

(SI 1970/1941)

NOTES

Made: 17 December 1970.
Authority: International Organisations Act 1968, s 5.
Commencement: see art 1(2).

PART I
GENERAL

1 Citation and Entry into Force

(1) This Order may be cited as the European Commission and Court of Human Rights (Immunities and Privileges) Order 1970.

(2) Parts I and II of this Order shall come into operation on the date when the Fourth Protocol to the General Agreement on Privileges and Immunities of the Council of Europe opened for signature in Paris on 16th December 1961 enters into force with respect to the United Kingdom, and Part III of this Order shall come into operation on the date when the European Agreement relating to Persons participating in Proceedings of the European Commission and Court of Human Rights opened for signature in London on 6th May 1969 enters into force with respect to the United Kingdom. These dates shall be notified in the London, Edinburgh and Belfast Gazettes.

[2389]

2 Interpretation

(1) The Interpretation Act 1889 shall apply for the interpretation of this Order as it applies for the interpretation of an Act of Parliament.

(2) In this Order—

"the Convention" means the Convention for the Protection of Human Rights and Fundamental Freedoms signed at Rome on 4th November 1950;

"the Commission" means the European Commission of Human Rights established by Article 19 of the Convention or any Sub-Commission, member or members of the Commission carrying out their duties under the terms of the Convention or rules of the Commission;

"the Committee of Ministers" means the Committee of Ministers of the Council of Europe when exercising its functions under Article 32 of the Convention;

"the Court" means the European Court of Human Rights established by Article 19 of the Convention or any Chamber, judge or judges of the Court carrying out their duties under the terms of the Convention or the rules of the Court;

"judges of the Court" means judges elected under Article 39 or appointed under Article 43 of the Convention;

["members of the Commission" means members elected under Article 21 of the Convention;]

"persons participating in proceedings" means—

(a) agents of States parties to the European Agreement relating to Persons participating in Proceedings of the European Commission and Court of Human Rights opened for signature in Paris on 6th May 1969, and advisers and advocates assisting them;

(b) persons taking part in proceedings instituted before the Commission under Article 25 of the Convention, whether in their own name or as representatives of one of the applicants enumerated in the said Article 25;

(c) barristers, solicitors or professors of law, taking part in proceedings in order to assist one of the persons referred to in sub-paragraph (b) of this paragraph;

(d) persons chosen by the delegates of the Commission to assist them in proceedings before the Court;

(e) witnesses, experts and other persons called upon by the Commission or the Court to take part in proceedings before the Commission or the Court;

(f) any person mentioned in sub-paragraphs (a) to (e) of this paragraph who is called upon to appear before or to submit written statements to the Committee of Ministers;

"tribunal to which this Order applies" means the Commission, the Court or the Committee of Ministers.

(3) For the purposes of this Order any petition, complaint or other communication which, with a view to action to be taken by or before a tribunal to which this Order applies,—

(a) is made to the tribunal, or

(b) is made to a person through whom, in accordance with the constitution, rules or practice of the tribunal, such a communication can be received by the tribunal,

shall be deemed to be proceedings before the tribunal, and the person making any such communication shall be deemed to be a party to such proceedings.

[2390]

NOTES

Para (2): words in square brackets inserted by the European Commission and Court of Human Rights (Immunities and Privileges) (Amendment) Order 1990, SI 1990/2290, art 2.

PART II
THE COURT

3 The judges of the Court, the Registrar of the Court and the Deputy Registrar of the Court shall have inviolability in respect of their documents and papers in so far as they relate to the business of the Court.

[2391]

4 Except in so far as in any particular case any privilege or immunity is waived by the Court sitting in plenary session, judges of the Court, the Registrar of the Court and, when he is acting as the Registrar, the Deputy Registrar of the Court shall enjoy:—

(a) in respect of words spoken or written and all acts done or omitted to be done by them in their official capacity, the like immunity from suit and legal process as is accorded to the head of a diplomatic mission;

(b) while exercising their functions and during journeys made in the exercise of their functions, the like immunity from personal arrest or detention as is accorded to the head of a diplomatic mission;

(c) while exercising their functions and during journeys made in the exercise of their functions, the like exemptions and privileges in respect of their personal baggage as in accordance with Article 36 in Schedule 1 to the Diplomatic Privileges Act 1964 are accorded to a diplomatic agent;

provided that the provisions of paragraph (c) of this Article shall not apply to any person who is a citizen of the United Kingdom and Colonies, a British subject by virtue of section 2, 13 or 16 of the British Nationality Act 1948 or the British Nationality Act 1965, or a British protected person within the meaning of the said Act of 1948.

[2392]

PART III
PERSONS PARTICIPATING IN PROCEEDINGS

5 Except in so far as in any particular case any immunity is waived by the tribunal, persons participating in proceedings shall have:—

(a) in respect of words spoken or written and documents or other evidence submitted by them before or to a tribunal to which this Order applies (but not where such words, documents or evidence or any part thereof are communicated by them or on their behalf outside the tribunal) the like immunity from suit and legal process as is accorded to the head of a diplomatic mission;

(b) while passing in transit through the United Kingdom during their journeys to and from the proceedings or while in the United Kingdom for the purpose of such proceedings there, immunity from criminal proceedings and, except for the purpose of detaining a person who has escaped from legal custody, from personal arrest in respect of acts or convictions prior to the commencement of the journey, provided that their presence at the proceedings has been authorised in advance by the tribunal and that fifteen days have not elapsed from the date when their presence is no longer required by the tribunal.

[2393]

[PART IV
EXEMPTION FROM INCOME TAX

6 Members of the Commission and judges of the Court shall enjoy exemption from income tax in respect of emoluments paid to them by the Council of Europe as holders of those offices.]

[2394]

NOTES

Inserted by the European Commission and Court of Human Rights (Immunities and Privileges) (Amendment) Order 1990, SI 1990/2290, art 2.

ORGANISATION FOR ECONOMIC CO-OPERATION AND DEVELOPMENT (IMMUNITIES AND PRIVILEGES) ORDER 1974

(SI 1974/1258)

NOTES

Made: 25 July 1974.
Authority: International Organisations Act 1968, s 1.
Commencement: 1 August 1974.

PART I
GENERAL

1 This Order may be cited as the Organisation for Economic Co-operation and Development (Immunities and Privileges) Order 1974 and shall come into operation on 1st August 1974.

[2395]

2(1) In this Order "the 1961 Convention Articles" means the Articles (being certain Articles of the Vienna Convention on Diplomatic Relations signed in 1961) which are set out in Schedule 1 to the Diplomatic Privileges Act 1964.

(2) The Interpretation Act 1889 shall apply for the interpretation of this Order as it applies for the interpretation of an Act of Parliament, and as if this Order and the Order hereby revoked were Acts of Parliament.

[2396]

3 (*Revokes the Organisation for Economic Co-operation and Development (Immunities and Privileges) Order 1961, SI 1961/836.*)

PART II
THE ORGANISATION

4 The Organisation for Economic Co-operation and Development (hereinafter referred to as the Organisation) is an organisation of which the United Kingdom and foreign sovereign Powers are members.

[2397]

5 The Organisation shall have the legal capacities of a body corporate.

[2398]

6 Except in so far as in any particular case it has expressly waived its immunity, the Organisation shall have immunity from suit and legal process. No waiver of immunity shall be deemed to extend to any measure of execution.

[2399]

7 The Organisation shall have the like inviolability of official archives and premises as in accordance with the 1961 Convention Articles is accorded in respect of the official archives and premises of a diplomatic mission.

[2400]

8 The Organisation shall have the like exemption or relief from taxes, other than customs duties and taxes on the importation of goods, as is accorded to a foreign sovereign Power.

[2401]

9 The Organisation shall have the like relief from rates as in accordance with Article 23 of the 1961 Convention Articles is accorded in respect of the premises of a diplomatic mission.

[2402]

10 The Organisation shall have exemption from customs duties and taxes on the importation of goods imported by the Organisation for its official use in the United Kingdom and on the importation of publications of the Organisation imported by it, such exemption to be subject to compliance with such conditions as the Commissioners of Customs and Excise may prescribe for the protection of the Revenue.

[2403]

11 The Organisation shall have exemption from prohibitions and restrictions on importation or exportation in the case of goods imported or exported by the Organisation for its official use and in the case of any publications of the Organisation imported or exported by it.

[2404]

12 The Organisation shall have relief, under arrangements made by the Commissioners of Customs and Excise, by way of refund of customs duty paid on [or value added tax paid on the importation of] any hydrocarbon oil (within the meaning of the Hydrocarbon Oil (Customs & Excise) Act 1971) which is bought in the United Kingdom and used for the official purposes of the Organisation, such relief to be subject to compliance with such conditions as may be imposed in accordance with the arrangements.

[2405]

NOTES

Words in square brackets inserted by the International Organisations (Immunities and Privileges) Miscellaneous Provisions Order 1975, SI 1975/1209, art 3, Schedule.

13 The Organisation shall have relief, under arrangements made by the Secretary of State, by way of refund of car tax paid on any vehicles and value added tax paid on the supply of any goods which are used for the official purposes of the Organisation, such relief to be subject to compliance with such conditions as may be imposed in accordance with the arrangements.

[2406]

PART III
REPRESENTATIVES

14(1) Except in so far as in any particular case any privilege or immunity is waived by the Government of the member which he represents, any representative of a member to the principal and subsidiary organs of the Organisation shall, while exercising his functions and during his journeys to and from the place of meeting, enjoy:—

(a) the like immunity from suit and legal process, the like inviolability of residence and the like exemption or relief from taxes, other than customs duties and taxes on the importation of goods, and rates as are accorded to or in respect of a diplomatic agent;

(b) the like exemption from customs duties and taxes on the importation of articles imported for his personal use or the use of members of his family forming part of his household, including articles intended for his establishment, as in accordance with paragraph 1 of Article 36 of the 1961 Convention Articles is accorded to a diplomatic agent;

(c) the like exemption and privileges in respect of his personal baggage as in accordance with paragraph 2 of Article 36 of the 1961 Convention Articles are accorded to a diplomatic agent;

(d) relief, under arrangements made by the Commissioners of Customs and Excise, by way of refund of customs duty paid on [or value added tax paid on the importation of] any hydrocarbon oil (within the meaning of the Hydrocarbon Oil (Customs & Excise) Act 1971) which is bought in the United Kingdom by him or on his behalf, such relief to be subject to compliance with such conditions as may be imposed in accordance with the arrangements; and

(e) exemptions whereby, for the purposes of the enactments relating to national insurance and social security, including enactments in force in Northern Ireland,—

(i) services rendered for the Organisation by the representative shall be deemed to be excepted from any class of employment in respect of which contributions or premiums under those enactments are payable, but

(ii) no person shall be rendered liable to pay any contribution or premium which he would not be required to pay if those services were not deemed to be so excepted;

provided that until the day appointed for the coming into force of section 2 of the Social Security Act 1973 the following shall apply in substitution for the foregoing provisions of this subparagraph—

"exemptions whereby for the purposes of the National Insurance Acts 1965 to 1973, the National Insurance (Industrial Injuries) Acts 1965 to 1973, any enactment for the time being in force amending any of those Acts, and any enactment of the Parliament of Northern Ireland corresponding to any of those Acts or to any enactment amending any of those Acts,—

(i) services rendered for the Organisation by the representative shall be deemed to be excepted from any class of employment which is insurable employment, or in respect of which contributions are required to be paid, but

(ii) no person shall be rendered liable to pay any contribution which he would not be required to pay if those services were not deemed to be so excepted.".

(2) Part IV of Schedule 1 to the Act shall not operate so as to confer any privilege or immunity on:—

(a) the official staff of a representative other than delegates, alternates, advisers, technical experts and secretaries of delegations, or

(b) the family of a representative or of a member of the official staff of a representative.

(3) Neither this Article nor Part IV of Schedule 1 to the Act shall operate so as to confer any privilege or immunity on any person as the representative of the United Kingdom or as a member of the official staff of such a representative or on any person who is a citizen of the United Kingdom and Colonies.

[2407]

NOTES

Para (1): words in square brackets in sub-para (d) inserted by the International Organisations (Immunities and Privileges) Miscellaneous Provisions Order 1975, SI 1975/1209, art 3, Schedule.

PART IV
OFFICERS

15 High Officers

(1) Except in so far as in any particular case any privilege or immunity is waived by the Council of the Organisation, and subject to the provisions of paragraph (2) of this Article, the Secretary-General of the Organisation and any Deputy Secretary-General shall enjoy:—

(a) the like immunity from suit and legal process, the like inviolability of residence and the like exemption or relief from taxes, other than customs duties and taxes on the importation of goods, and rates as are accorded to or in respect of the head of a diplomatic mission;

(b) the like exemption from customs duties and taxes on the importation of articles imported for their personal use or the use of members of their families forming part of their households, including articles intended for their establishment, as in accordance with paragraph 1 of Article 36 of the 1961 Convention Articles is accorded to a diplomatic agent;

(c) the like exemption and privileges in respect of their personal baggage as in accordance with paragraph 2 of Article 36 of the 1961 Convention Articles are accorded to a diplomatic agent;

(d) relief, under arrangements made by the Commissioners of Customs and Excise, by way of refund of customs duty paid on [or value added tax paid on the importation of] any hydrocarbon oil (within the meaning of the Hydrocarbon Oil (Customs & Excise) Act 1971) which is bought in the United Kingdom by them or on their behalf, such relief to be subject to compliance with such conditions as may be imposed in accordance with the arrangements; and

(e) exemptions whereby, for the purposes of the enactments relating to national insurance and social security, including enactments in force in Northern Ireland,—

(i) services rendered by them for the Organisation shall be deemed to be excepted from any class of employment in respect of which contributions or premiums under those enactments are payable, but

(ii) no person shall be rendered liable to pay any contribution or premium which he would not be required to pay if those services were not deemed to be so excepted;

provided that until the day appointed for the coming into force of section 2 of the Social Security Act 1973 the following shall apply in substitution for the foregoing provisions of this subparagraph—

"exemptions whereby for the purposes of the National Insurance Acts 1965 to 1973, the National Insurance (Industrial Injuries) Acts 1965 to 1973, any enactment for the time being in force amending any of those Acts, and any enactment of the Parliament of Northern Ireland corresponding to any of those Acts or to any enactment amending any of those Acts,—

(i) services rendered by them for the Organisation shall be deemed to be excepted from any class of employment which is insurable employment, or in respect of which contributions are required to be paid, but

(ii) no person shall be rendered liable to pay any contribution which he would not be required to pay if those services were not deemed to be so excepted.".

(2) This Article shall not apply to any person who is a citizen of the United Kingdom and Colonies or a permanent resident of the United Kingdom.

(3) Part IV of Schedule 1 to the Act shall not operate so as to confer any privilege or immunity on any member of the family of the Secretary-General other than [his spouse or civil partner] and children under the age of 21 or on any member of the family of any Deputy Secretary-General.

[2408]

NOTES

Para (1): words in square brackets in sub-para (d) inserted by the International Organisations (Immunities and Privileges) Miscellaneous Provisions Order 1975, SI 1975/1209, art 3, Schedule.

Para (3): words in square brackets substituted by the International Organisations (Immunities and Privileges) Miscellaneous Provisions Order 2006, SI 2006/1075, art 2, Schedule.

16 All Officers

Except in so far as in any particular case any privilege or immunity is waived by the Secretary-General, Assistant Secretaries-General and established members of the staff of the Organisation shall enjoy:—

(a) immunity from suit and legal process in respect of things done or omitted to be done by them in their official capacity;

(b) exemption from income tax in respect of emoluments received by them as officers of the Organisation; and

(c) the like exemption from customs duties and taxes on the importation of articles which—

(i) at or about the time when they first enter the United Kingdom to take up their posts as officers of the Organisation are imported for their personal use or that of members of their families forming part of their household, including articles intended for their establishment, and

(ii) are articles which were in their ownership or possession or that of such members of their families, or which they or such members of their families were under contract to purchase, immediately before they so entered the United Kingdom,

as in accordance with paragraph 1 of Article 36 of the 1961 Convention Articles is accorded to a diplomatic agent.

[2409]

PART V
EXPERTS

17 Except in so far as in any particular case any privilege or immunity is waived by the Secretary-General, experts (other than officers of the Organisation) performing missions for the Organisation shall enjoy:—

(a) immunity from suit and legal process in respect of things done or omitted to be done by them in the course of the performance of their missions;

(b) during the period of their missions, including the time spent on journeys in connection with their missions, the like immunity from personal arrest or detention and from seizure of their baggage and the like inviolability for all papers and documents as is accorded to a diplomatic agent.

[2410]

PART VI
THE TRIBUNAL

18(1) In this Article "the Tribunal" means the Tribunal established by the Convention on the Establishment of a Security Control in the field of Nuclear Energy.

(2) Except in so far as in any particular case any immunity is waived by the Tribunal, the judges of the Tribunal shall enjoy immunity from suit and legal process in respect of things done or omitted to be done by them in their judicial capacity.

(3) Except in so far as in any particular case any immunity is waived by the Tribunal, the representatives, counsel and advocates appearing before the Tribunal shall enjoy:—

(a) immunity from suit and legal process in regard to statements made and writings produced by them in connection with the performance of their duties as representatives, counsel or advocates before the Tribunal; and

(b) inviolability for their documents.

[2411]

SPECIALIZED AGENCIES OF THE UNITED NATIONS (IMMUNITIES AND PRIVILEGES) ORDER 1974

(SI 1974/1260)

NOTES

Made: 25 July 1974.
Authority: International Organisations Act 1968, s 1.
Commencement: 1 August 1974.

PART I
GENERAL

1 This Order may be cited as the Specialized Agencies of the United Nations (Immunities and Privileges) Order 1974 and shall come into operation on 1st August 1974.

[2412]

2(1) In this Order "the 1961 Convention Articles" means the Articles (being certain Articles of the Vienna Convention on Diplomatic Relations signed in 1961) which are set out in Schedule 1 to the Diplomatic Privileges Act 1964.

(2) The Interpretation Act 1889 shall apply for the interpretation of this Order as it applies for the interpretation of an Act of Parliament and as if this Order and the Orders hereby revoked were Acts of Parliament.

[2413]

3 The Orders listed in Schedule 3 to this Order are hereby revoked.

[2414]

PART II
THE ORGANISATION

4 The organisations listed in Schedule 1 to this Order (each of which is hereinafter referred to as the Organisation) are organisations of which the United Kingdom and foreign sovereign Powers are members.

[2415]

5 The Organisation shall have the legal capacities of a body corporate.

[2416]

6 Except in so far as in any particular case it has expressly waived its immunity, the Organisation shall have immunity from suit and legal process. No waiver of immunity shall be deemed to extend to any measure of execution.

[2417]

7 The Organisation shall have the like inviolability of official archives and premises as in accordance with the 1961 Convention Articles is accorded in respect of the official archives and premises of a diplomatic mission.

[2418]

8 The Organisation shall have the like exemption or relief from taxes, other than customs duties and taxes on the importation of goods, as is accorded to a foreign sovereign Power.

[2419]

9 The Organisation shall have the like relief from rates as in accordance with Article 23 of the 1961 Convention Articles is accorded in respect of the premises of a diplomatic mission.

[2420]

10 The Organisation shall have exemption from customs duties and taxes on the importation of goods imported by the Organisation for its official use in the United Kingdom and on the importation of publications of the Organisation imported by it, such exemption to be subject to compliance with such conditions as the Commissioners of Customs and Excise may prescribe for the protection of the Revenue.

[2421]

11 The Organisation shall have exemption from prohibitions and restrictions on importation or exportation in the case of goods imported or exported by the Organisation for its official use and in the case of any publications of the Organisation imported or exported by it.

[2422]

12 The Organisation shall have relief, under arrangements made by the Commissioners of Customs and Excise, by way of refund of customs duty paid on [or value added tax paid on the importation of] any hydrocarbon oil (within the meaning of the Hydrocarbon Oil (Customs & Excise) Act 1971) which is bought in the United Kingdom and used for the official purposes of the Organisation, such relief to be subject to compliance with such conditions as may be imposed in accordance with the arrangements.

[2423]

NOTES

Words in square brackets inserted by the International Organisations (Immunities and Privileges) Miscellaneous Provisions Order 1975, SI 1975/1209, art 3, Schedule.

13 The Organisation shall have relief, under arrangements made by the Secretary of State, by way of refund of car tax paid on any vehicle and value added tax paid on the supply of any goods [or services] which are used for the official purposes of the Organisation, such relief to be subject to compliance with such conditions as may be imposed in accordance with the arrangements.

[2424]

NOTES

Words in square brackets inserted by the International Organisations (Immunities and Privileges) Miscellaneous Provisions Order 1975, SI 1975/1209, art 3, Schedule.

[13A The International Labour Organization shall have relief, under arrangements made by the Secretary of State, by way of refund of insurance premium tax and air passenger duty paid by the Organization in the exercise of its official activities.]

[2425]

NOTES

Inserted by the Specialized Agencies of the United Nations (Immunities and Privileges) (Amendment) Order 2002, SI 2002/1827, art 2.

PART III
REPRESENTATIVES AND OTHER PERSONS

14(1) Except in so far as in any particular case any privilege or immunity is waived by the Government of the member which they represent, representatives of members of the Organisation (and representatives of Associate Members of the Food and Agriculture Organization and of the World Health Organization) at the meetings of any organ, committee or other subordinate body of the Organisation (including any sub-committee or other subordinate body of a subordinate body) shall enjoy:—

(a) immunity from suit and legal process in respect of things done or omitted to be done by them in their official capacity;

(b) while exercising their functions and during their journeys to and from the place of meeting, the like immunity from personal arrest or detention and from seizure of their personal baggage and the like inviolability for all papers and documents as is accorded to a diplomatic agent; and

(c) while exercising their functions and during their journeys to and from the place of meeting, the like exemptions and privileges in respect of their personal baggage as in accordance with Article 36 of the 1961 Convention Articles are accorded to a diplomatic agent.

(2) Where the incidence of any form of taxation depends upon residence, a representative shall not be deemed to be resident in the United Kingdom during any period when he is present in the United Kingdom for the discharge of his duties.

(3) Part IV of Schedule 1 to the Act shall not operate so as to confer any privilege or immunity on:—

(a) the official staff of a representative other than alternates, advisers, technical experts and secretaries of delegations, or

(b) the family of a representative or of a member of the official staff of a representative.

(4) Neither the preceding paragraphs of this Article nor Part IV of Schedule 1 to the Act shall operate so as to confer any privilege or immunity on any person as the representative of the United Kingdom or as a member of the official staff of such a representative or on any person who is a citizen of the United Kingdom and Colonies.

(5) Except in so far as in any particular case any privilege or immunity is waived by the organ indicated in Schedule 2 to this Order, the additional persons specified in that Schedule shall, unless they are representatives of the United Kingdom or citizens of the United Kingdom and Colonies, enjoy the privileges and immunities provided for in paragraphs (1) and (2) of this Article.

(6) Part IV of Schedule 1 to the Act shall not operate so as to confer any privilege or immunity on the official staffs or families of any person to whom paragraph (5) of this Article applies.

[2426]

PART IV
OFFICERS

15 High Officers

(1) Except in so far as in any particular case any privilege or immunity is waived by or on behalf of the Organisation, and subject to the provisions of paragraph (2) of this Article, any person mentioned in Schedule 1 to this Order shall enjoy:—

(a) the like immunity from suit and legal process, the like inviolability of residence and the like exemption or relief from taxes, other than customs duties and taxes on the importation of goods, and rates as are accorded to or in respect of the head of a diplomatic mission;

(b) the like exemption from customs duties and taxes on the importation of articles imported for his personal use or the use of members of his family forming part of his household, including articles intended for his establishment, as in accordance with paragraph 1 of Article 36 of the 1961 Convention Articles is accorded to a diplomatic agent;

(c) the like exemption and privileges in respect of his personal baggage as in accordance with paragraph 2 of Article 36 of the 1961 Convention Articles are accorded to a diplomatic agent;

(d) relief, under arrangements made by the Commissioners of Customs and Excise, by way of refund of customs duty paid on [or value added tax paid on the importation of] any hydrocarbon oil (within the meaning of the Hydrocarbon Oil (Customs & Excise) Act 1971) which is bought in the United Kingdom by him or on his behalf, such relief to be subject to compliance with such conditions as may be imposed in accordance with the arrangements; and

(e) exemptions whereby, for the purposes of the enactments relating to national insurance and social security, including enactments in force in Northern Ireland,—

(i) services rendered for the Organisation by the officer shall be deemed to be excepted from any class of employment in respect of which contributions or premiums under those enactments are payable, but

(ii) no person shall be rendered liable to pay any contribution or premium which he would not be required to pay if those services were not deemed to be so excepted;

provided that until the day appointed for the coming into force of section 2 of the Social Security Act 1973 the following shall apply in substitution for the foregoing provisions of this sub-paragraph—

PART III
STATUTORY INSTRUMENTS

"exemptions whereby for the purposes of the National Insurance Acts 1965 to 1973, the National Insurance (Industrial Injuries) Acts 1965 to 1973, any enactment for the time being in force amending any of those Acts, and any enactment of the Parliament of Northern Ireland corresponding to any of those Acts or to any enactment amending any of those Acts,—

(i) services rendered for the Organisation by the officer shall be deemed to be excepted from any class of employment which is insurable employment, or in respect of which contributions are required to be paid, but

(ii) no person shall be rendered liable to pay any contribution which he would not be required to pay if those services were not deemed to be so excepted".

(2) This Article shall not apply to any person who is a citizen of the United Kingdom and Colonies or a permanent resident of the United Kingdom.

(3) Part IV of Schedule 1 of the Act shall not operate so as to confer any privilege or immunity on any member of the family of any officer to whom this Article applies other than [his spouse or civil partner] and minor children.

[2427]

NOTES

Words in square brackets inserted by the International Organisations (Immunities and Privileges) Miscellaneous Provisions Order 1975, SI 1975/1209, art 3, Schedule.

Para (3): words in square brackets substituted by the International Organisations (Immunities and Privileges) Miscellaneous Provisions Order 2006, SI 2006/1075, art 2, Schedule.

---

16 All Officers

Except in so far as in any particular case any privilege or immunity is waived by or on behalf of the Organisation, officers of the Organisation (other than those who are locally recruited and assigned to hourly rates of pay) shall enjoy:—

(a) immunity from suit and legal process in respect of things done or omitted to be done by them in their official capacity;

(b) exemption from income tax in respect of emoluments received by them as officers of the Organisation; and

(c) the like exemption from customs duties and taxes on the importation of articles which—

(i) at or about the time when they first enter the United Kingdom to take up their posts as officers of the Organisation are imported for their personal use or that of members of their families forming part of their households, including articles intended for their establishment, and

(ii) are articles which were in their ownership or possession or that of such members of their families, or which they or such members of their families were under contract to purchase, immediately before they so entered the United Kingdom.

as in accordance with paragraph 1 of Article 36 of the 1961 Convention Articles is accorded to a diplomatic agent.

[2428]

[16A Unless they are British citizens, [British overseas territories citizens] or British Overseas citizens or permanently resident in the United Kingdom, officers of the World Health Organization (other than those who are locally recruited and assigned to hourly rates of pay) shall enjoy exemptions whereby, for the purposes of the enactments relating to social security, including enactments in force in Northern Ireland—

(a) services rendered for the World Health Organization by them shall be deemed to be excepted from any class of employment in respect of which contributions or premiums under those enactments are payable, but

(b) no person shall be rendered liable to pay any contribution or premium which he would not be required to pay if those services were not deemed to be so excepted.]

[2429]

NOTES

Inserted by the Specialized Agencies of the United Nations (Immunities and Privileges) (Amendment) (No 2) Order 1985, SI 1985/753, art 2.

Words in square brackets substituted by virtue of the British Overseas Territories Act 2002, s 2(3).

PART V
EXPERTS

17 Except in so far as in any particular case any privilege or immunity is waived by or on behalf of the Organisation, experts (other than officers of the Organisation) serving on committees of, or performing missions for, the Organisation shall enjoy:—

(a) immunity from suit and legal process in respect of things done or omitted to be done by them in the exercise of their functions;

(b) during the period of their service on committees or missions, including the time spent on journeys in connection with service on such committees or missions, the like immunity from personal arrest or detention and from seizure of their personal baggage and the like inviolability for all papers and documents as is accorded to a diplomatic agent; and

(c) during the period of their service on committees or missions, including the time spent on journeys in connection with service on such committees or missions, the like exemptions and privileges in respect of their personal baggage as in accordance with Article 36 of the 1961 Convention Articles are accorded to a diplomatic agent.

Provided that this Article shall not apply to experts serving on committees of, or performing missions for, the Universal Postal Union, the International Telecommunication Union or the World Meteorological Organization.

[2430]

SCHEDULE 1
INTERNATIONAL ORGANISATIONS TO WHICH THIS ORDER APPLIES, AND HIGH OFFICERS OF SUCH ORGANISATIONS ENJOYING PRIVILEGES AND IMMUNITIES UNDER ARTICLE 15 OF THIS ORDER

Food and Agriculture Organization

The Director General

The Deputy Director-General

Any Assistant Director-General

Any official acting on behalf of the Director-General during his absence from duty

International Civil Aviation Organization

The Secretary-General

The President of the Council

Any official acting on behalf of the Secretary-General during his absence from duty.

International Labour Organization

The Director-General

Any Deputy Director-General

Any Assistant Director-General

Any official acting on behalf of the Director-General during his absence from duty

International Telecommunication Union

The Secretary-General

Any official acting on behalf of the Secretary-General during his absence from duty

United Nations Educational, Scientific and Cultural Organization

The Director-General

The Deputy Director-General

Any official acting on behalf of the Director-General during his absence from duty

Universal Postal Union

The Director of the International Bureau

Any official acting on behalf of the Director during his absence from duty

World Health Organization

The Director-General

Any Deputy Director-General

Any Assistant Director-General

Any Regional Director

Any official acting on behalf of the Director-General during his absence from duty

World Meteorological Organization

The Secretary-General

Any official acting on behalf of the Secretary-General during his absence from duty

[World Intellectual Property Organization

The Director-General

Any Deputy Director-General

Any official acting on behalf of the Director-General during his absence from duty]

[2431]

NOTES

Entries relating to the World Intellectual Property Organization substituted by the Specialized Agencies of the United Nations (Immunities and Privileges) (Amendment) Order 1985, SI 1985/451, art 2.

SCHEDULE 2
ADDITIONAL PERSONS ENJOYING PRIVILEGES AND IMMUNITIES UNDER ARTICLE 14 OF THIS ORDER

Organisation	Additional Persons	Organ with power to waive
International Labour Organization.	The employers' and workers' members and deputy members of the Governing Body and their substitutes.	The Governing Body.
Food and Agriculture Organization.	The Chairman of the Council.	The Council.
United Nations Educational Scientific and Cultural Organization.	The President of the Conference and members of the Executive Board, their substitutes and advisers.	The Executive Board.
World Health Organization.	Persons designated to serve on the Executive Board, their alternates and advisers.	The Executive Board.

[2432]

UNITED NATIONS AND INTERNATIONAL COURT OF JUSTICE (IMMUNITIES AND PRIVILEGES) ORDER 1974

(SI 1974/1261)

NOTES

Made: 25 July 1974.
Authority: International Organisations Act 1968, s 1.
Commencement: 1 August 1974.

ARRANGEMENT OF ARTICLES

PART I
GENERAL

PART II
THE UNITED NATIONS

PART III
THE INTERNATIONAL COURT OF JUSTICE

PART I
GENERAL

1 This Order may be cited as the United Nations and International Court of Justice (Immunities and Privileges) Order 1974 and shall come into operation on 1st August 1974.

[2433]

2(1) In this Order "the 1961 Convention Articles" means the Articles (being certain Articles of the Vienna Convention on Diplomatic Relations signed in 1961) which are set out in Schedule 1 to the Diplomatic Privileges Act 1964.

(2) The Interpretation Act 1889 shall apply for the interpretation of this Order as it applies for the interpretation of an Act of Parliament, and as if this Order and the Orders hereby revoked were Acts of Parliament.

[2434]

3 (*Revokes the Diplomatic Privileges* (*United Nations and International Court of Justice*) *Order in Council 1947, SR & O 1947/1772, and the amending SI 1949/1428 and SI 1950/515.*)

PART III
STATUTORY INSTRUMENTS

PART II
THE UNITED NATIONS

The United Nations

4 The United Nations is an organisation of which the United Kingdom and foreign sovereign Powers are members.

[2435]

5 The United Nations shall have the legal capacities of a body corporate.

[2436]

6 Except in so far as in any particular case it has expressly waived its immunity, the United Nations shall have immunity from suit and legal process. No waiver of immunity shall be deemed to extend to any measure of execution.

[2437]

7 The United Nations shall have the like inviolability of official archives and premises as in accordance with the 1961 Convention Articles is accorded in respect of the official archives and premises of a diplomatic mission.

[2438]

8 The United Nations shall have the like exemption or relief from taxes, other than customs duties and taxes on the importation of goods, as is accorded to a foreign sovereign Power.

[2439]

[**8A** The United Nations shall have relief, under arrangements made by the Secretary of State, by way of refund of insurance premium tax and air passenger duty paid by the Organization in the exercise of its official activities.]

[2440]

NOTES

Commencement: 17 July 2002.

Inserted by the United Nations and International Court of Justice (Immunities and Privileges) (Amendment) Order 2002, SI 2002/1828, art 2.

9 The United Nations shall have the like relief from rates as in accordance with Article 23 of the 1961 Convention Articles is accorded in respect of the premises of a diplomatic mission.

[2441]

10 The United Nations shall have exemption from customs duties and taxes on the importation of goods imported by the United Nations for its official use in the United Kingdom and on the importation of publications of the United Nations imported by it, such exemption to be subject to compliance with such conditions as the Commissioners of Customs and Excise may prescribe for the protection of the Revenue.

[2442]

11 The United Nations shall have exemption from prohibitions and restrictions on importation or exportation in the case of goods imported or exported by the United Nations for its official use and in the case of any publications of the United Nations imported or exported by it.

[2443]

12 The United Nations shall have relief, under arrangements made by the Commissioners of Customs and Excise, by way of refund of customs duty paid on [or value added tax paid on the importation of] any hydrocarbon oil (within the meaning of the Hydrocarbon Oil (Customs & Excise) Act 1971) which is bought in the United Kingdom and used for the official purposes of the United Nations, such relief to be subject to compliance with such conditions as may be imposed in accordance with the arrangements.

[2444]

NOTES

Words in square brackets inserted by the International Organisations (Immunities and Privileges) Miscellaneous Provisions Order 1975, SI 1975/1209, art 3, Schedule.

13 The United Nations shall have relief, under arrangements made by the Secretary of State, by way of refund of car tax paid on any vehicles and value added tax paid on the supply of any goods [or services] which are used for the official purposes of the United Nations, such relief to be subject to compliance with such conditions as may be imposed in accordance with the arrangements.

[2445]

NOTES

Words in square brackets inserted by the International Organisations (Immunities and Privileges) Miscellaneous Provisions Order 1975, SI 1975/1209, art 3, Schedule.

14 Representatives

(1) Except in so far as in any particular case any privilege or immunity is waived by the Government of the member which they represent, representatives of members to any organ, committee or other subordinate body of the United Nations (including any sub-committee or other subordinate body of a subordinate body of the United Nations) shall enjoy:—

(a) immunity from suit and legal process in respect of things done or omitted to be done by them in their capacity as representatives;

(b) while exercising their functions and during their journeys to and from the place of meeting, the like inviolability of residence, the like immunity from personal arrest or detention and from seizure of their personal baggage, the like inviolability of all papers and documents and the like exemption or relief from taxes (other than customs and excise duties, car tax and value added tax) and rates as is accorded to the head of a diplomatic mission;

(c) while exercising their functions and during their journeys to and from the place of meeting, the like exemptions and privileges in respect of their personal baggage as in accordance with Article 36 of the 1961 Convention Articles are accorded to a diplomatic agent; and

(d) while exercising their functions and during their journeys to and from the place of meeting, exemptions whereby, for the purposes of the enactments relating to national insurance and social security, including enactments in force in Northern Ireland,—

(i) services rendered for the United Nations by them shall be deemed to be excepted from any class of employment in respect of which contributions or premiums under those enactments are payable, but

(ii) no person shall be rendered liable to pay any contribution or premium which he would not be required to pay if those services were not deemed to be so excepted;

provided that until the day appointed for the coming into force of section 2 of the Social Security Act 1973 the following shall apply in substitution for the foregoing provisions of this subparagraph—

"while exercising their functions and during their journeys to and from the place of meeting, exemptions whereby for the purposes of the National Insurance Acts 1965 to 1973, the National Insurance (Industrial Injuries) Acts 1965 to 1973, any enactment for the time being in force amending any of those Acts, and any enactment of the Parliament of Northern Ireland corresponding to any of those Acts or to any enactment amending any of those Acts,—

(i) services rendered for the United Nations by them shall be deemed to be excepted from any class of employment which is insurable employment, or in respect of which contributions are required to be paid, but

(ii) no person shall be rendered liable to pay any contribution which he would not be required to pay if those services were not deemed to be so excepted.".

(2) Where the incidence of any form of taxation depends upon residence, a representative shall not be deemed to be resident in the United Kingdom during any period when he is present in the United Kingdom for the discharge of his duties.

PART III STATUTORY INSTRUMENTS

(3) Part IV of Schedule 1 to the Act shall not operate so as to confer any privilege or immunity on:—

(a) the official staff of a representative other than delegates, deputy delegates, advisers, technical experts and secretaries of delegations, or

(b) the family of a representative or of a member of the official staff of a representative.

(4) Neither this Article nor Part IV of Schedule 1 to the Act shall operate so as to confer any privilege or immunity on any person as the representative of the United Kingdom or as a member of the official staff of such a representative or on any person who is a citizen of the United Kingdom and Colonies.

[2446]

NOTES

The Northern Ireland Act 1998 makes new provision for the government of Northern Ireland for the purpose of implementing the Belfast Agreement (the agreement reached at multi-party talks on Northern Ireland and set out in Command Paper 3883). As a consequence of that Act, any reference in this article to the Parliament of Northern Ireland or the Assembly established under the Northern Ireland Assembly Act 1973, s 1, certain office-holders and Ministers, and any legislative act and certain financial dealings thereof, shall, for the period specified, be construed in accordance with Sch 12, paras 1–11 to the 1998 Act.

15 High Officers

(1) Except in so far as in any particular case any privilege or immunity is waived in the case of the Secretary-General by the Security Council and in the case of an Assistant Secretary-General by the Secretary-General, and subject to the provisions of paragraph (2) of this Article, the Secretary-General of the United Nations and any Assistant Secretary-General shall enjoy:—

(a) the like immunity from suit and legal process, the like inviolability of residence and the like exemption or relief from taxes, other than customs duties and taxes on the importation of goods, and rates as are accorded to or in respect of the head of a diplomatic mission;

(b) the like exemption from customs duties and taxes on the importation of articles imported for his personal use or the use of members of his family forming part of his household, including articles intended for his establishment, as in accordance with paragraph 1 of Article 36 of the 1961 Convention Articles is accorded to a diplomatic agent;

(c) the like exemption and privileges in respect of his personal baggage as in accordance with paragraph 2 of Article 36 of the 1961 Convention Articles are accorded to a diplomatic agent;

(d) relief, under arrangements made by the Commissioners of Customs and Excise, by way of refund of customs duty paid on [or value added tax paid on the importation of] any hydrocarbon oil (within the meaning of the Hydrocarbon Oil (Customs & Excise) Act 1971) which is bought in the United Kingdom by him or on his behalf, such relief to be subject to compliance with such conditions as may be imposed in accordance with the arrangements; and

(e) exemptions whereby, for the purposes of the enactments relating to national insurance and social security, including enactments in force in Northern Ireland,—

(i) services rendered for the United Nations by the officer shall be deemed to be excepted from any class of employment in respect of which contributions or premiums under those enactments are payable, but

(ii) no person shall be rendered liable to pay any contribution or premium which he would not be required to pay if those services were not deemed to be so excepted;

provided that until the day appointed for the coming into force of section 2 of the Social Security Act 1973 the following shall apply in substitution for the foregoing provisions of this subparagraph—

"exemptions whereby for the purposes of the National Insurance Acts 1965 to 1973, the National Insurance (Industrial Injuries) Acts 1965 to 1973, any enactment for the time being in force amending any of those Acts, and any enactment of the Parliament of Northern Ireland corresponding to any of those Acts or to any enactment amending any of those Acts,—

(i) services rendered for the United Nations by the officer shall be deemed to be excepted from any class of employment which is insurable employment, or in respect of which contributions are required to be paid, but

(ii) no person shall be rendered liable to pay any contribution which he would not be required to pay if those services were not deemed to be so excepted.".

(2) This Article shall not apply to any person who is a citizen of the United Kingdom and Colonies or a permanent resident of the United Kingdom.

(3) Part IV of Schedule 1 to the Act shall not operate so as to confer any privilege or immunity on any member of the family of the Secretary-General or any Assistant Secretary-General other than [his spouse or civil partner] and minor children.

[2447]

NOTES

Para (1): words in square brackets inserted by the International Organisations (Immunities and Privileges) Miscellaneous Provisions Order 1975, SI 1975/1209, art 3, Schedule.

Para (3): words in square brackets substituted by the International Organisations (Immunities and Privileges) Miscellaneous Provisions Order 2006, SI 2006/1075, art 2, Schedule.

The Northern Ireland Act 1998 makes new provision for the government of Northern Ireland for the purpose of implementing the Belfast Agreement (the agreement reached at multi-party talks on Northern Ireland and set out in Command Paper 3883). As a consequence of that Act, any reference in this article to the Parliament of Northern Ireland or the Assembly established under the Northern Ireland Assembly Act 1973, s 1, certain office-holders and Ministers, and any legislative act and certain financial dealings thereof, shall, for the period specified, be construed in accordance with Sch 12, paras 1–11 to the 1998 Act.

16 All Officers

Except in so far as in any particular case any privilege or immunity is waived by the Secretary-General, officers of the United Nations (other than those who are locally recruited and assigned to hourly rates of pay) shall enjoy:—

(a) immunity from suit and legal process in respect of things done or omitted to be done by them in their official capacity;

(b) exemption from income tax in respect of emoluments received by them as officers of the United Nations; and

(c) the like exemption from customs duties and taxes on the importation of articles which—

(i) at or about the time when they first enter the United Kingdom to take up their posts as officers of the United Nations are imported for their personal use or that of members of their families forming part of their household, including articles intended for their establishment, and

(ii) are articles which were in their ownership or possession or that of such members of their families, or which they or such members of their families were under contract to purchase, immediately before they so entered the United Kingdom,

as in accordance with paragraph 1 of Article 36 of the 1961 Convention Articles is accorded to a diplomatic agent.

[2448]

17 Experts

Except in so far as in any particular case any privilege or immunity is waived by the Secretary-General, experts (other than officers of the United Nations) performing missions on behalf of the United Nations shall enjoy:—

(a) immunity from suit and legal process in respect of things done or omitted to be done by them in the course of the performance of their missions;

(b) during the period of their missions, including the time spent on journeys in connection with service on such missions, the like immunity from personal arrest or detention and the like inviolability for all papers and documents as is accorded to a diplomatic agent; and

(c) during the period of their missions, including the time spent on journeys in connection with service on such missions, the like exemptions and privileges in respect of their personal baggage as in accordance with Article 36 of the 1961 Convention Articles are accorded to a diplomatic agent.

[2449]

PART III
THE INTERNATIONAL COURT OF JUSTICE

Judges and Registrar

18 Except in so far as in any particular case any privilege or immunity is waived by the Court, the judges and Registrar of the Court and any officer of the Court acting as Registrar shall enjoy, when engaged on the business of the Court and on journeys in connection with the exercise of their functions and, in the case of judges who are not citizens of the United Kingdom and Colonies, when residing in the United Kingdom for the purpose of holding themselves permanently at the disposal of the Court, the like privileges and immunities as in accordance with the 1961 Convention Articles are accorded to the head of a diplomatic mission.

[2450]

19 The judges and Registrar shall have exemption from income tax in respect of emoluments received by them as judges or Registrar.

[2451]

20 All Officers

Except in so far as in any particular case any privilege or immunity is waived by the Registrar of the Court with the approval of the President of the Court, officers of the Court shall enjoy:—

(a) immunity from suit and legal process in respect of things done or omitted to be done by them in the exercise of their functions; and

(b) exemption from income tax in respect of emoluments received by them as officers of the Court.

[2452]

21 Agents, counsel and advocates

(1) Except in so far as in any particular case any privilege or immunity is waived, in the case of persons representing States by the government of the State which they represent and in the case of persons representing international organisations by the organisation which they represent, the agents, counsel and advocates appearing before the Court shall enjoy:—

(a) immunity from suit and legal process in respect of things done or omitted to be done by them in their capacity as agents, counsel or advocates;

(b) during the period of their missions, including the time spent on journeys in connection with their missions, the like inviolability of residence, the like immunity from personal arrest or detention, the inviolability for all papers and documents and the like exemption or relief from taxes (other than customs and excise duties, car tax and value added tax) and rates as are accorded to the head of a diplomatic mission; and

(c) during the period of their missions, including the time spent on journeys in connection with their missions, the like exemptions and privileges in respect of their personal baggage as in accordance with Article 36 of the 1961 Convention Articles are accorded to a diplomatic agent.

(2) Where the incidence of any form of taxation depends upon residence, an agent, counsel or advocate shall not be deemed to be resident in the United Kingdom during any period when he is present in the United Kingdom for the discharge of his duties.

(3) This Article shall not apply to any agent, counsel or advocate representing the United Kingdom or to any person who is a citizen of the United Kingdom and Colonies.

[2453]

22 Assessors, witnesses, experts and persons performing missions

Except in so far as in any particular case any privilege or immunity is waived by the Court or, when the Court is not sitting, by the President of the Court, assessors, witnesses, experts and persons performing missions by order of the Court shall enjoy:—

(a) immunity from suit and legal process in respect of things done or omitted to be done by them in the course of the performance of their missions;

(b) during the period of their missions, including the time spent on journeys in connection with their missions, the like immunity from personal arrest or detention and from seizure of their personal baggage and the like inviolability for all papers and documents as are accorded to a diplomatic agent; and

(c) during the period of their missions, including the time spent on journeys in connection with their missions, the like exemptions and privileges in respect of their personal baggage as in accordance with Article 36 of the 1961 Convention Articles are accorded to a diplomatic agent.

[2454]

INTERNATIONAL MONETARY FUND (IMMUNITIES AND PRIVILEGES) ORDER 1977

(SI 1977/825)

NOTES

Made: 11 May 1977.

Authority: Bretton Woods Agreement Act 1945, s 3(3) (now repealed), International Organisations Act 1968, s 1; in so far as made under the 1945 Act, s 3(3), this Order now takes effect as if made under the International Monetary Fund Act 1979, s 5.

Commencement: 1 April 1978 (save for provisions relating to Council representatives, which come into operation when that Council is established).

1(1) This Order may be cited as the International Monetary Fund (Immunities and Privileges) Order 1977.

(2)

(a) Articles 1 to 6 of this Order shall come into operation on the date on which the Second Amendment to the Articles of Agreement of the International Monetary Fund enters into force. This date shall be notified in the London, Edinburgh and Belfast Gazettes.

(b) Article 7 of this Order shall come into operation on the date on which a Council is established under Article XII, Section 1 of the Articles of Agreement of the International Monetary Fund as amended (hereinafter referred to as the Fund Agreement). This date shall be notified in the London, Edinburgh and Belfast Gazettes.

[2455]

2 The Interpretation Act 1889 shall apply for the interpretation of this Order as it applies for the interpretation of an Act of Parliament.

[2456]

3 (*Revokes section 8 of Art IX of the Fund Agreement in Pt I of the Schedule to the Bretton Woods Agreements Order in Council 1946, SR & O 1946/36 at* **[2362]**.)

4 The International Monetary Fund (hereinafter referred to as the Fund) is an organisation of which the United Kingdom and foreign sovereign Powers are members.

[2457]

Representatives

5(1) All Governors, Executive Directors, Alternates, members of committees, and representatives of Member States appointed to attend a meeting of the Executive Board under Article XII, Section 3(j) of the Fund Agreement shall enjoy immunity from suit and legal process with respect to acts performed by them in their official capacity except when the Fund waives this immunity.

(2) Part IV of Schedule I to the Act shall not operate so as to confer any immunity on the families of persons to whom this Article applies.

(3) Part IV of Schedule I to the Act shall not operate so as to confer any immunity on the official staff, other than advisers, of persons to whom this Article applies.

(4) This Article shall not operate so as to confer any immunity on any person as the representative of Her Majesty's Government in the United Kingdom or as a member of the staff of such a representative.

[2458]

Officers

6 All officers and employees of the Fund shall enjoy immunity from suit and legal process with respect to acts performed by them in their official capacity except when the Fund waives this immunity.

[2459]

Representatives to the Council

7(1) All Councillors, their Alternates and Associates shall enjoy immunity from suit and legal process with respect to acts performed by them in their official capacity except when the Fund waives this immunity.

(2) Part IV of Schedule I to the Act shall not operate so as to confer any immunity on the families of persons to whom this Article applies.

(3) Part IV of Schedule I to the Act shall not operate so as to confer any immunity on the official staff, other than advisers, of persons to whom this Article applies.

(4) This Article shall not operate so as to confer any immunity on any person as the representative of Her Majesty's Government in the United Kingdom or as a member of the staff of such a representative.

[2460]

STATE IMMUNITY (FEDERAL STATES) ORDER 1979

(SI 1979/457)

NOTES

Made: 11 April 1979.
Authority: State Immunity Act 1978, s 14(5).
Commencement: 2 May 1979.

1 This Order may be cited as the State Immunity (Federal States) Order 1979 and shall come into operation on 2nd May 1979.

[2461]

2 The provisions of Part 1 of the State Immunity Act 1978 shall apply to the following constituent territories of the Republic of Austria as they apply to a State: Burgenland, Carinthia, Lower Austria, Upper Austria, Salzburg, Styria, Tyrol, Vorarlberg and Vienna.

[2462]

EUROPEAN BANK FOR RECONSTRUCTION AND DEVELOPMENT (IMMUNITIES AND PRIVILEGES) ORDER 1991

(SI 1991/757)

NOTES

Made: 20 March 1991.
Authority: International Organisations Act 1968, s 1.
Commencement: 15 April 1991.

PART I
GENERAL

1 Citation, Entry into Force and Revocation

(1) This Order may be cited as the European Bank for Reconstruction and Development (Immunities and Privileges) Order 1991 and shall come into force on the date on which the Headquarters Agreement between the Government of the United Kingdom of Great Britain and Northern Ireland and the European Bank for Reconstruction and Development enters into force. That date will be notified in the London, Edinburgh and Belfast Gazettes.

(2) (*Revokes the European Bank for Reconstruction and Development* (*Immunities and Privileges*) *Order 1990, SI 1990/2142.*)

[2463]

2 Interpretation

In this Order—

(a) "the 1961 Convention Articles" means the Articles (being certain Articles of the Vienna Convention on Diplomatic Relations signed in 1961) which are set out in Schedule 1 to the Diplomatic Privileges Act 1964;

(b) "Agreement Establishing the Bank" means the Agreement Establishing the European Bank for Reconstruction and Development signed in Paris on 29th May 1990, and any amendments thereto;

(c) "Bank" means the European Bank for Reconstruction and Development;

(d) the terms "Member", "President", "Vice-President", "Governor", "Alternate Governor", "Temporary Alternate Governor", "Board of Governors", "Director", "Alternate Director" and "Temporary Alternate Director", "Board of Directors", have the same meaning as in the Agreement Establishing the Bank, its By-laws or Rules of Procedure;

(e) "Premises of the Bank" means the land, buildings and parts of buildings, including access facilities, used for the Official Activities of the Bank;

(f) "Representatives of Members" means heads of delegations of Members participating in meetings convened by the Bank other than meetings of the Board of Governors or the Board of Directors;

(g) "Members of Delegation" means alternates, advisers, technical experts and secretaries of delegations of Representatives of Members;

(h) "Officers" means the President, the Vice-President and other persons appointed by the President to be Officers of the Bank;

(i) "Employees of the Bank" means the staff of the Bank excluding those staff both recruited locally and assigned to hourly rates of pay;

(j) "Archives of the Bank" includes all records, correspondence, documents, manuscripts, still and moving pictures and films, sound recordings, computer programmes and written materials, video tapes or discs, and discs or tapes containing data belonging to, or held by, the Bank;

(k) "Official Activities of the Bank" includes all activities undertaken pursuant to the Agreement Establishing the Bank, and all activities appropriate to fulfil its purpose and functions under Articles 1 and 2 of that Agreement, or undertaken in exercise of its powers under Article 20 of that Agreement including its administrative activities; and

(l) "Persons Connected with the Bank" means Governors, Alternate Governors, Temporary Alternate Governors, Representatives of Members, Members of Delegations, Directors, Alternate Directors, Temporary Alternate Directors, the President, the Vice-Presidents, Officers and Employees of the Bank, and experts performing missions for the Bank.

[2464]

PART II
THE BANK

3 The Bank is an organisation of which the United Kingdom and other sovereign Powers are members.

[2465]

4 The Bank shall have the legal capacities of a body corporate.

[2466]

5(1) Except to the extent that the Board of Directors of the Bank shall have waived immunity, the Bank shall have immunity from suit and legal process—

(a) where the Bank has no office in the United Kingdom, nor has appointed an agent in the United Kingdom for the purpose of accepting service or notice of process, nor has issued or guaranteed securities in the United Kingdom; or

(b) where actions are brought by any member of the Bank or by any person acting for or deriving claims from any member of the Bank; or

(c) in respect of any form of seizure of, or restraint, attachment or execution on, the property or assets of the Bank, wheresoever located or by whomsoever held, before the delivery of final judgment against the Bank; or

(d) in respect of the search, requisition, confiscation or expropriation of, or any other form of interference with, or taking of or foreclosure on, the property or assets of the Bank, wheresoever located and by whomsoever held.

(2) Without prejudice to paragraph (1), the Bank shall, within the scope of its Official Activities, have immunity from suit and legal process, except that the immunity of the Bank shall not apply—

(a) to the extent that the Bank shall have expressly waived any such immunity in any particular case or in any written document;

(b) in respect of a civil action arising out of the exercise of its powers to borrow money, to guarantee obligations and to buy or sell or underwrite the sale of any securities;

(c) in respect of a civil action by a third party for damage arising from a road traffic accident caused by an Officer or an Employee of the Bank acting on behalf of the Bank;

(d) in respect of a civil action relating to death or personal injury caused by an act or omission in the United Kingdom;

(e) in respect of the enforcement of an arbitration award made against the Bank as a result of an express submission to arbitration by or on behalf of the Bank; or

(f) in respect of any counter-claim directly connected with court proceedings initiated by the Bank.

[2467]

6(1) The Premises of the Bank and the Archives of the Bank shall have the like inviolability as, in accordance with the 1961 Convention Articles, is accorded in respect of the official archives and premises of a diplomatic mission, except that the Premises of the Bank may be entered with the consent of and under conditions approved by the President; such consent may be assumed in the case of fire or other disasters requiring prompt action.

(2) The Premises of the Bank may be entered in connection with fire prevention, sanitary regulations or emergencies without the prior consent of the Bank in such circumstances and in such a manner as may have been determined by any agreement for that purpose entered into between the Government and the Bank.

[2468]

7 Within the scope of its Official Activities the Bank, its property, assets, income and profits shall have exemption from income tax, capital gains tax and corporation tax.

[2469]

8 The Bank shall have the like relief from rates on the Premises of the Bank as in accordance with Article 23 of the 1961 Convention Articles is accorded in respect of the premises of a diplomatic mission.

[2470]

9 The Bank shall have exemption from duties (whether of customs or excise) and taxes on the importation by it or on its behalf of goods necessary for the exercise of the Official Activities of the Bank and on the importation of any publications of the Bank imported by it or on its behalf, such exemption to be subject to compliance with such conditions as the Commissioners of Customs and Excise may prescribe for the protection of the Revenue.

[2471]

10 The Bank shall have exemption from prohibitions and restrictions on importation or exportation in the case of goods imported or exported by the Bank and necessary for the exercise of its Official Activities and in the case of any publications of the Bank imported or exported by it.

[2472]

11 The Bank shall have relief, under arrangements made by the Commissioners of Customs and Excise, by way of refund of duty (whether of customs or excise) paid on imported hydrocarbon oil (within the meaning of the Hydrocarbon Oil Duties Act 1979) or value added tax paid on the importation of such oil which is bought in the United Kingdom and is necessary for the exercise of its Official Activities, such relief to be subject to compliance with such conditions as may be imposed in accordance with the arrangements.

[2473]

12 The Bank shall have relief, under arrangements made by Secretary of State, by way of refund of car tax and value added tax paid on any official vehicle and value added tax paid on the supply of any goods or services which are supplied for the Official Activities of the Bank, such relief to be subject to compliance with such conditions as may be imposed in accordance with the arrangements.

[2474]

[12A The Bank shall have relief, under arrangements made by the Secretary of State, by way of refund of Insurance Premium Tax and Air Passenger Duty paid by the Bank in the exercise of its official activities.]

[2475]

NOTES

Inserted by the International Organisations (Immunities and Privileges) Miscellaneous Provisions Order 1999, SI 1999/2034, art 2, Schedule.

PART III
PERSONS CONNECTED WITH THE BANK

13(1) A Person Connected with the Bank shall enjoy—

(a) immunity from suit and legal process, even after the termination of his mission or service, in respect of acts performed by him in his official capacity including words written or spoken by him, except in respect of civil liability in the case of damage arising from a road traffic accident caused by him;

(b) such immunity from suit and legal process as is necessary to ensure that all their official papers and documents have the like inviolability as, in accordance with the 1961 Convention Articles, is accorded in respect of official archives of a diplomatic mission.

(2) In addition to the immunities set out in paragraph (1), Directors, Alternate Directors, Officers and Employees, and experts performing missions for the Bank under contract longer than 18 months shall, at the time of first taking up their post in the United Kingdom, be exempt from duties (whether of customs or excise) and taxes on the importation of articles (except payments for services) in respect of import of their furniture and personal effects (including one motor car each), and the furniture and personal effects of members of their family forming part of their household, which are in their ownership or possession or already ordered by them and intended for their personal use or for their establishment.

(3) In addition to the privileges and immunities set out in paragraph (1), Governors, Alternate Governors, and Representatives of Members shall enjoy—

(i) the like exemption from duties (whether of customs or excise) and taxes on the importation of their personal baggage and the like privilege as to the importation of such articles, as In accordance with paragraph 1 of Article 36 of the 1961 Convention Articles is accorded to a diplomatic agent;

(ii) the like exemption and privileges in respect of their personal baggage as in accordance with paragraph 2 of Article 36 of the 1961 Convention Articles are accorded to a diplomatic agent;

(iii) such immunity from suit and legal process as is necessary to ensure that their personal baggage cannot be seized;

(iv) immunity from arrest or detention.

(4) In addition to the immunities set out in paragraph (1), the President and five Vice-Presidents, as nominated by the President, shall enjoy—

(a) the like immunity from suit and legal process, the like inviolability of residence and the like exemption or relief from taxes (other than income tax in respect of their emoluments and duties and taxes on the importation of goods) as are accorded to or in respect of a diplomatic agent;

(b) the like exemption or relief from being subject to a community charge, or being liable to pay anything in respect of a community charge or anything by way of contribution in respect of a collective community charge, as is accorded to or in respect of a diplomatic agent;

(c) the like exemption from duties and taxes on the importation of articles imported for their personal use, including articles intended for their establishment, as in accordance with paragraph 1 of Article 36 of the 1961 Convention Articles is accorded to a diplomatic agent;

(d) the like exemption and privileges in respect of their personal baggage as in accordance with paragraph 2 of Article 36 of the 1961 Convention Articles are accorded to a diplomatic agent;

(e) relief, under arrangements made by the Commissioners of Customs and Excise, by way of refund of duty (whether of customs or excise) or value added tax paid on any hydrocarbon oil (within the meaning of the Hydrocarbon Oil Duties Act 1979) which is bought in the United Kingdom by them or on their behalf and which is for the personal use or for that of members of their family forming part of their household, such relief to be subject to compliance with such conditions as may be imposed in accordance with the arrangements.

(5) Paragraphs (2), (3) and (4) of this Article shall not apply to any person who is a British citizen, a [British overseas territories citizen], a British Overseas citizen, or a British National (Overseas), or who is a permanent resident of the United Kingdom.

(6) Part IV of Schedule 1 to the Act shall not operate so as to confer any privilege or immunity on the official staff of representatives other than Members of Delegations, nor so as to confer any privilege or immunity on the family of any person to whom this Article applies.

(7) Neither the provisions of the preceding paragraphs of this Article, nor those of Part IV of Schedule 1 to the Act, shall operate so as to confer any privilege or immunity on any persons as the representative of the United Kingdom or as a member of the delegation of such a representative.

(8) Any privilege or immunity conferred by the preceding paragraphs of this Article may be waived as follows:—

(i) in the case of any privilege or immunity conferred on any officer or employee of the Bank (other than the President or a Vice-President), or on an expert performing a mission for the Bank, by the President;

(ii) in the case of any privilege or immunity conferred on the President or a Vice-President, by the Board of Directors;

(iii) in the case of any privilege or immunity conferred on a Representative of a Member or a member of his delegation, by the Member concerned.

[2476]

NOTES

Para (5): words in square brackets substituted by virtue of the British Overseas Territories Act 2002, s 2(3).

14(1) As from the date on which an internal effective tax for the benefit of the Bank on the salaries and emoluments paid to him by the Bank is applied, any Director, Alternate, Officer and Employee of the Bank shall enjoy exemption from income tax in respect of such salaries and emoluments, provided that nothing in this paragraph shall be interpreted as precluding such salaries and emoluments from being taken into account for the purpose of assessing the amount of taxation to be applied to income from other sources.

(2) Paragraph (1) of this Article shall not apply to pensions or annuities paid by the Bank.

[2477]

15 As from the date on which the Bank establishes or joins a social security scheme, the Directors, Alternate Directors, Officers and Employees of the Bank shall enjoy exemptions whereby for the purposes of the enactments relating to social security, including enactments in force in Northern Ireland—

(i) services rendered for the Bank by them shall be deemed to be excepted from any class of employment in respect of which contributions or premiums under those enactments are payable, but

(ii) no person shall be rendered liable to pay any contribution or premium which he would not be required to pay if those services were not deemed to be so excepted.

[2478]

STATE IMMUNITY (FEDERAL STATES) ORDER 1993

(SI 1993/2809)

NOTES

Made: 16 November 1993.
State Immunity Act 1978, s 14(5).
Commencement: 7 December 1993.

1 This Order may be cited as the State Immunity (Federal States) Order 1993 and shall come into force on 7th December 1993.

[2479]

2 The provisions of Part I of the State Immunity Act 1978 shall apply to the following constituent territories of the Federal Republic of Germany as they apply to a State: Baden-Württemberg, Bavaria, Berlin, Brandenburg, Bremen, Hamburg, Hesse, Mecklenburg-Western Pomerania, Lower Saxony, North-Rhine/Westphalia, Rhineland-Palatinate, Saarland, Saxony, Saxony-Anhalt, Schleswig-Holstein and Thuringia.

[2480]

WORLD TRADE ORGANISATION (IMMUNITIES AND PRIVILEGES) ORDER 1995

(SI 1995/266)

NOTES

Made: 8 February 1995.
Authority: International Organisations Act 1968, s 1.
Commencement: see art 1.

PART I
GENERAL

1 Citation and Entry into Force

This Order may be cited as the World Trade Organisation (Immunities and Privileges) Order 1995 and shall come into force on the date on which the Agreement Establishing the World Trade Organisation (hereinafter referred to as the Agreement) enters into force in the United Kingdom. This date will be notified in the London, Edinburgh and Belfast Gazettes.

[2481]

2 Interpretation

In this Order:

(a) "the 1961 Convention Articles" means the Articles (being certain Articles of the Vienna Convention on Diplomatic Relations signed in 1961) which are set out in Schedule 1 to the Diplomatic Privileges Act 1964;

(b) "Organisation" means the World Trade Organisation;

(c) "Member" means a member of the Organisation;

(d) "representatives of Members" means representatives, alternates, advisers, technical experts and secretaries of delegations of Members.

[2482]

PART III STATUTORY INSTRUMENTS

PART II
THE ORGANISATION

3 The Organisation is an organisation of which the United Kingdom and other sovereign Powers are members.

[2483]

4 The Organisation shall have the legal capacities of a body corporate.

[2484]

5 Except in so far as in any particular case it has expressly waived its immunity, the Organisation shall have immunity from suit and legal process. No waiver of immunity shall be deemed to extend to any measure of execution.

[2485]

6 The Organisation shall have the like inviolability of official archives and premises as in accordance with the 1961 Convention Articles is accorded in respect of the official archives and premises of a diplomatic mission.

[2486]

7 The Organisation, its assets, income and other property shall have exemption from income tax, capital gains tax and corporation tax.

[2487]

8 The Organisation shall have the like relief from rates as in accordance with Article 23 of the 1961 Convention Articles is accorded in respect of the premises of a diplomatic mission.

[2488]

9 The Organisation shall have exemption from customs duties and taxes on the importation by it of goods for its official use in the United Kingdom and on the importation of publications of the Organisation imported by it, such exemption to be subject to compliance with such conditions as the Commissioners of Customs and Excise may prescribe for the protection of the Revenue.

[2489]

10 The Organisation shall have exemption from prohibitions and restrictions on importation or exportation in the case of goods imported or exported by the Organisation for its official use and in the case of any publications of the Organisation imported or exported by it.

[2490]

11 The Organisation shall have relief, under arrangements made by the Commissioners of Customs and Excise, by way of refund of customs duty paid on imported hydrocarbon oil (within the meaning of the Hydrocarbon Oil Duties Act 1979 or value added tax paid on the importation of such oil which is bought in the United Kingdom and used for the official purposes of the Organisation, such relief to be subject to compliance with such conditions as may be imposed in accordance with the arrangements.

[2491]

12 The Organisation shall have relief, under arrangements made by the Secretary of State, by way of refund of value added tax paid on the purchase of new motor vehicles of United Kingdom manufacture and of value added tax paid on the supply of any goods or services which are used for the official purposes of the Organisation, such relief to be subject to compliance with such conditions as may be imposed in accordance with the arrangements.

[2492]

PART III
REPRESENTATIVES

13(1) Except in so far as in any particular case any privilege or immunity is waived by the Member which they represent, representatives of Members at the meetings of the Organisation shall enjoy—

(a) immunity from suit and legal process in respect of things done or omitted to be done by them in their official capacity;

(b) while exercising their functions and during their journeys to and from the place of meeting, the like immunity from personal arrest or detention and from seizure of their personal baggage and the like inviolability for all papers and documents as is accorded to a diplomatic agent; and

(c) while exercising their functions and during their journeys to and from the place of meeting, the like exemptions and privileges in respect of their personal baggage as in accordance with Article 36 of the 1961 Convention Articles are accorded to a diplomatic agent.

(2) Where the incidence of any form of taxation depends upon residence, a representative shall not be deemed to be resident in the United Kingdom during any period when he is present in the United Kingdom for the discharge of his duties.

(3) Part IV of Schedule 1 to the Act shall not operate so as to confer any privilege or immunity on—

(a) the official staff of a representative other than alternates, advisers, technical experts and secretaries of delegations, or

(b) the family of a representative or of a member of the official staff of a representative.

(4) Neither the preceding paragraphs of this Article nor Part IV of Schedule 1 to the Act shall operate so as to confer any privilege or immunity on any person as the representative of the United Kingdom or as a member of the official staff of such a representative or on any person who is a British citizen, a [British overseas territories citizen], a British Overseas citizen, or a British National (Overseas).

[2493]

NOTES

Para (4): words in square brackets substituted by virtue of the British Overseas Territories Act 2002, s 2(3).

PART IV
OFFICIALS

14 High Officials

(1) Except in so far as in any particular case any privilege or immunity is waived by or on behalf of the Organisation, and subject to the provisions of paragraph (2) of this Article, the Director-General, any Deputy Director-General or Assistant Director-General and any official acting on behalf of the Director-General during his absence from duty, shall enjoy—

(a) the like immunity from suit and legal process, the like inviolability of residence and the like exemption or relief from taxes, other than customs duties and taxes on the importation of goods, as are accorded to or in respect of the head of a diplomatic mission;

(b) the like exemption or relief from being liable to pay anything in respect of council tax as is accorded to or in respect of a diplomatic agent;

(c) the like exemption from customs duties and taxes on the importation of articles imported for his personal use or the use of members of his family forming part of his household, including articles intended for his establishment, as in accordance with paragraph 1 of Article 36 of the 1961 Convention Articles is accorded to a diplomatic agent;

(c) the like exemption and privileges in respect of his personal baggage as in accordance with paragraph 2 of Article 36 of the 1961 Convention Articles are accorded to a diplomatic agent;

(d) relief, under arrangements made by the Commissioners of Customs and Excise, by way of refund of customs duty paid on imported hydrocarbon oil (within the meaning of the Hydrocarbon Oil Duties Act 1979) or value added tax paid on the importation of such oil which is bought in the United Kingdom by him or on his behalf, such relief to be subject to compliance with such conditions as may be imposed in accordance with the arrangements; and

(e) exemptions whereby, for the purposes of the enactments relating to national insurance and social security, including enactments in force in Northern Ireland,—

(i) services rendered for the Organisation by the officer shall be deemed to be excepted from any class of employment in respect of which contributions or premiums under those enactments are payable, but
(ii) no person shall be rendered liable to pay any contribution or premium which he would not be required to pay if those services were not deemed to be so excepted.

(2) This Article shall not apply to any person who is a British citizen, a [British overseas territories citizen], a British Overseas citizen, or a British National (Overseas) or who is a permanent resident of the United Kingdom.

(3) Part IV of Schedule 1 of the Act shall not operate so as to confer any privilege or immunity on any member of the family of any officer to whom this Article applies other than [his spouse or civil partner] and minor children.

[2494]

NOTES

Para (2): words in square brackets substituted by virtue of the British Overseas Territories Act 2002, s 2(3).

Para (3): words in square brackets substituted by the International Organisations (Immunities and Privileges) Miscellaneous Provisions Order 2006, SI 2006/1075, art 2, Schedule.

15 All Officials

Except in so far as in any particular case any privilege or immunity is waived by or on behalf of the Organisation, officials of the Organisation (other than those who are locally recruited and assigned to hourly rates of pay) shall enjoy—

(a) immunity from suit and legal process in respect of things done or omitted to be done by them in their official capacity;
(b) exemption from income tax in respect of emoluments received by them as officials of the Organisation; and
(c) the like exemption from customs duties and taxes on the importation of articles which—
  (i) at or about the time when they first enter the United Kingdom to take up their posts as officials of the Organisation are imported for their personal use or that of members of their families forming part of their households, including articles intended for their establishment, and
  (ii) are articles which were in their ownership or possession or that of such members of their families, or which they or such members of their families were under contract to purchase, immediately before they so entered the United Kingdom,

as in accordance with paragraph 1 of Article 36 of the 1961 Convention Articles is accorded to a diplomatic agent.

[2495]

EUROPEAN COURT OF HUMAN RIGHTS (IMMUNITIES AND PRIVILEGES) ORDER 2000

(SI 2000/1817)

NOTES

Made: 12 July 2000.
Authority: International Organisations Act 1968, s 5.
Commencement: 10 December 2001; see art 1(2).

PART I
GENERAL

1(1) This Order may be cited as the European Court of Human Rights (Immunities and Privileges) Order 2000.

(2) Parts I and II of this Order shall come into force on the date on which the Sixth Protocol to the General Agreement on Privileges and Immunities of the Council of Europe done at Strasbourg on 5th March 1996 enters into force with respect to the United Kingdom. Part III of this Order shall come into force on the date on which the European Agreement relating to Persons Participating in Proceedings of the European Court of Human Rights done at Strasbourg on 5th March 1996 enters into force with respect to the United Kingdom. These dates shall be notified in the London, Edinburgh and Belfast Gazettes.

[2496]

NOTES

Commencement: 10 December 2001.

2(1) In this Order—

"the Convention" means the Convention for the Protection of Human Rights and Fundamental Freedoms signed at Rome on 4th November 1950 as amended by Protocol No 11 to the Convention for the Protection of Human Rights and Fundamental Freedoms restructuring the control machinery established thereby;

"the Committee of Ministers" means the Committee of Ministers of the Council of Europe when exercising its functions under Article 46(2) of the Convention;

"the Court" means the European Court of Human Rights established by Article 19 of the Convention or any Chamber, judge or judges of the Court carrying out their duties under the terms of the Convention or the rules of the Court;

"judges of the Court" means judges elected under Article 22 or appointed under Article 27 of the Convention;

"persons participating in proceedings" means—

(a) any persons taking part in proceedings instituted before the Court as parties, their representatives and advisors.

(b) witnesses and experts called upon by the Court and other persons invited by the President of the Court to take part in proceedings.

(c) any person mentioned in sub-paragraph (a) or (b) of this paragraph who is called upon to appear before or to submit written statements to the Committee of Ministers;

"the 1961 Convention Articles" means the Articles (being certain Articles of the Vienna Convention on Diplomatic Relations signed in 1961) which are set out in Schedule 1 to the Diplomatic Privileges Act 1964.

(2) For the purposes of this Order any petition, complaint or other communication which, with a view to action to be taken by or before the Court—

(a) is made to the Court, or

(b) is made to a person through whom, in accordance with the constitution, rules or practice of the Court, such a communication can be received,

shall be deemed to be proceedings before the Court, and the person making any such communication shall be deemed to be a party to such proceedings.

[2497]

NOTES

Commencement: 10 December 2001.

PART II
THE COURT

3 The judges of the Court, the Registrar of the Court and the Deputy Registrar of the Court shall have inviolability in respect of their documents and papers in so far as they relate to the business of the Court.

[2498]

NOTES

Commencement: 10 December 2001.

4(1) Except in so far as in any particular case any privilege or immunity is waived by the Court sitting in plenary session, judges of the Court, the Registrar of the Court and, when he is acting as the Registrar, the Deputy Registrar of the Court shall enjoy:—

(a) unless they are British citizens, [British overseas territories citizens], British Overseas citizens, British Nationals (Overseas) or permanently resident in the United Kingdom the like immunity from suit and legal process, the like inviolability of residence and the like exemption or relief from taxes, other than customs duties and taxes on the importation of goods, and rates as are accorded to or in respect of the head of a diplomatic mission;

(b) immunity from suit and legal process in respect of words spoken or written and things done or omitted to be done by them in their official capacity;

(c) exemption from income tax in respect of the salaries and emoluments received by them;

(d) the like exemption from duties and taxes on the importation of articles imported for their personal use, including articles intended for their establishment, as in accordance with paragraph 1 of Article 36 of the 1961 Convention Articles is accorded to a diplomatic agent;

(e) unless they are British citizens, British Dependent Territories citizens, British Overseas citizens, British Nationals (Overseas) or permanently resident in the United Kingdom the like exemption and privileges in respect of their personal baggage as in accordance with paragraph 2 of Article 36 of the 1961 Convention Articles are accorded to a diplomatic agent;

(f) unless they are British citizens, British Territories citizens, British Overseas citizens, British Nationals (Overseas) or permanently resident in the United Kingdom relief under arrangements made by the Commissioners of Customs and Excise, by way of refund of customs duty paid on imported hydrocarbon oil (within the meaning of the Hydrocarbon Oil Duties Act 1979) or value added tax paid on the importation of such oil which is bought in the United Kingdom by or on their behalf, such relief to be subject to compliance with such conditions as may be imposed in accordance with the arrangements; and

(g) exemptions whereby, for the purposes of the enactments relating to national insurance and social security, including enactments in force in Northern Ireland,

(i) services rendered for the Court by them shall be deemed to be excepted from any class of employment in respect of which contributions or premiums under those enactments are payable, but

(ii) no person shall be rendered liable to pay any contribution or premium which he would not be required to pay if those services were not deemed to be so excepted.

(2) Paragraph 1(c) of this Article shall not apply to pensions or annuities paid by the Court.

[2499]

NOTES

Commencement: 10 December 2001.

Para (1): in sub-para (a) words in square brackets substituted by virtue of the British Overseas Territories Act 2002, s 2(3).

[4A(1) Except in so far as in any particular case any privilege or immunity is waived by the Court sitting in plenary session, [spouses or civil partners] and minor children of judges of the Court shall enjoy—

(a) the like immunity from suit and legal process, the like inviolability of residence and the like exemption or relief from taxes, other than customs duties and taxes on the importation of goods, and rates as are accorded to or in respect of the head of a diplomatic mission;

(b) the like exemption from duties and taxes on the importation of articles imported for their personal use, including articles intended for their establishment, as in accordance with paragraph 1 of Article 36 of the 1961 Convention Articles is accorded to a diplomatic agent;

(c) the like exemption and privileges in respect of their personal baggage as in accordance with paragraph 2 of Article 36 of the 1961 Convention Articles are accorded to a diplomatic agent;

(d) relief, under arrangements made by the Commissioners for Her Majesty's Revenue and Customs, by way of refund of duty (whether of customs or excise) paid on imported hydrocarbon oil (within the meaning of the Hydrocarbon Oil Duties Act 1979) or value added tax paid on the importation of such oil which is bought in the United Kingdom by or on their behalf, such relief to be subject to compliance with such conditions as may be imposed in accordance with the arrangements.

(2) This article shall not apply to any person who is a British citizen, British Overseas territories citizen, British Overseas citizen or British National (Overseas).]

[2500]

NOTES

Commencement: 2 January 2006.

Inserted by the European Court of Human Rights (Immunities and Privileges) (Amendment) Order 2005, SI 2005/3425, art 2.

Para (1): words in square brackets substituted by the International Organisations (Immunities and Privileges) Miscellaneous Provisions Order 2006, SI 2006/1075, art 2, Schedule.

PART III
PERSONS PARTICIPATING IN PROCEEDINGS

5 Except in so far as in any particular case any immunity is waived by the Court, persons participating in proceedings shall have:—

(a) in respect of words spoken or written and documents or other evidence submitted by them before or to the Court (but not where such words, documents or evidence or any part thereof are communicated by them or on their behalf outside the Court) the like immunity from suit and legal process as is accorded to the head of a diplomatic mission;

(b) while passing in transit through the United Kingdom during their journeys to and from the proceedings or while in the United Kingdom for the purpose of such proceedings there, immunity from criminal proceedings and, except for the purpose of detaining a person who has escaped from legal custody, from personal arrest in respect of acts or convictions prior to the commencement of the journey, provided that their presence at the proceedings has been authorised in advance by the Court and that fifteen days have not elapsed from the date when their presence is no longer required by the Court.

[2501]

NOTES

Commencement: 10 December 2001.

H. CROSS-BORDER INSOLVENCY

NOTES

See also the provisions relating to insolvency in the Financial Markets and Insolvency (Settlement Finality) Regulations 1999, SI 1999/2979 at **[2179]** and the Financial Collateral Arrangements (No 2) Regulations 2003, SI 2003/3226 at **[2190]**.

INSOLVENCY (SCOTLAND) RULES 1986

(SI 1986/1915 (S 139))

NOTES

Made: 10 November 1986.

Authority: Insolvency Act 1986, s 411.

Commencement: 29 December 1986.

Application: these Rules are applied to limited liability partnerships with such modifications as the context requires for the purpose of giving effect to the provisions of the Insolvency Act 1986, by the Limited Liability Partnerships Regulations 2001, SI 2001/1090, reg 10, Sch 6, Pt II (except in so far as they relate to the exceptions to the reserved matters specified in the Scotland Act 1998, Sch 5, Pt II, C 2), and by the Limited Liability Partnerships (Scotland) Regulations 2001, SSI 2001/128, reg 6.

Only the rules relevant to cross-border aspects of insolvency proceedings are reproduced here.

ARRANGEMENT OF THE RULES

INTRODUCTORY PROVISIONS

PART 1
COMPANY VOLUNTARY ARRANGEMENTS

CHAPTER 8
EC REGULATION—CONVERSION OF VOLUNTARY ARRANGEMENT INTO WINDING UP

CHAPTER 9
EC REGULATION—MEMBER STATE LIQUIDATOR

PART 2
ADMINISTRATION PROCEDURE

CHAPTER 12
EC REGULATION—CONVERSION OF ADMINISTRATION TO WINDING UP

INTRODUCTORY PROVISIONS

0.1 Citation and commencement

These Rules may be cited as the Insolvency (Scotland) Rules 1986 and shall come into operation on 29th December 1986.

[2502]

0.2 Interpretation

(1) In these Rules—

"the Act" means the Insolvency Act 1986;

"the Companies Act" means the Companies Act 1985;

["the Banking Act" means the Banking Act 1987;]

"the Bankruptcy Act" means the Bankruptcy (Scotland) Act 1985;

"the Rules" means the Insolvency (Scotland) Rules 1986;

"accounting period" in relation to the winding up of a company, shall be construed in accordance with section 52(1) and (6) of the Bankruptcy Act as applied by Rule 4.68;

["authorised person" is a reference to a person who is authorised pursuant to section 389A of the Act to act as nominee or supervisor of a voluntary arrangement proposed or approved under Part I or Part VIII of the Act.]

"business day" means any day other than a Saturday, a Sunday, Christmas Day, Good Friday or a day which is a bank holiday in any part of Great Britain;

["centre of main interests" has the same meaning as in the EC Regulation;]

"company" means a company which the courts in Scotland have jurisdiction to wind up;

["EC Regulation" means Council Regulation (EC) No 1346/2000 of 29th May 2000 on insolvency proceedings;]

["establishment" has the meaning given by Article 2(h) of the EC Regulation;]

"insolvency proceedings" means any proceedings under the first group of Parts in the Act or under these Rules;

["main proceedings" means proceedings opened in accordance with Article 3 (1) of the EC Regulation and falling within the definition of insolvency proceedings in Article 2(a) of the EC Regulation, and

(a) in relation to England and Wales and Scotland set out in Annex A to the EC Regulation under the heading "United Kingdom"; and

(b) in relation to another member State, set out in Annex A to the EC Regulation under the heading relating to that member State;]

["member State liquidator" means a person falling within the definition of liquidator in Article 2(b) of the EC Regulation appointed in proceedings to which it applies in a member State other than the United Kingdom;]

["prescribed part" has the same meaning as it does in section 176A(2)(a) of the Act]

["proxy-holder" shall be construed in accordance with Rule 7.14;]

"receiver" means a receiver appointed under section 51 (Receivers (Scotland)); and

"responsible insolvency practitioner" means, in relation to any insolvency proceedings, the person acting as supervisor of a voluntary arrangement under Part I of the Act, or as administrator, receiver, liquidator or provisional liquidator.

["secondary proceedings" means proceedings opened in accordance with Articles 3(2) and 3(3) of the EC Regulation and falling within the definition of winding-up proceedings in Article 2(c) of the EC Regulation, and

(a) in relation to England and Wales and Scotland, set out in Annex B to the EC Regulation under the heading "United Kingdom"; and

(b) in relation to another member State, set out in Annex B to the EC Regulation under the heading relating to that member State;]

["territorial proceedings" means proceedings opened in accordance with Articles 3(2) and 3(4) of the EC Regulation and falling within the definition of insolvency proceedings in Article 2(a) of the EC Regulation, and

(a) in relation to England and Wales and Scotland, set out in Annex A to the EC Regulation under the heading "United Kingdom"; and

(b) in relation to another member State, set out in Annex A to the EC Regulation under the heading relating to that member State.]

(2) In these Rules, unless the context otherwise requires, any reference—

(a) to a section is a reference to a section of the Act;

(b) to a Rule is a reference to a Rule of the Rules;

(c) to a Part or a Schedule is a reference to a Part of, or Schedule to, the Rules;

(d) to a Chapter is a reference to a Chapter of the Part in which that reference is made.
[2503]

NOTES

Para (1): definitions "the Banking Act" and "proxy-holder" inserted by the Insolvency (Scotland) Amendment Rules 1987, SI 1987/1921, r 3(1), Schedule, Pt I, para 1; definition "authorised person" inserted by the Insolvency (Scotland) Amendment Rules 2002, SI 2002/2709, r 3; definitions "centre of main interests", "EC Regulation", "establishment", "main proceedings", "member State liquidator", "secondary proceedings" and "territorial proceedings" inserted by the Insolvency (Scotland) Regulations 2003, SI 2003/2109, regs 23, 24, subject to the saving that anything done under or for the purposes of any provision of these Rules before 8 September 2003 has effect as if done under or for the purposes of the provision as amended; definition "prescribed part" inserted by the Enterprise Act 2002 (Consequential Amendments) (Prescribed Part) (Scotland) Order 2003, SI 2003/2108, art 3.

0.3 Application

These Rules apply—

(a) to receivers appointed, and

(b) to all other insolvency proceedings which are commenced,

on or after the date on which the Rules come into operation.
[2504]

PART 1
COMPANY VOLUNTARY ARRANGEMENTS

[CHAPTER 8
EC REGULATION—CONVERSION OF VOLUNTARY ARRANGEMENT INTO WINDING UP

1.46 Application for conversion into winding up

(1) Where a member State liquidator proposes to apply to the court for the conversion under Article 37 of the EC Regulation (conversion of earlier proceedings) of a voluntary arrangement into a winding up, an affidavit complying with Rule 1.47 must be prepared and sworn, and lodged in court in support of the application.

(2) The application and the affidavit required under this Rule shall be served upon—
- (a) the company; and
- (b) the supervisor.]

[2505]

NOTES

Commencement: 8 September 2003.

Chapter heading preceding this Rule, and this Rule, together with rr 1.47–1.49, inserted by the Insolvency (Scotland) Regulations 2003, SI 2003/2109, regs 23, 25(4), subject to the saving that anything done under or for the purposes of any provision of these Rules before 8 September 2003 has effect as if done under or for the purposes of the provision as amended.

[1.47 Contents of affidavit

(1) The affidavit shall state—
- (a) that main proceedings have been opened in relation to the company in a member State other than the United Kingdom;
- (b) the deponent's belief that the conversion of the voluntary arrangement into a winding up would prove to be in the interests of the creditors in the main proceedings;
- (c) the deponent's opinion as to whether the company ought to enter voluntary winding up or be wound up by the court; and
- (d) all other matters that, in the opinion of the member State liquidator, would assist the court—
  - (i) in deciding whether to make such an order, and
  - (ii) if the court were to do so, in considering the need for any consequential provision that would be necessary or desirable.

(2) An affidavit under this Rule shall be sworn by, or on behalf of, the member State liquidator.]

[2506]

NOTES

Commencement: 8 September 2003.

Inserted as noted to r 1.46 at **[2505]**.

[1.48 Power of court

(1) On hearing the application for conversion into winding up, the court may make such order as it thinks fit.

(2) If the court makes an order for conversion into winding up, the order may contain all such consequential provisions as the court deems necessary or desirable.

(3) Without prejudice to the generality of paragraph (1), an order under that paragraph may provide that the company be wound up as if a resolution for voluntary winding up under section 84 were passed on the day on which the order is made.

(4) Where the court makes an order for conversion into winding up under paragraph (1), any expenses properly incurred as expenses of the administration of the voluntary arrangement in question shall be a first charge on the company's assets.]

[2507]

NOTES

Commencement: 8 September 2003.
Inserted as noted to r 1.46 at **[2505]**.

[CHAPTER 9
EC REGULATION—MEMBER STATE LIQUIDATOR

1.49 Notice to member State liquidator

(1) This Rule applies where a member State liquidator has been appointed in relation to the company.

(2) Where the supervisor is obliged to give notice to, or provide a copy of a document (including an order of court) to, the court or the registrar of companies, the supervisor shall give notice or provide a copy, as appropriate, to the member State liquidator.

(3) Paragraph (2) is without prejudice to the generality of the obligations imposed by Article 31 of the EC Regulation (duty to co operate and communicate information).]

[2508]

NOTES

Commencement: 8 September 2003.
Inserted, together with chapter heading preceding this Rule, as noted to r 1.46 at **[2505]**.

[PART 2
ADMINISTRATION PROCEDURE]

NOTES

This Part (Pt 2 (rr 2.1–2.60)) substituted for existing Pt 2 (rr 2.1–2.25) by the Insolvency (Scotland) Amendment Rules 2003, SI 2003/2111, r 3, Sch 1, Pt 1, subject to savings in r 7 thereof.

[CHAPTER 12
EC REGULATION—CONVERSION OF ADMINISTRATION TO WINDING UP

2.57 Application for conversion into winding up

(1) Where a member State liquidator proposes to apply to the court for the conversion under Article 37 of the EC Regulation (conversion of earlier proceedings) of an administration into a winding up[, whether by entering voluntary winding up, being wound up by the court or wound up through the administration], there shall be lodged in support of his application an affidavit complying with Rule 2.58.

(2) The application and the affidavit required under this Rule shall be served upon—

(a) the company; and
(b) the administrator.]

[2509]

NOTES

Commencement: 15 September 2003.
This Part (Pt 2 (rr 2.1–2.60)) substituted for existing Pt 2 (rr 2.1–2.25) by the Insolvency (Scotland) Amendment Rules 2003, SI 2003/2111, r 3, Sch 1, Pt 1, subject to savings in r 7 thereof.
Para (1): words in square brackets inserted by the Insolvency (Scotland) Amendment Rules 2006, SI 2006/734, rr 3, 11.

[2.58 Contents of affidavit

(1) The affidavit shall state—

(a) that main proceedings have been opened in relation to the company in a member State other than the United Kingdom;
(b) the deponent's belief that the conversion of the administration into a winding up would prove to be in the interests of the creditors in the main proceedings;
(c) the deponent's opinion as to whether the company ought to enter voluntary

winding up[, be wound up by the court or be wound up through the administration] or be wound up by the court; and

(d) all other matters that, in the opinion of the member State liquidator, would assist the court—

(i) in deciding whether to make such an order; and

(ii) if the court were to do so, in considering the need for any consequential provision that would be necessary or desirable.

(2) An affidavit under this rule shall be sworn by, or on behalf of, the member State liquidator.]

[2510]

NOTES

Commencement: 15 September 2003.

Substituted as noted to r 2.57 at **[2509]**.

Para (1): words in square brackets in para (c) substituted by the Insolvency (Scotland) Amendment Rules 2006, SI 2006/734, rr 3, 12.

Para (1): see further Sch 5, Form 2.30B (Scot), and the notes to that Schedule.

[2.59 Power of court

(1) On hearing the application for conversion into winding up the court may make such order as it thinks fit.

(2) If the court makes an order for conversion into winding up the order may contain all such consequential provisions as the court deems necessary or desirable.

(3) Without prejudice to the generality of paragraph (1) of this Rule, an order under that paragraph may provide that the company be wound up as if a resolution for voluntary winding up under section 84 were passed on the day on which the order is made.]

[2511]

NOTES

Commencement: 15 September 2003.

Substituted as noted to r 2.57 at **[2509]**.

[CHAPTER 13
EC REGULATION—MEMBER STATE LIQUIDATOR

2.60 Interpretation of creditor and notice to member State liquidator

(1) This Rule applies where a member State liquidator has been appointed in relation to the company.

(2) For the purposes of Chapters 6, 7 and 8 of these Rules, (and except where the context otherwise requires) the member State liquidator is deemed to be a creditor.

(3) Paragraph (2) of this Rule is without prejudice to the generality of the right to participate referred to in paragraph 3 of Article 32 of the EC Regulation (exercise of creditor's rights).

(4) Where the administrator is obliged to give notice to, or provide a copy of a document (including an order of court) to, the court, the registrar of companies, or a provisional liquidator or liquidator, the administrator shall also give notice or provide copies, as the case may be, to the member State liquidator.

(5) Paragraph (4) is without prejudice to the generality of the obligations imposed by Article 31 of the EC Regulation (duty to co-operate and communicate information).]

[2512]

NOTES

Commencement: 15 September 2003.

Substituted as noted to r 2.57 at **[2509]**.

PART 4
WINDING UP BY THE COURT

[CHAPTER 14
EC REGULATION—MEMBER STATE LIQUIDATOR

4.83 Interpretation of creditor and notice to member State liquidator

(1) This Rule applies where a member State liquidator has been appointed in relation to the company.

(2) For the purposes of the provisions referred to in paragraph (3) the member State liquidator is deemed to be a creditor.

(3) The provisions referred to in paragraph (2) are—

(a) Rules 4.10(1) (report to creditors and contributories), 4.10(3) (summary of statement of affairs), 4.13 (other meetings of creditors), 4.15 (submission of claims), 4.17 (claims in foreign currency), 4.18(4) (appointment of liquidator by court), 4.23(2) and (4) (summoning of meeting for removal of liquidator), 4.31 (final meeting), 4.35 (creditors' claim that remuneration is excessive), 4.41(1), (2) and (3) (membership of liquidation committee), 4.52(3) (vacancy (creditor members)), 4.62(1) (membership of committee), 4.74 (notice of order for public examination), 7.3 (notice of meeting) (insofar as it applies to a notice of meeting of creditors under section 138(3) or (4) for the purposes of rule 4.12 and to a meeting requisitioned under rule 7.6 insofar as it applies in a winding up by the court), 7.6(2) (meetings requisitioned) (insofar as it applies in a winding up by the court) and 7.9 (entitlement to vote (creditors)) (insofar as it applies in a winding up by the court); and

(b) sections 48(5), (6) and (8) and 49 of the Bankruptcy Act as applied by Rule 4.16 and section 52(3) of that Act as applied by rule 4.68(1).

(4) Paragraphs (2) and (3) are without prejudice to the generality of the right to participate referred to in paragraph 3 of Article 32 of the EC Regulation (exercise of creditors' rights).

(5) Where the liquidator is obliged to give notice to, or provide a copy of a document (including an order of court) to, the court or the registrar of companies, the liquidator shall give notice or provide copies, as the case may be, to the member State liquidator.

(6) Paragraph (5) is without prejudice to the generality of the obligations imposed by Article 31 of the EC Regulation (duty to co operate and communicate information).]

[2513]

NOTES

Commencement: 8 September 2003.

Inserted, together with the Chapter heading preceding this Rule and rr 4.84, 4.85, by the Insolvency (Scotland) Regulations 2003, SI 2003/2109, regs 23, 27(3), subject to the saving that anything done under or for the purposes of any provision of these Rules before 8 September 2003 has effect as if done under or for the purposes of the provision as amended.

[CHAPTER 15
EC REGULATION—CREDITORS' VOLUNTARY WINDING UP—CONFIRMATION BY THE COURT

4.84 Application for confirmation

(1) Where a company has passed a resolution for voluntary winding up, and no declaration under section 89 has been made, the liquidator may apply to the court for an order confirming the creditors' voluntary winding up for the purposes of the EC Regulation.

(2) The application shall be in writing in the form required by Rule 7.30 and Schedule 5 and verified by affidavit by the liquidator (using the same form) and shall state—

(a) the name of the applicant;

(b) the name of the company and its registered number;

(c) the date on which the resolution for voluntary winding up was passed;

(d) that the application is accompanied by all of the documents required under paragraph (3) which are true copies of the documents required; and

(e) that the EC Regulation will apply to the company and whether the proceedings will be main proceedings, territorial proceedings or secondary proceedings.

(3) The liquidator shall lodge in court two copies of the application, together with one copy of the following:—

(a) the resolution for voluntary winding up referred to by section 84(3);
(b) evidence of his appointment as liquidator of the company; and
(c) the statement of affairs required under section 99.

(4) It shall not be necessary to serve the application on, or give notice of it to, any person.

(5) On an application under this Rule the court may confirm the creditors' voluntary winding up.

(6) If the court confirms the creditor's voluntary winding up it may do so without a hearing.

(7) This Rule applies in relation to a UK insurer (within the meaning of the Insurers (Reorganisation and Winding Up) Regulations 2003) with the modification specified in paragraph (8) below.

(8) For the purposes of paragraph (7), this Rule has effect as if there were substituted for paragraph (1) above—

"(1) Where a UK Insurer (within the meaning of the Insurers (Reorganisation and Winding Up) Regulations 2003) has passed a resolution for voluntary winding up, and no declaration under section 89 has been made, the liquidator may apply to court for an order confirming the creditors' voluntary winding up for the purposes of Articles 9 and 27 of Directive 2001/17/EC of the European Parliament and of the Council of 19th March 2001 on the reorganisation and winding up of insurance undertakings.".]

[2514]

NOTES

Commencement: 8 September 2003.
Inserted as noted to r 4.83 at **[2513]**.
Para (2): see Sch 5, Form 4.30 (Scot), and the notes to that Schedule.

[4.85 Notice to member State liquidator and creditors in member States

Where the court has confirmed the creditors' voluntary winding up, the liquidator shall forthwith give notice—

(a) if there is a member State liquidator in relation to the company, to the member State liquidator;
(b) in accordance with Article 40 of the EC Regulation (duty to inform creditors).]

[2515]

NOTES

Commencement: 8 September 2003.
Inserted as noted to r 4.83 at **[2513]**.

PART III STATUTORY INSTRUMENTS

PART 7
PROVISIONS OF GENERAL APPLICATION

CHAPTER 3
MISCELLANEOUS

7.21 Giving of notices, etc

(1) All notices required or authorised by or under the Act or the Rules to be given, sent or delivered must be in writing, unless it is otherwise provided, or the court allows the notice to be sent or given in some other way.

(2) Any reference in the [Act or the] Rules to giving, sending or delivering a notice or any such document means, without prejudice to any other way and unless it is otherwise provided, that the notice or document may be sent by post, and that, subject to Rule 7.22, any form of post may be used. Personal service of the notice or document is permissible in all cases.

(3) Where under the Act or the Rules a notice or other document is required or authorised to be given, sent or delivered by a person ("the sender") to another ("the recipient"), it may be given, sent or delivered by any person duly authorised by the sender to do so to any person duly authorised by the recipient to receive or accept it.

(4) Where two or more persons are acting jointly as the responsible insolvency practitioner in any proceedings, the giving, sending or delivering of a notice or document to one of them is to be treated as the giving, sending or delivering of a notice or document to each or all.

[2516]

NOTES

Para (2): words in square brackets inserted by the Insolvency (Scotland) Amendment Rules 1987, SI 1987/1921, r 3(1), Schedule, Pt I, para 47.

7.22 Sending by post

(1) For a document to be properly sent by post, it must be contained in an envelope addressed to the person to whom it is to be sent, and pre-paid for either first or second class post.

[(1A) Any document to be sent by post may be sent to the last known address of the person to whom the document is to be sent.]

(2) Where first class post is used, the document is to be deemed to be received on the second business day after the date of posting, unless the contrary is shown.

(3) Where second class post is used, the document is to be deemed to be received on the fourth business day after the date of posting, unless the contrary is shown.

[2517]

NOTES

Para (1A): inserted by the Insolvency (Scotland) Amendment Rules 1987, SI 1987/1921, r 3(1), Schedule, Pt I, para 48.

7.23 Certificate of giving notice, etc

(1) Where in any proceedings a notice or document is required to be given, sent or delivered by the responsible insolvency practitioner, the date of giving, sending or delivery of it may be proved by means of a certificate signed by him or on his behalf by his solicitor, or a partner or an employee of either of them, that the notice or document was duly given, posted or otherwise sent, or delivered on the date stated in the certificate.

(2) In the case of a notice or document to be given, sent or delivered by a person other than the responsible insolvency practitioner, the date of giving, sending or delivery of it may be proved by means of a certificate by that person that he gave, posted or otherwise sent or delivered the notice or document on the date stated in the certificate, or that he instructed another person (naming him) to do so.

(3) A certificate under this Rule may be endorsed on a copy of the notice to which it relates.

(4) A certificate purporting to be signed by or on behalf of the responsible insolvency practitioner, or by the person mentioned in paragraph (2), shall be deemed, unless the contrary is shown, to be sufficient evidence of the matters stated therein.

[2518]

7.32 Power of court to cure defects in procedure

(1) Section 63 of the Bankruptcy Act (power of court to cure defects in procedure) shall apply in relation to any insolvency proceedings as it applies in relation to sequestration, subject to the modifications specified in paragraph (2) and to any other necessary modifications.

(2) For any reference in the said section 63 to any expression in column 1 below, there shall be substituted a reference to the expression in column 2 opposite thereto—

Column 1	*Column 2*
This Act or any regulations made under it	The Act or the Rules
Permanent trustee	Responsible insolvency practitioner
Sequestration process	Insolvency proceedings
Debtor	Company
Sheriff	The court
Person who would be eligible to be elected under section 24 of this Act	Person who would be eligible to act as a responsible insolvency practitioner

[2519]

INSOLVENCY RULES 1986

(SI 1986/1925)

NOTES

Made: 10 November 1986.
Authority: Insolvency Act 1986, ss 411, 412.
Commencement: 29 December 1986.
Only the rules relevant to cross-border aspects of insolvency proceedings are reproduced here.

ARRANGEMENT OF THE RULES

INTRODUCTORY PROVISIONS

THE FIRST GROUP OF PARTS
COMPANY INSOLVENCY; COMPANIES WINDING UP

PART 1
COMPANY VOLUNTARY ARRANGEMENTS

CHAPTER 7
EC REGULATION—CONVERSION OF VOLUNTARY ARRANGEMENT INTO WINDING UP

CHAPTER 8
EC REGULATION—MEMBER STATE LIQUIDATOR

PART 2
ADMINISTRATION PROCEDURE

CHAPTER 14
EC REGULATION: CONVERSION OF ADMINISTRATION INTO WINDING UP

CHAPTER 15
EC REGULATION: MEMBER STATE LIQUIDATOR

PART 4
COMPANIES WINDING UP

CHAPTER 23
EC REGULATION—MEMBER STATE LIQUIDATOR

THE THIRD GROUP OF PARTS

PART 7
COURT PROCEDURE AND PRACTICE

CHAPTER 11
EC REGULATION—MEMBER STATE LIQUIDATOR

PART 12
MISCELLANEOUS AND GENERAL

INTRODUCTORY PROVISIONS

0.1 Citation and commencement

These Rules may be cited as the Insolvency Rules 1986 and shall come into force on 29th December 1986.

[2520]

[0.2 Construction and interpretation

(1) In these Rules—

"the Act" means the Insolvency Act 1986 (any reference to a numbered section being to a section of that Act);

"the Companies Act" means the Companies Act 1985;

"CPR" means the Civil Procedure Rules 1998 and "CPR" followed by a Part or rule by number means the Part or rule with that number in those Rules;

"RSC" followed by an Order by number means the Order with that number set out in Schedule 1 to the CPR; and

"the Rules" means the Insolvency Rules 1986.

(2) References in the Rules to ex parte hearings shall be construed as references to hearings without notice being served on any other party; references to applications made ex parte as references to applications made without notice being served on any other party and other references which include the expression "ex parte" shall be similarly construed.

(3) Subject to paragraphs (1) and (2), Part 13 of the Rules has effect for their interpretation and application.]

[2521]

NOTES

Substituted by the Insolvency (Amendment) (No 2) Rules 1999, SI 1999/1022, r 3, Schedule, para 1.

0.3 Extent

(1) Parts 1, 2 and 4 of the Rules, and Parts 7 to 13 as they relate to company insolvency, apply in relation to companies which the courts in England and Wales have jurisdiction to wind up.

[(2) Rule 3.1 applies to all receivers to whom Part III of the Act applies, Rule 3.39 and 3.40 apply to all receivers who are not administrative receivers, and the remainder of Part 3 of the Rules applies to administrative receivers appointed otherwise than under section 51 (Scottish Receivership).]

(3) Parts 5 and 6 of the Rules, and Parts 7 to 13 as they relate to individual insolvency, extend to England and Wales only.

[2522]

NOTES

Para (2): substituted by the Insolvency (Amendment) Rules 2003, SI 2003/1730, r 3.

THE FIRST GROUP OF PARTS
COMPANY INSOLVENCY; COMPANIES WINDING UP

PART 1
COMPANY VOLUNTARY ARRANGEMENTS

[CHAPTER 7
EC REGULATION—CONVERSION OF VOLUNTARY ARRANGEMENT INTO WINDING UP]

NOTES

Commencement: 31 May 2002.
Chapter heading: inserted by the Insolvency (Amendment) Rules 2002, SI 2002/1307, rr 3(1), 4(4).

[1.31 Application for conversion into winding up

(1) Where a member State liquidator proposes to apply to the court for the conversion under Article 37 of the EC Regulation (conversion of earlier proceedings) of a voluntary arrangement into a winding up, an affidavit complying with Rule 1.32 must be prepared and sworn, and filed in court in support of the application.

(2) An application under this Rule shall be by originating application.

(3) The application and the affidavit required under this Rule shall be served upon—
(a) the company; and
(b) the supervisor.]

[2523]

NOTES

Commencement: 31 May 2002.
Chapters 7, 8 (rr 1.31–1.34) inserted by the Insolvency (Amendment) Rules 2002, SI 2002/1307, rr 3(1), 4(4).

[1.32 Contents of affidavit

(1) The affidavit shall state—
(a) that main proceedings have been opened in relation to the company in a member State other than the United Kingdom;
(b) the deponent's belief that the conversion of the voluntary arrangement into a winding up would prove to be in the interests of the creditors in the main proceedings;

PART III STATUTORY INSTRUMENTS

(c) the deponent's opinion as to whether the company ought to enter voluntary winding up or be wound up by the court; and

(d) all other matters that, in the opinion of the member State liquidator, would assist the court—

(i) in deciding whether to make such an order, and

(ii) if the court were to do so, in considering the need for any consequential provision that would be necessary or desirable.

(2) An affidavit under this Rule shall be sworn by, or on behalf of, the member State liquidator.]

[2524]

NOTES

Commencement: 31 May 2002.

Inserted as noted to r 1.31 at **[2523]**.

[1.33 Power of court

(1) On hearing the application for conversion into winding up the court may make such order as it thinks fit.

(2) If the court makes an order for conversion into winding up the order may contain all such consequential provisions as the court deems necessary or desirable.

(3) Without prejudice to the generality of paragraph (1), an order under that paragraph may provide that the company be wound up as if a resolution for voluntary winding up under section 84 were passed on the day on which the order is made.

(4) Where the court makes an order for conversion into winding up under paragraph (1), any expenses properly incurred as expenses of the administration of the voluntary arrangement in question shall be a first charge on the company's assets.]

[2525]

NOTES

Commencement: 31 May 2002.

Inserted as noted to r 1.31 at **[2523]**.

[CHAPTER 8

EC REGULATION—MEMBER STATE LIQUIDATOR]

NOTES

Commencement: 31 May 2002.

Chapter heading: inserted by the Insolvency (Amendment) Rules 2002, SI 2002/1307, rr 3(1), 4(4).

[1.34 Interpretation of creditor and notice to member State liquidator]

[(1) This Rule applies where a member State liquidator has been appointed in relation to the company.

(2) Where the supervisor is obliged to give notice to, or provide a copy of a document (including an order of court) to, the court, the registrar of companies or the official receiver, the supervisor shall give notice or provide copies, as appropriate, to the member State liquidator.

(3) Paragraph (2) is without prejudice to the generality of the obligations imposed by Article 31 of the EC Regulation (duty to cooperate and communicate information).]

[2526]

NOTES

Commencement: 31 May 2002.

Inserted as noted to r 1.31 at **[2523]**.

[PART 2
ADMINISTRATION PROCEDURE]

NOTES

Part heading: substituted by the Insolvency (Amendment) Rules 2003, SI 2003/1730, r 5(1), Sch 1, Pt 2, para 9; for effect and the continuing operation of this Part where a provision made by or under any enactment preserves the Insolvency Act 1986, old Pt II after that date see r 5(2)–(4) thereof.

[CHAPTER 14
EC REGULATION: CONVERSION OF ADMINISTRATION INTO WINDING UP]

NOTES

Chapter heading: substituted by the Insolvency (Amendment) Rules 2003, SI 2003/1730, r 5(1), Sch 1, Pt 2, para 9; for effect and the continuing operation of this Part where a provision made by or under any enactment preserves the Insolvency Act 1986, old Pt II after that date see r 5(2)–(4) thereof.

[2.130 Application for conversion into winding up

(1) Where a member State liquidator proposes to apply to the court for the conversion under Article 37 of the EC Regulation (conversion of earlier proceedings) of an administration into a winding up, an affidavit complying with Rule 2.131 must be prepared and sworn, and filed with the court in support of the application.

(2) An application under this Rule shall be by originating application.

(3) The application and the affidavit required under this Rule shall be served upon—

(a) the company; and

(b) the administrator.]

[2527]

NOTES

Commencement: 15 September 2003.

Pt 2 (rr 2.1–2.133) substituted by the Insolvency (Amendment) Rules 2003, SI 2003/1730, r 5(1), Sch 1, Pt 2, para 9; for effect and the continuing operation of this Part where a provision made by or under any enactment preserves the Insolvency Act 1986, old Pt II after that date see r 5(2)–(4) thereof.

[2.131 Contents of affidavit

(1) The affidavit shall state—

(a) that main proceedings have been opened in relation to the company in a member State other than the United Kingdom;

(b) the deponent's belief that the conversion of the administration into a winding up would prove to be in the interests of the creditors in the main proceedings;

(c) the deponent's opinion as to whether the company ought to enter voluntary winding up or be wound up by the court; and

(d) all other matters that, in the opinion of the member State liquidator, would assist the court—

(i) in deciding whether to make such an order; and

(ii) if the court were to do so, in considering the need for any consequential provision that would be necessary or desirable.

(2) An affidavit under this rule shall be sworn by, or on behalf of, the member State liquidator.]

[2528]

NOTES

Commencement: 15 September 2003.

Substituted as noted to r 2.130 at **[2527]**.

[2.132 Power of court

(1) On hearing the application for conversion into winding up the court may make such order as it thinks fit.

PART III
STATUTORY INSTRUMENTS

(2) If the court makes an order for conversion into winding up the order may contain all such consequential provisions as the court deems necessary or desirable.

(3) Without prejudice to the generality of paragraph (1), an order under that paragraph may provide that the company be wound up as if a resolution for voluntary winding up under section 84 were passed on the day on which the order is made.]

[2529]

NOTES

Commencement: 15 September 2003.
Substituted as noted to r 2.130 at **[2527]**.

[CHAPTER 15
EC REGULATION: MEMBER STATE LIQUIDATOR]

NOTES

Commencement: 15 September 2003.
Substituted as noted to r 2.130 at **[2527]**.

[2.133 Interpretation of creditor and notice to member State liquidator

(1) This Rule applies where a member State liquidator has been appointed in relation to the company.

(2) For the purposes of the Rules referred to in paragraph (3) the member State liquidator is deemed to be a creditor.

(3) The Rules referred to in paragraph (2) are Rules 2.34 (notice of creditors' meeting), 2.35(4) (creditors' meeting), 2.37 (requisitioning of creditors' meeting), 2.38 (entitlement to vote), 2.39 (admission and rejection of claims), 2.40 (secured creditors), 2.41 (holders of negotiable instruments), 2.42 (hire-purchase, conditional sale and chattel leasing agreements), 2.46 (notice to creditors), 2.47 (reports to creditors), 2.48 (correspondence instead of creditors' meeting), 2.50(2) (creditors' committee), 2.57(1)(b) and (c) (termination of membership of creditors' committee), 2.59(3) (vacancies in creditors' committee), 2.108(3) (administrator's remuneration—recourse to court) and 2.109 (challenge to administrator's remuneration).

(4) Paragraphs (2) and (3) are without prejudice to the generality of the right to participate referred to in paragraph 3 of Article 32 of the EC Regulation (exercise of creditor's rights).

(5) Where the administrator is obliged to give notice to, or provide a copy of a document (including an order of court) to, the court, the registrar of companies or the official receiver, the administrator shall give notice or provide copies, as the case may be, to the member State liquidator.

(6) Paragraph (5) is without prejudice to the generality of the obligations imposed by Article 31 of the EC Regulation (duty to co-operate and communicate information).]

[2530]

NOTES

Commencement: 15 September 2003.
Substituted as noted to r 2.130 at **[2527]**.

PART 4
COMPANIES WINDING UP

[CHAPTER 23
EC REGULATION—MEMBER STATE LIQUIDATOR]

NOTES

Commencement: 31 May 2002.
Inserted by the Insolvency (Amendment) Rules 2002, SI 2002/1307, rr 3(1), 6(9).

[4.231 Interpretation of creditor and notice to member State liquidator

(1) This Rule applies where a member State liquidator has been appointed in relation to the company.

(2) For the purposes of the Rules referred to in paragraph (3) the member State liquidator is deemed to be a creditor.

(3) The Rules referred to in paragraph (2) are Rules 4.43(1) (official receiver's report), 4.45(1) (report on statement of affairs), 4.46(2) (report where no statement of affairs), 4.47(2) (general rule on reporting), 4.48(2) (winding up stayed), 4.49 (information to creditors), 4.50(2) (notice of meetings), 4.51(2) (notice of creditors' meeting—CVL), 4.54 (power to call meetings), 4.57(1) (requisitioned meetings), 4.57(3), 4.67 (entitlement to vote (creditors)), 4.68 (chairman's discretion to allow vote—CVL), 4.70 (admission and rejection of proof (creditors' meeting)), 4.73 (meaning of "prove"), 4.74 (supply of forms), 4.75 (contents of proof), 4.76 (particulars of creditor's claim), 4.77 (claim established by affidavit), 4.78 (cost of proving), 4.79 (inspection of proofs), 4.82 (admission and rejection of proofs for dividend), 4.83(1) (appeal against decision in relation to proof), 4.83(2), 4.84 (withdrawal or variation of proof), 4.85(1) (expunging of proof), 4.86 (estimate of quantum), 4.87 (negotiable instruments, etc), 4.88 (secured creditors), 4.89 (discounts), 4.90 (mutual credit and set-off), 4.91 (debt in foreign currency), 4.92 (payment of a periodical nature), 4.93 (interest), 4.94 (debt payable at future time), 4.101A (power to fill vacancy in office of liquidator), 4.102(5) (appointment by court), 4.103(4) (appointment by court), 4.113(1) (meeting of creditors to remove liquidator), 4.114(1) (meeting of creditors to remove liquidator), 4.115 (regulation of meetings), 4.124(1) (release of official receiver), 4.125(1) (final meeting), [4.125A(2) (rule on reporting),] 4.126(1) (final meeting), 4.131(1) (challenge to liquidator's remuneration), 4.152(1) (liquidation committee), 4.152(3) (eligibility for liquidation committee), 4.163(3) (vacancy on liquidation committee), 4.175(1) (liquidation committee), 4.180 (notice of dividend) and 4.212(2) (notice of public examination hearing).

(4) Paragraphs (2) and (3) are without prejudice to the generality of the right to participate referred to in paragraph 3 of Article 32 of the EC Regulation (exercise of creditor's rights).

(5) Where the liquidator is obliged to give notice to, or provide a copy of a document (including an order of court) to, the court, the registrar of companies or the official receiver, the liquidator shall give notice or provide copies, as the case may be, to the member State liquidator.

(6) Paragraph (5) is without prejudice to the generality of the obligations imposed by Article 31 of the EC Regulation (duty to cooperate and communicate information).]

[2531]

NOTES

Commencement: 31 May 2002.
Chapter 23 (r 4.231) inserted by the Insolvency (Amendment) Rules 2002, SI 2002/1307, rr 3(1), 6(9).
Para (3): words in square brackets inserted by the Insolvency (Amendment) Rules 2004, SI 2004/584, r 23.

THE THIRD GROUP OF PARTS

PART 7
COURT PROCEDURE AND PRACTICE

[CHAPTER 11
EC REGULATION—MEMBER STATE LIQUIDATOR]

NOTES

Chapter heading: inserted by the Insolvency (Amendment) Rules 2002, SI 2002/1307, rr 3(1), 9(1).

[7.64 Interpretation of creditor

(1) This Rule applies where a member State liquidator has been appointed in relation to a person subject to insolvency proceedings.

(2) For the purposes of the Rules referred to in paragraph (3) a member State liquidator appointed in main proceedings is deemed to be a creditor.

(3) The Rules referred to in paragraph (2) are Rules 7.31(1) (right to inspect court file) and 7.53(1) (right of attendance).

(4) Paragraphs (2) and (3) are without prejudice to the generality of the right to participate referred to in paragraph 3 of Article 32 of the EC Regulation (exercise of creditor's rights).]

[2532]

NOTES

Commencement: 31 May 2002.

Chapter 11 (r 7.64) inserted by the Insolvency (Amendment) Rules 2002, SI 2002/1307, rr 3(1), 9(1).

PART 12
MISCELLANEOUS AND GENERAL

12.10 Service by post

(1) For a document to be properly served by post, it must be contained in an envelope addressed to the person on whom service is to be effected, and pre-paid for either first or second class post.

[(1A) A document to be served by post may be sent to the last known address of the person to be served.]

(2) Where first class post is used, the document is treated as served on the second business day after the date of posting, unless the contrary is shown.

(3) Where second class post is used, the document is treated as served on the fourth business day after the date of posting, unless the contrary is shown.

(4) The date of posting is presumed, unless the contrary is shown, to be the date shown in the post-mark on the envelope in which the document is contained.

[2533]

NOTES

Para (1A): inserted by the Insolvency (Amendment) Rules 1987, SI 1987/1919, r 3(1), Schedule, Pt 1, para 146.

[12.11 General provisions as to service

Subject to Rule 12.10 [and Rule 12.12], CPR Part 6 (service of documents) applies as regards any matter relating to the service of documents and the giving of notice in insolvency proceedings.]

[2534]

NOTES

Substituted by the Insolvency (Amendment) (No 2) Rules 1999, SI 1999/1022, r 3, Schedule, para 12; words in square brackets inserted by the Insolvency (Amendment) Rules 2005, SI 2005/527, r 45.

12.12 Service outside the jurisdiction

[(1) [CPR Part 6, paragraphs 6.17 to 6.35] (service of process, etc, out of the jurisdiction) [do] not apply in insolvency proceedings.]

(2) A bankruptcy petition may, with the leave of the court, be served outside England and Wales in such manner as the court may direct.

(3) Where for the purposes of insolvency proceedings any process or order of the court, or other document, is required to be served on a person who is not in England and Wales, the court may order service to be effected within such time, on such person, at such place and in such manner as it thinks fit, and may also require such proof of service as it thinks fit.

(4) An application under this Rule shall be supported by an affidavit stating—

(a) the grounds on which the application is made, and

(b) in what place or country the person to be served is, or probably may be found.

[(5) Leave of the court is not required to serve anything referred to in this Rule on a member State liquidator.]

[2535]

NOTES

Para (1): substituted by the Insolvency (Amendment) (No 2) Rules 1999, SI 1999/1022, r 3, Schedule, para 13; words in square brackets substituted by the Insolvency (Amendment) Rules 2005, SI 2005/527, r 46.

Para (5): added by the Insolvency (Amendment) Rules 2002, SI 2002/1307, rr 3(1), 10(5).

ACT OF SEDERUNT (SHERIFF COURT COMPANY INSOLVENCY RULES) 1986

(SI 1986/2297 (S 169))

NOTES

Made: 19 December 1986.
Authority: Sheriff Courts (Scotland) Act 1971, s 32.
Commencement: 29 December 1986.
Only the rules relevant to this work are reproduced here.

ARRANGEMENT OF RULES

PART V
GENERAL PROVISIONS

1 Citation and commencement

(1) This Act of Sederunt may be cited as the Act of Sederunt (Sheriff Court Company Insolvency Rules) 1986 and shall come into operation on 29th December 1986.

(2) This Act of Sederunt shall be inserted in the Books of Sederunt.

[2536]

2 (*Revokes the Act of Sederunt (Sheriff Court Liquidations) 1930 in relation to proceedings commenced on or after 29 December 1986.*)

3 Interpretation

(1) In these rules—

"the Act of 1986" means the Insolvency Act 1986;

"the Insolvency Rules" means the Insolvency (Scotland) Rules 1986;

["the Model Law" means the Model Law on Cross-Border Insolvency as set out in Schedule 1 to the Cross-Border Insolvency Regulations 2006;]

"registered office" means—

(a) the place specified, in the statement of the company delivered to the registrar of companies under section 10 of the Companies Act 1985, as the intended place of its registered office on incorporation; or

(b) where notice has been given by the company to the registrar of companies under section 287 of the Companies Act 1985 of a change of registered office, the place specified in the last such notice;

"sheriff-clerk" has the meaning assigned to it in section 3(f) of the Sheriff Courts (Scotland) Act 1907.

(2) Unless the context otherwise requires, words and expressions used in these rules which are also used in the Act of 1986 or the Insolvency Rules have the same meaning as in that Act or those Rules.

[2537]

NOTES

Para (1): definition "the Model Law" in square brackets inserted by the Act of Sederunt (Sheriff Court Company Insolvency Rules 1986) Amendment (UNCITRAL Model Law on Cross-Border Insolvency) 2006, SSI 2006/200, r 2(1), (2).

PART II
ADMINISTRATION [PROCEDURE]

NOTES

Part heading: word in square brackets substituted by the Act of Sederunt (Sheriff Court Company Insolvency Rules 1986) Amendment 2003, SSI 2003/388, r 2(1), (2).

10 Petitions for administration orders

(1) A petition for an administration order [or any other order in an administration] shall include averments in relation to—

(a) the petitioner and the capacity in which he presents the petition, if other than the company;

(b) whether it is believed that the company is, or is likely to become, unable to pay its debts and the grounds of that belief;

[(c) how the making of that order will achieve—

(i) any of the purposes specified in section 8(3) of the Act of 1986; or

(ii) an objective specified in paragraph 3 of Schedule B1 to the Act of 1986;]

(d) the company's financial position, specifying (so far as known) assets and liabilities, including contingent and prospective liabilities;
(e) any security known or believed to be held by creditors of the company, whether in any case the security confers power on the holder to appoint a receiver, and whether a receiver has been appointed;
(f) so far as known to the petitioner, whether any steps have been taken for the winding up of the company, giving details of them;
(g) other matters which, in the opinion of the petitioner, will assist the court in deciding whether to grant [that] order;
[(h) Council Regulation (EC) 1346/2000 of 29th May 2000 on insolvency proceedings—
  (i) that so far as known to the petitioner, there are no other proceedings; or
  (ii) whether the present proceedings are main or territorial proceedings;]
(i) the person proposed to be appointed as administrator, giving his name and address and that he is qualified to act as an insolvency practitioner in relation to the company.

(2) There shall be produced with the petition—
(a) any document instructing the facts relied on, or otherwise founded on, by the petitioner; and
(b) …

[2538]

NOTES

Para (1): words in first pair of square brackets inserted, sub-paras (c), (h) substituted, and word in square brackets in sub-para (g) substituted, by the Act of Sederunt (Sheriff Court Company Insolvency Rules 1986) Amendment 2003, SSI 2003/388, r 2(1), (3)(a)–(d).

Para (2): sub-para (b) revoked by SSI 2003/388, r 2(1), (3)(e).

11 Notice of petition

Notice of the petition on the persons to whom notice is to be given under rule [2.3] of the Insolvency Rules shall be made in such manner as the court shall direct.

[2539]

NOTES

Rule reference in square brackets substituted by the Act of Sederunt (Sheriff Court Company Insolvency Rules 1986) Amendment 2003, SSI 2003/388, r 2(1), (4).

[12 Applications during an administration

An application or appeal under any provision of the Act of 1986[, the Insolvency Rules or an application to participate under article 12 of the Model Law in an administration] during an administration shall be—
(a) where no previous application or appeal has been made, by petition; or
(b) where a petition for an order in respect of an administration has been made, by note in the process of that petition.]

[2540]

NOTES

Commencement: 15 September 2003.

Substituted by the Act of Sederunt (Sheriff Court Company Insolvency Rules 1986) Amendment 2003, SSI 2003/388, r 2(1), (5).

Words in square brackets substituted by the Act of Sederunt (Sheriff Court Company Insolvency Rules 1986) Amendment (UNCITRAL Model Law on Cross-Border Insolvency) 2006, SSI 2006/200, r 2(1), (3).

PART III
RECEIVERS

16 Intimation, service and advertisement

(1) Intimation, service and advertisement of the petition shall be made, in accordance with the following provisions of this rule unless the court otherwise directs.

(2) There shall be included in the order for service, a requirement to serve—
- (a) upon the company; …
- (b) where a petition for [an order in respect of an administration] has been presented, on that petitioner and any respondent to that petition[; and
- (c) upon an administrator.]

(3) Subject to paragraph (5), service of a petition on the company shall be effected at its registered office—
- (a) by registered or recorded delivery post addressed to the company; or
- (b) by sheriff officer—
  - (i) leaving the citation in the hands of a person who, after due inquiry, he has reasonable grounds for believing to be a director, other officer or responsible employee of the company or authorised to accept service on behalf of the company; or
  - (ii) if there is no such person as is mentioned in head (i) present, depositing it in the registered office in such a way that it is likely to come to the attention of such a person attending at that office.

(4) Where service is effected in accordance with paragraph (3)(b)(ii), the sheriff officer thereafter shall send a copy of the petition and citation by ordinary first class post to the registered office of the company.

(5) Where service cannot be effected at the registered office of the company or the company has no registered office—
- (a) service may be effected at the last known principal place of business of the company in Scotland or at some place in Scotland at which the company carries on business, by leaving the citation in the hands of such a person as is mentioned in paragraph (3)(b)(i) or by depositing it as specified in paragraph (3)(b)(ii); and
- (b) where the citation is deposited as is specified in paragraph (3)(b)(ii), the sheriff officer thereafter shall send a copy of the petition and citation by ordinary first class post to such place mentioned in sub-paragraph (a) of this paragraph in which the citation was deposited.

(6) The petition shall be advertised forthwith—
- (a) once in the Edinburgh Gazette; and
- (b) once in one or more newspapers as the court shall direct for ensuring that it comes to the notice of the creditors of the company.

(7) The advertisement under paragraph (6) shall state—
- (a) the name and address of the petitioner;
- (b) the name and address of the solicitor for the petitioner;
- (c) the date on which the petition was presented;
- (d) the precise order sought;
- (e) the period of notice; and
- (f) that any person who intends to appear in the petition must lodge answers to the petition within the period of notice.

(8) The period of notice within which answers to the petition may be lodged and after which further consideration of the petition may proceed shall be 8 days after such intimation, service and advertisement as the court may have ordered.

[2541]

NOTES

Para (2): word omitted from sub-para (a) revoked, words in first pair of square brackets in sub-para (b) substituted, and sub-para (c) and word "; and" immediately preceding it added, by the Act of Sederunt (Sheriff Court Company Insolvency Rules 1986) Amendment 2003, SSI 2003/388, r 4, Schedule, paras 1, 9.

17 Form of certain applications where receiver appointed

(1) An application under any of the following sections of the Act of 1986 shall be made by petition or, where the receiver was appointed by the court, by note in the process of the petition for appointment of a receiver:—
- (a) section 61(1) (by receiver for authority to dispose of interest in property);
- (b) section 62 (for removal or resignation of receiver);
- (c) section 63(1) (by receiver for directions);
- (d) section 69(1) (to enforce receiver to make returns, etc); and

(e) any other section relating to receivers not specifically mentioned in this Part.

(2) An application under any of the following provisions of the Act of 1986 or the Insolvency Rules shall be made by motion in the process of the petition:—

(a) section 67(1) or (2) (by receiver to extend time for sending report); and
(b) rule 3.9(2) (by receiver to extend time for sending abstract of receipts and payments).

[2542]

PART IV
WINDING UP BY THE COURT OF COMPANIES REGISTERED UNDER THE COMPANIES ACTS AND OF UNREGISTERED COMPANIES

18 Petitions to wind up a company

(1) A petition to wind up a company under the Act of 1986 shall include—

(a) particulars of the petitioner, if other than the company;
(b) in respect of the company—
  (i) the registered name;
  (ii) the address of the registered office and any change of that address within the last 6 months so far as known to the petitioner;
  (iii) a statement of the nature and objects, the amount of its capital (nominal and issued) and indicating what part is called up, paid up or credited as paid, and the amount of the assets of the company so far as known to the petitioner;
(c) a narrative of the facts on which the petitioner relies and any particulars required to instruct the title of the petitioner to present the petition;
(d) the name and address of the person to be appointed as interim liquidator and a statement that he is qualified to act as an insolvency practitioner in relation to the company; and
(e) a crave setting out the orders applied for, including any intimation, service and advertisement and any appointment of an interim liquidator.

(2) There shall be lodged with the petition any document—

(a) instructing the title of the petitioner; and
(b) instructing the facts relied on, or otherwise founded on, by the petitioner.

[2543]

19 Intimation, service and advertisement

(1) Intimation, service and advertisement shall be in accordance with the following provisions of this rule unless the court—

(a) summarily dismisses the petition; or
(b) otherwise directs.

(2) There shall be included in the order for intimation and service, a requirement—

(a) to intimate on the walls of the court;
(b) where the petitioner is other than the company, to serve upon the company;
(c) where the company is being wound up voluntarily and a liquidator has been appointed, to serve upon the liquidator;
(d) where a receiver has been appointed for the company, to serve upon the receiver;
[(dd) where a company is in administration, to serve upon the administrator;]
(e) where the company is—
  (i) a recognised bank or licensed institution within the meaning of the Banking Act 1979; or
  (ii) an institution to which sections 16 and 18 of that Act apply as if it were licensed,

and the petitioner is not the Bank of England, to serve upon the Bank of England.

(3) Subject to paragraph (5), service of a petition on the company shall be executed at its registered office—

(a) by registered or recorded delivery post addressed to the company; or
(b) by sheriff officer—
  (i) leaving the citation in the hands of a person who, after due inquiry, he has

PART III STATUTORY INSTRUMENTS

reasonable grounds for believing to be a director, other officer or responsible employee of the company or authorised to accept service on behalf of the company; or

(ii) if there is no such person as is mentioned in head (i) present, depositing it in the registered office in such a way that it is likely to come to the attention of such a person attending at that office.

(4) Where service is effected in accordance with paragraph (3)(b)(ii), the sheriff officer thereafter shall send a copy of the petition and citation by ordinary first class post to the registered office of the company.

(5) Where service cannot be effected at the registered office or the company has no registered office—

(a) service may be effected at the last known principal place of business of the company in Scotland or at some place in Scotland at which the company carries on business, by leaving the citation in the hands of such a person as is mentioned in paragraph (3)(b)(i) or by depositing it as specified in paragraph (3)(b)(ii); and

(b) where the citation is deposited as is specified in paragraph (3)(b)(ii), the sheriff officer thereafter shall send a copy of the petition and the citation by ordinary first class post to such place mentioned in sub-paragraph (a) of this paragraph in which the citation was deposited.

(6) The petition shall be advertised forthwith—

(a) once in the Edinburgh Gazette; and

(b) once in one or more newspapers as the court shall direct for ensuring that it comes to the notice of the creditors of the company.

(7) The advertisement under paragraph (6) shall state—

(a) the name and address of the petitioner and, where the petitioner is the company, the registered office;

(b) the name and address of the solicitor for the petitioner;

(c) the date on which the petition was presented;

(d) the precise order sought;

(e) where a provisional liquidator has been appointed, his name, address and the date of his appointment;

(f) the period of notice; and

(g) that any person who intends to appear in the petition must lodge answers to the petition within the period of notice.

(8) The period of notice within which answers to the petition may be lodged and after which further consideration of the petition may proceed shall be 8 days after such intimation, service and advertisement as the court may have ordered.

[2544]

NOTES

Para (2): sub-para (dd) inserted by the Act of Sederunt (Sheriff Court Company Insolvency Rules 1986) Amendment 2003, SSI 2003/388, r 4, Schedule, paras 1, 10.

20 Lodging of caveats

(1) A company, debenture holder, holder of a floating charge, receiver, shareholder of a company or other person claiming an interest, apprehensive that a petition to wind up that company may be presented and wishing to be heard by the court before an order for intimation, service and advertisement is pronounced, may lodge a caveat with the sheriff-clerk.

(2) A caveat shall endure for 12 months on the expiry of which a new caveat may be lodged.

(3) Where a caveat has been lodged and has not expired, no order may be pronounced without the person lodging the caveat having been given an opportunity to be heard by the court.

[2545]

21 Substitution of creditor or contributory for petitioner

(1) This rule applies where a petitioner—

(a) is subsequently found not entitled to present the petition;

(b) fails to make intimation, service and advertisement as directed by the court;
(c) consents to withdraw the petition or to allow it to be dismissed or refused;
(d) fails to appear when the petition is called for hearing; or
(e) appears, but does not move for an order in terms of the prayer of the petition.

(2) The court may, on such terms as it considers just, sist as petitioner in room of the original petitioner any creditor or contributory who, in the opinion of the court, is entitled to present a petition.

(3) An application by a creditor or contributory to be sisted under paragraph (2)—
(a) may be made at any time before the petition is dismissed or refused; and
(b) shall be made by note in the process of the petition, and if necessary the court may continue the cause for a specified period to allow a note to be presented.

[2546]

22 Advertisement of appointment of liquidator

Where a liquidator is appointed by the court, the court may order that the liquidator shall advertise his appointment once in one or more newspapers as the court shall direct for ensuring that it comes to the notice of creditors of the company.

[2547]

23 Provisional liquidators

(1) An application to appoint a provisional liquidator under section 135 of the Act of 1986 may be made—
(a) by the petitioner, in the crave of the petition or subsequently by note in the process of the petition; or
(b) by a creditor or contributory of the company, the company, Secretary of State or a person entitled under any enactment to present a petition to wind up the company, in a note in the process of the petition.

(2) The petition or note, as the case may be, shall include averments in relation to—
(a) the grounds on which it is proposed that a provisional liquidator should be appointed;
(b) the name and address of the person to be appointed as provisional liquidator and that he is qualified to act as an insolvency practitioner in relation to the company; and
(c) whether, to the knowledge of the applicant, there is a receiver [or administrator] for the company or a liquidator has been appointed for the voluntary winding up of the company.

(3) Where the court is satisfied that sufficient grounds exist for the appointment of a provisional liquidator, it shall, on making the appointment, specify the functions to be carried out by him in relation to the affairs of the company.

(4) The applicant shall send a certified copy of the interlocutor appointing a provisional liquidator forthwith to the person appointed.

(5) On receiving a certified copy of his appointment on an application by note, the provisional liquidator shall intimate his appointment forthwith—
(a) once in the Edinburgh Gazette; and
(b) once in one or more newspapers as the court shall direct for ensuring that it comes to the notice of creditors of the company.

(6) An application for discharge of a provisional liquidator shall be by note in the process of the petition.

[2548]

NOTES

Para (2): words in square brackets in sub-para (c) inserted by the Act of Sederunt (Sheriff Court Company Insolvency Rules 1986) Amendment 2003, SSI 2003/388, r 4, Schedule, paras 1, 11.

---

24 Applications and appeals in relation to a statement of affairs

(1) An application under section 131(5) of the Act of 1986 for—
(a) release from an obligation imposed under section 131(1) or (2) of the Act of 1986; or

(b) an extension of time for the submission of a statement of affairs, shall be made by note in the process of the petition.

(2) A note under paragraph (1) shall be served on the liquidator or provisional liquidator, as the case may be.

(3) The liquidator or provisional liquidator may lodge answers to the note or lodge a report of any matters which he considers should be drawn to the attention of the court.

(4) Where the liquidator or provisional liquidator lodges a report under paragraph (3), he shall send a copy of it to the noter forthwith.

(5) Where the liquidator or provisional liquidator does not appear, a certified copy of the interlocutor pronounced by the court disposing of the note shall be sent by the noter forthwith to him.

(6) An appeal under rule 4.9(6) of the Insolvency Rules against a refusal by the liquidator of an allowance towards the expense of preparing a statement of affairs shall be made by note in the process of the petition.

[2549]

25 Appeals against adjudication of claims

(1) An appeal under section 49(6) of the Bankruptcy (Scotland) Act 1985, as applied by rule 4.16 of the Insolvency Rules, by a creditor or contributory of the company against a decision of the liquidator shall be made by note in the process of the petition.

(2) A note under paragraph (1) shall be served on the liquidator.

(3) On receipt of the note served on him under this rule, the liquidator forthwith shall send to the court the claim in question and a copy of his adjudication for lodging in process.

(4) After the note has been disposed of, the court shall return the claim and the adjudication to the liquidator together with a copy of the interlocutor.

[2550]

26 Appointment of liquidator by the court

(1) An application to appoint a liquidator under section 139(4) of the Act of 1986 shall be made by note in the process of the petition.

(2) Where the court appoints a liquidator under section 138(5) of the Act of 1986, the sheriff-clerk shall send a certified copy of the interlocutor pronounced by the court to the liquidator forthwith.

[2551]

27 Removal of liquidator

An application by a creditor of the company for removal of a liquidator or provisional liquidator from office under section 172 of the Act of 1986 or for an order under section 171(3) of the Act of 1986 directing a liquidator to summon a meeting of creditors for the purpose of removing him shall be made by note in the process of the petition.

[2552]

28 Applications in relation to remuneration of liquidator

(1) An application by a liquidator under rule 4.34 of the Insolvency Rules shall be made by note in the process of the petition.

(2) An application by a creditor of the company under rule 4.35 of the Insolvency Rules shall be made by note in the process of the petition.

(3) A note under paragraph (2) shall be served on the liquidator.

[2553]

29 Application to appoint a special manager

(1) An application under section 177 of the Act of 1986 by a liquidator or provisional liquidator for the appointment of a special manager shall be made by note in the process of the petition.

(2) The cautioner, for the caution to be found by the special manager within such time as the court shall direct, may be—

(a) a private person, if approved by the court; or
(b) a guarantee company, chosen from a list of such companies prepared for this purpose annually by the Accountant of Court and approved by the Lord President of the Court of Session.

(3) A bond of caution certified by the noter under rule 4.70(4) of the Insolvency Rules shall be delivered to the sheriff-clerk by the noter, marked as received by him and transmitted forthwith by him to the Accountant of Court.

(4) On receipt of the bond of caution, the sheriff-clerk shall issue forthwith to the person appointed to be special manager a certified copy of the interlocutor appointing him.

(5) An application by a special manager to extend the time within which to find caution shall be made by motion.

[2554]

30 Other applications

An application under the Act of 1986 or rules made under that Act in relation to a winding up by the court not specifically mentioned in this Part [or an application to participate under article 12 of the Model Law in a winding up by the court] shall be made by note in the process of the petition.

[2555]

NOTES

Words in square brackets inserted by the Act of Sederunt (Sheriff Court Company Insolvency Rules 1986) Amendment (UNCITRAL Model Law on Cross-Border Insolvency) 2006, SSI 2006/200, r 2(1), (4).

PART V
GENERAL PROVISIONS

31 Application

This Part applies to Parts I to IV of these rules.

[2556]

[31A Applications under section 176A of the Act of 1986

(1) An application by a liquidator, administrator or receiver under section 176A of the Act of 1986 shall be—
(a) where there is no existing process in relation to any liquidation, administration or receivership, by petition; or
(b) where a process exists in relation to any liquidation, administration or receivership, by note in that process.

(2) The sheriff clerk shall—
(a) after lodging of any petition or note fix a hearing for the sheriff to consider an application under paragraph (1); and
(b) give notice of the hearing fixed under paragraph (2)(a) to the petitioner or noter.

(3) The petitioner or noter shall not be required to give notice to any person of the hearing fixed under paragraph (2)(a), unless the sheriff directs otherwise.]

[2557]

NOTES

Commencement: 15 September 2003.
Inserted by the Act of Sederunt (Sheriff Court Company Insolvency Rules 1986) Amendment 2003, SSI 2003/388, r 3.

[31B UNCITRAL Model Law on Cross-Border Insolvency

On receipt of a certified copy interlocutor of a Lord Ordinary ordering proceedings under these rules to be transferred to the Court of Session under paragraph 11 of Schedule 3 to the Cross-Border Insolvency Regulations 2006, the sheriff clerk shall within four days transmit the process to the deputy principal clerk of session.]

[2558]

NOTES

Commencement: 6 April 2006.

Inserted by the Act of Sederunt (Sheriff Court Company Insolvency Rules 1986) Amendment (UNCITRAL Model Law on Cross-Border Insolvency) 2006, SSI 2006/200, r 2(1), (5).

32 Intimation, service and advertisement of notes and appeals

An application by note, or an appeal, to the court under these rules shall be intimated, served and, if necessary, advertised as the court shall direct.

[2559]

33 Affidavits

The court may accept as evidence an affidavit lodged in support of a petition or note.

[2560]

34 Notices, reports and other documents sent to the court

Where, under the Act of 1986 or rules made under that Act—

(a) notice of a fact is to be given to the court;
(b) a report is to be made, or sent, to the court; or
(c) some other document is to be sent to the court;

it shall be sent or delivered to the sheriff-clerk of the court, who shall cause it to be lodged in the appropriate process.

[2561]

35 Failure to comply with rules

(1) The court may, in its discretion, relieve a party from the consequences of any failure to comply with the provisions of a rule shown to be due to mistake, oversight or other cause, which is not wilful non-observance of the rule, on such terms and conditions as the court considers just.

(2) Where the court relieves a party from the consequences of failure to comply with a rule under paragraph 1, the court may pronounce such interlocutor as may be just so as to enable the cause to proceed as if the failure to comply with the rule had not occurred.

[2562]

PART VI
APPEALS

36 Appeals to the Sheriff Principal or Court of Session

(1) Where an appeal to the Sheriff Principal or the Court of Session is competent, it shall be taken by note of appeal which shall—

(a) be written by the appellant or his solicitor on—
 (i) the interlocutor sheet or other written record containing the interlocutor appealed against; or
 (ii) a separate document lodged with the sheriff-clerk;
(b) be as nearly as may be in the following terms:—
 "The (*petitioner, noter, respondent or other party*) appeals to the Sheriff Principal [*or* Court of Session]"; and
(c) be signed by the appellant or his solicitor and bear the date on which it is signed.

(2) Such an appeal shall be marked within 14 days of the date of the interlocutor appealed against.

(3) Where the appeal is to the Court of Session, the note of appeal shall specify the name and address of the solicitor in Edinburgh who will be acting for the appellant.

(4) On an appeal being taken, the sheriff-clerk shall within 4 days—

(a) transmit the process—
 (i) where the appeal is to Sheriff Principal, to him; or
 (ii) where the appeal is to the Court of Session, to the Deputy Principal Clerk of Session; and

(b) send written notice of the appeal to any other party to the cause and certify in the interlocutor sheet, or other written record containing the interlocutor appealed against, that he has done so.

(5) Failure of the sheriff-clerk to give notice under paragraph 4(b) shall not invalidate the appeal.

[2563]

CO-OPERATION OF INSOLVENCY COURTS (DESIGNATION OF RELEVANT COUNTRIES AND TERRITORIES) ORDER 1986

(SI 1986/2123)

NOTES

Made: 2 December 1986.
Authority: Insolvency Act 1986, s 426(11).
Commencement: 29 December 1986.

1

This Order may be cited as the Co-operation of Insolvency Courts (Designation of Relevant Countries and Territories) Order 1986 and shall come into force on 29th December 1986.

[2564]

2

The countries and territories specified in the Schedule to this Order are hereby designated relevant countries and territories for the purposes of section 426 of the Insolvency Act 1986.

[2565]

SCHEDULE
RELEVANT COUNTRIES AND TERRITORIES

Article 2

Anguilla

Australia

The Bahamas

Bermuda

Botswana

Canada

Cayman Islands

Falkland Islands

Gibraltar

Hong Kong

Republic of Ireland

Montserrat

New Zealand

St Helena

Turks and Caicos Islands

Tuvalu

Virgin Islands

[2566]

ACT OF SEDERUNT (RULES OF THE COURT OF SESSION 1994) 1994

(SI 1994/1443 (S 69))

NOTES

Made: 31 May 1994.
Authority: Court of Session Act 1988, s 5.
Commencement: 5 September 1994.
Only provisions of this Act of Sederunt relevant to this work are reproduced here.

ARRANGEMENT OF RULES

SCHEDULE 2

CHAPTER 74
COMPANIES

PART I
GENERAL PROVISIONS

PART III
ADMINISTRATION PROCEDURE

PART V
WINDING UP OF COMPANIES

SCHEDULE 2

CHAPTER 74
COMPANIES

PART I
GENERAL PROVISIONS

74.1 Application and interpretation of this Chapter

(1) This Chapter applies to causes under—

[(a) the Insolvency Act 1986; and]
(b) the Company Directors Disqualification Act 1986.

(2) In this Chapter—
"the Act of 1986" means the Insolvency Act 1986;
"the Insolvency Rules" means the Insolvency (Scotland) Rules 1986;
["the EC Regulation" means Council Regulation (EC) 1346/2000 of 29th May 2000 on insolvency proceedings;]
"registered office" means—
(i) the place specified in the statement of the company delivered to the register of companies under section 10 of the Companies Act 1985 as the intended place of its registered office on incorporation, or
(ii) where notice has been given by the company to the registrar of companies under section 287 of the Companies Act 1985 of a change of registered office, the place specified in the last such notice.

(3) Unless the context otherwise requires, words and expressions used in this Chapter which are also used in the Act of 1986 or the Insolvency Rules have the same meaning as in that Act or those Rules, as the case may be.

[2567]

NOTES

Para (1): sub-para (a) substituted by the Act of Sederunt (Rules of the Court of Session Amendment No 3) (Miscellaneous) 1996, SI 1996/1756, r 2(42).

Para (2): definition "the EC Regulation" inserted by the Act of Sederunt (Rules of the Court of Session Amendment No 5) (Insolvency Proceedings) 2003, SSI 2003/385, r 2(1), (2).

74.2 Proceedings before insolvency judge

All proceedings in the Outer House in a cause under or by virtue of the Act of 1986 or the Company Directors Disqualification Act 1986 shall be brought before a judge of the court nominated by the Lord President as the insolvency judge or, where the insolvency judge is not available, any other judge of the court (including the vacation judge); and "insolvency judge" shall be construed accordingly.

[2568]

74.3 Notices and reports, etc, sent to the court

Where, under the Act of 1986 or the Insolvency Rules—
(a) notice of a fact is to be given to the court,
(b) a report is to be made, or sent, to the court, or
(c) any other document is to be sent to the court,
it shall be sent to the Deputy Principal Clerk who shall cause it to be lodged in the process to which it relates.

[2569]

PART III
ADMINISTRATION [PROCEDURE]

NOTES

Part Heading: word in square brackets substituted by the Act of Sederunt (Rules of the Court of Session Amendment No 5) (Insolvency Proceedings) 2003, SSI 2003/385, r 2(1), (6).

74.10 Form of petition [in administration procedure]

(1) In this Part, "the petition" means a petition under section 9 of the Act of 1986 (petition for an administration order).

(2) The petition shall include averments in relation to—
(a) the petitioner and the capacity in which he presents the petition, if other than the company;
(b) whether it is believed that the company is, or is likely to become, unable to pay its debts and the grounds of that belief;
[(c) how the making of that order will achieve—
(i) any of the purposes specified in section 8(3) of the Act of 1986; or
(ii) an objective specified in paragraph 3 of Schedule B1 to the Act of 1986;]

(d) the company's financial position specifying, so far as known, assets and liabilities, including contingent and prospective liabilities;

(e) any security known or believed to be held by creditors of the company, whether in any case the security confers power on the holder to appoint a receiver, and whether a receiver has been appointed;

(f) so far as known to the petitioner, whether any steps have been taken for the winding up [of] the company;

(g) other matters which, in the opinion of the petitioner, will assist the court in deciding whether to grant an [order in respect of an administration];

(h) whether an independent report on the affairs of the company has been prepared under rule 2.1 of the Insolvency Rules and, if not, an explanation why not …

(i) the name and address of the person proposed to be appointed, and his qualification to act, as administrator[; and

(j) whether—

(i) the EC Regulation applies; and

(ii) if so, whether the proceedings are main proceedings or territorial proceedings.]

(2) Where a report has been prepared under rule 2.1 of the Insolvency Rules, a copy of that report shall be lodged with the petition.

[2570]

NOTES

Rule heading: words in square brackets substituted by the Act of Sederunt (Rules of the Court of Session Amendment No 5) (Insolvency Proceedings) 2003, SSI 2003/385, r 2(1), (7)(a).

Para (2): sub-para (c) substituted, words in square brackets in sub-para (g) substituted for words "administration order", word "; and" omitted from sub-para (h) revoked, and sub-para (j) and word "; and" immediately preceding it added, by SSI 2003/385, r 2(1), (7)(b); word in square brackets in sub-para (f) inserted by the Act of Sederunt (Rules of the Court of Session 1994 Amendment No 3) (Miscellaneous) 1994, SI 1994/2901, r 2(20).

[74.10A Interim orders

(1) On making an interim order under paragraph 13(1)(d) of Schedule B1 to the Act of 1986 the Lord Ordinary shall fix a hearing on the By Order Roll for a date after the expiry of the period of notice mentioned in rule 14.6 (period of notice for lodging answers).

(2) At the hearing under paragraph (1) the Lord Ordinary shall make such order as to further procedure as he thinks fit.]

[2571]

NOTES

Commencement: 7 June 2005.

Inserted by the Act of Sederunt (Rules of the Court of Session Amendment No 7) (Miscellaneous) 2005, SSI 2005/268, r 2(1), (9).

74.11 Notice of petition

Where—

(a) the petition is to be served on a person mentioned in rule [2.3] of the Insolvency Rules, and

(b) by virtue of paragraph (2) of that rule, notice requires to be given to that person,

it shall be sufficient for the petitioner, where such notice and service is to be executed by post, to enclose the statutory notice and a copy of the petition in one envelope and to certify the giving of such notice and the execution of such service by one certificate.

[2572]

NOTES

Rule reference in square brackets in para (a) substituted for rule reference "2.2" by the Act of Sederunt (Rules of the Court of Session Amendment No 5) (Insolvency Proceedings) 2003, SSI 2003/385, r 2(1), (8).

74.12 Report of proposals of administrator

(1) A report of the meeting to approve the proposals of the administrator to be sent to the court under section 24(4) of the Act of 1986 shall be sent to the Deputy Principal Clerk of Session, who shall—

(a) cause it to be lodged in the process of the petition to which it relates; and
(b) give written intimation to the parties of the receipt and lodging of the report.

(2) Where a report under section 24(4) of the Act of 1986 discloses that the meeting has declined to approve the proposals of the administrator, the Keeper of the Rolls shall put the cause out on the By Order Roll for determination by the insolvency judge for any order he may make under section 24(5) of that Act.

[2573]

[74.13 Report of administrator's proposals: Schedule B1 to the Act of 1986

(1) Paragraph (2) shall apply where a report under paragraphs 53(2) or 54(6) of Schedule B1 to the Act of 1986 discloses a failure to approve, or to approve a revision of, an administrator's proposals.

(2) The Deputy Principal Clerk shall fix a hearing for determination by the insolvency judge of any order that may be made under paragraph 55(2) of Schedule B1 to the Act of 1986.]

[2574]

NOTES

Commencement: 15 September 2003.

Substituted, together with rr 74.14, 74.15, for original rr 74.13–74.15, by the Act of Sederunt (Rules of the Court of Session Amendment No 5) (Insolvency Proceedings) 2003, SSI 2003/385, r 2(1), (9).

[74.14 Time and date of lodging in an administration

(1) The time and date of lodging of a notice or document relating to an administration under the Act of 1986 or the Insolvency Rules shall be noted by the Deputy Principal Clerk upon the notice or document.

(2) Subject to any provision of the Insolvency Rules—
(a) where the time of lodging of a notice or document cannot be ascertained by the Deputy Principal Clerk, the notice or document shall be deemed to be lodged at 10 a.m. on the date of lodging; and
(b) where a notice or document under paragraph (1) is delivered on any day other than a business day, the date of lodging shall be the first business day after such delivery.]

[2575]

NOTES

Commencement: 15 September 2003.

Substituted as noted to r 74.13 at **[2574]**.

[74.15 Applications during an administration

An application on appeal under any provision of the Act of 1986 or the Insolvency Rules during an administration shall be—
(a) where no previous application or appeal has been made, by petition; or
(b) where a petition for an order in respect of an administration has been lodged, by note in the process of that petition.]

[2576]

NOTES

Commencement: 15 September 2003.

Substituted as noted to r 74.13 at **[2574]**.

PART V
WINDING UP OF COMPANIES

74.20 Interpretation of this Part

In this Part, "the petition" means a petition under section 124 of the Act of 1986 (petition to wind up a company).

[2577]

74.21 Petition to wind up a company

(1) The petition shall include averments in relation to
- (a) the petitioner, if other than the company, and his title to present the petition;
- (b) in respect of the company—
  - (i) its current and any previous registered name;
  - (ii) the address of its registered office, and any previous such address within 6 months immediately before the presentation of the petition so far as known to the petitioner;
  - (iii) a statement of the nature of its business and objects, the amount of its capital (nominal and issued) indicating what part is called up, paid up or credited as paid up, and the amount of the assets of the company so far as known to the petitioner;
- (c) whether, to the knowledge of the petitioner, a receiver has been appointed in respect of any part of the property of the company or a liquidator has been appointed for the voluntary winding up of the company;
- (d) the grounds on which the petition proceeds; and
- (e) the name and address of the person proposed to be appointed, and his qualification to act, as interim liquidator.

[2578]

74.22 Intimation, service and advertisement under this Part

(1) Unless the court otherwise directs, the order under rule 14.5 (first order in petitions) for intimation, service and advertisement of the petition shall include a requirement—
- (a) to serve the petition—
  - (i) where the petitioner is not the company, on the company;
  - (ii) where the company is being wound up voluntarily and a liquidator has been appointed, on the liquidator; and
  - (iii) where a receiver or administrator has been appointed, on the receiver or administrator, as the case may be;
- (b) where the company is an authorised institution or former authorised institution within the meaning assigned in section 106(1) of the Banking Act 1987 and the petitioner is not the Bank of England, to serve the petition on the Bank of England; and
- (c) to advertise the petition forthwith—
  - (i) once in the Edinburgh Gazette; and
  - (ii) once in one or more of such newspapers as the court shall direct.

(2) Subject to rule 14.6(2) (application to shorten or extend the period of notice), the period of notice for lodging answers to the petition shall be 8 days.

(3) An advertisement under paragraph (1) shall include—
- (a) the name and address of the petitioner and, where the petitioner is the company, its registered office;
- (b) the name and address of the agent for the petitioner;
- (c) the date on which the petition was presented—
- (d) the nature of the order sought;
- (e) where a provisional liquidator has been appointed by the court, his name, address and the date of his appointment;
- (f) the period of notice for lodging answers; and
- (g) a statement that any person who intends to appear in the petition must lodge answers within the period of notice.

[2579]

74.23 Remits from one court to another

(1) An application under section 120(3)(a)(i) of the Act of 1986 (application for remit of petition to a sheriff court) shall be made by motion.

(2) An application under—
- (a) section 120(3)(a)(ii) of the Act of 1986 (application for remit of petition from a sheriff court to the court), or
- (b) section 120(3)(b) of that Act (application for remit of petition from one sheriff court to another), shall be made by petition.

[2580]

74.24 Substitution of creditor or contributory for petitioner

(1) Where a petitioner in the petition—
(a) is subsequently found not entitled to present the petition,
(b) fails to make intimation, service and advertisement as directed by the court,
(c) moves or consents to withdraw the petition or to allow it to be dismissed or refused,
(d) fails to appear when the petition is called for hearing, or
(e) appears, but does not move for an order in terms of the prayer of the petition,

the court may, on such terms as it thinks fit, sist as petitioner in place of the original petitioner any creditor or contributory who, in the opinion of the court, is entitled to present the petition.

[(1A) Where a member State liquidator has been appointed in main proceedings in relation to the company, without prejudice to paragraph (1) the court may, on such terms as it thinks fit, substitute the member State liquidator as petitioner, where he is desirous of prosecuting the petition.]

(2) An application by a creditor or a contributory to be sisted under paragraph (1)—
(a) may be made at any time before the petition is dismissed or refused, and
(b) shall be made by note;

and, if necessary, the court may continue the petition for a specified period to allow a note to be presented.

[2581]

NOTES

Para (1A): inserted by the Act of Sederunt (Rules of the Court of Session Amendment No 5) (Insolvency Proceedings) 2003, SSI 2003/385, r 2(1), (11).

74.25 Provisional liquidator

(1) An application to appoint a provisional liquidator under section 135 of the Act of 1986 may be made—
(a) by the petitioner, in the prayer of the petition or, if made after the petition has been presented, by note; or
(b) by a creditor or contributory of the company, the company, the Secretary of State[, a member State liquidator appointed in main proceedings] or a person entitled under any enactment to present a petition, by note.

(2) The application mentioned in paragraph (1) shall include averments in relation to—
(a) the grounds for the appointment of the provisional liquidator;
(b) the name and address of the person proposed to be appointed, and his qualification to act, as provisional liquidator; and
(c) whether, to the knowledge of the applicant, an administrator has been appointed to the company or a receiver has been appointed in respect of any part of its property or a liquidator has been appointed voluntarily to wind it up.

(3) Where the court decides to appoint a provisional liquidator—
(a) it shall pronounce an interlocutor making the appointment and specifying the functions to be carried out by him in relation to the affairs of the company; and
(b) the applicant shall forthwith send a certified copy of such interlocutor to the person appointed.

(4) On receiving a certified copy of an interlocutor pronounced under paragraph (3), the provisional liquidator shall intimate his appointment forthwith—
(a) once in the Edinburgh Gazette; and
(b) once in one or more of such newspapers as the court has directed.

(5) An application for the discharge of a provisional liquidator shall be made by note.

[2582]

NOTES

Para (1): in sub-para (b), words in square brackets inserted by the Act of Sederunt (Rules of the Court of Session Amendment No 5) (Insolvency Proceedings) 2003, SSI 2003/385, r 2(1), (12).

74.26 Appointment of a liquidator

(1) Where the court pronounces an interlocutor appointing a liquidator—

(a) the Deputy Principal Clerk shall send a certified copy of that interlocutor to the liquidator;

(b) the court may, for the purposes of rule 4.18(4) of the Insolvency Rules (liquidator to give notice of appointment), give such direction as it thinks fit as to advertisement of such appointment.

(2) An application to appoint a liquidator under section 139(4) of the Act of 1986 shall be made by note.

[2583]

74.27 Applications and appeals in relation to a statement of affairs

(1) An application under section 131(5) of the Act of 1986 for—

(a) release from an obligation imposed under section 131(1) or (2) of that Act, or

(b) an extension of time for the submission of a statement of affairs,

shall be made by note.

(2) A note under paragraph (1) shall be served on the liquidator or provisional liquidator, as the case may be, who may lodge—

(a) answers to the note; or

(b) a report on any matters which he considers should be drawn to the attention of the court.

(3) Where the liquidator or provisional liquidator lodges a report under paragraph (2), he shall forthwith send a copy of it to the noter.

(4) Where the liquidator or the provisional liquidator does not appear at any hearing on the note, a certified copy of the interlocutor disposing of the note shall be sent to him forthwith by the noter.

(5) An appeal under rule 4.9(6) of the Insolvency Rules (appeal against refusal by liquidator of allowance towards expenses of preparing statement of affairs) shall be made by note.

[2584]

74.28 Appeals against adjudication of claims

(1) An appeal under section 49(6) of the Bankruptcy (Scotland) Act 1985 as applied by rule 4.16 of the Insolvency Rules (appeal by a creditor or contributory of the company against a decision of the liquidator), shall be made by note.

(2) A note under paragraph (1) shall be served on the liquidator.

(3) On such a note being served on him, the liquidator shall send the claim in question, and a copy of his adjudication, forthwith to the Deputy Principal Clerk who shall cause them to be lodged in process.

(4) After the note has been disposed of, the Deputy Principal Clerk shall return the claim and the adjudication to the liquidator with a copy of the interlocutor disposing of the note.

[2585]

74.29 Removal of liquidator

An application by a creditor of the company for an order—

(a) under section 171(3) of the Act of 1986 (order directing a liquidator to summon a meeting of creditors for the purpose of removing him), or

(b) under section 172 of that Act (order for removal of a liquidator),

shall be made by note.

[2586]

74.30 Application in relation to remuneration of liquidator

(1) An application—

(a) by a liquidator under rule 4.34 of the Insolvency Rules (application to increase remuneration), or

(b) by a creditor of the company under rule 4.35 of those Rules (application to reduce liquidator's remuneration),

shall be made by note.

(2) A note under paragraph (1)(b) shall be served on the liquidator.

[2587]

[74.30A Applications under section 176A of the Act of 1986

(1) An application by a liquidator, administrator or receiver under section 176A of the Act of 1986 shall be—

(a) where there is no existing process in relation to any liquidation, administration or receivership, by petition; or

(b) where a process exists in relation to any liquidation, administration or receivership, by note in that process.

(2) The Deputy Principal Clerk shall—

(a) after the lodging of any petition or note fix a hearing for the insolvency judge to consider an application under paragraph (1); and

(b) give notice of the hearing fixed under paragraph (2)(a) to the petitioner or noter.

(3) The petitioner or noter shall not be required to give notice to any person of the hearing fixed under paragraph (2)(a), unless the insolvency judge directs otherwise.]

[2588]

NOTES

Commencement: 15 September 2003.

Inserted by the Act of Sederunt (Rules of the Court of Session Amendment No 5) (Insolvency Proceedings) 2003, SSI 2003/385, r 2(1), (13).

74.31 Application to appoint a special manager

(1) An application under section 177 of the Act of 1986 (application for the appointment of a special manager) shall be made by note.

(2) A bond of caution certified by the noter under rule 4.70(4) of the Insolvency Rules shall be sent to the Petition Department by the noter.

(3) After the Deputy Principal Clerk has satisfied himself as to the sufficiency of caution under rule 33.7(1) of these Rules, the clerk of session shall issue to the person appointed to be special manager a certified copy of the interlocutor appointing him.

(4) A special manager may, before the expiry of the period for finding caution, apply to the insolvency judge for an extension of that period.

[2589]

74.32 Other applications

(1) An application under the Act of 1986 or any subordinate legislation made under that Act, or Part VII of the Companies Act 1989, in relation to a winding up by the court not mentioned in this Part shall—

(a) if made by a party to the petition, be made by motion; or

(b) in any other case, be made by note.

(2) At the hearing of a motion under paragraph (1)(a), the court may order that the application be made by note; and, in such a case, shall make an order for the lodging of answers to the note in process within such period as it thinks fit.

[2590]

CO-OPERATION OF INSOLVENCY COURTS (DESIGNATION OF RELEVANT COUNTRIES) ORDER 1996

(SI 1996/253)

NOTES

Made: 8 February 1996.

Authority: Insolvency Act 1986, s 426(11).

Commencement: 1 March 1996.

Application: this Order is applied to limited liability partnerships with such modifications as the context requires for the purpose of giving effect to the provisions of the Insolvency Act 1986, by the Limited Liability Partnerships Regulations 2001, SI 2001/1090, reg 10, Sch 6, Pt II.

1 This Order may be cited as the Co-operation of Insolvency Courts (Designation of Relevant Countries) Order 1996 and shall come into force on 1st March 1996.

[2591]

2 The countries specified in the Schedule to this Order are hereby designated relevant countries for the purposes of section 426 of the Insolvency Act 1986.

[2592]

SCHEDULE
RELEVANT COUNTRIES

Article 2

Malaysia

Republic of South Africa

[2593]

CO-OPERATION OF INSOLVENCY COURTS (DESIGNATION OF RELEVANT COUNTRY) ORDER 1998

(SI 1998/2766)

NOTES

Made: 11 November 1998.
Authority: Insolvency Act 1986, s 426(11).
Commencement: 11 December 1998.
Application: this Order is applied to limited liability partnerships with such modifications as the context requires for the purpose of giving effect to the provisions of the Insolvency Act 1986, by the Limited Liability Partnerships Regulations 2001, SI 2001/1090, reg 10, Sch 6, Pt II.

1 This Order may be cited as the Co-operation of Insolvency Courts (Designation of Relevant Country) Order 1998 and shall come into force on 11th December 1998.

[2594]

2 Brunei Darussalam is hereby designated a relevant country for the purposes of section 426 of the Insolvency Act 1986.

[2595]

INSURERS (REORGANISATION AND WINDING UP) REGULATIONS 2004

(SI 2004/353)

NOTES

Made: 12 February 2004.
Authority: European Communities Act 1972, s 2(2).
Commencement: 18 February 2004.

ARRANGEMENT OF REGULATIONS

PART I
GENERAL

PART II
INSOLVENCY MEASURES AND PROCEEDINGS:
JURISDICTION IN RELATION TO INSURERS

PART III
MODIFICATIONS OF THE LAW OF INSOLVENCY:
NOTIFICATION AND PUBLICATION

PART IV
PRIORITY OF PAYMENT OF INSURANCE
CLAIMS IN WINDING UP ETC

PART V
REORGANISATION OR WINDING UP OF UK INSURERS:
RECOGNITION OF EEA RIGHTS

PART III
STATUTORY INSTRUMENTS

PART I
GENERAL

1 Citation and Commencement

These Regulations may be cited as the Insurers (Reorganisation and Winding Up) Regulations 2004, and come into force on 18th February 2004.

[2596]

NOTES

Commencement: 18 February 2004.

2 Interpretation

(1) In these Regulations—

"the 1985 Act" means the Companies Act 1985;

"the 1986 Act" means the Insolvency Act 1986;

"the 2000 Act" means the Financial Services and Markets Act 2000;

"the 1989 Order" means the Insolvency (Northern Ireland) Order 1989;

"administrator" has the meaning given by paragraph 13 of Schedule B1;

"Article 418 compromise or arrangement" means a compromise or arrangement sanctioned by the court in relation to a UK insurer under Article 418 of the Companies Order, but does not include a compromise or arrangement falling within Article 420 or Articles 420A of that Order (reconstruction and amalgamations);

"the Authority" means the Financial Services Authority;

"branch", in relation to an EEA or UK insurer has the meaning given by Article 1(b) of the life insurance directive or the third non-life insurance directive;

"claim" means a claim submitted by a creditor of a UK insurer in the course of—

(a) a winding up,

(b) an administration, or

(c) a voluntary arrangement,

with a view to recovering his debt in whole or in part, and includes a proof of debt, within the meaning of Rule 4.73(4) of the Insolvency Rules, Rule 4.079(4) of the Insolvency Rules (Northern Ireland) or in Scotland a claim made in accordance with rule 4.15 of the Insolvency (Scotland) Rules;

"the Companies Order" means the Companies (Northern Ireland) Order 1986;

"creditors' voluntary winding up" has the meaning given by section 90 of the 1986 Act or Article 76 of the 1989 Order;

"debt"—

(a) in England and Wales and Northern Ireland—

(i) in relation to a winding up or administration of a UK insurer, has the meaning given by Rule 13.12 of the Insolvency Rules or Article 5 of the 1989 Order, and

(ii) in a case where a voluntary arrangement has effect, in relation to a UK insurer, means a debt which would constitute a debt in relation to the winding up of that insurer, except that references in paragraph (1) of Rule 13.12 or paragraph (1) of Article 5 of the 1989 Order to the date on which the company goes into liquidation are to be read as references to the date on which the voluntary arrangement has effect;

(b) in Scotland—

(i) in relation to a winding up of a UK insurer, shall be interpreted in accordance with Schedule 1 to the Bankruptcy (Scotland) Act 1985 as applied by Chapter 5 of Part 4 of the Insolvency (Scotland) Rules, and

(ii) in a case where a voluntary arrangement has effect in relation to a UK insurer, means a debt which would constitute a debt in relation to the winding up of that insurer, except that references in Chapter 5 of Part 4 of the Insolvency (Scotland) Rules to the date of commencement of winding up are to be read as references to the date on which the voluntary arrangement has effect;

"directive reorganisation measure" means a reorganisation measure as defined in Article 2(c) of the reorganisation and winding-up directive which was adopted or imposed on or after 20th April 2003;

"directive winding up proceedings" means winding up proceedings as defined in Article 2(d) of the reorganisation and winding-up directive which were opened on or after 20th April 2003;

"EEA creditor" means a creditor of a UK insurer who—

(a) in the case of an individual, is ordinarily resident in an EEA State, and

(b) in the case of a body corporate or unincorporated association of persons, has its head office in an EEA State;

"EEA insurer" means an undertaking, other than a UK insurer, pursuing the activity of direct insurance (within the meaning of Article 1 of the first life insurance directive or the first non-life insurance directive) which has received authorisation under Article 6 from its home state regulator;

"EEA regulator" means a competent authority (within the meaning of Article 1(1) of the life insurance directive or Article 1(k) of the third non-life insurance directive, as the case may be) of an EEA State;

"EEA State" means a State, other than the United Kingdom, which is a contracting party to the agreement on the European Economic Area signed at Oporto on 2 May 1992;

"the first non-life insurance directive" means the Council Directive (73/239/EEC) of 24 July 1973 on the co-ordination of laws, regulations and administrative provisions relating to the taking up and pursuit of the business of direct insurance other than life assurance;

"home state regulator", in relation to an EEA insurer, means the relevant EEA regulator in the EEA State where its head office is located;

"the Insolvency Rules" means the Insolvency Rules 1986;

"the Insolvency Rules (Northern Ireland)" means the Insolvency Rules (Northern Ireland) 1991;

"the Insolvency (Scotland) Rules" means the Insolvency (Scotland) Rules 1986;

"insurance claim" means any claim in relation to an insurance debt;

"insurance creditor" means a person who has an insurance claim against a UK insurer (whether or not he has claims other than insurance claims against that insurer);

"insurance debt" means a debt to which a UK insurer is, or may become liable, pursuant to a contract of insurance, to a policyholder or to any person who has a direct right of action against that insurer, and includes any premium paid in connection with a contract of insurance (whether or not that contract was concluded) which the insurer is liable to refund;

"life insurance directive" means the Directive (2002/83/EC) of the European Parliament and of the Council concerning life assurance;

"officer", in relation to a company, has the meaning given by section 744 of the 1985 Act or Article 2 of the Companies Order;

"official language" means a language specified in Article 1 of Council Regulation No 1 of 15th April 1958 determining the languages to be used by the European Economic

Community (Regulation 1/58/EEC), most recently amended by paragraph (a) of Part XVIII of Annex I to the Act of Accession 1994 (194 N);

"policyholder" has the meaning given by the Financial Services and Markets Act 2000 (Meaning of "Policy" and "Policyholder") Order 2001;

"the reorganisation and winding-up directive" means the Directive (2001/17/EC) of the European Parliament and of the Council of 19 March 2001 on the reorganisation and winding-up of insurance undertakings;

"Schedule B1" means Schedule B1 to the 1986 Act as inserted by section 248 of the Enterprise Act 2002;

"section 425 compromise or arrangement" means a compromise or arrangement sanctioned by the court in relation to a UK insurer under section 425 of the 1985 Act, but does not include a compromise or arrangement falling within section 427 or section 427A of that Act (reconstructions or amalgamations);

"section 425 or Article 418 compromise or arrangement" means a section 425 compromise or arrangement or an Article 418 compromise or arrangement;

"supervisor" has the meaning given by section 7 of the 1986 Act or Article 20 of the 1989 Order;

"the third non-life insurance directive" means the Council Directive (92/49/EEC) of 18th June 1992 on the co-ordination of laws, etc, and amending directives 73/239/EEC and 88/357/EEC;

"UK insurer" means a person who has permission under Part IV of the 2000 Act to effect or carry out contracts of insurance, but does not include a person who, in accordance with that permission, carries on that activity exclusively in relation to reinsurance contracts;

"voluntary arrangement" means a voluntary arrangement which has effect in relation to a UK insurer in accordance with section 4A of the 1986 Act or Article 17A of the 1989 Order; and

"winding up" means—

(a) winding up by the court, or

(b) a creditors' voluntary winding up.

(2) In paragraph (1)—

(a) for the purposes of the definition of "directive reorganisation measure", a reorganisation measure is adopted or imposed at the time when it is treated as adopted or imposed by the law of the relevant EEA State; and

(b) for the purposes of the definition of "directive winding up proceedings", winding up proceedings are opened at the time when they are treated as opened by the law of the relevant EEA State,

and in this paragraph "relevant EEA State" means the EEA State under the law of which the reorganisation is adopted or imposed, or the winding up proceedings are opened, as the case may be.

(3) In these Regulations, references to the general law of insolvency of the United Kingdom include references to every provision made by or under the 1986 Act or the 1989 Order; and in relation to friendly societies or to industrial and provident societies references to the law of insolvency or to any provision of the 1986 Act or the 1989 Order are to that law as modified by the Friendly Societies Act 1992 or by the Industrial and Provident Societies Act 1965 or the Industrial and Provident Societies Act (Northern Ireland) 1969 (as the case may be).

(4) References in these Regulations to a "contract of insurance" must be read with—

(a) section 22 of the 2000 Act;

(b) any relevant order made under that section; and

(c) Schedule 2 to that Act,

but for the purposes of these Regulations a contract of insurance does not include a reinsurance contract.

(5) Functions imposed or falling on the Authority by or under these Regulations shall be deemed to be functions under the 2000 Act.

[2597]

NOTES

Commencement: 18 February 2004.

3 Scope

For the purposes of these Regulations, neither the Society of Lloyd's nor the persons specified in section 316(1) of the 2000 Act are UK insurers.

[2598]

NOTES

Commencement: 18 February 2004.

PART II
INSOLVENCY MEASURES AND PROCEEDINGS: JURISDICTION IN RELATION TO INSURERS

4 Prohibition against winding up etc EEA insurers in the United Kingdom

(1) On or after the relevant date a court in the United Kingdom may not, in relation to an EEA insurer or any branch of an EEA insurer—

(a) make a winding up order pursuant to section 221 of the 1986 Act or Article 185 of the 1989 Order;

(b) appoint a provisional liquidator;

(c) make an administration order.

(2) Paragraph (1)(a) does not prevent—

(a) the court from making a winding up order after the relevant date in relation to an EEA insurer if—

(i) a provisional liquidator was appointed in relation to that insurer before the relevant date, and

(ii) that appointment continues in force until immediately before that winding up order is made;

(b) the winding up of an EEA insurer after the relevant date pursuant to a winding up order which was made, and has not been discharged, before that date.

(3) Paragraph (1)(b) does not prevent a provisional liquidator of an EEA insurer appointed before the relevant date from acting in relation to that insurer after that date.

(4) Paragraph (1)(c) does not prevent an administrator appointed before the relevant date from acting after that date in a case in which the administration order under which he or his predecessor was appointed remains in force after that date.

(5) An administrator may not, in relation to an EEA insurer, be appointed under paragraphs 14 or 22 of Schedule B1.

(6) A proposed voluntary arrangement shall not have effect in relation to an EEA insurer if a decision, under section 4 of the 1986 Act or Article 17 of the 1989 Order, with respect to the approval of that arrangement was made after the relevant date.

(7) Section 377 of the 2000 Act (reducing the value of contracts instead of winding up) does not apply in relation to an EEA insurer.

(8) An order under section 253 of the Enterprise Act 2002 (application of insolvency law to a foreign company) may not provide for any of the following provisions of the 1986 Act to apply in relation to an EEA insurer—

(a) Part I (company voluntary arrangements);

(b) Part II (administration);

(c) Chapter VI of Part IV (winding up by the Court).

(9) In this regulation and regulation 5, "relevant date" means 20th April 2003.

[2599]

NOTES

Commencement: 18 February 2004.

5 Schemes of arrangement: EEA insurers

(1) For the purposes of section 425(6)(a) of the 1985 Act or Article 418(5)(a) of the Companies Order, an EEA insurer or a branch of an EEA insurer is to be treated as a company

liable to be wound up under the 1986 Act or the 1989 Order if it would be liable to be wound up under that Act or Order but for the prohibition in regulation 4(1)(a).

(2) But a court may not make a relevant order under section 425(2) of the 1985 Act or Article 418(2) of the Companies Order in relation to an EEA insurer which is subject to a directive reorganisation measure or directive winding up proceedings, or a branch of an EEA insurer which is subject to such a measure or proceedings unless the conditions set out in paragraph (3) are satisfied.

(3) Those conditions are—

(a) the person proposing the section 425 or Article 418 compromise or arrangement ("the proposal") has given—
   (i) the administrator or liquidator, and
   (ii) the relevant competent authority,

reasonable notice of the details of that proposal; and

(b) no person notified in accordance with sub-paragraph (a) has objected to the proposal.

(4) Nothing in this regulation invalidates a compromise or arrangement which was sanctioned by the court by an order made before the relevant date.

(5) For the purposes of paragraph (2), a relevant order means an order sanctioning a section 425 or Article 418 compromise or arrangement which—

(a) is intended to enable the insurer, and the whole or any part of its undertaking, to survive as a going concern and which affects the rights of persons other than the insurer or its contributories; or

(b) includes among its purposes a realisation of some or all of the assets of the EEA insurer to which the order relates and the distribution of the proceeds to creditors, with a view to terminating the whole or any part of the business of that insurer.

(6) For the purposes of this regulation—

(a) "administrator" means an administrator, as defined by Article 2(i) of the reorganisation and winding up directive, who is appointed in relation to the EEA insurer in relation to which the proposal is made;

(b) "liquidator" means a liquidator, as defined by Article 2(j) of the reorganisation and winding up directive, who is appointed in relation to the EEA insurer in relation to which the proposal is made;

(c) "competent authority" means the competent authority, as defined by Article 2(g) of the reorganisation and winding up directive, which is competent for the purposes of the directive reorganisation measure or directive winding up proceedings mentioned in paragraph (2).

[2600]

NOTES

Commencement: 18 February 2004.

6 Reorganisation measures and winding up proceedings in respect of EEA insurers effective in the United Kingdom

(1) An EEA insolvency measure has effect in the United Kingdom in relation to—

(a) any branch of an EEA insurer,

(b) any property or other assets of that insurer,

(c) any debt or liability of that insurer

as if it were part of the general law of insolvency of the United Kingdom.

(2) Subject to paragraph (4)—

(a) a competent officer who satisfies the condition mentioned in paragraph (3); or

(b) a qualifying agent appointed by a competent officer who satisfies the condition mentioned in paragraph (3),

may exercise in the United Kingdom, in relation to the EEA insurer which is subject to an EEA insolvency measure, any function which, pursuant to that measure, he is entitled to exercise in relation to that insurer in the relevant EEA State.

(3) The condition mentioned in paragraph (2) is that the appointment of the competent officer is evidenced—

(a) by a certified copy of the order or decision by a judicial or administrative authority in the relevant EEA State by or under which the competent officer was appointed; or

(b) by any other certificate issued by the judicial or administrative authority which has jurisdiction in relation to the EEA insolvency measure,

and accompanied by a certified translation of that order, decision or certificate (as the case may be).

(4) In exercising functions of the kind mentioned in paragraph (2), the competent officer or qualifying agent—

(a) may not take any action which would constitute an unlawful use of force in the part of the United Kingdom in which he is exercising those functions;

(b) may not rule on any dispute arising from a matter falling within Part V of these Regulations which is justiciable by a court in the part of the United Kingdom in which he is exercising those functions; and

(c) notwithstanding the way in which functions may be exercised in the relevant EEA State, must act in accordance with relevant laws or rules as to procedure which have effect in the part of the United Kingdom in which he is exercising those functions.

(5) For the purposes of paragraph (4)(c), "relevant laws or rules as to procedure" mean—

(a) requirements as to consultation with or notification of employees of an EEA insurer;

(b) law and procedures relevant to the realisation of assets;

(c) where the competent officer is bringing or defending legal proceedings in the name of, or on behalf of, an EEA insurer, the relevant rules of court.

(6) In this regulation—

"competent officer" means a person appointed under or in connection with an EEA insolvency measure for the purpose of administering that measure;

"qualifying agent" means an agent validly appointed (whether in the United Kingdom or elsewhere) by a competent officer in accordance with the relevant law in the relevant EEA State;

"EEA insolvency measure" means, as the case may be, a directive reorganisation measure or directive winding up proceedings which has effect in relation to an EEA insurer by virtue of the law of the relevant EEA State;

"relevant EEA State", in relation to an EEA insurer, means the EEA State in which that insurer has been authorised in accordance with Article 4 of the life insurance directive or Article 6 of the first non-life insurance directive.

[2601]

NOTES

Commencement: 18 February 2004.

7 Confirmation by the court of a creditors' voluntary winding up

(1) Rule 7.62 of the Insolvency Rules or Rule 7.56 of the Insolvency Rules (Northern Ireland) applies in relation to a UK insurer with the modification specified in paragraph (2) or (3).

(2) In Rule 7.62 paragraph (1), after the words

"the Insurers (Reorganisation and Winding Up) Regulations 2003" insert the words "or the Insurers (Reorganisation and Winding Up) Regulations 2004".

In Rule 7.56 of the Insolvency Rules (Northern Ireland) paragraph (1), after the words "the Insurers (Reorganisation and Winding Up) Regulations 2003" insert the words "or the Insurers (Reorganisation and Winding Up) Regulations 2004".

[2602]

NOTES

Commencement: 18 February 2004.

PART III STATUTORY INSTRUMENTS

PART III
MODIFICATIONS OF THE LAW OF INSOLVENCY: NOTIFICATION AND PUBLICATION

8 Modifications of the law of insolvency

The general law of insolvency has effect in relation to UK insurers subject to the provisions of this Part.

[2603]

NOTES

Commencement: 18 February 2004.

9 Notification of relevant decision to the Authority

(1) Where on or after [3rd March 2004] the court makes a decision, order or appointment of any of the following kinds—

(a) an administration order under paragraph 13 of Schedule B1;

(b) a winding up order under section 125 of the 1986 Act or Article 105 of the 1989 Order;

(c) the appointment of a provisional liquidator under section 135(1) of the 1986 Act or Article 115(1) of the 1989 Order;

(d) an interim order under paragraph 13(1)(d) of Schedule B1;

(e) a decision to reduce the value of one or more of the insurer's contracts, in accordance with section 377 of the 2000 Act,

it must immediately inform the Authority, or cause the Authority to be informed of the decision, order or appointment which has been made.

(2) Where a decision with respect to the approval of a voluntary arrangement has effect, and the arrangement which is the subject of that decision is a qualifying arrangement, the supervisor must forthwith inform the Authority of the arrangement.

(3) Where a liquidator is appointed as mentioned in section 100 of the 1986 Act, paragraph 83 of Schedule B1 or Article 86 of the 1989 Order (appointment of liquidator in a creditors' voluntary winding up), the liquidator must inform the Authority forthwith of his appointment.

(4) Where in the case of a members' voluntary winding up, section 95 of the 1986 Act (effect of company's insolvency) or Article 81 of the 1989 Order applies, the liquidator must inform the Authority forthwith that he is of that opinion.

(6) Paragraphs (1), (2) and (3) do not apply in any case where the Authority was represented at all hearings in connection with the application in relation to which the decision, order or appointment is made.

(7) For the purposes of paragraph (2), a "qualifying arrangement" means a voluntary arrangement which—

(a) varies the rights of creditors as against the insurer and is intended to enable the insurer, and the whole or any part of its undertaking, to survive as a going concern; or

(b) includes a realisation of some or all of the assets of the insurer and distribution of the proceeds to creditors, with a view to terminating the whole or any part of the business of that insurer.

(8) An administrator, supervisor or liquidator who fails without reasonable excuse to comply with paragraph (2), (3), or (4) (as the case may be) commits an offence and is liable on summary conviction to a fine not exceeding level 3 on the standard scale.

[2604]

NOTES

Commencement: 18 February 2004.

Para (1): words in square brackets substituted by the Insurers (Reorganisation and Winding Up) (Amendment) Regulations 2004, SI 2004/546, reg 2(1), (2).

10 Notification of relevant decision to EEA regulators

(1) Where the Authority is informed of a decision, order or appointment in accordance with regulation 9, the Authority must as soon as is practicable inform the EEA regulators in every EEA State—

(a) that the decision, order or appointment has been made; and

(b) in general terms, of the possible effect of a decision, order or appointment of that kind on—

(i) the business of an insurer, and

(ii) the rights of policyholders under contracts of insurance effected and carried out by an insurer.

(2) Where the Authority has been represented at all hearings in connection with the application in relation to which the decision, order or appointment has been made, the Authority must inform the EEA regulators in every EEA State of the matters mentioned in paragraph (1) as soon as is practicable after that decision, order or appointment has been made.

[2605]

NOTES

Commencement: 18 February 2004.

11 Publication of voluntary arrangement, administration order, winding up order or scheme of arrangement

(1) This regulation applies where a qualifying decision has effect, or a qualifying order or qualifying appointment is made, in relation to a UK insurer on or after 20th April 2003.

(2) For the purposes of this regulation—

(a) a qualifying decision means a decision with respect to the approval of a proposed voluntary arrangement, in accordance with section 4A of the 1986 Act or Article 17A of the 1989 Order;

(b) a qualifying order means—

(i) an administration order under paragraph 13 of Schedule B1,

(ii) an order appointing a provisional liquidator in accordance with section 135 of the 1986 Act or Article 115 of the 1989 Order, or

(iii) a winding up order made by the court under Part IV of the 1986 Act or Part V of the 1989 Order.

(c) a qualifying appointment means the appointment of a liquidator as mentioned in section 100 of the 1986 Act or Article 86 of the 1989 Order (appointment of liquidator in a creditors' voluntary winding up).

(3) Subject to paragraph (8), as soon as is reasonably practicable after a qualifying decision has effect, or a qualifying order or a qualifying appointment has been made, the relevant officer must publish, or cause to be published, in the Official Journal of the European Communities the information mentioned in paragraph (4) and (if applicable) paragraphs (5), (6) or (7).

(4) That information is—

(a) a summary of the terms of the qualifying decision or qualifying appointment or the provisions of the qualifying order (as the case may be);

(b) the identity of the relevant officer; and

(c) the statutory provisions in accordance with which the qualifying decision has effect or the qualifying order or appointment has been made or takes effect.

(5) In the case of a qualifying appointment falling within paragraph (2)(c), that information includes the court to which an application under section 112 of the 1986 Act (reference of questions to the court) or Article 98 of the 1989 Order (reference of questions to the High Court) may be made.

(6) In the case of a qualifying decision, that information includes the court to which an application under section 6 of the 1986 Act or Article 19 of the 1989 Order (challenge of decisions) may be made.

(7) Paragraph (3) does not apply where a qualifying decision or qualifying order falling within paragraph (2)(b)(i) affects the interests only of the members, or any class of members, or employees of the insurer (in their capacity as members or employees).

(8) This regulation is without prejudice to any requirement to publish information imposed upon a relevant officer under any provision of the general law of insolvency.

(9) A relevant officer who fails to comply with paragraph (3) of this regulation commits an offence and is liable on summary conviction to a fine not exceeding level 3 on the standard scale.

(10) A qualifying decision, qualifying order or qualifying appointment is not invalid or ineffective if the relevant official fails to comply with paragraph (3) of this regulation.

(11) In this regulation, "relevant officer" means—

(a) in the case of a voluntary arrangement, the supervisor;

(b) in the case of an administration order or the appointment of an administrator, the administrator;

(c) in the case of a creditors' voluntary winding up, the liquidator;

(d) in the case of winding up order, the liquidator;

(e) in the case of an order appointing a provisional liquidator, the provisional liquidator.

[2606]

NOTES

Commencement: 18 February 2004.

12 Notification to creditors: winding up proceedings

(1) When a relevant order or appointment is made, or a relevant decision is taken, in relation to a UK insurer on or after 20th April 2003, the appointed officer must as soon as is reasonably practicable—

(a) notify all known creditors of that insurer in writing of—

(i) the matters mentioned in paragraph (4), and

(ii) the matters mentioned in paragraph (5); and

(b) notify all known insurance creditors of that insurer in writing of the matters mentioned in paragraph 6,

in any case.

(2) The appointed officer may comply with the requirement in paragraph (1)(a)(i) and the requirement in paragraph (1)(a)(ii) by separate notifications.

(3) For the purposes of this regulation—

(a) "relevant order" means—

(i) an administration order made under section 8 of the 1986 Act before 15th September 2003, or made on or after that date under paragraph 13 of Schedule B1 in the prescribed circumstances,

(ii) a winding up order under section 125 of the 1986 Act (powers of the court on hearing a petition) or Article 105 of the 1989 Order (powers of High Court on hearing of petition),

(iii) the appointment of a liquidator in accordance with section 138 of the 1986 Act (appointment of a liquidator in Scotland), and

(iv) an order appointing a provisional liquidator in accordance with section 135 of that Act or Article 115 of the 1989 Order;

(b) "relevant appointment" means the appointment of a liquidator as mentioned in section 100 of the 1986 Act or Article 86 of the 1989 Order (appointment of liquidator in a creditors' voluntary winding up); and

(c) "relevant decision" means a decision as a result of which a qualifying voluntary arrangement has effect.

(4) The matters which must be notified to all known creditors in accordance with paragraph (1)(a)(i) are as follows—

(a) that a relevant order or appointment has been made, or a relevant decision taken, in relation to the UK insurer; and

(b) the date from which that order, appointment or decision has effect.

(5) The matters which must be notified to all known creditors in accordance with paragraph (1)(a)(ii) are as follows—

(a) if applicable, the date by which a creditor must submit his claim in writing;

(b) the matters which must be stated in a creditor's claim;

(c) details of any category of debt in relation to which a claim is not required;

(d) the person to whom any such claim or any observations on a claim must be submitted; and

(e) the consequences of any failure to submit a claim by any specified deadline.

(6) The matters which must be notified to all known insurance creditors, in accordance with paragraph (1)(b), are as follows—

(a) the effect which the relevant order, appointment or decision will, or is likely, to have on the kind of contract of insurance under, or in connection with, which that creditor's insurance claim against the insurer is founded; and

(b) the date from which any variation (resulting from the relevant order or relevant decision) to the risks covered by, or the sums recoverable under, that contract has effect.

(7) Subject to paragraph (8), where a creditor is notified in accordance with paragraph (1)(a)(ii), the notification must be headed with the words "Invitation to lodge a claim: time limits to be observed", and that heading must be given in—

(a) the official language, or one of the official languages, of the EEA State in which that creditor is ordinarily resident; or

(b) every official language.

(8) Where a creditor notified in accordance with paragraph (1) is—

(a) an insurance creditor; and

(b) ordinarily resident in an EEA State,

the notification must be given in the official language, or one of the official languages, of that EEA State.

(9) The obligation under paragraph (1)(a)(ii) may be discharged by sending a form of proof in accordance with Rule 4.74 of the Insolvency Rules, Rule 4.080 of the Insolvency Rules (Northern Ireland) or Rule 4.15(2) of the Insolvency (Scotland) Rules as applicable in cases where any of those rules applies, provided that the form of proof complies with paragraph (7) or (8) (whichever is applicable).

(10) The prescribed circumstances are where the administrator includes in the statement of required under Rule 2.2 of the Insolvency Rules 1986 a statement to the effect that the objective set out in paragraph 3(1)(a) of Schedule BI is not reasonably likely to be achieved.

(11) Where, after the appointment of an administrator, the administrator concludes that it is not reasonably practicable to achieve the objective specified in paragraph 3(1)(a) of Schedule B1, he shall inform the court and the Authority in writing of that conclusion and upon so doing the order by which he was appointed shall be a relevant order for the purposes of this regulation and the obligation under paragraph (1) shall apply as from the date on which he so informs the court and the Authority.

(12) An appointed officer commits an offence if he fails without reasonable excuse to comply with an applicable requirement under this regulation, and is liable on summary conviction to a fine not exceeding level 3 on the standard scale.

(13) For the purposes of this regulation—

(a) "appointed officer" means—

(i) in the case of a relevant order falling within paragraph (3)(a)(i) or a relevant appointment falling within paragraph (3)(b)(i), the administrator,

(ii) in the case of a relevant order falling within paragraph (3)(a)(ii) or (iii) or a relevant appointment falling within paragraph (3)(b)(ii), the liquidator,

(iii) in the case of a relevant order falling within paragraph (3)(a)(iv), the provisional liquidator, or

(iv) in the case of a relevant decision, the supervisor; and

(b) a creditor is a "known" creditor if the appointed officer is aware, or should reasonably be aware of—

(i) his identity,

(ii) his claim or potential claim, and

(iii) a recent address where he is likely to receive a communication.

(14) For the purposes of paragraph (3), and of regulations 13 and 14, a voluntary arrangement is a qualifying voluntary arrangement if its purposes include a realisation of some or all of the assets of the UK insurer to which the order relates and a distribution of the proceeds to creditors, with a view to terminating the whole or any part of the business of that insurer.

[2607]

NOTES

Commencement: 18 February 2004.

13 Submission of claims by EEA creditors

(1) An EEA creditor who on or after 20th April 2003 submits a claim or observations relating to his claim in any relevant proceedings (irrespective of when those proceedings were commenced or had effect) may do so in his domestic language, provided that the requirements in paragraphs (3) and (4) are complied with.

(2) For the purposes of this regulation, "relevant proceedings" means—

(a) a winding up;
(b) a qualifying voluntary arrangement;
(c) administration.

(3) Where an EEA creditor submits a claim in his domestic language, the document must be headed with the words "Lodgement of claim" (in English).

(4) Where an EEA creditor submits observations on his claim (otherwise than in the document by which he submits his claim), the observations must be headed with the words "Submission of observations relating to claims" (in English).

(5) Paragraph (3) does not apply where an EEA creditor submits his claim using—

(a) in the case of a winding up, a form of proof supplied by the liquidator in accordance with Rule 4.74 of the Insolvency Rules, Rule 4.080 of the Insolvency Rules (Northern Ireland) or rule 4.15(2) of the Insolvency (Scotland) Rules as the case may be;
(b) in the case of a qualifying voluntary arrangement, a form approved by the court for that purpose.

(6) In this regulation—

(a) "domestic language", in relation to an EEA creditor, means the official language, or one of the official languages, of the EEA State in which he is ordinarily resident or, if the creditor is not an individual, in which the creditor's head office is located; and
(b) "qualifying voluntary arrangement" has the meaning given by regulation 12(12).

[2608]

NOTES

Commencement: 18 February 2004.

14 Reports to creditors

(1) This regulation applies where, on or after 20th April 2003—

(a) a liquidator is appointed in accordance with section 100 of the 1986 Act or Article 86 of the 1989 Order (creditors' voluntary winding up: appointment of liquidator) or, on or after 15th September 2003, paragraph 83 of Schedule B1 (moving from administration to creditors' voluntary liquidation);
(b) a winding up order is made by the court;
(c) a provisional liquidator is appointed; or
(d) [an administrator is appointed under paragraph 13 of Schedule B1].

(2) The liquidator or provisional liquidator (as the case may be) must send to every known creditor a report once in every 12 months beginning with the date when his appointment has effect.

(3) The requirement in paragraph (2) does not apply where a liquidator or provisional liquidator is required by order of the court to send a report to creditors at intervals which are more frequent than those required by this regulation.

(4) This regulation is without prejudice to any requirement to send a report to creditors, imposed by the court on the liquidator or provisional liquidator, which is supplementary to the requirements of this regulation.

(5) A liquidator or provisional liquidator commits an offence if he fails without reasonable excuse to comply with an applicable requirement under this regulation, and is liable on summary conviction to a fine not exceeding level 3 on the standard scale.

(6) For the purposes of this regulation—

(a) "known creditor" means—

(i) a creditor who is known to the liquidator or provisional liquidator, and

(ii) in a case falling within paragraph (1)(b) or (c), a creditor who is specified in the insurer's statement of affairs (within the meaning of section 131 of the 1986 Act or Article 111 of the 1989 Order); and

(b) "report" means a written report setting out the position generally as regards the progress of the winding up or provisional liquidation (as the case may be).

[2609]

NOTES

Commencement: 18 February 2004.

Para (1): words in square brackets substituted by the Insurers (Reorganisation and Winding Up) (Amendment) Regulations 2004, SI 2004/546, reg 2(1), (3).

15 Service of notices and documents

(1) This regulation applies to any notification, report or other document which is required to be sent to a creditor of a UK insurer by a provision of this Part ("a relevant notification").

(2) A relevant notification may be sent to a creditor by either of the following methods—

(a) posting it to the proper address of the creditor;

(b) transmitting it electronically, in accordance with paragraph (4).

(3) For the purposes of paragraph (2)(a), the proper address of a creditor is any current address provided by that creditor as an address for service of a relevant notification or, if no such address is provided—

(a) the last known address of that creditor (whether his residence or a place where he carries on business);

(b) in the case of a body corporate, the address of its registered or principal office; or

(c) in the case of an unincorporated association, the address of its principal office.

(4) A relevant notification may be transmitted electronically only if it is sent to—

(a) an electronic address notified to the relevant officer by the creditor for this purpose; or

(b) if no such address has been notified, an electronic address at which the relevant officer reasonably believes the creditor will receive the notification.

(5) Any requirement in this part to send a relevant notification to a creditor shall also be treated as satisfied if—

(a) the creditor has agreed with—

(i) the UK insurer which is liable under the creditor's claim, or

(ii) the relevant officer,

that information which is required to be sent to him (whether pursuant to a statutory or contractual obligation, or otherwise) may instead be accessed by him on a web site;

(b) the agreement applies to the relevant notification in question;

(c) the creditor is notified of—

(i) the publication of the relevant notification on a web site,

(ii) the address of that web site,

(iii) the place on that web site where the relevant notification may be accessed, and how it may be accessed; and

(d) the relevant notification is published on that web site throughout a period of at least one month beginning with the date on which the creditor is notified in accordance with sub-paragraph (c):

(6) Where, in a case in which paragraph (5) is relied on for compliance with a requirement of regulation 12 or 14—

(a) a relevant notification is published for a part, but not all, of the period mentioned in paragraph (5)(d); but

(b) the failure to publish it throughout that period is wholly attributable to circumstances which it would not be reasonable to have expected the relevant officer to prevent or avoid,

no offence is committed under regulation 12(10) or regulation 14(5) (as the case may be) by reason of that failure.

(7) In this regulation—

(a) "electronic address" includes any number or address used for the purposes of receiving electronic communications;

(b) "electronic communication" means an electronic communication within the meaning of the Electronic Communications Act 2000 the processing of which on receipt is intended to produce writing; and

(c) "relevant officer" means (as the case may be) an administrator, liquidator, provisional liquidator or supervisor who is required to send a relevant notification to a creditor by a provision of this Part.

[2610]

NOTES

Commencement: 18 February 2004.

16 Disclosure of confidential information received from an EEA regulator

(1) This regulation applies to information ("insolvency information") which—

(a) relates to the business or affairs of any other person; and

(b) is supplied to the Authority by an EEA regulator acting in accordance with Articles 5, 8 or 30 of the reorganisation and winding up directive.

(2) Subject to paragraphs (3) and (4), sections 348, 349 and 352 of the 2000 Act apply in relation to insolvency information in the same way as they apply in relation to confidential information within the meaning of section 348(2) of the 2000 Act.

(3) Insolvency information is not subject to the restrictions on disclosure imposed by section 348(1) of the 2000 Act (as it applies by virtue of paragraph (2)) if it satisfies any of the criteria set out in section 348(4) of the 2000 Act.

(4) The Disclosure Regulations apply in relation to insolvency information as they apply in relation to single market directive information (within the meaning of those Regulations).

(5) In this regulation, "the Disclosure Regulations" means the Financial Services and Markets Act 2000 (Disclosure of Confidential Information) Regulations 2001.

[2611]

NOTES

Commencement: 18 February 2004.

PART IV
PRIORITY OF PAYMENT OF INSURANCE CLAIMS IN WINDING UP ETC

17 Interpretation of this Part

(1) For the purposes of this Part—

"composite insurer" means a UK insurer who is authorised to carry on both general business and long term business, in accordance with article 18(2) of the life insurance directive;

"floating charge" has the meaning given by section 251 of the 1986 Act or paragraph (1) of Article 5 of the 1989 Order;

"general business" means the business of effecting or carrying out a contract of general insurance;

"general business assets" means the assets of a composite insurer which are, or should properly be, apportioned to that insurer's general business, in accordance with the requirements of Article 18(3) of the life insurance directive (separate management of long term and general business of a composite insurer);

"general business liabilities" means the debts of a composite insurer which are attributable to the general business carried on by that insurer;

"general insurer" means a UK insurer who carries on exclusively general business;

"long term business" means the business of effecting or carrying out a contract of long term insurance;

"long term business assets" means the assets of a composite insurer which are, or should properly be, apportioned to that insurer's long term business, in accordance with the requirements of Article 18(3) of the first life insurance directive (separate management of long term and general business of a composite insurer);

"long term business liabilities" means the debts of a composite insurer which are attributable to the long term business carried on by that insurer;

"long term insurer" means a UK insurer who—

(a) carries on long term business exclusively, or

(b) carries on long term business and permitted general business;

"non-transferring composite insurer" means a composite insurer the long term business of which has not been, and is not to be, transferred as a going concern to a person who may lawfully carry out those contracts, in accordance with section 376(2) of the 2000 Act;

"other assets" means any assets of a composite insurer which are not long term business assets or general business assets;

"other business", in relation to a composite insurer, means such of the business (if any) of the insurer as is not long term business or general business;

"permitted general business" means the business of effecting or carrying out a contract of general insurance where the risk insured against relates to either accident or sickness;

"preferential debt" means a debt falling into any of categories 4 or 5 of the debts listed in Schedule 6 to the 1986 Act or Schedule 4 to the 1989 Order, that is—

(a) contributions to occupational pension schemes, etc, and

(b) remuneration etc of employees;

"society" means—

(a) a friendly society incorporated under the Friendly Societies Act 1992,

(b) a society which is a friendly society within the meaning of section 7(1)(a) of the Friendly Societies Act 1974, and registered within the meaning of that Act, or

(c) an industrial and provident society registered or deemed to be registered under the Industrial and Provident Societies Act 1965 or the Industrial and Provident Societies Act (Northern Ireland) 1969.

(2) In this Part, references to assets include a reference to proceeds where an asset has been realised, and any other sums representing assets.

(3) References in paragraph (1) to a contract of long term or of general insurance must be read with—

(a) section 22 of the 2000 Act;

(b) any relevant order made under that section; and

(c) Schedule 2 to that Act.

[2612]

NOTES

Commencement: 18 February 2004.

---

18 Application of regulations 19 to 27

(1) Subject to paragraph (2), regulations 19 to 27 apply in the winding up of a UK insurer where—

(a) in the case of a winding up by the court, the winding up order is made on or after 20th April 2003; or

(b) in the case of a creditors' voluntary winding up, the liquidator is appointed, as mentioned in section 100 of the 1986 Act, paragraph 83 of Schedule B1 or Article 86 of the 1989 Order, on or after 20th April 2003.

(2) Where a relevant section 425 or Article 418 compromise or arrangement is in place,

(a) no winding up proceedings may be opened without the permission of the court, and

(b) the permission of the court is to be granted only if required by the exceptional circumstances of the case.

(3) For the purposes of paragraph (2), winding up proceedings include proceedings for a winding up order or for a creditors' voluntary liquidation with confirmation by the court.

(4) Regulations 20 to 27 do not apply to a winding up falling within paragraph (1) where, in relation to a UK insurer—

(a) an administration order was made before 20th April 2003, and that order is not discharged until the commencement date; or

(b) a provisional liquidator was appointed before 20th April 2003, and that appointment is not discharged until the commencement date.

(5) For purposes of this regulation, "the commencement date" means the date when a UK insurer goes into liquidation within the meaning given by section 247(2) of the 1986 Act or Article 6(2) of the 1989 Order.

[2613]

NOTES

Commencement: 18 February 2004.

19 Application of this Part: assets subject to a section 425 or Article 418 compromise or arrangement

(1) For the purposes of this Part, the insolvent estate of a UK insurer shall not include any assets which at the commencement date are subject to a relevant section 425 or Article 418 compromise or arrangement.

(2) In this regulation—

(a) "assets" has the same meaning as "property" in section 436 of the 1986 Act or Article 2(2) of the 1989 Order;

(b) "commencement date" has the meaning given in [regulation 18(5)];

(c) "insolvent estate"—

(i) in England, Wales and Northern Ireland has the meaning given by Rule 13.8 of the Insolvency Rules or Rule 0.2 of the Insolvency Rules (Northern Ireland), and

(ii) in Scotland means the company's assets;

(d) "relevant section 425 or Article 418 compromise or arrangement" means

(i) a section 425 or Article 418 compromise or arrangement which was sanctioned by the court before 20th April 2003, or

(ii) any subsequent section 425 or Article 418 compromise or arrangement sanctioned by the court to amend or replace a compromise or arrangement of a kind mentioned in paragraph (i).

[2614]

NOTES

Commencement: 18 February 2004.

Para (2): words in square brackets in sub-para (b) substituted by the Insurers (Reorganisation and Winding Up) (Lloyd's) Regulations 2005, SI 2005/1998, reg 49.

20 Preferential debts: disapplication of section 175 of the 1986 Act or Article 149 of the 1989 Order

Except to the extent that they are applied by regulation 27, section 175 of the 1986 Act or Article 149 of the 1989 Order (preferential debts (general provision)) does not apply in the case of a winding up of a UK insurer, and instead the provisions of regulations 21 to 26 have effect.

[2615]

NOTES

Commencement: 18 February 2004.

21 Preferential debts: long term insurers and general insurers

(1) This regulation applies in the case of a winding up of—

(a) a long term insurer;

(b) a general insurer;

(c) a composite insurer, where the long term business of that insurer has been or is to be transferred as a going concern to a person who may lawfully carry out the contracts in that long term business in accordance with section 376(2) of the 2000 Act.

(2) Subject to paragraph (3), the debts of the insurer must be paid in the following order of priority—

(a) preferential debts;

(b) insurance debts;
(c) all other debts.

(3) Preferential debts rank equally among themselves [after the expenses of the winding up] and must be paid in full, unless the assets are insufficient to meet them, in which case they abate in equal proportions.

(4) Insurance debts rank equally among themselves and must be paid in full, unless the assets available after the payment of preferential debts are insufficient to meet them, in which case they abate in equal proportions.

(5) Subject to paragraph (6), so far as the assets of the insurer available for the payment of unsecured creditors are insufficient to meet the preferential debts, those debts (and only those debts) have priority over the claims of holders of debentures secured by, or holders of, any floating charge created by the insurer, and must be paid accordingly out of any property comprised in or subject to that charge.

(6) The order of priority specified in paragraph (2)(a) and (b) applies for the purposes of any payment made in accordance with paragraph (5).

(7) Section 176A of the 1986 Act has effect with regard to an insurer so that insurance debts must be paid out of the prescribed part in priority to all other unsecured debts.

[2616]

NOTES

Commencement: 18 February 2004.

Para (3): words in square brackets inserted by the Insurers (Reorganisation and Winding Up) (Amendment) Regulations 2004, SI 2004/546, reg 2(1), (4).

22 Composite insurers: preferential debts attributable to long term and general business

(1) This regulation applies in the case of the winding up of a non-transferring composite insurer.

(2) Subject to the payment of costs in accordance with regulation 30, the long term business assets and the general business assets must be applied separately in accordance with paragraphs (3) and (4).

(3) Subject to paragraph (6), the long term business assets must be applied in discharge of the long term business preferential debts in the order of priority specified in regulation 23(1).

(4) Subject to paragraph (8), the general business assets must be applied in discharge of the general business preferential debts in the order of priority specified in regulation 24(1).

(5) Paragraph (6) applies where the value of the long term business assets exceeds the long term business preferential debts and the general business assets are insufficient to meet the general business preferential debts.

(6) Those long term business assets which represent the excess must be applied in discharge of the outstanding general business preferential debts of the insurer, in accordance with the order of priority specified in regulation 24(1).

(7) Paragraph (8) applies where the value of the general business assets exceeds the general business preferential debts, and the long term business assets are insufficient to meet the long term business preferential debts.

(8) Those general business assets which represent the excess must be applied in discharge of the outstanding long term business preferential debts of the insurer, in accordance with the order of priority specified in regulation 23(1).

(9) For the purposes of this regulation and regulations 23 and 24—

"long term business preferential debts" means those debts mentioned in regulation 23(1) and, unless the court orders otherwise, any expenses of the winding up which are apportioned to the long term business assets in accordance with regulation 30;

"general business preferential debts" means those debts mentioned in regulation 24(1) and, unless the court orders otherwise, any expenses of the winding up which are apportioned to the general business assets in accordance with regulation 30.

(10) For the purposes of paragraphs (6) and (8)—

"outstanding long term business preferential debts" means those long term business preferential debts, if any, which remain unpaid, either in whole or in part, after the application of the long term business assets, in accordance with paragraph (3);

"outstanding general business preferential debts" means those general business preferential debts, if any, which remain unpaid, either in whole or in part, after the application of the general business assets, in accordance with paragraph (3).

[2617]

NOTES

Commencement: 18 February 2004.

23 Preferential debts: long term business of a non-transferring composite insurer

(1) For the purpose of compliance with the requirement in regulation 22(3), the long term business assets of a non-transferring composite insurer must be applied in discharge of the following debts and in the following order of priority—

(a) relevant preferential debts;

(b) long term insurance debts.

(2) Relevant preferential debts rank equally among themselves, unless the long term business assets, any available general business assets and other assets (if any) applied in accordance with regulation 24 are insufficient to meet them, in which case they abate in equal proportions.

(3) Long term insurance debts rank equally among themselves, unless the long term business assets available after the payment of relevant preferential debts and any available general business assets and other assets (if any) applied in accordance with regulation 25 are insufficient to meet them, in which case they abate in equal proportions.

(4) So far as the long term business assets, and any available general business assets, which are available for the payment of unsecured creditors are insufficient to meet the relevant preferential debts, those debts (and only those debts) have priority over the claims of holders of debentures secured by, or holders of, any floating charge created by the insurer over any of its long term business assets, and must be paid accordingly out of any property comprised in or subject to that charge.

(5) The order of priority specified in paragraph (1) applies for the purposes of any payment made in accordance with paragraph (4).

(6) For the purposes of this regulation—

"available general business assets" means those general business assets which must be applied in discharge of the insurer's outstanding long term business preferential debts, in accordance with regulation 22(8);

"long term insurance debt" means an insurance debt which is attributable to the long term business of the insurer;

"relevant preferential debt" means a preferential debt which is attributable to the long term business of the insurer.

[2618]

NOTES

Commencement: 18 February 2004.

24 Preferential debts: general business of a composite insurer

(1) For the purpose of compliance with the requirement in regulation 22(4), the long term business assets of a non-transferring composite insurer must be applied in discharge of the following debts and in the following order of priority—

(a) relevant preferential debts;

(b) general insurance debts.

(2) Relevant preferential debts rank equally among themselves, unless the general business assets, any available long term business assets, and other assets (if any) applied in accordance with regulation 25 are insufficient to meet them, in which case they abate in equal proportions.

(3) General insurance debts rank equally among themselves, unless the general business assets available after the payment of relevant preferential debts, any available long term

business assets, and other assets (if any) applied in accordance with regulation 26 are insufficient to meet them, in which case they abate in equal proportions.

(4) So far as the other business assets and available long term assets of the insurer which are available for the payment of unsecured creditors are insufficient to meet relevant preferential debts, those debts (and only those debts) have priority over the claims of holders of debentures secured by, or holders of, any floating charge created by the insurer, and must be paid accordingly out of any property comprised in or subject to that charge.

(5) The order of priority specified in paragraph (1) applies for the purposes of any payment made in accordance with paragraph (4).

(6) For the purposes of this regulation—

"available long term business assets" means those long term business assets which must be applied in discharge of the insurer's outstanding general business preferential debts, in accordance with regulation 22(6);

"general insurance debt" means an insurance debt which is attributable to the general business of the insurer;

"relevant preferential debt" means a preferential debt which is attributable to the general business of the insurer.

[2619]

NOTES

Commencement: 18 February 2004.

25 Insufficiency of long term business assets and general business assets

(1) This regulation applies in the case of the winding up of a non-transferring composite insurer where the long term business assets and the general business assets, applied in accordance with regulation 22, are insufficient to meet in full the preferential debts and insurance debts.

(2) In a case in which this regulation applies, the other assets (if any) of the insurer must be applied in the following order of priority—

(a) outstanding preferential debts;
(b) unattributed preferential debts;
(c) outstanding insurance debts;
(d) all other debts.

(3) So far as the long term business assets, and any available general business assets, which are available for the payment of unsecured creditors are insufficient to meet the outstanding preferential debts and the unattributed preferential debts, those debts (and only those debts) have priority over the claims of holders of debentures secured by, or holders of, any floating charge created by the insurer over any of its other assets, and must be paid accordingly out of any property comprised in or subject to that charge.

(4) For the purposes of this regulation—

"outstanding insurance debt" means any insurance debt, or any part of an insurance debt, which was not discharged by the application of the long term business assets and the general business assets in accordance with regulation 22;

"outstanding preferential debt" means any preferential debt attributable either to the long term business or the general business of the insurer which was not discharged by the application of the long term business assets and the general business assets in accordance with regulation 23;

"unattributed preferential debt" means a preferential debt which is not attributable to either the long term business or the general business of the insurer.

[2620]

NOTES

Commencement: 18 February 2004.

26 Composite insurers: excess of long term business assets and general business assets

(1) This regulation applies in the case of the winding up of a non-transferring composite insurer where the value of the long term business assets and the general business assets, applied in accordance with regulation 22, exceeds the value of the sum of the long term business preferential debts and the general business preferential debts.

(2) In a case to which this regulation applies, long term business assets or general business assets which have not been applied in discharge of long term business preferential debts or general business preferential debts must be applied in accordance with regulation 27.

(3) In this regulation, "long term business preferential debts" and "general business preferential debts" have the same meaning as in regulation 22.

[2621]

NOTES

Commencement: 18 February 2004.

27 Composite insurers: application of other assets

(1) This regulation applies in the case of the winding up of a non-transferring composite insurer where regulation 25 does not apply.

(2) The other assets of the insurer, together with any outstanding business assets, must be paid in discharge of the following debts in accordance with section 175 of the 1986 Act or Article 149 of the 1989 Order—

(a) unattributed preferential debts;

(b) all other debts.

(3) In this regulation—

"unattributed preferential debt" has the same meaning as in regulation 25;

"outstanding business assets" means assets of the kind mentioned in regulation 26(2).

[2622]

NOTES

Commencement: 18 February 2004.

28 Composite insurers: proof of debts

(1) This regulation applies in the case of the winding up of a non-transferring composite insurer in compliance with the requirement in regulation 23(2).

(2) The liquidator may in relation to the insurer's long term business assets and its general business assets fix different days on or before which the creditors of the company who are required to prove their debts or claims are to prove their debts or claims, and he may fix one of those days without at the same time fixing the other.

(3) In submitting a proof of any debt a creditor may claim the whole or any part of such debt as is attributable to the company's long term business or to its general business, or he may make no such attribution.

(4) When he admits any debt, in whole or in part, the liquidator must state in writing how much of what he admits is attributable to the company's long term business, how much is attributable to the company's general business, and how much is attributable to its other business (if any).

(5) Paragraph (2) does not apply in Scotland.

[2623]

NOTES

Commencement: 18 February 2004.

29 Composite insurers: general meetings of creditors

(1) This regulation applies in the same circumstances as regulation 28.

(2) The creditors mentioned in section 168(2) of the 1986 Act, Article 143(2) of the 1989 Order or rule 4.13 of the Insolvency (Scotland) Rules (power of liquidator to summon general meetings of creditors) are to be—

(a) in relation to the long term business assets of that insurer, only those who are creditors in respect of long term business liabilities; and

(b) in relation to the general business assets of that insurer, only those who are creditors in respect of general business liabilities;

and, accordingly, any general meetings of creditors summoned for the purposes of that section, Article or rule are to be separate general meetings of creditors in respect of long term business liabilities and general business liabilities.

[2624]

NOTES

Commencement: 18 February 2004.

30 Composite insurers: apportionment of costs payable out of the assets

(1) In the case of the winding up of a non-transferring composite insurer, Rule 4.218 of the Insolvency Rules or Rule 4.228 of the Insolvency Rules (Northern Ireland) (general rules as to priority) or rule 4.67 (order of priority of expenses of liquidation) of the Insolvency (Scotland) Rules applies separately to long-term business assets and to the general business assets of that insurer.

(2) But where any fee, expense, cost, charge, or remuneration does not relate exclusively to the long-term business assets or to the general business assets of that insurer, the liquidator must apportion it amongst those assets in such manner as he shall determine.

[2625]

NOTES

Commencement: 18 February 2004.

31 Summary remedy against liquidators

Section 212 of the 1986 Act or Article 176 of the 1989 Order (summary remedy against delinquent directors, liquidators etc) applies in relation to a liquidator who is required to comply with regulations 21 to 27, as it applies in relation to a liquidator who is required to comply with section 175 of the 1986 Act or Article 149 of the 1989 Order.

[2626]

NOTES

Commencement: 18 February 2004.

32 Priority of subrogated claims by the Financial Services Compensation Scheme

(1) This regulation applies where an insurance creditor has assigned a relevant right to the scheme manager ("a relevant assignment").

(2) For the purposes of regulations 21, 23 and 24, where the scheme manager proves for an insurance debt in the winding up of a UK insurer pursuant to a relevant assignment, that debt must be paid to the scheme manager in the same order of priority as any other insurance debt.

(3) In this regulation—

"relevant right" means any direct right of action against a UK insurer under a contract of insurance, including the right to prove for a debt under that contract in a winding up of that insurer;

"scheme manager" has the meaning given by section 212(1) of the 2000 Act.

[2627]

NOTES

Commencement: 18 February 2004.

33 Voluntary arrangements: treatment of insurance debts

(1) The modifications made by paragraph (2) apply where a voluntary arrangement is proposed under section 1 of the 1986 Act or Article 14 of the 1989 Order in relation to a UK insurer, and that arrangement includes—

(a) a composition in satisfaction of any insurance debts; and

(b) a distribution to creditors of some or all of the assets of that insurer in the course of, or with a view to, terminating the whole or any part of the business of that insurer.

(2) Section 4 of the 1986 Act (decisions of meetings) has effect as if—
(a) after subsection (4) there were inserted—

"(4A) A meeting so summoned and taking place on or after 20th April 2003 shall not approve any proposal or modification under which any insurance debt of the company is to be paid otherwise than in priority to such of its debts as are not insurance debts or preferential debts.

(4B) Paragraph (4A) does not apply where—
(a) a winding up order made before 20th April 2003 is in force; or
(b) a relevant insolvency appointment made before 20th April 2003 has effect,

in relation to the company.";
(b) for subsection (7) there were substituted—

"(7) References in this section to preferential debts mean debts falling into any of categories 4 and 5 of the debts listed in Schedule 6 to this Act; and references to preferential creditors are to be construed accordingly."; and
(c) after subsection (7) as so substituted there were inserted—

"(8) For the purposes of this section—
(a) "insurance debt" has the meaning it has in the Insurers (Reorganisation and Winding up) Regulations 2004; and
(b) "relevant insolvency measure" means—
(i) the appointment of a provisional liquidator, or
(ii) the appointment of an administrator,

where an effect of the appointment will be, or is intended to be, a realisation of some or all of the assets of the insurer and the distribution of the proceeds to creditors, with a view to terminating the whole or any part of the business of that insurer."

(3) Article 17 of the 1989 Order (decisions of meetings) has effect as if—
(a) after paragraph (4) there were inserted—

"(4A) A meeting so summoned and taking place on or after 20th April 2003 shall not approve any proposal or modification under which any insurance debt of the company is to be paid otherwise than in priority to such of its debts as are not insurance debts or preferential debts.

(4B) Paragraph (4A) does not apply where—
(a) a winding up order made before 20th April 2003 is in force; or
(b) a relevant insolvency appointment made before 20th April 2003 has effect, in relation to the company.";
(b) for paragraph (7) there were substituted—

"(7) References in this Article to preferential debts mean debts falling into any of categories 4 and 5 of the debts listed in Schedule 4 to this Order, and references to preferential creditors are to be construed accordingly."; and
(c) after paragraph (7) as so substituted there were inserted—

"(8) For the purposes of this section—
(a) "insurance debt" has the meaning it has in the Insurers (Reorganisation and Winding Up) Regulations 2004 and
(b) "relevant insolvency measure" means—
(i) the appointment of a provisional liquidator, or
(ii) the appointment of an administrator,

where an effect of the appointment will be, or is intended to be, a realisation of some or all of the assets of the insurer and the distribution of the proceeds to creditors, with a view to terminating the whole or any part of the business of that insurer.".

[2628]

NOTES

Commencement: 18 February 2004.

PART V
REORGANISATION OR WINDING UP OF UK INSURERS: RECOGNITION OF EEA RIGHTS

34 Application of this Part

(1) This Part applies—

(a) where a decision with respect to the approval of a proposed voluntary arrangement having a qualifying purpose is made under section 4A of the 1986 Act or Article 17A of the 1989 Order on or after 20th April 2003 in relation to a UK insurer;

(b) where an administration order made under section 8 of the 1986 Act on or after 20th April 2003 or, on or after 15th September 2003, made under paragraph 13 of Schedule B1 is in force in relation to a UK insurer;

(c) where on or after 20th April 2003 the court reduces the value of one or more of the contracts of a UK insurer under section 377 of the 2000 Act or section 24(5) of the Friendly Societies Act 1992;

(d) where a UK insurer is subject to a relevant winding up;

(e) where a provisional liquidator is appointed in relation to a UK insurer on or after 20th April 2003.

(2) For the purposes of paragraph (1)(a), a voluntary arrangement has a qualifying purpose if it—

(a) varies the rights of the creditors as against the insurer and is intended to enable the insurer, and the whole or any part of its undertaking, to survive as a going concern; or

(b) includes a realisation of some or all of the assets of the insurer to which it relates and the distribution of the proceeds to creditors, with a view to terminating the whole or any part of the business of that insurer.

(3) For the purposes of paragraph (1)(d), a winding up is a relevant winding up if—

(a) in the case of a winding up by the court, the winding up order is made on or after 20th April 2003; or

(b) in the case of a creditors' voluntary winding up, the liquidator is appointed in accordance with section 100 of the 1986 Act, paragraph 83 of Schedule B1 or Article 86 of the 1989 Order on or after 20th April 2003.

[2629]

NOTES

Commencement: 18 February 2004.

35 Application of this Part: assets subject to a section 425 or Article 418 compromise or arrangement

(1) For the purposes of this Part, the insolvent estate of a UK insurer shall not include any assets which at the commencement date are subject to a relevant section 425 or Article 418 compromise or arrangement.

(2) In this regulation—

(a) "assets" has the same meaning as "property" in section 436 of the 1986 Act or Article 2(2) of the 1989 Order;

(b) "commencement date" has the meaning given in regulation 18(4);

(c) "insolvent estate" in England and Wales and Northern Ireland has the meaning given by Rule 13.8 of the Insolvency Rules or Rule 0.2 of the Insolvency Rules (Northern Ireland) and in Scotland means the company's assets;

(d) "relevant section 425 or Article 418 compromise or arrangement" means—

(i) a section 425 or Article 418 compromise or arrangement which was sanctioned by the court before 20th April 2003, or

(ii) any subsequent section 425 or Article 418 compromise or arrangement sanctioned by the court to amend or replace a compromise or arrangement of the kind mentioned in paragraph (i).

[2630]

NOTES

Commencement: 18 February 2004.

PART III
STATUTORY INSTRUMENTS

36 Interpretation of this Part

(1) For the purposes of this Part—

(a) "affected insurer" means a UK insurer which is the subject of a relevant reorganisation or a relevant winding up;

(b) "relevant reorganisation or a relevant winding up" means any voluntary arrangement, administration order, winding up, or order referred to in regulation 34(1)(d) t o which this Part applies; and

(c) "relevant time" means the date of the opening of a relevant reorganisation or a relevant winding up.

(2) In this Part, references to the opening of a relevant reorganisation or a relevant winding up mean—

(a) in the case of winding up proceedings—

(i) in the case of a winding up by the court, the date on which the winding up order is made, or

(ii) in the case of a creditors' voluntary winding up, the date on which the liquidator is appointed in accordance with section 100 of the 1986 Act, paragraph 83 of Schedule B1 or Article 86 of the 1989 Order;

(b) in the case of a voluntary arrangement, the date when a decision with respect to that voluntary arrangement has effect in accordance with section 4A(2) of the 1986 Act or Article 17A(2) of the 1989 Order;

(c) in a case where an administration order under paragraph 13 of Schedule B1 is in force, the date of the making of that order;

(d) in a case where an administrator is appointed under paragraphs 14 or 22 of Schedule B1 the date on which that appointment takes effect;

(e) in a case where the court reduces the value of one or more of the contracts of a UK insurer under section 377 of the 2000 Act or section 24(5) of the Friendly Societies Act 1992, the date the court exercises that power; and

(f) in a case where a provisional liquidator has been appointed, the date of that appointment,

and references to the time of an opening must be construed accordingly.

[2631]

NOTES

Commencement: 18 February 2004.

37 EEA rights: applicable law in the winding up of a UK insurer

(1) This regulation is subject to the provisions of regulations 38 to 47.

(2) In a relevant winding up, the matters mentioned in paragraph (3) in particular are to be determined in accordance with the general law of insolvency of the United Kingdom.

(3) Those matters are—

(a) the assets which form part of the estate of the affected insurer;

(b) the treatment of assets acquired by, or devolving on, the affected insurer after the opening of the relevant winding up;

(c) the respective powers of the affected insurer and the liquidator or provisional liquidator;

(d) the conditions under which set-off may be revoked;

(e) the effects of the relevant winding up on current contracts to which the affected insurer is a party;

(f) the effects of the relevant winding up on proceedings brought by creditors;

(g) the claims which are to be lodged against the estate of the affected insurer;

(h) the treatment of claims against the affected insurer arising after the opening of the relevant winding up;

(i) the rules governing—

(i) the lodging, verification and admission of claims,

(ii) the distribution of proceeds from the realisation of assets,

(iii) the ranking of claims,

(iv) the rights of creditors who have obtained partial satisfaction after the opening of the relevant winding up by virtue of a right in rem or through set-off;

(j) the conditions for and the effects of the closure of the relevant winding up, in particular by composition;

(k) the rights of creditors after the closure of the relevant winding up;
(l) who is to bear the cost and expenses incurred in the relevant winding up;
(m) the rules relating to the voidness, voidability or unenforceability of legal acts detrimental to all the creditors.

(4) In this regulation, "relevant winding up" has the meaning given by regulation 34(3).

[2632]

NOTES

Commencement: 18 February 2004.

38 Employment contracts and relationships

(1) The effects of a relevant reorganisation or a relevant winding up on any EEA employment contract and any EEA employment relationship are to be determined in accordance with the law of the EEA State to which that contract or that relationship is subject.

(2) In this regulation, an employment contract is an EEA employment contract, and an employment relationship is an EEA employment relationship, if it is subject to the law of an EEA State.

[2633]

NOTES

Commencement: 18 February 2004.

39 Contracts in connection with immovable property

The effects of a relevant reorganisation or a relevant winding up on a contract conferring the right to make use of or acquire immovable property situated within the territory of an EEA State are to be determined in accordance with the law of that State.

[2634]

NOTES

Commencement: 18 February 2004.

40 Registrable rights

The effects of a relevant reorganisation or a relevant winding up on rights of the affected insurer with respect to—

(a) immovable property,
(b) a ship, or
(c) an aircraft

which is subject to registration in a public register kept under the authority of an EEA State are to be determined in accordance with the law of that State.

[2635]

NOTES

Commencement: 18 February 2004.

41 Third parties' rights in rem

(1) A relevant reorganisation or a relevant winding up shall not affect the rights in rem of creditors or third parties in respect of tangible or intangible, movable or immovable assets (including both specific assets and collections of indefinite assets as a whole which change from time to time) belonging to the affected insurer which are situated within the territory of an EEA State at the relevant time.

(2) The rights in rem referred to in paragraph (1) shall in particular include—

(a) the right to dispose of the assets in question or have them disposed of and to obtain satisfaction from the proceeds of or the income from those assets, in particular by virtue of a lien or a mortgage;
(b) the exclusive right to have a claim met out of the assets in question, in particular a right guaranteed by a lien in respect of the claim or by assignment of the claim by way of guarantee;

(c) the right to demand the assets in question from, or to require restitution by, any person having possession or use of them contrary to the wishes of the party otherwise entitled to the assets;

(d) a right in rem to the beneficial use of assets.

(3) A right, recorded in a public register and enforceable against third parties, under which a right in rem within the meaning of paragraph (1) may be obtained, is also to be treated as a right in rem for the purposes of this regulation.

(4) Paragraph (1) does not preclude actions for voidness, voidability or unenforceability of legal acts detrimental to creditors under the general law of insolvency of the United Kingdom, as referred to in regulation 37(3)(m).

[2636]

NOTES

Commencement: 18 February 2004.

42 Reservation of title agreements etc

(1) The opening of a relevant reorganisation or a relevant winding up in relation to an insurer purchasing an asset shall not affect the seller's rights based on a reservation of title where at the time of that opening the asset is situated within the territory of an EEA State.

(2) The opening of a relevant reorganisation or a relevant winding up in relation to an insurer selling an asset, after delivery of the asset, shall not constitute grounds for rescinding or terminating the sale and shall not prevent the purchaser from acquiring title where at the time of that opening the asset sold is situated within the territory of an EEA State.

(3) Paragraphs (1) and (2) do not preclude actions for voidness, voidability or unenforceability of legal acts detrimental to creditors under the general law of insolvency of the United Kingdom, as referred to in regulation 37(3)(m).

[2637]

NOTES

Commencement: 18 February 2004.

43 Creditors' rights to set off

(1) A relevant reorganisation or a relevant winding up shall not affect the right of creditors to demand the set-off of their claims against the claims of the affected insurer, where such a set-off is permitted by the applicable EEA law.

(2) In paragraph (1), "applicable EEA law" means the law of the EEA State which is applicable to the claim of the affected insurer.

(3) Paragraph (1) does not preclude actions for voidness, voidability or unenforceability of legal acts detrimental to creditors under the general law of insolvency of the United Kingdom, as referred to in regulation 37(3)(m).

[2638]

NOTES

Commencement: 18 February 2004.

44 Regulated markets

(1) Without prejudice to regulation 40, the effects of a relevant reorganisation measure or winding up on the rights and obligations of the parties to a regulated market operating in an EEA State must be determined in accordance with the law applicable to that market.

(2) Paragraph (1) does not preclude actions for voidness, voidability or unenforceability of legal acts detrimental to creditors under the general law of insolvency of the United Kingdom, as referred to in regulation 37(3)(m).

(3) For the purposes of this regulation, "regulated market" has the meaning given by Council Directive (93/22/EEC) of 10th May 1993 on investment services in the securities field.

[2639]

NOTES
Commencement: 18 February 2004.

45 Detrimental acts pursuant to the law of an EEA State

(1) In a relevant reorganisation or a relevant winding up, the rules relating to detrimental transactions shall not apply where a person who has benefited from a legal act detrimental to all the creditors provides proof that—

(a) the said act is subject to the law of an EEA State; and
(b) that law does not allow any means of challenging that act in the relevant case.

(2) For the purposes of paragraph (1), "the rules relating to detrimental transactions" means any provisions of the general law of insolvency relating to the voidness, voidability or unenforceability of legal acts detrimental to all the creditors, as referred to in regulation 37(3)(m).

[2640]

NOTES
Commencement: 18 February 2004.

46 Protection of third party purchasers

(1) This regulation applies where, by an act concluded after the opening of a relevant reorganisation or a relevant winding up, an affected insurer disposes for a consideration of—

(a) an immovable asset situated within the territory of an EEA State;
(b) a ship or an aircraft subject to registration in a public register kept under the authority of an EEA State; or
(c) securities whose existence or transfer presupposes entry into a register or account laid down by the law of an EEA State or which are placed in a central deposit system governed by the law of an EEA State.

(2) The validity of that act is to be determined in accordance with the law of the EEA State within whose territory the immovable asset is situated or under whose authority the register, account or system is kept, as the case may be.

[2641]

NOTES
Commencement: 18 February 2004.

47 Lawsuits pending

(1) The effects of a relevant reorganisation or a relevant winding up on a relevant lawsuit pending in an EEA State shall be determined solely in accordance with the law of that EEA State.

(2) In paragraph (1), "relevant lawsuit" means a lawsuit concerning an asset or right of which the affected insurer has been divested.

[2642]

NOTES
Commencement: 18 February 2004.

PART VI
THIRD COUNTRY INSURERS

48 Interpretation of this Part

(1) In this Part—

(a) "relevant measure", in relation to a third country insurer, means
 (i) a winding up;
 (ii) an administration order made under paragraph 13 of Schedule B1; or

(iii) a decision of the court to reduce the value of one or more of the insurer's contracts, in accordance with section 377 of the 2000 Act;

(b) "third country insurer" means a person—
(i) who has permission under the 2000 Act to effect or carry out contracts of insurance; and
(ii) whose head office is not in the United Kingdom or an EEA State.

(2) In paragraph (1), the definition of "third country insurer" must be read with—
(a) section 22 of the 2000 Act;
(b) any relevant order made under that section; and
(c) Schedule 2 to that Act.

[2643]

NOTES
Commencement: 18 February 2004.

49 Application of these Regulations to a third country insurer

Parts III, IV and V of these Regulations apply where a third country insurer is subject to a relevant measure, as if references in those Parts to a UK insurer included a reference to a third country insurer.

[2644]

NOTES
Commencement: 18 February 2004.

50 Disclosure of confidential information: third country insurers

(1) This regulation applies to information ("insolvency practitioner information") which—
(a) relates to the business or other affairs of any person; and
(b) is information of a kind mentioned in paragraph (2).

(2) Information falls within paragraph (1)(b) if it is supplied to—
(a) the Authority by an EEA regulator; or
(b) an insolvency practitioner by an EEA administrator or liquidator,

in accordance with or pursuant to Article 30 of the reorganisation and winding up directive.

(3) Subject to paragraphs (4), (5) and (6), sections 348, 349 and 352 of the 2000 Act apply in relation to insolvency practitioner information in the same way as they apply in relation to confidential information within the meaning of section 348(2) of that Act.

(4) For the purposes of this regulation, sections 348, 349 and 352 of the 2000 Act and the Disclosure Regulations have effect as if the primary recipients specified in subsection (5) of section 348 of the 2000 Act included an insolvency practitioner.

(5) Insolvency practitioner information is not subject to the restrictions on disclosure imposed by section 348(1) of the 2000 Act (as it applies by virtue of paragraph (3)) if it satisfies any of the criteria set out in section 348(4) of the 2000 Act.

(6) The Disclosure Regulations apply in relation to insolvency practitioner information as they apply in relation to single market directive information (within the meaning of those Regulations).

(7) In this regulation—
"the Disclosure Regulations" means the Financial Services and Markets Act 2000 (Disclosure of Confidential Information) Regulations 2001;
"EEA administrator" and "EEA liquidator" mean respectively an administrator or liquidator within the meaning of the reorganisation and winding up directive;
"insolvency practitioner" means an insolvency practitioner, within the meaning of section 388 of the 1986 Act or Article 3 of the 1989 Order, who is appointed or acts in relation to a third country insurer.

[2645]

NOTES
Commencement: 18 February 2004.

PART VII
REVOCATION AND AMENDMENTS

51, 52 *(Reg 51 amends the Insurers (Winding Up) Rules 2001, SI 2001/3635, r 24 and the Insurers (Winding Up) (Scotland) Rules 2001, SI 2001/4040, r 23; reg 52 amends the Financial Services and Markets Act 2000 (Administration Orders Relating to Insurers) Order 2002, SI 2002/1242, reg 3.)*

53 Revocation and Transitional

(1) Except as provided in this regulation, the Insurers (Reorganisation and Winding Up) Regulations 2003 are revoked.

(2) Subject to (3), the provisions of Parts III and IV shall continue in force in respect of decisions orders or appointments referred to therein and made before the coming into force of these Regulations.

(3) Where an administrator has been appointed in respect of a UK insurer on or after 15th September 2003, he shall be treated as being so appointed on the date these regulations come into force.

[2646]

NOTES

Commencement: 18 February 2004.

CREDIT INSTITUTIONS (REORGANISATION AND WINDING UP) REGULATIONS 2004

(SI 2004/1045)

NOTES

Made: 1 April 2004.
Authority: European Communities Act 1972, s 2(2).
Commencement: 5 May 2004.

ARRANGEMENT OF REGULATIONS

PART 1
GENERAL

PART 2
INSOLVENCY MEASURES AND PROCEEDINGS: JURISDICTION IN RELATION TO CREDIT INSTITUTIONS

PART 3
MODIFICATIONS OF THE LAW OF INSOLVENCY: NOTIFICATION AND PUBLICATION

PART III
STATUTORY INSTRUMENTS

PART 1
GENERAL

1 Citation and commencement

These Regulations may be cited as the Credit Institutions (Reorganisation and Winding up) Regulations 2004, and come into force on 5th May 2004.

[2647]

NOTES

Commencement: 5 May 2004.

2 Interpretation

(1) In these Regulations—

"the 1985 Act" means the Companies Act 1985;

"the 1986 Act" means the Insolvency Act 1986;

"the 2000 Act" means the Financial Services and Markets Act 2000;

"the 1989 Order" means the Insolvency (Northern Ireland) Order 1989;

"administrator" has the meaning given by paragraph 13 of Schedule B1 to the 1986 Act or section 8(2) of the 1986 Act as the case may be;

"Article 418 compromise or arrangement" means a compromise or arrangement sanctioned by the court in relation to a UK credit institution under Article 418 of the Companies Order, but does not include a compromise or arrangement falling within Article 420 or Article 420A of that Order (reconstructions or amalgamations);

"the Authority" means the Financial Services Authority;

"banking consolidation directive" means the directive of the European Parliament and the Council of 20 March 2000 relating to the taking up and pursuit of the business of credit institutions (2000/12/EC) as most recently amended by the directive of the European Parliament and the Council of 16 December 2002 on the supplementary supervision of credit institutions, insurance undertakings and investment firms in a financial conglomerate (2002/87/EC);

"branch", in relation to an EEA or UK credit institution has the meaning given by Article 1(3) of the banking consolidation directive;

"claim" means a claim submitted by a creditor of a UK credit institution in the course of—

(a) a winding up,
(b) an administration, or
(c) a voluntary arrangement,

with a view to recovering his debt in whole or in part, and includes a proof, within the meaning of rule 2.72 of the Insolvency Rules, or a proof of debt within the meaning of rule 4.73(4) of the Insolvency Rules or Rule 4.079(4) of the Insolvency Rules (Northern Ireland), as the case may be, or in Scotland a claim made in accordance with rule 4.15 of the Insolvency (Scotland) Rules;

"the Companies Order" means the Companies (Northern Ireland) Order 1986;

"creditors' voluntary winding up" has the meaning given by section 90 of the 1986 Act or Article 76 of the 1989 Order as the case may be;

"debt"—

(a) in relation to a winding up or administration of a UK credit institution, has the meaning given by rule 13.12 of the Insolvency Rules or Article 5(1) of the 1989 Order except that where the credit institution is not a company, references in rule 13.12 or Article 5(1) to a company are to be read as references to the credit institution, and
(b) in a case where a voluntary arrangement has effect, in relation to a UK credit institution, means a debt which would constitute a debt in relation to the winding up of that credit institution, except that references in paragraph (1) of rule 13.12 or paragraph (1) of Article 5 of the 1989 Order to the date on which the company goes into liquidation are to be read as references to the date on which the voluntary arrangement has effect;
(c) in Scotland—
    (i) in relation to the winding up of a UK credit institution, shall be interpreted in accordance with Schedule 1 of the Bankruptcy (Scotland) Act 1985 as applied by Chapter 5 of Part 4 of the Insolvency (Scotland) Rules; and
    (ii) in a case where a voluntary arrangement has effect in relation to a UK credit institution, means a debt which would constitute a debt in relation to the winding up of that credit institution, except that references in Chapter 5 of Part 4 of the Insolvency (Scotland) Rules to the date of commencement of winding up are to be read as references to the date on which the voluntary arrangement has effect;

"directive reorganisation measure" means a reorganisation measure as defined in Article 2 of the reorganisation and winding up directive which was adopted or imposed on or after the 5th May 2004;

"directive winding-up proceedings" means winding-up proceedings as defined in Article 2 of the reorganisation and winding up directive which were opened on or after the 5th May 2004;

"Disclosure Regulations" means the Financial Services and Markets Act 2000 (Disclosure of Confidential Information) Regulations 2001;

"EEA credit institution" means an EEA undertaking, other than a UK credit institution, of the kind mentioned in Article 1(1) and (3) and subject to the conditions in Article 2(3) of the banking consolidation directive;

"EEA creditor" means a creditor of a UK credit institution who—

(a) in the case of an individual, is ordinarily resident in an EEA State; and
(b) in the case of a body corporate or unincorporated association of persons, has its head office in an EEA State;

"EEA regulator" means a competent authority (within the meaning of Article 1(4) of the banking consolidation directive) of an EEA State;

"EEA State" means a State, other than the United Kingdom, which is a contracting party to the agreement on the European Economic Area signed at Oporto on 2 May 1992;

"home state regulator", in relation to an EEA credit institution, means the relevant EEA regulator in the EEA State where its head office is located;

"the Insolvency Rules" means the Insolvency Rules 1986;

"the Insolvency Rules (Northern Ireland)" means the Insolvency Rules (Northern Ireland) 1991;

"the Insolvency (Scotland) Rules" means the Insolvency (Scotland) Rules 1986;

"liquidator", except for the purposes of regulation 4, includes any person or body appointed by the administrative or judicial authorities whose task is to administer winding-up proceedings in respect of a UK credit institution which is not a body corporate;

"officer", in relation to a company, has the meaning given by section 744 of the 1985 Act or Article 2 of the Companies Order;

"official language" means a language specified in Article 1 of Council Regulation No 1 of 15 April 1958 determining the languages to be used by the European Economic Community (Regulation 1/58/EEC), most recently amended by paragraph (a) of Part XVIII of Annex I to the Act of Accession 1994 (194 N);

"the reorganisation and winding up directive" means the directive of the European Parliament and of the Council of 4 April 2001 on the reorganisation and winding up of credit institutions (2001/24/EC);

"section 425 compromise or arrangement" means a compromise or arrangement sanctioned by the court in relation to a UK credit institution under section 425 of the 1985 Act, but does not include a compromise or arrangement falling within section 427 or section 427A of that Act (reconstructions or amalgamations);

"supervisor" has the meaning given by section 7 of the 1986 Act or Article 20 of the 1989 Order as the case may be;

"UK credit institution" means an undertaking whose head office is in the United Kingdom with permission under Part 4 of the 2000 Act to accept deposits or to issue electronic money as the case may be but does not include—

(a) an undertaking which also has permission under Part 4 of the 2000 Act to effect or carry out contracts of insurance; or

(b) a credit union within the meaning of section 1 of the Credit Unions Act 1979;

"voluntary arrangement" means a voluntary arrangement which has effect in relation to a UK credit institution in accordance with section 4A of the 1986 Act or Article 17A of the 1989 Order as the case may be; and

"winding up" means—

(a) winding up by the court, or

(b) a creditors' voluntary winding up.

(2) In paragraph (1)—

(a) for the purposes of the definition of "directive reorganisation measure", a reorganisation measure is adopted at the time when it is treated as adopted or imposed by the law of the relevant EEA State; and

(b) for the purposes of the definition of "directive winding-up proceedings", winding-up proceedings are opened at the time when they are treated as opened by the law of the relevant EEA State,

and in this paragraph "relevant EEA State" means the EEA State under the law of which the reorganisation is adopted or imposed, or the winding-up proceedings are opened, as the case may be.

(3) In these Regulations, references to the law of insolvency of the United Kingdom include references to every provision made by or under the 1986 Act or the 1989 Order as the case may be; and in relation to partnerships, limited liability partnerships or building societies, references to the law of insolvency or to any provision of the 1986 Act or the 1989 Order are to that law as modified by the Insolvent Partnerships Order 1994, the Insolvent Partnerships Order (Northern Ireland) 1995, the Limited Liability Partnerships Regulations 2001 or the Building Societies Act 1986 (as the case may be).

(4) References in these Regulations to "accepting deposits" and a "contract of insurance" must be read with—

(a) section 22 of the 2000 Act;

(b) any relevant order made under that section; and

(c) Schedule 2 to that Act.

(5) For the purposes of the 2000 Act, functions imposed or falling on the Authority under these Regulations shall be deemed to be functions under the 2000 Act.

[2648]

NOTES

Commencement: 5 May 2004.

PART 2
INSOLVENCY MEASURES AND PROCEEDINGS: JURISDICTION IN RELATION TO CREDIT INSTITUTIONS

3 Prohibition against winding up etc EEA credit institutions in the United Kingdom

(1) On or after the relevant date a court in the United Kingdom may not, in relation to an EEA credit institution or any branch of an EEA credit institution—

(a) make a winding-up order pursuant to section 221 of the 1986 Act or Article 185 of the 1989 Order;
(b) appoint a provisional liquidator;
(c) make an administration order.

(2) Paragraph (1)(a) does not prevent—

(a) the court from making a winding-up order on or after the relevant date in relation to an EEA credit institution if—
  (i) a provisional liquidator was appointed in relation to that credit institution before the relevant date, and
  (ii) that appointment continues in force until immediately before that winding-up order is made;
(b) the winding up of an EEA credit institution on or after the relevant date pursuant to a winding-up order which was made, and has not been discharged, before that date.

(3) Paragraph (1)(b) does not prevent a provisional liquidator of an EEA credit institution appointed before the relevant date from acting in relation to that credit institution on or after that date.

(4) Paragraph (1)(c) does not prevent an administrator appointed before the relevant date from acting on or after that date in a case in which the administration order under which he or his predecessor was appointed remains in force after that date.

(5) On or after the relevant date, an administrator may not, in relation to an EEA credit institution, be appointed under paragraphs 14 or 22 of Schedule B1 of the 1986 Act.

(6) A proposed voluntary arrangement shall not have effect in relation to an EEA credit institution if a decision under section 4 of the 1986 Act or Article 17 of the 1989 Order with respect to the approval of that arrangement was taken on or after the relevant date.

(7) An order under section 254 of the Enterprise Act 2002 (application of insolvency law to a foreign company) may not provide for any of the following provisions of the 1986 Act to apply in relation to an incorporated EEA credit institution—

(a) Part 1 (company voluntary arrangements);
(b) Part 2 (administration);
(c) Chapter 4 of Part 4 (creditors' voluntary winding up);
(d) Chapter 6 of Part 4 (winding up by the Court).

(8) In this regulation and regulation 4, "relevant date" means the 5th May 2004.

[2649]

NOTES

Commencement: 5 May 2004.

4 Schemes of arrangement

(1) For the purposes of section 425(6)(a) of the 1985 Act or Article 418(5)(a) of the Companies Order, an EEA credit institution or a branch of an EEA credit institution is to be

treated as a company liable to be wound up under the 1986 Act or the 1989 Order if it would be liable to be wound up under that Act or Order but for the prohibition in regulation 3(1)(a).

(2) But a court may not make a relevant order under section 425(2) of the 1985 Act or Article 418(2) of the Companies Order in relation to an EEA credit institution which is subject to a directive reorganisation measure or directive winding-up proceedings, or a branch of an EEA credit institution which is subject to such a measure or proceedings, unless the conditions set out in paragraph (3) are satisfied.

(3) Those conditions are—

(a) the person proposing the section 425 or Article 418 compromise or arrangement ("the proposal") has given—

(i) the administrator or liquidator, and

(ii) the relevant administrative or judicial authority,

reasonable notice of the details of that proposal; and

(b) no person notified in accordance with sub-paragraph (a) has objected to the proposal.

(4) Nothing in this regulation invalidates a compromise or arrangement which was sanctioned by the court by an order made before the relevant date.

(5) For the purposes of paragraph (2), a relevant order means an order sanctioning a section 425 or Article 418 compromise or arrangement which—

(a) is intended to enable the credit institution, and the whole or any part of its undertaking, to survive as a going concern and which affects the rights of persons other than the credit institution or its contributories; or

(b) includes among its purposes a realisation of some or all of the assets of the EEA credit institution to which the order relates and the distribution of the proceeds to creditors, with a view to terminating the whole or any part of the business of that credit institution.

(6) For the purposes of this regulation—

(a) "administrator" means an administrator, as defined by Article 2 of the reorganisation and winding up directive, who is appointed in relation to the EEA credit institution in relation to which the proposal is made;

(b) "liquidator" means a liquidator, as defined by Article 2 of the reorganisation and winding up directive, who is appointed in relation to the EEA credit institution in relation to which the proposal is made;

(c) "administrative or judicial authority" means the administrative or judicial authority, as defined by Article 2 of the reorganisation and winding up directive, which is competent for the purposes of the directive reorganisation measure or directive winding-up proceedings mentioned in paragraph (2).

[2650]

NOTES

Commencement: 5 May 2004.

5 Reorganisation measures and winding-up proceedings in respect of EEA credit institutions effective in the United Kingdom

(1) An EEA insolvency measure has effect in the United Kingdom in relation to—

(a) any branch of an EEA credit institution,

(b) any property or other assets of that credit institution,

(c) any debt or liability of that credit institution,

as if it were part of the general law of insolvency of the United Kingdom.

(2) Subject to paragraph (4)—

(a) a competent officer who satisfies the condition mentioned in paragraph (3); or

(b) a qualifying agent appointed by a competent officer who satisfies the condition mentioned in paragraph (3),

may exercise in the United Kingdom, in relation to the EEA credit institution which is subject to an EEA insolvency measure, any function which, pursuant to that measure, he is entitled to exercise in relation to that credit institution in the relevant EEA State.

(3) The condition mentioned in paragraph (2) is that the appointment of the competent officer is evidenced—

(a) by a certified copy of the order or decision by a judicial or administrative authority in the relevant EEA State by or under which the competent officer was appointed; or

(b) by any other certificate issued by the judicial or administrative authority which has jurisdiction in relation to the EEA insolvency measure,

and accompanied by a certified translation of that order, decision or certificate (as the case may be).

(4) In exercising the functions of the kind mentioned in paragraph (2), the competent officer or qualifying agent—

(a) may not take any action which would constitute an unlawful use of force in the part of the United Kingdom in which he is exercising those functions;

(b) may not rule on any dispute arising from a matter falling within Part 4 of these Regulations which is justiciable by a court in the part of the United Kingdom in which he is exercising those functions; and

(c) notwithstanding the way in which functions may be exercised in the relevant EEA State, must act in accordance with relevant laws or rules as to procedure which have effect in the part of the United Kingdom in which he is exercising those functions.

(5) For the purposes of paragraph (4)(c), "relevant laws or rules as to procedure" means—

(a) requirements as to consultation with or notification of employees of an EEA credit institution;

(b) law and procedures relevant to the realisation of assets;

(c) where the competent officer is bringing or defending legal proceedings in the name of, or on behalf of an EEA credit institution, the relevant rules of court.

(6) In this regulation—

"competent officer" means a person appointed under or in connection with an EEA insolvency measure for the purpose of administering that measure;

"qualifying agent" means an agent validly appointed (whether in the United Kingdom or elsewhere) by a competent officer in accordance with the relevant law in the relevant EEA State;

"EEA insolvency measure" means, as the case may be, a directive reorganisation measure or directive winding-up proceedings which have effect in relation to an EEA credit institution by virtue of the law of the relevant EEA State;

"relevant EEA State", in relation to an EEA credit institution, means the EEA State in which that credit institution has been authorised in accordance with Article 4 of the banking consolidation directive.

[2651]

NOTES

Commencement: 5 May 2004.

6 Confirmation by the court of a creditors' voluntary winding up

(1) Rule 7.62 of the Insolvency Rules or Rule 7.56 of the Insolvency Rules (Northern Ireland) applies in relation to a UK credit institution with the modification specified in paragraph (2) or (3).

(2) For the purposes of this regulation, rule 7.62 has effect as if there were substituted for paragraph (1)—

"(1) Where a UK credit institution (within the meaning of the Credit Institutions (Reorganisation and Winding up) Regulations 2004) has passed a resolution for voluntary winding up, and no declaration under section 89 has been made, the liquidator may apply to court for an order confirming the creditors' voluntary winding up for the purposes of Articles 10 and 28 of directive 2001/24/EC of the European Parliament and of the Council of 4 April 2001 on the reorganisation and winding up of credit institutions.".

(3) For the purposes of this regulation, Rule 7.56 of the Insolvency Rules (Northern Ireland) has effect as if there were substituted for paragraph (1)—

"(1) Where a UK credit institution (within the meaning of the Credit Institutions (Reorganisation and Winding up) Regulations 2004) has passed a resolution for voluntary winding up, and no declaration under Article 75 has been made, the liquidator may apply to court for an order confirming the creditors' voluntary winding up for the purposes of Articles 10 and 28 of directive 2001/24/EC of the European Parliament and of the Council of 4 April 2001 on the reorganisation and winding up of credit institutions.".

[2652]

NOTES

Commencement: 5 May 2004.

PART 3
MODIFICATIONS OF THE LAW OF INSOLVENCY: NOTIFICATION AND PUBLICATION

7 Modifications of the law of insolvency

The general law of insolvency has effect in relation to UK credit institutions subject to the provisions of this Part.

[2653]

NOTES

Commencement: 5 May 2004.

8 Consultation of the Authority prior to a voluntary winding up

(1) Where, on or after 5th May 2004, a UK credit institution ("the institution") intends to pass a resolution to wind up the institution under paragraph (b) or (c) of section 84(1) of the 1986 Act or sub-paragraph (b) or (c) of Article 70(1) of the 1989 Order, the institution must give written notice of the resolution to the Authority before it passes the resolution.

(2) Where notice is given under paragraph (1), the resolution may be passed only after the end of the period of five business days beginning with the day on which the notice was given.

[2654]

NOTES

Commencement: 5 May 2004.

9 Notification of relevant decision to the Authority

(1) Where on or after 5th May 2004 the court makes a decision, order or appointment of any of the following kinds—

- (a) an administration order under paragraph 13 of Schedule B1 to the 1986 Act or section 8(1) of the 1986 Act;
- (b) a winding-up order under section 125 of the 1986 Act or Article 105 of the 1989 Order;
- (c) the appointment of a provisional liquidator under section 135(1) of the 1986 Act or Article 115(1) of the 1989 Order;
- (d) the appointment of an administrator in an interim order under paragraph 13(1)(d) of Schedule B1 to the 1986 Act or Article 22(4) of the 1989 Order,

it must immediately inform the Authority, or cause the Authority to be informed, of the order or appointment which has been made.

(2) Where a decision with respect to the approval of a voluntary arrangement has effect, and the arrangement which is the subject of that decision is a qualifying arrangement, the supervisor must forthwith inform the Authority of the arrangement which has been approved.

(3) Where a liquidator is appointed as mentioned in section 100 of the 1986 Act, paragraph 83 of Schedule B1 to the 1986 Act or Article 86 of the 1989 Order (appointment of liquidator in a creditors' voluntary winding up), the liquidator must inform the Authority forthwith of his appointment.

(4) Where in the case of a members' voluntary winding up, section 95 of the 1986 Act (effect of company's insolvency) or Article 81 of the 1989 Order applies, the liquidator must inform the Authority forthwith that he is of that opinion.

(5) Paragraphs (1), (2) and (3) do not apply in any case where the Authority was represented at all hearings in connection with the application in relation to which the order or appointment is made.

(6) For the purposes of paragraph (2), a "qualifying arrangement" means a voluntary arrangement which—

(a) varies the rights of creditors as against the credit institution and is intended to enable the credit institution, and the whole or any part of its undertaking, to survive as a going concern; or

(b) includes a realisation of some or all of the assets of the credit institution, with a view to terminating the whole or any part of the business of that credit institution.

(7) A supervisor, administrator or liquidator who fails without reasonable excuse to comply with paragraph (2), (3), or (4) (as the case may be) commits an offence and is liable on summary conviction to a fine not exceeding level 3 on the standard scale.

[2655]

NOTES

Commencement: 5 May 2004.

10 Notification to EEA regulators

(1) Where the Authority is informed of a decision, order or appointment in accordance with regulation 9, the Authority must as soon as is practicable inform the relevant person—

(a) that the decision, order or appointment has been made; and

(b) in general terms, of the possible effect of a decision, order or appointment of that kind on the business of a credit institution.

(2) Where the Authority has been represented at all hearings in connection with the application in relation to which the decision, order or appointment has been made, the Authority must inform the relevant person of the matters mentioned in paragraph (1) as soon as is practicable after that decision, order or appointment has been made.

(3) Where, on or after 5th May 2004, it appears to the Authority that a directive reorganisation measure should be adopted in relation to or imposed on an EEA credit institution which has a branch in the United Kingdom, it will inform the home state regulator as soon as is practicable.

(4) In this regulation, the "relevant person" means the EEA regulator of any EEA State in which the UK credit institution has a branch.

[2656]

NOTES

Commencement: 5 May 2004.

11 Withdrawal of authorisation

(1) For the purposes of this regulation—

(a) a qualifying decision means a decision with respect to the approval of a voluntary arrangement where the voluntary arrangement includes a realisation of some or all of the assets of the credit institution with a view to terminating the whole or any part of the business of that credit institution;

(b) a qualifying order means—

(i) a winding-up order under section 125 of the 1986 Act or Article 105 of the 1989 Order; or

(ii) an administration order under paragraph 13 of Schedule B1 to the 1986 Act in the prescribed circumstances;

(c) a qualifying appointment means—

(i) the appointment of a provisional liquidator under section 135(1) of the 1986 Act or Article 115(1) of the 1989 Order; or

(ii) the appointment of a liquidator as mentioned in section 100 of the 1986 Act, Article 86 of the 1989 Order (appointment of liquidator in a creditors' voluntary winding up) or paragraph 83 of Schedule B1 to the 1986 Act (moving from administration to creditors' voluntary liquidation).

(2) The prescribed circumstances are where, after the appointment of an administrator, the administrator concludes that it is not reasonably practicable to achieve the objective specified in paragraph 3(1)(a) of Schedule B1 to the 1986 Act.

(3) When the Authority is informed of a qualifying decision, qualifying order or qualifying appointment, the Authority will as soon as reasonably practicable exercise its power under section 45 of the 2000 Act to vary or to cancel the UK credit institution's permission under Part 4 of that Act to accept deposits or to issue electronic money as the case may be.

[2657]

NOTES

Commencement: 5 May 2004.

12 Publication of voluntary arrangement, administration order, winding-up order or scheme of arrangement

(1) This regulation applies where a qualifying decision is approved, or a qualifying order or qualifying appointment is made, in relation to a UK credit institution on or after 5th May 2004.

(2) For the purposes of this regulation—

(a) a qualifying decision means a decision with respect to the approval of a proposed voluntary arrangement, in accordance with section 4A of the 1986 Act or Article 17A of the 1989 Order;

(b) a qualifying order means—

(i) an administration order under paragraph 13 of Schedule B1 to the 1986 Act or section 8(1) of the 1986 Act,

(ii) an order appointing a provisional liquidator in accordance with section 135 of that Act or Article 115 of that Order, or

(iii) a winding-up order made by the court under Part 4 of that Act or Part V of the 1989 Order;

(c) a qualifying appointment means the appointment of a liquidator as mentioned in section 100 of the 1986 Act or Article 86 of the 1989 Order (appointment of liquidator in a creditors' voluntary winding up).

(3) Subject to paragraph (7), as soon as is reasonably practicable after a qualifying decision has effect or a qualifying order or a qualifying appointment has been made, the relevant officer must publish, or cause to be published, in the Official Journal of the European Communities and in 2 national newspapers in each EEA State in which the UK credit institution has a branch the information mentioned in paragraph (4) and (if applicable) paragraphs (5) or (6).

(4) That information is—

(a) a summary of the terms of the qualifying decision, qualifying appointment or the provisions of the qualifying order (as the case may be);

(b) the identity of the relevant officer;

(c) the statutory provisions in accordance with which the qualifying decision has effect or the qualifying order or appointment has been made or takes effect.

(5) In the case of a qualifying appointment, that information includes the court to which an application under section 112 of the 1986 Act (reference of questions to the court), section 27 of the 1986 Act or Article 98 of the 1989 Order (reference of questions to the High Court) may be made.

(6) In the case of a qualifying decision, that information includes the court to which an application under section 6 of the 1986 Act or Article 19 of the 1989 Order (challenge of decisions) may be made.

(7) Paragraph (3) does not apply where a qualifying decision or qualifying order falling within paragraph (2)(b)(i) affects the interests only of the members, or any class of members, or employees of the credit institution (in their capacity as members or employees).

(8) This regulation is without prejudice to any requirement to publish information imposed upon a relevant officer under any provision of the general law of insolvency.

(9) A relevant officer who fails to comply with paragraph (3) of this regulation commits an offence and is liable on summary conviction to a fine not exceeding level 3 on the standard scale.

(10) A qualifying decision, qualifying order or qualifying appointment is not invalid or ineffective if the relevant official fails to comply with paragraph (3) of this regulation.

(11) In this regulation, "relevant officer" means—

(a) in the case of a voluntary arrangement, the supervisor;

(b) in the case of an administration order, the administrator;

(c) in the case of a creditors' voluntary winding up, the liquidator;

(d) in the case of winding-up order, the liquidator; or

(e) in the case of an order appointing a provisional liquidator, the provisional liquidator.

(12) The information to be published in accordance with paragraph (3) of this regulation shall be—

(a) in the case of the Official Journal of the European Communities, in the official language or languages of each EEA State in which the UK credit institution has a branch;

(b) in the case of the national newspapers of each EEA State in which the UK credit institution has a branch, in the official language or languages of that EEA State.

[2658]

NOTES

Commencement: 5 May 2004.

13 Honouring of certain obligations

(1) This regulation applies where, on or after 5th May 2004, a relevant obligation has been honoured for the benefit of a relevant credit institution by a relevant person.

(2) Where a person has honoured a relevant obligation for the benefit of a relevant credit institution, he shall be deemed to have discharged that obligation if he was unaware of the winding up of that credit institution.

(3) For the purposes of this regulation—

(a) a relevant obligation is an obligation which, after the commencement of the winding up of a relevant credit institution, should have been honoured for the benefit of the liquidator of that credit institution;

(b) a relevant credit institution is a UK credit institution which—

(i) is not a body corporate; and

(ii) is the subject of a winding up;

(c) a relevant person is a person who at the time the obligation is honoured—

(i) is in the territory of an EEA State; and

(ii) is unaware of the winding up of the relevant credit institution.

(4) For the purposes of paragraph (3)(c)(ii) of this regulation—

(a) a relevant person shall be presumed, in the absence of evidence to the contrary, to have been unaware of the winding up of a relevant credit institution where the relevant obligation was honoured before date of the publication provided for in regulation 12 in relation to that winding up;

(b) a relevant person shall be presumed, in the absence of evidence to the contrary, to have been aware of the winding up of the relevant credit institution where the relevant obligation was honoured on or after the date of the publication provided for in regulation 12 in relation to that winding up.

[2659]

NOTES

Commencement: 5 May 2004.

14 Notification to creditors: winding-up proceedings

(1) When a relevant order or appointment is made, or a relevant decision is taken, in relation to a UK credit institution on or after 5th May 2004, the appointed officer must, as soon as is reasonably practicable, notify in writing all known creditors of that credit institution—

(a) of the matters mentioned in paragraph (4); and

(b) of the matters mentioned in paragraph (5).

(2) The appointed officer may comply with the requirement in paragraphs (1)(a) and the requirement in paragraph (1)(b) by separate notifications.

(3) For the purposes of this regulation—
(a) "relevant order" means—
(i) an administration order under paragraph 13 of Schedule B1 to the 1986 Act in the prescribed circumstances or an administration order made for the purposes set out in section 8(3)(b) or (d) of the 1986 Act, as the case may be,
(ii) a winding-up order under section 125 of the 1986 Act (powers of the court on hearing a petition) or Article 105 of the 1989 Order (powers of High Court on hearing of petition),
(iii) the appointment of a liquidator in accordance with section 138 of the 1986 Act (appointment of a liquidator in Scotland), or
(iv) an order appointing a provisional liquidator in accordance with section 135 of that Act or Article 115 of the 1989 Order;
(b) a "relevant appointment" means the appointment of a liquidator as mentioned in section 100 of the 1986 Act or Article 86 of the 1989 Order (appointment of liquidator in a creditors' voluntary winding up); and
(c) a "relevant decision" means a decision as a result of which a qualifying voluntary arrangement has effect.

(4) The matters which must be notified to all known creditors in accordance with paragraph (1)(a) are as follows—
(a) that a relevant order or appointment has been made, or a relevant decision taken, in relation to the UK credit institution; and
(b) the date from which that order, appointment or decision has effect.

(5) The matters which must be notified to all known creditors in accordance with paragraph (1)(b) are as follows—
(a) if applicable, the date by which a creditor must submit his claim in writing;
(b) the matters which must be stated in a creditor's claim;
(c) details of any category of debt in relation to which a claim is not required;
(d) the person to whom any such claim or any observations on a claim must be submitted; and
(e) the consequences of any failure to submit a claim by any specified deadline.

(6) Where a creditor is notified in accordance with paragraph (1)(b), the notification must be headed with the words "Invitation to lodge a claim. Time limits to be observed", and that heading must be given in every official language.

(7) The obligation under paragraph (1)(b) may be discharged by sending a form of proof in accordance with rule 4.74 of the Insolvency Rules, Rule 4.080 of the Insolvency Rules (Northern Ireland) or Rule 4.15(2) of the (Insolvency) Scotland Rules as applicable in cases where any of those rules applies, provided that the form of proof complies with paragraph (6).

(8) The prescribed circumstances are where, after the appointment of an administrator, the administrator concludes that it is not reasonably practicable to achieve the objective specified in paragraph 3(1)(a) of Schedule B1 to the 1986 Act.

(9) Where, after the appointment of an administrator, the administrator concludes that it is not reasonably practicable to achieve the objective specified in paragraph 3(1)(a) of Schedule B1 to the 1986 Act, he shall inform the court and the Authority in writing of that conclusion and upon so doing the order by which he was appointed shall be a relevant order for the purposes of this regulation and the obligation under paragraph (1) shall apply as from the date on which he so informs the court and the Authority.

(10) An appointed officer commits an offence if he fails without reasonable excuse to comply with a requirement under paragraph (1) of this regulation, and is liable on summary conviction to a fine not exceeding level 3 on the standard scale.

(11) For the purposes of this regulation—
(a) "appointed officer" means—
(i) in the case of a relevant order falling within paragraph (3)(a)(i), the administrator,
(ii) in the case of a relevant order falling within paragraph (3)(a)(ii) or (iii) or a relevant appointment falling within paragraph (3)(b), the liquidator,
(iii) in the case of a relevant order falling within paragraph (3)(a)(iv), the provisional liquidator, or

(iv) in the case of a relevant decision, the supervisor; and

(b) a creditor is a "known" creditor if the appointed officer is aware of—

(i) his identity,

(ii) his claim or potential claim, and

(iii) a recent address where he is likely to receive a communication.

(12) For the purposes of paragraph (3), a voluntary arrangement is a qualifying voluntary arrangement if its purposes include a realisation of some or all of the assets of the UK credit institution to which the order relates with a view to terminating the whole or any part of the business of that credit institution.

[2660]

NOTES

Commencement: 5 May 2004.

15 Submission of claims by EEA creditors

(1) An EEA creditor who, on or after 5th May 2004, submits a claim or observations relating to his claim in any relevant proceedings (irrespective of when those proceedings were commenced or had effect) may do so in his domestic language, provided that the requirements in paragraphs (3) and (4) are complied with.

(2) For the purposes of this regulation, "relevant proceedings" means—

(a) a winding up;

(b) a qualifying voluntary arrangement; or

(c) administration.

(3) Where an EEA creditor submits a claim in his domestic language, the document must be headed with the words "Lodgement of claim" (in English).

(4) Where an EEA creditor submits observations on his claim (otherwise than in the document by which he submits his claim), the observations must be headed with the words "Submission of observations relating to claims" (in English).

(5) Paragraph (3) does not apply where an EEA creditor submits his claim using—

(a) in the case of a winding up, a form of proof supplied by the liquidator in accordance with rule 4.74 of the Insolvency Rules, Rule 4.080 of the Insolvency Rules (Northern Ireland) or rule 4.15(2) of the Insolvency (Scotland) Rules;

(b) in the case of a qualifying voluntary arrangement, a form approved by the court for that purpose.

(6) In this regulation—

(a) "domestic language", in relation to an EEA creditor, means the official language, or one of the official languages, of the EEA State in which he is ordinarily resident or, if the creditor is not an individual, in which the creditor's head office is located; and

(b) "qualifying voluntary arrangement" means a voluntary arrangement whose purposes include a realisation of some or all of the assets of the UK credit institution to which the order relates with a view to terminating the whole or any part of the business of that credit institution.

[2661]

NOTES

Commencement: 5 May 2004.

16 Reports to creditors

(1) This regulation applies where, on or after 5th May 2004—

(a) a liquidator is appointed in accordance with section 100 of the 1986 Act, Article 86 of the 1986 Order (creditors' voluntary winding up: appointment of liquidator) or paragraph 83 of Schedule B1 to the 1986 Act (moving from administration to creditors' voluntary liquidation);

(b) a winding-up order is made by the court;

(c) a provisional liquidator is appointed; or

(d) administration.

(2) The liquidator, provisional liquidator or administrator (as the case may be) must send a report to every known creditor once in every 12 months beginning with the date when his appointment has effect.

(3) The requirement in paragraph (2) does not apply where a liquidator, provisional liquidator or administrator is required by order of the court to send a report to creditors at intervals which are more frequent than those required by this regulation.

(4) This regulation is without prejudice to any requirement to send a report to creditors, imposed by the court on the liquidator, provisional liquidator or administrator, which is supplementary to the requirements of this regulation.

(5) A liquidator, provisional liquidator or administrator commits an offence if he fails without reasonable excuse to comply with an applicable requirement under this regulation, and is liable on summary conviction to a fine not exceeding level 3 on the standard scale.

(6) For the purposes of this regulation—
- (a) "known creditor" means—
  - (i) a creditor who is known to the liquidator, provisional liquidator or administrator, and
  - (ii) in a case falling within paragraph (1)(b) or (c), a creditor who is specified in the credit institution's statement of affairs (within the meaning of section 131 of the 1986 Act or Article 111 of the 1989 Order);
- (b) "report" means a written report setting out the position generally as regards the progress of the winding up, provisional liquidation or administration (as the case may be).

[2662]

NOTES

Commencement: 5 May 2004.

17 Service of notices and documents

(1) This regulation applies to any notification, report or other document which is required to be sent to a creditor of a UK credit institution by a provision of this Part ("a relevant notification").

(2) A relevant notification may be sent to a creditor by one of the following methods—
- (a) by posting it to the proper address of the creditor;
- (b) by transmitting it electronically, in accordance with paragraph (4).

(3) For the purposes of paragraph (2)(a), the proper address of a creditor is any current address provided by that person as an address for service of a relevant notification and, if no such address is provided—
- (a) the last known address of that creditor (whether his residence or a place where he carries on business);
- (b) in the case of a body corporate, the address of its registered or principal office; or
- (c) in the case of an unincorporated association, the address of its principal office.

(4) A relevant notification may be transmitted electronically only if it is sent to—
- (a) an electronic address notified to the relevant officer by the creditor for this purpose; or
- (b) if no such address has been notified, to an electronic address at which the relevant officer reasonably believes the creditor will receive the notification.

(5) Any requirement in this Part to send a relevant notification to a creditor shall also be treated as satisfied if the conditions set out in paragraph (6) are satisfied.

(6) The conditions of this paragraph are satisfied in the case of a relevant notification if—
- (a) the creditor has agreed with—
  - (i) the UK credit institution which is liable under the creditor's claim, or
  - (ii) the relevant officer,

  that information which is required to be sent to him (whether pursuant to a statutory or contractual obligation, or otherwise) may instead be accessed by him on a web site;
- (b) the agreement applies to the relevant notification in question;
- (c) the creditor is notified of—
  - (i) the publication of the relevant notification on a web site,

(ii) the address of that web site,

(iii) the place on that web site where the relevant notification may be accessed, and how it may be accessed; and

(d) the relevant notification is published on that web site throughout a period of at least one month beginning with the date on which the creditor is notified in accordance with sub-paragraph (c).

(7) Where, in a case in which paragraph (5) is relied on for compliance with a requirement of regulation 14 or 16—

(a) a relevant notification is published for a part, but not all, of the period mentioned in paragraph (6)(d) but

(b) the failure to publish it throughout that period is wholly attributable to circumstances which it would not be reasonable to have expected the relevant officer to prevent or avoid,

no offence is committed under regulation 14(10) or regulation 16(5) (as the case may be) by reason of that failure.

(8) In this regulation—

(a) "electronic address" includes any number or address used for the purposes of receiving electronic communications which are sent electronically;

(b) "electronic communication" means an electronic communication within the meaning of the Electronic Communications Act 2000 the processing of which on receipt is intended to produce writing; and

(c) "relevant officer" means (as the case may be) an administrator, liquidator, provisional liquidator or supervisor who is required to send a relevant notification to a creditor by a provision of this Part.

[2663]

NOTES

Commencement: 5 May 2004.

18 Disclosure of confidential information received from an EEA regulator

(1) This regulation applies to information ("insolvency information") which—

(a) relates to the business or affairs of any other person; and

(b) is supplied to the Authority by an EEA regulator acting in accordance with Articles 4, 5, 9, or 11 of the reorganisation and winding up directive.

(2) Subject to paragraphs (3) and (4), sections 348, 349 and 352 of the 2000 Act apply in relation to insolvency information as they apply in relation to confidential information within the meaning of section 348(2) of the 2000 Act.

(3) Insolvency information is not subject to the restrictions on disclosure imposed by section 348(1) of the 2000 Act (as it applies by virtue of paragraph (2)) if it satisfies any of the criteria set out in section 348(4) of the 2000 Act.

(4) The Disclosure Regulations apply in relation to insolvency information as they apply in relation to single market directive information (within the meaning of those Regulations).

[2664]

NOTES

Commencement: 5 May 2004.

PART 4
REORGANISATION OR WINDING UP OF UK CREDIT INSTITUTIONS: RECOGNITION OF EEA RIGHTS

19 Application of this Part

(1) This Part applies as follows—

(a) where a decision with respect to the approval of a proposed voluntary arrangement having a qualifying purpose is made under section 4A of the 1986 Act or Article 17A of the 1989 Order on or after 5th May 2004 in relation to a UK credit institution;

(b) where an administration order made under paragraph 13 of Schedule B1 to the 1986 Act or section 8(1) of the 1986 Act on or after 5th May 2004 is in force in relation to a UK credit institution;

(c) where a UK credit institution is subject to a relevant winding up; or

(d) where a provisional liquidator is appointed in relation to a UK credit institution on or after 5th May 2004.

(2) For the purposes of paragraph (1)(a), a voluntary arrangement has a qualifying purpose if it—

(a) varies the rights of the creditors as against the credit institution and is intended to enable the credit institution, and the whole or any part of its undertaking, to survive as a going concern; or

(b) includes a realisation of some or all of the assets of the credit institution to which the compromise or arrangement relates, with a view to terminating the whole or any part of the business of that credit institution.

(3) For the purposes of paragraph (1)(c), a winding up is a relevant winding up if—

(a) in the case of a winding up by the court, the winding-up order is made on or after 5th May 2004; or

(b) in the case of a creditors' voluntary winding up, the liquidator is appointed in accordance with section 100 of the 1986 Act, Article 86 of the 1989 Order or paragraph 83 of Schedule B1 to the 1986 Act on or after 5th May 2004.

[2665]

NOTES

Commencement: 5 May 2004.

20 Application of this Part: assets subject to a section 425 or Article 418 compromise or arrangement

(1) For the purposes of this Part, the insolvent estate of a UK credit institution shall not include any assets which at the commencement date are subject to a relevant section 425 or Article 418 compromise or arrangement.

(2) In this regulation—

(a) "assets" has the same meaning as "property" in section 436 of the 1986 Act or Article 2(2) of the 1989 Order;

(b) "commencement date" means the date when a UK credit institution goes into liquidation within the meaning given by section 247(2) of the 1986 Act or Article 6(2) of the 1989 Order;

(c) "insolvent estate" has the meaning given by rule 13.8 of the Insolvency Rules or Rule 0.2 of the Insolvency Rules (Northern Ireland) and in Scotland means the company's assets;

(d) "relevant section 425 or Article 418 compromise or arrangement" means—

(i) a section 425 or Article 418 compromise or arrangement which was sanctioned by the court before 5th May 2004, or

(ii) any subsequent section 425 or Article 418 compromise or arrangement sanctioned by the court to amend or replace a compromise or arrangement of a kind mentioned in paragraph (i).

[2666]

NOTES

Commencement: 5 May 2004.

21 Interpretation of this Part

(1) For the purposes of this Part—

(a) "affected credit institution" means a UK credit institution which is the subject of a relevant reorganisation or winding up;

(b) "relevant reorganisation" or "relevant winding up" means any voluntary arrangement, administration, winding up, or order referred to in regulation 19(1) to which this Part applies; and

(c) "relevant time" means the date of the opening of a relevant reorganisation or a relevant winding up.

(2) In this Part, references to the opening of a relevant reorganisation or a relevant winding up mean—

(a) in the case of winding-up proceedings—

(i) in the case of a winding up by the court, the date on which the winding-up order is made, or

(ii) in the case of a creditors' voluntary winding up, the date on which the liquidator is appointed in accordance with section 100 of the 1986 Act, Article 86 of the 1989 Order or paragraph 83 of Schedule B1 to the 1986 Act;

(b) in the case of a voluntary arrangement, the date when a decision with respect to the approval of that voluntary arrangement has effect in accordance with section 4A(2) of the 1986 Act or Article 17A(2) of the 1989 Order;

(c) in a case where an administration order under paragraph 13 of Schedule B1 to the 1986 Act or section 8(1) of the 1986 Act is in force, the date of the making of that order; and

(d) in a case where a provisional liquidator has been appointed, the date of that appointment,

and references to the time of an opening must be construed accordingly.

[2667]

NOTES

Commencement: 5 May 2004.

22 EEA rights: applicable law in the winding up of a UK credit institution

(1) This regulation is subject to the provisions of regulations 23 to 35.

(2) In a relevant winding up, the matters mentioned in paragraph (3) are to be determined in accordance with the general law of insolvency of the United Kingdom.

(3) Those matters are—

(a) the assets which form part of the estate of the affected credit institution;

(b) the treatment of assets acquired by the affected credit institution after the opening of the relevant winding up;

(c) the respective powers of the affected credit institution and the liquidator or provisional liquidator;

(d) the conditions under which set-off may be invoked;

(e) the effects of the relevant winding up on current contracts to which the affected credit institution is a party;

(f) the effects of the relevant winding up on proceedings brought by creditors;

(g) the claims which are to be lodged against the estate of the affected credit institution;

(h) the treatment of claims against the affected credit institution arising after the opening of the relevant winding up;

(i) the rules governing—

(i) the lodging, verification and admission of claims,

(ii) the distribution of proceeds from the realisation of assets,

(iii) the ranking of claims,

(iv) the rights of creditors who have obtained partial satisfaction after the opening of the relevant winding up by virtue of a right in rem or through set-off;

(j) the conditions for and the effects of the closure of the relevant winding up, in particular by composition;

(k) the rights of creditors after the closure of the relevant winding up;

(l) who is to bear the cost and expenses incurred in the relevant winding up;

(m) the rules relating to the voidness, voidability or unenforceability of legal acts detrimental to all the creditors.

[2668]

NOTES

Commencement: 5 May 2004.

PART III
STATUTORY INSTRUMENTS

23 Employment contracts and relationships

(1) The effects of a relevant reorganisation or a relevant winding up on EEA employment contracts and EEA employment relationships are to be determined in accordance with the law of the EEA State to which that contract or that relationship is subject.

(2) In this regulation, an employment contract is an EEA employment contract, and an employment relationship is an EEA employment relationship if it is subject to the law of an EEA State.

[2669]

NOTES

Commencement: 5 May 2004.

24 Contracts in connection with immovable property

(1) The effects of a relevant reorganisation or a relevant winding up on a contract conferring the right to make use of or acquire immovable property situated within the territory of an EEA State shall be determined in accordance with the law of that State.

(2) The law of the EEA State in whose territory the property is situated shall determine whether the property is movable or immovable.

[2670]

NOTES

Commencement: 5 May 2004.

25 Registrable rights

The effects of a relevant reorganisation or a relevant winding up on rights of the affected UK credit institution with respect to—

(a) immovable property,
(b) a ship, or
(c) an aircraft

which is subject to registration in a public register kept under the authority of an EEA State are to be determined in accordance with the law of that State.

[2671]

NOTES

Commencement: 5 May 2004.

26 Third parties' rights in rem

(1) A relevant reorganisation or a relevant winding up shall not affect the rights in rem of creditors or third parties in respect of tangible or intangible, movable or immovable assets (including both specific assets and collections of indefinite assets as a whole which change from time to time) belonging to the affected credit institution which are situated within the territory of an EEA State at the relevant time.

(2) The rights in rem referred to in paragraph (1) shall mean—

(a) the right to dispose of assets or have them disposed of and to obtain satisfaction from the proceeds of or the income from those assets, in particular by virtue of a lien or a mortgage;
(b) the exclusive right to have a claim met, in particular a right guaranteed by a lien in respect of the claim or by assignment of the claim by way of guarantee;
(c) the right to demand the assets from, or to require restitution by, any person having possession or use of them contrary to the wishes of the party so entitled;
(d) a right in rem to the beneficial use of assets.

(3) A right, recorded in a public register and enforceable against third parties, under which a right in rem within the meaning of paragraph (1) may be obtained, is also to be treated as a right in rem for the purposes of this regulation.

(4) Paragraph (1) does not preclude actions for voidness, voidability or unenforceability of legal acts detrimental to creditors under the general law of insolvency of the United Kingdom.

[2672]

NOTES

Commencement: 5 May 2004.

27 Reservation of title agreements etc

(1) The adoption of a relevant reorganisation or opening of a relevant winding up in relation to a credit institution purchasing an asset shall not affect the seller's rights based on a reservation of title where at the time of that adoption or opening the asset is situated within the territory of an EEA State.

(2) The adoption of a relevant reorganisation or opening of a relevant winding up in relation to a credit institution selling an asset, after delivery of the asset, shall not constitute grounds for rescinding or terminating the sale and shall not prevent the purchaser from acquiring title where at the time of that adoption or opening the asset sold is situated within the territory of an EEA State.

(3) Paragraphs (1) and (2) do not preclude actions for voidness, voidability or unenforceability of legal acts detrimental to creditors under the general law of insolvency of the United Kingdom.

[2673]

NOTES

Commencement: 5 May 2004.

28 Creditors' rights to set off

(1) A relevant reorganisation or a relevant winding up shall not affect the right of creditors to demand the set-off of their claims against the claims of the affected credit institution, where such a set-off is permitted by the law applicable to the affected credit institution's claim.

(2) Paragraph (1) does not preclude actions for voidness, voidability or unenforceability of legal acts detrimental to creditors under the general law of insolvency of the United Kingdom.

[2674]

NOTES

Commencement: 5 May 2004.

29 Regulated markets

(1) Subject to regulation 33, the effects of a relevant reorganisation or winding up on transactions carried out in the context of a regulated market operating in an EEA State must be determined in accordance with the law applicable to those transactions.

(2) For the purposes of this regulation, "regulated market" has the meaning given by the Council Directive of 10th May 1993 on investment services in the securities field (No 93/22/EEC).

[2675]

NOTES

Commencement: 5 May 2004.

30 Detrimental acts pursuant to the law of an EEA State

(1) In a relevant reorganisation or a relevant winding up, the rules relating to detrimental transactions shall not apply where a person who has benefited from a legal act detrimental to all the creditors provides proof that—

(a) the said act is subject to the law of an EEA State; and

(b) that law does not allow any means of challenging that act in the relevant case.

(2) For the purposes of paragraph (1), "the rules relating to detrimental transactions" means any provision of the general law of insolvency relating to the voidness, voidability or unenforceability of legal acts detrimental to all the creditors.

[2676]

NOTES
Commencement: 5 May 2004.

31 Protection of third party purchasers

(1) This regulation applies where, by an act concluded after the adoption of a relevant reorganisation or opening of a relevant winding up, an affected credit institution disposes for a consideration of—

(a) an immovable asset situated within the territory of an EEA State;
(b) a ship or an aircraft subject to registration in a public register kept under the authority of an EEA State;
(c) relevant instruments or rights in relevant instruments whose existence or transfer presupposes entry into a register or account laid down by the law of an EEA State or which are placed in a central deposit system governed by the law of an EEA State.

(2) The validity of that act is to be determined in accordance with the law of the EEA State within whose territory the immoveable asset is situated or under whose authority the register, account or system is kept, as the case may be.

(3) In this regulation, "relevant instruments" means the instruments referred to in Section B of the Annex to the Council Directive of 10th May 1993 on investment services in the securities field (No 93/22/EEC).

[2677]

NOTES
Commencement: 5 May 2004.

32 Lawsuits pending

(1) The effects of a relevant reorganisation or a relevant winding up on a relevant lawsuit pending in an EEA State shall be determined solely in accordance with the law of that EEA State.

(2) In paragraph (1), "relevant lawsuit" means a lawsuit concerning an asset or right of which the affected credit institution has been divested.

[2678]

NOTES
Commencement: 5 May 2004.

33 Lex rei sitae

(1) The effects of a relevant reorganisation or a relevant winding up on the enforcement of a relevant proprietary right shall be determined by the law of the relevant EEA State.

(2) In this regulation—

"relevant proprietary right" means proprietary rights in relevant instruments or other rights in relevant instruments the existence or transfer of which is recorded in a register, an account or a centralised deposit system held or located in an EEA state;

"relevant EEA State" means the Member State where the register, account or centralised deposit system in which the relevant proprietary right is recorded is held or located;

"relevant instrument" has the meaning given by regulation 31(3).

[2679]

NOTES
Commencement: 5 May 2004.

34 Netting agreements

The effects of a relevant reorganisation or a relevant winding up on a netting agreement shall be determined in accordance with the law applicable to that agreement.

[2680]

NOTES
Commencement: 5 May 2004.

35 Repurchase agreements

Subject to regulation 33, the effects of a relevant reorganisation or a relevant winding up on a repurchase agreement shall be determined in accordance with the law applicable to that agreement.

[2681]

NOTES
Commencement: 5 May 2004.

PART 5
THIRD COUNTRY CREDIT INSTITUTIONS

36 Interpretation of this Part

(1) In this Part—
- (a) "relevant measure", in relation to a third country credit institution, means—
  - (i) a winding up;
  - (ii) a provisional liquidation; or
  - (iii) an administration order made under paragraph 13 of Schedule B1 to the 1986 Act or section 8(1) of the 1986 Act as the case may be.
- (b) "third country credit institution" means a person—
  - (i) who has permission under the 2000 Act to accept deposits or to issue electronic money as the case may be; and
  - (ii) whose head office is not in the United Kingdom or an EEA State.

(2) In paragraph (1), the definition of "third country credit institution" must be read with—
- (a) section 22 of the 2000 Act;
- (b) any relevant order made under that section; and
- (c) Schedule 2 to that Act.

[2682]

NOTES
Commencement: 5 May 2004.

37 Application of these Regulations to a third country credit institution

Regulations 9 and 10 apply where a third country credit institution is subject to a relevant measure, as if references in those regulations to a UK credit institution included a reference to a third country credit institution.

[2683]

NOTES
Commencement: 5 May 2004.

38 Disclosure of confidential information: third country credit institution

(1) This regulation applies to information ("insolvency practitioner information") which—
- (a) relates to the business or other affairs of any person; and
- (b) is information of a kind mentioned in paragraph (2).

(2) Information falls within paragraph (1)(b) if it is supplied to—
- (a) the Authority by an EEA regulator; or
- (b) an insolvency practitioner by an EEA administrator or liquidator,

in accordance with or pursuant to Articles 8 or 19 of the reorganisation and winding up directive.

(3) Subject to paragraphs (4), (5) and (6), sections 348, 349 and 352 of the 2000 Act apply in relation to insolvency practitioner information in the same way as they apply in relation to confidential information within the meaning of section 348(2) of that Act.

(4) For the purposes of this regulation, sections 348, 349 and 352 of the 2000 Act and the Disclosure Regulations have effect as if the primary recipients specified in subsection (5) of section 348 of the 2000 Act included an insolvency practitioner.

(5) Insolvency practitioner information is not subject to the restrictions on disclosure imposed by section 348(1) of the 2000 Act (as it applies by virtue of paragraph (2)) if it satisfies any of the criteria set out in section 348(4) of the 2000 Act.

(6) The Disclosure Regulations apply in relation to insolvency practitioner information as they apply in relation to single market directive information (within the meaning of those Regulations).

(7) In this regulation—

"EEA administrator" and "EEA liquidator" mean an administrator or liquidator of a third country credit institution as the case may be within the meaning of the reorganisation and winding up directive;

"insolvency practitioner" means an insolvency practitioner, within the meaning of section 388 of the 1986 Act or Article 3 of the 1989 Order, who is appointed or acts in relation to a third country credit institution.

[2684]

NOTES

Commencement: 5 May 2004.

INSURERS (REORGANISATION AND WINDING UP) (LLOYD'S) REGULATIONS 2005

(SI 2005/1998)

NOTES

Made: 19 July 2005.
Authority: European Communities Act 1972, s 2(2).
Commencement: 10 August 2005.

ARRANGEMENT OF REGULATIONS

PART 1
GENERAL

PART 2
LLOYD'S MARKET REORGANISATION ORDER

PART 3
MODIFICATION OF LAW OF INSOLVENCY:
NOTIFICATION AND PUBLICATION

PART 4
APPLICATION OF PARTS 4 AND 5
OF THE PRINCIPAL REGULATIONS

PART 1
GENERAL

1 Citation and commencement

These Regulations may be cited as the Insurers (Reorganisation and Winding Up) (Lloyd's) Regulations 2005, and come into force on 10 August 2005.

[2685]

NOTES

Commencement: 10 August 2005.

2 Interpretation

(1) In these Regulations—

"the Administration for Insurers Order" means the Financial Services and Markets Act 2000 (Administration Orders Relating to Insurers) Order 2002;

"affected market participant" means any member, former member, managing agent, members' agent, Lloyd's broker, approved run-off company or coverholder to whom the Lloyd's market reorganisation order applies;

"approved run-off company" means a company with the permission of the Society to perform executive functions, insurance functions or administrative and processing functions on behalf of a managing agent;

"the association of underwriters known as Lloyd's" has the meaning it has for the purposes of the First Council Directive of 24 July 1973 on the coordination of laws, regulations and administrative provisions relating to the taking and pursuit of the business of direct insurance other than life assurance (73/239/EEC) and Directive 2002/83/EC of the European Parliament and of the Council of 5 November 2002 concerning life assurance;

"central funds" means the New Central Fund as provided for in the New Central Fund Byelaw (No 23 of 1996) and the Central Fund as provided for in the Central Fund Byelaw (No 4 of 1986);

"company" means a company within the meaning of section 735 of the 1985 Act or Article 3 of the Companies Order or a company incorporated elsewhere than in Great Britain that is a member of Lloyd's;

"corporate member" means a company admitted to membership of Lloyd's as an underwriting member;

"coverholder" means a company or partnership authorised by a managing agent to enter into, in accordance with the terms of a binding authority, a contract or contracts of insurance to be underwritten by the members of a syndicate managed by that managing agent;

"former member" means a person who has ceased to be a member, whether by resignation or otherwise, in accordance with Lloyd's Act 1982 and any byelaw made under it or in accordance with the provisions of Lloyd's Acts 1871–1982 then in force at the time the person ceased to be a member;

"Gazette" means the London Gazette, the Edinburgh Gazette and the Belfast Gazette;

"individual member" means a member or former member who is an individual;

"insurance market activity" has the meaning given by section 316(3) of the 2000 Act;

"insurance market debt" means an insurance debt under or in connection with a contract of insurance written at Lloyd's;

"Lloyd's Acts 1871–1982" means Lloyd's Act 1871, Lloyd's Act 1911, Lloyd's Act 1951 and Lloyd's Act 1982;

"Lloyd's broker" has the meaning given by section 2(1) of Lloyd's Act 1982;

"managing agent" has the meaning given by article 3(1) of the Financial Services and Markets Act 2000 (Regulated Activities) Order 2001;

"member" means an underwriting member of the Society;

"members' agent" means a person who carries out the activity of advising a person to become, or continue or cease to be, a member of a particular Lloyd's syndicate;

"overseas business regulatory deposit" means a deposit provided or maintained in respect of the overseas insurance and reinsurance business carried on by members in accordance with binding legal or regulatory requirements from time to time in force in the country or territory in which the deposit is held;

"overseas insurance business" means insurance business and reinsurance business transacted by members in a country or territory that is not or is not part of an EEA State;

"the principal Regulations" means the Insurers (Reorganisation and Winding Up) Regulations 2004;

"relevant trust fund" means any funds held on trust under a trust deed entered into by the member in accordance with the requirements of the Authority and the Byelaws of the Society for the payment of an obligation arising in connection with insurance market activity carried on by the member or for the establishment of a Lloyd's deposit and includes funds held on further trusts declared by the Society or the trustee of such a trust deed in respect of any class of insurance market activity;

"the Room" has the meaning given by section 2(1) of Lloyd's Act 1982;

"the Society" means the Society incorporated by Lloyd's Act 1871;

"subsidiary of the Society" means a company that is a subsidiary of the Society within the meaning of section 736 of the 1985 Act or Article 4 of the Companies Order;

"syndicate" has the meaning given by article 3(1) of the Financial Services and Markets Act 2000 (Regulated Activities) Order 2001.

(2) Subject to paragraph (3), words and phrases used in these Regulations have the same meaning as in the principal Regulations except where otherwise specified or where the context requires otherwise.

(3) For the purposes of these Regulations, "UK insurer" is to be treated as including a member or a former member.

(4) These Regulations have effect notwithstanding the provisions of section 360 of the 2000 Act.

[2686]

NOTES

Commencement: 10 August 2005.

PART 2
LLOYD'S MARKET REORGANISATION ORDER

3 Lloyd's market reorganisation order

(1) In these Regulations "Lloyd's market reorganisation order" means an order which—

(a) is made by the court in relation to the association of underwriters known as Lloyd's;

(b) appoints a reorganisation controller; and

(c) on the making of which there comes into force a moratorium on the commencement of—

(i) proceedings, or

(ii) other legal processes

set out in regulation 8 in respect of affected market participants, the Society and subsidiaries of the Society.

(2) A Lloyd's market reorganisation order applies to—

(a) every member, former member, managing agent, members' agent, Lloyd's broker and approved run-off company who has not been excluded from the order in accordance with regulation 7;

(b) every coverholder who has been included in the order in accordance with regulation 7;

(c) the Society; and

(d) subsidiaries of the Society.

[2687]

NOTES

Commencement: 10 August 2005.

4 Condition for making order

(1) The court may make a Lloyd's market reorganisation order if it is satisfied that—

(a) any regulatory solvency requirement is not, or may not be, met; and

(b) an order is likely to achieve one or both of the objectives in regulation 5.

(2) In paragraph (1), "regulatory solvency requirement" means a requirement to maintain adequate financial resources in respect of insurance business at Lloyd's, imposed under the 2000 Act, whether on a member or former underwriting member, either singly or together with other members or former underwriting members, or on the Society and includes a requirement to maintain a margin of solvency.

(3) In paragraph (2), "former underwriting member" has the meaning given by section 324(1) of the 2000 Act.

[2688]

NOTES

Commencement: 10 August 2005.

5 Objectives of a Lloyd's market reorganisation order

The objectives of a Lloyd's market reorganisation order are—

(a) to preserve or restore the financial situation of, or market confidence in, the association of underwriters known as Lloyd's in order to facilitate the carrying on of insurance market activities by members at Lloyd's;

(b) to assist in achieving an outcome that is in the interests of creditors of members, and insurance creditors in particular.

[2689]

NOTES

Commencement: 10 August 2005.

6 Application for a Lloyd's market reorganisation order

(1) An application for a Lloyd's market reorganisation order may be made by the Authority or by the Society, or by both.

(2) If the application is made by only one of those bodies it must inform the other body of its intention to make the application as soon as possible, and in any event before the application is lodged at the court.

(3) The Authority and the Society are entitled to be heard at the hearing of the application, regardless of which body makes the application.

(4) An application must clearly designate—

(a) any member, former member, managing agent, members' agent, Lloyd's broker, or approved run-off company to whom the order should not apply; and

(b) every coverholder to whom the order should apply.

(5) The applicant must give notice of the application by—

(a) ensuring the posting of a copy in the Room,

(b) displaying a copy on its website, and

(c) publishing a copy

(i) in the Gazette, and

(ii) in such newspaper or newspapers within the United Kingdom and elsewhere as the applicant considers appropriate to bring the application to the attention of those likely to be affected by it.

(6) The notice must be given as soon as reasonably practicable after the making of the application, unless the court orders otherwise.

[2690]

NOTES

Commencement: 10 August 2005.

7 Powers of the court

(1) On hearing an application for a Lloyd's market reorganisation order, the court may make—

(a) a Lloyd's market reorganisation order, and

(b) any other order in addition to a Lloyd's market reorganisation order which the court thinks appropriate for the attainment of either or both of the objectives in regulation 5.

(2) A Lloyd's market reorganisation order comes into force—

(a) at the time appointed by the court; or

(b) if no time is so appointed, when the order is made

and remains in force until revoked by the court.

(3) The court may on an application made by the Authority or the Society at the same time as an application under regulation 6 or the reorganisation controller, the Authority, the Society, a subsidiary of the Society or any affected market participant at any time while the Lloyd's market reorganisation order is in force, amend or vary a Lloyd's market reorganisation order so that it—

(a) does not apply to—

(i) particular assets, or

(ii) particular members, former members, member's agents, managing agents, Lloyd's brokers, approved run-off companies or subsidiaries of the Society,

specified in the order; and

(b) does apply to any coverholder specified in the order.

(4) The court—

(a) must appoint one or more persons to be the reorganisation controller;

(b) must specify the powers and duties of the reorganisation controller;

(c) may establish or approve the respective duties and functions of two or more persons appointed to be the reorganisation controller, including specifying that one of them shall have precedence; and

(d) may from time to time vary the powers of a reorganisation controller.

(5) An application made under paragraph (3) other than at the time of the application under regulation 6 shall be served on the reorganisation controller and the Authority who shall each be entitled to attend and be heard at a hearing of such an application.

[2691]

NOTES

Commencement: 10 August 2005.

8 Moratorium

(1) Except with the permission of the court, for the period during which a Lloyd's market reorganisation order is in force, no proceedings or other legal process may be commenced or continued against:

(a) an affected market participant;

(b) the Society; or

(c) a subsidiary of the Society to which the order applies.

(2) In paragraph (1),

(a) "court" means in England and Wales the High Court, in Northern Ireland the High Court and in Scotland the Court of Session; and

(b) "proceedings" means proceedings of every description and includes:

(i) a petition under section 124 or 124A of the 1986 Act or Article 104 or 104A of the 1989 Order for the appointment of a liquidator or provisional liquidator;

(ii) an application under section 252 of the 1986 Act or Article 226 of the 1989 Order for an interim order;

(iii) a petition for a bankruptcy order under Part 9 of the 1986 Act or Part 9 of the 1989 Order; and

(iv) a petition for sequestration under section 5 or 6 of the Bankruptcy (Scotland) Act, but

does not include prosecution for a criminal offence.

(3) Except with the permission of the court, for the period during which a Lloyd's market reorganisation order is in force, no execution may be commenced or continued, no security may be enforced, and no distress may be levied, against (or against the assets of or in the possession of):

(a) any person specified in paragraph (1);

(b) a relevant trust fund (or the trustees of a relevant trust fund); and

(c) an overseas business regulatory deposit.

(4) Paragraph (3) does not prevent the enforcement of—

(a) approved security granted to secure payment of approved debts of a member incurred in connection with an overseas regulatory deposit arrangement; or

(b) security granted by a Lloyd's broker over assets not being assets constituting or representing assets received or held by the Lloyd's broker as intermediary in respect of any contract of insurance or reinsurance written at Lloyd's or any contract of reinsurance reinsuring a member of Lloyd's in respect of a contract or contracts of insurance or reinsurance written by that member at Lloyd's.

(5) In the application of paragraph (3) to Scotland, references to execution being commenced or continued include references to diligence being carried out or continued, and references to distress being levied shall be omitted.

(6) For the period during which a Lloyd's market reorganisation order is in force, no action or step may be taken in respect of any of the persons specified in paragraph (1) by any person who is or may be entitled—

(a) under any provision in Schedule B1 to appoint an administrator;

(b) to appoint an administrative receiver or receiver;

(c) under section 425 of the 1985 Act or Article 418 of the Companies Order to propose a compromise or arrangement,

unless he has complied with paragraph (7).

(7) A person intending to take any such action or step shall give notice to the reorganisation controller before doing so.

(8) Where a person fails to comply with paragraph (7),

(a) an appointment to which sub-paragraph (6)(a) or (b) applies shall be void, and

(b) no application under section 425 or Article 418 may be entertained by the court,

except where the court, having heard the reorganisation controller, orders otherwise.

(9) Every application pursuant to paragraph (1) or paragraph (3) must be served on the reorganisation controller.

(10) For the period during which a Lloyd's market reorganisation order is in force, an affected market participant in Scotland may not grant a trust deed for his creditors without the consent of the reorganisation controller.

(11) Where a person who is subject to a Lloyd's market reorganisation order is, at the date of the order, in administration or liquidation or has been adjudged bankrupt or is a person whose estate is being sequestrated or who has granted a trust deed for his creditors—

(a) any application to the court for permission to take any action that would be subject to a moratorium arising in those earlier proceedings shall be served on the reorganisation controller and the reorganisation controller shall be entitled to be heard on the application; and

(b) the court shall take into account the achievement of the objectives for which the Lloyd's market reorganisation order was made.

(12) In this regulation—

(a) "approved debt" means a debt approved by the Society at the time it is incurred;

(b) "approved security" means security approved by the Society at the time it is granted over or in respect of assets comprised in the member's premiums trust funds or liable in the future to become comprised therein;

(c) "overseas regulatory deposit arrangement" means an arrangement approved by the Society and notified to the Authority whose purpose is to facilitate funding of any overseas business regulatory deposit.

[2692]

NOTES

Commencement: 10 August 2005.

9 Reorganisation controller

(1) The reorganisation controller is an officer of the court.

(2) A person may be appointed as reorganisation controller only if he is qualified to act as an insolvency practitioner under Part 13 of the 1986 Act and the court considers that he has appropriate knowledge, expertise and experience.

(3) On an application by the reorganisation controller, the court may appoint one or more additional reorganisation controllers to act jointly or severally with the first reorganisation controller on such terms as the court sees fit.

[2693]

NOTES
Commencement: 10 August 2005.

10 Announcement of appointment of controller

(1) This regulation applies when the court makes a Lloyd's market reorganisation order.

(2) As soon as is practicable after the order has been made, the Authority must inform the EEA regulators in every EEA State—

(a) that the order has been made; and

(b) in general terms, of the possible effect of a Lloyd's market reorganisation order on—

(i) the effecting or carrying out of contracts of insurance at Lloyd's, and

(ii) the rights of policyholders under or in respect of contracts of insurance written at Lloyd's.

(3) As soon as is reasonably practicable after a person becomes the reorganisation controller, he must—

(a) procure that notice of his appointment is posted—

(i) in the Room,

(ii) on the Society's website, and

(iii) on the Authority's website; and

(b) publish a notice of his appointment—

(i) once in the Gazette, and

(ii) once in such newspapers as he thinks most appropriate for securing so far as possible that the Lloyd's market reorganisation order comes to the notice of those who may be affected by it.

[2694]

NOTES
Commencement: 10 August 2005.

11 Market reorganisation plan

(1) The reorganisation controller may require any affected market participant, and any Lloyd's broker, approved run-off company, coverholder, the Society, subsidiary of the Society or trustee of a relevant trust fund—

(a) to provide him with any information he considers useful to him in the achievement of the objectives set out in regulation 5; and

(b) to carry out such work as may be necessary to prepare or organise information as the reorganisation controller may consider useful to him in the achievement of those objectives.

(2) As soon as is reasonably practicable and in any event by such date as the court may require, the reorganisation controller must prepare a plan ("the market reorganisation plan") for achieving the objectives of the Lloyd's market reorganisation order.

(3) The reorganisation controller must send a copy of the market reorganisation plan to the Authority and to the Society.

(4) Before the end of a period of one month beginning with the day on which it receives the market reorganisation plan, the Authority must notify the reorganisation controller and the Society in writing of its decision to—

(a) approve the plan;

(b) reject the plan; or

(c) approve the plan provisionally, subject to modifications set out in the notification.

(5) Where the Authority rejects the plan, the notification must—

(a) give reasons for its decision; and

(b) specify a date by which the reorganisation controller may submit a new market reorganisation plan.

(6) Where the reorganisation controller submits a new market reorganisation plan, he must send a copy to the Authority and to the Society.

(7) Before the end of a period of one month beginning with the day on which the Authority receives that plan, the Authority must—

(a) accept it;
(b) reject it; or
(c) accept it provisionally subject to modifications.

(8) Before the end of a period of one month beginning with the day on which he receives the notification from the Authority of the modifications required by it, the reorganisation controller must—

(a) accept the plan as modified by the Authority; or
(b) reject the plan as so modified.

(9) The reorganisation controller must—

(a) file with the court the market reorganisation plan that has been approved by him and the Authority, and
(b) send a copy of it to—
 (i) every member, former member, managing agent and member's agent who requests it, and
 (ii) every other person who requests it, on payment of a reasonable charge.

(10) Paragraph (11) applies if—

(a) the Authority rejects the market reorganisation plan and the reorganisation controller decides not to submit a new market reorganisation plan;
(b) the Authority rejects the new market reorganisation plan submitted by the reorganisation controller; or
(c) the reorganisation controller rejects the modifications made by the Authority to a new market reorganisation plan.

(11) As soon as is reasonably practicable after any such rejection, the reorganisation controller must apply to the court for directions.

(12) The Authority or the reorganisation controller as the case may be may apply to the court for an extension of the period specified in paragraph (4), (7) or (8) by a period of not more than one month. The court may not grant more than one such extension in respect of each period.

(13) Where any person is under an obligation to publish anything under this regulation, that obligation is subject to the provisions of sections 348 and 349 of the 2000 Act.

[2695]

NOTES

Commencement: 10 August 2005.

12 Remuneration of the reorganisation controller

(1) The reorganisation controller shall be entitled to receive remuneration and to recover expenses properly incurred in connection with the performance of his functions under or in connection with a Lloyd's market reorganisation order.

(2) Subject to paragraph (3), the remuneration so charged is payable by—

(a) members,
(b) former members,
(c) the Society, and
(d) managing agents.

(3) The court must give directions as to the payment of the remuneration and expenses of the reorganisation controller and in particular may provide for—

(a) apportionment of the amounts so charged between the classes of persons set out in paragraph (2) and between groups of persons within those classes; and
(b) payment of such remuneration and expenses out of relevant trust funds.

(4) Amounts of such remuneration and expenses paid by any of the persons described in paragraph (2) are to be treated as payments of the expenses of a liquidator, administrator, trustee in bankruptcy or in Scotland an interim or permanent trustee.

(5) The reorganisation controller may pay the reasonable charges of those to whom he has addressed a request for assistance or information under regulation 11 or anyone else from whom he has requested assistance in the performance of his functions.

(6) The provision of such information or assistance in good faith does not constitute a breach of

(a) any duty owed by any person involved in its preparation or delivery to any company or partnership of which he is an officer, member or employee,

(b) any duty owed by an agent to his principal, or

(c) any duty of confidence, subject to sections 348 and 349 of the 2000 Act.

[2696]

NOTES

Commencement: 10 August 2005.

13 Treatment of members

(1) Paragraph (2) applies where, after the making of a Lloyd's market reorganisation order, any of the following occurs pursuant to the 1986 Act, the 1989 Order or the Bankruptcy (Scotland) Act—

(a) a person seeks to exercise an entitlement to appoint an administrator,

(b) an application is made to the court for the appointment of an administrator,

(c) a petition for the winding up of a corporate member is presented to the court,

(d) a petition for a bankruptcy order or sequestration is presented to the court,

in respect of a member.

(2) These Regulations, the principal Regulations and the Administration for Insurers Order shall apply to the member and—

(a) for the purposes of the principal Regulations (notwithstanding regulation 3 of those Regulations), the member shall be treated as if it, he or she were a UK insurer; and

(b) for the purposes of the Administration for Insurers Order, a member that is a company shall be treated as if it were an insurance company.

(3) Paragraph (2) does not apply where the court so orders, on the application of the administrator, liquidator, provisional liquidator, receiver or trustee in bankruptcy, the Accountant in Bankruptcy or trustee under a trust deed for creditors or the person referred to in paragraph (1)(b) or (c) seeking the appointment or presenting the petition.

(4) A person who exercises an entitlement, makes an application or submits a petition to which paragraph (1) applies shall—

(a) if he intends to make an application under paragraph (3) make the application before doing any of those things; and

(b) include in any statement to be made under Schedule B1, or in any application or petition, a statement as to whether an order under paragraph (3) has been made in respect of the member concerned.

(5) An application under paragraph (3) must be notified to the reorganisation controller.

(6) The court must take account of any representation made by the reorganisation controller in relation to the application.

(7) The court may not make an order under paragraph (3) unless the court considers it likely that the insurance market debts of the member will be satisfied.

(8) In this regulation and regulation 14, references to a member include references to a former member.

[2697]

NOTES

Commencement: 10 August 2005.

14 Revocation of an order under regulation 13

(1) This regulation applies in the case of a member in respect of whom an order has been made under regulation 13(3).

(2) If the Society does not meet any request for payment of a cash call made by or on behalf of such a member, it must so inform the reorganisation controller, the Authority and the court.

(3) If it appears to the reorganisation controller that, in respect of any such member, the insurance market debts of the member are not likely to be satisfied, he must apply to the court for the revocation of that order.

(4) If the court revokes an order made under regulation 13(3), the provisions of these Regulations, the principal Regulations and the Administration for Insurers Order apply to the member and from the date of the revocation a relevant officer is to be treated as having been appointed by the court.

(5) For the purposes of paragraph (4), a relevant officer means—

(a) an administrator,
(b) a liquidator,
(c) a receiver,
(d) a trustee in bankruptcy, or
(e) in Scotland, an interim or permanent trustee,

as the case may be.

(6) For the purposes of this regulation, a "cash call" means a request or demand made by a managing agent to a member of a syndicate to make payments to the trustees of any relevant trust fund to be held for the purpose of discharging or providing for the liabilities incurred by that member as a member of the syndicate.

[2698]

NOTES

Commencement: 10 August 2005.

15 Reorganisation controller's powers: voluntary arrangements in respect of a member

(1) The directors of a corporate member or former corporate member may make a proposal for a voluntary arrangement under Part 1 of the 1986 Act (or Part 2 of the 1989 Order) in relation to the member only if the reorganisation controller consents to the terms of that arrangement.

(2) Section 1A of that Act or Article 14A of that Order do not apply to a corporate member or former corporate member if—

(a) a Lloyd's market reorganisation order applies to it; and

(b) there is no order under regulation 13(3) in force in relation to it.

(3) The reorganisation controller is entitled to be heard at any hearing of an application relating to the arrangement.

[2699]

NOTES

Commencement: 10 August 2005.

16 Reorganisation controller's powers: individual voluntary arrangements in respect of a member

(1) The reorganisation controller is entitled to be heard on an application under section 253 of the 1986 Act (or Article 227 of the 1989 Order) by an individual member or former member.

(2) When considering such an application the court shall have regard to the objectives of the Lloyd's market reorganisation order.

(3) Paragraphs (4) to (7) apply if an interim order is made on the application of such a person.

(4) The reorganisation controller, or a person appointed by him for that purpose, may attend any meeting of creditors of the member or former member summoned under section 257 of the 1986 Act (or Article 231 of the 1989 Order) (summoning of creditors meeting).

(5) Notice of the result of a meeting so summoned must be given to the reorganisation controller by the chairman of the meeting.

(6) The reorganisation controller may apply to the court under section 262 (challenge of meeting's decision) or 263 (implementation and supervision of approved voluntary arrangement) of the 1986 Act (or Article 236 or 237 or the 1989 Order).

(7) If a person other than the reorganisation controller makes an application to the court under any provision mentioned in paragraph (6), the reorganisation controller is entitled to be heard at any hearing relating to the application.

[2700]

NOTES

Commencement: 10 August 2005.

17 Reorganisation controller's powers: trust deeds for creditors in Scotland

(1) This regulation applies to the granting at any time by a debtor who is a member or former member of a trust deed for creditors.

(2) The debtor must inform the person who is or is proposed to be the trustee at or before the time that the trust deed is granted that he is a member or former member of Lloyd's.

(3) As soon as practicable after the making of the Lloyd's market reorganisation order the trustee must send to the reorganisation controller—

(a) in every case, a copy of the trust deed;

(b) where any other document or information is sent to every creditor known to the trustee in pursuance of paragraph 5(1)(c) of Schedule 5 to the Bankruptcy (Scotland) Act 1985, a copy of such document or information.

(4) If the debtor or the trustee fails without reasonable excuse to comply with any obligation in paragraph (2) or (3) he shall be guilty of an offence and shall be liable on summary conviction to a fine not exceeding level 5 on the statutory scale or to imprisonment for a term not exceeding 3 months or both.

(5) Paragraph 7 of that Schedule applies to the reorganisation controller as if he were a qualified creditor who has not been sent a copy of the notice as mentioned in paragraph 5(1)(c) of the Schedule.

(6) The reorganisation controller must be given the same notice as the creditors of any meeting of creditors held in relation to the trust deed.

(7) The reorganisation controller, or a person appointed by him for the purpose, is entitled to attend and participate in (but not to vote at) any such meeting of creditors as if the reorganisation controller were a creditor under the deed.

(8) Expressions used in this regulation and in the Bankruptcy (Scotland) Act 1985 have the same meaning in this regulation as in that Act.

[2701]

NOTES

Commencement: 10 August 2005.

18 Powers of reorganisation controller: section 425 or Article 418 compromise or arrangement

(1) The reorganisation controller may apply to the court for an order that a meeting or meetings be summoned under section 425(1) of the 1985 Act or Article 418(1) of the Companies Order (power of company to compromise with creditors and members) in connection with a compromise or arrangement in relation to a member or former member.

(2) Where a member, its creditors or members make an application under section 425(1) or Article 418 the reorganisation controller is entitled to attend and be heard at any hearing.

(3) Where a meeting is summoned under section 425(1) or Article 418(1), the reorganisation controller is entitled to attend the meeting so summoned and to participate in it (but not to vote at it).

[2702]

NOTES

Commencement: 10 August 2005.

19 Appointment of an administrator, receiver or interim trustee in relation to a member

(1) Where a Lloyd's market reorganisation order is in force, the following appointments may be made in relation to a member or former member only where an order has been made under regulation 13(3) and has not been revoked and shall be notified to the reorganisation controller—

(a) the appointment of an administrator under paragraph 14 of Schedule B1;

(b) the appointment of an administrator under paragraph 22 of Schedule B1;

(c) the appointment of an administrative receiver;

(d) the appointment of an interim receiver; and

(e) the appointment of an interim trustee, within the meaning of the Bankruptcy (Scotland) Act 1985.

(2) The notification to the reorganisation controller under paragraph (1) must be in writing.

(3) If the requirement to notify the reorganisation controller in paragraph (1) is not complied with the administrator, administrative receiver, interim receiver or interim trustee is guilty of an offence and is liable on conviction to a fine not exceeding level 3 on the standard scale.

[2703]

NOTES

Commencement: 10 August 2005.

20 Reorganisation controller's powers: administration orders in respect of members

(1) The reorganisation controller may make an administration application under paragraph 12 of Schedule B1 in respect of a member or former member.

(2) Paragraphs (3) to (5) apply if—

(a) a person other than the reorganisation controller makes an administration application under Schedule B1 in relation to a member or former member; and

(b) an order under regulation 13(3) is not in force in respect of that member.

(3) The reorganisation controller is entitled to be heard—

(a) at the hearing of the administration application; and

(b) at any other hearing of the court in relation to the member under Schedule B1 (or Part 3 of the 1989 Order).

(4) Any notice or other document required to be sent to a creditor of the member must also be sent to the reorganisation controller.

(5) The reorganisation controller, or a person appointed by him for the purpose, may—

(a) attend any meeting of creditors of the member summoned under any enactment;

(b) attend any meeting of a committee established under paragraph 57 of Schedule B1; and

(c) make representations as to any matter for decision at such a meeting.

(6) If, during the course of the administration of a member, a compromise or arrangement is proposed between the member and its creditors, or any class of them, the reorganisation controller may apply to court under section 425 of the 1985 Act (or Article 418 of the Companies Order).

[2704]

NOTES

Commencement: 10 August 2005.

21 Reorganisation controller's powers: receivership in relation to members

(1) This regulation applies if a receiver has been appointed in relation to a member or former member.

(2) The reorganisation controller may be heard on an application made under section 35 or 63 of the 1986 Act (or Article 45 of the 1989 Order).

(3) The reorganisation controller may make an application under section 41(1)(a) or 69(1)(a) of the 1986 Act (or Article 51(1)(a) of the 1989 Order).

(4) A report under section 48(1) or 67(1) of the 1986 Act (or Article 58(1) of the 1989 Order) must be sent by the person making it to the reorganisation controller.

(5) The reorganisation controller, or a person appointed by him for the purpose, may—
- (a) attend any meeting of creditors of the member or former member summoned under any enactment;
- (b) attend any meeting of a committee established under section 49 or 68 of the 1986 Act (or Article 58 of the 1989 Order);
- (c) attend any meeting of a committee of creditors of a member or former member in Scotland; and
- (d) make representations as to any matter for decision at such a meeting.

(6) Where an administration application is made in respect of a member by the reorganisation controller (and there is an administrative receiver, or in Scotland a receiver, of that member), paragraph 39 of Schedule B1 does not require the court to dismiss the application if it thinks that—
- (a) the objectives of the Lloyd's market reorganisation order are more likely to be achieved by the appointment of an administrator than by the appointment or continued appointment of a receiver in respect of that member, and
- (b) the interests of the person by or on behalf of whom the receiver was appointed will be adequately protected.

[2705]

NOTES
Commencement: 10 August 2005.

22 Syndicate set-off

(1) This regulation applies where—
- (a) a member ("the debtor") is subject to a relevant insolvency proceeding; and
- (b) no order under regulation 13(3) is in effect in relation to the debtor.

(2) In the application of section 323 of the 1986 Act or Article 296 of the 1989 Order, Rule 2.85 and Rule 4.90 of the Insolvency Rules or R4.096 of the Insolvency Rules (Northern Ireland) to the debtor, the following paragraphs apply in relation to each syndicate of which the debtor is a member, and for that purpose each reference to the debtor is to the debtor as a member of that syndicate only.

(3) Subject to paragraphs (4) and (5), where there have been mutual credits, mutual debts or other mutual dealings between the debtor in the course of his business as a member of the syndicate ("syndicate A") and a creditor, an account shall be taken of what is due from the debtor to that creditor, and of what is due from that creditor to the debtor, such account to be taken in respect of business transacted by the debtor as a member of syndicate A only and the sums due from one party shall be set off against the sums due from the other.

(4) Where the creditor is a member (whether or not a member of syndicate A) and there have been mutual credits, mutual debts or other mutual dealings between the debtor as a member of syndicate A and the creditor in the course of the creditor's business as a member of syndicate A or of another syndicate of which he is a member, paragraph (5) applies.

(5) A separate account must be taken in relation to each syndicate of which the creditor is a member of what is due from the debtor to the creditor, and of what is due from the creditor to the debtor, in respect only of business transacted between the debtor as a member of syndicate A and the creditor as a member of the syndicate in question (and not in respect of business transacted by the creditor as a member of any other syndicate or otherwise), and the sums due from one party shall be set off against the sums due from the other.

(6) In this regulation—
- (a) references to a member include references to a former member; and
- (b) "relevant insolvency proceedings" means proceedings in respect of an application or petition referred to in regulation 13(1).

[2706]

NOTES
Commencement: 10 August 2005.

23 Voluntary winding up of members: consent of reorganisation controller

(1) During any period in which a Lloyd's market reorganisation order is in force, a member or former member that is a company may not be wound up voluntarily without the consent of the reorganisation controller.

(2) Before a member or former member passes a resolution for voluntary winding up it must give written notice to the reorganisation controller.

(3) Where notice is given under paragraph (2), a resolution for voluntary winding up may be passed only—

(a) after the end of a period of five business days beginning with the day on which the notice was given, if the reorganisation controller has not refused his consent, or

(b) if the reorganisation controller has consented in writing to the passing of the resolution.

(4) A copy of a resolution for the voluntary winding up of a member forwarded to the registrar of companies in accordance with section 380 of the 1985 Act (or Article 388 of the Companies Order) must be accompanied by a certificate issued by the reorganisation controller stating that he consents to the voluntary winding up of the member.

(5) If paragraph (4) is complied with, the voluntary winding up is to be treated as having commenced at the time the resolution was passed.

(6) If paragraph (4) is not complied with, the resolution has no effect.

[2707]

NOTES

Commencement: 10 August 2005.

24 Voluntary winding up of members: powers of reorganisation controller

(1) This regulation applies in relation to a member or former member that is a company and which is being wound up voluntarily with the consent of the reorganisation controller.

(2) The reorganisation controller may apply to the court under section 112 of the 1986 Act (reference of questions to court) (or Article 98 of the 1989 Order) in respect of the member.

(3) The reorganisation controller is entitled to be heard at any hearing of the court in relation to the voluntary winding up of the member.

(4) Any notice or other document required to be sent to a creditor of the member must also be sent to the reorganisation controller.

(5) The reorganisation controller, or a person appointed by him for the purpose, is entitled—

(a) to attend any meeting of creditors of the member summoned under any enactment;

(b) to attend any meeting of a committee established under section 101 of the 1986 Act (or Article 87 of the 1989 Order); and

(c) to make representations as to any matter for decision at such a meeting.

(6) If, during the course of the winding up of the member, a compromise or arrangement is proposed between the member and its creditors, or any class of them, the reorganisation controller may apply to court under section 425 of the 1985 Act (or Article 418 of the Companies Order).

[2708]

NOTES

Commencement: 10 August 2005.

25 Petition for winding up of a member by reorganisation controller

(1) The reorganisation controller may present a petition to the court for the winding up of a member or former member that is a company.

(2) The petition is to be treated as made under section 124 of the 1986 Act or Article 104 of the 1989 Order.

(3) Section 122(1) of the 1986 Act, or Article 102(1) of the 1989 Order must, in the case of an application made by the reorganisation controller be read as if they included the following grounds—

(a) the member is in default of an obligation to pay an insurance market debt which is due and payable; or

(b) the court considers that the member is or is likely to be unable to pay insurance market debts as they fall due; and

(c) in the case of either (a) or (b), the court thinks that the winding up of the member is necessary or desirable for achieving the objectives of the Lloyd's market reorganisation order.

[2709]

NOTES

Commencement: 10 August 2005.

26 Winding up of a member: powers of reorganisation controller

(1) This regulation applies if a person other than the reorganisation controller presents a petition for the winding up of a member or former member that is a company.

(2) Any notice or other document required to be sent to a creditor of the member must also be sent to the reorganisation controller.

(3) The reorganisation controller may be heard—

(a) at the hearing of the petition; and

(b) at any other hearing of the court in relation to the member under or by virtue of Part 4 or 5 of the 1986 Act (or Part 5 or 6 of the 1989 Order).

(4) The reorganisation controller, or a person appointed by him for the purpose, may—

(a) attend any meeting of the creditors of the member;

(b) attend any meeting of a committee established for the purposes of Part 4 or 5 of the 1986 Act under section 101 of that Act or under section 141 or 142 of that Act;

(c) attend any meeting of a committee established for the purposes of Part 5 or 6 of the 1989 Order under Article 87 or Article 120 of that Order;

(d) make representations as to any matter for decision at such a meeting.

(5) If, during the course of the winding up of a member, a compromise or arrangement is proposed between the member and its creditors, or any class of them, the reorganisation controller may apply to the court under section 425 of the 1985 Act (or Article 418 of the Companies Order).

[2710]

NOTES

Commencement: 10 August 2005.

27 Petition for bankruptcy of a member by reorganisation controller

(1) The reorganisation controller may present a petition to the court for a bankruptcy order to be made against an individual member or, in Scotland, for the sequestration of the estate of an individual.

(2) The application shall be treated as made under section 264 of the 1986 Act (or Article 238 of the 1989 Order) or in Scotland under section 5 or 6 of the Bankruptcy (Scotland) Act 1985.

(3) On such a petition, the court may make a bankruptcy order or in Scotland an award of sequestration if (and only if)—

(a) the member is in default of an obligation to pay an insurance market debt which is due and payable; and

(b) the court thinks that the making of a bankruptcy order or award of sequestration in respect of that member is necessary or desirable for achieving the objectives of the Lloyd's market reorganisation order.

[2711]

NOTES

Commencement: 10 August 2005.

28 Bankruptcy of a member: powers of reorganisation controller

(1) This regulation applies if a person other than the reorganisation controller presents a petition to the court—

(a) under section 264 of the 1986 Act (or Article 238 of the 1989 Order) for a bankruptcy order to be made against an individual member;

(b) under section 5 of the Bankruptcy (Scotland) Act 1985 for the sequestration of the estate of an individual member; or

(c) under section 6 of that Act for the sequestration of the estate belonging to or held for or jointly by the members of an entity mentioned in subsection (1) of that section.

(2) The reorganisation controller is entitled to be heard—

(a) at the hearing of the petition, and

(b) at any other hearing in relation to the individual member or entity under—

(i) Part 9 of the 1986 Act,

(ii) Part 9 of the 1989 Order; or

(iii) the Bankruptcy (Scotland) Act 1985.

(3) A copy of the report prepared under section 274 of the 1986 Act (or Article 248 of the 1989 Order) must also be sent to the reorganisation controller.

(4) The reorganisation controller, or a person appointed by him for the purpose, is entitled—

(a) to attend any meeting of the creditors of the individual member or entity;

(b) to attend any meeting of a committee established under section 301 of the 1986 Act (or Article 274 of the 1989 Order);

(c) to attend any meeting of commissioners held under paragraph 17 or 18 of Schedule 6 to the Bankruptcy (Scotland) Act; and

(d) to make representations as to any matter for decision at such a meeting.

(5) In this regulation—

(a) references to an individual member include references to a former member who is an individual;

(b) "entity" means an entity which is a member or a former member.

[2712]

NOTES

Commencement: 10 August 2005.

29 Petition for winding up of the Society by reorganisation controller

(1) The reorganisation controller may present a petition to the court for the winding up of the Society in the circumstances set out in section 221(5) (winding up of unregistered companies) of the 1986 Act.

(2) Section 221(1) of that Act shall apply in respect of a petition presented by the reorganisation controller.

[2713]

NOTES

Commencement: 10 August 2005.

30 Winding up of the Society: service of petition etc on reorganisation controller

(1) This regulation applies if a person other than the reorganisation controller presents a petition for the winding up of the Society.

(2) The petitioner must serve a copy of the petition on the reorganisation controller.

(3) Any notice or other document required to be sent to a creditor of the Society must also be sent to the reorganisation controller.

(4) The reorganisation controller is entitled to be heard—

(a) at the hearing of the petition; and

(b) at any other hearing of the court in relation to the Society under or by virtue of Part 5 of the 1986 Act (winding up of unregistered companies).

(5) The reorganisation controller, or a person appointed by him for the purpose, is entitled—

(a) to attend any meeting of the creditors of the Society;

(b) to attend any meeting of a committee established for the purposes of Part 5 of the 1986 Act under section 101 of that Act (appointment of liquidation committee);

(c) to make representations as to any matter for decision at such a meeting.

(6) If, during the course of the winding up of the Society, a compromise or arrangement is proposed between the Society and its creditors, or any class of them, the reorganisation controller may apply to the court under section 425 of the 1985 Act.

[2714]

NOTES

Commencement: 10 August 2005.

31 Payments from central funds

(1) Unless otherwise agreed in writing between the Society, the reorganisation controller and the Authority, before making a payment from central funds during the period of the Lloyd's market reorganisation order, the Society must give 5 working days notice to the reorganisation controller.

(2) Notice under paragraph (1) must specify—

(a) the amount of the proposed payment;

(b) the purpose for which it is proposed to be made;

(c) the recipient of the proposed payment.

(3) An agreement under paragraph (1) may in particular provide for payments—

(a) to a specified person;

(b) to a specified class of person;

(c) for a specified purpose;

(d) for a specified class of purposes,

to be made without the notice provided for in paragraph (1)

(4) If before the end of the period of 5 working days from the date on which he receives the notice under paragraph (1) the reorganisation controller considers that the payment should not be made, he must within that period—

(a) apply to the court for a determination that the payment not be made; and

(b) give notice of his application to the Society and the Authority on or before the making of the application,

and the Society must not make payment without the permission of the court.

(5) The Society and the Authority may be heard at any hearing in connection with any such application.

(6) Where the reorganisation controller makes an application under paragraph (4), the Society commits an offence if it makes a payment from central funds without the permission of the court.

(7) If an offence under paragraph (6) is shown to have been committed with the consent or connivance of an officer of the Society, the officer as well as the Society is guilty of the offence.

(8) A person guilty of an offence under this regulation is liable—

(a) on summary conviction, to a fine not exceeding the statutory maximum;

(b) on conviction on indictment, to a fine.

(9) In this regulation "working day" means any day other than a Saturday, a Sunday, Christmas Day, Good Friday or a day which is a bank holiday under the Banking and Financial Dealings Act 1971 in any part of the United Kingdom.

(10) In paragraph (7), "officer", in relation to the Society, means the Chairman of Lloyd's, a Deputy Chairman of Lloyd's, the Chairman of the Committee established by section 5 of Lloyd's Act 1982, a deputy Chairman of the Committee, or a member of the Council established by section 3 of that Act.

[2715]

NOTES

Commencement: 10 August 2005.

PART 3

MODIFICATION OF LAW OF INSOLVENCY: NOTIFICATION AND PUBLICATION

32 Application of Parts 3 and 4

Parts 3 and 4 of these Regulations apply where a Lloyd's market reorganisation order is in force and in respect of a member or former member in relation to whom no order under regulation 13(3) is in force.

[2716]

NOTES

Commencement: 10 August 2005.

33 Notification of relevant decision to Authority

(1) Regulation 9 of the principal Regulations applies to a member or former member in the circumstances set out in paragraph (2) and has effect as if the modifications set out in paragraphs (3) and (4) were included in it as regards members or former members.

(2) The circumstances are where—

(a) the member or former member is subject to a Lloyd's market reorganisation order which remains in force; and

(b) no order has been made in respect of that member or former member under regulation 13(3) of these Regulations and has not been revoked.

(3) In paragraph (1) of regulation 9 of the principal Regulations, insert—

(a) after sub-paragraph (b)—

"(ba) a bankruptcy order under section 264 of the 1986 Act or under Article 245 or 247 of the 1989 Order;

(bb) an award of sequestration under the Bankruptcy (Scotland) Act 1985;";

(b) after paragraph (c)—

"(ca) the appointment of an interim trustee under section 286 or 287 of the 1986 Act or under Article 259 or 260 of the 1989 Order;

(cb) the appointment of a trustee in bankruptcy under sections 295, 296 or 300 of that Act or under Articles 268, 269 or 273 of that Order;

(cc) the appointment of an interim or permanent trustee under the Bankruptcy (Scotland) Act 1985;".

(4) In paragraph (2) of that regulation after "voluntary arrangement", insert "or individual voluntary arrangement" and after "supervisor" insert "or nominee (as the case may be)".

(5) In paragraph (7) of that regulation, in the definition of "qualifying arrangement",

(a) after "voluntary arrangement" insert "or individual voluntary arrangement"; and

(b) for "insurer", wherever appearing substitute "member or former member".

(6) In paragraph (8), after "supervisor" insert ", nominee, trustee in bankruptcy, trustee under a trust deed for creditors".

[2717]

NOTES

Commencement: 10 August 2005.

34 Notification of relevant decision to EEA Regulators

Regulation 10 of the principal Regulations applies as if—

(a) in paragraph (1)(b)(i) for "the business of an insurer" there were substituted "the insurance business of a member or former member"; and

(b) in paragraph (1)(b)(ii) for "an insurer" there were substituted "a member or former member".

[2718]

NOTES

Commencement: 10 August 2005.

35 Application of certain publication requirements in the principal Regulations to members

(1) Regulation 11 of the principal Regulations (publication of voluntary arrangement, administration order, winding up order or scheme of arrangement) applies, with the following, where a qualifying decision has effect, or a qualifying order or appointment is made, in relation to a member or former member.

(2) References in regulation 11(2) to a "qualifying decision", a "qualifying order" and a "qualifying appointment" have the same meaning as in that regulation, subject to the modifications set out in paragraphs (3) and (5).

(3) Regulation 11(2)(a) has effect as if a qualifying decision included a decision with respect to the approval of a proposed individual voluntary arrangement in relation to a member in accordance with section 258 of the 1986 Act or Article 232 of the 1989 Order (decisions of creditors' meeting: individual voluntary arrangements) or in Scotland the grant of a trust deed (within the meaning of the Bankruptcy (Scotland) Act 1985).

(4) In the case of a qualifying decision of a kind mentioned in paragraph (3) above, regulation 11(4) has effect as if the information mentioned therein included the court to which an application under sections 262 (challenge of the meeting's decision) and 263(3) (implementation and supervision of approved voluntary arrangement) of the 1986 Act may be made or Articles 236 (challenge of the meeting's decision) and 237(3) (implementation and supervision of approved voluntary arrangement) of the 1989 Order, or in Scotland under paragraph 12 of Schedule 5 to the Bankruptcy (Scotland) Act 1985.

(5) Regulation 11(2)(b) has effect as if a qualifying order included in relation to a member or former member a bankruptcy order under Part 9 of the 1986 Act or Part 9 of the 1989 Order, or in Scotland, an award of sequestration under the Bankruptcy (Scotland) Act.

(6) In the case of a qualifying order of the kind mentioned in paragraph (5) above, regulation 11(4) has effect as if the information mentioned therein included the court to which an application may be made under section 303 or 375 of the 1986 Act or Article 276 of the 1989 Order, or in Scotland included the court having jurisdiction to sequestrate.

(7) Regulation 11(11) has effect as if the meaning of "relevant officer" included—

- (a) in the case of a voluntary arrangement under Part 9 of the 1986 Act or Part 9 of the 1989 Order, the nominee;
- (b) in the case of a bankruptcy order, the trustee in bankruptcy;
- (c) in Scotland,
  - (i) the trustee acting under a trust deed;
  - (ii) in the case of an award of sequestration, the interim or permanent trustee, as the case may be.

[2719]

NOTES

Commencement: 10 August 2005.

36 Notification to creditors: winding up proceedings relating to members

(1) Regulation 12 of the principal Regulations (notification to creditors: winding up proceedings) applies, with the following modifications, where a relevant order or appointment is made, or a relevant decision is taken, in relation to a member or former member.

(2) References in paragraph (3) of that regulation to a "relevant order", a "relevant appointment" and a "relevant decision" have the meaning they have in that regulation, subject to the modifications set out in paragraphs (3) and (7).

(3) Paragraph (3) of that regulation has effect, for the purposes of this regulation, as if—

- (a) a relevant order included a bankruptcy order made in relation to a member or former member under Part 9 of the 1986 Act or Part 9 of the 1989 Order or an award of sequestration under the Bankruptcy (Scotland) Act 1985; and
- (b) a relevant decision included a decision as a result of which a qualifying individual

voluntary arrangement in relation to a member or former member has effect in accordance with section 258 of the 1986 Act or Article 232 of the 1989 Order (decisions of creditors' meeting: individual voluntary arrangements) or in Scotland the grant of a qualifying trust deed.

(4) Paragraph (4)(a) of that regulation has effect as if the reference to a UK insurer included a reference to a member or former member who is to be treated as a UK insurer for the purposes of the application of the principal Regulations.

(5) Paragraph (9) of that regulation has effect as if, in a case where a bankruptcy order is made in relation to a member or former member, it permitted the obligation under paragraph (1)(a)(ii) of that regulation to be discharged by sending a form of proof in accordance with rule 6.97 of the Insolvency Rules or Rule 6.095 of the Insolvency Rules (Northern Ireland) or submitting a claim in accordance with section 48 of the Bankruptcy (Scotland) Act 1985, provided that the form of proof or submission of claim complies with paragraph (7) or (8) of that regulation (whichever is applicable).

(6) Paragraph (13)(a) of that regulation has effect as if the meaning of "appointed officer" included—

(a) in the case of a qualifying individual voluntary arrangement approved in relation to a member or former member, the nominee;

(b) in the case of a bankruptcy order in relation to an individual member or former member, the trustee in bankruptcy;

(c) in Scotland in the case of a sequestration, the interim or permanent trustee; and

(d) in Scotland in the case of a relevant decision, the trustee.

(7) For the purposes of paragraph (3) of that regulation, an individual voluntary arrangement approved in relation to an individual member or former member is a qualifying individual voluntary arrangement and a trust deed within section 5(4A) of the Bankruptcy (Scotland) Act 1985 is a qualifying trust deed if its purposes or objects, as the case may be, include a realisation of some or all of the assets of that member or former member and a distribution of the proceeds to creditors, with a view to terminating the whole or any part of the business of that member carried on or formerly carried on in connection with contracts of insurance written at Lloyd's.

[2720]

NOTES

Commencement: 10 August 2005.

37 Submission of claims by EEA creditor

(1) Regulation 13 of the principal Regulations (submission of claims by EEA creditors) applies, with the modifications set out in paragraphs (3) to (6) below, in the circumstances set out in paragraph (2) below, in the same way as it applies where an EEA creditor submits a claim or observations in the circumstances set out in paragraph (1) of that regulation.

(2) Those circumstances are where, after the date these Regulations come into force an EEA creditor submits a claim or observations relating to his claim in any relevant proceedings in respect of a member or former member (irrespective of when those proceedings were commenced or had effect).

(3) Paragraph (2) of that regulation has effect as if the "relevant proceedings" included—

(a) bankruptcy or sequestration; or

(b) a qualifying individual voluntary arrangement or in Scotland a qualifying trust deed for creditors.

(4) Paragraph (5) of that regulation has effect as if it also provided that paragraph (3) of that regulation does not apply where an EEA creditor submits his claim using—

(a) in a case of a bankruptcy or an award of sequestration of a member or former member, a form of proof in accordance with Rule 6.97 of Insolvency Rules or Rule 4.080 of the Insolvency Rules (Northern Ireland) or section 48 of the Bankruptcy (Scotland) Act 1985;

(b) in the case of a qualifying trust deed, the form prescribed by the trustee; and

(c) in the case of a qualifying individual voluntary arrangement, a form approved by the court for that purpose.

(5) For the purposes of that regulation (as applied in the circumstances set out in paragraph (2) above), an individual voluntary arrangement approved in relation to an

individual member is a qualifying individual voluntary arrangement and a trust deed for creditors within section 5(4A) of the Bankruptcy (Scotland) Act 1985 is a qualifying trust deed for creditors if its purposes or objects as the case may be include a realisation of some or all of the assets of that member or former member and a distribution of the proceeds to creditors including insurance creditors, with a view to terminating the whole or any part of the business of that member carried on in connection with effecting or carrying out contracts of insurance written at Lloyd's.

[2721]

NOTES

Commencement: 10 August 2005.

38 Reports to creditors

(1) Regulation 14 of the principal Regulations (reports to creditors) applies with the modifications set out in paragraphs (2) to (4) where—

(a) a liquidator is appointed in respect of a member or former member in accordance with—

(i) section 100 of the 1986 Act or Article 86 of the 1989 Order (creditors' voluntary winding up: appointment of a liquidator), or

(ii) paragraph 83 of Schedule B1 (moving from administration to creditors' voluntary liquidation);

(b) a winding up order is made by the court in respect of a member or former member;

(c) a provisional liquidator is appointed in respect of a member or former member;

(d) an administrator of a member or former member (within the meaning given by paragraph 1(1) of Schedule B1) includes in the statement required by Rule 2.2 of the Insolvency Rules a statement to the effect that the objective set out in paragraph 3(1)(a) of Schedule B1 is not reasonably likely to be achieved; or

(e) a bankruptcy order or award of sequestration is made in respect of a member or former member.

(2) Paragraphs (2) to (5) of that regulation have effect as if they each included a reference to—

(a) an administrator who has made a statement to the effect that the objective set out in paragraph 3(1)(a) of Schedule B1 is not reasonably likely to be achieved;

(b) the official receiver or a trustee in bankruptcy; and

(c) in Scotland, an interim or permanent trustee.

(3) Paragraph (6)(a) of that regulation has effect as if the meaning of "known creditor" included—

(a) a creditor who is known to the administrator, the trustee in bankruptcy or the trustee, as the case may be;

(b) in a case where a bankruptcy order is made in respect of a member or former member, a creditor who is specified in a report submitted under section 274 of the 1986 Act or Article 149 of the 1989 Order or a statement of affairs submitted under section 288 or Article 261 in respect of the member or former member;

(c) in a case where an administrator of a member has made a statement to the effect that the objective set out in paragraph 3(1)(a) of Schedule B1 is not reasonably likely to be achieved, a creditor who is specified in the statement of the member's affairs required by the administrator under paragraph 47(1) of that Schedule;

(d) in a case where a sequestration has been awarded, a creditor who is specified in a statement of assets and liabilities under section 19 of the Bankruptcy (Scotland) Act 1985.

(4) Paragraph (6)(b) of that regulation has effect as if "report" included a written report setting out the position generally as regards the progress of—

(a) the bankruptcy or sequestration; or

(b) the administration.

[2722]

NOTES

Commencement: 10 August 2005.

39 Service of notices and documents

(1) Regulation 15 of the principal Regulations (service of notices and documents) applies, with the modifications set out in paragraphs (2) and (3) below, to any notification, report or other document which is required to be sent to a creditor of a member or former member by a provision of Part III of those Regulations as applied and modified by regulations 33 to 35 above.

(2) Paragraph 15(5)(a)(i) of that regulation has effect as if the reference to the UK insurer which is liable under the creditor's claim included a reference to the member or former member who or which is liable under the creditor's claim.

(3) Paragraph (7)(c) of that regulation has effect as if "relevant officer" included a trustee in bankruptcy, nominee, receiver or, in Scotland, an interim or permanent trustee under a trust deed within the meaning of section 5(4A) of the Bankruptcy (Scotland) Act who is required to send a notification to a creditor by a provision of Part III of the principal Regulations as applied and modified by regulations 33 to 37 above.

[2723]

NOTES

Commencement: 10 August 2005.

PART 4
APPLICATION OF PARTS 4 AND 5 OF THE PRINCIPAL REGULATIONS

40 Priority for insurance claims

(1) Part 4 of the principal Regulations applies with the modifications set out in paragraphs (2) to (11).

(2) References, in relation to a UK insurer, to a winding up by the court have effect as if they included a reference to the bankruptcy or sequestration of a member or former member.

(3) References to the making of a winding up order in relation to a UK insurer have effect as if they included a reference to the making of a bankruptcy order or, in Scotland, an award of sequestration in relation to an individual member or a member or former member that is a Scottish limited partnership.

(4) References to an administration order in relation to a UK insurer have effect as if they included a reference to an individual voluntary arrangement in relation to an individual member and a trust deed for creditors within the meaning of section 5(4A) of the Bankruptcy (Scotland) Act.

(5) Regulation 20 (preferential debts: disapplication of section 175 of the 1986 Act or Article 149 of the 1989 Order) has effect as if the references to section 175 of the 1986 Act and Article 149 of the 1989 Order included a reference to section 328 of that Act, Article 300 of that Order and section 51(1) (d) to (h) of the Bankruptcy (Scotland) Act 1985.

(6) Regulation 21(3) (preferential debts: long term insurers and general insurers) has effect as if after the words "rank equally among themselves" there were inserted the words "after the expenses of the bankruptcy or sequestration".

(7) Regulation 27 (composite insurers: application of other assets) has effect as if the reference to section 175 of the 1986 Act or Article 149 of the 1989 Order included a reference to section 328 of that Act, Article 300 of that Order and section 51(1) (e) to (h) of the Bankruptcy (Scotland) Act.

(8) Regulation 29 (composite insurers: general meetings of creditors) has effect as if after paragraph (2) there were inserted—

"(3) If the general meeting of the bankrupt's creditors proposes to establish a creditors' committee pursuant to section 301(1) of the 1986 Act or Article 274(1) of the 1989 Order, it must establish separate committees of creditors in respect of long-term business liabilities and creditors in respect of general business liabilities.

(4) The committee of creditors in respect of long-term business liabilities may exercise the functions of a creditors' committee under the 1986 Act or the 1989 Order in relation to long term business liabilities only.

(5) The committee of creditors in respect of general business liabilities may exercise the functions of a creditors' committee under the 1986 Act or the 1989 Order in relation to general business liabilities only.

(6) If, in terms of section 30(1) of the Bankruptcy (Scotland) Act 1985, at the statutory meeting or any subsequent meeting of creditors it is proposed to elect one or more commissioners (or new or additional commissioners) in the sequestration, it shall elect separate commissioners in respect of the long-term business liabilities and the general business liabilities.

(7) Any commissioner elected in respect of the long-term business liabilities shall exercise his functions under the Bankruptcy (Scotland) Act 1985 in respect of the long-term business liabilities only.

(8) Any commissioner elected in respect of the general business liabilities shall exercise his functions under the Bankruptcy (Scotland) Act 1985 in respect of the general business liabilities only.".

(9) Regulation 30 (composite insurers: apportionment of costs payable out of the assets) has effect as if in its application to members or former members who are individuals or Scottish limited partnerships—

- (a) in England and Wales, the reference to Rule 4.218 of the Insolvency Rules (general rule as to priority) included a reference to Rule 6.224 of the Insolvency Rules (general rule as to priority (bankruptcy));
- (b) in Northern Ireland, the reference to Rule 4.228 of the Insolvency Rules (Northern Ireland) (general rule as to priority) included a reference to Rule 6.222 of the Insolvency Rules (Northern Ireland) (general rule as to priority (bankruptcy)); and
- (c) in Scotland, the reference to Rule 4.67 of the Insolvency (Scotland) Rules includes reference to—
  - (i) any finally determined outlays or remuneration in a sequestration within the meaning of section 53 of the Bankruptcy (Scotland) Act 1985 and shall be calculated and applied separately in respect of the long-term business assets and the general business assets of that member; and
  - (ii) the remuneration and expenses of a trustee under a trust deed for creditors within the meaning of the Bankruptcy (Scotland) Act 1985,

and references to a liquidator include references to a trustee in bankruptcy, interim or permanent trustee, trustee under a trust deed for creditors, Accountant in Bankruptcy or Commissioners where appropriate.

(10) Regulation 31 (summary remedies against liquidators) has effect as if—

- (a) the reference to section 212 of the 1986 Act or Article 176 of the 1989 Order included a reference to section 304 of that Act or Article 277 of that Order (liability of trustee);
- (b) the references to a liquidator included a reference to a trustee in bankruptcy in respect of a qualifying insolvent member; and
- (c) the reference to section 175 of the 1986 Act or Article 149 of the 1989 Order included a reference to section 328 of that Act or Article 300 of that Order.

(11) Regulation 33 (voluntary arrangements: treatment of insurance debts) has effect as if after paragraph (3) there were inserted—

"(4) The modifications made by paragraph (5) apply where an individual member proposes an individual voluntary arrangement in accordance with Part 8 of the 1986 Act or Part 8 of the 1989 Order, and that arrangement includes—

- (a) a composition in satisfaction of any insurance debts; and
- (b) a distribution to creditors of some or all of the assets of that member in the course of, or with a view to, terminating the whole or any part of the insurance business of that member carried on at Lloyd's.

(5) Section 258 of the 1986 Act (decisions of creditors' meeting) has effect as if—

- (a) after subsection (5) there were inserted—

"(5A) A meeting so summoned in relation to an individual member and taking place when a Lloyd's market reorganisation order is in force shall not approve any proposal or modification under which any insurance debt of that member is to be paid otherwise than in priority to such of his debts as are not insurance debts or preferential debts.";

- (b) after subsection (7) there were inserted—

"(8) For the purposes of this section—

(a) "insurance debt" has the meaning it has in the Insurers (Reorganisation and Winding Up) Regulations 2004;

(b) "Lloyd's market reorganisation order" and "individual member" have the meaning they have in the Insurers (Reorganisation and Winding Up) (Lloyd's) Regulations 2005.".

(6) Article 232 of the 1989 Order (Decisions of creditors' meeting) has effect as if—

(a) after paragraph (6) there were inserted—

"(6A) A meeting so summoned in relation to an individual member and taking place when a Lloyd's market reorganisation order is in force shall not approve any proposal or modification under which any insurance debt of that member is to be paid otherwise than in priority to such of his debts as are not insurance debts or preferential debts.";

(b) after paragraph (9) there were inserted—

"(10) For the purposes of this Article—

(a) "insurance debt" has the meaning it has in the Insurers (Reorganisation and Winding Up) Regulations 2004;

(b) "Lloyd's market reorganisation order" and "individual member" have the meaning they have in the Insurers (Reorganisation and Winding Up) (Lloyd's) Regulations 2005.".

(7) In Scotland, where a member or former member grants a trust deed for creditors, Schedule 5 to the Bankruptcy (Scotland) Act 1985 shall be read as if after paragraph 4 there were included paragraphs 4A and 4B as follows—

"4A. Whether or not provision is made in any trust deed, where such a trust deed includes a composition in satisfaction of any insurance debts of a member or former member and a distribution to creditors of some or all of the assets of that member or former member in the course of or with a view to meeting obligations of his insurance business carried on at Lloyd's, the trustee may not provide for any insurance debt to be paid otherwise than in priority to such of his debts as are not insurance debts or preferred debts within the meaning of section 51(2).

4B. For the purposes of paragraph 4A,

(a) "insurance debt" has the meaning it has in the Insurance (Reorganisation and Winding Up) Regulations 2004; and

(b) "member " and "former member" have the meaning given in regulation 2(1) of the Insurers (Reorganisation and Winding Up) (Lloyd's) Regulations 2005."".

(12) The power to apply to court in section 303 of the 1986 Act or Article 276 of the 1989 Order or section 63 of the Bankruptcy (Scotland) Act (general control of trustee by court) may be exercised by the reorganisation controller if it appears to him that any act, omission or decision of a trustee of the estate of a member contravenes the provisions of Part 4 of the principal Regulations (as applied by this regulation).

[2724]

NOTES

Commencement: 10 August 2005.

41 Treatment of liabilities arising in connection with a contract subject to reinsurance to close

(1) Where in respect of a member or former member who is subject to a Lloyd's market reorganisation order any of the events specified in paragraph (2)(a) have occurred, for the purposes of the application of Part 4 of the principal Regulations to that member (and only for those purposes), an obligation of that member under a reinsurance to close contract in respect of a debt due or treated as due under a contract of insurance written at Lloyd's is to be treated as an insurance debt.

(2) For the purposes of this regulation—

(a) The events are—

(i) in respect of a member which is a corporation the appointment of a liquidator, provisional liquidator or administrator;

(ii) in respect of an individual member, the appointment of a receiver or trustee in bankruptcy; and

(iii) in respect of a member in Scotland being either an individual or a Scottish limited partnership, the making of a sequestration order or the appointment of an interim or permanent trustee;

(b) "reinsurance to close contract" means a contract under which, in accordance with the rules or practices of Lloyd's, underwriting members ("the reinsured members") who are members of a syndicate for a year of account ("the closed year") agree with underwriting members who constitute that or another syndicate for a later year of account ("the reinsuring members") that the reinsuring members will indemnify the reinsured members against all known and unknown liabilities of the reinsured members arising out of the insurance business underwritten through that syndicate and allocated to the closed year (including liabilities under any reinsurance to close contract underwritten by the reinsured members).

[2725]

NOTES

Commencement: 10 August 2005.

42 Assets of members

(1) This regulation applies where a member or former member is treated as a UK insurer in accordance with regulations 13 and 40 above.

(2) Subject to paragraphs (3) and (4), the undistributed assets of the member are to be treated as assets of the insurer for the purposes of the application of Part 4 of the principal Regulations in accordance with regulation 43 below.

(3) For the purposes of this regulation, the undistributed assets of the member so treated do not include any asset held in a relevant trust fund.

(4) But any asset released from a relevant trust fund and received by such a member is to be treated as an asset of the insurer for the purposes of the application of Part 4 of the principal Regulations.

[2726]

NOTES

Commencement: 10 August 2005.

43 Application of Part 4 of the principal Regulations: protection of settlements

(1) This regulation applies where a member or former member is subject to an insolvency measure mentioned in paragraph (4) at the time that a Lloyd's market reorganisation order comes into force.

(2) Nothing in these Regulations or Part 4 of the principal Regulations affects the validity of any payment or disposition made, or any settlement agreed, by the relevant officer before the date when the Lloyd's market reorganisation order came into force.

(3) For the purposes of the application of Part 4 of the principal Regulations, the insolvent estate of the member or former member shall not include any assets which are subject to a relevant section 425 or Article 418 compromise or arrangement, a relevant individual voluntary arrangement, or a relevant trust deed for creditors.

(4) In paragraph (2) "relevant officer" means—

(a) where the insolvency measure is a voluntary arrangement, the nominee;

(b) where the insolvency measure is administration, the administrator;

(c) where the insolvency measure is the appointment of a provisional liquidator, the provisional liquidator;

(d) where the insolvency measure is a winding up, the liquidator;

(e) where the insolvency measure is an individual voluntary arrangement, the nominee or supervisor;

(f) where the insolvency measure is bankruptcy, the trustee in bankruptcy;

(g) where the insolvency measure is sequestration, the interim or permanent trustee; and

(h) where the insolvency measure is a trust deed for creditors, the trustee.

(5) For the purposes of paragraph (3)—

(a) "assets" has the same meaning as "property" in section 436 of the 1986 Act or Article 2(2) of the 1989 Order;

(b) "insolvent estate" in England and Wales and Northern Ireland has the meaning given by Rule 13.8 of the Insolvency Rules or Rule 0.2 of the Insolvency Rules (Northern Ireland), and in Scotland means the whole estate of the member;

(c) "a relevant section 425 or Article 418 compromise or arrangement" means—

(i) a section 425 or Article 418 compromise or arrangement which was sanctioned by the court before the date on which an application for a Lloyd's market reorganisation order was made, or

(ii) any subsequent section 425 or Article 418 compromise or arrangement sanctioned by the court to amend or replace a compromise or arrangement of the kind mentioned in paragraph (i);

(d) "a relevant individual voluntary arrangement" and "a relevant trust deed for creditors" mean an individual voluntary arrangement or trust deed for creditors which was sanctioned by the court or entered into before the date on which an application for a Lloyd's market reorganisation order was made.

[2727]

NOTES

Commencement: 10 August 2005.

44 Challenge by reorganisation controller to conduct of insolvency practitioner

(1) The reorganisation controller may apply to the court claiming that a relevant officer is acting, has acted, or proposes to act in a way that fails to comply with a requirement of Part 4 of the principal Regulations.

(2) The reorganisation controller must send a copy of an application under paragraph (1) to the relevant officer in respect of whom the application is made.

(3) In the case of a relevant officer who is acting in respect of a member or former member subject to the jurisdiction of a Scottish court, the application must be made to the Court of Session.

(4) The court may—

(a) dismiss the application;

(b) make an interim order;

(c) make any other order it thinks appropriate.

(5) In particular, an order under this regulation may—

(a) regulate the relevant officer's exercise of his functions;

(b) require that officer to do or not do a specified thing;

(c) make consequential provision.

(6) An order may not be made under this regulation if it would impede or prevent the implementation of—

(a) a voluntary arrangement approved under Part 1 of the 1986 Act or Part 2 of the 1989 Order before the date when the Lloyd's market reorganisation order was made;

(b) an individual voluntary arrangement approved under Part 8 of that Act or Part 8 of that Order before the date when the Lloyd's market reorganisation order was made; or

(c) a section 425 or Article 418 compromise or arrangement which was sanctioned by the court before the date when the Lloyd's market reorganisation order was made.

(7) In this regulation "relevant officer" means—

(a) a liquidator,

(b) a provisional liquidator,

(c) an administrator

(d) the official receiver or a trustee in bankruptcy, or

(e) in Scotland, an interim or permanent trustee or a trustee for creditors,

who is appointed in relation to a member or former member.

[2728]

NOTES

Commencement: 10 August 2005.

45 Application of Part 5 of the principal Regulations

(1) Part 5 of the principal Regulations (reorganisation or winding up of UK insurers: recognition of EEA rights) applies with the modifications set out in regulation 46 where, on or after the date that a Lloyd's market reorganisation order comes into force, a member or former member is or becomes subject to a reorganisation or insolvency measure.

(2) For the purposes of this regulation a "reorganisation or insolvency measure" means—

- (a) a voluntary arrangement, having a qualifying purpose, approved in accordance with section 4A of the 1986 Act or Article 17A of the 1989 Order;
- (b) administration pursuant to an order under paragraph 13 of Schedule B1;
- (c) the reduction by the court of the value of one or more relevant contracts of insurance under section 377 of the 2000 Act or section 24(5) of the Friendly Societies Act 1992;
- (d) winding up;
- (e) the appointment of a provisional liquidator in accordance with section 135 of the 1986 Act or Article 115 of the 1989 Order;
- (f) an individual voluntary arrangement, having a qualifying purpose, approved in accordance with section 258 of the 1986 Act or Article 232 of the 1989 Order;
- (g) in Scotland a qualifying trust deed for creditors within the meaning of section 5(4A) of the Bankruptcy (Scotland) Act 1985;
- (h) bankruptcy, in accordance with Part 9 of the 1986 Act or Part 9 of the 1989 Order; or
- (i) sequestration under the Bankruptcy (Scotland) Act 1985.

(3) A measure imposed under the law of a State or country other than the United Kingdom is not a reorganisation or insolvency measure for the purposes of this regulation.

(4) For the purposes of sub-paragraphs (a), (f) and (g) of paragraph (2), a voluntary arrangement or individual voluntary arrangement has a qualifying purpose and a trust deed is a qualifying trust deed if it—

- (a) varies the rights of creditors as against the member and is intended to enable the member to continue to carry on an insurance market activity at Lloyd's; or
- (b) includes a realisation of some or all of the assets of the member and the distribution of proceeds to creditors, with a view to terminating the whole or any part of that member's business at Lloyd's.

[2729]

NOTES

Commencement: 10 August 2005.

46 Modification of provisions in Part 5 of the principal Regulations

(1) The modifications mentioned in regulation 45(1) are as follows.

(2) Regulation 35 is disapplied.

(3) Regulation 36 (interpretation of Part 5) has effect as if—

- (a) in paragraph (1)—
  - (i) the meaning of "affected insurer" included a member or former member who, on or after the date that a Lloyd's market reorganisation order comes into force, is or becomes subject to a reorganisation or insolvency measure within the meaning given by regulation 44(2)of these Regulations;
  - (ii) the meaning of "relevant reorganisation or relevant winding up" included any reorganisation or insolvency measure, in respect of a member or former member, to which Part 5 of the principal Regulations applies by virtue of regulation 45(1) of these Regulations;
  - (iii) in the case of sequestration, the date of sequestration within the meaning of section 12 of the Bankruptcy (Scotland) Act 1985; and
- (b) in paragraph (2) references to the opening of a relevant reorganisation or a relevant winding up meant (in addition to the meaning in the cases set out in that paragraph)—

(i) in the case of an individual voluntary arrangement, the date when a decision with respect to that arrangement has effect in accordance with section 258 of the 1986 Act or Article 232 of the 1989 Order;

(ii) in the case of bankruptcy, the date on which the bankruptcy order is made under Part 9 of the 1986 Act or Part 9 of the 1989 Order;

(iii) in the case of a trust deed for creditors under the Bankruptcy (Scotland) Act 1985 the date when the trust deed was granted.

(4) Regulation 37 of the principal Regulations (EEA rights: applicable law in the winding up of a UK insurer) has effect as if—

(a) references to a relevant winding up included (in each case) a reference to a reorganisation or insolvency measure within the meaning given by sub-paragraphs (d), (g) (h) and (i) of regulation 45(2) of these Regulations (winding up and bankruptcy) in respect of a member or former member; and

(b) the reference in paragraph (3)(c) to the liquidator included a reference to the trustee in bankruptcy or in Scotland to the interim or permanent trustee.

(5) Regulation 42 (reservation of title agreements etc) has effect as if the reference to an insurer in paragraphs (1) and (2) included a reference to a member or former member.

[2730]

NOTES

Commencement: 10 August 2005.

47 Application of Part 5 of the principal Regulations: protection of dispositions etc made before a Lloyd's market reorganisation order comes into force

(1) This regulation applies where—

(a) a member or former member is subject to a reorganisation or insolvency measure on the date when a Lloyd's market reorganisation order comes into force; and

(b) Part 5 of the principal Regulations applies in relation to that reorganisation or insolvency measure by virtue of regulation 45 above.

(2) Nothing in Part 5 of the principal Regulations affects the validity of any payment or disposition made, or any settlement agreed, by the relevant officer before the date when the Lloyd's market reorganisation order came into force.

(3) For the purposes of the application of Part 5 of the principal Regulations, the insolvent estate of the member does not include any assets which are subject to a relevant section 425 or Article 418 compromise or arrangement, a relevant individual voluntary arrangement, or a relevant trust deed for creditors.

(4) In paragraph (2) "relevant officer" means—

(a) where the member is subject to a voluntary arrangement in accordance with section 4A of the 1986 Act or Article 17A of the 1989 Order, the supervisor;

(b) where the member is in administration in accordance with Schedule B1, the administrator;

(c) where a provisional liquidator has been appointed in relation to a member in accordance with section 135 of the 1986 Act or Article 115 of the 1989 Order, the provisional liquidator;

(d) where the member is being wound up under Part 4 of the 1986 Act or Part 5 of the 1989 Order, the liquidator;

(e) where the member has made a voluntary arrangement in accordance with Part 8 of the 1986 Act or Part 8 of the 1989 Order, the nominee;

(f) where the member is bankrupt within the meaning of Part 9 of the 1986 Act or Part 9 of the 1989 Order, the official receiver or trustee in bankruptcy;

(g) where the member is being sequestrated, the interim or permanent trustee; and

(h) where a trust deed for creditors has been granted, the trustee.

(5) For the purposes of paragraph (3)—

(a) "assets" has the same meaning as "property" in section 436 of the 1986 Act or Article 2(2) of the 1989 Order, except in relation to relevant trust deeds;

(b) "insolvent estate" in England and Wales and Northern Ireland has the meaning given by Rule 13.8 of the Insolvency Rules or Rule 0.2 of the Insolvency Rules (Northern Ireland), and in Scotland means the assets of the member;

(c) "relevant section 425 or Article 418 compromise or arrangement" means—

(i) a section 425 or Article 418 compromise or arrangement which was

sanctioned by the court before the date when the Lloyd's market reorganisation order came into force, or
(ii) any subsequent section 425 or Article 418 compromise or arrangement sanctioned by the court to amend or replace a compromise or arrangement of the kind mentioned in paragraph (i);

(d) "relevant individual voluntary arrangement" means—
(i) an individual voluntary arrangement approved under Part 8 of the 1986 Act before the date when a Lloyd's market reorganisation order came in to force, and
(ii) any subsequent individual voluntary arrangement sanctioned by the court to amend or replace an arrangement of the kind mentioned in paragraph (i); and

(e) "relevant trust deed" means a trust deed granted by a member or former member before the date when the Lloyd's market reorganisation order entered into force.

[2731]

NOTES
Commencement: 10 August 2005.

48 Non-EEA countries

In respect of a member or former member who is established in a country outside the EEA, the court or the Authority may, subject to sections 348 and 349 of the 2000 Act, make such disclosures as each considers appropriate to a court or to a regulator with a role equivalent to that of the Authority for the purpose of facilitating the work of the reorganisation controller.

[2732]

NOTES
Commencement: 10 August 2005.

49 (*Amends the Insurers* (*Reorganisation and Winding Up*) *Regulations 2004, SI 2004/353, reg 19 at* **[2614]**.)

CROSS-BORDER INSOLVENCY REGULATIONS 2006

(SI 2006/1030)

NOTES
Made: 3 April 2006.
Authority: Insolvency Act 2000, s 14.
Commencement: 4 April 2006.

ARRANGEMENT OF REGULATIONS

PART III STATUTORY INSTRUMENTS

1 Citation, commencement and interpretation

(1) These Regulations may be cited as the Cross-Border Insolvency Regulations 2006 and shall come into force on the day after the day on which they are made.

(2) In these Regulations "the UNCITRAL Model Law" means the Model Law on cross-border insolvency as adopted by the United Nations Commission on International Trade Law on 30th May 1997.

[2733]

NOTES

Commencement: 4 April 2006.

2 UNCITRAL Model Law to have force of law

(1) The UNCITRAL Model Law shall have the force of law in Great Britain in the form set out in Schedule 1 to these Regulations (which contains the UNCITRAL Model Law with certain modifications to adapt it for application in Great Britain).

(2) Without prejudice to any practice of the courts as to the matters which may be considered apart from this paragraph, the following documents may be considered in ascertaining the meaning or effect of any provision of the UNCITRAL Model Law as set out in Schedule 1 to these Regulations—

(a) the UNCITRAL Model Law;

(b) any documents of the United Nations Commission on International Trade Law and its working group relating to the preparation of the UNCITRAL Model Law; and

(c) the Guide to Enactment of the UNCITRAL Model Law (UNCITRAL document A/CN 9/442) prepared at the request of the United Nations Commission on International Trade Law made in May 1997.

[2734]

NOTES

Commencement: 4 April 2006.

3 Modification of British insolvency law

(1) British insolvency law (as defined in article 2 of the UNCITRAL Model Law as set out in Schedule 1 to these Regulations) and Part 3 of the Insolvency Act 1986 shall apply with such modifications as the context requires for the purpose of giving effect to the provisions of these Regulations.

(2) In the case of any conflict between any provision of British insolvency law or of Part 3 of the Insolvency Act 1986 and the provisions of these Regulations, the latter shall prevail.

[2735]

NOTES

Commencement: 4 April 2006.

4 Procedural matters in England and Wales

Schedule 2 to these Regulations (which makes provision about procedural matters in England and Wales in connection with the application of the UNCITRAL Model Law as set out in Schedule 1 to these Regulations) shall have effect.

[2736]

NOTES

Commencement: 4 April 2006.

5 Procedural matters in Scotland

Schedule 3 to these Regulations (which makes provision about procedural matters in Scotland in connection with the application of the UNCITRAL Model Law as set out in Schedule 1 to these Regulations) shall have effect.

[2737]

NOTES

Commencement: 4 April 2006.

6 Notices delivered to the registrar of companies

Schedule 4 to these Regulations (which makes provision about notices delivered to the registrar of companies under these Regulations) shall have effect.

[2738]

NOTES

Commencement: 4 April 2006.

7 Co-operation between courts exercising jurisdiction in relation to cross-border insolvency

(1) An order made by a court in either part of Great Britain in the exercise of jurisdiction in relation to the subject matter of these Regulations shall be enforced in the other part of Great Britain as if it were made by a court exercising the corresponding jurisdiction in that other part.

(2) However, nothing in paragraph (1) requires a court in either part of Great Britain to enforce, in relation to property situated in that part, any order made by a court in the other part of Great Britain.

(3) The courts having jurisdiction in relation to the subject matter of these Regulations in either part of Great Britain shall assist the courts having the corresponding jurisdiction in the other part of Great Britain.

[2739]

NOTES

Commencement: 4 April 2006.

8 Disapplication of section 388 of the Insolvency Act 1986

Nothing in section 388 of the Insolvency Act 1986 applies to anything done by a foreign representative—

(a) under or by virtue of these Regulations;

(b) in relation to relief granted or cooperation or coordination provided under these Regulations.

NOTES

Commencement: 4 April 2006.

[2740]

(*Sch 1 contains the text of the UNCITRAL Model Law on Cross-Border Insolvency, reproduced in Pt V(H) of this work at* **[4448]**.)

SCHEDULE 2
PROCEDURAL MATTERS IN ENGLAND AND WALES

Regulation 4

PART 1
INTRODUCTORY PROVISIONS

Interpretation

1(1) In this Schedule—

"the 1986 Act" means the Insolvency Act 1986;

"article 21 relief application" means an application to the court by a foreign representative under article 21(1) or (2) of the Model Law for relief;

"business day" means any day other than a Saturday, a Sunday, Christmas Day, Good Friday or a day which is a bank holiday in England and Wales under or by virtue of the Banking and Financial Dealings Act 1971;

"CPR" means the Civil Procedure Rules 1998 and "CPR" followed by a Part or rule by number means the Part or rule with that number in those Rules;

"enforcement officer" means an individual who is authorised to act as an enforcement officer under the Courts Act 2003;

"file in court" and "file with the court" means deliver to the court for filing;

"the Gazette" means the London Gazette;

"interim relief application" means an application to the court by a foreign representative under article 19 of the Model Law for interim relief;

"main proceedings" means proceedings opened in accordance with Article 3(1) of the EC Insolvency Regulation and falling within the definition of insolvency proceedings in Article 2(a) of the EC Insolvency Regulation;

"member State liquidator" means a person falling within the definition of liquidator in Article 2(b) of the EC Insolvency Regulation appointed in proceedings to which it applies in a member State other than the United Kingdom;

"the Model Law" means the UNCITRAL Model Law as set out in Schedule 1 to these Regulations;

"modification or termination order" means an order by the court pursuant to its powers under the Model Law modifying or terminating recognition of a foreign proceeding, the stay and suspension referred to in article 20(1) or any part of it or any relief granted under article 19 or 21 of the Model Law;

"originating application" means an application to the court which is not an application in pending proceedings before the court;

"ordinary application" means any application to the court other than an originating application;

"practice direction" means a direction as to the practice and procedure of any court within the scope of the CPR;

"recognition application" means an application to the court by a foreign representative in accordance with article 15 of the Model Law for an order recognising the foreign proceeding in which he has been appointed;

"recognition order" means an order by the court recognising a proceeding the subject of a recognition application as a foreign main proceeding or foreign non-main proceeding, as appropriate;

"relevant company" means a company within the meaning of section 735(1) of the Companies Act 1985 or an unregistered company within the meaning of Part 5 of the 1986 Act which is subject to a requirement imposed by virtue of section 690A, 691(1) or 718 of the Companies Act 1985;

"review application" means an application to the court for a modification or termination order;

"the Rules" means the Insolvency Rules 1986 and "Rule" followed by a number means the rule with that number in those Rules;

"secondary proceedings" means proceedings opened in accordance with Articles 3(2) and 3(3) of the EC Insolvency Regulation and falling within the definition of winding up proceedings in Article 2(c) of the EC Insolvency Regulation;

"territorial proceedings" means proceedings opened in accordance with Articles 3(2) and 3(4) of the EC Insolvency Regulation and falling within the definition of insolvency proceedings in Article 2(a) of the EC Insolvency Regulation.

(2) Expressions defined in the Model Law have the same meaning when used in this Schedule.

(3) In proceedings under these Regulations, "Registrar" means—

(a) a Registrar in Bankruptcy of the High Court; and

(b) where the proceedings are in a district registry, the district judge.

(4) References to the "venue" for any proceedings or attendance before the court, are to the time, date and place for the proceedings or attendance.

(5) References in this Schedule to ex parte hearings shall be construed as references to hearings without notice being served on any other party, and references to applications made ex parte as references to applications made without notice being served on any other party; and other references which include the expression "ex parte" shall be similarly construed.

(6) References in this Schedule to a debtor who is of interest to the Financial Services Authority are references to a debtor who—

(a) is, or has been, an authorised person within the meaning of section 31 of the Financial Services and Markets Act 2000 (authorised persons);

(b) is, or has been, an appointed representative within the meaning of section 39 (exemption of appointed representatives) of that Act; or

(c) is carrying on, or has carried on, a regulated activity in contravention of the general prohibition.

(7) In sub-paragraph (6) "the general prohibition" has the meaning given by section 19 of the Financial Services and Markets Act 2000 and the reference to a "regulated activity" must be construed in accordance with—

(a) section 22 of that Act (classes of regulated activity and categories of investment);

(b) any relevant order under that section; and

(c) Schedule 2 to that Act (regulated activities).

(8) References in this Schedule to a numbered form are to the form that bears that number in Schedule 5.

[2741]

NOTES

Commencement: 4 April 2006.

PART 2
APPLICATIONS TO COURT FOR RECOGNITION OF FOREIGN PROCEEDINGS

Affidavit in support of recognition application

2 A recognition application shall be in Form ML1 and shall be supported by an affidavit sworn by the foreign representative complying with paragraph 4.

Form and content of application

3 The application shall state the following matters—

(a) the name of the applicant and his address for service within England and Wales;

(b) the name of the debtor in respect of which the foreign proceeding is taking place;

(c) the name or names in which the debtor carries on business in the country where the foreign proceeding is taking place and in this country, if other than the name given under sub-paragraph (b);

(d) the principal or last known place of business of the debtor in Great Britain (if any) and, in the case of an individual, his usual or last known place of residence in Great Britain (if any);

PART III STATUTORY INSTRUMENTS

(e) any registered number allocated to the debtor under the Companies Act 1985;
(f) brief particulars of the foreign proceeding in respect of which recognition is applied for, including the country in which it is taking place and the nature of the proceeding;
(g) that the foreign proceeding is a proceeding within the meaning of article 2(i) of the Model Law;
(h) that the applicant is a foreign representative within the meaning of article 2(j) of the Model Law;
(i) the address of the debtor's centre of main interests and, if different, the address of its registered office or habitual residence, as appropriate; and
(j) if the debtor does not have its centre of main interests in the country where the foreign proceeding is taking place, whether the debtor has an establishment within the meaning of article 2(e) of the Model Law in that country, and if so, its address.

Contents of affidavit in support

4(1) There shall be attached to the application an affidavit in support which shall contain or have exhibited to it—
(a) the evidence and statement required under article 15(2) and (3) respectively of the Model Law;
(b) any other evidence which in the opinion of the applicant will assist the court in deciding whether the proceeding the subject of the application is a foreign proceeding within the meaning of article 2(i) of the Model Law and whether the applicant is a foreign representative within the meaning of article 2(j) of the Model Law;
(c) evidence that the debtor has its centre of main interests or an establishment, as the case may be, within the country where the foreign proceeding is taking place; and
(d) any other matters which in the opinion of the applicant will assist the court in deciding whether to make a recognition order.

(2) The affidavit shall state whether, in the opinion of the applicant, the EC Insolvency Regulation applies to any of the proceedings identified in accordance with article 15(3) of the Model Law and, if so, whether those proceedings are main proceedings, secondary proceedings or territorial proceedings.

(3) The affidavit shall also have exhibited to it the translations required under article 15(4) of the Model Law and a translation in English of any other document exhibited to the affidavit which is in a language other than English.

(4) All translations referred to in sub-paragraph (3) must be certified by the translator as a correct translation.

The hearing and powers of court

5(1) On hearing a recognition application the court may in addition to its powers under the Model Law to make a recognition order—
(a) dismiss the application;
(b) adjourn the hearing conditionally or unconditionally;
(c) make any other order which the court thinks appropriate.

(2) If the court makes a recognition order, it shall be in Form ML2.

Notification of subsequent information

6(1) The foreign representative shall set out any subsequent information required to be given to the court under article 18 of the Model Law in a statement which he shall attach to Form ML3 and file with the court.

(2) The statement shall include—
(a) details of the information required to be given under article 18 of the Model Law; and
(b) in the case of any proceedings required to be notified to the court under that article, a statement as to whether, in the opinion of the foreign representative, any of those proceedings are main proceedings, secondary proceedings or territorial proceedings under the EC Insolvency Regulation.

(3) The foreign representative shall send a copy of the Form ML3 and attached statement filed with the court to the following—

(a) the debtor; and
(b) those persons referred to in paragraph 26(3).

[2742]

NOTES

Commencement: 4 April 2006.

PART 3
APPLICATIONS FOR RELIEF UNDER THE MODEL LAW

Application for interim relief—affidavit in support

[2743]

7(1) An interim relief application must be supported by an affidavit sworn by the foreign representative stating—

(a) the grounds on which it is proposed that the interim relief applied for should be granted;
(b) details of any proceeding under British insolvency law taking place in relation to the debtor;
(c) whether, to the foreign representative's knowledge, an administrative receiver or receiver or manager of the debtor's property is acting in relation to the debtor;
(d) an estimate of the value of the assets of the debtor in England and Wales in respect of which relief is applied for;
(e) whether, to the best of the knowledge and belief of the foreign representative, the interests of the debtor's creditors (including any secured creditors or parties to hire-purchase agreements) and any other interested parties, including if appropriate the debtor, will be adequately protected;
(f) whether, to the best of the foreign representative's knowledge and belief, the grant of any of the relief applied for would interfere with the administration of a foreign main proceeding; and
(g) all other matters that in the opinion of the foreign representative will assist the court in deciding whether or not it is appropriate to grant the relief applied for.

Service of interim relief application not required

8 Unless the court otherwise directs, it shall not be necessary to serve the interim relief application on, or give notice of it to, any person.

The hearing and powers of court

9 On hearing an interim relief application the court may in addition to its powers under the Model Law to make an order granting interim relief under article 19 of the Model Law—

(a) dismiss the application;
(b) adjourn the hearing conditionally or unconditionally;
(c) make any other order which the court thinks appropriate.

Application for relief under article 21 of the Model Law—affidavit in support

10 An article 21 relief application must be supported by an affidavit sworn by the foreign representative stating—

(a) the grounds on which it is proposed that the relief applied for should be granted;
(b) an estimate of the value of the assets of the debtor in England and Wales in respect of which relief is applied for;
(c) in the case of an application by a foreign representative who is or believes that he is a representative of a foreign non-main proceeding, the reasons why the applicant believes that the relief relates to assets that, under the law of Great Britain, should be administered in the foreign non-main proceeding or concerns information required in that proceeding;
(d) whether, to the best of the knowledge and belief of the foreign representative, the interests of the debtor's creditors (including any secured creditors or parties to hire-purchase agreements) and any other interested parties, including if appropriate the debtor, will be adequately protected; and
(e) all other matters that in the opinion of the foreign representative will assist the court in deciding whether or not it is appropriate to grant the relief applied for.

The hearing and powers of court

11 On hearing an article 21 relief application the court may in addition to its powers under the Model Law to make an order granting relief under article 21 of the Model Law—

(a) dismiss the application;
(b) adjourn the hearing conditionally or unconditionally;
(c) make any other order which the court thinks appropriate.

[2743]

NOTES

Commencement: 4 April 2006.

PART 4
REPLACEMENT OF FOREIGN REPRESENTATIVE

Application for confirmation of status of replacement foreign representative

12(1) This paragraph applies where following the making of a recognition order the foreign representative dies or for any other reason ceases to be the foreign representative in the foreign proceeding in relation to the debtor.

(2) In this paragraph "the former foreign representative" shall mean the foreign representative referred to in sub-paragraph (1).

(3) If a person has succeeded the former foreign representative or is otherwise holding office as foreign representative in the foreign proceeding in relation to the debtor, that person may apply to the court for an order confirming his status as replacement foreign representative for the purpose of proceedings under these Regulations.

Contents of application and affidavit in support

13(1) An application under paragraph 12(3) shall in addition to the matters required to be stated by paragraph 19(2) state the following matters—

(a) the name of the replacement foreign representative and his address for service within England and Wales;
(b) details of the circumstances in which the former foreign representative ceased to be foreign representative in the foreign proceeding in relation to the debtor (including the date on which he ceased to be the foreign representative);
(c) details of his own appointment as replacement foreign representative in the foreign proceeding (including the date of that appointment).

(2) The application shall be accompanied by an affidavit in support sworn by the applicant which shall contain or have attached to it—

(a) a certificate from the foreign court affirming—
    (i) the cessation of the appointment of the former foreign representative as foreign representative; and
    (ii) the appointment of the applicant as the foreign representative in the foreign proceeding; or
(b) in the absence of such a certificate, any other evidence acceptable to the court of the matters referred to in paragraph (a); and
(c) a translation in English of any document exhibited to the affidavit which is in a language other than English.

(3) All translations referred to in paragraph (c) must be certified by the translator as a correct translation.

The hearing and powers of court

14(1) On hearing an application under paragraph 12(3) the court may—

(a) make an order confirming the status of the replacement foreign representative as foreign representative for the purpose of proceedings under these Regulations;
(b) dismiss the application;
(c) adjourn the hearing conditionally or unconditionally;
(d) make an interim order;
(e) make any other order which the court thinks appropriate, including in particular an

order making such provision as the court thinks fit with respect to matters arising in connection with the replacement of the foreign representative.

(2) If the court dismisses the application, it may also if it thinks fit make an order terminating recognition of the foreign proceeding and—

(a) such an order may include such provision as the court thinks fit with respect to matters arising in connection with the termination; and

(b) paragraph 15 shall not apply to such an order.

[2744]

NOTES

Commencement: 4 April 2006.

PART 5
REVIEWS OF COURT ORDERS

Reviews of court orders—where court makes order of its own motion

15(1) The court shall not of its own motion make a modification or termination order unless the foreign representative and the debtor have either—

(a) had an opportunity of being heard on the question; or

(b) consented in writing to such an order.

(2) Where the foreign representative or the debtor desires to be heard on the question of such an order, the court shall give all relevant parties notice of a venue at which the question will be considered and may give directions as to the issues on which it requires evidence.

(3) For the purposes of sub-paragraph (2), all relevant parties means the foreign representative, the debtor and any other person who appears to the court to have an interest justifying his being given notice of the hearing.

(4) If the court makes a modification or termination order, the order may include such provision as the court thinks fit with respect to matters arising in connection with the modification or termination.

Review application—affidavit in support

16 A review application must be supported by an affidavit sworn by the applicant stating—

(a) the grounds on which it is proposed that the relief applied for should be granted;

(b) whether, to the best of the knowledge and belief of the applicant, the interests of the debtor's creditors (including any secured creditors or parties to hire-purchase agreements) and any other interested parties, including if appropriate the debtor, will be adequately protected; and

(c) all other matters that in the opinion of the applicant will assist the court in deciding whether or not it is appropriate to grant the relief applied for.

Hearing of review application and powers of the court

17 On hearing a review application, the court may in addition to its powers under the Model Law to make a modification or termination order—

(a) dismiss the application;

(b) adjourn the hearing conditionally or unconditionally;

(c) make an interim order;

(c) make any other order which the court thinks appropriate, including an order making such provision as the court thinks fit with respect to matters arising in connection with the modification or termination.

[2745]

NOTES

Commencement: 4 April 2006.

PART III STATUTORY INSTRUMENTS

PART 6
COURT PROCEDURE AND PRACTICE WITH REGARD TO PRINCIPAL APPLICATIONS AND ORDERS

Preliminary and interpretation

18(1) This Part applies to—

(a) any of the following applications made to the court under these Regulations—

(i) a recognition application;

(ii) an article 21 relief application;

(iii) an application under paragraph 12(3) for an order confirming the status of a replacement foreign representative;

(iv) a review application; and

(b) any of the following orders made by the court under these Regulations—

(i) a recognition order;

(ii) an order granting interim relief under article 19 of the Model Law;

(iii) an order granting relief under article 21 of the Model Law;

(iv) an order confirming the status of a replacement foreign representative; and

(v) a modification or termination order.

Form and contents of application

19(1) Subject to sub-paragraph (4) every application to which this Part applies shall be an ordinary application and shall be in Form ML5.

(2) Each application shall be in writing and shall state—

(a) the names of the parties;

(b) the nature of the relief or order applied for or the directions sought from the court;

(c) the names and addresses of the persons (if any) on whom it is intended to serve the application;

(d) the names and addresses of all those persons on whom these Regulations require the application to be served (so far as known to the applicant); and

(e) the applicant's address for service.

(3) The application must be signed by the applicant if he is acting in person, or, when he is not so acting, by or on behalf of his solicitor.

(4) This paragraph does not apply to a recognition application.

Filing of application

20(1) The application (and all supporting documents) shall be filed with the court, with a sufficient number of copies for service and use as provided by paragraph 21(2).

(2) Each of the copies filed shall have applied to it the seal of the court and be issued to the applicant; and on each copy there shall be endorsed the date and time of filing.

(3) The court shall fix a venue for the hearing of the application and this also shall be endorsed on each copy of the application issued under sub-paragraph (2).

Service of the application

21(1) In sub-paragraph (2), references to the application are to a sealed copy of the application issued by the court together with any affidavit in support of it and any documents exhibited to the affidavit.

(2) Unless the court otherwise directs, the application shall be served on the following persons, unless they are the applicant—

(a) on the foreign representative;

(b) on the debtor;

(c) if a British insolvency officeholder is acting in relation to the debtor, on him;

(d) if any person has been appointed an administrative receiver of the debtor or, to the knowledge of the foreign representative, as a receiver or manager of the property of the debtor in England and Wales, on him;

(e) if a member State liquidator has been appointed in main proceedings in relation to the debtor, on him;

(f) if to the knowledge of the foreign representative a foreign representative has been appointed in any other foreign proceeding regarding the debtor, on him;

(g) if there is pending in England and Wales a petition for the winding up or bankruptcy of the debtor, on the petitioner;

(h) on any person who to the knowledge of the foreign representative is or may be entitled to appoint an administrator of the debtor under paragraph 14 of Schedule B1 to the 1986 Act (appointment of administrator by holder of qualifying floating charge); and

(i) if the debtor is a debtor who is of interest to the Financial Services Authority, on that Authority.

Manner in which service to be effected

22(1) Service of the application in accordance with paragraph 21(2) shall be effected by the applicant, or his solicitor, or by a person instructed by him or his solicitor, not less than 5 business days before the date fixed for the hearing.

(2) Service shall be effected by delivering the documents to a person's proper address or in such other manner as the court may direct.

(3) A person's proper address is any which he has previously notified as his address for service within England and Wales; but if he has not notified any such address or if for any reason service at such address is not practicable, service may be effected as follows—

(a) (subject to sub-paragraph (4)) in the case of a company incorporated in England and Wales, by delivery to its registered office;

(b) in the case of any other person, by delivery to his usual or last known address or principal place of business in Great Britain.

(4) If delivery to a company's registered office is not practicable, service may be effected by delivery to its last known principal place of business in Great Britain.

(5) Delivery of documents to any place or address may be made by leaving them there or sending them by first class post in accordance with the provisions of paragraphs 70 and 75(1).

Proof of service

23(1) Service of the application shall be verified by an affidavit of service in Form ML6, specifying the date on which, and the manner in which, service was effected.

(2) The affidavit of service, with a sealed copy of the application exhibited to it, shall be filed with the court as soon as reasonably practicable after service, and in any event not less than 1 business day before the hearing of the application.

In case of urgency

24 Where the case is one of urgency, the court may (without prejudice to its general power to extend or abridge time limits)—

(a) hear the application immediately, either with or without notice to, or the attendance of, other parties; or

(b) authorise a shorter period of service than that provided for by paragraph 22(1),

and any such application may be heard on terms providing for the filing or service of documents, or the carrying out of other formalities, as the court thinks fit.

The hearing

25(1) At the hearing of the application, the applicant and any of the following persons (not being the applicant) may appear or be represented—

(a) the foreign representative;

(b) the debtor and, in the case of any debtor other than an individual, any one or more directors or other officers of the debtor, including—

  (i) where applicable, any person registered under Part 23 of the Companies Act 1985 as authorised to represent the debtor in respect of its business in England and Wales;

  (ii) in the case of a debtor which is a partnership, any person who is an officer of the partnership within the meaning of article 2 of the Insolvent Partnerships Order 1994;

(c) if a British insolvency officeholder is acting in relation to the debtor, that person;

(d) if any person has been appointed an administrative receiver of the debtor or as a receiver or manager of the property of the debtor in England and Wales, that person;
(e) if a member State liquidator has been appointed in main proceedings in relation to the debtor, that person;
(f) if a foreign representative has been appointed in any other foreign proceeding regarding the debtor, that person;
(g) any person who has presented a petition for the winding up or bankruptcy of the debtor in England and Wales;
(h) any person who is or may be entitled to appoint an administrator of the debtor under paragraph 14 of Schedule B1 to the 1986 Act (appointment of administrator by holder of qualifying floating charge);
(i) if the debtor is a debtor who is of interest to the Financial Services Authority, that Authority; and
(j) with the permission of the court, any other person who appears to have an interest justifying his appearance.

Notification and advertisement of order

26(1) If the court makes any of the orders referred to in paragraph 18(1)(b), it shall as soon as reasonably practicable send two sealed copies of the order to the foreign representative.

(2) The foreign representative shall send a sealed copy of the order as soon as reasonably practicable to the debtor.

(3) The foreign representative shall, as soon as reasonably practicable after the date of the order give notice of the making of the order—
(a) if a British insolvency officeholder is acting in relation to the debtor, to him;
(b) if any person has been appointed an administrative receiver of the debtor or, to the knowledge of the foreign representative, as a receiver or manager of the property of the debtor, to him;
(c) if a member State liquidator has been appointed in main proceedings in relation to the debtor, to him;
(d) if to his knowledge a foreign representative has been appointed in any other foreign proceeding regarding the debtor, that person;
(e) if there is pending in England and Wales a petition for the winding up or bankruptcy of the debtor, to the petitioner;
(f) to any person who to his knowledge is or may be entitled to appoint an administrator of the debtor under paragraph 14 of Schedule B1 to the 1986 Act (appointment of administrator by holder of qualifying floating charge);
(g) if the debtor is a debtor who is of interest to the Financial Services Authority, to that Authority;
(h) to such other persons as the court may direct.

(4) In the case of an order recognising a foreign proceeding in relation to the debtor as a foreign main proceeding, or an order under article 19 or 21 of the Model Law staying execution, distress or other legal process against the debtor's assets, the foreign representative shall also, as soon as reasonably practicable after the date of the order give notice of the making of the order—
(a) to any enforcement officer or other officer who to his knowledge is charged with an execution or other legal process against the debtor or its property; and
(b) to any person who to his knowledge is distraining against the debtor or its property.

(5) In the application of sub-paragraphs (3) and (4) the references to property shall be taken as references to property situated within England and Wales.

(6) Where the debtor is a relevant company, the foreign representative shall send notice of the making of the order to the registrar of companies before the end of the period of 5 business days beginning with the date of the order. The notice to the registrar of companies shall be in Form ML7.

(7) The foreign representative shall advertise the making of the following orders once in the Gazette and once in such newspaper as he thinks most appropriate for ensuring that the making of the order comes to the notice of the debtor's creditors—
(a) a recognition order;
(b) an order confirming the status of a replacement foreign representative; and

(c) a modification or termination order which modifies or terminates recognition of a foreign proceeding,

and the advertisement shall be in Form ML8.

Adjournment of hearing; directions

27(1) This paragraph applies in any case where the court exercises its power to adjourn the hearing of the application.

(2) The court may at any time give such directions as it thinks fit as to—
(a) service or notice of the application on or to any person, whether in connection with the venue of a resumed hearing or for any other purpose;
(b) the procedure on the application;
(c) the manner in which any evidence is to be adduced at a resumed hearing and in particular as to—
(i) the taking of evidence wholly or in part by affidavit or orally;
(ii) the cross-examination on the hearing in court or in chambers, of any deponents to affidavits;
(d) the matters to be dealt with in evidence.

[2746]

NOTES

Commencement: 4 April 2006.

PART 7
APPLICATIONS TO THE CHIEF LAND REGISTRAR

Applications to Chief Land Registrar following court orders

28(1) Where the court makes any order in proceedings under these Regulations which is capable of giving rise to an application or applications under the Land Registration Act 2002, the foreign representative shall, as soon as reasonably practicable after the making of the order or at the appropriate time, make the appropriate application or applications to the Chief Land Registrar.

(2) In sub-paragraph (1) an appropriate application is—
(a) in any case where—
(i) a recognition order in respect of a foreign main proceeding or an order suspending the right to transfer, encumber or otherwise dispose of any assets of the debtor is made, and
(ii) the debtor is the registered proprietor of a registered estate or registered charge and holds it for his sole benefit,

an application under section 43 of the Land Registration Act 2002 for a restriction of the kind referred to in sub-paragraph (3) to be entered in the relevant registered title; and
(b) in any other case, an application under the Land Registration Act 2002 for such an entry in the register as shall be necessary to reflect the effect of the court order under these Regulations.

(3) The restriction referred to in sub-paragraph (2)(a) is a restriction to the effect that no disposition of the registered estate or registered charge (as appropriate) by the registered proprietor of that estate or charge is to be completed by registration within the meaning of section 27 of the Land Registration Act 2002 except under a further order of the court.

[2747]

NOTES

Commencement: 4 April 2006.

PART 8
MISFEASANCE

Misfeasance by foreign representative

29(1) The court may examine the conduct of a person who—

PART III
STATUTORY INSTRUMENTS

(a) is or purports to be the foreign representative in relation to a debtor; or
(b) has been or has purported to be the foreign representative in relation to a debtor.

(2) An examination under this paragraph may be held only on the application of—
(a) a British insolvency officeholder acting in relation to the debtor;
(b) a creditor of the debtor; or
(c) with the permission of the court, any other person who appears to have an interest justifying an application.

(3) An application under sub-paragraph (2) must allege that the foreign representative—
(a) has misapplied or retained money or other property of the debtor;
(b) has become accountable for money or other property of the debtor;
(c) has breached a fiduciary or other duty in relation to the debtor; or
(d) has been guilty of misfeasance.

(4) On an examination under this paragraph into a person's conduct the court may order him—
(a) to repay, restore or account for money or property;
(b) to pay interest;
(c) to contribute a sum to the debtor's property by way of compensation for breach of duty or misfeasance.

(4) In sub-paragraph (3) "foreign representative" includes a person who purports or has purported to be a foreign representative in relation to a debtor.

[2748]

NOTES

Commencement: 4 April 2006.

PART 9
GENERAL PROVISION AS TO COURT PROCEDURE AND PRACTICE

Principal court rules and practice to apply with modifications

30(1) The CPR and the practice and procedure of the High Court (including any practice direction) shall apply to proceedings under these Regulations in the High Court with such modifications as may be necessary for the purpose of giving effect to the provisions of these Regulations and in the case of any conflict between any provision of the CPR and the provisions of these Regulations, the latter shall prevail.

(2) All proceedings under these Regulations shall be allocated to the multi-track for which CPR Part 29 (the multi-track) makes provision, and accordingly those provisions of the CPR which provide for allocation questionnaires and track allocation shall not apply.

Applications other than the principal applications—preliminary

31 Paragraphs 32 to 37 of this Part apply to any application made to the court under these Regulations, except any of the applications referred to in paragraph 18(1)(a).

Form and contents of application

32(1) Every application shall be in the form appropriate to the application concerned. Forms ML4 and ML5 shall be used for an originating application and an ordinary application respectively under these Regulations.

(2) Each application shall be in writing and shall state—
(a) the names of the parties;
(b) the nature of the relief or order applied for or the directions sought from the court;
(c) the names and addresses of the persons (if any) on whom it is intended to serve the application or that no person is intended to be served;
(d) where these Regulations require that notice of the application is to be given to specified persons, the names and addresses of all those persons (so far as known to the applicant); and
(e) the applicant's address for service.

(3) An originating application shall set out the grounds on which the applicant claims to be entitled to the relief or order sought.

(4) The application must be signed by the applicant if he is acting in person or, when he is not so acting, by or on behalf of his solicitor.

Filing and service of application

33(1) The application shall be filed in court, accompanied by one copy and a number of additional copies equal to the number of persons who are to be served with the application.

(2) Subject as follows in this paragraph and in paragraph 34, or unless the court otherwise orders, upon the presentation of the documents mentioned in sub-paragraph (1), the court shall fix a venue for the application to be heard.

(3) Unless the court otherwise directs, the applicant shall serve a sealed copy of the application, endorsed with the venue of the hearing, on the respondent named in the application (or on each respondent if more than one).

(4) The court may give any of the following directions—

(a) that the application be served upon persons other than those specified by the relevant provision of these Regulations;

(b) that the giving of notice to any person may be dispensed with;

(c) that notice be given in some way other than that specified in sub-paragraph (3).

(5) Subject to sub-paragraph (6), the application must be served at least 10 business days before the date fixed for the hearing.

(6) Where the case is one of urgency, the court may (without prejudice to its general power to extend or abridge time limits)—

(a) hear the application immediately, either with or without notice to, or the attendance of, other parties; or

(b) authorise a shorter period of service than that provided for by sub-paragraph (5);

and any such application may be heard on terms providing for the filing or service of documents, or the carrying out of other formalities, as the court thinks fit.

Other hearings *ex parte*

34(1) Where the relevant provisions of these Regulations do not require service of the application on, or notice of it to be given to, any person, the court may hear the application *ex parte*.

(2) Where the application is properly made *ex parte*, the court may hear it forthwith, without fixing a venue as required by paragraph 33(2).

(3) Alternatively, the court may fix a venue for the application to be heard, in which case paragraph 33 applies (so far as relevant).

Use of affidavit evidence

35(1) In any proceedings evidence may be given by affidavit unless the court otherwise directs; but the court may, on the application of any party, order the attendance for cross-examination of the person making the affidavit.

(2) Where, after such an order has been made, the person in question does not attend, his affidavit shall not be used in evidence without the permission of the court.

Filing and service of affidavits

36(1) Unless the court otherwise allows—

(a) if the applicant intends to rely at the first hearing on affidavit evidence, he shall file the affidavit or affidavits (if more than one) in court and serve a copy or copies on the respondent, not less than 10 business days before the date fixed for the hearing; and

(b) where a respondent to an application intends to oppose it and to rely for that purpose on affidavit evidence, he shall file the affidavit or affidavits (if more than one) in court and serve a copy or copies on the applicant, not less than 5 business days before the date fixed for the hearing.

(2) Any affidavit may be sworn by the applicant or by the respondent or by some other person possessing direct knowledge of the subject matter of the application.

Adjournment of hearings; directions

37 The court may adjourn the hearing of an application on such terms (if any) as it thinks fit and in the case of such an adjournment paragraph 27(2) shall apply.

Transfer of proceedings within the High Court

38(1) The High Court may, having regard to the criteria in CPR rule 30.3(2), order proceedings in the Royal Courts of Justice or a district registry, or any part of such proceedings (such as an application made in the proceedings), to be transferred—

(a) from the Royal Courts of Justice to a district registry; or

(b) from a district registry to the Royal Courts of Justice or to another district registry.

(2) The High Court may order proceedings before a district registry for the detailed assessment of costs to be transferred to another district registry if it is satisfied that the proceedings could be more conveniently or fairly taken in that other district registry.

(3) An application for an order under sub-paragraph (1) or (2) must, if the claim is proceeding in a district registry, be made to that registry.

(4) A transfer of proceedings under this paragraph may be ordered—

(a) by the court of its own motion; or

(b) on the application of a person appearing to the court to have an interest in the proceedings.

(5) Where the court orders proceedings to be transferred, the court from which they are to be transferred must give notice of the transfer to all the parties.

(6) An order made before the transfer of the proceedings shall not be affected by the order to transfer.

Transfer of proceedings—actions to avoid acts detrimental to creditors

39(1) If—

(a) in accordance with article 23(6) of the Model Law, the court grants a foreign representative permission to make an application in accordance with paragraph 1 of that article; and

(b) the relevant proceedings under British insolvency law taking place regarding the debtor are taking place in the county court,

the court may also order those proceedings to be transferred to the High Court.

(2) Where the court makes an order transferring proceedings under sub-paragraph (1)—

(a) it shall send sealed copies of the order to the county court from which the proceedings are to be transferred, and to the official receivers attached to that court and the High Court respectively; and

(b) the county court shall send the file of the proceedings to the High Court.

(3) Following compliance with this paragraph, if the official receiver attached to the court to which the proceedings are transferred is not already, by virtue of directions given by the Secretary of State under section 399(6)(a) of the 1986 Act, the official receiver in relation to those proceedings, he becomes, in relation to those proceedings, the official receiver in place of the official receiver attached to the other court concerned.

Shorthand writers

40(1) The judge may in writing nominate one or more persons to be official shorthand writers to the court.

(2) The court may, at any time in the course of proceedings under these Regulations, appoint a shorthand writer to take down the evidence of a person examined in pursuance of a court order under article 19 or 21 of the Model Law.

(3) The remuneration of a shorthand writer appointed in proceedings under these Regulations shall be paid by the party at whose instance the appointment was made or otherwise as the court may direct.

(4) Any question arising as to the rates of remuneration payable under this paragraph shall be determined by the court in its discretion.

Enforcement procedures

41 In any proceedings under these Regulations, orders of the court may be enforced in the same manner as a judgment to the same effect.

Title of proceedings

42(1) Every proceeding under these Regulations shall, with any necessary additions, be intituled "IN THE MATTER OF … (naming the debtor to which the proceedings relate) AND IN THE MATTER OF THE CROSS-BORDER INSOLVENCY REGULATIONS 2006".

(2) Sub-paragraph (1) shall not apply in respect of any form prescribed under these Regulations.

Court records

43 The court shall keep records of all proceedings under these Regulations, and shall cause to be entered in the records the taking of any step in the proceedings, and such decisions of the court in relation thereto, as the court thinks fit.

Inspection of records

44(1) Subject as follows, the court's records of proceedings under these Regulations shall be open to inspection by any person.

(2) If in the case of a person applying to inspect the records the Registrar is not satisfied as to the propriety of the purpose for which inspection is required, he may refuse to allow it. That person may then apply forthwith and *ex parte* to the judge, who may refuse the inspection or allow it on such terms as he thinks fit.

(3) The decision of the judge under sub-paragraph (2) is final.

File of court proceedings

45(1) In respect of all proceedings under these Regulations, the court shall open and maintain a file for each case; and (subject to directions of the Registrar) all documents relating to such proceedings shall be placed on the relevant file.

(2) No proceedings under these Regulations shall be filed in the Central Office of the High Court.

Right to inspect the file

46(1) In the case of any proceedings under these Regulations, the following have the right, at all reasonable times, to inspect the court's file of the proceedings—

- (a) the Secretary of State;
- (b) the person who is the foreign representative in relation to the proceedings;
- (c) if a foreign representative has been appointed in any other foreign proceeding regarding the debtor to which the proceedings under these Regulations relate, that person;
- (d) if a British insolvency officeholder is acting in relation to the debtor to which the proceedings under these Regulations relate, that person;
- (e) any person stating himself in writing to be a creditor of the debtor to which the proceedings under these Regulations relate;
- (f) if a member State liquidator has been appointed in relation to the debtor to which the proceedings under these Regulations relate, that person; and
- (g) the debtor to which the proceedings under these Regulations relate, or, if that debtor is a company, corporation or partnership, every person who is, or at any time has been—
    - (i) a director or officer of the debtor;
    - (ii) a member of the debtor; or

(iii) where applicable, a person registered under Part 23 of the Companies Act 1985 as authorised to represent the debtor in respect of its business in England and Wales.

(2) The right of inspection conferred as above on any person may be exercised on his behalf by a person properly authorised by him.

(3) Any person may, by leave of the court, inspect the file.

(4) The right of inspection conferred by this paragraph is not exercisable in the case of documents, or parts of documents, as to which the court directs (either generally or specially) that they are not to be made open to inspection without the court's permission. An application for a direction of the court under this sub-paragraph may be made by the foreign representative or by any party appearing to the court to have an interest.

(5) If, for the purpose of powers conferred by the 1986 Act or the Rules, the Secretary of State or the official receiver wishes to inspect the file of any proceedings under these Regulations, and requests the transmission of the file, the court shall comply with such request (unless the file is for the time being in use for the court's purposes).

(6) Paragraph 44(2) and (3) apply in respect of the court's file of any proceedings under these Regulations as they apply in respect of court records.

(7) Where these Regulations confer a right for any person to inspect documents on the court's file of proceedings, the right includes that of taking copies of those documents on payment of the fee chargeable under any order made under section 92 of the Courts Act 2003.

Copies of court orders

47(1) In any proceedings under these Regulations, any person who under paragraph 46 has a right to inspect documents on the court file also has the right to require the foreign representative in relation to those proceedings to furnish him with a copy of any court order in the proceedings.

(2) Sub-paragraph (1) does not apply if a copy of the court order has been served on that person or notice of the making of the order has been given to that person under other provisions of these Regulations.

Filing of Gazette notices and advertisements

48(1) In any court in which proceedings under these Regulations are pending, an officer of the court shall file a copy of every issue of the Gazette which contains an advertisement relating to those proceedings.

(2) Where there appears in a newspaper an advertisement relating to proceedings under these Regulations pending in any court, the person inserting the advertisement shall file a copy of it in that court.

The copy of the advertisement shall be accompanied by, or have endorsed on it, such particulars as are necessary to identify the proceedings and the date of the advertisement's appearance.

(3) An officer of any court in which proceedings under these Regulations are pending shall from time to time file a memorandum giving the dates of, and other particulars relating to, any notice published in the Gazette, and any newspaper advertisements, which relate to proceedings so pending.

The officer's memorandum is prima facie evidence that any notice or advertisement mentioned in it was duly inserted in the issue of the newspaper or the Gazette which is specified in the memorandum.

Persons incapable of managing their affairs—introductory

49(1) Paragraphs 50 to 52 apply where in proceedings under these Regulations it appears to the court that a person affected by the proceedings is one who is incapable of managing and administering his property and affairs either—

(a) by reason of mental disorder within the meaning of the Mental Health Act 1983; or

(b) due to physical affliction or disability.

(2) The person concerned is referred to as "the incapacitated person".

Appointment of another person to act

50(1) The court may appoint such person as it thinks fit to appear for, represent or act for the incapacitated person.

(2) The appointment may be made either generally or for the purpose of any particular application or proceeding, or for the exercise of particular rights or powers which the incapacitated person might have exercised but for his incapacity.

(3) The court may make the appointment either of its own motion or on application by—
- (a) a person who has been appointed by a court in the United Kingdom or elsewhere to manage the affairs of, or to represent, the incapacitated person; or
- (b) any relative or friend of the incapacitated person who appears to the court to be a proper person to make the application; or
- (c) in any case where the incapacitated person is the debtor, the foreign representative.

(4) Application under sub-paragraph (3) may be made *ex parte*; but the court may require such notice of the application as it thinks necessary to be given to the person alleged to be incapacitated, or any other person, and may adjourn the hearing of the application to enable the notice to be given.

Affidavit in support of application

51 An application under paragraph 50(3) shall be supported by an affidavit of a registered medical practitioner as to the mental or physical condition of the incapacitated person.

Service of notices following appointment

52 Any notice served on, or sent to, a person appointed under paragraph 50 has the same effect as if it had been served on, or given to, the incapacitated person.

Rights of audience

53 Rights of audience in proceedings under these Regulations are the same as obtain in proceedings under British insolvency law.

Right of attendance

54(1) Subject as follows, in proceedings under these Regulations, any person stating himself in writing, in records kept by the court for that purpose, to be a creditor of the debtor to which the proceedings relate, is entitled at his own cost, to attend in court or in chambers at any stage of the proceedings.

(2) Attendance may be by the person himself, or his solicitor.

(3) A person so entitled may request the court in writing to give him notice of any step in the proceedings; and, subject to his paying the costs involved and keeping the court informed as to his address, the court shall comply with the request.

(4) If the court is satisfied that the exercise by a person of his rights under this paragraph has given rise to costs for the estate of the debtor which would not otherwise have been incurred and ought not, in the circumstances, to fall on that estate, it may direct that the costs be paid by the person concerned, to an amount specified.

The rights of that person under this paragraph shall be in abeyance so long as those costs are not paid.

(5) The court may appoint one or more persons to represent the creditors of the debtor to have the rights conferred by this paragraph, instead of the rights being exercised by any or all of them individually.

If two or more persons are appointed under this paragraph to represent the same interest, they must (if at all) instruct the same solicitor.

Right of attendance for member State liquidator

55 For the purposes of paragraph 54(1), a member State liquidator appointed in relation to a debtor subject to proceedings under these Regulations shall be deemed to be a creditor.

British insolvency officeholder's solicitor

56 Where in any proceedings the attendance of the British insolvency officeholder's solicitor is required, whether in court or in chambers, the British insolvency officeholder himself need not attend, unless directed by the court.

Formal defects

57 No proceedings under these Regulations shall be invalidated by any formal defect or by any irregularity, unless the court before which objection is made considers that substantial injustice has been caused by the defect or irregularity, and that the injustice cannot be remedied by any order of the court.

Restriction on concurrent proceedings and remedies

58 Where in proceedings under these Regulations the court makes an order staying any action, execution or other legal process against the property of a debtor, service of the order may be effected by sending a sealed copy of the order to whatever is the address for service of the claimant or other party having the carriage of the proceedings to be stayed.

Affidavits

59(1) Where in proceedings under these Regulations, an affidavit is made by any British insolvency officeholder acting in relation to the debtor, he shall state the capacity in which he makes it, the position which he holds and the address at which he works.

(2) Any officer of the court duly authorised in that behalf, may take affidavits and declarations.

(3) Subject to sub-paragraph (4), where these Regulations provide for the use of an affidavit, a witness statement verified by a statement of truth may be used as an alternative.

(4) Sub-paragraph (3) does not apply to paragraphs 4 (affidavit in support of recognition application), 7 (affidavit in support of interim relief application), 10 (affidavit in support of article 21 relief application), 13 (affidavit in support of application regarding status of replacement foreign representative) and 16 (affidavit in support of review application).

Security in court

60(1) Where security has to be given to the court (otherwise than in relation to costs), it may be given by guarantee, bond or the payment of money into court.

(2) A person proposing to give a bond as security shall give notice to the party in whose favour the security is required, and to the court, naming those who are to be sureties to the bond.

(3) The court shall forthwith give notice to the parties concerned of a venue for the execution of the bond and the making of any objection to the sureties.

(4) The sureties shall make an affidavit of their sufficiency (unless dispensed with by the party in whose favour the security is required) and shall, if required by the court, attend the court to be cross-examined.

Further information and disclosure

61(1) Any party to proceedings under these Regulations may apply to the court for an order—

(a) that any other party—

(i) clarify any matter which is in dispute in the proceedings; or

(ii) give additional information in relation to any such matter,

in accordance with CPR Part 18 (further information); or

(b) to obtain disclosure from any other party in accordance with CPR Part 31 (disclosure and inspection of documents).

(2) An application under this paragraph may be made without notice being served on any other party.

Office copies of documents

62(1) Any person who has under these Regulations the right to inspect the court file of proceedings may require the court to provide him with an office copy of any document from the file.

(2) A person's right under this paragraph may be exercised on his behalf by his solicitor.

(3) An office copy provided by the court under this paragraph shall be in such form as the Registrar thinks appropriate, and shall bear the court's seal.

"The court"

63(1) Anything to be done in proceedings under these Regulations by, to or before the court may be done by, to or before a judge of the High Court or a Registrar.

(2) Where these Regulations require or permit the court to perform an act of a formal or administrative character, that act may be performed by a court officer.

[2749]

NOTES

Commencement: 4 April 2006.

PART 10
COSTS AND DETAILED ASSESSMENT

Requirement to assess costs by the detailed procedure

64 In any proceedings before the court, the court may order costs to be decided by detailed assessment.

Costs of officers charged with execution of writs or other process

65(1) Where by virtue of article 20 of the Model Law or a court order under article 19 or 21 of the Model Law an enforcement officer, or other officer, charged with execution of the writ or other process—

(a) is required to deliver up goods or money; or

(b) has deducted costs from the proceeds of an execution or money paid to him,

the foreign representative may require in writing that the amount of the enforcement officer's or other officer's bill of costs be decided by detailed assessment.

(2) Where such a requirement is made, if the enforcement officer or other officer does not commence detailed assessment proceedings within 3 months of the requirement under sub-paragraph (1), or within such further time as the court, on application, may permit, any claim by the enforcement officer or other officer in respect of his costs is forfeited by such failure to commence proceedings.

(3) Where, in the case of a deduction of costs by the enforcement officer or other officer, any amount deducted is disallowed at the conclusion of the detailed assessment proceedings, the enforcement officer or other officer shall forthwith pay a sum equal to that disallowed to the foreign representative for the benefit of the debtor.

Final costs certificate

66(1) A final costs certificate of the costs officer is final and conclusive as to all matters which have not been objected to in the manner provided for under the rules of the court.

(2) Where it is proved to the satisfaction of a costs officer that a final costs certificate has been lost or destroyed, he may issue a duplicate.

[2750]

NOTES

Commencement: 4 April 2006.

PART III
STATUTORY INSTRUMENTS

PART 11
APPEALS IN PROCEEDINGS UNDER THESE REGULATIONS

Appeals from court orders

67(1) An appeal from a decision of a Registrar of the High Court in proceedings under these Regulations lies to a single judge of the High Court; and an appeal from a decision of that judge on such an appeal lies, with the permission of the Court of Appeal, to the Court of Appeal.

(2) An appeal from a decision of a judge of the High Court in proceedings under these Regulations which is not a decision on an appeal made to him under sub-paragraph (1) lies, with the permission of that judge or the Court of Appeal, to the Court of Appeal.

Procedure on appeals

68(1) Subject as follows, CPR Part 52 (appeals to the Court of Appeal) and its practice direction apply to appeals in proceedings under these Regulations.

(2) The provisions of Part 4 of the practice direction on Insolvency Proceedings supporting CPR Part 49 relating to first appeals (as defined in that Part) apply in relation to any appeal to a single judge of the High Court under paragraph 67, with any necessary modifications.

(3) In proceedings under these Regulations, the procedure under CPR Part 52 is by ordinary application and not by appeal notice.

[2751]

NOTES

Commencement: 4 April 2006.

PART 12
GENERAL

Notices

69(1) All notices required or authorised by or under these Regulations to be given must be in writing, unless it is otherwise provided, or the court allows the notice to be given in some other way.

(2) Where in proceedings under these Regulations a notice is required to be sent or given by any person, the sending or giving of it may be proved by means of a certificate by that person that he posted the notice, or instructed another person (naming him) to do so.

(3) A certificate under this paragraph may be endorsed on a copy or specimen of the notice to which it relates.

"Give notice" etc

70(1) A reference in these Regulations to giving notice, or to delivering, sending or serving any document, means that the notice or document may be sent by post.

(2) Subject to paragraph 75, any form of post may be used.

(3) Personal service of a document is permissible in all cases.

(4) Notice of the venue fixed for an application may be given by service of the sealed copy of the application under paragraph 33(3).

Notice, etc to solicitors

71 Where in proceedings under these Regulations a notice or other document is required or authorised to be given to a person, it may, if he has indicated that his solicitor is authorised to accept service on his behalf, be given instead to the solicitor.

Notice to joint British insolvency officeholders

72 Where two or more persons are acting jointly as the British insolvency officeholder in proceedings under British insolvency law, delivery of a document to one of them is to be treated as delivery to them all.

Forms for use in proceedings under these Regulations

73(1) The forms contained in Schedule 5 to these Regulations shall be used in, and in connection with, proceedings under these Regulations.

(2) The forms shall be used with such variations, if any, as the circumstances may require.

Time limits

74(1) The provisions of CPR Rule 2.8 (time) apply, as regards computation of time, to anything required or authorised to be done by these Regulations.

(2) The provisions of CPR rule 3.1(2)(a) (the court's general powers of management) apply so as to enable the court to extend or shorten the time for compliance with anything required or authorised to be done by these Regulations.

Service by post

75(1) For a document to be properly served by post, it must be contained in an envelope addressed to the person on whom service is to be effected, and pre-paid for first class post.

(2) A document to be served by post may be sent to the last known address of the person to be served.

(3) Where first class post is used, the document is treated as served on the second business day after the date of posting, unless the contrary is shown.

(4) The date of posting is presumed, unless the contrary is shown, to be the date shown in the post-mark on the envelope in which the document is contained.

General provisions as to service and notice

76 Subject to paragraphs 22, 75 and 77, CPR Part 6 (service of documents) applies as regards any matter relating to the service of documents and the giving of notice in proceedings under these Regulations.

Service outside the jurisdiction

77(1) Sections III and IV of CPR Part 6 (service out of the jurisdiction and service of process of foreign court) do not apply in proceedings under these Regulations.

(2) Where for the purposes of proceedings under these Regulations any process or order of the court, or other document, is required to be served on a person who is not in England and Wales, the court may order service to be effected within such time, on such person, at such place and in such manner as it thinks fit, and may also require such proof of service as it thinks fit.

(3) An application under this paragraph shall be supported by an affidavit stating—

(a) the grounds on which the application is made; and

(b) in what place or country the person to be served is, or probably may be found.

False claim of status as creditor

78(1) Rule 12.18 (false claim of status as creditor, etc) shall apply with any necessary modifications in any case where a person falsely claims the status of a creditor of a debtor, with the intention of obtaining a sight of documents whether on the court's file or in the hands of the foreign representative or other person, which he has not under these Regulations any right to inspect.

(2) Rule 21.21 and Schedule 5 of the Rules shall apply to an offence under Rule 12.18 as applied by sub-paragraph (1) as they apply to an offence under Rule 12.18.

The Gazette

79(1) A copy of the Gazette containing any notice required by these Regulations to be gazetted is evidence of any fact stated in the notice.

(2) In the case of an order of the court notice of which is required by these Regulations to be gazetted, a copy of the Gazette containing the notice may in any proceedings be produced as conclusive evidence that the order was made on the date specified in the notice.
[2752]

NOTES

Commencement: 4 April 2006.

SCHEDULE 3
PROCEDURAL MATTERS IN SCOTLAND

Regulation 5

PART 1
INTERPRETATION

Interpretation

1(1) In this Schedule—

"the 1986 Act" means the Insolvency Act 1986;

"article 21 remedy application" means an application to the court by a foreign representative under article 21(1) or (2) of the Model Law for remedy;

"business day" means any day other than a Saturday, a Sunday, Christmas Day, Good Friday or a day which is a bank holiday in Scotland under or by virtue of the Banking and Financial Dealings Act 1971;

"the Gazette" means the Edinburgh Gazette;

"main proceedings" means proceedings opened in accordance with Article 3(1) of the EC Insolvency Regulation and falling within the definition of insolvency proceedings in Article 2(a) of the EC Insolvency Regulation;

"member State liquidator" means a person falling within the definition of liquidator in Article 2(b) of the EC Insolvency Regulation appointed in proceedings to which it applies in a member State other than the United Kingdom;

"the Model Law" means the UNCITRAL Model Law as set out in Schedule 1 to these Regulations;

"modification or termination order" means an order by the court pursuant to its powers under the Model Law modifying or terminating recognition of a foreign proceeding, the sist, restraint or suspension referred to in article 20(1) or any part of it or any remedy granted under article 19 or 21 of the Model Law;

"recognition application" means an application to the court by a foreign representative in accordance with article 15 of the Model Law for an order recognising the foreign proceeding in which he has been appointed;

"recognition order" means an order by the court recognising a proceeding the subject of a recognition application as a foreign main proceeding or foreign non-main proceeding, as appropriate;

"relevant company" means a company within the meaning of section 735(1) of the Companies Act 1985 or an unregistered company within the meaning of Part 5 of the 1986 Act which is subject to a requirement imposed by virtue of section 690A, 691(1) or 718 of the Companies Act 1985;

"review application" means an application to the court for a modification or termination order.

(2) Expressions defined in the Model Law have the same meaning when used in this Schedule.

(3) References in this Schedule to a debtor who is of interest to the Financial Services Authority are references to a debtor who—

(a) is, or has been, an authorised person within the meaning of section 31 of the Financial Services and Markets Act 2000 (authorised persons);

(b) is, or has been, an appointed representative within the meaning of section 39 (exemption of appointed representatives) of that Act; or

(c) is carrying, or has carried on, a regulated activity in contravention of the general prohibition.

(4) In sub-paragraph (3) "the general prohibition" has the meaning given by section 19 of the Financial Services and Markets Act 2000 and the reference to a "regulated activity" must be construed in accordance with—

(a) section 22 of that Act (classes of regulated activity and categories of investment);
(b) any relevant order under that section; and
(c) Schedule 2 to that Act (regulated activities).

(4) References in this Schedule to a numbered form are to the form that bears that number in Schedule 5.

[2753]

NOTES

Commencement: 4 April 2006.

PART 2
THE FOREIGN REPRESENTATIVE

Application for confirmation of status of replacement foreign representative

2(1) This paragraph applies where following the making of a recognition order the foreign representative dies or for any other reason ceases to be the foreign representative in the foreign proceedings in relation to the debtor.

(2) In this paragraph "the former foreign representative" means the foreign representative referred to in sub-paragraph (1).

(3) If a person has succeeded the former foreign representative or is otherwise holding office as foreign representative in the foreign proceeding in relation to the debtor, that person may apply to the court for an order confirming his status as replacement foreign representative for the purpose of proceedings under these Regulations.

(4) If the court dismisses an application under sub-paragraph (3) then it may also, if it thinks fit, make an order terminating recognition of the foreign proceeding and—

(a) such an order may include such provision as the court thinks fit with respect to matters arising in connection with the termination; and
(b) paragraph 5 shall not apply to such an order.

Misfeasance by a foreign representative

3(1) The court may examine the conduct of a person who—

(a) is or purports to be the foreign representative in relation to a debtor, or
(b) has been or has purported to be the foreign representative in relation to a debtor.

(2) An examination under this paragraph may be held only on the application of—

(a) a British insolvency officeholder acting in relation to the debtor,
(b) a creditor of the debtor, or
(c) with the permission of the court, any other person who appears to have an interest justifying an application.

(3) An application under sub-paragraph (2) must allege that the foreign representative—

(a) has misapplied or retained money or other property of the debtor,
(b) has become accountable for money or other property of the debtor,
(c) has breached a fiduciary duty or other duty in relation to the debtor, or
(d) has been guilty of misfeasance.

(4) On an examination under this paragraph into a person's conduct the court may order him—

(a) to repay, restore or account for money or property;
(b) to pay interest;
(c) to contribute a sum to the debtor's property by way of compensation for breach of duty or misfeasance.

(5) In sub-paragraph (3), "foreign representative" includes a person who purports or has purported to be a foreign representative in relation to a debtor.

[2754]

NOTES

Commencement: 4 April 2006.

PART 3
COURT PROCEDURE AND PRACTICE

Preliminary and interpretation

4(1) This Part applies to—
- (a) any of the following applications made to the court under these Regulations—
  - (i) a recognition application;
  - (ii) an article 21 remedy application;
  - (iii) an application under paragraph 2(3) for an order confirming the status of a replacement foreign representative;
  - (iv) a review application; and
- (b) any of the following orders made by the court under these Regulations—
  - (i) a recognition order;
  - (ii) an order granting interim remedy under article 19 of the Model Law;
  - (iii) an order granting remedy under article 21 of the Model Law;
  - (iv) an order confirming the status of a replacement foreign representative; or
  - (v) a modification or termination order.

Reviews of court orders—where court makes order of its own motion

5(1) The court shall not of its own motion make a modification or termination order unless the foreign representative and the debtor have either—
- (a) had an opportunity of being heard on the question, or
- (b) consented in writing to such an order.

(2) If the court makes a modification or termination order, the order may include such provision as the court thinks fit with respect to matters arising in connection with the modification or termination.

The hearing

6(1) At the hearing of the application, the applicant and any of the following persons (not being the applicant) may appear or be represented—
- (a) the foreign representative;
- (b) the debtor and, in the case of any debtor other than an individual, any one or more directors or other officers of the debtor, including—
  - (i) where applicable, any person registered under Part 23 of the Companies Act 1985 as authorised to represent the debtor in respect of its business in Scotland;
  - (ii) in the case of a debtor which is a partnership, any person who is a member of the partnership;
- (c) if a British insolvency officeholder is acting in relation to the debtor, that person;
- (d) if any person has been appointed an administrative receiver of the debtor or as a receiver or manager of the property of the debtor, that person;
- (e) if a member State liquidator has been appointed in main proceedings in relation to the debtor, that person;
- (f) if a foreign representative has been appointed in any other foreign proceeding regarding the debtor, that person;
- (g) any person who has presented a petition for the winding up or sequestration of the debtor in Scotland;
- (h) any person who is or may be entitled to appoint an administrator of the debtor under paragraph 14 of Schedule B1 to the 1986 Act (appointment of administrator by holder of qualifying floating charge);
- (i) if the debtor is a debtor who is of interest to the Financial Services Authority, that Authority; and
- (j) with the permission of the court, any other person who appears to have an interest justifying his appearance.

Notification and advertisement of order

7(1) This paragraph applies where the court makes any of the orders referred to in paragraph 4(1)(b).

(2) The foreign representative shall send a certified copy of the interlocutor as soon as reasonably practicable to the debtor.

(3) The foreign representative shall, as soon as reasonably practicable after the date of the order, give notice of the making of the order—

(a) if a British insolvency officeholder is acting in relation to the debtor, to him;
(b) if any person has been appointed an administrative receiver of the debtor or, to the knowledge of the foreign representative, as a receiver or manager of the property of the debtor, to him;
(c) if a member State liquidator has been appointed in main proceedings in relation to the debtor, to him;
(d) if to his knowledge a foreign representative has been appointed in any other foreign proceeding regarding the debtor, that person;
(e) if there is pending in Scotland a petition for the winding up or sequestration of the debtor, to the petitioner;
(f) to any person who to his knowledge is or may be entitled to appoint an administrator of the debtor under paragraph 14 of Schedule B1 to the 1986 Act (appointment of administrator by holder of qualifying floating charge);
(g) if the debtor is a debtor who is of interest to the Financial Services Authority, to that Authority; and
(h) to such persons as the court may direct.

(4) Where the debtor is a relevant company, the foreign representative shall send notice of the making of the order to the registrar of companies before the end of the period of 5 business days beginning with the date of the order. The notice to the registrar of companies shall be in Form ML7.

(5) The foreign representative shall advertise the making of the following orders once in the Gazette and once in such newspaper as he thinks most appropriate for ensuring that the making of the order comes to the notice of the debtor's creditors—

(a) a recognition order,
(b) an order confirming the status of a replacement foreign representative, and
(c) a modification or termination order which modifies or terminates recognition of a foreign proceeding,

and the advertisement shall be in Form ML8.

Registration of court order

8(1) Where the court makes a recognition order in respect of a foreign main proceeding or an order suspending the right to transfer, encumber or otherwise dispose of any assets of the debtor being heritable property, the clerk of the court shall send forthwith a certified copy of the order to the keeper of the register of inhibitions and adjudications for recording in that register.

(2) Recording under sub-paragraph (1) or (3) shall have the effect as from the date of the order of an inhibition and of a citation in an adjudication of the debtor's heritable estate at the instance of the foreign representative.

(3) Where the court makes a modification or termination order, the clerk of the court shall send forthwith a certified copy of the order to the keeper of the register of inhibitions and adjudications for recording in that register.

(4) The effect mentioned in sub-paragraph (2) shall expire—

(a) on the recording of a modification or termination order under sub-paragraph (3); or
(b) subject to sub-paragraph (5), if the effect has not expired by virtue of paragraph (a), at the end of the period of 3 years beginning with the date of the order.

(5) The foreign representative may, if recognition of the foreign proceeding has not been modified or terminated by the court pursuant to its powers under the Model Law, before the end of the period of 3 years mentioned in sub-paragraph (4)(b), send a memorandum in a form prescribed by the Court of Session by act of sederunt to the keeper of the register of inhibitions and adjudications for recording in that register, and such recording shall renew the effect mentioned in sub-paragraph (2); and thereafter the said effect shall continue to be preserved only if such memorandum is so recorded before the expiry of every subsequent period of 3 years.

Right to inspect court process

9(1) In the case of any proceedings under these Regulations, the following have the right, at all reasonable times, to inspect the court process of the proceedings—

(a) the Secretary of State;

(b) the person who is the foreign representative in relation to the proceedings;

(c) if a foreign representative has been appointed in any other foreign proceeding regarding the debtor, that person;

(d) if a British insolvency officeholder is acting in relation to the debtor, that person;

(e) any person stating himself in writing to be a creditor of the debtor to which the proceedings under these Regulations relate;

(f) if a member State liquidator has been appointed in relation to a debtor which is subject to proceedings under these Regulations, that person; and

(g) the debtor to which the proceedings under these Regulations relate, or, if that debtor is a company, corporation or partnership, every person who is, or at any time has been—

(i) a director or officer of the debtor,

(ii) a member of the debtor, or

(iii) where applicable, a person registered under Part 23 of the Companies Act 1985 as authorised to represent the debtor in respect of its business in Scotland.

(2) The right of inspection conferred as above on any person may be exercised on his behalf by a person properly authorised by him.

Copies of court orders

10(1) In any proceedings under these Regulations, any person who under paragraph 9 has a right to inspect documents in the court process also has the right to require the foreign representative in relation to those proceedings to furnish him with a copy of any court order in the proceedings.

(2) Sub-paragraph (1) does not apply if a copy of the court order has been served on that person or notice of the making of the order has been given to that person under other provisions of these Regulations.

Transfer of proceedings—actions to avoid acts detrimental to creditors

11 If, in accordance with article 23(6) of the Model Law, the court grants a foreign representative permission to make an application in accordance with paragraph (1) of that article, it may also order the relevant proceedings under British insolvency law taking place regarding the debtor to be transferred to the Court of Session if those proceedings are taking place in Scotland and are not already in that court.

[2755]

NOTES

Commencement: 4 April 2006.

PART 3
GENERAL

NOTES

This Schedule has two Parts numbered as Part 3. It is believed that this Part should have been numbered as Part 4.

Giving of notices, etc

12(1) All notices required or authorised by or under these Regulations to be given, sent or delivered must be in writing, unless it is otherwise provided, or the court allows the notice to be sent or given in some other way.

(2) Any reference in these Regulations to giving, sending or delivering a notice or any such document means, without prejudice to any other way and unless it is otherwise provided, that the notice or document may be sent by post, and that, subject to paragraph 13, any form of post may be used. Personal service of the notice or document is permissible in all cases.

(3) Where under these Regulations a notice or other document is required or authorised to be given, sent or delivered by a person ("the sender") to another ("the recipient"), it may be given, sent or delivered by any person duly authorised by the sender to do so to any person duly authorised by the recipient to receive or accept it.

(4) Where two or more persons are acting jointly as the British insolvency officeholder in proceedings under British insolvency law, the giving, sending or delivering of a notice or document to one of them is to be treated as the giving, sending or delivering of a notice or document to each or all.

Sending by post

13(1) For a document to be properly sent by post, it must be contained in an envelope addressed to the person to whom it is to be sent, and pre-paid for either first or second class post.

(2) Any document to be sent by post may be sent to the last known address of the person to whom the document is to be sent.

(3) Where first class post is used, the document is to be deemed to be received on the second business day after the date of posting, unless the contrary is shown.

(4) Where second class post is used, the document is to be deemed to be received on the fourth business day after the date of posting, unless the contrary is shown.

Certificate of giving notice, etc

14(1) Where in any proceedings under these Regulations a notice or document is required to be given, sent or delivered by any person, the date of giving, sending or delivery of it may be proved by means of a certificate by that person that he gave, posted or otherwise sent or delivered the notice or document on the date stated in the certificate, or that he instructed another person (naming him) to do so.

(2) A certificate under this paragraph may be endorsed on a copy of the notice to which it relates.

(3) A certificate purporting to be signed by or on behalf of the person mentioned in sub-paragraph (1) shall be deemed, unless the contrary is shown, to be sufficient evidence of the matters stated therein.

Forms for use in proceedings under these Regulations

15(1) Forms ML7 and ML8 contained in Schedule 5 to these Regulations shall be used in, and in connection with, proceedings under these Regulations.

(2) The forms shall be used with such variations, if any, as the circumstances may require.

[2756]

NOTES

Commencement: 4 April 2006.

SCHEDULE 4

NOTICES DELIVERED TO THE REGISTRAR OF COMPANIES

Regulation 6

Interpretation

1(1) In this Schedule—

"the 1985 Act" means the Companies Act 1985;

"electronic communication" means the same as in the Electronic Communications Act 2000;

"Model Law notice" means a notice delivered to the registrar of companies under paragraph 26(6) of Schedule 2 or paragraph 7(4) of Schedule 3.

(2) Expressions defined in the Model Law or Schedule 2 or 3, as appropriate, have the same meaning when used in this Schedule.

(3) References in this Schedule to delivering a notice include sending, forwarding, producing or giving it.

Functions of the registrar of companies

2(1) Where a Model Law notice is delivered to the registrar of companies in respect of a relevant company, the registrar shall enter a note in the register relating to that company.

(2) The note referred to in sub-paragraph (1) shall contain the following particulars, in each case as stated in the notice delivered to the registrar—

(a) brief details of the court order made;
(b) the date of the court order; and
(c) the name and address for service of the person who is the foreign representative in relation to the company.

Registrar of companies to whom notices to be delivered

3(1) References in Schedules 2 and 3 to the registrar of companies in relation to a relevant company shall be construed in accordance with the following provisions.

(2) The notices which a relevant company is required to deliver to the registrar of companies shall be delivered—

(a) to the registrar for England and Wales if the company has a relevant presence in England and Wales, and
(b) to the registrar for Scotland if the company has a relevant presence in Scotland,

and if the relevant company has a relevant presence in both parts of Great Britain, the notices shall be delivered to both registrars.

(3) For the purposes of this paragraph a "relevant presence" means—

(a) in the case of a company within the meaning of section 735(1) of the 1985 Act, its registered office,
(b) in the case of an unregistered company within the meaning of Part 5 of the 1986 Act which is subject to a requirement imposed by virtue of section 690A of the 1985 Act, a branch,
(c) in the case of an unregistered company within the meaning of Part 5 of the 1986 Act which is subject to a requirement imposed by virtue of section 691(1) of the 1985 Act, an established place of business, and
(d) in the case of an unregistered company within the meaning of Part 5 of the 1986 Act which is subject to a requirement imposed by virtue of section 718 of the 1985 Act, a principal place of business.

Delivery to registrar of notices

4(1) Electronic communications may be used for the delivery of any Model Law notice, provided that such delivery is in such form and manner as is directed by the registrar.

(2) Where the Model Law notice is required to be signed, it shall instead be authenticated in such manner as is directed by the registrar.

(3) If a Model Law notice is delivered to the registrar which does not comply with the requirements of these Regulations, he may serve on the person by whom the notice was delivered (or, if there are two or more such persons, on any of them) a notice (a non-compliance notice) indicating the respect in which the Model Law notice does not comply.

(4) Where the registrar serves a non-compliance notice, then, unless a replacement Model Law notice—

(a) is delivered to him within 14 days after the service of the non-compliance notice, and
(b) complies with the requirements of these Regulations or is not rejected by him for failure to comply with those requirements,

the original Model Law notice shall be deemed not to have been delivered to him.

Enforcement of foreign representative's duty to give notice to registrar

5(1) If a foreign representative, having made default in complying with paragraph 26(6) of Schedule 2 or paragraph 7(4) of Schedule 3 fails to make good the default within 14 days after the service of a notice on the foreign representative requiring him to do so, the court may, on an application made to it by any creditor, member, director or other officer of the debtor or by the registrar of companies, make an order directing the foreign representative to make good the default within such time as may be specified in the order.

(2) The court's order may provide that all costs of and incidental to the application shall be borne by the foreign representative.

Rectification of the register under court order

6(1) The registrar shall remove from the register any note, or part of a note—

(a) that relates to or is derived from a court order that the court has declared to be invalid or ineffective, or

(b) that the court declares to be factually inaccurate or derived from something that is factually inaccurate or forged,

and that the court directs should be removed from the register.

(2) The court order must specify what is to be removed from the register and indicate where on the register it is and the registrar shall carry out his duty under sub-paragraph (1) within a reasonable time of receipt by him of the relevant court order.

[2757]

NOTES

Commencement: 4 April 2006.

PART III
STATUTORY INSTRUMENTS

SCHEDULE 5
FORMS

Sch 2, para 73 and Sch 3, para 15

FORM ML1

Schedule 2, paragraph 2

Form ML 1

The Cross-Border Insolvency Regulations 2006
Recognition application

Name of Debtor	Company number *where applicable*
In the [full name of court]	*For court use only* Court case number

(a) Insert full name(s) of applicant(s)

1. The application of (a) ______

being the foreign representative(s) appointed in relation to the above named debtor in a foreign proceeding, in reliance on article 15 of the UNCITRAL Model Law on cross-border insolvency as set out in Schedule 1 to the Cross-Border Insolvency Regulations 2006 ("the Model law")

(b) insert full name of the debtor

2. The application is in respect of a foreign proceeding in relation to (b) ______

(c) Insert name of country where the foreign proceeding the subject of the application is taking place

("the debtor") [[lately] carrying on business in(c) ______

(d) Insert any trading name of the debtor if different from the full name given above and any former trading names in respect of any business in respect of which the debtor may have incurred debts or other liabilities still unsatisfied

as(d) ______]

(e) Insert any trading name of the debtor in Great Britain if different from the full name given above and any former trading names in respect of any business in great Britain in respect of which the debtor may have incurred debts or other liabilties still unsatisfied

[and [lately] carrying on business in Great Britain as(e) ______].

(f) Delete any statements in paragraph 3 which do not apply and insert full address details, where applicable

* Delete as applicable

3. (f)[The debtor's principal/last known* place of business in Great Britain is

______]

(SI 2006/1030)

Form ML 1 continued

(g) If the debtor's principal/last known place of business is in Scotland insert details of any place of business in England and Wales	(g)[and the debtor's principal/last known* place of business in England and Wales is_________ ____]
* Delete as applicable	[The debtor's usual/last known* place of residence in Great Britain is_________ ____]
(h) If the debtor's usual/last known place of residence is in Scotland insert details of any place of residence in England and Wales	(h)[and the debtor's usual/last known* place of residence in England and Wales is_____ ____]
	[The debtor has no place of business in Great Britain]
	[The debtor has no place of residence in Great Britain]
	[The debtor has assets situated within England and Wales]
(i) Insert date of incorporation	4. The debtor was incorporated on(i) _______________
(j) Insert registered number	under the Companies Act 19 ______, and the registered number of the debtor is(j) ________ _______________________
	OR
(k) If the debtor has a registered branch or place of business include applicable statement(s) and insert required details	(k)[The debtor has one or more branches registered under Schedule 21A of the Companies Act 1985. The registered numbers of the branch(es) are_______________ ____]
	[The debtor has delivered to the registrar of companies for the relevant part of Great Britain documents in respect of one or more places of business established by it in Great Britain.]
	OR

Form ML 1 continued

The debtor is not registered under the Companies Act 19______, nor does it have any branches registered under that Act or places of business of which particulars have been delivered to the registrar of companies.

(l) Give details of any business carried on by the debtor in respect of which the debtor may have incurred debts or other liabilities still unsatisfied

5. (l) The principal business [lately] carried on by the debtor in Great Britain is______________

OR

The debtor does not carry on business in Great Britain.

(m) Insert name of country where the foreign proceeding is taking place

6. The foreign proceeding in respect of which recognition is applied for is taking place in(m)____

(n) Insert brief details of the foreign proceedings

The foreign proceeding is(n)______________

7. The foreign proceeding in respect of which recognition is applied for is a proceeding within the meaning of article 2(i) of the Model Law,

and the applicant is the foreign representative of the debtor within the meaning of article 2(j) of the Model Law in relation to that proceeding.

and the evidence referred to in article 15(2) of the Model Law is contained in or exhibited to the affidavit in support attached to this application.

8. The address of the debtor's centre of main interests is ______________

Form ML1 continued

and

(o) Delete whichever of the two statements does not apply and insert address details. where applicable

(o)**EITHER**

* Delete as applicable

that is the address of the debtor's registered office/habitual residence*

OR

the address of the debtor's registered office/habitual residence* is ____________________

____

(p) If the application is for recognition of a foreign non-main proceeding include this statement, giving the name of the country where the foreign proceeding the subject of this application is taking place and the address of the establishment in that country

(p)[and the debtor has an establishment within the meaning of article 2(e) of the Model Law in ___

____

and the address of that establishment is ____________________

____

____________________]

Note: The terms centre of main interests, habitual residence and establishment have the meaning given to them under the Model Law.

9. The debtor is not a person falling within any of the exceptions set out in article 1(2) of the Model Law.

10. An affidavit in support of this application is attached.

11. The statement referred to in article 15(3) of the Model Law is exhibited to the affidavit in support attached to this application.

(q) Insert address for service
* Delete as applicable

12. The applicant's/applicant's solicitor's* address for service is(q)____________________

____

____

Form ML 1 continued

13. The applicant(s) therefore request(s) as follows:

* Delete as applicable

(a) that the court make an order recognising the foreign proceeding the subject of this application as a foreign main/non main* proceeding

(r) Insert details of any ancillary orders sought

(b) (r)____

____

OR

(c) that such other order may be made as the court thinks appropriate.

Signed____

* Delete as applicable

Applicant/Applicant's solicitor*
(If signing on behalf of firm or company state position or office held)

Dated____

[2758]

FORM ML2

Schedule 2,
paragraph 5(2)

Form ML 2

The Cross-Border Insolvency Regulations 2006

Recognition order

Name of Debtor	Company number *where applicable*
In the [full name of court]	*For court use only* Court case number

(a) Insert full name(s) and address(es) for service of applicant(s) — UPON THE APPLICATION OF (a) ______

______

(b) insert date — presented to the court on (b) ______

(c) Insert full name and address for service of the debtor — in respect of (c) ______

______

and upon hearing

(d) Insert details of any other parties (including the debtor) appearing and by whom represented — and for (d) ______

______

and upon reading the evidence

(e) Insert details of foreign proceeding — IT IS ORDERED that (e) ______

______

* Delete as applicable — be recognised as a foreign main proceeding/foreign non-main proceeding* in accordance with the UNCITRAL Model Law on cross-border insolvency as set out in Schedule 1 to the Cross-Border Insolvency Regulations 2006

(f) insert particulars of any further order made by the court — AND it is ordered that (f) ______

______

______

(g) Insert terms of order for costs — AND it is ordered that the costs of the said application (g) ______

______

(h) Insert date and time — This order shall take effect from (h) ______

(SI 2006/1030)

[2759]

FORM ML3

Schedule 2,
paragraph 6

Form ML 3

The Cross-Border Insolvency Regulations 2006

Statement of subsequent information

Name of Debtor	Company number *where applicable*
In the [full name of court]	Court case number

(a) Insert full name(s) and address(es) of foreign representatives

I/We(a) ____

attach a statement providing information in accordance with article 18 of the UNCITRAL Model Law on cross-border insolvency, as set out in Schedule 1 to the Cross-Border Insolvency Regulations 2006, and paragraph 6(2)(b) of Schedule 2 to those Regulations.

Signed ____
Joint/Foreign Representative(s)

Dated ____

(SI 2006/1030)

[2760]

FORM ML4

Schedule 2, paragraph 32

Form ML 4

The Cross-Border Insolvency Regulations 2006

Originating application

In the [full name of court]	*For court use only* Court case number

Between

Applicant ______

and

Respondent ______

(a) Insert full name and address of respondent

Let(a) ______

______

attend before the Judge on:

Date ______

Time ______ hours

Place ______

(b) Insert name of applicant

On the hearing of an application by(b) ______

(c) State the terms of the order to which the applicant claims to be entitled

the applicant for an order in the following terms:(c) ______

______

(d) Set out grounds or refer to a witness statement or affidavit in support

The grounds on which the applicant claims to be entitled to the order are:(d) ______

______

(e) State the name(s) and address(es) of the person(s) intended to be served

The names and addresses of the persons upon whom it is intended to serve this application are:(e)

______

______

______

OR

(SI 2006/1030)

Form ML 4 continued

It is not intended to serve any person with this application.

(f) State the applicant's address for service

The applicant's address for service is:(f) ____________________

____

Dated ____________________

Signed ____________________
(Solicitor for the) Applicant

If you do not attend, the court may make such order as it thinks fit.

[2761]

FORM ML5

Schedule 2,
paragraphs 19 and 32

Form ML 5

The Cross-Border Insolvency Regulations 2006
Ordinary application

In the [full name of court]	Court case number

Between

Applicant ______

and

Respondent ______

Take notice that I intend to apply to the Judge on:

Date ______

Time ______ hours

Place ______

(a) State nature and grounds of application

for(a) ______

Signed ______
(SOLICITOR FOR THE) APPLICANT

My/Our address for service is: ______

(b) Give the name(s) and address(es) of the person(s) (including the respondent) on whom it is intended to serve the application

To:(b) ______

OR

It is not intended to serve any person with this application.

If you do not attend, the court may make such order as it thinks fit.

(SI 2006/1030)

[2762]

PART III
STATUTORY INSTRUMENTS

FORM ML6

Schedule 2,
paragraph 23

Form ML 6

The Cross-Border Insolvency Regulations 2006

Affidavit of service of application under the Cross-Border Insolvency Regulations 2006

Name of Debtor	Company number *where applicable*
In the [full name of court]	Court case number

(a) Insert full name and address of person making affidavit

I, (a)____

____

* Delete as applicable

the applicant/acting on behalf of the applicant* state on oath:

1. That I did on______day the__________day of__________________20____

(b) insert details of application

serve the above-named debtor with a copy of an application for (b)________________

____

("the application") duly sealed with the seal of the court and its supporting documents by leaving

(c) Insert address where served

the same at the debtor's proper address at(c)____________________

____

OR by posting the same on______day the____________day of__________________20____

by ordinary post first class mail an envelope duly pre-paid and properly addressed to the said debtor at (c)________________________________

2. That I did on______day the____________day of______________20____

(d) Insert name

serve(d)____

the foreign representative in relation to the said debtor with a copy of the application duly sealed with the seal of the court and its supporting documents by leaving the same at his proper address at(c)____

____

(SI 2006/1030)

Form ML 6 continued

OR by posting the same on______ day the______________ day of______________ 20___

by ordinary post first class mail in an envelope duly pre-paid and properly addressed to the said(d) ____________________

at(c)____________________

____

3. That I did on______ day the______________ day of______________ 20___

serve(d)____________________

a British insolvency officeholder acting in relation to the said debtor with a copy of the application duly sealed with the seal of the court and its supporting documents by leaving the same at his proper address at(c) ____________________

____

OR by posting the same on ______day the______________ day of______________ 20___

by ordinary post first class mail in an envelope duly pre-paid and properly addressed to the said(d)____________________

at(c)____________________

____

4. That I did on______ day the______________ day of______________ 20___

serve(d) ____________________

* Delete as applicable

the administrative receiver/receiver or manager of the property of the debtor in England and Wales* with a copy of the application duly sealed with the seal of the court and its supporting documents by leaving the same at his proper address at(c)____________________

____

OR by posting the same on______ day the______________ day of______________ 20___

by ordinary post first class mail in an envelope duly prepraid and properly addressed to the said(d)

____

at(c)____________________

____

Form ML 6 continued

5. That I did on ______ day the ______________ day of ______________________ 20____

serve(d)____

a member State liquidator of the said debtor with a copy of the application duly sealed with the seal of the court and its supporting documents by leaving the same at his proper address at(c)__________

____

OR by posting the same on ______ day the ______________ day of ______________ 20____

by ordinary post first class mail in an envelope duly pre-praid and properly addressed to the said(d)____

at(c)____

____

6. That I did on ________ day the ______________ day of ____________________ 20______

serve(d)____

a foreign representative of the said debtor appointed in another foreign proceeding regarding the said debtor with a copy of the application duly sealed with the seal of the court and its supporting documents by leaving the same at his proper address at(c)______________________________

____

OR by posting the same on ______ day the ______________ day of ______________ 20____

by ordinary post first class mail in an envelope duly pre-praid and properly addressed to the said(d)____

at(c)____

7. That I did on ________ day the ______________ day of ____________________ 20______

serve(d)____

who has presented a petition to wind up the said debtor/for a bankruptcy order to be made against the said debtor* with a copy of the application duly sealed with the seal of the court and its supporting documents by leaving the same at his proper address at(c)______________________

____

OR by posting the same on ______ day the ______________ day of ______________ 20____

* Delete as applicable

Form ML 6 continued

by ordinary post first class mail in an envelope duly pre-paid and properly addressed to the

said(d) ______________________________

at(c) ______________________________

____

8. That I did on ______ day the ______________ day of ______________ 20____

serve(d) ______________________________

a person who is or may be entitled to appoint an administrator of the said debtor under paragraph 14 of Schedule B1 to the Insolvency Act 1986 with a copy of the application duly sealed with the seal of the court and its supporting documents by leaving the same at his proper address at(c) ______________________________

____

OR by posting the same on ______ day the ______________ day of ______________ 20____

by ordinary post first class mail in an envelope duly pre-praid and properly addressed to the

said(d) ______________________________

at(c) ______________________________

____

9. That I did on ________ day the ______________ day of ______________ 20____

serve the Financial Services Authority with a copy of the application duly sealed with the seal of the court and its supporting documents by leaving the same at its proper address at(c) ________

____

OR by posting the same on ______ day the ______________ day of ______________ 20____

by ordinary post first class mail in an envelope duly pre-praid and properly addressed to the Financial Services Authority at(c) ______________________________

____

A sealed copy of the application and its supporting documents are now produced to me marked "A".

SWORN ______________________________

[2763]

FORM ML7

Schedule 2,
paragraph 26(6)
and Schedule 3,
paragraph 7(4)

Form ML 7

The Cross-Border Insolvency Regulations 2006

Notice to registrar of companies of order under the Cross-border Insolvency Regulations 2006

ML 7

Name of Debtor	Company number *where applicable*
In the [full name of court]	Court case number

(a) Insert name(s) and address(es) for service of foreign representative(s)

Notice is hereby given by(a) ____________________

____

____

(b) Insert brief details of court order

the foreign representative(s) in relation to the above named debtor that the following order has been made under the Cross-border Insolvency Regulations 2006(b):

____

____

____

(c) Insert date

The order made on(c) ____________________

Signed ____________________
Joint/Foreign Representative(s)

Dated ____________________

(SI 2006/1030)

Form ML 7 continued

(a) If the debtor is an oversea company with branches in Great Britain, please complete requested details of branches. If this form is delivered in respect of more than one branch in the same part of Great Britain, the branch number and name (where different) must be given for each branch

(d) This return is delivered in respect of all the branches listed below.

Registration number	Branch name

Contact details:

You do not have to give any contact information in the box opposite but if you do, it will help Companies House to contact you if there is a query on the form.

	Tel
DX Number	DX Exchange

Companies House receipt barcode

When you have completed and signed this form please send it to the Registrar of Companies at:

for companies or branches registered or places of business established in England and Wales:

Companies House, Crown Way, Cardiff, CF14 3UZ **DX 33050 Cardiff**

for companies or branches registered or places of business established in Scotland:

Companies House, 37 Castle Terrace, Edinburgh, EH1 2EB **DX 325 Edinburgh** or **LP-4 Edinburgh 2**

[2764]

FORM ML8

Schedule 2, paragraph 26(7) and Schedule 3, paragraph 7(5)

Form ML 8

The Cross-Border Insolvency Regulations 2006

Notification of order under the Cross-border Insolvency Regulations 2006 (for newspaper and London or Edinburgh Gazette)

Name of Debtor	Company number *where applicable*
In the [full name of court]	Court case number

Nature of business (where applicable) ____________________

(a) Insert any trading names used by the debtor in Great Britain within the last 12 months, if different from the full name given above

Trading name(s) (a) ____________________

____

(b) Insert address of principal/last known place of business of debtor, or alternatively, in the case of a debtor who is an individual, the usual/last known place of residence of the debtor

Address of debtor (b) ____________________

____

____

(c) Insert brief details of order

The following order has been made in relation to the above debtor under the Cross-border Insolvency Regulations 2006 (c) ____________________

____

(d) Insert date

Order made on (d) ____________________

(c) Insert address for service

Name(s) and address(es) of foreign representative(s) (e) ____________________

____

____

(SI 2006/1030)

[2765]

I. OTHER

PROTECTION OF TRADING INTERESTS (US RE-EXPORT CONTROL) ORDER 1982

(SI 1982/885)

NOTES

Made: 30 June 1982.
Authority: Protection of Trading Interests Act 1980, s 1(1).
Commencement: 1 July 1982.

1 This Order may be cited as the Protection of Trading Interests (US Re-export Control) Order 1982 and shall come into operation on 1st July 1982.

[2766]

2 The Secretary of State hereby directs that section 1 of the 1980 Act shall apply to the measures referred to in the following Article.

[2767]

3 The measures to which this Order relates are those provisions of parts 374, 376, 379, 385 and 399 of the Export Administration Regulations, as amended, made by the United States Secretary of Commerce under the powers conferred on him by the United States Export Administration Act 1979 which affect the re-export or export of goods from the United Kingdom.

[2768]

PROTECTION OF TRADING INTERESTS (US ANTITRUST MEASURES) ORDER 1983

(SI 1983/900)

NOTES

Made: 23 June 1983.
Authority: Protection of Trading Interests Act 1980, s 1(1).
Commencement: 27 June 1983.

1—(1) This Order may be cited as the Protection of Trading Interests (US Antitrust Measures) Order 1983 and shall come into operation on 27th June 1983.

(2) In this Order—

"the Bermuda 2 Agreement" means the Agreement between the Government of the United Kingdom of Great Britain and Northern Ireland and the Government of the United States signed at Bermuda on 23rd July 1977, concerning air services;

"air service" and "tariff" shall be construed in accordance with the Bermuda 2 Agreement;

"UK designated airline" means a British airline (within the meaning of section 4(2) of the Civil Aviation Act 1982) designated by the Government of the United Kingdom under the Bermuda 2 Agreement.

[2769]

2—(1) The Secretary of State hereby directs that section 1 of the 1980 Act shall apply to sections 1 and 2 of the United States' Sherman Act and sections 4 and 4A of the United States' Clayton Act in their application to the cases described in the following paragraph.

(2) The cases mentioned in paragraph (1) of this Article are—

(i) an agreement or arrangement (whether legally enforceable or not) to which a UK designated airline is a party,

(ii) a discussion or communication to which a UK designated airline is a party,

(iii) any act done by a UK designated airline,

which, in respect of each case, concerns the tariffs charged or to be charged by any such airline or otherwise relates to the operation by it of an air service authorised pursuant to the Bermuda 2 Agreement.

[2770]

PROTECTION OF TRADING INTERESTS (AUSTRALIAN TRADE PRACTICES) ORDER 1988

(SI 1988/569)

NOTES

Made: 23 March 1988.
Authority: Protection of Trading Interests Act 1980, s 5(4).
Commencement: 24 March 1988.

1 This Order may be cited as the Protection of Trading Interests (Australian Trade Practices) Order 1988 and shall come into force on 24th March 1988.

[2771]

2 For the purposes of section 5(2)(b) of the 1980 Act the Secretary of State hereby specifies section 81(1A) of the Trade Practices Act 1974 of Australia.

[2772]

PROTECTION OF TRADING INTERESTS (US CUBAN ASSETS CONTROL REGULATIONS) ORDER 1992

(SI 1992/2449)

NOTES

Made: 14 October 1992.
Authority: Protection of Trading Interests Act 1980, s 1(1).
Commencement: 14 October 1992.

1 This Order may be cited as the Protection of Trading Interests (US Cuban Assets Control Regulations) Order 1992 and shall come into force at 11.40 am on 14th October 1992.

[2773]

2 The Secretary of State hereby directs that section 1 of the 1980 Act shall apply to the measures taken under the law of the United States referred to in the following Article.

[2774]

3 The measures to which this Order applies are those provisions of part 515 (entitled Cuban Assets Control Regulations) of title 31 of the Code of Federal Regulations which affect trading activities carried on in the United Kingdom or the import of goods to or the export of goods from the United Kingdom.

[2775]

4 In this Order "trading activities" includes any activity carried on in the course of a business of any description.

[2776]

EXTRATERRITORIAL US LEGISLATION (SANCTIONS AGAINST CUBA, IRAN AND LIBYA) (PROTECTION OF TRADING INTERESTS) ORDER 1996

(SI 1996/3171)

NOTES

Made: 19 December 1996.
Authority: European Communities Act 1972, s 2(2).
Commencement: 28 January 1997.

1—(1) This Order may be cited as the Extraterritorial US Legislation (Sanctions against Cuba, Iran and Libya) (Protection of Trading Interests) Order 1996 and shall come into force on 28th January 1997.

(2) In this Order, unless the context otherwise requires, expressions used in Council Regulation (EC) No 2271/96 of 22nd November 1996 protecting against the effects of the extraterritorial application of legislation adopted by a third country and actions based thereon or resulting therefrom ("the EC Counter-measures Regulation") shall have the same meaning as in that Regulation.

[2777]

2—(1) Subject to paragraph (2) below, any person referred to in Article 11 of the EC Counter-measures Regulation (that is to say)—

(i) any natural person being a resident in the Community and a national of a member state, or
(ii) any legal person incorporated within the Community, or
(iii) any natural or legal person referred to in Article 1(2) of Council Regulation (EEC) No 4055/86, or
(iv) any other natural person being a resident in the Community, unless that person is in the country of which he is a national, or
(v) any other natural person within the Community, including its territorial waters and air space and in any aircraft or on any vessel under the jurisdiction or control of a member state, acting in a professional capacity)

who commits a breach of Article 2 or the first paragraph of Article 5 of that Regulation, and any director, manager or other person with management responsibilities to whom the obligation in the first paragraph of Article 2 of that Regulation applies who commits a breach of that paragraph, shall be guilty of an offence and liable—

(a) on conviction on indictment, to a fine;
(b) on summary conviction, to a fine not exceeding the statutory maximum.

(2) Paragraph (1) above shall not apply in respect of anything done or omitted to be done—

(a) within the territorial jurisdiction of a member state other than the United Kingdom, or
(b) outside the territorial jurisdiction of any member state by—
  (i) a national of a member state other than the United Kingdom who is not also a British person, or
  (ii) a legal person incorporated in a member state other than the United Kingdom, or
  (iii) any person falling within paragraph (1)(iii) above unless—
    (aa) he is a British person, or
    (bb) it is a shipping company controlled by a British person or by nationals of a member state at least one of which is a British person, or
    (cc) the vessel, or at least one of the vessels, of that person is registered in the United Kingdom, or
  (iv) any person falling within paragraph (1)(iv) above unless he was established within the United Kingdom at some time during the period of at least six months referred to in footnote 1 to Article 11(1) of the EC Counter-measures Regulation;

and in this paragraph—

PART III STATUTORY INSTRUMENTS

"British person" means a British citizen, [British overseas territories citizen], British Overseas citizen, British National (Overseas), British subject or British protected person, and

the "territorial jurisdiction" of a member state means the territory of that member state within the European Community, including its territorial waters and air space, and any aircraft or vessel under the jurisdiction or control of that member state.

(3) No proceedings for an offence under paragraph (1) above shall be instituted in England, Wales or Northern Ireland except by the Secretary of State or with the consent of the Attorney General or, as the case may be, the Attorney General for Northern Ireland.

(4) Proceedings against any person for an offence under this section may be taken before the appropriate court in the United Kingdom having jurisdiction in the place where that person is for the time being.

[2778]

NOTES

Para (2): in definition "British person" words "British overseas territories citizen" in square brackets substituted by virtue of the British Overseas Territories Act 2002, s 2(3).

3—(1) Sections 1(1) and (3) and 2 of the Protection of Trading Interests Act 1980 and orders made and directions given thereunder shall not apply in respect of any matter to the extent that Article 5 of the EC Counter-measures Regulation applies in respect of it.

(2) Section 6 of that Act shall not apply in respect of a judgment to the extent that Article 6 of that Regulation provides for recovery of damages as a result thereof.

[2779]–[3000]

PART IV
EC MATERIALS

A. EC TREATIES

CONSOLIDATED VERSION OF THE TREATY ESTABLISHING THE EUROPEAN COMMUNITY

NOTES

Date of publication in OJ: OJ C325, 4.12.2002.

Please note that only European Union legislation published in the paper editions of the Official Journal of the European Communities is deemed authentic.

Only the provisions relevant to this work are reproduced here.

HIS MAJESTY THE KING OF THE BELGIANS, THE PRESIDENT OF THE FEDERAL REPUBLIC OF GERMANY, THE PRESIDENT OF THE FRENCH REPUBLIC, THE PRESIDENT OF THE ITALIAN REPUBLIC, HER ROYAL HIGHNESS THE GRAND DUCHESS OF LUXEMBOURG, HER MAJESTY THE QUEEN OF THE NETHERLANDS,[1]

DETERMINED to lay the foundations of an ever closer union among the peoples of Europe,

RESOLVED to ensure the economic and social progress of their countries by common action to eliminate the barriers which divide Europe,

AFFIRMING as the essential objective of their efforts the constant improvements of the living and working conditions of their peoples,

RECOGNISING that the removal of existing obstacles calls for concerted action in order to guarantee steady expansion, balanced trade and fair competition,

ANXIOUS to strengthen the unity of their economies and to ensure their harmonious development by reducing the differences existing between the various regions and the backwardness of the less favoured regions,

DESIRING to contribute, by means of a common commercial policy, to the progressive abolition of restrictions on international trade,

INTENDING to confirm the solidarity which binds Europe and the overseas countries and desiring to ensure the development of their prosperity, in accordance with the principles of the Charter of the United Nations,

RESOLVED by thus pooling their resources to preserve and strengthen peace and liberty, and calling upon the other peoples of Europe who share their ideal to join in their efforts,

DETERMINED to promote the development of the highest possible level of knowledge for their peoples through a wide access to education and through its continuous updating,

HAVE DECIDED to create a EUROPEAN COMMUNITY and to this end have designated as their Plenipotentiaries:

(*List of plenipotentiaries not reproduced*)

WHO, having exchanged their full powers, found in good and due form, have agreed as follows.

[3001]

NOTES

1 The Kingdom of Denmark, the Hellenic Republic, the Kingdom of Spain, Ireland, the Republic of Austria, the Portuguese Republic, the Republic of Finland, the Kingdom of Sweden and the United Kingdom of Great Britain and Northern Ireland have since become members of the European Community.

PART ONE
PRINCIPLES

Article 1

By this Treaty, the HIGH CONTRACTING PARTIES establish among themselves a EUROPEAN COMMUNITY.

Article 2

The Community shall have as its task, by establishing a common market and an economic and monetary union and by implementing common policies or activities referred to in Articles 3 and 4, to promote throughout the Community a harmonious, balanced and sustainable development of economic activities, a high level of employment and of social protection, equality between men and women, sustainable and non-inflationary growth, a high degree of competitiveness and convergence of economic performance, a high level of protection and improvement of the quality of the environment, the raising of the standard of living and quality of life, and economic and social cohesion and solidarity among Member States.

Article 3

1. For the purposes set out in Article 2, the activities of the Community shall include, as provided in this Treaty and in accordance with the timetable set out therein:

(a) the prohibition, as between Member States, of customs duties and quantitative restrictions on the import and export of goods, and of all other measures having equivalent effect;
(b) a common commercial policy;
(c) an internal market characterised by the abolition, as between Member States, of obstacles to the free movement of goods, persons, services and capital;
(d) measures concerning the entry and movement of persons as provided for in Title IV;
(e) a common policy in the sphere of agriculture and fisheries;
(f) a common policy in the sphere of transport;
(g) a system ensuring that competition in the internal market is not distorted;
(h) the approximation of the laws of Member States to the extent required for the functioning of the common market;
(i) the promotion of coordination between employment policies of the Member States with a view to enhancing their effectiveness by developing a coordinated strategy for employment;
(j) a policy in the social sphere comprising a European Social Fund;
(k) the strengthening of economic and social cohesion;
(l) a policy in the sphere of the environment;
(m) the strengthening of the competitiveness of Community industry;
(n) the promotion of research and technological development;
(o) encouragement for the establishment and development of trans-European networks;
(p) a contribution to the attainment of a high level of health protection;
(q) a contribution to education and training of quality and to the flowering of the cultures of the Member States;
(r) a policy in the sphere of development cooperation;
(s) the association of the overseas countries and territories in order to increase trade and promote jointly economic and social development;
(t) a contribution to the strengthening of consumer protection;
(u) measures in the spheres of energy, civil protection and tourism.

2. In all the activities referred to in this Article, the Community shall aim to eliminate inequalities, and to promote equality, between men and women.

Article 4

1. For the purposes set out in Article 2, the activities of the Member States and the Community shall include, as provided in this Treaty and in accordance with the timetable set out therein, the adoption of an economic policy which is based on the close coordination of Member States' economic policies, on the internal market and on the definition of common objectives, and conducted in accordance with the principle of an open market economy with free competition.

2. Concurrently with the foregoing, and as provided in this Treaty and in accordance with the timetable and the procedures set out therein, these activities shall include the irrevocable fixing of exchange rates leading to the introduction of a single currency, the ecu, and the definition and conduct of a single monetary policy and exchange-rate policy the primary objective of both of which shall be to maintain price stability and, without prejudice to this objective, to support the general economic policies in the Community, in accordance with the principle of an open market economy with free competition.

3. These activities of the Member States and the Community shall entail compliance with the following guiding principles: stable prices, sound public finances and monetary conditions and a sustainable balance of payments.

Article 5

The Community shall act within the limits of the powers conferred upon it by this Treaty and of the objectives assigned to it therein.

Article 10

Member States shall take all appropriate measures, whether general or particular, to ensure fulfilment of the obligations arising out of this Treaty or resulting from action taken by the institutions of the Community. They shall facilitate the achievement of the Community's tasks.

They shall abstain from any measure which could jeopardise the attainment of the objectives of this Treaty.

Article 12

Within the scope of application of this Treaty, and without prejudice to any special provisions contained therein, any discrimination on grounds of nationality shall be prohibited.

The Council, acting in accordance with the procedure referred to in Article 251, may adopt rules designed to prohibit such discrimination.

Article 14

1. The Community shall adopt measures with the aim of progressively establishing the internal market over a period expiring on 31 December 1992, in accordance with the provisions of this Article and of Articles 15, 26, 47(2), 49, 80, 93 and 95 and without prejudice to the other provisions of this Treaty.

2. The internal market shall comprise an area without internal frontiers in which the free movement of goods, persons, services and capital is ensured in accordance with the provisions of this Treaty.

3. The Council, acting by a qualified majority on a proposal from the Commission, shall determine the guidelines and conditions necessary to ensure balanced progress in all the sectors concerned.

[3002]

PART THREE
COMMUNITY POLICIES

TITLE I
FREE MOVEMENT OF GOODS

Article 23

1. The Community shall be based upon a customs union which shall cover all trade in goods and which shall involve the prohibition between Member States of customs duties on imports and exports and of all charges having equivalent effect, and the adoption of a common customs tariff in their relations with third countries.

2. The provisions of Article 25 and of Chapter 2 of this title shall apply to products originating in Member States and to products coming from third countries which are in free circulation in Member States.

[3003]

CHAPTER 2
PROHIBITION OF QUANTITATIVE RESTRICTIONS BETWEEN MEMBER STATES

Article 28

Quantitative restrictions on imports and all measures having equivalent effect shall be prohibited between Member States.

Article 29

Quantitative restrictions on exports, and all measures having equivalent effect, shall be prohibited between Member States.

Article 30

The provisions of Articles 28 and 29 shall not preclude prohibitions or restrictions on imports, exports or goods in transit justified on grounds of public morality, public policy or public security; the protection of health and life of humans, animals or plants; the protection of national treasures possessing artistic, historic or archaeological value; or the protection of industrial and commercial property. Such prohibitions or restrictions shall not, however, constitute a means of arbitrary discrimination or a disguised restriction on trade between Member States.

[3004]

TITLE III
FREE MOVEMENT OF PERSONS, SERVICES AND CAPITAL

CHAPTER 1
WORKERS

Article 39

1. Freedom of movement for workers shall be secured within the Community.

2. Such freedom of movement shall entail the abolition of any discrimination based on nationality between workers of the Member States as regards employment, remuneration and other conditions of work and employment.

3. It shall entail the right, subject to limitations justified on grounds of public policy, public security or public health:
   (a) to accept offers of employment actually made;
   (b) to move freely within the territory of Member States for this purpose;
   (c) to stay in a Member State for the purpose of employment in accordance with the provisions governing the employment of nationals of that State laid down by law, regulation or administrative action;
   (d) to remain in the territory of a Member State after having been employed in that State, subject to conditions which shall be embodied in implementing regulations to be drawn up by the Commission.

4. The provisions of this article shall not apply to employment in the public service.

[3005]

CHAPTER 2
RIGHT OF ESTABLISHMENT

Article 43

Within the framework of the provisions set out below, restrictions on the freedom of establishment of nationals of a Member State in the territory of another Member State shall be prohibited. Such prohibition shall also apply to restrictions on the setting-up of agencies, branches or subsidiaries by nationals of any Member State established in the territory of any Member State. Freedom of establishment shall include the right to take up and pursue activities as self-employed persons and to set up and manage undertakings, in particular companies or firms within the meaning of the second paragraph of Article 48, under the conditions laid down for its own nationals by the law of the country where such establishment is effected, subject to the provisions of the chapter relating to capital.

[3006]

CHAPTER 3
SERVICES

Article 49

Within the framework of the provisions set out below, restrictions on freedom to provide services within the Community shall be prohibited in respect of nationals of Member States who are established in a State of the Community other than that of the person for whom the services are intended.

The Council may, acting by a qualified majority on a proposal from the Commission, extend the provisions of the Chapter to nationals of a third country who provide services and who are established within the Community.

Article 50

Services shall be considered to be 'services' within the meaning of this Treaty where they are normally provided for remuneration, in so far as they are not governed by the provisions relating to freedom of movement for goods, capital and persons.

'Services' shall in particular include:

(a) activities of an industrial character;
(b) activities of a commercial character;
(c) activities of craftsmen;
(d) activities of the professions.

Without prejudice to the provisions of the chapter relating to the right of establishment, the person providing a service may, in order to do so, temporarily pursue his activity in the State where the service is provided, under the same conditions as are imposed by that State on its own nationals.

[3007]

CHAPTER 4
CAPITAL AND PAYMENTS

Article 56

1. Within the framework of the provisions set out in this chapter, all restrictions on the movement of capital between Member States and between Member States and third countries shall be prohibited.

2. Within the framework of the provisions set out in this chapter, all restrictions on payments between Member States and between Member States and third countries shall be prohibited.

[3008]

TITLE IV
VISAS, ASYLUM, IMMIGRATION AND OTHER POLICIES RELATED TO FREE MOVEMENT OF PERSONS

Article 61

In order to establish progressively an area of freedom, security and justice, the Council shall adopt:

(a) within a period of five years after the entry into force of the Treaty of Amsterdam, measures aimed at ensuring the free movement of persons in accordance with Article 14, in conjunction with directly related flanking measures with respect to external border controls, asylum and immigration, in accordance with the provisions of Article 62(2) and (3) and Article 63(1)(a) and (2)(a), and measures to prevent and combat crime in accordance with the provisions of Article 31(e) of the Treaty on European Union;
(b) other measures in the fields of asylum, immigration and safeguarding the rights of nationals of third countries, in accordance with the provisions of Article 63;
(c) measures in the field of judicial cooperation in civil matters as provided for in Article 65;
(d) appropriate measures to encourage and strengthen administrative cooperation, as provided for in Article 66;
(e) measures in the field of police and judicial cooperation in criminal matters aimed at a high level of security by preventing and combating crime within the Union in accordance with the provisions of the Treaty on European Union.

Article 65

Measures in the field of judicial cooperation in civil matters having cross-border implications, to be taken in accordance with Article 67 and in so far as necessary for the proper functioning of the internal market, shall include:

(a) improving and simplifying:
— the system for cross-border service of judicial and extrajudicial documents,

PART IV
EC MATERIALS

— cooperation in the taking of evidence,
— the recognition and enforcement of decisions in civil and commercial cases, including decisions in extrajudicial cases;

(b) promoting the compatibility of the rules applicable in the Member States concerning the conflict of laws and of jurisdiction;

(c) eliminating obstacles to the good functioning of civil proceedings, if necessary by promoting the compatibility of the rules on civil procedure applicable in the Member States.

Article 67[1]

1. During a transitional period of five years following the entry into force of the Treaty of Amsterdam, the Council shall act unanimously on a proposal from the Commission or on the initiative of a Member State and after consulting the European Parliament.

2. After this period of five years:

— the Council shall act on proposals from the Commission; the Commission shall examine any request made by a Member State that it submit a proposal to the Council,

— the Council, acting unanimously after consulting the European Parliament, shall take a decision with a view to providing for all or parts of the areas covered by this title to be governed by the procedure referred to in Article 251 and adapting the provisions relating to the powers of the Court of Justice.

3. By derogation from paragraphs 1 and 2, measures referred to in Article 62(2)(b) (i) and (iii) shall, from the entry into force of the Treaty of Amsterdam, be adopted by the Council acting by a qualified majority on a proposal from the Commission and after consulting the European Parliament.

4. By derogation from paragraph 2, measures referred to in Article 62(2)(b) (ii) and (iv) shall, after a period of five years following the entry into force of the Treaty of Amsterdam, be adopted by the Council acting in accordance with the procedure referred to in Article 251.

5. By derogation from paragraph 1, the Council shall adopt, in accordance with the procedure referred to in Article 251:

— the measures provided for in Article 63(1) and (2)(a) provided that the Council has previously adopted, in accordance with paragraph 1 of this article, Community legislation defining the common rules and basic principles governing these issues,

— the measures provided for in Article 65 with the exception of aspects relating to family law.

NOTES

1 Article amended by the Treaty of Nice.

Article 68

1. Article 234 shall apply to this title under the following circumstances and conditions: where a question on the interpretation of this title or on the validity or interpretation of acts of the institutions of the Community based on this title is raised in a case pending before a court or a tribunal of a Member State against whose decisions there is no judicial remedy under national law, that court or tribunal shall, if it considers that a decision on the question is necessary to enable it to give judgment, request the Court of Justice to give a ruling thereon.

2. In any event, the Court of Justice shall not have jurisdiction to rule on any measure or decision taken pursuant to Article 62(1) relating to the maintenance of law and order and the safeguarding of internal security.

3. The Council, the Commission or a Member State may request the Court of Justice to give a ruling on a question of interpretation of this title or of acts of the institutions of the Community based on this title. The ruling given by the Court of Justice in response to such a request shall not apply to judgments of courts or tribunals of the Member States which have become *res judicata*.

Article 69

The application of this title shall be subject to the provisions of the Protocol on the position of the United Kingdom and Ireland and to the Protocol on the position of Denmark and without prejudice to the Protocol on the application of certain aspects of Article 14 of the Treaty establishing the European Community to the United Kingdom and to Ireland.

[3009]

TITLE VI
COMMON RULES ON COMPETITION, TAXATION AND APPROXIMATION OF LAWS

CHAPTER 3
APPROXIMATION OF LAWS

Article 94

The Council shall, acting unanimously on a proposal from the Commission and after consulting the European Parliament and the Economic and Social Committee, issue directives for the approximation of such laws, regulations or administrative provisions of the Member States as directly affect the establishment or functioning of the common market.

Article 95

1. By way of derogation from Article 94 and save where otherwise provided in this Treaty, the following provisions shall apply for the achievement of the objectives set out in Article 14. The Council shall, acting in accordance with the procedure referred to in Article 251 and after consulting the Economic and Social Committee, adopt the measures for the approximation of the provisions laid down by law, regulation or administrative action in Member States which have as their object the establishment and functioning of the internal market.

2. Paragraph 1 shall not apply to fiscal provisions, to those relating to the free movement of persons nor to those relating to the rights and interests of employed persons.

3. The Commission, in its proposals envisaged in paragraph 1 concerning health, safety, environmental protection and consumer protection, will take as a base a high level of protection, taking account in particular of any new development based on scientific facts. Within their respective powers, the European Parliament and the Council will also seek to achieve this objective.

4. If, after the adoption by the Council or by the Commission of a harmonisation measure, a Member State deems it necessary to maintain national provisions on grounds of major needs referred to in Article 30, or relating to the protection of the environment or the working environment, it shall notify the Commission of these provisions as well as the grounds for maintaining them.

5. Moreover, without prejudice to paragraph 4, if, after the adoption by the Council or by the Commission of a harmonisation measure, a Member State deems it necessary to introduce national provisions based on new scientific evidence relating to the protection of the environment or the working environment on grounds of a problem specific to that Member State arising after the adoption of the harmonisation measure, it shall notify the Commission of the envisaged provisions as well as the grounds for introducing them.

6. The Commission shall, within six months of the notifications as referred to in paragraphs 4 and 5, approve or reject the national provisions involved after having verified whether or not they are a means of arbitrary discrimination or a disguised restriction on trade between Member States and whether or not they shall constitute an obstacle to the functioning of the internal market. In the absence of a decision by the Commission within this period the national provisions referred to in paragraphs 4 and 5 shall be deemed to have been approved. When justified by the complexity of the matter and in the absence of danger for human health, the Commission may notify the Member State concerned that the period referred to in this paragraph may be extended for a further period of up to six months.

7. When, pursuant to paragraph 6, a Member State is authorised to maintain or introduce national provisions derogating from a harmonisation measure, the Commission shall immediately examine whether to propose an adaptation to that measure.

8. When a Member State raises a specific problem on public health in a field which has been the subject of prior harmonisation measures, it shall bring it to the attention of the Commission which shall immediately examine whether to propose appropriate measures to the Council.

9. By way of derogation from the procedure laid down in Articles 226 and 227, the Commission and any Member State may bring the matter directly before the Court of Justice if it considers that another Member State is making improper use of the powers provided for in this Article.

10. The harmonisation measures referred to above shall, in appropriate cases, include a safeguard clause authorising the Member States to take, for one or more of the non-economic reasons referred to in Article 30, provisional measures subject to a Community control procedure.

Article 96

Where the Commission finds that a difference between the provisions laid down by law, regulation or administrative action in Member States is distorting the conditions of competition in the common market and that the resultant distortion needs to be eliminated, it shall consult the Member States concerned.

If such consultation does not result in an agreement eliminating the distortion in question, the Council shall, on a proposal from the Commission, acting by a qualified majority, issue the necessary directives.

The Commission and the Council may take any other appropriate measures provided for in this Treaty.

Article 97

1. Where there is a reason to fear that the adoption or amendment of a provision laid down by law, regulation or administrative action may cause distortion within the meaning of Article 96, a Member State desiring to proceed therewith shall consult the Commission. After consulting the Member States, the Commission shall recommend to the States concerned such measures as may be appropriate to avoid the distortion in question.

2. If a State desiring to introduce or amend its own provisions does not comply with the recommendation addressed to it by the Commission, other Member States shall not be required, pursuant to Article 96, to amend their own provisions in order to eliminate such distortion. If the Member State which has ignored the recommendation of the Commission causes distortion detrimental only to itself, the provisions of Article 96 shall not apply.

[3010]

PART FIVE
INSTITUTIONS OF THE COMMUNITY

TITLE I
PROVISIONS GOVERNING THE INSTITUTIONS

CHAPTER 1
THE INSTITUTIONS

SECTION 4
THE COURT OF JUSTICE

Article 234

The Court of Justice shall have jurisdiction to give preliminary rulings concerning:

(a) the interpretation of this Treaty;
(b) the validity and interpretation of acts of the institutions of the Community and of the ECB;
(c) the interpretation of the statutes of bodies established by an act of the Council, where those statutes so provide.

Where such a question is raised before any court or tribunal of a Member State, that court or tribunal may, if it considers that a decision on the question is necessary to enable it to give judgment, request the Court of Justice to give a ruling thereon.

Where any such question is raised in a case pending before a court or tribunal of a Member State against whose decisions there is no judicial remedy under national law, that court or tribunal shall bring the matter before the Court of Justice.

[3011]

PART SIX
GENERAL AND FINAL PROVISIONS

Article 281

The Community shall have legal personality.

Article 282

In each of the Member States, the Community shall enjoy the most extensive legal capacity accorded to legal persons under their laws; it may, in particular, acquire or dispose of movable and immovable property and may be a party to legal proceedings. To this end, the Community shall be represented by the Commission.

Article 288

The contractual liability of the Community shall be governed by the law applicable to the contract in question.

In the case of non-contractual liability, the Community shall, in accordance with the general principles common to the laws of the Member States, make good any damage caused by its institutions or by its servants in the performance of their duties.

The preceding paragraph shall apply under the same conditions to damage caused by the ECB or by its servants in the performance of their duties.

The personal liability of its servants towards the Community shall be governed by the provisions laid down in their Staff Regulations or in the Conditions of employment applicable to them.

Article 293

Member States shall, so far as is necessary, enter into negotiations with each other with a view to securing for the benefit of their nationals:

— the protection of persons and the enjoyment and protection of rights under the same conditions as those accorded by each State to its own nationals,
— the abolition of double taxation within the Community,
— the mutual recognition of companies or firms within the meaning of the second paragraph of Article 48, the retention of legal personality in the event of transfer of their seat from one country to another, and the possibility of mergers between companies or firms governed by the laws of different countries,
— the simplification of formalities governing the reciprocal recognition and enforcement of judgments of courts or tribunals and of arbitration awards.

Article 299

1. This Treaty shall apply to the Kingdom of Belgium, the Kingdom of Denmark, the Federal Republic of Germany, the Hellenic Republic, the Kingdom of Spain, the French Republic, Ireland, the Italian Republic, the Grand Duchy of Luxembourg, the Kingdom of the Netherlands, the Republic of Austria, the Portuguese Republic, the Republic of Finland, the Kingdom of Sweden and the United Kingdom of Great Britain and Northern Ireland.

2. The provisions of this Treaty shall apply to the French overseas departments, the Azores, Madeira and the Canary Islands. However, taking account of the structural social and economic situation of the French overseas departments, the Azores, Madeira and the Canary Islands, which is compounded by their remoteness, insularity, small size, difficult topography and climate, economic dependence on a few products, the permanence and combination of which severely restrain their development, the Council, acting by a qualified majority on a proposal from the Commission and after consulting the European Parliament, shall adopt specific measures aimed, in particular, at laying down the conditions of application of the present Treaty to those regions, including common policies.

The Council shall, when adopting the relevant measures referred to in the second subparagraph, take into account areas such as customs and trade policies, fiscal policy, free zones, agriculture and fisheries policies, conditions for supply of raw materials and essential consumer goods, State aids and conditions of access to structural funds and to horizontal Community programmes.

The Council shall adopt the measures referred to in the second subparagraph taking into account the special characteristics and constraints of the outermost regions without undermining the integrity and the coherence of the Community legal order, including the internal market and common policies.

3. The special arrangements for association set out in part four of this Treaty shall apply to the overseas countries and territories listed in Annex II to this Treaty.

This Treaty shall not apply to those overseas countries and territories having special relations with the United Kingdom of Great Britain and Northern Ireland which are not included in the aforementioned list.

4. The provisions of this Treaty shall apply to the European territories for whose external relations a Member State is responsible.

5. The provisions of this Treaty shall apply to the Åland Islands in accordance with the provisions set out in Protocol 2 to the Act concerning the conditions of accession of the Republic of Austria, the Republic of Finland and the Kingdom of Sweden.

6. Notwithstanding the preceding paragraphs:
(a) this Treaty shall not apply to the Faeroe Islands;
(b) this Treaty shall not apply to the sovereign base areas of the United Kingdom of Great Britain and Northern Ireland in Cyprus;
(c) this Treaty shall apply to the Channel Islands and the Isle of Man only to the extent necessary to ensure the implementation of the arrangements for those islands set out in the Treaty concerning the accession of new Member States to the European Economic Community and to the European Atomic Energy Community signed on 22 January 1972.

[3012]

PROTOCOL ON THE POSITION OF THE UNITED KINGDOM AND IRELAND 1997

THE HIGH CONTRACTING PARTIES,

DESIRING to settle certain questions relating to the United Kingdom and Ireland,

HAVING REGARD to the Protocol on the application of certain aspects of Article 7a of the Treaty establishing the European Community to the United Kingdom and to Ireland,

HAVE AGREED UPON the following provisions which shall be annexed to the Treaty establishing the European Community and to the Treaty on European Union,

Article 1

Subject to Article 3, the United Kingdom and Ireland shall not take part in the adoption by the Council of proposed measures pursuant to Title IIIa of the Treaty establishing the European Community. By way of derogation from Article 148(2) of the Treaty establishing the European Community, a qualified majority shall be defined as the same proportion of the weighted votes of the members of the Council concerned as laid down in the said Article 148(2). The unanimity of the members of the Council, with the exception of the representatives of the governments of the United Kingdom and Ireland, shall be necessary for decisions of the Council which must be adopted unanimously.

Article 2

In consequence of Article 1 and subject to Articles 3, 4 and 6, none of the provisions of Title IIIa of the Treaty establishing the European Community, no measure adopted pursuant to that Title, no provision of any international agreement concluded by the Community pursuant to that Title, and no decision of the Court of Justice interpreting any such provision or measure shall be binding upon or applicable in the United Kingdom or Ireland; and no such provision, measure or decision shall in any way affect the competences, rights and obligations of those States; and no such provision, measure or decision shall in any way affect the acquis communautaire nor form part of Community law as they apply to the United Kingdom or Ireland.

Article 3

1. The United Kingdom or Ireland may notify the President of the Council in writing, within three months after a proposal or initiative has been presented to the Council pursuant to Title IIIa of the Treaty establishing the European Community, that it wishes to take part in the adoption and application of any such proposed measure, whereupon that State shall be entitled to do so. By way of derogation from Article 148(2) of the Treaty establishing the European Community, a qualified majority shall be defined as the same proportion of the weighted votes of the members of the Council concerned as laid down in the said Article 148(2).

The unanimity of the members of the Council, with the exception of a member which has not made such a notification, shall be necessary for decisions of the Council which must be adopted unanimously. A measure adopted under this paragraph shall be binding upon all Member States which took part in its adoption.

2. If after a reasonable period of time a measure referred to in paragraph 1 cannot be adopted with the United Kingdom or Ireland taking part, the Council may adopt such measure in accordance with Article 1 without the participation of the United Kingdom or Ireland. In that case Article 2 applies.

Article 4

The United Kingdom or Ireland may at any time after the adoption of a measure by the Council pursuant to Title IIIa of the Treaty establishing the European Community notify its intention to the Council and to the Commission that it wishes to accept that measure. In that case, the procedure provided for in Article 5a(3) of the Treaty establishing the European Community shall apply mutatis mutandis.

Article 5

A Member State which is not bound by a measure adopted pursuant to Title IIIa of the Treaty establishing the European Community shall bear no financial consequences of that measure other than administrative costs entailed for the institutions.

Article 6

Where, in cases referred to in this Protocol, the United Kingdom or Ireland is bound by a measure adopted by the Council pursuant to Title IIIa of the Treaty establishing the European Community, the relevant provisions of that Treaty, including Article 73p, shall apply to that State in relation to that measure.

Article 7

Articles 3 and 4 shall be without prejudice to the Protocol integrating the Schengen acquis into the framework of the European Union.

Article 8

Ireland may notify the President of the Council in writing that it no longer wishes to be covered by the terms of this Protocol. In that case, the normal treaty provisions will apply to Ireland.

[3013]

PROTOCOL ON THE POSITION OF DENMARK 1997

THE HIGH CONTRACTING PARTIES,

RECALLING the Decision of the Heads of State or Government, meeting within the European Council at Edinburgh on 12 December 1992, concerning certain problems raised by Denmark on the Treaty on European Union,

HAVING NOTED the position of Denmark with regard to Citizenship, Economic and Monetary Union, Defence Policy and Justice and Home Affairs as laid down in the Edinburgh Decision,

BEARING IN MIND Article 3 of the Protocol integrating the Schengen acquis into the framework of the European Union,

HAVE AGREED UPON the following provisions, which shall be annexed to the Treaty establishing the European Community and to the Treaty on European Union,

[3014]

PART I

Article 1

Denmark shall not take part in the adoption by the Council of proposed measures pursuant to Title IIIa of the Treaty establishing the European Community. By way of derogation from Article 148(2) of the Treaty establishing the European Community, a qualified majority shall be defined as the same proportion of the weighted votes of the members of the Council concerned as laid down in the said Article 148(2). The unanimity of the members of the Council, with the exception of the representative of the government of Denmark, shall be necessary for the decisions of the Council which must be adopted unanimously.

Article 2

None of the provisions of Title IIIa of the Treaty establishing the European Community, no measure adopted pursuant to that Title, no provision of any international agreement concluded by the Community pursuant to that Title, and no decision of the Court of Justice interpreting any such provision or measure shall be binding upon or applicable in Denmark; and no such provision, measure or decision shall in any way affect the competences, rights and obligations of Denmark; and no such provision, measure or decision shall in any way affect the acquis communautaire nor form part of Community law as they apply to Denmark.

Article 3

Denmark shall bear no financial consequences of measures referred to in Article 1, other than administrative costs entailed for the institutions.

Article 4

Articles 1, 2 and 3 shall not apply to measures determining the third countries whose nationals must be in possession of a visa when crossing the external borders of the Member States, or measures relating to a uniform format for visas.

Article 5

1. Denmark shall decide within a period of 6 months after the Council has decided on a proposal or initiative to build upon the Schengen acquis under the provisions of Title IIIa of the Treaty establishing the European Community, whether it will implement this decision in its national law. If it decides to do so, this decision will create an obligation under international law between Denmark and the other Member States referred to in Article 1 of the Protocol integrating the Schengen acquis into the framework of the European Union as well as Ireland or the United Kingdom if those Member States take part in the areas of cooperation in question.

2. If Denmark decides not to implement a decision of the Council as referred to in paragraph 1, the Member States referred to in Article 1 of the Protocol integrating the Schengen acquis into the framework of the European Union will consider appropriate measures to be taken.

[3015]

PART II

Article 6

With regard to measures adopted by the Council in the field of Articles J.3(1) and J.7 of the Treaty on European Union, Denmark does not participate in the elaboration and the implementation of decisions and actions of the Union which have defence implications, but will not prevent the development of closer cooperation between Member States in this area. Therefore Denmark shall not participate in their adoption. Denmark shall not be obliged to contribute to the financing of operational expenditure arising from such measures.

[3016]

PART III

Article 7

At any time Denmark may, in accordance with its constitutional requirements, inform the other Member States that it no longer wishes to avail itself of all or part of this Protocol. In that event, Denmark will apply in full all relevant measures then in force taken within the framework of the European Union.

[3017]

PROTOCOL ON THE APPLICATION OF THE PRINCIPLES OF SUBSIDIARITY AND PROPORTIONALITY 1997

THE HIGH CONTRACTING PARTIES,

DETERMINED to establish the conditions for the application of the principles of subsidiarity and proportionality enshrined in Article 3b of the Treaty establishing the European Community with a view to defining more precisely the criteria for applying them and to ensure their strict observance and consistent implementation by all institutions;

WISHING to ensure that decisions are taken as closely as possible to the citizens of the Union;

TAKING ACCOUNT of the Interinstitutional Agreement of 25 October 1993 between the European Parliament, the Council and the Commission on procedures for implementing the principle of subsidiarity;

HAVE CONFIRMED that the conclusions of the Birmingham European Council on 16 October 1992 and the overall approach to the application of the subsidiarity principle agreed by the European Council meeting in Edinburgh on 11–12 December 1992 will continue to guide the action of the Union's institutions as well as the development of the application of the principle of subsidiarity, and, for this purpose,

HAVE AGREED UPON the following provisions which shall be annexed to the Treaty establishing the European Community:

(1) In exercising the powers conferred on it, each institution shall ensure that the principle of subsidiarity is complied with. It shall also ensure compliance with the principle of proportionality, according to which any action by the Community shall not go beyond what is necessary to achieve the objectives of the Treaty.

(2) The application of the principles of subsidiarity and proportionality shall respect the general provisions and the objectives of the Treaty, particularly as regards the maintaining in full of the acquis communautaire and the institutional balance; it shall not affect the principles developed by the Court of Justice regarding the relationship between national and Community law, and it should take into account Article F(4) of the Treaty on European Union, according to which 'the Union shall provide itself with the means necessary to attain its objectives and carry through its policies'.

(3) The principle of subsidiarity does not call into question the powers conferred on the European Community by the Treaty, as interpreted by the Court of Justice. The criteria referred to in the second paragraph of Article 3b of the Treaty shall relate to areas for which the Community does not have exclusive competence. The principle of subsidiarity provides a guide as to how those powers are to be exercised at the Community level. Subsidiarity is a dynamic concept and should be applied in the light of the objectives set out in the Treaty. It allows Community action within the limits of its powers to be expanded where circumstances so require, and conversely, to be restricted or discontinued where it is no longer justified.

(4) For any proposed Community legislation, the reasons on which it is based shall be stated with a view to justifying its compliance with the principles of subsidiarity and proportionality; the reasons for concluding that a Community objective can be better achieved by the Community must be substantiated by qualitative or, wherever possible, quantitative indicators.

(5) For Community action to be justified, both aspects of the subsidiarity principle shall be met: the objectives of the proposed action cannot be sufficiently achieved by Member States' action in the framework of their national constitutional system and can therefore be better achieved by action on the part of the Community.

The following guidelines should be used in examining whether the abovementioned condition is fulfilled:

— the issue under consideration has transnational aspects which cannot be satisfactorily regulated by action by Member States;
— actions by Member States alone or lack of Community action would conflict with the requirements of the Treaty (such as the need to correct distortion of competition or avoid disguised restrictions on trade or strengthen economic and social cohesion) or would otherwise significantly damage Member States' interests;
— action at Community level would produce clear benefits by reason of its scale or effects compared with action at the level of the Member States.

(6) The form of Community action shall be as simple as possible, consistent with satisfactory achievement of the objective of the measure and the need for effective

enforcement. The Community shall legislate only to the extent necessary. Other things being equal, directives should be preferred to regulations and framework directives to detailed measures. Directives as provided for in Article 189 of the Treaty, while binding upon each Member State to which they are addressed as to the result to be achieved, shall leave to the national authorities the choice of form and methods.

(7) Regarding the nature and the extent of Community action, Community measures should leave as much scope for national decision as possible, consistent with securing the aim of the measure and observing the requirements of the Treaty. While respecting Community law, care should be taken to respect well established national arrangements and the organisation and working of Member States' legal systems. Where appropriate and subject to the need for proper enforcement, Community measures should provide Member States with alternative ways to achieve the objectives of the measures.

(8) Where the application of the principle of subsidiarity leads to no action being taken by the Community, Member States are required in their action to comply with the general rules laid down in Article 5 of the Treaty, by taking all appropriate measures to ensure fulfilment of their obligations under the Treaty and by abstaining from any measure which could jeopardise the attainment of the objectives of the Treaty.

(9) Without prejudice to its right of initiative, the Commission should:

— except in cases of particular urgency or confidentiality, consult widely before proposing legislation and, wherever appropriate, publish consultation documents;

— justify the relevance of its proposals with regard to the principle of subsidiarity; whenever necessary, the explanatory memorandum accompanying a proposal will give details in this respect. The financing of Community action in whole or in part from the Community budget shall require an explanation;

— take duly into account the need for any burden, whether financial or administrative, falling upon the Community, national governments, local authorities, economic operators and citizens, to be minimised and proportionate to the objective to be achieved;

— submit an annual report to the European Council, the European Parliament and the Council on the application of Article 3b of the Treaty. This annual report shall also be sent to the Committee of the Regions and to the Economic and Social Committee.

(10) The European Council shall take account of the Commission report referred to in the fourth indent of point 9 within the report on the progress achieved by the Union which it is required to submit to the European Parliament in accordance with Article D of the Treaty on European Union.

(11) While fully observing the procedures applicable, the European Parliament and the Council shall, as an integral part of the overall examination of Commission proposals, consider their consistency with Article 3b of the Treaty. This concerns the original Commission proposal as well as amendments which the European Parliament and the Council envisage making to the proposal.

(12) In the course of the procedures referred to in Articles 189b and 189c of the Treaty, the European Parliament shall be informed of the Council's position on the application of Article 3b of the Treaty, by way of a statement of the reasons which led the Council to adopt its common position. The Council shall inform the European Parliament of the reasons on the basis of which all or part of a Commission proposal is deemed to be inconsistent with Article 3b of the Treaty.

(13) Compliance with the principle of subsidiarity shall be reviewed in accordance with the rules laid down by the Treaty.

[3018]

PROTOCOL ON ARTICLE 67 OF THE TREATY ESTABLISHING THE EUROPEAN COMMUNITY

THE HIGH CONTRACTING PARTIES

HAVE AGREED UPON the following provision, which shall be annexed to the Treaty establishing the European Community:

Sole Article

From 1 May 2004, the Council shall act by a qualified majority, on a proposal from the Commission and after consulting the European Parliament, in order to adopt the measures referred to in Article 66 of the Treaty establishing the European Community.

[3019]

PROTOCOL ON THE PRIVILEGES AND IMMUNITIES OF THE EUROPEAN COMMUNITIES

NOTES

Date of publication in OJ: OJ C325, 4.12.2002, p. 13, as amended by the Treaty of Amsterdam and the Treaty of Nice. This is the unofficial consolidated version from the European Central Bank website at www.ecb.int.

The High Contracting Parties,

Considering that, in accordance with Art. 28 of the Treaty establishing a Single Council and a Single Commission of the European Communities, these Communities and the European Investment Bank shall enjoy in the territories of the Member States such privileges and immunities as are necessary for the performance of their tasks,

Have agreed upon the following provisions, which shall be annexed to this Treaty:

CHAPTER I PROPERTY, FUNDS, ASSETS AND OPERATIONS OF THE EUROPEAN COMMUNITIES

Article 1

The premises and buildings of the Communities shall be inviolable. They shall be exempt from search, requisition, confiscation or expropriation. The property and assets of the Communities shall not be the subject of any administrative or legal measure of constraint without the authorisation of the Court of Justice.

Article 2

The archives of the Communities shall be inviolable.

Article 3

The Communities, their assets, revenues and other property shall be exempt from all direct taxes.

The Governments of the Member States shall, wherever possible, take the appropriate measures to remit or refund the amount of indirect taxes or sales taxes included in the price of movable or immovable property, where the Communities make, for their official use, substantial purchases the price of which includes taxes of this kind. These provisions shall not be applied, however, so as to have the effect of distorting competition within the Communities.

No exemption shall be granted in respect of taxes and dues which amount merely to charges for public utility services.

Article 4

The Communities shall be exempt from all customs duties, prohibitions and restrictions on imports and exports in respect of articles intended for their official use; articles so imported shall not be disposed of, whether or not in return for payment, in the territory of the country into which they have been imported, except under conditions approved by the Government of that country.

The Communities shall also be exempt from any customs duties and any prohibitions and restrictions on imports and exports in respect of their publications.

Article 5

The European Coal and Steel Community may hold currency of any kind and operate accounts in any currency.

[3020]

CHAPTER II
COMMUNICATIONS AND LALSSEZ-PASSER

Article 6

For their official communications and the transmission of all their documents, the institutions of the Communities shall enjoy in the territory of each Member State the treatment accorded by that State to diplomatic missions.

Official correspondence and other official communications of the institutions of the Communities shall not be subject to censorship.

Article 7

1. Laissez-passer in a form to be prescribed by the Council, which shall be recognised as valid travel documents by the authorities of the Member States, may be issued to members and servants of the institutions of the Communities by the Presidents of these institutions. These laissez-passer shall be issued to officials and other servants under conditions laid down in the Staff Regulations of officials and the Conditions of Employment of other servants of the Communities.

The Commission may conclude agreements for these laissez-passer to be recognised as valid travel documents within the territory of third countries.

2. The provisions of Art. 6 of the Protocol on the Privileges and Immunities of the European Coal and Steel Community shall, however, remain applicable to members and servants of the institutions who are at the date of entry into force of this Treaty in possession of the laissez-passer provided for in that Article, until the provisions of paragraph 1 of this Article are applied.

[3021]

CHAPTER III
MEMBERS OF THE EUROPEAN PARLIAMENT

Article 8

No administrative or other restriction shall be imposed on the free movement of members of the European Parliament travelling to or from the place of meeting of the European Parliament.

Members of the European Parliament shall, in respect of customs and exchange control, be accorded:

(a) by their own Government, the same facilities as those accorded to senior officials travelling abroad on temporary official missions;

(b) by the Governments of other Member States, the same facilities as those accorded to representatives of foreign Governments on temporary official missions.

Article 9

Members of the European Parliament shall not be subject to any form of inquiry, detention or legal proceedings in respect of opinions expressed or votes cast by them in the performance of their duties.

Article 10

During the sessions of the European Parliament, its members shall enjoy:

(a) in the territory of their own State, the immunities accorded to members of their parliament;

(b) in the territory of any other Member State, immunity from any measure of detention and from legal proceedings.

Immunity shall likewise apply to members while they are travelling to and from the place of meeting of the European Parliament.

Immunity cannot be claimed when a member is found in the act of committing an offence and shall not prevent the European Parliament from exercising its right to waive the immunity of one of its members.

[3022]

CHAPTER IV
REPRESENTATIVES OF MEMBER STATES TAKING PART IN THE WORK OF THE INSTITUTIONS OF THE EUROPEAN COMMUNITIES

Article 11

Representatives of Member States taking part in the work of the institutions of the Communities, their advisers and technical experts shall, in the performance of their duties and during their travel to and from the place of meeting, enjoy the customary privileges, immunities and facilities.

This Article shall also apply to members of the advisory bodies of the Communities.

[3023]

CHAPTER V
OFFICIALS AND OTHER SERVANTS OF THE EUROPEAN COMMUNITIES

Article 12

In the territory of each Member State and whatever their nationality, officials and other servants of the Communities shall:

(a) subject to the provisions of the Treaties relating, on the one hand, to the rules on the liability of officials and other servants towards the Communities and, on the other hand, to the jurisdiction of the Court in disputes between the Communities and their officials and other servants, shall be immune from legal proceedings in respect of acts performed by them in their official capacity, including their words spoken or written. They shall continue to enjoy this immunity after they have ceased to hold office;

(b) together with their spouses and dependent members of their families, not be subject to immigration restrictions or to formalities for registration of aliens;

(c) in respect of currency or exchange regulations, be accorded the same facilities as are customarily accorded to officials of international organisations;

(d) enjoy the right to import free of duty their furniture and effects at the time of first taking up their post in the country concerned, and the right to re-export free of duty their furniture and effects, on termination of their duties in that country, subject in either case to the conditions considered to be necessary by the Government of the country in which this right is exercised;

(e) have the right to import free of duty a motor car for their personal use, acquired either in the country of their last residence or in the country of which they are nationals on the terms ruling in the home market in that country, and to re-export it free of duty, subject in either case to the conditions considered to be necessary by the Government of the country concerned.

Article 13

Officials and other servants of the Communities shall be liable to a tax for the benefit of the Communities on salaries, wages and emoluments paid to them by the Communities, in accordance with the conditions and procedure laid down by the Council, acting on a proposal from the Commission.

They shall be exempt from national taxes on salaries, wages and emoluments paid by the Communities.

Article 14

In the application of income tax, wealth tax and death duties and in the application of conventions on the avoidance of double taxation concluded between Member States of the Communities, officials and other servants of the Communities who, solely by reason of the performance of their duties in the services of the Communities, establish their residence in the territory of a Member State other than their country of domicile for tax purposes at the time of entering the service of the Communities, shall be considered, both in the country of their actual residence and in the country of domicile for tax purposes, as having maintained their domicile in the latter country provided that it is a member of the Communities. This provision shall also apply to a spouse to the extent that the latter is not separately engaged in a gainful occupation, and to children dependent on and in the care of the persons referred to in this Article.

Movable property belonging to persons referred to in the first paragraph and situated in the territory of the country where they are staying shall be exempt from death duties in that country; such property shall, for the assessment of such duty, be considered as being in the country of domicile for tax purposes, subject to the rights of third countries and to the possible application of provisions of international conventions on double taxation.

Any domicile acquired solely by reason of the performance of duties in the service of other international organisations shall not be taken into consideration in applying the provisions of this Article.

Article 15

The Council shall, acting unanimously on a proposal from the Commission, lay down the scheme of social security benefits for officials and other servants of the Communities.

Article 16

The Council shall, acting on a proposal from the Commission and after consulting the other institutions concerned, determine the categories of officials and other servants of the Communities to whom the provisions of Art. 12, the second paragraph of Art. 13, and Art. 14 shall apply, in whole or in part.

The names, grades and addresses of officials and other servants included in such categories shall be communicated periodically to the Governments of the Member States.

[3024]

CHAPTER VI
PRIVILEGES AND IMMUNITIES OF MISSIONS OF THIRD COUNTRIES ACCREDITED TO THE EUROPEAN COMMUNITIES

Article 17

The Member State in whose territory the Communities have their seat shall accord the customary diplomatic immunities and privileges to missions of third countries accredited to the Communities.

[3025]

CHAPTER VII
GENERAL PROVISIONS

Article 18

Privileges, immunities and facilities shall be accorded to officials and other servants of the Communities solely in the interests of the Communities.

Each institution of the Communities shall be required to waive the immunity accorded to an official or other servant wherever that institution considers that the waiver of such immunity is not contrary to the interests of the Communities.

Article 19

The institutions of the Communities shall, for the purpose of applying this Protocol, co-operate with the responsible authorities of the Member States concerned.

Article 20

Arts. 12 to 15 and Art. 18 shall apply to members of the Commission.

Article 21

Arts. 12 to 15 and Art. 18 shall apply to the Judges, the Advocates-General, the Registrar and the Assistant Rapporteurs of the Court of Justice and to the Members and Registrar of the Court of First Instant, without prejudice to the provisions of Art. 3 of the Protocols on the Statute of the Court of Justice concerning immunity from legal proceedings of Judges and Advocates-General. [1]

NOTES

1 As amended by Art 6 of the Treaty of Nice.

Article 22

This Protocol shall also apply to the European Investment Bank, to the members of its organs, to its staff and to the representatives of the Member States taking part in its activities, without prejudice to the provisions of the Protocol on the Statute of the Bank.

The European Investment Bank shall in addition be exempt from any form of taxation or imposition of a like nature on the occasion of any increase in its capital and from the various formalities which may be connected therewith in the State where the Bank has its seat. Similarly, its dissolution or liquidation shall not give rise to any imposition. Finally, the activities of the Bank and of its organs carried on in accordance with its Statute shall not be subject to any turnover tax.

Article 23[1]

This Protocol shall also apply to the European Central Bank, to the members of its organs and to its staff, without prejudice to the provisions of the Protocol on the Statute of the European System of Central Banks and the European Central Bank.

The European Central Bank shall, in addition, be exempt from any form of taxation or imposition of a like nature on the occasion of any increase in its capital and from the various formalities which may be connected therewith in the State where the bank has its seat. The activities of the Bank and of its organs carried on in accordance with the Statute of the European System of Central Banks and of the European Central Bank shall not be subject to any turnover tax.

The above provisions shall also apply to the European Monetary Institute. Its dissolution or liquidation shall not give rise to any imposition.

NOTES

[1] Added by Art 9(5) of the Treaty of Amsterdam.

[3026]

IN WITNESS WHEREOF, the undersigned Plenipotentiaries have signed this Protocol.

Done at Brussels this 8 April 1965.

[Here follow the signatures.]

TREATY ESTABLISHING A CONSTITUTION FOR EUROPE

NOTES

The Treaty must be ratified by all 25 Member States. For a summary of the position regarding the processes for ratification of the Treaty, see http://www.europa.eu/constitution/ratification_en.htm.

The English version of this Treaty is published at http://europa.eu/constitution/index_en.htm. Only the provisions relevant to this work are reproduced here.

Please note that only European Union legislation published in the paper editions of the Official Journal of the European Communities is deemed authentic.

PART III
THE POLICIES AND FUNCTIONING OF THE UNION

TITLE III
INTERNAL POLICIES AND ACTION

CHAPTER IV
AREA OF FREEDOM, SECURITY AND JUSTICE

SECTION 1
GENERAL PROVISIONS

Article III

257

1. The Union shall constitute an area of freedom, security and justice with respect for fundamental rights and the different legal systems and traditions of the Member States

2. It shall ensure the absence of internal border controls for persons and shall frame a common policy on asylum, immigration and external border control, based on solidarity between Member States, which is fair towards third-country nationals. For the purpose of this Chapter, stateless persons shall be treated as third-country nationals.

3. The Union shall endeavour to ensure a high level of security through measures to prevent and combat crime, racism and xenophobia, and through measures for coordination and cooperation between police and judicial authorities and other competent authorities, as well as through the mutual recognition of judgments in criminal matters and, if necessary, through the approximation of criminal laws.

4. The Union shall facilitate access to justice, in particular through the principle of mutual recognition of judicial and extrajudicial decisions in civil matters.

[3027]

SECTION 3
JUDICIAL COOPERATION IN CIVIL MATTERS

Article III

269

1. The Union shall develop judicial cooperation in civil matters having cross-border implications, based on the principle of mutual recognition of judgments and decisions in extrajudicial cases. Such cooperation may include the adoption of measures for the approximation of the laws and regulations of the Member States.

2. For the purposes of paragraph 1, European laws or framework laws shall establish measures, particularly when necessary for the proper functioning of the internal market, aimed at ensuring:

(a) the mutual recognition and enforcement between Member States of judgments and decisions in extrajudicial cases;
(b) the cross-border service of judicial and extrajudicial documents;
(c) the compatibility of the rules applicable in the Member States concerning conflict of laws and of jurisdiction;
(d) cooperation in the taking of evidence;
(e) effective access to justice;
(f) the elimination of obstacles to the proper functioning of civil proceedings, if necessary by promoting the compatibility of the rules on civil procedure applicable in the Member States;
(g) the development of alternative methods of dispute settlement;
(h) support for the training of the judiciary and judicial staff.

Notwithstanding paragraph 2, a European law or framework law of the Council shall establish measures concerning family law with cross-border implications. The Council shall act unanimously after consulting the European Parliament.

The Council, on a proposal from the Commission, may adopt a European decision determining those aspects of family law with cross-border implications which may be the subject of acts adopted by the ordinary legislative procedure. The Council shall act unanimously after consulting the European Parliament.

[3028]

B. JURISDICTION AND FOREIGN JUDGMENTS

NOTES

With effect from 1 March 2002, the 1968 Brussels Convention has been largely superseded by Council Regulation 44/2001/EC on jurisdiction and the recognition and enforcement of judgments in civil and commercial matters (see Council Regulation 44/2001/EC, Art 68.1 at **[3146]**). The Brussels Convention continues to apply to relations between Denmark and the other Contracting States (see Council Regulation 44/2001/EC, recital (22) at **[3079]**) and to certain non-European territories of the Contracting States (see Table 1 at **[4676]**). Upon the coming into force of the agreement between the EC and Denmark on jurisdiction and the recognition and enforcement of judgments in civil and commercial matters reproduced at **[3204]** (date uncertain), the Brussels Convention will no longer apply to relations between Denmark and the Contracting States.

The relationship between Council Regulation 44/2001/EC and the 1988 Lugano Convention is less straightforward. It would seem, however, that the Lugano Convention (and not Council Regulation 44/2001/EC) will apply if (a) the defendant is domiciled in a Contracting State which is not an EC Member State (i e Iceland, Norway or Switzerland), (b) the Lugano Convention, Art 16 or 17 at **[3063]** confers jurisdiction on the courts of such a State, (c) the matter relates to a *lis pendens* or related actions (see the Lugano Convention, Arts 21, 22 at **[3063]**) if proceedings are instituted both in such a State and in a Contracting State which is an EC Member State, and (d) in matters of recognition or enforcement, where either the State of origin or the State addressed is not an EC Member State (see the Lugano Convention, Art 54B at **[3063]**, Council Regulation 44/2001/EC, Art 68.2 at **[3146]** and the Civil Jurisdiction and Judgments Act 1982, s 1(4) at **[135]**).

1968 BRUSSELS CONVENTION ON JURISDICTION AND THE ENFORCEMENT OF JUDGMENTS IN CIVIL AND COMMERCIAL MATTERS

NOTES

The text of the following Convention and the Protocol annexed thereto appear as set out in the Civil Jurisdiction and Judgments Act 1982, Sch 1. This version reflects amendments made by the Conventions on the Accession of Denmark, Ireland and the United Kingdom (Luxembourg, 1978), Greece (Luxembourg, 1982), Spain and Portugal (San Sebastian, 1989) and Austria, Finland and Sweden (Brussels, 1996). (A consolidated version of the 1968 Brussels Convention is also set out at OJ C27, 26.1.1998, p 1.)

See also the Introductory Note at the beginning of Pt IV(B).

For current status of the 1968 Brussels Convention, see Table 1 at **[4676]**.

[ARRANGEMENT OF PROVISIONS

PREAMBLE

THE HIGH CONTRACTING PARTIES TO THE TREATY ESTABLISHING THE EUROPEAN ECONOMIC COMMUNITY,

Desiring to implement the provisions of Article 220 of that Treaty by virtue of which they undertook to secure the simplification of formalities governing the reciprocal recognition and enforcement of judgments of courts or tribunals;

Anxious to strengthen in the Community the legal protection of persons therein established;

Considering that it is necessary for this purpose to determine the international jurisdiction of their courts, to facilitate recognition and to introduce an expeditious procedure for securing the enforcement of judgments, authentic instruments and court settlements;

Have decided to conclude this Convention and to this end have designated as their Plenipotentiaries;

(*Designations of Plenipotentiaries of the original six Contracting States*)

WHO, meeting within the Council, having exchanged their Full Powers, found in good and due form,

HAVE AGREED AS FOLLOWS:

TITLE 1
SCOPE

Article 1

This Convention shall apply in civil and commercial matters whatever the nature of the court or tribunal. It shall not extend, in particular, to revenue, customs or administrative matters.

The Convention shall not apply to—

1 The status or legal capacity of natural persons, rights in property arising out of a matrimonial relationship, wills and succession.

2 Bankruptcy, proceedings relating to the winding-up of insolvent companies or other legal persons, judicial arrangements, compositions and analogous proceedings.

3 Social security.

4 Arbitration.

TITLE II
JURISDICTION

SECTION 1
GENERAL PROVISIONS

Article 2

Subject to the provisions of this Convention, persons domiciled in a Contracting State shall, whatever their nationality, be sued in the courts of that State.

Persons who are not nationals of the State in which they are domiciled shall be governed by the rules of jurisdiction applicable to nationals of that State.

Article 3

Persons domiciled in a Contracting State may be sued in the courts of another Contracting State only by virtue of the rules set out in Sections 2 to 6 of this Title.

In particular the following provisions shall not be applicable as against them—

- — in Belgium: Article 15 of the civil code (Code civil—Burgerlijk Wetboek) and Article 638 of the judicial code (Code judiciaire—Gerechtelijk Wetboek),
- — in Denmark: Article 246(2) and (3) of the law on civil procedure (Lov om rettens pleje),
- — in the Federal Republic of Germany: Article 23 of the code of civil procedure (Zivilprozessordnung)
- — in Greece, Article 40 of the code of civil procedure (Κωδικας Πολιτινης Δικοκομιας),
- — in France: Articles 14 and 15 of the civil code (Code civil),

PART IV EC MATERIALS

— in Ireland: the rules which enable jurisdiction to be founded on the document instituting the proceedings having been served on the defendant during his temporary presence in Ireland,
— in Italy: Articles 2 and 4, nos 1 and 2 of the code of civil procedure (Codice di procedura civile),
— in Luxembourg: Articles 14 and 15 of the civil code (Code civil),
— in the Netherlands: Articles 126(3) and 127 of the code of civil procedure (Wetboek vanBurgerlijke Rechtsvordering),
— in Austria: Article 99 of the Law on Court Jurisdiction (Jurisdiktionsnorm),
— in Portugal: Article 65(1)(c), article 65(2) and article 65A(c) of the code of civil procedure (Código Processo Civil) and Article 11 of the code of labour procedure (Código de Processo de Trabalho),
— in Finland: the second, third and fourth sentences of the first paragraph of Section 1 of Chapter 10 of the Code of Judicial Procedure (oikeudenkäymiskaari/rättegångsbalken),
— in Sweden: the first sentence of the first paragraph of Section 3 of Chapter 10 of the Code of Judicial Procedure (rättegångsbalken),
— in the United Kingdom: the rules which enable jurisdiction to be founded on:
  (a) the document instituting the proceedings having been served on the defendant during his temporary presence in the United Kingdom; or
  (b) the presence within the United Kingdom of property belonging to the defendant; or
  (c) the seizure by the plaintiff of property situated in the United Kingdom.

Article 4

If the defendant is not domiciled in a Contracting State, the jurisdiction of the courts of each Contracting State shall, subject to the provisions of Article 16, be determined by the law of that State.

As against such a defendant, any person domiciled in a Contracting State may, whatever his nationality, avail himself in that State of the rules of jurisdiction there in force, and in particular those specified in the second paragraph of Article 3, in the same way as the nationals of that State.

SECTION 2
SPECIAL JURISDICTION

Article 5

A person domiciled in a Contracting State may, in another Contracting State, be sued—

1 In matters relating to a contract, in the courts for the place of performance of the obligation in question; in matters relating to individual contracts of employment, this place is that where the employee habitually carries out his work, or if the employee does not habitually carry out his work in any one country, the employer may also be sued in the courts for the place where the business which engaged the employee was or is now situated.

2 In matters relating to maintenance, in the courts for the place where the maintenance creditor is domiciled or habitually resident or, if the matter is ancillary to proceedings concerning the status of a person, in the court which, according to its own law, has jurisdiction to entertain those proceedings, unless that jurisdiction is based solely on the nationality of one of the parties.

3 In matters relating to tort, delict or quasi-delict, in the courts for the place where the harmful event occurred.

4 As regards a civil claim for damages or restitution which is based on an act giving rise to criminal proceedings, in the court seised of those proceedings, to the extent that that court has jurisdiction under its own law to entertain civil proceedings.

5 As regards a dispute arising out of the operations of a branch, agency or other establishment, in the courts for the place in which the branch, agency or other establishment is situated.

6 As settlor, trustee or beneficiary of a trust created by the operation of a statute, or by a written instrument, or created orally and evidenced in writing, in the courts of the Contracting State in which the trust is domiciled.

7 As regards a dispute concerning the payment of remuneration claimed in respect of the salvage of cargo or freight, in the court under the authority of which the cargo or freight in question—

(a) has been arrested to secure such payment, or

(b) could have been so arrested, but bail or other security has been given;

provided that this provision shall apply only if it is claimed that the defendant has an interest in the cargo or freight or had such an interest at the time of salvage.

Article 6

A person domiciled in a Contracting State may also be sued—

1 Where he is one of a number of defendants, in the courts for the place where any one of them is domiciled.

2 As a third party in an action on a warranty or guarantee or in any other third party proceedings, in the court seised of the original proceedings, unless these were instituted solely with the object of removing him from the jurisdiction of the court which would be competent in his case.

3 On a counter-claim arising from the same contract or facts on which the original claim was based, in the court in which the original claim is pending.

4 In matters relating to a contract, if the action may be combined with an action against the same defendant in matters relating to rights *in rem* in immovable property, in the court of the Contracting State in which the property is situated.

Article 6a

Where by virtue of this Convention a court of a Contracting State has jurisdiction in actions relating to liability from the use or operation of a ship, that court, or any other court substituted for this purpose by the internal law of that State, shall also have jurisdiction over claims for limitation of such liability.

SECTION 3
JURISDICTION IN MATTERS RELATING TO INSURANCE

Article 7

In matters relating to insurance, jurisdiction shall be determined by this Section, without prejudice to the provisions of Articles 4 and 5 point 5.

Article 8

An insurer domiciled in a Contracting State may be sued—

1. in the courts of the State where he is domiciled, or
2. in another Contracting State, in the courts for the place where the policy-holder is domiciled, or
3. if he is a co-insurer, in the courts of a Contracting State in which proceedings are brought against the leading insurer.

An insurer who is not domiciled in a Contracting State but has a branch, agency or other establishment in one of the Contracting States shall, in disputes arising out of the operations of the branch, agency or establishment, be deemed to be domiciled in that State.

Article 9

In respect of liability insurance or insurance of immovable property, the insurer may in addition be sued in the courts for the place where the harmful event occurred. The same applies if movable and immovable property are covered by the same insurance policy and both are adversely affected by the same contingency.

Article 10

In respect of liability insurance, the insurer may also, if the law of the court permits it, be joined in proceedings which the injured party had brought against the insured.

The provisions of Articles 7, 8 and 9 shall apply to actions brought by the injured party directly against the insurer, where such direct actions are permitted.

If the law governing such direct actions provides that the policy-holder or the insured may be joined as a party to the action, the same court shall have jurisdiction over them.

Article 11

Without prejudice to the provisions of the third paragraph of Article 10, an insurer may bring proceedings only in the courts of the Contracting State in which the defendant is domiciled, irrespective of whether he is the policy-holder, the insured or a beneficiary.

The provisions of this Section shall not affect the right to bring a counterclaim in the court in which, in accordance with this Section, the original claim is pending.

Article 12

The provisions of this Section may be departed from only by an agreement on jurisdiction—

1. which is entered into after the dispute has arisen, or
2. which allows the policy-holder, the insured or a beneficiary to bring proceedings in courts other than those indicated in this Section, or
3. which is concluded between a policy-holder and an insurer, both of whom are domiciled in the same Contracting State, and which has the effect of conferring jurisdiction on the courts of that State even if the harmful event were to occur abroad, providing that such an agreement is not contrary to the law of that State, or
4. which is concluded with a policy-holder who is not domiciled in a Contracting State, except in so far as the insurance is compulsory or relates to immovable property in a Contracting State, or
5. which relates to a contract of insurance in so far as it covers one or more of the risks set out in Article 12a.

Article 12a

The following are the risks referred to in point 5 of Article 12—

1. Any loss of or damage to—
   (a) sea-going ships, installations situated offshore or on the high seas, or aircraft, arising from perils which relate to their use for commercial purposes;
   (b) goods in transit other than passengers' baggage where the transit consists of or includes carriage by such ships or aircraft.
2. Any liability, other than for bodily injury to passengers or loss of or damage to their baggage—
   (a) arising out of the use or operation of ships, installations or aircraft as referred to in point 1(a) above in so far as the law of the Contracting State in which such aircraft are registered does not prohibit agreements on jurisdiction regarding insurance of such risks;
   (b) for loss or damage caused by goods in transit as described in point 1(b) above.
3. Any financial loss connected with the use or operation of ships, installations or aircraft as referred to in point 1(a) above, in particular loss of freight or charter-hire.
4. Any risk or interest connected with any of those referred to in points 1 to 3 above.

SECTION 4
JURISDICTION OVER CONSUMER CONTRACTS

Article 13

In proceedings concerning a contract concluded by a person for a purpose which can be regarded as being outside his trade or profession, hereinafter called "the consumer", jurisdiction shall be determined by this section, without prejudice to the provisions of Article 4 and point 5 of Article 5, if it is—

1. a contract for the sale of goods on instalment credit terms, or
2. a contract for a loan repayable by instalments, or for any other form of credit, made to finance the sale of goods, or
3. any other contract for the supply of goods or a contract for the supply of services, and
   (a) in the State of the consumer's domicile the conclusion of the contract was preceded by a specific invitation addressed to him or by advertising; and
   (b) the consumer took in that State the steps necessary for the conclusion of the contract.

Where a consumer enters into a contract with a party who is not domiciled in a Contracting State but has a branch, agency or other establishment in one of the Contracting States, that party shall, in disputes arising out of the operations of the branch, agency or establishment, be deemed to be domiciled in that State.

This Section shall not apply to contracts of transport.

Article 14

A consumer may bring proceedings against the other party to a contract either in the courts of the Contracting State in which that party is domiciled or in the courts of the Contracting State in which he is himself domiciled.

Proceedings may be brought against a consumer by the other party to the contract only in the courts of the Contracting State in which the consumer is domiciled.

These provisions shall not affect the right to bring a counter-claim in the court in which, in accordance with this Section, the original claim is pending.

Article 15

The provisions of this Section may be departed from only by an agreement—

1. which is entered into after the dispute has arisen, or
2. which allows the consumer to bring proceedings in courts other than those indicated in this Section, or
3. which is entered into by the consumer and the other party to the contract, both of whom are at the time of conclusion of the contract domiciled or habitually resident in the same Contracting State, and which confers jurisdiction on the courts of that State, provided that such an agreement is not contrary to the law of that State.

SECTION 5
EXCLUSIVE JURISDICTION

Article 16

The following courts shall have exclusive jurisdiction, regardless of domicile:

1—(a) in proceedings which have as their object rights *in rem* in immovable property or tenancies of immovable property, the courts of the Contracting State in which the property is situated;

(b) however, in proceedings which have as their object tenancies of immovable property concluded for temporary private use for a maximum period of six consecutive months, the courts of the Contracting State in which the defendant is domiciled shall also have jurisdiction, provided that the landlord and the tenant are natural persons and are domiciled in the same Contracting State.

2 In proceedings which have as their object the validity of the constitution, the nullity or the dissolution of companies or other legal persons or associations of natural or legal persons, or the decisions of their organs, the courts of the Contracting State in which the company, legal person or association has its seat.

3 In proceedings which have as their object the validity of entries in public registers, the courts of the Contracting State in which the register is kept.

4 In proceedings concerned with the registration or validity of patents, trade marks, designs, or other similar rights required to be deposited or registered, the courts of the Contracting State in which the deposit or registration has been applied for, has taken place or is under the terms of an international convention deemed to have taken place.

5 In proceedings concerned with the enforcement of judgments, the courts of the Contracting State in which the judgment has been or is to be enforced.

SECTION 6
PROROGATION OF JURISDICTION

Article 17

If the parties, one or more of whom is domiciled in a Contracting State, have agreed that a court or the courts of a Contracting State are to have jurisdiction to settle any disputes which have arisen or which may arise in connection with a particular legal relationship, that court or those courts shall have exclusive jurisdiction. Such an agreement conferring jurisdiction shall be either—

(a) in writing or evidenced in writing, or

(b) in a form which accords with practices which the parties have established between themselves, or

(c) in international trade or commerce, in a form which accords with a usage of which the parties are or ought to have been aware and which in such trade or commerce is widely known to, and regularly observed by, parties to contracts of the type involved in the particular trade or commerce concerned.

Where such an agreement is concluded by parties, none of whom is domiciled in a Contracting State, the courts of other Contracting States shall have no jurisdiction over their disputes unless the court or courts chosen have declined jurisdiction.

The court or courts of a Contracting State on which a trust instrument has conferred jurisdiction shall have exclusive jurisdiction in any proceedings brought against a settlor, trustee or beneficiary, if relations between these persons or their rights or obligations under the trust are involved.

Agreement or provisions of a trust instrument conferring jurisdiction shall have no legal force if they are contrary to the provisions of Articles 12 or 15, or if the courts whose jurisdiction they purport to exclude have exclusive jurisdiction by virtue of Article 16.

If an agreement conferring jurisdiction was concluded for the benefit of only one of the parties, that party shall retain the right to bring proceedings in any other court which has jurisdiction by virtue of this Convention.

In matters relating to individual contracts of employment an agreement conferring jurisdiction shall have legal force only if it is entered into after the dispute has arisen or if the employee invokes it to seise courts other than those for the defendant's domicile or those specified in Article 5(1).

Article 18

Apart from jurisdiction derived from other provisions of this Convention a court of a Contracting State before whom a defendant enters an appearance shall have jurisdiction. This rule shall not apply where appearance was entered solely to contest the jurisdiction, or where another court has exclusive jurisdiction by virtue of Article 16.

SECTION 7
EXAMINATION AS TO JURISDICTION AND ADMISSABILITY

Article 19

Where a court of a Contracting State is seised of a claim which is principally concerned with a matter over which the courts of another Contracting State have exclusive jurisdiction by virtue of Article 16, it shall declare of its own motion that it has no jurisdiction.

Article 20

Where a defendant domiciled in one Contracting State is sued in a court of another Contracting State and does not enter an appearance, the court shall declare of its own motion that it has no jurisdiction unless its jurisdiction is derived from the provisions of the Convention.

The court shall stay the proceedings so long as it is not shown that the defendant has been able to receive the document instituting the proceedings or an equivalent document in sufficient time to enable him to arrange for his defence, or that all necessary steps have been taken to this end.

The provisions of the foregoing paragraph shall be replaced by those of Article 15 of the Hague Convention of 15th November 1965 on the service abroad of judicial and extrajudicial documents in civil or commercial matters, if the documents instituting the proceedings or notice thereof had to be transmitted abroad in accordance with that Convention.

SECTION 8
LIS PENDENS—RELATED ACTIONS

Article 21

Where proceedings involving the same cause of action and between the same parties are brought in the courts of different Contracting States, any court other than the court first seised shall of its own motion stay its proceedings until such time as the jurisdiction of the court first seised is established.

Where the jurisdiction of the court first seised is established, any court other than the court first seised shall decline jurisdiction in favour of that court.

Article 22

Where related actions are brought in the courts of different Contracting States, any court other than the court first seised may, while the actions are pending at first instance, stay its proceedings.

A court other than the court first seised may also, on the application of one of the parties, decline jurisdiction if the law of that court permits the consolidation of related actions and the court first seised has jurisdiction over both actions.

For the purposes of this Article, actions are deemed to be related where they are so closely connected that it is expedient to hear and determine them together to avoid the risk of irreconcilable judgments resulting from separate proceedings.

Article 23

Where actions come within the exclusive jurisdiction of several courts, any court other than the court first seised shall decline jurisdiction in favour of that court.

SECTION 9
PROVISIONAL, INCLUDING PROTECTIVE, MEASURES

Article 24

Application may be made to the courts of a Contracting State for such provisional, including protective, measures as may be available under the law of that State, even if, under this Convention, the courts of another Contracting State have jurisdiction as to the substance of the matter.

TITLE III
RECOGNITION AND ENFORCEMENT

Article 25

For the purpose of this Convention, "judgment" means any judgment given by a court or tribunal of a Contracting State, whatever the judgment may be called, including a decree, order, decision or writ of execution, as well as the determination of costs or expenses by an officer of the court.

SECTION 1
RECOGNITION

Article 26

A judgment given in a Contracting State shall be recognized in the other Contracting States without any special procedure being required.

Any interested party who raises the recognition of a judgment as the principal issue in a dispute may, in accordance with the procedures provided for in Section 2 and 3 of this Title, apply for a decision that the judgment be recognised.

If the outcome of proceedings in a court of a Contracting State depends on the determination of an incidental question of recognition that court shall have jurisdiction over that question.

Article 27

A judgment shall not be recognized—

1. If such recognition is contrary to public policy in the State in which recognition is sought.
2. Where it was given in default of appearance, if the defendant was not duly served with the document which instituted the proceedings or with an equivalent document in sufficient time to enable him to arrange for his defence.
3. If the judgment is irreconcilable with a judgment given in a dispute between the same parties in the State in which recognition is sought.
4. If the court of the State of origin, in order to arrive at its judgment, has decided a preliminary question concerning the status or legal capacity of natural persons, rights in property arising out of a matrimonial relationship, wills or succession in a way that conflicts with a rule of the private international law of the State in which the recognition is sought, unless the same result would have been reached by the application of the rules of private international law of that State.
5. If the judgment is irreconcilable with an earlier judgment given in a non-contracting State involving the same cause of action and between the same parties, provided that this latter judgment fulfils the conditions necessary for its recognition in the state addressed.

Article 28

Moreover, a judgment shall not be recognised if it conflicts with the provisions of Sections 3, 4 or 5 of Title II, or in a case provided for in Article 59.

In its examination of the grounds of jurisdiction referred to in the foregoing paragraph, the court or authority applied to shall be bound by the findings of fact on which the court of the State of origin based its jurisdiction.

Subject to the provisions of the first paragraph, the jurisdiction of the court of the State of origin may not be reviewed; the test of public policy referred to in point 1 of Article 27 may not be applied to the rules relating to jurisdiction.

Article 29

Under no circumstances may a foreign judgment be reviewed as to its substance.

Article 30

A court of a Contracting State in which recognition is sought of a judgment given in another Contracting State may stay the proceedings if an ordinary appeal against the judgment has been lodged.

A court of a Contracting State in which recognition is sought of a judgment given in Ireland or the United Kingdom may stay the proceedings if enforcement is suspended in the State of origin, by reason of an appeal.

SECTION 2
ENFORCEMENT

Article 31

A judgment given in a Contracting State and enforceable in that State shall be enforced in another Contracting State when, on the application of any interested party, it has been declared enforceable there.

However, in the United Kingdom, such a judgment shall be enforced in England and Wales, in Scotland, or in Northern Ireland when, on the application of any interested party, it has been registered for enforcement in that part of the United Kingdom.

Article 32

1 The application shall be submitted—

— in Belgium, to the tribunal de première instance or rechtbank van eerste aanleg,
— in Denmark, to the byret,
— in the Federal Republic of Germany, to the presiding judge of a chamber of the Landgericht,
— in Greece, to the Μονομελες Πρωτοδικειο,
— in Spain, to the Juzgado de Primera Instancia,
— in France, to the presiding judge of the tribunal de grande instance,
— in Ireland, to the High Court,
— in Italy, to the corte d'appello,
— in Luxembourg, to the presiding judge of the tribunal d'arrondisement,
— in the Netherlands, to the presiding judge of the d'arrondissementsrechtbank,
— in Austria, to the Bezirksgericht,
— in Portugal, to the Tribunal Judicial de Circulo,
— in Finland, to the Käräjäoikeus/tingsrätt,
— in Sweden, in the Svea hovrätt,
— in the United Kingdom—
  (a) in England and Wales, to the High Court of Justice, or in the case of a maintenance judgment to the Magistrates' Court on transmission by the Secretary of State;
  (b) in Scotland, to the Court of Session, or in the case of a maintenance judgment to the Sheriff Court on transmission by the Secretary of State;
  (c) in Northern Ireland, to the High Court of Justice, or in the case of a maintenance judgment to the Magistrates' Court on transmission by the Secretary of State.

2 The jurisdiction of local courts shall be determined by reference to the place of domicile of the party against whom enforcement is sought. If he is not domiciled in the State in which enforcement is sought, it shall be determined by reference to the place of enforcement.

Article 33

The procedure for making the application shall be governed by the law of the State in which enforcement is sought.

The applicant must give an address for service of process within the area of jurisdiction of the court applied to. However, if the law of the State in which enforcement is sought does not provide for the furnishing of such an address, the applicant shall appoint a representative *ad litem*.

The documents referred to in Articles 46 and 47 shall be attached to the application.

Article 34

The court applied to shall give its decision without delay; the party against whom enforcement is sought shall not at this stage of the proceedings be entitled to make any submissions on the application.

The application may be refused only for one of the reasons specified in Articles 27 and 28.
Under no circumstances may the foreign judgment be reviewed as to its substance.

Article 35

The appropriate officer of the court shall without delay bring the decision given on the application to the notice of the applicant in accordance with the procedure laid down by the law of the State in which enforcement is sought.

Article 36

If enforcement is authorised, the party against whom enforcement is sought may appeal against the decision within one month of service thereof.

If that party is domiciled in a Contracting State other than that in which the decision authorising enforcement was given, the time for appealing shall be two months and shall run from the date of service, either on him in person or at his residence. No extension of time may be granted on account of distance.

Article 37

1 An appeal against the decision authorising enforcement shall be lodged in accordance with the rules governing procedure in contentious matters—

— in Belgium, with the tribunal de première instance or rechtbank van eerste aanleg,
— in Denmark, with the landsret,
— in the Federal Republic of Germany, with the Oberlandesgericht,
— in Greece, with the Εφετειο,
— in Spain, with the Audiencia Provincial,
— in France, with the cour d'appel,
— in Ireland, with the High Court,
— in Italy, with the corte d'appello,
— in Luxembourg, with the Court supérieure de justice sitting as a court of civil appeal,
— in the Netherlands, with the arrondissementsrechtbank,
— in Austria, with the Bezirksgericht,
— in Portugal, with the Tribunal de Relacção,
— in Finland, with the hovioikeus/hovrätt,
— in Sweden, with the Svea hovrätt,
— in the United Kingdom—
(a) in England and Wales, with the High Court of Justice, or in the case of a maintenance judgment with the Magistrates' Court;
(b) in Scotland, with the Court of Session, or in the case of a maintenance judgment with the Sheriff Court;
(c) in Northern Ireland, with the High Court of Justice, or in the case of a maintenance judgment with the Magistrates' Court.

2 The judgment given on the appeal may be contested only—

— in Belgium, Greece, Spain, France, Italy, Luxembourg and in the Netherlands, by an appeal in cassation,
— in Denmark, by an appeal to the højesteret, with the leave of the Minister of Justice,
— in the Federal Republic of Germany, by a Rechtsbeschwerde,
— in Ireland, by an appeal on a point of law to the Supreme Court,
— in Austria, in the case of an appeal by a Revisionsrekurs and, in the case of opposition proceedings, by a Berufung with the possibility of a revision,
— in Portugal, by an appeal on a point of law,
— in Finland, by an appeal to korkein oikeus/högsta domstolen,
— in Sweden, by an appeal to Högsta domstolen,
— in the United Kingdom, by a single further appeal on a point of law.

Article 38

The court with which the appeal under Article 37(1) is lodged may, on the application of the appellant, stay the proceedings if an ordinary appeal has been lodged against the judgment in the State of origin or if the time for such an appeal has not yet expired; in the latter case, the court may specify the time within which such an appeal is to be lodged.

Where the judgement was given in Ireland or the United Kingdom, any form of appeal available in the State of origin shall be treated as an ordinary appeal for the purposes of the first paragraph.

The court may also make enforcement conditional on the provision of such security as it shall determine.

Article 39

During the time specified for an appeal pursuant to Article 36 and until any such appeal has been determined, no measures of enforcement may be taken other than protective measures taken against the property of the party against whom enforcement is sought.

The decision authorising enforcement shall carry with it the power to proceed to any such protective measures.

Article 40

1 If the application for enforcement is refused, the applicant may appeal—

— in Belgium, to the cour d'appel or hof van beroep,
— in Denmark, to the landsret,
— in the Federal Republic of Germany, to the Oberlandesgericht,
— in Greece, to the Εφετειο,
— in Spain, to the Audiencia Provincial,
— in France, to the cour d'appel,
— in Ireland, to the High Court,
— in Italy, to the corte d'appello,
— in Luxembourg, to the Cour supérieure de justice sitting as a court of civil appeal,
— in the Netherlands, to the gerechtshof,
— in Austria, to the Bezirksgericht,
— in Portugal, to the Tribunal de Relacão,
— in Finland, to the hovioikeus/hovrätten,
— in Sweden, to the Svea hovrätt,
— in the United Kingdom—
(a) in England and Wales, to the High Court of Justice, or in the case of a maintenance judgment to the Magistrates' Court;
(b) in Scotland, to the Court of Session, or in the case of a maintenance judgment to the Sheriff Court;
(c) in Northern Ireland, to the High Court of Justice, or in the case of a maintenance judgment to the Magistrates' Court.

2 The party against whom enforcement is sought shall be summoned to appear before the appellate court. If he fails to appear, the provisions of the second and third paragraphs of Article 20 shall apply even where he is not domiciled in any of the Contracting States.

Article 41

A judgment given on appeal provided for in Article 40 may be contested only—

— in Belgium, Greece, Spain, France, Italy, Luxembourg and in the Netherlands, by an appeal in cassation,
— in Denmark, by an appeal to the højesteret, with the leave of the Minister of Justice,
— in the Federal Republic of Germany, by a Rechtsbeschwerde,
— in Ireland, by an appeal on a point of law to the Supreme Court,
— in Austria, by a Revisionsrekurs,
— in Portugal, by an appeal on a point of law,
— in Finland, by an appeal to korkein oikeus/högsta domstolen,
— in Sweden, by an appeal to Högsta domstolen,
— in the United Kingdom, by a single further appeal on a point of law.

Article 42

Where a foreign judgment has been given in respect of several matters and enforcement cannot be authorized for all of them, the court shall authorize enforcement for one or more of them.

An applicant may request partial enforcement of a judgment.

Article 43

A foreign judgment which orders a periodic payment by way of a penalty shall be enforceable in the State in which enforcement is sought only if the amount of the payment has been finally determined by the courts of the State of origin.

Article 44

An applicant who, in the State of origin has benefited from complete or partial legal aid or exemption from costs or expenses, shall be entitled, in the procedures provided for in Articles 32 to 35, to benefit from the most favourable legal aid or the most extensive exemption from costs or expenses provided for by the law of the State addressed.

However, an applicant who requests the enforcement of a decision given by an administrative authority in Denmark in respect of a maintenance order may, in the State addressed, claim the benefits referred to in the first paragraph if he presents a statement from the Danish Ministry of Justice to the effect that he fulfils the economic requirements to qualify for the grant of complete or partial legal aid or exemption from costs or expenses.

Article 45

No security, bond or deposit, however described, shall be required of a party who in one Contracting State applies for enforcement of a judgment given in another Contracting State on the ground that he is a foreign national or that he is not domiciled or resident in the State in which enforcement is sought.

SECTION 3
COMMON PROVISIONS

Article 46

A party seeking recognition or applying for enforcement of a judgment shall produce—

1. a copy of the judgment which satisfies the conditions necessary to establish its authenticity;
2. in the case of a judgment given in default, the original or a certified true copy of the document which establishes that the party in default was served with the document instituting the proceedings or with an equivalent document.

Article 47

A party applying for enforcement shall also produce—

1. documents which establish that, according to the law of the State of origin the judgment is enforceable and has been served;
2. where appropriate, a document showing that the applicant is in receipt of legal aid in the State of origin.

Article 48

If the documents specified in point 2 of Articles 46 and 47 are not produced, the court may specify a time for their production, accept equivalent documents or, if it considers that it has sufficient information before it, dispense with their production.

If the court so requires, a translation of the documents shall be produced; the translation shall be certified by a person qualified to do so in one of the Contracting States.

Article 49

No legalization or other similar formality shall be required in respect of the documents referred to in Articles 46 or 47 or the second paragraph of Article 48, or in respect of a document appointing a representative *ad litem*.

TITLE IV
AUTHENTIC INSTRUMENTS AND COURT SETTLEMENTS

Article 50

A document which has been formally drawn up or registered as an authentic instrument and is enforceable in one Contracting State shall, in another Contracting State, be declared enforceable there, on application made in accordance with the procedures provided for in Article 31 *et seq*. The application may be refused only if enforcement of the instrument is contrary to public policy in the State addressed.

The instrument produced must satisfy the conditions necessary to establish its authenticity in the State of origin.

The provisions of Section 3 of Title III shall apply as appropriate.

Article 51

A settlement which has been approved by a court in the course of proceedings and is enforceable in the State in which is was concluded shall be enforceable in the State addressed under the same conditions as authentic instruments.

TITLE V
GENERAL PROVISIONS

Article 52

In order to determine whether a party is domiciled in the Contracting State whose courts are seised of a matter, the Court shall apply its internal law.

If a party is not domiciled in the State whose courts are seised of the matter, then, in order to determine whether the party is domiciled in another Contracting State, the court shall apply the law of that State.

Article 53

For the purposes of this Convention, the seat of a company or other legal person or association of natural or legal persons shall be treated as its domicile. However, in order to determine that seat, the court shall apply its rules of private international law.

In order to determine whether a trust is domiciled in the Contracting State whose courts are seised of the matter, the court shall apply its rules of private international law.

TITLE VI
TRANSITIONAL PROVISIONS

Article 54

The provisions of the Convention shall apply only to legal proceedings instituted and to documents formally drawn up or registered as authentic instruments after its entry into force in the State of origin and, where recognition or enforcement of a judgment or authentic instruments is sought, in the State addressed.

However, judgments given after the date of entry into force of this Convention between the State of origin and the State addressed in proceedings instituted before that date shall be recognized and enforced in accordance with the provisions of Title III if jurisdiction was founded upon rules which accorded with those provided for either in Title II of this Convention or in a convention concluded between the State of origin and the State addressed which was in force when the proceedings were instituted.

If the parties to a dispute concerning a contract had agreed in writing before 1st June 1988 for Ireland or before 1st January 1987 for the United Kingdom that the contract was to be governed by the law of Ireland or of a part of the United Kingdom, the courts of Ireland or of that part of the United Kingdom shall retain the right to exercise jurisdiction in the dispute.

Article 54a

For a period of three years from 1st November 1987 for Denmark and from 1st June 1988 for Ireland, jurisdiction in maritime matters shall be determined in these States not only in accordance with the provisions of Title II, but also in accordance with the provisions of paragraphs 1 to 6 following. However, upon the entry into force of the International Convention relating to the arrest of sea-going ships, signed at Brussels on 10th May 1952, for one of these States, these provisions shall cease to have effect for that State.

1 A person who is domiciled in a Contracting State may be sued in the Courts of one of the States mentioned above in respect of a maritime claim if the ship to which the claim relates or any other ship owned by him has been arrested by judicial process within the territory of the latter State to secure the claim, or could have been so arrested there but bail or other security has been given, and either—

- (a) the claimant is domiciled in the latter State, or
- (b) the claim arose in the latter State, or
- (c) the claim concerns the voyage during which the arrest was made or could have been made, or
- (d) the claim arises out of a collision or out of damage caused by a ship to another ship or to goods or persons on board either ship, either by the execution or non-execution of a manoeuvre or by the non-observance of regulations, or
- (e) the claim is for salvage, or
- (f) the claim is in respect of a mortgage or hypothecation of the ship arrested.

2 A claimant may arrest either the particular ship to which the maritime claim relates, or any other ship which is owned by the person who was, at the time when the maritime claim arose, the owner of the particular ship. However, only the particular ship to which the maritime claim relates may be arrested in respect of the maritime claims set out in 5(o), (p) or (q) of this Article.

3 Ships shall be deemed to be in the same ownership when all the shares therein are owned by the same person or persons.

4 When in the case of a charter by demise of a ship the charterer alone is liable in respect of a maritime claim relating to that ship, the claimant may arrest that ship or any other ship owned by the charterer, but no other ship owned by the owner may be arrested in respect of such claim. The same shall apply to any case in which a person other than the owner of a ship is liable in respect of a maritime claim relating to that ship.

5 The expression "maritime claim" means a claim arising out of one or more of the following—

- (a) damage caused by any ship either in collision or otherwise;
- (b) loss of life or personal injury caused by any ship or occurring in connection with the operation of any ship;
- (c) salvage;
- (d) agreement relating to the use or hire of any ship whether by charterparty or otherwise;
- (e) agreement relating to the carriage of goods in any ship whether by charterparty or otherwise;
- (f) loss of or damage to goods including baggage carried in any ship;
- (g) general average;
- (h) bottomry;
- (i) towage;
- (j) pilotage;
- (k) goods or materials wherever supplied to a ship for her operation or maintenance;
- (l) construction, repair or equipment of any ship or dock charges and dues;
- (m) wages of master, officers or crew;
- (n) master's disbursements, including disbursements made by shippers, charterers or agents on behalf of a ship or her owner;
- (o) dispute as to the title to or ownership of any ship;
- (p) disputes between co-owners of any ship as to the ownership, possession, employment or earnings of that ship;
- (q) the mortgage or hypothecation of any ship.

6 In Denmark, the expression "arrest" shall be deemed as regards the maritime claims referred to in 5(o) and (p) of this Article, to include a "forbud", where that is the only procedure allowed in respect of such a claim under Articles 646 to 653 of the law on civil procedure (lov om rettens pleje).

TITLE VII
RELATIONSHIP TO OTHER CONVENTIONS

Article 55

Subject to the provisions of the second subparagraph of Article 54, and of Article 56, this Convention shall, for the States which are parties to it, supersede the following conventions concluded between two or more of them—

- the Convention between Belgium and France on jurisdiction and the validity and enforcement of judgments, arbitration awards and authentic instruments, signed at Paris on 8th July 1899,
- the Convention between Belgium and the Netherlands on jurisdiction, bankruptcy, and the validity and enforcement of judgments, arbitration awards and authentic instruments, signed at Brussels on 28th March 1925,
- the Convention between France and Italy on the enforcement of judgments in civil and commercial matters, signed at Rome on 3rd June 1930,
- the Convention between the United Kingdom and the French Republic providing for the reciprocal enforcement of judgments in civil and commercial matters, with Protocol, signed at Paris on 18th January 1934,
- the Convention between the United Kingdom and the Kingdom of Belgium providing for the reciprocal enforcement of judgments in civil and commercial matters, with Protocol, signed at Brussels on 2nd May 1934,
- the Convention between Germany and Italy on the recognition and enforcement of judgments in civil and commercial matters, signed at Rome on 9th March 1936,
- the Convention between the Kingdom of Belgium and Austria on the reciprocal recognition and enforcement of judgments and authentic instruments relating to maintenance obligations, signed at Vienna on 25th October 1957,
- the Convention between the Federal Republic of Germany and the Kingdom of Belgium on the mutual recognition and enforcement of judgments, arbitration awards and authentic instruments in civil and commercial matters, signed at Bonn on 30th June 1958,
- the Convention between the Kingdom of the Netherlands and the Italian Republic on the recognition and enforcement of judgments in civil and commercial matters, signed at Rome on 17th April 1959,
- the Convention between the Federal Republic of Germany and Austria on the reciprocal recognition and enforcement of judgments, settlements and authentic instruments in civil and commercial matters, signed at Vienna on 6th June 1959,
- the Convention between the Kingdom of Belgium and Austria on the reciprocal recognition and enforcement of judgments, arbitral awards and authentic instruments in civil and commercial matters, signed at Vienna on 16th June 1959,
- the Convention between the United Kingdom and the Federal Republic of Germany for the reciprocal recognition and enforcement of judgments in civil and commercial matters, signed at Bonn on 14th July 1960,
- the Convention between the Kingdom of Greece and the Federal Republic of Germany for the reciprocal recognition and enforcement of judgments, settlements and authentic instruments in civil and commercial matters, signed in Athens on 4th November 1961,
- the Convention between the Kingdom of Belgium and the Italian Republic on the recognition and enforcement of judgments and other enforceable instruments in civil and commercial matters, signed at Rome on 6th April 1962,
- the Convention between the Kingdom of the Netherlands and the Federal Republic of Germany on the mutual recognition and enforcement of judgments and other enforceable instruments in civil and commercial matters, signed at The Hague on 30th August 1962,
- the Convention between the Kingdom of the Netherlands and Austria on the reciprocal recognition and enforcement of judgments and authentic instruments in civil and commercial matters, signed at The Hague on 6th February 1963,
- the Convention between France and Austria on the recognition and enforcement of judgments and authentic instruments in civil and commercial matters, signed at Vienna on 15th July 1966,
- the Convention between the United Kingdom and the Republic of Italy for the reciprocal recognition and enforcement of judgments in civil and commercial matters, signed at Rome on 7th February 1964, with amending Protocol signed at Rome on 14th July 1970,
- the Convention between the United Kingdom and the Kingdom of the Netherlands providing for the reciprocal recognition and enforcement of judgments in civil matters, signed at The Hague on 17th November 1967,

- the Convention between Spain and France on the recognition and enforcement of judgment arbitration awards in civil and commercial matters, signed at Paris on 28th May 1969,
- the Convention between the United Kingdom and Austria providing for the reciprocal recognition and enforcement of judgments in civil and commercial matters, signed at Vienna on 14th July 1961, with amending Protocol signed at London on 6th March 1970,
- the Convention between Luxembourg and Austria on the recognition and enforcement of judgments and authentic instruments in civil and commercial matters, signed at Luxembourg on 29th July 1971,
- the Convention between Italy and Austria on the recognition and enforcement of judgments in civil and commercial matters, of judicial settlements and of authentic instruments, signed at Rome on 16th November 1971,
- the Convention between Spain and Italy regarding legal aid and the recognition and enforcement of judgments in civil and commercial matters, signed at Madrid on 22nd May 1973,
- the Convention between Finland, Iceland, Norway, Sweden and Denmark on the recognition and enforcement of judgments in civil matters, signed at Copenhagen on 11th October 1977,
- the Convention between Austria and Sweden on the recognition and enforcement of judgments in civil matters, signed at Stockholm on 16th September 1982,
- the Convention between Spain and the Federal Republic of Germany on the recognition and enforcement of judgments, settlements and enforceable authentic instruments in civil and commercial matters, signed at Bonn on 14th November 1983,
- the Convention between Austria and Spain on the recognition and enforcement of judgments, settlements and enforceable authentic instruments in civil and commercial matters, signed at Vienna on 17th February 1984, and
- the Convention between Finland and Austria on the recognition and enforcement of judgments in civil matters, signed at Vienna on 17th November 1986,

and, in so far as it is in force—

- the Treaty between Belgium, the Netherlands and Luxembourg on jurisdiction, bankruptcy, and the validity and enforcement of judgments, arbitration awards and authentic instruments, signed at Brussels on 24th November 1961.

Article 56

The Treaty and the conventions referred to in Article 55 shall continue to have effect in relation to matters to which this Convention does not apply.

They shall continue to have effect in respect of judgments given and documents formally drawn up or registered as authentic instruments before the entry into the force of this Convention.

Article 57

1 This Convention shall not affect any conventions to which the Contracting States are or will be parties and which in relation to particular matters, govern jurisdiction or the recognition or enforcement of judgments.

2 With a view to its uniform interpretation, paragraph 1 shall be applied in the following manner—

(a) this Convention shall not prevent a court of a Contracting State which is a party to a convention on a particular matter from assuming jurisdiction in accordance with that Convention, even where the defendant is domiciled in another Contracting State which is not a party to that Convention. The court hearing the action shall, in any event, apply Article 20 of this Convention.

(b) judgments given in a Contracting State by a court in the exercise of jurisdiction provided for in a convention on a particular matter shall be recognized and enforced in the other Contracting State in accordance with this Convention.

Where a convention on a particular matter to which both the State of origin and the State addressed are parties lays down conditions for the recognition or enforcement of judgments, those conditions shall apply. In any event, the provisions of this Convention which concern the procedure for recognition and enforcement of judgments may be applied.

3 This Convention shall not affect the application of provisions which, in relation to particular matters govern jurisdiction or the recognition or enforcement of judgments and which are or will be contained in acts of the institutions of the European Communities or in national laws harmonized in implementation of such acts.

Article 58

Until such time as the Convention on jurisdiction and the enforcement of judgments in civil and commercial matters, signed at Lugano on 16th September 1988 takes effect with regard to France and the Swiss Confederation, this Convention shall not affect the rights granted to Swiss nationals by the Convention between France and the Swiss Confederation on jurisdiction and enforcement of judgments in civil matters, signed at Paris on 15th June 1869.

Article 59

This Convention shall not prevent a Contracting State from assuming, in a convention on the recognition and enforcement of judgments, an obligation towards a third State not to recongize judgments given in other Contracting States against defendants domiciled or habitually resident in the third State where, in cases provided for in Article 4, the judgment could only be founded on a ground of jurisdiction specified in the second paragraph of Article 3.

However, a Contracting State may not assume an obligation towards a third State not to recognize a judgment given in another Contracting State by a court basing its jurisdiction on the presence within that State of property, belonging to the defendant, or the seizure by the plantiff of property situated there—

1. if the action is brought to assert or declare proprietary or possessory rights in that property, seeks to obtain authority to dispose of it, or arises from another issue relating to such property, or
2. if the property constitutes the security for a debt which is the subject-matter of the action.

TITLE VIII
FINAL PROVISIONS

Article 60

[Deleted]

Article 61

This Convention shall be ratified by the signatory States. The instruments of ratification shall be deposited with the Secretary-General of the Council of the European Communities.

Article 62

This Convention shall enter into force on the first day of the third month following the deposit of the instrument of ratification by the last signatory State to take this step.

Article 63

The Contracting States recognise that any State which becomes a member of the European Economic Community shall be required to accept this Convention as a basis for the negotiations between the Contracting States and that State necessary to ensure the implementation of the last paragraph of Article 220 of the Treaty establishing the European Economic Community.

The necessary adjustments may be the subject of a special convention between the Contracting States of the one part and the new Member States of the other part.

Article 64

The Secretary-General of the Council of the European Communities shall notify the signatory States of—

(a) the deposit of each instrument of ratification;
(b) the date of entry into force of this Convention;
(c) [Deleted]
(d) any declaration received pursuant to Article IV of the Protocol;
(e) any communication made pursuant to Article VI of the Protocol;

Article 65

The Protocol annexed to this Convention by common accord of the Contracting States shall form an integral part thereof.

Article 66

This Convention is concluded for an unlimited period.

Article 67

Any Contracting State may request the revision of this Convention. In this event, a revision conference shall be convened by the President of the Council of the European Communities.

Article 68

This Convention, drawn up in a single original in the Dutch, French, German and Italian languages, all four texts being equally authentic, shall be deposited in the archives of the Secretariat of the Council of the European Communities. The Secretary-General shall transmit a certified copy to the Government of each signatory State.

(Signatures of Plenipotentiaries of the original six Contracting States).

[3029]

ANNEXED PROTOCOL

The High Contracting Parties have agreed upon the following provisions, which shall be annexed to the Convention.

Article I

Any person domiciled in Luxembourg who is sued in a court of another Contracting State pursuant to Article 5(1) may refuse to submit to the jurisdiction of that court. If the defendant does not enter an appearance the court shall declare of its own motion that it has no jurisdiction.

An agreement conferring jurisdiction, within the meaning of Article 17, shall be valid with respect to a person domiciled in Luxembourg only if that person has expressly and specifically so agreed.

Article II

Without prejudice to any more favourable provisions of national laws, persons domiciled in a Contracting State who are being prosecuted in the criminal courts of another Contracting State of which they are not nationals for an offence which was not intentionally committed may be defended by persons qualified to do so, even if they do not appear in person.

However, the court seized of the matter may order appearance in person; in the case of failure to appear, a judgment given in the civil action without the person concerned having had the opportunity to arrange for his defence need not be recognised or enforced in the other Contracting States.

Article III

In proceedings for the issue of an order for enforcement, no charge, duty or fee calculated by reference to the value of the matter in issue may be levied in the State in which enforcement is sought.

Article IV

Judicial and extrajudicial documents drawn up in one Contracting State which have to be served on persons in another Contracting State shall be transmitted in accordance with the procedures laid down in the conventions and agreements concluded between the Contracting States.

Unless the State in which service is to take place objects by declaration to the Secretary-General of the Council of the European Communities, such documents may also be sent by the appropriate public officers of the State in which the document has been drawn up directly to the appropriate public officers of the State in which the addressee is to be found. In this case the officer of the State of origin shall send a copy of the document to the officer of the State applied to who is competent to forward it to the addressee. The document shall be forwarded in the manner specified by the law of the State applied to. The forwarding shall be recorded by a certificate sent directly to the officer of the State of origin.

Article V

The jurisdiction specified in Articles 6(2) and 10 in actions on a warranty or guarantee or in any other third party proceedings may not be resorted to in the Federal Republic of Germany or in Austria. Any person domiciled in another Contracting State may be sued in the courts:

— of the Federal Republic of Germany, pursuant to Articles 68, 72, 73 and 74 of the code of civil procedure (*Zivilprozessordnung*) concerning third-party notices;
— of Austria, pursuant to Article 21 of the code of civil procedure (*Zivilprozessordnung*) concerning third-party notices.

Judgments given in the other Contracting States by virtue of Articles 6(2) or 10 shall be recognised and enforced in the Federal Republic of Germany and in Austria in accordance with Title III. Any effects which judgments given in those States may have on third parties by application of the provisions in the preceding paragraph shall also be recognised in the other Contracting States.

Article Va

In matters relating to maintenance, the expression "court" includes the Danish administrative authorities.

In Sweden, in summary proceedings concerning orders to pay (*betalningsföreläggande*) and assistance (*handräckning*), the expression "court" includes the "Swedish enforcement service" (*kronofogdemyndighet*).

Article Vb

In proceedings involving a dispute between the master and a member of the crew of a sea-going ship registered in Denmark, in Greece, in Ireland or in Portugal, concerning remuneration or other conditions of service, a court in a Contracting State shall establish whether the diplomatic or consular officer responsible for the ship has been notified of the dispute. It shall stay the proceedings so long as he has not been notified. It shall of its own motion decline jurisdiction if the officer, having been duly notified, has exercised the powers accorded to him in the matter by a consular convention, or in the absence of such a convention has, within the time allowed, raised any objection to the exercise of such jurisdiction.

Article Vc

Articles 52 and 53 of this Convention shall, when applied by Article 69(5) of the Convention for the European patent for the common market, signed at Luxembourg on 15 December 1975, to the provisions relating to "residence" in the English text of that Convention, operate as if "residence" in that text were the same as "domicile" in Articles 52 and 53.

Article Vd

Without prejudice to the jurisdiction of the European Patent Office under the Convention on the grant of European patents, signed at Munich on 5 October 1973, the courts of each Contracting State shall have exclusive jurisdiction, regardless of domicile, in proceedings concerned with the registration or validity of any European patent granted for that State which is not a Community patent by virtue of the provisions of Article 86 of the Convention for the European patent for the common market, signed at Luxembourg on 15 December 1975.

Article Ve

Arrangements relating to maintenance obligations concluded with administrative authorities or authenticated by them shall also be regarded as authentic instruments within the meaning of the first paragraph of Article 50 of the Convention.

Article VI

The Contracting States shall communicate to the Secretary-General of the Council of the European Communities the text of any provisions of their laws which amend either those articles of their laws mentioned in the Convention or the lists of courts specified in Section 2 of Title III of the Convention.

(Signatures of Plenipotentiaries of the original six Contracting States).]

[3030]

NOTES

Commencement: 1 January 2001.

Substituted by the Civil Jurisdiction and Judgments Act 1982 (Amendment) Order 2000, SI 2000/1824, art 8(1), Sch 1.

JOINT DECLARATION

The Governments of the Kingdom of Belgium, the Federal Republic of Germany, the French Republic, the Italian Republic, the Grand Duchy of Luxembourg and the Kingdom of the Netherlands,

On signing the Convention on jurisdiction and the enforcement of judgments in civil and commercial matters,

Desiring to ensure that the Convention is applied as effectively as possible,

Anxious to prevent differences of interpretation of the Convention from impairing its unifying effect,

Recognizing that claims and disclaimers of jurisdiction may arise in the application of the Convention,

Declare themselves ready—

1. to study these questions and in particular to examine the possibility of conferring jurisdiction in certain matters on the Court of Justice of the European Communities and, if necessary, to negotiate an agreement to this effect;
2. to arrange meetings at regular intervals between their representatives.

[3031]

NOTES

The text of this Declaration appears in the consolidated version of the 1968 Brussels Convention at OJ C27, 26.1.1998, p 26.

JOINT DECLARATION
OF 9 OCTOBER 1978

THE REPRESENTATIVES OF THE GOVERNMENTS OF THE MEMBER STATES OF THE EUROPEAN ECONOMIC COMMUNITY, MEETING WITHIN THE COUNCIL,

Desiring to ensure that in the spirit of the Convention of 27 September 1968 uniformity of jurisdiction should also be achieved as widely as possible in maritime matters,

Considering that the International Convention relating to the arrest of sea-going ships, signed at Brussels on 10 May 1952, contains provisions relating to such jurisdiction,

Considering that all of the Member States are not parties to the said Convention,

Express the wish that Member States which are coastal States and have not already become parties to the Convention of 10 May 1952 should do so as soon as possible.

[3032]

NOTES

The text of this Declaration does not appear in the consolidated version of the 1968 Brussels Convention at OJ C27, 26.1.1998, p.1 but appears in OJ C189, 28.7.90, p 30.

[TEXT OF 1971 PROTOCOL, AS AMENDED

NOTES

The text of the following Protocol appears as set out in the Civil Jurisdiction and Judgments Act 1982, Sch 2.

This version reflects amendments made by the Conventions on the Accession of Denmark, Ireland and the United Kingdom (Luxembourg, 1978), Greece (Luxembourg, 1982), Spain and Portugal (San Sebastian, 1989) and Austria, Finland and Sweden (Brussels, 1996). (The text of this Protocol also appears in the consolidated version of the 1968 Brussels Convention at OJ C27, 26.1.1998, p 28.)

Article 1

The Court of Justice of the European Communities shall have jurisdiction to give rulings on the interpretation of the Convention on jurisdiction and the enforcement of judgments in civil and commercial matters and of the Protocol annexed to that Convention, signed at Brussels on 27th September 1968, and also on the interpretation of the present Protocol.

The Court of Justice of the European Communities shall also have jurisdiction to give rulings on the interpretation of the Convention on the accession of the Kingdom of Denmark, Ireland and the United Kingdom of Great Britain and Northern Ireland to the Convention of 27 September 1968 and to this Protocol.

The Court of Justice of the European Communities shall also have jurisdiction to give rulings on the interpretation of the Convention on the accession of the Hellenic Republic to the Convention of 27 September 1968 and to this Protocol, as adjusted by the 1978 Convention.

The Court of Justice of the European Communities shall also have jurisdiction to give rulings on the interpretation of the Convention on the accession of the Kingdom of Spain and the Portuguese Republic to the Convention of 27 September 1968 and to this Protocol, as adjusted by the 1978 Convention and the 1982 Convention.

The Court of Justice of the European Communities shall also have jurisdiction to give rulings on the interpretation of the Convention on the accession of the Republic of Austria, the Republic of Finland and the Kingdom of Sweden to the Convention of 27 September 1968 and to this Protocol, as adjusted by the 1978 Convention, the 1982 Convention and the 1989 Convention.

Article 2

The following courts may request the Court of Justice to give preliminary rulings on questions of interpretation—

1— in Belgium: la Cour de Cassation—het Hof van Cassatie and le Conseil d'État—de Raad van State,

— in Denmark: højesteret,

PART IV
EC MATERIALS

— in the Federal Republic of Germany: die obersten Gerichtshöfe des Bundes,

— in Greece: the ανωτατα δικαστηρια,

— in Spain: el Tribunal Supremo,

— in France: la Cour de Cassation and le Conseil d'État,

— in Ireland: the Supreme Court,

— in Italy: la Corte Suprema di Cassazione,

— in Luxembourg: la Cour Supérieure de Justice when sitting as Cour de Cassation,

— in Austria: the Oberste Gerichtshof, the Verwaltungsgerichtshof and the Verfassungsgerichtshof,

— in the Netherlands: de Hoge Raad,

— in Portugal: o Supremo Tribunal de Justiça and o Supremo Tribunal Administrativo.

— in Finland: Korkein oikeus/högsta domstolen and korkein hallintooikeus/högsta förvaltningsdomstolen,

— in Sweden: Högsta domstolen, Regeringsrätten, Arbetsdomstolen and Marknadsdomstolen,

— in the United Kingdom: the House of Lords and courts to which application has been made under the second paragraph of Article 37 or under Article 41 of the Convention.

2 The courts of the Contracting States when they are sitting in an appellate capacity.

3 In the cases provided for in Article 37 of the Convention, the courts referred to in that Article.

Article 3

1 Where a question of interpretation of the Convention or of one of the other instruments referred to in Article 1 is raised in a case pending before one of the courts listed in point 1 of Article 2, that court shall, if it considers that a decision on the question is necessary to enable it to give judgment, request the Court of Justice to give a ruling thereon.

2 Where such a question is raised before any court referred to in point 2 or 3 of Article 2, that court may, under the conditions laid down in paragraph 1, request the Court of Justice to give a ruling thereon.

Article 4

1 The competent authority of a Contracting State may request the Court of Justice to give a ruling on a question of interpretation of the Convention or of one of the other instruments referred to in Article 1 if judgments given by courts of that State conflict with the interpretation given either by the Court of Justice or in a judgment of one of the courts of another Contracting State referred to in point 1 or 2 of Article 2. The provisions of this paragraph shall apply only to judgments which have become *res judicata*.

2 The interpretation given by the Court of Justice in response to such a request shall not affect the judgments which gave rise to the request for interpretation.

3 The Procurators-General of the Courts of Cassation of the Contracting States, or any other authority designated by a Contracting State, shall be entitled to request the Court of Justice for a ruling on interpretation in accordance with paragraph 1.

4 The Registrar of the Court of Justice shall give notice of the request to the Contracting States, to the Commission and to the Council of the European Communities; they shall then be entitled within two months of the notification to submit statements of case or written observations to the Court.

5 No fees shall be levied or any costs or expenses awarded in respect of the proceedings provided for in this Article.

Article 5

1 Except where this Protocol otherwise provides, the provisions of the Treaty establishing the European Economic Community and those of the Protocol on the Statute of the Court of Justice annexed thereto, which are applicable when the Court is requested to give a preliminary ruling, shall also apply to any proceedings for the interpretation of the Convention and the other instruments referred to in Article 1.

2 The Rules of Procedure of the Court of Justice shall, if necessary, be adjusted and supplemented in accordance with Article 188 of the Treaty establishing the European Economic Community.

Article 6

[Deleted]

Article 7

This Protocol shall be ratified by the signatory States. The instruments of ratification shall be deposited with the Secretary-General of the Council of the European Communities.

Article 8

This Protocol shall enter into force on the first day of the third month following the deposit of the instrument of ratification by the last signatory State to take this step; provided that it shall at the earliest enter into force at the same time as the Convention of 27 September 1968 on jurisdiction and the enforcement of judgments in civil and commercial matters.

Article 9

The Contracting States recognise that any State which becomes a member of the European Economic Community, and to which Article 63 of the Convention on jurisdiction and the enforcement of judgments in civil and commercial matters applies, must accept the provisions of this Protocol, subject to such adjustments as may be required.

Article 10

The Secretary-General of the Council of the European Communities shall notify the signatory States of—

(a) the deposit of each instrument of ratification;
(b) the date of entry into force of this Protocol;
(c) any designation received pursuant to Article 4(3);
(d) [Deleted]

Article 11

The Contracting States shall communicate to the Secretary-General of the Council of the European Communities the texts of any provisions of their laws which necessitate an amendment to the list of courts in point 1 of Article 2.

Article 12

This Protocol is concluded for an unlimited period.

Article 13

Any Contracting State may request the revision of this Protocol. In this event, a revision conference shall be convened by the President of the Council of the European Communities.

Article 14

This Protocol, drawn up in a single original in the Dutch, French, German and Italian languages, all four texts being equally authentic, shall be deposited in the archives of the Secretariat of the Council of the European Communities. The Secretary-General shall transmit a certified copy to the Government of each signatory State.]

[3033]

NOTES

Commencement: 1 January 2001.

Substituted by the Civil Jurisdiction and Judgments Act 1982 (Amendment) Order 2000, SI 2000/1824, art 8(2), Sch 2.

JOINT DECLARATION

The Governments of the Kingdom of Belgium, the Federal Republic of Germany, the French Republic, the Italian Republic, the Grand Duchy of Luxembourg and the Kingdom of the Netherlands,

On signing the Protocol on the interpretation by the Court of Justice of the Convention of 27 September 1968 on jurisdiction and the enforcement of judgments in civil and commercial matters,

Desiring to ensure that the provisions of that Protocol are applied as effectively and as uniformly as possible,

Declare themselves ready to organize, in cooperation with the Court of Justice, an exchange of information on the judgments given by the courts referred to in Article 2(1) of that Protocol in application of the Convention and the Protocol of 27 September 1968.

[3034]

NOTES

The text of this Declaration appears in the consolidated version of the Brussels Convention at OJ C27, 26.1.1998, p 33.

COUNCIL REPORT

on the Convention on jurisdiction and the enforcement of judgments in civil and commercial matters

(Signed at Brussels, 27 September 1968)

NOTES

The Jenard Reports on the 1968 Brussels Convention and Annexed Protocol are set out at OJ C59, 5.3.79, p 1. References to the original pagination in the Official Journals are noted above the text to which they refer.

by Mr P Jenard

Director in the Belgian Ministry of Foreign Affairs and External Trade.

A committee of experts set up in 1960 by decision of the Committee of Permanent Representatives of the Member States, following a proposal by the Commission, prepared a draft Convention, in pursuance of Article 220 of the EEC Treaty, on jurisdiction and the enforcement of judgments in civil and commercial matters. The committee was composed of governmental experts from the six Member States, representatives of the Commission, and observers. Its rapporteur, Mr P Jenard, Directeur d'Administration in the Belgian Ministry for Foreign Affairs and External Trade, wrote the explanatory report, which was submitted to the governments at the same time as the draft prepared by the committee of experts. The following is the text of that report. It takes the form of a commentary on the Convention, which was signed in Brussels on 27 September 1968.

CONTENTS

[OJ C59, 5.3.79, p 3]

CHAPTER I
PRELIMINARY REMARKS

1. By Article 220 of the Treaty establishing the European Economic Community, the Member States agreed to enter into negotiations with each other, so far as necessary, with a view to securing for the benefit of their nationals the simplification of formalities governing the reciprocal recognition and enforcement of judgments of courts or tribunals and of arbitration awards.

The fact that the Treaty of Rome requires the Member States to resolve this problem shows that it is important. In a note sent to the Member States on 22 October 1959 inviting them to commence negotiations, the Commission of the European Economic Community pointed out that

> "a true internal market between the six States will be achieved only if adequate legal protection can be secured. The economic life of the Community may be subject to disturbances and difficulties unless it is possible, where necessary by judicial means, to ensure the recognition and enforcement of the various rights arising from the existence of a multiplicity of legal relationships. As jurisdiction in both civil and commercial matters is derived from the sovereignty of Member States, and since the effect of judicial acts is confined to each national territory, legal protection and, hence, legal certainty in the common market are essentially dependent on the adoption by the Member States of a satisfactory solution to the problem of recognition and enforcement of judgments."

PART IV EC MATERIALS

On receiving this note the Committee of Permanent Representatives decided on 18 February 1960 to set up a committee of experts. The committee, consisting of delegates from the six Member countries, observers from the Benelux Committee on the unification of law and from the Hague Conference on private international law, and representatives from the EEC Commission departments concerned, met for the first time from 11 to 13 July 1960 and appointed as its chairman Professor Bülow then Ministerialdirigent and later Staatssekretär in the Federal Ministry of Justice in Bonn, and as its rapporteur Mr Jenard, directeur in the Belgian Ministry for Foreign Affairs.

At its 15th meeting, held in Brussels from 7 to 11 December 1964, the committee adopted a "Preliminary Draft Convention on jurisdiction and the recognition and enforcement of judgments in civil and commercial matters, and the enforcement of authentic instruments (document 14371/IV/64). This preliminary draft, with an explanatory report (document 2449/IV/65), was submitted to the Governments for comment.

The comments of the Governments, and those submitted by the Union of the Industries of the European Community, the Permanent Conference of Chambers of Commerce and Industry of the EEC, the Banking Federation of the EEC, the Consultative Committee of the Barristers' and Lawyers' Associations of the six EEC countries (a committee of the International Association of Lawyers), were studied by the Committee at its meeting of 5 to 15 July 1966. The draft Convention was finally adopted by the experts at that meeting.

The names of the governmental experts who took part in the work of the committee are set out in the annex to this report.

[3035]

CHAPTER II
BACKGROUND TO THE CONVENTION

It is helpful to consider, first, the rules in each of the six countries governing the recognition and enforcement of foreign judgments.

[OJ C59, 5.3.79, p 4]

A. THE LAW IN FORCE IN THE SIX STATES

In Belgium, until the entry into force of the Judicial Code (Code Judiciaire), the relevant provisions as regards enforcement are to be found in Article 10 of the Law of 25 March 1876, which contains Title I of the Introductory Book of the Code of Civil Procedure.[1]

Where there is no reciprocal convention, a court seised of an application for an order for enforcement "has jurisdiction over a foreign judgment as to both form and substance, and can re-examine both the facts and the law. In other words, it has power to review the matter fully".[2, 3]

As regards recognition, text-book authorities and case-law draw a distinction between foreign judgments relating to status and legal capacity and those relating to other matters. The position at present is that foreign judgments not relating to the status and legal capacity of persons are not regarded by the courts as having the force of *res judicata*.

However, foreign judgments relating to a person's status or legal capacity may be taken as evidence of the status acquired by that person.[4] Such a foreign judgment thus acts as a bar to any new proceedings for divorce or separation filed before a Belgian court if the five conditions listed in Article 10 of the Law of 1876 are fulfilled, as they "constitute no more than the application to foreign judgments of rules which the legislature considers essential for any judgment to be valid".

In the *Federal Republic of Germany*, foreign judgments are recognized and enforced on the basis of reciprocity.[5] The conditions for recognition of foreign judgments are laid down in paragraph 328 of the Code of Civil Procedure (Zivilprozeßordnung):

"I. A judgment given by a foreign court may not be recognized:

1. where the courts of the State to which the foreign court belongs have no jurisdiction under German law;
2. where the unsuccessful defendant is German and has not entered an appearance, if the document instituting the proceedings was not served on him in person either in the State to which the court belongs, or by a German authority under the system of mutual assistance in judicial matters;
3. where, to the detriment of the German party, the judgment has not complied with the provisions of Article 13(1) and (3) or of Articles 17, 18, and 22 of

the Introductory Law to the Civil Code (Einführungsgesetz zum Bürgerlichen Gesetzbuch), or with the provisions of Article 27 of that Law which refer to Article 13(1), nor where, in matters falling within the scope of Article 12(3) of the Law of 4 July 1939 on disappearances, certifications of death, and establishment of the date of decease (RGBI. I, p 1186), there has been a failure to comply with the provisions of Article 13(2) of the Introductory Law to the Civil Code, to the detriment of the wife of a foreigner who has been declared dead by judgment of the court;[6]

[OJ C59, 5.3.79, p 5]

4. where recognition of the judgment would be contrary to "good morals" (gegen die guten Sitten) or the objectives of a German law;
5. where there is no guarantee of reciprocity.

II. The provision in (5) above shall not prevent recognition of a judgment given in a matter not relating to property rights where no court in Germany has jurisdiction under German law."

The procedure for recognizing judgments delivered in actions relating to matrimonial matters is governed by a special Law (Familienrechtsänderungsgesetz) of 11 August 1961 (BGBI. I, p 1221, Article 7).

Enforcement is governed by Articles 722 and 723 of the Code of Civil Procedure, which read as follows:

Article 722

"I. A foreign judgment may be enforced only where this is authorized by virtue of an order for enforcement.

II. An application for an order for enforcement shall be heard either by the Amtsgericht or the Landgericht having general jurisdiction in relation to the defendant, or otherwise by the Amtsgericht or the Landgericht before which the defendant may be summoned under Article 23."

Article 723

"I. An order for enforcement shall be granted without re-examination of the substance of the judgment.

II. An order for enforcement shall be granted only if the foreign judgment has become *res judicata* under the law of the court in which it was given. No order for enforcement shall be granted where recognition of the judgment is excluded by Article 328."

In France, Article 546 of the Code of Civil Procedure (Code de procédure civile) provides that judgments given by foreign courts and instruments recorded by foreign officials can be enforced only after being declared enforceable by a French court (Articles 2123 and 2128 of the Civil Code).

The courts have held that four conditions must be satisfied for an order for enforcement to be granted: the foreign court must have had jurisdiction; the procedure followed must have been in order; the law applied must have been that which is applicable under the French system of conflict of laws; and due regard must have been paid to public policy.[7]

The Cour de cassation recently held (Cass. civ. 1er Section, 7 January 1964—Munzer case) that the substance of the original action could not be reviewed by the court hearing the application for an order for enforcement. This judgment has since been followed.

In Italy, on the other hand, the Code of Civil Procedure (Codice di procedura civile) in principle allows foreign judgments to be recognized and enforced.

Under Article 796 of the Code of Civil Procedure, any foreign judgment may be declared enforceable in Italy by the Court of Appeal (Corte d'appello) for the place in which enforcement is to take place (Dichiarazione di efficacia).

Under Article 797 of the Code of Civil Procedure, the Court of Appeal examines whether the foreign judgment was given by a judicial authority having jurisdiction under the rules in force in Italy; whether in the proceedings abroad the document instituting the proceedings was properly served and whether sufficient notice was given; whether the parties properly entered an appearance in the proceedings or whether their default was duly recognized; whether the judgment has become *res judicata*; whether the judgment conflicts with a judgment given by an Italian judicial authority; whether proceedings between the same parties and concerning the same claim are pending before an Italian judicial authority; and whether the judgment contains anything contrary to Italian public policy.

However, if the defendant failed to appear in the foreign proceedings, he may request the Italian court to review the substance of the case (Article 798). In such a case, the Court may either order enforcement, or hear the substance of the case and give judgment.

[OJ C59, 5.3.79, p 6]

There is also in Italian law the "delibazione incidentale" (Article 799 of the Code of Civil Procedure) which, however, applies only to proceedings in which it is sought to invoke a foreign judgment.

Luxembourg. Under Article 546 of the Luxembourg Code of Civil Procedure (Code de procédure civile), judgments given by foreign courts and instruments recorded by foreign officials can be enforced in the Grand Duchy only after being declared enforceable by a Luxembourg court (see Articles 2123 and 2128 of the Civil Code).

Luxembourg law requires seven conditions to be satisfied before an order for enforcement can be granted: the judgment must be enforceable in the country in which it was given; the foreign court must have had jurisdiction; the law applied must have been that applicable under the Luxembourg rules of conflict of laws; the rules of procedure of the foreign law must have been observed; the rights of the defendant must have been observed; due regard must have been paid to public policy; the law must not have been contravened (Luxembourg, 5. 2. 64, Pasicrisie luxembourgeoise XIX, 285).

Luxembourg law no longer permits any review of a foreign judgment as to the merits.

In the *Netherlands,* the Code of Civil Procedure (Wetboek van Burgerlijke Rechtsvordering) lays down the principle that judgments of foreign courts are not enforceable in the Kingdom. Matters settled by foreign courts may be reconsidered by Netherlands courts (see Article 431 of the Code of Civil Procedure).

The national laws of the Member States thus vary considerably.

NOTES

1 Article 10 of the Law of 1876 provides that: They (courts of first instance) shall also have jurisdiction in relation to judgments given by foreign courts in civil and commercial matters. Where there exists a treaty concluded on a basis of reciprocity between Belgium and the country in which the judgment was given, they shall review only the following five points:

1. whether the judgment contains anything contrary to public policy or to the principles of Belgian public law;
2. whether, under the law of the country in which the judgment was given, it has become *res judicata*;
3. whether, under that law, the certified copy of the judgment satisfies the conditions necessary to establish its authenticity;
4. whether the rights of the defendant have been observed;
5. whether the jurisdiction of the foreign court is based solely on the nationality of the plaintiff.

Article 570 of the Judicial Code contained in the Law of 10 October 1967 (supplement to the Moniteur belge of 31 October 1967) reads as follows:

"Courts of first instance shall adjudicate on applications for orders for the enforcement of judgments given by foreign courts in civil matters, regardless of the amount involved. Except where the provisions of a treaty between Belgium and the country in which the judgment was given are to be applied, the court shall examine, in addition to the substance of the matter:
1. whether the judgment contains anything contrary to public policy or to the principles of Belgian public law;
2. whether the rights of the defendant have been observed;
3. whether the jurisdiction of the foreign court is based solely on the nationality of the plaintiff;
4. whether, under the law of the country in which the judgment was given, it has become *res judicata*;
5. whether, under the law, the certified copy of the judgment satisfies the conditions necessary to establish its authenticity."

These provisions will enter into force on 31 October 1970 at the latest. Before that date an *arrêté royal* (Royal Decree) will determine the date on which the provisions of the Judicial Code enter into force.

2 GRAULICH, Principes de droit international privé, No 248 *et seq.*

3 RIGAUX, L'efficacité des jugements étrangers en Belgique, Journal des tribunaux, 10.4.1960, p 287.

4 Cass. 16.1.1953—Pas. I. 335.

5 Riezler, Internationales Zivilprozeßrecht, 1949, p 509 *et seq.*

6 These Articles of the Introductory Law to the Civil Code provide for the application of German law in many cases: condition of validity of marriage, form of marriage, divorce, legitimate and illegitimate paternity, adoption, certification of death.

7 Batiffol, Traité élémentaire de droit international privé, No 741 *et seq.*

B. EXISTING CONVENTIONS

Apart from conventions dealing with particular matters (see p 10), various conventions on enforcement exist between the Six; they are listed in Article 55 of the Convention. However, relations between France and the Federal Republic of Germany, France and the Netherlands, France and Luxembourg, Germany and Luxembourg, and Luxembourg and Italy are hampered by the absence of such conventions.[1]

There are also striking differences between the various conventions. Some, like those between France and Belgium, and between Belgium and the Netherlands, and the Benelux Treaty, are based on "direct" jurisdiction; but all the others are based on "indirect" jurisdiction. The Convention between France and Italy is based on indirect jurisdiction, but nevertheless contains some rules of direct jurisdiction. Some conventions allow only those judgments which have become *res judicata* to be recognized and enforced, whilst others such as the Benelux Treaty and the Conventions between Belgium and the Netherlands, Germany and Belgium, Italy and Belgium and Germany and the Netherlands apply to judgments which are capable of enforcement.[2] Some cover judgments given in civil matters by criminal courts, whilst others are silent on this point or expressly exclude such judgments from their scope (Conventions between Italy and the Netherlands, Article 10, and between Germany and Italy, Article 12).

There are various other differences between these treaties and conventions which need not be discussed in detail; they relate in particular to the determination of competent courts and to the conditions governing recognition and enforcement. It should moreover be stressed that these conventions either do not lay down the enforcement procedure or give only a summary outline of it.

The present unsatisfactory state of affairs as regards the recognition and enforcement of judgments could have been improved by the conclusion of new bilateral conventions between Member States not yet bound by such conventions.

[OJ C59, 5.3.79, p 7]

However, the Committee has decided in favour of the conclusion of a multilateral convention between the countries of the European Economic Community, in accordance with the views expressed in the Commission's letter of 22 October 1959. The Committee felt that the differences between the bilateral conventions would hinder the "free movement" of judgments and lead to unequal treatment of the various nationals of the Member States, such inequality being contrary to the fundamental EEC principle of non-discrimination, set out, in particular, in Article 7 of the Treaty of Rome.

In addition, the European Economic Community provided the conditions necessary for a modern, liberal law on the recognition and enforcement of judgments, which would satisfy both legal and commercial interests.

NOTES

1 It should be noted that at the time of writing this report, the Benelux Treaty has not yet entered into force and there is no agreement existing between Luxembourg on the one hand and Belgium and the Netherlands on the other.

2 The Franco-Belgian convention, in spite of the provisions of Article 11(2) which impose the condition of *res judicata*, nevertheless applies to enforceable judgments even if there is still a right of appeal (see Niboyet, Droit international privé français, T. VII 2022).

C. THE NATURE OF THE CONVENTION

Some of the bilateral conventions concluded between the Member States, such as the Convention between France and Belgium of 8 July 1899, the Convention between Belgium and the Netherlands of 28 March 1925, and the Benelux Treaty of 24 November 1961, are based on rules of direct jurisdiction, whilst in the others the rules of jurisdiction are indirect. Under conventions of the first type, known also as "double treaties", the rules of jurisdiction laid down are applicable in the State of origin, i e the State in which the proceedings originally took place; they therefore apply independently of any proceedings for recognition and enforcement, and permit a defendant who is summoned before a court which under the convention in question would not have jurisdiction to refuse to accept its jurisdiction.

Rules of jurisdiction in a convention are said to be "indirect" when they do not affect the courts of the State in which the judgment was originally given, and are to be considered only in relation to recognition and enforcement. They apply only in determining cases in which the court of the State in which recognition or enforcement of a judgment is sought (the State addressed) is obliged to recognize the jurisdiction of the court of the State of origin. They can therefore be taken as conditions governing the recognition and enforcement of foreign judgments and, more specifically, governing supervision of the jurisdiction of foreign courts.

The Committee spent a long time considering which of these types of convention the EEC should have. It eventually decided in favour of a new system based on direct jurisdiction but differing in several respects from existing bilateral conventions of that type.

Although the Committee of experts did not underestimate the value and importance of "single" conventions, (ie conventions based on rules of indirect jurisdiction) it felt that within the EEC a convention based on rules of direct jurisdiction as a result of the adoption of common rules of jurisdiction would allow increased harmonization of laws, provide greater legal certainty, avoid discrimination and facilitate the "free movement" of judgments, which is after all the ultimate objective.

Conventions based on direct jurisdiction lay down common rules of jurisdiction, thus bringing about the harmonization of laws, whereas under those based on indirect jurisdiction, national provisions apply, without restriction, in determining international jurisdiction in each State.

Legal certainty is most effectively secured by conventions based on direct jurisdiction since, under them, judgments are given by courts deriving their jurisdiction from the conventions themselves; however, in the case of conventions based on indirect jurisdiction, certain judgments cannot be recognized and enforced abroad unless national rules of jurisdiction coincide with the rules of the convention.[1]

Moreover, since it establishes, on the basis of mutual agreement, an autonomous system of international jurisdiction in relations between the Member States, the Convention makes it easier to abandon certain rules of jurisdiction which are generally regarded as exorbitant.

Finally, by setting out rules of jurisdiction which may be relied upon as soon as proceedings are begun in the State of origin, the Convention regulates the problem of *lis pendens* and also helps to minimize the conditions governing recognition and enforcement.

[OJ C59, 5.3.79, p 8]

As already stated, the Convention is based on direct jurisdiction, but differs fundamentally from treaties and conventions of the same type previously concluded. This is not the place to undertake a detailed study of the differences, or to justify them; it will suffice merely to list them:

1. the criterion of domicile replaces that of nationality;
2. the principle of equality of treatment is extended to any person domiciled in the Community, whatever his nationality;
3. rules of exclusive jurisdiction are precisely defined;
4. the right of the defendant to defend himself in the original proceedings is safeguarded;
5. the number of grounds for refusal of recognition and enforcement is reduced.

In addition, the Convention is original in that:

1. the procedure for obtaining enforcement is standardized;
2. rules of procedure are laid down for cases in which recognition is at issue; 3. provision is made for cases of conflict with other conventions.

[3036]

NOTES

1 WESER, Les conflits de juridictions dans le cadre du Marché Commun, Revue Critique de droit international privé 1960, pp 161–172.

CHAPTER III
SCOPE OF THE CONVENTION

The scope of the Convention is determined by the preamble and Article 1.

It governs international legal relationships, applies automatically, and covers all civil and commercial matters, apart from certain exceptions which are exhaustively listed.

I. INTERNATIONAL LEGAL RELATIONSHIPS

As is stressed in the fourth paragraph of the preamble, the Convention determines the international jurisdiction of the courts of the Contracting States.

It alters the rules of jurisdiction in force in each Contracting State only where an international element is involved. It does not define this concept, since the international element in a legal relationship may depend on the particular facts of the proceedings of which the court is seised. Proceedings instituted in the courts of a Contracting State which involves only persons domiciled in that State will not normally be affected by the Convention; Article 2 simply refers matters back to the rules of jurisdiction in force in that State. It is possible, however, that an international element may be involved in proceedings of this type. This would be the case, for example, where the defendant was a foreign national, a situation in which the principle of equality of treatment laid down in the second paragraph of Article 2 would apply, or where the proceedings related to a matter over which the courts of another State had exclusive jurisdiction (Article 16), or where identical or related proceedings had been brought in the courts of another State (Article 21 to 23).

It is clear that at the recognition and enforcement stage, the Convention governs only international legal relationships, since *ex hypothesi* it concerns the recognition and enforcement in one Contracting State of judgments given in another Contracting State.[1]

NOTES

1 A. BÜLOW, Vereinheitlichtes internationales Zivilprozeßrecht in der Europäischen Wirtschaftsgemeinschaft—Rabels Zeitschrift für ausländisches und internationales Privatrecht, 1965, p 473 *et seq.*

II. THE BINDING NATURE OF THE CONVENTION

It was decided by the committee of experts that the Convention should apply automatically. This principle is formally laid down in Articles 19 and 20 which deal with the matter of examination by the courts of the Contracting States of their international jurisdiction. The courts must apply the rules of the Convention whether or not they are pleaded by the parties. It follows from this, for example, that if a person domiciled in Belgium is sued in a French court on the basis of Article 14 of the French Civil Code, and contests the jurisdiction of that court but without pleading the provisions of the Convention, the court must nevertheless apply Article 3 and declare that it has no jurisdiction.[1]

NOTES

1 Tribunal civil de Lille, 9.11.1953, Revue critique de droit international privé, 1954, p 832.

[OJ C59, 5.3.79, p 9]

III. CIVIL AND COMMERCIAL MATTERS

The Committee did not specify what is meant by "civil and commercial matters", nor did it point to a solution of the problem of classification by determining the law according to which that expression should be interpreted.

In this respect it followed the practice of existing conventions.[1]

However, it follows from the text of the Convention that civil and commercial matters are to be classified as such according to their nature, and irrespective of the character of the court or tribunal which is seised of the proceedings or which has given judgment. This emerges from Article 1, which provides that the Convention shall apply in civil and commercial matters "whatever the nature of the court or tribunal". The Convention also applies irrespective of whether the proceedings are contentious or non-contentious. It likewise applies to labour law in so far as this is regarded as a civil or commercial matter (see also under contracts of employment, page 24).

The Convention covers civil proceedings brought before criminal courts, both as regards decisions relating to jurisdiction, and also as regards the recognition and enforcement of judgments given by criminal courts in such proceedings. It thereby takes into account certain laws in force in the majority of the Contracting States,[2] tends to rule out any differences of interpretation such as have arisen in applying the Convention between Belgium and the Netherlands[3] and, finally, meets current requirements arising from the increased number of road accidents.

The relevant provisions of the treaty and conventions already concluded between the Member States vary widely, as has already been pointed out in Chapter I(A).

The formula adopted by the Committee reflects the current trend in favour of inserting in conventions clauses specifying that they apply to judgments given in civil or commercial

PART IV
EC MATERIALS

matters by criminal courts. This can in particular be seen in the Benelux Treaty of 24 November 1961 and in the work of the Hague Conference on private international law.

It should be noted that the provisions of Article 5(4) of the Convention in no way alter the penal jurisdiction of criminal courts and tribunals as laid down in the various codes of criminal procedure.

As regards both jurisdiction and recognition and enforcement, the Convention affects only civil proceedings of which those courts are seised, and judgments given in such proceedings.

However, in order to counter the objection that a party against whom civil proceedings have been brought might be obstructed in conducting his defence if criminal sanctions could be imposed on him in the same proceedings, the Committee decided on a solution identical to that adopted in the Benelux Treaty. Article II of the Protocol provides that such persons may be defended or represented in criminal courts. Thus they will not be obliged to appear in person to defend their civil interests.

The Convention also applies to civil or commercial matters brought before administrative tribunals.

The formula adopted by the Committee is identical to that envisaged by the Commission which was given the task at the fourth session of the Hague Conference on private international law of examining the Convention of 14 November 1896 in order to draw up common rules on a number of aspects of private international law relating to civil procedure. It reported as follows:

> "The expression 'civil or commercial matters' is very wide and does not include only those matters which fall within the jurisdiction of civil tribunals and commercial tribunals in countries where administrative tribunals also exist. Otherwise there would be a wholly unjustifiable inequality between the Contracting States: service abroad of judicial instruments could take place on a wider scale for countries which do not have administrative tribunals than for countries which have them. In brief, the Convention is applicable from the moment when private interests become involved …".[4]

[OJ C59, 5.3.79, p 10]

Thus, for example, decisions of the French Conseil d'État given on such matters may be recognized and enforced.[5]

NOTES

1 This problem is not dealt with in any treaty on enforcement. See also the report by Professor Fragistas on the Preliminary Draft Convention adopted by the Special Commission of the Hague Conference on private international law, preliminary document No 4 for the tenth session, p 11.

2 In *Belgium*, see Article 4 of the Law of 17 April 1878 containing the Introductory Title of the Code of Criminal Procedure.

In the *Federal Republic of Germany*, see Article 403 *et seq* of the Code of Criminal Procedure.

In *France*, see Article 4 of the Code of Criminal Procedure.

In *Luxembourg*, any person who claims to have suffered loss or injury as a result of a crime or other wrongful act may, under Article 63 of the Code of Criminal Procedure, be joined as a civil party.

In the *Netherlands*, see Articles 332 to 337 of the Code of Criminal Procedure, and Articles 44 and 56 of the Law of Judicial Procedure, which gives jurisdiction to the justices of the peace or to the courts up to Fl 200 and 500 respectively.

3 In interpreting the 1925 Convention between Belgium and the Netherlands, the Netherlands Court of Cassation held in its judgment of 16.3.1931 (N.J. 1931, p 689) that Articles 11 and 12 did not affect orders by criminal courts to pay compensation for injury or loss suffered by a party.

4 See The Hague Conference on private international law—documents of the fourth session (May to June 1904) p 84.

5 WESER, Traité franco-belge du 8.7.1899, No 235.

IV. MATTERS EXCLUDED FROM THE SCOPE OF THE CONVENTION

The ideal solution would certainly have been to apply the Convention to all civil and commercial matters. However, the Committee did not feel able to adopt this approach, and limited the scope of the Convention to matters relating to property rights for reasons similar to those which prevailed when the Hague Convention on the recognition and enforcement of foreign judgments in civil and commercial matters was drafted, the main reason being the difficulties resulting from the absence of any overall solution to the problem of conflict of laws.

The disparity between rules of conflict of laws is particularly apparent in respect of matters not relating to property rights, since in general the intention of the parties cannot regulate matters independently of considerations of public policy.

The Committee, like the Hague Conference on private international law, preferred a formula which excluded certain matters to one which would have involved giving a positive definition of the scope of the Convention. The solution adopted implies that all litigation and all judgments relating to contractual or non-contractual obligations which do not involve the status or legal capacity of natural persons, wills or succession, rights in property arising out of a matrimonial relationship, bankruptcy or social security must fall within the scope of the Convention, and that in this respect the Convention should be interpreted as widely as possible.

However, matters falling outside the scope of the Convention do so only if they constitute the principal subject-matter of the proceedings. They are thus not excluded when they come before the court as a subsidiary matter either in the main proceedings or in preliminary proceedings.[1]

NOTES

1 BELLET, "L'élaboration d'une convention sur la reconnaissance des jugements dans le cadre du Marché commun", Clunet, 1965.

A. Status, legal capacity, rights in property arising out of a matrimonial relationship, wills, succession

Apart from the desirability of bringing the Convention into force as soon as possible, the Committee was influenced by the following considerations. Even assuming that the Committee managed to unify the rules of jurisdiction in this field, and whatever the nature of the rules selected, there was such disparity on these matters between the various systems of law, in particular regarding the rules of conflict of laws, that it would have been difficult not to re-examine the rules of jurisdiction at the enforcement stage. This in turn would have meant changing the nature of the Convention and making it much less effective. In addition, if the Committee had agreed to withdraw from the court of enforcement all powers of examination, even in matters not relating to property rights, that court would surely have been encouraged to abuse the notion of public policy, using it to refuse recognition to foreign judgments referred to it. The members of the Committee chose the lesser of the two evils, retaining the unity and effectiveness of their draft while restricting its scope. The most serious difficulty with regard to status and legal capacity is obviously that of divorce, a problem which is complicated by the extreme divergences between the various systems of law: Italian law prohibits divorce, while Belgian law not only provides for divorce by consent (Articles 223, 275 *et seq* of the Civil Code), which is unknown under the other legal systems apart from that of Luxembourg, but also, by the Law of 27 June 1960 on the admissibility of divorce when at least one of the spouses is a foreign national, incorporates provisions governing divorces by foreign nationals who ordinarily reside in Belgium.

The wording used, "status or legal capacity of natural persons", differs slightly from that adopted in the Hague Convention, which excludes from its scope judgments concerning "the status or capacity of persons or questions of family law, including personal or financial rights and obligations between parents and children or between spouses" (Article 1(1)). The reason for this is twofold. Firstly, family law in the six Member States of the Community is not a concept distinct from questions of status or capacity; secondly, the EEC Convention, unlike the Hague Convention, applies to maintenance (Article 5(2)) even where the obligation stems from the status of the persons and irrespective of whether rights and duties between spouses or between parents and children are involved.

[OJ C59, 5.3.79, p 11]

Moreover, in order to avoid differences of interpretation, Article 1 specifies that the Convention does not apply to the status or legal capacity of natural persons, thereby constituting a further distinction between this Convention and the Hague Convention, which specifies that it does not apply to judgments dealing principally with "the existence or constitution of legal persons or the powers of their organs" (Article 1(2) third indent).

With regard to matters relating to succession, the Committee concurred in the opinion of the International Union of Latin Notaries.

This body, when consulted by the Committee, considered that it was necessary, and would become increasingly so as the EEC developed in the future, to facilitate the recognition and enforcement of judgments given in matters relating to succession, and that it was therefore desirable for the six Member States to conclude a convention on the subject. However, the Union considered that it was essential first to unify the rules of conflict of laws.

As is pointed out in the Memorandum of the Permanent Bureau of the Hague Conference on private international law,[1] from which this commentary has been taken, there are fairly marked differences between the various States on matters of succession and of rights in property arising out of a matrimonial relationship.

1. As regards succession, some systems of law make provision for a portion of the estate to devolve compulsorily upon the heirs, whereas others do not. The share allocated to the surviving spouse (a question which gives rise to the greatest number of proceedings in matters of succession because of the clash of interests involved) differs enormously from country to country. Some countries place the spouse on the same footing as a surviving child, or grant him or her a certain reserved portion (Italy), while others grant the spouse only a limited life interest (for example, Belgium).

The disparities as regards rules of conflict of laws are equally marked. Some States (Germany, Italy and the Netherlands) apply to succession the national law of the *de cujus*; others (Belgium and France) refer succession to the law of the domicile as regards movable property and, as regards immovable property, to the law of the place where the property is situated; or (as in Luxembourg) refer to the law of the place where the property is situated in the case of immovable property, but subject movable property to national law.

2. As regards rights in property arising out of a matrimonial relationship, the divergences between the legal systems are even greater, ranging from joint ownership of all property (Netherlands) through joint ownership of movable property and all property acquired during wedlock (France, Belgium and Luxembourg) or joint ownership of the increase in capital value of assets (Federal Republic of Germany) to the complete separation of property (Italy).

There are also very marked divergences between the rules of conflict of laws, and this provokes positive conflicts between the systems. In some States the rules governing matrimonial property, whether laid down by law or agreed between the parties, are subject to the national law of the husband (Germany, Italy and the Netherlands); in the other States (Belgium, France, and Luxembourg) matrimonial property is subject to the rules impliedly chosen by the spouses at the time of their marriage.

Unlike the preliminary draft the Convention does not expressly exclude gifts from its scope. In this respect it follows the Hague Convention, though gifts will of course be excluded in so far as they relate to succession.

However, the Committee was of the opinion that there might possibly be grounds for resuming discussion of these problems after the Judgments Convention had entered into force, depending on the results of the work currently being done by the Hague Conference and by the International Commission on Civil Status.

It should be stressed that these matters will still be governed, temporarily at least, by existing bilateral conventions, in so far as these conventions apply (see Article 56).

NOTES

1 The Hague Conference on private international law, recognition and enforcement of foreign judgments in matters relating to property rights. Memorandum, with Annexes, by the Permanent Bureau. Preliminary document No 1 of January 1962 for the Special Committee, p 10.

B. Bankruptcy

Bankruptcy is also excluded from the scope of this Convention.

A separate Convention is currently being drafted, since the peculiarities of this branch of law require special rules.

Article 1(2) excludes bankruptcy, proceedings relating to the winding-up of insolvent companies or other legal persons, judicial arrangements, compositions and analogous proceedings, i e those proceedings which, depending on the system of law involved, are based on the suspension of payments, the insolvency of the debtor or his inability to raise credit, and which involve the judicial authorities for the purpose either of compulsory and collective liquidation of the assets or simply of supervision.

[OJ C59, 5.3.79, p 12]

Thus the Convention will cover proceedings arising from schemes of arrangement out of court, since the latter depend on the intention of the parties and are of a purely contractual nature. The insolvency of a non-trader (déconfiture civile) under French law, which does not involve organized and collective proceedings, cannot be regarded as falling within the category of "analogous proceedings" within the meaning of Article 1(2).

Proceedings relating to a bankruptcy are not necessarily excluded from the Convention. Only proceedings arising directly from the bankruptcy[1] and hence falling within the scope of the Bankruptcy Convention of the European Economic Community are excluded from the scope of the Convention.[2]

Pending the conclusion of the separate Convention covering bankruptcy, proceedings arising directly from bankruptcy will be governed by the legal rules currently in force, or by the conventions which already exist between certain Contracting States, as provided in Article 56.[3]

NOTES

1 Benelux Treaty, Article 22(4), and the report annexed thereto. The Convention between France and Belgium is interpreted in the same way. See WESER, Convention franco-belge 1899, in the Jurisclasseur de droit international, Vol 591, Nos 146 to 148.

2 A complete list of the proceedings involved will be given in the Bankruptcy Convention of the European Economic Community.

3 These are the Conventions between Belgium and France, between France and Italy, and between Belgium and the Netherlands, unless the latter convention has been abrogated by the Benelux Treaty on its entry into force.

C. Social Security

The Committee decided, like the Hague Conference,[1] to exclude social security from the scope of the Convention. The reasons were as follows.

In some countries, such as the Federal Republic of Germany, social security is a matter of public law, and in others it falls in the borderline area between private law and public law.

In some States, litigation on social security matters falls within the jurisdiction of the ordinary courts, but in others it falls within the jurisdiction of administrative tribunals; sometimes it lies within the jurisdiction of both.[2]

NOTES

1 The Hague Conference on private international law, extraordinary session. Final Act, see Article 1 of the Convention.

2 Étude de la physionomie actuelle de la sécurité sociale dans les pays de la CEE. Série politique sociale 3—1962, Services des publications des Communautés européennes. 8058/1/IX/1962/5.

The Committee was moreover anxious to allow current work within the EEC pursuant to Articles 51, 117 and 118 of the Treaty of Rome to develop independently, and to prevent any overlapping on matters of social security between the Convention and agreements already concluded, whether bilaterally or under the auspices of other international organizations such as the International Labour Organization or the Council of Europe.

Social security has not in fact hitherto given rise to conflicts of jurisdiction, since judicial jurisdiction has been taken as coinciding with legislative jurisdiction, which is determined by Community regulations adopted pursuant to Article 51 of the Treaty of Rome; however, the recovery of contributions due to social security bodies still raises problems of enforcement. This matter should therefore be the subject of a special agreement between the Six.

What is meant by social security?

Since this is a field which is in a state of constant development, it did not seem desirable to define it expressly in the Convention, nor even to indicate in an annex what this concept covers, especially as Article 117 of the Treaty of Rome states that one of the Community's objectives is the harmonization of social security systems.

Nevertheless, it should be pointed out that in the six countries benefits are paid in the circumstances listed in Convention No 102 of the International Labour Organization on minimum standards of social security, namely: medical care, sickness benefits, maternity allowances, invalidity benefits, old age and survivors' pensions, benefits for accidents at work and occupational diseases, family allowances and unemployment benefits.[3] It may also be useful to refer to the definition given in Articles 1(c) and 2 of Council Regulation No 3 on social security for migrant workers which, moreover, corresponds to that laid down in Convention No 102 of the ILO.

[OJ C59, 5.3.79, p 13]

However, the litigation on social security which is excluded from the scope of the Convention is confined to disputes arising from relationships between the administrative authorities concerned and employers or employees. On the other hand, the Convention is applicable when the authority concerned relies on a right of direct recourse against a third party responsible for injury or damage, or is subrogated as against a third party to the rights of an injured party insured by it, since, in doing so, it is acting in accordance with the ordinary legal rules.[4]

NOTES

1 The Hague Conference on private international law, extraordinary session. Final Act, see Article 1 of the Convention.

2 Étude de la physionomie actuelle de la sécurité sociale dans les pays de la CEE. Série politique sociale 3—1962, Services des publications des Communautés européennes. 8058/1/IX/1962/5.

3 Tableaux comparatifs des régimes de sécurité sociale applicables dans les États membres des Communautés européennes. Third edition, Services des publications des Communautés européennes 8122/1/VII/1964/5.

4 See Michel Voirin, note under Cass 16.2.1965, Recueil Dalloz 1965, p 723.

D. Arbitration

There are already many international agreements on arbitration. Arbitration is, of course, referred to in Article 220 of the Treaty of Rome. Moreover, the Council of Europe has prepared a European Convention providing a uniform law on arbitration, and this will probably be accompanied by a Protocol which will facilitate the recognition and enforcement of arbitral awards to an even greater extent than the New York Convention. This is why it seemed preferable to exclude arbitration. The Brussels Convention does not apply to the recognition and enforcement of arbitral awards (see the definition in Article 25); it does not apply for the purpose of determining the jurisdiction of courts and tribunals in respect of litigation relating to arbitration—for example, proceedings to set aside an arbitral award; and, finally, it does not apply to the recognition of judgments given in such proceedings.

[3037]

CHAPTER IV
JURISDICTION

A. GENERAL CONSIDERATIONS

1. Preliminary remarks

Underlying the Convention is the idea that the Member States of the European Economic Community wanted to set up a common market with characteristics similar to those of a vast internal market. Everything possible must therefore be done not only to eliminate any obstacles to the functioning of this market, but also to promote its development. From this point of view, the territory of the Contracting States may be regarded as forming a single entity: it follows, for the purpose of laying down rules on jurisdiction, that a very clear distinction can be drawn between litigants who are domiciled within the Community and those who are not.

Starting from this basic concept, Title II of the Convention makes a fundamental distinction, in particular in Section 1, between defendants who are domiciled in a Contracting State and those who are domiciled elsewhere.

1. If a person is domiciled in a Contracting State, he must in general be sued in the courts of that State in accordance with the rules of jurisdiction in force in that State (Article 2).
2. If a person is domiciled in a Contracting State, he may be sued in the courts of another Contracting State only if the courts of that State are competent by virtue of the Convention (Article 3).
3. If a person is not domiciled in a Contracting State, that is, if he is domiciled outside the Community, the rules of jurisdiction in force in each Contracting State, including those regarded as exorbitant, are applicable (Article 4).

The instances in which a person domiciled in a Contracting State may be sued in the courts of another Contracting State—or must be so sued, in cases of exclusive jurisdiction or prorogation of jurisdiction—are set out in Sections 2 to 6. Section 7, entitled "Examination as to jurisdiction … and admissibility", is mainly concerned with safeguarding the rights of the defendant.

Section 8 concerns *lis pendens* and related actions. The very precise rules of this Section are intended to prevent as far as possible conflicting judgments being given in relation to the same dispute in different States.

[OJ C59, 5.3.79, p 14]

Section 9 relates to provisional and protective measures and provides that application for these may be made to any competent court of a Contracting State, even if, under the Convention, that court does not have jurisdiction over the substance of the matter.

2. Rationale of the basic principles of Title II

The far-reaching nature of the Convention may at first seem surprising. The rules of jurisdiction which it lays down differ fundamentally from those of bilateral conventions which are based on direct jurisdiction (the Conventions between France and Belgium, and between Belgium and the Netherlands, the Benelux Treaty, the Convention between France and Switzerland) and apply not only to nationals of the Contracting States but also to any person, whatever his nationality, who is domiciled in one of those States.

The radical nature of the Convention may not only evoke surprise but also give rise to the objection that the Committee has gone beyond its terms of reference, since Article 220 of the Treaty of Rome provides that States should enter into negotiations with a view to securing "for the benefit of their nationals" the simplification of formalities governing the recognition and enforcement of judgments. The obvious answer to this is that the extension of the scope of the Convention certainly does not represent a departure from the Treaty of Rome provided the Convention ensures, for the benefit of nationals, the simplification of formalities governing the recognition and enforcement of judgments. Too strict an interpretation of the Treaty of Rome would, moreover, have led to the Convention providing for the recognition and enforcement only of those judgments given in favour of nationals of the Contracting States. Such a limitation would have considerably reduced the scope of the Convention, which would in this regard have been less effective than existing bilateral conventions.

There are several reasons for widening the scope of the Convention by extending in particular the rules of jurisdiction under Title II to all persons, whatever their nationality, who are domiciled in a Contracting State.

First, it would be a retrograde step if common rules of jurisdiction were to be dependent on the nationality of the parties; the connecting factor in international procedure is usually the domicile or residence of the parties (see, for example, Article 3(1) and (2) of the Hague Convention of 15 April 1958 concerning the recognition and enforcement of decisions relating to maintenance obligations towards children; the Hague Convention of 15 April 1958 on the jurisdiction of the contractual forum in matters relating to the international sale of goods; Article 11 of the Benelux Treaty; and Article 10(1) of the Hague Convention on the recognition and enforcement of foreign judgments in civil and commercial matters).

Next, the adoption of common rules based on nationality would have caused numerous difficulties in applying the Convention. This method would have necessitated the introduction of different rules of jurisdiction depending on whether the litigation involved nationals of Contracting States, a national of a Contracting State and a foreign national, or two foreign nationals.

In some situations the rules of jurisdiction of the Convention would have had to be applied; in others, national rules of jurisdiction. Under this system the court would, at the commencement of proceedings, automatically have had to carry out an examination of the nationality of the parties, and it is not difficult to imagine the practical problems involved in, for example, establishing the nationality of a defendant who has failed to enter an appearance.

If the Convention had adopted the nationality of the parties as a connecting factor, it might well have been necessary to introduce a special provision to deal with the relatively frequent cases of dual nationality.

The Convention would thus have had to solve many problems which do not strictly speaking fall within its scope. Using nationality as a criterion would inevitably have led to a considerable increase in the effect of those rules of jurisdiction which may be termed exorbitant. Thus, for example, a judgment given in France or Luxembourg on the basis of Article 14 of the Civil Code in an action between a national of France or Luxembourg and a national of a non-Member State of the Community would have had to be recognized and enforced in Germany even if the foreign national was domiciled in Germany and a generally recognized jurisdiction, that of the defendant's domicile, thus existed.

By ruling out the criterion of nationality, the Committee is anxious not only to simplify the application of the Convention by giving it a unity which allows a uniform interpretation, but also, in fairness, to allow foreign nationals domiciled in the Community, who are established there and who thereby contribute to its economic activity and prosperity, to benefit from the provisions of the Convention.

[OJ C59, 5.3.79, p 15]

Moreover, the purpose of the Convention is also, by establishing common rules of jurisdiction, to achieve, in relations between the Six and in the field which it was required to cover, a genuine legal systematization which will ensure the greatest possible degree of legal certainty. To this end, the rules of jurisdiction codified in Title II determine which State's courts are most appropriate to assume jurisdiction, taking into account all relevant matters; the approach here adopted means that the nationality of the parties is no longer of importance.

3. Determination of domicile

As already shown, the rules of jurisdiction are based on the defendant's domicile. Determining that domicile is therefore a matter of the greatest importance.

The Committee was faced with numerous questions which proved difficult to resolve. Should the Convention include a common definition of domicile? Should domicile possibly be replaced by the concept of habitual residence? Should both domicile and habitual residence be used? Should the term domicile be qualified?

1. Should the Convention include a common definition of domicile?

The first point to note is that the concept of domicile is not defined in the Conventions between France and Belgium, Belgium and the Netherlands, Germany and Belgium, and Italy and Belgium, nor in the Benelux Treaty.

It is, however, defined in the Conventions between France and Italy (Article 28), between Italy and the Netherlands (Article 11), and between Germany and Italy (Article 13); but these Conventions are all based on indirect jurisdiction.

At first, the Committee thought of defining domicile in the Convention itself, but it finally rejected this course of action. Such a definition would have fallen outside the scope of the Convention, and properly belongs in a uniform law.[1] To define the concept of domicile in international conventions might even be dangerous, as this could lead to a multiplicity of definitions and so to inconsistency.

Moreover, such definitions run the risk of being superseded by developments in national law.

NOTES

1 The concept of domicile has been specified by the European Committee for Legal Cooperation, set up by the Council of Europe, as one of the basic legal concepts which should be defined.

2. Should domicile be replaced by habitual residence?

This course was similarly rejected. It was pointed out that the term "habitual" was open to conflicting interpretations, since the laws of some of the Member States provide that an entry in the population registers is conclusive proof of habitual residence.

The adoption of this course would, moreover, represent a divergence from that followed under the laws of the Contracting States, the majority of which use domicile as a basis of jurisdiction.[1]
[OJ C59, 5.3.79, p 16]

Adopting habitual residence as the sole criterion would have raised new problems as regards jurisdiction over persons whose domicile depends or may depend on that of another person or on the location of an authority (e g minors or married women).

Finally, in a treaty based on direct jurisdiction, it is particularly important that jurisdiction should have a secure legal basis for the court seised of the matter. The concept of domicile, while not without drawbacks, does however introduce the idea of a more fixed and stable place of establishment on the part of the defendant than does the concept of habitual residence.

NOTES

1 *Belgium*
Law of 25 March 1876 containing Title I of the Introductory Book of the Code of Civil Procedure.
Article 39: Except in the case of amendments and exceptions provided for under the law, the court of the defendant's domicile shall be the only court having jurisdiction.
Judicial Code:
Article 624: Except in cases where the law expressly determines the court having jurisdiction a plaintiff may institute proceedings:
1. in the court of the domicile of the defendant or one of the defendants.
Federal Republic of Germany
Code of Civil Procedure, Article 13: A person shall in general be subject to the jurisdiction of the courts of his domicile.
France
Code of Civil Procedure, Article 59(1): In actions in personam, the defendant shall be sued in the court of his domicile or, where he has no domicile, in the court of his place of residence.

Italy
Code of Civil Procedure, Article 18: Except where the law otherwise provides, the competent court shall be the court for the place where the defendant has his habitual residence or his domicile or, where these are not known, the court for the place where the defendant is resident.
Luxembourg
Article 59 of the Code of Civil Procedure corresponds to Article 59 of the French Code of Civil Procedure.
Netherlands
Code of Civil Procedure, Article 126:
1. In actions *in personam* or actions relating to movable property, the defendant shall be sued in the court of his domicile.

3. Should both domicile and habitual residence be adopted?

In a treaty based on direct jurisdiction, the inclusion of both criteria would result in the major disadvantage that the number of competent courts would be increased. If the domicile and the place of habitual residence happened to be in different States, national rules of jurisdiction of both the States concerned would be applicable by virtue of Article 2 of the Convention, thus defeating the object of the Convention. Moreover, the inclusion of both criteria could increase the number of cases of *lis pendens* and related actions. For these reasons, the Committee preferred finally to adopt only the concept of domicile.

4. Should the concept of domicile be qualified?

In view of the varied interpretations of the concept of domicile, the Committee considered that the implementation of the Convention would be facilitated by the inclusion of a provision specifying the law to be applied in determining domicile. The absence of such a provision might give rise to claims and disclaimers of jurisdiction; the purpose of Article 52 is to avoid this.

Article 52 deals with three different situations:
(i) where the court of a Contracting State must determine whether a person is domiciled in that State;
(ii) where the court must determine whether a person is domiciled in another Contracting State; and finally,
(iii) where the court must determine whether a person's domicile depends on that of another person or on the seat of an authority.

Article 52 does not deal with the case of a person domiciled outside the Community. In this case the court seised of the matter must apply its rules of private international law.

Nor does Article 52 attempt to resolve the conflicts which might arise if a court seised of a matter ruled that a defendant were to be considered as having his domicile in two other Contracting States, or in one Contracting State and a third country. According to the basic principles of Title II the court, having found that a person is domiciled in some other Contracting State, must, in order to determine its own jurisdiction, apply the rules set out in Article 3 and in Sections 2 to 6 of the Convention.

In most disputed cases it will be necessary to determine where the defendant is domiciled. However, when applying certain provisions of the Convention, in particular Article 5(2) and the first paragraph of Article 8, the rules set out will be used to determine the plaintiff's domicile. For this reason Article 52 does not specify either the defendant or the plaintiff since, in the opinion of the Committee, the same provisions for determining domicile must apply to both parties.

Under the first paragraph of Article 52, only the internal law of the court seised of the matter can determine whether a domicile exists in that State. It follows that, if there is a conflict between the *lex fori* and the law of another Contracting State when determining the domicile of a party, the *lex fori* prevails. For example, if a defendant sued in a French court is domiciled both in France, because he has his principal place of business there, and in Belgium, because his name is entered there in the official population registers, where the laws conflict the French court must apply only French law. If it is established under that law that the defendant is in fact domiciled in France, the court need take no other law into consideration. This is justified on various grounds. First, to take the example given, a defendant, by establishing his domicile in a given country, subjects himself to the law of that country. Next, only if the *lex fori* prevails can the court examine whether it has jurisdiction; as the Convention requires it to do, in cases where the defendant fails to enter an appearance (Article 20).

Where the courts of different Contracting States are properly seised of a matter—for example, the Belgian court because it is the court for the place where the defendant's name is entered in the population registers, and the French court because it is the court for the place where he has his principal place of business—the conflict may be resolved by applying the rules governing *lis pendens* or related actions.

[OJ C59, 5.3.79, p 17]

The second paragraph covers the case of a defendant who is not domiciled in the State whose courts are seised of the matter. The court must then determine whether he is domiciled in another Contracting State, and to do this the internal law of that other State must be applied.

This rule will be applied in particular where a defendant is sued in the courts of a Contracting State in which he is not domiciled. If the jurisdiction of the court is contested, then, following the basic principles of Title II, whether or not the court has jurisdiction will vary according to whether the defendant is domiciled in another Contracting State or outside the Community. Thus, for example, a person domiciled outside the Community may properly be sued in Belgium in the court for the place where the contract was concluded[1] while a person domiciled in another Contracting State and sued in the same court may refuse to accept its jurisdiction, since Article 5(1) of the Convention provides that only the courts for the place of performance of the obligation in question have jurisdiction. Thus if a defendant wishes to contest the jurisdiction of the Belgian court, he must establish that he is domiciled in a Contracting State.

Under the second paragraph of Article 52 the Belgian court must, in order to determine whether the defendant is domiciled in another Contracting State, apply the internal law of that State.

The Committee considered it both more equitable and more logical to apply the law of the State of the purported domicile rather than the *lex fori*.

If a court, seised of a matter in which the defendant was domiciled in another Contracting State, applied its own law to determine the defendant's domicile, the defendant might under that law not be regarded as being domiciled in the other Contracting State even though under the law of that other State he was in fact domiciled there. This solution becomes all the more untenable when one realises that a person establishing his domicile in a Contracting State can obviously not be expected to consider whether this domicile is regarded as such under a foreign law.[2]

On the other hand, where the law of the State of the purported domicile has two definitions of domicile,[3] that of the Civil Code and that of the Code of Civil Procedure, the latter should obviously be used since the problem is one of jurisdiction.

The third principle laid down by Article 52 concerns persons such as minors or married women whose domicile depends on that of another person or on the seat of an authority.

Under this provision national law is applied twice. For example, the national law of a minor first determines whether his domicile is dependent on that of another person. If it is, the national law of the minor similarly determines where that domicile is situated (e g where his guardian is domiciled). If, however, the domicile of the dependent person is under his national law not dependent on that of another person or on the seat of an authority, the first or second paragraph of Article 52 may be applied to determine the domicile of the dependent person. These two paragraphs also apply for the purpose of determining the domicile from which that of the dependent person derives.

The members of the Committee were alive to the difficulties which may arise in the event of dual nationality, and more especially in determining the domicile of a married woman. For example, where a German woman marries a Frenchman and acquires French nationality while retaining her German nationality, her domicile under French law[4] is that of her husband, whereas under German law she can have a separate domicile, since German law no longer provides that a married woman has the domicile of her husband.[5] In cases of this kind, the Committee considered that the usual rules relating to dual nationality should be applied. Thus, even if she has a separate domicile in Germany, that person may be sued in France in the court for the husband's domicile, since the French court must apply French law. If, however, she is sued in Germany in the court for the place of her own domicile, the German court will apply German law and declare that it has jurisdiction.

[OJ C59, 5.3.79, p 18]

Finally, it should be made clear that the concept of domicile within the meaning of the Convention does not extend to the legal fiction of an address for service of process.

NOTES

1 See Article 634 of the Judicial Code and Article 4 of the Convention.

2 NIBOYET, Traité de droit international privé français, Vol. VI, No 1723: "It is submitted that domicile is not systematically determined according to the *lex fori*, but according to the law of the country where the domicile is alleged to be. French law alone can therefore determine whether a person is domiciled in France, but whether a person is domiciled in any particular foreign country is a matter, not for French law, but for the law of the country concerned."

3 Such might for example be the case in Belgium, where Article 102 of the Civil Code provides that the domicile of a Belgian in so far as the exercise of his civil rights is concerned is where he has his principal establishment, while Article 36 of the Judicial Code provides that, for the purpose of that Code, a person is deemed to be domiciled in the place where his name is entered in the official population registers.

4 French Civil Code, Article 108: "A married woman has no domicile other than that of her husband."

5 BGB, Article 10, repealed by the Gleichberechtigungsgesetz (Law on equal rights of men and women in the field of civil law) of 18 June 1957.

B. COMMENTARY ON THE SECTIONS OF TITLE II

Section 1
General Provisions

Section 1 sets out the main principles on which the rules of jurisdiction laid down by the Convention are founded:

1. the rule that a defendant domiciled in a Contracting State is in general to be sued in the courts of that State (Article 2);
2. the rule that a person domiciled in a Contracting State may in certain circumstances be sued in the courts of another Contracting State (Article 3);
3. the rule that a person domiciled outside the Community is subject to all applicable national rules of jurisdiction (Article 4).

This Section also embodies the widely applied principle of equality of treatment,[1] which is already enshrined in Article 1 of the Convention between France and Belgium of 8 July 1899, Article 1 of the Convention between Belgium and the Netherlands of 28 March 1925 and Article 1 of the Benelux Treaty of 24 November 1961. Whilst this principle thus forms an integral part of treaties based on direct jurisdiction, in this Convention it also ensures implementation of the mandatory rules of the Treaty of Rome. Article 7 of that Treaty lays down the principle of non-discrimination between nationals of Member States of the Community.

Specific provisions applying the general principle set out in Article 7 of the Treaty of Rome to the right of establishment are laid down in Article 52 *et seq* of that Treaty.

During the preparation of the General Programme on establishment, the Economic and Social Committee of the European Communities drew particular attention to this aspect of the problem by requesting that equality of treatment as regards legal protection be achieved in full as quickly as possible.

NOTES

1 WESER, Revue critique de droit international privé, 1960, pp 29–35.

Article 2

The maxim "*actor sequitur forum rei*", which expresses the fact that law leans in favour of the defendant, is even more relevant in the international sphere than it is in national law.[1] It is more difficult, generally speaking, to defend oneself in the courts of a foreign country than in those of another town in the country where one is domiciled.

A defendant domiciled in a Contracting State need not necessarily be sued in the court for the place where he is domiciled or has his seat. He may be sued in any court of the State where he is domiciled which has jurisdiction under the law of that State.

As a result, if a defendant is sued in one of the courts of the State in which he is domiciled, the internal rules of jurisdiction of that State are fully applicable. Here the Convention requires the application of the national law of the court seised of the matter; the Convention determines whether the courts of the State in question have jurisdiction, and the law of that State in turn determines whether a particular court in that State has jurisdiction. This solution

PART IV
EC MATERIALS

seems equitable since it is usual for a defendant domiciled in a State to be subject to the internal law of that State without it being necessary for the Convention to provide special rules for his protection. It is, moreover, an extremely practical solution because it means that in most cases the court will not have to take the Convention any further into consideration.

[OJ C59, 5.3.79, p 19]

Defendants are usually sued in the courts of the State in which they are domiciled. This is true of proceedings in which there is no international element. It is also true of proceedings with an international element in which, by application of the traditionally accepted maxim "*actor sequitur forum rei*", the defendant is sued in the courts of the State of his domicile. The Convention does not therefore involve a general reversal of national rules of jurisdiction nor of the practice of judges and lawyers. In fact, judges and lawyers will need to take account of the changes effected by the Convention only in cases where a defendant is sued in a court of a State where he is not domiciled, or in one of the few cases in which the Convention has laid down common rules of exclusive jurisdiction.

The second paragraph of Article 2 embodies the principle of equality of treatment where a foreigner is domiciled in the State of the forum. Such foreigner, whether he is defendant or plaintiff, is governed in that State by the same rules of jurisdiction as its nationals, or more precisely, as its nationals who are domiciled in that State, where, as in Italy, the law of that State determines the jurisdiction of its courts according to whether the national concerned is domiciled in its territory.

As a result, Article 52 of the Belgian Law of 25 March 1876 will no longer be applicable as such to foreigners domiciled in Belgium.[2]

The positive aspect of equality of treatment is set out in the second paragraph of Article 4.

NOTES

1 See report by Professor FRAGISTAS—Hague Convention on private international law—preliminary doc No 4, May 1964, for the tenth session.

2 This Article provides, in particular, that foreigners who are domiciled or resident in Belgium may be sued before the court of the Kingdom either by a Belgian or by a foreigner.

Article 3

Article 3 deals with those cases in which a defendant domiciled in a Contracting State may be sued in another Contracting State. This Article lays down the principle that a defendant may be sued otherwise than in the courts of the State where he is domiciled only in the cases expressly provided for in the Convention. The rule sets aside the rules of exorbitant jurisdiction in force in each of the Contracting States. However, these rules of jurisdiction are not totally excluded; they are excluded only in respect of persons who are domiciled in another Contracting State. Thus they remain in force with respect to persons who are not domiciled within the Community.

The second paragraph of Article 3 prohibits the application of the most important and best known of the rules of exorbitant jurisdiction. While this paragraph is not absolutely essential it will nevertheless facilitate the application of certain provisions of the Convention (see, in particular, Article 59).

The following are the rules of exorbitant jurisdiction in question in each of the States concerned.

In Belgium

Articles 52, 52bis and 53 of the Law of 25 March 1876, which govern territorial jurisdiction in actions brought by Belgians[1] or by foreigners against foreigners before Belgian courts, and Article 15 of the Civil Code which corresponds to Article 15 of the French Civil Code.

NOTES

1 Répertoire pratique du droit belge, under "compétence"—No 17518 *et seq*—(see Judicial Code, Articles 635, 637 and 638).

In Germany

The nationality of the parties does not in general affect the rules of jurisdiction. Article 23 of the Code of Civil Procedure lays down that, where no other German court has jurisdiction, actions relating to property instituted against a person who is not domiciled in the national territory come under the jurisdiction of the court for the place where the property or subject of the dispute is situated.

German courts have in a number of cases given a very liberal interpretation to this provision, thereby leading some authors to state that Article 23 "can be likened to Article 14 of the French Civil Code".[1]

NOTES

[1] WESER, Revue critique de droit international privé, 1959, p 636; ROSENBURG, Lehrbuch des deutschen Zivilprozeßrechts, ninth edition, paragraph 35 I 3.

In France

1. Article 14 of the Civil Code provides that any French plaintiff may sue a foreigner or another Frenchman in the French courts, even if there is no connection between the cause of action and those courts.

[OJ C59, 5.3.79, p 20]

2. Article 15 of the Civil Code provides that a Frenchman may always be sued in the French courts by a Frenchman or by a foreigner, and can even insist on this.

Despite the fact that Articles 14 and 15 in terms refer only to contractual obligations, case law has extended their scope beyond contractual obligations to all actions whether or not relating to property rights. There are thus only two limitations to the general application of Articles 14 and 15: French courts are never competent to hear either actions *in rem* concerning immovable property situated abroad, or actions concerning proceedings for enforcement which is to take place abroad.[1]

NOTES

[1] BATIFFOL, *op cit*, No 684 *et seq.*

In Italy

1. Article 2 of the Code of Civil Procedure provides that an agreement to substitute for the jurisdiction of Italian courts the jurisdiction of a foreign court or arbitral tribunal will be valid only in the case of litigation between foreigners, or between a foreigner and an Italian citizen who is neither resident nor domiciled in Italy, and only if the agreement is evidenced in writing.

2.—

(a) Under Article 4(1) of the Code of Civil Procedure, a foreigner may be sued in an Italian court if he is resident or domiciled in Italy, or if he has an address for service there or has a representative who is authorized to bring legal proceedings in his name, or if he has accepted Italian jurisdiction, unless the proceedings concern immovable property situated abroad.

(b) Under Article 4(2) of the Code of Civil Procedure, a foreigner may be sued in the courts of the Italian Republic if the proceedings concern property situated in Italy, or succession to the estate of an Italian national, or an application for probate made in Italy, or obligations which arose in Italy or which must be performed there.

3. The interpretation given to Article 4 by Italian case law means that an Italian defendant may always be sued in the Italian courts.[1]

NOTES

[1] MORELLI, Diritto processuale civile internazionale, pp 108–112.

In Luxembourg

Articles 14 and 15 of the Civil Code correspond to Articles 14 and 15 of the French Civil Code.

Luxembourg case law applies the same principles of interpretation as French case law.

In the Netherlands

Article 126(3) of the Code of Civil Procedure provides that, in personal matters or matters concerning movable property, a defendant who has no known domicile or residence in the Kingdom shall be sued in the court for the domicile of the plaintiff. This provision applies whether or not the plaintiff is a Netherlands national.[1]

Article 127 provides that a foreigner, even if he does not reside in the Netherlands, may be sued in a Netherlands court for the performance of obligations contracted towards a Netherlander either in the Netherlands or abroad.

NOTES

1 WESER, Revue critique de droit international privé, 1959, p 632.

Article 4

Article 4 applies to all proceedings in which the defendant is not domiciled in a Contracting State, and provides that the rules of internal law remain in force.

This is justified on two grounds:

First, in order to ensure the free movement of judgments, this Article prevents refusal of recognition or enforcement of a judgment given on the basis of rules of internal law relating to jurisdiction. In the absence of such a provision, a judgment debtor would be able to prevent execution being levied on his property simply by transferring it to a Community country other than that in which judgment was given.

Secondly, this Article may perform a function in the case of *lis pendens*. Thus, for example, if a French court is seised of an action between a Frenchman and a defendant domiciled in America, and a German court is seised of the same matter on the basis of Article 23 of the Code of Civil Procedure, one of the two courts must in the interests of the proper administration of justice decline jurisdiction in favour of the other. This issue cannot be settled unless the jurisdiction of these courts derives from the Convention.

[OJ C59, 5.3.79, p 21]

In the absence of an article such as Article 4, there would be no rule in the Convention expressly recognizing the jurisdiction of the French and German courts in a case of this kind.

The only exception to the application of the rules of jurisdiction of internal law is the field of exclusive jurisdiction (Article 16).[1] The rules which grant exclusive jurisdiction to the courts of a State are applicable whatever the domicile of the defendant.

However, the question arises why the Committee did not extend the scope of the provision limiting the application of rules of exorbitant jurisdiction to include in particular nationals of Member States regardless of their place of domicile.

In other words, and to take another example based on Article 14 of the French Civil Code, why will it still be possible for a French plaintiff to sue in the French courts a foreigner, or even a national of a Member State of the Community, who is domiciled outside the Community?

The Committee thought that it would have been unreasonable to prevent the rules of exorbitant jurisdiction from applying to persons, including Community nationals, domiciled outside the Community. Thus, for example, a Belgian national domiciled outside the Community might own assets in the Netherlands. The Netherlands courts have no jurisdiction in the matter since the Convention does not recognize jurisdiction based on the presence of assets within a State. If Article 14 of the French Civil Code could not be applied, a French plaintiff would have to sue the Belgian defendant in a court outside the Community, and the judgment could not be enforced in the Netherlands if there were no enforcement treaty between the Netherlands and the non-member State in which judgment was given.

This, moreover, was the solution adopted in the Conventions between France and Belgium, and between Belgium and the Netherlands, and in the Benelux Treaty, which, however, take nationality as their criterion.[2]

The second paragraph of Article 4 of the Convention constitutes a positive statement of the principle of equality of treatment already laid down in the second paragraph of Article 2. An express provision was considered necessary in order to avoid any uncertainty.[3] Under this provision, any person domiciled in a Contracting State has the right, as plaintiff, to avail himself in that State of the same rules of jurisdiction as a national of that State.

This principle had already been expressly laid down in the Convention between France and Belgium of 8 July 1899 (Article 1(2)).

This positive aspect of the principle of equality of treatment was regarded as complementing the right of establishment (Article 52 *et seq* of the Treaty of Rome), the existence of which implies, as was stated in the General Programme for the abolition of restrictions on freedom of establishment of 18 December 1961,[4] that any natural or legal person established in a Member State should enjoy the same legal protection as a national of that State.

The provision is also justified on economic grounds. Since rules of exorbitant jurisdiction can still be invoked against foreigners domiciled outside the European Economic Community, persons who are domiciled in the Member State concerned and who thus contribute to the economic life of the Community should be able to invoke such rules in the same way as the nationals of that State.

It may be thought surprising that the Convention extends the "privileges of jurisdiction" in this way, since equality of treatment is granted in each of the States to all persons, whatever their nationality, who are domiciled in that State.

[OJ C59, 5.3.79, p 22]

It should first be noted that such treatment is already granted to foreigners in Belgium, the Federal Republic of Germany, Italy and the Netherlands, where the rules of exorbitant jurisdiction may be invoked by foreigners as well as by nationals. The second paragraph of Article 4 therefore merely brings into line with these laws the French and Luxembourg concepts, according to which Article 14 of the Civil Code constitutes a privilege of nationality.

Secondly, the solution adopted in the Convention follows quite naturally from the fact that, for the reasons already given, the Convention uses domicile as the criterion for determining jurisdiction. In this context it must not be forgotten that it will no longer be possible to invoke the privileges of jurisdiction against persons domiciled in the Community, although it will be possible to invoke them against nationals of the Community countries who have established their domicile outside the territory of the Six.

NOTES

1. The third paragraph of Article 8, which concerns jurisdiction in respect of insurers who are not domiciled in the Community but have a branch or agency there, may also be regarded as an exception.
2. The Convention between France and Belgium is interpreted to mean that a Frenchman may not rely on Article 14 of the Civil Code to sue in France a Belgian domiciled in Belgium, but may do so to sue a Belgian domiciled abroad. BATIFFOL, Traité élémentaire de droit international privé, No 714.
3. According to French case law on the Treaty of 9 February 1842 between France and Denmark, a Danish national may not rely on Article 14 of the French Civil Code.
4. *Official Journal of the European Communities*, 15.1.1962, p 36 *et seq.*

Section 2
Special jurisdiction

Articles 5 and 6

Articles 5 and 6 list the situations in which a defendant may be sued in a Contracting State other than that of his domicile. The forums provided for in these Articles supplement those which apply under Article 2. In the case of proceedings for which a court is specifically recognized as having jurisdiction under these Articles, the plaintiff may, at his option, bring the proceedings either in that court or in the competent courts of the State in which the defendant is domiciled.

One problem which arose here was whether it should always be possible to sue the defendant in one of the courts provided for in these Articles, or whether this should be allowed only if the jurisdiction of that court was also recognized by the internal law of the State concerned.

In other words, in the first case, jurisdiction would derive directly from the Convention and in the second there would need to be dual jurisdiction: that of the Convention and that of the internal law on local jurisdiction. Thus, for example, where Netherlands law on jurisdiction does not recognize the court for the place of performance of the obligation, can the plaintiff nevertheless sue the defendant before that court in the Netherlands? In addition, would there be any obligation on the Netherlands to adapt its national laws in order to give that court jurisdiction?

By adopting "special" rules of jurisdiction, that is by directly designating the competent court without referring to the rules of jurisdiction in force in the State where such a court might be situated, the Committee decided that a plaintiff should always be able to sue a defendant in one of the forums provided for without having to take the internal law of the State concerned into consideration. Further, in laying down these rules, the Committee intended to facilitate implementation of the Convention. By ratifying the Convention, the Contracting States will avoid having to take any other measures to adapt their internal legislation to the criteria laid down in Articles 5 and 6. The Convention itself determines which court has jurisdiction.

Adoption of the "special" rules of jurisdiction is also justified by the fact that there must be a close connecting factor between the dispute and the court with jurisdiction to resolve it. Thus, to take the example of the *forum delicti commissi*, a person domiciled in a Contracting State other than the Netherlands who has caused an accident in The Hague may, under the Convention, be sued in a court in The Hague. This accident cannot give other Netherlands courts jurisdiction over the defendant. On this point there is thus a distinct difference between Article 2 and Articles 5 and 6, due to the fact that in Article 2 domicile is the connecting factor.

Forum contractus (Article 5(1)) including contracts of employment

There are great differences between the laws of the Six in their attitude to the jurisdiction of the *forum contractus*; in some countries this jurisdiction is not recognized (the Netherlands, Luxembourg), while in others it exists in varying degrees. Belgian law recognizes the jurisdiction of the courts for the place where the obligation arose, and also that of the courts for the place where the obligation has been or is to be performed;[1] Italian law recognizes only the jurisdiction of the courts for the place where the obligation arose and where it has been performed;[2] German law in general recognizes only the jurisdiction of the courts for the place where the obligation has been performed;[3] and, finally. French law recognizes the jurisdiction of the *forum contractus* only to a limited extent and subject to certain conditions.[4]

[OJ C59, 5.3.79, p 23]

Some of the conventions concluded between the Six reject this forum, while others accept it in varying degrees. Article 2(1) of the Convention between *France and Belgium* provides that, where a defendant is neither domiciled nor resident in France or Belgium, a Belgian or French plaintiff may institute proceedings in the courts for the place where the obligation arose or where it has been or is to be performed.[5]

Article 4 of the Convention between *Belgium and the Netherlands* provides that in civil or commercial matters a plaintiff may bring a personal action concerning movable property in the courts for the place where the obligation arose or where it has been or is to be performed.

In Article 3(5) of the Convention between *Belgium and Germany*, jurisdiction is recognized where, in matters relating to a contract, proceedings are instituted in a court of the State where the obligation has been or is to be performed.

Article 14 of the Convention between *France and Italy* provides that if the action concerns a contract which is considered as a commercial matter by the law of the country in which the action is brought, a French or Italian plaintiff may seise the courts of either of the two countries in which the contract was concluded or is to be performed.

The Convention between *Belgium and Italy* (Article 2(5)) recognizes jurisdiction where, in matters relating to a contract, an action is brought before the courts of the State where the obligation arose, or where it has been or should have been performed.

There are no provisions on this subject in the Conventions between *Italy and the Netherlands, Germany and Italy*, and *Germany and the Netherlands*.

Finally, the Benelux Treaty adopts Article 4 of the Convention between Belgium and the Netherlands, but includes a Protocol which in Article 1 lays down that Article 4 shall not apply where Luxembourg is concerned if the defendant is domiciled or resident in the country of which he is a national.[6]

Article 5(1) provides a compromise between the various national laws.

The jurisdiction of the forum is, as in German law, limited to matters relating to contract. It could have been restricted to commercial matters, but account must be taken of the fact that European integration will mean an increase in the number of contractual relationships entered into. To have confined it to commercial matters would moreover have raised the problem of classification.

Only the jurisdiction of the *forum solutionis* has been retained, that is to say the jurisdiction of the courts for the place of performance of the obligation on which the claim is based. The reasons for this are as follows.

The Committee considered that it would be unwise to give jurisdiction to a number of courts, and thus possibly create conflicts of jurisdiction. A plaintiff already has a choice, in matters relating to a contract, between the competent courts of the State where the defendant is domiciled, or, where there is more than one defendant, the courts for the place where any one of them is domiciled, or finally, the courts for the place of performance of the obligation in question.

If the Committee had adopted as wide-ranging a provision as that of the Benelux Treaty, which recognizes also the jurisdiction of the courts for the place where the obligation arose, this would have involved very considerable changes for those States whose laws do not recognize that forum, or do so only with certain restrictions.

There was also concern that acceptance of the jurisdiction of the courts for the place where the obligation arose might sanction, by indirect means, the jurisdiction of the forum of the plaintiff. To have accepted this forum would have created tremendous problems of classification, in particular in the case of contracts concluded by parties who are absent.

The court for the place of performance of the obligation will be useful in proceedings for the recovery of fees: the creditor will have a choice between the courts of the State where the defendant is domiciled and the courts of another State within whose jurisdiction the services were provided, particularly where, according to the appropriate law, the obligation to pay must be performed where the services were provided. This forum can also be used where expert evidence or inquiries are required. The special position of Luxembourg justified, as in the Benelux Treaty, the inclusion of a special provision in the Protocol (Article I).

[OJ C59, 5.3.79, p 24]

NOTES

1 Articles 41 and 52 of the Law of 25 March 1876, Article 624 of the Judicial Code.

2 Articles 4 and 20 of the Code of Civil Procedure.

3 Article 29 of the Code of Civil Procedure.

4 Articles 59(3) and 420 of the Code of Civil Procedure.

5 On the serious controversy to which this Article has given rise, see WESER, Traité franco-belge du 8 juillet 1899. Étude critique, p 63 *et seq*; also Jurisclasseur de droit international, vol 591, Nos 42 and 45.

6 For the reasons for this limitation, see the report on the negotiations.

Contracts of employment

In matters relating to contracts of employment in the broadest sense of the term, the preliminary draft of the Convention contained a provision attributing exclusive jurisdiction to the courts of the Contracting State either in which the undertaking concerned was situated, or in which the work was to have been or had been performed. After prolonged consideration, the Committee decided not to insert in the Convention any special provisions on jurisdiction in this field. Its reasoning was as follows.

First, work is at present in progress within the Commission of the EEC to harmonize the provisions of labour law in the Member States. It is desirable that disputes over contracts of employment should as far as possible be brought before the courts of the State whose law governs the contract. The Committee therefore did not think that rules of jurisdiction should be laid down which might not coincide with those which may later be adopted for determining the applicable law.

In order to lay down such rules of jurisdiction, the Committee would have had to take into account not only the different ways in which work can be carried out abroad, but also the various categories of worker: wage-earning or salaried workers recruited abroad to work permanently for an undertaking, or those temporarily transferred abroad by an undertaking to work for it there; commercial agents, management, etc. Any attempt by the Committee to draw such distinctions might have provided a further hindrance to the Commission's work.

Next, in most Member States of the Community the principle of freedom of contract still plays an important part; a rule of exclusive jurisdiction such as that previously provided for in Article 16 would have nullified any agreements conferring jurisdiction.

The general rules of the Convention will therefore apply to contracts of employment. Thus, in litigation between employers and employees, the following courts have jurisdiction: the courts of the State where the defendant is domiciled (Article 2); the courts for the place of performance of the obligation, if that place is in a State other than that of the domicile of the defendant (Article 5(1)); and any court on which the parties have expressly or impliedly agreed (Articles 17 and 18). In the case of proceedings based on a tort committed at work (Article 2, Nos 2 and 3 of the Arbeitsgerichtsgesetz), Article 5(3), which provides for the jurisdiction of the courts for the place where the harmful event occurred, could also apply. It seems that these rules will, for the time being, prove of greater value to the persons concerned than a provision similar to that of the former Article 16(2), which could not be derogated from because it prohibited any agreement conferring jurisdiction.

The rules on the recognition and enforcement of judgments will probably ensure additional protection for employees. If the law of the State addressed had to be applied to a contract of employment, the courts of that State, upon being seised of an application for recognition or enforcement of a foreign judgment, would, on the basis of Article 27(1), which permits refusal of recognition (or enforcement) on grounds of public policy in the State addressed, be able to refuse the application if the court of the State of origin had failed to apply, or had misapplied, an essential provision of the law of the State addressed.

Once the work of the Commission in this field has been completed, it will always be possible to amend the provisions of the Convention, either by means of an additional Protocol, or by the drafting of a convention governing the whole range of problems relating to contracts of employment, which would, under Article 57, prevail over the Convention.

Maintenance obligations (Article 5(2))

Matters relating to maintenance are governed by the Convention.

The Convention is in a sense an extension of the Hague Convention of 15 April 1958 concerning the recognition and enforcement of decisions relating to maintenance obligations in respect of children,[1] since it ensures the recognition and enforcement of judgments granting maintenance to creditors other than children, and also of the New York Convention of 20 June 1956 on the recovery abroad of maintenance.[2]

[OJ C59, 5.3.79, p 25]

The Committee decided that jurisdiction should be conferred on the forum of the creditor, for the same reasons as the draftsmen of the Hague Convention.[3] For one thing, a convention which did not recognize the forum of the maintenance creditor would be of only limited value, since the creditor would be obliged to bring the claim before the court having jurisdiction over the defendant.

If the Convention did not confer jurisdiction on the forum of the maintenance creditor, it would apply only in those situations where the defendant against whom an order had been made subsequently changed residence, or where the defendant possessed property in a country other than that in which the order was made.

Moreover the court for the place of domicile of the maintenance creditor is in the best position to know whether the creditor is in need and to determine the extent of such need.

However, in order to align the Convention with the Hague Convention, Article 5(2) also confers jurisdiction on the courts for the place of habitual residence of the maintenance creditor. This alternative is justified in relation to maintenance obligations since it enables in particular a wife deserted by her husband to sue him for payment of maintenance in the courts for the place where she herself is habitually resident, rather than the place of her legal domicile.

The Convention also supplements the New York Convention of 20 June 1956 on the recovery abroad of maintenance. The latter is limited to providing that a forwarding authority will transmit to an intermediate body any judgment already given in favour of a maintenance creditor, and that body will then have to begin proceedings for enforcement or registration of the judgment, or institute new proceedings altogether.

This Convention, by simplifying the formalities governing enforcement, will thus facilitate implementation of the New York Convention.

As regards maintenance payments, the Committee did not overlook the problems which might be raised by preliminary issues (for example, the question of affiliation). However, it considered that these were not properly problems of jurisdiction, and that any difficulties should be considered in the chapter on recognition and enforcement of judgments.

It was suggested that, in order to avoid conflicting judgments, it might be desirable to provide that the court which had fixed the amount of a maintenance payment should be the only court to have jurisdiction to vary it. The Committee did not think it necessary to adopt such a solution. This would have obliged parties, neither of whom had any further connection with the original court, to bring proceedings before courts which could be very far away. Moreover, any judgment by a second court, in order to vary that of the first court, would have to be based on changed facts, and in those circumstances it could not be maintained that the judgments were in conflict.[4]

NOTES

1 In force on 1.9.1966 between Belgium, France, Germany, Italy and the Netherlands.
2 In force on 1.9.1966 between Belgium, France, Germany, Italy and the Netherlands.
3 Hague Conference on private international law, documents for the eighth session, p 315.
4 For a similar view, see the Hague Conference on private international law, documents for the ninth session. Report on the draft Convention concerning the recognition and enforcement of decisions relating to maintenance obligations in respect of children, p 321.

Forum delicti commissi (Article 5(3) and (4))

This jurisdiction is recognized by the national laws of the Member States with the exception of Luxembourg and the Netherlands, where it exists only in respect of collisions of ships and of road accidents.

The following are applicable in Belgium, Articles 41, and 52(3) of the Law of 1876;[1] in Germany, Article 32 of the Code of Civil Procedure; in France, Article 59(12) of the Code of Civil Procedure and Article 21 of the Decree of 22 December 1958; and in Italy, Article 20 of the Code of Civil Procedure.

This jurisdiction is incorporated in the bilateral conventions by the following provisions: Article 4 of the Convention between Belgium and the Netherlands and Article 4 of the Benelux Treaty, which cover all obligations concerning movable property, whether statutory, contractual or non-contractual;[2] Article 2(b) of the Convention between Belgium and Italy; Article 3(1)(6) of the Convention between Germany and Belgium; Article 15 of the Convention between France and Italy; Article 2(4) of the Convention between Germany and Italy; and Article 4(1)(e) of the Convention between Germany and the Netherlands.
[OJ C59, 5.3.79, p 26]

The fact that this jurisdiction is recognized under most of the legal systems, and incorporated in the majority of the bilateral conventions, was a ground for including it in the Convention, especially in view of the high number of road accidents.

Article 5(3) uses the expression "the place where the harmful event occurred". The Committee did not think it should specify whether that place is the place where the event which resulted in damage or injury occurred, or whether it is the place where the damage or injury was sustained. The Committee preferred to keep to a formula which has already been adopted by number of legal systems (Germany, France).

Article 5(4) provides that a civil claim may be brought before a court seised of criminal proceedings; this is in order to take into account the rules of jurisdiction laid down by the various codes of criminal procedure. A civil claim can thus always be brought, whatever the domicile of the defendant, in the criminal court having jurisdiction to entertain the criminal proceedings even if the place where the court sits (place of arrest, for example) is not the same as that where the harmful event occurred.

NOTES

1 Article 626 of the Judicial Code.
2 Report on the negotiations, p 17.

Jurisdiction based on a dispute arising out of the operations of a branch, agency or other establishment (Article 5(5))

This jurisdiction exists in the bilateral conventions already concluded between the Contracting States: the Conventions between Italy and Belgium (Article 2(3)), between Belgium and Germany (Article 2(1) (4)), between France and Belgium (Article 3(2)), between France and Italy (Article 13), between Italy and the Netherlands (Article 2(3)), and between Belgium and the Netherlands (Article 5(3)); the Benelux Treaty (Article 5(4)); and the Conventions between Germany and the Netherlands (Article 4(1)(d)), and between Germany and Italy (Article 2(3)).

This provision concerns only defendants domiciled in a Contracting State (Article 5), that is, companies or firms having their seat in one Contracting State and having a branch, agency or other establishment in another Contracting State. Companies or firms which have their seat outside the Community but have a branch, etc in a Contracting State are governed by Article 4, even as regards disputes relating to the activities of their branches, but without prejudice to the provisions of Article 8 relating to insurance.

More than one defendant (Article 6(1))

Where there is more than one defendant, the courts for the place where any one of the defendants is domiciled are recognized as having jurisdiction. This jurisdiction is provided for in the internal law of Belgium,[1] France,[2] Italy,[3] Luxembourg[4] and the Netherlands.[5]

It is not in general provided for in German law. Where an action must be brought in Germany against a number of defendants and there is no jurisdiction to which they are all subject, the court having jurisdiction may, subject to certain conditions, be designated by the superior court which is next above it (Article 36(3) of the German Code of Civil Procedure).

This jurisdiction is also provided for in the Conventions between Italy and the Netherlands (Article 2(1)), between Italy and Belgium (Article 2(1)), between France and Italy (Article 11(2)), and between Germany and Italy (Article 2(1)). However, under the latter Convention, jurisdiction depends on the existence of a procedural requirement that the various defendants be joined.

It follows from the text of the Convention that, where there are several defendants domiciled in different Contracting States, the plaintiff can at his option sue them all in the courts for the place where any one of them is domiciled.

In order for this rule to be applicable there must be a connection between the claims made against each of the defendants, as for example in the case of joint debtors.[6] It follows that action cannot be brought solely with the object of ousting the jurisdiction of the courts of the State in which the defendant is domiciled.[7]

[OJ C59, 5.3.79, p 27]

Jurisdiction derived from the domicile of one of the defendants was adopted by the Committee because it makes it possible to obviate the handing down in the Contracting States of judgments which are irreconcilable with one another.

NOTES

1. Articles 39 and 52(10) of the Law of 25 March 1876, and Article 624 of the Judicial Code.
2. Article 59(4) of the Code of Civil Procedure.
3. Article 33 of the Code of Civil Procedure.
4. Article 59(2) of the Code of Civil Procedure.
5. Article 126(7) of the Code of Civil Procedure.
6. MOREL, Traité élémentaire de procédure civile, No 264.
7. Cass. française 1924, D.P. 1925, Vol 13.

Actions on a warranty or guarantee, third party proceedings, counterclaims

(a) Actions on a warranty or guarantee (Article 6(2))

An action on a warranty or guarantee brought against a third party by the defendant in an action for the purpose of being indemnified against the consequences of that action, is available in Belgian,[1] French,[2] Italian,[3] Luxembourg[4] and Netherlands[5] law.

The proceeding which corresponds to an action on a warranty or guarantee in Germany is governed by Articles 72, 73 and 74 and Article 68 of the Code of Civil Procedure.

A party who in any proceedings considers that, if he is unsuccessful, he has a right of recourse on a warranty or guarantee against a third party, may join that third party in the proceedings (Article 72) (Streitverkündung—*litis denunciatio*).

The notice joining the third party must be served on that party and a copy must be sent to the other party (Article 73). No judgment can be given as regards the third party, but the judgment given in the original proceedings is binding in the sense that the substance of the judgment cannot be contested in the subsequent action which the defendant may bring against the third party (Article 68). Under the German Code of Civil Procedure the defendant can exercise his right of recourse against the third party only in separate proceedings.

Actions on a warranty or guarantee are governed by the bilateral Conventions between Belgium and Germany (Article 3(10)), between France and Belgium (Article 4(2)), between Belgium and the Netherlands (Article 6(2)), between Italy and the Netherlands (Article 2(4)), between Belgium and Italy (Article 2(10)), and between Germany and the Netherlands (Article 4(1)(c)), and also by the Benelux Treaty (Article 6(3)).

This jurisdiction is, in the opinion of the Committee, of considerable importance in commercial dealings, as can be seen from the following example: A German exporter delivers goods to Belgium and the Belgian importer resells them. The purchaser sues the importer for damages in the court for the place of his domicile, for example in Brussels. The Belgian importer has a right of recourse against the German exporter and consequently brings an action for breach of warranty against that exporter in the court in Brussels, since it has jurisdiction over the original action. The jurisdiction over the action on the warranty is allowed by the Convention although the warrantor is domiciled in Germany, since this is in the interests of the proper administration of justice.

However, under Article 17, the court seised of the original action will not have jurisdiction over the action on the warranty where the warrantor and the beneficiary of the warranty have agreed to confer jurisdiction on another court, provided that the agreement covers actions on the warranty.

Moreover, the court seised of the original action will not have jurisdiction over an action on the warranty if the original proceedings were instituted solely with the object of ousting the jurisdiction of the courts of the State in which the warrantor is domiciled.[6]

The special position of German law is covered by Article V of the Protocol.

Under this provision, the jurisdiction specified in Article 6(2) in actions on a warranty or guarantee may not be resorted to in the Federal Republic of Germany, but any person domiciled in another Contracting State may be summoned before the German courts on the basis of Articles 72 to 74 of the Code of Civil Procedure.

Judgments given against a guarantor or warrantor in the other Contracting States will be recognized and enforced in Germany.

Judgments given in Germany pursuant to Articles 72 to 74 will have the same effect in the other Contracting States as in Germany.

Thus, for example, a guarantor or warrantor domiciled in France can be sued in the German court having jurisdiction over the original action. The German law judgment given in Germany affects only the parties to the action, but it can be invoked against the guarantor or warrantor. Where the beneficiary of the guarantee or warranty proceeds against the guarantor or warrantor in the competent French courts, he will be able to apply for recognition of the German judgment, and it will no longer be possible to re-examine that judgment as to the merits.

[OJ C59, 5.3.79, p 28]

It is clear that, following the principles which apply to enforcement, a judgment given in an action on a guarantee or warranty will have no effects in the State in which enforcement is sought other than those which it had in the country of origin.

This principle, which already applied under the Conventions between Germany and Belgium (Article 3(10)) and between Germany and the Netherlands (Article 4(1)(i)), is thus incorporated in the provision governing relations between the Federal Republic of Germany and the other Member States of the Community.

(b) Third party proceedings

While a third party warranty or guarantee necessarily involves the intervention of an outsider, it seemed preferable to make separate provision for guarantors or warrantors and for other third parties. The simplest definition of third party proceedings is to be found in Articles 15 and 16 of the Belgian Judicial Code, which provides that:

> "Third party proceedings are those in which a third party is joined as a party to the action.
>
> They are intended either to safeguard the interests of the third party or of one of the parties to the action, or to enable judgment to be entered against a party, or to allow an order to be made for the purpose of giving effect to a guarantee or warranty (Article 15).
>
> The third party's intervention is voluntary where he appears in order to defend his interests.
>
> It is not voluntary where the third party is sued in the course of the proceedings by one or more of the parties (Article 16)."

(c) Counterclaims (Article 6(3))

The bilateral conventions on enforcement all recognize jurisdiction over counterclaims: see the Convention between Belgium and Germany (Article 3(1), (10)) (counterclaims); the Convention between Italy and Belgium (Article 2(1), (10)) (dependent counterclaims); the

PART IV EC MATERIALS

Convention between France and Belgium (Article 4(2)) (counterclaims); the Convention between Belgium and the Netherlands (Article 6) (counterclaims, third party proceedings and interlocutory proceedings); the Convention between France and Italy (Article 18) (claims for compensation, interlocutory or dependent proceedings, counterclaims); the Convention between Italy and the Netherlands (Article 2(4)) dependent proceedings, counterclaims); the Convention between Germany and Italy (Article 2(5)) (counterclaims); the Benelux Treaty (Article 6) (counterclaims, third party proceedings and interlocutory proceedings); and the Convention between Germany and the Netherlands (Article 4(1)(i)) (counterclaims and actions on a warranty or guarantee).

It has been made clear that in order to establish this jurisdiction the counterclaim must be related to the original claim. Since the concept of related actions is not recognized in all the legal systems, the provision in question, following the draft Belgian Judicial Code, states that the counterclaim must arise from the contract or from the facts on which the original claim was based.

NOTES

1 Articles 50 and 52 of the Law of 25 March 1876, Article 181 of the Code of Civil Procedure.
2 Articles 59(10) and 181 to 185 of the Code of Civil Procedure.
3 Articles 32 and 36 of the Code of Civil Procedure.
4 Articles 59(8) and 181 to 185 of the Code of Civil Procedure.
5 Article 126(14) of the Code of Civil Procedure.
6 See Article 181 of the Belgian, French and Luxembourg Code of Civil Procedure, and Article 74 of the Netherlands Code of Civil Procedure.

Sections 3 to 5
Insurance, instalment sales, exclusive jurisdiction

General remarks

In each of the six Contracting States, the rules of territorial jurisdiction are not as a rule part of public policy and it is therefore permissible for the parties to agree on a different jurisdiction.

There are, however, exceptions to this principle: certain rules of jurisdiction are mandatory or form part of public policy, either in order to further the efficient administration of justice by reducing the number of jurisdictions and concentrating certain forms of litigation in a single forum, or else out of social considerations for the protection of certain categories of persons, such as insured persons or buyers of goods on instalment credit terms.

In view of the Convention's structure and objectives, it was necessary to deal with this matter under the Convention. Failure to take account of the problem raised by these rules of jurisdiction might not only have caused recognition and enforcement to be refused in certain cases on grounds of public policy, which would be contrary to the principle of free movement of judgments, but also result, indirectly, in a general re-examination of the jurisdiction of the court of the State of origin.

[OJ C59, 5.3.79, p 29]

Several solutions were open to the Committee.

The first is found in many bilateral Conventions, and enables the court of the State in which recognition of enforcement is sought to refuse to recognize the jurisdiction of the court of the State of origin where, in the former State, there are "rules attributing exclusive jurisdiction to the courts of that State in the proceedings which led to the judgment".[1]

This system would have been unsatisfactory not only because it gives rise to the objections already set out above, but because it would have introduced into the Convention an element of insecurity incompatible with its basic principles. It is no solution to the problem, and only postpones the difficulties, deferring them until the recognition and enforcement stage.

Another possible solution would have been a general clause like that contained in the Convention between Belgium and the Netherlands or the Benelux Treaty (Article 5(1)), which takes into consideration the internal law of the Contracting States.[2] Such a clause could, however, lead to difficulties of interpretation, since the court of the State of origin must, where its jurisdiction is contested, apply the internal law of the State which claims to have exclusive jurisdiction.

Moreover, while such a solution might be acceptable in a Treaty between three States, it would be much more difficult to incorporate it in a Convention between six States where it is not always possible to determine in advance the State or States in which recognition or enforcement may be sought.

A third solution would have been to draw up a list of the individual jurisdictions which would be exclusive and which would thus be binding on all the Contracting States. Such a list would answer the need of the parties for information regarding the legal position, allow the court to give judgment on the basis of a definite common rule, remove any element of uncertainty and ensure a balance between the parties to contractual arrangements.

The considerations underlying the various provisions of the Convention are complex. Sections 3 and 4, for example, concerning insurance and instalment sales and loans, are dictated by social considerations and are aimed in particular at preventing abuses which could result from the terms of contracts in standard form.

Section 5 (Article 16) contains a list of situations in which the courts of a Contracting State are acknowledged as having exclusive jurisdiction, since the proper administration of justice requires that actions should be brought before the courts of a single State.

The Convention deals with the two categories differently. The first category has been placed in an intermediate position between the general rules of jurisdiction and the rules which are wholly exclusive.

The following system adopted:

1. For matters falling within Section 3 and 4 there is no single jurisdiction. A choice, albeit a limited one, exists between the courts of different Contracting States where the plaintiff is a protected person, that is, a policy-holder, a buyer or a borrower. In matters falling under exclusive jurisdictions pursuant to Section 5, the parties have no choice between the courts of several Contracting States.
2. The parties may, in certain circumstances, derogate from the provisions of Sections 3 and 4 (Articles 12, 15, and 18). The provisions of Section 5 may not, however, be derogated from, either by an agreement conferring jurisdiction (second paragraph of Article 17) or by an implied submission to the jurisdiction (Article 18).
3. The rules in Section 3 and 4 are applicable only where the defendant is domiciled in a Contracting State, whereas those in Section 5 apply regardless of domicile.

However, contravention of the provisions of Sections 3 and 4, as well as of those of Section 5, constitutes a ground for refusing recognition and enforcement (Articles 28 and 34).

NOTES

1 Convention between Germany and Belgium, Article 3(2); Convention between Italy and the Netherlands (end of Article 2); Convention between Italy and Belgium (end of Article 2).

2 Article 5(1) of the convention between Belgium and the Netherlands reads as follows: "Where a domicile conferring jurisdiction has been chosen in one of the two countries for the enforcement of an instrument, the courts for the place of domicile chosen shall have exclusive jurisdiction over litigation relating to that instrument, save for exceptions and modifications enacted or to be enacted under the national law of one of the two States or by international agreement."

[OJ C59, 5.3.79, p 30]

Section 3

Jurisdiction in matters relating to insurance

Rules of exclusive or special jurisdiction relating to insurance exist in France (Article 3 of the Law of 13 July 1930 concerning contracts of insurance), in Belgium (Law of 20 May 1920, added as Article 43 bis to the Law of 25 March 1876 on jurisdiction), in Germany (§48 of the Gesetz über den Versicherungsvertrag (Law on contracts of insurance)), and in Italy (Article 1903 (2) of the Civil Code, Article 124 of the Consolidated Law on private insurance). In Luxembourg, the Law of 16 May 1891 on contracts of insurance does not include any provision on jurisdiction. This is due to the small size of the Grand Duchy, which comprises only two judicial arrondissements. However, the Law of 16 May 1891 concerning the supervision of insurance matters governs jurisdiction in regard to foreign insurance companies. This Law requires an insurer resident abroad who is transacting insurance business in the Grand Duchy to appoint a general representative domiciled in Luxembourg who will represent him there judicially and extrajudicially. This representative must give an address for service of process in the judicial arrondissement in which he is not domiciled.

Either the domicile of the general representative or his address for service founds jurisdiction in respect of actions arising from contracts of insurance. In the Netherlands, there are no special provisions concerning the jurisdiction of the courts in insurance matters. As regards foreign life-assurance companies, the Netherlands Law of 22 December 1922 recognizes rules analogous to those of the Luxembourg Law of 16 May 1891. The rules are approximately the same in Germany.

Section 3 was drawn up in cooperation with the European Insurance Committee.

The provisions of this Section may be summarized as follows: in matters relating to insurance, actions against an insurer domiciled in a Contracting State may be brought in the following courts, i e either:

(i) In the courts of the State where he is domiciled (Article 8), or, subject to certain conditions, in the courts for the place where he has a branch (Articles 7 and 8); or

(ii)

- (a) in the courts for the place where the policy-holder is domiciled (Article 8);
- (b) in the courts of the State where one of the insurers is domiciled, if two or more insurers are the defendants (Article 8);
- (c) in the courts for the place where the agent who acted as intermediary in the making of the contract of insurance has his domicile, if there is provision for such jurisdiction under the law of the court seised of the matter (Article 8);
- (d)
  1. in respect of liability insurance, the insurer may in addition be sued:
     - (1) in the courts for the place where the harmful event occurred (Articles 9 and 10),
     - (2) as a third party, in the court seised of the action brought by the injured party against the insured if, under its own law, that court has jurisdiction in the third party proceedings (Article 10);
  2. in respect of insurance of immovable property, the insurer may in addition be sued in the courts for the place where the harmful event occurred. The same applies if movable and immovable property are covered by the same insurance policy and both are adversely affected by the same contingency (Article 9).

Where an insurer is the plaintiff, he may in general bring an action only in the courts of the State in which the defendant is domiciled, irrespective of whether the latter is the policy-holder, the insured or a beneficiary.

Agreements conferring jurisdiction which depart from these rules have no legal force if they were entered into before the dispute arose (Article 12).

Article 7

Article 7 specifies that jurisdiction in matters relating to insurance is governed solely by Section 3 of Title II.

Specific exceptions are made by the references to Articles 4 and 5(5), which concern respectively defendants domiciled outside the Community and disputes arising out of the operations of a branch, agency or other establishment.

It follows from the first of these exceptions that jurisdiction is determined by the law of the court seised of the matter, including the rules of exorbitant jurisdiction, where the defendant, whether he is the insurer or the policy-holder, is domiciled outside the Community. However, as an exception to the general rules of the Convention, an insurer domiciled outside the Community who has a branch or an agency in a Contracting State is, in disputes relating to the operations of the branch or agency, deemed to be domiciled in that State. This exception, which is contained in the last paragraph of Article 8, was adopted because foreign insurance companies can establish branches or agencies in other States only by putting up guarantees which in practice place them in the same position as national companies. However, the exception applies only to branches or agencies, i e when the foreign company is represented by a person able to conclude contracts with third parties on behalf of the company.

[OJ C59, 5.3.79, p 31]

The second exception again relates to branches or agencies, and also to other establishments, which, as appears from the reference back to Article 5(5), depend from a company whose seat is in a Contracting State. The result is that such a company may be sued in the courts for the place in which the branch, agency or establishment is situated, in all disputes arising out of their operations.

Article 8

Article 8 lays down general rules of jurisdiction in proceedings instituted against an insurer in matters relating to insurance.

First, the courts of the State where the insurer is domiciled have jurisdiction. This provision determines only general jurisdiction, namely the jurisdiction of the courts of the State where the insurer is domiciled. Each State must then apply its internal law to determine which court has jurisdiction. However, if the insurer is sued outside the State in which he is domiciled, the proceedings must be instituted in a specifically determined court, in accordance with the principles already adopted in Article 5.

Secondly, an action may be brought in a State other than that in which the insurer is domiciled, in the courts for the place where the policy-holder is domiciled. "Policy-holder" is to be taken to mean the other party to the contract of insurance. Where the insured or the beneficiary is not the same person as the policy-holder, their place of domicile is not taken into consideration. As was noted in particular by the European Insurance Committee, the insurer, as a supplier of services, enters into a business relationship with the other contracting party (the policy-holder). Because of their direct contact it is right and proper that the insurer can be sued in the courts for the place where the policy-holder is domiciled. But it would be unreasonable to expect the insurer to appear in the court of the insured or of a beneficiary, since he will not necessarily know their exact domicile at the time when the cause of action arises.

The domicile of the policy-holder which is relevant here is the domicile existing at the time when the proceedings are instituted.

Thirdly, if two or more insurers are defendants in the same action, they may be sued in the courts of the State where any one of them is domiciled. This provision is identical to that in Article 6(1), which does not apply here since the Section relating to insurance applies independently of the rest of the Convention.

Furthermore, an insurer may be sued in a State other than that in which he is domiciled, in the courts for the place where the agent who acted as intermediary in the making of the contract of insurance is domiciled, but subject to two conditions: first, that the domicile of the agent who acted as intermediary is mentioned in the insurance policy or proposal, and, secondly, that the law of the court seised of the matter recognizes this jurisdiction. It is not recognized in Belgium or in France, although it is in Germany[1] and in Italy (Article 1903 of the Civil Code). The reference to the insurance proposal takes account of the usual practice in Germany. Insurance companies there in general use data-processing systems, so that the place of the agency often appears in the policy only in the form of a number referring back to the insurance proposal. The insurance proposal, within the meaning of the Convention, means, of course, the final proposal which forms the basis of the contract.

The expression "the agent, who acted as intermediary in the making of the contract of insurance" includes both an agent through whom the contract was directly concluded between the company and the policy-holder, and also an agent who negotiated the contract to conclusion on behalf of the company. The significance of the last paragraph of Article 8 is made clear in the commentary on Article 7.

[OJ C59, 5.3.79, p 32]

NOTES

1 § 48 of the Gesetz über den Versicherungsvertrag:

"1. If an insurance agent has acted as intermediary in the making of the contract, or has concluded the contract, then in actions against the insurer arising out of the insurance contract the court for the place where, at the time when the contract was negotiated through the agent or concluded, the agent had his agency or, in the absence of an agency, has domicile, shall have jurisdiction.

2. The jurisdiction defined in paragraph 1 may not be excluded by agreement."

[OJ C59, 5.3.79, p 32]

Article 9

Article 9 allows an insurer to be sued in a State other than that in which he is domiciled in the courts for the place where the harmful event occurred, but without prejudice to the application

PART IV EC MATERIALS

of Article 12(3). This jurisdiction applies only in respect of liability insurance and insurance of immovable property. It extends to movable property in cases where a building and the movable property it contains are covered by the same insurance policy. This also applies if the movables are covered by an endorsement to the policy covering the immovable property.

Article 10

Article 10 contains rules of special jurisdiction for liability insurance cases. This provision is of particular importance in relation to road accidents.

Under the first paragraph of Article 10, in an action brought by the injured party against the insured, the latter may join the insurer as a third party if the court seised of the matter has jurisdiction in such a case under its own law. This is not possible in the Federal Republic of Germany.[1]

The problem arose whether consolidation of the two actions should be allowed even where the insurer and the insured are both domiciled in the same State, which, it must be assumed for the purposes of this argument, is different from the State of the court seised of the matter. For example, where an accident is caused in France by a German domiciled in Germany who is insured with a German company, should third party proceedings, which are recognized under French law, be possible even though the litigation concerns a contract of insurance between a German insured person and a German insurer? As it is subject to German law, should this contract not be litigated in a German court? The contractual relationship between the insurer and the policy-holder would then fall outside the scope of the proceedings relating to personal liability.

While acknowledging the relevance of this question, the Committee was of the opinion that it would be unwise to introduce rules of jurisdiction which would depart from national laws and which could also jeopardize the system in force following the introduction of the green card.[2]

The compromise solution adopted by the Committee is to reduce the scope of the first paragraph of Article 10 by inserting, under Article 12(3), a provision that, if the policy-holder and the insurer are both domiciled in the same Contracting State, when the contract is concluded, they may agree to confer jurisdiction on the courts of that State. Such an agreement must not, however, be contrary to the law of that State.

Under the second paragraph of Article 10 the insurer may also, in respect of liability insurance, be sued directly by the injured party[3] outside the State in which he is domiciled in any court which, under Articles 7 to 9, has jurisdiction over actions brought by the policy-holder against the insurer.

Where, however, under the first paragraph of Article 8, the court for the place where the policy-holder is domiciled has jurisdiction, there is no provision giving jurisdiction to the court for the place where the injured party is domiciled. The phrase "where such direct actions are permitted" has been used specifically to include the conflict of laws rules of the court seised of the matter.[4]

Under the last paragraph of Article 10, the insurer may join the policy-holder or the insured as parties to the action brought against him by the injured party. In the interests of the proper administration of justice, it must be possible for the actions to be brought in the same court in order to prevent different courts from giving judgments which are irreconcilable. This procedure will in addition protect the insurer against fraud.[5]

[OJ C59, 5.3.79, p 33]

NOTES

1 See Article V of the Protocol.

2 Insurance against civil liability in respect of motor vehicles is compulsory in all Community countries except Italy.
Belgium: Law of 1 July 1956.
France: Law of 27 February 1958, Decree of 7 January 1959.
Germany: Law of 7 November 1939.
Luxembourg: Law of 10 June 1932, Implementing Regulations of 28 October 1932 and 24 December 1932.
Netherlands: Law of 30 May 1963, Decree of 23 June 1964.

3 Direct actions are recognized under Belgian, French and Luxembourg law. Under German and Netherlands law they are recognized only with regard to compulsory insurance against civil liability in respect of motor vehicles.

[4] The rules of conflict must be used to decide whether the law to be applied is the law of the place where the harmful event occurred, the law governing the contract of insurance or the *lex fori*.

[5] J WAUTIER, L'assurance automobile obligatoire, Brussels 1947.

Article 11

Article 11 relates to actions brought by the insurer against the policy-holder, the insured or a beneficiary.

The courts of the State in which the defendant is domiciled when the proceedings are instituted have exclusive jurisdiction.

Again, this is a provision dealing with international jurisdiction; local jurisdiction within each State will be determined by the internal law of that State.

Article 11 does not apply where the defendant is domiciled outside a Contracting State, that is to say, outside the Community. In such cases Article 4 applies.

The second paragraph corresponds to the provisions of Article 6(3).

Article 12

Article 12 relates to agreements conferring jurisdiction. Agreements concluded before a dispute arises will have no legal force if they are contrary to the rules of jurisdiction laid down in the Convention.

The purpose of this Article is to prevent the parties from limiting the choice offered by this Convention to the policy-holder, and to prevent the insurer from avoiding the restrictions imposed under Article 11.

A number of exceptions are, however, permitted. After a dispute has arisen, that is to say "as soon as the parties disagree on a specific point and legal proceedings are imminent or contemplated",[1] the parties completely regain their freedom.

Certain agreements conferring jurisdiction which were concluded before the dispute arose are also permissible. First, there are those made to the advantage of the policy-holder, the insured or a beneficiary, which allow them to bring proceedings in courts other than those specified in the preceding Articles.

Certain other agreements conferring jurisdiction are allowed under Article 12(3), but only in the strictly defined circumstances therein specified which have been explained in the commentary on Article 10.

NOTES

[1] BRAAS, Précis de procédure civile, Vol I, No 795.

Section 4
Jurisdiction in matters relating to instalment sales and loans

This Section relates to the sale of goods where the price is payable in a series of instalments, and to the sale of goods where the sale is contractually linked to a loan (Abzahlungsgeschäfte). The rules here adopted are similar to those applicable in the national law of several of the Member States and, like them, stem from a desire to protect certain categories of persons. Article 13 provides that this Section applies independently of the rest of the Convention and, like Article 7, without prejudice to the provisions of Articles 4 and 5(5).

Article 14 determines the rules of jurisdiction.

In actions against a seller or a lender, proceedings may be instituted by the buyer or borrower either in the courts of the State in which the defendant is domiciled, or in the courts of the State in which the buyer or borrower is domiciled.

Actions by a seller or a lender may in general be brought only in the courts for the place where the buyer or borrower is domiciled when the proceedings are instituted.

The third paragraph, relating to counterclaims, corresponds to Article 6(3).

Article 15, which relates to agreements conferring jurisdiction, contains under (3) a provision analogous to that of Article 12(3), but for different reasons. In actions brought by a seller or a lender, it is rather difficult to determine jurisdiction where the buyer or borrower establishes himself abroad after the contract has been concluded. To protect these persons, they should ideally be sued only in the courts of the State where they have established their new domicile. For reasons of equity the Committee has however provided that where a seller and a buyer, or a lender and a borrower, are both domiciled or at least habitually resident in the same State when the contract is concluded, they may confer on the courts of that State jurisdiction over all disputes arising out of the contract, on condition that such agreements are not contrary to the law of that State.

The criterion of habitual residence allows agreements conferring jurisdiction to be concluded even where a buyer or borrower remains domiciled in a Contracting State other than that in which he is resident. It follows, for example, that a seller or lender need not sue the defendant abroad in the courts of the State in which the defendant is domiciled, if, when the proceedings are instituted, the defendant is still resident in the State in which the contract was concluded.

[OJ C59, 5.3.79, p 34]

Section 5
Exclusive jurisdiction

Article 16

Article 16 lists the circumstances in which the six States recognize that the courts of one of them have exclusive jurisdiction. The matters referred to in this Article will normally be the subject of exclusive jurisdiction only if they constitute the principal subject-matter of the proceedings of which the court is to be seised.

The provisions of Article 16 on jurisdiction may not be departed from either by an agreement purporting to confer jurisdiction on the courts of another Contracting State, or by an implied submission to the jurisdiction (Articles 17 and 18). Any court of a State other than the State whose courts have exclusive jurisdiction must declare of its own motion that it has no jurisdiction (Article 19). Failure to observe these rules constitutes a ground for refusal of recognition or enforcement (Articles 28 and 34).

These rules, which take as their criterion the subject-matter of the action, are applicable regardless of the domicile or nationality of the parties. In view of the reasons for laying down rules of exclusive jurisdiction, it was necessary to provide for their general application, even in respect of defendants domiciled outside the Community. Thus, for example, a Belgian court will not, on the basis of Article 53 of the Law of 1876 or of Article 637 of the draft Judicial Code, which in actions against foreigners recognize the jurisdiction of the courts of the plaintiff, have jurisdiction in proceedings between a Belgian and a person domiciled, for example, in Argentina, if the proceedings concern immovable property situated in Germany. Only the German courts will have jurisdiction.

Immovable property

Under Article 16(1), only the courts of the Contracting State in which the immovable property is situated have jurisdiction in proceedings concerning rights *in rem* in, or tenancies of, immovable property.

The importance of matters relating to immovable property had already been taken into consideration by the authors of the Treaty of Rome since, under Article 54(3)(c) of that Treaty, the Commission and the Council must enable "a national of one Member State to acquire and use land and buildings situated in the territory of another Member State", in so far as this does not conflict with the principles laid down in Article 39(2) relating to agricultural policy.

The problems which the Committee faced in this connection did not in fact relate to the recognition and enforcement of judgments, since these questions are governed by the provisions of the conventions already concluded between Member States, all of which apply in civil and commercial matters, including immovable property, but rather to the choice of rules of jurisdiction.

The laws of all the Member States include in this respect special rules of jurisdiction[1] which, generally speaking, have been incorporated in the bilateral conventions, whether they are based on direct[2] or indirect[3] jurisdiction.

However, the rules laid down in the Convention differ from those in the bilateral agreements in that the Convention lays down rules of exclusive jurisdiction. The Convention follows in this respect the Treaty between France and Germany settling the question of the Saar, Article 49 of which provides that the courts "of the country in which the immovable property is situated shall have exclusive jurisdiction in all disputes regarding the possession or ownership of such property and in all disputes regarding rights *in rem* in such property".

As in that Treaty, the exclusive jurisdiction established by Article 16(1) applies only in international relations; the internal rules of jurisdiction in force in each of the States are thus not affected.

[OJ C59, 5.3.79, p 35]

In other words, the Convention prohibits the courts of one Contracting State from assuming jurisdiction in disputes relating to immovable property situated in another Contracting State; it does not, in the State in which the immovable property is situated, prevent courts other than that for the place where the property is situated from having jurisdiction in such disputes if the jurisdiction of those other courts is recognized by the law of that State.

A number of considerations led the Committee to provide a rule of exclusive jurisdiction in this matter. In the Federal Republic of Germany and in Italy, the court for the place where the immovable property is situated has exclusive jurisdiction, this being considered a matter of public policy. It follows that, in the absence of a rule of exclusive jurisdiction, judgments given in other States by courts whose jurisdiction might have been derived from other provisions of the Convention (the court of the defendant's domicile, or an agreed forum) could have been neither recognized nor enforced in Germany or Italy.

Such a system would have been contrary to the principle of "free movement of judgments".

The Committee was all the more inclined to extend to international relations the rules of jurisdiction in force in the Federal Republic of Germany and in Italy, since it considered that to do so was in the interests of the proper administration of justice. This type of dispute often entails checks, enquiries and expert examinations which have to be made on the spot. Moreover, the matter is often governed in part by customary practices which are not generally known except in the courts of the place, or possibly of the country, where the immovable property is situated. Finally, the system adopted also takes into account the need to make entries in land registers located where the property is situated.

The wording adopted covers not only all disputes concerning rights *in rem* in immovable property, but also those relating to tenancies of such property. This will include tenancies of dwellings and of premises for professional or commercial use, and agricultural holdings. In providing for the courts of the State in which the property is situated to have jurisdiction as regards tenancies in immovable property, the Committee intended to cover disputes between landlord and tenant over the existence or interpretation of tenancy agreements, compensation for damage caused by the tenant, eviction, etc. The rule was not intended by the Committee to apply to proceedings concerned only with the recovery of rent, since such proceedings can be considered to relate to a subject-matter which is quite distinct from the rented property itself.

The adoption of this provision was dictated by the fact that tenancies of immovable property are usually governed by special legislation which, in view of its complexity, should preferably be applied only by the courts of the country in which it is in force. Moreover, several States provide for exclusive jurisdiction in such proceedings, which is usually conferred on special tribunals.

NOTES

1 Belgium: Article 8 of the Law of 25 March 1876, amended by the Arrêté royal of 3 January 1935; Article 52 of the Law of 1876; Federal Republic of Germany, Article 24 of the Code of Civil Procedure; France, Article 59(5) of the Code of Civil Procedure; Italy, Articles 4 and 21 of the Code of Civil Procedure; Luxembourg, Articles 59(3) and (4) of the Code of Civil Procedure; Netherlands, Article 126(8) of the Code of Civil Procedure.

2 Convention between Belgium and the Netherlands (Article 10).

3 Conventions between Germany and Belgium (Article 10); between France and Italy (Article 16); between Italy and the Netherlands (Article 2(6)); between Germany and Italy (Article 2(7)); between Belgium and Italy (Article 2(8)); and between Germany and the Netherlands (Article 4(1)(f)).

Companies and associations of natural or legal persons

Article 16(2) provides that the courts of the State in which a company or other legal person, or an association of natural or legal persons, has its seat, have exclusive jurisdiction in proceedings which are in substance concerned either with the validity of the constitution, the nullity or the dissolution of the company, legal person or association, or with the decisions of its organs.

It is important, in the interests of legal certainty, to avoid conflicting judgments being given as regards the existence of a company or association or as regards the validity of the decisions of its organs. For this reason, it is obviously preferable that all proceedings should take place in the courts of the State in which the company or association has its seat. It is in that State that information about the company or association will have been notified and made public. Moreover, the rule adopted will more often than not result in the application of the traditional maxim "*actor sequitur forum rei*". Such jurisdiction is recognized in particular in German law and, as regards non-profit making organizations, in Luxembourg law.

Public registers

Article 16(3) lays down that the courts of the State in which a public register is kept have exclusive jurisdiction in proceedings relating to the validity or effects of entries in that register.

This provision does not require a lengthy commentary. It corresponds to the provisions which appear in the internal laws of most of the Contracting States; it covers in particular entries in land registers, land charges registers and commercial registers.

[OJ C59, 5.3.79, p 36]

Patents

Article 16(4) applies to proceedings concerned with the registration or validity of patents, trade marks, designs or other similar rights, such as those which protect fruit and vegetable varieties, and which are required to be deposited or registered.

A draft convention has been drawn up by the EEC countries relating to patent law. The draft includes rules of jurisdiction for the Community patent, but it will not apply to national patents, which thus fall within the scope of the Judgments Convention.

Since the grant of a national patent is an exercise of national sovereignty, Article 16(4) of the Judgments Convention provides for exclusive jurisdiction in proceedings concerned with the validity of patents.

Other actions, including those for infringement of patents, are governed by the general rules of the Convention.

The expression "the deposit or registration has been applied for" takes into account internal laws which, like German law, make the grant of a patent subject to the results of an examination. Thus, for example, German courts will have exclusive jurisdiction in the case of an application to the competent authorities for a patent to be granted where, during the examination of the application, a dispute arises over the rights relating to the grant of that patent.

The phrase "is under the terms of an international convention deemed to have taken place" refers to the system introduced by the Madrid Agreement of 14 April 1891 concerning international registration of trade marks, revised at Brussels on 14 December 1900, at Washington on 2 June 1911, at The Hague on 6 November 1925 and at London on 2 June 1934, and also to the Hague Arrangement of 6 November 1925 for the international registration of industrial designs, revised at London on 2 June 1934. Under this system, the deposit of a trade mark, design or model at the International Office in Berne through the registry of the country of origin has the same effect in the other Contracting States as if that trade mark, design or model had been directly registered there. Thus where a trade mark is deposited at the International Office at the request of the German authorities, the French courts will have exclusive jurisdiction in disputes relating, for example, to whether the mark should be deemed to have been registered in France.

Enforcement of judgments

Article 16(5) provides that the courts of the State in which a judgment has been or is to be enforced have exclusive jurisdiction in proceedings concerned with the enforcement of that judgment.

What meaning is to be given to the expression "proceedings concerned with the enforcement of judgments"?

It means those proceedings which can arise from "recourse to force, constraint or distraint on movable or immovable property in order to ensure the effective implementation of judgments and authentic instruments".[1]

Problems arising out of such proceedings come within the exclusive jurisdiction of the courts for the place of enforcement.

Provisions of this kind appear in the internal law of many Member States.[2]

NOTES

1 BRAAS, Précis de procédure civile, Vol I, No 808.

2 See LEREBOURS-PIGEONNIÈRE, Droit international privé, seventh edition, p 9; LOUSSOUARN, No 411: French courts have exclusive jurisdiction over measures for enforcement which is to take place in France (preventive measures, distress levied on a tenant's chattels, writs of attachment and applications for enforcement of a foreign judgment); over distraint levied on immovable or movable property, and over proceedings concerned with the validity of measures for enforcement."

Section 6
Prorogation of jurisdiction

This section includes Article 17, on jurisdiction by consent, and Article 18, which concerns jurisdiction implied from submission.

Article 17

Jurisdiction deriving from agreements conferring jurisdiction is already a feature of all the Conventions concluded between Member States of the Community, whether the rules of jurisdiction are direct or indirect: see the Convention between France and Belgium (Article 3), and between Belgium and the Netherlands (Article 5); the Benelux Treaty (Article 5); the Convention between France and Italy (Article 12), between Germany and Italy (Article 2(2)), between Italy and the Netherlands (Article 2(2)), between Italy and Belgium (Article 2(1), (2)), between Germany and Belgium (Article 3(2)), and between Germany and the Netherlands (Article 4(1)(b)).

[OJ C59, 5.3.79, p 37]

This jurisdiction is also the subject of international conventions, namely the Hague Convention of 15 April 1958 on the jurisdiction of the contractual forum in matters relating to the international sale of goods, and the Hague Convention of 25 November 1965 on the choice of court.[1]

It is unnecessary to stress the importance of this jurisdiction, particularly in commercial relations.

However, although agreement was readily reached on the basic principle of including such a jurisdiction in the Convention, the Committee spent much time in drafting Article 17.

Like the draftsmen of the Convention between Germany and Belgium, the report of which may usefully be quoted, the Committee's first concern was "not to impede commercial practice, yet at the same time to cancel out the effects of clauses in contracts which might go unread. Such clauses will therefore be taken into consideration only if they are the subject of an agreement, and this implies the consent of all the parties. Thus, clauses in printed forms for business correspondence or in invoices will have no legal force if they are not agreed to by the party against whom they operate."

The Committee was further of the opinion that, in order to ensure legal certainty, the formal requirements applicable to agreements conferring jurisdiction should be expressly prescribed, but that "excessive formality which is incompatible with commercial practice"[2] should be avoided.

In this respect, the version adopted is similar to that of the Convention between Germany and Belgium, which was itself based on the rules of the Hague Convention of 15 April 1958, in that a clause conferring jurisdiction is valid only if it is in writing, or if at least one of the parties has confirmed in writing an oral agreement.[3]

Since there must be true agreement between the parties to confer jurisdiction, the court cannot necessarily deduce from a document in writing adduced by the party seeking to rely on it that there was an oral agreement. The special position of the Grand Duchy of Luxembourg in this matter necessitated an additional restriction which is contained in the second paragraph of Article I of the Protocol.

The question of how much weight is to be attached to the written document was left open by the Committee. In certain countries, a document in writing will be required only as evidence of the existence of the agreement; in others, however, it will go to the validity of the agreement.

Like the Conventions between Belgium and the Netherlands and between France and Belgium, and also the Benelux Treaty and the Hague Convention, the first paragraph of Article 17 provides that the court agreed on by the parties shall have exclusive jurisdiction. This solution is essential to avoid different courts from being properly seised of the matter and giving conflicting or at least differing judgments. In order to meet practical realities, the first paragraph of Article 17 also covers specifically cases of agreement that a particular court in a Contracting State or the courts of a Contracting State are to have jurisdiction, and is similar in this to the 1958 Hague Convention. As Professor Batiffol pointed out in his report on that Convention, an agreement conferring jurisdiction generally on the courts of a Contracting State "may have no legal effect if, in the absence of any connecting factor between the contractual situation and the State whose courts have been agreed on as having jurisdiction, the law of that State provides no way of determining which court can or should be seised of the matter".[4] But as Batiffol remarks, this is a matter which the parties should consider at the appropriate time.

The first paragraph of Article 17 applies only if at least one of the parties is domiciled in a Contracting State. It does not apply where two parties who are domiciled in the same Contracting State have agreed that a court of that State shall have jurisdiction, since the Convention, under the general principle laid down in the preamble, determines only the international jurisdiction of courts (see Commentary, Chapter III, Section 1, International legal relationships).

[OJ C59, 5.3.79, p 38]

Article 17 applies where the agreement conferring jurisdiction was made either between a person domiciled in one Contracting State and a person domiciled in another Contracting State, or between a person domiciled in a Contracting State and a person domiciled outside the Community, if the agreement confers jurisdiction on the courts of a Contracting State; it also applies where two persons domiciled in one Contracting State agree that a particular court of another Contracting State shall have jurisdiction.

The second paragraph of Article 17 provides that agreements conferring jurisdiction shall have no legal force if they are contrary to the provisions of Article 12 (insurance) or Article 15 (instalment sales), or if the courts whose jurisdiction they purport to exclude have exclusive jurisdiction by virtue of Article 16.

The intention behind the Convention is to obviate cases of refusal of recognition and enforcement on the basis of Articles 28 and 34, and so, as already stated, to promote the free movement of judgments.

The third paragraph of Article 17 provides that if the agreement conferring jurisdiction was concluded for the benefit of only one of the contracting parties, that party shall retain the right to bring proceedings in any other court which has jurisdiction.[5] Agreements conferring jurisdiction cannot of course affect the substantive jurisdiction of the courts.

NOTES

1. By 1 September 1966 neither of these Conventions had entered into force.
2. Hague Conference on private international law, documents of the eighth session. FRÉDERICQ, Report on the work of the Second Committee, p 303.
3. Hague Conference on private international law, Final Act of the tenth session. Convention on the choice of court, Article 4.
4. Hague Conference on private international law, documents of the eighth session, p 305.
5. See also the Conventions between France and Belgium, Article 3, between France and Italy, Article 2, and between Belgium and the Netherlands, Article 5 and the Benelux Treaty, Article 5.

Article 18

Article 18 governs jurisdiction implied from submission. If a defendant domiciled in a Contracting State is sued in a court of another Contracting State which does not have jurisdiction under the Convention, two situations may arise: the defendant may either, as he is entitled to do, plead that the court has no jurisdiction under the Convention, in which case the court must declare that it does not have jurisdiction; or he may elect not to raise this plea, and enter an appearance. In the latter case, the court will have jurisdiction.

Unlike the case of conventions based on indirect jurisdiction, the defendant may, by virtue of the Convention, rely on its provisions in the court seised of the proceedings and plead lack of jurisdiction. It will be necessary to refer to the rules of procedure in force in the State of the court seised of the proceedings in order to determine the point in time up to which the defendant will be allowed to raise this plea, and to determine the legal meaning of the term "appearance".

Moreover, by conferring jurisdiction on a court in circumstances where the defendant does not contest that court's jurisdiction, the Convention extends the scope of Title II and avoids any uncertainty. The main consequence of this rule is that if a defendant domiciled in a Contracting State is, notwithstanding the provisions of the second paragraph of Article 3, sued in another Contracting State on the basis of a rule of exorbitant jurisdiction, for example in France on the basis of Article 14 of the Civil Code, the court will have jurisdiction if this is not contested. The only cases in which a court must declare that it has no jurisdiction and where jurisdiction by submission will not be allowed are those in which the courts of another State have exclusive jurisdiction by virtue of Article 16.

Section 7
Examination as to jurisdiction and admissibility

Article 19

As has already been stated (page 8), a court must of its own motion examine whether it has jurisdiction. Article 19 emphasizes that the court must of its own motion declare that it has no jurisdiction if it is seised of a matter in which the courts of another Contracting State have exclusive jurisdiction by virtue of Article 16.

This rule is essential since the exclusive jurisdictions are conceived to be matters of public policy which cannot be departed from by the free choice of the parties. Moreover, it corresponds to Article 171 of the French Code of Civil Procedure, by virtue of which territorial jurisdiction is automatically examined where the parties are not permitted to reach a settlement.[1]

[OJ C59, 5.3.79, p 39]

If this Article deserves particular attention, it is mainly because, in order that the general rules of jurisdiction are observed, it grants wide powers to the court seised of the proceedings, since that court will of its own motion have to examine whether it has jurisdiction.

The words "principally concerned" have the effect that the court is not obliged to declare of its own motion that it has no jurisdiction if an issue which comes within the exclusive jurisdiction of another court is raised only as a preliminary or incidental matter.

NOTES

[1] The same is true in the Federal Republic of Germany: see ROSENBURG, *op cit* paragraph 38(I)(3).

Article 20

Article 20 is one of the most important Articles in the Convention: it applies where the defendant does not enter an appearance; here the court must of its own motion examine whether it has jurisdiction under the Convention. If it finds no basis for jurisdiction, the court must declare that it has no jurisdiction. It is obvious that the court is under the same obligation even where there is no basis for exclusive jurisdiction. Failure on the part of the defendant to enter an appearance is not equivalent to a submission to the jurisdiction. It is not sufficient for the court to accept the submissions of the plaintiff as regards jurisdiction; the court must itself ensure that the plaintiff proves that it has international jurisdiction.[1]

The object of this provision is to ensure that in cases of failure to enter an appearance the court giving judgment does so only if it has jurisdiction, and so to safeguard the defendant as fully as possible in the original proceedings. The rule adopted is derived from Article 37(2) of the Italian Code of Civil Procedure, by virtue of which the court must of its own motion examine whether it has jurisdiction where the defendant is a foreigner and does not enter an appearance.

The second paragraph of Article 20 is also designed to safeguard the rights of the defendant, by recognizing the international importance of the service of judicial documents. The service of judicial documents abroad, although governed differently in each of the Member States, can broadly be separated into two main systems. The German system is based on the cooperation of the public authorities of the place of residence of the addressee which have jurisdiction to deliver to him a copy of the instrument. A German court cannot in general give judgment in default of appearance unless it receives conclusive evidence that the instrument has been delivered to the addressee.[2, 3] The system contrasts with those in force in Belgium, France, Italy, Luxembourg and the Netherlands,[4] all of which are characterized by

PART IV
EC MATERIALS

the "desire to localize in the territory of the State of the forum all the formalities connected with the judicial document whose addressee resides abroad".[5]

Under the laws of these countries, service is properly effected, and causes time to begin to run, without there being any need to establish that the document instituting the proceedings has actually been served on its addressee. It is not impossible in these circumstances that, in some cases, a defendant may have judgment entered against him in default of appearance without having any knowledge of the action.

The Hague Convention of 1 March 1954 on civil procedure, to which the six Member States are party, does not solve the difficulties which arise under such legislation.

The Committee also tried to solve the problems arising when service is effected late, bearing in mind that the aim of the Convention is to promote, so far as possible, the free movement of judgments.

The search for a solution was obviously helped by the drafting at the tenth session of the Hague Conference on private international law of the Convention on the service abroad of judicial and extrajudicial documents in civil or commercial matters, which was opened for signature on 15 November 1965. This is the reason why the solution adopted in the second paragraph of Article 20 is only transitional.

This provision summarizes Article 15 of the Hague Convention, which is in fact derived from Article 20 of this present Convention, since the work of the Committee served as a basis for discussion at the meetings of the Special Commission which was established by the Hague Conference and which drew up the preliminary draft which was submitted for discussion at the tenth session.

[OJ C59, 5.3.79, p 40]

Under the second paragraph of Article 20, where a defendant domiciled in one Contracting State is sued in the courts of another State and does not enter an appearance, the court must stay the proceedings so long as it is not shown that the defendant has been able to receive the document instituting the proceedings in sufficient time to enable him to arrange for his defence, or that all necessary steps have been taken to this end.

This provision is based on the old Article 8 of the Netherlands Law of 12 June 1909, Stb No 141.[6]

The second paragraph of Article 20 requires first that notification of the proceedings has been given to the party who has not entered an appearance, that is either to him in person or at his domicile, and secondly that it has been delivered in sufficient time to enable the defendant to arrange for his defence. It does not require that the defendant should actually have been notified in sufficient time. The defendant must be responsible for any delay caused by his own negligence or by that of his relations or servants. The critical time is thus the time at which service was properly effected, and not the time at which the defendant received actual knowledge of the institution of proceedings.

The question of "sufficient time" is obviously a question of fact for the discretion of the court seised of the matter.

The court may give judgment in default against a defendant if it is shown that "all necessary steps have been taken" for him actually to have received in sufficient time the document instituting the proceedings.

This means that a court will be able to give judgment in default against a defendant even if no affidavit can be produced to confirm service on the defendant of the document instituting the proceedings, provided it is shown that all the necessary approaches have been made to the competent authorities of the State in which the defendant is domiciled in order to reach him in sufficient time. Where necessary, it must also be shown that "all the investigations required by good conscience and good faith have been undertaken to discover the defendant".[7]

As already stated, the second paragraph of Article 20 is only a transitional provision. Under the third paragraph of that Article, where the State of the forum and the State in which the document had to be transmitted have both ratified the new Hague Convention, the court seised of the matter will no longer apply the second paragraph of Article 20 but will be exclusively bound by Article 15 of the Hague Convention. Thus any possibility of conflict between Article 15 of the Hague Convention and the second paragraph of Article 20 of the EEC Judgments Convention is resolved in favour of the Hague Convention.

The Committee also considered it important to ensure certainty and speed in the transmission of judicial documents. In order to achieve this, it considered as a possible solution the transmission of such documents by registered post. However, it did not adopt this system for, although it meets the requirement of speed, it does not offer all the necessary safeguards from the point of view of certainty. In the end the Committee adopted the system which is set out in Article IV of the Protocol.

This Article simply adds a new method of transmission to those already provided for by the Hague Convention of 1 March 1954 on civil procedure, or by the agreements concluded between the Contracting States in application of that Convention. It corresponds, moreover, to the facility provided for by Article 10(b) of the new Hague Convention.

Under the system adopted in the Protocol, documents can be transmitted by public officers in one Contracting State directly to their colleagues in another Contracting State, who will deliver them to the addressee in person or to his domicile.

According to the assurances which were given to the Committee by a representative of the "Union internationale des huissiers de justice et d'officiers judiciaires", it will be easy for a public officer in one country to correspond with the appropriate public officer in another country. In case of difficulty it would moreover be possible for the officer in the State in which judgment was given to invoke the assistance of the national associations of public officers, or on the central office of the "Union" which has its headquarters in Paris.
[OJ C59, 5.3.79, p 41]

In the opinion of the Committee these arrangements meet the requirements of speed and certainty. Direct communication between public officers allows a considerable gain in time by avoiding any recourse to intermediary bodies such as Ministries for Foreign Affairs, Ministries of Justice or prosecutors' offices.

Certainty is further guaranteed since if, for example, the address is incomplete or inaccurate, the officer in the State in which service is to be effected may well be able to undertake investigations in order to find the addressee.

As for the linguistic difficulties which could arise in the context of a grouping of the six countries, these could be overcome by attaching to the instrument a summary in the language of the addressee.

Like Article 10(b) of the Hague Convention, Article IV of the Protocol allows a Contracting State to object to this method of transmission.

NOTES

1 BÜLOW, *op cit.*
2 RIGAUX, La signification des actes judiciaires à l'étranger. Revue critique de droit international privé, p 448 *et seq.*
3 See German Code of Civil Procedure, Article 335(1) (2) and Article 202.
4 Belgium: Code of Civil Procedure, Article 69bis, and Judgment of the Cour de cassation of 4 March 1954. Revue des huissiers de Belgique, May-June 1954, p 15.
France: Code of Civil Procedure, Article 69(10), as interpreted by the French Cour de cassation. See Revue critique de droit international privé, No 1, January-March 1961, p 174 *et seq.*
Italy: Code of Civil Procedure, Articles 142 and 143.
Luxembourg: Arrêté-loi of 1 April 1814.
Netherlands: Code of Civil Procedure, Article 4(8).
5 RIGAUX, id, p 454.
6 This Article reads as follows: "Where the defendant does not enter an appearance, the court may not give judgment in default if the plaintiff does not show that the defendant received the writ of summons. The plaintiff may ask for a new date to be fixed for the hearing."
7 Cour d'appel de POITIERS, 9.7.1959 (Gazette du Palais, 1959.II.183); cf GAVALDA, Revue critique de droit international privé, 1960, No 1, p 174.

Section 8
Lis pendens—related actions

Article 21

As there may be several concurrent international jurisdictions, and the courts of different States may properly be seised of a matter (see in particular Articles 2 and 5), it appeared to be necessary to regulate the question of *lis pendens*. By virtue of Article 21, the courts of a Contracting State must decline jurisdiction, if necessary of their own motion, where proceedings involving the same cause of action and between the same parties are already pending in a court of another State. In cases of *lis pendens* the court is therefore obliged to decline jurisdiction, either on the application of one of the parties, or of its own motion, since this will facilitate the proper administration of justice within the Community. A court will not

PART IV
EC MATERIALS

always have to examine of its own motion whether the same proceedings are pending in the courts of another country, but only when the circumstances are such as to lead the court to believe that this may be the case.

Instead of declining jurisdiction, the court which is subsequently seised of a matter may, however, stay its proceedings if the jurisdiction of the court first seised is contested. This rule was introduced so that the parties would not have to institute new proceedings if, for example, the court first seised of the matter were to decline jurisdiction. The risk of unnecessary disclaimers of jurisdiction is thereby avoided.

Jurisdiction is declined in favour of the court first seised of the matter. The Committee decided that there was no need to specify in the text the point in time from which the proceedings should be considered to be pending, and left this question to be settled by the internal law of each Contracting State.

Article 22

The solution offered by this Article to the problem of related actions differs in several respects from that adopted to regulate the question of *lis pendens*, although it also serves to avoid the risk of conflicting judgments and thus to facilitate the proper administration of justice in the Community.

Where actions are related, the first duty of the court is to stay its proceedings. The proceedings must, however, be pending at the same level of adjudication, for otherwise the object of the proceedings would be different and one of the parties might be deprived of a step in the hierarchy of the courts.

Furthermore, to avoid disclaimers of jurisdiction, the court may decline jurisdiction only if it appears that the court first seised has jurisdiction over both actions, that is to say, in addition, only if that court has not jurisdiction over the second action. The court may decline jurisdiction only on the application of one of the parties, and only if the law of the court first seised permits the consolidation of related actions which are pending in different courts. This last condition takes into account the specific problems of German and Italian law. In German law, consolidation is in general permitted only if both actions are pending in the same court. In Italian law, the constitution does not permit a court to decide whether it will hear an action itself or refer it to another court. It will, however, always be possible for a German or Italian court which is subsequently seised of a matter to stay its proceedings.

[OJ C59, 5.3.79, p 42]

Finally, since the expression "related actions" does not have the same meaning in all the Member States, the third paragraph of Article 22 provides a definition. This is based on the new Belgian Judicial Code (Article 30).

The Convention does not regulate the procedure for the consolidation of related actions. This is a question which is left to the internal laws of the individual States.

Article 23

This Article deals with a situation which will occur only very rarely, namely where an action comes within the exclusive jurisdiction of several courts. To avoid conflicts of jurisdiction, any court other than the court first seised of the action is required under Article 21 or Article 22 to decline jurisdiction in favour of that court.

Section 9
Provisional and protective measures

Article 24

Article 24 provides that application may be made to the courts of a Contracting State for such provisional measures, including protective measures, as may be available under the internal law of that State, irrespective of which court has jurisdiction as to the substance of the case. A corresponding provision will be found in nearly all the enforcement conventions.[1]

In each State, application may therefore be made to the competent courts for provisional or protective measures to be imposed or suspended, or for rulings on the validity of such measures, without regard to the rules of jurisdiction laid down in the Convention.

As regards the measures which may be taken, reference should be made to the internal law of the country concerned.

NOTES

[1] Benelux Treaty and Convention between Belgium and the Netherlands (Article 8); Convention between Germany and Belgium (Article 15(2)); between France and Belgium (Article 9); between Italy and Belgium (Article 14); between Italy and the Netherlands (Article 10); between France and Italy (Article 32); and between Germany and the Netherlands (Article 18(2)).

[3038]

CHAPTER V
RECOGNITION AND ENFORCEMENT

A. GENERAL CONSIDERATIONS

As a result of the safeguards granted to the defendant in the original proceedings, Title III of the Convention is very liberal on the question of recognition and enforcement. As already stated, it seeks to facilitate as far as possible the free movement of judgments, and should be interpreted in this spirit. This liberal approach is evidenced in Title III first by a reduction in the number of grounds which can operate to prevent the recognition and enforcement of judgments and, secondly, by the simplification of the enforcement procedure which will be common to the six countries.

It will be recalled that Article 1, which governs the whole of the Convention, provides that the Convention shall apply in civil and commercial matters whatever the nature of the court or tribunal. It follows that judgments given in a Contracting State in civil or commercial matters by criminal courts or by administrative tribunals must be recognized and enforced in the other Contracting States. Under Article 25, the Convention applies to any judgment, whatever the judgment may be called. It also applies to writs of execution (Vollstreckungsbefehl, Article 699 of the German Code of Civil Procedure)[1] and to the determination of costs (Kostenfestsetzungsbeschluß des Urkundsbeamten, Article 104 of the German Code of Civil Procedure) which, in the Federal Republic, are decisions of the registrar acting as an officer of the court. In decisions based on Article 104 of the German Code of Civil Procedure, the costs are determined in accordance with a schedule laid down by law and on the basis of the judgment of the court deciding on the substance of the matter.[2] In the event of a dispute as to the registrar's decision, a fully constituted court decides the issue.

[OJ C59, 5.3.79, p 43]

It follows from Article 1 that Title III cannot be invoked for the recognition and enforcement of judgments given on matters excluded from the scope of the Convention (status and legal capacity of persons, rules governing rights in property arising out of a matrimonial relationship, wills and succession, bankruptcy and other similar proceedings, social security, and arbitration, including arbitral awards).

On the other hand, Title III applies to any judgment given by a court or tribunal of a Contracting State in those civil and commercial matters which fall within the scope of the Convention, whether or not the parties are domiciled within the Community and whatever their nationality.

NOTES

[1] The Vollstrecknungsbefehl is issued by the court registrar.
[2] See also Article 18(2) of the Hague Convention of March 1954 on Civil Procedure.

B. COMMENTARY ON THE SECTIONS

Section 1
Recognition

Article 26

Recognition must have the result of conferring on judgments the authority and effectiveness accorded to them in the State in which they were given.

The words "*res judicata*" which appear in a number of conventions have expressly been omitted, since judgments given in interlocutory proceedings and *ex parte* may be recognized, and these do not always have the force of *res judicata*. Under the rules laid down in Article 26:

1. judgments are to be recognized automatically;
2. in the event of a dispute, if recognition is itself the principal issue, the procedure for enforcement provided for in the Convention may be applied;
3. if the outcome of proceedings depends on the determination of an incidental question of recognition, the court entertaining those proceedings has jurisdiction on the question of recognition.

The first of these rules lays down the principle that judgments are to be recognized; recognition is to be accorded without the need for recourse to any prior special procedure. It is thus automatic, and does not require a judicial decision in the State in which recognition is sought to enable the party in whose favour judgment has been given to invoke that judgment against any party concerned, for example an administrative authority, in the same way as a judgment given in that State. This provision means that certain legal provisions which in some countries, such as Italy, make the recognition of a foreign judgment subject to a special procedure (dichiarazione di efficacia) will be abolished. The Italian delegation stated that it was able to concur in this solution since the scope of the Convention was limited to matters relating to property rights.

Furthermore, this system is the opposite of that adopted in numerous conventions, according to which foreign judgments are recognized only if they fulfil a certain number of conditions. Under Article 26 there is a presumption in favour of recognition, which can be rebutted only if one of the grounds for refusal listed in Article 27 is present.

The second rule concerns the case where the recognition of a judgment is itself the point at issue, there being no other proceedings involved and no question of enforcement. For example, a negotiable instrument is declared invalid in Italy by reason of fraud. The negotiable instrument is presented to a bank in Belgium. Reliance is placed on the Italian judgment. The bank is faced with two contradictory instruments. The Italian judgment would normally have to be recognized, but it may be that one of the grounds for refusal set out in Article 27 applies. In the event of a dispute it is hardly the task of the bank to decide on the grounds for refusal, and in particular on the scope of Belgian "international public policy". The second rule of Article 26 offers a solution in cases of this kind. It allows the party seeking recognition to make use of the simplified procedure provided by the Convention for enforcement of the judgment. There is thus unification at the stage of recognition not only of the legal or administrative procedures which govern this matter in a number of States, but also in those countries which, like Belgium, do not allow actions for a declaration that a judgment is not to be recognized. Only the party seeking recognition may make use of this simplified procedure, which was evolved solely to promote the enforcement of judgments, and hence their recognition. It would moreover be difficult to apply the procedure laid down if the party opposing recognition could also avail himself of it; the latter will have to submit his claims in accordance with the ordinary rules of the internal law of the State in which recognition is sought.
[OJ C59, 5.3.79, p 44]

The third rule concerns the case where recognition of a judgment is raised as an incidental question in the course of other proceedings. To simplify matters, the Committee provided that the court entertaining the principal proceedings shall also have jurisdiction on the question of recognition.

It will immediately be noticed that two conditions which are frequently inserted in enforcement treaties are not referred to in the Convention: it is not necessary that the foreign judgment should have become *res judicata*,[1] and the jurisdiction of the court which gave the original judgment does not have to be verified by the court of the State in which the recognition is sought unless the matter in question falls within the scope of Sections 3, 4 or 5 of Title II.

NOTES

1 The condition of *res judicata* is required by the Conventions between Germany and Italy, France and Italy, and Italy and the Netherlands. It is not required in the Conventions between Belgium and the Netherlands, Belgium and Italy, Germany and Belgium and Germany and the Netherlands, in the Benelux Treaty, or in the application of the Convention between France and Belgium, in spite of the wording of this last Convention (Article 11(2)).

Article 27

Public policy

Recognition may be refused if it is contrary to public policy in the State in which the recognition is sought. In the opinion of the Committee this clause ought to operate only in exceptional cases. As has already been shown in the commentary on Article 4, public policy is not to be invoked as a ground for refusing to recognize a judgment given by a court of a Contracting State which has based its jurisdiction over a defendant domiciled outside the Community on a provision of its internal law, such as the provisions listed in the second paragraph of Article 3 (Article 14 of the French Civil Code, etc).

Furthermore, it follows from the last paragraph of Article 27 that public policy is not to be used as a means of justifying refusal of recognition on the grounds that the foreign court applied a law other than that laid down by the rules of private international law of the court in which the recognition is sought.

The wording of the public policy provision is similar to that adopted in the most recent conventions,[1] in that it is made clear that there are grounds for refusal, not of the foreign judgment itself, but if recognition of it is contrary to public policy in the State in which the recognition is sought. It is no part of the duty of the court seised of the matter to give an opinion as to whether the foreign judgment is, or is not, compatible with the public policy of its country. Indeed, this might be taken as criticism of the judgment. Its duty is rather to verify whether recognition of the judgment would be contrary to public policy.

NOTES

1 Conventions between Germany and Belgium, Italy and Belgium; Hague Convention on the recognition and enforcement of foreign judgments in civil and commercial matters.

Safeguarding the rights of the defendant

Where judgment is given in default of appearance, recognition must be refused if the defendant was not duly served with the document which instituted the proceedings in sufficient time to enable him to arrange for his defence. Where judgment is given abroad in default of appearance, the Convention affords the defendant double protection.

First, the document must have been duly served. In this connection reference must be made to the internal law of the State in which the judgment was given, and to the international conventions on the service abroad of judicial instruments. Thus, for example, a German court in which recognition of a Belgian judgment given in default of appearance against a person who is in Germany is sought could, on the basis of the Agreement between Belgium and Germany of 25 April 1959, which was entered into to simplify application of the Hague Convention of 1 March 1954 on civil procedure, refuse recognition if the document instituting the proceedings was sent from Belgium to Germany by registered post, since the Federal Republic of Germany does not permit this method of transmitting documents.

Secondly, even where service has been duly effected, recognition can be refused if the court in which recognition is sought considers that the document was not served in sufficient time to enable the defendant to arrange for his defence.

Looking at the second paragraph of Article 20, which lays down that the court of the State in which judgment is given must stay the proceedings if the document instituting the proceedings was not served on the defendant in sufficient time, it might be assumed that Article 27(2) would apply only in exceptional cases. It must not be forgotten, however, that the second paragraph of Article 20 requires the court of the State in which judgment is given to stay proceedings only where the defendant is domiciled in another Contracting State.

[OJ C59, 5.3.79, p 45]

Incompatibility with a judgment already given in the State in which recognition is sought

There can be no doubt that the rule of law in a State would be disturbed if it were possible to take advantage of two conflicting judgments.[1]

The case where a foreign judgment is irreconcilable with a judgment given by a national court is, in the existing conventions, either treated as a matter of public policy,[2] as in the Convention between France and Belgium, the Benelux Treaty and the Convention between Belgium and Germany, or is regulated by a special provision.

In the opinion of the Committee, to treat this as a matter of public policy would involve the danger that the concept of public policy would be interpreted too widely. Furthermore, the

Italian courts have consistently held that foreign judgments whose recognition is sought in Italy and which conflict with an Italian judgment do not fall within the scope of public policy. This is why the enforcement conventions concluded by Italy always contain two provisions, one referring to public policy, which serves the purpose of providing a safeguard in exceptional cases, and the other whereby the judgment must not conflict with an Italian judgment already given, or be prejudicial to proceedings pending in an Italian court.[3]

There are also several other conventions which contain a clause providing for refusal of recognition of a judgment which conflicts with another judgment already given by the courts of the State in which recognition is sought.

In certain conventions, the judgment given in the State in which recognition is sought has to have become *res judicata*,[4] in others it is sufficient for the judgment to be final and conclusive at that stage of procedure,[5] and finally there are some which do not regulate the point.[6]

The Committee preferred a form of wording which does not decide whether the judgment should have become *res judicata* or should merely be final and conclusive, and left this question to the discretion of the court in which recognition is sought.

The Committee also considered that, for refusal of recognition, it would be sufficient if the judgment whose recognition was sought were irreconcilable with a judgment given between the same parties in the State in which recognition was sought. It is therefore not necessary for the same cause of action to be involved. Thus, for example, a French court in which recognition of a Belgian judgment awarding damages for failure to perform a contract is sought will be able to refuse recognition if a French court has already given judgment in a dispute between the same parties declaring that the contract was invalid.

The form of words used also covers the situation referred to in Article 5(3)(c) of the Hague Convention on the recognition and enforcement of foreign judgments, under which recognition may be refused if the proceedings which gave rise to the judgment whose recognition is sought have already resulted in a judgment which was given in a third State and which would be entitled to recognition and enforcement under the law of the State in which recognition is sought.

It is to be anticipated that the application of the provisions of Title II regarding *lis pendens* and related actions will greatly reduce the number of irreconcilable judgments.

[OJ C59, 5.3.79, p 46]

NOTES

1 NIBOYET, Traité de droit international privé français, Paris 1949, Vol VI, No 2028.

2 BATIFFOL, Traité élémentaire de droit international privé, Paris 1959, No 761: "... any judgment which is irreconcilable with a French judgment previously given is contrary to public policy. This rule holds good even if the judgment is not final" (Civ 23 March 1936, Sirey 1936.1.175, R 1937–198); Riezler, *op cit* pp 521 and 547.

3 Conventions between Germany and Italy, Article 4; between France and Italy, Article 1(5); between Belgium and Italy, Article 1(4); and between the Netherlands and Italy, Article 1(3).

4 Hague Convention on the jurisdiction of the contractual forum in matters relating to the international sales of goods, Article 5(3).

5 Conventions between France and the United Kingdom, Article 3(1)(a); between the United Kingdom and Belgium, Article 3(1)(a); between France and Germany on the Saar, Article 30(I)(d); between Austria and Belgium on maintenance, Article 2(2)(b); between Austria and Belgium (general), Article 2(2)(b).

6 Hague Convention of 15 April 1958 concerning the recognition and enforcement of decisions relating to maintenance obligations towards children, Article 2(4), and the Conventions concluded by Italy. Hague Convention on the recognition and enforcement of foreign judgments in civil and commercial matters (Article 5).

PRELIMINARY QUESTIONS

Recognition is not to be refused on the sole ground that the court which gave the original judgment applied a law other than that which would have been applicable under the rules of private international law of the State in which recognition is sought. However, the Convention makes an exception for preliminary questions regarding the status or legal capacity of natural persons, rules governing rights in property arising out of a matrimonial relationship, wills and succession, unless the same result would have been reached by the application of the rules of private international law of the State in which recognition is sought.

The Convention between Belgium and Germany contains a rule which is similar, but confined to cases where the judgment concerns a national of the State in which it is sought to give effect to that judgment. It is pointed out in the report of the negotiators of that Convention that this exception is justified by the fact that States reserve to themselves the right to regulate the status of their nationals. The wording used is similar to that of Article 7 of the Hague Convention on the recognition and enforcement of foreign judgments in civil and commercial matters.

Article 28

The very strict rules of jurisdiction laid down in Title II, and the safeguards granted in Article 20 to defendants who do not enter an appearance, make it possible to dispense with any review, by the court in which recognition or enforcement is sought, of the jurisdiction of the court in which the original judgment was given.

The absence of any review of the substance of the case implies complete confidence in the court of the State in which judgment was given; it is similarly to be assumed that that court correctly applied the rules of jurisdiction of the Convention. The absence of any review as to whether the court in which the judgment was given had jurisdiction avoids the possibility that an alleged failure to comply with those rules might again be raised as an issue at the enforcement stage. The only exceptions concern, first, the matters for which Title II lays down special rules of jurisdiction (insurance, instalment sales and loans) or exclusive rules, and which, as has been shown, are in the six countries either of a binding character or matters of public policy, and, secondly, the case provided for in Article 59; reference should be made to the commentary on that Article.

The second paragraph contains a provision which is already included in a number of conventions (Convention between Germany and Belgium; Hague Convention, Article 9) and avoids recourse to time-wasting duplication in the exceptional cases where re-examination of the jurisdiction of the court of origin is permitted.

The last paragraph of Article 28 specifies that the rules of jurisdiction are not matters of public policy within the meaning of Article 27; in other words, public policy is not to be used as a means of justifying a review of the jurisdiction of the court of origin.[1] This again reflects the Committee's desire to limit so far as possible the concept of public policy.

NOTES

[1] For a similar provision, see Article 13(2) of the Benelux Treaty.

REVIEW AS TO SUBSTANCE

Article 29

It is obviously an essential provision of enforcement conventions that foreign judgments must not be reviewed.

The court of a State in which recognition of a foreign judgment is sought is not to examine the correctness of that judgment; "it may not substitute its own discretion for that of the foreign court[1] nor refuse recognition" if it considers that a point of fact or of law has been wrongly decided.[2]

NOTES

[1] P GRAULICH, Principes de droit international privé. Conflits de lois. Conflits de juridictions. No 254.

[2] BATIFFOL, Traité élémentaire de droit international privé, No 763.

STAY OF PROCEEDINGS

Article 30

Article 30 postulates the following situation: a party may, in the course of litigation, wish to plead a judgment which has been given in another Contracting State but has not yet become *res judicata*. In order to remedy the inconvenience which would result if such judgment were reversed, Article 30 allows the court to stay the proceedings upon the principal issue of which it is seised, until the foreign judgment whose recognition is sought has become *res judicata* in the State in which it was given.

[OJ C59, 5.3.79, p 47]

This power does not prevent the court from examining, before staying the proceedings, whether the foreign judgment fulfils the conditions for recognition laid down in Article 27.

PART IV
EC MATERIALS

Section 2
Enforcement

(a) Preliminary remarks

As has already been shown, the Committee endeavoured to give the Convention a progressive and pragmatic character by means of rules of jurisdiction which break new ground as compared with the enforcement conventions concluded hitherto.

This means, of course, that at the enforcement stage solutions must be found which follow from the rules of jurisdiction.

The progress achieved by Title II of the Convention would be rendered nugatory if a party seeking enforcement in a Contracting State of a judgment given in his favour were impeded by procedural obstacles.

The aim of Title II of the Convention is to strengthen the role of the court of the State in which the judgment was given. It must not be forgotten that that court must declare that it does not have jurisdiction if there are rules of exclusive jurisdiction which give jurisdiction to the courts of another State (Article 19); the court must also declare that it does not have jurisdiction, in cases where the defendant does not enter an appearance, if its jurisdiction is not derived from the Convention (first paragraph of Article 20).

Moreover, the court must stay the proceedings in the absence of proof that the defendant has been able to arrange for his defence (second paragraph of Article 20).

This role, as set out in Title II, is thus of prime importance.

It follows that the intervention of the court in which enforcement is sought is more limited than is usual under enforcement conventions. That court has in practice only two points to examine: public policy and whether the defendant has had the opportunity of defending himself. The other reasons for refusal—conflicting judgments, preliminary questions, review of jurisdiction in relation to certain specific topics—can, in fact, be regarded as akin to public policy. Since, moreover, the Convention is confined to matters relating to property rights, public policy will only very seldom have any part to perform.

This limitation on the powers of the court in which enforcement is sought led to a simplification of the enforcement procedure. Furthermore, as the position of the defendant in the original proceedings is well protected, it is proper that the applicant for enforcement be enabled to proceed rapidly with all the necessary formalities in the State in which enforcement is sought, that he be free to act without prior warning and that enforcement be obtained without unnecessary complications.

The Committee discussed the enforcement procedure at length before adopting it. There were several possibilities open to it: reference back to national laws but subject to certain rules of the Convention, ordinary contentious procedure, summary contentious procedure or *ex parte* application.

Each of these solutions had its advantages and disadvantages. The Committee finally adopted a system for the whole Community based on *ex parte* application. This rapid and simple procedure will apply in all six States.

This uniform solution has the advantage of creating a proper balance as between the various provisions of the Convention: uniform rules of jurisdiction in the six countries and identical procedures for enforcement.

(b) Conditions for enforcement

As has been shown, the Convention is based on the principle that a foreign judgment is presumed to be in order. It must, in principle, be possible to enforce it in the State in which enforcement is sought. Enforcement can be refused only if there is a ground for refusing recognition.[1] The foreign judgment must, however, be enforceable in the State in which it was given in order to be enforceable in the State in which enforcement is sought.

[OJ C59, 5.3.79, p 48]

If a judgment from which an appeal still lies or against which an appeal has been lodged in the State in which it was given cannot be provisionally enforced in that State, it cannot be enforced in the State in which enforcement is sought. It is an essential requirement of the instrument whose enforcement is sought that it should be enforceable in the State in which it originates. As Niboyet points out, there is no reason for granting to a foreign judgment rights which it does not have in the country in which it was given.[2]

Under no circumstances may a foreign judgment be reviewed as to its substance (Article 34).

NOTES

1 On the disadvantages resulting from a difference between the conditions for recognition and for enforcement, see RIGAUX, *op cit*, p 207, No 39.

2 NIBOYET, Droit international privé français. Vol VI, No 1974.

(c) Enforcement procedure

Before examining the Articles of the section on enforcement it seems appropriate to give on outline of the procedure which will be applicable in the six States.

1. The application, accompanied by the documents required under Articles 46 and 47, must be submitted to the authority specified in Article 32. The procedure for making the application is governed by the law of the State in which enforcement is sought.
   The applicant must give an address for service of process or appoint a representative *ad litem* in the jurisdiction of the court applied to.
2. The court applied to must give its decision without delay, and is not able to summon the other party. At this stage no contentious proceedings are allowed.
   The application may be refused only for one of the reasons specified in Articles 27 and 28.
3. If enforcement is authorized:
   (a) the party against whom enforcement is sought may appeal against the decision within one month of service of the decision (Article 36);
   (b) the appeal must be lodged, in accordance with the rules governing procedure in contentious matters, with the court specified in Article 37;
   (c) if an appeal has been lodged against the foreign judgment in the State in which it was given, or if the time for such an appeal has not yet expired, the court seised of the appeal against the decision authorizing enforcement may stay the proceedings or make enforcement conditional on the provision of security (Article 38);
   (d) the judgment given on the appeal against the decision authorizing enforcement may not be contested by an ordinary appeal. It may be contested only by an appeal in cassation[1] (Article 37);
   (e) during the time specified for an appeal against the decision authorizing enforcement, the applicant may take only protective measures; the decision authorizing enforcement carries with it the power to proceed to such measures (Article 39).
4. If enforcement is refused:
   (a) the applicant may appeal to the court specified in Article 40;
   (b) the procedure before that court is contentious, the other party being summoned to appear (Article 40);
   (c) the judgment given on this appeal may be contested only by an appeal in cassation[1] (Article 41).

NOTES

1 In the Federal Republic of Germany by a "Rechtsbeschwerde".

Article 31

Under this Article "a judgment given in a Contracting State and enforceable in that State shall be enforced in another Contracting State when, on the application of any interested party, the order for its enforcement has been issued there".

As can be seen, this provision is almost identical with that contained in the European Convention providing a uniform law on arbitration.[1] The Committee did, in fact, take the view that judgments given in one Contracting State should be enforceable in any other Contracting State as easily as arbitral awards.

[OJ C59, 5.3.79, p 49]

The legal systems of the Member States are already familiar with authorization of enforcement by means of an enforcement order. This is so, for example, in the case of judgments and decisions given by the European Community institutions (Article 92 of the ECSC Treaty, Article 192 of the EEC Treaty, Article 164 of the Euratom Treaty). It is also true of judgments and decisions falling within the scope of the Mannheim Convention.[2]

The Convention of 30 August 1962 between Germany and the Netherlands also provides that judgments given in one of the two States are to be enforced in the other if enforcement is authorized by means of an enforcement order.

A rule similar to that in Article 31, that is to say an *ex parte* procedure, was contained in the Franco-German Treaty on the Saar of 27 October 1956. Business circles in the Saar have said that the rule has proved entirely satisfactory.

About 80% of enforcement proceedings have been successfully completed by means of the first *ex parte* written phase of the procedure. In the majority of cases, judgment debtors have refrained from contesting the proceedings by means of an appeal. This is easily explained by the fact that cases of refusal of enforcement are exceptional, and the risk of having to bear the costs of the proceedings restrains the judgment debtor, unless he feels certain of winning his case.

Article 31 does not purport to determine whether it is the judgment given in the State of origin, or the decision authorizing the issue of the enforcement order, which is enforceable in the State in which enforcement is sought.

The expression "on the application of any interested party" implies that any person who is entitled to the benefit of the judgment in the State in which it was given has the right to apply for an order for its enforcement.

NOTES

1 European Convention providing a uniform law on arbitration, Strasbourg, 20 January 1966. Article 29 of Annex I: "An arbitral award may be enforced only when it can no longer be contested before arbitrators and when an enforcement formula has been apposed to it by the competent authority on the application of the interested party."

2 Revised Convention for the Navigation of the Rhine signed at Mannheim on 17 October 1868.

Article 32

Article 32 specifies the authority in each of the Contracting States to which the application must be submitted and which will have jurisdiction. It was considered to be in the interests of the parties that each relevant authority be indicated in the Convention itself.

The court to which local jurisdiction is given is that for the place of domicile of the party against whom enforcement is sought, or, if that party is not domiciled in the State in which enforcement is sought, the court for the place of enforcement, that is, where the judgment debtor has assets. The jurisdiction of the court for the place of enforcement is thus of minor importance.

The provision requiring applications to be submitted to the court for the place where the judgment debtor is domiciled was included for the following reason. It is quite possible that in the State in which enforcement is sought the judgment debtor may possess property situated in the jurisdiction of different courts. If jurisdiction had been given only to the court for the place of enforcement, a choice between several courts would have been open to the applicant. Thus an applicant who was unsuccessful in one court could, instead of availing himself of the methods of appeal provided for in the Convention, have applied to another court which would not necessarily have come to the same decision as the first court, and this without the knowledge of the other party, since the procedure is *ex parte*.

Article 33

Under Article 33, the procedure and formalities for making the application are to be governed by the law of the State in which enforcement is sought.

Reference must therefore be made to the national laws for the particulars which the application must contain, the number of copies which must be submitted to the court, the authority to which the application must be submitted, also, where necessary, the language in which it must be drawn up, and whether a lawyer should be instructed to appear.

The provisions to which reference must be made are the following:

Belgium:

The matter will be governed by the Judicial Code (see Articles 1025 and 1027);

Federal Republic of Germany, Netherlands and Italy:

The question will be governed by the law implementing the Convention;

France:

Code of Civil Procedure, Article 1040;

[OJ C59, 5.3.79, p 50]

Luxembourg:

A lawyer must be instructed in accordance with the general law under which no one can officially address the court except through an *avoué*. Article 856 or Article 512 of the Code of Civil Procedure is generally invoked in support of this proposition.

The application must be accompanied by the documents required to be produced under Articles 46 and 47.

In the view of the Committee, if the applicant does not produce the required documents, enforcement should not be refused, but the court may stay the proceedings and allow the applicant time to produce the documents. If the documents produced are not sufficient and the court cannot obtain sufficient information, it may refuse to entertain the application.

Finally, the applicant must, in accordance with the law of the State in which enforcement is sought, either give an address for service of process or appoint a representative *ad litem* within the area of jurisdiction of the court applied to. This provision is important in two respects: first for communicating to the applicant the decision given on the application (Article 35), and secondly in case the party against whom enforcement is sought wishes to appeal, since such an appeal must be lodged "in accordance with the rules governing procedure in contentious matters" (Article 37).

The respondent must therefore summon the applicant to appear; the furnishing of an address for service or the appointment of a representative enables the summons to be served rapidly, in accordance with the law of the country in which enforcement is sought, without risk of error and without all the hazards connected with the service of legal documents abroad. It will in fact usually happen that the applicant is domiciled outside the State in which enforcement is sought.

The appointment of a representative *ad litem* has been provided for because the furnishing of an address for service is unknown in German law.

The two methods will, of course, produce the same result.

Article 34

Article 34 provides that the court applied to shall give its decision without delay; "the party against whom enforcement is sought shall not at this stage of the proceedings be entitled to make any submissions on the application."

The Committee considered but rejected the idea of imposing on the court to which application is made a fixed period for giving its decision. Such a time limit is unknown in judicial practice, and there would in any case be no way of enforcing it.

The Convention does not allow the court to which application is made to ask the respondent to make submissions, even in exceptional cases. Such a possibility would have meant that the proceedings were not fully *ex parte*. Certain courts might be inclined to hear the respondent, which would in fact result in the *ex parte* procedure systematically becoming *inter partes*. Moreover, there would be a reduction in the element of surprise which is necessary in an enforcement procedure if the respondent is not to have the opportunity of withdrawing his assets from any measure of enforcement.

The rights of the respondent are safeguarded, since he can institute contentious proceedings by appealing against the decision authorizing enforcement.

As has been shown above, the application may be refused only for one of the reasons specified in Articles 27 and 28, and the foreign judgment may not be reviewed as to its substance. Consequently, fresh claims which have not been submitted to the foreign court are inadmissible; the court seised of the application may authorize or refuse enforcement, but it cannot alter the foreign judgment.

The court may, however, refuse the application if it does not satisfy the requirements of Articles 32 and 33.

Article 35

Article 35 provides that the appropriate officer of the court shall without delay bring the decision given on the application to the notice of the applicant in accordance with the procedure laid down by the law of the State in which enforcement is sought. It is important that the applicant be informed of the decision taken. This demonstrates the value of an address for service or of the appointment of a representative *ad litem*, particularly where the applicant is domiciled abroad.

The manner in which the decision is communicated to the applicant will be a matter for the national law of the State in which enforcement is sought, irrespective of whether enforcement is authorized or refused.

[OJ C59, 5.3.79, p 51]

Article 36

If enforcement is authorized, the decision must be notified to the party against whom enforcement has been granted. That party may appeal against the decision from the time it is served on him. As regards the period within which an appeal may be lodged and the moment from which it begins to run, Article 36 makes a distinction between the following situations:

(a) if the party is domiciled in the State in which the decision was given, the period is one month; the moment from which time begins to run is determined by the law of that State, from which there is no reason to derogate;

(b) if the party is domiciled in another Contracting State, the period is two months, and runs from the date when the decision was served, either on him in person or at his residence.[1]

In France and the Netherlands, the day of delivery to the prosecutor's office is not counted for purposes of computation of time. In Belgium, the day of delivery to the postal authorities is not counted (Article 40 of the Judicial Code), nor is the day on which an instrument is dispatched by a Belgian Consul to a foreign authority.[2]

The purpose of this rule, which derogates from some national laws, is to protect the respondent and to prevent his being deprived of a remedy because he had not been informed of the decision in sufficient time to contest it.

No extension of time may be granted on account of distance, as the time allowed is sufficient to enable the party concerned to contest the decision, if he is so minded;

(c) if the party is domiciled outside the Community, the period within which an appeal may be lodged runs from the date when the decision is served or is deemed to have been served according to the law of the State in which the decision was given. In this case the period of one month may be extended on account of distance in accordance with the law of that State.

Computation of time is governed by the internal law of the State in which the decision was given.

NOTES

1. Service on a party at his residence means delivering the instrument to a person who is present and empowered by law to receive a copy of the instrument or, if there is no such person, to a competent authority.
2. Belgian Court of Cassation, 4 March 1954; Revue des huissiers de Belgique, May to June 1954, p 15.

Article 37

Article 37 specifies for each country the court with which an appeal can be lodged.

In that court the proceedings are contentious. Accordingly it is incumbent upon the person against whom enforcement has been authorized to summon the other party to appear.

The court seised of the appeal will have to examine whether it was properly lodged and will have to decide upon the merits of the appeal, taking account of the additional information supplied by the appellant. It will therefore be open to the appellant to establish, in the case of a judgment originally given in default of appearance, that the rights of the defendant were disregarded, or that a judgment has already been given in a dispute between the same parties in the State in which enforcement is sought which is irreconcilable with the foreign judgment. The appellant may also plead Article 38 if he has lodged an appeal against the judgment whose enforcement is sought in the State in which it was given.

It is no part of the duty of the court with which the appeal against the decision authorizing enforcement is lodged to review the foreign judgment as to its substance. This would be contrary to the spirit of the Convention. The appellant could, however, effectively adduce grounds which arose after the foreign judgment was given. For example, he may establish that he has since discharged the debt. As Batiffol points out, such grounds are admissible in enforcement proceedings.[1, 2]

The second paragraph of Article 37 provides that the judgment given on the appeal may be contested only by an appeal in cassation and not by any other form of appeal or review.

This rule was requisite for the following reasons. First, the grounds for refusing enforcement are very limited and involve public policy in the State in which enforcement is sought. No useful purpose is served by further argument on this concept. Next, the situation is different from that in which purely national proceedings are involved. The proceedings on the merits of the case itself have already taken place in the State in which the judgment was given, and the Convention in no way interferes with the rights of appeal. It is true that the Convention applies to judgments which are enforceable only provisionally, but in this case the court with which the appeal is lodged may, as provided in Article 38, stay the proceedings. An excessive number of avenues of appeal might be used by the losing party purely as delaying tactics, and this would constitute an obstacle to the free movement of judgments which is the object of the Convention.

[OJ C59, 5.3.79, p 52]

Since appeals in cassation are unknown in the Federal Republic of Germany, it has been provided, in order to establish a certain parity amongst the Contracting States, that an appeal on a point of law (Rechtsbeschwerde) shall lie against a judgment of the Court of Appeal (Oberlandesgericht).

NOTES

1 BATIFFOL, *op cit*, p 863, note 57.

2 For the Federal Republic of Germany, see Article 767 of the Code of Civil Procedure; see also BAUMBACH-LAUTERBACH, Zivilprozeßordnung, paragraph 723, note 1.

Article 38

Article 38 covers cases where an ordinary appeal has been lodged against the judgment in the State in which that judgment was given, and also cases where the period within which such an appeal may be lodged has not yet expired. The court with which the appeal against enforcement under the first paragraph of Article 37 is lodged may either stay the proceedings, authorize enforcement, make enforcement conditional on the provision of such security as it thinks fit, or specify the time within which the defendant must lodge his appeal.

This provision originates in the Convention between Germany and Belgium (Article 10), and its "object is to protect the judgment debtor against any loss which could result from the enforcement of a judgment which has not yet become *res judicata* and may be amended".[1]

Article 38 deals only with judgments which, notwithstanding that they may be appealed against, are enforceable in the State in which they were given.

Only the court seised of the appeal has the power to stay the proceedings, and such a stay can be granted only on the application of the party against whom enforcement is sought. This is because that party does not appear at the first stage of the proceedings and cannot be required to do so.

NOTES

1 Convention between Germany and Belgium. See Report of the negotiators.

Article 39

Article 39 contains two very important rules. First it provides that during the time specified for the lodging of an appeal the applicant for enforcement may take no enforcement measures other than protective measures—namely those available under the law of the State in which enforcement is sought. Similarly, if an appeal has actually been lodged, this rule applies until the appeal has been determined. Secondly it provides that the decision authorizing enforcement carries with it the power to proceed to any such protective measures. Article 39 also allows the judgment creditor in certain States, for example in the Federal Republic of Germany, to initiate the first phase of the enforcement of the foreign instrument. The object of this provision is to ensure at the enforcement stage a balance between the rights and interests of the parties concerned, in order to avoid either of them suffering any loss as a result of the operation of the rules of procedure.

On the one hand, an applicant who, in consequence of a foreign judgment, is in possession of an enforceable instrument, must be able to take quickly all measures necessary to prevent the judgment debtor from removing the assets on which execution is to be levied. This is made possible by the *ex parte* procedure and by the provision in Article 39 that the decision authorizing enforcement carries with it the power to proceed to such protective measures. The power arises automatically. Even in those States whose law requires proof that the case calls for prompt action or that there is any risk in delay the applicant will not have to establish that either of those elements is present; power to proceed to protective measures is not a matter for the discretion of the court.

On the other hand, the fact that the enforcement procedure is *ex parte* makes it essential that no irreversible measures of execution can be taken against the defendant. The latter may be in a position to establish that there are grounds for refusal of enforcement; he may, for example, be able to show that the question of public policy was not examined in sufficient detail. To safeguard his rights it accordingly appeared to be necessary to delay enforcement, which is usually carried out by sequestration of the movable and immovable property of the defendant, until the end of the time specified for appeal (see Article 36) or, if an appeal is actually lodged, until it has been determined. In other words, this is a counterbalance to the *ex parte* procedure; the effect of the decision authorizing enforcement given pursuant to Article 31 is limited in that during the time specified for an appeal, or if an appeal has been lodged, no enforcement measures can be taken on the basis of that decision against the assets of the judgment debtor.
[OJ C59, 5.3.79, p 53]

Articles 40 and 41

These Articles relate to the case where an application for enforcement is refused.

Article 40 provides that the applicant may appeal to the appeal court which has jurisdiction in the State in which enforcement is sought.

The Committee did not think it necessary that the Convention should fix the period within which appeals would have to be lodged. If the applicant has had his application refused, it is for him to give notice of appeal within such time as he considers suitable. He will have regard, no doubt, to the length of time it will take him to assemble all the relevant documents.

Upon appeal the proceedings are contentious, since the party against whom enforcement is sought is summoned to appear. The *inter partes* procedure is necessary in order to avoid numerous appeals. If the procedure on appeal had remained *ex parte*, it would have been essential to provide for additional proceedings to enable the defendant to make his submissions if the appellate court were to reverse the decision at first instance and authorize enforcement. The Committee wished to avoid a plethora of appeals. Moreover, the dismissal of the application reverses the presumption of validity of the foreign judgment.

The summoning of the party against whom enforcement is sought is to be effected in manner prescribed by the national laws.

The appellate court can give judgment only if the judgment debtor has in fact been given an opportunity to make his submissions. The object of this provision is to protect the rights of the defendant and to mitigate the disadvantages which result from certain systems of serving instruments abroad. These disadvantages are all the more serious in that a party against whom enforcement is sought and who is not notified in time to arrange for his defence no longer has any judicial remedy against the judgment given on the appeal other than by way of an appeal in cassation, and then only to the extent that this is allowed by the law of the State in which enforcement is sought (Article 41).

Because of the safeguards contained in Article 40, Article 41 provides that the judgment given on the appeal may not be contested by an ordinary appeal, but only by an appeal in cassation. The reason why a special form of appeal (Rechtsbeschwerde) is provided for in the Federal Republic of Germany has already been explained (Article 37).

The procedure for the forms of appeal provided for in Articles 40 and 41 is to be determined by the national laws which may, where necessary, prescribe time limits.

Article 42

Article 42 covers two different situations.

The first paragraph of Article 42 empowers the court of the State in which enforcement is sought to authorize enforcement in respect of certain matters dealt with in a judgment and to refuse it in respect of others.[1] As explained in the report annexed to the Benelux Treaty, which contains a similar provision, "this discretion exists in all cases where a judgment deals with separate and independent heads of claim, and the decision on some of these is contrary to the public policy of the country in which enforcement is sought, while the decision on others is not."

The second paragraph of Article 42 allows an applicant to request the partial enforcement of a judgment, and *ex hypothesi* allows the court addressed to grant such a request. As mentioned in the report on the Benelux Treaty, "it is possible that the applicant for enforcement himself wants only partial enforcement, e g where the judgment whose enforcement is sought orders the payment of a sum of money, part of which has been paid since the judgment was given."[2]

As is made clear in the Conventions between Germany and Belgium, and between Belgium and Italy, which contain similar provisions, the applicant may exercise this option whether the judgment covers one or several heads of claim.

NOTES

1 See Benelux Treaty (Articles 14(4)); the Conventions between France and Italy (Article 3); between Italy and the Netherlands (Article 3); between Germany and Belgium (Article 11); between Belgium and Italy (Article 10) and between Germany and the Netherlands (Article 12).

2 See also the Conventions between Germany and Belgium (Article 11) and between Belgium and Italy (Article 10).

Article 43

Article 43 relates to judgments which order a periodic payment by way of a penalty. Some enforcement conventions contain a clause on this subject (see Benelux Treaty, Article 14; Convention between and the Germany and the Netherlands, Article 7).

[OJ C59, 5.3.79, p 54]

It follows from the wording adopted that judgments given in a Contracting State which order the payment of a sum of money for each day of delay, with the intention of getting the judgment debtor to fulfil his obligations, will be enforced in another Contracting State only if the amount of the payment has been finally determined by the courts of the State in which judgment was given.

Article 44

Article 44 deals with legal aid.

A number of enforcement conventions deal with this matter.[1]

The provisions adopted by the Committee supplements the Hague Convention of 1 March 1954 on civil procedure, which has been ratified by the six States, so that a party who has been granted legal aid in the State in which judgment was given also qualifies automatically for legal aid in the State in which enforcement is sought, but only as regards the issuing of the order for enforcement. Thus the automatic extension of legal aid achieved by the Convention does not apply in relation to enforcement measures or to proceedings arising from the exercise of rights of appeal.

The reasoning underlying Article 44 is as follows.

First, as maintenance obligations fall within the scope of the Convention, consideration was given to the humanitarian issues which were the basis for a similar provision in the 1958 Hague Convention.

Above all it must not be forgotten that if a needy applicant were obliged, before making his application for enforcement, to institute in the State in which enforcement is sought proceedings for recognition of the decision granting him legal aid in the State in which the judgment was given, he would be in a less favourable position than other applicants. He would in particular not have the advantage of the rapidity of the procedure and the element of surprise which Title III is designed to afford to any party seeking the enforcement of a foreign judgment.

It is moreover because of this consideration that the automatic extension of legal aid has been limited to the procedure for issuing the order for enforcement, and has not been extended to the proceedings on appeal. Once these proceedings have been set in motion, the applicant for enforcement, or, in case of appeal, the respondent, may, in accordance with the 1954 Hague Convention, take the necessary steps, in the State in which enforcement is sought, to obtain legal aid, in the same way as nationals of that State.

Under Article 47(2) an applicant must, on making his application, produce documents showing that he is in receipt of legal aid in the State in which judgment was given.

NOTES

[1] Hague Convention of 15 April 1958 concerning the recognition and enforcement of decisions relating to maintenance obligations towards children (Article 9); convention between Italy and the Netherlands (Article 6) and between Germany and the Netherlands (Article 15).

Article 45

This Article deals with security for costs. A similar rule is included in the Hague Convention of 1 March 1954 but as regards the obligation to provide security it exempts only nationals of the Contracting States who are also domiciled in one of those States (Article 17). Under Article 45, any party, irrespective of nationality or domicile, who seeks enforcement in one Contracting State of a judgment given in another Contracting State, may do so without providing security. The two conditions—nationality and domicile—prescribed by the 1954 Convention do not apply.

The Committee considered that the provision of security in relation to proceedings for the issuing of an order for enforcement was unnecessary.

As regards the proceedings which take place in the State in which judgment was given, the Committee did not consider it necessary to depart from the rules of the 1954 Convention.

Section 3
Common provisions

This Section deals with the documents which must be produced when application is made for the recognition or enforcement of a judgment.

Article 46 applies to both recognition and enforcement. Article 47 applies only to applications for enforcement. It should be noted that at the recognition stage there is no reason to require production of the documents referred to in Article 47.
[OJ C59, 5.3.79, p 55]

Article 47(1) provides for the production of documents which establish that the judgment is enforceable in the State in which it was given. The requirement that the judgment be, in law, enforceable in that State applies only in relation to its enforcement (not to its recognition) abroad. (Article 31).

Article 47(2), which relates to documents showing that the applicant is receiving legal aid in the State in which judgment was given, is also relevant only in enforcement proceedings. The documents are in fact intended to enable a party receiving legal aid in the State in which judgment was given to qualify for it automatically in the proceedings relating to the issue of the order for enforcement (Article 44). However, recognition requires no special procedure (Article 26). If recognition were itself the principal issue in an action, Article 44 and, consequently, Article 47(2) would apply, since Article 26 refers to Sections 2 and 3 of Title III.

Under Article 46(1), a copy of the judgment which satisfies the conditions necessary to establish its authenticity must be produced, whether it is recognition or enforcement which is sought.

This provision is found in all enforcement treaties and does not require any special comment. The authenticity of a judgment will be established in accordance with the maxim *locus regit actum*; it is therefore the law of the place where the judgment was given which prescribes the conditions which the copy of the judgment must satisfy in order to be valid.[1]

Under Article 46(2), if the judgment was given in default, a document which establishes that the party in default was served with the document instituting the proceedings must also be produced.

The court in which recognition or enforcement is sought must, if the foreign judgment was given in default, be in a position to verify that the defendant's right to defend himself was safeguarded.

Article 47 provides that the following documents must be produced:

(a) documents which establish that the judgment is enforceable according to the law of the State in which it was given. This does not mean that a separate document certifying that the judgment has become enforceable in that State is necessarily required. Thus, in France, "provisional enforceability" would be deduced from an express reference to it in judgments given pursuant to Article 135a of the Code of Civil Procedure. Decisions given in summary proceedings will be provisionally enforceable (Article 809 of the Code of Civil Procedure); and so will decisions in *ex parte* proceedings (Article 54 of the Decree of 30 March 1808). But whether other judgments are enforceable can be determined only when the date on which they were given has been considered in relation to the date on which they were served and the time allowed for lodging an appeal.[2] Documents which establish that the judgment has been served will also have to be produced, since some judgments may be enforceable and consequently fall within the scope of the Convention even if they have not been served on the other party. However, before enforcement can be applied for, that party must at least have been informed of the judgment given against him and also have had the opportunity to satisfy the judgment voluntarily;

(b) where appropriate, a document showing, in accordance with the law of the State in which the judgment was given, that the applicant is in receipt of legal aid in that State.

NOTES

1 WESER. Traité franco-belge du 8 juillet 1899. Étude critique No 247.

2 *Belgium*: Judicial Code: see Article 1029 for decisions in *ex parte* proceedings, Article 1039 for decisions in summary proceedings, and Articles 1398 and 1496 for judgments.

Federal Republic of Germany: "Vollstreckungsklausel"—Under Article 725 of the Code of Civil Procedure, the order for enforcement is worded as follows:

"This copy of the judgment shall be given to ... (name of the party) for the purpose of enforcement."

This order must be added at the end of the copy of the judgment and must be signed by the appropriate officer of the court and sealed with the seal of the court.

Luxembourg: see Articles 135, 136 and 137 of the Code of Civil Procedure, Article 164 for judgments in default, Article 439 for Commercial Courts (tribunaux de commerce) and Article 5 of the Law of 23 March 1893 on summary jurisdiction.

Netherlands: see Articles 339, 350, 430 and 433 of the Code of Civil Procedure, also Articles 82 and 85 of that Code.

Article 48

In order to avoid unnecessary formalities, this Article authorizes the court to allow time for the applicant to produce the documentary evidence proving service of the document instituting the proceedings, required under Article 46(2), and the documentary evidence showing that the applicant was in receipt of legal aid in the State in which judgment was given (Article 47(2)).

[OJ C59, 5.3.79, p 56]

The court may dispense with the production of these documents by the applicant (the Committee had in mind the case where the documents had been destroyed) if it considers that it has sufficient information before it from other evidence.

The second paragraph relates to the translation of the documents to be produced. Again with the object of simplifying the procedure, it is here provided that the translation may be certified by a person qualified to do so in any one of the Contracting States.

Article 49

This Article provides that legalization or other like formality is not necessary as regards the documents to be produced and, in particular, that the certificate provided for in the Hague Convention of 5 October 1961 abolishing the requirement of legalization for foreign public documents is not required. The same applies to the document whereby an applicant appoints a representative, perhaps a lawyer, to act for him in proceedings for the issue of an order for enforcement.

[3039]

CHAPTER VI
AUTHENTIC INSTRUMENTS AND COURT SETTLEMENTS

Article 50

In drawing up rules for the enforcement of authentic instruments, the Committee has broken no new ground. Similar provisions are, in fact, contained in the Conventions already concluded by the six States,[1] with the sole exception of the Convention between Germany and Italy.

Since Article 1 governs the whole Convention, Article 50 applies only to authentic instruments which have been drawn up or registered in matters falling within the scope of the Convention.

In order that an authentic instrument which has been drawn up or registered in one Contracting State may be the subject of an order for enforcement issued in another Contracting State, three conditions must be satisfied:

(a) the instrument must be enforceable in the State in which it was drawn up or registered;
(b) it must satisfy the conditions necessary to establish its authenticity in that State;
(c) its enforcement must not be contrary to public policy in the State in which enforcement is sought.

The provisions of Section 3 of Title III are applicable as appropriate. It follows in particular that no legalization or similar formality is required.

NOTES

1 Conventions between France and Belgium (Article 16); between Belgium and the Netherlands (Article 16); Benelux Treaty (Article 18); Conventions between Germany and Belgium (Article 14); between Italy and Belgium (Article 13); between Germany and the Netherlands (Article 16); between Italy and the Netherlands (Article 8); and between France and Italy (Article 6).

Article 51

A provision covering court settlements was considered necessary on account of the German and Netherlands legal systems,[1] under German and Netherlands law, settlements approved by a court in the course of proceedings are enforceable without further formality (Article 794(1) of the German Code of Civil Procedure, and Article 19 of the Netherlands Code of Civil Procedure).

The Convention, like the Convention between Germany and Belgium, makes court settlements subject to the same rules as authentic instruments, since both are contractual in nature. Enforcement can therefore be refused only if it is contrary to public policy in the State in which it is sought.

[3040]

NOTES

1 See the Conventions between Germany and Belgium (Article 14(1)); between Germany and the Netherlands (Article 16); between Germany and Italy (Article 9); and the Hague Convention on the choice of court (Article 10).

[OJ C59, 5.3.79, p 57]

CHAPTER VII
GENERAL PROVISIONS

Article 52

As regards the determination of domicile (Article 52), reference should be made to Chapter IV(A)(3) which deals with the matter.

Article 53

Article 53 provides that, for the purposes of this Convention, the seat of a company or other legal person or association of natural or legal persons shall be treated as its domicile.

The Convention does not define what is meant by the seat of a legal person or of a company or association of natural or legal persons any more than it defines domicile.

In determining the location of the seat, the court will apply its rules of private international law. The Committee did not think it possible to particularize the concept of seat in any other way, and considered that it could not be achieved by making a reference to Article 52, in view of the different approaches which the various Member States of the Community adopt in this matter. Moreover, the Committee did not wish to encroach upon the work on company law which is now being carried out within the Community.

It did not escape the attention of the Committee that the application of Article 16(2) of the Convention could raise certain difficulties. This would be the case, for example, where a court in one State ordered the dissolution of a company whose seat was in that State and application was then made for recognition of that order in another State under whose law the location of the company's seat was determined by its statutes, if, when so determined, it was in that other State. In the opinion of the Committee, the court of the State in which recognition were sought would be entitled, under the first paragraph of Article 28, to refuse recognition on the ground that the courts of that State had exclusive jurisdiction.

Article 53 does not deal with the preliminary question of the recognition of companies or other legal persons or associations of natural or legal persons; this must be resolved either by national law or by the Hague Convention of 1 June 1956 on the recognition of the legal personality of companies, firms, associations and foundations,[1] pending the entry into force of the Convention which is at present being prepared within the EEC on the basis of Article 220 of the Treaty of Rome.

Article 53 refers to companies or other legal persons and to associations of natural or legal persons; to speak only of legal persons would have been insufficient, since this expression would not have covered certain types of company, such as the "offene Handelsgesellschaft" under German law, which are not legal persons. Similarly, it would not have been sufficient to speak only of companies, since certain bodies, such as associations and foundations, would then not have been covered by this Convention.

[3041]

NOTES

[1] Ratified on 20 April 1966 by Belgium, France and the Netherlands.

CHAPTER VIII
TRANSITIONAL PROVISIONS

Article 54

As a general rule, enforcement treaties have no retroactive effect,[1] in order "not to alter a state of affairs which has been reached on the basis of legal relations other than those created between the two States as a result of the introduction of the Convention".[2]

So far as the author is aware only the Benelux Treaty applies to judgments given before its entry into force.

[OJ C59, 5.3.79, p 58]

A solution as radical as that of the Benelux Treaty did not seem acceptable. In the first place, the conditions which a judgment must fulfil in order to be recognized and enforced are much stricter under the Benelux Treaty (Article 13) than under the EEC Convention. Secondly, the ease with which recognition and enforcement can be granted under the EEC Convention is balanced by the provisions of Title II which safeguard the interests of the defendant. In particular, those provisions have made it possible, at the stage of recognition or enforcement, to dispense with any review of the jurisdiction of the court of origin (Article 28). But, of course, a defendant in the State in which judgment was originally given will be able to rely on these protective provisions only when the Convention has entered into force. Only then will he be able to invoke the Convention to plead lack of jurisdiction.

Although Article 54 was not modelled on the Benelux Treaty, its effect is not very different.

The rules adopted are as follows:

1. The Convention applies to proceedings which are instituted—and in which, therefore, judgment is given—after the entry into force of the Convention.
2. The Convention does not apply if the proceedings were instituted and judgment given before the entry into force of the Convention.

3. The Convention does apply, but subject to certain reservations, to judgments given after its entry into force in proceedings instituted before its entry into force.

In this case, the court of the State addressed may review the jurisdiction of the court of origin, since the defendant originally had no opportunity to contest that jurisdiction in that court on the basis of the Convention.

Enforcement will be authorized if the jurisdiction of the court of origin:

(i) either was based on a rule which accords with one of the rules of jurisdiction in the Convention; for example, if the defendant was domiciled in the State in which the judgment was given;

(ii) or was based on a multilateral or bilateral convention in force between the State of origin and the State addressed. Thus if, for example, an action relating to a contract were brought in a German court, the judgment given could be recognized and enforced in Belgium if the obligation had been or was to be performed in the Federal Republic since the jurisdiction of the German court would be founded on Article 3(1)(5) of the Convention between Germany and Belgium.[2]

If the jurisdiction of the court of origin is founded on one of those bases, the judgment must be recognized and enforced, provided of course that there is no ground for refusal under Article 27 or 28. Recognition will be accorded without any special procedure being required (Article 26); enforcement will be authorized in accordance with the rules of Section 2 of Title III, that is to say, on *ex parte* application.

It follows from Article 54, which provides that the Convention applies only to legal proceedings instituted after its entry into force, that the Convention will have no effect on proceedings in progress at the time of its entry into force. If, for example, before the entry into force of the Convention, proceedings were instituted in France in accordance with Article 14 of the Civil Code against a person domiciled in another Contracting State, that person could not plead the Convention for the purpose of contesting the jurisdiction of the French court.

[3042]

NOTES

1 Conventions between France and Belgium (Article 19); between Belgium and the Netherlands (Article 27); between Germany and Belgium (Article 17); between Germany and Italy (Article 18); between Germany and the Netherlands (Article 20); between Italy and Belgium (Article 17); and between Italy and the Netherlands (Article 16).

2 See Report of the negotiators of the Convention between Germany and Belgium.

CHAPTER IX
RELATIONSHIP TO OTHER INTERNATIONAL CONVENTIONS

Title VII deals with the relationship between the Convention and other international instruments governing jurisdiction, recognition and the enforcement of judgments. It covers the following matters:

[OJ C59, 5.3.79, p 59]

1. the relationship between the Convention and the bilateral agreements already in force between certain Member States of the Community (Article 55 and 56):[1]
2. the relationship between the Convention and those international agreements which, in relation to particular matters, govern—or will govern—jurisdiction and the recognition or enforcement of judgments (Article 57);
3. the relationship between the Convention and the Convention of 15 June 1869 between France and Switzerland, which is the only enforcement convention concluded between a Member State of the EEC and a non-member State to contain rules of direct jurisdiction (Article 58);
4. the relationship between the Convention and any other instruments, whether bilateral or multilateral, which may in the future govern the recognition and enforcement of judgments (Article 59).

It was not thought necessary to regulate the relationship between the Convention and the bilateral conventions already concluded between Member States of the EEC and non-member States since, with the exception of the Convention between France and Switzerland, such conventions all contain rules of indirect jurisdiction. There is, therefore, no conflict between those conventions and the rules of jurisdiction laid down in Title II of the Convention. Recognition and enforcement would seem to raise no problem, since judgments given in those non-member States must be recognized in accordance with the provisions of the bilateral conventions.

NOTES

[1] Mention has been made of the Benelux Treaty although, as this has not yet been ratified by Luxembourg, it has not yet entered into force; this is to avoid any conflict between the Convention and that Treaty should it enter into force.

Articles 55 and 56

Article 55 contains a list of the Conventions which will be superseded on the entry into force of the EEC Convention. This will, however, be subject to:

1. the provisions of the second paragraph of Article 54, as explained in the commentary on that Article;
2. the provisions of the first paragraph of Article 56, the consequence of which is that these conventions will continue to have effect in relation to matters to which the EEC Convention does not apply (status, legal capacity etc);
3. the provisions of the second paragraph of Article 56 concerning the recognition and enforcement of judgments given before the EEC Convention enters into force. Thus a judgment given in France before the EEC Convention enters into force and to which by virtue of Article 54 this Convention would therefore not apply, could be recognized and enforced in Italy after the entry into force of the EEC Convention under the terms of the Convention of 3 June 1930 between France and Italy. Without such a rule, judgments given before the Convention enters into force could be recognized and enforced only in accordance with the general law, and this would in several Contracting States involve the possibility of a review of the substance of the judgment, which would unquestionably be a retrograde step.

Article 57

The Member States of the Community, or some of them, are already parties to numerous international agreements which, in relation to particular matters, govern jurisdiction or the recognition or enforcement of judgments. Those agreements include the following:

1. The revised Convention for the navigation of the Rhine signed at Mannheim on 17 October 1868;[1]
2. The International Convention for the unification of certain rules relating to international carriage by air, and Additional Protocol, signed at Warsaw on 12 October 1929;[2]
3. The International Convention on certain rules concerning civil jurisdiction in matters of collision, signed at Brussels on 10 May 1952;[3]
4. The International Convention relating to the arrest of sea-going ships, signed at Brussels on 10 May 1952;[4]
5. The Convention on damage caused by foreign aircraft to third parties on the surface, signed at Rome on 7 October 1952;[5]

[OJ C59, 5.3.79, p 60]

6. The International Convention concerning the carriage of goods by rail (CIM), and Annexes, signed at Berne on 25 October 1952;[6]
7. The International Convention concerning the carriage of passengers and luggage by rail (CIV) and Annexes, signed at Berne on 25 October 1952;[7]
8. The Agreement on German external debts, signed at London on 27 February 1953;[7]
9. The Convention on civil procedure concluded at The Hague on 1 March 1954;[8]
10. The Convention on the contract for the International carriage of goods by road (CMR) and Protocol of Signature, signed at Geneva on 19 May 1956;[9]
11. The Convention concerning the recognition and enforcement of decisions relating to maintenance obligations in respect of children, concluded at The Hague on 15 April 1958;[10]
12. The Convention on the jurisdiction of the contractual forum in matters relating to the international sale of goods, concluded at The Hague on 15 April 1958;[11]
13. The Convention on third party liability in the field of nuclear energy, signed at Paris on 29 July 1960,[12a] and the Additional Protocol, signed at Paris on 28 January 1964,[12b] the Supplementary Convention to the Paris Convention of 29 July 1960, and Annex, signed at Brussels on 31 January 1963,[12c] and Additional Protocol to the Supplementary Convention signed at Paris on 28 January 1964;[12d]
14. The Convention on the liability of operators of nuclear ships, and Additional Protocol, signed at Brussels on 25 May 1962;[13]

PART IV EC MATERIALS

15. The Convention of 27 October 1956 between the Grand Duchy of Luxembourg, the Federal Republic of Germany and the French Republic on the canalization of the Moselle.[14]

The structure of these agreements varies considerably. Some of them govern only jurisdiction, like the Warsaw Convention of 12 October 1929 for the unification of certain rules relating to international carriage by air, or are based on indirect jurisdiction, like the Hague Convention of 15 April 1958 concerning the recognition and enforcement of decisions relating to maintenance obligations in respect of children, or contain rules of direct or even exclusive jurisdiction, such as the International Convention of 25 October 1952 concerning the carriage of goods by rail (CIM), which lays down in Article 43(5) that actions arising from the contract of carriage may be brought only in the courts of the State to which the defendant railway belongs.

The approach adopted by the Committee means that agreements relating to particular matters prevail over the Convention. It follows that, where those agreements lay down rules of direct or exclusive jurisdiction, the court of the State of origin will have to apply those rules to the exclusion of any others; where they contain provisions concerning the conditions governing the recognition and enforcement of judgments given in matters to which the agreements apply, only those conditions need be satisfied, so that the enforcement procedure set up by the EEC Convention will not apply to those judgments.

The Committee adopted this approach in view of the fact that the Member States of the Community, when they entered into these agreements, had for the most part contracted obligations towards non-Member States which should not be modified without the consent of those States.

Moreover, the following points must be borne in mind:

1. The rules of jurisdiction laid down in these agreements have been dictated by particular considerations relating to the matters of which they treat, e g the flag or port of registration of a vessel in the maritime conventions; the criterion of domicile is not often used to establish jurisdiction in such agreements.
2. The EEC Convention lays down that judgments are in principle to be recognized, whereas agreements relating to particular matters usually subject the recognition and enforcement of judgments to a certain number of conditions. These conditions may well differ from the grounds for refusal set out in Articles 27 and 28; moreover they usually include a requirement, which the Convention has dropped, that the court of origin had jurisdiction.

[OJ C59, 5.3.79, p 61]

3. The simplified enforcement procedure laid down by the Convention is the counterpart of Title II, the provisions of which will not necessarily have to be observed where the court of the State of origin has to apply another convention. Consequently, where agreements relating to particular matters refer for the enforcement procedure back to the ordinary law of the State in which enforcement is sought, it is that law which must be applied. There is, however, nothing to prevent a national legislature from substituting the Convention procedure for its ordinary civil procedure for the enforcement of judgments given in application of agreements governing particular matters.

NOTES

1 These Conventions have been ratified by the following Member States of the European Economic Community (list drawn up on 15 September 1966): Belgium, the Federal Republic of Germany, France and the Netherlands.
2 Belgium, the Federal Republic of Germany, France, Italy, Luxembourg and the Netherlands.
3 Belgium and France.
4 Belgium and France.
5 Belgium and Luxembourg.
6 Belgium, the Federal Republic of Germany, France, Luxembourg and the Netherlands.
7 Belgium, the Federal Republic of Germany, France, Luxembourg and the Netherlands.
8 The six States.
9 The six States.
10 Belgium, the Federal Republic of Germany, France, Italy and the Netherlands.
11 Italy.
12 (a) and (b) France and Belgium; (c) and (d) France.
13 Not ratified.
14 Ratified by the three States concerned.

Article 58

This Article deals only with certain problems of jurisdiction raised by the Convention of 15 June 1869 between France and Switzerland.

Under Article 1 of that Convention, a Swiss national domiciled in France may sue in the French courts a French national domiciled in a third State.

This option, granted by that Convention to Swiss nationals domiciled in France, might, in the absence of Article 58, conflict with the EEC Convention, according to which a defendant domiciled in a Contracting State may be sued in the courts of another Contracting State only in certain defined situations, and in any case not on the basis of rules of exorbitant jurisdiction such as those of Article 14 of the French Civil Code.

Under Article 58, a Swiss national domiciled in France can exercise the option which the Convention between France and Switzerland grants him to sue in France a Frenchman domiciled in another Contracting State, without there being any conflict with the EEC Convention, since the jurisdiction of the French Court will be recognized under the terms of Article 58. As a result of this provision, the rights secured by Swiss nationals domiciled in France are safeguarded, and France can continue to honour the obligations which it has entered into with respect to Switzerland. This is, of course, only an option which is granted to Swiss nationals, and there is nothing to prevent them from making use of the other provisions of the EEC Convention.

Article 59

It will be recalled that under Article 3 of the Convention, what are known as the rules of "exorbitant" jurisdiction are no longer to be applied in cases where the defendant is domiciled in the Community, but that under Article 4 they are still fully applicable where the defendant is domiciled outside the Community, and that, in such cases, judgments given by a court whose jurisdiction derives from those rules are to be recognized and enforced in the other Contracting States.

It must first be stressed that Article 59 does not reduce the effect of Article 4 of the Convention, for the latter Article does not prevent a State, in an agreement with a third State, from renouncing its rules of exorbitant jurisdiction either in whole or only in certain cases, for example, if the defendant is a national of that third State or if he is domiciled in that State. Each State party to the EEC Convention remains quite free to conclude agreements of this type with third States, just as it is free to amend the provisions of its legislation which contain rules of exorbitant jurisdiction; Article 4 of the Convention imposes no common rule, but merely refers back to the internal law of each State.

The only objective of Article 59 is to lessen the effects, within the Community, of judgments given on the basis of rules of exorbitant jurisdiction. Under the combined effect of Articles 59 and 28, recognition or enforcement of a judgment given in a State party to the Convention can be refused in any other Contracting State:

1. where the jurisdiction of the court of origin could only be based on one of the rules of exorbitant jurisdiction specified in the second paragraph of Article 3. It would therefore be no ground for refusal that the court of origin founded its jurisdiction on one of those rules, if it could equally well have founded its jurisdiction on other provisions of its law. For example, a judgment given in France on the basis of Article 14 of the Civil Code could be recognized and enforced if the litigation related to a contract which was to be performed in France;

[OJ C59, 5.3.79, p 62]

2. where a convention on the recognition and enforcement of judgments exists between the State addressed and a third State, under the terms of which judgments given in any other State on the basis of a rule of exorbitant jurisdiction will be neither recognized nor enforced where the defendant was domiciled or habitually resident in the third State. Belgium would thus not be obliged to recognize or enforce a judgment given in France against a person domiciled or habitually resident in Norway where the jurisdiction of the French courts over that person could be based only on Article 14 of the Civil Code since a convention between Belgium and Norway exists under which those two countries undertook not to recognize or enforce such judgments. Article 59 includes a reference not only to the defendant's domicile but also to his habitual residence, since in many non-member States this criterion is in practice equivalent to the concept of domicile as this is understood in the Member States of the Community (see also

Article 10(1)) of the Hague Convention on the recognition and enforcement of foreign judgments in civil and commercial matters).

As regards the recognition and enforcement of judgments. Article 59 thus opens the way towards regulating the relations between the Member States of the EEC and other States, in particular the increasing number which are members of the Hague Conference. This seemed to justify a slight encroachment on the principle of free movement of judgments.

[3043]

CHAPTER X
FINAL PROVISIONS

Articles 60 to 62 and 64 to 68

These Articles give rise to no particular comment.

Article 63

Article 63 deals with the accession of new Member States to the European Economic Community.

It is desirable, in the opinion of the Committee, that, in order to be able to fulfil the obligations laid down in Article 220 of the Treaty establishing the European Economic Community, such States should accede to the Convention. The legal systems of such States might, however, prevent the acceptance of the Convention as it stands, and negotiations might be necessary. If such were the case, any agreement concluded between the Six and a new Member State should not depart from the basic principles of the Convention. That is why Article 63 provides that the Convention must be taken as a basis for the negotiations, which should be concerned only with such adjustments as are essential for the new Member State to be able to accede to the Convention.

The negotiations with that State would not necessarily have to precede its admission to the Community.

Since the adjustments would be the subject of a special agreement between the Six and the new Member State, it follows from the second paragraph of Article 63 that these negotiations could not be used as an opportunity for the Six to reopen debate on the Convention.

[3044]

CHAPTER XI
PROTOCOL

Article I

Article I of the Protocol takes account of the special position of the Grand Duchy of Luxembourg. It provides that any person domiciled in Luxembourg who is sued in a court of another Contracting State pursuant to Article 5(1) (which provides, in matters relating to a contract, that the courts for the place of performance of the obligation shall have jurisdiction), may refuse the jurisdiction of those courts. A similar reservation is included in the Benelux Treaty (Protocol, Article I), and it is justified by the particular nature of the economic relations between Belgium and Luxembourg, in consequence of which the greater part of the contractual obligations between persons resident in the two countries are performed or are to be performed in Belgium. It follows from Article 5(1) that a plaintiff domiciled in Belgium could in most cases bring an action in the Belgian courts.

[OJ C59, 5.3.79, p 63]

Another characteristic of Luxembourg economic relations is that a large number of the contracts concluded by persons resident in Luxembourg are international contracts. In view of this, it was clearly necessary that agreements conferring jurisdiction which could be invoked against persons domiciled in Luxembourg should be subject to stricter conditions than those of Article 17. The text adopted is based on that of the Benelux Treaty (Article 5(3)).

Article II

Article II of the Protocol also has its origin in the Benelux Treaty. The latter applies *inter alia* to judgments given in civil matters by criminal courts, and thus puts an end to a controversy between Belgium and the Netherlands on the interpretation of the 1925 Convention between Belgium and the Netherlands. As the report annexed to the Treaty explains,[1] the reluctance of the Netherlands authorities to enforce judgments given by foreign criminal courts in civil claims is due to the fact that a Netherlander charged with a punishable offence committed in a foreign country may be obliged to appear in person before the foreign criminal court in order to defend himself even in relation to the civil claim, although the Netherlands does not extradite its nationals. This objection is less pertinent than would appear at first sight under certain systems of law, and in particular in France, Belgium and Luxembourg, the judgment in a criminal case has the force of *res judicata* in any subsequent civil action.

In view of this, the subsequent civil action brought against a Netherlander convicted of a criminal offence will inevitably go against him. It is therefore essential that he should be able to conduct his defence during the criminal stage of the proceedings.

For this reason the Convention, like the Benelux Treaty, provides (see the Protocol) that a person domiciled in a Contracting State may arrange for his defence in the criminal courts of any other Contracting State.

Under Article II of the Protocol, that person will enjoy this right even if he does not appear in person and even if the code of criminal procedure of the State in question does not allow him to be represented. However, if the court seised of the matter should specifically order appearance in person, the judgment given without the person concerned having had the opportunity to arrange for his defence, because he did not appear in person, need not be recognized or enforced in the other Contracting States.

This right is, however, accorded by Article II of the Protocol only to persons who are prosecuted for an offence which was not intentionally committed; this includes road accidents.

NOTES

[1] Benelux Treaty: see the commentary on Article 13 and Article II of the Protocol.

Article III

This Article is also based on the Benelux Treaty (Article III of the Protocol).

It abolishes the levying, in the State in which enforcement is sought, of any charge, duty or fee which is calculated by reference to the value of the matter in issue, and seeks to remedy the distortion resulting from the fact that enforcement gives rise to the levying of fixed fees in certain countries and proportional fees in others.

This Article is not concerned with lawyers' fees.

In the opinion of the Committee, while it was desirable to abolish proportional fees on enforcement, there was no reason to suppress the fixed charges, duties and fees which are payable, even under the internal laws of the Contracting States, whenever certain procedural acts are performed, and which in some respects can be regarded as fees charged for services rendered to the parties.

Article IV

(See the commentary on Article 20(2) page 66 *et seq.*)

[OJ C59, 5.3.79, p 64]

Article V

(See the commentary on Article 6(2), page 27 *et seq.*)

Article VI

This Article relates to the case where legislative amendments to national laws affect either the provisions of the laws mentioned in the Convention—as might happen in the case of the provisions specified in the second paragraph of Article 3—or affect the courts listed in Section 2 of Title III. Information on these matters must be passed to the Secretary General of the Council of the European Communities to enable him, in accordance with Article 64(e), to notify the other Contracting States.

[3045]

ANNEX
COMMITTEE OF EXPERTS WHO DRAFTED THE CONVENTION ON JURISDICTION AND THE ENFORCEMENT OF JUDGMENTS IN CIVIL AND COMMERCIAL MATTERS

CHAIRMAN	
Professor A. Bülow	Staatssekretär a.D. im Bundesministerium der Justiz der Bundesrepublik Deutschland
Belgium	
Mr P Jenard, *Chairman of the Working Party*	Directeur au ministère des affaires étrangères et du commerce extérieur
Mr H Meuleman	Directeur général au ministère de la justice
Mr M Rouserez	Magistrat délégué au ministère de la justice
Mr Ch van Reepinghen (†)	Commissaire royal à la réforme judiciaire
Mr E Krings	Commissaire royal à la réforme judiciaire
Professor R van der Elst	Avocat, professeur à l'université libre de Bruxelles
Germany	
Mr H Arnold	Ministerialrat in Bundesministerium der Justiz
France	
Mr J Baudoin	Sous-directeur des affaires civiles et du sceau—Ministère de la justice
Mr P Bellet	Premier vice-président du tribunal de grande instance de la Seine
Mr Y Cotte	Chef de bureau "Droit européen et international"—Ministère de la justice
Italy	
Professor L Marmo (†)	Consigliere di Corre di cassazione—Ministero di grazia e giustizia
Mr Caldarera	Consigliere di Corte di cassazione addetto al servizio del contenzioso diplomatico del ministero degli affari esteri
Mr G di Blasi	Magistrato, ministero degli affari esteri
Professor R Miccio	Consigliere di Corte d'appello, ministero di grazia e giustizia
[OJ C59, 5.3.79, p 65]	
Luxembourg	
Mr A Huss	Procureur général d'État
Mr F Goerens	Avocat général
Netherlands	
Mr Th van Sasse van Ysselt	Directeur, Afdelingschef bij het ministerie van justitie
Mr C W Dubbink	Raadsheer in de Hoge raad der Nederlanden
Observers	
Benelux Committee on the unification of law	
Mrs M Weser	Member of the Committee
Hague Conference on private international law	

Mr M H van Hoogstraten	Secretary-General to the Conference
Mr G Droz	First Secretary to the Permanent Bureau of the Conference
Commission of the European Economic Community	
—Directorate-General for Competition	
Mr W Hauschild	*Head of Division*
Miss M Van Es	*Member of Division*

[3046]

REPORT

on the Protocols on the interpretation by the Court of Justice of the Convention of 29 February 1968 on the mutual recognition of companies and legal persons and of the Convention of 27 September 1968 on jurisdiction and the enforcement of judgments in civil and commercial matters

(Signed at Luxembourg, 3 June 1971)

NOTES

The Jenard Reports on the 1968 Brussels Convention and Annexed Protocol are set out at OJ C59, 5.3.79, p 1. References to the original pagination in the Official Journals are noted above the text to which they refer.

By Mr P JENARD

Directeur in the Belgian Ministry of Foreign Affairs and External Trade

[OJ C59, 5.3.79, p 66]

I. GENERAL REMARKS

1. In Joint Declaration No 3, annexed to the Convention on the mutual recognition of companies and legal persons, signed at Brussels on 29 February 1968, the Governments of the Member States of the European Communities expressed their willingness to study means of avoiding differences in the interpretation of the Convention. To this end, they agreed to examine the possibility of conferring jurisdiction in certain matters on the Court of Justice of the European Communities and, if necessary, to negotiate an agreement to that effect.

A similar Joint Declaration was annexed to the Convention on jurisdiction and the enforcement of judgments in civil and commercial matters, signed at Brussels on 27 September 1968. This Declaration envisages the possibility of assigning to the Court of Justice jurisdiction both to interpret the Convention and to settle any conflicting claims and disclaimers of jurisdiction which may arise in applying it.

2. In the course of negotiations to give effect to these Declarations, it was soon agreed to give the Court additional jurisdiction, and to use for the purpose a system based on Article 177 of the Treaty. The further question nevertheless arose as to whether it would be appropriate to draft a general convention applicable to all the conventions which had been or were to be concluded on the basis of Article 220, or whether it would not be preferable to seek solutions which took into account the individual characteristics of each of these conventions.

This question was approached in an entirely pragmatic manner. A detailed study was made of the two Conventions already signed, the Convention on the mutual recognition of companies and legal persons, and the Convention on jurisdiction and the enforcement of judgments in civil and commercial matters.

3. This study led to the conclusion that these two Conventions have distinct features which justify different arrangements for their interpretation by the Court of Justice. Although it had been suggested that a single convention might determine the jurisdiction of the Court to

PART IV EC MATERIALS

interpret all the conventions concluded on the basis of Article 220 of the Treaty, in the end it was thought preferable to conclude separate Protocols which would be better adapted to the requirements of each of the Conventions.

4. There was no need to apply the procedure of Article 236 of the Treaty for the purposes of concluding these Protocols since they deal with the interpretation of Conventions drawn up pursuant to Article 220 of the Treaty and in no way aim at revising the Treaty itself.

They merely confer on the Court of Justice further jurisdiction which is additional to, but does not affect, its existing jurisdiction.[1]

NOTES

1 On various occasions, jurisdiction has been conferred on the Court of Justice without reference to the revision procedure set out in Article 236 (internal agreements under Conventions of Association—see OJ No 93 11.6.1964, p 1490/64; provisions of Council Regulation No 17 on appeal to the Court—see OJ No 13, 21.2.1962, p 204/62.

II. PROTOCOL ON THE INTERPRETATION OF THE CONVENTION ON THE MUTUAL RECOGNITION OF COMPANIES AND LEGAL PERSONS

5. As regards the interpretation of the Convention on the mutual recognition of companies and legal persons, there was thought to be no reason for departing from the preliminary ruling system laid down in Article 177 of the Treaty; and this system was therefore adopted in the draft Protocol in question.

[OJ C59, 5.3.79, p 67]

Article 1 of the Protocol confers on the Court jurisdiction to interpret the Convention of 29 February 1968, Joint Declaration No 1 contained in the Protocol annexed to that Convention, and the Protocol which is the subject of this report. Article 2 repeats, in identical terms, the second and third paragraphs of Article 177, defining the circumstances in which references may be made to the Court by courts which have to decide questions of interpretation.

6. Since the Convention sometimes refers back to national law, the problem arose as to whether it might be necessary expressly to exclude the jurisdiction of the Court to interpret such law. It was thought unnecessary expressly to exclude jurisdiction in this respect, for the cases decided by the Court of Justice have already firmly established that it has no jurisdiction to interpret national law.

7. Article 3 concerns the procedure to be followed before the Court of Justice when, in accordance with the Protocol, the Court is asked to give a ruling.

It was thought appropriate to provide that the Rules of Procedure of the Court should be supplemented to take account of the new jurisdiction. Article 3(2) indicated that Article 188 of the Treaty is to be used for this purpose.

It was considered that, in order to ensure that the Convention would be applied as effectively and as uniformly as possible, an exchange of information should be organized on judgments of national courts against whose decision there is no remedy under national law.

A Joint Declaration to this effect is annexed to the Protocol.

III. PROTOCOL ON THE INTERPRETATION OF THE CONVENTION ON JURISDICTION AND THE ENFORCEMENT OF JUDGMENTS IN CIVIL AND COMMERCIAL MATTERS

8. The study of the Convention on jurisdiction and the enforcement of judgments in civil and commercial matters showed that it has features sufficiently distinctive to justify a separate system for its interpretation by the Court of Justice.

There was unanimous agreement on the need to ensure uniform interpretation of the Convention, and hence to confer new jurisdiction on the Court of Justice, using a system based on Article 177. But it was feared that, in view of the number and diversity of the disputes to which the Convention applies, an application for a preliminary ruling on the lines of Article 177 might be made by one of the parties either as a delaying tactic or as a means of putting pressure on an opponent of modest financial means. In short, the application might be made for improper purposes.

(1) This Convention will be applicable in a large number of cases. It governs not only recognition and enforcement of judgments, but also the international jurisdiction of the courts, and in particular all cases where a person is sued in the courts of a Contracting State in which he is not domiciled. Moreover, it is not confined to a limited field such as the recognition of companies, but extends to all civil and commercial matters relating to rights in property (litigation over all kinds of contract, non-contractual liability, maintenance, etc).

(2) At the stage of recognition and enforcement, Article 34 of the Convention provides that the court to which application is made for the issue of an order for enforcement shall give its decision without delay, and without the party against whom enforcement is sought being entitled at that stage of the proceedings to make any submissions.

Plainly, an application to the Court of Justice for a preliminary ruling would, if made at this stage, undermine the object of the Convention which, by introducing a new, standardized, *ex parte* procedure for enforcement, aims at eliminating delaying tactics and preventing the respondent from withdrawing his assets from any measure of enforcement.

(3) Finally it must be stressed that decisions of the Court of Justice on the interpretation of the Convention differ from decisions on the interpretation of other conventions, as regards the consequences for the parties.

Thus, if the court were to interpret a provision of the Convention so as to rule that the courts seised of a matter had no jurisdiction, the proceedings might well have to be instituted again from the outset, either in a State other than that whose courts were originally seised or, perhaps, in other courts in the same State (see, for example, Article 5 of the Convention which lays down special rules of jurisdiction).

[OJ C59, 5.3.79, p 68]

9. The Protocol therefore follows the system of Article 177, but subject to such adjustments as were thought necessary to deal with the matters set out above. The system may be summarized as follows:

(a) the courts which are allowed to refer questions to the court are expressly specified;

(b) the right to apply to the court for a preliminary ruling is not given to courts of first instance;

(c) the Protocol provides that the Courts of Cassation and other courts of last instance are required to refer a question of interpretation to the court if they consider that a decision of the Court on that question is necessary to enable them to give judgment;

(d) in addition to requests for a preliminary ruling, there is a novel provision for interpretation by the Court of Justice, similar to the "pourvoi dans l'intérêt de la loi".

10. Article 1, which is similar to Article 1 of the Protocol on the interpretation of the Convention on the mutual recognition of companies and legal persons, confers on the Court jurisdiction to interpret the Convention of 27 September 1968 and its Protocol, as well as the Protocol which is the subject of this report.

11. Article 2 lists the national courts which may ask the Court to give a preliminary ruling.

(1) Courts of first instance are not included in this list. Their exclusion is designed mainly to prevent the interpretation of the Court being requested in too many cases, and particularly in trivial matters. Moreover, it was thought that where two courts of first instance, for example a "justice de paix" and an Amtsgericht, gave judgments which became *res judicata* and showed differences of interpretation in the application of the Convention, this should not necessitate further action, any more than would similar differences of interpretation between two inferior courts of the same country. Similarly, it was argued that the Court of Justice should not be required to give rulings unless it was fully informed. In order to achieve this, questions of interpretation should, in the first place, be dealt with by the national courts, especially in view of the fact that in the interests of legal certainty the Court of Justice can only seldom depart from the principles established by its previous judgments.

(2) Article 2(1) specifies by name the courts which are allowed to refer questions to the Court of Justice, including those which, pursuant to Article 3(1), are required to do so. Such a list seemed to be essential, since the present wording of the third paragraph of Article 177 has given rise to conflicting interpretations as to which are the courts and tribunals against whose decisions there is no judicial remedy under national law (for example, the theoretical and pragmatic schools of thought in Germany).

PART IV
EC MATERIALS

It seemed all the more necessary to make this point clear because, under the Protocol, inferior courts have no jurisdiction to refer a question to the Court of Justice.

This list also takes into account the fact that the Convention of 27 September 1968 governs only civil and commercial matters concerning property rights; the list therefore includes only those Courts which have jurisdiction in such cases.

(3) Article 2(2) states that the power to refer a question to the Court is also given to the courts of the Contracting States when they are sitting in an appellate capacity. The Courts in question thus include courts of appeal, save for the exceptional cases when they are sitting at first instance when sitting in an appellate capacity.

In the Federal Republic of Germany the expression "appeal" includes "Beschwerde".

(4) Article 2(3) lays down that in the cases provided for in Article 37 of the Convention of 27 September 1968, the courts referred to in that Article may also refer a question to the Court of Justice. It will be remembered that Article 37 governs appeals against judgments authorizing the enforcement of a foreign judgment.

[OJ C59, 5.3.79, p 69]

12. Article 3 lays down that a court of last instance is bound to refer a question to the Court of Justice only "if it considers that a decision on the question is necessary to enable it to give judgment". In Article 177 of the Treaty of Rome this provision appears only in the second paragraph, governing cases in which other courts are entitled to refer a question to the Court of Justice.

The provision contained in Article 3(1) of the Protocol accords with the interpretation now generally given to Article 177: it is generally agreed to be beyond dispute that a court of last instance has discretion to assess the relevance of questions put to it for interpretation.

Nevertheless, this provision seemed necessary to avoid conflicting interpretations; for it will be remembered that, as has already been pointed out in paragraph 8(3) of this report, decisions of the Court of Justice on the interpretation of the Judgments Convention differ, in their consequences, from decisions of the interpretation of other conventions.

Thus if the jurisdiction of a court were challenged on appeal, and the Court of Justice ruled that the Convention had been misinterpreted by the first court, the proceedings might have to be instituted again from the very beginning, either in another State or, perhaps, in another court in the same State.

A party to an action might accordingly be greatly tempted to raise a question of interpretation of the Convention before an appellate court merely in order to gain time, and the temptation would be all the greater if that court were automatically required to refer the question to the Court of Justice.

A number of other solutions were considered, including giving the highest courts only a power, rather than a duty, to refer a question to the Court, or requiring them to refer a question only if they would otherwise give to a provision an interpretation different from the interpretation already given either by the Court of Justice or by other courts. Finally, however, a provision very close to Article 177 was adopted in order to achieve the greatest possible uniformity in Community law.

For the reasons set out above, it was thought necessary to confirm the discretion of courts of last instance by means of a clear and unambiguous text, and above all to make it proof against any possible subsequent tendency automatically to refer questions to the Court.

As regards its form, Article 3 differs from Article 177, in that it sets out first of all the rule for the courts of last instance, and thereafter for the other courts. The object of this modified form was to emphasize that the Protocol was designed solely to provide a specific solution to problems of interpretation of the Convention on jurisdiction and the enforcement of judgments in civil and commercial matters.

13. Since the Convention also refers back to national law, reference should be made to what was said in this connection in the commentary on the protocol on the interpretation of the Convention on the mutual recognition of companies (see paragraph 6).

14. Article 4 lays down a new procedure based in part on the "pourvoi dans l'intérêt de la loi" and in part on the procedure for giving advisory opinions. All the countries of the Community, with the exception of the Federal Republic of Germany, have a form of appeal for the clarification of a point of law which enables the competent judicial authority, in this instance the Procurators-General of the Courts of Cassation, to appeal against a final decision which misunderstands or misapplies either the letter or the spirit of the law. The purpose of

this appeal is to avoid perpetuating an erroneous interpretation of the law where the parties have omitted to appeal against the decision which includes that interpretation (see Dalloz, Encyclopédie juridique under Cassation No 2509).

Article 4 is designed to make for a uniform interpretation of the Convention by introducing a procedure complementary to the request for a preliminary ruling provided for in Article 3. The purpose is to ensure a uniform interpretation for the future wherever existing judgments are in conflict.

In the last analysis, this procedure occupies an intermediate position between the "pourvoi dans l'intérêt de la loi", from which it differs in that it does not entail the setting aside of a judgment which is ultimately shown to have misinterpreted the Convention, and that of an advisory appeal. The procedure is, however, limited to cases in which a court has already given judgment.

Paragraph 1 defines the cases in which the competent authority of a State may apply to the Court of Justice. It will be for that authority to decide whether it is advisable to refer a matter to the Court, and it will presumably not do so unless the national judgment includes reasons which might lead to an interpretation different from that previously given by the Court of Justice or by a foreign court. If there are no factors involved which make it likely that the principles established in the decided cases would be changed, the national authority could always seek to clarify the point of law by appealing in its own country in accordance with the procedure there in force.

[OJ C59, 5.3.79, p 70]

Paragraph 2 lays down that rulings given by the Court shall not affect the decisions submitted to it, in the same way that the setting aside of a judgment following an appeal to clarify a point of law in no way influences the position of the parties.

It follows that the judgments of the Court cannot give rise to any fresh proceedings, even where otherwise an extraordinary avenue of appeal might be appropriate.

Paragraph 3 lays down that the Procurators-General of the Courts of Cassation (who, in the countries which know the "pourvoi dans l'intérêt de la loi", are competent) or any other authority designated by a State, are entitled to request the Court of Justice for a ruling. The designation of the Procurators-General is further evidence that the appeal procedure laid down in Article 4 is intended solely to clarify points of law.

The wording of paragraph 3 takes account of the situation obtaining in Germany, where the "pourvoi dans l'intérêt de la loi" is unknown. It furthermore empowers any of the Contracting States to designate any other authority or even to designate two authorities, as for example the Procurator-General for appeals against judgments of civil, commercial or criminal courts in civil matters, and the Minister of Justice for appeals against decisions of administrative tribunals.

Paragraph 4 amends Article 20 of the Statute of the Court of Justice to deal with the procedure provided for in Article 4. The amendment takes account of the fact that the parties to the original proceedings will have no interest in intervening at this stage.

It may be wondered what are the implications of a ruling on interpretation given on the basis of Article 4. The ruling certainly is not binding on the parties. It must be acknowledged that such a ruling has no force in law, and that accordingly nobody is bound by it. But clearly it will have the greatest persuasive authority and will for the future constitute the guideline for all Community courts. In this respect it may be compared with the decision on a "pourvoi dans l'intérêt de la loi". Such a decision is binding on nobody, but constitutes a decision of principle of the greatest importance for the future, and one which judges will generally follow.

15. Article 5 of the Protocol, like Article 3 of the Protocol on the interpretation of the Convention on the mutual recognition of companies, extends the provisions governing the jurisdiction of the Court of Justice to cover the exercise of the new jurisdiction conferred on it.

However, these provisions are extended only in so far as the Protocol does not otherwise provide; this reservation chiefly concerns Article 177 of the Treaty, whose provisions, even if they should be modified, are not applicable to the Protocol, which has its own separate provisions on this point.

16. Article 11 provides for any relevant amendment to the jurisdiction of the courts of the Contracting States.

17. The other Articles of the Protocol, which contain the final provisions, give rise to no particular comment. Again, an exchange of information is to be organized on the decisions of

the courts referred to in Article 2(1) in order to ensure that the Convention is applied as effectively and as uniformly as possible. A Joint Declaration to this effect is annexed to the Protocol.

18. The provisions of the Convention on *lis pendens* and related actions should go a long way, if not all the way, towards resolving any problems which may arise from conflicting claims and disclaimers of jurisdiction. Where, however, such problems arise from conflicting interpretations, they will be solved by applying the Protocol.

[3047]

REPORT

on the Convention on the Association of the Kingdom of Denmark, Ireland and the United Kingdom of Great Britain and Northern Ireland to the Convention on jurisdiction and the enforcement of judgments in civil and commercial matters and to the Protocol on its interpretation by the Court of Justice

(Signed at Luxembourg, 9 October 1978)

NOTES

The Schlosser Report on the accession of Denmark, Ireland and the United Kingdom is set out at OJ C59, 5.3.79, p 71. References to the original pagination in the Official Journal are noted above the text to which they refer.

by Professor Dr Peter SCHLOSSER,

of the Chair of German, international and foreign civil procedure, of the general theory of procedure and of civil law at the University of Munich

Pursuant to Article 3(2) of the Act of Accession of 22 January 1972 a Council working party, convened as a result of a decision taken by the Committee of Permanent Representatives of the Member States, prepared a draft Convention on the accession of the Kingdom of Denmark, Ireland and the United Kingdom of Great Britain and Northern Ireland to the Convention of 27 September 1968 on jurisdiction and the enforcement of judgments in civil and commercial matters and to the Protocol of 3 June 1971 on its interpretation by the Court of Justice. This working party was composed of government experts from the nine Member States and representatives from the Commission. The rapporteur, Mr P Schlosser, Professor of Law at the University of Munich, drafted the explanatory report which was submitted to the governments at the same time as the draft prepared by the experts. The text of this report, which is a commentary on the Convention of Accession signed at Luxembourg on 9 October 1978, is now being published in this issue of the Official Journal.

INDEX

[OJ C59, 5.3.79, p 77]

CHAPTER 1
PRELIMINARY REMARKS

1. Under Article 3(2) of the Act of Accession, the new Member States undertook "to accede to the Conventions provided for in Article 220 of the EEC Treaty, and to the Protocols on the interpretation of those Conventions by the Court of Justice, signed by the original Member States and to this end to enter into negotiations with the original Member States in order to make the necessary adjustments thereto". As a first step the Commission of the European Communities made preparations for the impending discussions on the contemplated adjustments. On 29 November 1971, it submitted to the Council an interim report on the additions considered necessary to the two Conventions signed in 1968, namely the Convention on jurisdiction and the enforcement of judgments in civil and commercial matters (hereinafter referred to as "the 1968 Convention") and the Convention on the mutual recognition of companies and legal persons. Following consultations with the new Member States, the Commission on 15 September 1972 drew up a comprehensive report to the Council on the main problems arising from adjusting both Conventions to the legal institutions and systems of the new Member States. On the basis of this report, the Committee of Permanent Representatives decided on 11 October 1972 to set up a Working Party which was to be composed of delegates of the original and the new Member States of the Community and of a representative of the Commission. The Working Party held its inaugural meeting on 16 November 1972 under the chairmanship of the Netherlands delegate in accordance with the rota. On this occasion, it decided to focus its attention initially on negotiations concerning adjustments to the 1968 Convention which had already been ratified by the original Member States of the EEC and to the Protocol of 3 June 1971 on its interpretation ("the Interpretation Protocol of 1971"), and to postpone the work entrusted to it regarding the Convention on the mutual recognition of companies and legal persons. At its second meeting, the Working Party elected the author of this report as its rapporteur. On the basis of a request made by the Working Party at its third meeting in June 1973, the Committee of Permanent Representatives appointed Mr Jenard, the "Directeur d'administration auprès du ministère belge des Affaires Étrangères", as its permanent chairman.

2. The Working Party initially considered proposing the legal form of a Protocol for the accession of the new Member States to the 1968 Convention, and that the adjustments contemplated should be annexed thereto. However, this method would have introduced some confusion into the subject. A distinction would then have had to be made between three different Protocols, ie the Protocol referred to in Article 65 of the 1968 Convention, the Interpretation Protocol of 1971 and the new Protocol on accession. Furthermore, there were no grounds for dividing the new provisions required in consequence of the accession of the new Member States to the 1968 Convention by putting some into a protocol and others into an act of accession annexed to it. The Working Party therefore presented the outcome of its discussions in the form of a draft Convention between the original Member States and the new Member States of the EEC. This draft Convention makes provision for accession both to the 1968 Convention and to the Interpretation Protocol of 1971 (Title I) as well as for the necessary changes to them (Titles II and IV). The accession of Denmark, Ireland and the United Kingdom to the 1968 Convention extends also to the Protocol referred to in Article 65 which is an integral part of the 1968 Convention. The Working Party also proposed adjustments to this Protocol (Title III).

The decision of the Working Party to adopt the legal form of a Convention incorporating adjustments instead of replacing the 1968 Convention by a new Convention has the advantage that the unchanged provisions of the 1968 Convention do not require renewed ratification.

Accordingly three different "Conventions" will in future have to be distinguished:

The Convention on jurisdiction and the enforcement of judgments in civil and commercial matters in its original form will be referred to as "the 1968 Convention".[1]

The expression "Accession Convention" refers to the draft Convention proposed by the Working Party.

After ratification of the Accession Convention certain provisions of the 1968 Convention will exist in an amended form. References in this report to the amended form will be indicated by the addition of that word, e g "Article 5(2) as amended".

[OJ C59, 5.3.79, p 78]

3. The structure of this report does not closely follow the structure of the proposed new Accession Convention. In many places, this report can only be understood, or at any rate is easier to understand, if it is read in conjunction with the corresponding parts of the reports on the 1968 Convention and on the Interpretation Protocol of 1971 which were drawn up by the present permanent chairman and erstwhile rapporteur of the Working Party (hereinafter referred to as "the Jenard report"). The structure of this report is based on that of these earlier reports.

[3047A]

CHAPTER 2
REASONS FOR THE CONVENTION

4. The second chapter of the Jenard report sets out the reasons for concluding a Convention. They apply with at least as much force to the new Member States as they did to the relationships between the original Member States of the EEC, but they do not call for further close examination here. The obligation on the new Member States to accede to the 1968 Convention is laid down in Article 3(2) of the Act of Accession to the EEC Treaty. However, in order to give a clear view of the legal position, it may be helpful to supplement the references in the Jenard report to the laws in force in the original Member States of the EEC and to the existing Conventions between these States with details concerning the new Member States.

A. THE LAW IN FORCE IN THE NEW MEMBER STATES

1. United Kingdom

5. The legal position in the United Kingdom is characterized by six significant features.

6. (a) In the first place, there is a distinction between recognition and enforcement at common law on the one hand and under the Foreign Judgments (Reciprocal Enforcement) Act 1933 on the other.

At common law, a judgment given in a foreign State may serve as a basis for proceedings before courts in the United Kingdom, if the adjudicating court was competent to assume jurisdiction. This legal consequence follows irrespective of whether or not there is reciprocity. In this connection, recognition and enforceability are not limited to the use of the foreign judgment as evidence. The United Kingdom court dealing with the case may not in general review the substance of the foreign judgment. There are, of course, a limited number of grounds for refusing recognition.

For recognition and enforcement under the Foreign Judgments (Reciprocal Enforcement) Act 1933 on the other hand the successful party does not have to institute fresh proceedings before courts in the United Kingdom on the basis of the foreign judgment. The successful party merely has to have the judgment registered with the appropriate court. However, this simplified recognition and enforcement procedure is available only where the judgment to be recognized was given by a Superior Court, and, more important, where a convention on the reciprocal recognition and enforcement of judgments is in force between the State of origin and the United Kingdom. Once the foreign judgment is registered, it has the same legal force and effect as a judgment given by the court of registration.

7. (b) Both these methods are available in the United Kingdom only for the enforcement of judgments which order payment of a specific sum of money. Consequently maintenance orders made by foreign courts which stipulate periodic payments are not generally enforceable in the United Kingdom. However, the Maintenance Orders (Reciprocal Enforcement) Act which came into force in 1972 makes it possible for international treaty obligations to be concluded in this field.

[OJ C59, 5.3.79, p 79]

8. (c) Both at common law and under the 1933 Act, it is a requirement for recognition and enforcement that the judgment should be "final and conclusive between the parties". This requirement is clearly satisfied where the adjudicating court can no longer alter its judgment

or can only do so in very exceptional circumstances. Similarly, neither the fact that the period during which an appeal may be made is still running nor even a pending appeal prevent this requirement from being satisfied. However, maintenance orders which stipulate periodic payments are excluded from recognition since they may be varied to take account of changed circumstances unless they are covered by the abovementioned Maintenance Orders (Reciprocal Enforcement) Act 1972.

9. (d) It is possible to institute proceedings on the basis of a foreign judgment or to make an application for its registration under the 1933 Act during a period of six years from the date on which the judgment was given.

10. (e) United Kingdom law distinguishes between the recognition and enforcement of foreign judgments in the same way as the other States of the Community. If a foreign judgment fulfils the common law requirements for its recognition or if it is registered with a United Kingdom court, it becomes effective also in fields other than enforcement. A clear distinction is made between recognition and enforcement of foreign judgments in, for example, the bilateral Conventions with France and Germany.

The requirements mentioned in paragraphs 7 and 9 are not set out in those Conventions as requirements for recognition.

11. (f) Finally, it should be noted that the United Kingdom although not a federal State, is not a single legal and judicial area. It consists of three areas with different legal systems: England and Wales, Scotland and Northern Ireland. Whilst the common law rules described in paragraph 6 apply uniformly to the whole of the United Kingdom, the different judicial systems in each of the three legal areas of this State have to be taken into consideration when the 1933 Act is applied. Applications for registration have to be made in England and Wales to the High Court of Justice, in Scotland to the Court of Session, and in Northern Ireland to the High Court of Justice of Northern Ireland. If registration is granted, the judgment can be enforced only in the area in which the relevant courts have jurisdiction, which extends to the whole of England and Wales, of Scotland or of Northern Ireland respectively (see paragraph 209; for maintenance orders, see paragraphs 210 and 218). Recognition of a judgment is, nevertheless, independent of its registration.

2. Ireland

12. The common law provisions of Irish law are similar to those which apply in the United Kingdom. The only statutory provisions of Irish law on the recognition and enforcement of foreign judgments are contained in the Maintenance Orders (Reciprocal Enforcement) Act 1974. This Act gives effect to an international agreement between Ireland and the United Kingdom for the reciprocal recognition of maintenance orders made by courts in those States. The agreement is expressed to terminate on the coming into force of the 1968 Convention for both States.

3. Denmark

13. Under paragraph 223a of the Law of 11 April 1916, foreign judgments can be recognized only if a treaty providing reciprocity has been concluded with the State of origin, or if binding effect has been given to judgments of a foreign State by Royal Decree. Denmark has concluded no bilateral conventions on recognition and enforcement. There is only one Royal Decree of the type referred to and it concerns judgments given by German courts.[2]

B. EXISTING CONVENTIONS

14. Apart from Conventions relating to particular matters (see paragraph 238 *et seq*), the United Kingdom is the only new Member State to be bound to other Member States of the EEC by bilateral Conventions on the recognition and enforcement of judgments. These are the Conventions with France, Belgium, the Federal Republic of Germany, Italy and the Netherlands listed in the new version of Article 55 (see paragraph 237). These bilateral Conventions serve to implement the Foreign Judgments (Reciprocal Enforcement) Act for the United Kingdom (see paragraph 6) and therefore contain provisions which more or less follow the same pattern. The requirements for recognition and enforcement correspond to the criteria mentioned in paragraphs 6 to 11 above. Rules providing for "direct" jurisdiction[3] are not included.

[OJ C59, 5.3.79, p 80]

C. GENERAL ARRANGEMENT OF THE PROPOSED ADJUSTMENTS

15. Neither Article 3(2) of the Act of Accession nor the terms of reference given to the Working Party provide any clear guide of what is meant by "necessary adjustments".

The term could be given a very narrow interpretation. The emphasis would then have to be laid above all on the requirement of necessity, in the sense of indispensability. At the beginning of the Working Party's discussions it became clear, however, that such a narrow view of the contemplated adjustments was bound to make it more difficult for the 1968 Convention to take root in the legal systems of the new Member States. There are a variety of reasons for this.

1. Special structural features of the legal systems of the new Member States

16. The 1968 Convention implicitly proceeded from a legal background common to the original Member States of the EEC. By contrast the legal systems of the new Member States unmistakably contain certain special structural features. It would hardly have been reasonable to expect these States to adjust their national law to the legal position on which the 1968 Convention is based.

On the contrary, adjustment of the Convention seemed the more obvious course on occasion. This applies, for example, to the distinction made in Articles 30 and 38 between ordinary and extraordinary appeals (see paragraph 195 *et seq*), which does not exist in United Kingdom and Irish law, to the system of registering judgments in the United Kingdom instead of the system of granting enforcement orders (see paragraph 208) and to the concept of the trust which is a characteristic feature of the common law[4] (see paragraph 109 *et seq*). The same also applies to the inter-relation existing in Denmark between judicial and administrative competence in maintenance cases (see paragraph 66 *et seq*).

2. Ambiguities in the existing text

17. In certain cases, enquiries about the precise meaning of some provisions of the 1968 Convention by the States obliged to accede to it clearly showed that their interpretation was often uncertain and controversial. The Working Party decided therefore to propose that certain provisions of the 1968 Convention should be given a more precise wording or an authoritative interpretation. This applies, for example, to the provisions about granting legal aid in enforcement proceedings (see paragraph 223). The Working Party also dealt in this way with the provisions of Article 57 on the relation between the 1968 Convention and other Conventions, (see paragraph 238 *et seq*). In most cases, however, the information requested could be given in a sufficiently clear and uniform way, so that this report need do no more than refer to it.

3. Further developments in the law of the original Member States of the EEC

18. In yet other cases, enquiries by the new Member States about the content of some provisions of the 1968 Convention revealed that in the original Member States of the EEC too the law had in the meantime evolved in such a way that general adjustments rather than adjustments restricted to relations with the new Member States seemed advisable. This applies particularly to proceedings in matters of family law in which ancillary relief, and especially maintenance claims, are now often combined with the main proceedings concerning status. In family and matrimonial matters, such combined proceedings have replaced the traditional system of separating status proceedings from subsequent proceedings in many countries during the years following the signing of the 1968 Convention. This is the reason for the revised Article 5(2) proposed by the Working Party (see paragraphs 32 and 90). The development of consumer protection law in the Member States led to a completely new version of Section 4 of Title II, and in one case the 1968 Convention was amended as a result of judgments of the Court of Justice of the European Communities (see paragraph 179).

[OJ C59, 5.3.79, p 81]

4. Specific economic effects

19. Finally, it became apparent that certain provisions of the 1968 Convention in their application to the new Member States would have economic repercussions unequalled in the original Member States. Thus, the worldwide significance of the British insurance market

prompted the Working Party to recommend amendments concerning jurisdiction in insurance matters (see paragraph 136). The new paragraph (7) of Article 5 (see paragraph 122) is justified by the special position occupied by British maritime jurisdiction.

[3047B]

CHAPTER 3
SCOPE OF THE CONVENTION

20. As already discussed in the Jenard report, the provisions governing the scope of the 1968 Convention contain four significant elements. These required some further explanation in the context of the relationship of the original Member States to each other. They are:

1. Limitation to proceedings and judgments on matters involving international legal relationships (I).
2. Duty of the national courts to observe the provisions governing the scope of the 1968 Convention of their own motion (II).
3. Limitation of the Convention to civil and commercial matters (III).
4. A list (Article 1, second paragraph) of matters excluded from the scope of the Convention (IV).

In the relationship of the original Member States to each other there was no problem about a fifth criterion which is much more clearly brought out in the title of the 1968 Convention than in Article 1 which defines its scope. The 1968 Convention only applies where court proceedings and court decisions are involved. Proceedings and decisions of administrative authorities do not come within the scope of the 1968 Convention. This gave rise to a particular problem of adjustment in relation to Denmark (V).

I. MATTERS INVOLVING INTERNATIONAL LEGAL RELATIONSHIPS

21. The accession of the new Member States to the 1968 Convention in no way affects the application of the principle that only proceedings and judgments about matters involving international legal relationships are affected, so that reference need only be made to Section I of Chapter III of the Jenard report.

II. BINDING NATURE OF THE CONVENTION

22. Under Articles 19 and 20 of the 1968 Convention the provisions concerning "direct jurisdiction" are to be observed by the court of its own motion: in some cases, ie where exclusive jurisdiction exists, irrespective of whether the defendant takes any steps; in other cases only where the defendant challenges the jurisdiction. Similarly, a court must also of its own motion consider whether there exists an agreement on jurisdiction which excludes the court's jurisdiction and which is valid in accordance with Article 17.

An obligation to observe the rules of jurisdiction of its own motion is by no means an unusual duty for a court in the original Member States. However, the United Kingdom delegation pointed out that such a provision would mean a fundamental change for its courts. Hitherto United Kingdom courts had been able to reach a decision only on the basis of submissions of fact or law made by the parties. Without infringing this principle, no possibility existed of examining their jurisdiction of their own motion.

However, Article 3(2) of the Act of Accession cannot be interpreted as requiring the amendment of any provisions of the Conventions referred to on the ground that introduction of those provisions into the legal system of a new Member State would necessitate certain changes in its long-established legal practices and procedures.

[OJ C59, 5.3.79, p 82]

It does not necessarily follow from Articles 19 and 20 of the 1968 Convention that the courts must, of their own motion, investigate the facts relevant to deciding the question of jurisdiction, that they must for example inquire where the defendant is domiciled. The only essential factor is that uncontested assertions by the parties should not bind the court. For this reason the following rule is reconcilable with the 1968 Convention: a court may assume jurisdiction only if it is completely satisfied of all the facts on which such jurisdiction is based; if it is not so satisfied it can and must request the parties to provide the necessary evidence, in default of which the action will be dismissed as inadmissible. In such circumstances the lack of jurisdiction would be declared by the court of its own motion, and not as a result of a challenge by one of the parties. Whether a court is itself obliged to investigate the facts relevant to jurisdiction, or whether it can, or must, place the burden of proof in this respect on the party interested in the jurisdiction of the court concerned, is determined solely by national law. Indeed some of the legal systems of the original Member States, for example Germany, do not require the court itself to undertake factual investigations in a case of exclusive jurisdiction, even though lack of such jurisdiction has to be considered by the court of its own motion.

III. CIVIL AND COMMERCIAL MATTERS

23. The scope of the 1968 Convention is limited to legal proceedings and judgments which relate to civil and commercial matters. All such proceedings not expressly excluded fall within its scope.

In particular, it is irrelevant whether an action is brought "against" a named defendant (see paragraphs 124 *et seq*). It is true that in such a case Article 2 *et seq* cannot operate; but otherwise the 1968 Convention remains applicable.

The distinction between civil and commercial matters on the one hand and matters of public law on the other is well recognized in the legal systems of the original Member States and is, in spite of some important differences, on the whole arrived at on the basis of similar criteria. Thus the term "civil law" also includes certain important special subjects which are not public law, especially, for example, parts of labour law.

For this reason the draftsmen of the original text of the 1968 Convention, and the Jenard report, did not include a definition of civil and commercial matters and merely stated that the 1968 Convention also applies to decisions of criminal and administrative courts, provided they are given in a civil or commercial matter, which occasionally happens. In this last respect, the accession of the three new Member States presents no additional problems. But as regards the main distinction referred to earlier considerable difficulties arise.

In the United Kingdom and Ireland the distinction commonly made in the original EEC States between private law and public law is hardly known. This meant that the problems of adjustment could not be solved simply by a reference to these classifications. In view of the Judgment of the Court of Justice of the European Communities of 14 October 1976,[5] which was delivered during the final stages of the discussions and which decided in favour of an interpretation which made no reference to the "applicable" national law, the Working Party restricted itself to declaring, in Article 1, paragraph 1, that revenue, customs or administrative matters are not civil or commercial matters within the meaning of the Convention. Moreover, the legal practice in the Member States of the Community, including the new Member States, must take account of the above judgment which states that, in interpreting the concept of civil and commercial matters, reference must be made "first, to the objectives and scheme of the Convention and, secondly, to the general principles which stem from the corpus of the national legal systems".

As a result of this all that this report can do is to throw light on the Court's instructions by setting out some details of comparative law.

A. Administrative law in Ireland and the United Kingdom

[OJ C59, 5.3.79, p 83]

24. In the United Kingdom and in Ireland the expression "civil law" is not a technical term and has more than one meaning. It is used mainly as the opposite of criminal law. Except in this limited sense, no distinction is made between "private" and "public" law which is in any way comparable to that made in the legal systems of the original Member States, where it is of fundamental importance. Constitutional law, administrative law and tax law are all included in "civil law". Admittedly the United Kingdom is already a party to several Conventions which expressly apply only to "civil and commercial matters". These include all the bilateral Conventions on the enforcement of foreign judgments concluded by the United Kingdom. None of these, however, contains any rules which decide the circumstances under which an original court before which an issue is brought may assume jurisdiction. They govern only the recognition and enforcement of judgments and deal with questions of jurisdiction only indirectly as a condition of recognition. Moreover, these Conventions generally only apply to judgments ordering the payment of a specific sum of money (see paragraph 7). In drafting them, a pragmatic approach dispensing with a definition of "civil and commercial matters" proved, therefore, quite adequate.

B. Administrative Law in the Continental Member States

25. In the legal systems of the original Member States, the State itself and corporations exercising public functions such as local authorities may become involved in legal

transactions in two ways. Having regard to their special functions and the fact that they are formally part of public law they may act outside private law in a "sovereign" capacity. If they do this, their administrative act ("Verwaltungsakt", "décision exécutoire") is of a special nature. The State and some other public corporations may, however, also engage in legal transactions in the same way as private individuals. They can conclude contracts subject to private law, for example with transport undertakings for the carriage of goods or persons in accordance with tariffs generally in force or with a property owner for the lease of premises. The State and public corporations can also incur tortious liability in the same way as private individuals, for example as a result of a traffic accident in which an official car is involved. The real difficulty arises from distinguishing between instances in which the State and its independent organs act in a private law capacity and those in which they act in a public law capacity. A few guidelines on how this difficulty may be overcome are set out below.

The difficulties of finding a dividing line are of three kinds. The field of activities governed by public law differs in the various continental Member States (1). Public authorities frequently have a choice of the form in which they wish to act (2). The position is relatively clear only regarding the legal relations between the State and its independent organs (3).

1. The varying extent of public law

26. The most important difference between national administrative laws on the continent consists in the legal rules governing the duties of public authorities to provide supplies for themselves and for public tasks. For this purpose the French legal system has established the separate concept of administrative contracts which are governed independently of the "Code civil" by a special law, the "Code des marchés publics". The administrative contract is used both when public authorities wish to cover their own requirements and when public works, such as surface or underground construction, land development, etc, have to be undertaken. In such situations the French State and public corporations do not act in the capacity of private persons. The characteristic result of this is that, if the other parties to the contract do not perform their obligations, the State and public corporations do not have to bring an action before the courts, but may impose unilaterally enforceable sanctions by an administrative act ("décision exécutoire"). The legal situation in Germany is quite different. There the administrative contract plays a completely subordinate role. Supplies to the administrative agencies, and in particular the placing of contracts for public works, are carried out solely on the basis of private law. Even where the State undertakes large projects like the construction of a dam or the channelling of a river, it concludes its contracts with the firms concerned like a private individual.

[OJ C59, 5.3.79, p 84]

2. Choice of type of law

27. However, the borderline between the public law and the private law activities of public agencies is not rigidly prescribed in some of the legal systems. Public authorities have, within certain limits, a right to choose whether in carrying out their functions they wish to use the method of a "sovereign act", i e an administrative contract, or merely to conclude a private transaction.

In respect of those areas where public authorities may act either under private or public law, it is not always easy to decide whether or not they have acted as private individuals. In practice a clear indication is often lacking.

3. Relationship of public authorities to one another

28. Relations between public authorities may also be governed either by private or by public law. If governed by public law, such relations are not subject to the 1968 Convention, even if, as in Italy, they are not considered part of administrative law. However, relations of States and public corporations with each other would fall almost without exception within the sphere of private law, if they contain international aspects (and are not subject to public international law). It is hard to imagine how, for example, it would be possible for relations under public law to exist between two local authorities in different States. However, such relations could, of course, be established in future by treaties.

C. Civil and Criminal Law

29. The Working Party considered it obvious that criminal proceedings and criminal judgments of all kinds are excluded from the scope of the 1968 Convention, and that this matter needed, therefore, no clarification in the revised text (see paragraph 17). This applies not only to criminal proceedings *stricto sensu*. Other proceedings imposing sanctions for

breaches of orders or prohibitions intended to safeguard the public interest also fall outside the scope of civil law. Certain difficulties may arise in some cases in classifying private penalties known to some legal systems like contractual penalty clauses, penalties imposed by associations, etc. Since in many legal systems criminal proceedings may be brought by a private plaintiff, a distinction cannot be made by reference to the party which instituted the proceedings. The decisive factor is whether the penalty is for the benefit of the private plaintiff or some other private individual. Thus the decisions of the Danish industrial courts imposing fines, which are for the benefit of the plaintiff or some other aggrieved party, certainly fall within the scope of the 1968 Convention.

IV. MATTERS EXPRESSLY EXCLUDED

30. The second paragraph of Article 1 sets out under four points the civil matters excluded from the scope of the 1968 Convention. The accession of the new Member States raises problems in respect of all four points.

A. Status or legal capacity of natural persons, rights in property arising out of a matrimonial relationship, wills and succession

31. The Working Party encountered considerable difficulties when dealing with two problems relating to point (1) of the second paragraph of Article 1. The first problem was that of maintenance proceedings ancillary to status proceedings (1) and the second problem was the meaning of the term "régimes matrimoniaux" (rights in property arising out of a matrimonial relationship) (2). Apart from these two problems, the enquiries directed to the Working Party by the new Member States in respect of point (1) of the second paragraph of Article 1 were relatively easy to answer (3).

1. Maintenance judgments ancillary to status proceedings (ancillary maintenance judgments)

[OJ C59, 5.3.79, p 85]

32. When the 1968 Convention was drawn up, the principle still applied in the original Member States that disputes relating to property could not be combined with status proceedings, nor could maintenance proceedings be combined with proceedings for the dissolution of a marriage or paternity proceedings. It was therefore possible, without running the risk of creating disadvantages caused by artificially separating proceedings which in reality belonged together, to exclude status matters, but not maintenance proceedings, from the scope of the 1968 Convention. Once this rule comes up against national legislation which allows combined proceedings comprising maintenance claims and status matters, it will perforce give rise to great difficulties. These difficulties had already become serious in the original Member States, as soon as the widespread reform of family law had led to an increasing number of combined proceedings in those countries. Accordingly a mere adjustment of the 1968 Convention as between the original and new Member States would have provided only a piecemeal solution. Time and opportunity were ripe for an adjustment of the 1968 Convention, even as regards the relationships between the original Member States, to take account of the developments in the law which had taken place (see paragraph 18).

33. (a) The solution proposed by the Working Party is the outcome of a lengthy and intensive study of the possible alternatives. A distinctive feature of the 1968 Convention is the inter-relation of the application of its rules of jurisdiction at the adjudicating stage and the prohibition against reopening the question of jurisdiction at the recognition stage. Consequently, on the basis of the original text of the Convention only two completely clear-cut solutions present themselves as regards the treatment of ancillary maintenance judgments. The first is that the adjudicating court dealing with a status matter may give an ancillary maintenance judgment only when it has jurisdiction under the 1968 Convention; the maintenance judgment must then be recognized by the foreign court which may not re-examine whether the original adjudicating court had jurisdiction. The second possible solution is that ancillary maintenance judgments should also be excluded from the scope of the 1968 Convention under point (1) of the second paragraph of Article 1 as being ancillary to status judgments. However, both solutions have practical drawbacks. The second would result in ancillary maintenance judgments being generally excluded from recognition and enforcement under the 1968 Convention, even though the great majority of cases are decided by courts which would have had jurisdiction under its provisions. In an unacceptably high number of cases established maintenance claims would then no longer be able to move freely. The first solution would constitute a retrograde step from the progressive and widely acclaimed achievement of combined proceedings and judgments in status and maintenance matters.

34. In view of the above, the simplest solution would have been to include rules of jurisdiction covering status proceedings in the 1968 Convention. However, the reasons given earlier against taking that course are still valid. Therefore, the only way out is to opt for one of the two alternatives outlined above, whilst mitigating its drawbacks as far as possible. In the view of the Working Party, to deprive maintenance judgments ancillary to status proceedings of the guarantee of their enforceability abroad, or to recognize them only to a severely limited extent, would be the greater evil.

35. The Working Party therefore tried first of all to find a solution along the following lines. National courts dealing with status matters should have unrestricted power to decide also on maintenance claims, even when they cannot use their jurisdiction in respect of the maintenance claim on any provision of the 1968 Convention; ancillary maintenance judgments should in principle be recognized and enforced, but the court addressed may, contrary to the principles of the 1968 Convention which would otherwise apply, re-examine whether the court which gave judgment on the maintenance claims had jurisdiction under the provisions of Title II. However, the principle that the jurisdiction of the court of origin should not be reexamined during the recognition and enforcement stages was one of the really decisive achievements of the 1968 Convention. Any further restriction of this principle, even if limited to one area, would be justifiable only if all other conceivable alternatives were even more unacceptable.

36. The proposed addition to Article 5 would on the whole have most advantages. It prevents maintenance judgments which are ancillary to status judgments being given on the basis of the rule of exorbitant jurisdiction which generally applies in family law matters, namely the rule which declares the nationality of only one of the two parties as sufficient. One can accept that maintenance proceedings may not be combined with status proceedings where the competence of the court concerned is based solely on such exorbitant jurisdiction. For status proceedings, jurisdiction will continue to depend on the nationality of one of the two parties. The maintenance proceedings will have to be brought before another court with jurisdiction under the 1968 Convention.

[OJ C59, 5.3.79, p 86]

(b) The significance of the new approach is as follows:

37. It applies uniformly to the original and to the new Member States alike.

38. The jurisdiction of the court of origin may not be re-examined during the recognition and enforcement stages. This still follows from the third paragraph of Article 28 even after the addition made to Article 5. The court of origin has a duty to examine very carefully whether it has jurisdiction under the 1968 Convention, because a wrong decision on the question of jurisdiction cannot be corrected later on.

39. Similar rules apply in respect of *lis pendens*. It was not necessary to amend Articles 21 and 23. As long as the maintenance claim is pending before the court seised of the status proceedings it may not validly be brought before the courts of another State.

40. The question whether the court seised of the status proceedings has indeed jurisdiction also in respect of the maintenance proceedings, without having to rely solely on the nationality of one of the parties to the proceedings, is to be determined solely by the *lex fori*, including of course its private international law and procedural law. Even where the courts of a State may not as a rule combine a status matter with a maintenance claim, but can do so if a foreign legal system applicable under the provisions of their private international law so provides, they have jurisdiction in respect of the maintenance claim under the provisions of Article 5(2) of the 1968 Convention as amended. This is subject to the proviso that the court concerned in fact had jurisdiction in respect of both the status proceedings and the maintenance claim under the current provisions of its own national law.

41. The 1968 Convention prohibits the assumption of a combined jurisdiction which may be provided for under the national law to cover both status and maintenance proceedings only where the court's jurisdiction would be based solely on the nationality of one of the two parties. This concerns principally the exorbitant jurisdictions which are referred to in the second paragraph of Article 3, and provided for in Article 15 of the Belgian Civil Code (Code civil), and Articles 14 and 15 of the French and Luxembourg Civil Code (Code civil), governing proceedings which do not relate only to status and are therefore not excluded pursuant to point (1) of the second paragraph of Article 1. Maintenance actions combined with status proceedings continue to be permitted, even if the jurisdiction of the court is based on grounds other than those which are normally excluded by the 1968 Convention as being exorbitant. Jurisdiction on the basis of both parties having the same nationality is excluded by

the 1968 Convention in respect of ordinary civil and commercial matters, (Article 3, second paragraph), but in respect of combined status and maintenance proceedings, it cannot be considered as exorbitant, and consequently should not be inadmissible. The plaintiff's domicile is recognized in any case as a basis for jurisdiction in maintenance actions.

Finally, the proposed addition to Article 5(2) deprives courts of jurisdiction to entertain maintenance claims in combined family law proceedings only where their jurisdiction in respect of the status proceedings is based solely on the nationality of one of the two parties. Where the jurisdiction of a court depends on the fulfilment of several conditions, only one of which is that one of the parties should possess the nationality of the country concerned, jurisdiction does not depend solely on the nationality of the two parties.

Article 606(3) of the German Code of Civil Procedure is intended to ensure, in conjunction with Article 606a, that in matrimonial matters a German court always has jurisdiction, even when only one of the spouses is German. The fact that this provision is only supplementary to other provisions governing jurisdiction does not change the fact that jurisdiction may be based solely on the nationality of one of the parties. Once Article 5(2) of the 1968 Convention comes into force in its amended form maintenance claims can no longer be brought and decided under that particular jurisdiction.

42. Article 5(2) does not apply where the defendant is not domiciled in a Contracting State, or where maintenance questions can be decided without the procedural requirement of a claim or petition by one spouse against the other (see paragraph 66).

[OJ C59, 5.3.79, p 87]

2. Rights in property arising out of a matrimonial relationship

43. The exclusion of "rights in property arising out of a matrimonial relationship" from the scope of the Convention (Article 1 second paragraph, point (1)) raises a problem for the United Kingdom and Ireland.

Neither of these countries has an equivalent legal concept, although the expression "matrimonial property" is used in legal literature. In principle, property rights as between spouses are governed by general law. Agreements between spouses regulating their property rights are no different in law from agreements with third parties. Occasionally, however, there are special statutory provisions affecting the rights of spouses. Under English law (Matrimonial Homes Act 1967) and Irish law (Family Home Protection Act 1976), a spouse is entitled to certain rights of occupation of the matrimonial home. Moreover, divorce courts in the United Kingdom have, under the Matrimonial Causes Act 1973, considerable powers, though varying in extent in the different parts of the country, to order the payment of capital sums by one former spouse to the other. In England even a general redistribution of property as between former spouses and their children is possible.

The concept of "rights in property arising out of a matrimonial relationship" can also give rise to problems in the legal systems of the original Member States. It does not cover the same legal relations in all the systems concerned.

For a better understanding of the problems involved, they are set out more fully below (a), before the solution proposed by the Working Party is discussed (b).

44. (a) Three observations may give an indication of what is meant by "matrimonial regimes" (rights in property arising out of a matrimonial relationship) in the legal systems of the seven continental Member States. They will deal with the character of the concept which is confined exclusively to relationships between spouses (paragraph 45), with the relationship with the provisions which apply to all marriages irrespective of the particular "matrimonial regime" between the spouses (paragraph 46), and finally with the possibility of third parties becoming involved (paragraph 47).

45. For the purpose of governing the relations between spouses in respect of property, these legal systems do not, or at least not predominantly, employ the legal concepts and institutions otherwise used in their civil law. Instead, they have developed exclusive legal institutions the application of which is limited to relations between spouses, and whose most important feature is a comprehensive set of rules governing property. However, there is not merely one such set of rules in each legal system. Instead, spouses have a choice between several, ranging from general "community of property" to strict "separation of property". Even the latter, when chosen by the spouses, is a special form of "property regime", although special features arising from marriage can then hardly be said to exist any longer. The choice of a "property regime" must take the form of a "marriage contract" which is a special legal concept and should not be confused with the conclusion of the marriage itself. If the spouses do not make a choice, one of the sets of rules governing property rights applies to them by law (known as the "statutory matrimonial regime").

In some legal systems (France and Belgium) the "matrimonial regime" existing at the beginning of a marriage can subsequently be changed only in exceptional circumstances. In others (Germany) the spouses are free to alter their "matrimonial regime" at any time.

Disputes concerning "matrimonial regimes" can arise in various forms. There may be a dispute about the existence and interpretation of a marriage contract. In certain circumstances, a spouse may apply to the court for conversion of one "matrimonial regime" into a different one. Some "matrimonial regimes" provide for different rules in respect of different types of property. A dispute may then arise as to the type of property to which a particular object belongs. Where the "matrimonial regime" in question differentiates between the management of different types of property, there may be disagreement as to which spouse may manage which items of property. The most frequent type of dispute relating to "matrimonial regimes" concerns the winding up of the "matrimonial regime" after termination of the marriage, particularly after divorce. The "statutory matrimonial regime" under German law ("Zugewinngemeinschaft" or community of acquisitions) then results in an equalization claim by the spouse whose property has not increased in value to the same extent as that of his partner.

[OJ C59, 5.3.79, p 88]

46. Some provisions apply to all marriages, irrespective of the particular "matrimonial régime" under which spouses live, especially in Germany and France. Significantly the German and French texts of the 1968 Convention use the term in the plural ("die Güterstände", "les régimes matrimoniaux").

This can be explained as follows: the Code civil, for instance, deals with property aspects of marriage in two different parts of the code. Title V of the third book (on the acquisition of property) refers in detail to the "contrat de mariage" and then "régimes matrimoniaux", while property aspects of the relations between spouses are also covered by Articles 212 to 226 in Title V of the first book. The new French divorce law of 11 July 1975[6] introduced into the new version of Article 270 *et seq* of the Code civil equalization payments normally in the form of lump sum compensation (Article 274) which are independent of the particular "regime" applicable between the spouses. German law in the fourth book of the Bürgerliches Gesetzbuch makes a similar distinction between the legal consequences in respect of property rights which generally follow from marriage (Title V, Article 1353 *et seq*) and those which follow from "matrimonial property law", which varies according to the various "matrimonial regimes". Under both systems (Article 1357(2) of the Bürgerliches Gesetzbuch, Article 220(2) of the French Code civil) it is possible, for example, to prevent a spouse from engaging in certain legal transactions which he is normally entitled to engage in his capacity as spouse. According to Article 285 of the Code civil[7] the court can, after divorce, make orders concerning the matrimonial home irrespective of the "matrimonial regime" previously applicable. Similar possibilities exist in other States.

French legal literature refers to provisions concerning property rights which apply to all marriages as "régime matrimonial primaire". Other legal systems have no such special expression. It is within the spirit of Article 1, second paragraph, point (1) of the 1968 Convention to exclude those provisions concerning property rights affecting all marriages from its scope of application, in so far as they are not covered by the term "maintenance claims" (see paragraph 91 *et seq*).

In all legal systems of the Community it is possible to conceive of relations affecting rights between spouses which are governed by the general law of contract, law of tort or property law. Some laws contain provisions specifically intended to govern cases where such relations exist between spouses. For example, Article 1595 of the French Code civil contains restrictions on the admissibility of contracts of sale between spouses. Case law has sometimes developed special rules in this field which are designed to take account of the fact that such transactions commonly occur in relations between spouses. All this does not alter the position that legal relations governed by the general law of contract or tort remain subject to the provisions of the 1968 Convention, even if they are between spouses.

47. Finally, legal provisions comprised in the term "matrimonial regimes" are not limited to relations between the spouses themselves. For example, in Italian law, in connection with the liquidation of a "fondo patrimoniale" disputes may arise between parents and children (Article 171(3) of the Codice civile), which under Italian law unequivocally concern relations arising our of "matrimonial property law" ("il regime patrimoniale della famiglia"). German law contains the regime of "continued community of property" ("fortgesetzte Gütergemeinschaft"), which forms a link between a surviving spouse and the issue of the marriage.

48. (b) These findings raise problems similar to those with which the Working Party was faced in connection with the concept "civil and commercial matters". It was, however,

possible to define the concept of "matrimonial regimes" not only in a negative manner (paragraph 49), but also positively, albeit rather broadly. This should enable implementing legislation in the United Kingdom and Ireland, in reliance on these statements, to indicate to the courts which legal relations form part of "matrimonial regimes" within the meaning of the 1968 Convention (paragraph 50). Consequently no formal adjustment of the 1968 Convention became necessary.

49. As a negative definition, it can be said with certainty that in no legal system do maintenance claims between spouses derive from rules governing "matrimonial regimes"; nor are maintenance claims confined to claims for periodic payments (see paragraph 93).

[OJ C59, 5.3.79, p 89]

50. The mutual rights of spouses arising from "matrimonial régimes" correspond largely with what are best described in English as "rights in property arising out of a matrimonial relationship". Apart from maintenance matters property relations between spouses which are governed by the differing legal systems of the original Member States otherwise than as "matrimonial regimes" only seldom give rise to court proceedings with international aspects.

Thus the following can be said in respect of the scope of point (1) of the second paragraph of Article 1 as far as "matrimonial regimes" are concerned:

The Convention does not apply to the assumption of jurisdiction by United Kingdom and Irish courts, nor to the recognition and enforcement of foreign judgments by those courts, if the subject matter of the proceedings concerns issues which have arisen between spouses, or exceptionally between a spouse and a third party, during or after dissolution of their marriage, and which affect rights in property arising out of the matrimonial relationship. The expression "rights in property" includes all rights of administration and disposal—whether by marriage contract or by statute—of property belonging to the spouses.

3. The remaining contents of article 1, second paragraph, point (1) of the 1968 Convention

51. (a) The non-applicability of the 1968 Convention in respect of the status or legal capacity of natural persons concerns in particular proceedings and judgments relating to:

— the voidability and nullity of marriages, and judicial separation,
— the dissolution of marriages,
— the death of a person,
— the status and legal capacity of a minor and the legal representation of a person who is mentally ill; the status and legal capacity of a minor also includes judgments on the right to custody after the divorce or legal separation of the parents; this was the Working Party's unanimous reply to the express question put by the Irish delegation,
— the nationality or domicile (see paragraph 71 *et seq*) of a person,
— the care, custody and control of children, irrespective of whether these are in issue in divorce, guardianship, or other proceedings,
— the adoption of children.

However, the 1968 Convention is only inapplicable when the proceedings are concerned directly with legal consequences arising from these matters. It is not sufficient if the issues raised are merely of a preliminary nature, even if their preliminary nature is, or has been, of some importance in the main proceedings.

52. (b) The expression "wills and succession" covers all claims to testate or intestate succession to an estate. It includes disputes as to the validity or interpretation of the terms of a will setting up a trust, even where the trust takes effect on a date subsequent to the death of the testator. The same applies to proceedings in respect of the application and interpretation of statutory provisions establishing trusts in favour of persons or institutions as a result of a person dying intestate. The 1968 Convention does not, therefore, apply to any disputes concerning the creation, interpretation and administration of trusts arising under the law of succession including wills. On the other hand, disputes concerning the relations of the trustee with persons other than beneficiaries, in other words the "external relations" of the trust, come within the scope of the 1968 Convention (see paragraph 109 *et seq*).

B. Bankruptcy and Similar Proceedings

53. Article 1, second paragraph, point (2), occupies a special position among the provisions concerning the legal matters excluded from the 1968 Convention. It was drafted with reference to a special Convention on bankruptcy which was being discussed at the same time as the 1968 Convention.

[OJ C59, 5.3.79, p 90]

Leaving aside special bankruptcy rules for very special types of business undertakings, the two Conventions were intended to dovetail almost completely with each other. Consequently, the preliminary draft Convention on bankruptcy, which was first drawn up in 1970, submitted in an amended form in 1975,[8] deliberately adopted the principal terms "bankruptcy", "compositions" and "analogous proceedings"[9] in the provisions concerning its scope in the same way[10] as they were used in the 1968 Convention. To avoid, as far as possible, leaving lacunae between the scope of the two Conventions, efforts are being made in the discussions on the proposed Convention on bankruptcy to enumerate in detail all the principal and secondary proceedings involved[11] and so to eliminate any problems of interpretation. As long as the proposed Convention on bankruptcy has not yet come into force, the application of Article 1, second paragraph, point (2) of the 1968 Convention remains difficult. The problems, including the matters arising from the accession of the new Member States, are of two kinds. First, it is necessary to define what proceedings are meant by bankruptcy, compositions or analogous proceedings as well as their constituent parts (1). Secondly, the legal position in the United Kingdom poses a special problem as the bankruptcy of "incorporated companies" is not a recognized concept in that country (2).

1. General and individual types of proceedings excluded from the scope of the 1968 Convention

54. It is relatively easy to define the basic types of proceedings that are subject to bankruptcy law and therefore fall outside the scope of the 1968 Convention. Such proceedings are defined in almost identical terms in both the Jenard and the Noël-Lemontey reports[12] as those

"which, depending on the system of law involved, are based on the suspension of payments, the insolvency of the debtor or his inability to raise credit, and which involve the judicial authorities for the purpose either of compulsory and collective liquidation of the assets or simply of supervision by those authorities."

In the legal systems of the original States of the EEC there are only a very few examples of proceedings of this kind, ranging from two (in Germany) to four (Italy and Luxembourg). In its 1975 version[8] the Protocol to the preliminary draft Convention on bankruptcy enumerates the proceedings according to types of proceedings and States concerned. A list is reproduced in Annex I to this report. Naturally, the 1968 Convention does not, *a fortiori*, cover global insolvency proceedings which do not take place before a court as, for example, can be the case in France when authorization can be withdrawn from an insurance undertaking for reasons of insolvency.

The enumeration in Article 17 of the preliminary draft Convention on bankruptcy cannot, before that Convention has come into force, be used for the interpretation of Article 1, second paragraph, point (2) of the 1968 Convention. Article 17 mentions the kind of proceedings especially closely connected with bankruptcy where the courts of the State where the bankruptcy proceedings are opened are to have exclusive jurisdiction.

It is not desirable at this stage to prescribe this list, or even an amended list, as binding. Further amendments may well have to be made during the discussions on the Convention on bankruptcy. To prescribe a binding list would cause confusion, even though the list to be included in the Protocol to the Convention on bankruptcy will, after the latter's entry into force, prevail over the 1968 Convention pursuant to Article 57, since it is part of a special Convention. Moreover, the list, as already mentioned, does not include all bankruptcies, compositions and analogous proceedings. For instance, it has become clear during the discussions on the Convention on bankruptcy that the list will not cover insurance undertakings which only undertake direct insurance,[13] without thereby bringing the bankruptcy of such undertakings within the scope of the 1968 Convention. Finally the Working Party was not sure whether all the proceedings included in the list as it stood at the beginning of 1976 could properly be regarded as bankruptcies, compositions or analogous proceedings, before the list formally comes into force. This applied particularly to the proceedings mentioned in connection with the liquidation of companies (see paragraph 57).

2. Bankruptcy law and the dissolution of companies

[OJ C59, 5.3.79, p 91]

55. As far as dissolution, whether or not by decision of a court, and the capacity to be made bankrupt are concerned, the legal treatment of a partnership[14] established under United Kingdom or Irish law is comparable in every respect to the treatment of companies established under continental legal systems. Companies[15] within the meaning of United Kingdom or Irish law, however, are dealt with in a fundamentally different way. The Bankruptcy Acts do not apply to them,[16] but instead they are subject to the winding-up procedure of the Companies Acts;[17] even if they are not registered companies. Winding-up is not a special bankruptcy procedure, but a legal concept which can take different forms and serves different purposes. A common feature of all winding-up proceedings is a disposal of assets and the distribution of their proceeds amongst the persons entitled thereto with a view of bringing the company to an end. The start of winding-up proceedings corresponds, therefore, to what is understood by "dissolution" on the continent. The dissolution of a company on the other hand is identical with the final result of a liquidation under continental legal systems.

A distinction is made between winding-up by the court, voluntary winding-up and winding-up subject to the supervision of the court. The second kind of winding-up takes place basically without the intervention of the court, either at the instance of the members alone or of the members together with the creditors. Only as a subsidiary measure and exceptionally can the court appoint a liquidator. The third kind of winding-up is only a variation on the second. The court has certain supervisory powers. A winding-up of a company by the court requires an application either by the company or by a creditor which is possible in a number of circumstances of which insolvency is only one. Other grounds for a winding-up include: the number of members falling below the required minimum, failure to commence, or a lengthy suspension of, business and the general ground "that the court is of the opinion that it is just and equitable that the company should be wound up".

56. The legal position outlined has the following consequences for the application of Article 1, second paragraph, point (2), and Article 16(2) of the 1968 Convention in the Continental (b) and other (a) Member States:

57. (a) A voluntary winding-up under United Kingdom or Irish law cannot be equated with court proceedings. The same applies to the non-judicial proceedings under Danish law for the dissolution of a company. Legal disputes incidental to or consequent upon such proceedings are therefore normal civil or commercial disputes and as such are not excluded from the scope of the 1968 Convention. This also applies in the case of a winding-up subject to the supervision of the court. The powers of the court in such a case are not sufficiently clearly defined for the proceedings to be classed as judicial.

A winding-up by the court cannot, of course, be automatically excluded from the scope of the 1968 Convention. For although most proceedings of this kind serve the purpose of the liquidation of an insolvent company, this is not always the case. The Working Party decided to exclude from the scope of the 1968 Convention only those proceedings which are or were based on Section 222(e) of the British Companies Act[18] or the equivalent provisions in the legislation of Ireland and Northern Ireland. This would, however, involve too narrow a definition of the proceedings to be excluded, as the liquidation of an insolvent company is frequently based on one of the other grounds referred to in Section 222 of the British Companies Act, notably in (a), which states that a special resolution of the members is sufficient to set proceedings in motion. There is no alternative therefore to ascertaining the determining factor in the dissolution in each particular case. The English version of Article 1, second paragraph, point (2), of the 1968 Convention has been worded accordingly. It was not, however, necessary to alter the text of the Convention in the other languages. If a winding-up in the United Kingdom or Ireland is based on a ground other than the insolvency of the company, the court concerned with recognition and enforcement in another Contracting State will have to examine whether the company was not in fact insolvent. Only if it is of the opinion that the company was solvent will the 1968 Convention apply.

58. Only in that event does the problem arise of whether exclusive jurisdiction exists for the courts at the seat of the company pursuant to Article 16(2) of the 1968 Convention. In the United Kingdom and Ireland this is the case for proceedings which involve or have involved a solvent company.

The term "dissolution" in Article 16(2) of the 1968 Convention is not to be understood in the narrow technical sense in which it is used in legal systems on the Continent. It also covers proceedings concerning the liquidation of a company after "dissolution". These include disputes about the amount to be paid out to a member; such proceedings are nothing more than stages on the way towards terminating the legal existence of a company.

[OJ C59, 5.3.79, p 92]

59. (b) If a company established under a Continental legal system is dissolved, i e enters the stage of liquidation, because it has become insolvent, court proceedings relating to the "dissolution of the company" are only conceivable as disputes concerning the admissibility of, or the mode and manner of conducting, winding-up proceedings. All this is outside the scope of the 1968 Convention. On the other hand, all other proceedings intended to declare or to bring about the dissolution of a company are not the concern of the law of winding-up. It is unnecessary to examine whether the company concerned is solvent or insolvent. It also makes no difference, if bankruptcy law questions arise as a preliminary issue. For instance, when litigation ensues as to whether a company should be dissolved, because a person who allegedly belongs to it has gone bankrupt, the dispute is not about a matter of bankruptcy law, but of a type which falls within the scope of the 1968 Convention. The Convention also applies if, in connection with the dissolution of a company not involving the courts, third parties contend in legal proceedings that they are creditors of the company and consequently entitled to satisfaction out of assets of the company.

C. Social security

60. Matters relating to social security were expressly excluded from the scope of the 1968 Convention. This was intended to avoid the difficulties which would arise from the fact that in some Member States this area of law comes under public law, whereas in others it is on the border-line between public and private law. Legal proceedings by social security authorities against third parties, for example against wrongdoers, in exercise of rights of action which they have acquired by subrogation or by operation of law, do come within the scope of the 1968 Convention.

D. Arbitration

61. The United Kingdom requested information on matters regarding the effect of the exclusion of "arbitration" from the scope of the 1968 Convention, which were not dealt with in the Jenard report. Two divergent basic positions which it was not possible to reconcile emerged from the discussion on the interpretation of the relevant provisions of Article 1, second paragraph, point (4). The point of view expressed principally on behalf of the United Kingdom was that this provision covers all disputes which the parties had effectively agreed should be settled by arbitration, including any secondary disputes connected with the agreed arbitration. The other point of view, defended by the original Member States of the EEC, only regards proceedings before national courts as part of "arbitration" if they refer to arbitration proceedings, whether concluded, in progress or to be started. It was nevertheless agreed that no amendment should be made to the text. The new Member States can deal with this problem of interpretation in their implementing legislation. The Working Party was prepared to accept this conclusion, because all the Member States of the Community, with the exception of Luxembourg and Ireland, had in the meantime become parties to the United Nations Convention of 10 June 1958 on the recognition and enforcement of foreign arbitral awards, and Ireland is willing to give sympathetic consideration to the question of her acceding to it. In any event, the differing basic positions lead to a different result in practice only in one particular instance (see paragraph 62).

1. Decisions of national courts on the subject matter of a dispute despite the existence of an arbitration agreement

62. If a national court adjudicates on the subject matter of a dispute, because it overlooked an arbitration agreement or considered it inapplicable, can recognition and enforcement of that judgment be refused in another State of the Community on the ground that the arbitration agreement was after all valid and that therefore, pursuant to Article 1, second paragraph, point (4), the judgment falls outside the scope of the 1968 Convention? Only if the first interpretation (see paragraph 61) is accepted can an affirmative answer be given to this question.

[OJ C59, 5.3.79, p 93]

In support of the view that this would be the correct course, it is argued that since a court in the State addressed is free, contrary to the view of the court in the State of origin, to regard a dispute as affecting the status of an individual, or the law of succession, or as falling outside the scope of civil law, and therefore as being outside the scope of the 1968 Convention, it must in the same way be free to take the opposite view to that taken by the court of origin and to reject the applicability of the 1968 Convention because arbitration is involved.

Against this, it is contended that the literal meaning of the word "arbitration" itself implies that it cannot extend to every dispute affected by an arbitration agreement; that "arbitration" refers only to arbitration proceedings. Proceedings before national courts would therefore be affected by Article 1, second paragraph, point (4) of the 1968 Convention only if they dealt with arbitration as a main issue and did not have to consider the validity of an arbitration agreement merely as a matter incidental to an examination of the competence of the court of origin to assume jurisdiction. It has been contended that the court in the State addressed can no longer re-open the issue of classification; if the court of the State of origin, in assuming jurisdiction, has taken a certain view as to the applicability of the 1968 Convention, this becomes binding on the court in the State addressed.

2. Other proceedings connected with arbitration before national courts

63. (a) The 1968 Convention as such in no way restricts the freedom of the parties to submit disputes to arbitration. This applies even to proceedings for which the 1968 Convention has established exclusive jurisdiction. Nor, of course, does the Convention prevent national legislation from invalidating arbitration agreements affecting disputes for which exclusive jurisdiction exists under national law or pursuant to the 1968 Convention.

64. (b) The 1968 Convention does not cover court proceedings which are ancillary to arbitration proceedings, for example the appointment or dismissal of arbitrators, the fixing of the place of arbitration, the extension of the time limit for making awards or the obtaining of a preliminary ruling on questions of substance as provided for under English law in the procedure known as "statement of a special case" (Section 21 of the Arbitration Act 1950). In the same way a judgment determining whether an arbitration agreement is valid or not, or because it is invalid, ordering the parties not to continue the arbitration proceedings, is not covered by the 1968 Convention.

65. (c) Nor does the 1968 Convention cover proceedings and decisions concerning applications for the revocation, amendment, recognition and enforcement of arbitration awards. This also applies to court decisions incorporating arbitration awards—a common method of recognition under United Kingdom law. If an arbitration award is revoked and the revoking court or another national court itself decides the subject matter in dispute, the 1968 Convention is applicable.

V. JUDICIAL NATURE OF PROCEEDINGS AND JUDGMENTS

66. As between the original Member States, and also as between those States and the United Kingdom and Ireland, the 1968 Convention could and can in one particular respect be based on a surprisingly uniform legal tradition. Almost everywhere the same tasks pertaining to the field of private law are assigned to the courts. The authorities which constitute "courts" can everywhere be recognized easily and with certainty. This is also true in cases where proceedings are being conducted in "court" which are not the result of an action by one party "against" another party (see paragraphs 23 and 124 *et seq*). The accession of Denmark raised new problems.

Although the Working Party had no difficulty in confirming that the Industrial Court under the Danish Industrial Court Act of 21 April 1964 (Bulletin No 124) was, in spite of its unusual structure, clearly to be considered a court within the meaning of the 1968 Convention, it was more difficult to decide how to classify proceedings in maintenance matters, which, in Denmark, failing an amicable settlement, are almost always held before administrative authorities and terminate with a decision by the latter.

[OJ C59, 5.3.79, p 94]

1. The legal position in Denmark

67. The legal position may be summed up as follows. Maintenance matters are determined as regards the obligation to pay either by agreement or by a court judgment. The amount of the payment and the scale of any necessary modifications are, however, determined by an authority known as the "Amtmand", which under Danish law is clearly not a court but an administrative authority which in this case plays a judicial role. It is true that decisions given in such proceedings come under The Hague Convention on the recognition and enforcement of decisions relating to maintenance obligations, but this is only because under that Convention the matter does not specifically require a court judgment.

2. Article Va of the Protocol and its effect

68. There would, however, be an imbalance in the scope of the 1968 Convention, if it excluded maintenance proceedings of the type found in Denmark on the sole ground that they do not take place before courts.

The amendment to the 1968 Convention thus made necessary is contained in the proposal for the adoption of a new Article Va in the Protocol. This method appeared simpler than attempting to amend a large number of separate provisions of the 1968 Convention.

Wherever the 1968 Convention refers to "court" or "judge" it must in the future be taken to include Danish administrative authorities when dealing with maintenance matters (as in Article 2, first paragraph, Article 3, first paragraph, Article 4, first paragraph, Article 5(2), Article 17, Article 18, Articles 20 to 22, Article 27(4), Article 28, third paragraph and Article 52). This applies in particular to Article 4, first paragraph, even though in the French, Italian and Dutch texts, unlike the German version, the word "court" does not appear.

Similarly, wherever the 1968 Convention refers to "judgments", the decisions arrived at by the Danish administrative authorities in maintenance matters will in future be included in the legal definition of the term "judgment" contained in Article 25. Its content is extended in this respect by the addition of Article Va to the Protocol, so that it is now to be understood as reading:

"For the purposes of this Convention, "judgment" means any judgment given by a court or tribunal of a Contracting State—including in matters relating to maintenance, the Danish administrative authorities—whatever the judgment may be called ... ."

[3047C]

CHAPTER 4
JURISDICTION

A. GENERAL REMARKS

69. In section A of Chapter 4 of his report, Mr Jenard sets out the main ideas underlying the rules of jurisdiction of the 1968 Convention. None of this is affected by the accession of the new Member States. The extent to which three features of the law in the United Kingdom and in Ireland are consistent with the application of the 1968 Convention must, however, be clarified. These features are: the far-reaching jurisdiction of the Superior Courts (1), the concept of domicile (2) and, lastly, the discretionary powers enjoyed by the courts to determine territorial jurisdiction (3).

1. First instance jurisdiction of the Superior Courts

70. The Continental Member States of the Community have geographically defined jurisdictions where courts of first instance are competent to give judgments even in the most important civil disputes. There are many courts of equal status: approximately 50 "Landgerichte" in Germany, and an equal number of "tribunaux de grande instance" in France and "Tribunali" in Italy. Where the 1968 Convention itself lays down both the international and local jurisdiction of the courts, as for example in Articles 5 and 6, jurisdiction is given to only one of the many courts with equal status in a State. There is little room for such a distinction in the judicial systems of Ireland and the United Kingdom in so far as a Superior Court has jurisdiction as a court of first instance.

[OJ C59, 5.3.79, p 95]

In Ireland, the High Court is the only court of first instance with unlimited jurisdiction. It can, exceptionally, sit outside Dublin. Nothing in the 1968 Convention precludes this. In addition to the High Court, there is a Circuit Court and a District Court. In respect of these courts too, the expression "the Court" is used in the singular and there is only one Court for the whole country but each of its judges is permanently assigned to a specific circuit or district. The local jurisdiction laid down in the 1968 Convention means, in the case of Ireland, the judge assigned to a certain "circuit" or "district".

In the United Kingdom three Superior Courts have jurisdiction at first instance: the High Court of Justice for England and Wales, the Outer House of the Court of Session for Scotland and the High Court for Northern Ireland. Each of these courts has, however, exclusive jurisdiction for the entire territory of the relevant part of the United Kingdom (see paragraph 11). Thus the same comments as those made in connection with the territorial jurisdiction of the Irish High Court apply also to each judicial area. The possibility of transferring a case from London to a district registry of the High Court does not mean transfer to another court. Bearing in mind that foreign judgments have to be registered separately in respect of each of the judicial areas of the United Kingdom in order to become enforceable therein (see paragraph 208), the distinction between international and local jurisdiction becomes largely irrelevant in the United Kingdom. The rules in the 1968 Convention governing local jurisdiction are relevant to the Superior Courts of first instance in the United Kingdom only in so far as a distinction has to be made between the courts of England and Wales, Scotland and Northern Ireland. The competence of the other courts (County Courts, Magistrates' Courts, and, in Scotland, the Sheriff Courts) presents no particular problems.

2. The concept of "domicile" and the application of the Convention

71. (a) The concept of domicile is of fundamental importance for the 1968 Convention in determining jurisdiction (e g Articles 2 to 6, 8, 11, 12(3), 14, 17 and 32). In the legal systems of the original Member States of the EEC, its meaning differs to some extent. In the Federal Republic of Germany, it expresses a person's connection with a local community within the national territory. In France and Luxembourg, it denotes a person's exact address. In Belgium, for purposes of jurisdiction the term denotes the place where a person is entered in the register of population as having his principal residence (Article 36 of the Code judiciaire). These differences explain why, in determining a person's domicile, e g German law places greater emphasis on the stability of the connection with a specific place than do some of the other legal systems.

Notwithstanding these differences the basic concept of "domicile" is the same in all the legal systems of the original Member States of the EEC, namely the connection of a person with a smaller local unit within the State. This made it possible in Article 52 of the 1968 Convention to leave a more precise definition of the term to the law of the State in which the "domicile" of a person had to be ascertained. It did not lead to an uneven application of the provisions of the 1968 Convention. Clearly, for the purposes of applying them in the original Member States of the Community it is irrelevant whether the concept of domicile refers to a specific address or to a local community.

72. (b) The concept of domicile under the law in Ireland and the United Kingdom differs considerably in several respects from the Continental concept.

First, this concept does not refer to a person's connection with a particular place and even less with a particular residence within a place, but to his having his roots within a territory covered by a particular legal system (see paragraph 11). A person's domicile only indicates whether he comes under the legal system of England and Wales, Scotland, Northern Ireland, or possibly under a foreign legal system. A person's legal connection with a particular place is denoted by the word "residence", not "domicile".

According to United Kingdom law, a person always has one "domicile" and can never have more than one. At birth a legitimate child acquires the domicile of its father, an illegitimate child that of its mother. A child retains its domicile of its parents throughout its minority.

[OJ C59, 5.3.79, p 96]

After it reaches its majority, it may acquire another domicile but for this there are very strict requirements: the usual place of residence must have been transferred to another country—with the intention of keeping it there permanently or at least for an unlimited period.

73. (c) Article 52 of the 1968 Convention does not expressly provide for the linking of the concept of domicile with a particular place or a particular residence, nor does it expressly prohibit it from being connected with a particular national territory. The United Kingdom and Ireland would, consequently, be free to retain their traditional concept of domicile when the jurisdiction of their courts is invoked. The Working Party came to the conclusion that this would lead to a certain imbalance in the application of the 1968 Convention. In certain cases, the courts of the United Kingdom or Ireland could assume jurisdiction on the basis of their rules on the retention of domicile, although by the law of all the other Member States of the Community, such a person would be domiciled at his actual place of residence within their territory.

The Working Party therefore requested the United Kingdom and Ireland to provide in their legislation implementing the 1968 Convention (see paragraph 256), at any rate for the purposes of that Convention, for a concept of domicile which would depart from their traditional rules and would tend to reflect more the concept of "domicile" as understood in the original States of the EEC.

In Article 69(5) of the Convention for the European patent for the common market which was drawn up concurrently with the Working Party's discussions, the concept of "Wohnsitz" is translated as "residence" and for the meaning of the expression reference is made to Articles 52 and 53 of the 1968 Convention. To prevent confusion, the proposed new Article Vc of the Protocol makes it clear that the concept of "residence" within the meaning of the Community Patent Convention should be ascertained in the same way as the concept of "domicile" in the 1968 Convention.

74. (d) It should be noted that the application of the third paragraph of Article 52 raises the problem of different concepts of domicile, when considering which system of law determines whether a person's domicile depends on that of another person. The relevant factor, in such a case, may be where the dependent person is domiciled. Under United Kingdom private international law, the question whether a person has a dependent domicile is not determined by that person's nationality, but by his domicile in the traditional sense of that concept. The re-definition of "domicile" in connection with the first paragraph of Article 52 in no way affects this.

If a foreigner under age who has settled in England is sued in an English court, that court must take account of the different concepts of domicile. As a first step it must establish where the defendant had his "domicile" before settling in England. This is decided in accordance with the traditional meaning of that concept. The law thus found to be applicable will then determine whether the minor was in a position to acquire a "domicile" in England within the meaning of the 1968 Convention. The English court must then ascertain whether the requirements for a "domicile" in the area covered by the English court concerned are satisfied.

75. (e) There is no equivalent in the law of the United Kingdom to the concept of the "seat" of a company in Continental law. In order to achieve the results which under private international law are linked on the continent with the "seat" of a company, the United Kingdom looks to the legal system where the company was incorporated ("law of incorporation", Section 406 of the Companies Act, 1948). The "domicile" of a company in the traditional sense of the term (see paragraph 72) is taken to be the judicial area in which it was incorporated. The new Member States of the Community are not obliged to introduce a legal concept which corresponds to that of a company's "seat" within the meaning of the continental legal systems, just as in general they are not obliged to adapt their concept of domicile. However, should the United Kingdom and Ireland not change their law on this point, the result would again be an imbalance in the application of the 1968 Convention. It would, therefore, be desirable for the United Kingdom to introduce for the purposes of the Convention an appropriate concept in its national legislation such as "domicile of a company", which would correspond more closely to the Continental concept of the "seat" of a company than the present United Kingdom concept of "law of incorporation".

[OJ C59, 5.3.79, p 97]

Such a provision would not preclude a company from having a "domicile" in the United Kingdom in accordance with legislation in the United Kingdom and a "seat" in a Continental State in accordance with the legislation of that State. As a result of the second sentence of Article 53, a company is enabled under the laws of several of the original States of the EEC to have a "seat" in more than one State. The problems which might arise from such a situation can be overcome by the provisions in the 1968 Convention on *lis pendens* and related actions (see paragraph 162).

3. Discretionary powers regarding jurisdiction and transfer of proceedings

76. The idea that a national court has discretion in the exercise of its jurisdiction either territorially or as regards the subject matter of a dispute does not generally exist in Continental legal systems. Even where, in the rules relating to jurisdiction, tests of an exceptionally flexible nature are laid down, no room is left for the exercise of any discretionary latitude. It is true that Continental legal systems recognize the power of a court to transfer proceedings from one court to another. Even then the court has no discretion in determining whether or not this power should be exercised. In contrast, the law in the United Kingdom and in Ireland has evolved judicial discretionary powers in certain fields. In some cases, these correspond in practice to legal provisions regarding jurisdiction which are more detailed in the Continental States, while in others they have no counterpart on the Continent. It is therefore difficult to evaluate such powers within the context of the 1968 Convention. A distinction has to be made between the international and national application of this legal concept.

77. (a) In relationships with the courts of other States and also, within the United Kingdom, as between the courts of different judicial areas (see paragraph 11) the doctrine of *forum conveniens*—in Scotland, *forum non conveniens*—is of relevance.

The courts are allowed, although only in very rare and exceptional cases, to disregard the fact that proceedings may already be pending before foreign courts, or courts of another judicial area.

Exceptionally, the courts may refuse to hear or decide a case, if they believe it would be better for the case to be heard before a court having equivalent jurisdiction in another State (or another judicial area) because this would increase the likelihood of an efficient and impartial hearing of the particular case.

There are several special reasons why in practice such discretionary powers are exercised: the strict requirements traditionally imposed by the laws of the United Kingdom and Ireland regarding changes of domicile (see paragraph 72); the rules allowing establishment of jurisdiction by merely serving a writ or originating summons in the territory of the State concerned (see paragraphs 85 and 86); the principles developed particularly strongly in the procedural law of these States requiring directness in the taking of evidence with the consequent restrictions on making use of evidence taken abroad or merely in another judicial area; and finally, the considerable difficulties arising in the application of foreign law by United Kingdom or Irish courts.

78. According to the views of the delegations from the Continental Member States of the Community such possibilities are not open to the courts of those States when, under the 1968 Convention, they have jurisdiction and are asked to adjudicate.

Article 21 expressly prohibits a court from disregarding the fact that proceedings are already pending abroad. For the rest the view was expressed that under the 1968 Convention the Contracting States are not only entitled to exercise jurisdiction in accordance with the provisions laid down in Title 2; they are also obliged to do so. A plaintiff must be sure which court has jurisdiction. He should not have to waste his time and money risking that the court concerned may consider itself less competent than another. In particular, in accordance with the general spirit of the 1968 Convention, the fact that foreign law has to be applied, either generally or in a particular case, should not constitute a sufficient reason for a court to decline jurisdiction. Where the courts of several States have jurisdiction, the plaintiff has deliberately been given a right of choice, which should not be weakened by application of the doctrine of *forum conveniens*. The plaintiff may have chosen another apparently "inappropriate" court from among the competent courts in order to obtain a judgment in the State in which he also wishes to enforce it. Furthermore, the risk of a negative conflict of jurisdiction should not be disregarded: despite the United Kingdom court's decision, the judge on the Continent could likewise decline jurisdiction. The practical reasons in favour of the doctrine of *forum conveniens* will lose considerably in significance, as soon as the 1968 Convention becomes applicable in the United Kingdom and Ireland. The implementing legislation will necessitate not inconsiderable changes in the laws of those States, both in respect of the definition of the concept of domicile (see paragraph 73) and on account of the abolition of jurisdictional competence based merely on service of a writ within the area of the court (see paragraph 86). To correct rules of jurisdiction in a particular case by means of the concept of *forum conveniens* will then be largely unnecessary. After considering these arguments the United Kingdom and Irish delegations did not press for a formal adjustment of the 1968 Convention on this point.

[OJ C59, 5.3.79, p 98]

79. (b) A concept similar to the doctrine of *forum conveniens* is also applied within the territory of the State, though the term itself is not used in that context. This may be due to the fact that the same result can be achieved by the device of transferring the case to another court having alternative jurisdiction within the same State or the same legal area (see paragraph 11). The Working Party had to examine to what extent the 1968 Convention restricted such powers of transfer. In this connection certain comments made earlier may be repeated: the powers of the Superior Courts in Ireland or in a judicial area of the United Kingdom (see paragraph 70) to decide as a court of first instance remain unchanged. For the rest, the following applies:

80. (aa) The previous legal position in Ireland and the United Kingdom remains essentially the same. Each court can transfer proceedings to another court, if that court has equivalent jurisdiction and can better deal with the matter. For example, if an action is brought before the High Court, the value of which is unlikely to exceed the amount which limits the jurisdiction of the lower court, the High Court has power to transfer the proceedings to such a court, but it is not obliged to do so. A Circuit Court in Ireland, a County Court or Magistrates' Court in England and a Sheriff Court in Scotland—but not an Irish District Court (see paragraph 70)—

may transfer proceedings to another court of the same category or exceptionally to a court of another category, if the location of the evidence or the circumstances for a fair hearing should make such a course desirable in the interest of the parties.

Some Continental legal systems also provide for the possibility, albeit on a much smaller scale, of a judge having discretion to confer jurisdiction on a court which would not otherwise have it. This is the case under, for instance, Article 36 of the German Code of Civil Procedure, if proper proceedings are not possible before the court which originally had jurisdiction. Under Section 356 of the new French Code of Civil Procedure[19] proceedings may be transferred to another court of the same type, if a risk of lack of impartiality exists.

81. (bb) The 1968 Convention in no way affects the competence as regards subject matter of the courts of a State. The national legal systems are thus free to provide for the possibility of transfer of cases between courts of different categories.

For the most part, the 1968 Convention does not affect the territorial jurisdiction of the courts within a State, but only their international jurisdiction. This is clearly reflected by the basic rule on jurisdiction contained in Article 2. Unless the jurisdiction of a court where proceedings are instituted against a person domiciled in the United Kingdom or Ireland is derived from a provision of the 1968 Convention which at the same time determines local jurisdiction, as for example Article 5, the 1968 Convention does not prevent a transfer of the proceedings to another court in the same State. Even in respect of exclusive jurisdiction, Article 16 only lays down the international jurisdiction of the courts of a State, and does not prevent a transfer within that State.

Finally, the 1968 Convention does not of course prevent a transfer to the court which actually has local jurisdiction under the Convention. This would occur where both parties agree to the transfer and the requirements for jurisdiction by consent pursuant to Article 17 are satisfied.

[OJ C59, 5.3.79, p 99]

The only type of case which remains problematic is where an action is brought before a court in circumstances where the 1968 Convention gives the plaintiff a choice of jurisdiction. An action in tort or a liability insurance claim is brought at the place where the harmful event occurred or a maintenance claim at the domicile of the maintenance creditor. It appears obvious that in special exceptional cases a transfer to another court of the same State must be permitted, when proper proceedings are not possible before the court which would otherwise have jurisdiction. However, the Working Party did not feel justified in incorporating these matters expressly in the 1968 Convention. They could be covered by a rule of interpretation to the effect that the court having local jurisdiction may, in exceptional cases, include the court which is designated as having local jurisdiction by the decision of another court. The courts for the place "where the harmful event occurred" could thus be a neighbouring court designated by another court, if the courts for the place of the harmful event should be unable to hear the proceedings.

In so far as a court's discretionary powers to confer jurisdiction on other courts and in particular to transfer proceedings to another court are not defined in detail such discretionary powers should, of course, only be used in the spirit of the 1968 Convention, if the latter has determined, not only international but also local jurisdiction. A transfer merely on account of the cost of the proceedings or in order to facilitate the taking of evidence would be possible only with the consent of the plaintiff, who had the choice of jurisdiction.

B. COMMENTS ON THE SECTIONS OF TITLE II

Section 1
General provisions

82. The proposed adjustments to Articles 2[20] to 4 are confined to inserting certain exorbitant jurisdictions in the legal systems of the new Member States into the second paragraph of Article 3. The occasion has been taken to adjust the text of that Article to take account also of an amendment to the law which has been introduced in Belgium. Detailed comments on the proposed alterations (I) precede two more general remarks on the relevance of this provision to the whole structure of the 1968 Convention (II).

I. Detailed comments

83. 1. Belgium

In Belgium, Articles 52, 52 bis and 53 of the law of 25 March 1876 had already been superseded before the coming into force of the 1968 Convention by Articles 635, 637 and 638 of the Judicial Code. Nevertheless only Article 638 of the Judicial Code is mentioned in the second paragraph of Article 3 in its revised version. It corresponds to Article 53 of the law of 25 March 1876 and provides that where Belgian courts do not possess jurisdiction based on other provisions, a plaintiff resident in Belgium may sue any person before the court of his place of residence. The version of Article 3, valid hitherto, erroneously classed the jurisdiction based on Articles 52 and 52 bis of the abovementioned law as exorbitant.

84. 2. Denmark

The provisions of Danish law included in the second paragraph of Article 3 state that a foreigner may be sued before any Danish court in whose district he is resident or has property when the document instituting the proceedings is served. On this last point the provision corresponds to similar German provisions included in the list of exorbitant jurisdictions. On the first point reference may be made to what follows concerning Ireland (see paragraph 85). There is a separate Code of Civil Procedure for Greenland (see paragraph 253); special reference had therefore to be made to the corresponding provisions affecting that country.

85. 3. Ireland

According to the principles of common law which are unwritten and apply equally in the United Kingdom and Ireland, a court has jurisdiction in principle if the plaintiff has been properly served with the court process. The jurisdiction of Irish (and United Kingdom) courts is indirectly restricted to the extent of the limits imposed on the service of a writ of summons. Service is available without special leave only within the territory of Ireland (or the United Kingdom). However, every service validly effected there is sufficient to establish jurisdiction; even a short stay by the defendant in the territory concerned will suffice. Service abroad will be authorized only where certain specified conditions are satisfied. As regards legal relations within the EEC—especially because of the possibility of free movement of judgments resulting from the 1968 Convention—there is no longer any justification for founding the jurisdiction of a court on the mere temporary presence of a person in the State of the court concerned. This common law jurisdiction, for which of course no statutory enactment can be cited, had therefore to be classed as exorbitant.

[OJ C59, 5.3.79, p 100]

86. 4. United Kingdom

As regards the United Kingdom it will suffice for point (a) of Article 3, second paragraph, of the 1968 Convention as amended, to refer to what has been said above in the case of Ireland. Points (b) and (c) deal with some characteristic features of Scottish law. To establish jurisdiction merely by service of a writ of summons during the temporary presence of the defendant is a rare, though not totally unknown, practice in Scotland. Scottish courts usually base their jurisdiction in respect of a defendant not permanently resident there on other factors, namely that he has been in Scotland for at least 40 days, or that he owns immovable property in Scotland or that he owns movable property which has been impounded in Scotland. In such cases service on the defendant is also required, but this may be effected by post or, exceptionally, by posting it on the court notice board. In the case of Germany, the 1968 Convention has already classed jurisdiction based solely on the existence of property in Germany as exorbitant. Any jurisdiction based solely on the seizure of property within a country must be treated in the same way.

II. The relevance of the second paragraph of Article 3 to the whole structure of the 1968 Convention

87. 1. The special significance of the second paragraph of Article 3

The rejection as exorbitant of jurisdictional bases hitherto considered to be important in the new Member States should not, any more than the original version of the second paragraph of Article 3, mislead anyone into thinking that the scope of the first paragraph of Article 3 would thereby be more closely circumscribed. Only particularly extravagant claims to international jurisdiction by the courts of a Member State are expressly underlined. Other rules founding jurisdiction in the national laws of the new Member States are compatible with the 1968 Convention also only to the extent that they do not offend against Article 2 and Articles 4 to 18. Thus, for example, the jurisdiction of English courts in respect of persons domiciled in the

Community can no longer be based on the ground that the claim concerns a contract which was concluded in England or is governed by English law. On the other hand, the rules on the jurisdiction of English courts in connection with breaches of contract in England or claims connected with the commission or omission of an act in England largely correspond to the provisions in Article 5(1) to (3).

2. Impossibility of founding jurisdiction on the location of property

88. With regard to Germany, Denmark and the United Kingdom the list in the second paragraph of Article 3 contains provisions rejecting jurisdiction derived solely from the existence of property in the territory of the State in which the court is situated. Such jurisdiction cannot be asserted even if the proceedings concern a dispute over rights of ownership, or possession, or the capacity to dispose of the specific property in question. Persons domiciled on the Continent of Europe may not be sued in Scotland, even if the aim of the action is to recover movable property situated or seized there or to determine its ownership. Interpleader actions (England and Wales) and multiple poinding (Scotland) are no longer permissible in the United Kingdom in respect of persons domiciled in another Member State of the Community, in so far as the international jurisdiction of the English or Scottish courts does not result from other provisions of the 1968 Convention. This applies, for example, to actions brought by an auctioneer to establish whether ownership of an article sent to him for disposal belongs to his customer or a third party claiming the article.

[OJ C59, 5.3.79, p 101]

There is, however, no reason why United Kingdom legislation should not introduce appropriate measures pursuant to Article 24, to provide protection to persons (such as auctioneers) faced with conflicting legal claims. This might, for instance, take the form of a court order authorizing an article to be temporarily withdrawn from auction.

As regards persons who are domiciled outside the Community, the provisions which hitherto governed the jurisdiction of courts in the new Member States remains unaffected. Even the rules of jurisdiction mentioned in the second paragraph of Article 3 may continue to apply to such persons. Judgments delivered by courts which thus have jurisdiction must also be recognized and enforced in other States of the Community unless one of the exceptions in the new paragraph 5 of Article 27 or in Article 59 as amended applies.

This latter provision is the only one concerning which the list in Article 3, second paragraph is not only of illustrative significance but has direct and restrictive importance.

Section 2
Special jurisdictions[21]

89. In the sphere of special, non-exclusive jurisdictions the problems of adjustment were confined to judicial competence as regards maintenance claims (I), questions raised by trusts in United Kingdom and Irish law (II) and problems in connection with jurisdiction in maritime cases (III). In addition, the Working Party dealt with a few less important individual questions (IV).

Reference should be made here to the Judgments of the Court of Justice of the European Communities of 6 October 1976 (12/76; 14/76) and of 30 November 1976 (21/76) which were delivered shortly before or after the end of the negotiations.[22] (see paragraph 249).

I. Maintenance claims

90. The need for an adjustment of Article 5(2) arose because the laws of the new Member States—as was also by then the case with the laws of many of the original States of the EEC—allow status proceedings to be combined with proceedings concerning maintenance claims (see paragraphs 32 to 42). As far as other problems were concerned no formal adjustment was required. However, certain special features of United Kingdom and Irish law give rise to questions of interpretation; the views of the Working Party as to their solutions should be recorded. They concern a more precise definition of the term "maintenance" (1) and how maintenance entitlements are to be adjusted to changed circumstances in accordance with the system of jurisdiction and recognition established by the 1968 Convention (2).

1. The term "maintenance"

91. (a) The 1968 Convention refers simply to "maintenance" in Article 5(2), the only Article which uses the expression. Several legal concepts used within one and the same national legal system can be covered by this term. For example, Italian law speaks of "alimenti" (Article 433 *et seq* of the codice civile) to indicate payments amongst relations and spouses,

PART IV EC MATERIALS

but payments after divorce are "assegni".[23] The new French divorce law,[24] too, does not speak of "aliments", but of "devoir de secours". In addition French legal terminology uses the expressions "devoir d'entretien" and "contribution aux charges du ménage". All those are "maintenance" within the meaning of Article 5(2) of the 1968 Convention.

92. (b) The Article says nothing, however, about the legal basis from which maintenance claims can emanate. The wording differs markedly from that of the Hague Convention of 2 October 1973 on the recognition and enforcement of decisions relating to maintenance obligations. Article 1 of that Convention excludes from its scope maintenance claims arising from tort, contract and the law of succession. However, there is no significant difference regarding the concept of maintenance as used in the two Conventions. The 1968 Convention is in any case not applicable to maintenance claims under the law of succession (second paragraph, point (1) of Article 1). "Maintenance" claims as the legal consequence of a tortious act are, in legal theory, claims for damages, even if the amount of compensation depends on the needs of the injured party. Contracts creating a "maintenance" obligation which previously did not exist are, according to the form employed, gifts, contracts of sale or other contracts for a consideration. Obligations arising therefrom, even where they consist in the payment of "maintenance", are to be treated like other contractual obligations. In such cases Article 5(1) rather than 5(2) of the 1968 Convention applies as far as jurisdiction is concerned; the outcome hardly differs from an application of Article 5(2). "Maintenance" obligations created by contract are generally to be fulfilled at the domicile or habitual residence of the maintenance creditor. Thus actions may also be brought there. Article 5(2) is applicable, however, where a maintenance contract merely crystallizes an existing maintenance obligation which originated from a family relationship.

[OJ C59, 5.3.79, p 102]

Judicial proceedings concerning "maintenance" claims are still civil and commercial matters even where Article 5(2) is not applicable because the claim arises from a tortious act or a contract.

93. (c) The concept of maintenance does not stipulate that the claim must be for periodic payments. Under Article 1613(2) of the German Civil Code, for example, the maintenance creditor may in addition to regular payments, claim payment of a lump sum on the ground of exceptional need. Under Article 1615(e) of the Code a father may agree with his illegitimate child on the payment of a lump sum settlement. Article 5(4), third sentence, of the Italian divorce law of 1 December 1970 allows divorced spouses to agree on the payment of maintenance in the form of a lump sum settlement. Finally, under Article 285 of the French Civil Code, as amended by the divorce law of 11 July 1975, the French courts can order maintenance in the form of a single capital payment even without the agreement of the spouses. The mere fact that the courts in the United Kingdom have power to order not only periodic payments by one spouse to the other after a divorce, but also the payment of a single lump sum of money, does not therefore prevent the proceedings or a judgment from being treated as a maintenance matter. Even the creation of charges on property and the transfer of property as provided on the Continent, for example in Article 8 of the Italian divorce law, can be in the nature of maintenance.

94. (d) It is difficult to distinguish between claims for maintenance on the one hand and claims for damages and the division of property on the other.

95. (aa) In Continental Europe a motivating factor in assessing the amount of maintenance due to a divorced spouse by his former partner is to compensate an innocent spouse for his loss of matrimonial status. A typical example is contained in Article 301 of the Civil Code in its original form, which still applies in Luxembourg. In its two paragraphs a sharp distinction is drawn in respect of post-matrimonial relations between a claim for maintenance and compensation for material and non-material damages. Yet material damages generally consist in the loss of the provision of maintenance which the divorced party would have enjoyed as a spouse. Thus the claims deriving from the two paragraphs of Article 301 of the Civil Code overlap in practice especially since they can both take the form of a pension or a single capital payment. It remains to be seen whether the new French divorce law of 11 July 1975, which makes a clearer distinction between "prestations compensatoires" and "devoir de secours", will change this situation.

Under Section 23(1)(c) and (f) and Section 27(6)(c) of the English Matrimonial Causes Act 1973, an English divorce court, too, may order a lump sum to be paid by one divorced spouse to the other or to a child. However, English law, which is characterized by judicial discretionary powers and which does not favour inflexible systematic rules, does not make a distinction as to whether the payments ordered by the Court are intended as damages or as maintenance.

96. (bb) The 1968 Convention is not applicable at all where the payments claimed or ordered are governed by matrimonial property law (see paragraph 45 *et seq*). Where claims for damages are involved, Article 5(2) is not relevant. Whether or not that provision applies depends, in the case of a lump sum payment, solely on whether a payment under family law is in the nature of maintenance.

[OJ C59, 5.3.79, p 103]

The maintenance nature of the payment is likely to predominate in relation to children. As between spouses, a division of property or damages may well be the underlying factor. Where both spouses are earning well, payment of a lump sum can only serve the purpose of a division of property or compensation for non-material damage. In that case the obligation to pay is not in the nature of maintenance. If payment is in pursuance of a division of property, the 1968 Convention does not apply at all. If it is to compensate for non-material damage, there is no scope for the application of Article 5(2). A divorce court may not adjudicate in the matter in either case, unless it has jurisdiction under Article 2 or Article 5(1).

97. (e) All legal systems have to deal with the problems of how the needs of a person requiring financial support are to be met when the maintenance debtor defaults. Others also liable to provide maintenance, if necessary a public authority, may have to step in temporarily. They, in turn, should be able to obtain a refund of their outlay from the (principal) maintenance debtor. Legal systems have therefore evolved various methods to overcome this problem. Some of them provide for the maintenance claim to be transferred to the payer, thereby giving it a new creditor, but not otherwise changing its nature. Others confer on the payer an independent right to compensation. United Kingdom law makes particular use of the latter method in cases where the Supplementary Benefits Commission has paid maintenance. As already mentioned in the Jenard report[25] claims of this type are covered by the 1968 Convention, even where claims for compensation are based on a payment made by a public authority in accordance with administrative law or under provisions of social security legislation. It is not, however, the purpose of the special rules of jurisdiction in Article 5(2) to confer jurisdiction in respect of compensation claims on the courts of the domicile of the maintenance creditor or even those of the seat of the public authority—whichever of the two abovementioned methods a legal system may have opted for.

2. *Adjustment of maintenance orders*

98. Economic circumstances in general and the particular economic position of those obliged to pay and those entitled to receive maintenance are constantly changing. The need for periodical adjustments of maintenance orders arises particularly in times of creeping inflation. Jurisdiction to order adjustments depends on the general provisions of the 1968 Convention. Since this is a problem of great practical importance it may be appropriate to preface its discussion in detail with a brief comparative legal survey.

99. (a) Continental legal systems differ according to whether the emphasis of the relevant legal provisions is placed on the concept of an infringement of the principle of finality of a maintenance judgment or more on the concept of an adjustment of the question of the claim (aa). In this respect, as in many others, the provisions of United Kingdom (bb) and Irish (cc) law do not fit into this scheme.

100. (aa) The provisions of German law relating to adjustments of maintenance orders are based on the concept of a special procedural remedy in the nature of a review of the proceedings (Wiederaufnahmeklage).

Since there are no special provisions governing jurisdiction, the general provisions governing jurisdiction in maintenance claims are considered applicable. This means that the original court making the maintenance order may have lost its competence to adjust it. Enforcement authorities, even when they are courts, have no power, either in general or in maintenance cases, to adjust a judgment to changed circumstances. Provisions giving protection against enforcement of a judgment for social reasons apply irrespective of whether or not the amount ordered to be paid in the judgment is subject to variation. This is also true regarding the subsidiary provision of Article 765(a) of the Zivilprozessordnung (Code of Civil Procedure),[26] which is of general application and states that enforcement measures may be rescinded or disallowed in very special circumstances, if they constitute an undue hardship for the debtor.

Accordingly legal theory and case law accept that a foreign maintenance order may be adjusted by a German court, if the latter has jurisdiction.[27]

[OJ C59, 5.3.79, p 104]

In the legal systems in the other original Member States of the EEC the problem has always been regarded as one of substantive law and not as a remedy providing protection against enforcement of judicial decisions. Accordingly jurisdiction depends on the general principles applying to maintenance cases.[28] Indirect adjustments cannot be obtained by invoking, as a defence against measures of enforcement, a change in the circumstances which were taken into account in determining the amount of the maintenance.

In general, the 1968 Convention is based on a similar legal position obtaining in all the original Member States: in the case of proceedings for adjustment of a maintenance order the jurisdiction of the court concerned has to be examined afresh.

101. (bb) In the United Kingdom, the most important legal basis for amendment of maintenance orders is Section 53 of the Magistrates' Courts Act of 1952 in conjunction with Sections 8 to 10 of the Matrimonial Proceedings (Magistrates' Courts) Act 1960 which will be suspended in 1979 by the Domestic Proceedings and Magistrates' Courts Act 1978. According to these Acts, the Court may revoke or vary maintenance orders, or revive them after they have been revoked or varied. In addition, the court in whose district the applicant is now resident also has jurisdiction in such matters.[29] In principle, the court's discretion is unfettered in such cases, but an application for variation may not be based on facts or evidence which could have been relied on when the original order was made.[30] The same applies under Section 31 of the Matrimonial Causes Act 1973. A divorce court can vary or discharge an order it has made with regard to maintenance, irrespective of whether the original basis for its jurisdiction still exists or not.

102. To these possibilities must be added another characteristic aspect of the British judicial system. Enforcement of judgments is linked much more closely than on the Continent to the jurisdiction of the particular court which gave the judgment (see paragraph 208). Before a judgment can be enforced by the executive organs of another court, it must be registered with that other court. After registration, it is regarded as a judgment of that court. A further consequence is that, after such registration, the court with which it is registered is empowered to amend it. Hitherto, the United Kingdom has also applied this system in cases where foreign maintenance judgments have been registered with a British court to be enforced in the United Kingdom.[31]

103. (cc) In Ireland the District Court has jurisdiction to make maintenance orders in respect of spouses and children of a marriage and also in respect of illegitimate children. The Court also has power to vary or revoke its maintenance orders. The jurisdiction of the Court is exercised by the judge for the district where either of the parties to the proceedings is ordinarily resident or carries on any profession or occupation or, in the case of illegitimate children, the judge for the district in which the mother of the child resides. A judge who makes a maintenance order loses jurisdiction to vary it if these requirements as to residence, etc, are no longer fulfilled. Apart from the possibility of having a maintenance order varied there is a right of appeal to the Circuit Court from such orders made by the District Court. The Circuit Court also has jurisdiction to make maintenance orders in proceedings relating to the guardianship of infants. It may also vary or revoke its maintenance orders. Its jurisdiction is exercised by the judge for the circuit in which the defendant is ordinarily resident at the date of application for maintenance or at the date of application for a variation of a maintenance order, as the case may be. An appeal lies to the High Court.

The High Court may order maintenance to be paid, including alimony pending suit and permanent alimony following the granting of divorce *a mensa et thoro*. It has jurisdiction to vary its own maintenance orders and appeals against its orders lie to the Supreme Court.

104. (b) Although it nowhere states this expressly, the 1968 Convention is based on the principle that all judgments given in a Member State can be contested in that State by all the legal remedies available under the law of that State, even when the basis on which the competence of the courts of that State was founded no longer exists. In France, a French judgment may be contested by an appeal, appeal in cassation and an application to set aside a conviction, even if the defendant has long since ceased to be domiciled in France. It follows from the obligation of recognition that no Contracting State can claim jurisdiction with regard to appeals against judgments given in another Contracting State. This also covers proceedings similar to an appeal, such as an action of reduction in Scotland or a "Wiederaufnahmeklage" in Germany. Conversely, every claim to jurisdiction which is not based on proceedings to pursue a remedy by way of appeal must satisfy the provisions of the 1968 Convention. This has three important consequences (see paragraphs 105 to 107) for decisions concerning jurisdiction for the adjustment of maintenance orders. A fourth concerns recognition and enforcement and is mentioned now as a connected matter. (See paragraph 108).

[OJ C59, 5.3.79, p 105]

105. On no account may the court of the State addressed examine whether the amount awarded is still appropriate, without having regard to the jurisdiction provisions of the 1968

Convention. If the proceedings are an appeal, the courts of the State of origin will remain competent. Alternatively the new action may be quite distinct from the original proceedings, in which case the jurisdiction provisions of the 1978 Convention must be observed.

106. (bb) Under the legal systems of all six original EEC States, the adjustment of maintenance orders, at any rate as far as jurisdiction is concerned, is not regarded as a remedy by way of appeal (see paragraph 100). Accordingly the courts of the State of origin lose their competence to adjust maintenance orders within the original scope of the 1968 Convention, if the conditions on which their jurisdiction was based no longer exist. The 1968 Convention could not, however, be applied consistently, if the courts in the United Kingdom were to claim jurisdiction to adjust decisions irrespective of the continued existence of the facts on which jurisdiction was originally based.

107. Applications for the adjustment of maintenance claims can only be made in courts with jurisdiction under Article 2 or Article 5(2), as amended, of the 1968 Convention. For example, if the maintenance creditor claims adjustment due to increases in the cost of living, he may choose between the international jurisdiction of the domicile of the maintenance debtor and the local jurisdiction of the place where he himself is domiciled or habitually resident. However, if the maintenance debtor seeks adjustment because of a deterioration in his financial circumstances, he can only apply under the international jurisdiction referred to in Article 2, i e the jurisdiction of the domicile of the maintenance creditor, even where the original judgment (pursuant to Article 2 where it is applicable) was given in the State of his own domicile and the parties have retained their places of residence.

108. If a maintenance debtor wishes effect to be given in another State to an adjusted order, account must be taken of the reversed roles of the parties. Adjustment at the instance of the maintenance debtor can only be aimed at a remission or reduction of the amount of maintenance. Reliance on such a decision in another Contracting State does not therefore involve "enforcement" within the meaning of Sections 2 and 3 of Title III, but rather recognition as referred to in Section 1 of that Title. It is true that the second paragraph of Article 26 makes provision for a special application to obtain recognition of a judgment, and the provisions of Sections 2 and 3 of Title III concerning enforcement are applicable to such an application. If, in these circumstances, recognition is to be granted to a judgment which has been amended on the application of the maintenance debtor, the position is as follows: the applicant within the meaning of Articles 34 and 36 is not the creditor but the debtor, and therefore, according to Article 34, the creditor is the party who is not entitled to make any submissions. The right of appeal of the party against whom enforcement is sought, provided for in Article 36, lies with the creditor in this case. As applicant, the maintenance debtor has the right laid down in the second paragraph of Article 42, read together with the second paragraph of Article 26, to request recognition of part only of an adjusting order. For the application of Article 44 it has to be determined whether, as plaintiff, he was granted legal aid in the original proceedings.

II. Trusts

1. Problems which the Convention in its present form would create with regard to trusts
[OJ C59, 5.3.79, p 106]

109. A distinguishing feature of United Kingdom and Irish law is the trust. In these two States it provides the solution to many problems which Continental legal systems overcome in an altogether different way. The basic structure of a trust may be described as the relationship which arises when a person or persons (the trustees) hold rights of any kind for the benefit of one or more persons (the beneficiaries) or for some object permitted by law, in such a way that the real benefit of the property accrues, not to the trustees, but to the beneficiaries (who may, however, include one or more of the trustees) or other object of the trust. Basically two kinds of legal relationships can be distinguished in a trust; they may be defined as the internal relationships and the external relationships.

110. (a) In his external relationships, i e in legal dealings with persons who are not beneficiaries of the trust, the trustee acts like any other owner of property. He can dispose of and acquire rights, enter into commitments binding on the trust and acquire rights for its benefit. As far as these acts are concerned no adjustments to the 1968 Convention are necessary. Its provisions on jurisdiction are applicable, as in legal dealings between persons who are not acting as trustees. If a Belgian lessee of property situated in Belgium, but belonging to an English trust, sues to be allowed into occupation, Article 16(1) is applicable, irrespective of the fact that the property belongs to a trust.

111. (b) Problems arise in connection with the internal relationships of a trust, i e as between the trustees themselves, between persons claiming the status of trustees and, above all,

between trustees on the one hand and the beneficiaries of a trust on the other. Disputes may occur among a number of persons as to who has been properly appointed as a trustee; among a number of trustees doubts may arise as to the extent of their respective rights to one another; there may be disputes between the trustees and the beneficiaries as to the rights of the latter to or in connection with the trust property, as to whether for example, the trustee is obliged to hand over assets to a child beneficiary of the trust after the child has attained a certain age. Disputes may also arise between the settlor and other parties involved in the trust.

112. The internal relationships of a trust are not necessarily covered by the 1968 Convention. They are excluded from its scope when the trust deals with one of the matters referred to in the second paragraph of Article 1. Thus as a legal institution the trust plays a significant role in connection with the law of succession. If a trust has been established by a will, disputes arising from the internal relationships are outside the scope of the 1968 Convention (see paragraph 52). The same applies when a trustee is appointed in bankruptcy proceedings; he would correspond to a liquidator ("Konkursverwalter") in Continental legal systems.

113. Where the 1968 Convention is applicable to the internal relationships of a trust, its provisions on jurisdiction were in their original form not always well adapted to this legal institution. To base jurisdiction on the domicile of the defendant trustee would not be appropriate in trust matters. A trust has no legal personality as such. If, however, an action is brought against a defendant in his capacity as trustee, his domicile would not necessarily be a suitable basis for determining jurisdiction. If a person leaves the United Kingdom to go to Corsica, it is right and proper that, in the absence of any special jurisdiction, claims directed against him personally should be brought only before Corsican courts. If, however, he is a sole or joint trustee or co-trustee of trust property situated in the United Kingdom and hitherto administered there, the beneficiaries and the other trustees cannot be expected to seek redress in a Corsican court.

Moreover, the legal relationships between trustees *inter se*, and between the trustees and the beneficiaries, are not of a contractual nature; in most cases, the trustees are not even authorized to conclude agreements conferring jurisdiction by consent. Jurisdiction for actions arising from the internal relationships of a trust can be based, therefore, neither on Article 5(1) nor—as a rule—on agreements conferring jurisdiction by consent pursuant to Article 17. To overcome this difficulty simply by amending the 1968 Convention so as to allow a settlor to stipulate which courts are to have jurisdiction would only partly solve the problem. Such an amendment would not include already existing trusts, and the most suitable jurisdiction for possible disputes cannot always be foreseen when creating a trust.

2. *The solution proposed*

[OJ C59, 5.3.79, p 107]

114. (a) The solution proposed in the new paragraph (6) of Article 5 is based on the argument that trusts, even though they have no legal personality, may be said to have a geographical centre of operation. This would fulfil functions similar to those fulfilled by the "seat" of business associations without legal personality. It is true that United Kingdom and Irish law have so far provided only a tentative definition of such a central point of a trust. However, the concept of the domicile of a trust is not, at present, unknown in legal practice and theory.[32] In his manual on Private International Law the Scottish Professor Anton gives the following definition:[33]

> "The domicile of a trust is thought to be basically a matter depending upon the wishes of a truster and his expressed intentions will usually be conclusive. In their absence the truster's intentions will be inferred from such circumstances as the administrative centre of the trust, the place of residence of the trustees, the situs of the assets of the trust, the nature of the trust purposes and the place where these are to be fulfilled."

No doubt these notions about the domicile of a trust were developed mainly for the purpose of determining the legal system to be applied, usually either English or Scottish law. The principal characteristics of "domicile" so defined and some of the factors on which it is based would also justify making it the basis for founding jurisdiction. The proposed new provision does not, strictly speaking, create a special jurisdiction. It covers only a very limited number of cases and is, therefore, added to Article 5 rather than to Article 2. For the non-exclusive character of the new provision see paragraph 118.

115. (b) The following are some detailed comments on the Working Party's proposal (see paragraph 181).

116. The concepts "trust", "trustee" and "domicile" have not been translated into the other Community languages, since they relate to a distinctive feature of United Kingdom and

Irish law. However, the Member States can give a more detailed definition of the concept of a trust in their national language in their legislation implementing the Accession Convention.

117. The phrase "created by the operation of a statute, or by a written instrument, or created orally and evidenced in writing" is intended to indicate clearly that the new rules on jurisdiction apply only to cases in which under United Kingdom or Irish law a trust has been expressly constituted, or for which provision is made by Statute. This is important, because these legal systems solve many problems with which Continental systems have to deal in a completely different way, by means of so-called "constructive" or "implied" trusts. Where the latter are involved, the new Article 5(6) is not applicable, as for instance where, after conclusion of a contract of sale, but prior to the transfer of title, the vendor is treated as holding the property on trust for the purchaser (see paragraph 172). Trusts resulting from the operation of a statutory provision are unlikely to fall within the scope of the 1968 Convention. Since in the United Kingdom, for example, children cannot own real property, a trust in their favour arises by operation of statute, if the circumstances are such that adult persons would have acquired ownership.

118. It should be noted that the new provision is not exclusive. It merely establishes an additional jurisdiction. The trustee who has gone to Corsica (see paragraph 113) can also be sued in the courts there. However, a settlor would be free to stipulate an exclusive jurisdiction (see paragraph 174).

119. If proceedings are brought in a Contracting State, relating to a trust which is subject to a foreign legal system, the question arises as to which law determines the domicile of that trust. The new version of Article 53 proposes the same criterion as that adopted in the 1968 Convention for ascertaining the "seat" of a company. As far as the legal systems of England and Wales, Scotland, Northern Ireland and Ireland are concerned, application of this provision should present no serious difficulty. There are at present no rules of private international law in the legal systems of the Continental Member States of the Community for determining the domicile of a trust. The courts of those States will have to evolve such rules to enable them to apply the trust provisions of the 1968 Convention. Two possibilities exist. It could be contended that the domicile of a trust should be determined by the legal system to which the trust is subject. One could, however, also contend that the court concerned should decide the issue in accordance with its own *lex fori* which would have to evolve its own appropriate criteria.

[OJ C59, 5.3.79, p 108]

120. In principle, the exclusive jurisdictions provided for by Article 16 take priority over the new Article 5(6). However, it is not easy to establish the precise extent of that priority.

In legal disputes arising from internal trust relationships, the legal relations referred to in the provisions in question usually play only an incidental role, if any. The trustee requires court approval for certain acts of management. Even where the management of immovable property is concerned, any such applications to the court do not affect the proprietary rights of the trustee, but only his fiduciary obligations under the trust. Article 16(1) does not apply. One could, however, envisage a dispute arising between two people as to which of them was trustee of certain property. If one of them instituted proceedings against the other in a German court claiming the cancellation of the entry in the land register showing the defendant as the owner of the property and the substitution of an entry showing the plaintiff as the true owner, there can be no doubt that, under Article 16(1) or (3), the German court would have exclusive jurisdiction. However, if a declaration is sought that a particular person is a trustee of a particular trust which includes certain property, Article 16(1) does not become applicable merely because that property includes immovable property.

III. Admiralty jurisdiction

121. The exercise of jurisdiction in maritime matters has traditionally played a far greater role in the United Kingdom than in the Continental States of the Community. The scope of the international competence of the courts, as it has been developed in the United Kingdom, has become of worldwide significance for admiralty jurisdiction. This factor is reflected not least in the Brussels Conventions of 1952 and 1957 (see paragraph 238 *et seq*). It would have been inappropriate to limit the exercise of admiralty jurisdiction to the basis of jurisdiction included in the 1968 Convention in its original form. If a ship is arrested in a State because of an internationally recognized maritime claim, it would be unreasonable to expect the creditor to seek a decision on his claim before the courts of the shipowner's domicile. For this reason, the Working Party gave lengthy consideration to the possible inclusion of a special section on admiralty jurisdiction in Title II. Article 36 of the Accession Convention is derived from an earlier draft prepared for that purpose (see paragraph 131). Parallel negotiations on Article 57

of the 1968 Convention did, however, lead to a generally acceptable interpretation which will enable States party to a Convention on maritime law to assume jurisdiction on any particular matter dealt with in that Convention, even in respect of persons domiciled in a Community State which is not a party to that Convention (see paragraph 236 *et seq*). Furthermore, all delegations are in support of a Joint Declaration urging the Community States to accede to the most important of all the Conventions on maritime law, namely the Brussels Conventions of 10 May 1952 (see paragraph 238). The Working Party, confident that this Joint Declaration will be adopted and implemented, finally dropped its plans for a section dealing with admiralty jurisdiction. This would also avoid interfering with the general principles of the 1968 Convention, and maintain a clear dividing line between its scope and that of other Conventions.

Two issues remain outstanding, however, since they are not fully covered by the Brussels Conventions of 1952 and 1957: jurisdiction in the event of the arrest of salvaged cargo or freight (the new Article 5(7)) (1) and actions for limitation of liability in maritime matters (the new Article 6(a) (2). Moreover, until Denmark and Ireland accede to the Brussels Arrest Convention of 10 May 1952, transitional provisions had also to be introduced (3). Finally, a particularity affecting only Denmark and Ireland (4) still remained to be settled.

1. Jurisdiction in connection with the arrest of salvaged cargo or freight

122. (a) The Brussels Convention of 1952 allows a claimant, *inter alia*, to invoke the jurisdiction of a State in which a ship has been arrested on account of a salvage claim (Article 7(1)(b)). Implicit in this provision is a rule of substantive law. A claim to remuneration for salvage entitles the salvage firm to a maritime lien on the ship. A similar lien in favour of a salvage firm can also exist on the cargo; this can be of some economic importance, if it is the cargo rather than the ship which was salvaged, or if the salvaged ship is so badly damaged that its value is less than the cost of the salvage operation. The value of the cargo of a modern supertanker can amount to a considerable sum. Finally, prior rights can also arise in regard to freight. If freight is payable solely in the event of the safe arrival of the cargo at the place of destination, it is appropriate that the salvage firm should have a prior right to be satisfied out of the claim to freight which was preserved due to the salvage of the cargo.

[OJ C59, 5.3.79, p 109]

Accordingly United Kingdom law provides that a salvage firm may apply for the arrest of the salvaged cargo or the freight claim preserved due to its intervention and may also apply to the court concerned for a final decision on its claims to remuneration for salvage. Jurisdiction of this kind is similar in scope to the provisions of Article 7 of the Brussels Convention of 1952. As there is no other Convention on the arrest of salvaged cargo and freight which would remain applicable under Article 57, the United Kingdom would, on acceding to the 1968 Convention, have suffered an unacceptable loss of jurisdiction if a special provision had not been introduced.

123. (b) The proposed solution applies the underlying principle of Article 7 of the Brussels Convention of 1952 to jurisdiction after the arrest of salvaged cargo or freight claims.

Under Article 24 of the 1968 Convention, there is no limitation on national laws with regard to the granting of provisional legal safeguards including arrest. However, they could not provide that arrest, whether authorized or effected, should suffice to found jurisdiction as to the substance of the matter. The exception introduced in Article 5(7)(a) is confined to arrest to safeguard a salvage claim.

Article 5(7)(b) introduces an extension of jurisdiction not expressly modelled on the Brussels Convention of 1952. It is a result of practical experience. After salvage operations—whether involving a ship, cargo or freight—arrest is sometimes ordered, but not actually carried into effect, because bail or other security has been provided. This must be sufficient to confer jurisdiction on the arresting court to decide also on the substance of the matter.

The object of the provision is to confer jurisdiction only with regard to those claims which are secured by a maritime lien. If the owner of a ship in difficulties has concluded a contract for its salvage, as his contract with the cargo owner frequently obliges him to do, any disputes arising from the former contract will not be governed by this provision.

2. Jurisdiction to order a limitation of liability

124. It is not easy to say precisely how the application of Article 57 of the 1968 Convention links up with that of the International Convention of 10 October 1957 relating to the limitation of the liability of owners of seagoing ships[34] (see end of paragraph 128) and with relevant national laws. The latter Convention contains no express provisions directly affecting international jurisdiction or the enforcement of judgments. The Working Party did

not consider that it was its task to deal systematically with the issues raised by that Convention and to devise proposals for solving them. It would, however, be particularly unfortunate in certain respects if the jurisdictional lacunae of the 1957 Convention on the limitation of liability were carried over into the 1968 Convention and were supplemented in accordance with the general provisions on jurisdiction of that Convention.

A distinction needs to be drawn between three differing aspects arising in connection with the limitation of liability in matters of maritime law. First, a procedure exists for setting up and allocating the liability fund. Secondly, the entitlement to damages against the shipowner must be judicially determined. Finally, and distinct from both, there is the assessment of limitation of liability regarding a given claim.

[OJ C59, 5.3.79, p 110]

The procedural details giving effect to these three aspects vary in the different legal systems of the Community.

125. Under one system, which is followed in particular in the United Kingdom, limitation of liability necessitates an action against one of the claimants—either by way of originating proceedings or, if an action has already been brought against the shipowner, as a counterclaim. The liability fund is set up at the court dealing with the limitation of liability issue, and other claimants must also lodge their claims with the same court.

126. Under the system obtaining in Germany, for example, proceedings for the limitation of liability are started not by means of an action brought against a claimant, but by a simple application which is not directed "against" any person, and which leads to the setting up of the fund.

If the application is successful, all claimants must lodge their claims with that court. If any disputes arise about the validity of any of the claims lodged, they have to be dealt with by special proceedings taking the form of an action by the claimant against the fund administrator, creditor or shipowner contesting the claim. Under this system an independent action by the shipowner against the claimant in connection with limitation of liability is also possible. Such an action leads not to the setting up of a liability fund or to an immediately effective limitation of liability, but merely establishes whether liability is subject to potential limitation, in case of future proceedings to assess the extent of such liability.

127. The new Article 6a does not apply to an action by a claimant against the shipowner, fund administrator or other competing claimants, nor to the collective proceedings for creating and allocating the liability fund, but only to the independent action brought by a shipowner against a claimant (a). Otherwise the present provisions of the 1968 Convention which are relevant to limitation of maritime liability apply (b).

128. (a) The actual or potential limitation of the liability of a shipowner can, however, in all legal systems of the Community be used otherwise than as a defence. If a shipowner anticipates a liability claim, it may be in his interest to take the initiative by asking for a declaration that he has only limited or potentially limited liability for the claim. In that case he can choose from one of the jurisdictions which are competent by virtue of Articles 2 to 6. According to these provisions, he cannot bring an action in the courts of his domicile. Since, however, he could be sued in those courts, it would be desirable also to allow him to have recourse to this jurisdiction. It is the purpose of Article 6a to provide for this. Moreover, apart from the Brussels Convention of 1952, this is the only jurisdiction where the shipowner could reasonably concentrate all actions affecting limitation of his liability. The result for English law (see paragraph 125) is that the fund can be set up and allocated by that same court. In addition, Article 6a makes it clear that proceedings for limitation of liability can also be brought by the shipowner in any other court which has jurisdiction over the claim. It also enables national legislations to give jurisdiction to a court within their territory other than the court which would normally have jurisdiction.

129. (b) For proceedings concerning the validity as such of a claim against a shipowner, Articles 2 to 6 are exclusively applicable.

In addition, Article 22 is always applicable. If proceedings to limit liability have been brought in one State, a court in another State which has before it an application to establish or to limit liability may stay the proceedings or even decline jurisdiction.

130. (c) A clear distinction must be drawn between the question of jurisdiction and the question which substantive law on limitation of liability is to be applied. This need not be the law of the State whose courts have jurisdiction for assessing the limitation of liability. The law applicable for the limitation of liability also defines more precisely the type of case in which limitation of liability can be claimed at all.

[OJ C59, 5.3.79, p 111]

131. 3. Transitional provisions

All the delegations hope that Denmark and Ireland will accede to the Brussels Convention of 10 May 1952 (see paragraph 121). This will, however, naturally take some time, and it is reasonable to allow a transitional period of three years after the entry into force of the Accession Convention. It would be harsh if, within that period, in the two States concerned jurisdiction in maritime matters were to be limited to what is authorized under the terms of Articles 2 to 6a. Article 36 of the Accession Convention therefore contains transitional provisions in favour of those States. These provisions correspond, apart from variations in the drafting, to the provisions which the Working Party originally proposed to recommend for the special section on maritime law as general rules of jurisdiction regarding the arrest of seagoing ships. In preparing these provisions the Working Party drew heavily, in fact almost exclusively, on the rules of the 1952 Brussels Convention relating to the arrest of seagoing ships (see paragraph 121).

Since they are temporary, the transitional provisions do not merit detailed comments on how they differ from the text of that Convention.

132. 4. Disputes between a shipmaster and crew members

The new Article Vb of the Protocol annexed to the 1968 Convention is based on a request by Denmark founded on Danish tradition. This has become part of the Danish Seamen's Law No 420 of 18 June 1973 which states that disputes between a crew member and a shipmaster of a Danish vessel may not be brought before foreign courts. The same principle is also embodied in some consular conventions between Denmark and other States. Following a specific request from the Irish delegation, the scope of this provision has also been extended to Irish ships.

IV. Other special matters

133. 1. Jurisdiction based on the place of performance

In the course of the negotiations it emerged that the French and Dutch texts of Article 5(1) were less specific than the German and Italian texts on the question of the designation of the obligation. The former could be misinterpreted as including other contractual obligations than those which were the subject of the legal proceedings in question. The revised versions of the French and Dutch texts should clear up this misunderstanding.[35]

134. 2. Jurisdiction in matters relating to tort

Article 5(3) deals with the special tort jurisdiction. It presupposes that the wrongful act has already been committed and refers to the place where the harmful event has occurred. The legal systems of some States provide for preventive injunctions in matters relating to tort. This applies, for example, in cases where it is desired to prevent the publication of a libel or the sale of goods which have been manufactured or put on the market in breach of the law on patents or industrial property rights. In particular the laws of the United Kingdom and Germany provide for measures of this nature. No doubt Article 24 is applicable when courts have an application for provisional protective measures before them, even if their decision has, in practice, final effect. There is much to be said for the proposition that the courts specified in Article 5(3) should also have jurisdiction in proceedings whose main object is to prevent the imminent commission of a tort.

135. 3. Third party proceedings and claims for redress

In Article 6(2), the term "third party proceedings" relates to a legal institution which is common to the legal systems of all the original Member States, with the exception of Germany. However, a jurisdictional basis which rests solely on the capacity of a third party to be joined as such in the proceedings cannot exist by itself. It must necessarily be supplemented by legal criteria which determine which parties may in which capacity and for what purpose be joined in legal proceedings. Thus the provisions already existing in, or which may in future be introduced into, the legal systems of the new Member States with reference to the joining of third parties in legal proceedings, remain unaffected by the 1968 Convention.

[OJ C59, 5.3.79, p 112]

Section 3
Jurisdiction in insurance matters

136. The accession of the United Kingdom introduced a totally new dimension to the insurance business as it had been practised hitherto within the European Community. Lloyds of London has a substantial share of the market in the international insurance of large risks.[36]

In view of this situation the United Kingdom requested a number of adjustments. Its main argument was that the protection afforded by Articles 7 to 12 was unnecessary for policy-holders domiciled outside the Community (I) or of great economic importance (II). The United Kingdom expressed concern that, without an adjustment of the 1968 Convention, insurers within the Community might be forced to demand higher premiums than their competitors in other States.

There were additional reasons for each particular request for an adjustment. As regards contracts of insurance with policy-holders domiciled outside the Community the United Kingdom sought the unrestricted admissibility of agreements conferring jurisdiction to be vouchsafed so that appropriate steps could be taken with regard to the binding provisions contained in the national laws of many policy-holders insuring with English insurers (I). Requests for adjustments also referred, in conjunction with the other requests for adjustments, to the scope of Articles 9 and 10 which seemed to require clarification (III). Finally there were requests for a few minor adjustments (IV).

The original request of the United Kingdom in respect of the first two problems, namely that the insurance matters in question should be excluded from the scope of Articles 7 to 12 was too far-reaching in view of the general objectives of the 1968 Convention. In particular a number of features of the mandatory rules of jurisdiction, which differ for the various types of insurance, had to be retained (see paragraphs 138, 139 and 143). However, the special structure of the British insurance market had to be taken into account—not least so that it would not be driven to resort systematically to arbitration. Although the 1968 Convention does not restrict the possibility of settling disputes by arbitration (see paragraph 63), national law should be careful not to encourage arbitration simply by making proceedings before national courts too complicated and uncertain for the parties. The Working Party therefore endeavoured to extend the possibilities of conferring jurisdiction by consent. For the form of such agreements see paragraph 176.

I. Insurance contracts taken out by policy-holders domiciled outside the Community

137. As already indicated earlier (see note 36), insurance contracts with policy-holders domiciled outside the Community account for a very large part of the British insurance business. The 1968 Convention does not expressly stipulate to what extent such contracts may provide for jurisdiction by consent. Article 4 applies only to the comparatively rare case where the policy-holder is the defendant in subsequent proceedings. In so far as the jurisdiction of courts outside the Community can be determined by agreement, the general question arises as to what restrictions should be imposed on such agreements having regard to the exclusive jurisdictions provided for by the 1968 Convention (see paragraphs 148, 162 *et seq*). The main problem in this connection was the jurisdiction under Articles 9 and 10 which, it was thought, could not be excluded. However, this difficulty did not affect insurance contracts only with policy-holders domiciled outside the Community. It also affects, more generally, agreements on jurisdiction which are authorized by Article 12.

In view of the great importance for the United Kingdom of the question of agreements on jurisdiction with policy-holders domiciled outside the Community, it was necessary to incorporate the admissibility in principle of such agreements on jurisdiction expressly in the 1968 Convention. If, therefore, a policy-holder domiciled outside the Community insures a risk in England, exclusive jurisdiction may be conferred by agreement on English courts as well as on the courts of the policy-holder's domicile or others.

[OJ C59, 5.3.79, p 113]

This basic rule had however to be limited again in two ways in the new paragraph (4) of Article 12.

138. 1. Compulsory insurance

Where a statutory obligation exists to take out insurance no departure from the provisions of Articles 8 to 11 on compulsory insurance can be permitted, even if the policy-holder is domiciled outside the Community. If a person domiciled in Switzerland owns a motor car which is normally based in Germany, then the car must, under German law, be insured against liability. Such an insurance contract may not contain provisions for jurisdiction by consent concerning accidents occurring in Germany.

The possibility of invoking the jurisdiction of German courts (Article 8) cannot be contractually excluded. This is so even although the relevant German law of 5 April 1965 on compulsory insurance (Bundesgesetzblatt I, page 213) does not expressly prohibit agreements on jurisdiction. However, in practice German law prevents the conclusion of agreements on jurisdiction in the area of compulsory insurance because approval of conditions of insurance containing such a provision would be withheld.

Compulsory insurance exists in the following Member States of the Community for the following articles, installations, activities and occupations, although this list does not claim to be complete:

Federal Republic of Germany[37]

1. Federal

Liability insurance compulsory for owners of motor vehicles, airline companies, hunters, owners of nuclear installations and handling of nuclear combustible materials and other radioactive materials, road haulage, accountants and tax advisers, security firms, those responsible for schools for nursing, infant and child care and midwifery, automobile experts, notaries' professional organizations, those responsible for development aid, exhibitors, pharmaceutical firms;

Life insurance for master chimney sweeps;

Accident insurance for airline companies and usufructuaries;

Fire insurance for owners of buildings which are subject to a charge, usufructuaries, warehouse occupiers, pawnbrokers;

Goods insurance for pawnbrokers;

Pension funds for theatres, cultural orchestras, district master chimney sweeps, supplementary pension funds for the public service.

2. Länder

There is no uniformity as between the Länder of the Federal Republic of Germany, but there is in particular compulsory fire insurance for buildings, compulsory pension funds for agricultural workers, the liberal professions (doctors, chemists, architects, notaries) and (in Bavaria, for example) members of the Honourable Company of Chimney Sweeps and, for example, a supplementary pension fund for workers in the Free and Hanseatic City of Bremen. In Bavaria there is compulsory insurance for livestock intended for slaughter.

Belgium

Motor vehicles, hunting, nuclear installations, accidents at work, transport accidents (for paying transport by motor vehicles).

Denmark

Motor vehicles, dogs, nuclear installations, accountants.

France

Operators of ships and nuclear installations, sand motor vehicles, operators of cable-cars, chair-lifts and other such mechanical units, hunting, estate agents, managers of property, syndics of co-owners, business managers, operators of sports centres, accountants, agricultural mutual assistance schemes, legal advisers, physical education establishments and pupils, operators of dance halls, managers of pharmacists' shops in the form of a private limited liability company (S.à.r.l.), blood transfusion centres, architects, motor vehicle experts, farmers.

Luxembourg

Motor vehicles, hunting and hunting organizations, hotel establishments, nuclear installations, fire and theft insurance for hotel establishments;

[OJ C59, 5.3.79, p 114]

Insurance against the seizure of livestock in slaughterhouses.

Netherlands

Motor vehicles, nuclear installations, tankers.

United Kingdom

Third party liability in respect of motor vehicles;

Employers' liability in respect of accidents at work;

Insurance of nuclear installations;

Insurance of British registered ships against oil pollution;

Compulsory insurance scheme for a number of professions, e g solicitors and insurance brokers.

139. 2. Insurance of immovable property

The second exception referred to at the end of paragraph 137 is particularly designed to ensure that Article 9 continues to apply even when the policy-holder is domiciled outside the Community. However, this exception has further implications. It prohibits jurisdiction agreements conferring exclusive jurisdiction on the courts mentioned in Article 9. This applies even where the national law of the State in which the immovable property is situated allows agreements conferring jurisdiction in such circumstances.

II. Insurance of large risks, in particular marine and aviation insurance

140. The United Kingdom's request for special rules for the insurance of large risks was probably the most difficult problem for the Working Party. The request was based on the realization that the concept of social protection underlying a restriction on the admissibility of provisions conferring jurisdiction in insurance matters is no longer justified where the policy-holders are powerful undertakings. The problem was one of finding a suitable demarcation line. Discussions on the second Directive on insurance had already revealed the impossibility of taking as criteria abstract, general factors like company capital or turnover. The only solution was to examine which types of insurance contracts were in general concluded only by policy-holders who did not require social protection. On this basis, special treatment could not be conceded to industrial insurance as a whole.

Accordingly, the Working Party directed its attention to the various classes of insurance connected with the transport industry. In this area there is an additional justification for special treatment for agreements on jurisdiction: the risks insured are highly mobile and insurance policies tend to change hands several times in quick succession. This leads to uncertainty as to which courts will have jurisdiction and the difficulties in calculating risks are thereby greatly increased. On the other hand, there are here, too, certain areas requiring social protection. Particular complications were caused by the fact that there is a well integrated insurance market for the transport industry. The various types of risk for different means of transport are usually covered under one single policy. The British insurance industry in particular has developed standard policies which only require for their completion a notification by the insured that the means of transport (which can be of many different types) have set off.

The result of a consideration of all these matters is the solution which figures in the new paragraph (5) of Article 12, as supplemented by Article 12a: agreements on jurisdiction are in principle to be given special treatment in marine insurance and in some sectors of aviation insurance. In the case of insurance of transport by land alone no exceptional rules of any kind appeared justified.

In order to avoid difficulties and differences of interpretation, a list had to be drawn up of the types of policy for which the admissibility of agreements on jurisdiction was to be extended. The idea of referring for this purpose to the list of classes of insurance appearing in the Annex to the First Council Directive of 24 July 1973 (73/239/EEC) proved inadequate. The classification used there took account of the requirements of State administration of insurance, and was not directed towards a fair balancing of private insurance interests. There was thus no alternative but to draw up a separate list for the purposes of the 1968 Convention. The following comments apply to the list and the classes of insurance not included in it.

[OJ C59, 5.3.79, p 115]

141. 1. Article 12a(1)(a)

This provision applies only to hull insurance and not to liability insurance. The term "seagoing ships" means all vessels intended to travel on the sea. This includes not only ships in the traditional sense of the word but also hovercraft, hydrofoils, barges and lighters used at sea. It also covers floating apparatus which cannot move under its own power, eg oil exploration and extraction installations which are moved about on water. Installations firmly moored or to be moored on the seabed are in any event expressly included in the text of the provision. The provision also covers ships in the course of construction, but only in so far as the damage is the result of a maritime risk. This is damage caused by the fact that the ship is on the water and not therefore, damage which occurs in dry-dock or in the workshops of shipyards.

142. 2. Article 12a(1)(b)

In the same way as (1)(a) covers the value of the hull of a ship or of an aeroplane, (1)(b) covers the value of goods destroyed or lost in transit, but not liability insurance for any loss or damage caused by those goods. The most important single decision taken on the provision was the addition of the words "consists of or includes". The reason for this is that goods in transit are frequently not conveyed by the same means of transport right to their final destination. There may be a sequence of journeys by land, sea and air. There would be unwarranted complications for the insurance industry in drafting policies and settling claims, if a fine distinction had always to be drawn as to the section of transit in which loss or damage had occurred. Moreover it is often impossible to ascertain this. One has only to think of container transport to realize how easily a loss may be discovered only at the destination. Practical considerations therefore required that agreements on jurisdiction be permitted, even where goods are carried by sea or by air for only part of their journey. Even if it can be proved that the loss occurred in the course of transport on land, agreements on jurisdiction permitted by the new paragraph (5) of Article 12 remain effective. The provision applies even if the shipment does not cross any national border.

143. The exception in respect of injury to passengers and loss of or damage to their baggage, which is repeated in Article 12a(2)(a) and (b), is justified by the fact that such persons as a group tend to have a weaker economic position and less bargaining power.

144. 3. Article 12a(2)(a)

Whether these provisions also cover all liability arising in connection with the construction, modification and repair of a ship; whether therefore the provision includes all liability which the shipyard incurs towards third parties and which was caused by the ship; or whether the expression "use or operation" has to be construed more narrowly as applying only to liability arising in the course of a trial voyage—all these are questions of interpretation which still await an answer. The exception for compulsory aircraft insurance is intended to leave the Member States free to provide for such protection as they consider necessary for the policy-holder and for the victim.

145. 4. Article 12a(2)(b)

As there is no reason to treat combined transport any differently for liability insurance than for hull insurance, it is equally irrelevant during which section of the transport the circumstances causing the liability occurred (see paragraphs 142 and 143).

146. 5. Article 12a(3)

The most important application of this provision is stated in the text itself. In the absence of a provision to the contrary in the charter party, an air crash would cause the carrier to lose his entitlement to freight and the owner his charter-fee from the charterer. Another example might be loss caused by the late arrival of a ship. For the rest the notion is the same as that used in Directive 73/239/EEC.

147. 6. Article 12a(4)

Insurance against ancillary risks is a familiar practice, especially in United Kingdom insurance contracts. An example would be "shipowner's disbursements" consisting of exceptional operational costs, e g harbour dues accruing whilst a ship remains disabled. Another example is insurance against "increased value", providing protection against loss arising from the fact that a destroyed or damaged cargo had increased in value during transit.

[OJ C59, 5.3.79, p 116]

The provision does not require an ancillary risk to be insured under the same policy as the main risk to which it relates. The Working Party therefore deliberately opted for a somewhat different wording from that in Directive 73/239/EEC for the "ancillary risks" referred to in that Directive. The definition in that Directive could not be used since it is concerned with a different subject, the authorization of insurance undertakings.

148. **III. The remaining scope of Articles 9 and 10**

The revised text of Article 12, like the original text, does not expressly deal with the effect of agreements on jurisdiction or the special jurisdictions for insurance matters set out in Section 3. Nevertheless, the legal position is clear from the systematic construction of Section 3 of the 1968 Convention, as amended. Agreements on jurisdiction cover all legal proceedings between insurer and policyholder, even where the latter wishes, pursuant to the first paragraph of Article 10, to join the insurer in the court in which he himself is sued by the injured party. However, jurisdiction clauses in insurance contracts cannot be binding upon third parties. The provisions of the second paragraph of Article 10 concerning a direct action by the injured party are thus not affected by such jurisdiction clauses. The same is true of the third paragraph of Article 10.

IV. Other problems of adjustment and clarification in insurance law

149. 1. Co-insurance

The substantive amendment in the first paragraph of Article 8 covers jurisdiction where several co-insurers are parties to a contract of insurance. What usually happens is that one insurer acts as leader for the other co-insurers and each of them underwrites a part of the risk, possibly a very small part. In such cases, however, there is no justification for permitting all the insurers, including the leader, to be sued in the courts of each State in which any one of the many co-insurers is domiciled. The only additional international jurisdiction which can be justified would be one which relates to the circumstances of the leading insurer. The Working Party considered at length whether to refer to the leading insurer's domicile, but the effect of this would have been that the remaining co-insurers could be sued there even if the leader was sued elsewhere. An additional jurisdiction based on the leading insurer's circumstances is justifiable only if it leads to a concentration of actions arising out of an insured event. The new version of the first paragraph of Article 8 therefore refers to the court where proceedings are brought against the leading insurer. Co-insurers can thus be sued for their share of the insurance in that court, at the same time as the leading insurer or subsequently. However, the provision does not impose an obligation for proceedings to be concentrated in one court; there is nothing to prevent a policy-holder from suing the various co-insurers in different courts. If the leading insurer has settled the claim out of court, the policy-holder must bring any action against the other co-insurers in one of the courts having jurisdiction under points (1) or (2) of the new version of the first paragraph of Article 8.

The remaining amendments to the first paragraph of Article 8 merely rephrase it for the sake of greater clarity.

150. 2. Insurance agents, the setting up of branches

There was discussion on the present text of the second paragraph of Article 8 of the 1968 Convention because its wording might give rise to the misunderstanding that jurisdiction could be founded not only on the intervention of an agent of the insurer, but also on that of an independent insurance broker of the type common in the United Kingdom. The discussion revealed that this provision was unnecessary in view of Article 5(5). The Working Party therefore changed the present paragraph three into paragraph two. The addition of the words "or other establishment" is intended merely to ensure consistency between Article 5(5) and the third paragraph of the new Article 13. The latter provision is necessary in addition to the former in order to prevent Article 4 being applicable.

[OJ C59, 5.3.79, p 117]

151. 3. Reinsurance

Reinsurance contracts cannot be equated with insurance contracts. Accordingly, Articles 7 to 12 do not apply to reinsurance contracts.

152. 4. The term "policy-holder"

The previous authentic texts of the 1968 Convention use the term "preneur d'assurance" and the equivalent in German, Italian and Dutch; the nearest English equivalent of the term proved to be "the policy-holder". However, this should not give rise to the misunderstanding that the problems arising from a transfer of legal rights are now any different from those existing before the accession of the new Member States to the Convention. The rightful possessor of the policy document is not always the "preneur d'assurance". It is of course conceivable that the whole legal status of the other party to the contract with the insurer might pass to another person by inheritance or some other means, in which case the new party to the contract would become the "preneur d'assurance". However, this case must be clearly distinguished from the transfer of individual rights arising out of the contract of insurance, especially in the form of assignment of the sum assured to a beneficiary. Such an assignment may be made in advance and may be contingent, for instance, upon the occurrence of a claim. In this event it is conceivable that the insurance policy might be passed on to the beneficiary at the same time as the assignment of the right to the sum assured so that he can claim his entitlement from the insurer, if the case arises. The beneficiary would not thereby become the "preneur d'assurance". Hence, where a court's jurisdiction is dependent on individual characteristics of the "preneur d'assurance", the situation remains unchanged as a result of prior assignment of any claim to the sum assured which might arise, even if the policy document is transferred at the same time.

152. (a) 5. Agreements on jurisdiction between parties to a contract from the same State

For the amendment to Article 12(3) ("at the time of conclusion of the contract"), see paragraph 161(a).

Section 4
Jurisdiction over consumer contracts

153. **I. Principles**

Leaving aside insurance matters, the 1968 Convention pays heed to consumer protection considerations only in one small section, that dealing with instalment sales and loans. This was consistent with the law as it then stood in the original Member States of the Community since it was in fact at first only in the field of instalment sales and loans that awareness of the need to protect the consumer against unfairly worded contracts became widespread. Since that time legislation in the Member States of the Community has become concerned with much broader-based consumer protection. In particular there has been a general move in consumer protection legislation to ensure appropriate jurisdictions for the consumer. Intolerable tensions would be bound to develop between national legislation and the 1968 Convention in the long run if the Convention did not afford the consumer much the same protection in the case of transfrontier contracts as he received under national legislation. The Working Party therefore decided to propose that the previous Section 4 of Title II be extended into a section on jurisdiction over consumer contracts, establishing at the same time for future purposes that only final consumers acting in a private capacity should be given special protection and not those contracting in the course of their business to pay by instalments for goods and services used. The Working Party was influenced on this last point by the proceedings in the Court of Justice of the European Communities in response to a reference from the French Cour de cassation concerning the interpretation of "instalment sales and loans", proceedings which centred on the question of whether the existing Section 4 of Title II covered instalment sales contracts concluded by businessmen (Case 150/77: Société Bertrand v Paul Ott KG).

The basic principle underlying the provisions of the new section is to draw upon ideas emerging from European Community law as it has evolved and is currently evolving. Consequently, most of the existing provisions on instalment sales and loans have been incorporated in the new section, which also draws on Article 5 of the preliminary draft Convention on the law applicable to contractual and non-contractual obligations. On points of drafting detail, however, improvements were made on the wording of the preliminary draft Convention. One substantive change was necessary, since to accord with the general structure of the 1968 Convention reference had to be made to the place where the parties are domiciled, rather than habitually resident. Details are as follows:
[OJ C59, 5.3.79, p 118]

154. **II. The scope of the new Section**

Using the device of an introductory provision defining the scope of the Section, the proposal follows the practice previously adopted at the beginning of Sections 3 and 4 of Title II.

1. Persons covered

155. The only new point of principle is a provision governing the persons covered by the section, including in particular the legal definition of the section's central term, the "consumer". The substances of the definition is taken from Article 5 of the preliminary draft Convention on the law applicable to contractual and non-contractual obligations the most recent version of which was used by the Working Party. The amendments made were only drafting improvements.

2. Subject matter covered

156. As regards the subject matter covered by the new section, a clear distinction is drawn between instalment sales, including the financing of such sales, and other consumer contracts. The consequent effect on the precedence of the provisions of Sections 3 and 4 is as follows: Section 3 is a more specific provision than Section 4 and hence takes precedence over it. A contract of insurance is not a contract for the supply of services within the meaning of the 1968 Convention. Within Section 4, the provisions on instalment sales are more specific than the general reference to consumer sales in the first paragraph of Article 13.

157. (a) As in the past, instalment sales are subject to the special provisions without any further preconditions. The sole change lies in the stipulation that the special provisions apply only where the purchaser is a private consumer. The rules governing instalment sales also apply automatically to the legal institution of hire purchase, which has developed into the commonest legal form for transacting instalment sales in the United Kingdom and Ireland. For reasons which are not material for jurisdiction purposes, instalment sales in those countries usually take the form in law of a contract of hire with an option to purchase for the hirer. In form the instalments represent the hire fee, whereas in substance they form the

purchase price. At the end of the prescribed "hire" period, once all the prescribed instalments of the "hire fee" have been paid, the "hirer" is entitled to purchase the article for a nominal price. As the term "instalment sale" under the continental legal systems by no means implies that ownership of the article must necessarily pass to the purchaser at the same time as physical possession, hire purchase is in practice tantamount to an instalment sale.

Contracts to finance instalment sales to private consumers are also subject to the special provisions without any further preconditions. Contrary to the legal position obtaining hitherto, the Working Party has made actions arising out of a loan contract to finance the purchase of movable property subject to the special provision, even if the loan itself is not repayable by instalments or if the article is purchased with a single payment (normally with the funds lent). Credit contracts are not, moreover, contracts for the supply of services, so that, apart from point (2) of the first paragraph of Article 13, the whole of Section 4 does not apply to such contracts. Contracts of sale not falling under point (1) of the first paragraph of Article 13 do not, for instance, come under point (2) of that paragraph, although Section 4 may be applicable to them subject to the further conditions contained in point (3) (see paragraph 158).

158. (b) On the other hand, consumer contracts other than those referred to in paragraph 157 are subject to the special provisions only if there is a sufficiently strong connection with the place where the consumer is domiciled. In this, the new provisions once again follow the preliminary draft Convention on the law applicable to contractual and non-contractual obligations. Both the conditions referred to in point (3) of the first paragraph of Article 13—an offer or advertising in the State of the consumer's domicile, and steps necessary for the conclusion of the contract taken by the consumer in that State—must be satisfied. The introductory phrase should, moreover, ensure that Articles 4 and 5(5) will apply to all consumer contracts, as has until now been the case only for instalment sales and for loans repayable by instalments. One particular consequence of this is that, subject to the second paragraph of Article 13, Section 4 does not apply where the defendant is not domiciled in the EEC.

[OJ C59, 5.3.79, p 119]

For further details of what is meant by "a specific invitation" or "advertising" in the State of the consumer's domicile and by "the steps necessary for the conclusion of the contract", see the report currently being drawn up by Professor Giuliano on the Convention on the law applicable to contractual and non-contractual obligations.

3. Only a branch, agency or other establishment within the Community

159. The exclusion from the scope of Section 4 of contracts between consumers and firms domiciled outside the EEC would not be reasonable where such firms have a branch, agency or other establishment within the EEC. Under the national laws upon which jurisdiction is to be founded in such cases pursuant to Article 4, it would often be impossible for the consumer to sue in the courts which would be guaranteed to have jurisdiction for his purposes in the case of contracts with parties domiciled within the EEC. Insurers with branches, agencies or other establishments in the EEC are treated as regards jurisdiction in like manner to those domiciled within the Community (Article 8) and for the same reasons the other parties to contracts with consumers must also be deemed to be domiciled within the EEC if they have a branch, agency or other establishment in the Community. It is, however, only logical that it should not be possible to invoke exorbitant jurisdictions against such parties simply because their head office lies outside the EEC.

4. Contracts of transport

160. The last paragraph of Article 13 is again taken from Article 5 of the preliminary draft Convention on the law applicable to contractual and non-contractual obligations. The reason for leaving contracts of transport out of the scope of the special consumer protection provisions in the 1968 Convention is that such contracts are subject under international agreements to special sets of rules with very considerable ramifications, and the inclusion of those contracts in the 1968 Convention purely for jurisdictional purposes would merely complicate the legal position. Moreover, the total exclusion of contracts of transport from the scope of Section 4 means that Sections 1 and 2 and hence in particular Article 5(1) remain applicable.

161. **III. The substance of the provisions of Section 4**

There are only a few points requiring a brief explanation of the substance of the new provisions.

1. Subsequent change of domicile by the consumer

In substance, the new Article 14 closely follows the existing Article 14, while extending it to actions arising from all consumer contracts. The rearrangement of the text is merely a rewording due to the availability of a convenient description for one party to the contract, the "consumer", which was better placed at the beginning of the text so as to make it more easily comprehensible. The Working Party's decision means in substance that, as in the case with the existing Article 14, the consumer may sue in the courts of his new State of domicile if he moves to another Community State after concluding the contract out of which an action subsequently arises. This only becomes practical, however, in the case of the instalment sales and credit contracts referred to in points (1) and (2) of the first paragraph of Article 13. For actions arising out of other consumer contracts the new Section 4 will in virtually all cases cease to be applicable if the consumer transfers his domicile to another State after conclusion of the contract. This is because the steps necessary for the conclusion of the contract will almost always not have been taken in the new State of domicile. The cross-frontier advertising requirement also ensures that the special provisions will in practice not be applicable to contracts between two persons neither of whom is acting in a professional or trading capacity.

2. *Agreements on jurisdiction*

161a. The new version of Article 15, too, is in substance based on the existing version relating to instalment sales and loans. The only addition is intended to make it clear that it is at the time of conclusion of the contract, and not when proceedings are subsequently instituted, that the parties must be domiciled in the same State. It was then necessary to align and clarify Article 12(3) in the same way.

[OJ C59, 5.3.79, p 120]

Although Article 13 is not expressed to be subject to Article 17, the Working Party was unanimously of the opinion that agreements on jurisdiction must, in so far as they are permitted at all, comply with the formal requirements of Article 17. Since the form of such agreements is not governed by Section 4, it must be governed by Article 17.

Section 5
Exclusive jurisdiction

162. The only amendment proposed by the Working Party to the cases of exclusive jurisdiction provided for in Article 16 is a technical amendment in Article Vd of the Protocol annexed to the 1968 Convention, to clarify Article 16(4). The Working Party did, however, spend some time discussing paragraphs (1) and (2) of that Article. Details of the information supplied to the new Member States regarding exclusive jurisdiction in actions relating to the validity of the constitution of companies or to their dissolution have already been given elsewhere (see paragraph *56 et seq*). It is only necessary to add that a company may have more than one seat. Where under a legal system it is possible for a company to have two seats, and it is that system which, pursuant to Article 53 of the 1968 Convention, is to determine the seat of the company, the existence of two seats has to be accepted. It is then open to the plaintiff to choose which of the two seats he will use to base the jurisdiction of the court for his action. Finally, it should be pointed out that Article 16(2) also applies to partnerships established under United Kingdom and Irish law (see paragraph 55).

Thus essentially the only exclusive jurisdiction left to be dealt with more fully here is that in respect of actions relating to rights *in rem* in, or tenancies of, immovable property. There were five problems with regard to which the new Member States had requested explanations.

163. There was no difficulty in clarifying that actions for damages based on infringement of rights *in rem* or in damage to property in which rights *in rem* exist do not fall within the scope of Article 16(1). In that context the existence and content of such rights *in rem*, usually rights of ownership, are only of marginal significance.

164. The Working Party was unable to agree whether actions concerned only with rent, i e dealing simply with the recovery of a debt, are excluded from the scope of Article 16(1) as, according to the Jenard report, was the opinion of the Committee which drafted the 1968 Convention.[38] However, the underlying principle of the provision quite clearly does not require its application to short-term agreements for use and occupation such as, for example, holiday accommodation.

165. Two of the three remaining problems which the Working Party examined relate to the differences between the law of immovable property on the continent and the corresponding law in the United Kingdom and Ireland; they require therefore somewhat more detailed comments. There is, first, the question what are rights *in rem* (1) within the meaning

of Article 16(1), and, secondly, the problem of disputes arising in connection with the transfer of immovable property (2). Certain other problems emerged as a result of developments which have taken place in the meantime in international patent law (3).

1. Rights "in rem" in immovable property in the Member States of the Community

166. (a) The concept of a right *in rem*—as distinct from a right *in personam*—is common to the legal systems of the original Member States of the EEC, even though the distinction does not appear everywhere with the same clarity.

A right *in personam* can only be claimed against a particular person; thus only the purchaser is obliged to pay the purchase price and only the lessor of an article is obliged to permit its use.

A right *in rem*, on the other hand, is available against the whole world. The most important legal consequence flowing from the nature of a right *in rem* is that its owner is entitled to demand that the thing in which it exists be given up by anyone not enjoying a prior right.

[OJ C59, 5.3.79, p 121]

In the legal systems of all the original Member States of the EEC without exception, there are only a restricted number of rights *in rem*, even though they do not rigidly apply the principle. Some rights *in rem* are defined only in outline, with freedom for the parties to agree the details. The typical rights *in rem* are listed under easily identifiable heads of the civil law, which in all six countries is codified.[39] In addition, a few rights *in rem* are included in some special laws, the most important of which are those on the co-ownership of real property. Apart from ownership as the most comprehensive right *in rem*, a distinction can be made between certain rights of enjoyment and certain priority rights to secure liabilities. All the legal systems know the concept of usufruct, which confers extensive rights to enjoyment of a property. More restricted rights of enjoyment can also exist in these legal systems in various ways.

167. (b) At first glance there appears to be in United Kingdom and Irish law too a small, strictly circumscribed group of statutory rights corresponding to the Continental rights *in rem*. However, the position is more complicated, because these legal systems distinguish between law and equity.

In this connection it has always to be borne in mind that equity also constitutes law and not something merely akin to fairness lying outside the concept of law. As a consequence of these special concepts of law and equity in the United Kingdom and in Ireland, equitable interests can exist in immovable property in addition to the legal rights.

In the United Kingdom the system of legal rights has its origin in the idea that all land belongs to the Crown and that the citizen can only have limited rights in immovable property. This is the reason why the term "ownership" does not appear in the law of immovable property. However, the estate in fee simple absolute in possession is equivalent to full ownership under the Continental legal systems. In addition the Law of Property Act 1925 provides for full ownership for a limited period of time ("term of years absolute"). The same Act limits restricted rights in immovable property ("interests or charges in or over land") to five. All the others are equitable interests, whose number and content are not limited by the Act. Equitable interests are not, however, merely the equivalent of personal rights on the Continent. Some can be registered and then, like legal rights, have universal effect, even against purchasers in good faith. Even if not registered they operate in principle against all the world; only purchasers in good faith who had no knowledge of them are protected in such a case.[40] If the owner of an estate in fee simple absolute in possession grants another person a right of way over his property for the period of that person's life, this cannot amount to a legal right. It can only be an equitable interest, though capable of registration.[41] Equitable interests can thus fulfil the same functions as rights *in rem* under the Continental legal systems, in which case they must be treated as such under Article 16(1). There is no limit to the number of such interests. The granting of equitable interests is on the contrary the method used for achieving any number of subdivisions of proprietary rights.[42]

168. (c) If an action relating to immovable property is brought in a particular State and the question whether the action is concerned with a right *in rem* within the meaning of Article 16(1) arises, the answer can hardly be derived from any law other than that of the *situs*.

2. Actions in connection with obligations to transfer immovable property

169. The legal systems of the original and the new Member States of the Community also differ as regards the manner in which ownership of immovable property is transferred on sale. Admittedly the legal position even within the original Member States differs in this respect.

PART IV EC MATERIALS

170. (a) German law distinguishes most clearly between the transfer itself and the contract of sale (or other contract designed to bring about a transfer). The legal position in the case of immovable property is no different from that obtaining in the case of movable property. The transfer is a special type of legal transaction which in the case of immovable property is called "Auflassung" (conveyance) and which even between the parties becomes effective only on entry in the land register. Where a purchaser of German immovable property brings proceedings on the basis of a contract for sale of immovable property which is governed by German law, the subject matter of such proceedings is never a right *in rem* in the property. The only matter in issue is the defendant's personal obligation to carry out all acts necessary to transfer and hand over the property. If one of the parties fails to fulfil its obligations under a contract for sale of immovable property, the remedy in German law is not a court order for rescission, but a claim for damages and the right to rescind the contract.
[OJ C59, 5.3.79, p 122]

Admittedly it is possible with the vendor's consent to protect the contractual claim for a transfer of ownership by means of a caution in the land register. In that case the claim has, as against third parties, effects which normally only attach to a right *in rem*. The consequence for German domestic law is that nowadays rights secured by such a caution may be claimed against third parties in the jurisdiction competent to deal with the property concerned.[43] However, any proceedings for a transfer of ownership against the vendor himself would remain an action based on a personal obligation.

171. (b) Under French, Belgian and Luxembourg law, which is largely followed by Italian law, the ownership, at any rate as between the parties, passes to the purchaser as soon as the contract of sale is concluded, just as it does in the case of movable property, unless the parties have agreed a later date (see eg Article 711 and 1583 of the French Civil Code and Article 1376 of the Italian Civil Code). The purchaser need only enter the transfer of ownership in the land register ("transcription") to acquire a legal title which is also effective against third parties. For the purchaser to bring proceedings for performance of the contract is therefore normally equivalent to a claim that the property be handed over to him. Admittedly this claim is based not only on the obligation which the vendor undertook by the contract of sale, but also on ownership which at that point has already passed to the purchaser. This means that the claim for handing over the property has as its basis both a personal obligation and a right *in rem*. The system of remedies which is available in the event of one party to a contract not complying with its obligations is fully in accordance with this. Accordingly, French domestic law has treated such actions as a "matière mixte" and given the plaintiff the right to choose between the jurisdiction applicable to the right *in rem* and the jurisdiction applicable to the personal obligation arising from the contract, ie the law of the defendant's domicile or of the place of performance of the contract.[44]

The 1968 Convention does not deal with this problem. It would seem that the personal aspect of such claims predominates and Article 16(1) is inapplicable.

172. (c) In the United Kingdom ownership passes on the conclusion of a contract of sale only in the case of movable property. In the case of a sale of immovable property the transfer of ownership follows the conclusion of the contract of sale and is effected by means of a separate document, the conveyance. If necessary, the purchaser has to bring an action for all necessary acts to be performed by the vendor. However, except in Scotland, in contrast with German law, the purchaser's rights prior to the transfer of ownership are not limited to a personal claim against the vendor. In fact the purchaser has an equitable interest (see paragraph 167) in the property which, provided the contract is protected by a notice on the Land Register, is also effective against third parties. Admittedly the new paragraph (6) of Article 5 does not apply (see paragraph 114 *et seq*), because a contract of sale does not create a trust within the meaning of Article 5(6), even if it is in writing. It is only in one respect that a purchaser's equitable interest does not place him in as strong a position as the French owner of immovable property prior to "transcription" (see paragraph 171): the vendor's cooperation is still required to make the new owner's legal title fully effective.

This legal position would justify application of the exclusive jurisdiction referred to in Article 16(1) even less than the corresponding position under French law. The common law has developed the concept of equitable interests so as to confer on parties to an agreement which originally gave them nothing more than merely personal rights a certain protection as against third parties not acting in good faith. As against the other party to the contract the claim remains purely a personal one, as does a claim, under German law, to transfer of ownership (see paragraph 170) secured by a caution in the Land Register. In Scotland contracts in favour of a third party are enforceable by that party (*jus quaesitum tertii*).

Actions based on contracts for the transfer of ownership or other rights *in rem* affecting immovable property do not therefore have as their object rights *in rem*. Accordingly they may also be brought before courts outside the United Kingdom. Admittedly, care will have to be exercised in that case to ensure that the plaintiff clearly specifies the acts to be done by the defendant so that the transfer of ownership (governed by United Kingdom law) does indeed become effective.

[OJ C59, 5.3.79, p 123]

173. 3. Jurisdiction in connection with patent disputes

Since the 1968 Convention entered into force, two Conventions on patents have been signed which are of the greatest international importance. The Munich Convention on the grant of European patents was signed on 5 October 1973 and the Luxembourg Convention for the European patent for the common market was signed on 15 December 1975. The purpose of the Munich Convention is to introduce a common patent application procedure for the Contracting States, though the patent subsequently granted is national in scale. It is valid for one or more States, its substance in each case being basically that of a corresponding patent granted nationally. The aim of the Luxembourg Convention is to institute in addition a patent granted *ab initio* for all States of the Community in a standard manner and with the same substance, based on Community law; such a patent necessarily remains valid or expires uniformly throughout the EEC.

Both instruments contain specific provisions on jurisdiction which take precedence over the 1968 Convention. However, the special jurisdiction provisions relate only to specific matters, such as applications for the revocation of patents pursuant to the Luxembourg Convention. Article 16(4) of the 1968 Convention remains relevant for actions for which no specific provision is made. In the case of European patents under the Munich Convention it is conceivable that this provision might be construed as meaning that actions must be brought in the State in which the patent was applied for and not in the State for which it is valid and in which it is challenged. The new Article Vd of the Protocol annexed to the 1968 Convention is designed to prevent this interpretation and ensure that only the courts of the State in which the patent is valid have jurisdiction, unless the Munich Convention itself lays down special provisions.

Clearly, such a provision cannot cover a Community patent under the Luxembourg Convention, since the governing principle is that the patent is granted, not for a given State, but for all the Member States of the EEC. Hence the exception at the end of the new provision. However, even in the area covered by the Luxembourg Convention patents valid for one or more, but not all, States of the Community are possible. Article 86 of that Convention allows this for a transitional period to which no term has yet been set. Where the applicant for a patent takes up the option available to him under this provision and applies for a patent for one or more, but not all, States of the EEC, the patent is not a Community patent even though it comes under some of the provisions of the Luxembourg Convention but merely a patent granted for one or more States. Accordingly, the courts of that State have exclusive jurisdiction under Article Vd of the Protocol annexed to the 1968 Convention. The same is true for any case in which a national patent is granted in response to an international application, e g under the Patent Cooperation Treaty opened for signature at Washington on 19 June 1970.

It only remains to be made clear that Article 16(4) of the 1968 Convention and the new Article Vd of the Protocol annexed to the Convention also cover actions which national legislation allows to be brought at the patent application stage, so as to reduce the risk of a patent being granted, and the correctness of the grant being subsequently challenged.

Section 6
Jurisdiction by consent[45]

174. Article 17, applying as it does only if the transaction in question is international in character (see paragraph 21), which the mere fact of choosing a court in a particular State is by no means sufficient to establish, presented the Working Party with four problems. First, account had to be taken of the practice of courts in the United Kingdom (excluding Scotland) and Ireland of deducing from the choice of law to govern the main issue an agreement as to the courts having jurisdiction. Secondly, there was the problem, previously ignored by the 1968 Convention, of agreements conferring jurisdiction upon a court outside the Community or agreements conferring jurisdiction upon courts within the Community by two parties both domiciled outside the Community. Thirdly, special rules had to be made for provisions in trusts. And finally, the Working Party had to consider whether it was reasonable to let Article 17 stand in view of the interpretation which had been placed upon it by the Court of Justice of the European Communities. It should be repeated (see paragraph 22) that the

existence of an agreement conferring jurisdiction on a court other than the court seised of the proceedings is one of the points to be taken into account by the court of its own motion.

[OJ C59, 5.3.79, p 124]

1. Choice-of-law clause and international jurisdiction

175. Nowhere in the 1968 Convention is there recognition of a connection between the law applicable to a particular issue and the international jurisdiction of the courts over that issue. However, persons who, relying on the practice of United Kingdom or Irish courts, have agreed on choice-of-law clauses before the entry into force of the Accession Convention, are entitled to expect protection. This explains the transitional provision contained in Article 35 of the proposed Accession Convention. The term 'entry into force' within the meaning of this provision refers to the date on which the Accession Convention comes into effect in the State in question. For the various systems of law applying in the United Kingdom, see paragraph 11.

2. Agreements conferring jurisdiction on courts outside the Community

176. (a) In cases where parties agree to bring their disputes before the courts of a State which is not a party to the 1968 Convention there is obviously nothing in the 1968 Convention to prevent such courts from declaring themselves competent, if their law recognizes the validity of such an agreement. The only question is whether and, if so, in what form such agreements are capable of depriving Community courts of jurisdiction which is stated by the 1968 Convention to be exclusive or concurrent. There is nothing in the 1968 Convention to support the conclusion that such agreements must be inadmissible in principle.[46] However, the 1968 Convention does not contain any rules as to their validity either. If a court within the Community is applied to despite such an agreement, its decision on the validity of the agreement depriving it of jurisdiction must be taken in accordance with its own *lex fori*. In so far as the local rules of conflict of laws support the authority of provisions of foreign law, the latter will apply. If, when these tests are applied, the agreement is found to be invalid, then the jurisdictional provisions of the 1968 Convention become applicable.

177. (b) On the other hand, proceedings can be brought before a court within the Community by parties who, although both domiciled outside the Community, have agreed that that court should have jurisdiction. There is no reason for the Convention to include rules on the conditions under which the court stipulated by such parties must accept jurisdiction. It is however important for the Community to ensure, by means of more detailed conditions, that the effect of such an agreement on jurisdiction is recognized throughout the EEC. The new third sentence of the first paragraph of Article 17 is designed to cater for this. It covers the situation where, despite the fact that both parties are domiciled outside the Community, a court in a Community State ("X") would, were it not for a jurisdiction agreement, have jurisdiction, e g on the ground that the place of performance lies within that State. If in such a case the parties agree that the courts of another Community State are to have exclusive jurisdiction, that agreement must be observed by the courts of State X, provided the agreement meets the formal requirements of Article 17. Strictly speaking, it is true, this is not a necessary adjustment. Such situations were possible before, in relations between the original Member States of the Community. However, owing to the frequency with which jurisdiction is conferred upon United Kingdom courts in international trade, the problem takes on considerably greater importance with the United Kingdom's accession to the Convention than hitherto.

3. Jurisdiction clauses in trusts

178. A trust (see paragraph 111) need not be established by contract. A unilateral legal instrument is sufficient. As the previous version of Article 17 dealt only with "agreements" on jurisdiction, it needed to be expanded.

4. The form of agreements on jurisdiction in international trade

[OJ C59, 5.3.79, p 125]

179. Some of the first judgments given by the Court of Justice of the European Communities since it was empowered to interpret the 1968 Convention were concerned with the form of jurisdiction clauses incorporated in standardized general conditions of trade.[47] The Court of Justice's interpretation of Article 17 of the 1968 Convention does protect the other party to a contract with anyone using such general conditions of trade from the danger of inadvertently finding himself bound by standard forms of agreement containing jurisdiction clauses without realizing it. However, the Court's interpretation of that Article, which many national courts have also shown a tendency to follow,[45] does not cater adequately for the

customs and requirements of international trade. In particular, the requirement that the other party to a contract with anyone employing general conditions of trade has to give written confirmation of their inclusion in the contract before any jurisdiction clause in those conditions can be effective is unacceptable in international trade. International trade is heavily dependent on standard conditions which incorporate jurisdiction clauses. Nor are those conditions in many cases unilaterally dictated by one set of interests in the market; they have frequently been negotiated by representatives of the various interests. Owing to the need for calculations based on constantly fluctuating market prices, it has to be possible to conclude contracts swiftly by means of a confirmation of order incorporating sets of conditions. These are the factors behind the relaxation of the formal provisions for international trade in the amended version of Article 17. This is however, as should be clearly emphasized, only a relaxation of the formal requirements. It must be proved that a consensus existed on the inclusion in the contract of the general conditions of trade and the particular provisions, though this is not the place to pass comment on whether questions of consensus other than the matter of form should be decided according to the national laws applicable or to unified EEC principles. Dealing with the form of jurisdiction agreements in a separate second sentence in the first paragraph of Article 17, rather than in passing in the first sentence as hitherto, is designed merely to obviate rather cumbersome wording.

Section 7
Examination of own motion

Adjustments and further clarification were not necessary.

Section 8
"Lis pendens" and related actions[48]

180. As regards *lis pendens*, there are two structural differences between the laws of the United Kingdom and Ireland, on the one hand, and the Continental legal systems on the other. However, neither of them necessitated a technical amendment of the 1968 Convention.

1. Discretion of the court

181. The rules governing *lis pendens* in England and Wales, and to some extent in Scotland, are more flexible than those on the Continent. Basically, it is a question for the court's discretion whether a stay should be granted. The doctrine of *lis pendens* is therefore less fully developed there than in the Continental States. The practice is in a sense an application of the doctrine of *forum conveniens* (see paragraph *77 et seq*). Generally a court will in fact grant an application for a stay of proceedings, where the matter in dispute is already pending before another court. Where proceedings are pending abroad, the courts in England and Wales exercise great caution, and if they grant a stay of proceedings at all, they will do so only if the plaintiff in England or Wales is also the plaintiff in the proceedings abroad. Scottish courts take into account to a considerable extent any conflicting proceedings which a Scottish defendant may have instituted abroad, or which are pending against him abroad.

After the United Kingdom has acceded to the 1968 Convention, it will no longer be possible for this practice to be maintained in relation to the other Member States of the Community. United Kingdom courts will have to acknowledge the existence of proceedings instituted in the other Member States, and even to take notice of them of their own motion (see paragraph 22).

2. Moment at which proceedings become pending

182. The fact that the moment at which proceedings become pending is determined differently in the United Kingdom and Ireland from the way it is determined on the Continent is due to peculiarities of procedural law in those States. In the original Member States of the Community a claim becomes pending when the document instituting the proceedings is served.[49] Filing with the court is sometimes sufficient. In the United Kingdom, except Scotland, and in Ireland, proceedings become pending as soon as the originating document has been issued. In Scotland, however, proceedings become pending only when service of the summons has been effected on the defender. The moment at which proceedings become pending under the national procedural law concerned is the deciding factor for the application of Article 21 of the 1968 Convention. The addition to the text of Article 20 does not concern this point. It is justified by the fact that in the United Kingdom and in Ireland foreigners who are abroad do not receive the original writ but only notification of the order of the court authorizing service.

[OJ C59, 5.3.79, p 126]

Section 9
Provisional measures

183. No particular adjustments had to be made to the provisions of the 1968 Convention concerning provisional measures. The change in emphasis which the accession of further Member States introduced into the 1968 Convention consists in this field entirely in the wide variety of provisional measures available in the law of Ireland and of the United Kingdom. This will involve certain difficulties where provisional judgments given in these States have to be given effect by the enforcement procedures of the original Member States of the Community. However, this problem does not affect only provisional measures. The integration of judgments on the main issue into the respective national enforcement procedures also involves difficulties in the relationship between Ireland and the United Kingdom on the one hand and the original Member States of the Community on the other (see paragraph 221 *et seq*).

[3047D]

CHAPTER 5
RECOGNITION AND ENFORCEMENT

A. GENERAL REMARKS—INTERLOCUTORY COURT DECISIONS

184. Article 25 emphasizes in terms which could hardly be clearer that every type of judgment given by a court in a Contracting State must be recognized and enforced throughout the rest of the Community. The provision is not limited to a judgment terminating the proceedings before the court, but also applies to provisional court orders. Nor does the wording of the provision indicate that interlocutory court decisions should be excluded from its scope where they do not provisionally regulate the legal relationships between the parties, but are for instance concerned only with the taking of evidence. What is more, the legal systems of the original Member States of the Community describe such interlocutory decisions in a way which corresponds to the terms given, by way of example, in Article 25. Thus, in France court decisions which order the taking of evidence are also called "jugements (d'avant dire droit)". In Germany they are termed "(Beweis) beschlüsse" of the court. Nevertheless, the provisions of the 1968 Convention governing recognition and enforcement are in general designed to cover only court judgments which either determine or regulate the legal relationships of the parties. An answer to the question whether, and if so which, interlocutory decisions intended to be of procedural assistance fall within the scope of the 1968 Convention cannot be given without further consideration.

1. Relationship of the continental states with each other

185. This matter is of no great significance as between the original Member States of the EEC, or as between the latter and Denmark. All seven States are parties to the 1954 Hague Convention relating to civil procedure. The latter governs the question of judicial assistance, particularly in the case of evidence to be taken abroad, and its provisions take precedence over the 1968 Convention by virtue of Article 57. In any case, it is always advisable in practice to make use of the machinery of the Hague Convention, which is particularly suited to the processes required for obtaining judicial assistance. See paragraph 238, and note 59 (7) on the Hague Convention of 15 November 1965 on the service abroad of judicial and extrajudicial documents in civil or commercial matters and on the Hague Convention of 18 March 1970 on the taking of evidence abroad in civil or commercial matters.

2. Relationship of the United Kingdom and Ireland with the other Member States

[OJ C59, 5.3.79, p 127]

186. It is only with the accession of the United Kingdom and Ireland to the 1968 Convention that the problem assumes any degree of importance. Ireland has concluded no convention judicial assistance of any kind with the other States of the European Community. Agreements on judicial assistance do, however, exist between the United Kingdom and the following States: the Federal Republic of Germany (Agreement of 20 March 1928), the Netherlands (Agreement of 17 November 1967). The United Kingdom is also party to the Hague Conventions of 1965 and 1970 referred to in paragraph 185. It has concluded no other agreements with Member States of the Community.

3. Precise scope of Title III of the 1968 Convention

187. If it were desired that interlocutory decisions by courts on the further conduct of the proceedings, and particularly on the taking of evidence, should be covered by Article 25 of the 1968 Convention, this would also affect decisions with which the parties would be totally unable to comply without the court's cooperation, and the enforcement of which would concern third parties, particularly witnesses. It would therefore be impossible to "enforce" such decisions under the 1968 Convention. It can only be concluded from the foregoing that interlocutory decisions which are not intended to govern the legal relationships of the parties, but to arrange the further conduct of the proceedings, should be excluded from the scope of Title III of the 1968 Convention.

B. COMMENTS ON THE INDIVIDUAL SECTIONS

Section 1
Recognition

188. With two exceptions (4), no formal amendments were required to Articles 26 to 30. The Working Party did, however, answer some questions raised by the new Member States regarding the interpretation of these provisions. Basically, these concerned problems arising in connection with the application of the public policy reservation in Article 27 (1)–(2), the right to a hearing—Article 27 (2)–(3), and the nature of the obligation to confer recognition, as district from enforceability (1). The fact that Article 28 makes no reference to the provisions of Section 60 of Title II on jurisdiction agreements is intentional and deserves mention. When considering such agreements it must be borne in mind that the court seised of the proceedings in the State of origin must of its own motion take note of any agreement to the contrary (see paragraphs 22 and 174).

1. Article 26

189. Article 26, second paragraph, introduces a special simplified procedure for seeking recognition, modelled on the provisions governing the issue of orders for enforcement. However, this is not the only way in which recognition may be sought. Every court and public authority must take account of judgments which qualify for recognition, and must decide whether the conditions for recognition exist in a particular case, unless this question has already been determined under Article 26, second paragraph. In particular, every court must itself decide whether there is an obligation to grant recognition, if the principal issue in a foreign judgment concerns a question which in the fresh proceedings emerges as a preliminary issue. Each of these two recognition procedures involves a problem which the Working Party discussed.

190. (a) If proceedings are conducted in accordance with Article 26, second paragraph, the court may of its own motion take into account grounds for refusing recognition if they appear from the judgment or are known to the court. It may not, however, make enquiries to establish whether such grounds exist, at this would not be compatible with the summary nature of the proceedings. Only if further proceedings are instituted by way of an appeal lodged pursuant to Article 36 can the court examine whether the requirements for recognition have been satisfied.

191. (b) The effects of a court decision are not altogether uniform under the legal systems obtaining in the Member States of the Community. A judgment delivered in one State as a decision on a procedural issue may, in another State, be treated as a decision on an issue of substance. The same type of judgment may be of varying scope and effect in different countries. In France, a judgment against the principal debtor is also effective against the surety, whereas in the Netherlands and Germany it is not.[50]

[OJ C59, 5.3.79, p 128]

The Working Party did not consider it to be its task to find a general solution to the problems arising from these differences in the national legal systems. However, one fact seemed obvious.

Judgments dismissing an action as unfounded must be recognized. If a German court declares that it has no jurisdiction, an English court cannot disclaim its own jurisdiction on the ground that the German court was in fact competent. Clearly, however, German decisions on procedural matters are not binding, as to the substance, in England. An English court may at any time allow (or, for substantive reasons, disallow) an action, if proceedings are started in England after such a decision has been given by a German court.

2. Article 27(1)—public policy

192. (a) The 1968 Convention does not state in terms whether recognition may be refused pursuant to Article 27(1) on the ground that the judgment has been obtained by fraud. Not even in the legal systems of the original Contracting States to the 1968 Convention is it expressly stated that fraud in obtaining a judgment constitutes a ground for refusing recognition. Such conduct is, however, generally considered as an instance for applying the doctrine of public policy.[51] The legal situation in the United Kingdom and Ireland is different inasmuch as fraud constitutes a special ground for refusing recognition in addition to the principle of public policy. In the conventions on enforcement which the United Kingdom concluded with Community States, a middle course was adopted by expressly referring to fraudulent conduct, but treating it as a special case of public policy.[52]

As a result there is no doubt that to obtain a judgment by fraud can in principle constitute an offence against the public policy of the State addressed. However, the legal systems of all Member States provide special means of redress by which it can be contended, even after the expiry of the normal period for an appeal, that the judgment was the result of a fraud (see paragraph 197 *et seq*). A court in the State addressed must always, therefore, ask itself, whether a breach of its public policy still exists in view of the fact that proceedings for redress can be, or could have been, lodged in the courts of the State of origin against the judgment allegedly obtained by fraud.

193. (b) Article 41(3) of the Irish Constitution prohibits divorce and also provides, as regards marriages dissolved abroad:

> "No person whose marriage has been dissolved under the civil law of any other State but is a subsisting valid marriage under the law for the time being in force within the jurisdiction of the Government and Parliament established by this Constitution shall be capable of contracting a valid marriage within that jurisdiction during the lifetime of the other party to the marriage so dissolved."

In so far as the jurisdiction of the 1968 Convention is concerned, this Article of the Constitution is of importance for maintenance orders made upon a divorce. The Irish courts have not yet settled whether the recognition of such maintenance orders would, in view of the constitutional provisions cited, be contrary to Irish public policy.

3. The right to a hearing (Article 27(2))

194. Article 27(2) is amended for the same reason as Article 20 (see paragraph 182). The object of the addition to Article 20 was to specify the moment when proceedings became pending before the Irish or British courts; in Article 27(2) it is intended to indicate which documents must have been served for the right to a hearing to be respected.

4. Ordinary and extraordinary appeals

195. The 1968 Convention makes a distinction in Articles 30 and 38 between ordinary and extraordinary appeals. No equivalent for this could be found in the Irish and United Kingdom legal systems. Before discussing the reason for this and explaining the implications of the solutions proposed by the Working Party (b), something should be said about the distinction between ordinary and extraordinary appeals in the Continental Member States of the EEC, since judges in the United Kingdom and Ireland will have to come to terms with these concepts which to them are unfamiliar (a).

[OJ C59, 5.3.79, p 129]

196. (a) A clearly defined distinction between ordinary and extraordinary appeals is nowhere to be found.

Legal literature and case law[53] have pointed out two criteria. In the first place neither an appeal ("Berufung") nor an objection to a default judgment ("Einspruch") has to be based on specific grounds; a party may challenge a judgment by alleging any kind of defect. Secondly execution is postponed during the period allowed for an appeal or objection, or after an appeal or objection has been lodged, unless the court otherwise directs or unless, exceptionally, different legal provisions apply.

Some legal systems contain a list of ordinary appeal procedures.

197. Part 1, Book 4 of the French Code de procédure civile of 1806, which still applies in Luxembourg, referred to extraordinary forms of appeal by which a judgment could be contested. It did not say, however, what was meant by ordinary appeals. Book 3 referred merely to "courts of appeal". However, in legal literature and case law appeals ("appel") and objections to default judgments ("opposition") have consistently been classified as ordinary

appeals. The new French Code de procédure civile of 1975 now expressly clarifies the position. In future only objections (Article 76) and appeals (Article 85) are to be classified as ordinary appeals.

198. The Belgian Code judiciaire of 1967 has retained the French system which previously applied in Belgium. Only appeals and objections are considered as ordinary appeals (Article 21).

199. There is no distinction in Netherlands law between ordinary and extraordinary appeals. Academic writers classify the forms of appeal as follows: objections ("Verzet"—where a judgment is given in default), appeals ("Hoger beroep"), appeals in cassation ("Beroep in cassatie") and appeals on a point of law ("Revisie") are classed as ordinary appeals. "Revisie" is a special form of appeal which lies only against certain judgments of the Hoge Raad sitting as a court of first instance.

200. The Italian text of Articles 30 and 38 refers to "impugnazione" without distinguishing between ordinary and extraordinary appeals. However, Italian legal literature distinguishes very clearly between ordinary and extraordinary appeals. Article 324 of the Codice di procedura civile states that a judgment does not become binding as between the parties until the periods within which the following forms of appeal may be lodged have expired: appeals on grounds of jurisdiction ("regolamento di competenza"), appeals ("appello"), appeals in cassation "ricorso per cassazione"), or petitions for review ("revocazione"), where these are based on one of the grounds provided for in Article 395(4) and (5). These forms of appeal are classified as ordinary.

201. In Denmark, too, the distinction between ordinary and extraordinary appeals is recognized only in legal literature. The deciding factor mentioned there is whether a form of appeal may be lodged within a given period without having to be based on particular grounds, or whether its admissibility depends on special consent by a court or ministry. Accordingly, appeals ("Anke") and objections to default judgments ("Genoptagelse af sager, i hvilke der er afsagt udeblivelsesdom") are classified as ordinary appeals.

202. Book 3 of the German Code of Civil Procedure ("Zivilprozeßordnung") is headed "Rechtsmittel" ("means of redress") and it governs "Berufung" (appeals) "Beschwerde" (complaints) and "Revision" (appeals on a point of law). These are frequently said to have in common the fact that the decision appealed against does not become binding ("rechtskräftig") until the period within which these means of redress may be lodged has expired. However Article 705 of the Code defines "Rechtskraft" as the stage when these means of redress are no longer available. The material difference between the means of redress and other forms of appeal is that the former need not be based on particular grounds of appeal, that they are addressed to a higher court and that, as long as the decision has not become binding, enforcement is also postponed pursuant to Article 704 unless the court, as is almost invariably the case, allows provisional enforcement. If the expression "ordinary appeal" is used at all, a reference to "Rechtsmittel" (means of redress) is intended.

German legal writers, in accordance with the phraseology used by the law, do not classify objections to default judgments as a means of redress ("Rechtsmittel").[54] It does not involve the competence of a higher court. However, it has the effect of suspending execution and is not tied to specific grounds of appeal, just like an objection in the other original Member States of the Community. It must therefore, be included under "ordinary appeals" within the meaning of Articles 30 and 38 of the 1968 Convention.

[OJ C59, 5.3.79, p 130]

203. In its judgment of 22 November 1977[55] the European Court held that the concept of an "ordinary appeal" was to be uniformly determined in the original Member States according to whether there was a specific period of time for appealing, which started to run "by virtue of" the judgment.

204. (b) In Ireland and the United Kingdom nothing which would enable a distinction to be drawn between ordinary and extraordinary appeals can be found in either statutes, cases or systematic treaties on procedural law. The basic method of redress is the appeal. Not only is this term used where review of a judgment can be sought within a certain period, without being subject to special grounds for appeal; it is also the name given to other means of redress. Some have special names such as; for default judgments, "reponing" (in Scotland) or "application to set the judgment aside" (in England, Wales and Ireland); or again "motion" (in Scotland) or "application" (in England, Wales and Ireland) "for a new trial", which correspond roughly to a petition for review in Continental legal systems. They are the only forms of redress against a verdict by a jury. A further distinctive feature of the appeal system

in these States is the fact that the enforceability of a judgment is not automatically affected by the appeal period or even by the lodging of an appeal. However, the appellate court will usually grant a temporary stay of execution, if security is given. Finally there do exist in the United Kingdom legal procedures whose function corresponds to the ordinary legal procedures of Continental legal systems, but which are not subject to time limits. The judge exercises his discretion in deciding on the admissibility of each particular case. This is the case, for example, with default judgments. The case law of the European Court could therefore not be applied to the new Member States.

The Working Party therefore made prolonged efforts to work out an equivalent for the United Kingdom and Ireland of the Continental distinction between ordinary and extraordinary appeals, but reached no satisfactory result. This failure was due in particular to the fact that the term "appeal" is so many-sided and cannot be regarded, like similar terms in Continental law, as a basis for "ordinary appeals". The Working Party therefore noted that the legal consequences resulting from the distinction drawn in Articles 30 and 38 between ordinary and extraordinary appeals do not have to be applied rigidly, but merely confer a discretion on the court. Accordingly, in the interests of practicality and clarity, a broad definition of appeal seemed justified in connection with judgments of Irish and United Kingdom courts. Continental courts will have to use their discretion in such a way that an equal balance in the application of Articles 30 and 38 in all Contracting States will be preserved. To this effect they will have to make only cautious use of their discretionary power to stay proceedings, if the appeal is one which is available in Ireland or the United Kingdom only against special defects in a judgment or which may still be lodged after a long period. A further argument in favour of this pragmatic solution was that, in accordance with Article 38, a judgment is in any event no longer enforceable if it was subject to appeal in the State of origin and the appellate court suspended execution or granted a temporary stay of execution.

5. Conflicts with judgments given in non-contracting States which qualify for recognition

205. In one respect the provisions of the 1968 Convention governing recognition required formal amendment. A certain lack of clarity in some of these provisions can be accepted since the European Court of Justice has jurisdiction to interpret them. However, Member States cannot be expected to accept lack of clarity where this might give rise to diplomatic complications with non-contracting States. The new Article 27(5) is designed to avoid such complications.

This may be explained by way of an example. A decision dismissing an action against a person domiciled in the Community is given in non-contracting State A. A Community State, B, is obliged to recognize the judgment under a bilateral convention. The plaintiff brings fresh proceedings in another Community State, C, which is not obliged to recognize the judgment given in the non-contracting State. If he is successful, the existing text of the 1968 Convention leaves it open to doubt whether the judgment has to be recognized in State B.

[OJ C59, 5.3.79, p 131]

In future, it is certain that this is not the case. In order to avoid unnecessary discrepancies, the text of the new provision is based on Article 5 of the Hague Convention of 1 February 1971 on the recognition and enforcement of foreign judgments in civil and commercial matters. Its wording is slightly wider in scope than would have been required to avoid diplomatic complications. A judgment given in a non-contracting State takes priority even where it has to be recognized, not by virtue of an international convention but merely under national law. For obligations under conventions not to recognize certain judgments, see paragraph 249 *et seq.*

Section 2
Enforcement

1. Preliminary remarks

206. The Working Party's efforts were almost entirely confined to deciding which courts in the new Member States should have jurisdiction in enforcement proceedings, and what appeal procedures should be provided in this context. In this connection four peculiarities of United Kingdom and, to a certain extent, Irish law had to be considered.

The Working Party took no decision on amendments to deal with the costs of the enforcement procedure. On this point, however, reference should be made to the judgment of the Court of Justice of the European Communities of 30 November 1976 (Case 42/76). According to that decision, Article 31 prohibits a successful plaintiff from bringing fresh proceedings in the State in which enforcement is sought. But the Contracting States are obliged to adopt rules on costs which take into account the desire to simplify the enforcement procedure.

207. The Working Party also abandoned attempts to draft provisions in the Convention on seizure for international claims, although it was clear that problems would occur to a certain extent if debtors and third party debtors were domiciled in different States. If, in one State, the court of the debtor's domicile has jurisdiction over seizure for such claims, then the State of domicile of the third party debtor may regard the making of the order for seizure applicable to the latter as a violation of its sovereignty, and refuse to enforce it. In such a situation the creditor can seek assistance by obtaining a declaration that the judgment is enforceable in the State of domicile of the third party debtor, and enforcing the debtor's claim against the third party in that State, provided that this State assumes international jurisdiction over such a measure.

208. (a) United Kingdom and Irish law does not have the *exequatur* system for foreign judgments. In these countries an action on the basis of the foreign judgment is necessary unless, as in the United Kingdom, a system of registration applies to the judgments of certain States (including the six original Member States with the exception of Luxembourg) (see paragraph 6). In that case the foreign judgments, if they are to be enforced, must be registered with a court in the United Kingdom. They then have the same force as judgments of the registering court itself. The application has to be lodged by the creditor in person or by a solicitor on his behalf. Personal appearance is essential; lodging by post will not suffice. If the application is granted, an order to that effect will be entered in the register kept at the court.

Except in Scotland, however, the United Kingdom has no independent enforcement officer like the French "huissier" or the German "Gerichtsvollzieher" (see paragraph 221). Only the court which gave the judgment or where the judgment was registered can direct enforcement measures. Since this system of registration affords the same protection to a foreign judgment creditor as does the *exequatur* system on the Continent, the United Kingdom registration system could also be accepted for applying the provisions of the 1968 Convention.

[OJ C59, 5.3.79, p 132]

209. (b) A special feature of the constitution of the United Kingdom has already been mentioned in the introductory remarks (see paragraph 11): England and Wales, Scotland and Northern Ireland are independent judicial areas. A new paragraph had to be added to Article 31 to cover this. Similarly the appeal possibilities provided for in Articles 37 and 40 apply separately to each registration. If a judgment has been validly registered with the High Court in London, another appeal is again possible against a subsequent registration with the Court of Session in Edinburgh.

210. (c) As far as the enforcement of foreign judgments is concerned the United Kingdom traditionally concedes special treatment to maintenance orders (see paragraph 7). Until now they have been enforced only in respect of a few Commonwealth countries and Ireland, and their enforcement is entrusted to courts different from those responsible for enforcing other judgments. Since the 1968 Convention contains no provisions precluding different recognition procedures for different types of judgment, there is no reason why maintenance orders cannot be covered by a special arrangement within the scope of the 1968 Convention. This will permit the creation of a uniform system for the recognition of maintenance orders from the Community and the Commonwealth and, in view of the type of court having jurisdiction, the setting up of a central agency to receive applications for enforcement (see paragraph 218). For agreements concerning maintenance see paragraph 226.

211. (d) Finally there were still problems in connection with judgments ordering performance other than the payment of money. Judgments directing a person to do a particular act are not generally enforceable under United Kingdom and Irish law, but only in pursuance of special legal provisions. These provisions cover judgments ordering the delivery of movable property or the transfer of ownership or possession of immovable property, and injunctions by which the court may in its discretion order an individual to do or refrain from doing a certain act. Enforcement is possible either by the sheriff's officer using direct compulsion or indirectly by means of fines or imprisonment for contempt of court. In Scotland, in addition to judgments for the transfer of possession or ownership of immovable property and preventative injunctions, there are also "decrees *ad factum prestandum*" by means of which the defendant can be ordered to perform certain acts, particularly to hand back movable property.

212. (aa) If an application is made in the Federal Republic of Germany for the enforcement of such a judgment given in Ireland or the United Kingdom, the court must apply the same means of compulsion as would be applicable in the case of a corresponding German judgment, i e a fine or imprisonment. In the reverse situation, the United Kingdom and Irish courts may have to impose penalties for contempt of court in the same way as when their own orders are disregarded.

PART IV
EC MATERIALS

213. (bb) The system for enforcing orders requiring the performance of a specific act is fundamentally different in other States of the Community, eg Belgium, France and Luxembourg. The defendant is ordered to perform the act and at the same time to pay a sum of money to the plaintiff to cover a possible non-compliance with the order. In France he is initially only threatened with a fine ("astreinte"). In case of non-compliance, a separate judgment is required and is hardly ever as high as the fine originally threatened. In Belgium the amount of the fine is already fixed in the judgment ordering the act to be performed.[56] With a view to overcoming the difficulties which this could cause for the inter-State enforcement of judgments ordering specific acts. Article 43 provides that, if the sanction takes the form of a fine ("astreinte"), the original court should itself fix the amount. Enforcement abroad is then limited to the "astreinte". French, Belgian, Dutch and Luxembourg judgments can be enforced without difficulty in Germany, the United Kingdom and Italy if the original court has proceeded on that basis.

However, the 1968 Convention leaves open the question whether such a fine for disregarding a court order can also be enforced when it accrues not to the judgment creditor but to the State. Since this is not a new problem arising out of the accession of the new Member States, the Working Party did not express a view on the matter.

[OJ C59, 5.3.79, p 133]

2. *Formal adjustments as regards courts having jurisdiction and authorized appeals*

214. Apart from the inclusion of a term equivalent in the Irish and United Kingdom legal systems to ordinary appeal (see paragraph 195), and apart from Article 44 which deals with legal aid (see paragraph 223), the formal adjustments to Articles 32 to 45 relate exclusively to the courts having jurisdiction and the possible types of appeal against their decisions. (See paragraph 108 for adjustments relating to maintenance.)

215. (a) For applications for a declaration of enforceability (see paragraph 208) of judgments other than maintenance orders only one court has been given jurisdiction in each of Ireland, England and Wales, Scotland and Northern Ireland. This is due to the peculiarities of the court systems in these countries (see paragraphs 11, 208 and 209).

216. If the judgment debtor wishes to argue against the authorization of enforcement, he must lodge his application to set the registration aside not with a higher court, as in Germany, France and Italy, but, as in Belgium and the Netherlands, with the court which registered the judgment. The proceedings will take the form of an ordinary contentious civil action.

A corresponding position applies regarding the appeal which the applicant may lodge if his application is refused, although in such a case it is a higher court which has jurisdiction in all seven Continental Member States of the Community.

217. The adjustment of the second paragraph of Article 37 and of Article 41 gave rise to difficulties with regard to the solution adopted for Articles 32 and 40.

In the original Member States of the Community an appeal against judgments of courts on which jurisdiction is conferred by Articles 37 and 40 could only be lodged on a point of law and with the highest court in the State. It was therefore sufficient to make the same provision apply to the appeals provided for in the 1968 Convention and, in the case of Belgium, simply to bypass the Cour d'appel. The purpose of this arrangement is to limit the number of appeals, in the interests of rapid enforcement, to a single appeal which may involve a full review of the facts and a second one limited to points of law. It would therefore not have been enough to stipulate for the new Member States that only one further appeal would be permitted against the judgment of the court which had ruled on an appeal made by either the debtor or the creditor. Instead, the second appeal had to be limited to points of law.

Ireland and the United Kingdom will have to adapt their appeal system to the requirements of the 1968 Convention. In the case of Ireland, which has only a two-tier superior court system, the Supreme Court is the only possibility. Implementing legislation in the United Kingdom will have to determine whether the further appeals should go direct to the House of Lords or, depending on the judicial area concerned (see paragraph 11), to the Court of Appeal in England and Wales, to the court of the same name in Northern Ireland or to the Inner House of the Court of Session in Scotland. The concept of "appeal on a point of law" is the nearest equivalent as far as United Kingdom law is concerned to the "Rechtsbeschwerde" of German law and the appeal in cassation in the legal systems of the other original Member States of the Community, the common feature of which is a restriction of the grounds of appeal to an incorrect application of the law (as opposed to an incorrect assessment of the facts). Even in relation to appeals in cassation and "Rechtsbeschwerde" the distinction between points of law and matters of fact is not identical; for the United Kingdom and Ireland, too, this will remain a matter for its own legislation and case law to clarify.

Traditionally the leave of the Minister for Justice is required for an appeal to the highest Danish court at third instance. The Working Party was initially doubtful whether it should accept this in the context of the 1968 Convention. It emerged, however, that the Convention does not guarantee a third instance in all circumstances. In order to relieve the burden on their highest courts, Member States may limit the admissibility of the appeals provided for in Article 41. The Danish solution is only one manifestation of this idea. There was also no need in the case of Denmark to stipulate that the appeal to the highest court should be limited to a point of law. When granting leave the Ministry of Justice can ensure that the appeal concerns only questions of law requiring further elucidation. Denmark has given an assurance that leave will always be granted, if the court of second instance has not made use of its discretion to refer a matter to the European Court of Justice or if enforcement of a foreign judgment has been refused on legal grounds.

[OJ C59, 5.3.79, p 134]

218. (b) In Ireland the proposed arrangement also applies to maintenance orders. In the United Kingdom, however, maintenance orders are subject to a special arrangement (see paragraph 210). In England and Wales and in Northern Ireland registration is a matter for the Magistrates' Courts, and in Scotland for the Sheriff Courts. These courts also have jurisdiction in respect of other maintenance matters including the enforcement of foreign maintenance orders. Foreign maintenance creditors cannot, however, have recourse to any of the above courts directly, but must apply to the Secretary of State,[57] who will transmit the order to the appropriate court. This arrangement was made in the interest of the foreign maintenance creditors, because Magistrates' Courts and Sheriff Courts have lay justices and no administrative machinery.

As regards jurisdiction in respect of appeals which may be brought by either the creditor or the debtor under the 1968 Convention, the usual system will continue to apply, i e the appeal is decided by the court which registered the order or refused such registration. It is impossible for a maintenance order to be amended during registration proceedings, even if it is claimed that the circumstances have changed (see paragraph 104 *et seq*).

The special situation regarding maintenance orders in the United Kingdom offers a series of advantages to the maintenance creditor. After forwarding the order to the Secretary of State, he has virtually no further need to concern himself with the progress of the proceedings or with their enforcement. The rest will be done free of charge. The Secretary of State transmits the order to the appropriate court and, unless the maintenance creditor otherwise requests, the clerk of that court will be regarded as the representative *ad litem* within the meaning of Article 33, second paragraph, second sentence. In England and Wales and in Northern Ireland the clerk in question will also be responsible for taking the necessary enforcement measures and for ensuring that the creditor receives the proceeds obtained. Only in Scotland need the creditor under the order seek the services of a solicitor when applying for enforcement following registration of an order. The Law Society of Scotland undertakes to provide solicitors whose fees are, if necessary, paid in accordance with the principles of legal aid. Should the maintenance debtor move to another judicial area in the United Kingdom (see paragraph 11), a maintenance order will, unlike other judgments, be automatically registered with the court which then has jurisdiction. For agreements concerning maintenance, see paragraph 226.

3. *Other adjustment problems*

219. (a) The United Kingdom asked whether Article 34 excludes the possibility of notifying the debtor that an application for registration of a foreign judgment has been lodged. One of the aims of Article 34 is to secure the element of surprise, which is essential if measures of enforcement are to be effective. Therefore, although this provision does not expressly forbid notifying the debtor in the proceedings of the application for the grant of an enforcement order, such notification should be confined to very exceptional cases. An example might be an application for registration made a long time after the original judgment was given. In any case, the court may not consider submissions from the debtor, whether or not he was notified in advance.

220. (b) The appeal provided for in Article 36 can be based, *inter alia*, on the grounds that the judgment does not come within the scope of the 1968 Convention, that it is not yet enforceable, or that the obligation imposed by the judgment has already been complied with. However, the substance of the judgment to be enforced or the procedure by which it came into existence can be reviewed only within the limits of Articles 27 and 28. For the adjustment of maintenance orders, see paragraph 108.

221. (c) The Working Party discussed Article 39 at length. The provision in question is modelled on the French legal system and legal systems related to it, to which the institution of

"huissier" is familiar. Under these systems, measures of enforcement in respect of movable property or contractual claims belonging to the debtor can be taken, without involving the court, by instructing a "huissier" to deal with their execution. It is for the creditor to choose between the available methods of enforcement. The enforcing agency has no discretion whatsoever in the matter. The legal position obtaining in the United Kingdom (especially in England and Wales and also in Scotland) and Ireland is quite different. In the United Kingdom it is the court which has given or registered the judgment which has jurisdiction over measures of enforcement. In Ireland it is the court which has given or enforced the judgment. The court also has some discretion as to which enforcement measures it will sanction. Protective measures confined to securing enforcement of a claim do not yet exist.
[OJ C59, 5.3.79, p 135]

This position will have to be altered by the implementing legislation of these States, which will have to introduce protective measures, in so far as this consequence does not arise as an automatic result of the entry into force of the 1968 Convention for one of these States (see paragraph 256).

The 1968 Convention does not guarantee specific measures of enforcement to the creditor. Neither is it in any way incompatible with the 1968 Convention to leave the measures of enforcement entirely to the court. The 1968 Convention contains no express provision obliging the Member States to employ an institution similar to the French "huissier". Even within its original scope, creditors have to apply directly to the court in the case of certain measures of enforcement; in Germany, for example, they would be required to do so in the case of enforcement against immovable property. It is certain however that in the German text the phrase "in das Vermögen des Schuldners" ("against the property of the party against whom enforcement is sought") does not mean that measures of enforcement are permissible as against third parties. The words quoted above could be omitted without changing the meaning of the provision. The question under what conditions measures of enforcement are possible against persons other than the judgment debtor is to be answered solely on the basis of national law. But the qualifications contained in Article 39 must also be observed.

The court enforcing the judgment need not be the one which grants the order of enforcement or registers the foreign judgment. Therefore, for the purposes of enforcement under the 1968 Convention, Denmark can retain its present system, by which execution is entrusted to a special enforcement judge.

222. (d) For the problems presented by the system of "*astreintes*", which applies in some Member States, see paragraph 213.

223. (e) In its present form, Article 44 does not provide for the case of a party who had been granted only partial legal aid in the State in which the judgment was given. Although this did not involve an adjustment problem specifically due to the accession of the new Member States, the Working Party decided to propose an amendment. The Working Party's discussions revealed that if the text were to remain in force in its present form, it could result in some undesirable complications. The Working Party's proposal was largely based on the formulation of Article 15 of the Hague Convention of 2 October 1973 on the recognition and enforcement of decisions relating to maintenance obligations which has now come into force. This provision opts for a generous solution: even if only partial legal aid was granted in the State of origin, full aid is to be granted in the enforcement proceedings.

This has a number of further advantages:

As the main application of Article 44 as amended relates to maintenance claims, the amended version contributes to the harmonization of provisions in international conventions.

Moreover, it leads to a general simplification of applications.

Since the rules concerning the granting of partial legal aid are not the same in all the Contracting States, the amended version also ensures a uniform application of the legal aid provisions.

Lastly, it secures the surprise effect of enforcement measures abroad, by avoiding procedural delays caused by difficult calculations concerning the applicant's share in the costs.

The first paragraph of Article 44 does not, however, oblige States which do not at present have a system of legal aid in civil matters to introduce such a system.

224. (f) The reason for the new second paragraph of Article 44 relates to the jurisdiction of the Danish administrative authorities (see paragraph 67) whose services are free. No question of legal aid therefore arises. The new provision is designed to ensure that the enforcement of

Danish maintenance orders is not, for this reason, at a disadvantage in the other EEC countries by comparison with maintenance orders from EEC countries other than Denmark.

[OJ C59, 5.3.79, p 135]

Section 3
Common provisions

225. The discussion of Articles 46 to 49 centred on whether the new Member States, in accordance with their legal tradition, could require an affidavit, in particular to the effect that none of the grounds for refusing recognition, specified in Articles 27 and 28, obtain. Affidavit evidence is certainly admissible in appellate proceedings, where the debtor appeals against registration or against a declaration of enforceability, or the creditor against a refusal to register. However, all the other means of giving evidence which are normally admissible must also be available in those proceedings.

The addition to Article 46(2) is proposed for the reasons given in paragraphs 182 and 194.

[3047E]

CHAPTER 6
AUTHENTIC INSTRUMENTS AND COURT SETTLEMENTS

226. In England and Ireland there is no equivalent of enforceable instruments. In Scotland, instruments establishing a clearly defined obligation to perform a contract can be entered in a public register. An extract from the public register can then serve as a basis for enforcement in the same way as a court judgment. Such extracts are covered by Article 50.

In the United Kingdom, the courts having jurisdiction for recognition and enforcement of maintenance orders are different from those concerned with other kinds of judgment (see paragraphs 210 and 218). It is for the internal law of the United Kingdom to determine whether foreign court settlements concerning maintenance should be treated as maintenance orders or as other judgments.

[3047F]

CHAPTER 7
GENERAL PROVISIONS

227. The outcome of the discussion of Articles 52 and 53 has already been recorded elsewhere (see paragraphs 73 *et seq*, and 119).

[3047G]

CHAPTER 8
TRANSITIONAL PROVISIONS

228. Article 54 continues to apply to the relationships between the original Member States. For their relationships with the new Member States, and the relationships of the new Member States with each other, an appropriate transitional provision is included in Article 34 of the proposed Accession Convention. It is closely modelled on Article 54 of the 1968 Convention, but takes into account the fact that the latter has already been in force in its present form between the original Member States since 1 February 1973, and also the fact that some amendments are to be made to it. Finally, the Interpretation Protocol of 3 June 1971 also had to be taken into account in the transitional rules. The detailed provisions are as follows:[58]

[OJ C59, 5.3.79, p 137]

I. JURISDICTION

229. 1. The provisions on jurisdiction in the 1968 Convention apply in the new Member States only in their amended version and only to proceedings instituted after the Accession Convention has come into force, and hence after the 1968 Convention has come into force, in the State in question (Article 34(1)).

230. 2. The amended version also applies to proceedings instituted in the original Member States after that date. Jurisdiction in respect of proceedings instituted in the original Member States before that date but after 1 February 1973 will continue to be determined in accordance with the original text of the 1968 Convention (Article 34(1)). It is to be noted, as

regards the relationships of the old Member States with each other, that under Article 39 of the Accession Convention the amended version can only come into force simultaneously for all six of them.

II. RECOGNITION AND ENFORCEMENT

1. End of the transitional period

231. The recognition and enforcement of judgments are in all respects governed by the Convention as amended, provided the transitional period had already ended at the time of institution of the proceedings. For this purpose, the Accession Convention must have come into force by that time both in the State of origin and in the State subsequently addressed (Article 34(1)). It is not sufficient for the Accession Convention to be in force in the former State only, since rules of exorbitant jurisdiction may still be invoked under Article 4 of the 1968 Convention against domiciliaries of the State subsequently addressed if that State was not also a party to the Accession Convention at the time of institution of the proceedings. This would render an obligation to recognize and enforce a judgment in that State without any preliminary review unacceptable. If we assume that the Accession Convention comes into force for the original Member States of the Community and Denmark on 1 January 1981 and an action is brought in Germany against a person domiciled in Denmark on 3 January 1981, then a judgment on 1 July 1981 finding in favour of the plaintiff would be enforceable irrespective of transitional provisions, even if, say, the United Kingdom did not become a party to the Convention until 1 December 1981. However, if in this example the action was brought and judgment given against a person domiciled in the United Kingdom, Article 34(1) would not govern recognition and enforcement in the United Kingdom. That would be a true transitional case.

Paragraphs (2) and (3) of Article 34 deal with judgments during the transitional period, i e judgments given after the Accession Convention has come into force in the State addressed, but in proceedings which were instituted at a time when, either in the State of origin or in the State addressed, the Accession Convention was not yet in force. In Article 34(2) and (3) a distinction is drawn between cases involving only the original Member States of the Community and those involving new Member States as well.

2. Among the original Member States of the Community

232. Article 34(2) makes the recognition and enforcement of judgments among the original Member States of the Community subject without any restriction to the 1968 Convention as amended, even if the actions were started before the entry into force of the Accession Convention, which will necessarily be simultaneous in those States (see the end of paragraph 230). This amounts indirectly to a statement that the situation as regards the recognition and enforcement of judgments among those States remains that in Article 54 of the 1968 Convention in the case of judgments given before the entry into force of the Accession Convention. The most important implication of Article 34(2) is that in proceedings for the recognition of judgments among the original Member States of the Community there is to be no consideration of whether the court giving the judgment whose recognition is sought would have had jurisdiction after the entry into force of the Accession Convention. If the action was started after 1 February 1973 then the jurisdiction of the court giving the judgment whose recognition is sought may no longer be examined. The point is of note since that court's jurisdiction could still have been founded on exorbitant jurisdictional rules where domiciliaries of the new Member States are concerned.

[OJ C59, 5.3.79, p 138]

To illustrate the point with an example, if a Frenchman were in 1978 to bring an action in the French courts pursuant to Article 14 of the Civil Code against a person domiciled in Ireland, which would be possible under Article 4 of the 1968 Convention, and judgment was given in favour of the plaintiff in 1982; then, assuming the Accession Convention came into force for the original Member States of the Community and Ireland in 1981, the judgment would have to be recognized and enforced in Germany, but not in Ireland.

3. Where new Member States are involved

233. The arrangements obtaining under Article 34(3) for the recognition and enforcement of judgments between the original Member States and the new Member States, or as between the new Member States, differ somewhat from those applying among the

original Member States. Article 34(3) is concerned with the possibility of recognition and enforcement being sought in one of the new Contracting States of a judgment from an original Contracting State or from another new Contracting State. Apart from the cases referred to in paragraph 231, this is possible after the end of the transitional period, subject to three requirements being met.

234. (a) The judgment must have been given after the Accession Convention came into force in both States.

235. (b) In addition, the proceedings must have been instituted, in the words of the Convention, before "the date of entry into force of this Convention, between the State of origin and the State addressed". The purport of this is that, at the time when the proceedings were instituted, the Accession Convention may have come into force either in the State of the court giving the judgment for which recognition is sought, or in the State in which recognition and enforcement are subsequently sought, but not in both of these States.

236. (c) Finally, the jurisdiction of the court giving the judgment for which recognition is sought must satisfy certain criteria which the court in the State addressed must check. These criteria exactly match what Article 54 of the 1968 Convention laid down regarding transitional cases which were pending when that Convention came into force between the six original Member States. In proceedings for recognition, the jurisdiction of the court which gave judgment is to be accepted as having been valid, provided one of two requirements is met:

(aa) The judgment must be recognized where the court in the State of origin would have had jurisdiction if the Accession Convention had already been in force as between the two States at the time when the proceedings were instituted.

(bb) The judgment must also be recognized where the court's jurisdiction was covered at the time when the proceedings were instituted by another international convention which was in force between the two States.

Reverting to the example in paragraph 232, the position would be as follows: the French judgment would indeed have been given after the Accession Convention had come into force in Ireland and France. The proceedings would have been instituted at a time when the Accession Convention was not yet in force in France (or in Ireland). Had this Convention already been in force as between France and Ireland at that time, the French courts would no longer have been able to found their jurisdiction on Article 14 of the Civil Code and hence, it must further be assumed, would have been unable to assume jurisdiction. Lastly, there is no bilateral convention between France and Ireland concerning the direct or indirect jurisdiction of the courts. Consequently, the judgment would not have had to be recognized in Ireland.

If one changes the example so that it now concerns France and the United Kingdom, one has to take into consideration the Convention between those two States of 18 January 1934 providing for the reciprocal enforcement of judgments. However, jurisdiction deriving from Article 14 of the Civil Code is not admitted under that Convention; thus the judgment would not have to be recognized in the United Kingdom either.

[OJ C59, 5.3.79, p 139]

If the example concerned Germany and the United Kingdom, and the defendant resident in the United Kingdom had agreed orally before the commencement of the proceedings that the German courts should have jurisdiction, then under the 1968 Convention the judgment would have to be recognized and enforced in the United Kingdom. Under ArticeI V(1)(a) of the Convention between the United Kingdom and Germany of 14 July 1960, oral agreement is sufficient to give grounds for jurisdiction for the purposes of recognition ("indirect" jurisdiction). However, the German court would have had to be a "Landgericht", since "Amtsgericht" judgments are not required to be recognized under that Convention (Article I(2)). In the event of a written agreement on jurisdiction, even the judgment of an "Amtsgericht" would have to be recognized, under Article 34(3) of the Accession Convention, as the "Amtsgericht" would in that case have assumed jurisdiction under circumstances in which jurisdiction would also have had to be assumed if the Accession Convention had been in force between Germany and the United Kingdom.

[3047H]

CHAPTER 9
RELATIONSHIP TO OTHER CONVENTIONS

I. ARTICLES 55 AND 56

237. The Working Party included in Article 55 the bilateral conventions between the United Kingdom and other Member States of the Community. No such conventions have been concluded by Ireland and Denmark.

II. ARTICLE 57[59]

1. The basic structure of the proposed provision

238. Great difficulties arose when an attempt was made to explain to the new Member States the exact scope of Article 57, the main reason being the statement that the Convention "shall not affect" any conventions in relation to particular matters, without stating how the provisions in such conventions could be reconciled with those of the 1968 Convention where they covered only part of the matters governed by the latter, which is usually the case. Special conventions can be divided into three groups. Many of them contain only provisions on direct jurisdiction, as in the case with the Warsaw Convention of 12 October 1929 for the unification of certain rules relating to international carriage by air and the Additional Protocols thereto,* and the Brussels Convention relating to the arrest of seagoing ships which is of great importance for maritime law (Article 7) (see paragraph 121). Most conventions govern only the recognition and enforcement of judgments, and merely refer indirectly to jurisdiction in so far as it constitutes a precondition for recognition. This is the case with the Hague Convention of 15 April 1958 on the recognition and enforcement of decisions relating to maintenance obligations towards children. Finally, there are also Conventions which contain provisions directly regulating jurisdiction as well as recognition and enforcement, as for example the Berne Convention on carriage by rail and the Mannheim Convention for the navigation of the Rhine. It is irrelevant for present purposes whether the conventions contain additional provisions on the applicable law or rules of substantive law.

NOTES

* Not to be confused with the Brussels Convention of the same date for the unification of certain rules relating to penal jurisdiction in matters of collision.

[OJ C59, 5.3.79, p 140]

239. (a) It is clear beyond argument that where a special convention contains no provisions directly governing jurisdiction, the jurisdiction provisions of the 1968 Convention apply. It is equally clear that where all the Contracting States are parties to a special convention containing provisions on jurisdiction, those provisions prevail. But for situations between these two extremes the solution provided by Article 57 is a great deal less clear. This is particularly the case for a number of questions, which arise where only the State of origin and the State addressed are parties to the special convention. The problems become acute where only one of these two States is a party. If both States are parties to a special convention which governs only direct jurisdiction, will the provisions of the 1968 Convention regarding examination of jurisdiction by the court of its own motion (Article 20), *lis pendens* (Article 21) and enforcement apply? Do the provisions of the 1968 Convention on the procedure for recognition and enforcement apply, if a special convention on the recognition and enforcement of judgments does not deal with procedure? Can a person domiciled in a Contracting State which is not a party to a special convention be sued in the courts of another Contracting State on the basis of jurisdiction provisions in the special conventions, or can the State of domicile which is not a party to the special convention claim that the jurisdiction rules of the 1968 Convention must be observed? Must a judgment given in a court which has jurisdiction only under a special convention be recognized and enforced even in a Contracting State which is not a party to that particular special convention? And, finally, what is the position where the special convention does not claim to be exclusive?

240. (b) Tentative and conflicting views were expressed within the Working Party as to how these problems were to be solved in interpreting Article 57 in its original form. It become clear that it would not be practicable to provide a precise solution to all of them, particularly since it is impossible to predict the form of future conventions. It was however appropriate, in the interests of clarifying the obligations about to be assumed by the new Member States, to include in the Accession Convention an authentic interpretation which concerns some problems which are of especial importance. The opportunity was taken to make a drafting improvement to the present Article 57 of the 1968 Convention—the new paragraph 1 of this Article—which will speak of recognition or enforcement. By reason of the purely drafting nature of the amendment to the text, the provision laying down the authentic interpretation of the new Article 57(1) also applies to the present version.

The solution arrived at is based on the following principles. The 1968 Convention contains the rules generally applicable in all Member States; provisions in special conventions are special rules which every State may make prevail over the 1968 Convention by becoming a party to such a convention. In so far as a special convention does not contain rules covering a particular matter the 1968 Convention applies. This is also the case where the special convention includes rules of jurisdiction which do not altogether fit the inter-connecting provisions of the various parts of the 1968 Convention, especially those governing the relationship between jurisdiction and enforcement. The overriding considerations are simplicity and clarity of the legal position.

The most important consequence of this is that provisions on jurisdiction contained in special conventions are to be regarded as if they were provisions of the 1968 Convention itself, even if only one Member State is a Contracting Party to such a special convention. Even Member States which are not Contracting Parties to the special convention must therefore recognize and enforce decisions given by courts which have jurisdiction only under the special convention. Furthermore, in the context of two States which are parties to a special convention, a person who wishes to obtain the recognition or enforcement of a judgment may rely upon the procedural provisions of the 1968 Convention on recognition and enforcement.

At the same time, the Working Party did not wish to reach a final conclusion on the question whether the general principle outlined above could be consistently applied in all its ramifications. To take a critical example, it was left open whether exclusive jurisdiction under the provisions of a special convention must invariably be applied. The same applies to the question whether a case of *lis pendens* arising from a special convention is covered by Article 21 of the 1968 Convention. The Working Party therefore preferred to provide expressly for the application of Article 20 and to leave the solution of the outstanding problems to legal literature and case law. For the implications of an authentic interpretation of Article 57 for maritime jurisdiction, see paragraph 121.

2. *Examples*

241. A river boatman domiciled in the Netherlands is liable for damages arising from an accident which occurred on the upper Rhine. It is however no longer possible to determine whether the harmful event occurred on German or French territory or from where the damage emanated.

[OJ C59, 5.3.79, p 141]

242. It is not possible in such a case for either German or French courts to assume jurisdiction under Article 5(3) or any other provision of the 1968 Convention. According to Article 34(2)(c) and Article 35a of the revised Rhine navigation Convention of 17 October 1868 in the version of the Protocol of 25 October 1972,[60] jurisdiction in such cases belongs to the court of the State which was the first or only one seised of the matter. That court must, however, take into account Article 20 of the 1968 Convention, even though no equivalent of this Article exists in the Rhine Navigation Convention. For example, if the defendant fails to enter an appearance, the court must of its own motion (see paragraph 22) ascertain whether all means have been exhausted of determining exactly where the accident occurred, for only if this cannot be determined does the court have jurisdiction under the abovementioned provisions of the Rhine Navigation Convention.

243. If the court first seised of the matter was French, then any judgment of that court must be recognized in Germany. The Rhine Navigation Convention is even stricter than the 1968 Convention in forbidding any re-examination of the original judgment in the State addressed. According to the correct interpretation of Article 57 of the 1968 Convention the judgment creditor has the choice of availing himself of the enforcement procedure provided by the Rhine Navigation Convention or by the 1968 Convention. However, if he proceeds under the 1968 Convention the court may not refuse recognition on any of the grounds given in Article 27 or Article 28 of the 1968 Convention. Unlike the enforcement procedure itself, the conditions for recognition and enforcement are exclusively governed by the special conventions—in this example, the Rhine Navigation Convention.

244. If, however, a judgment has been given in the court with jurisdiction at the place of destination pursuant to Article 28(1) of the Warsaw Convention of 12 October 1929 for the unification of certain rules relating to international carriage by air, the 1968 Convention applies fully to both recognition and enforcement, because the Warsaw Convention contains no provisions at all on these matters. The same applies where in maritime law the jurisdiction of the court of origin was based on the provisions governing arrest contained in the 1952 Brussels Convention (see paragraph 121).

245. If the boatman in the above example on Rhine Navigation had been domiciled in Luxembourg, which is not a party to the Rhine Navigation Convention, the position would be as follows: any jurisdiction assumed in France or Germany pursuant to the Rhine navigation

Convention can no longer be regarded in Luxembourg as an infringement of the 1968 Convention. Under the provisions and procedure of the 1968 Convention, Luxembourg is obliged to recognize and enforce a judgment given by the German or French Rhine navigation courts. If, conversely, the boatman is sued in the court of his Luxembourg domicile, which is also permissible, under the 1968 Convention, Germany and France would have to accept this, even though they are parties to the Rhine Navigation Convention which does not recognize jurisdiction based on domicile.

3. Undertakings in Conventions between States not to recognize judgments

246. Whether Article 57 also covers conventions under which one Member State of the Community undertakes not to recognize judgments given in another Member State remains an open question. It could be argued that the admissible scope of such conventions was governed exclusively by Article 59.

International obligations of this sort can result from a special convention which provides for the exclusive jurisdiction of the courts of one of the Contracting Parties. Such an obligation can however also result indirectly from the fact that the exercise of jurisdiction under the special convention is linked to a special regime of liability. For example, the Paris Convention of 1960 on third party liability in the field of nuclear energy, apart from laying down rules of jurisdiction, recognition and enforcement:

1. places the sole liability for damage on the operator of a nuclear installation;
2. makes his liability an absolute one;
3. sets maximum limits to his liability;

[OJ C59, 5.3.79, p 142]

4. requires him to insure against his liability;
5. allows a Contracting State to provide additional compensation from public funds.

The recognition and enforcement of a judgment which is given in a State not party to such a special convention and which is based on legal principles quite different from those outlined above could seriously undermine the operation of that special convention.

The 1968 Convention should always be interpreted in such a way that no limitations of liability contained in international conventions are infringed. The question however remains open whether this result is to be achieved by applying the public policy provision of Article 27(1), by analogy with the new paragraph (5) of Article 27, or by a broad interpretation of Article 57.

For conventions limiting liability in maritime law, see paragraph 124 *et seq.*

4. Precedence of secondary community law

247. Within the Working Party opinion was divided as to whether secondary Community law, or national laws adopted pursuant to secondary Community law, prevail over international agreements concluded between the Member States, in particular in the case of a convention provided for in Article 220 of the Treaty of Rome. There was, however, agreement that national and Community law referred to above should prevail over the 1968 Convention. This decision is embodied in Article 57; the provision is based on Article 25 of the preliminary draft Convention on the law applicable to contractual and non-contractual obligations.

5. Consultations before the future accession by Member States of the community to further agreements

248. By their accession to the Convention, the new Member States are also bound by the Joint Declaration made by the Contracting States at the time of the signing of the 1968 Convention. In the Declaration the States declare that they will arrange for regular periodic contacts between their representatives. The Working Party was unanimously of the opinion that consultations should also take place when a Member State intended to accede to a convention which would prevail over the 1968 Convention by virtue of Article 57.

III. ARTICLE 59

249. This provision refers only to judgments given against persons domiciled or habitually resident outside the Community. Such persons may also be sued on the basis of

jurisdictional provisions which could not be invoked in the case of persons domiciled within the Community, and which are classed as exorbitant and disallowed pursuant to the second paragraph of Article 3. Nevertheless, any judgment which may have been given is to be recognized and enforced in accordance with the 1968 Convention. As the Jenard report explains, it is intended that the Contracting States should remain free to conclude conventions with third States excluding the recognition and enforcement of judgments based on exorbitant jurisdictions—even though the 1968 Convention permits this in exceptional cases. The aim of the proposed amendment to Article 59 is further to limit the possibility of recognition and enforcement.

250. The way this will work may be illustrated by an example. If a creditor has a claim to be satisfied in France against a debtor domiciled in that country, then Danish courts have no jurisdiction under any circumstances to decide this issue, even if the debtor has property in Denmark and even if the claim is secured on immovable property there. Supposing the debtor is domiciled in Norway, then if Danish national law so allows Danish courts may very well claim jurisdiction, e g on the basis of the presence in Denmark of property owned by the debtor. Normally, the judgment given in such a case would also be enforceable in the United Kingdom. The United Kingdom could however undertake in a convention with Norway an obligation to refuse recognition and enforcement of such a judgment. This kind of treaty obligation may not however extend to a case where the jurisdiction of the Danish courts is based on the ground that immovable property in, Denmark constitutes security for the debt. In such circumstances, the judgment would be enforceable even in the United Kingdom.

[3047I]

[OJ C59, 5.3.79, p 143]

CHAPTER 10
FINAL PROVISIONS

1. IRELAND

251. Ireland has no territorial possessions outside the integral parts of its territory.

2. UNITED KINGDOM

252. The term “United Kingdom” does not include the Channel Islands, the Isle of Man, Gibraltar or the Sovereign Base Areas in Cyprus. There is no obligation on the United Kingdom to extend the scope of the 1968 Convention to include these territories, even though it is responsible for their external relations. It might, however, be useful if the United Kingdom were to extend the 1968 Convention and it should be authorized to do so. It would have to undertake the necessary “adjustments” itself, and there was no need to provide for them in the Accession Convention. The following adjustments would be required: indication of any exorbitant jurisdictions in the second paragraph of Article 3; a declaration as to whether in the newly included territories every appeal should be regarded as an ordinary appeal for the purposes of Articles 30 and 38; a declaration as to whether registration in any such territory in accordance with the second paragraph of Article 31 is effective only within its area; establishing which courts are competent under Articles 32, 37 and 40, the form in which the application should be made, and whether the adjustments in respect of the United Kingdom contained in the second paragraph of Article 37 as amended and in Article 41 as amended should also apply in the newly included territories. If any international conventions should apply to any one of the territories in question, appropriate adjustments would also have to be made to Article 55.

The penultimate paragraph of the proposed addition to Article 60 relates to the fact that judgments of courts in these territories which do not belong to the United Kingdom can be challenged in the last instance before the Judicial Committee of the Privy Council. It would be illogical to bring Privy Council decisions within the scope of the 1968 Convention if they related to disputes arising in territories to which the 1968 Convention does not apply.

3. DENMARK

253. For the purposes of EEC law, Greenland is included in the European territory of Denmark. The special constitutional positions of the Faroe Islands led to a solution corresponding closely to that proposed for the territories for whose foreign relations the United Kingdom is responsible. This had to allow for the fact that both appellate and first

instance proceedings which relate to the Faroes and are therefore conducted under the Code of Civil Procedure specially enacted for these islands can be brought in Copenhagen.

4. CHANGES IN A STATE'S TERRITORY

254. The Working Party was unanimous that any territory which becomes independent of the mother country thereby ceases to be a member of the European Community and, consequently, can no longer be a party to the 1968 Convention. It was unnecessary to provide for this expressly and, in any case, to have drafted such a provision would have gone beyond the Working Party's terms of reference.

[3047J]

CHAPTER 11
ADJUSTMENTS TO THE PROTOCOL OF 3 JUNE 1971 ON THE INTERPRETATION BY THE COURT OF JUSTICE OF THE EUROPEAN COMMUNITIES OF THE 1968 CONVENTION

1. FORMAL ADJUSTMENTS

[OJ C59, 5.3.79, p 144]

255. Formal adjustments to the Interpretation Protocol were few and fairly obvious. It became necessary to make only one short addition to its provisions: the courts in the new Member States which, in accordance with Article 2(1) and Article 3, are required to request the Court of Justice to give preliminary rulings on questions of interpretation, had to be designated.[61] In the United Kingdom, unlike the other Member States, not only the highest court within the country has been included, as it is more difficult to refer a matter to the House of Lords than it is to have recourse to the highest courts on the continent. Therefore, at least the appellate proceedings provided for in the second paragraph of Article 37 and in Article 41 of the 1968 Convention should in the United Kingdom also terminate in a court which is obliged to request a preliminary ruling from the Court of Justice. The expression "appellate capacity" in Article 2(2) should not be construed in a narrow technical sense, but in the sense of any challenge before a higher jurisdiction, so that it might be taken also to include the French "contredit".

The remaining formal adjustments concerned merely the scope (Article 1) and territorial application of the Protocol. Article 6, which deals with the latter point, is wholly based on Article 60 of the 1968 Convention (see paragraphs 251 to 254). Which authorities are to be designated as competent within the meaning of the third paragraph of Article 4 is a question to be decided entirely by the new Member States.

2. THE SPECIAL NATURE OF IMPLEMENTING LEGISLATION IN THE UNITED KINGDOM AND IRELAND

256. The extension of the Interpretation Protocol to the United Kingdom and Ireland will, however, in all probability also present a procedural problem. A long-standing legal tradition in these States does not allow provisions of international treaties to become directly applicable as national law. In the United Kingdom legislation has to be passed transforming such provisions into national law. In many cases the legislative enactment does not follow precisely the wording of the treaty. The usual form of legislation in this State often calls for a more detailed phraseology than that used in a treaty. The treaty and the corresponding national law are, therefore, to be carefully distinguished.

If the implementing legislation in the United Kingdom follows the usual pattern, courts in that country would only rarely be concerned with the interpretation of the 1968 Convention, but mostly with interpretation of the national implementing legislation. Only when the latter is not clear would it be open to a court, under the existing rules of construction in that country, to refer to the treaty on which the legislation is based, and only when the court is then faced with a problem of interpretation of the treaty may it turn to the European Court of Justice. If the provisions of implementing legislation are clear in themselves, the courts in the United Kingdom may as a rule refer neither to the text of the treaty nor to any decision by an international court on its interpretation.

This would undoubtedly lead to a certain disparity in the application of the Interpretation Protocol of 3 June 1971. The Working Party was of the opinion that this disparity could best be redressed if the United Kingdom could in some way ensure in its implementing legislation that the 1968 Convention will there too be endowed with the status of a source of law, or may at any rate be referred to directly when applying the national implementing legislation.

In the event of a judgment of the European Court of Justice being inconsistent with a provision of the United Kingdom implementing legislation, the latter would have to be amended.

It is also the case in Ireland that international agreements to which that State is a party are not directly applicable as national law. Lately, however, a number of Acts putting international agreements into force in national law have taken the form of an incorporation of the text of the agreement into national law. If the Act putting into force the 1968 Convention as amended by the Accession Convention were to take this form, the problems described above in relation to the United Kingdom would not arise in the case of Ireland.

[3047K]

[OJ C59, 5.3.79, p 145]

ANNEX I
EXTRACT FROM THE PROTOCOL TO THE PRELIMINARY DRAFT BANKRUPTCY CONVENTION (1975) (SEE PARAGRAPH 54)

Certain details of this list have been amended by later documents which, however, are not themselves final.

(aa) *Bankruptcy proceedings:*
Belgium:
"faillite"—"faillissement";
Denmark:
"Konkurs";
Federal Republic of Germany:
"Konkurs";
France:
"liquidation des biens";
Ireland:
"bankruptcy", "winding-up in bankruptcy of partnerships", "winding-up by the court under Sections 213, 344 and 345 of the Companies Act 1963", "creditors' voluntary winding-up under Section 256 of the Companies Act 1963",
Italy:
"fallimento";
Luxembourg:
"faillite";
Netherlands:
"faillissement",
United Kingdom:
"bankruptcy" (England, Wales and Northern Ireland), "sequestration" (Scotland), "administration in bankruptcy of the estates of persons dying insolvent" (England, Wales and Northern Ireland), "compulsory winding-up of companies", winding-up of companies under the supervision of the court".

(bb) *Other proceedings:*
Belgium:
"concordat judiciaire"—"gerechtelijk akkoord",
"sursis de paiement"—"uitstel van betaling";
Denmark:
"tvangsakkord",
"likvidation af insolvente aktieselskaber eller anpartsselskaber",
"likvidation af banker eller sparekasser, der har standset deres betalinger";
Federal Republic of Germany:
"gerichtliches Vergleichsverfahren";
France:
"règlement judiciaire",
"procédure de suspension provisoire des poursuites et d'apurement collectif du passif de certaines entreprises";
Ireland:
"arrangements under the control of the court", "arrangements, reconstructions and compositions of companies whether or not in the course of liquidation where sanction of the court is required and creditors' rights are affected";

Italy:
"concordato preventivo",
"amministrazione controllata",
"liquidazione coatta amministrativa"—in its judicial stage;
Luxembourg:
"concordat préventif de la faillite",
"sursis de paiement",
"régime spécial de liquidation applicable aux notaires",
Netherlands:
"surséance van betaling",
"regeling, vervat in de wet op de vergadering van houders van schuldbrieven aan toonder",
United Kingdom:
"compositions and schemes of arrangement" (England and Wales),
"compositions" (Northern Ireland),
"arrangements under the control of the court" (Northern Ireland),
"judicial compositions" (Scotland),
"arrangements, reconstructions and compositions of companies whether or not in the course of liquidation where sanction of the court is required and creditors' rights are involved",
"creditors' voluntary winding-up of companies",
"deeds of arrangement approved by the court" (Northern Ireland). **[3047L]**

[OJ C59, 5.3.79, p 147]

ANNEX II

1 When references are given to Articles without any further mention, reference is to the 1968 version of the Convention.
2 The Royal Decree of 13 April 1938, reproduced in "Bundesanzeiger" 1953, No 105, p 1 and in Bülow-Arnold, "Internationaler Rechtsverkehr", 925.5.
3 For this concept, see the Jenard report, Chapter II, B and C, and Chapter IV, A and B.
4 Zweigert-Kötz, "Einführung in die Rechtsvergleichung auf dem Gebiet des Privatrechts", Vol 1 (1971), p 78 *et seq.*
5 Case No 29/76 *[1976]* ECR 1541. The formal part of the Judgment reads as follows:
1. In the interpretation of the concept "civil and commercial matters" for the purposes of the application of the Convention of 27 September 1968 on jurisdiction and the enforcement of judgments in civil and commercial matters, in particular Title III thereof, reference must not be made to the law of one of the States concerned but, first, to the objectives and scheme of the Convention and, secondly, to the general principles which stem from the corpus of the national legal systems;
2. A judgment given in an action between a public authority and a person governed by private law, in which the public authority has acted in the exercise of its powers, is excluded from the area of application of the Convention.
6 Law No 75—617, JO 1975, 7171.
7 In the text of Law No 75—617 (note[6]).
8 Document of the Commission of the European Communities XI/449/75—F.
9 The word "analogous" does not appear in Article 1(1) simply because the proceedings in question are listed in a Protocol.
10 See the Report on the Convention on bankruptcy, winding-up arrangements, compositions and similar proceedings by Noël-Lemontey (16.775/XIV/70) Chapter 3, section I.
11 See preliminary draft Bankruptcy Convention, Article 17 and Protocol thereto, Articles 1 and 2 (note 8).
12 *op cit.*
13 1975 preliminary draft (see note[8]), Article 1(1), subparagraph (3), and Article II of the Protocol. See Noël-Lemontey report (note[10]) for reasons for exclusion.
14 Although it does not have its own legal personality it corresponds by and large to the "offene Handelsgesellschaft" in German law and the "société en nom collectif" in French law.
15 In the form of a "private company" it corresponds to the continental "Gesellschaft mit beschränkter Haftung" (company with limited liability) and in the form of a "public company" to the continental "Aktiengesellschaft" (joint stock company).
16 UK: Bankruptcy Act 1914, Sections 119 and 126. See Tridmann-Hicks-Johnson, "Bankruptcy Law and Practice" (1970), page 272.
17 In respect of Great Britain—Companies Act 1948; in respect of Northern Ireland—Companies Acts 1960 and Companies (Amendment) Act 1963; in respect of Ireland—Company Act 1963, Section 213.
18 "if ... the company is unable to pay its debts".
19 Decree No 75—1123 of 5 December 1975, (JO) 1975, 1251.
20 The adjustment proposed for Article 57 admittedly has certain repercussions on the scope of Article 20 (see paragraph 240).

21 The following cases may be mentioned with regard to difficulties of interpretation which have arisen hitherto in judicial practice in connection with the application of Articles 5 and 6: Corte Cassazione Italiana of 4 June 1974, "Giur. it." 1974, 18 (with regard to the concept of place of performance); Corte Cassazione Italiana No 3397 of 20 October 1975 (place of performance in the case of deliveries via a forwarding agent who has an obligation to instal); Tribunal de Grande Instance Paris D 1975, 638 with commentary by Droz (place where the harmful event occurred in cases of illegal publication in the press); Court of Justice of the European Communities, 6 October 1976, Case No 12/76 *[1976]* ECR 1473.

22 In the judgments referred to the formal parts of the judgments read as follows:

The "place of performance of the obligation in question" within the meaning of Article 5(1) of the Convention of 27 September 1968 on jurisdiction and the enforcement of judgments in civil and commercial matters is to be determined in accordance with the law which governs the obligation in question according to the rules of conflict of laws of the court before which the matter is brought (Case No 12/76).

In disputes in which the grantee of an exclusive sales concession is charging the grantor with having infringed the exclusive concession, the word "obligation" contained in Article 5(1) of the Convention of 27 September 1968 on jurisdiction and the enforcement of judgments in civil and commercial matters refers to the contractual obligation forming the basis of the legal proceedings, namely the obligation of the grantor which corresponds to the contractual right relied upon by the grantee in support of the application (Case No 14/76 [1976] ECR 1497).

In disputes concerning the consequences of the infringement by the grantor of a contract conferring an exclusive concession, such as the payment of damages or the dissolution of the contract, the obligation to which reference must be made for the purposes of applying Article 5(1) of the Convention is that which the contract imposes on the grantor and the non-performance of which is relied upon by the grantee in support of the application for damages or for the dissolution of the contract (Case No 14/76).

In the case of actions for payment of compensation by way of damages, it is for the national court to ascertain whether, under the law applicable to the contract, an independent contractual obligation or an obligation replacing the unperformed contractual obligation is involved (Case No 14/76).

When the grantee of an exclusive sales concession is not subject either to the control or to the direction of the grantor, he cannot be regarded as being at the head of a branch, agency or other establishment of the grantor within the meaning of Article 5(5) of the Convention of 27 September 1968 (Case No 14/76).

Where the place of the happening of the event which may give rise to liability in tort, delict or quasi-delict and the place where that event results in damage are not identical, the expression "place where the harmful event occurred" in Article 5(3) of the Convention of 27 September 1968 on jurisdiction and the enforcement of judgments in civil and commercial matters must be understood as being intended to cover both the place where the damage occurred and the place of the event giving rise to it (Case No 21/76 [1976] ECR 1735).

The result is that the defendant may be sued, at the option of the plaintiff, either in the courts for the place where the damage occurred or in the courts for the place of the event which gives rise to and is at the origin of that damage (Case No 21/76).

23 Divorce law of 1 December 1970, No 898, Article 5.

24 Law of 11 July 1975, new Article 281 of the Code civil.

25 Chapter III, end of Section IV.

26 Stein-Jonas (Münzberg) (note[27]), paragraph 765 a II 3 with reference to case law in note [28].

27 Stein-Jonas (Leipold) "Kommentar zur Zivilprozeßordnung", 19th ed, paragraph 323 II 2 c and other references.

28 In the case of France: Cour de Cassation of 21 July 1954 D 1955, 185.

29 Magistrates' Court Rules 1952, r 34 (2), and Rayden's "Law and Practice in Divorce and Family Matters" (1971), p 1181.

30 Bromley, "Family Law", 4th ed (1971), p 451 containing references to case-law.

31 Section 9 of the Maintenance Orders (Reciprocal Enforcement) Act 1972.

32 AE Anton, "Private International Law" (1967), p 470; Graveson, "The Conflict of Laws" (1969), p 565; Lord President Clyde in Clarks Trustee Petitioners 1966 SLT 249, p 251.

33 *op cit.*

34 The new Convention on limitation of liability for maritime claims, signed in London on 19 November 1976, was not yet in force at the end of the Working Party's discussions.

35 The Court of Justice of the European Communities has already decided in this sense: see judgment of 6 October 1976 (Case No 14/76).

36 In 1974 the premium income from overseas business amounted to no less than £3 045 million, £520 million of which consisted of business with Member States of the EEC, and 10% of which was accounted for by re-insurance business. A sizeable proportion of this insurance market consisted of marine and aviation insurance. For these classes alone the overseas premium income amounted to £535 million including £50 million worth of business with other EEC countries.

37 Extract from "Pflichtversicherung in den Europäischen Gemeinschaften", a study by Professor Ernst Steindorff, Munich.

38 The Landgericht of Aachen (NJW 76,487) refused to endorse this standpoint.

39 Germany: Bürgerliches Gesetzbuch, Book 3, Sections 3–8; France: Code civil, Book 2, and Book 3, Title XVII, Title XVIII, Chapters II and III; Italy: Codice civile, Book 3, Titles 4–6, Book 6, Title 3, Chapter 2, Section III, and Chapter 4.

40 Megarry and Baker, "The Law of Real Property", 5th ed (1969), p 71 *et seq*, p 79 *et seq.*

41 Megarry and Baker, *op cit*, p 546.

42 R David, "Les grands systèmes de droit contemporains", 5th ed (1973) No 311.

43 Stein-Jonas (Pohle) (note [27]), paragraph 24 III 2.

44 Code de procédure civile, Article 46, third indent; "Vincent, Procédure Civile", 16th ed (1973) No 291.

45 From past case law: Brunswick Landgericht, Recht der internationalen Wirtschaft/ Außenwirtschaftsdienst des Betriebsberaters (RIW/AWD) 74, 346 (written confirmation must actually be preceded by oral agreement); Hamburg Oberlandesgericht (RIW/AWD) 1975, 498 (no effective jurisdiction agreement where general terms of business are exchanged which are mutually contradictory); Munich Oberlandesgericht (RIW/AWD) 75,694; Italian Corte di Cassazione No 3397 of 20 October 1975 (written confirmation, containing a jurisdiction clause for the first time, is not of itself sufficient); Bundesgerichtshof, MDR 77, p 1013 (confirmation of an order by the seller not sufficient when the buyer has previously refused the incorporation); Heidelberg Landgericht (RIW/AWD) 76, p 532 (reference to general conditions of sale not sufficient); Frankfurt Oberlandesgericht (RIW/AWD) 76, p 532 (reference to general conditions of sale for the first time in the confirmation of the order from the supplier; reminder from the seller does not conclusively incorporate the jurisdiction clause included in the conditions); Düsseldorf Oberlandesgericht (RIW/AWD) 76, p 297 (jurisdiction clause contained in the condition of a bill of lading of no effect against persons who themselves have given no written declaration); Pretura of Brescia, Foro it. 1976 No 1, Column I 250 (subsequent national law prevails over Article 17); Tribunal of Aix-en-Provence of 10 May 1974, Dalloz 74, p 760 (jurisdiction agreements in favour of the courts of the employer's domicile may be entered into even in contracts of employment); Tribunal de commerce of Brussels, Journal des Tribunaux 1976, 210 (Article 17 has precedence over contrary national law).

46 As correctly stated by von Hoffmann (RIW/AWD) 1973, 57 (63); Droz ("Compétence judiciaire et effets des jugements dans le marché commun") No 216 *et seq*, Weser ("Convention communautaire sur la compétence judiciaire et l'exécution des décisions") No 265.

47 In the case of an orally concluded contract, the requirements of the first paragraph of Article 17 of the Convention of 27 September 1968 on jurisdiction and the enforcement of judgments in civil and commercial matters as to form are satisfied only if the vendor's confirmation in writing accompanied by notification of the general conditions of sale has been accepted in writing by the purchaser (Case No 25/76, [1976] ECR 1851.

The fact that the purchaser does not raise any objections against a confirmation issued unilaterally by the other party does not amount to acceptance on his part of the clause conferring jurisdiction unless the oral agreement comes within the framework of a continuing trading relationship between the parties which is based on the general conditions of one of them, and those conditions contain a clause conferring jurisdiction (Case No 25/76).

Where a clause conferring jurisdiction is included among the general conditions of sale of one of the parties, printed on the back of a contract, the requirement of a writing under the first paragraph of Article 17 of the Convention of 27 September 1968 on jurisdiction and the enforcement of judgments in civil and commercial matters is fulfilled only if the contract signed by both parties contains an express reference to those general conditions (Case No 24/76 [1976] ECR 1831).

In the case of a contract concluded by reference to earlier offers, which were themselves made with reference to the general conditions of one of the parties including a clause conferring jurisdiction, the requirement of a writing under the first paragraph of Article 17 of the Convention is satisfied only if the reference is express and can therefore be checked by a party exercising reasonable care (Case No 24/76).

48 For further questions in Section 8, see paragraphs 22 and 240.

49 Germany: Article 253 (1) of the Zivilprozeßordnung; France: Article 54 of the Code de procédure civile.

50 For details see Droz (note [46]) No 448.

51 Italy: Article 798(1) together with Article 395(1) of the Codice di procedura civile; France: Batiffol, "Droit international privé" 5th ed (1971), No 727.

52 Article 3(1)(c) (2) of the German-British Treaty of 14 July 1960; Article 3(1)(c)(ii) of the Franco-British Treaty of 18 January 1934.

53 From a comparative law point of view: Walther J Habscheid, "Introduction à la procédure judiciaire, les systèmes de procédures civiles", published by the Association internationale de droit comparé, Barcelona 1968.

54 Stein-Jonas (Grunsky) (note [27]), introduction to paragraph 511 I 1; Rosenberg-Schwab, "Zivilprozeßrecht", 11th ed, paragraph 135 I 1 b.

55 Case No 43/77 (Industrial Diamond Supplies v Riva).

56 Cour de Cassation, 25 February 1937 Pas. 1937 I 73.

57 Exact name and address: If the judgment is to be executed in Scotland—Secretary of State for Scotland, Scottish Office, New St Andrew's House, St James Centre, Edinburgh EH1 3 SX; Otherwise—Secretary of State for the Home Department, Home Office, 50 Queen Anne's Gate, London SW1H 9AT.

58 Typical case law examples for Article 54: Hamburg Landgericht (RIW/AWD) 74, 403 *et seq*; Frankfurt Oberlandesgericht (RIW/AWD) 76, 107.

59 The original and new Member States of the Community, or some of them, are already parties to numerous international conventions governing jurisdiction and the recognition and enforcement of judgments in particular areas of law. The following should be mentioned, including those already listed in the Jenard report:

1. The revised Mannheim Convention for the navigation of the Rhine of 17 October 1868 together with the Revised Agreement of 20 November 1963 and the Additional Protocol of 25 October 1972 (Belgium, Germany, France, Netherlands, United Kingdom);
2. The Warsaw Convention of 12 October 1929 for the unification of certain rules relating

to international carriage by air and the Amending Protocol of 28 September 1955 and Supplementary Convention of 18 September 1961 (all nine States) with the Additional Protocols of 8 March 1971 and 25 September 1975 (not yet in force);

3. The Brussels International Convention of 10 May 1952 on certain rules concerning civil jurisdiction in matters of collision (Belgium, Germany, France, United Kingdom);
4. The Brussels International Convention of 10 May 1952 relating to the arrest of seagoing ships (Belgium, Germany, France, United Kingdom);
5. The Rome Convention of 7 October 1952 relating to damage caused by foreign aircraft to third parties on the surface (Belgium, Luxembourg);
6. The London Agreement of 27 February 1953 on German external debts (all nine States);
7.
   (a) The Hague Convention of 1 March 1954 on civil procedure (Belgium, Denmark, Germany, France, Italy, Luxembourg, Netherlands),
   (b) The Hague Convention of 15 November 1965 on the service abroad of judicial and extrajudicial documents in civil and commercial matters (Belgium, Denmark, France, Italy, Luxembourg, Netherlands, United Kingdom),
   (c) The Hague Convention of 18 March 1970 on the taking of evidence abroad in civil or commercial matters (Denmark, France, Italy, Luxembourg, United Kingdom);
8. The Geneva Convention of 19 May 1956 together with its Protocol of Signature on the contract for the international carriage of goods by road (CMR) (Belgium, Denmark, Germany, France, Italy, Luxembourg, Netherlands, United Kingdom);
9. The Convention of 27 October 1956 between the Grand Duchy of Luxembourg, the Federal Republic of Germany and the French Republic on the canalization of the Moselle, with the Additional Protocol of 28 November 1976 (the three signatory States);
10. The Hague Convention of 15 April 1958 on the recognition and enforcement of decisions relating to maintenance obligations in respect of children (Belgium, Denmark, Germany, France, Italy, Netherlands);
11. The Hague Convention of 15 April 1958 on the jurisdiction of the contractual forum in matters relating to the international sale of goods (not yet ratified);
12. The Paris Convention of 29 July 1960 on third party liability in the field of nuclear energy (Belgium, France, Germany), together with the Paris Additional Protocol of 28 January 1964 (Belgium, Denmark, France, Germany, Italy), and the Brussels Convention and Annex thereto of 31 January 1963 supplementary to the Paris Convention of 29 July 1960 and the Paris Additional Protocol to the Supplementary Convention of 28 January 1964 (Denmark, France, Germany, Italy, United Kingdom);
13. The Supplementary Convention of 26 February 1966 to the International Convention of 25 February 1961 concerning the carriage of passengers and luggage by rail (CIV) on the liability of railways for death or injury to passengers, amended by Protocol II of the Diplomatic Conference for the entry into force of the CIM and CIV International Agreements of 7 February 1970 concerning the extension of the period of validity of the Supplementary Convention of 26 February 1966 (all nine States);
14. The Brussels Convention of 25 May 1962 on the liability of operators of nuclear ships and Additional Protocol (Germany);
15. The Brussels International Convention of 27 May 1967 for the unification of rules relating to the carriage of passengers' luggage by sea (not yet in force);
16. The Brussels International Convention of 27 May 1967 for the unification of certain rules relating to maritime liens and mortgages (not yet in force);
17. The Brussels International Convention of 29 November 1969 on civil liability for oil pollution damage (Belgium, Denmark, France, Germany, Netherlands, United Kingdom) and the International Convention to supplement that Convention of 18 December 1971 on the establishment of an international fund for compensation for oil pollution damage (Denmark, France, Germany, United Kingdom);
18. The Berne International Conventions of 7 February 1970 on the carriage of goods by rail (CIM) and the carriage of passengers and luggage by rail (CIV), together with the Additional Protocol and Protocol I of 9 November 1973 of the Diplomatic Conference for the implementation of the Conventions (all nine States with the exception of Ireland for Protocol I);
19. The Athens Convention of 13 December 1974 on the carriage by sea of passengers and their luggage (not yet in force);
20. The European Agreement of 30 September 1957 covering the international carriage of dangerous goods by road (ADR) (United Kingdom) and the Additional Protocol of 21 August 1975 (United Kingdom) (not yet in force);
21. The Geneva Convention of 1 March 1973 on the contract for the international carriage of passengers and baggage by road (CUR) (not yet in force);
22. The Hague Convention of 2 October 1973 on the recognition and enforcement of decisions relating to maintenance obligations (no Community Member State is a party to this Convention).

[60] See note[59.1].

[61] The expression "court" should not be taken as meaning the opposite of other jurisdictions (such as tribunals) but means the legal body which is declared competent in each case.

[3047M]

PART IV
EC MATERIALS

COUNCIL REPORT

on the accession of the Hellenic Republic to the Community Convention on jurisdiction and the enforcement of judgments in civil and commercial matters

(86/C298/01)

NOTES

The Evrigenis and Kerameus Report on the accession of Greece to the 1968 Brussels Convention and Annexed Protocol is set out at OJ C298, 24.11.86, p 1. References to the original pagination in the Official Journals are noted above the text to which they refer.

FOREWORD

This report is the last work to flow from the pen of Professor Demetrios I Evrigenis, who, as always, was the moving spirit and a principal actor in its creation. It was almost complete when he died, in the prime of life, in Strasbourg on 27 January 1986 when about to return to Thessaloniki to discuss some final matters with me, his co-author. His sudden death obliged me to settle them alone, few in number and little of consequence as they were. The problems of international jurisdiction and the enforcement of the judgments of foreign courts, which absorbed his energies so productively throughout his academic life, have thus become the theme of his parting words at its inexorable end. This work is dedicated to his memory with gratitude and respect.

K D KERAMEUS

CONTENTS

[OJ C298, 24.11.86, p 3]

I. BACKGROUND TO AND STRUCTURE OF THE CONVENTION

1. On 25 October 1982, representatives of the ten Member States of the European Communities at that time signed the Convention on the accession of the Hellenic Republic to the Convention on jurisdiction and the enforcement of judgments in civil and commercial matters and to the Protocol on its interpretation by the Court of Justice with the amendments made to them by the Convention on the accession of the Kingdom of Denmark, of Ireland and of the United Kingdom of Great Britain and Northern Ireland. The conclusion of this Convention was provided for in Article 3(2) of the Act concerning the conditions of accession of the Hellenic Republic and the adjustments to the Treaties annexed to the Treaty of 28 May 1979 concerning the accession of the Hellenic Republic to the European Economic Community and to the European Atomic Energy Community. In accordance with that provision "the Hellenic Republic undertakes to accede to the conventions provided for in Article 220 of the EEC Treaty and to the protocols on the interpretation of those conventions by the Court of Justice, signed by the Member States of the Community as originally or at present constituted, and to this end it undertakes to enter into negotiations with the present Member States in order to make the necessary adjustments thereto". To date, the only existing convention based on Article 220 of the EEC Treaty is the Convention of 27 September 1968 on jurisdiction and the enforcement of judgments in civil and commercial matters.

2. In preparation for the negotiations for accession to this Convention, the Hellenic Republic drew up a memorandum with proposed adjustments which was forwarded in October 1981 to the other Member States via the Council. The Permanent Representatives Committee convened an *ad hoc* Working Party composed of experts from the Member States and Commission representatives which met on two occasions in Brussels, on 14 December 1981 and 5 April 1982. From these meetings there emerged a draft Convention on the accession of the Hellenic Republic, which was approved by the Permanent Representatives Committee on 11 June 1982 and was signed on 25 October 1982 by representatives of the Member States at a conference of the Ministers for Justice of the Member States in Luxembourg.

3. Before presenting and commenting on the Convention on Greece's accession, it will be useful to list all the individual texts making up the current version of the Convention on jurisdiction and the enforcement of judgments in civil and commercial matters. These texts are as follows:

3.1.1 Convention on jurisdiction and the enforcement of judgments in civil and commercial matters (hereinafter referred to as the "1968 Convention").

3.1.2 Protocol (hereinafter referred to as the "1968 Protocol").

3.1.3 Joint Declaration (hereinafter referred to as the "1968 Joint Declaration").

The texts referred to in points 3.1.1 to 3.1.3 were signed in Brussels on 27 September 1968 and entered into force on 1 February 1972. The Greek versions were published in *Official Journal of the European Communities* No L388 of 31 December 1982, page 7.

3.2.1 Protocol on the interpretation by the Court of Justice of the European Communities of the Convention of 27 September 1968 on jurisdiction and the enforcement of judgments in civil and commercial matters (hereinafter referred to as the "1971 Protocol").

3.2.2 Joint Declaration (hereinafter referred to as the "1971 Joint Declaration").

The texts referred to in points 3.2.1 and 3.2.2 were signed in Luxembourg on 3 June 1971 and entered into force on 1 September 1975. The Greek versions were published in *Official Journal of the European Communities* No L388 of 31 December 1982, page 20.

3.3.1 Convention on the accession of the Kingdom of Denmark, of Ireland and of the United Kingdom of Great Britain and Northern Ireland to the Convention on jurisdiction and the enforcement of judgments in civil and commercial matters, and the Protocol on its interpretation by the Court of Justice of the European Communities (hereinafter referred to as the "1978 Accession Convention").

3.3.2 Joint Declaration (hereinafter referred to as the "1978 Joint Declaration").

The texts referred to in points 3.3.1 and 3.3.2 were signed in Luxembourg on 9 October 1978.* The Greek versions were published in *Official Journal of the European Communities* No L388 of 31 December 1982, page 24.

3.4.1 Convention on the accession of the Hellenic Republic to the Convention on jurisdiction and the enforcement of judgments in civil and commercial matters and to the Protocol on its interpretation by the Court of Justice with the amendments made to them by the Convention on the accession of the Kingdom of Denmark, of Ireland and of the United Kingdom of Great Britain and Northern Ireland (hereinafter referred to as the "1982 Accession Convention").

[OJ C298, 24.11.86, p 4]

This Convention was signed in Luxembourg on 25 October 1982 and published in *Official Journal of the European Communities* No L388 of 31 December 1982, pages 1 to 6.

All the above texts were published in an unofficial consolidated version prepared by the General Secretariat of the Council, in *Official Journal of the European Communities* No C97 of 11 April 1983, pages 2 to 29. For the publication of the above texts in the other Community languages, see the table given on page 1 of *Official Journal of the European Communities* No C97 of 11 April 1983.

4. Explanatory reports were drawn up on the texts referred to in points 3.1.1. to 3.3.2. The report on the 1968 Convention, Protocol and Joint Declaration and the report on the 1971 Protocol and Joint Declaration were drawn up by Mr P Jenard, Director in the Belgian Ministry of Foreign Affairs and External Trade.[1] The report on the 1978 Accession Convention and Joint Declaration was drawn up by Mr P Schlosser, Professor at the University of Munich.[2] A Greek translation of these reports appears in the present edition of the Official Journal. The reports in question contain the background to the preparation of the texts and explain and elucidate the provisions of the texts in relation to the autonomous law of the Contracting Parties. They are of considerable assistance in interpreting the Convention.

5. **Technical legal aspects of accession to the Convention**

As in the case of the accession of Denmark, Ireland and the United Kingdom, in the case of the accession of Greece the Contracting Parties preferred to draft a Convention incorporating adjustments supplementing the existing 1968, 1971 and 1978 texts instead of directly revising them. This solution has clear advantages. It relieves the Contracting Parties of the obligation to ratify once more those parts of the existing Convention which have not been amended through the new accession and, at the same time, permits a clear distinction to be made between the successive stages in the development of the Convention. There are, however, disadvantages, as the result is a gradual accumulation of texts effecting repeated indirect changes to the original Convention. The number of such independent texts is bound to increase with each new enlargement of the Community and, consequently, with each further accession to the Convention. This multiplicity of sources will, of course, create further problems of interpretation in determining the law applicable in a particular case. Of assistance on this point are the consolidations of the texts of the Convention into a single corpus which are usually prepared after each new accession by the Council General Secretariat.[3] Anyone seeking to interpret the Convention must not forget, however, that these consolidations are unofficial and therefore do not have binding force.

6. **Brief description of the 1982 Convention**

In contrast to the 1978 Accession Convention, the 1982 Accession Convention did not involve any substantial changes to the text either of the 1968 Convention or the 1971 Protocol, as already amended by the 1978 Accession Convention. The adjustments made to those texts by the 1982 Convention are purely technical and are restricted to additions required as a result of the accession of the new Contracting Party. Greece, as shown by the memorandum which it submitted for the negotiations for its accession to the Convention,[4] felt that it could accept the Convention in its entirety, as already amended by the 1978 texts. Two points which might have led to substantial amendments were finally dealt with in the minutes of the ad hoc Committee. These points are dealt with below.[5]

7. **Structure of the 1968/1978/1982 Convention**

The Convention governs, on the one hand, the international jurisdiction of the courts, and, on the other, the recognition and enforcement of judgments, authentic instruments and court settlements. Given its content, it may be classified as a "double" convention. In other words, in addition to provisions governing the recognition and enforcement of foreign judgments, it contains direct rules on jurisdiction defining the court competent to deal with a dispute, in contrast to "single" conventions which deal with jurisdiction only indirectly as a pre-condition for the recognition and enforcement of foreign judgments. The Convention is divided into eight Titles and deals successively with the scope of the Convention itself (Title I, Article 1), jurisdiction (Title II, Articles 2 to 24), recognition and enforcement (Title III, Articles 25 to 49), authentic instruments and court settlements (Title IV, Articles 50 to 51). Title V (Articles 52 to 53) contains general provisions and Title VI (Article 54) transitional provisions to which must be added the provisions of Articles 34 to 36 of the 1978 Convention and of Article 12 of the 1982 Convention. Title VII (Articles 55 to 59) governs the relationship of the Convention to other conventions while Title VIII (Articles 60 to 68) contains the final provisions, to which must be added the corresponding provisions of the 1978 Convention (Articles 37 to 41) and the 1982 Convention (Articles 13 to 17). The 1968 Protocol contains a set of specific provisions.

For the 1971 Protocol on the interpretation of the Convention by the Court of Justice and the amendments thereto in the 1978 and 1982 texts, see Section III.D below, points 91 to 99. **[3048]**

[OJ C298, 24.11.86, p 5]

II. THE GREEK SYSTEM OF INTERNATIONAL JURISDICTION AND ENFORCEMENT OF JUDGMENTS OF FOREIGN COURTS

8. After the foundation of the modern Greek State (1830) positive legislation in respect of international jurisdiction and the recognition and enforcement of the judgments of foreign courts went through two major phases. These two phases are quite distinct as regards international jurisdiction[6] and less so as regards the recognition and enforcement of foreign judgments.[7] The following brief account concludes with a description of the international convention provisions governing these matters in force in Greece.[8]

9. The civil procedure of 1834, which was drawn up by the Bavarian jurist G L von Maurer and which applied from 25 January 1835 until 15 September 1968 followed French legal thinking (Articles 14 and 15 of the French Civil Code) in providing for the nationality of the litigants to be the main criterion of international jurisdiction. Thus, under Article 28 of the 1834 civil procedure, Greek courts possessed jurisdiction where *either* the plaintiff *or* the defendant were Greek. As a result, a Greek national could sue a foreign national, and *vice versa*, before the Greek courts irrespective of the geographical location of the dispute or of any other connecting factor providing a link with the Greek State. In addition, however, pursuant to Article 27 of the civil procedure, the international jurisdiction of the Greek civil courts also extended to actions between foreign nationals if they had agreed to submit their dispute to the Greek courts, or if certain, very few, special jurisdictions applied, or if considerations of public policy were involved.[9]

10. The basis of the system was changed by the introduction of the Civil Code (23 February 1946). Under Article 7(1) of the law introducing the Code, Articles 27 and 28 of the civil procedure were repealed; Article 126 of the law stipulated that foreign nationals were subject to the jurisdiction of Greek courts and could sue or be sued in the same manner as Greek nationals in accordance with the provisions governing jurisdiction. Thus, at least in the case of foreign nationals, jurisdiction was dissociated from the nationality of the litigants and became a function of place: in litigation between foreign nationals or where only the defendant was a foreign national the Greek civil courts had jurisdiction in every case, provided that any one such court had territorial competence for the dispute in question.

11. However, opinions differed regarding disputes under private international law where the defendant was a Greek national. According to the "resultant" theory,[10] the purpose of the legislator in drafting Article 126 of the law introducing the Civil Code was fully to equate foreign and Greek nationals as regards jurisdiction. Consequently, just as, under Article 126, international jurisdiction with regard to foreign nationals was nothing more nor less than the sum total, or the resultant of various particular jurisdictions, so in the case of Greek nationals international jurisdiction could not be exercised by the Greek State unless such nationals were also linked by some general or special jurisdiction to the area of jurisdiction of a Greek civil court, their Greek nationality being insufficient for this purpose. On the other hand, the "distinction" theory,[11] which finally prevailed in jurisprudence in the period up to 1968, distinguished between foreign and Greek defendants, requiring only in the case of the former that some form of jurisdiction should exist and in the case of the latter merely that they possess Greek nationality. This conception of jurisdiction as a function of nationality proved in practice to be an unfortunate privilege for Greeks in that it allowed them to be sued in Greek courts without there being any other connecting factor than their nationality, whereas possession of Greek nationality was not sufficient for a *plaintiff* to be able to bring proceedings against a foreign national in Greek courts.[12]

12. The introduction of the new Code of Civil Procedure (on 16 September 1968) marked the final break with the French system and led to the predominance of the "resultant" theory. Under Article 53 of the law introducing the Code, Article 126 of the Civil Code was repealed and Article 3(1) of the Code of Civil Procedure laid down that Greek and foreign nationals were subject to the jurisdiction of the civil courts in so far as a Greek court was competent. The fact that Greek and foreign nationals were referred to on the same basis and on the same level and that Article 3(1) of the Code of Civil Procedure was stated to be the prime source of international jurisdiction under Greek law resulted, to use the expression frequently encountered in jurisprudence, in Greek law switching from the principle of nationality to the principle of territoriality. Since that time, and irrespective of the nationality of any of the litigants, the pre-requisite for international jurisdiction to lie with the Greek State has been, as a rule, that the dispute must be subject to the general or special jurisdiction of a Greek civil court.[13] Only by way of exception, namely in matrimonial disputes and disputes between parents and children, will the Greek nationality of any of the litigants of itself constitute a basis of jurisdiction on the part of the Greek courts (Code of Civil Procedure, Articles 612 and 622).

[OJ C298, 24.11.86, p 6]

13. The various individual jurisdictions which thus together make up international jurisdiction under modern Greek law do not diverge all that much from general practice under the laws of the other Community countries.[14] General jurisdiction is based on the domicile or seat, and secondarily on the residence, of the defendant (Code of Civil Procedure, Articles 22 to 26 and 32). General jurisdiction is automatically set aside when any of the six *special exclusive jurisdictions* under the Code of Civil Procedure applies: jurisdiction of the court for the place where the property is situated in the case of disputes concerning rights *in rem* or

similar rights in, or tenancies of, immovable property (Code of Civil Procedure, Article 29); jurisdiction in matters relating to succession, vested in the court for the last place of domicile of the testator (Code of Civil Procedure, Article 30, see also Article 810); jurisdiction based on related actions, where the court hearing the main action has jurisdiction in respect of ancillary proceedings (Code of Civil Procedure, Article 31); jurisdiction in respect of company disputes, covering disputes between a company and its members and between the members themselves, in so far as they arise out of the company relationship, vested in the court for the place where the company has its seat (Code of Civil Procedure, Article 27); jurisdiction in respect of management under a court order, vested in the local court which made the order (Code of Civil Procedure, Article 28); jurisdiction in respect of counter-claims (Code of Civil Procedure, Article 34), although it should be noted that under Greek law the filing of a counter-claim is not obligatory, nor is any substantive connection required between the defendant's counter-claim and the claim brought by the plaintiff.

The general section of the Code of Civil Procedure also lays down six *concurrent special jurisdictions* with the plaintiff being able to choose between them and general jurisdiction (Code of Civil Procedure, Article 41): jurisdiction in respect of legal acts, with either the place where the act was drawn up or the place of performance being taken as connecting factors (Code of Civil Procedure, Article 33); jurisdiction in respect of criminal offences, which in the case of civil disputes arising from acts giving rise to criminal proceedings lies either with the court for the place where the offence was committed or with the court for the place where the consequences of the offence occurred (Code of Civil Procedure, Article 35, Criminal Code, Article 16); jurisdiction in respect of management other than under a court order, which lies with the court for the place of management (Code of Civil Procedure, Article 36); jurisdiction where identical law is applicable, which, mainly in case of jointly defended proceedings, allows the defendants to be sued in a court which has jurisdiction for any one of them (Code of Civil Procedure, Article 37); jurisdiction in matrimonial disputes, which vests in the court for the last place of joint residence of the spouses (Code of Civil Procedure, Article 39); jurisdiction in respect of claims relating to property, where proceedings may be instituted both before the court for the place where the defendant has resided for a reasonable length of time (Code of Civil Procedure, Article 38), and, mainly where proceedings involve a defendant not domiciled in Greece, before the court for the place where property belonging to the defendant or the object in litigation is situated (Code of Civil Procedure, Article 40). With regard to special procedures (Code of Civil Procedure, Articles 591 to 681) Articles 616, 664 and 678 provide for additional forms of concurrent special jurisdiction which in principle favour the plaintiff.

14. The possibility of basing jurisdiction on an agreement between the litigants is very widely recognized in disputes concerning property (Code of Civil Procedure, Articles 3, paragraphs 1, 42 to 44). The agreement may in principle be informal, an agreement in writing being required only where it relates to a potential future dispute. An informal agreement may in principle also be tacit, and be inferred from a defendant's failure to challenge the jurisdiction of the court when entering an appearance at the first hearing of the case. An express agreement is required only where special exclusive jurisdiction is to be set aside. There is a legal presumption that a court on which jurisdiction is conferred has exclusive jurisdiction. In addition, no substantive connecting factor is required between the dispute to which the conferral of jurisdiction relates and the Greek State. The only bar lies in the prohibition against submitting to Greek jurisdiction disputes concerning immovable property situated outside Greece (Code of Civil Procedure, Article 4, first subparagraph, *in fine*). Lastly, just as jurisdiction may be conferred, it may also be removed with the submission of a dispute to a foreign court; such agreements are not considered as infringements of Greek sovereignty or as contrary to public policy; recourse to foreign courts merely has to be possible so that there is no international denial of justice.

15. Jurisdiction of the Greek State with regard to the substance of a dispute is not a pre-condition for provisional measures to be taken. Of course, such measures may be ordered by the court before which the principal case is pending (Code of Civil Procedure, Articles 684 and 683(2)). However, they can also be ordered by the court with competence *ratione materiae* nearest to the place where they are to be implemented (Code of Civil Procedure, Article 683(3)). Hence, the fact that the principal action is pending before a foreign court or, even where not so pending, is subject to the international jurisdiction of a State other than Greece does not prevent provisional measures being taken in Greece.

16. Lack of jurisdiction is in general examined by the court of its own motion. However, since jurisdiction can in principle also be based on a defendant's failure to challenge when entering an appearance,[15] the question of lack of jurisdiction is only examined by the court of its own motion where the defendant *does not* enter an appearance at the first hearing or where

he appears and does not challenge but his silence cannot constitute a basis for implied jurisdiction because the dispute relates to immovable property situated outside Greece (Code of Civil Procedure, Article 4, first subparagraph), or because the object of the dispute is not property, or because the law provides for exclusive jurisdiction (Code of Civil Procedure, Article 4, first subparagraph, Article 42(1), first and second subparagraphs, Article 46, first subparagraph, Article 263(a)). Where jurisdiction is found to be lacking, the action will be dismissed as inadmissible (Code of Civil Procedure, Article 4, second subparagraph) and there will be no referral to a foreign court. However, if despite lack of jurisdiction a judgment is given in the case, it may be challenged in law but will not be void unless it infringes the rules of extraterritoriality (Code of Civil Procedure, Article 313(1)(e)).

[OJ C298, 24.11.86, p 7]

17. Under the old civil procedure of 1834 (Articles 858 to 860) a distinction was made in the enforcement in Greece of judgments of foreign courts according to the nationality of the party against whom enforcement was sought.[16] If that party was a foreigner, enforcement was authorized by the presiding judge of a court of first instance and three conditions had to be satisfied:

(a) the foreign instrument had to be enforceable in the State of origin;
(b) that State must have possessed jurisdiction (which was assessed according to Greek law);
(c) the instrument must not be contrary to Greek public policy.

On the other hand, if the party against whom enforcement was sought was Greek, jurisdiction to authorize enforcement was vested in the three member courts of first instance and two further conditions had to be satisfied:

(d) the judgment could not be in contradiction with proven fact, a requirement which led to a limited review of the foreign judgment as to its substance, and
(e) no events must have occurred to invalidate the claim included in the foreign instrument. These conditions, which were required by law for enforcement to be authorized, were also extended by judicial practice to the simple recognition of the *res judicata* status of foreign judgments.[17]

18. Here, too,[18] the new Code of Civil Procedure eliminated all distinction between Greek and foreign nationals.[19] Irrespective of the nationality of the party against whom enforcement is sought, the following conditions must now be satisfied for the enforcement of a foreign judgment to be authorized in Greece (Code of Civil Procedure, Articles 905(2)(3), 323, points 2 to 5):

(a) it must be enforceable under the law of the place where it was delivered;
(b) the dispute must have been subject in accordance with Greek law to the jurisdiction of the State in which the judgment originates;
(c) the party against whom the judgment has been given must not have been deprived of the right of defence, or the right of participation in general in the proceedings;
(d) the foreign judgment must not conflict with a judgment which has become *res judicata* delivered by a Greek court in proceedings between the same parties and in the same dispute;
(e) the foreign judgment must not conflict with public morality or public policy. Apart from these conditions, there is no requirement as to reciprocity or application of the substantive law defined as applicable under Greek private international law, nor may the procedural legality or the correctness as to substance of the foreign judgment be verified.[20] Lastly, as regards the enforcement of other foreign instruments, these need merely be enforceable under the law of the place where they were issued and must not be contrary to public morality or public policy (Code of Civil Procedure, Article 905(2)).

19. The distinction between Greek and foreign nationals has also been abolished as regards both jurisdiction[21] to authorize enforcement and the relevant procedure. In every case, jurisdiction is vested in the single-member court of first instance in the area of jurisdiction in which the debtor is domiciled or, where this is inapplicable, is resident; where neither connecting factor applies jurisdiction is vested in the single-member court of first instance in Athens. The procedure followed is that applicable in non-contentious proceedings (Code of Civil Procedure, Article 905(1)), and an enforcement order may be challenged by means of an ordinary appeal, reasoned appeal against a default judgment, judicial review and appeal in cassation (Code of Civil Procedure, Article 905(1), second subparagraph, Article 760 to 772), none of which have suspensive effect under the law (Code of Civil Procedure, Articles 763, 770, 771 and 774). A foreign instrument, the enforcement of which has been authorized, is enforced in accordance with the enforcement procedure and measures provided for under Greek law.[22]

20. *Recognition* of the *res judicata* status of foreign judgments is basically subject to the same conditions. The only difference is that instead of the judgment having to be enforceable under the law of the place where it was delivered,[23] it must have *res judicata* status under Greek law (Code of Civil Procedure, Article 323, point 1). Recognition of *res judicata* status is not subject to any special procedure (Code of Civil Procedure, Article 323 pr.) and such status may be recognized as an incidental matter by any judicial or administrative authority.[24] Only in the case of the recognition of the *res judicata* force of foreign judgments concerning the status of persons, in particular with respect to divorce, must the same procedure be followed as for authorization of enforcement (Code of Civil Procedure, Article 905(4)).

21. Greece is not a contracting party to any bilateral international conventions which directly govern jurisdiction.[25] Any clauses in agreements placing foreign nationals on the same legal footing as Greek nationals are no longer relevant,[26] from the point of view of jurisdiction, since such assimilation is now a rule of Greek internal law further to Article 126 of the law introducing the Civil Code and Article 3(1) of the Code of Civil Procedure.[27]

[OJ C298, 24.11.86, p 8]

22. Greece is a contracting party to eight "single"[28] bilateral conventions concerning recognition and the enforcement of judgments of foreign courts; these are with Czechoslovakia (1927, Law 3617/1928), Yugoslavia (1959, Decree 4007/1959), the Federal Republic of Germany (1961, Law 4305/1963), Romania (1972, Decree 429/1974), Hungary (1979, Law 1149/1981, Articles 24 to 31), Poland (1979, Law 1184/1981, Articles 21 to 31), Syria (1981, Law 1450/1984, Articles 21 to 29) and Cyprus (1984, Law 1548/1985, Articles 21 to 28). As regards their content, these conventions do not differ substantially from Greek internal law in the Code of Civil Procedure, and they apply irrespective of the nationality of the litigants. They do not permit review as to substance, and they do not make recognition dependent on the substantive law applied in the foreign judgment except in questions concerning the status of persons. The most detailed of these conventions, that between Greece and Germany,[29] covers the enforcement not only of court judgments but also of court settlements and authentic instruments (Articles 13 to 16); it also covers non-contentious proceedings (Article 1(1), subparagraph 1) and interim orders (Article 6) and allows recognition to be refused on grounds of lack of jurisdiction solely where the courts of the country in which recognition is sought have *exclusive* jurisdiction, or where the court which gave the judgment heard the case exclusively on the basis of jurisdiction in respect of matters relating to property (Article 3(3) (4)).

23. Multilateral conventions[30] which apply in Greece include the Vienna Convention on Diplomatic Relations of 18 April 1961 (Decree 503/1970) and the Vienna Convention on Consular Relations of 24 April 1963 (Law 90/1975), which deal in detail with extra-territoriality. Other conventions applicable include those of 7 February 1970 on the International Carriage of Goods (CIM), Passengers and Luggage (CIV) by Rail (Emergency Law 365/1968), which contain provisions governing jurisdiction (Article 44) and the enforcement of judgments of foreign courts (Article 56). The New York Multilateral Convention of 20 June 1956 on the Recovery abroad of Maintenance, which applies in Greece (Decree 4421/1964), also contains provisions on the enforcement of foreign judgments (Articles 5 and 6). In the area of maritime law there are the Brussels Conventions of 10 May 1952 on Certain Rules concerning Civil Jurisdiction in matters of Collision (Law 4407/1964) and on the Unification of Certain Rules relating to the Arrest of Sea-going Ships (Decree 4570/1966, in particular Article 7 on international jurisdiction). As regards air law there is the Warsaw Convention on the Unification of Certain Rules relating to International Carriage by Air (Emergency Law 596/1937, in particular Article 28(1) and Article 32 on jurisdiction). In the area of arbitration law there is the New York Convention of 10 June 1958 on the Recognition and Enforcement of Foreign Arbitral Awards (Decree 4220/1961). However, Greece has not signed the International Conventions of The Hague of 1 February 1971 on the Recognition and Enforcement of Foreign Judgments in Civil and Commercial Matters, and of 2 October 1973 on the Recognition and Enforcement of Decisions relating to Maintenance Obligations; it has signed (but not yet ratified) the earlier Hague Convention of 15 April 1958 concerning the Recognition and Enforcement of Decisions relating to Maintenance Obligations towards Children. It has also signed, but not yet ratified, the Luxembourg European Convention of 20 May 1980 (within the framework of the Council of Europe) on the Recognition and Enforcement of Decisions concerning Custody of Children and on Restoration of Custody of Children.

[3049]

III. THE COMMUNITY CONVENTION ON JURISDICTION AND ENFORCEMENT OF JUDGMENTS IN CIVIL AND COMMERCIAL MATTERS

A. SCOPE OF THE CONVENTION

24. *The Convention concerns issues of international points of contact.* In so far as it governs the *international* jurisdiction of the courts the Convention obviously concerns international issues or, to use the normal definition, issues which contain a foreign element. This characteristic, which is inherent in the very nature of the Convention, is stressed in the third paragraph of the preamble; this refers in French to determining the "compétence de (…) juridictions dans l'ordre international" (jurisdiction of the courts at international level), which the Greek version of the Convention renders as "international jurisdiction". Furthermore, both in the title and in the text of the Convention the term "jurisdiction" (French: "compétence judiciaire") is translated in Greek as "international jurisdiction" in line with normal Greek terminology which distinguishes between international jurisdiction and internal competence. [OJ C298, 24.11.86, p 9]

25. The Convention also governs the recognition and enforcement of *foreign* judgments, ie judgments delivered in one Contracting State recognition or enforcement of which is sought in another Contracting State; the same applies as regards authentic instruments and court settlements.

26. *The Convention relates to civil and commercial matters.* The meaning of the expression "civil and commercial matters" (Article 1, first paragraph) is not defined in the Convention.

However, Article 1 specifies that civil or commercial matters are to be classified as such irrespective of the nature of the court before which they are heard or which gave judgment and of whether the proceedings are contentious or non-contentious. Hence the criterion which applies is substantive rather than procedural. According to the Court of Justice of the European Communities,[31] it is essentially determined by the legal relationships between the parties to the action or the subject-matter of the action.

27. Although the drafters of the Convention did not attempt to define or to give clear guidance as to the meaning of the expression "civil and commercial matters", there can be no doubt that it is to be determined on the basis of the Convention. The concept is therefore independent and is not determined by reference to any specific national legal order. Its meaning should accordingly not be sought in the law of the Contracting State of the court seised or even in the law of the State, whether a Contracting State or not, governing the substance of the action. The Court of Justice of the European Communities confirmed this principle of interpretation in its Judgment of 14 October 1976[32] when it emphasized the independent nature of the concept and stated that it should be interpreted by reference, on the one hand, to the objectives and scheme of the Convention and, on the other, to the general principles which stem from the corpus of the national legal systems. This in the Court's view makes it necessary to ensure, as far as possible, that the rights and obligations which derive from the Convention for the Contracting States and the persons to whom it applies are equal and uniform. The same approach as regards interpretation can be found in more recent judgments of the Court.[33]

28. Civil and commercial matters must be distinguished from disputes of public law, which do not come within the scope of the Convention. In the view of the Court of Justice, it would appear that these two categories can be distinguished on the basis of a traditional feature of public law in continental jurisprudence, namely the exercise of sovereign powers.[34] The problem assumed a new dimension when the Convention was opened for accession by States belonging to the family of Anglo-Saxon law which do not in principle recognize the distinction between private law and public law. The existence side-by-side in the Community of divergent approaches of this kind naturally creates difficulties in seeking an independent, generally applicable definition. The Court will be impeded in performing its interpretative function in the absence of general principles common to all the legal systems of the Contracting Parties from which a single criterion can be deduced for distinguishing matters which can be classified as coming under public law. A partial solution to the problem was attempted with the addition made by the 1978 Convention (Article 3) to the original text of the first paragraph of Article 1 of the Convention; the addition specifies that the Convention does not extend "in particular, to revenue, customs or administrative matters". This distinction, which may have been self-evident in the case of the majority of the Contracting Parties (including Greece), was necessary in the case of those States—Ireland and the United

Kingdom—where the distinction between private and public law is not as firmly and extensively established in positive law or in current jurisprudence.

29. Civil and commercial matters also include relationships arising from contracts of employment. This approach, which is in line with prevailing Greek legal thinking, has been confirmed by the Court of Justice of the European Communities.[35]

30. **Exclusions**

The second paragraph of Article 1 specifies a series of matters which are excluded from the scope of the Convention. Most represent a genuine limitation of the civil and commercial matters covered, with their exclusion being necessitated for different reasons in every instance. This is the case as regards the relationships listed in point 1 (status or legal capacity of natural persons, rights and property arising out of a matrimonial relationship and succession), point 2 (bankruptcy, proceedings relating to the winding up of insolvent companies or other legal persons, judicial arrangements, compositions and analogous proceedings), and point 4 (arbitration). The exclusion contained in point 3 (social security) is justified both by the fact that social security comes under public law in some countries whilst it falls in the borderline area between private law and public law in others, and because social security matters are increasingly governed by secondary Community legislation.

[OJ C298, 24.11.86, p 10]

31. Point 1 of the second paragraph of Article 1 refers to the status or legal capacity of natural persons, rights and property arising out of a matrimonial relationship and succession. The exclusion of these matters from the scope of the Convention was necessitated by their specific characteristics, which are reflected in the great variety of ways they are dealt with at national level in both substantive law and private international law. Their inclusion in the Convention would have meant either that these specific characteristics would have had to be levelled out or, alternatively, that such matters would have been dealt with in a rather inconsistent manner from the point of view of international jurisdiction, although consistency is one of the main aims of the Convention. Faced with this dilemma, the drafters of the Convention preferred to exclude these relationships from its scope.

32. Interpreting these exclusions, the Court of Justice of the European Communities has ruled that the enforcement of a judicial decision on the placing under seal or the freezing of the assets of the spouse as a provisional measure in the course of proceedings for divorce does not fall within the scope of the Convention.[36] The Court took the same view in the case of an application on the part of the wife for the Court to order the husband, as a provisional protective measure, to deliver up a document in order to prevent its use as evidence in a dispute concerning a husband's management of his wife's property, because the management was closely connected with the proprietary relationship resulting directly from the marriage bond.[37]

33. Matters relating to maintenance, however, come within the scope of the Convention, as is apparent from Article 5, point 2, which governs jurisdiction with regard to maintenance obligations. As was perhaps to be expected, problems have arisen from the common practice of linking maintenance claims with proceedings relating to the status of persons, and, in particular, with divorce proceedings. The Court of Justice of the European Communities has ruled that the Convention is applicable to an interim maintenance award under a divorce judgment.[38] This point is expressly dealt with in the 1978 amendment to Article 5, point 2, of the Convention.

34. Point 2 of the second paragraph of Article 1 excludes from the scope of the Convention bankruptcies, proceedings relating to the winding up of insolvent companies or other legal persons, judicial arrangements, composition and analogous proceedings. These matters had to be excluded given that the Member States of the Community intended, and still intend, to draft a separate Community bankruptcy convention. In relation to Article 16, point 2, which stipulates that, in proceedings which have as their object the dissolution of companies or other legal persons or associations of natural or legal persons, the courts of the Contracting State in which the company, legal person or association has its seat have exclusive jurisdiction, this exclusion may give rise to problems where the dissolution is a consequence of bankruptcy, winding up, judicial arrangement, composition, or analogous proceedings.[39]

35. Arbitration, a form of proceedings encountered in civil and, in particular, commercial matters, (Article 1, second paragraph, point 4) is excluded because of the existence of numerous multilateral international agreements in this area. Proceedings which are directly concerned with arbitration as the principal issue, e g cases where the court is instrumental in

setting up the arbitration body, judicial annulment or recognition of the validity or the defectiveness of an arbitration award, are not covered by the Convention. However, the verification, as an incidental question, of the validity of an arbitration agreement which is cited by a litigant in order to contest the jurisdiction of the court before which he is being sued pursuant to the Convention, must be considered as falling within its scope.

36. Social security, which is excluded from the Convention by point 3 of the second paragraph of Article 1, is regarded in some national legal systems as a matter of public law and in others as a mixed legal category on the borderline between public law and private law. Although it could perhaps be argued that this feature alone would be enough to exclude social security from the scope of the Convention as defined in the first paragraph of Article 1, its express exclusion was nevertheless thought to be desirable. There were, however, other reasons as well for excluding social security from the scope of the Convention, such as the fact that it is governed by the Treaties and by secondary Community legislation, and the fact that there are numerous bilateral social security agreements between the Community Member States. The drafters of the Convention considered that this legal situation should not be disturbed by extending the Convention to regulate social security.

37. It should, however, be noted that this exclusion concerns relationships directly connected with the insurance aspect and, particularly, relationships between the insuring body and the insured party, his successors in title and the employer. Ancillary matters, such as direct claims of the injured party against the insuring body or subrogation of the insuring body to the claims of an injured party as against a third party responsible for the injury or damage, are in principle covered by ordinary legal rules and come within the scope of the Convention.

[OJ C298, 24.11.86, p 11]

B. JURISDICTION

38. General state of the law

In common with Greek internal law (Code of Civil Procedure, Article 3, paragraph 1, 22) the Convention (Article 2, first paragraph) bases international jurisdiction on the domicile of the defendant. The fundamental provision in the first paragraph of Article 2 expressly dissociates jurisdiction from nationality and, secondly, *requires* proceedings against persons domiciled in the territory of a Contracting State to be brought before the courts of that State except where the Convention itself provides otherwise (specifically in Articles 5 to 18). Consequently, the domicile of a defendant in a Contracting State, irrespective of whether he is a national of such a State, also serves as the criterion for defining the application of the Convention externally. Given that the first paragraph of Article 2 excludes nationality as a factor in determining jurisdiction, the second paragraph provides for the positive assimilation of foreigners to nationals of the State concerned by making the former subject to the rules of jurisdiction applicable to the latter.[40]

39. The Convention does not itself define domicile; instead, reference is made to the internal law of the State in the territory of which domicile is being investigated for the case in point (Article 52). However, the mere place of residence of the defendant was rejected as a basis of jurisdiction.[41] Consequently, under the Convention, Article 38 of the Greek Code of Civil Procedure may not be invoked in order to extend the jurisdiction of the Greek courts. For the rest, however, the exclusion of residence as an independent basis of jurisdiction on a par with domicile does not affect the application of Article 23(1) of the Code of Civil Procedure: if the defendant is domiciled in a non-Contracting State but is resident in a Contracting State, Article 2 will of course not be applicable, but nor can recourse be had to Article 23(1) of the Code of Civil Procedure which consistently prefers domicile wherever it may be found to exist; if, however, a defendant has no domicile at all but has his place of residence in Greece, then, since such residence constitutes the party's closest geographical connecting factor and thus justifies the application of Article 23(1) of the Code of Civil Procedure, it must be regarded as satisfying the purpose of Article 2 and hence as constituting a basis of jurisdiction.

40. As is apparent from the first paragraph of Article 2, since the Convention governs solely international jurisdiction and not in principle territorial competence, it merely requires that the courts of the State of domicile of the defendant be responsible without stipulating that it be heard by the *particular* court for the place where the defendant is domiciled. The Convention, however, contains no particular provisions determining the legal domicile of certain parties because, as stated above, it generally refers that issue to the internal law of the State concerned. The third paragraph of Article 52 nevertheless stipulates the law applicable

when determining the dependent domicile in question. However, the Convention does not easily accommodate national provisions which displace the material time and replace the present domicile by a previous domicile. Thus, the Convention takes precedence over Article 24 of the Code of Civil Procedure, which applies to Greek public servants posted abroad without extraterritorial status (e g teachers at Greek schools or works supervisors for Greek workers in another Contracting State) and makes them subject to the jurisdiction of the courts of their place of domicile before being sent abroad. Accordingly, if a Greek teacher previously domiciled in Athens is posted to the Greek school in Munich and becomes domiciled there, general jurisdiction will henceforth be vested exclusively in the Munich courts, and no longer in the Athens courts.

41. The Convention treats the seat of companies and other legal persons as their domicile (Article 53, first paragraph, first sentence). The seat is determined in accordance with the rules of private international law of the court seised (Article 53, first paragraph, second sentence). The basic rule is the same as that in Article 25 of the Code of Civil Procedure, as regards including associations of natural persons who pursue a common aim without legal personality, since it was the intention when framing the Convention[42] that they should be covered by the "company".

42. *Special bases*

Article 3 enunciates the general principle of the Convention, that persons domiciled in a Contracting State may be sued in the courts of another Contracting State only to the extent permitted under the special jurisdictions stipulated in Articles 5 to 18 of the Convention.[43] Hence, as regards matters within its scope, the Convention does not allow of the existence of special jurisdictions other than those it itself specifies. However, the restriction applies only to matters within its scope.[44] In disputes involving no foreign element, it will therefore still be possible, after the Convention's entry into force, for persons domiciled in Greece to be sued in *Greek* courts other than the court of their place of domicile by virtue of special jurisdictions under the *Greek* courts other than the court of their place of domicile by virtue of special jurisdictions under the Greek Code of Civil Procedure, even where such jurisdictions are not provided for in the Convention. The exhaustive nature of the special jurisdictions which, according to the Convention, provide the basis for determining jurisdiction becomes apparent once a person is to be sued in a Contracting State other than his State of domicile. The Convention thus allows general jurisdiction of domicile as a basis for international jurisdiction to be set aside only in favour of special jurisdictions exhaustively enumerated in the Convention itself. This approach is not unknown in Greek internal law. Under Article 22 of the Code of Civil Procedure, a person may be sued before a court other than that of his place of domicile only where the law so provides, i e where special jurisdiction is stipulated.

[OJ C298, 24.11.86, p 12]

43. In this connection, the Convention gives a specific, but only indicative, list of bases of jurisdiction provided for under national procedural rules but considered under the Convention to be exorbitant (*règles de compétence exorbitantes*). These include rules which base jurisdiction on the fact that either the plaintiff or the defendant is a national of the State in question (Belgium, France, Luxembourg, Netherlands), on the service of a writ of summons on national territory on a defendant who is temporarily present there (Ireland, United Kingdom), on the seizure of property situated on national territory (United Kingdom), on the presence on national territory of property belonging to the defendant (Denmark, Federal Republic of Germany, Greece, United Kingdom) or on other forms of unfavourable treatment of foreign nationals (Italy). Consequently, Greek courts will in future be unable to base their jurisdiction on the special jurisdiction in respect of property under Article 40 of the Code of Civil Procedure, if the defendant is domiciled in any Contracting State. The existence, in a State, of property belonging to the defendant, and even the presence there of the object in litigation, are not regarded by the Convention as constituting a sufficient connecting factor to provide a basis of jurisdiction.

44. Both the general provisions of the Convention and the exclusion of exorbitant bases of jurisdiction in the second paragraph of Article 3 relate solely to defendants domiciled in a Contracting State, irrespective of the domicile and, of course, the nationality of the plaintiff. However, where a defendant is not domiciled in a Contracting State the Convention does not contain any rules of its own but refers to the internal law of the State of the court hearing the action (Article 4, first paragraph). As against such a defendant, the Convention permits any person domiciled in a Contracting State, whatever his nationality, to avail himself of the law of that State, including, of course, the rules of exorbitant jurisdiction which are excluded under the second paragraph of Article 3 (Article 4, second paragraph). Consequently,

although defendants are treated unequally according to whether or not they are domiciled in a Contracting State, plaintiffs at least enjoy equal treatment irrespective of nationality, provided they are domiciled in a Contracting State. However, the judgment handed down will, in any event, be recognized and enforced in accordance with the Convention. Apart from the possibility of prorogation of jurisdiction pursuant to Articles 17 and 18, an express exception to the principle that the application of the Convention is dependent on the defendant being domiciled in a Contracting State is constituted by the exclusive jurisdiction provided for under Article 16. In the five categories of proceedings listed in Article 16, the Convention considers that the very close link between the dispute and the territory of a Contracting State must prevail over the fact that the defendant is not domiciled in the territory of any of the Contracting States. Thus, in addition to the domicile of the defendant, the Convention also uses the situation of immovable property, the seat of legal persons, the place where entries have been made in public registers and the place where a judgment has been or is to be enforced as objective[45] connecting factors for defining its application.

45. The following sections 2 to 6 of Title II (Articles 5 to 18) contain special rules directly governing jurisdiction. They lay down special bases of jurisdiction, in some cases supplementing general jurisdiction based on domicile, (eg Article 5 dealing with certain categories of proceedings and Article 6 dealing with certain categories of persons, in particular defendants), and in others excluding such jurisdiction (Article 16). For certain categories of proceedings which, it was felt, required special procedural arrangements, such as matters relating to insurance and consumer contracts, the relevant Sections 3 (Articles 7 to 12a) and 4 (Articles 13 to 15) lay down self-contained rules on jurisdiction in the sense that, of all the other provisions of the Convention relating to jurisdiction, only Article 4 dealing with the case of defendants with no domicile in a Contracting State[46] and Article 5, point 5, dealing with disputes arising out of the operation of a branch, apply as well. Consequently, in the case of matters relating to insurance and in the case of consumer contracts, the domicile of the parties to the dispute is taken into account as a possible basis of jurisdiction only in so far as it is specifically referred to in the relevant section, and recourse may not be had to the general provision in Article 2.

46. **Special concurrent jurisdiction**

Articles 5 to 6a, which lay down a series of objective (Article 5) and subjective (Article 6) connecting factors, specify the cases in which the Convention allows a person domiciled in one Contracting State to be sued in another such State. In other words, they provide for "special jurisdiction", which, provided that a defendant is domiciled in a Contracting State and that the bases of the special jurisdiction exist, in the case in question, in the territory of another Contracting State, assign jurisdiction to the latter State as well as to the State of domicile of the defendant. The choice is a matter for the plaintiff and is expressed when proceedings are instituted.[47]

[OJ C298, 24.11.86, p 13]

47. Article 5 of the original Convention contained five cases of special jurisdiction (points 1 to 5), namely matters relating to contracts, to maintenance obligations, to tort, delict or quasi-delict, to civil claims for damages in criminal courts and to disputes arising out of the operations of a branch. With the accession of Denmark, Ireland and the United Kingdom, the 1978 Accession Convention added two further cases, namely disputes relating to trusts and disputes relating to the payment of remuneration in respect of salvage. Article 5 is one of the most important and most frequently applied articles of the Convention.

48. Article 5, point 1, regarding matters relating to contracts establishes the jurisdiction of the court of the place of performance of the obligation in question. The place of performance is thus recognized as a connecting factor which, for the purposes of jurisdiction, can apply with respect to all matters arising out of the operation of a contract. According to the case law of the Court of Justice of the European Communities, this special jurisdiction may be invoked even where the existence of the contract on which the claim is based is in dispute between the parties.[48] Matters relating to a contract can also include obligations in regard to the payment of a sum of money which have their basis in the relationship existing between an association and its members, irrespective of whether the obligations in question arise simply from the act of becoming a member or from that act in conjunction with one or more decisions made by organs of the association.[49] The definition of the courts referred to in the Article gives rise to greater difficulties than the delimitation of the matters covered. Thus, it has been held that the place of performance of an obligation is to be determined in accordance with the law which governs the obligation in question according to the rules of private international law of the court before which the matter is brought.[50] If the national law

applicable so permits, the place of performance may be specified by the parties without it being necessary for their agreement to fulfil the formal conditions required under Article 17 of the Convention for prorogation of jurisdiction.[51] Finally, as regards the obligation the place of performance of which constitutes the basis of special jurisdiction, whereas the Court previously defined it as the contractual obligation (of any kind) forming the basis of the legal proceedings,[52] it now appears to be limited, in the case of proceedings based on a number of obligations possibly to be performed in a number of places, to the obligation which characterizes the contract.[53]

49. Special jurisdiction based on the place of performance of a contractual obligation differs from current Greek internal law (Code of Civil Procedure, 33) in two respects. Firstly, it relates only to disputes concerning contracts, with unilateral legal acts not being covered by the actual wording of the provision. However, if the term "contract" in Article 5, point 1, is interpreted specifically within the framework of the Convention, it would probably include quasi-contractual obligations within the meaning of Article 33(2) of the Code of Civil Procedure, whereas it remains an open question whether disputes arising from unilateral legal acts are covered. Secondly, under Article 5 only the place of performance of the obligation is considered to be relevant and not also, as in Article 33(1) of the Greek Code of Civil Procedure, the place where the contract was concluded. Finally, in line with current Greek legal thinking, it is clear under the Convention that the place of performance means the place where the obligation has been or is to be performed, obviously as determined by the parties or under the law applicable.[54] It should be noted here that with regard to disputes between the master and a member of the crew of a sea-going ship registered in Denmark, in Greece or in Ireland, Article Vb of the 1968 Protocol provides for the possibility of intervention by the competent diplomatic or consular officers.

50. Article 5, point 2, basically provides that jurisdiction in respect of maintenance claims, whatever their legal origin or content,[55] can also be exercised by the courts for the place where the maintenance creditor is domiciled or habitually resident. This affords the latter a degree of legal protection since he is thus not obliged to call upon a court some distance away from the place where he is established. The 1978 Accession Convention extended this form of special jurisdiction. It now includes maintenance proceedings which are combined, or heard jointly, with proceedings concerning the status of a person—which do not, in themselves, come within the scope of the Convention—and the jurisdiction of the court hearing the main action is thus extended to ancillary maintenance proceedings, unless such jurisdiction is based solely on the nationality of one of the parties. The dependence of the maintenance claim on the main action concerning the status of a person will therefore extend jurisdiction in every case where the latter is not construed solely on the basis of the nationality of one of the parties. Accordingly, since Greek law provides by way of exception that in matrimonial disputes, and disputes between parents and children, international jurisdiction can be based simply on the nationality of any one of the parties (Code of Civil Procedure, Articles 612 and 622), the combining, or joint hearing, of such proceedings with maintenance proceedings (Code of Civil Procedure, Articles 592(2) and 614(2)) is not an option which can be exercised under the Convention unless there is a further criterion other than nationality on which international jurisdiction can be based.

[OJ C298, 24.11.86, p 14]

51. Article 5, point 3, provides for the special jurisdiction of the *forum delicti commissi*. This covers all obligations, pecuniary or otherwise, resulting from torts, delicts or quasi-delicts, and refers them to the courts for the place where the harmful event occurred. According to the Court of Justice of the European Communities,[56] this can be either the place where the damage occurred or the place of the event giving rise to it. While this interpretation of the Convention on the subject of the relevant place is in line with current Greek law, the Convention nevertheless differs from Greek law in that, as it does not require that an act giving rise to criminal proceedings must have been committed (Code of Civil Procedure, 35), it also covers claims resulting from purely civil delicts.

52. Civil claims for damages (or restitution) based on an *act giving rise to criminal proceedings* are covered by Article 5, point 4. Under this provision, the possibility of bringing a civil action in the context of criminal proceedings constitutes an independent basis of jurisdiction, with the result that the criminal court, even if sitting elsewhere than "the place where the harmful event occurred" (Article 5, point 3)[57] can acquire jurisdiction in respect of the civil action to the extent that its internal law so permits. While national legal systems thus remain free to determine whether civil actions in such circumstances are permissible and how criminal courts should proceed with respect to such actions, national codes of criminal procedure are directly affected by Article II of the 1968 Protocol. In particular, this Article

provides (in the first paragraph) for the possibility of representation ("by persons qualified to do so") for defendants domiciled in a Contracting State who are being prosecuted in the criminal courts of another Contracting State of which they are not nationals for an offence which was not intentionally committed. According to the Court of Justice of the European Communities, this provision applies if subsequent civil proceedings have been, or may be, brought.[58] By comparison with this provision, Greek law (Code of Criminal Procedure, 340, paragraph 2, first subparagraph) is in principle more strict, in that it permits a defendant to be represented only where he is accused of a petty offence or a minor crime carrying a financial penalty, a fine or a prison sentence of not more than three months, and not in every case of prosecution for an offence not intentionally committed. Consequently, under the Convention, Article 340, paragraph 2, first subparagraph, of the Code of Criminal Procedure will be replaced by Article II of the 1968 Protocol where it applies.[59]

53. Jurisdiction in the case of disputes arising out of the operations of a branch, agency or other establishment (Article 5, point 5) is recognized under Greek law only in the form of jurisdiction based on partial domicile for business purposes (Civil Code, Article 51, subparagraph 3, as amended by Article 2 of Law 1329/ 1983; Code of Civil Procedure, Article 23, paragraph 2) and has not been commonly applied as a basis of jurisdiction. However, as regards the application of the Convention, the Court of Justice of the European Communities has delivered three judgments clarifying the meaning of the provision in question. Firstly, it did not apply the provision to the case of a sole agent who was not subject either to the control or to the direction of the principal.[60] Secondly, it interpreted the meaning of a "branch", stressing in particular that it must have the appearance of permanency as a place of business and as an extension of a parent body, and the meaning of disputes arising out of "operations", which it considered as comprising contractual and non-contractual obligations concerning the management of the branch itself and undertakings entered into in the name of the parent body.[61] Thirdly, it did not apply the provision in the case of an independent commercial agent entitled to represent several undertakings at the same time and who being free to arrange his own time and work did no more than transmit orders to the parent undertaking.[62]

54. The provision contained in Article 5, point 6, is foreign to Greek law, which does not recognize trusts as such. This provision was added under the 1978 Accession Convention and it stipulates that the disputes to which it refers and which concern the creation or operation of a trust are subject to the jurisdiction of the Contracting State in which the trust is domiciled.

55. Article 5, point 7, introduces into the Convention as a basis of special jurisdiction the arrestment of cargo or freight in disputes concerning remuneration in respect of salvage at sea. Following the uncertainties which existed prior to the introduction of the Code of Civil Procedure, arrestment is not recognized as a basis of jurisdiction under modern Greek internal law. The latter, of course, recognizes jurisdiction based on property (Code of Civil Procedure, Article 40) in the more general sense, but precisely this jurisdiction is not allowed under the Convention[63]. Article 5, point 7, of the Convention has to some extent re-introduced jurisdiction based on property, but in a very restricted form, ie only in the case of disputes concerning remuneration in respect of the salvage of a cargo or freight and further subject, in accordance with the traditional approach under common law,[64] to the condition that the cargo or freight has been or could have been arrested.

[OJ C298, 24.11.86, p 15]

56. The bases of special jurisdiction under Article 6 of the Convention which arise from personal connecting factors are in substance known in Greek law. The main differences between the Convention and the Greek Code of Civil Procedure relate to the following three points which correspond to the three special jurisdictions under the Convention:

(a) Jurisdiction in the case of joint proceedings is confined under the Convention to the courts for the place where any one of the defendants is *domiciled*. Greek law goes further and permits the institution of joint proceedings before the court which is vested with either general or some special form of jurisdiction in respect of any one of the defendants.

(b) Article 6, point 2, of the Convention limits jurisdiction based on related actions (see Code of Civil Procedure, Article 31) as a basis of international jurisdiction to third party proceedings. However, even in such instances it is not allowed as a basis of jurisdiction if it is found that the sole purpose of the third party proceedings was to distort the normal limits of international jurisdiction by removing the third party from the jurisdiction of the court which would be competent in his case. As third party proceedings are not recognized under German law, the Federal Republic of Germany preferred not to recognize this basis of jurisdiction in the case of its courts and instead to retain the requirements of notice of proceedings (German Code of Civil Procedure, 72 to 74, 1968 Protocol, Article V).

(c) Whereas jurisdiction based on a counter-claim does not, under Greek law, require that the opposing claims be related (Code of Civil Procedure, Articles 34 and 268), the Convention limits this jurisdictional basis and requires that the counter-claim must arise "from the same contract or facts on which the original claim was based".

57. Under Article 6a, which was added by the 1978 Accession Convention, a court with jurisdiction in actions relating to liability arising from the use or operation of a ship also has jurisdiction over claims for limitation of such liability. This makes it legally easier for shipowners to limit their liability since they will be able to institute proceedings for such limitation before the courts of their place of domicile.

58. **Matters relating to insurance**

The whole of Section 3 (Articles 7 to 12a) which governs international jurisdiction in matters relating to insurance, is essentially concerned with the legal protection of policy-holders *vis-à-vis* insurers. It provides for proceedings to be brought against an insurer before the courts for the place where the policy-holder is domiciled (Article 8, point 2), or, in the case of liability insurance or insurance of immovable property, before the courts for the place where the harmful event occurred (Article 9). The same points of contact also apply in the case of actions brought by an injured party directly against the insurer, where such direct actions are permitted (Article 10, second paragraph). In addition, in so far as the law of the court permits third party proceedings, the Convention extends jurisdiction to cover the case of an insurer being joined in proceedings which an injured party has brought against the insured (Article 10, first paragraph), obviously without there being the restriction laid down by Article 6, point 2, in respect of false third party proceedings. There is also a corresponding legal requirement imposed on the insurer in cases where it is he who institutes proceedings. An insurer "may bring proceedings only in the courts of the Contracting State in which the defendant is domiciled, irrespective of whether he is the policy-holder, the insured or a beneficiary" (Article 11, first paragraph). Lastly, Articles 12 and 12a provide limited scope for prorogation by permitting agreements between the parties provided that they are entered into after the dispute has arisen (Article 12, point 1) or that they are to the advantage of the party in dispute with the insurer (Article 12, points 2 and 3).

59. **Consumer contracts**

The content in Section 4 (Articles 13 to 15) dealing with jurisdiction over consumer contracts (it has been found that sale of a machine on instalment credit terms by one company to another is not a contract of this nature)[65] is in substance similar and are also unknown in Greek internal law. Thus, a seller or a lender may be sued in the courts for the place where the buyer or borrower (the consumer) is domiciled (Article 14, first paragraph), whereas a seller suing a buyer, or a lender suing a borrower, can only do so in the courts where the defendant is domiciled (Article 14, second paragraph).

[OJ C298, 24.11.86, p 16]

Here too there is limited scope for prorogation, agreements between the parties being permitted only if they are entered into after the dispute has arisen (Article 15, point 1) or if they are to the advantage of the buyer or borrower (ie the consumer) (Article 15, point 2, see also point 3).

60. **Special exclusive jurisdiction**

As in the case of Greek internal law (Code of Civil Procedure, Articles 27 to 31 and Article 34), the Convention (Article 16) specifies a number of bases of exclusive jurisdiction in the sense that if the pre-conditions for any one of them are fulfilled, a plaintiff may not sue before the courts of the Contracting State in which the defendant is domiciled as in the case of the matters covered by Articles 5 and 6, and, irrespective of whether or not the defendant is domiciled in a Contracting State, may sue only before the courts of the State vested with the relevant exclusive jurisdiction. The list of bases of exclusive jurisdiction given in the Convention (Article 16) is in several respects more restrictive than under Greek internal law. Under the Convention (Article 16, point 1), "proceedings which have as their object rights *in rem* in, or tenancies of, immovable property are subject to the jurisdiction of the *forum rei sitae* but, unlike Article 29(1) of the Greek Code of Civil Procedure, this does not appear to cover claims against any person in possession (*actiones in rem scriptae*), proceedings for compensation for expropriation[66] or disputes relating to the transfer of a usufructuary right in immovable property.[67]

In contrast to the generalized jurisdiction in respect of company disputes under Greek law (Code of Civil Procedure, Article 27), which includes disputes arising out of the relationship between a company and its members and between the members themselves, the Convention (Article 16, point 2) limits the corresponding exclusive jurisdiction to proceedings concerned with validity, nullity or dissolution—albeit not only as regards companies but as regards legal persons in general—and not only as regards the existence of the legal persons as such but also as regards the validity of the decisions of their organs. Similarly, in Article 16, point 5 (enforcement of judgments), the Convention is narrower than Greek internal law, not as regards the proceedings covered but as regards the courts stated to have jurisdiction; reference is made only to the courts of the Contracting State in which the judgment has been or is to be enforced[68] and not also to the courts vested with general jurisdiction in respect of the third party entering the objection, which courts may be competent under Greek law pursuant to Article 933(2) in conjunction with Article 584 of the Code of Civil Procedure in cases where an order has been granted but other enforcement measures have not (yet) been taken. Nor does this point cover, under the enforcement procedure, objections which are based on claims over which the courts of the State of enforcement have no jurisdiction.[69] Lastly, the Convention does not recognize jurisdiction based on related actions to the extent provided in Article 31(1) of the Code of Civil Procedure: it confines such jurisdiction to third party proceedings (Article 6, point 2; but see also Article 22)[70] and assigns it concurrent status only. By contrast with these restrictive features, the Convention (Article 16, points 3 and 4) confers exclusive jurisdiction in proceedings which have as their object the validity of entries in public registers and proceedings concerned with the registration or validity of patents, trademarks, designs or other similar rights upon the courts of the State in which the relevant records are kept. The former category, namely entries in public registers, may be considered, at least as regards rights *in rem* in immovable property, as covered in Greek internal law by Articles 29(1) and 791(2) of the Code of Civil Procedure taken together. As regards the latter category, relating to proceedings concerned with industrial property,[71] Greek internal law provides for wider, and not exclusive, jurisdiction, with competence in respect of trademarks devolving upon the normal administrative tribunals. With particular reference to European (as opposed to Community) patents which are not valid throughout the Community, it is specified that exclusive jurisdiction rests with the courts of the particular Contracting State with respect to which the validity of the patent in the particular case is challenged (Article Vd of the 1968 Protocol).[72]

61. **Prorogation of jurisdiction**

The rules on prorogation of jurisdiction occupy a central position in the Convention and have repeatedly been the subject of interpretations by the Court of Justice of the European Communities. Exactly as in the presumption in Article 44 of the Code of Civil Procedure, the Convention firstly recognizes the exclusive nature of agreements conferring jurisdiction (Article 17, first paragraph, first sentence in fine) and allows either a specific court or the courts in general of a Contracting State to be designated as having jurisdiction.[73] Again in common with Greek internal law (Code of Civil Procedure, Article 43), the Convention allows jurisdiction to be conferred in respect of disputes which may arise in the future only where they are in connection "with a particular legal relationship" (Article 17, first paragraph, first sentence). However, in contrast to Greek law (Code of Civil Procedure, Articles 42 and 43) no distinction is made as regards the form of the agreement conferring jurisdiction according to whether it relates to present or future disputes (Article 17, first paragraph, first sentence: "… disputes which have arisen or which may arise …").

[OJ C298, 24.11.86, p 17]

62. The Convention is more strict in its requirements as to the form an agreement conferring jurisdiction must take than Greek internal law, which does not in principle require that the agreement be in writing (Code of Civil Procedure, Article 42, see also the exception in Article 43). The Convention is basically oriented towards such agreements being formulated in writing and requires them to be in one of the following three forms:

(a) agreement in writing;
(b) oral agreement evidenced in writing;

and

(c) in international trade or commerce, a form which accords with practices in that trade or commerce of which the parties are or ought to have been aware.

With regard to forms (a) and (b), the Court of Justice of the European Communities has ruled that the requirement as to written form is fulfilled if the clause conferring jurisdiction is included among the general conditions printed on the back of a contract, provided that the contract contains an express reference to those general conditions;[74] it has also ruled that in the case of an orally concluded contract, the vendor's written confirmation must have been accepted in writing by the purchaser, oral acceptance by the purchaser being sufficient only within the framework of a continuing trading relationship between the parties which is based on the general conditions of one of them, which conditions must contain a clause conferring jurisdiction.[75] Recent judgments of the Court of Justice have become even more liberal. The Court has ruled that the second form, i e oral agreement evidenced in writing, can be complied with if the clause conferring jurisdiction is printed on a bill of lading which has been signed by only the carrier[76] and, more generally, if the clause has been confirmed in writing by one party only, provided that the document concerned has been received by the other and that the latter has raised no objection.[77] In addition, agreements conferring jurisdiction which pre-date the entry into force of the Convention, and which would have been void under the national law in force at that time, can be regarded as valid if the proceedings were instituted after the entry into force of the Convention, the existence of jurisdiction being assessed, pursuant to Article 54, in accordance with Title II of the Convention.[78] Finally, prorogation of jurisdiction is also rendered easier by the Court of Justice's view that agreement between the parties with regard to the place of performance, which constitutes a basis of jurisdiction pursuant to Article 5, point 1,[79] is clearly a substantive agreement and is not subject to the formal conditions laid down in Article 17 for prorogation of jurisdiction.[80]

63. The Court of Justice of the European Communities has also widened the subjective and objective limits of agreements conferring jurisdiction. Thus, in the case of a contract of insurance for the benefit of a third party, it has ruled that the third party (the insured) may rely on conferral of jurisdiction even where he was not a party to the contract and did not sign the clause conferring jurisdiction provided that the consent of the insurer in that respect has been clearly manifested.[81] The same holds true in the case of a third party holding a bill of lading *vis-à-vis* the carrier, provided that the national law applicable considers the third party to have succeeded to the shipper's rights and obligations.[82] Further, as regards the objective scope of agreements conferring jurisdiction, the Court of Justice has found that the court before which a dispute has thereby been brought is not prohibited from taking into account a set-off connected with the legal relationship in dispute.[83]

64. The effect of agreements conferring jurisdiction is limited by two factors under the Convention. The existence of exclusive jurisdiction under Article 16 cannot, in the case in point, simply be circumvented, as in Greek law (Code of Civil Procedure, Article 42(1), second paragraph), by an express agreement conferring jurisdiction, but is a bar to *any form* of prorogation. This is also true in the case of conflict with Articles 12 or 15 of the Convention which permit agreements conferring jurisdiction in the case of matters relating to insurance and in the case of consumer contracts, provided that they are entered into after the dispute has arisen, or that they are to the advantage of the policyholder, buyer or borrower.[84] An agreement conferring jurisdiction is however not invalidated by the fact that it is drawn up in a language other than that prescribed by the legislation of a Contracting State.[85] Under the Convention, the effect of agreements conferring jurisdiction also differs according to the domicile of the parties. The rules of the Convention apply in full if at least one of the parties is domiciled in a Contracting State (Article 17, first paragraph, first sentence). If none of the parties is so domiciled and the agreement confers jurisdiction on the courts of a Contracting State, its effect will be determined according to the law of that State, and the courts of other Contracting States might as a result lose any legitimate jurisdiction they might otherwise have. The third sentence of the first paragraph of Article 17 is specifically aimed at ensuring that this effect of loss of jurisdiction is dealt with in a uniform manner: it allows the courts of other Contracting States to have jurisdiction only if the courts chosen in the agreement have declined it,[86] which means that the courts of other Contracting Parties may not examine the validity of the agreement conferring jurisdiction as an incidental issue.

[OJ C298, 24.11.86, p 18]

65. As in the case of Greek internal law (Code of Civil Procedure, Article 42(2), 3(1)) the Convention (Article 18) also provides for tacit conferral of jurisdiction where a defendant enters an appearance before a court which lacks jurisdiction and he does not plead the court's lack of jurisdiction. The Court of Justice of the European Communities[87] has widened this basis of jurisdiction to cover unrelated counter-claims which, though not subject to the jurisdiction of the court, are lodged by the defendant and contested by the plaintiff in court in proceedings on the substance of the case. There can be tacit conferral even if jurisdiction has already been expressly conferred on another court pursuant to Article 17.[88] Furthermore, as in

the case of Greek law, according to the consistent judicial practice of the Court of Justice of the European Communities,[89] a defendant wishing to challenge a tacit conferral of jurisdiction is not obliged to confine his defence to contesting the court's jurisdiction, but may also make subsidiary submissions on the substance of the action in order not to be left without a defence in case the court finds that it has jurisdiction.

66. **Examination as to jurisdiction**

As in the case of Greek internal law (Code of Civil Procedure, Articles 4, 46, first subparagraph and 263(a)), under the Convention (Articles 19 and 20) a court must in principle examine of its own motion whether it has jurisdiction. This rule applies without exception where, by virtue of Article 16, the courts of another Contracting State have exclusive jurisdiction (Article 19) which cannot be set aside either by an express (Article 17, third paragraph) or tacit (Article 18 *in fine*) agreement conferring jurisdiction; the rule is indeed so strict that it requires the national court to declare of its own motion that it has no jurisdiction where the courts of another Contracting State have exclusive jurisdiction, even if, as in the case of ordinary appeals (Code of Civil Procedure, Articles 522, 533(1) and 535(1)) and further appeals (in cassation) (Code of Civil Procedure, Article 562(4) by implication and 577(3)), the national rules of procedure limit the court's reviewal to the grounds raised by the parties and these do not include a claim of lack of jurisdiction.[90] However, if the defendant is domiciled in a Contracting State—the classic case to which the Convention applies[91]—the fact that jurisdiction may be implied where a defendant enters an appearance before a court without contesting its jurisdiction (Article 18) means that, as under Greek law (Code of Civil Procedure, Article 4, first subparagraph, see also Article 263(a)), a court will of its own motion examine jurisdiction only where the defendant does not enter an appearance (Article 20, first paragraph). As for the subject-matter itself, the court's examination will of course be confined to the grounds from which jurisdiction may be derived pursuant to the Convention (Article 20, first paragraph *in fine*). The Convention adds the rule, which is new to Greek law[92] that before giving a judgment in default, the court must verify that the defendant has been able to receive the document instituting the proceedings in sufficient time to enable him to arrange for his defence, or at least that all necessary steps have been taken to this end (Article 20, second paragraph). This transitional provision has, however, already been replaced (Article 20, third paragraph) by Article 15 of the Hague Convention of 15 November 1965 on the service abroad of judicial and extrajudicial documents in civil and commercial matters, which Greece has ratified.[93] As well as this, and on a more general basis, the second paragraph of Article IV of the 1968 Protocol provides that documents for service may also be sent by the appropriate public officers of the State in which they have been drawn up directly to the appropriate public officers of the State in which the addressee is to be found, thus enabling there to be direct communication between public officers in the Contracting States.[94]

67. **Lis pendens**

Article 21 of the Convention expressly regulates jurisdiction in cases of *lis pendens* in a way which corresponds to Greek internal law (Code of Civil Procedure, Article 222(1)), but instead of obliging courts other than that first seised to stay their proceedings (as under the Code of Civil Procedure, Article 222(2)), it requires them to dismiss the action on the grounds that they lack jurisdiction (Article 21, first paragraph, directly, and Article 21, second paragraph, by implication). Only as an exception may a court which would be required to decline jurisdiction stay its proceedings if the jurisdiction of the other court is contested (Article 21, second paragraph). However, the question of when proceedings may be regarded as having been instituted, and thus as definitively pending, in particular whether the filing of an action is enough, or whether notice must also be served, is one to be determined in accordance with the national law of each of the courts concerned.[95]

68. **Related actions**

The Convention also provides for a corresponding possibility of stay of proceedings in the case of related actions (Article 22). Under the Convention, related actions do not constitute an independent basis of jurisdiction, but possible grounds for staying proceedings before any court other than that first seised where proceedings are pending before the courts of two or more Contracting States.[96] In addition to a stay of proceedings, the Convention also allows a court other than that first seised to decline jurisdiction in respect of a related action pending before it if the following three conditions are all fulfilled:

[OJ C298, 24.11.86, p 19]

(a) one of the parties so requests;

(b) the court first seised has jurisdiction over both actions; such jurisdiction cannot however be based on the fact that they are related except in the cases covered by Article 6, point 2[97]

(c) the law of the court other than that first seised permits the consolidation of related actions pending in different courts.[98]

This last condition is not recognized by Greek law, which allows actions to be heard jointly if they are in principle pending in the same court (Code of Civil Procedure, Article 246). Under the Convention, Greek courts would therefore be able to stay their proceedings, but not to decline jurisdiction in favour of the courts of another Contracting State. Lastly, the Convention gives a quasi-legislative definition of related actions (Article 22, third paragraph) which is vaguer and thus broader than the definition given to the concept in Greek internal law (Code of Civil Procedure, Article 31(1)).

69. The rule that the court first seised takes precedence, as contained in Greek law (Code of Civil Procedure, Article 41, 221(1), point (c)) and expressed in the provisions on *lis pendens* and related actions in the Convention, also applies under the latter in particular in the rare instances where several courts have exclusive jurisdiction (Article 23). In such cases, exclusive jurisdiction as to the subject-matter gives way to the criterion as to time, ie to the rule of precedence of the court first seised of the action.

70. **Provisional and protective measures**

Although, in matters falling within its scope,[99] the Convention does not prevent the court vested with international jurisdiction as to the substance from ordering provisional and protective measures, it also allows the simultaneous application of the various national laws in respect of provisional or protective measures in order not to impede the operation of interim judicial protection. Thus, Article 24 of the Convention leaves the courts of a Contracting State free to order provisional or protective measures available under the law of that State even if, under the Convention, the courts of another Contracting State have jurisdiction as to the substance of the matter; this is in line with the principle that jurisdiction in respect of provisional or protective measures is separate, as expressed in Greek internal law in Articles 683(3) and 889(1) of the Code of Civil Procedure: the limitation that a particular court has jurisdiction as to the substance of the dispute does not in principle affect the possibility of provisional or protective measures being taken by other courts.

C. RECOGNITION AND ENFORCEMENT

71. Recognition and enforcement of judgments is dealt with in Title III (Articles 25 to 49). Title IV (Articles 50 and 51) deals with the enforcement of authentic instruments and court settlements.

72. Title III begins with a definition of judgments which are to be recognized or enforced in accordance with the Convention (Article 25) and is divided into three sections, the first of which (Articles 26 to 30) covers the recognition of judgments, the second (Articles 31 to 45) the enforcement of judgments, while the third (Articles 46 to 49) contains common provisions concerning the whole Title.

73. Such judgments will be recognized and enforced as fall within the scope of the Convention, ie judgments in civil and commercial matters subject to the qualifications and exceptions laid down in Article 1.[100] Moreover, in accordance with Article 25, the judgments concerned must have been delivered by a court in a Contracting State, whatever such judgments may be called nationally (eg decree, order, decision or writ of execution) and irrespective of the nationality or domicile of the parties. Under the same provision, the determination of costs or expenses by an officer of the court is also deemed to be a judgment. The Court of Justice of the European Communities has, however, found that judicial decisions authorizing provisional or protective measures which have been delivered without the party against which they are directed having been summoned to appear and which are intended to be enforced in their country of issue without prior service cannot be recognized or enforced under the Convention.[101]

74. The Convention draws a distinction between the recognition and enforcement of judgments. This distinction, which has always been known in Greek procedural law, is legally enshrined in the Code of Civil Procedure (Articles 323, 780, 905; see also Articles 903, 906).

75. **Recognition**

[OJ C298, 24.11.86, p 20]

By its recognition a judgment generates the same legal effects in the State addressed as those conferred on it by the State in which the judgment was given. The Convention facilitates considerably the free movement of judgments in the Contracting States to a reasonable degree. As regards the recognition of judgments, this principle is expressed at two levels: firstly, at procedural level, by providing for automatic recognition, ie without any prior special assessment by a judicial body (Article 26, first paragraph). This solution is also known in Greek law, in respect of the recognition of the res judicata force of foreign judgments (Code of Civil Procedure, Article 323).[102] It should be noted that the Convention allows the recognition of foreign judgments at whatever stage in the judicial proceedings, including, therefore, decisions which have not acquired the force of res judicata. However, if an ordinary appeal has been lodged against a judgment or, in particular in the case of judgments given in Ireland or the United Kingdom, if enforcement is suspended in the State in which the judgment was given by reason of an appeal, the court of the State addressed may stay the proceedings for recognition of the judgment. Secondly, the principle applies in respect of the conditions for recognition, which are comparatively limited and are negatively framed, thereby constituting grounds for refusing recognition rather than positive conditions (Articles 27 and 28; see also Code of Civil Procedure, Article 323).

76. The automatic recognition of judgments at procedural level obviously operates in cases where there is no dispute between the interested parties as to the validity of the judgment in the State addressed. If, as often happens in commerce, the validity of the judgment is disputed, the party wishing to rely on it may seek recognition either as a principal or incidental issue. Where the application for recognition is the principal issue, the rules of Sections 1 and 2 of Title III governing the enforcement of judgments apply. If the recognition of a judgment is sought as an incidental question, the court of the Contracting State entertaining the principal proceedings will also have jurisdiction over the question of recognition (Article 26, second and third paragraphs). These rules also successfully resolve in a more general context the problems which arose in Greece from the lack of a special procedure for the recognition of foreign judgments and which led to the addition of paragraph 4 to Article 905 of the Code of Civil Procedure.

77. Articles 27 and 28 set forth a series of grounds for refusing recognition. A comparison of these grounds with the corresponding conditions in Article 323 of the Code of Civil Procedure shows similarities and differences which it is not possible to detail in this report.[103] The point to be emphasized is that as a consequence of its character as a "double" convention,[104] the Convention does not in principle allow the State addressed to review the jurisdiction of the court which gave the judgment (Article 28, third paragraph), in contrast to the provisions in point 2 of Article 323 of the Code of Civil Procedure. To the list of grounds for refusing recognition of foreign judgments must be added that laid down by Article II of the 1968 Protocol.

78. This solution can be explained if two facts are taken into account: firstly, that jurisdiction both in the State in which the judgment was given and in the State addressed is dealt with in a uniform manner by the Convention and, secondly that, in as much as Article 29 (see also Article 34, third paragraph) contains the general rule that foreign judgments may not be reviewed as to their substance, the court of the State addressed does not have the power to carry out a substantive examination of the findings on which the court of the State in which the judgment was given based its jurisdiction.[105] There is a basically irrefutable presumption that the judgment to be recognized was given by a court which had jurisdiction in accordance with the Convention. The Convention also rules out the possibility of the court in the State addressed invoking public policy as a ground for reviewing any breach of the rules on jurisdiction by the court of the State in which the judgment was given. Thus, according to the second phrase in the third paragraph of Article 28, "the test of public policy referred to in point 1 of Article 27 may not be applied to the rules relating to jurisdiction".

79. To a limited degree, however, the Convention does allow the State addressed to review the jurisdiction of the Court which delivered the judgment. According to the first paragraph of Article 28, a judgment will not be recognized if it conflicts with the provisions of Sections 3, 4 and 5 of Title II, ie the rules on jurisdiction relating to insurance matters (Articles 7 to 12a), consumer contracts (Articles 13 to 15) and cases of exclusive jurisdiction (Article 16). The case provided for in Article 59 also requires there to be a possibility of reviewing the jurisdiction of the court which delivered the judgment and for that reason it has been included in the exceptions listed in the first paragraph of Article 28. It should nevertheless be noted that in its examination of jurisdiction in cases covered by this exhaustive list of exceptions, the court or authority in the State addressed which is called upon to recognize the judgment "shall be bound by the findings of fact on which the court of the

State in which the judgment was given based its jurisdiction" (Article 28, second paragraph). Consequently, the examination carried out in the State addressed will concern the legal aspects of the considerations on which the court of the State in which the judgment was given based its jurisdiction.

[OJ C298, 24.11.86, p 21]

80. As has already been pointed out, the Convention does not allow a foreign judgment to be reviewed as to its substance (Article 29). The court or authority of the State addressed which is called upon to recognize the judgment is not entitled to review the substantive or legal soundness of the conclusions of the court which gave the judgment or to refuse to recognize the judgment if it discovers a substantive or legal defect. The rule prohibiting reviews as to substance is, however, subject to certain restrictions: as was observed above, the first and second paragraphs of Article 28 permit a legal review of the judgment as regards certain bases of jurisdiction.[106] The possibility of review must, out of logical necessity, also be accepted with respect to point 4 of Article 27, which requires in each case an examination both of the factual and legal aspects of the judgment to be recognized. Moreover, examination of the judgment to ensure that recognition is not contrary to public policy in the State addressed (Article 27, point 1) may lead to a re-assessment of its factual or legal considerations. Subject to these reservations, the rule that a judgment may not be reviewed as to its substance is one of the principles of the Convention.

81. Article 30 provides for the possibility of staying recognition proceedings if an ordinary appeal has been lodged against the judgment in the State in which it was given. The meaning of the concept of "ordinary appeal" is to be interpreted on an autonomous basis and covers any appeal which is such that it may result in the annulment or the amendment of the judgment under appeal, and the lodging of which is bound to a period which is laid down by law and which is linked to the actual judgment.[107]

82. *Enforcement*

While the recognition of foreign judgments does not require a specific procedure to be followed, enforcement of such judgments is only possible if an order for enforcement has been issued in the State addressed or, in the case of the United Kingdom, if the judgments are registered for enforcement. The order for enforcement and, *mutatis mutandis*, registration for enforcement presuppose that a judgment has been given in a Contracting State and is enforceable in that State; the order is then issued or registration effected by the court (specifically defined in the Convention) of the State in which enforcement is sought, following an application which any interested party may submit for the enforcement of the judgment.

83. The procedure for making such applications is governed by the law of the State in which enforcement is sought. If the applicant is not domiciled within the area of jurisdiction of the court applied to, he must, in accordance with the requirements laid down by the law of the State in which enforcement is sought, either give an address for service of process or appoint a representative *ad litem* in that area; the choice of domicile must, as a matter of principle, be made in accordance with the procedures laid down under the law of the State in which enforcement is sought, or, failing this, at the latest on service of the enforcing judgment and the sanctions provided for under this law can in no case adversely affect the objectives of the Convention.[108] The documents which are to accompany the application are specified in Articles 46 and 47 (Article 33).

84. The procedure for obtaining enforcement of foreign judgments is exclusive in the sense that a successful party must resort to it in order to obtain satisfaction of his claim and cannot, instead, initiate the same proceedings anew in any other State in which the Convention applies.[109] The procedure operates on three levels of jurisdiction:

(a) The application is submitted to the court specifically designated for each State of enforcement. For Greece the Μουομελες Πρωτοδικειο has jurisdiction (Article 32, first paragraph). The jurisdiction of local courts is determined by reference to the place of domicile of the party against whom enforcement is sought or by reference to the place of enforcement where that party is not domiciled in the State of enforcement (Article 32, second paragraph).
The procedure for issuing the order for enforcement is simple and rapid. There is no obligation to inform the party against whom enforcement is sought of the submission of the application or of the date of the proceedings, and even if that party learns of the proceedings, he is not entitled at this stage to appear or make submissions on the application. The court must give its decision without delay. The foreign judgment may not be reviewed as to its substance and the application

may be refused only for one of the reasons specified in Articles 27 and 28 (Article 34). The appropriate officer of the court will without delay bring the decision to the notice of the applicant in accordance with the procedure laid down by the law of the State in which enforcement is sought (Article 35).

[OJ C298, 24.11.86, p 22]

(b) The party against whom enforcement is sought has the right to lodge an appeal against the decision granting the application with the court designated for each Contracting State in Article 37. The appeal must be lodged within one month of service of the decision authorizing enforcement if the party against whom enforcement is sought is domiciled in the State of enforcement (Article 36, first paragraph).This time limit will be two months from the date on which the decision is served on that party in person or at his residence if the latter is in a Contracting State other than that in which the decision authorizing enforcement is given. No extension of time may be granted on account of distance (Article 36, second paragraph). The Convention does not deal with the situation where the party against whom enforcement is sought is domiciled outside the territory of the Contracting States. In such cases it is accepted that the time limit will be one month which may be extended on account of distance in accordance with the law of the State authorizing enforcement of the foreign judgment.[110] The Court of Justice of the European Communities has ruled that appeals under Article 31 are the only appeals which may be lodged against decisions authorizing enforcement of foreign judgments and has excluded the possibility of lodging any other appeals available under national law.[111] In Greece the Εφετειο has jurisdiction to hear appeals. Appeals are to be lodged and heard in accordance with the rules governing procedure in contentious matters (Article 37). The court having jurisdiction to hear an appeal by the party against whom enforcement is sought may, on the application of that party, stay the proceedings if an ordinary appeal[112] has been lodged against the judgment in the State in which that judgment was given or if the time for such an appeal has not yet expired. The same court may make enforcement conditional on the provision of a security (Article 38); the provision of a security will be ordered in the judgment on the appeal.[113]

(c) The second paragraph of Article 37 gives an exhaustive list, for each Contracting State, of the types of further appeal which may be filed against the judgment given on the appeal lodged, in accordance with Article 36 and the first paragraph of Article 37, by the party against whom enforcement is sought. In Greece only an appeal in cassation is allowed.

85. A party seeking enforcement of a foreign judgment also has the right to lodge an appeal if an application submitted in accordance with Articles 31 *et seq* is refused. The courts with jurisdiction to hear such appeals are specified for each Contracting State in the first paragraph of Article 40. In Greece such appeals are heard by the Εφετειο. When the appeal is heard, the person against whom enforcement is sought must be summoned,[114] and if he fails to appear the provisions of the second and third paragraphs of Article 20 of the Convention apply. A judgment given on such an appeal may be contested only by one form of appeal in each Contracting State, as specified in Article 41. In Greece this may only be by an appeal in cassation.

86. Throughout the time specified for an appeal against the decision authorizing enforcement of the foreign judgment[115] and until any such appeal has been determined, no measures of enforcement may be taken other than protective measures taken against the property of the party against whom enforcement is sought. The decision authorizing enforcement of the foreign judgment constitutes the legal basis for taking such measures (Article 39), without any special leave or subsequent confirmation being required of the national court.[116]

87. The court of the State in which enforcement is sought may authorize partial enforcement of the foreign judgment if that judgment was given in respect of several matters and enforcement cannot be authorized for all of them, or if the applicant requests partial enforcement of the judgment (Article 42). Articles 44 and 45 deal with legal aid and prohibit any sort of security being required of a party applying for enforcement of a foreign judgment, in accordance with the Convention, on the grounds of his status as a foreigner or because he is not domiciled or resident in the State in which enforcement is sought. It should also be noted that Article III of the 1968 Protocol prohibits any charge, duty or fee calculated by reference to the value of the matter in issue from being levied in the State in which enforcement is sought in proceedings for the issue of an order for enforcement.

88. Articles 46 to 49 specify, in the interests of simplification, the supporting documents which a party seeking authorization of enforcement of a foreign judgment must produce before the court. Translation of such documents into the language of the proceedings is not obligatory, although it may be required by the court. The translation may be certified by any person qualified to do so in any of the Contracting States. In particular, it should be noted that Article 49 relieves the party concerned of any obligation to legalize documents which he submits.

89. **Enforcement of authentic instruments and court settlements**

Title IV contains provisions governing enforcement of authentic instruments (Article 50) and court settlements (Article 51). This concerns authentic instruments which have been drawn up or registered and are enforceable in a Contracting State. They will be declared enforceable in another Contracting State in accordance with the procedures laid down in Articles 31 *et seq.* An application for a foreign authentic instrument to be declared enforceable may be refused only if enforcement of the instrument is contrary to public policy in the State in which enforcement is sought (Article 50, first paragraph). The same rules also apply for the enforcement of court settlements approved by a court in a Contracting State and enforceable in that State (Article 51). These provisions of the Convention lay down arrangements which are in substance identical to those under Greek law (Articles 904 and 905 of the Code of Civil Procedure).

90. **General provisions**

Title V (Articles 52 and 53) lays down rules and connecting factors establishing the law applicable for determining the domicile of natural persons and the seat of a company or other legal person and also the domicile of trusts. In order to determine whether a party is domiciled in a Contracting State, including the State in which the proceedings were initiated, the court will apply the internal law of that State. It will apply the internal law of the relevant Contracting State, to the exclusion of the rules of private international law (Article 52, first and second paragraphs).[117] If however, in accordance with a party's national law his domicile depends on that of another person or on the seat of an authority, his domicile will be determined in accordance with his national law (Article 52, third paragraph). The Convention does not, however, contain rules governing the domicile of a party outside the territory of the Contracting States. In this case the court seised of the matter will rule on the basis of the lex fori.[118] Finally, in order to determine the seat of a company or other legal person or the domicile of a trust, the court seised of the matter will apply its rules of private international law (Article 53).[119]

[OJ C298, 24.11.86, p 23]

D. THE 1971 PROTOCOL ON INTERPRETATION

91. Aware of the need to ensure that the Convention was applied as effectively as possible, to prevent differences of interpretation from restricting its unifying effect, and to avoid possible claims and disclaimers of jurisdiction, the Contracting States, in the Joint Declaration of 1968, expressed their intention to study these questions and in particular to examine the possibility of conferring jurisdiction in certain matters of interpretation on the Court of Justice of the European Communities and, if necessary, to negotiate an agreement to that effect. This undertaking resulted in the 1971 Protocol which confers jurisdiction on the Court of Justice of the European Communities to interpret the Convention. The Protocol has, of course, been adjusted by the 1978 and 1982 Accession Conventions.

92. The arrangements provided for in the 1971 Protocol are largely in line with the provisions of Article 177 of the EEC Treaty; that Article lays down that the national court can, or, in appropriate cases, must, refer questions on the interpretation of Community law and of the validity of acts by Community institutions to the Court of Justice for preliminary rulings. However, certain modifications were necessary in view of the particular nature of the matters governed by the Convention. The authors of the Protocol attempted to keep these changes to a minimum in their desire to maintain unity in the judicial practice of the Court of Justice of the European Communities in giving preliminary rulings on interpretation, as laid down by the Treaty, and not to disturb the system of cooperation which had been established over a period of many years between the Community Court and national courts. This intention is also clear from Article 5(1) of the Protocol, which states that the provisions of the Treaty and of the Protocol on the Statute of the Court of Justice relating to preliminary rulings also apply to any proceedings for the interpretation of the Convention and the other instruments referred to in Article 1 of the Protocol, except where the latter provides otherwise.

93. The jurisdiction conferred upon the Court of Justice of the European Communities to give rulings on interpretation concerns the instruments referred to in Article 1 of the Protocol. These instruments are the 1968 Convention, the 1968 Protocol and the 1971 Protocol, together with the instruments adjusting them, i e the 1978 and 1982 Accession Conventions.

94. The Protocol provides for three types of referral for preliminary rulings to the Court of Justice of the European Communities: firstly, optional referral by certain courts; secondly, obligatory referral by certain courts and, thirdly, referral "in the interests of the law" by the competent national authorities.

95. Under Article 3 of the Protocol, both optional and obligatory referrals for a preliminary ruling are provided for where a question of interpretation of the Convention or of one of the other instruments referred to in Article 1 of the Protocol is raised in a case pending and a decision on the question of interpretation is necessary to enable the national court to give judgment.

96. Referrals may be made by the courts of the Contracting States when they are sitting in an appellate capacity (Article 2, point 2, and Article 3(2) of the Protocol), and the courts of the Contracting States mentioned in Article 37 of the Convention where they are exercising the jurisdiction laid down in that provision (Article 2, point 3, and Article 3(2) of the Protocol).

97. Referrals for a preliminary ruling on questions of interpretation must be made by the national courts mentioned in Article 2, point 1, of the Protocol. These are the national supreme courts which are specifically listed for the majority of Contracting States, with the exception of the United Kingdom and Greece. These two exceptions were made on the grounds of the judicial structure of the countries in question. In particular in the case of Greece it was considered advisable not to refer exclusively by name to the two main supreme courts, the Αρειος Παγος and the Συμβουλιο της Επικρατειας, in order to extend the power to submit requests for preliminary rulings to the other supreme judicial bodies with general or specific jurisdiction, such as the special supreme court referred to in Article 100 of the Constitution and the Ελεγκτικο Συνεδριο. If only exceptionally, the matters falling within the jurisdiction of such courts may involve questions of interpretation of the Convention.

[OJ C298, 24.11.86, p 24]

98. A request for the interpretation of the Convention or of one of the other instruments referred to in Article 1 of the Protocol may be submitted to the Court of Justice of the European Communities by the competent national authorities in accordance with Article 4(1). In accordance with Article 4(3), these authorities are the Procurators-General of the Courts of Cassation of the Contracting States or any other authority designated by a Contracting State (see also Article 10(c)). This possibility of obtaining an interpretation "in the interests of the law" may be exercised by the national authorities when judgments by courts in their country conflict with the interpretation already given either by the Court of Justice of the European Communities or by one of the courts of another Contracting State referred to in point 1 or 2 of Article 2. This power, however, only exists in respect of judgments which have become *res judicata*. Article 4(2) of the Protocol specifies that the interpretation given in such cases by the Court of Justice of the European Communities does not affect the judgments by national courts which gave rise to the request for interpretation. Finally, in accordance with Article 4(4), requests for interpretation submitted to the Court of Justice of the European Communities pursuant to Article 4 are to be notified to the Contracting States, to the Commission and to the Council of the European Communities, which are then entitled within two months of the notification to submit statements of case or written observations to the Court; new Member States who have not yet signed the Convention but will accede to it in the future are also entitled to submit observations.[120] To accommodate the particular nature of requests for interpretation submitted pursuant to Article 4 of the Protocol, Article 4(4) thus amends Article 20 of the Protocol on the Statute of the Court of Justice annexed to the Treaty establishing the European Economic Community, in accordance with which the decision of a national court or tribunal which submits a request for a preliminary ruling is notified by the Registrar of the Court of Justice of the European Communities to the parties, to the Member States and to the Commission, and also to the Council if the act the validity or interpretation of which is in dispute, originates from the Council.

99. The frequency with which national courts submit requests for interpretation to the Court of Justice of the European Communities may be described as satisfactory. Application of the Protocol has already led to nearly fifty rulings being given by the Court of Justice.

E. TRANSITIONAL AND FINAL PROVISIONS: PROBLEMS OF TERMINOLOGY

100. Transitional provisions

The 1968 Convention (Title VI, Article 54) and the 1978 Accession Convention (Title V, Articles 34 to 36) contain a number of transitional provisions. Transitional provisions are also contained in the 1982 Convention on the Accession of Greece. In accordance in particular with Article 12 of the 1982 Accession Convention, the 1968 Convention and the 1971 Protocol, as amended by the 1978 and 1982 Accession Conventions, apply only to legal proceedings instituted and to authentic instruments formally drawn up or registered after the entry into force of the 1982 Convention in the State of origin and, where recognition or enforcement of a judgment or authentic instrument is sought, in the State addressed. Paragraph 2 of the Article, however, states that the provisions on recognition and enforcement in the Convention (Title III) also apply to judgments given in proceedings instituted before the entry into force of the 1982 Accession Convention, such entry into force being defined in particular in Article 12(1) of that Convention, if jurisdiction was founded upon rules of the Community Convention or any other convention which was in force between the State of origin and the State addressed when the proceedings were instituted.

101. Relationship between the Convention and other conventions and Community law

Title VII (Articles 55 to 59) contains a number of provisions regarding the position of the numerous, in particular bilateral, conventions on jurisdiction and enforcement of judgments previously concluded between the Contracting States. The Convention, as a Community instrument, naturally supersedes these more particular conventions (Article 55) to the extent that it coincides with them in terms of date of application and the subject matter covered (Article 56).[121] Moreover, the Convention does not affect the validity, or prevent the conclusion by the Contracting Parties, of conventions which, in relation to particular matters, govern jurisdiction or the recognition or enforcement of judgments, nor does it affect corresponding existing or possible future legal acts of Community bodies or provisions of national law harmonized in implementation of such acts (Article 57).

102. Language versions of the Convention

All the texts of the Convention[122] have drawn up in the eight official languages of the Community, as constituted after the accession of Greece: Danish, Dutch, English, French, German, Greek, Irish and Italian (Article 68 of the 1968 Convention, Article 37, first paragraph, and Article 41 of the 1978 Accession Convention, Article 13, first paragraph, and Article 17 of the 1982 Accession Convention). All the language versions are equally authentic (Article 68 of the 1968 Convention, Article 37, second paragraph, and Article 41 of the 1978 Accession Convention, Article 13, second paragraph, and Article 17 of the 1982 Accession Convention).

[OJ C298, 24.11.86, p 25]

103. Terminological problems in the Greek version of the Convention

There follows a list of points in the Greek version of the Convention which require clarification or correction:

(a) In the first sentence of the first paragraph of Article 1, the word "δικαστηριο" (court) was preferred to the word "δικαιοδοσια" (jurisdiction) in order to avoid the suggestion that a distinction is being made between contentious and non-contentious proceedings, when in fact the provision relates to the nature of the court itself (eg civil, criminal, administrative).

(b) In the section on lis pendens (Articles 21 to 23), a general rather than a technical term, "επιλαμβανεται", was used for the court "seised", in order not to prejudge the solution to the question which has already been referred to the Court of Justice of the European Communities 123 as to whether this is a term with its own specific meaning in the Convention, or a general reference to the internal rules on jurisdiction of the Contracting States. Similar considerations led to the use of the more general expression "αναστολη της διαδικασιας" (stay of proceedings) in preference to "αναστολη της αποΦασεως" (stay of judgment) (Article 21, second paragraph, Article 22, first paragraph).

(c) In Article 24, "provisional, including protective, measures" has been rendered by the general and established term "ασΦαλιστικα μετρα" instead of "προσωρινα" or "συντηρητικα μετρα" (provisional or safeguard measures) to avoid giving the impression that distinctions previously made in Greek procedural law are being revived.

(d) In the second paragraph of Article 26 and the first paragraph of Article 31, reference is made to "καθε ενδιαΦερομενος" (any interested party) rather than to "καθε διαδικος" (any litigant) as being entitled to apply for the recognition or enforcement of a judgment. The general term has been used in order to avoid the impression that the text of the Convention itself confines such entitlement to the litigants in the original proceedings before the foreign court.

(e) In point 2 of Article 16 clearly "ακυροτητα" (nullity) and not "εγκυροτητα" is meant in contrast to the immediately following term "κυρος" (validity).

(f) The meaning of "καταχωριση" (article 16, point 4, of the Convention) and of "εγγραΦη" (Article Vd of the 1968 Protocol) of patents is the same. What is involved in both cases is the public act which formally protects the right of the inventor. Both terms render the term "registration" into Greek.

104. **Entry into force of the Convention**

The 1968 Convention entered into force on 1 February 1973 and the 1971 Protocol on 1 September 1975. As at 31 March 1986 the 1978 Accession Convention had been ratified by five States; it has not yet entered into force.[124] The entry into force of the 1982 Accession Convention is governed by Article 15, in accordance with which the Convention "shall enter into force, as between the States which have ratified it, on the first day of the third month following the deposit of the last instrument of ratification by the Hellenic Republic and those States which have put into force the 1978 Convention in accordance with Article 39 of that Convention". The entry into force of the 1982 Accession Convention therefore depends on the entry into force of the 1978 Accession Convention and on the ratification of the 1982 Accession Convention by Greece.

[3050]

ANNEX

1 OJ No C59, 5.3.1979, pp. 1 to 65 and pp. 66 to 70.
2 OJ No C59, 5.3.1979, pp. 71 to 151.
3 See point 3 *in fine*.
4 See point 2.
5 See points 49 and 52.
6 See points 9 to 16.
7 See points 17 to 20.
8 See points 21 to 23.
9 On all these questions, see Frangistas, Δικαιοδοσια επι διεθνων διαΦορων ιδιω τικου δικαιου (1934), passim, in particular 26 to 96.
10 Frangistas, in Ερμηνεια του αστικου κωδικος ΕισΝ 126 αριθ. 12–22; Rammos, Στοιχεια εγγηνικης πολιτικης δικονομιας I/15 (1961) 148, 146; Mitsopoulos, Problèmes de juridiction internationale en droit grec, Ερανιον προσ Γ. Σ. Μαριδακην II (1963) 301–312.
11 Maridakis, Η δικαιοδοσια της εγγηνικης Πολιτειας επι ελληνων κατοικουντων εις τη ν αλλοδαπην, Νεον δικαιον 1956, 1–5; P Valindras, ΕΦημερις των Ελληνων Νομικων 1950, 532–533.
12 See Evrigenis, Το ιδιωτικον διεθνες δικαιον εις την ελληνικην νομολογιαν, Armenopoulos 1964, 409 et seq (465–490), in particular 470–478).
13 See however, Maridakis, Ιδιωτικον διεθνες δικαιον καθα ισχυει εις την Ελλαδα II2 (1968) 188–191, in which he continues to defend the "distinction" theory under the Code of Civil Procedure.
14 For the following, see Rammos, Εγχειριδιον αστικου δικονομικου δικαιου I (1978) 185–233; Mitsopoulos, Πολιτικη δικονομια Α (1972) 204–261; Kerameas, Αστικο δικονομικο δικαιο. Γενικο Μερος (1986) 48–85.
15 See point 14.
16 For the following; see Maridakis, Η εκτελεσις αλλοδαπων αποΦασεων κατα το ιοχυον εις την Ελλαλα δικαιον[2] 2 (1946), in particular 60–120; by the same author, Η αντιΦασις των αλλοδαπων αποΦασεων εις αποδεδειγμενα πραγματα (1930). Ευρυγενη, Ζητηματα εκ της εκτελεσεως και αναγνωρισεως αλλοδαπων αποΦασεων, Επιστημονικη Επετηρις της Σχολης των Νομικων και Οικονομικων Επιστομων του Αριστοτελειου Πανεπιστημιου Θεσσαλονικης III: Μνημοσυνον Γεωργιομ Σ. Στμωνετου (1957) 323–360.
17 Evrigenis, ibid., 329 and point 8.
18 See point 12.
19 For the following, see principally Maridakis, Η εκτελεσις αλλοδαπων αποΦασεων κατα το ισχυον εις την Ελλαδα δικαιον[3] (1970), passim, in particular 54–109.
20 Maridakis, *ibid*, 66–99.
21 See point 17.
22 See Maridakis, (footnote 19) 83–85.
23 See point 18, condition (a).
24 See Maridakis (footnote 19) 107.

[25] In specific areas, jurisdiction is directly governed by certain *multilateral* conventions; see point 23 below.
[26] Frangistas and Gesiou-Faltsi, Αι διεθνεις συβασεις τηζ Ελλαδος εις το αστικον δικονομικον δικαιον, Συμβατικα κειμενα και ερμηνευτικαι συμβολαι (1976) ιστ'—ιθ".
[27] See points 10 and 12.
[28] See point 7.
[29] For this Convention in particular, see Kerameus, Rechtsmittelfestigkeit und Vollstreckung von ausländischen Entscheidungen, *Multitudo legum ius unum: Festschrift für Wilhelm Wengler* II (1973) 383–395. P Gesiou-Faltsi, Zeitschrift für Zivilprozess 96 (1983) 67–89. Pouliadis, Die Bedeutung des deutsch-griechischen Vertrages vom 4.11.1961 für die Anerkennung und Vollstreckung deutscher Entscheidungen in der griechischen Praxis, IPrax 5 (1985) 357–369.
[30] See Frangistas and Gesiou-Faltsi (footnote 26), p. 241–292.
[31] Judgment of 16.12.1980, Case 814/79, Ruffer v Netherlands, paragraph 14.
[32] Judgment of Case 29/76, LTU v Eurocontrol.
[33] Judgment of 14.10.1976, 22.2.1979, Case 133/78, Gourdain v Nadler. See also Judgment of 22.11.1978, Case 33/78, Somafer v Saar-Ferngas.
[34] Judgments of 14.10.1976 and 16.12.1980 referred to above in footnotes 32 and 31.
[35] Judgment of 13.11.1979, Case 25/79, Sanicentral v Collin.
[36] Judgment of 27.3.1979, Case 143/78, de Cavel v de Cavel I.
[37] Judgment of 31.3.1982, Case 25/81, CHW v GJH.
[38] Judgment of 6.3.1980, Case 120/79, de Cavel v de Cavel II.
[39] Jenard, report, page 10, section IV in fine; Schlosser, report, paragraphs 55 et seq.
[40] Cf Code of Civil Procedure, 3, paragraph 1, and, previously, the Law introducing the Civil Code, Article 126.
[41] See Jenard, report, pages 15 and 16.
[42] Jenard, report, page 57, re Article 53.
[43] See point 38.
[44] See point 24.
[45] See point 38.
[46] See point 44.
[47] See Code of Civil Procedure, Articles 41 and 221 paragraph 1, subparagraph c.
[48] Judgment of 4.3.1982, Case 38/81, Effer v Kanter.
[49] Judgment of 22.3.1983, Case 34/82, Martin Peters v ZNAV.
[50] Judgment of 6.10.1976, Case 12/76, Tessili v Dunlop.
[51] Judgment of 17.1.1980, Case 56/79, Zelger v Salinitri.
[52] Judgment of 6.10.1976, Case 14/76, de Bloos v Bouyer.
[53] Judgment of 26.5.1982, Case 133/81, Ivenell v Schwab. If, however, the obligation which characterises the contract does not form the subject of the dispute, all depends on the obligation which provides the basis for the action; Judgment of 15.1.1987, Case 266/85, Shenavi v Kreischer.
[54] See Judgment of 6.10.1976, referred to in footnote 52.
[55] Schlosser, report, pages 101 to 103, points 91 to 97.
[56] Judgment of 30.11.1976, Case 21/76, Bier v Mines de potasse d'Alsace.
[57] See Jenard, report, page 26 I.
[58] Judgment of 26.5.1981, Case 157/80, Rinkau.
[59] The possibility of the defendant's being represented was extended, by Article 6(3) of Law 1653 of 8 November 1986 to offences liable to up to six months imprisonment.
[60] Judgment of 6.10.1976, see footnote 52.
[61] Judgment of 22.11.1978, see footnote 33.
[62] Judgment of 18.3.1981, Case 139/80, Blanckaert & Willems v Trost.
[63] See point 43 in fine.
[64] See Schlosser, report, pages 108 and 109, points 121, 122; Collins, The Civil Jurisdiction and Judgments Act 1982 (1983) 65.
[65] Judgment of 21.6.1978, Case 150/77, Bertrand v Orr.
[66] See Schlosser, report, page 120, point 163.
[67] Despite the restrictive interpretation of this provision (Judgment of 14.12.1977, Case 73/77, Sanders v Van der Putte), the Court of Justice of the EC recently ruled that the exclusive jurisdiction provided for in Article 16, point 1, also applies to proceedings in respect of the payment of rent, and that this includes short-term lettings of holiday homes: Judgment of 15.1.1985, Case 241/83, Rösler v Rottwinkel.
[68] As in the case of third party objections under Greek law: Code of Civil Procedure, 936, paragraph 1, third subparagraph.
[69] "Clear abuse of the process", Judgment of 4.7.1985, Case 220/84, Autoteile v Malhé.
[70] See point 68.
[71] But not including disputes between employees and employers over their respective patent rights arising out of the contract of employment: Judgment of 15.11.1983, Case 288/82, Duijnstee v Goderbauer.
[72] See Schlosser, report, page 123, point 173.
[73] Each party may also designate a different group of courts in which it may be sued: Judgment of 9.11.1978, Case 23/78, Meeth v Glacetal. If an agreement conferring jurisdiction has been stipulated in favour of only one of the parties, the convention (Article 17, fourth paragraph) allows this party to bring the matter before any other court with jurisdiction under the Convention. At all events, the Court of Justice of the EC took the view (in its Judgment given on 24.6.1987 in Case 22/85, Anterist v Crédit Lyonnais) that, for such an agreement to exist in favour of only one of the parties, it would not be enough for the parties to have agreed on the international jurisdiction of a

court or courts of a contracting State in the territory of which the "advantaged" party is domiciled, but the common desire to favour the party must be clearly brought to light.

74 Judgment of 14.12.1976, Case 24/76, Estasis Salotti v RÜWA. However, in the particular case of persons domiciled in Luxembourg, the second paragraph of Article I of the 1968 Protocol requires that an express and specific clause conferring jurisdiction, which the Court of Justice of the European Communities has held to be the case (Judgment of 6.5.1980, Case 784/79, Porta-Leasing v Prestige International) when the provision in question is separate, has been signed and is contained in the same document as the principal contract between the parties.

75 Judgment of 14.12.1976, Case 25/76, Segoura v Bonakdarian.

76 Judgment of 19.6.1984, Case 71/83, Tilly Russ v Haven.

77 Judgment of 11.7.1985, Case 221/84, Berghoefer v ASA. Along the same lines, now also Judgment of 11.11.1986 in Case 313/85, Iveco Fiat v Van Hool, concerning the written prorogation of an agreement conferring jurisdiction.

78 Judgment of 13.11.1979, see footnote 35.

79 See points 48 and 49.

80 Judgment of 17.1.1980, see footnote 51.

81 Judgment of 14.7.1983, Case 201/82, Gerling v Amministrazione del Tesoro dello Stato.

82 Judgment of 19.6.1984, see footnote 76.

83 Judgment of 9.11.1978, see footnote 73.

84 See above, point 58 in fine and point 59 in fine.

85 Judgment of 24.6.1981, Case 150/80, Elefanten Schuh v Jacqmain.

86 See Schlosser, report, page 124, paragraphs 176 and 177.

87 Judgment of 7.3.1985, Case 38/84, Spitzley v Sommer.

88 Judgments of 24.6.1981, see footnote 84 and 7.3.1985, see footnote 87.

89 Judgments of 24.6.1981, see footnote 84; 22.10.1981, Case 27/81, Rohr v Ossberger; 31.3.1982, see footnote 37; 14.7.1983, see footnote 81.

90 Judgment of 15.11.1983, see footnote 71.

91 See points 38 and 44.

92 See Jenard, report, pp. 39 to 41.

93 Law No 1334/1983.

94 See Jenard, report, pp. 40 and 41.

95 Judgment of 7.6.1984, Case 129/83, Zelger v Salinitri.

96 Judgment of 24.6.1981, see footnote 84; a similar rule exists in Greek law in the Code of Civil Procedure, Articles 249 and 250.

97 See point 56.

98 See Jenard, report, page 41.

99 Judgment of 31.3.1982, see footnote 37.

100 See points 24 to 37.

101 Judgment of 21.5.1980, Case 125/79, Denilauler v Coucher Frères.

102 However, as regards the recognition of the res judicata force of foreign judgments concerning status, see Code of Civil Procedure, Article 905, point 4, AII (supreme court) 569/1972, Legal Gazette, 1972, 1427, AII 1007/1982, Legal Gazette 1983, 1006.

103 The question of whether, in the case of a judgment given in default, the document which instituted the proceedings was served on the defendant in sufficient time to enable him to arrange for his defence (Article 27, point 2, of the Convention) is, according to the case law of the Court of Justice of the European Communities, to be examined by the court of the State in which enforcement is sought separately and without reference to the law on service applicable in the State of origin (Judgment of 16.6.1981, Case 166/80, Klomps v. Michel; the point was made more clearly recently: Judgment of 11.6.1985, Case 49/84, Debaecker v Bouwman) or to the opinion of the court which delivered the judgment recognition or enforcement of which is sought (Judgment of 15.7.1982, Case 228/81, Pendy Plastic v Pluspunkt).

104 See point 7.

105 Jenard, report, page 46.

106 See point 79.

107 Judgment of 22.11.1977, Case 43/77, Industrial Diamond Supplies v Riva.

108 Judgment of 10.7.1986, Case 198/85, Carron v Federal Republic of Germany.

109 Judgment of 30.11.1976, Case 42/76, De Wolf v Cox.

110 Jenard, report, page 51.

111 Judgment of 2.7.1985, Case 148/84, Deutsche Genossenschaftsbank v Brasserie du Pêcheur.

112 See point 81 and footnote 107.

113 Judgment of 27.11.1984, Case 258/83, Brennero v Wendel.

114 See Judgment of 12.7.1984, Case 178/83, P. v K.

115 See point 84(b).

116 Judgment of 3.10.1985, Case 119/84, Capelloni v Pelkmans.

117 Jenard, report, page 17.

118 Jenard, report, page 16.

119 See also point 41.

120 Judgment of 6.10.1976, see footnote 50.

121 Judgment of 14.7.1977, Cases 9 and 10/77, Bavaria v Eurocontrol.

122 See point 3.

123 See footnote 95.

* Editor's note

Since this report was drawn up the 1978 Accession Convention entered into force, in relations between the six original Member States of the European Communities and the Kingdom of

Denmark, on 1 November 1986. It will enter into force, with regard to the United Kingdom of Great Britain and Northern Ireland, on 1 January 1987.

[3051]

REPORT

on the Convention on the accession of the Kingdom of Spain and the Portuguese Republic to the Convention on jurisdiction and the enforcement of judgments in civil and commercial matters and to the Protocol on its interpretation by the Court of Justice with the adjustments made to them by the Convention on the accession of the Kingdom of Denmark, of Ireland and of the United Kingdom of Great Britain and Northern Ireland and the adjustments made to them by the Convention on the accession of the Hellenic Republic

(90/C189/06)

(Signed at Donostia/San Sebastián on 26 May 1989)

NOTES

The Cruz, Real and Jenard Report on the accession of Spain and Portugal to the 1968 Brussels Convention and Annexed Protocol is set out at OJ C189, 28.7.90, p 35. References to the original pagination in the Official Journals are noted above the text to which they refer.

by

Mr Martinho de ALMEIDA CRUZ

Judge at First Instance, Legal Counsellor at the Permanent Representation of Portugal to the European Communities

Mr Manuel DESANTES REAL

Professor, Law Faculty, University of Alicante

and Mr Paul JENARD

Honorary Director of Administration at the Belgian Ministry of Foreign Affairs

In addition to the draft Convention and the other instruments drawn up by the government experts, the draft explanatory report was submitted to the Governments of the Member States of the European Communities prior to the Conference of representatives of the Governments of the Member States held in San Sebastián on 26 May 1989.

This report takes account of the comments made by certain Governments. It takes the form of an authorized commentary on the Convention of 26 May 1989.

LIST OF CONTENTS

NB: References are to the Articles of the Brussels Convention and are followed in brackets by the relevant Articles of the Accession Convention.

[OJ C189, 28.7.90, p 38]

CHAPTER 1
GENERAL CONSIDERATIONS

1. Introductory remarks

1. By Article 220 of the Treaty establishing the European Economic Community, the Member States agreed to enter into negotiations with each other, so far as necessary, "with a view to securing for the benefit of their nationals the simplification of formalities governing the reciprocal recognition and enforcement of judgments of courts or tribunals and of arbitration awards".

From this provision has developed, in this specific field, a genuine European legal area which, as will be seen, is destined to extend well beyond the relations between the Member States of the European Communities.

2. Three Conventions have been concluded under Article 220 of the Treaty of Rome prior to the Convention on the accession of Spain and Portugal—

1. the Brussels Convention of 27 September 1968 on jurisdiction and the enforcement of judgments in civil and commercial matters, supplemented by the Protocol of 3 June 1971 on its interpretation by the Court of Justice;
2. the Luxembourg Convention of 9 October 1978 on the accession of Denmark, of Ireland and of the United Kingdom of Great Britain and Northern Ireland to the Brussels Convention and to the 1971 Protocol;
3. the Luxembourg Convention of 25 October 1982 on the accession of Greece to the Brussels Convention as adjusted by the 1978 Convention and the 1971 Protocol.

In addition, negotiations with the Member States of the European Free Trade Association resulted in the Lugano Convention of 16 September 1988, based very largely on the 1968 Brussels Convention as adjusted by the Accession Conventions of 1978 and 1982.

Before entering on a detailed commentary on the Convention on the accession of Spain and Portugal, a brief description of the previous Conventions is helpful.

2. Previous conventions concluded under Article 220 of the Treaty of Rome

1. Brussels Convention of 27 September 1968

3. This Convention on jurisdiction and the enforcement of judgments in civil and commercial matters was concluded between the six original Member States of the European Communities, the Six being Belgium, the Federal Republic of Germany, France, Italy,

Luxembourg and the Netherlands.[1] The Convention entered into force between the six Member States concerned on 1 February 1973.

The Brussels Convention is supplemented by a Protocol signed in Luxembourg on 3 June 1971 conferring on the Court of Justice of the European Communities jurisdiction to interpret the Convention.[2] This Protocol entered into force on 1 September 1975.

4. The Brussels Convention is based on a number of fundamental principles—[3]

— it applies only to matters relating to property,
— it lays down rules of direct jurisdiction, ie applying from the beginning of proceedings,
— the defendant's domicile, and not his nationality, is considered to be the basic rule for determining the jurisdiction of the courts,
— no derogation from this rule is allowed, unless expressly provided for in the Convention,
— the defendant's rights must have been respected in the State of origin,
— the grounds for refusing recognition and enforcement are limited in the interests of ensuring the greatest possible freedom of movement of judgments in the Community,
— the *exequatur* procedure is unified and simplified,
— any State which becomes a member of the European Economic Community is required to accept the Convention as a basis for the negotiations necessary to ensure the implementation of Article 220 of the Treaty of Rome; however, the necessary adjustments may be the subject of special conventions (Article 63).

[OJ C189, 28.7.90, p 39]

NOTES

1 The Convention was published in OJ L299, 31.12.1972. It was accompanied by an explanatory report drawn up by Mr P Jenard, published in OJ C59, 5.3.1979, hereinafter referred to as the Jenard Report.
2 The Protocol was published in OJ L204, 2.8.1975. For its scope, see Jenard Report, pp 66 to 70.
3 For a fuller account of these principles, see Jenard-Möller Report, paragraph 13. Details of that report are given in [para 9, fn 2 below].

2. *Luxembourg Convention of 9 October 1978*

5. After Denmark, Ireland and the United Kingdom of Great Britain and Northern Ireland joined the European Communities (Europe of Nine), a new Convention was concluded on the accession of those three States to the 1968 Convention and to the 1971 Protocol.[1]

6. That Convention, which is in conformity with Article 220 of the Treaty of Rome and Article 63 of the Brussels Convention, entered into force for Denmark on 1 November 1986, for the United Kingdom on 1 January 1987 and for Ireland on 1 June 1988.

7. The Convention of 9 October 1978 is thus currently in force between nine Member States of the Communities. While it introduced into the Brussels Convention a number of quite significant amendments, it left unchanged the basic principles of that Convention, as summarized in paragraph 4 above.

NOTES

1 This Convention, signed in Luxembourg on 9 October 1978, was published in OJ L304, 30.10.1978. It was the subject of a report drawn up by Prof P Schlosser, published in OJ C59, 5.3.1979, hereinafter referred to as the Schlosser Report.

3. *Luxembourg Convention of 25 October 1982*

8. After Greece became a member of the Communities (Europe of Ten) the Luxembourg Convention of 25 October 1982[1] was concluded on its accession to the 1968 Brussels Convention and to the 1971 Protocol, with the adjustments made to them by the 1978 Convention.

That Convention entered into force between Greece and the other States parties to the 1978 Convention on 1 April 1989, with the exception of the United Kingdom, for which it entered into force on 1 October 1989.

The amendments made by the Luxembourg Convention to the Brussels Convention and to the 1971 Protocol are technical only.[2]

NOTES

[1] Published in OJ L388, 31.12.1982. It is accompanied by an explanatory report drawn up by Professors D Evrigenis and K D Kerameus, published in OJ C298, 24.11.1986, hereinafter referred to as the Evrigenis-Kerameus Report.

[2] For the convenience of practitioners, an unofficial consolidated version of the three Conventions (1968, 1978 and 1982) was drawn up by the Council General Secretariat and published in OJ C97, 11.4.1983. A table giving the dates of publication of the various instruments is provided in Annex I to this report.

3. Lugano Convention of 16 September 1988

9. The Member States of the European Free Trade Association[1] were desirous of concluding with the Member States of the European Communities a Convention based on the principles of the 1968 Brussels Convention.

Preparatory proceedings began in 1985 and were completed relatively quickly. They resulted in a Convention on jurisdiction and the enforcement of judgments in civil and commercial matters, which was opened for signature in Lugano on 16 September 1988, at the close of a diplomatic conference held at the invitation of the Swiss Government.[2]

10. Without entering into great detail, it is important here to note that the Lugano Convention is also based on the fundamental principles of the Brussels Convention[3] and that many of its Articles are identical to those of that Convention.

Where amendments have been made to the Brussels Convention, these can often be regarded as improvements. It was therefore natural that they should be taken into account in the preparatory negotiations, within the Communities, for the accession of Spain and Portugal to the Brussels Convention (see Chapter V).

The relationship between the Brussels and Lugano Conventions is dealt with in a specific Article (Article 54b)[4] of the Lugano Convention.

[OJ C189, 28.7.90, p 40]

The Jenard-Möller Report (paragraphs 14 to 17) has the following to say on the subject—

"As shown above, although the structure of the two Conventions is identical and they contain a great number of comparable provisions, they remain separate Conventions.

Application of the two Conventions is governed by Article 54b. The first point to note is that this Article primarily concerns the courts of member countries of the European Communities, these being the only courts which may be required to deliver judgments pursuant to either Convention. Courts in EFTA Member States are not bound by the Brussels Convention since the EFTA States are not parties to that Convention.

However, Article 54b is relevant for the courts of EFTA countries since it was felt advantageous that Article 54b should, for reasons of clarity, contain details relating to *lis pendens*, related actions, recognition and enforcement of judgments.

The philosophy of Article 54b is as follows—

According to paragraph 1, the Brussels Convention continues to apply in relations between Member States of the European Communities.

This applies in particular where—

(a) a person, of whatever nationality, domiciled in one Community State, e g France, is summoned to appear before a court in another such State, e g Italy. The plaintiff's nationality and domicile are immaterial;

(b) a judgment has been delivered in one European Community Member State, e g France, and must be recognized or enforced in another such State, e g Italy.

The Brussels Convention also applies where a person domiciled outside the territory of a European Community Member State and outside the territory of any other State party to the Lugano Convention, e g in the United States, is summoned to appear before a court in a European Community Member State (Article 4 of the Brussels Convention).

In each of these three instances, the Court of Justice of the European Communities has jurisdiction under the 1971 Protocol to rule on problems which may arise with regard to the interpretation of the Brussels Convention.

However, under paragraph 2, the court of a European Community Member State must apply the Lugano Convention where—

PART IV

1. a defendant is domiciled in the territory of a State which is party to the Lugano Convention and an EFTA member or is deemed to be so domiciled under Articles 8 or 13 of the Convention. For instance, if a person domiciled in Norway is summoned before a French court, jurisdiction will be vested in that court only in the cases for which the Lugano Convention provides. In particular the rules of exorbitant jurisdiction provided for in Article 4 of the Brussels Convention may not be relied on as against that person;
2. the courts of an EFTA Member State possess exclusive jurisdiction (Article 16) or jurisdiction by prorogation (Article 17). The courts of Member States of the European Communities may not, for instance, be seised of a dispute relating to real rights in immovable property situated in the territory of a State party to the Lugano Convention and an EFTA Member State, notwithstanding Article 16(1) of the Brussels Convention, which does not apply unless the immovable property is situated in the territory of a State party to the 1968 Convention;
3. recognition or enforcement of a judgment delivered in a State party to the Lugano Convention and an EFTA Member State is being sought in a Community Member State (paragraph 2(c)).

[OJ C189, 28.7.90, p 41]

Paragraph 2 also provides that the Lugano Convention applies where a judgment delivered in a Community Member State is to be enforced in an EFTA Member State party to the Lugano Convention.

This does not resolve potential conflicts between the two Conventions, but it does define their respective scope. Obviously, if a judgment has been delivered in a State party to the Lugano Convention and an EFTA Member State and is to be enforced either in a Community Member State or in an EFTA Member State, the Brussels Convention does not apply;

4. Article 54b also contains provisions relating to *lis pendens* (Article 21) and related actions (Article 22). Under Article 54b(2)(b) a court in a Community Member State must apply these Articles of the Lugano Convention if a court in an EFTA Member State is seised of the same dispute or a related application.

   Apart from the greater clarity which they bring, these provisions serve a double purpose: to remove all uncertainty, and to ensure that judgments delivered in the different States concerned do not conflict;
5. Article 54b(3) lays down that a court in an EFTA Member State may refuse recognition or enforcement of a judgment delivered by a court in a Community Member State if the grounds on which the latter court has based its jurisdiction are not provided for in the Lugano Convention and if recognition or enforcement is being sought against a party who is domiciled in any EFTA Contracting State.

   These grounds for refusal are additional to those provided for in Article 28, and arise essentially from a guarantee sought by the EFTA Member States. The cases involved can be expected to arise relatively seldom, since with regard to rules of jurisdiction the Conventions are extremely similar. The possibility nevertheless remains. The case would arise in the event of a judgment on a contract of employment delivered by a court in a Community Member State which had erroneously based its jurisdiction with regard to a person domiciled in an EFTA Member State either on Article 4 or Article 5(1) of the Brussels Convention, i e in a manner inconsistent with Article 5(1) of the Lugano Convention, which includes a specific provision on contracts of employment, or on an agreement conferring jurisdiction which predated the origin of the dispute (Article 17).

   However, in the interests of freedom of movement of judgments, the judgment will be recognized and enforced provided that this can be done in accordance with the rules of common law of the State addressed, in particular its common law rules on the jurisdiction of foreign courts;
6. For convenience, we have used the term "EFTA Member States" in the above examples. Obviously, the same arrangements would apply to States which are not members of either the EEC or EFTA but accede to the Lugano Convention (see Article 62(1)(b)).

[3052]

NOTES

1 Present EFTA membership: Austria, Finland, Iceland, Norway, Sweden and Switzerland.

2 Published in OJ L319, 25.11.1988. The Convention is accompanied by an explanatory report drawn up jointly by Mr P Jenard and Mr G Möller, hereinafter referred to as the Jenard-Möller Report.

3 See paragraph 4 above.

4 Article 54b states—

"1. This Convention shall not prejudice the application by the Member States of the European Communities of the Convention on jurisdiction and the enforcement of judgments in civil and commercial matters, signed at Brussels on 27 September 1968 and of the Protocol on interpretation of that Convention by the Court of Justice, signed at Luxembourg on 3 June 1971, as amended by the Conventions of Accession to the said Convention and the said Protocol by the States acceding to the European Communities, all of these Conventions and the Protocol being hereinafter referred to as the "Brussels Convention".

2. However, this Convention shall in any event be applied—
   (a) in matters of jurisdiction, where the defendant is domiciled in the territory of a Contracting State which is not a member of the European Communities, or where Articles 16 or 17 of this Convention confer a jurisdiction on the courts of such a Contracting State;
   (b) in relation to a *lis pendens* or to related actions as provided for in Articles 21 and 22, when proceedings are instituted in a Contracting State which is not a member of the European Communities and in a Contracting State which is a member of the European Communities;
   (c) in matters of recognition and enforcement, where either the State of origin or the State addressed is not a member of the European Communities.

3. In addition to the grounds provided for in Title III, recognition or enforcement may be refused if the ground of jurisdiction on which the judgment has been based differs from that resulting from this Convention and recognition or enforcement is sought against a party who is domiciled in a Contracting State which is not a member of the European Communities, unless the judgment may otherwise be recognized or enforced under any rule of law in the State addressed".

CHAPTER II
ACCESSION OF SPAIN AND PORTUGAL TO THE 1968 CONVENTION

11. Article 3(2) of the Act concerning the conditions of accession of the Kingdom of Spain and the Portuguese Republic to the European Communities states that "the new Member States undertake to accede to the conventions provided for in Article 220 of the EEC Treaty … and also to the protocols on the interpretation of those conventions by the Court of Justice, signed by the Member States of the Community as originally constituted or as enlarged and to this end they undertake to enter into negotiations with the present Member States in order to make the necessary adjustments thereto".[1]

The only Convention in force that is based on Article 220 is the Brussels Convention of 27 September 1968 as adjusted by the 1978 and 1982 Conventions.

[OJ C189, 28.7.90, p 42]

12. At the request of the two Governments concerned, an *ad hoc* working party was set up and held its first meeting in Brussels on 20 February 1989 under the chairmanship of Mr A Boixareu Carrera, First Secretary at the Permanent Representation of Spain to the European Communities.

As rapporteurs, the Permanent Representatives Committee appointed Mr Martinho de Almeida Cruz, Judge at First Instance, Legal Counsellor at the Permanent Representation of Portugal to the European Communities. Mr Manuel Desantes Real, Professor in the Law Faculty of the University of Alicante and Mr Paul Jenard, Honorary Director of Administration at the Belgian Ministry of Foreign Affairs.

The *ad hoc* working party met three times between 20 February and 10 April 1989.[2]

13. This report deals with—
— the technical adjustments to the Brussels Convention (Chapter IV),
— the adjustments which take account of the Lugano Convention (Chapter V).

In addition, particular attention is given to the final provisions of the Accession Convention, especially as regards its entry into force and territorial application (Chapter VI).

The amendments to the 1971 Protocol on the interpretation of the Convention by the Court of Justice, although only technical, are dealt with in a separate chapter (Chapter VII).

[3053]

NOTES

1 See OJ L302, 15.11.1985.
2 For the list of participants, see Annex II.

CHAPTER III
INTRODUCTORY REMARKS

In the interests of clarity, we have referred in the report to the corresponding Articles of the Brussels Convention. However, Articles 1 and 2 of Accession Convention have no equivalent in the Brussels Convention.

Article 1 containing the undertaking by Spain and Portugal to accede to the Brussels Convention as adjusted by the subsequent Conventions gives rise to no particular comment.

Article 2 includes the provision that the formal adjustments to those Conventions are set out in Annex I to the 1989 Convention, of which it forms an integral part. This provision is designed, in the interests of legal security, to align the various language versions on those of the Lugano Convention, as a number of minor errors in the earlier Conventions were discovered during these negotiations. As Annex I forms an integral part of the Convention, it is the adjusted texts that will be authentic.

[3054]

CHAPTER IV
TECHNICAL ADJUSTMENTS MADE TO THE BRUSSELS CONVENTION BY THE CONVENTION ON THE ACCESSION OF SPAIN AND PORTUGAL

14. The adjustments concern only—

— exorbitant jurisdictional bases [Article 3 (Article 3)],
— the list of Spanish and Portuguese courts with jurisdiction to apply Title III regarding the recognition and enforcement of judgments,
— bilateral Conventions concerned by the Accession Convention.

1. Exorbitant jurisdictional bases
[Article 3 (Article 3)]

15. *Portugal*:

Articles 65(1)(c), 65(2) and 65a(c) of the Code of Civil Procedure and Article 11 of the Code of Labour Procedure.

This provision, inserted in Article 3 of the Accession Convention, is included in the Lugano Convention; on the basis of information provided by the Portuguese delegation, the Jenard-Möller Report comments as follows (paragraph 31)—

[OJ C189, 28.7.90, p 43]

"Article 65 of Chapter II of the Code of Civil Procedure provides that a foreign national may be sued in a Portuguese court where—

— (paragraph 1 (c)) the plaintiff is Portuguese and, if the situation were reversed, he could be sued in the courts of the State of which the defendant is a national,
— (paragraph 2) under Portuguese law, the court with jurisdiction would be that of the defendant's domicile, if the latter is a foreigner who has been resident in Portugal for more than six months or who is fortuitously on Portuguese territory provided that, in the latter case, the obligation which is the subject of the dispute was entered into in Portugal.

Article 65a(c) of the Code of Civil Procedure confers exclusive jurisdiction on Portuguese courts for actions relating to employment relationships if any of the parties is of Portuguese nationality.

Article 11 of the Code of Labour Procedure gives jurisdiction to Portuguese labour courts for disputes concerning a Portuguese worker where the contract was concluded in Portugal."

16. *Spain:*

Articles 21 and 25 of the Spanish Ley Orgánica del Poder Judicial of 1 July 1985 governing the international jurisdiction of Spanish civil and social courts are directly based on the Brussels Convention, although drafted unilaterally. There are thus no such exorbitant bases in Spain.

In any event, the particulars for insertion in Article 3 of the Convention are not exhaustive since neither is the list contained in that Article, which merely cites examples, thus if there were any exorbitant jurisdiction, it, too, would be inapplicable.

2. Spanish and Portuguese courts having jurisdiction to apply Title III of the Convention

17. The additions are essentially technical in nature.

The formal adjustments to Articles 32 to 41 (Articles 10 to 13) relate exclusively to the courts having jurisdiction and the types of appeal that may be lodged against their judgments.

With regard to Portugal, it should be pointed out that the term "appeal on a point of law" used in Articles 37 and 41 relates to the restriction of the grounds of appeal to an incorrect application of the law as opposed to an incorrect assessment of the facts.

3. Relationship to existing conventions and community acts

(a) *Bilateral Conventions* [Article 55 (Article 18)]

18. The list of bilateral Conventions on the recognition and the enforcement of judgments (of general scope) covers the Conventions concluded by Spain with France, Italy and the Federal Republic of Germany. Portugal has concluded no such Conventions with the Member States of the European Communities.

For the scope of Article 55 of the Brussels Convention the reader is referred to page 59 of the Jenard Report.

Article 58 (Article 20): Franco-Swiss Convention

19. During the negotiations on the Accession Convention it was considered advisable to specify the scope of Article 58 of the 1968 Convention with regard to the application of the Franco-Swiss Convention on jurisdiction and enforcement of judgments in civil matters, signed at Paris on 15 June 1869.

The attention accorded to this Convention is due not to its age but to the fact that it will cease to have effect once the Lugano Convention enters into force between France and the Swiss Confederation. The aim here was to prevent any conflict between the Brussels Convention and the Lugano Convention.

(b) *Multilateral Conventions* [Article 57 (Article 19)]

20. This matter is covered by Article 57. Article 57(2) lays down a much more detailed system for settling conflicts of convention between the Brussels Convention and Conventions concluded on a particular matter. This provision was adopted in the 1978 Accession Convention (see Schlosser Report, paragraphs 238 to 246). In the interests of clarity it was thought preferable that it should be reproduced as such in Article 57(2), just as it was included in the Lugano Convention, although with some differences from that Convention in order to ensure greater freedom of movement of judgments in the Community (see Jenard-Möller Report, paragraphs 81 to 83).

[OJ C189, 28.7.90, p 44]

(c) *Community acts* [Article 57(3) (Article 19]

21. This provision, which appears in the 1978 Convention, has been incorporated as such.

It should be noted that no Community act (Regulation or Directive) has so far contained any provision relating to jurisdiction and the recognition and enforcement of judgments.

The problem of Community acts in relations between the Member States of the European Communities, i e in the Convention on the accession of Spain and Portugal, undoubtedly differs considerably from that which arises in relations with third countries. It is thus normal that on this point the Accession Convention should depart from the Lugano Convention (see Protocol 3 and relevant Declaration, and Jenard-Möller Report, paragraphs 120 to 128).

4. Special consideration regarding Spain: actions on a warranty or guarantee

22. Third party intervention in proceedings is not governed by explicit rules in the Spanish legal system and the want of proper procedures is the source of procedural uncertainty. This legal hiatus has been severely criticized in the works of legal experts, who have recommended that it be remedied in the near future. However, this has not prevented acceptance of third party proceedings in some fields of jurisprudence or in civil laws governing certain specific cases, e g Article 124(3) of Law No 11 of 20 March 1986 on patents and Article 1482[1] of the Civil Code, regarding eviction. Generally speaking, it is the latter rule which is applicable in cases of non-voluntary third party proceedings; in the negotiations between the Member States of the European Communities and those of the European Free Trade Association, it was therefore judged advisable to include it in Article V of Protocol 1. Article 1482 is referred to, albeit indirectly, in Articles 638 (gift), 1145 (joint and several

PART IV EC MATERIALS

obligations), 1529 (assignment of claims), 1540 (exchange), 1553 (tenancy) 1681 (obligations of partners), 1830 (surety), 1831 (co-surety), etc of the Civil Code.

When the problem arose during the negotiations for Spanish and Portuguese accession to the Brussels Convention, the Spanish delegation concluded that jurisprudence in this area could soon develop beyond the limited case of Article 1482 of the Civil Code. It therefore seemed wiser to omit any reference to Spain in Article V of Protocol 1, with there to be no difference in interpretation between the Lugano Convention and the Brussels Convention.

[3055]

NOTES

1 Article 1482 of the Spanish Civil Code—

"The purchaser against whom an action for eviction is brought shall request, within the period specified by the Code of Civil Procedure for replying to this action, that it be served on the vendor(s) as soon as possible.

Service shall be in the manner specified in the said Code for service on defendants.

The time limit for reply by the purchaser shall be suspended until the expiry of the period notified to the vendor(s) for appearing and replying to the action, which shall correspond to the periods laid down for all defendants by the Code of Civil Procedure and shall run from the date of the service referred to in the first paragraph of this Article.

If those cited in eviction proceedings fail to appear in the manner and time specified, the period allowed for replying to the action shall be extended in respect of the purchaser."

CHAPTER V
AMENDMENTS INCORPORATED FROM THE LUGANO CONVENTION

1. Article 5(1) (Article 4): Contract of employment

23.

(a) In negotiations for the Lugano Convention, the EFTA Member States requested that the question of the contract of employment should, where Article 5 and Article 17 were concerned (on the latter Article, see 27 below), be covered by independent provisions in order to ensure that the interpretation of it was that given on a number of occasions by the Court of Justice (see in particular the judgment of the Court of 26 May 1982 in Ivenel v Schwab, Case 133/81, ECR 1982, p 1891, and that given on 15 January 1987 in Shenavai v Kreischer, Case 266/85, ECR 1987, pp 239 to 257). Under the new Article 5(1) of the Lugano Convention on the question of the contract of employment, the place of performance of the obligation in question is taken to mean that where the employee habitually carries out his work; if he does not habitually carry out his work in any one country, this place is the place of business through which he was engaged (see Jenard-Möller Report, paragraphs 35 to 44).

(b) Following signature of the Lugano Convention, the working party took cognizance of the judgment given by the Court of Justice on 15 February 1989 (Six Constructions v Humbert, Case 32/88). In the case, the French Cour de Cassation (Court of Cassation) had requested a ruling, *inter alia*, on the following question: "what is the obligation to be taken into account for the purposes of the application of Article 5(1) of the Brussels Convention of 27 September 1968 where the court is faced with claims based on obligations arising under a contract of employment binding an employee resident in France to a company having its registered office in Belgium which sent him to several countries outside Community territory?"

Although in the operative part of this judgment the Court of Justice restricts itself to pointing out that "Article 5(1) of the Convention must be interpreted as meaning that, as regards contracts of employment, the obligation to be taken into consideration is that which characterizes the contract, in particular the obligation to carry out the duties agreed", it stresses *obiter dictum* the need to ensure adequate protection for the contracting party in the weaker position from the social point of view—ie the employee—concluding that "the particular characteristics of contracts of employment do not justify an interpretation under which Article 5(1) of the Convention would allow the place where the business which engaged the employee is situated to be taken into consideration in cases where it would be difficult or impossible to say in which State the work had been carried out".

(c) The solution adopted attempts to improve on that adopted by the Lugano Convention without departing from it too greatly, while following the guidelines laid down by the Court of Justice on the protection of the weaker party in the contractual relationship (note the same concern for protection in Article 17(5) at 27 below). It was therefore agreed that, where the employee does not habitually carry out his work in any one country, the assumption contained in the last part of Article 5(1) of the Lugano Convention is to operate in favour of the employee only. In order to avoid all ambiguity, the text states that the employee may bring proceedings before the courts for the place where the business[1] which engaged him was situated either at the time of engagement or at the time when proceedings are brought. This stipulation was found necessary following discussions held within the working party on the degree to which the Six Constructions v Humbert ruling should be taken into account.

(d) It follows from the same concern to protect the employee that the expression "in any one country" also includes cases where the work has been carried out, in whole or in part, outside Community territory.

(e) The effect of this provision is that, in any dispute between an employer and an employee, where the employee does not habitually carry out his work in any one country (whether or not within the Community)—

1. the employer can only bring an action before the courts indicated in general terms in Article 2;
2. the employee can bring proceedings before the courts indicated in general terms in Article 2 or those in the last part of Article 5(1) (the courts within the jurisdiction of which the business which engaged the employee is or was situated).

NOTES

[1] The term "place of business", as in the Lugano Convention, is to be understood in the broad sense; in particular, it covers any entity such as a branch or agency with no legal personality (see Jenard-Möller Report, paragraph 43). On the concept of "place of business" see also the judgments of the Court of Justice of 22 November 1978 (Somafer v Ferngas, Case 33/78, pp 2183–2195) and 19 December 1987 (Schotte v Rothschild, Case 218/86, OJ C2, 6.1.1988, p 3).

2. Article 6(4) (Article 5): Combinations of actions *in rem* and *in personam*

24. This provision is taken directly from the text of the Lugano Convention. The Jenard-Möller Report (paragraphs 46 and 47) gives the following commentary on it—

"When a person has a mortgage on immovable property the owner of that property is quite often also personally liable for the secured debt. Therefore it has in some States been made possible to combine an action concerning the personal liability of the owner with an action for the enforced sale of the immovable property. This presupposes of course that the court for the place where the immovable property is situated also has jurisdiction as to actions concerning the personal liability of the owner.

[OJ C189, 28.7.90, p 46]

It was agreed that it was practical that an action concerning the personal liability of the owner of an immovable property could be combined with an action for the enforced sale of the immovable property in those States where such a combination of actions was possible. Therefore it was deemed appropriate to include in the Convention a provision according to which a person domiciled in a Contracting State also may be sued in matters relating to a contract, if the action may be combined with an action against the same defendant in matters relating to rights *in rem* in immovable property, in the court of the Contracting State in which the property is situated.

To illustrate, let us assume that a person domiciled in France is the owner of an immovable property situated in Norway. This person has raised a loan which is secured through a mortgage on his immovable property in Norway. In the eventuality of the loan not being repaid when due, if the creditor wants to bring an action for the enforced sale of the immovable property, the Norwegian court has exclusive jurisdiction under Article 16(1). This court has however, under the present provision, moreover jurisdiction as to an action against the owner of the property concerning his personal liability for the debt, if the creditor wants to combine the latter action with an action for the enforced sale of the property.

It goes without saying that this jurisdictional basis cannot exist by itself. It must necessarily be supplemented by legal criteria which determine on which conditions such a combination is possible. Thus the provisions already existing in or which in the future may be introduced into the legal systems of the Contracting States with reference to the combining of the abovementioned actions remain unaffected by the Lugano Convention.

It goes without saying however that the combination of the two actions which this paragraph deals with have to be instituted by the "same claimant". The "same claimant" includes of course also a person to whom another person has transferred his rights or his successor."

3. Article 16(1) (Article 6): Tenancies

25.

(a) Taking into consideration the Lugano Convention and the intention, according to the Jenard (page 35) and Schlosser (paragraph 164) Reports, of the drafters of the Brussels Convention, the working party decided to insert a new subparagraph (b) in Article 16(1), containing a special provision on short-term tenancies. This insertion was necessary in view of the fact that, in giving a ruling on the provision as drafted in 1968, the Court had been obliged to interpret literally Article 16(1) of the Convention and to decide that it applied to all proceedings concerning the payment of rent, including cases of short-term rental of holiday accommodation (judgment of 15 January 1985, Rösler v Rottwinkel, Case 241/83, ECR 1985, pp 99 to 129).

(b) Because of the interpretation given by the Court to Article 16(1), the Member States of EFTA and a number of Member States of the Communities expressed interest in including in the Lugano Convention a provision relating to tenancies of immovable property for limited periods. An agreement covering this was reached by which Article 16(1) would be supplemented by the addition of a new subparagraph (b) (see Jenard-Möller Report, paragraph 49 *et seq*).

(c) The solution adopted by the Accession Convention differs from that contained in the Lugano Convention. In the first place, it is more restrictive: under subparagraph (b), the plaintiff may also bring an action before the courts of the Contracting State in the territory of which the defendant has his domicile where the proceedings concern tenancies of immovable property concluded for temporary private use for a maximum period of six consecutive months—this refers in particular to contracts agreed for holiday purposes—if (and only if) the tenant and the landlord are natural persons domiciled in the same Contracting State. Legal persons are excluded on the grounds that they are generally concerned with commercial transactions.

Secondly, this provision is not accompanied by any reservation option, since the introduction of a reservation was considered hardly conceivable in connection with a Convention based on Article 220 of the Treaty of Rome. It should be noted that Article 1b in Protocol 1 to the Lugano Convention allows for the possibility of entering a reservation by which any Contracting State may declare that it will not recognize or enforce a decision on tenancies of immovable property if the property concerned is situated on the territory of the State entering the reservation, even where the tenancy is of the type referred to in Article 16(1)(b) and where the jurisdiction of the court of the State of origin is based on the domicile of the defendant (see Jenard-Möller Report, paragraph 53).

[OJ C189, 28.7.90, p 47]

(d) As already pointed out in the Jenard-Möller Report (paragraph 54), "Article 16(1) applies only if the property is situated in the territory of a Contracting State. The text is sufficiently explicit on this point. If the property is situated in the territory of a third State, the other provisions of the Convention apply, e g Article 2 if the defendant is domiciled in the territory of a Contracting State, and Article 4 if he is domiciled in the territory of a third State, etc".

4. Article 17 (Article 7): Agreements conferring jurisdiction

(*a*) *Form of agreements conferring jurisdiction*

26. Paragraph 1 of Article 17 is once again directly from the text of the Lugano Convention.

The Jenard-Möller Report deals with this point at some length (see paragraphs 55 to 59); in summary, it says that, under the new arrangements adopted, agreements conferring jurisdiction should be—

— in writing or evidenced in writing; this is in accordance with the terms of the 1968 Convention,

— or in a form which accords with practices which the parties have established between themselves; on this, see the judgment of the Court of Justice of 14 December 1976, Case 25/76, Segoura v Bonakdarian, ECR 1976, pp 1851 to 1863,

— or, in international trade or commerce, in a form which accords with a usage of which the parties are or ought to have been aware (this is in accordance with the amendments made by the 1978 Convention to the 1968 Convention), but in addition this usage in such trade or commerce must be widely known to, and regularly observed by parties to contracts of the type involved in the particular trade or commerce concerned.

These conditions supplementary to the text of the 1978 Convention were taken from Article 9(2) of the 1980 Vienna Convention on International Contracts for the Sale of Goods.

(*b*) *Agreements conferring jurisdiction relating to contracts of employment* [Article 17(5) (Article 7)]

27.

(a) This paragraph relates to agreements conferring jurisdiction in matters relating to contracts of employment.
There is no one provision of the 1968 Brussels Convention, as modified by the 1978 and 1982 Conventions, which expressly deals with this subject, although it has given rise to a judgment of the Court of Justice.[1]

(b) During negotiations for the Lugano Convention, the representatives of the Member States of EFTA proposed the addition of a new paragraph to Article 17 to the effect that agreements conferring jurisdiction in the matter of an individual contract of employment should only have legal force if they are entered into after the dispute has arisen. The addition was accepted in view of the fact that the idea underlying this provision was the protection of the employee who from the socioeconomic point of view is regarded as the weaker in the contractual relationship (see Jenard-Möller Report, paragraph 60).

(c) It was natural that this amendment made by the Lugano Convention to the Brussels Convention should be the subject of particularly careful study during the negotiations on the Accession Convention, having regard also to the judgment given on 15 February 1989 by the Court of Justice, in which the Court, too, in its grounds for judgment gave particular attention to the protection of the weaker party, i e the employee (Case 32/88, Six Constructions v P Humbert, OJ No C62, 11.3.1979, p 7; see also 23 above).

(d) The solution adopted by the Accession Convention differs from that contained in the Lugano Convention in its emphasis on protection of the employee.
In other words, the solution incorporated in the Lugano Convention was considered too radical: this would be the case in particular where the agreement conferring jurisdiction while entered into prior to the dispute arising, could in the employee's own view be favourable to him. For this reason the new paragraph 5 in Article 17 of the Convention provides that the agreement conferring jurisdiction may only take effect where it is entered into after the dispute has arisen—as in the Lugano Convention—or if "the employee invokes it to seise courts other than those for the defendant's domicile or those specified in Article 5(1)", which moderates the radicality of the Lugano Convention.

[OJ C189, 28.7.90, p 48]

(e) It follows from this provision that—

1. The employee, in any dispute with the employer, may refer the dispute to the agreed courts having jurisdiction, even if the agreement conferring jurisdiction was entered into prior to the dispute arising.
2. Under the terms of the new provision this option is only open to the employee so that he may himself refer the dispute to the court to which prorogation is made; he could not make use of it in exceptional circumstances, e g if he were summoned to appear before the courts of his domicile. The latter possibility is denied him for the sake of protecting legal security and avoiding delaying action.
3. Finally, if the clause conferring jurisdiction attributes it to a court in the State of the defendant's domicile, the court to which prorogation has specially been made would have jurisdiction if the Convention is invoked by the employee. This should be the case, given that the deciding factor is the employee's choice and that where protection of employees is concerned the legal systems of different Contracting States are not all in agreement.

(f) In this new construction, the choice between the courts having jurisdiction (courts of the State of the defendant's domicile, place of performance of the contract of employment or to which prorogation has been made) thus lies entirely at the discretion of the employee in his capacity as plaintiff.

NOTES

[1] See judgment of the Court of Justice of 13 November 1979 in Case 25/79, Sanicentral v Collin, ECR 1979, pp 3423 to 3431.

5. Article 21 (Article 8) *Lis pendens*

28. Article 21 of the Brussels Convention has been brought into line with Article 21 of the Lugano Convention, which lays down that in cases of *lis pendens* a court other than the one first seised, instead of declining jurisdiction of its own motion, must stay its proceedings of its own motion until the jurisdiction of the first court seised has been established. The Jenard-Möller Report (paragraph 64) contains the following commentary on this—

"Only this Article has been amended in Section 8.

Article 21 of the Brussels Convention provides that in cases of *lis pendens*, any court other than the court first seised must of its own motion decline jurisdiction in favour of that court and may stay its proceedings if the jurisdiction of the other court is contested.

The representatives of the EFTA Member States thought this solution was too radical.

They observed that an action often had to be brought in order to comply with a time limit or stop further time from running, and that opinions differed as to whether a time limit had been complied with where an action had been brought before a court lacking jurisdiction internationally.

Thus, in their view, if an action was brought before a judge who would have had jurisdiction, but was not the first to be seised, that judge would of his own motion have to decline jurisdiction in favour of the court first seised. However, that court might perhaps decide that it did not have jurisdiction. In that case, both actions would have been dismissed with the result that the time limits might have run out and the action be time barred.

These remarks have been taken into consideration.

Article 21 has been amended so that the court other than the court first seised will of its own motion stay its proceedings until the jurisdiction of the other court has been established.

A court other than the one first seised will not decline jurisdiction in favour of the court first seised until the jurisdiction of the latter has been established (see Schlosser Report, paragraph 176).

The Court of Justice has ruled that the concepts employed in Article 21 to define a case of *lis pendens* should be considered to be "independent" (point 11 of the grounds for judgment) and that the term *lis pendens* to which Article 21 refers covers a case where a party brings an action before a court in a Contracting State for a declaration that an international sales contract is inoperative or for the termination thereof whilst an action by the other party to secure performance of the said contract is pending before a court in another Contracting State" (judgment of 8 December 1987 in Case 144/86, Gubisch v Palumbo, OJ No C8, 13.1.1988, p 3).

6. Articles 31 and 50 (Articles 9 and 14)

29. The expression "when the order for its enforcement has been issued", used in the Brussels Convention has been replaced by "when it has been declared enforceable", as in the Lugano Convention. This amendment to the Brussels Convention was adopted in order to bring the two Conventions into line, particularly since the two expressions may be considered virtually equivalent (see also the Jenard-Möller Report, paragraph 68 and 69, on this).

7. Article 52, third paragraph (Article 15)

30. The third paragraph of Article 52 has been deleted, in line with the Lugano Convention, as pointed out in the Jenard-Möller Report. This course was taken in view particularly of developments since the 1968 Convention was drafted as regards the domicile of married women (for further explanation, see the Jenard-Möller Report, paragraph 53).

[OJ C189, 28.7.90, p 49]

8. Article 54 (Article 16): Transitional provisions

31.

1. Only technical adjustments have been made to the first and second paragraphs of this Article. No modification to the substance has been made (see Jenard Report, pp 57 and 58, Schlosser Report, paragraphs 228 to 235 and Jenard-Möller Report, paragraph 74).
2. During negotiations for the 1989 Accession Convention it was considered appropriate to reproduce the third paragraph of Article 54 of the Lugano Convention and specify the scope of the words "this Convention". This paragraph corresponds to Article 35 of the 1978 Accession Convention (see Schlosser Report, paragraphs 121 *et seq*) and was declared to extend to the accession of the Hellenic Republic by virtue of Article 1(2) of the 1982 Accession Convention. For reasons of clarity, the 1989 Accession Convention defines what is to be understood by "date of entry into force". It was agreed that the provision shall only apply to agreements in writing dating from before 1 January 1987 where the United Kingdom is concerned and 1 June 1988 where Ireland is concerned.

9. Article 54a (Article 17)

32. This Article corresponds to Article 36 of the 1978 Accession Convention and Article 54a of the Lugano Convention (see Schlosser Report, paragraphs 121 *et seq*, and Jenard-Möller Report, paragraph 75).

It should be noted that despite the wording of Article 54a of the Lugano Convention this provision does not apply to Greece, as Greece has ratified the Brussels Convention of 10 May 1952 on the Arrest of Seagoing Ships. That Convention will also shortly be ratified by Denmark, and the approval procedure is under way in Ireland.

[3056]

CHAPTER VI
FINAL PROVISIONS

1. Territorial application

33. This question was specifically dealt with by Article 60 of the 1968 Convention, as amended by Article 27 of the 1978 Accession Convention. Those two Articles are rescinded by Article 21 of this Accession Convention.

Under those Articles 60 and 27, the 1968 and 1978 Conventions applied to the European territory of the Contracting States, but special provisions applied to France, Denmark, the Netherlands and the United Kingdom.

In accordance with those provisions and with statements made, where in existence, the situation at the date of signature of the Convention on the accession of Spain and Portugal is as follows—

(a) *France*: the 1968 Convention as modified by the 1978 Convention applies to all territories which are an integral part of the French Republic (see Articles 71 *et seq* of the Constitution), including therefore the French Overseas Departments (Guadeloupe, Martinique, Guiana, Réunion), the Overseas Territories (Polynesia, New Caledonia, Southern and Antarctic Territories) and the individual territorial collectivities (Saint Pierre and Miquelon, Mayotte).

(b) *Denmark*: The 1978 Convention does not apply—
- — either to the Faroe Islands, in the absence of any declaration to that effect.
- — or to Greenland, as Denmark declared upon deposit of its instrument of ratification that the Convention did not extend to Greenland.

(c) *The Netherlands*: Since 1 January 1986, the Kingdom of the Netherlands consists of three countries, namely: the Netherlands, the Netherlands Antilles (the islands of Bonaire, Curaçao, Sint Maarten (Netherlands part of the island), Sint Eustatius and Saba) and Aruba.
It should be noted here that the 1968 Convention stated that the Government of the Netherlands could declare the Convention applicable to Surinam and the Netherlands Antilles and that, in the absence of such declaration with respect to the Netherlands Antilles, proceedings taking place in the European territory of the Kingdom as a result of an appeal in cassation against the judgment of a court in the Netherlands Antilles should be deemed to be proceedings in the latter court.

[OJ C189, 28.7.90, p 50]

In the 1978 Convention, the same provision was adopted except in relation to Surinam (Article 27 of the Accession Convention). The Convention therefore does not extend to Surinam. Upon deposit of the Netherlands' instrument of ratification regarding the 1978 Convention, it was expressly stated that the instrument included the declaration that the *ratification applied only to the Kingdom in Europe*.

As regards other territories which since 1986 have been part of the Kingdom of the Netherlands, it should be noted that the Convention's application was extended to Aruba on 30 June 1986.

(d) *United Kingdom:* The 1978 Convention (Article 27) providing that the Convention applied only to the European territory of the Contracting States specified that it did not apply to European territories situated outside the United Kingdom for the international relations of which the United Kingdom was responsible, in the absence of a declaration to the contrary by the United Kingdom with respect to such a territory (on these territories, see Schlosser Report, paragraph 252). No such declaration has been made by the United Kingdom.

34. In conclusion, on the date of the opening for signature of the Convention on the accession of Spain and Portugal, the 1968 Convention as modified by the 1978 and 1982 Conventions—

(a) applied to all territories which are an integral part of the French Republic;
(b) in the case of Denmark, did not apply to Greenland or the Faroe Islands;
(c) in the case of the Netherlands, applied only to the Kingdom's territory in Europe and to Aruba;
(d) in the case of the United Kingdom, did not apply to European territories situated outside the United Kingdom for the international relations of which the United Kingdom was responsible.

2. Effect of depletion of Article 60

35. The deletion of Article 60 is in agreement with the solution adopted in the Lugano Convention which also includes no clause on territorial application (see Jenard-Möller Report, paragraphs 91 to 96). The Convention could therefore be applicable to non-European territories.

36.(a) *Territories affected*

France: See 33 above.

Spain: The Convention applies to the whole territory of the Kingdom of Spain.

Portugal: The Convention applies to the whole territory of the Portuguese Republic. An extension of the Convention to Macao and East Timor would be possible.

Denmark: Denmark could extend the application of the Convention to the Faroe Islands and Greenland.

The Netherlands: The Netherlands could extend application to the Netherlands Antilles, extension to Aruba having already been accomplished.

United Kingdom: The list of non-European territories for the international relations of which the United Kingdom is responsible is given in Annex III.

It should be noted that in the negotiations leading up to the Lugano Convention, the United Kingdom indicated that, of its non-European territories, Anguilla, Bermuda, the British Virgin Islands, Montserrat, the Turks and Caicos Islands and Hong Kong were ones to which there might be a real prospect of the Convention being extended.

37.(b) *Transitional situations*

1. It could happen that before entry into force of the Accession Convention with regard to one of the States concerned (e g Denmark or the United Kingdom), that State might make declarations of extension on the basis of Article 60 of the 1978 Convention.

   In our view, such declarations would become effective with regard to the States which were parties to the 1978 Convention and would continue to apply with regard to Spain and Portugal as from the entry into force of the Accession Convention between those countries and the territory concerned.

2. The effect of the progressive implementation of the Convention on the accession of Spain and Portugal is that for a transitional period this Convention and the 1968 Convention, as modified by the 1978 and 1982 Conventions will be governing relations between the Member States of the Communities simultaneously. To illustrate this, the following example may be taken: if Spain and the Netherlands are the first two States ratifying the Convention on the accession of Spain and Portugal, that Convention will govern relations between them, but between the

Netherlands and the other States which have ratified the 1978 and 1982 Conventions it will be the provisions of those two Conventions which will remain applicable.

[OJ C189, 28.7.90, p 51]

This duality is not without implications for the territorial application of the Conventions. If it is supposed that after ratifying the Convention on the accession of Spain and Portugal the Netherlands wishes to extend it to the Netherlands Antilles, its declaration of extension would have to be made not only on the basis of Article 60 of the 1968 Convention[1] so that the extension will be effective with regard to the other States which are party to that Convention, but also in conformity with the rules of public international law so that it will be effective with regard to Spain and Portugal.

3. Concerning the United Kingdom, under Article 60(16) of the 1978 Convention, the United Kingdom may extend the Convention's application "to *European* territories" situated outside the United Kingdom for the international relations of which it is responsible.

The 1978 Convention does not give the United Kingdom the right to extend the application of this Convention to non-European territories for the international relations of which it is responsible.

Extension of the Convention even to non-European territories for the international relations of which the United Kingdom is responsible will therefore be governed in accordance with the rules of public international law.

38. The situation might prove somewhat complex for a time, but this demonstrates that there is every incentive to ensure that the Convention on the accession of Spain and Portugal is ratified as soon as possible by all the Member States of the Communities.

NOTES

[1] Article 60 here means Article 60 of the 1968 Convention, as modified by Article 27 of the 1978 Convention.

3. Entry into force

39.

1. Under Article 32 of the 1989 Accession Convention, it will enter into force when it has been ratified by two signatory States one of which is the Kingdom of Spain or the Portuguese Republic.
2. An accelerated entry into force of the Convention has been intentionally sought after. This intention was confirmed by the Declaration annexed to the Convention, which establishes a link between the Brussels Convention and the completion of the internal market and urges the States to adopt appropriate measures for ratification as soon as possible and, if possible, by 31 December 1992.
   The effect of Article 32 is that the Convention could enter into force between Spain and Portugal if they were the first countries to ratify it.
3. It was understood that even in such circumstances the Court of Justice would have jurisdiction to give a ruling on the interpretation of the Accession Convention.

[3057]

CHAPTER VII
LUXEMBOURG PROTOCOL OF 3 JUNE 1971

40. In general it may be said that the 1971 Protocol has been adapted to successive Accession Conventions. Its basic structure, which falls within the framework of Article 177 of the Treaty of Rome has not been altered.

The considerations contained in the Jenard Report (OJ No C59, 5.3.1979, p 66), Schlosser Report (paragraphs 255 and 256) and Evrigenis-Kerameus Report (paragraphs 91 to 99) are therefore appropriate for consultation purposes. The necessary technical adjustments consequent upon the accession of Spain and Portugal were made.

Articles 26 and 27 of the 1989 Accession Convention have deleted Articles 6 and 10(d) of the Protocol relating to the Convention's territorial application.

[3058]

[OJ C189, 28.7.90, p 52]

CHAPTER VIII
CONCLUSIONS

1. The situation as revealed in this report may appear to be fairly complex, as the specialist finds himself confronted with a number of international instruments applying to a single area.

2. Without denying this complexity, one should not lose sight of the fact that this is a process which involves a very great effort on the part of 18 European States for the purpose of achieving, in the specific area of jurisdiction and recognition and enforcement of judgments in civil and commercial matters, a true European judicial area resting on common foundations. This creation has been brought about by successive accretions resulting from the extension of the Communities and from the interest shown by the EFTA countries in the Brussels Convention.

3. As a remedy, consideration should first be given to early ratification by all the States concerned of the Convention on the accession of Spain and Portugal, in accordance with the terms of the Declaration and because of the links between the Convention and the single market to which it draws attention. The situation would then certainly be clearer with the Brussels Convention brought up to date, as it were, by all the Member States of the Communities. This apart, arrangements have been adopted—as we described in our discussion of the final provisions (Chapter VI)—to speed up the implementation of this Accession Convention.

4. An early ratification of the Lugano Convention is of no less interest. At a practical level, it would protect persons domiciled in a Member State of the Communities in that they could no longer be required to appear before the courts of EFTA Member States on exorbitant bases, and it would also ensure free movement of judgments. In economic terms, the EFTA countries are the European Communities' principal customer ahead even of the United States and Japan together; conversely, the Communities represent the EFTA countries, most important market. The Lugano Convention should resolve any disputes that may arise in the course of such trade.

5. Since 1 October 1989 the Brussels Convention has been in force between 10 Member States of the Communities.

The following summary indicates the various stages which have been reached—

1. *The 1968 Brussels Convention* entered into force on 1 February 1973 between Belgium, the Federal Republic of Germany, France, Italy, Luxembourg and the Netherlands. The Protocol of 3 June 1971 entered into force between those six countries on 1 September 1975.
2. The 1968 Convention was replaced by the 1978 Convention in relations between those six States and Denmark with effect from 1 November 1986, between all of those and the United Kingdom with effect from 1 January 1987 and between all of those and Ireland with effect from 1 June 1988.
3. The 1982 Convention on the accession of Greece entered into force on 1 April 1989 between Greece and Belgium, the Federal Republic of Germany, Denmark, France, Ireland, Italy, Luxembourg and the Netherlands. It has applied to the United Kingdom since 1 October 1989.
4. The 1989 Accession Convention will enter into force when it has been ratified by two signatory States one of which is the Kingdom of Spain or the Portuguese Republic.
5. The Lugano Convention of 16 September 1988 will enter into force when it has been ratified by two States one of which is a member of the Communities and the other a member of EFTA.

[3059]

[OJ C189, 28.7.90, p 53]

ANNEX I

Convention Protocol Report	*Publication in OJ*	*Entry into force Notification in OJ*	*Declaration of territorial application*
1968 Convention Brussels: 27.9.1968	L299, 31.12.1972	Between the six original Member States:[1] (L299, 31.12.1972)	Federal Republic of Germany: to Berlin Netherlands: Kingdom in Europe + Aruba
1971 Protocol Luxembourg: 3.6.1971	L204, 2.8.1975	Between the Six: 1.9.1975 (L204, 2.8.1975)	Federal Republic of Germany: to Berlin
1978 Convention Luxembourg: 9.10.1978	L304, 30.10.1978 (Irish special edition L388)	Between the Six and Denmark: 1.11.1986 (C285, 12.11.1986) Between the Six + Denmark and United Kingdom: 1.1.1987 (C285, 12.11.1986) Between the Six + Denmark + United Kingdom and Ireland: 1.6.1988 (C125, 12.5.1988)	Denmark: not to Greenland Federal Republic of Germany: to Berlin
1982 Convention Luxembourg: 25.10.1982	L388, 31.12.1982	Between the Six + Denmark + Ireland and Greece: 1.4.1989 (C37, 14.2.1989) Between the Six + Denmark + Ireland + Greece and United Kingdom: 1.10.1989 (C249, 30.9.1989)	Denmark: not to Greenland Federal Republic of Germany: to Berlin
1989 Convention San Sebastián: 26.5.1989	L285, 3.10.1989 (Irish special edition L285)		
Consolidated text of — 1968/1978 Conventions 1971 Protocol — 1968/1978/1982 Conventions 1971 Protocol	L304, 30.10.1978 C97, 11.4.1983		
Lugano Convention Lugano: 16.9.1988	L319, 25.11.1988		
Jenard Report 1968 Convention 1971 Protocol Schlosser Report 1978 Convention	C59, 5.3.1979		

PART IV EC MATERIALS

Convention Protocol Report	*Publication in OJ*	*Entry into force Notification in OJ*	*Declaration of territorial application*
Evrigenis-Kerameus Report 1982 Convention + Greek versions of Jenard and Schlosser Reports	C298, 24.11.1986		

[3060]

NOTES

[1] The Six: Belgium, Federal Republic of Germany, France, Italy, Luxembourg and the Netherlands.

[OJ C189, 28.7.90, p 54]

ANNEX II
LIST OF PARTICIPANTS

CHAIRMAN

Mr A BOIXAREU CARRERA	First Secretary Permanent Representation of Spain to the European Communities

BELGIUM

Mr G GENOT	Counsellor Ministry of Foreign Affairs
Mr J MATTHIJS	Administrative Secretary Ministry of Justice

DENMARK

Mr HC STØVLBÆK	Ministry of Justice
Miss H LINDEGAARD	Legal Attaché Permanent Representation to the European Communities

FEDERAL REPUBLIC OF GERMANY

Mr C BÖHMER	Federal Ministry of Justice
Mr D WELP	Federal Ministry of Justice
Mr B SCHMIDT-STEINHAUSER	Permanent Representation to the European Communities

GREECE

Mrs M TOUSSIS-SCORDAMAGLIA	First Secretary, Legal Affairs Permanent Representation to the European Communities
Mrs C SAMONI-RANTOY	Ministry of Foreign Affairs
Mrs H RIGA	Director Ministry of Justice

SPAIN

Mr J DE MIGUAL ZARAGOZA	Assistant Director

	Ministry of Justice
Mr M DESANTES REAL	Professor, Law Faculty,
	University of Alicante
	Ministry of Justice
FRANCE	
Mr CORMAILLE DE VALBRAY	Ministry of Justice
Mr JP BERAUDO	Magistrate
	Ministry of Justice
IRELAND	
Mr CÓ HUIGINN	Principal
	Department of Justice
ITALY	
Mr A SAGGIO	Consigliere di Cassazione
	Ministry of Justice
Mr R FOGLIA	Consigliere di Cassazione
	Ministry of Justice
Mrs A D'ALESSANDRO	Ministry of Industry

[OJ C189, 28.7.90, p 55]

LUXEMBOURG	
Mrs A CLEMANG	Justice Attaché
	Ministry of Justice

NETHERLANDS

Herr P MEIJKNECHT	Ministry of Justice
Mr G BORCHARDT	Permanent Representation to the European Communities

PORTUGAL

Mr M DE ALMEIDA CRUZ	Judge at First Instance, Legal Counsellor Permanent Representation to the European Communities
Mr L FERNANDEZ	Director Ministry of Foreign Affairs
Mr A RIBEIRO	Director Ministry of Justice

UNITED KINGDOM

Mr D GLADWELL	Lord Chancellor's Department
Mr R WHITE	Lord Chancellor's Department

COMMISSION OF THE EUROPEAN COMMUNITIES

Mr P JENARD	Counsellor Honorary Director of Administration, Belgian Ministry of Foreign Affairs
Mr F DANIS	Administrator, DG III

GENERAL SECRETARIAT OF THE COUNCIL OF THE EUROPEAN COMMUNITIES

Mr V SCORDAMAGLIA	Director DG C Internal Market
Mr O PETERSEN	Principal administrator DG C Internal Market
Miss G MALESY	Principal secretary DG C Internal Market

[3061]

[OJ C189, 28.7.90, p 56]

ANNEX III

LIST OF NON-EUROPEAN TERRITORIES FOR WHOSE INTERNATIONAL RELATIONS THE UNITED KINGDOM IS RESPONSIBLE

— Caribbean and North Atlantic: Anguilla, Bermuda, Cayman Islands, Montserrat, Turks and Caicos Islands, British Virgin Islands;

— South Atlantic: British Antarctic Territory, Falkland Islands, South Georgia and the South Sandwich Islands, St Helena and dependencies (Ascension Island) (Tristan da Cunha);

— Indian Ocean: British Indian Ocean Territory;

— South Pacific: Pitcairn Island, Henderson, Ducie and Oeno;

— Hong Kong.

[3062]

1988 LUGANO CONVENTION ON JURISDICTION AND THE ENFORCEMENT OF JUDGMENTS IN CIVIL AND COMMERCIAL MATTERS

NOTES

Please note that this Handbook is not an official publication by the Swiss authorities. The official text of the Lugano Convention is published in the Swiss Collection of Federal Law. The text of the following Convention and the Protocols annexed thereto appear as set out in the Civil Jurisdiction and Judgments Act 1982, Sch 3C. They are also set out in OJ L319, 25.11.1988, p 9. For current status of the 1988 Lugano Convention, see Table 1 at **[4676]**. See also the Introductory Note at the beginning of Pt IV(B) above.

[ARRANGEMENT OF PROVISIONS

PREAMBLE

The High Contracting Parties to this Convention,

Anxious to strengthen in their territories the legal protection of persons therein established,

Considering that it is necessary for this purpose to determine the international jurisdiction of their courts, to facilitate recognition and to introduce an expeditious procedure for securing the enforcement of judgments, authentic instruments and court settlements,

Aware of the links between them, which have been sanctioned in the economic field by the free trade agreements concluded between the European Economic Community and the States members of the European Free Trade Association,

Taking into account the Brussels Convention of 27 September 1968 on jurisdiction and the enforcement of judgments in civil and commercial matters, as amended by the Accession Conventions under the successive enlargements of the European Communities,

Persuaded that the extension of the principles of that Convention to the States parties to this instrument will strengthen legal and economic co-operation in Europe,

Desiring to ensure as uniform an interpretation as possible of this instrument,

Have in this spirit decided to conclude this Convention and

Have agreed as follows—

TITLE I
SCOPE

Article 1

This Convention shall apply in civil and commercial matters whatever the nature of the court or tribunal. It shall not extend, in particular, to revenue, customs or administrative matters.1

The Convention shall not apply to—

1. the status or legal capacity of natural persons, rights in property arising out of a matrimonial relationship, wills and succession;
2. bankruptcy, proceedings relating to the winding-up of insolvent companies or other legal persons, judicial arrangements, compositions and analogous proceedings;
3. social security;
4. arbitration.

TITLE II
JURISDICTION

SECTION 1
GENERAL PROVISIONS

Article 2

Subject to the provisions of this Convention, persons domiciled in a Contracting State shall, whatever their nationality, be sued in the courts of that State.

Persons who are not nationals of the State in which they are domiciled shall be governed by the rules of jurisdiction applicable to nationals of that State.

Article 3

Persons domiciled in a Contracting State may be sued in the courts of another Contracting State only by virtue of the rules set out in Sections 2 to 6 of this Title.

In particular the following provisions shall not be applicable as against them—

— in Belgium: Article 15 of the civil code (Code civil—Burgerlijk Wetboek) and Article 638 of the judicial code (Code judiciaire—Gerechtelijk Wetboek),
— in Denmark: Article 246(2) and (3) of the law on civil procedure (Lov om rettens pleje),
— in the Federal Republic of Germany: Article 23 of the code of civil procedure (Zivilprozeßordnung),
— in Greece: Article 40 of the code of civil procedure (Κωδικας πολιτικης δικονομιας),
— in France: Articles 14 and 15 of the civil code (Code civil),
— in Ireland: the rules which enable jurisdiction to be founded on the document instituting the proceedings having been served on the defendant during his temporary presence in Ireland,
— in Iceland: Article 77 of the Civil Proceedings Act (lög um međferđ einkamála í héradi),
— in Italy: Articles 2 and 4, Nos 1 and 2 of the code of civil procedure (Codice di procedura civile),
— in Luxembourg: Articles 14 and 15 of the civil code (Code civil),
— in the Netherlands: Articles 126(3) and 127 of the code of civil procedure (Wetboek van Burgerlijke Rechtsvordering),
— in Norway: Section 32 of the Civil Proceedings Act (tvistemålsloven),
— in Austria: Article 99 of the Law on Court Jurisdiction (Jurisdiktionsnorm),
[— in Poland: Articles 1103 and 1110, of the Code of Civil Procedure,]
— in Portugal: Articles 65(1)(c), 65(2) and 65A(c) of the code of civil procedure (Código de Processo Civil) and Article 11 of the code of labour procedure (Código de Processo de Trabalho),
— in Switzerland: le for du lieu du séquestre/Gerichtsstand des Arrestortes/foro del luogo del sequestro within the meaning of Article 4 of the loi fédérale sur le droit international privé/Bundesgesetz über das internationale Privatrecht/legge federale sul diritto internazionale privato,

— in Finland: the second, third and fourth sentences of Section 1 of Chapter 10 of the Code of Judicial Procedure (oikeudenkäymiskaari/rättegångsbalken),

— in Sweden: the first sentence of Section 3 of Chapter 10 of the Code of Judicial Procedure (Rättegångsbalken),

— in the United Kingdom: the rules which enable jurisdiction to be founded on—
  (a) the document instituting the proceedings having been served on the defendant during his temporary presence in the United Kingdom; or
  (b) the presence within the United Kingdom of property belonging to the defendant; or
  (c) the seizure by the plaintiff of property situated in the United Kingdom.

Article 4

If the defendant is not domiciled in a Contracting State, the jurisdiction of the courts of each Contracting State shall, subject to the provisions of Article 16, be determined by the law of that State.

As against such a defendant, any person domiciled in a Contracting State may, whatever his nationality, avail himself in that State of the rules of jurisdiction there in force, and in particular those specified in the second paragraph of Article 3, in the same way as the nationals of that State.

SECTION 2
SPECIAL JURISDICTION

Article 5

A person domiciled in a Contracting State may, in another Contracting State, be sued—

1. in matters relating to a contract, in the courts for the place of performance of the obligation in question; in matters relating to individual contracts of employment, this place is that where the employee habitually carries out his work, or if the employee does not habitually carry out his work in any one country, this place shall be the place of business through which he was engaged;
2. in matters relating to maintenance, in the courts for the place where the maintenance creditor is domiciled or habitually resident or, if the matter is ancillary to proceedings concerning the status of a person, in the court which, according to its own law, has jurisdiction to entertain those proceedings, unless that jurisdiction is based solely on the nationality of one of the parties;
3. in matters relating to tort, delict or quasi-delict, in the courts for the place where the harmful event occurred;
4. as regards a civil claim for damages or restitution which is based on an act giving rise to criminal proceedings, in the court seised of those proceedings, to the extent that that court has jurisdiction under its own law to entertain civil proceedings;
5. as regards a dispute arising out of the operations of a branch, agency or other establishment, in the courts for the place in which the branch, agency or other establishment is situated;
6. in his capacity as settlor, trustee or beneficiary of a trust created by the operation of a statute, or by a written instrument, or created orally and evidenced in writing, in the courts of the Contracting State in which the trust is domiciled;
7. as regards a dispute concerning the payment of remuneration claimed in respect of the salvage of a cargo or freight, in the court under the authority of which the cargo or freight in question—
   (a) has been arrested to secure such payment, or
   (b) could have been so arrested, but bail or other security has been given;

provided that this provision shall apply only if it is claimed that the defendant has an interest in the cargo or freight or had such an interest at the time of salvage.

Article 6

A person domiciled in a Contracting State may also be sued—

1. where he is one of a number of defendants, in the courts for the place where any of one of them is domiciled;
2. as a third party in an action on a warranty or guarantee or in any other third party

PART IV
EC MATERIALS

proceedings, in the court seised of the original proceedings, unless these were instituted solely with the object of removing him from the jurisdiction of the court which would be competent in his case;

3. on a counterclaim arising from the same contract or facts on which the original claim was based, in the court in which the original claim is pending;
4. in matters relating to a contract, if the action may be combined with an action against the same defendant in matters relating to rights *in rem* in immovable property, in the court of the Contracting State in which the property is situated.

Article 6A

Where by virtue of this Convention a court of a Contracting State has jurisdiction in actions relating to liability arising from the use or operation of a ship, that court, or any other court substituted for this purpose by the internal law of that State, shall also have jurisdiction over claims for limitation of such liability.

SECTION 3
JURISDICTION IN MATTERS RELATING TO INSURANCE

Article 7

In matters relating to insurance, jurisdiction shall be determined by this Section, without prejudice to the provisions of Articles 4 and 5(5).

Article 8

An insurer domiciled in a Contracting State may be sued—

1. in the courts of the State where he is domiciled; or
2. in another Contracting State, in the courts for the place where the policyholder is domiciled; or
3. if he is a co-insurer, in the courts of a Contracting State in which proceedings are brought against the leading insurer.

An insurer who is not domiciled in a Contracting State but has a branch, agency or other establishment in one of the Contracting States shall, in disputes arising out of the operations of the branch, agency or establishment, be deemed to be domiciled in that State.

Article 9

In respect of liability insurance or insurance of immovable property, the insurer may in addition be sued in the courts for the place where the harmful event occurred. The same applies if movable and immovable property are covered by the same insurance policy and both are adversely affected by the same contingency.

Article 10

In respect of liability insurance, the insurer may also, if the law of the court permits it, be joined in proceedings which the injured party has brought against the insured.

The provisions of Articles 7, 8 and 9 shall apply to actions brought by the injured party directly against the insurer, where such direct actions are permitted.

If the law governing such direct actions provides that the policy-holder or the insured may be joined as a party to the action, the same court shall have jurisdiction over them.

Article 11

Without prejudice to the provisions of the third paragraph of Article 10, an insurer may bring proceedings only in the courts of the Contracting State in which the defendant is domiciled, irrespective of whether he is the policy-holder, the insured or a beneficiary.

The provisions of this Section shall not affect the right to bring a counterclaim in the court in which, in accordance with this Section, the original claim is pending.

Article 12

The provisions of this Section may be departed from only by an agreement on jurisdiction—

1. which is entered into after the dispute has arisen; or
2. which allows the policy-holder, the insured or a beneficiary to bring proceedings in courts other than those indicated in this Section; or
3. which is concluded between a policy-holder and an insurer, both of whom are at the time of conclusion of the contract domiciled or habitually resident in the same Contracting State, and which has the effect of conferring jurisdiction on the courts of that State even if the harmful event were to occur abroad, provided that such an agreement is not contrary to the law of the State; or
4. which is concluded with a policy-holder who is not domiciled in a Contracting State, except in so far as the insurance is compulsory or relates to immovable property in a Contracting State; or
5. which relates to a contract of insurance in so far as it covers one or more of the risks set out in Article 12A.

Article 12A

The following are the risks referred to in Article 12(5)—

1. any loss of or damage to—
   (a) sea-going ships, installations situated offshore or on the high seas, or aircraft, arising from perils which relate to their use for commercial purposes;
   (b) goods in transit other than passengers' baggage where the transit consists of or includes carriage by such ships or aircraft;
2. any liability, other than for bodily injury to passengers or loss of or damage to their baggage;
   (a) arising out of the use or operation of ships, installations or aircraft as referred to in (1)(a) above in so far as the law of the Contracting State in which such aircraft are registered does not prohibit agreements on jurisdiction regarding insurance of such risks;
   (b) for loss or damage caused by goods in transit as described in (1)(b) above;
3. any financial loss connected with the use or operation of ships, installations or aircraft as referred to in (1)(a) above, in particular loss of freight or charter-hire;
4. any risk or interest connected with any of those referred to in (1) to (3) above.

SECTION 4
JURISDICTION OVER CONSUMER CONTRACTS

Article 13

In proceedings concerning a contract concluded by a person for a purpose which can be regarded as being outside his trade or profession, hereinafter called "the consumer", jurisdiction shall be determined by this Section, without prejudice to the provisions of Articles 4 and 5(5), if it is—

1. a contract for the sale of goods on instalment credit terms; or
2. a contract for a loan repayable by instalments, or for any other form of credit, made to finance the sale of goods; or
3. any other contract for the supply of goods or a contract for the supply of services, and
   (a) in the State of the consumer's domicile the conclusion of the contract was preceded by a specific invitation addressed to him or by advertising, and
   (b) the consumer took in that State the steps necessary for the conclusion of the contract.

Where a consumer enters into a contract with a party who is not domiciled in a Contracting State but has a branch, agency or other establishment in one of the Contracting States, that party shall, in disputes arising out of the operations of the branch, agency or establishment, be deemed to be domiciled in that State.

This Section shall not apply to contracts of transport.

Article 14

A consumer may bring proceedings against the other party to a contract either in the courts of the Contracting State in which that party is domiciled or in the courts of the Contracting State in which he is himself domiciled.

Proceedings may be brought against a consumer by the other party to the contract only in the courts of the Contracting State in which the consumer is domiciled.

These provisions shall not affect the right to bring a counterclaim in the court in which, in accordance with this Section, the original claim is pending.

Article 15

The provisions of this Section may be departed from only by an agreement—

1. which is entered into after the dispute has arisen; or
2. which allows the consumer to bring proceedings in courts other than those indicated in this Section; or
3. which is entered into by the consumer and the other party to the contract, both of whom are at the time of conclusion of the contract domiciled or habitually resident in the same Contracting State, and which confers jurisdiction on the courts of that State, provided that such an agreement is not contrary to the law of that State.

SECTION 5
EXCLUSIVE JURISDICTION

Article 16

The following courts shall have exclusive jurisdiction, regardless of domicile—

1.
   (a) in proceedings which have as their object rights *in rem* in immovable property or tenancies of immovable property, the courts of the Contracting State in which the property is situated;
   (b) however, in proceedings which have as their object tenancies of immovable property concluded for temporary private use for a maximum period of six consecutive months, the courts of the Contracting State in which the defendant is domiciled shall also have jurisdiction, provided that the tenant is a natural person and neither party is domiciled in the Contracting State in which the property is situated;
2. in proceedings which have as their object the validity of the constitution, the nullity or the dissolution of companies or other legal persons or associations of natural or legal persons, or the decisions of their organs, the courts of the Contracting State in which the company, legal person or association has its seat;
3. in proceedings which have as their object the validity of entries in public registers, the courts of the Contracting State in which the register is kept;
4. in proceedings concerned with the registration or validity of patents, trade marks, designs, or other similar rights required to be deposited or registered, the courts of the Contracting State in which the deposit or registration has been applied for, has taken place or is under the terms of an international convention deemed to have taken place;
5. in proceedings concerned with the enforcement of judgments, the courts of the Contracting State in which the judgment has been or is to be enforced.

SECTION 6
PROROGATION OF JURISDICTION

Article 17

1. If the parties, one or more of whom is domiciled in a Contracting State, have agreed that a court or the courts of a Contracting State are to have jurisdiction to settle any disputes which have arisen or which may arise in connection with a particular legal relationship, that court or those courts shall have exclusive jurisdiction. Such an agreement conferring jurisdiction shall be either—
   (a) in writing or evidenced in writing, or
   (b) in a form which accords with practices which the parties have established between themselves, or
   (c) in international trade or commerce, in a form which accords with a usage of which the parties are or ought to have been aware and which in such trade or commerce is widely known to, and regularly observed by, parties to contracts of the type involved in the particular trade or commerce concerned.

Where such an agreement is concluded by parties, none of whom is domiciled in a Contracting State, the courts of other Contracting States shall have no jurisdiction over their disputes unless the court or courts chosen have declined jurisdiction.

2. The court or courts of a Contracting State on which a trust instrument has conferred jurisdiction shall have exclusive jurisdiction in any proceedings brought against a settlor, trustee or beneficiary, if relations between these persons or their rights or obligations under the trust are involved.

3. Agreements or provisions of a trust instrument conferring jurisdiction shall have no legal force if they are contrary to the provisions of Article 12 or 15, or if the courts whose jurisdiction they purport to exclude have exclusive jurisdiction by virtue of Article 16.

4. If an agreement conferring jurisdiction was concluded for the benefit of only one of the parties, that party shall retain the right to bring proceedings in any other court which has jurisdiction by virtue of this Convention.

5. In matters relating to individual contracts of employment an agreement conferring jurisdiction shall have legal force only if it is entered into after the dispute has arisen.

Article 18

Apart from jurisdiction derived from other provisions of this Convention, a court of a Contracting State before whom a defendant enters an appearance shall have jurisdiction. This rule shall not apply where appearance was entered solely to contest the jurisdiction, or where another court has exclusive jurisdiction by virtue of Article 16.

SECTION 7
EXAMINATION AS TO JURISDICTION AND ADMISSIBILITY

Article 19

Where a court of a Contracting State is seised of a claim which is principally concerned with a matter over which the courts of another Contracting State have exclusive jurisdiction by virtue of Article 16, it shall declare of its own motion that it has no jurisdiction.

Article 20

Where a defendant domiciled in one Contracting State is sued in a court of another Contracting State and does not enter an appearance, the court shall declare of its own motion that it has no jurisdiction unless its jurisdiction is derived from the provisions of this Convention.

The court shall stay the proceedings so long as it is not shown that the defendant has been able to receive the document instituting the proceedings or an equivalent document in sufficient time to enable him to arrange for his defence, or that all necessary steps have been taken to this end.

The provisions of the foregoing paragraph shall be replaced by those of Article 15 of the Hague Convention of 15 November 1965 on the service abroad of judicial and extrajudicial documents in civil or commercial matters, if the document instituting the proceedings or notice thereof had to be transmitted abroad in accordance with that Convention.

SECTION 8
LIS PENDENS—RELATED ACTIONS

Article 21

Where proceedings involving the same cause of action and between the same parties are brought in the courts of different Contracting States, any court other than the court first seised shall of its own motion stay its proceedings until such time as the jurisdiction of the court first seised is established.

Where the jurisdiction of the court first seised is established, any court other than the court first seised shall decline jurisdiction in favour of that court.

Article 22

Where related actions are brought in the courts of different Contracting States, any court other than the court first seised may, while the actions are pending at first instance, stay its proceedings.

A court other than the court first seised may also, on the application of one of the parties, decline jurisdiction if the law of that court permits the consolidation of related actions and the court first seised has jurisdiction over both actions.

For the purposes of this Article, actions are deemed to be related where they are so closely connected that it is expedient to hear and determine them together to avoid the risk of irreconcilable judgments resulting from separate proceedings.

Article 23

Where actions come within the exclusive jurisdiction of several courts, any court other than the court first seised shall decline jurisdiction in favour of that court.

SECTION 9
PROVISIONAL, INCLUDING PROTECTIVE, MEASURES

Article 24

Application may be made to the courts of a Contracting State for such provisional, including protective, measures as may be available under the law of that State, even if, under this Convention, the courts of another Contracting State have jurisdiction as to the substance of the matter.

TITLE III
RECOGNITION AND ENFORCEMENT

Article 25

For the purposes of this Convention, "judgment" means any judgment given by a court or tribunal of a Contracting State, whatever the judgment may be called, including a decree, order, decision or writ of execution, as well as the determination of costs or expenses by an officer of the court.

SECTION 1
RECOGNITION

Article 26

A judgment given in a Contracting State shall be recognised in the other Contracting State without any special procedure being required.

Any interested party who raises the recognition of a judgment as the principal issue in a dispute may, in accordance with the procedures provided for in Sections 2 and 3 of this Title, apply for a decision that the judgment be recognised.

If the outcome of proceedings in a court of a Contracting State depends on the determination of an incidental question of recognition that court shall have jurisdiction over that question.

Article 27

A judgment shall not be recognised—

1. if such recognition is contrary to public policy in the State in which recognition is sought;
2. where it was given in default of appearance, if the defendant was not duly served with the document which instituted the proceedings or with an equivalent document in sufficient time to enable him to arrange for his defence;
3. if the judgment is irreconcilable with a judgment given in a dispute between the same parties in the State in which recognition is sought;
4. if the court of the State of origin, in order to arrive at its judgment, has decided a preliminary question concerning the status or legal capacity of natural persons, rights in property arising out of a matrimonial relationship, wills or succession in a way that conflicts with a rule of the private international law of the State in which the recognition is sought, unless the same result would have been reached by the application of the rules of private international law of that State;

5. if the judgment is irreconcilable with an earlier judgment given in a non-contracting State involving the same cause of action and between the same parties, provided that this latter judgment fulfils the conditions necessary for its recognition in the State addressed.

Article 28

Moreover, a judgment shall not be recognised if it conflicts with the provisions of Section 3, 4 or 5 of Title II or in a case provided for in Article 59.

A judgment may furthermore be refused recognition in any case provided for in Article 54B(3) or 57(4).

In its examination of the grounds of jurisdiction referred to in the foregoing paragraphs, the court or authority applied to shall be bound by the findings of fact on which the court of the State of origin based its jurisdiction.

Subject to the provisions of the first and second paragraphs, the jurisdiction of the court of the State of origin may not be reviewed; the test of public policy referred to in Article 27(1) may not be applied to the rules relating to jurisdiction.

Article 29

Under no circumstances may a foreign judgment be reviewed as to its substance.

Article 30

A court of a Contracting State in which recognition is sought of a judgment given in another Contracting State may stay the proceedings if an ordinary appeal against the judgment has been lodged.

A court of a Contracting State in which recognition is sought of a judgment given in Ireland or the United Kingdom may stay the proceedings if enforcement is suspended in the State of origin by reason of an appeal.

SECTION 2
ENFORCEMENT

Article 31

A judgment given in a Contracting State and enforceable in that State shall be enforced in another Contracting State when, on the application of any interested party, it has been declared enforceable there.

However, in the United Kingdom, such a judgment shall be enforced in England and Wales, in Scotland, or in Northern Ireland when, on the application of any interested party, it has been registered for enforcement in that part of the United Kingdom.

Article 32

1. The application shall be submitted—
   - — in Belgium, to the tribunal de première instance or rechtbank van eerste aanleg,
   - — in Denmark, to the byret,
   - — in the Federal Republic of Germany, to the presiding judge of a chamber of the Landgericht,
   - — in Greece, to the μονομελες πρωτοδικειο,
   - — in Spain, to the Juzgado de Primera Instancia,
   - — in France, to the presiding judge of the tribunal de grande instance,
   - — in Ireland, to the High Court,
   - — in Iceland, to the héraðsdómari,
   - — in Italy, to the corte d'appello,
   - — in Luxembourg, to the presiding judge of the tribunal d'arrondissement,
   - — in the Netherlands, to the presiding judge of the arrondissementsrechtbank,
   - — in Norway, to the herredsrett or byrett as namsrett,
   - — in Austria, to the Landesgericht or the Kreisgericht,
   - [— in Poland, to the sad okregowy,]
   - — in Portugal, to the Tribunal Judicial de Círculo,
   - — in Switzerland—

PART IV
EC MATERIALS

(a) in respect of judgments ordering the payment of a sum of money, to the juge de la mainlevée/Rechtsöffnungsrichter/giudice competente a pronunciare sul rigetto dell'opposizione, within the framework of the procedure governed by Articles 80 and 81 of the loi fédérale sur la poursuite pour dettes et la faillite/Bundesgesetz über Schuldbetreibung und Konkurs/legge federale sulla esecuzione e sul fallimento;

(b) in respect of judgments ordering a performance other than the payment of a sum of money, to the juge cantonal d'exequatur compétent/zuständiger kantonaler Vollstreckungsrichter/giudice cantonale competente a pronunciare l'exequatur,

— in Finland, to the ulosotonhaltija/överexekutor,
— in Sweden, to the Svea hovrätt,
— in the United Kingdom—

(a) in England and Wales, to the High Court of Justice, or in the case of a maintenance judgment to the Magistrates' Court on transmission by the Secretary of State;

(b) in Scotland, to the Court of Session, or in the case of a maintenance judgment to the Sheriff Court on transmission by the Secretary of State;

(c) in Northern Ireland, to the High Court of Justice, or in the case of a maintenance judgment to the Magistrates' Court on transmission by the Secretary of State.

2. The jurisdiction of local courts shall be determined by reference to the place of domicile of the party against whom enforcement is sought. If he is not domiciled in the State in which enforcement is sought, it shall be determined by reference to the place of enforcement.

Article 33

The procedure for making the application shall be governed by the law of the State in which enforcement is sought.

The applicant must give an address for service of process within the area of jurisdiction of the court applied to. However, if the law of the State in which enforcement is sought does not provide for the furnishing of such an address, the applicant shall appoint a representative *ad litem.*

The documents referred to in Articles 46 and 47 shall be attached to the application.

Article 34

The court applied to shall give its decision without delay; the party against whom enforcement is sought shall not at this stage of the proceedings be entitled to make any submissions on the application.

The application may be refused only for one of the reasons specified in Articles 27 and 28.

Under no circumstances may the foreign judgment be reviewed as to its substance.

Article 35

The appropriate officer of the court shall without delay bring the decision given on the application to the notice of the applicant in accordance with the procedure laid down by the law of the State in which enforcement is sought.

Article 36

If enforcement is authorised, the party against whom enforcement is sought may appeal against the decision within one month of service thereof.

If that party is domiciled in a Contracting State other than that in which the decision authorising enforcement was given, the time for appealing shall be two months and shall run from the date of service, either on him in person or at his residence. No extension of time may be granted on account of distance.

Article 37

1. An appeal against the decision authorising enforcement shall be lodged in accordance with the rules governing procedure in contentious matters—

— in Belgium, with the tribunal de première instance or rechtbank van eerste aanleg,
— in Denmark, with the landsret,
— in the Federal Republic of Germany, with the Oberlandesgericht,
— in Greece, with the εφετειο,
— in Spain, with the Audiencia Provincial,
— in France, with the cour d'appel,
— in Ireland, with the High Court,
— in Iceland, with the héraðsdómari,
— in Italy, with the corte d'appello,
— in Luxembourg, with the Cour supérieure de justice sitting as a court of civil appeal,
— in the Netherlands, with the arrondissementsrechtbank,
— in Norway, with the lagmannsrett,
— in Austria, with the Landesgericht or the Kreisgericht,
[— in Poland, to the sad okregowy by an appeal in cassation,]
— in Portugal, with the Tribunal da Relacao,
— in Switzerland, with the tribunal cantonal/Kantonsgericht/tribunale cantonale,
— in Finland, with the hovioikeus/hovrätt,
— in Sweden, with the Svea hovrätt,
— in the United Kingdom—
 (a) in England and Wales, with the High Court of Justice, or in the case of a maintenance judgment with the Magistrates' Court;
 (b) in Scotland, with the Court of Session, or in the case of a maintenance judgment with the Sheriff Court;
 (c) in Northern Ireland, with the High Court of Justice, or in the case of a maintenance judgment with the Magistrates' Court.

2. The judgment given on the appeal may be contested only—
— in Belgium, Greece, Spain, France, Italy, Luxembourg and in the Netherlands, by an appeal in cassation,
— in Denmark, by an appeal to the højesteret, with the leave of the Minister of Justice,
— in the Federal Republic of Germany, by a Rechtsbeschwerde,
— in Ireland, by an appeal on a point of law to the Supreme Court,
— in Iceland, by an appeal to the Hæstiréttur,
— in Norway, by an appeal (kjæremål or anke) to the Hoyesteretts Kjæremålsutvalg or Hoyesterett,
— in Austria, in the case of an appeal, by a Revisionsrekurs and, in the case of opposition proceedings, by a Berufung with the possibility of a Revision,
— in Portugal, by an appeal on a point of law,
— in Switzerland, by a recours de droit public devant le tribunal fédéral/staatsrechtliche Beschwerde beim Bundesgericht/ricorso di diritto pubblico davanti al tribunale federale,
— in Finland, by an appeal to the korkein oikeus/högsta domstolen,
— in Sweden, by an appeal to the högsta domstolen,
— in the United Kingdom, by a single further appeal on a point of law.

Article 38

The court with which the appeal under the first paragraph of Article 37(1) is lodged may, on the application of the appellant, stay the proceedings if an ordinary appeal has been lodged against the judgment in the State of origin or if the time for such an appeal has not yet expired; in the latter case, the court may specify the time within which such an appeal is to be lodged.

Where the judgment was given in Ireland or the United Kingdom, any form of appeal available in the State of origin shall be treated as an ordinary appeal for the purposes of the first paragraph.

The court may also make enforcement conditional on the provision of such security as it shall determine.

Article 39

During the time specified for an appeal pursuant to Article 36 and until any such appeal has been determined, no measures of enforcement may be taken other than protective measures taken against the property of the party against whom enforcement is sought.

The decision authorising enforcement shall carry with it the power to proceed to any such protective measures.

Article 40

1. If the application for enforcement is refused, the applicant may appeal—
— in Belgium, to the cour d'appel or hof van beroep,
— in Denmark, to the landsret,
— in the Federal Republic of Germany, to the Oberlandesgericht,
— in Greece, to the εφετειο,
— in Spain, to the Audiencia Provincial,
— in France, to the cour d'appel,
— in Ireland, to the High Court,
— in Iceland, to the héraðsdómari,
— in Italy, to the corte d'appello,
— in Luxembourg, to the Cour supérieure de justice sitting as a court of civil appeal,
— in the Netherlands, to the gerechtshof,
— in Norway, to the lagmannsrett,
— in Austria, to the Landesgericht or the Kreisgericht,
[— in Poland, to the sad apelacyjny,]
— in Portugal, to the Tribunal da Relação,
— in Switzerland, to the tribunal cantonal/Kantonsgericht/tribunale cantonale,
— in Finland, to the hovioikeus/hovrätt,
— in Sweden, to the Svea hovrätt,
— in the United Kingdom—
(a) in England and Wales, to the High Court of Justice, or in the case of a maintenance judgment to the Magistrates' Court;
(b) in Scotland, to the Court of Session, or in the case of a maintenance judgment to the Sheriff Court;
(c) in Northern Ireland, to the High Court of Justice or in the case of a maintenance judgment to the Magistrates' Court.

2. The party against whom enforcement is sought shall be summoned to appear before the appellate court. If he fails to appear, the provisions of the second and third paragraphs of Article 20 shall apply even where he is not domiciled in any of the Contracting States.

Article 41

A judgment given on an appeal provided for in Article 40 may be contested only—
— in Belgium, Greece, Spain, France, Italy, Luxembourg and in the Netherlands, by an appeal in cassation,
— in Denmark, by an appeal to the højesteret, with the leave of the Minister of Justice,
— in the Federal Republic of Germany, by a Rechtsbeschwerde,
— in Ireland, by an appeal on a point of law to the Supreme Court,
— in Iceland, by an appeal to the Hæstiréttur,
— In Norway, by an appeal (kjaeremål or anke) to the Hoyesteretts kjaeremålsutvalg or Hoyesterett,
— in Austria, by a Revisionsrekurs,
[— in Poland, by an appeal in cassation,]
— in Portugal, by an appeal on a point of law,
— in Switzerland, by a recours de droit public devant le tribunal fédéral/ staatsrechtliche Beschwerde beim Bundesgericht/ricorso di diritto pubblico davanti al tribunale federale,
— in Finland, by an appeal to the korkein oikeus/högsta domstolen,
— in Sweden, by an appeal to the högsta domstolen,
— in the United Kingdom, by a single further appeal on a point of law.

Article 42

Where a foreign judgment has been given in respect of several matters and enforcement cannot be authorised for all of them, the court shall authorise enforcement for one or more of them.

An applicant may request partial enforcement of a judgment.

Article 43

A foreign judgment which orders a periodic payment by way of a penalty shall be enforceable in the State in which enforcement is sought only if the amount of the payment has been finally determined by the courts of the State of origin.

Article 44

An applicant who, in the State of origin, has benefited from complete or partial legal aid or exemption from costs or expenses, shall be entitled, in the procedures provided for in Articles 32 to 35, to benefit from the most favourable legal aid or the most extensive exemption from costs or expenses provided for by the law of the State addressed.

However, an applicant who requests the enforcement of a decision given by an administrative authority in Denmark or in Iceland in respect of a maintenance order may, in the State addressed, claim the benefits referred to in the first paragraph if he presents a statement from, respectively, the Danish Ministry of Justice or the Icelandic Ministry of Justice to the effect that he fulfils the economic requirements to qualify for the grant of complete or partial legal aid or exemption from costs or expenses.

Article 45

No security, bond or deposit, however described, shall be required of a party who in one Contracting State applies for enforcement of a judgment given in another Contracting State on the ground that he is a foreign national or that he is not domiciled or resident in the State in which enforcement is sought.

SECTION 3
COMMON PROVISIONS

Article 46

A party seeking recognition or applying for enforcement of a judgment shall produce—

1. a copy of the judgment which satisfies the conditions necessary to establish its authenticity;
2. in the case of a judgment given in default, the original or a certified true copy of the document which establishes that the party in default was served with the document instituting the proceedings or with an equivalent document.

Article 47

A party applying for enforcement shall also produce—

1. documents which establish that, according to the law of the State of origin, the judgment is enforceable and has been served;
2. where appropriate, a document showing that the applicant is in receipt of legal aid in the State of origin.

Article 48

If the documents specified in Article 46(2) and Article 47(2) are not produced, the court may specify a time for their production, accept equivalent documents or, if it considers that it has sufficient information before it, dispense with their production.

If the court so requires, a translation of the documents shall be produced; the translation shall be certified by a person qualified to do so in one of the Contracting States.

Article 49

No legalisation or other similar formality shall be required in respect of the documents referred to in Article 46 or 47 or the second paragraph of Article 48, or in respect of a document appointing a representative *ad litem*.

TITLE IV
AUTHENTIC INSTRUMENTS AND COURT SETTLEMENTS

Article 50

A document which has been formally drawn up or registered as an authentic instrument and is enforceable in one Contracting State shall, in another Contracting State, be declared enforceable there, on application made in accordance with the procedures provided for in Articles 31 *et seq.* The application may be refused only if enforcement of the instrument is contrary to public policy in the State addressed.

The instrument produced must satisfy the conditions necessary to establish its authenticity in the State of origin.

The provisions of Section 3 of Title III shall apply as appropriate.

Article 51

A settlement which has been approved by a court in the course of proceedings and is enforceable in the State in which it was concluded shall be enforceable in the State addressed under the same conditions as authentic instruments.

TITLE V
GENERAL PROVISIONS

Article 52

In order to determine whether a party is domiciled in the Contracting State whose courts are seised of a matter, the court shall apply its internal law.

If a party is not domiciled in the State whose courts are seised of the matter, then, in order to determine whether the party is domiciled in another Contracting State, the court shall apply the law of that State.

Article 53

For the purposes of this Convention, the seat of a company or other legal person or association of natural or legal persons shall be treated as its domicile. However, in order to determine that seat, the court shall apply its rules of private international law.

In order to determine whether a trust is domiciled in the Contracting State whose courts are seised of the matter, the court shall apply its rules of private international law.

TITLE VI
TRANSITIONAL PROVISIONS

Article 54

The provisions of this Convention shall apply only to legal proceedings instituted and to documents formally drawn up or registered as authentic instruments after its entry into force in the State of origin and, where recognition or enforcement of a judgment or authentic instrument is sought, in the State addressed.

However, judgments given after the date of entry into force of this Convention between the State of origin and the State addressed in proceedings instituted before that date shall be recognised and enforced in accordance with the provisions of Title III if jurisdiction was founded upon rules which accorded with those provided for either in Title II of this Convention or in a convention concluded between the State of origin and the State addressed which was in force when the proceedings were instituted.

If the parties to a dispute concerning a contract had agreed in writing before the entry into force of this Convention that the contract was to be governed by the law of Ireland or of a part of the United Kingdom, the courts of Ireland or of that part of the United Kingdom shall retain the right to exercise jurisdiction in the dispute.

Article 54A

For a period of three years from the entry into force of this Convention for Denmark, Greece, Ireland, Iceland, Norway, Finland and Sweden, respectively, jurisdiction in maritime matters shall be determined in these States not only in accordance with the provisions of Title II, but also in accordance with the provisions of paragraphs 1 to 7 following. However, upon the entry into force of the International Convention relating to the arrest of sea-going ships, signed at Brussels on 10 May 1952, for one of these States, these provisions shall cease to have effect for that State.

1. A person who is domiciled in a Contracting State may be sued in the courts of one of the States mentioned above in respect of a maritime claim if the ship to which the claim relates or any other ship owned by him has been arrested by judicial process within the territory of the latter State to secure the claim, or could have been so arrested there but bail or other security has been given, and either—
   (a) the claimant is domiciled in the latter State; or
   (b) the claim arose in the latter State; or
   (c) the claim concerns the voyage during which the arrest was made or could have been made; or
   (d) the claim arises out of a collision or out of damage caused by a ship to another ship or to goods or persons on board either ship, either by the execution or non-execution of a manoeuvre or by the non-observance of regulations; or
   (e) the claim is for salvage; or
   (f) the claim is in respect of a mortgage or hypothecation of the ship arrested.

2. A claimant may arrest either the particular ship to which the maritime claim relates, or any other ship which is owned by the person who was, at the time when the maritime claim arose, the owner of the particular ship. However, only the particular ship to which the maritime claim relates may be arrested in respect of the maritime claims set out in 5(o), (p) or (q) of this Article.

3. Ships shall be deemed to be in the same ownership when all the shares therein are owned by the same person or persons.

4. When in the case of a charter by demise of a ship the charterer alone is liable in respect of a maritime claim relating to that ship, the claimant may arrest that ship or any other ship owned by the charterer, but no other ship owned by the owner may be arrested in respect of such claim. The same shall apply to any case in which a person other than the owner of a ship is liable in respect of a maritime claim relating to that ship.

5. The expression "maritime claim" means a claim arising out of one or more of the following—
   (a) damage caused by any ship either in collision or otherwise;
   (b) loss of life or personal injury caused by any ship or occurring in connection with the operation of any ship;
   (c) salvage;
   (d) agreement relating to the use or hire of any ship whether by charterparty or otherwise;
   (e) agreement relating to the carriage of goods in any ship whether by charterparty or otherwise;
   (f) loss of or damage to goods including baggage carried in any ship;
   (g) general average;
   (h) bottomry;
   (i) towage;
   (j) pilotage;
   (k) goods or materials wherever supplied to a ship for her operation or maintenance;
   (l) construction, repair or equipment of any ship or dock charges and dues;
   (m) wages of masters, officers or crew;
   (n) master's disbursements, including disbursements made by shippers, charterers or agents on behalf of a ship or her owner;
   (o) dispute as to the title to or ownership of any ship;
   (p) disputes between co-owners of any ship as to the ownership, possession, employment or earnings of that ship;
   (q) the mortgage or hypothecation of any ship.

6. In Denmark, the expression "arrest" shall be deemed, as regards the maritime claims referred to in 5.(o) and (p) of this Article, to include a "forbud", where that is the only procedure allowed in respect of such a claim under Articles 646 to 653 of the law on civil procedure (lov om rettens pleje).

7. In Iceland, the expression "arrest" shall be deemed, as regards the maritime claims referred to in 5(o) and (p) of this Article, to include a "lögbann", where that is the only procedure allowed in respect of such a claim under Chapter III of the law on arrest and injunction (lög um kyrrsetningu og lögbann).

TITLE VII
RELATIONSHIP TO THE BRUSSELS CONVENTION AND TO OTHER CONVENTIONS

Article 54B

1. This Convention shall not prejudice the application by the Member States of the European Communities of the Convention on Jurisdiction and the Enforcement of Judgments in Civil and Commercial Matters, signed at Brussels on 27 September 1968 and of the Protocol on interpretation of that Convention by the Court of Justice, signed at Luxembourg on 3 June 1971, as amended by the Conventions of Accession to the said Convention and the said Protocol by the States acceding to the European Communities, all of these Conventions and the Protocol being hereinafter referred to as the "Brussels Convention".

2. However, this Convention shall in any event be applied—
   (a) in matters of jurisdiction, where the defendant is domiciled in the territory of a Contracting State which is not a member of the European Communities, or where Article 16 or 17 of this Convention confers a jurisdiction on the courts of such a Contracting State;
   (b) in relation to a *lis pendens* or to related actions as provided for in Articles 21 and 22, when proceedings are instituted in a Contracting State which is not a member of the European Communities and in a Contracting State which is a member of the European Communities;
   (c) in matters of recognition and enforcement, where either the State of origin or the State addressed is not a member of the European Communities.

3. In addition to the grounds provided for in Title III recognition or enforcement may be refused if the ground of jurisdiction on which the judgment has been based differs from that resulting from this Convention and recognition or enforcement is sought against a party who is domiciled in a Contracting State which is not a member of the European Communities, unless the judgment may otherwise be recognised or enforced under any rule of law in the State addressed.

Article 55

Subject to the provisions of the second paragraph of Article 54(2) and 56, this Convention shall, for the States which are parties to it, supersede the following conventions concluded between two or more of them—

— the Convention between the Swiss Confederation and France on jurisdiction and enforcement of judgments in civil matters, signed at Paris on 15 June 1869,
— the Treaty between the Swiss Confederation and Spain on the mutual enforcement of judgments in civil or commercial matters, signed at Madrid on 19 November 1896,
— the Convention between the Swiss Confederation and the German Reich on the recognition and enforcement of judgments and arbitration awards, signed at Berne on 2 November 1929,
— the Convention between Denmark, Finland, Iceland, Norway and Sweden on the recognition and enforcement of judgments, signed at Copenhagen on 16 March 1932,
— the Convention between the Swiss Confederation and Italy on the recognition and enforcement of judgments, signed at Rome on 3 January 1933,
— the Convention between Sweden and the Swiss Confederation on the recognition and enforcement of judgments and arbitral awards, signed at Stockholm on 15 January 1936,
— the Convention between the Kingdom of Belgium and Austria on the reciprocal recognition and enforcement of judgments and authentic instruments relating to maintenance obligations, signed at Vienna on 25 October 1957,
— the Convention between the Swiss Confederation and Belgium on the recognition and enforcement of judgments and arbitration awards, signed at Berne on 29th April 1959,

— the Convention between the Federal Republic of Germany and Austria on the reciprocal recognition and enforcement of judgments, settlements, and authentic instruments in civil and commercial matters, signed at Vienna on 6 June 1959,
— the Convention between the Kingdom of Belgium and Austria on the reciprocal recognition and enforcement of judgments, arbitral awards and authentic instruments in civil and commercial matters, signed at Vienna on 16 June 1959,
— the Convention between Austria and the Swiss Confederation on the recognition and enforcement of judgments, signed at Berne on 16 December 1960,
— the Convention between Norway and the United Kingdom providing for the reciprocal recognition and enforcement of judgments in civil matters, signed at London on 12 June 1961,
[— the Convention between Poland and Austria on Bilateral Relations in Civil Matters and on Documents signed at Vienna on December 11 1963,
— the Convention between Poland and France on Applicable Law, Jurisdiction and the Enforcement of Judgments in the Field of Personal and Family Law, signed at Warsaw on April 5 1967,]
— the Convention between the United Kingdom and Austria providing for the reciprocal recognition and enforcement of judgments in civil and commercial matters, signed at Vienna on 14 July 1961, with amending Protocol signed at London on 6 March 1970,
— the Convention between the Kingdom of the Netherlands and Austria on the reciprocal recognition and enforcement of judgments and authentic instruments in civil and commercial matters, signed at The Hague on 6 February 1963,
— the Convention between France and Austria on the recognition and enforcement of judgments and authentic instruments in civil and commercial matters, signed at Vienna on 15 July 1966,
— the Convention between Luxembourg and Austria on the recognition and enforcement of judgments and authentic instruments in civil and commercial matters, signed at Luxembourg on 29 July 1971,
— the Convention between Italy and Austria on the recognition and enforcement of judgments in civil and commercial matters, of judicial settlements and of authentic instruments, signed at Rome on 16 November 1971,
— the Convention between Norway and the Federal Republic of Germany on the recognition and enforcement of judgments and enforceable documents, in civil and commercial matters, signed at Oslo on 17 June 1977,
— the Convention between Denmark, Finland, Iceland, Norway and Sweden on the recognition and enforcement of judgments in civil matters, signed at Copenhagen on 11 October 1977,
[— the Convention between Poland and Greece on Mutual Assistance in Civil and Criminal Matters, signed at Athens on October 24 1979,]
— the Convention between Austria and Sweden on the recognition and enforcement of judgments in civil matters, signed at Stockholm on 16 September 1982,
— the Convention between Austria and Spain on the recognition and enforcement of judgments, settlements and enforceable authentic instruments in civil and commercial matters, signed at Vienna on 17 February 1984,
— the Convention between Norway and Austria on the recognition and enforcement of judgments in civil matters, signed at Vienna on 21 May 1984, and
— the Convention between Finland and Austria on the recognition and enforcement of judgments in civil matters, signed at Vienna on 17 November 1986
[— the Convention between Poland and Italy on Mutual Assistance and the Recognition and Enforcement of Judgments in Civil Matters, signed at Warsaw on April 28 1989.]

Article 56

The Treaty and the conventions referred to in Article 55 shall continue to have effect in relation to matters to which this Convention does not apply.

They shall continue to have effect in respect of judgments given and documents formally drawn up or registered as authentic instruments before the entry into force of this Convention.

Article 57

1. This Convention shall not affect any conventions to which the Contracting States are or will be parties and which, in relation to particular matters, govern jurisdiction or the recognition or enforcement of judgments.

2. This Convention shall not prevent a court of a Contracting State which is party to a convention referred to in the first paragraph from assuming jurisdiction in accordance with that convention, even where the defendant is domiciled in a Contracting State which is not a party to that convention. The court hearing the action shall, in any event, apply Article 20 of this Convention.

3. Judgments given in a Contracting State by a court in the exercise of jurisdiction provided for in a convention referred to in the first paragraph shall be recognised and enforced in the other Contracting States in accordance with Title III of this Convention.

4. In addition to the grounds provided for in Title III, recognition or enforcement may be refused if the State addressed is not a contracting party to a convention referred to in the first paragraph and the person against whom recognition or enforcement is sought is domiciled in that State, unless the judgment may otherwise be recognised or enforced under any rule of law in the State addressed.

5. Where a convention referred to in the first paragraph to which both the State of origin and the State addressed are parties lays down conditions for the recognition or enforcement of judgments, those conditions shall apply. In any event, the provisions of this Convention which concern the procedures for recognition and enforcement of judgments may be applied.

Article 58

(*None*)

Article 59

This Convention shall not prevent a Contracting State from assuming, in a convention on the recognition and enforcement of judgments, an obligation towards a third State not to recognise judgments given in other Contracting States against defendants domiciled or habitually resident in the third State where, in cases provided for in Article 4, the judgment could only be founded on a ground of jurisdiction specified in the second paragraph of Article 3.

However, a Contracting State may not assume an obligation towards a third State not to recognise a judgment given in another Contracting State by a court basing its jurisdiction on the presence within that State of property belonging to the defendant, or the seizure by the plaintiff of property situated there—

1. if the action is brought to assert or declare proprietary or possessory rights in that property, seeks to obtain authority to dispose of it, or arises from another issue relating to such property, or
2. if the property constitutes the security for a debt which is the subject-matter of the action.

TITLE VIII
FINAL PROVISIONS

Article 60

The following may be parties to this Convention—

(a) States which, at the time of the opening of this Convention for signature, are members of the European Communities or of the European Free Trade Association;

(b) States which, after the opening of this Convention for signature, become members of the European Communities or of the European Free Trade Association;

(c) States invited to accede in accordance with Article 62(1)(b).

Article 61

1. This Convention shall be opened for signature by the States members of the European Communities or of the European Free Trade Association.

2. The Convention shall be submitted for ratification by the signatory States. The instruments of ratification shall be deposited with the Swiss Federal Council.

3. The Convention shall enter into force on the first day of the third month following the date on which two States, of which one is a member of the European Communities and the other a member of the European Free Trade Association, deposit their instruments of ratification.

4. The Convention shall take effect in relation to any other signatory State on the first day of the third month following the deposit of its instrument of ratification.

Article 62

1. After entering into force this Convention shall be open to accession by—
   (a) the States referred to in Article 60(b);
   (b) other States which have been invited to accede upon a request made by one of the Contracting States to the depositary State. The depositary State shall invite the State concerned to accede only if, after having communicated the contents of the communications that this State intends to make in accordance with Article 63, it has obtained the unanimous agreement of the signatory States and the Contracting States referred to in Article 60(a) and (b).

2. If an acceding State wishes to furnish details for the purposes of Protocol No 1, negotiations shall be entered into to that end. A negotiating conference shall be convened by the Swiss Federal Council.

3. In respect of an acceding State, the Convention shall take effect on the first day of the third month following the deposit of its instrument of accession.

4. However, in respect of an acceding State referred to in paragraph 1(a) or (b), the Convention shall take effect only in relations between the acceding State and the Contracting States which have not made any objections to the accession before the first day of the third month following the deposit of the instrument of accession.

Article 63

Each acceding State shall, when depositing its instrument of accession, communicate the information required for the application of Articles 3, 32, 37, 40, 41 and 55 of this Convention and furnish, if need be, the details prescribed during the negotiations for the purposes of Protocol No 1.

Article 64

1. This Convention is concluded for an initial period of five years from the date of its entry into force in accordance with Article 61(3), even in the case of States which ratify it or accede to it after that date.

2. At the end of the initial five-year period, the Convention shall be automatically renewed from year to year.

3. Upon the expiry of the initial five-year period, any Contracting State may, at any time, denounce the Convention by sending a notification to the Swiss Federal Council.

4. The denunciation shall take effect at the end of the calendar year following the expiry of a period of six months from the date of receipt by the Swiss Federal Council of the notification of denunciation.

Article 65

The following are annexed to this Convention—

- — a Protocol No 1, on certain questions of jurisdiction, procedure and enforcement,
- — a Protocol No 2, on the uniform interpretation of the Convention,
- — a Protocol No 3, on the application of Article 57.

These Protocols shall form an integral part of the Convention.

Article 66

Any Contracting State may request the revision of this Convention. To that end, the Swiss Federal Council shall issue invitations to a revision conference within a period of six months from the date of the request for revision.

Article 67

The Swiss Federal Council shall notify the States represented at the Diplomatic Conference of Lugano and the States who have later acceded to the Convention of—

(a) the deposit of each instrument of ratification or accession;
(b) the dates of entry into force of this Convention in respect of the Contracting States;
(c) any denunciation received pursuant to Article 64;
(d) any declaration received pursuant to Article Ia of Protocol No 1;
(e) any declaration received pursuant to Article Ib of Protocol No 1;
(f) any declaration received pursuant to Article IV of Protocol No 1;
(g) any communication made pursuant to Article VI of Protocol No 1.

Article 68

This Convention, drawn up in a single original in the Danish, Dutch, English, Finnish, French, German, Greek, Icelandic, Irish, Italian, Norwegian, Portuguese, Spanish and Swedish languages, all fourteen texts being equally authentic, shall be deposited in the archives of the Swiss Federal Council. The Swiss Federal Council shall transmit a certified copy to the Government of each State represented at the Diplomatic Conference of Lugano and to the Government of each acceding State.

[3063]

PROTOCOL NO 1
ON CERTAIN QUESTIONS OF JURISDICTION, PROCEDURE AND ENFORCEMENT

The High Contracting Parties have agreed upon the following provisions, which shall be annexed to the Convention—

Article I

Any person domiciled in Luxembourg who is sued in a court of another Contracting State pursuant to Article 5(1) may refuse to submit to the jurisdiction of that court. If the defendant does not enter an appearance the court shall declare of its own motion that it has no jurisdiction.

An agreement conferring jurisdiction, within the meaning of Article 17, shall be valid with respect to a person domiciled in Luxembourg only if that person has expressly and specifically so agreed.

Article Ia

1. Switzerland reserves the right to declare, at the time of depositing its instrument of ratification, that a judgment given in another Contracting State shall be neither recognised nor enforced in Switzerland if the following conditions are met—

(a) the jurisdiction of the court which has given the judgment is based only on Article 5(1) of this Convention; and
(b) the defendant was domiciled in Switzerland at the time of the introduction of the proceedings; for the purposes of this Article, a company or other legal person is considered to be domiciled in Switzerland if it has its registered seat and the effective centre of activities in Switzerland; and
(c) the defendant raises an objection to the recognition or enforcement of the judgment in Switzerland, provided that he has not waived the benefit of the declaration foreseen under this paragraph.

2. This reservation shall not apply to the extent that at the time recognition or enforcement is sought a derogation has been granted from Article 59 of the Swiss Federal Constitution. The Swiss Government shall communicate such derogations to the signatory States and the acceding States.

3. This reservation shall cease to have effect on 31 December 1999. It may be withdrawn at any time.

Article Ib

Any Contracting State may, by declaration made at the time of signing or of deposit of its instrument of ratification or of accession, reserve the right, notwithstanding the provisions of Article 28, not to recognise and enforce judgments given in the other Contracting States if the jurisdiction of the court of the State of origin is based, pursuant to Article 16(1)(b), exclusively on the domicile of the defendant in the State of origin, and the property is situated in the territory of the State which entered the reservation.

Article II

Without prejudice to any more favourable provisions of national laws, persons domiciled in a Contracting State who are being prosecuted in the criminal courts of another Contracting State of which they are not nationals for an offence which was not intentionally committed may be defended by persons qualified to do so, even if they do not appear in person.

However, the court seised of the matter may order appearance in person; in the case of failure to appear, a judgment given in the civil action without the person concerned having had the opportunity to arrange for his defence need not be recognised or enforced in the other Contracting States.

Article III

In proceedings for the issue of an order for enforcement, no charge, duty or fee calculated by reference to the value of the matter in issue may be levied in the State in which enforcement is sought.

Article IV

Judicial and extrajudicial documents drawn up in one Contracting State which have to be served on persons in another Contracting State shall be transmitted in accordance with the procedures laid down in the conventions and agreements concluded between the Contracting States.

Unless the State in which service is to take place objects by declaration to the Swiss Federal Council, such documents may also be sent by the appropriate public officers of the State in which the document has been drawn up directly to the appropriate public officers of the State in which the addressee is to be found. In this case the officer of the State of origin shall send a copy of the document to the officer of the State applied to who is competent to forward it to the addressee. The document shall be forwarded in the manner specified by the law of the State applied to. The forwarding shall be recorded by a certificate sent directly to the officer of the State of origin.

Article V

The jurisdiction specified in Articles 6(2) and 10 in actions on a warranty or guarantee or in any other third party proceedings may not be resorted to in the Federal Republic of Germany, in Spain, in Austria and in Switzerland. Any person domiciled in another Contracting State may be sued in the courts—

- — of the Federal Republic of Germany, pursuant to Articles 68, 72, 73 and 74 of the code of civil procedure (Zivilprozeßordnung) concerning third-party notices,
- — of Spain, pursuant to Article 1482 of the civil code,
- — of Austria, pursuant to Article 21 of the code of civil procedure (Zivilprozeßordnung) concerning third-party notices,
- — of Switzerland, pursuant to the appropriate provisions concerning third-party notices of the cantonal codes of civil procedure.

Judgments given in the other Contracting States by virtue of Article 6(2) or Article 10 shall be recognised and enforced in the Federal Republic of Germany, in Spain, in Austria and in Switzerland in accordance with Title III. Any effects which judgments given in these States may have on third parties by application of the provisions in the preceding paragraph shall also be recognised in the other Contracting States.

Article Va

In matters relating to maintenance, the expression "court" includes the Danish, Icelandic and Norwegian administrative authorities.

In civil and commercial matters, the expression "court" includes the Finnish ulosotonhaltija/överexekutor.

Article Vb

In proceedings involving a dispute between the master and a member of the crew of a sea-going ship registered in Denmark, in Greece, in Ireland, in Iceland, in Norway, in Portugal or in Sweden concerning remuneration or other conditions of service, a court in a Contracting State shall establish whether the diplomatic or consular officer responsible for the ship has been notified of the dispute. It shall stay the proceedings so long as he has not been notified. It shall of its own motion decline jurisdiction if the officer, having been duly notified, has exercised the powers accorded to him in the matter by a consular convention, or in the absence of such a convention has, within the time allowed, raised any objection to the exercise of such jurisdiction.

Article Vc

(*None*)

Article Vd

Without prejudice to the jurisdiction of the European Patent Office under the Convention on the grant of European patents, signed at Munich on 5 October 1973, the courts of each Contracting State shall have exclusive jurisdiction, regardless of domicile, in proceedings concerned with the registration or validity of any European patent granted for that State which is not a Community patent by virtue of the provision of Article 86 of the Convention for the European patent for the common market, signed at Luxembourg on 15 December 1975.

Article VI

The Contracting States shall communicate to the Swiss Federal Council the text of any provisions of their laws which amend either those provisions of their laws mentioned in the Convention or the lists of courts specified in Section 2 of Title III.

[3064]

PROTOCOL NO 2
ON THE UNIFORM INTERPRETATION OF THE CONVENTION

PREAMBLE

The High Contracting Parties,

Having regard to Article 65 of this Convention,

Considering the substantial link between this Convention and the Brussels Convention,

Considering that the Court of Justice of the European Communities by virtue of the Protocol of 3 June 1971 has jurisdiction to give rulings on the interpretation of the provisions of the Brussels Convention,

Being aware of the rulings delivered by the Court of Justice of the European Communities on the interpretation of the Brussels Convention up to the time of signature of this Convention,

Considering that the negotiations which led to the conclusion of the Convention were based on the Brussels Convention in the light of these rulings,

Desiring to prevent, in full deference to the independence of the courts, divergent interpretations and to arrive at as uniform an interpretation as possible of the provisions of the Convention, and of these provisions and those of the Brussels Convention which are substantially reproduced in this Convention,

Have agreed as follows—

Article 1

The courts of each Contracting State shall, when applying and interpreting the provisions of the Convention, pay due account to the principles laid down by any relevant decision delivered by courts of the other Contracting States concerning provisions of this Convention.

Article 2

1. The Contracting Parties agree to set up a system of exchange of information concerning judgments delivered pursuant to this Convention as well as relevant judgments under the Brussels Convention. This system shall comprise—

— transmission to a central body by the competent authorities of judgments delivered by courts of last instance and the Court of Justice of the European Communities as well as judgments of particular importance which have become final and have been delivered pursuant to this Convention or the Brussels Convention,

— classification of these judgments by the central body including, as far as necessary, the drawing-up and publication of translations and abstracts,

— communication by the central body of the relevant documents to the competent national authorities of all signatories and acceding States to the Convention and to the Commission of the European Communities.

2. The central body is the Registrar of the Court of Justice of the European Communities.

Article 3

1. A Standing Committee shall be set up for the purposes of this Protocol.

2. The Committee shall be composed of representatives appointed by each signatory and acceding State.

3. The European Communities (Commission, Court of Justice and General Secretariat of the Council) and the European Free Trade Association may attend the meetings as observers.

Article 4

1. At the request of a Contracting Party, the depositary of the Convention shall convene meetings of the Committee for the purpose of exchanging views on the functioning of the Convention and in particular on—

— the development of the case-law as communicated under the first paragraph first indent of Article 2,

— the application of Article 57 of the Convention.

2. The Committee, in the light of these exchanges, may also examine the appropriateness of starting on particular topics a revision of the Convention and make recommendations.

[3065]

PROTOCOL NO 3
ON THE APPLICATION OF ARTICLE 57

The High Contracting Parties have agreed as follows—

1. For the purposes of the Convention, provisions which, in relation to particular matters, govern jurisdiction or the recognition or enforcement of judgments and which are, or will be, contained in acts of the institutions of the European Communities shall be treated in the same way as the conventions referred to in paragraph 1 of Article 57.
2. If one Contracting State is of the opinion that a provision contained in an act of the institutions of the European Communities is incompatible with the Convention, the Contracting States shall promptly consider amending the Convention pursuant to Article 66, without prejudice to the procedure established by Protocol No 2.]

[3066]

NOTES

Inserted by the Civil Jurisdiction and Judgments Act 1991, s 1(3), Sch 1.

Arts 3, 32, 37, 40, 41, 55: entries in square brackets inserted by the Civil Jurisdiction and Judgments Act 1982 (Amendment) Order 2000, SI 2000/1824, art 12.

DECLARATION
BY THE REPRESENTATIVES OF THE GOVERNMENTS OF THE STATE SIGNATORIES TO THE LUGANO CONVENTION WHICH ARE MEMBERS OF THE EUROPEAN COMMUNITIES ON PROTOCOL 3 ON THE APPLICATION OF ARTICLE 57 OF THE CONVENTION

Upon signature of the Convention on jurisdiction and the enforcement of judgments in civil and commercial matters done at Lugano on 16 September 1988,

THE REPRESENTATIVES OF THE GOVERNMENTS OF THE MEMBER STATES OF THE EUROPEAN COMMUNITIES,

taking into account the undertakings entered into *vis-a-vis* the member states of the European Free Trade Association,

anxious not to prejudice the unity of the legal system set up by the Convention,

declare that they will take all measures in their power to ensure, when Community acts referred to in paragraph 1 of Protocol 3 on the application of Article 57 are being drawn up, respect for the rules of jurisdiction and recognition and enforcement of judgments established by the Convention. **[3067]**

NOTES

The text of this Declaration appears in OJ L319, 25.11.88, p 34.

DECLARATION
BY THE REPRESENTATIVES OF THE GOVERNMENTS OF THE STATES SIGNATORIES TO THE LUGANO CONVENTION WHICH ARE MEMBERS OF THE EUROPEAN COMMUNITIES

Upon signature of the Convention on jurisdiction and the enforcement of judgments in civil and commercial matters done at Lugano on 16 September 1988,

THE REPRESENTATIVES OF THE GOVERNMENTS OF THE MEMBER STATES OF THE EUROPEAN COMMUNITIES

declare that they consider as appropriate that the Court of Justice of the European Communities, when interpreting the Brussels Convention, pay due account to the rulings contained in the case-law of the Lugano Convention. **[3068]**

NOTES

The text of this Declaration appears in OJ L319, 25.11.1988, p 37.

DECLARATION
BY THE REPRESENTATIVES OF THE GOVERNMENTS OF THE STATES SIGNATORIES TO THE LUGANO CONVENTION WHICH ARE MEMBERS OF THE EUROPEAN FREE TRADE ASSOCIATION

Upon signature of the Convention on jurisdiction and the enforcement of judgments in civil and commercial matters done at Lugano on 16 September 1988,

THE REPRESENTATIVES OF THE GOVERNMENTS OF THE MEMBER STATES OF THE EUROPEAN FREE TRADE ASSOCIATION

declare that they consider as appropriate that their courts, when interpreting the Lugano Convention, pay due account to the rulings contained in the case law of the Court of Justice of the European Communities and of courts of the Member States of the European Communities in respect of provisions of the Brussels Convention which are substantially reproduced in the Lugano Convention. **[3069]**

NOTES

The text of this Declaration appears in OJ L319, 25.11.1988, p 40.

CONVENTION

on jurisdiction and the enforcement of judgments in civil and commercial matters done at Lugano on 16 September 1988

(90/C189/07)

NOTES

The Jenard and Möller Report on the 1988 Lugano Convention is set out at OJ C189, 28.7.90, p 57. References to the original pagination in the Official Journals are noted above the text to which they refer.

REPORT

by Mr P JENARD

Honorary Director of Administration at the Belgian Ministry of Foreign Affairs,

and Mr G MÖLLER

President of the Court of First Instance in Toijala

In addition to the draft Convention and the other instruments drawn up by the government experts, the draft explanatory report was submitted to the Governments of the Member States of the European Communities and of the European Free Trade Association before the Diplomatic Conference held in Lugano from 12 to 16 September 1988.

This report takes account of the comments made by certain Governments and of the amendments made by the Diplomatic Conference to the drafts before it. It takes the form of a commentary on the Convention signed in Lugano on 16 September 1988.

LIST OF CONTENTS

[OJ C189, 28.7.90, p 61]

CHAPTER I
GENERAL CONSIDERATIONS

1. INTRODUCTORY REMARKS

1. The Lugano Convention, opened for signature on 16 September 1988, is concluded between the Member States of the European Communities and the Member States of the European Free Trade Association (EFTA).

It will be referred to in this report as the "Lugano Convention" although during the preparatory proceedings it was known as the "Parallel Convention". It was given that name because it corresponds very closely to the Brussels Convention of 27 September 1968 on jurisdiction and the enforcement of judgments in civil and commercial matters, which was concluded between the six original Community Member States[1] and adopted consequent upon the accession of new Member States to the Communities.[2] For convenience, that Convention, in its adopted form, will be referred to as the "Brussels Convention".

Although the Lugano Convention takes not only its structure but also numerous provisions from the Brussels Convention, it is nevertheless a separate instrument.

2. This report does not contain a detailed commentary on all the provisions of the Lugano Convention.

Where provisions are identical to those of the Brussels Convention, the reader should refer to the existing reports by Mr P Jenard on the 1968 Convention, by Mr P Schlosser on the 1978 Convention on the accession of Denmark, Ireland and the United Kingdom and by Messrs Evrigenis and Kerameus on the 1982 Convention on the accession of Greece.[3]

The provisions in force in each of the EFTA Member States on the recognition and enforcement of foreign judgments and an account of the relevant conventions concluded by those States with one another or with Member States of the Communities are not included in the body of this report but are given in Annexes I and II. This different layout from previous reports has been adopted so as not to complicate the text.

2. JUSTIFICATION FOR AND BACKGROUND TO THE LUGANO CONVENTION

3. The European Communities and EFTA are at present made up of a great many European countries who share very similar conceptions of constitutional (separation of powers between the legislature, the executive and the judiciary), legal (primacy of the rule of law and the rights of the individual) and economic matters (market economy).

The two organizations differ however with regard to their objectives and institutions. That is why we felt it useful to give a brief outline.

A. THE EUROPEAN COMMUNITIES

4. The European Communities differ substantially from the other international or European organizations on account of their particular aims and the originality of their institutional machinery.

They pursue the specific objectives assigned to them by the three Treaties establishing them (ECSC, EEC and Euratom) but their ultimate objective is to establish a real European union.

The economic dimension of this union in the making is complemented by a political discussion which is expressed through the medium of European Political Cooperation, by means of which the Twelve endeavour to harmonize their foreign policies.

The construction of Europe initiated by the six founding States (Belgium, the Federal Republic of Germany, France, Italy, the Grand Duchy of Luxembourg and the Netherlands) took a step forward with the signing first of all of the Treaty of Paris (18 April 1951) which established the European Coal and Steel Community (ECSC) and subsequently (on 25 March 1957) of the two Treaties of Rome which laid the foundations of the European Economic Community (EEC) and the European Atomic Energy Community (Euratom).

Denmark, Ireland and the United Kingdom acceded to those three Treaties on 1 January 1973 (the Nine), Greece on 1 January 1981 (the Ten), Spain and Portugal on 1 January 1986 (the Twelve).

The European Communities therefore currently comprise twelve European countries which are bound together by jointly undertaken commitments.

5. With the Single European Act, which entered into force on 1 July 1987, a new stage was reached on the path towards a European union. This new Community legal instrument aims in particular at the progressive establishment, over a period expiring on 31 December 1992, of a real internal market providing for the free movement of goods, persons, services and capital. It also aims at promoting significant progress in both the monetary field and new policy sectors (in particular the environment and new technologies). It makes Community decision-making machinery more flexible in a number of fields and, by means of treaty provisions, institutionalizes European Political Cooperation.

[OJ C189, 28.7.90, p 62]

6. The institutional architecture of the Communities rests on four pillars—

1. The Council of Ministers

The Council consists of the representatives of the Member States and each Government delegates one of its members to it, depending on the field of competence and the nature of the subjects under discussion.

The Ministers of Foreign Affairs coordinate general Community policy.

The Council of Ministers is the Communities' decision-making body. It participates in legislative power and as such is empowered to take binding measures in the form of Regulations or Directives which are directly binding on the Member States and/or their nationals. The Regulations are directly applicable in the Member States, whereas Directives have to be incorporated into national legislation.

The Council's decisions are prepared by the Permanent Representatives Committee (Coreper), composed of the Permanent Representatives of the Member States to the European Communities.

The Council's decisions are taken unanimously, by a simple majority or by a qualified majority, depending on the legal provisions on which they are based.

The Single Act aims at multiplying the cases in which a majority vote becomes standard practice, so as to expedite the proceedings of an enlarged Community.

Twice a year the European Council brings together the Heads of State or of Government of the Member States. This body, set up at the highest level on a political basis in 1975, was given Treaty recognition following the adoption of the Single Act.

Its main task is to work out guidelines and give the necessary impetus to the development of the Community process.

2. The Commission

The Commission currently consists of 17 members chosen by common agreement by the Governments.

The Commission is the most original institution in the Community's institutional machinery. It cannot be likened to a secretariat because the authors of the Treaties chose to make it the prime mover of European integration. It participates actively in the preparation and formulation of the acts of the Council by virtue of its power of initiative.

3. The Court of Justice

The role of the Court of Justice is to ensure that Community law is obeyed in the implementation of the three Treaties establishing the European Communities. Its powers are manifold and it has *inter alia* the power to give rulings in the form of judgments on the validity of the acts of Community authorities and on the interpretation of the Treaties and Community acts.

In its decisions, the Court has affirmed the precedence of Community law over Member States' constitutional and legislative provisions.

Under the Luxembourg Protocol of 3 June 1971, the Member States of the Communities conferred jurisdiction upon the Court of Justice for giving judgment on the interpretation of the 1968 Brussels Convention, which is of particular concern to us.

4. The European Parliament

Since 1979 the Members of the European Parliament have been elected by direct universal suffrage for a five-year term of office.

Although the European Parliament has quite extensive powers of political supervision in respect of the action of the Council and the Commission and in the budgetary field, it does not however have legislative powers similar to those of national Parliaments.

The Single Act contains new cooperation arrangements designed to involve the Parliament more closely in the exercise of the legislative power conferred jointly upon the Council and the Commission.

7. In conclusion, in the field under review, it should be noted that—
   1. the Lugano Convention is linked to the 1968 Brussels Convention which is based on Article 220 of the Treaty establishing the European Economic Community;
   2. with regard to Community acts, legislative power is mainly conferred upon the Council;

[OJ C189, 28.7.90, p 63]

   3. the European Communities have created a very dense network of relations with the outside world which are embodied in agreements of various kinds, either with States or with organisations.

B. EFTA

8. The European Free Trade Association is a group of six European countries which share with the European Communities the aim of creating a dynamic, homogeneous European economic area embracing the Member States of the EEC and EFTA. That aim was laid down in the Luxembourg Declaration adopted on 9 April 1984 by the Ministers of all EEC and EFTA Member States.

EFTA's goal is the removal of import duties, quotas and other obstacles to trade in Western Europe and the upholding of liberal, non-discriminatory practices in international trade. Set up in 1960, the Association now has six member countries: Austria, Finland, Iceland, Norway, Sweden and Switzerland.

EFTA's establishment and evolution form part of the story of economic integration in Western Europe. Its founder members, which included Denmark, Portugal and the United Kingdom, adopted as their *first objective* the introduction of free trade between themselves in industrial goods. This objective was realised three years ahead of schedule at the end of 1966.

9. The trade between the EFTA countries accounts for only 13 to 14% of their overall trade. Much more important is their trade with the EEC which is the source of more than half of their imports and the destination of more than half of their exports. The EFTA countries are also important trading partners for the EEC, providing markets for between a fifth and a quarter of EEC exports (excluding trade between the EEC countries).

The closeness of the commercial links between the EFTA and the EEC countries was one of the reasons for the attempt in the 1950s to negotiate a free trade area embracing the original six-nation EEC and the other Western European countries. The attempt failed. But when seven of these countries resolved to strengthen their own links by founding EFTA they saw the Association as, among other things, a means of preparing the way for the eventual fulfilment of their hopes of a single European market. Thus EFTA was born with the ambition of bringing about a larger market including all the countries of Western Europe. This was the *second objective* of EFTA's founder members.

This second goal was in effect achieved in the 1970s through negotiations which brought each of the present EFTA countries into a new relationship with the EEC, and at the same time the EEC was enlarged by the entry of two former EFTA countries, Denmark and the United Kingdom, and of Ireland. Free trade agreements came into force between the enlarged EEC and Austria, Portugal, Sweden and Switzerland on 1 January 1973, and the EEC and Iceland on 1 April 1973. Similar agreements came into force between Norway and the EEC on 1 July 1973 and between Finland and the EEC on 1 January 1974. Under these agreements the import duties on almost all industrial products were abolished from July 1977. These free trade agreements also apply to trade between the EFTA countries and three countries which joined the EEC at later dates: Greece from 1 January 1981, Portugal and Spain from 1 January 1986.

As mentioned above, the extension and intensification of EEC-EFTA cooperation have given rise since 1984 to talks between the two groups of States in many areas connected, directly or indirectly, with the EEC's ambitious programme for the creation of a genuine internal market in 1992. They concern matters such as technical barriers to trade, competition rules, intellectual property rights, product liability, etc.

The negotiations for the Lugano Convention came within that context.

C. JUSTIFICATION FOR THE CONVENTION

10. According to a report produced by Mr Johnsen for the Parliamentary Assembly of the Council of Europe (document 5774 of 9 September 1987—FDO C5774), "the Member States of EFTA and the EEC now make up a vast market of 350 million European consumers. With a few exceptions, industrial products circulate within this area without being subject to custom duties or quantitative restrictions. It is the largest market in the world, surpassing the United States market (240 million) and the Japanese market (120 million)."

It thus became apparent that this economic cooperation between the two groupings of European States ought to be strengthened through a convention on jurisdiction and the recognition and enforcement of judgments.

In this connection, the Brussels Convention was considered to embody a number of principles which could serve to strengthen judicial and economic cooperation between the States involved.

[OJ C189, 28.7.90, p 64]

The aim of the Brussels Convention is to simplify the formalities needed for mutual recognition and enforcement of court decisions. For this reason the Convention begins by specifying the rules of jurisdiction regarding the courts before which proceedings are to be brought in civil and commercial matters relating to property. The Convention goes on to lay down a procedure for the enforcement of judgments given in another Member State which is simpler than traditional arrangements and swift because the initial stages are non-adversarial.

The Brussels Convention and the 1971 Protocol on its interpretation by the Court of Justice have both assumed considerable practical importance: hundreds of decisions based on the Convention have been given in the Member States and there is a series of interpretative judgments of the Court (see Chapter VI).

Because of the magnitude of trade between the EEC Member States and EFTA, it was to be expected that the need would arise for a judgment given in a Community Member State to be enforced in an EFTA country, or for a judgment given in an EFTA member country to be enforced in a Member State of the European Communities.

D. BACKGROUND TO THE CONVENTION

11. In 1973, when discussions over the accession of Denmark, Ireland and the United Kingdom to the Brussels Convention were under way, the Swedish Government indicated its interest in the creation of contractual links between the Community Member States on the one hand, and Sweden plus other countries which might be interested on the other hand, with a view to facilitating the recognition and enforcement of judgments in civil and commercial matters.

In 1981, the Swiss Mission to the European Communities took up the Swedish Government's initiative and inquired of the competent authorities of the Commission whether and on what terms the recognition and enforcement of judgments in civil and commercial matters between the Member States of the Communities and Switzerland could be facilitated along the lines of the Brussels Convention of 27 September 1968. The inquiry was renewed in April 1982 to Mr Thorn, President of the Commission, by Mr Furgler, Member of the Swiss Federal Council.

In January 1985, acting on the instructions of the Council of the European Communities, an *ad hoc* working party met to examine, on the basis of a paper submitted by the Commission, the possibility of organizing negotiations with the EFTA countries with a view to extending the Brussels Convention.

With the assistance of the Council Secretariat and the Commission departments, preliminary talks were entered into with the Member States of EFTA in order to establish whether an extension of the Brussels Convention could be envisaged.

It emerged that Norway, Sweden, Switzerland, Finland, and subsequently Iceland, were in favour of opening negotiations on the drafting of a parallel Convention to the Brussels Convention.

At the end of this exploratory stage, the representatives of the Governments of the EEC Member States, meeting in the Permanent Representatives Committee in May 1985, noted that all the conditions obtained for negotiations to be initiated. They therefore agreed to issue an invitation to the EFTA Member States to take part in such negotiations.

A working party made up of governmental experts from the Member States of the European Communities and experts appointed by the EFTA Member States was set up to this end. The working party met for the first time on 8 and 9 October 1985 under the alternating chairmanship of Mr Voyame, Director at the Ministry of Justice of the Swiss Confederation, and Mr Saggio, Counsellor at the Italian Court of Appeal. A delegation sent by the Austrian Government attended the negotiations in an observer capacity, as did representatives of The Hague Conference. The working party also appointed two rapporteurs, Mr P Jenard, at the time Director of Administration at the Belgian Ministry of Foreign Affairs, for the Member States of the European Communities and Mr Möller, at that time Counsellor on Legislation to the Finnish Ministry of Justice and now President of the Court of First Instance in Toijala, for the EFTA Member States.

The working party's discussions lasted two years, during which a preliminary draft Convention was prepared for use as the basic document for a diplomatic conference.

An overall assessment of the results achieved by the working party can be nothing if not positive, since wide consensus was reached with regard to the draft Convention, to the Protocols which supplement it and are an integral part thereof, and to three Declarations.

At all events, the conclusion of a multilateral Convention between a number of States offers better prospects of legal certainty and practical convenience than a series of bilateral, and inescapably divergent, agreements. The Convention also opens the way towards implementation of a common system of interpretation, a point which is specifically mentioned in Protocol 2.

[OJ C189, 28.7.90, p 65]

Another possibility might have been for the EFTA Member States to accede to the Brussels Convention. This possibility was not followed up because, being based on Article 220 of the Treaty of Rome and being the subject of the Protocol of 3 June 1971 which entrusted the Court of Justice of the European Communities with the power to interpret the Convention, the Brussels Convention is a Community instrument and it would have been difficult to ask non-Member States to become signatories.

12. The draft Convention and the other instruments drawn up by the working party were submitted to a diplomatic conference held, at the invitation of the Swiss Federal Government, in Lugano from 12 to 16 September 1988. All the Member States of the European Communities and of the European Free Trade Association were represented at this conference. Certain amendments were made to the drafts prepared by the working party. In accordance with the Final Act of the conference (see Annex III), the representatives of all the States concerned adopted the final texts of the Convention, the three Protocols and the three Declarations.

On 16 September 1988, the date of opening for signature, the required signatures were appended by the representatives of 10 States, that is, for the Member States of the European Communities, Belgium, Denmark, Greece, Italy, Luxembourg and Portugal, and for the Member States of EFTA, Iceland, Norway, Sweden and Switzerland. The Convention was signed by Finland on 30 November 1988 and by the Netherlands on 7 February 1989.

3. IDENTITY OF STRUCTURE BETWEEN THE BRUSSELS CONVENTION AND THE LUGANO CONVENTION—FUNDAMENTAL PRINCIPLES

13. The two Conventions are based on identical fundamental principles which can be summarized as follows—

First principle:

The scope of the two Conventions as determined *ratione materiae* is confined to civil and commercial matters relating to property. The two Conventions have the same Article 1.

Second principle:

Both Conventions fall into the "double treaty" category, that is to say they contain rules of direct jurisdiction. These rules are applicable in the State in which the initial proceedings are brought and serve to determine the court vested with jurisdiction, whereas "simple treaties" merely contain rules of indirect jurisdiction which do not apply until the stage of recognition and enforcement has been reached.

Third principle:

A defendant's domicile is the point on which the rules on jurisdiction hinge. For the purposes of the 1978 Accession Convention, the United Kingdom and Ireland adjusted their legislation to align their concept of domicile on that of many continental countries.[4] Proceedings against any person domiciled in the territory of a Contracting State must, save where the Conventions provide otherwise, be brought before the courts of that State. Under no circumstances may rules of exorbitant jurisdiction be involved as arguments (Articles 2 and 3).

However, where a defendant is not domiciled in the territory of a Contracting State jurisdiction continues to be determined in each State by the law of that State. Furthermore, persons domiciled in the territory of a Contracting State may, regardless of their nationality, avail themselves of the rules of jurisdiction which apply in that State, including exorbitant jurisdiction (Article 4), in the same way as nationals of that State.

Fourth principle:

Both Conventions contain precise and detailed rules of jurisdiction specifying the instances in which a person domiciled in a Contracting State may be sued in the courts of another Contracting State.

In this respect, the structures of the two Conventions are again identical, these rules being contained in the following sections.

(*a*) *Additional rules of jurisdiction*

Title II, Section 2 (Articles 5 and 6) contains additional rules of jurisdiction in that the courts therein specified are not mentioned in Article 2. The section relates to proceedings which can be considered as having a particularly close link with the court before which proceedings are brought.

The rules of jurisdiction set out in this section are special because, in general, both Conventions directly specify which court has jurisdiction.

As will be seen below, there are certain differences between the Brussels Convention and the Lugano Convention with regard to the provisions contained in this section (see Article 5(1) and Article 6(4), points 36 to 44, 46 and 47).

[OJ C189, 28.7.90, p 66]

(b) Mandatory rules

Both Conventions contain mandatory rules on jurisdiction in matters relating to insurance (Section 3) and consumer contracts (Section 4), the primary objective of which is to protect the weaker party. The rules are mandatory in that the parties are not permitted to depart from them before a dispute has arisen. These sections are the same in both Conventions.

(c) Exclusive jurisdiction

Both Conventions contain rules of exclusive jurisdiction (Section 5, Article 16)—

(a) in some cases, disputes must be brought before the courts of a given State (rights *in rem* in, or tenancies of, immovable property; validity, nullity or dissolution of companies; validity of entries in public registers; registration or validity of patents, trade marks and designs; proceedings concerned with the enforcement of judgments);

(b) the parties are not permitted to waive the jurisdiction of the competent courts, either by an agreement conferring jurisdiction even if entered into after a dispute has arisen (Article 17), or by submission to the jurisdiction (Article 18);

(c) a court of a State other than the State whose courts have exclusive jurisdiction must declare, of its own motion, that it has no jurisdiction (Article 19);

(d) breach of the rules constitutes grounds for refusing recognition and enforcement (Articles 28 and 34);

(e) the rules apply whether or not the defendant is domiciled in a Contracting State.

The only difference between the two Conventions relates to tenancies of immovable property (see points 49 to 54).

(d) Prorogation of jurisdiction

The two Conventions also contain rules of prorogation of jurisdiction by agreement or tacitly (Title II, Section 6, Articles 17 and 18). The Conventions differ in the case of Article 17 (prorogation by agreement—see points 55 to 61) but not in the case of Article 18 (submission to jurisdiction).

(e) Lis pendens and related actions

Both Conventions contain provisions on the case of a *lis pendens* (Article 21) and related actions (Article 22) in Section 8, the aim of which is to avoid conflicting judgments. The wordings differ slightly here with regard to a *lis pendens* (see point 62).

Fifth principle:

The defendant's rights must have been respected in the State of origin.

Both Conventions provide in the first paragraph of Article 20, the importance of which should be emphasized, that if a defendant does not enter an appearance the court must declare of its own motion that it has no jurisdiction unless its jurisdiction is derived from the provisions of the Convention.

The second and third paragraphs of Article 20 cover the problem of notification of legal documents to the defendant, the court being obliged to stay its proceedings so long as it has not been shown that the defendant was able to receive the document instituting the proceedings in sufficient time to enable him to arrange for his defence. This Article has not been amended.

Sixth principle:

Grounds for refusing recognition and enforcement are limited.

Pursuant to the first paragraph of Article 26 of both Conventions, judgments given in a Contracting State must be recognized in the other Contracting States without any special procedure being required. In other words, judgments are entitled to automatic recognition: the Conventions establish the presumption in favour of recognition and the only grounds for refusal are those listed in Articles 27 and 28.

There are two conditions which agreements such as this usually contain but which these two Conventions omit: recognition does not require that the foreign judgment should have become *res judicata*, and the jurisdiction of the court in the State of origin is no longer examined by the court of the State in which enforcement is being sought. In this respect there are some differences between the two Conventions with regard to Article 28 (see points 16 and 82).

[OJ C189, 28.7.90, p 67]

Seventh principle:

The enforcement procedure is unified and simplified.

It is unified in that, in every Contracting State, the procedure is initiated by submission of an application.

It is simplified in particular with reference to the appeals procedure.

The Lugano Convention makes a number of technical adjustments as against the 1968 Convention (see points 68 to 70).

Eighth principle:

The Conventions govern relations with other international Conventions. On this point, and with regard to Conventions concluded on particular matters, there are a few differences between the two Conventions (see points 79 to 82).

Ninth principle:

Steps are taken to ensure that interpretation of the two Conventions is uniform.

Interpretation of the 1968 Convention is entrusted to the Court of Justice by the Luxembourg Protocol of 3 June 1971.

Interpretation of the Lugano Convention is governed by Protocol 2 to that Convention (see points 110 to 119).

[3070]

CHAPTER II
RESPECTIVE SCOPE OF THE BRUSSELS CONVENTION AND THE LUGANO CONVENTION

(Article 54b)

14. As shown above, although the structure of the two Conventions is identical and they contain a great number of comparable provisions, they remain separate Conventions.

15. The respective application of the two Conventions is governed by Article 54b. The first point to note is that this Article primarily concerns the courts of member countries of the European Communities, these being the only courts which may be required to deliver judgments pursuant to either Convention. Courts in EFTA Member States are not bound by the Brussels Convention since the EFTA States are not parties to that Convention.

However, Article 54b is relevant for the courts of EFTA countries since it was felt advantageous that Article 54b should, for reasons of clarity, contain details relating to the case of a *lis pendens*, related actions and recognition and enforcement of judgments.

The philosophy of Article 54b is as follows—

According to paragraph 1, the Brussels Convention continues to apply in relations between Member States of the European Communities.

This applies in particular where—

(a) a person, of whatever nationality, domiciled in one Community State, e g France, is summoned to appear before a court in another such State, e g Italy. The plaintiff's nationality and domicile are immaterial;

(b) a judgment has been delivered in one European Community Member State, e g France, and must be recognized or enforced in another such State, e g Italy.

The Brussels Convention also applies where a person domiciled outside the territory of a European Community Member State and outside the territory of any other State party to the Lugano Convention, e g in the United States, is summoned to appear before a court in a European Community Member State (Article 4 of the Brussels Convention).

In each of these three instances, the Court of Justice of the European Communities has jurisdiction under the 1971 Protocol to rule on problems which may arise with regard to the interpretation of the Brussels Convention.

16. However, under paragraph 2, the court of a European Community Member State must apply the Lugano Convention where—

PART IV EC MATERIALS

(1) a defendant is domiciled in the territory of a State which is party to the Lugano Convention and an EFTA member or is deemed to be so domiciled under Articles 8 or 13 of the Convention. For instance, if a person domiciled in Norway is summoned before a French court, jurisdiction will be vested in that court only in the cases for which the Lugano Convention provides. In particular the rules of exorbitant jurisdiction provided for in Article 4 of the Brussels Convention may not be relied on as against that person;

[OJ C189, 28.7.90, p 68]

(2) the courts of an EFTA Member State possess exclusive jurisdiction (Article 16) or jurisdiction by prorogation (Article 17). The courts of Member States of the European Communities may not, for instance, be seised of a dispute relating to rights *in rem* in immovable property situated in the territory of a State party to the Lugano Convention and an EFTA Member State, notwithstanding Article 16 (1) of the Brussels Convention, which will apply only if the immovable property is situated in the territory of a State party to the 1968 Convention;

(3) recognition or enforcement of a judgment delivered in a State party to the Lugano Convention and an EFTA Member State is being sought in a Community Member State (paragraph 2(c)).
Paragraph 2 also provides that the Lugano Convention applies where a judgment delivered in a Community Member State is to be enforced in an EFTA Member State party to the Lugano Convention.
This does not resolve potential conflicts between the two Conventions, but it does define their respective scope. Obviously if a judgment has been delivered in a State party to the Lugano Convention and an EFTA Member State and is to be enforced either in a Community Member State or in an EFTA Member State, the Brussels Convention does not apply;

(4) Article 54b also contains provisions relating to a *lis pendens* (Article 21) and related actions (Article 22). Under Article 54b(2)(b) a court in a Community Member State must apply these Articles of the Lugano Convention if a court in an EFTA Member State is seised of the same dispute or a related claim.
Apart from the greater clarity which they bring, these provisions serve a double purpose: to remove all uncertainty, and to ensure that judgments delivered in the different States concerned do not conflict;

(5) Article 54b(3) provides that a court in an EFTA Member State may refuse recognition or enforcement of a judgment delivered by a court in a Community Member State if the grounds on which the latter court has based its jurisdiction are not provided for in the Lugano Convention and if recognition or enforcement is being sought against a party who is domiciled in any EFTA Contracting State.
These grounds for refusal are additional to those provided for in Article 28, and arise essentially from a guarantee sought by the EFTA Member States. The cases involved can be expected to arise relatively seldom, since the Conventions are so similar in respect of their rules of jurisdiction. The possibility nevertheless remains. The case would arise in the event of a judgment on a contract of employment delivered by a court in a Community Member State which had erroneously based its jurisdiction with regard to a person domiciled in an EFTA Member State either on Article 4 or Article 5(1) of the Brussels Convention, i e in a manner inconsistent with Article 5(1) of the Lugano Convention, which includes a specific provision on contracts of employment, or on an agreement conferring jurisdiction which predated the origin of the dispute (Article 17).
However, in the interests of freedom of movement of judgments, the judgment will be recognized and enforced provided that this can be done in accordance with the rules of common law of the State addressed, in particular its common law rules on the jurisdiction of foreign courts;

(6) for convenience, we have used the term "EFTA Member States" in the above examples. Obviously, the same arrangements would apply to States which are not members of either the EEC or EFTA but accede to the Lugano Convention (see Article 62(1)(b)).

17. The question remained unresolved as to how the Lugano Convention would apply between Community Member States one of which was not a party to the Brussels Convention such as, for instance, Spain or Portugal, while both were parties to the Lugano Convention. The issue would, for example, arise should both Belgium and Spain become parties to the Lugano Convention before the Treaty on the accession of Spain to the Brussels Convention has been concluded or has entered into force and should enforcement of a judgment delivered in one of these States be requested in the other. In the rapporteurs' opinion, the Lugano

Convention would, as a source of law, apply in the case in point pending entry into force between Belgium and Spain of the Treaty on the accession of Spain to the Brussels Convention.

[3071]

[OJ C189, 28.7.90, p 69]

CHAPTER III
PROVISIONS WHICH DISTINGUISH THE LUGANO CONVENTION FROM THE BRUSSELS CONVENTION

1. SUMMARY OF THESE PROVISIONS

18. The amendments are not numerous. Before considering them in detail it might be helpful to list the Articles in the Lugano Convention which differ from the corresponding Articles in the Brussels Convention.

Article 3

This Article adds the rules of exorbitant jurisdiction current in the EFTA Member States and in Portugal. It should be noted that no such rules exist in Spain.

Article 5(1)

A special provision has been inserted covering matters relating to contracts of employment.

Article 6

A new paragraph 4 relates to the combination of proceedings *in rem* with proceedings *in personam.*

Article 16

Matters relating to tenancies in immovable property are the subject of a new provision (paragraph 1(b)) and of a reservation (Protocol No 1, Article Ib).

Article 17

This Article has been amended with regard to the reference to commercial practices and contracts of employment.

Article 21

The reference in this Article to lis pendens has been somewhat amended.

Article 28

This Article now contains further grounds for refusing recognition and enforcement.

Articles 31 to 41

Technical modifications have been made to some of these Articles with regard to procedure for enforcement and modes of appeal.

Article 50

The wording of this Article, which concerns authentic instruments, has been slightly altered.

Article 54

This Article has been clarified with regard to the transitional provisions.

Article 54A

This Article is based on Article 36 of the 1978 Accession Convention and contains additions.

Article 54B

This is a new Article governing the respective scope of the Brussels Convention and the Lugano Convention.

Article 55

This Article concerns relations with other conventions and refers only to conventions to which EFTA Member States are party.

Article 57

This Article governs implementation of conventions concluded with regard to particular matters and differs appreciably from Article 57 of the Brussels Convention.

Articles 60 to 68 (Final provisions)

These Articles have been amended.

19. **Protocol 1**

Article Ia

This new Article contains a reservation requested by the Swiss delegation.

[OJ C189, 28.7.90, p 70]

Article Ib

This new Article contains a reservation resulting from the amendment of Article 16(1) relating to tenancies in immovable property.

Article V

This Article covers actions on a warranty or guarantee and contains additions covering current legislation in several States.

Article Va

The Article covers maintenance matters in particular and contains additions to take account of the situation in several States.

Article Vb

This Article covers disputes between the master and a member of the crew of a vessel and again contains additions to take account of the laws in a number of States.

20. **Protocol 2**

This Protocol has been added in order to ensure that, as far as possible, the Lugano Convention and the provisions therein which are identical to the Brussels Convention are interpreted uniformly.

21. **Protocol 3**

This Protocol deals with the problem of Community acts.

22. **Declarations**

First Declaration: supplementary to Protocol 3.

Second and Third Declarations: supplementary to Protocol 2 on the uniform interpretation of the Lugano Convention.

2. DETAILED EXAMINATION

TITLE I
SCOPE OF THE LUGANO CONVENTION
(ARTICLE 1)

23. Since this differs in no respect from the Brussels Convention, the reader is referred to the Jenard and Schlosser reports.

TITLE II
JURISDICTION (ARTICLES 2 TO 24)

Section 1
General provisions (Article 2 to 4)

(a) Introductory remarks

24. The proposed adaptations to Articles 2 to 4 are confined to mentioning, in the second paragraph of Article 3, certain exorbitant jurisdictions in the legal systems of the EFTA Member States and of Portugal. A brief explanation of the proposed additional provisions (see point 1) precedes, as in the *Schlosser* report, two more general remarks on the relevance of these provisions to the whole structure of the Lugano Convention.

(b) Exorbitant jurisdictional bases in force in the EFTA Member States and Portugal

1. Austria

25. Article 99 of the Law on Court Jurisdiction (Jurisdiktionsnorm) provides that any person neither domiciled nor ordinarily resident in Austria may, in matters relating to property, be sued in the court for any place where he has assets or where the disputed property is located. The value of the assets located in Austria may, however, not be considerably lower than the value of the matter in dispute.

Foreign establishments, foundations, companies, cooperatives and associations may, according to the abovementioned Article (paragraph 3), also be sued in the court for the place where they have their permanent representation for Austria or an agency.

2. Finland

26. The second sentence of Article 1 of Chapter 10 of the Finnish Code of Judicial Procedure provides that a person who has no habitual residence in Finland may be sued in the court of the place where the documents instituting the proceeding were served on him or in the court of the place where he has assets. The third sentence of the same Article provides that a Finnish national who is staying abroad may also be sued in the court for the place where he had his last residence in Finland. The fourth sentence of the same Article provides that a foreign national, having neither domicile nor residence in Finland may, unless there is a special provision to the contrary as to nationals of a particular State, be sued in the court for the place where the documents instituting the proceedings were served on him or in the court for the place where he has assets.

[OJ C189, 28.7.90, p 71]

3. Iceland

27. Article 77 of the Icelandic Civil Proceedings Act provides that in matters relating to property obligations to Icelandic citizens, firms etc any person not domiciled in that country may be sued in the court for the place where the person was when the documents instituting the proceedings were served on him or where he has assets.

4. Norway

28. Article 32 of the Norwegian Civil Proceedings Act provides that any person not domiciled in Norway may be sued, in matters relating to property, in the court for the place where he has assets or where the disputed property is located at the time when the documents instituting the proceedings were served on him.

5. Sweden

29. The first sentence of Section 3 of Chapter 10 of the Swedish Code of Judicial Procedure provides that anyone without a known domicile in Sweden may be sued, in matters concerning payment of a debt, in the court for the place where he has assets.

6. Switzerland

30. Article 40 of the Federal Law on Private International Law states that if there is no other provision on jurisdiction in Swiss law an action concerning sequestration may be brought before the court for the place where the goods were attached in Switzerland.

7. Portugal

31. Article 65 of Chapter II of the Code of Civil Procedure provides that a foreign national may be sued in a Portuguese court where—

- (paragraph 1(c)) the plaintiff is Portuguese and, if the situation were reversed, he could be sued in the courts of the State of which the defendant is a national,
- (paragraph 2) under Portuguese law, the court with jurisdiction would be that of the defendant's domicile, if the latter is a foreigner who has been resident in Portugal for more than six months or who is fortuitously on Portuguese territory provided that, in the latter case, the obligation which is the subject of the dispute was entered into in Portugal.

Article 65a(c) of the Code of Civil Procedure confers exclusive jurisdiction on Portuguese courts for actions relating to employment relationships if any of the parties is of Portuguese nationality.

Article 11 of the Code of Labour Procedure gives jurisdiction to Portuguese labour courts for disputes concerning a Portuguese worker where the contract was concluded in Portugal.

(c) The relevance of the second paragraph of Article 3 to the whole structure of the Lugano Convention

1. Scope of the second paragraph of Article 3

32. The rejection as exorbitant of jurisdictional bases hitherto considered to be important in the various States should not, any more than the second paragraph of Article 3 of the 1968 Brussels Convention, mislead anyone as regards the scope of the first paragraph of Article 3. Only particularly extravagant claims to international jurisdiction for the courts of a Contracting State are expressly underlined. Other rules founding jurisdiction in the national laws of the Contracting States also remain compatible with the Lugano Convention only to the extent that they do not offend against Article 2 and Articles 4 to 18. Thus, for example, the jurisdiction of Swedish courts in respect of persons domiciled in a Contracting State can no longer be based, in contractual matters, on the fact that the contract was entered into in Sweden.

2. Impossibility of founding jurisdiction on the location of property

33. With regard to Austria, Denmark, Finland, Germany, Iceland, Norway, Sweden and the United Kingdom, the list in the second paragraph of Article 3 contains provisions rejecting jurisdiction derived solely from the existence of property in the territory of the State in which the court is situated. Such jurisdiction cannot be invoked even if the proceedings concern a dispute over rights of ownership, or possession or the capacity to dispose of the specific property in question.

[OJ C189, 28.7.90, p 72]

34. With regard to Switzerland, the list in the second paragraph contains a provision rejecting jurisdiction derived solely from an attachment of property located in Switzerland. There is, however, no obstacle for Swiss courts pursuant to Article 24, to grant such provisional, including protective, measures as may be available under the law of Switzerland, even if, under the Convention, the courts of another Contracting State have jurisdiction as to the substance of the matter.

35. As regards persons who are domiciled outside the Contracting States, the provisions which hitherto governed the jurisdiction of courts in the Contracting States remain unaffected. Even the rules on jurisdiction mentioned in the second paragraph of Article 3 may continue to apply to such persons. Judgments delivered by courts which thus have jurisdiction must also be recognized and enforced in other Contracting States unless one of the exceptions in paragraph 5 of Article 27 or in Article 59 of the Convention applies.

The latter provision is the only one concerning which the list in Article 3 second paragraph is not only of illustrative significance, but has direct and restrictive importance.

Section 2
Special jurisdiction (Articles 5 and 6)

(a) Article 5(1)—Contract of employment

36. The domicile of the defendant constitutes the basic rule of both the Brussels Convention and the Lugano Convention.

However, Section 2 (Articles 5 and 6) of Title II on jurisdiction contains a number of supplementary provisions. Under these provisions, the plaintiff may choose to bring the action in the court specified in Section 2, or in the courts of the State in which the defendant is domiciled (Article 2).

Article 5(1) of the Brussels Convention provides that the defendant may be sued "in matters relating to a contract, in the courts for the place of performance of the obligation in question".

37. This paragraph is applicable with regard to a contract of employment (see Jenard report, p 24 and Chapter VI: judgment of the Court of Justice of 13 November 1979 in Sanicentral v Collin, according to which employment legislation comes within the Convention's scope). When asked to give a ruling on this matter, the Court of Justice ruled that the obligation to be taken into account in the case of claims based on different obligations arising under a contract of employment as a representative binding a worker to an undertaking was the obligation which characterized the contract, i e that of the place where the work was carried out (judgment of the Court of 26 May 1982 in Ivenel v Schwab, see Chapter VI).

This ruling was based, amongst other things, on Article 6 of the Rome Convention on the law applicable to contractual obligations (OJ No L266, 1980, p 1), which provides that in matters relating to an employment contract, the contract "is to be governed, in the absence of choice of the applicable law, by the law of the country in which the employee habitually carries out his work in performance of the contract, unless it appears that the contract is more closely connected with another country". In the above judgment, the Court commented that the aim of this provision was to secure adequate protection for the party who from the socioeconomic point of view was to be regarded as the weaker in the contractual relationship (see also Giuliano-Lagarde report, OJ No C282, 1982, p 25).

In another ruling, the Court of Justice observed that contracts of employment, like other contracts for work other than on a self-employed basis, differed from other contracts—even those for the provision of services—by virtue of certain particularities: they created a lasting bond which brought the worker to some extent within the organizational framework of the business of the undertaking or employer, and they were linked to the place where the activities were pursued, which determined the application of mandatory rules and collective agreements (judgment of 15 January 1987 in Shenavai v Kreischer, see Chapter VI).

During negotiation of the Lugano Convention the EFTA Member States requested that, in respect of Article 5 and Article 17 (for this last Article, see point 60), matters relating to employment contracts should be the subject of a separate provision.

This request was granted.

38. Under the new Article 5(1) on matters relating to contracts of employment, the place of performance of the obligation in question is deemed to be that where the employee habitually carries out his work. If he does not habitually carry out his work in any one country, the place is that in which is situated the place of business through which he was engaged. It should be noted that such an issue is currently before the Court of Justice (see Chapter VI, Six Constructions v Humbert case).

[OJ C189, 28.7.90, p 73]

As we have seen, this provision is in line with the previous judgments of the Court of Justice corresponding quite closely to Article 6 of the Rome Convention.[5]

39. The stipulation in Article 5(1) gives rise to the following comments—

According to the general structure of the Lugano Convention, the following have jurisdiction where there are disputes between employers and employees—

— the courts of the State in which the defendant is domiciled (Article 2),
— the courts specified in Article 5(1). If an employee habitually carries out his work in the same country, but not in any particular place, the internal law of that country will determine the court which has jurisdiction,
— courts on which jurisdiction has been conferred by an agreement entered into after the dispute has arisen (see Article 17(5)),
— courts whose jurisdiction is implied by submission (Article 18).

However, these rules do not apply unless the dispute contains an extraneous element. The Conventions only lay down rules of international jurisdiction (see preamble). They have no effect if the contract (domicile of the employer, domicile of the employee and place of work) is actually situated in a single country. In this connection, the employee's nationality must not be taken into account, as the employee must be treated in the same way as other employees.

On the other hand, if the defendant is domiciled outside the territory of one of the Contracting States, Article 4 is applicable.

40. Where the defendant does not habitually carry out his work in any one country, the courts of the place in which the place of business through which he was engaged is situated will have jurisdiction. This system is in keeping with that laid down by Article 6(2)(b) of the Rome Convention on the law applicable to contractual obligations.

The purpose of the provision is to avoid increasing the number of courts with jurisdiction in disputes between employers and employees where the employee is required to carry out his work in several countries. In addition, for States parties to the Rome Convention and the Lugano Convention, jurisdiction will be congruent with the applicable law. The same applies in some States which are not parties to the Rome Convention.

41. The question whether a contract of employment exists is not settled by the Convention. If the judge to whom the matter has been referred gives an affirmative reply to this question, he will have to apply the second part of Article 5(1), which constitutes a specific provision. Although there is as yet no independent concept of what constitutes a contract of employment, it may be considered that it presupposes a relationship of subordination of the employee to the employer (see Chapter VI, judgments in Shenavai v Kreischer, cited earlier, and in Arcado v Haviland of 8 March 1988).

42. Article 5(1) refers only to individual employment relationships, and not to collective agreements between employers and workers' representatives.

43. The term "place of business" is to be understood in the broad sense; in particular, it covers any entity such as a branch or an agency with no legal personality.

44. In conclusion, it may be considered that although the texts of the Brussels Convention and the Lugano Convention are not identical, they do converge, particularly by reason of the interpretation by the Court of Justice of Article 5(1) of the Brussels Convention.

(b) Article 6(1)—Co-defendants

45. No change has been made to the text of the Brussels Convention which provides that "a person domiciled in a Contracting State may be sued, where he is one of a number of defendants, in the courts for the place where any one of them is domiciled". However, this provision was taken over verbatim only in the light of the comments made in the Jenard report on the 1968 Convention (OJ No C59/79, p 26) to the effect that "in order for this rule to be applicable there must be a connection between the claims made against each of the defendants, as for example in the case of joint debtors. It follows that action cannot be brought solely with the object of ousting the jurisdiction of the courts of the State in which the defendant is domiciled." A few days after the diplomatic conference ended, the Court of Justice delivered a judgment along these lines (judgment of 27 September 1988 in Kalfelis v Schroder, see Chapter VI, OJ No C281, 4.11.1988, p 18).

[OJ C189, 28.7.90, p 74]

(c) Article 6(4)—Combination of actions in rem and in personam

46. When a person has a mortgage on immovable property the owner of that property is quite often also personally liable for the secured debt. Therefore it has been made possible in some States to combine an action concerning the personal liability of the owner with an action for the enforced sale of the immovable property. This presupposes of course that the court for the place where the immovable property is situated also has jurisdiction as to actions concerning the personal liability of the owner.

It was agreed that it was practical that an action concerning the personal liability of the owner of an immovable property could be combined with an action for the enforced sale of the immovable property in those States where such a combination of actions was possible. Therefore it was deemed appropriate to include in the Convention a provision according to which a person domiciled in a Contracting State also may be sued in matters relating to a contract, if the action may be combined with an action against the same defendant in matters relating to rights *in rem* in immovable property, in the court of the Contracting State in which the property is situated.

To illustrate, let us assume that a person domiciled in France is the owner of an immovable property situated in Norway. This person has raised a loan which is secured through a mortgage on his immovable property in Norway. In the eventuality of the loan not being repaid when due, if the creditor wishes to bring an action for the enforced sale of the immovable property, the Norwegian court has exclusive jurisdiction under Article 16(1). However, under the present provision, this court also has jurisdiction as to an action against the owner of the property concerning his personal liability for the debt, if the creditor wishes to combine the latter action with an action for the enforced sale of the property.

47. It is evident that this jurisdictional basis cannot exist by itself. It must necessarily be supplemented by legal criteria which determine on which conditions such a combination is possible. Thus the provisions already existing in or which in the future may be introduced into the legal systems of the Contracting States with reference to the combining of the abovementioned actions remain unaffected by the Lugano Convention. It goes without saying however that the combination of the two actions which this paragraph deals with have to be instituted by the "same claimant". The "same claimant" includes of course also a person to whom another person has transferred his rights or his successor.

Sections 3 and 4

Jurisdiction in matters relating to insurance (Articles 7 to 12a) and over consumer contracts (Articles 13 to 15)

48. Since no amendments have been made to these sections, reference should be made to the Jenard and Schlosser reports.

Section 5

Exclusive jurisdiction

Article 16(1)—Tenancies

49. Under Article 16(1) of the Brussels Convention, only courts of the Contracting State in which the immovable property is situated have jurisdiction concerning rights *in rem* in, or

tenancies of, immovable property. Thus the wording covers not only all disputes concerning rights *in rem* in immovable property, but also those relating to tenancies of such property. According to the Jenard report (p 35), the Committee which drafted the Brussels Convention intended to cover disputes between landlord and tenant over the existence or interpretation of tenancy agreements, compensation for damage caused by the tenant, eviction, etc The rule was, according to the same report, not intended by the Committee to apply to proceedings concerned only with the recovery of rent, since such proceedings can be considered to relate to a subject-matter which is quite distinct from the rented property itself.

The working party which drafted the Convention on the accession of Denmark, Ireland and the United Kingdom of Great Britain and Northern Ireland to the Brussels Convention and to the Protocol on its interpretation by the Court of Justice was, however, according to the Schlosser report (paragraph 164), unable to agree whether actions concerned only with rent, i e dealing simply with recovery of a debt, are excluded from the scope of Article 16(1).

As stated in the Jenard report, the reference to tenancies in Article 16(1) of the Brussels Convention includes tenancies of dwellings and of premises for professional or commercial use, and agricultural holdings. According to the Schlosser report, the underlying principle of the provision quite clearly does not require its application to short-term agreements for use and occupation such as, for example, holiday accommodation.

[OJ C189, 28.7.90, p 75]

50. The Court of Justice of the European Communities has ruled that Article 16(1) does not cover disputes relating to transfer of an usufructuary right in immovable property (judgment of 14 December 1977 in Sanders v Van der Putte, see Chapter VI). The Court held that Article 16(1) must not be interpreted as including an agreement to rent under a usufructuary lease a retail business carried on in immovable property rented from a third person by the lessor. However, departing from the intentions of the authors of the 1968 Convention, the Court of Justice recently ruled that the exclusive jurisdiction provided for in Article 16(1) also applies to proceedings in respect of the payment of rent, and that this includes short-term lettings of holiday homes (judgment of 18 January 1985 in Rösler v Rottwinkel, see Chapter VI). The Court held that this exclusive jurisdiction applies to all lettings of immovable property, even for short term and even where they relate only to the use and occupation of a holiday home and that this jurisdiction covers all disputes concerning the obligations of the landlord or the tenant under a tenancy, in particular those concerning the existence of tenancies or the interpretation of the terms thereof, their duration, the giving up of possession to the landlord, the repairing of damage caused by the tenant or the recovery of rent and of incidental charges for the consumption of water, gas and electricity. This decision seems at least partially to be in contradiction with what, according to the Jenard and Schlosser reports, was the intention of those who drafted the Brussels Convention.

51. Having regard especially to the ruling given by the Court of Justice in the case of Rösler v Rottwinkel, the EFTA Member States insisted on the inclusion of a special provision concerning short-term tenancies of immovable property in the Lugano Convention. As an alternative, these States put forward the idea of excluding tenancies totally from the scope of the Convention or particularly from Article 16. The working party agreed that it was inappropriate to exclude tenancies altogether from the scope of the Convention, in view of the importance of this matter. As to the proposal for excluding tenancies from Article 16 especially, the delegations of the Community Member States found such a solution totally unacceptable as the normal jurisdiction rules of the Convention would have been applicable to tenancies of immovable property, which was alien to the whole philosophy existing in this respect at least in the Community States. Thus the working party decided to include in Article 16(1) a new subparagraph (b) containing a special provision concerning short-term tenancies.

52. The result of this change is that, where tenancies are concerned, there will be two exclusive jurisdictions, which might be described as alternative exclusive jurisdictions. Under subparagraph (a), the courts of the Contracting State in which the immovable property is situated will always have jurisdiction without restriction. However, under subparagraph (b), in proceedings which have as their object tenancies of immovable property concluded for temporary private use for a maximum period of six consecutive months—which covers particularly holiday lettings—the plaintiff may also apply to the courts of the Contracting State in which the defendant is domiciled. This option is open to him only if the tenant (and not the owner) is a natural person and if, in addition, neither party is domiciled in the Contracting State in which the property is situated.

Legal persons holding tenancies were excluded since they are generally engaged in commercial transactions.

Furthermore, where one of the parties is domiciled in the Contracting State in which the property is situated, it was considered appropriate to retain the rule in Article 16(1) which lays down the principle of the jurisdiction of the courts of that State.

53. Article 16(1)(b) did, however, create serious political difficulties for certain Community Member States. In order to overcome these difficulties, the working party agreed that this provision be accompanied by the possibility of a reservation. By means of this, any Contracting State may declare that it will neither recognize nor enforce a judgment in respect of a case concerning tenancies of immovable property, if the immovable property concerned is situated on its territory even if the tenancy is such as referred to in Article 16 paragraph 1(b) and the jurisdiction of the court which has given the judgment has been based on the domicile of the defendant. This reservation is given in Article Ib of Protocol No 1.

[OJ C189, 28.7.90, p 76]

This possibility of a reservation only concerns such cases in which the immovable property is situated in the State where recognition and enforcement are sought. If, thus, for instance, Spain makes use of this possibility, that does not mean that Spain is entitled to refuse the recognition or enforcement of a judgment given in proceedings which had as their object a tenancy referred to in Article 16(1)(b) if the immovable property is situated in another State eg Italy, and the judgment is given by a court in a third State, where the defendant has his domicile, eg Sweden. Whether the State where the immovable property is situated has made use of the reservation is in this case completely irrelevant.

It was however understood that any State which wishes to use this reservation may make a narrower reservation than that provided for. Thus a State may, for instance, declare that the reservation is limited to the case where the landlord is a legal person.

54. Article 16(1) applies only if the property is situated in the territory of a Contracting State. The text is sufficiently explicit on this point. If the property is situated in the territory of a third State, the other provisions of the Convention apply, eg Article 2 if the defendant is domiciled in the territory of a Contracting State, and Article 4 if he is domiciled in the territory of a third State, etc

Section 6

Prorogation of jurisdiction (Articles 17 and 18)

(a) Article 17—Prorogation by an agreement

55. *1.* Paragraph 1 of this Article essentially concerns the formal requirements for agreements conferring jurisdiction. The question of whether an agreement on jurisdiction has been validly entered into (eg lack of due consent) is to be regulated by the applicable law (judgment of the Court of Justice of 11 November 1986 in Iveco Fiat v Van Hool, see Chapter VI). As to whether such an agreement can be validly entered into in specific matters it should be pointed out that the Court of Justice (judgment of 13 November 1979 in Sanicentral v Collin, see Chapter VI) ruled that in matters governed by the Convention national procedural law was set aside in favour of the Convention's provisions.

56. According to the original version of Article 17 of the Brussels Convention, an agreement conferring jurisdiction must be in writing or evidenced in writing. In the light of the interpretation of the Court of Justice of the European Communities in some of its first judgments concerning Article 17 of the Brussels Convention (see Chapter VI), the working party preparing the 1978 Convention on the accession of the Kingdom of Denmark, Ireland and the United Kingdom of Great Britain and Northern Ireland to the Brussels Convention and to the Protocol of 3 June 1971 on its interpretation by the Court of Justice was of the opinion that these formal requirements did not cater adequately for the customs and needs of international trade. Therefore a relaxation of these formal requirements as far as agreements on jurisdiction in international trade or commerce are concerned was felt necessary. According to Article 17 of the Brussels Convention as amended by the 1978 Accession Convention, an agreement conferring jurisdiction may in international trade or commerce be in a form which accords with practices in that trade or commerce of which the parties are or ought to have been aware.

57. During the negotiations on the Lugano Convention, the EFTA Member States, however, felt that this provision was too vague and might create legal uncertainty. Those States feared that Article 17(1), as far as agreements on jurisdiction in international commerce or trade are concerned, might make it possible to consider an agreement established by the mere fact that no protest has been launched against a jurisdiction clause in certain unilateral statements by one party, for instance in an invoice or in terms of trade presented as a confirmation of the contract. Therefore the EFTA Member States proposed the following amendment of the second sentence of Article 17(1)—

"Such an agreement conferring jurisdiction shall be either

(a) in writing (or clearly evidenced in writing) including an exchange of letters, telegrams and telexes (or other modern means of technical communications), or

(b) included or incorporated by reference in a bill of lading or a similar transport document."

The representatives of the Community Member States found however that this proposal would not only lead to an excessive amount of rigidity but would also be in contradiction with the rulings of the Court of Justice of the European Communities, according to which it should be possible to take into account particular practices (judgment of 14 December 1976 in Segoura v Bonakdarian, see Chapter VI).
[OJ C189, 28.7.90, p 77]

58. Article 17(1)(a) of the Lugano Convention is based on Article 9 paragraph 2 of the 1980 United Nations Convention on Contracts for the International Sale of Goods (the so-called Vienna Convention). Since the Member States of the EEC and the EFTA States may become parties to that Convention, the working party found it desirable to align in this respect the text of Article 17 on the text of Article 9 paragraph 2 of the Vienna Convention. The provision can be seen as a compromise between the two groups of States.

First, according to Article 17(1)(b) of the Lugano Convention, an agreement conferring jurisdiction fulfils the formal requirements if it is in a form that accords with practices which the parties have established between themselves. This is not provided for in the wording of Article 17 of the Brussels Convention. In the light of the case law of the Court of Justice of the European Communities (see Chapter VI), this seems, however, to be the understanding of Article 17 of the Brussels Convention. The working party was of the opinion that this understanding should be explicitly reflected in the text of the Lugano Convention.

Secondly, in international trade or commerce an agreement conferring jurisdiction fulfils the formal requirements if it is in a form that accords with a usage of which the parties are or ought to have been aware and which in such trade is widely known to, and regularly observed by, parties to contracts of the type involved in the particular trade or commerce concerned.

Thus, even in international trade or commerce, it is not sufficient that an agreement conferring jurisdiction be in a form which accords with practices (or a usage) in such trade or commerce of which the parties are or ought to have been aware. It is moreover required that the usage shall be, on the one hand, widely known in international trade or commerce and, on the other, regularly observed by parties to contracts of the type involved in the particular trade or commerce concerned.

In particular, having regard to the words "internationale Handelsbräuche" and "usages" which are used in the German and French versions of Article 17 of the Brussels Convention, it seems that there are at least no major differences in substance between the provisions concerned in the two Conventions. In order to ensure a uniform interpretation it was, however, felt by the EFTA States that the present wording of paragraph 1(c) was necessary in the Lugano Convention.

59. Article 17 of the Brussels Convention has given rise to a considerable number of judgments by the Court of Justice of the European Communities. In this connection, readers are referred to Chapter VI.2, point 12 "Article 17", paragraphs 1 to 12.

However, it should be mentioned in this context that the Court of Justice has ruled that an agreement between the parties with regard to the place of performance, which constitutes a ground of jurisdiction pursuant to Article 5(1), is sufficient to confer jurisdiction without being subject to the formal requirements laid down in Article 17 for prorogation of jurisdiction (judgment of 17 January 1980 in Zelger v Salinitri, see Chapter VI).

60. 2. Article 17(5) was proposed by the EFTA Member States. It provides that in matters relating to contracts of employment an agreement conferring jurisdiction within the meaning of the first paragraph shall have legal force only if it is entered into after the dispute has arisen. The background of this provision is the same as that for Article 5(1), i e the protection of the employee, who from the socioeconomic point of view is regarded as the weaker in the contractual relationship. It seemed desirable that it should not be possible for the protection intended to be given to employees by virtue of Article 5(1) to be taken away by prorogation agreements entered into before the dispute arose. As in the case of Article 5(1) this provision applies only to individual employment relationships and not to collective agreements concluded between employers and employees' representatives.

61. During the Diplomatic Conference, stress was laid on the difference between the Brussels and Lugano Conventions as regards agreements conferring jurisdiction with respect

to contracts of employment, and a number of problems were highlighted. The example given was that of an agreement conferring jurisdiction which, at the time, was concluded between parties domiciled in the territory of two States which had ratified the Brussels Convention. Under that Convention, prorogation of jurisdiction by agreement may, as regards a contract of employment, be effected before the dispute arises.

What happens if, at a later stage, one of the parties transfers his domicile to an EFTA Member State? What would be the attitude either of the court in a Community Member State to which a dispute is referred on the basis of that agreement conferring jurisdiction, or of a court in an EFTA Member State to which a dispute is referred despite the agreement?

The question was left open and, although the solutions adopted by the Brussels and the Lugano Conventions are not without their merits, might possibly be resolved in the Convention on the accession of Spain and Portugal to the Brussels Convention by aligning the Brussels Convention on the Lugano Convention.

[OJ C189, 28.7.90, p 78]

(b) Article 18—Submission to jurisdiction

62. Discrepancies have been noted between the various versions of the Brussels Convention. A number of versions, for example the English and the German ones, provide that the rule whereby the court of the Contracting State has jurisdiction does not apply where appearance was entered "solely" to contest the jurisdiction, which restriction is not included in the French text.

However, no amendment was made to the various texts in view of a judgment given by the Court of Justice to the effect that Article 18 applies under certain conditions where the defendant contests the court's jurisdiction and also makes submissions on the substance of the action (judgment of 24 June 1981 in Elefanten Schuh v Jacqmain, see Chapter VI).

Section 7
Examination as to jurisdiction and admissibility
(Articles 19 and 20)

63. Although these Articles correspond to Articles 19 and 20 of the Brussels Convention, Article 20 requires some comment, given that it is a particularly important provision where the defendant fails to enter an appearance (see Jenard report, page 39).

A judge required to apply the Lugano Convention must declare of his own motion that he has no jurisdiction unless his jurisdiction is derived from the provisions of Sections 2 to 6 of Title II of that Convention. For example, a French judge before whom a person domiciled in Norway is required to appear on the basis of Article 14 of the Code Civil (jurisdiction derived from the French nationality of the applicant) must declare of his own motion that he has no jurisdiction if the defendant fails to enter an appearance.

Likewise, the judge must declare of his own motion that he has no jurisdiction unless his jurisdiction is derived from the provisions of an international convention governing jurisdiction in particular matters, as stipulated in Article 57(2). In this connection reference should be made to the comments on Article 57.

It should be noted that almost all the Community and EFTA Member States are currently parties to the Hague Convention of 15 November 1965 on the service abroad of judicial and extra-judicial documents in civil or commercial matters since, at 1 June 1988, the sole exceptions are Austria, Ireland, Iceland and Switzerland.

Section 8
***Lis pendens*—related actions** (Articles 21 to 23)

64. *Article 21*

Only this Article has been amended in Section 8.

Article 21 of the Brussels Convention provides that in case of a *lis alibi pendens*, any court other than the court first seised must of its own motion decline jurisdiction in favour of that court and may stay its proceedings if the jurisdiction of the other court is contested.

The representatives of the EFTA Member States thought this solution was too radical.

They observed that an action often had to be brought in order to comply with a time limit or stop further time from running, and that opinions differed as to whether a time limit had been complied with where an action had been brought before a court lacking jurisdiction internationally.

Thus, in their view, if an action was brought before a judge who would have had jurisdiction, but was not the first to be seised, that judge would of his own motion have to decline jurisdiction in favour of the court first seised. However, that court might perhaps decide that it did not have jurisdiction. In that case, both actions would have been dismissed with the result that the time limits might have run out and the action be time barred.

These remarks have been taken into consideration.

Article 21 has been amended so that the court other than the court first seised will of its own motion stay its proceedings until the jurisdiction of the other court has been established.

A court other than the one first seised will not decline jurisdiction in favour of the court first seised until the jurisdiction of the latter has been established (see Schlosser report, paragraph 176).

The Court of Justice has ruled that the term *lis pendens* used in Article 21 covers a case where a party brings an action before a court in a Contracting State for a declaration that an international sales contract is inoperative or for the termination thereof whilst an action by the other party to secure performance of the said contract is pending before a court in another Contracting State (judgment of 8 December 1987 in Gubisch v Palumbo).

[OJ C189, 28.7.90, p 79]

Section 9

65. *Article 24—Provisional, including protective, measures*

As this provision has not been amended, reference should be made to the Jenard report, page 42 and the Schlosser report, paragraph 183.

TITLE III
RECOGNITION AND ENFORCEMENT (ARTICLES 25 TO 49)

Section 1
Recognition (Articles 26 to 30)

(*a*) *Article 27(5)*

66. Article 27(5) refers only to cases where the judgment recognition of which is requested is irreconcilable in the State addressed with an earlier judgment given in a *non-Contracting* State and recognizable in the State addressed.

The case of a judgment given in a *Contracting State* which is irreconcilable with an earlier judgment given in another Contracting State and recognizable in the State addressed is not specifically dealt with, nor is it covered in the Brussels Convention. It was felt that such cases would be extremely exceptional given the mechanisms provided for in Title II and in particular Articles 21 and 22 with a view to avoiding contradictory decisions. Should such a case, however, arise it would be for the court in the State addressed to apply its rules of procedure and the general principles arising out of the Convention and to refuse to recognize and enforce the judgment given after the first judgment had been recognized. It might, indeed, be argued that, since it has already been recognized in the State addressed, the first judgment should produce the same effects there as a judgment given by the courts in that State, the situation covered by Article 27(3).

(*b*) *Article 28*

67. Two grounds for refusal have been added. They concern the cases provided in Articles 54B and 57; reference should be made to the comments on those Articles.

Section 2
Enforcement (Articles 31 to 45)

(*a*) *Article 31*

68. Under the first paragraph of this Article in the Brussels Convention, "A judgment given in a Contracting State and enforceable in that State shall be enforced in another Contracting State when, on the application of any interested party, the order for its enforcement has been issued there". Since United Kingdom law does not have the exequatur system for foreign judgments, paragraph 2 of this Article provides that such a judgment shall be enforced in England and Wales, in Scotland, or in Northern Ireland where, on the application of any interested party, it has been registered for enforcement in that part of the United Kingdom (see Schlosser report, paragraphs 208 *et seq*).

69. In Switzerland, a distinction must be drawn between judgments ordering the payment of a sum of money and those ordering performance other than the payment of money. The enforcement of judgments ordering the payment of a sum of money is governed by Articles 69 *et seq* of the federal law on suit for bankruptcy debts (LP). Articles 80 and 81 LP require, for the purposes of enforcement, the production of an enforceable judgment in a civil case. In the case of foreign judgments, involving an order for payment of money, an order for its enforcement is necessary only if the judgment was given in a State which has not concluded a treaty on recognition and enforcement with Switzerland. If such a treaty exists, a foreign judgment involving an order for payment of money is enforceable in the same way as a Swiss judgment. The only objections which can be raised are those provided for in the convention in question (third paragraph of Article 81 LP).

A foreign judgment ordering performance other than the payment of money is enforced under cantonal law, even if there is a treaty with the State concerned. In general, the cantonal rules governing orders for enforcement are then applicable. With the convention in mind, Switzerland declared that it intends to continue to grant the preferential treatment it gives to judgments involving an order for payment of money.

The working party agreed that the wording of Article 31(1) of the Brussels Convention had been chosen to comply with the legal system of the original six Member States of the European Communities and acknowledged that this wording could create problems for States with different enforcement procedures than those existing in these six States. Therefore and in order to take account, in particular, of the Swiss position the words "the order for its enforcement has been issued" in the first paragraph of Article 31 of the Brussels Convention have been replaced in the Lugano Convention by the words "it has been declared enforceable".

[OJ C189, 28.7.90, p 80]

(*b*) *Articles 32 to 45*

70. The formal adjustments to Articles 32 to 45 relate exclusively to the courts having jurisdiction and possible types of appeal against their decisions.

For applications for a declaration of enforceability of judgments only one court has been given jurisdiction in Iceland and in Sweden. In Sweden, this is due to the practice according to which the "Svea hovrätt" is competent to declare enforceable foreign judgments and arbitral awards.

If the judgment debtor wishes to argue against the authorization of enforcement, he must lodge his application to set the enforcement order aside not with the higher court, as in most other Contracting States, but as in Austria, Belgium, Ireland, Italy, the Netherlands and the United Kingdom, with the same court as declared the judgment enforceable. The proceedings will take the form of an ordinary contentious civil action. This applies also regarding the appeal which the applicant may lodge if his application is refused.

Section 3

Common provisions (Articles 46 to 48)

71. Since no amendments have been made to the provisions of this section, reference should be made to the Jenard report (pp 54 to 56) and the Schlosser report (paragraph 225).

TITLE IV
AUTHENTIC INSTRUMENTS AND COURT SETTLEMENTS (ARTICLES 50 AND 51)

Article 50—Authentic instruments

72. The representatives of the EFTA Member States were able to agree to the text of Article 50, although the concept of an authentic instrument is contained only in Austria's legislation.

However, they did request that the report should specify the conditions which had to be fulfilled by an authentic instrument in order to be regarded as authentic within the meaning of Article 50 (see Schlosser report, paragraph 226).

The conditions are as follows—

— the authenticity of the instrument should have been established by a public authority,
— this authenticity should relate to the content of the instrument and not only, for example, the signature,

— the instrument has to be enforceable in itself in the State in which it originates.

Thus, for example, settlements occurring outside courts which are known in Danish law and enforceable under that law (udenretlig forlig) do not fall under Article 50.

Likewise, commercial bills and cheques are not covered by Article 50.

As in Article 31 (see point 69), the phrase "have an order for its enforcement issued there" has been replaced by the words "be declared enforceable".

It should be noted that the application of Article 50 of the Brussels Convention appears to be relatively uncommon.

TITLE V
GENERAL PROVISIONS

Article 52—Domicile

73. The third paragraph of Article 52 of the Brussels Convention relates to persons whose domicile depends on that of another person or on the seat of an authority.

It adopts a common rule of conflicts based on the personal status of the person making the application, in the case in point, the national law of the person.

The EFTA Member States challenged this rule, particularly in view of the developments regarding the domicile of married women that have taken place since the 1968 Convention was drawn up.

It was decided to delete the third paragraph.

It follows that in order to determine whether the defendant is a minor or legally incapacitated, the judge will apply the law specified by the conflicts rules applied in his country.

In the affirmative case, either the first paragraph or the second paragraph of Article 52, depending on the case, will be applied to determine the legal domicile. Thus, to determine whether a minor is domiciled in the territory of the State whose courts are seised of a matter, the judge will apply his internal law.

[OJ C189, 28.7.90, p 81]

When the minor is domiciled in the territory of the State whose courts are seised of the matter, the judge will, in order to determine whether the minor is domiciled in another Contracting State, apply the law of that State.

TITLE VI
TRANSITIONAL PROVISIONS
(ARTICLES 54 AND 54A)

(*a*) *Article 54—Temporal application*

74. The adjustments made to this Article are only technical ones, given that the procedures for entry into force of the two Conventions are not identical, but that no substantive changes have been made (see Jenard report, pp 57 and 58 and Schlosser report, paragraphs 228 to 235).

(*b*) *Article 54a* (*Maritime claims*)

75. Article 54a corresponds to Article 36 of the 1978 Accession Convention (see Schlosser report, paragraphs 121 *et seq*).

Paragraph 5 of this Article defines the expression "maritime claim". A maritime claim, according to this definition, is *inter alia* a claim arising out of dock charges and dues (point (1)). The German version of this Convention as well as of the Brussels Convention uses the word "Hafenabgaben" for dock charges and dues. This should however not mislead anybody into thinking that port charges, dues or tolls or similar public fees are regarded as dock charges or dues for the purposes of this Article.

TITLE VII
RELATIONSHIP TO THE BRUSSELS CONVENTION AND OTHER CONVENTIONS

(*a*) *Article 54b* (*Relationship to the Brussels Convention*)

76. Reference should be made to the comments in Chapter II.

(b) Articles 55 and 56 (Conventions concerning the EFTA Member States)

77. Article 55 lists conventions concluded between the EFTA Member States and conventions concluded between EFTA Member States and Community Member States (see Annex II).

Conventions between Community Member States have not been included since they are already covered by Article 55 of the Brussels Convention and, where Spain and Portugal are concerned, will be covered by the Conventions on Accession to the Brussels Convention.

78. Article 56 has not been amended.

(c) Article 57 (Conventions in relation to particular matters)

79. It may be said that the problem of conflicts of law, together with the problem of conflicts of jurisdiction, are the chief concern of private international law.

However, the problem of conflicts of convention also requires attention, since nowadays, with so many international organizations drawing up international conventions, the number which deal directly or indirectly with the same subject is considerable. As for solving the problem, several systems could perfectly well be contemplated under international law. Some are based on the principle *specialia generalibus derogant*, others on the rule of antecedence. Lastly, yet others advocate taking the effectiveness criterion into consideration. For example, where a judgment is to be recognized and enforced, the conventions which exist might be considered and the one selected which, translating the aim sought by the authors of the conventions, gives the party to whom judgment has been delivered in one country the best possibility of getting it recognized and enforced in another.

As noted by Professor Schlosser in his report (paragraphs 238 to 246), this question was dealt with at length during the negotiations on the 1978 Accession Convention.

The solution was enshrined in Article 25 of that Convention.

80. The problem was taken up again during negotiation of the Lugano Convention. The same basic principle has been adopted in both Conventions: namely, that the Convention will not affect any conventions to which the Contracting States are or will be parties and which, in relation to particular matters, govern jurisdiction or the recognition or enforcement of judgments.[6]

[OJ C189, 28.7.90, p 82]

The arrangements adopted are set out in Article 57. They may be examined on two levels: firstly, the level of jurisdiction, and secondly, that of recognition and enforcement.

81. *Regarding jurisdiction*, the two Conventions, i e the 1968 Convention as amended by the 1978 Convention, and the Lugano Convention, both contain similar provisions.

Article 57(2) of the Lugano Convention, like Article 25(2) of the 1978 Accession Convention, provides that the Convention will not prevent a court of a Contracting State which is party to a convention relating to a particular matter from assuming jurisdiction in accordance with that convention, even where the defendant is domiciled in a State party to the Lugano Convention, but not to the convention on the particular matter.

In this respect, Article 57 provides another exception to Article 2, which lays down the principle that the defendant must be sued in the courts of his domicile.

Take the following example—

The International Convention for the unification of certain rules relating to international carriage by air, signed at Warsaw on 12 October 1929, has not been ratified by Luxembourg. The carrier is domiciled in Luxembourg, but the Warsaw Convention provides that the court with jurisdiction is that of the place of "destination" (a court not adopted *as such* by the Lugano Convention, nor, for that matter, by the Brussels Convention).

Article 57 enables the applicant to sue the Luxembourg carrier in the court of a State party to the Lugano Convention and to the Warsaw Convention, since that court is allowed under that Convention.

Exactly the same arrangement is adopted in the Brussels Convention. It is the special convention which prevails, in the interests, as stated by Professor Schlosser in his report on the 1978 Convention (paragraph 240(b)), of "simplicity and clarity of the legal position" and, let us add, so as not to fail to recognize the rights that nationals of third States might hold under the special convention.

However, the court seised will have to apply Article 20 of the Lugano Convention in order to ensure respect for the rights of the defence.

In the case in point, if the defendant fails to enter an appearance, the judge must of his own motion examine whether he does indeed have jurisdiction under the special convention and whether the defendant has been sued properly, and in sufficient time to enable him to arrange his defence.

82. *Regarding recognition and enforcement*, the arrangements in the Brussels Convention (as adjusted on this point by the 1978 Convention) and the Lugano Convention are not the same. Unlike the Brussels Convention, the Lugano Convention provides that recognition or enforcement may be refused if the State addressed is not a contracting party to the special convention and if the person against whom recognition or enforcement is sought is domiciled in that State.

The reason for this difference is that the Brussels Convention applies between Member States of the same Community, while the Lugano Convention is not based on a similar principle.

The EFTA Member States therefore requested that the courts of the State addressed should be able to refuse recognition or enforcement if the person against whom they were sought was domiciled in that State, on the grounds that such a guarantee should be granted the defendant, particularly for fear that the special convention might contain grounds for jurisdiction considered as exorbitant by the State addressed in accordance with the law of that State.

It must be emphasized that this ground for refusal is an exception, given that paragraph 3 establishes the principle of recognition and enforcement. It does not therefore apply automatically, but is left to the discretion of the judge in the State addressed under the law of that State.

It goes without saying that a judgment delivered in an EFTA Member State on the basis of a rule of jurisdiction provided for in a special convention might be refused recognition or enforcement, under the same terms, in a Community Member State.

83. In the opinion of the rapporteurs, although the question is not expressly dealt with in the text of Article 57, if a court in a Contracting State having jurisdiction under a special convention is seised first, the rules on *lis pendens* and related actions in Articles 21 and 22 are applicable. Hence, for instance, in the case of *lis pendens*, the courts of another Contracting State would, even though that State was not party to the special convention, have to stay their proceedings of their own motion if seised subsequently. The jurisdiction of the court first seised is recognized by the Lugano Convention through the conjunction of Articles 21 and 57, with the latter recognizing the jurisdiction of the court first seised on the basis of a special convention.

[OJ C189, 28.7.90, p 83]

84. For the purposes of the Lugano Convention, Community acts are to be treated in the same way as special conventions. Reference should be made here to the comments on Protocol 3.

TITLE VIII
FINAL PROVISIONS
(ARTICLES 60 TO 68)

(a) Introductory remarks

85. Although final provisions are usually fairly standard, those in the present Convention are somewhat different and therefore require quite detailed comment. This is a Convention which first and foremost requires the Contracting States to have extremely similar thinking on constitutional and economic matters (see Chapter I.2, point 3). Moreover, the Convention was negotiated between States all of which belong to European organizations, either the European Communities or EFTA.

The drafters of the Convention had to deal with several questions. The first was the general one of deciding which States could become parties to the Convention. Other more specific questions were—

What was the position of those States which, after the opening of the Convention for signature, became members either of the European Communities or EFTA?

What was the position of third States, i e countries which did not belong to either of these two organizations but wished to become parties to the Convention?

What was the territorial application of the Convention?

What, finally, was the position if one of the territories for whose international relations a Contracting State was responsible were to become independent?

PART IV EC MATERIALS

Each of these questions was examined in detail and a series of solutions was found.[7]

(b) Article 60—States which may become parties to the Convention

86. *Article 60* deals with this question, while Articles 61 and 62 define the relevant procedures involving either signature and ratification (Article 61) or accession (Article 62).

The following may in any case become parties to the Convention—

1. States which, at the date of the opening of the Convention for signature, are members either of the European Communities or of EFTA;
2. States which, after that date, become members of one or other of the two organizations. In view of the origins of the Convention, this solution was virtually self-evident since neither of the two organizations could remain fixed in time;
3. third States. This was undoubtedly the most delicate question. There are, in addition to Member States of the two organizations, States which share the same fundamental conceptions even though they are not European. As we shall see in the comments on Article 62, provision has been made for fairly strict conditions for the accession of such States to the Convention. In brief, although the Convention reflects a desire for openness, its approach is clearly a cautious one.

(c) Article 61—Signature, ratification and entry into force

87. According to Article 61, the Lugano Convention shall be opened for signature by those States which were members of one or other of the two organizations on the date—16 September 1988—on which it was opened for signature.

This was agreed because it was at the diplomatic conference that the final text was drawn up and adopted by the persons empowered to do so by their States.

On that date, the Convention was signed by 10 States: for the Community Member States: Belgium, Denmark, Greece, Italy, Luxembourg and Portugal, and for the EFTA Member States: Iceland, Norway, Sweden and Switzerland. The Convention was subsequently signed by Finland on 30 November 1988 and by the Netherlands on 7 February 1989.

The Convention may be signed at any subsequent time by the other six States (Federal Republic of Germany, Spain, France, Ireland and the United Kingdom on the one hand and Austria on the other).

88. Pursuant to Article 61(3), the Convention shall enter into force when it has been ratified by one Community Member State and one Member State of EFTA.

[OJ C189, 28.7.90, p 84]

Since this is a multilateral Convention, such a method of entry into force might seem somewhat surprising.

The intention was deliberately to speed up entry into force of the Lugano Convention. For persons domiciled in a Member State of EFTA, the Convention offers a number of guarantees when they are sued in the courts of a Community Member State. Thus, for example, Article 4 of the Brussels Convention will cease to apply to such persons. Moreover, persons domiciled in a Community Member State will not be able to be sued in the courts of a Member State of EFTA on the basis of exorbitant rules of jurisdiction.

Furthermore, ratification procedures can be quite slow and this would delay the entry into force of a multilateral Convention where a certain number of ratifications are required.

Examples of this are the 1968 Convention, which only entered into force in 1973, and the 1978 Accession Convention, which only entered into force between the six original Member States and Denmark on 1 October 1986, the United Kingdom on 1 January 1987 and Ireland on 1 June 1988. The Convention on the accession of Greece of 25 October 1982 entered into force on 1 April 1989 with regard to Belgium, Denmark, the Federal Republic of Germany, Greece, France, Ireland, Italy, Luxembourg and the Netherlands and on 1 October 1989 with regard to the United Kingdom.

In brief, it is sufficient therefore for one Community Member State and one EFTA Member State to ratify the Lugano Convention in order to bring it into force between those two States as from the first day of the third month following the deposit of the second instrument of ratification.

(d) Articles 62 and 63—Accession

1. New Member States

89. Those States which, after the opening of the Convention for signature, become members of either the Communities or EFTA may accede to the Convention.

Under Article 62(4), a Contracting State may, however, consider that it is not bound by such an accession.

This clause was adopted in view of the fact that a Member State of one of the two organizations has no say in the accession of new States to the other organization and, for reasons of its own, might feel it cannot have ties with that new State which are as close as those created by the Lugano Convention. This is a safeguard clause which also applies to third States.

2. Third States

90. A cautious attitude to such States is reflected in specific conditions.

Firstly, their wish to accede to the Lugano Convention must be "sponsored" by a Contracting State, ie a State which has either ratified the Convention or acceded to it, which will inform the depositary State of the third State's intention.

Secondly, the third State will have to inform the depositary State of the contents of any declarations it intends to make in order to apply the Convention and of any details it would like to furnish in order to apply Protocol No 1, and the depositary State will then communicate that information to the other signatory States and States which have acceded. Negotiations may be held on this subject: they may not, in any circumstances, call into question the provisions of the Lugano Convention itself. The device envisaged therefore differs from that in Article 63 of the Brussels Convention, which stipulates that a new Member State of the European Economic Community may ask for "necessary adjustments" to be the subject of a special convention. This procedure, which was followed notably when drawing up the 1978 Accession Convention, is not therefore applicable in the present case.

Thirdly, the States referred to in Article 60(a) and (b) must, when they have thus been informed of the declarations and details envisaged by the State applying for accession, decide unanimously whether that State should be invited to accede.

The States referred to in Article 60(a) and (b) are either those States which were members of one or other of the two organizations on the date on which the Convention was opened for signature, ie 16 September 1988, or States which became members of one or other of the two organizations after that date. The agreement of any third States which have acceded to the Convention is not therefore required. This was agreed because the Convention is essentially a Convention between Community and EFTA Member States and consequently it did not seem advisable to give a third State which has become a party to the Convention the right to veto the accession of another third State.

[OJ C189, 28.7.90, p 85]

Fourthly, once the decision has been taken to look at the application of a third State, negotiations can be started, either at that State's request or at the request of other States concerned, regarding the details it intends to furnish for the purposes of Protocol No 1.

Finally, it should be noted that a last safeguard clause allows any Contracting State (pursuant to paragraph 4) to refuse application of the Convention in its relations with a third State which has acceded to the Convention. This system, which is based on various Conventions drawn up pursuant to The Hague Conference on Private International Law, takes account of the (possibly political) problems which might arise between a Contracting State and a third State.

(e) Territorial application

91. Article 60 of the 1968 Convention and Article 27 of the 1978 Convention deal with the territorial application of those Conventions, limiting it to the European territory of the Contracting States, subject to clearly defined exceptions.

92. In the negotiations leading up to the Lugano Convention it was found that application of the Convention to non-European territories forming an integral part of the national territory of Contracting States or for whose international relations the latter assume responsibility needed to be envisaged on a broader basis. A number of these territories are frequently important financial centres having close relations with Contracting States. Given the speed with which means of communication are developing, assets could be transferred to such territories, and if the Convention could not be applied to them, this would create a situation which would defeat the desired aim, since judgments given in a State which was party to the Convention could not be enforced in such territories under these provisions.

93. It was agreed at the diplomatic conference that it would be better if, like many other international conventions, the Convention contained no provision on territorial application.

The limitation to European territories laid down in principle in the 1968 and 1978 Conventions is thus not included in the Lugano Convention.

94. However, it was clear from the negotiations that in the absence of any specific clause the Lugano Convention applies automatically to—

- the entire territory of the Kingdom of Spain,
- the entire territory of the Portuguese Republic,
- in the case of France: all territories which are an integral part of the French Republic (see Article 71 *et seq* of the Constitution), including therefore the French Overseas Departments (Guadeloupe, Martinique, Guiana, Réunion), the Overseas Territories (Polynesia, New Caledonia, Southern and Antarctic Territories) and the individual territorial collectivities (Saint Pierre and Miquelon, Mayotte).

95. The situation is slightly different where Denmark and the Netherlands are concerned.

Denmark:

With a view to ratification of the Lugano Convention, Denmark made known its wish to reserve the right to extend the scope of the Convention at a later stage to the Faroe Islands and Greenland which are part of the Kingdom of Denmark but enjoy autonomy in their internal affairs (Law No 137 of 23 March 1948 for the Faroe Islands and No 577 of 29 November 1978 for Greenland) and which must be consulted on draft laws affecting their territories. In the light of the outcome of such consultations, Denmark will be able to state, in a declaration to be addressed at any time to the depositary State, what the situation is with respect to the application of the Convention to these territories.

The Netherlands:

Since 1 January 1986, the Kingdom of the Netherlands consists of three countries, namely: the Netherlands, the Netherlands Antilles (the islands of Bonaire, Curaçao, Sint Maarten (Netherlands part of the island), Sint Eustatius and Saba) and Aruba. Following the necessary consultations, the Netherlands, just like Denmark in the case of the Faroe Islands and Greenland, will be able to state in a declaration which may be addressed at any time to the depositary State, what the situation is with respect to the application of the Convention to the Netherlands Antilles and to Aruba.

96. On the other hand, other Contracting States (the United Kingdom and Portugal in the case of Macao and Timor-Leste) comprise entities which are separate from the metropolitan territory. International agreements cannot be concluded on behalf of these entities other than by the United Kingdom and Portugal.

United Kingdom:

During the negotiations, the United Kingdom, like the other States, provided a full list of non-European territories for whose international relations it is responsible.[8] For the European territories, see Schlosser report, paragraph 252.

[OJ C189, 28.7.90, p 86]

This list of non-European territories is included in the acts of the diplomatic conference. The United Kingdom also gave an indication of the territories to which it might consider making the Convention actually apply. It was agreed that provision of such information did not imply any binding obligation that other extensions could not be made, but the information provided was intended to assist the other States in assessing the practical consequences for them of an extension of the application of the Convention.

For this purpose, the United Kingdom indicated that, of its non-European territories, Anguilla, Bermuda, British Virgin Islands, Montserrat, Turks and Caicos Islands and Hong Kong were ones to which there might be a real prospect of the Convention being extended.

Portugal:

The question of extending the Convention to Macao and Timor-Leste has not yet been settled.

(f) Territories which become independent

97. The question of what would happen regarding application of the Lugano Convention to territories gaining independence was also considered.

The Convention contains no provisions on this subject. Such a clause is not usual in international Conventions. On the other hand, this is a familiar problem in public international law and it is generally accepted that, if a country gains independence, any Contracting State is free to decide whether or not it is bound by the Convention in question in respect of the new State and vice versa (on this point, see Schlosser report, paragraph 254).

In any event, a State which has become independent may, if it wishes to become a party to the Lugano Convention, make use of the accession procedure provided for third States in Article 62 of the Lugano Convention (see point 90).

[3072]

CHAPTER IV PROTOCOLS

98. Under Article 65, the three supplementary Protocols form an integral part of the Convention.

PROTOCOL 1 ON CERTAIN QUESTIONS OF JURISDICTION, PROCEDURE AND ENFORCEMENT

1. Introductory remarks

99. This Protocol corresponds to the Protocol annexed to the Brussels Convention. The provisions contained in Articles I, II, III and Vd of that Protocol are reproduced unmodified in Protocol 1 to the Lugano Convention. The provisions contained in Article Vc of the Protocol annexed to the Brussels Convention are not reproduced in this Protocol. Those provisions were inserted into the Protocol annexed to the Brussels Convention only to make it clear that the concept of "residence" in the English text of the Convention for the European patent for the common market, signed at Luxembourg on 15 December 1975, should be deemed to have the same scope as the concept of "domicile" in the Brussels Convention. Such provisions were, however, redundant in the Lugano Convention. The other provisions of the Protocol annexed to the Brussels Convention are reproduced in this Protocol with minor amendments most of which are due to the law in force in various EFTA Member States. Furthermore, the Protocol contains two Articles (Ia and Ib) which have no equivalent in the Protocol annexed to the Brussels Convention.

2. Article Ia—Swiss reservation

100. This Article contains a reservation asked for by Switzerland. It provides that Switzerland may declare, at the time of depositing its instrument of ratification, that a judgment given in another Contracting State shall neither be recognized nor enforced in Switzerland if the jurisdiction of the court which has given the judgment is based only on Article 5(1) (place of performance of contract) of the Lugano Convention and if certain other conditions are met. As this head of jurisdiction is regarded by many States as the most commercially significant of all the special bases of jurisdiction in the Lugano Convention, the terms of this part of Protocol No 1 were the subject of close discussion.

[OJ C189, 28.7.90, p 87]

For Switzerland the need for a reservation arose from the provisions of Article 59 of the Swiss Federal Constitution[9] which reserves the right for a person of Swiss domicile, whatever his nationality, to be sued over a contract in the courts of his domicile. Whilst some exceptions existed to this general principle, it became clear that a provision such as Article 5(1) of the Convention could involve a conflict with the constitutional rule in Switzerland and make Swiss participation in the Convention impossible. The compromise reached limits the effect of the reservation to the minimum necessary.

101. In the first place, any reservation will only apply if the defendant was domiciled in Switzerland at the time of the introduction of the proceedings. In the application of the reservation the question of domicile will be determined and acknowledged in accordance with the general principles and rules of the Convention. However, a company or other legal person is considered to be domiciled in Switzerland only if it has its registered seat and the effective centre of activities in Switzerland. The reservation will thus not apply if the effective centre of activities of a company or other legal person is outside Switzerland even if the company or other legal person has its registered seat in Switzerland. Furthermore, the reservation will never apply unless the company or legal person concerned has its registered seat in Switzerland.

Secondly, recognition and enforcement may only be refused under the reservation if the jurisdiction of the court which has given the judgment was based solely on Article 5(1). If, for example, a defendant domiciled in Switzerland were to submit to the jurisdiction in the other

PART IV EC MATERIALS

Contracting State the reservation would not apply, because in that event jurisdiction would not have been based solely on Article 5(1), but also on Article 18. Equally, the reservation will not apply if the jurisdiction of the original court is based on an agreement to confer jurisdiction over contractual disputes, since in that case jurisdiction would have been derived from Article 17.

Thirdly, the reservation will not apply unless the defendant raises an objection to the recognition and enforcement of the judgment in Switzerland. The objection must be raised in good faith. It was explained by the Swiss delegation that it was entirely possible under Swiss law for the defendant to waive the protection available under Article 59 of the Constitution and that this waiver could validly be made at any time. Thus this waiver can be made even before Switzerland has made any declaration. This is reflected in the text of the Article by the words "the declaration *foreseen* under this paragraph". It will therefore be possible for persons contracting with persons enjoying Swiss domicile to stipulate a waiver of the protection provided for in Article 59 of the Swiss Federal Constitution which would otherwise be available. An agreement between the parties on the waiver of such protection could be made orally or in writing as long as there is sufficient proof that the waiver has been made. In the event that such an agreement has been made, or if the Swiss court is otherwise satisfied as a matter of fact that the defendant has waived his rights, then recognition and enforcement will not be refused in Switzerland even if a reservation has been made.

Fourthly, the reservation will not apply to contracts in respect of which, at the time recognition and enforcement is sought, a derogation has been granted from Article 59 of the Swiss Federal Constitution. The Swiss Government is obliged to communicate such derogations to the signatory States and the acceding States.

Fifthly, the Swiss delegation has declared that a reservation envisaged in this Article will not apply to contracts of employment. Thus Switzerland will in no event refuse the recognition or enforcement of a judgment given in a matter relating to an individual contract of employment on the ground that the jurisdiction of the court which has given the judgment is based only on the second part of Article 5(1) of the Convention.

Finally, any declaration made by Switzerland under this Article is to expire on a fixed date, ie on 31 December 1999. If, by that time, the Swiss Federal Constitution has not been amended so as to remove the constitutional difficulty, one possibility would be for Switzerland to consider denouncing the Convention, and become a party to it again when the constitutional difficulty has been removed.

102. If Switzerland makes the reservation provided for in this Article it will be open to other Contracting States to reciprocate the effect of that reservation by refusing to enforce judgments originating in Switzerland if the jurisdiction of the Swiss court is based solely on Article 5(1) of the Convention and if conditions corresponding to those mentioned in Article Ia of the Protocol are fulfilled.
[OJ C189, 28.7.90, p 88]

By reason of the difference in constitutional systems, a reciprocity clause was not inserted in the Protocol. The result is that the matter of reciprocity will be left to the normal rules of public international law. In view of the fact that such rules may be incorporated differently into national law, solutions to the question of reciprocity may vary from country to country.

In countries applying the "dualist" system the question of reciprocity will be dealt with at a legislative level, thus settling the question of reciprocity in a general manner. In those countries where the "monist" system exists it is for the courts or other authorities to decide on the question of reciprocity. For instance in France, where the "monist" system exists, a treaty, according to the French constitution, has a higher level than law provided that the treaty is applied in a reciprocal manner. If the question of whether a treaty is applied in a reciprocal manner is raised before a court and the answer is not clear, the judge will submit the question to the Ministry of Foreign Affairs which is competent for the interpretation of treaties.

As far as the aspect of application of Article 7 of the Treaty establishing the European Economic Community is concerned (non-discrimination on grounds of nationality), the judge in a Community Member State can, if the question arises before him, submit it to the Court of Justice of the European Communities for a preliminary ruling under Article 177 of the EEC Treaty.

From the discussions it is apparent that certain States will not reciprocate.

3. Article Ib—Reservation on tenancies

103. This Article provides that any Contracting State may, by a declaration made at the time of signing or deposit of its instrument of ratification or accession, reserve the right not to

recognize and enforce judgments given in other Contracting States if the jurisdiction of the court of origin is based, pursuant to Article 16(1)(b), exclusively on the domicile of the defendant in the State of origin.

This provision has been commented on above (see point 53).

4. Article IV—Judicial and extra-judicial documents

104. This Article reproduces Article IV of the Protocol annexed to the Brussels Convention. The declaration referred to in paragraph 2 of this Article will, however, not be made to the Secretary-General of the Council of the European Communities but to the depositary of the Lugano Convention.

5. Article V—Actions on a warranty or guarantee

105. Under Austrian, Spanish and Swiss law, as under German law, the function performed by an action on a warranty or guarantee or any other third party proceedings is fulfilled by means of third-party notices. A rule analogous to that contained in Article V of the Protocol annexed to the Brussels Convention (see Jenard report, page 27, comments on Article 6(2)) has accordingly been applied to Austria, Spain and Switzerland in this Article. Unlike the case of Austria, the Federal Republic of Germany and Spain, it has not been possible to refer to a single legislative source in Swiss law. Provisions on third-party notices are to be found both in the federal law of civil procedure and in the 26 cantonal codes of civil procedure.

Third party intervention in proceedings is not governed by explicit rules in the Spanish legal system and the want of proper procedures is the source of procedural uncertainty. This legal hiatus has been severely criticized in the works of legal experts, who have recommended that it be remedied in the near future. However, this has not prevented acceptance of third party proceedings in some fields of jurisprudence or in civil laws governing certain specific cases, e g Article 124(3) of Law No 11 of 20 March 1986 on patents and Article 1482* of the Civil Code, regarding eviction. Generally speaking, it is the latter rule which is applicable in cases of non-voluntary third party proceedings; in the negotiations between the Member States of the European Communities and those of the European Free Trade Association, it was therefore judged advisable to include it in Article V of Protocol No 1.
[OJ C189, 28.7.90, p 89]

Article 1482 is referred to, albeit indirectly, in Article 638 (gift), 1145 (joint and several obligations), 1529 (assignment of claims), 1540 (exchange), 1553 (tenancy), 1681 (obligations of partners), 1830 (surety), 1831 (co-surety), etc of the Civil Code.

6. Article Va—Jurisdiction of administrative authorities

106. In Iceland and Norway administrative authorities are, as in Denmark, competent in matters relating to maintenance. Thus Iceland and Norway have been included in this Article in addition to Denmark.

107. In Finland, for historical reasons the "ulosoton-haltija/överexekutor" (regional chief enforcement authority) is competent for protective measures referred to in Article 24 of the Lugano Convention. Furthermore, a documentary procedure for collecting debts based on a promissory note or a similar document, as well as some other summary proceedings e g eviction, take place before that authority. These proceedings are an optional alternative to court proceedings. The "ulosoton-haltija/överexekutor" is clearly not a court but an administrative authority, which in the aforementioned cases plays a judicial role. The abolition of the "ulosotonhaltija/ överexekutor" is envisaged and its functions as far as civil and commercial matters are concerned will be transferred to the courts.

In order to avoid any imbalance a second paragraph has been inserted in this Article according to which the expression "court" in civil and commercial matters includes the Finnish "ulosoton-haltija/överexekutor".

7. Article Vb—Dispute between the master and a member of a ship's crew

108. Following specific requests from the Icelandic, Norwegian, Portuguese and Swedish delegations, Iceland, Norway, Portugal and Sweden have been included in this Article.

8. Article VI—Amendment of national legislation

109. This Article reproduces Article VI of the Protocol annexed to the Brussels Convention. The communication provided for in this Article will, however, not be made to the Secretary-General of the Council of the European Communities but to the depositary of the Lugano Convention.

PROTOCOL 2 ON THE UNIFORM INTERPRETATION OF THE CONVENTION

1. Introductory remarks

110. Without uniform interpretation, the unifying force of the Lugano Convention would be considerably reduced. In addition, a considerable number, if not the majority, of its provisions are reproduced from the Brussels Convention, which posed a further problem. As we know, in order to avoid such differences of interpretation, the Community Member States concluded a Protocol on 3 June 1971 giving jurisdiction to the Court of Justice of the European Communities to rule on the interpretation of the Brussels Convention. When applying that Convention, the courts of the Community Member States must comply with the interpretation given by the Court of Justice.

However, the Court of Justice could not be assigned jurisdiction to interpret the Lugano Convention which is not a source of Community law. Furthermore, the EFTA Member States could not have accepted a solution according to which an institution of the Communities would, as a court of last resort, rule on the Lugano Convention. Nor was it conceivable to assign such jurisdiction to any other international court or to create a new court since, *inter alia,* the Court of Justice of the European Communities already had jurisdiction under the 1971 Protocol to rule on the interpretation of the Brussels Convention and conflicts of jurisdiction between international courts had at all events to be avoided.

111. The solution adopted to resolve this somewhat complex situation (ie ensuring uniform interpretation of the Lugano Convention while taking account of the powers of the Court of Justice of the European Communities as regards the interpretation of the Brussels Convention, many of the provisions of which were reproduced in the Lugano Convention) is based on the principle of consultation and not on judicial hierarchy.

It was thus agreed that judgments delivered pursuant to the Lugano Convention or the Brussels Convention are to be communicated through a central body to each signatory State and acceding State and that meetings of representatives appointed by each such State are to be convened to exchange views on the functioning of the Convention. As regards legal technique, it was decided that the provisions aiming at uniform interpretation should be included in a Protocol annexed to the Convention, the provisions of which would form an integral part thereof. It was furthermore agreed that two Declarations would be annexed to the Protocol. One of these Declarations was to be signed by the representatives of the Governments of the States signatories to the Lugano Convention which were members of the European Communities and the other by the representatives of the Governments of the States signatories to the Lugano Convention which were members of EFTA.

[OJ C189, 28.7.90, p 90]

2. Preamble

112. The *first* recital in the preamble makes reference to Article 65 of the Lugano Convention. According to this Article, a Protocol 2 on the uniform interpretation of the Convention by the courts will form an integral part of the Convention.

The *second* recital refers to the substantial link between the Lugano Convention and the Brussels Convention.

As has already been mentioned, the Court of Justice of the European Communities has, under the Protocol of 3 June 1971, been entrusted with jurisdiction to give rulings on the interpretation of the provisions of the Brussels Convention. A starting point for the negotiations for the conclusion of the Lugano Convention was that those provisions of the Brussels Convention which were to be substantially reproduced in the Lugano Convention should be understood in the light of these rulings given up to the date of opening for signature of the latter Convention. The working party which drafted the Convention was aware of all those rulings delivered up to that date. The intention was to arrive at as uniform as possible an interpretation where the provisions in question were identical in the two Conventions. On the other hand, insofar as a provision of the Brussels Convention as interpreted by the Court of Justice of the European Communities, e g Article 16(1), was found not to be acceptable, it was not reproduced unmodified in the Convention (for judgments of the Court of Justice, see Chapter VI).

The *third, fourth* and *fifth* recitals were included in the Preamble in order to stress the relevance of the rulings on the interpretation of the Brussels Convention given by the Court of Justice of the European Communities up to the time of the signature of the Lugano Convention.

The *sixth* recital confirms the wish of the Contracting States to prevent, in full deference to the independence of the courts, divergent interpretations.

3. Article 1

113. This Article relates only to decisions concerning provisions of the Lugano Convention. It provides that the courts of each Contracting Party shall, when applying and interpreting that Convention, pay due account to the principles laid down by any *relevant decision* delivered by courts of the other Contracting Parties concerning provisions of the Lugano Convention. The expression "any relevant decision" means in this Article those decisions delivered by courts of the Contracting Parties which according to Article 2(1), first indent, have been transmitted to a central body, i e judgments delivered by courts of last instance and other judgments of particular importance which have become final.

114. This Article does not *explicitly* refer to decisions concerning the application and interpretation of those provisions of the Brussels Convention which are substantially reproduced in the Lugano Convention.

It must be remembered that the courts of the Community Member States are the only courts required to apply the Brussels Convention and that when they interpret provisions of that Convention, they must respect the judgments of the Court of Justice. The Community Member States were, however, not in a position to commit the Court of Justice, a separate institution, to pay due regard to judgments of national courts in EFTA Member States. For their part, the representatives of the EFTA Member States thought that it would not be entirely fair to include a provision in the Protocol which expressly stipulated that the courts of these States had to take account not only of the decisions given by the courts of the other Contracting States but also of the judgments of the Court of Justice of the European Communities, while the latter would not be subject to any undertaking as regards the interpretation of the provisions of the Brussels Convention which were reproduced in the Lugano Convention.

115. It was, however, recognized that the courts of the Community Member States, when interpreting provisions of the Lugano Convention which are reproduced from the Brussels Convention, would understand those provisions in the same way as the identical provisions of the Brussels Convention and in accordance with the interpretations given in the rulings of the Court of Justice of the European Communities. It was therefore essential, in order to ensure as uniform an interpretation as possible of the Lugano Convention, that the courts of the EFTA Member States apply it in the same way as the courts of the Community Member States. But it was equally necessary for the Court of Justice, when interpreting provisions of the Brussels Convention which were reproduced in the Lugano Convention to pay due account in particular to the case law of the courts of the EFTA Member States.

[OJ C189, 28.7.90, p 91]

116. In order to achieve this twofold objective two Declarations accompany the Convention. In one of them the representatives of the Governments of the States signatories to the Lugano Convention which are members of the Communities declare that they consider as appropriate that the Court of Justice, when interpreting the Brussels Convention, pay due account to the rulings contained in the case law of the Lugano Convention. In the other, the representatives of the EFTA States declare that they consider as appropriate that their courts, when interpreting the Lugano Convention, pay due account to the rulings contained in the case law of the Court of Justice of the European Communities and of the courts of the Member States of the European Communities in respect of provisions of the Brussels Convention which are substantially reproduced in the Lugano Convention.

At the request of the representatives of the EFTA States, a list and the contents of the judgments delivered by the Court of Justice when interpreting the 1968 Convention is given in this report (see Chapter VI).

4. Article 2

117. As we have already said, it was agreed that a uniform interpretation of the common provisions of the Lugano and Brussels Conventions would be achieved by means of information and consultation. According to the first paragraph of this Article the Contracting States agree to set up a system of exchange of information concerning judgments delivered pursuant to the Lugano Convention as well as *relevant* judgments under the Brussels Convention. The expression "relevant judgments" means, in this context, those judgments delivered pursuant to the Brussels Convention which are relevant for the interpretation of the Lugano Convention as well.

This system of exchange of information comprises—

— transmission to a central body by the competent national authorities of judgments delivered pursuant to the Lugano Convention or the Brussels Convention,

PART IV EC MATERIALS

— classification of these judgments by the central body including, as far as necessary, the drawing up and publication of translations and abstracts,

— communication by the central body of the relevant documents to the competent national authorities of all signatories and acceding States to the Lugano Convention and to the Commission of the European Communities.

The abovementioned central body will, according to paragraph 2 of this Article, be the Registrar of the Court of Justice of the European Communities. The Registrar has signified his agreement to this, provided that the detailed arrangements for the system of exchange of information, and in particular the question of the translation of judgments not drawn up in an official language of the Communities, are worked out with the Court after the Diplomatic Conference and that the department of the Court receive the necessary aid and budgetary support. The competent national authorities referred to in the first and third indent of paragraph 1 of this Article are to be designated by each Member State concerned.

This system of exchange of information will, however, not include every judgment delivered by a national court pursuant to the Lugano Convention or every relevant judgment delivered pursuant to the Brussels Convention. For the purposes of the objective which the Protocol is aiming at it will suffice that judgments delivered by courts of last instance and the Court of Justice as well as judgments of other courts which are of particular importance and have become final are transmitted to the central body referred to in this Article (paragraph 1 first indent). Only those judgments will thus be classified by the central body and communicated pursuant to the third indent of paragraph 1 of this Article.

To the extent that the communication of documentation implies publication of translations and abstracts by the central body, it was agreed that such publication, in the interests of economy, could take a simplified form.

5. Article 3

118. In order to ensure a uniform interpretation of the common provisions of the Lugano and Brussels Conventions, it was deemed necessary that representatives appointed by each signatory or acceding State meet to exchange views on the functioning of the Lugano Convention. To this end Article 3 provides that a Standing Committee composed of representatives appointed by each signatory or acceding State shall be set up. This Standing Committee is not intended to be a bureaucratic body but rather a forum where national experts could exchange their views on the functioning of the Convention and in particular on the case law as it develops in the various Contracting States, with the aim of fostering in that manner, as far as possible, uniformity in the interpretation of the Convention. No regular meetings of the Committee are provided for in the Protocol. Meetings of the Committee will, according to Article 4(1) of the Protocol, be convened only at the request of a Contracting Party.

[OJ C189, 28.7.90, p 92]

In this context it deserves to be emphasized that not only States which have already become parties to the Convention (either by ratifying it or by acceding to it), but also States which have signed the Convention but not yet become parties to it may appoint their representatives as members of the Standing Committee. This solution was adopted since a distinction between signatory and Contracting States would suggest that certain States might sign the Lugano Convention without any intention of ratifying it.

Divergent views were expressed as to whether the Standing Committee should be composed of judges or civil servants. It was decided that it would be for each State to appoint its representatives on the Committee. Thus, it may well be that certain States will appoint judges whereas other States may appoint civil servants or others. It goes without saying that each State is free to decide how and for which period of time anyone is appointed to represent it on the Committee.

Because of the links between the Lugano Convention and the Brussels Convention, paragraph 3 of this Article provides that representatives of the European Communities (ie of the Commission, the Court of Justice and the General Secretariat of the Council) and of EFTA may attend the meetings of the Committee as observers.

If necessary, it will be for the Committee to establish its own rules of procedure.

6. Article 4

119. The provisions of paragraph 1 of this Article concern the convocation and the tasks of the Standing Committee. As already mentioned, the meetings of the Committee will be convened at the request of a Contracting Party for the purpose of exchanging views on the functioning of the Convention. In this context it deserves to be emphasized that a meeting of

the Committee cannot be convened at the request of a State which has only signed the Convention but not yet become a party to it, even though the Committee, according to Article 3(2), will be composed of representatives appointed by each signatory State or acceding State. The task of convening the Committee has been entrusted to the depositary of the Convention.

There are no limitations as to the questions relating to the functioning of the Convention which oblige the depositary to convene meetings of the Committee at the request of a Contracting Party.

In view of the purpose of the Protocol, Article 4 provides that meetings of the Committee will be convened for the purpose of exchanging views in particular on the development of the case law as communicated under the first indent of Article 2(1). The purpose of this provision is not, however, to invest the Committee with the role of a higher body which would assess the judgments given by national courts. It is rather a body, which, by examining such judgments, would identify divergences of interpretation and, as far as possible, foster uniformity in the interpretation of the Convention.

Article 57(1) of the Convention provides that it will not affect any conventions to which the Contracting States are or will be parties and which, in relation to particular matters, govern jurisdiction or the recognition or enforcement of judgments. According to Protocol No 3, provisions which govern jurisdiction or the recognition or enforcement of judgments and which are or will be contained in acts of the institutions of the European Communities will be treated in the same way as conventions referred to in Article 57(1).

Provisions which in relation to particular matters govern jurisdiction may, irrespective of whether such provisions are contained in a convention or in a Community act, amount to a change of the rules of jurisdiction contained in the Convention without the agreement of all the Contracting Parties. Therefore paragraph 1 of this Article further provides that meetings of the Committee will be convened for exchanging views on the application of Article 57 of the Convention. Paragraph 2 of Protocol No 3 on Community acts makes provision for a similar procedure. Thus the Committee will provide a forum where views can be exchanged *inter alia* on the provisions governing jurisdiction in particular matters adopted or envisaged in Community acts.

In the light of these exchanges of views it may appear that an amendment of the Convention would be appropriate. This may be the case if the Committee, when examining the case law communicated under Article 2, were to identify divergences of interpretation arising from a lack of clarity in one or more of the provisions of the Convention. Therefore, paragraph 2 of the Article provides that the Committee may also examine the appropriateness of starting on particular topics a revision of the Convention and make recommendations.
[OJ C189, 28.7.90, p 93]

This power of the Committee should not be confused with the right for any Contracting State under Article 66 of the Convention to request the revision of the Convention. The powers and procedures in that Article differ radically from those provided for in Article 4(2) of the Protocol. A recommendation made by the Committee is thus not to be assimilated with a request by a Contracting State under Article 67 of the Convention for a revision conference. Only a Contracting State but not the Committee may request the depositary of the Convention to convene a revision conference. Neither is a recommendation of the Committee a prerequisite for the right of a Contracting State to request the revision of the Convention.

PROTOCOL 3 ON THE APPLICATION OF ARTICLE 57

120. This Protocol is in response to the problems which might arise from any provisions on jurisdiction and the recognition and enforcement of judgments appearing in Community acts.

1. Concern of the States party to the Lugano Convention

121. The entirely justified concern of both Community and EFTA Member States has been vigorously expressed in regard to Community acts. Why is this?

(a) For the Community Member States, it is because they have, in a manner of speaking, a dual personality. They are sovereign States. But they are also members of the Communities and are thus bound, by virtue of this latter point, to comply with the obligations to which they have subscribed under the Treaties establishing the European Communities (ECSC, EEC and Euratom). Under those Treaties, it is the Council which is competent to adopt Regulations and Directives which in specific matters may possibly concern jurisdiction and the recognition and enforcement of judgments, according to the requirements of those Communities.[10]

The concern of these States was threefold—
— the need to comply with the obligations they have entered into by becoming party to the Treaties establishing the Communities,
— the need to avoid hampering any development taking place in the context of the Treaties and relating to the powers of the Community institutions,
— the need to respect the commitments entered into by the Lugano Convention *vis-à-vis* the EFTA Member States.

(b) For the EFTA Member States, because they feared that the guarantees offered them by the Lugano Convention regarding jurisdiction and the recognition and enforcement of judgments could, in certain areas, be practically wiped out by a Community act. In particular, the representatives of the EFTA Member States voiced the fear that the protection guaranteed by the Lugano Convention, particularly by Article 3, to defendants domiciled in an EFTA Member State might be undermined by a Community act. Such defendants might thus be treated differently from defendants domiciled in a Community Member State, or even be put in the same situation as defendants domiciled in third States. For example, for the representatives of these States it was inconceivable to accept that it should be possible for a person domiciled in the territory of an EFTA Member State (e g Norway) to be required to appear before the courts of a Member State of the Communities (such as France) on the basis of a Community act which they had played no part in drawing up and on the basis of a criterion of jurisdiction not provided for in the Lugano Convention. In any event, for these States, it was unacceptable that it should be possible for a judgment delivered on the basis of such a rule of jurisdiction to be recognized and enforced in their territory under the Lugano Convention. These fears would seem to be as well-founded as those of the Member States of the Communities.

In short, for the EFTA Member States, the inclusion of rules of jurisdiction and of recognition and enforcement of judgments in Community acts could, in the absence of any correcting mechanism, be regarded as empowering the Community Member States to amend the Lugano Convention unilaterally.

[OJ C189, 28.7.90, p 94]

2. Response to this concern

122. The question for the authors of the Convention was how to respond to these various concerns, all equally justified, and to work out a solution that could be accepted by all the Contracting Parties. We shall try and answer two questions, the problem having been resolved: Why was it possible to solve the problem? How was it solved?

It was possible to respond to this concern because there existed on both sides a conviction or, one might prefer to say, a deep awareness that despite its difficulties the problem posed could and had to be resolved, in accordance with the principles of public international law, because of the fundamental objectives of the Lugano Convention, ie the granting of guarantees to a defendant domiciled in the territory of a Contracting State and the free movement of judgments.

In addition, it emerged during the discussions that despite its theoretical aspect the problem had only a very relative impact in practice; thus the Member States of the Communities stressed the fact that in 30 years no Community act containing provisions on jurisdiction had been adopted. It should however be noted that a draft Regulation on the Community trade mark containing such jurisdiction rules is currently in preparation.

Also, some Community Member States made it clear that for practical reasons they were not in favour of Community acts including provisions relating to jurisdiction and to the recognition and enforcement of judgments. For these States, the issue had to be settled by the Brussels Convention, even if that meant its being revised, amended or supplemented, since for the practitioner (lawyers, judges, and others) this Convention constituted a Community code which was becoming well known. If these provisions were scattered throughout numerous Community instruments it would weaken the scope of this code and make it more difficult to apply. These States were well aware of the importance that Community acts might have in this matter and they considered that any resort to these instruments, in the areas in question, should continue to be entirely exceptional.

3. Solution adopted

123. How was the problem resolved?

The solution is to be found in Protocol 3 and in the Declaration by the Member States of the Communities which supplements it.

What is involved in this solution that has given satisfaction to both sides?

Protocol 3 and the Declaration supplementing it form a whole.

(*a*) *Protocol 3*

124. *In paragraph 1*, for the purposes of the Lugano Convention, Protocol No 3 treats Community acts in the same way as the conventions which have been concluded on particular matters and whose effect on the Lugano Convention is determined by Article 57 of the Convention (see points 79 to 83). In the view of the representatives of the Community Member States, there is no difference, except as regards the way they were drawn up, between these two types of instrument.

They pointed out that if the EFTA Member States were willing to entertain the possibility for the States party to the Lugano Convention of the rules of that Convention being amended by conventions concluded in particular areas (transport, etc) they could also agree to the Community amending the Convention by means of Community acts. These representatives also stressed that to be approved a Community act required in principle the agreement of the 12 Member States, whereas a convention on a particular matter, whose rules could depart from those of the Lugano Convention, could be concluded between two States only. In their view, there was accordingly no substantive difference between the two types of instrument: conventions on particular matters and Community acts.

The representatives of the EFTA Member States were able to accept this view only for the purposes of this Convention and in conjunction with paragraph 2 of Protocol 3 and the Declaration supplementing it (see point 127 below). They also said that their States had no wish to obstruct the Communities' proper and specific demands that they preserve a certain freedom to develop Community law.

125. What are the consequences of paragraph 1 of Protocol 3 which, for the purposes of this Convention, treats Community acts in the same way as conventions concluded on particular matters?

It will be possible for a person domiciled in the territory of a Contracting State (such as Switzerland) to be summoned to appear in the territory of another Contracting State belonging to the European Communities (such as Belgium) on the basis of a rule of jurisdiction which is not laid down in the Lugano Convention but results from a Community act (just like a convention on a particular matter).

[OJ C189, 28.7.90, p 95]

A judgment handed down by a court in a Community Member State—which has jurisdiction by virtue of the Community act which derogates, as regards jurisdiction, from the Lugano Convention—will be recognized and enforced in the other Community Member States. However, recognition and enforcement may be refused under the conditions laid down in Article 57(4), i e in an EFTA Member State where the person against whom recognition or enforcement of the decision is being sought is domiciled, unless such recognition and enforcement are permitted under the law of the State.

It should be noted that paragraph 1 of the Protocol refers only to Community acts and not to the legislation of the Community Member States where this has been harmonized pursuant to those acts, in this case by Directives. The assimilation of Community acts to conventions concluded on particular matters can only refer to an act which is equivalent to such a convention and cannot therefore extend to national legislation.

Moreover, if a national legislation, departing from a Directive, were to introduce rules of jurisdiction derogating from the Lugano Convention, the situation would be different, i e it would be a question of the responsibility of the State which had taken such measures.

As explained above, the representatives of the EFTA Member States were able to agree to Community acts being treated in the same way as conventions concluded on particular matters only subject to a Declaration by the Community Member States that they will comply with the rules on jurisdiction and recognition and enforcement of judgments established by the Lugano Convention (for comments on that Declaration, see point 127 below).

126. *Paragraph 2 of Protocol 3* refers to the case where, notwithstanding the precautions taken, in the view of one of the Contracting Parties, a provision of a Community act is not compatible with the Lugano Convention. For example, this is the situation that might arise if the Community act provided for the jurisdiction of the court of the plaintiff's domicile *vis-à-vis* a defendant who was domiciled outside the Community and therefore in an EFTA Member State.

Paragraph 2 has the effect of a *pactum de negotiando*. If one of the Contracting Parties considers there is incompatibility between the Community act and the Lugano Convention, negotiations will be initiated to amend, if necessary, the Lugano Convention. To this end the review procedure provided for in Article 66 of the Lugano Convention will apply without prejudice to the possibility of a meeting of the Standing Committee set up by Article 3 of Protocol 2 being convened to hear this request in accordance with Article 4 of that Protocol.

Negotiations will have to begin immediately to establish rapidly whether or not there is any need to amend the Lugano Convention. Paragraph 2 contains only an undertaking to contemplate an amendment rather than actually to amend the Convention.

Moreover, paragraph 2 of Protocol 3 does not contain any undertaking, nor could it, to contemplate an amendment to a Community act. Such negotiations would lie outside relations between the States party to the Convention and should be undertaken with the Community institutions, as Community acts fall within the competence of the latter.

It should be noted that the procedure laid down in paragraph 2 could be instigated equally well by a Community Member State or by an EFTA Member State. An EFTA Member State will be able in particular to request the amendment of the Lugano Convention to avoid derogating measures being taken through a Community act in respect of persons domiciled in its territory. On the other hand, a Community Member State could have an interest in adapting the Lugano Convention so that judgments delivered in its territory can be recognized and executed in all EFTA Member States, to which Article 57(4) might prove an obstacle.

(b) The Declaration by the Governments of the Member States of the Communities

127. Protocol 3 is accompanied by an important Declaration by the Community Member States. This unilateral Declaration represents an essential element of the solution adopted, the other two being the placing of Community acts on the same footing as conventions on particular matters and the undertaking to negotiate if there is any divergence between a Community act and the Lugano Convention.

[OJ C189, 28.7.90, p 96]

As we have explained, the Community Member States are caught between two stools. On the one hand, they have to respect the institutional machinery laid down by the Treaties establishing the Communities while on the other they must respect the undertakings they entered into under the Lugano Convention in respect of the EFTA Member States.

The Declaration is important because the Community Member States, without forgetting that they belong to the Communities and with due respect for its institutions—

(a) take into consideration the undertakings which they have entered into with regard to the EFTA Member States. For those States the Lugano Convention is therefore an instrument to be complied with. On their side there is therefore what was regarded as a "best efforts" clause aimed at avoiding as far as possible any divergence between the provisions of Community acts and those of the Lugano Convention;

(b) indicate their concern not to jeopardize the unity of the legal system established by the Lugano Convention. This is an obvious concern if we consider that the Lugano Convention, through rules based firmly on the Brussels Convention, is intended to guarantee the free movement of judgments among the great majority of West European States, i e including judgments delivered by the courts of the Member States of the Communities;

(c) the Community Member States consequently undertake, when drafting Community acts, to take all the steps in their power to ensure that the rules contained in the Lugano Convention are complied with, particularly as regards the protection which the Convention gives a defendant domiciled in a Contracting State. The result is that when a Community act is discussed in the Council of the Communities, particular attention will have to be paid by each of the Member States to the rules of the Lugano Convention.

To sum up, the Declaration represents a moral and political undertaking, made in good faith by the Community Member States, to keep intact the efforts towards unification which are being made by the Lugano Convention.

4. Conclusion

128. The questions raised by Community acts were amongst the most difficult with which the drafters of the Lugano Convention had to deal. A solution was reached thanks to the constructive will of the representatives of all the States concerned. This compromise solution appears to us to allay the concern shown on both sides. To summarize, it may be said to be a three-storey edifice—

(a) it places Community acts on the same footing as conventions on particular matters, which corresponds to the wishes of the Community Member States;
(b) the Community Member States have given a unilateral undertaking to make every effort to ensure that the unity of the legal system established by the Lugano Convention is not put in jeopardy, which satisfies the EFTA Member States;
(c) as a corrective, there is the undertaking to seek a negotiated solution in the case of a divergence between a Community act and the Lugano Convention. As we have stated, this satisfies both sides.

The compromise thus appears to be perfectly balanced.

[3073]

CHAPTER V
DECLARATIONS ANNEXED TO THE CONVENTION

129. The Lugano Convention is supplemented by three Declarations. The first concerns Protocol 3 which relates to Community acts (see points 120 to 128) and the two others Protocol 2 on the uniform interpretation of the Convention (see points 110 to 119).

[3074]

[OJ C189, 28.7.90, p 97]

CHAPTER VI
JUDGMENTS OF THE COURT OF JUSTICE OF THE EUROPEAN COMMUNITIES CONCERNING THE INTERPRETATION OF THE BRUSSELS CONVENTION OF 27 SEPTEMBER 1968

1. General

130. The Protocol of 3 June 1971 confers on the Court of Justice of the European Communities jurisdiction to rule on the interpretation of the Brussels Convention.

Article 30 of the Accession Convention of 9 October 1978 (Denmark, Ireland, United Kingdom) provides that the Court of Justice also has jurisdiction to rule on the interpretation of that Convention. Article 10 of the Convention of 25 October 1982 on the accession of Greece contains a similar provision.

As at 1 June 1988 the six original Member States of the Communities together with Denmark, Ireland and the United Kingdom are parties to the Protocol.

On the scope of the Protocol, reference should be made to the Jenard report (pp 66 to 70) and the Schlosser report (paragraphs 255 and 256).

It should be noted, however, that the Protocol makes provision for two forms of reference: reference for a preliminary ruling and reference in the interests of the law. The latter possibility has not so far been used. Reference for a preliminary ruling means that a national court required to rule on a question of interpretation of the Convention or the Protocol refers the matter to the Court of Justice and stays its proceedings, pending the latter's decision.

Since the Protocol came into force on 1 September 1975, nearly 60 judgments have been handed down by the Court (see point 3 below) and a number of case are currently pending (see point 4 below).

As stated in the comments on Protocol 2 (see points 112 and 116), in the negotiations on the Lugano Convention it was agreed that the provisions of the Brussels Convention should be construed as interpreted by the Court of Justice and that the report would mention the various judgments handed down by the Court.

This Chapter meets the latter stipulation.

The judgments are given not in chronological order but by reference to those Articles of the Brussels Convention, the Protocol annexed thereto and the 1971 Protocol which have been interpreted, since this seems a more convenient arrangement.

This Chapter gives only the operative part of the decision and not, barring exceptions, the grounds. For it is not the purpose of this report to study the judgments of the Court of Justice but merely to indicate how it has interpreted a number or Articles.

2. Content of the judgments[11]

131.

(*1*) *Application of the Convention*

PART IV EC MATERIALS

National procedural laws are set aside in the matters governed by the Convention in favour of the provisions thereof (judgment of 13 November 1979 in Case 25/79 Sanicentral v Collin (1979) ECR 3423–3431).

(2) Article 1, first paragraph: Civil and commercial matters

1. The Court held that the concept of civil and commercial matters must be regarded as autonomous. It ruled that a judgment given in an action between a public authority and a person governed by private law, in which the public authority has acted "in the exercise of its powers", is excluded from the area of application of the Convention (judgment of 14 October 1976 in Case 29/76 LTU v Eurocontrol (1976) ECR 1541–1552).

2. It confirmed its decision in its judgment of 16 December 1980 in Case 814/79 Netherlands State v Rüffer to the effect that the concept of civil and commercial matters does not include the recovery of the costs incurred by the agent responsible for administering public waterways, in this instance the Netherlands State, in the removal of a wreck pursuant to an international Convention ((1980) ECR 3807–3822).

3. Contracts of employment come within the scope of the Convention (judgment of 13 November 1979 in Case 25/79 Sanicentral v Collin (1979) ECR 3423–3431).

(3) Article 1, second paragraph

(1)

(a) Status of persons

1. Judicial decisions authorizing provisional measures in the course of proceedings for divorce do not fall within the scope of the Convention "if those measures concern or are closely connected with either questions of the status of the persons involved in the divorce proceedings or proprietary legal relations resulting directly from the matrimonial relationship or the dissolution thereof" (judgment of 27 March 1979 in Case 143/78 J De Cavel v L De Cavel (1979) ECR 1055–1068).

[OJ C189, 28.7.90, p 98]

2. However, the Convention is applicable, on the one hand, to the enforcement of an interlocutory order made by a French court in divorce proceedings whereby one of the parties to the proceedings is awarded a monthly maintenance allowance and, on the other hand, to an interim compensation payment, payable monthly, awarded to one of the parties by a French divorce judgment pursuant to Article 270 *et seq* of the French Civil Code.

The Court held that the scope of the Convention extends to maintenance obligations and that the treatment of an ancillary claim is not necessarily linked to that of the principal claim.

Ancillary claims come within the scope of the Convention according to the subject matter with which they are concerned and not according to the subject matter involved in the principal claim (judgment of 6 March 1980 in Case 120/79 L De Cavel v J De Cavel (1980) ECR 731).

(b) Matrimonial relationships

1. The term "rights in property arising out of a matrimonial relationship" includes not only property arrangements specifically and exclusively envisaged by certain national legal systems in the case of marriage but also any proprietary relationships resulting directly from the matrimonial relationship or the dissolution thereof (judgment of 27 March 1979 in Case 143/78 J De Cavel v L De Cavel (1979) ECR 1055–1068).

2. An application for provisional measures to secure the delivery up of a document in order to prevent it from being used as evidence in an action concerning a husband's management of his wife's property does not fall within the scope of the Convention if such management is closely connected with the proprietary relationship resulting directly from the marriage bond (judgment of 31 March 1982 in Case 25/81 CHW v GJH (1982) ECR 1189–1205).

(2) Bankruptcy

A decision such as that of a French civil court based on Article 99 of the French Law of 13 July 1967, ordering the de facto manager of a legal person to pay a certain sum into the assets of a company must be considered as given in the context of bankruptcy or analogous proceedings (judgment of 22 February 1979 in Case 133/78 Gourdain v Nadler (1979) ECR 733–746).

(4) Article 5(1): Contractual matters

1. The place of performance of the obligation in question is to be determined in accordance with the law which governs the obligations in question according to the rules of conflict of laws of the court before which the matter is brought (judgment of 6 October 1978 in Case 12/76 Tessili v Dunlop (1976) ECR 1473–1487).

2. If the place of performance of a contractual obligation has been specified by the parties in a clause which is valid according to the national law applicable to the contract, the court for that place has jurisdiction to take cognizance of disputes relating to that obligation under Article 5(1), irrespective of whether the formal conditions provided for under Article 17 have been observed (judgment of 17 January 1980 in Case 56/79 Zelger v Salinitri (1980) ECR 89–98).

3. The word "obligation" contained in Article 5 (1) refers to the contractual obligation forming the basis of the legal proceedings, namely the obligation of the grantor in the case of an exclusive sales contract (judgment of 6 October 1976 in Case 14/76 De Bloos v Bouyer).

4. The plaintiff may invoke the jurisdiction of the courts of the place of performance in accordance with Article 5(1) of the Convention even when the existence of the contract is in dispute between the parties (judgment of 4 March 1982 in Case 38/81 Effer v Kantner (1982) ECR 825–836).

5. The obligation to be taken into account for the purposes of the application of Article 5(1) of the Convention in the case of claims based on different obligations arising under a contract of employment as a representative binding a worker to an undertaking is the obligation which characterizes the contract, i e that of the place where the work is carried out (judgment of 26 May 1982 in Case 133/82 Ivenel v Schwab (1982) ECR 1891–1902).

6. The concept of matters relating to a contract is an autonomous concept. Obligations in regard to the payment of a sum of money which have their basis in the relationship existing between an association and its members by virtue of membership are "matters relating to a contract", whether the obligations in question arise simply from the act of becoming a member or from decisions made by organs of the association (judgment of 22 March 1983 in Case 34/82 Peters v Znav (1983) ECR 987–1004).
[OJ C189, 28.7.90, p 99]

7. For the purpose of determining the place of performance within the meaning of Article 5(1), the obligation to be taken into consideration in an action for the recovery of fees, commenced by an architect commissioned to prepare plans for the building of houses, is the contractual obligation actually forming the basis of the legal proceedings.

In the case in point that obligation consists of a debt for a sum of money payable at the defendant's permanent address.

The place of payment is determined by the law applicable to the contract (judgment of 15 January 1987 in Case 266/85 Shenavai v Kreischer, OJ No C39, 17.2.1987, p 3).

8.

(a) On the question of whether a claim for compensation for sudden and premature termination of an agreement was a matter relating to a contract or to quasi-delict, the Court of Justice replied that "proceedings relating to the wrongful repudiation of an independent commercial agency agreement and the payment of commission due under such an agreement are proceedings in matters relating to a contract within the meaning of Article 5(1) of the Brussels Convention".

(b) It repeated that matters relating to a contract should be regarded as an "autonomous" concept (judgment of 22 March 1983 in Case 34/82 Peters v Znav).

(c) Compensation for wrongful repudiation of an agreement is based on failure to comply with a contractual obligation.

(d) Lastly, the Court referred to the Rome Convention of 19 June 1980 on the law applicable to contractual obligations, which includes (Article 10) within the field of the law applicable to a contract the consequences of total or partial non-performance of the obligations arising from it and hence the contractual liability of the party responsible for non-performance (judgment of 8 March 1988 in Case 9/87 Arcado v Haviland, OJ No C89, 6.4.1988, p 9).

(5) Article 5(2): Maintenance

The subject of maintenance obligations falls within the scope of the Convention even if the claim in question is ancillary to divorce proceedings (judgment of 6 March 1980 in Case 120/79 L De Cavel v J De Cavel (1980) ECR 731).

(6) Article 5(3): Tort or delict

1. The expression "place where the harmful event occurred" must be understood as being intended to cover both the place where the damage occurred and the place of the event giving rise to it.

The result is that the defendant may be sued, at the option of the plaintiff, either in the courts for the place where the damage occurred or in the courts for the place of the event which gives rise to and is at the origin of that damage (judgment of 30 November 1976 in Case 21/76 Bier, Reinwater v Mines de potasse d'Alsace (1976) ECR 1735–1748).

2.

(a) The term "tort delict or quasi-delict" in Article 5(3) of the Convention must be regarded as an autonomous concept covering all actions which seek to establish the liability of a defendant and which are not related to a "contract" within the meaning of Article 5(1).

(b) A court which has jurisdiction under Article 5(3) to entertain an action with regard to tortious matters does not have jurisdiction to entertain that action with regard to other matters not based on tort (judgment of 27 September 1988 in Case 189/87 Kalfelis v Schröder, OJ No C281, 4.11.1988, p 18).

(7) Article 5(5): Branch, agency or other establishment

1. When the grantee of an exclusive sales concession is not subject either to the control or to the direction of the grantor, he cannot be regarded as being at the head of a branch, agency or other establishment of the grantor within the meaning of Article 5(5) (judgment of 6 October 1976 in Case 14/76 De Bloos v Bouyer (1976) ECR 1497–1511).

[OJ C189, 28.7.90, p 100]

2. The Court has given an *autonomous* interpretation to the concepts of "operations of a branch, agency or other establishment"—

(a) the concept of branch, agency or other establishment implies a place of business which has the appearance of permanency, such as the extension of a parent body, has a management and is materially equipped to negotiate business with third parties so that the latter, although knowing that there will if necessary be a legal link with the parent body, the head office of which is abroad, do not have to deal directly with such parent body but may transact business at the place of business constituting the extension;

(b) the concept of "operations" comprises—

(1) actions relating to rights and contractual or non-contractual obligations concerning the management properly so-called of the agency, branch or other establishment itself such as those concerning the situation of the building where such entity is established or the local engagement of staff to work there,

(2) actions relating to undertakings which have been entered into at the abovementioned place of business in the name of the parent body and which must be performed in the Contracting State where the place of business is established,

(3) actions concerning non-contractual obligations arising from the activities in which the branch, agency or other establishment has engaged at the place in which it is established on behalf of the parent body (judgment of 22 November 1978 in Case 33/78 Somafer v Ferngas (1978) ECR 2183–2195).

3. An "independent commercial agent", inasmuch as he is free to arrange his own work and the undertaking which he represents may not prevent him from representing several firms at the same time and he merely transmits orders to the parent undertaking without being involved in either their terms or their execution, does not have the character of a branch (judgment of 18 March 1981 in Case 139/80 Blanckaert & Willems v Trost (1981) ECR 819–830).

4. Article 5(5) must be interpreted as applying to a case in which a legal person established in a Contracting State does not operate any dependent branch, agency or other establishment in another Contracting State but nevertheless pursues its activities there by means of an independent undertaking which has the same name and identical management, which negotiates and conducts business in its name and which it uses as an extension of itself (judgment of 9 December 1987 in Case 218/86 Schotte v Rothschild, OJ No C2, 6.1.1988, p 3).

(7a) Article 6(1): Co-defendants

For the application of Article 6(1) of the Convention there must exist between the various actions brought by the same plaintiff against different defendants a link such that it is expedient to determine those actions together in order to avoid the risk of irreconcilable judgments resulting from separate proceedings (judgment of 27 September 1988 in Case 189/87 Kalfelis v Schröder, OJ No C281, 4.11.1988, p 18).

(8) Article 13: Sale of goods on instalment credit terms and loans repayable by instalments

The Court ruled in favour of an autonomous concept of the sale of goods on instalment credit terms albeit implicitly in that it is not to be understood to extend to the sale of a machine which one company agrees to make to another company on the basis of a price to be paid by way of bills of exchange spread over a period.

The jurisdictional advantage is to be restricted to buyers who are in need of protection (judgment of 21 June 1978 in Case 150/77 Bertrand v Ott (1978) ECR 1431–1447).

It should be noted that this Article was amended in the 1978 Convention in line with the judgment.

(9) Article 16(1): Immovable property

1. The concept of "matters relating to … tenancies of immovable property" must not be interpreted as including an agreement to rent under a usufructuary lease a retail business carried on in immovable property rented from a third person by the lessor.

Article 16(1) must not be given a wider interpretation than is required by its objective (judgment of 14 December 1977 in Case 73/77 Sanders v Van Der Putte).

2. Article 16(1) applies to all lettings of immovable property (judgment of 15 January 1985 in Case 241/83 Rösler v Rottwinkel (1985) ECR 99–129).

[OJ C189, 28.7.90, p 101]

This not uncontroversial judgment was not followed in the Lugano Convention (see points 50 and 51). Nor was it in line with the views of those who framed the 1968 Convention (see Jenard report, page 35 and Schlosser report, paragraph 164).

3. Article 16(1) must be interpreted as meaning that in a dispute as to the existence of a lease relating to immovable property situated in two Contracting States (Belgium and the Netherlands in the case in point), exclusive jurisdiction over the property situated in each Contracting State is held by the courts of that State (judgment of 6 July 1988 in Case 158/87 Scherens v Maenhout and Van Poucke, OJ No C211, 11.8.1988, p 7).

(10) Article 16(4): Patents

See the judgment of 15 November 1983 in Case 288/82 Duijnstee v Goderbauer (1983) ECR 3663–3679.

(11) Article 16(5): Applications to oppose enforcement

Applications to oppose enforcement, as provided for under paragraph 767 of the German Code of Civil Procedure, fall, as such, within the jurisdiction provision contained in Article 16 (5) of the Convention; that provision does not however make it possible, in an application to oppose enforcement made to the courts of the Contracting State in which enforcement is to take place, to plead a set-off between the right whose enforcement is being sought and a claim over which the courts of that State would have no jurisdiction if it were raised independently.

The Court held that this amounts to a clear abuse of the process on the part of the plaintiff for the purpose of obtaining indirectly from the German courts a decision regarding a claim over which those courts have no jurisdiction under the Convention (judgment of 4 July 1985 in Case 220/84 AS-Autoteile v Malhe (1985) ECR 2267–2279).

(12) Article 17: Agreements conferring jurisdiction

1.

(a) Where a clause conferring jurisdiction is included among the general conditions of sale of one of the parties, printed on the back of a contract, the requirement of a writing under the first paragraph on Article 17 is fulfilled only if the contract signed by both parties contains an express reference to those general conditions and

(b) in the case of a contract concluded by reference to earlier offers, which were themselves made with reference to the general conditions of one of the parties

PART IV EC MATERIALS

including a clause conferring jurisdiction, the requirement of a writing under the first paragraph of Article 17 is satisfied only if the reference is express and can therefore be checked by a party exercising reasonable care (judgment of 14 December 1976 in Case 24/76 Colzani v Ruwa (1976) ECR 1831–1843).

2.

(a) In the case of an orally concluded contract, the requirements of the first paragraph of Article 17 as to form are satisfied only if the vendor's confirmation in writing accompanied by notification of the general conditions of sale has been accepted in writing by the purchaser and

(b) the fact that the purchaser does not raise any objections against a confirmation issued unilaterally by the other party does not amount to acceptance on his part of the clause conferring jurisdiction unless the oral agreement comes within the framework of a continuing trading relationship between the parties which is based on the general conditions of one of them, and those conditions contain a clause conferring jurisdiction (judgment of 14 December 1976 in Case 25/76 Segoura v Bonakdarian (1976) ECR 1851–1863).

3.

(a) The first paragraph of Article 17 cannot be interpreted as prohibiting an agreement under which the two parties to a contract for sale, who are domiciled in different States, can be sued only in the courts of their respective States and

(b) in the above case the Article cannot be interpreted as prohibiting the court before which a dispute has been brought in pursuance of such a clause from taking into account a set-off connected with the legal relationship in dispute (judgment of 9 November 1978 in Case 23/78 Meeth v Glacetal (1978) ECR 2133–2144).

[OJ C189, 28.7.90, p 102]

4.

(a) National procedural laws are set aside in the matters governed by the Convention in favour of the provisions thereof and

(b) in judicial proceedings instituted after the coming into force of the Convention, clauses conferring jurisdiction included in contracts of employment concluded prior to that date must be considered valid even in cases in which they would have been regarded as void under the national law in force at the time when the contract was entered into (judgment of 13 November 1979 in Case 25/79 Sanicentral v Collin (1979) ECR 3423–3431).

5. If the place of performance of a contractual obligation has been specified by the parties in a clause which is valid according to the national law applicable to the contract, the court for that place has jurisdiction to take cognizance of disputes relating to that obligation under Article 5(1) of the Convention, irrespective of whether the formal conditions provided for under Article 17 have been observed (judgment of 17 January 1980 in Case 56/79 Zelger v Salinitri (1980) ECR 89–98).

6. Article 17 must be interpreted as meaning that the legislation of a Contracting State may not allow the validity of an agreement conferring jurisdiction to be called in question solely on the ground that the language used is not that prescribed by that legislation (judgment of 24 June 1981 in Case 150/81 Elefanten Schuh v Jacqmain (1981) ECR 1671–1690).

7. Article 17 must be interpreted as meaning that where a contract of insurance, entered into between an insurer and a policy-holder and stipulated by the latter to be for his benefit and to enure for the benefit for third parties, contains a clause conferring jurisdiction relating to proceedings which might be brought by such third parties, the latter, even if they have not expressly signed the said clause, may rely upon it (judgment of 14 July 1983 in Case 201/82 Gerling v Amministrazione del tesoro dello Stato (1983) ECR 2503–2518).

8. On bills of lading, the Court handed down a judgment to the effect that—

(a) the bill of lading issued by the carrier to the shipper may be regarded as an "agreement" "evidenced in writing" between the parties, within the meaning of Article 17. The jurisdiction clause applies if the parties have signed the bill of lading. If the clause conferring jurisdiction appears in the general conditions, the shipper must have expressly accepted it in writing. The wording of the bill of lading signed by both parties must expressly refer to the general conditions. However, if the carrier and the shipper have a continuing business relationship, which is governed as a whole by the carrier's general conditions, the clause conferring jurisdiction applies even without acceptance in writing;

(b) the bill of lading issued by the carrier to the shipper may be regarded as an "agreement" "evidenced in writing", within the meaning of Article 17, *vis-à-vis* a third party holding the bill only if that third party is bound by an agreement with the carrier under the relevant national law and if the bill of lading, as "evidence in writing" of the "agreement", satisfies the formal conditions in Article 17 (judgment of 19 June 1984 in Case 71/83 Russ v Nova, Goeminne (1984) ECR 2417–2436).

9. The court of a Contracting State before which the applicant, without raising any objection as to the court's jurisdiction, enters an appearance in proceedings relating to a claim for a set-off which is not based on the same contract or subject-matter as the claims in his application and in respect of which there is a valid agreement conferring exclusive jurisdiction on the courts of another Contracting State within the meaning of Article 17 has jurisdiction by virtue of Article 18 (judgment of 7 March 1985 in Case 48/84 Spitzley v Sommer (1985) ECR 787–800).

10. The first paragraph of Article 17 must be interpreted as meaning that the formal requirements therein laid down are satisfied if it is established that jurisdiction was conferred by express oral agreement, that written confirmation of that agreement by *one* of the parties was received by the other and that the latter raised no objection (judgment of 11 July 1985 in Case 221/84 Berghoefer v ASA (1985) ECR 2699–2710).

11. An agreement conferring jurisdiction is not to be regarded as having been concluded for the benefit of only one of the parties, within the meaning of the third paragraph of Article 17 of the Convention, where all that is established is that the parties have agreed that a court or the courts of the Contracting State in which that party is domiciled are to have jurisdiction.

The Court held that clauses which expressly state the name of the party for whose benefit they were agreed and those which, whilst specifying the courts in which either party may sue the other, give one of them a wider choice of courts must be regarded as clauses whose wording shows that they were agreed for the exclusive benefit of one of the parties (judgment of 24 June 1986 in Case 22/85 Anterist v Credit Lyonnais, OJ No C196, 5.8.1986).

[OJ C189, 28.7.90, p 103]

12. Article 17 must be interpreted as meaning that where a written agreement containing a jurisdiction clause and stipulating that the agreement can be renewed only in writing has expired but has continued to serve as the legal basis for the contractual relations between the parties, the jurisdiction clause satisfies the formal requirements in Article 17 if, under the law applicable, the parties could validly renew the original contract otherwise than in writing, or if, conversely, either party has confirmed in writing either the jurisdiction clause or the group of clauses which have been tacitly renewed and of which the jurisdiction clause forms part, without any objection on the part of the other party to whom such confirmation has been notified (judgment of 11 November 1986 in Case 313/85 Iveco Fiat v Van Hool, OJ No C308, 2.12.1986, p 4).

(13) Article 18: Submission to the jurisdiction

1.

(a) Article 18 applies even where the parties have by agreement designated a court in another State since Article 17 is not one of the exceptions laid down in Article 18 and

(b) Article 18 is applicable where the defendant not only contests the court's jurisdiction but also makes submissions on the substance of the action, provided that, if the challenge to jurisdiction is not preliminary to any defence as to the substance, it does not occur after the making of the submissions which under national procedural law are considered to be the first defence addressed to the court seised (judgment of 24 June 1981 in Case 150/81 Elefanten Schuh v Jacqmain (1981) ECR 1671–1690).
(See also the judgments of 22 October 1981 in Case 27/81 Rohr v Ossberger, 31 March 1982 in Case 25/81 CHW v GJH and 14 July 1983 in Case 201/82 Gerling v Amministrazione del tesoro dello Stato.)

2. The court of a Contracting State before which the applicant, without raising any objection as to the court's jurisdiction, enters an appearance in proceedings relating to a claim for a set-off which is not based on the same contract or subject matter as the claims in his application and in respect of which there is a valid agreement conferring exclusive jurisdiction on the courts of another Contracting State within the meaning of Article 17 of the Convention of 27 September 1968 on jurisdiction and the enforcement of judgments in civil and

commercial matters has jurisdiction by virtue of Article 18 of that Convention (judgment of 7 March 1985 in Case 48/84 Spitzley v Sommer (1985) ECR 787–800).

(14) Article 19: Examination of jurisdiction

Article 19 requires the national court to declare of its own motion that it has no jurisdiction whenever it finds that a court of another Contracting State has exclusive jurisdiction under Article 16 of the Convention, even in an appeal in cassation where the national rules of procedure limit the court's review to the grounds raised by the parties (judgment of 15 November 1983 in Case 288/82 Duijnstee v Goderbauer (1983) ECR 3663–3679).

(15) Article 21: Lis pendens

1. See the judgment of 7 June 1984 in Case 129/83 Zelger v Salinitri.

2. The term *lis pendens* used in Article 21 covers a case where a party brings an action before a court in a Contracting State for a declaration that an international sales contract is inoperative or for the termination thereof whilst an action by the other party to secure performance of the said contract is pending before a court in another Contracting State.

The Court also ruled that the terms used in Article 21 to determine a situation of *lis pendens* are to be regarded as *autonomous* concepts (judgment of 8 December 1987 in Case 144/86 Gubisch v Palumbo, OJ No C8, 13.1.1988, p 3).

(16) Article 22: Related actions

Article 22 does not confer jurisdiction.

It applies only where related actions are brought before courts of two or more Contracting States (judgment of 24 June 1981 in Case 150/81 Elefanten Schuh v Jacqmain (1981) ECR 1671–1690).

[OJ C189, 28.7.90, p 104]

(17) Article 24: Provisional, including protective, measures

1. The inclusion of provisional measures in the scope of the Convention is determined not by their own nature but by the nature of the rights which they serve to protect (judgment of 27 March 1979 in Case 143/78 J De Cavel v L De Cavel (1979) ECR 1055–1068).

2. On the enforcement of judicial decisions authorizing provisional and protective measures, see Article 27 below (judgment of 21 May 1980 in Case 125/ 79 Denilauler v Couchet (1980) ECR 1553).

3. Article 24 may not be relied on to bring within the scope of the Convention provisional measures relating to matters which are excluded from it (judgment of 31 March 1982 in Case 25/81 CHW v GJH (1982) ECR 1189–1205).

(18) Article 26: Recognition

A foreign judgment recognized by virtue of Article 26 must *in principle* have the same effects in the State in which enforcement is sought as it does in the State in which the judgment was given.

Subject, however, it should be added, to the grounds for non-recognition laid down in the Convention (judgment of 4 February 1988 in Case 145/86 Hoffmann v Krieg. See also in the same case the Court's interpretation of Articles 27(1) and (3), 31 and 36, OJ No C63, 8.3.1988, p 6).

(19) Article 27(1): Public policy

Recourse to the public policy clause, which is to be had only in exceptional cases, … is in any event not possible where the problem is one of compatibility of a foreign judgment with a domestic judgment. That problem must be resolved on the basis of Article 27(3), which covers the case of a foreign judgment irreconcilable with a judgment given between the same parties in the State in which enforcement is sought (judgment of 4 February 1988 in Case 145/86 Hoffmann v Klieg, OJ No C63, 8.3.1988, p 6).

(20) Article 27(2): Rights of the defence

1. Judicial decisions authorizing provisional or protective measures, which are delivered without the party against which they are directed having been summoned to appear and which are intended to be enforced without prior service do not come within the system of recognition and enforcement provided for by Title III of the Convention (judgment of 21 May 1980 in Case 125/79 Denilauler v Couchet (1980) ECR 1553).

2. Article 27(2) must be interpreted as follows—

(a) the words "the document which instituted the proceedings" cover any document, such as the order for payment (Zahlungsbefehl) in German law;

(b) a decision such as the enforcement order (Vollstreckungsbefehl) in German law is not covered by the words "the document which instituted the proceedings";

(c) in order to determine whether the defendant has been enabled to arrange for his defence as required by Article 27(2) the court in which enforcement is sought must take account only of the time, such as that allowed under German law for submitting an objection (Widerspruch), available to the defendant for the purposes of preventing the issue of a judgment in default which is enforceable under the Convention;

(d) Article 27(2) remains applicable where the defendant has lodged an objection against the decision given in default and a court of the State in which the judgment was given has held the objection to be inadmissible on the ground that the time for lodging an objection has expired;

(e) even if a court of the State in which the judgment was given has held, in separate adversary proceedings, that service was duly effected, Article 27(2) still requires the court in which enforcement is sought to examine whether service was effected in sufficient time to enable the defendant to arrange for his defence;

(f) the court in which enforcement is sought may as a general rule confine itself to examining whether the period, reckoned from the date on which service was duly effected, allowed the defendant sufficient time for his defence; it must, however, consider whether, in a particular case, there are exceptional circumstances such as the fact that, although service was duly effected, it was inadequate for the purposes of causing that time to begin to run;

[OJ C189, 28.7.90, p 105]

(g) Article 52 of the Convention and the fact that the court of the State in which enforcement is sought concluded that under the law of that State the defendant was habitually resident within its territory at the date of service of the document which instituted the proceedings do not affect the replies given above (judgment of 16 June 1981 in Case 166/80 Klomps v Michel (1981) ECR 1593–1612).

3. The court of the State in which enforcement is sought may, if it considers that the conditions laid down by Article 27(2) are fulfilled, refuse to grant recognition and enforcement of a judgment, even though the court of the State in which the judgment was given regarded it as proven, in accordance with the third paragraph of Article 20 of that Convention in conjunction with Article 15 of the Hague Convention of 15 November 1965, that the defendant, who failed to enter an appearance, had an opportunity to receive service of the document instituting the proceedings in sufficient time to enable him to make arrangements for his defence (judgment of 15 July 1982 in Case 288/81 Pendy Plastic Products v Pluspunkt (1982) ECR 2723–2737).

4.

(a) Article 27(2) is also applicable, in respect of its requirement that service of the document which instituted the proceedings should have been effected in sufficient time, where service was effected within a period prescribed by the court of the State in which the judgment was given or where the defendant resided, exclusively or otherwise, within the jurisdiction of that court or in the same country as that court.

(b) In examining whether service was effected in sufficient time, the court in which enforcement is sought may take account of exceptional circumstances which arose *after* service was duly effected.

(c) The fact that the plaintiff was apprised of the defendant's new address, after service was effected, and the fact that the defendant was responsible for the failure of the duly served document to reach him are matters which the court in which enforcement is sought may take into account in assessing whether service was effected in sufficient time (judgment of 11 June 1985 in Case 49/84 Debaecker and Plouvier v Bouwman (1985) ECR 1779–1803).

(21) *Article 27(3): Irreconcilable judgments*

A foreign judgment ordering a person to make maintenance payments to his spouse by virtue of his obligations, arising out of the marriage, to support her is irreconcilable for the purposes of Article 27(3) with a national judgment which has decreed the divorce of the spouses in question (judgment of 4 February 1988 in Case 145/86 Hoffmann v Krieg, OJ No C63, 8.3.1988, p 6).

(22) *Articles 30 and 38: Ordinary appeal*

The Court ruled in favour of an *autonomous* concept of ordinary appeal. An "ordinary appeal" is constituted by any appeal—

(a) which is such that it may result in the annulment or the amendment of the judgment which is the subject matter of the procedure for recognition or enforcement and

(b) the lodging of which is bound, in the State in which the judgment was given, to a period which is laid down by the law and starts to run by virtue of that same judgment (judgment of 22 November 1977 in Case 43/77 Industrial Diamond v Riva (1977) ECR 2175–2191).

(23) Article 31: Enforcement

1. The provisions of the Convention prevent a party who has obtained a judgment in his favour in a Contracting State, being a judgment for which an order for enforcement under Article 31 may issue in another Contracting State, from making an application to a court in that other State for a judgment against the other party in the same terms as the judgment delivered in the first State (judgment in Case 42/76 De Wolf v Cox).

2. A foreign judgment the enforcement of which has been ordered in a Contracting State pursuant to Article 31, and which remains enforceable in the State in which it was given, need not remain enforceable in the State in which enforcement is sought when, under the legislation of the latter State, it ceases to be enforceable for reasons which lie outside the scope of the Convention.

In the case in point a foreign judgment ordering a person to make maintenance payments to his spouse by virtue of his obligations, arising out of the marriage, to support her is irreconcilable with a national judgment which has decreed the divorce of the spouses in question (judgment of 4 February 1988 in Case 145/86 Hoffman v Krieg, OJ No C63, 8.3.1988, p 6).

[OJ C189, 28.7.90, p 106]

(24) Article 33: Address for service

1.

(a) The second paragraph of Article 33 must be interpreted as meaning that the requirement to give an address for service laid down in that provision must be complied with in accordance with the rules laid down by the law of the State in which enforcement is sought or, if those rules do not specify when that requirement must be complied with, *no later than* the date on which the enforcement order is served.

(b) The consequences of an infringement of the rules concerning the choice of an address for service are, by virtue of Article 33 of the Convention, governed by the law of the State in which enforcement is sought, provided that the aims of the Convention are respected, i e the law of the latter State remains subject to the aims of the Convention; the penalty cannot therefore call into question the validity of the judgment granting enforcement or allow the rights of the party against whom enforcement is sought to be prejudiced (judgment of 10 July 1986 in Case 198/85 Carron v FRG, OJ No C209, 20.8.1986, p 5).

(25) Article 36: Enforcement procedure

1.

(a) Article 36 of the Convention excludes any procedure whereby interested third parties may challenge an enforcement order, even where such a procedure is available to third parties under the domestic law of the State in which the enforcement order is granted.

(b) The Court held that the Convention has established an enforcement procedure which constitutes an *autonomous* and complete *system*, including the matter of appeals. It follows that Article 36 of the Convention excludes procedures whereby interested third parties may challenge an enforcement order under domestic law.

(c) The Convention merely regulates the procedure for obtaining an order for the enforcement of foreign enforceable instruments and does not deal with execution itself, which continues to be governed by the domestic law of the court in which execution is sought, so that interested third parties may contest execution by means of the procedures available to them under the law of the State in which execution is levied (judgment of 2 July 1985 in Case 148/84 Deutsche Genossenschaftsbank v Brasserie du Pecheur (1985) ECR 1981–1993).

2. The Article must be interpreted as meaning that the party who has failed to appeal against the enforcement order referred to in Article 31 (in the case in point within one month

of service of the enforcement order) is thereafter precluded, at the stage at which the judgment is enforced, from relying upon a valid reason which he could have invoked in such appeal. That rule is to be applied ex officio by the courts of the State in which enforcement is sought. *However*, that rule does not apply when it has the effect of obliging the national court to make the effects of a national judgment lying outside the scope of the Convention (divorce) conditional on that judgment being recognized in the State in which the foreign judgment whose enforcement is at issue was given (judgment of 4 February 1988 in Case 145/86 Hoffman v Krieg, OJ No C63, 8.3.1988, p 6).

(26) Article 37: Enforcement procedure

1.

(a) The second paragraph of Article 37 must be interpreted as meaning that an appeal in cassation and, in the Federal Republic of Germany, a "Rechtsbeschwerde" may be lodged only against the judgment given on the appeal.

(b) That provision cannot be extended so as to enable an appeal to be lodged against a judgment other than that given on the appeal, for instance against a preliminary or interlocutory order requiring preliminary inquiries to be made (judgment of 27 November 1984 in Case 258/83 Brennero v Wendel (1984) ECR 3971–3984).

(27) Article 38: Enforcement procedure

1. See (20) above on "ordinary appeal".

2. The second paragraph of Article 38 of the Convention of 27 September 1968 on jurisdiction and the enforcement of judgments in civil and commercial matters must be interpreted as meaning that a court with which an appeal has been lodged against a decision authorizing enforcement, given pursuant to the Convention, may make enforcement conditional on the provision of security only when it gives judgment on the appeal (judgment of 27 November 1984 in Case 258/ 83 Brennero v Wendel (1984) ECR 3971–3984).

[OJ C189, 28.7.90, p 107]

(28) Article 39: Enforcement procedure

1.

(a) By virtue of Article 39 of the Convention, a party who has applied for and obtained authorization for enforcement may, within the period mentioned in that Article, proceed directly with protective measures against the property of the party against whom enforcement is sought and is under no obligation to obtain specific authorization.

(b) A party who has obtained authorization for enforcement may proceed with the protective measures referred to in Article 39 until the expiry of the period prescribed in Article 36 for lodging an appeal and, if such an appeal is lodged, until a decision is given thereon.

(c) A party who has proceeded with the protective measures referred to in Article 39 of the Convention is under no obligation to obtain, in respect of those measures, any confirmatory judgment required by the national law of the court in question (judgment of 3 October 1985 in Case 119/84 Capelloni v Pelkmans (1985) ECR 3147–3164).

(29) Article 40: Enforcement procedure

The court hearing an appeal by a party seeking enforcement is required to hear the party against whom enforcement is sought, pursuant to the first sentence of the second paragraph of Article 40 of the Convention, even though the application for an enforcement order was dismissed in the lower court simply because documents were not produced at the appropriate time.

This is because the Convention formally requires that both parties should be given a hearing at the appellate level, without regard to the scope of the decision in the lower court (judgment of 12 July 1984 in Case 178/83 P v K (1984) ECR 3033–3043).

(30) Article 54: Temporal application

The effect of Article 54 is that the only essential for the rules of the Convention to be applicable to litigation relating to legal relationships created before the date of the coming into force of the Convention is that the judicial proceedings should have been instituted subsequently to that date. This is true even if an agreement conferring jurisdiction was concluded before the Convention came into force and could be regarded as void under the law applicable to it; the case in point concerns a contract of employment between a French employee and a German firm, to which French law was applicable (judgment of 13 November 1979 in Case 25/79 Sanicentral v Collin (1979) ECR 3423–3431).

(31) Articles 55 and 56: Bilateral Conventions

As the first paragraph of Article 56 of the Convention states that the bilateral Conventions listed in Article 55 continue to have effect in relation to matters to which the Convention does not apply, the court of the State in which enforcement is sought may apply them to decisions which, without coming under the second paragraph of Article 1, are excluded from the Convention's scope. This is the case as regards application of the German-Belgian Convention of 1958, which may continue to have effect in "civil and commercial matters", irrespective of the autonomous construction placed upon that concept by the Court for the purposes of interpretation of the 1968 Convention (judgment of 14 July 1977 in joined Cases 9/ 77 and 10/77 Bavaria and Germanair v Eurocontrol (1977) ECR 1517–1527).

(32) Article I, second paragraph, of the Protocol annexed to the Convention (Luxembourg)

A clause conferring jurisdiction is not binding upon a person domiciled in Luxembourg unless that clause is mentioned in a provision—

(a) specially and exclusively meant for this purpose;

(b) specifically signed by that party; in this respect the signing of the contract as a whole does not suffice. It is not necessary for that clause to be mentioned in a separate document (judgment of 6 May 1980 in Case 784/79 Porta-Leasing v Prestige International (1980) ECR 1517).

(33) Article II of the Protocol annexed to the Convention

1. The expression "an offence which was not intentionally committed" should be understood as meaning any offence the legal definition of which does not require the existence of intent, and

[OJ C189, 28.7.90, p 108]

2. Article II of the Protocol applies in all criminal proceedings concerning offences which were not intentionally committed, "in which the accused's liability at civil law, arising from the elements of the offence for which he is being prosecuted, is in question or on which such liability might subsequently be based" (judgment of 26 May 1981 in Case 157/80 Rinkau (1981) ECR 1391–1484).

(34) Article 2 of the Protocol of 3 June 1971

Lower courts not sitting in an appellate capacity are not empowered to seek a preliminary ruling from the Court of Justice on a question of interpretation of the Convention.

See the Court of Justice's order of 9 November 1983 in Case 80/83 Habourdin v Italocremona (1983) ECR 3639–3641) and order of 28 March 1984 in Case 56/84 Von Gallera v Maitre ((1984) ECR 1769–1772).

132. 3. **List of judgments of the Court of Justice** (from 6 October 1976 to 27 September 1988)

I	6.10.1976	Case 12/76	Tessili v Dunlop	Article 5(1)	(1976) ECR 1473–1487
II	6.10.1976	Case 14/76	De Bloos v Bouyer	Article 5(1) and Article 5(5)	(1976) ECR 1497–1511
III	14.10.1976	Case 29/76	LTU v Eurocontrol	Article 1	(1976) ECR 1541–1552
IV	30.11.1976	Case 21/76	Reinwater v Potasse d'Alsace	Article 5(3)	(1976) ECR 1735–1748
V	30.11.1976	Case 42/76	De Wolf v Cox	Article 31	(1976) ECR 1759–1768
VI	14.12.1976	Case 24/76	Colzani v Ruwa	Article 17, paragraph 1	(1976) ECR 1831–1843
VII	14.12.1976	Case 25/76	Segoura v Bonakdarian	Article 17, paragraph 1	(1976) ECR 1851–1863

VIII	14.7.1977	Case 9/77 and 10/77	Bavaria-Germanair v Eurocontrol	Article 56	(1977) ECR 1517–1527
IX	22.11.1977	Case 43/77	Diamond v Riva	Articles 30 and 38	(1977) ECR 2175–2191
X	14.12.1977	Case 73/77	Sanders v Van der Putte	Article 16(1)	(1977) ECR 2382–2392
XI	21.6.1978	Case 150/77	Bertrand v Ott	Article 13	(1978) ECR 1431–1447
XII	9.11.1978	Case 23/78	Meeth v Glacetal	Article 17	(1978) ECR 2133–2144
XIII	22.11.1978	Case 33/78	Somafer v Ferngas	Article 5(5)	(1978) ECR 2183–2195
XIV	22.9.1979	Case 133/78	Gourdain v Nadler	Article 1, paragraph 2, point 2	(1979) ECR 733–746
XV	27.3.1979	Case 143/78	J De Cavel v L De Cavel	Articles 1, paragraph 2, and 24	(1979) ECR 1055–1068
XVI	13.11.1979	Case 25/79	Sanicentral v Collin	Articles 17 and 54	(1979) ECR 3423–3431
XVII	17.1.1980	Case 56/79	Zelger v Salinitri	Articles 5(1) and 17	(1980) ECR 89–98
XVIII	6.3.1980	Case 120/79	L De Cavel v J De Cavel	Articles 5(2) and 24	(1980) ECR 731
XIX	6.5.1980	Case 784/79	Porta-Leasing v Prestige International	Article I, paragraph 2 of Protocol	(1980) ECR1517
XX	21.5.1980	Case 125/79	Denilauler v Couchet	Title III	(1980) ECR1553

[OJ C189, 28.7.90, p 109]

XXI	16.12.1980	Case 814/79	Netherlands State v Rüffer	Article 1	(1980) ECR 3807–3822
XXII	18.3.1981	Case 139/80	Blanckaert & Willems v Trost	Article 5(5)	(1981) ECR 819–830
XXIII	26.5.1981	Case 157/80	Rinkau	Article II of Protocol	(1981) ECR 1391–1404
XXIV	16.6.1981	Case 166/80	Klomps v Michel	Article 27(2)	(1981) ECR 1593–1612
XXV	24.6.1981	Case 150/80	Elefenten Schuh v Jacqmain	Articles 17, 18 and 22, paragraph 1 (1981) ECR 1671–1698	
XXVI	22.10.1981	Case 27/81	Rohr v Ossberger	Article 18	(1981) ECR 2431–2448
XXVII	4.3.1982	Case 38/81	Effer v Kantner	Article 5(1)	(1982) ECR 825–836
XXVIII	31.3.1982	Case 25/81	CHW v GJH.	Articles 1, 18 and 24	(1982) ECR 1189–1205

PART IV EC MATERIALS

XXIX	26.5.1982	Case 133/81	Ivenel v Schwab	Article 5(1)	(1982) ECR 1891–1902
XXX	15.7.1982	Case 228/81	Pendy Plastic Products v Pluspunkt	Articles 20, paragraph 3 and 27(2)	(1982) ECR 2723/2737
XXXI	22.3.1983	Case 34/82	Peters v ZNAV	Article 5(1)	(1983) ECR 987–1004
XXXII	14.7.1983	Case 201/82	Gerling v Amminist-razione del Tesoro dello Stato	Articles 17 and 18	(1983) ECR 2503–2518
XXXIII	21.9.1983	(order) Case 157/82	Verheezen v Müller	Articles 1 and 50	—
XXXIV	15.11.1983	Case 288/82	Duijnstee v Goderbauer	Articles 16(4) and 19	(1983) ECR 3663–3679
XXXV	9.11.1983	(order) Case 80/83	Habourdin v Italocremona	Article 2 of Protocol of 3.6.1971	(1983) ECR 3639–3641
XXXVI	7.6.1984	Case 129/83	Zelger v Salinitri	Article 21	(1984) ECR 2397–2409
XXXVII	19.6.1984	Case 71/83	Russ v Goeminne	Article 17	(1984) ECR 2417–2436
XXXVIII	12.7.1984	Case 178/83	P v K	Article 40	(1984) ECR 3033–3043
XXXIX	27.11.1984	Case 258/83	Brennero v Wendel	Articles 37 and 38	(1984) ECR 3971–3984
XL	15.1.1985	Case 241/83	Rösler v Rottwinkel	Article 16(1)	(1985) ECR 99–129
XLI	7.3.1985	Case 48/84	Spitzley v Sommer	Articles 17 and 18	(1985) ECR 787–800
XLII	11.6.1985	Case 49/84	Debaecker & Plouvier v Bouwman	Article 27	(1985) ECR 1779–1803
XLIII	2.7.1985	Case 148/84	Genossenschaftsbank v Brasserie du Pêcheur	Article 36	(1985) ECR 1981–1993
XLIV	4.7.1985	Case 228/84	AS-Autoteile v Malhé	Article 16(5)	(1985) ECR 2267–2279
XLV	11.7.1985	Case 221/84	Berghoefer v ASA	Article 17	(1985) ECR 2699–2710
XLVI	3.10.1985	Case 119/84	Capelloni-Aquilini v Pelkmans	Article 39	(1985) ECR 3147–3164
XLVII	24.6.1986	Case 22/85	Anterist v Crédit Lyonnais	Article 17	OJ No C196, 5.8.1986, p 5
XLVIII	10.7.1986	Case 198/85	Carron v FRG	Article 33	OJ No C209, 20.8.1986, p 5

[OJ C189, 28.7.90, p 110]

XLIX	11.11.1986	Case 313/85	Iveco Fiat v Van Hool	Article 17	OJ No C308, 2.12.1986, p 4.
L	15.1.1987	Case 266/85	Shenavai v Kreischer	Article 5(1)	OJ No C39, 17.2.1987, p 3
LI	8.12.1987	Case 144/86	Gubisch v Palumbo	Article 21	OJ No C8, 13.1.1988, p 3.
LII	9.12.1987	Case 218/86	Schotte v Rothschild	Article 5(5)	OJ No C2, 6.1.1988, p 3
LIII	4.2.1988	Case 145/86	Hoffman v Krieg	Articles 26, 27, 31 and 36	OJ No C63, 8.3.1988, p 6
LIV	8.3.1988	Case 9/87	Arcado v Haviland	Article 5(1)	OJ No C89, 6.4.1988, p 9
LV	6.7.1988	Case 158/87	Scherens v Maenhout	Article 16(1)	OJ No C211, 11.8.1988, p 7
LVI	27.9.1988	Case 189/87	Kalfelis v Schröder	Articles 5(3) and 6(1)	OJ No C281, 4.11.1988, p 18.

4. Cases pending as at 1 February 1989

133. A number of applications for preliminary rulings are currently before the Court of Justice. The cases involved are as follows—

(a) Case 32/88 Six Constructions v Humbert
Article 5(1)—Contract of employment
What if a contract of employment is performed in a number of countries?
OJ No C55, 26.2.1988, p 12.

(b) Case 36/88 Schilling v Merbes
Article 27(2)
What if the defaulting defendant was not served with the document instituting proceedings in due form, albeit in sufficient time to enable him to arrange for his defence?
OJ No C79, 26.3.1988, p 4.
This case has been removed from the register following the withdrawal of the appeal.

(c) Case 115/88 Reichert-Kockler v Dresdner Bank
Article 16(1)—Concept of rights *in rem* in immovable property
OJ No C125, 12.5.1988, p 13.

(d) Case 220/88 Dumez Bâtiment SA v Hessische Landesbank
Article 5(3)
OJ No C226, 1.9.1988, p 6.

(e) Case 305/88 Lancray SA v Peters & Sickert KG
Article 27(2)
OJ No C300, 25.11.1988, p 10.

(f) Case 365/88 Congress Agentur Hagen GmbH/Zeehaghe BV
Article 5 (beginning) and point 1 and Article 6 (beginning) and point 2
OJ No C20, 26.1.1989, p 8.

[3075]

[OJ C189, 28.7.90, p 111]

ANNEX I

THE LAW IN FORCE IN THE EFTA MEMBER STATES CONCERNING THE RECOGNITION AND ENFORCEMENT OF FOREIGN JUDGMENTS

A. AUSTRIA

134. Foreign judgments in civil and commercial matters are not recognized and cannot be enforced in Austria unless a treaty is in force with the State in which the judgment was

given. However, foreign judgments concerning the status or legal capacity of persons are in most cases recognized even if there are no statutory provisions requiring such recognition. A foreign judgment which is neither recognized nor enforced in Austria may however have a certain evidential value there. The evidential value of a foreign judgment will depend on the circumstances in each particular case.

B. FINLAND AND SWEDEN

135. The main principle of Finnish and of Swedish law is that foreign judgments are neither recognized nor enforced, unless there is a statutory provision to the contrary. Such statutory provisions are very few and they are almost always based on international conventions or agreements. Most of these provisions cover only decisions dealing with rather special matters, such as some aspects of international carriage, maintenance or civil liability in the field of nuclear energy.

What has been mentioned above does, however, not apply to decisions relating to status and legal capacity. Those decisions are in most cases recognized even where there is no statutory provision ordering recognition.

The fact that a foreign judgment is, in the absence of a statutory provision to the contrary, neither recognized nor enforced in Finland and Sweden does not mean that such a foreign judgment is completely without value in those countries. Firstly a foreign judgment can be invoked as evidence concerning certain facts or the contents of applicable foreign law. According to Finnish and Swedish law there is, generally speaking, no "inadmissible" evidence at all. Within the framework of this principle, the court may take into consideration the facts established in foreign proceedings and the foreign courts' legal reasoning. Naturally this evidential value of a foreign judgment will depend on the circumstances in each particular case, especially on the degree of confidence in the foreign court. In some situations, particularly when according to the rules on conflict of laws the dispute is to be decided by the substantive law of the foreign court and the foreign court has applied the same law (*lex fori*), the foreign judgment may shift the burden of proof to the party challenging its outcome. If the judgment of a foreign court relates to immovable property within its jurisdiction there will—at least in most cases—be no review of the substance of the dispute.

Secondly, a foreign judgment may be of great value in Finland and Sweden also in those cases where Finnish and Swedish courts do not have jurisdiction and where a party nevertheless has an interest to rely upon the judgment in the country concerned, e g in order to obtain enforcement of a money judgment. If, for instance, a foreign court according to a forum-selection clause has exclusive jurisdiction for a dispute, Finnish and Swedish courts will usually decline jurisdiction. The judgment of the chosen foreign court (*forum prorogatum*) cannot, however, be enforced in Finland or Sweden as such. The plaintiff (the creditor) can in this situation sue in a Finnish or Swedish court invoking the foreign judgment. The court will, under such circumstances, most probably abstain from considering the merits of the case and base its decision on the foreign judgment. In any case there will be no complete review of the merits (révision au fond) of the foreign judgment.

C. ICELAND

136. The main principle of Icelandic law is that foreign judgments are neither recognized nor enforced, unless there is a statutory provision to the contrary. Such provisions have hitherto always been based on international conventions. However, foreign judgments concerning the status or legal capacity of a natural person are usually recognized even if there is no statutory provision ordering recognition. Foreign judgments which are neither recognized nor enforced in Iceland can, however, have a certain evidential value there. This is mainly due to the fact that there is, generally speaking, no inadmissible evidence in Icelandic courts. The findings of fact in a foreign judgment are therefore likely to have a certain relevance.

[OJ C189, 28.7.90, p 112]

D. NORWAY

137. Foreign judgments in civil and commercial matters are not recognized and may not be enforced in Norway unless there is a treaty with the State in which the judgment in question was rendered.

However, foreign judgments concerning the status or legal capacity of a natural person are recognized in Norway even if there is no treaty with the State in question, provided that certain criteria are fulfilled.

As regards jurisdiction and enforcement of judgments based on a convention conferring jurisdiction, Norway operates a procedure similar to those applying in Finland and Sweden (see point 135 above).

The remarks in point 135 above on the evidential validity of a foreign judgment also apply to Norway.

E. SWITZERLAND

138. In Switzerland, the rules relating to international jurisdiction and the principles governing the recognition and enforcement of foreign judgments were until very recently scattered among several legal sources, these being partly federal and partly cantonal. On a number of matters relevant to international jurisdiction, neither federal law nor cantonal law contained explicit rules. In such situations the principles of intercantonal law were applied by analogy to international cases.

On 18 December 1987, the Swiss Parliament passed a new Act on Private International Law. The new law, which will come into force on 1 January 1989, contains provisions on the international jurisdiction of Swiss Courts and on the recognition and enforcement of judgments in civil and commercial matters. These provisions replace the present provisions of cantonal and federal law concerning jurisdiction and recognition and enforcement of judgments. Thus, the recognition and enforcement of judgments in civil and commercial matters will in its entirety be governed by federal law, which prevails over the cantonal laws. According to the APIL, reciprocity will no longer be a formal requirement for obtaining recognition or enforcement of foreign judgments. In fact, the effects of the reciprocity-test are replaced by the new system of control of jurisdiction of the State of origin.

— According to Article 25 of the APIL, a foreign judgment will be recognized in Switzerland—

(a) if the courts of the State of origin had jurisdiction according to the APIL;
(b) if the judgment is no longer subject to ordinary forms of review or if the judgment is final;
(c) if there is no ground for refusal mentioned in APIL Article 27.

— A foreign court is according to APIL Article 26 considered to have jurisdiction—

(a) if this follows from a provision in the APIL (eg Articles 112 to 115 as regards contracts and civil liability, and Articles 151 to 153 as regards company law) or, in the absence of such a provision, if the defendant had his domicile in the State of origin;
(b) in the case of dispute concerning a sum of money, if the parties have agreed that the court which has given the judgment had jurisdiction and this agreement was not invalid according to the provisions of the APIL,
(c) in the case of a dispute concerning a sum of money, if the defendant has argued the merits without challenging the jurisdiction of the court or making any reservation thereon (*exceptio incompetentiae internationalis*),

[OJ C189, 28.7.90, p 113]

(d) in the case of a counterclaim, if the court had jurisdiction to try the principal claim and the principal claim and the counterclaim were interrelated.

— A foreign judgment will, according to Article 27, paragraph 1 of the APIL, not be recognized if recognition would be manifestly incompatible with the public policy of Switzerland.

— Recognition of a judgment will, according to Article 27, paragraph 2, also be refused at the request of a party against whom it is invoked if that party furnishes proof—

(a) that he was, neither according to the law of his domicile nor according to the law of his habitual residence, duly served with the document which instituted the proceedings, unless he has argued the merits without reservation;
(b) that the judgment resulted from proceedings incompatible with fundamental principles of the Swiss law of procedure, especially that the party concerned has not had an opportunity to defend himself;
(c) that proceedings between the same parties and concerning the same matter
    (i) are already pending before a court in Switzerland,
    (ii) have resulted in a decision by a Swiss court, or
    (iii) have resulted in an earlier judgment by a court of a third State which fulfills the conditions for recognition in Switzerland.

— Under Article 29, paragraph 1, a judgment which is recognized according to Articles 25 to 27 of the APIL will be enforced in Switzerland, on the application of any interested party. The application for enforcement must be submitted to the competent authority of the canton where the foreign judgment is invoked. The following documents must be attached to the application—

(a) a complete and authenticated copy of the decision;
(b) an attestation according to which the judgment is no longer subject to the ordinary forms of review in the State of origin or that it is final;
(c) if the judgment was rendered by default, an official document establishing that the defaulting party was served with the document instituting the proceedings and had an opportunity to defend himself.

In the proceedings for recognition and enforcement the party against whom enforcement is sought must be heard (Article 29, paragraph 2).

[3076]

[OJ C189, 28.7.90, p 114]

ANNEX II
EXISTING CONVENTIONS WHICH CONCERN THE EFTA MEMBER STATES

139. Apart from conventions dealing with particular matters, various conventions on recognition and enforcement of judgments exist between certain EFTA Member States and certain States of the European Communities. These are the conventions listed in Article 55 of the Lugano Convention between Denmark, Finland, Iceland, Norway and Sweden, the bilateral treaties concluded between Austria and Belgium, Spain, France, Italy, Luxembourg, the Netherlands, the Federal Republic of Germany and the United Kingdom, and the bilateral treaties concluded between the Swiss Confederation and Belgium, Spain, France, Italy, Norway and the Federal Republic of Germany and between Norway and the United Kingdom and the Federal Republic of Germany.

In addition to conventions dealing with particular matters, various conventions on recognition and enforcement also exist between the EFTA Member States. These are the abovementioned convention between Denmark, Finland, Iceland, Norway and Sweden, the bilateral conventions concluded by Austria with Finland, Norway, Sweden and the Swiss Confederation and the bilateral convention between Sweden and the Swiss Confederation listed in Article 55 of the Lugano Convention. Thus, relations between Switzerland on the one hand, and Finland, Iceland and Norway on the other hand, as well as relations between Austria and Iceland, are hampered by the absence of such conventions.

There are also differences between the various conventions. The convention between Switzerland and France is based on "direct" jurisdiction; but all the others are based on "indirect" jurisdiction. There are also various other differences between these conventions which need not be discussed in detail; they relate in particular to the determination of courts with jurisdiction and to the conditions governing recognition and enforcement.

[3077]

[OJ C189, 28.7.90, p 115]

ANNEX III
FINAL ACT

The representatives of

THE GOVERNMENT OF THE KINGDOM OF BELGIUM,

THE GOVERNMENT OF THE KINGDOM OF DENMARK,

THE GOVERNMENT OF THE FEDERAL REPUBLIC OF GERMANY,

THE GOVERNMENT OF THE HELLENIC REPUBLIC,

THE GOVERNMENT OF THE KINGDOM OF SPAIN,

THE GOVERNMENT OF THE FRENCH REPUBLIC,

THE GOVERNMENT OF IRELAND,

THE GOVERNMENT OF THE REPUBLIC OF ICELAND,

THE GOVERNMENT OF THE ITALIAN REPUBLIC,

THE GOVERNMENT OF THE GRAND DUCHY OF LUXEMBOURG,

THE GOVERNMENT OF THE KINGDOM OF THE NETHERLANDS,

THE GOVERNMENT OF THE KINGDOM OF NORWAY,

THE GOVERNMENT OF THE REPUBLIC OF AUSTRIA,

THE GOVERNMENT OF THE PORTUGUESE REPUBLIC,

THE GOVERNMENT OF THE KINGDOM OF SWEDEN,

THE GOVERNMENT OF THE SWISS CONFEDERATION,

THE GOVERNMENT OF THE REPUBLIC OF FINLAND,

THE GOVERNMENT OF THE UNITED KINGDOM OF GREAT BRITAIN AND NORTHERN IRELAND,

Assembled at Lugano on the sixteenth day of September in the year one thousand nine hundred and eighty-eight on the occasion of the Diplomatic Conference on jurisdiction in civil matters, have placed on record the fact that the following texts have been drawn up and adopted within the Conference—

I. the Convention on jurisdiction and the enforcement of judgments in civil and commercial matters;

II. the following Protocols, which form an integral part of the Convention—
— 1, on certain questions of jurisdiction, procedure and enforcement,
— 2, on the uniform interpretation of the Convention,
— 3, on the application of Article 57;

III. (*Contains the declarations by the representatives and their signatures.*)

[3078]

NOTES

1 Belgium, Federal Republic of Germany, France, Italy, Luxembourg and the Netherlands.

2 Convention of 9 October 1978 on the accession of Denmark, Ireland and the United Kingdom of Great Britain and Northern Ireland (OJ No L304, 30.10.1978) and Convention of 25 October 1982 on the accession of Greece (OJ No L388, 31.12.1982).

3 The Jenard and Schlosser reports were published on OJ No C59, 15.3.1979. The report by Mr Evrigenis and Mr Kerameus was published in OJ No C298, 24.11.1986.

4 In order to align the United Kingdom concept of domicile on that of many continental countries the Civil Jurisdiction Act 1982, introducing the Convention into United Kingdom law, deals with the matter in Section 41. According to the Act, a person is deemed to have his domicile in the United Kingdom if he resides there and the nature and circumstances of his residence show there to be an effective link between his residence and the United Kingdom. For Ireland, see the Jurisdiction of Courts and Enforcement of Judgments (European Communities) Act 1988, Sections 13 and 5 in the Schedule.

5 Article 6 of the Rome Convention provides that—

"1. Notwithstanding the provisions of Article 3, in a contract of employment a choice of law made by the parties shall not have the result of depriving the employee of the protection afforded to him by the mandatory rules of the law which would be applicable under paragraph 2 in the absence of choice.

2. Notwithstanding the provisions of Article 4, a contract of employment shall, in the absence of choice in accordance with Article 3, be governed—

(a) by the law of the country in which the employee habitually carries out his work in performance of the contract, even if he is temporarily employed in another country; or

(b) if the employee does not habitually carry out his work in any one country, by the law of the country in which the place of business through which he was engaged is situated—

unless it appears from the circumstances as a whole that the contract is more closely connected with another country, in which case the contract shall be governed by the law of that country.

If the persons against whom eviction proceedings are brought fail to appear in the manner and time specified, the period allowed for replying to the action shall be extended in respect of the purchaser."

6 These international agreements are numerous and relate to fields as varied as inland waterway transport, transport by sea, air, road and rail, and maintenance obligations. See, for instance, Jenard report, pp 59 and 60.

7 In the course of the negotiations no account was taken of the distinction between "Contracting State" and "party" made in the Vienna Convention on the Law of Treaties (Article 2(f) and (g)). As in the Brussels Convention, the term "Contracting State" refers both to a State which has consented to be bound by the Convention, either by ratifying it or by acceding to it, and to a State in respect of which the Convention has entered into force.

8

— Non-European dependent territories of the United Kingdom, which have expressed interest in participating in the EEC/EFTA Convention on jurisdiction and the

PART IV EC MATERIALS

enforcement of judgments in civil and commercial matters: Anguilla, Bermuda, British Virgin Islands, Montserrat and Turks and Caicos Islands, Hong Kong.

— Non-European dependent territories of the United Kingdom other than those mentioned above—

— Caribbean and North Atlantic: Cayman Islands,

— South Atlantic: British Antarctic Territory, Falkland Islands, South Georgia and the South Sandwich Islands, St Helena and dependencies (Ascension Island) (Tristan da Cunha),

— Indian Ocean: British Indian Ocean Territory,

— South Pacific: Pitcairn Island, Henderson, Ducie and Oeno.

9 Article 59 of the Federal Constitution states that—

"1. For the purposes of personal claims a solvent debtor domiciled in Switzerland must be sued before the court for his domicile; his property may not therefore be seized or sequestrated outside the canton in which he is domiciled, in pursuance of personal claims.

2. In the case of foreign nationals this is without prejudice to the provisions of international treaties."

* Article 1482 of the Spanish Civil Code: by the Code of Civil Procedure for replying to the action, that it be served on the vendor(s) as soon as possible.

Service shall be in the manner specified in the said Code for service on defendants.

The time limit for reply by the purchaser shall be suspended until the expiry of the period notified to the vendor(s) for appearing and replying to the action, which shall correspond to the periods laid down for all defendants by the Code of Civil Procedure and shall run from the date of the service referred to in paragraph 1 of this Article.

If the persons against whom eviction proceedings are brought fail to appear in the manner and time specified, the period allowed for replying to the action shall be extended in respect of the purchaser."

10 It should be noted that to date one draft Regulation contains such provisions.

11 Much of this section is taken from Weser-Jenard: Manuel de droit international privé Van der Elst, Volume II: Les conflits de juridictions, Bruylant, Brussels, 1985.

COUNCIL REGULATION

of 22 December 2000

on jurisdiction and the recognition and enforcement of judgments in civil and commercial matters

(44/2001/EC)

NOTES

Date of original publication in OJ: OJ L12, 16.1.2001, p 1, reproduced as corrected by corrigendum at OJ L307, 24.11.2001, p 28 and as subsequently amended.

For current status of Council Regulation 44/2001/EC, see Table 1 at **[4676]**.

THE COUNCIL OF THE EUROPEAN UNION,

Having regard to the Treaty establishing the European Community, and in particular Article 61(c) and Article 67(1) thereof,

Having regard to the proposal from the Commission,[1]

Having regard to the opinion of the European Parliament,[2]

Having regard to the opinion of the Economic and Social Committee,[3]

Whereas:

(1) The Community has set itself the objective of maintaining and developing an area of freedom, security and justice, in which the free movement of persons is ensured. In order to establish progressively such an area, the Community should adopt, amongst other things, the measures relating to judicial cooperation in civil matters which are necessary for the sound operation of the internal market.

(2) Certain differences between national rules governing jurisdiction and recognition of judgments hamper the sound operation of the internal market. Provisions to unify the rules of conflict of jurisdiction in civil and commercial matters and to simplify the formalities with a view to rapid and simple recognition and enforcement of judgments from Member States bound by this Regulation are essential.

(3) This area is within the field of judicial cooperation in civil matters within the meaning of Article 65 of the Treaty.

(4) In accordance with the principles of subsidiarity and proportionality as set out in Article 5 of the Treaty, the objectives of this Regulation cannot be sufficiently achieved by the Member States and can therefore be better achieved by the Community. This Regulation confines itself to the minimum required in order to achieve those objectives and does not go beyond what is necessary for that purpose.

(5) On 27 September 1968 the Member States, acting under Article 293, fourth indent, of the Treaty, concluded the Brussels Convention on Jurisdiction and the Enforcement of Judgments in Civil and Commercial Matters, as amended by Conventions on the Accession of the New Member States to that Convention (hereinafter referred to as the "Brussels Convention").[4] On 16 September 1988 Member States and EFTA States concluded the Lugano Convention on Jurisdiction and the Enforcement of Judgments in Civil and Commercial Matters, which is a parallel Convention to the 1968 Brussels Convention. Work has been undertaken for the revision of those Conventions, and the Council has approved the content of the revised texts. Continuity in the results achieved in that revision should be ensured.

(6) In order to attain the objective of free movement of judgments in civil and commercial matters, it is necessary and appropriate that the rules governing jurisdiction and the recognition and enforcement of judgments be governed by a Community legal instrument which is binding and directly applicable.

(7) The scope of this Regulation must cover all the main civil and commercial matters apart from certain well-defined matters.

(8) There must be a link between proceedings to which this Regulation applies and the territory of the Member States bound by this Regulation. Accordingly common rules on jurisdiction should, in principle, apply when the defendant is domiciled in one of those Member States.

(9) A defendant not domiciled in a Member State is in general subject to national rules of jurisdiction applicable in the territory of the Member State of the court seised, and a defendant domiciled in a Member State not bound by this Regulation must remain subject to the Brussels Convention.

(10) For the purposes of the free movement of judgments, judgments given in a Member State bound by this Regulation should be recognised and enforced in another Member State bound by this Regulation, even if the judgment debtor is domiciled in a third State.

(11) The rules of jurisdiction must be highly predictable and founded on the principle that jurisdiction is generally based on the defendant's domicile and jurisdiction must always be available on this ground save in a few well-defined situations in which the subject-matter of the litigation or the autonomy of the parties warrants a different linking factor. The domicile of a legal person must be defined autonomously so as to make the common rules more transparent and avoid conflicts of jurisdiction.

(12) In addition to the defendant's domicile, there should be alternative grounds of jurisdiction based on a close link between the court and the action or in order to facilitate the sound administration of justice.

(13) In relation to insurance, consumer contracts and employment, the weaker party should be protected by rules of jurisdiction more favourable to his interests than the general rules provide for.

(14) The autonomy of the parties to a contract, other than an insurance, consumer or employment contract, where only limited autonomy to determine the courts having jurisdiction is allowed, must be respected subject to the exclusive grounds of jurisdiction laid down in this Regulation.

(15) In the interests of the harmonious administration of justice it is necessary to minimise the possibility of concurrent proceedings and to ensure that irreconcilable judgments will not be given in two Member States. There must be a clear and effective mechanism for resolving cases of lis pendens and related actions and for obviating problems flowing from national differences as to the determination of the time when a case is regarded as pending. For the purposes of this Regulation that time should be defined autonomously.

(16) Mutual trust in the administration of justice in the Community justifies judgments given in a Member State being recognised automatically without the need for any procedure except in cases of dispute.

(17) By virtue of the same principle of mutual trust, the procedure for making enforceable in one Member State a judgment given in another must be efficient and rapid. To that end, the declaration that a judgment is enforceable should be issued virtually automatically after purely formal checks of the documents supplied, without there being any possibility for the court to raise of its own motion any of the grounds for non-enforcement provided for by this Regulation.

(18) However, respect for the rights of the defence means that the defendant should be able to appeal in an adversarial procedure, against the declaration of enforceability, if he

considers one of the grounds for non-enforcement to be present. Redress procedures should also be available to the claimant where his application for a declaration of enforceability has been rejected.

(19) Continuity between the Brussels Convention and this Regulation should be ensured, and transitional provisions should be laid down to that end. The same need for continuity applies as regards the interpretation of the Brussels Convention by the Court of Justice of the European Communities and the 1971 Protocol[5] should remain applicable also to cases already pending when this Regulation enters into force.

(20) The United Kingdom and Ireland, in accordance with Article 3 of the Protocol on the position of the United Kingdom and Ireland annexed to the Treaty on European Union and to the Treaty establishing the European Community, have given notice of their wish to take part in the adoption and application of this Regulation.

(21) Denmark, in accordance with Articles 1 and 2 of the Protocol on the position of Denmark annexed to the Treaty on European Union and to the Treaty establishing the European Community, is not participating in the adoption of this Regulation, and is therefore not bound by it nor subject to its application.

(22) Since the Brussels Convention remains in force in relations between Denmark and the Member States that are bound by this Regulation, both the Convention and the 1971 Protocol continue to apply between Denmark and the Member States bound by this Regulation.

(23) The Brussels Convention also continues to apply to the territories of the Member States which fall within the territorial scope of that Convention and which are excluded from this Regulation pursuant to Article 299 of the Treaty.

(24) Likewise for the sake of consistency, this Regulation should not affect rules governing jurisdiction and the recognition of judgments contained in specific Community instruments.

(25) Respect for international commitments entered into by the Member States means that this Regulation should not affect conventions relating to specific matters to which the Member States are parties.

(26) The necessary flexibility should be provided for in the basic rules of this Regulation in order to take account of the specific procedural rules of certain Member States. Certain provisions of the Protocol annexed to the Brussels Convention should accordingly be incorporated in this Regulation.

(27) In order to allow a harmonious transition in certain areas which were the subject of special provisions in the Protocol annexed to the Brussels Convention, this Regulation lays down, for a transitional period, provisions taking into consideration the specific situation in certain Member States.

(28) No later than five years after entry into force of this Regulation the Commission will present a report on its application and, if need be, submit proposals for adaptations.

(29) The Commission will have to adjust Annexes I to IV on the rules of national jurisdiction, the courts or competent authorities and redress procedures available on the basis of the amendments forwarded by the Member State concerned; amendments made to Annexes V and VI should be adopted in accordance with Council Decision 1999/468/EC of 28 June 1999 laying down the procedures for the exercise of implementing powers conferred on the Commission,[6]

[3079]

NOTES

1 OJ C376, 28.12.1999, p 1.
2 Opinion delivered on 21 September 2000 (not yet published in the Official Journal).
3 OJ C117, 26.4.2000, p 6.
4 OJ L299, 31.12.1972, p 32; OJ L304, 30.10.1978, p 1; OJ L388, 31.12.1982, p 1; OJ L285, 3.10.1989, p 1; OJ C15, 15.1.1997, p 1. For a consolidated text, see OJ C27, 26.1.1998, p 1.
5 OJ L204, 2.8.1975, p 28; OJ L304, 30.10.1978, p 1; OJ L388, 31.12.1982, p 1; OJ L285, 3.10.1989, p 1; OJ C15, 15.1.1997, p 1. For a consolidated text see OJ C27, 26.1.1998, p 28.
6 OJ L184, 17.7.1999, p 23.

HAS ADOPTED THIS REGULATION—

CHAPTER I
SCOPE

Article 1

1. This Regulation shall apply in civil and commercial matters whatever the nature of the court or tribunal. It shall not extend, in particular, to revenue, customs or administrative matters.

2. The Regulation shall not apply to:

(a) the status or legal capacity of natural persons, rights in property arising out of a matrimonial relationship, wills and succession;

(b) bankruptcy, proceedings relating to the winding-up of insolvent companies or other legal persons, judicial arrangements, compositions and analogous proceedings;

(c) social security;

(d) arbitration.

3. In this Regulation, the term "Member State" shall mean Member States with the exception of Denmark.

[3080]

CHAPTER II
JURISDICTION

SECTION 1
GENERAL PROVISIONS

Article 2

1. Subject to this Regulation, persons domiciled in a Member State shall, whatever their nationality, be sued in the courts of that Member State.

2. Persons who are not nationals of the Member State in which they are domiciled shall be governed by the rules of jurisdiction applicable to nationals of that State.

[3081]

Article 3

1. Persons domiciled in a Member State may be sued in the courts of another Member State only by virtue of the rules set out in Sections 2 to 7 of this Chapter.

2. In particular the rules of national jurisdiction set out in Annex I shall not be applicable as against them.

[3082]

Article 4

1. If the defendant is not domiciled in a Member State, the jurisdiction of the courts of each Member State shall, subject to Articles 22 and 23, be determined by the law of that Member State.

2. As against such a defendant, any person domiciled in a Member State may, whatever his nationality, avail himself in that State of the rules of jurisdiction there in force, and in particular those specified in Annex I, in the same way as the nationals of that State.

[3083]

SECTION 2
SPECIAL JURISDICTION

Article 5

A person domiciled in a Member State may, in another Member State, be sued:

1.

(a) in matters relating to a contract, in the courts for the place of performance of the obligation in question;

(b) for the purpose of this provision and unless otherwise agreed, the place of performance of the obligation in question shall be:
—in the case of the sale of goods, the place in a Member State where, under the contract, the goods were delivered or should have been delivered,
—in the case of the provision of services, the place in a Member State where, under the contract, the services were provided or should have been provided,

(c) if subparagraph (b) does not apply then subparagraph (a) applies;

2. in matters relating to maintenance, in the courts for the place where the maintenance creditor is domiciled or habitually resident or, if the matter is ancillary to proceedings concerning the status of a person, in the court which, according to its own law, has jurisdiction to entertain those proceedings, unless that jurisdiction is based solely on the nationality of one of the parties;

3. in matters relating to tort, delict or quasi-delict, in the courts for the place where the harmful event occurred or may occur;

4. as regards a civil claim for damages or restitution which is based on an act giving rise to criminal proceedings, in the court seised of those proceedings, to the extent that that court has jurisdiction under its own law to entertain civil proceedings;

5. as regards a dispute arising out of the operations of a branch, agency or other establishment, in the courts for the place in which the branch, agency or other establishment is situated;

6. as settlor, trustee or beneficiary of a trust created by the operation of a statute, or by a written instrument, or created orally and evidenced in writing, in the courts of the Member State in which the trust is domiciled;

7. as regards a dispute concerning the payment of remuneration claimed in respect of the salvage of a cargo or freight, in the court under the authority of which the cargo or freight in question:

(a) has been arrested to secure such payment, or

(b) could have been so arrested, but bail or other security has been given;

provided that this provision shall apply only if it is claimed that the defendant has an interest in the cargo or freight or had such an interest at the time of salvage.

[3084]

Article 6

A person domiciled in a Member State may also be sued:

1. where he is one of a number of defendants, in the courts for the place where any one of them is domiciled, provided the claims are so closely connected that it is expedient to hear and determine them together to avoid the risk of irreconcilable judgments resulting from separate proceedings;

2. as a third party in an action on a warranty or guarantee or in any other third party proceedings, in the court seised of the original proceedings, unless these were instituted solely with the object of removing him from the jurisdiction of the court which would be competent in his case;

3. on a counter-claim arising from the same contract or facts on which the original claim was based, in the court in which the original claim is pending;

4. in matters relating to a contract, if the action may be combined with an action against the same defendant in matters relating to rights in rem in immovable property, in the court of the Member State in which the property is situated.

[3085]

Article 7

Where by virtue of this Regulation a court of a Member State has jurisdiction in actions relating to liability from the use or operation of a ship, that court, or any other court substituted for this purpose by the internal law of that Member State, shall also have jurisdiction over claims for limitation of such liability.

[3086]

SECTION 3
JURISDICTION IN MATTERS RELATING TO INSURANCE

Article 8

In matters relating to insurance, jurisdiction shall be determined by this Section, without prejudice to Article 4 and point 5 of Article 5.

[3087]

Article 9

1. An insurer domiciled in a Member State may be sued:
   (a) in the courts of the Member State where he is domiciled, or
   (b) in another Member State, in the case of actions brought by the policyholder, the insured or a beneficiary, in the courts for the place where the plaintiff is domiciled,
   (c) if he is a co-insurer, in the courts of a Member State in which proceedings are brought against the leading insurer.

2. An insurer who is not domiciled in a Member State but has a branch, agency or other establishment in one of the Member States shall, in disputes arising out of the operations of the branch, agency or establishment, be deemed to be domiciled in that Member State.

[3088]

Article 10

In respect of liability insurance or insurance of immovable property, the insurer may in addition be sued in the courts for the place where the harmful event occurred. The same applies if movable and immovable property are covered by the same insurance policy and both are adversely affected by the same contingency.

[3089]

Article 11

1. In respect of liability insurance, the insurer may also, if the law of the court permits it, be joined in proceedings which the injured party has brought against the insured.

2. Articles 8, 9 and 10 shall apply to actions brought by the injured party directly against the insurer, where such direct actions are permitted.

3. If the law governing such direct actions provides that the policyholder or the insured may be joined as a party to the action, the same court shall have jurisdiction over them.

[3090]

Article 12

1. Without prejudice to Article 11(3), an insurer may bring proceedings only in the courts of the Member State in which the defendant is domiciled, irrespective of whether he is the policyholder, the insured or a beneficiary.

2. The provisions of this Section shall not affect the right to bring a counter-claim in the court in which, in accordance with this Section, the original claim is pending.

[3091]

Article 13

The provisions of this Section may be departed from only by an agreement:

1. which is entered into after the dispute has arisen, or
2. which allows the policyholder, the insured or a beneficiary to bring proceedings in courts other than those indicated in this Section, or
3. which is concluded between a policyholder and an insurer, both of whom are at the time of conclusion of the contract domiciled or habitually resident in the same Member State, and which has the effect of conferring jurisdiction on the courts of that State even if the harmful event were to occur abroad, provided that such an agreement is not contrary to the law of that State, or
4. which is concluded with a policyholder who is not domiciled in a Member State, except in so far as the insurance is compulsory or relates to immovable property in a Member State, or

5. which relates to a contract of insurance in so far as it covers one or more of the risks set out in Article 14.

[3092]

Article 14

The following are the risks referred to in Article 13(5):

1. any loss of or damage to:
   (a) seagoing ships, installations situated offshore or on the high seas, or aircraft, arising from perils which relate to their use for commercial purposes;
   (b goods in transit other than passengers' baggage where the transit consists of or includes carriage by such ships or aircraft;

2. any liability, other than for bodily injury to passengers or loss of or damage to their baggage:
   (a) arising out of the use or operation of ships, installations or aircraft as referred to in point 1(a) in so far as, in respect of the latter, the law of the Member State in which such aircraft are registered does not prohibit agreements on jurisdiction regarding insurance of such risks;
   (b) for loss or damage caused by goods in transit as described in point 1(b);

3. any financial loss connected with the use or operation of ships, installations or aircraft as referred to in point 1(a), in particular loss of freight or charter-hire;

4. any risk or interest connected with any of those referred to in points 1 to 3;

5. notwithstanding points 1 to 4, all "large risks" as defined in Council Directive 73/239/EEC,[1] as amended by Council Directives 88/357/EEC[2] and 90/618/EEC,[3] as they may be amended.

[3093]

NOTES

[1] OJ L228, 16.8.1973, p 3. Directive as last amended by Directive 2000/26/EC of the European Parliament and of the Council (OJ L181, 20.7.2000, p 65).
[2] OJ L172, 4.7.1988, p 1. Directive as last amended by Directive 2000/26/EC.
[3] OJ L330, 29.11.1990, p 44.

SECTION 4
JURISDICTION OVER CONSUMER CONTRACTS

Article 15

1. In matters relating to a contract concluded by a person, the consumer, for a purpose which can be regarded as being outside his trade or profession, jurisdiction shall be determined by this Section, without prejudice to Article 4 and point 5 of Article 5, if:
   (a) it is a contract for the sale of goods on instalment credit terms; or
   (b) it is a contract for a loan repayable by instalments, or for any other form of credit, made to finance the sale of goods; or
   (c) in all other cases, the contract has been concluded with a person who pursues commercial or professional activities in the Member State of the consumer's domicile or, by any means, directs such activities to that Member State or to several States including that Member State, and the contract falls within the scope of such activities.

2. Where a consumer enters into a contract with a party who is not domiciled in the Member State but has a branch, agency or other establishment in one of the Member States, that party shall, in disputes arising out of the operations of the branch, agency or establishment, be deemed to be domiciled in that State.

3. This Section shall not apply to a contract of transport other than a contract which, for an inclusive price, provides for a combination of travel and accommodation.

[3094]

Article 16

1. A consumer may bring proceedings against the other party to a contract either in the courts of the Member State in which that party is domiciled or in the courts for the place where the consumer is domiciled.

2. Proceedings may be brought against a consumer by the other party to the contract only in the courts of the Member State in which the consumer is domiciled.

3. This Article shall not affect the right to bring a counter-claim in the court in which, in accordance with this Section, the original claim is pending.

[3095]

Article 17

The provisions of this Section may be departed from only by an agreement:

1. which is entered into after the dispute has arisen; or

2. which allows the consumer to bring proceedings in courts other than those indicated in this Section; or

3. which is entered into by the consumer and the other party to the contract, both of whom are at the time of conclusion of the contract domiciled or habitually resident in the same Member State, and which confers jurisdiction on the courts of that Member State, provided that such an agreement is not contrary to the law of that Member State.

[3096]

SECTION 5
JURISDICTION OVER INDIVIDUAL CONTRACTS OF EMPLOYMENT

Article 18

1. In matters relating to individual contracts of employment, jurisdiction shall be determined by this Section, without prejudice to Article 4 and point 5 of Article 5.

2. Where an employee enters into an individual contract of employment with an employer who is not domiciled in a Member State but has a branch, agency or other establishment in one of the Member States, the employer shall, in disputes arising out of the operations of the branch, agency or establishment, be deemed to be domiciled in that Member State.

[3097]

Article 19

An employer domiciled in a Member State may be sued:

1. in the courts of the Member State where he is domiciled; or

2. in another Member State:
   (a) in the courts for the place where the employee habitually carries out his work or in the courts for the last place where he did so, or
   (b) if the employee does not or did not habitually carry out his work in any one country, in the courts for the place where the business which engaged the employee is or was situated.

[3098]

Article 20

1. An employer may bring proceedings only in the courts of the Member State in which the employee is domiciled.

2. The provisions of this Section shall not affect the right to bring a counter-claim in the court in which, in accordance with this Section, the original claim is pending.

[3099]

Article 21

The provisions of this Section may be departed from only by an agreement on jurisdiction:

1. which is entered into after the dispute has arisen; or

2. which allows the employee to bring proceedings in courts other than those indicated in this Section.

[3100]

SECTION 6
EXCLUSIVE JURISDICTION

Article 22

The following courts shall have exclusive jurisdiction, regardless of domicile:

1. in proceedings which have as their object rights in rem in immovable property or tenancies of immovable property, the courts of the Member State in which the property is situated.

However, in proceedings which have as their object tenancies of immovable property concluded for temporary private use for a maximum period of six consecutive months, the courts of the Member State in which the defendant is domiciled shall also have jurisdiction, provided that the tenant is a natural person and that the landlord and the tenant are domiciled in the same Member State;

2. in proceedings which have as their object the validity of the constitution, the nullity or the dissolution of companies or other legal persons or associations of natural or legal persons, or of the validity of the decisions of their organs, the courts of the Member State in which the company, legal person or association has its seat. In order to determine that seat, the court shall apply its rules of private international law;

3. in proceedings which have as their object the validity of entries in public registers, the courts of the Member State in which the register is kept;

4. in proceedings concerned with the registration or validity of patents, trade marks, designs, or other similar rights required to be deposited or registered, the courts of the Member State in which the deposit or registration has been applied for, has taken place or is under the terms of a Community instrument or an international convention deemed to have taken place.

Without prejudice to the jurisdiction of the European Patent Office under the Convention on the Grant of European Patents, signed at Munich on 5 October 1973, the courts of each Member State shall have exclusive jurisdiction, regardless of domicile, in proceedings concerned with the registration or validity of any European patent granted for that State;

5. in proceedings concerned with the enforcement of judgments, the courts of the Member State in which the judgment has been or is to be enforced.

[3101]

SECTION 7
PROROGATION OF JURISDICTION

Article 23

1. If the parties, one or more of whom is domiciled in a Member State, have agreed that a court or the courts of a Member State are to have jurisdiction to settle any disputes which have arisen or which may arise in connection with a particular legal relationship, that court or those courts shall have jurisdiction. Such jurisdiction shall be exclusive unless the parties have agreed otherwise. Such an agreement conferring jurisdiction shall be either:

(a) in writing or evidenced in writing; or

(b) in a form which accords with practices which the parties have established between themselves; or

(c) in international trade or commerce, in a form which accords with a usage of which the parties are or ought to have been aware and which in such trade or commerce is widely known to, and regularly observed by, parties to contracts of the type involved in the particular trade or commerce concerned.

2. Any communication by electronic means which provides a durable record of the agreement shall be equivalent to "writing".

3. Where such an agreement is concluded by parties, none of whom is domiciled in a Member State, the courts of other Member States shall have no jurisdiction over their disputes unless the court or courts chosen have declined jurisdiction.

4. The court or courts of a Member State on which a trust instrument has conferred jurisdiction shall have exclusive jurisdiction in any proceedings brought against a settlor, trustee or beneficiary, if relations between these persons or their rights or obligations under the trust are involved.

5. Agreements or provisions of a trust instrument conferring jurisdiction shall have no legal force if they are contrary to Articles 13, 17 or 21, or if the courts whose jurisdiction they purport to exclude have exclusive jurisdiction by virtue of Article 22.

[3102]

Article 24

Apart from jurisdiction derived from other provisions of this Regulation, a court of a Member State before which a defendant enters an appearance shall have jurisdiction. This rule shall not apply where appearance was entered to contest the jurisdiction, or where another court has exclusive jurisdiction by virtue of Article 22.

[3103]

SECTION 8
EXAMINATION AS TO JURISDICTION AND ADMISSIBILITY

Article 25

Where a court of a Member State is seised of a claim which is principally concerned with a matter over which the courts of another Member State have exclusive jurisdiction by virtue of Article 22, it shall declare of its own motion that it has no jurisdiction.

[3104]

Article 26

1. Where a defendant domiciled in one Member State is sued in a court of another Member State and does not enter an appearance, the court shall declare of its own motion that it has no jurisdiction unless its jurisdiction is derived from the provisions of this Regulation.

2. The court shall stay the proceedings so long as it is not shown that the defendant has been able to receive the document instituting the proceedings or an equivalent document in sufficient time to enable him to arrange for his defence, or that all necessary steps have been taken to this end.

3. Article 19 of Council Regulation (EC) No 1348/2000 of 29 May 2000 on the service in the Member States of judicial and extrajudicial documents in civil or commercial matters[1] shall apply instead of the provisions of paragraph 2 if the document instituting the proceedings or an equivalent document had to be transmitted from one Member State to another pursuant to this Regulation.

4. Where the provisions of Regulation (EC) No 1348/2000 are not applicable, Article 15 of the Hague Convention of 15 November 1965 on the Service Abroad of Judicial and Extrajudicial Documents in Civil or Commercial Matters shall apply if the document instituting the proceedings or an equivalent document had to be transmitted pursuant to that Convention.

[3105]

NOTES

[1] OJ L160, 30.6.2000, p 37.

SECTION 9
LIS PENDENS – RELATED ACTIONS

Article 27

1. Where proceedings involving the same cause of action and between the same parties are brought in the courts of different Member States, any court other than the court first seised shall of its own motion stay its proceedings until such time as the jurisdiction of the court first seised is established.

2. Where the jurisdiction of the court first seised is established, any court other than the court first seised shall decline jurisdiction in favour of that court.

[3106]

Article 28

1. Where related actions are pending in the courts of different Member States, any court other than the court first seised may stay its proceedings.

2. Where these actions are pending at first instance, any court other than the court first seised may also, on the application of one of the parties, decline jurisdiction if the court first seised has jurisdiction over the actions in question and its law permits the consolidation thereof.

3. For the purposes of this Article, actions are deemed to be related where they are so closely connected that it is expedient to hear and determine them together to avoid the risk of irreconcilable judgments resulting from separate proceedings.

[3107]

Article 29

Where actions come within the exclusive jurisdiction of several courts, any court other than the court first seised shall decline jurisdiction in favour of that court.

Article 30

For the purposes of this Section, a court shall be deemed to be seised:

1. at the time when the document instituting the proceedings or an equivalent document is lodged with the court, provided that the plaintiff has not subsequently failed to take the steps he was required to take to have service effected on the defendant, or

2. if the document has to be served before being lodged with the court, at the time when it is received by the authority responsible for service, provided that the plaintiff has not subsequently failed to take the steps he was required to take to have the document lodged with the court.

[3108]

SECTION 10
PROVISIONAL, INCLUDING PROTECTIVE, MEASURES

Article 31

Application may be made to the courts of a Member State for such provisional, including protective, measures as may be available under the law of that State, even if, under this Regulation, the courts of another Member State have jurisdiction as to the substance of the matter.

[3109]

CHAPTER III
RECOGNITION AND ENFORCEMENT

Article 32

For the purposes of this Regulation, "judgment" means any judgment given by a court or tribunal of a Member State, whatever the judgment may be called, including a decree, order, decision or writ of execution, as well as the determination of costs or expenses by an officer of the court.

[3110]

SECTION 1
RECOGNITION

Article 33

1. A judgment given in a Member State shall be recognised in the other Member States without any special procedure being required.

2. Any interested party who raises the recognition of a judgment as the principal issue in a dispute may, in accordance with the procedures provided for in Sections 2 and 3 of this Chapter, apply for a decision that the judgment be recognised.

3. If the outcome of proceedings in a court of a Member State depends on the determination of an incidental question of recognition that court shall have jurisdiction over that question.

[3111]

Article 34

A judgment shall not be recognised:

1. if such recognition is manifestly contrary to public policy in the Member State in which recognition is sought;

2. where it was given in default of appearance, if the defendant was not served with the document which instituted the proceedings or with an equivalent document in sufficient time and in such a way as to enable him to arrange for his defence, unless the defendant failed to commence proceedings to challenge the judgment when it was possible for him to do so;

3. if it is irreconcilable with a judgment given in a dispute between the same parties in the Member State in which recognition is sought;

4. if it is irreconcilable with an earlier judgment given in another Member State or in a third State involving the same cause of action and between the same parties, provided that the earlier judgment fulfils the conditions necessary for its recognition in the Member State addressed.

[3112]

Article 35

1. Moreover, a judgment shall not be recognised if it conflicts with Sections 3, 4 or 6 of Chapter II, or in a case provided for in Article 72.

2. In its examination of the grounds of jurisdiction referred to in the foregoing paragraph, the court or authority applied to shall be bound by the findings of fact on which the court of the Member State of origin based its jurisdiction.

3. Subject to the paragraph 1, the jurisdiction of the court of the Member State of origin may not be reviewed. The test of public policy referred to in point 1 of Article 34 may not be applied to the rules relating to jurisdiction.

[3113]

Article 36

Under no circumstances may a foreign judgment be reviewed as to its substance.

[3114]

Article 37

1. A court of a Member State in which recognition is sought of a judgment given in another Member State may stay the proceedings if an ordinary appeal against the judgment has been lodged.

2. A court of a Member State in which recognition is sought of a judgment given in Ireland or the United Kingdom may stay the proceedings if enforcement is suspended in the State of origin, by reason of an appeal.

[3115]

SECTION 2
ENFORCEMENT

Article 38

1. A judgment given in a Member State and enforceable in that State shall be enforced in another Member State when, on the application of any interested party, it has been declared enforceable there.

2. However, in the United Kingdom, such a judgment shall be enforced in England and Wales, in Scotland, or in Northern Ireland when, on the application of any interested party, it has been registered for enforcement in that part of the United Kingdom.

[3116]

Article 39

1. The application shall be submitted to the court or competent authority indicated in the list in Annex II.

2. The local jurisdiction shall be determined by reference to the place of domicile of the party against whom enforcement is sought, or to the place of enforcement.

[3117]

Article 40

1. The procedure for making the application shall be governed by the law of the Member State in which enforcement is sought.

2. The applicant must give an address for service of process within the area of jurisdiction of the court applied to. However, if the law of the Member State in which enforcement is sought does not provide for the furnishing of such an address, the applicant shall appoint a representative ad litem.

3. The documents referred to in Article 53 shall be attached to the application.

[3118]

Article 41

The judgment shall be declared enforceable immediately on completion of the formalities in Article 53 without any review under Articles 34 and 35. The party against whom enforcement is sought shall not at this stage of the proceedings be entitled to make any submissions on the application.

[3119]

Article 42

1. The decision on the application for a declaration of enforceability shall forthwith be brought to the notice of the applicant in accordance with the procedure laid down by the law of the Member State in which enforcement is sought.

2. The declaration of enforceability shall be served on the party against whom enforcement is sought, accompanied by the judgment, if not already served on that party.

[3120]

Article 43

1. The decision on the application for a declaration of enforceability may be appealed against by either party.

2. The appeal is to be lodged with the court indicated in the list in Annex III.

3. The appeal shall be dealt with in accordance with the rules governing procedure in contradictory matters.

4. If the party against whom enforcement is sought fails to appear before the appellate court in proceedings concerning an appeal brought by the applicant, Article 26(2) to (4) shall apply even where the party against whom enforcement is sought is not domiciled in any of the Member States.

5. An appeal against the declaration of enforceability is to be lodged within one month of service thereof. If the party against whom enforcement is sought is domiciled in a Member State other than that in which the declaration of enforceability was given, the time for appealing shall be two months and shall run from the date of service, either on him in person or at his residence. No extension of time may be granted on account of distance.

[3121]

Article 44

The judgment given on the appeal may be contested only by the appeal referred to in Annex IV.

[3122]

Article 45

1. The court with which an appeal is lodged under Article 43 or Article 44 shall refuse or revoke a declaration of enforceability only on one of the grounds specified in Articles 34 and 35. It shall give its decision without delay.

2. Under no circumstances may the foreign judgment be reviewed as to its substance.

[3123]

Article 46

1. The court with which an appeal is lodged under Article 43 or Article 44 may, on the application of the party against whom enforcement is sought, stay the proceedings if an ordinary appeal has been lodged against the judgment in the Member State of origin or if the time for such an appeal has not yet expired; in the latter case, the court may specify the time within which such an appeal is to be lodged.

2. Where the judgment was given in Ireland or the United Kingdom, any form of appeal available in the Member State of origin shall be treated as an ordinary appeal for the purposes of paragraph 1.

3. The court may also make enforcement conditional on the provision of such security as it shall determine.

[3124]

Article 47

1. When a judgment must be recognised in accordance with this Regulation, nothing shall prevent the applicant from availing himself of provisional, including protective, measures in accordance with the law of the Member State requested without a declaration of enforceability under Article 41 being required.

2. The declaration of enforceability shall carry with it the power to proceed to any protective measures.

3. During the time specified for an appeal pursuant to Article 43(5) against the declaration of enforceability and until any such appeal has been determined, no measures of enforcement may be taken other than protective measures against the property of the party against whom enforcement is sought.

[3125]

Article 48

1. Where a foreign judgment has been given in respect of several matters and the declaration of enforceability cannot be given for all of them, the court or competent authority shall give it for one or more of them.

2. An applicant may request a declaration of enforceability limited to parts of a judgment.

[3126]

Article 49

A foreign judgment which orders a periodic payment by way of a penalty shall be enforceable in the Member State in which enforcement is sought only if the amount of the payment has been finally determined by the courts of the Member State of origin.

[3127]

Article 50

An applicant who, in the Member State of origin has benefited from complete or partial legal aid or exemption from costs or expenses, shall be entitled, in the procedure provided for in this Section, to benefit from the most favourable legal aid or the most extensive exemption from costs or expenses provided for by the law of the Member State addressed.

[3128]

Article 51

No security, bond or deposit, however described, shall be required of a party who in one Member State applies for enforcement of a judgment given in another Member State on the ground that he is a foreign national or that he is not domiciled or resident in the State in which enforcement is sought.

[3129]

Article 52

In proceedings for the issue of a declaration of enforceability, no charge, duty or fee calculated by reference to the value of the matter at issue may be levied in the Member State in which enforcement is sought.

[3130]

SECTION 3
COMMON PROVISIONS

Article 53

1. A party seeking recognition or applying for a declaration of enforceability shall produce a copy of the judgment which satisfies the conditions necessary to establish its authenticity.

2. A party applying for a declaration of enforceability shall also produce the certificate referred to in Article 54, without prejudice to Article 55.

[3131]

Article 54

The court or competent authority of a Member State where a judgment was given shall issue, at the request of any interested party, a certificate using the standard form in Annex V to this Regulation.

[3132]

Article 55

1. If the certificate referred to in Article 54 is not produced, the court or competent authority may specify a time for its production or accept an equivalent document or, if it considers that it has sufficient information before it, dispense with its production.

2. If the court or competent authority so requires, a translation of the documents shall be produced. The translation shall be certified by a person qualified to do so in one of the Member States.

[3133]

Article 56

No legalisation or other similar formality shall be required in respect of the documents referred to in Article 53 or Article 55(2), or in respect of a document appointing a representative ad litem.

[3134]

CHAPTER IV
AUTHENTIC INSTRUMENTS AND COURT SETTLEMENTS

Article 57

1. A document which has been formally drawn up or registered as an authentic instrument and is enforceable in one Member State shall, in another Member State, be declared enforceable there, on application made in accordance with the procedures provided for in Articles 38, et seq. The court with which an appeal is lodged under Article 43 or Article 44 shall refuse or revoke a declaration of enforceability only if enforcement of the instrument is manifestly contrary to public policy in the Member State addressed.

2. Arrangements relating to maintenance obligations concluded with administrative authorities or authenticated by them shall also be regarded as authentic instruments within the meaning of paragraph 1.

3. The instrument produced must satisfy the conditions necessary to establish its authenticity in the Member State of origin.

4. Section 3 of Chapter III shall apply as appropriate. The competent authority of a Member State where an authentic instrument was drawn up or registered shall issue, at the request of any interested party, a certificate using the standard form in Annex VI to this Regulation.

[3135]

Article 58

A settlement which has been approved by a court in the course of proceedings and is enforceable in the Member State in which it was concluded shall be enforceable in the State addressed under the same conditions as authentic instruments. The court or competent authority of a Member State where a court settlement was approved shall issue, at the request of any interested party, a certificate using the standard form in Annex V to this Regulation.

[3136]

CHAPTER V
GENERAL PROVISIONS

Article 59

1. In order to determine whether a party is domiciled in the Member State whose courts are seised of a matter, the court shall apply its internal law.

2. If a party is not domiciled in the Member State whose courts are seised of the matter, then, in order to determine whether the party is domiciled in another Member State, the court shall apply the law of that Member State.

[3137]

Article 60

1. For the purposes of this Regulation, a company or other legal person or association of natural or legal persons is domiciled at the place where it has its:
(a) statutory seat, or
(b) central administration, or
(c) principal place of business.

2. For the purposes of the United Kingdom and Ireland "statutory seat" means the registered office or, where there is no such office anywhere, the place of incorporation or, where there is no such place anywhere, the place under the law of which the formation took place.

3. In order to determine whether a trust is domiciled in the Member State whose courts are seised of the matter, the court shall apply its rules of private international law.

[3138]

Article 61

Without prejudice to any more favourable provisions of national laws, persons domiciled in a Member State who are being prosecuted in the criminal courts of another Member State of which they are not nationals for an offence which was not intentionally committed may be defended by persons qualified to do so, even if they do not appear in person. However, the court seised of the matter may order appearance in person; in the case of failure to appear, a judgment given in the civil action without the person concerned having had the opportunity to arrange for his defence need not be recognised or enforced in the other Member States.

[3139]

Article 62

In Sweden, in summary proceedings concerning orders to pay (betalningsföreläggande) and assistance (handräckning), the expression "court" includes the "Swedish enforcement service" (kronofogdemyndighet).

[3140]

Article 63

1. A person domiciled in the territory of the Grand Duchy of Luxembourg and sued in the court of another Member State pursuant to Article 5(1) may refuse to submit to the jurisdiction of that court if the final place of delivery of the goods or provision of the services is in Luxembourg.

2. Where, under paragraph 1, the final place of delivery of the goods or provision of the services is in Luxembourg, any agreement conferring jurisdiction must, in order to be valid, be accepted in writing or evidenced in writing within the meaning of Article 23(1)(a).

3. The provisions of this Article shall not apply to contracts for the provision of financial services.

4. The provisions of this Article shall apply for a period of six years from entry into force of this Regulation.

[3141]

Article 64

1. In proceedings involving a dispute between the master and a member of the crew of a seagoing ship registered in Greece or in Portugal, concerning remuneration or other conditions of service, a court in a Member State shall establish whether the diplomatic or consular officer responsible for the ship has been notified of the dispute. It may act as soon as that officer has been notified.

2. The provisions of this Article shall apply for a period of six years from entry into force of this Regulation.

[3142]

[Article 65

1. The jurisdiction specified in Article 6(2) and Article 11 in actions on a warranty of guarantee or in any other third party proceedings may not be resorted to Germany, Austria and Hungary. Any person domiciled in another Member State may be sued in the courts:

(a) of Germany, pursuant to Articles 68 and 72 to 74 of the Code of Civil Procedure (Zivilprozessordnung) concerning third-party notices;

(b) of Austria, pursuant to Article 21 of the Code of Civil Procedure (Zivilprozessordnung) concerning third-party notices;

(c) of Hungary, pursuant to Articles 58 to 60 of the Code of Civil Procedure (Polgári perrendtartás) concerning third-party notices.

2. Judgments given in other Member States by virtue of Article 6(2), or Article 11 shall be recognised and enforced in Germany, Austria and Hungary in accordance with Chapter III. Any effects which judgments given in these States may have on third parties by application of the provisions in paragraph 1 shall also be recognised in the other Member States.]

[3143]

NOTES

Substituted by the Act concerning the conditions of accession of the Czech Republic, the Republic of Estonia, the Republic of Cyprus, the Republic of Latvia, the Republic of Lithuania, the Republic of Hungary, the Republic of Malta, the Republic of Poland, the Republic of Slovenia and Slovak Republic and the adjustments of the Treaties on which the European Union is founded (OJ L236, 23.9.2003, p 33).

CHAPTER VI
TRANSITIONAL PROVISIONS

Article 66

1. This Regulation shall apply only to legal proceedings instituted and to documents formally drawn up or registered as authentic instruments after the entry into force thereof.

2. However, if the proceedings in the Member State of origin were instituted before the entry into force of this Regulation, judgments given after that date shall be recognised and enforced in accordance with Chapter III,

(a) if the proceedings in the Member State of origin were instituted after the entry into force of the Brussels or the Lugano Convention both in the Member State or origin and in the Member State addressed;

(b) in all other cases, if jurisdiction was founded upon rules which accorded with those provided for either in Chapter II or in a convention concluded between the Member State of origin and the Member State addressed which was in force when the proceedings were instituted.

[3144]

CHAPTER VII
RELATIONS WITH OTHER INSTRUMENTS

Article 67

This Regulation shall not prejudice the application of provisions governing jurisdiction and the recognition and enforcement of judgments in specific matters which are contained in Community instruments or in national legislation harmonised pursuant to such instruments.

[3145]

Article 68

1. This Regulation shall, as between the Member States, supersede the Brussels Convention, except as regards the territories of the Member States which fall within the territorial scope of that Convention and which are excluded from this Regulation pursuant to Article 299 of the Treaty.

2. In so far as this Regulation replaces the provisions of the Brussels Convention between Member States, any reference to the Convention shall be understood as a reference to this Regulation.

[3146]

Article 69

Subject to Article 66(2) and Article 70, this Regulation shall, as between Member States, supersede the following conventions and treaty concluded between two or more of them:

— the Convention between Belgium and France on Jurisdiction and the Validity and Enforcement of Judgments, Arbitration Awards and Authentic Instruments, signed at Paris on 8 July 1899,

— the Convention between Belgium and the Netherlands on Jurisdiction, Bankruptcy, and the Validity and Enforcement of Judgments, Arbitration Awards and Authentic Instruments, signed at Brussels on 28 March 1925,

— the Convention between France and Italy on the Enforcement of Judgments in Civil and Commercial Matters, signed at Rome on 3 June 1930,

— the Convention between the United Kingdom and the French Republic providing for the reciprocal enforcement of judgments in civil and commercial matters, with Protocol, signed at Paris on 18 January 1934,

— the Convention between the United Kingdom and the Kingdom of Belgium providing for the reciprocal enforcement of judgments in civil and commercial matters, with Protocol, signed at Brussels on 2 May 1934,

— the Convention between Germany and Italy on the Recognition and Enforcement of Judgments in Civil and Commercial Matters, signed at Rome on 9 March 1936,

— the Convention between Belgium and Austria on the Reciprocal Recognition and Enforcement of Judgments and Authentic Instruments relating to Maintenance Obligations, signed at Vienna on 25 October 1957,

— the Convention between Germany and Belgium on the Mutual Recognition and Enforcement of Judgments, Arbitration Awards and Authentic Instruments in Civil and Commercial Matters, signed at Bonn on 30 June 1958,

— the Convention between the Netherlands and Italy on the Recognition and Enforcement of Judgments in Civil and Commercial Matters, signed at Rome on 17 April 1959,

— the Convention between Germany and Austria on the Reciprocal Recognition and Enforcement of Judgments, Settlements and Authentic Instruments in Civil and Commercial Matters, signed at Vienna on 6 June 1959,

— the Convention between Belgium and Austria on the Reciprocal Recognition and Enforcement of Judgments, Arbitral Awards and Authentic Instruments in Civil and Commercial Matters, signed at Vienna on 16 June 1959,

— the Convention between the United Kingdom and the Federal Republic of Germany for the reciprocal recognition and enforcement of judgments in civil and commercial matters, signed at Bonn on 14 July 1960,

— the Convention between the United Kingdom and Austria providing for the reciprocal recognition and enforcement of judgments in civil and commercial matters, signed at Vienna on 14 July 1961, with amending Protocol signed at London on 6 March 1970,

— the Convention between Greece and Germany for the Reciprocal Recognition and Enforcement of Judgments, Settlements and Authentic Instruments in Civil and Commercial Matters, signed in Athens on 4 November 1961,

— the Convention between Belgium and Italy on the Recognition and Enforcement of Judgments and other Enforceable Instruments in Civil and Commercial Matters, signed at Rome on 6 April 1962,

— the Convention between the Netherlands and Germany on the Mutual Recognition and Enforcement of Judgments and Other Enforceable Instruments in Civil and Commercial Matters, signed at The Hague on 30 August 1962,

— the Convention between the Netherlands and Austria on the Reciprocal Recognition and Enforcement of Judgments and Authentic Instruments in Civil and Commercial Matters, signed at The Hague on 6 February 1963,

— the Convention between the United Kingdom and the Republic of Italy for the reciprocal recognition and enforcement of judgments in civil and commercial matters, signed at Rome on 7 February 1964, with amending Protocol signed at Rome on 14 July 1970,

— the Convention between France and Austria on the Recognition and Enforcement of Judgments and Authentic Instruments in Civil and Commercial Matters, signed at Vienna on 15 July 1966,

— the Convention between the United Kingdom and the Kingdom of the Netherlands providing for the reciprocal recognition and enforcement of judgments in civil matters, signed at The Hague on 17 November 1967,

— the Convention between Spain and France on the Recognition and Enforcement of Judgment Arbitration Awards in Civil and Commercial Matters, signed at Paris on 28 May 1969,

— the Convention between Luxembourg and Austria on the Recognition and Enforcement of Judgments and Authentic Instruments in Civil and Commercial Matters, signed at Luxembourg on 29 July 1971,
— the Convention between Italy and Austria on the Recognition and Enforcement of Judgments in Civil and Commercial Matters, of Judicial Settlements and of Authentic Instruments, signed at Rome on 16 November 1971,
— the Convention between Spain and Italy regarding Legal Aid and the Recognition and Enforcement of Judgments in Civil and Commercial Matters, signed at Madrid on 22 May 1973,
— the Convention between Finland, Iceland, Norway, Sweden and Denmark on the Recognition and Enforcement of Judgments in Civil Matters, signed at Copenhagen on 11 October 1977,
— the Convention between Austria and Sweden on the Recognition and Enforcement of Judgments in Civil Matters, signed at Stockholm on 16 September 1982,
— the Convention between Spain and the Federal Republic of Germany on the Recognition and Enforcement of Judgments, Settlements and Enforceable Authentic Instruments in Civil and Commercial Matters, signed at Bonn on 14 November 1983,
— the Convention between Austria and Spain on the Recognition and Enforcement of Judgments, Settlements and Enforceable Authentic Instruments in Civil and Commercial Matters, signed at Vienna on 17 February 1984,
— the Convention between Finland and Austria on the Recognition and Enforcement of Judgments in Civil Matters, signed at Vienna on 17 November 1986, and
— the Treaty between Belgium, the Netherlands and Luxembourg in Jurisdiction, Bankruptcy, and the Validity and Enforcement of Judgments, Arbitration Awards and Authentic Instruments, signed at Brussels on 24 November 1961, in so far as it is in force,
[— the Convention between the Czechoslovak Republic and Portugal on the Recognition and Enforcement of Court Decisions, signed at Lisbon on 23 November 1927, still in force between the Czech Republic and Portugal,
— the Convention between the Federative People's Republic of Yugoslavia and the Republic of Austria on Mutual Judicial Cooperation, signed at Vienna on 16 December 1954,
— the Convention between the Polish People's Republic and the Hungarian People's Republic on the Legal Assistance in Civil, Family and Criminal Matters, signed at Budapest on 6 March 1959,
— the Convention between the Federative People's Republic of Yugoslavia and the Kingdom of Greece on the Mutual Recognition and Enforcement of Judgments, signed at Athens on 18 June 1959,
— the Convention between the Polish People's Republic and the Federative People's Republic of Yugoslavia on the Legal Assistance in Civil and Criminal Matters, signed at Warsaw on 6 February 1960, now in force between Poland and Slovenia,
— the Agreement between the Federative People's Republic of Yugoslavia and the Republic of Austria on the Mutual Recognition and Enforcement of Arbitral Awards and Arbitral Settlements in Commercial Matters, signed at Belgrade on 18 March 1960,
— the Agreement between the Federative People's Republic of Yugoslavia and the Republic of Austria on the Mutual Recognition and Enforcement of Decisions in Alimony Matters, signed at Vienna on 10 October 1961,
— the Convention between Poland and Austria on Mutual Relations in Civil Matters and on Documents, signed at Vienna on 11 December 1963,
— the Treaty between the Czechoslovak Socialist Republic and the Socialist Federative Republic of Yugoslavia on Settlement of Legal Relations in Civil, Family and Criminal Matters, signed at Belgrade on 20 January 1964, still in force between the Czech Republic, Slovakia and Slovenia,
— the Convention between Poland and France on Applicable Law, Jurisdiction and the Enforcement of Judgments in the Field of Personal and Family Law, concluded in Warsaw on 5 April 1967,
— the Convention between the Governments of Yugoslavia and France on the Recognition and Enforcement of Judgments in Civil and Commercial Matters, signed at Paris on 18 May 1971,
— the Convention between the Federative Socialist Republic of Yugoslavia and the Kingdom of Belgium on the Recognition and Enforcement of Court Decisions in Alimony Matters, signed at Belgrade on 12 December 1973,
— the Convention between Hungary and Greece on Legal Assistance in Civil and Criminal Matters, signed at Budapest on 8 October 1979,

- the Convention between Poland and Greece on Legal Assistance in Civil and Criminal Matters, signed at Athens on 24 October 1979,
- the Convention between Hungary and France on Legal Assistance in Civil and Family Law, on the Recognition and Enforcement of Decisions and on Legal Assistance in Criminal Matters and on Extradition, signed at Budapest on 31 July 1980,
- the Treaty between the Czechoslovak Socialist Republic and the Hellenic Republic on Legal Aid in Civil and Criminal Matters, signed at Athens on 22 October 1980, still in force between the Czech Republic, Slovakia and Greece,
- the Convention between the Republic of Cyprus and the Hungarian People's Republic on Legal Assistance in Civil and Criminal Matters, signed at Nicosia on 30 November 1981,
- the Treaty between the Czechoslovak Socialistic Republic and the Republic of Cyprus on Legal Aid in Civil and Criminal Matters, signed at Nicosia on 23 April 1982, still in force between the Czech Republic, Slovakia and Cyprus,
- the Agreement between the Republic of Cyprus and the Republic of Greece on Legal Cooperation in Matters of Civil, Family, Commercial and Criminal Law, signed at Nicosia on 5 March 1984,
- the Treaty between the Government of the Czechoslovak Socialist Republic and the Government of the Republic of France on Legal Aid and the Recognition and Enforcement of Judgments in Civil, Family and Commercial Matters, signed at Paris on 10 May 1984, still in force between the Czech Republic, Slovakia and France,
- the Agreement between the Republic of Cyprus and the Socialist Federal Republic of Yugoslavia on Legal Assistance in Civil and Criminal Matters, signed at Nicosia on 19 September 1984, now in force between Cyprus and Slovenia,
- the Treaty between the Czechoslovak Socialist Republic and the Italian Republic on Legal Aid in Civil and Criminal Matters, signed at Prague on 6 December 1985, still in force between the Czech Republic, Slovakia and Italy,
- the Treaty between the Czechoslovak Socialist Republic and the Kingdom of Spain on Legal Aid, Recognition and Enforcement of Court Decisions in Civil Matters, signed at Madrid on 4 May 1987, still in force between the Czech Republic, Slovakia and Spain,
- the Treaty between the Czechoslovak Socialist Republic and the Polish People's Republic on Legal Aid and Settlement of Legal Relations in Civil, Family, Labour and Criminal Matters, signed at Warsaw on 21 December 1987, still in force between the Czech Republic, Slovakia and Poland,
- the Treaty between the Czechoslovak Socialist Republic and the Hungarian People's Republic on Legal Aid and Settlement of Legal Relations in Civil, Family and Criminal Matters, signed at Bratislava on 28 March 1989, still in force between the Czech Republic, Slovakia and Hungary,
- the Convention between Poland and Italy on Judicial Assistance and the Recognition and Enforcement of Judgments in Civil Matters, signed at Warsaw on 28 April 1989,
- the Treaty between the Czech Republic and the Slovak Republic on Legal Aid provided by Judicial Bodies and on Settlements of Certain Legal Relations in Civil and Criminal Matters, signed at Prague on 29 October 1992,
- the Agreement between the Republic of Latvia, the Republic of Estonia and the Republic of Lithuania on Legal Assistance and Legal Relationships, signed at Tallinn on 11 November 1992,
- the Agreement between the Republic of Poland and the Republic of Lithuania on Legal Assistance and Legal Relations in Civil, Family, Labour and Criminal Matters, signed in Warsaw on 26 January 1993,
- the Agreement between the Republic of Latvia and the Republic of Poland on Legal Assistance and Legal Relationships in Civil, Family, Labour and Criminal Matters, signed at Riga on 23 February 1994,
- the Agreement between the Republic of Cyprus and the Republic of Poland on Legal Cooperation in Civil and Criminal Matters, signed at Nicosia on 14 November 1996,
- the Agreement between Estonia and Poland on Granting Legal Assistance and Legal Relations on Civil, Labour and Criminal Matters, signed at Tallinn on 27 November 1998.]

[3147]

NOTES

Entries in square brackets added by the Act concerning the conditions of accession of the Czech Republic, the Republic of Estonia, the Republic of Cyprus, the Republic of Latvia, the Republic of Lithuania, the Republic of Hungary, the Republic of Malta, the Republic of Poland, the Republic of Slovenia and Slovak Republic and the adjustments of the Treaties on which the European Union is founded (OJ L236, 23.9.2003, p 33).

Article 70

1. The Treaty and the Conventions referred to in Article 69 shall continue to have effect in relation to matters to which this Regulation does not apply.

2. They shall continue to have effect in respect of judgments given and documents formally drawn up or registered as authentic instruments before the entry into force of this Regulation.

[3148]

Article 71

1. This Regulation shall not affect any conventions to which the Member States are parties and which in relation to particular matters, govern jurisdiction or the recognition or enforcement of judgments.

2. With a view to its uniform interpretation, paragraph 1 shall be applied in the following manner:

(a) this Regulation shall not prevent a court of a Member State, which is a party to a convention on a particular matter, from assuming jurisdiction in accordance with that convention, even where the defendant is domiciled in another Member State which is not a party to that convention. The court hearing the action shall, in any event, apply Article 26 of this Regulation;

(b) judgments given in a Member State by a court in the exercise of jurisdiction provided for in a convention on a particular matter shall be recognised and enforced in the other Member States in accordance with this Regulation.

Where a convention on a particular matter to which both the Member State of origin and the Member State addressed are parties lays down conditions for the recognition or enforcement of judgments, those conditions shall apply. In any event, the provisions of this Regulation which concern the procedure for recognition and enforcement of judgments may be applied.

[3149]

Article 72

This Regulation shall not affect agreements by which Member States undertook, prior to the entry into force of this Regulation pursuant to Article 59 of the Brussels Convention, not to recognise judgments given, in particular in other Contracting States to that Convention, against defendants domiciled or habitually resident in a third country where, in cases provided for in Article 4 of that Convention, the judgment could only be founded on a ground of jurisdiction specified in the second paragraph of Article 3 of that Convention.

[3150]

CHAPTER VIII
FINAL PROVISIONS

Article 73

No later than five years after the entry into force of this Regulation, the Commission shall present to the European Parliament, the Council and the Economic and Social Committee a report on the application of this Regulation. The report shall be accompanied, if need be, by proposals for adaptations to this Regulation.

[3151]

Article 74

1. The Member States shall notify the Commission of the texts amending the lists set out in Annexes I to IV. The Commission shall adapt the Annexes concerned accordingly.

2. The updating or technical adjustment of the forms, specimens of which appear in Annexes V and VI, shall be adopted in accordance with the advisory procedure referred to in Article 75(2).

[3152]

Article 75

1. The Commission shall be assisted by a committee.

2. Where reference is made to this paragraph, Articles 3 and 7 of Decision 1999/468/EC shall apply.

3. The Committee shall adopt its rules of procedure.

[3153]

Article 76

This Regulation shall enter into force on 1 March 2002.

This Regulation is binding in its entirety and directly applicable in the Member States in accordance with the Treaty establishing the European Community.

[3154]

Done at Brussels, 22 December 2000.

ANNEX I

RULES OF JURISDICTION REFERRED TO IN ARTICLE 3(2) AND ARTICLE 4(2)

The rules of jurisdiction referred to in Article 3(2) and Article 4(2) are the following:

— in Belgium: Article 15 of the Civil Code (Code civil/Burgerlijk Wetboek) and Article 638 of the Judicial Code (Code judiciaire/Gerechtelijk Wetboek);

[— in the Czech Republic: Article 86 of Act No 99/1963 Coll., the Code of Civil Procedure (občanskí soudní řád), as amended,]

— in Germany: Article 23 of the Code of Civil Procedure (Zivilprozessordnung),

[— in Estonia: Article 139, paragraph 2 of the Code of Civil Procedure (tsiviilkohtumenetluse seadustik),]

— in Greece, Article 40 of the Code of Civil Procedure (Κώδικας Πολιτικής Δικονομίας);

— in France: Articles 14 and 15 of the Civil Code (Code civil),

— in Ireland: the rules which enable jurisdiction to be founded on the document instituting the proceedings having been served on the defendant during his temporary presence in Ireland,

— in Italy: Articles 3 and 4 of Act 218 of 31 May 1995,

[— in Cyprus: section 21(2) of the Courts of Justice Law No 14 of 1960, as amended,

[— in Latvia: section 27 and paragraphs 3, 5, 6 and 9 of section 28 of the Civil Procedure Law (Civilprocesa likums),]

— in Lithuania: Article 31 of the Code of Civil Procedure (Civilinio proceso kodeksas),]

— in Luxembourg: Articles 14 and 15 of the Civil Code (Code civil),

[— in Hungary: Article 57 of Law Decree No. 13 of 1979 on International Private Law (a nemzetközi magánjogról szóló 1979. évi 13. törvényereju rendelet),

— in Malta: Articles 742, 743 and 744 of the Code of Organisation and Civil Procedure – Cap 12 (Kodici ta' Organizzazzjoni u Procedura Civili – Kap 12) and Article 549 of the Commercial Code – Cap 13 (Kodici tal-kummerc – Kap 13)]

— …

— in Austria: Article 99 of the Court Jurisdiction Act (Jurisdiktionsnorm),

[— in Poland: Articles 1103 and 1110 of the Code of Civil Procedure (Kodeks postępowania cywilnego),]

— in Portugal: Articles 65 and 65A of the Code of Civil Procedure (Código de Processo Civil) and Article 11 of the Code of Labour Procedure (Código de Processo de Trabalho),

[[— in Slovenia: Article 48(2) of the Private International Law and Procedure Act (Zakon o medarodnem zasebnem pravu in postopku) in relation to Article 47(2) of Civil Procedure Act (Zakon o pravdnem postopku) and Article 58(1) of the Private International Law and Procedure Act (Zakon o medarodnem zasebnem pravu in postopku) in relation to Article 57(1) and 47(2) of Civil Procedure Act (Zakon o pravdnem postopku),]

[— in Slovakia: Articles 37 to 37e of the Act No 97/1963 on Private International Law and the Rules of Procedure Relating Thereto,]]

— in Finland: the second, third and fourth sentences of the first paragraph of Section 1 of Chapter 10 of the Code of Judicial Procedure (oikeudenkäymiskaari/rättegångsbalken),

— in Sweden: the first sentence of the first paragraph of Section 3 of Chapter 10 of the Code of Judicial Procedure (rättegångsbalken),

— in the United Kingdom: rules which enable jurisdiction to be founded on:

(a) the document instituting the proceedings having been served on the defendant during his temporary presence in the United Kingdom; or

(b) the presence within the United Kingdom of property belonging to the defendant; or

(c) the seizure by the plaintiff of property situated in the United Kingdom.

[3155]

NOTES

Indents relating to the Czech Republic, Estonia, Cyprus, Lithuania, Hungary, Malta, Poland, inserted by the Act concerning the conditions of accession of the Czech Republic, the Republic of Estonia, the Republic of Cyprus, the Republic of Latvia, the Republic of Lithuania, the Republic of Hungary, the Republic of Malta, the Republic of Poland, the Republic of Slovenia and Slovak Republic and the adjustments of the Treaties on which the European Union is founded (OJ L236, 23.9.2003, p 33).

Indents relating to Latvia, Slovenia, Slovakia inserted by the 2004 Act of Accession (see note above), substituted by Commission Regulation 2245/2004/EC, Art 1(1) (OJ L381, 28.12.2004, p 10).

Indent omitted repealed by Commission Regulation 1496/2002/EC, Art 1 (OJ l225, 22.8.2002, p 13).

ANNEX II

The courts or competent authorities to which the application referred to in Article 39 may be submitted are the following:

— in Belgium, the "tribunal de première instance" or "rechtbank van eerste aanleg" or "erstinstanzliches Gericht",

[— in the Czech Republic, the "okresní soud" or "soudní exekutor",]

— [in Germany:

(a) the presiding Judge of a chamber of the "Landgericht";

(b) a notary ("…") in a procedure of declaration of enforceability of an authentic instrument.]

[— in Estonia, the "maakohus" or the "linnakohus",]

— in Greece, the "Μονομελές Πρωτοδικείο",

— in Spain, the "Juzgado de Primera Instancia",

[— in France:

(a) the "greffier en chef du tribunal de grande instance",

(b) the "président de la chambre départementale des notaires" in the case of application for a declaration of enforceability of a notarial authentic instrument.]

— in Ireland, the High Court,

— in Italy, the "Corte d'appello",

[— in Cyprus, the "Επαρχιακό Δικαστήριο" or in the case of a maintenance judgment the "Οικογενειακό Δικαστήριο",

— in Latvia, the "rajona (pilsetas) tiesa",

— in Lithuania, the "Lietuvos apeliacinis teismas",]

— in Luxembourg, the presiding judge of the "tribunal d'arrondissement",

[— in Hungary, the "megyei bíróság székhelyén muködo helyi bíróság", and in Budapest the "Budai Központi Kerületi Bíróság",

— in Malta, the "Prim' Awla tal-Qorti Civili" or "Qorti tal-Magistrati ta' Ghawdex fil-gurisdizzjoni superjuri taghha", or, in the case of a maintenance judgment, the "Registratur tal-Qorti" on transmission by the "Ministru responsabbli ghall-Gustizzja",]

— [in the Netherlands, the "voorzieningenrechter van de rechtbank"];

— in Austria, the "Bezirksgericht",

[— in Poland, the "Sąd Okręgowy",]

— in Portugal, the "Tribunal de Comarca",

[[— in Slovenia, the "okrožno sodišče",]

[— in Slovakia, the "okresný súd",]]

— in Finland, the "käräjäoikeus/tingsrätt",

— in Sweden, the "Svea hovrätt",

— in the United Kingdom:

(a) in England and Wales, the High Court of Justice, or in the case of a maintenance judgment, the Magistrate's Court on transmission by the Secretary of State;
(b) in Scotland, the Court of Session, or in the case of a maintenance judgment, the Sheriff Court on transmission by the Secretary of State;
(c) in Northern Ireland, the High Court of Justice, or in the case of a maintenance judgment, the Magistrate's Court on transmission by the Secretary of State;
(d) in Gibraltar, the Supreme Court of Gibraltar, or in the case of a maintenance judgment, the Magistrates' Court on transmission by the Attorney General of Gibraltar.

[3156]

NOTES

Indents relating to the Czech Republic, Estonia, Cyprus, Latvia, Lithuania, Hungary, Malta, Poland inserted by the Act concerning the conditions of accession of the Czech Republic, the Republic of Estonia, the Republic of Cyprus, the Republic of Latvia, the Republic of Lithuania, the Republic of Hungary, the Republic of Malta, the Republic of Poland, the Republic of Slovenia and Slovak Republic and the adjustments of the Treaties on which the European Union is founded (OJ L236, 23.9.2003, p 33).

Indent relating to France substituted by Commission Regulation 2245/2004/EC, Art 1(2)(a).

In indents relating to Germany and the Netherlands, words in square brackets substituted by Commission Regulation 1496/2002/EC, Arts 2, 3 (OJ L225, 22.8.2002, p 13).

Indents relating to Slovenia, Slovakia inserted by the 2003 Act of Accession (see note above); substituted by Commission Regulation 2245/2004/EC (OJ L381, 28.12.2004, p 10), Art 1(2)(b), (c).

ANNEX III

The courts with which appeals referred to in Article 43(2) may be lodged are the following:

— in Belgium,
(a) as regards appeal by the defendant: the "tribunal de première instance" or "rechtbank van eerste aanleg" or "erstinstanzliches Gericht",
(b) as regards appeal by the applicant: the "Cour d'appel" or "hof van beroep",
[— in the Czech Republic, the "okresní soud",]
— in the Federal Republic of Germany, the "Oberlandesgericht",
[— in Estonia, the "ringkonnakohus",]
— in Greece, the "Εφετείο",
— in Spain, the "Audiencia Provincial",
[— in France:
(a) the "cour d'appel" on decisions allowing the application,
(b) the presiding judge of the "tribunal de grande instance", on decisions rejecting the application,]
— in Ireland, the High Court,
— in Italy, the "corte d'appello",
[— in Cyprus, the "Επαρχιακό Δικαστήριο" or in the case of a maintenance judgment the "Οικογενειακό Δικαστήριο",
— in Latvia, the "Apgabaltiesa",
[— in Lithuania, the "Lietuvos apeliacinis teismas",]]
— in Luxembourg, the "Cour supérieure de Justice" sitting as a court of civil appeal,
[— in Hungary, the "megyei bíróság"; in Budapest, the "Fovárosi Bíróság",
— in Malta, the "Qorti ta' l-Appell" in accordance with the procedure laid down for appeals in the Kodici ta' Organizzazzjoni u Procedura Civili – Kap.12 or in the case of a maintenance judgment by "citazzjoni" before the "Prim' Awla tal-Qorti Civili jew il-Qorti tal-Magistrati ta' Ghawdex fil-gurisdizzjoni superjuri taghha"',]
— in the Netherlands:
(a) for the defendant: the "arrondissementsrechtbank",
(b) for the applicant: the "gerechtshof",
— in Austria, the "Bezirksgericht",
[— in Poland, the "Sąd Apelacyjny",]
— in Portugal, the "Tribunal de Relação",
[[— in Slovenia, the "okrožno sodišče",]
[— in Slovakia, "okresný súd",]]
— in Finland, the "hovioikeus/hovrätt",
— in Sweden, the "Svea hovrätt",
— in the United Kingdom:
(a) in England and Wales, the High Court of Justice, or in the case of a maintenance judgment, the Magistrate's Court;

(b) in Scotland, the Court of Session, or in the case of a maintenance judgment, the Sheriff Court;
(c) in Northern Ireland, the High Court of Justice, or in the case of a maintenance judgment, the Magistrate's Court;
(d) in Gibraltar, the Supreme Court of Gibraltar, or in the case of a maintenance judgment, the Magistrates' Court.

[3157]

NOTES

Indents relating to the Czech Republic, Estonia, Cyprus, Latvia, Hungary, Malta, Poland inserted by the Act concerning the conditions of accession of the Czech Republic, the Republic of Estonia, the Republic of Cyprus, the Republic of Latvia, the Republic of Lithuania, the Republic of Hungary, the Republic of Malta, the Republic of Poland, the Republic of Slovenia and Slovak Republic and the adjustments of the Treaties on which the European Union is founded (OJ L236, 23.9.2003, p 33).

Indent relating to France substituted by Commission Regulation 2245/2004/EC (OJ L381, 28.12.2004, p 10), Art 1(3)(a).

Indents relating to Lithuania, Slovenia, Slovakia inserted by the 2003 Act of Accession (see note above); substituted by Commission Regulation 2245/2004/EC (OJ L381, 28.12.2004, p 10), Art 1(3)(b)–(d).

ANNEX IV

The appeals which may be lodged pursuant to Article 44 are the following

— in Belgium, Greece, Spain, France, Italy, Luxembourg and the Netherlands, an appeal in cassation,
[— in the Czech Republic, a "dovolání" and a "žaloba pro zmatečnost",]
— in Germany, a "Rechtsbeschwerde",
[— in Estonia, a "kassatsioonkaebus",]
— in Ireland, an appeal on a point of law to the Supreme Court,
[— in Cyprus, an appeal to the Supreme Court,
— in Latvia, an appeal to the "Augstākātiesa",
[— in Lithuania, an appeal to the "Lietuvos Aukščiausiasis Teismas",]
— in Hungary, "felülvizsgálati kérelem",
— in Malta, no further appeal lies to any other court; in the case of a maintenance judgment the "Qorti ta' l-Appell" in accordance with the procedure laid down for appeal in the "kodici ta' Organizzazzjoni u Procedura Civili – Kap. 12",]
— in Austria, a "Revisionsrekurs",
[— in Poland, by an appeal in cassation to the "Sąd Najwyższy",]
— in Portugal, an appeal on a point of law,
[[— in Slovenia, an appeal to the "Vrhovno sodišče Republike Slovenije",]
[— in Slovakia, the "dovolanie".]]
— in Finland, an appeal to the "korkein oikeus/högsta domstolen",
— in Sweden, an appeal to the "Högsta domstolen",
— in the United Kingdom, a single further appeal on a point of law.

[3158]

NOTES

Indents relating to the Czech Republic, Estonia, Cyprus, Latvia, Hungary, Malta, Poland inserted by the Act concerning the conditions of accession of the Czech Republic, the Republic of Estonia, the Republic of Cyprus, the Republic of Latvia, the Republic of Lithuania, the Republic of Hungary, the Republic of Malta, the Republic of Poland, the Republic of Slovenia and Slovak Republic and the adjustments of the Treaties on which the European Union is founded (OJ L236, 23.9.2003, p 33).

Indents relating to Lithuania, Slovenia, Slovakia inserted by AA5; substituted by Commission Regulation 2245/2004/EC, Art 1(4) (OJ L381, 28.12.2004, p 10).

ANNEX V

CERTIFICATE REFERRED TO IN ARTICLES 54 AND 58 OF THE REGULATION ON JUDGMENTS AND COURT SETTLEMENTS

(English, inglés, anglais, inglese, …)

1. Member State of origin

2. Court or competent authority issuing the certificate
   2.1. Name
   2.2. Address
   2.3. Tel/fax/e-mail

3. Court which delivered the judgment/approved the court settlement*
   3.1. Type of court
   3.2. Place of court

4. Judgment/court settlement*
   4.1. Date
   4.2. Reference number
   4.3. The parties to the judgment/court settlement*
      4.3.1. Name(s) of plaintiff(s)
      4.3.2. Name(s) of defendant(s)
      4.3.3. Name(s) of other party(ies), if any
   4.4. Date of service of the document instituting the proceedings where judgment was given in default of appearance
   4.5. Text of the judgment/court settlement* as annexed to this certificate

5. Names of parties to whom legal aid has been granted

The judgment/court settlement* is enforceable in the Member State of origin (Articles 38 and 58 of the Regulation) against:

Name:

Done at .... , date ....

Signature and/or stamp ....

[3159]

* Delete as appropriate.

ANNEX VI

CERTIFICATE REFERRED TO IN ARTICLE 57(4) OF THE REGULATION ON AUTHENTIC INSTRUMENTS

(English, inglés, anglais, inglese ....)

1. Member State of origin
2. Competent authority issuing the certificate
   2.1. Name
   2.2. Address
   2.3. Tel/fax/e-mail
3. Authority which has given authenticity to the instrument
   3.1. Authority involved in the drawing up of the authentic instrument (if applicable)
      3.1.1. Name and designation of authority
      3.1.2. Place of authority
   3.2. Authority which has registered the authentic instrument (if applicable)
      3.2.1. Type of authority
      3.2.2. Place of authority
4. Authentic instrument
   4.1. Description of the instrument
   4.2. Date
      4.2.1. on which the instrument was drawn up
      4.2.2. if different: on which the instrument was registered
   4.3. Reference number
   4.4. Parties to the instrument
      4.4.1. Name of the creditor
      4.4.2. Name of the debtor
5. Text of the enforceable obligation as annexed to this certificate

The authentic instrument is enforceable against the debtor in the Member State of origin (Article 57(1) of the Regulation)

Done at .... , date ....

Signature and/or stamp ....

[3160]

PART IV EC MATERIALS

REGULATION OF THE EUROPEAN PARLIAMENT AND OF THE COUNCIL

of 21 April 2004

creating a European Enforcement Order for uncontested claims

(805/2004/EC)

NOTES

Date of original publication in OJ: OJ L143, 30.4.2004, p 15, reproduced as corrected by corrigendum (OJ L97, 15.4.2005, p 64) and subsequently amended.

THE EUROPEAN PARLIAMENT AND THE COUNCIL OF THE EUROPEAN UNION,

Having regard to the Treaty establishing the European Community, and in particular Articles 61(c) and the second indent of Article 67(5) thereof,

Having regard to the proposal from the Commission,[1]

Having regard to the Opinion of the European Economic and Social Committee,[2]

Acting in accordance with the procedure laid down in Article 251 of the Treaty,[3]

Whereas:

(1) The Community has set itself the objective of maintaining and developing an area of freedom, security and justice, in which the free movement of persons is ensured. To this end, the Community is to adopt, inter alia, measures in the field of judicial cooperation in civil matters that are necessary for the proper functioning of the internal market.

(2) On 3 December 1998, the Council adopted an Action Plan of the Council and the Commission on how best to implement the provisions of the Treaty of Amsterdam on an area of freedom, security and justice[4] (the Vienna Action Plan).

(3) The European Council meeting in Tampere on 15 and 16 October 1999 endorsed the principle of mutual recognition of judicial decisions as the cornerstone for the creation of a genuine judicial area.

(4) On 30 November 2000, the Council adopted a programme of measures for implementation of the principle of mutual recognition of decisions in civil and commercial matters.[5] This programme includes in its first stage the abolition of exequatur, that is to say, the creation of a European Enforcement Order for uncontested claims.

(5) The concept of "uncontested claims" should cover all situations in which a creditor, given the verified absence of any dispute by the debtor as to the nature or extent of a pecuniary claim, has obtained either a court decision against that debtor or an enforceable document that requires the debtor's express consent, be it a court settlement or an authentic instrument.

(6) The absence of objections from the debtor as stipulated in Article 3(1)(b) can take the shape of default of appearance at a court hearing or of failure to comply with an invitation by the court to give written notice of an intention to defend the case.

(7) This Regulation should apply to judgments, court settlements and authentic instruments on uncontested claims and to decisions delivered following challenges to judgments, court settlements and authentic instruments certified as European Enforcement Orders.

(8) In its Tampere conclusions, the European Council considered that access to enforcement in a Member State other than that in which the judgment has been given should be accelerated and simplified by dispensing with any intermediate measures to be taken prior to enforcement in the Member State in which enforcement is sought. A judgment that has been certified as a European Enforcement Order by the court of origin should, for enforcement purposes, be treated as if it had been delivered in the Member State in which enforcement is sought. In the United Kingdom, for example, the registration of a certified foreign judgment will therefore follow the same rules as the registration of a judgment from another part of the United Kingdom and is not to imply a review as to the substance of the foreign judgment. Arrangements for the enforcement of judgments should continue to be governed by national law.

(9) Such a procedure should offer significant advantages as compared with the exequatur procedure provided for in Council Regulation (EC) No 44/2001 of 22 December 2000 on jurisdiction and the recognition and enforcement of judgments in civil and commercial matters,[6] in that there is no need for approval by the judiciary in a second Member State with the delays and expenses that this entails.

(10) Where a court in a Member State has given judgment on an uncontested claim in the absence of participation of the debtor in the proceedings, the abolition of any checks in the

Member State of enforcement is inextricably linked to and dependent upon the existence of a sufficient guarantee of observance of the rights of the defence.

(11) This Regulation seeks to promote the fundamental rights and takes into account the principles recognised in particular by the Charter of Fundamental Rights of the European Union. In particular, it seeks to ensure full respect for the right to a fair trial as recognised in Article 47 of the Charter.

(12) Minimum standards should be established for the proceedings leading to the judgment in order to ensure that the debtor is informed about the court action against him, the requirements for his active participation in the proceedings to contest the claim and the consequences of his non-participation in sufficient time and in such a way as to enable him to arrange for his defence.

(13) Due to differences between the Member States as regards the rules of civil procedure and especially those governing the service of documents, it is necessary to lay down a specific and detailed definition of those minimum standards. In particular, any method of service that is based on a legal fiction as regards the fulfilment of those minimum standards cannot be considered sufficient for the certification of a judgment as a European Enforcement Order.

(14) All the methods of service listed in Articles 13 and 14 are characterised by either full certainty (Article 13) or a very high degree of likelihood (Article 14) that the document served has reached its addressee. In the second category, a judgment should only be certified as a European Enforcement Order if the Member State of origin has an appropriate mechanism in place enabling the debtor to apply for a full review of the judgment under the conditions set out in Article 19 in those exceptional cases where, in spite of compliance with Article 14, the document has not reached the addressee.

(15) Personal service on certain persons other than the debtor himself pursuant to Article 14(1)(a) and (b) should be understood to meet the requirements of those provisions only if those persons actually accepted/received the document in question.

(16) Article 15 should apply to situations where the debtor cannot represent himself in court, as in the case of a legal person, and where a person to represent him is determined by law as well as situations where the debtor has authorised another person, in particular a lawyer, to represent him in the specific court proceedings at issue.

(17) The courts competent for scrutinising full compliance with the minimum procedural standards should, if satisfied, issue a standardised European Enforcement Order certificate that makes that scrutiny and its result transparent.

(18) Mutual trust in the administration of justice in the Member States justifies the assessment by the court of one Member State that all conditions for certification as a European Enforcement Order are fulfilled to enable a judgment to be enforced in all other Member States without judicial review of the proper application of the minimum procedural standards in the Member State where the judgment is to be enforced.

(19) This Regulation does not imply an obligation for the Member States to adapt their national legislation to the minimum procedural standards set out herein. It provides an incentive to that end by making available a more efficient and rapid enforceability of judgments in other Member States only if those minimum standards are met.

(20) Application for certification as a European Enforcement Order for uncontested claims should be optional for the creditor, who may instead choose the system of recognition and enforcement under Regulation (EC) No 44/2001 or other Community instruments.

(21) When a document has to be sent from one Member State to another for service there, this Regulation and in particular the rules on service set out herein should apply together with Council Regulation (EC) No 1348/2000 of 29 May 2000 on the service in the Member States of judicial and extrajudicial documents in civil or commercial matters,[7] and in particular Article 14 thereof in conjunction with Member States declarations made under Article 23 thereof.

(22) Since the objectives of the proposed action cannot be sufficiently achieved by the Member States and can therefore, by reason of the scale or effects of the action, be better achieved at Community level, the Community may adopt measures, in accordance with the principle of subsidiarity as set out in Article 5 of the Treaty. In accordance with the principle of proportionality, as set out in that Article, this Regulation does not go beyond what is necessary in order to achieve those objectives.

(23) The measures necessary for the implementation of this Regulation should be adopted in accordance with Council Decision 1999/468/EC of 28 June 1999 laying down the procedures for the exercise of implementing powers conferred on the Commission.[8]

(24) In accordance with Article 3 of the Protocol on the position of the United Kingdom and Ireland annexed to the Treaty on European Union and the Treaty establishing the European Community, the United Kingdom and Ireland have notified their wish to take part in the adoption and application of this Regulation.

(25) In accordance with Articles 1 and 2 of the Protocol on the position of Denmark annexed to the Treaty on European Union and the Treaty establishing the European Community, Denmark does not take part in the adoption of this Regulation, and is therefore not bound by it or subject to its application.

(26) Pursuant to the second indent of Article 67(5) of the Treaty, the codecision procedure is applicable from 1 February 2003 for the measures laid down in this Regulation,

[3161]

NOTES

1 OJ C203 E, 27.8.2002, p 86.
2 OJ C85, 8.4.2003, p 1.
3 Opinion of the European Parliament of 8 April 2003 (OJ C64 E, 12.3.2004, p 79), Council Common Position of 6.2.2004 (not yet published in the Official Journal) and Position of the European Parliament of 30.3.2004 (not yet published in the Official Journal).
4 OJ C19, 23.1.1999, p 1.
5 OJ C12, 15.1.2001, p 1.
6 OJ L12, 16.1.2001, p 1. Regulation as last amended by Commission Regulation (EC) No 1496/2002 (OJ L225, 22.8.2002, p 13).
7 OJ L160, 30.6.2000, p 37.
8 OJ L184, 17.7.1999, p 23.

HAVE ADOPTED THIS REGULATION:

CHAPTER I
SUBJECT MATTER, SCOPE AND DEFINITIONS

Article 1

Subject matter

The purpose of this Regulation is to create a European Enforcement Order for uncontested claims to permit, by laying down minimum standards, the free circulation of judgments, court settlements and authentic instruments throughout all Member States without any intermediate proceedings needing to be brought in the Member State of enforcement prior to recognition and enforcement.

[3162]

Article 2

Scope

1. This Regulation shall apply in civil and commercial matters, whatever the nature of the court or tribunal. It shall not extend, in particular, to revenue, customs or administrative matters or the liability of the State for acts and omissions in the exercise of State authority ("acta iure imperii").

2. This Regulation shall not apply to:

(a) the status or legal capacity of natural persons, rights in property arising out of a matrimonial relationship, wills and succession;
(b) bankruptcy, proceedings relating to the winding-up of insolvent companies or other legal persons, judicial arrangements, compositions and analogous proceedings;
(c) social security;
(d) arbitration.

3. In this Regulation, the term "Member State" shall mean Member States with the exception of Denmark.

[3163]

Article 3

Enforcement titles to be certified as a European Enforcement Order

1. This Regulation shall apply to judgments, court settlements and authentic instruments on uncontested claims.

A claim shall be regarded as uncontested if:

(a) the debtor has expressly agreed to it by admission or by means of a settlement which has been approved by a court or concluded before a court in the course of proceedings; or

(b) the debtor has never objected to it, in compliance with the relevant procedural requirements under the law of the Member State of origin, in the course of the court proceedings; or

(c) the debtor has not appeared or been represented at a court hearing regarding that claim after having initially objected to the claim in the course of the court proceedings, provided that such conduct amounts to a tacit admission of the claim or of the facts alleged by the creditor under the law of the Member State of origin; or

(d) the debtor has expressly agreed to it in an authentic instrument.

2. This Regulation shall also apply to decisions delivered following challenges to judgments, court settlements or authentic instruments certified as European Enforcement Orders.

[3164]

Article 4

Definitions

For the purposes of this Regulation, the following definitions shall apply:

1. "judgment": any judgment given by a court or tribunal of a Member State, whatever the judgment may be called, including a decree, order, decision or writ of execution, as well as the determination of costs or expenses by an officer of the court;
2. "claim": a claim for payment of a specific sum of money that has fallen due or for which the due date is indicated in the judgment, court settlement or authentic instrument;
3. "authentic instrument":
   (a) a document which has been formally drawn up or registered as an authentic instrument, and the authenticity of which:
      (i) relates to the signature and the content of the instrument; and
      (ii) has been established by a public authority or other authority empowered for that purpose by the Member State in which it originates;

   or

   (b) an arrangement relating to maintenance obligations concluded with administrative authorities or authenticated by them;
4. "Member State of origin": the Member State in which the judgment has been given, the court settlement has been approved or concluded or the authentic instrument has been drawn up or registered, and is to be certified as a European Enforcement Order;
5. "Member State of enforcement": the Member State in which enforcement of the judgment, court settlement or authentic instrument certified as a European Enforcement Order is sought;
6. "court of origin": the court or tribunal seised of the proceedings at the time of fulfilment of the conditions set out in Article 3(1)(a), (b) or (c);
7. in Sweden, in summary proceedings concerning orders to pay (betalningsföreläggande), the expression "court" includes the Swedish enforcement service (kronofogdemyndighet).

[3165]

CHAPTER II
EUROPEAN ENFORCEMENT ORDER

Article 5

Abolition of exequatur

A judgment which has been certified as a European Enforcement Order in the Member State of origin shall be recognised and enforced in the other Member States without the need for a declaration of enforceability and without any possibility of opposing its recognition.

[3166]

PART IV

Article 6

Requirements for certification as a European Enforcement Order

1. A judgment on an uncontested claim delivered in a Member State shall, upon application at any time to the court of origin, be certified as a European Enforcement Order if:
   (a) the judgment is enforceable in the Member State of origin; and
   (b) the judgment does not conflict with the rules on jurisdiction as laid down in sections 3 and 6 of Chapter II of Regulation (EC) No 44/2001; and
   (c) the court proceedings in the Member State of origin met the requirements as set out in Chapter III where a claim is uncontested within the meaning of Article 3(1)(b) or (c); and
   (d) the judgment was given in the Member State of the debtor's domicile within the meaning of Article 59 of Regulation (EC) No 44/2001, in cases where
   — a claim is uncontested within the meaning of Article 3(1)(b) or (c); and
   — it relates to a contract concluded by a person, the consumer, for a purpose which can be regarded as being outside his trade or profession; and
   — the debtor is the consumer.

2. Where a judgment certified as a European Enforcement Order has ceased to be enforceable or its enforceability has been suspended or limited, a certificate indicating the lack or limitation of enforceability shall, upon application at any time to the court of origin, be issued, using the standard form in Annex IV.

3. Without prejudice to Article 12(2), where a decision has been delivered following a challenge to a judgment certified as a European Enforcement Order in accordance with paragraph 1 of this Article, a replacement certificate shall, upon application at any time, be issued, using the standard form in Annex V, if that decision on the challenge is enforceable in the Member State of origin.

[3167]

Article 7

Costs related to court proceedings

Where a judgment includes an enforceable decision on the amount of costs related to the court proceedings, including the interest rates, it shall be certified as a European Enforcement Order also with regard to the costs unless the debtor has specifically objected to his obligation to bear such costs in the course of the court proceedings, in accordance with the law of the Member State of origin.

[3168]

Article 8

Partial European Enforcement Order certificate

If only parts of the judgment meet the requirements of this Regulation, a partial European Enforcement Order certificate shall be issued for those parts.

[3169]

Article 9

Issue of the European Enforcement Order certificate

1. The European Enforcement Order certificate shall be issued using the standard form in Annex I.

2. The European Enforcement Order certificate shall be issued in the language of the judgment.

[3170]

Article 10

Rectification or withdrawal of the European Enforcement Order certificate

1. The European Enforcement Order certificate shall, upon application to the court of origin, be
   (a) rectified where, due to a material error, there is a discrepancy between the judgment and the certificate;

(b) withdrawn where it was clearly wrongly granted, having regard to the requirements laid down in this Regulation.

2. The law of the Member State of origin shall apply to the rectification or withdrawal of the European Enforcement Order certificate.

3. An application for the rectification or withdrawal of a European Enforcement Order certificate may be made using the standard form in Annex VI.

4. No appeal shall lie against the issuing of a European Enforcement Order certificate.

[3171]

Article 11

Effect of the European Enforcement Order certificate

The European Enforcement Order certificate shall take effect only within the limits of the enforceability of the judgment.

[3172]

CHAPTER III

MINIMUM STANDARDS FOR UNCONTESTED CLAIMS PROCEDURES

Article 12

Scope of application of minimum standards

1. A judgment on a claim that is uncontested within the meaning of Article 3(1)(b) or (c) can be certified as a European Enforcement Order only if the court proceedings in the Member State of origin met the procedural requirements as set out in this Chapter.

2. The same requirements shall apply to the issuing of a European Enforcement Order certificate or a replacement certificate within the meaning of Article 6(3) for a decision following a challenge to a judgment where, at the time of that decision, the conditions of Article 3(1)(b) or (c) are fulfilled.

[3173]

Article 13

Service with proof of receipt by the debtor

1. The document instituting the proceedings or an equivalent document may have been served on the debtor by one of the following methods:

(a) personal service attested by an acknowledgement of receipt, including the date of receipt, which is signed by the debtor;

(b) personal service attested by a document signed by the competent person who effected the service stating that the debtor has received the document or refused to receive it without any legal justification, and the date of the service;

(c) postal service attested by an acknowledgement of receipt including the date of receipt, which is signed and returned by the debtor;

(d) service by electronic means such as fax or e-mail, attested by an acknowledgement of receipt including the date of receipt, which is signed and returned by the debtor.

2. Any summons to a court hearing may have been served on the debtor in compliance with paragraph 1 or orally in a previous court hearing on the same claim and stated in the minutes of that previous court hearing.

[3174]

Article 14

Service without proof of receipt by the debtor

1. Service of the document instituting the proceedings or an equivalent document and any summons to a court hearing on the debtor may also have been effected by one of the following methods:

(a) personal service at the debtor's personal address on persons who are living in the same household as the debtor or are employed there;

(b) in the case of a self-employed debtor or a legal person, personal service at the debtor's business premises on persons who are employed by the debtor;
(c) deposit of the document in the debtor's mailbox;
(d) deposit of the document at a post office or with competent public authorities and the placing in the debtor's mailbox of written notification of that deposit, provided that the written notification clearly states the character of the document as a court document or the legal effect of the notification as effecting service and setting in motion the running of time for the purposes of time limits;
(e) postal service without proof pursuant to paragraph 3 where the debtor has his address in the Member State of origin;
(f) electronic means attested by an automatic confirmation of delivery, provided that the debtor has expressly accepted this method of service in advance.

2. For the purposes of this Regulation, service under paragraph 1 is not admissible if the debtor's address is not known with certainty.

3. Service pursuant to paragraph 1, (a) to (d), shall be attested by:
(a) a document signed by the competent person who effected the service, indicating:
(i) the method of service used; and
(ii) the date of service; and
(iii) where the document has been served on a person other than the debtor, the name of that person and his relation to the debtor,

or
(b) an acknowledgement of receipt by the person served, for the purposes of paragraphs 1(a) and (b).

[3175]

Article 15

Service on the debtor's representatives

Service pursuant to Articles 13 or 14 may also have been effected on a debtor's representative.

[3176]

Article 16

Provision to the debtor of due information about the claim

In order to ensure that the debtor was provided with due information about the claim, the document instituting the proceedings or the equivalent document must have contained the following:
(a) the names and the addresses of the parties;
(b) the amount of the claim;
(c) if interest on the claim is sought, the interest rate and the period for which interest is sought unless statutory interest is automatically added to the principal under the law of the Member State of origin;
(d) a statement of the reason for the claim.

[3177]

Article 17

Provision to the debtor of due information about the procedural steps necessary to contest the claim

The following must have been clearly stated in or together with the document instituting the proceedings, the equivalent document or any summons to a court hearing:
(a) the procedural requirements for contesting the claim, including the time limit for contesting the claim in writing or the time for the court hearing, as applicable, the name and the address of the institution to which to respond or before which to appear, as applicable, and whether it is mandatory to be represented by a lawyer;
(b) the consequences of an absence of objection or default of appearance, in particular, where applicable, the possibility that a judgment may be given or enforced against the debtor and the liability for costs related to the court proceedings.

[3178]

Article 18

Cure of non-compliance with minimum standards

1. If the proceedings in the Member State of origin did not meet the procedural requirements as set out in Articles 13 to 17, such non-compliance shall be cured and a judgment may be certified as a European Enforcement Order if:

(a) the judgment has been served on the debtor in compliance with the requirements pursuant to Article 13 or Article 14; and

(b) it was possible for the debtor to challenge the judgment by means of a full review and the debtor has been duly informed in or together with the judgment about the procedural requirements for such a challenge, including the name and address of the institution with which it must be lodged and, where applicable, the time limit for so doing; and

(c) the debtor has failed to challenge the judgment in compliance with the relevant procedural requirements.

2. If the proceedings in the Member State of origin did not comply with the procedural requirements as set out in Article 13 or Article 14, such non-compliance shall be cured if it is proved by the conduct of the debtor in the court proceedings that he has personally received the document to be served in sufficient time to arrange for his defence.

[3179]

Article 19

Minimum standards for review in exceptional cases

1. Further to Articles 13 to 18, a judgment can only be certified as a European Enforcement Order if the debtor is entitled, under the law of the Member State of origin, to apply for a review of the judgment where:

(a)

(i) the document instituting the proceedings or an equivalent document or, where applicable, the summons to a court hearing, was served by one of the methods provided for in Article 14; and

(ii) service was not effected in sufficient time to enable him to arrange for his defence, without any fault on his part;

or

(b) the debtor was prevented from objecting to the claim by reason of force majeure, or due to extraordinary circumstances without any fault on his part,

provided in either case that he acts promptly.

2. This Article is without prejudice to the possibility for Member States to grant access to a review of the judgment under more generous conditions than those mentioned in paragraph 1.

[3180]

CHAPTER IV
ENFORCEMENT

Article 20

Enforcement procedure

1. Without prejudice to the provisions of this Chapter, the enforcement procedures shall be governed by the law of the Member State of enforcement.

A judgment certified as a European Enforcement Order shall be enforced under the same conditions as a judgment handed down in the Member State of enforcement.

2. The creditor shall be required to provide the competent enforcement authorities of the Member State of enforcement with:

(a) a copy of the judgment which satisfies the conditions necessary to establish its authenticity; and

(b) a copy of the European Enforcement Order certificate which satisfies the conditions necessary to establish its authenticity; and

(c) where necessary, a transcription of the European Enforcement Order certificate or a translation thereof into the official language of the Member State of enforcement or, if there are several official languages in that Member State, the official language or one of the official languages of court proceedings of the place where enforcement is sought, in conformity with the law of that Member State, or into another language that the Member State of enforcement has indicated it can accept. Each Member State may indicate the official language or languages of the institutions of the European Community other than its own which it can accept for the completion of the certificate. The translation shall be certified by a person qualified to do so in one of the Member States.

3. No security, bond or deposit, however described, shall be required of a party who in one Member State applies for enforcement of a judgment certified as a European Enforcement Order in another Member State on the ground that he is a foreign national or that he is not domiciled or resident in the Member State of enforcement. **[3181]**

Article 21

Refusal of enforcement

1. Enforcement shall, upon application by the debtor, be refused by the competent court in the Member State of enforcement if the judgment certified as a European Enforcement Order is irreconcilable with an earlier judgment given in any Member State or in a third country, provided that:

(a) the earlier judgment involved the same cause of action and was between the same parties; and

(b) the earlier judgment was given in the Member State of enforcement or fulfils the conditions necessary for its recognition in the Member State of enforcement; and

(c) the irreconcilability was not and could not have been raised as an objection in the court proceedings in the Member State of origin.

2. Under no circumstances may the judgment or its certification as a European Enforcement Order be reviewed as to their substance in the Member State of enforcement. **[3182]**

Article 22

Agreements with third countries

This Regulation shall not affect agreements by which Member States undertook, prior to the entry into force of Regulation (EC) No 44/2001, pursuant to Article 59 of the Brussels Convention on jurisdiction and the enforcement of judgments in civil and commercial matters, not to recognise judgments given, in particular in other Contracting States to that Convention, against defendants domiciled or habitually resident in a third country where, in cases provided for in Article 4 of that Convention, the judgment could only be founded on a ground of jurisdiction specified in the second paragraph of Article 3 of that Convention. **[3183]**

Article 23

Stay or limitation of enforcement

Where the debtor has

— challenged a judgment certified as a European Enforcement Order, including an application for review within the meaning of Article 19, or

— applied for the rectification or withdrawal of a European Enforcement Order certificate in accordance with Article 10,

the competent court or authority in the Member State of enforcement may, upon application by the debtor:

(a) limit the enforcement proceedings to protective measures; or

(b) make enforcement conditional on the provision of such security as it shall determine; or

(c) under exceptional circumstances, stay the enforcement proceedings. **[3184]**

CHAPTER V
COURT SETTLEMENTS AND AUTHENTIC INSTRUMENTS

Article 24

Court settlements

1. A settlement concerning a claim within the meaning of Article 4(2) which has been approved by a court or concluded before a court in the course of proceedings and is enforceable in the Member State in which it was approved or concluded shall, upon application to the court that approved it or before which it was concluded, be certified as a European Enforcement Order using the standard form in Annex II.

2. A settlement which has been certified as a European Enforcement Order in the Member State of origin shall be enforced in the other Member States without the need for a declaration of enforceability and without any possibility of opposing its enforceability.

3. The provisions of Chapter II, with the exception of Articles 5, 6(1) and 9(1), and of Chapter IV, with the exception of Articles 21(1) and 22, shall apply as appropriate.

[3185]

Article 25

Authentic instruments

1. An authentic instrument concerning a claim within the meaning of Article 4(2) which is enforceable in one Member State shall, upon application to the authority designated by the Member State of origin, be certified as a European Enforcement Order, using the standard form in Annex III.

2. An authentic instrument which has been certified as a European Enforcement Order in the Member State of origin shall be enforced in the other Member States without the need for a declaration of enforceability and without any possibility of opposing its enforceability.

3. The provisions of Chapter II, with the exception of Articles 5, 6(1) and 9(1), and of Chapter IV, with the exception of Articles 21(1) and 22, shall apply as appropriate.

[3186]

CHAPTER VI
TRANSITIONAL PROVISION

Article 26

Transitional provision

This Regulation shall apply only to judgments given, to court settlements approved or concluded and to documents formally drawn up or registered as authentic instruments after the entry into force of this Regulation.

[3187]

CHAPTER VII
RELATIONSHIP WITH OTHER COMMUNITY INSTRUMENTS

Article 27

Relationship with Regulation (EC) No 44/2001

This Regulation shall not affect the possibility of seeking recognition and enforcement, in accordance with Regulation (EC) No 44/2001, of a judgment, a court settlement or an authentic instrument on an uncontested claim.

[3188]

Article 28

Relationship with Regulation (EC) No 1348/2000

This Regulation shall not affect the application of Regulation (EC) No 1348/2000.

[3189]

CHAPTER VIII
GENERAL AND FINAL PROVISIONS

Article 29

Information on enforcement procedures and authorities

The Member States shall cooperate to provide the general public and professional circles with information on:

(a) the methods and procedures of enforcement in the Member States; and
(b) the competent authorities for enforcement in the Member States,

in particular via the European Judicial Network in civil and commercial matters established in accordance with Decision 2001/470/EC.[9]

[3190]

Article 30

Information relating to redress procedures, languages and authorities

1. The Member States shall notify the Commission of:

(a) the procedures for rectification and withdrawal referred to in Article 10(2) and for review referred to in Article 19(1);
(b) the languages accepted pursuant to Article 20(2)(c);
(c) the lists of the authorities referred to in Article 25;

and any subsequent changes thereof.

2. The Commission shall make the information notified in accordance with paragraph 1 publicly available through publication in the Official Journal of the European Union and through any other appropriate means.

[3191]

Article 31

Amendments to the Annexes

Any amendment to the standard forms in the Annexes shall be adopted in accordance with the advisory procedure referred to in Article 32(2).

[3192]

Article 32

Committee

1. The Commission shall be assisted by the committee provided for by Article 75 of Regulation (EC) No 44/2001.

2. Where reference is made to this paragraph, Articles 3 and 7 of Decision 1999/468/EC shall apply, having regard to the provisions of Article 8 thereof.

3. The Committee shall adopt its Rules of Procedure.

[3193]

Article 33

Entry into force

This Regulation shall enter into force on 21 January 2005.

It shall apply from 21 October 2005, with the exception of Articles 30, 31 and 32, which shall apply from 21 January 2005.

This Regulation shall be binding in its entirety and directly applicable in the Member States in accordance with the Treaty establishing the European Community.

[3194]

NOTES

[9] OJ L174, 27.6.2001, p 25.

Done at Strasbourg, 21 April 2004.

[ANNEX I
EUROPEAN ENFORCEMENT ORDER
CERTIFICATE—JUDGMENT

1. Member State of origin:

Belgium___Czech Republic___Germany___Estonia___Greece___

Spain___France___Ireland___Italy___Cyprus___Latvia___

Lithuania___Luxembourg___Hungary___Malta___Netherlands___

Austria___Poland___Portugal___Slovakia___Slovenia___Finland___

Sweden___United Kingdom___

2. Court/Tribunal issuing the certificate:

2.1. Name:

2.2. Address:

2.3. Tel/fax/e-mail:

3. If different, Court/Tribunal giving the judgment:

3.1. Name:

3.2. Address:

3.3. Tel/fax/e-mail:

4. Judgment:

4.1. Date:

4.2. Reference number:

4.3. The parties

4.3.1. Name and address of creditor(s):

4.3.2. Name and address of debtor(s):

5. Monetary claim as certified:

5.1. Principal amount:

5.1.1. Currency:

Euro___Cyprus pound___Czech koruna___Estonian kroon___

Pound sterling___Hungarian forint___Lithuanian litas___Latvian lats___

Maltese lira___Polish zloty___Swedish kronor___Slovak koruna___

Slovenian tolar___

other (explain)___

5.1.2. If the claim is for periodical payments

5.1.2.1. Amount of each instalment:

5.1.2.2. Due date of first instalment:

5.1.2.3. Due dates of following instalments
weekly___monthly___other (explain)___

5.1.2.4. Period of the claim

5.1.2.4.1. Currently indefinite ___ or

5.1.2.4.2. Due date of last instalment:

5.2. Interest

5.2.1. Interest rate

5.2.1.1. … % or

5.2.1.2. … % above the base rate of the ECB[1]

5.2.1.3. Other (explain)

5.2.2. Interest to be collected as from:

5.3. Amount of reimbursable costs if specified in the judgment:

6. Judgment is enforceable in the Member State of origin ___

7. Judgment is still subject to the possibility of a challenge

Yes ___ No ___

8. Judgment is on an uncontested claim under Article 3(1) ___

9. Judgment is in compliance with Article 6(1)(b) ___

10. The judgment concerns matters relating to consumer contracts
Yes ___ No ___

10.1. If yes:
The debtor is the consumer
Yes ___ No ___

10.2. If yes:
The debtor is domiciled in the Member State of origin (within the meaning of Article 59 of Regulation (EC) No 44/2001) ___

11. Service of the document instituting the proceedings under Chapter III, where applicable
Yes ___ No ___

11.1. Service was effected in compliance with Article 13 ___
or service was effected in compliance with Article 14 ___
or it is proved in accordance with Article 18(2) that the debtor has received the document ___

11.2. Due information
The debtor was informed in compliance with Articles 16 and 17 ___

12. Service of summons, where applicable
Yes ___ No ___

12.1. Service was effected in compliance with Article 13 ___
or service was effected in compliance with Article 14 ___
or it is proved in accordance with Article 18(2) that the debtor has received the summons ___

12.2. Due information
The debtor was informed in compliance with Article 17 ___

13. Cure of non-compliance with procedural minimum standards pursuant to Article 18(1)

13.1. Service of the judgment was effected in compliance with Article 13 ___
or service of the judgment was effected in compliance with Article 14 ___
or it is proved in accordance with Article 18(2) that the debtor has received the judgment ___

13.2. Due information
The debtor was informed in compliance with Article 18(1)(b) ___

13.3. It was possible for the debtor to challenge the judgment
Yes ___ No ___

13.4. The debtor failed to challenge the judgment in compliance with the relevant procedural requirements
Yes ___ No ___

Done at date

....

Signature and/or stamp..]

[3195]

---

[1] Interest rate applied by the European Central Bank to its main refinancing operations.

NOTES

Commencement: 24 November 2005.

Substituted by Commission Regulation 1869/2005/EC, Art 1, Annex I (OJ L300, 17.11.2005, p 6).

[ANNEX II

EUROPEAN ENFORCEMENT ORDER CERTIFICATE—COURT SETTLEMENT

1. Member State of origin:

Belgium___Czech Republic___Germany___Estonia___Greece___

Spain___France___Ireland___Italy___Cyprus___Latvia___

Lithuania___Luxembourg___Hungary___Malta___Netherlands___

Austria___Poland___Portugal___Slovakia___Slovenia___Finland___

Sweden___United Kingdom___

2. Court issuing the certificate

2.1. Name:

2.2. Address:

2.3. Tel/fax/e-mail:

3. If different, Court approving the settlement or before which is was concluded

3.1. Name:

3.2. Address:

3.3. Tel/fax/e-mail:

4. Court settlement

4.1. Date:

4.2. Reference number:

4.3. The parties

4.3.1. Name and address of creditor(s):

4.3.2. Name and address of debtor(s):

5. Monetary claim as certified

5.1. Principal Amount:

5.1.1. Currency:

Euro___Cyprus pound___Czech koruna___Estonian kroon___

Pound sterling___Hungarian forint___Lithuanian litas___Latvian lats___

Maltese lira___Polish zloty___Swedish kronor___Slovak koruna___

Slovenian tolar___

other (explain)___

5.1.2. If the claim is for periodical payments

5.1.2.1. Amount of each instalment:

5.1.2.2. Due date of first instalment:

5.1.2.3. Due dates of following instalments
weekly___monthly___other (explain)___

5.1.2.4. Period of the claim

5.1.2.4.1. Currently indefinite ___ or

5.1.2.4.2. Due date of last instalment:

5.2. Interest

5.2.1. Interest rate

5.2.1.1. … % or

5.2.1.2. … % above the base rate of the ECB[1]

5.2.1.3. Other (explain)

5.2.2. Interest to be collected as from:

5.3. Amount of reimbursable costs if specified in the court settlement:

6. The court settlement is enforceable in the Member State origin ___

Done at date

....

Signature and/or stamp..]

[3196]

---

1 Interest rate applied by the European Central Bank to its main refinancing operations.

NOTES

Commencement: 24 November 2005.

Substituted by Commission Regulation 1869/2005/EC, Art 1, Annex II (OJ L300, 17.11.2005, p 6).

[ANNEX III

EUROPEAN ENFORCEMENT ORDER CERTIFICATE—AUTHENTIC INSTRUMENT

1. Member State of origin:

Belgium___Czech Republic___Germany___Estonia___Greece___

Spain___France___Ireland___Italy___Cyprus___Latvia___

Lithuania___Luxembourg___Hungary___Malta___Netherlands___

Austria___Poland___Portugal___Slovakia___Slovenia___Finland___

Sweden___United Kingdom___

2. Court/Authority issuing the certificate

2.1. Name:

2.2. Address:

2.3. Tel/fax/e-mail:

3. If different, Court/Authority drawing up or registering the authentic instrument

3.1. Name:

3.2. Address:

3.3. Tel/fax/e-mail:

4. Authentic Instrument

4.1. Date:

4.2. Reference number:

4.3. The parties

4.3.1. Name and address of creditor(s):

4.3.2. Name and address of debtor(s):

5. Monetary claim as certified

5.1. Principal Amount:

5.1.1. Currency:

Euro___Cyprus pound___Czech koruna___Estonian kroon___

Pound sterling___Hungarian forint___Lithuanian litas___Latvian lats___

Maltese lira___Polish zloty___Swedish kronor___Slovak koruna___

Slovenian tolar___

other (explain)___

5.1.2. If the claim is for periodical payments

5.1.2.1. Amount of each instalment:

5.1.2.2. Due date of first instalment:

5.1.2.3. Due dates of following instalments
weekly___monthly___other (explain)___

5.1.2.4. Period of the claim

5.1.2.4.1. Currently indefinite ___ or

5.1.2.4.2. Due date of last instalment:

5.2. Interest

5.2.1. Interest rate

5.2.1.1. … % or

5.2.1.2. … % above the base rate of the ECB[1]

5.2.1.3. Other (explain)

5.2.2. Interest to be collected as from:

5.3. Amount of reimbursable costs if specified in the authentic instrument:

6. The authentic instrument is enforceable in the Member State origin___

Done at date

………………………………………………………………

Signature and/or stamp………………………………………]

[3197]

[1] Interest rate applied by the European Central Bank to its main refinancing operations.

NOTES

Commencement: 24 November 2005.
Substituted by Commission Regulation 1869/2005/EC, Art 1, Annex III (OJ L300, 17.11.2005, p 6).

[ANNEX IV
CERTIFICATE OF LACK OR LIMITATION OF ENFORCEABILITY

(Article 6(2))

1. Member State of origin:

Belgium___Czech Republic___Germany___Estonia___Greece___

Spain___France___Ireland___Italy___Cyprus___Latvia___

Lithuania___Luxembourg___Hungary___Malta___Netherlands___

Austria___Poland___Portugal___Slovakia___Slovenia___Finland___

Sweden___United Kingdom___

2. Court/Authority issuing the certificate

2.1. Name:

2.2. Address:

2.3. Tel/fax/e-mail:

3. If different, Court/Authority issuing the judgment/Court setlement/Authentic Instrument*

3.1. Name:

3.2. Address:

3.3. Tel/fax/e-mail:

4. Judgment/Court settlement/Authentic Instrument*

4.1. Date:

4.2. Reference number:

4.3. The parties

4.3.1. Name and address of creditor(s):

4.3.2. Name and address of debtor(s):

5. This judgment/Court settlement/Authentic instrument* was certified as a European Enforcement Order but

5.1. the judgment/Court settlement/Authentic instrument* is no longer enforeable ___

5.2 Enforcement is temporarily

5.2.1 stayed ___

5.2.2 limited to protective measures ___

5.2.3 conditional upon the provision of a security which is still outstanding ___

5.2.3.1 Amount of the security:

5.2.3.2 Currency:

Euro___Cyprus pound___Czech koruna___Estonian kroon___

Pound sterling___Hungarian forint___Lithuanian litas___Latvian lats___

Maltese lira___Polish zloty___Swedish kronor___Slovak koruna___

Slovenian tolar___

other (explain)___

5.2.4. Other (explain) ___

Done at date

....

Signature and/or stamp..]

* Delete as appropriate.

[3198]

NOTES

Commencement: 24 November 2005.
Substituted by Commission Regulation 1869/2005/EC, Art 1, Annex IV (OJ L300, 17.11.2005, p 6).

[ANNEX V
EUROPEAN ENFORCEMENT ORDER REPLACEMENT CERTIFICATE FOLLOWING A CHALLENGE

(Article 6(3))

A. The following judgment/court settlement/authentic instrument* certified as a European Enforcement Order was challenged

1. Member State of origin:

Belgium___Czech Republic___Germany___Estonia___Greece___

Spain___France___Ireland___Italy___Cyprus___Latvia___

Lithuania___Luxembourg___Hungary___Malta___Netherlands___

Austria___Poland___Portugal___Slovakia___Slovenia___Finland___

Sweden___United Kingdom___

2. Court/Authority issuing the certificate

2.1. Name:

2.2. Address:

2.3. Tel/fax/e-mail:

3. If different, Court/Authority issuing the judgment/Court settlement/Authentic Instrument*

3.1. Name:

3.2. Address:

3.3. Tel/fax/e-mail:

4. Judgment/Court settlement/Authentic Instrument*

4.1. Date:

4.2. Reference number:

4.3. The parties

4.3.1. Name and address of creditor(s):

4.3.2. Name and address of debtor(s):

B. Upon that challenge the following decision has been handed down and is hereby certified as a European Enforcement Order replacing the original European Enforcement Order.

1. Court

1.1. Name:

1.2. Address:

1.3. Tel/fax/e-mail:

2. Decision

2.1. Date:

2.2. Reference number:

3. Monetary claim as certified

3.1. Principal amount:

3.1.1. Currency

Euro___Cyprus pound___Czech koruna___Estonian kroon___

Pound sterling___Hungarian forint___Lithuanian litas___Latvian lats___

Maltese lira___Polish zloty___Swedish kronor___Slovak koruna___

Slovenian tolar___

other (explain)___

3.1.2. If the claim is for periodic payments

3.1.2.1. Amount of each instalment:

3.1.2.2. Due date of first instalment:

3.1.2.3. Due dates of following instalments
weekly___monthly___other (explain)___

3.1.2.4. Period of the claim

3.1.2.4.1. Currently indefinite ___ or

3.1.2.4.2. Due date of last instalment:

3.2. Interest

3.2.1. Interest rate

3.2.1.1. ... % or

3.2.1.2. ... % above the base rate of the ECB

PART IV
EC MATERIALS

3.2.1.3. Other (explain)

3.2.2. Interest to be collected as from:

3.3. Amount of reimbursable costs if specified in the decision:

4. Decision is enforceable in the Member State of origin ___

5. Decision is still subject to the possibility of a further appeal
Yes ___ No ___

6. Decision is in compliance with Article 6(1)(b) ___

7. The decision concerns matters relating to consumer contracts
Yes ___ No ___

7.1. If yes:
The debtor is the consumer
Yes ___ No ___

7.2. If yes:
The debtor is domiciled in the Member State of origin in the meaning of Article 59 of Regulation (EC) No 44/2001 ___

8. At the time of the decision following the challenge, the claim is uncontested within the meaning of Article 3(1)(b) or (c)
Yes ___ No ___

If yes:

8.1. Service of the document instituting the challenge
Did the creditor lodge the challenge?
Yes ___ No ___

If yes:

8.1.1. Service was effected in compliance with Article 13 ___
or service was effected in compliance with Article 14 ___
or it is proved in accordance with Article 18(2) that the debtor has received the document ___

8.1.2. Due information
The debtor was informed in compliance with Articles 16 and 17 ___

8.2. Service of summons, where applicable
Yes ___ No ___

If yes:

8.2.1. Service was effected in compliance with Article 13 ___
or service was effected in compliance with Article 14 ___
or it is proved in accordance with Article 18(2) that the debtor has received the summons ___

8.2.2. Due information
The debtor was informed in compliance with Article 17 ___

8.3. Cure of non-compliance with procedural minimum standards pursuant to Article 18(1)

8.3.1. Service of the decision was effected in compliance with Article 13 ___
or Service of the decision was effected in compliance with Article 14 ___
or it is proved in accordance with Article 18(2) that the debtor has received the decision ___

8.3.2. Due information
The debtor was informed in compliance with Article 18(1)(b) ___

Done at date

....

Signature and/or stamp..]

* Delete as appropriate.

[3199]

NOTES

Commencement: 24 November 2005.

Substituted by Commission Regulation 1869/2005/EC, Art 1, Annex V (OJ L300, 17.11.2005, p 6).

[ANNEX VI

APPLICATION FOR RECTIFICATION OR WITHDRAWAL OF THE EUROPEAN ENFORCEMENT ORDER CERTIFICATE

(Article 10(3))

THE FOLLOWING EUROPEAN ENFORCEMENT ORDER CERTIFICATE

1. Member State of origin:

Belgium___Czech Republic___Germany___Estonia___Greece___

Spain___France___Ireland___Italy___Cyprus___Latvia___

Lithuania___Luxembourg___Hungary___Malta___Netherlands___

Austria___Poland___Portugal___Slovakia___Slovenia___Finland___

Sweden___United Kingdom___

2. Court/Authority issuing the certificate

2.1. Name:

2.2. Address:

2.3. Tel/fax/e-mail:

3. If different, Court/Authority issuing the judgment/Court settlement/Authentic Instrument*

3.1. Name:

3.2. Address:

3.3. Tel/fax/e-mail:

4. Judgment/Court settlement/Authentic Instrument*

4.1. Date:

4.2. Reference number:

4.3. The parties

4.3.1. Name and address of creditor(s):

4.3.2. Name and address of debtor(s):

HAS TO BE

5. RECTIFIED as due to a material error there is the following discrepancy between the European Enforcement Order certificate and the underlying judgment/court settlement/ authentic instrument (explain) ___

6. WITHDRAWN because:

6.1 the certified judgment was related to a consumer contract but was given in a Member State where the consumer is not domiciled within the meaning of Article 59 of Regulation (EC) No 44/2001 ___

6.2 the European Enforcement Order certificate was clearly wrongly granted for another reason (explain) ___

Done at date

....

Signature and/or stamp..]

* Delete as appropriate.

[3200]

NOTES

Commencement: 24 November 2005.
Substituted by Commission Regulation 1869/2005/EC, Art 1, Annex VI.

COUNCIL DECISION

of 20 September 2005

on the signing, on behalf of the Community, of the Agreement between the European Community and the Kingdom of Denmark on jurisdiction and the recognition and enforcement of judgments in civil and commercial matters

(2005/790/EC)

Date of publication in OJ: OJ L299, 16.11.2005, p 61.
This Agreement between the European Community and Denmark (not a party to Council Regulation 44/2001/EC at **[3080]**) is not yet in force.
On 27 April 2006, the European Community and the Kingdom of Denmark concluded their Agreement on jurisdiction and the recognition and enforcement of judgments in civil and commercial matters. The text of the Council Decision concerning the conclusion of that Agreement is set out in OJ L120, 5.5.2006, p 22. It can also be viewed at http://eur-lex.europa.eu/LexUriServ/site/en/oj/2006/l_120/l_12020060505en00220022.pdf.

THE COUNCIL OF THE EUROPEAN UNION,

Having regard to the Treaty establishing the European Community, and in particular Article 61(c) thereof, in conjunction with the first sentence of the first subparagraph of Article 300(2) thereof,

Having regard to the proposal from the Commission,

Whereas:

(1) In accordance with Articles 1 and 2 of the Protocol on the position of Denmark annexed to the Treaty on European Union and the Treaty establishing the European Community, Denmark is not bound by the provisions of Council Regulation (EC) No 44/2001 of 22 December 2000 on jurisdiction and the recognition and enforcement of judgments in civil and commercial matters,[1] nor subject to their application.

(2) By Decision of 8 May 2003, the Council authorised exceptionally the Commission to negotiate an agreement between the European Community and the Kingdom of Denmark extending to Denmark the provisions of the abovementioned Regulation.

(3) The Commission has negotiated such agreement, on behalf of the Community, with the Kingdom of Denmark.

(4) The United Kingdom and Ireland, in accordance with Article 3 of the Protocol on the position of the United Kingdom and Ireland annexed to the Treaty on European Union and the Treaty establishing the European Community, are taking part in the adoption and application of this Decision.

(5) In accordance with Articles 1 and 2 of the abovementioned Protocol on the position of Denmark, Denmark is not taking part in the adoption of this Decision and is not bound by it or subject to its application.

(6) The Agreement, initialled at Brussels on 17 January 2005, should be signed,

[3201]

NOTES

1 OJ L12, 16.1.2001, p 1. Regulation as last amended by Commission Regulation (EC) No 2245/2004 (OJ L381, 28.12.2004, p 10).

HAS DECIDED AS FOLLOWS:

Article 1

The signing of the Agreement between the European Community and the Kingdom of Denmark on jurisdiction and the recognition and enforcement of judgments in civil and commercial matters is hereby approved on behalf of the Community, subject to the Council Decision concerning the conclusion of the said Agreement.

The text of the Agreement is attached to this Decision.

[3202]

Article 2

The President of the Council is hereby authorised to designate the person(s) empowered to sign the Agreement on behalf of the Community subject to its conclusion.

[3203]

Done at Brussels, 20 September 2005.

AGREEMENT BETWEEN THE EUROPEAN COMMUNITY AND THE KINGDOM OF DENMARK ON JURISDICTION AND THE RECOGNITION AND ENFORCEMENT OF JUDGMENTS IN CIVIL AND COMMERCIAL MATTERS

THE EUROPEAN COMMUNITY, hereinafter referred to as "the Community",

of the one part, and

THE KINGDOM OF DENMARK, hereinafter referred to as "Denmark",

of the other part,

HAVE AGREED AS FOLLOWS:

Article 1

Aim

1. The aim of this Agreement is to apply the provisions of the Brussels I Regulation and its implementing measures to the relations between the Community and Denmark, in accordance with Article 2(1) of this Agreement.

2. It is the objective of the Contracting Parties to arrive at a uniform application and interpretation of the provisions of the Brussels I Regulation and its implementing measures in all Member States.

3. The provisions of Articles 3(1), 4(1) and 5(1) of this Agreement result from the Protocol on the position of Denmark.

Article 2

Jurisdiction and the recognition and enforcement of judgments in civil and commercial matters

1. The provisions of the Brussels I Regulation, which is annexed to this Agreement and forms part thereof, together with its implementing measures adopted pursuant to Article 74(2) of the Regulation and, in respect of implementing measures adopted after the entry into force of this Agreement, implemented by Denmark as referred to in Article 4 of this Agreement, and the measures adopted pursuant to Article 74(1) of the Regulation, shall under international law apply to the relations between the Community and Denmark.

2. However, for the purposes of this Agreement, the application of the provisions of that Regulation shall be modified as follows:

(a) Article 1(3) shall not apply.

(b) Article 50 shall be supplemented by the following paragraph (as paragraph 2):

"2. However, an applicant who requests the enforcement of a decision given by an administrative authority in Denmark in respect of a maintenance order may, in the Member State addressed, claim the benefits referred to in the first paragraph if he presents a statement from the Danish Ministry of Justice to the effect that he fulfils the financial requirements to qualify for the grant of complete or partial legal aid or exemption from costs or expenses.".

(c) Article 62 shall be supplemented by the following paragraph (as paragraph 2):

"2. In matters relating to maintenance, the expression "court" includes the Danish administrative authorities.".

(d) Article 64 shall apply to seagoing ships registered in Denmark as well as in Greece and Portugal.

(e) The date of entry into force of this Agreement shall apply instead of the date of entry into force of the Regulation as referred to in Articles 70(2), 72 and 76 thereof.

(f) The transitional provisions of this Agreement shall apply instead of Article 66 of the Regulation.
(g) In Annex I the following shall be added: "in Denmark: Article 246(2) and (3) of the Administration of Justice Act (lov om rettens pleje)".
(h) In Annex II the following shall be added: "in Denmark, the "byret"".
(i) In Annex III the following shall be added: "in Denmark, the "landsret"".
(j) In Annex IV the following shall be added: "in Denmark, an appeal to the "Højesteret" with leave from the "Procesbevillingsnævnet"".

Article 3

Amendments to the Brussels I Regulation

1. Denmark shall not take part in the adoption of amendments to the Brussels I Regulation and no such amendments shall be binding upon or applicable in Denmark.

2. Whenever amendments to the Regulation are adopted Denmark shall notify the Commission of its decision whether or not to implement the content of such amendments. Notification shall be given at the time of the adoption of the amendments or within 30 days thereafter.

3. If Denmark decides that it will implement the content of the amendments the notification shall indicate whether implementation can take place administratively or requires parliamentary approval.

4. If the notification indicates that implementation can take place administratively the notification shall, moreover, state that all necessary administrative measures enter into force on the date of entry into force of the amendments to the Regulation or have entered into force on the date of the notification, whichever date is the latest.

5. If the notification indicates that implementation requires parliamentary approval in Denmark, the following rules shall apply:
(a) Legislative measures in Denmark shall enter into force on the date of entry into force of the amendments to the Regulation or within 6 months after the notification, whichever date is the latest;
(b) Denmark shall notify the Commission of the date upon which the implementing legislative measures enter into force.

6. A Danish notification that the content of the amendments has been implemented in Denmark, in accordance with paragraphs 4 and 5, creates mutual obligations under international law between Denmark and the Community. The amendments to the Regulation shall then constitute amendments to this Agreement and shall be considered annexed hereto.

7. In cases where:
(a) Denmark notifies its decision not to implement the content of the amendments; or
(b) Denmark does not make a notification within the 30-day time-limit set out in paragraph 2; or
(c) Legislative measures in Denmark do not enter into force within the time-limits set out in paragraph 5,

this Agreement shall be considered terminated unless the parties decide otherwise within 90 days or, in the situation referred to under (c), legislative measures in Denmark enter into force within the same period. Termination shall take effect three months after the expiry of the 90-day period.

8. Legal proceedings instituted and documents formally drawn up or registered as authentic instruments before the date of termination of the Agreement as set out in paragraph 7 are not affected hereby.

Article 4

Implementing measures

1. Denmark shall not take part in the adoption of opinions by the Committee referred to in Article 75 of the Brussels I Regulation. Implementing measures adopted pursuant to Article 74(2) of that Regulation shall not be binding upon and shall not be applicable in Denmark.

2. Whenever implementing measures are adopted pursuant to Article 74(2) of the Regulation, the implementing measures shall be communicated to Denmark. Denmark shall

notify the Commission of its decision whether or not to implement the content of the implementing measures. Notification shall be given upon receipt of the implementing measures or within 30 days thereafter.

3. The notification shall state that all necessary administrative measures in Denmark enter into force on the date of entry into force of the implementing measures or have entered into force on the date of the notification, whichever date is the latest.

4. A Danish notification that the content of the implementing measures has been implemented in Denmark creates mutual obligations under international law between Denmark and the Community. The implementing measures will then form part of this Agreement.

5. In cases where:

(a) Denmark notifies its decision not to implement the content of the implementing measures; or

(b) Denmark does not make a notification within the 30-day time-limit set out in paragraph 2,

this Agreement shall be considered terminated unless the parties decide otherwise within 90 days. Termination shall take effect three months after the expiry of the 90-day period.

6. Legal proceedings instituted and documents formally drawn up or registered as authentic instruments before the date of termination of the Agreement as set out in paragraph 5 are not affected hereby.

7. If in exceptional cases the implementation requires parliamentary approval in Denmark, the Danish notification under paragraph 2 shall indicate this and the provisions of Article 3(5) to (8) shall apply.

8. Denmark shall notify the Commission of texts amending the items set out in Article 2(2)(g) to (j) of this Agreement. The Commission shall adapt Article 2(2)(g) to (j) accordingly.

Article 5

International agreements which affect the Brussels I Regulation

1. International agreements entered into by the Community based on the rules of the Brussels I Regulation shall not be binding upon and shall not be applicable in Denmark.

2. Denmark will abstain from entering into international agreements which may affect or alter the scope of the Brussels I Regulation as annexed to this Agreement unless it is done in agreement with the Community and satisfactory arrangements have been made with regard to the relationship between this Agreement and the international agreement in question.

3. When negotiating international agreements that may affect or alter the scope of the Brussels I Regulation as annexed to this Agreement, Denmark will coordinate its position with the Community and will abstain from any actions that would jeopardise the objectives of a Community position within its sphere of competence in such negotiations.

Article 6

Jurisdiction of the Court of Justice of the European Communities in relation to the interpretation of the Agreement

1. Where a question on the validity or interpretation of this Agreement is raised in a case pending before a Danish court or tribunal, that court or tribunal shall request the Court of Justice to give a ruling thereon whenever under the same circumstances a court or tribunal of another Member State of the European Union would be required to do so in respect of the Brussels I Regulation and its implementing measures referred to in Article 2(1) of this Agreement.

2. Under Danish law, the courts in Denmark shall, when interpreting this Agreement, take due account of the rulings contained in the case law of the Court of Justice in respect of provisions of the Brussels Convention, the Brussels I Regulation and any implementing Community measures.

3. Denmark may, like the Council, the Commission and any Member State, request the Court of Justice to give a ruling on a question of interpretation of this Agreement. The ruling given by the Court of Justice in response to such a request shall not apply to judgments of courts or tribunals of the Member States which have become res judicata.

4. Denmark shall be entitled to submit observations to the Court of Justice in cases where a question has been referred to it by a court or tribunal of a Member State for a preliminary ruling concerning the interpretation of any provision referred to in Article 2(1).

5. The Protocol on the Statute of the Court of Justice of the European Communities and its Rules of Procedure shall apply.

6. If the provisions of the Treaty establishing the European Community regarding rulings by the Court of Justice are amended with consequences for rulings in respect of the Brussels I Regulation, Denmark may notify the Commission of its decision not to apply the amendments in respect of this Agreement. Notification shall be given at the time of the entry into force of the amendments or within 60 days thereafter.

In such a case this Agreement shall be considered terminated. Termination shall take effect three months after the notification.

7. Legal proceedings instituted and documents formally drawn up or registered as authentic instruments before the date of termination of the Agreement as set out in paragraph 6 are not affected hereby.

Article 7

Jurisdiction of the Court of Justice of the European Communities in relation to compliance with the Agreement

1. The Commission may bring before the Court of Justice cases against Denmark concerning non-compliance with any obligation under this Agreement.

2. Denmark may bring a complaint before the Commission as to the non-compliance by a Member State of its obligations under this Agreement.

3. The relevant provisions of the Treaty establishing the European Community governing proceedings before the Court of Justice as well as the Protocol on the Statute of the Court of Justice of the European Communities and its Rules of Procedure shall apply.

Article 8

Territorial application

1. This Agreement shall apply to the territories referred to in Article 299 of the Treaty establishing the European Community.

2. If the Community decides to extend the application of the Brussels I Regulation to territories currently governed by the Brussels Convention, the Community and Denmark shall cooperate in order to ensure that such an application also extends to Denmark.

Article 9

Transitional provisions

1. This Agreement shall apply only to legal proceedings instituted and to documents formally drawn up or registered as authentic instruments after the entry into force thereof.

2. However, if the proceedings in the Member State of origin were instituted before the entry into force of this Agreement, judgments given after that date shall be recognised and enforced in accordance with this Agreement,

(a) if the proceedings in the Member State of origin were instituted after the entry into force of the Brussels or the Lugano Convention both in the Member State of origin and in the Member State addressed;

(b) in all other cases, if jurisdiction was founded upon rules which accorded with those provided for either in this Agreement or in a convention concluded between the Member State of origin and the Member State addressed which was in force when the proceedings were instituted.

Article 10

Relationship to the Brussels I Regulation

1. This Agreement shall not prejudice the application by the Member States of the Community other than Denmark of the Brussels I Regulation.

2. However, this Agreement shall in any event be applied:

(a) in matters of jurisdiction, where the defendant is domiciled in Denmark, or where Article 22 or 23 of the Regulation, applicable to the relations between the Community and Denmark by virtue of Article 2 of this Agreement, confer jurisdiction on the courts of Denmark;

(b) in relation to a lis pendens or to related actions as provided for in Articles 27 and 28 of the Brussels I Regulation, applicable to the relations between the Community and Denmark by virtue of Article 2 of this Agreement, when proceedings are instituted in a Member State other than Denmark and in Denmark;

(c) in matters of recognition and enforcement, where Denmark is either the State of origin or the State addressed.

Article 11

Termination of the agreement

1. This Agreement shall terminate if Denmark informs the other Member States that it no longer wishes to avail itself of the provisions of Part I of the Protocol on the position of Denmark, in accordance with Article 7 of that Protocol.

2. This Agreement may be terminated by either Contracting Party giving notice to the other Contracting Party. Termination shall be effective six months after the date of such notice.

3. Legal proceedings instituted and documents formally drawn up or registered as authentic instruments before the date of termination of the Agreement as set out in paragraph 1 or 2 are not affected hereby.

Article 12

Entry into force

1. The Agreement shall be adopted by the Contracting Parties in accordance with their respective procedures.

2. The Agreement shall enter into force on the first day of the sixth month following the notification by the Contracting Parties of the completion of their respective procedures required for this purpose.

Article 13

Authenticity of texts

This Agreement is drawn up in duplicate in the Czech, Danish, Dutch, English, Estonian, Finnish, French, German, Greek, Hungarian, Italian, Latvian, Lithuanian, Maltese, Polish, Portuguese, Slovene, Slovak, Spanish and Swedish languages, each of these texts being equally authentic.

Done at Brussels on the nineteenth day of October in the year two thousand and five.

ANNEX

Council Regulation (EC) No 44/2001 of 22 December 2000 on jurisdiction and the recognition and enforcement of judgments in civil and commercial matters, as amended by Commission Regulation (EC) No 1496/2002 of 21 August 2002 amending Annex I (the rules of jurisdiction referred to in Article 3(2) and Article 4(2)) and Annex II (the list of competent courts and authorities) to Council Regulation (EC) No 44/2001 on jurisdiction and the recognition and enforcement of judgements in civil and commercial matters and by Commission Regulation (EC) No 2245/2004 of 27 December 2004 amending Annexes I, II, III and IV to Council Regulation (EC) No 44/2001 on jurisdiction and the recognition and enforcement of judgments in civil and commercial matters.

[3204]

C. APPLICABLE LAW

NOTES

See also European Parliament and Council Directives 1998/26/EC on settlement finality in payment and securities settlement systems and 2002/47/EC on financial collateral arrangements at **[3242]**, **[3292]**, which contain rules of applicable law.

1980 ROME CONVENTION ON THE LAW APPLICABLE TO CONTRACTUAL OBLIGATIONS

NOTES

The text of the following Convention and the Protocol annexed thereto appear as set out in the Contracts (Applicable Law) Act 1990, Sch 1. This version reflects changes made by the Conventions for the Accession of Greece (Luxembourg, 1984), Spain and Portugal (Funchal, 1992) and Austria, Finland and Sweden (Brussels, 1996). (A consolidated version of the 1980 Rome Convention, reflecting these amendments, is also set out at OJ C27, 26.1.1998, p 34.)

The United Kingdom has yet to ratify the 2005 Convention for the Accession to the 1980 Rome Convention of the 10 Member States which joined the European Community in 2004.

The High Contracting Parties to the Treaty establishing the European Economic Community,

ANXIOUS to continue in the field of private international law the work of unification of law which has already been done within the Community, in particular in the field of jurisdiction and enforcement of judgments,

WISHING to establish uniform rules concerning the law applicable to contractual obligations,

HAVE AGREED AS FOLLOWS—

TITLE I
SCOPE OF THE CONVENTION

Article 1
Scope of the Convention

1. The rules of this Convention shall apply to contractual obligations in any situation involving a choice between the laws of different countries.

2. They shall not apply to—

(a) questions involving the status or legal capacity of natural persons, without prejudice to Article 11;

(b) contractual obligations relating to—
- — wills and succession,
- — rights in property arising out of a matrimonial relationship,
- — rights and duties arising out of a family relationship, parentage, marriage or affinity, including maintenance obligations in respect of children who are not legitimate;

(c) obligations arising under bills of exchange, cheques and promissory notes and other negotiable instruments to the extent that the obligations under such other negotiable instruments arise out of their negotiable character;

(d) arbitration agreements and agreements on the choice of court;

(e) questions governed by the law of companies and other bodies corporate or unincorporate such as the creation, by registration or otherwise, legal capacity, internal organisation or winding up of companies and other bodies corporate or unincorporate and the personal liability of officers and members as such for the obligations of the company or body;

(f) the question whether an agent is able to bind a principal, or an organ to bind a company or body corporate or unincorporate, to a third party;

(g) the constitution of trusts and the relationship between settlors, trustees and beneficiaries;

(h) evidence and procedure, without prejudice to Article 14.

3. The rules of this Convention do not apply to contracts of insurance which cover risks situated in the territories of the Member States of the European Economic Community. In order to determine whether a risk is situated in these territories the court shall apply its internal law.

4. The preceding paragraph does not apply to contracts of re-insurance.

Article 2
Application of law of non-contracting States

Any law specified by this Convention shall be applied whether or not it is the law of a Contracting State.

TITLE II
UNIFORM RULES

Article 3
Freedom of choice

1. A contract shall be governed by the law chosen by the parties. The choice must be [expressed] or demonstrated with reasonable certainty by the terms of the contract or the circumstances of the case. By their choice the parties can select the law applicable to the whole or a part only of the contract.

2. The parties may at any time agree to subject the contract to a law other than that which previously governed it, whether as a result of an earlier choice under this Article or of other provisions of this Convention. Any variation by the parties of the law to be applied made after the conclusion of the contract shall not prejudice its formal validity under Article 9 or adversely affect the rights of third parties.

3. The fact that the parties have chosen a foreign law, whether or not accompanied by the choice of a foreign tribunal, shall not, where all the other elements relevant to the situation at the time of the choice are connected with one country only, prejudice the application of rules of the law of that country which cannot be derogated from by contract, hereinafter called "mandatory rules".

4. The existence and validity of the consent of the parties as to the choice of the applicable law shall be determined in accordance with the provisions of Articles 8, 9 and 11.

Article 4
Applicable law in the absence of choice

1. To the extent that the law applicable to the contract has not been chosen in accordance with Article 3, the contract shall be governed by the law of the country with which it is most closely connected. Nevertheless, a severable part of the contract which has a closer connection with another country may by way of exception be governed by the law of that other country.

2. Subject to the provisions of paragraph 5 of this Article, it shall be presumed that the contract is most closely connected with the country where the party who is to effect the performance which is characteristic of the contract has, at the time of conclusion of the contract, his habitual residence or, in the case of a body corporate or unincorporate, its central administration. However, if the contract is entered into in the course of that party's trade or profession, that country shall be the country in which the principal place of business is situated or, where under the terms of the contract the performance is to be effected through a place of business other than the principal place of business, the country in which that other place of business is situated.

3. Notwithstanding the provisions of paragraph 2 of this Article, to the extent that the subject matter of the contract is a right in immovable property or a right to use immovable property it shall be presumed that the contract is most closely connected with the country where the immovable property is situated.

4. A contract for the carriage of goods shall not be subject to the presumption in paragraph 2. In such a contract if the country in which, at the time the contract is concluded, the carrier has his principal place of business is also the country in which the place of loading

or the place of discharge or the principal place of business of the consignor is situated, it shall be presumed that the contract is most closely connected with that country. In applying this paragraph single voyage charter-parties and other contracts the main purpose of which is the carriage of goods shall be treated as contracts for the carriage of goods.

5. Paragraph 2 shall not apply if the characteristic performance cannot be determined, and the presumptions in paragraphs 2, 3 and 4 shall be disregarded if it appears from the circumstances as a whole that the contract is more closely connected with another country.

Article 5
Certain consumer contracts

1. This Article applies to a contract the object of which is the supply of goods or services to a person ("the consumer") for a purpose which can be regarded as being outside his trade or profession, or a contract for the provision of credit for that object.

2. Notwithstanding the provisions of Article 3, a choice of law made by the parties shall not have the result of depriving the consumer of the protection afforded to him by the mandatory rules of the law of the country in which he has his habitual residence—

— if in that country the conclusion of the contract was preceded by a specific invitation addressed to him or by advertising, and he had taken in that country all the steps necessary on his part for the conclusion of the contract, or
— if the other party or his agent received the consumer's order in that country, or
— if the contract is for the sale of goods and the consumer travelled from that country to another country and there gave his order, provided that the consumer's journey was arranged by the seller for the purpose of inducing the consumer to buy.

3. Notwithstanding the provisions of Article 4, a contract to which this Article applies shall, in the absence of choice in accordance with Article 3, be governed by the law of the country in which the consumer has his habitual residence if it is entered into in the circumstances described in paragraph 2 of this Article.

4. This Article shall not apply to—
(a) a contract of carriage;
(b) a contract for the supply of services where the services are to be supplied to the consumer exclusively in a country other than that in which he has his habitual residence.

5. Notwithstanding the provisions of paragraph 4, this Article shall apply to a contract which, for an inclusive price, provides for a combination of travel and accommodation.

Article 6
Individual employment contracts

1. Notwithstanding the provisions of Article 3, in a contract of employment a choice of law made by the parties shall not have the result of depriving the employee of the protection afforded to him by the mandatory rules of the law which would be applicable under paragraph 2 in the absence of choice.

2. Notwithstanding the provisions of Article 4, a contract of employment shall, in the absence of choice in accordance with Article 3, be governed—
(a) by the law of the country in which the employee habitually carries out his work in performance of the contract, even if he is temporarily employed in another country; or
(b) if the employee does not habitually carry out his work in any one country, by the law of the country in which the place of business through which he was engaged is situated;

unless it appears from the circumstances as a whole that the contract is more closely connected with another country, in which case the contract shall be governed by the law of that country.

Article 7
Mandatory rules

1. When applying under this Convention the law of a country, effect may be given to the mandatory rules of the law of another country with which the situation has a close connection,

if and in so far as, under the law of the latter country, those rules must be applied whatever the law applicable to the contract. In considering whether to give effect to these mandatory rules, regard shall be had to their nature and purpose and to the consequences of their application or non-application.

2. Nothing in this Convention shall restrict the application of the rules of the law of the forum in a situation where they are mandatory irrespective of the law otherwise applicable to the contract.

Article 8
Material validity

1. The existence and validity of a contract, or of any term of a contract, shall be determined by the law which would govern it under this Convention if the contract or term were valid.

2. Nevertheless a party may rely upon the law of the country in which he has his habitual residence to establish that he did not consent if it appears from the circumstances that it would not be reasonable to determine the effect of his conduct in accordance with the law specified in the preceding paragraph.

Article 9
Formal validity

1. A contract concluded between persons who are in the same country is formally valid if it satisfies the formal requirements of the law which governs it under this Convention or of the law of the country where it is concluded.

2. A contract concluded between persons who are in different countries is formally valid if it satisfies the formal requirements of the law which governs it under this Convention or of the law of one of those countries.

3. Where a contract is concluded by an agent, the country in which the agent acts is the relevant country for the purposes of paragraphs 1 and 2.

4. An act intended to have legal effect relating to an existing or contemplated contract is formally valid if it satisfies the formal requirements of the law which under this Convention governs or would govern the contract or of the law of the country where the act was done.

5. The provisions of the preceding paragraphs shall not apply to a contract to which Article 5 applies, concluded in the circumstances described in paragraph 2 of Article 5. The formal validity of such a contract is governed by the law of the country in which the consumer has his habitual residence.

6. Notwithstanding paragraphs 1 to 4 of this Article, a contract the subject matter of which is a right in immovable property or a right to use immovable property shall be subject to the mandatory requirements of form of the law of the country where the property is situated if by that law those requirements are imposed irrespective of the country where the contract is concluded and irrespective of the law governing the contract.

Article 10
Scope of the applicable law

1. The law applicable to a contract by virtue of Articles 3 to 6 and 12 of this Convention shall govern in particular—

(a) interpretation;
(b) performance;
(c) within the limits of the powers conferred on the court by its procedural law, the consequences of breach, including the assessment of damages in so far as it is governed by rules of law;
(d) the various ways of extinguishing obligations, and prescription and limitation of actions;
(e) the consequences of nullity of the contract.

2. In relation to the manner of performance and the steps to be taken in the event of defective performance regard shall be had to the law of the country in which performance takes place.

Article 11
Incapacity

In a contract concluded between persons who are in the same country, a natural person who would have capacity under the law of that country may invoke his incapacity resulting from another law only if the other party to the contract was aware of this incapacity at the time of the conclusion of the contract or was not aware thereof as a result of negligence.

Article 12
Voluntary assignment

1. The mutual obligations of assignor and assignee under a voluntary assignment of a right against another person ("the debtor") shall be governed by the law which under this Convention applies to the contract between the assignor and assignee.

2. The law governing the right to which the assignment relates shall determine its assignability, the relationship between the assignee and the debtor, the conditions under which the assignment can be invoked against the debtor and any question whether the debtor's obligations have been discharged.

Article 13
Subrogation

1. Where a person ("the creditor") has a contractual claim upon another ("the debtor"), and a third person has a duty to satisfy the creditor, or has in fact satisfied the creditor in discharge of that duty, the law which governs the third person's duty to satisfy the creditor shall determine whether the third person is entitled to exercise against the debtor the rights which the creditor had against the debtor under the law governing their relationship and, if so, whether he may do so in full or only to a limited extent.

2. The same rule applies where several persons are subject to the same contractual claim and one of them has satisfied the creditor.

Article 14
Burden of proof, etc

1. The law governing the contract under this Convention applies to the extent that it contains, in the law of contract, rules which raise presumptions of law or determine the burden of proof.

2. A contract or an act intended to have legal effect may be proved by any mode of proof recognised by the law of the forum or by any of the laws referred to in Article 9 under which that contract or act is formally valid, provided that such mode of proof can be administered by the forum.

Article 15
Exclusion of renvoi

The application of the law of any country specified by this Convention means the application of the rules of law in force in that country other than its rules of private international law.

Article 16
"Ordre public"

The application of a rule of the law of any country specified by this Convention may be refused only if such application is manifestly incompatible with the public policy ("ordre public") of the forum.

Article 17
No retrospective effect

This Convention shall apply in a Contracting State to contracts made after the date on which this Convention has entered into force with respect to that State.

Article 18
Uniform interpretation

In the interpretation and application of the preceding uniform rules, regard shall be had to their international character and to the desirability of achieving uniformity in their interpretation and application.

Article 19
States with more than one legal system

1. Where a State comprises several territorial units each of which has its own rules of law in respect of contractual obligations, each territorial unit shall be considered as a country for the purposes of identifying the law applicable under this Convention.

2. A State within which different territorial units have their own rules of law in respect of contractual obligations shall not be bound to apply this Convention to conflicts solely between the laws of such units.

Article 20
Precedence of Community Law

This Convention shall not affect the application of provisions which, in relation to particular matters, lay down choice of law rules relating to contractual obligations and which are or will be contained in acts of the institutions of the European Communities or in national laws harmonised in implementation of such acts.

Article 21
Relationship with other conventions

This Convention shall not prejudice the application of international conventions to which a Contracting State is, or becomes, a party.

Article 22
Reservations

1. Any Contracting State may, at the time of signature, ratification, acceptance or approval, reserve the right not to apply—
   (a) the provisions of Article 7(1);
   (b) the provisions of Article 10(1)(e).

2. …

3. Any Contracting State may at any time withdraw a reservation which it has made; the reservation shall cease to have effect on the first day of the third calendar month after notification of the withdrawal.

TITLE III
FINAL PROVISIONS

Article 23

1. If, after the date on which this Convention has entered into force for a Contracting State, that State wishes to adopt any new choice of law rule in regard to any particular category of contract within the scope of this Convention, it shall communicate its intention to the other signatory States through the Secretary-General of the Council of the European Communities.

2. Any signatory State may, within six months from the date of the communication made to the Secretary-General, request him to arrange consultations between signatory States in order to reach agreement.

3. If no signatory State has requested consultations within this period or if within two years following the communication made to the Secretary-General no agreement is reached in the course of consultations, the Contracting State concerned may amend its law in the manner

indicated. The measures taken by that State shall be brought to the knowledge of the other signatory States through the Secretary-General of the Council of the European Communities.

Article 24

1. If, after the date on which this Convention has entered into force with respect to a Contracting State, that State wishes to become a party to a multilateral convention whose principal aim or one of whose principal aims is to lay down rules of private international law concerning any of the matters governed by this Convention, the procedure set out in Article 23 shall apply. However, the period of two years, referred to in paragraph 3 of that Article, shall be reduced to one year.

2. The procedure referred to in the preceding paragraph need not be followed if a Contracting State or one of the European Communities is already a party to the multilateral convention, or if its object is to revise a convention to which the State concerned is already a party, or if it is a convention concluded within the framework of the Treaties establishing the European Communities.

Article 25

If a Contracting State considers that the unification achieved by this Convention is prejudiced by the conclusion of agreements not covered by Article 24(1), that State may request the Secretary-General of the Council of the European Communities to arrange consultations between the signatory States of this Convention.

Article 26

Any Contracting State may request the revision of this Convention. In this event a revision conference shall be convened by the President of the Council of the European Communities.

Article 27

…

Article 28

1. This Convention shall be open from 19 June 1980 for signature by the States party to the Treaty establishing the European Economic Community.

2. This Convention shall be subject to ratification, acceptance or approval by the signatory States. The instruments of ratification, acceptance or approval shall be deposited with the Secretary-General of the Council of the European Communities.

Article 29

1. This Convention shall enter into force on the first day of the third month following the deposit of the seventh instrument of ratification, acceptance or approval.

2. This Convention shall enter into force for each signatory State ratifying, accepting or approving at a later date on the first day of the third month following the deposit of its instrument of ratification, acceptance or approval.

Article 30

1. This Convention shall remain in force for 10 years from the date of its entry into force in accordance with Article 29(1), even for States for which it enters into force at a later date.

2. If there has been no denunciation it shall be renewed tacitly every five years.

3. A Contracting State which wishes to denounce shall, not less than six months before the expiration of the period of 10 or five years, as the case may be, give notice to the Secretary-General of the Council of the European Communities …

4. The denunciation shall have effect only in relation to the State which has notified it. The Convention will remain in force as between all other Contracting States.

Article 31

The Secretary-General of the Council of the European Communities shall notify the States party to the Treaty establishing the European Economic Community of—

(a) the signatures;
(b) the deposit of each instrument of ratification, acceptance or approval;
(c) the date of entry into force of this Convention;
[(d) communications made in pursuance of Articles 23, 24, 25, 26 and 30;]
(e) the reservations and withdrawals of reservations referred to in Article 22.

Article 32

The Protocol annexed to this Convention shall form an integral part thereof.

Article 33

This Convention, drawn up in a single original in the Danish, Dutch, English, French, German, Irish and Italian languages, these texts being equally authentic, shall be deposited in the archives of the Secretariat of the Council of the European Communities. The Secretary-General shall transmit a certified copy thereof to the Government of each signatory State.

[PROTOCOL

The High Contracting Parties have agreed upon the following provision which shall be annexed to the Convention—

Notwithstanding the provisions of the Convention, Denmark, Sweden and Finland may retain national provisions concerning the law applicable to questions relating to the carriage of goods by sea and may amend such provisions without following the procedure provided for in Article 23 of the Convention of Rome. The national provisions applicable in this respect are the following:

— in Denmark, paragraphs 252 and 321(3) and (4) of the "Sølov" (maritime law);
— in Sweden, Chapter 13, Article 2(1) and (2), and Chapter 14, Article 1(3), of "sjölagen" (maritime law);
— in Finland, Chapter 13, Article 2(1) and (2), and Chapter 14, Article 1(3) of "merilaki"/"sjölagen" (maritime law).]

[3205]

NOTES

Art 3: in the Official Journal version of this Convention the word "expressed" occurs in place of the word "express" in para 1. This is therefore assumed to be an error in the Queen's Printer's copy and substituted accordingly.

Art 22: para 2 repealed by the Contracts (Applicable Law) Act 1990 (Amendment) Order 1994, SI 1994/1900, art 7.

Art 27: repealed by the Contracts (Applicable Law) Act 1990 (Amendment) Order 1994, SI 1994/1900, art 7.

Art 30: words omitted from para 3 repealed by the Contracts (Applicable Law) Act 1990 (Amendment) Order 1994, SI 1994/1900, art 7.

Art 31: para (d) substituted by the Contracts (Applicable Law) Act 1990 (Amendment) Order 1994, SI 1994/1900, art 8.

Protocol: substituted by the Contracts (Applicable Law) Act 1990 (Amendment) Order 2000, SI 2000/1825, art 5.

Reservations under Art 22: the United Kingdom has entered reservations with respect to both Arts 7(1) and 10(1)(e). To date, it is the only Contracting State to have done so. Germany, Ireland, Luxembourg, Portugal and (more recently) Latvia and Slovenia have entered reservations with respect to Art 7(1) only. Italy has entered a reservation with respect to Art 10(1)(e) only. For the text of these reservations, see the website of the Council of Europe Agreements Office, at http://www.consilium.europa.eu/cms3_applications/Applications/accords/search.asp?lang=EN&cmsID=297).

JOINT DECLARATION

At the time of the signature of the Convention on the law applicable to contractual obligations, the Governments of the Kingdom of Belgium, the Kingdom of Denmark, the Federal Republic of Germany, the French Republic, Ireland, the Italian Republic, the Grand Duchy of Luxembourg, the Kingdom of the Netherlands and the United Kingdom of Great Britain and Northern Ireland,

I. anxious to avoid, as far as possible, dispersion of choice of law rules among several instruments and differences between these rules, express the wish that the institutions of the European Communities, in the exercise of their powers under the Treaties by which they were established, will, where the need arises, endeavour to adopt choice of law rules which are as far as possible consistent with those of this Convention;

II. declare their intention as from the date of signature of this Convention until becoming bound by Article 24, to consult with each other if any one of the signatory States wishes to become a party to any convention to which the procedure referred to in Article 24 would apply;

III. having regard to the contribution of the Convention on the law applicable to contractual obligations to the unification of choice of law rules within the European Communities, express the view that any State which becomes a member of the European Communities should accede to this Convention.

[3206]

NOTES

The text of this Declaration appears in the consolidated version of the 1980 Rome Convention at OJ C27, 26.1.98, p 45.

JOINT DECLARATION

The Governments of the Kingdom of Belgium, the Kingdom of Denmark, the Federal Republic of Germany, the French Republic, Ireland, the Italian Republic, the Grand Duchy of Luxembourg, the Kingdom of the Netherlands, and the United Kingdom of Great Britain and Northern Ireland,

On signing the Convention on the law applicable to contractual obligations;

Desiring to ensure that the Convention is applied as effectively as possible;

Anxious to prevent differences of interpretation of the Convention from impairing its unifying effect;

Declare themselves ready:

1. to examine the possibility of conferring jurisdiction in certain matters on the Court of Justice of the European Communities and, if necessary, to negotiate an agreement to this effect;
2. to arrange meetings at regular intervals between their representatives.

[3207]

NOTES

The text of this Declaration appears in the consolidated version of the 1980 Rome Convention at OJ C27, 26.1.98, p 46.

THE BRUSSELS PROTOCOL

NOTES

The text of the following Protocol appears as set out in the Contracts (Applicable Law) Act 1990, Sch 3. It is also set out at OJ C27, 26.1.1998, p 47.

The High Contracting Parties to the Treaty establishing the European Economic Community,

Having regard to the Joint Declaration annexed to the Convention on the law applicable to contractual obligations, opened for signature in Rome on 19 June 1980,

Have decided to conclude a Protocol conferring jurisdiction on the Court of Justice of the European Communities to interpret that Convention, and to this end have designated as their Plenipotentiaries—

(Designation of plenipotentiaries)

Who, meeting within the Council of the European Communities, having exchanged their full powers, found in good and due form,

HAVE AGREED AS FOLLOWS—

Article 1

The Court of Justice of the European Communities shall have jurisdiction to give rulings on the interpretation of—

(a) the Convention on the law applicable to contractual obligations, opened for signature in Rome on 19 June 1980, hereinafter referred to as "the Rome Convention";

(b) the Convention on accession to the Rome Convention by the States which have become Members of the European Communities since the date on which it was opened for signature;

(c) this Protocol.

Article 2

Any of the courts referred to below may request the Court of Justice to give a preliminary ruling on a question raised in a case pending before it and concerning interpretation of the provisions contained in the instruments referred to in Article 1 if that court considers that a decision on the question is necessary to enable it to give judgment—

(a)

— in Belgium:
la Cour de cassation (het Hof van Cassatie) and le Conseil d'Etat (de Raad van State),

— in Denmark:
Højesteret,

— in the Federal Republic of Germany:
die obersten Gerichtschöfe des Bundes,

— in Greece:
τα ανώτατα Δικαστήρια,

— in Spain:
el Tribunal Supremo,

— in France:
la Cour de cassation and le Conseil d'Etat,

— in Ireland:
the Supreme Court,

— in Italy:
la Corte suprema di cassazione and il Consiglio di Stato,

— in Luxembourg:
la Cour Supérieure de Justice, when sitting as Cour de cassation,

[— in Austria:
the Oberste Gerichtshof, the Verwaltungsgerichtshof and the Verfassungsgerichtshof]

— in the Netherlands:
de Hoge Raad,

— in Portugal:
o Supremo Tribunal de Justiça and o Supremo Tribunal Administrativo,

[— in Finland:
korkein oikeus/högsta domstolen, korkein hallinto-oikeus/högsta förvaltningsdomstolen, markkinatuomioistuin/marknadsdomstolen and työtuomioistuin/arbetsdomstolen,

— Sweden:
Högsta domstolen, Regeringsrätten, Arbetsdomstolen and Marknadsdomstolen,]

— in the United Kingdom:
the House of Lords and other courts from which no further appeal is possible;

(b) the courts of the Contracting States when acting as appeal courts.

Article 3

1. The competent authority of a Contracting State may request the Court of Justice to give a ruling on a question of interpretation of the provisions contained in the instruments referred to in Article 1 if judgments given by courts of that State conflict with the

interpretation given either by the Court of Justice or in a judgment of one of the courts of another Contracting State referred to in Article 2. The provisions of this paragraph shall apply only to judgments which have become res judicata.

2. The interpretation given by the Court of Justice in response to such a request shall not affect the judgments which gave rise to the request for interpretation.

3. The Procurators-General of the Supreme Courts of Appeal of the Contracting States, or any other authority designated by a Contracting State, shall be entitled to request the Court of Justice for a ruling on interpretation in accordance with paragraph 1.

4. The Registrar of the Court of Justice shall give notice of the request to the Contracting States, to the Commission and to the Council of the European Communities; they shall then be entitled within two months of the notification to submit statements of case or written observations to the Court.

5. No fees shall be levied or any costs or expenses awarded in respect of the proceedings provided for in this Article.

Article 4

1. Except where this Protocol otherwise provides, the provisions of the Treaty establishing the European Economic Community and those of the Protocol on the Statute of the Court of Justice annexed thereto, which are applicable when the Court is requested to give a preliminary ruling, shall also apply to any proceedings for the interpretation of the instruments referred to in Article 1.

2. The Rules of Procedure of the Court of Justice shall, if necessary, be adjusted and supplemented in accordance with Article 188 of the Treaty establishing the European Economic Community.

Article 5

This Protocol shall be subject to ratification by the Signatory States. The instruments of ratification shall be deposited with the Secretary-General of the Council of the European Communities.

Article 6

1. To enter into force, this Protocol must be ratified by seven States in respect of which the Rome Convention is in force. This Protocol shall enter into force on the first day of the third month following the deposit of the instrument of ratification by the last such State to take this step. If, however, the Second Protocol conferring on the Court of Justice of the European Communities certain powers to interpret the Convention on the law applicable to contractual obligations, opened for signature in Rome on 19 June 1980, concluded in Brussels on 19 December 1988, enters into force on a later date, this Protocol shall enter into force on the date of entry into force of the Second Protocol.

2. Any ratification subsequent to the entry into force of this Protocol shall take effect on the first day of the third month following the deposit of the instrument of ratification provided that the ratification, acceptance or approval of the Rome Convention by the State in question has become effective.

Article 7

The Secretary-General of the Council of the European Communities shall notify the Signatory States of—

(a) the deposit of each instrument of ratification;
(b) the date of entry into force of this Protocol;
(c) any designation communicated pursuant to Article 3(3);
(d) any communication made pursuant to Article 8.

Article 8

The Contracting States shall communicate to the Secretary-General of the Council of the European Communities the texts of any provisions of their laws which necessitate an amendment to the list of courts in Article 2(a).

Article 9

This Protocol shall have effect for as long as the Rome Convention remains in force under the conditions laid down in Article 30 of that Convention.

Article 10

Any Contracting State may request the revision of this Protocol. In this event, a revision conference shall be convened by the President of the Council of the European Communities.

Article 11

This Protocol, drawn up in a single original in the Danish, Dutch, English, French, German, Greek, Irish, Italian, Portuguese and Spanish languages, all 10 texts being equally authentic, shall be deposited in the archives of the General Secretariat of the Council of the European Communities. The Secretary-General shall transmit a certified copy to the Government of each Signatory State.

[3208]

JOINT DECLARATION

The Governments of the Kingdom of Belgium, the Kingdom of Denmark, the Federal Republic of Germany, the Hellenic Republic, the Kingdom of Spain, the French Republic, Ireland, the Italian Republic, the Grand Duchy of Luxembourg, the Kingdom of the Netherlands, the Portuguese Republic and the United Kingdom of Great Britain and Northern Ireland,

On signing the First Protocol on the interpretation by the Court of Justice of the European Communities of the Convention on the law applicable to contractual obligations, opened for signature in Rome on 19 June 1980,

Desiring to ensure that the Convention is applied as effectively and as uniformly as possible,

Declare themselves ready to organise, in cooperation with the Court of Justice of the European Communities, an exchange of information on judgments which have become *res judicata* and have been handed down pursuant to the Convention on the law applicable to contractual obligations by the courts referred to in Article 2 of the said Protocol. The exchange of information will comprise:

— the forwarding to the Court of Justice by the competent national authorities of judgments handed down by the courts referred to in Article 2(a) and significant judgments handed down by the courts referred to in Article 2(b),
— the classification and the documentary exploitation of these judgments by the Court of Justice including, as far as necessary, the drawing up of abstracts and translations, and the publication of judgments of particular importance,
— the communication by the Court of Justice of the documentary material to the competent national authorities of the States parties to the Protocol and to the Commission and the Council of the European Communities.

[3209]

NOTES

Art 2: entries in square brackets inserted by the Contracts (Applicable Law) Act 1990 (Amendment) Order 2000, SI 2000/1825, art 6.

The text of this Declaration appears in the consolidated version of the 1980 Rome Convention at OJ C27, 26.1.1998, p 50.

JOINT DECLARATION

The Government of the Kingdom of Belgium, the Kingdom of Denmark, the Federal Republic of Germany, the Hellenic Republic, the Kingdom of Spain, the French Republic, Ireland, the Italian Republic, the Grand Duchy of Luxembourg, the Kingdom of the Netherlands, the Portuguese Republic and the United Kingdom of Great Britain and Northern Ireland,

On signing the First Protocol on the interpretation by the Court of Justice of the European Communities of the Convention on the law applicable to contractual obligations, opened for signature in Rome on 19 June 1980,

Having regard to the Joint Declaration annexed to the Convention on the law applicable to contractual obligations,

Desiring to ensure that the Convention is applied as effectively and as uniformly as possible,

Anxious to prevent differences of interpretation of the Convention from impairing its unifying effect,

Express the view that any State which becomes a member of the European Communities should accede to this Protocol.

[3210]

NOTES

The text of this Declaration appears in the consolidated version of the 1980 Rome Convention at OJ C27, 26.1.1998, p 51.

SECOND PROTOCOL CONFERRING ON THE COURT OF JUSTICE OF THE EUROPEAN COMMUNITIES CERTAIN POWERS TO INTERPRET THE CONVENTION ON THE LAW APPLICABLE TO CONTRACTUAL OBLIGATIONS, OPENED FOR SIGNATURE IN ROME ON 19 JUNE 1980

(89/129/EEC)

THE HIGH CONTRACTING PARTIES TO THE TREATY ESTABLISHING THE EUROPEAN ECONOMIC COMMUNITY,

WHEREAS the Convention on the law applicable to contractual obligations, opened for signature in Rome on 19 June 1980, hereinafter referred to as "the Rome Convention", will enter into force after the deposit of the seventh instrument of ratification, acceptance or approval;

WHEREAS the uniform application of the rules laid down in the Rome Convention requires that machinery to ensure uniform interpretation be set up and whereas to that end appropriate powers should be conferred upon the Court of Justice of the European Communities, even before the Rome Convention enters into force with respect to all the Member States of the European Economic Community,

HAVE DECIDED to conclude this Protocol and to this end have designated as the Plenipotentiaries:

(Signatures of the Plenipotentiaries)

WHO, meeting within the Council of the European Communities, having exchanged their full powers, found in good and due form,

HAVE AGREED AS FOLLOWS:

Article 1

1. The Court of Justice of the European Communities shall, with respect to the Rome Convention, have the jurisdiction conferred upon it by the First Protocol on the interpretation by the Court of Justice of the European Communities of the Convention on the law applicable to contractual obligations, opened for signature in Rome on 19 June 1980, concluded in Brussels on 19 December 1988. The Protocol on the Statute of the Court of Justice of the European Communities and the Rules of Procedure of the Court of Justice shall apply.

2. The Rules of Procedure of the Court of Justice shall be adapted and supplemented as necessary in accordance with Article 188 of the Treaty establishing the European Economic Community.

Article 2

This Protocol shall be subject to ratification by the Signatory States. The instruments of ratification shall be deposited with the Secretary-General of the Council of the European Communities.

Article 3

This Protocol shall enter into force on the first day of the third month following the deposit of the instrument of ratification of the last Signatory State to complete that formality.

Article 4

This Protocol, drawn up in a single original in the Danish, Dutch, English, French, German, Greek, Irish, Italian, Portuguese and Spanish languages, all 10 texts being equally authentic, shall be deposited in the archives of the General Secretariat of the Council of the European Communities. The Secretary-General shall transmit a certified copy to the Government of each signatory.

[3211]

NOTES

The text of this Protocol appears in OJ C27, 26.1.1998, p 52.

COUNCIL REPORT

on the Convention on the law applicable to contractual obligations[1]

by Mario Giuliano

Professor, University of Milan

(who contributed the introduction and the comments on Articles 1, 3 to 8, 10, 12 and 13)

and Paul Lagarde

Professor, University of Paris I

(who contributed the comments on Articles 2, 9, 11, and 14 to 33)

NOTES

1 The text of the Convention on the law applicable to contractual obligations was published in Official Journal OJ L266 of 9 October 1980.

The Convention, open for signature in Rome on 19 June 1980, was signed on that day by the Plenipotentiaries of the following seven Member States: Belgium, Germany, France, Ireland, Italy, Luxembourg and the Netherlands.

CONTENTS

[OJ C282, 31.10.80, p 4]

INTRODUCTION

1. Proposal by the Governments of the Benelux countries to the Commission of the European communities

On 8 September 1967 the Permanent Representative of Belgium extended to the Commission, in the name of his own Government and those of the Kingdom of the Netherlands and the Grand Duchy of Luxembourg, an invitation to collaborate with the experts of the Member States, on the basis of the draft Benelux convention, in the unification of private international law and codification of the rules of conflict of laws within the Community.

The object of this proposal was to eliminate the inconveniences arising from the diversity of the rules of conflict, notably in the field of contract law. Added to this was "an element of urgency", having regard to the reforms likely to be introduced in some Member States and the consequent "danger that the existing divergences would become more marked".

In the words of Mr T Vogelaar, Director-General for the Internal Market and Approximation of Legislation at the Commission, in his opening address as chairman of the meeting of government experts on 26 to 28 February 1969: "This proposal should bring about a complete unification of the rules of conflict. Thus in each of our six countries, instead of the existing rules of conflict and apart from cases of application of international Agreements binding any Member State, identical rules of conflict would enter into force both in Member States' relations *inter se* and in relations with non-Community States. Such a development would give rise to a common corpus of unified legal rules covering the territory of the Community's Member States. The great advantage of this proposal is undoubtedly that the level of legal certainty would be raised, confidence in the stability of legal relationships fortified, agreements on jurisdiction according to the applicable law facilitated, and the protection of rights acquired over the whole field of private law augmented. Compared with the unification of substantive law, unification of the rules of conflict of laws is more practicable, especially in the field of property law, because the rules of conflict apply solely to legal relations involving an international element".[1]

2. Examination of the proposal by the Commission and its consequences

In examining the proposal by the Benelux countries the Commission arrived at the conclusion that at least in some special fields of private international law the harmonization of rules of conflict would be likely to facilitate the workings of the common market.

Mr Vogelaar's opening address reviews the grounds on which the Commission's conclusion was founded and is worth repeating here—

"According to both the letter and spirit of the Treaty establishing the EEC, harmonization is recognized as fulfilling the function of permitting or facilitating the creation in the economic field of legal conditions similar to those governing an internal market. I appreciate that opinions may differ as to the precise delimitation of the inequalities which directly affect the functioning of the common market and those having only an indirect effect. Yet there are still legal fields in which the differences between national legal systems and the lack of unified rules of conflict definitely impede the free movement of persons, goods, services and capital among the Member States.

Some will give preference to the harmonization or unification of substantive law rather than the harmonization of rules of conflict. As we know, the former has already been achieved in various fields. However, harmonization of substantive law does not always contrive to keep pace with the dismantling of economic frontiers. The problem of the law to be applied will therefore continue to arise as long as substantive law is not unified. The number of cases in which the question of applicable law must be resolved increases with the growth of private law relationships across frontiers.

At the same time there will be a growing number of cases in which the courts have to apply a foreign law. The Convention signed on 27 September 1968 on jurisdiction and the enforcement of judgments in civil and commercial matters uniformly governs the international jurisdiction of the courts within the Community. It should help to facilitate and expedite many civil actions and enforcement proceedings. It also enables the parties in many matters, to teach agreements assigning jurisdiction and to choose among several courts. The outcome may be that preference is given to the court of a State whose law seems to offer a better solution to the proceedings. To prevent this "forum shopping", increase legal certainty, and anticipate more easily the law which will be applied, it would be advisable for the rules of conflict to be unified in fields of particular economic importance so that the same law is applied irrespective of the State in which the decision is given.

[OJ C282, 31.10.80, p 5]

To sum up, there are three main considerations guiding our proposal for harmonizing the rules of conflict for a few well-defined types of legal relations. The first is dictated by the history of private international law: to try to unify everything is to attempt too much and would take too long. The second is the urgent necessity for greater legal certainty in some sectors of major economic importance the third is the wish to forestall any aggravation of the differences between the rules of private international law of the various Member States".[2]

These were in fact the motives which prompted the Commission to convene a meeting of experts from the Member States in order to obtain a complete picture of the present state of the law and to decide whether and to what extent a harmonization or unification of private international law within the Community should be undertaken. The invitation was accompanied by a questionnaire designed to facilitate the discussion.[3]

3. Favourable attitude of Member States to the search for uniform rules of conflict, the setting of priorities and establishment of the working group to study and work out these rules

The meeting in question took place on 26 to 28 February 1969. It produced a first survey of the situation with regard to prospects for and possible advantage of work in the field of unification of rules of conflict among Member States of the European Communities.[4]

However, it was not until the next meeting on 20 to 22 October 1969 that the government experts were able to give a precise opinion both on the advisability and scope of harmonization and on the working procedure and organization of work.

As regards advisability of harmonization the Member States' delegations (with the sole exception of the German delegation) declared themselves to be fundamentally in agreement on the value of the work in making the law more certain in the Community. The German delegation, while mentioning some hesitation on this point in professional and business circles, said that this difference of opinion was not such as to affect the course of the work at the present time.

As regards the scope of harmonization, it was recognized (without prejudice to future developments) that a start should be made on matters most closely involved in the proper functioning of the common market, more specifically—

1. the law applicable to corporeal and incorporeal property;
2. the law applicable to contractual and non-contractual obligations;

PART IV EC MATERIALS

3. the law applicable to the form of legal transactions and evidence;
4. general matters under the foregoing heads (renvoi, classification, application of foreign law, acquired rights, public policy, capacity, representation).

As for the legal basis of the work, it was the unanimous view that the proposed harmonization, without being specifically connected with the provisions of Article 220 of the EEC Treaty, would be a natural sequel to the Convention on jurisdiction and enforcement of judgments.

Lastly, on the procedure to be followed, all the delegations were in favour of that adopted for work on the Conventions already signed or in process of drafting under Article 220 and of seeking the most suitable ways of expediting the work.[5]

The results of the meeting were submitted through the Directorate-General for the Internal Market an Approximation of Legislation to the Commission with a proposal to seek the agreement of Member States for continuance of the work and preparation of a preliminary draft Convention establishing uniformity of law in certain relevant areas of private international law.

The Commission acceded to the proposal. At its meeting on 15 January 1970 the Committee of Permanent Representatives expressly authorized the Group to continue its work on harmonization of the rules of private international law, on the understanding that the preliminary draft or drafts would give priority to the four areas previously indicated.

[OJ C282, 31.10.90, p 6]

Following the abovementioned decision of the Permanent Representatives Committee, the Group met on 2 and 3 February 1970 and elected its chairman, Mr P Jenard, Director of Administration in the Belgian Ministry of Foreign Affairs and External Trade, and its vice-chairman, Prof Miccio, Counsellor to the Italian Court of Cassation.

Having regard to the decision of the previous meeting that the matters to be given priority should be divided into four sectors, the Group adopted the principle that each of the four sectors should have its own rapporteur appointed as follows, to speed up the work—

1. in the case of the law applicable to corporeal and incorporeal property, by the German delegation;
2. in the case of the law applicable to contractual and extracontractual obligations, by the Italian delegation—
3. in the case of the law applicable to the form of legal transactions and evidence, by the French delegation;
4. in general matters, by the Netherlands delegation, in agreement with the Belgian and Luxembourg delegations.

As a result the following were appointed: Prof K Arndt, Oberlandsgerichtspräsident ad; Prof M Giuliano, University of Milan; Prof P Lagarde, University of Paris I; Mr T van Sasse van Ysselt, Director in the Netherlands Ministry of Justice.

Other matters were dealt with at the same meeting, notably the kind of convention to be prepared, as to which the great majority of delegates favoured a universal convention not based upon reciprocity; the method of work; participation of observers from the Hague Conference on Private International Law and the Benelux Commission on Unification of Law.[6]

4. Organization, progress and initial results of the Group's work at the end of 1972

The Group took as its starting point the examination and discussion of the questionnaires prepared by the rapporteurs, Messrs Giuliano, Lagarde and van Sasse van Ysselt in their respective fields. They were discussed at a meeting of the rapporteurs chaired by Mr Jenard on 1 to 4 June 1970. The three questionnaires were subjected to a thorough analysis, extending both to the rules of conflict (national or established by convention) in force in the Community Member States and to the evolutionary trends already apparent in case law and legal theory in certain countries or worthy of consideration in relation to certain present-day requirements in international life. This oral analysis was further supplemented by the written replies given by each rapporteur on the basis of the statutes, case law and legal theory of his own country (of the three Benelux countries in the case of Mr van Sasse) to the questionnaires drawn up by his colleagues and himself.[7]

This preliminary work and material enable each of the rapporteurs to present an interim report, with draft articles on the matter considered, as a working basis for the Group meetings. It was agreed that these meetings would be devoted to an examination of Mr Giuliano's report on the law applicable to contractual and non-contractual obligations and to the subject matter of Mr Lagarde's and Mr van Sasse van Ysselt's report to the extent that this was relevant to Mr Giuliano's subject.

It was agreed that Mr Arndt's report on the law applicable to corporeal and incorporeal property would be discussed later, Mr Arndt having explained that a comparative study of the principal laws on security rights and interests should precede his report and that the need for such a study had been generally recognized.

Apart from the meeting of rapporteurs in June 1970, the work fully occupied 11 Group plenary sessions, each with an average duration of five days.[8]

At its meeting in June 1972 the Group completed the preliminary draft convention on the law applicable to contractual and non-contractual obligations and decided that it should be submitted, together with the reports finalized at a meeting of rapporteurs on 27 and 28 September 1972, to the Permanent Representatives Committee for transmission to the Governments of the Community Member States.[9]

5. Re-examination of Group work in the light of observations by the Governments of original and new Member States of the EEC and results achieved in February 1979

It follows from the foregoing observations that the 1972 draft dealt both with the law applicable to contractual obligations and with that applicable to non-contractual obligations. At the same time it provided solutions relating to the law governing the form of legal transactions and evidence, questions of interpretation of uniform rules and their relationship with other rules of conflict of international origin, to the extent to which these were connected with the subject of the preliminary draft.

[OJ C282, 31.10.80, p 7]

Following the accession of the United Kingdom, Denmark and Ireland to the EEC in 1973 the Commission extended the Group to include government experts from the new Member States and the Permanent Representatives Committee authorized the enlarged Group to re-examine in the light of observations from the Governments of the original and of the new Member States of the EEC, the preliminary draft convention which the Commission had submitted to it at the end of 1972. The Group elected Prof Philip as vice-chairman.

Nevertheless the preliminary draft was not re-examined immediately. The need to allow the experts from the new Member States time to consult their respective Governments and interested parties on the one hand and the political uncertainties in the United Kingdom concerning membership of the European Communities (which were not settled until the 1975 referendum) on the other, resulted in a significant reduction (if not suspension) of the Group's activities for about three years. It was not until the end of 1975 that the Group was able properly to resume its work and proceed with the preparation of the Convention on the law applicable to contractual obligations. In fact the Group decided at its meeting in March 1978 to limit the present convention to contracts alone and to begin negotiations for a second Convention, on non-contractual obligations, after the first had been worked out. Most delegations thought it better for reasons of time to finish the part relating to contractual obligations first.

The original preliminary draft, with the limitation referred to, was re-examined in the course of 14 plenary sessions of the Group and three special meetings on transport and insurance contracts; each of the plenary sessions lasted two to five days.[10] At the meeting in February 1979 the Group finished the draft convention, decided upon the procedure for transmitting the draft to the Council before the end of April and instructed Professors Giuliano and Lagarde to draw up the report; this was then finalized at a meeting of rapporteurs on 18 to 20 June 1979 in which one expert per delegation participated, and transmitted in turn to the Council and to the Governments by the chairman, Mr Jenard.

6. Finalization of the Convention within the Council of the European Communities

On 18 May 1979 the Group's chairman, Mr Jenard, sent the draft Convention to the President of the Council of the European Communities with a request that the Governments make their comments on the draft by the end of the year so that the Convention could then be concluded during 1980.

On 20 July 1979 Mr Jenard sent the President of the Council a draft report on the Convention, which was the predecessor of this report.

The General Secretariat of the Council received written comments from the Belgian, Netherlands, Danish, Irish, German, Luxembourg and United Kingdom Governments. In addition, on 17 March 1980, the Commission adopted an opinion on the draft Convention, which was published in *Official Journal of the European Communities* No L94 of 11 April 1980.

On 16 January 1980 the Permanent Representatives Committee set up an *ad hoc* working party on private international law, whose terms of reference were twofold—

— to finalize the Convention text in the light of the comments made by Member States' Governments,

— to consider whether, and if so within what limits, the Court of Justice of the European Communities should be given jurisdiction to interpret the Convention.

The *ad hoc* working party met twice, from 24 to 28 March and 21 to 25 April 1980, with Mr Brancaccio from the Italian Ministry of Justice in the chair.[11] Working from the Governments' written comments and others made orally during discussions, the working party reached general agreement on the substantive provisions of the Convention and on the accompanying report.

The only problems unresolved by the working party concerned the problem of where the Convention stood in relation to the Community legal order. They arose in particular in determining the number of ratifications required for the Convention to come into force and in drafting a statement by the Governments of the Member States on the conferral of jurisdiction on the Court of Justice.

Following a number of discussions in the Permanent Representatives Committee, which gradually brought agreement within sight, the Council Presidency deemed circumstances to be ripe politically for the points of disagreement to be discussed by the Ministers of Justice with a good chance of success at a special Council meeting on 19 June 1980 in Rome.

[OJ C282, 31.10.80, p 8]

At that meeting, a final round of negotiations produced agreement on a number of seven Member States required to ratify in order for the Convention to come into force. Agreement was also reached on the wording of a joint statement on the interpretation of the Convention by the Court of Justice, which followed word for word the matching statement made by the Governments of the original six Member States of the Community when the Convention on jurisdiction and enforcement was concluded on 27 September 1968 in Brussels. In adopting the statement, the Representatives of Governments of the Member States, meeting within the Council, also instructed the *ad hoc* Council working party on private international law to consider by what means point 1 of the statement could be implemented and report back by 30 June 1981.

With these points settled, the President-in-Office of the Council, Tommaso Morlino, Italian Minister of Justice, recorded the agreement of the Representatives of the Governments of the Member States, meeting within the Council, on the following—

— adoption of the text of the Convention and of the two joint statements annexed to it,

— the Convention would be open for signing from 19 June 1980,

— the Convention and accompanying report would be published in the *Official Journal of the European Communities* for information.

The Convention was signed on 19 June 1980 by the plenipotentiaries of Belgium, the Federal Republic of Germany, France, Ireland, Italy, Luxembourg and the Netherlands.

7. Review of the internal sources and nature of the rules in force in the EEC Member States relating to the law applicable to contractual obligations

The chief aim of the Convention is to introduce into the national laws of the EEC Member States a set of uniform rules on the law applicable to contractual obligations and on certain general points of private international law to the extent that these are linked with those obligations.

Without going here into details of positive law, though it may be necessary to return to it in the comments on the uniform rules, a short survey can now be given of the internal sources and the nature of the rules of conflict at present in force in the Community countries in the field covered by the Convention. This survey will bring out both the value and the difficulties of the unification undertaken by the Group and of which the convention is only the first fruit.

Of the nine Member States of the Community, Italy is the only one to have a set of rules of conflict enacted by the legislature covering almost all the matters with which the Convention is concerned. These rules are to be found for the most part in the second paragraph of Article 17 and in Articles 25, 26, 30 and 31 of the general provisions constituting the introduction to the 1942 Civil Code, and in Articles 9 and 10 of the 1942 Navigation Code.

In the other Member States of the Community, however, the body of rules of conflict on the law applicable to contractual obligations is founded only on customary rules or on rules originating in case law. Academic studies and writings have helped considerably to develop and harmonize these rules.

The position as just stated has not been altered substantially either by the French draft law supplementing the Civil Code in respect of private international law (1967) or by the Benelux Treaty establishing uniform rules of private international law signed in Brussels on 3 July 1969. These two texts are certainly an interesting attempt to codify the rules of conflict and also, in the case of the Benelux countries, to make these rules uniform on an inter-State level. The Group did not fail to take account of their results in its own work. However, the entry into force of the Benelux Treaty has not been pursued, and the French draft law seems unlikely to be adopted in the near future.

8. Universal application of the uniform rules

From the very beginning of its work the Group has professed itself to be in favour of uniform rules which would apply not only to the nationals of Member States and to persons domiciled or resident within the Community but also to the nationals of third States and to persons domiciled or resident therein. The provisions of Article 2 specify the universal application of the convention.

The Group took the view that its main purpose was to frame general rules such as those existing in legislative provisions currently in force in Italy and in the Benelux Treaty and the French draft law. In such a context these general rules, which would become the "common law" of each Member State for settling conflicts of laws, would not prejudice the detailed regulation of clearly delimited matters arising from other work, especially that of the Hague Conference on private international law. The application of these particular conventions is safeguarded by the provisions of Article 21.

[OJ C282, 31.10.80, p 9]

9. On the normally general nature of the uniform rules in the Convention and their significance in the unification of laws already undertaken in the field of private international law

At the outset of its work the Group had also to determine the nature and scope of the uniform rules of conflict to be formulated. Should they be general rules, to be applied indiscriminately to all contracts, or would it be better to regulate contractual obligations by means of a series of specific rules applicable to the various categories of contract, or again should an intermediate solution be envisaged, namely by adopting general rules and supplementing them by specific rules for certain categories of contract?

Initially the rapporteur advocated the latter method. This provided that, in default of an express of implied choice by the parties, the contract would be governed (subject to specific provisions for certain categories) by one system of law.

When the Group tackled the question of whether to supplement the general rules for determining the law applicable to the contract by some specific rules for certain categories of contract it became clear that the point was no longer as significant as it had been in the context of the rapporteur's initial proposals. The Group's final version of the text of Article 4 provided satisfactory solutions for most of the contracts whose applicable law was the subject of specific rules of conflict in the rapporteur's proposals, notably because of its flexibility. The Group therefore merely provided for some exceptions to the rule contained in Article 4, notably those in Articles 5 and 6 concerning the law applicable respectively to certain consumer contracts and to contracts of employment in default of an express or implied choice by the parties.

The normally general nature of the uniform rules made it necessary to provide for a few exceptions and to allow the judge a certain discretion as to their application in each particular case. This aspect will be dealt with in the comments on a number of Articles in Chapter III of this report.

As declared in the Preamble, in concluding this Convention the nine States which are parties to the Treaty establishing the European Economic Community show their desire to continue in the field of private international law the work of unification already undertaken in the Community, particularly in matters of jurisdiction and enforcement of judgments. The question of accession by third States is not dealt with in the Convention (see page 41, penultimate paragraph).

[3212]

[OJ C282, 31.10.80, p 10]

TITLE 1
SCOPE OF THE CONVENTION

Article 1
Scope of the Convention

1. As provided in Article 1(1) the uniform rules in this Convention apply generally to contractual obligations in situations involving a conflict of laws.

It must be stressed that the uniform rules apply to the abovementioned obligations only "in situations involving a choice between the laws of different countries". The purpose of this provision is to define the true aims of the uniform rules. We know that the law applicable to contracts and to the obligations arising from them is not always that of the country where the problems of interpretation or enforcement are in issue. There are situations in which this law is not regarded by the legislature or by the case law as that best suited to govern the contract and the obligations resulting from it. These are situations which involve one or more elements foreign to the internal social system of a country (for example, the fact that one or all of the parties to the contract are foreign nationals or persons habitually resident abroad, the fact that the contract was made abroad, the fact that one or more of the obligations of the parties are to be performed in a foreign country, etc), thereby giving the legal systems of several countries claims to apply. These are precisely the situations in which the uniform rules are intended to apply.

Moreover the present wording of paragraph 1 means that the uniform rules are to apply in all cases where the dispute would give rise to a conflict between two or more legal systems. The uniform rules also apply if those systems coexist within one State (cf Article 19(1)). Therefore the question whether a contract is governed by English or Scots law is within the scope of the Convention, subject to Article 19(2).

2. The principle embodied in paragraph 1 is however subject to a number of restrictions.

First, since the Convention is concerned only with the law applicable to contractual obligations, property rights and intellectual property are not covered by these provisions. An Article in the original preliminary draft had expressly so provided. However, the Group considered that such a provision would be superfluous in the present text, especially as this would have involved the need to recapitulate the differences existing as between the various legal system of the Member States of the Community.

3. There are also the restrictions set out in paragraph 2 of Article 1.

The first of these, at (a), is the status or legal capacity of natural persons, subject to Article 11; then, at (b), contractual obligations relating to wills and succession, to property rights arising out of matrimonial relationships, to rights and duties arising out of family relationships, parentage, marriage or affinity, including maintenance obligations in respect of illegitimate children. The Group intended this enumeration to exclude from the scope of the Convention all matters of family law.

As regards maintenance obligations, within the meaning of Article 1 of the Hague Convention on the law applicable to maintenance obligations, the Group considered that this exclusion should also extend to contracts which parties under a legal maintenance obligation make in performance of that obligation. All other contractual obligations, even if they provide for the maintenance of a member of the family towards whom there are no legal maintenance obligations, would fall within the scope of the Convention.

Contrary to the provisions of the second paragraph of Article 1 in the original preliminary draft, the current wording of subparagraph (b) does not in general exclude gifts. Most of the delegations favoured the inclusion of gifts where they arise from a contract within the scope of the Convention, even when made within the family, provided they are not covered by family law. Therefore the only contractual gifts left outside the scope of the uniform rules are those to which family law, the law relating to matrimonial property rights or the law of succession apply.

[OJ C282, 31.10.80, p 11]

The Group unanimously affirmed that matters relating to the custody of children are outside the scope of the Convention, since they fall within the sphere of personal status and capacity. However, the Group thought it inappropriate to specify this exclusion in the text of the Convention itself, thereby intending to avoid an *a contrario* interpretation of the Convention of 27 September 1968.

To obviate any possibility of misconstruction, the present wording of subparagraphs (a) and (b) uses the same terminology as the 1968 Convention on jurisdiction and enforcement of judgments.

4. Subparagraph (c) excludes from the scope of the uniform rules in the first instance obligations arising from bills of exchange, cheques, promissary notes.

In retaining this exclusion, for which provision had already been made in the original preliminary draft, the Group took the view that the provisions of the Convention were not suited to the regulation of obligations of this kind. Their inclusion would have involved rather complicated special rules. Moreover the Geneva Conventions to which several Member States of the Community are parties govern most of these areas. Also, certain Member States of the Community regard these obligations as non-contractual.

Subparagraph (c) excludes other negotiable instruments to the extent that the obligations under such other negotiable instruments arise out of their negotiable character. If a document, though the obligation under it is transferable, is not regarded as a negotiable instrument, it falls outside the exclusion. This has the effect that such documents as bills of lading, similar documents issued in connection with transport contracts, and bonds, debentures, guarantees, letters of indemnity, certificates of deposit, warrants and warehouse receipts are only excluded by subparagraph (c) if, they can be regarded as negotiable instruments; and even then the exclusion only applies with regard to obligations arising out of their negotiable character. Furthermore, neither the contracts pursuant to which such instruments are issued nor contracts for the purchase and sale of such instruments are excluded. Whether a document is characterized as a negotiable instrument is not governed by this Convention and is a matter for the law of the forum (including its rules of private international law).

5. Arbitration agreements and agreements on the choice of court are likewise excluded from the scope of the Convention (subparagraph (d)).

There was a lively debate in the Group on whether or not to exclude agreements on the choice of court. The majority in the end favoured exclusion for the following reasons: the matter lies within the sphere of procedure and forms part of the administration of justice (exercise of State authority); rules on this matter might have endangered the ratification of the Convention. It was also noted that rules on jurisdiction are a matter of public policy and there is only marginal scope for freedom of contract. Each court is obliged to determine the validity of the agreement on the choice of court in relation to its own law, not in relation to the law chosen. Given the nature of these provisions and their fundamental diversity, no rule of conflict can lead to a uniform solution. Moreover, these rules would in any case be frustrated if the disputes were brought before a court in a third country. It was also pointed out that so far as concerns relationships within the Community, the most important matters (validity of the clause and form) are governed by Article 17 of the Convention of 27 September 1968. The outstanding points, notably those relating to consent, do not arise in practice, having regard to the fact that Article 17 provides that these agreements shall be in writing. Those delegations who thought that agreements on choice of court should be included within the Convention pointed out that the validity of such an agreement would often be dealt with by the application of the same law that governed the rest of the contract in which the agreement was included and should therefore be governed by the same law as the contract. In some systems of law, agreement as to choice of court is itself regarded as a contract and the ordinary choice of law rules are applied to discover the law applicable to such a contract.

As regards arbitration agreements, certain delegations, notably the United Kingdom delegation, had proposed that these should not be excluded from the Convention. It was emphasized that an arbitration agreement does not differ from other agreements as regards the contractual aspects, and that certain international Conventions do not regulate the law applicable to arbitration agreements, while others are inadequate in this respect. Moreover the international Conventions have not been ratified by all the Member States of the Community and, even if they had been, the problem would not be solved because these Conventions are not of universal applications. It was added that there would not be unification within the Community on this important matter in international commerce.

[OJ C282, 31.10.80, p 12]

Other delegations, notably the German and French delegations, opposed the United Kingdom proposal, emphasizing particularly that any increase in the number of conventions in this area should be avoided, that severability is accepted in principle in the draft and the arbitration clause is independent, that the concept of "closest ties" difficult to apply to arbitration agreements, that procedural and contractual aspects are difficult to separate, that the matter is complex and the experts' proposals show great divergences; that since procedural matters and those relating to the question whether a dispute was arbitrable would in any case be excluded, the only matter to be regulated would be consent; that the International Chamber of Commerce—which, as everyone knows, has great experience in this matter—has not felt the need for further regulation.

Having regard to the fact that the solutions which can and have been considered generally for arbitration are very complex and show great disparity, a delegate proposed that this matter should be studied separately and any results embodied in a Protocol. The Group adopted this proposal and consequently excluded arbitration agreements from the scope of the uniform rules, subject to returning to an examination of these problems and of agreements on the choice of court once the Convention has been finally drawn up.

The exclusion of arbitration agreements does not relate to the procedural aspects, but also to the formation, validity and effects of such agreements. Where the arbitration clause forms an integral part of a contract, the exclusion relates only to the clause itself and not to the contract as a whole. This exclusion does not prevent such clauses being taken into consideration for the purposes of Article 3(1).

6. Subparagraph (e) provides that the uniform rules shall not apply to questions governed by the law of companies, and other bodies corporate or unincorporate such as the creation, by registration or otherwise, legal capacity, internal organization or winding-up of companies, and other bodies corporate or unincorporate and the personal legal liability of officers and members as such for the obligations of the company or body.

This exclusion in no way implies that this aspect was considered unimportant in the economic life of the Member States of the Community. Indeed, this is an area which, by virtue of its economic importance and the place which it occupies in many provisions of the Treaty establishing the EEC, appears to have the strongest possible reasons for not being separated from Community work in the field of unification of private international law, notably in conflicts of laws pertaining to economic relations.

Notwithstanding the foregoing considerations, the Group had thought it inadvisable, even in the original preliminary draft, to include companies, firms and legal persons within the scope of the Convention, especially in view of the work being done on this subject within the European Communities.[12] Confirming this exclusion, the Group stated that it affects all the complex acts (contractual, administrative, registration) which are necessary to the creation of a company or firm and to the regulation of its internal organization and winding-up, ie acts which fall within the scope of company law.

On the other hand, acts or preliminary contracts whose sole purpose is to create obligations between interested parties (promoters) with a view to forming a company or firm are not covered by exclusion.

The subject may be a body with or without legal personality, profit-making or non-profit-making. Having regard to the differences which exist, it may be that certain relationships will be regarded as within the scope of company law or might be treated as being governed by that law (for example, société de droit civil, nicht-rechtsfähiger Verein, partnership, Vennootschap onder firma, etc) in some countries but not in others. The rule has been made flexible in order to take account of the diversity of national laws.

Examples of "internal organization" are: the calling of meetings, the right to vote, the necessary quorum, the appointment of officers of the company or firm, etc "Winding-up" would cover either the termination of the company or firm as provided by its constitution or by operation of law, or its disappearance by merger or other similar process.

At the request of the German delegation the Group extended the subparagraph (e) exclusion to the personal liability of members and organs, and also to the legal capacity of companies or firms. On the other hand the Group did not adopt the proposal that mergers and groupings should also be expressly mentioned, most of the delegations being of the opinion that mergers and groupings were already covered by the present wording.

As regards legal capacity, it should be made clear that the reference is to limitations, which may be imposed by law on companies and firms, for example in respect of acquisition of immovable property, not to *ultra vires* acts by organs of the company or firm, which fall under subparagraph (f).

[OJ C282, 31.10.80, p 13]

7. The solution adopted in subparagraph (f) involves the exclusion from the scope of the uniform rules of the question whether an agent is able to bind a principal, or an organ to bind a company or body corporate or unincorporate, to a third party.

The exclusion affects only the relationships between the principal and third parties, more particularly the question whether the principal is bound *vis-à-vis* third parties by the acts of the agent in specific cases. It does not affect other aspects of the complex field of agency, which also extends to relationships between the principal and the agent and to agent-third party relationships. The exclusion is justified by the fact that it is difficult to accept the principle of freedom of contract on this point. On the other hand, principal-agent and agent-third party relationships in no way differ from other obligations and are therefore included within the scope of the Convention in so far as they are of a contractual nature.

8. The exception in subparagraph (g) concerns "trusts" in the sense in which they are understood in the common law countries. The English word "trust" is properly used to define the scope of the exclusion. On the other hand similar institutions under continental laws falls within the provisions of the Convention because they are normally contractual in origin. Nevertheless it will be open to the judge to treat them in the same way as the institutions of the common law countries when they exhibit the same characteristics.

9. Under subparagraph (h) the uniform rules do not apply to evidence and procedure, subject to Article 14.

This exclusion seems to require no comment. The scope and extent to which the exclusion is subject to limitation will be noted in the commentary on Article 14.

10. The question whether contracts of insurance should or should not be included in the scope of the uniform rules was discussed at length by the Group. The solution finally adopted was that which appears in paragraph 3.

Under this paragraph the provisions of the Convention do not apply to contracts of insurance covering risks situated in the territories of Member States of the European Economic Community. This exclusion takes account of work being done within the Community in the field of insurance. Thus the uniform rules apply to contracts of insurance covering risks situate outside those territories. The States are nevertheless free to apply rules based on those in the Convention even to risks situate in the Community, subject to the Community rules which are to be established.

Insurance contracts, where they cover risks situate outside the Community, may also, in appropriate cases, fall under Article 5 of the Convention.

To determine whether a risk is situate in the territories of the Member States of the Community the last phrase of paragraph 3 states that the judge is required to apply his own national law. This expression means the rules in force in the judge's country, to the exclusion of the rules of private international law as stated by Article 15 of the Convention.

11. By virtue of paragraph 4 of Article 1 the exclusion provided for in paragraph 3 does not affect reinsurance contracts. In fact these contracts do not raise the same problems as contracts of insurance, where the need to protect the persons insured must necessarily be taken into account. Thus the uniform rules apply to reinsurance contracts.

Article 2

Application of law of non-Contracting States

This Article underlines the universal character of the uniform rules laid down in this Convention. The Convention does not apply only in situations involving some form of connection with one or other of the Contracting States. It is of universal application in the sense that the choice of law which it lays down may result in the law of a State not party to the Convention being applied. By way of example, under Article 3, parties to a contract may opt for the law of a third State, and in the absence of any choice, that same law may be applied to the contract under Articles 4 and 5 if it is with that State that the contract has the closest links. In other words, the Convention is a uniform measure of private international law which will replace the rules of private international law in force in each of the Contracting States, with regard to the subject matter which it covers and subject to any other convention to which the Contracting States are party (see Article 21).

The solution is consistent with that adopted in most of the Hague Conventions on private international law that deal with choice of laws (*stricto sensu*). The text follows that of the Hague Convention drafted during the XIIIth session (Conventions of 14 March 1978 on the law applicable to matrimonial property regimes, Article 2, and on the law applicable to agency, Article 4).

[3213]

[OJ C282, 31.10.80, p 15]

TITLE II

UNIFORM RULES

Article 3

Freedom of choice

1. The rule stated in Article 3(1) under which the contract is governed by the law chosen by the parties simply reaffirms a rule currently embodied in the private international law of all the Member States of the Community and of most other countries.

In French law the rule conferring this power (or "autonomie de la volonté" as it is called) upon the parties is founded on case law dating back to the judgment delivered on 5 December 1910 by the Court of Cassation in *American Trading Company v Quebec Steamship Company Limited*. The French draft law of 1967 to supplement the Civil Code in matters of private international law merely confirms the state of French law in this matter by providing in the first paragraph of Article 2312: "Contracts of an international character and the obligations arising from them shall be subject to the law under which the parties intended to place themselves."

The firm establishment of the rule in French case law was accompanied by corresponding developments in legal theory. The most eminent contemporary writers declare themselves fundamentally in favour of the principle of the parties' freedom of contract in determining the law applicable to the contract, or, according to the opinion of some legal writers, the "localization" of the contract in a specific legal system.[13]

The same applies to the law of the German Federal Republic, where the subject of contractual obligations was not dealt with by the legislature in the final version of the "introductory law" of 1896. The rule conferring upon the parties the power to specify the law applicable to their contract is nevertheless founded on case law which has been developed and strengthened in recent decades despite the opposition of the great majority of earlier German legal theorists. At all events present-day theory is in entire agreement with the position taken by the case law.[14]

Unlike the situation in France and Germany, in Italy the principle of freedom of contract of the contracting parties was expressly enacted as early as 1865 in the preliminary provisions of the Civil Code. It is currently based upon the first paragraph of Article 25 of the preliminary provisions of the 1942 Civil Code, in which the freedom of the parties to choose the law applicable to their contract is formally accepted, as in Articles 9 and 10 of the Navigation Code, where it is provided that the power of the parties to designate the applicable law may also be exercised in seamen's contracts and in contracts for the use of ships, boats and aircraft. According to the preponderant view of theorists and consistent decisions by the Court of Cassation, the law applicable to the contract must be determined primarily on the basis of the express will of the parties; only in default of such a nomination will the law of the contract be determined by the connecting factors stipulated in the abovementioned provisions.[15]

As regards Belgium, Luxembourg and the Netherlands, the rule that the contracting parties enjoy freedom of contract in choosing the applicable law has also been sanctioned by judicial practice and by contemporary legal writers.

In its judgment of 24 February 1938 in *SA Antwerpia v Ville d'Anvers* the Belgian Court of Cassation stated for the first time, in terms clearly suggested by the French judgment of 5 December 1910, that: "the law applicable to contracts, both to their formation and their conditions and effects, (is) that adopted by the parties".[16] Several Belgian writers have contributed to the firm establishment of the rule in theory and in practice.[17]

In the Netherlands the Hoge Raad put the finishing touches to the developments in case law in this field in its judgment of 13 May 1966 in the Alnati case. The previous decisions of the Supreme Court and the differing views of writers on the precise scope of the freedom of contract rule would not have permitted definition of the state of Netherlands law in this matter with sufficient certainty.[18]

[OJ C282, 31.10.80, p 16]

At all events the 1969 Benelux Treaty on uniform rules for private international law, even though the signatory States have not pursued its entry into force, is clear evidence of their present views on this subject. Article 13(1) of the uniform law states: "Contracts shall be governed by the law chosen by the parties as regards both essential and ancillary provisions".

English law recognizes that the parties to a contract are free to choose the law which is to govern it ("the proper law of the contract"). This principle of freedom of choice is founded on judicial decisions.[19] In *Vita Food Products Inc v Unus Shipping Co Ltd*[20] Lord Wright indicated that the parties' choice must be *bona fide* and legal and could be avoided on the ground of public policy. In certain areas the parties' freedom of choice is subject to limitations imposed by statute,[20a] the most important of these being in the field of exemption clauses.[20b]

The law of Scotland is to similar effect[20c] and Irish law draws its inspiration from the same principles as the English and Scottish legal systems.

Under English law (and the situation is similar in Scots law and Irish law), in the case where the parties have not expressly chosen the law to govern their contract,[20d] the court will consider whether the parties' choice of law to be applied can be inferred from the terms of the contract. The most common case in which the court may infer a choice of the proper law is where the contract contains an arbitration or choice of jurisdiction clause naming a particular country as the seat of arbitration or litigation. Such a clause gives rise to an argument that the law of the country chosen should be applied as the proper law of the contract. This inference however is not conclusive and can be rebutted by any contrary inferences which may be drawn from the other provisions of the contract and the relevant surrounding circumstances.[20e]

Finally, as regards Denmark, the principle of the freedom of contracting parties to choose the law applicable to their contract already seems to have inspired several opinions by Supreme Court judges during this century. Today at all events this principle forms the basis of Danish case law, as can be seen from the judgment in 1957 in *Baltica v MJ Vermaas Scheepvaart bedrijf*, with full support from legal writers.[21]

2. The principle of the parties' freedom to choose the law applicable is also supported both by arbitration decisions and by international treaties designed to unify certain rules of conflict in relation to contracts.

The rule, which had already been cited in 1929 by the Permanent Court of International Justice in its judgment in the case of the Brazilian Loans,[22] very clearly underlay the award made by the arbitration tribunal on 29 August 1958 in *Saudi Arabia v Arabian American Oil Company* (*Aramco*) in which it was stated that the "principles of private international law to be consulted in order to find the law applicable are those relating to freedom of choice, by virtue of which, in an agreement which is international in character, the law expressly chosen by the parties must be applied first …".[23] Similarly in the arbitration findings given on 15 March 1963 in *Sapphire International Petroleums Ltd v National Iranian Oil Company*, the sole arbitrator, Mr Cavin, affirmed that it is the will of the parties that determines the law applicable in matters of contract.[24] The rule was reaffirmed even more recently by the sole arbitrator, Mr Dupuy, in the award which he made on 19 January 1977 in *Libyan Arab Republic v California Asiatic Oil Company and Texaco Overseas Petroleum Company*.[25]

As regards international treaties, the rule of freedom of choice has been adopted in the Convention on the law applicable to international sales of goods concluded at the Hague on 15 June 1955 which entered into force on 1 September 1964. Article 2 of this Convention, which is in force among several European countries, provides that: "The sale shall be governed by the internal law of the country nominated by the contracting parties."

Article VIII of the European Convention on international commercial arbitration concluded at Geneva on 21 April 1961, which entered into force on 7 January 1964, provides that the parties are free to determine the law which the arbitrators must apply in a dispute.

The same principle forms the basis of the 1965 Convention for the settlement of disputes relating to investments between States and nationals of other States, which entered into force on 14 October 1966, when it provides in Article 42 that "the Tribunal shall rule on the dispute in accordance with the rules of law adopted by the parties".

The Hague Convention of 14 March 1978 on the law applicable to agency provides in Article 5 that "the internal law chosen by the principal and the agent is to govern the agency relationship between them".[26]

[OJ C282, 31.10.80, p 17]

3. The parties' choice must be express or be demonstrated with reasonable certainty by the terms of the contract or the circumstances of the case. This interpretation, which emerges from the second sentence of Article 3(1), has an important consequence.

The choice of law by the parties will often be express but the Convention recognizes the possibility that the Court may, in the light of all the facts, find that the parties have made a real choice of law although this is not expressly stated in the contract. For example, the contract may be in a standard form which is known to be governed by a particular system of law even though there is no express statement to this effect, such as a Lloyd's policy of marine insurance. In other cases a previous course of dealing between the parties under contracts containing an express choice of law may leave the court in no doubt that the contract in question is to be governed by the law previously chosen where the choice of law clause has been omitted in circumstances which do not indicate a deliberate change of policy by the parties. In some cases the choice of a particular forum may show in no uncertain manner that the parties intend the contract to be governed by the law of that forum, but this must always be subject to the other terms of the contract and all the circumstances of the case. Similarly references in a contract to specific Articles of the French Civil Code may leave the court in no doubt that the parties have deliberately chosen French law, although there is no expressly stated choice of law. Other matters that may impel the court to the conclusion that a real choice of law has been made might include an express choice of law in related transactions between the same parties, or the choice of a place where disputes are to be settled by arbitration in circumstances indicating that the arbitrator should apply the law of that place.

This Article does not permit the court to infer a choice of law that the parties might have made where they had no clear intention of making a choice. Such a situation is governed by Article 4.

4. The last sentence of Article 3(1) acknowledges that the parties' choice of the law applicable may relate to the whole of the contract or to only part thereof. On the question whether severability (dépeçage) was to be allowed, some experts observed that the contract should in principle be governed by one law, unless that contract, although apparently a single contract, consists in reality of several contracts or parts which are separable and independent of each other from the legal and economic points of view. In the opinion of these experts, no reference to severability should have been made in the text of the Convention itself. In the view of others, on the contrary, severability is directly linked with the principle of freedom of contract and so would be difficult to prohibit. Nevertheless when the contract is severable the choice must be logically consistent, i e it must relate to elements in the contract which can be governed by different laws without giving rise to contradictions. For example, an "index-linking clause" may be made subject to a different law; on the other hand it is unlikely that repudiation of the contract for non-performance would be subjected to two different laws, one for the vendor and the other for the purchaser. Recourse must be had to Article 4 of the Convention if the chosen laws cannot be logically reconciled.

In the opinion of these experts the danger that the argument of severability might be used to avoid certain mandatory provisions is eliminated by the operation of Article 7. The experts concerned also emphasized that severability should not be limited to cases of express choice of law.

The solution adopted in the last sentence of Article 3(1) is prompted by exactly this kind of idea. The Group did not adopt the idea that the judge can use a partial choice of law as the basis for a presumption in favour of one law invoked to govern the contract in its entirety. Such an idea might be conducive to error in situations in which the parties had reached agreement on the choice of law solely on a specific point. Recourse must be had to Article 4 in the case of partial choice.

5. The first sentence of Article 3(2) leaves the parties maximum freedom as to the time at which the choice of applicable law can be made.

It may be made either at the time the contract is concluded or at an earlier or later date. The second sentence of paragraph 2 also leaves the parties maximum freedom as to amendment of the choice of applicable law previously made.

The solution adopted by the Group in paragraph 2 corresponds only in part to what seems to be the current state of the law on this point in the Member States of the Community.

In the Federal Republic of Germany and in France the choice of applicable law by the parties can apparently be made even after the contract has been concluded, and the courts sometimes deduce the applicable law from the parties' attitude during the proceedings when they refer with clear agreement to a specific law. The power of the parties to vary the choice of law applicable to their contract also seems to be very widely accepted.[27]

Case law in the Netherlands seems to follow the same line of interpretation.[28]

[OJ C282, 31.10.80, p 18]

In Italy, however, the Court of Cassation (sitting as a full court) stated in its judgment of 28 June 1966 No 1680 in Assael *Nissim v Crespi* that; "the parties', choice of applicable law is not admissible if made after the contract has been drawn up".[29]

According to this dictum, which Italian commentators do not wholly support[30] the choice can be made only at the time the contract is concluded. Once the choice is made, the parties no longer have the option of agreeing to nominate a law other than that nominated at the time of concluding the contract.

In the laws of England and Wales, Scotland, Northern Ireland and Ireland, there is no clear authority as to the law which governs the possibility of a change in the proper law.

6. The liberal solution adopted by the Group seems to be in accordance with the requirement of logical consistency. Once the principle of freedom of contract has been accepted, and having regard to the fact that the requirement of a choice of law by the parties may arise both at the time of conclusion of the contract and after that time, it seems quite logical that the power of the parties should not be limited solely to the time of conclusion of the contract. The same applies to a change (by a new agreement between the parties) in the applicable law previously chosen.

As to the way in which the choice of law can be changed, it is quite natural that this change should be subject to the same rules as the initial choice.

If the choice of law is made or changed in the course of proceedings the question arises as to the limits within which the choice or change can be effective. However, the question falls within the ambit of the national law of procedure, and can be settled only in accordance with that law.

7. The second sentence of Article 3(2) states that a change in the applicable law after the contract has been concluded shall not prejudice its formal validity under Article 9 or adversely affect the rights of third parties. The purpose of the reservation concerning the formal validity of the contract is to avoid a situation whereby the agreement between the parties to subject the contract to a law other than that which previously governed it could create doubts as to the validity of the contract during the period preceding the agreement between the parties. The preservation of third-party rights appears to be entirely justified. In certain legal systems, a third party may have acquired rights in consequence of a contract concluded between two other persons. These rights cannot be affected by a subsequent change in the choice of the applicable law.

8. Article 3(3) provides that the choice of a foreign law by the parties, whether or not accompanied by the choice of a foreign tribunal, shall not, where all other elements relevant to the situation at the time of the choice are connected with one country only, prejudice the application of the law of that country which cannot be derogated from by contract, hereinafter called "mandatory rules".

This solution is the result of a compromise between two lines of argument which have been diligently pursued within the Group: the wish on the one hand of certain experts to limit the parties' freedom of choice embodied in this Article by means of a correcting factor specifying that the choice of a foreign law would be insufficient *per se* to permit the application of that law if the situation at the moment of choice did not involve another foreign element, and on the other the concern of other experts, notably the United Kingdom experts, that such a correcting factor would be too great an obstacle to the freedom of the parties in situations in which their choice appeared justified, made in good faith, and capable of serving interests worthy of protection. In particular these experts emphasized that departures from the principle of the parties' freedom of choice should be authorized only in exceptional circumstances, such as the application of the mandatory rules of a law other than that chosen by the parties; they also gave several examples of cases in which the choice of a foreign law by the parties was fully justified, although there was apparently no other foreign element in the situation.

The Group recognized that this concern was well founded, while maintaining the principle that the choice by the parties of a foreign law where all the other elements relevant to the situation at the time of the choice are connected with one country only shall not prejudice the application of the mandatory rules of the law of that country.

9. Article 3(4) merely refers questions relating to the existence and validity of the parties' consent as to the choice of the law applicable to the provisions of Articles 8, 9 and 11. We will return to these matters in the comments on those Articles.

[OJ C282, 31.10.80, p 19]

Article 4

Applicable law in the absence of choice

1. In default of an express or implied choice by the parties, there is at present no uniform way of determining the law applicable to contracts in the legal systems of the Member States of the Community.[31]

In French and Belgian law no distinction is to be drawn between the express and hypothetical (or presumed) will of the parties. Failing an express choice of applicable law, the courts look for various "pointers" capable of showing that the contract is located in a particular country. This localization is sometimes regarded subjectively as equivalent to the probable wish of the parties had such a wish been expressed, sometimes objectively as equivalent to the country with which the transaction is most closely connected.[32]

The objective concept seems to be receiving more and more support from legal writers and from case law. Following this concept, the Paris Court stated in its judgment of 27 January 1955 (*Soc Jansen v Soc Heurtey*) that, in default of an indication of the will of the parties, the applicable law "is determined objectively by the fact that the contract is located by its context and economic aspects in a particular country, the place with which the transaction is most closely connected being that in which the contract is to be performed in fulfilment of the obligation characteristic of its nature".[33]

PART IV
EC MATERIALS

It is this concept of the location of the contracts that is referred to, in terms clearly modelled on the above judgment, in the second paragraph of Article 2313 of the French draft, which states that in default of the expressed will of the parties "the contract is governed by the law with which it is most closely connected by its economic aspects, and notably by the main place of performance".

Similarly, in German law the solution adopted by the courts in determining the law of the contract in the absence of choice by the parties is based largely upon the search for "pointers" capable of showing the "hypothetischer Parteiwille", the presumed will of the parties, having regard to the general interests at stake in each particular case. If this gives no result, the law applicable to the contract according to German case law is determined by the place of performance: more precisely, by the place of performance of each of the obligations arising from the contract, because the German courts take the view that if the various contractual obligations are to be performed in different countries, each shall be governed by the law of the country in which it is performed.[34]

In English law where the parties have not expressly chosen the proper law and no choice can be inferred, the law applicable to the contract is the system of law with which the transaction has its "closest and most real connection".[35] In such a case the judge does not seek to ascertain the actual intentions of the contracting parties, because that is non-existent, but seeks "to determine for the parties what is the proper law which, as just and reasonable persons, they ought to have intended if they had thought about the question when they made the contract".[36] In this inquiry, the court has to consider all the circumstances of the case. No one factor is decisive; instead a wide range of factors must be taken into account, such as for instance, the place of residence or business of the parties, the place of performance, the place of contracting and the nature and subject-matter of the contract.

Scots law adopts a similar approach,[36a] as does the law of Ireland.

In Italian law, where the presumed will of the parties plays no part, the matter is settled expressly and directly by the legislature. Failing a choice of law by the parties, the obligations arising from the contract are governed by the following—

(a) contracts for employment on board foreign ships or aircraft, by the national law of the ship or aircraft (Naval Code Article 9);

(b) marine, domestic and air hiring contracts, charters and transport contracts, by the national law of the ship or aircraft (Naval Code Article 10);

(c) all other contracts, by the national law of the contracting parties, if common to both; otherwise by the law of the place where the contract was concluded (preliminary provisions of the Civil Code, Article 25, first subparagraph).

The abovementioned laws are of subsidiary effect only; they apply only in default of an expression of the parties' will as to the law applicable. Italian case law so holds and legal writers concur with this view.[37]

To conclude this short survey, only the provisions of the third and fourth paragraphs of Article 13 of the 1969 Benelux Treaty which has not entered into force remain to be mentioned. According to the third paragraph, in default of a choice by the parties "the contract shall be governed by the law of the country with which it is most closely connected", and according to the fourth paragraph "when it is impossible to determine that country, the contract shall be governed by the law of the country in which it was concluded". One may note a tendency in Netherlands case law to formulate special rules of reference for certain types of contract (see "Journal du Droit Int. 1978, pp 336 to 344" and "Neth Int Law Rev 1974, pp 315 to 316"), i e contracts of employment, agency contracts and contracts of carriage.

[OJ C282, 31.10.80, p 20]

The foregoing survey has shown that, with the sole exception of Italy, where the subsidiary law applicable to the contract is determined once and for all by hard-and-fast connecting factors, all the other Community countries have preferred and continue to prefer a more flexible approach, leaving the judge to select the preponderant and decisive connecting factor for determining the law applicable to the contract in each specific case among the various elements of the contract and the circumstances of the case.

2. Having considered the advantages and disadvantages of the solutions adopted by the legislatures and the case law of the Member States of the Community and after analyzing a range of ideas and alternatives advanced both by the rapporteur and by several delegates, the Group agreed upon the uniform rule embodied in Article 4.

The first paragraph of this Article provides that, in default of a choice by the parties, the contract shall be governed by the law of the country with which it has the closest connection.

In order to determine the country with which the contract is most closely connected, it is also possible to take account of factors which supervened after the conclusion of the contract.

In fact the beginning of the first paragraph does not mention default of choice by the parties; the expression used is "to the extent that the law applicable to the contract has not been chosen in accordance with Article 3". The use of these words is justified by reference to what has been said in paragraph 4 of the commentary on Article 3.

However, the flexibility of the general principle established by paragraph 1 is substantially modified by the presumptions in paragraphs 2, 3 and 4, and by a strictly limited exception in favour of severability at the end of paragraph 1.

3. According to Article 4(2), it is presumed that the contract has the closest connection with the country in which the party who is to effect the performance which is characteristic of the contract has his habitual residence at the time when the contract is concluded, or, in the case of a body corporate or unincorporate, its central administration. If the contract is concluded by that party in the course of his trade or profession, the country concerned is that in which his principal place of business is situated or, if the contract is to be performed through a place of business other than the principal place of business, the country in which that other place of business is situated. Article 4(2) establishes a presumption which may be rebutted in accordance with Article 4(5).

The kind of idea upon which paragraph 2 is based is certainly not entirely unknown to some specialists. It gives effect to a tendency which has been gaining ground both in legal writings and in case law in many countries in recent decades.[38] The submission of the contract, in the absence of a choice by the parties, to the law appropriate to the characteristic performance defines the connecting factor of the contract from the inside, and not from the outside by elements unrelated to the essence of the obligation such as the nationality of the contracting parties or the place where the contract was concluded.

In addition it is possible to relate the concept of characteristic performance to an even more general idea, namely the idea that his performance refers to the function which the legal relationship involved fulfils in the economic and social life of any country. The concept of characteristic performance essentially links the contract to the social and economic environment of which it will form a part.

Identifying the characteristic performance of a contract obviously presents no difficulty in the case of unilateral contracts. By contrast, in bilateral (reciprocal) contracts whereby the parties undertake mutual reciprocal performance, the counterperformance by one of the parties in a modern economy usually takes the form of money. This is not, of course, the characteristic performance of the contract. It is the performance for which the payment is due, i e depending on the type of contract, the delivery of goods, the granting of the right to make use of an item of property, the provision of a service, transport, insurance, banking operations, security, etc, which usually constitutes the centre of gravity and the socio-economic function of the contractual transaction.

[OJ C282, 31.10.80, p 21]

As for the geographical location of the characteristic performance, it is quite natural that of the country in which the party liable for the performance is habitually resident or has his central administration (if a body corporate or unincorporate) or his place of business, according to whether the performance in question is in the course of his trade or profession or not, should prevail over the country of performance where, of course, the latter is a country other than that of habitual residence, central administration or the place of business. In the solution adopted by the Group the position is that only the place of habitual residence or of the central administration or of the place of business of the party providing the essential performance is decisive in locating the contract.

Thus, for example, in a banking contract the law of the country of the banking establishment with which the transaction is made will normally govern the contract. It is usually the case in a commercial contract of sale that the law of the vendor's place of business will govern the contract. To take another example, in an agency contract concluded in France between a Belgian commercial agent and a French company, the characteristic performance being that of the agent, the contract will be governed by Belgian law if the agent has his place of business in Belgium.[39]

In conclusion, Article 4(2) gives specific form and objectivity to the, in itself, too vague concept of "closest connection". At the same time it greatly simplifies the problem of determining the law applicable to the contract in default of choice by the parties. The place where the act was done becomes unimportant. There is no longer any need to determine where the contract was concluded, with all the difficulties and the problems of classification that arise in practice. Seeking the place of performance or the different places of performance and classifying them becomes superfluous.

For each category of contract it is the characteristic performance that is in principle the relevant factor in applying the presumption for determining the applicable law, even in situations peculiar to certain contracts, as for example in the contract of guarantee where the characteristic performance is always that of the guarantor, whether in relation to the principal debtor or the creditor.

To counter the possibility of changes in the connecting factor ("conflits mobiles") in the application of paragraph 2, it has been made clear that the country of habitual residence or of the principal place of business of the party providing the characteristic performance is the country in which he is habitually resident or has his central administration or place of business, as appropriate, "at the time of conclusion of the contract".

According to the last part of paragraph 2, if the contract prescribes performance by an establishment other than the principal place of business, it is presumed that the contract has the closest connection with the country of that other establishment.

4. Article 4(3) establishes that the presumption in paragraph 2 does not operate to the extent that the subject of the contract is a right in immovable property or a right to use immovable property. It is presumed in this case that the contract is most closely connected with the country in which the immovable property is situated.

It is advisable to state that the provision in question merely establishes a presumption in favour of the law of the country in which the immovable property is situate. In other words this is a presumption which, like that in paragraph 2, could also be rebutted if circumstances so required.

For example, this presumption could be rebutted if two persons resident in Belgium were to make a contract for renting a holiday home on the island of Elba (Italy). It might be thought in such a case that the contract was most closely connected with the country of the contracting parties' residence, not with Italy.

Finally it should be stressed that paragraph 3 does not extend to contracts for the construction or repair of immovable property. This is because the main subject-matter of these contracts is the construction or repair rather than the immovable property itself.

5. After a long and animated discussion the Group decided to include transport contracts within the scope of the convention. However, the Group deemed it inappropriate to submit contracts for the carriage of goods to the presumption contained in paragraph 2, having regard to the peculiarities of this type of transport. The contract for carriage of goods is therefore made subject to a presumption of its own, namely that embodied in paragraph 4. This presumption may be rebutted in accordance with Article 4(5).

According to this fourth paragraph it is presumed in the case of contracts for the carriage of goods that if the country in which the carrier has his principal place of business at the time the contract is concluded is also the country of the place of loading or unloading or of the principal place of business of the consignor, the contract is most closely connected with that country. The term "consignor" refers in general to any person who consigns goods to the carrier (Afzender, Aflader, Verzender, Mittente, Caricatore, etc).

[OJ C282, 31.10.80 p 22]

Thus the paragraph 4 presumption rests upon a combination of connecting factors. To counter the possibility of changes in the connecting factor in applying the paragraph, it has been made clear here also that the reference to the country in which the carrier has his principal place of business must be taken to refer to the carrier's place of business "at the time the contract is concluded".

It appears that for purposes of the application of this paragraph the places of loading and unloading which enter into consideration are those agreed at the time when the contract is concluded.

It often happens in contracts for carriage that a person who contracts to carry goods for another does not carry them himself but arranges for a third party to do so. In Article 4(4) the term "the carrier" means the party to the contract who undertakes to carry the goods, whether or not he performs the carriage himself.

In addition, the third sentence of paragraph 4 provides that in applying that paragraph single-voyage charterparties and other contracts whose main purpose is the carriage of goods shall be treated as contracts for the carriage of goods. The wording of paragraph 4 is intended to make it clear that charterparties may be considered to be contracts for the carriage of goods in so far as that is their substance.

6. Contracts for the carriage of passengers remain subject to the general presumption, ie that provided for in Article 4(2).

This solution was adopted by majority vote within the Group. Certain delegations favoured the special presumption embodied in paragraph 4, arguing that, as with other types of transport, the need was for a combination of connecting factors, in view of the fact that reference solely to the place where the carrier, who provides the characteristic performance, has his principal place of business may not be a significant connecting factor: by way of example they cited the case of transportation of French or English passengers between London and Paris by an American airline. It was also emphasized that in a mixed contract (passengers and goods) the difficulty of applying two different laws would arise.

Nevertheless the other delegations were against the special presumption, their principal arguments being: the application of several laws to passengers on the same journey would involve serious difficulties; the formulation of paragraph 4 is such that it would hardly ever apply to carriage of passengers, so recourse would usually be had to the first paragraph of Article 4, which does not give the judge sufficiently precise criteria for decision; contracts of carriage normally contain a clause conferring jurisdiction on the court of the carrier's principal place of business, and paragraph 2 would operate so that the law of the court of competent jurisdiction would coincide with the applicable law.

In any event it should be stated that the judge will not be able to exclude consideration of the country in which the carrier has his principal place of business in seeking the places with which the contract is most closely connected.

Finally it is useful to note that the Group repeatedly stressed in the course of the discussions on transport problems that the international conventions took precedence in this matter.

7. Article 4(2) does not apply when the characteristic performance cannot be determined. The case then falls under paragraph 1, ie the contract will be governed by the law of the country with which it is most closely connected.

The first part of Article 4(5) contains precisely that provision.

However, that paragraph also provides for the possibility of disregarding the presumptions in paragraphs 2, 3, and 4 when all the circumstances show the contract to have closer connections with another country. In this case the law of that other country is applied.

The grounds for the latter provision are as follows. Given the entirely general nature of the conflict rule contained in Article 4, the only exemptions to which are certain contracts made by consumers and contracts of employment, it seemed essential to provide for the possibility of applying a law other than those referred to in the presumptions in paragraphs 2, 3 and 4 whenever all the circumstances show the contract to be more closely connected with another country.

Article 4(5) obviously leaves the judge a margin of discretion as to whether a set of circumstances exists in each specific case justifying the non-application of the presumptions in paragraphs 2, 3 and 4. But this is the inevitable counterpart of a general conflict rule intended to apply to almost all types of contract.

[OJ C282, 31.10.80, p 23]

8. Article 4(1) allows parts of the contract to be severed under certain conditions. The last sentence of this paragraph provides that if one part of the contract can be separated from the rest and is more closely connected with another country, then by way of exception the law of that other country can be applied to that part of the contract.

Discussion of the matter within the Group revealed that no delegation wished to encourage the idea of severability (dépeçage). However, most of the experts were in favour of allowing the court to effect a severance, by way of exception, for a part of the contract which is independent and separable, in terms of the contract and not of the dispute, where that part has a closer connection with another country (for example, contracts for joint venture, complex contracts).

As to whether or not the possibility of severance should be mentioned in the text of the convention itself most delegations were in favour of its being mentioned. It was emphasized in particular that mere reference to the matter in the report would be insufficient by itself, because in some Member States of the Community it is not usual to take account of the report. It was also emphasized that to include it in the text would reduce the risk of variation in the application of the convention on this point, because the text would specify the conditions under which severance was allowed.

The wording of the last sentence in paragraph 1 embodies precisely this idea. The words "by way of exception" are therefore to be interpreted in the sense that the court must have recourse to severance as seldom as possible.

9. It should be noted that the presumptions mentioned in paragraphs 2, 3 and 4 of Article 4 are only rebuttable presumptions.

Article 5
Certain consumer contracts

1. Article 5 of the convention establishes a specific conflict rule for certain contracts made by consumers. Most of the experts who have participated in the Group's work since 1973 have taken the view that consumer protection, the present aim of several national legislatures, would entail a reversal of the connecting factor provided for in Article 4 or a modification of the principle of freedom of choice provided for in Article 3. On the one hand the choice of the parties should not adversely affect the mandatory provisions of the State in which the consumer is habitually resident; on the other, in this type of contract it is the law of the buyer (the weaker party) which should normally prevail over that of the seller.

2. The definition of consumer contracts corresponds to that contained in Article 13 of the Convention on jurisdiction and enforcement of judgments. It should be interpreted in the light of its purpose which is to protect the weaker party and in accordance with other international instruments with the same purpose such as the Judgments Convention. Thus, in the opinion of the majority of the delegations it will, normally, only apply where the person who supplies goods or services or provides credit acts in the course of his trade or profession. Similarly, the rule does not apply to contracts made by traders, manufacturers or persons in the exercise of a profession (doctors, for example) who buy equipment or obtain services for that trade or profession. If such a person acts partly within, partly outside his trade or profession the situation only falls within the scope of Article 5 if he acts primarily outside his trade or profession. Where the receiver of goods or services or credit in fact acted primarily outside his trade or profession but the other party did not know this and, taking all the circumstances into account should not reasonably have known it, the situation falls outside the scope of Article 5. Thus if the receiver of goods or services holds himself out as a professional, e g by ordering goods which might well be used in his trade or profession on his professional paper the good faith of the other party is protected and the case will not be governed by Article 5.

The rule extends to credit sales as well as to cash sales, but sales of securities are excluded. The Group has specifically avoided a more precise definition of "consumer contract" in order to avoid conflict with the various definitions already given by national legislation. The rule also applies to the supply of services, such as insurance, as well as supply of goods.

3. Paragraph 2 embodies the principle that a choice of law in a consumer contract cannot deprive the consumer of the protection afforded to him by the law of the country in which he has his habitual residence. This principle shall, however, only apply under certain conditions set out in the three indents of paragraph 2.

[OJ C282, 31.10.80, p 24]

The first indent relates to situations where the trader has taken steps to market his goods or services in the country where the consumer resides. It is intended to cover *inter alia* mail order and door-step selling. Thus the trader must have done certain acts such as advertising in the press, or on radio or television, or in the cinema or by catalogues aimed specifically at that country, or he must have made business proposals individually through a middleman or by canvassing. If, for example, a German makes a contract in response to an advertisement published by a French company in a German publication, the contract is covered by the special rule. If, on the other hand, the German replies to an advertisement in American publications, even if they are sold in Germany, the rule does not apply unless the advertisement appeared in special editions of the publication intended for European countries. In the latter case the seller will have made a special advertisement intended for the country of the purchaser.

The Group expressly adopted the words "steps necessary on his part" in order to avoid the classic problem of determining the place where the contract was concluded. This is a particularly delicate matter in the situations referred to, because it involves international contracts normally concluded by correspondence. The word "steps" includes *inter alia* writing or any action taken in consequence of an offer or advertisement.

According to the second indent Article 5 shall apply in all situations where the trader or his agent has received the order of the consumer in the country in which the consumer has his habitual residence. This provision is a parallel to Article 3(2) of the 1955 Hague Convention on international sales.

There is a considerable overlap between the first and the second indents. This overlap is, however, not complete. For example, the second indent applies in situations where the consumer has addressed himself to the stand of a foreign firm at a fair or exhibition taking place in the consumers country or to a permanent branch or agency of a foreign firm established in the consumer's country even though the foreign firm has not advertised in the consumer's country in a way covered by the first indent. The word "agent" is intended to cover all persons acting on behalf of the trader.

The third indent deals with a situation which is rather special but where, on the other hand, a majority of delegations found a clear need for protecting the consumer under the provisions of Article 5. It covers what one might describe as "border-crossing excursion-selling", ie for example, a situation where a store-owner in country A arranges one-day bus trips for consumers in a neighbouring country B with the main purpose of inducing the consumers to buy in his store. This is a practice well-known in some areas. The situation is not covered by the first indent because there it is required that the consumer has taken in his own country all the steps necessary on his part for the conclusion of the contract. The third indent is, unlike the rest of paragraph 2, limited to contracts for the sale of goods. The condition that the journey was arranged by the seller shall not be understood in the narrow way that the seller must himself have taken care of the transportation. It is sufficient that the seller has arranged the journey by way of an agreement with the transportation company.

In describing the situation in which Article 5 applies to consumer contracts, the Group has not followed the text of Article 13(1) of the Judgments Convention as amended by the Accession Convention. On the one hand Article 5 contains no special provision for hire purchase contracts and loans on deferred terms. On the other hand, Article 13 of the Judgments Convention has no provisions parallel to the second and third indents of Article 5(2).

4. Article 5(3) introduces an exception to Article 4 of the Convention. According to this paragraph, notwithstanding the provisions of Article 4 and in the absence of choice in accordance with Article 3, a contract made by a consumer shall "be governed by the law of the country in which the consumer has his habitual residence if it is entered into in the circumstances described in the second paragraph of Article 5".

The wording of paragraph 3 is sufficiently clear, and calls for no additional examination.

5. Under the terms of paragraph 4 thereof, Article 5 applies neither to contracts of carriage (a) nor to contracts relating to the supply of services provided exclusively in a country other than that in which the consumer is resident (b). The exclusion of contracts of carriage is justified by the fact that the special protective measures for which provision is made in Article 5 are not appropriate for governing contracts of this type. Similarly, in the case of contracts relating to the supply of services (for example, accommodation in a hotel, or a language course) which are supplied exclusively outside the State in which the consumer is resident, the latter cannot reasonably expect the law of his State of origin to be applied in derogation from the general rules of Articles 3 and 4. In the cases referred to under (b) the contract is more closely connected with the State in which the other contracting party is resident, even if the latter has performed one of the acts described in paragraph 2 (advertising, for example) in the State in which the consumer is resident.

[OJ C282, 31.10.90, p 25]

6. The intention of paragraph 5 is to ensure that Article 5, notwithstanding the exclusions made in on paragraph 4, shall apply to contracts providing for what is in English normally called a "package tour" ie an ordinary tourist arrangement consisting of a combination of travel and accommodation for an inclusive price. If a package tour starts with transportation from the country in which the consumer has his habitual residence the contract would not be excluded according to paragraph 4. The importance of paragraph 5 is, therefore that it ensures application of Article 5 also in situations where the services provided for under a package tour start with transportation from another country. However, Article 5 of course only applies to package tours where the general conditions of paragraphs 1 and 2 are fulfilled, ie that the contract can be regarded as a consumer contract and that it is entered into in one of the situations mentioned in paragraph 2.

When formulating paragraph 5, the Group met with difficulty in defining a "package tour". The Group confined itself to a definition which underlines the main elements of this type of contract well known in practice, leaving it to the courts to solve any possible doubt as to the exact delimitation. The accommodation which is a part of a package tour must normally be separate from the transportation, and so paragraph 5 would not apply to the provision of a sleeper on a train.

Article 6
Individual employment contracts

1. Re-examination of the specific conflict rule in the matter of contracts of employment led the Group to make fundamental changes to this Article, which already appeared (as Article 5) in the original preliminary draft, and to harmonize its approach with that of the present Article 5 on consumer contracts.

In both cases the question was one of finding a more appropriate arrangement for matters in which the interests of one of the contracting parties are not the same as those of the other, and at the same time to secure thereby more adequate protection for the party who from the socio-economic point of view is regarded as the weaker in the contractual relationship.

2. On this basis, Article 6(1) sets a limit on the on the parties' freedom to choose the applicable law, as permitted by Article 3 of the convention, affirming that this choice in contracts of employment "shall not have the result of depriving the employee of the protection afforded to him by the mandatory rules of the law which would be applicable under paragraph 2 in the absence of choice".

The purpose of this text is as follows—

if the law applicable pursuant to paragraph 2 grants employees protection which is greater than that resulting from the law chosen by the parties, the result is not that the choice of this law becomes completely without effect. On the contrary, in this case the law which was chosen continues in principle to be applicable. In so far as the provisions of the law applicable pursuant to paragraph 2 give employees better protection than the chosen law, for example by giving a longer period of notice, these provisions set the provisions of the chosen law aside and are applicable in their place.

The mandatory rules from which the parties may not derogate consist not only of the provisions relating to the contract of employment itself, but also provisions such as those concerning industrial safety and hygiene which are regarded in certain Member States as being provisions of public law.

It follows from this text that if the law of the country designated by Article 6(2) makes the collective employment agreements binding for the employer, the employee will not be deprived of the protection afforded to him by these collective employment agreements by the choice of law of another State in the individual employment contract.

Article 6 applies to individual employment contracts and not to collective agreements. Consequently, the fact that an employment contract is governed by a foreign law cannot affect the powers which an employee's trade union might derive from collective agreements in its own country.

The present wording of Article 6 speaks of "contract of employment" instead of "employment relationship" as in the original preliminary draft. It should be stated, however, that the rule in Article 6 also covers the case of void contracts and also *de facto* employment relationships in particular those characterized by failure to respect the contract imposed by law for the protection of employees.

[OJ C282, 31.10.80, p 26]

3. According to Article 6(2), in the absence of choice by the parties and notwithstanding the provisions of Article 4, the contract of employment is governed as follows—

(a) by the law of the country in which the employee habitually carries out his work in performance of his contract, even if he is temporarily employed in another country; or

(b) if the employee does not habitually carry out his work in any one country, by the law of the country in which the place of business through which he was engaged is situated,

unless it appears from the circumstances as a whole that the contract of employment is more closely connected with another country, in which case the law of that other country applies.

After a thorough examination of the various problems raised by contracts of employment in private international law, in the course of which particular consideration was given both to the draft Regulation prepared in this connection by the EEC Commission and to the latest trends in the legal literature and case law of the Member States of the Community, the Group finally adopted the following solution. If the employee habitually works in one and the same country the contract of employment is governed by the law of that country even if the employee is temporarily employed in another country. This is the rule which appears in subparagraph 2(a). On the other hand, if the employee does not habitually work in one and the same country the contract of employment is governed by the law of the country in which the place of business through which he was engaged is situated. This is the rule which appears in subparagraph 2(b).

These solutions obviously differ substantially from those which would have resulted from the Article 4 presumption.

However, the last sentence of Article 6(2) provides that if it appears from the cirumstances as a whole that the contract is more closely connected with another country, the law of the latter country is applied.

4. As regards work done outside the jurisdiction of any State, the Group considered that the rule adopted in Article 6 could in principle be applied. In the case of work on an oil-rig platform on the high seas, the law of the country of the undertaking which engaged the employee should be applied.

The Group did not seek a special rule for the work of members of the crew on board a ship.

Article 7
Mandatory rules

1. The wording of Article 7 of the original preliminary draft has been considerably improved in the course of the Group's re-examination of the text of the convention since 1973, in order to permit a better interpretation in the various situations in which it will have to be applied.

The Group reiterated at its last meeting that Article 7 merely embodies principles which already exist in the laws of the Member States of the Community.

The principle that national courts can give effect under certain conditions to mandatory provisions other than those applicable to the contract by virtue of the choice of the parties or by virtue of a subsidiary connecting factor, has been recognized for several years both in legal writings and in practice in certain of our countries and elsewhere.

For example, the principle was recognized in the abovementioned 1966 judgment of the Netherlands Supreme Court in the Alnati case (cited *supra*, commentary on Article 3(1)) in which the Court said that, although the law applicable to contracts of an international character can, as a matter of principle, only be that which the parties themselves have chosen, "it may be that, for a foreign State, the observance of certain of its rules, even outside its own territory, is of such importance that the courts must take account of them, and hence apply them in preference to the law of another State which may have been chosen by the parties to govern their contract".

This judgment formed the basis for the second paragraph of Article 13 of the non-entered-into-force Benelux Treaty of 1969 on uniform rules of private international law, which provides that "where the contract is manifestly connected with a particular country, the intention of the parties shall not have the effect of excluding the provisions of the law of that country which, by reason of their special nature and subject-matter, exclude the application of any other law".

[OJ C282, 31.10.80, p 27]

The same attitude, at any event, underlies Article 16 of the Hague Convention of 14 March 1978 on the law applicable to agency, whereby, in the application of that convention, effect may be given to the mandatory rules of any State with which the situation has a significant connection, if and to the extent that, by the law of that State, those rules are applicable irrespective of the law indicated by its conflict rules.

On the other hand, despite the opinion of some jurists, it must be frankly recognized that no clear indication in favour of the principle in question seems discernible in the English cases (*Ralli Bros v Sota y Aznar; Regazzoni v Sethia; Rossano v Manufacturers Life Insurance Co*).[40]

2. The wording of Article 7(1) specifically provides that in the application of the convention "effect may be given to the mandatory rules of the law of another country with which the situation has a close connection if and in so far as, under the law of the latter country, those rules must be applied whatever the law applicable to the contract."

The former text did not specify the nature of the "connection" which must exist between the contract and a country other than that whose law is applicable. Several experts have observed that this omission might oblige the court in certain cases to take a large number of different and even contradictory laws into account. This lack of precision could make the court's task difficult, prolong the proceedings, and lend itself to delaying tactics. Accepting

PART IV
EC MATERIALS

the force of these observations, the Group decided that it is essential that there be a genuine connection with the other country, and that a merely vague connection is not adequate. For example, there would be a genuine connection when the contract is to be performed in that other country or when one party is resident or has his main place of business in that other country. Among the suggested versions, the Group finally adopted the word "close" which seemed the most suitable to define the situation which it wished to cover.

The connection in question must exist between the contract as a whole and the law of a country other than that to which the contract is submitted. The Group rejected the proposal by one delegation designed to establish a connection between the point in dispute and a specific law. In fact this proposal would have given rise to a regrettable dismemberment of the contract and would have led to the application of mandatory laws not foreseeable by the parties. Nevertheless the Group preferred to replace the word "the contracts" by "the situation". Since the former text seemed to some delegations to be lacking in clarity, the Group decided to improve the wording. In the new text it has therefore stated that the legal system of the country of which these mandatory provisions are an integral part must be examined to find out whether these provisions apply in the particular case whatever the law applicable to the contract. Furthermore, in the French text the word "loi" has been replaced by the word "droi" in order to avoid any doubts as to the scope of the rule, which is to cover both "legislative" provisions of any other country and also common law rules. Finally, after a long discussion, the majority of the Group, in view of the concern expressed by certain delegations in relation to constitutional difficulties, decided that it was preferable to allow the courts a discretion in the application of this Article.

3. Article 7(1) adds in relation to the mandatory rules that their nature and purpose, and the consequences of their application or non-application, must be taken into account in order to decide whether effect should be given to them.

Thus the application of the mandatory provisions of any other country must be justified by their nature and by their purpose. One delegation had suggested that this should be defined by saying that the nature and purpose of the provisions in question should be established according to internationally recognized criteria (for example, similar laws existing in other countries or which serve a generally recognized interest). However, other experts pointed out that these international criteria did not exist and that consequently difficulties would be created for the court. Moreover this formula would touch upon the delicate matter of the credit to be given to foreign legal systems. For these reasons the Group, while not disapproving this idea, did not adopt this drafting proposal.

Additionally, in considering whether to give effect to these mandatory rules, regard must be had to "the consequences of their application or non-application".

Far from weakening the rule this subsequent element—which did not appear in the original preliminary draft—defines, clarifies and strengthens it. In fact, the judge must be given a power of discretion, in particular in the case where contradictory mandatory rules of two different countries both purport simultaneously to be applicable to one and the same situation, and where a choice must necessarily be made between them.

To complete the comments on Article 7(1) it only remains to emphasize that the words "effect may be given" impose on the court the extremely delicate task of combining the mandatory provisions with the law normally applicable to the contract in the particular situation in question. The novelty of this provision, and the fear of the uncertainty to which it could give rise, have led some delegations to ask that a reservation may be entered on Article 7(1) (see Article 22(1)(a)).
[OJ C282, 31.10.80, p 28]

4. Article 7(2) states that "nothing in this Convention shall restrict the application of the rules of the law of the forum in a situation where they are mandatory irrespective of the law otherwise applicable to the contract".

The origin of this paragraph is found in the concern of certain delegations to safeguard the rules of the law of the forum (notably rules on cartels, competition and restrictive practices, consumer protection and certain rules concerning carriage) which are mandatory in the situation whatever the law applicable to the contract may be.

Thus the paragraph merely deals with the application of mandatory rules (lois d'application immédiate; leggi di applicazione necessaria; etc) in a different way from paragraph 1.[40a]

Article 8

Material validity

1. Article 8(1) provides that the existence and validity of a contract, or of any term of a contract, shall be determined by the law which would govern it under this Convention if the contract or term were valid.

The paragraph is intended to cover all aspects of formation of the contract other than general validity. As we have emphasized previously in paragraph 9 of the comments on Article 3, this provision is also applicable with regard to the existence and validity of the parties' consent as to choice of the law applicable.

The word "term" has been adopted to cover cases in which there is a dispute as to the validity of a term of the contract, such as a choice of law clause.

2. Notwithstanding the general rule in paragraph 1, paragraph 2 provides a special rule which relates only to the existence and not to the validity of consent.

According to this special rule a party may rely upon the law of the country in which he has his habitual residence to establish that he did not consent if it appears from the circumstances that it would not be reasonable to determine the effect of his conduct in accordance with the law specified in paragraph 1.

The solution adopted by the Group in this respect is designed *inter alia* to solve the problem of the implications of silence by one party as to the formation of the contract.

The word "conduct" must be taken to cover both action and failure to act by the party in question; it does not, therefore, relate solely to silence.

The words "if it appears from the circumstances" mean that the court must have regard to all the circumstances of the case, not solely to those in which the party claiming that he has not consented to the contract has acted. The Court will give particular consideration to the practices followed by the parties *inter se* as well as their previous business relationships.

According to the circumstances, the words "a party" can relate either to the offeror or to the offeree.

The application of paragraph 2 can result in a decision releasing a party who would have been bound under the terms of paragraph 1, but it can never produce the opposite effect of holding that a contract exists which is non-existent by its proper law.

Article 9(4) contains a special rule relating to acts intended to have legal effect, such as, in accordance with the law of many countries, an offer. Such acts have not been mentioned in Article 8. Nonetheless, the rules in Article 8 apply to such acts by way of analogy.

Article 9
Formal validity

Article 9 deals with the formal validity of contracts and acts intended to have legal effect. The first four paragraphs lay down rules governing all contracts and acts intended to have legal effect. The last two paragraphs lay down special rules peculiar to certain types of contract. [OJ C282, 31.10.80, p 29]

I. General rules (paragraphs 1 to 4 inclusive)

The scope of these general rules needs to be specified before indicating the various laws which they declare to be applicable.

A. The scope of the general rules

1. Acts to which they apply

Article 9 applies to contracts and unilateral acts intended to have legal effect. The preliminary draft of 1972 used only the term "act intended to have legal effect" (acte juridique) which, in the terminology originating from Roman law, includes both categories. The inclusion in Article 9 of both contracts and acts intended to have legal effect, mentioned successively, is due merely to a wish to ensure clarity, since the rules to be applied are based on the same principles in both cases.

Unilateral acts intended to have legal effect which fall within the scope of the Article are those which are related to an existing or contemplated contract. Acts relating to a concluded contract can be extremely varied: notice of termination, remission of a debt, declaration of rescission or repudiation, etc.

But the act must be connected with a contract. A unilateral undertaking, unconnected with a contract, as for example, in some legal systems, a recognition of a debt not arising under a contract, or a unilateral act creating, transferring or extinguishing a right *in rem*, would not fall within the scope of Article 9 or of any other provision in the Convention since the latter is concerned only with contractual obligations.

Such an act must also, quite clearly, relate to a contract falling within the scope of the convention. Article 9 does not apply to the formal validity of acts relating to contracts excluded from the convention under Article 1(2) and (3).

There is no provision expressly referring to "public acts". This omission is intentional. First, the concept of a public act is not recognized in all the legal systems and could raise awkward problems of definition. Moreover, it seems wrong for there to be special provisions governing the formal validity of private law acts concluded before public officials. Indeed, as has recently been pointed out,[41] it is because a public official can draw up an instrument only in accordance with the law from which he derives his authority that the formal validity for the act concluded before him is necessarily subject to that law. If, for example, a notary has not observed the law from which he derives his authority, the contract he has drawn up will not of course be a valid notarial act. But it will not be entirely void if the law which governs its substance (and which may also determine its formal validity by virtue of Article 9) does not require a special form for that type of contract.

The general rules accordingly apply to "public acts". This has the advantage of validating acts drawn up by a public official who has thought it appropriate, as happens in the Netherlands, to follow the forms laid down by the foreign law which governs the substance of the contract.

2. Article 9 does not define what is to be understood by the "formal validity" of acts. It seemed realistic to leave open this difficult problem of definition, especially as its importance has been slightly reduced in consequence of the solutions found for the problem of the connecting factor which to some extent equate formal and material validity.

It is nevertheless permissible to consider "form", for the purposes of Article 9, as including every external manifestation required on the part of a person expressing the will to be legally bound, and in the absence of which such expression of will would not be regarded as fully effective.[42] This definition does not include the special requirements which have to be fulfilled where there are persons under a disability to be protected, such as the need in French law for the consent of a family council to an act for the benefit of a minor, or where an act is to be valid against third parties, for example the need in English law for a notice of a statutory assignment of a chose in action.

B. Laws to be applied

1. The principle of applying in the alternative the *lex causae* or the *lex loci actus*.

The system contained in Article 9 is a compromise between *favor negotii*, which tends to take a liberal attitude regarding the formalities required for acts, and the due observance of formalities which, most often, is merely giving effect to requirements of substance.

In supporting the former attitude, it did not seem possible to follow the example of the Hague Convention of 5 October 1961 concerning conflict of laws with regard to testamentary dispositions. *Favor testamenti* is justified by the fact that a will is an act of final disposition which by definition cannot be reenacted if its validity is challenged after the testator's death. This consideration does not affect other acts intended to have legal effect in the case of which excessive freedom with regard to formalities would result in robbing of all effect the requirements in this field which are specified by the various legal systems, very often with a legitimate aim in view. Moreover, the connection between questions of form and questions of evidence (Article 14) makes it desirable to limit the number of laws applicable to formal validity.

[OJ C282, 31.10.80, p 30]

On the other hand, in order to avoid parties being caught unawares by the annulment of their act on the ground of an unexpected formal defect Article 9 has, nonetheless, laid down a fairly flexible system based on applying in the alternative either the law of the place where the contract was entered into (or in the case of a unilateral act the law of the country where the act was done) or else the law which governs its substance.

This choice of applicable laws appears to be sufficient and this is why the possibility of applying the law of the common nationality or habitual residence of the parties was rejected.[43] On the other hand no priority has been accorded either to the *lex causae* or to the *lex loci actus*. If the act is valid to one of these two laws, that is enough to prevent defects of form under the other from affording grounds for nullity.[44]

The Group did not examine the question of which of the two laws would apply to an action brought to annul the contract for formal defect in a case where the contract would be null and void according to both these laws. If, for example, the limitation period for bringing an action for annulment on the ground of a formal defect is not the same in the two legal systems, it may seem to be in keeping with the spirit of this Article to apply the law which provides for the shorter period and, in this respect, is more favourable than the other to the validity of the act.

Renvoi must be rejected as regards formal validity as in all other matters governed by the Convention (cf Article 15).

2. Problems raised by applying the law governing the substance of the contract to the question of formal validity.

The *lex causae* is already recognized as applicable, either as the principal law or as a subsidiary option, to the question of formal validity by the law of the Contracting States and its application is fully justified by the logical connection between substance and form.[45]

The law governing the substance of the contract must be determined by reference to Articles 3, 4 and 6 of the Convention (for contracts provided for under Article 5, see II below, Special rules peculiar to certain contracts). Article 3(2) specifically governs the formal consequences of a voluntary change by the parties in the law governing the substance of the contract. This text means that, on this assumption of changes in the connecting facts, it is enough for the contract to be formally valid in accordance with one or other of the laws successively called upon to govern the substance of the contract.

A difficulty will arise when a contract is subject to several laws, either because the parties have selected the law applicable to a part only of their contract (Article 3(1)), or because the court itself, by way of exception, has proceeded to sever the contract (Article 4(1)). Which of the laws governing the substance of the contract is to determine its formal validity? In such a case it would seem reasonable to apply the law applicable to the part of the contract most closely connected with the disputed condition on which its formal validity depends.

Article 8(1), dealing with material validity, says that the existence and validity of a contract or of any term of a contract shall be determined by the law which would govern it under the Convention if the contract or term were valid. This is to avoid the circular argument that where there is a choice of the applicable law no law can be said to be applicable until the contract is found to be valid. A similar point arises in relation to formal validity under Article 9, and although the text does not expressly say so it is intended that "the law which governs it under this Convention" should be the law which would govern the contract if it were formally valid.

3. Problems raised by applying the *locus regitactum* rule to the question of formal validity.

The application of the law of the country in which a contract was entered into or in which a unilateral act was done, in order to determine the formal validity of the contract or act, results from the age-old maxim *locus regit actum*, recognized alike, usually as a principal rule, by the law of the Contracting States.[46]

However a classic difficulty arises in determining the country in which the contract was entered into when the contract has been made between persons in different countries.

To resolve this difficulty it is first necessary to describe exactly what is meant by persons being or not being in the same country. Where the contract is concluded through the offices of one or more agents, Article 9(3) indicates clearly that the place to be taken into consideration is where the agents are acting at the time when the contract is concluded. If the parties' agents (or one party and the agent of the other) meet in a given country and conclude the contract there, this contract is considered, within the meaning of paragraph 1, to be concluded between persons in that country, even if the party or parties represented were in another country at the time. Similarly, if the parties' agents (or one party and the agent of the other) are in different countries at the time when they conclude the contract, this contract is considered, within the meaning of paragraph 2, to be concluded between persons in different countries even if both the parties represented were in fact in the same country at the time.

[OJ C282, 31.10.80, p 31]

The question of finding which law is the law of the place where the contract was entered into and therefore determines the formal validity of a contract made between persons in different countries, in the sense just indicated, has been very widely debated. Solutions consisting in fixing the conclusion of the contract either in the place where the offer was made or in the place where the acceptance was made have been rejected as rather artificial.[47] The solution consisting in applying to offer and acceptance separately the law of the country in which each was made, directly based on the Frankenstein draft for a European code of private international law and retained in the preliminary draft of 1972, and by the 1978 Swiss draft of Federal law on private international law, Article 125(2), was also rejected. It is clear that there are numerous requirements as to formal validity which are laid down with regard to the contract itself, taken as a whole and not stage by stage. This is the case where, for example, two signatures are required or where the contract has to be made in duplicate. Accordingly, rather than split the law determining the formal validity of a contract, it seemed preferable to look for a law which would be applicable to the formal validity of the contract as a whole.

The choice was therefore between a liberal solution, retaining the application in the alternative of the law of one or other of the countries which the persons concluding the contract were at the time it was entered into, and a strict solution, requiring the cumulative application of these various laws. The liberal solution was adopted by Article 9(2). When a contract is concluded between persons in different countries, it is formally valid if it satisfies the requirements as to form laid down by the law of one of those countries or of the law governing the substance of the contract.

4. Reservation regarding mandatory rules.

Article 7 of the Convention, which contains a reservation in favour of the application of mandatory rules, may lead to the rejection of the liberal system based on the application in the alternative of either the law governing the substance of the contract or the law of the place where it was entered into. It may happen that certain formal requirements laid down by the law of the country with which a contract or act has a close connection have a mandatory character so marked that they could be applied even though the law of that country is not one of those which would normally determine formal validity under Article 9.

In this connection mention was .made of the rules regarding form laid down by the law of the country where an employment contract is to be carried out, especially the requirement that a non-competition clause should be in writing, even though the oral form is permitted by the law of the place where the contract was entered into or under the law chosen by the parties.

Of course, under the system established by Article 7, it will be for the court hearing the case to decide whether it is appropriate to give effect to these mandatory provisions and consequently to disregard the rules laid down in Article 9.

II. Special rules peculiar to certain contracts (paragraphs 5 and 6)

Paragraphs 5 and 6 provide special rules for the formal validity of certain contracts made by consumers and of contracts the subject matter of which is a right in immovable property or a right to use immovable property. It would have been conceivable with regard to such contracts merely to apply Article 7 quite simply and, as an exception to Article 9, to allow, for example, the application of certain formal provisions for consumer protection laid down by the law of the consumer's habitual place of residence, or of certain mandatory requirements as to form imposed by the law of the country where the immovable property is situated.

This solution, however, was not thought adequate to ensure the effective application of these laws because of the discretionary power which Article 7 gives to the court hearing the case. It was accordingly decided to exclude the first four paragraphs of Article 9 completely in the case of contracts of these kinds.

The fifth paragraph of Article 9 deals with the contracts mentioned in Article 5(1), entered into in the circumstances described in Article 5(2), taking into account Article 5(4) and (5).

Just as Article 5 protects the consumer, despite any choice of law specified in the contract, by imposing, as regards substance, the mandatory rules of the law of the country in which he has his habitual residence (Article 5(3)), Article 9(5) imposes the rules of that same country with regard to formal validity. This is justified by the very close connection, in the context of consumer protection, between mandatory rules of form and rules of substance.

[OJ C282, 31.10.80, p 32]

For the same reasons, it might have been expected that the formal validity of employment contracts would also have been made subject to mandatory attachment to the rules of a particular national law.

This idea, though at first contemplated, was finally rejected. Indeed, contrary to Article 5 which provides explicitly that consumer contracts, in the absence of any choice by the parties, shall be subject as regards formal validity to the law of the country where the consumer has his habitual residence, for the purpose of determining the connecting factors applying to employment contracts Article 6 of the Convention only introduces rebuttable presumptions which must been disregarded in cases where it appears from the circumstances that the employment contract is more closely connected with a country other than that indicated by these presumptions. Consequently, if it had been decided that the law governing the substance of the contract should be mandatory for determining the formal validity of employment contracts, it would have been impossible, at the time a contract was entered into, to determine the law governing its formal validity because of the uncertainty caused by Article 6. Therefore no special rule was laid down regarding the formal validity of employment contracts, but thanks to Article 7, it is to be expected that the mandatory rules regarding formal validity laid down by the law of the country where the work is to be carried out will frequently be found to apply.

The sixth paragraph of Article 9 deals with contracts the subject matter of which is a right in immovable property or a right to use immovable property. Such contracts are not subject to a mandatory connecting factor as regards substance, Article 4(3) merely raising a presumption in favour of the law of the country where the immovable property is situated. It is clear, however, that if the law of the country where the immovable property is situated lays down mandatory rules determining formal validity, these must be applied to the contract, but only in the probably rather rare cases where, according to that law, these formal rules must be applied even when the contract has been entered into abroad and is governed by a foreign law.

The scope of this provision is the same as that of Article 4(3).

Article 10
Scope of the applicable law

1. Article 10 defines the scope of the law applicable to the contract under the terms of this Convention.[48]

The original preliminary draft contained no specific rule on this point. It confined itself to the provision in Article 15 that the law which governs an obligation also governs the conditions for its performance, the various ways in which it can be discharged, and the consequences of non-performance. However, since Article 11 of the preliminary draft defined in detail the scope of the law applicable to non-contractual obligations, the principal subject of Article 15 was the scope of the law of the contract.

2. Article 10(1) lists the matters which fall within the scope of the law applicable to the contract. However, this list is not exhaustive, as is indicated by the words "in particular".

The law applicable to the contract under the terms of his Convention governs firstly its interpretation (subparagraph (a)).

Secondly the law applicable to the contract governs the performance of the obligations arising from the contract (subparagraph (b)).

This appears to embrace the totality of the conditions, resulting from the law or from the contract, in accordance with which the act is essential for the fulfilment of an obligation must be performed, but not the manner of its performance (in so far as this is referred to in the second paragraph of Article 10 or the conditions relating to the capacity of the persons who are to perform it (capacity being a matter excluded from the scope of the uniform rules, subject to the provisions of Article 11) or the conditions relating to the form of the act which is to be done in performance of the obligation.

The following therefore fall within the provisions of the first paragraph of Article 10: the diligence with which the obligation must be performed; conditions relating to the place and time of performance; the extent to which the obligation can be performed by a person other than the party liable; the conditions as to performance of the obligation both in general and in relation to certain categories of obligation (joint and several obligations, alternative obligations, divisible and indivisible obligations, pecuniary obligations); where performance consists of the payment of a sum of money, the conditions relating to the discharge of the debtor who has made the payment, the appropriation of the payment, the receipt, etc.

[OJ C282, 31.10.80, p 33]

Within the limits of the powers conferred upon the court by its procedural law, the law applicable to the contract also governs the consequences of total or partial failure to perform these obligations, including the assessment of damages insofar as this is governed by rules of law.

The assessment of damages has given rise to some difficulties. According to some delegations the assessment of the amount of damages is a question of fact and should not be covered by the Convention. To determine the amount of damages the court is obliged to take account of economic and social conditions in its country; there are some cases in which the amount of damages is fixed by a jury; some countries use methods of calculation which might not be accepted in others.

Other delegations countered these arguments, however, by pointing out that in several legal systems there are rules for determining the amount of damages; some international conventions fix limits as to the amount of compensation (for example, conventions relating to carriage); the amount of damages in case of nonperformance is often prescribed in the contract and grave difficulties would be created for the parties if these amounts had to be determined later by the court hearing the action.

By way of compromise the Group finally decided to refer in subparagraph (c) solely to rules of law in matters of assessment of damages, given that questions of fact will always be a matter for the court hearing the action.

The expression "consequences of breach" refers to the consequences which the law or the contract attaches to the breach of a contractual obligation, whether it is a matter of the liability of the party to whom the breach is attributable or of a claim to terminate the contract for breach. Any requirement of service of notice on the party to assume his liability also comes within this context.

According to subparagraph 1(d), the law applicable to the contract governs the various ways of extinguishing obligations, and prescription and limitation of actions. This Article must be applied with due regard to the limited admission of severability (dépeçage) in Articles 3 and 4.

Subparagraph (e) also makes the consequences of nullity subject to the applicable law. The working party's principal objective in introducing this provision was to make the refunds which the parties have to pay each other subsequent to a finding of nullity of the contract subject to the applicable law.

Some delegations have indicated their opposition to this approach on the grounds that, under their legal systems, the consequences of nullity of the contract are non-contractual in nature. The majority of delegations have nevertheless said they are in favour of including such consequences within the scope of the law of contracts, but in order to take account of the opposition expressed provision had been made for any Contracting State to enter a reservation on this matter (Article 22(1)(b)).

3. Article 10(2) states that in relation to the manner of performance and the steps to be taken in the event of defective performance regard shall be had to the law of the country in which performance takes place.

This is a restriction which is often imposed in the national law of many countries as well as in several international conventions. Many jurists have supported and continue to support this restriction on the scope of the law applicable to the contract even when the contractual obligation is performed in a country other than that whose law is applicable.

What is meant, however, by "manner of performance" of an obligation? It does not seem that any precise and uniform meaning is given to this concept in the various laws and in the differing views of learned writers. The Group did not for its part wish to give a strict definition of this concept. It will consequently be for the *lex fori* to determine what is meant by "manner of performance". Among the matters normally falling within the description of "manner of performance", it would seem that one might in any event mention the rules governing public holidays, the manner in which goods are to be examined, and the steps to be taken if they are refused.[49]

Article 10(2) says that a court may have regard to the law of the place of performance. This means that the court may consider whether such law has any relevance to the manner in which the contract should be performed and has a discretion whether to apply it in whole or in part so as to do justice between the parties.

Article 11
Incapacity

The legal capacity of natural persons or of bodies corporate or unincorporate is in principle excluded from the scope of the Convention (Article 1(2)(a) and (e)). This exclusion means that each Contracting State will continue to apply its own system of private international law to contractual capacity.

[OJ C282, 31.10.80, p 34]

However, in the case of natural persons, the question of capacity is not entirely excluded. Article 11 is intended to protect a party who in good faith believed himself to be contracting with a person of full capacity and who, after the contract has been entered into, is confronted by the incapacity of the other contracting party. This anxiety to protect a party in good faith against the risk of a contract being held voidable or void on the ground of the other party's incapacity on account of the application of a law other than that of the place where the contract was concluded is clearly present in the countries which subject capacity to the law of the nationality.[50]

A rule of the same kind is also thought necessary in the countries which make capacity subject to the law of the country of domicile. The only countries which could dispense with it are those which subject capacity to the law of the place where the contract was entered into or to the law governing the substance of the contract.

Article 11 subjects the protection of the other party to the contract to very stringent conditions. First, the contract must be concluded between persons who are in the same country. The Convention does not wish to prejudice the protection of a party under a disability where the contract is concluded at a distance, between persons who are in different countries, even if, under the law governing the contract, the latter is deemed to have been concluded in the country where the party with full capacity is.

Secondly, Article 11 is only to be applied where there is a conflict of laws. The law which, according to the private international law of the court hearing the case, governs the capacity of the person claiming to be under a disability must be different from the law of the country where the contract was concluded.

Thirdly, the person claiming to be under a disability must be deemed to have full capacity by the law of the country where the contract was concluded. This is because it is only in this case that the other party may rely on apparent capacity.

In principle these three conditions are sufficient to prevent the incapacitated person from pleading his incapacity against the other contracting party. This will not however be so "if the other party to the contract was aware of his incapacity at the time of the conclusion of the contract or was not aware thereof as a result of negligence". This wording implies that the burden of proof lies on the incapacitated party. It is he who must establish that the other party knew of his incapacity or should have known of it.

Article 12

Voluntary assignment

1. The subject of Article 12 is the voluntary assignment of rights.

Article 12(1) provides that the mutual obligations of assignor and assignee under a voluntary assignment of a right against another person (the debtor) shall be governed by the law which under this Convention applies to the contract between the assignor and assignee.

Interpretation of this provision gives rise to no difficulty. It is obvious that according to this paragraph the relationship between the assignor and assignee of a right is governed by the law applicable to the agreement to assign.

Although the purpose and meaning of the provision leave hardly any room for doubt, one wonders why the Group did not draft it more simply and probably more elegantly. For example, why not say that the assignment of a right by agreement shall be governed in relations between assignor and assignee by the law applicable to that agreement.

Such a form of words had in fact been approved initially by most of the delegations, but it was subsequently abandoned because of the difficulties of interpretation which might have arisen in German law, where the expression "assignment" of a right by agreement includes the effects of it upon the debtor: this was expressly excluded by Article 12(2).

The present wording was in fact finally adopted precisely to avoid a form which might lead to the idea that the law applicable to the agreement for assignment in a legal system in which it is understood as "Kausalgeschäft" also determines the conditions of validity of the assignment with respect to the debtor.

2. On the contrary, under the terms of Article 12(2) it is the law governing the right to which the assignment relates which determines its assignability, the relationship between the assignee and the debtor, the conditions under which the assignment can be invoked against the debtor and any question whether the debtor's obligations have been discharged.

The words "conditions under which the assignment can be invoked" cover the conditions of transferability of the assignment as well as the procedures required to give effect to the assignment in relation to the debtor.

[OJ C282, 31.10.80, p 35]

Notwithstanding the provisions of paragraph 2, the matters which it covers, with the sole exception of assignability, are governed, as regards relations between assignor and debtor if a contract exists between them, by the law which governs their contract in so far as the said matters are dealt with in that contract.

Subrogation

1. The substitution of one creditor for another may result both from the voluntary assignment of a right (or assignment properly so called) referred to in Article 12 and from the assignment of a right by operation of law following a payment made by a person other than the debtor.

According to the legislation in various Member States of the Community, "subrogration" involves the vesting of the creditor's rights in the person who, being obliged to pay the debt with or on behalf of others, had an interest in satisfying it: this is so under Article 1251–3 of the French Civil Code and Article 1203–3 of the Italian Civil Code. For example, in a contract of guarantee the guarantor who pays instead of the debtor succeeds to the rights of the creditor. The same occurs when a payment is made by one of a number of debtors who are jointly and severally liable or when an indivisible obligation is discharged.

Article 13 of the Convention embodies the conflict rule in matters of subrogation of a third party to the rights of a creditor. Having regard to the fact that the Convention applies only to contractual obligations, the Group thought it proper to limit the application of the rule adopted in Article 13 to assignments of rights which are contractual in nature. Therefore this rule does not apply to subrogation by operation of law when the debt to be paid has its origin in tort (for example, where the insurer succeeds to the rights of the insured against the person causing damage).

2. According to the wording of Article 13(1), where a person (the creditor) has a contractual claim upon another (the debtor), and a third person has a duty to satisfy the creditor, or has in fact satisfied the creditor in discharge of that duty, the law which governs the third person's duty to satisfy the creditor shall determine whether the third person is entitled to exercise against the debtor the rights which the creditor had against the debtor under the law governing their relationship and, if so, whether he may do so in full or only to a limited extent.

The law which governs the third person's duty to satisfy the creditor (for example, the law applicable to the contract of guarantee, where the guarantor has paid instead of the debtor) will therefore determine whether and to what extent the third person is entitled to exercise the rights of the creditor against the debtor according to the law governing their contractual relations.

In formulating the rule under analysis the Group made a point of considering situations in which a person has paid without being obliged so to do by contract or by law but having an economic interest recognized by law as anticipated by Article 1251–3 of the French Civil Code and Article 1203–3 of the Italian Civil Code. In principle the same rule applies to these situations, but the court has a discretion in this respect.

As regards the possibility of a partial subrogation such as that provided for by Article 1252 of the French Civil Code and by Article 1205 of the Italian Civil Code, it seems right that this should be subject to the law applicable to the subrogation.

In addition, when formulating Article 13 the Group envisaged the possibility that the legal relationship between the third party and the debtor was governed by a contract. This contract will obviously be governed by the law which is applicable to it by the terms of this Convention. Article 13 in no way affects this aspect of the relationship between the third party and the debtor.

3. Article 13(2) extends the same rule in paragraph 1 to cases in which several persons are liable for the same contractual obligation (co-debtors) and the creditor's interest has been discharged by one of them.

4. As well as the problem of voluntary assignment of rights and the problem of assignment of rights by operation of law (Articles 12 and 13), there exists the problem of assignment of duties. However, the Group did not wish to resolve this problem, because it is new and because there are still many uncertainties as to the solution to be given.

Article 14
Burden of proof, etc

Article 14 deals with the law to be applied to certain questions of evidence.

[OJ C282, 31.10.80, p 36]

There is no rule of principle dealing with evidence in general. In the legal systems of the Contracting States, except as regards the burden of proof, questions of evidence (both as regards facts and acts intended to have legal effect and as regards foreign law) are in principle subject to the law of the forum. This principle is, however, subject to a certain number of exceptions which are not the same in all these legal systems. Since it was decided that only certain questions of evidence should be covered in Article 14, it was thought better not to bind the interpretation thereof by a general provision making the rules of evidence subject to the law of the forum on questions not decided by the Convention, such as, for example, the taking of evidence abroad or the evidential value of legal acts. In order that there should be no doubt as to the freedom retained by the States regarding questions of evidence not decided by the Convention, Article 1(2)(h) excludes evidence and procedure from the scope of the Convention, expressly without prejudice to Article 14.

Two major questions have been covered and are each the subject of a separate paragraph. These are the burden of proof on the one hand and the recognition of modes of proving acts intended to have legal effect on the other. After considerable hesitation the Group decided not to deal with the problem of evidential value.

A. Burden of proof

The first paragraph of Article 14 provides for the application of the law of the contract "to the extent that it contains, in the law of contract, rules which raise presumptions of law or determine the burden of proof". Presumptions of law, relieving the party in whose favour they operate from the necessity of producing any evidence, are really rules of substance which in the law of contract contribute to making clear the obligations of the parties and therefore cannot be separated from the law which governs the contract. By way of example, where Article 1731 of the French Civil Code provides that "where no inventory of the state of the premises has been taken, the lessee shall be deemed to have received them in good tenantable repair and must, in the absence of proof to the contrary, restore them in such condition", the Article is in reality determining the obligation of the lessee to restore the let premises. It is therefore logical that the law of the contract should apply here.

The same observation applies to rules determining the burden of proof. By way of example, Article 1147 of the French Civil Code provides that a debtor who has failed to fulfil his obligation shall be liable for damages "unless he shows that this failure is due to an extraneous cause outside his control". This text determines the burden of proof between the parties. The creditor must prove that the obligation has not been fulfilled, the debtor must prove that the failure is due to an extraneous cause. But in dividing the burden, the text establishes the debtor's obligations on a vital point, since the debtor is liable for damages even if the failure to fulfil is not due to a proven fault on his part. The rule is accordingly a rule of substance which can only be subject to the law of the contract.

Nevertheless the text of the first paragraph of Article 14 does contain a restriction. The burden of proof is not totally subject to the law of the contract. It is only subject to it to the extent that the law of the contract determines it with regard to contractual obligations ("in the law of contract"), that is to say only to the extent to which the rules relating to the burden of proof are in effect rules of substance.

This is not always the case. Some legal systems recognize rules relating to the burden of proof, sometimes even classed as presumptions of law, which clearly are part of procedural law and which it would be wrong to subject to the law of the contract. This is the case, for example, with the rule whereby the claim of a party who appears is deemed to be substantiated if the other party fails to appear, or the rule making silence on the part of a party to an action with regard to facts alleged by the other party equivalent to an admission of those facts.

Such rules do not form part of "the law of contract" and accordingly do not fall within the choice of law rule established by Article 4(1).

B. Admissibility of modes of proving acts intended to have legal effect

Paragraph 2 of Article 14 deals with the admissibility of modes of proving acts intended to have legal effect (in the sense of *voluntas negotium*).

The text provides for the application in the alternative of the law of the forum or of the law which determines the formal validity of the act. This liberal solution favouring proof of the act is already recognized in France and in the Benelux countries.[51] It seems to be the only solution capable of reconciling the requirements of the law of the forum with the desire to respect the legitimate expectations of the parties at the time of concluding their act.

The law of the forum is normally employed to determine the means which may be used for proving an act intended to have legal effect, which in this context includes a contract. If, for example, that law allows a contract to be proved by witnesses, it should be followed, irrespective of any more stringent provisions on the point contained in the law governing the substance or formal validity of the act.

[OJ C282, 31.10.80, p 37]

On the other hand, in the opposite case, if the law governing the formal validity of the act only requires oral agreement and allows such an agreement to be proved by witnesses, the expectations of parties who had relied on that law would be disappointed if such proof were to be held inadmissible solely on the ground that the law of the trial court required written evidence of all acts intended to have legal effect. The parties must therefore be allowed to employ the modes of proof recognized by the law governing formal validity.

Nevertheless this liberalism should not lead to imposing on the trial court modes of proof which its procedural law does not enable it to administer. Article 14 does not deal with the administration of modes of proof, which the legal system of each Contracting State makes subject to the law of the trial court. Admitting the application of a law other than that of the forum to modes of proof ought not to lead to the rules of the law of the forum, as regards the administration of the modes of proof, being rendered nugatory.

This is the explanation of the proviso which in substance enables a court, without reference to public policy, to disregard modes of proof which the law of procedure cannot generally allow, such as an affidavit, the testimony of a party or common knowledge. Consideration was also given to the case of rights subject to registration in a public register, holding that the authority charged with keeping that register could, owing to that provision, only recognize the modes of proof provided for by its own law.

Such being the general system adopted, a proviso had to be added regarding the law determining formal validity applicable as an alternative to the law of the forum.

The text refers to "any of the laws referred to in Article 9 under which that contract or act is formally valid". This expression means that if, for example, the act is formally valid under the law governing the substance of the contract but is not formally valid under the law of the place where it was done, the parties may employ only the modes of proof provided for by the first of these two laws, even if the latter is more liberal as regards proof. The reference in Article 14(2) to the law governing formal validity is clearly based on the assumption that the law governing formal validity has been observed. On the other hand, if the act is formally valid according to both laws (*lex causae* and *lex loci actus*) mentioned in Article 9, the parties will be able to employ the modes of proof provided for by either of those laws.

C. There is no provision dealing with the evidential value of acts intended to have legal effect. The preliminary draft of 1972 contained a provision covering two questions derived, in Roman law countries, from the concept of evidential value; the question how far a written document affords sufficient evidence of the obligations contained in it and the question of the modes of proof to add to or contradict the contents of the document—"outside and against the content" of such a document, according to the old phraseology of the Code Napoléon (Article 1341). Despite long discussion, no agreement could be reached between the delegations and it was therefore decided to leave the question of evidential value outside the scope of the Convention.

Article 15
Exclusion of renvoi

This Article excludes renvoi.

It is clear that there is no place for renvoi in the law of contract if the parties have chosen the law to be applied to their contract. If they have made such a choice, it is clearly with the intention that the provisions of substance in the chosen law shall be applicable; their choice accordingly excludes any possibility of renvoi to another law.[52]

Renvoi is also excluded where the parties have not chosen the law to be applied. In this case the contract is governed, in accordance with Article 4(1), by the law of the country with which it is most closely connected. Paragraph 2 introduces a presumption that that country is the country where the party who is to effect the performance which is characteristic of the contract has his habitual residence. It would not be reasonable for a court, despite this express localization, to subject the contract to the law of another country by introducing renvoi, solely because the rule of conflict of laws in the country where the contract was localized contained other connecting factors. This is equally so where the last paragraph of Article 4 applies and the court has decided the place of the contract with the aid of indications which seem to it decisive.

More generally, the exclusion of renvoi is justified in international conventions regarding conflict of laws. If the Convention attempts as far as possible to localize the legal situation and to determine the country with which it is most closely connected, the law specified by the conflicts rule in the Convention should not be allowed to question this determination of place. Such, moreover, has been the solution adopted since 1951 in the conventions concluded at The Hague.

[OJ C282, 31.10.80, p 38]

Article 16
"Ordre public"

Article 16 contains a precise and restrictively worded reservation in favour of public policy ("ordre public").

First it is expressly stated that, in the abstract and taken as a whole, public policy is not to affect the law specified by the Convention. Public policy is only to be taken into account where a certain provision of the specified law, if applied in an actual case, would lead to consequences contrary to the public policy ("ordre public") of the forum. It may therefore happen that a foreign law, which might in the abstract be held to be contrary to the public policy of the forum, could nevertheless be applied, if the actual result of its being applied does not in itself offend the public policy of the forum.

Secondly, the result must be "manifestly" incompatible with the public policy of the forum. This condition, which is to be found in all the Hague Conventions since 1956, requires the court to find special grounds for upholding an objection.[53]

Article 16 provides that it is the public policy of the forum which must be offended by the application of the specified law. It goes without saying that this expression includes Community public policy, which has become an integral part of the public policy ("ordre public") of the Member States of the European Community.

Article 17
No retrospective effect

Article 17 means that the Convention has no retrospective effect on contracts already in existence. It applies only to contracts concluded after it enters into force, but the entry into force must be considered separately for each State since the Convention will not enter into force simultaneously in all the contracting States (see Article 29). Of course, there is no provision preventing a court of a contracting State with respect to which the Convention has not yet entered into force from applying it in advance under the concept of *ratio scripta*.

Article 18
Uniform interpretation

This Article is based on a formula developed by the United Nations Commission on International Trade Law.

The draft revision of the uniform law on international sales and the preliminary draft of the Convention on prescription and limitation of actions in international sales contained the following provision: "In the interpretation and application of this Convention, regard shall be had to its international character and to the necessity of promoting uniformity". This provision, whose wording was slightly amended, has been incorporated in the United Nations Convention on contracts for the international sale of goods (Article 7) signed in Vienna on 11 April 1980.

Article 18 operates as a reminder that in interpreting an international convention regard must be had to its international character and that, consequently, a court will not be free to assimilate the provisions of the Convention, in so far as concerns their interpretation, to provisions of law which are purely domestic. It seemed that one of the advantages of this Article might be to enable parties to rely in their actions on decisions given in other countries.

It is within the spirit of this Article that a solution must be found to the problem of classification, for which, following the example of the Benelux uniform law, the French draft and numerous conventions of The Hague, the Convention has refrained from formulating a special rule.

Article 18 will retain its importance even if a protocol subjecting the interpretation of the Convention to the Court of Justice of the European Communities is drawn up pursuant to the Joint Declaration of the Representatives of the Governments made when the Convention was opened for signature on 19 June 1980.

Article 19
States with more than one legal system

This Article is based on similar provisions contained in some of the Hague Conventions (see, for example, the Convention on the law applicable to matrimonial property regimes, Articles 17 and 18 and the Convention on the law applicable to agency, Articles 19 and 20).

According to the first paragraph, where a State has several territorial units each with its own rules of law in respect of contractual obligations, each of those units will be considered as a country for the purposes of the Convention. If, for example, in the case of Article 4, the party who is to effect the performance which is characteristic of the contract has his habitual residence in Scotland, it is with Scottish law that the contract will be deemed to be most closely connected.

[OJ C282, 31.10.80, p 39]

Paragraph 2, which is of special concern to the United Kingdom, covers the case where the situation is connected with several territorial units in a single country but not with another State. In such a case there is a conflict of laws, but it is a purely domestic matter for the State concerned which consequently is under no obligation to resolve it by applying the rules of the Convention.

Article 20

Precedence of Community law

This Article is intended to avoid the possibility of conflict between this Convention and acts of the Community institutions, by according precedence to the latter. The text is based on that of Article 52(2) of the Convention of 27 September 1968 as revised by the Accession Convention of 9 October 1978.

The Community provisions which will have precedence over the Convention are, as regards their object, those which, in relation to particular matters, lay down rules of private international law with regard to contractual obligations. For example, the Regulation on conflict of laws with respect to employment contracts will, when it has been finally adopted, take precedence over the Convention.

The Governments of the Member States have, nevertheless, in a joint declaration, expressed the wish that these Community instruments will be consistent with the provisions of the Convention.

As regards the form which these instruments are to take, the Community provisions contemplated by Article 20 are not only acts of the institutions of the European Communities, that is to say principally the Regulations and the Directives as well as the Conventions concluded by those Communities, but also national laws harmonized in implementation of such acts. A law or regulation adopted by a State in order to make its legislation comply with a Directive borrows, as it were, from the Directive its Community force, thus justifying the precedence accorded to it over this Convention.

Finally, the precedence which Article 20 accords to Community law applies not only to Community law in force at the date when this Convention enters into force, but also to that adopted after the Convention has entered into force.

Article 21

Relationship with other Conventions

This Article, which has its equivalent in the Hague Conventions on the law applicable to matrimonial property regimes (Article 20) and on the law applicable to agency (Article 22) means that this Convention will not prejudice the application of any other international agreement, present or future, to which a Contracting State is or becomes party, for example, to Conventions relating to carriage. This leaves open the possibility of a more far-reaching international unification with regard to all or part of the ground covered by this Convention.

This provision does not of course eliminate all possibility of difficulty arising from the combined application of this Convention and another concurrent Convention, especially if the latter contains a provision similar to that in Article 21. But the States which are parties to several Conventions must seek a solution to these difficulties of application without jeopardizing the observance of their international obligations.

Moreover, Article 21 must be read in conjunction with Articles 24 and 25. The former specifies the conditions under which a contracting State may become a party to a multilateral Convention after the date on which this Convention enters into force with respect thereto. The latter deals with the case where the conclusion of other Conventions would prejudice the unification achieved by this Convention.

Article 22

Reservations

This Article indicates the reservations which may be made to the Convention, the reasons for which have been set out in this report as regards Articles 7(1) and 10(1)(e). Following the practice generally applied, in particular in the Hague Conventions, it lays down the procedure by means of which these reservations can be made or withdrawn.

[3214]

[OJ C282, 31.10.80, p 40]

TITLE III
FINAL PROVISIONS
Article 23
Unilateral adoption by a contracting State of a new choice of law rule

Article 23 is an unusual text since it allows the contracting States to make unilateral derogations from the rules of the Convention. This weakening of its mandatory force was thought desirable because of the very wide scope of the Convention and the very general character of most of its rules. The case was envisaged where a State found it necessary for political, economic or social reasons to amend a choice of law rule and it was thought desirable to find a solution sufficiently flexible to enable States to ratify the Convention without having to denounce it as soon as they were forced to disregard its rules on a particular point.

The possibility of making unilateral derogations from the Convention is, however, subject to certain conditions and restrictions.

First, derogation is only possible if it consists in adopting a new choice of law rule in regard to a particular category of contract. For example, Article 23 would not authorize a State to abandon the general principle of the Convention. But it would enable it to adopt, under the conditions specified, a particular choice of law rule different from that of the Convention with respect, for example, to contracts made by travel agencies or to contracts for correspondence courses where the specialist nature of the contract could justify this derogation from the common rule. It is of course understood that the derogation procedure shall only be imposed on States if the contract for which they wish to adopt a new choice of law rule falls within the scope of the Convention.

Secondly, such a derogation is subject to procedural conditions. The State which wishes to derogate from the Convention must inform the other signatory States through the Secretary-General of the Council of the European Communities. The latter shall, if a State so requests, arrange for consultation between the signatory States in order to reach unanimous agreement. If, within a period of two years, no State has requested consultation or no agreement has been able to be reached, the State may then amend its law in the manner indicated.

The Group considered whether this procedure should apply to situations where the contracting States would wish to adopt a rule of the kind referred to in Article 7 of the Convention, ie a mandatory rule which must be applied whatever the law applicable to the contract. It was considered that the States should not be bound to submit themselves to the Article 23 procedure before adopting such a rule. But to escape the application of Article 23 the rule in question must meet the criteria of Article 7 and be explicable by the strong mandatory character of the rule of substantive law which it lays down. It is not the intention that the contracting States should be able to avoid the conditions of Article 23 by disguising under the form of a mandatory rule of the Article 7 kind a rule of conflict dealing with matters whose absolute mandatory nature is not established.

Articles 24 and 25
New Conventions

The procedure for consultation imposed under Article 23 on a State intending to derogate from the Convention by amending its national law is also imposed on a State which wishes to derogate from the Convention on becoming a party to another Convention.

This system of "freedom under supervision" imposed on contracting States applies only to conventions whose main object or whose principal aim or one of whose principal aims is to lay down rules of private international law concerning any of the matters governed by this Convention. Consequently the States are free to accede to a Convention which consolidates the material law of such and such a contract, with regard, for example, to transport and which contains, as an ancillary provision, a rule of private international law. But, within the area thus defined, the consultation procedure applied even to Conventions which were open for signature before the entry into force of the present Convention.

[OJ C282, 31.10.80, p 41]

Article 24(2) further restricts the scope of the obligation imposed on the States by specifying that the procedure in the first paragraph need not apply—

1. if the object of the new Convention is to revise a former Convention. The opposite solution would have had the unfortunate effect of obstructing the modernization of existing Conventions;

2. if one or more contracting States or the European Communities are already parties to the new Convention;
3. if the new Convention is concluded within the framework of the European Treaties particularly in the case of a multilateral Convention to which one of the Communities is already party. These rules are in harmony with the precedence of Community law provided for under Article 20.

Article 24 therefore establishes a clear distinction between Conventions to which contracting States may freely become parties and those to which they may become parties only upon condition that they submit to consultation procedure.

For Conventions of the former class, Article 25 provides for the case where the conclusion of such agreements prejudiced the unification achieved by this Convention. If a contracting State considers that such is the case, it may request the Secretary-General of the Council of the European Communities to open consultation procedure. The text of the Article implies that the Secretary-General of the Council possesses a certain discretionary power. The Joint Declaration annexed to this Convention in fact provides that, even before the entry into force of this Convention, the States will confer together if one of them wishes to become a party to such a Convention.

For Conventions of the latter class, the consultation procedure is the same as that of Article 23 except that the period of two years is here reduced to one year.

Article 26
Revision

This Article provides for a possible revision of the Convention. It is identical with Article 67 of the Convention of 27 September 1968.

Articles 27 to 33
Usual protocol clauses

Article 27 defines the territories of the Member States to which the Convention is to apply (cf Article 60 of the revised Convention of 27 September 1968). Articles 28 and 29 deal with the opening for signature of the Convention and its ratification. Article 28 does not make any statement on the methods by which each contracting State will incorporate the provisions of the Convention into its national law. This is a matter which by international custom is left to the sovereign discretion of States. Each contracting State may therefore give effect to the Convention either by giving it force of law directly or by including its provisions into its own national legislation in a form appropriate to that legislation. The most noteworthy provision is that of Article 29(1) which provides for entry into force after seven ratifications. It appeared that to require ratification by all nine contracting States might result in delaying entry into force for too long a period.

Article 30 lays down a duration of 10 years, automatically renewable for five-year periods. For States which ratify the Convention after its entry into force, the period of 10 years or five years to be taken into consideration is that which is running for the first States in respect of which the Convention entered into force (Article 29(1)). Article 30(3) makes provision for denunciation in manner similar to the Hague Conventions (see for example Article 28 Agency Convention). Such a denunciation will take effect on expiry of the period of 10 years or five years as the case may be (cf Article 30(3)). This Article has no equivalent in the Convention of 27 September 1968. The difference is explained by the fact that this Convention, unlike that of 1968, is not directly based on Article 220 of the Treaty of Rome. It is a Convention freely concluded between the States of the Community and not imposed by the Treaty.

Articles 31 and 33 entrust the management of the Convention (deposit of the Convention and notification to the signatory States) to the Secretary-General of the Council of the European Communities.

No provision is made for third States to accede to the Convention. The question was discussed by the Group but it was unable to reach agreement. In these circumstances, if a third State asked to accede to the Convention, there would have to be consultation among the Member States.

On the other hand a solution was found to the position, *vis-á-vis* the Convention, of States which might subsequently become members of the European Community.

[OJ C282, 31.10.80, p 42]

The Group considered that the Convention itself could not deal with this question as it is a matter which falls within the scope of the Accession Convention with new members. Accordingly it simply drew up a joint declaration by the contracting States expressing the view that new Member States should be under an obligation also to accede to this Convention.

Protocol relating to the Danish Statute on Maritime Law—Article 169

The Danish Statute on Maritime Law is a uniform law common to the Scandinavian countries. Due to the method applied in Scandinavian legal cooperation it is not based upon a Convention but a result of the simultaneous introduction in the Parliaments of identical bills.

Article 169 of the Statute embodies a number of choice of law rules. These rules are partly based upon the bills of lading Convention 1924 as amended by the 1968 Protocol (The Hague—Visby rules). To the extent that that is the case, they are upheld as a result of Article 21 of the present Convention, even after its ratification by Denmark.

The rule in Article 169, however, provides certain additional choice of law rules with respect to the applicable law in matters of contracts of carriage by sea. These could have been retained by Denmark under Article 21 if the Scandinavian countries had cooperated by means of Conventions. It has been accepted that the fact that another method of cooperation has been followed should not prevent Denmark from retaining this result of Scandinavian cooperation in the field of uniform legislation. The rule in the Protocol permitting revision of Article 169 without following the procedure prescribed in Article 23 corresponds to the rule in Article 24(2) of the Convention with respect to revision of other Conventions to which the States party to this Convention are also party.

[3215]

NOTES RELATING TO THE REPORT ON THE CONVENTION ON THE LAW APPLICABLE TO CONTRACTUAL OBLIGATIONS

1 Minutes of the meeting of 26 to 28 February 1969.

2 Minutes of the meeting of 26 to 28 February 1969, pages 3, 4 and 9.

3 Commission document 12.665/XIV/68.

4 Minutes of the meeting of 26 to 28 February 1969.

5 Minutes of the meeting of 20 to 22 October 1969.

6 Minutes of the meeting of 2 and 3 February 1970.

7 See the following Commission documents: 12.153/XIV/70 (questionnaire prepared by Professor Giuliano and replies of the rapporteurs); 6.975/XIV/70 (questionnaire prepared by Mr Van Sasse van Ysselt and replies of the rapporteurs); 15.393/XIV/70 (questionnaire prepared by Professor Lagarde and replies of the rapporteurs).

8 The meetings were held on the following dates: 28 September to 2 October 1970; 16 to 20 November 1970; 15 to 19 February 1971; 15 to 19 March 1971; 28 June to 2 July 1971; 4 to 8 October 1971; 29 November to 3 December 1971; 31 January to 3 February 1972; 20 to 24 March 1972; 29 to 31 May 1972; 21 to 23 June 1972.

9 Minutes of the meeting of 21 to 23 June 1972, page 29 *et seq.*

10 The meetings were held on the following dates: 22 to 23 September 1975; 17 to 19 December 1975; 1 to 5 March 1976; 23 to 30 June 1976; 16 to 17 December 1976; 21 to 23 February 1977; 3 to 6 May 1977; 27 to 28 June 1977; 19 to 23 September 1977; 12 to 15 December 1977; 6 to 10 March 1978; 5 to 9 June 1978; 25 to 28 September 1978; 6 to 10 November 1978; 15 to 16 January 1979; 19 to 23 February 1979.

11 The list of government experts who took part in the work of this *ad hoc* working party or in the work of the working party chaired by Mr Jenard is attached to this report.

12 The work done on company law by the European Communities falls into three categories. The first category consists of the Directives provided for by Article 54(3)(g) of the EEC Treaty. Four of these Directives are already in force. The first, issued on 9 March 1968 (OJ No L65, 14.3.1968), concerns disclosure, the extent to which the company is bound by acts done on its behalf, and nullity, in relation to public limited companies. The second, issued on 13 December 1976 (OJ No L26, 31.1.1977), concerns the formation of public limited companies and the maintenance and alteration of their capital. The third, issued on 9 October 1978 (OJ No L295, 20.10.1978), deals with company mergers, and the fourth, issued on 25 July 1978 (OJ No L222, 14.8.1978), relates to annual accounts. Four other proposals for Directives made by the Commission are currently before the Council. They concern the structure of "sociétés anonymes" (OJ No C131,13.12.1972), the admission of securities to quotation (OJ No C131, 13.12.1972), consolidated accounts (OJ No C121, 2.6.1976) and the minimum qualifications of persons who carry out legal audits of company accounts (OJ No C112, 13.5.1978). The second category comprises the Conventions provided for by Article 220 of the EEC Treaty. One of these concerns the mutual recognition of companies and legal persons. It was signed at Brussels on 29 February 1968 (the text was published in Supplement No 2 of 1969 to the Bulletin of the European Communities). The draft of a second Convention will shortly be submitted to the Council; it concerns international mergers. Finally, work has progressed with a view to creating a Statute for European companies. This culminated in the proposal for a Regulation on the Statute for European companies, dated 30 June 1970 (OJ No C124, 10.10.1970).

13 For the text of the judgment, see: *Rev crit*, 1911, p 395; Journal *dr int privé*, 1912, p 1156. For comments, cf Batiffol and Lagarde, *Droit international privé* (2 vol), sixth edition, Paris, 1974–1976, II, No 567–573, pp 229–241.

14 Kegel, *Internationales Privatrecht: Ein Studienbuch*, third edition, München-Berlin, 1971, § 18, pp 253–257; Kegel, *Das IPR im Einführungsgesetz zum BGB*, in Soergel/Siebert, *Kommentar zum BGB* (Band 7), 10th edition, 1970, Margin Notes 220–225; Reithmann, *Internationales*

Vertragsrecht. Das internationale Privatrecht der Schuldverträge, third edition, Köln, 1980, margin notes 5 and 6 Drobnig, *America-German Private International Law*, second edition, New York, 1972, pp 225–232.

15 Morelli, *Elementi di diritto internazionale privato italiano*, 10th edition, Napoli, 1971, Nos 97–98, pp 154–157; Vitta, Op cit, III, pp 229–290.

16 *Rev crit*, 1938, p 661.

17 Frederic, *La vente en droit international privé, in Recueil des Cours de l'Ac de La Haye*, Tome 93 (1958–1), pp 30–18; Rigaux, *Droit intenational privé*, Bruxelles, 1968, Nos 348–349; Vander Elst, *Droit international privé. Règles générales des conflits de lois dans les différentes matières de droit privé*, Bruxelles, 1977, No 56, p 100 *et seq.*

18 The text of the judgement in the Alnati case (Nederlandse Jurisprudentie 1967, p 3) is published in the French in Rev crit, 1967, p 522. (Struycken note on the Alnati decision). For the views of legal writers: cf: JEJ Th Deelen, Rechtskeuze in het Nederlands internationaal contractenrecht, Amsterdam, 1965; WLG. Lemaire, Nederlands internationaal privaatrecht, 1968, p 242 et ss; Jessurun d'Oliveira, Kotting, Bervoets en De Boer, Partij-invloed in het Internationaal Privaatrecht, Amsterdam 1974.

19 The principle of freedom of choice has been recognized in England since at least 1796: *Gienar v Mieyer* (1796), 2 Hy Bl 603.

20 [1939] AC 277, p 290.

20a See, eg, the Employment Protection (Consolidation) Act 1978, s 153(5) and the Trade Union and Labour Relations Act 1974, s 30 (6)).

20b Unfair Contract Terms Act 1977, s 27(2).

20c Anton, Private International Law, pp 187–192.

20d This includes cases where the parties have attempted to make an express choice but have not done so with sufficient clarity.

20e *Compagnie d'Armement Maritime SA v Compagnie Tunisienne de Navigation SA* [1971] AC 572, at pp 584, 587 to 591, 596 to 600, 604 to 607.

21 Lando, Contracts, in International Encyclopedia of Comparative Law, vol III, Private International Law (Lipstein, Chief editor), sections 51 and 54, pp 28 to 29; Philip, Dansk International Privat-og Procesret, second edition, Copenhagen, 1972, p 291.

22 CPJI, Publications, Série A, Nos 20 to 21, p 122.

23 International Law Reports, vol 27, pp 117 to 233, p 165; Riv dir int, 1963, pp 230 to 249, p 244.

24 For a summary of this award, including extensive quotations, see: Lalive, Un récent arbitrage suisse entre un organisme d'Etat et une société privée étrangère, in Annuaire suisse de dr int, 1963, pp 273 to 302, especially pp 284 to 288.

25 Int Legal Mat, 1979, pp 3 to 37, at p 11; Riv dir int, 1978, pp 514 to 517, at p 518.

26 The first Convention, dated 1 October 1976, was in force between the following eight European countries: Belgium, Denmark, Finland, France, Italy, Norway, Sweden, Switzerland. The Republic of Niger also acceded to the convention. For the text of the second and third conventions, see: *Associazione Italiana per l'Arbitrato, Conventions multilaterales et autres instruments en matière d'arbitrage*, Roma, 1974, pp 86 to 114. For the text of the fourth convention see: *Conf. de La Haye de droit international privé, Recueil des conventions (1951–1977)*, p 252. For the state of ratifications and accessions to these Conventions at 1 February 1976, see: Giuliano, Pocar and Treves, *Codice delle convenzioni di diritto internazionale privato e processuale*, Milano, 1977, pp 1404, 1466 *et seq*, 1497 *et seq.*

27 Kegel, Das IPR cit, margin notes 269 to 273 and notes 1 and 3; Batiffol and Lagarde, Droit international privé cit II, No 592, p 243; judgment of the French Cour de Cassation of 18 November 1959 in Soc. Deckardt c Etabl. Moatti, in Rev crit, 1960, p 83.

28 Cf Trib. Rotterdam, 2 April 1963, S § S 1963, 53; Kollewijn, De rechtskeuse achteraf, Neth Int Law Rev 1964 225; Lemaire Nederlands Internationaal Privaatrecht, 1968, 265.

29 Riv dir int priv proc, 1967, pp 126 et seq.

30 V Treves T, Sulla volontà delle parti di cui all'art. 25 delle preleggi e sul momento del suo sorgere, in Riv dir int priv proc, 1967, pp 315 et seq.

31 For a comparative survey c f Rabel, The Conflict of Laws. A comparative study, II, second edition, Ann Arbor, 1960, Chapter 30, pp 432 to 486.

32 Batiffol and Lagarde. Droit international privé, cit, II, Nos 572 et seq, pp 236 et seq, and the essay of Batiffol, Subjectivisme et objectivisme dans le droit international privé des contrats, reproduit dans choix d'articles rassemblés par ses amis, Paris 1976, pp 249 to 263.

33 Rev crit, 1955, p 330.

34 According to German case law, "hypothetischer-Parteiwille" does not involve seeking the supposed intentions of the parties, but evaluating the interests involved reasonably and equitably, on an objective basis, with a view to determing the law applicable (BGH, 14 April 1953, in IPRspr, 1952–53, No 40, pp 151 et seq). According to another case, "in making this evaluation of the interests involved, the essential question is where the centre of gravity of the contractual relationship is situated" (BGH, 14 July 1955, in IPRspr, 1954–1955, No 67, pp 206 et seq). The following may be consulted on this concept: Kegel, Internationales Privatrecht ct. § 18, pp 257 et seq; Kegel, Das IPR cit, Nos 240 to 268, and the numerous references to judicial decisions given in the notes; Reithmann, Internationales Vertragsrecht, cit, pp 42 et seq.

35 *See Bonython v Commonwealth of Australia* [1951] AC 201 at p 219; *Tomkinson v First Pennsylvania Banking and Trust Co* [1961] AC 1007 at pp 1068, 1081 and 1082; *James Miller and Partners Ltd v Whitworth Street Estates (Manchester) Ltd* [1970] AC 583 at pp 603, 605 and 606, 601 to 611; *Compagnie d'Armement Maritime SA v Compagnie Tunisienne de Navigation SA* [1971] AC 572 at pp 583, 587, 603; *Coast Lines Ltd v Hudig and Veder Chartering NV*, [1972] 2 QB 34 at pp 44, 46, 50.

36 *Mount Albert Borough Council v Australian Temperance and General Mutual Life Assurance Society* [1938] AC 224 at p 240 per Lord Wright; The Assunzione [1974] P 150 at pp 175 and 179 per Singleton LJ.

36a Anton, Private International Law, pp 192 to 197.

37 See to this effect: Cour de Cassation, judgment of 28 March 1953 (n 827), supra; Cour de Cassation (full court), judgment of 28 June 1966 (n 1680), supra; Cour de Cassation, judgment of 30 April 1969 (n 1403), in Offcina Musso c Société Sevplant (Riv dir int priv proc, 1970, pp 332 et seq. For comments: Morelli, Elementi di diritto internazionale privato, cit n 97, p 155; Vitta Dir intern privato (3 V) Torino 1972–1975 III, pp 229 to 290.

38 See especially Vischer, Internationales Vertragsrecht, Bern, 1962, especially pp 89 to 144. This work also contains a table of the decisions in which this connection has been upheld. See also the judgment of 1 April 1970 of the Court of Appeal of Amsterdam, in *NAP NV v Christophery*.

39 This is the solution adopted by the Court of Limoges in its judgment of 10 November 1970, and by the Tribunal de commerce of Paris in its judgment of 4 December 1970 (Rev crit, 1971, pp 703 et seq). The same principle underlies the judgment of the Supreme Court of the Netherlands of 6 April 1973 (NI 1973 N371). See also Article 6 of the Hague Convention of 14 March 1978 on the law applicable to agency.

40 For the judgments mentioned in the text see: Rev crit 1967 pp 521 to 523; [1920] 2 KB 287; [1958] AC 301; [1963] 2 QB 352 and more recently: R Van Rooij, De positie van publiekrechtelijke regels op het terrein van het internationaal privaatrecht, 1976, 236 et seq; L Strikwerda, Semipubliekrecht in het conflictenrecht, 1978, 76 et seq.

40a On this Article, see the reflections of Vischer, The antagonism between legal security and search of justice in the field of contract, in Recueil de l'Académie de La Haye, Tome 142 (1974 II) pp 21 to 30; Lando op cit n 200 to 203 pp 106 to 110; Segre (T), Il diritto comunitario della concorrenza come legge d'applicazione necessaria, in Riv dir. int. priv et proc. 1979 pp 75 to 79; Drobnig, comments on Article 7 of the draft convention in European Private International Law of obligations edited by Lando—Von Hoffman-Siehr, Tübingen 1975, pp 88 et seq.

41 V Delaporte, Recherches sur la forme des actes juridiques en droit international privé. Thesis Paris I, 1974, duplicated, No 123 et seq.

42 V Delaporte, op cit, No III.

43 The possibility of applying a common national law is expressly provided for by Article 26 of the preliminary provisions to the Italian Civil Code. See also Article 2315 of the French draft of 1967.

44 The solution adopted has been influenced by that approved, though in a wider setting, by the Corte di Cassazione italiana, 30 April 1969, Riv dir. int. priv e pro. 1970, 332 et seq. It is contrary to that given by the Cour de Cassation of France, 10 December 1974, Rev crit dr inter pr 1975, 474, note AP. The alternative solution also prevails in the United Kingdom, *Van Grutten v Digby* (1862), 31 Beav 561; cf Cheshire and North, PIL 10th edition, p 220.

45 Solution adopted in German (principal law), Article 11 EGB. GB; in Italy (subsidiary) Article 26 prel pro and in France (Cour de Cassation 26 May 1963, Rev crit dr int pr 1964, 513, note Loussouarn; 10 December 1974 see note 44 above), and implicitly allowed by the Benelux Treaty (Article 19).

46 See references cited in the previous note.

47 See, for example, Article 13(4) of the Benelux Treaty 1969 which has not entered into-force.

48 For a comparative outline on this subject, see: Toubiana: Le domaine de la loi du contrat en droit international privé (contrats internationaux et dirigisme économique) Paris 1972, spec pp 1 to 146; Lando: Contracts in International Encyclopedia of Comparative Law, vol III, Private international law (Lipstein, chief editor) sections 199 to 231 pp 106 to 125.

49 See on this subject Article 4 of the Hague Convention of 1955 on the law applicable to international sales of corporeal movables.

50 See the Benelux Treaty 1969 (Article 2) not entered into force, the preliminary provisions of the Italian Civil Code (Article 1), the law introducing the German Civil Code (Article 7) and French judicial decisions. Rec. 16 January 1861, Lizardi, DP 1861.1.193, S 1861.1.305.

51 See Article 20(3) of the Benelux Treaty 1969 not entered into force and, in France, Cass. 24 February 1959 (Isaac), D 1959 J 485; 12 February 1963 (*Ruffini v Sylvestre*), Rev crit dip, 1964, p 121.

52 Cf Kegel, IPR, fourth edition, p 173; Batiffol and Lagarde, sixth edition, p 394; Article 2 of the Convention of 15 June 1955 on the law applicable to international sales of corporeal movables; Article 5 of the Convention of 14 March 1978 on the law applicable to agency. Dicey and Morris, ninth edition pp 723 to 724.

53 See Acts and Documents of the Hague Conference, IXth Session vol III, Wills (1961) explanatory report, p 170.

[3216]

[OJ C282, 31.10.80, p 48]

LIST OF PARTICIPANTS[1]

WORK UNDER THE AUSPICES OF THE COMMISSION

Chairman

Mr P Jenard	Director d'administration, Ministère des Affaires étrangères et du Commerce extérieur, Brussels.

WORK UNDER THE AUSPICES OF THE COUNCIL

Chairman

Mr A Brancaccio	Ministero di Grazia e Giustizia, Rome.
BELGIUM	
Mr M Hanotiau	Chef de service, Ministère de la Justice, Brussels.
Mr P Gothot	Professeur à la Faculté de droit à l'Université de Liège.
Mr R Vander Elst	Professeur, Université libre de Bruxelles.
DENMARK	
Mr A Philip	Professor, Justitsministeriet, Copenhagen.
Mr P Blok	Professor, Justitsministeriet, Copenhagen.
Mr H C Abildtrup	Attaché (Justitsministeriet), Danmarks faste Repræsentation, Brussels.
Mr N Waage	Attaché (Justitsministeriet), Danmarks faste Repræsentation, Brussels.
Mr H Wendler-Pedersen	Fuldmægtig, Justitsministeriet, Copenhagen.
GERMANY	
Prof Dr Arndt	OLG Präsident iR, Sachverständiger, Bremen.
Dr B Klingsporn	Ministerialrat, Bundesministerium der Justiz, Bonn.
Mr E Rebmann	Regierungsdirektor, Bundesministerium der Justiz, Bonn.
Mr W Hantke	Regierungsrat, Bundesministerium für Wirtschaft, Bonn.
Mr H König	Richter AG, Bundesministerium der Justiz, Bonn.
FRANCE	
Mr H Batiffol	Doyen honoraire, Prof à la Faculté de Droit à Paris.
Mr P Lagarde	Professeur à l'Université de Paris I.
Mr T Cathala	Conseiller à la Cour d'Appel, Paris.
IRELAND	
The Hon J B Walsh	Senior Ordinary Judge of the Supreme Court of Ireland Law Reform Commission.

[OJ C282, 31.10.80, p 49]

Mr E Hanley	Legal Adviser, EEC Division, Department of Justice, Dublin.
Mr J Brennan	Assistant Legal Adviser, EEC Division, Department of Justice, Dublin.
Mr M G Gleeson	Administrative Officer, Department of Justice, EEC Division, Dublin.

Mr L Cahill	Administrative Officer, Department of Justice, EEC Division, Dublin.
Mrs M Gleeson	Assistant Principal Officer, Department of Tourism and Transport, Dublin.

ITALY

Mr M Giuliano	Esperto, Professore all'Università di Milano.
Mr L Battaglini	Magistrato di cassazione Ministero degli Affari Esteri—Rome.
Mr L Giampaolino	Vice-Capo di Gabinetto, Ministero del Lavoro, Rome.
Mr F Di Filippis	Magistrato administrativo, Ministero dell'Industria, del Commercio e del'Artigianato, Rome.
Mr L Rovelli	Magistrato Tribunale, Ministero di Grazia e Giustizia, Rome.
Mr De Renzis	Magistrato, Ministero dell'industria.
Mr G Fienga	Ministero Industria.

LUXEMBOURG

Mr A Huss	Procureur Général d'État Honoraire, Ministère de la Justice, Luxembourg.
Mr A Weitzel	Conseiller à la Cour Supérieure de Justice, Ministère de la Justice, Luxembourg.
Mr R Heiderscheid	Président Honoraire de Tribunal, Luxembourg.
Mr C Wampach	Conseiller à la Cour Supérieure de Justice, Ministère de la Justice, Luxembourg.

NETHERLANDS

Mr J van Rijn van Alkemade	Raadadviseur, Ministerie von Justitie, 's Gra-venhage.
Mr R van Rooy	Administrateur, Ministerie van Justitie, 's Gra-venhage.
Mr J C Schultsz	Hoogleraar, Ministerie van Justitie, 's Gra-venhage.
Mr J G Sauverplanne	Hoogleraar, Fakulteit van Rechtsgeleerdheid, Utrecht.
Mr A J van Duyne-Strobosch	Administrateur, Ministerie van Justitie, 's Gra-venhage.

UNITED KINGDOM

The Hon Lord P Maxwell	Judge, Court of Session, Edinburgh.
Mr A L Diamond	Director, Institute of Advanced Legal Studies, London.

[OJ C282 31.10.80 p 50]

Mr K M Newmann	Under-Secretary, Lord Chancellor's Office, London.
Mr P M North	Law Commissioner, Law Commission, London.
Mr A Akbar	Senior Legal Assistant, Law Commission, London.

HAGUE CONFERENCE

Mr M H van Hoogstraaten	Secretary-General of the Hague Conference on Private International law, 's Gravenhagen.

BENELUX COMMISSION

Mrs M Weser	Professeur, Membre de la Commission Benelux pour l'unification du droit, Brussels.

COMMISSION OF THE EUROPEAN COMMUNITIES

Directorate-General of Internal Market and Industrial affairs (DG III)

Mr W Hauschild	Head of division.
Mr G Di Marco	Principal administrator.
Mr O Czerny	Principal administrative assistant.

Legal Service

Mr P Leleux	Legal adviser.
Mr A McClellan	Legal adviser.
Mr J Seche	Legal adviser.

Directorate General of Employment and Social affairs (DG V)

Mr H Ollenhauer	Head of division.
Mr K M Schilz	Principal administrator.

Directorate General of Financial Institutions and Taxation (DG XV)

Mr G Imbert	Director.
Mr H Schlude	Administrator.

COMMISSION EXPERTS

Transport

Mr F Berlingieri	Professor at the University of Genoa.
Mr E Selvig	Professor of the University of Oslo.

Employment contracts

Mr G Schnorr	Professor at the University of Innsbruck.

GENERAL SECRETARIAT OF THE COUNCIL OF THE EUROPEAN COMMUNITIES

Mr R Fornasier	Director, Legal Service.
Mr V Scordamaglia	Head of division, DG Internal Market.
Mr O Petersen	Administrator, DG Internal Market.
Mr J-F Faure	Administrator, DG Internal Market.

[3217]

NOTES

1 Other specialist experts who do not appear on this list, have been consulted on the examination of certain specific questions, and in particular concerning insurance, labour law, interpretation of the Convention by the Court of Justice of the European Communities.

COUNCIL REPORT

on the Protocols on the interpretation by the Court of Justice of the Rome Convention of 19 June 1980 on the law applicable to contractual obligations

(signed in Brussels on 19 December 1988)

by Antonio TIZZANO,

Professor of European Community Law at the University of Naples

(90/C219/01)

CONTENTS

[OJ C219, 3.9.90, p 3]

INTRODUCTION

1. Some eight years after the signing of the Rome Convention on the law applicable to contractual obligations, and while the Convention has still not entered into force, the Member States of the European Communities have finally followed up the intentions they stated at the time and have given the Court of Justice specific powers to interpret the Convention.[1]

In their "joint declaration" attached to the Convention the Member States "desiring to ensure that the Convention is applied as effectively as possible" had said that they were "anxious to prevent differences of interpretation of the Convention from impairing its unifying effect". Consequently, they declared themselves ready "to examine the possibility of conferring jurisdiction in certain matters on the Court of Justice of the European Communities and, if necessary, to negotiate an agreement to this effect" (and "to arrange meetings at regular intervals between their representatives").

Negotiations were set in hand immediately, but only on 19 December 1988 did the Member States sign, in Brussels, two Protocols on the matter, viz: "the first Protocol on the interpretation by the Court of Justice of the European Communities of the Convention" and "the second Protocol conferring on the Court of Justice of the European Communities certain powers to interpret the Convention" (OJ No L48, 20.2.1989).

Thus the Rome Convention too, like other "Community" Conventions, was provided in advance with the formal instrument needed to give the Court of Justice of the European Communities interpretative powers and so strengthen the possibility of its uniform application.

At the same time, and indeed because of this, practical effect could be given to the Convention's "Community" connection, i e to its institutional link with the Community legal system. In this particular instance this result was even more significant, since the Rome Convention, unlike the precedents in the matter, falls outside the scope of application of Article 220 of the EEC Treaty.

Finally, it proved possible to give continuity and substance to a now increasingly significant procedure in this field and indeed to provide it with openings for further possibilities of development, thanks to the originality of the solutions adopted.

However, as for the precedents referred to, drawing up the Protocols on the interpretative powers of the Court of Justice in respect of the Rome Convention did not prove to be at all easy. Everything was discussed at length: the need and/or the desirability of providing for such powers; the technique to be followed in the matter; the scope and conditions for exercising such powers; the involvement of all the Member States, etc The duration and the vicissitudes of the negotiations, the use of two separate legal instruments, the specific solutions outlined within them, and so on, are clear confirmation of such difficulties.

However, while certain even quite important aspects of the two Protocols betray these difficulties and raise a number of doubts, the final result of the lengthy and tortuous negotiations may be considered favourable overall. This is not only because the way has nonetheless been cleared for interpretative action by the Court of Justice, with the more general implications which have been mentioned and which will be returned to, but also because such a result was achieved in respect of a more complex and controversial situation than those tackled in the past. In addition, the danger of a lull in the development of the procedure referred to has been avoided and indeed, in some respects, a contribution has been made to actually consolidating and strengthening the procedure.

2. In order to give a clearer picture of the special nature of the solution adopted in the Protocols under review this Report is divided into two parts. Part One (sections 3 to 30) looks back over the practice followed prior to the Protocols and discards the terms of the negotiations and the motives that led the Member States to make substantial changes *vis-à-vis* that practice. Part Two (sections 31 to 41) comments on the separate articles of the two Protocols.

[3218]

[OJ C219, 3.9.90, p 4]

PART ONE
PRELIMINARY REMARKS

I. THE PRACTICE PRIOR TO THE PROTOCOLS

A. Origins and Development

3. Precisely because the two Protocols being examined fall in with a practice which is unvarying with respect to its aims although multifarious in its outward forms, it would appear advisable to begin with a brief summary of the development of that practice.

It will be recalled that the practice concerned began to emerge in the 1960s, at the time of the negotiations for the preparation of certain Conventions between Member States in the framework of Article 220 of the EEC Treaty, in particular the Convention on the mutual recognition of companies and legal persons, the Convention on jurisdiction and the enforcement of judgements in civil and commercial matters and the Convention on bankruptcy, winding-up arrangements, compositions and similar proceedings.

As known, of these Conventions only the second is in force. The first, signed in Brussels by the then six Member States of the European Communities on 29 February 1968, subsequently came to grief over the ratification procedures. Negotiations on the third Convention led to an extensive preliminary draft in 1970, but after various ups and downs (some of which we shall shortly return to) these negotiations were shelved.[2]

The second Convention, however, was more successful, as already mentioned. After being signed in Brussels on 27 September 1968 by the original Member States, it was progressively extended to the new Member States with the Luxembourg Convention of 9 October 1978 for the accession of Denmark, the United Kingdom and Ireland; with the Luxembourg Convention of 25 October 1982 for the accession of Greece; and finally with the Donostia-San Sebastian Convention of 26 May 1989 for the accession of Spain and Portugal.[3]

4. In all the instances mentioned so far, a Declaration was attached to the Conventions (or draft Conventions) in which the Signatory States, in terms and for purposes substantially similar to those of the Declaration attached to the Rome Convention, said that they were ready "to examine the possibility of conferring jurisdiction in certain matters on the Court of Justice of the European Communities and, if necessary, to negotiate an agreement to this effect".

This subsequently happened for the two Brussels Conventions referred to of 29 February and 27 September 1968 as a result of the signing of the two Luxembourg Protocols of 3 June 1971, only one of which, as is known, has entered into force, viz the Protocol to the Brussels Convention on the enforcement of judgement.[4]

In both Protocols, however, the powers of the Court of Justice to interpret the texts of the Agreements are defined in accordance with the scheme laid out in Article 177 of the EEC Treaty. Indeed, the Protocol to the first of the Conventions in question involves barely more than a straightforward transposition of that provision. For the other, however, some modifications had to be made, for reasons not unlike those underlying the innovations introduced by the Protocols being examined.

5. Following the precedents referred to, further opportunities arose for providing that such powers be given to the Court of Justice in draft conventions and conventions drawn up subsequently, including some whose subject-matter lay outside the scope of Article 220 of the EEC Treaty.

This is the case, in particular, for the draft Convention on bankruptcy, winding-up arrangements, compositions and similar proceedings, established in 1980 as a subsequent development of the preliminary draft of 1970 mentioned above. However, instead of the aforementioned Declaration attached to the preliminary draft on the powers of the Court of Justice to interpret the Convention, the 1980 draft makes use of the precedent constituted by the 1971 Luxembourg Protocol and inserts directly in the Convention itself provisions corresponding almost word for word to those of the Protocol (Articles 70 to 74). As said, however, negotiations on the Community Convention on bankruptcy are deadlocked for the time being.[5]

This is also the case for the Community Patent Convention, signed in Luxembourg on 15 December 1975 (OJ No L17, 26.1.1976), which directly embodies a provision giving the Court of Justice powers to interpret the Convention (Article 73). As is known, however, the entry into force of the Convention ran into numerous difficulties, with the result that in order to improve the chances of success it was considered desirable to make certain changes and additions to the Convention at conferences held in Luxembourg from 4 to 18 December 1985 and from 11 to 15 December 1989. The latter led to the Agreement on the Community patent, concluded in Luxembourg on 15 December 1989.[6]

[OJ C219, 3.9.90, p 5]

As regards the aspect which interests us here, these recent additions also have a significant bearing on the Court of Justice's interpretative powers, which are now partially replaced by those of the Common Appeal Court, set up on that occasion. The latter is, however, also required, in certain cases, to submit questions for preliminary rulings to the Court of Justice, while in other cases the national courts have the responsibility for so doing, in accordance with the schemes defined in the 1971 Luxembourg Protocol (Articles 2 to 5 of the 1989 Agreement). It should also be pointed out that the idea—subsequently taken over and actually put into effect for the Rome Convention—of providing for not one but two separate texts on the powers of the Court of Justice was first defined precisely in connection with the Community Patent Convention, and for exactly the same reasons as will be seen later in respect of the Protocols being examined.

B. Reasons

6. The reasons underlying the practice referred to above are so obvious that they require no more than a brief reference.

As is known, this practice has been developing mainly in relation to "Community" Conventions, the term used roughly to describe those Conventions between Member States intended to achieve objectives of importance for the European Communities. It is also known that while they may deal with matters which are not directly the subject of Community treaties and while they retain essential characteristics peculiar to international agreements of the traditional kind, there are aspects to those Conventions which link them to the Community legal system in a special way. They are in fact aimed at setting up between the Member States of the European Communities a complex of common rules (substantive or procedural), which in a way seek to supplement the system of rules already established or to be established, pursuant to the Community Treaties and "secondary" legislation, in line with, and with a view to, the general process of integration, in respect of which the creation of as uniform a "legal area" as is possible obviously constitutes a useful and, in some respects, indispensable instrument.

It is unlikely that this will be disputed as regards the Conventions which refer to Article 220, since the same rule links them to the Community legal system by making provision for them to be concluded between all Member States (and only between them) "so far as is necessary", i e in accordance with the achievement of the objectives of the EEC.

The same may, however, be said in respect of other Conventions between Member States which, although they go beyond the provisions of Article 220, may also be regarded as contributing towards the achievement of Community objectives. This is particularly so if such objectives are understood in a broad sense and in the dynamic and evolving prospect of the process of Community integration. In fact, in the light of the developments which have taken place in that process over a period and of its obvious tendency to grow, the listing of fields given in Article 220 appears less and less crucial for a Convention to be described as a "Community" Convention.

Moreover, various indications, albeit of different kinds and degrees of importance, provide evidence of the Community link in such Conventions. Reference may be made, for example, to the Commission's role in taking the initiative and providing a constant impetus for negotiations in this respect (in the case of the Rome Convention, that role has even taken the form of the Commission adopting official positions).[7]

It may also be recalled that such Conventions are concluded between all the Member States, between the Member States alone and between the Member States "meeting within the Council". Attention may also be drawn to the tendency to seek legal bases in the Treaty itself in order to provide rules on the matter by a Community act rather than through the Convention (see references in the Commission opinion referred to above as regards the harmonization of private international law; the trend has, however, already affected other sectors).

Finally, these links are also formally confirmed by those Community texts in which express reference is made, in addition to the Conventions provided for in Article 220 of the EEC Treaty, to "Conventions … that are inseparable from the attainment of the objectives" of the Treaty "and thus linked to the Community legal order".[8]

7. But above all what stands out, in respect of the aims mentioned, is the tendency to give the Court of Justice specific powers to interpret the Conventions referred to.

Such a trend undoubtedly corresponds in the first place to a requirement common to uniform-law Conventions. It is in fact generally acknowledged that the interpretation of such Conventions must take account of their international nature and of their specific unifying function. In the case of the Rome Convention, but not only for that Convention, the requirement mentioned above is actually expressed formally in a provision.[9]

It is also known, however, that despite this the effective application of those Conventions and their unifying function are often at risk of being thwarted as a result of differences in the way they are interpreted in the national legal systems of the Contracting States. The specific features of national legal traditions, the tendency of judges to use the legal categories most familiar to them, variations in the different language versions, the different techniques for transposing a Convention into the national legal systems, to mention only the main reasons, invariably lead to differences in the interpretative process, with the unfortunate consequences referred to. Hence the usefulness of setting up machinery capable of ensuring that the Conventions concerned are interpreted in terms which are as uniform as possible.

[OJ C219, 3.9.90, p 6]

The point, however, which needs to be given most emphasis here is that in the cases being discussed giving the Court jurisdiction is not intended merely to meet such concerns. The aim is in fact also, if not above all, to give formal expression and authentic substance to that aforementioned Community connection in the Conventions being examined. The aim is then not merely the general one of setting up a single centre for interpretation, but above all to entrust that task to the body which is the main guarantor of the uniform interpretation of the entire Community legal system and which, because of its position in the institutional hierarchy and the nature of its functions, is more capable than any other body of ensuring the organic link between the Conventions and that system. Moreover, it is precisely because of the role thus given the Court in this matter that in legal doctrine there is a growing tendency to construe Conventions and Community law as a single body of rules, in the sense that the Conventions become incorporated as fully-fledged elements in the Community legal system, as sub-systems present in it.[10]

If we then add to all these considerations the positive experiences gained over the past few years in the practical application both of Article 177 of the EEC Treaty and of the 1971 Protocol, the reasons for the growing trend to give the Court of Justice jurisdiction in the matter will appear more obvious still.[11]

C. Attempts to Provide an Institutional Framework

8. As has been said, approval for such a trend was already apparent on the occasion of the two 1968 Brussels Conventions. The fact that with these Conventions the era of the Conventions based on Article 220 was beginning (or was thought to be beginning) and that the problem of the powers of the Court arose simultaneously for two Conventions even raised the

question whether it was preferable to take a decision on conferring those powers on a case-by-case basis or to draw up a general act applicable to all Conventions concluded or to be concluded on the basis of Article 220.[12]

The latter hypothesis was rejected because it was thought preferable to define the Court's powers in each case according to its specific requirements.

However, the idea that continuity and stability should be given to the procedure remained and indeed grew stronger with the emergence of new requirements: the extension of Community Conventions beyond the area defined by Article 220; the recurrent difficulty in achieving the consensus of the Member States; the existence of problems peculiar to some States, and so on.

9. Amongst the first pressing requests along these lines were those made by the Court of Justice itself, which on various occasions expressed an opinion in favour of being given the powers in question, as it considered them necessary to "ensure both the unified nature of Community jurisdiction and the uniform application of Conventions in all Member States".

Nor did the Court seem to be discouraged by the well-known difficulties deriving from the increasing workload with which it was already faced at that time. Indeed, the clearest indication of support for those powers in the terms just referred to was officially expressed in a memorandum which the Court sent to the Council of the European Communities on 21 July 1978 to ask for a series of measures to be taken which were needed to improve the way the Court operated, with a view, likewise, to the conferring on it of such powers.

The Court's request met with immediate sympathy within the Council, in which the German delegation proposed endowing the Court of Justice with general jurisdiction in the field of private and commercial law Conventions to which all the Member States were parties, but not third countries, and which were related to the aims of the Community. The Council took note of the proposal at its meeting on 9 October 1978, but no further action was taken.

10. The idea that such powers should be conferred in general terms, albeit under arrangements to be defined, was not, however, abandoned. It reappeared on various occasions, even in official texts.

Thus the "Solemn Declaration on European Union", approved by the European Council in Stuttgart on 19 June 1983, proclaimed in point 2.5 that "taking account of the respective constitutional provisions in their States, the Heads of State or Government agree to consider, on a case-by-case basis, the inclusion, as appropriate, in international Conventions between Member States, of a clause conferring on the Court of Justice appropriate jurisdiction with regard to the interpretation of the texts".

In turn, the report prepared by the ad hoc Committee for Institutional Affairs (the "Dooge" Committee) suggested that the Court of Justice "must be given jurisdiction for the interpretation of agreements concluded within the ambit of the Treaties as far as possible by means of a standard clause" (point III, paragraph D).

[OJ C219, 3.9.90, p 7]

Finally, the idea also resurfaced to some extent during the Intergovernmental Conference which drew up the Single European Act, where there was talk of following up the statements mentioned.

But in the end no proposals were put forward in this connection.

11. The preparatory work for the Protocols being examined was thus carried out without any opportunity to refer, for those aspects just mentioned, to a legal framework already defined in general terms. Consequently the usual problems in the matter had to be faced, although obviously the abovementioned procedure had significant effects.

II. NEGOTIATIONS ON THE TWO PROTOCOLS

A. Introductory comments

12. In point of fact the first signs of the difficulties attending the negotiations were already apparent before the signing of the Rome Convention. When work on the draft Convention was finally concluded, after more than 10 years' discussions, the text contained no reference to the Court's jurisdiction, nor did it have annexed to it, as the other "Community" Conventions did, the aforementioned joint declaration on that jurisdiction.

The Commission then considered it necessary to draw up an opinion on the matter (see section 6), drawing attention to a number of shortcomings in the draft and especially the one just mentioned. In particular it said that it regarded it as essential not only that the Court be given jurisdiction, but also that the rules governing that jurisdiction be enacted in the body of the Convention by incorporating a provision based on Article 177 of the EEC Treaty. It was willing to accept a Protocol on the lines of that of 1971 concerning the Brussels Convention on jurisdiction and enforcement only as an alternative.

13. The Joint Declaration was adopted in partial accommodation of the Commission's request. However, as is normally the case, it contains no commitment on the part of the Member States to confer jurisdiction on the Court of Justice but merely a statement of their readiness to do so.

Specific negotiations were therefore necessary to give practical effect to the declared readiness; these began in June 1980, immediately after the signing of the Rome Convention and extended over many years in the various Council bodies, in particular the ad hoc Working Party on Private International Law.

14. Certain differences which proved difficult to bridge emerged during the negotiations, even though the Court of Justice itself, whose opinion had been expressly sought, had from the outset been favourable to extending the solution adopted for the 1971 Luxembourg Protocol to this case.

Moreover, certain Member States made it clear that they would not ratify the Convention until it was certain that jurisdiction would be conferred on the Court of Justice.

After various vicissitudes and periods of stalemate, the deadlock was finally broken in 1987. It was then possible fairly rapidly to draw up the two Protocols and for them to be signed at the end of 1988.

B. General problems

15. Some of the problems discussed during the negotiations bore specifically on the Protocols under examination or were posed in specific terms in relation to them; however, others were substantially the same as those that had arisen over the previous Protocols and had thus already been solved.

This meant that the discussion of those problems could be circumscribed and indeed in a number of cases the problems taken as solved.

16. Firstly, there was little doubt about whether conferral on the Court of Justice of powers not provided for in the Treaties required recourse to the relevant procedure for revision of the EEC Treaty laid down in Article 236, or whether other means could be used, in particular that of unanimous agreement among the Member States.

This issue had already arisen during negotiations on the 1971 Luxembourg Protocol and the solution then adopted had been that recourse to Article 236 was unnecessary. It was considered that application of Article 236 was necessary only where there was direct amendment to the text of the Treaty and/or an effect on the structure and operation of the Court. In this case, there was to be no amendment to the Treaty provisions relating to the Court of Justice, but rather an "extension" of the Court's jurisdiction: something was thus being "added", but the existing situation was not being changed. This also applied to the nature and subject of the jurisdiction being established, since this was wholly consistent with another already existing jurisdiction and related to a Convention which bore on the objectives of the EEC Treaty.[13]

It must, however, be objected that this solution appears somewhat forced and shows scant regard for Article 4 of the EEC Treaty ("each institution shall act within the limits of the powers conferred upon it by this Treaty"). Indeed, it seems difficult to deny the existence, in the cases under scrutiny, of an actual change in the overall picture of the Court's powers as defined by the EEC Treaty, since the powers being conferred are "new", "different" and far from insubstantial. On a more general level too the subtle and arguable distinction between "changing" and "extending" the Court's powers led to the risk, given its ambiguity, of making the interpretation of Article 236 still more uncertain, and even of restricting its scope. It is, however, a well-known fact that the Court of Justice favours the broadest application of that provision, inasmuch as the procedure it establishes offers specific institutional guarantees and lies wholly within the Community system.[14]

[OJ C219, 3.9.90, p 8]

Nevertheless, the above solution, adopted for the 1971 Protocol, prevailed, in particular because of the scope it allows for procedural simplification. It should be emphasized that this solution subsequently received general acceptance, ie irrespective of the connection between the Conventions concerned and Article 220, which could also to some extent have mitigated the requirement to apply Article 236. It is for this reason that it has been extended, without further discussion, to the subsequent agreements and hence also to the Protocols under examination.

17. Neither has there been any challenge to the principle whereby even where an ad hoc agreement is used rather than the Article 236 procedure, powers are conferred on the Court of Justice by *all* Member States, since the powers of a Community institution, as defined by the Treaty, are affected.

While there were some reservations on the argument that Conventions in the areas mentioned in Article 220 of the EEC Treaty (and a *fortiori* others) may, if it is impossible to proceed under the terms of that Article, be concluded within the time specified between Member States only, it is undisputed that the unanimous agreement of the Member States is required for Court of Justice jurisdiction to be established. However, this does not preclude, as will be seen for the Protocols under examination, more sophisticated solutions in cases where unanimity is more difficult to achieve.

18. In the absence of a general solution regarding the techniques for conferring jurisdiction on the Court of Justice (see section 8 *et seq*), account was taken of the specific nature of the case and as a result here, too, the procedure was to draw up special Protocols.

There was also in fact a suggestion that an ad hoc provision should be inserted in the body of the Rome Convention. This was the solution openly favoured by the Commission itself in its opinion of 17 March 1980 (see section 6), and there was no lack of precedents for it (see section 5).

However, this idea was soon dismissed: in view of the continuing reservations on the proposed establishment of Court of Justice jurisdiction it seemed advisable not to prejudice the negotiations on the Rome Convention for the sake of a point which clearly required further discussion and consideration.

19. Lastly, as regards the arrangements and conditions governing the exercise by the Court of the jurisdiction conferred on it, the possibility of merely extending Article 177 of the EEC Treaty, as was substantially the case for the Convention on the mutual recognition of companies and legal persons, was not even considered.

It was decided instead to follow the precedent of the 1971 Protocol to the Brussels Convention on jurisdiction and enforcement, which contains various adaptations to the model provided by Article 177 of the EEC Treaty. The Protocols under examination in fact depart even more substantially from that model, as we shall see.

C. Problems specific to the Rome Convention

20. As already noted, however, the Member States' discussions on the preparation of the Protocols under scrutiny focused not so much on the general questions so far presented as on issues more strictly related to the special nature of the case in point, and in particular the following—

(a) whether it was necessary or desirable to confer on the Court of Justice the task of uniform interpretation of the Rome Convention; and, if so, on what particular conditions to effect the conferral so as to take account of the specific nature of the Convention;

(b) how to overcome some Member States' objective difficulties in agreeing to that conferral; these related to problems which were not new but which were rendered more complex by certain aspects of this case, in particular the fact that there was no connection between the Rome Convention and Article 220.

21. (a) On this first point it has already been stated that from the outset, in the negotiations on the preparation of the Convention, the misgivings on the proposal to provide for Court of Justice jurisdiction had been stronger than in other cases. The last-minute addition of the oft-mentioned Joint Declaration smoothed out the immediate difficulties but did not remove a number of Member States' reservations.

22. Apart from reservations regarding the premature nature of the exercise (the Rome Convention was not, and is still not, in force), the main objection raised was that the Convention did not fall within the scope of Article 220 of the EEC Treaty. Thus the connection with Community objectives was to be considered more tenuous and above all it appeared less urgent to provide for interpretative machinery to reflect that connection than had been the case for the 1971 Protocols which related to Conventions based on Article 220.

[OJ C219, 3.9.90, p 9]

It was argued in reply to this objection that the choices made with regard to those Protocols had not been exclusively, or indeed even chiefly, based on the relationship between the individual Conventions and Article 220, because the main purpose seemed to be to ensure the uniform interpretation of the Convention and to achieve this through the Court of Justice. Subsequent practice has in fact confirmed the justice of this view, since there has been a growing tendency, also as regards the aspects examined here, to narrow the differences between Conventions based on Article 220 and those which are not so based but nevertheless relate to the achievement of Community objectives (see section 6 *et seq*). It has also been seen that in the proposals under discussion here regarding institutionalization of the Court's jurisdiction, no distinction was made between those Conventions (see section 8 *et seq*).

A more specific argument was that the Rome Convention was "the logical complement" to the Brussels Convention on jurisdiction and enforcement and that it was "precisely because of the numerous framework provisions and the imprecision of many of the legal concepts employed" that it needed to be interpreted in a uniform manner.[13]

23. Another, more specific, objection was that the subject and characteristics of the Rome Convention made provision for Court of Justice jurisdiction undesirable.

In particular, it was pointed out that the Convention was universal in nature (Article 2), i e it was also applicable to contracts having no connection with the Community Member States, except in that the disputes arising from them were subject to the Courts of one of those States. The jurisdiction of the Court of Justice should not therefore be imposed on parties who might not even be aware of the Court's existence.

In some way related to this objection were the fears expressed by some Member States that the tendency, widespread in international commercial practice, to accord their courts jurisdiction in disputes relating to "international contracts" might be undermined. It was thought that the prospect of such disputes having to undergo further trial (i e in the Court of Justice) might encourage traditional clients of those Community fora to go elsewhere in order to avoid more protracted, expensive and risky proceedings.

To counter the first of these objections, it was argued that the situations envisaged were in principle to be regarded as exceptional and did not constitute the Convention's main frame of reference.

In reply to both objections, it was pointed out that while they could lead, as in fact they did, to a search for appropriate solutions to the difficulties raised, they could not be allowed to result in failure to meet the requirements necessitating the conferral of jurisdiction on the Court of Justice.

24. Less weight was given to certain objections which had received particularly close attention during the negotiations on the 1971 Luxembourg Protocol.

We refer in particular to the fear that Court of Justice intervention might give scope for the parties to engage in delaying tactics or for other abuse and lead to overly-protracted proceedings. In practice, the application of the 1971 Protocol had already shown such fears to be groundless.

We also refer to the objections that had led the authors of the 1971 Protocol to exclude referrals to the Court of Justice by courts of first instance. The main purpose of that exclusion had been to prevent too many cases, unimportant rulings and minor points being submitted for the Court's interpretation.[16] Although legal authors had countered point by point the grounds for those fears, and the Commission and some delegations challenged the wisdom of the exclusion, it was virtually never seriously questioned for the Protocols under examination.[17]

25. (b) The other problem referred to [section 20(b)] arose from the difficulties encountered by some Member States in agreeing to the conferral of the new jurisdiction on the Court of Justice.

This was the case, in particular, for Ireland; the Irish Constitution [Article 34(1)] is generally interpreted to mean that it is not possible to refer to courts other than the national courts (hence also to supranational courts) matters which fall within the jurisdiction of the national courts.

This problem had, when the Treaties were ratified, been expressly resolved with regard to the jurisdiction conferred on the Court of Justice under the Community Treaties but of course only insofar as that jurisdiction was concerned. In the case of the 1971 Luxembourg Protocol, it had been possible to rely on the fact that this referred to a Convention formally based on the EEC Treaty. This reasoning could clearly not be used for the Rome Convention, nor for all the other Conventions (eg the Community Patent Convention) which likewise have no formal connection with Article 220 or any other Treaty provision which could constitute their legal basis. Nor did it seem feasible to regard the Rome Convention for these purposes as a mere extension of the Brussels Convention.

[OJ C219, 3.9.90, p 10]

The problem thus appeared difficult to solve, since on the one hand amendment of the Irish Constitution did not, and does not, seem an immediate possibility (see section 36) and on the other, the Court's jurisdiction under discussion could only be established, as already mentioned (see section 17), with the unanimous agreement of the Member States.

D. Solutions proposed

26. In the course of the long negotiations, various solutions were proposed, nearly all comprising variants, to overcome the difficulties described above.

(a) On the first of the above mentioned problems, as referrals to the Court of Justice by courts of first instance were excluded and as everyone accepted the procedure of petition for review in the interest of the law, discussion focused on possible referral by courts of last instance and appeal courts.

There were naturally attempts to put forward again *as such* the solution adopted in the 1971 Protocol (mandatory referral for the former, only optional referral for the latter). However, these came up against the difficulties described earlier and, despite the persistence of certain delegations, it was very soon apparent that they had no real chance of success.

Attention focused instead on the search for solutions which could reconcile the coherence of the system established by that Protocol with the need to overcome the objections to its extension to this case. In this connection it did in fact become immediately clear that some delegations were willing to withdraw their reservations only if the demands they had put forward (see section 23) were suitably met. These involved either restricting the range of courts empowered to refer a question of interpretation to the Court of Justice, or limiting the number of situations in which such referral was compulsory, and in any event making referral conditional on the prior agreement of the parties to the proceedings.

Various solutions were proposed, viz that such agreement should be required only in the case of appeal courts and/or courts of last instance; that compulsory referral should apply only to the latter category of courts or not at all; that in the context of a general system along the lines of that of the 1971 Protocol, the agreement of the parties should be required only in the case of courts of the common-law States and for a limited, 10-year period, hence with scope for review of the derogation with a view to possible alignment on the general system; that the agreement of the parties should be required in all Member States and limited to Supreme Courts, where neither of the parties was resident in a Contracting State of the Convention, etc.

A further solution was proposed for the problem under consideration, which was also designed to help solve the difficulty referred to in the preceding section; although it would not necessarily be an alternative to those indicated. This consisted in conferring on the Court of Justice the task of delivering opinions or non-binding decisions, rather than interpretative rulings which would be formally binding on the referring court. This solution could also perhaps involve strengthening the normal machinery for petitions for review in the interest of the law, with the Member States jointly appointing another body competent on the same footing as national bodies to lodge such appeals.

(b) Turning now to the second problem mentioned, when it came to considering practicalities (principally in the final stages of the negotiations), the most convincing solution was that which had been suggested and developed in relation to other Community Conventions in preparation which had raised or were raising similar difficulties. This was the idea of providing for two separate legal instruments: one to confer the jurisdiction in question on the Court of Justice, which, as noted earlier (see section 17), required ratification by all the Member States; the other, an instrument accepting that jurisdiction, admitting of a more limited number of ratifications.

27. However, the solutions proposed met with strong resistance, particularly from the delegations favouring the "traditional" system.

First and foremost, many Member States considered it contrary to the principles of their legal systems and to the actual authority of the judiciary to make judges' decisions formally conditional on the prior consent of the parties. Moreover, such a condition appeared to be at odds with the principle of cooperation between Member States' judiciaries and the Court of Justice, which underlay Article 177 of the EEC Treaty and the 1971 Protocol.

[OJ C219, 3.9.90, p 11]

The proposal that courts of last resort should merely have the option of referral appeared less liable to "subvert" the system after the *Cilfit* judgement, which had given those courts greater scope to exercise their discretion.[18] However, that judgement had also attenuated the urgent need, which lay behind the proposal, to allow those courts a wider margin of discretion.

The idea of establishing a separate system for the common-law States prompted the comment that this amounted to introducing, without clear objective grounds, a major exception to the general system, which would also have institutional repercussions. Moreover, such a derogation was at variance with the "universal" nature of the Rome Convention and liable to encourage the practice of "forum shopping".

The idea that the Court of Justice should be reduced to a sort of consultative body was vigorously rejected not only by the Court of Justice and the Commission but also by most Member States. It was felt that this solution would in general be liable to weaken the role of the Court and was in practice ill-suited to achieving uniform interpretation of the Convention, given that any pronouncements by the Court of Justice would bear little weight in relation to the referring judge's decisions.[19]

28. In addition to these specific objections, there were also some important general points of concern.

These resulted primarily from a reluctance to amend the system laid down in the 1971 Protocol, which had proved its worth, had not given rise to any abuse and had by now become familiar to national courts. This reluctance was reinforced by the fear of creating a precedent which would pave the way for the proliferation of formulae other than the formulae laid down in the Protocol. Moreover, as has already been stated, both the Court of Justice and the Commission had openly endorsed these assessments.

To this was then added the consideration that all the solutions envisaged would have had the ultimate effect of substantially restricting the scope of the unifying activities of the Court of Justice and consequently the overall efficiency of the system. In fact, the courts of first instance were already excluded from the system. In addition, it was now being suggested that the highest courts should simply have the option of referring cases, and furthermore that such referral should be subject to the consensus of the parties. Under these circumstances, the cases of "authorized" evasion of the Court's jurisdiction would obviously increase considerably.

This would be all the more likely to happen if the two Protocol system were used. In fact Member States who were parties to the Convention would then, if they ratified only the general Protocol, be entitled not to accept the Court's jurisdiction and therefore to prevent their own courts having any possibility of referral. This would also cause undesirable differentiation between Member States and encourage forum shopping.

29. For a long time the approval of several delegations hinged on the abovementioned objections. More or less wholehearted agreement was reached only at the last minute, thanks to a number of arguments put forward in support of the solution being proposed.

It was pointed out first of all that such a solution appeared to be the only practicable one in the circumstances and that the alternative would be simply not to establish the Court's jurisdiction.

Furthermore, unlike the 1968 Brussels Convention which established a system applicable only between the Member States, The Rome Convention is based, as has been pointed out many times, on universally applicable rules.

In addition, the purpose of the, so to speak, optional nature of one of the two Protocols was not to establish a permanent situation in advance, but merely to allow the system to get started, so as to encourage the later accession of such States as might have declined to join it. After all, even for the Rome Convention, entry into force was subject to only seven ratifications.

Lastly, it was pointed out, in keeping with the conclusions shared by most of the interpretations of Article 177 of the EEC Treaty and of the 1971 Protocol, that the rulings of the Court of Justice have a "persuasive effect" which transcends individual cases. The Court itself had stated that its interpretation of a Community Convention should be applied generally and uniformly.[20] Practice has confirmed this trend, as shown by the attention generally given even by courts of first instance to the Court's interpretative rulings. In its turn the Rome Convention made a certain contribution to this trend, because Article 18 of that Convention is clearly also based on the Court's jurisprudence.

In other words, failure to ratify the first Protocol rules out the possibility of referral to the Court, but not the Court's interpretative jurisdiction and above all the general and indirect effects of exercising such jurisdiction, which tend to favour that uniform application of the Convention which the second Protocol itself states to be necessary. Therefore, in conclusion, serious problems of differentiation for certain Member States should not arise, provided, of course, that they have ratified the Rome convention.

[OJ C219, 3.9.90, p 12]

E. Summary of solutions adopted

30. The reasons for the particular nature of the Protocols under examination cannot be grasped without having the terms of the discussions at hand in summary form. To avoid the difficulties mentioned and to achieve at least in part (and certainly as far as the principles are concerned) the desired result, it became necessary to work out comprise solutions, sometimes relating to key aspects of the problem.

The result is a system which presents a number of original features. Limiting ourselves to the main elements, and subject to further analytical examination, it may be summarized as follows—

(a) The jurisdiction of the Court is governed by two distinct Protocols, for the purposes and within the terms already mentioned. In the case of the Protocol establishing this jurisdiction, ratification by all the Member States is needed; in the other case, a minimum of seven ratifications is required, the same number as that necessary for the entry into force of the Rome Convention.
The nature of the Court's jurisdiction is defined in the latter Protocol.

(b) Referral to the Court is optional not only for appeal Courts, but also for Courts of last instance, with the further important stipulations which we will deal with later. It is not open to judges of first instance.
Courts of last instance are, here too, designated by name.

(c) The procedure governing petition for review in the interest of the law remains unchanged.

(d) Likewise, the system of exchange of information on the application of the Convention on the part of national courts is retained.

[3219]

PART TWO
COMMENTARY

I. THE FIRST PROTOCOL

A. Introduction

31. This Protocol defines the scope of the Court's jurisdiction and the conditions under which that jurisdiction is exercised.

To this end, it reproduces in very general terms the arrangements for referrals for a preliminary ruling first set out in Article 177 of the EEC Treaty and subsequently in the Luxembourg Protocol of 1971, but it adds further important changes to the innovations already introduced into the original system by that 1971 Protocol.

This will be seen clearly from the following analysis; it should be noted that, for any aspect also applying to the 1971 Protocol, reference will in principle be made to the comments made on that Protocol and the later adjustments to it (see note 3).

B. Preamble

32. *The preamble* to the Protocol is substantially the same as the preambles to the Luxembourg Protocol of 1971: it refers to the Joint Declaration annexed to the Rome Convention, and expresses the decision to draw up the Protocol.

C. Scope of the Court's jurisdiction

33. *Article 1* defines the scope of the jurisdiction of the Court of Justice in terms analogous to the precedents mentioned.

The following may therefore be the subject of interpretation by the Court: first of all, the Rome Convention, including the Protocol annexed thereto, which forms an integral part of it (Article 32 of the Convention); then the Conventions on the accession of the Member States to the Rome Convention [such as the Luxembourg Convention of 10 April 1984 concerning the accession of Greece: (see note 1)]; lastly, the Protocol actually under consideration (however, there is no mention of the second Protocol).

It should be emphasized here, however, that the references made in subsequent Articles to the abovementioned acts as a subject of interpretation by the Court of Justice are expressed in unusual detail compared with the precedents on the subject. In defining the questions of interpretation which may be put to the Court of Justice, the first sentence of Article 2 and paragraph 1 of Article 3 of the Protocol do not confine themselves, as do the precedents, to providing that such questions must concern the interpretation of the texts listed in Article 1, but refer to "the provisions contained in the instruments referred to in Article 1".

[OJ C219, 3.9.90, p 13]

This difference in wording relates to a question which is in fact not new and not confined to the Protocol under scrutiny; this question arose in the course of the negotiations with reference to a specific situation.

In certain Member States domestic law is, in fact, adapted to international Conventions through the issuing of appropriate laws which reproduce the content of the Conventions, adapting them to the particular style of the national legislation if necessary. This, of course, raises a few problems from our point of view, since, for judges in the States in question, the reference will be dictated more often by the national law than the Convention, with the consequent risk of excluding the actual premises for action by the Court of Justice.[21]

In the case of the Protocol under examination the question arose in connection with the procedure followed by the Federal Republic of Germany for incorporating the Rome Convention into domestic law. The rules of the Convention were not absorbed in their organic entirety but were distributed, so to speak, among the introductory provisions of the Civil Code in accordance with the system applied to those provisions, and were also adjusted as regards their content.

The Commission of the European Communities was concerned about the repercussions of this approach, when it was still at the planning stage, and sent the Federal Republic an appropriate recommendation on 15 January 1985 (see note 7).

In the recommendation it stated that this approach could undermine full and integral compliance with the Rome Convention, prejudicing the uniformity of the interpretation and application of the Convention and even the exercise of the powers which were intended to be conferred on the Court of Justice. National judges would have to identify one by one the provisions derived from the Convention on which it might be necessary to seek an interpretative ruling from the Court.

The Commission's action did not change the Federal Republic's decisions. The law ratifying the Convention expressly excluded the direct effect of the rules of the Convention (Law of 25 July 1986, BGBI, 1986, II, 809); these rules were distributed among the introductory provisions mentioned above when these were simultaneously amended (BGBI, 1986. I, 1142).[22]

During negotiations on the Protocol in question, however, it was the German delegation itself that suggested wording Articles 2 and 3 of the Protocol along the lines indicated above, omitting any direct reference to the Convention. As the German delegation subsequently explained in a statement in the minutes, the aim of this was precisely to overcome the problem already mentioned. The statement in fact says that by virtue of the wording proposed "if a question relates directly to the interpretation of a national rule which has transposed into national law a provision of one of the instruments referred to in Article 1 or corresponds to such a provision, the indirectly related question of interpretation of the rule on which the provision is based may be submitted to the Court of Justice for a preliminary ruling. The Rome Convention does not stipulate how the individual Contracting States have to transpose the provisions of the Convention into national law. This is a question which, according to international practice, it is left to the responsibility of the States concerned to settle. Any Contracting State may therefore bring the Rome Convention into force either by directly giving it force of law or by adopting its provisions in appropriate form in its national legislation". The statement also points out that Article 36 of the introductory provisions to the German Civil Code explicitly provides that those introductory provisions which concern contractual obligations based on the rules of the Convention must be interpreted and applied in a uniform manner.

The wording proposed by the German delegation was subsequently approved by the other Member States, leading eventually to the text as it now stands.

D. Conditions for referral and courts empowered to do so

34. *Article 2* states the conditions under which a question of interpretation may be referred to the Court of Justice and lists the national courts which are allowed to make such referrals.

On both points the provisions restates nearly all the amendments to the system outlined in Article 177 of the EEC Treaty which were already made by the Luxembourg Protocol of 1971

(Articles 2 and 3). This applies in particular to the analytical list of courts of last instance, the inversion of the order of presentation between these and the others, and the exclusion—mentioned several times already—of the courts of first instance.

The Protocol differs from its immediate predecessor in other respects as well.

(a) The most substantial differences concern the conditions of referral to the Court of Justice.

The main difference, pointed out several times already, clearly lies in the fact that in this connection it does away with the usual distinction between national courts of last instance and the others, in the sense that even the former now merely have the option of making referrals, not an obligation to do so.

[OJ C219, 3.9.90, p 14]

The reasons for this change and the concerns which underlie it have already been indicated (see section 26 *et seq*) and so there is no need to return to them. Rather it may be noted that the fact that the aforementioned diversity of system has been removed means that the conditions of referral are now laid down in a single provision for all the relevant courts, rather than in two separate provisions, as is done both in Article 177 of the EEC Treaty (second and third paragraphs) and, in reverse order, in the 1971 Protocol [Article 3(1) and (2)].

Otherwise, the conditions in question are not substantively different from the usual ones: the question requiring interpretation must have arisen in a case pending before one of the courts mentioned; it must concern the interpretation of the legal instruments mentioned in Article 1 or rather—as stated in the previous paragraph—the "provisions contained" in those instruments; the court making the referral must consider that a preliminary ruling from the Court on the question put is necessary to enable it to give its own judgment.

On this last point it should be noted, in connection with the discussions held on this subject during the preparatory work (see sections 23, 26 *et seq*), that in agreeing on the solution adopted in the Protocol, the representatives of the Member States said that they wanted to ensure that the courts empowered to apply to the Court of Justice for a preliminary ruling were allowed a discretionary power which they would exercise taking into consideration—subject to the national rules governing their operation—any appropriate factor, such as the position of the parties on the question of referral to the Court of Justice.

(b) As to the indication of the courts empowered to apply to the Court of Justice, Article 2 of the Protocol gives a specific list of courts of last instance.

To a large extent the list reproduces the list in Article 2 of the 1971 Protocol, as adjusted following the various accessions. Attention should also be drawn to the following differences—

— In the case of Italy, there has now been added a reference to the Consiglio di Stato, since it was considered that the provisions of the Rome Convention could also be invoked before the highest administrative court.

— For the United Kingdom, in addition to the House of Lords, reference is now made to "other courts from which no further appeal is possible", in such a way as to give the Protocol a broader field of application.

The fact that a distinction is no longer made between courts which are obliged to make a referral and those which simply have the option of doing so has not invalidated the listing of the courts of last instance. This is because this listing fulfils other requirements and, in particular, is intended to remove the doubts which had arisen with regard to the interpretation of Article 177 of the EEC Treaty in respect of the identification of those courts, and which had led to the changes introduced by the 1971 Protocol.

As regards appeal courts, it need only be pointed out that, as was already made clear in the report on this last Protocol, it is not the formal description which matters but the fact that the above courts act as appeal courts in this specific case.

It should also be pointed out with regard to the United Kingdom that, subject to a declaration to the contrary by that State, the courts empowered to hear appeals should exclude those which rule on appeals against decisions handed down by courts operating in European territories situated outside the United Kingdom, for the international relations of which that country is responsible [see Article 27(2)(b) and (4) of the Rome Convention].

Finally, as previously stated, Article 2 of the Protocol makes no mention of courts of first instance, despite the strong criticism which this same omission had provoked in respect of the 1971 Luxembourg Protocol (see section 24), especially because of the potential risks which this might involve for the uniform interpretation of the Convention.

It was at least partly to meet this concern that the provision concerning "petition for review in the interest of the law", referred to in Article 3 of the Protocol in question and Article 4 of the 1971 Protocol, was introduced. It is in fact no accident that no provision has been made for such a procedure either in Article 177 of the EEC Treaty or in the 1971 Protocol, relating to the Convention on the mutual recognition of companies (see section 4), both of which permit the referral of cases by courts of first instance.

E. "Petition for review in the interest of the law"—Other rules applicable

35. *Articles 3 and 4* of the Protocol concern respectively "petition for review in the interest of the law" and the applicability of the rules of the EEC Treaty and the Court of Justice Protocol, as well as possible adjustments to the Rules of Procedure.

Both the provisions reiterate word-for-word the corresponding provisions of the 1971 Protocol (Articles 4 and 5) and there is therefore no need to comment at length.

With regard to petition for review in the interest of the law, suffice it to point out that despite what has just been said about its specific aims (see previous section), it has never yet been applied in practice. It should also be remembered that the Protocol under scrutiny does not merely rule out reference to the Court for courts of first instance; it also makes such referral optional for courts of last instance. And that could increase the likelihood of petition for review in the interest or the law.

[OJ C219, 3.9.90, p 15]

As for Article 4 of the Protocol, it should be considered that it also includes the applicability, for the proceedings instituted by virtue of the Protocol itself, of Article 20 of the Court's Statute. This means, among other things, that even the Member States that have not ratified the Protocol can submit statements of case or written observations during these proceedings.

F. Ratification and entry into force of the Protocol

36. *Articles 5 and 6* are concerned respectively with the ratification and entry into force of the Protocol. The first corresponds exactly to Article 7 of the 1971 Protocol and does not require further comment.

Article 6, however, represents a considerable innovation with respect to Article 8 of that Protocol, for the reasons mentioned several times. The entry into force of the Protocol in hand is now linked not to ratification by all the Member States, but by seven of those States in respect of which the Rome Convention is in force (the Convention itself, of course, requiring the same minimum number of ratifications).

This enables the entry into force of the Protocol to be linked to that of the Convention (and successive ratifications must apply to both), while also permitting circumvention of the requirement for unanimity, which raises grave difficulties in this case, as has been noted, although other difficulties might be created by the solution adopted (see sections 25 and 28).

In fact, at the signing of the Protocols, the Irish delegation made the following statement—

> "At the time of signature of the First Protocol on the interpretation by the Court of Justice of the European Communities of the Convention on the law applicable to contractual obligations, opened for signature in Rome on 19 June 1980, the Irish delegation states that because of certain provisions of the Constitution of Ireland concerning the jurisdiction of, and the administration of justice by, the Courts of Ireland, Ireland is not at present in a position to ratify this Protocol, adherence to which is not an obligation of the Treaties establishing the European Communities, and will not be in a position to proceed to ratification until such time as the constitutional impediment has been removed."

Of course, in view of the fact that this Protocol cannot become effective if the Court's jurisdiction has not been established by unanimous agreement among the Member States, its entry into force is conditional on that of the second Protocol.

G. Other standard clauses—Duration of the Protocol

37. *Articles 7 to 11* contain standard clauses, or clauses which in any event already exist in almost identical terms in the 1971 Luxembourg Protocol.

Article 9, however, differs from the corresponding provision in that Protocol. Whereas the latter was concluded for an unlimited period like the Brussels Convention to which it refers (Article 12), this Protocol follows the model of the Rome Convention, which was concluded for ten years with tacit renewal every five years if there has been no denunciation (Article 30 of the Convention).

H. The question of territorial scope

38. It should be noted that, like the second Protocol, this Protocol contains no clause on the field of its territorial scope, whereas the Rome Convention does include a special provision on the subject (Article 27).

The absence of any such provision from the two Protocols is in fact in line with more recent practice in Community conventions and those associated with them. Indeed, the Convention of Accession of Spain and Portugal to the 1968 Brussels Convention not only contains no clause on territorial application, but also deletes those contained in the Brussels Convention itself (Article 60) and in the 1971 Protocol (Article 6) (see respectively Article 21 and Articles 26 and 27 of the Donostia-San Sebastian Convention). A similar omission is to be found in the 1988 Lugano Convention (see note 3).

In considering the implications of this lack of any definition of the scope of the Protocols, it is sufficient to refer to the reports on the aforementioned Conventions of Donostia-San Sebastian and Lugano, given their similarity.

The fact that the Rome Convention contains a territorial clause should not have any repercussion for the two Protocols in hand, in terms of authorizing any extension of the scope of the Convention to the Protocols. In fact, although closely linked, these contractual instruments are formally independent. In any event, in cases where it was desired that the territorial scope of a Protocol should coincide with that of the "main" Convention, appropriate clauses were inserted into both texts (as indeed occurred with the Brussels Convention and the Protocol relating to it, before the aforementioned deletion).

[OJ C219, 3.9.90, p 16]

I. Accession of new members

39. The Protocol also omits any provision on the accession of any new members of the EEC, whereas Article 9 of the 1971 Protocol requires them to accede. This is because the Rome Convention is not based on Article 220 of the EEC Treaty and so, unlike the Brussels Convention, it necessarily left open the matter of the accession of future Community members. However, the Protocol resembles the Rome Convention in having a "*Joint Declaration*" annexed to it, in which the signatory countries state their conviction that "any State which becomes a member of the European Communities should accede to this Protocol".

It should be noted that the Protocol was also signed by Spain and Portugal, which are not yet parties to the Rome Convention.

J. Exchange of information

40. Lastly, it is worth pointing out that this Protocol, like the 1971 Protocol, has annexed to it a "*Joint Declaration*" in which Member States declare themselves ready to organize an exchange of information on judgements which have become *res judicata* and have been handed down pursuant to the Rome Convention by the courts referred to in Article 2 of this Protocol.

However, in relation to the corresponding Declaration annexed to the Luxembourg Protocol, the Declaration currently being considered gives a far more analytical description of the information concerned. It is likely that this was achieved to some extent thanks to the specific precedent provided by Article 2(1) of Protocol 2 annexed to the abovementioned 1988 Lugano Convention.

II. THE SECOND PROTOCOL

41. The examination of this Protocol requires little comment.

The *preamble* describes the reasons why the instrument was drawn up. It refers to the fact that the Rome Convention enters into force after the seventh ratification and stresses that, even before its entry into force, in order to ensure uniform application of the Convention, a mechanism needs to be introduced in order to ensure its uniform interpretation, and that this could be achieved by conferring the appropriate powers on the Court of Justice.

Article 1 therefore confers those powers according to the terms and conditions laid down in the first Protocol. The reference to the application of the Protocol on the Statute of the Court of Justice and of the Rules of Procedure, and to any necessary adaptation of the latter, is restated here, although already included in the First Protocol, in order to base the provision on the unanimous agreement of the Member States.

With regard to *Articles 2 to 4*, it only needs to be stressed that, for the reasons given on a number of occasions, the Protocol can enter into force only after ratification by all the Member States (Article 3). **[3220]**

NOTES

1 As is known, the Rome Convention was concluded on 19 June 1980. On that occasion it was signed by seven States at that time Members of the Community. Denmark signed on 10 March 1981 and the United Kingdom on 7 December of the same year. (The text of the Convention can be found in OJ No L266, 9.10.1980. The report on the Convention by Professors Giuliano and Lagarde was published in OJ No C282, 31.10.1980).

Seven ratifications are required for the Convention to enter into force. So far, six countries have ratified it, in order of date: France, Italy, Denmark, Luxembourg, Federal Republic of Germany and Belgium.

After Greece's entry into the Community, the Convention for the accession of that State to the Rome Convention (OJ No L146, 31.5.1984) was signed in Luxembourg on 10 April 1984. Its entry into force is dependent on it being ratified by Greece and at least seven other signatory States. So far, the following have deposited the instruments of ratification, in order of date: France, Italy, Denmark, Luxembourg, Greece, Federal Republic of Germany.

Spain and Portugal are required by Article 3(2) of the Act of Accession of those States to the Community to accede, with whatever adjustments may be necessary, to the "Community" Conventions (see OJ No L302, 15.11.1985, also below, note 6). Up to now, however, negotiations for accession to the Rome Convention have not yet begun.

On the subject of that Convention see in particular—already shortly after it was signed—T Treves (ed), *Verso una disciplina comunitaria della legge applicabile ai contratti*, Cedam, Padua, 1983; and more recently, with ample bibliography, M Virgos Soriano, *El Convenio de Roma de 19 de junio 1980 sobre la ley aplicable a las obligaciones contractuales*, in E García de Enterria, JD González Campos and S Muñoz Machado, *Tratado de Derecho Comunitario Europeo*, Civitas, Madrid, 1986, vol III, pp 753 *et seq.*

Specifically on the Protocols covered by this report, see M Virgos Soriano, *La interpretación del Convenio de Roma de 1980 sobre la ley aplicable a las obligaciones contractuales y el Tribunal de Justicia de las Comunidades Europeas*, in *Noticias*/CEE 1990, pp 83 *et seq.*

2 See note 5 below. For the text of the preliminary draft, see *Les problèmes internationaux de la faillite et le Marché Commun*, Cedam, Padua, 1971, which covers the proceedings of a conference held in Milan on 12 to 15 June 1970. For the aspect which is of interest here, see, in the same volume, A Tizzano, *La déclaration commune et la compétence de la Cour de Justice des Communautés européennes*, pp 170 *et seq.*

3 The texts of the Brussels Convention of 1968 and the Luxembourg Conventions of 1978 and 1982 all in force can be found respectively in OJ No L299, 31.12.1972; OJ No L304, 30.10.1978 and OJ No L388, 31.12.1982.

The Donostia-San Sebastian Convention was published in OJ No L285, 3.10.1989. It will enter into force after ratification by two States, of which one must be the Kingdom of Spain or the Portuguese Republic.

A consolidated text has been published in OJ No C189, 28.7.1990.

The reports on the above Conventions were drawn up by, in order of date: Mr Jenard (OJ No C59, 5.3.1979), Mr Schlosser (*ibid*), Messrs Evrigenis and Kerameus (OJ No C298, 24.11.1986); Messrs Almeida Cruz, Desantes Real and Jenard (OJ No C189, 28.7.1990).

To complete the picture, it should be pointed out that a Convention on jurisdiction and the enforcement of judgements in civil and commercial matters (OJ No L319, 25.11.1988, p 9) was opened for signature by the Member States of the European Communities and EFTA in Lugano on 16 September 1988. This so-to-speak parallel Convention to the Brussels Convention of 1968 has been signed by seven Member States of the European Communities (Belgium, Denmark, Greece, Italy, Luxembourg, Netherlands and Portugal) and five Member States of EFTA (Finland, Iceland, Norway, Sweden and Switzerland). It will enter into force after the deposit of the instruments of ratification of two signatory States, one a member of the European Communities and the other of EFTA. The report on the Convention was drawn up by Messrs Jenard and Möller (OJ No C189, 28.7.1990).

4 See OJ No L204, 2.8.1975. The Protocol entered into force on 1 September 1975 for the original six Member States of the European Communities. For the others, accession to the Protocol proceeded *pari passu* with accession to the Brussels Convention (see previous note). Similarly, the reports on the Protocol are incorporated in those on the Brussels Convention and on the other Conventions which have amended it (*ibid*).

The Protocol relating to the Convention on the mutual recognition of companies, on the other hand, suffered the same fate as that Convention which, as has been noted, never gained the required number of ratifications.

5 The hypothesis now under consideration by the Member States, given the difficulties still existing in this matter, involves adopting the Convention in preparation within the Council of Europe "on certain international aspects of insolvency" and subsequently carrying out further harmonization within the Community framework.

For the text of the 1980 draft see *Bulletin of the European Communities*, Supplement 2/82, which also contains the report of the Chairman of the Working Party, Mr Lemontey (*ibid*). For a more recent analysis, see also L Daniele, *Il fallimento nel diritto internazionale privato e processuale*, Cedam, Padua, 1987, pp 22 *et seq.*

6 See OJ No L401, 31.12.1989. For the first of the abovementioned conferences see the volume published by the Council of the European Communities: *Texts established by the Luxembourg Conference on the Community Patent* 1985, Luxembourg, 1985.

7 In particular: with the opinion of 17 March 1980 regarding the draft Convention (OJ No L94, 11.4.1980, p 39), to which we shall return later (but see especially note 12) and the recommendation of 15 January 1985 regarding the Convention (OJ No L44, 14.2.1985, p 42) (on which see section 33).

8 These are the terms defining, in its own preamble, the Convention on the Community patent of 15 December 1975 (see note 5). But these are also the terms defining, in Article 3(2) of the Act of accession of Spain and Portugal to the European Communities, the conventions to which, in addition to the conventions based on Article 220, those two States undertake to accede.

9 The reference is of course to Article 18, according to which "In the interpretation and application of the preceding uniform rules, regard shall be had to their international character and to the desirability of achieving uniformity in their interpretation and application". On the significance of such rules and on analogous provisions in other uniform law conventions [see the Giuliano and Lagarde Report, pp 37 *et seq* (see note 1)].

10 Thus, with specific reference to the Rome Convention, R Luzzatto, *L'interpretazione della Convenzione e il problema della competenza della Corte di Giustizia delle Comunità* in T Treves (ed), *Verso una disciplina comunitaria della legge applicabile ai contratti* (op cit, pp 58 *et seq* and 62).

11 In regard to this, it should be pointed out that in some 13 years of application of the Protocol, the Court has delivered more than 60 judgements, that is to say an average of around five pronouncements a year. For a summary of this jurisprudence and a list of the judgements, updated to 27 September 1988 (see the Jenard-Möller Report, note 3 above). For a recent analysis, see P Vlas, *The Protocol on Interpretation of the EEC Convention on jurisdiction and enforcement of judgements: Over 10 years in legal practice (1975 to 1985)*, in *Netherlands International Law Rev*, 1986, pp 84 *et seq.*

12 See the Jenard Report, point 2, note 3 above.

13 See the Jenard Report, point 4.

14 See e g the Judgement of 8 April 1976, Case 43/75, *Defrenne/Sabena, Court Reports* 1976, p 478 ("... apart from any specific provisions, the Treaty can only be modified by means of the amendment procedure carried out in accordance with Article 236").

15 Thus, *inter alia*, the Commission in the opinion of 17 March 1980 cited above (note 7), and, with abundant examples, M Virgos Soriano, *La interpretación* ..., pp 89 *et seq.* Note also that the Court of Justice had, albeit indirectly, already had occasion to interpret the Rome Convention; see the Judgements of 26 May 1982, Case 133/81, *Ivenel/Schwab, Court Reports* 1982, p 1900; and 8 March 1988, Case 9/87, *Arcado/Haviland, Court Reports* 1988, p 1555. See also the Judgement of 15 February 1989, Case 32/88, *Six Constructions/Humbert*, not yet published.

16 See the Jenard Report, point 11. See also T Cathala, *L'interprétation uniforme des conventions conclues entre États membres de la CEE en matière de droit privé*, in *Recueil Dalloz Sirey* 1972, *Chronique VII*, pp 32 *et seq.*

17 On this point, see also section 34. On the criticisms referred to in the text, see *inter alia* H Rasmussen, *A New Generation of Community Law?*, in *Common Market Law Rev*, XV, 1978, pp 249 *et seq.*; F Pocar, *Il protocollo sull'interpretazione uniforme della Convenzione di Bruxelles sulla competenza giurisdizionale e l'esecuzione delle sentenze*, in *Rivista di diritto internazionale privato e processuale* 1978, pp 281 *et seq* and pp 285 *et seq*; E Metzger, note in *Revue critique de droit international privé* 1979, pp 130 *et seq.*

18 See the Judgements of 6 October 1982, Case 283/81, *Court Reports* 1982, pp 3415 *et seq* and pp 3429 *et seq.* In this judgement, of course, the Court began by confirming that, in the framework of Article 177 of the EEC Treaty, even courts of last instance may use their discretion to decide whether an interpretative pronouncement from the Court of Justice is necessary for deciding the case pending before them. But above all, it stated that such courts may, albeit with all due circumspection, refrain from referral where the Community law to be applied has such a clear meaning as not to raise any doubt in reality as to its interpretation.

19 See again the opinion of 17 March 1980 cited above (note 7), and R Luzzatto (note 10), pp 65 *et seq.*

20 See especially the Judgement of 14 July 1977, joined Cases 9 and 10/77, *Bavaria Fluggesellschaft* and *Germanair/Eurocontrol, Court Reports* 1977, p 1517, in which the Court states that "The principle of legal certainty in the Community legal system and the objectives of the Brussels Convention (of 1968) in accordance with Article 220 of the EEC Treaty, which is at its origin, require in all Member States a uniform application of the legal concepts and legal classifications developed by the Court in the context of the Brussels Convention."

21 See the Schlosser Report, p 144, point 256, note 3 above.

22 In this connection see E Jayme and C Kohler, *Das internationale Privat- und Verfahrensrecht der Europäischen Gemeinschaft. Jüngste Entwicklungen*, in IPRax 1988, n 3, pp 133 *et seq* and pp 137 *et seq.*

COUNCIL CONVENTION

of 14 April 2005

On the Accession of the Czech Republic, the Republic of Estonia, the Republic of Cyprus, the Republic of Latvia, the Republic of Lithuania, the Republic of Hungary, the Republic of Malta, the Republic of Poland, the Republic of Slovenia And the Slovak Republic to the Convention on the Law Applicable to Contractual Obligations Opened for Signature in Rome on 19 June 1980, and to the First and Second Protocols on its Interpretation by the Court of Justice of the European Communities

(2005/C169/01)

NOTES

Date of publication in OJ: OJ C169, 8.7.2005, p 1.

THE HIGH CONTRACTING PARTIES TO THE TREATY ESTABLISHING THE EUROPEAN COMMUNITY,

BEARING IN MIND the Act concerning the conditions of accession of the Czech Republic, the Republic of Estonia, the Republic of Cyprus, the Republic of Latvia, the Republic of Lithuania, the Republic of Hungary, the Republic of Malta, the Republic of Poland, the Republic of Slovenia and the Slovak Republic, and the adjustments to the Treaties on which the European Union is founded, and in particular Article 5(2) thereof,

RECALLING that by becoming Members of the European Union, the new Member States undertook to accede to the Convention on the Law applicable to Contractual Obligations, opened for signature in Rome on 19 June 1980, and to the First and Second Protocols on its interpretation by the Court of Justice as modified by the Convention signed in Luxembourg on 10 April 1984, on the accession of the Hellenic Republic, the Convention signed in Funchal on 18 May 1992 on the accession of the Kingdom of Spain and the Portuguese Republic, and the Convention signed in Brussels on 29 November 1996 on the accession of the Republic of Austria, the Republic of Finland and the Kingdom of Sweden,

HAVE AGREED AS FOLLOWS:

TITLE I
GENERAL PROVISIONS

Article 1

The Czech Republic, the Republic of Estonia, the Republic of Cyprus, the Republic of Latvia, the Republic of Lithuania, the Republic of Hungary, the Republic of Malta, the Republic of Poland, the Republic of Slovenia and the Slovak Republic hereby accede to:

(a) the Convention on the Law applicable to Contractual Obligations, opened for signature in Rome on 19 June 1980, hereinafter referred to as 'the Convention of 1980', as it stands following incorporation of the adjustments and amendments made thereto by:

— the Convention signed in Luxembourg on 10 April 1984, hereinafter referred to as 'the Convention of 1984', on the accession of the Hellenic Republic to the Convention on the Law applicable to Contractual Obligations,

— the Convention signed in Funchal on 18 May 1992, hereinafter referred to as 'the Convention of 1992', on the accession of the Kingdom of Spain and the Portuguese Republic to the Convention on the Law applicable to Contractual Obligations,

— the Convention signed in Brussels on 29 November 1996, hereinafter referred to as 'the Convention of 1996', on the accession of the Republic of Austria, the Republic of Finland and the Kingdom of Sweden to the Convention on the Law applicable to Contractual Obligations;

(b) the First Protocol, signed on 19 December 1988, hereinafter referred to as 'the First Protocol of 1988' on the interpretation by the Court of Justice of the European Communities of the Convention on the Law applicable to Contractual Obligations, as it stands following incorporation of the adjustments and amendments made thereto by the Convention of 1992 and the Convention of 1996;

(c) the Second Protocol, signed on 19 December 1988, hereinafter referred to as 'the Second Protocol of 1988', conferring on the Court of Justice of the European Communities certain powers to interpret the Convention on the Law applicable to Contractual Obligations.

[3221]

TITLE II
ADJUSTMENTS TO THE FIRST PROTOCOL OF 1988

Article 2

The following indents shall be inserted in Article 2(a):

(a) between the first and the second indents:
'– in the Czech Republic:
Nejvyšší soud České republiky
Nejvyšší správní soud'

(b) between the third and the fourth indents:
'– in Estonia:
Riigikohus'

(c) between the eighth and the ninth indents:
'– in Cyprus:
Ανώτατο Δικαστήριο
– in Latvia:
Augstākās Tiesas Senāts
– in Lithuania:
Lietuvos Aukščiausiasis Teismas
Lietuvos vyriausiasis administracinis teismas'

(d) between the ninth and the tenth indents:
'– in Hungary:
Legfelsõbb Bíróság
– in Malta:
Qorti ta' l-Appell'

(e) between the eleventh and the twelfth indents:
'– in Poland:
Sąd Najwyższy
Naczelny Sąd Administracyjny'

(f) between the twelfth and the thirteenth indents:
'– in Slovenia:
Ustavno sodišče Republike Slovenije
Vrhovno sodišče Republike Slovenije
– in Slovakia:
Najvyšší súd Slovenskej republiky'.

[3222]

TITLE III
FINAL PROVISIONS

Article 3

1. The Secretary-General of the Council of the European Union shall transmit a certified copy of the Convention of 1980, the Convention of 1984, the First Protocol of 1988, the Second Protocol of 1988, the Convention of 1992 and the Convention of 1996 in the Danish, Dutch, English, Finnish, French, German, Greek, Irish, Italian, Portuguese, Spanish and Swedish languages to the Governments of the Czech Republic, the Republic of Estonia, the Republic of Cyprus, the Republic of Latvia, the Republic of Lithuania, the Republic of Hungary, the Republic of Malta, the Republic of Poland, the Republic of Slovenia and the Slovak Republic.

2. The texts of the Convention of 1980, the Convention of 1984, the First Protocol of 1988, the Second Protocol of 1988, the Convention of 1992 and the Convention of 1996 in the Czech, Estonian, Hungarian, Latvian, Lithuanian, Maltese, Polish, Slovakian and Slovenian languages shall be authentic under the same conditions as the other texts of the Convention of 1980, the Convention of 1984, the First Protocol of 1988, the Second Protocol of 1988, the Convention of 1992 and the Convention of 1996.

[3223]

Article 4

This Convention shall be ratified by the signatory States. The instruments of ratification shall be deposited with the Secretary-General of the Council of the European Union.

[3224]

Article 5

1. This Convention shall enter into force between the States which have ratified it, on the first day of the third month following the deposit of the second instrument of ratification.

2. Thereafter, this Convention shall enter into force, for each signatory State which subsequently ratifies it, on the first day of the third month following the deposit of its instrument of ratification.

[3225]

Article 6

The Secretary-General of the Council of the European Union shall notify the signatory States of:

(a) the deposit of each instrument of ratification;
(b) the dates of entry into force of this Convention for the Contracting States.

[3226]

Article 7

This Convention, drawn up in a single original in the Czech, Danish, Dutch, English, Estonian, Finnish, French, German, Greek, Hungarian, Irish, Italian, Latvian, Lithuanian, Maltese, Polish, Portuguese, Slovakian, Slovene, Spanish and Swedish languages, all 21 texts being equally authentic, shall be deposited in the archives of the General Secretariat of the Council of the European Union. The Secretary-General shall transmit a certified copy to the Government of each signatory state.

[3227]

Done at Luxembourg on the fourteenth day of April in the year two thousand and five.

[Signatures appear here]

Joint declaration by the High Contracting Parties concerning the deadlines set for ratification of the Accession Convention

'The High Contracting Parties, meeting in the Council at the time of the signature of the Convention on the accession of the Czech Republic, the Republic of Estonia, the Republic of Cyprus, the Republic of Latvia, the Republic of Lithuania, the Republic of Hungary, the Republic of Malta, the Republic of Poland, the Republic of Slovenia and the Slovak Republic to the 1980 Rome Convention on the law applicable to contractual obligations, declare that they will take the necessary steps to ratify this Convention within a reasonable time and, if possible, before December 2005.'

Declaration by the Member States concerning the timing of the submission of a proposal for a Regulation on the law applicable to contractual obligations

'The Member States request that the Commission submit, as soon as possible and at the latest by the end of 2005, a proposal for a Regulation on the law applicable to contractual obligations.'

Joint Declaration by the Member States on the exchange of information

The Governments of the Kingdom of Belgium, the Czech Republic, the Kingdom of Denmark, the Federal Republic of Germany, the Republic of Estonia, the Hellenic Republic, the Kingdom of Spain, the French Republic, Ireland, the Italian Republic, the Republic of Cyprus, the Republic of Latvia, the Republic of Lithuania, the Grand Duchy of Luxembourg, the Republic of Hungary, the Republic of Malta, the Kingdom of the Netherlands, the Republic of Austria, the Republic of Poland, the Portuguese Republic, the Republic of Slovenia, the Slovak Republic, the Republic of Finland, the Kingdom of Sweden and the United Kingdom of Great Britain and Northern Ireland,

On signing the 2005 Convention on accession to the Convention on the law applicable to contractual obligations, opened for signature in Rome on 19 June 1980, and to the First and Second Protocols on interpretation by the Court of Justice of the European Communities, as amended,

Desiring to ensure that the provisions of the First Protocol are applied as effectively and as uniformly as possible,

Declare themselves ready to organise, in cooperation with the Court of Justice of the European Communities, an exchange of information on judgments which have become res judicata and have been handed down pursuant to the Convention on the law applicable to contractual obligations by the courts referred to in Article 2 of the said Protocol. The exchange of information will comprise:

— the forwarding to the Court of Justice by the competent national authorities of judgments handed down by the courts referred to in Article 2(a) of the First Protocol and significant judgments handed down by the courts referred to in Article 2(b) of that Protocol,

— the classification and the documentary exploitation of these judgments by the Court of Justice including, as far as necessary, the drawing up of abstracts and translations, and the publication of judgments of particular importance,

— the communication by the Court of Justice of the documentary material to the competent national authorities of the States parties to the Protocol and to the Commission and the Council of the European Communities.

[3228]

PART IV EC MATERIALS

D. INTERNATIONAL COMMERCIAL AND FINANCIAL LAW

COUNCIL DIRECTIVE

of 5 April 1993

on unfair terms in consumer contracts

(93/13/EEC)

NOTES

This Directive has been implemented in the UK by the Unfair Terms in Consumer Contracts Regulations 1999, SI 1999/2083 at **[2191]**.

Date of publication in OJ: OJ L95, 21.4.1993, p 29.

THE COUNCIL OF THE EUROPEAN COMMUNITIES,

Having regard to the Treaty establishing the European Economic Community, and in particular Article 100A thereof,

Having regard to the proposal from the Commission,[1]

In co-operation with the European Parliament,[2]

Having regard to the opinion of the Economic and Social Committee,[3]

Whereas it is necessary to adopt measures with the aim of progressively establishing the internal market before 31 December 1992; whereas the internal market comprises an area without internal frontiers in which goods, persons, services and capital move freely;

Whereas the laws of Member States relating to the terms of contract between the seller of goods or supplier of services, on the one hand, and the consumer of them, on the other hand, show many disparities, with the result that the national markets for the sale of goods and services to consumers differ from each other and that distortions of competition may arise amongst the sellers and suppliers, notably when they sell and supply in other Member States;

Whereas, in particular, the laws of Member States relating to unfair terms in consumer contracts show marked divergences;

Whereas it is the responsibility of the Member States to ensure that contracts concluded with consumers do not contain unfair terms;

Whereas, generally speaking, consumers do not know the rules of law which, in Member States other than their own, govern contracts for the sale of goods or services; whereas this lack of awareness may deter them from direct transactions for the purchase of goods or services in another Member State;

Whereas, in order to facilitate the establishment of the internal market and to safeguard the citizen in his role as consumer when acquiring goods and services under contracts which are governed by the laws of Member States other than his own, it is essential to remove unfair terms from those contracts;

Whereas sellers of goods and suppliers of services will thereby be helped in their task of selling goods and supplying services, both at home and throughout the internal market; whereas competition will thus be stimulated, so contributing to increased choice for Community citizens as consumers;

Whereas the two Community programmes for a consumer protection and information policy[4] underlined the importance of safeguarding consumers in the matter of unfair terms of contract; whereas this protection ought to be provided by laws and regulations which are either harmonised at Community level or adopted directly at that level;

Whereas in accordance with the principle laid down under the heading "Protection of the economic interests of the consumers", as stated in those programmes: "acquirers of goods and services should be protected against the abuse of power by the seller or supplier, in particular against one-sided standard contracts and the unfair exclusion of essential rights in contracts";

Whereas more effective protection of the consumer can be achieved by adopting uniform rules of law in the matter of unfair terms; whereas those rules should apply to all contracts concluded between sellers or suppliers and consumers; whereas as a result inter alia contracts relating to employment, contracts relating to succession rights, contracts relating to rights under family law and contracts relating to the incorporation and organisation of companies or partnership agreements must be excluded from this Directive;

Whereas the consumer must receive equal protection under contracts concluded by word of mouth and written contracts regardless, in the latter case, of whether the terms of the contract are contained in one or more documents;

Whereas, however, as they now stand, national laws allow only partial harmonisation to be envisaged; whereas, in particular, only contractual terms which have not been individually negotiated are covered by this Directive; whereas Member States should have the option, with due regard for the Treaty, to afford consumers a higher level of protection through national provisions that are more stringent than those of this Directive;

Whereas the statutory or regulatory provisions of the Member States which directly or indirectly determine the terms of consumer contracts are presumed not to contain unfair terms; whereas, therefore, it does not appear to be necessary to subject the terms which reflect mandatory statutory or regulatory provisions and the principles or provisions of international conventions to which the Member States or the Community are party; whereas in that respect the wording "mandatory statutory or regulatory provisions" in Article 1(2) also covers rules which, according to the law, shall apply between the contracting parties provided that no other arrangements have been established;

Whereas Member States must however ensure that unfair terms are not included, particularly because this Directive also applies to trades, business or professions of a public nature;

Whereas it is necessary to fix in a general way the criteria for assessing the unfair character of contract terms;

Whereas the assessment, according to the general criteria chosen, of the unfair character of terms, in particular in sale or supply activities of a public nature providing collective services which take account of solidarity among users, must be supplemented by a means of making an overall evaluation of the different interests involved; whereas this constitutes the requirement of good faith; whereas, in making an assessment of good faith, particular regard shall be had to the strength of the bargaining positions of the parties, whether the consumer had an inducement to agree to the term and whether the goods or services were sold or supplied to the special order of the consumer; whereas the requirement of good faith may be satisfied by the seller or supplier where he deals fairly and equitably with the other party whose legitimate interests he has to take into account;

Whereas, for the purposes of this Directive, the annexed list of terms can be of indicative value only and, because of the cause of the minimal character of the Directive, the scope of these terms may be the subject of amplification or more restrictive editing by the Member States in their national laws;

Whereas the nature of goods or services should have an influence on assessing the unfairness of contractual terms;

Whereas, for the purposes of this Directive, assessment of unfair character shall not be made of terms which describe the main subject matter of the contract nor the quality/price ratio of the goods or services supplied; whereas the main subject matter of the contract and the price/quality ratio may nevertheless be taken into account in assessing the fairness of other terms; whereas it follows, inter alia, that in insurance contracts, the terms which clearly define or circumscribe the insured risk and the insurer's liability shall not be subject to such assessment since these restrictions are taken into account in calculating the premium paid by the consumer;

Whereas contracts should be drafted in plain, intelligible language, the consumer should actually be given an opportunity to examine all the terms and, if in doubt, the interpretation most favourable to the consumer should prevail;

Whereas Member States should ensure that unfair terms are not used in contracts concluded with consumers by a seller or supplier and that if, nevertheless, such terms are so used, they will not bind the consumer, and the contract will continue to bind the parties upon those terms if it is capable of continuing in existence without the unfair provisions;

Whereas there is a risk that, in certain cases, the consumer may be deprived of protection under this Directive by designating the law of a non-Member country as the law applicable to the contract; whereas provisions should therefore be included in this Directive designed to avert this risk;

Whereas persons or organisations, if regarded under the law of a Member State as having a legitimate interest in the matter, must have facilities for initiating proceedings concerning terms of contract drawn up for general use in contracts concluded with consumers, and in particular unfair terms, either before a court or before an administrative authority competent to decide upon complaints or to initiate appropriate legal proceedings; whereas this possibility does not, however, entail prior verification of the general conditions obtaining in individual economic sectors;

Whereas the courts or administrative authorities of the Member States must have at their disposal adequate and effective means of preventing the continued application of unfair terms in consumer contracts,

[3229]

NOTES

[1] OJ C73, 24.3.1992, p 7.
[2] OJ C326, 16.12.1991, p 108 and OJ C21, 25.1.1993.
[3] OJ C159, 17.6.1991, p 34.
[4] OJ C92, 25.4.1975 and OJ C133, 3.6.1981, p 1.

HAS ADOPTED THIS DIRECTIVE—

Article 1

1. The purpose of this Directive is to approximate the laws, regulations and administrative provisions of the Member States relating to unfair terms in contracts concluded between a seller or supplier and a consumer.

2. The contractual terms which reflect mandatory statutory or regulatory provisions and the provisions or principles of international conventions to which the Member States or the Community are party, particularly in the transport area, shall not be subject to the provisions of this Directive.

[3230]

Article 2

For the purposes of this Directive—

(a) "unfair terms" means the contractual terms defined in Article 3;
(b) "consumer" means any natural person who, in contracts covered by this Directive, is acting for purposes which are outside his trade, business or profession;
(c) "seller or supplier" means any natural or legal person who, in contracts covered by this Directive, is acting for purposes relating to his trade, business or profession, whether publicly owned or privately owned.

[3231]

Article 3

1. A contractual term which has not been individually negotiated shall be regarded as unfair if, contrary to the requirement of good faith, it causes a significant imbalance in the parties' rights and obligations arising under the contract, to the detriment of the consumer.

2. A term shall always be regarded as not individually negotiated where it has been drafted in advance and the consumer has therefore not been able to influence the substance of the term, particularly in the context of a pre-formulated standard contract.

The fact that certain aspects of a term or one specific term have been individually negotiated shall not exclude the application of this Article to the rest of a contract if an overall assessment of the contract indicates that it is nevertheless a pre-formulated standard contract.

Where any seller or supplier claims that a standard term has been individually negotiated, the burden of proof in this respect shall be incumbent on him.

3. The Annex shall contain an indicative and non-exhaustive list of the terms which may be regarded as unfair.

[3232]

Article 4

1. Without prejudice to Article 7, the unfairness of a contractual term shall be assessed, taking into account the nature of the goods or services for which the contract was concluded and by referring, at the time of conclusion of the contract, to all the circumstances attending the conclusion of the contract and to all the other terms of the contract or of another contract on which it is dependent.

2. Assessment of the unfair nature of the terms shall relate neither to the definition of the main subject matter of the contract nor to the adequacy of the price and remuneration, on the one hand, as against the services or goods supplies in exchange, on the other, in so far as these terms are in plain intelligible language.

[3233]

Article 5

In the case of contracts where all or certain terms offered to the consumer are in writing, these terms must always be drafted in plain, intelligible language. Where there is doubt about the meaning of a term, the interpretation most favourable to the consumer shall prevail. This rule on interpretation shall not apply in the context of the procedures laid down in Article 7(2).

[3234]

Article 6

1. Member States shall lay down that unfair terms used in a contract concluded with a consumer by a seller or supplier shall, as provided for under their national law, not be binding on the consumer and that the contract shall continue to bind the parties upon those terms if it is capable of continuing in existence without the unfair terms.

2. Member States shall take the necessary measures to ensure that the consumer does not lose the protection granted by this Directive by virtue of the choice of the law of a non-Member country as the law applicable to the contract if the latter has a close connection with the territory of the Member States.

[3235]

Article 7

1. Member States shall ensure that, in the interests of consumers and of competitors, adequate and effective means exist to prevent the continued use of unfair terms in contracts concluded with consumers by sellers or suppliers.

2. The means referred to in paragraph 1 shall include provisions whereby persons or organisations, having a legitimate interest under national law in protecting consumers, may take action according to the national law concerned before the courts or before competent administrative bodies for a decision as to whether contractual terms drawn up for general use are unfair, so that they can apply appropriate and effective means to prevent the continued use of such terms.

3. With due regard for national laws, the legal remedies referred to in paragraph 2 may be directed separately or jointly against a number of sellers or suppliers from the same economic sector or their associations which use or recommend the use of the same general contractual terms or similar terms.

[3236]

Article 8

Member States may adopt or retain the most stringent provisions compatible with the Treaty in the area covered by this Directive, to ensure a maximum degree of protection for the consumer.

[3237]

Article 9

The Commission shall present a report to the European Parliament and to the Council concerning the application of this Directive five years at the latest after the date in Article 10(1).

[3238]

Article 10

1. Member States shall bring into force the laws, regulations and administrative provisions necessary to comply with this Directive no later than 31 December 1994. They shall forthwith inform the Commission thereof.

These provisions shall be applicable to all contracts concluded after 31 December 1994.

2. When Member States adopt these measures, they shall contain a reference to this Directive or shall be accompanied by such reference on the occasion of their official publication. The methods of making such a reference shall be laid down by the Member States.

3. Member States shall communicate the main provisions of national law which they adopt in the field covered by this Directive to the Commission.

[3239]

Article 11

This Directive is addressed to the Member States.

[3240]

Done at Luxembourg, 5 April 1993.

ANNEX
TERMS REFERRED TO IN ARTICLE 3(3)

1. Terms which have the object or effect of—
   (a) excluding or limiting the legal liability of a seller or supplier in the event of the death of a consumer or personal injury to the latter resulting from an act or omission of that seller or supplier;
   (b) inappropriately excluding or limiting the legal rights of the consumer *vis-à-vis* the seller or supplier or another party in the event of total or partial non-performance or inadequate performance by the seller or supplier of any of the contractual obligations, including the option of offsetting a debt owed to the seller or supplier against any claim which the consumer may have against him;
   (c) making an agreement binding on the consumer whereas provision of services by the seller or supplier is subject to a condition whose realisation depends on his own will alone;
   (d) permitting the seller or supplier to retain sums paid by the consumer where the latter decides not to conclude or perform the contract, without providing for the consumer to receive compensation of an equivalent amount from the seller or supplier where the latter is the party cancelling the contract;
   (e) requiring any consumer who fails to fulfil his obligation to pay a disproportionately high sum in compensation;
   (f) authorising the seller or supplier to dissolve the contract on a discretionary basis where the same facility is not granted to the consumer, or permitting the seller or supplier to retain the sums paid for services not yet supplied by him where it is the seller or supplier himself who dissolves the contract;
   (g) enabling the seller or supplier to terminate a contract of indeterminate duration without reasonable notice except where there are serious grounds for doing so;
   (h) automatically extending a contract of fixed duration where the consumer does not indicate otherwise, when the deadline fixed for the consumer to express this desire not to extend the contract is unreasonably early;
   (i) irrevocably binding the consumer to terms with which he had no real opportunity of becoming acquainted before the conclusion of the contract;
   (j) enabling the seller or supplier to alter the terms of the contract unilaterally without a valid reason which is specified in the contract;
   (k) enabling the seller or supplier to alter unilaterally without a valid reason any characteristics of the product or service to be provided;
   (l) providing for the price of goods to be determined at the time of delivery or allowing a seller of goods or supplier of services to increase their price without in both cases giving the consumer the corresponding right to cancel the contract if the final price is too high in relation to the price agreed when the contract was concluded;
   (m) giving the seller or supplier the right to determine whether the goods or services supplied are in conformity with the contract, or giving him the exclusive right to interpret any term of the contract;
   (n) limiting the seller's or supplier's obligation to respect commitments undertaken by his agents or making his commitments subject to compliance with a particular formality;
   (o) obliging the consumer to fulfil all his obligations where the seller or supplier does not perform his;
   (p) giving the seller or supplier the possibility of transferring his rights and obligations under the contract, where this may serve to reduce the guarantees for the consumer, without the latter's agreement;
   (q) excluding or hindering the consumer's right to take legal action or exercise any other legal remedy, particularly by requiring the consumer to take disputes exclusively to arbitration not covered by legal provisions, unduly restricting the evidence available to him or imposing on him a burden of proof which, according to the applicable law, should lie with another party to the contract.

2. Scope of subparagraphs (g), (j) and (l)—
   (a) Subparagraph (g) is without hindrance to terms by which a supplier of financial services reserves the right to terminate unilaterally a contract of indeterminate duration without notice where there is a valid reason, provided that the supplier is required to inform the other contracting party or parties thereof immediately.
   (b) Subparagraph (j) is without hindrance to terms under which a supplier of financial

services reserves the right to alter the rate of interest payable by the consumer or due to the latter, or the amount of other charges for financial services without notice where there is a valid reason, provided that the supplier is required to inform the other contracting party or parties thereof at the earliest opportunity and that the latter are free to dissolve the contract immediately.

Subparagraph (j) is also without hindrance to terms under which a seller or supplier reserves the right to alter unilaterally the conditions of a contract of indeterminate duration, provided that he is required to inform the consumer with reasonable notice and that the consumer is free to dissolve the contract.

(c) Subparagraphs (g), (j) and (l) do not apply to—

— transactions in transferable securities, financial instruments and other products or services where the price is linked to fluctuations in a stock exchange quotation or index or a financial market rate that the seller or supplier does not control;

— contracts for the purchase or sale of foreign currency, traveller's cheques or international money orders denominated in foreign currency.

(d) Subparagraph (l) is without hindrance to price-indexation clauses, where lawful, provided that the method by which prices vary is explicitly described.

[3241]

EUROPEAN PARLIAMENT AND COUNCIL DIRECTIVE

of 19 May 1998

on settlement finality in payment and securities settlement systems

(98/26/EC)

NOTES

Date of publication in OJ: OJ L166, 11.6.1998, p 45.

THE EUROPEAN PARLIAMENT AND THE COUNCIL OF THE EUROPEAN UNION,

Having regard to the Treaty establishing the European Community, and in particular Article 100a thereof,

Having regard to the proposal from the Commission,[1]

Having regard to the opinion of the European Monetary Institute,[2]

Having regard to the opinion of the Economic and Social Committee,[3]

Acting in accordance with the procedure laid down in Article 189b of the Treaty,[4]

(1) Whereas the Lamfalussy report of 1990 to the Governors of the central banks of the Group of Ten Countries demonstrated the important systemic risk inherent in payment systems which operate on the basis of several legal types of payment netting, in particular multilateral netting; whereas the reduction of legal risks associated with participation in real time gross settlement systems is of paramount importance, given the increasing development of these systems;

(2) Whereas it is also of the utmost importance to reduce the risk associated with participation in securities settlement systems, in particular where there is a close connection between such systems and payment systems;

(3) Whereas this Directive aims at contributing to the efficient and cost effective operation of cross-border payment and securities settlement arrangements in the Community, which reinforces the freedom of movement of capital in the internal market; whereas this Directive thereby follows up the progress made towards completion of the internal market, in particular towards the freedom to provide services and liberalisation of capital movements, with a view to the realisation of Economic and Monetary Union;

(4) Whereas it is desirable that the laws of the Member States should aim to minimise the disruption to a system caused by insolvency proceedings against a participant in that system;

(5) Whereas a proposal for a Directive on the reorganisation and winding-up of credit institutions submitted in 1985 and amended on 8 February 1988 is still pending before the Council; whereas the Convention on Insolvency Proceedings drawn up on 23 November 1995 by the Member States meeting within the Council explicitly excludes insurance undertakings, credit institutions and investment firms;

(6) Whereas this Directive is intended to cover payment and securities settlement systems of a domestic as well as of a cross-border nature; whereas the Directive is applicable to

PART IV
EC MATERIALS

Community systems and to collateral security constituted by their participants, be they Community or third country participants, in connection with participation in these systems;

(7) Whereas Member States may apply the provisions of this Directive to their domestic institutions which participate directly in third country systems and to collateral security provided in connection with participation in such systems;

(8) Whereas Member States should be allowed to designate as a system covered by this Directive a system whose main activity is the settlement of securities even if the system to a limited extent also deals with commodity derivatives;

(9) Whereas the reduction of systemic risk requires in particular the finality of settlement and the enforceability of collateral security; whereas collateral security is meant to comprise all means provided by a participant to the other participants in the payment and/or securities settlement systems to secure rights and obligations in connection with that system, including repurchase agreements, statutory liens and fiduciary transfers; whereas regulation in national law of the kind of collateral security which can be used should not be affected by the definition of collateral security in this Directive;

(10) Whereas this Directive, by covering collateral security provided in connection with operations of the central banks of the Member States functioning as central banks, including monetary policy operations, assists the European Monetary Institute in its task of promoting the efficiency of cross-border payments with a view to the preparation of the third stage of Economic and Monetary Union and thereby contributes to developing the necessary legal framework in which the future European central bank may develop its policy;

(11) Whereas transfer orders and their netting should be legally enforceable under all Member States' jurisdictions and binding on third parties;

(12) Whereas rules on finality of netting should not prevent systems testing, before the netting takes place, whether orders that have entered the system comply with the rules of that system and allow the settlement of that system to take place;

(13) Whereas nothing in this Directive should prevent a participant or a third party from exercising any right or claim resulting from the underlying transaction which they may have in law to recovery or restitution in respect of a transfer order which has entered a system, e g in case of fraud or technical error, as long as this leads neither to the unwinding of netting nor to the revocation of the transfer order in the system;

(14) Whereas it is necessary to ensure that transfer orders cannot be revoked after a moment defined by the rules of the system;

(15) Whereas it is necessary that a Member State should immediately notify other Member States of the opening of insolvency proceedings against a participant in the system;

(16) Whereas insolvency proceedings should not have a retroactive effect on the rights and obligations of participants in a system;

(17) Whereas, in the event of insolvency proceedings against a participant in a system, this Directive furthermore aims at determining which insolvency law is applicable to the rights and obligations of that participant in connection with its participation in a system;

(18) Whereas collateral security should be insulated from the effects of the insolvency law applicable to the insolvent participant;

(19) Whereas the provisions of Article 9(2) should only apply to a register, account or centralised deposit system which evidences the existence of proprietary rights in or for the delivery or transfer of the securities concerned;

(20) Whereas the provisions of Article 9(2) are intended to ensure that if the participant, the central bank of a Member State or the future European central bank has a valid and effective collateral security as determined under the law of the Member State where the relevant register, account or centralised deposit system is located, then the validity and enforceability of that collateral security as against that system (and the operator thereof) and against any other person claiming directly or indirectly through it, should be determined solely under the law of that Member State;

(21) Whereas the provisions of Article 9(2) are not intended to prejudice the operation and effect of the law of the Member State under which the securities are constituted or of the law of the Member State where the securities may otherwise be located (including, without limitation, the law concerning the creation, ownership or transfer of such securities or of rights in such securities) and should not be interpreted to mean that any such collateral security will be directly enforceable or be capable of being recognised in any such Member State otherwise than in accordance with the law of that Member State;

(22) Whereas it is desirable that Member States endeavour to establish sufficient links between all the securities settlement systems covered by this Directive with a view towards promoting maximum transparency and legal certainty of transactions relating to securities;

(23) Whereas the adoption of this Directive constitutes the most appropriate way of realising the abovementioned objectives and does not go beyond what is necessary to achieve them,

[3242]

NOTES

[1] OJ C207, 18.7.1996, p 13, and OJ C259, 26.8.1997, p 6.
[2] Opinion delivered on 21 November 1996.
[3] OJ C56, 24.2.1997, p 1.
[4] Opinion of the European Parliament of 9 April 1997 (OJ C132, 28.4.1997, p 74), Council Common Position of 13 October 1997 (OJ C375, 10.12.1997, p 34) and Decision of the European Parliament of 29 January 1998 (OJ C56, 23.2.1998). Council Decision of 27 April 1998.

HAVE ADOPTED THIS DIRECTIVE—

SECTION I
SCOPE AND DEFINITIONS

Article 1

The provisions of this Directive shall apply to—

(a) any system as defined in Article 2(a), governed by the law of a Member State and operating in any currency, the ecu or in various currencies which the system converts one against another;
(b) any participant in such a system;
(c) collateral security provided in connection with—
 — participation in a system, or
 — operations of the central banks of the Member States in their functions as central banks.

[3243]

Article 2

For the purpose of this Directive—

(a) 'system' shall mean a formal arrangement—
 — between three or more participants, without counting a possible settlement agent, a possible central counterparty, a possible clearing house or a possible indirect participant, with common rules and standardised arrangements for the execution of transfer orders between the participants,
 — governed by the law of a Member State chosen by the participants; the participants may, however, only choose the law of a Member State in which at least one of them has its head office, and
 — designated, without prejudice to other more stringent conditions of general application laid down by national law, as a system and notified to the Commission by the Member State whose law is applicable, after that Member State is satisfied as to the adequacy of the rules of the system.

 Subject to the conditions in the first subparagraph, a Member State may designate as a system such a formal arrangement whose business consists of the execution of transfer orders as defined in the second indent of (i) and which to a limited extent executes orders relating to other financial instruments, when that Member State considers that such a designation is warranted on grounds of systemic risk.

 A Member State may also on a case-by-case basis designate as a system such a formal arrangement between two participants, without counting a possible settlement agent, a possible central counterparty, a possible clearing house or a possible indirect participant, when that Member State considers that such a designation is warranted on grounds of systemic risk;

(b) 'institution' shall mean—
 — a credit institution as defined in the first indent of Article 1 of Directive 77/780/EEC[1] including the institutions set out in the list in Article 2(2) thereof, or
 — an investment firm as defined in point 2 of Article 1 of Directive 93/22/EEC[2] excluding the institutions set out in the list in Article 2(2)(a) to (k) thereof, or
 — public authorities and publicly guaranteed undertakings, or
 — any undertaking whose head office is outside the Community and whose functions correspond to those of the Community credit institutions or investment firms as defined in the first and second indent,

 which participates in a system and which is responsible for discharging the financial obligations arising from transfer orders within that system.

PART IV EC MATERIALS

If a system is supervised in accordance with national legislation and only executes transfer orders as defined in the second indent of (i), as well as payments resulting from such orders, a Member State may decide that undertakings which participate in such a system and which have responsibility for discharging the financial obligations arising from transfer orders within this system, can be considered institutions, provided that at least three participants of this system are covered by the categories referred to in the first subparagraph and that such a decision is warranted on grounds of systemic risk;

(c) 'central counterparty' shall mean an entity which is interposed between the institutions in a system and which acts as the exclusive counterparty of these institutions with regard to their transfer orders;

(d) 'settlement agent' shall mean an entity providing to institutions and/or a central counterparty participating in systems, settlement accounts through which transfer orders within such systems are settled and, as the case may be, extending credit to those institutions and/or central counterparties for settlement purposes;

(e) 'clearing house' shall mean an entity responsible for the calculation of the net positions of institutions, a possible central counterparty and/or a possible settlement agent;

(f) 'participant' shall mean an institution, a central counterparty, a settlement agent or a clearing house.

According to the rules of the system, the same participant may act as a central counterparty, a settlement agent or a clearing house or carry out part or all of these tasks.

A Member State may decide that for the purposes of this Directive an indirect participant may be considered a participant if it is warranted on the grounds of systemic risk and on condition that the indirect participant is known to the system;

(g) 'indirect participant' shall mean a credit institution as defined in the first indent of (b) with a contractual relationship with an institution participating in a system executing transfer orders as defined in the first indent of (i) which enables the abovementioned credit institution to pass transfer orders through the system;

(h) 'securities' shall mean all instruments referred to in section B of the Annex to Directive 93/22/EEC;

(i) 'transfer order' shall mean—

— any instruction by a participant to place at the disposal of a recipient an amount of money by means of a book entry on the accounts of a credit institution, a central bank or a settlement agent, or any instruction which results in the assumption or discharge of a payment obligation as defined by the rules of the system, or

— an instruction by a participant to transfer the title to, or interest in, a security or securities by means of a book entry on a register, or otherwise;

(j) 'insolvency proceedings' shall mean any collective measure provided for in the law of a Member State, or a third country, either to wind up the participant or to reorganise it, where such measure involves the suspending of, or imposing limitations on, transfers or payments;

(k) 'netting' shall mean the conversion into one net claim or one net obligation of claims and obligations resulting from transfer orders which a participant or participants either issue to, or receive from, one or more other participants with the result that only a net claim can be demanded or a net obligation be owed;

(l) 'settlement account' shall mean an account at a central bank, a settlement agent or a central counterparty used to hold funds and securities and to settle transactions between participants in a system;

(m) 'collateral security' shall mean all realisable assets provided under a pledge (including money provided under a pledge), a repurchase or similar agreement, or otherwise, for the purpose of securing rights and obligations potentially arising in connection with a system, or provided to central banks of the Member States or to the future European central bank.

[3244]

NOTES

1 First Council Directive 77/780/EEC of 12 December 1977 on the coordination of the laws, regulations and administrative provisions relating to the taking up and pursuit of the business of credit institutions (OJ L322, 17.12.1977, p 30). Directive as last amended by Directive 96/13/EC (OJ L66, 16.3.1996, p 15).

2 Council Directive 93/22/EEC of 10 May 1993 on investment services in the securities field (OJ L141, 11.6.1993, p 27). Directive as last amended by Directive 97/9/EC (OJ L84, 26.3.1997, p 22).

SECTION II
NETTING AND TRANSFER ORDERS

Article 3

1. Transfer orders and netting shall be legally enforceable and, even in the event of insolvency proceedings against a participant, shall be binding on third parties, provided that transfer orders were entered into a system before the moment of opening of such insolvency proceedings as defined in Article 6(1).

Where, exceptionally, transfer orders are entered into a system after the moment of opening of insolvency proceedings and are carried out on the day of opening of such proceedings, they shall be legally enforceable and binding on third parties only if, after the time of settlement, the settlement agent, the central counterparty or the clearing house can prove that they were not aware, nor should have been aware, of the opening of such proceedings.

2. No law, regulation, rule or practice on the setting aside of contracts and transactions concluded before the moment of opening of insolvency proceedings, as defined in Article 6(1) shall lead to the unwinding of a netting.

3. The moment of entry of a transfer order into a system shall be defined by the rules of that system. If there are conditions laid down in the national law governing the system as to the moment of entry, the rules of that system must be in accordance with such conditions.

[3245]

Article 4

Member States may provide that the opening of insolvency proceedings against a participant shall not prevent funds or securities available on the settlement account of that participant from being used to fulfil that participant's obligations in the system on the day of the opening of the insolvency proceedings. Furthermore, Member States may also provide that such a participant's credit facility connected to the system be used against available, existing collateral security to fulfil that participant's obligations in the system.

[3246]

Article 5

A transfer order may not be revoked by a participant in a system, nor by a third party, from the moment defined by the rules of that system.

[3247]

SECTION III
PROVISIONS CONCERNING INSOLVENCY PROCEEDINGS

Article 6

1. For the purpose of this Directive, the moment of opening of insolvency proceedings shall be the moment when the relevant judicial or administrative authority handed down its decision.

2. When a decision has been taken in accordance with paragraph 1, the relevant judicial or administrative authority shall immediately notify that decision to the appropriate authority chosen by its Member State.

3. The Member State referred to in paragraph 2 shall immediately notify other Member States.

[3248]

Article 7

Insolvency proceedings shall not have retroactive effects on the rights and obligations of a participant arising from, or in connection with, its participation in a system earlier than the moment of opening of such proceedings as defined in Article 6(1).

[3249]

Article 8

In the event of insolvency proceedings being opened against a participant in a system, the rights and obligations arising from, or in connection with, the participation of that participant shall be determined by the law governing that system.

[3250]

SECTION IV
INSULATION OF THE RIGHTS OF HOLDERS OF COLLATERAL SECURITY FROM THE EFFECTS OF THE INSOLVENCY OF THE PROVIDER

Article 9

1. The rights of—

— a participant to collateral security provided to it in connection with a system, and

— central banks of the Member States or the future European central bank to collateral security provided to them,

shall not be affected by insolvency proceedings against the participant or counterparty to central banks of the Member States or the future European central bank which provided the collateral security. Such collateral security may be realised for the satisfaction of these rights.

2. Where securities (including rights in securities) are provided as collateral security to participants and/or central banks of the Member States or the future European central bank as described in paragraph 1, and their right (or that of any nominee, agent or third party acting on their behalf) with respect to the securities is legally recorded on a register, account or centralised deposit system located in a Member State, the determination of the rights of such entities as holders of collateral security in relation to those securities shall be governed by the law of that Member State.

[3251]

SECTION V
FINAL PROVISIONS

Article 10

Member States shall specify the systems which are to be included in the scope of this Directive and shall notify them to the Commission and inform the Commission of the authorities they have chosen in accordance with Article 6(2).

The system shall indicate to the Member State whose law is applicable the participants in the system, including any possible indirect participants, as well as any change in them.

In addition to the indication provided for in the second subparagraph, Member States may impose supervision or authorisation requirements on systems which fall under their jurisdiction.

Anyone with a legitimate interest may require an institution to inform him of the systems in which it participates and to provide information about the main rules governing the functioning of those systems.

[3252]

Article 11

1. Member States shall bring into force the laws, regulations and administrative provisions necessary to comply with this Directive before 11 December 1999. They shall forthwith inform the Commission thereof.

When Member States adopt these measures, they shall contain a reference to this Directive or shall be accompanied by such reference on the occasion of their official publication. The methods of making such a reference shall be laid down by the Member States.

2. Member States shall communicate to the Commission the text of the provisions of domestic law which they adopt in the field governed by this Directive. In this Communication, Member States shall provide a table of correspondence showing the national provisions which exist or are introduced in respect of each Article of this Directive.

[3253]

Article 12

No later than three years after the date mentioned in Article 11(1), the Commission shall present a report to the European Parliament and the Council on the application of this Directive, accompanied where appropriate by proposals for its revision.

[3254]

Article 13

This Directive shall enter into force on the day of its publication in the *Official Journal of the European Communities*.

[3255]

Article 14

This Directive is addressed to the Member States.

[3256]

Done at Brussels, 19 May 1998.

DIRECTIVE OF THE EUROPEAN PARLIAMENT AND OF THE COUNCIL

of 8 June 2000

on certain legal aspects of information society services, in particular electronic commerce, in the Internal Market (Directive on electronic commerce)

(2000/31/EC)

NOTES

Date of publication in OJ: OJ L178, 17.7.2000, p 1.

THE EUROPEAN PARLIAMENT AND THE COUNCIL OF THE EUROPEAN UNION,

Having regard to the Treaty establishing the European Community, and in particular Articles 47(2), 55 and 95 thereof,

Having regard to the proposal from the Commission,[1]

Having regard to the opinion of the Economic and Social Committee,[2]

Acting in accordance with the procedure laid down in Article 251 of the Treaty,[3]

Whereas—

(1) The European Union is seeking to forge ever closer links between the States and peoples of Europe, to ensure economic and social progress; in accordance with Article 14(2) of the Treaty, the internal market comprises an area without internal frontiers in which the free movements of goods, services and the freedom of establishment are ensured; the development of information society services within the area without internal frontiers is vital to eliminating the barriers which divide the European peoples.

(2) The development of electronic commerce within the information society offers significant employment opportunities in the Community, particularly in small and medium-sized enterprises, and will stimulate economic growth and investment in innovation by European companies, and can also enhance the competitiveness of European industry, provided that everyone has access to the Internet.

(3) Community law and the characteristics of the Community legal order are a vital asset to enable European citizens and operators to take full advantage, without consideration of borders, of the opportunities afforded by electronic commerce; this Directive therefore has the purpose of ensuring a high level of Community legal integration in order to establish a real area without internal borders for information society services.

(4) It is important to ensure that electronic commerce could fully benefit from the internal market and therefore that, as with Council Directive 89/552/EEC of 3 October 1989 on the coordination of certain provisions laid down by law, regulation or administrative action in Member States concerning the pursuit of television broadcasting activities,[4] a high level of Community integration is achieved.

(5) The development of information society services within the Community is hampered by a number of legal obstacles to the proper functioning of the internal market which make less attractive the exercise of the freedom of establishment and the freedom to provide services; these obstacles arise from divergences in legislation and from the legal uncertainty as to which national rules apply to such services; in the absence of coordination and adjustment of legislation in the relevant areas, obstacles might be justified in the light of the case-law of the Court of Justice of the European Communities; legal uncertainty exists with regard to the extent to which Member States may control services originating from another Member State.

(6) In the light of Community objectives, of Articles 43 and 49 of the Treaty and of secondary Community law, these obstacles should be eliminated by coordinating certain national laws and by clarifying certain legal concepts at Community level to the extent necessary for the proper functioning of the internal market; by dealing only with certain

specific matters which give rise to problems for the internal market, this Directive is fully consistent with the need to respect the principle of subsidiarity as set out in Article 5 of the Treaty.

(7) In order to ensure legal certainty and consumer confidence, this Directive must lay down a clear and general framework to cover certain legal aspects of electronic commerce in the internal market.

(8) The objective of this Directive is to create a legal framework to ensure the free movement of information society services between Member States and not to harmonise the field of criminal law as such.

(9) The free movement of information society services can in many cases be a specific reflection in Community law of a more general principle, namely freedom of expression as enshrined in Article 10(1) of the Convention for the Protection of Human Rights and Fundamental Freedoms, which has been ratified by all the Member States; for this reason, directives covering the supply of information society services must ensure that this activity may be engaged in freely in the light of that Article, subject only to the restrictions laid down in paragraph 2 of that Article and in Article 46(1) of the Treaty; this Directive is not intended to affect national fundamental rules and principles relating to freedom of expression.

(10) In accordance with the principle of proportionality, the measures provided for in this Directive are strictly limited to the minimum needed to achieve the objective of the proper functioning of the internal market; where action at Community level is necessary, and in order to guarantee an area which is truly without internal frontiers as far as electronic commerce is concerned, the Directive must ensure a high level of protection of objectives of general interest, in particular the protection of minors and human dignity, consumer protection and the protection of public health; according to Article 152 of the Treaty, the protection of public health is an essential component of other Community policies.

(11) This Directive is without prejudice to the level of protection for, in particular, public health and consumer interests, as established by Community acts; amongst others, CouncilDirective 93/13/EEC of 5 April 1993 on unfair terms in consumer contracts[5] and Directive 97/7/EC of the European Parliament and of the Council of 20 May 1997 on the protection of consumers in respect of distance contracts[6] form a vital element for protecting consumers in contractual matters; those Directives also apply in their entirety to information society services; that same Community acquis, which is fully applicable to information society services, also embraces in particular Council Directive 84/450/EEC of 10 September 1984 concerning misleading and comparative advertising,[7] Council Directive 87/102/EEC of 22 December 1986 for the approximation of the laws, regulations and administrative provisions of the Member States concerning consumer credit,[8] Council Directive 93/22/EEC of 10 May 1993 on investment services in the securities field,[9] Council Directive 90/314/EEC of 13 June 1990 on package travel, package holidays and package tours,[10] Directive 98/6/EC of the European Parliament and of the Council of 16 February 1998 on consumer production in the indication of prices of products offered to consumers,[11] Council Directive 92/59/EEC of 29 June 1992 on general product safety,[12] Directive 94/47/EC of the European Parliament and of the Council of 26 October 1994 on the protection of purchasers in respect of certain aspects on contracts relating to the purchase of the right to use immovable properties on a timeshare basis,[13] Directive 98/27/EC of the European Parliament and of the Council of 19 May 1998 on injunctions for the protection of consumers' interests,[14] Council Directive 85/374/EEC of 25 July 1985 on the approximation of the laws, regulations and administrative provisions concerning liability for defective products,[15] Directive 1999/44/EC of the European Parliament and of the Council of 25 May 1999 on certain aspects of the sale of consumer goods and associated guarantees,[16] the future Directive of the European Parliament and of the Council concerning the distance marketing of consumer financial services and Council Directive 92/28/EEC of 31 March 1992 on the advertising of medicinal products;[17] this Directive should be without prejudice to Directive 98/43/EC of the European Parliament and of the Council of 6 July 1998 on the approximation of the laws, regulations and administrative provisions of the Member States relating to the advertising and sponsorship of tobacco products[18] adopted within the framework of the internal market, or to directives on the protection of public health; this Directive complements information requirements established by the abovementioned Directives and in particular Directive 97/7/EC.

(12) It is necessary to exclude certain activities from the scope of this Directive, on the grounds that the freedom to provide services in these fields cannot, at this stage, be guaranteed under the Treaty or existing secondary legislation; excluding these activities does not preclude any instruments which might prove necessary for the proper functioning of the internal market; taxation, particularly value added tax imposed on a large number of the services covered by this Directive, must be excluded from the scope of this Directive.

(13) This Directive does not aim to establish rules on fiscal obligations nor does it pre-empt the drawing up of Community instruments concerning fiscal aspects of electronic commerce.

(14) The protection of individuals with regard to the processing of personal data is solely governed by Directive 95/46/EC of the European Parliament and of the Council of 24 October 1995 on the protection of individuals with regard to the processing of personal data and on the free movement of such data[19] and Directive 97/66/EC of the European Parliament and of the Council of 15 December 1997 concerning the processing of personal data and the protection of privacy in the telecommunications sector[20] which are fully applicable to information society services; these Directives already establish a Community legal framework in the field of personal data and therefore it is not necessary to cover this issue in this Directive in order to ensure the smooth functioning of the internal market, in particular the free movement of personal data between Member States; the implementation and application of this Directive should be made in full compliance with the principles relating to the protection of personal data, in particular as regards unsolicited commercial communication and the liability of intermediaries; this Directive cannot prevent the anonymous use of open networks such as the Internet.

(15) The confidentiality of communications is guaranteed by Article 5 Directive 97/66/EC; in accordance with that Directive, Member States must prohibit any kind of interception or surveillance of such communications by others than the senders and receivers, except when legally authorised.

(16) The exclusion of gambling activities from the scope of application of this Directive covers only games of chance, lotteries and betting transactions, which involve wagering a stake with monetary value; this does not cover promotional competitions or games where the purpose is to encourage the sale of goods or services and where payments, if they arise, serve only to acquire the promoted goods or services.

(17) The definition of information society services already exists in Community law in Directive 98/34/EC of the European Parliament and of the Council of 22 June 1998 laying down a procedure for the provision of information in the field of technical standards and regulations and of rules on information society services[21] and in Directive 98/84/EC of the European Parliament and of the Council of 20 November 1998 on the legal protection of services based on, or consisting of, conditional access;[22] this definition covers any service normally provided for remuneration, at a distance, by means of electronic equipment for the processing (including digital compression) and storage of data, and at the individual request of a recipient of a service; those services referred to in the indicative list in Annex V to Directive 98/34/EC which do not imply data processing and storage are not covered by this definition.

(18) Information society services span a wide range of economic activities which take place on-line; these activities can, in particular, consist of selling goods on-line; activities such as the delivery of goods as such or the provision of services off-line are not covered; information society services are not solely restricted to services giving rise to on-line contracting but also, in so far as they represent an economic activity, extend to services which are not remunerated by those who receive them, such as those offering non-line information or commercial communications, or those providing tools allowing for search, access and retrieval of data; information society services also include services consisting of the transmission of information via a communication network, in providing access to a communication network or in hosting information provided by a recipient of the service; television broadcasting within the meaning of Directive EEC/89/552 and radio broadcasting are not information society services because they are not provided at individual request; by contrast, services which are transmitted point to point, such as video-on-demand or the provision of commercial communications by electronic mail are information society services; the use of electronic mail or equivalent individual communications for instance by natural persons acting outside their trade, business or profession including their use for the conclusion of contracts between such persons is not an information society service; the contractual relationship between an employee and his employer is not an information society service; activities which by their very nature cannot be carried out at a distance and by electronic means, such as the statutory auditing of company accounts or medical advice requiring the physical examination of a patient are not information society services.

(19) The place at which a service provider is established should be determined in conformity with the case-law of the Court of Justice according to which the concept of establishment involves the actual pursuit of an economic activity through a fixed establishment for an indefinite period; this requirement is also fulfilled where a company is constituted for a given period; the place of establishment of a company providing services via an Internet website is not the place at which the technology supporting its website is located or the place at which its website is accessible but the place where it pursues its economic activity; in cases where a provider has several places of establishment it is important to determine from which place of establishment the service concerned is provided; in cases

where it is difficult to determine from which of several places of establishment a given service is provided, this is the place where the provider has the centre of his activities relating to this particular service.

(20) The definition of "recipient of a service" covers all types of usage of information society services, both by persons who provide information on open networks such as the Internet and by persons who seek information on the Internet for private or professional reasons.

(21) The scope of the coordinated field is without prejudice to future Community harmonisation relating to information society services and to future legislation adopted at national level in accordance with Community law; the coordinated field covers only requirements relating to on-line activities such as on-line information, on-line advertising, on-line shopping, on-line contracting and does not concern Member States' legal requirements relating to goods such as safety standards, labelling obligations, or liability for goods, or Member States' requirements relating to the delivery or the transport of goods, including the distribution of medicinal products; the coordinated field does not cover the exercise of rights of pre-emption by public authorities concerning certain goods such as works of art.

(22) Information society services should be supervised at the source of the activity, in order to ensure an effective protection of public interest objectives; to that end, it is necessary to ensure that the competent authority provides such protection not only for the citizens of its own country but for all Community citizens; in order to improve mutual trust between Member States, it is essential to state clearly this responsibility on the part of the Member State where the services originate; moreover, in order to effectively guarantee freedom to provide services and legal certainty for suppliers and recipients of services, such information society services should in principle be subject to the law of the Member State in which the service provider is established.

(23) This Directive neither aims to establish additional rules on private international law relating to conflicts of law nor does it deal with the jurisdiction of Courts; provisions of the applicable law designated by rules of private international law must not restrict the freedom to provide information society services as established in this Directive.

(24) In the context of this Directive, notwithstanding the rule on the control at source of information society services, it is legitimate under the conditions established in this Directive for Member States to take measures to restrict the free movement of information society services.

(25) National courts, including civil courts, dealing with private law disputes can take measures to derogate from the freedom to provide information society services in conformity with conditions established in this Directive.

(26) Member States, in conformity with conditions established in this Directive, may apply their national rules on criminal law and criminal proceedings with a view to taking all investigative and other measures necessary for the detection and prosecution of criminal offences, without there being a need to notify such measures to the Commission.

(27) This Directive, together with the future Directive of the European Parliament and of the Council concerning the distance marketing of consumer financial services, contributes to the creating of a legal framework for the on-line provision of financial services; this Directive does not pre-empt future initiatives in the area of financial services in particular with regard to the harmonisation of rules of conduct in this field; the possibility for Member States, established in this Directive, under certain circumstances of restricting the freedom to provide information society services in order to protect consumers also covers measures in the area of financial services in particular measures aiming at protecting investors.

(28) The Member States' obligation not to subject access to the activity of an information society service provider to prior authorisation does not concern postal services covered by Directive 97/67/EC of the European Parliament and of the Council of 15 December 1997 on common rules for the development of the internal market of Community postal services and the improvement of quality of service[23] consisting of the physical delivery of a printed electronic mail message and does not affect voluntary accreditation systems, in particular for providers of electronic signature certification service.

(29) Commercial communications are essential for the financing of information society services and for developing a wide variety of new, charge-free services; in the interests of consumer protection and fair trading, commercial communications, including discounts, promotional offers and promotional competitions or games, must meet a number of transparency requirements; these requirements are without prejudice to Directive 97/7/EC; this Directive should not affect existing Directives on commercial communications, in particular Directive 98/43/EC.

(30) The sending of unsolicited commercial communications by electronic mail may be undesirable for consumers and information society service providers and may disrupt the smooth functioning of interactive networks; the question of consent by recipient of certain

forms of unsolicited commercial communications is not addressed by this Directive, but has already been addressed, in particular, by Directive 97/7/EC and by Directive 97/66/EC; in Member States which authorise unsolicited commercial communications by electronic mail, the setting up of appropriate industry filtering initiatives should be encouraged and facilitated; in addition it is necessary that in any event unsolicited commercial communities are clearly identifiable as such in order to improve transparency and to facilitate the functioning of such industry initiatives; unsolicited commercial communications by electronic mail should not result in additional communication costs for the recipient.

(31) Member States which allow the sending of unsolicited commercial communications by electronic mail without prior consent of the recipient by service providers established in their territory have to ensure that the service providers consult regularly and respect the opt-out registers in which natural persons not wishing to receive such commercial communications can register themselves.

(32) In order to remove barriers to the development of cross-border services within the Community which members of the regulated professions might offer on the Internet, it is necessary that compliance be guaranteed at Community level with professional rules aiming, in particular, to protect consumers or public health; codes of conduct at Community level would be the best means of determining the rules on professional ethics applicable to commercial communication; the drawing-up or, where appropriate, the adaptation of such rules should be encouraged without prejudice to the autonomy of professional bodies and associations.

(33) This Directive complements Community law and national law relating to regulated professions maintaining a coherent set of applicable rules in this field.

(34) Each Member State is to amend its legislation containing requirements, and in particular requirements as to form, which are likely to curb the use of contracts by electronic means; the examination of the legislation requiring such adjustment should be systematic and should cover all the necessary stages and acts of the contractual process, including the filing of the contract; the result of this amendment should be to make contracts concluded electronically workable; the legal effect of electronic signatures is dealt with by Directive 1999/93/EC of the European Parliament and of the Council of 13 December 1999 on a Community framework for electronic signatures;[24] the acknowledgement of receipt by a service provider may take the form of the on-line provision of the service paid for.

(35) This Directive does not affect Member States' possibility of maintaining or establishing general or specific legal requirements for contracts which can be fulfilled by electronic means, in particular requirements concerning secure electronic signatures.

(36) Member States may maintain restrictions for the use of electronic contracts with regard to contracts requiring by law the involvement of courts, public authorities, or professions exercising public authority; this possibility also covers contracts which require the involvement of courts, public authorities, or professions exercising public authority in order to have an effect with regard to third parties as well as contracts requiring by law certification or attestation by a notary.

(37) Member States' obligation.to remove obstacles to the use of electronic contracts concerns only obstacles resulting from legal requirements and not practical obstacles resulting from the impossibility of using electronic means in certain cases.

(38) Member States' obligation to remove obstacles to the use of electronic contracts is to be implemented in conformity with legal requirements for contracts enshrined in Community law.

(39) The exceptions to the provisions concerning the contracts concluded exclusively by electronic mail or by equivalent individual communications provided for by this Directive, in relation to information to be provided and the placing of orders, should not enable, as a result, the by-passing of those provisions by providers of information society services.

(40) Both existing and emerging disparities in Member States' legislation and case-law concerning liability of service providers acting as intermediaries prevent the smooth functioning of the internal market, in particular by impairing the development of cross-border services and producing distortions of competition; service providers have a duty to act, under certain circumstances, with a view to preventing or stopping illegal activities; this Directive should constitute the appropriate basis for the development of rapid and reliable procedures for removing and disabling access to illegal information; such mechanisms could be developed on the basis of voluntary agreements between all parties concerned and should be encouraged by Member States; it is in the interest of all parties involved in the provision of information society services to adopt and implement such procedures; the provisions of this Directive relating to liability should not preclude the development and effective operation, by the different interested parties, of technical systems of protection and identification and of technical surveillance instruments made possible by digital technology within the limits laid down by Directives 95/46/EC and 97/66/EC.

(41) This Directive strikes a balance between the different interests at stake and establishes principles upon which industry agreements and standards can be based.

(42) The exemptions from liability established in this Directive cover only cases where the activity of the information society service provider is limited to the technical process of operating and giving access to a communication network over which information made available by third parties is transmitted or temporarily stored, for the sole purpose of making the transmission more efficient; this activity is of a mere technical, automatic and passive nature, which implies that the information society service provider has neither knowledge of nor control over the information which is transmitted or stored.

(43) A service provider can benefit from the exemptions for "mere conduit" and for "caching" when he is in no way involved with the information transmitted; this requires among other things that he does not modify the information that he transmits; this requirement does not cover manipulations of a technical nature which take place in the course of the transmission as they do not alter the integrity of the information contained in the transmission.

(44) A service provider who deliberately collaborates with one of the recipients of his service in order to undertake illegal acts goes beyond the activities of "mere conduit" or "caching" and as a result cannot benefit from the liability exemptions established for these activities.

(45) The limitations of the liability of intermediary service providers established in this Directive do not affect the possibility of injunctions of different kinds; such injunctions can in particular consist of orders by courts or administrative authorities requiring the termination or prevention of any infringement, including the removal of illegal information or the disabling of access to it.

(46) In order to benefit from a limitation of liability, the provider of an information society service, consisting of the storage of information, upon obtaining actual knowledge or awareness of illegal activities has to act expeditiously to remove or to disable access to the information concerned; the removal or disabling of access has to be undertaken in the observance of the principle of freedom of expression and of procedures established for this purpose at national level; this Directive does not affect Member States' possibility of establishing specific requirements which must be fulfilled expeditiously prior to the removal or disabling of information.

(47) Member States are prevented from imposing a monitoring obligation on service providers only with respect to obligations of a general nature; this does not concern monitoring obligations in a specific case and, in particular, does not affect orders by national authorities in accordance with national legislation.

(48) This Directive does not affect the possibility for Member States of requiring service providers, who host information provided by recipients of their service, to apply duties of care, which can reasonably be expected from them and which are specified by national law, in order to detect and prevent certain types of illegal activities.

(49) Member States and the Commission are to encourage the drawing-up of codes of conduct; this is not to impair the voluntary nature of such codes and the possibility for interested parties of deciding freely whether to adhere to such codes.

(50) It is important that the proposed directive on the harmonisation of certain aspects of copyright and related rights in the information society and this Directive come into force within a similar time scale with a view to establishing a clear framework of rules relevant to the issue of liability of intermediaries for copyright and relating rights infringements at Community level.

(51) Each Member State should be required, where necessary, to amend any legislation which is liable to hamper the use of schemes for the out-of-court settlement of disputes through electronic channels; the result of this amendment must be to make the functioning of such schemes genuinely and effectively possible in law and in practice, even across borders.

(52) The effective exercise of the freedoms of the internal market makes it necessary to guarantee victims effective access to means of settling disputes; damage which may arise in connection with information society services is characterised both by its rapidity and by its geographical extent; in view of this specific character and the need to ensure that national authorities do not endanger the mutual confidence which they should have in one another, this Directive requests Member States to ensure that appropriate court actions are available; Member States should examine the need to provide access to judicial procedures by appropriate electronic means.

(53) Directive 98/27/EC, which is applicable to information society services, provides a mechanism relating to actions for an injunction aimed at the protection of the collective interests of consumers; this mechanism will contribute to the free movement of information society services by ensuring a high level of consumer protection.

(54) The sanctions provided for under this Directive are without prejudice to any other sanction or remedy provided under national law; Member States are not obliged to provide criminal sanctions for infringement of national provisions adopted pursuant to this Directive.

(55) This Directive does not affect the law applicable to contractual obligations relating to consumer contracts; accordingly, this Directive cannot have the result of depriving the consumer of the protection afforded to him by the mandatory rules relating to contractual obligations of the law of the Member State in which he has his habitual residence.

(56) As regards the derogation contained in this Directive regarding contractual obligations concerning contracts concluded by consumers, those obligations should be interpreted as including information on the essential elements of the content of the contract, including consumer rights, which have a determining influence on the decision to contract.

(57) The Court of Justice has consistently held that a Member State retains the right to take measures against a service provider that is established in another Member State but directs all or most of his activity to the territory of the first Member State if the choice of establishment was made with a view to evading the legislation that would have applied to the provider had he been established on the territory of the first Member State.

(58) This Directive should not apply to services supplied by service providers established in a third country; in view of the global dimension of electronic commerce, it is, however, appropriate to ensure that the Community rules are consistent with international rules; this Directive is without prejudice to the results of discussions within international organisations (amongst others WTO, OECD, Uncitral) on legal issues.

(59) Despite the global nature of electronic communications, coordination of national regulatory measures at European Union level is necessary in order to avoid fragmentation of the internal market, and for the establishment of an appropriate European regulatory framework; such coordination should also contribute to the establishment of a common and strong negotiating position in international forums.

(60) In order to allow the unhampered development of electronic commerce, the legal framework must be clear and simple, predictable and consistent with the rules applicable at international level so that it does not adversely affect the competitiveness of European industry or impede innovation in that sector.

(61) If the market is actually to operate by electronic means in the context of globalisation, the European Union and the major non-European areas need to consult each other with a view to making laws and procedures compatible.

(62) Cooperation with third countries should be strengthened in the area of electronic commerce, in particular with applicant countries, the developing countries and the European Union's other trading partners.

(63) The adoption of this Directive will not prevent the Member States from taking into account the various social, societal and cultural implications which are inherent in the advent of the information society; in particular it should not hinder measures which Member States might adopt in conformity with Community law to achieve social, cultural and democratic goals taking into account their linguistic diversity, national and regional specificities as well as their cultural heritage, and to ensure and maintain public access to the widest possible range of information society services; in any case, the development of the information society is to ensure that Community citizens can have access to the cultural European heritage provided in the digital environment.

(64) Electronic communication offers the Member States an excellent means of providing public services in the cultural, educational and linguistic fields.

(65) The Council, in its resolution of 19 January 1999 on the consumer dimension of the information society,[25] stressed that the protection of consumers deserved special attention in this field; the Commission will examine the degree to which existing consumer protection rules provide insufficient protection in the context of the information society and will identify, where necessary, the deficiencies of this legislation and those issues which could require additional measures; if need be, the Commission should make specific additional proposals to resolve such deficiencies that will thereby have been identified,

[3257]

NOTES

1. OJ C30, 5.2.1999, p 4.
2. OJ C169, 16.6.1999, p 36.
3. Opinion of the European Parliament of 6 May 1999 (OJ C279, 1.10.1999, p 389), Council common position of 28 February 2000 (OJ C128, 8.5.2000, p 32) and Decision of the European Parliament of 4 May 2000 (not yet published in the Official Journal).
4. OJ L298, 17.10.1989, p 23. Directive as amended by Directive 97/36/EC of the European Parliament and of the Council (OJ L202, 30.7.1997, p 60).
5. OJ L95, 21.4.1993, p 29.
6. OJ L144, 4.6.1999, p 19.

7 OJ L250, 19.9.1984, p 17. Directive as amended by Directive 97/55/EC of the European Parliament and of the Council (OJ L290, 23.10.1997, p 18).
8 OJ L42, 12.2.1987, p 48. Directive as last amended by Directive 98/7/EC of the European Parliament and of the Council (OJ L101, 1.4.1998, p 17).
9 OJ L141, 11.6.1993, p 27. Directive as last amended by Directive 97/9/EC of the European Parliament and of the Council (OJ L84, 26.3.1997, p 22).
10 OJ L158, 23.6.1990, p 59.
11 OJ L80, 18.3.1998, p 27.
12 OJ L228, 11.8.1992, p 24.
13 OJ L280, 29.10.1994, p 83.
14 OJ L166, 11.6.1998, p 51. Directive as amended by Directive 1999/44/EC (OJ L171, 7.7.1999, p 12).
15 OJ L210, 7.8.1985, p 29. Directive as amended by Directive 1999/34/EC (OJ L141, 4.6.1999, p 20).
16 OJ L171, 7.7.1999, p 12.
17 OJ L113, 30.4.1992, p 13.
18 OJ L213, 30.7.1998, p 9.
19 OJ L281, 23.11.1995, p 31.
20 OJ L24, 30.1.1998, p 1.
21 OJ L204, 21.7.1998, p 37. Directive as amended by Directive 98/48/EC (OJ L217, 5.8.1998, p 18).
22 OJ L320, 28.11.1998, p 54.
23 OJ L15, 21.1.1998, p 14.
24 OJ L13, 19.1.2000, p 12.
25 OJ C23, 28.1.1999, p 1.

HAVE ADOPTED THIS DIRECTIVE—

CHAPTER I
GENERAL PROVISIONS

Article 1

Objective and scope

1. This Directive seeks to contribute to the proper functioning of the internal market by ensuring the free movement of information society services between the Member States.

2. This Directive approximates, to the extent necessary for the achievement of the objective set out in paragraph 1, certain national provisions on information society services relating to the internal market, the establishment of service providers, commercial communications, electronic contracts, the liability of intermediaries, codes of conduct, out-of-court dispute settlements, court actions and cooperation between Member States.

3. This Directive complements Community law applicable to information society services without prejudice to the level of protection for, in particular, public health and consumer interests, as established by Community acts and national legislation implementing them in so far as this does not restrict the freedom to provide information society services.

4. This Directive does not establish additional rules on private international law nor does it deal with the jurisdiction of Courts.

5. This Directive shall not apply to—
   (a) the field of taxation;
   (b) questions relating to information society services covered by Directives 95/46/EC and 97/66/EC;
   (c) questions relating to agreements or practices governed by cartel law;
   (d) the following activities of information society services—
      — the activities of notaries or equivalent professions to the extent that they involve a direct and specific connection with the exercise of public authority,
      — the representation of a client and defence of his interests before the courts,
      — gambling activities which involve wagering a stake with monetary value in games of chance, including lotteries and betting transactions.

6. This Directive does not affect measures taken at Community or national level, in the respect of Community law, in order to promote cultural and linguistic diversity and to ensure the defence of pluralism.

[3258]

Article 2

Definitions

For the purpose of this Directive, the following terms shall bear the following meanings—

(a) "information society services": services within the meaning of Article 1(2) of Directive 98/34/EC as amended by Directive 98/48/EC;

(b) "service provider": any natural or legal person providing an information society service;

(c) "established service provider": a service provider who effectively pursues an economic activity using a fixed establishment for an indefinite period. The presence and use of the technical means and technologies required to provide the service do not, in themselves, constitute an establishment of the provider;

(d) "recipient of the service": any natural or legal person who, for professional ends or otherwise, uses an information society service, in particular for the purposes of seeking information or making it accessible;

(e) "consumer": any natural person who is acting for purposes which are outside his or her trade, business or profession;

(f) "commercial communication": any form of communication designed to promote, directly or indirectly, the goods, services or image of a company, organisation or person pursuing a commercial, industrial or craft activity or exercising a regulated profession. The following do not in themselves constitute commercial communications—

— information allowing direct access to the activity of the company, organisation or person, in particular a domain name or an electronic-mail address,

— communications relating to the goods, services or image of the company, organisation or person compiled in an independent manner, particularly when this is without financial consideration;

(g) "regulated profession": any profession within the meaning of either Article 1(d) of Council Directive 89/48/EEC of 21 December 1988 on a general system for the recognition of higher-education diplomas awarded on completion of professional education and training of at least three-years duration[1] or of Article 1(f) of Council Directive 92/51/EEC of 18 June 1992 on a second general system for the recognition of professional education and training to supplement Directive 89/48/EEC;[2]

(h) "coordinated field": requirements laid down in Member States' legal systems applicable to information society service providers or information society services, regardless of whether they are of a general nature or specifically designed for them.

(i) The coordinated field concerns requirements with which the service provider has to comply in respect of—

— the taking up of the activity of an information society service, such as requirements concerning qualifications, authorisation or notification,

— the pursuit of the activity of an information society service, such as requirements concerning the behaviour of the service provider, requirements regarding the quality or content of the service including those applicable to advertising and contracts, or requirements concerning the liability of the service provider;

(ii) The coordinated field does not cover requirements such as—

— requirements applicable to goods as such,

— requirements applicable to the delivery of goods,

— requirements applicable to services not provided by electronic means.

[3259]

NOTES

[1] OJ L19, 24.1.1989, p 16.

[2] OJ L209, 24.7.1992, p 25. Directive as last amended by Commission Directive 97/38/EC (OJ L184, 12.7.1997, p 31).

Article 3

Internal market

1. Each Member State shall ensure that the information society services provided by a service provider established on its territory comply with the national provisions applicable in the Member State in question which fall within the coordinated field.

2. Member States may not, for reasons falling within the coordinated field, restrict the freedom to provide information society services from another Member State.

3. Paragraphs 1 and 2 shall not apply to the fields referred to in the Annex.

4. Member States may take measures to derogate from paragraph 2 in respect of a given information society service if the following conditions are fulfilled—

(a) the measures shall be—

(i) necessary for one of the following reasons—

— public policy, in particular the prevention, investigation, detection and prosecution of criminal offences, including the protection of minors and the fight against any incitement to hatred on grounds of race, sex, religion or nationality, and violations of human dignity concerning individual persons,

— the protection of public health,

— public security, including the safeguarding of national security and defence,

— the protection of consumers, including investors;

(ii) taken against a given information society service which prejudices the objectives referred to in point (i) or which presents a serious and grave risk of prejudice to those objectives;

(iii) proportionate to those objectives;

(b) before taking the measures in question and without prejudice to court proceedings, including preliminary proceedings and acts carried out in the framework of a criminal investigation, the Member State has—

— asked the Member State referred to in paragraph 1 to take measures and the latter did not take such measures, or they were inadequate,

— notified the Commission and the Member State referred to in paragraph 1 of its intention to take such measures.

5. Member States may, in the case of urgency, derogate from the conditions stipulated in paragraph 4(b). Where this is the case, the measures shall be notified in the shortest possible time to the Commission and to the Member State referred to in paragraph 1, indicating the reasons for which the Member State considers that there is urgency.

6. Without prejudice to the Member State's possibility of proceeding with the measures in question, the Commission shall examine the compatibility of the notified measures with Community law in the shortest possible time; where it comes to the conclusion that the measure is incompatible with Community law, the Commission shall ask the Member State in question to refrain from taking any proposed measures or urgently to put an end to the measures in question.

[3260]

CHAPTER II
PRINCIPLES

Section 1: Establishment and information requirements

Article 4

Principle excluding prior authorisation

1. Member States shall ensure that the taking up and pursuit of the activity of an information society service provider may not be made subject to prior authorisation or any other requirement having equivalent effect.

2. Paragraph 1 shall be without prejudice to authorisation schemes which are not specifically and exclusively targeted at information society services, or which are covered by Directive 97/13/EC of the European Parliament and of the Council of 10 April 1997 on a common framework for general authorisations and individual licences in the field of telecommunications services.[1]

[3261]

NOTES

[1] OJ L117, 7.5.1997, p 15.

Article 5

General information to be provided

1. In addition to other information requirements established by Community law, Member States shall ensure that the service provider shall render easily, directly and permanently accessible to the recipients of the service and competent authorities, at least the following information—

(a) the name of the service provider;

(b) the geographic address at which the service provider is established;

(c) the details of the service provider, including his electronic mail address, which allow him to be contacted rapidly and communicated with in a direct and effective manner;

(d) where the service provider is registered in a trade or similar public register, the trade register in which the service provider is entered and his registration number, or equivalent means of identification in that register;

(e) where the activity is subject to an authorisation scheme, the particulars of the relevant supervisory authority;

(f) as concerns the regulated professions—

— any professional body or similar institution with which the service provider is registered,

— the professional title and the Member State where it has been granted,

— a reference to the applicable professional rules in the Member State of establishment and the means to access them;

(g) where the service provider undertakes an activity that is subject to VAT, the identification number referred to in Article 22(1) of the sixth Council Directive 77/388/EEC of 17 May 1977 on the harmonisation of the laws of the Member States relating to turnover taxes—Common system of value added tax: uniform basis of assessment.[1]

2. In addition to other information requirements established by Community law, Member States shall at least ensure that, where information society services refer to prices, these are to be indicated clearly and unambiguously and, in particular, must indicate whether they are inclusive of tax and delivery costs.

[3262]

NOTES

[1] OJ L145, 13.6.1977, p 1. Directive as last amended by Directive 1999/85/EC (OJ L277, 28.10.1999, p 34).

Section 2: Commercial communications

Article 6

Information to be provided

In addition to other information requirements established by Community law, Member States shall ensure that commercial communications which are part of, or constitute, an information society service comply at least with the following conditions—

(a) the commercial communication shall be clearly identifiable as such;

(b) the natural or legal person on whose behalf the commercial communication is made shall be clearly identifiable;

(c) promotional offers, such as discounts, premiums and gifts, where permitted in the Member State where the service provider is established, shall be clearly identifiable as such, and the conditions which are to be met to qualify for them shall be easily accessible and be presented clearly and unambiguously;

(d) promotional competitions or games, where permitted in the Member State where the service provider is established, shall be clearly identifiable as such, and the conditions for participation shall be easily accessible and be presented clearly and unambiguously.

[3263]

Article 7

Unsolicited commercial communication

1. In addition to other requirements established by Community law, Member States which permit unsolicited commercial communication by electronic mail shall ensure that such commercial communication by a service provider established in their territory shall be identifiable clearly and unambiguously as such as soon as it is received by the recipient.

2. Without prejudice to Directive 97/7/EC and Directive 97/66/EC, Member States shall take measures to ensure that service providers undertaking unsolicited commercial communications by electronic mail consult regularly and respect the opt-out registers in which natural persons not wishing to receive such commercial communications can register themselves.

[3264]

Article 8

Regulated professions

1. Member States shall ensure that the use of commercial communications which are part of, or constitute, an information society service provided by a member of a regulated profession is permitted subject to compliance with the professional rules regarding, in particular, the independence, dignity and honour of the profession, professional secrecy and fairness towards clients and other members of the profession.

2. Without prejudice to the autonomy of professional bodies and associations, Member States and the Commission shall encourage professional associations and bodies to establish codes of conduct at Community level in order to determine the types of information that can be given for the purposes of commercial communication in conformity with the rules referred to in paragraph 1.

3. When drawing up proposals for Community initiatives which may become necessary to ensure the proper functioning of the Internal Market with regard to the information referred to in paragraph 2, the Commission shall take due account of codes of conduct applicable at Community level and shall act in close cooperation with the relevant professional associations and bodies.

4. This Directive shall apply in addition to Community Directives concerning access to, and the exercise of, activities of the regulated professions.

[3265]

Section 3: Contracts concluded by electronic means

Article 9

Treatment of contracts

1. Member States shall ensure that their legal system allows contracts to be concluded by electronic means. Member States shall in particular ensure that the legal requirements applicable to the contractual process neither create obstacles for the use of electronic contracts nor result in such contracts being deprived of legal effectiveness and validity on account of their having been made by electronic means.

2. Member States may lay down that paragraph 1 shall not apply to all or certain contracts falling into one of the following categories—

- (a) contracts that create or transfer rights in real estate, except for rental rights;
- (b) contracts requiring by law the involvement of courts, public authorities or professions exercising public authority;
- (c) contracts of suretyship granted and on collateral securities furnished by persons acting for purposes outside their trade, business or profession;
- (d) contracts governed by family law or by the law of succession.

3. Member States shall indicate to the Commission the categories referred to in paragraph 2 to which they do not apply paragraph 1. Member States shall submit to the Commission every five years a report on the application of paragraph 2 explaining the reasons why they consider it necessary to maintain the category referred to in paragraph 2(b) to which they do not apply paragraph 1.

[3266]

Article 10

Information to be provided

1. In addition to other information requirements established by Community law, Member States shall ensure, except when otherwise agreed by parties who are not consumers, that at least the following information is given by the service provider clearly, comprehensibly and unambiguously and prior to the order being placed by the recipient of the service—
   (a) the different technical steps to follow to conclude the contract;
   (b) whether or not the concluded contract will be filed by the service provider and whether it will be accessible;
   (c) the technical means for identifying and correcting input errors prior to the placing of the order;
   (d) the languages offered for the conclusion of the contract.

2. Member States shall ensure that, except when otherwise agreed by parties who are not consumers, the service provider indicates any relevant codes of conduct to which he subscribes and information on how those codes can be consulted electronically.

3. Contract terms and general conditions provided to the recipient must be made available in a way that allows him to store and reproduce them.

4. Paragraphs 1 and 2 shall not apply to contracts concluded exclusively by exchange of electronic mail or by equivalent individual communications.

[3267]

Article 11

Placing of the order

1. Member States shall ensure, except when otherwise agreed by parties who are not consumers, that in cases where the recipient of the service places his order through technological means, the following principles apply—
   — the service provider has to acknowledge the receipt of the recipient's order without undue delay and by electronic means,
   — the order and the acknowledgement of receipt are deemed to be received when the parties to whom they are addressed are able to access them.

2. Member States shall ensure that, except when otherwise agreed by parties who are not consumers, the service provider makes available to the recipient of the service appropriate, effective and accessible technical means allowing him to identify and correct input errors, prior to the placing of the order.

3. Paragraph 1, first indent, and paragraph 2 shall not apply to contracts concluded exclusively by exchange of electronic mail or by equivalent individual communications.

[3268]

Section 4: Liability of intermediary service providers

Article 12

"Mere conduit"

1. Where an information society service is provided that consists of the transmission in a communication network of information provided by a recipient of the service, or the provision of access to a communication network, Member States shall ensure that the service provider is not liable for the information transmitted, on condition that the provider—
   (a) does not initiate the transmission;
   (b) does not select the receiver of the transmission; and
   (c) does not select or modify the information contained in the transmission.

2. The acts of transmission and of provision of access referred to in paragraph 1 include the automatic, intermediate and transient storage of the information transmitted in so far as this takes place for the sole purpose of carrying out the transmission in the communication network, and provided that the information is not stored for any period longer than is reasonably necessary for the transmission.

3. This Article shall not affect the possibility for a court or administrative authority, in accordance with Member States' legal systems, of requiring the service provider to terminate or prevent an infringement.

[3269]

Article 13

"Caching"

1. Where an information society service is provided that consists of the transmission in a communication network of information provided by a recipient of the service, Member States shall ensure that the service provider is not liable for the automatic, intermediate and temporary storage of that information, performed for the sole purpose of making more efficient the information's onward transmission to other recipients of the service upon their request, on condition that—

(a) the provider does not modify the information;

(b) the provider complies with conditions on access to the information;

(c) the provider complies with rules regarding the updating of the information, specified in a manner widely recognised and used by industry;

(d) the provider does not interfere with the lawful use of technology, widely recognised and used by industry, to obtain data on the use of the information; and

(e) the provider acts expeditiously to remove or to disable access to the information it has stored upon obtaining actual knowledge of the fact that the information at the initial source of the transmission has been removed from the network, or access to it has been disabled, or that a court or an administrative authority has ordered such removal or disablement.

2. This Article shall not affect the possibility for a court or administrative authority, in accordance with Member States' legal systems, of requiring the service provider to terminate or prevent an infringement.

[3270]

Article 14

Hosting

1. Where an information society service is provided that consists of the storage of information provided by a recipient of the service, Member States shall ensure that the service provider is not liable for the information stored at the request of a recipient of the service, on condition that—

(a) the provider does not have actual knowledge of illegal activity or information and, as regards claims for damages, is not aware of facts or circumstances from which the illegal activity or information is apparent; or

(b) the provider, upon obtaining such knowledge or awareness, acts expeditiously to remove or to disable access to the information.

2. Paragraph 1 shall not apply when the recipient of the service is acting under the authority or the control of the provider.

3. This Article shall not affect the possibility for a court or administrative authority, in accordance with Member States' legal systems, of requiring the service provider to terminate or prevent an infringement, nor does it affect the possibility for Member States of establishing procedures governing the removal or disabling of access to information.

[3271]

Article 15

No general obligation to monitor

1. Member States shall not impose a general obligation on providers, when providing the services covered by Articles 12, 13 and 14, to monitor the information which they transmit or store, nor a general obligation actively to seek facts or circumstances indicating illegal activity.

2. Member States may establish obligations for information society service providers promptly to inform the competent public authorities of alleged illegal activities undertaken or information provided by recipients of their service or obligations to communicate to the competent authorities, at their request, information enabling the identification of recipients of their service with whom they have storage agreements.

[3272]

CHAPTER III
IMPLEMENTATION

Article 16

Codes of conduct

1. Member States and the Commission shall encourage—
   (a) the drawing up of codes of conduct at Community level, by trade, professional and consumer associations or organisations, designed to contribute to the proper implementation of Articles 5 to 15;
   (b) the voluntary transmission of draft codes of conduct at national or Community level to the Commission;
   (c) the accessibility of these codes of conduct in the Community languages by electronic means;
   (d) the communication to the Member States and the Commission, by trade, professional and consumer associations or organisations, of their assessment of the application of their codes of conduct and their impact upon practices, habits or customs relating to electronic commerce;
   (e) the drawing up of codes of conduct regarding the protection of minors and human dignity.

2. Member States and the Commission shall encourage the involvement of associations or organisations representing consumers in the drafting and implementation of codes of conduct affecting their interests and drawn up in accordance with paragraph 1(a). Where appropriate, to take account of their specific needs, associations representing the visually impaired and disabled should be consulted.

[3273]

Article 17

Out-of-court dispute settlement

1. Member States shall ensure that, in the event of disagreement between an information society service provider and the recipient of the service, their legislation does not hamper the use of out-of-court schemes, available under national law, for dispute settlement, including appropriate electronic means.

2. Member States shall encourage bodies responsible for the out-of-court settlement of, in particular, consumer disputes to operate in a way which provides adequate procedural guarantees for the parties concerned.

3. Member States shall encourage bodies responsible for out-of-court dispute settlement to inform the Commission of the significant decisions they take regarding information society services and to transmit any other information on the practices, usages or customs relating to electronic commerce.

[3274]

Article 18

Court actions

1. Member States shall ensure that court actions available under national law concerning information society services' activities allow for the rapid adoption of measures, including interim measures, designed to terminate any alleged infringement and to prevent any further impairment of the interests involved.

2. …

[3275]

NOTES

Para 2: amends Directive 98/27/EC, Annex.

Article 19

Cooperation

1. Member States shall have adequate means of supervision and investigation necessary to implement this Directive effectively and shall ensure that service providers supply them with the requisite information.

2. Member States shall cooperate with other Member States; they shall, to that end, appoint one or several contact points, whose details they shall communicate to the other Member States and to the Commission.

3. Member States shall, as quickly as possible, and in conformity with national law, provide the assistance and information requested by other Member States or by the Commission, including by appropriate electronic means.

4. Member States shall establish contact points which shall be accessible at least by electronic means and from which recipients and service providers may—

(a) obtain general information on contractual rights and obligations as well as on the complaint and redress mechanisms available in the event of disputes, including practical aspects involved in the use of such mechanisms;

(b) obtain the details of authorities, associations or organisations from which they may obtain further information or practical assistance.

5. Member States shall encourage the communication to the Commission of any significant administrative or judicial decisions taken in their territory regarding disputes relating to information society services and practices, usages and customs relating to electronic commerce. The Commission shall communicate these decisions to the other Member States.

[3276]

Article 20

Sanctions

Member States shall determine the sanctions applicable to infringements of national provisions adopted pursuant to this Directive and shall take all measures necessary to ensure that they are enforced. The sanctions they provide for shall be effective, proportionate and dissuasive.

[3277]

CHAPTER IV
FINAL PROVISIONS

Article 21

Re-examination

1. Before 17 July 2003, and thereafter every two years, the Commission shall submit to the European Parliament, the Council and the Economic and Social Committee a report on the application of this Directive, accompanied, where necessary, by proposals for adapting it to legal, technical and economic developments in the field of information society services, in particular with respect to crime prevention, the protection of minors, consumer protection and to the proper functioning of the internal market.

2. In examining the need for an adaptation of this Directive, the report shall in particular analyse the need for proposals concerning the liability of providers of hyperlinks and location tool services, “notice and take down” procedures and the attribution of liability following the taking down of content. The report shall also analyse the need for additional conditions for the exemption from liability, provided for in Articles 12 and 13, in the light of technical developments, and the possibility of applying the internal market principles to unsolicited commercial communications by electronic mail.

[3278]

Article 22

Transposition

1. Member States shall bring into force the laws, regulations and administrative provisions necessary to comply with this Directive before 17 January 2002. They shall forthwith inform the Commission thereof.

2. When Member States adopt the measures referred to in paragraph 1, these shall contain a reference to this Directive or shall be accompanied by such reference at the time of their official publication. The methods of making such reference shall be laid down by Member States.

[3279]

Article 23

Entry into force

This Directive shall enter into force on the day of its publication in the *Official Journal of the European* Communities.

[3280]

Article 24

Addressees

This Directive is addressed to the Member States.

[3281]

Done at Luxembourg, 8 June 2000.

ANNEX

DEROGATIONS FROM ARTICLE 3

As provided for in Article 3(3), Article 3(1) and (2) do not apply to—

— copyright, neighbouring rights, rights referred to in Directive 87/54/EEC[1] and Directive 96/9/EC[2] as well as industrial property rights,

— the emission of electronic money by institutions in respect of which Member States have applied one of the derogations provided for in Article 8(1) of Directive 2000/46/EC,[3]

— Article 44(2) of Directive 85/611/EEC,[4]

— Article 30 and Title IV of Directive 92/49/EEC,[5] Title IV of Directive 92/96/EEC,[6] Articles 7 and 8 of Directive 88/357/EEC[7] and Article 4 of Directive 90/619/EEC,[8]

— the freedom of the parties to choose the law applicable to their contract,

— contractual obligations concerning consumer contacts,

— formal validity of contracts creating or transferring rights in real estate where such contracts are subject to mandatory formal requirements of the law of the Member State where the real estate is situated,

— the permissibility of unsolicited commercial communications by electronic mail.

[3282]

NOTES

1 OJ L24, 27.1.1987, p 36.
2 OJ L77, 27.3.1996, p 20.
3 Not yet published in the Official Journal.
4 OJ L375, 31.12.1985, p 3. Directive as last amended by Directive 95/26/EC (OJ L168, 18.7.1995, p 7).
5 OJ L228, 11.8.1992, p 1. Directive as last amended by Directive 95/26/EC.
6 OJ L360, 9.12.1992, p 2. Directive as last amended by Directive 95/26/EC.
7 OJ L172, 4.7.1988, p 1. Directive as last amended by Directive 92/49/EC.
8 OJ L330, 29.11.1990, p 50. Directive as last amended by Directive 92/96/EC.

DIRECTIVE OF THE EUROPEAN PARLIAMENT AND OF THE COUNCIL

of 29 June 2000

on combating late payment in commercial transactions

(2000/35/EC)

NOTES

Date of publication in OJ: OJ L200, 8.8.2000, p 35.

THE EUROPEAN PARLIAMENT AND THE COUNCIL OF THE EUROPEAN UNION,

Having regard to the Treaty establishing the European Community, and in particular Article 95 thereof,

PART IV

Having regard to the proposal from the Commission,[1]

Having regard to the opinion of the Economic and Social Committee,[2]

Acting in accordance with the procedure laid down in Article 251 of the Treaty,[3] in the light of the joint text approved by the Conciliation Committee on 4 May 2000,

Whereas:

(1) In its resolution on the integrated programme in favour of SMEs and the craft sector[4] the European Parliament urged the Commission to submit proposals to deal with the problem of late payment.

(2) On 12 May 1995 the Commission adopted a recommendation on payment periods in commercial transactions.[5]

(3) In its resolution on the Commission recommendation on payment periods in commercial transactions,[6] the European Parliament called on the Commission to consider transforming its recommendation into a proposal for a Council directive to be submitted as soon as possible.

(4) On 29 May 1997 the Economic and Social Committee adopted an opinion on the Commission's Green Paper on Public procurement in the European Union: Exploring the way forward.[7]

(5) On 4 June 1997 the Commission published an action plan for the single market, which underlined that late payment represents an increasingly serious obstacle for the success of the single market.

(6) On 17 July 1997 the Commission published a report on late payments in commercial transactions,[8] summarising the results of an evaluation of the effects of the Commission's recommendation of 12 May 1995.

(7) Heavy administrative and financial burdens are placed on businesses, particularly small and medium-sized ones, as a result of excessive payment periods and late payment. Moreover, these problems are a major cause of insolvencies threatening the survival of businesses and result in numerous job losses.

(8) In some Member States contractual payment periods differ significantly from the Community average.

(9) The differences between payment rules and practices in the Member States constitute an obstacle to the proper functioning of the internal market.

(10) This has the effect of considerably limiting commercial transactions between Member States. This is in contradiction with Article 14 of the Treaty as entrepreneurs should be able to trade throughout the internal market under conditions which ensure that transborder operations do not entail greater risks than domestic sales. Distortions of competition would ensue if substantially different rules applied to domestic and transborder operations.

(11) The most recent statistics indicate that there has been, at best, no improvement in late payments in many Member States since the adoption of the recommendation of 12 May 1995.

(12) The objective of combating late payments in the internal market cannot be sufficiently achieved by the Member States acting individually and can, therefore, be better achieved by the Community. This Directive does not go beyond what is necessary to achieve that objective. This Directive complies therefore, in its entirety, with the requirements of the principles of subsidiarity and proportionality as laid down in Article 5 of the Treaty.

(13) This Directive should be limited to payments made as remuneration for commercial transactions and does not regulate transactions with consumers, interest in connection with other payments, e.g. payments under the laws on cheques and bills of exchange, payments made as compensation for damages including payments from insurance companies.

(14) The fact that the liberal professions are covered by this Directive does not mean that Member States have to treat them as undertakings or merchants for purposes not covered by this Directive.

(15) This Directive only defines the term "enforceable title" but does not regulate the various procedures of forced execution of such a title and the conditions under which forced execution of such a title can be stopped or suspended.

(16) Late payment constitutes a breach of contract which has been made financially attractive to debtors in most Member States by low interest rates on late payments and/or slow procedures for redress. A decisive shift, including compensation of creditors for the costs incurred, is necessary to reverse this trend and to ensure that the consequences of late payments are such as to discourage late payment.

(17) The reasonable compensation for the recovery costs has to be considered without prejudice to national provisions according to which a national judge can award to the creditor any additional damage caused by the debtor's late payment, taking also into account that such incurred costs may be already compensated for by the interest for late payment.

(18) This Directive takes into account the issue of long contractual payment periods and, in particular, the existence of certain categories of contracts where a longer payment period in combination with a restriction of freedom of contract or a higher interest rate can be justified.

(19) This Directive should prohibit abuse of freedom of contract to the disadvantage of the creditor. Where an agreement mainly serves the purpose of procuring the debtor additional liquidity at the expense of the creditor, or where the main contractor imposes on his suppliers and subcontractors terms of payment which are not justified on the grounds of the terms granted to himself, these may be considered to be factors constituting such an abuse. This Directive does not affect national provisions relating to the way contracts are concluded or regulating the validity of contractual terms which are unfair to the debtor.

(20) The consequences of late payment can be dissuasive only if they are accompanied by procedures for redress which are rapid and effective for the creditor. In conformity with the principle of non-discrimination contained in Article 12 of the Treaty, those procedures should be available to all creditors who are established in the Community.

(21) It is desirable to ensure that creditors are in a position to exercise a retention of title on a non-discriminatory basis throughout the Community, if the retention of title clause is valid under the applicable national provisions designated by private international law.

(22) This Directive should regulate all commercial transactions irrespective of whether they are carried out between private or public undertakings or between undertakings and public authorities, having regard to the fact that the latter handle a considerable volume of payments to business. It should therefore also regulate all commercial transactions between main contractors and their suppliers and subcontractors.

(23) Article 5 of this Directive requires that the recovery procedure for unchallenged claims be completed within a short period of time in conformity with national legislation, but does not require Member States to adopt a specific procedure or to amend their existing legal procedures in a specific way,

[3283]

NOTES

1 OJ C168, 3.6.1998, p 13, and OJ C374, 3.12.1998, p 4.
2 OJ C407, 28.12.1998, p 50.
3 Opinion of the European Parliament of 17 September 1998 (OJ C313, 12.10.1998, p 142), Council Common Position of 29 July 1999 (OJ C284, 6.10.1999, p 1) and decision of the European Parliament of 16 December 1999 (not yet published in the Official Journal). Decision of the European Parliament of 15 June 2000 and Decision of the Council of 18 May 2000.
4 OJ C323, 21.11.1994, p 19.
5 OJ L127, 10.6.1995, p 19.
6 OJ C211, 22.7.1996, p 43.
7 OJ C287, 22.9.1997, p 92.
8 OJ C216, 17.7.1997, p 10.

HAVE ADOPTED THIS DIRECTIVE:

Article 1

Scope

This Directive shall apply to all payments made as remuneration for commercial transactions.

[3284]

Article 2

Definitions

For the purposes of this Directive:

1. "commercial transactions" means transactions between undertakings or between undertakings and public authorities which lead to the delivery of goods or the provision of services for remuneration,

"public authority" means any contracting authority or entity, as defined by the Public Procurement Directives (92/50/EEC,[9] 93/36/EEC),[10] 93/37/EEC[11] and 93/38/EEC[12]),

"undertaking" means any organisation acting in the course of its independent economic or professional activity, even where it is carried on by a single person;

2. "late payment" means exceeding the contractual or statutory period of payment;

3. "retention of title" means the contractual agreement according to which the seller retains title to the goods in question until the price has been paid in full;

4. "interest rate applied by the European Central Bank to its main refinancing operations" means the interest rate applied to such operations in the case of fixed-rate tenders. In the event

that a main refinancing operation was conducted according to a variable-rate tender procedure, this interest rate refers to the marginal interest rate which resulted from that tender. This applies both in the case of single-rate and variable-rate auctions;

5. "enforceable title" means any decision, judgment or order for payment issued by a court or other competent authority, whether for immediate payment or payment by instalments, which permits the creditor to have his claim against the debtor collected by means of forced execution; it shall include a decision, judgment or order for payment that is provisionally enforceable and remains so even if the debtor appeals against it.

[3285]

Article 3

Interest in case of late payment

1. Member States shall ensure that:

(a) interest in accordance with point (d) shall become payable from the day following the date or the end of the period for payment fixed in the contract;

(b) if the date or period for payment is not fixed in the contract, interest shall become payable automatically without the necessity of a reminder:

(i) 30 days following the date of receipt by the debtor of the invoice or an equivalent request for payment; or

(ii) if the date of the receipt of the invoice or the equivalent request for payment is uncertain, 30 days after the date of receipt of the goods or services; or

(iii) if the debtor receives the invoice or the equivalent request for payment earlier than the goods or the services, 30 days after the receipt of the goods or services; or

(iv) if a procedure of acceptance or verification, by which the conformity of the goods or services with the contract is to be ascertained, is provided for by statute or in the contract and if the debtor receives the invoice or the equivalent request for payment earlier or on the date on which such acceptance or verification takes place, 30 days after this latter date;

(c) the creditor shall be entitled to interest for late payment to the extent that:

(i) he has fulfilled his contractual and legal obligations; and

(ii) he has not received the amount due on time, unless the debtor is not responsible for the delay;

(d) the level of interest for late payment ("the statutory rate"), which the debtor is obliged to pay, shall be the sum of the interest rate applied by the European Central Bank to its most recent main refinancing operation carried out before the first calendar day of the half-year in question ("the reference rate"), plus at least seven percentage points ("the margin"), unless otherwise specified in the contract. For a Member State which is not participating in the third stage of economic and monetary union, the reference rate referred to above shall be the equivalent rate set by its national central bank. In both cases, the reference rate in force on the first calendar day of the half-year in question shall apply for the following six months;

(e) unless the debtor is not responsible for the delay, the creditor shall be entitled to claim reasonable compensation from the debtor for all relevant recovery costs incurred through the latter's late payment. Such recovery costs shall respect the principles of transparency and proportionality as regards the debt in question. Member States may, while respecting the principles referred to above, fix maximum amounts as regards the recovery costs for different levels of debt.

2. For certain categories of contracts to be defined by national law, Member States may fix the period after which interest becomes payable to a maximum of 60 days provided that they either restrain the parties to the contract from exceeding this period or fix a mandatory interest rate that substantially exceeds the statutory rate.

3. Member States shall provide that an agreement on the date for payment or on the consequences of late payment which is not in line with the provisions of paragraphs 1(b) to (d) and 2 either shall not be enforceable or shall give rise to a claim for damages if, when all circumstances of the case, including good commercial practice and the nature of the product, are considered, it is grossly unfair to the creditor. In determining whether an agreement is grossly unfair to the creditor, it will be taken, inter alia, into account whether the debtor has any objective reason to deviate from the provisions of paragraphs 1(b) to (d) and 2. If such an agreement is determined to be grossly unfair, the statutory terms will apply, unless the national courts determine different conditions which are fair.

4. Member States shall ensure that, in the interests of creditors and of competitors, adequate and effective means exist to prevent the continued use of terms which are grossly unfair within the meaning of paragraph 3.

5. The means referred to in paragraph 4 shall include provisions whereby organisations officially recognised as, or having a legitimate interest in, representing small and medium-sized enterprises may take action according to the national law concerned before the courts or before competent administrative bodies on the grounds that contractual terms drawn up for general use are grossly unfair within the meaning of paragraph 3, so that they can apply appropriate and effective means to prevent the continued use of such terms.

[3286]

Article 4

Retention of title

1. Member States shall provide in conformity with the applicable national provisions designated by private international law that the seller retains title to goods until they are fully paid for if a retention of title clause has been expressly agreed between the buyer and the seller before the delivery of the goods.

2. Member States may adopt or retain provisions dealing with down payments already made by the debtor.

[3287]

Article 5

Recovery procedures for unchallenged claims

1. Member States shall ensure that an enforceable title can be obtained, irrespective of the amount of the debt, normally within 90 calendar days of the lodging of the creditor's action or application at the court or other competent authority, provided that the debt or aspects of the procedure are not disputed. This duty shall be carried out by Member States in conformity with their respective national legislation, regulations and administrative provisions.

2. The respective national legislation, regulations and administrative provisions shall apply the same conditions for all creditors who are established in the European Community.

3. The 90 calendar day period referred to in paragraph 1 shall not include the following:
(a) periods for service of documents;
(b) any delays caused by the creditor, such as periods devoted to correcting applications.

4. This Article shall be without prejudice to the provisions of the Brussels Convention on jurisdiction and enforcement of judgments in civil and commercial matters.[13]

[3288]

Article 6

Transposition

1. Member States shall bring into force the laws, regulations and administrative provisions necessary to comply with this Directive before 8 August 2002. They shall forthwith inform the Commission thereof.

When Member States adopt these measures, they shall contain a reference to this Directive or shall be accompanied by such reference on the occasion of their official publication. The methods of making such reference shall be laid down by Member States.

2. Member States may maintain or bring into force provisions which are more favourable to the creditor than the provisions necessary to comply with this Directive.

3. In transposing this Directive, Member States may exclude:
(a) debts that are subject to insolvency proceedings instituted against the debtor;
(b) contracts that have been concluded prior to 8 August 2002; and
(c) claims for interest of less than EUR 5.

4. Member States shall communicate to the Commission the text of the main provisions of national law which they adopt in the field covered by this Directive.

5. The Commission shall undertake two years after 8 August 2002 a review of, inter alia, the statutory rate, contractual payment periods and late payments, to assess the impact on

commercial transactions and the operation of the legislation in practice. The results of this review and of other reviews will be made known to the European Parliament and the Council, accompanied where appropriate by proposals for improvement of this Directive.

[3289]

Article 7

Entry into force

This Directive shall enter into force on the day of its publication in the Official Journal of the European Communities.

[3290]

Article 8

Addressees

This Directive is addressed to the Member States.

[3291]

NOTES

9 OJ L209, 24.7.1992, p 1.
10 OJ L199, 9.8.1993, p 1.
11 OJ L199, 9.8.1993, p 54.
12 OJ L199, 9.8.1993, p 84.
13 Consolidated version in OJ C27, 26.1.1998, p 3.

Done at Luxembourg, 29 June 2000.

For the European Parliament

The President

N Fontaine

For the Council

The President

M Marques da Costa

DIRECTIVE OF THE EUROPEAN PARLIAMENT AND OF THE COUNCIL

of 6 June 2002

on financial collateral arrangements

(2002/47/EC)

NOTES

Date of publication in OJ: OJ L168, 27.6.2002, p 43.

THE EUROPEAN PARLIAMENT AND THE COUNCIL OF THE EUROPEAN UNION,

Having regard to the Treaty establishing the European Community, and in particular Article 95 thereof,

Having regard to the proposal from the Commission,[1]

Having regard to the opinion of the European Central Bank,[2]

Having regard to the opinion of the Economic and Social Committee,[3]

Acting in accordance with the procedure laid down in Article 251 of the Treaty,[4]

Whereas:

(1) Directive 98/26/EC of the European Parliament and of the Council of 19 May 1998 on settlement finality in payment and securities settlement systems[5] constituted a milestone in establishing a sound legal framework for payment and securities settlement systems. Implementation of that Directive has demonstrated the importance of limiting systemic risk

inherent in such systems stemming from the different influence of several jurisdictions, and the benefits of common rules in relation to collateral constituted to such systems.

(2) In its communication of 11 May 1999 to the European Parliament and to the Council on financial services: implementing the framework for financial markets: action plan, the Commission undertook, after consultation with market experts and national authorities, to work on further proposals for legislative action on collateral urging further progress in the field of collateral, beyond Directive 98/26/EC.

(3) A Community regime should be created for the provision of securities and cash as collateral under both security interest and title transfer structures including repurchase agreements (repos). This will contribute to the integration and cost-efficiency of the financial market as well as to the stability of the financial system in the Community, thereby supporting the freedom to provide services and the free movement of capital in the single market in financial services. This Directive focuses on bilateral financial collateral arrangements.

(4) This Directive is adopted in a European legal context which consists in particular of the said Directive 98/ 26/EC as well as Directive 2001/24/EC of the European Parliament and of the Council of 4 April 2001 on the reorganisation and winding up of credit institutions,[6] Directive 2001/17/EC of the European Parliament and of the Council of 19 March 2001 on the reorganisation and winding-up of insurance undertakings[7] and Council Regulation (EC) No 1346/2000 of 29 May 2000 on insolvency proceedings.[8] This Directive is in line with the general pattern of these previous legal acts and is not opposed to it. Indeed, this Directive complements these existing legal acts by dealing with further issues and going beyond them in connection with particular matters already dealt with by these legal acts.

(5) In order to improve the legal certainty of financial collateral arrangements, Member States should ensure that certain provisions of insolvency law do not apply to such arrangements, in particular, those that would inhibit the effective realisation of financial collateral or cast doubt on the validity of current techniques such as bilateral close-out netting, the provision of additional collateral in the form of top-up collateral and substitution of collateral.

(6) This Directive does not address rights which any person may have in respect of assets provided as financial collateral, and which arise otherwise than under the terms of the financial collateral arrangement and otherwise than on the basis of any legal provision or rule of law arising by reason of the commencement or continuation of winding-up proceedings or reorganisation measures, such as restitution arising from mistake, error or lack of capacity.

(7) The principle in Directive 98/26/EC, whereby the law applicable to book entry securities provided as collateral is the law of the jurisdiction where the relevant register, account or centralised deposit system is located, should be extended in order to create legal certainty regarding the use of such securities held in a cross-border context and used as financial collateral under the scope of this Directive.

(8) The *lex rei sitae* rule, according to which the applicable law for determining whether a financial collateral arrangement is properly perfected and therefore good against third parties is the law of the country where the financial collateral is located, is currently recognised by all Member States. Without affecting the application of this Directive to directly-held securities, the location of book entry securities provided as financial collateral and held through one or more intermediaries should be determined. If the collateral taker has a valid and effective collateral arrangement according to the governing law of the country in which the relevant account is maintained, then the validity against any competing title or interest and the enforceability of the collateral should be governed solely by the law of that country, thus preventing legal uncertainty as a result of other unforeseen legislation.

(9) In order to limit the administrative burdens for parties using financial collateral under the scope of this Directive, the only perfection requirement which national law may impose in respect of financial collateral should be that the financial collateral is delivered, transferred, held, registered or otherwise designated so as to be in the possession or under the control of the collateral taker or of a person acting on the collateral taker's behalf while not excluding collateral techniques where the collateral provider is allowed to substitute collateral or to withdraw excess collateral.

(10) For the same reasons, the creation, validity, perfection, enforceability or admissibility in evidence of a financial collateral arrangement, or the provision of financial collateral under a financial collateral arrangement, should not be made dependent on the performance of any formal act such as the execution of any document in a specific form or in a particular manner, the making of any filing with an official or public body or registration in a public register, advertisement in a newspaper or journal, in an official register or publication or in any other matter, notification to a public officer or the provision of evidence in a particular form as to the date of execution of a document or instrument, the amount of the relevant financial obligations or any other matter. This Directive must however provide a balance between market efficiency and the safety of the parties to the arrangement and third parties, thereby avoiding *inter alia* the risk of fraud. This balance should be achieved through

the scope of this Directive covering only those financial collateral arrangements which provide for some form of dispossession, i.e. the provision of the financial collateral, and where the provision of the financial collateral can be evidenced in writing or in a durable medium, ensuring thereby the traceability of that collateral. For the purpose of this Directive, acts required-under the law of a Member State as conditions for transferring or creating a security interest on financial instruments, other than book entry securities, such as endorsement in the case of instruments to order, or recording on the issuer's register in the case of registered instruments, should not be considered as formal acts.

(11) Moreover, this Directive should protect only financial collateral arrangements which can be evidenced. Such evidence can be given in writing or in any other legally enforceable manner provided by the law which is applicable to the financial collateral arrangement.

(12) The simplification of the use of financial collateral through the limitation of administrative burdens promotes the efficiency of the cross-border operations of the European Central Bank and the national central banks of Member States participating in the economic and monetary union, necessary for the implementation of the common monetary policy. Furthermore, the provision of limited protection of financial collateral arrangements from some rules of insolvency law in addition supports the wider aspect of the common monetary policy, where the participants in the money market balance the overall amount of liquidity in the market among themselves, by cross-border transactions backed by collateral.

(13) This Directive seeks to protect the validity of financial collateral arrangements which are based upon the transfer of the full ownership of the financial collateral, such as by eliminating the so-called re-characterisation of such financial collateral arrangements (including repurchase agreements) as security interests.

(14) The enforceability of bilateral close-out netting should be protected, not only as an enforcement mechanism for title transfer financial collateral arrangements including repurchase agreements but more widely, where close-out netting forms part of a financial collateral arrangement. Sound risk management practices commonly used in the financial market should be protected by enabling participants to manage and reduce their credit exposures arising from all kinds of financial transactions on a net basis, where the credit exposure is calculated by combining the estimated current exposures under all outstanding transactions with a counterparty, setting off reciprocal items to produce a single aggregated amount that is compared with the current value of the collateral.

(15) This Directive should be without prejudice to any restrictions or requirements under national law on bringing into account claims, on obligations to set-off, or on netting, for example relating to their reciprocity or the fact that they have been concluded prior to when the collateral taker knew or ought to have known of the commencement (or of any mandatory legal act leading to the commencement) of winding-up proceedings or reorganisation measures in respect of the collateral provider.

(16) The sound market practice favoured by regulators whereby participants in the financial market use top-up financial collateral arrangements to manage and limit their credit risk to each other by mark-to-market calculations of the current market value of the credit exposure and the value of the financial collateral and accordingly ask for top-up financial collateral or return the surplus of financial collateral should be protected against certain automatic avoidance rules. The same applies to the possibility of substituting for assets provided as financial collateral other assets of the same value. The intention is merely that the provision of top-up or substitution financial collateral cannot be questioned on the sole basis that the relevant financial obligations existed before that financial collateral was provided, or that the financial collateral was provided during a prescribed-period. However, this does not prejudice the possibility of questioning under national law the financial collateral arrangement and the provision of financial collateral as part of the initial provision, top-up or substitution of financial collateral, for example where this has been intentionally done to the detriment of the other creditors (this covers *inter alia* actions based on fraud or similar avoidance rules which may apply in a prescribed period).

(17) This Directive provides for rapid and non-formalistic enforcement procedures in order to safeguard financial stability and limit contagion effects in case of a default of a party to a financial collateral arrangement. However, this Directive balances the latter objectives with the protection of the collateral provider and third-parties by explicitly confirming the possibility for Member States to keep or introduce in their national legislation an *a posteriori* control which the Courts can exercise in relation to the realisation or valuation of financial collateral and the calculation of the relevant financial obligations. Such control should allow for the judicial authorities to verify that the realisation or valuation has been conducted in a commercially reasonable manner.

(18) It should be possible to provide cash as collateral under both title transfer and secured structures respectively protected by the recognition of netting or by the pledge of cash

collateral. Cash refers only to money which is represented by a credit to an account, or similar claims on repayment of money (such as money market deposits), thus explicitly excluding banknotes.

(19) This Directive provides for a right of use in case of security financial collateral arrangements, which increases liquidity in the financial market stemming from such reuse of pledged securities. This reuse however should be without prejudice to national legislation about separation of assets and unfair treatment of creditors.

(20) This Directive does not prejudice the operation and effect of the contractual terms of financial instruments provided as financial collateral, such as rights and obligations and other conditions contained in the terms of issue and any other rights and obligations and other conditions which apply between the issuers and holders of such instruments.

(21) This Act complies with the fundamental rights and follows the principles laid down in particular in the Charter of Fundamental Rights of the European Union.

(22) Since the objective of the proposed action, namely to create a minimum regime relating to the use of financial collateral, cannot be sufficiently achieved by the Member States and can therefore, by reason of the scale and effects of the action, be better achieved at Community level, the Community may adopt measures, in accordance with the principle of subsidiarity as set out in Article 5 of the Treaty. In accordance with the principle of proportionality, as set out in that Article, this Directive does not go beyond what is necessary in order to achieve that objective,

[3292]

NOTES

1 OJ C180 E, 26.6.2001, p 312.
2 OJ C196, 12.7.2001, p 10.
3 OJ C48, 21.2.2002, p 1.
4 Opinion of the European Parliament of 13 December 2001 (not yet published in the Official Journal), Council Common Position of 5 March 2002 (not yet published in the Official Journal) and Decision of the European Parliament of 15 May 2002.
5 OJ L166, 11.6.1998, p 45.
6 OJ L125, 5.5.2001, p 15.
7 OJ L110, 20.4.2001, p 28.
8 OJ L160, 30.6.2000, p 1.

HAVE ADOPTED THIS DIRECTIVE:

Article 1

Subject matter and scope

1. This Directive lays down a Community regime applicable to financial collateral arrangements which satisfy the requirements set out in paragraphs 2 and 5 and to financial collateral in accordance with the conditions set out in paragraphs 4 and 5.

2. The collateral taker and the collateral provider must each belong to one of the following categories:

(a) a public authority (excluding publicly guaranteed undertakings unless they fall under points (b) to (e)) including:
  (i) public sector bodies of Member States charged with or intervening in the management of public debt, and
  (ii) public sector bodies of Member States authorised to hold accounts for customers;

(b) a central bank, the European Central Bank, the Bank for International Settlements, a multilateral development bank as defined in Article 1(19) of Directive 2000/12/EC of the European Parliament and of the Council of 20 March 2000 relating to the taking up and pursuit of the business of credit institutions,[1] the International Monetary Fund and the European Investment Bank;

(c) a financial institution subject to prudential supervision including:
  (i) a credit institution as defined in Article 1(1) of Directive 2000/12/EC, including the institutions listed in Article 2(3) of that Directive;
  (ii) an investment firm as defined in Article 1(2) of Council Directive 93/22/EEC of 10 May 1993 on investment services in the securities field;[2]
  (iii) a financial institution as defined in Article 1(5) of Directive 2000/12/EC;
  (iv) an insurance undertaking as defined in Article 1(a) of Council Directive 92/49/EEC of 18 June 1992 on the coordination of laws, regulations and administrative provisions relating to direct insurance other than life

PART IV

assurance[3] and a life assurance undertaking as defined in Article 1(a) of Council Directive 92/96/EEC of 10 November 1992 on the coordination of laws, regulations and administrative provisions relating to direct life assurance;[4]

(v) an undertaking for collective investment in transferable securities (UCITS) as defined in Article 1(2) of Council Directive 85/611/EEC of 20 December 1985 on the coordination of laws, regulations and administrative provisions relating to undertakings for collective investment in transferable securities (UCITS);[5]

(vi) a management company as defined in Article 1a(2) of Directive 85/611/EEC;

(d) a central counterparty, settlement agent or clearing house, as defined respectively in Article 2(c), (d) and (e) of Directive 98/26/EC, including similar institutions regulated under national law acting in the futures, options and derivatives markets to the extent not covered by that Directive, and a person, other than a natural person, who acts in a trust or representative capacity on behalf of any one or more persons that includes any bondholders or holders of other forms of securitised debt or any institution as defined in points (a) to (d);

(e) a person other than a natural person, including unincorporated firms and partnerships, provided that the other party is an institution as defined in points (a) to (d).

If they make use of this option Member States shall inform the Commission which shall inform the other Member States thereof.

3. Member States may exclude from the scope of this Directive financial collateral arrangements where one of the parties is a person mentioned in paragraph 2(e).

4.—

(a) The financial collateral to be provided must consist of cash or financial instruments.

(b) Member States may exclude from the scope of this Directive financial collateral consisting of the collateral provider's own shares, shares in affiliated undertakings within the meaning of seventh Council Directive 83/ 349/EEC of 13 June 1983 on consolidated accounts,[6] and shares in undertakings whose exclusive purpose is to own means of production that are essential for the collateral provider's business or to own real property.

5. This Directive applies to financial collateral once it has been provided and if that provision can be evidenced in writing.

The evidencing of the provision of financial collateral must allow for the identification of the financial collateral to which it applies. For this purpose, it is sufficient to prove that the book entry securities collateral has been credited to, or forms a credit in, the relevant account and that the cash collateral has been credited to, or forms a credit in, a designated account.

This Directive applies to financial collateral arrangements if that arrangement can be evidenced in writing or in a legally equivalent manner.

[3293]

NOTES

1 OJ L126, 26.5.2000, p 1. Directive as amended by Directive 2000/28/EC (OJ L275, 27.10.2000, p 37).

2 OJ L141, 11.6.1993, p 27. Directive as last amended by Directive 2000/64/EC of the European Parliament and of the Council (OJ L290, 17.11.2000, p 27).

3 OJ L228, 11.8.1992, p 1. Directive as last amended by Directive 2000/64/EC of the European Parliament and of the Council.

4 OJ L360, 9.12.1992, p 1. Directive as last amended by Directive 2000/64/EC of the European Parliament and of the Council.

5 OJ L375, 31.12.1985, p 3. Directive as last amended by Directive 2001/108/EC of the European Parliament and of the Council (OJ L41, 13.2.2002, p 35).

6 OJ L193, 18.7.1983, p 1. Directive as last amended by Directive 2001/65/EC of the European Parliament and of the Council (OJ L283, 27.10.2001, p 28).

Article 2

Definitions

1. For the purpose of this Directive:

(a) financial collateral arrangement means a title transfer financial collateral arrangement or a security financial collateral arrangement whether or not these are covered by a master agreement or general terms and conditions;

(b) title transfer financial collateral arrangement means an arrangement, including repurchase agreements, under which a collateral provider transfers full ownership of financial collateral to a collateral taker for the purpose of securing or otherwise covering the performance of relevant financial obligations;

(c) security financial collateral arrangement means an arrangement under which a collateral provider provides financial collateral by way of security in favour of, or to, a collateral taker, and where the full ownership of the financial collateral remains with the collateral provider when the security right is established;

(d) cash means money credited to an account in any currency, or similar claims for the repayment of money, such as money market deposits;

(e) financial instruments means shares in companies and other securities equivalent to shares in companies and bonds and other forms of debt instruments if these are negotiable on the capital market, and any other securities which are normally dealt in and which give the right to acquire any such shares, bonds or other securities by subscription, purchase or exchange or which give rise to a cash settlement (excluding instruments of payment), including units in collective investment undertakings, money market instruments and claims relating to or rights in or in respect of any of the foregoing;

(f) relevant financial obligations means the obligations which are secured by a financial collateral arrangement and which give a right to cash settlement and/or delivery of financial instruments.

Relevant financial obligations may consist of or include:

- (i) present or future, actual or contingent or prospective obligations (including such obligations arising under a master agreement or similar arrangement);
- (ii) obligations owed to the collateral taker by a person other than the collateral provider; or
- (iii) obligations of a specified class or kind arising from time to time;

(g) book entry securities collateral means financial collateral provided under a financial collateral arrangement which consists of financial instruments, title to which is evidenced by entries in a register or account maintained by or on behalf of an intermediary;

(h) relevant account means in relation to book entry securities collateral which is subject to a financial collateral arrangement, the register or account which may be maintained by the collateral taker i which the entries are made by which that book entry securities collateral is provided to the collateral taker;

(i) equivalent collateral:

- (i) in relation to cash, means a payment of the same amount and in the same currency;
- (ii) in relation to financial instruments, means financial instruments of the same issuer or debtor, forming part of the same issue or class and of the same nominal amount, currency and description or, where a financial collateral arrangement provides for the transfer of other assets following the occurrence of any event relating to or affecting any financial instruments provided as financial collateral, those other assets;

(j) winding-up proceedings means collective proceedings involving realisation of the assets and distribution of the proceeds among the creditors, shareholders or members as appropriate, which involve any intervention by administrative or judicial authorities, including where the collective proceedings are terminated by a composition or other analogous measure, whether or not they are founded on insolvency or are voluntary or compulsory;

(k) reorganisation measures means measures which involve any intervention by administrative or judicial authorities which are intended to preserve or restore the financial situation and which affect pre-existing rights of third-parties, including but not limited to measures involving a suspension of payments, suspension of enforcement measures or reduction of claims;

(l) enforcement event means an event of default or any similar event as agreed between the parties on the occurrence of which, under the terms of a financial collateral arrangement or by operation of law, the collateral taker is entitled to realise or appropriate financial collateral or a close-out netting provision comes into effect;

(m) right of use means the right of the collateral taker to use and dispose of financial collateral provided under a security financial collateral arrangement as the owner of it in accordance with the terms of the security financial collateral arrangement;

(n) close-out netting provision means a provision of a financial collateral arrangement, or of an arrangement of which a financial collateral arrangement forms part, or, in the absence of any such provision, any statutory rule by which, on the occurrence of an enforcement event, whether through the operation of netting or set-off or otherwise:

(i) the obligations of the parties are accelerated so as to be immediately due and expressed as an obligation to pay an amount representing their estimated current value, or are terminated and replaced by an obligation to pay such an amount; and/or

(ii) an account is taken of what is due from each party to the other in respect of such obligations, and a net sum equal to the balance of the account is payable by the party from whom the larger amount is due to the other party.

2. References in this Directive to financial collateral being provided , or to the provision of financial collateral, are to the financial collateral being delivered, transferred, held, registered or otherwise designated so as to be in the possession or under the control of the collateral taker or of a person acting on the collateral taker's behalf. Any right of substitution or to withdraw excess financial collateral in favour of the collateral provider shall not prejudice the financial collateral having been provided to the collateral taker as mentioned in this Directive.

3. References in this Directive to writing include recording by electronic means and any other durable medium.

[3294]

Article 3

Formal requirements

1. Member States shall not require that the creation, validity, perfection, enforceability or admissibility in evidence of a financial collateral arrangement or the provision of financial collateral under a financial collateral arrangement be dependent on the performance of any formal act.

2. Paragraph 1 is without prejudice to the application of this Directive to financial collateral only once it has been provided and if that provision can be evidenced in writing and where the financial collateral arrangement can be evidenced in writing or in a legally equivalent manner.

[3295]

Article 4

Enforcement of financial collateral arrangements

1. Member States shall ensure that on the occurrence of an enforcement event, the collateral taker shall be able to realise in the following manners, any financial collateral provided under, and subject to the terms agreed in, a security financial collateral arrangement:

(a) financial instruments by sale or appropriation and by setting off their value against, or applying their value in discharge of, the relevant financial obligations;

(b) cash by setting off the amount against or applying it in discharge of the relevant financial obligations.

2. Appropriation is possible only if:

(a) this has been agreed by the parties in the security financial collateral arrangement; and

(b) the parties have agreed in the security financial collateral arrangement on the valuation of the financial instruments.

3. Member States which do not allow appropriation on 27 June 2002 are not obliged to recognise it.

If they make use of this option, Member States shall inform the Commission which in turn shall inform the other Member States thereof.

4. The manners of realising the financial collateral referred to in paragraph 1 shall, subject to the terms agreed in the security financial collateral arrangement, be without any requirement to the effect that:

(a) prior notice of the intention to realise must have been given;

(b) the terms of the realisation be approved by any court, public officer or other person;

(c) the realisation be conducted by public auction or in any other prescribed manner; or

(d) any additional time period must have elapsed.

5. Member States shall ensure that a financial collateral arrangement can take effect in accordance with its terms notwithstanding the commencement or continuation of winding-up proceedings or reorganisation measures in respect of the collateral provider or collateral taker.

6. This Article and Articles 5, 6 and 7 shall be without prejudice to any requirements under national law to the effect that the realisation or valuation of financial collateral and the calculation of the relevant financial obligations must be conducted in a commercially reasonable manner.

[3296]

Article 5

Right of use of financial collateral under security financial collateral arrangements

1. If and to the extent that the terms of a security financial collateral arrangement so provide, Member States shall ensure that the collateral taker is entitled to exercise a right of use in relation to financial collateral provided under the security financial collateral arrangement.

2. Where a collateral taker exercises a right of use, he thereby incurs an obligation to transfer equivalent collateral to replace the original financial collateral at the latest on the due date for the performance of the relevant financial obligations covered by the security financial collateral arrangement.

Alternatively, the collateral taker shall, on the due date for the performance of the relevant financial obligations, either transfer equivalent collateral, or, if and to the extent that the terms of a security financial collateral arrangement so provide, set off the value of the equivalent collateral against or apply it in discharge of the relevant financial obligations.

3. The equivalent collateral transferred in discharge of an obligation as described in paragraph 2, first subparagraph, shall be subject to the same security financial collateral agreement to which the original financial collateral was subject and shall be treated as having been provided under the security financial collateral arrangement at the same time as the original financial collateral was first provided.

4. Member States shall ensure that the use of financial collateral by the collateral taker according to this Article does not render invalid or unenforceable the rights of the collateral taker under the security financial collateral arrangement in relation to the financial collateral transferred by the collateral taker in discharge of an obligation as described in paragraph 2, first subparagraph.

5. If an enforcement event occurs while an obligation as described in paragraph 2 first subparagraph remains outstanding, the obligation may be the subject of a close-out netting provision.

[3297]

Article 6

Recognition of title transfer financial collateral arrangements

1. Member States shall ensure that a title transfer financial collateral arrangement can take effect in accordance with its terms.

2. If an enforcement event occurs while any obligation of the collateral taker to transfer equivalent collateral under a title transfer financial collateral arrangement remains outstanding, the obligation may be the subject of a close-out netting provision.

[3298]

Article 7

Recognition of close-out netting provisions

1. Member States shall ensure that a close-out netting provision can take effect in accordance with its terms:

(a) notwithstanding the commencement or continuation of winding-up proceedings or reorganisation measures in respect of the collateral provider and/or the collateral taker; and/or

(b) notwithstanding any purported assignment, judicial or other attachment or other disposition of or in respect of such rights.

2. Member States shall ensure that the operation of a close-out netting provision may not be subject to any of the requirements that are mentioned in Article 4(4), unless otherwise agreed by the parties.

[3299]

Article 8

Certain insolvency provisions disapplied

1. Member States shall ensure that a financial collateral arrangement, as well as the provision of financial collateral under such arrangement, may not be declared invalid or void or be reversed on the sole basis that the financial collateral arrangement has come into existence, or the financial collateral has been provided:

(a) on the day of the commencement of winding-up proceedings or reorganisation measures, but prior to the order or decree making that commencement; or

(b) in a prescribed period prior to, and defined by reference to, the commencement of such proceedings or measures or by reference to the making of any order or decree or the taking of any other action or occurrence of any other event in the course of such proceedings or measures.

2. Member States shall ensure that where a financial collateral arrangement or a relevant financial obligation has come into existence, or financial collateral has been provided on the day of, but after the moment of the commencement of, winding-up proceedings or reorganisation measures, it shall be legally enforceable and binding on third parties if the collateral taker can prove that he was not aware, nor should have been aware, of the commencement of such proceedings or measures.

3. Where a financial collateral arrangement contains:

(a) an obligation to provide financial collateral or additional financial collateral in order to take account of changes in the value of the financial collateral or in the amount of the relevant financial obligations, or

(b) a right to withdraw financial collateral on providing, by way of substitution or exchange, financial collateral of substantially the same value,

Member States shall ensure that the provision of financial collateral, additional financial collateral or substitute or replacement financial collateral under such an obligation or right shall not be treated as invalid or reversed or declared void on the sole basis that:

(i) such provision was made on the day of the commencement of winding-up proceedings or reorganisation measures, but prior to the order or decree making that commencement or in a prescribed period prior to, and defined by reference to, the commencement of winding-up proceedings or reorganisation measures or by reference to the making of any order or decree or the taking of any other action or occurrence of any other event in the course of such proceedings or measures; and/or

(ii) the relevant financial obligations were incurred prior to the date of the provision of the financial collateral, additional financial collateral or substitute or replacement financial collateral.

4. Without prejudice to paragraphs 1, 2 and 3, this Directive leaves unaffected the general rules of national insolvency law in relation to the violence of transactions entered into during the prescribed period referred to in paragraph 1(b) and in paragraph 3(i).

[3300]

Article 9

Conflict of laws

1. Any question with respect to any of the matters specified in paragraph 2 arising in relation to book entry securities collateral shall be governed by the law of the country in which the relevant account is maintained. The reference to the law of a country is a reference to its domestic law, disregarding any rule under which, in deciding the relevant question, reference should be made to the law of another country.

2. The matters referred to in paragraph 1 are:

(a) the legal nature and proprietary effects of book entry securities collateral;

(b) the requirements for perfecting a financial collateral arrangement relating to book entry securities collateral and the provision of book entry securities collateral under such an arrangement, and more generally the completion of the steps necessary to render such an arrangement and provision effective against third parties;

(c) whether a person's title to or interest in such book entry securities collateral is overridden by or subordinated to a competing title or interest, or a good faith acquisition has occurred;

(d) the steps required for the realisation of book entry securities collateral following the occurrence of an enforcement event.

[3301]

Article 10

Report by the Commission

Not later than 27 December 2006, the Commission shall present a report to the European Parliament and the Council on the application of this Directive, in particular on the application of Article 1(3), Article 4(3) and Article 5, accompanied where appropriate by proposals for its revision.

[3302]

Article 11

Implementation

Member States shall bring into force the laws, regulations and administrative provisions necessary to comply with this Directive by 27 December 2003 at the latest. They shall forthwith inform the Commission thereof.

When Member States adopt those provisions, they shall contain a reference to this Directive or be accompanied by such reference on the occasion of their official publication. Member States shall determine how such reference is to be made.

[3303]

Article 12

Entry into force

This Directive shall enter into force on the day of its publication in the *Official Journal of the European Communities*.

[3304]

Article 13

Addressees

This Directive is addressed to the Member States.

[3305]

Done at Brussels, 6 June 2002.

COUNCIL DIRECTIVE

of 11 May 2005

concerning unfair business-to-consumer commercial practices in the internal market and amending Council Directive 84/450/EEC, Directives 97/7/EC, 98/27/EC and 2002/65/EC of the European Parliament and of the Council and Regulation (EC) No 2006/2004 of the European Parliament and of the Council ('Unfair Commercial Practices Directive')

(2005/29/EC)

(Text with EEA relevance)

NOTES

Date of publication in OJ: OJ L149, 11.6.2005, p 22.

THE EUROPEAN PARLIAMENT AND THE COUNCIL OF THE EUROPEAN UNION,

Having regard to the Treaty establishing the European Community, and in particular Article 95 thereof,

Having regard to the proposal from the Commission,

Having regard to the opinion of the European Economic and Social Committee,[1]

Acting in accordance with the procedure laid down in Article 251 of the Treaty,[2]

Whereas:

(1) Article 153(1) and (3)(a) of the Treaty provides that the Community is to contribute to the attainment of a high level of consumer protection by the measures it adopts pursuant to Article 95 thereof.

(2) In accordance with Article 14(2) of the Treaty, the internal market comprises an area without internal frontiers in which the free movement of goods and services and freedom of establishment are ensured. The development of fair commercial practices within the area without internal frontiers is vital for the promotion of the development of crossborder activities.

(3) The laws of the Member States relating to unfair commercial practices show marked differences which can generate appreciable distortions of competition and obstacles to the smooth functioning of the internal market. In the field of advertising, Council Directive 84/450/EEC of 10 September 1984 concerning misleading and comparative advertising[3] establishes minimum criteria for harmonising legislation on misleading advertising, but does not prevent the Member States from retaining or adopting measures which provide more extensive protection for consumers. As a result, Member States' provisions on misleading advertising diverge significantly.

(4) These disparities cause uncertainty as to which national rules apply to unfair commercial practices harming consumers' economic interests and create many barriers affecting business and consumers. These barriers increase the cost to business of exercising internal market freedoms, in particular when businesses wish to engage in cross border marketing, advertising campaigns and sales promotions. Such barriers also make consumers uncertain of their rights and undermine their confidence in the internal market.

(5) In the absence of uniform rules at Community level, obstacles to the free movement of services and goods across borders or the freedom of establishment could be justified in the light of the case-law of the Court of Justice of the European Communities as long as they seek to protect recognised public interest objectives and are proportionate to those objectives. In view of the Community's objectives, as set out in the provisions of the Treaty and in secondary Community law relating to freedom of movement, and in accordance with the Commission's policy on commercial communications as indicated in the Communication from the Commission entitled 'The follow-up to the Green Paper on Commercial Communications in the Internal Market', such obstacles should be eliminated. These obstacles can only be eliminated by establishing uniform rules at Community level which establish a high level of consumer protection and by clarifying certain legal concepts at Community level to the extent necessary for the proper functioning of the internal market and to meet the requirement of legal certainty.

(6) This Directive therefore approximates the laws of the Member States on unfair commercial practices, including unfair advertising, which directly harm consumers' economic interests and thereby indirectly harm the economic interests of legitimate competitors. In line with the principle of proportionality, this Directive protects consumers from the consequences of such unfair commercial practices where they are material but recognises that in some cases the impact on consumers may be negligible. It neither covers nor affects the national laws on unfair commercial practices which harm only competitors' economic interests or which relate to a transaction between traders; taking full account of the principle of subsidiarity, Member States will continue to be able to regulate such practices, in conformity with Community law, if they choose to do so. Nor does this Directive cover or affect the provisions of Directive 84/450/EEC on advertising which misleads business but which is not misleading for consumers and on comparative advertising. Further, this Directive does not affect accepted advertising and marketing practices, such as legitimate product placement, brand differentiation or the offering of incentives which may legitimately affect consumers' perceptions of products and influence their behaviour without impairing the consumer's ability to make an informed decision.

(7) This Directive addresses commercial practices directly related to influencing consumers' transactional decisions in relation to products. It does not address commercial practices carried out primarily for other purposes, including for example commercial communication aimed at investors, such as annual reports and corporate promotional literature. It does not address legal requirements related to taste and decency which vary widely among the Member States. Commercial practices such as, for example, commercial solicitation in the streets, may be undesirable in Member States for cultural reasons. Member States should accordingly be able to continue to ban commercial practices in their territory, in

conformity with Community law, for reasons of taste and decency even where such practices do not limit consumers' freedom of choice. Full account should be taken of the context of the individual case concerned in applying this Directive, in particular the general clauses thereof.

(8) This Directive directly protects consumer economic interests from unfair business-to-consumer commercial practices. Thereby, it also indirectly protects legitimate businesses from their competitors who do not play by the rules in this Directive and thus guarantees fair competition in fields coordinated by it. It is understood that there are other commercial practices which, although not harming consumers, may hurt competitors and business customers. The Commission should carefully examine the need for Community action in the field of unfair competition beyond the remit of this Directive and, if necessary, make a legislative proposal to cover these other aspects of unfair competition.

(9) This Directive is without prejudice to individual actions brought by those who have been harmed by an unfair commercial practice. It is also without prejudice to Community and national rules on contract law, on intellectual property rights, on the health and safety aspects of products, on conditions of establishment and authorisation regimes, including those rules which, in conformity with Community law, relate to gambling activities, and to Community competition rules and the national provisions implementing them. The Member States will thus be able to retain or introduce restrictions and prohibitions of commercial practices on grounds of the protection of the health and safety of consumers in their territory wherever the trader is based, for example in relation to alcohol, tobacco or pharmaceuticals. Financial services and immovable property, by reason of their complexity and inherent serious risks, necessitate detailed requirements, including positive obligations on traders. For this reason, in the field of financial services and immovable property, this Directive is without prejudice to the right of Member States to go beyond its provisions to protect the economic interests of consumers. It is not appropriate to regulate here the certification and indication of the standard of fineness of articles of precious metal.

(10) It is necessary to ensure that the relationship between this Directive and existing Community law is coherent, particularly where detailed provisions on unfair commercial practices apply to specific sectors. This Directive therefore amends Directive 84/450/EEC, Directive 97/7/EC of the European Parliament and of the Council of 20 May 1997 on the protection of consumers in respect of distance contracts,[4] Directive 98/27/EC of the European Parliament and of the Council of 19 May 1998 on injunctions for the protection of consumers' interests[5] and Directive 2002/65/EC of the European Parliament and of the Council of 23 September 2002 concerning the distance marketing of consumer financial services.[6] This Directive accordingly applies only in so far as there are no specific Community law provisions regulating specific aspects of unfair commercial practices, such as information requirements and rules on the way the information is presented to the consumer. It provides protection for consumers where there is no specific sectoral legislation at Community level and prohibits traders from creating a false impression of the nature of products. This is particularly important for complex products with high levels of risk to consumers, such as certain financial services products. This Directive consequently complements the Community acquis, which is applicable to commercial practices harming consumers' economic interests.

(11) The high level of convergence achieved by the approximation of national provisions through this Directive creates a high common level of consumer protection. This Directive establishes a single general prohibition of those unfair commercial practices distorting consumers' economic behaviour. It also sets rules on aggressive commercial practices, which are currently not regulated at Community level.

(12) Harmonisation will considerably increase legal certainty for both consumers and business. Both consumers and business will be able to rely on a single regulatory framework based on clearly defined legal concepts regulating all aspects of unfair commercial practices across the EU. The effect will be to eliminate the barriers stemming from the fragmentation of the rules on unfair commercial practices harming consumer economic interests and to enable the internal market to be achieved in this area.

(13) In order to achieve the Community's objectives through the removal of internal market barriers, it is necessary to replace Member States' existing, divergent general clauses and legal principles. The single, common general prohibition established by this Directive therefore covers unfair commercial practices distorting consumers' economic behaviour. In order to support consumer confidence the general prohibition should apply equally to unfair commercial practices which occur outside any contractual relationship between a trader and a consumer or following the conclusion of a contract and during its execution. The general prohibition is elaborated by rules on the two types of commercial practices which are by far the most common, namely misleading commercial practices and aggressive commercial practices.

(14) It is desirable that misleading commercial practices cover those practices, including misleading advertising, which by deceiving the consumer prevent him from making an informed and thus efficient choice. In conformity with the laws and practices of Member

States on misleading advertising, this Directive classifies misleading practices into misleading actions and misleading omissions. In respect of omissions, this Directive sets out a limited number of key items of information which the consumer needs to make an informed transactional decision. Such information will not have to be disclosed in all advertisements, but only where the trader makes an invitation to purchase, which is a concept clearly defined in this Directive. The full harmonisation approach adopted in this Directive does not preclude the Member States from specifying in national law the main characteristics of particular products such as, for example, collectors' items or electrical goods, the omission of which would be material when an invitation to purchase is made. It is not the intention of this Directive to reduce consumer choice by prohibiting the promotion of products which look similar to other products unless this similarity confuses consumers as to the commercial origin of the product and is therefore misleading. This Directive should be without prejudice to existing Community law which expressly affords Member States the choice between several regulatory options for the protection of consumers in the field of commercial practices. In particular, this Directive should be without prejudice to Article 13(3) of Directive 2002/58/EC of the European Parliament and of the Council of 12 July 2002 concerning the processing of personal data and the protection of privacy in the electronic communications sector.[7]

(15) Where Community law sets out information requirements in relation to commercial communication, advertising and marketing that information is considered as material under this Directive. Member States will be able to retain or add information requirements relating to contract law and having contract law consequences where this is allowed by the minimum clauses in the existing Community law instruments. A non-exhaustive list of such information requirements in the acquis is contained in Annex II. Given the full harmonisation introduced by this Directive only the information required in Community law is considered as material for the purpose of Article 7(5) thereof. Where Member States have introduced information requirements over and above what is specified in Community law, on the basis of minimum clauses, the omission of that extra information will not constitute a misleading omission under this Directive. By contrast Member States will be able, when allowed by the minimum clauses in Community law, to maintain or introduce more stringent provisions in conformity with Community law so as to ensure a higher level of protection of consumers' individual contractual rights.

(16) The provisions on aggressive commercial practices should cover those practices which significantly impair the consumer's freedom of choice. Those are practices using harassment, coercion, including the use of physical force, and undue influence.

(17) It is desirable that those commercial practices which are in all circumstances unfair be identified to provide greater legal certainty. Annex I therefore contains the full list of all such practices. These are the only commercial practices which can be deemed to be unfair without a case-by-case assessment against the provisions of Articles 5 to 9. The list may only be modified by revision of the Directive.

(18) It is appropriate to protect all consumers from unfair commercial practices; however the Court of Justice has found it necessary in adjudicating on advertising cases since the enactment of Directive 84/450/EEC to examine the effect on a notional, typical consumer. In line with the principle of proportionality, and to permit the effective application of the protections contained in it, this Directive takes as a benchmark the average consumer, who is reasonably well informed and reasonably observant and circumspect, taking into account social, cultural and linguistic factors, as interpreted by the Court of Justice, but also contains provisions aimed at preventing the exploitation of consumers whose characteristics make them particularly vulnerable to unfair commercial practices. Where a commercial practice is specifically aimed at a particular group of consumers, such as children, it is desirable that the impact of the commercial practice be assessed from the perspective of the average member of that group It is therefore appropriate to include in the list of practices which are in all circumstances unfair a provision which, without imposing an outright ban on advertising directed at children, protects them from direct exhortations to purchase. The average consumer test is not a statistical test. National courts and authorities will have to exercise their own faculty of judgement, having regard to the case-law of the Court of Justice, to determine the typical reaction of the average consumer in a given case.

(19) Where certain characteristics such as age, physical or mental infirmity or credulity make consumers particularly susceptible to a commercial practice or to the underlying product and the economic behaviour only of such consumers is likely to be distorted by the practice in a way that the trader can reasonably foresee, it is appropriate to ensure that they are adequately protected by assessing the practice from the perspective of the average member of that group.

(20) It is appropriate to provide a role for codes of conduct, which enable traders to apply the principles of this Directive effectively in specific economic fields. In sectors where there are specific mandatory requirements regulating the behaviour of traders, it is appropriate that

these will also provide evidence as to the requirements of professional diligence in that sector. The control exercised by code owners at national or Community level to eliminate unfair commercial practices may avoid the need for recourse to administrative or judicial action and should therefore be encouraged. With the aim of pursuing a high level of consumer protection, consumers' organisations could be informed and involved in the drafting of codes of conduct.

(21) Persons or organisations regarded under national law as having a legitimate interest in the matter must have legal remedies for initiating proceedings against unfair commercial practices, either before a court or before an administrative authority which is competent to decide upon complaints or to initiate appropriate legal proceedings. While it is for national law to determine the burden of proof, it is appropriate to enable courts and administrative authorities to require traders to produce evidence as to the accuracy of factual claims they have made.

(22) It is necessary that Member States lay down penalties for infringements of the provisions of this Directive and they must ensure that these are enforced. The penalties must be effective, proportionate and dissuasive.

(23) Since the objectives of this Directive, namely to eliminate the barriers to the functioning of the internal market represented by national laws on unfair commercial practices and to provide a high common level of consumer protection, by approximating the laws, regulations and administrative provisions of the Member States on unfair commercial practices, cannot be sufficiently achieved by the Member States and can therefore be better achieved at Community level, the Community may adopt measures, in accordance with the principle of subsidiarity as set out in Article 5 of the Treaty. In accordance with the principle of proportionality, as set out in that Article, this Directive does not go beyond what is necessary in order to eliminate the internal market barriers and achieve a high common level of consumer protection.

(24) It is appropriate to review this Directive to ensure that barriers to the internal market have been addressed and a high level of consumer protection achieved. The review could lead to a Commission proposal to amend this Directive, which may include a limited extension to the derogation in Article 3(5), and/or amendments to other consumer protection legislation reflecting the Commission's Consumer Policy Strategy commitment to review the existing acquis in order to achieve a high, common level of consumer protection.

(25) This Directive respects the fundamental rights and observes the principles recognised in particular by the Charter of Fundamental Rights of the European Union,

[3306]

NOTES

1 OJ C108, 30.4.2004, p 81.

2 Opinion of the European Parliament of 20 April 2004 (OJ C104 E, 30.4.2004, p 260), Council Common Position of 15 November 2004 (OJ C38 E, 15.2.2005, p 1), Position of the European Parliament of 24 February 2005 (not yet published in the Official Journal) and Council Decision of 12 April 2005.

3 OJ L250, 19.9.1984, p 17. Directive as amended by Directive 97/55/EC of the European Parliament and of the Council (OJ L290, 23.10.1997, p 18).

4 OJ L144, 4.6.1997, p 19. Directive as amended by Directive 2002/65/EC (OJ L271, 9.10.2002, p 16).

5 OJ L166, 11.6.1998, p 51. Directive as last amended by Directive 2002/65/EC.

6 OJ L271, 9.10.2002, p 16.

7 OJ L201, 31.7.2002, p 37. L149/24 EN Official Journal of the European Union 11.6.2005.

HAS ADOPTED THIS DIRECTIVE—

CHAPTER 1
GENERAL PROVISIONS

Article 1

Purpose

The purpose of this Directive is to contribute to the proper functioning of the internal market and achieve a high level of consumer protection by approximating the laws, regulations and administrative provisions of the Member States on unfair commercial practices harming consumers' economic interests.

[3307]

Article 2

Definitions

For the purposes of this Directive:

(a) 'consumer' means any natural person who, in commercial practices covered by this Directive, is acting for purposes which are outside his trade, business, craft or profession;

(b) 'trader' means any natural or legal person who, in commercial practices covered by this Directive, is acting for purposes relating to his trade, business, craft or profession and anyone acting in the name of or on behalf of a trader;

(c) 'product' means any goods or service including immovable property, rights and obligations;

(d) 'business-to-consumer commercial practices' (hereinafter also referred to as commercial practices) means any act, omission, course of conduct or representation, commercial communication including advertising and marketing, by a trader, directly connected with the promotion, sale or supply of a product to consumers;

(e) 'to materially distort the economic behaviour of consumers' means using a commercial practice to appreciably impair the consumer's ability to make an informed decision, thereby causing the consumer to take a transactional decision that he would not have taken otherwise;

(f) 'code of conduct' means an agreement or set of rules not imposed by law, regulation or administrative provision of a Member State which defines the behaviour of traders who undertake to be bound by the code in relation to one or more particular commercial practices or business sectors;

(g) 'code owner' means any entity, including a trader or group of traders, which is responsible for the formulation and revision of a code of conduct and/or for monitoring compliance with the code by those who have undertaken to be bound by it;

(h) 'professional diligence' means the standard of special skill and care which a trader may reasonably be expected to exercise towards consumers, commensurate with honest market practice and/or the general principle of good faith in the trader's field of activity;

(i) 'invitation to purchase' means a commercial communication which indicates characteristics of the product and the price in a way appropriate to the means of the commercial communication used and thereby enables the consumer to make a purchase;

(j) 'undue influence' means exploiting a position of power in relation to the consumer so as to apply pressure, even without using or threatening to use physical force, in a way which significantly limits the consumer's ability to make an informed decision;

(k) 'transactional decision' means any decision taken by a consumer concerning whether, how and on what terms to purchase, make payment in whole or in part for, retain or dispose of a product or to exercise a contractual right in relation to the product, whether the consumer decides to act or to refrain from acting;

(l) 'regulated profession' means a professional activity or a group of professional activities, access to which or the pursuit of which, or one of the modes of pursuing which, is conditional, directly or indirectly, upon possession of specific professional qualifications, pursuant to laws, regulations or administrative provisions.

[3308]

Article 3

Scope

1. This Directive shall apply to unfair business-to-consumer commercial practices, as laid down in Article 5, before, during and after a commercial transaction in relation to a product.

2. This Directive is without prejudice to contract law and, in particular, to the rules on the validity, formation or effect of a contract.

3. This Directive is without prejudice to Community or national rules relating to the health and safety aspects of products.

4. In the case of conflict between the provisions of this Directive and other Community rules regulating specific aspects of unfair commercial practices, the latter shall prevail and apply to those specific aspects.

5. For a period of six years from 12 June 2007, Member States shall be able to continue to apply national provisions within the field approximated by this Directive which are more restrictive or prescriptive than this Directive and which implement directives containing minimum harmonisation clauses. These measures must be essential to ensure that consumers are adequately protected against unfair commercial practices and must be proportionate to the attainment of this objective. The review referred to in Article 18 may, if considered appropriate, include a proposal to prolong this derogation for a further limited period.

6. Member States shall notify the Commission without delay of any national provisions applied on the basis of paragraph 5.

7. This Directive is without prejudice to the rules determining the jurisdiction of the courts.

8. This Directive is without prejudice to any conditions of establishment or of authorisation regimes, or to the deontological codes of conduct or other specific rules governing regulated professions in order to uphold high standards of integrity on the part of the professional, which Member States may, in conformity with Community law, impose on professionals.

9. In relation to 'financial services', as defined in Directive 2002/65/EC, and immovable property, Member States may impose requirements which are more restrictive or prescriptive than this Directive in the field which it approximates.

10. This Directive shall not apply to the application of the laws, regulations and administrative provisions of Member States relating to the certification and indication of the standard of fineness of articles of precious metal.

[3309]

Article 4

Internal market

Member States shall neither restrict the freedom to provide services nor restrict the free movement of goods for reasons falling within the field approximated by this Directive.

[3310]

CHAPTER 2
UNFAIR COMMERCIAL PRACTICES

Article 5

Prohibition of unfair commercial practices

1. Unfair commercial practices shall be prohibited.

2. A commercial practice shall be unfair if:
(a) it is contrary to the requirements of professional diligence, and
(b) it materially distorts or is likely to materially distort the economic behaviour with regard to the product of the average consumer whom it reaches or to whom it is addressed, or of the average member of the group when a commercial practice is directed to a particular group of consumers.

3. Commercial practices which are likely to materially distort the economic behaviour only of a clearly identifiable group of consumers who are particularly vulnerable to the practice or the underlying product because of their mental or physical infirmity, age or credulity in a way which the trader could reasonably be expected to foresee, shall be assessed from the perspective of the average member of that group This is without prejudice to the common and legitimate advertising practice of making exaggerated statements or statements which are not meant to be taken literally.

4. In particular, commercial practices shall be unfair which:
(a) are misleading as set out in Articles 6 and 7, or
(b) are aggressive as set out in Articles 8 and 9.

5. Annex I contains the list of those commercial practices which shall in all circumstances be regarded as unfair. The same single list shall apply in all Member States and may only be modified by revision of this Directive.

[3311]

SECTION 1
MISLEADING COMMERCIAL PRACTICES

Article 6

Misleading actions

1. A commercial practice shall be regarded as misleading if it contains false information and is therefore untruthful or in any way, including overall presentation, deceives or is likely to deceive the average consumer, even if the information is factually correct, in relation to one or more of the following elements, and in either case causes or is likely to cause him to take a transactional decision that he would not have taken otherwise:

(a) the existence or nature of the product;

(b) the main characteristics of the product, such as its availability, benefits, risks, execution, composition, accessories, aftersale customer assistance and complaint handling, method and date of manufacture or provision, delivery, fitness for purpose, usage, quantity, specification, geographical or commercial origin or the results to be expected from its use, or the results and material features of tests or checks carried out on the product;

(c) the extent of the trader's commitments, the motives for the commercial practice and the nature of the sales process, any statement or symbol in relation to direct or indirect sponsorship or approval of the trader or the product;

(d) the price or the manner in which the price is calculated, or the existence of a specific price advantage;

(e) the need for a service, part, replacement or repair;

(f) the nature, attributes and rights of the trader or his agent, such as his identity and assets, his qualifications, status, approval, affiliation or connection and ownership of industrial, commercial or intellectual property rights or his awards and distinctions;

(g) the consumer's rights, including the right to replacement or reimbursement under Directive 1999/44/EC of the European Parliament and of the Council of 25 May 1999 on certain aspects of the sale of consumer goods and associated guarantees,[1] or the risks he may face.

2. A commercial practice shall also be regarded as misleading if, in its factual context, taking account of all its features and circumstances, it causes or is likely to cause the average consumer to take a transactional decision that he would not have taken otherwise, and it involves:

(a) any marketing of a product, including comparative advertising, which creates confusion with any products, trade marks, trade names or other distinguishing marks of a competitor;

(b) non-compliance by the trader with commitments contained in codes of conduct by which the trader has undertaken to be bound, where:

  (i) the commitment is not aspirational but is firm and is capable of being verified, and

  (ii) the trader indicates in a commercial practice that he is bound by the code.

[3312]

NOTES

1 OJ L171, 7.7.1999, p 12.

Article 7

Misleading omissions

1. A commercial practice shall be regarded as misleading if, in its factual context, taking account of all its features and circumstances and the limitations of the communication medium, it omits material information that the average consumer needs, according to the context, to take an informed transactional decision and thereby causes or is likely to cause the average consumer to take a transactional decision that he would not have taken otherwise.

2. It shall also be regarded as a misleading omission when, taking account of the matters described in paragraph 1, a trader hides or provides in an unclear, unintelligible, ambiguous or untimely manner such material information as referred to in that paragraph or fails to identify the commercial intent of the commercial practice if not already apparent from the context, and

where, in either case, this causes or is likely to cause the average consumer to take a transactional decision that he would not have taken otherwise.

3. Where the medium used to communicate the commercial practice imposes limitations of space or time, these limitations and any measures taken by the trader to make the information available to consumers by other means shall be taken into account in deciding whether information has been omitted.

4. In the case of an invitation to purchase, the following information shall be regarded as material, if not already apparent from the context:

(a) the main characteristics of the product, to an extent appropriate to the medium and the product;

(b) the geographical address and the identity of the trader, such as his trading name and, where applicable, the geographical address and the identity of the trader on whose behalf he is acting;

(c) the price inclusive of taxes, or where the nature of the product means that the price cannot reasonably be calculated in advance, the manner in which the price is calculated, as well as, where appropriate, all additional freight, delivery or postal charges or, where these charges cannot reasonably be calculated in advance, the fact that such additional charges may be payable;

(d) the arrangements for payment, delivery, performance and the complaint handling policy, if they depart from the requirements of professional diligence;

(e) for products and transactions involving a right of withdrawal or cancellation, the existence of such a right.

5. Information requirements established by Community law in relation to commercial communication including advertising or marketing, a non-exhaustive list of which is contained in Annex II, shall be regarded as material.

[3313]

SECTION 2
AGGRESSIVE COMMERCIAL PRACTICES

Article 8

Aggressive commercial practices

A commercial practice shall be regarded as aggressive if, in its factual context, taking account of all its features and circumstances, by harassment, coercion, including the use of physical force, or undue influence, it significantly impairs or is likely to significantly impair the average consumer's freedom of choice or conduct with regard to the product and thereby causes him or is likely to cause him to take a transactional decision that he would not have taken otherwise.

[3314]

Article 9

Use of harassment, coercion and undue influence

In determining whether a commercial practice uses harassment, coercion, including the use of physical force, or undue influence, account shall be taken of:

(a) its timing, location, nature or persistence;

(b) the use of threatening or abusive language or behaviour;

(c) the exploitation by the trader of any specific misfortune or circumstance of such gravity as to impair the consumer's judgement, of which the trader is aware, to influence the consumer's decision with regard to the product;

(d) any onerous or disproportionate non-contractual barriers imposed by the trader where a consumer wishes to exercise rights under the contract, including rights to terminate a contract or to switch to another product or another trader;

(e) any threat to take any action that cannot legally be taken.

[3315]

CHAPTER 3
CODES OF CONDUCT

Article 10

Codes of conduct

This Directive does not exclude the control, which Member States may encourage, of unfair commercial practices by code owners and recourse to such bodies by the persons or organisations referred to in Article 11 if proceedings before such bodies are in addition to the court or administrative proceedings referred to in that Article. Recourse to such control bodies shall never be deemed the equivalent of foregoing a means of judicial or administrative recourse as provided for in Article 11.

[3316]

CHAPTER 4
FINAL PROVISIONS

Article 11

Enforcement

1. Member States shall ensure that adequate and effective means exist to combat unfair commercial practices in order to enforce compliance with the provisions of this Directive in the interest of consumers.

Such means shall include legal provisions under which persons or organisations regarded under national law as having a legitimate interest in combating unfair commercial practices, including competitors, may:

(a) take legal action against such unfair commercial practices; and/or
(b) bring such unfair commercial practices before an administrative authority competent either to decide on complaints or to initiate appropriate legal proceedings.

It shall be for each Member State to decide which of these facilities shall be available and whether to enable the courts or administrative authorities to require prior recourse to other established means of dealing with complaints, including those referred to in Article 10.

These facilities shall be available regardless of whether the consumers affected are in the territory of the Member State where the trader is located or in another Member State. It shall be for each Member State to decide:

(a) whether these legal facilities may be directed separately or jointly against a number of traders from the same economic sector; and
(b) whether these legal facilities may be directed against a code owner where the relevant code promotes non-compliance with legal requirements.

2. Under the legal provisions referred to in paragraph 1, Member States shall confer upon the courts or administrative authorities powers enabling them, in cases where they deem such measures to be necessary taking into account all the interests involved and in particular the public interest:

(a) to order the cessation of, or to institute appropriate legal proceedings for an order for the cessation of, unfair commercial practices; or
(b) if the unfair commercial practice has not yet been carried out but is imminent, to order the prohibition of the practice, or to institute appropriate legal proceedings for an order for the prohibition of the practice,

even without proof of actual loss or damage or of intention or negligence on the part of the trader.

Member States shall also make provision for the measures referred to in the first subparagraph to be taken under an accelerated procedure:

— either with interim effect, or
— with definitive effect, on the understanding that it is for each Member State to decide which of the two options to select.

Furthermore, Member States may confer upon the courts or administrative authorities powers enabling them, with a view to eliminating the continuing effects of unfair commercial practices the cessation of which has been ordered by a final decision:

(a) to require publication of that decision in full or in part and in such form as they deem adequate;
(b) to require in addition the publication of a corrective statement.

3. The administrative authorities referred to in paragraph 1 must:

(a) be composed so as not to cast doubt on their impartiality;
(b) have adequate powers, where they decide on complaints, to monitor and enforce the observance of their decisions effectively;
(c) normally give reasons for their decisions. Where the powers referred to in paragraph 2 are exercised exclusively by an administrative authority, reasons for

its decisions shall always be given. Furthermore, in this case, provision must be made for procedures whereby improper or unreasonable exercise of its powers by the administrative authority or improper or unreasonable failure to exercise the said powers can be the subject of judicial review.

[3317]

Article 12

Courts and administrative authorities: substantiation of claims

Member States shall confer upon the courts or administrative authorities powers enabling them in the civil or administrative proceedings provided for in Article 11:

(a) to require the trader to furnish evidence as to the accuracy of factual claims in relation to a commercial practice if, taking into account the legitimate interest of the trader and any other party to the proceedings, such a requirement appears appropriate on the basis of the circumstances of the particular case; and

(b) to consider factual claims as inaccurate if the evidence demanded in accordance with (a) is not furnished or is deemed insufficient by the court or administrative authority.

[3318]

Article 13

Penalties

Member States shall lay down penalties for infringements of national provisions adopted in application of this Directive and shall take all necessary measures to ensure that these are enforced. These penalties must be effective, proportionate and dissuasive.

[3319]

Arts 14–16 (*Art 14 substitutes Directive 84/450/EEC, Arts 1, 3a, 4, 7(1) and amends Art 2 of that Directive; Art 15 amends Directive 97/7/EC, Art 9 and Directive 2002/65/EC, Art 9; Art 16 amends Directive 98/27/EC, Annex and Regulation 2006/2004/EC, Annex.*)

Article 17

Information

Member States shall take appropriate measures to inform consumers of the national law transposing this Directive and shall, where appropriate, encourage traders and code owners to inform consumers of their codes of conduct.

[3320]

Article 18

Review

1. By 12 June 2011 the Commission shall submit to the European Parliament and the Council a comprehensive report on the application of this Directive, in particular of Articles 3(9) and 4 and Annex I, on the scope for further harmonisation and simplification of Community law relating to consumer protection, and, having regard to Article 3(5), on any measures that need to be taken at Community level to ensure that appropriate levels of consumer protection are maintained. The report shall be accompanied, if necessary, by a proposal to revise this Directive or other relevant parts of Community law.

2. The European Parliament and the Council shall endeavour to act, in accordance with the Treaty, within two years of the presentation by the Commission of any proposal submitted under paragraph 1.

[3321]

Article 19

Transposition

Member States shall adopt and publish the laws, regulations and administrative provisions necessary to comply with this Directive by 12 June 2007. They shall forthwith inform the Commission thereof and inform the Commission of any subsequent amendments without delay.

They shall apply those measures by 12 December 2007. When Member States adopt those measures, they shall contain a reference to this Directive or be accompanied by such a reference on the occasion of their official publication. Member States shall determine how such reference is to be made.

[3322]

Article 20

Entry into force

This Directive shall enter into force on the day following its publication in the *Official Journal of the European Union*.

Article 21

Addressees

This Directive is addressed to the Member States.

[3323]

Done at Strasbourg, 11 May 2005.

ANNEX I
COMMERCIAL PRACTICES WHICH ARE IN ALL CIRCUMSTANCES CONSIDERED UNFAIR

Misleading commercial practices

1. Claiming to be a signatory to a code of conduct when the trader is not.

2. Displaying a trust mark, quality mark or equivalent without having obtained the necessary authorisation.

3. Claiming that a code of conduct has an endorsement from a public or other body which it does not have.

4. Claiming that a trader (including his commercial practices) or a product has been approved, endorsed or authorised by a public or private body when he/it has not or making such a claim without complying with the terms of the approval, endorsement or authorisation.

5. Making an invitation to purchase products at a specified price without disclosing the existence of any reasonable grounds the trader may have for believing that he will not be able to offer for supply or to procure another trader to supply, those products or equivalent products at that price for a period that is, and in quantities that are, reasonable having regard to the product, the scale of advertising of the product and the price offered (bait advertising).

6. Making an invitation to purchase products at a specified price and then:
   (a) refusing to show the advertised item to consumers; or
   (b) refusing to take orders for it or deliver it within a reasonable time; or
   (c) demonstrating a defective sample of it,

with the intention of promoting a different product (bait and switch)

7. Falsely stating that a product will only be available for a very limited time, or that it will only be available on particular terms for a very limited time, in order to elicit an immediate decision and deprive consumers of sufficient opportunity or time to make an informed choice.

8. Undertaking to provide after-sales service to consumers with whom the trader has communicated prior to a transaction in a language which is not an official language of the Member State where the trader is located and then making such service available only in another language without clearly disclosing this to the consumer before the consumer is committed to the transaction.

9. Stating or otherwise creating the impression that a product can legally be sold when it cannot.

10. Presenting rights given to consumers in law as a distinctive feature of the trader's offer.

11. Using editorial content in the media to promote a product where a trader has paid for the promotion without making that clear in the content or by images or sounds clearly identifiable by the consumer (advertorial). This is without prejudice to Council Directive 89/552/EEC.[1]

12. Making a materially inaccurate claim concerning the nature and extent of the risk to the personal security of the consumer or his family if the consumer does not purchase the product.

13. Promoting a product similar to a product made by a particular manufacturer in such a manner as deliberately to mislead the consumer into believing that the product is made by that same manufacturer when it is not.

14. Establishing, operating or promoting a pyramid promotional scheme where a consumer gives consideration for the opportunity to receive compensation that is derived primarily from the introduction of other consumers into the scheme rather than from the sale or consumption of products.

15. Claiming that the trader is about to cease trading or move premises when he is not.

16. Claiming that products are able to facilitate winning in games of chance.

17. Falsely claiming that a product is able to cure illnesses, dysfunction or malformations.

18. Passing on materially inaccurate information on market conditions or on the possibility of finding the product with the intention of inducing the consumer to acquire the product at conditions less favourable than normal market conditions.

19. Claiming in a commercial practice to offer a competition or prize promotion without awarding the prizes described or a reasonable equivalent.

20. Describing a product as 'gratis', 'free', 'without charge' or similar if the consumer has to pay anything other than the unavoidable cost of responding to the commercial practice and collecting or paying for delivery of the item.

21. Including in marketing material an invoice or similar document seeking payment which gives the consumer the impression that he has already ordered the marketed product when he has not.

22. Falsely claiming or creating the impression that the trader is not acting for purposes relating to his trade, business, craft or profession, or falsely representing oneself as a consumer.

23. Creating the false impression that after-sales service in relation to a product is available in a Member State other than the one in which the product is sold.

Aggressive commercial practices

24. Creating the impression that the consumer cannot leave the premises until a contract is formed.

25. Conducting personal visits to the consumer's home ignoring the consumer's request to leave or not to return except in circumstances and to the extent justified, under national law, to enforce a contractual obligation.

26. Making persistent and unwanted solicitations by telephone, fax, e-mail or other remote media except in circumstances and to the extent justified under national law to enforce a contractual obligation. This is without prejudice to Article 10 of Directive 97/7/EC and Directives 95/46/EC[2] and 2002/58/EC.

27. Requiring a consumer who wishes to claim on an insurance policy to produce documents which could not reasonably be considered relevant as to whether the claim was valid, or failing systematically to respond to pertinent correspondence, in order to dissuade a consumer from exercising his contractual rights.

28. Including in an advertisement a direct exhortation to children to buy advertised products or persuade their parents or other adults to buy advertised products for them. This provision is without prejudice to Article 16 of Directive 89/552/EEC on television broadcasting.

29. Demanding immediate or deferred payment for or the return or safekeeping of products supplied by the trader, but not solicited by the consumer except where the product is a substitute supplied in conformity with Article 7(3) of Directive 97/7/EC (inertia selling).

30. Explicitly informing a consumer that if he does not buy the product or service, the trader's job or livelihood will be in jeopardy.

31. Creating the false impression that the consumer has already won, will win, or will on doing a particular act win, a prize or other equivalent benefit, when in fact either: — there is no prize or other equivalent benefit, or — taking any action in relation to claiming the prize or other equivalent benefit is subject to the consumer paying money or incurring a cost.

[3324]

NOTES

1 Council Directive 89/552/EEC of 3 October 1989 on the coordination of certain provisions laid down by Law, Regulation or Administrative Action in Member States concerning the pursuit of television broadcasting activities (OJ L298, 17.10.1989, p 23). Directive as amended by Directive 97/36/EC of the European Parliament and of the Council (OJ L202, 30.7.1997, p 60).

2 Directive 95/46/EC of the European Parliament and of the Council of 24 October 1995 on the protection of individuals with regard to the processing of personal data and on the free movement of such data (OJ L281, 23.11.1995, p 31). Directive as amended by Regulation (EC) No 1882/2003 (OJ L284, 31.10.2003, p 1).

ANNEX II
COMMUNITY LAW PROVISIONS SETTING OUT RULES FOR ADVERTISING AND COMMERCIAL COMMUNICATION

Articles 4 and 5 of Directive 97/7/EC

Article 3 of Council Directive 90/314/EEC of 13 June 1990 on package travel, package holidays and package tours[1]

Article 3(3) of Directive 94/47/EC of the European Parliament and of the Council of 26 October 1994 on the protection of purchasers in respect of certain aspects of contracts relating to the purchase of a right to use immovable properties on a timeshare basis[2]

Article 3(4) of Directive 98/6/EC of the European Parliament and of the Council of 16 February 1998 on consumer protection in the indication of the prices of products offered to consumers[3]

Articles 86 to 100 of Directive 2001/83/EC of the European Parliament and of the Council of 6 November 2001 on the Community code relating to medicinal products for human use[4]

Articles 5 and 6 of Directive 2000/31/EC of the European Parliament and of the Council of 8 June 2000 on certain legal aspects of information society services, in particular electronic commerce, in the Internal Market (Directive on electronic commerce)[5]

Article 1(d) of Directive 98/7/EC of the European Parliament and of the Council of 16 February 1998 amending Council Directive 87/102/EEC for the approximation of the laws, regulations and administrative provisions of the Member States concerning consumer credit[6]

Articles 3 and 4 of Directive 2002/65/EC

Article 1(9) of Directive 2001/107/EC of the European Parliament and of the Council of 21 January 2002 amending Council Directive 85/611/EEC on the coordination of laws, regulations and administrative provisions relating to undertakings for collective investment in transferable securities (UCITS) with a view to regulating management companies and simplified prospectuses[7]

Articles 12 and 13 of Directive 2002/92/EC of the European Parliament and of the Council of 9 December 2002 on insurance mediation[8]

Article 36 of Directive 2002/83/EC of the European Parliament and of the Council of 5 November 2002 concerning life assurance[9]

Article 19 of Directive 2004/39/EC of the European Parliament and of the Council of 21 April 2004 on markets in financial instruments[10]

Articles 31 and 43 of Council Directive 92/49/EEC of 18 June 1992 on the coordination of laws, regulations and administrative provisions relating to direct insurance other than life assurance[11] (third non-life insurance Directive)

Articles 5, 7 and 8 of Directive 2003/71/EC of the European Parliament and of the Council of 4 November 2003 on the prospectus to be published when securities are offered to the public or admitted to trading[12]

[3325]

NOTES

1 OJ L158, 23.6.1990, p 59.
2 OJ L280, 29.10.1994, p 83.
3 OJ L80, 18.3.1998, p 27.
4 OJ L311, 28.11.2001, p 67. Directive as last amended by Directive 2004/27/EC (OJ L136, 30.4.2004, p 34).
5 OJ L178, 17.7.2000, p 1.
6 OJ L101, 1.4.1998, p 17.
7 OJ L41, 13.2.2002, p 20.
8 OJ L9, 15.1.2003, p 3.
9 OJ L345, 19.12.2002, p 1. Directive as amended by Council Directive 2004/66/EC. (OJ L168, 1.5.2004, p 35).
10 OJ L145, 30.4.2004, p 1.
11 OJ L228, 11.8.1992, p 1. Directive as last amended by Directive 2002/87/EC of the European Parliament and of the Council (OJ L35, 11.2.2003, p 1).
12 OJ L345, 31.12.2003, p 64.

E. INTERNATIONAL CARRIAGE: AIR

[COUNCIL REGULATION

of 9 October 1997

on air carrier liability in respect of the carriage of passengers and their baggage by air]

(2027/97/EC)

NOTES

Title: substituted by Regulation 889/2002/EC of the European Parliament and of the Council, Art 1(1).
Date of publication in OJ: OJ L285, 17.10.1997, p 1.

THE COUNCIL OF THE EUROPEAN UNION,

Having regard to the Treaty establishing the European Community, and in particular Article 84(2) thereof,

Having regard to the proposal from the Commission,[1]

Having regard to the opinion of the Economic and Social Committee,[2]

Acting in accordance with the procedure laid down in Article 189(c) of the Treaty,[3]

(1) Whereas, in the framework of the common transport policy, it is necessary to improve the level of protection of passangers involved in air accidents;

(2) Whereas the rules on liability in the event of accidents are governed by the Convention for the Unification of Certain Rules Relating to International Carriage by Air, signed at Warsaw on 12 October 1929, or that Convention as amended at The Hague on 28 September 1955 and the Convention done at Guadalajara on 18 September 1961, whichever may be applicable each being hereinafter referred to, as applicable, as the "Warsaw Convention"; whereas the Warsaw Convention is applied worldwide for the benefit of both passengers and air carriers;

(3) Whereas the limit set on liability by the Warsaw Convention is too low by today's economic and social standards and often leads to lengthy legal actions which damage the image of air transport; whereas as a result Member States have variously increased the liability limit, thereby leading to different terms and conditions of carriage in the internal aviation market;

(4) Whereas in addition the Warsaw Convention applies only to international transport; whereas, in the internal aviation market, the distinction between national and international transport has been eliminated; whereas it is therefore appropriate to have the same level and nature of liability in both national and international transport;

(5) Whereas a full review and revision of the Warsaw Convention is long overdue and would represent, in the long term, a more uniform and applicable response, at an international level, to the issue of air carrier liability in the event of accidents; whereas efforts to increase the limits of liability imposed in the Warsaw Convention should continue through negotiation at multilateral level;

(6) Whereas, in compliance with the principle of subsidiarity, action at Community level is desirable in order to achieve harmonization in the field of air carrier liability and could serve as a guideline for improved passenger protection on a global scale;

(7) Whereas it is appropriate to remove all monetary limits of liability within the meaning of Article 22(1) of the Warsaw Convention or any other legal or contractual limits, in accordance with present trends at international level;

(8) Whereas, in order to avoid situations where victims of accidents are not compensated, Community air carriers should not, with respect of any claim arising out of the death, wounding or other bodily injury of a passenger under Article 17 of the Warsaw Convention, avail themselves of any defence under Article 20(1) of the Warsaw Convention up to a certain limit;

(9) Whereas Community air carriers may be exonerated from their liability in cases of contributory negligence of the passenger concerned;

(10) Whereas it is necessary to clarify the obligations of this Regulation in the light of Article 7 of Council Regulation (EEC) No 2407/92 of 23 July 1992 on licensing of air carriers;[4] whereas, in this regard, Community air carriers should be insured up to a certain limit laid down in this Regulation;

(11) Whereas Community air carriers should always be entitled to claim against third parties;

(12) Whereas prompt advance payments can considerably assist the injured passengers or natural persons entitled to compensation in meeting the immediate costs following an air accident;

(13) Whereas the rules on the nature and limitation of liability in the event of death, wounding or any other bodily injury suffered by a passenger form part of the terms and conditions of carriage in the air transport contract between carrier and passenger; whereas, in order to reduce the risk of distorting competition, third-country carriers should adequately inform passengers of their conditions of carriage;

(14) Whereas it is appropriate and necessary that the monetary limits expressed in this Regulation be reviewed in order to take into account economic developments and developments in international fora;

(15) Whereas the International Civil Aviation Organization (ICAO) is at present engaged in a review of the Warsaw Convention; whereas, pending the outcome of such review, actions on an interim basis by the Community will enhance the protection of passengers; whereas the Council should review this Regulation as soon as possible after the review by ICAO,

[3326]

NOTES

1 OJ C104, 10.4.1996, p 18 and OJ No C29, 30.1.1997, p 10.
2 OJ C212, 22.7.1996, p 38.
3 Opinion of the European Parliament of 17 September 1996 (OJ No C320, 28.10.1996, p 30), Council Common Position of 24 February 1997 (OJ No C123, 21.4.1997, p 89) and Decision of the European Parliament of 29 May 1997 (OJ C182, 16.6.1997).
4 OJ L240, 24.8.1992, p 1.

HAS ADOPTED THIS REGULATION:

[Article 1

This Regulation implements the relevant provisions of the Montreal Convention in respect of the carriage of passengers and their baggage by air and lays down certain supplementary provisions. It also extends the application of these provisions to carriage by air within a single Member State.]

[3327]

NOTES

Commencement: 30 May 2002.
Substituted by Regulation 889/2002/EC of the European Parliament and of the Council, Art 1(2).

[Article 2

1. For the purpose of this Regulation:

(a) "air carrier" shall mean an air transport undertaking with a valid operating licence; (b) "Community air carrier" shall mean an air carrier with a valid operating licence granted by a Member State in accordance with the provisions of Regulation (EEC) No 2407/92;

(b) "Community air carrier" shall mean an air carrier with a valid operating licence granted by a Member State in accordance with the provisions of Regulation (EEC) No 2407/92;

(c) "person entitled to compensation" shall mean a passenger or any person entitled to claim in respect of that passenger, in accordance with applicable law;

(d) "baggage", unless otherwise specified, shall mean both checked and unchecked baggage with the meaning of Article 17(4) of the Montreal Convention;

(e) "SDR" shall mean a special drawing right as defined by the International Monetary Fund;

(f) "Warsaw Convention" shall mean the Convention for the Unification of Certain Rules Relating to International Carriage by Air, signed at Warsaw on 12 October 1929, or the Warsaw Convention as amended at The Hague on 28 September 1955 and the Convention supplementary to the Warsaw Convention done at Guadalajara on 18 September 1961;

(g) "Montreal Convention" shall mean the "Convention for the Unification of Certain Rules Relating to International Carriage by Air", signed at Montreal on 28 May 1999.

2. Concepts contained in this Regulation which are not defined in paragraph 1 shall be equivalent to those used in the Montreal Convention.]

[3328]

NOTES

Commencement: 30 May 2002.
Substituted by Regulation 889/2002/EC of the European Parliament and of the Council, Art 1(3).

[Article 3

1. The liability of a Community air carrier in respect of passengers and their baggage shall be governed by all provisions of the Montreal Convention relevant to such liability.

2. The obligation of insurance set out in Article 7 of Regulation (EEC) No 2407/92 as far as it relates to liability for passengers shall be understood as requiring that a Community air carrier shall be insured up to a level that is adequate to ensure that all persons entitled to compensation receive the full amount to which they are entitled in accordance with this Regulation.]

[3329]

NOTES

Commencement: 30 May 2002.
Substituted by Regulation 889/2002/EC of the European Parliament and of the Council, Art 1(4).

[Article 3a

The supplementary sum which, in accordance with Article 22(2) of the Montreal Convention, may be demanded by a Community air carrier when a passenger makes a special declaration of interest in delivery of their baggage at destination, shall be based on a tariff which is related to the additional costs involved in transporting and insuring the baggage concerned over and above those for baggage valued at or below the liability limit. The tariff shall be made available to passengers on request.]

[3330]

NOTES

Commencement: 30 May 2002.
Inserted by Regulation 889/2002/EC of the European Parliament and of the Council, Art 1(5).

Art 4 *(Revoked by Regulation 889/2002/EC of the European Parliament and of the Council, Art 1(6).)*

[Article 5

1. The Community air carrier shall without delay, and in any event not later than fifteen days after the identity of the natural person entitled to compensation has been established, make such advance payments as may be required to meet immediate economic needs on a basis proportional to the hardship suffered.

2. Without prejudice to paragraph 1, an advance payment shall not be less than the equivalent in euro of 16 000 SDRs per passenger in the event of death.

3. An advance payment shall not constitute recognition of liability and may be offset against any subsequent sums paid on the basis of Community air carrier liability, but is not returnable, except in the cases prescribed in Article 20 of the Montreal Convention or where the person who received the advance payment was not the person entitled to compensation.]

[3331]

NOTES

Commencement: 30 May 2002.
Substituted by Regulation 889/2002/EC of the European Parliament and of the Council, Art 1(7).

[Article 6

1. All air carriers shall, when selling carriage by air in the Community, ensure that a summary of the main provisions governing liability for passengers and their baggage, including deadlines for filing an action for compensation and the possibility of making a special declaration for baggage, is made available to passengers at all points of sale, including sale by telephone and via the Internet. In order to comply with this information requirement,

Community air carriers shall use the notice contained in the Annex. Such summary or notice cannot be used as a basis for a claim for compensation, nor to interpret the provisions of this Regulation or the Montreal Convention.

2. In addition to the information requirements set out in paragraph 1, all air carriers shall in respect of carriage by air provided or purchased in the Community, provide each passenger with a written indication of:

— the applicable limit for that flight on the carrier's liability in respect of death or injury, if such a limit exists,

— the applicable limit for that flight on the carrier's liability in respect of destruction, loss of or damage to baggage and a warning that baggage greater in value than this figure should be brought to the airline's attention at check-in or fully insured by the passenger prior to travel;

— the applicable limit for that flight on the carrier's liability for damage occasioned by delay.

3. In the case of all carriage performed by Community air carriers, the limits indicated in accordance with the information requirements of paragraphs 1 and 2 shall be those established by this Regulation unless the Community air carrier applies higher limits by way of voluntary undertaking. In the case of all carriage performed by non- Community air carriers, paragraphs 1 and 2 shall apply only in relation to carriage to, from or within the Community.]

[3332]

NOTES

Commencement: 30 May 2002.
Substituted by Regulation 889/2002/EC of the European Parliament and of the Council, Art 1(8).

[Article 7

No later than three years after the date on which Regulation (EC) No 889/2002[1] begins to apply, the Commission shall draw up a report on the application of this Regulation. In particular, the Commission shall examine the need to revise the amounts mentioned in the relevant Articles of the Montreal Convention in the light of economic developments and the notifications of the ICAO Depositary.]

[3333]

NOTES

Commencement: 30 May 2002.
Substituted by Regulation 889/2002/EC of the European Parliament and of the Council, Art 1(9).
[1] OJ L140, 30.5.2002, p 2.

Article 8

This Regulation shall enter into force one year after the date of its publication in the *Official Journal of the European Communities*.

This Regulation shall be binding in its entirety and directly applicable in all Member States.

[3334]

Done at Luxembourg, 9 October 1997.

For the Council

The President

M DELVAUX-STEHRES

[ANNEX

Air carrier liability for passengers and their baggage

This information notice summarises the liability rules applied by Community air carriers as required by Community legislation and the Montreal Convention.

Compensation in the case of death or injury

There are no financial limits to the liability for passenger injury or death. For damages up to 100 000 SDRs (approximate amount in local currency) the air carrier cannot contest claims

PART IV EC MATERIALS

for compensation. Above that amount, the air carrier can defend itself against a claim by proving that it was not negligent or otherwise at fault.

Advance payments

If a passenger is killed or injured, the air carrier must make an advance payment, to cover immediate economic needs, within 15 days from the identification of the person entitled to compensation. In the event of death, this advance payment shall not be less than 16 000 SDRs (approximate amount in local currency).

Passenger delays

In case of passenger delay, the air carrier is liable for damage unless it took all reasonable measures to avoid the damage or it was impossible to take such measures. The liability for passenger delay is limited to 4 150 SDRs (approximate amount in local currency).

Baggage delays

In case of baggage delay, the air carrier is liable for damage unless it took all reasonable measures to avoid the damage or it was impossible to take such measures.

The liability for baggage delay is limited to 1 000 SDRs (approximate amount in local currency).

Destruction, loss or damage to baggage

The air carrier is liable for destruction, loss or damage to baggage up to 1 000 SDRs (approximate amount in local currency). In the case of checked baggage, it is liable even if not at fault, unless the baggage was defective. In the case of unchecked baggage, the carrier is liable only if at fault.

Higher limits for baggage

A passenger can benefit from a higher liability limit by making a special declaration at the latest at check-in and by paying a supplementary fee.

Complaints on baggage

If the baggage is damaged, delayed, lost or destroyed, the passenger must write and complain to the air carrier as soon as possible. In the case of damage to checked baggage, the passenger must write and complain within seven days, and in the case of delay within 21 days, in both cases from the date on which the baggage was placed at the passenger's disposal.

Liability of contracting and actual carriers

If the air carrier actually performing the flight is not the same as the contracting air carrier, the passenger has the right to address a complaint or to make a claim for damages against either. If the name or code of an air carrier is indicated on the ticket, that air carrier is the contracting air carrier.

Time limit for action

Any action in court to claim damages must be brought within two years from the date of arrival of the aircraft, or from the date on which the aircraft ought to have arrived.

Basis for the information

The basis for the rules described above is the Montreal Convention of 28 May 1999, which is implemented in the Community by Regulation (EC) No 2027/97 (as amended by Regulation (EC) No 889/2002) and national legislation of the Member States.]

[3335]

NOTES

Commencement: 30 May 2002.
Inserted by Regulation 889/2002/EC of the European Parliament and of the Council, Art 1(10).

F. CROSS-BORDER INSOLVENCY

NOTES

See also European Parliament and Council Directives 1998/26/EC on settlement finality in payment and securities settlement systems and 2002/47/EC on financial collateral arrangements at **[3242]**, **[3292]**, which contain rules applicable in insolvency situations.

COUNCIL REGULATION

of 29 May 2000

on insolvency proceedings

(1346/2000/EC)

NOTES

Date of publication in OJ: OJ L160, 30.6.2000, p 1, reproduced as subsequently amended.

THE COUNCIL OF THE EUROPEAN UNION,

Having regard to the Treaty establishing the European Community, and in particular Articles 61(c) and 67(1) thereof,

Having regard to the initiative of the Federal Republic of Germany and the Republic of Finland,

Having regard to the opinion of the European Parliament,[1]

Having regard to the opinion of the Economic and Social Committee,[2]

Whereas:

(1) The European Union has set out the aim of establishing an area of freedom, security and justice.

(2) The proper functioning of the internal market requires that cross-border insolvency proceedings should operate efficiently and effectively and this Regulation needs to be adopted in order to achieve this objective which comes within the scope of judicial cooperation in civil matters within the meaning of Article 65 of the Treaty.

(3) The activities of undertakings have more and more cross-border effects and are therefore increasingly being regulated by Community law. While the insolvency of such undertakings also affects the proper functioning of the internal market, there is a need for a Community act requiring coordination of the measures to be taken regarding an insolvent debtor's assets.

(4) It is necessary for the proper functioning of the internal market to avoid incentives for the parties to transfer assets or judicial proceedings from one Member State to another, seeking to obtain a more favourable legal position (forum shopping).

(5) These objectives cannot be achieved to a sufficient degree at national level and action at Community level is therefore justified.

(6) In accordance with the principle of proportionality this Regulation should be confined to provisions governing jurisdiction for opening insolvency proceedings and judgments which are delivered directly on the basis of the insolvency proceedings and are closely connected with such proceedings. In addition, this Regulation should contain provisions regarding the recognition of those judgments and the applicable law which also satisfy that principle.

(7) Insolvency proceedings relating to the winding-up of insolvent companies or other legal persons, judicial arrangements, compositions and analogous proceedings are excluded from the scope of the 1968 Brussels Convention on Jurisdiction and the Enforcement of Judgments in Civil and Commercial Matters,[3] as amended by the Conventions on Accession to this Convention.[4]

(8) In order to achieve the aim of improving the efficiency and effectiveness of insolvency proceedings having cross-border effects, it is necessary, and appropriate, that the provisions on jurisdiction, recognition and applicable law in this area should be contained in a Community law measure which is binding and directly applicable in Member States.

(9) This Regulation should apply to insolvency proceedings, whether the debtor is a natural person or a legal person, a trader or an individual. The insolvency proceedings to which this Regulation applies are listed in the Annexes. Insolvency proceedings concerning insurance undertakings, credit institutions, investment undertakings holding funds or securities for third parties and collective investment undertakings should be excluded from the scope of this Regulation. Such undertakings should not be covered by this Regulation since

they are subject to special arrangements and, to some extent, the national supervisory authorities have extremely wide-ranging powers of intervention.

(10) Insolvency proceedings do not necessarily involve the intervention of a judicial authority; the expression "court" in this Regulation should be given a broad meaning and include a person or body empowered by national law to open insolvency proceedings. In order for this Regulation to apply, proceedings (comprising acts and formalities set down in law) should not only have to comply with the provisions of this Regulation, but they should also be officially recognised and legally effective in the Member State in which the insolvency proceedings are opened and should be collective insolvency proceedings which entail the partial or total divestment of the debtor and the appointment of a liquidator.

(11) This Regulation acknowledges the fact that as a result of widely differing substantive laws it is not practical to introduce insolvency proceedings with universal scope in the entire Community. The application without exception of the law of the State of opening of proceedings would, against this background, frequently lead to difficulties. This applies, for example, to the widely differing laws on security interests to be found in the Community. Furthermore, the preferential rights enjoyed by some creditors in the insolvency proceedings are, in some cases, completely different. This Regulation should take account of this in two different ways. On the one hand, provision should be made for special rules on applicable law in the case of particularly significant rights and legal relationships (eg rights in rem and contracts of employment). On the other hand, national proceedings covering only assets situated in the State of opening should also be allowed alongside main insolvency proceedings with universal scope.

(12) This Regulation enables the main insolvency proceedings to be opened in the Member State where the debtor has the centre of his main interests. These proceedings have universal scope and aim at encompassing all the debtor's assets. To protect the diversity of interests, this Regulation permits secondary proceedings to be opened to run in parallel with the main proceedings. Secondary proceedings may be opened in the Member State where the debtor has an establishment. The effects of secondary proceedings are limited to the assets located in that State. Mandatory rules of coordination with the main proceedings satisfy the need for unity in the Community.

(13) The "centre of main interests" should correspond to the place where the debtor conducts the administration of his interests on a regular basis and is therefore ascertainable by third parties.

(14) This Regulation applies only to proceedings where the centre of the debtor's main interests is located in the Community.

(15) The rules of jurisdiction set out in this Regulation establish only international jurisdiction, that is to say, they designate the Member State the courts of which may open insolvency proceedings. Territorial jurisdiction within that Member State must be established by the national law of the Member State concerned.

(16) The court having jurisdiction to open the main insolvency proceedings should be enabled to order provisional and protective measures from the time of the request to open proceedings. Preservation measures both prior to and after the commencement of the insolvency proceedings are very important to guarantee the effectiveness of the insolvency proceedings. In that connection this Regulation should afford different possibilities. On the one hand, the court competent for the main insolvency proceedings should be able also to order provisional protective measures covering assets situated in the territory of other Member States. On the other hand, a liquidator temporarily appointed prior to the opening of the main insolvency proceedings should be able, in the Member States in which an establishment belonging to the debtor is to be found, to apply for the preservation measures which are possible under the law of those States.

(17) Prior to the opening of the main insolvency proceedings, the right to request the opening of insolvency proceedings in the Member State where the debtor has an establishment should be limited to local creditors and creditors of the local establishment or to cases where main proceedings cannot be opened under the law of the Member State where the debtor has the centre of his main interest. The reason for this restriction is that cases where territorial insolvency proceedings are requested before the main insolvency proceedings are intended to be limited to what is absolutely necessary. If the main insolvency proceedings are opened, the territorial proceedings become secondary.

(18) Following the opening of the main insolvency proceedings, the right to request the opening of insolvency proceedings in a Member State where the debtor has an establishment is not restricted by this Regulation. The liquidator in the main proceedings or any other person empowered under the national law of that Member State may request the opening of secondary insolvency proceedings.

(19) Secondary insolvency proceedings may serve different purposes, besides the protection of local interests. Cases may arise where the estate of the debtor is too complex to administer as a unit or where differences in the legal systems concerned are so great that

difficulties may arise from the extension of effects deriving from the law of the State of the opening to the other States where the assets are located. For this reason the liquidator in the main proceedings may request the opening of secondary proceedings when the efficient administration of the estate so requires.

(20) Main insolvency proceedings and secondary proceedings can, however, contribute to the effective realisation of the total assets only if all the concurrent proceedings pending are coordinated. The main condition here is that the various liquidators must cooperate closely, in particular by exchanging a sufficient amount of information. In order to ensure the dominant role of the main insolvency proceedings, the liquidator in such proceedings should be given several possibilities for intervening in secondary insolvency proceedings which are pending at the same time. For example, he should be able to propose a restructuring plan or composition or apply for realisation of the assets in the secondary insolvency proceedings to be suspended.

(21) Every creditor, who has his habitual residence, domicile or registered office in the Community, should have the right to lodge his claims in each of the insolvency proceedings pending in the Community relating to the debtor's assets. This should also apply to tax authorities and social insurance institutions. However, in order to ensure equal treatment of creditors, the distribution of proceeds must be coordinated. Every creditor should be able to keep what he has received in the course of insolvency proceedings but should be entitled only to participate in the distribution of total assets in other proceedings if creditors with the same standing have obtained the same proportion of their claims.

(22) This Regulation should provide for immediate recognition of judgments concerning the opening, conduct and closure of insolvency proceedings which come within its scope and of judgments handed down in direct connection with such insolvency proceedings. Automatic recognition should therefore mean that the effects attributed to the proceedings by the law of the State in which the proceedings were opened extend to all other Member States. Recognition of judgments delivered by the courts of the Member States should be based on the principle of mutual trust. To that end, grounds for non-recognition should be reduced to the minimum necessary. This is also the basis on which any dispute should be resolved where the courts of two Member States both claim competence to open the main insolvency proceedings. The decision of the first court to open proceedings should be recognised in the other Member States without those Member States having the power to scrutinise the court's decision.

(23) This Regulation should set out, for the matters covered by it, uniform rules on conflict of laws which replace, within their scope of application, national rules of private international law. Unless otherwise stated, the law of the Member State of the opening of the proceedings should be applicable (lex concursus). This rule on conflict of laws should be valid both for the main proceedings and for local proceedings; the lex concursus determines all the effects of the insolvency proceedings, both procedural and substantive, on the persons and legal relations concerned. It governs all the conditions for the opening, conduct and closure of the insolvency proceedings.

(24) Automatic recognition of insolvency proceedings to which the law of the opening State normally applies may interfere with the rules under which transactions are carried out in other Member States. To protect legitimate expectations and the certainty of transactions in Member States other than that in which proceedings are opened, provisions should be made for a number of exceptions to the general rule.

(25) There is a particular need for a special reference diverging from the law of the opening State in the case of rights in rem, since these are of considerable importance for the granting of credit. The basis, validity and extent of such a right in rem should therefore normally be determined according to the lex situs and not be affected by the opening of insolvency proceedings. The proprietor of the right in rem should therefore be able to continue to assert his right to segregation or separate settlement of the collateral security. Where assets are subject to rights in rem under the lex situs in one Member State but the main proceedings are being carried out in another Member State, the liquidator in the main proceedings should be able to request the opening of secondary proceedings in the jurisdiction where the rights in rem arise if the debtor has an establishment there. If a secondary proceeding is not opened, the surplus on sale of the asset covered by rights in rem must be paid to the liquidator in the main proceedings.

(26) If a set-off is not permitted under the law of the opening State, a creditor should nevertheless be entitled to the set-off if it is possible under the law applicable to the claim of the insolvent debtor. In this way, set-off will acquire a kind of guarantee function based on legal provisions on which the creditor concerned can rely at the time when the claim arises.

(27) There is also a need for special protection in the case of payment systems and financial markets. This applies for example to the position-closing agreements and netting agreements to be found in such systems as well as to the sale of securities and to the guarantees provided for such transactions as governed in particular by Directive 98/26/EC of the European Parliament and of the Council of 19 May 1998 on settlement finality in payment

and securities settlement systems.[5] For such transactions, the only law which is material should thus be that applicable to the system or market concerned. This provision is intended to prevent the possibility of mechanisms for the payment and settlement of transactions provided for in the payment and set-off systems or on the regulated financial markets of the Member States being altered in the case of insolvency of a business partner. Directive 98/26/EC contains special provisions which should take precedence over the general rules in this Regulation.

(28) In order to protect employees and jobs, the effects of insolvency proceedings on the continuation or termination of employment and on the rights and obligations of all parties to such employment must be determined by the law applicable to the agreement in accordance with the general rules on conflict of law. Any other insolvency-law questions, such as whether the employees' claims are protected by preferential rights and what status such preferential rights may have, should be determined by the law of the opening State.

(29) For business considerations, the main content of the decision opening the proceedings should be published in the other Member States at the request of the liquidator. If there is an establishment in the Member State concerned, there may be a requirement that publication is compulsory. In neither case, however, should publication be a prior condition for recognition of the foreign proceedings.

(30) It may be the case that some of the persons concerned are not in fact aware that proceedings have been opened and act in good faith in a way that conflicts with the new situation. In order to protect such persons who make a payment to the debtor because they are unaware that foreign proceedings have been opened when they should in fact have made the payment to the foreign liquidator, it should be provided that such a payment is to have a debt-discharging effect.

(31) This Regulation should include Annexes relating to the organisation of insolvency proceedings. As these Annexes relate exclusively to the legislation of Member States, there are specific and substantiated reasons for the Council to reserve the right to amend these Annexes in order to take account of any amendments to the domestic law of the Member States.

(32) The United Kingdom and Ireland, in accordance with Article 3 of the Protocol on the position of the United Kingdom and Ireland annexed to the Treaty on European Union and the Treaty establishing the European Community, have given notice of their wish to take part in the adoption and application of this Regulation.

(33) Denmark, in accordance with Articles 1 and 2 of the Protocol on the position of Denmark annexed to the Treaty on European Union and the Treaty establishing the European Community, is not participating in the adoption of this Regulation, and is therefore not bound by it nor subject to its application,

[3336]

NOTES

1 Opinion delivered on 2 March 2000 (not yet published in the Official Journal).
2 Opinion delivered on 26 January 2000 (not yet published in the Official Journal).
3 OJ L299, 31.12.1972, p 32.
4 OJ L204, 2.8.1975, p 28; OJ L304, 30.10.1978, p 1; OJ L388, 31.12.1982, p 1; OJ L285, 3.10.1989, p 1; OJ C15, 15.1.1997, p 1.
5 OJ L166, 11.6.1998, p 45.

HAS ADOPTED THIS REGULATION—

CHAPTER I
GENERAL PROVISIONS

Article 1

Scope

1. This Regulation shall apply to collective insolvency proceedings which entail the partial or total divestment of a debtor and the appointment of a liquidator.

2. This Regulation shall not apply to insolvency proceedings concerning insurance undertakings, credit institutions, investment undertakings which provide services involving the holding of funds or securities for third parties, or to collective investment undertakings.

[3337]

Article 2

Definitions

For the purposes of this Regulation—

(a) "insolvency proceedings" shall mean the collective proceedings referred to in Article 1(1). These proceedings are listed in Annex A;

(b) "liquidator" shall mean any person or body whose function is to administer or liquidate assets of which the debtor has been divested or to supervise the administration of his affairs. Those persons and bodies are listed in Annex C;

(c) "winding-up proceedings" shall mean insolvency proceedings within the meaning of point (a) involving realising the assets of the debtor, including where the proceedings have been closed by a composition or other measure terminating the insolvency, or closed by reason of the insufficiency of the assets. Those proceedings are listed in Annex B;

(d) "court" shall mean the judicial body or any other competent body of a Member State empowered to open insolvency proceedings or to take decisions in the course of such proceedings;

(e) "judgment" in relation to the opening of insolvency proceedings or the appointment of a liquidator shall include the decision of any court empowered to open such proceedings or to appoint a liquidator;

(f) "the time of the opening of proceedings" shall mean the time at which the judgment opening proceedings becomes effective, whether it is a final judgment or not;

(g) "the Member State in which assets are situated" shall mean, in the case of:

— tangible property, the Member State within the territory of which the property is situated,

— property and rights ownership of or entitlement to which must be entered in a public register, the Member State under the authority of which the register is kept,

— claims, the Member State within the territory of which the third party required to meet them has the centre of his main interests, as determined in Article 3(1);

(h) "establishment" shall mean any place of operations where the debtor carries out a non-transitory economic activity with human means and goods.

[3338]

Article 3

International jurisdiction

1. The courts of the Member State within the territory of which the centre of a debtor's main interests is situated shall have jurisdiction to open insolvency proceedings. In the case of a company or legal person, the place of the registered office shall be presumed to be the centre of its main interests in the absence of proof to the contrary.

2. Where the centre of a debtor's main interests is situated within the territory of a Member State, the courts of another Member State shall have jurisdiction to open insolvency proceedings against that debtor only if he possesses an establishment within the territory of that other Member State. The effects of those proceedings shall be restricted to the assets of the debtor situated in the territory of the latter Member State.

3. Where insolvency proceedings have been opened under paragraph 1, any proceedings opened subsequently under paragraph 2 shall be secondary proceedings. These latter proceedings must be winding-up proceedings.

4. Territorial insolvency proceedings referred to in paragraph 2 may be opened prior to the opening of main insolvency proceedings in accordance with paragraph 1 only:

(a) where insolvency proceedings under paragraph 1 cannot be opened because of the conditions laid down by the law of the Member State within the territory of which the centre of the debtor's main interests is situated; or

(b) where the opening of territorial insolvency proceedings is requested by a creditor who has his domicile, habitual residence or registered office in the Member State within the territory of which the establishment is situated, or whose claim arises from the operation of that establishment.

[3339]

Article 4

Law applicable

1. Save as otherwise provided in this Regulation, the law applicable to insolvency proceedings and their effects shall be that of the Member State within the territory of which such proceedings are opened, hereafter referred to as the "State of the opening of proceedings".

2. The law of the State of the opening of proceedings shall determine the conditions for the opening of those proceedings, their conduct and their closure. It shall determine in particular:

(a) against which debtors insolvency proceedings may be brought on account of their capacity;
(b) the assets which form part of the estate and the treatment of assets acquired by or devolving on the debtor after the opening of the insolvency proceedings;
(c) the respective powers of the debtor and the liquidator;
(d) the conditions under which set-offs may be invoked;
(e) the effects of insolvency proceedings on current contracts to which the debtor is party;
(f) the effects of the insolvency proceedings on proceedings brought by individual creditors, with the exception of lawsuits pending;
(g) the claims which are to be lodged against the debtor's estate and the treatment of claims arising after the opening of insolvency proceedings;
(h) the rules governing the lodging, verification and admission of claims;
(i) the rules governing the distribution of proceeds from the realisation of assets, the ranking of claims and the rights of creditors who have obtained partial satisfaction after the opening of insolvency proceedings by virtue of a right in rem or through a set-off;
(j) the conditions for and the effects of closure of insolvency proceedings, in particular by composition;
(k) creditors' rights after the closure of insolvency proceedings;
(l) who is to bear the costs and expenses incurred in the insolvency proceedings;
(m) the rules relating to the voidness, voidability or unenforceability of legal acts detrimental to all the creditors.

[3340]

Article 5

Third parties' rights in rem

1. The opening of insolvency proceedings shall not affect the rights in rem of creditors or third parties in respect of tangible or intangible, moveable or immoveable assets—both specific assets and collections of indefinite assets as a whole which change from time to time—belonging to the debtor which are situated within the territory of another Member State at the time of the opening of proceedings.

2. The rights referred to in paragraph 1 shall in particular mean:

(a) the right to dispose of assets or have them disposed of and to obtain satisfaction from the proceeds of or income from those assets, in particular by virtue of a lien or a mortgage;
(b) the exclusive right to have a claim met, in particular a right guaranteed by a lien in respect of the claim or by assignment of the claim by way of a guarantee;
(c) the right to demand the assets from, and/or to require restitution by, anyone having possession or use of them contrary to the wishes of the party so entitled;
(d) a right in rem to the beneficial use of assets.

3. The right, recorded in a public register and enforceable against third parties, under which a right in rem within the meaning of paragraph 1 may be obtained, shall be considered a right in rem.

4. Paragraph 1 shall not preclude actions for voidness, voidability or unenforceability as referred to in Article 4(2)(m).

[3341]

Article 6

Set-off

1. The opening of insolvency proceedings shall not affect the right of creditors to demand the set-off of their claims against the claims of the debtor, where such a set-off is permitted by the law applicable to the insolvent debtor's claim.

2. Paragraph 1 shall not preclude actions for voidness, voidability or unenforceability as referred to in Article 4(2)(m).

[3342]

Article 7

Reservation of title

1. The opening of insolvency proceedings against the purchaser of an asset shall not affect the seller's rights based on a reservation of title where at the time of the opening of proceedings the asset is situated within the territory of a Member State other than the State of opening of proceedings.

2. The opening of insolvency proceedings against the seller of an asset, after delivery of the asset, shall not constitute grounds for rescinding or terminating the sale and shall not prevent the purchaser from acquiring title where at the time of the opening of proceedings the asset sold is situated within the territory of a Member State other than the State of the opening of proceedings.

3. Paragraphs 1 and 2 shall not preclude actions for voidness, voidability or unenforceability as referred to in Article 4(2)(m).

[3343]

Article 8

Contracts relating to immoveable property

The effects of insolvency proceedings on a contract conferring the right to acquire or make use of immoveable property shall be governed solely by the law of the Member State within the territory of which the immoveable property is situated.

[3344]

Article 9

Payment systems and financial markets

1. Without prejudice to Article 5, the effects of insolvency proceedings on the rights and obligations of the parties to a payment or settlement system or to a financial market shall be governed solely by the law of the Member State applicable to that system or market.

2. Paragraph 1 shall not preclude any action for voidness, voidability or unenforceability which may be taken to set aside payments or transactions under the law applicable to the relevant payment system or financial market.

[3345]

Article 10

Contracts of employment

The effects of insolvency proceedings on employment contracts and relationships shall be governed solely by the law of the Member State applicable to the contract of employment.

[3346]

Article 11

Effects on rights subject to registration

The effects of insolvency proceedings on the rights of the debtor in immoveable property, a ship or an aircraft subject to registration in a public register shall be determined by the law of the Member State under the authority of which the register is kept.

[3347]

Article 12

Community patents and trade marks

For the purposes of this Regulation, a Community patent, a Community trade mark or any other similar right established by Community law may be included only in the proceedings referred to in Article 3(1).

[3348]

Article 13

Detrimental acts

Article 4(2)(m) shall not apply where the person who benefited from an act detrimental to all the creditors provides proof that:

— the said act is subject to the law of a Member State other than that of the State of the opening of proceedings, and
— that law does not allow any means of challenging that act in the relevant case.

[3349]

Article 14

Protection of third-party purchasers

Where, by an act concluded after the opening of insolvency proceedings, the debtor disposes, for consideration, of:
— an immoveable asset, or
— a ship or an aircraft subject to registration in a public register, or
— securities whose existence presupposes registration in a register laid down by law,
the validity of that act shall be governed by the law of the State within the territory of which the immoveable asset is situated or under the authority of which the register is kept.

[3350]

Article 15

Effects of insolvency proceedings on lawsuits pending

The effects of insolvency proceedings on a lawsuit pending concerning an asset or a right of which the debtor has been divested shall be governed solely by the law of the Member State in which that lawsuit is pending.

[3351]

CHAPTER II
RECOGNITION OF INSOLVENCY PROCEEDINGS

Article 16

Principle

1. Any judgment opening insolvency proceedings handed down by a court of a Member State which has jurisdiction pursuant to Article 3 shall be recognised in all the other Member States from the time that it becomes effective in the State of the opening of proceedings.

This rule shall also apply where, on account of his capacity, insolvency proceedings cannot be brought against the debtor in other Member States.

2. Recognition of the proceedings referred to in Article 3(1) shall not preclude the opening of the proceedings referred to in Article 3(2) by a court in another Member State. The latter proceedings shall be secondary insolvency proceedings within the meaning of Chapter III.

[3352]

Article 17

Effects of recognition

1. The judgment opening the proceedings referred to in Article 3(1) shall, with no further formalities, produce the same effects in any other Member State as under this law of the State of the opening of proceedings, unless this Regulation provides otherwise and as long as no proceedings referred to in Article 3(2) are opened in that other Member State.

2. The effects of the proceedings referred to in Article 3(2) may not be challenged in other Member States. Any restriction of the creditors' rights, in particular a stay or discharge, shall produce effects vis-à-vis assets situated within the territory of another Member State only in the case of those creditors who have given their consent.

[3353]

Article 18

Powers of the liquidator

1. The liquidator appointed by a court which has jurisdiction pursuant to Article 3(1) may exercise all the powers conferred on him by the law of the State of the opening of

proceedings in another Member State, as long as no other insolvency proceedings have been opened there nor any preservation measure to the contrary has been taken there further to a request for the opening of insolvency proceedings in that State. He may in particular remove the debtor's assets from the territory of the Member State in which they are situated, subject to Articles 5 and 7.

2. The liquidator appointed by a court which has jurisdiction pursuant to Article 3(2) may in any other Member State claim through the courts or out of court that moveable property was removed from the territory of the State of the court of the opening of proceedings to the territory of that other Member State after the opening of the insolvency proceedings. He may also bring any action to set aside which is in the interests of the creditors.

3. In exercising his powers, the liquidator shall comply with the law of the Member State within the territory of which he intends to take action, in particular with regard to procedures for the realisation of assets. Those powers may not include coercive measures or the right to rule on legal proceedings or disputes.

[3354]

Article 19

Proof of the liquidator's appointment

The liquidator's appointment shall be evidenced by a certified copy of the original decision appointing him or by any other certificate issued by the court which has jurisdiction.

A translation into the official language or one of the official languages of the Member State within the territory of which he intends to act may be required. No legalisation or other similar formality shall be required.

[3355]

Article 20

Return and imputation

1. A creditor who, after the opening of the proceedings referred to in Article 3(1) obtains by any means, in particular through enforcement, total or partial satisfaction of his claim on the assets belonging to the debtor situated within the territory of another Member State, shall return what he has obtained to the liquidator, subject to Articles 5 and 7.

2. In order to ensure equal treatment of creditors a creditor who has, in the course of insolvency proceedings, obtained a dividend on his claim shall share in distributions made in other proceedings only where creditors of the same ranking or category have, in those other proceedings, obtained an equivalent dividend.

[3356]

Article 21

Publication

1. The liquidator may request that notice of the judgment opening insolvency proceedings and, where appropriate, the decision appointing him, be published in any other Member State in accordance with the publication procedures provided for in that State. Such publication shall also specify the liquidator appointed and whether the jurisdiction rule applied is that pursuant to Article 3(1) or Article 3(2).

2. However, any Member State within the territory of which the debtor has an establishment may require mandatory publication. In such cases, the liquidator or any authority empowered to that effect in the Member State where the proceedings referred to in Article 3(1) are opened shall take all necessary measures to ensure such publication.

[3357]

Article 22

Registration in a public register

1. The liquidator may request that the judgment opening the proceedings referred to in Article 3(1) be registered in the land register, the trade register and any other public register kept in the other Member States.

2. However, any Member State may require mandatory registration. In such cases, the liquidator or any authority empowered to that effect in the Member State where the proceedings referred to in Article 3(1) have been opened shall take all necessary measures to ensure such registration.

[3358]

Article 23

Costs

The costs of the publication and registration provided for in Articles 21 and 22 shall be regarded as costs and expenses incurred in the proceedings.

[3359]

Article 24

Honouring of an obligation to a debtor

1. Where an obligation has been honoured in a Member State for the benefit of a debtor who is subject to insolvency proceedings opened in another Member State, when it should have been honoured for the benefit of the liquidator in those proceedings, the person honouring the obligation shall be deemed to have discharged it if he was unaware of the opening of proceedings.

2. Where such an obligation is honoured before the publication provided for in Article 21 has been effected, the person honouring the obligation shall be presumed, in the absence of proof to the contrary, to have been unaware of the opening of insolvency proceedings; where the obligation is honoured after such publication has been effected, the person honouring the obligation shall be presumed, in the absence of proof to the contrary, to have been aware of the opening of proceedings.

[3360]

Article 25

Recognition and enforceability of other judgments

1. Judgments handed down by a court whose judgment concerning the opening of proceedings is recognised in accordance with Article 16 and which concern the course and closure of insolvency proceedings, and compositions approved by that court shall also be recognised with no further formalities. Such judgments shall be enforced in accordance with Articles 31 to 51, with the exception of Article 34(2), of the Brussels Convention on Jurisdiction and the Enforcement of Judgments in Civil and Commercial Matters, as amended by the Conventions of Accession to this Convention.

The first subparagraph shall also apply to judgments deriving directly from the insolvency proceedings and which are closely linked with them, even if they were handed down by another court.

The first subparagraph shall also apply to judgments relating to preservation measures taken after the request for the opening of insolvency proceedings.

2. The recognition and enforcement of judgments other than those referred to in paragraph 1 shall be governed by the Convention referred to in paragraph 1, provided that that Convention is applicable.

3. The Member States shall not be obliged to recognise or enforce a judgment referred to in paragraph 1 which might result in a limitation of personal freedom or postal secrecy.

[3361]

Article 26[1]

Public policy

Any Member State may refuse to recognise insolvency proceedings opened in another Member State or to enforce a judgment handed down in the context of such proceedings where the effects of such recognition or enforcement would be manifestly contrary to that State's public policy, in particular its fundamental principles or the constitutional rights and liberties of the individual.

[3362]

NOTES

1 Note the Declaration by Portugal concerning the application of Articles 26 and 37 (OJ C183, 30.6.2000, p 1).

CHAPTER III
SECONDARY INSOLVENCY PROCEEDINGS

Article 27

Opening of proceedings

The opening of the proceedings referred to in Article 3(1) by a court of a Member State and which is recognised in another Member State (main proceedings) shall permit the opening in that other Member State, a court of which has jurisdiction pursuant to Article 3(2), of secondary insolvency proceedings without the debtor's insolvency being examined in that other State. These latter proceedings must be among the proceedings listed in Annex B. Their effects shall be restricted to the assets of the debtor situated within the territory of that other Member State.

[3363]

Article 28

Applicable law

Save as otherwise provided in this Regulation, the law applicable to secondary proceedings shall be that of the Member State within the territory of which the secondary proceedings are opened.

[3364]

Article 29

Right to request the opening of proceedings

The opening of secondary proceedings may be requested by:

(a) the liquidator in the main proceedings;

(b) any other person or authority empowered to request the opening of insolvency proceedings under the law of the Member State within the territory of which the opening of secondary proceedings is requested.

[3365]

Article 30

Advance payment of costs and expenses

Where the law of the Member State in which the opening of secondary proceedings is requested requires that the debtor's assets be sufficient to cover in whole or in part the costs and expenses of the proceedings, the court may, when it receives such a request, require the applicant to make an advance payment of costs or to provide appropriate security.

[3366]

Article 31

Duty to cooperate and communicate information

1. Subject to the rules restricting the communication of information, the liquidator in the main proceedings and the liquidators in the secondary proceedings shall be duty bound to communicate information to each other. They shall immediately communicate any information which may be relevant to the other proceedings, in particular the progress made in lodging and verifying claims and all measures aimed at terminating the proceedings.

2. Subject to the rules applicable to each of the proceedings, the liquidator in the main proceedings and the liquidators in the secondary proceedings shall be duty bound to cooperate with each other.

3. The liquidator in the secondary proceedings shall give the liquidator in the main proceedings an early opportunity of submitting proposals on the liquidation or use of the assets in the secondary proceedings.

[3367]

Article 32

Exercise of creditors' rights

1. Any creditor may lodge his claim in the main proceedings and in any secondary proceedings.

2. The liquidators in the main and any secondary proceedings shall lodge in other proceedings claims which have already been lodged in the proceedings for which they were appointed, provided that the interests of creditors in the latter proceedings are served thereby, subject to the right of creditors to oppose that or to withdraw the lodgement of their claims where the law applicable so provides.

3. The liquidator in the main or secondary proceedings shall be empowered to participate in other proceedings on the same basis as a creditor, in particular by attending creditors' meetings.

[3368]

Article 33

Stay of liquidation

1. The court, which opened the secondary proceedings, shall stay the process of liquidation in whole or in part on receipt of a request from the liquidator in the main proceedings, provided that in that event it may require the liquidator in the main proceedings to take any suitable measure to guarantee the interests of the creditors in the secondary proceedings and of individual classes of creditors. Such a request from the liquidator may be rejected only if it is manifestly of no interest to the creditors in the main proceedings. Such a stay of the process of liquidation may be ordered for up to three months. It may be continued or renewed for similar periods.

2. The court referred to in paragraph 1 shall terminate the stay of the process of liquidation:

— at the request of the liquidator in the main proceedings,

— of its own motion, at the request of a creditor or at the request of the liquidator in the secondary proceedings if that measure no longer appears justified, in particular, by the interests of creditors in the main proceedings or in the secondary proceedings.

[3369]

Article 34

Measures ending secondary insolvency proceedings

1. Where the law applicable to secondary proceedings allows for such proceedings to be closed without liquidation by a rescue plan, a composition or a comparable measure, the liquidator in the main proceedings shall be empowered to propose such a measure himself.

Closure of the secondary proceedings by a measure referred to in the first subparagraph shall not become final without the consent of the liquidator in the main proceedings; failing his agreement, however, it may become final if the financial interests of the creditors in the main proceedings are not affected by the measure proposed.

2. Any restriction of creditors' rights arising from a measure referred to in paragraph 1 which is proposed in secondary proceedings, such as a stay of payment or discharge of debt, may not have effect in respect of the debtor's assets not covered by those proceedings without the consent of all the creditors having an interest.

3. During a stay of the process of liquidation ordered pursuant to Article 33, only the liquidator in the main proceedings or the debtor, with the former's consent, may propose measures laid down in paragraph 1 of this Article in the secondary proceedings; no other proposal for such a measure shall be put to the vote or approved.

[3370]

Article 35

Assets remaining in the secondary proceedings

If by the liquidation of assets in the secondary proceedings it is possible to meet all claims allowed under those proceedings, the liquidator appointed in those proceedings shall immediately transfer any assets remaining to the liquidator in the main proceedings.

[3371]

Article 36

Subsequent opening of the main proceedings

Where the proceedings referred to in Article 3(1) are opened following the opening of the proceedings referred to in Article 3(2) in another Member State, Articles 31 to 35 shall apply to those opened first, in so far as the progress of those proceedings so permits.

[3372]

Article 37[1]

Conversion of earlier proceedings

The liquidator in the main proceedings may request that proceedings listed in Annex A previously opened in another Member State be converted into winding-up proceedings if this proves to be in the interests of the creditors in the main proceedings.

The court with jurisdiction under Article 3(2) shall order conversion into one of the proceedings listed in Annex B.

[3373]

NOTES

1 Note the Declaration by Portugal concerning the application of Articles 26 and 37 (OJ C183, 30.6.2000, p 1).

Article 38

Preservation measures

Where the court of a Member State which has jurisdiction pursuant to Article 3(1) appoints a temporary administrator in order to ensure the preservation of the debtor's assets, that temporary administrator shall be empowered to request any measures to secure and preserve any of the debtor's assets situated in another Member State, provided for under the law of that State, for the period between the request for the opening of insolvency proceedings and the judgment opening the proceedings.

[3374]

CHAPTER IV
PROVISION OF INFORMATION FOR CREDITORS AND LODGEMENT OF THEIR CLAIMS

Article 39

Right to lodge claims

Any creditor who has his habitual residence, domicile or registered office in a Member State other than the State of the opening of proceedings, including the tax authorities and social security authorities of Member States, shall have the right to lodge claims in the insolvency proceedings in writing.

[3375]

Article 40

Duty to inform creditors

1. As soon as insolvency proceedings are opened in a Member State, the court of that State having jurisdiction or the liquidator appointed by it shall immediately inform known creditors who have their habitual residences, domiciles or registered offices in the other Member States.

2. That information, provided by an individual notice, shall in particular include time limits, the penalties laid down in regard to those time limits, the body or authority empowered to accept the lodgement of claims and the other measures laid down. Such notice shall also indicate whether creditors whose claims are preferential or secured in rem need lodge their claims.

[3376]

Article 41

Content of the lodgement of a claim

A creditor shall send copies of supporting documents, if any, and shall indicate the nature of the claim, the date on which it arose and its amount, as well as whether he alleges preference, security in rem or a reservation of title in respect of the claim and what assets are covered by the guarantee he is invoking.

[3377]

Article 42

Languages

1. The information provided for in Article 40 shall be provided in the official language or one of the official languages of the State of the opening of proceedings. For that purpose a form shall be used bearing the heading "Invitation to lodge a claim. Time limits to be observed" in all the official languages of the institutions of the European Union.

2. Any creditor who has his habitual residence, domicile or registered office in a Member State other than the State of the opening of proceedings may lodge his claim in the official language or one of the official languages of that other State. In that event, however, the lodgement of his claim shall bear the heading "Lodgement of claim" in the official language or one of the official languages of the State of the opening of proceedings. In addition, he may be required to provide a translation into the official language or one of the official languages of the State of the opening of proceedings.

[3378]

CHAPTER V
TRANSITIONAL AND FINAL PROVISIONS

Article 43

Applicability in time

The provisions of this Regulation shall apply only to insolvency proceedings opened after its entry into force. Acts done by a debtor before the entry into force of this Regulation shall continue to be governed by the law which was applicable to them at the time they were done.

[3379]

Article 44

Relationship to Conventions

1. After its entry into force, this Regulation replaces, in respect of the matters referred to therein, in the relations between Member States, the Conventions concluded between two or more Member States, in particular:

(a) the Convention between Belgium and France on Jurisdiction and the Validity and Enforcement of Judgments, Arbitration Awards and Authentic Instruments, signed at Paris on 8 July 1899;

(b) the Convention between Belgium and Austria on Bankruptcy, Winding-up, Arrangements, Compositions and Suspension of Payments (with Additional Protocol of 13 June 1973), signed at Brussels on 16 July 1969;

(c) the Convention between Belgium and the Netherlands on Territorial Jurisdiction, Bankruptcy and the Validity and Enforcement of Judgments, Arbitration Awards and Authentic Instruments, signed at Brussels on 28 March 1925;

(d) the Treaty between Germany and Austria on Bankruptcy, Winding-up, Arrangements and Compositions, signed at Vienna on 25 May 1979;

(e) the Convention between France and Austria on Jurisdiction, Recognition and Enforcement of Judgments on Bankruptcy, signed at Vienna on 27 February 1979;

(f) the Convention between France and Italy on the Enforcement of Judgments in Civil and Commercial Matters, signed at Rome on 3 June 1930;

(g) the Convention between Italy and Austria on Bankruptcy, Winding-up, Arrangements and Compositions, signed at Rome on 12 July 1977;

(h) the Convention between the Kingdom of the Netherlands and the Federal Republic of Germany on the Mutual Recognition and Enforcement of Judgments and other Enforceable Instruments in Civil and Commercial Matters, signed at The Hague on 30 August 1962;

(i) the Convention between the United Kingdom and the Kingdom of Belgium providing for the Reciprocal Enforcement of Judgments in Civil and Commercial Matters, with Protocol, signed at Brussels on 2 May 1934;

(j) the Convention between Denmark, Finland, Norway, Sweden and Iceland on Bankruptcy, signed at Copenhagen on 7 November 1933;

(k) the European Convention on Certain International Aspects of Bankruptcy, signed at Istanbul on 5 June 1990;

[(l) the Convention between the Federative People's Republic of Yugoslavia and the Kingdom of Greece on the Mutual Recognition and Enforcement of Judgments, signed at Athens on 18 June 1959;

(m) the Agreement between the Federative People's Republic of Yugoslavia and the Republic of Austria on the Mutual Recognition and Enforcement of Arbitral Awards and Arbitral Settlements in Commercial Matters, signed at Belgrade on 18 March 1960;

(n) the Convention between the Federative People's Republic of Yugoslavia and the Republic of Italy on Mutual Judicial Cooperation in Civil and Administrative Matters, signed at Rome on 3 December 1960;

(o) the Agreement between the Socialist Federative Republic of Yugoslavia and the Kingdom of Belgium on Judicial Cooperation in Civil and Commercial Matters, signed at Belgrade on 24 September 1971;

(p) the Convention between the Governments of Yugoslavia and France on the Recognition and Enforcement of Judgments in Civil and Commercial Matters, signed at Paris on 18 May 1971;

(q) the Agreement between the Czechoslovak Socialist Republic and the Hellenic Republic on Legal Aid in Civil and Criminal Matters, signed at Athens on 22 October 1980, still in force between the Czech Republic and Greece;

(r) the Agreement between the Czechoslovak Socialist Republic and the Republic of Cyprus on Legal Aid in Civil and Criminal Matters, signed at Nicosia on 23 April 1982, still in force between the Czech Republic and Cyprus;

(s) the Treaty between the Government of the Czechoslovak Socialist Republic and the Government of the Republic of France on Legal Aid and the Recognition and Enforcement of Judgments in Civil, Family and Commercial Matters, signed at Paris on 10 May 1984, still in force between the Czech Republic and France;

(t) the Treaty between the Czechoslovak Socialist Republic and the Italian Republic on Legal Aid in Civil and Criminal Matters, signed at Prague on 6 December 1985, still in force between the Czech Republic and Italy; signed at Tallinn on 27 November 1998;

(w) the Agreement between the Republic of Lithuania and the Republic of Poland on Legal Assistance and Legal Relations in Civil, Family, Labour and Criminal Matters, signed in Warsaw on 26 January 1993.]

2. The Conventions referred to in paragraph 1 shall continue to have effect with regard to proceedings opened before the entry into force of this Regulation.

3. This Regulation shall not apply:

(a) in any Member State, to the extent that it is irreconcilable with the obligations arising in relation to bankruptcy from a convention concluded by that State with one or more third countries before the entry into force of this Regulation;

(b) in the United Kingdom of Great Britain and Northern Ireland, to the extent that is irreconcilable with the obligations arising in relation to bankruptcy and the winding-up of insolvent companies from any arrangements with the Commonwealth existing at the time this Regulation enters into force.

[3380]

NOTES

Para 1: words in square brackets added by the Act concerning the conditions of accession of the Czech Republic, the Republic of Estonia, the Republic of Cyprus, the Republic of Latvia, the Republic of Lithuania, the Republic of Hungary, the Republic of Malta, the Republic of Poland, the Republic of Slovenia and Slovak Republic and the adjustments of the Treaties on which the European Union is founded (OJ L236, 23.9.2003, p 33).

Article 45

Amendment of the Annexes

The Council, acting by qualified majority on the initiative of one of its members or on a proposal from the Commission, may amend the Annexes.

[3381]

Article 46

Reports

No later than 1 June 2012, and every five years thereafter, the Commission shall present to the European Parliament, the Council and the Economic and Social Committee a report on the application of this Regulation. The report shall be accompanied if need be by a proposal for adaptation of this Regulation.

[3382]

Article 47

Entry into force

This Regulation shall enter into force on 31 May 2002.

This Regulation shall be binding in its entirety and directly applicable in the Member States in accordance with the Treaty establishing the European Community. **[3383]**

Done at Brussels, 29 May 2000.

[ANNEX A
INSOLVENCY PROCEEDINGS REFERRED TO IN ARTICLE 2(A)

BELGIË/BELGIQUE

— Het faillissement/La faillite
— Het gerechtelijk akkoord/Le concordat judiciaire
— De collectieve schuldenregeling/Le règlement collectif de dettes
— De vrijwillige vereffening/La liquidation volontaire
— De gerechtelijke vereffening/La liquidation judiciaire
— De voorlopige ontneming van beheer, bepaald in artikel 8 van de faillissementswet/Le dessaisissement provisoire, visé à l'article 8 de la loi sur les faillites

ČESKÁ REPUBLIKA

— Konkurs
— Nucené vyrovnání
— Vyrovnání

DEUTSCHLAND

— Das Konkursverfahren
— Das gerichtliche Vergleichsverfahren
— Das Gesamtvollstreckungsverfahren
— Das Insolvenzverfahren

EESTI

— Pankrotimenetlus

ΕΛΛΑΣ

— Η πτώχευση
— Η ειδική εκκαθάριση
— Η προσωρινή διαχείριση εταιρείας. Η διοίκηση και διαχείριση των πιστωτών
— Η υπαγωγή επιχείρησης υπό επίτροπο με σκοπό τη σύναψη συμβιβασμούμε τους πιστωτές

ESPAÑA

— Concurso

FRANCE

— Sauvegarde
— Redressement judiciaire
— Liquidation judiciaire

IRELAND

— Compulsory winding up by the court
— Bankruptcy
— The administration in bankruptcy of the estate of persons dying insolvent
— Winding-up in bankruptcy of partnerships
— Creditors' voluntary winding up (with confirmation of a Court)
— Arrangements under the control of the court which involve the vesting of all or part of the property of the debtor in the Official Assignee for realisation and distribution
— Company examinership

ITALIA

— Fallimento
— Concordato preventivo
— Liquidazione coatta amministrativa
— Amministrazione straordinaria

ΚΥΠΡΟΣ
— Υποχρεωτική εκκαθάριση από το Δικαστήριο
— Εκούσια εκκαθάριση από πιστωτές κατόπιν Δικαστικού Διατάγματος
— Εκούσια εκκαθάριση από μέλη
— Εκκαθάριση με την εποπτεία του Δικαστηρίου
— Πτώχευση κατόπιν Δικαστικού Διατάγματος
— Διαχείριση της περιουσίας προσώπων που απεβίωσαν αφερέγγυα

LATVIJA
— Bankrots
— Izlīgums
— Sanācija

LIETUVA
— įmonės restrukt rizavimo byla
— įmonės bankroto byla
— įmonės bankroto procesas ne teismo tvarka

LUXEMBOURG
— Faillite
— Gestion contrôlée
— Concordat préventif de faillite (par abandon d'actif)
— Régime spécial de liquidation du notariat

MAGYARORSZÁG
— Csődeljárás
— Felszámolási eljárás

MALTA
— Xoljiment
— Amministrazzjoni
— Stralċvolontarju mill-membri jew mill-kredituri
— Stralċmill-Qorti
— Falliment f'każ ta' negozjant

NEDERLAND
— Het faillissement
— De surséance van betaling
— De schuldsaneringsregeling natuurlijke personen

ÖSTERREICH
— Das Konkursverfahren
— Das Ausgleichsverfahren

POLSKA
— Postępowanie upadlościowe
— Postępowanie ukladowe
— Upadlość obejmująca likwidację
— Upadlość z możliwością zawarcia ukladu

PORTUGAL
— O processo de insolvência
— O processo de falência
— Os processos especiais de recuperação de empresa, ou seja:
  — À concordata
  — A reconstituição empresarial
  — A reestruturação financeira
  — A gestão controlada

SLOVENIJA
— Stečajni postopek
— Skrajšani stečajni postopek
— Postopek prisilne poravnave
— Prisilna poravnava v stečaju

SLOVENSKO
— Konkurzné konanie
— Reštrukturalizačné konanie

SUOMI/FINLAND
— Konkurssi/konkurs

— Yrityssaneeraus/företagssanering

SVERIGE
— Konkurs
— Företagsrekonstruktion

UNITED KINGDOM
— Winding up by or subject to the supervision of the court
— Creditors' voluntary winding up (with confirmation by the court)
— Administration, including appointments made by filing prescribed documents with the court
— Voluntary arrangements under insolvency legislation
— Bankruptcy or sequestration.]

[3384]

NOTES

Commencement: 7 May 2006.
Substituted by Council Regulation 694/2006/EC, Art 1(1), Annex I (OJ L121, 6.5.2006, p 1).

[ANNEX B
WINDING-UP PROCEEDINGS REFERRED TO IN ARTICLE 2(C)

BELGIË/BELGIQUE
— Het faillissement/La faillite
— De vrijwillige vereffening/La liquidation volontaire
— De gerechtelijke vereffening/La liquidation judiciaire

ČESKÁ REPUBLIKA
— Konkurs
— Nucené vyrovnání

DEUTSCHLAND
— Das Konkursverfahren
— Das Gesamtvollstreckungsverfahren
— Das Insolvenzverfahren

EESTI
— Pankrotimenetlus

ΕΛΛΑΣ
— Η πτώχευση
— Η ειδική εκκαθάριση

ESPAÑA
— Concurso

FRANCE
— Liquidation judiciaire

IRELAND
— Compulsory winding up
— Bankruptcy
— The administration in bankruptcy of the estate of persons dying insolvent
— Winding-up in bankruptcy of partnerships
— Creditors' voluntary winding up (with confirmation of a court)
— Arrangements under the control of the court which involve the vesting of all or part of the property of the debtor in the Official Assignee for realisation and distribution

ITALIA
— Fallimento
— Liquidazione coatta amministrativa
— Concordato preventivo con cessione dei beni

ΚΥΠΡΟΣ
— Υποχρεωτική εκκαθάριση από το Δικαστήριο
— Εκκαθάριση με την εποπτεία του Δικαστηρίου
— Εκούσια εκκαθάριση από πιστωτές (με την επικύρωση του Δικαστηρίου)
— Πτώχευση
— Διαχείριση της περιουσίας προσώπων που απεβίωσαν αφερέγγυα

LATVIJA
— Bankrots

LIETUVA
— įmonės bankroto byla
— įmonės bankroto procesas ne teismo tvarka

LUXEMBOURG
— Faillite
— Régime spécial de liquidation du notariat

MAGYARORSZÁG
— Felszámolási eljárás

MALTA
— Stralċvolontarju
— Stralċmill-Qorti
— Falliment inkluż il-hruġta' mandat ta' qbid mill-Kuratur f'każ ta' negozjant fallut

NEDERLAND
— Het faillissement
— De schuldsaneringsregeling natuurlijke personen

ÖSTERREICH
— Das Konkursverfahren

POLSKA
— Postępowanie upadlościowe
— Upadlośc obejmująca likwidację

PORTUGAL
— O processo de insolvência
— O processo de falência

SLOVENIJA
— Stečajni postopek
— Skrajšani stečajni postopek

SLOVENSKO
— Konkurzné konanie
— Reštrukturalizačné konanie

SUOMI/FINLAND
— Konkurssi/konkurs

SVERIGE
— Konkurs

UNITED KINGDOM
— Winding up by or subject to the supervision of the court
— Winding up through administration, including appointments made by filing prescribed documents with the court
— Creditors' voluntary winding up (with confirmation by the court)
— Bankruptcy or sequestration.]

[3385]

NOTES

Commencement: 7 May 2006.
Substituted by Council Regulation 694/2006/EC, Art 1(2), Annex II (OJ L121, 6.5.2006, p 1).

[ANNEX C
LIQUIDATORS REFERRED TO IN ARTICLE 2(B)

BELGIË/BELGIQUE
— De curator/Le curateur
— De commissaris inzake opschorting/Le commissaire au sursis
— De schuldbemiddelaar/Le médiateur de dettes
— De vereffenaar/Le liquidateur
— De voorlopige bewindvoerder/L'administrateur provisoire

ČESKÁ REPUBLIKA
— Správce podstaty

PART IV EC MATERIALS

— Předběžní správce
— Vyrovnací správce
— Zvláštní správce
— Zástupce správce

DEUTSCHLAND
— Konkursverwalter
— Vergleichsverwalter
— Sachwalter (nach der Vergleichsordnung)
— Verwalter
— Insolvenzverwalter
— Sachwalter (nach der Insolvenzordnung)
— Treuhänder
— Vorläufiger Insolvenzverwalter

EESTI
— Pankrotihaldur
— Ajutine pankrotihaldur
— Usaldusisik

ΕΛΛΑΣ
— Ο σύνδικος
— Ο προσωρινός διαχειριστής. Η διοικούσα επιτροπή των πιστωτών
— Ο ειδικός εκκαθαριστής
— Ο επίτροπος

ESPAÑA
— Administradores concursales

FRANCE
— Mandataire judiciaire
— Liquidateur
— Administrateur judiciaire
— Commissaire à l'exécution du plan

IRELAND
— Liquidator
— Official Assignee
— Trustee in bankruptcy
— Provisional Liquidator
— Examiner

ITALIA
— Curatore
— Commissario
— Liquidatore giudiziale

ΚΥΠΡΟΣ
— Εκκαθαριστής και Προσωρινός Εκκαθαριστής
— Επίσημος Παραλήπτης
— Διαχειριστής της Πτώχευσης
— Εξεταστής

LATVIJA
— Maksātnespējas procesa administrators

LIETUVA
— Bankrutuojančių įmonių administratorius
— Restruktūrizuojamų įmonių administratorius

LUXEMBOURG
— Le curateur
— Le commissaire
— Le liquidateur
— Le conseil de gérance de la section d'assainissement du notariat

MAGYARORSZÁG
— Csődeljárás
— Felszámolási eljárás

MALTA
— Amministratur Proviżorju

— Riċevitur Uffiċjali
— Stralċjarju
— Manager Speċjali
— Kuraturi f'każ ta' proċeduri ta' falliment

NEDERLAND

— De curator in het faillissement
— De bewindvoerder in de surséance van betaling
— De bewindvoerder in de schuldsaneringsregeling natuurlijke personen

ÖSTERREICH

— Masseverwalter
— Ausgleichsverwalter
— Sachverwalter
— Treuhänder
— Besondere Verwalter
— Konkursgericht

POLSKA

— Syndyk
— Nadzorca sądowy
— Zarządca

PORTUGAL

— Administrador da insolvência
— Gestor judicial
— Liquidatário judicial
— Comissão de credores

SLOVENIJA

— Upravitelj prisilne poravnave
— Stečajni upravitelj
— Sodišče, pristojno za postopek prisilne poravnave
— Sodišče, pristojno za stečajni postopek

SLOVENSKO

— Predbežný správca
— Správca

SUOMI/FINLAND

— Pesänhoitaja/boförvaltare
— Selvittäjä/utredare

SVERIGE

— Förvaltare
— God man
— Rekonstruktör

UNITED KINGDOM

— Liquidator
— Supervisor of a voluntary arrangement
— Administrator
— Official Receiver
— Trustee
— Provisional Liquidator
— Judicial factor.]

[3386]

NOTES

Commencement: 7 May 2006.
Substituted by Council Regulation 694/2006/EC, Art 1(3), Annex III (OJ L121, 6.5.2006, p 1).

PART IV EC MATERIALS

REPORT ON THE CONVENTION ON INSOLVENCY PROCEEDINGS[1]

(Virgos and Schmit), Brussels, 3 May 1996

6500/96
DRS 8 (CFC)

NOTES
Reproduced by kind permission of Professor Miguel Virgos.

by Miguel VIRGOS:

Professor, Universidad Autonoma of Madrid (who contributed the background and general introduction and the comments on Articles 1 to 26, 43 to 46, territorial application and Article 48)

and Etienne SCHMIT:

Magistrate, Deputy Public Prosecutor, Luxembourg (who contributed the comments on Article 3(2) to 3(4) and Articles 27 to 42, 47 and 49 to 55)

NOTES

1 The text of the Convention on insolvency proceedings was published in Official Journal No L . The Convention, open for signature in Brussels on 23 November 1995, was signed on that day by the Plenipotentiaries of the following twelve Member States: Belgium, Denmark, Germany, Greece, Spain, France, Italy, Luxembourg, Austria, Portugal, Finland and Sweden.

I. BACKGROUND TO THE CONVENTION

1. The absence of a Convention on insolvency proceedings within the framework of the Community is viewed as a shortcoming in the completion of the internal market. It seems hard to accept that undertakings' activities are increasingly being regulated by Community law while national law alone continues to apply in the event of the failure of an undertaking. This consideration prompted Community Ministers for Justice, meeting informally in San Sebastian from 25 to 27 May 1989, to express the wish that a solution be found and to relaunch the negotiations on a Convention on this matter between the Member States and to give instructions to that effect to an ad hoc Working Party on the Bankruptcy Convention set up within the Council of the European Communities, as it then was.

A number of national experts (see the list in Annex 1) was therefore designated. The ad hoc Working Party met from 1991 until the conclusion of the definitive text of the Convention in 1995. Dr Manfred Balz (from Germany) was nominated chairman of the committee of experts. He was also the main author of the various drafts discussed during the negotiations.

2. A limited number of bilateral conventions do indeed exist between some Member States (see Article 48 of the Convention); however, Member States should be linked by a multilateral convention which, through mutual recognition of proceedings opened in each of the Member States, would permit coordination of the measures to be taken regarding an insolvent debtor's assets. To date, attempts to draw up a suitable instrument have been unsuccessful.

3. Bankruptcy, proceedings relating to the winding-up of insolvent companies or other legal persons, judicial arrangements, compositions and analogous proceedings were excluded from the scope of the Convention on Jurisdiction and the Enforcement of Judgments in Civil and Commercial Matters, signed in Brussels on 27 September 1968 and revised for the accession of new Community Member States in 1978, 1982 and 1989 (see OJCE No C189 of 28 July 1990) hereafter referred to as the "1968 Brussels Convention". Regarding those proceedings, a committee of experts met, under the auspices of the Commission of the European Communities, between 1963 and 1980 to draw up a first, and subsequently (following the Community's enlargement as from 1973) a second, draft Convention (see Bulletin of the European Communities, Supplement 2/82, containing both the Draft Convention and the explanatory report). The latter Convention was studied by an EC Council Working Party from 1982 until 1985, when work was suspended for lack of sufficient consensus.

That draft Convention provided for single proceedings (with exclusive competence to decree bankruptcy conferred on the Courts of State in which the debtor's centre of administration was located) which would be recognized in the other Contracting States, and parallel local proceedings were not permitted in those other States. The principles of "unity" (a single proceeding for the whole territory of the Community) and "universality" (the proceedings comprise all debtor's assets, wherever located) which governed the proceedings were therefore scrupulously followed in this text.

4. In the meantime, negotiations had been initiated within the Council of Europe which culminated in the adoption of a "European Convention on Certain International Aspects of Bankruptcy", opened for signing in Istanbul on 5 June 1990 hereafter referred to as the "1990 Istanbul Convention" (see the Convention and its explanatory report in Council of Europe, International aspects of bankruptcy, Strasbourg 1990).

It must be pointed out, however, that it is not certain that any Member State will ratify the 1990 Istanbul Convention. Moreover, Article 40 thereof allows scope for reservations on either Chapter II (Exercise of certain powers of the liquidator) or Chapter III (Secondary insolvency proceedings), which involves a serious risk of disparity as between Contracting States.

Notwithstanding, the text of the 1990 Istanbul Convention remains important since it introduced more flexibility into the underlying principles of unity and universality.

5. The earlier Community draft ran into a number of obstacles. The principles of unity of the bankruptcy proceedings, on which it was based, led in particular to some complex provisions needed to take account of safeguards and privileges existing only in one or other Member State. Those provisions included the possibility of forming national "sub-estates" with regard to security interests, privileges and priority claims. Overall, the system proved to be too complicated and ambitious.

For that reason, the new Community Convention on insolvency proceedings offers solutions which are as simple and flexible as possible. Above all, it is based on the principle of the universality of the proceedings limited, however, by the possible opening of one or more sets of secondary proceedings the effects of which are confined to the Member State or Member States in which they were opened.

The parallelism between the main proceedings (recognized elsewhere) and the secondary proceedings (enabling creditors in another Contracting State to invoke a local instrument in order to safeguard their interests) has made it possible to avoid over-rigid centralization, which hitherto appeared to be unacceptable to some Member States. Mandatory rules of coordination with the main proceedings guarantee the needs of unity in the Community.

[3387]

II. GENERAL INTRODUCTION TO THE CONVENTION

A. SCHEME OF THE CONVENTION

6. The Convention is divided into six Chapters with a total of 55 Articles. A Preamble, which contains important information about the scope and character of the Convention, and three Annexes, which form an integral part of it, complement its provisions.

Chapter I (Articles 1–15) defines the scope of application of the Convention (Articles 1–2), lays down the rules of direct international jurisdiction (Article 3), and determines the national law applicable through uniform conflict of laws rules (Articles 4–15).

Chapter II (Articles 16–26) addresses the recognition and enforcement of insolvency proceedings opened in other Contracting States and the recognition of the liquidator's powers.

Chapter III (Articles 27–38) contains the rules on secondary proceedings and on their coordination with the main proceedings and with other secondary proceedings.

Chapter IV (Articles 39–42) introduces several uniform rules on the right to lodge claims, the duty to provide information and the language to be used.

Chapter V (Articles 43–46) confers jurisdiction to interpret the Convention on the Court of Justice of the European Communities.

Chapter VI (Articles 47–55) contains the transitional and final provisions, including those regarding the applicability in time of the Convention (Article 47), its relationship to other Conventions (Article 48) and the procedures to amend the Annexes (Article 54), which list the insolvency proceedings to which the Convention applies and the persons who or organs which may be recognised as liquidator under the Convention.

[3388]

B. REASONS FOR THE CONVENTION

7. To date, from a Private International Law perspective, the situation in the Community in the field of insolvency has been far from encouraging. There was a conflict of laws at both the internal level, with divergent national substantive rules, and the international level, with different Private International Law solutions.

Unlike contracts, insolvencies do not form an area of the law where private spontaneous cooperation can compensate for the lack of a common legal framework at the international level. Institutional co-operation is needed to provide a certain legal order to avoid incentives for the parties to transfer disputes or goods from one country to another, seeking to obtain a more favourable legal position ("forum shopping"), or to realise their individual claims independently of the costs which this may entail for the creditors as a whole or to the going-concern value of the debtor's firm.

Only a multilateral Convention among all the Member States may discourage the opportunistic conduct of debtors or creditors from taking place and allow for the efficient administration of the financial crisis of firms and individuals within the Community. The Convention on insolvency proceedings provides such a mandatory legal framework of intra-Community cooperation.

The Convention implements Article 220 of the Treaty establishing the European Community (hereafter referred to as the "EC Treaty") and complements the 1968 Brussels Convention. It also confers on the Court of Justice of the European Communities jurisdiction to rule on the interpretation of its provisions. But, unlike the 1968 Brussels Convention, it also contains conflict of law rules. There are important grounds which justify this difference.

8. Insolvency proceedings are collective proceedings. Collective action needs clearly determined legal positions to provide for an adequate bargaining environment. This is true not only once the insolvency proceedings have been opened, but also before they have been opened (when the debtor is already in economic difficulties), as the rights "in bankruptcy" will influence negotiations for a possible "pre-bankruptcy" reorganization.

Furthermore, international insolvency proceedings can be effectively conducted only if the States concerned recognize the jurisdiction of the courts of the State of the opening of the proceedings, the powers of their liquidators and the effects of their judgements. They may accept it only if the rules on conflict of laws are also harmonized, because harmonized conflict of law rules prove a degree of certainty that, in the event of insolvency, rights created or granted in their jurisdictions will be recognized throughout the Contracting States.

[3389]

C. SCOPE

9. The Convention applies to collective insolvency proceedings which entail the partial or total divestment of a debtor and the appointment of a liquidator. Two Annexes to the Convention determine the national proceedings covered by the Convention. These Annexes form an integral part of the Convention.

10. Insurance undertakings, credit institutions, investment undertakings holding funds or securities for third parties and collective investment undertakings are all excluded from the scope of the Convention. Community discussions are under way regarding reorganization and winding-up proceedings for these entities.

11. The Convention deals only with the intra-Community effects of insolvency proceedings. It applies only when the centre of the debtor's main interests lies within the territory of a Contracting State (i e the Community). Even then, the Convention does not regulate the effect of the proceedings vis-à-vis third States. In relation to third States, the Convention does not impair the freedom of the Contracting States to adopt the appropriate rules.

[3390]

D. THE MAIN AND SECONDARY MODEL OF INSOLVENCY PROCEEDINGS

12. The Convention tries to provide a "neutral mechanism" for international cooperation, honouring the basic expectations of the parties, independently of the Contracting State in which they are situated. For this purpose, it follows a combined model of the existing principles of regulation of international bankruptcies (universality or territoriality of effects and unity or plurality of proceedings).

The idea of a single exclusive universal form of insolvency proceedings for the whole of the Community is difficult to implement without modifying, by the application of the law of the State of the opening of proceedings, pre-existing rights created before insolvency under the different national laws of other Contracting States. The reason for this lies in the absence of a uniform system of security rights in Europe, and in the great diversity of national insolvency laws as regards criteria for the priority to be given to the different classes of creditors.

13. In this legal context, the Convention seeks to reconcile the advantages of the principle of universality and the necessary protection of local interests. This explains why a combined model has been adopted which permits local proceedings to coexist with the main universal proceedings.

14. Insolvency proceedings may be opened in the Contracting State where the debtor has the centre of his main interests. Insolvency proceedings opened in that State will be main proceedings of universal character; "main", because if local proceedings are opened, they will be subject to mandatory rules of coordination and subordination to it, and "universal", because, unless local proceedings are opened, all assets of the debtor will be encompassed therein, wherever located.

Single main proceedings are always possible within the Community but the Convention does not exclude the opening of local proceedings, controlled and governed by the national law concerned, to protect those local interests. Local proceedings have only territorial scope, limited to the assets located in the State concerned. To open such local proceedings it is necessary that the debtor possesses an establishment in the territory of the State of the opening of proceedings (hereafter referred to as the "State of the opening"). In relation to the main proceedings, local insolvency proceedings can only be "secondary proceedings", since the latter are to be coordinated with and subordinated to the main proceedings.

[3391]

E. THE MAIN INSOLVENCY PROCEEDINGS

15. The "main insolvency proceedings" can be opened only in the Contracting State where the debtor has established the "centre of his main interests" (hereinafter "F1 State"). Normally it will be the place of the registered office in the case of legal persons. There can be only one main set of insolvency proceedings.

16. The main insolvency proceedings may be winding-up or reorganization proceedings, as listed in Annex A to the Convention.

17. The law of the State of the opening (lex fori concursus) is generally applicable to the insolvency proceedings. It governs the opening of the proceedings, their conduct and their closure.

18. Some aspects are regulated directly by the Convention, which provides a uniform system of individual notification, lodgement of claims and use of language:

(a) Creditors abroad must be duly informed of the opening of the proceedings. An individual notice must be sent to all known creditors domiciled in other Contracting States;
Where necessary, a notice of the opening of the proceedings shall be published in other Contracting States in accordance with their national publication procedures (F2 laws). Contracting States within the territory of which the debtor has an establishment may demand mandatory publication.

(b) Creditors who have their habitual residence, domicile or registered office in a Contracting State may participate in the main proceedings, whatever the nature (public or private) of their claims.

19. Main proceedings are always universal. This has a number of important legal consequences:

(a) Assets located outside the State of opening are also included in the proceedings and sequestrated as from the opening of proceedings on a world-wide basis;
(b) All creditors are encompassed;
(c) Proceedings opened in one Member State will produce effects throughout the whole territory of the Contracting States (i e the Community). The recognition of the effects of the proceedings in other Contracting States is automatic, by force of law, without the need for an exequatur, and is independent of publication;
However, enforcement of judgments will require prior limited control by the national courts, through an exequatur. If the conditions set out by the Convention are satisfied, the national Courts are obliged to grant it.
The Convention follows the model of "extension" to the other States (to F2, F3, etc) of the effects laid down by the national law of the State where the main proceedings have been opened (F1).

(d) The liquidator appointed in the main proceedings has authority to act in all the other Contracting States, without the need for an exequatur. He may remove assets from the State in which they are located. In exercising these powers (granted by F1 laws), the liquidator must comply with the laws of the State concerned (F2). This is particularly the case if coercion is necessary to gain control of the assets (he must then request the assistance of the local authorities);

(e) Individual execution is not possible against the assets of a debtor located in any Contracting State;

(f) There is a legal duty to surrender to the insolvency proceedings the proceeds recovered by individual execution or obtained from the debtor's voluntary payment out of assets located abroad.

20. Local insolvency proceedings opened in accordance with the Convention limit the universal scope of the main proceedings. Assets located in the Contracting State where a court opens local insolvency proceedings are subject only to the local proceedings. However, the universal character of the main proceedings reveals itself through the mandatory rules of coordination of the local proceedings with the main proceedings, which include some specific powers of intervention given by the Convention to the liquidator of the main proceedings (see points 36(3) and 38) and the transfer of any surplus in the local proceedings to the main proceedings.

[3392]

F. PROTECTION OF LOCAL INTEREST WITHIN THE MAIN PROCEEDINGS

21. The application by the State of the opening of proceedings of its law and the automatic extension of the effects of those proceedings to all Community Member States may interfere with the rules under which local market transactions are carried out in other States. For this reason, in the provisions governing the main proceedings, the Convention gives due attention to important local interests: protection of legitimate expectations and security of transactions.

22. To this end, the Convention excludes certain rights located abroad from the effects of the main proceedings or declares that those effects must be decided by the insolvency laws of the States concerned, and not by the law of the State of the opening of the proceedings.

23.

1. Exclusion from the effects of the main proceedings:

   (a) The opening of insolvency proceedings will not affect pre-existing rights in rem of creditors or other third parties over assets situated in a different State at the time of the opening of the proceedings. The same rule is also applicable to reservations of title. Firms may obtain credit under conditions which could not be offered without this kind of guarantee.
   If the law of the State in which the security is located permits these rights to be affected, the liquidator (or any authorized creditor) has to request the opening of local insolvency proceedings to achieve this result. The position of the secured creditors will then be the same as in a purely domestic bankruptcy. Only security rights which are in the legal form of a "right in rem" qualify for this benefit.

   (b) Set-off rights governed by the law of a Contracting State other than the State of the opening receive a solution parallel to that of rights in rem.

2. In other cases, the Convention amends the rule that the law of the State of opening (F1) is applicable and provides that the law of the State concerned (F2) shall govern certain specific effects of the insolvency. In this way, the effects in a given State of insolvency proceedings opened in another Contracting State will be the same as in a domestic case.

   (a) To protect the local systems of registration of property rights, the admissible effects of the insolvency proceedings on rights of the debtor in respect of immovable assets, ships or aircraft subject to registration are determined by the bankruptcy laws of the State of registration.

   (b) Furthermore, in order to protect bona-fide third-party purchasers the Convention provides that the law of the Contracting State in which the assets are situated applies in the case where the debtor disposes for consideration of immovable assets after the opening of insolvency proceedings in another Contracting State. In the case of aircraft, ships or securities subject to registration, the law of the State of registration applies.

   (c) To avoid disruptions in payment systems and financial markets, which may be protected by national law against the normal rules of insolvency law, the effects of the insolvency proceedings are determined by the law of the State the law of which governs the payment system or financial market.

(d) The effects of the insolvency proceedings on contracts conferring rights to make use of or acquire immovable property, and on employment contracts and relationships are governed respectively by the laws of the State in which they are situated and by the law applicable to the contract.

[3393]

G. LOCAL INSOLVENCY PROCEEDINGS: "INDEPENDENT" AND "SECONDARY" TERRITORIAL PROCEEDINGS

24. Local insolvency proceedings may be opened in the Contracting State where the debtor has an establishment. The effects of local proceedings are limited to the assets located in that State. Local insolvency proceedings are always "territorial".

25. The Convention permits the opening of local proceedings both before and after main proceedings have been opened in the Member State where the debtor has his centre of main interests.

Local insolvency proceedings are considered as "independent" territorial insolvency proceedings in the first case (since there are as yet no main proceedings to which they are subordinated) and as "secondary" territorial insolvency proceedings in the latter case.

Independent proceedings become secondary proceedings once main proceedings have been opened, subject to some special rules (see points 31, 37 and 38).

26. Both types of proceedings are subject to rules of coordination with the main proceedings (in the case of independent territorial proceedings, after the opening of the main proceedings) and with other local proceedings.

27. The law of the State of the opening of the local proceedings is applicable to the local insolvency proceedings (see point 17).

The right to participate in local insolvency proceedings is not limited to local creditors. Once local proceedings have been opened, all creditors (whether local or not) may participate directly or through the liquidator in the main proceedings. This openness guarantees respect for the principle of equal treatment of creditors throughout the Community. As the Community forms an internal market, there can be no restrictions on participation in local proceedings based on the place of origin of the creditor's claim, or on the place of residence of the creditor.

28. The Convention does not restrict the right of any creditor to demand the opening of secondary territorial insolvency proceedings.

29. Secondary territorial insolvency proceedings may only be winding-up proceedings (see also point 31).

30. The right to request the opening of independent territorial proceedings is limited to local creditors and creditors of the local establishment or to cases where main proceedings cannot be opened under the applicable law. The purpose of these restrictions is to avoid the existence of parallel local proceedings which are not coordinated in the framework of the main Community proceedings.

Such limitations would not impair the individual rights of the creditors to recover debts: if no collective insolvency proceedings are opened, they may resort to individual enforcement measures.

31. Independent territorial proceedings may be winding-up or reorganization proceedings as listed in Annex A or Annex B to the Convention.

In the case of reorganization proceedings, the subsequent opening of the main proceedings makes them subject to the possibility of conversion into winding-up proceedings, if the liquidator in the main proceedings so requests. If such a conversion is not requested, the local proceedings may continue as reorganization proceedings.

[3394]

H. FUNCTIONS OF THE LOCAL PROCEEDINGS

32. The first function of local proceedings is the "protection of local interests". Creditors may request the opening of local territorial proceedings to protect themselves against the effects of the law of another Contracting State. They can thus be certain that, even if the debtor's centre

of interests is located in another Contracting State, their legal position will be the same as in domestic proceedings. This possibility makes sense for creditors who cannot rely on the recognition of their rights (or their preferential rank) in proceedings in another Contracting State. Further, it also makes sense for creditors who cannot count on the application of the law of another Contracting State (for instance, small creditors who participated only in domestic transactions with the local establishment of an undertaking of another Contracting State, etc).

33. The second function of local proceedings is to serve as "auxiliary proceedings" to the main proceedings.

The liquidator in the main proceedings may request the opening of secondary proceedings when the efficient administration of the estate so requires. This may be, for instance, the case where the estate of the debtor is too complex to administer as a unit, where differences in the legal systems concerned are so great that difficulties may arise from the extension of effects deriving from the law of the State of the opening to the other States where the assets are located. It will be always the case where the liquidator in the main proceedings seeks to affect the rights in rem of creditors or other third parties in respect of assets situated in another State at the time of the opening.

[3395]

I. COORDINATION OF LOCAL INSOLVENCY PROCEEDINGS

34. Parallel main and local insolvency proceedings represent an intermediate stage between the individual actions undertaken by the creditors and the "collective action" in the full sense of the term, represented by single universal proceedings. Cooperation is made easier, since the liquidators' role of intermediary limits the number of parties, reducing the overall complexity.

However, the method of coordination established between the local proceedings is as important as their existence. In order to encourage cooperation, the Convention permits all creditors, irrespective of the State of origin of their claims, to participate in the local proceedings (local proceedings are not reserved for local creditors).

35. Secondary insolvency proceedings are subject to coordination with the main proceedings in a number of ways to ensure that due attention is given to the interests of the main insolvency without encroaching on the specific functions of the secondary proceedings. Some of these rules of coordination apply also to secondary proceedings inter se (see points 36(1), (2) and (5)).

36.

1. The Convention imposes a duty of reciprocal cooperation and exchange of information on all liquidators in both the main and secondary proceedings.
2. All liquidators are empowered to:
   (a) lodge in other proceedings the claims already lodged in the proceedings for which they have responsibility; this power is very important for small creditors, whose claims may thus be lodged in proceedings in another Contracting State without great expense, and also for the liquidator in the main proceedings, since it can reinforce his powers to influence the secondary proceedings;
   (b) participate in those proceedings.
3. The liquidator in the main proceedings is, as such, empowered to:
   (a) request the opening of secondary insolvency proceedings;
   (b) make proposals with a view to the winding-up or other use of the assets in the secondary proceedings;
   (c) propose any rescue plan, composition or comparable measure in the secondary proceedings or require such arrangements to be subject to conditions, his consent being in principle required to that effect;
   (d) request a stay on the liquidation of the assets in the secondary proceedings. Such request may be rejected by the local court only if it is manifestly of no interest to the creditors in the main proceedings. The reason behind this is a desire to provide time for a reorganization or composition to be concluded in the main proceedings, or for the sale of the whole undertaking or establishment.
4. Any assets remaining after winding-up and distribution in local proceedings pass to the main proceedings.
5. Any creditor may keep what he has obtained in secondary proceedings but may not participate in the distribution of the estate in the main insolvency proceedings until the other creditors with the same ranking (according to the law of the main proceedings) have obtained, in percentage, an equivalent dividend. The same rule

is applicable when the creditor seeks to participate in other secondary proceedings. A consolidated account of dividends must be drawn up for all of the Contracting States (i e the Community.)

37. Independent territorial insolvency proceedings also become "subordinated" proceedings as soon as main proceedings are opened within the Community. In this case, the same coordination rules to which secondary proceedings are subject apply to the extent that the progress of the independent proceedings so permits. After the opening of main proceedings, local insolvency proceedings may therefore continue not as independent proceedings but as secondary proceedings.

38. In addition, the liquidator in the main proceedings has the specific right to request the conversion of the previously opened independent territorial proceedings of a reorganizational nature (see points 31, 86 and 210) into winding-up proceedings (with a view to easier coordination with the main insolvency proceedings).

39. The Convention does not address the exceptional situation of two parallel independent territorial proceedings taking place at the same time in the Community, without main proceedings having been opened in the Contracting State where the debtor has his centre of main interests. It should be possible to apply, by analogy, the same conventional rules which serve to coordinate secondary insolvency proceedings inter se (see points 36(1), (2) and (5)). **[3396]**

III. ANALYSIS OF THE PROVISIONS

A. PREAMBLE

40. The preamble to the Convention contains several important items of information regarding the role of the Convention within the Community system.

41. The first concerns the legal basis of the Convention. The preamble cites Article 220 of the EC Treaty as that basis.

Consequently, the characteristics of the Convention on insolvency proceedings are as follows:

— all Member States must ratify the Convention,

— powers to give rulings on interpretation are conferred on the Court of Justice of the European Communities. Unlike the 1968 Brussels Convention and the Rome Convention of 19 June 1980 on the Law applicable to Contractual Obligations, hereafter referred to as the "1980 Rome Convention", these powers are granted in the text of the Convention itself and not in additional protocols,

— there can be no reservations, except as regards the conferral of powers on the Court of Justice of the European Communities (see Article 46) (see points 57 et seq).

42. The Convention on insolvency proceedings complements the system of international jurisdiction and recognition and enforcement of judgments set up in the 1968 Brussels Convention, which is also based on Article 220 of the EC Treaty.

However, the Convention on insolvency proceedings goes beyond the scope of the 1968 Brussels Convention, since it not only governs international jurisdiction and the recognition of judgments but also contains rules on conflicts regarding the law applicable to the proceedings and effects thereof. A Convention on the mutual recognition of insolvency proceedings would not be possible without the guarantee of respect for acquired rights offered by a uniform system of rules on conflict of laws. Harmonized conflict of law rules guarantee acquired rights so that, in the event of insolvency, rights created in each state will be recognized in other Contracting States.

43. The Convention on insolvency proceedings does not contain any explicit provision regarding its interpretation. In the same way as in the 1968 Brussels Convention and the 1980 Rome Convention, two principles should be followed when interpreting its provisions: the principle of respect for the international character of the rule, and the principle of uniformity.

The Convention is a self-contained legal structure, and its concepts cannot be placed in the same category as concepts belonging to national law. The Convention must retain the same meaning within different national systems. Its concepts may not therefore be interpreted simply as referring to the national law of one or other of the States concerned.

When the substance of a problem is directly governed by the Convention, the international character of the Convention requires an autonomous interpretation of its concepts. An autonomous interpretation implies that the meaning of its concepts should be determined by reference to the objectives and system of the Convention, taking into account the specific function of those concepts within this system and the general principles which can be inferred from all the national laws of the Contracting States.

However, the Convention itself may require the meaning of a concept to be found in the applicable national law, when it does not wish to interfere with the national laws or when the function of a specific provision of the Convention so requires. This is the case, for example, with the concept of insolvency in Article 1 or the concept of rights in rem as laid down in Article 5 of the Convention.

Uniformity of interpretation is required in order to ensure equality in the rights and obligations derived from the Convention for the Contracting States and for the persons concerned irrespective of the Contracting State in which they are located. To this end, the Convention confers powers of interpretation on the Court of Justice of the European Communities.

44. The second important piece of information concerns the territorial framework of the Convention, which covers only the "intra-Community effects" of insolvency proceedings. The Convention governs only internal conflicts of the Community, with two further limitations:

(a) the Convention does not govern all intra-Community conflicts. It covers only cases where the centre of the debtor's main interests is located in a Contracting State. When the centre of the debtor's main interests is outside the territory of a Contracting State, the Convention does not apply. In such a case, it is up to the private international law of Member States to decide whether insolvency proceedings may be opened against the debtor and on the rules and conditions to be applied;
This holds true regardless of whether the debtor has assets or creditors in other Member States and whether the question of the effects of such proceedings in other Member States is raised (see point 82);

(b) Even when the centre of a debtor's main interests is in a Contracting State and the Convention is applicable, its provisions are restricted to relations with other Contracting States. Where non-Member States are concerned, it is the responsibility of each Member State to define the appropriate conflict rules.
Hence, for example, Article 8 governs the effects of insolvency proceedings on contracts relating to the immovable property of the debtor, as an exception to the general applicability of the law of the State of the opening (ex Article 4), but is applicable only when the immovable property is located in a Contracting State. If the asset in question is situated in a non-Contracting State, the Convention does not govern the case. It is for the State opening the proceedings to decide whether or not an exception to the general applicability of its law is advisable, and under what terms.

45. As the Convention provides only partial (intra-Community) rules, it needs to be supplemented by the private international law provisions of the State in which the insolvency proceedings were opened.

When incorporating the Convention into their legislations, the Contracting States will therefore have to examine whether their current rules can appropriately implement the rules of the Convention or whether they should establish new rules to that end. In this respect, nothing prevents Contracting States from extending all or some of the solutions of the Convention unilaterally on an extra-Community basis, as part of their national law.

46. The third important item of information relates to the relations between this Convention and Community law. The Convention represents the general framework of intra-Community cooperation in the area of insolvency proceedings. However, as in the 1968 Brussels Convention (Article 57(3)) and the 1980 Rome Convention (Article 20), the principle of the primacy of secondary Community law is explicitly enshrined in it. For this reason, the preamble stresses that the Convention does not affect the possible application of the provisions of Community law, or of national law harmonized in accordance with those provisions, which govern insolvency proceedings in particular areas.

This principle does not prevent certain rules of the Convention from directly amending the solutions contained in previous Community acts (see Article 12).

47. The fourth item of information concerns the binding nature of the Convention, the provisions of which, including the rules on conflicts of law, should be applied by the court of its own motion even if they are not invoked by the parties concerned.

Although there is no specific mention of this point in the Convention, this was the solution adopted in the 1968 Brussels Convention. Substantial grounds for the binding nature do exist in the Convention on insolvency proceedings, since it deals with collective proceedings which by their very nature are likely to affect multiple interests and individuals. This binding nature is necessary to strengthen the legal protection of individuals established in the Community, since the Convention represents the basic guarantee of their rights vis-à-vis insolvency proceedings opened in other Contracting States.

However, it is for the national law to determine whether the judge is himself bound to establish the facts or whether it is for the interested parties to establish them (see Schlosser Report on the 1968 Brussels Convention, point 22).

[3397]

B. CHAPTER I: GENERAL PROVISIONS

Article 1
Scope

48. Article 1(1) defines the scope of the Convention by means of the concept of "collective insolvency proceedings". Given that it has to encompass widely differing national proceedings, Article 1 restricts itself to providing a very broad framework. Paragraph 1 defines this framework, requiring four cumulative conditions, which will be described below.

It should be pointed out here that, for the Convention to be applied, it is not sufficient that the proceedings in question meet these conditions in a generic way. Under Article 2(a) and (c), for insolvency proceedings to be covered by the Convention the proceedings concerned must also have been expressly entered by the State concerned in the lists of proceedings in the Annexes, which form an integral part of this Convention. Only those proceedings expressly entered in the list will be considered "insolvency proceedings" as covered by the Convention and will be able to benefit from its provisions. In an area where national laws differ considerably, the lists are aimed at providing legal certainty regarding the proceedings to which the Convention may be applied.

In short, Article 1(1) lays down the conditions which enable proceedings to be added to the lists in the Convention by Contracting States, and only when the proceedings are included in the appropriate list will the Convention be applicable (see Article 2 (a) and (c)).

49. Article 1(1) defines the proceedings to which the Convention applies on the basis of four fundamental conditions:

(a) proceedings must be "collective", ie all the creditors concerned may seek satisfaction only through the insolvency proceedings, as individual action will be precluded;

(b) the proceedings must be based on the debtor's "insolvency" and not on any other grounds.
The Convention is based on the idea of financial crisis, but does not provide its own definition of insolvency. It takes this from the national law of the country in which proceedings are opened.
There is no test of insolvency other than that demanded by the national legislation of the State in which proceedings are opened. Thus, if a national law is based on the occurrence of an act of bankruptcy listed in the bankruptcy law or on the evidence that the debtor has ceased to pay his debts, it is sufficient for one of these facts to be established in order that insolvency proceedings be opened and the Convention applied.
By way of exception, it may happen that one of the forms of proceedings listed in Annex A or Annex B to the Convention is not confined to bankruptcy law but serves several purposes. Such a proceeding falls within the scope of the Convention only if it is based on the debtor's insolvency (where appropriate the 1968 Brussels Convention will be applied). This is the case with winding-up proceedings under British and Irish law (see points 55 et seq of the Schlosser Report to the 1968 Brussels Convention).
Thus, States which list proceedings which can be used for purposes other than insolvency, must provide sufficient means of identification of the proceedings to facilitate the application of the Convention. For instance, requiring their courts or competent bodies to specify clearly the grounds on which the decision to open proceedings is based, so that these can then be used as an identification "label";

(c) the proceedings must entail the total or partial divestment of the debtor, that is to say the transfer to another person, the liquidator, of the powers of administration and of disposal over all or part of his assets, or the limitation of these powers through the intervention and control of his actions. It should be remembered that partial divestment, whether of his assets or his power of administration, is

PART IV

sufficient. The legal nature that such divestment may take, depending on the national legislation applicable, has no bearing on the application of the Convention to the proceedings in question;

(d) the proceedings should entail the appointment of a liquidator. This requirement is directly linked to the previous condition. The concept of liquidator used by the Convention is, once again, a very broad concept. Under Article 2(b) it includes any person or body whose function is to administer or realize the assets or supervise the management of the debtor's business. The court itself may fulfil this role. The persons or bodies considered to be liquidators by the Convention are set out in the list in Annex C to the Convention.

50. All the proceedings listed in Annex A have two ultimate consequences: the total or partial divestment of the debtor and the appointment of a liquidator. However, distortions would arise if the Convention were to apply only from the time when these consequences occur. The initial stages of insolvency proceedings could be excluded from the Convention's system of international cooperation. These consequences are necessary for proceedings to appear in the lists in Annex A. However, once the proceedings have been included, it is sufficient to open proceedings in order that the Convention should apply from the outset.

51. Article 1(1) of the Convention does not include in its final version the condition that the proceedings may entail the realization of the debtor's assets.

Limiting the application of the Convention to winding-up proceedings would have had the advantage of simplifying the resulting rules. The disadvantage would have been that it would have excluded from European cooperation very important proceedings in bankruptcy practice in certain Contracting States, such as the "suspensión de pagos" in Spain or the "surséance van betaling" in the Netherlands.

Economic analysis shows that retaining the option between two possibilities in insolvency law (winding-up or reorganization) is in itself a sound decision. The same should hold true in the international arena. There is no economic reason to justify the exclusion of reorganization proceedings from international cooperation. The Convention also contains sufficient mechanisms to protect creditors' interests (e g the possibility of opening territorial insolvency proceedings in accordance with local law). For some Contracting States the exclusion of reorganization proceedings would therefore be unjustified.

The outcome of the negotiations was a compromise to extend the Convention system to insolvency proceedings the main aim of which was not winding-up but reorganization.

As part of this compromise, however, local territorial proceedings opened after the main proceedings may only be winding-up proceedings (see points 83 and 86). If opened before, local territorial proceedings are subject to conversion into winding-up proceedings if the liquidator of the main proceedings so requests. The complications of compatibility and coordination between secondary reorganization proceedings (of which there could be several, if the debtor was based in several different Contracting States) and the main proceedings have led to restriction.

52. The Convention is drawn up on the basis of insolvency proceedings conducted by the courts. This will be the general rule.

However, Article 1 does not require the proceedings necessarily to involve the intervention of a judicial authority (or of an authority with an equivalent role). They must be proceedings (comprising a minimum number of acts and formalities as set down in law) which are officially recognized and legally effective in the State in which the proceedings are opened and which fulfil the four conditions set out in Article 1(1).

The requirement of intervention by a judicial authority was deliberately excluded to allow the Convention to be applied to ordinary non-judicial collective proceedings in countries such as the United Kingdom and Ireland (especially the creditor's voluntary winding-up). These proceedings offer sufficient guarantees (including access to the courts, for the legality of the proceedings to be supervised and for any questions which may arise to be settled) in order that they be brought under the Convention. Their practical significance justifies this: they represent an important percentage of all corporate insolvency cases. Once again, the Convention has enough mechanisms to defend the positions of the creditors (the possibility of secondary proceedings, public order exceptions, safeguard of acquired rights, etc) to enable these proceedings to benefit from the Convention system.

The fact that non-judicial proceedings are covered in the Convention does not mean that they are dealt with as if they were judicial proceedings or that the decisions adopted in the course of these proceedings are regarded as having the effect of a court ruling. It simply means the rules of the Convention must be applied with flexibility taking into account that they were drawn up on the basis of proceedings conducted by a court.

From this point of view, the Convention guarantees a positive answer to two essential questions:

1. these proceedings have to be recognized as collective insolvency proceedings pursuant to Article 1. Once proceedings have been opened in a Contracting State in accordance with Article 3, the creditors must seek payment of their debts through these collective proceedings, even if they are not conducted by the courts. Any question relating to the conduct of the proceedings or the decisions taken in the course of those proceedings, should be referred to the courts of that State;
2. the appointment of the liquidator and the powers conferred on him by the law of the State where proceedings were opened must be recognized in other Contracting States. However if the liquidator wishes to exercise his powers in another Contracting State, it is necessary for the Contracting States having proceedings of this type (the United Kingdom and Ireland) to introduce into their national legislation a system of confirmation by the courts of the nature of the proceedings and the appointment of the liquidator. This condition is shown in the list in Annex A which contains the proceedings designated by each country. In both cases these are termed proceedings "with confirmation of or by a court".

53. Finally, Article 1(1) does not require that a debtor have a particular status. The Convention applies equally to all proceedings, whether these involve a natural person or a legal person, a trader or an individual (see comments on Article 4).

54. Article 1(2): The Convention does not cover insolvency proceedings concerning insurance undertakings, credit institutions, investment undertakings which provide services involving the holding of funds or securities for third parties, or collective investment undertakings.

Contracting States subject these entities to prudential supervision through national regulatory authorities in order to minimize the risk to the relevant industries and to the financial system as a whole. All these entities are subject to specific Community regulations in the exercise of freedom of establishment and freedom to provide services, which are founded on the principle of control by the authorities of the State of origin of the entity in question. Negotiations are under way for Directives on reorganization measures and winding-up proceedings for credit institutions and insurance undertakings and Directives concerning insolvency proceedings relating to other entities described in this point are expected to follow. It has been agreed, therefore, that insolvency proceedings relating to the aforementioned entities should be excluded from the scope of this Convention.

55. The exclusion of credit institutions and insurance undertakings was agreed to by all Member States only after a statement by the Council and the Commission regarding the need to step up work on insolvency proceedings involving institutions and undertakings referred to in Article 1(2).

56. The excluded entities and undertakings are defined not in the Convention but by other instruments of Community law. The provisions currently applicable are mentioned in points 57 to 60.

The entities and undertakings which fall under the definitions given by the relevant Community Regulations and Directives are excluded from the Convention. Once an entity or an undertaking falls under the said definitions, the fact that the specific rules laid down by those Community Regulations or Directives are not, for any other reason, applicable to them does not alter this rule.

57. An "insurance undertaking" is any entity covered by the First Council Directive 73/239/EEC of 24 July 1973 on the coordination of laws, regulations and administrative provisions relating to the taking up and pursuit of the business of direct insurance other than life assurance as last amended by Directive 95/26/EC and by the First Council Directive 79/267/EEC of 5 March 1979 on the coordination of laws, regulations and administrative provisions relating to the taking up and pursuit of the business of direct life assurance, as last amended by Directive 95/26/EC.

58. A "credit institution" is any entity covered by the definition in the First Council Directive 77/780/EEC of 12 December 1977 the coordination of the laws, regulations and administrative provisions relating to the taking up and pursuit of the business of credit institutions as last amended by Directive 95/26/EC, which is an enterprise whose activity consists of receiving deposits or other reimbursable funds from the public and granting loans on its own account.

59. An "investment undertaking" is any entity covered by the definition in Council Directive 93/22/EEC of 10 May 1993 on investment services in the securities field as amended by Directive 95/26/EC (Article 1); in other words, any enterprise which regularly carries out a

professional activity consisting of supplying third parties with an investment service concerning securities (and money-market instruments). Examples of an investment service are: the receiving, transfer and buying or selling of securities on behalf of another person, dealing in these securities on one's own behalf, management on a discretionary and individualized basis of investment portfolios of securities in accordance with a mandate given by the investors.

60. A "collective investment undertaking" is any undertaking covered by the definition set out in Council Directive 85/611/EEC of 20 December 1985 on the coordination of laws, regulations and administrative provisions relating to undertakings for collective investment in transferable securities (UCITS) as last amended by Directive 95/26/EC; in other words, any body whose sole aim is the joint investment of securities from capital collected from the public, whose operations are subject to the principles of risk sharing, and the shares of which are, on the bearer's request, bought or paid back, directly or indirectly, from the assets of those bodies. **[3398]**

Article 2
Definitions

61. Article 2 provides definitions of a series of concepts which appear throughout the Convention.

62. Article 2(a) indicates that, for the purposes of the Convention, "insolvency proceedings" refer to proceedings which meet the conditions in Article 1(1) and are included in Annex A to the Convention which forms an integral part thereof. Hence only the proceedings included in the Annex may benefit from the system of recognition in the Convention.

Contracting States may amend the list of their proceedings by using the revision mechanism laid down in Article 54.

63. Article 2(b): the concept of "liquidator" is understood in a broad sense, to encompass any person or body who or which is appointed to administer or realize the bankrupt's assets, or to supervise the management of the debtor's affairs (the full or partial divestment of the debtor being one of the pre-conditions if the proceedings are to fall under the Convention).

The identification of those persons or bodies of national law who or which may be characterized as "liquidator" for the purposes of the Convention is established by means of their inclusion in the list of Annex C of the Convention.

When the court itself performs, according to the national law, functions of administration of the debtor's assets, it may qualify as "liquidator" within the meaning of the Convention. It is, however, necessary that the State in question states in Annex C of the Convention that its courts may act as liquidator.

64. Article 2(c): the concept of "winding-up proceedings" aims to define the type of proceedings acceptable as secondary proceedings.

For the reasons given in point 51, only insolvency proceedings within the meaning of Article 1 which, in addition, may entail the realization of the debtor's assets can be secondary proceedings after the main proceedings have been opened.

The fact that winding-up proceedings may be brought to a close through agreement with the creditors, or in some other way, thus putting an end to the debtor's insolvency, does not alter this qualification if the essential aim of the proceedings is to proceed with winding-up.

The Contracting States must enter in the list in Annex B those proceedings which serve as secondary proceedings. If a State fails to include specific proceedings in the list in Annex B, these proceedings may not then benefit from the provisions of the Convention. All Contracting States must include at least one type of proceedings in the list in Annex B.

65. The Convention does not restrict the types of proceedings which can serve as independent territorial proceedings opened before the main proceedings in accordance with Article 3(4).

These proceedings may be those included in Annex A (including reorganization proceedings) or Annex B (only winding-up proceedings). However, once the main proceedings are opened, the liquidator in the main proceedings is empowered to request the conversion of any local insolvency proceedings opened in accordance with Article 3(4) into winding-up proceedings listed in Annex B.

66. Article 2(d): the expression "court" is taken in a very broad sense. It covers not only the judiciary or an authority which plays a role similar to that of a court or public authority (as

was the case with earlier versions of the draft), but also a person or body empowered by national law to open proceedings or make decisions in the course of those proceedings (see point 52).

This wording brings this Convention close to the concept of "competent authority" in Article 4 of the 1990 Istanbul Convention, where the explanatory report (in point 23) states that the term "competent authority" for the opening of proceedings may include the competent body of a legal person which decides on its own winding-up for reasons of insolvency as is the case in Ireland and the United Kingdom.

67. Article 2(e): "judgment" must be taken in a broad sense to mean "decision", consistent with what is said in point 66.

68. Article 2(f): "the time of the opening of proceedings" is very important, since many questions are settled by reference to it. The time of the opening of proceedings is deemed to be the time when the decision begins to be effective under the law of the State of the opening of the proceedings.

The Convention does not require the decision to open insolvency proceedings to be final. It is sufficient for it to have effect in the State of opening and for its effects not to have been stayed.

In the case of non-judicial proceedings of the "creditors voluntary winding-up" type, the working party discussed whether, in order to fix the time of opening, the same rule should be used or whether the date of confirmation by the court of the nature of the proceedings and the appointment of the liquidator should be taken as the reference point. Only in order to allow the liquidator to exercise his powers on the territory of another Contracting State would it be necessary to take the date of confirmation by the court as the reference (see point 52). For all other matters, the general rule given above in this point stands.

69. Article 2(g): "the Contracting State in which assets are situated". This definition is important insofar as the main proceedings do not affect certain rights on assets located abroad (see Articles 5 and 7) and territorial proceedings can only affect the assets located in the State in which proceedings are opened. To this extent the Convention must help to determine what criteria regarding location are to be followed. In reality, the Convention does no more than stress traditional solutions of private international law which are well known in all the Contracting States.

Thus, tangible property is considered to be located in the place in which it is physically situated.

Property and rights ownership of or entitlement to which must be entered in a public register are considered to be located in the State under the authority of which the register is kept. This provision is applicable, for example, in the case of ship and aircraft registers, and also extends to intangible property, such as patents or securities. The State under whose authority the register is kept is not necessarily the State in which the register is physically situated (eg it may be a consular register or centralized international register).

"Public register" does not mean a register kept by a public authority, but rather a register for public access, an entry in which produces effects vis-à-vis third parties. It also includes private registers with these characteristics, recognized by the national legal system concerned.

In the case of Community patents, trademarks and other similar rights of Community origin, Article 12 states that these can only be included in main proceedings based on Article 3(1) (see point 133).

Finally, claims are deemed to be situated in the State where the debtor required to meet the claim in question (and not the insolvent debtor) has his centre of main interests. The concept of "centre of main interests" is the same as that specified in Article 3(1) (see point 75).

70. Article 2(h): The concept of "establishment" is linked to the basis of international jurisdiction to open territorial proceedings. In this regard, it should be mentioned that Article 3(2), in which the jurisdiction to open such territorial proceedings is dealt with, was one of the most debated provisions throughout the negotiations.

Several Contracting States wished to have the possibility of basing territorial proceedings not only on the presence of an establishment, but also on the mere presence of assets of the debtor (assigned to an economic activity) without the debtor having an establishment.

For the sake of an overall consensus on the Convention, those States agreed to abandon the presence of assets as a basis for international competence provided that the concept of establishment is interpreted in a broad manner but consistently with the text of the Convention. This explains the very open definition given in Article 2(h).

In the Convention, the mere presence of assets (e g the existence of a bank account) does not enable local territorial proceedings to be opened. The presence of an establishment of the debtor within the jurisdiction concerned is necessary.

Though defended by one State, the possibility of adopting the same concept of establishment in the Convention as that given by the Court of Justice of the European Communities in its interpretation of Article 5(5) of the 1968 Brussels Convention was ruled out. The majority of States preferred an independent concept to be developed.

Indeed, the Court of Justice of the European Communities emphasized that the special powers laid down in Article 5 of the 1968 Brussels Convention must be strictly interpreted vis-à-vis the general forum of the place of domicile of the defendant. Under these conditions, to import a concept from the 1968 Brussels Convention involved the risk of conveying a possibly restrictive interpretation of the concept of establishment to the Convention on insolvency proceedings, which was precisely the opposite of what most of the working party intended. For this reason, they opted to give the Convention its own definition, which is contained in Article 2.

71. For the Convention on insolvency proceedings, "establishment" is understood to mean a place of operations through which the debtor carries out an economic activity on a non-transitory basis, and where he uses human resources and goods.

Place of operations means a place from which economic activities are exercised on the market (i e externally), whether the said activities are commercial, industrial or professional.

The emphasis on an economic activity having to be carried out using human resources shows the need for a minimum level of organization. A purely occasional place of operations cannot be classified as an "establishment". A certain stability is required. The negative formula ("non-transitory") aims to avoid minimum time requirements. The decisive factor is how the activity appears externally, and not the intention of the debtor.

The rationale behind the rule is that foreign economic operators conducting their economic activities through a local establishment should be subject to the same rules as national economic operators as long as they are both operating in the same market. In this way, potential creditors concluding a contract with a local establishment will not have to worry about whether the company is a national or foreign one. Their information costs and legal risks in the event of insolvency of the debtor will be the same whether they conclude a contract with a national undertaking or a foreign undertaking with a local presence on that market.

Naturally, the possibility of opening local territorial insolvency proceedings makes sense only if the debtor possesses sufficient assets within the jurisdiction. Whether or not these assets are linked to the economic activities of the establishment is of no relevance.

[3399]

Article 3

International jurisdiction

72. The rules of jurisdiction set out in the Convention establish only international jurisdiction, that is to say, they designate the Contracting State the courts of which may open insolvency proceedings. Territorial jurisdiction within that Contracting State must be established by the national law of the State concerned.

73. Main insolvency proceedings:

Article 3(1) enables main insolvency universal proceedings to be opened in the Contracting State where the debtor has his centre of main interests. Main insolvency proceedings have universal scope. They aim at encompassing all the debtor's assets on a world-wide basis and at affecting all creditors, wherever located.

Only one set of main proceedings may be opened in the territory covered by the Convention.

74. Which persons or legal entities may be subject to insolvency proceedings is determined by national law. Where the international jurisdiction rule mentions the debtor, this means the natural persons or legal entity (whether a legal person or not) concerned.

75. The concept of "centre of main interests" must be interpreted as the place where the debtor conducts the administration of his interests on a regular basis and is therefore ascertainable by third parties.

The rationale of this rule is not difficult to explain. Insolvency is a foreseeable risk. It is therefore important that international jurisdiction (which, as we will see, entails the application of the insolvency laws of that Contracting State) be based on a place known to the debtor's potential creditors. This enables the legal risks which would have to be assumed in the case of insolvency to be calculated.

By using the term "interests", the intention was to encompass not only commercial, industrial or professional activities, but also general economic activities, so as to include the activities of private individuals (e g consumers). The expression "main" serves as a criterion for the cases where these interests include activities of different types which are run from different centres.

In principle, the centre of main interests will in the case of professionals be the place of their professional domicile and for natural persons in general, the place of their habitual residence.

Where companies and legal persons are concerned, the Convention presumes, unless proved to the contrary, that the debtor's centre of main interests is the place of his registered office. This place normally corresponds to the debtor's head office.

76. The Convention offers no rule for groups of affiliated companies (parent-subsidiary schemes).

The general rule to open or to consolidate insolvency proceedings against any of the related companies as a principal or jointly liable debtor is that jurisdiction must exist according to the Convention for each of the concerned debtors with a separate legal entity.

Naturally, the drawing up of a European norm on associated companies may affect this answer.

77. Article 3(1) gives the courts in the State of the opening of proceedings jurisdiction in relation to insolvency proceedings. However, the Convention contains no rule defining the limits of this jurisdiction.

This is a fundamental question since it raises the issue of the relationship between the Convention on insolvency proceedings and the 1968 Brussels Convention and their respective scope.

Certain Contracting States recognize a "vis attractiva concursus" in their national law, by virtue of which the Court which opens the insolvency proceedings has within its jurisdiction not only the actual insolvency proceedings but also all the actions arising from the insolvency.

Although the projection of this principle in the international domain is controversial, the 1982 Community Draft Convention contained a provision in Article 15 which, according to the Lemontey Report, was inspired by the "vis attractiva" theory. This Article conferred on the courts of the State of the opening of insolvency proceedings jurisdiction over a wide series of actions resulting from the insolvency.

Neither this precept nor this philosophy has been adopted in this Convention. There is no provision in Article 3 of the Convention addressing this problem. However, the Convention's silence on the matter is only partial. Article 25 thereof contains the delimitation criterion between both the 1968 Brussels Convention and this Convention.

This criterion is directly taken from the Court of Justice of the European Communities. It was outlined by the Court of Justice in the interpretation of Article 1(2) of the 1968 Brussels Convention in its Judgment of 22 February 1979 (Case 133/78, Gourdain-v-Nadler [1979] ECR p 733).

Article 1(2) of the 1968 Brussels Convention excludes "bankruptcy, proceedings relating to the winding-up of insolvent companies or other legal persons, judicial arrangements, compositions and analogous proceedings" from its scope. In that Judgment the Court of Justice of the European Communities used the nature of the action taken as the criterion for determining whether or not the jurisdiction rules of the 1968 Brussels Convention applied. According to this criterion, actions directly derived from insolvency and in close connection with the insolvency proceedings are excluded from the 1968 Brussels Convention. Logically, to avoid unjustifiable loopholes between the two Conventions, these actions are now subject to the Convention on insolvency proceedings and to its rules of jurisdiction.

78. The rule on international jurisdiction in Article 3(1) enables the court having jurisdiction to open main insolvency proceedings to order provisional and protective measures from the time of the request to open proceedings.

Preservation measures both prior to and after the commencement of the insolvency proceedings are very important to guarantee the effectiveness of the insolvency proceedings. They may be ordered by the court having jurisdiction according to Article 3(1) irrespective of the Contracting State where the assets or persons concerned (either debtor or a creditor) are located. Such measures may adopt a wide-range of forms, according to the national law of the court ordering them (e g interlocutory orders to do or not to do, appointment of a temporary administrator, attachment of assets).

These preservation measures shall be recognised and enforced in other Contracting States, according to the conditions set out in Article 25 of the Convention (see point 198).

Article 3(1) does not prevent the liquidator, or any other empowered person, from going to the place where the preservation is to be carried out (e g the State in which the assets are located) and asking the local courts to adopt provisional measures available under the national law. This possibility presupposes that the courts of that State enjoy jurisdiction to adopt such measures under their national law (as should usually be the case), and the fulfilment of the subject-matter requirements of that law (evidence of a good prima facie case, sufficient urgency, security to cover damages which may be caused, etc).

These preservation measures are ancillary to the main proceedings. Logically, they remain subordinated to the decisions taken in the course of the main proceedings by the court having jurisdiction under Article 3(1) and which benefit from the system of recognition and enforcement of the Convention. Hence, under Articles 16 and 25, such a court may even stipulate that those preservation measures are to be lifted, modified or continued (see point 198).

The possibility of going to the court of the place where the measures are to take effect is referred to again in Article 38, although with a different purpose. Article 38 empowers the temporary administrator appointed after the request for the opening of main insolvency proceedings, but before such opening, to call directly on the authorities of any other Contracting State to adopt preservation measures provided under the insolvency law of this State for winding-up proceedings on the debtor's assets situated in its territory, as a pre-opening stage of secondary proceedings (see point 262).

79. The Convention does not provide any express rule to resolve cases where the courts of two Contracting States concurrently claim jurisdiction in accordance with Article 3(1). Such conflicts of jurisdiction must be an exception, given the necessarily uniform nature of the criteria of jurisdiction used.

Where disputes do arise, to solve them, the courts will be able to take account of:

1. the Convention's system according to which:
   (a) each court is obliged to verify its own international jurisdiction in accordance with the Convention;
   (b) the principle of Community trust, according to which once the first court of a Contracting State has adopted a decision, the other States are required to recognize it (see points 202 and 220);
2. the possibility of a request for a preliminary ruling to the Court of Justice of the European Communities, guaranteeing the uniformity of the contents of the criteria for international jurisdiction and its appropriate interpretation in the given case;
3. the general principles of procedural law which are valid in all Contracting States; these principles include those derived from other Community Conventions such as the 1968 Brussels Convention.

80. Local insolvency proceedings

Article 3(2) enables territorial proceedings to be opened in the State in which the debtor has an establishment, as defined in Article 2(h), under the following conditions.

In cases where the debtor's centre of main interests is located in a Contracting State, the courts of other Contracting States have no power to open main insolvency proceedings.

However, any of these Contracting States may open territorial proceedings, the effectiveness of which is restricted to the assets situated in that State, if the debtor has an establishment in the territory of that State. The mere presence of assets is not sufficient to open territorial proceedings.

Depending on whether or not main proceedings have been opened, the proceedings shall be secondary or independent territorial proceedings.

81. Article 3(2) does not grant jurisdiction to open territorial proceedings to the courts of a State where the debtor does not have an establishment. The assets located in that State cannot, therefore, be included in territorial proceedings, but revert to the main proceedings, if such have been opened.

82. Should the debtor's centre of main interests be located outside the territory of the Contracting States, it is not within the jurisdiction of any Contracting State to open insolvency proceedings within the scope of the Convention. Article 3(1) and (2) assumes that the centre of main interests is in a Contracting State.

When the centre of main interest does not lie in a Contracting State, national law determines the international jurisdiction of its courts. The effects of such proceedings are not governed by this Convention (see point 44).

83. Secondary territorial insolvency proceedings

Article 3(3) requires that after main proceedings have been opened by the competent court within the meaning of Article 3(1), the subsequent proceedings opened by the court of the State where the establishment is located, in accordance with Article 3(2), are secondary proceedings, subject to Chapter III.

In the event of there being a number of establishments located in different Contracting States, several sets of secondary proceedings may be opened.

The secondary proceedings under Article 3(3) may not be reorganization proceedings, rather they must be winding-up proceedings as mentioned in Annex B. This rule is reaffirmed in Article 27 (see comments re Article 27 (points 211 et seq)).

84. Independent territorial insolvency proceedings

Article 3(4) deals with situations which exist prior to the opening of main proceedings. This is the result of efforts to reconcile two essentially conflicting approaches.

In line with the philosophy expressed most particularly in Articles 3(1) and (2) and Article 27, the court of the debtor's centre of main interests is the only one having jurisdiction to open main proceedings. These proceedings should naturally encompass all the debtor's assets regardless of the State in which the property is located.

It is only as an exception to the universal proceedings that territorial proceedings may be opened in advance, in order to satisfy "local" creditors as to the assets present in that State. Indeed, it is difficult to imagine that "local" creditors who hold a favourable ranking in the State where the property is located would want to transfer all the assets to another State where their ranking would be less favourable. It is likewise difficult for States without any creditors holding a preferential ranking to accept the transfer of all the assets abroad.

The other approach involves seeking to protect local creditors by allowing national rules on the opening of proceedings to follow their normal course, even in a State where an establishment is located, and even at all times, prior to and regardless of the opening of proceedings in the State of the centre of main interests. This approach takes into account the insolvency of an establishment and the creditors' interest in territorial proceedings or the general interest in territorial proceedings to reorganize an establishment of social and economic importance within that State, and grants less consideration to the principle of the universality of insolvency proceedings.

85. Article 3(4) adopts the following rule:

The courts of a Contracting State having jurisdiction under Article 3(2) may open, prior to the main proceedings, territorial insolvency proceedings called for this reason independent territorial proceedings, in only two cases:

1. The conditions for opening the insolvency proceedings, as set out by the law of the State where the centre of main interests is located, do not allow main proceedings to be opened.
   That will be the case if, for example, the debtor cannot be subject to insolvency proceedings, e g where the applicable law requires the debtor to be a trader, and this is not the case, or where the debtor is a public company which the law of the State of the centre of main interests does not allow to be declared insolvent.
2. A local creditor or a creditor of the local establishment, within the meaning of Article 3(4)(b), requests territorial proceedings be opened.
   The protected creditor to whom this right to request the opening of territorial proceedings is granted is one:
   (a) whose habitual residence, domicile and registered office is in the State where the establishment is located,
   (b) or whose claim arises from the operation of that establishment (e g an employee working for that establishment; a person who entered through the establishment into an undertaking which must be performed in that State; the tax authorities and social security bodies).

Outside these two possible cases, the court having jurisdiction to open the territorial proceedings cannot open proceedings prior to the opening of proceedings in the centre of main interests.

86. The territorial proceedings mentioned in Article 3(4) may be winding-up proceedings or reorganization proceedings mentioned in Annex A or Annex B.

PART IV

In the event of the subsequent opening of the main proceedings, independent territorial proceedings become secondary proceedings, in accordance with the special rules of Articles 36 and 37 of the Convention.

Furthermore, reorganization proceedings as mentioned in Annex A will, at the request of the liquidator in the main proceedings, be converted into secondary winding-up proceedings, in accordance with Articles 36 and 37 (see points 210, 254 to 261). If the liquidator in the main proceedings does not request this conversion, the territorial proceedings may continue as reorganization proceedings.

[3400]

Article 4
Law applicable

87. The Convention sets out, for the matters covered by it, uniform rules on conflict of laws which replace national rules of private international law.

When these rules on conflict of laws talk of the "applicable law", they refer to the internal law of the Contracting State designated by the rule, excluding its rules of private international law.

88. General rule on conflict of laws

Article 4 lays down the basic rule on conflict of laws of the Convention. This Article determines the law applicable to the insolvency proceedings, the conduct thereof and their material effects: unless otherwise stated by this Convention, the law of the Contracting State of the opening of the proceedings is applicable (lex concursus).

89. This rule on conflict of laws is valid both for the main proceedings and for local proceedings (secondary or independent territorial proceedings).

To avoid any doubts, Article 28 reiterates this solution for the secondary proceedings. Although Article 28 only considers the secondary proceedings, it is clear that the application of the law of the State of the opening of the proceedings operates as the general conflict of laws rule of the Convention and is also valid for independent territorial proceedings.

90. The law of the State of the opening of proceedings determines all the effects of the insolvency proceedings, both procedural and substantive, on the persons and legal relations concerned.

This law governs all the conditions for the opening, conduct and closure of the insolvency proceedings. It stipulates, inter alia, who may be subject to insolvency proceedings, the requirements to open them and who may present the petition; it determines the nature and the extent of the debtor's divestment and the assets covered by it; it outlines the organization of the administration of the estate and regulates the designation of the liquidator and his powers; it decides the admissibility of claims and the rules on distribution and preferences; it governs the closure of the proceedings and its consequences, etc.

The substantive effects referred to the competence of the law of the State of the opening by Article 4, are those typical of insolvency law, i e effects which are necessary for the insolvency proceedings to fulfil its aims. To this extent, the law of the State of the opening may displace (unless the Convention provides otherwise), the law normally applicable, under the common pre-insolvency rules on conflict of laws, to the act concerned. This happens for instance when Article 4 makes applicable the law of the State of opening of proceedings to invalidate any act (e g a contract) detrimental to all the creditors, even if that act is governed under the general rules on conflict of laws (if a contract, those of the 1980 Rome Convention), by the law of a different State.

91. To facilitate its interpretation, Article 4(2) contains a non-exhaustive list of questions that are governed by the law of the State of the opening.

(a) whether a particular debtor by virtue of his status (e g trader/non-trader, public law company) may be subject to insolvency proceedings (Article 4(2)(a)). This rule is valid for both the main proceedings and for secondary proceedings, where the solution to the case may be different. This paragraph is linked to Article 3(4)(a) and Article 16(2) (see points 85 and 148);

(b) which assets form part of the estate and the treatment of assets acquired by the debtor after the opening of proceedings;

(c) the respective powers of the debtor and the liquidator. This paragraph is linked to Article 14 (see point 141);

(d) the conditions under which set-offs may be invoked. This paragraph is linked to Articles 6 and 9 (see points 107 to 111 and 120 et seq);

(e) the effects of the proceedings on current contracts to which the debtor is party (paragraph (e)). To the extent necessary, the law of the State of the opening displaces the law of the contract determined in accordance with the 1980 Rome Convention. This paragraph is linked to Articles 8 and 10 (see points 116 to 119; 125 et seq);

(f) the effects of the insolvency proceedings on executions brought by individual creditors, their suspension or prohibition after the opening of collective insolvency proceedings. However, the effects of the proceedings on lawsuits pending remain subject to the law of the Contracting State where the lawsuit is pending, ex Article 15 (see point 142);

(g) the claims which are to be lodged against the debtor's estate and the treatment of claims arising after the opening of insolvency proceedings (ie claims arising in the administration and management of the assets which in many systems benefit from preferential payment);

(h) the rules governing the lodging, verification and admission of claims. It must be borne in mind that Chapter IV of the Convention sets out a number of uniform rules on this subject. As regards claims that are admissible, Article 39 acknowledges "iure conventionis" that Contracting States' public law claims can be lodged in insolvency proceedings opened in other Contracting States. This precept expressly stipulates the right of the tax and social security authorities of any Contracting State to submit their claims in insolvency proceedings opened pursuant to the Convention;

(i) the ranking (privileges, preferences, etc) and the rules on distribution of the assets realized. As in all main or secondary proceedings the national law of the State of the opening is applicable, the ranking of a claim may vary for each of the proceedings in which it is lodged;

(j) the conditions and effects of the closure of proceedings, including closure by composition or equivalent measure;

(k) the rights of the creditors subsequent to the closure of the proceedings, including any possible discharge of the debtor;

(l) the costs and expenses of the proceedings;

(m) the voidness, voidability or unenforceability of legal acts that may be detrimental to all the creditors. The applicable national law determines whether action must be taken to obtain their invalidation or whether the decision to open proceedings automatically entails invalidation. To the extent necessary, the law of the State of the opening displaces the law normally applicable to the act in question. This paragraph is to be taken in conjunction with Article 13 (see point 135).

In the case of secondary proceedings, the local rules on invalidation of a detrimental act shall be applicable only insofar as damage has been caused to the debtor's assets which are in this State (eg to the estate of the secondary proceedings). For instance, the act in question (sale, establishment of a right in rem) involves an asset which was located in this State at the relevant time.

92. Exceptions to the general rule on conflicts of law of Article 4

The application, by the courts in the State of the opening of proceedings, of their national insolvency law and the automatic extension of its effects to all the Contracting States (see Articles 16 and 25) may interfere with the rules under which transactions are carried out in these States.

To protect legitimate expectations and the certainty of transactions in States other than that in which proceedings are opened (for in the latter State all the operators have to count on the application of its laws) the Convention provides for a number of exceptions to the general rule:

1. In certain cases, the Convention excludes some rights over assets located abroad from the effects of the insolvency proceedings (as in Articles 5, 6 and 7).
2. In other cases, it ensures that certain effects of the insolvency proceedings are governed not by the law of the State of the opening (F1), but by the law of the State concerned (see Articles 8, 9, 10, 11, 14 and 15). In such cases, the effects to be given to the proceedings opened in other Contracting States are the same effects attributed to a domestic proceedings of equivalent nature (liquidation, composition, or reorganization proceedings) by the law of the State concerned (F2).

93. The exceptions to the application of the law of the State of the opening (Article 4) are referred to in Articles 5 to 15 of the Convention. Apart from Articles 6 and 14, which by systemic arguments must be interpreted in the same way, the exception is made in favour of the law of a "Contracting State".

This does not mean that, by a contrario interpretation, the law of the State of the opening of proceedings is applicable where the State concerned is not a Contracting State. The need to protect legitimate expectations and the certainty of transactions is equally valid in relations with non-Contracting States. The group's intention was simply to regulate these cases in line with the general restriction of the Convention to the intra-Community effect of insolvency proceedings (see point 44). Contracting States are, therefore, free to decide which rules they deem most appropriate in other cases (the same ones as in Articles 5 to 15 of the Convention, or others). **[3401]**

Article 5
Third parties' rights in rem

94. This provision excludes from the effects of the proceedings rights in rem of third parties and creditors in respect of assets belonging to the debtor which, at the time of the opening of proceedings, are situated within the territory of another Contracting State.

If the assets are situated in a non-Contracting State, Article 5 does not govern the issue (see points 44 and 93).

95. In order to understand the functioning of Article 5, account should be taken of the fact that main insolvency proceedings based on Article 3(1) have a universal scope. All the assets of the debtor shall be subject to the main proceedings irrespective of the State where they are situated unless territorial proceedings are opened. The law of the State of the opening of the main proceedings shall determine which of those assets shall be regarded as forming a part of the estate in the main proceedings and which shall be excluded (see Article 4(2)(b)).

A part of those assets may be subject to third parties' rights in rem. The Convention does not make it obligatory for these assets to be included in or excluded from the estate in the main proceedings. The Convention imposes only an obligation to respect third parties' rights in rem over assets located within the territory of a Contracting State different from the State of the opening of proceedings.

The creation, validity and scope of these rights in rem are governed by their own applicable law (in general, the "lex rei sitae" at the relevant time) and cannot be affected by the opening of insolvency proceedings.

This means that although the law of the State of the opening stipulates that all assets are part of the estate, the holder of the right in rem retains all his rights in respect of the assets in question. For instance, the holder of the right in rem may exercise the right to separate the security from the estate and, where necessary, to realize the asset individually to satisfy the claim. On the other hand, the liquidator, even if he is in possession of the asset, cannot take any decision on that asset which might affect the right in rem created on it, without the consent of its holder (see also point 161).

96. Article 5 only applies to the rights in rem created before the opening of proceedings. If they are created after the opening, Article 4 shall apply without exception (without prejudice to Article 14).

97. The fundamental policy pursued is to protect the trade in the State where the assets are situated and legal certainty of the rights over them. Rights in rem have a very important function with regard to credit and the mobilization of wealth. They insulate their holders against the risk of insolvency of the debtor and the interference of third parties. They allow credit to be obtained under conditions that would not be possible without this type of guarantee.

Rights in rem can only properly fulfil their function insofar as they are not more affected by the opening of insolvency proceedings in other Contracting States than they would be by the opening of national insolvency proceedings. This aim could be achieved through alternative solutions which were in fact discussed in the working party. However, to facilitate the administration of the estate the simplicity of the formula laid down in the current Article 5 was preferred by the majority: insolvency proceedings do not affect rights in rem on assets located in other Contracting States.

98. The rule does not "immunize" rights in rem against the debtor's insolvency. If the law of the State where the assets are located allows these rights in rem to be affected in some way, the liquidator (or any other person empowered to do so) may request secondary insolvency proceedings be opened in that State if the debtor has an establishment there. The secondary proceedings are conducted according to national law and allow the liquidator to affect these rights under the same conditions as in purely domestic proceedings.

99. Article 5 states that the proceedings shall not affect rights in rem in respect of assets located in other Contracting States and not that the proceedings shall not affect assets located in another State. As main proceedings are universal (ex. Article 3(1)) they encompass all the debtor's assets.

This is important if the value of the security is greater than the value of the claim guaranteed by the right in rem. The creditor will be then obliged to surrender to the estate any surplus of the proceeds of sale.

Without affecting the economic value of the right or its immediate realisability, it also gives the liquidator the power to decide on the immediate payment of the claim guaranteed, and thus avoid the loss in value that certain assets could suffer when they are realized separately.

100. Article 5 refers to "rights in rem" but does not define what these are. The Convention does not intend to impose its own definition of a right in rem, running the risk of describing as rights in rem legal positions which the law of the State where the assets are located does not consider to be rights in rem, or of not encompassing rights in rem which do not fulfil the conditions of that definition.

The Convention acknowledges the interest of each State in protecting its market's trade, in the form of respect of rights in rem acquired over assets of the debtor located in that country under the law that is applicable before the opening of the insolvency proceedings.

For this reason, the characterization of a right as a right in rem must be sought in the national law which, according to the normal pre-insolvency conflict of law rules, governs rights in rem (in general, the lex rei sitae at the relevant time). In this sense, the Convention adopts a "lege causae" characterization.

101. The only departure from the above statement is found in Article 5(3), which for the purposes of Article 5, directly and independently of national law, considers as a right in rem any right entered in a public register and enforceable against third parties, allowing a right in rem to be obtained.

102. However, the rationale of Article 5 imposes certain limits to the national qualification of a right in rem. It must be borne in mind that Article 5 represents an important exception as regards the application of the law of the State of the opening and the universal effect of the main proceedings. It must equally be remembered that secondary proceedings are only possible if the debtor has an establishment in that Contracting State. The mere presence of assets is not enough in order to open such proceedings.

An unreasonably wide interpretation of the national concept of a right in rem to include, for instance, rights simply reinforced by a right to claim preferential payment, as is the case for a certain number of privileges, would make the Convention meaningless, and such a wide interpretation is not to be attributed to Article 5.

103. In order to facilitate the application of the Convention and avoid doubts Article 5(2) provides a list of types of rights that are normally considered by national laws as rights in rem.

This list is inspired in two main considerations. The first, that a right which exists only after insolvency proceedings have been opened, but not before, is not a right in rem for the purposes of Article 5 (which protect pre-existing rights).

The second, that a right in rem basically has two characteristics (see also the concept of rights in rem in the Member States in point 166 of the Schlosser Report on the 1968 Brussels Convention):

(a) its direct and immediate relationship with the asset it covers, which remains linked to its satisfaction, without depending on the asset belonging to a person's estate or on the relationship between the holder of the right in rem and another person;

(b) the absolute nature of the allocation of the right to the holder. This means that the person who holds a right in rem can enforce it against anyone who breaches or harms his right without his assent (eg such rights are typically protected by actions to recover); that the right can resist the alienation of the asset to a third party (it can be claimed erga omnes, with the restrictions characteristic of the protection of the bona fide purchaser); and that the right can thus resist individual enforcement by third parties and in collective insolvency proceedings (by its separation or individual satisfaction).

104. A right in rem may not only be established with regard to specific assets but also with regard to assets as a whole. Security rights such as the "floating charge" recognised in United Kingdom and Irish law can, therefore, be characterized as a right in rem for the purposes of

the Convention. Likewise, rights characterized under national law as rights in rem over intangible assets or over rights are also included (see Article 5(1)).

105. This provision is based on non-fraudulent location of the assets.

106. The establishment of a right in rem in favour of a particular creditor or third party could be an act detrimental to all the creditors. In this case, the general rules of the Convention governing actions for voidness, voidability or unenforceability of legal acts are applicable (see Article 4(2)(m), and Article 13). **[3402]**

Article 6
Set-off

107. This Article deals with set-off in the same way as Article 5 dealt with rights in rem. When under the normally applicable rules on conflict of laws the right to demand the set-off stems from a national law other than the "lex concursus", Article 6 allows the creditor to retain this possibility as an acquired right against the insolvency proceedings: the right to set-off is not affected by the opening of proceedings.

108. Set-off is a part of the law of obligations governed by the relevant rules of private international law regarding the law applicable to obligations. By including two claims which offset each other, the question arises whether the right to set-off stems from:

(a) the cumulative application of laws applicable to the two claims or

(b) the law applicable to the claim of the debtor ("passive" claim in the set-off) against which the creditor intends to set off his counter-claim against the debtor ("active" claim in the set-off).
The Convention opts for this second interpretation when it derives the right to set-off from "the law applicable to the insolvent debtor's claim", (ie from the law applicable to the claim where the insolvent debtor is the creditor in relation to the other party).

109. The laws of some Member States altogether restrict or prohibit set-off in insolvency. Article 4 subjects insolvency set-off to the competence of the law of the State of the opening of the insolvency proceedings.

If insolvency proceedings are opened, it falls therefore to the "lex concursus" to govern admissibility and the conditions under which set-off can be exercised against a claim of the debtor.

If the "lex concursus" allows for set-off, no problem will arise and Article 4 should be applied in order to claim the set-off as provided for by the law. On the other hand, if the "lex concursus" does not allow for set-off (eg since it requires both claims to be liquidated, matured and payable prior to a certain date), then Article 6 constitutes an exception to the general application of that law in this respect, by permitting the set-off according to the conditions established for insolvency set-off by the law applicable to the insolvent debtor's claim ("passive" claim).

In this way, set-off becomes, in substance, a sort of guarantee governed by a law on which the creditor concerned can rely at the moment of contracting or incurring the claim.

110. Article 6 covers only rights to set-off arising in respect of mutual claims incurred prior to the opening of the insolvency proceedings. After this time, Article 4 is applied without exception to decide whether or not the set-off is admissible.

Contractual set-off implies an agreement subject to its own applicable law according to the 1980 Rome Convention. The same rationale on which Article 5 is based explains that in the event of a contractual set-off agreement covering different claims between two parties, the law of the Contracting State applicable to that agreement will continue to govern the set-off of claims covered by the agreement and incurred prior to the opening of the insolvency proceedings.

111. As in the case of Article 5, any actions detrimental to all the creditors may be corrected by bringing actions for voidness, voidability or unenforceability as set out in Article 4(2)(m). **[3403]**

Article 7
Reservation of title

112. In the same way as Article 5, this provision seeks to protect trade by excluding from the scope of insolvency proceedings the reservation of title on property which, at the time the proceedings were opened, was located in a Contracting State other than the State of the opening.

The remarks made with regard to Article 5 apply here mutatis mutandis. The biggest difference between Article 5 and Article 7 concerns Article 7(2) which contains a uniform substantive rule.

113. The first paragraph governs the insolvency of the purchaser of an asset, by allowing the seller to preserve his rights based on the reservation of title. For this to occur, the asset must be located at the time when the insolvency proceedings are opened in a Contracting State other than the one where the proceedings are opened. If its location changes after the opening of the proceedings, this does not affect the application of the provision.

114. The second paragraph covers the insolvency of the seller of an asset after delivery of the asset, allowing the sale to remain valid. If the purchaser continues to make payments, he shall acquire title at the end of the period set out in the contract. For this rule to be applied, it is also a requirement that at the time the insolvency proceedings are opened the asset is located within a State other than the State of the opening of proceedings.

115. Of course, actions for voidness, voidability or unenforceability, as provided for in Article 4(2)(m) can also be brought against these reservations of title.

[3404]

Article 8
Contracts relating to immovable property

116. Insolvency law may have an impact on current contracts. Thus, for instance, in the case of mutual obligations pending fulfilment, the liquidator may be empowered to decide either on the performance or termination of the contract. The aim of rules of this kind is to protect the estate from the obligation to perform contracts which may be disadvantageous in these new circumstances.

117. The general rule on conflicts of law is that it falls to the law of the Contracting State of the opening of proceedings to regulate the effects of the proceedings on current contracts to which the debtor is a party (Article 4(2)(e)).

To this extent, the applicable national insolvency law interferes with and overlaps the rules applicable to contracts, which derive from the law applicable under the 1980 Rome Convention.

118. This rule, which overall is positive for the general interests of the creditors may be detrimental to other interests. In all the Contracting States, contracts covering immoveable property are subject to special rules, both of conflict of laws as well as of international jurisdiction, in order to take into account several interests: those of the parties to the contract (eg tenants) and the general interests protected by the State in which the immoveable property is to be found.

Protection of these specific interests justify an exception to the application of the law of the State of the opening of proceedings. Hence Article 8 makes the effects of the insolvency proceedings exclusively subject to the law of the Contracting State where the immovable property is located.

Solely means that only the law of the Contracting State of location of the immovable (including its insolvency law), and not the "lex concursus" under Article 4, is applicable to establish these effects.

119. Article 8 not only covers contracts for the use of immovable property (rental, leasing) but also includes contracts covering the transfer of the immovable property (sale).

[3405]

Article 9
Payment systems and financial markets

120. The intention of Article 9 is for any effects on transactions subject to a payment or settlement system or to a financial market of insolvency proceedings opened in another

PART IV EC MATERIALS

Contracting State to be the same as those in proceedings under national law. By making the effects of insolvency exclusively subject to the law applicable to the payment system and the financial market, general confidence in these mechanisms is protected.

The aim of this provision is to avoid any modification of the mechanisms for regulating and settling transactions provided for in payment or settlement systems or on the organized financial markets operating in Contracting States, in the event of insolvency of a party to a transaction which would otherwise result if the "lex concursus" applied. The relevant mechanisms include closing out contracts and netting, and insofar as the security is situated in that Contracting State, the realization of securities.

Payment systems and markets involve large-scale transactions and as a consequence have been found to require special rules to guarantee their smooth operation and security. That is why the law governing the particular system or market concerned remains applicable.

A financial market is not defined but is understood to be a market in a Contracting State where financial instruments, other financial assets or commodity futures and options are traded. It is characterized by regular trading and conditions of operation and access and it is subject to the law of the relevant Contracting State, including appropriate supervision, if any, by the regulatory authorities of that Contracting State.

121. Article 9 means that only the law governing the system or market in question can be applied to the relevant transactions affected by an insolvency and not the "lex concursus" as provided by Article 4. Thus, the complex problems of potential conflicts of the two laws are avoided and the certainty of transactions is preserved.

122. For the same reason, any possible voidness, voidability or unenforceability of a payment or transaction carried out under this system or market and which may be detrimental to all the creditors, remains subject to the same solution: the law applicable to the payment system or financial market governs these cases.

123. To determine the law applicable to European payment systems account must be taken of the work in progress in the Community on those systems.

124. The reference to Article 5 means that protection of rights in rem of any kind of creditors or third parties over assets belonging to the debtor is always carried out in the same way under the Convention: by reference to the location of the assets, regardless of the type of creditor or institution which may benefit from its function as a guarantee. Rights in rem affect third parties and uniform treatment of them is essential in order to protect trade. **[3406]**

Article 10
Contracts of employment

125. Article 10 derogates from the general application of the law of the State of the opening of proceedings (Article 4) and makes the effects of the proceedings on employment contracts and on labour relations subject to the law of the Contracting State applicable to the contract of employment, including its law on insolvency.

This Article aims to protect employees and labour relations from the application of a foreign law, different from that which governs the contractual relations between employer and employees. For this reason, effects of the insolvency proceedings on the continuation or termination of the employment relationship and on the rights and obligations of each party under such relationship are to be determined by the law applicable to the contract under the general conflict of laws rules.

126. The 1980 Rome Convention will determine the law applicable to employment contracts (see, in particular, its Articles 6 and 7).

127. The word "solely" emphasizes that only the law applicable to the employment contract is applied in order to establish these effects and not the "lex concursus" as provided by Article 4. Any problem regarding possible conflicts between the two laws is therefore avoided.

128. Insolvency questions other than those relating to the impact of the opening of proceedings on contract and employment relationships remain subject to the general competence of the law of the State of the opening, ex Article 4. Thus, for instance, the following would be covered, the question of whether or not workers' claims arising out of their employment shall be protected by a privilege, the prescribed amount protected and the rank of the privilege if any, etc. In the same way as lodgement, verification and admission of claims, all these questions are subject to the law of the State of the opening (Article 4(2)(h)).

Guaranteed payments of workers' claims in cases of insolvency of the employer, ensured by a national institution under a wage guarantee scheme in the event of insolvency governed by the national law of a Contracting State, are subject to the law of that State.

[3407]

Article 11
Effects on rights subject to registration

129. The application of the law of the State of the opening (F1) to determine the effects of the insolvency proceedings also on the assets of debtors located in another Contracting State may come into conflict with national registration systems, when this law provides for effects or consequences different from or unknown to the system of the State of registration (eg a statutory lien of the general body of creditors over the debtor's property).

130. The Convention does not try to modify the systems either of registration or of rights in rem of the Contracting States. The systems for the registration of property play a significant role in protecting trade and legal certainty. General confidence in its contents and consequences should be protected under the same conditions, whether the insolvency proceedings are opened in the State of registration or in another Contracting State.

To preserve these systems, Article 11 establishes an exception to the application of the law of the State of the opening. This exception is, however, more limited than the exceptions contained in Articles 8, 9 and 10 of the Convention. Contrary to these provisions, Article 11 does not submit the effects of the insolvency proceedings "solely" to the law of the Contracting State under the authority of which the register is kept. This means that the general applicability of the law of the State of the opening in accordance with Article 4 is not displaced. Hence, a sort of cumulative application of both laws is necessary.

Under Article 11, the law of the Contracting State of registration will therefore determine the modifications which, required by the law of the State of the opening, may be prompted by the insolvency proceedings and affect the rights of the debtor over immovable property, ships and aircraft subject to registration, the requisite entries in the register and the consequences thereof. In consequence, the law of the Contracting State of registration decides which effects of the insolvency proceedings are admissible and affect the rights of the debtor subject to registration in that State.

However, this rule does have certain disadvantages. While it makes access to different national registers easier, it means that the effects may be different for each Contracting State. The administration of the insolvency proceedings by a liquidator thus becomes more complex, although it increases in certainty. With that in mind, this rule is limited to registers on immovable property, ships and aircraft.

131. Article 11 does not refer to assets but to rights subject to registration in public registers, the purpose of which is to determine who is the holder or which are the rights in rem over the assets. It also includes systems of registration of deeds relating to immovable property to effect priorities such as the Registry of Deeds which exists in Ireland.

Article 11 refers only to the effects on the rights of the debtor over immovable property, ships or aircraft. For rights in rem, whether registered or not, of creditors or third parties acquired before the opening of the insolvency proceedings, see Article 5.

132. For the concept of "public register", see comments on Article 2.

[3408]

Article 12
Community patents and trademarks

133. The Agreement relating to Community patents (1989 Luxembourg Agreement), Council Regulation (EC) No 40/94 of 20 December 1993 on the Community trademark and Council Regulation (EC) No 2100/94 of 27 July 1994 on Community plant variety rights all create rights which cover the whole territory of the European Community.

This Convention opens up the possibility of insolvency proceedings with universal effect (thus encompassing the whole Community territory) if the debtor's centre of main interests is located in a Contracting State.

However, the Patent Convention contained in the 1989 Luxembourg Agreement (Article 41), the 1993 Regulation on the Community trademark (Article 21), and the 1994 Regulation on Community plant variety rights (Article 25), contain a rule to the effect that a

Community right derived therefrom may be included only in the first proceedings (regardless of whether these are main or territorial proceedings) opened in a Contracting State. This rule was logical insofar as common regulations on international insolvency proceedings were lacking. With this Convention it is logical to allocate those Community rights to the main proceedings. Article 12 of the Convention seeks to modify the rule established by the Patent Convention, the Regulation on the Community trademark and the Regulation on Community plant variety rights and to replace it with Article 12.

134. As may be concluded from Article 3(1), Article 12 is operative only when the debtor has his centre of main interests in a Contracting State. In all other cases, i e when this centre is located outside the Community, the provisions of the Patent Convention (Article 41), the Regulation on the Community trademark (Article 21) and the Regulation on Community plant variety rights (Article 25) shall be applied.

[3409]

Article 13

Detrimental acts

135. This provision must be taken in conjunction with Article 4(2)(m). The basic rule of the Convention is that the law of the State of the opening governs, under Article 4, any possible voidness, voidability or unenforceability of acts which may be detrimental to all the creditors' interests. This same law determines the conditions to be met, the manner in which the nullity and voidability function (automatically, by allocating retrospective effects to the proceedings or pursuant to an action taken by the liquidator, etc) and the legal consequences of nullity and voidability.

136. Article 13 represents a defence against the application of the law of the State of the opening, which must be pursued by the interested party, who must claim it.

It acts as a "veto" against the invalidity of the act decreed by the law of the State of the opening. This mechanism is easier to apply than other possible solutions based on the cumulative application of the two laws. It is now clear that all the conditions, content and the consequences of the voidability are borrowed from the law of the State of the opening. The only purpose of Article 13 and the law governing the act concerned is to reject the application of that law in a given case.

137. In this respect, Article 13 provides that the rules of the law of the State of the opening shall not apply when the person who has benefited from the contested act provides proof that:

1. the act in question (e g a contract) is subject to the law of a Contracting State other than the State of the opening of the proceedings;
2. the law of that other State does not allow for this act to be challenged by any means. By "any means" it is understood that the act must not be capable of being challenged using either rules on insolvency or general rules of the national law applicable to the act (e g to the contract referred to in paragraph (1)).

"In the relevant case" means that the act should not be capable of being challenged in fact i e after taking into account all the concrete circumstances of the case. It is not sufficient to determine whether it can be challenged in the abstract.

138. The aim of Article 13 is to uphold legitimate expectations of creditors or third parties of the validity of the act in accordance to the normally applicable national law, against interference from a different "lex concursus".

From the perspective of the protection of legitimate expectations, the operation of Article 13 is justified with regard to acts carried out prior to the opening of the insolvency proceedings, and threatened by either the retroactive nature of the insolvency proceedings opened in another country or actions to set aside previous acts of the debtor brought by the liquidator in those proceedings.

After the proceedings have been opened in a Contracting State, the creditor's reliance on the validity of the transaction under the national law applicable in non-insolvency situations is no longer justified. Thenceforth, all unauthorised disposals by the debtor are in principle ineffective by virtue of the divestment of his powers to dispose of the assets and such effect is recognised in all Contracting States. Article 13 does not protect against such an effect of the insolvency proceedings and it is not applicable to disposals occurring after the opening of the insolvency proceedings.

139. This rule covers both the main proceedings and the secondary proceedings (in each case with regard to the law of the State of the opening of the respective proceedings).

[3410]

Article 14
Protection of third-party purchasers

140. This provision was initially based on the desire to protect the confidence of third parties in the content of property registers when the debtor, after the insolvency proceedings have been opened, disposes for consideration of an asset from the estate, and the opening of proceedings or the restrictions on the debtor have not yet been entered or referred to in the register in question. The final drafting of this Article goes further and covers all acts of disposal concerning immovable assets which take place after the opening of the insolvency proceedings.

To be protected by Article 14, it is necessary that the debtor dispose of the asset for consideration (e g not gratuitously).

141. In principle, any act of disposal by the debtor after the proceedings have been opened shall be ineffective in accordance with the law of the State of the opening (as this law deprives the debtor of his powers of disposal).

However, in order to protect trade and reliance on systems of publication of rights in rem, the protection of bona fide third parties should be no different in respect of proceedings in another Contracting State as compared to domestic proceedings.

If the proceedings opened in another Contracting State do not appear in the local register, the only way adequately to protect confidence in the system of publication regarding rights in rem over assets, without any loopholes, is to make the effects of disposal subject to the law of the Contracting State under the authority of which the register is kept or, in the case of immovable property, to the law of the Contracting State where the immovable property is located.

Property covered by this Article means an immovable asset, ships or aircraft subject to registration in a public register and securities the existence of which presupposes registration (see point 69).

An act of disposal must be understood to include not only transfers of ownership but also the constitution of a right in rem relating to such property.

[3411]

Article 15
Effects of the insolvency procedure on lawsuits pending

142. The Convention distinguishes between the effects of insolvency on individual enforcement proceedings and those on lawsuits pending.

The effects on individual enforcement actions are governed by the law of the State of the opening (see Article 4(2)(f)) so that the collective insolvency proceedings may stay or prevent any individual enforcement action brought by creditors against the debtor's assets.

Effects of the insolvency proceedings on other legal proceedings concerning the assets or rights of the estate are governed (ex Article 15) by the law of the Contracting State where these proceedings are under way. The procedural law of this State shall decide whether or not the proceedings are to be suspended, how they are to be continued and whether any appropriate procedural modifications are needed in order to reflect the loss or the restriction of the powers of disposal and administration of the debtor and the intervention of the liquidator in his place.

[3412]

C. CHAPTER II: RECOGNITION OF INSOLVENCY PROCEEDINGS

Article 16
Principle

143. To recognize foreign judgments is to admit for the territory of the recognising State the authority which they enjoy in the State where they were handed down.

The Convention accords immediate recognition of judgments concerning the opening, course and closure of insolvency proceedings which come within its scope and of judgments handed down in direct connection with such insolvency proceedings.

Recognition is automatic within the system of the Convention. It requires no preliminary decision by a court of the requested State.

144. Article 16 establishes the general principle of recognition, in the territory of the Contracting States (eg the Community), of a judgment opening insolvency proceedings adopted by the competent authorities of a Contracting State under Article 3 of the Convention.

145. Only insolvency proceedings within the scope of the Convention benefit from the system of recognition of the Convention. To fall within such scope, the proceedings must be listed in the Annexes to the Convention.

Proceedings not listed in those Annexes shall not be eligible for recognition under the Convention nor shall they prevent the recognition of proceedings provided for in the Convention even though they were opened earlier.

146. The general principle of recognition is valid for all proceedings opened in a Contracting State under Article 3, ie for both main proceedings and territorial, either secondary or independent. Obviously, in the second case recognition will be limited to the territorial effects of the proceedings.

147. A judgment opening proceedings need not necessarily be a final judgment (not subject to ordinary appeal) in order to enjoy recognition. Such judgment whether final or provisional shall have effect in the whole territory covered by the Convention as long as it is effective in the State of the opening of proceedings.

The Convention is based on the principle of Community trust and on the "favor recognitionis", so that national borders are no obstacle to the efficient administration of international insolvency proceedings throughout the Community.

148. The Convention imposes an obligation to recognize insolvency proceedings opened in another Contracting State, even when such proceedings cannot be brought against the debtor in that State, due to his professional capacity or to his public or private nature, as in the case of non-traders in certain countries.

Main insolvency proceedings may be opened in a State (F1) in accordance with its own law, although in another Contracting State (F2) insolvency proceedings cannot be brought against the debtor by virtue of his professional capacity (ie a non-trader). The second State (F2) in such a case is obliged to recognize and, where appropriate, enforce the foreign judgment. The State requested (F2) cannot invoke public policy in its territory to oppose recognition on those grounds (under Article 26).

Since the main proceedings can be opened only if the debtor has his centre of main interests in the State of the opening, it seems logical that the decision of the law of that State to allow collective insolvency proceedings against that debtor should be respected by the other Member States, whose connection with the debtor is restricted to the existence of an establishment or assets.

However, these other States (ie F2) will not be obliged to open local secondary proceedings against that debtor, since the conditions laid down by their insolvency law, which is applicable pursuant to Article 28, have not been fulfilled.

The opposite hypothesis, ie the impossibility of opening main proceedings because the law of the contracting State competent under Article 3(1) does not allow it, presents no difficulties. The Convention expressly recognizes the possibility of opening territorial proceedings. Where the law of a State which has jurisdiction under Article 3(2) allows insolvency proceedings against that kind of debtor, it will be possible to open independent territorial proceedings (see Article 3(4)).

Naturally, the territorial proceedings have effects only in the State of the opening of proceedings and do not extend them to the territory of other States (see point 156); they do not therefore affect the situation of the debtor in other States. Only the main proceedings have that effect (see point 212).

149. The relationship between the recognition of main proceedings under Article 3(1) and the possibility of opening territorial proceedings under Article 3(2) is referred to in Article 16(2). The recognition of main proceedings does not preclude the subsequent opening of secondary territorial proceedings (see point 212).

[3413]

Article 17
Effects of recognition

150. Whereas Article 16 establishes the general principle of the recognition of a judgment opening insolvency proceedings, Article 17 distinguishes between the recognition of main proceedings and that of territorial proceedings.

151. Recognition of the main proceedings

The universality of main proceedings opened under Article 3(1), embracing all the debtor's assets and creditors, implies recognition of the proceedings and their effects in the States in which those assets or creditors are situated. The Convention guarantees this universality through the setting up of a system of mandatory automatic recognition in all Contracting States. The Convention reinforces this by making the consequence of recognition the "extension" to all other Contracting States of the effects attributed to those proceedings by the law of the State of the opening of proceedings.

152. "Automatic recognition" means immediate recognition by virtue of the Convention (ipso iure recognition) without any need to resort to preliminary proceedings to declare it effective.

Since recognition is not subject to prior proceedings, the authorities of the requested State which may be confronted with the judgment opening proceedings may determine incidentally whether it is a judgment under the Convention and whether grounds for refusal under Article 26 exist.

153. Article 17 lays down a model of recognition based on the extension of the effects of the judgment in a Contracting State to the whole territory covered by the Convention. Proceedings opened in another Contracting State will not, as regards their effects, be equated with national proceedings but will be recognized in other Contracting States with the same effects attributed to them by the law of the State of the opening (= "extension model").

The law of the State of the opening (and not the law of the requested State) shall be applicable to determine those effects. This shall apply to all the effects of the proceedings in another Contracting State, both procedural and substantive (see point 90). The substantive effects are included by virtue of the general applicability which the Convention attributes to the law of the State of the opening (see Article 4) and they are therefore subject to the same exceptions as are provided for by the Convention in respect of that law (see Articles 5 et seq).

154. The system of automatic recognition and the extension model reinforce the universality of the main proceedings. From the time fixed by the law of the State of the opening, the judgment opening proceedings produces its effects with equal force in all Contracting States. The divestment of the debtor, the appointment of the liquidator, the prohibition on individual executions, the inclusion of the debtor's assets in the estate regardless of the State in which they are situated, the obligation to return what has been obtained by individual creditors after opening, etc, are all effects laid down by the law of the State of the opening which are simultaneously applicable in all Contracting States.

155. The recognition of main proceedings under Article 3(1) shall be limited by the opening of territorial proceedings in accordance with Article 3(2).

The main proceedings cannot produce its effects in respect of the assets and legal situations which come within the jurisdiction of territorial proceedings opened. The territorial proceedings protect local interests and for this purpose the national law applies. However, the main proceedings may influence the conduct of territorial proceedings as a result of coordination and subordination rules which derive from the Convention and to which territorial proceedings are subject.

156. Recognition of territorial proceedings

Territorial proceedings can affect only the assets situated in the State of the opening. Recognition cannot imply, therefore, the extension of the effects of those proceedings to property situated in other Contracting States. Recognition of territorial proceedings means admitting the validity of the opening of the local proceedings and of the effects which they produce over the assets located in the territory of the State of the opening, which cannot be challenged in other Contracting States.

This is the case, for example, where the liquidator in those proceedings has to demand the return of assets belonging to the estate in the secondary proceedings which were transferred abroad without authorization after the opening of proceedings.

Moreover the opening of the territorial proceedings limits the extra-territorial effects of the main proceedings which may no longer include the assets situated in the State where those territorial proceedings were opened, except for the surplus assets in the secondary proceedings under Article 35. The main proceedings must observe that limitation.

157. Article 17(2), second sentence, covers the case of territorial proceedings, either secondary or independent, which may conclude by authorizing the debtor to postpone payment or even by discharging the remaining debt.

It may be clearly seen that, in the case of proceedings under Article 3(2), this reduction of creditors' rights can apply only to the debtor's estate situated in the State of the opening of the territorial proceedings. The creditors concerned will, therefore, be able to seek unlimited satisfaction of all their debts from the assets situated in other Contracting States. Naturally, nothing prevents the creditors from voluntarily agreeing to a further reduction of their rights affecting assets situated outside the State of opening of territorial proceedings. However, that supplementary restriction can be relied on only against creditors who have accepted it personally and not by a majority vote. This principle should be seen in conjunction with Article 34(2).

[3414]

Article 18
Powers of the liquidator

158. The main effect of the recognition of insolvency proceedings opened in a Contracting State is the recognition of the appointment of the liquidator and of his powers in all other Contracting States. The term "liquidator" must be understood in the wide sense of the definition given in Article 2 of the Convention.

159. By virtue of that recognition, the liquidator appointed in proceedings in a Contracting State will be able, in other Contracting States, to exercise the powers conferred on him by the law of the State of the opening.

The liquidator's powers, their nature and their scope will be determined by the law of the State of the opening of the proceedings in respect of which he was appointed. That law also establishes the liquidator's obligations.

160. As the Convention provides for a system of automatic recognition of insolvency proceedings, the appointment of the liquidator and the exercise of his powers are covered by that same automatic effect. Neither the exequatur nor the publication provided for in Article 21 is necessary for the liquidator to be able to exercise his powers in other Contracting States.

161. Within the limits laid down in the Convention, the liquidator in the main proceedings may exercise all his powers in the other Contracting States (i e in the whole of the territory of the Community).

In order to remove any doubts, Article 18 expressly stipulates that the liquidator may even transfer assets out of the State in which they are situated. In doing so, the liquidator must respect Articles 5 and 7 of the Convention, since the proceedings cannot affect rights in rem of creditors or third parties over assets situated, at the time of the opening, in a Contracting State other than the State of the opening of proceedings. To the extent that it is required by the right in rem, the removal of those assets to another State may be subject to the consent of the holder of the right in rem.

The creditors can prevent such transfer by requesting the opening of secondary proceedings concerning those assets (provided that the conditions laid down in Article 3(2) and (3) are fulfilled).

162. The powers of the liquidator in the main proceedings are subject to two general restrictions.

163. The first derives from the possible opening of territorial insolvency proceedings in another Contracting State (under Article 3(2)).

This restriction is logical, since the assets cannot be subject to the powers of two different liquidators. Once territorial proceedings have been opened, the direct powers of the liquidator in the main proceedings no longer apply to assets situated in the State of the opening of the territorial proceedings. The liquidator in the territorial proceedings has exclusive powers over those assets. This does not imply that the main liquidator loses all influence over the debtor's estate situated in the other Contracting State, but that that influence must be exercised through the powers conferred on that liquidator by the Convention to coordinate the territorial proceedings and the main proceedings (see Articles 31 to 37).

Article 18 extends this first restriction to cases where provisional protective measures incompatible with the exercise of those powers have been already adopted as a consequence of the request to open territorial proceedings.

The liquidator in the main proceedings is entitled under the Convention to request secondary proceedings (Article 29).

164. The second restriction provided for in Article 18(3) derives from the liquidator's obligation, when exercising his powers, to comply with the law of the State within the territory of which he intends to take action.

(a) The general principle of prohibiting the exercise of coercive power in another State also applies to a foreign liquidator. The latter can take action only in other States if he complies with that principle. Hence Article 18 expressly prohibits direct recourse to coercive measures. Any use of force or coercive action is excluded.

If persons affected by a liquidator's acts do not voluntarily agree to their performance and if coercive measures are required with regard to assets or persons, the liquidator must apply to the authorities of the State where the assets or persons are located to have them adopted and implemented. The Convention allows a foreign liquidator from another Contracting State, on the basis of the automatic recognition of his appointment and his powers, to petition those authorities to adopt distraint measures against such assets or persons in accordance with national law.

(b) The liquidator shall exercise his powers without infringing the laws of the State in which he takes action.

For example, the liquidator may transfer the assets belonging to the estate to another Contracting State. This power may be subject to rules limiting the free movement of goods. Thus, if an asset is part of the historical and cultural heritage of a Contracting State, it may be subject to an export ban protected under Article 36 of the EC Treaty. This prohibition naturally also applies to the liquidator. With regard to this type of asset, he may not exercise his general power to transfer assets.

(c) With regards to procedures for the realisation of assets, the liquidator shall comply with the law of the State where the assets are located. The law of the State of the opening shall establish the extent of the powers of the liquidator and the manners in which they may be exercised. Only that law can determine, for example, whether the sale of immovable property can be private (person-to-person) or if sale by public auction is necessary. However, once the form of sale has been decided according to that law, the procedures by which the assets are realized must be in accordance with the provisions of national law. In our example, if the law of the State of the opening requires a sale by public auction, the procedure of carrying out the sale in the State where the immovable property is situated shall be determined by the law of the latter State.

165. The liquidator in territorial proceedings is subject to a supplementary restriction. His powers of administration and disposal have the same scope as the proceedings from which they derive, i e they are territorial. However, assets subject to these proceedings may have been removed to other Contracting States after the opening of proceedings.

In this case, Article 18(2) clearly states that the liquidator may apply to these other Contracting States and request from their courts the return of the asset or may insist on such transfer for any other purpose useful to the local proceedings. He may also bring any action to set aside which is in the interest of the creditors (see point 224).

166. The Convention contains no rule regarding opposition to the exercise of powers by the liquidator. General rules shall therefore be applicable.

Consequently, the authorities of the State in which the powers are intended to be exercised shall have jurisdiction to take a decision if the grounds for opposition lie in the non-recognition, in accordance with the Convention, of the proceedings opened in another Contracting State or of the judgment appointing the liquidator. This is also the case where the grounds for opposition are a breach by the liquidator of the provisions of the Convention which govern the exercise of his powers in other States, for instance, Article 18(1) or Article 3(3).

If the opposition concerns the substance of the exercise of those powers, i e the justification for a measure which the liquidator intends to take, jurisdiction lies with the judicial authorities of the State of the opening of proceedings.

[3415]

Article 19
Proof of the liquidator's appointment

167. This provision derives from Article 2 of the 1990 Istanbul Convention. In contrast to the draft Community Convention of 1982, it was not thought necessary to establish a uniform model for the certificate attesting the appointment of the liquidator.

168. The proof of the liquidator's appointment may be established by a duly certified copy of the original decision, issued by a person authorized by the State in which the decision originated or by any other certificate issued by the competent court attesting the appointment.

169. The certified copy of the decision or the official certificate of the appointment shall require no legalization or other similar formality, such as the certificate ("apostille") provided for by the 1961 Hague Convention abolishing the requirement of legalization for foreign public documents.

A translation into the official language or languages of the Contracting State in which the liquidator intends to act may be required. This translation shall take into account the requirements established in this State regarding translations of official documents. For example, if we accept the parallel with the provisions of Article 48, second subparagraph, of the 1968 Brussels Convention the translation is certified by a person authorized for that purpose by one of the Contracting States, whether that of the opening of proceedings or that in which the liquidator intends to exercise his powers.

170. The Convention contains no rules regarding the means of proving the scope of the powers of the liquidator.

It seems reasonable that, in the case of doubt or opposition, these powers, based on the law of another Contracting State, are established by the person who invokes them. Proof may be by means of a certificate issued by the Court appointing the liquidator, which shall define his powers, or by any other means of evidence admitted by the law of the State where the liquidator intends to exercise his powers.

[3416]

Article 20
Return and imputation

171. The Convention considers its geographical scope (the Community) to be a single economic area. The main proceedings shall therefore produce effects within the whole of the territory of the Contracting States. Also for this reason, where the Convention allows for the opening of secondary proceedings, the whole area should be taken as a reference for the distribution of dividends, making it compulsory to take into account the sum obtained in each set of proceedings by means of a sort of consolidated account of the dividends obtained on a European scale. The aim of this Article is to guarantee the equal treatment of all the creditors of a single debtor.

172. Rule regarding return (Article 20(1))

The rule on return is the consequence of the universality of the main proceedings, which encompass all the debtor's assets, wherever they are situated, and affect all the creditors. As a result of this principle of universality, it is evident that a creditor who, after the opening of proceedings, obtains total or partial satisfaction of his claim individually (by means of payment by the debtor or execution of assets situated in other States) breaches the principle of collective satisfaction on which the insolvency proceedings are based. Hence, the obligation to return "what has been obtained". The liquidator may demand either the return of the assets received or the equivalent in money.

173. The previous rule operates within the limits of Articles 5 and 7, which exclude from the scope of the main proceedings rights in rem of creditors and third parties in respect of the debtor's assets situated outside the State of the opening of proceedings at that time. As long as these Articles apply, a creditor who obtains satisfaction of claims guaranteed by rights in rem by realization of the security does not enrich himself to the detriment of the estate and does not breach the principle of collective satisfaction (see comment on Article 5).

174. Rule regarding imputation (Article 20(2))

The Convention allows for the opening of parallel insolvency proceedings (see Article 3). Thus, when a creditor obtains satisfaction in insolvency proceedings opened in another Contracting State, he does not breach a law, but simply exercises a right (see Article 32(1)).

For this reason, Article 20(2) allows a creditor to keep what he has obtained in the first proceedings in which distribution took place. Nevertheless, in order to guarantee the equality of all creditors on a Community level, they may not, once this payment has been received, participate in other distributions until all creditors of the same ranking have obtained equal satisfaction.

175. The method of calculation is relatively simple. It comprises four rules:

1. Nobody may obtain more than 100% of his claims.
2. The total original amount of the claim (100% of its initial value) shall be taken into account, and not the remaining amount (satisfaction obtained in other proceedings is not deducted).

If claims were not taken into account in each of the proceedings at 100% of their amount (without deducting the part satisfied in other proceedings), it would not be possible to guarantee the equal treatment of creditors participating in several proceedings.

The only exception to the second rule is that of claims secured by rights in rem or through a set-off, the secured parts of which are not affected by insolvency proceedings (see Articles 5, 6 and 7). The Convention lays down no rule on whether the amount of the original claim or the remaining claim shall be taken into account; this question is left to the rules of the law of the State of the opening (see Article 4(2)(i)).

3. A claim is not taken into account in the distribution until such time as the creditors with the same ranking have obtained an equal percentage of satisfaction in these proceedings as that obtained by its holder in the first proceedings.

For example, if creditor X in proceedings opened in a Contracting State F1 has obtained 5% on an ordinary unsecured claim with an amount of 75, he cannot take part in the distribution in the proceedings opened in another Contracting State F2 (where he has also lodged his claim) until the ordinary unsecured creditors have obtained 5%. If in F2 the percentage of satisfaction attains 8% for ordinary unsecured creditors, creditor X may participate in it only with regard to the difference, ie up to 3% (8% minus 5% already obtained in F1 = 3%). This 3% shall apply to the whole claim (to the 100% of its initial amount of 75), in accordance with the second rule mentioned above.

Conversely, if the first proceedings are in F2 where the creditors obtain a percentage of satisfaction of 8%, despite also having lodged their claims in the proceedings opened in F1, they shall not participate in the distribution in F1, since the ordinary unsecured creditors there obtain only 5%, whereas they have already obtained 8% in F2.

Thus, regardless of which proceedings take place first, the creditors of both F1 and F2 who have lodged their claims in both proceedings shall obtain an equal final dividend (8% of the total claim).

4. The ranking or category of each claim is determined for each of the proceedings by the law of the State of the opening (Article 4(2)(i)). Since different insolvency laws apply to the different proceedings (each is governed by its own national law), the ranking of the same claim lodged in two different proceedings may not be the same in both. The only ranking or category which is taken into account in order to apply Article 20(2) is that given to the claim by the law governing proceedings in which distribution is to be effected.

Hence, for the calculation of the dividend, only the percentage of satisfaction obtained in other proceedings, and not the rank or category which the claim enjoyed in those other proceedings, is taken into account. Thus in our example, if the claim of creditor X is an ordinary unsecured claim in F1 but it benefits from a preference in F2, it follows that it has already obtained 5% in F1, no matter what the ranking was; this percentage is, for the purposes of calculation, compared to the dividend which the rules in force in F2 apply to preferential claims. If these claims obtain a dividend of 25% in F2, creditor X shall benefit from a dividend of 20% in F2 (25% minus 5% already obtained in F1 = 20%).

176. In practice, if a number of claims have been lodged both in the insolvency proceedings opened in F1 and F2, the liquidator in the F2 proceedings may calculate the distribution in F2 by stages, for each rank. In our example, up to 5% (dividend obtained in F1) he will not take into account the claims already satisfied in F1. Once the claims lodged only in F2 have attained 5%, if there are remaining assets to be distributed he will make a further calculation introducing also the claims already satisfied in F1 together with the claims lodged only in F2, in order to determine the new dividend.

[3417]

Article 21
Publication

177. The publication of the opening of insolvency proceedings in another Contracting State is not a precondition for the recognition of those proceedings or for the recognition and exercise of the powers of the liquidator appointed in such proceedings.

The principal aim of publication is to contribute to the security of trade in the States where the debtor has assets or where he conducts business, by drawing his creditors' and future contracting parties' attention to the legal situation of the debtor.

178. Although recognition is not dependent on publication of the opening of the proceedings, publication may produce significant legal effects in relation to the evaluation of the behaviour of the persons concerned, within the framework of either the Convention (for example Article 24) or the national law to be applied.

179. The initiative to publish in other States is vested in the liquidator. For this purpose, he will have to evaluate all the circumstances, (e g individual creditors cannot be identified) and the need for trade security (e g an establishment remains in operation in another State where future creditors should be informed).

This rule shall not prevent the courts of the State of the opening from ordering publication if its national insolvency law provides for this.

180. Any Contracting State in which the debtor has an establishment may provide for mandatory publication of the opening of insolvency proceedings. In no cases may this mandatory publication constitute a precondition for recognition (this would breach the rules of the Convention).

Article 21(2) explicitly states that in the case of mandatory publication, the latter must be arranged by the liquidator or the authority designated by the State of the opening of proceedings. Where necessary, the national law of the State which provides for such mandatory publication will determine the liquidator's liability when the latter has not taken the necessary measures to arrange publication.

181. The Convention establishes no uniform mechanism for publication but stipulates that it should be in accordance with the arrangements laid down by the law of the State in which it is to take place. On the other hand, the Convention does determine what information is to be published: the basic content of the judgment opening proceedings and, where necessary (for example, if there are a number of appointments), the basic content of the decision appointing the liquidator. In both cases, it should always indicate the identity of the liquidator appointed and specify the jurisdiction rule applied (Article 3(1) or Article 3(2)). This does not exclude other items of information which may be of interest to third parties or creditors (deadlines for lodging claims, etc).

In the case of publication as referred to in Article 21(2), the compulsory information required may not go beyond the information mentioned in paragraph 1 of that Article.

[3418]

Article 22

Registration in a public register

182. Registration in a public register is not a precondition for recognition of foreign insolvency proceedings or for recognition of the powers conferred on the liquidator appointed in another Contracting State. Nevertheless, the registers play a significant role for the trade security. The trust of third parties acting in good faith on the basis of information contained in these registers is protected in all Member States. For this reason, but also to guarantee the full effectiveness of the insolvency proceedings, the Convention empowers the liquidator to request the registration of the judgment opening insolvency proceedings in another Contracting State.

This rule shall not prevent the courts of the State of the opening from ordering the liquidator to register in other States, if its national insolvency law so provides.

The form and content of the registration shall be subject to the law of the Contracting State under the authority of which the register is kept. Such Contracting State should allow registration of proceedings in another Contracting State under conditions similar to those applied for the registration of national proceedings.

183. The Contracting States cannot demand an exequatur as a precondition for access to the registration of a foreign judgment. Recognition shall be automatic.

Each State may, however, decide if the authority responsible for the register at the time of registration should, incidentally, check whether the decision is recognizable under the Convention.

184. The registration requirement relates to the main proceedings, since by definition the territorial proceedings cannot affect assets situated outside the State of the opening of proceedings.

185. The Contracting States may request mandatory registration in their registers (when the debtor is a holder of registered assets, for example). In no case may such mandatory publication be a precondition for recognition.

Where necessary, the national law of the State of registration will determine the liquidator's liability when the latter has not taken the necessary measures to ensure such registration.

[3419]

Article 23
Costs

186. The Convention considers the expenditure arising from the publication and registration measures laid down in Articles 21 and 22 as costs incurred in the proceedings. The proposal by some delegations to limit this definition to the expenditure arising from action by the liquidator (Article 21(1) and Article 22(1)) and not to that arising from the mandatory publication or registration requested by a State different from the State of the opening and conduct of proceedings was not approved.

[3420]

Article 24
Honouring of an obligation to a debtor

187. The automatic recognition of insolvency proceedings opened in another Contracting State, and the lack of any general system of prior publication, guarantee the immediate effectiveness of the judgment opening proceedings in all the Contracting States.

Nevertheless, in some cases, a number of those persons may be unaware of the opening of proceedings and may act in good faith in contradiction with these new circumstances. In this connection, Article 24 provides for a solution to the problem where an obligation is honoured in good faith for the benefit of a debtor, when it should have been honoured for the benefit of the liquidator in the proceedings in another Contracting State. This Article establishes that the person honouring the obligation shall be deemed to have discharged it if he was unaware of the opening of proceedings.

Article 24 is therefore based on a double presumption. If the obligation is honoured before the publication provided for in Article 21 has occurred in the State concerned (e g the State in which the person honouring the obligation is established or the State in which the obligation is honoured, as the case may be), there shall be a presumption of ignorance. If the obligation is honoured after publication has taken place, there shall be a presumption of awareness. These two presumptions are rebuttable, but under each of them the burden of proof shifts from one party to the other. So, for instance, once publication has taken place, it shall be for the debtor honouring the obligation in question to provide evidence rebutting the presumptions.

188. In Article 24(1) the place where an obligation is honoured means the place where the obligation has been performed in fact by the debtor of the obligation.

[3421]

Article 25
Recognition and enforceability of other judgments

189. Introduction

The Convention refers firstly to the recognition of the opening of insolvency proceedings (Article 16) and to its effects (Articles 17 to 24).

The recognition of judgments relating to the conduct and closure of the insolvency proceedings and of judgments adopted in the framework of those proceedings is dealt with generally in Article 25. This provision also regulates the enforcement of all judgments, including, where necessary, the judgment opening proceedings, as regards all its consequences except the opening itself (see point 143).

190. To enforce is to put into execution. Enforcement implies the exercise of the State's coercive power to ensure compliance.

The principle of exclusive territorial sovereignty precludes the direct exercise of a State's power within the territory of other States. By virtue of this principle, direct application of coercive powers is limited to the authorities of the State where the assets or persons to which this action relates are situated. The Convention has not altered this state of affairs.

As a consequence, the enforcement of judgments of other Contracting States shall depend on prior authorization by the authorities of the State in which it must be carried out. This authorization is obtained by means of a special procedure: the procedure called exequatur.

The exequatur does not deal with the enforcement itself, but with the prior authorization needed for enforcement. Enforcement in the strict sense shall be carried out by the competent national authorities by means of the procedures established by the national law for the enforcement of equivalent domestic judgments. The Convention on insolvency proceedings, like the 1968 Brussels Convention, deals only with the first aspect (prior authorization and its conditions).

If the conditions laid down by the Convention are fulfilled, the authorities of the requested State shall be obliged to grant this authorization, pursuant to the Convention. National law thereafter determines the methods by which the judgment of another Contracting State is enforced by the national authorities. The usual methods of coercive enforcement of the national law will be used, adapted, where necessary, to guarantee the "effet utile" of the Convention, ie to render effective in other States the specific decision taken by the foreign court.

191. Judgments relating to insolvency proceedings (Article 25(1), first subparagraph)

Judgments relating to the conduct and closure of insolvency proceedings present no specific problem of characterization.

The recognition of these judgments operates in the same way and with the same effects as the judgment opening proceedings which we have already mentioned (see Articles 16 and 17).

The Convention subjects any composition approved by the competent court of the State of the opening to the same system of recognition.

192. As regards the enforcement of all these judgments and, where necessary, of the composition, various possibilities were examined at the negotiations. The idea finally adopted was to use the same system for the enforcement of judgments in civil and commercial matters, as provided for by the 1968 Brussels Convention. This explains the reference in Article 25(1) to the rules on enforcement in the 1968 Brussels Convention.

Thus, the simplified system of exequatur provided for in that Convention will be used for the enforcement of judgments adopted in the framework of insolvency proceedings (see Articles 31 to 51 of the 1968 Brussels Convention; for a thorough analysis of that system see also the reports on that Convention).

As under the 1968 Brussels Convention (see Article 31 thereof), in order for enforcement to take effect in the State requested, the judgment should be already enforceable in the State in which it was given (State of origin) and that effect should not have been suspended there. A judgment cannot produce more effects in other States than in the State of origin.

However, grounds for rejection of the exequatur are taken not from the 1968 Brussels Convention (Article 34(2) of the 1968 Brussels Convention is expressly excluded), but from the Convention on insolvency proceedings (see Article 26).

193. It is important to stress that Article 25(3) excludes from the obligation to recognize and enforce those foreign judgments which might result in a limitation of the personal freedom or postal secrecy of the insolvent debtor or of any other person who may be affected by the limitations derived from the insolvency proceedings.

This is an area which relates directly to fundamental rights and the Contracting States preferred to retain their freedom as to the recognition and enforcement of such decisions, regardless of the Convention on insolvency proceedings. Each State will decide autonomously on the treatment of such decisions when they originate in another Contracting State.

194. Judgments arising from insolvency proceedings (Article 25(1), second subparagraph)

The Convention also governs the recognition and enforcement of judgments arising from insolvency proceedings. These are judgments directly deriving from bankruptcy law which have a direct link to the insolvency proceedings but do not relate to the opening, conduct and closure of insolvency proceedings.

Recognition and enforcement of such judgments are always governed by the Convention whether they are adopted by the bankruptcy court or by an ordinary court, as could be the case under national law.

195. The raison d'être of this provision derives from the Judgment of the Court of Justice of 22 February 1979 (Case 133/78) (Gourdain v Nadler [1979] ECR p 733). Called upon to interpret Article 1(2) of the 1968 Brussels Convention (which excludes the field of bankruptcy, winding-up of insolvent companies, compositions and analogous proceedings from its scope), the Court of Justice adopted a criterion to define bankruptcy based on the nature of the action undertaken. According to this criterion, actions the direct legal basis of

which is the insolvency law and which are closely linked with the insolvency proceedings are not covered by the 1968 Brussels Convention. The character of the judicial body which decides on this action is of no importance.

In accordance with this decision of the Court of Justice, such actions should be subject to the Convention on insolvency proceedings or, otherwise, in the overall Convention rules there might be unjustifiable gaps between the general Convention and the specific Convention. For this reason, Article 25(1), second subparagraph, of the Convention on insolvency proceedings expressly adopts the same criterion of delimitation.

196. In order for the Convention on insolvency proceedings to apply it is necessary that the action undertaken directly derives from insolvency law and be closely connected with the insolvency proceedings.

Such is the case of actions which are based on (and not only affected by) insolvency law and are only possible during the insolvency proceedings or in direct relation with them. It includes actions to set aside acts detrimental to the general body of creditors (see Article 13); actions on the personal liability of directors based upon insolvency law, i e the "action en comblement pour insuffisance d'actif" vis-à-vis the managers of the company provided by the French Law, which the Court of Justice of the European Communities considered as a bankruptcy action in its Judgment of 22 February 1978, Case 133/78; actions relating to the admission or the ranking of a claim; disputes between the liquidator and the debtor on whether an asset belongs to the bankrupt's estate, etc.

However, actions deriving from law other than that relating to insolvency should not be included, even though they may be affected by the opening of proceedings (actively or passively). Such is the case of actions on the existence or the validity under general law of a claim (e g a contract) or relating to its amount; actions to recover another's property the holder of which is the debtor; and, in general, actions that the debtor could have undertaken even without the opening of insolvency proceedings.

197. The purpose of Article 25(2) is to avoid gaps between the Convention on insolvency proceedings and the 1968 Brussels Convention. The exclusion of insolvency proceedings as provided for in Article 1(2) of the 1968 Brussels Convention should be interpreted in accordance with the definition of insolvency proceedings given by the Convention on insolvency proceedings and the criteria incorporated in Article 25 thereof.

198. Preservation measures (Article 25(1), third subparagraph)

The same system of recognition and enforcement shall apply to preservation measures ordered by a court having jurisdiction under Article 3(1) after the request for the opening of insolvency proceedings.

Article 25 covers preservation measures adopted both before and after the opening of insolvency proceedings, Article 25(1) third subparagraph ensures that from the moment of the request of the opening of insolvency proceedings covered by the Convention, all preservation measures necessary to protect the future effectiveness of those proceedings fall under the system of this Convention.

199. The reason for this rule lies in the case law of the Court of Justice of the European Communities. According to the judgment of 27 March 1979 (Case 143/78, De Cavel v De Cavel [1979] ECR p 1055), provisional orders and protective measures shall be included in the scope of the 1968 Brussels Convention, not by virtue of "their own nature" but of "the nature of the rights which they serve to protect". Since insolvency proceedings are expressly excluded from the scope of the 1968 Brussels Convention (Article 1 subparagraph 2), that Convention cannot apply to measures adopted prior to the opening of insolvency proceedings to guarantee its future effectiveness. In view of the practical significance of preservation measures in insolvency matters it seemed logical to establish a rule expressly including those measures in the scope of the Convention.

200. The resulting system for preservation measures is similar to the one laid down by the 1968 Brussels Convention for preservation measures in civil and commercial matters (see, however, point 207). This solution is of immediate practical importance. There are many examples of preservation measures that should have extraterritorial scope and cover the whole Community (e g after the request for the opening of proceedings and with sufficient grounds, attempted fraudulent concealment of assets, the judge who has jurisdiction under Article 3(1) issues a provisional injunction prohibiting the disposal of assets by the debtor).

201. To understand the recognition and enforcement system for preservation measures, it must be taken into account that this Convention (as well as the 1968 Brussels Convention) governs both jurisdiction for adopting binding judgments (which is attributed to the courts of the State

where the centre of the debtor's main interests is situated (F1)) and the recognition and enforcement of such judgments in other Contracting States.

The court having jurisdiction under Article 3(1) also has jurisdiction to decide, for example, the seizure of the debtor's assets, even though they are situated abroad, or any other preservation measure. This decision shall be entitled, according to Article 25, to its recognition and enforcement in the Contracting State where the assets concerned are situated (F2).

Recognition and enforcement of that decision always fall under the exclusive authority of the courts of the State where the measure is to be carried out (F2).

The courts in F2 will only verify that it is a decision covered by the Convention, that it emanates from the judge who claims jurisdiction under Article 3(1) and that the said measure does not breach public policy. It is not necessary, nor may it be requested, that the requirements laid down by the national law of F2 for the direct adoption of equivalent preservation measures be fulfilled.

Once the exequatur has been granted according to the Convention, the enforcement itself shall be done using the mechanisms of enforcement available under the domestic law of F2 (see point 190).

[3422]

Article 26
Public policy

202. Defences against recognition and enforcement – Introduction

The Convention is based on the principle of Community trust and on the general legal presumption that the foreign judgment is valid. For this reason it establishes that the only ground for opposing recognition is that the foreign judgment is contrary to the public policy of the requested State. As a consequence:

1. The foreign judgment cannot be the subject of review as regards its substance (révision au fond). All questions regarding the substance must be discussed before the courts of the State of the opening of proceedings. In the State where recognition or enforcement is requested, the court may only decide whether the foreign judgment will have effects contrary to its public policy.
2. The Convention contains no provisions as to the verification of the international jurisdiction of the court of the State of origin (the court in the State of the opening of proceedings which has jurisdiction under Article 3 of the Convention). The courts of the requested States may not review the jurisdiction of the court of the State of origin, but only verify that the judgment emanates from a court of a Contracting State which claims jurisdiction under Article 3 of the Convention. It is for the judicial authorities of the State in which the judgment originated (F1) to verify and control its international jurisdiction under the Convention. Any interested party seeking to challenge the jurisdiction of a national court must go to the State of the opening of proceedings to appeal against the decision asserting jurisdiction. The court may refer the interpretation of Article 3 (international jurisdiction) to the Court of Justice of the European Communities for a preliminary ruling (see Article 44).

203. Public Policy

The exception in Article 26 is the traditional exception that a judgment of a foreign court need not be recognised or enforced if such recognition or enforcement is contrary to the public policy in the Contracting State in which recognition or enforcement is sought.

204. The public policy exception ought to operate only in exceptional cases. For this reason Article 26 requires recognition or enforcement of the foreign judgment to be "manifestly" contrary to public policy.

Furthermore, Article 26 does not require the compatibility with public policy of the rule or principle applied by the foreign court to be ascertained in the abstract, but that the result of recognition or enforcement of the judgment offends against public policy. Verification of conformity with public policy is directed towards the result of the recognition or enforcement, which means that all the circumstances peculiar to the case, including the connection with the requested State, are relevant.

205. Public policy derives from national law, and therefore the concept does not necessarily have a uniform content throughout the Community. Public policy is based on the fundamental

principles of the law of the recognizing State. It involves, in particular, constitutionally protected rights and freedoms, and fundamental policies of the requested State, including those of the Community.

However, public policy cannot be used by Contracting States to unilaterally challenge the system of the Convention. Unreasonably wide interpretations of public policy are not covered by Article 26. (See also point 208).

206. Public policy operates as a general clause as regards recognition and enforcement, covering fundamental principles of both substance and procedure.

Public policy may thus protect participants or persons concerned by the proceedings against failures to observe due process. Public policy does not involve a general control of the correctness of the procedure followed in another Contracting State, but rather of essential procedural guarantees such as the adequate opportunity to be heard and the rights of participation in the proceedings. Rights of participation and non-discrimination play a special role in the case of plans to reorganize businesses or compositions, in relation to creditors whose participation is hindered or who are the subject of unfounded discrimination.

The 1968 Brussels Convention deals separately, in Article 27, with the conditions concerning the serving of documents and the time necessary to prepare the defence, which form part of (but do not exhaust) the guarantees of the right of defence. However, in view of the special nature of insolvency proceedings, which are collective proceedings with special rules of individual notice (Article 40) and publicity (Article 21), and taking into account that the most important criterion of international jurisdiction is the State of the debtor's centre of main interests, which in principle will normally be that of the domicile or seat of the debtor, the group preferred to leave these conditions to case law.

However, if within the context of insolvency proceedings individual decisions are taken vis-à-vis a specific creditor, it seems reasonable to provide guarantees equivalent to those laid down in Article 27 of the 1968 Brussels Convention.

207. All the Contracting States provide for the possibility of taking, under certain urgent circumstances, ex parte preservation measures without an ex ante hearing of the party concerned. Naturally, for these measures to be constitutional, in most States they are subject to special requirements guaranteeing respect of due process (e g cumulatively, evidence of a good prima facie case, serious urgency, lodging of a guarantee by the applicant, immediate notification of the person concerned and the real possibility of challenging the adoption of the measures).

The Convention does not rule out the possibility of such measures being recognized "by virtue of their nature". Whether they are recognized (and, where appropriate, enforced) or not depends on whether or not they are compatible with the public policy of the requested State in which the judgment is to take effect (F2).

208. For the reasons explained in point 193, the Convention excludes judgments affecting personal freedom or postal secrecy from the obligation of recognition and enforcement, so that the States will not be obliged to resort to this exemption clause (Article 25(3)).

Conversely, as stated in point 148, in order to prevent the use of public policy to paralyse such recognition or enforcement, the Convention does not allow the use of the status of the debtor (e g trader/non-trader) to prevent recognition of a foreign judgment (second subparagraph of Article 16(1)).

209. Public policy may result in total or partial rejection of the foreign judgments.

210. The Portuguese Republic indicated in a unilateral statement made at the meeting of the Council of the European Union on 25 September 1995 that, under the conditions set out in Article 26, Portuguese public policy might be invoked to defend important local interests against the application of Article 37, which concerns the conversion of territorial proceedings opened before the main proceedings, where those interests are not sufficiently taken into account in such conversion.

[3423]

D. CHAPTER III: SECONDARY INSOLVENCY PROCEEDINGS

Article 27
Opening of insolvency proceedings

211. The Convention permits the opening of local proceedings by the courts of the State where the debtor has an establishment (Article 3(2)).

After main proceedings have been opened in a Contracting State, those local proceedings can only be "secondary" proceedings.

Secondary proceedings are governed by national law. The Convention, however, modifies the conditions established by the national law for the opening of insolvency proceedings in two aspects:

1. The national law requirement of insolvency of the debtor need not be met, insofar as the judgment opening main insolvency proceedings in another Contracting State is recognized.
2. The right to request the opening of insolvency proceedings is directly given by the Convention to the liquidator of the main proceedings.

The remaining conditions are those of the national law (see Articles 28 and 29(2)) without modifications, i e if local insolvency proceedings can be opened on account of the status of the debtor, persons empowered to request the opening, etc.

212. The judgment opening insolvency proceedings by the court of the State in which the centre of the debtor's main interests is situated has the specific effect of allowing territorial proceedings to be opened in the State where the debtor has an establishment, without the court of the State in which the establishment is situated having to examine the insolvency of the debtor.

213. The court where the opening of secondary proceedings is requested examines whether the proceedings opened in another Contracting State and by virtue of which the opening of territorial proceedings is requested are covered by Article 16: i e the judgment opens a set of insolvency proceedings as listed in Annex A, it is delivered by a court which has declared that it has jurisdiction within the meaning of Article 3(1) and it is effective.

Moreover, the court examines its international jurisdiction for opening territorial proceedings, as well as its domestic jurisdiction, and, concerning those aspects not covered by the Convention, the conditions for opening proceedings provided for by national legislation.

214. The proceedings by virtue of which the opening of secondary proceedings is requested must be proceedings included in Annex A to the Convention.

They must be proceedings based on the debtor's insolvency (see point 49(b), fourth and fifth subparagraphs for the problem posed by winding-up proceedings in Ireland and the United Kingdom).

215. The proceedings by virtue of which the opening of secondary proceedings is requested must be opened by a court of a Contracting State which has jurisdiction, as provided for in Article 3(1): such a court has verified that the centre of the debtor's main interests is situated in that State and it bases its jurisdiction on those grounds to open proceedings which may claim to be the main proceedings.

The court which is required to open secondary proceedings cannot verify the correctness of the appraisal of the first court, whose judgment benefits from the trust placed in judgments delivered by Community courts.

216. The court where the opening of secondary proceedings is requested also examines whether the foreign judgment is effective.

217. If the judgment opens an insolvency proceeding mentioned in Annex A, acknowledges that it constitutes the opening of main proceedings and has begun to be effective, that judgment is recognized within the meaning of Article 16.

The requirement for opening secondary proceedings laid down by the Convention is thus met.

218. In consequence, the court where the opening of secondary proceedings is requested does not have to examine the debtor's insolvency.

219. Furthermore, the court requested to open secondary proceedings examines its jurisdiction within the meaning of Article 3(2).

The debtor must have an establishment as defined in Article 2(h) on the territory in question. If there is no establishment, no secondary proceedings will be opened.

In the latter case, the main proceedings will produce their full effects on the territory where the debtor does not have an establishment, but does have assets. Chapter II of the Convention comes into play and the liquidator in the main proceedings may exercise all his powers on that territory. Thus, for instance, as the mere existence of a credit balance in a bank account does not constitute an establishment, the liquidator in the main proceedings may, subject in particular to the rights in rem of third parties referred to in Article 5, order the transfer of such money to the State of the opening in order to distribute it amongst the creditors involved in the main proceedings.

220. In examining its international jurisdiction within the meaning of Article 3(2), the court appraises the facts to determine whether the debtor has an establishment in that territory. In fact, the court may be led to consider that the debtor's activities in that territory constitute more than a simple establishment and could have been considered as the centre of the debtor's main interests.

The principle of trust attached to decisions of courts within the Community does not allow those courts to call into question the appraisal of the court that has declared itself competent in accordance with Article 3(1) (see point 215).

A court which establishes that the judgment opening the main proceedings has the quality of a recognized judgment and that the debtor has a place of activity in its territory that can be considered to be an establishment will be led to open territorial secondary proceedings.

221. In accordance with Article 3(3), secondary insolvency proceedings opened after the main proceedings must be winding-up proceedings within the meaning of Article 2(c). Their purpose is to realize the debtor's assets. The proceedings are mentioned in Annex B to the Convention.

The court cannot open insolvency proceedings the purpose of which is the reorganization of the debtor's business or of his financial situation.

The discussions on the Convention have finally resulted in the inclusion of both winding-up proceedings and reorganization proceedings in the main insolvency proceedings.

In the case of proven insolvency at the centre of the debtor's main interests, it is difficult to conceive, under certain legal systems in the Community, of an establishment dependent on the insolvent person being separately the subject of reorganization. On the other hand, coordination between the main proceedings and the secondary reorganization proceedings was regarded by most Contracting States as so complex technically as to be difficult to carry out.

In order to confer the widest possible scope on the Convention by recognizing not only winding-up proceedings – accepted from the beginning of discussion as proceedings to be recognized – but also reorganization proceedings, it was decided to allow only secondary winding-up proceedings.

This solution shows the dependency of the secondary proceedings vis-à-vis the main proceedings of a universal nature.

222. National legislation determines more specifically the court which has territorial jurisdiction.

It should be noted that the Convention deals with international jurisdiction but does not specify which court has jurisdiction among the courts of the Contracting State in which an establishment is situated.

States shall ensure that their legislation designates the court which has territorial jurisdiction to open secondary proceedings.

223. The court also applies its national law regarding the conditions for opening proceedings which are not the subject of a rule of the Convention (Article 4(2)).

National law determines the persons against whom insolvency proceedings may be brought (Article 4(2)(a)). Where, for example, national legislation does not permit insolvency proceedings against a person who does not have the capacity of a trader, or against a public undertaking, the possibility of secondary proceedings is excluded.

224. In accordance with Article 3(2), secondary proceedings only produce effects with regard to the debtor's assets situated in the territory of the State where the establishment is situated.

The secondary liquidator has, however, the right to act outside his territory in order to recover an asset moved out of that State after the opening of the secondary proceedings or in fraud against the creditors of those proceedings. (Article 18(2)). He is also allowed to bring actions in other States for the voidness, voidability or unenforceability of detrimental legal acts (Article 4(2)(m) and Article 13). The purpose of these actions outside the territory is, in fact, the return of assets which were legally situated in the territory of the proceedings at the time of the opening or which, without fraud, would have been situated in the territory of the proceedings at the time of the opening.

The action of the secondary liquidator in the matter of the return of assets which are actually situated abroad but which should normally be included in the secondary proceedings is to be assessed on the basis of the law of the secondary proceedings, pursuant in particular to Article 4(2)(m), subject to Article 13 (see points 91(l) and 135 to 139).

[3424]

Article 28
Applicable law

225. This Article expressly stipulates that, save as otherwise provided by the Convention, the law of the State in which secondary proceedings are opened shall apply to those proceedings.

In fact, this reiterates Article 4, which is interpreted as meaning that the law applicable to the main proceedings is the law of the State where the main proceedings are opened, and the law applicable to the secondary proceedings is the law of the State of the opening of the secondary proceedings.

[3425]

Article 29
Right to request the opening of proceedings

226. The Convention authorizes the liquidator in the main proceedings to request the opening of secondary proceedings. The temporary administrator who, according to national law, may be appointed after the request of the opening of the main insolvency proceedings but before the opening itself, is not covered by Article 29(a) (see point 262).

The liquidator in secondary proceedings has, however, no right derived from the Convention to request the opening of other secondary proceedings.

This rule states the relationship of dependence of the secondary proceedings upon the main proceedings.

227. Furthermore, the persons and authorities empowered by national law to request the opening of the insolvency proceedings referred to in Annex B are also entitled to request the opening of secondary proceedings.

The right of these persons and therefore the right of the creditors to bring about proceedings is not limited by the requirement of a specific interest.

The provision envisaged in the discussions, whereby only the creditors who would benefit from a more favourable legal status in the secondary proceedings than in the main proceedings (for example, a more favourable ranking) could request the opening of secondary proceedings, has been deleted.

On the other hand, Article 29(b) confers the right to have proceedings opened on any person, without distinction.

It should be noted that the right to request the opening of territorial proceedings before the opening of the main proceedings is limited to those proceedings referred to in Article 3(4)(b) (see point 85).

[3426]

Article 30
Advance payment of costs and expenses

228. Various legislations rule out the possibility of insolvency proceedings where the debtor's assets are insufficient to cover in whole or in part the costs and expenses of the proceedings.

The Convention takes these legislations into account.

The provision in Article 30 is understood to mean that where national law does not require sufficient assets in order to open insolvency proceedings, it cannot introduce such a requirement for secondary proceedings only.

Should national law rule out insolvency proceedings where assets are insufficient, the Convention upholds this law and allows the court to require from the applicant, including the liquidator, an advance payment of costs, or an appropriate security. The terms "may require" do not confer a power on the court but mean that national legislation continues to apply.

[3427]

Article 31
Duty to cooperate and communicate information

229. The main proceedings and the secondary proceedings are interdependent proceedings which concern a debtor with several centres of activity and assets spread over several territories.

The debtor's creditors participate, or may have an interest in participating, in several proceedings. Cooperation and information between the liquidators is thus necessary to ensure the smooth course of operations in the various proceedings.

230. The exchange of information between the liquidators concerns in particular:

- the assets,
- the actions planned or under way in order to recover assets: actions to obtain payment or actions for set aside,
- possibilities for liquidating assets,
- claims lodged,
- verification of claims and disputes concerning them,
- the ranking of creditors,
- planned reorganization measures,
- proposed compositions,
- plans for the allocation of dividends,
- the progress of operations in the proceedings.

231. The duty to communicate information may be limited by national legislation on data exchange, e g by legislation relating to the protection of computerized personal data.

232. The duty of the liquidators to exchange information is complemented by the obligation to cooperate with each other. The liquidators have a duty to act in concert with a view to the development of proceedings and their coordination, and to facilitate their respective work.

233. Article 31(3) expressly mentions a specific obligation of information and cooperation that affects the liquidator in the secondary proceedings, on the grounds of primacy of the main proceedings over the secondary proceedings. The liquidator in the secondary proceedings must give the liquidator in the main proceedings the opportunity to submit proposals on the realization or use of the assets in the secondary proceedings. The secondary liquidator must therefore inform the main liquidator of any use or realization of these assets.

This obligation may enable the main liquidator, for example, to prevent the sale of assets involved in the secondary proceedings, the preservation of which may be deemed advisable from the viewpoint of the reorganization of the business at the centre of main interests and to request a stay of the liquidation through the application of Article 33.

The obligation considered in Article 31(3) refers to important assets or decisions (such as continuation or cessation of the activities of the establishment) in the secondary proceedings. It should not be interpreted in such a broad way as in practice to paralyse the work of the liquidator in the secondary proceedings.

234. Where appropriate, the applicable national law will determine the liquidator's liability when the latter has not respected the duties arising from Article 31.

[3428]

Article 32
Exercise of creditors' rights

235. Pursuant to Article 4(2)(h), the law of the State of the opening of the proceedings determines the rules governing the lodging of claims.

However, national law concerning the creditors entitled to lodge claims is replaced by the provision in Article 32(1), which entitles any creditor to lodge his claim in the main proceedings and in any secondary proceedings.

The creditor is entitled to lodge claims in the proceedings of his choice, even in several proceedings.

The right to lodge claims of creditors with their domicile, habitual residence, or registered office in a Contracting State other than the State of the opening of the proceedings is restated in Article 39. For comments on the scope of that Article, (see points 265–270).

236. Article 32(2) establishes the liquidator's right to lodge in other proceedings claims which have already been lodged in his proceedings. The Convention modifies national legislation concerning the lodging of claims, simply by adding a right for the liquidator to lodge claims (see point 237).

Both the liquidator in the main proceedings and each liquidator in secondary proceedings may lodge claims in the other proceedings.

The aim of this provision is to facilitate the exercise of the rights of those creditors who lodge claims in certain proceedings and to facilitate that their claims are also lodged by the liquidator in other proceedings, and finally, to permit the liquidators to reinforce their influence in other proceedings.

237. The rights of the creditors are preserved insofar as they may oppose the lodging of their claims in other proceedings by the liquidator or withdraw any previous lodgement in other proceedings.

The Convention allows creditors the right to oppose a claim lodged in other proceedings by the liquidator.

On the other hand, the right to withdraw a claim lodged by the liquidator is governed by the law applicable to the proceedings in which the claim has been presented: creditors' rights are subject to the law of the State in which the proceedings are opened and it is a question of determining the rights of creditors in the proceedings in which the claim has been presented.

Insofar as the liquidator's claim is lodged on behalf of the creditor, the issue of withdrawal is not a new one, and national laws establish the creditor's right to withdraw the claim lodged.

238. The lodging of a claim by the liquidator has the same effects as the lodging of a claim by the creditor: the liquidator acts on behalf of the creditor and in his stead. The Convention mentions this right of the liquidator to lodge claims.

However, national rules concerning the period for lodging, the consequences of delayed lodging, the admissibility and well-foundedness of the lodging and the expenses linked to the verification of the claims remain unchanged (see point 267).

239. Under Article 32(2), liquidators should lodge in other proceedings claims which have already been lodged in their own proceedings. The obligation to lodge such claims exists insofar as it is in the general interests of all the creditors or of a class of creditors.

It is effective subject to the individual creditor's right to oppose the lodging of the claim.

The creditor may have various reasons for opposing the lodging of his claim in proceedings other than those he has selected. For example, as the liquidator's claim is lodged on his behalf, and as national law determines the rules for the lodging and verification of claims, including the costs, the creditor may run the risk in the other proceedings of incurring costs which he is not willing to bear.

Appraisal of the specific interest in lodging claims rests with the creditor, who must defend his interests himself. In a way, he has already made a choice when lodging his claim in a certain State.

Specific appraisal of the interest involves an examination in accordance with the law applicable to the claim and, as regards the status of the claim, in accordance with the legislation of the State in which the lodging is envisaged (Article 4(2)(h)).

This specific appraisal for each claim would involve a difficult task for the liquidator, and would be a costly and lengthy procedure.

However, the aim of the Convention is different. Under Article 32(2) the liquidator's task to lodge exists only when it is in the general interest of all creditors in his proceedings or of a class of them.

For example, if the liquidator finds that the assets to be distributed in other proceedings are so significant that even the ordinary unsecured creditors in his proceedings may receive a dividend, in competition with the ordinary unsecured creditors lodging claims in the other proceedings, the lodging of the claim may be useful and will take place.

Moreover, he will also lodge a claim where a creditor, rather than lodging a claim himself, has informed the liquidator of the interest of the lodging of his claim.

He will obviously not lodge a claim if the lodgement would be irrevocably delayed and therefore not appropriate.

The liquidator's task, thus delimited, may improve the situation of the creditors, without complicating the proceedings to the detriment of creditors.

240. Article 32(3) empowers any liquidator to participate in other proceedings. The aim of the provision is to better ensure the presence of creditors and the expression of their interests through the liquidator.

In order to resolve the frequent absence of creditors, the Convention allows the liquidator to attend creditors' meetings.

The text stipulates that the liquidator shall participate in other proceedings "on the same basis as a creditor". Obviously, the liquidator has the right to express his opinion in the course of the proceedings, and more specifically at the meeting of creditors involved in the other proceedings. However, the Convention does not establish the specific content of the liquidator's right to participate and does not determine how the liquidator shall exercise the rights of the creditors in his proceedings.

It should be noted that the provisions permitting the liquidator who lodges claims already lodged in the other proceedings to exercise the voting right deriving from a claim lodged, and the provisions concerning the simultaneous exercise by several liquidators of the voting right arising from a claim, were rejected in the course of negotiations.

Participation by the liquidator may be regulated by national law.

[3429]

Article 33
Stay of liquidation

241. At the request of the liquidator in the main proceedings, the process of liquidation in the secondary proceedings may be stayed in whole or in part.

This provision establishes the primacy of the main proceedings, but it equally takes into account the interests of the creditors in the secondary proceedings.

242. The liquidator in the main proceedings submits a request for the stay of liquidation in the secondary proceedings.

The court may not refuse the stay except if it is manifestly not in the interests of the creditors in the main proceedings.

The grounds for request of a stay may be appraised only in relation to the interests of the creditors in the main proceedings.

243. The interests of the creditors in the main proceedings in the stay of liquidation that the court takes into consideration can assume different aspects. For example, the preservation of the estate situated in the State of the secondary proceedings may be useful with a view to selling the main business or the secondary establishment to a purchaser or with a view to a composition. The safeguarding of some of the elements of the assets, useful within a reorganization, or with a view to a sale "en masse" together with some of the assets involved in the main proceedings may justify a partial stay on the liquidation.

244. The court may take into account the interests of all the creditors in the secondary proceedings, as well as those of certain groups of creditors, imposing on the liquidator in the main proceedings a guarantee which it determines as appropriate, before ordering the stay.

245. The stay is limited to a maximum of three months. Once this period is over, it may be extended for another three months maximum each time. The number of successive extensions is not limited.

The liquidation process which is restarted after a stay can be stayed again, and the stay can be renewed. The number of new stays is not limited.

246. The decision on a stay does not terminate the liquidation process. The effects brought about by the opening of proceedings pursuant to the law of the State of the opening of proceedings, e g as regards the exercise of individual actions, come into play. The liquidation process simply does not continue.

247. Where the stay no longer appears to be justified, the court terminates it.

A stay may be terminated at any moment.

The court may act:

— at the request of the liquidator in the main proceedings, or
— of its own motion, or
— at the request of the liquidator in the secondary proceedings, or
— at the request of a creditor.

If, in particular, the interests of the creditors in the main proceedings, or those of the creditors in the secondary proceedings no longer appear to justify the stay, it is to be terminated.

Consideration of the interests of the creditors in the secondary proceedings may lead by themselves to an end to the stay.

[3430]

Article 34
Measures ending secondary insolvency proceedings

248. If the law of the State in which the secondary proceedings are opened allows insolvency proceedings to be closed by means of a rescue plan, a composition, or a comparable measure, all those stipulated by that law, may propose such a measure. In addition, the Convention empowers the liquidator in the main proceedings to propose it himself.

249. Under rescue plans, compositions or comparable measures, the creditors may accept a rescheduling of debts or waive some of their rights and the debtor may undertake to meet certain conditions. All of which may affect the interests in the main proceedings. For this reason, the Convention requires that, to become final, such a measure must obtain the consent of the liquidator in the main proceedings.

In adopting his decision, the liquidator may take into consideration all the interests of the creditors in the main proceedings, including the interests in reorganizing and continuing the main business.

Should, however, the liquidator in the main proceedings oppose the rescue plan, the composition or a comparable measure in the secondary proceedings, the Convention permits his agreement to be waived, and the secondary proceedings may be closed if the financial interests of the creditors in the main proceedings are not affected by the measure proposed.

The concept of financial interests is more restrictive than that of the interest of the creditors in the main proceedings, which may, for instance, justify a stay on secondary proceedings and which is examined in point 243.

The financial interests are estimated by evaluating the effects which the rescue plan or the composition has on the dividend to be paid to the creditors in the main proceedings. If those creditors could not reasonably have expected to receive more, after the transfer of any surplus of the assets remaining in the secondary proceedings (ex Article 35), in the absence of a rescue plan or a composition, their financial interests are not thereby affected.

250. The effects of secondary proceedings are confined to assets situated within the territory of the State in which they have been opened.

Consequently, a rescue plan or a composition restricting creditors' rights may apply only to the assets covered by the secondary proceedings and not to the debtor's other assets situated outside that State.

A composition confined in its effects to the assets involved in the proceedings shall be arrived at under the conditions laid down by the applicable law and, where appropriate, by a majority decision of the creditors. The rights of all the creditors, including the minority creditors who disagree with the measure, would be affected as regards the assets relevant to those proceedings.

A composition restricting creditors' rights may be reached in the secondary proceedings with effects on assets not covered by those proceedings, provided that it is agreed to by every creditor concerned by that measure, ie having an interest affected by the measure.

251. In the event of a stay of the process of liquidation in the secondary proceedings only a measure for a composition proposed by the liquidator in the main proceedings, or by the debtor with that liquidator's agreement, may be put to the vote or approved.

The stay is ordered at the request of the liquidator in the main proceedings on account of the interests of the creditors in those proceedings. During this period, the course of the main proceedings must not be disrupted by measures not agreed to by the liquidator.

Efforts to bring about the reorganization of the main business may have led to a stay. Article 34(3), prohibiting for the duration of the stay any composition not proposed by the liquidator in the main proceedings or by the debtor with his agreement, enables the interests of the creditors who brought about the stay to be taken into consideration (see point 243).

[3431]

Article 35
Assets remaining in the secondary proceedings

252. If the assets in the secondary proceedings are sufficient to meet all claims allowed in them, any assets not distributed are to be transferred to the main proceedings.

The liquidator shall transfer the remaining assets to the liquidator in the main proceedings.

The transfer of any remaining assets to the main proceedings reflects the primary nature of those proceedings.

253. Assets will be distributed amongst all creditors whose claims are allowed in the secondary proceedings. The Convention allows creditors to lodge claims in any proceedings, so that even creditors with preferential claims in the main proceedings who might be ordinary unsecured creditors in the secondary proceedings will have an incentive to lodge claims in order, at least, to have their claims met in the same way and at the same time as other ordinary unsecured creditors.

The scale of the assets to be distributed will attract creditors. If the assets were such that any surplus remains after distribution amongst all creditors whose claims were admitted to these proceedings, only those claims not lodged or not admitted will remain unsatisfied and may be affected by the transfer of the remaining assets to the main proceedings.

[3432]

Article 36
Subsequent opening of the main proceedings

254. Should a court in the State in which the centre of the debtor's main interests is located, open insolvency proceedings in accordance with Article 3(1), after independent territorial proceedings have been opened by a court in a State in which there is an establishment, pursuant to Article 3(2), the proceedings opened at the place of the centre of main interests will be the main proceedings, while the proceedings previously opened at the place of the establishment will have to be necessarily regarded as secondary proceedings.

255. Insofar as the progress of the independent territorial proceedings, opened first, so permits, the rules for coordination between the main proceedings and the secondary proceedings as laid down in Articles 31 to 35 are to be followed.

[3433]

Article 37
Conversion of earlier proceedings

256. Pursuant to Articles 3(3) and 27, secondary proceedings opened at the place in which an establishment is situated after the main proceedings, are to be winding-up proceedings within the meaning of Article 2(c), as listed in Annex B.

Where, prior to the opening of main proceedings, independent territorial insolvency proceedings listed in Annex A but not in Annex B are opened, these latter proceedings may be converted into winding-up proceedings listed in Annex B in the event of main proceedings being opened.

257. Under the Convention, the liquidator in the main proceedings shall be entitled to request that independent territorial reorganization proceedings, as mentioned in Annex A, be converted into secondary winding-up proceedings.

The Convention does not prohibit the law of a Contracting State competent under Article 3(4) from allowing the liquidator in the main proceedings simply to request the closure of independent territorial reorganization proceedings under the conditions laid down by that law.

258. The court is not obliged to order conversion of the proceedings at the liquidator's request. It is necessary that the conversion proves to be in the interests of the creditors in the main proceedings.

This provision reflects the primary nature of the main proceedings. (See also point 210).

259. If conversion is not requested by the liquidator or ordered by the court, territorial proceedings may continue as reorganization proceedings.

260. As a result of conversion, the proceedings will be conducted as secondary winding-up insolvency proceedings in accordance with Article 36.

261. Should any territorial proceedings opened prior to main proceedings in a State where an establishment is situated not be proceedings listed in Annex A, they will not be covered by the Convention.

Main proceedings that are opened after the territorial proceedings have all the effects laid down in the Convention; the liquidator in the main proceedings is allowed to exercise his powers in other Contracting States and to request the opening of secondary proceedings. Consequently, these territorial proceedings may not continue. The national law must adopt the appropriate solution that would conform with the provisions of the Convention: that could for example be the closing of the territorial proceedings.

[3434]

Article 38
Preservation measures

262. In order to avoid any change in the debtor's estate to the detriment of creditors from the date on which the opening of insolvency proceedings is requested to the date on which the judgment opening them is handed down, certain laws provide for the appointment of a temporary administrator.

Article 29 authorizes the liquidator in the main proceedings, but not such temporary administrator, to request the opening of secondary proceedings in any other Contracting State where the debtor possesses an establishment.

However, as a pre-opening stage of secondary insolvency proceedings, Article 38 allows the temporary administrator designated by a court competent to open main proceedings to request measures to secure and preserve the debtor's assets situated in any other Contracting State, provided for under the law of this State for the period between the request for the opening of insolvency proceedings and the opening itself. As a pre-opening stage of secondary proceedings, Article 38 presupposes the existence of an establishment of the debtor in that Contracting State (see Article 3(2)). For the same reason, the preservation measures available will be those which, under the national insolvency law of that State, correspond to winding-up proceedings.

Once appointed, the liquidator in the main proceedings will decide whether or not to request the opening of secondary proceedings.

If the request is made, the national courts of the State of the opening of secondary proceedings will decide on the continuation or modification of such measures. Until that moment or, also, if the opening of secondary proceedings is not finally requested, the preservation measures taken over the assets of the debtor situated in that country will be subordinated to the decisions taken by the court competent under Article 3(1), which benefit from the system of recognition and enforcement of the Convention, in similar terms as those already explained in point 78 of this report.

263. The position of a temporary administrator appointed after the request, but before the opening, of the main insolvency proceedings has to be seen in relation to the provisional task of preserving the assets which is entrusted to him. Such temporary administrator, whose task is more limited, does not correspond exactly with the definition in Article 2(b) of a liquidator in insolvency proceedings and is not necessarily listed in Annex C.

Article 38 allows the temporary administrator to request in the country where the debtor possesses an establishment preservation measures of a more general character than those contemplated in point 78, fourth paragraph, of this report.

[3435]

E. CHAPTER IV: PROVISION OF INFORMATION FOR CREDITORS AND LODGEMENT OF THEIR CLAIMS

264. Chapter IV specifies the information which the court or the liquidator is required to provide to creditors and the rules for lodging claims.

These provisions are applicable both to main proceedings and to territorial (independent or secondary) insolvency proceedings.

[3436]

Article 39
Right to lodge claims

265. Article 39 establishes a rule of substantive law, laying down the right of foreign creditors, ie of any creditor who has his habitual residence, domicile or registered office in another Contracting State, to lodge claims in writing in insolvency proceedings. This provision derogates, in the way specified below, from the application of national law, pursuant to Article 4(2)(h).

To clear up any doubts, it is specified that the right of any foreign creditor to lodge claims includes the tax authorities and social security authorities of other Contracting States.

It should be noted that Article 32 allows all creditors to participate in the main or secondary proceedings, as they choose, and even in several proceedings (see point 235).

266. Establishing the right of foreign creditors to lodge claims means that lodgement of their claims cannot be disallowed on the grounds that the creditor is situated abroad or that the claim is governed by foreign public law.

267. However, under Article 4(2)(h), the national law of the State of the opening will govern the time limit for lodging claims, the effect of a late lodgement, and the admissibility and well-foundedness of the lodgement.

268. In addition, the national law of each proceedings determines the costs, to the charge of a creditor, attached to the claim and to the verification of the debts.

The prudent creditor will take into account the rules relevant to the costs, and will appreciate the interest that a claim presents. He will examine the ranking that the law of the proceedings accords to his claim and the importance of the assets that will be distributed.

269. The right to lodge claims for creditors situated in the State in which proceedings are opened is governed by national law.

Moreover, the Convention does not concern itself with the rights of creditors situated outside the Contracting States. The right of creditors from outside the Community to lodge claims is governed by national law.

270. The Convention gives creditors the right to lodge claims in writing, but it does not prevent national law from permitting claims to be lodged in any other more favourable form for creditors.

[3437]

Article 40
Duty to inform creditors

271. The court having jurisdiction or the liquidator must, without delay, inform known creditors who have their habitual residence, domicile or registered office in the other Contracting States of the opening of insolvency proceedings and of the need to lodge their claims.

The Convention aims to improve the situation of intra-Community creditors situated outside the State in which proceedings are opened.

The liquidator's duty to inform creditors situated in the State in which proceedings are opened is governed by national law.

The Convention does not take into consideration creditors from outside the Community to whom the national law of the State in which the proceedings are opened applies.

272. Article 40(2) lays down the form and the content to be taken by the information provided for creditors.

The liquidator is required to send a notice to each creditor. This notice has to state the time limits for lodging claims, the legal consequences laid down for failing to meet those time limits and the person or body with whom claims must be lodged. It must specify whether creditors with preferential claims or claims secured in rem are required to lodge them.

The compulsory contents of the notice as laid down in the Convention are designed to protect foreign creditors; national laws may not reduce the contents of the notice. A national law may stipulate additional information in the interests of creditors.

[3438]

Article 41
Content of the lodgement of a claim

273. Under Article 4(2)(h), the lodging of claims is subject to the law of the State of the opening of proceedings.

Article 41 constitutes, together with Articles 39 and 42(2), an exception to that rule insofar as it stipulates the content of claims lodged by creditors situated in another Contracting State.

The requirements set out in Article 41 are intended to identify the claim which is sought to be lodged. As this provision is meant to facilitate the exercise of intra-Community creditors' rights, national legislation may impose no additional conditions on the content of the lodgement of claims by foreign creditors protected by the Convention.

According to the Convention, a creditor may lodge his claim in writing (Article 39), supplying copies of supporting documents, if any, stating:

— the nature of the claim,
— the date on which it arose,
— its amount.

It must also specify any preference, security right or reservation of title alleged, as well as the assets covered by the guarantee invoked.

274. Under Article 4(2)(h), however, national law governs the verification and admission of claims and determines the procedure by which a creditor must establish his claim in order to have it admitted to the proceedings.

[3439]

Article 42
Languages

275. The information for creditors regarding the opening of proceedings for their debtor's insolvency and the lodging of claims is to be given in an official language of the State of the opening of proceedings.

In order to help those creditors who do not understand the language of the State in which proceedings are opened, the information notice has to be headed "Invitation to lodge a claim. Time limits to be observed". This heading is to be given in all the official languages of the Community.

The heading, drawn up by the Secretariat of the Council of the European Union, will be published together with the Convention and the report.

276. Creditors from other Contracting States are allowed to lodge claims in an official language of the State in which they have their habitual residence, domicile or registered office.

However, their written statement must be headed "Lodgement of claim" in a language of the State in which proceedings are opened.

In order to avoid delay in lodging claims and unnecessary lodgement costs, claims may be lodged in the creditor's language or, to be more exact, in the language of the State in which he lives or carries on his business.

277. Bearing in mind the scale of intra-Community trade and interpenetration of economies, especially in border regions, as well as the understanding of one another's languages, a systematic requirement that claims be lodged in an official language of the State of the proceedings may run counter to the interests of creditors without being really necessary.

Use of the creditor's language is therefore the rule; a translation into the official language may be required in the course of the proceedings if this proves necessary.

[3440]

F. CHAPTER V: INTERPRETATION BY THE COURT OF JUSTICE OF THE EUROPEAN COMMUNITIES

278. The conferral of jurisdiction on the Court of Justice to give rulings on interpretation is not an innovation of the Convention on insolvency proceedings. The system of conferral follows the system established by Article 177 of the EC Treaty and adopted by the Protocols of 3 June 1971 concerning the interpretation by the Court of Justice of the 1968 Brussels Convention, and the Protocols of 19 December 1988 concerning the interpretation of the 1980 Rome Convention. Both Protocols were examined in the reports by Mr P Jenard and Mr A Tizziano (see OJ No C189 of 28 July 1990 and No C219 of 3 September 1990). We refer to those reports for further details.

[3441]

Article 43
Jurisdiction of the Court of Justice

279. By virtue of this rule new powers of interpretation are conferred on the Court of Justice of the European Communities, supplementing its existing powers. In addition to this

Convention and its Annexes, this jurisdiction also applies to future Conventions on accession by States which become Members of the European Union. Article 50 requires the new Members to follow the system of the Convention on insolvency proceedings and to make such adjustments and amendments as may be necessary. This explains the reference to future Conventions.

This jurisdiction covers the actual rules for the conferral of powers, so that it is for the Court of Justice to interpret the rules determining the scope of its jurisdiction or the procedures by which it may be exercised.

280. Jurisdiction in matters of interpretation means that the Court of Justice rules only on the interpretation of the text of the Convention and it is for the national court to apply the rules according to this interpretation and to give a judgment on the substance of the matter.

281. In contrast to the 1968 Brussels Convention and the 1980 Rome Convention, the conferral of jurisdiction to interpret is to be found in the text of the Convention and not in a separate Protocol. This emphasizes the close relationship between this Convention and the Community legal system and the significance of the uniform interpretation of those rules.

282. Both the Protocol on the Statute of the Court of Justice and the Rules of Procedure of the Court of Justice shall apply.

283. The Convention provides for two procedural channels through which the Court of Justice can resolve any problem of interpretation. The first involves preliminary ruling proceedings, as laid down by Article 44 of the Convention following the model of Article 177 of the EC Treaty. The second, included in Article 45 of the Convention, could be termed "proceedings in the interests of the law".

[3442]

Article 44
Preliminary ruling proceedings

284. These are proceedings whereby a national court before which a case is brought requests the Court of Justice of the European Communities to give a preliminary ruling on the interpretation of a provision of the Convention or its Annexes, the application of which in the case in point has raised questions which must be resolved in order for a decision to be given on the substance of the matter.

285. The Convention determines the national courts which make such a request to the Court of Justice. Only the expressly designated courts are duly empowered, i e the higher law courts (such as the Tribunal Supremo in Spain, the Cour de Cassation in France, etc) which are listed in Article 44(a), and other courts when acting as courts of appeal. In the second case it is not necessary for the court to be officially entitled a "Court of Appeal". However, it must be involved in hearing appeals against judgments of a lower court. The power to request a preliminary ruling on interpretation is not granted to the courts of first instance.

286. The question must be one raised in a case pending before the court which submits the request for interpretation. The Court of Justice therefore resolves the questions of interpretation concerning cases pending before a national court.

287. It must be a question on which the national court considers a decision on interpretation to be "necessary" for the judgment, i e it must be a problem of interpretation on which the solution to the case depends. If the different possibilities of interpretation lead to the same result, this requirement would not be fulfilled. The national court must assess in each individual case whether or not this need exists.

288. National courts have the power to submit questions of interpretation of their own motion to the Court of Justice. A request by a party is not necessary. If such a request is made the national court is not obliged to refer to the Court of Justice.

289. This Convention does not oblige national courts to submit questions of interpretation to the Court of Justice but it simply allows them to make such requests if all the abovementioned requirements are fulfilled.

The need for speed in the conduct of insolvency proceedings explains the choice of a flexible formula which allows the national courts to decide on whether a preliminary ruling is appropriate. The Convention does not impose any criteria.

The national court may take into account the estimated time needed for a ruling by the Court of Justice, the general significance of the question for the proceedings, the formal request of the parties directly affected (as we know, this does not bind the national court), etc.

290. The Convention does not mention a possible suspensive effect of the preliminary ruling on the insolvency proceedings until such time as the Court of Justice settles the problem of interpretation.

The question of the average time for obtaining preliminary rulings is a serious problem in the area of insolvency proceedings.

291. In order to solve the question of suspensive effect, several facts should be taken into account:

1. The jurisdiction of the Court of Justice derives directly from the powers conferred on it by the Convention on insolvency proceedings and its scope is defined by the latter.
2. This conferral of jurisdiction is aimed at better fulfilling the specific objectives of the Convention on insolvency proceedings. The advantages of uniformity of interpretation must be counterbalanced by the need for efficiency in insolvency proceedings.
3. Time is a crucial factor in insolvency proceedings. They are opened as a consequence of a financial crisis. Promptness of action is imperative in order to avoid a depreciation of existing assets. The suspension of the insolvency proceedings may even preclude the possibility of reorganization. For this reason, many national legislations exclude the suspensive effect of appeals to higher courts in the case of insolvency proceedings. In addition, the collective nature of insolvency proceedings implies that a partial problem should not necessarily alter the main course of the proceedings.

292. In this context, the Convention leaves it to the national law of the State of the opening of proceedings to determine whether preliminary ruling proceedings before the Court of Justice should have suspensive effect. As there is no formal obligation to submit the question of interpretation to the Court of Justice, the most appropriate solution seems to be to confer on the national court the power to decide on whether or not it is necessary to interrupt the insolvency proceedings.

[3443]

Article 45
Proceedings brought by a competent authority

293. These proceedings can be described as proceedings brought "in the interests of the law", since the solution to proceedings under way does not depend on the ruling; it is designed to guarantee uniformity of interpretation in the future, when the national courts of different Contracting States have handed down contradictory interpretations of the rules of the Convention.

294. The request to the Court of Justice shall be brought by the Procurators-General of the Supreme Courts of Appeal of the Contracting States or any other authority designated by a Contracting State.

295. In order that this national authority may make a request to the Court of Justice of the European Communities, it is necessary for a national court of the same State to have given a final judgment (res judicata) which contradicts the interpretation given by the Court of Justice or by the courts of other Contracting States mentioned in Article 44 (the higher courts or those acting as appeal courts).

296. The ruling on the interpretation given by the Court of Justice of the European Communities does not affect the judgments which gave rise to it. Its aim is merely to clarify the interpretation for the future, without creating definitive binding precedent.

297. Article 45 incorporates proceedings established by the 1971 Protocols on the 1968 Brussels Convention and by the 1988 Protocols on the 1980 Rome Convention. Further comments may be found in the respective reports (see point 278).

[3444]

Article 46
Reservations

298. The possibility of entering a reservation is not at the discretion of the State, but depends on the existence of an impediment for constitutional reasons relating to the conferral of jurisdiction.

299. The rationale of this reservation is to allow one Member State to minimize the risk of constitutional difficulties at the ratification stage of the Convention, which it felt might arise through the conferral of jurisdiction on the Court of Justice of the European Communities. The difficulties would arise in the event of the Convention being deemed to go beyond the limits of the objectives defined by Article 220 of the EC Treaty.

On the other hand, it was felt by other Contracting States that conferral of jurisdiction for interpretation on the Court of Justice is fundamental to the proper functioning of the system set up by the Convention on insolvency proceedings. A uniform interpretation by this Court is necessary to ensure that the rights and obligations deriving from the Convention are the same for all persons, irrespective of the Contracting State in which the party or person concerned is located. Hence, to mitigate as far as possible such risk, it was agreed that the scope of the Convention should be strictly limited to the intra-Community effects of the insolvency proceedings covered by the Convention. Thus, the perfect adaptation of the Convention to the scope of Article 220 of the Treaty of Rome would counterbalance the extension of its content to the rules on conflict of laws, without which the system of recognition of insolvency proceedings would distort legal certainty within the Community (see point 42).

[3445]

G. CHAPTER VI: TRANSITIONAL AND FINAL PROVISIONS TERRITORIAL APPLICATION

300. The Convention has no provisions governing territorial application. Consequently, the general rules of public international law, i e Article 29 of the 1969 Vienna Convention on the Law of Treaties are applicable.

301. This means that, in principle, the Convention on insolvency proceedings applies to the whole territory of the Contracting States. This includes non-European territories which are an integral part of the territory of these States. However, the autonomy of these territories can vary widely. Consequently, the Contracting States may exclude or reserve the application of the Convention to these territories by means of a declaration to that effect. This is the case, for example, with the Netherlands in relation to the Netherlands Antilles and Aruba.

302. For the same reason, the Convention does not apply to those territories whose international relations are assumed by any of the Contracting States, but which are not an integral part of their territory, being a separate entity. In principle, the Convention does not apply to them, no matter whether they are European or non-European territories. Should a Contracting State with such responsibility wish to extend the scope of the Convention to those territories, extension would only take effect if no other Contracting State opposed it.

[3446]

Article 47
Applicability in time

303. Article 47 establishes two rules concerning the time of the application of the Convention.

The Convention is applicable only to insolvency proceedings opened after the entry into force of the Convention. Acts done by the debtor before the entry into force of the Convention shall continue to be governed by the law which was applicable to them at the time they were done.

These two rules were prompted by the concern not to alter existing situations and relations which were governed by specific legal rules at the time of the introduction of the new rules of the Convention into the legal systems of the Contracting States.

304. The Convention applies to insolvency proceedings opened after the entry into force of the Convention; it does not apply to proceedings opened beforehand.

The Convention allows the opening of several sets of proceedings some of which may be opened before and some after entry into force.

If proceedings are opened on the basis of the debtor's centre of main interests after the entry into force of the Convention, it could have been thought that, in view of the primacy of the main proceedings in the operation of the Convention, the latter would apply even if proceedings had previously been opened away from the centre of main interests. This solution was not adopted, because it might disturb the course of proceedings opened in accordance with the law applicable at the time of opening. Reorganization proceedings opened in a State where the debtor's centre of main interests is not situated would have to be converted. Rules on conflict of laws would where appropriate have to be modified in the course of proceedings by the application of those in the Convention. Proceedings of a universal nature opened in accordance with the criteria of international jurisdiction laid down in the national law applicable would, where appropriate, be classified as territorial proceedings if, within the meaning of the Convention, the centre of main interests was not situated in the State of the opening of the earlier proceedings.

If earlier proceedings were opened in the State considered by the Convention as being the State where the debtor's centre of main interests is located, those proceedings will not be covered by the Convention. Before the entry into force of the Convention these proceedings may produce effects outside the State of the opening pursuant to the rules applicable under the different national laws. In the case of the earlier opening of proceedings in the State of the centre of main interests, proceedings opened after entry into force in the State where the debtor has an establishment are not subject to the Convention.

The rule in Article 47 has an absolute character: if insolvency proceedings are opened against a given debtor prior to the entry into force of the Convention in a Contracting State, any proceedings opened after the entry into force are not subject to the Convention, irrespective of whether such later proceedings are main or secondary proceedings within the meaning of the Convention.

305. In order to determine whether proceedings are opened before or after the entry into force of the Convention, the concept of the time of opening of proceedings, as established by the Convention, applies (see also point 68). Insolvency proceedings opened in advance do not come within the scope of the Convention if the judgment opening proceedings produced effects before the entry into force of the Convention.

306. The law applicable to the acts done by the debtor before the entry into force of the Convention continues to govern these acts.

This rule is prompted by the concern to avoid making the acts of the debtor subject to new rules and is aimed at keeping the relations to which the debtor is party subject to the law which governed his acts.

As regards the purpose of the rule, the determination of the acts done by the debtor and the time at which they are done are governed by the applicable law.

[3447]

Article 48
Relationship to other Conventions

307. Article 48 establishes the relationship between the new Convention on insolvency proceedings and other international instruments which govern the Private International Law questions of international insolvencies, i e jurisdiction to open insolvency proceedings, law applicable to the proceedings and their effects, and the recognition and enforcement in other States of such proceedings. Article 48 deals with:

1. the relationship between the Convention and Treaties already concluded between certain Contracting States, in Article 48(1);
2. the relationship between the Convention and Treaties already concluded with third States, in Article 48(3).

308. Article 48(1) contains a list of the Conventions which will be superseded after the entry into force of the Convention on Insolvency Proceedings as between the States which are party to it. Such replacement will be subject to:

1. the provisions of Article 48(1) itself, pursuant to which these Conventions will continue to take effect in matters to which this Convention does not apply;
2. the provisions of Article 48(2) relating to insolvency proceedings opened before the entry into force of this Convention, which shall continue to be governed by the Conventions referred to in the list of Article 48(1), where applicable (see also Article 47).

309. The list of previous Conventions superseded, as between the Contracting States, by this Convention includes the 1990 Istanbul Convention, and the Convention between Denmark, Finland, Norway, Sweden and Iceland on Bankruptcy, signed at Copenhagen on 11 November 1933.

310. Article 48(3) concerns the problem of the compatibility of the Convention on Insolvency Proceedings with Treaties already concluded between a Contracting State and a third State.

To the extent that the application of this Convention would be irreconcilable with obligations arising out of Conventions or other international Agreements already concluded with a third State, the Convention on Insolvency Proceedings will not apply. To determine if the application of this Convention is or not irreconcilable with the obligations arising out of another existing Convention, it should be examined whether they entail legal consequences which are mutually exclusive.

The Convention on Insolvency Proceedings is only applicable when the debtor's centre of main interests is in the territory of a Contracting State. Furthermore, its provisions are restricted to relations with other Contracting States (see point 44). Hence, conflicts with other Conventions will seldom arise.

[3448]

Article 49
Ratification and entry into force

311. The Convention shall be deposited with the Secretary-General of the Council of the European Union.

312. The decision-making process allowing a State to bind itself by the Convention shall be governed by the national law of each State. The Convention shall be subject to ratification, acceptance or approval by the signatory States.

313. The Convention shall enter into force on the first day of the sixth month following that of the last deposit of the instrument of ratification, acceptance or approval.

[3449]

Article 50
Accession to the Convention

314. The future Member States of the European Union shall be required to accept this Convention as a basis for the negotiations necessary to ensure the implementation of Article 220 of the EC Treaty.

A special Convention may be concluded between the Contracting States and the future Member State for the purpose of introducing the necessary adjustments.

[3450]

Article 51
Notification by the depositary

315. The Secretary-General of the Council of the European Union shall notify the signatory States of the deposit of each instrument of ratification, acceptance or approval of the Convention, the date of entry into force, and any other act, notification or communication relating to this Convention.

[3451]

Article 52
Duration of the Convention

316. The Convention shall remain in force for an unlimited duration.

It does not contain any particular provision governing withdrawal of a State from the Convention. Any withdrawal is subject to the general law of international treaties.

[3452]

Article 53
Revision or evaluation of the Convention

317. The Convention shall be the subject of a conference for the revision or evaluation of this Convention if any Contracting State so requests.

In the case of such request from a State the President of the Council of the European Union must convene the conference.

318. If no evaluation conference is held at the request of a Contracting State in the ten years that follow entry into force, the President of the Council of the European Union shall convene such a conference.

[3453]

Article 54
Amendment of the Annexes

319. Each Contracting State may amend Annexes A, B and C which list the insolvency proceedings that may be the subject of main proceedings (list A: reorganization proceedings and winding-up proceedings) or of secondary proceedings (list B: winding-up proceedings), as well as the persons or organs which can assume the functions of a liquidator (list C).

The right of the States to amend the lists is subject to two restrictions.

The new proceedings included in lists A or B must correspond to the definitions of the proceedings given in Article 1(1) and Article 2(a) (list A, see points 48 and 62) and Article 2(c) (list B, see point 64).

320. Each Contracting State may amend the Annexes at any time.

The State shall address to the Secretary-General of the Council of the European Union, the depositary of the Convention under Article 49(1), a declaration containing the amendment which it wishes to make to an Annex.

321. The depositary of the Convention will notify the signatory States and the Contracting States of the content of any such declaration.

322. The amendment that a State wishes to make to an Annex must be subject to the acceptance by the Contracting or signatory States. It is not necessary for the States to communicate their acceptance expressly: if any State has not objected to the amendment within three months from the date of notification of the amending declaration, the amendment of the Annex shall be deemed to be accepted.

Even if the Convention does not expressly stipulate this, the objection of a State should be notified to the depositary of the Convention who received the amending declaration. The depositary shall notify the communicated objection to the Contracting States (see Article 51(c)). Where an objection is communicated by a State, the amendment will not come into force. A solution to a divergence between two States could be sought by convening of a conference for revision.

323. The declaration for the amendment of an Annex which was not objected to shall come into force on the first day of the month after the three-month period following the notification of the amending declaration to the Contracting and signatory States by the depositary.

[3454]

Article 55
Deposit of the Convention

324. The Convention shall be drawn up in twelve languages; all texts shall be equally authentic.

The Convention shall be deposited with the Secretary-General of the Council of the European Union.

[3455]

COUNCIL DIRECTIVE

of 19 March 2001

on the reorganisation and winding-up of insurance undertakings

(2001/17/EC)

NOTES

Date of publication in OJ: OJ L110, 20.4.2001, p 28.

This Directive was implemented in the UK with effect from 20 April 2003 by the Insurers (Reorganisation and Winding Up) Regulations 2003, SI 2003/1102. Those Regulations were revoked and replaced as from 18 February 2004 by the Insurers (Reorganisation and Winding Up) Regulations 2004, SI 2004/353, reg 53(1) at **[2646]**, subject to transitional provisions in reg 53(2), (3) thereof. See also the Insurers (Reorganisation and Winding Up) (Lloyd's) Regulations 2005, SI 2005/1998 at **[2685]**.

THE EUROPEAN PARLIAMENT AND THE COUNCIL OF THE EUROPEAN UNION,

Having regard to the Treaty establishing the European Community, and in particular Articles 47(2) and 55 thereof,

Having regard to the proposal from the Commission,[1]

Having regard to the opinion of the Economic and Social Committee,[2]

Acting in accordance with the procedure laid down in Article 251 of the Treaty,[3]

Whereas:

(1) First Council Directive 73/239/EEC of 24 July 1973 on the coordination of laws, regulations and administrative provisions relating to the taking up and pursuit of the business of direct insurance other than life assurance,[4] as supplemented by Directive 92/49/EEC,[5] and the First Council Directive 79/267/EEC of 5 March 1979 on the coordination of laws, regulations and administrative provisions relating to the taking up and pursuit of the business of direct life assurance,[6] as supplemented by Directive 92/96/EEC,[7] provide for a single authorisation of the insurance undertakings granted by the home Member State supervisory authority. This single authorisation allows the insurance undertaking to carry out its activities in the Community by means of establishment or free provision of services without any further authorisation by the host Member State and under the sole prudential supervision of the home Member State supervisory authorities.

(2) The insurance directives providing a single authorisation with a Community scope for the insurance undertakings do not contain coordination rules in the event of winding-up proceedings. Insurance undertakings as well as other financial institutions are expressly excluded from the scope of Council Regulation (EC) No 1346/2000 of 29 May 2000 on insolvency proceedings.[8] It is in the interest of the proper functioning of the internal market and of the protection of creditors that coordinated rules are established at Community level for winding-up proceedings in respect of insurance undertakings.

(3) Coordination rules should also be established to ensure that the reorganisation measures, adopted by the competent authority of a Member State in order to preserve or restore the financial soundness of an insurance undertaking and to prevent as much as possible a winding-up situation, produce full effects throughout the Community. The reorganisation measures covered by this Directive are those affecting pre-existing rights of parties other than the insurance undertaking itself. The measures provided for in Article 20 of Directive 73/239/EEC and Article 24 of Directive 79/267/EEC should be included within the scope of this Directive provided that they comply with the conditions contained in the definition of reorganisation measures.

(4) This Directive has a Community scope which affects insurance undertakings as defined in Directives 73/239/EEC and 79/267/EEC which have their head office in the Community, Community branches of insurance undertakings which have their head office in third countries and creditors resident in the Community. This Directive should not regulate the effects of the reorganisation measures and winding-up proceedings vis-à-vis third countries.

(5) This Directive should concern winding-up proceedings whether or not they are founded on insolvency and whether they are voluntary or compulsory. It should apply to collective proceedings as defined by the home Member State's legislation in accordance with Article 9 involving the realisation of the assets of an insurance undertaking and the distribution of their proceeds. Winding-up proceedings which, without being founded on insolvency, involve for the payment of insurance claims a priority order in accordance with Article 10 should also be included in the scope of this Directive. Claims by the employees of an insurance undertaking arising from employment contracts and employment relationships should be capable of being subrogated to a national wage guarantee scheme; such subrogated claims should benefit from the treatment determined by the home Member State's law (lex concursus) according to the principles of this Directive. The provisions of this Directive should apply to the different cases of winding-up proceedings as appropriate.

(6) The adoption of reorganisation measures does not preclude the opening of winding-up proceedings. Winding-up proceedings may be opened in the absence of, or following, the adoption of reorganisation measures and they may terminate with composition or other analogous measures, including reorganisation measures.

(7) The definition of branch, in accordance with existing insolvency principles, should take account of the single legal personality of the insurance undertaking. The home Member State's legislation should determine the way in which the assets and liabilities held by independent persons who have a permanent authority to act as agent for an insurance undertaking should be treated in the winding-up of an insurance undertaking.

(8) A distinction should be made between the competent authorities for the purposes of reorganisation measures and winding-up proceedings and the supervisory authorities of the insurance undertakings. The competent authorities may be administrative or judicial authorities depending on the Member State's legislation. This Directive does not purport to harmonise national legislation concerning the allocation of competences between such authorities.

(9) This Directive does not seek to harmonise national legislation concerning reorganisation measures and winding-up proceedings but aims at ensuring mutual recognition of Member States' reorganisation measures and winding-up legislation concerning insurance undertakings as well as the necessary cooperation. Such mutual recognition is implemented in this Directive through the principles of unity, universality, coordination, publicity, equivalent treatment and protection of insurance creditors.

(10) Only the competent authorities of the home Member State should be empowered to take decisions on winding-up proceedings concerning insurance undertakings (principle of unity). These proceedings should produce their effects throughout the Community and should be recognised by all Member States. All the assets and liabilities of the insurance undertaking should, as a general rule, be taken into consideration in the winding-up proceedings (principle of universality).

(11) The home Member State's law should govern the winding-up decision concerning an insurance undertaking, the winding-up proceedings themselves and their effects, both substantive and procedural, on the persons and legal relations concerned, except where this Directive provides otherwise. Therefore all the conditions for the opening, conduct and closure of winding-up proceedings should in general be governed by the home Member State's law. In order to facilitate its application this Directive should include a non-exhaustive list of aspects which, in particular, are subject to the general rule of the home Member State's legislation.

(12) The supervisory authorities of the home Member State and those of all the other Member States should be informed as a matter of urgency of the opening of winding-up proceedings (principle of coordination).

(13) It is of utmost importance that insured persons, policy-holders, beneficiaries and any injured party having a direct right of action against the insurance undertaking on a claim arising from insurance operations be protected in winding-up proceedings. Such protection should not include claims which arise not from obligations under insurance contracts or insurance operations but from civil liability caused by an agent in negotiations for which, according to the law applicable to the insurance contract or operation, the agent himself is not responsible under such insurance contract or operation. In order to achieve this objective Member States should ensure special treatment for insurance creditors according to one of two optional methods provided for in this Directive. Member States may choose between granting insurance claims absolute precedence over any other claim with respect to assets representing the technical provisions or granting insurance claims a special rank which may only be preceded by claims on salaries, social security, taxes and rights in rem over the whole assets of the insurance undertaking. Neither of the two methods provided for in this Directive impedes a Member State from establishing a ranking between different categories of insurance claims.

(14) This Directive should ensure an appropriate balance between the protection of insurance creditors and other privileged creditors protected by the Member State's legislation and not harmonise the different systems of privileged creditors existing in the Member States.

(15) The two optional methods for treatment of insurance claims are considered substantially equivalent. The first method ensures the affectation of assets representing the technical provisions to insurance claims, the second method ensures insurance claims a position in the ranking of creditors which not only affects the assets representing the technical provisions but all the assets of the insurance undertaking.

(16) Member States which, in order to protect insurance creditors, opt for the method of granting insurance claims absolute precedence with respect to the assets representing the technical provisions should require their insurance undertakings to establish and keep up to date a special register of such assets. Such a register is a useful instrument for identifying the assets affected to such claims.

(17) In order to strengthen equivalence between both methods of treatment of insurance claims, this Directive should oblige the Member States which apply the method set out in Article 10(1)(b) to require every insurance undertaking to represent, at any moment and independently of a possible winding-up, claims, which according to that method may have precedence over insurance claims and which are registered in the insurance undertaking's accounts, by assets allowed by the insurance directives in force to represent the technical provisions.

(18) The home Member State should be able to provide that, where the rights of insurance creditors have been subrogated to a guarantee scheme established in such home Member State, claims by that scheme should not benefit from the treatment of insurance claims under this Directive.

(19) The opening of winding-up proceedings should involve the withdrawal of the authorisation to conduct business granted to the insurance undertaking unless such authorisation has previously been withdrawn.

(20) The decision to open winding-up proceedings, which may produce effects throughout the Community according to the principle of universality, should have appropriate publicity within the Community. In order to protect interested parties, the decision should be published in accordance with the home Member State's procedures and in the *Official Journal of the European Communities* and, further, by any other means decided by the other Member States' supervisory authorities within their respective territories. In addition to publication of the decision, known creditors who are resident in the Community should be individually informed of the decision and this information should contain at least the elements specified in this Directive. Liquidators should also keep creditors regularly informed of the progress of the winding-up proceedings.

(21) Creditors should have the right to lodge claims or to submit written observations in winding-up proceedings. Claims by creditors resident in a Member State other than the home Member State should be treated in the same way as equivalent claims in the home Member State without any discrimination on the grounds of nationality or residence (principle of equivalent treatment).

(22) This Directive should apply to reorganisation measures adopted by a competent authority of a Member State principles which are similar mutatis mutandis to those provided for in winding-up proceedings. The publication of such reorganisation measures should be limited to the case in which an appeal in the home Member State is possible by parties other than the insurance undertaking itself. When reorganisation measures affect exclusively the rights of shareholders, members or employees of the insurance undertaking considered in those capacities, the competent authorities should determine the manner in which the parties affected should be informed in accordance with relevant legislation.

(23) This Directive provides for coordinated rules to determine the law applicable to reorganisation measures and winding-up proceedings of insurance undertakings. This Directive does not seek to establish rules of private international law determining the law applicable to contracts and other legal relations. In particular, this Directive does not seek to govern the applicable rules on the existence of a contract, the rights and obligations of parties and the evaluation of debts.

(24) The general rule of this Directive, according to which reorganisation measures and the winding-up proceedings are governed by the law of the home Member State, should have a series of exceptions in order to protect legitimate expectations and the certainty of certain transactions in Member States other than the home Member State. Such exceptions should concern the effects of such reorganisation measures or winding-up proceedings on certain contracts and rights, third parties' rights in rem, reservations of title, set-off, regulated markets, detrimental acts, third party purchasers and lawsuits pending.

(25) The exception concerning the effects of reorganisation measures and winding-up proceedings on certain contracts and rights provided for in Article 19 should be limited to the effects specified therein and should not include any other issues related to reorganisation measures and winding-up proceedings such as the lodging, verification, admission and ranking of claims regarding such contracts and rights, which should be governed by the home Member State's legislation.

(26) The effects of reorganisation measures or winding-up proceedings on a lawsuit pending should be governed by the law of the Member States in which the lawsuit is pending concerning an asset or a right of which the insurance undertaking has been divested as an exception to the application of the law of the home Member State. The effects of such measures and proceedings on individual enforcement actions arising from these lawsuits should be governed by the home Member State's legislation, according to the general rule of this Directive.

(27) All persons required to receive or divulge information connected with the procedures of communication provided for in this Directive should be bound by professional secrecy in the same manner as that established in Article 16 of Directive 92/49/EEC and Article 15 of Directive 92/96/EEC, with the exception of any judicial authority to which specific national legislation applies.

(28) For the sole purpose of applying the provisions of this Directive to reorganisation measures and winding-up proceedings concerning branches situated in the Community of an insurance undertaking whose head office is located in a third country the home Member State should be defined as the Member State in which the branch is located and the supervisory authorities and competent authorities as the authorities of that Member State.

(29) Where there are branches in more than one Member State of an insurance undertaking whose head office is located outside the Community, each branch should be treated independently with regard to the application of this Directive. In that case the competent authorities, supervisory authorities, administrators and liquidators should endeavour to coordinate their actions,

[3456]

NOTES

1 OJ C71, 19.3.1987, p 5, and OJ C253, 6.10.1989, p 3.
2 OJ C319, 30.11.1987, p 10.
3 Opinion of the European Parliament of 15 March 1989 (OJ C96, 17.4.1989, p 99), confirmed on 27 October 1999, Council Common Position of 9 October 2000 (OJ C344, 1.12.2000, p 23) and Decision of the European Parliament of 15 February 2001.
4 OJ L228, 16.8.1973, p 3. Directive as last amended by European Parliament and Council Directive 95/26/EC (OJ L168, 18.7.1995, p 7).
5 Council Directive 92/49/EEC of 18 June 1992 on the coordination of laws, regulations and administrative provisions relating to direct insurance other than life assurance and amending Directives 73/239/EEC and 88/357/EEC (third non-life insurance directive) (OJ L228, 11.8.1992, p 1).
6 OJ L63, 13.3.1979, p 1. Directive as last amended by Directive 95/26/EC.
7 Council Directive 92/96/EEC of 10 November 1992 on the coordination of laws, regulations and administrative provisions relating to direct life assurance and amending Directives 79/267/EEC and 90/619/EEC (third life assurance directive) (OJ L360, 9.12.1992, p 1).
8 OJ L160, 30.6.2000, p 1.

HAVE ADOPTED THIS DIRECTIVE—

TITLE I
SCOPE AND DEFINITIONS

Article 1

Scope

1. This Directive applies to reorganisation measures and winding-up proceedings concerning insurance undertakings.

2. This Directive also applies, to the extent provided for in Article 30, to reorganisation measures and winding-up proceedings concerning branches in the territory of the Community of insurance undertakings having their head office outside the Community.

[3457]

Article 2

Definitions

For the purpose of this Directive—

(a) "insurance undertaking" means an undertaking which has received official authorisation in accordance with Article 6 of Directive 73/239/EEC or Article 6 of Directive 79/267/EEC;

(b) "branch" means any permanent presence of an insurance undertaking in the territory of a Member State other than the home Member State which carries out insurance business;

(c) "reorganisation measures" means measures involving any intervention by administrative bodies or judicial authorities which are intended to preserve or restore the financial situation of an insurance undertaking and which affect pre-existing rights of parties other than the insurance undertaking itself, including but not limited to measures involving the possibility of a suspension of payments, suspension of enforcement measures or reduction of claims;

(d) "winding-up proceedings" means collective proceedings involving realising the assets of an insurance undertaking and distributing the proceeds among the creditors, shareholders or members as appropriate, which necessarily involve any intervention by the administrative or the judicial authorities of a Member State, including where the collective proceedings are terminated by a composition or other analogous measure, whether or not they are founded on insolvency or are voluntary or compulsory;

(e) "home Member State" means the Member State in which an insurance undertaking has been authorised in accordance with Article 6 of Directive 73/239/EEC or Article 6 of Directive 79/267/EEC;

(f) "host Member State" means the Member State other than the home Member State in which an insurance undertaking has a branch;

(g) "competent authorities" means the administrative or judicial authorities of the

Member States which are competent for the purposes of the reorganisation measures or the winding-up proceedings;

(h) "supervisory authorities" means the competent authorities within the meaning of Article 1(k) of Directive 92/49/EEC and of Article 1(l) of Directive 92/96/EEC;

(i) "administrator" means any person or body appointed by the competent authorities for the purpose of administering reorganisation measures;

(j) "liquidator" means any person or body appointed by the competent authorities or by the governing bodies of an insurance undertaking, as appropriate, for the purpose of administering winding-up proceedings;

(k) "insurance claims" means any amount which is owed by an insurance undertaking to insured persons, policy holders, beneficiaries or to any injured party having direct right of action against the insurance undertaking and which arises from an insurance contract or from any operation provided for in Article 1(2) and (3), of Directive 79/267/EEC in direct insurance business, including amounts set aside for the aforementioned persons, when some elements of the debt are not yet known. The premiums owed by an insurance undertaking as a result of the non-conclusion or cancellation of these insurance contracts and operations in accordance with the law applicable to such contracts or operations before the opening of the winding-up proceedings shall also be considered insurance claims.

[3458]

TITLE II
REORGANISATION MEASURES

Article 3

Scope

This Title applies to the reorganisation measures defined in Article 2(c).

[3459]

Article 4

Adoption of reorganisation measures—applicable law

1. Only the competent authorities of the home Member State shall be entitled to decide on the reorganisation measures with respect to an insurance undertaking, including its branches in other Member States. The reorganisation measures shall not preclude the opening of winding-up proceedings by the home Member State.

2. The reorganisation measures shall be governed by the laws, regulations and procedures applicable in the home Member State, unless otherwise provided in Articles 19 to 26.

3. The reorganisation measures shall be fully effective throughout the Community in accordance with the legislation of the home Member State without any further formalities, including against third parties in other Member States, even if the legislation of those other Member States does not provide for such reorganisation measures or alternatively makes their implementation subject to conditions which are not fulfilled.

4. The reorganisation measures shall be effective throughout the Community once they become effective in the Member State where they have been taken.

[3460]

Article 5

Information to the supervisory authorities

The competent authorities of the home Member State shall inform as a matter of urgency the home Member State's supervisory authorities of their decision on any reorganisation measure, where possible before the adoption of such a measure and failing that immediately thereafter. The supervisory authorities of the home Member State shall inform as a matter of urgency the supervisory authorities of all other Member States of the decision to adopt reorganisation measures including the possible practical effects of such measures.

[3461]

Article 6

Publication

1. Where an appeal is possible in the home Member State against a reorganisation measure, the competent authorities of the home Member State, the administrator or any

person entitled to do so in the home Member State shall make public its decision on a reorganisation measure in accordance with the publication procedures provided for in the home Member State and, furthermore, publish in the *Official Journal of the European Communities* at the earliest opportunity an extract from the document establishing the reorganisation measure. The supervisory authorities of all the other Member States which have been informed of the decision on a reorganisation measure pursuant to Article 5 may ensure the publication of such decision within their territory in the manner they consider appropriate.

2. The publications provided for in paragraph 1 shall also specify the competent authority of the home Member State, the applicable law as provided in Article 4(2) and the administrator appointed, if any. They shall be carried out in the official language or in one of the official languages of the Member State in which the information is published.

3. The reorganisation measures shall apply regardless of the provisions concerning publication set out in paragraphs 1 and 2 and shall be fully effective as against creditors, unless the competent authorities of the home Member State or the law of that State provide otherwise.

4. When reorganisation measures affect exclusively the rights of shareholders, members or employees of an insurance undertaking, considered in those capacities, this Article shall not apply unless the law applicable to these reorganisation measures provides otherwise. The competent authorities shall determine the manner in which the interested parties affected by such reorganisation measures shall be informed in accordance with the relevant legislation.

[3462]

Article 7

Information to known creditors—right to lodge claims

1. Where the legislation of the home Member State requires lodgement of a claim with a view to its recognition or provides for compulsory notification of a reorganisation measure to creditors who have their normal place of residence, domicile or head office in that State, the competent authorities of the home Member State or the administrator shall also inform known creditors who have their normal place of residence, domicile or head office in another Member State, in accordance with the procedures laid down in Articles 15 and 17(1).

2. Where the legislation of the home Member State provides for the right of creditors who have their normal place of residence, domicile or head office in that State to lodge claims or to submit observations concerning their claims, creditors who have their normal place of residence, domicile or head office in another Member State shall have the same right to lodge claims or submit observations in accordance with the procedures laid down in Articles 16 and 17(2).

[3463]

TITLE III
WINDING-UP PROCEEDINGS

Article 8

Opening of winding-up proceedings—information to the supervisory authorities

1. Only the competent authorities of the home Member State shall be entitled to take a decision concerning the opening of winding-up proceedings with regard to an insurance undertaking, including its branches in other Member States. This decision may be taken in the absence, or following the adoption, of reorganisation measures.

2. A decision adopted according to the home Member State's legislation concerning the opening of winding-up proceedings of an insurance undertaking, including its branches in other Member States, shall be recognised without further formality within the territory of all other Member States and shall be effective there as soon as the decision is effective in the Member State in which the proceedings are opened.

3. The supervisory authorities of the home Member State shall be informed as a matter of urgency of the decision to open winding-up proceedings, if possible before the proceedings are opened and failing that immediately thereafter. The supervisory authorities of the home Member State shall inform as a matter of urgency the supervisory authorities of all other Member States of the decision to open winding-up proceedings including the possible practical effects of such proceedings.

[3464]

Article 9

Applicable law

1. The decision to open winding-up proceedings with regard to an insurance undertaking, the winding-up proceedings and their effects shall be governed by the laws, regulations and administrative provisions applicable in its home Member State unless otherwise provided in Articles 19 to 26.

2. The law of the home Member State shall determine in particular—

(a) the assets which form part of the estate and the treatment of assets acquired by, or devolving on, the insurance undertaking after the opening of the winding-up proceedings;

(b) the respective powers of the insurance undertaking and the liquidator;

(c) the conditions under which set-off may be invoked;

(d) the effects of the winding-up proceedings on current contracts to which the insurance undertaking is party;

(e) the effects of the winding-up proceedings on proceedings brought by individual creditors, with the exception of lawsuits pending as provided for in Article 26;

(f) the claims which are to be lodged against the insurance undertaking's estate and the treatment of claims arising after the opening of winding-up proceedings;

(g) the rules governing the lodging, verification and admission of claims;

(h) the rules governing the distribution of proceeds from the realisation of assets, the ranking of claims, and the rights of creditors who have obtained partial satisfaction after the opening of winding-up proceedings by virtue of a right in rem or through a set-off;

(i) the conditions for and the effects of closure of winding-up proceedings, in particular by composition;

(j) creditors' rights after the closure of winding-up proceedings;

(k) who is to bear the cost and expenses incurred in the winding-up proceedings;

(l) the rules relating to the voidness, voidability or unenforceability of legal acts detrimental to all the creditors.

[3465]

Article 10

Treatment of insurance claims

1. Member States shall ensure that insurance claims take precedence over other claims on the insurance undertaking according to one or both of the following methods—

(a) insurance claims shall, with respect to assets representing the technical provisions, take absolute precedence over any other claim on the insurance undertaking;

(b) insurance claims shall, with respect to the whole of the insurance undertaking's assets, take precedence over any other claim on the insurance undertaking with the only possible exception of—

(i) claims by employees arising from employment contracts and employment relationships,

(ii) claims by public bodies on taxes,

(iii) claims by social security systems,

(iv) claims on assets subject to rights in rem.

2. Without prejudice to paragraph 1, Member States may provide that the whole or a part of the expenses arising from the winding-up procedure, as defined by their national legislation, shall take precedence over insurance claims.

3. Member States which have opted for the method provided for in paragraph 1(a) shall require that insurance undertakings establish and keep up to date a special register in line with the provisions set out in the Annex.

[3466]

Article 11

Subrogation to a guarantee scheme

The home Member State may provide that, where the rights of insurance creditors have been subrogated to a guarantee scheme established in that Member State, claims by that scheme shall not benefit from the provisions of Article 10(1).

[3467]

Article 12

Representation of preferential claims by assets

By way of derogation from Article 18 of Directive 73/239/EEC and Article 21 of Directive 79/267/EEC, Member States which apply the method set out in Article 10(1)(b) of this Directive shall require every insurance undertaking to represent, at any moment and independently from a possible winding-up, the claims which may take precedence over insurance claims pursuant to Article 10(1)(b) and which are registered in the insurance undertaking's accounts, by assets mentioned in Article 21 of Directive 92/49/EEC and Article 21 of Directive 92/96/EEC.

[3468]

Article 13

Withdrawal of the authorisation

1. Where the opening of winding-up proceedings is decided in respect of an insurance undertaking, the authorisation of the insurance undertaking shall be withdrawn, except to the extent necessary for the purposes of paragraph 2, in accordance with the procedure laid down in Article 22 of Directive 73/239/EEC and Article 26 of Directive 79/267/EEC, if the authorisation has not been previously withdrawn.

2. The withdrawal of authorisation pursuant to paragraph 1 shall not prevent the liquidator or any other person entrusted by the competent authorities from carrying on some of the insurance undertakings' activities in so far as that is necessary or appropriate for the purposes of winding-up. The home Member State may provide that such activities shall be carried on with the consent and under the supervision of the supervisory authorities of the home Member State.

[3469]

Article 14

Publication

1. The competent authority, the liquidator or any person appointed for that purpose by the competent authority shall publish the decision to open winding-up proceedings in accordance with the publication procedures provided for in the home Member State and also publish an extract from the winding-up decision in the *Official Journal of the European Communities*. The supervisory authorities of all the other Member States which have been informed of the decision to open winding-up proceedings in accordance with Article 8(3) may ensure the publication of such decision within their territories in the manner they consider appropriate.

2. The publication of the decision to open winding-up proceedings provided for in paragraph 1 shall also specify the competent authority of the home Member State, the applicable law and the liquidator appointed. It shall be in the official language or in one of the official languages of the Member State in which the information is published.

[3470]

Article 15

Information to known creditors

1. When winding-up proceedings are opened, the competent authorities of the home Member State, the liquidator or any person appointed for that purpose by the competent authorities shall without delay individually inform by written notice each known creditor who has his normal place of residence, domicile or head office in another Member State thereof.

2. The notice referred to in paragraph 1 shall in particular deal with time limits, the penalties laid down with regard to those time limits, the body or authority empowered to accept the lodgement of claims or observations relating to claims and the other measures laid down. The notice shall also indicate whether creditors whose claims are preferential or secured in rem need to lodge their claims. In the case of insurance claims, the notice shall further indicate the general effects of the winding-up proceedings on the insurance contracts, in particular, the date on which the insurance contracts or the operations will cease to produce effects and the rights and duties of insured persons with regard to the contract or operation.

[3471]

Article 16

Right to lodge claims

1. Any creditor who has his normal place of residence, domicile or head office in a Member State other than the home Member State, including Member States' public authorities, shall have the right to lodge claims or to submit written observations relating to claims.

2. The claims of all creditors who have their normal place of residence, domicile or head office in a Member State other than the home Member State, including the aforementioned authorities, shall be treated in the same way and accorded the same ranking as claims of an equivalent nature lodgeable by creditors who have their normal place of residence, domicile or head office in the home Member State.

3. Except in cases where the law of the home Member State allows otherwise, a creditor shall send copies of supporting documents, if any, and shall indicate the nature of the claim, the date on which it arose and the amount, whether he alleges preference, security in rem or reservation of title in respect of the claim and what assets are covered by his security. The precedence granted to insurance claims by Article 10 need not be indicated.

[3472]

Article 17

Languages and form

1. The information in the notice referred to in Article 15 shall be provided in the official language or one of the official languages of the home Member State. For that purpose a form shall be used bearing the heading "Invitation to lodge a claim; time limits to be observed" or, where the law of the home Member State provides for the submission of observations relating to claims, "Invitation to submit observations relating to a claim; time limits to be observed", in all the official languages of the European Union.

However, where a known creditor is a holder of an insurance claim, the information in the notice referred to in Article 15 shall be provided in the official language or one of the official languages of the Member State in which the creditor has his normal place of residence, domicile or head office.

2. Any creditor who has his normal place of residence, domicile or head office in a Member State other than the home Member State may lodge his claim or submit observations relating to his claim in the official language or one of the official languages of that other Member State. However, in that event the lodgement of his claim or the submission of observations on his claim, as appropriate, shall bear the heading "Lodgement of claim" or "Submission of observations relating to claims", as appropriate, in the official language or one of the official languages of the home Member State.

[3473]

Article 18

Regular information to the creditors

1. Liquidators shall keep creditors regularly informed, in an appropriate manner, in particular regarding the progress of the winding-up.

2. The supervisory authorities of the Member States may request information on developments in the winding-up procedure from the supervisory authorities of the home Member State.

[3474]

TITLE IV
PROVISIONS COMMON TO REORGANISATION MEASURES AND WINDING-UP PROCEEDINGS

Article 19

Effects on certain contracts and rights

By way of derogation from Articles 4 and 9, the effects of the opening of reorganisation measures or of winding-up proceedings on the contracts and rights specified below shall be governed by the following rules—

(a) employment contracts and employment relationships shall be governed solely by the law of the Member State applicable to the employment contract or employment relationship;

(b) a contract conferring the right to make use of or acquire immovable property shall be governed solely by the law of the Member State in whose territory the immovable property is situated;

(c) rights of the insurance undertaking with respect to immovable property, a ship or an aircraft subject to registration in a public register shall be governed by the law of the Member State under whose authority the register is kept.

[3475]

Article 20

Third parties' rights in rem

1. The opening of reorganisation measures or winding-up proceedings shall not affect the rights in rem of creditors or third parties in respect of tangible or intangible, movable or immovable assets—both specific assets and collections of indefinite assets as a whole which change from time to time—belonging to the insurance undertaking which are situated within the territory of another Member State at the time of the opening of such measures or proceedings.

2. The rights referred to in paragraph 1 shall in particular mean—

(a) the right to dispose of assets or have them disposed of and to obtain satisfaction from the proceeds of or income from those assets, in particular by virtue of a lien or a mortgage;

(b) the exclusive right to have a claim met, in particular a right guaranteed by a lien in respect of the claim or by assignment of the claim by way of a guarantee;

(c) the right to demand the assets from, and/or to require restitution by, anyone having possession or use of them contrary to the wishes of the party so entitled;

(d) a right in rem to the beneficial use of assets.

3. The right, recorded in a public register and enforceable against third parties, under which a right in rem within the meaning of paragraph 1 may be obtained, shall be considered a right in rem.

4. Paragraph 1 shall not preclude actions for voidness, voidability or unenforceability referred to in Article 9(2)(l).

[3476]

Article 21

Reservation of title

1. The opening of reorganisation measures or winding-up proceedings against an insurance undertaking purchasing an asset shall not affect the seller's rights based on a reservation of title where at the time of the opening of such measures or proceedings the asset is situated within the territory of a Member State other than the State in which such measures or proceedings were opened.

2. The opening of reorganisation measures or winding-up proceedings against an insurance undertaking selling an asset, after delivery of the asset, shall not constitute grounds for rescinding or terminating the sale and shall not prevent the purchaser from acquiring title where at the time of the opening of such measures or proceedings the asset sold is situated within the territory of a Member State other than the State in which such measures or proceedings were opened.

3. Paragraphs 1 and 2 shall not preclude actions for voidness, voidability or unenforceability referred to in Article 9(2)(l).

[3477]

Article 22

Set-off

1. The opening of reorganisation measures or winding-up proceedings shall not affect the right of creditors to demand the set-off of their claims against the claims of the insurance undertaking, where such a set-off is permitted by the law applicable to the insurance undertaking's claim.

2. Paragraph 1 shall not preclude actions for voidness, voidability or unenforceability referred to in Article 9(2)(l).

[3478]

Article 23

Regulated markets

1. Without prejudice to Article 20 the effects of a reorganisation measure or the opening of winding-up proceedings on the rights and obligations of the parties to a regulated market shall be governed solely by the law applicable to that market.

2. Paragraph 1 shall not preclude any action for voidness, voidability, or unenforceability referred to in Article 9(2)(l) which may be taken to set aside payments or transactions under the law applicable to that market.

[3479]

Article 24

Detrimental acts

Article 9(2)(l) shall not apply, where a person who has benefited from a legal act detrimental to all the creditors provides proof that—

(a) the said act is subject to the law of a Member State other than the home Member State, and

(b) that law does not allow any means of challenging that act in the relevant case.

[3480]

Article 25

Protection of third-party purchasers

Where, by an act concluded after the adoption of a reorganisation measure or the opening of winding-up proceedings, an insurance undertaking disposes, for a consideration, of—

(a) an immovable asset,

(b) a ship or an aircraft subject to registration in a public register, or

(c) transferable or other securities whose existence or transfer presupposes entry in a register or account laid down by law or which are placed in a central deposit system governed by the law of a Member State,

the validity of that act shall be governed by the law of the Member State within whose territory the immovable asset is situated or under whose authority the register, account or system is kept.

[3481]

Article 26

Lawsuits pending

The effects of reorganisation measures or winding-up proceedings on a pending lawsuit concerning an asset or a right of which the insurance undertaking has been divested shall be governed solely by the law of the Member State in which the lawsuit is pending.

[3482]

Article 27

Administrators and liquidators

1. The administrator's or liquidator's appointment shall be evidenced by a certified copy of the original decision appointing him or by any other certificate issued by the competent authorities of the home Member State.

A translation into the official language or one of the official languages of the Member State within the territory of which the administrator or liquidator wishes to act may be required. No legalisation or other similar formality shall be required.

2. Administrators and liquidators shall be entitled to exercise within the territory of all the Member States all the powers which they are entitled to exercise within the territory of the home Member State. Persons to assist or, where appropriate, represent administrators and liquidators may be appointed, according to the home Member State's legislation, in the course

of the reorganisation measure or winding-up proceedings, in particular in host Member States and, specifically, in order to help overcome any difficulties encountered by creditors in the host Member State.

3. In exercising his powers according to the home Member State's legislation, an administrator or liquidator shall comply with the law of the Member States within whose territory he wishes to take action, in particular with regard to procedures for the realisation of assets and the informing of employees. Those powers may not include the use of force or the right to rule on legal proceedings or disputes.

[3483]

Article 28

Registration in a public register

1. The administrator, liquidator or any other authority or person duly empowered in the home Member State may request that a reorganisation measure or the decision to open winding-up proceedings be registered in the land register, the trade register and any other public register kept in the other Member States.

However, if a Member State prescribes mandatory registration, the authority or person referred to in subparagraph 1 shall take all the measures necessary to ensure such registration.

2. The costs of registration shall be regarded as costs and expenses incurred in the proceedings.

[3484]

Article 29

Professional secrecy

All persons required to receive or divulge information in connection with the procedures of communication laid down in Articles 5, 8 and 30 shall be bound by professional secrecy, in the same manner as laid down in Article 16 of Directive 92/49/EEC and Article 15 of Directive 92/96/EEC, with the exception of any judicial authorities to which existing national provisions apply.

[3485]

Article 30

Branches of third country insurance undertakings

1. Notwithstanding the definitions laid down in Article 2(e), (f) and (g) and for the purpose of applying the provisions of this Directive to the reorganisation measures and winding-up proceedings concerning a branch situated in a Member State of an insurance undertaking whose head office is located outside the Community—

(a) "home Member State" means the Member State in which the branch has been granted authorisation according to Article 23 of Directive 73/239/EEC and Article 27 of Directive 79/267/EEC, and

(b) "supervisory authorities" and "competent authorities" mean such authorities of the Member State in which the branch was authorised.

2. When an insurance undertaking whose head office is outside the Community has branches established in more than one Member State, each branch shall be treated independently with regard to the application of this Directive. The competent authorities and the supervisory authorities of these Member States shall endeavour to coordinate their actions. Any administrators or liquidators shall likewise endeavour to coordinate their actions.

[3486]

Article 31

Implementation of this Directive

1. Member States shall bring into force the laws, regulations and administrative provisions necessary to comply with this Directive before 20 April 2003. They shall forthwith inform the Commission thereof.

When Member States adopt these measures, they shall contain a reference to this Directive or shall be accompanied by such reference on the occasion of their official publication. The methods of making such reference shall be laid down by Member States.

2. National provisions adopted in application of this Directive shall apply only to reorganisation measures or winding-up proceedings adopted or opened after the date referred to in paragraph 1. Reorganisation measures adopted or winding-up proceedings opened before that date shall continue to be governed by the law that was applicable to them at the time of adoption or opening.

3. Member States shall communicate to the Commission the text of the main provisions of domestic law which they adopt in the field governed by this Directive.

[3487]

Article 32

Entry into force

This Directive shall enter into force on the day of its publication in the *Official Journal of the European Communities*.

[3488]

Article 33

Addressees

This Directive is addressed to the Member States.

[3489]

Done at Brussels, 19 March 2001.

ANNEX
SPECIAL REGISTER REFERRED TO IN ARTICLE 10(3)

1. Every insurance undertaking must keep at its head office a special register of the assets used to cover the technical provisions calculated and invested in accordance with the home Member State's rules.

2. Where an insurance undertaking transacts both non-life and life business, it must keep at its head office separate registers for each type of business. However, where a Member State authorises insurance undertakings to cover life and the risks listed in points 1 and 2 of Annex A to Directive 73/239/EEC, it may provide that those insurance undertakings must keep a single register for the whole of their activities.

3. The total value of the assets entered, valued in accordance with the rules applicable in the home Member State, must at no time be less than the value of the technical provisions.

4. Where an asset entered in the register is subject to a right in rem in favour of a creditor or a third party, with the result that part of the value of the asset is not available for the purpose of covering commitments, that fact is recorded in the register and the amount not available is not included in the total value referred to in point 3.

5. Where an asset employed to cover technical provisions is subject to a right in rem in favour of a creditor or a third party, without meeting the conditions of point 4, or where such an asset is subject to a reservation of title in favour of a creditor or of a third party or where a creditor has a right to demand the set-off of his claim against the claim of the insurance undertaking, the treatment of such asset in case of the winding-up of the insurance undertaking with respect to the method provided for in Article 10(1)(a) shall be determined by the legislation of the home Member State except where Articles 20, 21 or 22 apply to that asset.

6. The composition of the assets entered in the register in accordance with points 1 to 5, at the time when winding-up proceedings are opened, must not thereafter be changed and no alteration other than the correction of purely clerical errors must be made in the registers, except with the authorisation of the competent authority.

7. Notwithstanding point 6, the liquidators must add to the said assets the yield therefrom and the value of the pure premiums received in respect of the class of business concerned between the opening of the winding-up proceedings and the time of payment of the insurance claims or until any transfer of portfolio is effected.

8. If the product of the realisation of assets is less than their estimated value in the registers, the liquidators must be required to justify this to the home Member States' competent authorities.

9. The supervisory authorities of the Member States must take appropriate measures to ensure full application by the insurance undertakings of the provisions of this Annex. **[3490]**

DIRECTIVE OF THE EUROPEAN PARLIAMENT AND OF THE COUNCIL

of 4 April 2001

on the reorganisation and winding up of credit institutions

(2001/24/EC)

NOTES

Date of publication in OJ: OJ L125, 5.5.2001, p 15.

This Directive has been implemented in the UK with effect from 5 May 2004 by the Credit Institutions (Reorganisation and Winding up) Regulations 2004, SI 2004/1045 at **[2647]**.

THE EUROPEAN PARLIAMENT AND THE COUNCIL OF THE EUROPEAN UNION,

Having regard to the Treaty establishing the European Community, and in particular Article 47(2) thereof,

Having regard to the proposal from the Commission,[1]

Having regard to the opinion of the Economic and Social Committee,[2]

Having regard to the opinion of the European Monetary Institute,[3]

Acting in accordance with the procedure laid down in Article 251 of the Treaty,[4]

Whereas—

(1) In accordance with the objectives of the Treaty, the harmonious and balanced development of economic activities throughout the Community should be promoted through the elimination of any obstacles to the freedom of establishment and the freedom to provide services within the Community.

(2) At the same time as those obstacles are eliminated, consideration should be given to the situation which might arise if a credit institution runs into difficulties, particularly where that institution has branches in other Member States.

(3) This Directive forms part of the Community legislative framework set up by Directive 2000/12/EC of the European Parliament and of the Council of 20 March 2000 relating to the taking up and pursuit of the business of credit institutions.[5] It follows therefrom that, while they are in operation, a credit institution and its branches form a single entity subject to the supervision of the competent authorities of the State where authorisation valid throughout the Community was granted.

(4) It would be particularly undesirable to relinquish such unity between an institution and its branches where it is necessary to adopt reorganisation measures or open winding-up proceedings.

(5) The adoption of Directive 94/19/EC of the European Parliament and of the Council of 30 May 1994 on deposit-guarantee schemes,[6] which introduced the principle of compulsory membership by credit institutions of a guarantee scheme in their home Member State, brings out even more clearly the need for mutual recognition of reorganisation measures and winding-up proceedings.

(6) The administrative or judicial authorities of the home Member State must have sole power to decide upon and to implement the reorganisation measures provided for in the law and practices in force in that Member State. Owing to the difficulty of harmonising Member States' laws and practices, it is necessary to establish mutual recognition by the Member States of the measures taken by each of them to restore to viability the credit institutions which it has authorised.

(7) It is essential to guarantee that the reorganisation measures adopted by the administrative or judicial authorities of the home Member State and the measures adopted by persons or bodies appointed by those authorities to administer those reorganisation measures, including measures involving the possibility of a suspension of payments, suspension of enforcement measures or reduction of claims and any other measure which could affect third parties' existing rights, are effective in all Member States.

(8) Certain measures, in particular those affecting the functioning of the internal structure of credit institutions or managers' or shareholders' rights, need not be covered by this Directive to be effective in Member States insofar as, pursuant to the rules of private international law, the applicable law is that of the home State.

(9) Certain measures, in particular those connected with the continued fulfilment of conditions of authorisation, are already the subject of mutual recognition pursuant to Directive 2000/12/EC insofar as they do not affect the rights of third parties existing before their adoption.

(10) Persons participating in the operation of the internal structures of credit institutions as well as managers and shareholders of such institutions, considered in those capacities, are not to be regarded as third parties for the purposes of this Directive.

(11) It is necessary to notify third parties of the implementation of reorganisation measures in Member States where branches are situated when such measures could hinder the exercise of some of their rights.

(12) The principle of equal treatment between creditors, as regards the opportunities open to them to take action, requires the administrative or judicial authorities of the home Member State to adopt such measures as are necessary for the creditors in the host Member State to be able to exercise their rights to take action within the time limit laid down.

(13) There must be some coordination of the role of the administrative or judicial authorities in reorganisation measures and winding-up proceedings for branches of credit institutions having head offices outside the Community and situated in different Member States.

(14) In the absence of reorganisation measures, or in the event of such measures failing, the credit institutions in difficulty must be wound up. Provision should be made in such cases for mutual recognition of winding-up proceedings and of their effects in the Community.

(15) The important role played by the competent authorities of the home Member State before winding-up proceedings are opened may continue during the process of winding up so that these proceedings can be properly carried out.

(16) Equal treatment of creditors requires that the credit institution is wound up according to the principles of unity and universality, which require the administrative or judicial authorities of the home Member State to have sole jurisdiction and their decisions to be recognised and to be capable of producing in all the other Member States, without any formality, the effects ascribed to them by the law of the home Member State, except where this Directive provides otherwise.

(17) The exemption concerning the effects of reorganisation measures and winding-up proceedings on certain contracts and rights is limited to those effects and does not cover other questions concerning reorganisation measures and winding-up proceedings such as the lodging, verification, admission and ranking of claims concerning those contracts and rights and the rules governing the distribution of the proceeds of the realisation of the assets, which are governed by the law of the home Member State.

(18) Voluntary winding up is possible when a credit institution is solvent. The administrative or judicial authorities of the home Member State may nevertheless, where appropriate, decide on a reorganisation measure or winding-up proceedings, even after voluntary winding up has commenced.

(19) Withdrawal of authorisation to pursue the business of banking is one of the consequences which winding up a credit institution necessarily entails. Withdrawal should not, however, prevent certain activities of the institution from continuing insofar as is necessary or appropriate for the purposes of winding up. Such a continuation of activity may nonetheless be made subject by the home Member State to the consent of, and supervision by, its competent authorities.

(20) Provision of information to known creditors on an individual basis is as essential as publication to enable them, where necessary, to lodge their claims or submit observations relating to their claims within the prescribed time limits. This should take place without discrimination against creditors domiciled in a Member State other than the home Member State, based on their place of residence or the nature of their claims. Creditors must be kept regularly informed in an appropriate manner throughout winding-up proceedings.

(21) For the sole purpose of applying the provisions of this Directive to reorganisation measures and winding-up proceedings involving branches located in the Community of a credit institution of which the head office is situated in a third country, the definitions of "home Member State", "competent authorities" and "administrative or judicial authorities" should be those of the Member State in which the branch is located.

(22) Where a credit institution which has its head office outside the Community possesses branches in more than one Member State, each branch should receive individual treatment in regard to the application of this Directive. In such a case, the administrative or judicial authorities and the competent authorities as well as the administrators and liquidators should endeavour to coordinate their activities.

(23) Although it is important to follow the principle that the law of the home Member State determines all the effects of reorganisation measures or winding-up proceedings, both procedural and substantive, it is also necessary to bear in mind that those effects may conflict with the rules normally applicable in the context of the economic and financial activity of the

credit institution in question and its branches in other Member States. In some cases reference to the law of another Member State represents an unavoidable qualification of the principle that the law of the home Member State is to apply.

(24) That qualification is especially necessary to protect employees having a contract of employment with a credit institution, ensure the security of transactions in respect of certain types of property and protect the integrity of regulated markets functioning in accordance with the law of a Member State on which financial instruments are traded.

(25) Transactions carried out in the framework of a payment and settlement system are covered by Directive 98/26/EC of the European Parliament and of the Council of 19 May 1998 on settlement finality in payment and securities settlement systems.[7]

(26) The adoption of this Directive does not call into question the provisions of Directive 98/26/EC according to which insolvency proceedings must not have any effect on the enforceability of orders validly entered into a system, or on collateral provided for a system.

(27) Some reorganisation measures or winding-up proceedings involve the appointment of a person to administer them. The recognition of his appointment and his powers in all other Member States is therefore an essential factor in the implementation of decisions taken in the home Member State. However, the limits within which he may exercise his powers when he acts outside the home Member State should be specified.

(28) Creditors who have entered into contracts with a credit institution before a reorganisation measure is adopted or winding-up proceedings are opened should be protected against provisions relating to voidness, voidability or unenforceability laid down in the law of the home Member State, where the beneficiary of the transaction produces evidence that in the law applicable to that transaction there is no available means of contesting the act concerned in the case in point.

(29) The confidence of third-party purchasers in the content of the registers or accounts regarding certain assets entered in those registers or accounts and by extension of the purchasers of immovable property should be safeguarded, even after winding-up proceedings have been opened or a reorganisation measure adopted. The only means of safeguarding that confidence is to make the validity of the purchase subject to the law of the place where the immovable asset is situated or of the State under whose authority the register or account is kept.

(30) The effects of reorganisation measures or winding-up proceedings on a lawsuit pending are governed by the law of the Member State in which the lawsuit is pending, by way of exception to the application of the lex concursus. The effects of those measures and procedures on individual enforcement actions arising from such lawsuits are governed by the legislation of the home Member State, in accordance with the general rule established by this Directive.

(31) Provision should be made for the administrative or judicial authorities in the home Member State to notify immediately the competent authorities of the host Member State of the adoption of any reorganisation measure or the opening of any winding-up proceedings, if possible before the adoption of the measure or the opening of the proceedings, or, if not, immediately afterwards.

(32) Professional secrecy as defined in Article 30 of Directive 2000/12/EC is an essential factor in all information or consultation procedures. For that reason it should be respected by all the administrative authorities taking part in such procedures, whereas the judicial authorities remain, in this respect, subject to the national provisions relating to them,

[3491]

NOTES

1 OJ C356, 31.12.85, p 55 and OJ C36, 8.2.88, p 1.
2 OJ C263, 20.10.86, p 13.
3 OJ C332, 30.10.98, p 13.
4 Opinion of the European Parliament of 13 March 1987 (OJ C99, 13.4.87, p 211), confirmed on 2 December 1993 (OJ C342, 20.12.93, p 30), Council Common Position of 17 July 2000 (OJ C300, 20.10.2000, p 13) and Decision of the European Parliament of 16 January 2001 (not yet published in the Official Journal). Council Decision of 12 March 2001.
5 OJ L126, 26.5.2000, p 1.
6 OJ L135, 31.5.94, p 5.
7 OJ L166, 11.6.98, p 45.

HAVE ADOPTED THIS DIRECTIVE—

TITLE I
SCOPE AND DEFINITIONS

Article 1

Scope

1. This Directive shall apply to credit institutions and their branches set up in Member States other than those in which they have their head offices, as defined in points (1) and (3) of Article 1 of Directive 2000/12/EC, subject to the conditions and exemptions laid down in Article 2(3) of that Directive.

2. The provisions of this Directive concerning the branches of a credit institution having a head office outside the Community shall apply only where that institution has branches in at least two Member States of the Community.

[3492]

Article 2

Definitions

For the purposes of this Directive—

- "home Member State" shall mean the Member State of origin within the meaning of Article 1, point (6) of Directive 2000/12/EC;
- "host Member State" shall mean the host Member State within the meaning of Article 1, point (7) of Directive 2000/12/EC;
- "branch" shall mean a branch within the meaning of Article 1, point (3) of Directive 2000/12/EC;
- "competent authorities" shall mean the competent authorities within the meaning of Article 1, point (4) of Directive 2000/12/EC;
- "administrator" shall mean any person or body appointed by the administrative or judicial authorities whose task is to administer reorganisation measures;
- "administrative or judicial authorities" shall mean such administrative or judicial authorities of the Member States as are competent for the purposes of reorganisation measures or winding-up proceedings;
- "reorganisation measures" shall mean measures which are intended to preserve or restore the financial situation of a credit institution and which could affect third parties" pre-existing rights, including measures involving the possibility of a suspension of payments, suspension of enforcement measures or reduction of claims;
- "liquidator" shall mean any person or body appointed by the administrative or judicial authorities whose task is to administer winding-up proceedings;
- "winding-up proceedings" shall mean collective proceedings opened and monitored by the administrative or judicial authorities of a Member State with the aim of realising assets under the supervision of those authorities, including where the proceedings are terminated by a composition or other, similar measure;
- "regulated market" shall mean a regulated market within the meaning of Article 1, point (13) of Directive 93/22/EEC;
- "instruments" shall mean all the instruments referred to in Section B of the Annex to Directive 93/22/EEC.

[3493]

TITLE II
REORGANISATION MEASURES

A. Credit institutions having their head offices within the Community

Article 3

Adoption of reorganisation measures—applicable law

1. The administrative or judicial authorities of the home Member State shall alone be empowered to decide on the implementation of one or more reorganisation measures in a credit institution, including branches established in other Member States.

2. The reorganisation measures shall be applied in accordance with the laws, regulations and procedures applicable in the home Member State, unless otherwise provided in this Directive.

They shall be fully effective in accordance with the legislation of that Member State throughout the Community without any further formalities, including as against third parties in other Member States, even where the rules of the host Member State applicable to them do not provide for such measures or make their implementation subject to conditions which are not fulfilled.

The reorganisation measures shall be effective throughout the Community once they become effective in the Member State where they have been taken.

[3494]

Article 4

Information for the competent authorities of the host Member State

The administrative or judicial authorities of the home Member State shall without delay inform, by any available means, the competent authorities of the host Member State of their decision to adopt any reorganisation measure, including the practical effects which such a measure may have, if possible before it is adopted or otherwise immediately thereafter. Information shall be communicated by the competent authorities of the home Member State.

[3495]

Article 5

Information for the supervisory authorities of the home Member State

Where the administrative or judicial authorities of the host Member State deem it necessary to implement within their territory one or more reorganisation measures, they shall inform the competent authorities of the home Member State accordingly. Information shall be communicated by the host Member State's competent authorities.

[3496]

Article 6

Publication

1. Where implementation of the reorganisation measures decided on pursuant to Article 3(1) and (2) is likely to affect the rights of third parties in a host Member State and where an appeal may be brought in the home Member State against the decision ordering the measure, the administrative or judicial authorities of the home Member State, the administrator or any person empowered to do so in the home Member State shall publish an extract from the decision in the *Official Journal of the European Communities* and in two national newspapers in each host Member State, in order in particular to facilitate the exercise of the right of appeal in good time.

2. The extract from the decision provided for in paragraph 1 shall be forwarded at the earliest opportunity, by the most appropriate route, to the Office for Official Publications of the European Communities and to the two national newspapers in each host Member State.

3. The Office for Official Publications of the European Communities shall publish the extract at the latest within twelve days of its dispatch.

4. The extract from the decision to be published shall specify, in the official language or languages of the Member States concerned, in particular the purpose and legal basis of the decision taken, the time limits for lodging appeals, specifically a clearly understandable indication of the date of expiry of the time limits, and the full address of the authorities or court competent to hear an appeal.

5. The reorganisation measures shall apply irrespective of the measures prescribed in paragraphs 1 to 3 and shall be fully effective as against creditors, unless the administrative or judicial authorities of the home Member State or the law of that State governing such measures provide otherwise.

[3497]

Article 7

Duty to inform known creditors and right to lodge claims

1. Where the legislation of the home Member State requires lodgement of a claim with a view to its recognition or provides for compulsory notification of the measure to creditors

who have their domiciles, normal places of residence or head offices in that State, the administrative or judicial authorities of the home Member State or the administrator shall also inform known creditors who have their domiciles, normal places of residence or head offices in other Member States, in accordance with the procedures laid down in Articles 14 and 17(1).

2. Where the legislation of the home Member State provides for the right of creditors who have their domiciles, normal places of residence or head offices in that State to lodge claims or to submit observations concerning their claims, creditors who have their domiciles, normal places of residence or head offices in other Member States shall also have that right in accordance with the procedures laid down in Article 16 and Article 17(2).

[3498]

B. Credit institutions having their head offices outside the Community

Article 8

Branches of third-country credit institutions

1. The administrative or judicial authorities of the host Member State of a branch of a credit institution having its head office outside the Community shall without delay inform, by any available means, the competent authorities of the other host Member States in which the institution has set up branches which are included on the list referred to in Article 11 of Directive 2000/12/EC and published each year in the *Official Journal of the European Communities*, of their decision to adopt any reorganisation measure, including the practical effects which that measure may have, if possible before it is adopted or otherwise immediately thereafter. Information shall be communicated by the competent authorities of the host Member State whose administrative or judicial authorities decide to apply the measure.

2. The administrative or judicial authorities referred to in paragraph 1 shall endeavour to coordinate their actions.

[3499]

TITLE III
WINDING-UP PROCEEDINGS

A. Credit institutions having their head offices within the Community

Article 9

Opening of winding-up proceedings—Information to be communicated to other competent authorities

1. The administrative or judicial authorities of the home Member State which are responsible for winding up shall alone be empowered to decide on the opening of winding-up proceedings concerning a credit institution, including branches established in other Member States. A decision to open winding-up proceedings taken by the administrative or judicial authority of the home Member State shall be recognised, without further formality, within the territory of all other Member States and shall be effective there when the decision is effective in the Member State in which the proceedings are opened.

2. The administrative or judicial authorities of the home Member State shall without delay inform, by any available means, the competent authorities of the host Member State of their decision to open winding-up proceedings, including the practical effects which such proceedings may have, if possible before they open or otherwise immediately thereafter. Information shall be communicated by the competent authorities of the home Member State.

[3500]

Article 10

Law applicable

1. A credit institution shall be wound up in accordance with the laws, regulations and procedures applicable in its home Member State insofar as this Directive does not provide otherwise.

2. The law of the home Member State shall determine in particular—

(a) the goods subject to administration and the treatment of goods acquired by the credit institution after the opening of winding-up proceedings;
(b) the respective powers of the credit institution and the liquidator;
(c) the conditions under which set-offs may be invoked;
(d) the effects of winding-up proceedings on current contracts to which the credit institution is party;
(e) the effects of winding-up proceedings on proceedings brought by individual creditors, with the exception of lawsuits pending, as provided for in Article 32;
(f) the claims which are to be lodged against the credit institution and the treatment of claims arising after the opening of winding-up proceedings;
(g) the rules governing the lodging, verification and admission of claims;
(h) the rules governing the distribution of the proceeds of the realisation of assets, the ranking of claims and the rights of creditors who have obtained partial satisfaction after the opening of insolvency proceedings by virtue of a right *in re* or through a set-off;
(i) the conditions for, and the effects of, the closure of insolvency proceedings, in particular by composition;
(j) creditors' rights after the closure of winding-up proceedings;
(k) who is to bear the costs and expenses incurred in the winding-up proceedings;
(l) the rules relating to the voidness, voidability or unenforceability of legal acts detrimental to all the creditors.

[3501]

Article 11

Consultation of competent authorities before voluntary winding up

1. The competent authorities of the home Member State shall be consulted in the most appropriate form before any voluntary winding-up decision is taken by the governing bodies of a credit institution.

2. The voluntary winding up of a credit institution shall not preclude the adoption of a reorganisation measure or the opening of winding-up proceedings.

[3502]

Article 12

Withdrawal of a credit institution's authorisation

1. Where the opening of winding-up proceedings is decided on in respect of a credit institution in the absence, or following the failure, of reorganisation measures, the authorisation of the institution shall be withdrawn in accordance with, in particular, the procedure laid down in Article 22(9) of Directive 2000/12/EC.

2. The withdrawal of authorisation provided for in paragraph 1 shall not prevent the person or persons entrusted with the winding up from carrying on some of the credit institution's activities insofar as that is necessary or appropriate for the purposes of winding up.

The home Member State may provide that such activities shall be carried on with the consent, and under the supervision, of the competent authorities of that Member State.

[3503]

Article 13

Publication

The liquidators or any administrative or judicial authority shall announce the decision to open winding-up proceedings through publication of an extract from the winding-up decision in the *Official Journal of the European Communities* and at least two national newspapers in each of the host Member States.

[3504]

Article 14

Provision of information to known creditors

1. When winding-up proceedings are opened, the administrative or judicial authority of the home Member State or the liquidator shall without delay individually inform known

creditors who have their domiciles, normal places of residence or head offices in other Member States, except in cases where the legislation of the home State does not require lodgement of the claim with a view to its recognition.

2. That information, provided by the dispatch of a notice, shall in particular deal with time limits, the penalties laid down in regard to those time limits, the body or authority empowered to accept the lodgement of claims or observations relating to claims and the other measures laid down. Such a notice shall also indicate whether creditors whose claims are preferential or secured *in re* need lodge their claims.

[3505]

Article 15

Honouring of obligations

Where an obligation has been honoured for the benefit of a credit institution which is not a legal person and which is the subject of winding-up proceedings opened in another Member State, when it should have been honoured for the benefit of the liquidator in those proceedings, the person honouring the obligation shall be deemed to have discharged it if he was unaware of the opening of proceedings. Where such an obligation is honoured before the publication provided for in Article 13 has been effected, the person honouring the obligation shall be presumed, in the absence of proof to the contrary, to have been unaware of the opening of winding-up proceedings; where the obligation is honoured after the publication provided for in Article 13 has been effected, the person honouring the obligation shall be presumed, in the absence of proof to the contrary, to have been aware of the opening of proceedings.

[3506]

Article 16

Right to lodge claims

1. Any creditor who has his domicile, normal place of residence or head office in a Member State other than the home Member State, including Member States' public authorities, shall have the right to lodge claims or to submit written observations relating to claims.

2. The claims of all creditors whose domiciles, normal places of residence or head offices are in Member States other than the home Member State shall be treated in the same way and accorded the same ranking as claims of an equivalent nature which may be lodged by creditors having their domiciles, normal places of residence, or head offices in the home Member State.

3. Except in cases where the law of the home Member State provides for the submission of observations relating to claims, a creditor shall send copies of supporting documents, if any, and shall indicate the nature of the claim, the date on which it arose and its amount, as well as whether he alleges preference, security *in re* or reservation of title in respect of the claim and what assets are covered by his security.

[3507]

Article 17

Languages

1. The information provided for in Articles 13 and 14 shall be provided in the official language or one of the official languages of the home Member State. For that purpose a form shall be used bearing, in all the official languages of the European Union, the heading "Invitation to lodge a claim. Time limits to be observed" or, where the law of the home Member State provides for the submission of observations relating to claims, the heading "Invitation to submit observations relating to a claim. Time limits to be observed".

2. Any creditor who has his domicile, normal place of residence or head office in a Member State other than the home Member State may lodge his claim or submit observations relating to his claim in the official language or one of the official languages of that other Member State. In that event, however, the lodgement of his claim or the submission of observations on his claim shall bear the heading "Lodgement of claim" or "Submission of observations relating to claims" in the official language or one of the official languages of the home Member State. In addition, he may be required to provide a translation into that language of the lodgement of claim or submission of observations relating to claims. **[3508]**

Article 18

Regular provision of information to creditors

Liquidators shall keep creditors regularly informed, in an appropriate manner, particularly with regard to progress in the winding up.

[3509]

B. Credit institutions the head offices of which are outside the Community

Article 19

Branches of third-country credit institutions

1. The administrative or judicial authorities of the host Member State of the branch of a credit institution the head office of which is outside the Community shall without delay inform, by any available means, the competent authorities of the other host Member States in which the credit institution has set up branches on the list referred to in Article 11 of Directive 2000/12/EC and published each year in the *Official Journal of the European Communities*, of their decision to open winding-up proceedings, including the practical effects which these proceedings may have, if possible before they open or otherwise immediately thereafter. Information shall be communicated by the competent authorities of the first above-mentioned host Member State.

2. Administrative or judicial authorities which decide to open proceedings to wind up a branch of a credit institution the head office of which is outside the Community shall inform the competent authorities of the other host Member States that winding-up proceedings have been opened and authorisation withdrawn.

Information shall be communicated by the competent authorities in the host Member State which has decided to open the proceedings.

3. The administrative or judicial authorities referred to in paragraph 1 shall endeavour to coordinate their actions.

Any liquidators shall likewise endeavour to coordinate their actions.

[3510]

TITLE IV
PROVISIONS COMMON TO REORGANISATION MEASURES AND WINDING-UP PROCEEDINGS

Article 20

Effects on certain contracts and rights

The effects of a reorganisation measure or the opening of winding-up proceedings on—

(a) employment contracts and relationships shall be governed solely by the law of the Member State applicable to the employment contract;

(b) a contract conferring the right to make use of or acquire immovable property shall be governed solely by the law of the Member State within the territory of which the immovable property is situated. That law shall determine whether property is movable or immovable;

(c) rights in respect of immovable property, a ship or an aircraft subject to registration in a public register shall be governed solely by the law of the Member State under the authority of which the register is kept.

[3511]

Article 21

Third parties' rights in re

1. The adoption of reorganisation measures or the opening of winding-up proceedings shall not affect the rights *in re* of creditors or third parties in respect of tangible or intangible, movable or immovable assets—both specific assets and collections of indefinite assets as a whole which change from time to time—belonging to the credit institution which are situated within the territory of another Member State at the time of the adoption of such measures or the opening of such proceedings.

2. The rights referred to in paragraph 1 shall in particular mean—
(a) the right to dispose of assets or have them disposed of and to obtain satisfaction from the proceeds of or income from those assets, in particular by virtue of a lien or a mortgage;
(b) the exclusive right to have a claim met, in particular a right guaranteed by a lien in respect of the claim or by assignment of the claim by way of a guarantee;
(c) the right to demand the assets from, and/or to require restitution by, anyone having possession or use of them contrary to the wishes of the party so entitled;
(d) a right *in re* to the beneficial use of assets.

3. The right, recorded in a public register and enforceable against third parties, under which a right *in re* within the meaning of paragraph 1 may be obtained, shall be considered a right *in re*.

4. Paragraph 1 shall not preclude the actions for voidness, voidability or unenforceability laid down in Article 10(2)(l).

[3512]

Article 22

Reservation of title

1. The adoption of reorganisation measures or the opening of winding-up proceedings concerning a credit institution purchasing an asset shall not affect the seller's rights based on a reservation of title where at the time of the adoption of such measures or opening of such proceedings the asset is situated within the territory of a Member State other than the State in which the said measures were adopted or the said proceedings were opened.

2. The adoption of reorganisation measures or the opening of winding-up proceedings concerning a credit institution selling an asset, after delivery of the asset, shall not constitute grounds for rescinding or terminating the sale and shall not prevent the purchaser from acquiring title where at the time of the adoption of such measures or the opening of such proceedings the asset sold is situated within the territory of a Member State other than the State in which such measures were adopted or such proceedings were opened.

3. Paragraphs 1 and 2 shall not preclude the actions for voidness, voidability or unenforceability laid down in Article 10(2)(l).

[3513]

Article 23

Set-off

1. The adoption of reorganisation measures or the opening of winding-up proceedings shall not affect the right of creditors to demand the set-off of their claims against the claims of the credit institution, where such a set-off is permitted by the law applicable to the credit institution's claim.

2. Paragraph 1 shall not preclude the actions for voidness, voidability or unenforceability laid down in Article 10(2)(l).

[3514]

Article 24

Lex rei sitae

The enforcement of proprietary rights in instruments or other rights in such instruments the existence or transfer of which presupposes their recording in a register, an account or a centralised deposit system held or located in a Member State shall be governed by the law of the Member State where the register, account, or centralised deposit system in which those rights are recorded is held or located.

[3515]

Article 25

Netting agreements

Netting agreements shall be governed solely by the law of the contract which governs such agreements.

[3516]

Article 26

Repurchase agreements

Without prejudice to Article 24, repurchase agreements shall be governed solely by the law of the contract which governs such agreements.

[3517]

Article 27

Regulated markets

Without prejudice to Article 24, transactions carried out in the context of a regulated market shall be governed solely by the law of the contract which governs such transactions.

[3518]

Article 28

Proof of liquidators' appointment

1. The administrator or liquidator's appointment shall be evidenced by a certified copy of the original decision appointing him or by any other certificate issued by the administrative or judicial authority of the home Member State.

A translation into the official language or one of the official languages of the Member State within the territory of which the administrator or liquidator wishes to act may be required. No legalisation or other similar formality shall be required.

2. Administrators and liquidators shall be entitled to exercise within the territory of all the Member States all the powers which they are entitled to exercise within the territory of the home Member State. They may also appoint persons to assist or, where appropriate, represent them in the course of the reorganisation measure or winding-up proceedings, in particular in host Member States and, specifically, in order to help overcome any difficulties encountered by creditors in the host Member State.

3. In exercising his powers, an administrator or liquidator shall comply with the law of the Member States within the territory of which he wishes to take action, in particular with regard to procedures for the realisation of assets and the provision of information to employees. Those powers may not include the use of force or the right to rule on legal proceedings or disputes.

[3519]

Article 29

Registration in a public register

1. The administrator, liquidator or any administrative or judicial authority of the home Member State may request that a reorganisation measure or the decision to open winding-up proceedings be registered in the land register, the trade register and any other public register kept in the other Member States. A Member State may, however, prescribe mandatory registration. In that event, the person or authority referred to in the preceding subparagraph shall take all the measures necessary to ensure such registration.

2. The costs of registration shall be regarded as costs and expenses incurred in the proceedings.

[3520]

Article 30

Detrimental acts

1. Article 10 shall not apply as regards the rules relating to the voidness, voidability or unenforceability of legal acts detrimental to the creditors as a whole, where the beneficiary of these acts provides proof that—

— the act detrimental to the creditors as a whole is subject to the law of a Member State other than the home Member State, and

— that law does not allow any means of challenging that act in the case in point.

2. Where a reorganisation measure decided on by a judicial authority provides for rules relating to the voidness, voidability or unenforceability of legal acts detrimental to the

creditors as a whole performed before adoption of the measure, Article 3(2) shall not apply in the cases provided for in paragraph 1 of this Article.

[3521]

Article 31

Protection of third parties

Where, by an act concluded after the adoption of a reorganisation measure or the opening of winding-up proceedings, a credit institution disposes, for consideration, of—

— an immovable asset,
— a ship or an aircraft subject to registration in a public register, or
— instruments or rights in such instruments the existence or transfer of which presupposes their being recorded in a register, an account or a centralised deposit system held or located in a Member State,

the validity of that act shall be governed by the law of the Member State within the territory of which the immovable asset is situated or under the authority of which that register, account or deposit system is kept.

[3522]

Article 32

Lawsuits pending

The effects of reorganisation measures or winding-up proceedings on a pending lawsuit concerning an asset or a right of which the credit institution has been divested shall be governed solely by the law of the Member State in which the lawsuit is pending.

[3523]

Article 33

Professional secrecy

All persons required to receive or divulge information in connection with the information or consultation procedures laid down in Articles 4, 5, 8, 9, 11 and 19 shall be bound by professional secrecy, in accordance with the rules and conditions laid down in Article 30 of Directive 2000/12/EC, with the exception of any judicial authorities to which existing national provisions apply.

[3524]

TITLE V
FINAL PROVISIONS

Article 34

Implementation

1. Member States shall bring into force the laws, regulations and administrative provisions necessary to comply with this Directive on 5 May 2004. They shall forthwith inform the Commission thereof.

National provisions adopted in application of this Directive shall apply only to reorganisation measures or winding-up proceedings adopted or opened after the date referred to in the first subparagraph. Measures adopted or proceedings opened before that date shall continue to be governed by the law that was applicable to them at the time of adoption or opening.

2. When Member States adopt these measures, they shall contain a reference to this Directive or shall be accompanied by such reference on the occasion of their official publication. The methods of making such reference shall be laid down by Member States.

3. Member States shall communicate to the Commission the texts of the main provisions of national law which they adopt in the field governed by this Directive.

[3525]

Article 35

Entry into force

This Directive shall enter into force on the date of its publication.

[3526]

Article 36

Addressees

This Directive is addressed to the Member States.

[3527]

Done at Luxembourg, 4 April 2001.

G. SERVICE OF DOCUMENTS

COUNCIL REGULATION

of 29 May 2000

on the service in the Member States of judicial and extra-judicial documents in civil or commercial matters

(1348/2000/EC)

NOTES

Date of publication in OJ: OJ L160, 30.6.2000, p 37.

On 8 July 2005, the European Commission adopted a proposal for a Regulation of the European Parliament and of the Council amending Council Regulation 1348/2000/EC of 29 May 2000 on the service in the Member States of judicial and extrajudicial documents in civil or commercial matters (see http://eur-lex.europa.eu/LexUriServ/site/en/com/2005/com2005_0305en01.pdf).

The Commission has stated: "The aim of this proposal is to further improve and expedite the transmission and the service of documents, to simplify the application of certain provisions of the Regulation and to improve legal certainty for the applicant and for the addressee."

"The main modifications proposed are:

- Introduction of a rule providing that service should be effected in any event within one month of receipt by the receiving agency
- Introduction of a new standard form to inform the addressee about his right to refuse to accept a document within one week of service
- Introduction of a rule providing that costs occasioned by the employment of a judicial officer or of a person competent under the law of the Member State addressed must correspond to a fixed fee laid down by that Member State in advance which respects the principles of proportionality and non-discrimination
- Introduction of uniform conditions for service by postal services (registered letter with acknowledgement of receipt or equivalent)."

(Source: European Judicial Network website, http://ec.europa.eu/civiljustice/serv_doc/serv_doc_ec_en.htm).

THE COUNCIL OF THE EUROPEAN UNION,

Having regard to the Treaty establishing the European Community, and in particular Article 61(c) and Article 67(1) thereof,

Having regard to the proposal from the Commission,[1]

Having regard to the opinion of the European Parliament,[2]

Having regard to the opinion of the Economic and Social Committee,[3]

Whereas:

(1) The Union has set itself the objective of maintaining and developing the Union as an area of freedom, security and justice, in which the free movement of persons is assured. To establish such an area, the Community is to adopt, among others, the measures relating to judicial cooperation in civil matters needed for the proper functioning of the internal market.

(2) The proper functioning of the internal market entails the need to improve and expedite the transmission of judicial and extrajudicial documents in civil or commercial matters for service between the Member States.

(3) This is a subject now falling within the ambit of Article 65 of the Treaty.

(4) In accordance with the principles of subsidiarity and proportionality as set out in Article 5 of the Treaty, the objectives of this Regulation cannot be sufficiently achieved by the Member States and can therefore be better achieved by the Community. This Regulation does not go beyond what is necessary to achieve those objectives.

(5) The Council, by an Act dated 26 May 1997,[4] drew up a Convention on the service in the Member States of the European Union of judicial and extrajudicial documents in civil or commercial matters and recommended it for adoption by the Member States in accordance with their respective constitutional rules. That Convention has not entered into force. Continuity in the results of the negotiations for conclusion of the Convention should be ensured. The main content of this Regulation is substantially taken over from it.

(6) Efficiency and speed in judicial procedures in civil matters means that the transmission of judicial and extrajudicial documents is to be made direct and by rapid means between local bodies designated by the Member States. However, the Member States may indicate their intention of designating only one transmitting or receiving agency or one agency to perform both functions for a period of five years. This designation may, however, be renewed every five years.

(7) Speed in transmission warrants the use of all appropriate means, provided that certain conditions as to the legibility and reliability of the document received are observed. Security in transmission requires that the document to be transmitted be accompanied by a pre-printed form, to be completed in the language of the place where service is to be effected, or in another language accepted by the Member State in question.

(8) To secure the effectiveness of this Regulation, the possibility of refusing service of documents is confined to exceptional situations.

(9) Speed of transmission warrants documents being served within days of reception of the document. However, if service has not been effected after one month has elapsed, the receiving agency should inform the transmitting agency. The expiry of this period should not imply that the request be returned to the transmitting agency where it is clear that service is feasible within a reasonable period.

(10) For the protection of the addressee's interests, service should be effected in the official language or one of the official languages of the place where it is to be effected or in another language of the originating Member State which the addressee understands.

(11) Given the differences between the Member States as regards their rules of procedure, the material date for the purposes of service varies from one Member State to another. Having regard to such situations and the possible difficulties that may arise, this Regulation should provide for a system where it is the law of the receiving Member State which determines the date of service. However, if the relevant documents in the context of proceedings to be brought or pending in the Member State of origin are to be served within a specified period, the date to be taken into consideration with respect to the applicant shall be that determined according to the law of the Member State of origin. A Member State is, however, authorised to derogate from the aforementioned provisions for a transitional period of five years, for appropriate reasons. Such a derogation may be renewed by a Member State at five-year intervals due to reasons related to its legal system.

(12) This Regulation prevails over the provisions contained in bilateral or multilateral agreements or arrangements having the same scope, concluded by the Member States, and in particular the Protocol annexed to the Brussels Convention of 27 September 1968[5] and the Hague Convention of 15 November 1965 in relations between the Member States party thereto. This Regulation does not preclude Member States from maintaining or concluding agreements or arrangements to expedite or simplify the transmission of documents, provided that they are compatible with the Regulation.

(13) The information transmitted pursuant to this Regulation should enjoy suitable protection. This matter falls within the scope of Directive 95/46/EC of the European Parliament and of the Council of 24 October 1995 on the protection of individuals with regard to the processing of personal data and on the free movement of such data,[6] and of Directive 97/66/EC of the European Parliament and of the Council of 15 December 1997 concerning the processing of personal data and the protection of privacy in the telecommunications sector.[7]

(14) The measures necessary for the implementation of this Regulation should be adopted in accordance with Council Decision 1999/468/EC of 28 June 1999 laying down the procedures for the exercise of implementing powers conferred on the Commission.[8]

(15) These measures also include drawing up and updating the manual using appropriate modern means.

(16) No later than three years after the date of entry into force of this Regulation, the Commission should review its application and propose such amendments as may appear necessary.

(17) The United Kingdom and Ireland, in accordance with Article 3 of the Protocol on the position of the United Kingdom and Ireland annexed to the Treaty on European Union and the Treaty establishing the European Community, have given notice of their wish to take part in the adoption and application of this Regulation.

(18) Denmark, in accordance with Articles 1 and 2 of the Protocol on the position of Denmark annexed to the Treaty on European Union and the Treaty establishing the European Community, is not participating in the adoption of this Regulation, and is therefore not bound by it nor subject to its application,

[3528]

NOTES

1. OJ C247 E, 31.8.1999, p 11.
2. Opinion of 17 November 1999 (not yet published in the Official Journal).
3. OJ C368, 20.12.1999, p 47.
4. OJ C261, 27.8.1997, p 1. On the same day as the Convention was drawn up the Council took note of the explanatory report on the Convention which is set out on page 26 of the aforementioned Official Journal.

5 Brussels Convention of 27 September 1968 on Jurisdiction and the Enforcement of Judgments in Civil and Commercial Matters (OJ L299, 13.12.1972, p 32; consolidated version, OJ C27, 26.1.1998, p 1).
6 OJ L281, 23.11.1995, p 31.
7 OJ L24, 30.1.1998, p 1.
8 OJ L184, 17.7.1999, p 23.

HAS ADOPTED THIS REGULATION:

CHAPTER I
GENERAL PROVISIONS

Article 1
Scope

1. This Regulation shall apply in civil and commercial matters where a judicial or extrajudicial document has to be transmitted from one Member State to another for service there.

2. This Regulation shall not apply where the address of the person to be served with the document is not known.

[3529]

Article 2

Transmitting and receiving agencies

1. Each Member State shall designate the public officers, authorities or other persons, hereinafter referred to as "transmitting agencies", competent for the transmission of judicial or extrajudicial documents to be served in another Member State.

2. Each Member State shall designate the public officers, authorities or other persons, hereinafter referred to as "receiving agencies", competent for the receipt of judicial or extrajudicial documents from another Member State.

3. A Member State may designate one transmitting agency and one receiving agency or one agency to perform both functions. A federal State, a State in which several legal systems apply or a State with autonomous territorial units shall be free to designate more than one such agency. The designation shall have effect for a period of five years and may be renewed at five-year intervals.

4. Each Member State shall provide the Commission with the following information:

(a) the names and addresses of the receiving agencies referred to in paragraphs 2 and 3;
(b) the geographical areas in which they have jurisdiction;
(c) the means of receipt of documents available to them; and
(d) the languages that may be used for the completion of the standard form in the Annex.

Member States shall notify the Commission of any subsequent modification of such information.

[3530]

Article 3

Central body

Each Member State shall designate a central body responsible for:

(a) supplying information to the transmitting agencies;
(b) seeking solutions to any difficulties which may arise during transmission of documents for service;
(c) forwarding, in exceptional cases, at the request of a transmitting agency, a request for service to the competent receiving agency.

A federal State, a State in which several legal systems apply or a State with autonomous territorial units shall be free to designate more than one central body.

[3531]

CHAPTER II
JUDICIAL DOCUMENTS

SECTION 1
TRANSMISSION AND SERVICE OF JUDICIAL DOCUMENTS

Article 4

Transmission of documents

1. Judicial documents shall be transmitted directly and as soon as possible between the agencies designated on the basis of Article 2.

2. The transmission of documents, requests, confirmations, receipts, certificates and any other papers between transmitting agencies and receiving agencies may be carried out by any appropriate means, provided that the content of the document received is true and faithful to that of the document forwarded and that all information in it is easily legible.

3. The document to be transmitted shall be accompanied by a request drawn up using the standard form in the Annex. The form shall be completed in the official language of the Member State addressed or, if there are several official languages in that Member State, the official language or one of the official languages of the place where service is to be effected, or in another language which that Member State has indicated it can accept. Each Member State shall indicate the official language or languages of the European Union other than its own which is or are acceptable to it for completion of the form.

4. The documents and all papers that are transmitted shall be exempted from legalisation or any equivalent formality.

5. When the transmitting agency wishes a copy of the document to be returned together with the certificate referred to in Article 10, it shall send the document in duplicate.

[3532]

Article 5

Translation of documents

1. The applicant shall be advised by the transmitting agency to which he or she forwards the document for transmission that the addressee may refuse to accept it if it is not in one of the languages provided for in Article 8.

2. The applicant shall bear any costs of translation prior to the transmission of the document, without prejudice to any possible subsequent decision by the court or competent authority on liability for such costs.

[3533]

Article 6

Receipt of documents by receiving agency

1. On receipt of a document, a receiving agency shall, as soon as possible and in any event within seven days of receipt, send a receipt to the transmitting agency by the swiftest possible means of transmission using the standard form in the Annex.

2. Where the request for service cannot be fulfilled on the basis of the information or documents transmitted, the receiving agency shall contact the transmitting agency by the swiftest possible means in order to secure the missing information or documents.

3. If the request for service is manifestly outside the scope of this Regulation or if non-compliance with the formal conditions required makes service impossible, the request and the documents transmitted shall be returned, on receipt, to the transmitting agency, together with the notice of return in the standard form in the Annex.

4. A receiving agency receiving a document for service but not having territorial jurisdiction to serve it shall forward it, as well as the request, to the receiving agency having territorial jurisdiction in the same Member State if the request complies with the conditions laid down in Article 4(3) and shall inform the transmitting agency accordingly, using the standard form in the Annex. That receiving agency shall inform the transmitting agency when it receives the document, in the manner provided for in paragraph 1.

[3534]

Article 7

Service of documents

1. The receiving agency shall itself serve the document or have it served, either in accordance with the law of the Member State addressed or by a particular form requested by the transmitting agency, unless such a method is incompatible with the law of that Member State.

2. All steps required for service of the document shall be effected as soon as possible. In any event, if it has not been possible to effect service within one month of receipt, the receiving agency shall inform the transmitting agency by means of the certificate in the standard form in the Annex, which shall be drawn up under the conditions referred to in Article 10(2). The period shall be calculated in accordance with the law of the Member State addressed.

[3535]

Article 8

Refusal to accept a document

1. The receiving agency shall inform the addressee that he or she may refuse to accept the document to be served if it is in a language other than either of the following languages:

(a) the official language of the Member State addressed or, if there are several official languages in that Member State, the official language or one of the official languages of the place where service is to be effected; or

(b) a language of the Member State of transmission which the addressee understands.

2. Where the receiving agency is informed that the addressee refuses to accept the document in accordance with paragraph 1, it shall immediately inform the transmitting agency by means of the certificate provided for in Article 10 and return the request and the documents of which a translation is requested.

[3536]

Article 9

Date of service

1. Without prejudice to Article 8, the date of service of a document pursuant to Article 7 shall be the date on which it is served in accordance with the law of the Member State addressed.

2. However, where a document shall be served within a particular period in the context of proceedings to be brought or pending in the Member State of origin, the date to be taken into account with respect to the applicant shall be that fixed by the law of that Member State.

3. A Member State shall be authorised to derogate from the provisions of paragraphs 1 and 2 for a transitional period of five years, for appropriate reasons.

This transitional period may be renewed by a Member State at five-yearly intervals due to reasons related to its legal system. That Member State shall inform the Commission of the content of such a derogation and the circumstances of the case.

[3537]

Article 10

Certificate of service and copy of the document served

1. When the formalities concerning the service of the document have been completed, a certificate of completion of those formalities shall be drawn up in the standard form in the Annex and addressed to the transmitting agency, together with, where Article 4(5) applies, a copy of the document served.

2. The certificate shall be completed in the official language or one of the official languages of the Member State of origin or in another language which the Member State of origin has indicated that it can accept. Each Member State shall indicate the official language or languages of the European Union other than its own which is or are acceptable to it for completion of the form.

[3538]

Article 11

Costs of service

1. The service of judicial documents coming from a Member State shall not give rise to any payment or reimbursement of taxes or costs for services rendered by the Member State addressed.

2. The applicant shall pay or reimburse the costs occasioned by:

(a) the employment of a judicial officer or of a person competent under the law of the Member State addressed;

(b) the use of a particular method of service.

[3539]

SECTION 2

OTHER MEANS OF TRANSMISSION AND SERVICE OF JUDICIAL DOCUMENTS

Article 12

Transmission by consular or diplomatic channels

Each Member State shall be free, in exceptional circumstances, to use consular or diplomatic channels to forward judicial documents, for the purpose of service, to those agencies of another Member State which are designated pursuant to Article 2 or 3.

[3540]

Article 13

Service by diplomatic or consular agents

1. Each Member State shall be free to effect service of judicial documents on persons residing in another Member State, without application of any compulsion, directly through its diplomatic or consular agents.

2. Any Member State may make it known, in accordance with Article 23(1), that it is opposed to such service within its territory, unless the documents are to be served on nationals of the Member State in which the documents originate.

[3541]

Article 14

Service by post

1. Each Member State shall be free to effect service of judicial documents directly by post to persons residing in another Member State.

2. Any Member State may specify, in accordance with Article 23(1), the conditions under which it will accept service of judicial documents by post.

[3542]

Article 15

Direct service

1. This Regulation shall not interfere with the freedom of any person interested in a judicial proceeding to effect service of judicial documents directly through the judicial officers, officials or other competent persons of the Member State addressed.

2. Any Member State may make it known, in accordance with Article 23(1), that it is opposed to the service of judicial documents in its territory pursuant to paragraph 1.

[3543]

CHAPTER III

EXTRAJUDICIAL DOCUMENTS

Article 16

Transmission

Extrajudicial documents may be transmitted for service in another Member State in accordance with the provisions of this Regulation.

[3544]

CHAPTER IV
FINAL PROVISIONS

Article 17

Implementing rules

The measures necessary for the implementation of this Regulation relating to the matters referred to below shall be adopted in accordance with the advisory procedure referred to in Article 18(2):

(a) drawing up and annually updating a manual containing the information provided by Member States in accordance with Article 2(4);

(b) drawing up a glossary in the official languages of the European Union of documents which may be served under this Regulation;

(c) updating or making technical amendments to the standard form set out in the Annex.

[3545]

Article 18

Committee

1. The Commission shall be assisted by a committee.

2. Where reference is made to this paragraph, Articles 3 and 7 of Decision 1999/468/EC shall apply.

3. The Committee shall adopt its rules of procedure.

[3546]

Article 19

Defendant not entering an appearance

1. Where a writ of summons or an equivalent document has had to be transmitted to another Member State for the purpose of service, under the provisions of this Regulation, and the defendant has not appeared, judgment shall not be given until it is established that:

(a) the document was served by a method prescribed by the internal law of the Member State addressed for the service of documents in domestic actions upon persons who are within its territory; or

(b) the document was actually delivered to the defendant or to his residence by another method provided for by this Regulation;

and that in either of these cases the service or the delivery was effected in sufficient time to enable the defendant to defend.

2. Each Member State shall be free to make it known, in accordance with Article 23(1), that the judge, notwithstanding the provisions of paragraph 1, may give judgment even if no certificate of service or delivery has been received, if all the following conditions are fulfilled:

(a) the document was transmitted by one of the methods provided for in this Regulation;

(b) a period of time of not less than six months, considered adequate by the judge in the particular case, has elapsed since the date of the transmission of the document;

(c) no certificate of any kind has been received, even though every reasonable effort has been made to obtain it through the competent authorities or bodies of the Member State addressed.

3. Notwithstanding paragraphs 1 and 2, the judge may order, in case of urgency, any provisional or protective measures.

4. When a writ of summons or an equivalent document has had to be transmitted to another Member State for the purpose of service, under the provisions of this Regulation, and a judgment has been entered against a defendant who has not appeared, the judge shall have the power to relieve the defendant from the effects of the expiration of the time for appeal from the judgment if the following conditions are fulfilled:

(a) the defendant, without any fault on his part, did not have knowledge of the document in sufficient time to defend, or knowledge of the judgment in sufficient time to appeal; and

(b) the defendant has disclosed a prima facie defence to the action on the merits.

An application for relief may be filed only within a reasonable time after the defendant has knowledge of the judgment.

Each Member State may make it known, in accordance with Article 23(1), that such application will not be entertained if it is filed after the expiration of a time to be stated by it in that communication, but which shall in no case be less than one year following the date of the judgment.

5. Paragraph 4 shall not apply to judgments concerning status or capacity of persons.

[3547]

Article 20

Relationship with agreements or arrangements to which Member States are Parties

1. This Regulation shall, in relation to matters to which it applies, prevail over other provisions contained in bilateral or multilateral agreements or arrangements concluded by the Member States, and in particular Article IV of the Protocol to the Brussels Convention of 1968 and the Hague Convention of 15 November 1965.

2. This Regulation shall not preclude individual Member States from maintaining or concluding agreements or arrangements to expedite further or simplify the transmission of documents, provided that they are compatible with this Regulation.

3. Member States shall send to the Commission:
   (a) a copy of the agreements or arrangements referred to in paragraph 2 concluded between the Member States as well as drafts of such agreements or arrangements which they intend to adopt; and
   (b) any denunciation of, or amendments to, these agreements or arrangements.

[3548]

Article 21

Legal aid

This Regulation shall not affect the application of Article 23 of the Convention on Civil Procedure of 17 July 1905, Article 24 of the Convention on Civil Procedure of 1 March 1954 or Article 13 of the Convention on International Access to Justice of 25 October 1980 between the Member States Parties to these Conventions.

[3549]

Article 22

Protection of information transmitted

1. Information, including in particular personal data, transmitted under this Regulation shall be used by the receiving agency only for the purpose for which it was transmitted.

2. Receiving agencies shall ensure the confidentiality of such information, in accordance with their national law.

3. Paragraphs 1 and 2 shall not affect national laws enabling data subjects to be informed of the use made of information transmitted under this Regulation.

4. This Regulation shall be without prejudice to Directives 95/46/EC and 97/66/EC.

[3550]

Article 23

Communication and publication

1. Member States shall communicate to the Commission the information referred to in Articles 2, 3, 4, 9, 10, 13, 14, 15, 17(a) and 19.

2. The Commission shall publish in the Official Journal of the European Communities the information referred to in paragraph 1.

[3551]

NOTE

The consolidated information communicated by the member states to the European Commission under this Article is reproduced at **[3558]**.

Article 24

Review

No later than 1 June 2004, and every five years thereafter, the Commission shall present to the European Parliament, the Council and the Economic and Social Committee a report on the application of this Regulation, paying special attention to the effectiveness of the bodies designated pursuant to Article 2 and to the practical application of point (c) of Article 3 and Article 9. The report shall be accompanied if need be by proposals for adaptations of this Regulation in line with the evolution of notification systems.

[3552]

Article 25

Entry into force

This Regulation shall enter into force on 31 May 2001.

This Regulation shall be binding in its entirety and directly applicable in the Member States in accordance with the Treaty establishing the European Community.

[3553]

Done at Brussels, 29 May 2000.

For the Council

The President

A COSTA

ANNEX

REQUEST FOR SERVICE OF DOCUMENTS

(Article 4(3) of Council Regulation (EC) No 1348/2000 on the service in the Member States of judicial and extrajudicial documents in civil or commercial matters[1]**)**

Reference No: ....

1. TRANSMITTING AGENCY
   1.1. Identity:
   1.2. Address:
      1.2.1. Street and number/PO box:
      1.2.2. Place and code:
      1.2.3. Country:
   1.3. Tel:
   1.4. Fax*:
   1.5. E-mail*
2. RECEIVING AGENCY
   2.1. Identity:
   2.2. Address:
      2.2.1. Street and number/PO box:
      2.2.2. Place and code:
      2.2.3. Country:
   2.3. Tel:
   2.4. Fax*:
   2.5. E-mail*:
3. APPLICANT
   3.1. Identity:
   3.2. Address:
      3.2.1. Street and number/PO box:
      3.2.2. Place and code:
      3.2.3. Country:
   3.3. Tel*:
   3.4. Fax*:

PART IV
EC MATERIALS

3.5. E-mail*:

4. ADDRESSEE

4.1. Identity:
4.2. Address:
4.2.1. Street and number/PO box:
4.2.2. Place and code:
4.2.3. Country:
4.3. Tel*:
4.4. Fax*:
4.5. E-mail*:

4.6. Identification number/social security number/organisation number/or equivalent*:

5. METHOD OF SERVICE

5.1. In accordance with the law of the Member State addressed
5.2. By the following particular method:
5.2.1. If this method is incompatible with the law of the Member State addressed, the document(s) should be served in accordance with the law:
5.2.1.1. yes
5.2.1.2. no

6. DOCUMENT TO BE SERVED

(a) 6.1. Nature of the document
6.1.1. judicial
6.1.1.1. writ of summons
6.1.1.2. judgment
6.1.1.3. appeal
6.1.1.4. other
6.1.2. extrajudicial
(b) 6.2. Date or time limit stated in the document*:
(c) 6.3. Language of document:
6.3.1. original DE, EN, DK, EL, FI, FR, GR, IT, NL, PT, SV, others:
6.3.2. translation* DE, EN, DK, ES, FI, FR, EL, IT, NL, PT, SV, others:
6.4. Number of enclosures:

7. A COPY OF DOCUMENT TO BE RETURNED WITH THE CERTIFICATE OF SERVICE (Article 4(5) of the Regulation)

7.1. Yes (in this case send two copies of the document to be served)
7.2. No

1. You are required by Article 7(2) of the Regulation to effect all steps required for service of the document as soon as possible. In any event, if it is not possible for you to effect service within one month of receipt, you must inform this agency by means of the certificate provided for in point 13.
2. If you cannot fulfil this request for service on the basis of the information or documents transmitted, you are required by Article 6(2) of the Regulation to contact this agency by the swiftest possible means in order to secure the missing information or document.

Done at:

Date:

Signature and/or stamp:

NOTES

1 OJ L160, 30.6.2000, p 37.
* This item is optional.

Reference No of the receiving agency:

ACKNOWLEDGEMENT OF RECEIPT

(Article 6(1) of Council Regulation (EC) No 1348/2000)

This acknowledgement must be sent by the swiftest possible means of transmission as soon as possible after receipt of the document and in any event within seven days of receipt.

8. DATE OF RECEIPT:

Done at:

Date:

Signature and/or stamp:

NOTICE OF RETURN OF REQUEST AND DOCUMENT

(Article 6(3) of Council Regulation (EC) No 1348/2000)

The request and document must be returned on receipt.

9. REASON FOR RETURN:
   9.1. The request is manifestly outside the scope of the Regulation:
      9.1.1. the document is not civil or commercial
      9.1.2. the service is not from one Member State to another Member State
   9.2. Non-compliance with formal conditions required makes service impossible:
      9.2.1. the document is not easily legible
      9.2.2. the language used to complete the form is incorrect
      9.2.3. the document received is not a true and faithful copy
      9.2.4. other (please give details):
   9.3. The method of service is incompatible with the law of that Member State (Article 7(1) of the Regulation)

Done at:

Date:

Signature and/or stamp:

NOTICE OF RETRANSMISSION OF REQUEST AND DOCUMENT TO THE APPROPRIATE RECEIVING AGENCY

(Article 6(4) of Council Regulation (EC) No 1348/2000)

The request and document were forwarded on to the following receiving agency, which has territorial jurisdiction to serve it:

10.1. Identity:

10.2. Address:
   10.2.1. Street and number/PO box:
   10.2.2. Place and code:

10.2.3. Country:

10.3. Tel:

10.4. Fax*:

10.5. E-mail*:

Done at:

Date:

Signature and/or stamp:

---

* This item is optional.

Reference No of the appropriate receiving agency:

NOTICE OF RECEIPT BY THE APPROPRIATE RECEIVING AGENCY HAVING TERRITORIAL JURISDICTION TO THE TRANSMITTING AGENCY

(Article 6(4) of Council Regulation (EC) No 1348/2000)

This notice must be sent by the swiftest possible means of transmission as soon as possible after receipt of the document and in any event within seven days of receipt.

11. DATE OF RECEIPT:

Done at:

Date:

Signature and/or stamp:

CERTIFICATE OF SERVICE OR NON-SERVICE OF DOCUMENTS

(Article 10 of Council Regulation (EC) No 1348/2000)

The service shall be effected as soon as possible. In any event, if it has not been possible to effect service within one month of receipt, the receiving agency shall inform the transmitting agency (according to Article 7(2) of the Regulation)

12. COMPLETION OF SERVICE

(a) 12.1. Date and address of service:

(b) 12.2. The document was

(A) 12.2.1. served in accordance with the law of the Member State addressed, namely

12.2.1.1. handed to

12.2.1.1.1. the addressee in person

12.2.1.1.2. another person

12.2.1.1.2.1. Name:

12.2.1.1.2.2. Address:

12.2.1.1.2.2.1. Street and number/PO box:

12.2.1.1.2.2.2. Place and code:

12.2.1.1.2.2.3. Country:

12.2.1.1.2.3. Relation to the addressee:

family employee others

12.2.1.1.3. the addressee's address

12.2.1.2. served by post
12.2.1.2.1. without acknowledgement of receipt
12.2.1.2.2. with the enclosed acknowledgement of receipt
12.2.1.2.2.1. from the addressee
12.2.1.2.2.2. another person
12.2.1.2.2.2.1. Name:
12.2.1.2.2.2.2. Address:
12.2.1.2.2.2.2.1. Street and number/PO box:
12.2.1.2.2.2.2.2. Place and code:
12.2.1.2.2.2.2.3. Country:
12.2.1.2.2.2.3. Relation to the addressee:
family employee others
12.2.1.3. other method (please say how):
(B) 12.2.2. served by the following particular method (please say how):

(c) 12.3. The addressee of the document was informed (orally) (in writing) that he or she may refuse to accept it if it was not in an official language of the place of service or in an official language of the state of transmission which he or she understands.

13. INFORMATION IN ACCORDANCE WITH ARTICLE 7(2)

It was not possible to effect service within one month of receipt.

14. REFUSAL OF DOCUMENT

The addressee refused to accept the document on account of the language used. The documents are annexed to this certificate.

15. REASON FOR NON-SERVICE OF DOCUMENT
15.1. Address unknown
15.2. Addressee cannot be located
15.3. Document could not be served before the date or time limit stated in point 6.2.
15.4. Others (please specify):

The documents are annexed to this certificate.

Done at:

Date:

Signature and/or stamp:

[3554]

COMMISSION DECISION

of 3 April 2002

amending Decision 2001/781/EC adopting a manual of receiving agencies and a glossary of documents that may be served under Council Regulation (EC) No 1348/2000 on the service in the Member States of judicial and extrajudicial documents in civil or commercial matters

(2002/350/EC)

NOTES

Date of publication in OJ: OJ L125, 13.5.2002, p 1. Amending Commission Decision 2001/781/EC (OJ L298, 15.11.2001, p 1; not reproduced here). Annexes I and II, which contain the manual and glossary referred to in the recitals below, runs to several hundred pages and are not reproduced here. See http://ec.europa.eu/justice_home/judicialatlascivil/html/ds_docs_en.htm#manual

THE COMMISSION OF THE EUROPEAN COMMUNITIES,

Having regard to the Treaty establishing the European Community,

Having regard to Council Regulation (EC) No 1348/2000 of 29 May 2000 on the service in the Member States of judicial and extrajudicial documents in civil or commercial matters,[1] and in particular points (a) and (b) of Article 17 thereof,

Whereas:

PART IV EC MATERIALS

(1) In order to implement Regulation (EC) No 1348/2000 it was necessary to draw up and publish a manual containing information about the receiving agencies provided for in Article 2 of that Regulation.

(2) Point (b) of Article 17 of Regulation (EC) No 1348/2000 also provides for a glossary to be drawn up in the official languages of the European Union of documents that may be served on the basis of the Regulation.

(3) In accordance with Regulation (EC) No 1348/2000, Commission Decision 2001/781/EC of 25 September 2001 adopting a manual of receiving agencies and a glossary of documents that may be served under Council Regulation (EC) No 1348/2000 on the service in the Member States of judicial and extrajudicial documents in civil or commercial matters[2] has been published in the Official Journal of the European Communities.

(4) The manual and the glossary need to be amplified by the information sent to the Commission by Germany.

(5) The measures provided for in this Decision are in accordance with the opinion of the committee established by Article 18 of Regulation (EC) No 1348/2000,

NOTES

1 OJ L160, 30.6.2000, p 37.
2 OJ L298, 15.11.2001, p 1.

[3555]

HAS ADOPTED THIS DECISION:

Article 1

Annex I to Decision 2001/781/EC (manual referred to in point (a) of Article 17 of Regulation (EC) No 1348/2000) is amended in accordance with Annex I to this Decision.

[3556]

Article 2

Annex II to Decision 2001/781/EC (glossary referred to in point (b) of Article 17 of Regulation (EC) No 1348/2000) is amended in accordance with Annex II to this Decision.

[3557]

This Decision is addressed to the Member States.

Done at Brussels, 3 April 2002.

CONSOLIDATED VERSION

Information communicated by Member States under Article 23 of Council Regulation (EC) No 1348/2000 of 29 May 2000 on the service in the Member States of judicial and extrajudicial documents in civil or commercial matters

Disclaimer:

Consolidation entails the integration of basic instruments of Community legislation, their amendments and corrections in single, non-official documents. Each document is intended for use as a documentation tool and the Institutions do not assume any liability for its content.

INTRODUCTION

This Official Journal contains some of the information which must be published pursuant to Article 23(2) of Regulation (EC) No 1348/2000.[1] This is the information communicated by Member States pursuant to Articles 2 (transmitting agencies), 3, 4, 9, 10, 13, 14, 15 and 19 of Regulation (EC) No 1348/2000. The information concerning receiving agencies is published separately in a manual.[2]

It should be pointed out that the Regulation does not apply to Denmark.

As regards Article 14, the fact that a Member State has not communicated a specific language requirement means implicitly that the language requirements of Article 8 are applicable.

[3558]

NOTES

1 OJ L160, 30.6.2000, p 37.
2 OJ L298, 15.11.2001, p 1.

BELGIUM

Article 2 – Transmitting agencies

1. Clerks of cantonal courts and local criminal courts
2. Clerks of courts of first instance
3. Clerks of commercial courts
4. Clerks of labour tribunals
5. Clerks of courts of appeal and labour courts
6. Clerks of Court of Cassation
7. Public prosecutor's office including office representing the public interest in labour matters
8. Bailiffs.

Article 3 – Central body

The central body is the National Bailiffs' Association of Belgium.

Chambre Nationale des Huissiers de Justice de Belgique/Nationale Kamer van Gerechtsdeurwaarders van België
Avenue Henri Jaspar 93/Henri Jasparlaan 93
B-1060 Brussels

Tel (32–2) 538 00 92
Fax (32–2) 539 41 11
E-mail: Chambre.Nationale@huissiersdejustice.be
Nationale.Kamer@gerechtsdeurwaarders.be

Information may be sent by post, fax, e-mail or telephone.

Knowledge of languages: French, Dutch, German and English.

Article 4 – Transmission of documents

Apart from French, Dutch and German, Belgium will accept standard request forms which are completed in English.

Article 9 – Date of service

Belgium intends to derogate from the system provided for in Article 9(1) and (2) by extending the scope of paragraph 2, which would then read:

"However, regarding the service of a judicial or extrajudicial document, the date to be taken into account with respect to the applicant shall be that fixed by the law of the Member State of origin".

Justification

Belgium believes that fixing the date of notification of the document is justifiable on the ground of legal certainty from the applicant's point of view and that it is not prejudicial to the protection of the other party as stipulated by Article 9(1).

In its present form, paragraph 2 can adversely affect the rights of the applicant since, even where the law does not stipulate a time limit for action, it is important to acknowledge the effect of service of a judicial or extrajudicial document.

If a party to an action who has lost the case in a court of first instance wishes to appeal, for instance, they must be able to do so without awaiting formal notification of the judgment.

The same is true if a person wishing to interrupt a limitation period effects service of an extrajudicial document.

Article 10 – Certificate of service and copy of the document served

Apart from French, Dutch and German, Belgium will accept certificates completed in English.

Article 13 – Service by diplomatic or consular agents

Belgium is opposed to the exercise in its territory of the right conferred by Article 13(1).

Article 14 – Service by post

Belgium accepts service of judicial documents by post on the following conditions:

— registered letter with acknowledgement of receipt or equivalent;
— need for translation in accordance with Article 8;
— use of the following form:

"Service by post – Article 14 of Council Regulation (EC) No 1348/2000 on the service in the Member States of judicial and extrajudicial documents in civil or commercial matters.[3]

Reference number:

1. TRANSMITTING AGENCY
 1.1. Name:
 1.2. Address:
  1.2.1. Street and number/PO box:
  1.2.2. Place and post code:
  1.2.3. Country:
 1.3. Tel:
 1.4. Fax:[4]
 1.5. E-mail:[5]
2. APPLICANT
 2.1. Name:
 2.2. Address:
  2.2.1. Street and number/PO box:
  2.2.2. Place and post code:
  2.2.3. Country:
 2.3. Tel:
 2.4. Fax:[6]
 2.5. E-mail:[7]
3. ADDRESSEE
 3.1. Name:
 3.2. Address:
  3.2.1. Street and number/PO box:
  3.2.2. Place and post code
  3.2.3. Country
 3.3. Tel:
 3.4. Fax:[8]
 3.5. E-mail:[9]
 3.6. Identification number/social security number/organisation number/or equivalent:[10]
4. METHOD OF SERVICE: by post
5. DOCUMENT TO BE SERVED BY POST
 (a) 5.1. Nature of document
  5.1.1. judicial
   5.1.1.1. writ of summons
   5.1.1.2. judgment
   5.1.1.3. appeal
   5.1.1.4. other
  5.1.2. extrajudicial
 (b) 5.2. Language of document
  5.2.1. original; DE, EN, DA, ES, FI, FR, EL, IT, NL, PT, SV, other:
  5.2.2.[11] translation: DE, EN, DA, ES, FI, FR, EL, IT, NL, PT, SV, other:
 (c) Number of enclosures

6.1. USE OF LANGUAGES

L'entité d'origine informe le destinataire qu'il peut refuser l'acte s'il n'est pas rédigé dans la ou l'une des langues du lieu de signification ou de notification ou dans une langue de l'Etat d'origine qu'il comprend et qu'il y a lieu de renvoyer l'acte à l'entité d'origine en précisant la raison du refus.

El organismo transmisor informa al destinatario del documento de que puede negarse a aceptarlo si no está redactado en una lengua oficial del lugar de notificación o traslado o en una lengua del Estado de transmisión que el destinatario entienda, y que en tal caso procede devolver el documento al organismo transmisor, precisando la razón del rechazo.

Den fremsendende instans underretter modtageren om, at han kan afvise dokumentet, hvis det ikke er affattet på (et af) forkyndelsesstedets sprog, eller på et sprog i det fremsendende land, som han forstår, og at dokumentet skal sendes tilbage til den fremsendende instans med nærmere angivelse af årsagen til afvisningen.

Der Empfänger wird von der Übermittlungsstelle davon in Kenntnis gesetzt, dass er die Annahme des Schriftstücks verweigern darf, wenn es nicht in der oder einer der Sprache(n) des Zustellungsorts oder in einer Sprache des Übermittlungsstaats abgefasst ist, die er nicht versteht, und dass das Schriftstück an die Übermittlungsstelle unter Angabe des Annahmeverweigerungsgrunds zurückzusenden ist.

Η υπηρεσία διαβίβασης ενημερώνει τον παραλήπτη ότι μπορεί να αρνηθεί την παραλαβή της πράξης εφόσον αυτί δεν έχει συνταχθεί στη γλώςςα ή σε μία από τις γλώσσες του τόπου κοινοποίησης ή επίδοσης ή σε γλώσςα του κράτους μέλους διαβίβασης την οποία ο παραλήπτης κατανοεί και ότι μπορεί να παραπέμψει την πράξη στην υπηρεσία διαβίβασης διευκρινίζοντας το λόγο άρνησης της παραλαβής.

The transmitting agency informs addressees that they may reject the document if it is not drafted in the language or one of the languages of the place of service or in a language of the State of origin which they understand and that they should return the document to the transmitting agency explaining why it has been rejected.

L'organo mittente informa il destinatario dell'atto che può rifiutare di riceverlo se non è redatto in una delle lingue ufficiali del luogo di notificazione o comunicazione o in una lingua ufficiale dello Stato membro mittente di sua comprensione e che può rinviarlo all'organo mittente precisando le ragioni del suo rifiuto.

De verzendende instantie deelt de geadresseerde mede dat hij het stuk kan weigeren indien dit niet is gesteld in de taal of één van de talen van de plaats van betekening of kennisgeving of in een taal van de staat van herkomst die hij begrijpt, en dat het stuk aan de verzendende instantie moet worden teruggezonden met vermelding van de redenen van de weigering.

A entidade de origem informa o destinatário que pode recusar o acto se este não estiver redigido na língua ou numa das línguas do local da citação ou notificação ou numa língua do Estado de origem que o destinatário compreenda, devendo o acto ser remetido à entidade de origem, indicando-se a razão da recusa.

Lähettävän viranomaisen on ilmoitettava vastaanottajalle, että tämä voi kieltäytyä vastaanottamasta asiakirjaa, jollei sitä ole laadittu tiedoksiantomaan kielellä tai sellaisella lähettävän maan kielellä, jota vastaanottaja ymmärtää, ja että asiakirja on tällöin palautettava lähettävälle viranomaiselle ja perusteltava, miksi sitä ei ole otettu vastaan.

Det sändande organet skall upplysa mottagaren om att denne har rätt att vägra ta emot handlingen om den inte är avfattad på det eller de språk som används där delgivningen sker eller på språket i ursprungslandet, det senare under förutsättning att mottagaren förstår det språket. Det skall också anges att mottagaren skall skicka tillbaka handlingen till det sändande organet, med uppgift om varför han eller hon vägrat ta emot den.

Done at:
Date:
Signature and/or stamp:"

Article 15 – Direct service

Belgium does not oppose the possibility of direct service provided for by Article 15(1).

Article 19 – Defendant not entering an appearance

Courts in Belgium, notwithstanding paragraph 1, may give judgment if all the conditions of paragraph 2 are met.

An application for relief provided for by paragraph 4 may be entertained within one year after the judgment has been given.

[3559]

NOTES

[3] OJ C160, 30.6.2000, p 37.
[4] Optional.
[5] Optional.
[6] Optional.
[7] Optional.
[8] Optional.
[9] Optional.
[10] Optional.
[11] Optional.

CZECH REPUBLIC

Article 2 – Transmitting agencies

Transmitting agencies designated: District courts, regional courts, high courts, the Supreme Court, the Supreme Administrative Court, court executors, district state prosecution offices, regional state prosecution offices, high state prosecution offices, the Supreme State Prosecution Office.

Article 3 – Central body

Ministry of Justice
International Department

Address:
Ministerstvo spravedlnosti
mezinárodní odbor
Vyšehradská 16
128 10 Praha 2

Phone: +420-221-997-157
Fax: +420-224-911-365
Email: posta@msp.justice.cz

Article 4 – Transmission of documents

Apart from Czech, the Czech Republic will accept standard request forms that are completed in Slovak, English or German.

Article 9 – Date of service

The Czech Republic does not intend to derogate from Article 9(1) and 9(2).

Article 10 – Certificate of service and copy of the document served

Apart from Czech, the Czech Republic will accept certificates completed in Slovak, English or German.

Article 13 – Service by diplomatic or consular agents

The Czech Republic does not oppose the possibility of a Member State serving judicial documents on person residing in the Czech Republic, without any compulsion, direct through its diplomatic or consular agents together with translation of the document in the language of receiving person.

Article 14 – Service by post

The Czech Republic accepts service of judicial documents by post on the following conditions:

1. The documents are served in a registered letter with acknowledgment of receipt or equivalent.
2. The documents served are in Czech or accompanied with official translation into Czech or the documents are in one of the official languages of the Member State from which the documents are served where the addressee is a national of the Member State in question.

Article 15 – Direct service

The Czech Republic is opposed to this form of service in its territory.

Article 19 – Defendant not entering an appearance

Courts in the Czech Republic, notwithstanding Article 19(1) may give judgment even if no certificate of service or delivery has been received, if all the conditions of Art 19(2) are met.

There is no time limit within the meaning of the last subparagraph of the Article 19(4) for filling an application for relief from the effects of the expiration of the time for appeal.

Article 20 – Agreements or arrangements to which Member States are Parties

The Commission will be provided with the texts of the following treaties:

— Treaty between the Czechoslovak Socialist Republic and Polish Peoples' Republic on legal aid and settlement of legal relations in civil, family, labor and criminal matters, signed at Warsaw on 21 December 1987, in force between the Czech Republic and Poland

— Treaty between the Czechoslovak Socialist Republic and Hungarian Peoples' Republic on legal aid and settlement of legal relations in civil, family and criminal matters, signed at Bratislava on 28 March 1989, in force between the Czech Republic and Hungary

— Treaty between the Czech Republic and Slovak Republic on legal aid provided by judicial bodies and on settlements of certain legal relations in civil and criminal matters, signed at Prague on 29 October 1992

— Treaty between the Czech Republic and Germany on further facilitation of legal aid provision based on Hague Conventions relating to civil procedure, concluded on the 1st March 1954, and on the Service Abroad of Judicial and Extrajudicial Documents in Civil or Commercial Matters, concluded on the 15th November 1965, and on the Taking of Evidence Abroad in Civil or Commercial Matters, concluded on the 18th March 1970

[3560]

GERMANY

Article 2 – Transmitting agencies

The transmitting agency for judicial documents is the court serving the document (Section 1069(1), point 1, of the Zivilprozessordnung [ZPO]).

The transmitting agency for extrajudicial documents is the district court (Amtsgericht) of the district (Bezirk) in which the person serving the document is domiciled or habitually resident; in the case of notarised deeds, it is also the district court of the district in which the office of the notarising notary is located; in the case of legal persons, it is the district court of the district in which the head office is located; The Land Governments may, by statutory order, allocate the tasks of transmitting agency for the districts of several district courts to a single district court (Section 1069(1), point 1, of the Zivilprozessordnung).

Article 3 – Central bodies

The task of the central body is performed in each Land by one of the bodies determined by the Land Government (Section 1069(3) of the Zivilprozessordnung).

List of central bodies alongside the available means of communication

The postal address should first indicate – where available – the post code and locality and/or the post box number.

For letter post, the post code and locality should be indicated with, where available, the postal box number.

For express items and packages (including small packages), the street address should be used.

		Postal address	Street address
A.	**BADEN-WÜRTTEMBERG**		
Tel	(49–761) 205–0	Amtsgericht Freiburg	Amtsgericht Freiburg

PART IV EC MATERIALS

Fax (49–761) 205–18 04 e-mail: Poststelle@AGFreiburg.justiz.bwl.de	D-79095 Freiburg im Breisgau	Holzmarkt 2 D-79098 Freiburg im Breisgau
B. BAVARIA Tel (49–89) 55 97–01 Fax (49–89) 55 97–23 22 e-mail: poststelle@stmj.bayern.de	Bayerisches Staatsministerium der Justiz D-80097 München	Bayerisches Staatsministerium der Justiz Justizpalast Prielmayerstraße 7 D-80335 München
C. BERLIN Tel (49–30) 90 13–0 Fax (49 30) 90 13–20 00 e-mail: poststelle@senjust.verwalt-berlin.de	Senatsverwaltung für Justiz Salzburger Straße 21–25 D-10825 Berlin	Senatsverwaltung für Justiz Salzburger Straße 21–25 D-10825 Berlin
D. BRANDENBURG Tel (49–331) 866–0 Fax (49–331) 866–30 80/30 81 e-mail: Poststelle@mdje.brandenburg.de	Ministerium der Justiz und für Europaangelegenheiten des Landes Brandenburg D-14460 Potsdam	Ministerium der Justiz und für Europaangelegenheiten des Landes Brandenburg Heinrich-Mann-Allee 107 D-14473 Potsdam
E. BREMEN Tel (49–421) 361 42 04 Fax (49–421) 361 67 13 e-mail: office@landgericht.bremen.de	Landgericht Bremen Postfach 10 78 43 D-28078 Bremen	Landgericht Bremen Domsheide 16 D-28195 Bremen
F. HAMBURG Tel (49–40) 428 43–0 Fax (49–40) 428 43–23 83 e-mail: poststelle@ag.justiz.hamburg.de	Amtsgericht Hamburg D-20348 Hamburg	Amtsgericht Hamburg Sievekingplatz 1 D-20355 Hamburg
G. HESSE Tel (49–611) 32–0 Fax (49–611) 32–27 63 e-mail: poststelle@hmdj.hessen.de	Die Präsidentin oder der Präsident des Oberlandesgericht Frankfurt am Main Postfach 10 01 01 D-60313 Frankfurt am Main	Die Präsidentin oder der Präsident des Oberlandesgericht Frankfurt am Main Zeil 42 D-60313 Frankfurt am Main
H. MECKLENBURG-EASTERN POMERANIA Tel (49–385) 588–0	Justizministerium	Justizministerium

Fax	(49–611) 588–34 53	Mecklenburg-Vorpommern	Mecklenburg-Vorpommern
e-mail:	poststelle@jm.mv-regierung.de	D-19048 Schwerin	Demmlerplatz 14
			D-19053 Schwerin
I.	**LOWER SAXONY**		
Tel	(49–511) 120–0	Niedersächsisches	Niedersächsisches
Fax	(49–511) 120–51 70/51 85	Justizministerium	Justizministerium
e-mail:	Henning.Baum@mj.niedersachsen.de	Postfach 201	Waterlooplatz 1
		D-30002 Hannover	D-30169 Hannover
J.	**NORTH RHINE-WESTPHALIA**		
Tel	(49–211) 49 71–0	Oberlandesgericht Düsseldorf	Oberlandesgericht Düsseldorf
Fax	(49–211) 49 71–548	Postfach 30 02 10	Cecilienallee 3
e-mail:	poststelle@olg-duesseldorf.nrw.de	D-40402 Düsseldorf	D-40474 Düsseldorf
K.	**RHINELAND-PALATINATE**		
Tel	(49–6131) 16–0	Ministerium der Justiz	Ministerium der Justiz
Fax	(49–6131) 16–48 87	Postfach 32 60	Ernst-Ludwig-Straße 3
e-mail:	poststelle@min.jm.rlp.de	D-55022 Mainz	D-55116 Mainz
L.	**SAARLAND**		
Tel	(49–681) 501–00	Ministerium der Justiz	Ministerium der Justiz
Fax	(49–681) 501–58 55	Postfach 10 24 51	Zähringerstraße 12
e-mail:	poststelle@justiz.saarland.de	D-66024 Saarbrücken	D-66119 Saarbrücken
M.	**SAXONY**		
Tel	(49–351) 446–0	Oberlandesgericht Dresden	Oberlandesgericht Dresden
Fax	(49–351) 446–1299	Postfach 12 07 32	Schlossplatz 1
e-mail:	verwaltung-olg@olg.justiz.sachsen.de	D-01008 Dresden	D-01067 Dresden
N.	**SAXONY-ANHALT**		
Tel	(49–391) 567–01	Ministerium der Justiz	Ministerium der Justiz
Fax	(49–391) 567–61 80	Postfach 34 29	Hegelstr 40–42
e-mail:	Altrichter@mj.lsa-net.de	D-39043 Magdeburg	D-39104 Magdeburg
O.	**SCHLESWIG-HOLSTEIN**		
Tel	(49–431) 988–0	Ministerium für Justiz, Frauen, Jugend und Familie	Ministerium für Justiz, Frauen, Jugend und Familie
Fax	(49–431) 988–38 70	Lorentzendamm 35	Lorentzendamm 35
e-mail:	poststelle@jumi.landsh.de	D-24103 Kiel	D-24103 Kiel

P. THURINGIA	Thüringer Justizministerium	Thüringer Justizministerium
Tel (49–361) 37 95–000		
Fax (49–361) 37 95–888	Postfach 10 01 51	Werner-Seelenbinder-Straße 5
e-mail: poststelle@tjm.thueringen.de	D-99001 Erfurt	D-99096 Erfurt

Territorial competence

A. Baden-Württemberg

B. Bavaria

C. Berlin

D. Brandenburg

E. Bremen

F. Hamburg

G. Hesse

H. Mecklenburg-Eastern Pomerania

I. Lower Saxony

J. North Rhine-Westphalia

K. Rhineland-Palatinate

L. Saarland

M. Saxony

N. Saxony-Anhalt

O. Schleswig-Holstein

P. Thuringia

The following means of communication are available:

For receipt and dispatch: post, including private courier services, fax.

For other communications: telephone and e-mail.

Apart from German, English is permitted.

Article 4 – Transmission of documents

The form (request) may be completed in German or English.

Article 9 – Date of service

The Federal Republic of Germany does not currently intend to derogate from Article 9(1) or (2).

Article 10 – Certificate of service and copy of the document served

The form (certificate) may be completed in German or English.

Article 13 – Service by diplomatic or consular agents

In the territory of the Federal Republic of Germany, service by diplomatic or consular agents within the meaning of Article 13(1) of the Regulation is not allowed unless the document is to be served on a national of the transmitting State (Section 1067 of the Zivilprozessordnung).

Article 14 – Service by post

In the territory of the Federal Republic of Germany, direct service by post within the meaning of Article 14(1) of the Regulation is accepted only in the form of registered letter with advice of delivery and only on the further condition that the document to be served is in one of the following languages or accompanied by a translation into one of the following languages:

German or one of the official languages of the transmitting State, if the addressee is a national of that State (Section 1068(2) of the Zivilprozessordnung).

Article 15 – Direct service

In the territory of the Federal Republic of Germany, direct service within the meaning of Article 15(1) of the Regulation is not allowed (Section 1071 of the Zivilprozessordnung).

Article 19 – Defendant not entering an appearance

Where the conditions of Article 19(2) are fulfilled, German courts may give judgment where a writ of summons or equivalent document has been publicly served in the Federal Republic of Germany.

No application may be entertained for the restoration of the original situation within the meaning of Article 19(4) of the Regulation more than one year after the end of the missed deadline.

[3561]

ESTONIA

Article 2 – Transmitting agencies

The transmitting and receiving agency for judicial documents is the Ministry of Justice.

Ministry of Justice
Tõnismägi 5a
15191 Tallinn
Estonia

Tel (372) 6 208 100
Fax (372) 6 208 109
e-mail: info@just.ee

The following means of communication are available:

— for receipt and dispatch of documents: post, including private courier services,

— for other communications: telephone and e-mail.

Apart from Estonian, English is permitted.

Article 3 – Central body

The central authority is the Ministry of Justice.

Ministry of Justice
Tõnismägi 5a
15191 Tallinn
Estonia

Article 4 – Transmission of documents

The form (request) may be completed in Estonian or English.

Article 9 – Date of service

The Republic of Estonia does not currently intend to derogate from Article 9(1) or (2).

Article 10 – Certificate of service and copy of the document served

The Republic of Estonia accepts the form in English in addition to Estonian.

Article 13 – Service by diplomatic or consular agents

In the territory of the Republic of Estonia, service by diplomatic or consular agents within the meaning of Article 13(1) of the Regulation is allowed.

Article 14 – Service by post

In the territory of the Republic of Estonia, direct service by post within the meaning of Article 14(1) of the Regulation is accepted only in the form of registered letter with advice of delivery and only on the further condition that the document to be served is in one of the following languages or accompanied by a translation into one of the following languages: Estonian or one of the official languages of the transmitting State witch the addressee understands.

Article 15 – Direct service

In the territory of the Republic of Estonia, direct service within the meaning of Article 15(1) of the Regulation is not allowed.

Article 19 – Defendant not entering an appearance

Where the conditions of Article 19(2) are fulfilled, Estonian courts may give judgment.

According to Article 19(4) of the Regulation no application may be entertained more than one year after the end of the missed deadline.

[3562]

GREECE

Article 2 – Transmitting agencies

The transmitting agencies are the public prosecutors' offices of the Supreme Court, the courts of appeal and the courts of first instance.

Article 3 – Central body

The central body is the Ministry of Justice.

Ministry of Justice
Υπουργείο Δικαιοσύνης/Ipourgio Dikeosinis
Section of International Judicial Cooperation in Civil Cases
96 Mesogeion Av
11527 Athens Greece

Tel: (+30) 210 7767321
Fax: (+30) 210 7767499
e-mail: minjust8@otenet.gr

The persons responsible at the central body are Mrs Argyro Eleftheriadou.

Apart from Greek, they have a knowledge of English.

Article 4 – Transmission of documents

Apart from Greek, Greece will accept standard request forms which are completed in English or French.

Article 9 – Date of service

Greece will not be derogating from Article 9(1) and (2).

Article 10 – Certificate of service and copy of the document served

Apart from Greek, Greece will accept certificates completed in English or French.

Article 13 – Service by diplomatic or consular agents

Greece has no reservations to formulate regarding this Article.

Article 14 – Service by post

Service of judicial documents by post is accepted on the condition that the letter is registered and is delivered to the person to whom it is addressed or to his or her authorised legal representative or spouse, or to a child, a brother or sister, or a parent of the addressee.

Article 15 – Direct service

Greece has no reservations to formulate regarding this Article.

Article 19 – Defendant not entering an appearance

The courts in Greece, notwithstanding paragraph 1, are not bound to give judgment if all the conditions of paragraph 2 are met.

An application for relief provided for by paragraph 4 may be entertained within three years after the judgment has been given.

[3563]

SPAIN

Article 2 – Transmitting agencies

The transmitting agencies in Spain are the "*Secretarios Judiciales de los distintos Juzgados y Tribunales*".

Article 3 – Central body

The central body designated by Spain is the Directorate for International Legal Cooperation in the Ministry of Justice.

Subdirección General de Cooperación Jurídica Internacional
Ministerio de Justicia
C/San Bernardo, 62
E-28015 Madrid

Fax (34) 913 90 44 57

The means of receipt currently accepted is postal delivery.

Knowledge of languages: Spanish, English and French.

Article 4 – Transmission of documents

Apart from Spanish, Spain will accept standard request forms which are completed in English, French or Portuguese.

Article 9 – Date of service

In accordance with Article 9(3), Spain will not apply the provisions of Article 9(2).

The grounds for this derogation reside in the need for legal certainty and the right to effective legal protection. The Spanish legal system cannot allow a date of service to be taken other than that stipulated in Article 9(1), namely the date on which the document is served to the addressee in accordance with the law of the Member State addressed.

In Spain no civil action is subject to a specific time-limit; the time-limits for the action will run from the day after the date on which the document is served.

Article 10 – Certificate of service and copy of the document served

For the certificate referred to in Article 10 no other language is accepted.

Article 13 – Service by diplomatic or consular agents

Spain does not oppose the possibility of service through diplomatic or consular agents in the conditions laid down in Article 13(1).

Article 14 – Service by post

Spain accepts service of judicial documents by means of postal delivery, with acknowledgement of receipt. The translation rules in Articles 5 and 8 of the Regulation must also be complied with.

Article 15 – Direct service

Spain does not oppose the possibility of direct service provided for by Article 15(1).

Article 19 – Defendant not entering an appearance

Spain makes it known that the courts may lift the suspension of proceedings that has been decided and give judgment, notwithstanding Article 19(1), if the conditions of Article 19(2) are met.

With regard to the court's power to relieve the defendant from the effects of expiry of the time allowed for appeal, Spain makes it known that an application for such relief will not be entertained if it is filed more than one year following the date of the judgment.

[3564]

FRANCE

Article 2 – Transmitting agencies

1. Bailiffs

2. The court departments (registries, secretariats, etc.) responsible for the service of documents.

Article 3 – Central body

The central body is the Office for Judicial Cooperation in Civil and Commercial Matters.

Direction des Affaires Civiles et du Sceau
Bureau de l'entraide civile et commerciale internationale
13, place Vendôme
F-75042 Paris Cedex 01

Tel: 00 33 (0)1 44 77 61 05
Fax: 00 33 (0)1 44 77 61 22
E-Mail: Entraide-civile-internationale@justice.gouv.fr

Knowledge of languages: French and English.

Article 4 – Transmission of documents

Apart from French, France will accept standard request forms which are completed in English.

Article 9 – Date of service

France intends to derogate from Article 9(2).

Content of the derogation:

France intends to extend the scope of Article 9(2) by dispensing with the following two conditions:

— That the document is being served in the context of proceedings;
— That the document must be served within a specified period.

Consequently, Article 9(2) should read as follows: "However, regarding the service of a judicial or extrajudicial document, the date to be taken into account with respect to the applicant shall be that fixed by the law of the Member State of origin".

Grounds for the derogation:

For the applicant, the date of service will be the date of transmission of the document by the French transmitting agency.

That date applies in the case not only of procedural documents but of also of extrajudicial documents and bailiffs' documents specified by law in order to fix a definite date of service where that is a condition of the preservation or exercise of a right.

This applies in particular to commercial leases (notice of termination, continuation of lease, change of purpose of lease) or agricultural leases (notice of termination, right to recover the property, pre-emption) and to securities or execution procedures (execution or ejection).

Moreover, legal effects may flow from the date of a document where the date of notification is not fixed by law both in the case of judicial documents, where, for example, time-limits for appeals begin from the date of service, and of extrajudicial documents, for example, an order for payment, which can interrupt a limitation period or give rise to liability to interest on arrears.

In those cases it is important for legal certainty that applicants should be informed quickly of a definite date of service.

Article 10 – Certificate of service and copy of the document served

Apart from French, France will accept certificates completed in English.

Article 13 – Service by diplomatic or consular agents

France does not intend to oppose the exercise in its territory of the right conferred by Article 13(1).

Article 14 – Service by post

Service will be accepted by registered letter with a form for acknowledgement of receipt and a schedule of the documents being sent or any other method ensuring certainty as to the date of sending and receipt and the items sent.

Article 15 – Direct service

France does not oppose the possibility of direct service provided for by Article 15(1).

Article 19 – Defendant not entering an appearance

Courts in France, notwithstanding paragraph 1, may give judgment if all the conditions of paragraph 2 are met.

An application for relief provided for by paragraph 4 may be entertained within one year after the judgment has been given.

[3565]

IRELAND

Article 2 – Transmitting agencies

In Ireland, the transmitting agencies will be county registrars, who are 26 in number and who are attached to the Circuit Court office in each county.

Article 3 – Central body

The Master,
The High Court,
Four Courts
Dublin 7
Ireland

Communications in English or Irish may be effected by post, or by fax to the Central Office of the High Court at (353–1) 872 56 69. Communication by telephone to the Central Office of the High Court at (353–1) 888 60 00 is also possible.

Article 4 – Transmission of documents

Ireland accepts the application form (standard form) in English or Gaelic.

Article 9 – Date of service

Ireland intends to derogate from the provisions of this Article. There are difficulties associated with the idea that different dates of service may, in certain circumstances, apply as between applicant and addressee and the introduction at this time of a rule of the kind provided for in this Article, particularly in view of the lack of clarity which surrounds its formulation, would not accord with current legal practice.

Article 10 – Certificate of service and copy of the document served

Ireland accepts the certificate form in English or Gaelic.

Article 13 – Service by diplomatic or consular agents

Ireland does not oppose this.

Article 14 – Service by post

Ireland accepts the service of judicial documents by post where delivery is effected by pre-paid registered post by a company which returns undelivered mail.

Article 15 – Direct service

In relation to paragraph 2 of this Article, Ireland does not object to the possibility that any person interested in a judicial proceeding may effect service of judicial documents directly through a solicitor in Ireland.

Article 19 – Defendant not entering an appearance

Notwithstanding the provisions of paragraph 1, a court in Ireland may give judgment even if no certificate of service or delivery has been received, if all the conditions set out in paragraph 2 have been fulfilled.

In relation to Article 19(4), it is for the court to satisfy itself that the application for relief has been filed within a reasonable time after the defendant had knowledge of the judgment.
[3566]

ITALY

Article 2 – Transmitting agencies

1. Central offices of bailiffs at courts of appeal

2. Central offices of bailiffs at ordinary courts other than appeal courts and their separate chambers.

Article 3 – Central body

The central body is the Central Office of Bailiffs at the Rome Court of Appeal.

Ufficio Unico degli Ufficiali Giudiziari presso la Corte di Appello di Roma
Viale Giulio Cesare N. 52
I-00192 Roma

Tel (39)06.328361
Fax (39)06.328367933

Documents to be served in Italy must arrive by post and will be returned to the transmitting agencies by the same means.

Knowledge of languages: Italian, English and French.

Article 4 – Transmission of documents

Apart from Italian, Italy will accept standard request forms which are completed in English or French.

Article 9 – Date of service

No derogation is invoked.

Article 10 – Certificate of service and copy of the document served

Apart from Italian, Italy will accept certificates completed in English or French.

Article 13 – Service by diplomatic or consular agents

Italy is opposed to the service of judicial documents on persons residing in another Member State directly by diplomatic or consular agents (except where the document is served on an Italian national residing in another Member State).

Italy is opposed to the service of judicial documents by the diplomatic or consular agents of a Member State on persons residing in Italy, except where the document is to be served on a national of the Member State in question.

Article 14 – Service by post

Service of documents by post is accepted provided that they are accompanied by an Italian translation.

Article 15 – Direct service

There is nothing to prevent any person interested in a judicial proceeding effecting service of judicial documents directly through the competent officials of the Member State addressed.

Article 19 – Defendant not entering an appearance

Italy does not intend to make the statements provided for by paragraphs 2 and 4.
[3567]

CYPRUS

Article 2 – Transmitting agencies

(a) Names and addresses, telephone and fax numbers, email

Cyprus (all districts): Ministry of Justice and Public Order

Υπουργείο Δικαιοσύνης και Δημοσίας Τάξεως (Ministry of Justice and Public Order)
Λεωφόρος Αθαλάσσας (Athalassas Avenue 125)
CY-1461 Λευκωσία [Lefkosia (Nicosia)]
Κύπρος (Cyprus)

Tel: (357) 22 805928
Fax: (357) 22 518328
e-mail: emorphaki@mjpo.gov.cy

(b) Geographical areas of jurisdiction

All areas of the Republic of Cyprus

(c) Means of receipt of documents available to them

Post, fax, email

(d) Languages that may be used for completion of the standard form

Greek and English

Article 3 – Central body

(a) Name and Address, telephone and fax numbers, email

Ministry of Justice and Public Order

Υπουργείο Δικαιοσύνης και Δημοσίας Τάξεως (Ministry of Justice and Public Order)
Λεωφόρος Αθαλάσσας (Athalassas Avenue 125)
CY-1461 Λευκωσία [Lefkosia (Nicosia)]
Κύπρος (Cyprus)

Tel: (357) 22 805928
Fax: (357) 22 518328
E-mail: emorphaki@mjpo.gov.cy

(b) Geographical areas of jurisdiction: not applicable

(c) Means of receipt/communication available and language skills

Post, fax, email – Greek and English

Article 4 – Transmission of documents

English

Article 9 – Date of service

No

Article 10 – Certificate of service and copy of the document served

English

Article 13 – Service by diplomatic or consular agents

No opposition

Article 14 – Service by post

Service must be effected by registered post

Article 15 – Direct service

No opposition

Article 19 – Defendant not entering an appearance

— it would be possible at the Court's discretion, at he request of the applicant
— one year, as provided by para 4 of this Article, since at present there exists no specific period for such relief and it is left at the discretion of the Court provided that it is sought within a reasonable time after the defendant has knowledge of the judgment

Article 20 – Agreements or arrangements to which Member States are Parties

None

[3568]

LATVIA

Article 2 – Transmitting agencies

The transmitting and receiving agency for judicial documents is the Ministry of Justice.

Ministry of Justice
Bvld Brivibas 36
LV-1536, Riga
Latvia

Tel (371) 7036716
Fax (371) 7 210823
e-mail: tm.kanceleja@tm.gov.lv

Article 3 – Central body

The central body is the Ministry of Justice of the Republic of Latvia.

Postal address:

Ministry of Justice
Bvld Brivibas 36
LV-1536, Riga
Latvia

Tel (+371) 7036736
(+371) 7036738
Fax (+371) 210823
E-mail: tm.kanceleja@tm.gov.lv

Article 4 – Transmission of documents

Latvia accepts standard request forms, which are completed in Latvian or English.

Article 9 – Date of service

Latvia will not be derogating from Article 9 (1) and (2).

Article 10 – Certificate of service and copy of the document served

Apart from Latvian, Latvia will accept form completed in English.

Article 13 – Service by diplomatic or consular agents

Latvia accepts service by diplomatic or consular agents.

In the territory of the Republic of Latvia, service by diplomatic or consular agents within the meaning of Article 13 (1) of the Regulation is allowed.

Article 14 – Service by post

Latvia does not impose any specific conditions for accepting service by post.

Article 15 – Direct service

In the territory of the Republic of Latvia, direct service within the meaning of Article 15 (1) of the Regulation is not allowed.

Article 19 – Defendant not entering an appearance

Latvia does not intend to make the statements provided for by paragraphs 2 and 4.

[3569]

LITHUANIA

Article 2 – Transmitting agencies

The Republic of Lithuania has designated all courts of general competence of the Republic of Lithuania which deal with civil and commercial matters, ie all district courts of regions and cities, county courts, the Appeal Court of Lithuania and the Supreme Court of Lithuania as competent transmitting agencies according to Regulation 1348/2000.

Article 3 – Central body

The Central Authority is the Ministry of Justice of the Republic of Lithuania.

Centrin e i staiga yra Lietuvos Respublikos teisingumo ministerija.
Gedimino pr. 30/1
LT-01104 Vilnius

Tel: +370 5 2662980 / +370 5 2662938 / +370 5 2662942 / +370 5 2662941
Fax: +370 5 262 59 40 +370 5 2662854
E-mail: tminfo@tic.lt

Service of judicial and extra judicial documents is accepted by means of post and fax.

Language skills: English and French.

Article 4 – Transmission of documents

Apart from Lithuanian, the Republic of Lithuania will accept standard request forms, completed in English or French.

Article 9 – Date of service

The Republic of Lithuania intends to derogate from Article 9(2).

In Lithuanian law there are no specific time limits for the service of documents.

Article 10 – Certificate of service and copy of the document served

Apart from Lithuanian, the Republic of Lithuania will accept certificates completed in English or French.

Article 13 – Service by diplomatic or consular agents

The Republic of Lithuania declares that it opposes to the ways of service of documents provided in this Article, unless the documents are to be served upon a national of the State in which the documents originate.

Article 14 – Service by post

Service of judicial documents is accepted by registered post with acknowledgment of receipt and translation in accordance with Article 5 and Article 8.

Article 15 – Direct service

The Republic of Lithuania opposes the possibility of direct service, provided in Article 15(1).

Article 19 – Defendant not entering an appearance

Courts of the Republic of Lithuania may give judgment even if no certificate of service or delivery has been received, if all conditions of Article 19 (2) are fulfilled.

The application for relief will not be entertained if it is filed after the expiration of one year following the date of the judgment.

Article 20 – Agreements or arrangements to which Member States are Parties

(1) The agreement on Legal Assistance and Legal Relations in Civil, Family, Labour and Criminal Matters, between the Republic of Lithuania and the Republic of Poland (1993), done in Lithuanian and Polish.

(2) The Agreement on Legal Assistance and Legal Relations between the Republic of Lithuania, the Republic of Estonia and the Republic of Latvia (1992), done in Lithuanian, Latvian and Estonian.

[3570]

LUXEMBOURG

Article 2 – Transmitting agencies

Bailiffs empowered to serve documents. Court registrars empowered to serve documents.

Article 3 – Central body

The central body is the Public Prosecutor's Office at the High Court.

Parquet Général près la Cour supérieure de Justice
Boîte Postale 15
L-2010 Luxembourg

Tel (352) 47 59 81–336
Fax (352) 47 05 50
E-mail: Parquet.General@mj.etat.lu

Knowledge of languages: French and German.

Article 4 – Transmission of documents

Apart from French, Luxembourg will accept standard request forms which are completed in German.

Article 9 – Date of service

Luxembourg does not intend to derogate and will be applying Article 9(1) and (2) as worded in the Regulation.

Article 10 – Certificate of service and copy of the document served

Apart from French, Luxembourg will accept certificates completed in German.

Article 13 – Service by diplomatic or consular agents

Luxembourg is opposed to its diplomatic or consular agents serving judicial and extrajudicial documents in another Member State.

Luxembourg is also opposed to diplomatic or consular agents of other Member States serving such documents in its own territory, except where the document is to be served on a national of the Member State in which the document originates.

Article 14 – Service by post

Where service is to be by post, it must be by registered letter with advice of delivery and the rules governing translations in the Regulation must be applied.

Article 15 – Direct service

Luxembourg is not opposed to the possibility provided for by Article 15 regarding Member States that allow reciprocity, on the understanding that a bailiff in the requested State is not responsible for the proper form and content of the document sent to him direct by the person concerned but responsible solely for the service formalities and procedures that he applies in the requested State.

Article 19 – Defendant not entering an appearance

Luxembourg states that, notwithstanding Article 19(1), its courts may give judgement if the conditions of Article 19(2) are fulfilled.

Luxembourg states that, under Article 19(4), an application for relief may be rejected if it is not filed within a reasonable time, to be assessed by the court, either from the time when the defendant has knowledge of the judgment or from the time when the impossibility of taking action ended; applications may not be filed more than one year after the decision has been delivered.

[3571]

HUNGARY

Article 2 – Transmitting agencies

In accordance with Art 2 para 3 for a period of five years the Ministry of Justice is designated as transmitting agency. All requests shall be transmitted to:

Ministry of Justice. Department of Private International Law.

Igazságügyi Minisztérium
Nemzetközi Magánjogi Osztály
Budapest
Postafiók 54
1363

Tel: +36 1 4413110
Fax: +36 1 4413112
E-mail: nemzm@im.hu

Article 3 – Central body

(a) Names and addresses, telephone and fax numbers, email

Ministry of Justice. Department of Private International Law.
Igazságügyi Minisztérium
Nemzetközi Magánjogi Osztály
Budapest
Postafiók 54
1363

Tel: +36 1 4413110
Fax: +36 1 4413112
E-mail: nemzm@im.hu

(b) Geographical areas of jurisdiction (where several central bodies are designated)

(c) Means of receipt/communication available and language skills
- Mail, fax, e-mail
- Hungarian, German, English, French

Article 4 – Transmission of documents

German, English, French

Article 9 – Date of service

The Republic of Hungary intends to derogate from Article 9(2) as this rule is not applied in Hungarian law, it cannot be applied in the procedure of Hungarian courts.

Article 10 – Certificate of service and copy of the document served

German, English, French.

Article 13 – Service by diplomatic or consular agents

The Republic of Hungary does not oppose this possibility.

Article 14 – Service by post

The Republic of Hungary accepts use of the method referred to in Article 14(1) for serving judicial documents to persons residing in its own territory where the following conditions are met:

(a) the document being served must be sent by post as a registered letter with acknowledgement of receipt;

(b) the serving of a summons on the addressee must take place at least thirty days before the date of the hearing or other procedural act;

(c) where the document to be served is not provided with a Hungarian translation, the following information in Hungarian must be attached:
"The attached official document is being served on you on the basis of Regulation 1348/2000/EC on the service in the Member States of judicial and extrajudicial documents in civil or commercial matters (Official Journal of the European Communities L160, 30.6.2000, p 37). In view of the fact that the document is not provided with a Hungarian translation, you are entitled to refuse to receive it on the grounds that you do not understand the language of the document. You can avail yourself of this right by posting the document, within fifteen days of the date on which it was served by post, to the transmitting court (authority) stating that you do not accept it."
"A mellékelt hivatalos irat az Ön részére a polgári és kereskedelmi ügyekben keletkeztetett bírósági és bíróságon kívüli iratok tagállamokban történő kézbesítéséről szóló 1348/2000/EK rendelet (az Európai Közösségek Hivatalos Lapja, 2000. évi L160 sz 37 oldal) alapján került kézbesítésre. Figyelemmel arra, hogy az irat nincs ellátva magyar nyelven készült fordítással, Ön jogosult elutasítani annak átvételét arra való hivatkozással, hogy az irat nyelvét nem érti. E jogával oly módon élhet, hogy az iratot a postai kézbesítés napjától számított tizenöt napon belül postára adja a feladó bíróság (hatóság) részére azzal a nyilatkozattal, hogy azt nem fogadja el"

Article 15 – Direct service

The Republic of Hungary opposes the possibility of direct service (Art 15) in its territory.

Article 19 – Defendant not entering an appearance

The courts of the Republic of Hungary may give judgment on the question provided all the conditions of paragraph 2 have been met.

In the Republic of Hungary the period of time for making an application for relief provided for by paragraph 4 is one year.

[3572]

MALTA

Article 2 – Transmitting agencies

1. Transmitting agencies designated:

Agency:

Attorney General's office
The Palace
St George's Square
Valletta. CMR02

Public officers:

Cynthia Scerri De Bono
Attorney General's Office
The Palace, St George's Square
Valletta. CMR02

Tel: (00356) 2125683206
Fax: (00356) 21237281
Email: cynthia.scerri-debono@gov.mt

Heidi Testa
Attorney General's Office
The Palace
St George's Square
Valletta. CMR02

Tel: (00356) 2125683209 / (00356) 21225560
Fax: (00356) 21237281
Email: heidi.testa@gov.mt

Geographical areas of jurisdiction: Malta and Gozo

Means of receipt of documents available to them: Original documents to be sent by post. Documents may be advanced by fax/email.

Languages that may be used for completion of the standard form: English

Article 3 – Central body

Attorney General's office
The Palace
St George's Square
Valletta. CMR02

Tel: (00356) 2125683206 / (00356) 21225560
Fax: (00356) 21237281

Geographical areas of jurisdiction: Malta and Gozo

Means of receipt/communication available and language skills: English, Italian

Article 4 – Transmission of documents

Official Language: English

Article 9 – Date of service

Derogation from article 9(1)(2). Malta intends to derogate from article 9(2) as this would run counter to Maltese procedural law.

Article 10 – Certificate of service and copy of the document served

Official language: English

Article 13 – Service by diplomatic or consular agents

Yes we oppose.

Article 14 – Service by post

Service by post shall be accepted subject to the following conditions:—

— By leaving a copy at the place of residence, or business or place of work or postal address of such person, or with his attorney or person authorised to receive mail.

— There must be adequate proof of receipt.

Article 15 – Direct service

Service by interested persons: No opposition

Article 19 – Defendant not entering an appearance

It is not possible as proof of service is required. However if judgment is given against a person and such person has not in the first place been duly served with a writ of summons, within 3 months from the delivery of the judgment, he may proceed with by a claim for a new trial.

Article 20 – Agreements or arrangements to which Member States are Parties

Nil

[3573]

NETHERLANDS

Article 2 – Transmitting agencies

1. Bailiffs

2. The courts (cantonal courts, district courts, courts of justice and Supreme Court) where they have statutory tasks of summoning persons or serving documents.

Article 3 – Central body

The central body is the Koninklijke Beroepsorganisatie van Gerechtsdeurwaarders (Royal Federation of Bailiffs).

Street address:

Wilhelminalaan 3
3743 DB BAARN
Nederland

Postal address:

PO Box 12
3740 AA BAARN
Nederland

Tel +31 35 542 75 13
Fax +31 35 542 75 13
E-mail: kbvg@kbvg.nl
Web: www.kbvg.nl

The central body can receive and transmit documents by post, fax or e-mail, and can be contacted by telephone, in Dutch or English.

Article 4 – Transmission of documents

Apart from Dutch, the Netherlands will accept standard request forms which are completed in English.

Article 9 – Date of service

The Netherlands exercises the option under Article 9(3) of the Regulation of derogating from the provisions of Article 9(1) and (2).

Content of the derogation, as provided for in Article 56 of the Code of Civil Procedure: if a document has to be served within a given period of time, the date on which the document is sent shall be deemed to be the date of service in the case of the person at whose request the document is being served.

Explanation: although the Regulation is intended to speed up the service of documents in international cases there is as yet no assurance that service will be speeded up to such an extent that the derogation from Article 9(1) and (2) will prove superfluous. The cases at issue here are those (including matters external to cases that are about to open or are already pending) where the law sets short deadlines for serving particular documents, for example in the law on seizure of property, or cases where a decision is taken to enforce a time limit only shortly before its expiry, for example periods of limitation or peremptory time limits.

Article 10 – Certificate of service and copy of the document served

Apart from Dutch, the Netherlands will accept certificates completed in English.

Article 13 – Service by diplomatic or consular agents

The Netherlands does not oppose the possibility of a Member State serving judicial documents on persons residing in the Netherlands, without any compulsion, direct through its diplomatic or consular agents.

Article 14 – Service by post

The Netherlands accepts service of judicial documents by post on the following terms:

(a) Direct service by post on persons who are in the Netherlands must be by registered letter;

(b) Documents sent by post to persons residing in the Netherlands must be drafted or translated in Dutch or in a language that the recipient understands.

Article 15 – Direct service

The Netherlands does not oppose direct service.

Article 19 – Defendant not entering an appearance

The courts in the Netherlands will be empowered by implementing legislation now in the pipeline, notwithstanding the provisions of paragraph 1, to give judgment where all the conditions of paragraph 2 are met.

Once the judgment has been given, fresh time may be allowed if the application for it is made within one year running from the date when judgment is given.

[3574]

AUSTRIA

Article 2 – Transmitting agencies

The transmitting agencies are the district courts, the courts of first instance, the higher regional courts, the Vienna Labour and Social Affairs Court, the Vienna Commercial Court, the Vienna Juvenile Court and the Supreme Court.

Article 3 – Central body

The central body is the Federal Ministry of Justice.

Bundesministerium für Justiz
Postfach 63
A-1016 Vienna, or

Bundesministerium für Justiz
Museumstrasse 7
A-1070 Vienna, or

Bundesministerium für Justiz
Neustiftgasse 2
A-1070 Vienna

Tel (43–1) 521 52–2292
(43–1) 521 52–2115
(43–1) 521 52–2293

Fax (43–1) 521 52–2829
E-mail: ihor.tarko@bmj.gv.at
barbara.goeth@bmj.gv.at
barbara.makal@bmj.gv.at

Knowledge of languages: German and English.

Article 4 – Transmission of documents

Apart from German, Austria will accept standard request forms which are completed in English.

Article 9 – Date of service

Austria will not be derogating from Article 9(1) and (2).

Article 10 – Certificate of service and copy of the document served

Apart from German, Austria will accept certificates completed in English.

Article 13 – Service by diplomatic or consular agents

Austria does not intend to oppose the exercise in its territory of the right conferred by Article 13(1).

Article 14 – Service by post

Austria will accept the service of judicial documents by post from another Member State under Article 14(2) under the following conditions:

1. The documents to be served by post must be written in the official language of the place where they are served or accompanied by a certified translation into the language in question.

2. Where this provision is not adhered to, the recipient of the service may refuse to accept the documents. Should the recipient exercise this right, the documents may not be deemed to have been served.

Recipients must be informed in writing of their right to refuse acceptance of the documents.

3. Recipients may also exercise the right of refusal by informing the office that served the documents or the office of dispatch, within three days, that they are not prepared to accept the documents. The time begins when the document is served; the time taken for postal delivery is not included in this period and therefore the date as postmarked is decisive.

4. Postal deliveries must use the standard international advice of delivery.

The following text should be used to inform recipients of their rights:

"Das angeschlossene Schriftstück wird Ihnen unter Anwendung der Verordnung (EG) Nr. 1348/2000 des Rates vom 29. Mai 2000 über die Zustellung gerichtlicher und aussergerichtlicher Schriftstücke in Zivil- oder Handelssachen in den Mitgliedstaaten, ABl. L160 vom 30. Juni 2000, S. 37 ff, zugestellt.

Sie sind berechtigt, die Annahme des Schriftstückes zu verweigern, wenn dieses nicht in deutscher Sprache abgefasst oder nicht mit einer beglaubigten Übersetzung in diese Sprache versehen ist. Sollten Sie von diesem Annahmeverweigerungsrecht Gebrauch machen wollen, müssen Sie innerhalb von drei Tagen ab der Zustellung gegenüber der Stelle, die das Schriftstück zugestellt hat, oder gegenüber der Absendestelle unter Rücksendung des Schriftstückes an eine dieser Stellen erklären, dass Sie zur Annahme nicht bereit sind."

("The enclosed documents are being served under Council Regulation (EC) No 1348/2000 of 29 May 2000 on the service in the Member States of judicial and extrajudicial documents in civil or commercial matters. You have the right to refuse to accept the documents if they are not in German or accompanied by a certified German translation. Should you wish to exercise this right, you must, within three days of service, return the documents to the office which served them or to the office of dispatch stating that you are not prepared to accept them.")

Article 15 – Direct service

Austria is opposed to the direct service of judicial documents in its territory through the judicial officers, officials or other competent persons of the Member State addressed.

Article 19 – Defendant not entering an appearance

Courts in Austria, notwithstanding paragraph 1, may give judgment if the conditions of paragraph 2 are met.

Austria has not communicated any time-limit within the meaning of the last subparagraph of Article 19(4) for filing an application for relief from the effects of expiry of the time allowed for appeal.

[3575]

POLAND

Article 2 – Transmitting agencies

Transmitting agencies are:

— District Courts (*Sądy Rejonowe*)
— Regional Courts (*Sądy Okręgowe*)
— Courts of Appeal (*Sądy Apelacyjne*)
— Supreme Court (*Sąd Najwyższy*)

Article 3 – Central body

Ministry of Justice. Department of Judicial Assistance and European Law.

Ministerstwo Sprawiedliwości
Departament Współpracy Międzynarodowej i Prawa Europejskiego
Al. Ujazdowskie 11
00–950 Warszawa
Phone/fax: +48 22 6280949

Knowledge of languages: Polish, English, German.

Article 4 – Transmission of documents

Poland will accept standard form if completed in Polish or English or German.

Article 9 – Date of service

Poland intends to derogate from the provision of Article 9 (2) on the basis of the need for legal certainty and the right for legal protection. The Polish legal system cannot allow a date of service to be taken other than that stipulated in Article 9 (1). It is important that the date of service can be identified with certainty as it determines the time from which a party may enter default judgement. The meaning of this provision is not precise and clear. Therefore it could increase the potential for confusion.

Article 10 – Certificate of service and copy of the document served

Poland will accept the standard form (certificate of service) if completed in Polish or English or German.

Article 13 – Service by diplomatic or consular agents

Poland opposes service by consular or diplomatic agents within its territory, unless the document is to be served on the national of the MS in which the document originates.

Article 14 – Service by post

Poland accepts service of judicial documents by post on the following conditions:

— documents are served by registered letter with acknowledgement of receipt; and
— documents are drafted or translated into Polish or one of the official languages of the Member States of transmission if the addressee is a national of that State.

Article 15 – Direct service

Poland opposes service pursuant to article 15 (1) within its territory.

Article 19 – Defendant not entering an appearance

Poland will not make use of the possibility provided for by Article 19(2), and courts in Poland will therefore not be able to give judgment in the circumstances referred to therein.

Applications for relief provided for by Article 19 (4) will not be entertained if they are filed after the expiration of one year time following the date of the judgement.

[3576]

PORTUGAL

Article 2 – Transmitting agencies

The transmitting agencies designated by Portugal are the cantonal courts, in the person of the clerk of the court.

Article 3 – Central body

The central body is the Directorate-General for the Administration of Justice.

Direcção Geral da Administração da Justiça
Av. 5 de Outubro, no 125
P-1069 – 044 Lisbon
Portugal

Tel (351) 21 790 62 00 – (351) 21 790 62 23
Fax (351) 21 790 64 60 – (351) 21 790 62 29
E-mail: correio@dgaj.mj.pt
Website: www.dgaj.mj.pt

Knowledge of languages: Portuguese, Spanish, English and French.

Article 4 – Transmission of documents

Apart from Portuguese, Portugal will accept standard request forms which are completed in Spanish.

Article 9 – Date of service

Portugal intends to derogate from Article 9(2) on the grounds of the imprecision and uncertainty that can result from the determination of two different dates of service, set by reference to the laws of two different countries, to the detriment of legal certainty.

Article 10 – Certificate of service and copy of the document served

Apart from Portuguese, Portugal will accept certificates completed in Spanish.

Article 13 – Service by diplomatic or consular agents

Portugal has no reservations to formulate regarding this Article.

Article 14 – Service by post

Portugal states that it will accept service by post, provided it is made by registered letter with advice of delivery and accompanied by a translation in accordance with Article 8 of the Regulation.

Article 15 – Direct service

On grounds of legal certainty, Portugal is opposed to this form of service in its territory.

Article 19 – Defendant not entering an appearance

Portugal will not make use of the possibility provided for by Article 19(2), and courts in Portugal will therefore not be able to give judgment in the circumstances referred to therein.

The time-limit for filing an application for relief from the effects of expiry of the time allowed for appeal is one year following the date of the judgment being challenged (Article 19(4)).

[3577]

SLOVENIA

Article 2 – Transmitting agencies

Transmitting agencies:

Transmitting agencies are County Courts, District Courts, Labour and Social Affairs Court, Administrative Court, Higher Courts, Supreme Court ans and State Attorney's Office.

Article 3 – Central body

The central body is:

Ministry of Justice
Župančičeva 3
SLO-1000 Ljubljana

Tel: (++386)1369 53 38
Fax: (++386)136953 06
E-mail: gp.mp@gov.si

Article 4 – Transmission of documents

Apart from Slovenian, Slovenia will accept standard request forms which are completed in English.

Article 9 – Date of service

Slovenia will derogate from Article 9 (2). The grounds for this derogation are in the need for legal certainty. Slovenian legal system does not allow a date of service to be taken other than that stipulated in Art. 9 (1), namely the date on which the document is served to the addressee in accordance with the law of the Member State addressed.

Article 10 – Certificate of service and copy of the document served

Apart from Slovenian, Slovenia will accept certificates completed in English.

Article 13 – Service by diplomatic or consular agents

a. Slovenia does not oppose the possibility of service through diplomatic or consular agents under conditions laid down in Article 13 (1).

b. Slovenia is opposed to the service of judicial documents on persons residing in Slovenia through diplomatic or consular agents of another Member State, except where the document is to be served on a national of a Member State in which the documents originate.

Article 14 – Service by post

Slovenia will accept the service of judicial documents by post from another Member State under Article 14 (2) under following conditions:

1. The documents to be served by post must be written in or accompanied by a translation into Slovenian or one of the official languages of the Member States from which the documents are served if the addressee is the national of that Member State. Where this provision is not adhered to, the recepient of service may refuse to accept the documents and they may not be deemed to have been served.

2. The service by post is permitted only in a form of registered letter with acknowledgement of receipt.

Article 15 – Direct service

Slovenia is opposed to the direct service of judicial documents in its territory through the judicial officers, officials or other competent persons of the Member State addressed.

Article 19 – Defendant not entering an appearance

According to Slovenian law, Slovenian courts may not give judgement in the circumstances referred to in Article 19 (2). Thus, there is no need for communication referred to in Article 19 (4).

[3578]

SLOVAKIA

Article 2 – Transmitting agencies

Transmitting agencies:

District	Name and full address	Telephone, fax, e-mail
Slovakia	Ministry of Justice of the Slovak Republic Župné nám. 13 813 11 Bratislava Slovak Republic	(421) 259 353 347 (421) 259 353 604 inter.coop@justice.sk
Slovenská republika	Ministerstvo spravodlivosti Slovenskej republiky Župné nám. 13 813 11 Bratislava Slovenská republika	(421) 259 353 347 (421) 259 353 604 inter.coop@justice.sk
Bratislavský kraj	Krajský súd v Bratislave Záhradnícka 10 813 66 Bratislava	(421) 255 424 060 (421) 255 423 841 krajsudba@gtsi.sk
	Okresný súd Bratislava I. Záhradnícka 10 812 44 Bratislava	(421) 250 118 111 (421) 255 571 634 _sekretariat_os_ba1@justice.sk
	Okresný súd Bratislava II. Drie ń ová 5 827 02 Bratislava	(421) 243 335 880 (421) 243 410 446 _sekretariat_os_ba2@justice.sk
	Okresný súd Bratislava III. Námestie Biely kríž 7 832 50 Bratislava	(421) 249 204 511 (421) 244 450 332 _sekretariat_os_ba3@justice.sk
	Okresný súd Bratislava IV. Saratovská 1/a 844 54 Bratislava	(421) 264 284 624 (421) 264 284 945 _sekretariat_os_ba4@justice.sk
	Okresný súd Bratislava V. Prokofievova 12 852 38 Bratislava	(421) 263 811 378 (421) 263 825 828 _sekretariat_os_ba5@justice.sk
Trnavský kraj	Krajský súd v Trnave Vajanského 2 918 70 Trnava	(421) 335 511 057 (421) 335 512 662 kstrnava.brosova@bratislava.telecom.sk
	Okresný súd Trnava Hlavná 20 917 83 Trnava	(421) 335 913 511 (421) 335 511 443 _sekretariat_os_tt@justice.sk
	Okresný súd Dunajská Streda Alžbetínske nám. 8 929 27 Dunajská Streda	(421) 315 905 110 (421) 315 527 908 _sekretariat_os_ds@justice.sk
	Okresný súd Galanta Mierové nám. 1 924 23 Galanta	(421) 317 802 121 (421) 317 803 459 _sekretariat_ga_ds@justice.sk
	Okresný súd Senica Nám. Oslobodenia 1 905 30 Senica	(421) 346 512 003 (421) 346 513 803 _sekretariat_os_ds@justice.sk
Trenčiansky kraj	Krajskí súd v Trenčíne Nám. Sv. Anny 28 911 50 Trenčín	(421) 326 572 811 (421) 326 582 342 secretariat@kstn.sk
	Okresní súd Trenčín Piaristická 27 911 80 Trenčín	(421) 326 561 111 (421) 326 528 116 _sekretariat_os_tt@justice.sk
	Okresný súd Považská Bystrica Štúrova 1 / 2 017 33 Považská Bystrica	(421) 424 326 838 (421) 424 326 854 _sekretariat_os_pb@justice.sk

District	Name and full address	Telephone, fax, e-mail
	Okresný súd Prievidza Švernyho 5 971 72 Prievidza	(421) 465 422 022 (421) 465 423 501 _sekretariat_os_pd@justice.sk
Nitriansky kraj	Krajský súd v Nitre Štúrova 9 949 68 Nitra	(421) 376 526 880 (421) 376 526 878 cina@plastika.sk
	Okresný súd Nitra Štúrova 9 949 68 Nitra	(421) 376 525 221 (421) 376 526 633 _sekretariat_os_nr@justice.sk
	Okresný súd Komárno Pohraničná 6 945 35 Komárno	(421) 357 701 767 (421) 357 701 724 _sekretariat_os_kn@justice.sk
	Okresný súd Levice Kalvínske nám. 7 934 31 Levice	(421) 366 312 205 (421) 366 222 214
	Okresný súd Nové Zámky Rákocziho 15 940 16 Nové Zámky	(421) 356 400 380 (421) 356 401 763 _sekretariat_os_nz@justice.sk
	Okresní súd Topol'čany M.R.Štefánika 55 955 15 Topol'čany	(421) 385 369 111 (421) 385 327 702 _sekretariat_os_to@justice.sk
Žilinský kraj	Krajský súd v Žiline Orolská 3 010 01 Žilina	(421) 415 626 367 (421) 415 626 355 kszilina@bb.telecom.sk
	Okresný súd Žilina Hviezdoslavova 28 010 59 Žilina	(421) 415 620 190 (421) 415 622 468 _sekretariat_os_za@justice.sk
	Okresní súd Čadca 17. novembra 1256 022 21 Čadca	(421) 414 331 590 (421) 414 331 594 _sekretariat_os_ca@justice.sk
	Okresný súd Dolný Kubín Radlinského 36 026 01 Dolný Kubín	(421) 435 862 281 (421) 435 863 126 _sekretariat_os_dk@justice.sk
	Okresný súd Liptovský Mikuláš Tomášikova 5 031 33 Liptovský Mikuláš	(421) 445 523 115 (421) 445 514 041 _sekretariat_os_lm@justice.sk
	Okresný súd Martin E. B. Luká č a 2A 036 61 Martin	(421) 434 008 401 (421) 434 008 333 _sekretariat_os_mi@justice.sk
	Okresní súd Ružomberok Dončova 8 034 01 Ružomberok	(421) 444 322 390 (421) 444 327 474 _sekretariat_os_rk@justice.sk
Banskobystrický kraj	Krajský súd v Banskej Bystrici Skuteckého 28 975 59 Banská Bystrica	(421) 484 125 326 (421) 484 124 976 ksudbb@isternet.sk
	Okresný súd Banská Bystrica Skuteckého 28 975 59 Banská Bystrica	(421) 484 145 601 (421) 484 145 606 _sekretariat_os_bb@justice.sk
	Okresní súd Lučenec Dr. Hereza 14 984 37 Lučenec	(421) 474 325 866 (421) 474 324 563 _sekretariat_os_lc@justice.sk

District	Name and full address	Telephone, fax, e-mail
	Okresný súd Rimavská Sobota Jesenského 2 979 01 Rimavská Sobota	(421) 475 631 141 (421) 475 624 103 _sekretariat_os_rs@justice.sk
	Okresní súd Vel'kí Krtíš SNP 714/2 990 14 Vel'kí Krtíš	(421) 474 831 015 (421) 474 831 473 _sekretariat_os_vk@justice.sk
	Okresní súd Zvolen Kozačekova 19 960 68 Zvolen	(421) 455 333 131 (421) 455 331 851 _sekretariat_os_zv@justice.sk
	Okresný súd Žiar nad Hronom Nám. Matice Slovenskej 5/1 965 35 Žiar nad Hronom	(421) 456 738 930 (421) 456 734 650 _sekretariat_os_zh@justice.sk
	Okresný súd Brezno Kuzmányho 4 977 01 Brezno	(421) 486 115 280 (421) 486 111 803 _sekretariat_os_br@justice.sk
Prešovský kraj	Krajský súd v Prešove Košická cesta 20 080 01 Prešov	(421) 517 733 206 (421) 517 724 782 infor@vadium.sk
	Okresný súd Prešov Grešova 3 080 01 Prešov	(421) 517 562 211 (421) 517 562 299 _sekretariat_os_po@justice.sk
	Okresný súd Bardejov Partizánska 1 085 75 Bardejov	(421) 544 722 091 (421) 544 724 331 _sekretariat_os_bj@justice.sk
	Okresný súd Humenné Laborecká 17 066 34 Humenné	(421) 577 865 201 (421) 577 752 756 _sekretariat_os_hn@justice.sk
	Okresný súd Kežmarok Trhovište 16 060 01 Kežmarok	(421) 524 525 080 (421) 524 525 081 _sekretariat_os_kk@justice.sk
	Okresný súd Poprad Štefánikova 100 058 01 Poprad	(421) 527 862 111 (421) 527 724 046 _sekretariat_os_pp@justice.sk
	Okresní súd Stará L'ubovňa 17. novembra 30 064 27 Stará L'ubovňa	(421) 524 322 871 (421) 524 369 063 _sekretariat_os_sl@justice.sk
	Okresný súd Svidník Sov. Hrdinov 200/35 089 01 Svidník	(421) 547 521 241 (421) 547 522 184 _sekretariat_os_sk@justice.sk
	Okresný súd Vranov nad Top l'ou M. R. Štefánika 874 093 32 Vranov nad Top l'ou	(421) 574 421 311 (421) 574 421 312 _sekretariat_os_vv@justice.sk
	Košický kraj Krajský súd v Košiciach Štúrova 29 041 51 Košice	(421) 557 269 111 (421) 557 269 221 secretariat@krajsudke.sk
	Okresný súd Košice I Štúrova 29 041 51 Košice	(421) 557 269 111 (421) 557 269 420 _sekretariat_os_ke i@justice.sk

District	Name and full address	Telephone, fax, e-mail
	Okresný súd Košice II Štúrova 29 041 51 Košice	(421) 557 269 111 (421) 557 269 520 _sekretariat_os_ke ii@justice.sk
	Okresný súd Košice-okolie Štúrova 29 041 51 Košice	(421) 557 269 111 (421) 557 269 620 _sekretariat_os_ke iii@justice.sk
	Okresný súd Michalovce Námestie Slobody 11 071 80 Michalovce	(421) 566 425 240 (421) 566 425 594 _sekretariat_os_mi@justice.sk
	Okresní súd Rožňava mája č. 1 048 80 Rožňava	(421) 587 324 246 (421) 587 343 687 _sekretariat_os_rv@justice.sk
	Okresný súd Spišská Nová Ves Stará cesta 3 052 80 Spišská Nová Ves	(421) 534 171 111 (421) 534 424 537 _sekretariat_os_sn@justice.sk
	Okresný súd Trebišov Nám. Mieru 638 075 01 trebišov	(421) 566 722 321 (421) 566 725 597 _sekretariat_os_tv@justice.sk

Article 3 – Central body

District	Name and full address	Telephone, fax, e-mail	Language skills
Slovakia	Ministry of Justice of the Slovak Republic Division for Private International Law and International Judicial Co-operation Župné nám. 13 813 11 Bratislava Slovak Republic	(421) 259 353 347 (421) 259 353 604 inter.coop@justice.sk	Slovak Czech English French German

Article 4 – Transmission of documents

Slovak language

Article 9 – Date of service

Slovakia does not intend to derogate from Article 9.

Article 10 – Certificate of service and copy of the document served

Slovakia does not intend to derogate from Article 10.

Article 13 – Service by diplomatic or consular agents

The Slovak Republic opposes the possibility of serving judicial documents through diplomatic or consular agents unless the documents are to be served on a national of the Member State in which the document originates.

Article 14 – Service by post

The Slovak Republic accepts the service of judicial document by post to person residing in its territory if the document is in the language specified in Article 8 para. 1, letters a/ or b/.

Article 15 – Direct service

The Slovak Republic opposes the possibility of any person interested in a judicial proceeding to effect service of judicial documents in its territory directly through the judicial officers, officials or other competent persons of the Slovak Republic.

Article 19 – Defendant not entering an appearance

The Slovak Republic does not intend to make any declaration in respect of Paragraph 2 of this Article.

Article 20 – Agreements or arrangements to which Member States are Parties

Treaties under paragraph 3 letter a/:

Treaty between the Slovak Republic and the Czech Republic on Mutual Legal Assistance Provided by Judicial Authorities and the Regulation of Certain Legal Relations in Civil and Criminal Matters with Final Protocol (Prague 29 October 1992)

Treaty between the Czechoslovak Socialist Republic and the Hungarian People's Republic on Mutual Legal Assistance and the Regulation of Legal Relations in Civil, Family and Criminal Matters (Bratislava 28 March 1989)

Treaty between the Czechoslovak Socialist Republic and the Polish People's Republic on Mutual Legal Assistance and the Regulation of Legal Relations in Civil, Family, Labour and Criminal Matters (Warsaw 21 December 1987)

[3579]

FINLAND

Article 2 – Transmitting agencies

The transmitting agencies are the courts of first instance, the appeal courts, the Supreme Court and the Ministry of Justice.

Article 3 – Central body

The central body is the Ministry of Justice.

Street address:
Oikeusministeriö
Eteläesplanadi 10
FIN-00130 Helsinki

Postal address:
Oikeusministeriö
PL 25
FIN-00023 Valtioneuvosto

Tel (358–9) 16 06 76 28
Fax (358–9) 16 06 75 24
E-mail: central.authority@om.fi

Documents can be transmitted by post, fax or e-mail.

Knowledge of languages: Finnish, Swedish and English.

Article 4 – Transmission of documents

Finland accepts the form in English in addition to Finnish and Swedish.

Article 9 – Date of service

In accordance with paragraph 3, Finland intends to derogate from the provisions of paragraphs 1 and 2. In their current form, these provisions have no explicable *ratio legis* in the context of the Finnish legal system, and therefore cannot be applied in practice.

Article 10 – Certificate of service and copy of the document served

Finland accepts the form in English in addition to Finnish and Swedish.

Article 13 – Service by diplomatic or consular agents

Finland does not oppose this form of service.

Article 14 – Service by post

Finland accepts the service of documents by post, provided that the recipient signs an advice of receipt or returns an acknowledgement of receipt. Any document other than a summons can be also delivered by post to an address specified by the recipient to the relevant authority.

Article 15 – Direct service

Finland does not oppose this form of service.

Article 19 – Defendant not entering an appearance

Finland does not intend to make the communication referred to in Article 19(2); thus, the Finnish courts may not give judgment in accordance with that provision. By the same token, there will be no need for the communication referred to in Article 19(4).

[3580]

SWEDEN

Article 2 – Transmitting agencies

Transmitting agencies are courts, enforcement authorities and other Swedish authorities which serve judicial and extrajudicial documents in civil or commercial matters.

Article 3 – Central body

The central body is the Ministry of Justice.

Justitiedepartementet
Enheten för brottmålsärenden och internationellt rättsligt samarbete
Centralmyndigheten
S-103 33 Stockholm

Tel (46–8)-405 45 00
Fax (46–8)-405 46 76
E-mail birs@justice.ministry.se

Documents may be received by post, fax or any other means agreed in the specific case. Contact may also be made by telephone.

Knowledge of languages: Swedish or English may be used.

Article 4 – Transmission of documents

Apart from Swedish, Sweden will accept standard request forms which are completed in English.

Article 9 – Date of service

Sweden does not intend to apply Article 9(2) concerning the date of service with respect to the applicant because under Swedish law service cannot be deemed to have taken place at different times with respect to the applicant and the addressee.

Article 10 – Certificate of service and copy of the document served

Apart from Swedish, Sweden will accept certificates completed in English.

Article 13 – Service by diplomatic or consular agents

Sweden accepts service by diplomatic or consular agents.

Article 14 – Service by post

Sweden does not impose any specific conditions for accepting service by post.

Article 15 – Direct service

Sweden is not opposed to any person interested in a judicial proceeding having the freedom to effect service of judicial documents directly through judicial officers, officials or other competent persons. However, the Swedish authorities are not required to provide assistance in such cases.

Article 19 – Defendant not entering an appearance

Swedish courts cannot give judgment if the conditions of Article 19(2), but not those of Article 19(1), are met. Sweden does not intend to issue any communication under Article 19(4).

[3581]

UNITED KINGDOM

Article 2 – Transmitting agencies

1. England and Wales:
the transmitting agency is the Senior Master, for the Attention of the Foreign Process Department, Royal Courts of Justice.

2. Scotland:
the transmitting agencies are the Messengers-at-Arms and accredited Solicitors.

3. Northern Ireland:
the transmitting agency is the Master (Queen's Bench and Appeals), Royal Courts of Justice.

4. Gibraltar:
the transmitting agency is "The Registrar of the Supreme Court of Gibraltar".

Article 3 – Central body

1. England and Wales:
The Senior Master
For the Attention of the Foreign Process Department (Room E10)
Royal Courts of Justice
Strand
London WC2A 2LL
United Kingdom
Tel (44–20) 79 47 66 91
Fax (44–20) 79 47 62 37

2. Scotland:
Scottish Executive
Justice Department
Civil and International Division
2nd Floor West
St Andrew's House
Regent Road
Edinburgh
EH1 3DG
Tel (44–131) 244 48 26
Fax (44–131) 244 48 48
E-mail: David.Berry@scotland.gsi.gov.uk

3. Northern Ireland:
The Master (Queen's Bench and Appeals)
Royal Courts of Justice
Chichester Street
Belfast BT1 3JF
United Kingdom
Tel (44–28) 90 72 47 06
Fax (44–28) 90 23 51 86

4. Gibraltar:
The Registrar of the Supreme Court of Gibraltar Supreme Court,
Law Courts
277 Main Street
Gibraltar
Tel: +350 78808
Fax: +350 77118
Formal communications with the receiving agency should be addressed to the Registrar at the above address but sent via:
The United Kingdom Government Gibraltar Liaison Unit for EU Affairs
Foreign and Commonwealth Office

King Charles Street
London
SW1A 2AH
Tel: +44 20 7008 1577
Fax: +44 20 7008 3629
e-mail: ukgglu@fco.gov.uk

Communication will be by means of letter, fax, e-mail and telephone and the central body will be responsible for checking translations.

Article 4 – Transmission of documents

Apart from English, the United Kingdom will accept standard request forms which are completed in French.

Article 9 – Date of service

The United Kingdom intends to derogate from these provisions on the basis that the complexities of its law on time-limits and limitation periods would only be exacerbated by this Article. It is important that the date of service can be identified with certainty as it determines the time from which a party may enter a default judgment. The UK does not consider that the precise meaning of this provision, and its intended operation in practice, is sufficiently clear; it could therefore increase the potential for confusion. Accordingly it believes that this matter is best left to national law, at least until it has had an opportunity to assess how it works in practice in the other Member States following implementation of the Regulation.

Article 10 – Certificate of service and copy of the document served

Apart from English, the United Kingdom will accept certificates completed in French.

Article 13 – Service by diplomatic or consular agents

The United Kingdom does not intend to oppose the exercise in its territory of the right conferred by Article 13(1).

Article 14 – Service by post

Service of a document by post is acceptable by means of registered mail or recorded mail only. A signature must be obtained from the addressee, or any other person who is prepared to accept receipt on behalf of the addressee, as proof of delivery of the document.

The addressee may refuse to accept service of the principal document unless it is accompanied by a certified English translation or by a certified translation into a language which the addressee understands.

Article 15 – Direct service

1. England, Wales and Northern Ireland:
England, Wales and Northern Ireland are opposed to the possibility of direct service provided for by Article 15(1).

2. Scotland:
Scotland does not oppose the possibility of direct service provided for by Article 15(1).

3. Gibraltar:
Gibraltar does not oppose the possibility of direct service provided for by Article 15(1).

Article 19 – Defendant not entering an appearance

In accordance with the existing provision of the Hague Convention, courts in the United Kingdom, notwithstanding paragraph 1, may give judgment if all the conditions of paragraph 2 have been met.

Period of time after the judgment has been given within which an application for relief provided for by paragraph 4 may be entertained:

1. England, Wales and Northern Ireland:
When considering setting aside a judgment in default, the court must have regard to whether the person seeking to set aside the judgment made an application to do so promptly.

2. Scotland:

No later than the expiry of one year from the date of decree – this would be in line with the Hague Convention and is the period incorporated in Scotland's court rules.

3. Gibraltar:
When considering setting aside a judgment in default, the court must have regard to whether the person seeking to set aside the judgment made an application to do so promptly.

[3582]

COUNCIL DECISION

of 20 September 2005

on the signing, on behalf of the Community, of the Agreement between the European Community and the Kingdom of Denmark on the service of judicial and extrajudicial documents in civil or commercial matters

(2005/794/EC)

NOTES

Date of publication in OJ: OJ L300, 17.11.2005, p 53.

This Agreement between the European Community and Denmark (not a party to Council Regulation 1348/2000/EC at **[3528]**) is not yet in force.

On 27 April 2006, the European Community and the Kingdom of Denmark concluded the Agreement on the service of judicial and extrajudicial documents in civil or commercial matters. The text of the Council Decision concerning the conclusion of that Agreement is set out in OJ L120, 5.5.2006, p 23. It can also be viewed at http://eur-lex.europa.eu/LexUriServ/site/en/oj/2006/l_120/l_12020060505en00230023.pdf

THE COUNCIL OF THE EUROPEAN UNION,

Having regard to the Treaty establishing the European Community, and in particular Article 61(c) thereof, in conjunction with the first sentence of the first subparagraph of Article 300(2) thereof,

Having regard to the proposal from the Commission,

Whereas:

(1) In accordance with Articles 1 and 2 of the Protocol on the position of Denmark annexed to the Treaty on European Union and the Treaty establishing the European Community, Denmark is not bound by the provisions of Council Regulation (EC) No 1348/2000 of 29 May 2000 on the service in the Member States of judicial and extrajudicial documents in civil or commercial matters,[1] nor subject to their application.

(2) By Decision of 8 May 2003, the Council authorised exceptionally the Commission to negotiate an agreement between the European Community and the Kingdom of Denmark extending to Denmark the provisions of the abovementioned Regulation.

(3) The Commission has negotiated such agreement, on behalf of the Community, with the Kingdom of Denmark.

(4) The United Kingdom and Ireland, in accordance with Article 3 of the Protocol on the position of the United Kingdom and Ireland annexed to the Treaty on European Union and the Treaty establishing the European Community, are taking part in the adoption and application of this Decision.

(5) In accordance with Articles 1 and 2 of the abovementioned Protocol on the position of Denmark, Denmark is not taking part in the adoption of this Decision and is not bound by it or subject to its application.

(6) The Agreement, initialled at Brussels on 17 January 2005, should be signed,

[3583]

NOTES

[1] OJ L160, 30.6.2000, p 37.

PART IV
EC MATERIALS

HAS DECIDED AS FOLLOWS:

Article 1

The signing of the Agreement between the European Community and the Kingdom of Denmark on the service of judicial and extrajudicial documents in civil or commercial matters is hereby approved on behalf of the Community, subject to the Council Decision concerning the conclusion of the said Agreement.

The text of the Agreement is attached to this Decision.

[3584]

Article 2

The President of the Council is hereby authorised to designate the person(s) empowered to sign the Agreement on behalf of the Community subject to its conclusion.

[3585]

Done at Brussels, 20 September 2005.

For the Council

The President

M BECKETT

AGREEMENT
BETWEEN THE EUROPEAN COMMUNITY AND THE KINGDOM OF DENMARK ON THE SERVICE OF JUDICIAL AND EXTRAJUDICIAL DOCUMENTS IN CIVIL OR COMMERCIAL MATTERS

THE EUROPEAN COMMUNITY, hereinafter referred to as 'the Community',

of the one part, and

THE KINGDOM OF DENMARK, hereinafter referred to as 'Denmark',

of the other part,

DESIRING to improve and expedite transmission between Denmark and the other Member States of the Community of judicial and extrajudicial documents in civil or commercial matters,

CONSIDERING that transmission for this purpose is to be made directly between local bodies designated by the Contracting Parties,

CONSIDERING that speed in transmission warrants the use of all appropriate means, provided that certain conditions as to the legibility and reliability of the documents received are observed,

CONSIDERING that security in transmission requires that the document to be transmitted be accompanied by a pre-printed form, to be completed in the language of the place where the service is to be effected, or in another language accepted by the receiving Member State,

CONSIDERING that to secure the effectiveness of this Agreement, the possibility of refusing service of documents should be confined to exceptional situations,

WHEREAS the Convention on the service in the Member States of the European Union of judicial and extrajudicial documents in civil or commercial matters drawn up by the Council of the European Union by Act of 26 May 1997[1] has not entered into force and that continuity in the results of the negotiations for conclusion of the Convention should be ensured,

WHEREAS the main content of that Convention has been taken over in Council Regulation (EC) No 1348/2000 of 29 May 2000 on the service in the Member States of judicial and extrajudicial documents in civil or commercial matters[2] (the Regulation on the service of documents),

REFERRING to the Protocol on the position of Denmark annexed to the Treaty on European Union and to the Treaty establishing the European Community (the Protocol on the position of Denmark) pursuant to which the Regulation on the service of documents shall not be binding upon or applicable in Denmark,

DESIRING that the provisions of the Regulation on the service of documents, future amendments hereto and the implementing measures relating to it should under international law apply to the relations between the Community and Denmark being a Member State with a special position with respect to Title IV of the Treaty establishing the European Community,

STRESSING the importance of proper coordination between the Community and Denmark with regard to the negotiation and conclusion of international agreements that may affect or alter the scope of the Regulation on the service of documents,

STRESSING that Denmark should seek to join international agreements entered into by the Community where Danish participation in such agreements is relevant for the coherent application of the Regulation on the service of documents and this Agreement,

STATING that the Court of Justice of the European Communities should have jurisdiction in order to secure the uniform application and interpretation of this Agreement including the provisions of the Regulation on the service of documents and any implementing Community measures forming part of this Agreement,

REFERRING to the jurisdiction conferred to the Court of Justice of the European Communities pursuant to Article 68(1) of the Treaty establishing the European Community to give rulings on preliminary questions relating to the validity and interpretation of acts of the institutions of the Community based on Title IV of the Treaty, including the validity and interpretation of this Agreement, and to the circumstance that this provision shall not be binding upon or applicable in Denmark, as results from the Protocol on the position of Denmark,

CONSIDERING that the Court of Justice of the European Communities should have jurisdiction under the same conditions to give preliminary rulings on questions concerning the validity and interpretation of this Agreement which are raised by a Danish court or tribunal, and that Danish courts and tribunals should therefore request preliminary rulings under the same conditions as courts and tribunals of other Member States in respect of the interpretation of the Regulation on the service of documents and its implementing measures,

REFERRING to the provision that, pursuant to Article 68(3) of the Treaty establishing the European Community, the Council of the European Union, the European Commission and the Member States may request the Court of Justice of the European Communities to give a ruling on the interpretation of acts of the institutions of the Community based on Title IV of the Treaty, including the interpretation of this Agreement, and the circumstance that this provision shall not be binding upon or applicable in Denmark, as results from the Protocol on the position of Denmark,

CONSIDERING that Denmark should, under the same conditions as other Member States in respect of the Regulation on the service of documents and its implementing measures, be accorded the possibility to request the Court of Justice of the European Communities to give rulings on questions relating to the interpretation of this Agreement,

STRESSING that under Danish law the courts in Denmark should—when interpreting this Agreement including the provisions of the Regulation on the service of documents and any implementing Community measures forming part of this Agreement—take due account of the rulings contained in the case law of the Court of Justice of the European Communities and of the courts of the Member States of the European Communities in respect of provisions of the Regulation on the service of documents and any implementing Community measures,

CONSIDERING that it should be possible to request the Court of Justice of the European Communities to rule on questions relating to compliance with obligations under this Agreement pursuant to the provisions of the Treaty establishing the European Community governing proceedings before the Court,

WHEREAS, by virtue of Article 300(7) of the Treaty establishing the European Community, this Agreement binds Member States; it is therefore appropriate that Denmark, in the case of non-compliance by a Member State, should be able to seize the Commission as guardian of the Treaty,

[3586]

NOTES

1 OJ C261, 27.8.1997, p 1. On the same day as the Convention was drawn up the Council took note of the explanatory report on the Convention which is set out on p 26 of the aforementioned Official Journal.

2 OJ L160, 30.6.2000, p 37.

HAVE AGREED AS FOLLOWS:

Article 1

Aim

1. The aim of this Agreement is to apply the provisions of the Regulation on the service of documents and its implementing measures to the relations between the Community and Denmark, in accordance with Article 2(1) of this Agreement.

2. It is the objective of the Contracting Parties to arrive at a uniform application and interpretation of the provisions of the Regulation on the service of documents and its implementing measures in all Member States.

3. The provisions of Articles 3(1), 4(1) and 5(1) of this Agreement result from the Protocol on the position of Denmark.

[3587]

Article 2

Cooperation on the service of documents

1. The provisions of the Regulation on the service of documents, which is annexed to this Agreement and forms part thereof, together with its implementing measures adopted pursuant to Article 17 of the Regulation and—in respect of implementing measures adopted after the entry into force of this Agreement—implemented by Denmark as referred to in Article 4 of this Agreement, and the information communicated by Member States under Article 23 of the Regulation, shall under international law apply to the relations between the Community and Denmark.

2. The date of entry into force of this Agreement shall apply instead of the date referred to in Article 25 of the Regulation.

[3588]

Article 3

Amendments to the Regulation on the service of documents

1. Denmark shall not take part in the adoption of amendments to the Regulation on the service of documents and no such amendments shall be binding upon or applicable in Denmark.

2. Whenever amendments to the Regulation are adopted Denmark shall notify the Commission of its decision whether or not to implement the content of such amendments. Notification shall be given at the time of the adoption of the amendments or within 30 days thereafter.

3. If Denmark decides that it will implement the content of the amendments the notification shall indicate whether implementation can take place administratively or requires parliamentary approval.

4. If the notification indicates that implementation can take place administratively the notification shall, moreover, state that all necessary administrative measures enter into force on the date of entry into force of the amendments to the Regulation or have entered into force on the date of the notification, whichever date is the latest.

5. If the notification indicates that implementation requires parliamentary approval in Denmark, the following rules shall apply:

(a) legislative measures in Denmark shall enter into force on the date of entry into force of the amendments to the Regulation or within 6 months after the notification, whichever date is the latest;

(b) Denmark shall notify the Commission of the date upon which the implementing legislative measures enter into force.

6. A Danish notification that the content of the amendments have been implemented in Denmark, in accordance with paragraph 4 and 5, creates mutual obligations under international law between Denmark and the Community. The amendments to the Regulation shall then constitute amendments to this Agreement and shall be considered annexed hereto.

7. In cases where:

(a) Denmark notifies its decision not to implement the content of the amendments; or

(b) Denmark does not make a notification within the 30-day time limit set out in paragraph 2; or

(c) legislative measures in Denmark do not enter into force within the time limits set out in paragraph 5,

this Agreement shall be considered terminated unless the parties decide otherwise within 90 days or, in the situation referred to under (c), legislative measures in Denmark enter into force within the same period. Termination shall take effect three months after the expiry of the 90-day period.

8. Requests that have been transmitted before the date of termination of the Agreement as set out in paragraph 7 are not affected hereby.

[3589]

Article 4

Implementing measures

1. Denmark shall not take part in the adoption of opinions by the Committee referred to in Article 18 of the Regulation on the service of documents. Implementing measures adopted pursuant to Article 17 of that Regulation shall not be binding upon and shall not be applicable in Denmark.

2. Whenever implementing measures are adopted pursuant to Article 17 of the Regulation, the implementing measures shall be communicated to Denmark. Denmark shall notify the Commission of its decision whether or not to implement the content of the implementing measures. Notification shall be given upon receipt of the implementing measures or within 30 days thereafter.

3. The notification shall state that all necessary administrative measures in Denmark enter into force on the date of entry into force of the implementing measures or have entered into force on the date of the notification, whichever date is the latest.

4. A Danish notification that the content of the implementing measures has been implemented in Denmark creates mutual obligations under international law between Denmark and the Community. The implementing measures will then form part of this Agreement.

5. In cases where:

(a) Denmark notifies its decision not to implement the content of the implementing measures; or

(b) Denmark does not make a notification within the 30-day time limit set out in paragraph 2,

this Agreement shall be considered terminated unless the parties decide otherwise within 90 days. Termination shall take effect three months after the expiry of the 90-day period.

6. Requests that have been transmitted before the date of termination of the Agreement as set out in paragraph 5 are not affected hereby.

7. If in exceptional cases the implementation requires parliamentary approval in Denmark, the Danish notification under paragraph 2 shall indicate this and the provisions of Article 3(5) to (8), shall apply.

8. Denmark shall communicate to the Commission the information referred to in Articles 2, 3, 4, 9, 10, 13, 14, 15, 17(a) and 19 of the Regulation on the service of documents. The Commission shall publish this information together with the relevant information concerning the other Member States. The manual and the glossary drawn up pursuant to Article 17 of that Regulation shall include also the relevant information on Denmark.

[3590]

Article 5

International agreements which affect the Regulation on the service of documents

1. International agreements entered into by the Community when exercising its external competence based on the rules of the Regulation on the service of documents shall not be binding upon and shall not be applicable in Denmark.

2. Denmark will abstain from entering into international agreements which may affect or alter the scope of the Regulation on the service of documents as annexed to this Agreement unless it is done in agreement with the Community and satisfactory arrangements have been made with regard to the relationship between this Agreement and the international agreement in question.

3. When negotiating international agreements that may affect or alter the scope of the Regulation on the service of documents as annexed to this Agreement, Denmark will coordinate its position with the Community and will abstain from any actions that would jeopardise the objectives of a coordinated position of the Community within its sphere of competence in such negotiations.

[3591]

Article 6

Jurisdiction of the Court of Justice of the European Communities in relation to the interpretation of the Agreement

1. Where a question on the validity or interpretation of this Agreement is raised in a case pending before a Danish court or tribunal, that court or tribunal shall request the Court of Justice to give a ruling thereon whenever under the same circumstances a court or tribunal of another Member State of the European Union would be required to do so in respect of the Regulation on the service of documents and its implementing measures referred to in Article 2(1) of this Agreement.

2. Under Danish law, the courts in Denmark shall, when interpreting this Agreement, take due account of the rulings contained in the case law of the Court of Justice in respect of provisions of the Regulation on the service of documents and any implementing Community measures.

3. Denmark may, like the Council, the Commission and any Member State, request the Court of Justice to give a ruling on a question of interpretation of this Agreement. The ruling given by the Court of Justice in response to such a request shall not apply to judgments of courts or tribunals of the Member States which have become *res judicata*.

4. Denmark shall be entitled to submit observations to the Court of Justice in cases where a question has been referred to it by a court or tribunal of a Member State for a preliminary ruling concerning the interpretation of any provision referred to in Article 2(1).

5. The Protocol on the Statute of the Court of Justice of the European Communities and its Rules of Procedure shall apply.

6. If the provisions of the Treaty establishing the European Community regarding rulings by the Court of Justice are amended with consequences for rulings in respect of the Regulation on the service of documents, Denmark may notify the Commission of its decision not to apply the amendments under this Agreement. Notification shall be given at the time of the entry into force of the amendments or within 60 days thereafter.

In such a case this Agreement shall be considered terminated. Termination shall take effect three months after the notification.

7. Requests that have been transmitted before the date of termination of the Agreement as set out in paragraph 6 are not affected hereby.

[3592]

Article 7

Jurisdiction of the Court of Justice of the European Communities in relation to compliance with the Agreement

1. The Commission may bring before the Court of Justice cases against Denmark concerning non-compliance with any obligation under this Agreement.

2. Denmark may bring a complaint before the Commission as to the non-compliance by a Member State of its obligations under this Agreement.

3. The relevant provisions of the Treaty establishing the European Community governing proceedings before the Court of Justice as well as the Protocol on the Statute of the Court of Justice of the European Communities and its Rules of Procedure shall apply.

[3593]

Article 8

Territorial application

This Agreement shall apply to the territories referred to in Article 299 of the Treaty establishing the European Community.

[3594]

Article 9

Termination of the Agreement

1. This Agreement shall terminate if Denmark informs the other Member States that it no longer wishes to avail itself of the provisions of Part I of the Protocol on the position of Denmark, in accordance with Article 7 of that Protocol.

2. This Agreement may be terminated by either Contracting Party giving notice to the other Contracting Party. Termination shall be effective six months after the date of such notice.

3. Requests that have been transmitted before the date of termination of the Agreement as set out in paragraph 1 or 2 are not affected hereby.

[3595]

Article 10

Entry into force

1. The Agreement shall be adopted by the Contracting Parties in accordance with their respective procedures.

2. The Agreement shall enter into force on the first day of the sixth month following the notification by the Contracting Parties of the completion of their respective procedures required for this purpose.

[3596]

Article 11

Authenticity of texts

This Agreement is drawn up in duplicate in the Czech, Danish, Dutch, English, Estonian, Finnish, French, German, Greek, Hungarian, Italian, Latvian, Lithuanian, Maltese, Polish, Portuguese, Slovene, Slovak, Spanish and Swedish languages, each of these texts being equally authentic.

[3597]

Done at Brussels on the nineteenth day of October in the year two thousand and five.

For the European Community

For the Kingdom of Denmark

PART IV

H. EVIDENCE

COUNCIL REGULATION

of 28 May 2001

on co-operation between the courts of the Member States in the taking of evidence in civil or commercial matters

(1206/2001/EC)

NOTES

Date of publication in OJ: OJ L174, 27.6.2001, p 1.

THE COUNCIL OF THE EUROPEAN UNION,

Having regard to the Treaty establishing the European Community, and in particular Article 61(c) and Article 67(1) thereof,

Having regard to the initiative of the Federal Republic of Germany,[1]

Having regard to the opinion of the European Parliament,[2]

Having regard to the opinion of the Economic and Social Committee,[3]

Whereas:

(1) The European Union has set itself the objective of maintaining and developing the European Union as an area of freedom, security and justice in which the free movement of persons is ensured. For the gradual establishment of such an area, the Community is to adopt, among others, the measures relating to judicial cooperation in civil matters needed for the proper functioning of the internal market.

(2) For the purpose of the proper functioning of the internal market, cooperation between courts in the taking of evidence should be improved, and in particular simplified and accelerated.

(3) At its meeting in Tampere on 15 and 16 October 1999, the European Council recalled that new procedural legislation in cross-border cases, in particular on the taking of evidence, should be prepared.

(4) This area falls within the scope of Article 65 of the Treaty.

(5) The objectives of the proposed action, namely the improvement of cooperation between the courts on the taking of evidence in civil or commercial matters, cannot be sufficiently achieved by the Member States and can therefore be better achieved at Community level. The Community may adopt measures in accordance with the principle of subsidiarity as set out in Article 5 of the Treaty. In accordance with the principle of proportionality, as set out in that Article, this Regulation does not go beyond what is necessary to achieve those objectives.

(6) To date, there is no binding instrument between all the Member States concerning the taking of evidence. The Hague Convention of 18 March 1970 on the taking of evidence abroad in civil or commercial matters applies between only 11 Member States of the European Union.

(7) As it is often essential for a decision in a civil or commercial matter pending before a court in a Member State to take evidence in another Member State, the Community's activity cannot be limited to the field of transmission of judicial and extrajudicial documents in civil or commercial matters which falls within the scope of Council Regulation (EC) No 1348/2000 of 29 May 2000 on the serving in the Member States of judicial and extrajudicial documents in civil or commercial matters.[4] It is therefore necessary to continue the improvement of cooperation between courts of Member States in the field of taking of evidence.

(8) The efficiency of judicial procedures in civil or commercial matters requires that the transmission and execution of requests for the performance of taking of evidence is to be made directly and by the most rapid means possible between Member States' courts.

(9) Speed in transmission of requests for the performance of taking of evidence warrants the use of all appropriate means, provided that certain conditions as to the legibility and reliability of the document received are observed. So as to ensure the utmost clarity and legal certainty the request for the performance of taking of evidence must be transmitted on a form to be completed in the language of the Member State of the requested court or in another language accepted by that State. For the same reasons, forms should also be used as far as possible for further communication between the relevant courts.

(10) A request for the performance of the taking of evidence should be executed expeditiously. If it is not possible for the request to be executed within 90 days of receipt by the requested court, the latter should inform the requesting court accordingly, stating the reasons which prevent the request from being executed swiftly.

(11) To secure the effectiveness of this Regulation, the possibility of refusing to execute the request for the performance of taking of evidence should be confined to strictly limited exceptional situations.

(12) The requested court should execute the request in accordance with the law of its Member State.

(13) The parties and, if any, their representatives, should be able to be present at the performance of the taking of evidence, if that is provided for by the law of the Member State of the requesting court, in order to be able to follow the proceedings in a comparable way as if evidence were taken in the Member State of the requesting court. They should also have the right to request to participate in order to have a more active role in the performance of the taking of evidence. However, the conditions under which they may participate should be determined by the requested court in accordance with the law of its Member State.

(14) The representatives of the requesting court should be able to be present at the performance of the taking of evidence, if that is compatible with the law of the Member State of the requesting court, in order to have an improved possibility of evaluation of evidence. They should also have the right to request to participate, under the conditions laid down by the requested court in accordance with the law of its Member State, in order to have a more active role in the performance of the taking of evidence.

(15) In order to facilitate the taking of evidence it should be possible for a court in a Member State, in accordance with the law of its Member State, to take evidence directly in another Member State, if accepted by the latter, and under the conditions determined by the central body or competent authority of the requested Member State.

(16) The execution of the request, according to Article 10, should not give rise to a claim for any reimbursement of taxes or costs. Nevertheless, if the requested court requires reimbursement, the fees paid to experts and interpreters, as well as the costs occasioned by the application of Article 10(3) and (4), should not be borne by that court. In such a case, the requesting court is to take the necessary measures to ensure reimbursement without delay. Where the opinion of an expert is required, the requested court may, before executing the request, ask the requesting court for an adequate deposit or advance towards the costs.

(17) This Regulation should prevail over the provisions applying to its field of application, contained in international conventions concluded by the Member States. Member States should be free to adopt agreements or arrangements to further facilitate cooperation in the taking of evidence.

(18) The information transmitted pursuant to this Regulation should enjoy protection. Since Directive 95/46/EC of the European Parliament and of the Council of 24 October 1995 on the protection of individuals with regard to the processing of personal data and on the free movement of such data,[5] and Directive 97/66/EC of the European Parliament and of the Council of 15 December 1997 concerning the processing of personal data and the protection of privacy in the telecommunications sector,[6] are applicable, there is no need for specific provisions on data protection in this Regulation.

(19) The measures necessary for the implementation of this Regulation should be adopted in accordance with Council Decision 1999/468/EC of 28 June 1999[7] laying down the procedures for the exercise of implementing powers conferred on the Commission.

(20) For the proper functioning of this Regulation, the Commission should review its application and propose such amendments as may appear necessary.

(21) The United Kingdom and Ireland, in accordance with Article 3 of the Protocol on the position of the United Kingdom and Ireland annexed to the Treaty on the European Union and to the Treaty establishing the European Community, have given notice of their wish to take part in the adoption and application of this Regulation.

(22) Denmark, in accordance with Articles 1 and 2 of the Protocol on the position of Denmark annexed to the Treaty on European Union and to the Treaty establishing the European Community, is not participating in the adoption of this Regulation, and is therefore not bound by it nor subject to its application,

[3598]

NOTES

1 OJ C314, 3.11.2000, p 2.
2 Opinion delivered on 14 March 2001 (not yet published in the Official Journal).
3 Opinion delivered on 28 February 2001 (not yet published in the Official Journal).
4 OJ L160, 30.6.2000, p 37.
5 OJ L281, 23.11.1995, p 31.
6 OJ L24, 30.1.1998, p 1.

7 OJ L184, 17.7.1999, p 23.

HAS ADOPTED THIS REGULATION:

CHAPTER I
GENERAL PROVISIONS

Article 1

Scope

1. This Regulation shall apply in civil or commercial matters where the court of a Member State, in accordance with the provisions of the law of that State, requests:
(a) the competent court of another Member State to take evidence; or
(b) to take evidence directly in another Member State.

2. A request shall not be made to obtain evidence which is not intended for use in judicial proceedings, commenced or contemplated.

3. In this Regulation, the term "Member State" shall mean Member States with the exception of Denmark.

[3599]

Article 2

Direct transmission between the courts

1. Requests pursuant to Article 1(1)(a), hereinafter referred to as "requests", shall be transmitted by the court before which the proceedings are commenced or contemplated, hereinafter referred to as the "requesting court", directly to the competent court of another Member State, hereinafter referred to as the "requested court", for the performance of the taking of evidence.

2. Each Member State shall draw up a list of the courts competent for the performance of taking of evidence according to this Regulation. The list shall also indicate the territorial and, where appropriate, the special jurisdiction of those courts.

[3600]

Article 3

Central body

1. Each Member State shall designate a central body responsible for:
(a) supplying information to the courts;
(b) seeking solutions to any difficulties which may arise in respect of a request;
(c) forwarding, in exceptional cases, at the request of a requesting court, a request to the competent court.

2. A federal State, a State in which several legal systems apply or a State with autonomous territorial entities shall be free to designate more than one central body.

3. Each Member State shall also designate the central body referred to in paragraph 1 or one or several competent authority(ies) to be responsible for taking decisions on requests pursuant to Article 17.

[3601]

CHAPTER II
TRANSMISSION AND EXECUTION OF REQUESTS

SECTION 1
TRANSMISSION OF THE REQUEST

Article 4

Form and content of the request

1. The request shall be made using form A or, where appropriate, form I in the Annex. It shall contain the following details:

(a) the requesting and, where appropriate, the requested court;
(b) the names and addresses of the parties to the proceedings and their representatives, if any;
(c) the nature and subject matter of the case and a brief statement of the facts;
(d) a description of the taking of evidence to be performed;
(e) where the request is for the examination of a person:
- the name(s) and address(es) of the person(s) to be examined,
- the questions to be put to the person(s) to be examined or a statement of the facts about which he is (they are) to be examined,
- where appropriate, a reference to a right to refuse to testify under the law of the Member State of the requesting court,
- any requirement that the examination is to be carried out under oath or affirmation in lieu thereof, and any special form to be used,
- where appropriate, any other information that the requesting court deems necessary;

(f) where the request is for any other form of taking of evidence, the documents or other objects to be inspected;
(g) where appropriate, any request pursuant to Article 10(3) and (4), and Articles 11 and 12 and any information necessary for the application thereof.

2. The request and all documents accompanying the request shall be exempted from authentication or any equivalent formality.

3. Documents which the requesting court deems it necessary to enclose for the execution of the request shall be accompanied by a translation into the language in which the request was written.

[3602]

Article 5

Language

The request and communications pursuant to this Regulation shall be drawn up in the official language of the requested Member State or, if there are several official languages in that Member State, in the official language or one of the official languages of the place where the requested taking of evidence is to be performed, or in another language which the requested Member State has indicated it can accept. Each Member State shall indicate the official language or languages of the institutions of the European Community other than its own which is or are acceptable to it for completion of the forms.

[3603]

Article 6

Transmission of requests and other communications

Requests and communications pursuant to this Regulation shall be transmitted by the swiftest possible means, which the requested Member State has indicated it can accept. The transmission may be carried out by any appropriate means, provided that the document received accurately reflects the content of the document forwarded and that all information in it is legible.

[3604]

SECTION 2
RECEIPT OF REQUEST

Article 7

Receipt of request

1. Within seven days of receipt of the request, the requested competent court shall send an acknowledgement of receipt to the requesting court using form B in the Annex. Where the request does not comply with the conditions laid down in Articles 5 and 6, the requested court shall enter a note to that effect in the acknowledgement of receipt.

2. Where the execution of a request made using form A in the Annex, which complies with the conditions laid down in Article 5, does not fall within the jurisdiction of the court to

which it was transmitted, the latter shall forward the request to the competent court of its Member State and shall inform the requesting court thereof using form A in the Annex. **[3605]**

Article 8

Incomplete request

1. If a request cannot be executed because it does not contain all of the necessary information pursuant to Article 4, the requested court shall inform the requesting court thereof without delay and, at the latest, within 30 days of receipt of the request using form C in the Annex, and shall request it to send the missing information, which should be indicated as precisely as possible.

2. If a request cannot be executed because a deposit or advance is necessary in accordance with Article 18(3), the requested court shall inform the requesting court thereof without delay and, at the latest, within 30 days of receipt of the request using form C in the Annex and inform the requesting court how the deposit or advance should be made. The requested Court shall acknowledge receipt of the deposit or advance without delay, at the latest within 10 days of receipt of the deposit or the advance using form D. **[3606]**

Article 9

Completion of the request

1. If the requested court has noted on the acknowledgement of receipt pursuant to Article 7(1) that the request does not comply with the conditions laid down in Articles 5 and 6 or has informed the requesting court pursuant to Article 8 that the request cannot be executed because it does not contain all of the necessary information pursuant to Article 4, the time limit pursuant to Article 10 shall begin to run when the requested court received the request duly completed.

2. Where the requested court has asked for a deposit or advance in accordance with Article 18(3), this time limit shall begin to run when the deposit or the advance is made. **[3607]**

SECTION 3
TAKING OF EVIDENCE BY THE REQUESTED COURT

Article 10

General provisions on the execution of the request

1. The requested court shall execute the request without delay and, at the latest, within 90 days of receipt of the request.

2. The requested court shall execute the request in accordance with the law of its Member State.

3. The requesting court may call for the request to be executed in accordance with a special procedure provided for by the law of its Member State, using form A in the Annex. The requested court shall comply with such a requirement unless this procedure is incompatible with the law of the Member State of the requested court or by reason of major practical difficulties. If the requested court does not comply with the requirement for one of these reasons it shall inform the requesting court using form E in the Annex.

4. The requesting court may ask the requested court to use communications technology at the performance of the taking of evidence, in particular by using videoconference and teleconference.

The requested court shall comply with such a requirement unless this is incompatible with the law of the Member State of the requested court or by reason of major practical difficulties.

If the requested court does not comply with the requirement for one of these reasons, it shall inform the requesting court, using form E in the Annex.

If there is no access to the technical means referred to above in the requesting or in the requested court, such means may be made available by the courts by mutual agreement. **[3608]**

Article 11

Performance with the presence and participation of the parties

1. If it is provided for by the law of the Member State of the requesting court, the parties and, if any, their representatives, have the right to be present at the performance of the taking of evidence by the requested court.

2. The requesting court shall, in its request, inform the requested court that the parties and, if any, their representatives, will be present and, where appropriate, that their participation is requested, using form A in the Annex. This information may also be given at any other appropriate time.

3. If the participation of the parties and, if any, their representatives, is requested at the performance of the taking of evidence, the requested court shall determine, in accordance with Article 10, the conditions under which they may participate.

4. The requested court shall notify the parties and, if any, their representatives, of the time when, the place where, the proceedings will take place, and, where appropriate, the conditions under which they may participate, using form F in the Annex.

5. Paragraphs 1 to 4 shall not affect the possibility for the requested court of asking the parties and, if any their representatives, to be present at or to participate in the performance of the taking of evidence if that possibility is provided for by the law of its Member State.

[3609]

Article 12

Performance with the presence and participation of representatives of the requesting court

1. If it is compatible with the law of the Member State of the requesting court, representatives of the requesting court have the right to be present in the performance of the taking of evidence by the requested court.

2. For the purpose of this Article, the term "representative" shall include members of the judicial personnel designated by the requesting court, in accordance with the law of its Member State. The requesting court may also designate, in accordance with the law of its Member State, any other person, such as an expert.

3. The requesting court shall, in its request, inform the requested court that its representatives will be present and, where appropriate, that their participation is requested, using form A in the Annex. This information may also be given at any other appropriate time.

4. If the participation of the representatives of the requesting court is requested in the performance of the taking of evidence, the requested court shall determine, in accordance with Article 10, the conditions under which they may participate.

5. The requested court shall notify the requesting court, of the time when, and the place where, the proceedings will take place, and, where appropriate, the conditions under which the representatives may participate, using form F in the Annex.

[3610]

Article 13

Coercive measures

Where necessary, in executing a request the requested court shall apply the appropriate coercive measures in the instances and to the extent as are provided for by the law of the Member State of the requested court for the execution of a request made for the same purpose by its national authorities or one of the parties concerned.

[3611]

Article 14

Refusal to execute

1. A request for the hearing of a person shall not be executed when the person concerned claims the right to refuse to give evidence or to be prohibited from giving evidence,

(a) under the law of the Member State of the requested court; or

(b) under the law of the Member State of the requesting court, and such right has been specified in the request, or, if need be, at the instance of the requested court, has been confirmed by the requesting court.

2. In addition to the grounds referred to in paragraph 1, the execution of a request may be refused only if:

(a) the request does not fall within the scope of this Regulation as set out in Article 1; or

(b) the execution of the request under the law of the Member State of the requested court does not fall within the functions of the judiciary; or

(c) the requesting court does not comply with the request of the requested court to complete the request pursuant to Article 8 within 30 days after the requested court asked it to do so; or

(d) a deposit or advance asked for in accordance with Article 18(3) is not made within 60 days after the requested court asked for such a deposit or advance.

3. Execution may not be refused by the requested court solely on the ground that under the law of its Member State a court of that Member State has exclusive jurisdiction over the subject matter of the action or that the law of that Member State would not admit the right of action on it.

4. If execution of the request is refused on one of the grounds referred to in paragraph 2, the requested court shall notify the requesting court thereof within 60 days of receipt of the request by the requested court using form H in the Annex.

[3612]

Article 15

Notification of delay

If the requested court is not in a position to execute the request within 90 days of receipt, it shall inform the requesting court thereof, using form G in the Annex. When it does so, the grounds for the delay shall be given as well as the estimated time that the requested court expects it will need to execute the request.

[3613]

Article 16

Procedure after execution of the request

The requested court shall send without delay to the requesting court the documents establishing the execution of the request and, where appropriate, return the documents received from the requesting court. The documents shall be accompanied by a confirmation of execution using form H in the Annex.

[3614]

SECTION 4
DIRECT TAKING OF EVIDENCE BY THE REQUESTING COURT

Article 17

1. Where a court requests to take evidence directly in another Member State, it shall submit a request to the central body or the competent authority referred to in Article 3(3) in that State, using form I in the Annex.

2. Direct taking of evidence may only take place if it can be performed on a voluntary basis without the need for coercive measures.

Where the direct taking of evidence implies that a person shall be heard, the requesting court shall inform that person that the performance shall take place on a voluntary basis.

3. The taking of evidence shall be performed by a member of the judicial personnel or by any other person such as an expert, who will be designated, in accordance with the law of the Member State of the requesting court.

4. Within 30 days of receiving the request, the central body or the competent authority of the requested Member State shall inform the requesting court if the request is accepted and, if necessary, under what conditions according to the law of its Member State such performance is to be carried out, using form J.

In particular, the central body or the competent authority may assign a court of its Member State to take part in the performance of the taking of evidence in order to ensure the proper application of this Article and the conditions that have been set out.

The central body or the competent authority shall encourage the use of communications technology, such as videoconferences and teleconferences.

5. The central body or the competent authority may refuse direct taking of evidence only if:

(a) the request does not fall within the scope of this Regulation as set out in Article 1;
(b) the request does not contain all of the necessary information pursuant to Article 4; or
(c) the direct taking of evidence requested is contrary to fundamental principles of law in its Member State.

6. Without prejudice to the conditions laid down in accordance with paragraph 4, the requesting court shall execute the request in accordance with the law of its Member State.

[3615]

SECTION 5
COSTS

Article 18

1. The execution of the request, in accordance with Article 10, shall not give rise to a claim for any reimbursement of taxes or costs.

2. Nevertheless, if the requested court so requires, the requesting court shall ensure the reimbursement, without delay, of:

— the fees paid to experts and interpreters, and
— the costs occasioned by the application of Article 10(3) and (4).

The duty for the parties to bear these fees or costs shall be governed by the law of the Member State of the requesting court.

3. Where the opinion of an expert is required, the requested court may, before executing the request, ask the requesting court for an adequate deposit or advance towards the requested costs. In all other cases, a deposit or advance shall not be a condition for the execution of a request.

The deposit or advance shall be made by the parties if that is provided for by the law of the Member State of the requesting court.

[3616]

CHAPTER III
FINAL PROVISIONS

Article 19

Implementing rules

1. The Commission shall draw up and regularly update a manual, which shall also be available electronically, containing the information provided by the Member States in accordance with Article 22 and the agreements or arrangements in force, according to Article 21.

2. The updating or making of technical amendments to the standard forms set out in the Annex shall be carried out in accordance with the advisory procedure set out in Article 20(2).

[3617]

Article 20

Committee

1. The Commission shall be assisted by a Committee.

2. Where reference is made to this paragraph, Articles 3 and 7 of Decision 1999/468/EC shall apply.

3. The Committee shall adopt its Rules of Procedure. **[3618]**

Article 21

Relationship with existing or future agreements or arrangements between Member States

1. This Regulation shall, in relation to matters to which it applies, prevail over other provisions contained in bilateral or multilateral agreements or arrangements concluded by the Member States and in particular the Hague Convention of 1 March 1954 on Civil Procedure and the Hague Convention of 18 March 1970 on the Taking of Evidence Abroad in Civil or Commercial Matters, in relations between the Member States party thereto.

2. This Regulation shall not preclude Member States from maintaining or concluding agreements or arrangements between two or more of them to further facilitate the taking of evidence, provided that they are compatible with this Regulation.

3. Member States shall send to the Commission:

(a) by 1 July 2003, a copy of the agreements or arrangements maintained between the Member States referred to in paragraph 2;

(b) a copy of the agreements or arrangements concluded between the Member States referred to in paragraph 2 as well as drafts of such agreements or arrangements which they intend to adopt; and

(c) any denunciation of, or amendments to, these agreements or arrangements.

[3619]

Article 22

Communication

By 1 July 2003 each Member State shall communicate to the Commission the following:

(a) the list pursuant to Article 2(2) indicating the territorial and, where appropriate, the special jurisdiction of the courts;

(b) the names and addresses of the central bodies and competent authorities pursuant to Article 3, indicating their territorial jurisdiction;

(c) the technical means for the receipt of requests available to the courts on the list pursuant to Article 2(2);

(d) the languages accepted for the requests as referred to in Article 5.

Member States shall inform the Commission of any subsequent changes to this information.

[3620]

Article 23

Review

No later than 1 January 2007, and every five years thereafter, the Commission shall present to the European Parliament, the Council and the Economic and Social Committee a report on the application of this Regulation, paying special attention to the practical application of Article 3(1)(c) and 3, and Articles 17 and 18.

[3621]

Article 24

Entry into force

1. This Regulation shall enter into force on 1 July 2001.

2. This Regulation shall apply from 1 January 2004, except for Articles 19, 21 and 22, which shall apply from 1 July 2001.

This Regulation shall be binding in its entirety and directly applicable in the Member States in accordance with the Treaty establishing the European Community.

[3622]

Done at Brussels, 28 May 2001.

For the Council

The President

T BODSTRÖM

I. OTHER

COUNCIL REGULATION

of 22 November 1996

protecting against the effects of the extra-territorial application of legislation adopted by a third country, and actions based thereon or resulting therefrom

(2271/96/EC)

NOTES

Date of publication in OJ: L309, 29.11.1996, p 1.

THE COUNCIL OF THE EUROPEAN UNION,

Having regard to the Treaty establishing the European Community, and in particular Articles 73c, 113 and 235 thereof,

Having regard to the proposal from the Commission,

Having regard to the opinion of the European Parliament,[1]

Whereas the objectives of the Community include contributing to the harmonious development of world trade and to the progressive abolition of restrictions on international trade;

Whereas the Community endeavours to achieve to the greatest extent possible the objective of free movement of capital between Member States and third countries, including the removal of any restrictions on direct investment—including investment in real estate—establishment, the provision of financial services or the admission of securities to capital markets;

Whereas a third country has enacted certain laws, regulations, and other legislative instruments which purport to regulate activities of natural and legal persons under the jurisdiction of the Member State;

Whereas by their extra-territorial application such laws, regulations and other legislative instruments violate international law and impede the attainment of the aforementioned objectives;

Whereas such laws, including regulations and other legislative instruments, and actions based thereon or resulting therefrom affect or are likely to affect the established legal order and have adverse effects on the interests of the Community and the interests of natural and legal persons exercising rights under the Treaty establishing the European Community;

Whereas, under these exceptional circumstances, it is necessary to take action at Community level to protect the established legal order, the interests of the Community and the interests of the said natural and legal persons, in particular by removing, neutralising, blocking or otherwise countering the effects of the foreign legislation concerned;

Whereas the request to supply information under this Regulation does not preclude a Member State from requiring information of the same kind to be provided to the authorities of that State;

Whereas the Council has adopted the Joint Action 96/668/CFSP of 22 November 1996[2] in order to ensure that the Member States take the necessary measures to protect those natural and legal persons whose interests are affected by the aforementioned laws and actions based thereon, insofar as those interests are not protected by this Regulation;

Whereas the Commission, in the implementation of this Regulation, should be assisted by a committee composed of representatives of the Member States;

Whereas the actions provided for in this Regulation are necessary to attain objectives of the Treaty establishing the European Community;

Whereas for the adoption of certain provisions of this Regulation the Treaty does not provide powers other than those of Article 235,

[3623]

NOTES

1 Opinion delivered on 25 October 1996 (OJ No C347, 18.11.1996).

2 See page 7 of this Official Journal.

HAS ADOPTED THIS REGULATION:

Article 1

This Regulation provides protection against and counteracts the effects of the extra-territorial application of the laws specified in the Annex of this Regulation, including regulations and other legislative instruments, and of actions based thereon or resulting therefrom, where such application affects the interests of persons, referred to in Article 11, engaging in international trade and/or the movement of capital and related commercial activities between the Community and third countries.

Acting in accordance with the relevant provisions of the Treaty and notwithstanding the provisions of Article 7(c), the Council may add or delete laws to or from the Annex to this Regulation.

[3624]

Article 2

Where the economic and/or financial interests of any person referred to in Article 11 are affected, directly or indirectly, by the laws specified in the Annex or by actions based thereon or resulting therefrom, that person shall inform the Commission accordingly within 30 days from the date on which it obtained such information; insofar as the interests of a legal person are affected, this obligation applies to the directors, managers and other persons with management responsibilities.[1]

At the request of the Commission, such person shall provide all information relevant for the purposes of this Regulation in accordance with the request from the Commission within 30 days from the date of the request.

All information shall be submitted to the Commission either directly or through the competent authorities of the Member States. Should the information be submitted directly to the Commission, the Commission will inform immediately the competent authorities of the Member States in which the person who gave the information is resident or incorporated.

[3625]

NOTES

1 Information should be supplied to the following address: European Commission, Directorate General I, Rue de la Loi/Wetstraat 200, B-1049 Brussels (fax (32–2) 295 65 05).

Article 3

All information supplied in accordance with Article 2 shall only be used for the purposes for which it was provided.

Information which is by nature confidential or which is provided on a confidential basis shall be covered by the obligation of professional secrecy. It shall not be disclosed by the Commission without the express permission of the person providing it.

Communication of such information shall be permitted where the Commission is obliged or authorized to do so, in particular in connection with legal proceedings. Such communication must take into account the legitimate interests of the person concerned that his or her business secrets should not be divulged.

This Article shall not preclude the disclosure of general information by the Commission. Such disclosure shall not be permitted if this is incompatible with the original purpose of such information.

In the event of a breach of confidentiality, the originator of the information shall be entitled to obtain that it be deleted, disregarded or rectified, as the case may be.

[3626]

Article 4

No judgment of a court or tribunal and no decision of an administrative authority located outside the Community giving effect, directly or indirectly, to the laws specified in the Annex or to actions based thereon or resulting there from, shall be recognized or be enforceable in any manner.

[3627]

Article 5

No person referred to in Article 11 shall comply, whether directly or through a subsidiary or other intermediary person, actively or by deliberate omission, with any requirement or prohibition, including requests of foreign courts, based on or resulting, directly or indirectly, from the laws specified in the Annex or from actions based thereon or resulting therefrom.

Persons may be authorized, in accordance with the procedures provided in Articles 7 and 8, to comply fully or partially to the extent that non-compliance would seriously damage their interests or those of the Community. The criteria for the application of this provision shall be established in accordance with the procedure set out in Article 8. When there is sufficient evidence that non-compliance would cause serious damage to a natural or legal person, the Commission shall expeditiously submit to the committee referred to in Article 8 a draft of the appropriate measures to be taken under the terms of the Regulation.

[3628]

Article 6

Any person referred to in Article 11, who is engaging in an activity referred to in Article 1 shall be entitled to recover any damages, including legal costs, caused to that person by the application of the laws specified in the Annex or by actions based thereon or resulting therefrom.

Such recovery may be obtained from the natural or legal person or any other entity causing the damages or from any person acting on its behalf or intermediary.

The Brussels Convention of 27 September 1968 on jurisdiction and the enforcement of judgments in civil and commercial matters shall apply to proceedings brought and judgments given under this Article. Recovery may be obtained on the basis of the provisions of Sections 2 to 6 of Title II of that Convention, as well as, in accordance with Article 57(3) of that Convention, through judicial proceedings instituted in the Courts of any Member State where that person, entity, person acting on its behalf or intermediary holds assets.

Without prejudice to other means available and in accordance with applicable law, the recovery could take the form of seizure and sale of assets held by those persons, entities, persons acting on their behalf or intermediaries within the Community, including shares held in a legal person incorporated within the Community.

[3629]

Article 7

For the implementation of this Regulation the Commission shall:

(a) inform the European Parliament and the Council immediately and fully of the effects of the laws, regulations and other legislative instruments and ensuing actions mentioned in Article 1, on the basis of the information obtained under this Regulation, and make regularly a full public report thereon;

(b) grant authorization under the conditions set forth in Article 5 and, when laying down the time limits with regard to the delivery by the Committee of its opinion, take fully into account the time limits which have to be complied with by the persons which are to be subject of an authorization;

(c) add or delete, where appropriate, references to regulations or other legislative instruments deriving from the laws specified in the Annex, and falling under the scope of this Regulation;

(d) publish a notice in the Official Journal of the European Communities on the judgments and decisions to which Articles 4 and 6 apply;

(e) publish in the Official Journal of the European Communities the names and addresses of the competent authorities of the Member States referred to in Article 2.

[3630]

[Article 8

1. For the purposes of the application of Article 7(b) and (c), the Commission shall be assisted by a committee.

2. Where reference is made to this Article, Articles 5 and 7 of Decision 1999/468/EC[1] shall apply.

The period laid down in Article 5(6) of Decision 1999/468/EC shall be set at two weeks.

3. The committee shall adopt its rules of procedure.]

[3631]

NOTES

Commencement: 5 June 2003.

Substituted by Council Regulation 807/2003/EC, Art 3, Annex III, para 50.

[1] OJ L184, 17.7.1999, p 23.

Article 9

Each Member State shall determine the sanctions to be imposed in the event of breach of any relevant provisions of this Regulation. Such sanctions must be effective, proportional and dissuasive.

[3632]

Article 10

The Commission and the Member States shall inform each other of the measures taken under this Regulation and of all other relevant information pertaining to this Regulation.

[3633]

Article 11

This Regulation shall apply to:

1. any natural person being a resident in the Community[1] and a national of a Member State,
2. any legal person incorporated within the Community,
3. any natural or legal person referred to in Article 1(2) of Regulation (EEC) No 4055/86,[2]
4. any other natural person being a resident in the Community, unless that person is in the country of which he is a national,
5. any other natural person within the Community, including its territorial waters and air space and in any aircraft or on any vessel under the jurisdiction or control of a Member State, acting in a professional capacity.

[3634]

NOTES

[1] For the purposes of this Regulation, "being a resident in the Community" means: being legally established in the Community for a period of at least six months within the 12-month period immediately prior to the date on which, under this Regulation, an obligation arises or a right is exercised.

[2] Council Regulation (EEC) No 4055/86 of 22 December 1986 applying the principle of freedom to provide services to maritime transport between Member States and between Member States and third countries (OJ No L378, 31.12.1986, p 1). Regulation as last amended by Regulation (EC) No 3573/90 (OJ No C353, 17.12.1990, p 16).

Article 12

This Regulation shall enter into force on the day of its publication in the Official Journal of the European Communities.

This Regulation shall be binding in its entirety and directly applicable in all Member States.

[3635]

Done at Brussels, 22 November 1996.

For the Council

The President

S BARRETT

ANNEX

LAWS, REGULATIONS AND OTHER LEGISLATIVE INSTRUMENTS[1] REFERRED TO IN ARTICLE 1

COUNTRY: UNITED STATES OF AMERICA

ACTS

1. "National Defense Authorization Act for Fiscal Year 1993", Title XVII "Cuban Democracy Act 1992", sections 1704 and 1706

Required compliance:

The requirements are consolidated in Title I of the "Cuban Liberty and Democratic Solidarity Act of 1996", see below.

Possible damages to EU interests:

The liabilities incurred are now incorporated within the "Cuban Liberty and Democratic Solidarity Act of 1996", see below.

2. "Cuban Liberty and Democratic Solidarity Act of 1996"

Title I

Required compliance:

To comply with the economic and financial embargo concerning Cuba by the USA, by, inter alia, not exporting to the USA any goods or services of Cuban origin or containing materials or goods originating in Cuba either directly or through third countries, dealing in merchandise that is or has been located in or transported from or through Cuba, re-exporting to the USA sugar originating in Cuba without notification by the competent national authority of the exporter or importing into the USA sugar products without assurance that those products are not products of Cuba, freezing Cuban assets, and financial dealings with Cuba.

Possible damages to EU interests:

Prohibition to load or unload freight from a vessel in any place in the USA or to enter a USA port; refusal to import any goods or services originating in Cuba and to import into Cuba goods or services originating in the USA, blocking of financial dealings involving Cuba.

Title III and Title IV:

Required compliance:

To terminate "trafficking" in property, formerly owned by US persons (including Cubans who have obtained US citizenship) and expropriated by the Cuban regime. (Trafficking includes: use, sale, transfer, control, management and other activities to the benefit of a person).

Possible damages to EU interests:

Legal proceedings in the USA, based upon liability already accruing, against EU citizens or companies involved in trafficking, leading to judgments/decisions to pay (multiple) compensation to the USA party. Refusal of entry into the USA for persons involved in trafficking, including the spouses, minor children and agents thereof.

3. "Iran and Libya Sanctions Act of 1996"

Required compliance:

Not to invest in Iran or Libya any amount greater than USD 40 million during a period of 12 months that directly and significantly contributes to the enhancement of the Iranian or Libyan ability to develop their petroleum resources. (Investment covering the entering into a contract for the said development, or the guaranteeing of it, or the profiting therefrom or the purchase of a share of ownership therein.)

NB: Investments under contracts existing before 5 August 1996 are exempted.

Respect of embargo concerning Libya established by Resolutions 748 (1992) and 883 (1993) of the Security Council of the United Nations.[2]

Possible damages to EU interests:

Measures taken by the US President to limit imports into USA or procurement to USA, prohibition of designation as primary dealer or as repository of USA Government funds, denial of access to loans from USA financial institutions, export restrictions by USA, or refusal of assistance by EXIM-Bank.

REGULATIONS

1.31 CFR (Code of Federal Regulations) Ch V (7-1-95 edition) Part 515 – Cuban Assets Control Regulations, subpart B (Prohibitions), E (Licenses, Authorizations and Statements of Licensing Policy) and G (Penalties)

Required compliance:

The prohibitions are consolidated in Title I of the "Cuban Liberty and Democratic Solidarity Act of 1996", see above. Furthermore, requires the obtaining of licences and/or authorizations in respect of economic activities concerning Cuba.

Possible damages to EU interests:

Fines, forfeiture, imprisonment in cases of violation.

[3636]

NOTES

1 Further information with regard to the aforementioned laws and regulations can be obtained from the European Commission, Directorate General I.E.3, Rue de la Loi/Wetstraat 200, B-1049 Brussels (fax: (32–2) 295 65 05).

2 See Community implementation of those Resolutions through Council Regulation (EC) No 3274/93 (OJ No L295, 30.11.1993, p 1).

COUNCIL REGULATION

of 15 December 2003

protecting against the effects of the application of the United States Anti-Dumping Act of 1916, and actions based thereon or resulting therefrom

(2238/2003/EC)

NOTES

Date of publication in OJ: OJ L333, 20.12.2003, p 1.

THE COUNCIL OF THE EUROPEAN UNION,

Having regard to the Treaty establishing the European Community, and in particular Article 133 thereof,

Having regard to the proposal from the Commission,

Whereas:

(1) The objectives of the Community include contributing to the harmonious development of world trade and to the progressive abolition of restrictions on international trade.

(2) In the United States of America ("USA"), the Anti-Dumping Act of 1916[1] provides for civil and criminal proceedings and penalties against dumping of any articles when conducted with an intent to destroy or injure an industry in the USA, or to prevent the establishment of an industry in the USA, or to restrain or monopolise any part of trade and commerce in such articles in the USA.

(3) On 26 September 2000, the Dispute Settlement Body of the World Trade Organisation (WTO), adopting the Appellate Body report[2] and the Panel report,[3] as upheld by the Appellate Body report, found the Anti-Dumping Act of 1916 to be incompatible with the US obligations under the WTO agreements, notably by providing remedies against dumping, such as the imposition of treble damages, fines and imprisonment, none of which is permitted by the General Agreement on Tariffs and Trade 1994 ("GATT 1994") or by the Agreement on Implementation of Article VI of the General Agreement on Tariffs and Trade 1994 ("AD Agreement").

(4) The USA failed to comply with the Panel and Appellate Body recommendations and rulings within the time limit of 20 December 2001. As a result, the Community requested authorisation to suspend the application to the USA of its obligations under GATT 1994 and the AD Agreement.

(5) In February 2002, the Community agreed to suspend the arbitration on its request, on the express understanding that a bill was pending in the US Congress to repeal the Anti-Dumping Act of 1916 and to terminate the on-going cases before US Courts.

(6) The Anti-Dumping Act of 1916 has yet to be repealed, and claims brought under this Act are pending before US Courts against persons under the jurisdiction of the Member States.

(7) These judicial proceedings are causing substantial litigation costs and may ultimately result in a judgment awarding treble damages.

(8) By its maintenance and application, the Anti-Dumping Act of 1916 impedes the attainment of the aforementioned objectives, affects the established legal order and has adverse effects on the interests of the Community and the interests of natural and legal persons exercising rights under the Treaty.

PART IV EC MATERIALS

(9) Under these exceptional circumstances, it is necessary to take action at Community level to protect the interests of the natural and legal persons under the jurisdiction of the Member States, in particular by removing, neutralising, blocking or otherwise counteracting the effects of the Anti-Dumping Act of 1916,

[3637]

NOTES

1 Enacted under the heading of "unfair competition" in Title VIII of the Revenue Act of 1916; Title VIII of that Act is codified at United States Code 71–74, cited as 15 U.S.C §72.

2 AB-2000–5 and AB-2000–6, 28 August 2000.

3 United States—Anti-Dumping Act of 1916, Panel report (WT/DS/136/R, 31 March 2000).

HAS ADOPTED THIS REGULATION:

Article 1

No judgment of a court or tribunal and no decision of an administrative authority located in the United States of America giving effect, directly or indirectly, to the Anti-Dumping Act of 1916 or to actions based thereon or resulting therefrom, shall be recognised or be enforceable in any manner.

[3638]

Article 2

1. Any person referred to in Article 3 shall be entitled to recover any outlays, costs, damages and miscellaneous expenses incurred by him or her as a result of the application of the Anti-Dumping Act of 1916 or by actions based thereon or resulting therefrom.

2. Recovery may be obtained as soon as an action under the Anti-Dumping Act of 1916 is commenced.

3. Recovery may be obtained from the natural or legal person or any other entity that brought a claim under the Anti-Dumping Act of 1916 or from any person or entity related to that person or entity. Persons or entities shall be deemed to be related if:

(a) they are officers or directors of one another's businesses;
(b) they are legally recognised partners in business;
(c) one of them controls directly or indirectly the other;
(d) both of them are directly or indirectly controlled by a third person.

4. Without prejudice to other means available and in accordance with applicable law, the recovery may take the form of seizure and sale of assets held by the defendant, including shares held in a legal person incorporated within the Community.

[3639]

Article 3

The persons referred to in Article 2(1) shall be:

(a) any natural person being a resident in the Community;
(b) any legal person incorporated within the Community;
(c) any natural or legal person referred to in Article 1(2) of Regulation (EEC) No 4055/86;[1]
(d) any other natural person acting in a professional capacity within the Community, including in territorial waters and air space and in any aircraft or on any vessel under the jurisdiction or control of a Member State.

For the purposes of point (a), "being a resident in the Community" shall mean being legally established in the Community for a period of at least six months within the 12-month period immediately prior to the date on which, under this Regulation, an obligation arises or a right is exercised.

[3640]

NOTES

1 OJ L378, 31.12.1986, p 1; Regulation as last amended by Regulation (EEC) No 3573/90 (OJ L353, 17.12.1990, p 16).

Article 4

This Regulation shall enter into force on the 20th day following that of its publication in the *Official Journal of the European Union*.

This Regulation shall be binding in its entirety and directly applicable in all Member States.

[3641]–[4000]

Done at Brussels, 15 December 2003.

For the Council

The President

A MARZANO

PART V
OTHER INTERNATIONAL MATERIALS

A. JURISDICTION AND FOREIGN JUDGMENTS

CONVENTION ON CHOICE OF COURT AGREEMENTS

(Concluded The Hague, 30 June 2005)

NOTES

The original source of this convention is Hague Conference on Private International Law, website http://www.hcch.net; to be published in the next edition of the "Collection of Conventions' (1951–2005).

Neither the United Kingdom nor the European Community has ratified this Convention, which is not yet in force.

The States Parties to the present Convention,

DESIRING to promote international trade and investment through enhanced judicial co-operation,

BELIEVING that such co-operation can be enhanced by uniform rules on jurisdiction and on recognition and enforcement of foreign judgments in civil or commercial matters,

BELIEVING that such enhanced co-operation requires in particular an international legal regime that provides certainty and ensures the effectiveness of exclusive choice of court agreements between parties to commercial transactions and that governs the recognition and enforcement of judgments resulting from proceedings based on such agreements,

HAVE RESOLVED to conclude this Convention and have agreed upon the following provisions—

CHAPTER I
SCOPE AND DEFINITIONS

Article 1

Scope

1. This Convention shall apply in international cases to exclusive choice of court agreements concluded in civil or commercial matters.

2. For the purposes of Chapter II, a case is international unless the parties are resident in the same Contracting State and the relationship of the parties and all other elements relevant to the dispute, regardless of the location of the chosen court, are connected only with that State.

3. For the purposes of Chapter III, a case is international where recognition or enforcement of a foreign judgment is sought.

[4001]

Article 2

Exclusions from scope

1. This Convention shall not apply to exclusive choice of court agreements—
   (a) to which a natural person acting primarily for personal, family or household purposes (a consumer) is a party;
   (b) relating to contracts of employment, including collective agreements.

2. This Convention shall not apply to the following matters—
   (a) the status and legal capacity of natural persons;
   (b) maintenance obligations;
   (c) other family law matters, including matrimonial property regimes and other rights or obligations arising out of marriage or similar relationships;
   (d) wills and succession;
   (e) insolvency, composition and analogous matters;
   (f) the carriage of passengers and goods;
   (g) marine pollution, limitation of liability for maritime claims, general average, and emergency towage and salvage;
   (h) anti-trust (competition) matters;

(i) liability for nuclear damage;
(j) claims for personal injury brought by or on behalf of natural persons;
(k) tort or delict claims for damage to tangible property that do not arise from a contractual relationship;
(l) rights in rem in immovable property, and tenancies of immovable property;
(m) the validity, nullity, or dissolution of legal persons, and the validity of decisions of their organs;
(n) the validity of intellectual property rights other than copyright and related rights;
(o) infringement of intellectual property rights other than copyright and related rights, except where infringement proceedings are brought for breach of a contract between the parties relating to such rights, or could have been brought for breach of that contract;
(p) the validity of entries in public registers.

3. Notwithstanding paragraph 2, proceedings are not excluded from the scope of this Convention where a matter excluded under that paragraph arises merely as a preliminary question and not as an object of the proceedings. In particular, the mere fact that a matter excluded under paragraph 2 arises by way of defence does not exclude proceedings from the Convention, if that matter is not an object of the proceedings.

4. This Convention shall not apply to arbitration and related proceedings.

5. Proceedings are not excluded from the scope of this Convention by the mere fact that a State, including a government, a governmental agency or any person acting for a State, is a party thereto.

6. Nothing in this Convention shall affect privileges and immunities of States or of international organisations, in respect of themselves and of their property.

[4002]

Article 3

Exclusive choice of court agreements

For the purposes of this Convention—

(a) "exclusive choice of court agreement" means an agreement concluded by two or more parties that meets the requirements of paragraph (c) and designates, for the purpose of deciding disputes which have arisen or may arise in connection with a particular legal relationship, the courts of one Contracting State or one or more specific courts of one Contracting State to the exclusion of the jurisdiction of any other courts;
(b) a choice of court agreement which designates the courts of one Contracting State or one or more specific courts of one Contracting State shall be deemed to be exclusive unless the parties have expressly provided otherwise;
(c) an exclusive choice of court agreement must be concluded or documented—
 (i) in writing; or
 (ii) by any other means of communication which renders information accessible so as to be usable for subsequent reference;
(d) an exclusive choice of court agreement that forms part of a contract shall be treated as an agreement independent of the other terms of the contract. The validity of the exclusive choice of court agreement cannot be contested solely on the ground that the contract is not valid.

[4003]

Article 4

Other definitions

1. In this Convention, "judgment" means any decision on the merits given by a court, whatever it may be called, including a decree or order, and a determination of costs or expenses by the court (including an officer of the court), provided that the determination relates to a decision on the merits which may be recognised or enforced under this Convention. An interim measure of protection is not a judgment.

2. For the purposes of this Convention, an entity or person other than a natural person shall be considered to be resident in the State—

(a) where it has its statutory seat;
(b) under whose law it was incorporated or formed;

(c) where it has its central administration; or
(d) where it has its principal place of business.

[4004]

CHAPTER II
JURISDICTION

Article 5

Jurisdiction of the chosen court

1. The court or courts of a Contracting State designated in an exclusive choice of court agreement shall have jurisdiction to decide a dispute to which the agreement applies, unless the agreement is null and void under the law of that State.

2. A court that has jurisdiction under paragraph 1 shall not decline to exercise jurisdiction on the ground that the dispute should be decided in a court of another State.

3. The preceding paragraphs shall not affect rules—
   (a) on jurisdiction related to subject matter or to the value of the claim;
   (b) on the internal allocation of jurisdiction among the courts of a Contracting State. However, where the chosen court has discretion as to whether to transfer a case, due consideration should be given to the choice of the parties.

[4005]

Article 6

Obligations of a court not chosen

A court of a Contracting State other than that of the chosen court shall suspend or dismiss proceedings to which an exclusive choice of court agreement applies unless—
   (a) the agreement is null and void under the law of the State of the chosen court;
   (b) a party lacked the capacity to conclude the agreement under the law of the State of the court seised;
   (c) giving effect to the agreement would lead to a manifest injustice or would be manifestly contrary to the public policy of the State of the court seised;
   (d) for exceptional reasons beyond the control of the parties, the agreement cannot reasonably be performed; or
   (e) the chosen court has decided not to hear the case.

[4006]

Article 7

Interim measures of protection

Interim measures of protection are not governed by this Convention. This Convention neither requires nor precludes the grant, refusal or termination of interim measures of protection by a court of a Contracting State and does not affect whether or not a party may request or a court should grant, refuse or terminate such measures.

[4007]

CHAPTER III
RECOGNITION AND ENFORCEMENT

Article 8

Recognition and enforcement

1. A judgment given by a court of a Contracting State designated in an exclusive choice of court agreement shall be recognised and enforced in other Contracting States in accordance with this Chapter. Recognition or enforcement may be refused only on the grounds specified in this Convention.

2. Without prejudice to such review as is necessary for the application of the provisions of this Chapter, there shall be no review of the merits of the judgment given by the court of origin. The court addressed shall be bound by the findings of fact on which the court of origin based its jurisdiction, unless the judgment was given by default.

3. A judgment shall be recognised only if it has effect in the State of origin, and shall be enforced only if it is enforceable in the State of origin.

4. Recognition or enforcement may be postponed or refused if the judgment is the subject of review in the State of origin or if the time limit for seeking ordinary review has not expired. A refusal does not prevent a subsequent application for recognition or enforcement of the judgment.

5. This Article shall also apply to a judgment given by a court of a Contracting State pursuant to a transfer of the case from the chosen court in that Contracting State as permitted by Article 5, paragraph 3. However, where the chosen court had discretion as to whether to transfer the case to another court, recognition or enforcement of the judgment may be refused against a party who objected to the transfer in a timely manner in the State of origin.

[4008]

Article 9

Refusal of recognition or enforcement

Recognition or enforcement may be refused if—

(a) the agreement was null and void under the law of the State of the chosen court, unless the chosen court has determined that the agreement is valid;

(b) a party lacked the capacity to conclude the agreement under the law of the requested State;

(c) the document which instituted the proceedings or an equivalent document, including the essential elements of the claim,

  (i) was not notified to the defendant in sufficient time and in such a way as to enable him to arrange for his defence, unless the defendant entered an appearance and presented his case without contesting notification in the court of origin, provided that the law of the State of origin permitted notification to be contested; or

  (ii) was notified to the defendant in the requested State in a manner that is incompatible with fundamental principles of the requested State concerning service of documents;

(d) the judgment was obtained by fraud in connection with a matter of procedure;

(e) recognition or enforcement would be manifestly incompatible with the public policy of the requested State, including situations where the specific proceedings leading to the judgment were incompatible with fundamental principles of procedural fairness of that State;

(f) the judgment is inconsistent with a judgment given in the requested State in a dispute between the same parties; or

(g) the judgment is inconsistent with an earlier judgment given in another State between the same parties on the same cause of action, provided that the earlier judgment fulfils the conditions necessary for its recognition in the requested State.

[4009]

Article 10

Preliminary questions

1. Where a matter excluded under Article 2, paragraph 2, or under Article 21, arose as a preliminary question, the ruling on that question shall not be recognised or enforced under this Convention.

2. Recognition or enforcement of a judgment may be refused if, and to the extent that, the judgment was based on a ruling on a matter excluded under Article 2, paragraph 2.

3. However, in the case of a ruling on the validity of an intellectual property right other than copyright or a related right, recognition or enforcement of a judgment may be refused or postponed under the preceding paragraph only where—

(a) that ruling is inconsistent with a judgment or a decision of a competent authority on that matter given in the State under the law of which the intellectual property right arose; or

(b) proceedings concerning the validity of the intellectual property right are pending in that State.

4. Recognition or enforcement of a judgment may be refused if, and to the extent that, the judgment was based on a ruling on a matter excluded pursuant to a declaration made by the requested State under Article 21.

[4010]

Article 11

Damages

1. Recognition or enforcement of a judgment may be refused if, and to the extent that, the judgment awards damages, including exemplary or punitive damages, that do not compensate a party for actual loss or harm suffered.

2. The court addressed shall take into account whether and to what extent the damages awarded by the court of origin serve to cover costs and expenses relating to the proceedings.

[4011]

Article 12

Judicial settlements (transactions judiciaires)

Judicial settlements (transactions judiciaires) which a court of a Contracting State designated in an exclusive choice of court agreement has approved, or which have been concluded before that court in the course of proceedings, and which are enforceable in the same manner as a judgment in the State of origin, shall be enforced under this Convention in the same manner as a judgment.

[4012]

Article 13

Documents to be produced

1. The party seeking recognition or applying for enforcement shall produce—
   (a) a complete and certified copy of the judgment;
   (b) the exclusive choice of court agreement, a certified copy thereof, or other evidence of its existence;
   (c) if the judgment was given by default, the original or a certified copy of a document establishing that the document which instituted the proceedings or an equivalent document was notified to the defaulting party;
   (d) any documents necessary to establish that the judgment has effect or, where applicable, is enforceable in the State of origin;
   (e) in the case referred to in Article 12, a certificate of a court of the State of origin that the judicial settlement or a part of it is enforceable in the same manner as a judgment in the State of origin.

2. If the terms of the judgment do not permit the court addressed to verify whether the conditions of this Chapter have been complied with, that court may require any necessary documents.

3. An application for recognition or enforcement may be accompanied by a document, issued by a court (including an officer of the court) of the State of origin, in the form recommended and published by the Hague Conference on Private International Law.

4. If the documents referred to in this Article are not in an official language of the requested State, they shall be accompanied by a certified translation into an official language, unless the law of the requested State provides otherwise.

[4013]

Article 14

Procedure

The procedure for recognition, declaration of enforceability or registration for enforcement, and the enforcement of the judgment, are governed by the law of the requested State unless this Convention provides otherwise. The court addressed shall act expeditiously.

[4014]

Article 15

Severability

Recognition or enforcement of a severable part of a judgment shall be granted where recognition or enforcement of that part is applied for, or only part of the judgment is capable of being recognised or enforced under this Convention.

[4015]

CHAPTER IV
GENERAL CLAUSES

Article 16

Transitional provisions

1. This Convention shall apply to exclusive choice of court agreements concluded after its entry into force for the State of the chosen court.

2. This Convention shall not apply to proceedings instituted before its entry into force for the State of the court seised.

[4016]

Article 17

Contracts of insurance and reinsurance

1. Proceedings under a contract of insurance or reinsurance are not excluded from the scope of this Convention on the ground that the contract of insurance or reinsurance relates to a matter to which this Convention does not apply.

2. Recognition and enforcement of a judgment in respect of liability under the terms of a contract of insurance or reinsurance may not be limited or refused on the ground that the liability under that contract includes liability to indemnify the insured or reinsured in respect of—

(a) a matter to which this Convention does not apply; or
(b) an award of damages to which Article 11 might apply.

[4017]

Article 18

No legalisation

All documents forwarded or delivered under this Convention shall be exempt from legalisation or any analogous formality, including an Apostille.

[4018]

Article 19

Declarations limiting jurisdiction

A State may declare that its courts may refuse to determine disputes to which an exclusive choice of court agreement applies if, except for the location of the chosen court, there is no connection between that State and the parties or the dispute.

[4019]

Article 20

Declarations limiting recognition and enforcement

A State may declare that its courts may refuse to recognise or enforce a judgment given by a court of another Contracting State if the parties were resident in the requested State, and the relationship of the parties and all other elements relevant to the dispute, other than the location of the chosen court, were connected only with the requested State.

[4020]

Article 21

Declarations with respect to specific matters

1. Where a State has a strong interest in not applying this Convention to a specific matter, that State may declare that it will not apply the Convention to that matter. The State making such a declaration shall ensure that the declaration is no broader than necessary and that the specific matter excluded is clearly and precisely defined.

2. With regard to that matter, the Convention shall not apply—

(a) in the Contracting State that made the declaration;

(b) in other Contracting States, where an exclusive choice of court agreement designates the courts, or one or more specific courts, of the State that made the declaration.

[4021]

Article 22

Reciprocal declarations on non-exclusive choice of court agreements

1. A Contracting State may declare that its courts will recognise and enforce judgments given by courts of other Contracting States designated in a choice of court agreement concluded by two or more parties that meets the requirements of Article 3, paragraph c), and designates, for the purpose of deciding disputes which have arisen or may arise in connection with a particular legal relationship, a court or courts of one or more Contracting States (a non-exclusive choice of court agreement).

2. Where recognition or enforcement of a judgment given in a Contracting State that has made such a declaration is sought in another Contracting State that has made such a declaration, the judgment shall be recognised and enforced under this Convention, if—

(a) the court of origin was designated in a non-exclusive choice of court agreement;
(b) there exists neither a judgment given by any other court before which proceedings could be brought in accordance with the non-exclusive choice of court agreement, nor a proceeding pending between the same parties in any other such court on the same cause of action; and
(c) the court of origin was the court first seised.

[4022]

Article 23

Uniform interpretation

In the interpretation of this Convention, regard shall be had to its international character and to the need to promote uniformity in its application.

[4023]

Article 24

Review of operation of the Convention

The Secretary General of the Hague Conference on Private International Law shall at regular intervals make arrangements for—

(a) review of the operation of this Convention, including any declarations; and
(b) consideration of whether any amendments to this Convention are desirable.

[4024]

Article 25

Non-unified legal systems

1. In relation to a Contracting State in which two or more systems of law apply in different territorial units with regard to any matter dealt with in this Convention—

(a) any reference to the law or procedure of a State shall be construed as referring, where appropriate, to the law or procedure in force in the relevant territorial unit;
(b) any reference to residence in a State shall be construed as referring, where appropriate, to residence in the relevant territorial unit;
(c) any reference to the court or courts of a State shall be construed as referring, where appropriate, to the court or courts in the relevant territorial unit;
(d) any reference to a connection with a State shall be construed as referring, where appropriate, to a connection with the relevant territorial unit.

2. Notwithstanding the preceding paragraph, a Contracting State with two or more territorial units in which different systems of law apply shall not be bound to apply this Convention to situations which involve solely such different territorial units.

3. A court in a territorial unit of a Contracting State with two or more territorial units in which different systems of law apply shall not be bound to recognise or enforce a judgment from another Contracting State solely because the judgment has been recognised or enforced in another territorial unit of the same Contracting State under this Convention.

4. This Article shall not apply to a Regional Economic Integration Organisation.

[4025]

Article 26

Relationship with other international instruments

1. This Convention shall be interpreted so far as possible to be compatible with other treaties in force for Contracting States, whether concluded before or after this Convention.

2. This Convention shall not affect the application by a Contracting State of a treaty, whether concluded before or after this Convention, in cases where none of the parties is resident in a Contracting State that is not a Party to the treaty.

3. This Convention shall not affect the application by a Contracting State of a treaty that was concluded before this Convention entered into force for that Contracting State, if applying this Convention would be inconsistent with the obligations of that Contracting State to any non-Contracting State. This paragraph shall also apply to treaties that revise or replace a treaty concluded before this Convention entered into force for that Contracting State, except to the extent that the revision or replacement creates new inconsistencies with this Convention.

4. This Convention shall not affect the application by a Contracting State of a treaty, whether concluded before or after this Convention, for the purposes of obtaining recognition or enforcement of a judgment given by a court of a Contracting State that is also a Party to that treaty. However, the judgment shall not be recognised or enforced to a lesser extent than under this Convention.

5. This Convention shall not affect the application by a Contracting State of a treaty which, in relation to a specific matter, governs jurisdiction or the recognition or enforcement of judgments, even if concluded after this Convention and even if all States concerned are Parties to this Convention. This paragraph shall apply only if the Contracting State has made a declaration in respect of the treaty under this paragraph. In the case of such a declaration, other Contracting States shall not be obliged to apply this Convention to that specific matter to the extent of any inconsistency, where an exclusive choice of court agreement designates the courts, or one or more specific courts, of the Contracting State that made the declaration.

6. This Convention shall not affect the application of the rules of a Regional Economic Integration Organisation that is a Party to this Convention, whether adopted before or after this Convention—

(a) where none of the parties is resident in a Contracting State that is not a Member State of the Regional Economic Integration Organisation;

(b) as concerns the recognition or enforcement of judgments as between Member States of the Regional Economic Integration Organisation.

[4026]

CHAPTER V
FINAL CLAUSES

Article 27

Signature, ratification, acceptance, approval or accession

1. This Convention is open for signature by all States.

2. This Convention is subject to ratification, acceptance or approval by the signatory States.

3. This Convention is open for accession by all States.

4. Instruments of ratification, acceptance, approval or accession shall be deposited with the Ministry of Foreign Affairs of the Kingdom of the Netherlands, depositary of the Convention.

[4027]

Article 28

Declarations with respect to non-unified legal systems

1. If a State has two or more territorial units in which different systems of law apply in relation to matters dealt with in this Convention, it may at the time of signature, ratification,

acceptance, approval or accession declare that the Convention shall extend to all its territorial units or only to one or more of them and may modify this declaration by submitting another declaration at any time.

2. A declaration shall be notified to the depositary and shall state expressly the territorial units to which the Convention applies.

3. If a State makes no declaration under this Article, the Convention shall extend to all territorial units of that State.

4. This Article shall not apply to a Regional Economic Integration Organisation.

[4028]

Article 29

Regional Economic Integration Organisations

1. A Regional Economic Integration Organisation which is constituted solely by sovereign States and has competence over some or all of the matters governed by this Convention may similarly sign, accept, approve or accede to this Convention. The Regional Economic Integration Organisation shall in that case have the rights and obligations of a Contracting State, to the extent that the Organisation has competence over matters governed by this Convention.

2. The Regional Economic Integration Organisation shall, at the time of signature, acceptance, approval or accession, notify the depositary in writing of the matters governed by this Convention in respect of which competence has been transferred to that Organisation by its Member States. The Organisation shall promptly notify the depositary in writing of any changes to its competence as specified in the most recent notice given under this paragraph.

3. For the purposes of the entry into force of this Convention, any instrument deposited by a Regional Economic Integration Organisation shall not be counted unless the Regional Economic Integration Organisation declares in accordance with Article 30 that its Member States will not be Parties to this Convention.

4. Any reference to a "Contracting State" or "State" in this Convention shall apply equally, where appropriate, to a Regional Economic Integration Organisation that is a Party to it.

[4029]

Article 30

Accession by a Regional Economic Integration Organisation without its Member States

1. At the time of signature, acceptance, approval or accession, a Regional Economic Integration Organisation may declare that it exercises competence over all the matters governed by this Convention and that its Member States will not be Parties to this Convention but shall be bound by virtue of the signature, acceptance, approval or accession of the Organisation.

2. In the event that a declaration is made by a Regional Economic Integration Organisation in accordance with paragraph 1, any reference to a "Contracting State" or "State" in this Convention shall apply equally, where appropriate, to the Member States of the Organisation.

[4030]

Article 31

Entry into force

1. This Convention shall enter into force on the first day of the month following the expiration of three months after the deposit of the second instrument of ratification, acceptance, approval or accession referred to in Article 27.

2. Thereafter this Convention shall enter into force—

(a) for each State or Regional Economic Integration Organisation subsequently ratifying, accepting, approving or acceding to it, on the first day of the month following the expiration of three months after the deposit of its instrument of ratification, acceptance, approval or accession;

(b) for a territorial unit to which this Convention has been extended in accordance with Article 28, paragraph 1, on the first day of the month following the expiration of three months after the notification of the declaration referred to in that Article.

[4031]

Article 32

Declarations

1. Declarations referred to in Articles 19, 20, 21, 22 and 26 may be made upon signature, ratification, acceptance, approval or accession or at any time thereafter, and may be modified or withdrawn at any time.

2. Declarations, modifications and withdrawals shall be notified to the depositary.

3. A declaration made at the time of signature, ratification, acceptance, approval or accession shall take effect simultaneously with the entry into force of this Convention for the State concerned.

4. A declaration made at a subsequent time, and any modification or withdrawal of a declaration, shall take effect on the first day of the month following the expiration of three months after the date on which the notification is received by the depositary.

5. A declaration under Articles 19, 20, 21 and 26 shall not apply to exclusive choice of court agreements concluded before it takes effect.

[4032]

Article 33

Denunciation

1. This Convention may be denounced by notification in writing to the depositary. The denunciation may be limited to certain territorial units of a non-unified legal system to which this Convention applies.

2. The denunciation shall take effect on the first day of the month following the expiration of twelve months after the date on which the notification is received by the depositary. Where a longer period for the denunciation to take effect is specified in the notification, the denunciation shall take effect upon the expiration of such longer period after the date on which the notification is received by the depositary.

[4033]

Article 34

Notifications by the depositary

The depositary shall notify the Members of the Hague Conference on Private International Law, and other States and Regional Economic Integration Organisations which have signed, ratified, accepted, approved or acceded in accordance with Articles 27, 29 and 30 of the following—

(a) the signatures, ratifications, acceptances, approvals and accessions referred to in Articles 27, 29 and 30;

(b) the date on which this Convention enters into force in accordance with Article 31;

(c) the notifications, declarations, modifications and withdrawals of declarations referred to in Articles 19, 20, 21, 22, 26, 28, 29 and 30;

(d) the denunciations referred to in Article 33.

In witness whereof the undersigned, being duly authorised thereto, have signed this Convention.

[4034]

Done at The Hague, on 30 June 2005, in the English and French languages, both texts being equally authentic, in a single copy which shall be deposited in the archives of the Government of the Kingdom of the Netherlands, and of which a certified copy shall be sent, through diplomatic channels, to each of the Member States of the Hague Conference on Private International Law as of the date of its Twentieth Session and to each State which participated in that Session.

ANNEX TO THE CONVENTION
RECOMMENDED FORM

Recommended Form under the Convention on Choice of Court Agreements ("The Convention")

(Sample form confirming the issuance and content of a judgement given by the court of origin for the purposes of recognition and enforcement under the Convention)

1. (THE COURT OF ORIGIN) ....
ADDRESS ....
TEL ....
FAX ....
E-MAIL ....
2. CASE/DOCKET NUMBER ....
3. ....(PLAINTIFF)
v
....(DEFENDANT)
4. (THE COURT OF ORIGIN) gave a judgment in the above-captioned matter on (DATE) in (CITY, STATE).
5. This court was designated in an exclusive choice of court agreement within the meaning of Article 3 of the Convention:

YES ___ NO ___

UNABLE TO CONFIRM ___

6. If yes, the exclusive choice of court agreement was concluded or documented in the following manner: ....
7. This court awarded the following payment of money (*please indicate, where applicable, any relevant categories of damages included*): ....
8. This court awarded interest as follows (*please specify the rate(s) of interest, the portion(s) of the award to which interest applies, the date from which interest is computed, and any further information regarding interest that would assist the court addressed*): ....
9. This court included within the judgment the following costs and expenses relating to the proceedings (*please specify the amounts of any such awards, including, where applicable, any amount(s) within a monetary award intended to cover costs and expenses relating to the proceedings*): ....
10. This court awarded the following non-monetary relief (*please describe the nature of such relief*): ....
11. This judgment is enforceable in the State of origin:

YES ___ NO ___

UNABLE TO CONFIRM ___

12. This judgment (or a part thereof) is currently the subject of review in the State of origin:

YES ___ NO ___

UNABLE TO CONFIRM ___

If "yes" please specify the nature and status of such review: ....
13. Any other relevant information: ....
14. Attached to this form are the documents marked in the following list (*if available*):
— a complete and certified copy of the judgment;
— the exclusive choice of court agreement, a certified copy thereof, or other evidence of its existence;
— if the judgment was given by default, the original or a certified copy of a document establishing that the document which instituted the proceedings or an equivalent document was notified to the defaulting party;
— any documents necessary to establish that the judgment has effect or, where applicable, is enforceable in the State of origin;
(*list if applicable*): ....
— in the case referred to in Article 12 of the Convention, a certificate of a court of the State of origin that the judicial settlement or a part of it is enforceable in the same manner as a judgment in the State of origin;
— other documents: ....
15. Dated this .... day of .... , 20...... at ....
16. Signature and/or stamp by the court or officer of the court:
CONTACT PERSON:

TEL:
FAX:
E-MAIL:

[4035]

B. APPLICABLE LAW

NOTES

See also the UN Receivables Convention at **[4071]** and the Cape Town Convention and Aircraft Equipment Protocol at **[4121]**, **[4184]**, which contain rules of applicable law.

CONVENTION ON THE LAW APPLICABLE TO TRUSTS AND ON THEIR RECOGNITION

(Concluded The Hague, 1 July 1985)

NOTES

The text of the following Convention appears as set out in the Recognition of Trusts Act 1987, Schedule. See also the Hague Conference on Private International Law website at http://www.hcch.net.

CHAPTER I
SCOPE

Article 1

This Convention specifies the law applicable to trusts and governs their recognition.

Article 2

For the purposes of this Convention, the term "trust" refers to the legal relationship created—inter vivos or on death—by a person, the settlor, when assets have been placed under the control of a trustee for the benefit of a beneficiary or for a specified purpose.

A trust has the following characteristics—

(a) the assets constitute a separate fund and are not a part of the trustee's own estate;
(b) title to the trust assets stands in the name of the trustee or in the name of another person on behalf of the trustee;
(c) the trustee has the power and the duty, in respect of which he is accountable, to manage, employ or dispose of the assets in accordance with the terms of the trust and the special duties imposed upon him by law.

The reservation by the settlor of certain rights and powers, and the fact that the trustee may himself have rights as a beneficiary, are not necessarily inconsistent with the existence of a trust.

Article 3

The Convention applies only to trusts created voluntarily and evidenced in writing.

Article 4

The Convention does not apply to preliminary issues relating to the validity of wills or of other acts by virtue of which assets are transferred to the trustee.

Article 5

The Convention does not apply to the extent that the law specified by Chapter II does not provide for trusts or the category of trusts involved.

[4036]

CHAPTER II
APPLICABLE LAW

Article 6

A trust shall be governed by the law chosen by the settlor. The choice must be express or be implied in the terms of the instrument creating or the writing evidencing the trust, interpreted, if necessary, in the light of the circumstances of the case.

Where the law chosen under the previous paragraph does not provide for trusts or the category of trust involved, the choice shall not be effective and the law specified in Article 7 shall apply.

Article 7

Where no applicable law has been chosen, a trust shall be governed by the law with which it is most closely connected.

In ascertaining the law with which a trust is most closely connected reference shall be made in particular to—

(a) the place of administration of the trust designated by the settlor;
(b) the situs of the assets of the trust;
(c) the place of residence or business of the trustee;
(d) the objects of the trust and the places where they are to be fulfilled.

Article 8

The law specified by Article 6 or 7 shall govern the validity of the trust, its construction, its effects and the administration of the trust.

In particular that law shall govern—

(a) the appointment, resignation and removal of trustees, the capacity to act as a trustee, and the devolution of the office of trustee;
(b) the rights and duties of trustees among themselves;
(c) the right of trustees to delegate in whole or in part the discharge of their duties or the exercise of their powers;
(d) the power of trustees to administer or to dispose of trust assets, to create security interests in the trust assets, or to acquire new assets;
(e) the powers of investment of trustees;
(f) restrictions upon the duration of the trust, and upon the power to accumulate the income of the trust;
(g) the relationships between the trustees and the beneficiaries including the personal liability of the trustees to the beneficiaries;
(h) the variation of termination of the trust;
(i) the distribution of the trust assets;
(j) the duty of trustees to account for their administration.

Article 9

In applying this Chapter a severable aspect of the trust, particularly matters of administration, may be governed by a different law.

Article 10

The law applicable to the validity of the trust shall determine whether that law or the law governing a severable aspect of the trust may be replaced by another law.

[4037]

CHAPTER III
RECOGNITION

Article 11

A trust created in accordance with the law specified by the preceding Chapter shall be recognised as a trust.

Such recognition shall imply, as a minimum, that the trust property constitutes a separate fund, that the trustee may sue and be sued in his capacity as trustee, and that he may appear or act in this capacity before a notary or any person acting in an official capacity.

In so far as the law applicable to the trust requires or provides, such recognition shall imply in particular—

(a) that personal creditors of the trustee shall have no recourse against the trust assets;

(b) that the trust assets shall not form part of the trustee's estate upon his insolvency or bankruptcy;

(c) that the trust assets shall not form part of the matrimonial property of the trustee or his spouse nor part of the trustee's estate upon his death;

(d) that the trust assets may be recovered when the trustee, in breach of trust, has mingled trust assets with his own property or has alienated trust assets. However, the rights and obligations of any third party holder of the assets shall remain subject to the law determined by the choice of law rules of the forum.

Article 12

Where the trustee desires to register assets, movable or immovable, or documents of title to them, he shall be entitled, in so far as this is not prohibited by or inconsistent with the law of the State where registration is sought, to do so in his capacity as trustee or in such other way that the existence of the trust is disclosed.

Article 14

The Convention shall not prevent the application of rules of law more favourable to the recognition of trusts.

[4038]

CHAPTER IV
GENERAL CLAUSES

Article 15

The Convention does not prevent the application of provisions of the law designated by the conflicts rules of the forum, in so far as those provisions cannot be derogated from by voluntary act, relating in particular to the following matters—

(a) the protection of minors and incapable parties;

(b) the personal and proprietary effects of marriage;

(c) succession rights, testate and intestate, especially the indefeasible shares of spouses and relatives;

(d) the transfer of title to property and security interests in property;

(e) the protection of creditors in matters of insolvency;

(f) the protection, in other respects, of third parties acting in good faith.

If recognition of a trust is prevented by application of the preceding paragraph, the court shall try to give effect to the objects of the trust by other means.

Article 16

The Convention does not prevent the application of those provisions of the law of the forum which must be applied even to international situations, irrespective of rules of conflict of laws.

Article 17

In the Convention the word 'law' means the rules of law in force in a State other than its rules of conflict of laws.

Article 18

The provisions of the Convention may be disregarded when their application would be manifestly incompatible with public policy.

Article 22

The Convention applies to trusts regardless of the date on which they were created.

[4039]

CONVENTION OF THE LAW APPLICABLE TO CERTAIN RIGHTS IN RESPECT OF SECURITIES HELD WITH AN INTERMEDIARY

NOTES

The original source of this convention is Hague Conference on Private International Law, website http://www.hcch.net; "Collection of Conventions 1951–2003"; "Proceedings of the Nineteenth Session (2002), Tome II, Securities held with an intermediary" (to be published in 2006); "Explanatory Report" (ISBN 90 04 14836 1).

As yet, neither the United Kingdom nor the European Community has ratified this Convention, which is not yet in force.

THE STATES PARTIES TO THE PRESENT CONVENTION,

AWARE of the urgent practical need in a large and growing global financial market to provide legal certainty and predictability as to the law applicable to securities that are now commonly held through clearing and settlement systems or other intermediaries,

CONSCIOUS of the importance of reducing legal risk, systemic risk and associated costs in relation to cross-border transactions involving securities held with an intermediary so as to facilitate the international flow of capital and access to capital markets,

DESIRING to establish common provisions on the law applicable to securities held with an intermediary beneficial to States at all levels of economic development,

RECOGNISING that the "Place of the Relevant Intermediary Approach" (or PRIMA) as determined by account agreements with intermediaries provides the necessary legal certainty and predictability,

HAVE RESOLVED to conclude a Convention to this effect, and have agreed upon the following provisions—

CHAPTER I
DEFINITIONS AND SCOPE OF APPLICATION

Article 1

Definitions and interpretation

1. In this Convention—
   - (a) "securities" means any shares, bonds or other financial instruments or financial assets (other than cash), or any interest therein;
   - (b) "securities account" means an account maintained by an intermediary to which securities may be credited or debited;
   - (c) "intermediary" means a person that in the course of a business or other regular activity maintains securities accounts for others or both for others and for its own account and is acting in that capacity;
   - (d) "account holder" means a person in whose name an intermediary maintains a securities account;
   - (e) "account agreement" means, in relation to a securities account, the agreement with the relevant intermediary governing that securities account;
   - (f) "securities held with an intermediary" means the rights of an account holder resulting from a credit of securities to a securities account;
   - (g) "relevant intermediary" means the intermediary that maintains the securities account for the account holder;
   - (h) "disposition" means any transfer of title whether outright or by way of security and any grant of a security interest, whether possessory or non-possessory;
   - (i) "perfection" means completion of any steps necessary to render a disposition effective against persons who are not parties to that disposition;
   - (j) "office" means, in relation to an intermediary, a place of business at which any of the activities of the intermediary are carried on, excluding a place of business which is intended to be merely temporary and a place of business of any person other than the intermediary;
   - (k) "insolvency proceeding" means a collective judicial or administrative proceeding, including an interim proceeding, in which the assets and affairs of the debtor are subject to control or supervision by a court or other competent authority for the purpose of reorganisation or liquidation;
   - (l) "insolvency administrator" means a person authorised to administer a reorganisation or liquidation, including one authorised on an interim basis, and includes a debtor in possession if permitted by the applicable insolvency law;

(m) "Multi-unit State" means a State within which two or more territorial units of that State, or both the State and one or more of its territorial units, have their own rules of law in respect of any of the issues specified in Article 2(1);

(n) "writing" and "written" mean a record of information (including information communicated by teletransmission) which is in tangible or other form and is capable of being reproduced in tangible form on a subsequent occasion.

2. References in this Convention to a disposition of securities held with an intermediary include—

(a) a disposition of a securities account;

(b) a disposition in favour of the account holder's intermediary;

(c) a lien by operation of law in favour of the account holder's intermediary in respect of any claim arising in connection with the maintenance and operation of a securities account.

3. A person shall not be considered an intermediary for the purposes of this Convention merely because—

(a) it acts as registrar or transfer agent for an issuer of securities; or

(b) it records in its own books details of securities credited to securities accounts maintained by an intermediary in the names of other persons for whom it acts as manager or agent or otherwise in a purely administrative capacity.

4. Subject to paragraph (5), a person shall be regarded as an intermediary for the purposes of this Convention in relation to securities which are credited to securities accounts which it maintains in the capacity of a central securities depository or which are otherwise transferable by book entry across securities accounts which it maintains.

5. In relation to securities which are credited to securities accounts maintained by a person in the capacity of operator of a system for the holding and transfer of such securities on records of the issuer or other records which constitute the primary record of entitlement to them as against the issuer, the Contracting State under whose law those securities are constituted may, at any time, make a declaration that the person which operates that system shall not be an intermediary for the purposes of this Convention.

[4040]

Article *2*

Scope of the Convention and of the applicable law

1. This Convention determines the law applicable to the following issues in respect of securities held with an intermediary—

(a) the legal nature and effects against the intermediary and third parties of the rights resulting from a credit of securities to a securities account;

(b) the legal nature and effects against the intermediary and third parties of a disposition of securities held with an intermediary;

(c) the requirements, if any, for perfection of a disposition of securities held with an intermediary;

(d) whether a person's interest in securities held with an intermediary extinguishes or has priority over another person's interest;

(e) the duties, if any, of an intermediary to a person other than the account holder who asserts in competition with the account holder or another person an interest in securities held with that intermediary;

(f) the requirements, if any, for the realisation of an interest in securities held with an intermediary;

(g) whether a disposition of securities held with an intermediary extends to entitlements to dividends, income, or other distributions, or to redemption, sale or other proceeds.

2. This Convention determines the law applicable to the issues specified in paragraph (1) in relation to a disposition of or an interest in securities held with an intermediary even if the rights resulting from the credit of those securities to a securities account are determined in accordance with paragraph (1)(a) to be contractual in nature.

3. Subject to paragraph (2), this Convention does not determine the law applicable to—

(a) the rights and duties arising from the credit of securities to a securities account to the extent that such rights or duties are purely contractual or otherwise purely personal;

(b) the contractual or other personal rights and duties of parties to a disposition of securities held with an intermediary; or

(c) the rights and duties of an issuer of securities or of an issuer's registrar or transfer agent, whether in relation to the holder of the securities or any other person. **[4041]**

Article 3

Internationality

This Convention applies in all cases involving a choice between the laws of different States. **[4042]**

CHAPTER II— APPLICABLE LAW

Article 4

Primary rule

1. The law applicable to all the issues specified in Article 2(1) is the law in force in the State expressly agreed in the account agreement as the State whose law governs the account agreement or, if the account agreement expressly provides that another law is applicable to all such issues, that other law. The law designated in accordance with this provision applies only if the relevant intermediary has, at the time of the agreement, an office in that State, which—

(a) alone or together with other offices of the relevant intermediary or with other persons acting for the relevant intermediary in that or another State—
   (i) effects or monitors entries to securities accounts;
   (ii) administers payments or corporate actions relating to securities held with the intermediary; or
   (iii) is otherwise engaged in a business or other regular activity of maintaining securities accounts; or

(b) is identified by an account number, bank code, or other specific means of identification as maintaining securities accounts in that State.

2. For the purposes of paragraph (1)(a), an office is not engaged in a business or other regular activity of maintaining securities accounts—

(*a*) merely because it is a place where the technology supporting the bookkeeping or data processing for securities accounts is located;

(b) merely because it is a place where call centres for communication with account holders are located or operated;

(c) merely because it is a place where the mailing relating to securities accounts is organised or files or archives are located; or

(d) if it engages solely in representational functions or administrative functions, other than those related to the opening or maintenance of securities accounts, and does not have authority to make any binding decision to enter into any account agreement.

3. In relation to a disposition by an account holder of securities held with a particular intermediary in favour of that intermediary, whether or not that intermediary maintains a securities account on its own records for which it is the account holder, for the purposes of this Convention—

(a) that intermediary is the relevant intermediary;

(b) the account agreement between the account holder and that intermediary is the relevant account agreement;

(c) the securities account for the purposes of Article 5(2) and (3) is the securities account to which the securities are credited immediately before the disposition. **[4043]**

Article 5

Fall-back rules

1. If the applicable law is not determined under Article 4, but it is expressly and unambiguously stated in a written account agreement that the relevant intermediary entered into the account agreement through a particular office, the law applicable to all the issues specified in Article 2(1) is the law in force in the State, or the territorial unit of a Multi-unit State, in which that office was then located, provided that such office then satisfied the condition specified in the second sentence of Article 4(1). In determining whether an account

agreement expressly and unambiguously states that the relevant intermediary entered into the account agreement through a particular office, none of the following shall be considered—

(a) a provision that notices or other documents shall or may be served on the relevant intermediary at that office;

(b) a provision that legal proceedings shall or may be instituted against the relevant intermediary in a particular State or in a particular territorial unit of a Multi-unit State;

(c) a provision that any statement or other document shall or may be provided by the relevant intermediary from that office;

(d) a provision that any service shall or may be provided by the relevant intermediary from that office;

(e) a provision that any operation or function shall or may be carried on or performed by the relevant intermediary at that office.

2. If the applicable law is not determined under paragraph (1), that law is the law in force in the State, or the territorial unit of a Multi-unit State, under whose law the relevant intermediary is incorporated or otherwise organised at the time the written account agreement is entered into or, if there is no such agreement, at the time the securities account was opened; if, however, the relevant intermediary is incorporated or otherwise organised under the law of a Multi-unit State and not that of one of its territorial units, the applicable law is the law in force in the territorial unit of that Multi-unit State in which the relevant intermediary has its place of business, or, if the relevant intermediary has more than one place of business, its principal place of business, at the time the written account agreement is entered into or, if there is no such agreement, at the time the securities account was opened.

3. If the applicable law is not determined under either paragraph (1) or paragraph (2), that law is the law in force in the State, or the territorial unit of a Multi-unit State, in which the relevant intermediary has its place of business, or, if the relevant intermediary has more than one place of business, its principal place of business, at the time the written account agreement is entered into or, if there is no such agreement, at the time the securities account was opened.

[4044]

Article 6

Factors to be disregarded

In determining the applicable law in accordance with this Convention, no account shall be taken of the following factors—

(a) the place where the issuer of the securities is incorporated or otherwise organised or has its statutory seat or registered office, central administration or place or principal place of business;

(b) the places where certificates representing or evidencing securities are located;

(c) the place where a register of holders of securities maintained by or on behalf of the issuer of the securities is located; or

(d) the place where any intermediary other than the relevant intermediary is located.

[4045]

Article 7

Protection of rights on change of the applicable law

1. This Article applies if an account agreement is amended so as to change the applicable law under this Convention.

2. In this Article—

(a) "the new law" means the law applicable under this Convention after the change;

(b) "the old law" means the law applicable under this Convention before the change.

3. Subject to paragraph (4), the new law governs all the issues specified in Article 2(1).

4. Except with respect to a person who has consented to a change of law, the old law continues to govern—

(a) the existence of an interest in securities held with an intermediary arising before the change of law and the perfection of a disposition of those securities made before the change of law;

(b) with respect to an interest in securities held with an intermediary arising before the change of law—

(i) the legal nature and effects of such an interest against the relevant intermediary and any party to a disposition of those securities made before the change of law;
(ii) the legal nature and effects of such an interest against a person who after the change of law attaches the securities;
(iii) the determination of all the issues specified in Article 2(1) with respect to an insolvency administrator in an insolvency proceeding opened after the change of law;

(c) priority as between parties whose interests arose before the change of law.

5. Paragraph (4)(c) does not preclude the application of the new law to the priority of an interest that arose under the old law but is perfected under the new law.

[4046]

Article 8

Insolvency

1. Notwithstanding the opening of an insolvency proceeding, the law applicable under this Convention governs all the issues specified in Article 2(1) with respect to any event that has occurred before the opening of that insolvency proceeding.

2. Nothing in this Convention affects the application of any substantive or procedural insolvency rules, including any rules relating to—

(a) the ranking of categories of claim or the avoidance of a disposition as a preference or a transfer in fraud of creditors; or
(b) the enforcement of rights after the opening of an insolvency proceeding.

[4047]

CHAPTER III—
GENERAL PROVISIONS

Article 9

General applicability of the Convention

This Convention applies whether or not the applicable law is that of a Contracting State.

[4048]

Article 10

Exclusion of choice of law rules (renvoi)

In this Convention, the term "law" means the law in force in a State other than its choice of law rules.

[4049]

Article 11

Public policy and internationally mandatory rules

1. The application of the law determined under this Convention may be refused only if the effects of its application would be manifestly contrary to the public policy of the forum.

2. This Convention does not prevent the application of those provisions of the law of the forum which, irrespective of rules of conflict of laws, must be applied even to international situations.

3. This Article does not permit the application of provisions of the law of the forum imposing requirements with respect to perfection or relating to priorities between competing interests, unless the law of the forum is the applicable law under this Convention.

[4050]

Article 12

Determination of the applicable law for Multi-unit States

1. If the account holder and the relevant intermediary have agreed on the law of a specified territorial unit of a Multi-unit State—

(a) the references to "State" in the first sentence of Article 4(1) are to that territorial unit;

(b) the references to "that State" in the second sentence of Article 4(1) are to the Multi-unit State itself.

2. In applying this Convention—

(a) the law in force in a territorial unit of a Multi-unit State includes both the law of that unit and, to the extent applicable in that unit, the law of the Multi-unit State itself;

(b) if the law in force in a territorial unit of a Multi-unit State designates the law of another territorial unit of that State to govern perfection by public filing, recording or registration, the law of that other territorial unit governs that issue.

3. A Multi-unit State may, at the time of signature, ratification, acceptance, approval or accession, make a declaration that if, under Article 5, the applicable law is that of the Multi-unit State or one of its territorial units, the internal choice of law rules in force in that Multi-unit State shall determine whether the substantive rules of law of that Multi-unit State or of a particular territorial unit of that Multi-unit State shall apply. A Multi-unit State that makes such a declaration shall communicate information concerning the content of those internal choice of law rules to the Permanent Bureau of the Hague Conference on Private International Law.

4. A Multi-unit State may, at any time, make a declaration that if, under Article 4, the applicable law is that of one of its territorial units, the law of that territorial unit applies only if the relevant intermediary has an office within that territorial unit which satisfies the condition specified in the second sentence of Article 4(1). Such a declaration shall have no effect on dispositions made before that declaration becomes effective.

[4051]

Article 13

Uniform interpretation

In the interpretation of this Convention, regard shall be had to its international character and to the need to promote uniformity in its application.

[4052]

Article 14

Review of practical operation of the Convention

The Secretary General of the Hague Conference on Private International Law shall at regular intervals convene a Special Commission to review the practical operation of this Convention and to consider whether any amendments to this Convention are desirable.

[4053]

CHAPTER IV— TRANSITION PROVISIONS

Article 15

Priority between pre-Convention and post-Convention interests

In a Contracting State, the law applicable under this Convention determines whether a person's interest in securities held with an intermediary acquired after this Convention entered into force for that State extinguishes or has priority over another person's interest acquired before this Convention entered into force for that State.

[4054]

Article 16

Pre-Convention account agreements and securities accounts

1. References in this Convention to an account agreement include an account agreement entered into before this Convention entered into force in accordance with Article 19(1). References in this Convention to a securities account include a securities account opened before this Convention entered into force in accordance with Article 19(1).

2. Unless an account agreement contains an express reference to this Convention, the courts of a Contracting State shall apply paragraphs (3) and (4) in applying Article 4(1) with respect to account agreements entered into before the entry into force of this Convention for that State in accordance with Article 19. A Contracting State may, at the time of signature, ratification, acceptance, approval or accession, make a declaration that its courts shall not apply those paragraphs with respect to account agreements entered into after the entry into force of this Convention in accordance with Article 19(1) but before the entry into force of this Convention for that State in accordance with Article 19(2). If the Contracting State is a Multi-unit State, it may make such a declaration with respect to any of its territorial units.

3. Any express terms of an account agreement which would have the effect, under the rules of the State whose law governs that agreement, that the law in force in a particular State, or a territorial unit of a particular Multi-unit State, applies to any of the issues specified in Article 2(1), shall have the effect that such law governs all the issues specified in Article 2(1), provided that the relevant intermediary had, at the time the agreement was entered into, an office in that State which satisfied the condition specified in the second sentence of Article 4(1). A Contracting State may, at the time of signature, ratification, acceptance, approval or accession, make a declaration that its courts shall not apply this paragraph with respect to an account agreement described in this paragraph in which the parties have expressly agreed that the securities account is maintained in a different State. If the Contracting State is a Multi-unit State, it may make such a declaration with respect to any of its territorial units.

4. If the parties to an account agreement, other than an agreement to which paragraph (3) applies, have agreed that the securities account is maintained in a particular State, or a territorial unit of a particular Multi-unit State, the law in force in that State or territorial unit is the law applicable to all the issues specified in Article 2(1), provided that the relevant intermediary had, at the time the agreement was entered into, an office in that State which satisfied the condition specified in the second sentence of Article 4(1). Such an agreement may be express or implied from the terms of the contract considered as a whole or from the surrounding circumstances.

[4055]

CHAPTER V—
FINAL CLAUSES

Article 17

Signature, ratification, acceptance, approval or accession

1. This Convention shall be open for signature by all States.

2. This Convention is subject to ratification, acceptance or approval by the signatory States.

3. Any State which does not sign this Convention may accede to it at any time.

4. The instruments of ratification, acceptance, approval or accession shall be deposited with the Ministry of Foreign Affairs of the Kingdom of the Netherlands, Depositary of this Convention.

[4056]

Article 18

Regional Economic Integration Organisations

1. A Regional Economic Integration Organisation which is constituted by sovereign States and has competence over certain matters governed by this Convention may similarly sign, accept, approve or accede to this Convention. The Regional Economic Integration Organisation shall in that case have the rights and obligations of a Contracting State, to the extent that that Organisation has competence over matters governed by this Convention. Where the number of Contracting States is relevant in this Convention, the Regional Economic Integration Organisation shall not count as a Contracting State in addition to its Member States which are Contracting States.

2. The Regional Economic Integration Organisation shall, at the time of signature, acceptance, approval or accession, notify the Depositary in writing specifying the matters governed by this Convention in respect of which competence has been transferred to that

Organisation by its Member States. The Regional Economic Integration Organisation shall promptly notify the Depositary in writing of any changes to the distribution of competence specified in the notice in accordance with this paragraph and any new transfer of competence.

3. Any reference to a "Contracting State" or "Contracting States" in this Convention applies equally to a Regional Economic Integration Organisation where the context so requires.

[4057]

Article 19

Entry into force

1. This Convention shall enter into force on the first day of the month following the expiration of three months after the deposit of the third instrument of ratification, acceptance, approval or accession referred to in Article 17.

2. Thereafter this Convention shall enter into force—

(a) for each State or Regional Economic Integration Organisation referred to in Article 18 subsequently ratifying, accepting, approving or acceding to it, on the first day of the month following the expiration of three months after the deposit of its instrument of ratification, acceptance, approval or accession;

(b) for a territorial unit to which this Convention has been extended in accordance with Article 20(1), on the first day of the month following the expiration of three months after the notification of the declaration referred to in that Article.

[4058]

Article 20

Multi-unit States

1. A Multi-unit State may, at the time of signature, ratification, acceptance, approval or accession, make a declaration that this Convention shall extend to all its territorial units or only to one or more of them.

2. Any such declaration shall state expressly the territorial units to which this Convention applies.

3. If a State makes no declaration under paragraph (1), this Convention extends to all territorial units of that State.

[4059]

Article 21

Reservations

No reservation to this Convention shall be permitted.

[4060]

Article 22

Declarations

For the purposes of Articles 1(5), 12(3) and (4), 16(2) and (3) and 20—

(a) any declaration shall be notified in writing to the Depositary;

(b) any Contracting State may modify a declaration by submitting a new declaration at any time;

(c) any Contracting State may withdraw a declaration at any time;

(d) any declaration made at the time of signature, ratification, acceptance, approval or accession shall take effect simultaneously with the entry into force of this Convention for the State concerned; any declaration made at a subsequent time and any new declaration shall take effect on the first day of the month following the expiration of three months after the date on which the Depositary made the notification in accordance with Article 24;

(e) a withdrawal of a declaration shall take effect on the first day of the month following the expiration of six months after the date on which the Depositary made the notification in accordance with Article 24.

[4061]

Article 23

Denunciation

1. A Contracting State may denounce this Convention by a notification in writing to the Depositary. The denunciation may be limited to certain territorial units of a Multi-unit State to which this Convention applies.

2. The denunciation shall take effect on the first day of the month following the expiration of twelve months after the date on which the notification is received by the Depositary. Where a longer period for the denunciation to take effect is specified in the notification, the denunciation shall take effect upon the expiration of such longer period after the date on which the notification is received by the Depositary.

[4062]

Article 24

Notifications by the Depositary

The Depositary shall notify the Members of the Hague Conference on Private International Law, and other States and Regional Economic Integration Organisations which have signed, ratified, accepted, approved or acceded in accordance with Articles 17 and 18, of the following—

(a) the signatures and ratifications, acceptances, approvals and accessions referred to in Articles 17 and 18;
(b) the date on which this Convention enters into force in accordance with Article 19;
(c) the declarations and withdrawals of declarations referred to in Article 22;
(d) the notifications referred to in Article 18(2);
(e) the denunciations referred to in Article 23.

In witness whereof the undersigned, being duly authorised thereto, have signed this Convention.

Done at The Hague, on the ...... day of .... 20.... , in the English and French languages, both texts being equally authentic, in a single copy which shall be deposited in the archives of the Government of the Kingdom of the Netherlands, and of which a certified copy shall be sent, through diplomatic channels, to each of the Member States of the Hague Conference on Private International Law as of the date of its Nineteenth Session and to each State which participated in that Session.

[4063]

C. INTERNATIONAL COMMERCIAL AND FINANCIAL LAW

THE UNIFORM LAW ON THE INTERNATIONAL SALE OF GOODS

(1964)

NOTES

The text of the following Law appears as set out in the Uniform Laws on International Sales Act 1967, Sch 1. See also the website of the International Institution for the Unification of Private Law (UNIDROIT) at http://www.unidroit.org.

CHAPTER I
SPHERE OF APPLICATION OF THE LAW

ARTICLE 1

1 The present Law shall apply to contracts of sale of goods entered into by parties whose places of business are in the territories of different Contracting States, in each of the following cases:

(a) where the contract involves the sale of goods which are at the time of the conclusion of the contract in the course of carriage or will be carried from the territory of one State to the territory of another;

(b) where the acts constituting the offer and the acceptance have been effected in the territories of different States;

(c) where delivery of the goods is to be made in the territory of a State other than that within whose territory the acts constituting the offer and the acceptance have been effected.

2 Where a party to the contract does not have a place of business, reference shall be made to his habitual residence.

3 The application of the present Law shall not depend on the nationality of the parties.

4 In the case of contracts by correspondence, offer and acceptance shall be considered to have been effected in the territory of the same State only if the letters, telegrams or other documentary communications which contain them have been sent and received in the territory of that State.

5 For the purpose of determining whether the parties have their places of business or habitual residences in "different States", any two or more States shall not be considered to be "different States" if a valid declaration to that effect made under Article II of the Convention dated the 1st day of July 1964 relating to a Uniform Law on the International Sale of Goods is in force in respect of them.

ARTICLE 2

Rules of private international law shall be excluded for the purposes of the application of the present Law, subject to any provision to the contrary in the said Law.

ARTICLE 3

The parties to a contract of sale shall be free to exclude the application thereto of the present Law either entirely or partially. Such exclusion may be express or implied.

ARTICLE 4

The present Law shall also apply where it has been chosen as the law of the contract by the parties, whether or not their places of business or their habitual residences are in different States and whether or not such States are Parties to the Convention dated the 1st day of July 1964 relating to the Uniform Law on the International Sale of Goods, to the extent that it does not affect the application of any mandatory provisions of law which would have been applicable if the parties had not chosen the Uniform Law.

ARTICLE 5

1 The present Law shall not apply to sales:

(a) of stocks, shares, investment securities, negotiable instruments or money;

(b) of any ship, vessel or aircraft, which is or will be subject to registration;

(c) of electricity;

(d) by authority of law or on execution or distress.

2 The present Law shall not affect the application of any mandatory provision of national law for the protection of a party to a contract which contemplates the purchase of goods by that party by payment of the price by instalments.

ARTICLE 6

Contracts for the supply of goods to be manufactured or produced shall be considered to be sales within the meaning of the present Law, unless the party who orders the goods undertakes to supply an essential and substantial part of the materials necessary for such manufacture or production.

ARTICLE 7

The present Law shall apply to sales regardless of the commercial or civil character of the parties or of the contracts.

ARTICLE 8

The present Law shall govern only the obligations of the seller and the buyer arising from a contract of sale. In particular, the present Law shall not, except as otherwise expressly provided therein, be concerned with the formation of the contract, nor with the effect which the contract may have on the property in the goods sold, nor with the validity of the contract or of any of its provisions or of any usage.

[4064]

CHAPTER II
GENERAL PROVISIONS

ARTICLE 9

1 The parties shall be bound by any usage which they have expressly or impliedly made applicable to their contract and by any practices which they have established between themselves.

2 They shall also be bound by usages which reasonable persons in the same situation as the parties usually consider to be applicable to their contract. In the event of conflict with the present Law, the usages shall prevail unless otherwise agreed by the parties.

3 Where expressions, provisions or forms of contract commonly used in commercial practice are employed, they shall be interpreted according to the meaning usually given to them in the trade concerned.

ARTICLE 10

For the purposes of the present Law, a breach of contract shall be regarded as fundamental wherever the party in breach knew, or ought to have known, at the time of the conclusion of the contract, that a reasonable person in the same situation as the other party would not have entered into the contract if he had foreseen the breach and its effects.

ARTICLE 11

Where under the present Law an act is required to be performed "promptly", it shall be performed within as short a period as possible, in the circumstances, from the moment when the act could reasonably be performed.

ARTICLE 12

For the purposes of the present Law, the expression "current price" means a price based upon an official market quotation, or, in the absence of such a quotation, upon those factors which, according to the usage of the market, serve to determine the price.

ARTICLE 13

For the purposes of the present Law, the expression "a party knew or ought to have known", or any similar expression, refers to what should have been known to a reasonable person in the same situation.

ARTICLE 14

Communications provided for by the present Law shall be made by the means usual in the circumstances.

ARTICLE 15

A contract of sale need not be evidenced by writing and shall not be subject to any other requirements as to form. In particular, it may be proved by means of witnesses.

ARTICLE 16

Where under the provisions of the present Law one party to a contract of sale is entitled to require performance of any obligation by the other party, a court shall not be bound to enter or enforce a judgment providing for specific performance except in accordance with the provisions of Article VII of the Convention dated the 1st day of July 1964 relating to a Uniform Law on the International Sale of Goods.

ARTICLE 17

Questions concerning matters governed by the present Law which are not expressly settled therein shall be settled in conformity with the general principles on which the present Law is based.

[4065]

CHAPTER III
OBLIGATIONS OF THE SELLER

ARTICLE 18

The seller shall effect delivery of the goods, hand over any documents relating thereto and transfer the property in the goods, as required by the contract and the present Law.

SECTION I—DELIVERY OF THE GOODS

ARTICLE 19

1 Delivery consists in the handing over of goods which conform with the contract.

2 Where the contract of sale involves carriage of the goods and no other place for delivery has been agreed upon, delivery shall be effected by handing over the goods to the carrier for transmission to the buyer.

3 Where the goods handed over to the carrier are not clearly appropriated to performance of the contract by being marked with an address or by some other means, the seller shall, in addition to handing over the goods, send to the buyer notice of the consignment and, if necessary, some document specifying the goods.

SUB-SECTION 1—OBLIGATIONS OF THE SELLER AS REGARDS THE DATE AND PLACE OF DELIVERY

A—DATE OF DELIVERY

ARTICLE 20

Where the parties have agreed upon a date for delivery or where such date is fixed by usage, the seller shall, without the need for any other formality, be bound to deliver the goods at that date, provided that the date thus fixed is determined or determinable by the calendar or is fixed in relation to a definite event, the date of which can be ascertained by the parties.

ARTICLE 21

Where by agreement of the parties or by usage delivery shall be effected within a certain period (such as a particular month or season), the seller may fix the precise date of delivery, unless the circumstances indicate that the fixing of the date was reserved to the buyer.

ARTICLE 22

Where the date of delivery has not been determined in accordance with the provisions of Articles 20 or 21, the seller shall be bound to deliver the goods within a reasonable time after the conclusion of the contract, regard being had to the nature of the goods and to the circumstances.

B—PLACE OF DELIVERY

ARTICLE 23

1 Where the contract of sale does not involve carriage of the goods, the seller shall deliver the goods at the place where he carried on business at the time of the conclusion of the contract, or, in the absence of a place of business, at his habitual residence.

2 If the sale relates to specific goods and the parties knew that the goods were at a certain place at the time of the conclusion of the contract, the seller shall deliver the goods at that place. The same rule shall apply if the goods sold are unascertained goods to be taken from a specified stock or if they are to be manufactured or produced at a place known to the parties at the time of the conclusion of the contract.

C—REMEDIES FOR THE SELLER'S FAILURE TO PERFORM HIS OBLIGATIONS AS REGARDS THE DATE AND PLACE OF DELIVERY

ARTICLE 24

1 Where the seller fails to perform his obligations as regards the date or the place of delivery, the buyer may, as provided in Articles 25 to 32:

- (a) require performance of the contract by the seller;
- (b) declare the contract avoided.

2 The buyer may also claim damages as provided in Article 82 or in Articles 84 to 87.

3 In no case shall the seller be entitled to apply to a court or arbitral tribunal to grant him a period of grace.

ARTICLE 25

The buyer shall not be entitled to require performance of the contract by the seller, if it is in conformity with usage and reasonably possible for the buyer to purchase goods to replace those to which the contract relates. In this case the contract shall be *ipso facto* avoided as from the time when such purchase should be effected.

(a) Remedies as regards the date of delivery

ARTICLE 26

1 Where the failure to deliver the goods at the date fixed amounts to a fundamental breach of the contract, the buyer may either require performance by the seller or declare the contract avoided. He shall inform the seller of his decision within a reasonable time; otherwise the contract shall be *ipso facto* avoided.

2 If the seller requests the buyer to make known his decision under paragraph 1 of this Article and the buyer does not comply promptly, the contract shall be *ipso facto* avoided.

3 If the seller has effected delivery before the buyer has made known his decision under paragraph 1 of this Article and the buyer does not exercise promptly his right to declare the contract avoided, the contract cannot be avoided.

4 Where the buyer has chosen performance of the contract and does not obtain it within a reasonable time, he may declare the contract avoided.

ARTICLE 27

1 Where failure to deliver the goods at the date fixed does not amount to a fundamental breach of the contract, the seller shall retain the right to effect delivery and the buyer shall retain the right to require performance of the contract by the seller.

2 The buyer may however grant the seller an additional period of time of reasonable length. Failure to deliver within this period shall amount to a fundamental breach of the contract.

ARTICLE 28

Failure to deliver the goods at the date fixed shall amount to a fundamental breach of the contract whenever a price for such goods is quoted on a market where the buyer can obtain them.

ARTICLE 29

Where the seller tenders delivery of the goods before the date fixed, the buyer may accept or reject delivery; if he accepts, he may reserve the right to claim damages in accordance with Article 82.

(b) Remedies as regards the place of delivery

ARTICLE 30

1 Where failure to deliver the goods at the place fixed amounts to a fundamental breach of the contract, and failure to deliver the goods at the date fixed would also amount to a fundamental breach, the buyer may either require performance of the contract by the seller or declare the contract avoided. The buyer shall inform the seller of his decision within a reasonable time; otherwise the contract shall be *ipso facto* avoided.

2 If the seller requests the buyer to make known his decision under paragraph 1 of this Article and the buyer does not comply promptly, the contract shall be *ipso facto* avoided.

3 If the seller has transported the goods to the place fixed before the buyer has made known his decision under paragraph 1 of this Article and the buyer does not exercise promptly his right to declare the contract avoided, the contract cannot be avoided.

ARTICLE 31

1 In cases not provided for in Article 30, the seller shall retain the right to effect delivery at the place fixed and the buyer shall retain the right to require performance of the contract by the seller.

2 The buyer may however grant the seller an additional period of time of reasonable length. Failure to deliver within this period at the place fixed shall amount to a fundamental breach of the contract.

ARTICLE 32

1 If delivery is to be effected by handing over the goods to a carrier and the goods have been handed over at a place other than that fixed, the buyer may declare the contract avoided, whenever the failure to deliver the goods at the place fixed amounts to a fundamental breach of the contract. He shall lose this right if he has not promptly declared the contract avoided.

2 The buyer shall have the same right, in the circumstances and on the conditions provided in paragraph 1 of this Article, if the goods have been despatched to some place other than that fixed.

3 If despatch from a place or to a place other than that fixed does not amount to a fundamental breach of the contract, the buyer may only claim damages in accordance with Article 82.

SUB-SECTION 2—OBLIGATIONS OF THE SELLER AS REGARDS THE CONFORMITY OF THE GOODS

A—LACK OF CONFORMITY

ARTICLE 33

1 The seller shall not have fulfilled his obligation to deliver the goods, where he has handed over:

(a) part only of the goods sold or a larger or a smaller quantity of the goods than he contracted to sell;

(b) goods which are not those to which the contract relates or goods of a different kind;

(c) goods which lack the qualities of a sample or model which the seller has handed over or sent to the buyer, unless the seller has submitted it without any express or implied undertaking that the goods would conform therewith;

(d) goods which do not possess the qualities necessary for their ordinary or commercial use;

(e) goods which do not possess the qualities for some particular purpose expressly or impliedly contemplated by the contract;

(f) in general, goods which do not possess the qualities and characteristics expressly or impliedly contemplated by the contract.

2 No difference in quantity, lack of part of the goods or absence of any quality or characteristic shall be taken into consideration where it is not material.

ARTICLE 34

In the cases to which Article 33 relates, the rights conferred on the buyer by the present Law exclude all other remedies based on lack of conformity of the goods.

Article 35

1 Whether the goods are in conformity with the contract shall be determined by their conditions at the time when risk passes. However, if risk does not pass because of a declaration of avoidance of the contract or of a demand for other goods in replacement, the conformity of the goods with the contract shall be determined by their condition at the time when risk would have passed had they been in conformity with the contract.

2 The seller shall be liable for the consequences of any lack of conformity occurring after the time fixed in paragraph 1 of this Article if it was due to an act of the seller or of a person for whose conduct he is responsible.

Article 36

The seller shall not be liable for the consequences of any lack of conformity of the kind referred to in sub-paragraphs (d), (e) or (f) of paragraph 1 of Article 33, if at the time of the conclusion of the contract the buyer knew, or could not have been unaware of, such lack of conformity.

Article 37

If the seller has handed over goods before the date fixed for delivery he may, up to that date, deliver any missing part or quantity of the goods or deliver other goods which are in conformity with the contract or remedy any defects in the goods handed over, provided that the exercise of this right does not cause the buyer either unreasonable inconvenience or unreasonable expense.

B—ASCERTAINMENT AND NOTIFICATION OF LACK OF CONFORMITY

Article 38

1 The buyer shall examine the goods, or cause them to be examined, promptly.

2 In case of carriage of the goods the buyer shall examine them at the place of destination.

3 If the goods are redespatched by the buyer without transhipment and the seller knew or ought to have known, at the time when the contract was concluded, of the possibility of such redespatch, examination of the goods may be deferred until they arrive at the new destination.

4 The methods of examination shall be governed by the agreement of the parties or, in the absence of such agreement, by the law or usage of the place where the examination is to be effected.

Article 39

1 The buyer shall lose the right to rely on a lack of conformity of the goods if he has not given the seller notice thereof promptly after he has discovered the lack of conformity or ought to have discovered it. If a defect which could not have been revealed by the examination of the goods provided for in Article 38 is found later, the buyer may nonetheless rely on that defect, provided that he gives the seller notice thereof promptly after its discovery. In any event, the buyer shall lose the right to rely on a lack of conformity of the goods if he has not given notice thereof to the seller within a period of two years from the date on which the goods were handed over, unless the lack of conformity constituted a breach of a guarantee covering a longer period.

2 In giving notice to the seller of any lack of conformity, the buyer shall specify its nature and invite the seller to examine the goods or to cause them to be examined by his agent.

3 Where any notice referred to in paragraph 1 of this Article has been sent by letter, telegram or other appropriate means, the fact that such notice is delayed or fails to arrive at its destination shall not deprive the buyer of the right to rely thereon.

ARTICLE 40

The seller shall not be entitled to rely on the provisions of Articles 38 and 39 if the lack of conformity relates to facts of which he knew, or of which he could not have been unaware, and which he did not disclose.

C—REMEDIES FOR LACK OF CONFORMITY

ARTICLE 41

1 Where the buyer has given due notice to the seller of the failure of the goods to conform with the contract, the buyer may, as provided in Articles 42 to 46:

(a) require performance of the contract by the seller;

(b) declare the contract avoided;

(c) reduce the price.

2 The buyer may also claim damages as provided in Article 82 or in Articles 84 to 87.

ARTICLE 42

1 The buyer may require the seller to perform the contract:

(a) if the sale relates to goods to be produced or manufactured by the seller, by remedying defects in the goods, provided the seller is in a position to remedy the defects;

(b) if the sale relates to specific goods, by delivering the goods to which the contract refers or the missing part thereof;

(c) if the sale relates to unascertained goods, by delivering other goods which are in conformity with the contract or by delivering the missing part or quantity, except where the purchase of goods in replacement is in conformity with usage and reasonably possible.

2 If the buyer does not obtain performance of the contract by the seller within a reasonable time, he shall retain the rights provided in Articles 43 to 46.

ARTICLE 43

The buyer may declare the contract avoided if the failure of the goods to conform to the contract and also the failure to deliver on the date fixed amount to fundamental breaches of the contract. The buyer shall lose his right to declare the contract avoided if he does not exercise it promptly after giving the seller notice of the lack of conformity or, in the case to which paragraph 2 of Article 42 applies, after the expiration of the period referred to in that paragraph.

ARTICLE 44

1 In cases not provided for in Article 43, the seller shall retain, after the date fixed for the delivery of the goods, the right to deliver any missing part or quantity of the goods or to deliver other goods which are in conformity with the contract or to remedy any defect in the goods handed over, provided that the exercise of this right does not cause the buyer either unreasonable inconvenience or unreasonable expense.

2 The buyer may however fix an additional period of time of reasonable length for the further delivery or for the remedying of the defect. If at the expiration of the additional period the seller has not delivered the goods or remedied the defect, the buyer may choose between requiring the performance of the contract or reducing the price in accordance with Article 46 or, provided that he does so promptly, declare the contract avoided.

Article 45

1 Where the seller has handed over part only of the goods or an insufficient quantity or where part only of the goods handed over is in conformity with the contract, the provisions of Articles 43 and 44 shall apply in respect of the part or quantity which is missing or which does not conform with the contract.

2 The buyer may declare the contract avoided in its entirety only if the failure to effect delivery completely and in conformity with the contract amounts to a fundamental breach of the contract.

Article 46

Where the buyer has neither obtained performance of the contract by the seller nor declared the contract avoided, the buyer may reduce the price in the same proportion as the value of the goods at the time of the conclusion of the contract has been diminished because of their lack of conformity with the contract.

Article 47

Where the seller has proffered to the buyer a quantity of unascertained goods greater than that provided for in the contract, the buyer may reject or accept the excess quantity. If the buyer rejects the excess quantity, the seller shall be liable only for damages in accordance with Article 82. If the buyer accepts the whole or part of the excess quantity, he shall pay for it at the contract rate.

Article 48

The buyer may exercise the rights provided in Articles 43 to 46, even before the time fixed for delivery, if it is clear that goods which would be handed over would not be in conformity with the contract.

Article 49

1 The buyer shall lose his right to rely on lack of conformity with the contract at the expiration of a period of one year after he has given notice as provided in Article 39, unless he has been prevented from exercising his right because of fraud on the part of the seller.

2 After the expiration of this period, the buyer shall not be entitled to rely on the lack of conformity, even by way of defence to an action. Nevertheless, if the buyer has not paid for the goods and provided that he has given due notice of the lack of conformity promptly, as provided in Article 39, he may advance as a defence to a claim for payment of the price a claim for a reduction in the price or for damages.

SECTION II—HANDING OVER OF DOCUMENTS

Article 50

Where the seller is bound to hand over to the buyer any documents relating to the goods, he shall do so at the time and place fixed by the contract or by usage.

Article 51

If the seller fails to hand over documents as provided in Article 50 at the time and place fixed or if he hands over documents which are not in conformity with those which he was bound to hand over, the buyer shall have the same rights as those provided under Articles 24 to 32 or under Articles 41 to 49, as the case may be.

SECTION III—TRANSFER OF PROPERTY

ARTICLE 52

1 Where the goods are subject to a right or claim of a third person, the buyer, unless he agreed to take the goods subject to such right or claim, shall notify the seller of such right or claim, unless the seller already knows thereof, and request that the goods should be freed therefrom within reasonable time or that other goods free from all rights and claims of third persons be delivered to him by the seller.

2 If the seller complies with a request made under paragraph 1 of this Article and the buyer nevertheless suffers a loss, the buyer may claim damages in accordance with Article 82.

3 If the seller fails to comply with a request made under paragraph 1 of this Article and a fundamental breach of the contract results thereby, the buyer may declare the contract avoided and claim damages in accordance with Articles 84 to 87. If the buyer does not declare the contract avoided or if there is no fundamental breach of the contract, the buyer shall have the right to claim damages in accordance with Article 82.

4 The buyer shall lose his right to declare the contract avoided if he fails to act in accordance with paragraph 1 of this Article within a reasonable time from the moment when he became aware or ought to have become aware of the right or claim of the third person in respect of the goods.

ARTICLE 53

The rights conferred on the buyer by Article 52 exclude all other remedies based on the fact that the seller has failed to perform his obligation to transfer the property in the goods or that the goods are subject to a right or claim of a third person.

SECTION IV—OTHER OBLIGATIONS OF THE SELLER

ARTICLE 54

1 If the seller is bound to despatch the goods to the buyer, he shall make, in the usual way and on the usual terms, such contracts as are necessary for the carriage of the goods to the place fixed.

2 If the seller is not bound by the contract to effect insurance in respect of the carriage of the goods, he shall provide the buyer, at his request, with all information necessary to enable him to effect such insurance.

ARTICLE 55

1 If the seller fails to perform any obligation other than those referred to in Articles 20 to 53, the buyer may:

(a) where such failure amounts to a fundamental breach of the contract, declare the contract avoided, provided that he does so promptly, and claim damages in accordance with Articles 84 to 87, or

(b) in any other case, claim damages in accordance with Article 82.

2 The buyer may also require performance by the seller of his obligation, unless the contract is avoided.

[4066]

CHAPTER IV
OBLIGATIONS OF THE BUYER

ARTICLE 56

The buyer shall pay the price for the goods and take delivery of them, as required by the contract and the present law.

SECTION I—PAYMENT OF THE PRICE

A—FIXING THE PRICE

ARTICLE 57

Where a contract has been concluded but does not state a price or make provision for the determination of the price, the buyer shall be bound to pay the price generally charged by the seller at the time of the conclusion of the contract.

ARTICLE 58

Where the price is fixed according to the weight of the goods, it shall, in case of doubt, be determined by the net weight.

B—PLACE AND DATE OF PAYMENT

ARTICLE 59

1 The buyer shall pay the price to the seller at the seller's place of business or, if he does not have a place of business, at his habitual residence, or, where the payment is to be made against the handing over of the goods or of documents, at the place where such handing over takes place.

2 Where, in consequence of a change in the place of business or habitual residence of the seller subsequent to the conclusion of the contract, the expenses incidental to payment are increased, such increase shall be borne by the seller.

ARTICLE 60

Where the parties have agreed upon a date for the payment of the price or where such date is fixed by usage, the buyer shall, without the need for any other formality, pay the price at that date.

C—REMEDIES FOR NON-PAYMENT

ARTICLE 61

1 If the buyer fails to pay the price in accordance with the contract and with the present law, the seller may require the buyer to perform his obligation.

2 The seller shall not be entitled to require payment of the price by the buyer if it is in conformity with usage and reasonably possible for the seller to resell the goods. In that case the contract shall be *ipso facto* avoided as from the time when such resale should be effected.

ARTICLE 62

1 Where the failure to pay the price at the date fixed amounts to a fundamental breach of the contract, the seller may either require the buyer to pay the price or declare the contract avoided. He shall inform the buyer of his decision within a reasonable time; otherwise the contract shall be *ipso facto* avoided.

2 Where the failure to pay the price at the date fixed does not amount to a fundamental breach of the contract, the seller may grant to the buyer an additional period of time of reasonable length. If the buyer has not paid the price at the expiration of the additional period, the seller may either require the payment of the price by the buyer or, provided that he does so promptly, declare the contract avoided.

ARTICLE 63

1 Where the contract is avoided because of failure to pay the price, the seller shall have the right to claim damages in accordance with Articles 84 to 87.

2 Where the contract is not avoided, the seller shall have the right to claim damages in accordance with Articles 82 and 83.

ARTICLE 64

In no case shall the buyer be entitled to apply to a court or arbitral tribunal to grant him a period of grace for the payment of the price.

SECTION II—TAKING DELIVERY

ARTICLE 65

Taking delivery consists in the buyer's doing all such acts as are necessary in order to enable the seller to hand over the goods and actually taking them over.

ARTICLE 66

1 Where the buyer's failure to take delivery of the goods in accordance with the contract amounts to a fundamental breach of the contract or gives the seller good grounds for fearing that the buyer will not pay the price, the seller may declare the contract avoided.

2 Where the failure to take delivery of the goods does not amount to a fundamental breach of the contract, the seller may grant to the buyer an additional period of time of reasonable length. If the buyer has not taken delivery of the goods at the expiration of the additional period, the seller may declare the contract avoided, provided that he does so promptly.

ARTICLE 67

1 If the contract reserves to the buyer the right subsequently to determine the form, measurement or other features of the goods (sale by specification) and he fails to make such specification either on the date expressly or impliedly agreed upon or within a reasonable time after receipt of a request from the seller, the seller may declare the contract avoided, provided that he does so promptly, or make the specification himself in accordance with the requirements of the buyer in so far as these are known to him.

2 If the seller makes the specification himself, he shall inform the buyer of the details thereof and shall fix a reasonable period of time within which the buyer may submit a different specification. If the buyer fails to do so the specification made by the seller shall be binding.

ARTICLE 68

1 Where the contract is avoided because of the failure of the buyer to accept delivery of the goods or to make a specification, the seller shall have the right to claim damages in accordance with Articles 84 to 87.

2 Where the contract is not avoided, the seller shall have the right to claim damages in accordance with Article 82.

SECTION III—OTHER OBLIGATIONS OF THE BUYER

ARTICLE 69

The buyer shall take the steps provided for in the contract, by usage or by laws and regulations in force, for the purpose of making provision for or guaranteeing payment of the price, such as the acceptance of a bill of exchange, the opening of a documentary credit or the giving of a banker's guarantee.

ARTICLE 70

1 If the buyer fails to perform any obligation other than those referred to in Sections I and II of this Chapter, the seller may:

(a) where such failure amounts to a fundamental breach of the contract, declare the contract avoided, provided that he does so promptly, and claim damages in accordance with Articles 84 to 87; or

(b) in any other case, claim damages in accordance with Article 82.

2 The seller may also require performance by the buyer of his obligation, unless the contract is avoided.

[4067]

CHAPTER V
PROVISIONS COMMON TO THE OBLIGATIONS OF THE SELLER AND OF THE BUYER

SECTION I—CONCURRENCE BETWEEN DELIVERY OF THE GOODS AND PAYMENT OF THE PRICE

ARTICLE 71

Except as otherwise provided in Article 72, delivery of the goods and payment of the price shall be concurrent conditions. Nevertheless, the buyer shall not be obliged to pay the price until he has had an opportunity to examine the goods.

ARTICLE 72

1 Where the contract involves carriage of the goods and where delivery is, by virtue of paragraph 2 of Article 19, effected by handing over the goods to the carrier, the seller may either postpone despatch of the goods until he receives payment or proceed to despatch them on terms that reserve to himself the right of disposal of the goods during transit. In the latter case, he may require that the goods shall not be handed over to the buyer at the place of destination except against payment of the price and the buyer shall not be bound to pay the price until he has had an opportunity to examine the goods.

2 Nevertheless, when the contract requires payment against documents, the buyer shall not be entitled to refuse payment of the price on the ground that he has not had the opportunity to examine the goods.

ARTICLE 73

1 Each party may suspend the performance of his obligations whenever, after the conclusion of the contract, the economic situation of the other party appears to have become so difficult that there is good reason to fear that he will not perform a material part of his obligations.

2 If the seller has already despatched the goods before the economic situation of the buyer described in paragraph 1 of this Article becomes evident, he may prevent the handing over of the goods to the buyer even if the latter holds a document which entitles him to obtain them.

3 Nevertheless, the seller shall not be entitled to prevent the handing over of the goods if they are claimed by a third person who is a lawful holder of a document which entitles him to obtain the goods, unless the document contains a reservation concerning the effects of its transfer or unless the seller can prove that the holder of the document, when he acquired it, knowingly acted to the detriment of the seller.

SECTION II—EXEMPTIONS

ARTICLE 74

1 Where one of the parties has not performed one of his obligations, he shall not be liable for such non-performance if he can prove that it was due to circumstances which, according to the intention of the parties at the time of the conclusion of the contract, he was not bound to take into account or to avoid or to overcome; in the absence of any expression of the intention of the parties, regard shall be had to what reasonable persons in the same situation would have intended.

2 Where the circumstances which gave rise to the non-performance of the obligation constituted only a temporary impediment to performance, the party in default shall nevertheless be permanently relieved of his obligation if, by reason of the delay, performance would be so radically changed as to amount to the performance of an obligation quite different from that contemplated by the contract.

3 The relief provided by this Article for one of the parties shall not include the avoidance of the contract under some other provision of the present Law or deprive the other party of any right which he has under the present Law to reduce the price, unless the circumstances which entitled the first party to relief were caused by the act of the other party or of some person for whose conduct he was responsible.

SECTION III—SUPPLEMENTARY RULES CONCERNING THE AVOIDANCE OF THE CONTRACT

A—SUPPLEMENTARY GROUNDS FOR AVOIDANCE

ARTICLE 75

1 Where, in the case of contracts for delivery of goods by instalments, by reason of any failure by one party to perform any of his obligations under the contract in respect of any instalment, the other party has good reason to fear failure of performance in respect of future instalments, he may declare the contract avoided for the future, provided that he does so promptly.

2 The buyer may also, provided that he does so promptly, declare the contract avoided in respect of future deliveries or in respect of deliveries already made or both, if by reason of their interdependence such deliveries would be worthless to him.

ARTICLE 76

Where prior to the date fixed for performance of the contract it is clear that one of the parties will commit a fundamental breach of the contract, the other party shall have the right to declare the contract avoided.

ARTICLE 77

Where the contract has been avoided under Article 75 or Article 76, the party declaring the contract avoided may claim damages in accordance with Articles 84 to 87.

B—EFFECTS OF AVOIDANCE

ARTICLE 78

1 Avoidance of the contract releases both parties from their obligations thereunder, subject to any damages which may be due.

2 If one party has performed the contract either wholly or in part, he may claim the return of whatever he has supplied or paid under the contract. If both parties are required to make restitution, they shall do so concurrently.

ARTICLE 79

1 The buyer shall lose his right to declare the contract avoided where it is impossible for him to return the goods in the condition in which he received them.

2 Nevertheless, the buyer may declare the contract avoided:

(a) if the goods or part of the goods have perished or deteriorated as a result of the defect which justifies the avoidance;

(b) if the goods or part of the goods have perished or deteriorated as a result of the examination prescribed in Article 38;

(c) if part of the goods have been consumed or transformed by the buyer in the course of normal use before the lack of conformity with the contract was discovered;

(d) if the impossibility of returning the goods or of returning them in the condition in which they were received is not due to the act of the buyer or of some other person for whose conduct he is responsible;

(e) if the deterioration or transformation of the goods is unimportant.

ARTICLE 80

The buyer who has lost the right to declare the contract avoided by virtue of Article 79 shall retain all the other rights conferred on him by the present Law.

ARTICLE 81

1 Where the seller is under an obligation to refund the price, he shall also be liable for the interest thereon at the rate fixed by Article 83, as from the date of payment.

2 The buyer shall be liable to account to the seller for all benefits which he has derived from the goods or part of them, as the case may be:

(a) where he is under an obligation to return the goods or part of them,

(b) where it is impossible for him to return the goods or part of them, but the contract is nevertheless avoided.

SECTION IV—SUPPLEMENTARY RULES CONCERNING DAMAGES

A—DAMAGES WHERE THE CONTRACT IS NOT AVOIDED

ARTICLE 82

Where the contract is not avoided, damages for a breach of contract by one party shall consist of a sum equal to the loss, including loss of profit, suffered by the other party. Such damages shall not exceed the loss which the party in breach ought to have foreseen at the time of the conclusion of the contract, in the light of the facts and matters which then were known or ought to have been known to him, as a possible consequence of the breach of the contract.

ARTICLE 83

Where the breach of contract consists of delay in the payment of the price, the seller shall in any event be entitled to interest on such sum as is in arrear at a rate equal to the official discount rate in the country where he has his place of business or, if he has no place of business, his habitual residence, plus 1 per cent.

B—DAMAGES WHERE THE CONTRACT IS AVOIDED

ARTICLE 84

1 In case of avoidance of the contract, where there is a current price for the goods, damages shall be equal to the difference between the price fixed by the contract and the current price on the date on which the contract is avoided.

2 In calculating the amount of damages under paragraph 1 of this Article, the current price to be taken into account shall be that prevailing in the market in which the transaction took place or, if there is no such current price or if its application is inappropriate, the price in a market which serves as a reasonable substitute, making due allowance for differences in the cost of transporting the goods.

ARTICLE 85

If the buyer has bought goods in replacement or the seller has resold goods in a reasonable manner, he may recover the difference between the contract price and the price paid for the goods bought in replacement or that obtained by the resale.

ARTICLE 86

The damages referred to in Articles 84 and 85 may be increased by the amount of any reasonable expenses incurred as a result of the breach or up to the amount of any loss, including loss of profit, which should have been foreseen by the party in breach, at the time of the conclusion of the contract, in the light of the facts and matters which were known or ought to have been known to him, as a possible consequence of the breach of the contract.

ARTICLE 87

If there is no current price for the goods, damages shall be calculated on the same basis as that provided in Article 82.

C—GENERAL PROVISIONS CONCERNING DAMAGES

ARTICLE 88

The party who relies on a breach of the contract shall adopt all reasonable measures to mitigate the loss resulting from the breach. If he fails to adopt such measures, the party in breach may claim a reduction in the damages.

ARTICLE 89

In case of fraud, damages shall be determined by the rules applicable in respect of contracts of sale not governed by the present law.

SECTION V—EXPENSES

ARTICLE 90

The expenses of delivery shall be borne by the seller; all expenses after delivery shall be borne by the buyer.

SECTION VI—PRESERVATION OF THE GOODS

ARTICLE 91

Where the buyer is in delay in taking delivery of the goods or in paying the price, the seller shall take reasonable steps to preserve the goods; he shall have the right to retain them until he has been reimbursed his reasonable expenses by the buyer.

ARTICLE 92

1 Where the goods have been received by the buyer, he shall take reasonable steps to preserve them if he intends to reject them; he shall have the right to retain them until he has been reimbursed his reasonable expenses by the seller.

2 Where goods despatched to the buyer have been put at his disposal at their place of destination and he exercises the right to reject them, he shall be bound to take possession of them on behalf of the seller, provided that this may be done without payment of the price and without unreasonable inconvenience or unreasonable expense. This provision shall not apply where the seller or a person authorised to take charge of the goods on his behalf is present at such destination.

ARTICLE 93

The party who is under an obligation to take steps to preserve the goods may deposit them in the warehouse of a third person at the expense of the other party provided that the expense incurred is not unreasonable.

ARTICLE 94

1 The party who, in the cases to which Articles 91 and 92 apply, is under an obligation to take steps to preserve the goods may sell them by any appropriate means, provided that there has been unreasonable delay by the other party in accepting them or taking them back or in paying the costs of preservation and provided that due notice has been given to the other party of the intention to sell.

2 The party selling the goods shall have the right to retain out of the proceeds of sale an amount equal to the reasonable costs of preserving the goods and of selling them and shall transmit the balance to the other party.

ARTICLE 95

Where, in the cases to which Articles 91 and 92 apply, the goods are subject to loss or rapid deterioration or their preservation would involve unreasonable expense, the party under the duty to preserve them is bound to sell them in accordance with Article 94.

[4068]

CHAPTER VI
PASSING OF THE RISK

ARTICLE 96

Where the risk has passed to the buyer, he shall pay the price notwithstanding the loss or deterioration of the goods, unless this is due to the act of the seller or of some other person for whose conduct the seller is responsible.

ARTICLE 97

1 The risk shall pass to the buyer when delivery of the goods is effected in accordance with the provisions of the contract and the present Law.

2 In the case of the handing over of goods which are not in conformity with the contract, the risk shall pass to the buyer from the moment when the handing over has, apart from the lack of conformity, been effected in accordance with the provisions of the contract and of the present Law, where the buyer has neither declared the contract avoided nor required goods in replacement.

ARTICLE 98

1 Where the handing over of the goods is delayed owing to the breach of an obligation of the buyer, the risk shall pass to the buyer as from the last date when, apart from such breach, the handing over could have been made in accordance with the contract.

2 Where the contract relates to a sale of unascertained goods, delay on the part of the buyer shall cause the risk to pass only when the seller has set aside goods manifestly appropriated to the contract and has notified the buyer that this has been done.

3 Where unascertained goods are of such a kind that the seller cannot set aside a part of them until the buyer takes delivery, it shall be sufficient for the seller to do all acts necessary to enable the buyer to take delivery.

ARTICLE 99

1 Where the sale is of goods in transit by sea, the risk shall be borne by the buyer as from the time at which the goods were handed over to the carrier.

2 Where the seller, at the time of the conclusion of the contract, knew or ought to have known that the goods had been lost or had deteriorated, the risk shall remain with him until the time of the conclusion of the contract.

ARTICLE 100

If, in a case to which paragraph 3 of Article 19 applies, the seller, at the time of sending the notice or other document referred to in that paragraph knew or ought to have known that the goods had been lost or had deteriorated after they were handed over to the carrier, the risk shall remain with the seller until the time of sending such notice or document.

ARTICLE 101

The passing of the risk shall not necessarily be determined by the provisions of the contract concerning expenses. **[4069]**

THE UNIFORM LAW ON THE FORMATION OF CONTRACTS FOR THE INTERNATIONAL SALE OF GOODS

(1965)

NOTES

The text of the following Law appears as set out in the Uniform Laws on International Sales Act 1967, Sch 2. See also the website of the International Institution for the Unification of Private Law (UNIDROIT) at http://www.unidroit.org.

ARTICLE 1

The present Law shall apply to the formation of contracts of sale of goods which, if they were concluded, would be governed by the Uniform Law on the International Sale of Goods.

ARTICLE 2

1 The provisions of the following Articles shall apply except to the extent that it appears from the preliminary negotiations, the offer, the reply, the practices which the parties have established between themselves or usage, that other rules apply.

2 However, a term of the offer stipulating that silence shall amount to acceptance is invalid.

ARTICLE 3

An offer or an acceptance need not be evidenced by writing and shall not be subject to any other requirement as to form. In particular, they may be proved by means of witnesses.

ARTICLE 4

1 The communication which one person addresses to one or more specific persons with the object of, concluding a contract of sale shall not constitute an offer unless it is sufficiently definite to permit the conclusion of the contract by acceptance and indicates the intention of the offeror to be bound.

2 This communication may be interpreted by reference to and supplemented by the preliminary negotiations, any practices which the parties have established between themselves, usage and the provisions of the Uniform Law on the International Sale of Goods.

ARTICLE 5

1 The offer shall not bind the offeror until it has been communicated to the offeree; it shall lapse if its withdrawal is communicated to the offeree before or at the same time as the offer.

2 After an offer has been communicated to the offeree it can be revoked unless the revocation is not made in good faith or in conformity with fair dealing or unless the offer states a fixed time for acceptance or otherwise indicates that it is firm or irrevocable.

3 An indication that the offer is firm or irrevocable may be express or implied from the circumstances, the preliminary negotiations, any practices which the parties have established between themselves or usage.

4 A revocation of an offer shall only have effect if it has been communicated to the offeree before he has despatched his acceptance or has done any act treated as acceptance under paragraph 2 of Article 6.

ARTICLE 6

1 Acceptance of an offer consists of a declaration by any means whatsoever to the offeror.

2 Acceptance may also consist of the despatch of the goods or of the price or of any other act which may be considered to be equivalent to the declaration referred to in paragraph 1 of this Article either by virtue of the offer or as a result of practices which the parties have established between themselves or usage.

ARTICLE 7

1 An acceptance containing additions, limitations or other modifications shall be a rejection of the offer and shall constitute a counter-offer.

2 However, a reply to an offer which purports to be an acceptance but which contains additional or different terms which do not materially alter the terms of the offer shall constitute an acceptance unless the offeror promptly objects to the discrepancy; if he does not so object, the terms of the contract shall be the terms of the offer with the modifications contained in the acceptance.

ARTICLE 8

1 A declaration of acceptance of an offer shall have effect only if it is communicated to the offeror within the time he has fixed or, if no such time is fixed, within a reasonable time, due account being taken of the circumstances of the transaction, including the rapidity of the means of communication employed by the offeror, and usage. In the case of an oral offer, the acceptance shall be immediate, if the circumstances do not show that the offeree shall have time for reflection.

2 If a time for acceptance is fixed by an offeror in a letter or in a telegram, it shall be presumed to begin to run from the day the letter was dated or the hour of the day the telegram was handed in for despatch.

3 If an acceptance consists of an act referred to in paragraph 2 of Article 6, the act shall have effect only if it is done within the period laid down in paragraph 1 of the present Article.

ARTICLE 9

1 If the acceptance is late, the offeror may nevertheless consider it to have arrived in due time on condition that he promptly so informs the acceptor orally or by despatch of a notice.

2 If however the acceptance is communicated late, it shall be considered to have been communicated in due time, if the letter or document which contains the acceptance shows that it has been sent in such circumstances that if its transmission had been normal it would have been communicated in due time; this provision shall not however apply if the offeror has promptly informed the acceptor orally or by despatch of a notice that he considers his offer as having lapsed.

ARTICLE 10

An acceptance cannot be revoked except by a revocation which is communicated to the offeror before or at the same time as the acceptance.

ARTICLE 11

The formation of the contract is not affected by the death of one of the parties or by his becoming incapable of contracting before acceptance unless the contrary results from the intention of the parties, usage or the nature of the transaction.

ARTICLE 12

1 For the purposes of the present Law, the expression "to be communicated" means to be delivered at the address of the person to whom the communication is directed.

2 Communications provided for by the present Law shall be made by the means usual in the circumstances.

ARTICLE 13

1 "Usage" means any practice or method of dealing which reasonable persons in the same situation as the parties usually consider to be applicable to the formation of their contract.

2 Where expressions, provisions or forms of contract commonly used in commercial practice are employed, they shall be interpreted according to the meaning usually given to them in the trade concerned. **[4070]**

UNITED NATIONS CONVENTION ON THE ASSIGNMENT OF RECEIVABLES IN INTERNATIONAL TRADE

(2001)

NOTES

The original source for this convention is the United Nations: UN Convention on the Assignment of Receivables in International Trade (2001), © United Nations. Reprinted with the permission of the publisher. The text of the Convention appears on the United Nations Commission on International Trade Law (UNCITRAL) website at www.uncitral.org.

As yet, neither the United Kingdom nor the European Community has ratified this Convention.

PREAMBLE

The Contracting States,

Reaffirming their conviction that international trade on the basis of equality and mutual benefit is an important element in the promotion of friendly relations among States,

Considering that problems created by uncertainties as to the content and the choice of legal regime applicable to the assignment of receivables constitute an obstacle to international trade,

Desiring to establish principles and to adopt rules relating to the assignment of receivables that would create certainty and transparency and promote the modernization of the law relating to assignments of receivables, while protecting existing assignment practices and facilitating the development of new practices,

Desiring also to ensure adequate protection of the interests of debtors in assignments of receivables,

Being of the opinion that the adoption of uniform rules governing the assignment of receivables would promote the availability of capital and credit at more affordable rates and thus facilitate the development of international trade,

Have agreed as follows:

CHAPTER I
SCOPE OF APPLICATION

Article 1

Scope of application

1. This Convention applies to:
   (a) Assignments of international receivables and to international assignments of receivables as defined in this chapter, if, at the time of conclusion of the contract of assignment, the assignor is located in a Contracting State; and
   (b) Subsequent assignments, provided that any prior assignment is governed by this Convention.

2. This Convention applies to subsequent assignments that satisfy the criteria set forth in paragraph 1(a) of this article, even if it did not apply to any prior assignment of the same receivable.

3. This Convention does not affect the rights and obligations of the debtor unless, at the time of conclusion of the original contract, the debtor is located in a Contracting State or the law governing the original contract is the law of a Contracting State.

4. The provisions of chapter V apply to assignments of international receivables and to international assignments of receivables as defined in this chapter independently of paragraphs 1 to 3 of this article. However, those provisions do not apply if a State makes a declaration under article 39.

5. The provisions of the annex to this Convention apply as provided in article 42.

[4071]

Article 2

Assignment of receivables

For the purposes of this Convention:

(a) "Assignment" means the transfer by agreement from one person ("assignor") to another person ("assignee") of all or part of or an undivided interest in the assignor's contractual right to payment of a monetary sum ("receivable") from a third person ("the debtor"). The creation of rights in receivables as security for indebtedness or other obligation is deemed to be a transfer;

(b) In the case of an assignment by the initial or any other assignee ("subsequent assignment"), the person who makes that assignment is the assignor and the person to whom that assignment is made is the assignee.

[4072]

Article 3

Internationality

A receivable is international if, at the time of conclusion of the original contract, the assignor and the debtor are located in different States. An assignment is international if, at the time of conclusion of the contract of assignment, the assignor and the assignee are located in different States.

[4073]

Article 4

Exclusions and other limitations

1. This Convention does not apply to assignments made:
   (a) To an individual for his or her personal, family or household purposes;
   (b) As part of the sale or change in the ownership or legal status of the business out of which the assigned receivables arose.

2. This Convention does not apply to assignments of receivables arising under or from:
   (a) Transactions on a regulated exchange;
   (b) Financial contracts governed by netting agreements, except a receivable owed on the termination of all outstanding transactions;
   (c) Foreign exchange transactions;
   (d) Inter-bank payment systems, inter-bank payment agreements or clearance and settlement systems relating to securities or other financial assets or instruments;
   (e) The transfer of security rights in, sale, loan or holding of or agreement to repurchase securities or other financial assets or instruments held with an intermediary;
   (f) Bank deposits;
   (g) A letter of credit or independent guarantee.

3. Nothing in this Convention affects the rights and obligations of any person under the law governing negotiable instruments.

4. Nothing in this Convention affects the rights and obligations of the assignor and the debtor under special laws governing the protection of parties to transactions made for personal, family or household purposes.

5. Nothing in this Convention:
   (a) Affects the application of the law of a State in which real property is situated to either:
      (i) An interest in that real property to the extent that under that law the assignment of a receivable confers such an interest; or
      (ii) The priority of a right in a receivable to the extent that under that law an interest in the real property confers such a right; or
   (b) Makes lawful the acquisition of an interest in real property not permitted under the law of the State in which the real property is situated.

[4074]

CHAPTER II
GENERAL PROVISIONS

Article 5

Definitions and rules of interpretation

For the purposes of this Convention:

(a) "Original contract" means the contract between the assignor and the debtor from which the assigned receivable arises;

(b) "Existing receivable" means a receivable that arises upon or before conclusion of the contract of assignment and "future receivable" means a receivable that arises after conclusion of the contract of assignment;

(c) "Writing" means any form of information that is accessible so as to be usable for subsequent reference. Where this Convention requires a writing to be signed, that requirement is met if, by generally accepted means or a procedure agreed to by the person whose signature is required, the writing identifies that person and indicates that person's approval of the information contained in the writing;

(d) "Notification of the assignment" means a communication in writing that reasonably identifies the assigned receivables and the assignee;

(e) "Insolvency administrator" means a person or body, including one appointed on an interim basis, authorized in an insolvency proceeding to administer the reorganization or liquidation of the assignor's assets or affairs;

(f) "Insolvency proceeding" means a collective judicial or administrative proceeding, including an interim proceeding, in which the assets and affairs of the assignor are subject to control or supervision by a court or other competent authority for the purpose of reorganization or liquidation;

(g) "Priority" means the right of a person in preference to the right of another person and, to the extent relevant for such purpose, includes the determination whether the right is a personal or a property right, whether or not it is a security right for indebtedness or other obligation and whether any requirements necessary to render the right effective against a competing claimant have been satisfied;

(h) A person is located in the State in which it has its place of business. If the assignor or the assignee has a place of business in more than one State, the place of business is that place where the central administration of the assignor or the assignee is exercised. If the debtor has a place of business in more than one State, the place of business is that which has the closest relationship to the original contract. If a person does not have a place of business, reference is to be made to the habitual residence of that person;

(i) "Law" means the law in force in a State other than its rules of private international law;

(j) "Proceeds" means whatever is received in respect of an assigned receivable, whether in total or partial payment or other satisfaction of the receivable. The term includes whatever is received in respect of proceeds. The term does not include returned goods;

(k) "Financial contract" means any spot, forward, future, option or swap transaction involving interest rates, commodities, currencies, equities, bonds, indices or any other financial instrument, any repurchase or securities lending transaction, and any other transaction similar to any transaction referred to above entered into in financial markets and any combination of the transactions mentioned above;

(l) "Netting agreement" means an agreement between two or more parties that provides for one or more of the following:

  (i) The net settlement of payments due in the same currency on the same date whether by novation or otherwise;

  (ii) Upon the insolvency or other default by a party, the termination of all outstanding transactions at their replacement or fair market values, conversion of such sums into a single currency and netting into a single payment by one party to the other; or

  (iii) The set-off of amounts calculated as set forth in subparagraph (l)(ii) of this article under two or more netting agreements;

(m) "Competing claimant" means:

  (i) Another assignee of the same receivable from the same assignor, including a person who, by operation of law, claims a right in the assigned receivable as a result of its right in other property of the assignor, even if that receivable is not an international receivable and the assignment to that assignee is not an international assignment;

  (ii) A creditor of the assignor; or

  (iii) The insolvency administrator.

[4075]

Article 6

Party autonomy

Subject to article 19, the assignor, the assignee and the debtor may derogate from or vary by agreement provisions of this Convention relating to their respective rights and obligations. Such an agreement does not affect the rights of any person who is not a party to the agreement.

[4076]

Article 7

Principles of interpretation

1. In the interpretation of this Convention, regard is to be had to its object and purpose as set forth in the preamble, to its international character and to the need to promote uniformity in its application and the observance of good faith in international trade.

2. Questions concerning matters governed by this Convention that are not expressly settled in it are to be settled in conformity with the general principles on which it is based or, in the absence of such principles, in conformity with the law applicable by virtue of the rules of private international law.

[4077]

CHAPTER III
EFFECTS OF ASSIGNMENT

Article 8

Effectiveness of assignments

1. An assignment is not ineffective as between the assignor and the assignee or as against the debtor or as against a competing claimant, and the right of an assignee may not be denied priority, on the ground that it is an assignment of more than one receivable, future receivables or parts of or undivided interests in receivables, provided that the receivables are described:

(a) Individually as receivables to which the assignment relates; or

(b) In any other manner, provided that they can, at the time of the assignment or, in the case of future receivables, at the time of conclusion of the original contract, be identified as receivables to which the assignment relates.

2. Unless otherwise agreed, an assignment of one or more future receivables is effective without a new act of transfer being required to assign each receivable.

3. Except as provided in paragraph 1 of this article, article 9 and article 10, paragraphs 2 and 3, this Convention does not affect any limitations on assignments arising from law.

[4078]

Article 9

Contractual limitations on assignments

1. An assignment of a receivable is effective notwithstanding any agreement between the initial or any subsequent assignor and the debtor or any subsequent assignee limiting in any way the assignor's right to assign its receivables.

2. Nothing in this article affects any obligation or liability of the assignor for breach of such an agreement, but the other party to such agreement may not avoid the original contract or the assignment contract on the sole ground of that breach. A person who is not party to such an agreement is not liable on the sole ground that it had knowledge of the agreement.

3. This article applies only to assignments of receivables:

(a) Arising from an original contract that is a contract for the supply or lease of goods or services other than financial services, a construction contract or a contract for the sale or lease of real property;

(b) Arising from an original contract for the sale, lease or licence of industrial or other intellectual property or of proprietary information;

(c) Representing the payment obligation for a credit card transaction; or

(d) Owed to the assignor upon net settlement of payments due pursuant to a netting agreement involving more than two parties.

[4079]

Article 10

Transfer of security rights

1. A personal or property right securing payment of the assigned receivable is transferred to the assignee without a new act of transfer. If such a right, under the law governing it, is transferable only with a new act of transfer, the assignor is obliged to transfer such right and any proceeds to the assignee.

2. A right securing payment of the assigned receivable is transferred under paragraph 1 of this article notwithstanding any agreement between the assignor and the debtor or other person granting that right, limiting in any way the assignor's right to assign the receivable or the right securing payment of the assigned receivable.

3. Nothing in this article affects any obligation or liability of the assignor for breach of any agreement under paragraph 2 of this article, but the other party to that agreement may not avoid the original contract or the assignment contract on the sole ground of that breach. A person who is not a party to such an agreement is not liable on the sole ground that it had knowledge of the agreement.

4. Paragraphs 2 and 3 of this article apply only to assignments of receivables:

(a) Arising from an original contract that is a contract for the supply or lease of goods or services other than financial services, a construction contract or a contract for the sale or lease of real property;

(b) Arising from an original contract for the sale, lease or licence of industrial or other intellectual property or of proprietary information;

(c) Representing the payment obligation for a credit card transaction; or

(d) Owed to the assignor upon net settlement of payments due pursuant to a netting agreement involving more than two parties.

5. The transfer of a possessory property right under paragraph 1 of this article does not affect any obligations of the assignor to the debtor or the person granting the property right with respect to the property transferred existing under the law governing that property right.

6. Paragraph 1 of this article does not affect any requirement under rules of law other than this Convention relating to the form or registration of the transfer of any rights securing payment of the assigned receivable.

[4080]

CHAPTER IV
RIGHTS, OBLIGATIONS AND DEFENCES

SECTION I
ASSIGNOR AND ASSIGNEE

Article 11

Rights and obligations of the assignor and the assignee

1. The mutual rights and obligations of the assignor and the assignee arising from their agreement are determined by the terms and conditions set forth in that agreement, including any rules or general conditions referred to therein.

2. The assignor and the assignee are bound by any usage to which they have agreed and, unless otherwise agreed, by any practices they have established between themselves.

3. In an international assignment, the assignor and the assignee are considered, unless otherwise agreed, implicitly to have made applicable to the assignment a usage that in international trade is widely known to, and regularly observed by, parties to the particular type of assignment or to the assignment of the particular category of receivables.

[4081]

Article 12

Representations of the assignor

1. Unless otherwise agreed between the assignor and the assignee, the assignor represents at the time of conclusion of the contract of assignment that:

(a) The assignor has the right to assign the receivable;
(b) The assignor has not previously assigned the receivable to another assignee; and
(c) The debtor does not and will not have any defences or rights of set-off.

2. Unless otherwise agreed between the assignor and the assignee, the assignor does not represent that the debtor has, or will have, the ability to pay.

[4082]

Article 13

Right to notify the debtor

1. Unless otherwise agreed between the assignor and the assignee, the assignor or the assignee or both may send the debtor notification of the assignment and a payment instruction, but after notification has been sent only the assignee may send such an instruction.

2. Notification of the assignment or a payment instruction sent in breach of any agreement referred to in paragraph 1 of this article is not ineffective for the purposes of article 17 by reason of such breach. However, nothing in this article affects any obligation or liability of the party in breach of such an agreement for any damages arising as a result of the breach.

[4083]

Article 14

Right to payment

1. As between the assignor and the assignee, unless otherwise agreed and whether or not notification of the assignment has been sent:

(a) If payment in respect of the assigned receivable is made to the assignee, the assignee is entitled to retain the proceeds and goods returned in respect of the assigned receivable;
(b) If payment in respect of the assigned receivable is made to the assignor, the assignee is entitled to payment of the proceeds and also to goods returned to the assignor in respect of the assigned receivable; and
(c) If payment in respect of the assigned receivable is made to another person over whom the assignee has priority, the assignee is entitled to payment of the proceeds and also to goods returned to such person in respect of the assigned receivable.

2. The assignee may not retain more than the value of its right in the receivable.

[4084]

SECTION II
DEBTOR

Article 15

Principle of debtor protection

1. Except as otherwise provided in this Convention, an assignment does not, without the consent of the debtor, affect the rights and obligations of the debtor, including the payment terms contained in the original contract.

2. A payment instruction may change the person, address or account to which the debtor is required to make payment, but may not change:

(a) The currency of payment specified in the original contract; or
(b) The State specified in the original contract in which payment is to be made to a State other than that in which the debtor is located.

[4085]

Article 16

Notification of the debtor

1. Notification of the assignment or a payment instruction is effective when received by the debtor if it is in a language that is reasonably expected to inform the debtor about its contents. It is sufficient if notification of the assignment or a payment instruction is in the language of the original contract.

2. Notification of the assignment or a payment instruction may relate to receivables arising after notification.

3. Notification of a subsequent assignment constitutes notification of all prior assignments.

[4086]

Article 17

Debtor's discharge by payment

1. Until the debtor receives notification of the assignment, the debtor is entitled to be discharged by paying in accordance with the original contract.

2. After the debtor receives notification of the assignment, subject to paragraphs 3 to 8 of this article, the debtor is discharged only by paying the assignee or, if otherwise instructed in the notification of the assignment or subsequently by the assignee in a writing received by the debtor, in accordance with such payment instruction.

3. If the debtor receives more than one payment instruction relating to a single assignment of the same receivable by the same assignor, the debtor is discharged by paying in accordance with the last payment instruction received from the assignee before payment.

4. If the debtor receives notification of more than one assignment of the same receivable made by the same assignor, the debtor is discharged by paying in accordance with the first notification received.

5. If the debtor receives notification of one or more subsequent assignments, the debtor is discharged by paying in accordance with the notification of the last of such subsequent assignments.

6. If the debtor receives notification of the assignment of a part of or an undivided interest in one or more receivables, the debtor is discharged by paying in accordance with the notification or in accordance with this article as if the debtor had not received the notification. If the debtor pays in accordance with the notification, the debtor is discharged only to the extent of the part or undivided interest paid.

7. If the debtor receives notification of the assignment from the assignee, the debtor is entitled to request the assignee to provide within a reasonable period of time adequate proof that the assignment from the initial assignor to the initial assignee and any intermediate assignment have been made and, unless the assignee does so, the debtor is discharged by paying in accordance with this article as if the notification from the assignee had not been received. Adequate proof of an assignment includes but is not limited to any writing emanating from the assignor and indicating that the assignment has taken place.

8. This article does not affect any other ground on which payment by the debtor to the person entitled to payment, to a competent judicial or other authority, or to a public deposit fund discharges the debtor.

[4087]

Article 18

Defences and rights of set-off of the debtor

1. In a claim by the assignee against the debtor for payment of the assigned receivable, the debtor may raise against the assignee all defences and rights of set-off arising from the original contract, or any other contract that was part of the same transaction, of which the debtor could avail itself as if the assignment had not been made and such claim were made by the assignor.

2. The debtor may raise against the assignee any other right of set-off, provided that it was available to the debtor at the time notification of the assignment was received by the debtor.

3. Notwithstanding paragraphs 1 and 2 of this article, defences and rights of set-off that the debtor may raise pursuant to article 9 or 10 against the assignor for breach of an agreement limiting in any way the assignor's right to make the assignment are not available to the debtor against the assignee.

[4088]

Article 19

Agreement not to raise defences or rights of set-off

1. The debtor may agree with the assignor in a writing signed by the debtor not to raise against the assignee the defences and rights of set-off that it could raise pursuant to article 18. Such an agreement precludes the debtor from raising against the assignee those defences and rights of set-off.

2. The debtor may not waive defences:
(a) Arising from fraudulent acts on the part of the assignee; or
(b) Based on the debtor's incapacity.

3. Such an agreement may be modified only by an agreement in a writing signed by the debtor. The effect of such a modification as against the assignee is determined by article 20, paragraph 2.
[4089]

Article 20

Modification of the original contract

1. An agreement concluded before notification of the assignment between the assignor and the debtor that affects the assignee's rights is effective as against the assignee, and the assignee acquires corresponding rights.

2. An agreement concluded after notification of the assignment between the assignor and the debtor that affects the assignee's rights is ineffective as against the assignee unless:
(a) The assignee consents to it; or
(b) The receivable is not fully earned by performance and either the modification is provided for in the original contract or, in the context of the original contract, a reasonable assignee would consent to the modification.

3. Paragraphs 1 and 2 of this article do not affect any right of the assignor or the assignee arising from breach of an agreement between them.
[4090]

Article 21

Recovery of payments

Failure of the assignor to perform the original contract does not entitle the debtor to recover from the assignee a sum paid by the debtor to the assignor or the assignee.
[4091]

SECTION III
THIRD PARTIES

Article 22

Law applicable to competing rights

With the exception of matters that are settled elsewhere in this Convention and subject to articles 23 and 24, the law of the State in which the assignor is located governs the priority of the right of an assignee in the assigned receivable over the right of a competing claimant.
[4092]

Article 23

Public policy and mandatory rules

1. The application of a provision of the law of the State in which the assignor is located may be refused only if the application of that provision is manifestly contrary to the public policy of the forum State.

2. The rules of the law of either the forum State or any other State that are mandatory irrespective of the law otherwise applicable may not prevent the application of a provision of the law of the State in which the assignor is located.

3. Notwithstanding paragraph 2 of this article, in an insolvency proceeding commenced in a State other than the State in which the assignor is located, any preferential right that

arises, by operation of law, under the law of the forum State and is given priority over the rights of an assignee in insolvency proceedings under the law of that State may be given priority notwithstanding article 22. A State may deposit at any time a declaration identifying any such preferential right.

[4093]

Article 24

Special rules on proceeds

1. If proceeds are received by the assignee, the assignee is entitled to retain those proceeds to the extent that the assignee's right in the assigned receivable had priority over the right of a competing claimant in the assigned receivable.

2. If proceeds are received by the assignor, the right of the assignee in those proceeds has priority over the right of a competing claimant in those proceeds to the same extent as the assignee's right had priority over the right in the assigned receivable of that claimant if:

(a) The assignor has received the proceeds under instructions from the assignee to hold the proceeds for the benefit of the assignee; and

(b) The proceeds are held by the assignor for the benefit of the assignee separately and are reasonably identifiable from the assets of the assignor, such as in the case of a separate deposit or securities account containing only proceeds consisting of cash or securities.

3. Nothing in paragraph 2 of this article affects the priority of a person having against the proceeds a right of set-off or a right created by agreement and not derived from a right in the receivable.

[4094]

Article 25

Subordination

An assignee entitled to priority may at any time subordinate its priority unilaterally or by agreement in favour of any existing or future assignees.

[4095]

CHAPTER V
AUTONOMOUS CONFLICT-OF-LAWS RULES

Article 26

Application of chapter V

The provisions of this chapter apply to matters that are:

(a) Within the scope of this Convention as provided in article 1, paragraph 4; and

(b) Otherwise within the scope of this Convention but not settled elsewhere in it.

[4096]

Article 27

Form of a contract of assignment

1. A contract of assignment concluded between persons who are located in the same State is formally valid as between them if it satisfies the requirements of either the law which governs it or the law of the State in which it is concluded.

2. A contract of assignment concluded between persons who are located in different States is formally valid as between them if it satisfies the requirements of either the law which governs it or the law of one of those States.

[4097]

Article 28

Law applicable to the mutual rights and obligations of the assignor and the assignee

1. The mutual rights and obligations of the assignor and the assignee arising from their agreement are governed by the law chosen by them.

2. In the absence of a choice of law by the assignor and the assignee, their mutual rights and obligations arising from their agreement are governed by the law of the State with which the contract of assignment is most closely connected.

[4098]

Article 29

Law applicable to the rights and obligations of the assignee and the debtor

The law governing the original contract determines the effectiveness of contractual limitations on assignment as between the assignee and the debtor, the relationship between the assignee and the debtor, the conditions under which the assignment can be invoked against the debtor and whether the debtor's obligations have been discharged.

[4099]

Article 30

Law applicable to priority

1. The law of the State in which the assignor is located governs the priority of the right of an assignee in the assigned receivable over the right of a competing claimant.

2. The rules of the law of either the forum State or any other State that are mandatory irrespective of the law otherwise applicable may not prevent the application of a provision of the law of the State in which the assignor is located.

3. Notwithstanding paragraph 2 of this article, in an insolvency proceeding commenced in a State other than the State in which the assignor is located, any preferential right that arises, by operation of law, under the law of the forum State and is given priority over the rights of an assignee in insolvency proceedings under the law of that State may be given priority notwithstanding paragraph 1 of this article.

[4100]

Article 31

Mandatory rules

1. Nothing in articles 27 to 29 restricts the application of the rules of the law of the forum State in a situation where they are mandatory irrespective of the law otherwise applicable.

2. Nothing in articles 27 to 29 restricts the application of the mandatory rules of the law of another State with which the matters settled in those articles have a close connection if and insofar as, under the law of that other State, those rules must be applied irrespective of the law otherwise applicable.

[4101]

Article 32

Public policy

With regard to matters settled in this chapter, the application of a provision of the law specified in this chapter may be refused only if the application of that provision is manifestly contrary to the public policy of the forum State.

[4102]

CHAPTER VI
FINAL PROVISIONS

Article 33

Depositary

The Secretary-General of the United Nations is the depositary of this Convention.

[4103]

Article 34

Signature, ratification, acceptance, approval, accession

1. This Convention is open for signature by all States at the Headquarters of the United Nations in New York until 31 December 2003.

2. This Convention is subject to ratification, acceptance or approval by the signatory States.

3. This Convention is open to accession by all States that are not signatory States as from the date it is open for signature.

4. Instruments of ratification, acceptance, approval and accession are to be deposited with the Secretary-General of the United Nations.

[4104]

Article 35

Application to territorial units

1. If a State has two or more territorial units in which different systems of law are applicable in relation to the matters dealt with in this Convention, it may at any time declare that this Convention is to extend to all its territorial units or only one or more of them, and may at any time substitute another declaration for its earlier declaration.

2. Such declarations are to state expressly the territorial units to which this Convention extends.

3. If, by virtue of a declaration under this article, this Convention does not extend to all territorial units of a State and the assignor or the debtor is located in a territorial unit to which this Convention does not extend, this location is considered not to be in a Contracting State.

4. If, by virtue of a declaration under this article, this Convention does not extend to all territorial units of a State and the law governing the original contract is the law in force in a territorial unit to which this Convention does not extend, the law governing the original contract is considered not to be the law of a Contracting State.

5. If a State makes no declaration under paragraph 1 of this article, the Convention is to extend to all territorial units of that State.

[4105]

Article 36

Location in a territorial unit

If a person is located in a State which has two or more territorial units, that person is located in the territorial unit in which it has its place of business. If the assignor or the assignee has a place of business in more than one territorial unit, the place of business is that place where the central administration of the assignor or the assignee is exercised. If the debtor has a place of business in more than one territorial unit, the place of business is that which has the closest relationship to the original contract. If a person does not have a place of business, reference is to be made to the habitual residence of that person. A State with two or more territorial units may specify by declaration at any time other rules for determining the location of a person within that State.

[4106]

Article 37

Applicable law in territorial units

Any reference in this Convention to the law of a State means, in the case of a State which has two or more territorial units, the law in force in the territorial unit. Such a State may specify by declaration at any time other rules for determining the applicable law, including rules that render applicable the law of another territorial unit of that State.

[4107]

Article 38

Conflicts with other international agreements

1. This Convention does not prevail over any international agreement that has already been or may be entered into and that specifically governs a transaction otherwise governed by this Convention.

2. Notwithstanding paragraph 1 of this article, this Convention prevails over the Unidroit Convention on International Factoring ("the Ottawa Convention"). To the extent that this

Convention does not apply to the rights and obligations of a debtor, it does not preclude the application of the Ottawa Convention with respect to the rights and obligations of that debtor.

[4108]

Article 39

Declaration on application of chapter V

A State may declare at any time that it will not be bound by chapter V.

[4109]

Article 40

Limitations relating to Governments and other public entities

A State may declare at any time that it will not be bound or the extent to which it will not be bound by articles 9 and 10 if the debtor or any person granting a personal or property right securing payment of the assigned receivable is located in that State at the time of conclusion of the original contract and is a Government, central or local, any subdivision thereof, or an entity constituted for a public purpose. If a State has made such a declaration, articles 9 and 10 do not affect the rights and obligations of that debtor or person. A State may list in a declaration the types of entity that are the subject of a declaration.

[4110]

Article 41

Other exclusions

1. A State may declare at any time that it will not apply this Convention to specific types of assignment or to the assignment of specific categories of receivables clearly described in a declaration.

2. After a declaration under paragraph 1 of this article takes effect:
   (a) This Convention does not apply to such types of assignment or to the assignment of such categories of receivables if the assignor is located at the time of conclusion of the contract of assignment in such a State; and
   (b) The provisions of this Convention that affect the rights and obligations of the debtor do not apply if, at the time of conclusion of the original contract, the debtor is located in such a State or the law governing the original contract is the law of such a State.

3. This article does not apply to assignments of receivables listed in article 9, paragraph 3.

[4111]

Article 42

Application of the annex

1. A State may at any time declare that it will be bound by:
   (a) The priority rules set forth in section I of the annex and will participate in the international registration system established pursuant to section II of the annex;
   (b) The priority rules set forth in section I of the annex and will effectuate such rules by use of a registration system that fulfils the purposes of such rules, in which case, for the purposes of section I of the annex, registration pursuant to such a system has the same effect as registration pursuant to section II of the annex;
   (c) The priority rules set forth in section III of the annex;
   (d) The priority rules set forth in section IV of the annex; or
   (e) The priority rules set forth in articles 7 and 9 of the annex.

2. For the purposes of article 22:
   (a) The law of a State that has made a declaration pursuant to paragraph 1 (a) or (b) of this article is the set of rules set forth in section I of the annex, as affected by any declaration made pursuant to paragraph 5 of this article;
   (b) The law of a State that has made a declaration pursuant to paragraph 1 (c) of this article is the set of rules set forth in section III of the annex, as affected by any declaration made pursuant to paragraph 5 of this article;
   (c) The law of a State that has made a declaration pursuant to paragraph 1 (d) of this

article is the set of rules set forth in section IV of the annex, as affected by any declaration made pursuant to paragraph 5 of this article; and

(d) The law of a State that has made a declaration pursuant to paragraph 1 (e) of this article is the set of rules set forth in articles 7 and 9 of the annex, as affected by any declaration made pursuant to paragraph 5 of this article.

3. A State that has made a declaration pursuant to paragraph 1 of this article may establish rules pursuant to which contracts of assignment concluded before the declaration takes effect become subject to those rules within a reasonable time.

4. A State that has not made a declaration pursuant to paragraph 1 of this article may, in accordance with priority rules in force in that State, utilize the registration system established pursuant to section II of the annex.

5. At the time a State makes a declaration pursuant to paragraph 1 of this article or thereafter, it may declare that:

(a) It will not apply the priority rules chosen under paragraph 1 of this article to certain types of assignment or to the assignment of certain categories of receivables; or

(b) It will apply those priority rules with modifications specified in that declaration.

6. At the request of Contracting or Signatory States to this Convention comprising not less than one third of the Contracting and Signatory States, the depositary shall convene a conference of the Contracting and Signatory States to designate the supervising authority and the first registrar and to prepare or revise the regulations referred to in section II of the annex.

[4112]

Article 43

Effect of declaration

1. Declarations made under articles 35, paragraph 1, 36, 37 or 39 to 42 at the time of signature are subject to confirmation upon ratification, acceptance or approval.

2. Declarations and confirmations of declarations are to be in writing and to be formally notified to the depositary.

3. A declaration takes effect simultaneously with the entry into force of this Convention in respect of the State concerned. However, a declaration of which the depositary receives formal notification after such entry into force takes effect on the first day of the month following the expiration of six months after the date of its receipt by the depositary.

4. A State that makes a declaration under articles 35, paragraph 1, 36, 37 or 39 to 42 may withdraw it at any time by a formal notification in writing addressed to the depositary. Such withdrawal takes effect on the first day of the month following the expiration of six months after the date of the receipt of the notification by the depositary.

5. In the case of a declaration under articles 35, paragraph 1, 36, 37 or 39 to 42 that takes effect after the entry into force of this Convention in respect of the State concerned or in the case of a withdrawal of any such declaration, the effect of which in either case is to cause a rule in this Convention, including any annex, to become applicable:

(a) Except as provided in paragraph 5 (b) of this article, that rule is applicable only to assignments for which the contract of assignment is concluded on or after the date when the declaration or withdrawal takes effect in respect of the Contracting State referred to in article 1, paragraph 1 (a);

(b) A rule that deals with the rights and obligations of the debtor applies only in respect of original contracts concluded on or after the date when the declaration or withdrawal takes effect in respect of the Contracting State referred to in article 1, paragraph 3.

6. In the case of a declaration under articles 35, paragraph 1, 36, 37 or 39 to 42 that takes effect after the entry into force of this Convention in respect of the State concerned or in the case of a withdrawal of any such declaration, the effect of which in either case is to cause a rule in this Convention, including any annex, to become inapplicable:

(a) Except as provided in paragraph 6 (b) of this article, that rule is inapplicable to assignments for which the contract of assignment is concluded on or after the date when the declaration or withdrawal takes effect in respect of the Contracting State referred to in article 1, paragraph 1 (a);

(b) A rule that deals with the rights and obligations of the debtor is inapplicable in respect of original contracts concluded on or after the date when the declaration or withdrawal takes effect in respect of the Contracting State referred to in article 1, paragraph 3.

7. If a rule rendered applicable or inapplicable as a result of a declaration or withdrawal referred to in paragraph 5 or 6 of this article is relevant to the determination of priority with respect to a receivable for which the contract of assignment is concluded before such declaration or withdrawal takes effect or with respect to its proceeds, the right of the assignee has priority over the right of a competing claimant to the extent that, under the law that would determine priority before such declaration or withdrawal takes effect, the right of the assignee would have priority.

[4113]

Article 44

Reservations

No reservations are permitted except those expressly authorized in this Convention.

[4114]

Article 45

Entry into force

1. This Convention enters into force on the first day of the month following the expiration of six months from the date of deposit of the fifth instrument of ratification, acceptance, approval or accession with the depositary.

2. For each State that becomes a Contracting State to this Convention after the date of deposit of the fifth instrument of ratification, acceptance, approval or accession, this Convention enters into force on the first day of the month following the expiration of six months after the date of deposit of the appropriate instrument on behalf of that State.

3. This Convention applies only to assignments if the contract of assignment is concluded on or after the date when this Convention enters into force in respect of the Contracting State referred to in article 1, paragraph 1(a), provided that the provisions of this Convention that deal with the rights and obligations of the debtor apply only to assignments of receivables arising from original contracts concluded on or after the date when this Convention enters into force in respect of the Contracting State referred to in article 1, paragraph 3.

4. If a receivable is assigned pursuant to a contract of assignment concluded before the date when this Convention enters into force in respect of the Contracting State referred to in article 1, paragraph 1 (a), the right of the assignee has priority over the right of a competing claimant with respect to the receivable to the extent that, under the law that would determine priority in the absence of this Convention, the right of the assignee would have priority.

[4115]

Article 46

Denunciation

1. A Contracting State may denounce this Convention at any time by written notification addressed to the depositary.

2. The denunciation takes effect on the first day of the month following the expiration of one year after the notification is received by the depositary. Where a longer period is specified in the notification, the denunciation takes effect upon the expiration of such longer period after the notification is received by the depositary.

3. This Convention remains applicable to assignments if the contract of assignment is concluded before the date when the denunciation takes effect in respect of the Contracting State referred to in article 1, paragraph 1 (a), provided that the provisions of this Convention that deal with the rights and obligations of the debtor remain applicable only to assignments of receivables arising from original contracts concluded before the date when the denunciation takes effect in respect of the Contracting State referred to in article 1, paragraph 3.

4. If a receivable is assigned pursuant to a contract of assignment concluded before the date when the denunciation takes effect in respect of the Contracting State referred to in

article 1, paragraph 1 (a), the right of the assignee has priority over the right of a competing claimant with respect to the receivable to the extent that, under the law that would determine priority under this Convention, the right of the assignee would have priority.

[4116]

Article 47

Revision and amendment

1. At the request of not less than one third of the Contracting States to this Convention, the depositary shall convene a conference of the Contracting States to revise or amend it.

2. Any instrument of ratification, acceptance, approval or accession deposited after the entry into force of an amendment to this Convention is deemed to apply to the Convention as amended.

ANNEX TO THE CONVENTION

SECTION I
PRIORITY RULES BASED ON REGISTRATION

Article 1

Priority among several assignees

As between assignees of the same receivable from the same assignor, the priority of the right of an assignee in the assigned receivable is determined by the order in which data about the assignment are registered under section II of this annex, regardless of the time of transfer of the receivable. If no such data are registered, priority is determined by the order of conclusion of the respective contracts of assignment.

Article 2

Priority between the assignee and the insolvency administrator or creditors of the assignor

The right of an assignee in an assigned receivable has priority over the right of an insolvency administrator and creditors who obtain a right in the assigned receivable by attachment, judicial act or similar act of a competent authority that gives rise to such right, if the receivable was assigned, and data about the assignment were registered under section II of this annex, before the commencement of such insolvency proceeding, attachment, judicial act or similar act.

[4117]

SECTION II
REGISTRATION

Article 3

Establishment of a registration system

A registration system will be established for the registration of data about assignments, even if the relevant assignment or receivable is not international, pursuant to the regulations to be promulgated by the registrar and the supervising authority. Regulations promulgated by the registrar and the supervising authority under this annex shall be consistent with this annex. The regulations will prescribe in detail the manner in which the registration system will operate, as well as the procedure for resolving disputes relating to that operation.

Article 4

Registration

1. Any person may register data with regard to an assignment at the registry in accordance with this annex and the regulations. As provided in the regulations, the data registered shall be the identification of the assignor and the assignee and a brief description of the assigned receivables.

2. A single registration may cover one or more assignments by the assignor to the assignee of one or more existing or future receivables, irrespective of whether the receivables exist at the time of registration.

3. A registration may be made in advance of the assignment to which it relates. The regulations will establish the procedure for the cancellation of a registration in the event that the assignment is not made.

4. Registration or its amendment is effective from the time when the data set forth in paragraph 1 of this article are available to searchers. The registering party may specify, from options set forth in the regulations, a period of effectiveness for the registration. In the absence of such a specification, a registration is effective for a period of five years.

5. Regulations will specify the manner in which registration may be renewed, amended or cancelled and regulate such other matters as are necessary for the operation of the registration system.

6. Any defect, irregularity, omission or error with regard to the identification of the assignor that would result in data registered not being found upon a search based on a proper identification of the assignor renders the registration ineffective.

Article 5

Registry searches

1. Any person may search the records of the registry according to identification of the assignor, as set forth in the regulations, and obtain a search result in writing.

2. A search result in writing that purports to be issued by the registry is admissible as evidence and is, in the absence of evidence to the contrary, proof of the registration of the data to which the search relates, including the date and hour of registration.

[4118]

SECTION III
PRIORITY RULES BASED ON THE TIME OF THE CONTRACT OF ASSIGNMENT

Article 6

Priority among several assignees

As between assignees of the same receivable from the same assignor, the priority of the right of an assignee in the assigned receivable is determined by the order of conclusion of the respective contracts of assignment.

Article 7

Priority between the assignee and the insolvency administrator or creditors of the assignor

The right of an assignee in an assigned receivable has priority over the right of an insolvency administrator and creditors who obtain a right in the assigned receivable by attachment, judicial act or similar act of a competent authority that gives rise to such right, if the receivable was assigned before the commencement of such insolvency proceeding, attachment, judicial act or similar act.

Article 8

Proof of time of contract of assignment

The time of conclusion of a contract of assignment in respect of articles 6 and 7 of this annex may be proved by any means, including witnesses.

[4119]

SECTION IV
PRIORITY RULES BASED ON THE TIME
OF NOTIFICATION OF ASSIGNMENT

Article 9

Priority among several assignees

As between assignees of the same receivable from the same assignor, the priority of the right of an assignee in the assigned receivable is determined by the order in which notification of the respective assignments is received by the debtor. However, an assignee may not obtain priority over a prior assignment of which the assignee had knowledge at the time of conclusion of the contract of assignment to that assignee by notifying the debtor.

Article 10

Priority between the assignee and the insolvency administrator or creditors of the assignor

The right of an assignee in an assigned receivable has priority over the right of an insolvency administrator and creditors who obtain a right in the assigned receivable by attachment, judicial act or similar act of a competent authority that gives rise to such right, if the receivable was assigned and notification was received by the debtor before the commencement of such insolvency proceeding, attachment, judicial act or similar act.

DONE at New York, this 12th day of December two thousand one, in a single original, of which the Arabic, Chinese, English, French, Russian and Spanish texts are equally authentic.

IN WITNESS WHEREOF the undersigned plenipotentiaries, being duly authorized by their respective Governments, have signed the present Convention.

[4120]

CONVENTION ON INTERNATIONAL INTERESTS IN MOBILE EQUIPMENT

(2001)

The Convention is reproduced with the kind permission of the International Institute for the Unification of Private Law (UNIDROIT) (see website at http://www.unidroit.org) and the International Civil Aviation Organization (http://www.icao.int). No unauthorised reproduction of the texts of the Convention on International Interests in Mobile Equipment, the Protocol to the Convention on International Interests in Mobile Equipment on Matters Specific to Aircraft Equipment and the Consolidated text, other than for personal use, is permitted. Any requests for such permission should be addressed to the UNIDROIT Secretariat and the Director of the Bureau of Administration and Services of the International Civil Aviation Organization (ICAO).

As yet, neither the United Kingdom not the European Community has ratified this Convention.

THE STATES PARTIES TO THIS CONVENTION,

AWARE of the need to acquire and use mobile equipment of high value or particular economic significance and to facilitate the financing of the acquisition and use of such equipment in an efficient manner,

RECOGNISING the advantages of asset-based financing and leasing for this purpose and desiring to facilitate these types of transaction by establishing clear rules to govern them,

MINDFUL of the need to ensure that interests in such equipment are recognised and protected universally,

DESIRING to provide broad and mutual economic benefits for all interested parties,

BELIEVING that such rules must reflect the principles underlying asset-based financing and leasing and promote the autonomy of the parties necessary in these transactions,

CONSCIOUS of the need to establish a legal framework for international interests in such equipment and for that purpose to create an international registration system for their protection,

TAKING INTO CONSIDERATION the objectives and principles enunciated in existing Conventions relating to such equipment,

HAVE AGREED upon the following provisions:

CHAPTER I
SPHERE OF APPLICATION AND GENERAL PROVISIONS

Article 1

Definitions

In this Convention, except where the context otherwise requires, the following terms are employed with the meanings set out below:

(a) "agreement" means a security agreement, a title reservation agreement or a leasing agreement;

(b) "assignment" means a contract which, whether by way of security or otherwise, confers on the assignee associated rights with or without a transfer of the related international interest;

(c) "associated rights" means all rights to payment or other performance by a debtor under an agreement which are secured by or associated with the object;

(d) "commencement of the insolvency proceedings" means the time at which the insolvency proceedings are deemed to commence under the applicable insolvency law;

(e) "conditional buyer" means a buyer under a title reservation agreement;

(f) "conditional seller" means a seller under a title reservation agreement;

(g) "contract of sale" means a contract for the sale of an object by a seller to a buyer which is not an agreement as defined in (a) above;

(h) "court" means a court of law or an administrative or arbitral tribunal established by a Contracting State;

(i) "creditor" means a chargee under a security agreement, a conditional seller under a title reservation agreement or a lessor under a leasing agreement;

(j) "debtor" means a chargor under a security agreement, a conditional buyer under a title reservation agreement, a lessee under a leasing agreement or a person whose interest in an object is burdened by a registrable non-consensual right or interest;

(k) "insolvency administrator" means a person authorised to administer the reorganisation or liquidation, including one authorised on an interim basis, and includes a debtor in possession if permitted by the applicable insolvency law;

(l) "insolvency proceedings" means bankruptcy, liquidation or other collective judicial or administrative proceedings, including interim proceedings, in which the assets and affairs of the debtor are subject to control or supervision by a court for the purposes of reorganisation or liquidation;

(m) "interested persons" means:
   (i) the debtor;
   (ii) any person who, for the purpose of assuring performance of any of the obligations in favour of the creditor, gives or issues a suretyship or demand guarantee or a standby letter of credit or any other form of credit insurance;
   (iii) any other person having rights in or over the object;

(n) "internal transaction" means a transaction of a type listed in Article 2(2)(a) to (c) where the centre of the main interests of all parties to such transaction is situated, and the relevant object located (as specified in the Protocol), in the same Contracting State at the time of the conclusion of the contract and where the interest created by the transaction has been registered in a national registry in that Contracting State which has made a declaration under Article 50(1);

(o) "international interest" means an interest held by a creditor to which Article 2 applies;

(p) "International Registry" means the international registration facilities established for the purposes of this Convention or the Protocol;

(q) "leasing agreement" means an agreement by which one person (the lessor) grants a right to possession or control of an object (with or without an option to purchase) to another person (the lessee) in return for a rental or other payment;

(r) "national interest" means an interest held by a creditor in an object and created by an internal transaction covered by a declaration under Article 50(1);

(s) "non-consensual right or interest" means a right or interest conferred under the law of a Contracting State which has made a declaration under Article 39 to secure the performance of an obligation, including an obligation to a State, State entity or an intergovernmental or private organisation;

(t) "notice of a national interest" means notice registered or to be registered in the International Registry that a national interest has been created;

(u) "object" means an object of a category to which Article 2 applies;

(v) "pre-existing right or interest" means a right or interest of any kind in or over an object created or arising before the effective date of this Convention as defined by Article 60(2)(a);
(w) "proceeds" means money or non-money proceeds of an object arising from the total or partial loss or physical destruction of the object or its total or partial confiscation, condemnation or requisition;
(x) "prospective assignment" means an assignment that is intended to be made in the future, upon the occurrence of a stated event, whether or not the occurrence of the event is certain;
(y) "prospective international interest" means an interest that is intended to be created or provided for in an object as an international interest in the future, upon the occurrence of a stated event (which may include the debtor's acquisition of an interest in the object), whether or not the occurrence of the event is certain;
(z) "prospective sale" means a sale which is intended to be made in the future, upon the occurrence of a stated event, whether or not the occurrence of the event is certain;
(aa) "Protocol" means, in respect of any category of object and associated rights to which this Convention applies, the Protocol in respect of that category of object and associated rights;
(bb) "registered" means registered in the International Registry pursuant to Chapter V;
(cc) "registered interest" means an international interest, a registrable non-consensual right or interest or a national interest specified in a notice of a national interest registered pursuant to Chapter V;
(dd) "registrable non-consensual right or interest" means a non-consensual right or interest registrable pursuant to a declaration deposited under Article 40;
(ee) "Registrar" means, in respect of the Protocol, the person or body designated by that Protocol or appointed under Article 17(2)(b);
(ff) "regulations" means regulations made or approved by the Supervisory Authority pursuant to the Protocol;
(gg) "sale" means a transfer of ownership of an object pursuant to a contract of sale;
(hh) "secured obligation" means an obligation secured by a security interest;
(ii) "security agreement" means an agreement by which a chargor grants or agrees to grant to a chargee an interest (including an ownership interest) in or over an object to secure the performance of any existing or future obligation of the chargor or a third person;
(jj) "security interest" means an interest created by a security agreement;
(kk) "Supervisory Authority" means, in respect of the Protocol, the Supervisory Authority referred to in Article 17(1);
(ll) "title reservation agreement" means an agreement for the sale of an object on terms that ownership does not pass until fulfilment of the condition or conditions stated in the agreement;
(mm) "unregistered interest" means a consensual interest or non-consensual right or interest (other than an interest to which Article 39 applies) which has not been registered, whether or not it is registrable under this Convention; and
(nn) "writing" means a record of information (including information communicated by teletransmission) which is in tangible or other form and is capable of being reproduced in tangible form on a subsequent occasion and which indicates by reasonable means a person's approval of the record.

[4121]

Article 2

The international interest

1. This Convention provides for the constitution and effects of an international interest in certain categories of mobile equipment and associated rights.

2. For the purposes of this Convention, an international interest in mobile equipment is an interest, constituted under Article 7, in a uniquely identifiable object of a category of such objects listed in paragraph 3 and designated in the Protocol:
(a) granted by the chargor under a security agreement;
(b) vested in a person who is the conditional seller under a title reservation agreement; or
(c) vested in a person who is the lessor under a leasing agreement.

An interest falling within sub-paragraph (a) does not also fall within sub-paragraph (b) or (c).

3. The categories referred to in the preceding paragraphs are:
   (a) airframes, aircraft engines and helicopters;
   (b) railway rolling stock; and
   (c) space assets.

4. The applicable law determines whether an interest to which paragraph 2 applies falls within sub-paragraph (a), (b) or (c) of that paragraph.

5. An international interest in an object extends to proceeds of that object.

[4122]

Article 3

Sphere of application

1. This Convention applies when, at the time of the conclusion of the agreement creating or providing for the international interest, the debtor is situated in a Contracting State.

2. The fact that the creditor is situated in a non-Contracting State does not affect the applicability of this Convention.

[4123]

Article 4

Where debtor is situated

1. For the purposes of Article 3(1), the debtor is situated in any Contracting State:
   (a) under the law of which it is incorporated or formed;
   (b) where it has its registered office or statutory seat;
   (c) where it has its centre of administration; or
   (d) where it has its place of business.

2. A reference in sub-paragraph (d) of the preceding paragraph to the debtor's place of business shall, if it has more than one place of business, mean its principal place of business or, if it has no place of business, its habitual residence.

[4124]

Article 5

Interpretation and applicable law

1. In the interpretation of this Convention, regard is to be had to its purposes as set forth in the preamble, to its international character and to the need to promote uniformity and predictability in its application.

2. Questions concerning matters governed by this Convention which are not expressly settled in it are to be settled in conformity with the general principles on which it is based or, in the absence of such principles, in conformity with the applicable law.

3. References to the applicable law are to the domestic rules of the law applicable by virtue of the rules of private international law of the forum State.

4. Where a State comprises several territorial units, each of which has its own rules of law in respect of the matter to be decided, and where there is no indication of the relevant territorial unit, the law of that State decides which is the territorial unit whose rules shall govern. In the absence of any such rule, the law of the territorial unit with which the case is most closely connected shall apply.

[4125]

Article 6

Relationship between the Convention and the Protocol

1. This Convention and the Protocol shall be read and interpreted together as a single instrument.

2. To the extent of any inconsistency between this Convention and the Protocol, the Protocol shall prevail.

[4126]

CHAPTER II
CONSTITUTION OF AN INTERNATIONAL INTEREST

Article 7

Formal requirements

An interest is constituted as an international interest under this Convention where the agreement creating or providing for the interest:

(a) is in writing;

(b) relates to an object of which the chargor, conditional seller or lessor has power to dispose;

(c) enables the object to be identified in conformity with the Protocol; and

(d) in the case of a security agreement, enables the secured obligations to be determined, but without the need to state a sum or maximum sum secured.

[4127]

CHAPTER III
DEFAULT REMEDIES

Article 8

Remedies of chargee

1. In the event of default as provided in Article 11, the chargee may, to the extent that the chargor has at any time so agreed and subject to any declaration that may be made by a Contracting State under Article 54, exercise any one or more of the following remedies:

(a) take possession or control of any object charged to it;

(b) sell or grant a lease of any such object;

(c) collect or receive any income or profits arising from the management or use of any such object.

2. The chargee may alternatively apply for a court order authorising or directing any of the acts referred to in the preceding paragraph.

3. Any remedy set out in sub-paragraph (a), (b) or (c) of paragraph 1 or by Article 13 shall be exercised in a commercially reasonable manner. A remedy shall be deemed to be exercised in a commercially reasonable manner where it is exercised in conformity with a provision of the security agreement except where such a provision is manifestly unreasonable.

4. A chargee proposing to sell or grant a lease of an object under paragraph 1 shall give reasonable prior notice in writing of the proposed sale or lease to:

(a) interested persons specified in Article 1(m)(i) and (ii); and

(b) interested persons specified in Article 1(m)(iii) who have given notice of their rights to the chargee within a reasonable time prior to the sale or lease.

5. Any sum collected or received by the chargee as a result of exercise of any of the remedies set out in paragraph 1 or 2 shall be applied towards discharge of the amount of the secured obligations.

6. Where the sums collected or received by the chargee as a result of the exercise of any remedy set out in paragraph 1 or 2 exceed the amount secured by the security interest and any reasonable costs incurred in the exercise of any such remedy, then unless otherwise ordered by the court the chargee shall distribute the surplus among holders of subsequently ranking interests which have been registered or of which the chargee has been given notice, in order of priority, and pay any remaining balance to the chargor.

[4128]

Article 9

Vesting of object in satisfaction; redemption

1. At any time after default as provided in Article 11, the chargee and all the interested persons may agree that ownership of (or any other interest of the chargor in) any object covered by the security interest shall vest in the chargee in or towards satisfaction of the secured obligations.

2. The court may on the application of the chargee order that ownership of (or any other interest of the chargor in) any object covered by the security interest shall vest in the chargee in or towards satisfaction of the secured obligations.

3. The court shall grant an application under the preceding paragraph only if the amount of the secured obligations to be satisfied by such vesting is commensurate with the value of the object after taking account of any payment to be made by the chargee to any of the interested persons.

4. At any time after default as provided in Article 11 and before sale of the charged object or the making of an order under paragraph 2, the chargor or any interested person may discharge the security interest by paying in full the amount secured, subject to any lease granted by the chargee under Article 8(1)(b) or ordered under Article 8(2). Where, after such default, the payment of the amount secured is made in full by an interested person other than the debtor, that person is subrogated to the rights of the chargee.

5. Ownership or any other interest of the chargor passing on a sale under Article 8(1)(b) or passing under paragraph 1 or 2 of this Article is free from any other interest over which the chargee's security interest has priority under the provisions of Article 29.

[4129]

Article 10

Remedies of conditional seller or lessor

In the event of default under a title reservation agreement or under a leasing agreement as provided in Article 11, the conditional seller or the lessor, as the case may be, may:

(a) subject to any declaration that may be made by a Contracting State under Article 54, terminate the agreement and take possession or control of any object to which the agreement relates; or

(b) apply for a court order authorising or directing either of these acts.

[4130]

Article 11

Meaning of default

1. The debtor and the creditor may at any time agree in writing as to the events that constitute a default or otherwise give rise to the rights and remedies specified in Articles 8 to 10 and 13.

2. Where the debtor and the creditor have not so agreed, "default" for the purposes of Articles 8 to 10 and 13 means a default which substantially deprives the creditor of what it is entitled to expect under the agreement.

[4131]

Article 12

Additional remedies

Any additional remedies permitted by the applicable law, including any remedies agreed upon by the parties, may be exercised to the extent that they are not inconsistent with the mandatory provisions of this Chapter as set out in Article 15.

[4132]

Article 13

Relief pending final determination

1. Subject to any declaration that it may make under Article 55, a Contracting State shall ensure that a creditor who adduces evidence of default by the debtor may, pending final determination of its claim and to the extent that the debtor has at any time so agreed, obtain from a court speedy relief in the form of such one or more of the following orders as the creditor requests:

(a) preservation of the object and its value;

(b) possession, control or custody of the object;

(c) immobilisation of the object; and

(d) lease or, except where covered by sub-paragraphs (a) to (c), management of the object and the income therefrom.

2. In making any order under the preceding paragraph, the court may impose such terms as it considers necessary to protect the interested persons in the event that the creditor:

(a) in implementing any order granting such relief, fails to perform any of its obligations to the debtor under this Convention or the Protocol; or

(b) fails to establish its claim, wholly or in part, on the final determination of that claim.

3. Before making any order under paragraph 1, the court may require notice of the request to be given to any of the interested persons.

4. Nothing in this Article affects the application of Article 8(3) or limits the availability of forms of interim relief other than those set out in paragraph 1.

[4133]

Article 14

Procedural requirements

Subject to Article 54(2), any remedy provided by this Chapter shall be exercised in conformity with the procedure prescribed by the law of the place where the remedy is to be exercised.

[4134]

Article 15

Derogation

In their relations with each other, any two or more of the parties referred to in this Chapter may at any time, by agreement in writing, derogate from or vary the effect of any of the preceding provisions of this Chapter except Articles 8(3) to (6), 9(3) and (4), 13(2) and 14.

[4135]

CHAPTER IV
THE INTERNATIONAL REGISTRATION SYSTEM

Article 16

The International Registry

1. An International Registry shall be established for registrations of:

(a) international interests, prospective international interests and registrable non-consensual rights and interests;

(b) assignments and prospective assignments of international interests;

(c) acquisitions of international interests by legal or contractual subrogations under the applicable law;

(d) notices of national interests; and

(e) subordinations of interests referred to in any of the preceding sub-paragraphs.

2. Different international registries may be established for different categories of object and associated rights.

3. For the purposes of this Chapter and Chapter V, the term "registration" includes, where appropriate, an amendment, extension or discharge of a registration.

[4136]

Article 17

The Supervisory Authority and the Registrar

1. There shall be a Supervisory Authority as provided by the Protocol.

2. The Supervisory Authority shall:

(a) establish or provide for the establishment of the International Registry;

(b) except as otherwise provided by the Protocol, appoint and dismiss the Registrar;

(c) ensure that any rights required for the continued effective operation of the International Registry in the event of a change of Registrar will vest in or be assignable to the new Registrar;

(d) after consultation with the Contracting States, make or approve and ensure the publication of regulations pursuant to the Protocol dealing with the operation of the International Registry;
(e) establish administrative procedures through which complaints concerning the operation of the International Registry can be made to the Supervisory Authority;
(f) supervise the Registrar and the operation of the International Registry;
(g) at the request of the Registrar, provide such guidance to the Registrar as the Supervisory Authority thinks fit;
(h) set and periodically review the structure of fees to be charged for the services and facilities of the International Registry;
(i) do all things necessary to ensure that an efficient notice-based electronic registration system exists to implement the objectives of this Convention and the Protocol; and
(j) report periodically to Contracting States concerning the discharge of its obligations under this Convention and the Protocol.

3. The Supervisory Authority may enter into any agreement requisite for the performance of its functions, including any agreement referred to in Article 27(3).

4. The Supervisory Authority shall own all proprietary rights in the data bases and archives of the International Registry.

5. The Registrar shall ensure the efficient operation of the International Registry and perform the functions assigned to it by this Convention, the Protocol and the regulations.
[4137]

CHAPTER V
OTHER MATTERS RELATING TO REGISTRATION

Article 18

Registration requirements

1. The Protocol and regulations shall specify the requirements, including the criteria for the identification of the object:
(a) for effecting a registration (which shall include provision for prior electronic transmission of any consent from any person whose consent is required under Article 20);
(b) for making searches and issuing search certificates, and, subject thereto;
(c) for ensuring the confidentiality of information and documents of the International Registry other than information and documents relating to a registration.

2. The Registrar shall not be under a duty to enquire whether a consent to registration under Article 20 has in fact been given or is valid.

3. Where an interest registered as a prospective international interest becomes an international interest, no further registration shall be required provided that the registration information is sufficient for a registration of an international interest.

4. The Registrar shall arrange for registrations to be entered into the International Registry data base and made searchable in chronological order of receipt, and the file shall record the date and time of receipt.

5. The Protocol may provide that a Contracting State may designate an entity or entities in its territory as the entry point or entry points through which the information required for registration shall or may be transmitted to the International Registry. A Contracting State making such a designation may specify the requirements, if any, to be satisfied before such information is transmitted to the International Registry.
[4138]

Article 19

Validity and time of registration

1. A registration shall be valid only if made in conformity with Article 20.

2. A registration, if valid, shall be complete upon entry of the required information into the International Registry data base so as to be searchable.

3. A registration shall be searchable for the purposes of the preceding paragraph at the time when:
   (a) the International Registry has assigned to it a sequentially ordered file number; and
   (b) the registration information, including the file number, is stored in durable form and may be accessed at the International Registry.

4. If an interest first registered as a prospective international interest becomes an international interest, that international interest shall be treated as registered from the time of registration of the prospective international interest provided that the registration was still current immediately before the international interest was constituted as provided by Article 7.

5. The preceding paragraph applies with necessary modifications to the registration of a prospective assignment of an international interest.

6. A registration shall be searchable in the International Registry data base according to the criteria prescribed by the Protocol.

[4139]

Article 20

Consent to registration

1. An international interest, a prospective international interest or an assignment or prospective assignment of an international interest may be registered, and any such registration amended or extended prior to its expiry, by either party with the consent in writing of the other.

2. The subordination of an international interest to another international interest may be registered by or with the consent in writing at any time of the person whose interest has been subordinated.

3. A registration may be discharged by or with the consent in writing of the party in whose favour it was made.

4. The acquisition of an international interest by legal or contractual subrogation may be registered by the subrogee.

5. A registrable non-consensual right or interest may be registered by the holder thereof.

6. A notice of a national interest may be registered by the holder thereof.

[4140]

Article 21

Duration of registration

Registration of an international interest remains effective until discharged or until expiry of the period specified in the registration.

[4141]

Article 22

Searches

1. Any person may, in the manner prescribed by the Protocol and regulations, make or request a search of the International Registry by electronic means concerning interests or prospective international interests registered therein.

2. Upon receipt of a request therefor, the Registrar, in the manner prescribed by the Protocol and regulations, shall issue a registry search certificate by electronic means with respect to any object:
   (a) stating all registered information relating thereto, together with a statement indicating the date and time of registration of such information; or
   (b) stating that there is no information in the International Registry relating thereto.

3. A search certificate issued under the preceding paragraph shall indicate that the creditor named in the registration information has acquired or intends to acquire an international interest in the object but shall not indicate whether what is registered is an international interest or a prospective international interest, even if this is ascertainable from the relevant registration information.

[4142]

Article 23

List of declarations and declared non-consensual rights or interests

The Registrar shall maintain a list of declarations, withdrawals of declaration and of the categories of non- consensual right or interest communicated to the Registrar by the Depositary as having been declared by Contracting States in conformity with Articles 39 and 40 and the date of each such declaration or withdrawal of declaration. Such list shall be recorded and searchable in the name of the declaring State and shall be made available as provided in the Protocol and regulations to any person requesting it.

[4143]

Article 24

Evidentiary value of certificates

A document in the form prescribed by the regulations which purports to be a certificate issued by the International Registry is prima facie proof:

(a) that it has been so issued; and
(b) of the facts recited in it, including the date and time of a registration.

[4144]

Article 25

Discharge of registration

1. Where the obligations secured by a registered security interest or the obligations giving rise to a registered non-consensual right or interest have been discharged, or where the conditions of transfer of title under a registered title reservation agreement have been fulfilled, the holder of such interest shall, without undue delay, procure the discharge of the registration after written demand by the debtor delivered to or received at its address stated in the registration.

2. Where a prospective international interest or a prospective assignment of an international interest has been registered, the intending creditor or intending assignee shall, without undue delay, procure the discharge of the registration after written demand by the intending debtor or assignor which is delivered to or received at its address stated in the registration before the intending creditor or assignee has given value or incurred a commitment to give value.

3. Where the obligations secured by a national interest specified in a registered notice of a national interest have been discharged, the holder of such interest shall, without undue delay, procure the discharge of the registration after written demand by the debtor delivered to or received at its address stated in the registration.

4. Where a registration ought not to have been made or is incorrect, the person in whose favour the registration was made shall, without undue delay, procure its discharge or amendment after written demand by the debtor delivered to or received at its address stated in the registration.

[4145]

Article 26

Access to the international registration facilities

No person shall be denied access to the registration and search facilities of the International Registry on any ground other than its failure to comply with the procedures prescribed by this Chapter.

[4146]

CHAPTER VI
PRIVILEGES AND IMMUNITIES OF THE SUPERVISORY AUTHORITY AND THE REGISTRAR

Article 27

Legal personality; immunity

1. The Supervisory Authority shall have international legal personality where not already possessing such personality.

2. The Supervisory Authority and its officers and employees shall enjoy such immunity from legal or administrative process as is specified in the Protocol.

3.
   (a) The Supervisory Authority shall enjoy exemption from taxes and such other privileges as may be provided by agreement with the host State.
   (b) For the purposes of this paragraph, "host State" means the State in which the Supervisory Authority is situated.

4. The assets, documents, data bases and archives of the International Registry shall be inviolable and immune from seizure or other legal or administrative process.

5. For the purposes of any claim against the Registrar under Article 28(1) or Article 44, the claimant shall be entitled to access to such information and documents as are necessary to enable the claimant to pursue its claim.

6. The Supervisory Authority may waive the inviolability and immunity conferred by paragraph 4.

[4147]

CHAPTER VII
LIABILITY OF THE REGISTRAR

Article 28

Liability and financial assurances

1. The Registrar shall be liable for compensatory damages for loss suffered by a person directly resulting from an error or omission of the Registrar and its officers and employees or from a malfunction of the international registration system except where the malfunction is caused by an event of an inevitable and irresistible nature, which could not be prevented by using the best practices in current use in the field of electronic registry design and operation, including those related to back-up and systems security and networking.

2. The Registrar shall not be liable under the preceding paragraph for factual inaccuracy of registration information received by the Registrar or transmitted by the Registrar in the form in which it received that information nor for acts or circumstances for which the Registrar and its officers and employees are not responsible and arising prior to receipt of registration information at the International Registry.

3. Compensation under paragraph 1 may be reduced to the extent that the person who suffered the damage caused or contributed to that damage.

4. The Registrar shall procure insurance or a financial guarantee covering the liability referred to in this Article to the extent determined by the Supervisory Authority, in accordance with the Protocol.

[4148]

CHAPTER VIII
EFFECTS OF AN INTERNATIONAL INTEREST AS AGAINST THIRD PARTIES

Article 29

Priority of competing interests

1. A registered interest has priority over any other interest subsequently registered and over an unregistered interest.

2. The priority of the first-mentioned interest under the preceding paragraph applies:
   (a) even if the first-mentioned interest was acquired or registered with actual knowledge of the other interest; and
   (b) even as regards value given by the holder of the first-mentioned interest with such knowledge.

3. The buyer of an object acquires its interest in it:
   (a) subject to an interest registered at the time of its acquisition of that interest; and
   (b) free from an unregistered interest even if it has actual knowledge of such an interest.

4. The conditional buyer or lessee acquires its interest in or right over that object:
   (a) subject to an interest registered prior to the registration of the international interest held by its conditional seller or lessor; and
   (b) free from an interest not so registered at that time even if it has actual knowledge of that interest.

5. The priority of competing interests or rights under this Article may be varied by agreement between the holders of those interests, but an assignee of a subordinated interest is not bound by an agreement to subordinate that interest unless at the time of the assignment a subordination had been registered relating to that agreement.

6. Any priority given by this Article to an interest in an object extends to proceeds.

7. This Convention:
   (a) does not affect the rights of a person in an item, other than an object, held prior to its installation on an object if under the applicable law those rights continue to exist after the installation; and
   (b) does not prevent the creation of rights in an item, other than an object, which has previously been installed on an object where under the applicable law those rights are created.

[4149]

Article 30

Effects of insolvency

1. In insolvency proceedings against the debtor an international interest is effective if prior to the commencement of the insolvency proceedings that interest was registered in conformity with this Convention.

2. Nothing in this Article impairs the effectiveness of an international interest in the insolvency proceedings where that interest is effective under the applicable law.

3. Nothing in this Article affects:
   (a) any rules of law applicable in insolvency proceedings relating to the avoidance of a transaction as a preference or a transfer in fraud of creditors; or
   (b) any rules of procedure relating to the enforcement of rights to property which is under the control or supervision of the insolvency administrator.

[4150]

CHAPTER IX
ASSIGNMENTS OF ASSOCIATED RIGHTS AND INTERNATIONAL INTERESTS; RIGHTS OF SUBROGATION

Article 31

Effects of assignment

1. Except as otherwise agreed by the parties, an assignment of associated rights made in conformity with Article 32 also transfers to the assignee:
   (a) the related international interest; and
   (b) all the interests and priorities of the assignor under this Convention.

2. Nothing in this Convention prevents a partial assignment of the assignor's associated rights. In the case of such a partial assignment the assignor and assignee may agree as to their respective rights concerning the related international interest assigned under the preceding paragraph but not so as adversely to affect the debtor without its consent.

3. Subject to paragraph 4, the applicable law shall determine the defences and rights of set-off available to the debtor against the assignee.

4. The debtor may at any time by agreement in writing waive all or any of the defences and rights of set-off referred to in the preceding paragraph other than defences arising from fraudulent acts on the part of the assignee.

5. In the case of an assignment by way of security, the assigned associated rights revest in the assignor, to the extent that they are still subsisting, when the obligations secured by the assignment have been discharged.

[4151]

Article 32

Formal requirements of assignment

1. An assignment of associated rights transfers the related international interest only if it:
   (a) is in writing;
   (b) enables the associated rights to be identified under the contract from which they arise; and
   (c) in the case of an assignment by way of security, enables the obligations secured by the assignment to be determined in accordance with the Protocol but without the need to state a sum or maximum sum secured.

2. An assignment of an international interest created or provided for by a security agreement is not valid unless some or all related associated rights also are assigned.

3. This Convention does not apply to an assignment of associated rights which is not effective to transfer the related international interest.

[4152]

Article 33

Debtor's duty to assignee

1. To the extent that associated rights and the related international interest have been transferred in accordance with Articles 31 and 32, the debtor in relation to those rights and that interest is bound by the assignment and has a duty to make payment or give other performance to the assignee, if but only if:
   (a) the debtor has been given notice of the assignment in writing by or with the authority of the assignor; and
   (b) the notice identifies the associated rights.

2. Irrespective of any other ground on which payment or performance by the debtor discharges the latter from liability, payment or performance shall be effective for this purpose if made in accordance with the preceding paragraph.

3. Nothing in this Article shall affect the priority of competing assignments.

[4153]

Article 34

Default remedies in respect of assignment by way of security

In the event of default by the assignor under the assignment of associated rights and the related international interest made by way of security, Articles 8, 9 and 11 to 14 apply in the relations between the assignor and the assignee (and, in relation to associated rights, apply in so far as those provisions are capable of application to intangible property) as if references:
   (a) to the secured obligation and the security interest were references to the obligation secured by the assignment of the associated rights and the related international interest and the security interest created by that assignment;
   (b) to the chargee or creditor and chargor or debtor were references to the assignee and assignor;
   (c) to the holder of the international interest were references to the assignee; and
   (d) to the object were references to the assigned associated rights and the related international interest.

[4154]

Article 35

Priority of competing assignments

1. Where there are competing assignments of associated rights and at least one of the assignments includes the related international interest and is registered, the provisions of Article 29 apply as if the references to a registered interest were references to an assignment of the associated rights and the related registered interest and as if references to a registered or unregistered interest were references to a registered or unregistered assignment.

2. Article 30 applies to an assignment of associated rights as if the references to an international interest were references to an assignment of the associated rights and the related international interest.

[4155]

Article 36

Assignee's priority with respect to associated rights

1. The assignee of associated rights and the related international interest whose assignment has been registered only has priority under Article 35(1) over another assignee of the associated rights:

(a) if the contract under which the associated rights arise states that they are secured by or associated with the object; and

(b) to the extent that the associated rights are related to an object.

2. For the purposes of sub-paragraph (b) of the preceding paragraph, associated rights are related to an object only to the extent that they consist of rights to payment or performance that relate to:

(a) a sum advanced and utilised for the purchase of the object;

(b) a sum advanced and utilised for the purchase of another object in which the assignor held another international interest if the assignor transferred that interest to the assignee and the assignment has been registered;

(c) the price payable for the object;

(d) the rentals payable in respect of the object; or

(e) other obligations arising from a transaction referred to in any of the preceding sub- paragraphs.

3. In all other cases, the priority of the competing assignments of the associated rights shall be determined by the applicable law.

[4156]

Article 37

Effects of assignor's insolvency

The provisions of Article 30 apply to insolvency proceedings against the assignor as if references to the debtor were references to the assignor.

[4157]

Article 38

Subrogation

1. Subject to paragraph 2, nothing in this Convention affects the acquisition of associated rights and the related international interest by legal or contractual subrogation under the applicable law.

2. The priority between any interest within the preceding paragraph and a competing interest may be varied by agreement in writing between the holders of the respective interests but an assignee of a subordinated interest is not bound by an agreement to subordinate that interest unless at the time of the assignment a subordination had been registered relating to that agreement.

[4158]

CHAPTER X
RIGHTS OR INTERESTS SUBJECT TO DECLARATIONS BY CONTRACTING STATES

Article 39

Rights having priority without registration

1. A Contracting State may at any time, in a declaration deposited with the Depositary of the Protocol declare, generally or specifically:

(a) those categories of non-consensual right or interest (other than a right or interest to which Article 40 applies) which under that State's law have priority over an interest in an object equivalent to that of the holder of a registered international interest and which shall have priority over a registered international interest, whether in or outside insolvency proceedings; and

(b) that nothing in this Convention shall affect the right of a State or State entity, intergovernmental organisation or other private provider of public services to arrest or detain an object under the laws of that State for payment of amounts owed to such entity, organisation or provider directly relating to those services in respect of that object or another object.

2. A declaration made under the preceding paragraph may be expressed to cover categories that are created after the deposit of that declaration.

3. A non-consensual right or interest has priority over an international interest if and only if the former is of a category covered by a declaration deposited prior to the registration of the international interest.

4. Notwithstanding the preceding paragraph, a Contracting State may, at the time of ratification, acceptance, approval of, or accession to the Protocol, declare that a right or interest of a category covered by a declaration made under sub-paragraph (a) of paragraph 1 shall have priority over an international interest registered prior to the date of such ratification, acceptance, approval or accession.

[4159]

Article 40

Registrable non-consensual rights or interests

A Contracting State may at any time in a declaration deposited with the Depositary of the Protocol list the categories of non-consensual right or interest which shall be registrable under this Convention as regards any category of object as if the right or interest were an international interest and shall be regulated accordingly. Such a declaration may be modified from time to time.

[4160]

CHAPTER XI
APPLICATION OF THE CONVENTION TO SALES

Article 41

Sale and prospective sale

This Convention shall apply to the sale or prospective sale of an object as provided for in the Protocol with any modifications therein.

[4161]

CHAPTER XII
JURISDICTION

Article 42

Choice of forum

1. Subject to Articles 43 and 44, the courts of a Contracting State chosen by the parties to a transaction have jurisdiction in respect of any claim brought under this Convention, whether or not the chosen forum has a connection with the parties or the transaction. Such jurisdiction shall be exclusive unless otherwise agreed between the parties.

2. Any such agreement shall be in writing or otherwise concluded in accordance with the formal requirements of the law of the chosen forum.

[4162]

Article 43

Jurisdiction under Article 13

1. The courts of a Contracting State chosen by the parties and the courts of the Contracting State on the territory of which the object is situated have jurisdiction to grant relief under Article 13(1)(a), (b), (c) and Article 13(4) in respect of that object.

2. Jurisdiction to grant relief under Article 13(1)(d) or other interim relief by virtue of Article 13(4) may be exercised either:

(a) by the courts chosen by the parties; or

(b) by the courts of a Contracting State on the territory of which the debtor is situated, being relief which, by the terms of the order granting it, is enforceable only in the territory of that Contracting State.

3. A court has jurisdiction under the preceding paragraphs even if the final determination of the claim referred to in Article 13(1) will or may take place in a court of another Contracting State or by arbitration.

[4163]

Article 44

Jurisdiction to make orders against the Registrar

1. The courts of the place in which the Registrar has its centre of administration shall have exclusive jurisdiction to award damages or make orders against the Registrar.

2. Where a person fails to respond to a demand made under Article 25 and that person has ceased to exist or cannot be found for the purpose of enabling an order to be made against it requiring it to procure discharge of the registration, the courts referred to in the preceding paragraph shall have exclusive jurisdiction, on the application of the debtor or intending debtor, to make an order directed to the Registrar requiring the Registrar to discharge the registration.

3. Where a person fails to comply with an order of a court having jurisdiction under this Convention or, in the case of a national interest, an order of a court of competent jurisdiction requiring that person to procure the amendment or discharge of a registration, the courts referred to in paragraph 1 may direct the Registrar to take such steps as will give effect to that order.

4. Except as otherwise provided by the preceding paragraphs, no court may make orders or give judgments or rulings against or purporting to bind the Registrar.

[4164]

Article 45

Jurisdiction in respect of insolvency proceedings

The provisions of this Chapter are not applicable to insolvency proceedings.

[4165]

CHAPTER XIII
RELATIONSHIP WITH OTHER CONVENTIONS

Article 45 *bis*

Relationship with the *United Nations Convention on the Assignment of Receivables in International Trade*

This Convention shall prevail over the *United Nations Convention on the Assignment of Receivables in International Trade*, opened for signature in New York on 12 December 2001, as it relates to the assignment of receivables which are associated rights related to international interests in aircraft objects, railway rolling stock and space assets.

[4166]

Article 46

Relationship with the *UNIDROIT Convention on International Financial Leasing*

The Protocol may determine the relationship between this Convention and the *UNIDROIT Convention on International Financial Leasing*, signed at Ottawa on 28 May 1988.

[4167]

CHAPTER XIV
FINAL PROVISIONS

Article 47

Signature, ratification, acceptance, approval or accession

1. This Convention shall be open for signature in Cape Town on 16 November 2001 by States participating in the Diplomatic Conference to Adopt a Mobile Equipment Convention

and an Aircraft Protocol held at Cape Town from 29 October to 16 November 2001. After 16 November 2001, the Convention shall be open to all States for signature at the Headquarters of the International Institute for the Unification of Private Law (UNIDROIT) in Rome until it enters into force in accordance with Article 49.

2. This Convention shall be subject to ratification, acceptance or approval by States which have signed it.

3. Any State which does not sign this Convention may accede to it at any time.

4. Ratification, acceptance, approval or accession is effected by the deposit of a formal instrument to that effect with the Depositary.

[4168]

Article 48

Regional Economic Integration Organisations

1. A Regional Economic Integration Organisation which is constituted by sovereign States and has competence over certain matters governed by this Convention may similarly sign, accept, approve or accede to this Convention. The Regional Economic Integration Organisation shall in that case have the rights and obligations of a Contracting State, to the extent that that Organisation has competence over matters governed by this Convention. Where the number of Contracting States is relevant in this Convention, the Regional Economic Integration Organisation shall not count as a Contracting State in addition to its Member States which are Contracting States.

2. The Regional Economic Integration Organisation shall, at the time of signature, acceptance, approval or accession, make a declaration to the Depositary specifying the matters governed by this Convention in respect of which competence has been transferred to that Organisation by its Member States. The Regional Economic Integration Organisation shall promptly notify the Depositary of any changes to the distribution of competence, including new transfers of competence, specified in the declaration under this paragraph.

3. Any reference to a "Contracting State" or "Contracting States" or "State Party" or "States Parties" in this Convention applies equally to a Regional Economic Integration Organisation where the context so requires.

[4169]

Article 49

Entry into force

1. This Convention enters into force on the first day of the month following the expiration of three months after the date of the deposit of the third instrument of ratification, acceptance, approval or accession but only as regards a category of objects to which a Protocol applies:

(a) as from the time of entry into force of that Protocol;
(b) subject to the terms of that Protocol; and
(c) as between States Parties to this Convention and that Protocol.

2. For other States this Convention enters into force on the first day of the month following the expiration of three months after the date of the deposit of their instrument of ratification, acceptance, approval or accession but only as regards a category of objects to which a Protocol applies and subject, in relation to such Protocol, to the requirements of sub-paragraphs (a), (b) and (c) of the preceding paragraph.

[4170]

Article 50

Internal transactions

1. A Contracting State may, at the time of ratification, acceptance, approval of, or accession to the Protocol, declare that this Convention shall not apply to a transaction which is an internal transaction in relation to that State with regard to all types of objects or some of them.

2. Notwithstanding the preceding paragraph, the provisions of Articles 8(4), 9(1), 16, Chapter V, Article 29, and any provisions of this Convention relating to registered interests shall apply to an internal transaction.

3. Where notice of a national interest has been registered in the International Registry, the priority of the holder of that interest under Article 29 shall not be affected by the fact that such interest has become vested in another person by assignment or subrogation under the applicable law.

[4171]

Article 51

Future Protocols

1. The Depositary may create working groups, in co-operation with such relevant non-governmental organisations as the Depositary considers appropriate, to assess the feasibility of extending the application of this Convention, through one or more Protocols, to objects of any category of high-value mobile equipment, other than a category referred to in Article 2(3), each member of which is uniquely identifiable, and associated rights relating to such objects.

2. The Depositary shall communicate the text of any preliminary draft Protocol relating to a category of objects prepared by such a working group to all States Parties to this Convention, all member States of the Depositary, member States of the United Nations which are not members of the Depositary and the relevant intergovernmental organisations, and shall invite such States and organisations to participate in intergovernmental negotiations for the completion of a draft Protocol on the basis of such a preliminary draft Protocol.

3. The Depositary shall also communicate the text of any preliminary draft Protocol prepared by such a working group to such relevant non-governmental organisations as the Depositary considers appropriate. Such non-governmental organisations shall be invited promptly to submit comments on the text of the preliminary draft Protocol to the Depositary and to participate as observers in the preparation of a draft Protocol.

4. When the competent bodies of the Depositary adjudge such a draft Protocol ripe for adoption, the Depositary shall convene a diplomatic conference for its adoption.

5. Once such a Protocol has been adopted, subject to paragraph 6, this Convention shall apply to the category of objects covered thereby.

6. Article 45 *bis* of this Convention applies to such a Protocol only if specifically provided for in that Protocol.

[4172]

Article 52

Territorial units

1. If a Contracting State has territorial units in which different systems of law are applicable in relation to the matters dealt with in this Convention, it may, at the time of ratification, acceptance, approval or accession, declare that this Convention is to extend to all its territorial units or only to one or more of them and may modify its declaration by submitting another declaration at any time.

2. Any such declaration shall state expressly the territorial units to which this Convention applies.

3. If a Contracting State has not made any declaration under paragraph 1, this Convention shall apply to all territorial units of that State.

4. Where a Contracting State extends this Convention to one or more of its territorial units, declarations permitted under this Convention may be made in respect of each such territorial unit, and the declarations made in respect of one territorial unit may be different from those made in respect of another territorial unit.

5. If by virtue of a declaration under paragraph 1, this Convention extends to one or more territorial units of a Contracting State:

(a) the debtor is considered to be situated in a Contracting State only if it is incorporated or formed under a law in force in a territorial unit to which this Convention applies or if it has its registered office or statutory seat, centre of administration, place of business or habitual residence in a territorial unit to which this Convention applies;

(b) any reference to the location of the object in a Contracting State refers to the location of the object in a territorial unit to which this Convention applies; and

(c) any reference to the administrative authorities in that Contracting State shall be construed as referring to the administrative authorities having jurisdiction in a territorial unit to which this Convention applies.

[4173]

Article 53

Determination of courts

A Contracting State may, at the time of ratification, acceptance, approval of, or accession to the Protocol, declare the relevant "court" or "courts" for the purposes of Article 1 and Chapter XII of this Convention.

[4174]

Article 54

Declarations regarding remedies

1. A Contracting State may, at the time of ratification, acceptance, approval of, or accession to the Protocol, declare that while the charged object is situated within, or controlled from its territory the chargee shall not grant a lease of the object in that territory.

2. A Contracting State shall, at the time of ratification, acceptance, approval of, or accession to the Protocol, declare whether or not any remedy available to the creditor under any provision of this Convention which is not there expressed to require application to the court may be exercised only with leave of the court.

[4175]

Article 55

Declarations regarding relief pending final determination

A Contracting State may, at the time of ratification, acceptance, approval of, or accession to the Protocol, declare that it will not apply the provisions of Article 13 or Article 43, or both, wholly or in part. The declaration shall specify under which conditions the relevant Article will be applied, in case it will be applied partly, or otherwise which other forms of interim relief will be applied.

[4176]

Article 56

Reservations and declarations

1. No reservations may be made to this Convention but declarations authorised by Articles 39, 40, 50, 52, 53, 54, 55, 57, 58 and 60 may be made in accordance with these provisions.

2. Any declaration or subsequent declaration or any withdrawal of a declaration made under this Convention shall be notified in writing to the Depositary.

[4177]

Article 57

Subsequent declarations

1. A State Party may make a subsequent declaration, other than a declaration authorised under Article 60, at any time after the date on which this Convention has entered into force for it, by notifying the Depositary to that effect.

2. Any such subsequent declaration shall take effect on the first day of the month following the expiration of six months after the date of receipt of the notification by the Depositary. Where a longer period for that declaration to take effect is specified in the notification, it shall take effect upon the expiration of such longer period after receipt of the notification by the Depositary.

3. Notwithstanding the previous paragraphs, this Convention shall continue to apply, as if no such subsequent declarations had been made, in respect of all rights and interests arising prior to the effective date of any such subsequent declaration.

[4178]

Article 58

Withdrawal of declarations

1. Any State Party having made a declaration under this Convention, other than a declaration authorised under Article 60, may withdraw it at any time by notifying the Depositary. Such withdrawal is to take effect on the first day of the month following the expiration of six months after the date of receipt of the notification by the Depositary.

2. Notwithstanding the previous paragraph, this Convention shall continue to apply, as if no such withdrawal of declaration had been made, in respect of all rights and interests arising prior to the effective date of any such withdrawal.

[4179]

Article 59

Denunciations

1. Any State Party may denounce this Convention by notification in writing to the Depositary.

2. Any such denunciation shall take effect on the first day of the month following the expiration of twelve months after the date on which notification is received by the Depositary.

3. Notwithstanding the previous paragraphs, this Convention shall continue to apply, as if no such denunciation had been made, in respect of all rights and interests arising prior to the effective date of any such denunciation.

[4180]

Article 60

Transitional provisions

1. Unless otherwise declared by a Contracting State at any time, the Convention does not apply to a pre-existing right or interest, which retains the priority it enjoyed under the applicable law before the effective date of this Convention.

2. For the purposes of Article 1(v) and of determining priority under this Convention:
   (a) "effective date of this Convention" means in relation to a debtor the time when this Convention enters into force or the time when the State in which the debtor is situated becomes a Contracting State, whichever is the later; and
   (b) the debtor is situated in a State where it has its centre of administration or, if it has no centre of administration, its place of business or, if it has more than one place of business, its principal place of business or, if it has no place of business, its habitual residence.

3. A Contracting State may in its declaration under paragraph 1 specify a date, not earlier than three years after the date on which the declaration becomes effective, when this Convention and the Protocol will become applicable, for the purpose of determining priority, including the protection of any existing priority, to pre-existing rights or interests arising under an agreement made at a time when the debtor was situated in a State referred to in sub-paragraph (b) of the preceding paragraph but only to the extent and in the manner specified in its declaration.

[4181]

Article 61

Review Conferences, amendments and related matters

1. The Depositary shall prepare reports yearly or at such other time as the circumstances may require for the States Parties as to the manner in which the international regimen established in this Convention has operated in practice. In preparing such reports, the Depositary shall take into account the reports of the Supervisory Authority concerning the functioning of the international registration system.

2. At the request of not less than twenty-five per cent of the States Parties, Review Conferences of States Parties shall be convened from time to time by the Depositary, in consultation with the Supervisory Authority, to consider:
   (a) the practical operation of this Convention and its effectiveness in facilitating the asset-based financing and leasing of the objects covered by its terms;

(b) the judicial interpretation given to, and the application made of the terms of this Convention and the regulations;
(c) the functioning of the international registration system, the performance of the Registrar and its oversight by the Supervisory Authority, taking into account the reports of the Supervisory Authority; and
(d) whether any modifications to this Convention or the arrangements relating to the International Registry are desirable.

3. Subject to paragraph 4, any amendment to this Convention shall be approved by at least a two- thirds majority of States Parties participating in the Conference referred to in the preceding paragraph and shall then enter into force in respect of States which have ratified, accepted or approved such amendment when ratified, accepted, or approved by three States in accordance with the provisions of Article 49 relating to its entry into force.

4. Where the proposed amendment to this Convention is intended to apply to more than one category of equipment, such amendment shall also be approved by at least a two-thirds majority of States Parties to each Protocol that are participating in the Conference referred to in paragraph 2.

[4182]

Article 62

Depositary and its functions

1. Instruments of ratification, acceptance, approval or accession shall be deposited with the International Institute for the Unification of Private Law (UNIDROIT), which is hereby designated the Depositary.

2. The Depositary shall:
(a) inform all Contracting States of:
(i) each new signature or deposit of an instrument of ratification, acceptance, approval or accession, together with the date thereof;
(ii) the date of entry into force of this Convention;
(iii) each declaration made in accordance with this Convention, together with the date thereof;
(iv) the withdrawal or amendment of any declaration, together with the date thereof; and
(v) the notification of any denunciation of this Convention together with the date thereof and the date on which it takes effect;
(b) transmit certified true copies of this Convention to all Contracting States;
(c) provide the Supervisory Authority and the Registrar with a copy of each instrument of ratification, acceptance, approval or accession, together with the date of deposit thereof, of each declaration or withdrawal or amendment of a declaration and of each notification of denunciation, together with the date of notification thereof, so that the information contained therein is easily and fully available; and
(d) perform such other functions customary for depositaries.

IN WITNESS WHEREOF the undersigned Plenipotentiaries, having been duly authorised, have signed this Convention.

[4183]

DONE at Cape Town, this sixteenth day of November, two thousand and one, in a single original in the English, Arabic, Chinese, French, Russian and Spanish languages, all texts being equally authentic, such authenticity to take effect upon verification by the Joint Secretariat of the Conference under the authority of the President of the Conference within ninety days hereof as to the conformity of the texts with one another.

PROTOCOL TO THE CONVENTION ON INTERNATIONAL INTERESTS IN MOBILE EQUIPMENT ON MATTERS SPECIFIC TO AIRCRAFT EQUIPMENT[1]

NOTES

The Protocol is reproduced with the kind permission of UNIDROIT (http://www.unidroit.org) and the International Civil Aviation Organization (http://www.icao.int).

As yet, neither the United Kingdom nor the European Community has ratified this Protocol.

THE STATES PARTIES TO THIS PROTOCOL,

CONSIDERING it necessary to implement the Convention on International Interests in Mobile Equipment (hereinafter referred to as "the Convention") as it relates to aircraft equipment, in the light of the purposes set out in the preamble to the Convention,

MINDFUL of the need to adapt the Convention to meet the particular requirements of aircraft finance and to extend the sphere of application of the Convention to include contracts of sale of aircraft equipment,

MINDFUL of the principles and objectives of the Convention on International Civil Aviation, signed at Chicago on 7 December 1944,

HAVE AGREED upon the following provisions relating to aircraft equipment:

CHAPTER I
SPHERE OF APPLICATION AND GENERAL PROVISIONS

Article I—Defined terms

1. In this Protocol, except where the context otherwise requires, terms used in it have the meanings set out in the Convention.

2. In this Protocol the following terms are employed with the meanings set out below:

(a) "aircraft" means aircraft as defined for the purposes of the Chicago Convention which are either airframes with aircraft engines installed thereon or helicopters;

(b) "aircraft engines" means aircraft engines (other than those used in military, customs or police services) powered by jet propulsion or turbine or piston technology and:

(i) in the case of jet propulsion aircraft engines, have at least 1750 lb of thrust or its equivalent; and

(ii) in the case of turbine-powered or piston-powered aircraft engines, have at least 550 rated take-off shaft horsepower or its equivalent, together with all modules and other installed, incorporated or attached accessories, parts and equipment and all data, manuals and records relating thereto;

(c) "aircraft objects" means airframes, aircraft engines and helicopters;

(d) "aircraft register" means a register maintained by a State or a common mark registering authority for the purposes of the Chicago Convention;

(e) "airframes" means airframes (other than those used in military, customs or police services) that, when appropriate aircraft engines are installed thereon, are type certified by the competent aviation authority to transport:

(i) at least eight (8) persons including crew; or

(ii) goods in excess of 2750 kilograms, together with all installed, incorporated or attached accessories, parts and equipment (other than aircraft engines), and all data, manuals and records relating thereto;

(f) "authorised party" means the party referred to in Article XIII(3);

(g) "Chicago Convention" means the Convention on International Civil Aviation, signed at Chicago on 7 December 1944, as amended, and its Annexes;

(h) "common mark registering authority" means the authority maintaining a register in accordance with Article 77 of the Chicago Convention as implemented by the Resolution adopted on 14 December 1967 by the Council of the International Civil Aviation Organization on nationality and registration of aircraft operated by international operating agencies;

(i) "de-registration of the aircraft" means deletion or removal of the registration of the aircraft from its aircraft register in accordance with the Chicago Convention;

(j) "guarantee contract" means a contract entered into by a person as guarantor;

(k) "guarantor" means a person who, for the purpose of assuring performance of any obligations in favour of a creditor secured by a security agreement or under an agreement, gives or issues a suretyship or demand guarantee or a standby letter of credit or any other form of credit insurance;

(l) "helicopters" means heavier-than-air machines (other than those used in military, customs or police services) supported in flight chiefly by the reactions of the air on one or more power-driven rotors on substantially vertical axes and which are type certified by the competent aviation authority to transport:

(i) at least five (5) persons including crew; or

(ii) goods in excess of 450 kilograms, together with all installed, incorporated or attached accessories, parts and equipment (including rotors), and all data, manuals and records relating thereto;

(m) "insolvency-related event" means:

(i) the commencement of the insolvency proceedings; or

(ii) the declared intention to suspend or actual suspension of payments by the debtor where the creditor's right to institute insolvency proceedings against the debtor or to exercise remedies under the Convention is prevented or suspended by law or State action;

(n) "primary insolvency jurisdiction" means the Contracting State in which the centre of the debtor's main interests is situated, which for this purpose shall be deemed to be the place of the debtor's statutory seat or, if there is none, the place where the debtor is incorporated or formed, unless proved otherwise;

(o) "registry authority" means the national authority or the common mark registering authority, maintaining an aircraft register in a Contracting State and responsible for the registration and de-registration of an aircraft in accordance with the Chicago Convention; and

(p) "State of registry" means, in respect of an aircraft, the State on the national register of which an aircraft is entered or the State of location of the common mark registering authority maintaining the aircraft register.

[4184]

Article II—Application of Convention as regards aircraft objects

1. The Convention shall apply in relation to aircraft objects as provided by the terms of this Protocol.

2. The Convention and this Protocol shall be known as the Convention on International Interests in Mobile Equipment as applied to aircraft objects.

[4185]

Article III—Application of Convention to Sales

The following provisions of the Convention apply as if references to an agreement creating or providing for an international interest were references to a contract of sale and as if references to an international interest, a prospective international interest, the debtor and the creditor were references to a sale, a prospective sale, the seller and the buyer respectively:

Articles 3 and 4;
Article 16(1)(a);
Article 19(4);
Article 20(1) (as regards registration of a contract of sale or a prospective sale);
Article 25(2) (as regards a prospective sale); and Article 30.

In addition, the general provisions of Article 1, Article 5, Chapters IV to VII, Article 29 (other than Article 29(3) which is replaced by Article XIV(1) and (2)), Chapter X, Chapter XII (other than Article 43), Chapter XIII and Chapter XIV (other than Article 60) shall apply to contracts of sale and prospective sales.

[4186]

Article IV—Sphere of application

1. Without prejudice to Article 3(1) of the Convention, the Convention shall also apply in relation to a helicopter, or to an airframe pertaining to an aircraft, registered in an aircraft register of a Contracting State which is the State of registry, and where such registration is made pursuant to an agreement for registration of the aircraft it is deemed to have been effected at the time of the agreement.

2. For the purposes of the definition of "internal transaction" in Article 1 of the Convention:

(a) an airframe is located in the State of registry of the aircraft of which it is a part;

(b) an aircraft engine is located in the State of registry of the aircraft on which it is installed or, if it is not installed on an aircraft, where it is physically located; and

(c) a helicopter is located in its State of registry, at the time of the conclusion of the agreement creating or providing for the interest.

3. The parties may, by agreement in writing, exclude the application of Article XI and, in their relations with each other, derogate from or vary the effect of any of the provisions of this Protocol except Article IX (2)–(4).

[4187]

Article V—Formalities, effects and registration of contract of sale

1. For the purposes of this Protocol, a contract of sale is one which:
   (a) is in writing;
   (b) relates to an aircraft object of which the seller has power to dispose; and
   (c) enables the aircraft object to be identified in conformity with this Protocol.

2. A contract of sale transfers the interest of the seller in the aircraft object to the buyer according to its terms.

3. Registration of a contract of sale remains effective indefinitely. Registration of a prospective sale remains effective unless discharged or until expiry of the period, if any, specified in the registration.

[4188]

Article VI—Representative capacities

A person may enter into an agreement or a sale, and register an international interest in, or a sale of, an aircraft object, in an agency, trust or other representative capacity. In such case, that person is entitled to assert rights and interests under the Convention.

[4189]

Article VII—Description of aircraft objects

A description of an aircraft object that contains its manufacturer's serial number, the name of the manufacturer and its model designation is necessary and sufficient to identify the object for the purposes of Articles 7(c) of the Convention and Article V(1)(c) of this Protocol.

[4190]

Article VIII—Choice of law

1. This Article applies only where a Contracting State has made a declaration pursuant to Article XXX(1).

2. The parties to an agreement, or a contract of sale, or a related guarantee contract or subordination agreement may agree on the law which is to govern their contractual rights and obligations wholly or in part.

3. Unless otherwise agreed, the reference in the preceding paragraph to the law chosen by the parties is to the domestic rules of law of the designated State or, where that State comprises several territorial units, to the domestic law of the designated territorial unit.

[4191]

CHAPTER II
DEFAULT REMEDIES, PRIORITIES AND ASSIGNMENTS

Article IX—Modification of default remedies provisions

1. In addition to the remedies specified in Chapter III of the Convention, the creditor may, to the extent that the debtor has at any time so agreed and in the circumstances specified in that Chapter:
   (a) procure the de-registration of the aircraft; and
   (b) procure the export and physical transfer of the aircraft object from the territory in which it is situated.

2. The creditor shall not exercise the remedies specified in the preceding paragraph without the prior consent in writing of the holder of any registered interest ranking in priority to that of the creditor.

3. Article 8(3) of the Convention shall not apply to aircraft objects. Any remedy given by the Convention in relation to aircraft objects shall be exercised in a commercially reasonable manner. A remedy shall be deemed to be exercised in a commercially reasonable manner where it is exercised in conformity with a provision of the agreement except where such a provision is manifestly unreasonable.

4. A chargee giving ten or more working days' prior written notice of a proposed sale or lease to interested persons shall be deemed to satisfy the requirement of providing "reasonable prior notice" specified in Article 8(4) of the Convention. The foregoing shall not prevent a chargee and a chargor or a guarantor from agreeing to a longer period of prior notice.

5. The registry authority in a Contracting State shall, subject to any applicable safety laws and regulations, honour a request for de-registration and export if:

(a) the request is properly submitted by the authorised party under a recorded irrevocable de-registration and export request authorisation; and

(b) the authorised party certifies to the registry authority, if required by that authority, that all registered interests ranking in priority to that of the creditor in whose favour the authorisation has been issued have been discharged or that the holders of such interests have consented to the de-registration and export.

6. A chargee proposing to procure the de-registration and export of an aircraft under paragraph 1 otherwise than pursuant to a court order shall give reasonable prior notice in writing of the proposed de-registration and export to:

(a) interested persons specified in Article 1(m)(i) and (ii) of the Convention; and

(b) interested persons specified in Article 1(m)(iii) of the Convention who have given notice of their rights to the chargee within a reasonable time prior to the de-registration and export.

[4192]

Article X—Modification of provisions regarding relief pending final determination

1. This Article applies only where a Contracting State has made a declaration under Article XXX(2) and to the extent stated in such declaration.

2. For the purposes of Article 13(1) of the Convention, "speedy" in the context of obtaining relief means within such number of working days from the date of filing of the application for relief as is specified in a declaration made by the Contracting State in which the application is made.

3. Article 13(1) of the Convention applies with the following being added immediately after sub-paragraph (d):

"(e) if at any time the debtor and the creditor specifically agree, sale and application of proceeds therefrom",

and Article 43(2) applies with the insertion after the words "Article 13(1)(d)" of the words "and (e)".

4. Ownership or any other interest of the debtor passing on a sale under the preceding paragraph is free from any other interest over which the creditor's international interest has priority under the provisions of Article 29 of the Convention.

5. The creditor and the debtor or any other interested person may agree in writing to exclude the application of Article 13(2) of the Convention.

6. With regard to the remedies in Article IX(1):

(a) they shall be made available by the registry authority and other administrative authorities, as applicable, in a Contracting State no later than five working days after the creditor notifies such authorities that the relief specified in Article IX(1) is granted or, in the case of relief granted by a foreign court, recognised by a court of that Contracting State, and that the creditor is entitled to procure those remedies in accordance with the Convention; and

(b) the applicable authorities shall expeditiously co-operate with and assist the creditor in the exercise of such remedies in conformity with the applicable aviation safety laws and regulations.

7. Paragraphs 2 and 6 shall not affect any applicable aviation safety laws and regulations.

[4193]

Article XI—Remedies on insolvency

1. This Article applies only where a Contracting State that is the primary insolvency jurisdiction has made a declaration pursuant to Article XXX(3).

Alternative A

2. Upon the occurrence of an insolvency-related event, the insolvency administrator or the debtor, as applicable, shall, subject to paragraph 7, give possession of the aircraft object to the creditor no later than the earlier of:
   (a) the end of the waiting period; and
   (b) the date on which the creditor would be entitled to possession of the aircraft object if this Article did not apply.

3. For the purposes of this Article, the "waiting period" shall be the period specified in a declaration of the Contracting State which is the primary insolvency jurisdiction.

4. References in this Article to the "insolvency administrator" shall be to that person in its official, not in its personal, capacity.

5. Unless and until the creditor is given the opportunity to take possession under paragraph 2:
   (a) the insolvency administrator or the debtor, as applicable, shall preserve the aircraft object and maintain it and its value in accordance with the agreement; and
   (b) the creditor shall be entitled to apply for any other forms of interim relief available under the applicable law.

6. Sub-paragraph (a) of the preceding paragraph shall not preclude the use of the aircraft object under arrangements designed to preserve the aircraft object and maintain it and its value.

7. The insolvency administrator or the debtor, as applicable, may retain possession of the aircraft object where, by the time specified in paragraph 2, it has cured all defaults other than a default constituted by the opening of insolvency proceedings and has agreed to perform all future obligations under the agreement. A second waiting period shall not apply in respect of a default in the performance of such future obligations.

8. With regard to the remedies in Article IX(1):
   (a) they shall be made available by the registry authority and the administrative authorities in a Contracting State, as applicable, no later than five working days after the date on which the creditor notifies such authorities that it is entitled to procure those remedies in accordance with the Convention; and
   (b) the applicable authorities shall expeditiously co-operate with and assist the creditor in the exercise of such remedies in conformity with the applicable aviation safety laws and regulations.

9. No exercise of remedies permitted by the Convention or this Protocol may be prevented or delayed after the date specified in paragraph 2.

10. No obligations of the debtor under the agreement may be modified without the consent of the creditor.

11. Nothing in the preceding paragraph shall be construed to affect the authority, if any, of the insolvency administrator under the applicable law to terminate the agreement.

12. No rights or interests, except for non-consensual rights or interests of a category covered by a declaration pursuant to Article 39(1), shall have priority in the insolvency proceedings over registered interests.

13. The Convention as modified by Article IX of this Protocol shall apply to the exercise of any remedies under this Article.

Alternative B

2. Upon the occurrence of an insolvency-related event, the insolvency administrator or the debtor, as applicable, upon the request of the creditor, shall give notice to the creditor within the time specified in a declaration of a Contracting State pursuant to Article XXX(3) whether it will:
   (a) cure all defaults other than a default constituted by the opening of insolvency proceedings and agree to perform all future obligations, under the agreement and related transaction documents; or

(b) give the creditor the opportunity to take possession of the aircraft object, in accordance with the applicable law.

3. The applicable law referred to in sub-paragraph (b) of the preceding paragraph may permit the court to require the taking of any additional step or the provision of any additional guarantee.

4. The creditor shall provide evidence of its claims and proof that its international interest has been registered.

5. If the insolvency administrator or the debtor, as applicable, does not give notice in conformity with paragraph 2, or when the insolvency administrator or the debtor has declared that it will give the creditor the opportunity to take possession of the aircraft object but fails to do so, the court may permit the creditor to take possession of the aircraft object upon such terms as the court may order and may require the taking of any additional step or the provision of any additional guarantee.

6. The aircraft object shall not be sold pending a decision by a court regarding the claim and the international interest.

[4194]

Article XII—Insolvency assistance

1. This Article applies only where a Contracting State has made a declaration pursuant to Article XXX(1).

2. The courts of a Contracting State in which an aircraft object is situated shall, in accordance with the law of the Contracting State, co-operate to the maximum extent possible with foreign courts and foreign insolvency administrators in carrying out the provisions of Article XI.

[4195]

Article XIII—De-registration and export request authorisation

1. This Article applies only where a Contracting State has made a declaration pursuant to Article XXX(1).

2. Where the debtor has issued an irrevocable de-registration and export request authorisation substantially in the form annexed to this Protocol and has submitted such authorisation for recordation to the registry authority, that authorisation shall be so recorded.

3. The person in whose favour the authorisation has been issued (the "authorised party") or its certified designee shall be the sole person entitled to exercise the remedies specified in Article IX(1) and may do so only in accordance with the authorisation and applicable aviation safety laws and regulations. Such authorisation may not be revoked by the debtor without the consent in writing of the authorised party. The registry authority shall remove an authorisation from the registry at the request of the authorised party.

4. The registry authority and other administrative authorities in Contracting States shall expeditiously co-operate with and assist the authorised party in the exercise of the remedies specified in Article IX.

[4196]

Article XIV—Modification of priority provisions

1. A buyer of an aircraft object under a registered sale acquires its interest in that object free from an interest subsequently registered and from an unregistered interest, even if the buyer has actual knowledge of the unregistered interest.

2. A buyer of an aircraft object acquires its interests in that object subject to an interest registered at the time of its acquisition.

3. Ownership of or another right or interest in an aircraft engine shall not be affected by its installation on or removal from an aircraft.

4. Article 29(7) of the Convention applies to an item, other than an object, installed on an airframe, aircraft engine or helicopter.

[4197]

Article XV—Modification of assignment provisions

Article 33(1) of the Convention applies as if the following were added immediately after sub-paragraph (b):

"and

(c) the debtor has consented in writing, whether or not the consent is given in advance of the assignment or identifies the assignee."

1. In the absence of a default within the meaning of Article 11 of the Convention, the debtor shall be entitled to the quiet possession and use of the object in accordance with the agreement as against:

(a) its creditor and the holder of any interest from which the debtor takes free pursuant to Article 29(4) of the Convention or, in the capacity of buyer, Article XIV(1) of this Protocol, unless and to the extent that the debtor has otherwise agreed; and

(b) the holder of any interest to which the debtor's right or interest is subject pursuant to Article 29(4) of the Convention or, in the capacity of buyer, Article XIV(2) of this Protocol, but only to the extent, if any, that such holder has agreed.

2. Nothing in the Convention or this Protocol affects the liability of a creditor for any breach of the agreement under the applicable law in so far as that agreement relates to an aircraft object.

[4198]

CHAPTER III
REGISTRY PROVISIONS RELATING TO INTERNATIONAL INTERESTS IN AIRCRAFT OBJECTS

Article XVII—The Supervisory Authority and the Registrar

1. The Supervisory Authority shall be the international entity designated by a Resolution adopted by the Diplomatic Conference to Adopt a Mobile Equipment Convention and an Aircraft Protocol.

2. Where the international entity referred to in the preceding paragraph is not able and willing to act as Supervisory Authority, a Conference of Signatory and Contracting States shall be convened to designate another Supervisory Authority.

3. The Supervisory Authority and its officers and employees shall enjoy such immunity from legal and administrative process as is provided under the rules applicable to them as an international entity or otherwise.

4. The Supervisory Authority may establish a com-mission of experts, from among persons nominated by Signatory and Contracting States and having the necessary qualifications and experience, and entrust it with the task of assisting the Supervisory Authority in the discharge of its functions.

5. The first Registrar shall operate the International Registry for a period of five years from the date of entry into force of this Protocol. Thereafter, the Registrar shall be appointed or reappointed at regular five-yearly intervals by the Supervisory Authority.

[4199]

Article XVIII—First regulations

The first regulations shall be made by the Supervisory Authority so as to take effect upon the entry into force of this Protocol.

[4200]

Article XIX—Designated entry points

1. Subject to paragraph 2, a Contracting State may at any time designate an entity or entities in its territory as the entry point or entry points through which there shall or may be transmitted to the International Registry information required for registration other than registration of a notice of a national interest or a right or interest under Article 40 in either case arising under the laws of another State.

2. A designation made under the preceding paragraph may permit, but not compel, use of a designated entry point or entry points for information required for registrations in respect of aircraft engines.

[4201]

Article XX—Additional modifications to Registry provisions

1. For the purposes of Article 19(6) of the Convention, the search criterion for an aircraft object shall be the name of its manufacturer, its manufacturer's serial number and its model designation, supplemented as necessary to ensure uniqueness. Such supplementary information shall be specified in the regulations.

2. For the purposes of Article 25(2) of the Convention and in the circumstances there described, the holder of a registered prospective international interest or a registered prospective assignment of an international interest or the person in whose favour a prospective sale has been registered shall take such steps as are within its power to procure the discharge of the registration no later than five working days after the receipt of the demand described in such paragraph.

3. The fees referred to in Article 17(2)(h) of the Convention shall be determined so as to recover the reasonable costs of establishing, operating and regulating the International Registry and the reasonable costs of the Supervisory Authority associated with the performance of the functions, exercise of the powers, and discharge of the duties contemplated by Article 17(2) of the Convention.

4. The centralised functions of the International Registry shall be operated and administered by the Registrar on a twenty-four hour basis. The various entry points shall be operated at least during working hours in their respective territories.

5. The amount of the insurance or financial guarantee referred to in Article 28(4) of the Convention shall, in respect of each event, not be less than the maximum value of an aircraft object as determined by the Supervisory Authority.

6. Nothing in the Convention shall preclude the Registrar from procuring insurance or a financial guarantee covering events for which the Registrar is not liable under Article 28 of the Convention.

[4202]

CHAPTER IV
JURISDICTION

Article XXI—Modification of jurisdiction provisions

For the purposes of Article 43 of the Convention and subject to Article 42 of the Convention, a court of a Contracting State also has jurisdiction where the object is a helicopter, or an airframe pertaining to an aircraft, for which that State is the State of registry.

[4203]

Article XXI—Waivers of sovereign immunity

1. Subject to paragraph 2, a waiver of sovereign immunity from jurisdiction of the courts specified in Article 42 or Article 43 of the Convention or relating to enforcement of rights and interests relating to an aircraft object under the Convention shall be binding and, if the other conditions to such jurisdiction or enforcement have been satisfied, shall be effective to confer jurisdiction and permit enforcement, as the case may be.

2. A waiver under the preceding paragraph must be in writing and contain a description of the aircraft object.

[4204]

CHAPTER V
RELATIONSHIP WITH OTHER CONVENTIONS

Article XXIII—Relationship with the Convention on the International Recognition of Rights in Aircraft

The Convention shall, for a Contracting State that is a party to the Convention on the International Recognition of Rights in Aircraft, signed at Geneva on 19 June 1948, supersede that Convention as it relates to aircraft, as defined in this Protocol, and to aircraft objects. However, with respect to rights or interests not covered or affected by the present Convention, the Geneva Convention shall not be superseded.

[4205]

Article XXIV—Relationship with the Convention for the Unification of Certain Rules Relating to the Precautionary Attachment of Aircraft

1. The Convention shall, for a Contracting State that is a Party to the Convention for the Unification of Certain Rules Relating to the Precautionary Attachment of Aircraft, signed at Rome on 29 May 1933, supersede that Convention as it relates to aircraft, as defined in this Protocol.

2. A Contracting State Party to the above Convention may declare, at the time of ratification, acceptance, approval of, or accession to this Protocol, that it will not apply this Article.

[4206]

Article XXV—Relationship with the UNIDROIT Convention on International Financial Leasing

The Convention shall supersede the UNIDROIT Convention on International Financial Leasing as it relates to aircraft objects.

[4207]

CHAPTER VI
FINAL PROVISIONS

Article XXVI—Signature, ratification, acceptance, approval or accession

1. This Protocol shall be open for signature in Cape Town on 16 November 2001 by States participating in the Diplomatic Conference to Adopt a Mobile Equipment Convention and an Aircraft Protocol held at Cape Town from 29 October to 16 November 2001. After 16 November 2001, this Protocol shall be open to all States for signature at the Headquarters of the International Institute for the Unification of Private Law (UNIDROIT) in Rome until it enters into force in accordance with Article XXVIII.

2. This Protocol shall be subject to ratification, acceptance or approval by States which have signed it.

3. Any State which does not sign this Protocol may accede to it at any time.

4. Ratification, acceptance, approval or accession is effected by the deposit of a formal instrument to that effect with the Depositary.

5. A State may not become a Party to this Protocol unless it is or becomes also a Party to the Convention.

[4208]

Article XXVII—Regional Economic Integration Organisations

1. A Regional Economic Integration Organisation which is constituted by sovereign States and has competence over certain matters governed by this Protocol may similarly sign, accept, approve or accede to this Protocol. The Regional Economic Integration Organisation shall in that case have the rights and obligations of a Contracting State, to the extent that Organisation has competence over matters governed by this Protocol. Where the number of

Contracting States is relevant in this Protocol, the Regional Economic Integration Organisation shall not count as a Contracting State in addition to its Member States which are Contracting States.

2. The Regional Economic Integration Organisation shall, at the time of signature, acceptance, approval or accession, make a declaration to the Depository specifying the matters governed by this Protocol in respect of which competence has been transferred to that Organisation by its Member States. The Regional Economic Integration Organisation shall promptly notify the Depository of any changes to the distribution of competence, including new transfers of competence, specified in the declaration under this paragraph.

3. Any reference to a "Contracting State" or "Contracting States" or "State Party" or "States Parties" in this Protocol applies equally to a Regional Economic Integration Organisation where the context so requires.

[4209]

Article XXVIII—Entry into force

1. This Protocol enters into force on the first day of the month following the expiration of three months after the date of the deposit of the eighth instrument of ratification, acceptance, approval or accession, between the States which have deposited such instruments.

2. For other States this Protocol enters into force on the first day of the month following the expiration of three months after the date of the deposit of its instrument of ratification, acceptance, approval or accession.

[4210]

Article XXIX—Territorial units

1. If a Contracting State has territorial units in which different systems of law are applicable in relation to the matters dealt with in this Protocol, it may, at the time of ratification, acceptance, approval or accession, declare that this Protocol is to extend to all its territorial units or only to one or more of them and may modify its declaration by submitting another declaration at any time.

2. Any such declaration shall state expressly the territorial units to which this Protocol applies.

3. If a Contracting State has not made any declaration under paragraph 1, this Protocol shall apply to all territorial units of that State.

4. Where a Contracting State extends this Protocol to one or more of its territorial units, declarations permitted under this Protocol may be made in respect of each such territorial unit, and the declarations made in respect of one territorial unit may be different from those made in respect of another territorial unit.

5. If by virtue of a declaration under paragraph 1, this Protocol extends to one or more territorial units of a Contracting State:

(a) the debtor is considered to be situated in a Contracting State only if it is incorporated or formed under a law in force in a territorial unit to which the Convention and this Protocol apply or if it has its registered office or statutory seat, centre of administration, place of business or habitual residence in a territorial unit to which the Convention and this Protocol apply;

(b) any reference to the location of the object in a Contracting State refers to the location of the object in a territorial unit to which the Convention and this Protocol apply; and

(c) any reference to the administrative authorities in that Contracting State shall be construed as referring to the administrative authorities having jurisdiction in a territorial unit to which the Convention and this Protocol apply and any reference to the national registry or to the registry authority in that Contracting State shall be construed as referring to the aircraft registry in force or to the registry authority having jurisdiction in the territorial unit or units to which the Convention and this Protocol apply.

[4211]

Article XXX—Declarations relating to certain provisions

1. A Contracting State may, at the time of ratification, acceptance, approval of, or accession to this Protocol, declare that it will apply any one or more of Articles VIII, XII and XIII of this Protocol.

2. A Contracting State may, at the time of ratification, acceptance, approval of, or accession to this Protocol, declare that it will apply Article X of this Protocol, wholly or in part. If it so declares with respect to Article X(2), it shall specify the time-period required thereby.

3. A Contracting State may, at the time of ratification, acceptance, approval of, or accession to this Protocol, declare that it will apply the entirety of Alternative A, or the entirety of Alternative B of Article XI and, if so, shall specify the types of insolvency proceeding, if any, to which it will apply Alternative A and the types of insolvency proceeding, if any, to which it will apply Alternative B. A Contracting State making a declaration pursuant to this paragraph shall specify the time-period required by Article XI.

4. The courts of Contracting States shall apply Article XI in conformity with the declaration made by the Contracting State which is the primary insolvency jurisdiction.

5. A Contracting State may, at the time of ratification, acceptance, approval of, or accession to this Protocol, declare that it will not apply the provisions of Article XXI, wholly or in part. The declaration shall specify under which conditions the relevant Article will be applied, in case it will be applied partly, or otherwise which other forms of interim relief that will be applied.

[4212]

Article XXXI—Declarations under the Convention

Declarations made under the Convention, including those made under Articles 39, 40, 50, 53, 54, 55, 57, 58 and 60 of the Convention, shall be deemed to have also been made under this Protocol unless stated otherwise.

[4213]

Article XXXII—Reservations and declarations

1. No reservations may be made to this Protocol but declarations authorised by Articles XXIV, XXIX, XXX, XXXI, XXXIII and XXXIV may be made in accordance with these provisions.

2. Any declaration or subsequent declaration or any withdrawal of a declaration made under this Protocol shall be notified in writing to the Depositary.

[4214]

Article XXXIII—Subsequent declarations

1. A State party may make a subsequent declaration, other than the declaration made in accordance with Article XXXI under Article 60 of the Convention, at any time after the date on which this Protocol has entered into force for it, by notifying the Depositary to that effect.

2. Any such subsequent declaration shall take effect on the first day of the month following the expiration of six months after the date of receipt of the notification by the Depositary. Where a longer period for that declaration to take effect is specified in the notification, it shall take effect upon the expiration of such longer period after receipt of the notification by the Depositary.

3. Notwithstanding the previous paragraphs, this Protocol shall continue to apply, as if no such subsequent declarations had been made, in respect of all rights and interests arising prior to the effective date of any such subsequent declaration.

[4215]

Article XXXIV—Withdrawal of declarations

1. Any State Party having made a declaration under this Protocol, other than a declaration made in accordance with Article XXXI under Article 60 of the Convention, may

withdraw it at any time by notifying the Depositary. Such withdrawal is to take effect on the first day of the month following the expiration of six months after the date of receipt of the notification by the Depositary.

2. Notwithstanding the previous paragraph, this Protocol shall continue to apply, as if no such withdrawal of declaration had been made, in respect of all rights and interests arising prior to the effective date of any such withdrawal.

[4216]

Article XXXV—Denunciations

1. Any State Party may denounce this Protocol by notification in writing to the Depositary.

2. Any such denunciation shall take effect on the first day of the month following the expiration of twelve months after the date of receipt of the notification by the Depositary.

3. Notwithstanding the previous paragraphs, this Protocol shall continue to apply, as if no such denunciation had been made, in respect of all rights and interests arising prior to the effective date of any such denunciation.

[4217]

Article XXXVI—Review Conferences, amendments and related matters

1. The Depositary, in consultation with the Supervisory Authority, shall prepare reports yearly, or at such other time as the circumstances may require, for the States Parties as to the manner in which the international regime established in the Convention as amended by the Protocol has operated in practice. In preparing such reports, the Depositary shall take into account the reports of the Supervisory Authority concerning the functioning of the international registration system.

2. At the request of not less than twenty-five per cent of the States Parties, Review Conferences of the States Parties shall be convened from time to time by the Depositary, in consultation with the Supervisory Authority, to consider:

(a) the practical operation of the Convention as amended by this Protocol and its effectiveness in facilitating the asset-based financing and leasing of the objects covered by its terms;

(b) the judicial interpretation given to, and the application made of the terms of this Protocol and the regulations;

(c) the functioning of the international registration system, the performance of the Registrar and its oversight by the Supervisory Authority, taking into account the reports of the Supervisory Authority; and

(d) whether any modifications to this Protocol or the arrangements relating to the International Registry are desirable.

3. Any amendment to this Protocol shall be approved by at least a two-thirds majority of States Parties participating in the Conference referred to in the preceding paragraph and shall then enter into force in respect of States which have ratified, accepted or approved such amendment when it has been ratified, accepted or approved by eight States in accordance with the provisions of Article XXVIII relating to its entry into force.

[4218]

Article XXXVII—Depositary and its functions

1. Instruments of ratification, acceptance, approval or accession shall be deposited with the International Institute for the Unification of Private Law (UNIDROIT), which is hereby designated the Depositary.

2. The Depositary shall:

(a) inform all Contracting States of:

(i) each new signature or deposit of an instrument of ratification, acceptance, approval or accession, together with the date thereof;

(ii) the date of entry into force of this Protocol;

(iii) each declaration made in accordance with this Protocol, together with the date thereof;

(iv) the withdrawal or amendment of any declaration, together with the date thereof; and

(v) the notification of any denunciation of this Protocol together with the date thereof and the date on which it takes effect;

(b) transmit certified true copies of this Protocol to all Contracting States;

(c) provide the Supervisory Authority and the Registrar with a copy of each instrument of ratification, acceptance, approval or accession, together with the date of deposit thereof, of each declaration or withdrawal or amendment of a declaration and of each notification of denunciation, together with the date of notification thereof, so that the information contained therein is easily and fully available; and

(d) perform such other functions customary for depositaries.

[4219]

[1] ICAO Doc 9794 (2002).

IN WITNESS WHEREOF the undersigned Plenipotentiaries, having been duly authorised, have signed this Protocol.

DONE at Cape Town, this sixteenth day of November, two thousand and one, in a single original in the English, Arabic, Chinese, French, Russian and Spanish languages, all texts being equally authentic, such authenticity to take effect upon verification by the Joint Secretariat of the Conference under the authority of the President of the Conference within ninety days hereof as to the conformity of the texts with one another.

D. INTERNATIONAL ARBITRATION

GENEVA CONVENTION ON THE EXECUTION OF FOREIGN ARBITRAL AWARDS SIGNED AT GENEVA ON BEHALF OF HIS MAJESTY ON THE TWENTY-SIXTH DAY OF SEPTEMBER, NINETEEN HUNDRED AND TWENTY-SEVEN

(1927)

NOTES

The text of the following Convention appears as set out in the Arbitration Act 1950, Sch 2.

Article 1

In the territories of any High Contracting Party to which the present Convention applies, an arbitral award made in pursuance of an agreement, whether relating to existing or future differences (hereinafter called "a submission to arbitration") covered by the Protocol on Arbitration Clauses, opened at Geneva on September 24, 1923, shall be recognised as binding and shall be enforced in accordance with the rules of the procedure of the territory where the award is relied upon, provided that the said award has been made in a territory of one of the High Contracting Parties to which the present Convention applies and between persons who are subject to the jurisdiction of one of the High Contracting Parties.

To obtain such recognition or enforcement, it shall, further, be necessary—

(a) That the award has been made in pursuance of a submission to arbitration which is valid under the law applicable thereto;

(b) That the subject-matter of the award is capable of settlement by arbitration under the law of the country in which the award is sought to be relied upon;

(c) That the award has been made by the Arbitral Tribunal provided for in the submission to arbitration or constituted in the manner agreed upon by the parties and in conformity with the law governing the arbitration procedure;

(d) That the award has become final in the country in which it has been made, in the sense that it will not be considered as such if it is open to *opposition*, *appel* or *pourvoi en cassation* (in the countries where such forms of procedure exist) of if it is proved that any proceedings for the purpose of contesting the validity of the award are pending;

(e) That the recognition or enforcement of the award is not contrary to the public policy or to the principles of the law of the country in which it is sought to be relied upon.

Article 2

Even if the conditions laid down in Article 1 hereof are fulfilled, recognition and enforcement of the award shall be refused if the Court is satisfied—

(a) That the award has been annulled in the country in which it was made;

(b) That the party against whom it is sought to use the award was not given notice of the arbitration proceedings in sufficient time to enable him to present his case; or that, being under a legal incapacity, he was not properly represented;

(c) That the award does not deal with the differences contemplated by or falling within the terms of the submission to arbitration or that it contains decisions on matters beyond the scope of the submission to arbitration.

If the award has not covered all the questions submitted to the arbitral tribunal, the competent authority of the country where recognition or enforcement of the award is sought can, if it think fit, postpone such recognition or enforcement or grant it subject to such guarantee as that authority may decide.

Article 3

If the party against whom the award has been made proves that, under the law governing the arbitration procedure, there is a ground, other than the grounds referred to in Article 1(a) and (c), and Article 2(b) and (c), entitling him to contest the validity of the award in a Court of Law, the Court may, if it thinks fit, either refuse recognition or enforcement of the award or adjourn the consideration thereof, giving such party a reasonable time within which to have the award annulled by the competent tribunal.

Article 4

The party relying upon an award or claiming its enforcement must supply, in particular—

(1) The original award or a copy thereof duly authenticated, according to the requirements of the law of the country in which it was made;
(2) Documentary or other evidence to prove that the award has become final, in the sense defined in Article 1(d), in the country in which it was made;
(3) When necessary, documentary or other evidence to prove that the conditions laid down in Article 1, paragraph 1 and paragraph 2(a) and (c), have been fulfilled.

A translation of the award and of the other documents mentioned in this Article into the official language of the country where the award is sought to be relied upon may be demanded. Such translation must be certified correct by a diplomatic or consular agent of the country to which the party who seeks to rely upon the award belongs or by a sworn translator of the country where the award is sought to be relied upon.

Article 5

The provisions of the above Articles shall not deprive any interested party of the right of availing himself of an arbitral award in the manner and to the extent allowed by the law or the treaties of the country where such award is sought to be relied upon.

Article 6

The present Convention applies only to arbitral awards made after the coming into force of the Protocol on Arbitration Clauses, opened at Geneva on September 24th 1923.

Article 7

The present Convention, which will remain open to the signature of all the signatories of the Protocol of 1923 on Arbitration Clauses, shall be ratified.

It may be ratified only on behalf of those Members of the League of Nations and non-Member States on whose behalf the Protocol of 1923 shall have been ratified.

Ratifications shall be deposited as soon as possible with the Secretary-General of the League of Nations, who will notify such deposit to all the signatories.

Article 8

The present Convention shall come into force three months after it shall have been ratified on behalf of two High Contracting Parties. Thereafter, it shall take effect, in the case of each High Contracting Party, three months after the deposit of the ratification on its behalf with the Secretary-General of the League of Nations.

Article 9

The present Convention may be denounced on behalf of any Member of the League or non-Member State. Denunciation shall be notified in writing to the Secretary-General of the League of Nations, who will immediately send a copy thereof, certified to be in conformity with the notification, to all the other Contracting Parties, at the same time informing them of the date on which he received it.

The denunciation shall come into force only in respect of the High Contracting Party which shall have notified it and one year after such notification shall have reached the Secretary-General of the League of Nations.

The denunciation of the Protocol on Arbitration Clauses shall entail ipso facto, the denunciation of the present Convention.

Article 10

The present Convention does not apply to the Colonies, Protectorates or territories under suzerainty or mandate of any High Contracting Party unless they are specially mentioned.

The application of this Convention to one or more of such Colonies, Protectorates or territories to which the Protocol on Arbitration Clauses, opened at Geneva on September 24th 1923, applies, can be effected at any time by means of a declaration addressed to the Secretary-General of the League of Nations by one of the High Contracting Parties.

Such declaration shall take effect three months after the deposit thereof.

The High Contracting Parties can at any time denounce the Convention for all or any of the Colonies, Protectorates or territories referred to above. Article 9 hereof applies to such denunciation.

Article 11

A certified copy of the present Convention shall be transmitted by the Secretary-General of the League of Nations to every Member of the League of Nations and to every non-Member State which signs the same.

[4220]

UN CONVENTION ON THE RECOGNITION AND ENFORCEMENT OF FOREIGN ARBITRAL AWARDS

(Concluded New York, 10 June 1958)

NOTES

This Convention is published as Cmnd 6419.

The original source for this convention is the United Nations: United Nations Convention on the Recognition and Enforcement of Foreign Arbitral Awards (10 June 1958), © United Nations. Reprinted with the permission of the publisher. See the website of the United Nations Commission on International Trade Law (http://www.uncitral.org).

For the status of the 1958 New York Convention, see Table 2 at **[4677]**.

Article I

1. This Convention shall apply to the recognition and enforcement of arbitral awards made in the territory of a State other than the State where the recognition and enforcement of such awards are sought, and arising out of differences between persons, whether physical or legal. It shall also apply to arbitral awards not considered as domestic awards in the State where their recognition and enforcement are sought.

2. The term "arbitral awards" shall include not only awards made by arbitrators appointed for each case but also those made by permanent arbitral bodies to which the parties have submitted.

3. When signing, ratifying or acceding to this Convention, or notifying extension under article X hereof, any State may on the basis of reciprocity declare that it will apply the Convention to the recognition and enforcement of awards made only in the territory of another Contracting State. It may also declare that it will apply the Convention only to differences arising out of legal relationships, whether contractual or not, which are considered as commercial under the national law of the State making such declaration.

Article II

1. Each Contracting State shall recognize an agreement in writing under which the parties undertake to submit to arbitration all or any differences which have arisen or which may arise between them in respect of a defined legal relationship, whether contractual or not, concerning a subject matter capable of settlement by arbitration.

2. The term "agreement in writing" shall include an arbitral clause in a contract or an arbitration agreement, signed by the parties or contained in an exchange of letters or telegrams.

3. The court of a Contracting State, when seized of an action in a matter in respect of which the parties have made an agreement within the meaning of this article, shall, at the request of one of the parties, refer the parties to arbitration, unless it finds that the said agreement is null and void, inoperative or incapable of being performed.

Article III

Each Contracting State shall recognize arbitral awards as binding and enforce them in accordance with the rules of procedure of the territory where the award is relied upon, under the conditions laid down in the following articles. There shall not be imposed substantially more onerous conditions or higher fees or charges on the recognition or enforcement of arbitral awards to which this Convention applies than are imposed on the recognition or enforcement of domestic arbitral awards.

Article IV

1. To obtain the recognition and enforcement mentioned in the preceding article, the party applying for recognition and enforcement shall, at the time of the application, supply—

(a) The duly authenticated original award or a duly certified copy thereof;

(b) The original agreement referred to in article II or a duly certified copy thereof.

2. If the said award or agreement is not made in an official language of the country in which the award is relied upon, the party applying for recognition and enforcement of the award shall produce a translation of these documents into such language. The translation shall be certified by an official or sworn translator or by a diplomatic or consular agent.

Article V

1. Recognition and enforcement of the award may be refused, at the request of the party against whom it is invoked, only if that party furnishes to the competent authority where the recognition and enforcement is sought, proof that—

(a) The parties to the agreement referred to in article II were, under the law applicable to them, under some incapacity, or the said agreement is not valid under the law to which the parties have subjected it or, failing any indication thereon, under the law of the country where the award was made; or

(b) The party against whom the award is invoked was not given proper notice of the appointment of the arbitrator or of the arbitration proceedings or was otherwise unable to present his case; or

(c) The award deals with a difference not contemplated by or not falling within the terms of the submission to arbitration, or it contains decisions on matters beyond the scope of the submission to arbitration, provided that, if the decisions on matters submitted to arbitration can be separated from those not so submitted, that part of the award which contains decisions on matters submitted to arbitration may be recognized and enforced; or

(d) The composition of the arbitral authority or the arbitral procedure was not in accordance with the agreement of the parties, or, failing such agreement, was not in accordance with the law of the country where the arbitration took place; or

(e) The award has not yet become binding on the parties, or has been set aside or suspended by a competent authority of the country in which, or under the law of which, that award was made.

2. Recognition and enforcement of an arbitral award may also be refused if the competent authority in the country where recognition and enforcement is sought finds that—

(a) The subject matter of the difference is not capable of settlement by arbitration under the law of that country; or

(b) The recognition or enforcement of the award would be contrary to the public policy of that country.

Article VI

If an application for the setting aside or suspension of the award has been made to a competent authority referred to in article V(1)(e), the authority before which the award is sought to be relied upon may, if it considers it proper, adjourn the decision on the enforcement of the award and may also, on the application of the party claiming enforcement of the award, order the other party to give suitable security.

Article VII

1. The provisions of the present Convention shall not affect the validity of multilateral or bilateral agreements concerning the recognition and enforcement of arbitral awards entered into by the Contracting States nor deprive any interested party of any right he may have to avail himself of an arbitral award in the manner and to the extent allowed by the law or the treaties of the country where such award is sought to be relied upon.

2. The Geneva Protocol on Arbitration Clauses of 1923[1] and the Geneva Convention on the Execution of Foreign Arbitral Awards of 1927[2] shall cease to have effect between Contracting States on their becoming bound and to the extent that they become bound, by this Convention.

NOTES

1 Treaty Series No 4 (1925), Cmd 2312.
2 Treaty Series No 28 (1930), Cmd 3655.

Article VIII

1. This Convention shall be open until 31 December 1958 for signature on behalf of any Member of the United Nations and also on behalf of any other State which is or hereafter becomes a member of any specialized agency of the United Nations, or which is or hereafter becomes a party to the Statute of the International Court of Justice,[1] or any other State to which an invitation has been addressed by the General Assembly of the United Nations.

2. This Convention shall be ratified and the instrument of ratification shall be deposited with the Secretary-General of the United Nations.

NOTES

1 Treaty Series No 67 (1946), Cmd 7015.

Article IX

1. This Convention shall be open for accession to all States referred to in article VIII.

2. Accession shall be effected by the deposit of an instrument of accession with the Secretary-General of the United Nations.

Article X

1. Any State may, at the time of signature, ratification or accession, declare that this Convention shall extend to all or any of the territories for the international relations of which it is responsible. Such a declaration shall take effect when the Convention enters into force for the State concerned.

2. At any time thereafter any such extension shall be made by notification addressed to the Secretary-General of the United Nations and shall take effect as from the ninetieth day after the day of receipt by the Secretary-General of the United Nations of this notification, or as from the date of entry into force of the Convention for the State concerned, whichever is the later.

3. With respect to those territories to which this Convention is not extended at the time of signature, ratification or accession, each State concerned shall consider the possibility of

taking the necessary steps in order to extend the application of this Convention to such territories, subject, where necessary for constitutional reasons, to the consent of the Governments of such territories.

Article XI

In the case of a federal or non-unitary State, the following provisions shall apply—

(a) With respect to those articles of this Convention that come within the legislative jurisdiction of the federal authority, the obligations of the federal Government shall to this extent be the same as those of Contracting States which are not federal States—

(b) With respect to those articles of this Convention that come within the legislative jurisdiction of constituent states or provinces which are not, under the constitutional system of the federation, bound to take legislative action, the federal Government shall bring such articles with a favourable recommendation to the notice of the appropriate authorities of constituent states or provinces at the earliest possible moment;

(c) A federal State Party to this Convention shall, at the request of any other Contracting State transmitted through the Secretary-General of the United Nations, supply a statement of the law and practice of the federation and its constituent units in regard to any particular provision of this Convention, showing the extent to which effect has been given to that provision by legislative or other action.

Article XII

1. This Convention shall come into force on the ninetieth day following the date of deposit of the third instrument of ratification or accession.[1]

2. For each State ratifying or acceding to this Convention after the deposit of the third instrument of ratification or accession, this Convention shall enter into force on the ninetieth day after deposit by such State of its instrument of ratification or accession.

NOTES

1 The Convention entered into force on 7 June 1959.

Article XIII

1. Any Contracting State may denounce this Convention by a written notification to the Secretary-General of the United Nations. Denunciation shall take effect one year after the date of receipt of the notification by the Secretary-General.

2. Any State which has made a declaration or notification under article X may, at any time thereafter, by notification to the Secretary-General of the United Nations, declare that this Convention shall cease to extend to the territory concerned one year after the date of the receipt of the notification by the Secretary-General.

3. This Convention shall continue to be applicable to arbitral awards in respect of which recognition or enforcement proceedings have been instituted before the denunciation takes effect.

Article XIV

A Contracting State shall not be entitled to avail itself of the present Convention against other Contracting States except to the extent that it is itself bound to apply the Convention.

Article XV

The Secretary-General of the United Nations shall notify the States contemplated in article VIII of the following—

(a) Signatures and ratifications in accordance with article VIII;

(b) Accessions in accordance with article IX;

(c) Declarations and notifications under articles I, X and XI;

(d) The date upon which this Convention enters into force in accordance with article XII;

(e) Denunciations and notifications in accordance with article XIII.

Article XVI

1. This Convention, of which the Chinese, English, French, Russian and Spanish texts shall be equally authentic, shall be deposited in the archives of the United Nations.

2. The Secretary-General of the United Nations shall transmit a certified copy of this Convention to the States contemplated in article VIII.

[4221]–[4222]

NOTES

For signatures and ratifications, see Table 2 at **[4677]**.

CONVENTION ON THE SETTLEMENT OF INVESTMENT DISPUTES BETWEEN STATES AND NATIONALS OF OTHER STATES

(1965)

NOTES

The text of the following Convention appears as set out in the Arbitration (International Investment Disputes) Act 1966, Schedule. See also the website of The World Bank Group (http://www.worldbank.org/icsid/index.html).

PREAMBLE

The Contracting States

Considering the need for international co-operation for economic development, and the role of private international investment therein;

Bearing in mind the possibility that from time to time disputes may arise in connection with such investment between Contracting States and nationals of other Contracting States;

Recognising that while such disputes would usually be subject to national legal processes, international methods of settlement may be appropriate in certain cases;

Attaching particular importance to the availability of facilities for international conciliation or arbitration to which Contracting States and nationals of other Contracting States may submit such disputes if they so desire;

Desiring to establish such facilities under the auspices of the International Bank for Reconstruction and Development;

Recognising that mutual consent by the parties to submit such disputes to conciliation or to arbitration through such facilities constitutes a binding agreement which requires in particular that due consideration be given to any recommendation of conciliators, and that any arbitral award be complied with; and

Declaring that no Contracting State shall by the mere fact of its ratification acceptance or approval of this Convention and without its consent be deemed to be under any obligation to submit any particular dispute to conciliation or arbitration.

Have agreed as follows:

CHAPTER I
INTERNATIONAL CENTRE FOR SETTLEMENT OF INVESTMENT DISPUTES

SECTION 1
ESTABLISHMENT AND ORGANISATION

Article 1

(1) There is hereby established the International Centre for Settlement of Investment Disputes (hereinafter called the Centre).

(2) The purpose of the Centre shall be to provide facilities for conciliation and arbitration of investment disputes between Contracting States and nationals of other Contracting States in accordance with the provisions of this Convention.

Article 2

The seat of the Centre shall be at the principal office of the International Bank for Reconstruction and Development (hereinafter called the Bank). The seat may be moved to another place by decision of the Administrative Council adopted by a majority of two-thirds of its members.

Article 3

The Centre shall have an Administrative Council and a Secretariat and shall maintain a Panel of Conciliators and a Panel of Arbitrators.

SECTION 2
THE ADMINISTRATIVE COUNCIL

Article 4

(1) The Administrative Council shall be composed of one representative of each Contracting State. An alternate may act as representative in case of his principal's absence from a meeting or inability to act.

(2) In the absence of a contrary designation, each governor and alternate governor of the Bank appointed by a Contracting State shall be *ex officio* its representative and its alternate respectively.

Article 5

The President of the Bank shall be *ex officio* Chairman of the Administrative Council (hereinafter called the Chairman) but shall have no vote. During his absence or inability to act and during any vacancy in the office of President of the Bank, the person for the time being acting as President shall act as Chairman of the Administrative Council.

Article 6

(1) Without prejudice to the powers and functions vested in it by other provisions of this Convention, the Administrative Council shall

- (a) adopt the administrative and financial regulations of the Centre;
- (b) adopt the rules of procedure for the institution of conciliation and arbitration proceedings;
- (c) adopt the rules of procedure for conciliation and arbitration proceedings (hereinafter called the Conciliation Rules and the Arbitration Rules);
- (d) approve arrangements with the Bank for the use of the Bank's administrative facilities and services;
- (e) determine the conditions of service of the Secretary-General and of any Deputy Secretary-General;
- (f) adopt the annual budget of revenues and expenditures of the Centre;
- (g) approve the annual report on the operation of the Centre.

The decisions referred to in sub-paragraphs (a), (b), (c) and (f) above shall be adopted by a majority of two-thirds of the members of the Administrative Council.

(2) The Administrative Council may appoint such committees as it considers necessary.

(3) The Administrative Council shall also exercise such other powers and perform such other functions as it shall determine to be necessary for the implementation of the provisions of this Convention.

Article 7

(1) The Administrative Council shall hold an annual meeting and such other meetings as may be determined by the Council, or convened by the Chairman, or convened by the Secretary-General at the request of not less than five members of the Council.

(2) Each member of the Administrative Council shall have one vote and, except as otherwise herein provided, all matters before the Council shall be decided by a majority of the votes cast.

(3) A quorum for any meeting of the Administrative Council shall be a majority of its members.

(4) The Administrative Council may establish, by a majority of two-thirds of its members, a procedure whereby the Chairman may seek a vote of the Council without convening a meeting of the Council. The vote shall be considered valid only if the majority of the members of the Council cast their votes within the time limit by the said procedure.

Article 8

Members of the Administrative Council and the Chairman shall serve without remuneration from the Centre.

SECTION 3
THE SECRETARIAT

Article 9

The Secretariat shall consist of a Secretary-General, one or more Deputy Secretaries-General and staff.

Article 10

(1) The Secretary-General and any Deputy Secretary-General shall be elected by the Administrative Council by a majority of two-thirds of its members upon the nomination of the Chairman for a term of service not exceeding six years and shall be eligible for re-election. After consulting the members of the Administrative Council, the Chairman shall propose one or more candidates for each such office.

(2) The offices of Secretary-General and Deputy Secretary-General shall be incompatible with the exercise of any political function. Neither the Secretary-General nor any Deputy Secretary-General may hold any other employment or engage in any other occupation except with the approval of the Administrative Council.

(3) During the Secretary-General's absence or inability to act, and during any vacancy of the office of Secretary-General, the Deputy Secretary-General shall act as Secretary-General. If there shall be more than one Deputy Secretary-General, the Administrative Council shall determine in advance the order in which they shall act as Secretary-General.

Article 11

The Secretary-General shall be the legal representative and the principal officer of the Centre and shall be responsible for its administration, including the appointment of staff, in accordance with the provisions of this Convention and the rules adopted by the Administrative Council. He shall perform the function of registrar and shall have the power to authenticate arbitral awards rendered pursuant to this Convention, and to certify copies thereof.

SECTION 4
THE PANELS

Article 12

The Panel of Conciliators and the Panel of Arbitrators shall each consist of qualified persons, designated as hereinafter provided, who are willing to serve thereon.

Article 13

(1) Each Contracting State may designate to each Panel four persons who may but need not be its nationals.

(2) The Chairman may designate ten persons to each Panel. The persons so designated to a Panel shall each have a different nationality.

Article 14

(1) Persons designated to serve on the Panels shall be persons of high moral character and recognised competence in the fields of law, commerce, industry or finance, who may be relied upon to exercise independent judgment. Competence in the field of law shall be of particular importance in the case of persons on the Panel of Arbitrators.

(2) The Chairman, in designating persons to serve on the Panels, shall in addition pay due regard to the importance of assuring representation on the Panels of the principal legal systems of the world and of the main forms of economic activity.

Article 15

(1) Panel members shall serve for renewable periods of six years.

(2) In case of death or resignation of a member of a Panel, the authority which designated the member shall have the right to designate another person to serve for the remainder of that member's term.

(3) Panel members shall continue in office until their successors have been designated.

Article 16

(1) A person may serve on both Panels.

(2) If a person shall have been designated to serve on the same Panel by more than one Contracting State, or by one or more Contracting States and the Chairman, he shall be deemed to have been designated by the authority which first designated him or, if one such authority is the State of which he is a national by that State.

(3) All designations shall be notified to the Secretary-General and shall take effect from the date on which the notification is received.

SECTION 5
FINANCING THE CENTRE

Article 17

If the expenditure of the Centre cannot be met out of charges for the use of its facilities, or out of other receipts, the excess shall be borne by Contracting States which are members of the Bank in proportion to their respective subscriptions to the capital stock of the Bank, and by Contracting States which are not members of the Bank in accordance with rules adopted by the Administrative Council.

SECTION 6
STATUS, IMMUNITIES AND PRIVILEGES

Article 18

The Centre shall have full international legal personality. The legal capacity of the Centre shall include the capacity

(a) to contract;
(b) to acquire and dispose of movable and immovable property;
(c) to institute legal proceedings.

Article 19

To enable the Centre to fulfil its functions, it shall enjoy in the territories of each Contracting State the immunities and privileges set forth in this Section.

Article 20

The Centre, its property and assets shall enjoy immunity from all legal process, except when the Centre waives this immunity.

Article 21

The Chairman, the members of the Administrative Council, persons acting as conciliators or arbitrators or members of a Committee appointed pursuant to paragraph (3) of Article 52, and the officers and employees of the Secretariat

(a) shall enjoy immunity from legal process with respect to acts performed by them in the exercise of their functions, except when the Centre waives this immunity;

(b) not being local nationals, shall enjoy the same immunities from immigration restrictions, alien registration requirements and national service obligations, the same facilities as regards exchange restrictions and the same treatment in respect of travelling facilities as are accorded by Contracting States to the representatives, officials and employees of comparable rank of other Contracting States.

Article 22

The provisions of Article 21 shall apply to persons appearing in proceedings under this Convention as parties, agents, counsel, advocates, witnesses or experts; provided, however, that sub-paragraph (b) thereof shall apply only in connection with their travel to and from, and their stay at, the place where the proceedings are held.

Article 23

(1) The archives of the Centre shall be inviolable, wherever they may be.

(2) With regard to its official communications, the Centre shall be accorded by each Contracting State treatment not less favourable than that accorded to other international organisations.

Article 24

(1) The Centre, its assets, property and income, and its operations and transactions authorised by this Convention shall be exempt from all taxation and customs duties. The Centre shall also be exempt from liability for the collection or payment of any taxes or customs duties.

(2) Except in the case of local nationals, no tax shall be levied on or in respect of expense allowances paid by the Centre to the Chairman or members of the Administrative Council, or on or in respect of salaries, expense allowances or other emoluments paid by the Centre to officials or employees of the Secretariat.

(3) No tax shall be levied on or in respect of fees or expense allowances received by persons acting as conciliators, or arbitrators, or members of a Committee appointed pursuant to paragraph (3) of Article 52, in proceedings under this Convention, if the sole jurisdictional basis for such tax is the location of the Centre or the place where such proceedings are conducted or the place where such fees or allowances are paid.

[4223]

CHAPTER II
JURISDICTION OF THE CENTRE

Article 25

(1) The jurisdiction of the Centre shall extend to any legal dispute arising directly out of an investment, between a Contracting State (or any constituent subdivision or agency of a

Contracting State designated to the Centre by that State) and a national of another Contracting State, which the parties to the dispute consent in writing to submit to the Centre. When the parties have given their consent, no party may withdraw its consent unilaterally.

(2) "National of another Contracting State" means:

(a) any natural person who had the nationality of a Contracting State other than the State party to the dispute on the date on which the parties consented to submit such dispute to conciliation or arbitration as well as on the date on which the request was registered pursuant to paragraph (3) of Article 28 or paragraph (3) of Article 36, but does not include any person who on either date also had the nationality of the Contracting State party to the dispute; and

(b) any juridical person which had the nationality of a Contracting State other than the State party to the dispute on the date on which the parties consented to submit such dispute to conciliation or arbitration and any juridical person which had the nationality of the Contracting State party to the dispute on that date and which, because of foreign control, the parties have agreed should be treated as a national of another Contracting State for the purposes of this Convention.

(3) Consent by a constituent subdivision or agency of a Contracting State shall require the approval of that State unless that State notifies the Centre that no such approval is required.

(4) Any Contracting State may, at the time of ratification, acceptance or approval of this Convention or at any time thereafter, notify the Centre of the class or classes of disputes which it would or would not consider submitting to the jurisdiction of the Centre. The Secretary-General shall forthwith transmit such notification to all Contracting States. Such notification shall not constitute the consent required by paragraph (1).

Article 26

Consent of the parties to arbitration under this Convention shall, unless otherwise stated, be deemed consent to such arbitration to the exclusion of any other remedy. A Contracting State may require the exhaustion of local administrative or judicial remedies as a condition of its consent to arbitration under this Convention.

Article 27

(1) No Contracting State shall give diplomatic protection, or bring an international claim, in respect of a dispute which one of its nationals and another Contracting State shall have consented to submit or shall have submitted to arbitration under this Convention, unless such other Contracting State shall have failed to abide by and comply with the award rendered in such dispute.

(2) Diplomatic protection, for the purposes of paragraph (1), shall not include informal diplomatic exchanges for the sole purpose of facilitating a settlement of the dispute.

[4224]

CHAPTER III
CONCILIATION

SECTION 1
REQUEST FOR CONCILIATION

Article 28

(1) Any Contracting State or any national of a Contracting State wishing to institute conciliation proceedings shall address a request to that effect in writing to the Secretary-General who shall send a copy of the request to the other party.

(2) The request shall contain information concerning the issues in dispute, the identity of the parties and their consent to conciliation in accordance with the rules of procedure for the institution of conciliation and arbitration proceedings.

(3) The Secretary-General shall register the request unless he finds, on the basis of the information contained in the request, that the dispute is manifestly outside the jurisdiction of the Centre. He shall forthwith notify the parties of registration or refusal to register.

SECTION 2
CONSTITUTION OF THE CONCILIATION COMMISSION

Article 29

(1) The Conciliation Commission (hereinafter called the Commission) shall be constituted as soon as possible after registration of a request pursuant to Article 28.

(2)

(a) The Commission shall consist of a sole conciliator or any uneven number of conciliators appointed as the parties shall agree.

(b) Where the parties do not agree upon the number of conciliators and the method of their appointment, the Commission shall consist of three conciliators, one conciliator appointed by each party and the third, who shall be the president of the Commission, appointed by agreement of the parties.

Article 30

If the Commission shall not have been constituted within 90 days after notice of registration of the request has been dispatched by the Secretary-General in accordance with paragraph (3) of Article 28, or such other period as the parties may agree, the Chairman shall, at the request of either party and after consulting both parties as far as possible, appoint the conciliator or conciliators not yet appointed.

Article 31

(1) Conciliators may be appointed from outside the Panel of Conciliators, except in the case of appointments by the Chairman pursuant to Article 30.

(2) Conciliators appointed from outside the Panel of Conciliators shall possess the qualities stated in paragraph (1) of Article 14.

SECTION 3
CONCILIATION PROCEEDINGS

Article 32

(1) The Commission shall be the judge of its own competence.

(2) Any objection by a party to the dispute that that dispute is not within the jurisdiction of the Centre, or for other reasons is not within the competence of the Commission, shall be considered by the Commission which shall determine whether to deal with it as a preliminary question or to join it to the merits of the dispute.

Article 33

Any conciliation proceeding shall be conducted in accordance with the provisions of this Section and, except as the parties otherwise agree, in accordance with the Conciliation Rules in effect on the date on which the parties consented to conciliation. If any question of procedure arises which is not covered by this Section or the Conciliation Rules or any rules agreed by the parties, the Commission shall decide the question.

Article 34

(1) It shall be the duty of the Commission to clarify the issues in dispute between the parties and to endeavour to bring about agreement between them upon mutually acceptable terms. To that end, the Commission may at any stage of the proceedings and from time to time recommend terms of settlement to the parties. The parties shall cooperate in good faith with the Commission in order to enable the Commission to carry out its functions, and shall give their most serious consideration to its recommendations.

(2) If the parties reach agreement, the Commission shall draw up a report noting the issues in dispute and recording that the parties have reached agreement. If, at any stage of the proceedings, it appears to the Commission that there is no likelihood of agreement between

the parties, it shall close the proceedings and shall draw up a report noting the submission of the dispute and recording the failure of the parties to reach agreement. If one party fails to appear or participate in the proceedings, the Commission shall close the proceedings and shall draw up a report noting that party's failure to appear or participate.

Article 35

Except as the parties to the dispute shall otherwise agree, neither party to a conciliation proceeding shall be entitled in any other proceeding, whether before arbitrators or in a court of law or otherwise, to invoke or rely on any views expressed or statements or admissions or offers of settlement made by the other party in the conciliation proceedings, or the report or any recommendations made by the Commission. **[4225]**

CHAPTER IV ARBITRATION

SECTION 1 REQUEST FOR ARBITRATION

Article 36

(1) Any Contracting State or any national of a Contracting State wishing to institute arbitration proceedings shall address a request to that effect in writing to the Secretary-General who shall send a copy of the request to the other party.

(2) The request shall contain information concerning the issues in dispute, the identity of the parties and their consent to arbitration in accordance with the rules of procedure for the institution of conciliation and arbitration proceedings.

(3) The Secretary-General shall register the request unless he finds, on the basis of the information contained in the request, that the dispute is manifestly outside the jurisdiction of the Centre. He shall forthwith notify the parties of registration or refusal to register.

SECTION 2 CONSTITUTION OF THE TRIBUNAL

Article 37

(1) The Arbitral Tribunal (hereinafter called the Tribunal) shall be constituted as soon as possible after registration of a request pursuant to Article 36.

(2)

(a) The Tribunal shall consist of a sole arbitrator or any uneven number of arbitrators appointed as the parties shall agree.

(b) Where the parties do not agree upon the number of arbitrators and the method of their appointment, the Tribunal shall consist of three arbitrators, one arbitrator appointed by each party and the third, who shall be the president of the Tribunal, appointed by agreement of the parties.

Article 38

If the Tribunal shall not have been constituted within 90 days after notice of registration of the request has been dispatched by the Secretary-General in accordance with paragraph (3) of Article 36, or such other period as the parties may agree, the Chairman shall, at the request of either party and after consulting both parties as far as possible, appoint the arbitrator or arbitrators not yet appointed. Arbitrators appointed by the Chairman pursuant to this Article shall not be nationals of the Contracting State party to the dispute or of the Contracting State whose national is a party to the dispute.

Article 39

The majority of the arbitrators shall be nationals of States other than the Contracting State party to the dispute and the Contracting State whose national is a party to the dispute; provided, however, that the foregoing provisions of this Article shall not apply if the sole arbitrator or each individual member of the Tribunal has been appointed by agreement of the parties.

Article 40

(1) Arbitrators may be appointed from outside the Panel of Arbitrators, except in the case of appointments by the Chairman pursuant to Article 38.

(2) Arbitrators appointed from outside the Panel of Arbitrators shall possess the qualities stated in paragraph (1) of Article 14.

SECTION 3
POWERS AND FUNCTIONS OF THE TRIBUNAL

Article 41

(1) The Tribunal shall be the judge of its own competence.

(2) Any objection by a party to the dispute that that dispute is not within the jurisdiction of the Centre, or for other reasons is not within the competence of the Tribunal, shall be considered by the Tribunal which shall determine whether to deal with it as a preliminary question or to join it to the merits of the dispute.

Article 42

(1) The Tribunal shall decide a dispute in accordance with such rules of law as may be agreed by the parties. In the absence of such agreement, the Tribunal shall apply the law of the Contracting State party to the dispute (including its rules on the conflict of laws) and such rules of international law as may be applicable.

(2) The Tribunal may not bring in a finding of *non liquet* on the ground of silence or obscurity of the law.

(3) The provisions of paragraphs (1) and (2) shall not prejudice the power of the Tribunal to decide a dispute *ex aequo et bono* if the parties so agree.

Article 43

Except as the parties otherwise agree, the Tribunal may, if it deems it necessary at any stage of the proceedings,

(a) call upon the parties to produce documents or other evidence, and
(b) visit the scene connected with the dispute, and conduct such enquires there as it may deem appropriate.

Article 44

Any arbitration proceeding shall be conducted in accordance with the provisions of this Section and, except as the parties otherwise agree, in accordance with the Arbitration Rules in effect on the date on which the parties consented to arbitration. If any question of procedure arises which is not covered by this Section or the Arbitration Rules or any rules agreed by the parties, the Tribunal shall decide the question.

Article 45

(1) Failure of a party to appear or to present his case shall not be deemed an admission of the other party's assertions.

(2) If a party fails to appear or to present his case at any stage of the proceedings the other party may request the Tribunal to deal with the questions submitted to it and to render an

award. Before rendering an award, the Tribunal shall notify, and grant a period of grace to, the party failing to appear or to present its case, unless it is satisfied that that party does not intend to do so.

Article 46

Except as the parties otherwise agree, the Tribunal shall, if requested by a party, determine any incidental or additional claims or counter-claims arising directly out of the subject-matter of the dispute provided that they are within the scope of the consent of the parties and are otherwise within the jurisdiction of the Centre.

Article 47

Except as the parties otherwise agree, the Tribunal may, if it considers that the circumstances so require, recommend any provisional measures which should be taken to preserve the respective rights of either party.

SECTION 4
THE AWARD

Article 48

(1) The Tribunal shall decide questions by a majority of the votes of all its members.

(2) The award of the Tribunal shall be in writing and shall be signed by the members of the Tribunal who voted for it.

(3) The award shall deal with every question submitted to the Tribunal, and shall state the reasons upon which it is based.

(4) Any member of the Tribunal may attach his individual opinion to the award, whether he dissents from the majority or not, or a statement of his dissent.

(5) The Centre shall not publish the award without the consent of the parties.

Article 49

(1) The Secretary-General shall promptly dispatch certified copies of the award to the parties. The award shall be deemed to have been rendered on the date on which the certified copies were dispatched.

(2) The Tribunal upon the request of a party made within 45 days after the date on which the award was rendered may after notice to the other party decide any question which it had omitted to decide in the award, and shall rectify any clerical, arithmetical or similar error in the award. Its decision shall become part of the award and shall be notified to the parties in the same manner as the award. The periods of time provided for under paragraph (2) of Article 51 and paragraph (2) of Article 52 shall run from the date on which the decision was rendered.

SECTION 5
INTERPRETATION, REVISION AND ANNULMENT OF THE AWARD

Article 50

(1) If any dispute shall arise between the parties as to the meaning or scope of an award, either party may request interpretation of the award by an application in writing addressed to the Secretary-General.

(2) The request shall, if possible, be submitted to the Tribunal which rendered the award. If this shall not be possible, a new Tribunal shall be constituted in accordance with Section 2 of this Chapter. The Tribunal may, if it considers that the circumstances so require, stay enforcement of the award pending its decision.

Article 51

(1) Either party may request revision of the award by an application in writing addressed to the Secretary-General on the ground of discovery of some fact of such a nature as decisively to affect the award, provided that when the award was rendered that fact was unknown to the Tribunal and to the applicant and that the applicant's ignorance of that fact was not due to negligence.

(2) The application shall be made within 90 days after the discovery of such fact and in any event within three years after the date on which the award was rendered.

(3) The request shall, if possible, be submitted to the Tribunal which rendered the award. If this shall not be possible, a new Tribunal shall be constituted in accordance with Section 2 of this Chapter.

(4) The Tribunal may, if it considers that the circumstances so require, stay enforcement of the award pending its decision. If the applicant requests stay of enforcement of the award in his application, enforcement shall be stayed provisionally until the Tribunal rules on such request.

Article 52

(1) Either party may request annulment of the award by an application in writing addressed to the Secretary-General on one or more of the following grounds:

(a) that the Tribunal was not properly constituted;
(b) that the Tribunal has manifestly exceeded its powers;
(c) that there was corruption on the part of a member of the Tribunal;
(d) that there has been a serious departure from a fundamental rule of procedure; or
(e) that the award has failed to state the reasons on which it is based.

(2) The application shall be made within 120 days after the date on which the award was rendered except that when annulment is requested on the ground of corruption such application shall be made within 120 days after discovery of the corruption and in any event within three years after the date on which the award was rendered.

(3) On receipt of the request the Chairman shall forthwith appoint from the Panel of Arbitrators an *ad hoc* Committee of three persons. None of the members of the Committee shall have been a member of the Tribunal which rendered the award, shall be of the same nationality as any such member, shall be a national of the State party to the dispute or of the State whose national is a party to the dispute, shall have been designated to the Panel of Arbitrators by either of those States, or shall have acted as a conciliator in the same dispute. The Committee shall have the authority to annul the award or any part thereof on any of the grounds set forth in paragraph (1).

(4) The provisions of Articles 41–45, 48, 49, 53 and 54, and of Chapters VI and VII shall apply *mutatis mutandis* to proceedings before the Committee.

(5) The Committee may, if it considers that circumstances so require, stay enforcement of the award pending its decision. If the applicant requests a stay of enforcement of the award in his application, enforcement shall be stayed provisionally until the Committee rules on such request.

(6) If the award is annulled the dispute shall, at the request of either party, be submitted to a new Tribunal constituted in accordance with Section 2 of this Chapter.

SECTION 6
RECOGNITION AND ENFORCEMENT OF THE AWARD

Article 53

(1) The award shall be binding on the parties and shall not be subject to any appeal or to any other remedy except those provided for in this Convention. Each party shall abide by and comply with the terms of the award except to the extent that enforcement shall have been stayed pursuant to the relevant provisions of this Convention.

(2) For the purposes of this Section, "award" shall include any decision interpreting, revising or annulling such award pursuant to Articles 50, 51 or 52.

Article 54

(1) Each Contracting State shall recognise an award rendered pursuant to this Convention as binding and enforce the pecuniary obligations imposed by that award within its territories as if it were a final judgment of a court in that State. A Contracting State with a federal constitution may enforce such an award in or through its federal courts and may provide that such courts shall treat the award as if it were a final judgment of the courts of a constituent state.

(2) A party seeking recognition or enforcement in the territories of a Contracting State shall furnish to a competent court or other authority which such State shall have designated for this purpose a copy of the award certified by the Secretary-General. Each Contracting State shall notify the Secretary-General of the designation of the competent court or other authority for this purpose and of any subsequent change in such designation.

(3) Execution of the award shall be governed by the laws concerning the execution of judgments in force in the State in whose territories such execution is sought.

Article 55

Nothing in Article 54 shall be construed as derogating from the law in force in any Contracting State relating to immunity of that State or of any foreign State from execution.

[4226]

CHAPTER V
REPLACEMENT AND DISQUALIFICATION OF CONCILIATORS AND ARBITRATORS

Article 56

(1) After a Commission or a Tribunal has been constituted and proceedings have begun, its composition shall remain unchanged; provided, however, that if a conciliator or an arbitrator should die, become incapacitated, or resign, the resulting vacancy shall be filled in accordance with the provisions of Section 2 of Chapter III or Section 2 of Chapter IV.

(2) A member of the Commission or Tribunal shall continue to serve in that capacity notwithstanding that he shall have ceased to be a member of the Panel.

(3) If a conciliator or arbitrator appointed by a party shall have resigned without the consent of the Commission or Tribunal of which he was a member, the Chairman shall appoint a person from the appropriate Panel to fill the resulting vacancy.

Article 57

A party may propose to a Commission or Tribunal the disqualification of any of its members on account of any fact indicating a manifest lack of the qualities required by paragraph (1) of Article 14. A party to arbitration proceedings may, in addition, propose the disqualification of an arbitrator on the ground that he was ineligible for appointment to the Tribunal under Section 2 of Chapter IV.

Article 58

The decision on any proposal to disqualify a conciliator or arbitrator shall be taken by the other members of the Commission or Tribunal as the case may be, provided that where those members are equally divided, or in the case of a proposal to disqualify a sole conciliator or arbitrator, or a majority of the conciliators or arbitrators, the Chairman shall take that decision. If it is decided that the proposal is well-founded the conciliator or arbitrator to whom the decision relates shall be replaced in accordance with the provisions of Section 2 of Chapter III or Section 2 of Chapter IV.

[4227]

CHAPTER VI
COST OF PROCEEDINGS

Article 59

The charges payable by the parties for the use of the facilities of the Centre shall be determined by the Secretary-General in accordance with the regulations adopted by the Administrative Council.

Article 60

(1) Each Commission and each Tribunal shall determine the fees and expenses of its members within limits established from time to time by the Administrative Council and after consultation with the Secretary-General.

(2) Nothing in paragraph (1) of this Article shall preclude the parties from agreeing in advance with the Commission or Tribunal concerned upon the fees and expenses of its members.

Article 61

(1) In the case of conciliation proceedings the fees and expenses of members of the Commission as well as the charges for the use of the facilities of the Centre, shall be borne equally by the parties. Each party shall bear any other expenses it incurs in connection with the proceedings.

(2) In the case of arbitration proceedings the Tribunal shall, except as the parties otherwise agree, assess the expenses incurred by the parties in connection with the proceedings, and shall decide how and by whom those expenses, the fees and expenses of the members of the Tribunal and the charges for the use of the facilities of the Centre shall be paid. Such decision shall form part of the award.

[4228]

CHAPTER VII
PLACE OF PROCEEDINGS

Article 62

Conciliation and arbitration proceedings shall be held at the seat of the Centre except as hereinafter provided.

Article 63

Conciliation and arbitration proceedings may be held, if the parties so agree,

(a) at the seat of the Permanent Court of Arbitration or of any other appropriate institution, whether private or public, with which the Centre may make arrangements for that purpose; or

(b) at any other place approved by the Commission or Tribunal after consultation with the Secretary-General.

[4229]

CHAPTER VIII
DISPUTES BETWEEN CONTRACTING STATES

Article 64

Any dispute arising between Contracting States concerning the interpretation or application of this Convention which is not settled by negotiation shall be referred to the International Court of Justice by the application of any party to such dispute, unless the States concerned agree to another method of settlement.

[4230]

CHAPTER IX
AMENDMENT

Article 65

Any Contracting State may propose amendment of this Convention. The text of a proposed amendment shall be communicated to the Secretary-General not less than 90 days prior to the meeting of the Administrative Council at which such amendment is to be considered and shall forthwith be transmitted by him to all the members of the Administrative Council.

Article 66

(1) If the Administrative Council shall so decide by a majority of two-thirds of its members, the proposed amendment shall be circulated to all Contracting States for ratification, acceptance or approval. Each amendment shall enter into force 30 days after dispatch by the depositary of this Convention of a notification to Contracting States that all Contracting States have ratified, accepted or approved the amendment.

(2) No amendment shall affect the rights and obligations under this Convention of any Contracting State or of any of its constituent subdivisions or agencies, or of any national of such State arising out of consent to the jurisdiction of the Centre given before the date of entry into force of the amendment. **[4231]**

CHAPTER X
FINAL PROVISIONS

Article 67

This Convention shall be open for signature on behalf of States members of the Bank. It shall also be open for signature on behalf of any other State which is a party to the Statute of the International Court of Justice and which the Administrative Council, by a vote of two-thirds of its members, shall have invited to sign the Convention.

Article 68

(1) This Convention shall be subject to ratification, acceptance or approval by the signatory States in accordance with their respective constitutional procedures.

(2) This Convention shall enter into force 30 days after the date of deposit of the twentieth instrument of ratification, acceptance or approval. It shall enter into force for each State which subsequently deposits its instrument of ratification, acceptance or approval 30 days after the date of such deposit.

Article 69

Each Contracting State shall take legislative or other measures as may be necessary for making the provisions of this Convention effective in its territories.

Article 70

This Convention shall apply to all territories for whose international relations a Contracting State is responsible, except those which are excluded by such State by written notice to the depositary of this Convention either at the time of ratification, acceptance or approval or subsequently.

Article 71

Any Contracting State may denounce this Convention by written notice to the depositary of this Convention. The denunciation shall take effect six months after receipt of such notice.

Article 72

Notice by a Contracting State pursuant to Article 70 or 71 shall not affect the rights or obligations under this Convention of that State or of any of its constituent subdivisions or agencies or of any national of that State arising out of consent to the jurisdiction of the Centre given by one of them before such notice was received by the depositary.

Article 73

Instruments of ratification, acceptance or approval of this Convention and of amendments thereto shall be deposited with the Bank which shall act as the depositary of this Convention. The depositary shall transmit certified copies of this Convention to States members of the Bank and to any other State invited to sign the Convention.

Article 74

The depositary shall register this Convention with the Secretariat of the United Nations in accordance with Article 102 of the Charter of the United Nations and the Regulations thereunder adopted by the General Assembly.

Article 75

The depositary shall notify all signatory States of the following:

(a) signatures in accordance with Article 67;
(b) deposits of instruments of ratification, acceptance and approval in accordance with Article 73;
(c) the date on which this Convention enters into force in accordance with Article 68;
(d) exclusions from territorial application pursuant to Article 70;
(e) the date on which any amendment of this Convention enters into force in accordance with Article 66; and
(f) denunciations in accordance with Article 71.

DONE at Washington in the English, French and Spanish languages, all three texts being equally authentic, in a single copy which shall remain deposited in the archives of the International Bank for Reconstruction and Development, which has indicated by its signature below its agreement to fulfil the functions with which it is charged under this Convention.

(Here follow the signatures)

[4232]

UNCITRAL MODEL LAW ON INTERNATIONAL COMMERCIAL ARBITRATION

(1985)

NOTES

The text of the following Convention appears as set out in the Law Reform (Miscellaneous Provisions) (Scotland) Act 1990, Sch 7. See also the website of the United Nations Commission on International Trade Law (UNCITRAL) at http://www.uncitral.org.

CHAPTER I
GENERAL PROVISIONS

Article 1
Scope of application

(1) This Law applies to international commercial arbitration, subject to any agreement in force between the United Kingdom and any other State or States which applies in Scotland.

(2) The provisions of this Law, except articles 8, 9, 35 and 36, apply only if the place of arbitration is in Scotland.

(3) An arbitration is international if—
- (a) the parties to an arbitration agreement have, at the time of the conclusion of that agreement, their places of business in different States; or
- (b) one of the following places is situated outside the State in which the parties have their places of business:
  - (i) the place of arbitration if determined in, or pursuant to, the arbitration agreement;
  - (ii) any place where a substantial part of the obligations of the commercial relationship is to be performed or the place with which the subject-matter of the dispute is most closely connected.

(4) For the purposes of paragraph (3) of this article—
- (a) if a party has more than one place of business, the place of business is that which has the closest relationship to the arbitration agreement;
- (b) if a party does not have a place of business, reference is to be made to his habitual residence.

(5) This Law shall not affect any other enactment or rule of law in force in Scotland by virtue of which certain disputes may not be submitted to arbitration or may be submitted to arbitration only according to provisions other than those of this Law.

Article 2
Definitions and rules of interpretation

For the purposes of this Law—
- (a) "arbitration" means any arbitration whether or not administered by a permanent arbitral institution;
- (b) "arbitral tribunal" means an arbitrator or a panel of arbitrators;
- (c) "arbitrator" includes an arbiter;
- (d) "commercial", in relation to an arbitration, includes matters arising form all relationships of a commercial nature, whether contractual or not;
- (e) "country" includes Scotland;
- (f) "court" means a body or organ of the judicial system of a State;
- (g) "relationships of a commercial nature" include, but are not limited to, the following transactions, namely any trade transaction for the supply or exchange of goods or services; distribution agreement; commercial representation or agency; factoring; leasing; construction of works; consulting; engineering; licensing; investment; financing; banking; insurance; exploitation agreement or concession; joint venture and other forms of industrial or business co-operation; carriage of goods or passengers by air, sea, rail or road;
- (h) "State", except in article 1(1), includes Scotland;
- (i) where a provision of this Law, except article 28, leaves the parties free to determine a certain issue, such freedom includes the right of the parties to authorise a third party, including an institution, to make that determination;
- (j) where a provision of this Law refers to the fact that the parties have agreed or that they may agree or in any other way refers to an agreement of the parties, such agreement includes any arbitration rules referred to in that agreement;
- (k) where a provision of this Law, other than in articles 25(a) and 32(2)(a), refers to a claim, it also applies to a counter-claim, and where it refers to a defence, it also applies to a defence to such counter-claim;
- (l) article headings are for reference purposes only and are not to be used for purposes of interpretation.

Article 3
Receipt of written communications

(1) Unless otherwise agreed by the parties—
- (a) any written communication is deemed to have been received if it is delivered to the addressee personally or if it is delivered at his place of business, habitual residence or mailing address; if none of these can be found after making a reasonable inquiry, a written communication is deemed to have been received if it is sent to the addressee's last known place of business, habitual residence or mailing address by registered letter or any other means which provides a record of the attempts to deliver it;
- (b) the communication is deemed to have been received on the day it is so delivered.

(2) The provisions of this article do not apply to communications in court proceedings.

Article 4
Waiver of right to object

A party who knows that any provision of this Law from which the parties may derogate or any requirement under the arbitration agreement has not been complied with and yet proceeds with the arbitration without stating his objections to such non-compliance without undue delay or, if a time-limit is provided therefor, within such period of time, shall be deemed to have waived his right to object.

Article 5
Extent of court intervention

In matters governed by this Law, no court shall intervene except where so provided in this Law.

Article 6
Court for certain functions of arbitration assistance, supervision and enforcement

The functions referred to in articles 11(3), 11(4), 13(3), 14, 16(3), 34(2), 35 and 36 shall be performed by:
(a) the Court of Session; or
(b) where it has jurisdiction, the sheriff court.

[4233]

CHAPTER II
ARBITRATION AGREEMENT

Article 7
Definition and form of arbitration agreement

(1) "Arbitration agreement" is an agreement by the parties to submit to arbitration all or certain disputes which have arisen or which may arise between them in respect of a defined legal relationship, whether contractual or not. An arbitration agreement may be in the form of an arbitration clause in a contract or in the form of a separate agreement.

(2) The arbitration agreement shall be in writing. An agreement is in writing if it is contained in a document signed by the parties or in an exchange of letters, telex, telegrams or other means of telecommunication which provide a record of the agreement, or in an exchange of statements of claim and defence in which the existence of an agreement is alleged by one party and not denied by another. The reference in contract to a document containing an arbitration clause constitutes an arbitration agreement provided that the contract is in writing and the reference is such as to make that clause part of the contract.

Article 8
Arbitration agreement and substantive claim before court

(1) A court before which an action is brought in a matter which is the subject of an arbitration agreement shall, if a party so requests at any time before the pleadings in the action are finalised, refer the parties to arbitration unless it finds that the agreement is null and void, inoperative or incapable of being performed.

(2) Where an action referred to in paragraph (1) of this article has been brought, arbitral proceedings may nevertheless be commenced or continued, and an award may be made, while the issue is pending before the court.

Article 9
Arbitration agreement and interim measures by court

(1) It is not incompatible with an arbitration agreement for a party to request, before or during arbitral proceedings, from a court an interim measure of protection and for a court to grant such measure.

(2) In paragraph (1) of this article "interim measure of protection" includes, but is not limited to, the following—
- (a) arrestment or inhibition to ensure that any award which may be made in the arbitral proceedings is not rendered ineffectual by the dissipation of assets by another party;
- (b) interim interdict or other interim order.

(3) Where—
- (a) a party applies to a court for an interim interdict or other interim order; and
- (b) an arbitral tribunal has already ruled on the matter,

the court shall treat the ruling or any finding of fact made in the course of the ruling as conclusive for the purposes of the application.

CHAPTER III
COMPOSITION OF ARBITRATION TRIBUNAL

Article 10
Number of arbitrators

(1) The parties are free to determine the number of arbitrators.

(2) Failing such determination, there shall be a single arbitrator.

Article 11
Appointment of arbitrators

(1) No person shall be precluded by reason of his nationality from acting as an arbitrator, unless otherwise agreed by the parties.

(2) The parties are free to agree on a procedure of appointing the arbitrator or arbitrators, subject to the provisions of paragraphs (4) and (5) of this article.

(3) Failing such agreement,
- (a) in an arbitration with three arbitrators, each party shall appoint one arbitrator, and the two arbitrators thus appointed shall appoint the third arbitrator; if a party fails to appoint the arbitrator within thirty days of receipt of a request to do so from the other party, or if the two arbitrators fail to agree on the third arbitrator within thirty days of their appointment, the appointment shall be made, upon request of a party, by the court specified in article 6;
- (b) in an arbitration with a single arbitrator, if the parties are unable to agree on the arbitrator, he shall be appointed, upon request of a party, by the court specified in article 6.

(4) Where, under an appointment procedure agreed upon by the parties:
- (a) a party fails to act as required under such procedure, or
- (b) the parties, or two arbitrators, are unable to reach an agreement expected of them under such procedure, or
- (c) a third party, including an institution, fails to perform any function entrusted to it under such procedure,

any party may request the court specified in article 6 to take the necessary measure, unless the agreement on the appointment procedure provides other means for securing the appointment.

(5) A decision on a matter entrusted by paragraph (3) or (4) of this article to the court specified in article 6 shall be subject to no appeal. The court, in appointing an arbitrator, shall have due regard to any qualifications required of the arbitrator by the agreement of the parties and to such considerations as are likely to secure the appointment of an independent and impartial arbitrator and, in the case of a sole or third arbitrator, shall take into account as well the advisability of appointing an arbitrator of a nationality other than those of the parties.

Article 12
Grounds for challenge

(1) When a person is approached in connection with his possible appointment as an arbitrator, he shall disclose any circumstances likely to give rise to justifiable doubts as to his impartiality or independence. An arbitrator, from the time of his appointment and throughout the arbitral proceedings, shall without delay disclose any such circumstances to the parties unless they have already been informed of them by him.

(2) An arbitrator may be challenged only if circumstances exist that give rise to justifiable doubts as to his impartiality or independence, or if he does not possess qualifications agreed to by the parties. A party may challenge an arbitrator appointed by him, or in whose appointment he has participated, only for reasons of which he becomes aware after the appointment has been made.

Article 13
Challenge procedure

(1) The parties are free to agree on a procedure for challenging an arbitrator, subject to the provisions of paragraph (3) of this article.

(2) Failing such agreement, a party who intends to challenge an arbitrator shall, within fifteen days after becoming aware of the constitution of the arbitral tribunal or after becoming aware of any circumstances referred to in article 12(2), send a written statement of the reasons for the challenge to the arbitral tribunal. Unless the challenged arbitrator withdraws from his office or the other party agrees to the challenge, the arbitral tribunal shall decide on the challenge.

(3) If a challenge under any procedure agreed upon by the parties or under the procedure of paragraph (2) of this article is not successful, the challenging party may, within thirty days after having received notice of the decision rejecting the challenge, request the court specified in article 6 to decide on the challenge, which decision shall be subject to no appeal. While such a request is pending, the arbitral tribunal, including the challenged arbitrator, may continue the arbitral proceedings and make an award.

Article 14
Failure or impossibility to act

(1) If an arbitrator becomes de jure or de facto unable to perform his functions or for other reasons fails to act without undue delay, his mandate terminates if he withdraws from his office or if the parties agree on the termination. Otherwise, if a controversy remains concerning any of these grounds, any party may request the court specified in article 6 to decide on the termination of the mandate, which decision shall be subject to no appeal.

(2) If, under this article or article 13(2), an arbitrator withdraws from his office or a party agrees to the termination of the mandate of an arbitrator, this does not imply acceptance of the validity of any ground referred to in this article or article 12(2).

Article 15
Appointment of substitute arbitrator

Where the mandate of an arbitrator terminates under article 13 or 14 or because of his withdrawal from office for any other reason or because of the revocation of his mandate by agreement of the parties or in any other case of termination of his mandate, a substitute arbitrator shall be appointed according to the rules that were applicable to the appointment of the arbitrator being replaced.

CHAPTER IV
JURISDICTION OF ARBITRAL TRIBUNAL

Article 16
Competence of arbitral tribunal to rule on its jurisdiction

(1) The arbitral tribunal may rule on its own jurisdiction, including any objections with respect to the existence or validity of the arbitration agreement. For that purpose, an

arbitration clause which forms part of a contract shall be treated as an agreement independent of the other terms of the contract. A decision by the arbitral tribunal that the contract is null and void shall not entail ipso jure the invalidity of the arbitration clause.

(2) A plea that the arbitral tribunal does not have jurisdiction shall be raised not later than the submission of the statement of defence. A party is not precluded from raising such a plea by the fact that he has appointed, or participated in the appointment of, an arbitrator. A plea that the arbitral tribunal is exceeding the scope of its authority shall be raised as soon as the matter alleged to be beyond the scope of its authority is raised during the arbitral proceedings. The arbitral tribunal may, in either case, admit a later plea if it considers the delay justified.

(3) The arbitral tribunal may rule on a plea referred to in paragraph (2) of this article either as a preliminary question or in an award on the merits. If the arbitral tribunal rules on such a plea as a preliminary question, any party may, within thirty days after having received notice of that ruling, request the court specified in article 6 to decide the matter, which decision shall be subject to no appeal. While such a request is pending, the arbitral tribunal may continue the arbitral proceedings and make an award.

Article 17
Power of arbitral tribunal to order interim measures

(1) Unless otherwise agreed by the parties, the arbitral tribunal may, at the request of a party, order any party to take such interim measures of protection as the arbitral tribunal may consider necessary in respect of the subject-matter of the dispute. The arbitral tribunal may require any party to provide appropriate security in connection with such measure.

(2) An order under paragraph (1) of this article shall take the form of an award and articles 31, 35 and 36 shall apply accordingly.

CHAPTER V
CONDUCT OF ARBITRAL PROCEEDINGS

Article 18
Equal treatment of parties

The parties shall be treated with equality and each party shall be given a full opportunity of presenting his case.

Article 19
Determination of rules of procedure

(1) Subject to the provisions of this Law, the parties are free to agree on the procedure to be followed by the arbitral tribunal in conducting the proceedings.

(2) Failing such agreement, the arbitral tribunal may, subject to the provisions of this Law, conduct the arbitration in such manner as it considers appropriate. The power conferred upon the arbitral tribunal includes the power to determine the admissibility, relevance, materiality and weight of any evidence.

Article 20
Place of arbitration

(1) The parties are free to agree on the place of arbitration. Failing such agreement, the place of arbitration shall be determined by the arbitral tribunal having regard to the circumstances of the case, including the convenience of the parties.

(2) Notwithstanding the provisions of paragraph (1) of this article, the arbitral tribunal may, unless otherwise agreed by the parties, meet at any place it considers appropriate for consultation among its members, for hearing witnesses, experts or the parties, or for inspection of goods, other property or documents.

Article 21
Commencement of arbitral proceedings

Unless otherwise agreed by the parties, the arbitral proceedings in respect of a particular dispute commence on the date on which a request for that dispute to be referred to arbitration is received by the respondent

Article 22
Language

(1) The parties are free to agree on the language or languages to be used in the arbitral proceedings. Failing such agreement, the arbitral tribunal shall determine the language or languages to be used in the proceedings. This agreement or determination, unless otherwise specified therein, shall apply to any written statement by a party, any hearing and any award, decision or other communication by the arbitral tribunal.

(2) The arbitral tribunal may order that any documentary evidence shall be accompanied by a translation into the language or languages agreed upon by the parties or determined by the arbitral tribunal.

Article 23
Statements of claim and defence

(1) Within the period of time agreed by the parties or determined by the arbitral tribunal, the claimant shall state the facts supporting his claim, the points at issue and the relief or remedy sought, and the respondent shall state his defence in respect of these particulars, unless the parties have otherwise agreed as to the required elements of such statements. The parties may submit with their statements all documents they consider to be relevant or may add a reference to the documents or other evidence they will submit.

(2) Unless otherwise agreed by the parties, either party may amend or supplement his claim or defence during the course of the arbitral proceedings, unless the arbitral tribunal considers it inappropriate to allow such amendment having regard to the delay in making it.

Article 24
Hearings and written proceedings

(1) Subject to any contrary agreement by the parties, the arbitral tribunal shall decide whether to hold oral hearings for the presentation of evidence or for oral argument, or whether the proceedings shall be conducted on the basis of documents and other materials. However, unless the parties have agreed that no hearings shall be held, the arbitral tribunal shall hold such hearings at an appropriate stage of the proceedings, if so requested by a party.

(2) The parties shall be given sufficient advance notice of any hearing and of any meeting of the arbitral tribunal for the purposes of inspection of goods, other property or documents.

(3) All statements, documents or other information supplied to the arbitral tribunal by one party shall be communicated to the other party. Also any expert report or evidentiary document on which the arbitral tribunal may rely in making its decision shall be communicated to the parties.

Article 25
Default of a party

Unless otherwise agreed by the parties, if, without showing sufficient cause,

(a) the claimant fails to communicate his statement of claim in accordance with article 23(1), the arbitral tribunal shall terminate the proceedings;

(b) the respondent fails to communicate his statement of defence in accordance with article 23(1), the arbitral tribunal shall continue the proceedings without treating such failure in itself as an admission of the claimant's allegations;

(c) any party fails to appear at a hearing or to produce documentary evidence, the arbitral tribunal may continue the proceedings and make the award on the evidence before it.

Article 26
Expert appointed by arbitral tribunal

(1) Unless otherwise agreed by the parties, the arbitral tribunal:

(a) may appoint one or more experts to report to it on specific issues to be determined by the arbitral tribunal;

(b) may require a party to give the expert any relevant information or to provide access to any relevant documents, goods or other property for his inspection.

(2) Unless otherwise agreed by the parties, if a party so requests or if the arbitral tribunal considers it necessary, the expert shall, after delivery of his written or oral report, participate in a hearing where the parties have the opportunity to put questions to him and to present expert witnesses in order to testify on the points at issue.

Article 27
Court assistance in taking evidence

The arbitral tribunal or a party with the approval of the arbitral tribunal may request from the Court of Session or the sheriff court assistance in taking evidence and recovering documents. The court may execute the request within its competence and according to its rules on taking evidence and recovery of documents.

CHAPTER VI
MAKING OF AWARD AND TERMINATION OF PROCEEDINGS

Article 28
Rules applicable to substance of dispute

(1) The arbitral tribunal shall decide the dispute in accordance with such rules of law as are chosen by the parties as applicable to the substance of the dispute. Any designation of the law or legal system of a given State shall be construed, unless otherwise expressed, as directly referring to the substantive law of that State and not to its conflict of laws rules.

(2) Failing any designation by the parties, the arbitral tribunal shall apply the law determined by the conflict of laws rules which it considers applicable.

(3) The arbitral tribunal shall decide ex aequo et bono or as amiable compositeur only if the parties have expressly authorised it to do so.

(4) In all cases, the arbitral tribunal shall decide in accordance with the terms of the contract and shall take into account the usages of the trade applicable to the transaction.

Article 29
Decision making by panel of arbitrators

In arbitral proceedings with more than one arbitrator, any decision of the arbitral tribunal shall be made, unless otherwise agreed by the parties, by a majority of all its members. However, questions of procedure may be decided by a presiding arbitrator, if so authorised by the parties or all members of the arbitral tribunal.

Article 30
Settlement

(1) If, during arbitral proceedings, the parties settle the dispute, the arbitral tribunal shall terminate the proceedings and, if so requested by the parties and not objected to by the arbitral tribunal, record the settlement in the form of an arbitral award on agreed terms.

(2) An award on agreed terms shall be made in accordance with the provisions of article 31 and shall state that it is an award. Such an award has the same status and effect as any other award on the merits of the case.

Article 31
Form and contents of award

(1) The award shall be made in writing and shall be signed by the arbitrator or arbitrators. In arbitral proceedings with more than one arbitrator, the signatures of the majority of all members of the arbitral tribunal shall suffice, provided that the reason for any omitted signature is stated.

(2) The award shall state the reasons upon which it is based, unless the parties have agreed that no reasons are to be given or the award is on agreed terms under article 30.

(3) The award shall state its date and the place of arbitration as determined in accordance with article 20(1). The award shall be deemed to have been made at that place.

(4) After the award is made, a copy signed by the arbitrators in accordance with paragraph (1) of this article shall be delivered to each party.

Article 32
Termination of proceedings

(1) The arbitral proceedings are terminated by the final award or by an order of the arbitral tribunal in accordance with paragraph (2) of this article.

(2) The arbitral tribunal shall issue an order for the termination of the arbitral proceedings when:

(a) the claimant withdraws his claim, unless the respondent objects thereto and the arbitral tribunal recognises a legitimate interest on his part in obtaining a final settlement of the dispute;
(b) the parties agree on the termination of the proceedings;
(c) the arbitral tribunal finds that the continuation of the proceedings has for any other reason become unnecessary or impossible.

(3) The mandate of the arbitral tribunal terminates with the termination of the arbitral proceedings, subject to the provisions of articles 33 and 34(4).

Article 33
Correction and interpretation of award and making of additional award

(1) Within thirty days of receipt of the award, unless another period of time has been agreed upon by the parties:

(a) a party, with notice to the other party, may request the arbitral tribunal to correct in the award any errors in computation, any clerical or typographical errors or any errors of similar nature;
(b) if so agreed by the parties, a party, with notice to the other party, may request the arbitral tribunal to give an interpretation of a specific point or part of the award.

If the arbitral tribunal considers the request to be justified, it shall make the correction or give the interpretation within thirty days of receipt of the request. The interpretation shall form part of the award.

(2) The arbitral tribunal may correct any error of the type referred to in paragraph (1)(a) of this article on its own initiative within thirty days of the date of the award.

(3) Unless otherwise agreed by the parties, a party, with notice to the other party, may, within thirty days of receipt of the award, request the arbitral tribunal to make an additional award as to claims presented in the arbitral proceedings but omitted from the award. If the arbitral tribunal considers the request to be justified, it shall make the additional award.

(4) The arbitral tribunal may extend, if necessary, the period of time within which it shall make a correction or interpretation under paragraph (1) of this article.

(5) The provisions of article 31 shall apply to a correction or interpretation of the award or to an additional award.

CHAPTER VII
RECOURSE AGAINST AWARD

Article 34
Application for setting aside as exclusive recourse against arbitral award

(1) Recourse to a court against an arbitral award may be made only by an application for setting aside in accordance with paragraphs (2) and (3) of this article.

(2) An arbitral award may be set aside by the court specified in article 6 only if:

(a) the party making the application furnishes proof that:

(i) a party to the arbitration agreement referred to in article 7 was under some incapacity, or the said agreement is not valid under the law to which the parties have subjected it or, failing any indication thereon, under the law of Scotland; or

(ii) the party making the application was not given proper notice of the appointment of an arbitrator or of the arbitral proceedings or was otherwise unable to present his case; or

(iii) the award deals with a dispute not contemplated by or not falling within the terms of the submission to arbitration, or contains decisions on matters beyond the scope of the submission to arbitration, provided that, if the decisions on matters submitted to arbitration can be separated from those not so submitted, only that part of the award which contains decisions on matters not submitted to arbitration may be set aside; or

(iv) the composition of the arbitral tribunal or the arbitral procedure was not in accordance with the agreement of the parties, unless such agreement was in conflict with a provision of this Law from which the parties cannot derogate, or, failing such agreement, was not in accordance with this Law; or

(v) the award was procured by fraud, bribery or corruption; or

(b) the court finds that:

(i) the subject-matter of the dispute is not capable of settlement by arbitration under the law of Scotland; or

(ii) the award is in conflict with public policy.

(3) An application for setting aside may not be made after three months have elapsed from the date on which the party making that application had received the award or, if a request had been made under article 33, from the date on which that request had been disposed of by the arbitral tribunal. This paragraph does not apply to an application for setting aside on the ground mentioned in paragraph (2)(a)(v) of this article.

(4) The court, when asked to set aside an award, may, where appropriate and so requested by a party, suspend the setting aside proceedings for a period of time determined by it in order to give the arbitral tribunal an opportunity to resume the arbitral proceedings or to take such other action as in the arbitral tribunal's opinion will eliminate the grounds for setting aside.

[4234]

CHAPTER VIII
RECOGNITION AND ENFORCEMENT OF AWARDS

Article 35
Recognition and enforcement

(1) An arbitral award, irrespective of the country in which it was made, shall be recognised as binding and, upon application in writing to the competent court, shall be enforced subject to the provisions of this article and of article 36.

(2) The party relying on an award or applying for its enforcement shall supply the duly authenticated original award or a duly certified copy thereof, and the original arbitration agreement referred to in article 7 or a duly certified copy thereof. If the award or agreement is not made in English, the party shall supply a duly certified translation thereof into English.

Article 36

Grounds for refusing recognition or enforcement

(1) Recognition or enforcement of an arbitral award, irrespective of the country in which it was made, may be refused only—

(a) at the request of the party against whom it is invoked, if that party furnishes to the competent court where recognition or enforcement is sought proof that—

(i) a party to the arbitration agreement referred to in article 7 was under some incapacity; or the said agreement is not valid under the law to which the parties have subjected it or, failing any indication thereon, under the law of the country where the award was made; or

(ii) the party against whom the award is invoked was not given proper notice of the appointment of an arbitrator or of the arbitral proceedings or was otherwise unable to present his case; or

(iii) the award deals with a dispute not contemplated by or not falling within the terms of the submission to arbitration, or it contains decisions on matters beyond the scope of the submission to arbitration, provided that, if the decision on matters submitted to arbitration can be separated from those not so submitted, that part of the award which contains decisions on matters submitted to arbitration may be recognised and enforced; or

(iv) the composition of the arbitral tribunal or the arbitral procedure was not in accordance with the agreement of the parties or, failing such agreement, was not in accordance with the law of the country where the arbitration took place; or

(v) the award has not yet become binding on the parties or has been set aside or suspended by a court of the country in which, or under the law of which, that award was made, or

(b) if the court finds that—

(i) the subject matter of the dispute is not capable of settlement by arbitration under the law of Scotland; or

(ii) the recognition or enforcement of the award would be contrary to public policy.

(2) If an application for setting aside or suspension of an award has been made to a court referred to in paragraph (1)(a)(v) of this article, the court where recognition or enforcement is sought may, if it considers it proper, adjourn its decision and also, on the application of the party claiming recognition or enforcement of the award, order the other party to provide appropriate security.

[4235]

UNITED NATIONS COMMISSION ON INTERNATIONAL TRADE LAW (UNCITRAL) ARBITRATION RULES

(1976)

NOTES

The Rules are reproduced with the kind permission of the United Nations. The original source of these Rules is the United Nations Commission on International Trade Law. See http://www.uncitral.org. See also the UNCITRAL Model Law, at **[4662]**.

THE GENERAL ASSEMBLY,

Recognizing the value of arbitration as a method of settling disputes arising in the context of international commercial relations,

Being convinced that the establishment of rules for ad hoc arbitration that are acceptable in countries with different legal, social and economic systems would significantly contribute to the development of harmonious international economic relations,

Bearing in mind that the Arbitration Rules of the United Nations Commission on International Trade Law have been prepared after extensive consultation with arbitral institutions and centres of international commercial arbitration,

Noting that the Arbitration Rules of the United Nations Commission on International Trade Law at its ninth session[1] after due deliberation,

1. Recommends the use of the Arbitration Rules of the United Nations Commission on International Trade Law in the settlement of disputes arising in the context of international commercial relations, particularly by reference to the Arbitration Rules in commercial contracts;

2. Requests the Secretary-General to arrange for the widest possible distribution of the Arbitration Rules.

[4236]

NOTES

1 Official Records of the General Assembly, Thirty-first Session, Supplement No 17 (A/31/17), chap V, sect C.

SECTION I
INTRODUCTORY RULES

Scope of Application

Article 1

1. Where the parties to a contract have agreed in writing* that disputes in relation to that contract shall be referred to arbitration under the UNCITRAL Arbitration Rules, then such disputes shall be settled in accordance with these Rules subject to such modification as the parties may agree in writing.

2. These Rules shall govern the arbitration except that where any of these Rules is in conflict with a provision of the law applicable to the arbitration from which the parties cannot derogate, that provision shall prevail.

**Model Arbitration Clause*

Any dispute, controversy or claim arising out of or relating to this contract, or the breach, termination or invalidity thereof, shall be settled by arbitration in accordance with the UNCITRAL arbitration Rules as at present in force.

Note – Parties may wish to consider adding:

(a) The appointing authority shall be … (name of institution or person);
(b) The number of arbitrators shall be … (one or three);
(c) The place of arbitration shall be … (town or country);
(d) The language(s) to be used in the arbitral proceedings shall be …

Notice, Calculation of Periods of Time

Article 2

1. For the purposes of these Rules, any notice, including a notification, communication or proposal, is deemed to have been received if it is physically delivered to the addressee or if it is delivered at his habitual residence, place of business or mailing address, or, if none of these can be found after making reasonable inquiry, then at the addressees last-known residence or place of business. Notice shall be deemed to have been received on the day it is so delivered.

2. For the purposes of calculating a period of time under these Rules, such period shall begin to run on the day following the day when a notice, notification, communication or proposal is received. If the last day of such period is an official holiday or a non-business day at the residence or place of business of the addressee, the period is extended until the first business day which follows. Official holidays or non-business days occurring during the running of the period of time are included in calculating the period.

Notice of Arbitration

Article 3

1. The party initiating recourse to arbitration (hereinafter called the "claimant") shall give to the other party (hereinafter called the respondent) a notice of arbitration.

2. Arbitral proceedings shall be deemed to commence on the date on which the notice of arbitration is received by the respondent.

3. The notice of arbitration shall include the following:
- (a) A demand that the dispute be referred to arbitration;
- (b) The names and addresses of the parties;
- (c) A reference to the arbitration clause or the separate arbitration agreement that is invoked;
- (d) A reference to the contract out of or in relation to which the dispute arises;
- (e) The general nature of the claim and an indication of the amount involved, if any;
- (f) The relief or remedy sought;
- (g) A proposal as to the number of arbitrators (i.e. one or three), if the parties have not previously agreed thereon.

4. The notice of arbitration may also include:
- (a) The proposals for the appointments of a sole arbitrator and an appointing authority referred to in article 6, paragraph 1;
- (b) The notification of the appointment of an arbitrator referred to in article 7;
- (c) The statement of claim referred to in article 18.

Representation and Assistance

Article 4

The parties may be represented or assisted by persons of their choice. The names and addresses of such persons must be communicated in writing to the other party; such communication must specify whether the appointment is being made for purposes of representation or assistance.

[4237]

SECTION II
COMPOSITION OF THE ARBITRAL TRIBUNAL

Number of Arbitrators

Article 5

If the parties have not previously agreed on the number of arbitrators (i.e. one or three), and if within 15 days after the receipt by the respondent of the notice of arbitration the parties have not agreed that there shall be only one arbitrator, three arbitrators shall be appointed.

Appointment of Arbitrators (Articles 6 to 8)

Article 6

1. If a sole arbitrator is to be appointed, either party may propose to the other:
- (a) The names of one or more persons, one of whom would serve as the sole arbitrator; and
- (b) If no appointing authority has been agreed upon by the parties, the name or names of one or more institutions or persons, one of whom would serve as appointing authority.

2. If within 30 days after receipt by a party of a proposal made in accordance with paragraph 1 the parties have not reached agreement on the choice of a sole arbitrator, the sole arbitrator shall be appointed by the appointing authority agreed upon by the parties. If no appointing authority has been agreed upon by the parties, or if the appointing authority agreed upon refuses to act or fails to appoint the arbitrator within 60 days of the receipt of a party's request therefor, either party may request the Secretary-General of the Permanent Court of Arbitration at The Hague to designate an appointing authority.

3. The appointing authority shall, at the request of one of the parties, appoint the sole arbitrator as promptly as possible. In making the appointment the appointing authority shall use the following list-procedure, unless both parties agree that the list-procedure should not be used or unless the appointing authority determines in its discretion that the use of the list-procedure is not appropriate for the case:
- (a) At the request of one of the parties the appointing authority shall communicate to both parties an identical list containing at least three names;
- (b) Within 15 days after the receipt of his list, each party may return the list to the

appointing authority after having deleted the name or names to which he objects and numbered the remaining names on the list in the order of his preference;

(c) After the expiration of the above period of time the appointing authority shall appoint the sole arbitrator from among the names approved on the lists returned to it and in accordance with the order of preference indicated by the parties;

(d) If for any reason the appointment cannot be made according to this procedure, the appointing authority may exercise its discretion in appointing the sole arbitrator.

4. In making the appointment, the appointing authority shall have regard to such considerations as are likely to secure the appointment of an independent and impartial arbitrator and shall take into account as well the advisability of appointing an arbitrator of a nationality other than the nationalities of the parties.

Article 7

1. If three arbitrators are to be appointed, each party shall appoint one arbitrator. The two arbitrators thus appointed shall choose the third arbitrator who will act as the presiding arbitrator of the tribunal.

2. If within 30 days after the receipt of a party's notification of the appointment of an arbitrator the other party has not notified the first party of the arbitrator he has appointed:

(a) The first party may request the appointing authority previously designated by the parties to appoint the second arbitrator; or

(b) If no such authority has been previously designated by the parties, or if the appointing authority previously designated refuses to act or fails to appoint the arbitrator within 30 days after receipt of a party's request therefor, the first party may request the Secretary-General of the Permanent Court of Arbitration at The Hague to designate the appointing authority. The first party may then request the appointing authority so designated to appoint the second arbitrator. In either case, the appointing authority may exercise its discretion in appointing the arbitrator.

3. If within 30 days after the appointment of the second arbitrator the two arbitrators have not agreed on the choice of the presiding arbitrator, the presiding arbitrator shall be appointed by an appointing authority in the same way as a sole arbitrator would be appointed under article 6.

Article 8

1. When an appointing authority is requested to appoint an arbitrator pursuant to article 6 or article 7, the party which makes the request shall send to the appointing authority a copy of the notice of arbitration, a copy of the contract out of or in relation to which the dispute has arisen and a copy of the arbitration agreement if it is not contained in the contract. The appointing authority may require from either party such information as it deems necessary to fulfil its function.

2. Where the names of one or more persons are proposed for appointment as arbitrators, their full names, addresses and nationalities shall be indicated, together with a description of their qualifications.

Challenge of Arbitrators (*Articles 9 to 12*)

Article 9

A prospective arbitrator shall disclose to those who approach him in connexion with his possible appointment any circumstances likely to give rise to justifiable doubts as to his impartiality or independence. An arbitrator, once appointed or chosen, shall disclose such circumstances to the parties unless they have already been informed by him of these circumstances.

Article 10

1. Any arbitrator may be challenged if circumstances exist that give rise to justifiable doubts as to the arbitrators impartiality or independence.

2. A party may challenge the arbitrator appointed by him only for reasons of which he becomes aware after the appointment has been made.

Article 11

1. A party who intends to challenge an arbitrator shall send notice of his challenge within 15 days after the appointment of the challenged arbitrator has been notified to the challenging party or within 15 days after the circumstances mentioned in articles 9 and 10 became known to that party.

2. The challenge shall be notified to the other party, to the arbitrator who is challenged and to the other members of the arbitral tribunal. The notification shall be in writing and shall state the reasons for the challenge.

3. When an arbitrator has been challenged by one party, the other party may agree to the challenge. The arbitrator may also, after the challenge, withdraw from his office. In neither case does this imply acceptance of the validity of the grounds for the challenge. In both cases the procedure provided in article 6 or 7 shall be used in full for the appointment of the substitute arbitrator, even if during the process of appointing the challenged arbitrator a party had failed to exercise his right to appoint or to participate in the appointment.

Article 12

1. If the other party does not agree to the challenge and the challenged arbitrator does not withdraw, the decision on the challenge will be made:

(a) When the initial appointment was made by an appointing authority, by that authority;

(b) When the initial appointment was not made by an appointing authority, but an appointing authority has been previously designated, by that authority;

(c) In all other cases, by the appointing authority to be designated in accordance with the procedure for designating an appointing authority as provided for in article 6.

2. If the appointing authority sustains the challenge, a substitute arbitrator shall be appointed or chosen pursuant to the procedure applicable to the appointment or choice of an arbitrator as provided in articles 6 to 9 except that, when this procedure would call for the designation of an appointing authority, the appointment of the arbitrator shall be made by the appointing authority which decided on the challenge.

Replacement of an Arbitrator

Article 13

1. In the event of the death or resignation of an arbitrator during the course of the arbitral proceedings, a substitute arbitrator shall be appointed or chosen pursuant to the procedure provided for in articles 6 to 9 that was applicable to the appointment or choice of the arbitrator being replaced.

2. In the event that an arbitrator fails to act or in the event of the de jure or de facto impossibility of his performing his functions, the procedure in respect of the challenge and replacement of an arbitrator as provided in the preceding articles shall apply.

Repetition of Hearings in the Event of the Replacement of an Arbitrator

Article 14

If under articles 11 to 13 the sole or presiding arbitrator is replaced, any hearings held previously shall be repeated; if any other arbitrator is replaced, such prior hearings may be repeated at the discretion of the arbitral tribunal.

[4238]

SECTION III
ARBITRAL PROCEEDINGS

General provisions

Article 15

1. Subject to these Rules, the arbitral tribunal may conduct the arbitration in such manner as it considers appropriate, provided that the parties are treated with equality and that at any stage of the proceedings each party is given a full opportunity of presenting his case.

2. If either party so requests at any stage of the proceedings, the arbitral tribunal shall hold hearings for the presentation of evidence by witnesses, including expert witnesses, or for oral argument. In the absence of such a request, the arbitral tribunal shall decide whether to hold such hearings or whether the proceedings shall be conducted on the basis of documents and other materials.

3. All documents or information supplied to the arbitral tribunal by one party shall at the same time be communicated by that party to the other party.

Place of Arbitration

Article 16

1. Unless the parties have agreed upon the place where the arbitration is to be held, such place shall be determined by the arbitral tribunal, having regard to the circumstances of the arbitration.

2. The arbitral tribunal may determine the locale of the arbitration within the country agreed upon by the parties. It may hear witnesses and hold meetings for consultation among its members at any place it deems appropriate, having regard to the circumstances of the arbitration.

3. The arbitral tribunal may meet at any place it deems appropriate for the inspection of goods, other property or documents. The parties shall be given sufficient notice to enable them to be present at such inspection.

4. The award shall be made at the place of arbitration.

Language

Article 17

1. Subject to an agreement by the parties, the arbitral tribunal shall, promptly after its appointment, determine the language or languages to be used in the proceedings. This determination shall apply to the statement of claim, the statement of defence, and any further written statements and, if oral hearings take place, to the language or languages to be used in such hearings.

2. The arbitral tribunal may order that any documents annexed to the statement of claim or statement of defence, and any supplementary documents or exhibits submitted in the course of the proceedings, delivered in their original language, shall be accompanied by a translation into the language or languages agreed upon by the parties or determined by the arbitral tribunal.

Statement of Claim

Article 18

1. Unless the statement of claim was contained in the notice of arbitration, within a period of time to be determined by the arbitral tribunal, the claimant shall communicate his statement of claim in writing to the respondent and to each of the arbitrators. A copy of the contract, and of the arbitration agreement if not contained in the contract, shall be annexed thereto.

2. The statement of claim shall include the following particulars:
   (a) The names and addresses of the parties;
   (b) A statement of the facts supporting the claim;
   (c) The points at issue;
   (d) The relief or remedy sought. The claimant may annex to his statement of claim all documents he deems relevant or may add a reference to the documents or other evidence he will submit.

Statement of Defence

Article 19

1. Within a period of time to be determined by the arbitral tribunal, the respondent shall communicate his statement of defence in writing to the claimant and to each of the arbitrators.

2. The statement of defence shall reply to the particulars (b), (c) and (d) of the statement of claim (article 18, para 2). The respondent may annex to his statement the documents on which he relies for his defence or may add a reference to the documents or other evidence he will submit.

3. In his statement of defence, or at a later stage in the arbitral proceedings if the arbitral tribunal decides that the delay was justified under the circumstances, the respondent may make a counter-claim arising out of the same contract or rely on a claim arising out of the same contract for the purpose of a set-off.

4. The provisions of article 18, paragraph 2, shall apply to a counter-claim and a claim relied on for the purpose of a set-off.

Amendments to the Claim or Defence

Article 20

During the course of the arbitral proceedings either party may amend or supplement his claim or defence unless the arbitral tribunal considers it inappropriate to allow such amendment having regard to the delay in making it or prejudice to the other party or any other circumstances. However, a claim may not be amended in such a manner that the amended claim falls outside the scope of the arbitration clause or separate arbitration agreement.

Pleas as to the Jurisdiction of the Arbitral Tribunal

Article 21

1. The arbitral tribunal shall have the power to rule on objections that it has no jurisdiction, including any objections with respect to the existence or validity of the arbitration clause or of the separate arbitration agreement.

2. The arbitral tribunal shall have the power to determine the existence or the validity of the contract of which an arbitration clause forms a part. For the purposes of article 21, an arbitration clause which forms part of a contract and which provides for arbitration under these Rules shall be treated as an agreement independent of the other terms of the contract. A decision by the arbitral tribunal that the contract is null and void shall not entail ipso jure the invalidity of the arbitration clause.

3. A plea that the arbitral tribunal does not have jurisdiction shall be raised not later than in the statement of defence or, with respect to a counter-claim, in the reply to the counter-claim.

4. In general, the arbitral tribunal should rule on a plea concerning its jurisdiction as a preliminary question. However, the arbitral tribunal may proceed with the arbitration and rule on such a plea in their final award.

Further Written Statements

Article 22

The arbitral tribunal shall decide which further written statements, in addition to the statement of claim and the statement of defence, shall be required from the parties or may be presented by them and shall fix the periods of time for communicating such statements.

Periods of Time

Article 23

The periods of time fixed by the arbitral tribunal for the communication of written statements (including the statement of claim and statement of defence) should not exceed 45 days. However, the arbitral tribunal may extend the time-limits if it concludes that an extension is justified.

Evidence and Hearings (Articles 24 and 25)

Article 24

1. Each party shall have the burden of proving the facts relied on to support his claim or defence.

2. The arbitral tribunal may, if it considers it appropriate, require a party to deliver to the tribunal and to the other party, within such a period of time as the arbitral tribunal shall decide, a summary of the documents and other evidence which that party intends to present in support of the facts in issue set out in his statement of claim or statement of defence.

3. At any time during the arbitral proceedings the arbitral tribunal may require the parties to produce documents, exhibits or other evidence within such a period of time as the tribunal shall determine.

Article 25

1. In the event of an oral hearing, the arbitral tribunal shall give the parties adequate advance notice of the date, time and place thereof.

2. If witnesses are to be heard, at least 15 days before the hearing each party shall communicate to the arbitral tribunal and to the other party the names and addresses of the witnesses he intends to present, the subject upon and the languages in which such witnesses will give their testimony.

3. The arbitral tribunal shall make arrangements for the translation of oral statements made at a hearing and for a record of the hearing if either is deemed necessary by the tribunal under the circumstances of the case, or if the parties have agreed thereto and have communicated such agreement to the tribunal at least 15 days before the hearing.

4. Hearings shall be held in camera unless the parties agree otherwise. The arbitral tribunal may require the retirement of any witness or witnesses during the testimony of other witnesses. The arbitral tribunal is free to determine the manner in which witnesses are examined.

5. Evidence of witnesses may also be presented in the form of written statements signed by them.

6. The arbitral tribunal shall determine the admissibility, relevance, materiality and weight of the evidence offered.

Interim Measures of Protection

Article 26

1. At the request of either party, the arbitral tribunal may take any interim measures it deems necessary in respect of the subject-matter of the dispute, including measures for the conservation of the goods forming the subject-matter in dispute, such as ordering their deposit with a third person or the sale of perishable goods.

2. Such interim measures may be established in the form of an interim award. The arbitral tribunal shall be entitled to require security for the costs of such measures.

3. A request for interim measures addressed by any party to a judicial authority shall not be deemed incompatible with the agreement to arbitrate, or as a waiver of that agreement.

Experts

Article 27

1. The arbitral tribunal may appoint one or more experts to report to it, in writing, on specific issues to be determined by the tribunal. A copy of the experts terms of reference, established by the arbitral tribunal, shall be communicated to the parties.

2. The parties shall give the expert any relevant information or produce for his inspection any relevant documents or goods that he may require of them. Any dispute between a party and such expert as to the relevance of the required information or production shall be referred to the arbitral tribunal for decision.

3. Upon receipt of the experts report, the arbitral tribunal shall communicate a copy of the report to the parties who shall be given the opportunity to express, in writing, their opinion on the report. A party shall be entitled to examine any document on which the expert has relied in his report.

4. At the request of either party the expert, after delivery of the report, may be heard at a hearing where the parties shall have the opportunity to be present and to interrogate the expert. At this hearing either party may present expert witnesses in order to testify on the points at issue. The provisions of article 25 shall be applicable to such proceedings.

Default

Article 28

1. If, within the period of time fixed by the arbitral tribunal, the claimant has failed to communicate his claim without showing sufficient cause for such failure, the arbitral tribunal shall issue an order for the termination of the arbitral proceedings. If, within the period of time fixed by the arbitral tribunal, the respondent has failed to communicate his statement of defence without showing sufficient cause for such failure, the arbitral tribunal shall order that the proceedings continue.

2. If one of the parties, duly notified under these Rules, fails to appear at a hearing, without showing sufficient cause for such failure, the arbitral tribunal may proceed with the arbitration.

3. If one of the parties, duly invited to produce documentary evidence, fails to do so within the established period of time, without showing sufficient cause for such failure, the arbitral tribunal may make the award on the evidence before it.

Closure of Hearings

Article 29

1. The arbitral tribunal may inquire of the parties if they have any further proof to offer or witnesses to be heard or submissions to make and, if there are none, it may declare the hearings closed.

2. The arbitral tribunal may, if it considers it necessary owing to exceptional circumstances, decide, on its own motion or upon application of a party, to reopen the hearings at any time before the award is made.

Waiver of Rules

Article 30

A party who knows that any provision of, or requirement under, these Rules has not been complied with and yet proceeds with the arbitration without promptly stating his objection to such non-compliance, shall be deemed to have waived his right to object.

[4239]

SECTION IV
THE AWARD

DECISIONS

Article 31

1. When there are three arbitrators, any award or other decision of the arbitral tribunal shall be made by a majority of the arbitrators.

2. In the case of questions of procedure, when there is no majority or when the arbitral tribunal so authorizes, the presiding arbitrator may decide on his own, subject to revision, if any, by the arbitral tribunal.

Form and Effect of the Award

Article 32

1. In addition to making a final award, the arbitral tribunal shall be entitled to make interim, interlocutory, or partial awards.

2. The award shall be made in writing and shall be final and binding on the parties. The parties undertake to carry out the award without delay.

3. The arbitral tribunal shall state the reasons upon which the award is based, unless the parties have agreed that no reasons are to be given.

4. An award shall be signed by the arbitrators and it shall contain the date on which and the place where the award was made. Where there are three arbitrators and one of them fails to sign, the award shall state the reason for the absence of the signature.

5. The award may be made public only with the consent of both parties.

6. Copies of the award signed by the arbitrators shall be communicated to the parties by the arbitral tribunal.

7. If the arbitration law of the country where the award is made requires that the award be filed or registered by the arbitral tribunal, the tribunal shall comply with this requirement within the period of time required by law.

Applicable Law, Amiable Compositeur

Article 33

1. The arbitral tribunal shall apply the law designated by the parties as applicable to the substance of the dispute. Failing such designation by the parties, the arbitral tribunal shall apply the law determined by the conflict of laws rules which it considers applicable.

2. The arbitral tribunal shall decide as amiable compositeur or ex aequo et bono only if the parties have expressly authorized the arbitral tribunal to do so and if the law applicable to the arbitral procedure permits such arbitration.

3. In all cases, the arbitral tribunal shall decide in accordance with the terms of the contract and shall take into account the usages of the trade applicable to the transaction.

Settlement or Other Grounds for Termination

Article 34

1. If, before the award is made, the parties agree on a settlement of the dispute, the arbitral tribunal shall either issue an order for the termination of the arbitral proceedings or, if requested by both parties and accepted by the tribunal, record the settlement in the form of an arbitral award on agreed terms. The arbitral tribunal is not obliged to give reasons for such an award.

2. If, before the award is made, the continuation of the arbitral proceedings becomes unnecessary or impossible for any reason not mentioned in paragraph 1, the arbitral tribunal shall inform the parties of its intention to issue an order for the termination of the proceedings. The arbitral tribunal shall have the power to issue such an order unless a party raises justifiable grounds for objection.

3. Copies of the order for termination of the arbitral proceedings or of the arbitral award on agreed terms, signed by the arbitrators, shall be communicated by the arbitral tribunal to the parties. Where an arbitral award on agreed terms is made, the provisions of article 32, paragraphs 2 and 4 to 7, shall apply.

Interpretation of the Award

Article 35

1. Within 30 days after the receipt of the award, either party, with notice to the other party, may request that the arbitral tribunal give an interpretation of the award.

2. The interpretation shall be given in writing within 45 days after the receipt of the request. The interpretation shall form part of the award and the provisions of article 32, paragraphs 2 to 7, shall apply.

Correction of the Award

Article 36

1. Within 30 days after the receipt of the award, either party, with notice to the other party, may request the arbitral tribunal to correct in the award any errors in computation, any clerical or typographical errors, or any errors of similar nature. The arbitral tribunal may within 30 days after the communication of the award make such corrections on its own initiative.

2. Such corrections shall be in writing, and the provisions of article 32, paragraphs 2 to 7, shall apply.

Additional Award

Article 37

1. Within 30 days after the receipt of the award, either party, with notice to the other party, may request the arbitral tribunal to make an additional award as to claims presented in the arbitral proceedings but omitted from the award.

2. If the arbitral tribunal considers the request for an additional award to be justified and considers that the omission can be rectified without any further hearings or evidence, it shall complete its award within 60 days after the receipt of the request.

3. When an additional award is made, the provisions of article 32, paragraphs 2 to 7, shall apply.

Costs (Articles 38 to 40)

Article 38

The arbitral tribunal shall fix the costs of arbitration in its award. The term "costs" includes only:

(a) The fees of the arbitral tribunal to be stated separately as to each arbitrator and to be fixed by the tribunal itself in accordance with article 39;
(b) The travel and other expenses incurred by the arbitrators;
(c) The costs of expert advice and of other assistance required by the arbitral tribunal;
(d) The travel and other expenses of witnesses to the extent such expenses are approved by the arbitral tribunal;
(e) The costs for legal representation and assistance of the successful party if such costs were claimed during the arbitral proceedings, and only to the extent that the arbitral tribunal determines that the amount of such costs is reasonable;
(f) Any fees and expenses of the appointing authority as well as the expenses of the Secretary-General of the Permanent Court of Arbitration at The Hague.

Article 39

1. The fees of the arbitral tribunal shall be reasonable in amount, taking into account the amount in dispute, the complexity of the subject-matter, the time spent by the arbitrators and any other relevant circumstances of the case.

2. If an appointing authority has been agreed upon by the parties or designated by the Secretary-General of the Permanent Court of Arbitration at The Hague, and if that authority has issued a schedule of fees for arbitrators in international cases which it administers, the arbitral tribunal in fixing its fees shall take that schedule of fees into account to the extent that it considers appropriate in the circumstances of the case.

3. If such appointing authority has not issued a schedule of fees for arbitrators in international cases, any party may at any time request the appointing authority to furnish a statement setting forth the basis for establishing fees which is customarily followed in international cases in which the authority appoints arbitrators. If the appointing authority consents to provide such a statement, the arbitral tribunal in fixing its fees shall take such information into account to the extent that it considers appropriate in the circumstances of the case.

4. In cases referred to in paragraphs 2 and 3, when a party so requests and the appointing authority consents to perform the function, the arbitral tribunal shall fix its fees only after consultation with the appointing authority which may make any comment it deems appropriate to the arbitral tribunal concerning the fees.

Article 40

1. Except as provided in paragraph 2, the costs of arbitration shall in principle be borne by the unsuccessful party. However, the arbitral tribunal may apportion each of such costs between the parties if it determines that apportionment is reasonable, taking into account the circumstances of the case.

2. With respect to the costs of legal representation and assistance referred to in article 38, paragraph (e), the arbitral tribunal, taking into account the circumstances of the case, shall be free to determine which party shall bear such costs or may apportion such costs between the parties if it determines that apportionment is reasonable.

3. When the arbitral tribunal issues an order for the termination of the arbitral proceedings or makes an award on agreed terms, it shall fix the costs of arbitration referred to in article 38 and article 39, paragraph 1, in the text of that order or award.

4. No additional fees may be charged by an arbitral tribunal for interpretation or correction or completion of its award under articles 35 to 37.

Deposit of Costs

Article 41

1. The arbitral tribunal, on its establishment, may request each party to deposit an equal amount as an advance for the costs referred to in article 38, paragraphs (a), (b) and (c).

2. During the course of the arbitral proceedings the arbitral tribunal may request supplementary deposits from the parties.

3. If an appointing authority has been agreed upon by the parties or designated by the Secretary-General of the Permanent Court of Arbitration at The Hague, and when a party so requests and the appointing authority consents to perform the function, the arbitral tribunal shall fix the amounts of any deposits or supplementary deposits only after consultation with the appointing authority which may make any comments to the arbitral tribunal which it deems appropriate concerning the amount of such deposits and supplementary deposits.

4. If the required deposits are not paid in full within 30 days after the receipt of the request, the arbitral tribunal shall so inform the parties in order that one or another of them may make the required payment. If such payment is not made, the arbitral tribunal may order the suspension or termination of the arbitral proceedings.

5. After the award has been made, the arbitral tribunal shall render an accounting to the parties of the deposits received and return any unexpended balance to the parties.

NOTE Official Records of the General

[4240]

RULES OF ARBITRATION OF THE INTERNATIONAL CHAMBER OF COMMERCE

(1998)

NOTES

The current Rules of Arbitration of the International Chamber of Commerce came into effect on 1 January 1998. They include the costs scales effective as of 1 July 2003. The publisher and copyright holder of these Rules is the International Chamber of Commerce (ICC). The Rules are available from the ICC International Court of Arbitration, 38 Cours Albert 1er, 75008 Paris, France, and on the website http://www.iccarbitration.org.

Introductory Provisions

Article 1

International Court of Arbitration

1. The International Court of Arbitration (the "Court") of the International Chamber of Commerce (the "ICC") is the arbitration body attached to the ICC. The statutes of the Court are set forth in Appendix I. Members of the Court are appointed by the World Council of the ICC. The function of the Court is to provide for the settlement by arbitration of business disputes of an international character in accordance with the Rules of Arbitration of the International Chamber of Commerce (the "Rules"). If so empowered by an arbitration agreement, the Court shall also provide for the settlement by arbitration in accordance with these Rules of business disputes not of an international character.

2. The Court does not itself settle disputes. It has the function of ensuring the application of these Rules. It draws up its own Internal Rules (Appendix II).

3. The Chairman of the Court or, in the Chairman's absence or otherwise at his request, one of its Vice-Chairmen shall have the power to take urgent decisions on behalf of the Court, provided that any such decision is reported to the Court at its next session.

4. As provided for in its Internal Rules, the Court may delegate to one or more committees composed of its members the power to take certain decisions, provided that any such decision is reported to the Court at its next session.

5. The Secretariat of the Court (the "Secretariat") under the direction of its Secretary General (the "Secretary General") shall have its seat at the headquarters of the ICC.

[4241]

Article 2

Definitions

In these Rules:

(i) "Arbitral Tribunal" includes one or more arbitrators.

(ii) "Claimant" includes one or more claimants and "Respondent" includes one or more respondents.

(iii) "Award" includes, *inter alia*, an interim, partial or final Award.

[4242]

Article 3

Written Notifications or Communications; Time Limits

1. All pleadings and other written communications submitted by any party, as well as all documents annexed thereto, shall be supplied in a number of copies sufficient to provide one copy for each party, plus one for each arbitrator, and one for the Secretariat. A copy of any communication from the Arbitral Tribunal to the parties shall be sent to the Secretariat.

2. All notifications or communications from the Secretariat and the Arbitral Tribunal shall be made to the last address of the party or its representative for whom the same are intended, as notified either by the party in question or by the other party. Such notification or communication may be made by delivery against receipt, registered post, courier, facsimile transmission, telex, telegram or any other means of telecommunication that provides a record of the sending thereof.

3. A notification or communication shall be deemed to have been made on the day it was received by the party itself or by its representative, or would have been received if made in accordance with the preceding paragraph.

4. Periods of time specified in or fixed under the present Rules, shall start to run on the day following the date a notification or communication is deemed to have been made in accordance with the preceding paragraph. When the day next following such date is an official holiday, or a non-business day in the country where the notification or communication is deemed to have been made, the period of time shall commence on the first following business day. Official holidays and non-business days are included in the calculation of the period of time. If the last day of the relevant period of time granted is an official holiday or a non-business day in the country where the notification or communication is deemed to have been made, the period of time shall expire at the end of the first following business day.

[4243]

Commencing the Arbitration

Article 4

Request for Arbitration

1. A party wishing to have recourse to arbitration under these Rules shall submit its Request for Arbitration (the "Request") to the Secretariat, which shall notify the Claimant and Respondent of the receipt of the Request and the date of such receipt.

2. The date on which the Request is received by the Secretariat shall, for all purposes, be deemed to be the date of the commencement of the arbitral proceedings.

3. The Request shall, *inter alia*, contain the following information:

(a) the name in full, description and address of each of the parties;

(b) a description of the nature and circumstances of the dispute giving rise to the claim(s);

(c) a statement of the relief sought, including, to the extent possible, an indication of any amount(s) claimed;
(d) the relevant agreements and, in particular, the arbitration agreement;
(e) all relevant particulars concerning the number of arbitrators and their choice in accordance with the provisions of Articles 8, 9 and 10, and any nomination of an arbitrator required thereby; and
(f) any comments as to the place of arbitration, the applicable rules of law and the language of the arbitration.

4. Together with the Request, the Claimant shall submit the number of copies thereof required by Article 3(1) and shall make the advance payment on administrative expenses required by Appendix III ("Arbitration Costs and Fees") in force on the date the Request is submitted. In the event that the Claimant fails to comply with either of these requirements, the Secretariat may fix a time limit within which the Claimant must comply, failing which the file shall be closed without prejudice to the right of the Claimant to submit the same claims at a later date in another Request.

5. The Secretariat shall send a copy of the Request and the documents annexed thereto to the Respondent for its Answer to the Request once the Secretariat has sufficient copies of the Request and the required advance payment.

6. When a party submits a Request in connection with a legal relationship in respect of which arbitration proceedings between the same parties are already pending under these Rules, the Court may, at the request of a party, decide to include the claims contained in the Request in the pending proceedings provided that the Terms of Reference have not been signed or approved by the Court. Once the Terms of Reference have been signed or approved by the Court, claims may only be included in the pending proceedings subject to the provisions of Article 19.

[4244]

Article 5

Answer to the Request; Counterclaims

1. Within 30 days from the receipt of the Request from the Secretariat, the Respondent shall file an Answer (the "Answer") which shall, *inter alia*, contain the following information:
(a) its name in full, description and address;
(b) its comments as to the nature and circumstances of the dispute giving rise to the claim(s);
(c) its response to the relief sought;
(d) any comments concerning the number of arbitrators and their choice in light of the Claimant's proposals and in accordance with the provisions of Articles 8, 9 and 10, and any nomination of an arbitrator required thereby; and
(e) any comments as to the place of arbitration, the applicable rules of law and the language of the arbitration.

2. The Secretariat may grant the Respondent an extension of the time for filing the Answer, provided the application for such an extension contains the Respondent's comments concerning the number of arbitrators and their choice and, where required by Articles 8, 9 and 10, the nomination of an arbitrator. If the Respondent fails to do so, the Court shall proceed in accordance with these Rules.

3. The Answer shall be supplied to the Secretariat in the number of copies specified by Article 3(1).

4. A copy of the Answer and the documents annexed thereto shall be communicated by the Secretariat to the Claimant.

5. Any counterclaim(s) made by the Respondent shall be filed with its Answer and shall provide:
(a) a description of the nature and circumstances of the dispute giving rise to the counterclaim(s); and
(b) a statement of the relief sought, including, to the extent possible, an indication of any amount(s) counterclaimed.

6. The Claimant shall file a reply to any counterclaim within 30 days from the date of receipt of the counterclaim(s) communicated by the Secretariat. The Secretariat may grant the Claimant an extension of time for filing the reply.

[4245]

Article 6

Effect of the Arbitration Agreement

1. Where the parties have agreed to submit to arbitration under the Rules, they shall be deemed to have submitted *ipso facto* to the Rules in effect on the date of commencement of the arbitration proceedings, unless they have agreed to submit to the Rules in effect on the date of their arbitration agreement.

2. If the Respondent does not file an Answer, as provided by Article 5, or if any party raises one or more pleas concerning the existence, validity or scope of the arbitration agreement, the Court may decide, without prejudice to the admissibility or merits of the plea or pleas, that the arbitration shall proceed if it is *prima facie* satisfied that an arbitration agreement under the Rules may exist. In such a case, any decision as to the jurisdiction of the Arbitral Tribunal shall be taken by the Arbitral Tribunal itself. If the Court is not so satisfied, the parties shall be notified that the arbitration cannot proceed. In such a case, any party retains the right to ask any court having jurisdiction whether or not there is a binding arbitration agreement.

3. If any of the parties refuses or fails to take part in the arbitration or any stage thereof, the arbitration shall proceed notwithstanding such refusal or failure.

4. Unless otherwise agreed, the Arbitral Tribunal shall not cease to have jurisdiction by reason of any claim that the contract is null and void or allegation that it is non-existent, provided that the Arbitral Tribunal upholds the validity of the arbitration agreement. The Arbitral Tribunal shall continue to have jurisdiction to determine the respective rights of the parties and to adjudicate their claims and pleas even though the contract itself may be non-existent or null and void.

[4246]

The Arbitral Tribunal

Article 7

General Provisions

1. Every arbitrator must be and remain independent of the parties involved in the arbitration.

2. Before appointment or confirmation, a prospective arbitrator shall sign a statement of independence and disclose in writing to the Secretariat any facts or circumstances which might be of such a nature as to call into question the arbitrator's independence in the eyes of the parties. The Secretariat shall provide such information to the parties in writing and fix a time limit for any comments from them.

3. An arbitrator shall immediately disclose in writing to the Secretariat and to the parties any facts or circumstances of a similar nature which may arise during the arbitration.

4. The decisions of the Court as to the appointment, confirmation, challenge or replacement of an arbitrator shall be final and the reasons for such decisions shall not be communicated.

5. By accepting to serve, every arbitrator undertakes to carry out his responsibilities in accordance with these Rules.

6. Insofar as the parties have not provided otherwise, the Arbitral Tribunal shall be constituted in accordance with the provisions of Articles 8, 9 and 10.

[4247]

Article 8

Number of Arbitrators

1. The disputes shall be decided by a sole arbitrator or by three arbitrators.

2. Where the parties have not agreed upon the number of arbitrators, the Court shall appoint a sole arbitrator, save where it appears to the Court that the dispute is such as to warrant the appointment of three arbitrators. In such case, the Claimant shall nominate an arbitrator within a period of 15 days from the receipt of the notification of the decision of the

Court, and the Respondent shall nominate an arbitrator within a period of 15 days from the receipt of the notification of the nomination made by the Claimant.

3. Where the parties have agreed that the dispute shall be settled by a sole arbitrator, they may, by agreement, nominate the sole arbitrator for confirmation. If the parties fail to nominate a sole arbitrator within 30 days from the date when the Claimant's Request for Arbitration has been received by the other party, or within such additional time as may be allowed by the Secretariat, the sole arbitrator shall be appointed by the Court.

4. Where the dispute is to be referred to three arbitrators, each party shall nominate in the Request and the Answer, respectively, one arbitrator for confirmation. If a party fails to nominate an arbitrator, the appointment shall be made by the Court. The third arbitrator, who will act as chairman of the Arbitral Tribunal, shall be appointed by the Court, unless the parties have agreed upon another procedure for such appointment, in which case the nomination will be subject to confirmation pursuant to Article 9. Should such procedure not result in a nomination within the time limit fixed by the parties or the Court, the third arbitrator shall be appointed by the Court.

[4248]

Article 9

Appointment and Confirmation of the Arbitrators

1. In confirming or appointing arbitrators, the Court shall consider the prospective arbitrator's nationality, residence and other relationships with the countries of which the parties or the other arbitrators are nationals and the prospective arbitrator's availability and ability to conduct the arbitration in accordance with these Rules. The same shall apply where the Secretary General confirms arbitrators pursuant to Article 9(2).

2. The Secretary General may confirm as co-arbitrators, sole arbitrators and chairmen of Arbitral Tribunals persons nominated by the parties or pursuant to their particular agreements, provided they have filed a statement of independence without qualification or a qualified statement of independence has not given rise to objections. Such confirmation shall be reported to the Court at its next session. If the Secretary General considers that a co-arbitrator, sole arbitrator or chairman of an Arbitral Tribunal should not be confirmed, the matter shall be submitted to the Court.

3. Where the Court is to appoint a sole arbitrator or the chairman of an Arbitral Tribunal, it shall make the appointment upon a proposal of a National Committee of the ICC that it considers to be appropriate. If the Court does not accept the proposal made, or if the National Committee fails to make the proposal requested within the time limit fixed by the Court, the Court may repeat its request or may request a proposal from another National Committee that it considers to be appropriate.

4. Where the Court considers that the circumstances so demand, it may choose the sole arbitrator or the chairman of the Arbitral Tribunal from a country where there is no National Committee, provided that neither of the parties objects within the time limit fixed by the Court.

5. The sole arbitrator or the chairman of the Arbitral Tribunal shall be of a nationality other than those of the parties. However, in suitable circumstances and provided that neither of the parties objects within the time limit fixed by the Court, the sole arbitrator or the chairman of the Arbitral Tribunal may be chosen from a country of which any of the parties is a national.

6. Where the Court is to appoint an arbitrator on behalf of a party which has failed to nominate one, it shall make the appointment upon a proposal of the National Committee of the country of which that party is a national. If the Court does not accept the proposal made, or if the National Committee fails to make the proposal requested within the time limit fixed by the Court, or if the country of which the said party is a national has no National Committee, the Court shall be at liberty to choose any person whom it regards as suitable. The Secretariat shall inform the National Committee, if one exists, of the country of which such person is a national.

[4249]

Article 10

Multiple Parties

1. Where there are multiple parties, whether as Claimant or as Respondent, and where the dispute is to be referred to three arbitrators, the multiple Claimants, jointly, and the multiple Respondents, jointly, shall nominate an arbitrator for confirmation pursuant to Article 9.

2. In the absence of such a joint nomination and where all parties are unable to agree to a method for the constitution of the Arbitral Tribunal, the Court may appoint each member of the Arbitral Tribunal and shall designate one of them to act as chairman. In such case, the Court shall be at liberty to choose any person it regards as suitable to act as arbitrator, applying Article 9 when it considers this appropriate.

[4250]

Article 11

Challenge of Arbitrators

1. A challenge of an arbitrator, whether for an alleged lack of independence or otherwise, shall be made by the submission to the Secretariat of a written statement specifying the facts and circumstances on which the challenge is based.

2. For a challenge to be admissible, it must be sent by a party either within 30 days from receipt by that party of the notification of the appointment or confirmation of the arbitrator, or within 30 days from the date when the party making the challenge was informed of the facts and circumstances on which the challenge is based if such date is subsequent to the receipt of such notification.

3. The Court shall decide on the admissibility and, at the same time, if necessary, on the merits of a challenge after the Secretariat has afforded an opportunity for the arbitrator concerned, the other party or parties and any other members of the Arbitral Tribunal to comment in writing within a suitable period of time. Such comments shall be communicated to the parties and to the arbitrators.

[4251]

Article 12

Replacement of Arbitrators

1. An arbitrator shall be replaced upon his death, upon the acceptance by the Court of the arbitrator's resignation, upon acceptance by the Court of a challenge or, upon the request of all the parties.

2. An arbitrator shall also be replaced on the Court's own initiative when it decides that he is prevented *de jure* or *de facto* from fulfilling his functions, or that he is not fulfilling his functions in accordance with the Rules or within the prescribed time limits.

3. When, on the basis of information that has come to its attention, the Court considers applying Article 12(2), it shall decide on the matter after the arbitrator concerned, the parties and any other members of the Arbitral Tribunal have had an opportunity to comment in writing within a suitable period of time. Such comments shall be communicated to the parties and to the arbitrators.

4. When an arbitrator is to be replaced, the Court has discretion to decide whether or not to follow the original nominating process. Once reconstituted, and after having invited the parties to comment, the Arbitral Tribunal shall determine if and to what extent prior proceedings shall be repeated before the reconstituted Arbitral Tribunal.

5. Subsequent to the closing of the proceedings, instead of replacing an arbitrator who has died or been removed by the Court pursuant to Articles 12(1) and 12(2), the Court may decide, when it considers it appropriate, that the remaining arbitrators shall continue the arbitration. In making such determination, the Court shall take into account the views of the remaining arbitrators and of the parties and such other matters that it considers appropriate in the circumstances.

[4252]

The Arbitral Proceedings

Article 13

Transmission of the File to the Arbitral Tribunal

The Secretariat shall transmit the file to the Arbitral Tribunal as soon as it has been constituted, provided the advance on costs requested by the Secretariat at this stage has been paid.

[4253]

Article 14

Place of the Arbitration

1. The place of the arbitration shall be fixed by the Court unless agreed upon by the parties.

2. The Arbitral Tribunal may, after consultation with the parties, conduct hearings and meetings at any location it considers appropriate unless otherwise agreed by the parties.

3. The Arbitral Tribunal may deliberate at any location it considers appropriate.

[4254]

Article 15

Rules Governing the Proceedings

1. The proceedings before the Arbitral Tribunal shall be governed by these Rules, and, where these Rules are silent by any rules which the parties or, failing them, the Arbitral Tribunal may settle on, whether or not reference is thereby made to the rules of procedure of a national law to be applied to the arbitration.

2. In all cases, the Arbitral Tribunal shall act fairly and impartially and ensure that each party has a reasonable opportunity to present its case.

[4255]

Article 16

Language of the Arbitration

In the absence of an agreement by the parties, the Arbitral Tribunal shall determine the language or languages of the arbitration, due regard being given to all relevant circumstances, including the language of the contract.

[4256]

Article 17

Applicable Rules of Law

1. The parties shall be free to agree upon the rules of law to be applied by the Arbitral Tribunal to the merits of the dispute. In the absence of any such agreement, the Arbitral Tribunal shall apply the rules of law which it determines to be appropriate.

2. In all cases the Arbitral Tribunal shall take account of the provisions of the contract and the relevant trade usages.

3. The Arbitral Tribunal shall assume the powers of an *amiable compositeur* or decide *ex aequo et bono* only if the parties have agreed to give it such powers.

[4257]

Article 18

Terms of Reference; Procedural Timetable

1. As soon as it has received the file from the Secretariat, the Arbitral Tribunal shall draw up, on the basis of documents or in the presence of the parties and in the light of their most recent submissions, a document defining its Terms of Reference. This document shall include the following particulars:

(a) the full names and descriptions of the parties;

(b) the addresses of the parties to which notifications and communications arising in the course of the arbitration may be made;
(c) a summary of the parties' respective claims and of the relief sought by each party, with an indication to the extent possible of the amounts claimed or counterclaimed;
(d) unless the Arbitral Tribunal considers it inappropriate, a list of issues to be determined;
(e) the full names, descriptions and addresses of the arbitrators;
(f) the place of the arbitration; and
(g) particulars of the applicable procedural rules and, if such is the case, reference to the power conferred upon the Arbitral Tribunal to act as *amiable compositeur* or to decide *ex aequo et bono*.

2. The Terms of Reference shall be signed by the parties and the Arbitral Tribunal. Within two months of the date on which the file has been transmitted to it, the Arbitral Tribunal shall transmit to the Court the Terms of Reference signed by it and by the parties. The Court may extend this time limit pursuant to a reasoned request from the Arbitral Tribunal or on its own initiative if it decides it is necessary to do so.

3. If any of the parties refuses to take part in the drawing up of the Terms of Reference or to sign the same, they shall be submitted to the Court for approval. When the Terms of Reference have been signed in accordance with Article 18(2) or approved by the Court, the arbitration shall proceed.

4. When drawing up the Terms of Reference, or as soon as possible thereafter, the Arbitral Tribunal, after having consulted the parties, shall establish in a separate document a provisional timetable that it intends to follow for the conduct of the arbitration and shall communicate it to the Court and the parties. Any subsequent modifications of the provisional timetable shall be communicated to the Court and the parties.

[4258]

Article 19

New Claims

After the Terms of Reference have been signed or approved by the Court, no party shall make new claims or counterclaims which fall outside the limits of the Terms of Reference unless it has been authorized to do so by the Arbitral Tribunal, which shall consider the nature of such new claims or counterclaims, the stage of the arbitration and other relevant circumstances.

[4259]

Article 20

Establishing the Facts of the Case

1. The Arbitral Tribunal shall proceed within as short a time as possible to establish the facts of the case by all appropriate means.

2. After studying the written submissions of the parties and all documents relied upon, the Arbitral Tribunal shall hear the parties together in person if any of them so requests or, failing such a request, it may of its own motion decide to hear them.

3. The Arbitral Tribunal may decide to hear witnesses, experts appointed by the parties or any other person, in the presence of the parties, or in their absence provided they have been duly summoned.

4. The Arbitral Tribunal, after having consulted the parties, may appoint one or more experts, define their terms of reference and receive their reports. At the request of a party, the parties shall be given the opportunity to question at a hearing any such expert appointed by the Tribunal.

5. At any time during the proceedings, the Arbitral Tribunal may summon any party to provide additional evidence.

6. The Arbitral Tribunal may decide the case solely on the documents submitted by the parties unless any of the parties requests a hearing.

7. The Arbitral Tribunal may take measures for protecting trade secrets and confidential information.

[4260]

Article 21

Hearings

1. When a hearing is to be held, the Arbitral Tribunal, giving reasonable notice, shall summon the parties to appear before it on the day and at the place fixed by it.

2. If any of the parties, although duly summoned, fails to appear without valid excuse, the Arbitral Tribunal shall have the power to proceed with the hearing.

3. The Arbitral Tribunal shall be in full charge of the hearings, at which all the parties shall be entitled to be present. Save with the approval of the Arbitral Tribunal and the parties, persons not involved in the proceedings shall not be admitted.

4. The parties may appear in person or through duly authorized representatives. In addition, they may be assisted by advisers.

[4261]

Article 22

Closing of the Proceedings

1. When it is satisfied that the parties have had a reasonable opportunity to present their cases, the Arbitral Tribunal shall declare the proceedings closed. Thereafter, no further submission or argument may be made, or evidence produced, unless requested or authorized by the Arbitral Tribunal.

2. When the Arbitral Tribunal has declared the proceedings closed, it shall indicate to the Secretariat an approximate date by which the draft Award will be submitted to the Court for approval pursuant to Article 27. Any postponement of that date shall be communicated to the Secretariat by the Arbitral Tribunal.

[4262]

Article 23

Conservatory and Interim Measures

1. Unless the parties have otherwise agreed, as soon as the file has been transmitted to it, the Arbitral Tribunal may, at the request of a party, order any interim or conservatory measure it deems appropriate. The Arbitral Tribunal may make the granting of any such measure subject to appropriate security being furnished by the requesting party. Any such measure shall take the form of an order, giving reasons, or of an Award, as the Arbitral Tribunal considers appropriate.

2. Before the file is transmitted to the Arbitral Tribunal, and in appropriate circumstances even thereafter, the parties may apply to any competent judicial authority for interim or conservatory measures. The application of a party to a judicial authority for such measures or for the implementation of any such measures ordered by an Arbitral Tribunal shall not be deemed to be an infringement or a waiver of the arbitration agreement and shall not affect the relevant powers reserved to the Arbitral Tribunal. Any such application and any measures taken by the judicial authority must be notified without delay to the Secretariat. The Secretariat shall inform the Arbitral Tribunal thereof.

[4263]

Awards

Article 24

Time Limit for the Award

1. The time limit within which the Arbitral Tribunal must render its final Award is six months. Such time limit shall start to run from the date of the last signature by the Arbitral Tribunal or by the parties of the Terms of Reference or, in the case of application of Article 18(3), the date of the notification to the Arbitral Tribunal by the Secretariat of the approval of the Terms of Reference by the Court.

2. The Court may extend this time limit pursuant to a reasoned request from the Arbitral Tribunal or on its own initiative if it decides it is necessary to do so.

[4264]

Article 25

Making of the Award

1. When the Arbitral Tribunal is composed of more than one arbitrator, an Award is given by a majority decision. If there be no majority, the Award shall be made by the chairman of the Arbitral Tribunal alone.

2. The Award shall state the reasons upon which it is based.

3. The Award shall be deemed to be made at the place of the arbitration and on the date stated therein.

[4265]

Article 26

Award by Consent

If the parties reach a settlement after the file has been transmitted to the Arbitral Tribunal in accordance with Article 13, the settlement shall be recorded in the form of an Award made by consent of the parties if so requested by the parties and if the Arbitral Tribunal agrees to do so.

[4266]

Article 27

Scrutiny of the Award by the Court

Before signing any Award, the Arbitral Tribunal shall submit it in draft form to the Court. The Court may lay down modifications as to the form of the Award and, without affecting the Arbitral Tribunal's liberty of decision, may also draw its attention to points of substance. No Award shall be rendered by the Arbitral Tribunal until it has been approved by the Court as to its form.

[4267]

Article 28

Notification, Deposit and Enforceability of the Award

1. Once an Award has been made, the Secretariat shall notify to the parties the text signed by the Arbitral Tribunal, provided always that the costs of the arbitration have been fully paid to the ICC by the parties or by one of them.

2. Additional copies certified true by the Secretary General shall be made available on request and at any time to the parties, but to no one else.

3. By virtue of the notification made in accordance with Paragraph 1 of this Article, the parties waive any other form of notification or deposit on the part of the Arbitral Tribunal.

4. An original of each Award made in accordance with the present Rules shall be deposited with the Secretariat.

5. The Arbitral Tribunal and the Secretariat shall assist the parties in complying with whatever further formalities may be necessary.

6. Every Award shall be binding on the parties. By submitting the dispute to arbitration under these Rules, the parties undertake to carry out any Award without delay and shall be deemed to have waived their right to any form of recourse insofar as such waiver can validly be made.

[4268]

Article 29

Correction and Interpretation of the Award

1. On its own initiative, the Arbitral Tribunal may correct a clerical, computational or typographical error, or any errors of similar nature contained in an Award, provided such correction is submitted for approval to the Court within 30 days of the date of such Award.

2. Any application of a party for the correction of an error of the kind referred to in Article 29(1), or for the interpretation of an Award, must be made to the Secretariat within 30 days of the receipt of the Award by such party, in a number of copies as stated in Article 3(1).

After transmittal of the application to the Arbitral Tribunal, the latter shall grant the other party a short time limit, normally not exceeding 30 days, from the receipt of the application by that party to submit any comments thereon. If the Arbitral Tribunal decides to correct, or interpret the Award, it shall submit its decision in draft form to the Court not later than 30 days following the expiration of the time limit for the receipt of any comments from the other party or within such other period as the Court may decide.

3. The decision to correct or to interpret the Award shall take the form of an addendum and shall constitute part of the Award. The provisions of Articles 25, 27 and 28 shall apply *mutatis mutandis*.

[4269]

Costs

Article 30

Advance to Cover the Costs of the Arbitration

1. After receipt of the Request, the Secretary General may request the Claimant to pay a provisional advance in an amount intended to cover the costs of arbitration until the Terms of Reference have been drawn up.

2. As soon as practicable, the Court shall fix the advance on costs in an amount likely to cover the fees and expenses of the arbitrators and the ICC administrative costs for the claims and counterclaims which have been referred to it by the parties. This amount may be subject to readjustment at any time during the arbitration. Where, apart from the claims, counterclaims are submitted, the Court may fix separate advances on costs for the claims and the counterclaims.

3. The advance on costs fixed by the Court shall be payable in equal shares by the Claimant and the Respondent. Any provisional advance paid on the basis of Article 30(1) will be considered as a partial payment thereof. However, any party shall be free to pay the whole of the advance on costs in respect of the principal claim or the counterclaim should the other party fail to pay its share. When the Court has set separate advances on costs in accordance with Article 30(2), each of the parties shall pay the advance on costs corresponding to its claims.

4. When a request for an advance on costs has not been complied with, and after consultation with the Arbitral Tribunal, the Secretary General may direct the Arbitral Tribunal to suspend its work and set a time limit, which must be not less than 15 days, on the expiry of which the relevant claims, or counterclaims, shall be considered as withdrawn. Should the party in question wish to object to this measure, it must make a request within the aforementioned period for the matter to be decided by the Court. Such party shall not be prevented, on the ground of such withdrawal, from reintroducing the same claims or counterclaims at a later date in another proceeding.

5. If one of the parties claims a right to a set-off with regard to either claims or counterclaims, such set-off shall be taken into account in determining the advance to cover the costs of arbitration in the same way as a separate claim insofar as it may require the Arbitral Tribunal to consider additional matters.

[4270]

Article 31

Decision as to the Costs of the Arbitration

1. The costs of the arbitration shall include the fees and expenses of the arbitrators and the ICC administrative expenses fixed by the Court, in accordance with the scale in force at the time of the commencement of the arbitral proceedings, as well as the fees and expenses of any experts appointed by the Arbitral Tribunal and the reasonable legal and other costs incurred by the parties for the arbitration.

2. The Court may fix the fees of the arbitrators at a figure higher or lower than that which would result from the application of the relevant scale should this be deemed necessary due to the exceptional circumstances of the case. Decisions on costs other than those fixed by the Court may be taken by the Arbitral Tribunal at any time during the proceedings.

3. The final Award shall fix the costs of the arbitration and decide which of the parties shall bear them or in what proportion they shall be borne by the parties.

[4271]

PART V

Miscellaneous

Article 32

Modified Time Limits

1. The parties may agree to shorten the various time limits set out in these Rules. Any such agreement entered into subsequent to the constitution of an Arbitral Tribunal shall become effective only upon the approval of the Arbitral Tribunal.

2. The Court, on its own initiative, may extend any time limit which has been modified pursuant to Article 32(1) if it decides that it is necessary to do so in order that the Arbitral Tribunal or the Court may fulfil their responsibilities in accordance with these Rules.

[4272]

Article 33

Waiver

A party which proceeds with the arbitration without raising its objection to a failure to comply with any provision of these Rules, or of any other rules applicable to the proceedings, any direction given by the Arbitral Tribunal, or any requirement under the arbitration agreement relating to the constitution of the Arbitral Tribunal, or to the conduct of the proceedings, shall be deemed to have waived its right to object.

[4273]

Article 34

Exclusion of Liability

Neither the arbitrators, nor the Court and its members, nor the ICC and its employees, nor the ICC National Committees shall be liable to any person for any act or omission in connection with the arbitration.

[4274]

Article 35

General Rule

In all matters not expressly provided for in these Rules, the Court and the Arbitral Tribunal shall act in the spirit of these Rules and shall make every effort to make sure that the Award is enforceable at law.

[4275]

APPENDIX I
STATUTES OF THE INTERNATIONAL COURT OF ARBITRATION

Article 1

Function

1. The function of the International Court of Arbitration of the International Chamber of Commerce (the "Court") is to ensure the application of the Rules of Arbitration of the International Chamber of Commerce, and it has all the necessary powers for that purpose.

2. As an autonomous body, it carries out these functions in complete independence from the ICC and its organs.

3. Its members are independent from the ICC National Committees.

Article 2

Composition of the Court

The Court shall consist of a Chairman, Vice-Chairmen, and members and alternate members (collectively designated as members). In its work it is assisted by its Secretariat (Secretariat of the Court).

Article 3

Appointment

1. The Chairman is elected by the ICC World Council upon the recommendation of the Executive Board of the ICC.

2. The ICC World Council appoints the Vice-Chairmen of the Court from among the members of the Court or otherwise.

3. Its members are appointed by the ICC World Council on the proposal of National Committees, one member for each Committee.

4. On the proposal of the Chairman of the Court, the World Council may appoint alternate members.

5. The term of office of all members is three years. If a member is no longer in a position to exercise his functions, his successor is appointed by the World Council for the remainder of the term.

Article 4

Plenary Session of the Court

The Plenary Sessions of the Court are presided over by the Chairman or, in his absence, by one of the Vice-Chairmen designated by him. The deliberations shall be valid when at least six members are present. Decisions are taken by a majority vote, the Chairman having a casting vote in the event of a tie.

Article 5

Committees

The Court may set up one or more Committees and establish the functions and organization of such Committees.

Article 6

Confidentiality

The work of the Court is of a confidential nature which must be respected by everyone who participates in that work in whatever capacity. The Court lays down the rules regarding the persons who can attend the meetings of the Court and its Committees and who are entitled to have access to the materials submitted to the Court and its Secretariat.

Article 7

Modification of the Rules of Arbitration

Any proposal of the Court for a modification of the Rules is laid before the Commission on Arbitration before submission to the Executive Board and the World Council of the ICC for approval.

[4276]

APPENDIX II
INTERNAL RULES OF THE INTERNATIONAL COURT OF ARBITRATION

Article 1

Confidential Character of the Work of the International Court of Arbitration

1. The sessions of the Court, whether plenary or those of a Committee of the Court, are open only to its members and to the Secretariat.

2. However, in exceptional circumstances, the Chairman of the Court may invite other persons to attend. Such persons must respect the confidential nature of the work of the Court.

3. The documents submitted to the Court, or drawn up by it in the course of its proceedings, are communicated only to the members of the Court and to the Secretariat and to persons authorized by the Chairman to attend Court sessions.

4. The Chairman or the Secretary General of the Court may authorize researchers undertaking work of a scientific nature on international trade law to acquaint themselves with awards and other documents of general interest, with the exception of memoranda, notes, statements and documents remitted by the parties within the framework of arbitration proceedings.

5. Such authorization shall not be given unless the beneficiary has undertaken to respect the confidential character of the documents made available and to refrain from any publication in their respect without having previously submitted the text for approval to the Secretary General of the Court.

6. The Secretariat will in each case submitted to arbitration under the Rules retain in the archives of the Court all Awards, Terms of Reference, and decisions of the Court, as well as copies of the pertinent correspondence of the Secretariat.

7. Any documents, communications or correspondence submitted by the parties or the arbitrators may be destroyed unless a party or an arbitrator requests in writing within a period fixed by the Secretariat the return of such documents. All related costs and expenses for the return of those documents shall be paid by such party or arbitrator.

Article 2

Participation of Members of the International Court of Arbitration in ICC Arbitration

1. The Chairman and the members of the Secretariat of the Court may not act as arbitrators or as counsel in cases submitted to ICC arbitration.

2. The Court shall not appoint Vice-Chairmen or members of the Court as arbitrators. They may, however, be proposed for such duties by one or more of the parties, or pursuant to any other procedure agreed upon by the parties, subject to confirmation.

3. When the Chairman, a Vice-Chairman or a member of the Court or of the Secretariat is involved in any capacity whatsoever in proceedings pending before the Court, such person must inform the Secretary General of the Court upon becoming aware of such involvement.

4. Such person must refrain from participating in the discussions or in the decisions of the Court concerning the proceedings and must be absent from the courtroom whenever the matter is considered.

5. Such person will not receive any material documentation or information pertaining to such proceedings.

Article 3

Relations between the Members of the Court and the ICC National Committees

1. By virtue of their capacity, the members of the Court are independent of the ICC National Committees which proposed them for appointment by the ICC World Council.

2. Furthermore, they must regard as confidential, vis-à-vis the said National Committees, any information concerning individual cases with which they have become acquainted in their capacity as members of the Court, except when they have been requested by the Chairman of the Court or by its Secretary General to communicate specific information to their respective National Committee.

Article 4

Committee of the Court

1. In accordance with the provisions of Article 1(4) of the Rules and Article 5 of its Statutes (Appendix I), the Court hereby establishes a Committee of the Court.

2. The members of the Committee consist of a Chairman and at least two other members. The Chairman of the Court acts as the Chairman of the Committee. If absent, the Chairman may designate a Vice-Chairman of the Court or, in exceptional circumstances, another member of the Court as Chairman of the Committee.

3. The other two members of the Committee are appointed by the Court from among the Vice-Chairmen or the other members of the Court. At each Plenary Session the Court appoints the members who are to attend the meetings of the Committee to be held before the next Plenary Session.

4. The Committee meets when convened by its Chairman. Two members constitute a quorum.

5.

(a) The Court shall determine the decisions that may be taken by the Committee.
(b) The decisions of the Committee are taken unanimously.

(c) When the Committee cannot reach a decision or deems it preferable to abstain, it transfers the case to the next Plenary Session, making any suggestions it deems appropriate.

(d) The Committee's decisions are brought to the notice of the Court at its next Plenary Session.

Article 5

Court Secretariat

1. In case of absence, the Secretary General may delegate to the General Counsel and Deputy Secretary General the authority to confirm arbitrators, to certify true copies of Awards and to request the payment of a provisional advance, respectively provided for in Articles 9(2), 28(2) and 30(1) of the Rules.

2. The Secretariat may, with the approval of the Court, issue notes and other documents for the information of the parties and the arbitrators, or as necessary for the proper conduct of the arbitral proceedings.

Article 6

Scrutiny of Arbitral Awards

When the Court scrutinizes draft Awards in accordance with Article 27 of the Rules, it considers, to the extent practicable, the requirements of mandatory law at the place of arbitration.

[4277]

APPENDIX III
ARBITRATION COSTS AND FEES

Article 1

Advance on Costs

1. Each request to commence an arbitration pursuant to the Rules must be accompanied by an advance payment of US$ 2,500 on the administrative expenses. Such payment is nonrefundable, and shall be credited to the Claimant's portion of the advance on costs.

2. The provisional advance fixed by the Secretary General according to Article 30(1) of the Rules shall normally not exceed the amount obtained by adding together the administrative expenses, the minimum of the fees (as set out in the scale hereinafter) based upon the amount of the claim and the expected reimbursable expenses of the Arbitral Tribunal incurred with respect to the drafting of the Terms of Reference. If such amount is not quantified, the provisional advance shall be fixed at the discretion of the Secretary General. Payment by the Claimant shall be credited to its share of the advance on costs fixed by the Court.

3. In general, after the Terms of Reference have been signed or approved by the Court and the provisional timetable has been established, the Arbitral Tribunal shall, in accordance with Article 30(4) of the Rules, proceed only with respect to those claims or counterclaims in regard to which the whole of the advance on costs has been paid.

4. The advance on costs fixed by the Court according to Article 30(2) of the Rules comprises the fees of the arbitrator or arbitrators (hereinafter referred to as "arbitrator"), any arbitration-related expenses of the arbitrator and the administrative expenses.

5. Each party shall pay in cash its share of the total advance on costs. However, if its share exceeds an amount fixed from time to time by the Court, a party may post a bank guarantee for this additional amount.

6. A party that has already paid in full its share of the advance on costs fixed by the Court may, in accordance with Article 30(3) of the Rules, pay the unpaid portion of the advance owed by the defaulting party by posting a bank guarantee.

7. When the Court has fixed separate advances on costs pursuant to Article 30(2) of the Rules, the Secretariat shall invite each party to pay the amount of the advance corresponding to its respective claim(s).

8. When, as a result of the fixing of separate advances on costs, the separate advance fixed for the claim of either party exceeds one half of such global advance as was previously

fixed (in respect of the same claims and counterclaims that are the subject of separate advances), a bank guarantee may be posted to cover any such excess amount. In the event that the amount of the separate advance is subsequently increased, at least one half of the increase shall be paid in cash.

9. The Secretariat shall establish the terms governing all bank guarantees which the parties may post pursuant to the above provisions.

10. As provided in Article 30(2) of the Rules, the advance on costs may be subject to readjustment at any time during the arbitration, in particular to take into account fluctuations in the amount in dispute, changes in the amount of the estimated expenses of the arbitrator, or the evolving difficulty or complexity of arbitration proceedings.

11. Before any expertise ordered by the Arbitral Tribunal can be commenced, the parties, or one of them, shall pay an advance on costs fixed by the Arbitral Tribunal sufficient to cover the expected fees and expenses of the expert as determined by the Arbitral Tribunal. The Arbitral Tribunal shall be responsible for ensuring the payment by the parties of such fees and expenses.

Article 2

Costs and Fees

1. Subject to Article 31(2) of the Rules, the Court shall fix the fees of the arbitrator in accordance with the scale hereinafter set out or, where the sum in dispute is not stated, at its discretion.

2. In setting the arbitrator's fees, the Court shall take into consideration the diligence of the arbitrator, the time spent, the rapidity of the proceedings, and the complexity of the dispute so as to arrive at a figure within the limits specified or, in exceptional circumstances (Article 31(2) of the Rules), at a figure higher or lower than those limits.

3. When a case is submitted to more than one arbitrator, the Court, at its discretion, shall have the right to increase the total fees up to a maximum which shall normally not exceed three times the fees of one arbitrator.

4. The arbitrator's fees and expenses shall be fixed exclusively by the Court as required by the Rules. Separate fee arrangements between the parties and the arbitrator are contrary to the Rules.

5. The Court shall fix the administrative expenses of each arbitration in accordance with the scale hereinafter set out or, where the sum in dispute is not stated, at its discretion. In exceptional circumstances, the Court may fix the administrative expenses at a lower or higher figure than that which would result from the application of such scale, provided that such expenses shall normally not exceed the maximum amount of the scale. Further, the Court may require the payment of administrative expenses in addition to those provided in the scale of administrative expenses as a condition to holding an arbitration in abeyance at the request of the parties or of one of them with the acquiescence of the other.

6. If an arbitration terminates before the rendering of a final Award, the Court shall fix the costs of the arbitration at its discretion, taking into account the stage attained by the arbitral proceedings and any other relevant circumstances.

7. In the case of an application under Article 29(2) of the Rules, the Court may fix an advance to cover additional fees and expenses of the Arbitral Tribunal and may make the transmission of such application to the Arbitral Tribunal subject to the prior cash payment in full to the ICC of such advance. The Court shall fix at its discretion any possible fees of the arbitrator when approving the decision of the Arbitral Tribunal.

8. When an arbitration is preceded by an attempt at amicable resolution pursuant to the ICC ADR Rules, one half of the administrative expenses paid for such ADR proceedings shall be credited to the administrative expenses of the arbitration.

9. Amounts paid to the arbitrator do not include any possible value added taxes (VAT) or other taxes or charges and imposts applicable to the arbitrator's fees. Parties have a duty to pay any such taxes or charges; however, the recovery of any such charges or taxes is a matter solely between the arbitrator and the parties.

Article 3

ICC as Appointing Authority

Any request received for an authority of the ICC to act as appointing authority will be treated in accordance with the Rules of ICC as Appointing Authority in UNCITRAL or Other Ad Hoc

Arbitration Proceedings and shall be accompanied by a non-refundable sum of US$ 2,500. No request shall be processed unless accompanied by the said sum. For additional services, ICC may at its discretion fix administrative expenses, which shall be commensurate with the services provided and shall not exceed the maximum sum of US$ 10,000.

Article 4

Scales of Administrative Expenses and Arbitrator's Fees

1. The Scales of Administrative Expenses and Arbitrator's Fees set forth below shall be effective as of 1 July 2003 in respect of all arbitrations commenced on or after such date, irrespective of the version of the Rules applying to such arbitrations.

2. To calculate the administrative expenses and the arbitrator's fees, the amounts calculated for each successive slice of the sum in dispute must be added together, except that where the sum in dispute is over US$ 80 million, a flat amount of US$ 88,800 shall constitute the entirety of the administrative expenses.

A. ADMINISTRATIVE EXPENSES

Sum in dispute (in US Dollars)	*Administrative expenses(*)*
up to 50 000	$ 2500
from 50 001 to 100 000	3.50%
from 100 001 to 500 000	1.70%
from 500 001 to 1 000 000	1.15%
from 1 000 001 to 2 000 000	0.70%
from 2 000 001 to 5 000 000	0.30%
from 5 000 001 to 10 000 000	0.20%
from 10 000 001 to 50 000 000	0.07%
from 50 000 001 to 80 000 000	0.06%
over 80 000 000	$ 88 800

(*) For illustrative purposes only, the table on the following page indicates the resulting administrative expenses in US$ when the proper calculations have been made.

B. ARBITRATOR'S FEES

Sum in dispute (in US Dollars)	*Fees(**)*	
	minimum	*maximum*
up to 50 000	$ 2500	17.00%
from 50 001 to 100 000	2.00%	11.00%
from 100 001 to 500 000	1.00%	5.50%
from 500 001 to 1 000 000	0.75%	3.50%
from 1 000 001 to 2 000 000	0.50%	2.75%
from 2 000 001 to 5 000 000	0.25%	1.12%
from 5 000 001 to 10 000 000	0.10%	0.616%
from 10 000 001 to 50 000 000	0.05%	0.193%

Sum in dispute (in US Dollars)	*Fees(**)*	
from 50 000 001 to 80 000 000	0.03%	0.136%
from 80 000 001 to 100 000 000	0.02%	0.112%
over 100 000 000	0.01%	0.056%

(**) *For illustrative purposes only, the table on the following page indicates the resulting range of fees when the proper calculations have been made.*

SUM IN DISPUTE (in US Dollars)	*A. ADMINISTRATIVE EXPENSES (in US Dollars)*
up to 50 000	2500
from 50 001 to 100 000	2500 + 3.50% of amt. over 50 000
from 100 001 to 500 000	4250 + 1.70% of amt. over 100 000
from 500 001 to 1 000 000	11 050 + 1.15% of amt. over 500 000
from 1 000 001 to 2 000 000	16 800 + 0.70% of amt. over 1 000 000
from 2 000 001 to 5 000 000	23 800 + 0.30% of amt. over 2 000 000
from 5 000 001 to 10 000 000	32 800 + 0.20% of amt. over 5 000 000
from 10 000 001 to 50 000 000	42 800 + 0.07% of amt. over 10 000 000
from 50 000 001 to 80 000 000	70 800 + 0.06% of amt. over 50 000 000
from 80 000 001 to 100 000 000	88 800
over 100 000 000	88 800

SUM IN DISPUTE (in US Dollars)	*B. ARBITRATOR'S FEES (in US Dollars)*	
	Minimum	*Maximum*
up to 50 000	2500	17.00% of amount in dispute
from 50 001 to 100 000	2500 + 2.00% of amt. over 50 000	8500 + 11.00% of amt. over 50 000
from 100 001 to 500 000	3500 + 1.00% of amt. over 100 000	14 000 + 5.50% of amt. over 100 000
from 500 001 to 1 000 000	7500+ 0.75% of amt. over 500 000	36 000 + 3.50% of amt. over 500 000
from 1 000 001 to 2 000 000	11 250 + 0.50% of amt. over 1 000 000	53 500 + 2.75% of amt. over 1 000 000
from 2 000 001 to 5 000 000	16 250 + 0.25% of amt. over 2 000 000	81 000 + 1.12% of amt. over 2 000 000
from 5 000 001 to 10 000 000	23 750 + 0.10% of amt. over 5 000 000	114 600 + 0.616% of amt. over 5 000 000
from 10 000 001 to 50 000 000	28 750 + 0.05% of amt. over 10 000 000	145 400 + 0.193% of amt. over 10 000 000
from 50 000 001 to 80 000 000	48 750 + 0.03% of amt. over 50 000 000	222 600 + 0.136% of amt. over 50 000 000
from 80 000 001 to 100 000 000	57 750 + 0.02% of amt. over 80 000 000	263 400+ 0.112% of amt. over 80 000 000

SUM IN DISPUTE (in US Dollars)	B. ARBITRATOR'S FEES (in US Dollars)	
over 100 000 000	61 750 + 0.01% of amt. over 100 000 000	285 800 + 0.056% of amt. over 100 000 000

[4278]

LCIA ARBITRATION RULES

(adopted to take effect for arbitrations commencing on or after 1 January 1998)

NOTES

The original source of these Rules is the LCIA. See http://www.lcia.org.

Where any agreement, submission or reference provides in writing and in whatsoever manner for arbitration under the rules of the LCIA or by the Court of the LCIA ("the LCIA Court"), the parties shall be taken to have agreed in writing that the arbitration shall be conducted in accordance with the following rules ("the Rules") or such amended rules as the LCIA may have adopted hereafter to take effect before the commencement of the arbitration. The Rules include the Schedule of Costs in effect at the commencement of the arbitration, as separately amended from time to time by the LCIA Court.

Article 1

The Request for Arbitration

1.1 Any party wishing to commence an arbitration under these Rules ("the Claimant") shall send to the Registrar of the LCIA Court ("the Registrar") a written request for arbitration ("the Request"), containing or accompanied by:

(a) the names, addresses, telephone, facsimile, telex and e-mail numbers (if known) of the parties to the arbitration and of their legal representatives;

(b) a copy of the written arbitration clause or separate written arbitration agreement invoked by the Claimant ("the Arbitration Agreement"), together with a copy of the contractual documentation in which the arbitration clause is contained or in respect of which the arbitration arises;

(c) a brief statement describing the nature and circumstances of the dispute, and specifying the claims advanced by the Claimant against another party to the arbitration ("the Respondent");

(d) a statement of any matters (such as the seat or language(s) of the arbitration, or the number of arbitrators, or their qualifications or identities) on which the parties have already agreed in writing for the arbitration or in respect of which the Claimant wishes to make a proposal;

(e) if the Arbitration Agreement calls for party nomination of arbitrators, the name, address, telephone, facsimile, telex and e-mail numbers (if known) of the Claimant's nominee;

(f) the fee prescribed in the Schedule of Costs (without which the Request shall be treated as not having been received by the Registrar and the arbitration as not having been commenced);

(g) confirmation to the Registrar that copies of the Request (including all accompanying documents) have been or are being served simultaneously on all other parties to the arbitration by one or more means of service to be identified in such confirmation.

1.2 The date of receipt by the Registrar of the Request shall be treated as the date on which the arbitration has commenced for all purposes. The Request (including all accompanying documents) should be submitted to the Registrar in two copies where a sole arbitrator should be appointed, or, if the parties have agreed or the Claimant considers that three arbitrators should be appointed, in four copies.

[4279]

Article 2

The Response

2.1 Within 30 days of service of the Request on the Respondent, (or such lesser period fixed by the LCIA Court), the Respondent shall send to the Registrar a written response to the Request ("the Response"), containing or accompanied by:

(a) confirmation or denial of all or part of the claims advanced by the Claimant in the Request;

(b) a brief statement describing the nature and circumstances of any counterclaims advanced by the Respondent against the Claimant;

(c) comment in response to any statements contained in the Request, as called for under Article 1.1(d), on matters relating to the conduct of the arbitration;

(d) if the Arbitration Agreement calls for party nomination of arbitrators, the name, address, telephone, facsimile, telex and e-mail numbers (if known) of the Respondent's nominee; and

(e) confirmation to the Registrar that copies of the Response (including all accompanying documents) have been or are being served simultaneously on all other parties to the arbitration by one or more means of service to be identified in such confirmation.

2.2 The Response (including all accompanying documents) should be submitted to the Registrar in two copies, or if the parties have agreed or the Respondent considers that three arbitrators should be appointed, in four copies.

2.3 Failure to send a Response shall not preclude the Respondent from denying any claim or from advancing a counterclaim in the arbitration. However, if the Arbitration Agreement calls for party nomination of arbitrators, failure to send a Response or to nominate an arbitrator within time or at all shall constitute an irrevocable waiver of that party's opportunity to nominate an arbitrator.

[4280]

Article 3

The LCIA Court and Registrar

3.1 The functions of the LCIA Court under these Rules shall be performed in its name by the President or a Vice President of the LCIA Court or by a division of three or five members of the LCIA Court appointed by the President or a Vice President of the LCIA Court, as determined by the President.

3.2 The functions of the Registrar under these Rules shall be performed by the Registrar or any deputy Registrar of the LCIA Court under the supervision of the LCIA Court.

3.3 All communications from any party or arbitrator to the LCIA Court shall be addressed to the Registrar.

[4281]

Article 4

Notices and Periods of Time

4.1 Any notice or other communication that may be or is required to be given by a party under these Rules shall be in writing and shall be delivered by registered postal or courier service or transmitted by facsimile, telex, e-mail or any other means of telecommunication that provide a record of its transmission.

4.2 A party's last-known residence or place of business during the arbitration shall be a valid address for the purpose of any notice or other communication in the absence of any notification of a change to such address by that party to the other parties, the Arbitral Tribunal and the Registrar.

4.3 For the purpose of determining the date of commencement of a time limit, a notice or other communication shall be treated as having been received on the day it is delivered or, in the case of telecommunications, transmitted in accordance with Articles 4.1 and 4.2.

4.4 For the purpose of determining compliance with a time limit, a notice or other communication shall be treated as having been sent, made or transmitted if it is dispatched in accordance with Articles 4.1 and 4.2 prior to or on the date of the expiration of the time-limit.

4.5 Notwithstanding the above, any notice or communication by one party may be addressed to another party in the manner agreed in writing between them or, failing such agreement, according to the practice followed in the course of their previous dealings or in whatever manner ordered by the Arbitral Tribunal.

4.6 For the purpose of calculating a period of time under these Rules, such period shall begin to run on the day following the day when a notice or other communication is received. If the last day of such period is an official holiday or a non-business day at the residence or place of business of the addressee, the period is extended until the first business day which follows. Official holidays or non-business days occurring during the running of the period of time are included in calculating that period.

4.7 The Arbitral Tribunal may at any time extend (even where the period of time has expired) or abridge any period of time prescribed under these Rules or under the Arbitration Agreement for the conduct of the arbitration, including any notice or communication to be served by one party on any other party. **[4282]**

Article 5

Formation of the Arbitral Tribunal

5.1 The expression "the Arbitral Tribunal" in these Rules includes a sole arbitrator or all the arbitrators where more than one. All references to an arbitrator shall include the masculine and feminine. (References to the President, Vice President and members of the LCIA Court, the Registrar or deputy Registrar, expert, witness, party and legal representative shall be similarly understood).

5.2 All arbitrators conducting an arbitration under these Rules shall be and remain at all times impartial and independent of the parties; and none shall act in the arbitration as advocates for any party. No arbitrator, whether before or after appointment, shall advise any party on the merits or outcome of the dispute.

5.3 Before appointment by the LCIA Court, each arbitrator shall furnish to the Registrar a written résumé of his past and present professional positions; he shall agree in writing upon fee rates conforming to the Schedule of Costs; and he shall sign a declaration to the effect that there are no circumstances known to him likely to give rise to any justified doubts as to his impartiality or independence, other than any circumstances disclosed by him in the declaration. Each arbitrator shall thereby also assume a continuing duty forthwith to disclose any such circumstances to the LCIA Court, to any other members of the Arbitral Tribunal and to all the parties if such circumstances should arise after the date of such declaration and before the arbitration is concluded.

5.4 The LCIA Court shall appoint the Arbitral Tribunal as soon as practicable after receipt by the Registrar of the Response or after the expiry of 30 days following service of the Request upon the Respondent if no Response is received by the Registrar (or such lesser period fixed by the LCIA Court). The LCIA Court may proceed with the formation of the Arbitral Tribunal notwithstanding that the Request is incomplete or the Response is missing, late or incomplete. A sole arbitrator shall be appointed unless the parties have agreed in writing otherwise, or unless the LCIA Court determines that in view of all the circumstances of the case a three-member tribunal is appropriate.

5.5 The LCIA Court alone is empowered to appoint arbitrators. The LCIA Court will appoint arbitrators with due regard for any particular method or criteria of selection agreed in writing by the parties. In selecting arbitrators consideration will be given to the nature of the transaction, the nature and circumstances of the dispute, the nationality, location and languages of the parties and (if more than two) the number of parties.

5.6 In the case of a three-member Arbitral Tribunal, the chairman (who will not be a party-nominated arbitrator) shall be appointed by the LCIA Court. **[4283]**

Article 6

Nationality of Arbitrators

6.1 Where the parties are of different nationalities, a sole arbitrator or chairman of the Arbitral Tribunal shall not have the same nationality as any party unless the parties who are not of the same nationality as the proposed appointee all agree in writing otherwise.

6.2 The nationality of parties shall be understood to include that of controlling shareholders or interests.

6.3 For the purpose of this Article, a person who is a citizen of two or more states shall be treated as a national of each state; and citizens of the European Union shall be treated as nationals of its different Member States and shall not be treated as having the same nationality.

[4284]

Article 7

Party and Other Nominations

7.1 If the parties have agreed that any arbitrator is to be appointed by one or more of them or by any third person, that agreement shall be treated as an agreement to nominate an arbitrator for all purposes. Such nominee may only be appointed by the LCIA Court as arbitrator subject to his prior compliance with Article 5.3. The LCIA Court may refuse to appoint any such nominee if it determines that he is not suitable or independent or impartial.

7.2 Where the parties have howsoever agreed that the Respondent or any third person is to nominate an arbitrator and such nomination is not made within time or at all, the LCIA Court may appoint an arbitrator notwithstanding the absence of the nomination and without regard to any late nomination. Likewise, if the Request for Arbitration does not contain a nomination by the Claimant where the parties have howsoever agreed that the Claimant or a third person is to nominate an arbitrator, the LCIA Court may appoint an arbitrator notwithstanding the absence of the nomination and without regard to any late nomination.

[4285]

Article 8

Three or More Parties

8.1 Where the Arbitration Agreement entitles each party howsoever to nominate an arbitrator, the parties to the dispute number more than two and such parties have not all agreed in writing that the disputant parties represent two separate sides for the formation of the Arbitral Tribunal as Claimant and Respondent respectively, the LCIA Court shall appoint the Arbitral Tribunal without regard to any party's nomination.

8.2 In such circumstances, the Arbitration Agreement shall be treated for all purposes as a written agreement by the parties for the appointment of the Arbitral Tribunal by the LCIA Court.

[4286]

Article 9

Expedited Formation

9.1 In exceptional urgency, on or after the commencement of the arbitration, any party may apply to the LCIA Court for the expedited formation of the Arbitral Tribunal, including the appointment of any replacement arbitrator under Articles 10 and 11 of these Rules.

9.2 Such an application shall be made in writing to the LCIA Court, copied to all other parties to the arbitration; and it shall set out the specific grounds for exceptional urgency in the formation of the Arbitral Tribunal.

9.3 The LCIA Court may, in its complete discretion, abridge or curtail any time-limit under these Rules for the formation of the Arbitral Tribunal, including service of the Response and of any matters or documents adjudged to be missing from the Request. The LCIA Court shall not be entitled to abridge or curtail any other time-limit.

[4287]

Article 10

Revocation of Arbitrator's Appointment

10.1 If either (a) any arbitrator gives written notice of his desire to resign as arbitrator to the LCIA Court, to be copied to the parties and the other arbitrators (if any) or (b) any arbitrator dies, falls seriously ill, refuses, or becomes unable or unfit to act, either upon challenge by a party or at the request of the remaining arbitrators, the LCIA Court may revoke that arbitrator's appointment and appoint another arbitrator. The LCIA Court shall decide upon the amount of fees and expenses to be paid for the former arbitrator's services (if any) as it may consider appropriate in all the circumstances.

10.2 If any arbitrator acts in deliberate violation of the Arbitration Agreement (including these Rules) or does not act fairly and impartially as between the parties or does not conduct or participate in the arbitration proceedings with reasonable diligence, avoiding unnecessary delay or expense, that arbitrator may be considered unfit in the opinion of the LCIA Court.

10.3 An arbitrator may also be challenged by any party if circumstances exist that give rise to justifiable doubts as to his impartiality or independence. A party may challenge an arbitrator it has nominated, or in whose appointment it has participated, only for reasons of which it becomes aware after the appointment has been made.

10.4 A party who intends to challenge an arbitrator shall, within 15 days of the formation of the Arbitral Tribunal or (if later) after becoming aware of any circumstances referred to in Article 10.1, 10.2 or 10.3, send a written statement of the reasons for its challenge to the LCIA Court, the Arbitral Tribunal and all other parties. Unless the challenged arbitrator withdraws or all other parties agree to the challenge within 15 days of receipt of the written statement, the LCIA Court shall decide on the challenge.

[4288]

Article 11

Nomination and Replacement of Arbitrators

11.1 In the event that the LCIA Court determines that any nominee is not suitable or independent or impartial or if an appointed arbitrator is to be replaced for any reason, the LCIA Court shall have a complete discretion to decide whether or not to follow the original nominating process.

11.2 If the LCIA Court should so decide, any opportunity given to a party to make a re-nomination shall be waived if not exercised within 15 days (or such lesser time as the LCIA Court may fix), after which the LCIA Court shall appoint the replacement arbitrator.

[4289]

Article 12

Majority Power to Continue Proceedings

12.1 If any arbitrator on a three-member Arbitral Tribunal refuses or persistently fails to participate in its deliberations, the two other arbitrators shall have the power, upon their written notice of such refusal or failure to the LCIA Court, the parties and the third arbitrator, to continue the arbitration (including the making of any decision, ruling or award), notwithstanding the absence of the third arbitrator.

12.2 In determining whether to continue the arbitration, the two other arbitrators shall take into account the stage of the arbitration, any explanation made by the third arbitrator for his non-participation and such other matters as they consider appropriate in the circumstances of the case. The reasons for such determination shall be stated in any award, order or other decision made by the two arbitrators without the participation of the third arbitrator.

12.3 In the event that the two other arbitrators determine at any time not to continue the arbitration without the participation of the third arbitrator missing from their deliberations, the two arbitrators shall notify in writing the parties and the LCIA Court of such determination; and in that event, the two arbitrators or any party may refer the matter to the LCIA Court for the revocation of that third arbitrator's appointment and his replacement under Article 10.

[4290]

Article 13

Communications between Parties and the Arbitral Tribunal

13.1 Until the Arbitral Tribunal is formed, all communications between parties and arbitrators shall be made through the Registrar.

13.2 Thereafter, unless and until the Arbitral Tribunal directs that communications shall take place directly between the Arbitral Tribunal and the parties (with simultaneous copies to the Registrar), all written communications between the parties and the Arbitral Tribunal shall continue to be made through the Registrar.

13.3 Where the Registrar sends any written communication to one party on behalf of the Arbitral Tribunal, he shall send a copy to each of the other parties. Where any party sends to the Registrar any communication (including Written Statements and Documents under Article 15), it shall include a copy for each arbitrator; and it shall also send copies direct to all other parties and confirm to the Registrar in writing that it has done or is doing so.

[4291]

Article 14

Conduct of the Proceedings

14.1 The parties may agree on the conduct of their arbitral proceedings and they are encouraged to do so, consistent with the Arbitral Tribunal's general duties at all times:

(i) to act fairly and impartially as between all parties, giving each a reasonable opportunity of putting its case and dealing with that of its opponent; and

(ii) to adopt procedures suitable to the circumstances of the arbitration, avoiding unnecessary delay or expense, so as to provide a fair and efficient means for the final resolution of the parties' dispute.

Such agreements shall be made by the parties in writing or recorded in writing by the Arbitral Tribunal at the request of and with the authority of the parties

14.2 Unless otherwise agreed by the parties under Article 14.1, the Arbitral Tribunal shall have the widest discretion to discharge its duties allowed under such law(s) or rules of law as the Arbitral Tribunal may determine to be applicable; and at all times the parties shall do everything necessary for the fair, efficient and expeditious conduct of the arbitration.

14.3 In the case of a three-member Arbitral Tribunal the chairman may, with the prior consent of the other two arbitrators, make procedural rulings alone.

[4292]

Article 15

Submission of Written Statements and Documents

15.1 Unless the parties have agreed otherwise under Article 14.1 or the Arbitral Tribunal should determine differently, the written stage of the proceedings shall be as set out below.

15.2 Within 30 days of receipt of written notification from the Registrar of the formation of the Arbitral Tribunal, the Claimant shall send to the Registrar a Statement of Case setting out in sufficient detail the facts and any contentions of law on which it relies, together with the relief claimed against all other parties, save and insofar as such matters have not been set out in its Request.

15.3 Within 30 days of receipt of the Statement of Case or written notice from the Claimant that it elects to treat the Request as its Statement of Case, the Respondent shall send to the Registrar a Statement of Defence setting out in sufficient detail which of the facts and contentions of law in the Statement of Case or Request (as the case may be) it admits or denies, on what grounds and on what other facts and contentions of law it relies. Any counterclaims shall be submitted with the Statement of Defence in the same manner as claims are to be set out in the Statement of Case.

15.4 Within 30 days of receipt of the Statement of Defence, the Claimant shall send to the Registrar a Statement of Reply which, where there are any counterclaims, shall include a Defence to Counterclaim in the same manner as a defence is to be set out in the Statement of Defence.

15.5 If the Statement of Reply contains a Defence to Counterclaim, within 30 days of its receipt the Respondent shall send to the Registrar a Statement of Reply to Counterclaim.

15.6 All Statements referred to in this Article shall be accompanied by copies (or, if they are especially voluminous, lists) of all essential documents on which the party concerned relies and which have not previously been submitted by any party, and (where appropriate) by any relevant samples and exhibits.

15.7 As soon as practicable following receipt of the Statements specified in this Article, the Arbitral Tribunal shall proceed in such manner as has been agreed in writing by the parties or pursuant to its authority under these Rules.

15.8 If the Respondent fails to submit a Statement of Defence or the Claimant a Statement of Defence to Counterclaim, or if at any point any party fails to avail itself of the opportunity to present its case in the manner determined by Article 15.2 to 15.6 or directed by the Arbitral Tribunal, the Arbitral Tribunal may nevertheless proceed with the arbitration and make an award. **[4293]**

Article 16

Seat of Arbitration and Place of Hearings

16.1 The parties may agree in writing the seat (or legal place) of their arbitration. Failing such a choice, the seat of arbitration shall be London, unless and until the LCIA Court determines in view of all the circumstances, and after having given the parties an opportunity to make written comment, that another seat is more appropriate.

16.2 The Arbitral Tribunal may hold hearings, meetings and deliberations at any convenient geographical place in its discretion; and if elsewhere than the seat of the arbitration, the arbitration shall be treated as an arbitration conducted at the seat of the arbitration and any award as an award made at the seat of the arbitration for all purposes.

16.3 The law applicable to the arbitration (if any) shall be the arbitration law of the seat of arbitration, unless and to the extent that the parties have expressly agreed in writing on the application of another arbitration law and such agreement is not prohibited by the law of the arbitral seat. **[4294]**

Article 17

Language of Arbitration

17.1 The initial language of the arbitration shall be the language of the Arbitration Agreement, unless the parties have agreed in writing otherwise and providing always that a non-participating or defaulting party shall have no cause for complaint if communications to and from the Registrar and the arbitration proceedings are conducted in English.

17.2 In the event that the Arbitration Agreement is written in more than one language, the LCIA Court may, unless the Arbitration Agreement provides that the arbitration proceedings shall be conducted in more than one language, decide which of those languages shall be the initial language of the arbitration.

17.3 Upon the formation of the Arbitral Tribunal and unless the parties have agreed upon the language or languages of the arbitration, the Arbitration Tribunal shall decide upon the language(s) of the arbitration, after giving the parties an opportunity to make written comment and taking into account the initial language of the arbitration and any other matter it may consider appropriate in all the circumstances of the case.

17.4 If any document is expressed in a language other than the language(s) of the arbitration and no translation of such document is submitted by the party relying upon the document, the Arbitral Tribunal or (if the Arbitral Tribunal has not been formed) the LCIA Court may order that party to submit a translation in a form to be determined by the Arbitral Tribunal or the LCIA Court, as the case may be. **[4295]**

Article 18

Party Representation

18.1 Any party may be represented by legal practitioners or any other representatives.

18.2 At any time the Arbitral Tribunal may require from any party proof of authority granted to its representative(s) in such form as the Arbitral Tribunal may determine. **[4296]**

Article 19

Hearings

19.1 Any party which expresses a desire to that effect has the right to be heard orally before the Arbitral Tribunal on the merits of the dispute, unless the parties have agreed in writing on documents-only arbitration.

19.2 The Arbitral Tribunal shall fix the date, time and physical place of any meetings and hearings in the arbitration, and shall give the parties reasonable notice thereof.

19.3 The Arbitral Tribunal may in advance of any hearing submit to the parties a list of questions which it wishes them to answer with special attention.

19.4 All meetings and hearings shall be in private unless the parties agree otherwise in writing or the Arbitral Tribunal directs otherwise.

19.5 The Arbitral Tribunal shall have the fullest authority to establish time-limits for meetings and hearings, or for any parts thereof.

[4297]

Article 20

Witnesses

20.1 Before any hearing, the Arbitral Tribunal may require any party to give notice of the identity of each witness that party wishes to call (including rebuttal witnesses), as well as the subject matter of that witness's testimony, its content and its relevance to the issues in the arbitration.

20.2 The Arbitral Tribunal may also determine the time, manner and form in which such materials should be exchanged between the parties and presented to the Arbitral Tribunal; and it has a discretion to allow, refuse, or limit the appearance of witnesses (whether witness of fact or expert witness).

20.3 Subject to any order otherwise by the Arbitral Tribunal, the testimony of a witness may be presented by a party in written form, either as a signed statement or as a sworn affidavit.

20.4 Subject to Article 14.1 and 14.2, any party may request that a witness, on whose testimony another party seeks to rely, should attend for oral questioning at a hearing before the Arbitral Tribunal. If the Arbitral Tribunal orders that other party to produce the witness and the witness fails to attend the oral hearing without good cause, the Arbitral Tribunal may place such weight on the written testimony (or exclude the same altogether) as it considers appropriate in the circumstances of the case.

20.5 Any witness who gives oral evidence at a hearing before the Arbitral Tribunal may be questioned by each of the parties under the control of the Arbitral Tribunal. The Arbitral Tribunal may put questions at any stage of his evidence.

20.6 Subject to the mandatory provisions of any applicable law, it shall not be improper for any party or its legal representatives to interview any witness or potential witness for the purpose of presenting his testimony in written form or producing him as an oral witness.

20.7 Any individual intending to testify to the Arbitral Tribunal on any issue of fact or expertise shall be treated as a witness under these Rules notwithstanding that the individual is a party to the arbitration or was or is an officer, employee or shareholder of any party.

[4298]

Article 21

Experts to the Arbitral Tribunal

21.1 Unless otherwise agreed by the parties in writing, the Arbitral Tribunal:

(a) may appoint one or more experts to report to the Arbitral Tribunal on specific issues, who shall be and remain impartial and independent of the parties throughout the arbitration proceedings; and

(b) may require a party to give any such expert any relevant information or to provide access to any relevant documents, goods, samples, property or site for inspection by the expert.

21.2 Unless otherwise agreed by the parties in writing, if a party so requests or if the Arbitral Tribunal considers it necessary, the expert shall, after delivery of his written or oral report to the Arbitral Tribunal and the parties, participate in one or more hearings at which the parties shall have the opportunity to question the expert on his report and to present expert witnesses in order to testify on the points at issue.

21.3 The fees and expenses of any expert appointed by the Arbitral Tribunal under this Article shall be paid out of the deposits payable by the parties under Article 24 and shall form part of the costs of the arbitration.

[4299]

Article 22

Additional Powers of the Arbitral Tribunal

22.1 Unless the parties at any time agree otherwise in writing, the Arbitral Tribunal shall have the power, on the application of any party or of its own motion, but in either case only after giving the parties a reasonable opportunity to state their views:

(a) to allow any party, upon such terms (as to costs and otherwise) as it shall determine, to amend any claim, counterclaim, defence and reply;

(b) to extend or abbreviate any time-limit provided by the Arbitration Agreement or these Rules for the conduct of the arbitration or by the Arbitral Tribunal's own orders;

(c) to conduct such enquiries as may appear to the Arbitral Tribunal to be necessary or expedient, including whether and to what extent the Arbitral Tribunal should itself take the initiative in identifying the issues and ascertaining the relevant facts and the law(s) or rules of law applicable to the arbitration, the merits of the parties' dispute and the Arbitration Agreement;

(d) to order any party to make any property, site or thing under its control and relating to the subject matter of the arbitration available for inspection by the Arbitral Tribunal, any other party, its expert or any expert to the Arbitral Tribunal;

(e) to order any party to produce to the Arbitral Tribunal, and to the other parties for inspection, and to supply copies of, any documents or classes of documents in their possession, custody or power which the Arbitral Tribunal determines to be relevant;

(f) to decide whether or not to apply any strict rules of evidence (or any other rules) as to the admissibility, relevance or weight of any material tendered by a party on any matter of fact or expert opinion; and to determine the time, manner and form in which such material should be exchanged between the parties and presented to the Arbitral Tribunal;

(g) to order the correction of any contract between the parties or the Arbitration Agreement, but only to the extent required to rectify any mistake which the Arbitral Tribunal determines to be common to the parties and then only if and to the extent to which the law(s) or rules of law applicable to the contract or Arbitration Agreement permit such correction; and

(h) to allow, only upon the application of a party, one or more third persons to be joined in the arbitration as a party provided any such third person and the applicant party have consented thereto in writing, and thereafter to make a single final award, or separate awards, in respect of all parties so implicated in the arbitration.

22.2 By agreeing to arbitration under these Rules, the parties shall be treated as having agreed not to apply to any state court or other judicial authority for any order available from the Arbitral Tribunal under Article 22.1, except with the agreement in writing of all parties.

22.3 The Arbitral Tribunal shall decide the parties' dispute in accordance with the law(s) or rules of law chosen by the parties as applicable to the merits of their dispute. If and to the extent that the Arbitral Tribunal determines that the parties have made no such choice, the Arbitral Tribunal shall apply the law(s) or rules of law which it considers appropriate.

22.4 The Arbitral Tribunal shall only apply to the merits of the dispute principles deriving from "ex aequo et bono", "amiable composition" or "honourable engagement" where the parties have so agreed expressly in writing.

[4300]

Article 23

Jurisdiction of the Arbitral Tribunal

23.1 The Arbitral Tribunal shall have the power to rule on its own jurisdiction, including any objection to the initial or continuing existence, validity or effectiveness of the Arbitration Agreement. For that purpose, an arbitration clause which forms or was intended to form part of another agreement shall be treated as an arbitration agreement independent of that other agreement. A decision by the Arbitral Tribunal that such other agreement is non-existent, invalid or ineffective shall not entail ipso jure the non-existence, invalidity or ineffectiveness of the arbitration clause.

23.2 A plea by a Respondent that the Arbitral Tribunal does not have jurisdiction shall be treated as having been irrevocably waived unless it is raised not later than the Statement of

Defence; and a like plea by a Respondent to Counterclaim shall be similarly treated unless it is raised no later than the Statement of Defence to Counterclaim. A plea that the Arbitral Tribunal is exceeding the scope of its authority shall be raised promptly after the Arbitral Tribunal has indicated its intention to decide on the matter alleged by any party to be beyond the scope of its authority, failing which such plea shall also be treated as having been waived irrevocably. In any case, the Arbitral Tribunal may nevertheless admit an untimely plea if it considers the delay justified in the particular circumstances.

23.3 The Arbitral Tribunal may determine the plea to its jurisdiction or authority in an award as to jurisdiction or later in an award on the merits, as it considers appropriate in the circumstances.

23.4 By agreeing to arbitration under these Rules, the parties shall be treated as having agreed not to apply to any state court or other judicial authority for any relief regarding the Arbitral Tribunal's jurisdiction or authority, except with the agreement in writing of all parties to the arbitration or the prior authorisation of the Arbitral Tribunal or following the latter's award ruling on the objection to its jurisdiction or authority.

[4301]

Article 24

Deposits

24.1 The LCIA Court may direct the parties, in such proportions as it thinks appropriate, to make one or several interim or final payments on account of the costs of the arbitration. Such deposits shall be made to and held by the LCIA and from time to time may be released by the LCIA Court to the arbitrator(s), any expert appointed by the Arbitral Tribunal and the LCIA itself as the arbitration progresses.

24.2 The Arbitral Tribunal shall not proceed with the arbitration without ascertaining at all times from the Registrar or any deputy Registrar that the LCIA is in requisite funds.

24.3 In the event that a party fails or refuses to provide any deposit as directed by the LCIA Court, the LCIA Court may direct the other party or parties to effect a substitute payment to allow the arbitration to proceed (subject to any award on costs). In such circumstances, the party paying the substitute payment shall be entitled to recover that amount as a debt immediately due from the defaulting party.

24.4 Failure by a claimant or counterclaiming party to provide promptly and in full the required deposit may be treated by the LCIA Court and the Arbitral Tribunal as a withdrawal of the claim or counterclaim respectively.

[4302]

Article 25

Interim and Conservatory Measures

25.1 The Arbitral Tribunal shall have the power, unless otherwise agreed by the parties in writing, on the application of any party:

(a) to order any respondent party to a claim or counterclaim to provide security for all or part of the amount in dispute, by way of deposit or bank guarantee or in any other manner and upon such terms as the Arbitral Tribunal considers appropriate. Such terms may include the provision by the claiming or counterclaiming party of a cross-indemnity, itself secured in such manner as the Arbitral Tribunal considers appropriate, for any costs or losses incurred by such respondent in providing security. The amount of any costs and losses payable under such cross-indemnity may be determined by the Arbitral Tribunal in one or more awards;

(b) to order the preservation, storage, sale or other disposal of any property or thing under the control of any party and relating to the subject matter of the arbitration; and

(c) to order on a provisional basis, subject to final determination in an award, any relief which the Arbitral Tribunal would have power to grant in an award, including a provisional order for the payment of money or the disposition of property as between any parties.

25.2 The Arbitral Tribunal shall have the power, upon the application of a party, to order any claiming or counterclaiming party to provide security for the legal or other costs of any other party by way of deposit or bank guarantee or in any other manner and upon such terms as the Arbitral Tribunal considers appropriate. Such terms may include the provision by that other party of a cross-indemnity, itself secured in such manner as the Arbitral Tribunal considers appropriate, for any costs and losses incurred by such claimant or counterclaimant in providing security. The amount of any costs and losses payable under such cross-indemnity may be determined by the Arbitral Tribunal in one or more awards. In the event that a claiming or counterclaiming party does not comply with any order to provide security, the Arbitral Tribunal may stay that party's claims or counterclaims or dismiss them in an award.

25.3 The power of the Arbitral Tribunal under Article 25.1 shall not prejudice howsoever any party's right to apply to any state court or other judicial authority for interim or conservatory measures before the formation of the Arbitral Tribunal and, in exceptional cases, thereafter. Any application and any order for such measures after the formation of the Arbitral Tribunal shall be promptly communicated by the applicant to the Arbitral Tribunal and all other parties. However, by agreeing to arbitration under these Rules, the parties shall be taken to have agreed not to apply to any state court or other judicial authority for any order for security for its legal or other costs available from the Arbitral Tribunal under Article 25.2. **[4303]**

Article 26

The Award

26.1 The Arbitral Tribunal shall make its award in writing and, unless all parties agree in writing otherwise, shall state the reasons upon which its award is based. The award shall also state the date when the award is made and the seat of the arbitration; and it shall be signed by the Arbitral Tribunal or those of its members assenting to it.

26.2 If any arbitrator fails to comply with the mandatory provisions of any applicable law relating to the making of the award, having been given a reasonable opportunity to do so, the remaining arbitrators may proceed in his absence and state in their award the circumstances of the other arbitrator's failure to participate in the making of the award.

26.3 Where there are three arbitrators and the Arbitral Tribunal fails to agree on any issue, the arbitrators shall decide that issue by a majority. Failing a majority decision on any issue, the chairman of the Arbitral Tribunal shall decide that issue.

26.4 If any arbitrator refuses or fails to sign the award, the signatures of the majority or (failing a majority) of the chairman shall be sufficient, provided that the reason for the omitted signature is stated in the award by the majority or chairman.

26.5 The sole arbitrator or chairman shall be responsible for delivering the award to the LCIA Court, which shall transmit certified copies to the parties provided that the costs of arbitration have been paid to the LCIA in accordance with Article 28.

26.6 An award may be expressed in any currency. The Arbitral Tribunal may order that simple or compound interest shall be paid by any party on any sum awarded at such rates as the Arbitral Tribunal determines to be appropriate, without being bound by legal rates of interest imposed by any state court, in respect of any period which the Arbitral Tribunal determines to be appropriate ending not later than the date upon which the award is complied with.

26.7 The Arbitral Tribunal may make separate awards on different issues at different times. Such awards shall have the same status and effect as any other award made by the Arbitral Tribunal.

26.8 In the event of a settlement of the parties' dispute, the Arbitral Tribunal may render an award recording the settlement if the parties so request in writing (a "Consent Award"), provided always that such award contains an express statement that it is an award made by the parties' consent. A Consent Award need not contain reasons. If the parties do not require a consent award, then on written confirmation by the parties to the LCIA Court that a settlement has been reached, the Arbitral Tribunal shall be discharged and the arbitration proceedings concluded, subject to payment by the parties of any outstanding costs of the arbitration under Article 28.

26.9 All awards shall be final and binding on the parties. By agreeing to arbitration under these Rules, the parties undertake to carry out any award immediately and without any delay (subject only to Article 27); and the parties also waive irrevocably their right to any form of appeal, review or recourse to any state court or other judicial authority, insofar as such waiver may be validly made. **[4304]**

Article 27

Correction of Awards and Additional Awards

27.1 Within 30 days of receipt of any award, or such lesser period as may be agreed in writing by the parties, a party may by written notice to the Registrar (copied to all other parties) request the Arbitral Tribunal to correct in the award any errors in computation, clerical or typographical errors or any errors of a similar nature. If the Arbitral Tribunal considers the request to be justified, it shall make the corrections within 30 days of receipt of the request. Any correction shall take the form of separate memorandum dated and signed by the Arbitral Tribunal or (if three arbitrators) those of its members assenting to it; and such memorandum shall become part of the award for all purposes.

27.2 The Arbitral Tribunal may likewise correct any error of the nature described in Article 27.1 on its own initiative within 30 days of the date of the award, to the same effect.

27.3 Within 30 days of receipt of the final award, a party may by written notice to the Registrar (copied to all other parties), request the Arbitral Tribunal to make an additional award as to claims or counterclaims presented in the arbitration but not determined in any award. If the Arbitral Tribunal considers the request to be justified, it shall make the additional award within 60 days of receipt of the request. The provisions of Article 26 shall apply to any additional award.

[4305]

Article 28

Arbitration and Legal Costs

28.1 The costs of the arbitration (other than the legal or other costs incurred by the parties themselves) shall be determined by the LCIA Court in accordance with the Schedule of Costs. The parties shall be jointly and severally liable to the Arbitral Tribunal and the LCIA for such arbitration costs.

28.2 The Arbitral Tribunal shall specify in the award the total amount of the costs of the arbitration as determined by the LCIA Court. Unless the parties agree otherwise in writing, the Arbitral Tribunal shall determine the proportions in which the parties shall bear all or part of such arbitration costs. If the Arbitral Tribunal has determined that all or any part of the arbitration costs shall be borne by a party other than a party which has already paid them to the LCIA, the latter party shall have the right to recover the appropriate amount from the former party.

28.3 The Arbitral Tribunal shall also have the power to order in its award that all or part of the legal or other costs incurred by a party be paid by another party, unless the parties agree otherwise in writing. The Arbitral Tribunal shall determine and fix the amount of each item comprising such costs on such reasonable basis as it thinks fit.

28.4 Unless the parties otherwise agree in writing, the Arbitral Tribunal shall make its orders on both arbitration and legal costs on the general principle that costs should reflect the parties' relative success and failure in the award or arbitration, except where it appears to the Arbitral Tribunal that in the particular circumstances this general approach is inappropriate. Any order for costs shall be made with reasons in the award containing such order.

28.5 If the arbitration is abandoned, suspended or concluded, by agreement or otherwise, before the final award is made, the parties shall remain jointly and severally liable to pay to the LCIA and the Arbitral Tribunal the costs of the arbitration as determined by the LCIA Court in accordance with the Schedule of Costs. In the event that such arbitration costs are less than the deposits made by the parties, there shall be a refund by the LCIA in such proportion as the parties may agree in writing, or failing such agreement, in the same proportions as the deposits were made by the parties to the LCIA.

[4306]

Article 29

Decisions by the LCIA Court

29.1 The decisions of the LCIA Court with respect to all matters relating to the arbitration shall be conclusive and binding upon the parties and the Arbitral Tribunal. Such decisions are to be treated as administrative in nature and the LCIA Court shall not be required to give any reasons.

29.2 To the extent permitted by the law of the seat of the arbitration, the parties shall be taken to have waived any right of appeal or review in respect of any such decisions of the LCIA Court to any state court or other judicial authority. If such appeals or review remain possible due to mandatory provisions of any applicable law, the LCIA Court shall, subject to the provisions of that applicable law, decide whether the arbitral proceedings are to continue, notwithstanding an appeal or review. **[4307]**

Article 30

Confidentiality

30.1 Unless the parties expressly agree in writing to the contrary, the parties undertake as a general principle to keep confidential all awards in their arbitration, together with all materials in the proceedings created for the purpose of the arbitration and all other documents produced by another party in the proceedings not otherwise in the public domain – save and to the extent that disclosure may be required of a party by legal duty, to protect or pursue a legal right or to enforce or challenge an award in bona fide legal proceedings before a state court or other judicial authority.

30.2 The deliberations of the Arbitral Tribunal are likewise confidential to its members, save and to the extent that disclosure of an arbitrator's refusal to participate in the arbitration is required of the other members of the Arbitral Tribunal under Articles 10, 12 and 26.

30.3 The LCIA Court does not publish any award or any part of an award without the prior written consent of all parties and the Arbitral Tribunal. **[4308]**

Article 31

Exclusion of Liability

31.1 None of the LCIA, the LCIA Court (including its President, Vice Presidents and individual members), the Registrar, any deputy Registrar, any arbitrator and any expert to the Arbitral Tribunal shall be liable to any party howsoever for any act or omission in connection with any arbitration conducted by reference to these Rules, save where the act or omission is shown by that party to constitute conscious and deliberate wrongdoing committed by the body or person alleged to be liable to that party.

31.2 After the award has been made and the possibilities of correction and additional awards referred to in Article 27 have lapsed or been exhausted, neither the LCIA, the LCIA Court (including its President, Vice Presidents and individual members), the Registrar, any deputy Registrar, any arbitrator or expert to the Arbitral Tribunal shall be under any legal obligation to make any statement to any person about any matter concerning the arbitration, nor shall any party seek to make any of these persons a witness in any legal or other proceedings arising out of the arbitration. **[4309]**

Article 32

General Rules

32.1 A party who knows that any provision of the Arbitration Agreement (including these Rules) has not been complied with and yet proceeds with the arbitration without promptly stating its objection to such non-compliance, shall be treated as having irrevocably waived its right to object.

32.2 In all matters not expressly provided for in these Rules, the LCIA Court, the Arbitral Tribunal and the parties shall act in the spirit of these Rules and shall make every reasonable effort to ensure that an award is legally enforceable. **[4310]**

The Schedule of Fees and the Recommended Arbitration Clauses are not reproduced here. They can be found at www.lcia.org.

E. INTERNATIONAL CARRIAGE: AIR, RAIL AND ROAD

THE WARSAW CONVENTION WITH THE AMENDMENTS MADE IN IT BY THE HAGUE PROTOCOL

NOTES

The text of the following Convention appears as set out in the Carriage by Air Act 1961, Sch 1.

The text is set out in italics to indicate that it is to be substituted, as from a day to be appointed, by the Carriage by Air and Road Act 1979, s 1(1), Sch 1, as set out at **[4303]**.

PART I
THE ENGLISH TEXT

CONVENTION
FOR THE UNIFICATION OF CERTAIN RULES RELATING TO INTERNATIONAL CARRIAGE BY AIR

CHAPTER I
SCOPE—DEFINITIONS

Article 1

(1) This Convention applies to all international carriage of persons, baggage or cargo performed by aircraft for reward. It applies equally to gratuitous carriage by aircraft performed by an air transport undertaking.

(2) For the purposes of this Convention, the expression international carriage means any carriage in which, according to the agreement between the parties, the place of departure and the place of destination, whether or not there be a break in the carriage or a transhipment, are situated either within the territories of two High Contracting Parties or within the territory of a single High Contracting Party if there is an agreed stopping place within the territory of another State, even if that State is not a High Contracting Party. Carriage between two points within the territory of a single High Contracting Party without an agreed stopping place within the territory of another State is not international carriage for the purposes of this Convention.

(3) Carriage to be performed by several successive air carriers is deemed, for the purposes of this Convention, to be one undivided carriage if it has been regarded by the parties as a single operation, whether it had been agreed upon under the form of a single contract or of a series of contracts, and it does not lose its international character merely because one contract or a series of contracts is to be performed entirely within the territory of the same State.

Article 2

(1) This Convention applies to carriage performed by the State or by legally constituted public bodies provided it falls within the conditions laid down in Article 1.

(2) This Convention shall not apply to carriage of mail and postal packages.

CHAPTER II
DOCUMENTS OF CARRIAGE

SECTION 1.—PASSENGER TICKET

Article 3

(1) In respect of the carriage of passengers a ticket shall be delivered containing—

(a) an indication of the places of departure and destination;

(b) if the places of departure and destination are within the territory of a single High Contracting Party, one or more agreed stopping places being within the territory of another State, an indication of at least one such stopping place;

(c) *a notice to the effect that, if the passenger's journey involves an ultimate destination or stop in a country other than the country of departure, the Warsaw Convention may be applicable and that the Convention governs and in most cases limits the liability of carriers for death or personal injury and in respect of loss of or damage to baggage.*

(2) *The passenger ticket shall constitute prima facie evidence of the conclusion and conditions of the contract of carriage. The absence, irregularity or loss of the passenger ticket does not affect the existence or the validity of the contract of carriage which shall, none the less, be subject to the rules of this Convention. Nevertheless, if, with the consent of the carrier, the passenger embarks without a passenger ticket having been delivered, or if the ticket does not include the notice required by paragraph (1)(c) of this Article, the carrier shall not be entitled to avail himself of the provisions of Article 22.*

SECTION 2.—BAGGAGE CHECK

Article 4

(*1*) *In respect of the carriage of registered baggage, a baggage check shall be delivered, which, unless combined with or incorporated in a passenger ticket which complies with the provisions of Article 3, paragraph (1), shall contain—*

(*a*) *an indication of the places of departure and destination;*

(*b*) *if the places of departure and destination are within the territory of a single High Contracting Party, one or more agreed stopping places being within the territory of another State, an indication of at least one such stopping place;*

(*c*) *a notice to the effect that, if the carriage involves an ultimate destination or stop in a country other than the country of departure, the Warsaw Convention may be applicable and that the Convention governs and in most cases limits the liability of carriers in respect of loss of or damage to baggage.*

(2) *The baggage check shall constitute prima facie evidence of the registration of the baggage and of the conditions of the contract of carriage. The absence, irregularity or loss of the baggage check does not affect the existence or the validity of the contract of carriage which shall, none the less, be subject to the rules of this Convention. Nevertheless, if the carrier takes charge of the baggage without a baggage check having been delivered or if the baggage check (unless combined with or incorporated in the passenger ticket which complies with the provisions of Article 3, paragraph (1) (c)) does not include the notice required by paragraph (1) (c) of this Article, he shall not be entitled to avail himself of the provisions of Article 22, paragraph (2).*

SECTION 3.—AIR WAYBILL

Article 5

(*1*) *Every carrier of cargo has the right to require the consignor to make out and hand over to him a document called an "air waybill"; every consignor has the right to require the carrier to accept this document.*

(2) *The absence, irregularity or loss of this document does not affect the existence or the validity of the contract of carriage which shall, subject to the provisions of Article 9, be none the less governed by the rules of this Convention.*

Article 6

(*1*) *The air waybill shall be made out by the consignor in three original parts and be handed over with the cargo.*

(2) *The first part shall be marked "for the carrier," and shall be signed by the consignor. The second part shall be marked "for the consignee"; it shall be signed by the consignor and by the carrier and shall accompany the cargo. The third part shall be signed by the carrier and handed by him to the consignor after the cargo has been accepted.*

(3) *The carrier shall sign prior to the loading of the cargo on board the aircraft.*

(4) *The signature of the carrier may be stamped; that of the consignor may be printed or stamped.*

(5) If, at the request of the consignor, the carrier makes out the air waybill, he shall be deemed, subject to proof to the contrary, to have done so on behalf of the consignor.

Article 7

The carrier of cargo has the right to require the consignor to make out separate waybills when there is more than one package.

Article 8

The air waybill shall contain—

(a) an indication of the places of departure and destination;

(b) if the places of departure and destination are within the territory of a single High Contracting Party, one or more agreed stopping places being within the territory of another State, an indication of at least one such stopping place;

(c) a notice to the consignor to the effect that, if the carriage involves an ultimate destination or stop in a country other than the country of departure, the Warsaw Convention may be applicable and that the Convention governs and in most cases limits the liability of carriers in respect of loss of or damage to cargo.

Article 9

If, with the consent of the carrier, cargo is loaded on board the aircraft without an air waybill having been made out, or if the air waybill does not include the notice required by Article 8, paragraph (c), the carrier shall not be entitled to avail himself of the provisions of Article 22, paragraph (2).

Article 10

(1) The consignor is responsible for the correctness of the particulars and statements relating to the cargo which he inserts in the air waybill.

(2) The consignor shall indemnify the carrier against all damage suffered by him, or by any other person to whom the carrier is liable, by reason of the irregularity, incorrectness or incompleteness of the particulars and statements furnished by the consignor.

Article 11

(1) The air waybill is prima facie evidence of the conclusion of the contract, of the receipt of the cargo and of the conditions of carriage.

(2) The statements in the air waybill relating to the weight, dimensions and packing of the cargo, as well as those relating to the number of packages, are prima facie evidence of the facts stated; those relating to the quantity, volume and condition of the cargo do not constitute evidence against the carrier except so far as they both have been, and are stated in the air waybill to have been, checked by him in the presence of the consignor, or relate to the apparent condition of the cargo.

Article 12

(1) Subject to his liability to carry out all his obligations under the contract of carriage, the consignor has the right to dispose of the cargo by withdrawing it at the aerodrome of departure or destination, or by stopping it in the course of the journey on any landing, or by calling for it to be delivered at the place of destination or in the course of the journey to a person other than the consignee named in the air waybill, or by requiring it to be returned to the aerodrome of departure. He must not exercise this right of disposition in such a way as to prejudice the carrier or other consignors and he must repay any expenses occasioned by the exercise of this right.

(2) If it is impossible to carry out the orders of the consignor the carrier must so inform him forthwith.

(3) If the carrier obeys the orders of the consignor for the disposition of the cargo without requiring the production of the part of the air waybill delivered to the latter, he will be

liable, without prejudice to his right of recovery from the consignor, for any damage which may be caused thereby to any person who is lawfully in possession of that part of the air waybill.

(4) *The right conferred on the consignor ceases at the moment when that of the consignee begins in accordance with Article 13. Nevertheless, if the consignee declines to accept the waybill or the cargo, or if he cannot be communicated with, the consignor resumes his right of disposition.*

Article 13

(1) *Except in the circumstances set out in the preceding Article, the consignee is entitled, on arrival of the cargo at the place of destination, to require the carrier to hand over to him the air waybill and to deliver the cargo to him, on payment of the charges due and on complying with the conditions of carriage set out in the air waybill.*

(2) *Unless it is otherwise agreed, it is the duty of the carrier to give notice to the consignee as soon as the cargo arrives.*

(3) *If the carrier admits the loss of the cargo, or if the cargo has not arrived at the expiration of seven days after the date on which it ought to have arrived, the consignee is entitled to put into force against the carrier the rights which flow from the contract of carriage.*

Article 14

The consignor and the consignee can respectively enforce all the rights given them by Articles 12 and 13, each in his own name, whether he is acting in his own interest or in the interest of another, provided that he carries out the obligations imposed by the contract.

Article 15

(1) *Articles 12, 13 and 14 do not affect either the relations of the consignor or the consignee with each other or the mutual relations of third parties whose rights are derived either from the consignor or from the consignee.*

(2) *The provisions of Articles 12, 13 and 14 can only be varied by express provision in the air waybill.*

(3) *Nothing in this Convention prevents the issue of a negotiable air waybill.*

Article 16

(1) *The consignor must furnish such information and attach to the air waybill such documents as are necessary to meet the formalities of customs, octroi or police before the cargo can be delivered to the consignee. The consignor is liable to the carrier for any damage occasioned by the absence, insufficiency or irregularity of any such information or documents, unless the damage is due to the fault of the carrier or his servants or agents.*

(2) *The carrier is under no obligation to enquire into the correctness or sufficiency of such information or documents.*

CHAPTER III
LIABILITY OF THE CARRIER

Article 17

The carrier is liable for damage sustained in the event of the death or wounding of a passenger or any bodily injury suffered by a passenger, if the accident which caused the damage so sustained took place on board the aircraft or in the course of any of the operations of embarking or disembarking.

Article 18

(1) *The carrier is liable for damage sustained in the event of the destruction or loss of, or of damage to, any registered baggage or any cargo, if the occurrence which caused the damage so sustained took place during the carriage by air.*

(2) The carriage by air within the meaning of the preceding paragraph comprises the period during which the baggage or cargo is in charge of the carrier, whether in an aerodrome or on board an aircraft, or, in the case of a landing outside an aerodrome, in any place whatsoever.

(3) The period of the carriage by air does not extend to any carriage by land, by sea or by river performed outside an aerodrome. If, however, such a carriage takes place in the performance of a contract for carriage by air, for the purpose of loading, delivery or transshipment, any damage is presumed, subject to proof to the contrary, to have been the result of an event which took place during the carriage by air.

Article 19

The carrier is liable for damage occasioned by delay in the carriage by air of passengers, baggage or cargo.

Article 20

The carrier is not liable if he proves that he and his servants or agents have taken all necessary measures to avoid the damage or that it was impossible for him or them to take such measures.

Article 21

If the carrier proves that the damage was caused by or contributed to by the negligence of the injured person the court may, in accordance with the provisions of its own law, exonerate the carrier wholly or partly from his liability.

Article 22

(1) In the carriage of persons the liability of the carrier for each passenger is limited to the sum of [16,600 special drawing rights]. Where, in accordance with the law of the court seised of the case, damages may be awarded in the form of periodical payments the equivalent capital value of the said payments shall not exceed [this limit]. Nevertheless, by special contract, the carrier and the passenger may agree to a higher limit of liability.

(2)

- (a) *In the carriage of registered baggage and of cargo, the liability of the carrier is limited to a sum of [17 special drawing rights] per kilogramme, unless the passenger or consignor has made, at the time when the package was handed over to the carrier, a special declaration of interest in delivery at destination and has paid a supplementary sum if the case so requires. In that case the carrier will be liable to pay a sum not exceeding the declared sum, unless he proves that that sum is greater than the passenger's or consignor's actual interest in delivery at destination.*
- (b) *In the case of loss, damage or delay of part of registered baggage or cargo, or of any object contained therein, the weight to be taken into consideration in determining the amount to which the carrier's liability is limited shall be only the total weight of the package or packages concerned. Nevertheless, when the loss, damage or delay of a part of the registered baggage or cargo, or of an object contained therein, affects the value of other packages covered by the same baggage check or the same air waybill, the total weight of such package or packages shall also be taken into consideration in determining the limit of liability.*

(3) As regards objects of which the passenger takes charge himself the liability of the carrier is limited to [332 special drawing rights] per passenger.

(4) The limits prescribed in this Article shall not prevent the court from awarding, in accordance with its own law, in addition, the whole or part of the court costs and of the other expenses of the litigation incurred by the plaintiff. The foregoing provision shall not apply if the amount of the damages awarded, excluding court costs and other expenses of the litigation, does not exceed the sum which the carrier has offered in writing to the plaintiff within a period of six months from the date of the occurrence causing the damage, or before the commencement of the action, if that is later.

[(5) The sums mentioned in terms of the special drawing right in this Article shall be deemed to refer to the special drawing right as defined by the International Monetary Fund. Conversion of the sums into national currencies shall, in case of judicial proceedings, be made according to the value of such currencies in terms of the special drawing right at the date of the judgment.]

Article 23

(1) Any provision tending to relieve the carrier of liability or to fix a lower limit than that which is laid down in this Convention shall be null and void, but the nullity of any such provision does not involve the nullity of the whole contract, which shall remain subject to the provisions of this Convention.

(2) Paragraph (1) of this Article shall not apply to provisions governing loss or damage resulting from the inherent defect, quality or vice of the cargo carried.

Article 24

(1) In the case covered by Articles 18 and 19 any action for damages, however founded, can only be brought subject to the conditions and limits set out in this Convention.

(2) In the cases covered by Article 17 the provisions of the preceding paragraph also apply, without prejudice to the questions as to who are the persons who have the right to bring suit and what are their respective rights.

Article 25

The limits of liability specified in Article 22 shall not apply if it is proved that the damage resulted from an act or omission of the carrier, his servants or agents, done with intent to cause damage or recklessly and with knowledge that damage would probably result; provided that, in the case of such act or omission of a servant or agent, it is also proved that he was acting within the scope of his employment.

Article 25A

(1) If an action is brought against a servant or agent of the carrier arising out of damage to which this Convention relates, such servant or agent, if he proves that he acted within the scope of his employment, shall be entitled to avail himself of the limits of liability which that carrier himself is entitled to invoke under Article 22.

(2) The aggregate of the amounts recoverable from the carrier, his servants and agents, in that case, shall not exceed the said limits.

(3) The provisions of paragraphs (1) and (2) of this Article shall not apply if it is proved that the damage resulted from an act or omission of the servant or agent done with intent to cause damage or recklessly and with knowledge that damage would probably result.

Article 26

(1) Receipt by the person entitled to delivery of baggage or cargo without complaint is prima facie evidence that the same has been delivered in good condition and in accordance with the document of carriage.

(2) In the case of damage, the person entitled to delivery must complain to the carrier forthwith after the discovery of the damage, and, at the latest, within seven days from the date of receipt in the case of baggage and fourteen days from the date of receipt in the case of cargo. In the case of delay the complaint must be made at the latest within twenty-one days from the date on which the baggage or cargo have been placed at his disposal.

(3) Every complaint must be made in writing upon the document of carriage or by separate notice in writing despatched within the times aforesaid.

(4) Failing complaint within the times aforesaid, no action shall lie against the carrier, save in the case of fraud on his part.

Article 27

In the case of the death of the person liable, an action for damages lies in accordance with the terms of this Convention against those legally representing his estate.

Article 28

(*1*) *An action for damages must be brought, at the option of the plaintiff, in the territory of one of the High Contracting Parties, either before the court having jurisdiction where the carrier is ordinarily resident, or has his principal place of business, or has an establishment by which the contract has been made or before the court having jurisdiction at the place of destination.*

(2) *Questions of procedure shall be governed by the law of the court seised of the case.*

Article 29

(*1*) *The right to damages shall be extinguished if an action is not brought within two years, reckoned from the date of arrival at the destination, or from the date on which the aircraft ought to have arrived, or from the date on which the carriage stopped.*

(2) *The method of calculating the period of limitation shall be determined by the law of the court seised of the case.*

Article 30

(*1*) *In the case of carriage to be performed by various successive carriers and falling within the definition set out in the third paragraph of Article 1, each carrier who accepts passengers, baggage or cargo is subjected to the rules set out in this Convention, and is deemed to be one of the contracting parties to the contract of carriage in so far as the contract deals with that part of the carriage which is performed under his supervision.*

(2) *In the case of carriage of this nature, the passenger or his representative can take action only against the carrier who performed the carriage during which the accident or the delay occurred, save in the case where, by express agreement, the first carrier has assumed liability for the whole journey.*

(3) *As regards baggage or cargo, the passenger or consignor will have a right of action against the first carrier, and the passenger or consignee who is entitled to delivery will have a right of action against the last carrier, and further, each may take action against the carrier who performed the carriage during which the destruction, loss, damage or delay took place. These carriers will be jointly and severally liable to the passenger or to the consignor or consignee.*

CHAPTER IV
PROVISIONS RELATING TO COMBINED CARRIAGE

Article 31

(*1*) *In the case of combined carriage performed partly by air and partly by any other mode of carriage, the provisions of this Convention apply only to the carriage by air, provided that the carriage by air falls within the terms of Article 1.*

(2) *Nothing in this Convention shall prevent the parties in the case of combined carriage from inserting in the document of air carriage conditions relating to other modes of carriage, provided that the provisions of this Convention are observed as regards the carriage by air.*

CHAPTER V
GENERAL AND FINAL PROVISIONS

Article 32

Any clause contained in the contract and all special agreements entered into before the damage occurred by which the parties purport to infringe the rules laid down by this Convention, whether by deciding the law to be applied, or by altering the rules as to jurisdiction, shall be null and void. Nevertheless for the carriage of cargo arbitration clauses are allowed, subject to this Convention, if the arbitration is to take place within one of the jurisdictions referred to in the first paragraph of Article 28.

Article 33

Nothing contained in this Convention shall prevent the carrier either from refusing to enter into any contract of carriage, or from making regulations which do not conflict with the provisions of this Convention.

Article 34

The provisions of Articles 3 to 9 inclusive relating to documents of carriage shall not apply in the case of carriage performed in extraordinary circumstances outside the normal scope of an air carrier's business.

Article 35

The expression "days" when used in this Convention means current days not working days.

Article 36

The Convention is drawn up in French in a single copy which shall remain deposited in the archives of the Ministry for Foreign Affairs of Poland and of which one duly certified copy shall be sent by the Polish Government to the Government of each of the High Contracting Parties.

Article 40A

(*1*) (This paragraph is not reproduced. It defines "High Contracting Party".)

(2) *For the purposes of the Convention the word territory means not only the metropolitan territory of a State but also all other territories for the foreign relations of which that State is responsible.*

(Articles 37, 38, 39, 40 and 41 and the concluding words of the Convention are not reproduced. They deal with the coming into force of the Convention.)

ADDITIONAL PROTOCOL

(*With Reference to Article* 2)

The High Contracting Parties reserve to themselves the right to declare at the time of ratification or of accession that the first paragraph of Article 2 of this Convention shall not apply to international carriage by air performed directly by the State, its colonies, protectorates or mandated territories or by any other territory under its sovereignty, suzerainty or authority.

[4311]

NOTES

Substituted, as from a day to be appointed, by the Carriage by Air and Road Act 1979, s 1(1), Sch 1, as set out at **[4303]**.

Art 22: words in square brackets in paras (1)–(3) and the whole of para (5) substituted by the Carriage by Air and Road Act 1979, s 4(1)(a).

PART II
THE FRENCH TEXT

CONVENTION
POUR L'UNIFICATION DE CERTAINES REGLES RELATIVES AU TRANSPORT AERIEN INTERNATIONAL

CHAPITRE IER
OBJET—DÉFINITIONS

Article 1er

(1) La présente Convention s'applique à tout transport international de personnes, bagages ou marchandises, effectué par aéronef contre rémunération. Elle s'applique également aux transports gratuits effectués par aéronef par une entreprise de transports aériens.

(2) Est qualifié transport international, au sens de la présente Convention, tout transport dans lequel, d'après les stipulations des parties, le point de départ et le point de destination, qu'il y ait ou non interruption de transport ou transbordement, sont situés soit sur le territoire de deux Hautes Parties Contractantes, soit sur le territoire d'une seule Haute Partie Contractante si une escale est prévue sur le territoire d'un autre Etat, même si cet Etat n'est pas une Haute Partie Contractante. Le transport sans une telle escale entre deux points du territoire d'une seule Haute Partie Contractante n'est pas considéré comme international au sens de la présente Convention.

(3) Le transport à exécuter par plusieurs transporteurs par air successifs est censé constituer pour l'application de la présente Convention un transport unique lorsqu'il a été envisagé par les parties comme une seule opération, qu'il ait été conclu sous la forme d'un seul contrat ou d'une série de contrats, et il ne perd pas son caractère international par le fait qu'un seul contrat ou une série de contrats doivent être exécutés intégralement dans le territoire d'un même Etat.

Article 2

(1) La Convention s'applique aux transports effectués par l'État ou les autres personnes juridiques de droit public, dans les conditions prévues à l'article 1er.

(2) La présente Convention ne s'applique pas au transport du courrier et des colis postaux.

CHAPITRE II
TITRE DE TRANSPORT

SECTION 1.—BILLET DE PASSAGE

Article 3

(1) Dans le transport de passagers, un billet de passage doit être délivré, contenant—

(a) l'indication des points de départ et de destination;

(b) si les points de départ et de destination sont situés sur le territoire d'une même Haute Partie Contractante et qu'une ou plusieurs escales soient prévues sur le territoire d'un autre Etat, l'indication d'une de ces escales;

(c) un avis indiquant que si les passagers entreprennent un voyage comportant une destination finale ou une escale dans un pays autre que le pays de départ, leur transport peut être régi par la Convention de Varsovie qui, en général, limite la responsabilité du transporteur en cas de mort ou de lésion corporelle, ainsi qu'en cas de perte ou d'avarie des bagages.

(2) Le billet de passage fait foi, jusqu'à preuve contraire, de la conclusion et des conditions du contrat de transport. L'absence, l'irrégularité ou la perte du billet n'affecte ni l'existence ni la validité du contrat de transport, qui n'en sera pas moins soumis aux règles de la présente Convention. Toutefois, si, du consentement du transporteur, le passager s'embarque sans qu'un billet de passage ait été délivré, ou si le billet ne comporte pas l'avis prescrit à l'alinéa 1(c) du présent article, le transporteur n'aura pas le droit de se prévaloir des dispositions de l'article 22.

SECTION 2.—BULLETIN DE BAGAGES

Article 4

(1) Dans le transport de bagages enregistrés, un bulletin de bagages doit être délivré qui, s'il n'est pas combiné avec un billet de passage conforme aux dispositions de l'article 3, alinéa 1er, ou n'est pas inclus dans un tel billet, doit contenir—

(*a*) *l'indication des points de départ et de destination;*

(*b*) *si les points de départ et de destination sont situés sur le territoire d'une même Haute Partie Contractante et qu'une ou plusieurs escales soient prévues sur le territoire d'un autre Etat, l'indication d'une de ces escales;*

(*c*) *un avis indiquant que, si le transport comporte une destination finale ou une escale dans un pays autre que le pays de départ, il peut être régi par la Convention de Varsovie qui, en général, limite la responsabilité du transporteur en cas de perte ou d'avarie des bagages.*

(2) Le bulletin de bagages fait foi, jusqu'à preuve contraire, de l'enregistrement des bagages et des conditions du contrat de transport. L'absence, l'irrégularité ou la perte du bulletin n'affecte ni l'existence ni la validité du contrat de transport, qui n'en sera pas moins soumis aux règles de la présente Convention. Toutefois, si le transporteur accepte la garde des bagages sans qu'un bulletin ait été délivré ou si, dans le cas où le bulletin n'est pas combiné avec un billet de passage conforme aux dispositions de l'article 3, alinéa 1(c), ou n'est pas inclus dans un tel billet, il ne comporte pas l'avis prescrit à l'alinéa 1(c) du présent article, le transporteur n'aura pas le droit de se prévaloir des dispositions de l'article 22, alinéa 2.

SECTION 3.—LETTRE DE TRANSPORT AÉRIEN

Article 5

(1) Tout transporteur de marchandises a le droit de demander à l'expéditeur l'établissement et la remise d'un titre appelé: "lettre de transport aérien"; tout expéditeur a le droit de demander au transporteur l'acceptation de ce document.

(2) Toutefois, l'absence, l'irrégularité ou la perte de ce titre n'affecte ni l'existence, ni la validité du contrat de transport qui n'en sera pas moins soumis aux règles de la présente Convention, sous réserve des dispositions de l'article 9.

Article 6

(1) La lettre de transport aérien est établie par l'expéditeur en trois exemplaires originaux et remise avec la marchandise.

(2) Le premier exemplaire porte la mention "pour le transporteur"; il est signé par l'expéditeur. Le deuxième exemplaire porte la mention "pour le destinataire"; il est signé par l'expéditeur et le transporteur et il accompagne la marchandise. Le troisième exemplaire est signé par le transporteur et remis par lui à l'expéditeur après acceptation de la marchandise.

(3) La signature du transporteur doit être apposée avant l'embarquement de la marchandise à bord de l'aéronef.

(4) La signature du transporteur peut être remplacée par un timbre; celle de l'expéditeur peut être imprimée ou remplacée par un timbre.

(5) Si, à la demande de l'expéditeur, le transporteur établit la lettre de transport aérien, il est considéré jusqu'à preuve contraire, comme agissant pour le compte de l'expéditeur.

Article 7

Le transporteur de marchandises a le droit de demander à l'expéditeur l'établissement de lettres de transport aérien différentes lorsqu'il y a plusieurs colis.

Article 8

La lettre de transport aérien doit contenir—

(*a*) *l'indication des points de départ et de destination;*

(*b*) *si les points de départ et de destination sont situés sur le territoire d'une même Haute Partie Contractante et qu'une ou plusieurs escales soient prévues sur le territoire d'un autre Etat, l'indication d'une de ces escales;*

(*c*) *un avis indiquant aux expéditeurs que, si le transport comporte une destination finale ou une escale dans un pays autre que le pays de départ, il peut être régi par la Convention de Varsovie qui, en général, limite la responsabilité des transporteurs en cas de perte ou d'avarie des marchandises.*

Article 9

Si, du consentement du transporteur, des marchandises sont embarquées à bord de l'aéronef sans qu'une lettre de transport aérien ait été établie ou si celle-ci ne comporte pas l'avis prescrit à l'article 8, alinéa (c), le transporteur n'aura pas le droit de se prévaloir des dispositions de l'article 22, alinéa 2.

Article 10

(*1*) *L'expéditeur est responsable de l'exactitude des indications et déclarations concernant la marchandise qu'il inscrit dans la lettre de transport aérien.*

(2) *Il supportera la responsabilité de tout dommage subi par le transporteur ou par toute autre personne à l'égard de laquelle la responsabilité du transporteur est engagée à raison de ses indications et déclarations irrégulières, inexactes ou incomplètes.*

Article 11

(*1*) *La lettre de transport aérien fait foi, jusqu'à preuve contraire, de la conclusion du contrat, de la réception de la marchandise et des conditions du transport.*

(2) *Les énonciations de la lettre de transport aérien, relatives au poids, aux dimensions et à l'emballage de la marchandise ainsi qu'au nombre des colis, font foi jusqu'à preuve contraire; celles relatives à la quantité au volume et à l'état de la marchandise ne font preuve contre le transporteur qu'autant que la vérification en a été faite par lui en présence de l'expéditeur, et constatée sur la lettre de transport aérien, ou qu'il s'agit d'énonciations relatives à l'état apparent de la marchandise.*

Article 12

(*1*) *L'expéditeur a le droit, sous la condition d'exécuter toutes les obligations résultant du contrat de transport, de disposer de la marchandise, soit en la retirant à l'aérodrome de départ ou de destination, soit en l'arrêtant en cours de route lors d'un atterrissage, soit en la faisant délivrer au lieu de destination ou en cours de route à une personne autre que le destinataire indiqué sur la lettre de transport aérien, soit en demandant son retour à l'aérodrome de départ, pour autant que l'exercice de ce droit ne port préjudice ni au transporteur, ni aux autres expéditeurs et avec l'obligation de rembourser les frais qui en résultent.*

(2) *Dans le cas où l'exécution des ordres de l'expéditeur est impossible, le transporteur doit l'en aviser immédiatement.*

(*3*) *Si le transporteur se conforme aux ordres de disposition de l'expéditeur, sans exiger la production de l'exemplaire de la lettre de transport aérien délivré à celui-ci, il sera responsable, sauf son recours contre l'expéditeur, du préjudice qui pourrait être causé par ce fait à celui qui est régulièrement en possession de la lettre de transport aérien.*

(4) *Le droit de l'expéditeur cesse au moment où celui du destinataire commence, conformément à l'article 13 ci-dessous. Toutefois, si le desinataire refuse la lettre de transport ou la marchandise, ou s'il ne peut être atteint, l'expéditeur reprend son droit de disposition.*

Article 13

(*1*) *Sauf dans les cas indiqués à l'article précédent, le destinataire a le droit, dès l'arrivée de la marchandise au point de destination, de demander au transporteur de lui remettre la lettre de transport aérien et de lui livrer la marchandise contre le paiement du montant des créances et contre l'exécution des conditions de transport indiquées dans la lettre de transport aérien.*

(2) *Sauf stipulation contraire, le transporteur doit aviser le destinataire dès l'arrivée de la marchandise.*

(3) *Si la perte de la marchandise est reconnue par le transporteur ou si, à l'expiration d'un délai de sept jours après qu'elle aurait dû arriver, la marchandise n'est pas arrivée, le destinataire est autorisé à faire valoir vis-à-vis du transporteur les droits résultant du contrat de transport.*

Article 14

L'expéditeur et le destinataire peuvent faire valoir tous les droits qui leur sont respectivement conférés par les articles 12 et 13, chacun en son propre nom, qu'il agisse dans son propre intérêt ou dans l'intérêt d'autrui, à condition d'exécuter les obligations que le contrat impose.

Article 15

(1) *Les articles 12, 13 et 14 ne portent aucun préjudice ni aux rapports de l'expéditeur et du destinataire entre eux, ni aux rapports des tiers dont les droits proviennent, soit de l'expéditeur, soit du destinataire.*

(2) *Toute clause dérogeant aux stipulations des articles 12, 13 et 14 doit être inscrite dans la lettre de transport aérien.*

(3) *Rien dans la présente Convention n'empêche l'établissement d'une lettre de transport aérien négociable.*

Article 16

(1) *L'expéditeur est tenu de fournir les renseignements et de joindre à la lettre de transport aérien les documents qui, avant la remise de la marchandise au destinataire, sont nécessaires à l'accomplissement des formalités de douane, d'octroi ou de police. L'expéditeur est responsable envers le transporteur de tous dommages qui pourraient résulter de l'absence, de l'insuffisance ou de l'irrégularité de ces renseignements et pièces, sauf le cas de faute de la part du transporteur ou de ses préposés.*

(2) *Le transporteur n'est pas tenu d'examiner si ces renseignements et documents sont exacts ou suffisants.*

CHAPITRE III
RESPONSABILITÉ DU TRANSPORTEUR

Article 17

Le transporteur est responsable du dommage survenu en cas de mort, de blessure ou de toute autre lésion corporelle subie par un voyageur lorsque l'accident qui a causé le dommage s'est produit à bord de l'aéronef ou au cours de toutes opérations d'embarquement et de débarquement.

Article 18

(1) *Le transporteur est responsable du dommage survenu en cas de destruction, perte ou avarie de bagages enregistrés ou de marchandises lorsque l'événement qui a causé le dommage s'est produit pendant le transport aérien.*

(2) *Le transport aérien, au sens de l'alinéa précédent, comprend la période pendant laquelle les bagages ou marchandises se trouvent sous la garde du transporteur, que ce soit dans un aérodrome ou à bord d'un aéronef ou dans un lieu quelconque en cas d'atterrissage en dehors d'un aérodrome.*

(3) *La période du transport aérien ne couvre aucun transport terrestre, maritime ou fluvial effectué en dehors d'un aérodrome. Toutefois lorsqu'un tel transport est effectué dans*

l'exécution du contrat de transport aérien en vue du chargement, de la livraison ou du transbordement, tout dommage est présumé, sauf preuve contraire, résulter d'un événement survenu pendant le transport aérien.

Article 19

Le transporteur est responsable du dommage résultant d'un retard dans le transport aérien de voyageurs, bagages ou marchandises.

Article 20

Le transporteur n'est pas responsable s'il prouve que lui et ses préposés ont pris toutes les mesures nécessaires pour éviter le dommage ou qu'il leur était impossible de les prendre.

Article 21

Dans le cas où le transporteur fait la preuve que la faute de la personne lésée a causé le dommage on y a contribué, le tribunal pourra, conformément aux dispositions de sa propre loi, écarter ou atténuer la responsabilité du transporteur.

Article 22

(1) Dans le transport des personnes, la responsabilité du transporteur relative à chaque passager est limitée à la somme de [16.600 Droits de Tirage spéciaux]. Dans le cas où, d'après la loi du tribunal saisi, l'indemnité peut être fixée sous forme de rente, le capital de la rente ne peut dépasser cette limite. Toutefois par une convention spéciale avec la transporteur, le passager pourra fixer une limite de responsabilité plus élevée.

(2)

(a) Dans le transport de bagages enregistrés et de marchandises, la responsabilité du transporteur est limité à la somme de [17 Droits de Tirage spéciaux] par kilogramme, sauf déclaration spéciale d'intérêt à la livraison faite par l'expéditeur au moment de la remise du colis au transporteur et moyennant le paiement d'une taxe supplémentaire éventuelle. Dans ce cas, le transporteur sera tenu de payer jusqu'à concurrence de la somme déclarée, à moins qu'il ne prouve qu'elle est supérieure à l'intérêt réel de l'expéditeur à la livraison.

(b) En cas de perte, d'avarie ou de retard d'une partie des bagages enregistrés ou des marchandises, ou de tout objet qui y est contenu, seul le poids total du ou des colis dont il s'agit est pris en considération pour déterminer la limite de responsabilité du transporteur. Toutefois, lorsque la perte, l'avarie ou le retard d'une partie des bagages enregistrés ou des marchandises, ou d'un objet qui y est contenu, affecte la valeur d'autres colis couverts par le même bulletin de bagages ou la même lettre de transport aérien, le poids total de ces colis doit être pris en considération pour déterminer la limite de responsabilité.

(3) En ce qui concerne les objets dont le passager conserve la garde, la responsabilité du transporteur est limitée à [332 Droits de Tirage spéciaux] par passager.

(4) Les limites fixées par le présent article n'ont pas pour effet d'enlever au tribunal la faculté d'allouer en outre, conformément à sa loi, une somme correspondant à tout ou partie des dépens et autres frais du procès exposés par le demandeur. La disposition précédente ne s'applique pas lorsque le montant de l'indemnité allouée, non compris les dépens et autres frais de procès, ne dépasse pas la somme que le transporteur a offerte par écrit au demandeur dans un délai de six mois à dater du fait qui a causé le dommage ou avant l'introduction de l'instance si celle-ci est postérieure à ce délai.

[(5) Les sommes indiquées en Droits de Tirage spéciaux dans le présent article sont considérées comme se rapportant au Droit de Tirage spécial tel que défini par le Fonds monétaire international. La conversion de ces sommes en monnaies nationales s'effectuera en cas d'instance judiciaire suivant la valeur de ces monnaies en Droit de Tirage spécial à la date du jugement.]

Article 23

(1) Toute clause tendant à exonérer le transporteur de sa responsabilité ou à établir une limite inférieure à celle qui est fixée dans la présente Convention est nulle et du nul effet, mais la nullité de cette clause n'entraîne pas la nullité du contrat qui reste soumis aux dispositions de la présente Convention.

(2) L'alinéa 1er du présent article ne s'applique pas aux clauses concernant le perte ou le dommage résultant de la nature ou du vice propre des marchandises transportées.

Article 24

(1) Dans les cas prévus aux articles 18 et 19 toute action en responsabilité, à quelque titre que ce soit, ne peut être exercée que dans les conditions et limites prévues par la présente Convention.

(2) Dans les cas prévus à l'article 17, s'appliquent également les dispositions de l'alinéa précédent, sans préjudice de la détermination des personnes qui ont le droit d'agir et de leurs droits respectifs.

Article 25

Les limites de responsabilité prévues à l'article 22 ne s'appliquent pas s'il est prouvé que le dommage résulte d'un acte ou d'une omission du transporteur ou de ses préposés fait, soit avec l'intention de provoquer un dommage, soit témérairement et avec conscience qu'un dommage en résultera probablement, pour autant que, dans le cas d'un acte ou d'une omission de préposés, la preuve soit également apportée que ceux-ci ont agi dans l'exercice de leur fonctions.

Article 25A

(1) Si une action est intentée contre un préposé du transporteur à la suite d'un dommage visé par la présente Convention, ce préposé, s'il prouve qu'il a agi dans l'exercice de ses fonctions, pourra se prévaloir des limites de responsabilité que peut invoquer ce transporteur en vertu de l'article 22.

(2) Le montant total de la réparation qui, dans ce cas, peur être obtenu du transporteur et de ses préposés ne doit pas dépasser lesdites limites.

(3) Les dispositions des alinéas 1 et 2 du présent article ne s'appliquent pas s'il est prouvé que le dommage résulte d'un acte ou d'une omission du préposé fait, soit avec l'intention de provoquer un dommage, soit témérairement et avec conscience qu'un dommage en résultera probablement.

Article 26

(1) La réception des bagages et marchandises sans protestation par le destinataire constituera présomption, sauf preuve contraire, que les marchandises ont été livrées en bon état et conformément au titre de transport.

(2) En cas d'avarie, le destinataire doit adresser au transporteur une protestation immédiatement après la découverte de l'avarie et, au plus tard, dans un délai de sept jours pour les bagages et de quatorze jours pour les marchandises à dater de leur réception. En cas de retard, la protestation devra être faite au plus tard dans les vingt et un jours à dater du jour où le bagage ou la marchandise auront été mis à sa disposition.

(3) Toute protestation doit être faite par réserve inscrite sur le titre de transport ou par un autre écrit expédié dans le délai prévu pour cette protestation.

(4) A défaut de protestation dans les délais prévus, toutes actions contre le transporteur sont irrecevables, sauf le cas de fraude de celui-ci.

Article 27

En cas de décès du débiteur, l'action en responsabilité, dans les limites prévues par la présente Convention, s'exerce contre ses ayants droit.

Article 28

(1) L'action en responsabilité devra être portée, au choix du demandeur, dans le territoire d'une des Hautes Parties Contractantes, soit devant le tribunal du domicile du transporteur, du siège principal de son exploitation ou du lieu où il possède un établissement par le soin duquel le contrat a été conclu, soit devant le tribunal du lieu de destination.

(2) La procédure sera réglée par la loi du tribunal saisi.

Article 29

(1) L'action en responsabilité doit être intentée, sous peine de déchéance, dans le délai de deux ans à compter de l'arrivée à destination ou du jour où l'aéronef aurait dû arriver, ou de l'arrêt du transport.

(2) Le mode du calcul du délai est déterminé par la loi du tribunal saisi.

Article 30

(1) Dans les cas de transport régis par la définition du troisième alinéa de l'article 1er, a exécuter par divers transporteurs successifs, chaque transporteur acceptant des voyageurs, des bagages ou des marchandises est soumis aux règles établies par cette Convention, et est censé être une des parties contractantes du contrat de transport, pour autant que ce contrat ait trait à la partie du transport effectuée sous son contrôle.

(2) Au cas d'un tel transport, le voyageur ou ses ayants droit ne pourront recourir que contre le transporteur ayant effectué le transport au cours duquel l'accident ou le retard s'est produit, sauf dans le cas où, par stipulation expresse, le premier transporteur aura assuré la responsabilité pour tout le voyage.

(3) S'il s'agit de bagages ou de marchandises, l'expéditeur aura recours contre le premier transporteur et le destinataire qui a le droit à la délivrance contre le dernier, et l'un et l'autre pourront, en outre, agir contre le transporteur ayant effectué le transport au cours duquel la destruction, la perte, l'avarie ou le retard se sont produits. Ces transporteurs seront solidairement responsables envers l'expéditeur et le destinataire.

CHAPITRE IV
DISPOSITIONS RELATIVES AUX TRANSPORTS COMBINÉS

Article 31

(1) Dans le cas de transports combinés effectués en partie par air et en partie par tout autre moyen de transport, les stipulations de la présente Convention ne s'appliquent qu'au transport aérien et si celui-ci répond aux conditions de l'article 1er.

(2) Rien dans la présente Convention n'empêche les parties, dans le cas de transports combinés, d'insérer dans le titre de transport aérien des conditions relatives à d'autres modes de transport, à condition que les stipulations de la présente Convention soient respectées en ce qui concerne le transport par air.

CHAPITRE V
DISPOSITIONS GÉNÉRALES ET FINALES

Article 32

Sont nulles toutes clauses du contrat de transport et toutes conventions particulières antérieures au dommage par lesquelles les parties dérogeraient aux règles de la présente Convention soit par une détermination de la loi applicable, soit par une modification des règles de compétence. Toutefois, dans le transport des marchandises, les clauses d'arbitrage sont admises, dans les limites de la présente Convention, lorsque l'arbitrage doit s'effectuer dans les lieux de compétence des tribunaux prévus à l'article 28, alinéa 1.

Article 33

Rien dans la présente Convention ne peut empêcher un transporteur de refuser la conclusion d'un contrat de transport ou de formuler des règlements qui ne sont pas en contradiction avec les dispositions de la présente Convention.

Article 34

Les dispositions des articles 3 à 9 inclus relative aux titres de transport ne sont pas applicables au transport effectué dans des circonstances extraordinaires en dehors de toute opération normale de l'exploitation aérienne.

Article 35

Lorsque dans la présente Convention il est question de jours, il s'agit de jours courants et non de jours ouvrables.

Article 36

La présente Convention est rédigée en français en un seul exemplaire qui restera déposé aux archives du Ministère des Affaires Etrangères de Pologne, et dont une copie certifiée conforme sera transmise par les soins du Gouvernement polonais au Gouvernement de chacune des Hautes Parties Contractantes.

Article 40A

(1) …

(2) *Aux fins de la Convention, le mot territoire signifie non seulement le territoire métropolitan d'un Etat, mais aussi tous les territoires qu'il représente dans les relations extérieures.*

PROTOCOLE ADDITIONNEL

Ad Article 2

Les Hautes Parties Contractantes se réservent le droit de déclarer au moment de la ratification ou de l'adhésion que l'article 2, alinéa premier, de la présente Convention ne s'appliquera pas aux transports internationaux aériens effectués directement par l'Etat, ses colonies, protectorats, territoires sous mandat ou tout autre territoire sous sa souveraineté, sa suzeraineté ou son autorité.

[4312]

NOTES

Substituted, as from a day to be appointed, by the Carriage by Air and Road Act 1979, s 1(1), Sch 1, as set out at **[4303]**.

Art 22: words in square brackets in paras (1)–(3) and the whole of para (5) substituted by the Carriage by Air and Road Act 1979, s 4(1)(b).

CONVENTION SUPPLEMENTARY TO THE WARSAW CONVENTION, FOR THE UNIFICATION OF CERTAIN RULES RELATING TO INTERNATIONAL CARRIAGE BY AIR PERFORMED BY A PERSON OTHER THAN THE CONTRACTING CARRIER

NOTES

The text of the following Convention appears as set out in the Carriage by Air (Supplementary Provisions) Act 1962, Schedule.

PART I
THE ENGLISH TEXT

CONVENTION
SUPPLEMENTARY TO THE WARSAW CONVENTION, FOR THE UNIFICATION OF CERTAIN RULES RELATING TO INTERNATIONAL CARRIAGE BY AIR PERFORMED BY A PERSON OTHER THAN THE CONTRACTING CARRIER

ARTICLE I

In this Convention—

(a) (*This paragraph is not reproduced. It defines "Warsaw Convention".*)

(b) "contracting carrier" means a person who as a principal makes an agreement for carriage governed by the Warsaw Convention with a passenger or consignor or with a person acting on behalf of the passenger or consignor;

(c) "actual carrier" means a person, other than the contracting carrier, who, by virtue of authority from the contracting carrier, performs the whole or part of the carriage contemplated in paragraph (b) but who is not with respect to such part a successive carrier within the meaning of the Warsaw Convention. Such authority is presumed in the absence of proof to the contrary.

ARTICLE II

If an actual carrier performs the whole or part of carriage which, according to the agreement referred to in Article I, paragraph (b), is governed by the Warsaw Convention, both the contracting carrier and the actual carrier shall, except as otherwise provided in this Convention, be subject to the rules of the Warsaw Convention, the former for the whole of the carriage contemplated in the agreement, the latter solely for the carriage which he performs.

ARTICLE III

1. The acts and omissions of the actual carrier and of his servants and agents acting within the scope of their employment shall, in relation to the carriage performed by the actual carrier, be deemed to be also those of the contracting carrier.

2. The acts and omissions of the contracting carrier and of his servants and agents acting within the scope of their employment shall, in relation to the carriage performed by the actual carrier, be deemed to be also those of the actual carrier. Nevertheless, no such act or omission shall subject the actual carrier to liability exceeding the limits specified in Article 22 [or Article 22A] of the Warsaw Convention. Any special agreement under which the contracting carrier assumes obligations not imposed by the Warsaw Convention or any waiver of rights conferred by that Convention or any special declaration of interest in delivery at destination contemplated in Article 22 [or Article 22A] of the said Convention, shall not affect the actual carrier unless agreed to by him.

ARTICLE IV

Any complaint to be made or order to be given under the Warsaw Convention to the carrier shall have the same effect whether addressed to the contracting carrier or to the actual carrier. Nevertheless, orders referred to in Article 12 of the Warsaw Convention shall only be effective if addressed to the contracting carrier.

ARTICLE V

In relation to the carriage performed by the actual carrier, any servant or agent of that carrier or of the contracting carrier shall, if he proves that he acted within the scope of his employment, be entitled to avail himself of the limits of liability which are applicable under this Convention to the carrier whose servant or agent he is unless it is proved that he acted in a manner which, under the Warsaw Convention, prevents the limits of liability from being invoked.

ARTICLE VI

In relation to the carriage performed by the actual carrier, the aggregate of the amounts recoverable from that carrier and the contracting carrier, and from their servants and agents acting within the scope of their employment, shall not exceed the highest amount which could be awarded against either the contracting carrier or the actual carrier under this Convention, but none of the persons mentioned shall be liable for a sum in excess of the limit applicable to him.

ARTICLE VII

In relation to the carriage performed by the actual carrier, an action for damages may be brought, at the option of the plaintiff, against that carrier or the contracting carrier, or against both together or separately. If the action is brought against only one of those carriers, that carrier shall have the right to require the other carrier to be joined in the proceedings, the procedure and effects being governed by the law of the court seised of the case.

ARTICLE VIII

Any action for damages contemplated in Article VII of this Convention must be brought, at the option of the plaintiff, either before a court in which an action may be brought against the contracting carrier, as provided in Article 28 of the Warsaw Convention, or before the court having jurisdiction at the place where the actual carrier is ordinarily resident or has his principal place of business.

ARTICLE IX

1. Any contractual provision tending to relieve the contracting carrier or the actual carrier of liability under this Convention or to fix a lower limit than that which is applicable according to this Convention shall be null and void, but the nullity of any such provision does not involve the nullity of the whole agreement, which shall remain subject to the provisions of this Convention.

2. In respect of the carriage performed by the actual carrier, the preceding paragraph shall not apply to contractual provisions governing loss or damage resulting from the inherent defect, quality or vice of the cargo carried.

3. Any clause contained in an agreement for carriage and all special agreements entered into before the damage occurred by which the parties purport to infringe the rules laid down by this Convention, whether by deciding the law to be applied, or by altering the rules as to jurisdiction, shall be null and void. Nevertheless, for the carriage of cargo arbitration clauses are allowed, subject to this Convention, if the arbitration is to take place in one of the jurisdictions referred to in Article VIII.

ARTICLE X

Except as provided in Article VII, nothing in this Convention shall affect the rights and obligations of the two carriers between themselves.

(*Articles XI to XVIII and the concluding words of the Convention are not reproduced. They deal with the coming into force of the Convention and provide that in the case of inconsistency the text in French shall prevail.*)

[4313]

NOTES

Article III: words in square brackets in para 2 inserted by the Carriage by Air and Road Act 1979, s 1(2), Sch 2, para 6, as from a day to be appointed.

PART II
THE FRENCH TEXT

CONVENTION

COMPLEMENTAIRE A LA CONVENTION DE VARSOVIE, POUR L'UNIFICATION DE CERTAINES REGLES RELATIVES AU TRANSPORT AERIEN INTERNATIONAL EFFECTUE PAR UNE PERSONNE AUTRE QUE LE TRANSPORTEUR CONTRACTUEL.

ARTICLE PREMIER

Dans la présente Convention—

(a) ...
(b) "transporteur contractuel" signifie une personne partie à un contrat de transport régi par la Convention de Varsovie et conclu avec un passager ou un expéditeur ou avec une personne agissant pour le compte du passager ou de l'expéditeur;
(c) "transporteur de fait" signifie une personne, autre que le transporteur contractuel, qui, en vertu d'une autorisation donnée par le transporteur contractuel, effectue tout ou partie du transport prévu à l'alinéa (b) mais n'est pas, en ce qui concerne cette partie, un transporteur successif au sens de la Convention de Varsovie. Cette autorisation est présumée, sauf preuve contraire.

ARTICLE II

Sauf disposition contraire de la présente Convention, si un transporteur de fait effectue tout ou partie du transport qui, conformément au contrat visé à l'article premier, alinéa (b), est régi par la Convention de Varsovie, le transporteur contractuel et le transporteur de fait sont soumis aux règles de la Convention de Varsovie, le premier pour la totalité du transport envisagé dans le contrat, le second seulement pour le transport qu'il effectue.

ARTICLE III

1. Les actes et omissions du transporteur de fait ou de ses préposés agissant dans l'exercice de leurs fonctions, relatifs au transport effectué par le transporteur de fait, sont réputés être également ceux du transporteur contractuel.

2. Les actes et omissions du transporteur contractuel ou de ses préposés agissant dans l'exercice de leurs fonctions, relatifs au transport effectué par le transporteur de tait, sont réputés être également ceux du transporteur de fait. Toutefois, aucun de ces actes ou omissions ne pourra soumettre le transporteur de fait à une responsabilité dépassant les limites prévues à l'article 22 [ou à l'article 22A] de la Convention de Varsovie. Aucun accord spécial aux termes duquel le transporteur contractuel assume des obligations que n'impose pas la Convention de Varsovie, aucune renonciation à des droits prévus par ladite Convention ou aucune déclaration spéciale d'intérêt à la livraison, visée à l'article 22 [ou à l'article 22A] de ladite Convention, n'auront d'effet à l'égard du transporteur de fait, sauf consentement de ce dernier.

ARTICLE IV

Les ordres ou protestations à notifier au transporteur, en application de la Convention de Varsovie, ont le même effet qu'ils soient adressés au transporteur contractuel ou au transporteur de fait. Toutefois, les ordres visés à l'article 12 de la Convention de Varsovie n'ont d'effet que s'ils sont adressés au transporteur contractuel.

ARTICLE V

En ce qui concerne le transport effectué par le transporteur de fait, tout préposé de ce transporteur ou du transporteur contractuel, s'il prouve qu'il a agi dans l'exercice de ses fonctions, peut se prévaloir des limites de responsabilité applicables, en vertu de la présente Convention, au transporteur dont il est préposé, sauf s'il est prouvé qu'il a agi de telle fa;accon que les limites de responsabilité ne puissent être invoquées aux termes de la Convention de Varsovie.

ARTICLE VI

En ce qui concerne le transport effectué par le transporteur de fait, le montant total de la réparation qui peut être obtenu de ce transporteur, du transporteur contractuel et de leurs préposés quand ils ont agi dans l'exercice de leurs fonctions, ne peut pas dépasser l'indemnité la plus élevée qui peut être mise à charge soit du transporteur contractuel, soit du transporteur de fait, en vertu de la présente Convention, sous réserve qu'aucune des personnes mentionnées dans le présent article ne puisse être tenue pour responsable au delà de la limite qui lui est applicable.

ARTICLE VII

Toute action en responsabilité, relative au transport effectuée par le transporteur de fait, peut être intentée, au choix du demandeur, contre ce transporteur ou le transporteur contractuel ou contre l'un et l'autre, conjointement ou séparément. Si l'action est intentée contre l'un seulement de ces transporteurs, ledit transporteur aura le droit d'appeler l'autre transporteur en intervention devant le tribunal saisi, les effets de cette intervention ainsi que la procédure qui lui est applicable étant réglés par la loi de ce tribunal.

ARTICLE VIII

Toute action en responsabilité, prévue à l'article VII de la présente Convention, doit être portée, au choix du demandeur, soit devant l'un des tribunaux où une action peut être intentée au transporteur contractuel, conformément à l'article 28 de la Convention de Varsovie, soit devant le tribunal du domicile du transporteur de fait ou du siège principal de son exploitation.

ARTICLE IX

1. Toute clause tendant à exonérer le transporteur contractuel ou le transporteur de fait de leur responsabilité en vertu de la présente Convention ou à établir une limite inférieure à celle qui est fixée dans la présente Convention est nulle et de nul effet, mais la nullité de cette clause n'entraîne pas la nullité du contrat qui reste soumis aux dispositions de la présente Convention.

2. En ce qui concerne le transport effectué par le transporteur de fait, le paragraphe précédent ne s'applique pas aux clauses concernant la perte ou le dommage résultant de la nature ou du vice propre des marchandises transportées.

3. Sont nulles toutes clauses du contrat de transport et toutes conventions particulières antérieures au dommage par lesquelles les parties dérogeraient aux règles de la présente Convention soit par une détermination de la loi applicable, soit par une modification des règles de compétence. Toutefois, dans le transport des marchandises, les clauses d'arbitrage sont admises, dans les limites de la présente Convention, lorsque l'arbitrage doit s'effectuer dans les lieux de compétence des tribunaux prévus à l'article VIII.

ARTICLE X

Sous réserve de l'article VII, aucune disposition de la présente Convention ne peut être interprétée comme affectant les droits et obligations existant entre les deux transporteurs.

[4314]

NOTES

Article III: words in square brackets in para 2 inserted by the Carriage by Air and Road Act 1979, s 1(2), Sch 2, para 6, as from a day to be appointed.

THE WARSAW CONVENTION AS AMENDED AT THE HAGUE IN 1955 AND BY PROTOCOLS NO 3 AND NO 4 SIGNED AT MONTREAL IN 1975

NOTES

The text of the following Convention appears as set out in the Carriage by Air and Road Act 1979, Sch 1.

PART I
THE ENGLISH TEXT

CHAPTER I
SCOPE—DEFINITIONS

Article 1

(1) This Convention applies to all international carriage of persons, baggage or cargo performed by aircraft for reward. It applies equally to gratuitous carriage by aircraft performed by an air transport undertaking.

(2) For the purposes of this Convention, the expression *international carriage* means any carriage in which, according to the agreement between the parties, the place of departure and the place of destination, whether or not there be a break in the carriage or a trans-shipment,

are situated either within the territories of two High Contracting Parties or within the territory of a single High Contracting Party if there is an agreed stopping place within the territory of another State, even if that State is not a High Contracting Party. Carriage between two points within the territory of a single High Contracting Party without an agreed stopping place within the territory of another State is not international carriage for the purposes of this Convention.

(3) Carriage to be performed by several successive air carriers is deemed, for the purposes of this Convention, to be one undivided carriage if it has been regarded by the parties as a single operation, whether it had been agreed upon under the form of a single contract or of a series of contracts, and it does not lose its international character merely because one contract or a series of contracts is to be performed entirely within the territory of the same State.

Article 2

(1) This Convention applies to carriage performed by the State or by legally constituted public bodies provided it falls within the conditions laid down in Article 1.

(2) In the carriage of postal items the carrier shall be liable only to the relevant postal administration in accordance with the rules applicable to the relationship between the carriers and the postal administrations.

(3) Except as provided in paragraph (2) of this Article, the provisions of this Convention shall not apply to the carriage of postal items.

CHAPTER II
DOCUMENTS OF CARRIAGE

SECTION 1—PASSENGER TICKET

Article 3

(1) In respect of the carriage of passengers an individual or collective document of carriage shall be delivered containing—

(a) an indication of the places of departure and destination;

(b) if the places of departure and destination are within the territory of a single High Contracting Party, one or more agreed stopping places being within the territory of another State, an indication of at least one such stopping place.

(2) Any other means which would preserve a record of the information indicated in (a) and (b) of the foregoing paragraph may be substituted for the delivery of the document referred to in that paragraph.

(3) Non-compliance with the provisions of the foregoing paragraphs shall not affect the existence or the validity of the contract of carriage, which shall, none the less, be subject to the rules of this Convention including those relating to limitation of liability.

Article 4

(1) In respect of the carriage of checked baggage, a baggage check shall be delivered, which, unless combined with or incorporated in a document of carriage which complies with the provisions of Article 3, paragraph (1), shall contain—

(a) an indication of the places of departure and destination;

(b) if the places of departure and destination are within the territory of a single High Contracting Party, one or more agreed stopping places being within the territory of another State, an indication of at least one such stopping place.

(2) Any other means which would preserve a record of the information indicated in (a) and (b) of the foregoing paragraph may be substituted for the delivery of the baggage check referred to in that paragraph.

(3) Non-compliance with the provisions of the foregoing paragraphs shall not affect the existence or the validity of the contract of carriage, which shall, none the less, be subject to the rules of this Convention including those relating to limitation of liability.

SECTION 3—DOCUMENTATION RELATING TO CARGO

Article 5

(1) In respect of the carriage of cargo an air waybill shall be delivered.

(2) Any other means which would preserve a record of the carriage to be performed may, with the consent of the consignor, be substituted for the delivery of an air waybill. If such other means are used, the carrier shall, if so requested by the consignor, deliver to the consignor a receipt for the cargo permitting identification of the consignment and access to the information contained in the record preserved by such other means.

(3) The impossibility of using, at points of transit and destination, the other means which would preserve the record of the carriage referred to in paragraph (2) of this Article does not entitle the carrier to refuse to accept the cargo for carriage.

Article 6

(1) The air waybill shall be made out by the consignor in three original parts.

(2) The first part shall be marked "for the carrier"; it shall be signed by the consignor. The second part shall be marked "for the consignee"; it shall be signed by the consignor and by the carrier. The third part shall be signed by the carrier and handed by him to the consignor after the cargo has been accepted.

(3) The signature of the carrier and that of the consignor may be printed or stamped.

(4) If, at the request of the consignor, the carrier makes out the air waybill, he shall be deemed, subject to proof to the contrary, to have done so on behalf of the consignor.

Article 7

When there is more than one package—

(a) the carrier of cargo has the right to require the consignor to make out separate air waybills;

(b) the consignor has the right to require the carrier to deliver separate receipts when the other means referred to in paragraph (2) of Article 5 are used.

Article 8

The air waybill and the receipt for the cargo shall contain—

(a) an indication of the places of departure and destination;

(b) if the places of departure and destination are within the territory of a single High Contracting Party, one or more agreed stopping places being within the territory of another State, an indication of at least one such stopping place; and

(c) an indication of the weight of the consignment.

Article 9

Non-compliance with the provisions of Articles 5 to 8 shall not affect the existence or the validity of the contract of carriage, which shall, none the less, be subject to the rules of this Convention including those relating to limitation of liability.

Article 10

(1) The consignor is responsible for the correctness of the particulars and statements relating to the cargo inserted by him or on his behalf in the air waybill or furnished by him or on his behalf to the carrier for insertion in the receipt for the cargo or for insertion in the record preserved by the other means referred to in paragraph (2) of Article 5.

(2) The consignor shall indemnify the carrier against all damage suffered by him, or by any other person to whom the carrier is liable, by reason of the irregularity, incorrectness or incompleteness of the particulars and statements furnished by the consignor or on his behalf.

(3) Subject to the provisions of paragraphs (1) and (2) of this Article, the carrier shall indemnify the consignor against all damage suffered by him, or by any other person to whom

the consignor is liable, by reason of the irregularity, incorrectness or incompleteness of the particulars and statements inserted by the carrier or on his behalf in the receipt for the cargo or in the record preserved by the other means referred to in paragraph (2) of Article 5.

Article 11

(1) The air waybill or the receipt for the cargo is prima facie evidence of the conclusion of the contract, of the acceptance of the cargo and of the conditions of carriage mentioned therein.

(2) Any statements in the air waybill or the receipt for the cargo relating to the weight, dimensions and packing of the cargo, as well as those relating to the number of packages, are prima facie evidence of the facts stated; those relating to the quantity, volume and condition of the cargo do not constitute evidence against the carrier except so far as they both have been, and are stated in the air waybill to have been, checked by him in the presence of the consignor, or relate to the apparent condition of the cargo.

Article 12

(1) Subject to his liability to carry out all his obligations under the contract of carriage, the consignor has the right to dispose of the cargo by withdrawing it at the airport of departure or destination, or by stopping it in the course of the journey on any landing, or by calling for it to be delivered at the place of destination or in the course of the journey to a person other than the consignee originally designated, or by requiring it to be returned to the airport of departure. He must not exercise this right of disposition in such a way as to prejudice the carrier or other consignors and he must repay any expenses occasioned by the exercise of this right.

(2) If it is impossible to carry out the orders of the consignor the carrier must so inform him forthwith.

(3) If the carrier obeys the orders of the consignor for the disposition of the cargo without requiring the production of the part of the air waybill or the receipt for the cargo delivered to the latter, he will be liable, without prejudice to his right of recovery from the consignor, for any damage which may be caused thereby to any person who is lawfully in possession of that part of the air waybill or the receipt for the cargo.

(4) The right conferred on the consignor ceases at the moment when that of the consignee begins in accordance with Article 13. Nevertheless, if the consignee declines to accept the cargo, or if he cannot be communicated with, the consignor resumes his right of disposition.

Article 13

(1) Except when the consignor has exercised his right under Article 12, the consignee is entitled, on arrival of the cargo at the place of destination, to require the carrier to deliver the cargo to him, on payment of the charges due and on complying with the conditions of carriage.

(2) Unless it is otherwise agreed, it is the duty of the carrier to give notice to the consignee as soon as the cargo arrives.

(3) If the carrier admits the loss of the cargo, or if the cargo has not arrived at the expiration of seven days after the date on which it ought to have arrived, the consignee is entitled to enforce against the carrier the rights which flow from the contract of carriage.

Article 14

The consignor and the consignee can respectively enforce all the rights given them by Articles 12 and 13, each in his own name, whether he is acting in his own interest or in the interest of another, provided that he carries out the obligations imposed by the contract of carriage.

Article 15

(1) Articles 12, 13 and 14 do not affect either the relations of the consignor and the consignee with each other or the mutual relations of third parties whose rights are derived either from the consignor or from the consignee.

(2) The provisions of Articles 12, 13 and 14 can only be varied by express provision in the air waybill or the receipt for the cargo.

Article 16

(1) The consignor must furnish such information and such documents as are necessary to meet the formalities of customs, octroi or police before the cargo can be delivered to the consignee. The consignor is liable to the carrier for any damage occasioned by the absence, insufficiency or irregularity of any such information or documents, unless the damage is due to the fault of the carrier, his servants or agents.

(2) The carrier is under no obligation to enquire into the correctness or sufficiency of such information or documents.

CHAPTER III
LIABILITY OF THE CARRIER

Article 17

(1) The carrier is liable for damage sustained in case of death or personal injury of a passenger upon condition only that the event which caused the death or injury took place on board the aircraft or in the course of any of the operations of embarking or disembarking. However, the carrier is not liable if the death or injury resulted solely from the state of health of the passenger.

(2) The carrier is liable for damage sustained in case of destruction or loss of, or of damage to, baggage upon condition only that the event which caused the destruction, loss or damage took place on board the aircraft or in the course of any of the operations of embarking or disembarking or during any period within which the baggage was in charge of the carrier. However, the carrier is not liable if the damage resulted solely from the inherent defect, quality or vice of the baggage.

(3) Unless otherwise specified, in this Convention the term "baggage" means both checked baggage and objects carried by the passenger.

Article 18

(1) The carrier is liable for damage sustained in the event of the destruction or loss of, or damage to, cargo upon condition only that the occurrence which caused the damage so sustained took place during the carriage by air.

(2) However, the carrier is not liable if he proves that the destruction, loss of, or damage to, the cargo resulted solely from one or more of the following—

(a) inherent defect, quality or vice of that cargo;

(b) defective packing of that cargo performed by a person other than the carrier or his servants or agents;

(c) an act of war or an armed conflict;

(d) an act of public authority carried out in connection with the entry, exit or transit of the cargo.

(3) The carriage by air within the meaning of paragraph (1) of this Article comprises the period during which the cargo is in the charge of the carrier, whether in an airport or on board an aircraft, or, in the case of a landing outside an airport, in any place whatsoever.

(4) The period of the carriage by air does not extend to any carriage by land, by sea or by river performed outside an airport. If, however, such carriage takes place in the performance of a contract for carriage by air, for the purpose of loading, delivery or transhipment, any damage is presumed, subject to proof to the contrary, to have been the result of an event which took place during the carriage by air.

Article 19

The carrier is liable for damage occasioned by delay in the carriage by air of passengers, baggage or cargo.

Article 20

In the carriage of passengers, baggage and cargo, the carrier shall not be liable for damage occasioned by delay if he proves that he and his servants and agents have taken all necessary measures to avoid the damage or that it was impossible for them to take such measures.

Article 21

(1) In the carriage of passengers and baggage, if the carrier proves that the damage was caused or contributed to by the negligence or other wrongful act or omission of the person claiming compensation, the carrier shall be wholly or partly exonerated from his liability to such person to the extent that such negligence or wrongful act or omission caused or contributed to the damage. When by reason of the death or injury of a passenger compensation is claimed by a person other than the passenger, the carrier shall likewise be wholly or partly exonerated from his liability to the extent that he proves that the damage was caused or contributed to by the negligence or other wrongful act or omission of that passenger.

(2) In the carriage of cargo, if the carrier proves that the damage was caused by or contributed to by the negligence or other wrongful act or omission of the person claiming compensation, or the person from whom he derives his rights, the carrier shall be wholly or partly exonerated from his liability to the claimant to the extent that such negligence or wrongful act or omission caused or contributed to the damage.

Article 22

(1)

(a) In the carriage of persons the liability of the carrier is limited to the sum of 100,000 special drawing rights for the aggregate of the claims, however founded, in respect of damage suffered as a result of the death or personal injury of each passenger. Where, in accordance with the law of the court seised of the case, damages may be awarded in the form of periodic payments, the equivalent capital value of the said payments shall not exceed 100,000 special drawing rights.

(b) In the case of delay in the carriage of persons the liability of the carrier for each passenger is limited to 4,150 special drawing rights.

(c) In the carriage of baggage the liability of the carrier in the case of destruction, loss, damage or delay is limited to 1,000 special drawing rights for each passenger.

(2)

(a) The courts of the High Contracting Parties which are not authorised under their law to award the costs of the action, including lawyers' fees, shall, in actions relating to the carriage of passengers and baggage to which this Convention applies, have the power to award, in their discretion, to the claimant the whole or part of the costs of the action, including lawyers' fees which the court considers reasonable.

(b) The costs of the action including lawyers' fees shall be awarded in accordance with subparagraph (a) only if the claimant gives a written notice to the carrier of the amount claimed including the particulars of the calculation of that amount and the carrier does not make, within a period of six months after his receipt of such notice, a written offer of settlement in an amount at least equal to the compensation awarded within the applicable limit. This period will be extended until the time of commencement of the action if that is later.

(c) The costs of the action including lawyers' fees shall not be taken into account in applying the limits under this Article.

(3) The sums mentioned in terms of special drawing right in this Article shall be deemed to refer to the special drawing right as defined by the International Monetary Fund. Conversion of the sums into national currencies shall, in case of judicial proceedings, be made according to the value of such currencies in terms of the special drawing right at the date of the judgment.

Article 22A

(1)

(a) In the carriage of cargo, the liability of the carrier is limited to a sum of 17 special drawing rights per kilogramme, unless the consignor has made, at the time when the package was handed over to the carrier, a special declaration of interest in delivery at destination and has paid a supplementary sum if the case so requires. In that case the carrier will be liable to pay a sum not exceeding the declared sum, unless he proves that that sum is greater than the consignor's actual interest in delivery at destination.

(b) In the case of loss, damage or delay of part of the cargo, or of any object contained therein, the weight to be taken into consideration in determining the amount to which the carrier's liability is limited shall be only the total weight of the package or packages concerned. Nevertheless, when the loss, damage or delay of a part of the cargo, or of an object contained therein, affects the value of other packages covered by the same air waybill, the total weight of such package or packages shall also be taken into consideration in determining the limit of liability.

(2) The limits prescribed in this Article shall not prevent the court in an action relating to the carriage of cargo from awarding in accordance with its own law, in addition, the whole or part of the court costs and of the other expenses of the litigation incurred by the plaintiff. The foregoing provision shall not apply if the amount of the damages awarded, excluding court costs and other expenses of the litigation, does not exceed the sum which the carrier had offered in writing to the plaintiff within a period of six months from the date of the occurrence causing the damage, or before the commencement of the action, if that is later.

(3) The sums mentioned in terms of special drawing right in this Article shall be deemed to refer to the special drawing right as defined by the International Monetary Fund. Conversion of the sums into national currencies shall, in case of judicial proceedings, be made according to the value of such currencies in terms of the special drawing right at the date of the judgment.

Article 23

(1) Any provision tending to relieve the carrier of liability or to fix a lower limit than that which is laid down in this Convention shall be null and void, but the nullity of any such provision does not involve the nullity of the whole contract, which shall remain subject to the provisions of this Convention.

(2) Paragraph (1) of this Article shall not apply to provisions governing loss or damage resulting from the inherent defect, quality or vice of the cargo carried.

Article 24

In the carriage of passengers, baggage and cargo, any action for damages, however founded, whether under this Convention or in contract or in tort or otherwise, can only be brought subject to the conditions and limits of liability set out in this Convention without prejudice to the question as to who are the persons who have the right to bring suit and what are their respective rights. Such limits of liability constitute maximum limits and may not be exceeded whatever the circumstances which gave rise to the liability.

Article 25A

(1) If an action is brought against a servant or agent of the carrier arising out of damage to which the Convention relates, such servant or agent, if he proves that he acted within the scope of his employment, shall be entitled to avail himself of the limits of liability which that carrier himself is entitled to invoke under this Convention.

(2) The aggregate of the amount recoverable from the carrier, his servants and agents, in that case, shall not exceed the said limits.

Article 26

(1) Receipt by the person entitled to delivery of baggage or cargo without complaint is prima facie evidence that the same has been delivered in good condition and in accordance with the document of carriage.

(2) In the case of damage, the person entitled to delivery must complain to the carrier forthwith after the discovery of the damage, and, at the latest, within seven days from the date

of receipt in the case of baggage and fourteen days from the date of receipt in the case of cargo. In the case of delay the complaint must be made at the latest within twenty-one days from the date on which the baggage or cargo have been placed at his disposal.

(3) Every complaint must be made in writing upon the document of carriage or by separate notice in writing despatched within the times aforesaid.

(4) Failing complaint within the times aforesaid, no action shall lie against the carrier, save in the case of fraud on his part.

Article 27

In the case of the death of the person liable, an action for damages lies in accordance with the terms of this Convention against those legally representing his estate.

Article 28

(1) An action for damages must be brought, at the option of the plaintiff, in the territory of one of the High Contracting Parties, either before the court having jurisdiction where the carrier is ordinarily resident, or has his principal place of business, or has an establishment by which the contract has been made or before the court having jurisdiction at the place of destination.

(2) In respect of damage resulting from the death, injury or delay of a passenger or the destruction, loss, damage or delay of baggage, the action may be brought before one of the courts mentioned in paragraph (1) of this Article, or in the territory of one of the High Contracting Parties, before the court within the jurisdiction of which the carrier has an establishment if the passenger has his ordinary or permanent residence in the territory of the same High Contracting Party.

(3) Questions of procedure shall be governed by the law of the court seised of the case.

Article 29

(1) The right to damages shall be extinguished if an action is not brought within two years, reckoned from the date of arrival at the destination, or from the date on which the aircraft ought to have arrived, or from the date on which the carriage stopped.

(2) The method of calculating the period of limitation shall be determined by the law of the court seised of the case.

Article 30

(1) In the case of carriage to be performed by various successive carriers and falling within the definition set out in the third paragraph of Article 1, each carrier who accepts passengers, baggage or cargo is subjected to the rules set out in this Convention, and is deemed to be one of the contracting parties to the contract of carriage in so far as the contract deals with that part of the carriage which is performed under his supervision.

(2) In the case of carriage of this nature, the passenger or his representative can take action only against the carrier who performed the carriage during which the accident or the delay occurred, save in the case where, by express agreement, the first carrier has assumed liability for the whole journey.

(3) As regards baggage or cargo, the passenger or consignor will have a right of action against the first carrier, and the passenger or consignee who is entitled to delivery will have a right of action against the last carrier, and further, each may take action against the carrier who performed the carriage during which the destruction, loss, damage or delay took place. These carriers will be jointly and severally liable to the passenger or to the consignor or consignee.

Article 30A

Nothing in this Convention shall prejudice the question whether a person liable for damage in accordance with its provisions has a right of recourse against any other person.

CHAPTER IV
PROVISIONS RELATING TO COMBINED CARRIAGE

Article 31

(1) In the case of combined carriage performed partly by air and partly by any other mode of carriage, the provisions of this Convention apply only to the carriage by air, provided that the carriage by air falls within the terms of Article 1.

(2) Nothing in this Convention shall prevent the parties in the case of combined carriage from inserting in the document of air carriage conditions relating to other modes of carriage, provided that the provisions of this Convention are observed as regards the carriage by air.

CHAPTER V
GENERAL AND FINAL PROVISIONS

Article 32

Any clause contained in the contract and all special agreements entered into before the damage occurred by which the parties purport to infringe the rules laid down by this Convention, whether by deciding the law to be applied, or by altering the rules as to jurisdiction, shall be null and void. Nevertheless for the carriage of cargo arbitration clauses are allowed, subject to this Convention, if the arbitration is to take place within one of the jurisdictions referred to in the first paragraph of Article 28.

Article 33

Except as provided in paragraph (3) of Article 5, nothing in this Convention shall prevent the carrier either from refusing to enter into any contract of carriage or from making regulations which do not conflict with the provisions of this Convention.

Article 34

The provisions of Articles 3 to 8 inclusive relating to documents of carriage shall not apply in the case of carriage performed in extraordinary circumstances outside the normal scope of an air carrier's business.

Article 35

The expression "days" when used in this Convention means current days not working days.

Article 35A

No provision contained in this Convention shall prevent a State from establishing and operating within its territory a system to supplement the compensation payable to claimants under the Convention in respect of death, or personal injury, of passengers. Such a system shall fulfil the following conditions—

(a) it shall not in any circumstances impose upon the carrier, his servants or agents, any liability in addition to that provided under this Convention;

(b) it shall not impose upon the carrier any financial or administrative burden other than collecting in that State contributions from passengers if required so to do;

(c) it shall not give rise to any discrimination between carriers with regard to the passengers concerned and the benefits available to the said passengers under the system shall be extended to them regardless of the carrier whose services they have used;

(d) if a passenger has contributed to the system, any person suffering damage as a consequence of death or personal injury of such passenger shall be entitled to the benefits of the system.

Article 40A

(*1*) (*This paragraph is not reproduced. It defines "High Contracting Party".*)

(2) For the purposes of the Convention the word *territory* means not only the metropolitan territory of a State but also all other territories for the foreign relations of which that State is responsible.

(*Articles 36, 37, 38, 39, 40, 41 and 42 and the concluding words of the Convention are not reproduced. They deal, among other things, with the coming into force of the Convention. The former Article 25 is superseded by Article 24.*)

ADDITIONAL PROTOCOL

(*With reference to Article 2*)

The High Contracting Parties reserve to themselves the right to declare at the time of ratification or of accession that the first paragraph of Article 2 of this Convention shall not apply to international carriage by air performed directly by the State, its colonies, protectorates or mandated territories or by any other territory under its sovereignty, suzerainty or authority.

[4315]

NOTES

Commencement: to be appointed.

PART II
THE FRENCH TEXT

CHAPITRE IER
OBJET—DÉFINITIONS

Article 1er

(1) La presente Convention s'applique à tout transport international de personnes, bagages ou marchandises, effectué par aéronef contre rémunération. Elle s'applique également aux transports gratuits effectues par aeronef par une entreprise de transports aériens.

(2) Est qualifié *transport international*, au sens de la présente Convention, tout transport dans lequel, d'après les stipulations des parties, le point de départ et le point de destination, qu'il y ait ou non interruption de transport ou transbordement, sont situés soit sur le territoire de deux Hautes Parties Contractantes, soit sur le territoire d'une seule Haute Partie Contractante si une escale est prévue sur le territoire d'un autre Etat, même si cet Etat n'est pas une Haute Partie Contractante. Le transport sans une telle escale entre deux points du territoire d'une seule Haute Partie Contractante n'est pas considéré comme international au sens de la présente Convention.

(3) Le transport à exécuter par plusieurs transporteurs par air successifs est censé constituer pour l'application de la présente Convention un transport unique lorsqu'il a été envisagé par les parties comme une seule opération, qu'il ait été conclu sous la forme d'un seul contrat ou d'une série de contrats, et il ne perd pas son caractère international par le fait qu'un seul contrat ou une série de contrats doivent être exécutés intégralement dans le territoire d'un même Etat.

Article 2

(1) La Convention s'applique aux transports effectués par l'Etat ou les autres personnes juridiques de droit public, dans les conditions prévues à l'article 1er.

(2) Dans le transport des envois postaux, le transporteur n'est responsable qu'envers l'administration postale compétente conformément aux règles applicables dans les rapports entre les transporteurs et les administration postales.

(3) Les dispositions de la présente Convention autres que celles de l'alinéa (2) ci-dessus ne s'appliquent pas au transport des envois postaux.

CHAPITRE II
TITRES DE TRANSPORT

SECTION 1—BILLET DE PASSAGE

Article 3

(1) Dans le transport de passagers, un titre de transport individuel ou collectif doit être délivré, contenant—

(a) l'indication des points de départ et de destination;

(b) si les points de départ et de destination sont situés sur le territoire d'une même Haute Partie Contractante et si une ou plusieurs escales sont prévues sur le territoire d'un autre Etat, l'indication d'une de ces escales.

(2) L'emploi de tout autre moyen constatant les indications qui figurent à l'alinéa (1)(a) et (b), peut se substituer à la délivrance du titre de transport mentionné audit alinéa.

(3) L'inobservation des dispositions de l'alinéa précédent n'affecte ni l'existence ni la validité du contrat de transport, qui n'en sera pas moins soumis aux règles de la présente Convention, y compris celles qui portent sur la limitation de responsabilité.

SECTION 2—SULLETIN DE BAGAGES

Article 4

(1) Dans le transport de bagages enregistrés, un bulletin de bagages doit être délivré qui, s'il n'est pas combiné avec un titre de transport conforme aux dispositions de l'article 3, alinéa 1er, ou n'est pas inclus dans un tel titre de transport, doit contenir—

(a) l'indication des points de départ et de destination;

(b) si les points de départ et de destination sont situés sur le territoire d'une même Haute Partie Contractante et si une ou plusieurs escales sont prévues sur le territoire d'un autre Etat, l'indication d'une de ces escales.

(2) L'emploi de tout autre moyen constatant les indications qui figurent à l'alinéa (1)(a) et (b), peut se substituer à la délivrance du bulletin de bagages mentionné audit alinéa.

(3) L'inobservation des dispositions de l'alinéa précédent n'affecte ni l'existence ni la validité du contrat de transport, qui n'en sera pas moins soumis aux règles de la présente Convention, y compris celles qui portent sur la limitation de responsabilité.

SECTION 3—DOCUMENTATION RELATIVE AUX MARCHANDISES

Article 5

(1) Pour le transport de marchandises une lettre de transport aérien est émise.

(2) L'emploi de tout autre moyen constatant les indications relatives au transport à exécuter peut, avec le consentement de l'expéditeur, se substituer à l'émission de la lettre de transport aérien. Si de tels autres moyens sont utilisés, le transporteur délivre à l'expéditeur, à la demande de ce dernier, un récépissé de la marchandise permettant l'identification de l'expédition et l'accès aux indications enregistrées par ces autres moyens.

(3) L'impossibilité d'utiliser, aux points de transit et de destination, les autres moyens permettant de constater les indications relatives au transport, visés à l'alinéa (2) ci-dessus, n'autorise pas le transporteur à refuser l'acceptation des marchandises en vue du transport.

Article 6

(1) La lettre de transport aérien est établie par l'expéditeur en trois exemplaires originaux.

(2) Le premier exemplaire porte la mention "pour le transporteur"; il est signé par l'expéditeur. Le deuxième exemplaire porte la mention "pour le destinaire"; il est signé par l'expéditeur et le transporteur. Le troisième exemplaire est signé par le transporteur et remis par lui à l'expéditeur après acceptation de la marchandise.

(3) La signature du transporteur et celle de l'expéditeur peuvent être imprimées ou remplacées par un timbre.

(4) Si, à la demande de l'expéditeur, le transporteur établit la lettre de transport aérien, il est considéré, jusqu'à preuve contraire, comme agissant au nom de l'expéditeur.

Article 7

Lorsqu'il y a plusieurs colis—

(a) le transporteur de marchandises a le droit de demander à l'expéditeur l'établissment de lettres de transport aérien distinctes;

(b) l'expéditeur a le droit de demander au transporteur le remise de récépissés distincts, lorsque les autres moyens visés à l'alinéa (2) de l'article 5 sont utilisés.

Article 8

La lettre de transport aérien et le récépissé de la marchandise contiennent—

(a) l'indication des points de départ et de destination;

(b) si les points de départ et de destination sont situes sur le territoire d'une même Haute Partie Contractante et qu'une ou plusieurs escales soient prévues sur le territoire d'un autre Etat, l'indication d'une de ces escales;

(c) la mention du poids de l'expédition.

Article 9

L'inobservation des dispositions des articles 5 à 8 n'affecte ni l'existence ni la validité du contrat de transport, qui n'en sera pas moins soumis aux règles de la présente Convention, y compris celles qui portent sur la limitation de responsabilité.

Article 10

(1) L'expéditeur est responsable de l'exactitude des indications et déclarations concernant la marchandise inscrites par lui ou en son nom dans la lettre de transport aérien, ainsi que de celles fournies et faites par lui ou en son nom au transporteur en vue d'être insérées dans le récépissé de la marchandise ou pour insertion dans les données enregistrées par les autres moyens prévus à l'alinéa (2) de l'article 5.

(2) L'expéditeur assume la responsabilité de tout dommage subi par le transporteur ou par toute autre personne à l'égard de laquelle la responsabilité du transporteur est engagée, à raison des indications et déclarations irrégulières, inexactes ou incomplètes fournies et faites par lui ou en son nom.

(3) Sous réserve des dispositions des alinéas (1) et (2) du présent article, le transporteur assume la responsabilité de tout dommage subi par l'expéditeur ou par toute autre personne à l'égard de laquelle la responsabilité de l'expéditeur est engagée, à raison des indications et déclarations irrégulières, inexactes ou incomplètes insérées par lui ou en son nom dans le récépissé de la marchandise ou dans les données enregistrées par les autres moyens prévus à l'alinéa (2) de l'article 5.

Article 11

(1) La lettre de transport aérien et le récépissé de la marchandise font foi, jusqu'à preuve contraire, de la conclusion du contrat, de la réception de la marchandise et des conditions du transport qui y figurent.

(2) Les énonciations de la lettre de transport aérien et du récépissé de la marchandise, relatives au poids, aux dimensions et à l'emballage de la marchandise ainsi qu'au nombre des colis font foi jusqu'à preuve contraire; celles relatives à la quantité, au volume et à l'état de la marchandise ne font preuve contre le transporteur qu'autant que la vérification en a été faite par lui en présence de l'expéditeur, et constatée sur la lettre de transport aérien, ou qu'il s'agit d'énonciations relatives à l'état apparent de la marchandise.

Article 12

(1) L'expéditeur a le droit, sous la condition d'exécuter toutes les obligations résultant du contrat de transport, de disposer de la marchandise, soit en la retirant à l'aérodrome de départ

ou de destination, soit en l'arrêtant en cours de route lors d'un atterrissage, soit en la faisant délivrer au lieu de destination ou en cours de route à une personne autre que le destinataire initialement désigné, soit en demandant son retour à l'aérodrome de départ, pour autant que l'exercice de ce droit ne porte préjudice ni au transporteur, ni aux autres expéditeurs et avec l'obligation de rembourser les frais qui en résultent.

(2) Dans le cas où l'exécution des ordres de l'expéditeur est impossible, le transporteur doit l'en aviser immédiatement.

(3) Si le transporteur se conforme aux ordres de disposition de l'expéditeur, sans exiger la production de l'exemplaire de la lettre de transport aérien ou du récépissé de la marchandise délivré à celui-ci, il sera responsable, sauf son recours contre l'expéditeur, du préjudice qui pourra être causé par ce fait à celui qui est régulièrement en possession de la lettre de transport aérien ou du récépissé de la marchandise.

(4) Le droit de l'expéditeur cesse au moment où celui du destinataire commence, conformément à l'article 13. Toutefois, si le destinataire refuse la marchandise, ou s'il ne peut être atteint, l'expéditeur reprend son droit de disposition.

Article 13

(1) Sauf lorsque l'expéditeur a exercé le droit qu'il tient de l'article 12, le destinataire a le droit, dès l'arrivée de la marchandise au point de destination, de demander au transporteur de lui livrer la marchandise contre le paiement du montant des créances et contre l'exécution des conditions de transport.

(2) Sauf stipulation contraire, le transporteur doit aviser le destinataire dès l'arrivée de la marchandise.

(3) Si la perte de la marchandise est reconnue par le transporteur ou si, à l'expiration d'un délai de sept jours après qu'elle aurait dû arriver, la marchandise n'est pas arrivée, le destinataire est authorisé à faire valoir vis-à-vis du transporteur les droits résultant du contrat de transport.

Article 14

L'expéditeur et le destinataire peuvent faire valoir tous les droits qui leur sont respectivement conférés par les articles 12 et 13, chacun en son propre nom, qu'il agisse dans son propre intérêt ou dans l'intérêt d'autrui, à condition d'exécuter les obligations que le contrat de transport impose.

Article 15

(1) Les articles 12, 13 et 14 ne portent aucun préjudice ni aux rapports de l'expéditeur et du destinataire entre eux, ni aux rapports des tiers dont les droits proviennent, soit de l'expéditeur, soit du destinataire.

(2) Toute clause dérogeant aux stipulations des articles 12, 13 et 14 doit être inscrite dans la lettre de transport aérien ou dans le récépissé de la marchandise.

Article 16

(1) L'expéditeur est tenu de fournir les renseignements et les documents qui, avant la remise de la marchandise au destinataire, sont nécessaires à l'accomplissement des formalités de douane, d'octroi ou de police. L'expéditeur est responsable envers le transporteur de tous dommages qui pourraient résulter de l'absence, de l'insuffisance ou de l'irrégularité de ces renseignements et pièces, sauf le cas de faute de la part du transporteur ou de ses préposés.

(2) Le transporteur n'est pas tenu d'examiner si ces renseignements et documents sont exacts ou suffisants.

CHAPITRE III
RESPONSABILITÉ DU TRANSPORTEUR

Article 17

(1) Le transporteur est responsable du préjudice survenu en cas de mort ou de toute lésion corporelle subie par un passager, par cela seul que le fait qui a causé la mort ou la

lésion corporelle s'est produit à bord de l'aéronef ou au cours de toutes opérations d'embarquement ou de débarquement. Toutefois, le transporteur n'est pas responsable si la mort ou la lésion corporelle résulte uniquement de l'état de santé du passager.

(2) Le transporteur est responsable du dommage survenu en cas de destruction, perte ou avarie de bagages, par cela seul que le fait qui a causé la destruction, la perte ou l'avarie s'est produit à bord de l'aéronef, au cours de toutes opérations d'embarquement ou de débarquement ou au cours de toute période durant laquelle le transporteur avait la garde des bagages. Toutefois, le transporteur n'est pas responsable si le dommage résulte uniquement de la nature ou du vice propre des bagages.

(3) Sous réserve de dispositions contraires, dans cette Convention le terme "bagages" désigne les bagages enregistrés aussi bien que les objets qu'emporte le passager.

Article 18

(1) Le transporteur est responsable du dommage survenue en cas de destruction, perte ou avarie de la marchandise par cela seul que le fait qui a causé le dommage s'est produit pendant le transport aérien.

(2) Toutefois, le transporteur n'est pas responsable s'il établit que la destruction, la perte ou l'avarie de la marchandise résulte uniquement de l'un ou de plusieurs des faits suivants—

(a) la nature ou le vice propre de la marchandise;
(b) l'emballage défectueux de la marchandise par une personne autre que le transporteur ou ses préposés;
(c) un fait de guerre ou un conflit armé;
(d) un acte de l'autorité publique accompli en relation avec l'entrée, la sortie ou le transit de la marchandise.

(3) Le transport aérien, au sens de l'alinéa (1) du présent article, comprend la période pendant laquelle les bagages ou marchandises se trouvent sous la garde du transporteur, que ce soit dans un aérodrome ou à bord d'un aéronef ou dans un lieu quelconque en cas d'atterrissage en dehors d'un aérodrome.

(4) La période du transport aérien ne couvre aucun transport terrestre, maritime ou fluvial effectué en dehors d'un aérodrome. Toutefois, lorsqu'un tel transport est effectué dans l'exécution du contrat de transport aérien en vue du chargement, de la livraison ou du transbordement, tout dommage est présumé, sauf preuve contraire, résulter d'un événement survenu pendant le transport aérien.

Article 19

Le transporteur est responsable du dommage résultant d'un retard dans le transport aérien de voyageurs, bagages ou marchandises.

Article 20

Dans le transport de passagers, de bagages et de marchandises, le transporteur n'est pas responsable du dommage résultant d'un retard s'il prouve que lui et ses préposés ont pris toutes les mesures nécessaires pour éviter le dommage ou qu'il leur était impossible de les prendre.

Article 21

(1) Dans le cas où il fait la preuve que la faute de la personne qui demande réparation a causé le dommage ou y a contribué, le transporteur est exonéré en tout ou en partie de sa responsabilité à l'égard de cette personne, dans la mesure où cette faute a causé le dommage ou y a contribué. Lorsqu'une demande en réparation est introduite par une personne autre que le passager, en raison de la mort ou d'une lésion corporelle subie par ce dernier, le transporteur est également exonéré en tout ou en partie de sa responsabilité dans la mesure où il prouve que la faute de ce passager a causé le dommage ou y a contribué.

(2) Dans le transport de marchandises, le transporteur est exonéré, en tout ou en partie, de sa responsabilité dans la mesure où il prouve que la faute de la personne qui demande réparation ou de la personne dont elle tient ses droits a causé le dommage ou y a contribué.

Article 22

(1)

(a) Dans le transport de personnes, la responsabilité du transporteur est limitée à la somme de 100.000 Droits de Tirage spéciaux pour l'ensemble des demandes présentées, à quelque titre que ce soit, en réparation du dommage subi en conséquence de la mort ou de lésions corporelles d'un passager. Dans le cas où, d'après la loi du tribunal saisi, l'indemnité peut être fixée sous forme de rente, le capital de la rente ne peut dépasser 100.000 Droits de Tirage spéciaux.

(b) En cas de retard dans le transport de personnes, la responsabilité du transporteur est limitée à la somme de 4.150 Droits de Tirage spéciaux par passager.

(c) Dans le transport de bagages, la responsabilité du transporteur en cas de destruction, perte, avarie ou retard est limitée à la somme de 1.000 Droits de Tirage spéciaux par passager.

(2)

(a) Les tribunaux des Hautes Parties Contractantes qui n'ont pas la faculté, en vertu de leur propre loi, d'allouer des frais de procès y compris des honoraires d'avocat auront, dans les instances auxquelles la présente Convention s'applique, le pouvoir d'allouer au demandeur, suivant leur appréciation, tout ou partie des frais de procès, y compris les honoraires d'avocat qu'ils jugent raisonnables.

(b) Les frais de procès y compris des honoraires d'avocat ne sont accordés, en vertu de l'alinéa (a), que si le demandeur a notifié par écrit au transporteur le montant de la somme réclamée, y compris les détails de calcul de cette somme, et si le transporteur n'a pas, dans un délai de six mois à compter de la réception de cette demande, fait par écrit une offre de règlement d'un montant au moins égal à celui des dommages-intérêts alloués par le tribunal à concurrence de la limite applicable. Ce délai est prorogé jusqu'au jour de l'introduction de l'instance si celle-ci est postérieure à l'expiration de ce délai.

(c) Les frais de procès y compris des honoraires d'avocat ne sont pas pris en considération pour l'application des limites prévues au présent article.

(3) Les sommes indiquées en Droits de Tirage spéciaux dans le présent article sont considérées comme se rapportant au Droit de Tirage spécial tel que défini par le Fonds monétaire international. La conversion de ces sommes en monnaies nationales s'effectuera en cas d'instance judiciaire suivant la valeur de ces monnaies en Droit de Tirage spécial à la date du jugement.

Article 22A

(1)

(a) Dans le transport de marchandises, la responsabilité du transporteur est limitée à la somme de 17 Droits de Tirage spéciaux par kilogramme, sauf déclaration spéciale d'intérêt à la livraison faite par l'expéditeur au moment de la remise du colis au transporteur et moyennant le paiement d'une taxe supplémentaire éventuelle. Dans ce cas, le transporteur sera tenu de payer jusqu'à concurrence de la somme déclarée, à moins qu'il ne prouve qu'elle est supérieure à l'intérêt réel de l'expéditeur à la livraison.

(b) En cas de perte, d'avarie ou de retard d'une partie des marchandises, ou de tout objet qui y est contenu, seul le poids total du ou des colis dont il s'agit est pris en considération pour déterminer la limite de responsabilité du transporteur. Toutefois, lorsque la perte, l'avarie ou le retard d'une partie des marchandises, ou d'un objet qui y est contenu, affecte la valeur d'autres colis couverts par le même lettre de transport aérien, le poids total de ces colis doit être pris en considération pour déterminer la limite de responsabilité.

(2) Les limites fixées par le présent article n'ont pas pour effet d'enlever au tribunal la faculté d'allouer en outre, conformément à sa loi, une somme correspondante à tout ou partie des dépens et autres frais du procès exposés par le demandeur. La disposition précédente ne s'applique pas lorsque le montant de l'indemnité allouée, non compris les dépens et autres frais de procès, ne dépasse pas la somme que le transporteur a offerte par écrit au demandeur dans un délai de six mois à dater du fait qui a causé le dommage ou avant l'introduction de l'instance si celle-ci est postérieure à ce délai.

(3) Les sommes indiquées en Droits de Tirage spéciaux dans le présent article sont considérées comme se rapportant au Droit de Tirage spécial tel que défini par le Fonds monétaire international. La conversion de ces sommes en monnaies nationales s'effectuera en cas d'instance judiciaire suivant la valeur de ces monnaies en Droit de Tirage spécial à la date du jugement.

Article 23

(1) Toute clause tendant à exonérer le transporteur de sa responsabilité ou à établir une limite inférieure à celle qui est fixée dans la présente Convention est nulle et de nul effet, mais la nullité de cette clause n'entraîne pas la nullité du contrat qui reste soumis aux dispositions de la présente Convention.

(2) L'alinéa 1er du présent article ne s'applique pas aux clauses concernant la perte ou le dommage resultant de la nature ou du vice propre des marchandises transportées.

Article 24

Dans le transport de passagers, de bagages et de marchandises, toute action en responsabilité introduite, à quelque titre que ce soit, que ce soit en vertu de la présente Convention, en raison d'un contrat ou d'un acte illicite ou pour toute autre cause, ne peut être exercée que dans les conditions et limites de responsabilité prévues par la présente Convention, sans préjudice de la détermination des personnes qui ont le droit d'agir et de leurs droits respectifs. Ces limites de responsabilité constituent un maximum et sont infranchissables, quelles que soient les circonstances qui sont à l'origine de la responsabilité.

Article 25A

(1) Si une action est intentée contre un préposé du transporteur à la suite d'un dommage visé par la Convention, ce préposé, s'il prouve qu'il a agi dans l'exercise de ses fonctions, pourra se prévaloir des limites de responsabilité que peut invoquer ce transporteur en vertue de la présente Convention.

(2) Le montant total de la réparation qui, dans ce cas, peut être obtenu du transporteur et de ses préposés ne doit pas dépasser lesdites limites.

Article 26

(1) La réception des bagages et marchandises sans protestation par le destinataire constituera présomption, sauf preuve contraire, que les marchandises ont été livrées en bon état et conformément au titre de transport.

(2) En cas d'avarie, le destinataire doit adresser au transporteur une protestation immédiatement après la découverte de l'avarie et, au plus tard, dans un délai de sept jours pour les bagages et de quatorze jours pour les marchandises à dater de leur réception. En cas de retard, la protestation devra ètre faite au plus tard dans les vingt et un jours à dater du jour où le bagage ou la marchandise auront été mis à sa disposition.

(3) Toute protestation doit être faite par réserve inscrite sur le titre de transport ou par un autre écrit expédié dans le délai prévu pour cette protestation.

(4) A défaut de protestation dans les délais prévus, toutes actions contre le transporteur sont irrecevables, sauf le cas de fraude de celui-ci.

Article 27

En cas de décès de débiteur, l'action en responsabilité, dans les limites prévues par la présente Convention, s'exerce contre ses ayants droit.

Article 28

(1) L'action en responsabilité devra être portée, au choix du demandeur, dans le territoire d'une des Hautes Parties Contractantes, soit devant le tribunal du domicile du transporteur, du siège principal de son exploitation ou du lieu où il possède un établissement par le soin duquel le contrat a été conclu, soit devant le tribunal du lieu de destination.

(2) En ce qui concerne le dommage résultant de la mort, d'une lésion corporelle ou du retard subi par un passager ainsi que de la destruction, perte, avarie ou retard des bagages, l'action en responsabilité peut être intentée devant l'un des tribunaux mentionnés à l'alinéa 1er du présent article ou, sur le territoire d'une Haute Partie Contractante, devant le tribunal dans le ressort duquel le transporteur possède un établissement, si le passager a son domicile ou sa résidence permanente sur le territoire de la même Haute Partie Contractante.

(3) La procédure sera réglée par la loi du tribunal saisi.

Article 29

(1) L'action en responsabilité doit être intentée, sous peine de déchéance, dans le délai de deux ans à compter de l'arrivée à destination ou du jour où l'aéronef aurait dû arriver, ou de l'arrêt du transport.

(2) Le mode de calcul du délai est déterminé par la loi du tribunal saisi.

Article 30

(1) Dans les cas de transport régis par la définition du troisième alinéa de l'article 1er, à exécuter par divers transporteurs successifs, chaque transporteur acceptant des voyageurs, des bagages ou des marchandises est soumis aux règles établies par cette Convention, et est censé être une des parties contractantes du contrat de transport, pour autant que ce contrat ait trait à la partie du transport effectuée sous son contrôle.

(2) Au cas d'un tel transport, le voyageur ou ses ayants droit ne pourront recourir que contre le transporteur ayant effectué le transport au cours duquel l'accident ou le retard s'est produit, sauf dans le cas où, par stipulation expresse, le premier transporteur aura assuré la responsabilité pour tout le voyage.

(3) S'il s'agit de bagages ou de marchandises, l'expéditeur aura recours contre le premier transporteur et le destinataire qui a le droit à la délivrance contre le dernier, et l'un et l'autre pourront, en outre, agir contre le transporteur ayant effectué le transport au cours duquel la destruction, la perte, l'avarie ou le retard se sont produits. Ces transporteurs seront solidairement responsables envers l'expéditeur et le destinataire.

Article 30A

La présente Convention ne préjuge en aucune manière la question de savoir si la personne tenue pour responsable en vertu de ses dispositions a ou non un recours contre toute autre personne.

CHAPITRE IV
DISPOSITIONS RELATIVES AUX TRANSPORTS COMBINÉS

Article 31

(1) Dans le cas de transports combinés effectués en partie par air et en partie par tout autre moyen de transport, les stipulations de la présente Convention ne s'appliquent qu'au transport aérien et si celui-ci répond aux conditions de l'article 1er.

(2) Rien dans la présente Convention n'empêche les parties, dans le cas de transports combinés, d'insérer dans le titre de transport aérien des conditions relatives à d'autres modes de transport, à condition que les stipulations de la présente Convention soient respectées en ce qui concerne le transport par air.

CHAPITRE V
DISPOSITIONS GÉNÉRALES ET FINALES

Article 32

Sont nulles toutes clauses du contrat de transport et toutes conventions particulières au dommage par lesquelles les parties dérogeraient aux règles de la présente Convention soit par une détermination de la loi applicable, soit par une modification des règles de compétence. Toutefois, dans le transport des marchandises, les clauses d'arbitrage sont admises, dans les limites de la présente Convention, lorsque l'arbitrage doit s'effectuer dans le lieux de compétence des tribunaux prévus à l'article 28, alinéa (1).

Article 33

Sous réserve des dispositions de l'alinéa (3) de l'article 5, rien dans la présente Convention ne peut empêcher un transporteur de refuser la conclusion d'un contrat de transport ou de formuler des règlements qui ne sont pas en contradiction avec les dispositions de la présente Convention.

Article 34

Les dispositions des articles 3 à 8 inclus relatives aux titres de transport ne sont pas applicables au transport effectué dans des circonstances extraordinaires en dehors de toute opération normale de l'exploitation aérienne.

Article 35

Lorsque dans la présente Convention il est question de jours, il s'agit de jours courants et non de jours ouvrables.

Article 35A

Rien dans la présente Convention ne prohibe l'institution par un Etat et l'application sur son territoire d'un système d'indemnisation complémentaire à celui prévu par la présente Convention en faveur des demandeurs dans le cas de mort ou de lésions corporelles d'un passager. Un tel systeme doit satisfaire aux conditions suivantes—

(a) en aucun cas il ne doit imposer au transporteur et à ses préposés une responsabilité quelconque s'ajoutant à celle stipulée par la Convention;

(b) il ne doit imposer au transporteur aucune charge financière ou administrative autre que la perception dans ledit Etat des contributions des passagers, s'il en est requis;

(c) il ne doit donner lieu à aucune discrimination entre les transporteurs en ce qui concerne les passagers intéressés et les avantages que ces derniers peuvent retirer du système doivent leur être accordés quel que soit le transporteur dont ils ont utilisé les services;

(d) lorsqu'un passager a contribué au système, toute personne ayant subi des dommages à la suite de la mort ou de lésions corporelles de ce passager pourra prétendre à bénéficier des avantages du système.

(1) …

(2) Aux fins de la Convention, le mot *territoire* signifie non seulement le territoire métropolitain d'un Etat, mais aussi tous les territoires qu'il représente dans les relations extérieures.

PROTOCOLE ADDITIONNEL

Ad Article 2

Les Hautes Parties Contractantes se réservent le droit de déclarer au moment de la ratification ou de l'adhésion que l'article 2, alinéa 1er, de la présente Convention ne s'appliquera pas aux transports internationaux aériens effectués directement par l'Etat, ses colonies, protectorats, territoires sous mandat ou tout autre territoire sous sa souveraineté, sa suzeraineté ou son autorité.

[4316]

NOTES

Commencement: to be appointed.

THE WARSAW CONVENTION WITH THE AMENDMENTS MADE IN IT BY THE HAGUE PROTOCOL AND PROTOCOL NO 4 OF MONTREAL, 1975

NOTES

The text of the following Convention appears as set out in the Carriage by Air Act 1961, Sch 1A.

[PART 1
THE ENGLISH TEXT

CONVENTION
FOR THE UNIFICATION OF CERTAIN RULES RELATING TO INTERNATIONAL CARRIAGE BY AIR

CHAPTER I
SCOPE—DEFINITIONS

Article 1

(1) This Convention applies to all international carriage of persons, baggage or cargo performed by aircraft for reward. It applies equally to gratuitous carriage by aircraft performed by an air transport undertaking.

(2) For the purposes of this Convention, the expression international carriage means any carriage in which, according to the agreement between the parties, the place of departure and the place of destination, whether or not there be a break in the carriage or a transhipment, are situated either within the territories of two High Contracting Parties or within the territory of a single High Contracting Party if there is an agreed stopping place within the territory of another State, even if that State is not a High Contracting Party. Carriage between two points within the territory of a single High Contracting Party without an agreed stopping place within the territory of another State is not international carriage for the purposes of this Convention.

(3) Carriage to be performed by several successive air carriers is deemed, for the purposes of this Convention, to be one undivided carriage if it has been regarded by the parties as a single operation, whether it had been agreed upon under the form of a single contract or a series of contracts, and it does not lose its international character merely because one contract or a series of contracts is to be performed entirely within the territory of the same State.

Article 2

(1) This Convention applies to carriage performed by the State or by legally constituted public bodies provided it falls within the conditions laid down in Article 1.

(2) In the carriage of postal items the carrier shall be liable only to the relevant postal administration in accordance with the rules applicable to the relationship between the carriers and the postal administrations.

(3) Except as provided in paragraph (2) of this Article, the provisions of this Convention shall not apply to the carriage of postal items.

CHAPTER II
DOCUMENTS OF CARRIAGE

SECTION 1—PASSENGER TICKET

Article 3

(1) In respect of the carriage of passengers a ticket shall be delivered containing:
- (a) an indication of the places of departure and destination;
- (b) if the places of departure and destination are within the territory of a single High Contracting Party, one or more agreed stopping places being within the territory of another State, an indication of at least one such stopping place;
- (c) a notice to the effect that, if the passenger's journey involves an ultimate destination or stop in a country other than the country of departure, the Warsaw Convention may be applicable and that the Convention governs and in most cases limits the liability of carriers for death or personal injury and in respect of loss of or damage to baggage.

(2) The passenger ticket shall constitute prima facie evidence of the conclusion and conditions of the contract of carriage. The absence, irregularity or loss of the passenger ticket does not affect the existence or the validity of the contract of carriage which shall, none the

less, be subject to the rules of this Convention. Nevertheless, if, with the consent of the carrier, the passenger embarks without a passenger ticket having been delivered, or if the ticket does not include the notice required by paragraph (1)(c) of this Article, the carrier shall not be entitled to avail himself of the provisions of Article 22.

SECTION 2—BAGGAGE CHECK

Article 4

(1) In respect of the carriage of registered baggage, a baggage check shall be delivered, which, unless combined with or incorporated in a passenger ticket which complies with the provisions of Article 3, paragraph (1), shall contain:

- (a) an indication of the places of departure and destination;
- (b) if the places of departure and destination are within the territory of a single High Contracting Party, one or more agreed stopping places being within the territory of another State, an indication of at least one such stopping place;
- (c) a notice to the effect that, if the carriage involves an ultimate destination or stop in a country other than the country of departure, the Warsaw Convention may be applicable and that the Convention governs and in most cases limits the liability of carriers in respect of loss or damage to baggage.

(2) The baggage check shall constitute prima facie evidence of the registration of the baggage and of the conditions of the contract of carriage. The absence, irregularity or loss of the baggage check does not affect the existence or the validity of the contract of carriage which shall, none the less, be subject to the rules of this Convention. Nevertheless, if the carrier takes charge of the baggage without a baggage check having been delivered or if the baggage check (unless combined with or incorporated in the passenger ticket which complies with the provisions of Article 3, paragraph (1)(c)) does not include the notice required by paragraph (1)(c) of this Article, he shall not be entitled to avail himself of the provisions of Article 22, paragraph (2).

SECTION 3—DOCUMENTATION RELATING TO CARGO

Article 5

(1) In respect of the carriage of cargo an air waybill shall be delivered.

(2) Any other means which would preserve a record of the carriage to be performed may, with the consent of the consignor, be substituted for the delivery of an air waybill. If such other means are used, the carrier shall, if so requested by the consignor, deliver to the consignor a receipt for the cargo permitting identification of the consignment and access to the information contained in the record preserved by such other means.

(3) The impossibility of using, at points of transit and destination, the other means which would preserve a record of the carriage referred to in paragraph (2) of this Article does not entitle the carrier to refuse to accept the cargo for carriage.

Article 6

(1) The air waybill shall be made out by the consignor in three original parts.

(2) The first part shall be marked "for the carrier"; it shall be signed by the consignor. The second part shall be marked "for the consignee"; it shall be signed by the consignor and the carrier. The third part shall be signed by the carrier and handed by him to the consignor after the cargo has been accepted.

(3) The signature of the carrier and that of the consignor may be printed or stamped.

(4) If, at the request of the consignor, the carrier makes out the air waybill, he shall be deemed, subject to proof to the contrary, to have done so on behalf of the consignor.

Article 7

Where there is more than one package:

- (a) the carrier of the cargo has the right to require the consignor to make out separate air waybills;

(b) the consignor has the right to require the carrier to deliver separate receipts when the other means referred to in paragraph (2) of Article 5 are used.

Article 8

The air waybill and receipt for the cargo shall contain:

(a) an indication of the places of departure and destination;
(b) if the places of departure and destination are within the territory of a single High Contracting Party, one or more agreed stopping places being within the territory of another State, an indication of at least one such stopping place; and
(c) an indication of the weight of the consignment.

Article 9

Non-compliance with the provisions of Articles 5 to 8 shall not affect the existence or the validity of the contract of carriage, which shall, none the less, be subject to the rules of this Convention including those relating to limitation of liability.

Article 10

(1) The consignor is responsible for the correctness of the particulars and statements relating to the cargo inserted by him or on his behalf in the air waybill or furnished by him or on his behalf to the carrier for insertion in the receipt for the cargo or for insertion in the record preserved by the other means referred to in paragraph (2) of Article 5.

(2) The consignor shall indemnify the carrier against all damage suffered by him, or by any other person to whom the carrier is liable, by reason of the irregularity, incorrectness or incompleteness of the particulars and statements furnished by the consignor or on his behalf.

(3) Subject to the provisions of paragraphs (1) and (2) of this Article, the carrier shall indemnify the consignor against all damage suffered by him, or by any other person to whom the consignor is liable, by reason of the irregularity, incorrectness or incompleteness of the particulars and statements inserted by the carrier or on his behalf in the receipt for the cargo or in the record preserved by the other means referred to in paragraph (2) of Article 5.

Article 11

(1) The air waybill or the receipt for the cargo is prima facie evidence of the conclusion of the contract, of the acceptance of the cargo and of the conditions of carriage mentioned therein.

(2) Any statements in the air waybill or the receipt for the cargo relating to the weight, dimensions and packing of the cargo, as well as those relating to the number of packages, are prima facie evidence of the facts stated; those relating to the quantity, volume and condition of the cargo do not constitute evidence against the carrier except so far as they both have been, and are stated in the air waybill to have been, checked by him in the presence of the consignor, or relate to the apparent condition of the cargo.

Article 12

(1) Subject to his liability to carry out all his obligations under the contract of carriage, the consignor has the right to dispose of the cargo by withdrawing it at the airport of departure or destination, or by stopping it in the course of the journey on any landing, or by calling for it to be delivered at the place of destination or in the course of the journey to a person other than the consignee originally designated, or by requiring it to be returned to the airport of departure. He must not exercise this right of disposition in such a way as to prejudice the carrier or other consignors and he must repay any expenses occasioned by the exercise of this right.

(2) If it is impossible to carry out the orders of the consignor the carrier must so inform him forthwith.

(3) If the carrier obeys the orders of the consignor for the disposition of the cargo without requiring the production of the part of the air waybill or the receipt for the cargo delivered to the latter, he will be liable, without prejudice to his right of recovery from the

consignor, for any damage which may be caused thereby to any person who is lawfully in possession of that part of the air waybill or the receipt for the cargo.

(4) The right conferred on the consignor ceases at the moment when that of the consignee begins in accordance with Article 13. Nevertheless, if the consignee declines to accept the cargo, or if he cannot be communicated with, the consignor resumes his right of disposition.

Article 13

(1) Except when the consignor has exercised his right under Article 12, the consignee is entitled, on the arrival of the cargo at the place of destination, to require the carrier to deliver the cargo to him, on payment of the charges due and on complying with the conditions of carriage.

(2) Unless it is otherwise agreed, it is the duty of the carrier to give notice to the consignee as soon as the cargo arrives.

(3) If the carrier admits the loss of the cargo, or if the cargo has not arrived at the expiration of seven days after the date on which it ought to have arrived, the consignee is entitled to enforce against the carrier the rights which flow from the contract of carriage.

Article 14

The consignor and the consignee can respectively enforce all the rights given them by Articles 12 and 13, each in his own name, whether he is acting in his own interest or in the interest of another, provided that he carries out the obligations imposed by the contract of carriage.

Article 15

(1) Articles 12, 13 and 14 do not affect the relations of the consignor and the consignee with each other or the mutual relations of third parties whose rights are derived either from the consignor or from the consignee.

(2) The provisions of Articles 12, 13 and 14 can only be varied by express provision in the air waybill or the receipt for the cargo.

Article 16

(1) The consignor must furnish such information and such documents as are necessary to meet the formalities of customs, octroi or police before the cargo can be delivered to the consignee. The consignor is liable to the carrier for any damage occasioned by the absence, insufficiency or irregularity of any such information or documents, unless the damage is due to the fault of the carrier, his servants or agents.

(2) The carrier is under no obligation to enquire into the correctness or sufficiency of such information or documents.

CHAPTER III
LIABILITY OF THE CARRIER

Article 17

The carrier is liable for damage sustained in the event of the death or wounding of a passenger or any other bodily injury suffered by a passenger, if the accident which caused the damage so sustained took place on board the aircraft or in the course of any of the operations of embarking or disembarking.

Article 18

(1) The carrier is liable for damage sustained in the event of the destruction or loss of, or damage to, any registered baggage, if the occurrence which caused the damage so sustained took place during the carriage by air.

(2) The carrier is liable for damage sustained in the event of the destruction or loss of, or damage to, cargo upon condition only that the occurrence which caused the damage so sustained took place during the carriage by air.

(3) However, the carrier is not liable if he proves that the destruction, loss of, or damage to, the cargo resulted solely from one or more of the following:

(a) inherent defect, quality or vice of that cargo;

(b) defective packing of that cargo performed by a person other than the carrier or his servants or agents;

(c) an act of war or an armed conflict;

(d) an act of a public authority carried out in connection with the entry, exit or transit of the cargo.

(4) The carriage by air within the meaning of the preceding paragraphs of this Article comprises the period during which the baggage or cargo is in the charge of the carrier, whether in an airport or on board an aircraft, or, in the case of a landing outside an airport, in any place whatsoever.

(5) The period of the carriage by air does not extend to any carriage by land, by sea or by river performed outside an airport. If, however, such carriage takes place in the performance of a contract for carriage by air, for the purpose of loading, delivery or transhipment, any damage is presumed, subject to proof to the contrary, to have been the result of an event which took place during the carriage by air.

Article 19

The carrier is liable for damage occasioned by delay in the carriage by air of passengers, baggage or cargo.

Article 20

In the case of passengers and baggage, and in the case of damage occasioned by delay in the carriage of cargo, the carrier shall not be liable if he proves that he and his servants and agents have taken all necessary measures to avoid the damage or that it was impossible for them to take such measures.

Article 21

(1) In the carriage of passengers and baggage, if the carrier proves that the damage was caused by or contributed to by the negligence of the person suffering the damage the Court may, in accordance with the provisions of its own law, exonerate the carrier wholly or partly from his liability.

(2) In the carriage of cargo, if the carrier proves that the damage was caused by or contributed to by the negligence or other wrongful act or omission of the person claiming compensation, or the person from whom he derives his rights, the carrier shall be wholly or partly exonerated from his liability to the claimant to the extent that such negligence or wrongful act or omission caused or contributed to the damage.

Article 22

(1) In the carriage of persons the liability of the carrier for each passenger is limited to the sum of 16,600 Special Drawing Rights. Where, in accordance with the law of the court seised of the case, damages may be awarded in the form of periodical payments, the equivalent capital value of the said payments shall not exceed this limit. Nevertheless, by special contract, the carrier and the passenger may agree to a higher limit of liability.

(2)

(a) In the carriage of registered baggage, the liability of the carrier is limited to a sum of 17 Special Drawing Rights per kilogramme, unless the passenger or consignor has made, at the same time when the package was handed over to the carrier, a special declaration or interest in delivery at destination and has paid a supplementary sum if the case so requires. In that case the carrier will be liable to pay a sum not exceeding the declared sum, unless he proves that that sum is greater than the passenger's or the consignor's actual interest in delivery at destination.

(b) In the carriage of cargo, the liability of the carrier is limited to a sum of 17 Special Drawing Rights per kilogramme, unless the consignor has made, at the same time when the package was handed over to the carrier, a special declaration of interest in delivery at destination and has paid a supplementary sum if the case so requires. In that case the carrier will be liable to pay a sum not exceeding the declared sum, unless he proves that that sum is greater than the consignor's actual interest in delivery at destination.

(c) In the case of loss, damage or delay of part of registered baggage or cargo, or of any object contained therein, the weight to be taken into consideration in determining the amount to which the carrier's liability is limited shall be only the total weight of the package or packages concerned. Nevertheless, when the loss, damage or delay of a part of the registered baggage or cargo, or of an object contained therein, affects the value of other packages covered by the same baggage check or the same air waybill, the total weight of such package or packages shall also be taken into consideration in determining the limit of liability.

(3) As regards objects of which the passenger takes charge himself the liability of the carrier is limited to 332 Special Drawing Rights per passenger.

(4) The limits prescribed in this Article shall not prevent the court from awarding, in accordance with its own law, in addition, the whole or part of the court costs and of the other expenses of the litigation incurred by the plaintiff. The foregoing provision shall not apply if the amount of the damages awarded, excluding court costs and other expenses of the litigation, does not exceed the sum which the carrier has offered in writing to the plaintiff within a period of six months from the date of the occurrence causing the damage, or before the commencement of the action, if that is later.

(5) The sums mentioned in terms of the Special Drawing Right in this Article shall be deemed to refer to the Special Drawing Right as defined by the International Monetary Fund. Conversion of the sums into national currencies shall, in case of judicial proceedings, be made according to the value of such currencies in terms of the Special Drawing Right at the date of judgment.

(6) The value of a national currency, in terms of the Special Drawing Right, of a High Contracting Party which is a Member of the International Monetary Fund, shall be calculated in accordance with the method of valuation applied by the International Monetary Fund, in effect at the date of the judgment for its operations and transactions. The value of a national currency, in terms of the Special Drawing Right, of a High Contracting Party which is not a Member of the International Monetary Fund, shall be calculated in a manner determined by that High Contracting Party. Nevertheless, those States which are not Members of the International Monetary Fund and whose law does not permit the application of the provisions of paragraph (2)(b) of Article 22 may, at the time of ratification or accession or at any time thereafter, declare that the limit of liability of the carrier in judicial proceedings in their territories is fixed at a sum of two hundred and fifty monetary units per kilogramme. This monetary unit corresponds to sixty-five and a half milligrammes of gold of millesimal fineness nine hundred. This sum may be converted into the national currency concerned in round figures. The conversion of this sum into national currency shall be made according to the law of the State concerned.

Article 23

(1) Any provision tending to relieve the carrier of liability or to fix a lower limit than that laid down in this Convention shall be null and void, but the nullity of any such provision does not involve the nullity of the whole contract, which shall remain subject to the provisions of this Convention.

(2) Paragraph (1) of this Article shall not apply to provisions governing loss or damage resulting from the inherent defect, quality or vice of the cargo carried.

Article 24

(1) In the carriage of passengers and baggage, any action for damages, however founded, can only be brought subject to the conditions and limits set out in this Convention, without prejudice to the question as to who are the persons who have the right to bring suit and what are their respective rights.

(2) In the carriage of cargo, any action for damages, however founded, whether under this Convention or in contract or in tort or otherwise, can only be brought subject to the conditions and limits of liability set out in this Convention without prejudice to the question as to who are the persons who have the right to bring suit and what are their respective rights. Such limits of liability constitute maximum limits and may not be exceeded whatever the circumstances which give rise to the liability.

Article 25

In the carriage of passengers and baggage, the limits of liability specified in Article 22 shall not apply if it is proved that the damage resulted from an act or omission of the carrier, his servants or agents, done with intent to cause damage or recklessly and with knowledge that damage would probably result; provided that, in the case of such act or omission of a servant or agent, it is also proved that he was acting within the scope of his employment.

Article 25A

(1) If an action is brought against a servant or agent of the carrier arising out of damage to which this Convention relates, such servant or agent, if he proves that he acted within the scope of his employment, shall be entitled to avail himself of the limits of liability which that carrier himself is able to invoke under Article 22.

(2) The aggregate of the amounts recoverable from the carrier, his servants or agents, in that case, shall not exceed the said limits.

(3) In the carriage of passengers and baggage, the provisions of paragraphs (1) and (2) of this Article shall not apply if it is proved that the damage resulted from an act or omission of the servant or agent done with intent to cause damage or recklessly and with knowledge that damage would probably result.

Article 26

(1) Receipt by the person entitled to delivery of baggage or cargo without complaint is prima facie evidence that the same have been delivered in good condition and in accordance with the document of carriage.

(2) In the case of damage, the person entitled to delivery must complain to the carrier forthwith after the discovery of the damage, and, at the latest, within seven days from the date of receipt in the case of baggage and fourteen days from the date of receipt in the case of cargo. In the case of delay the complaint must be made at the latest within twenty-one days from the date on which the baggage or cargo has been placed at his disposal.

(3) Every complaint must be made in writing upon the document of carriage or by separate notice in writing despatched within the times aforesaid.

(4) Failing complaint within the times aforesaid, no action shall lie against the carrier, save in the case of fraud on his part.

Article 27

In the case of the death of the person liable, an action for damages lies in accordance with the terms of this Convention against those legally representing his estate.

Article 28

(1) An action for damages must be brought, at the option of the plaintiff, in the territory of one of the High Contracting Parties, either before the court having jurisdiction where the carrier is ordinarily resident, or has his principal place of business, or has an establishment by which the contract has been made or before the court having jurisdiction at the place of destination.

(2) Questions of procedure shall be governed by the law of the court seised of the case.

Article 29

(1) The right to damages shall be extinguished if an action is not brought within two years, reckoned from the date of arrival at the destination, or from the date on which the aircraft ought to have arrived, or from the date on which the carriage stopped.

(2) The method of calculating the period of limitation shall be determined by the law of the court seised of the case.

Article 30

(1) In the case of carriage to be performed by various succesive carriers and falling within the definition set out in the third paragraph of Article 1, each carrier who accepts passengers, baggage or cargo is subjected to the rules set out in this Convention, and is deemed to be one of the contracting parties to the contract of carriage in so far as the contract deals with that part of the carriage which is performed under his supervision.

(2) In the case of carriage of this nature, the passenger or his representative can take action only against the carrier who performed the carriage during which the accident or the delay occurred, save in the case where, by express agreement, the first carrier has assumed liability for the whole journey.

(3) As regards baggage or cargo, the passenger or consignor will have a right of action against the first carrier, and the passenger or consignee who is entitled to delivery will have a right of action against the last carrier, and further, each may take action against the carrier who performed the carriage during which the destruction, loss, damage or delay took place. These carriers will be jointly and severally liable to the passenger or to the consignor or consignee.

Article 30A

Nothing in this Convention shall prejudice the question whether a person liable for damage in accordance with its provisions has a right of recourse against any other person.

CHAPTER IV
PROVISIONS RELATING TO COMBINED CARRIAGE

Article 31

(1) In the case of combined carriage performed partly by air and partly by any other mode of carriage, the provisions of this Convention apply only to the carriage by air, provided that carriage by air falls within the terms of Article 1.

(2) Nothing in this Convention shall prevent the parties in the case of combined carriage from inserting in the document of air carriage conditions relating to other modes of carriage, provided that the provisions of this Convention are observed as regards the carriage by air.

CHAPTER V
GENERAL AND FINAL PROVISIONS

Article 32

Any clause contained in the contract and all special agreements entered into before the damage occurred by which the parties purport to infringe the rules laid down by this Convention, whether by deciding the law to be applied, or by altering the rules as to jurisdiction shall be null and void. Nevertheless for the carriage of cargo arbitration clauses are allowed subject to this Convention, if the arbitration is to take place within one of the jurisdictions referred to in the first paragraph of Article 28.

Article 33

Except as provided in paragraph (3) of Article 5, nothing in this Convention shall prevent the carrier either from refusing to enter into any contract of carriage or from making regulations which do not conflict with the provisions of this Convention.

Article 34

The provisions of Articles 3 to 8 inclusive relating to documents of carriage shall not apply in the case of carriage performed in extraordinary circumstances outside the normal scope of an air carrier's business.

Article 35

The expression "days" when used in this Convention means current days not working days.

Article 36

The Convention is drawn up in French in a single copy which shall remain deposited in the archives of the Ministry of Foreign Affairs of Poland and of which one duly certified copy shall be sent by the Polish Government to the Government of each of the High Contracting Parties.

Article 40A

(1) [This paragraph is not reproduced. It defines "High Contracting Party".]

(2) For the purposes of the Convention the word territory means not only the metropolitan territory of a State but also all other territories for the foreign relations of which that state is responsible.

[Articles 37, 38, 39, 40 and 41 and the concluding words of the Convention are not reproduced. They deal with the coming into force of the Convention.]

ADDITIONAL PROTOCOL

With reference to Article 2

The High Contracting Parties reserve to themselves the right to declare at the time of ratification or of accession that the first paragraph of Article 2 of this Convention shall not apply to international carriage by air performed directly by the State, its colonies, protectorates or mandated territories or by any other territory under its sovereignty, suzerainty or authority.]

[4317]

NOTES

Inserted, together with Pt II, by the Carriage by Air Acts (Implementation of Protocol No 4 of Montreal, 1975) Order 1999, SI 1999/1312, art 2(1), (6), Schedule.

PART II
THE FRENCH TEXT

CONVENTION
POUR L'UNIFICATION DE CERTAINES RÉGLES RELATIVES AU TRANSPORT AÉRIEN INTERNATIONAL

CHAPITRE 1ER
OBJET—DEFINITIONS

Article 1er

(1) La présente Convention s'applique à tout transport international de personnes, bagages ou merchandises, effectué par aéronef contre rémunération. Elle s'applique également aux transports gratuits effectués par aéronef par une entreprise de transports aériens.

(2) Est qualifié transport international, au sens de la présente Convention, tout transport dans lequel, d'après les stipulations des parties, le point de départ et le point de destination, qu'il y ait ou non interruption de transport ou transbordement, sont situés soit sur le territoire de deux Hautes Parties Contractantes, soit sur le territoire d'une seule Haute Partie Contractante si une escale est prévue sur le territoire d'un autre Etat, même si cet Etat n'est pas une Haute Partie Contractante. Le transport sans une telle escale entre deux points du territoire d'une seule Haute Partie Contractante n'est pas considéré comme international au sens de la présente Convention.

(3) Le transport à exécuter par plusieurs transporteurs par air successifs est censé constituer pour l'application de la présente Convention un transport unique lorsqu'il a été

envisagé par les parties comme une seule opération, qu'il été conclu sous la forme d'un seul contrat ou d'une série de contrats, et il ne perd pas son caractère international par le fait qu'un seul contrat ou une série de contrats doivent être exécutés intégralement dans le territoire d'un même Etat.

Article 2

(1) La Convention s'applique aux transports effectués par l'Etat ou les autres personnes juridiques de droit public, dans les conditions prévues a l'article 1er.

(2) Dans le transport des envois postaux, le transporteur n'est responsable qu'envers l'administration postale compétente conformément aux règles applicables dans les rapports entre les transporteurs et les administrations postales.
{d2}{n2}(3)
{t2}Les dispositions de la présente Convention autres que celles de l'alinéa 2 ci-dessus ne s'appliquent pas au transport des envois postaux.

CHAPITRE II
TITRE DE TRANSPORT

SECTION I
BILLET DE PASSAGE

Article 3

(1) Dans le transport de passagers, un billet de passage doit être délivré, contenant:
- (a) l'indication des points de départ et de destination;
- (b) si les points de départ et de destination sont situés sur le territoire d'une même Haute Partie Contractante et qu'une ou plusieurs escales soient prévues sur le territoire d'un autre Etat, l'indication d'une de ces escales:
- (c) un avis indiquant que si les passagers entreprennent un voyage comportant une destination finale ou une escale dans un pays autre que le pays de départ, leur transport peut être régi par la Convention de Varsovie qui, en général, limite la responsabilité du transporteur en cas de mort ou de lésion corporelle, ainsi qu'en cas de perte ou d'avarie des bagages.

(2) Le billet de passage fait foi, jusqu'à preuve contraire, de la conclusion et des conditions du contrat de transport. L'absence, l'irrégularité ou la perte du billet n'affecte ni l'existence ni la validité du contrat de transport, qui n'en sera pas moins soumis aux règles de la présente Convention. Toutefois, si, du consentement du transporteur, le passager s'embarque sans qu'un billet de passage ait été delivré, ou si le billet ne comporte pas l'avis prescrit à l'alinéa I (c) du présent article, le transporteur n'aura pas le droit de se prévaloir des dispositions de l'article 22.

SECTION II
BULLETIN DE BAGAGES

Article 4

(1) Dans le transport de bagages enregistrés, un bulletin de bagages doit être délivré qui, s'il n'est pas combiné avec un billet de passage conforme aux dispositions de l'article 3, alinéa Ier, ou n'est pas inclus dans un tel billet, doit contenir:
- (a) l'indication des points de départ et de destination;
- (b) si les points de départ et de destination sont situés sur le territoire d'une même Haute Partie Contractante et qu'une ou plusieurs escales soient prévues sur le territoire d'un autre Etat, l'indication d'une de ces escales;
- (c) un avis indiquant que, si le transport comporte une destination finale ou une escale dans un pays autre que le pays de départ, il peut être régi par la Convention de Varsovie qui, en général, limite la responsabilité du transporteur en cas de perte ou d'avarie des bagages.

(2) Le bulletin de bagages fait foi, jusqu'à preuve contraire de l'enregistrement des bagages et des conditions du contrat de transport. L'absence, l'irrégularité ou la perte du bulletin n'affecte ni l'existence ni la validité du contrat de transport, qui n'en sera pas moins soumis aux règles de la présente Convention. Toutefois, si le transporteur accepte la garde des

bagages sans qu'un bulletin ait été délivré ou si, dans le cas où le bulletin n'est pas combiné avec un billet de passage conforme aux dispositions de l'article 3, alinéa I (c), ou n'est pas inclus dans un tel billet, il ne comporte pas l'avis prescrit a l'alinéa I (c) du présent article, le transporteur n'aura pas le droit de se prévaloir des dispositions de l'article 22, alinéa 2.

SECTION III
DOCUMENTATION RELATIVE AUX MARCHANDISES

Article 5

(1) Pour le transport de marchandises une lettre de transport aérien est émise.

(2) L'emploi de tout autre moyen constatant les indications relatives au transport à exécuter peut, avec le consentement de l'expéditeur, se substituer à l'emission de la lettre de transport aérien. Si de tels autres moyens sont utilisés, le transporteur délivre à l'expéditeur, à la demande de ce dernier, un récépissé de la merchandise permettant l'identification de l'expédition et l'accès aux indications enregistreés par ces autres moyens.

(3) L'impossibilité d'utiliser, aux points de transit et de destination, les autres moyens permettant de constater les indications relatives au transport, visés a l'alinéa 2 ci-dessus, n'autorise pas le transporteur à refuser l'acceptation des merchandises en vue du transport.

Article 6

(1) La lettre de transport aérien est établie par l'expéditeur en trois exemplaires originaux.

(2) Le premier exemplaire porte la mention "pour le transporteur"; il est signé par l'expéditeur. Le deuxième exemplaire porte la mention ^q^pour le destinataire^/q^; il est signé par l'expéditeur et le transporteur. Le troisième exemplaire ets signé par le transporteur et remis par lui à l'expéditeur après acceptation de la marchandise.

(3) La signature du transporteur et celle de l'expéditeur peuvent être imprimées ou remplacées par un timbre.

(4) Si, à la demande de l'expéditeur, le transporteur établit la lettre de transport aérien, il est considéré, jusqu'à preuve contraire, comme agissant au nom de l'expéditeur.

Article 7

Lorsqu'il y a plusieurs colis:

(a) le transporteur de marchandises a le droit de demander à l'expéditeur l'établissement de lettres de transport aérien distinctes;

(b) l'expéditeur a le droit de demander au transporteur la remise de récépissés distincts, lorsque les autres moyens visés a l'alinéa 2 de l'article 5 sont utilisés.

Article 8

La lettre de transport aérien et le récépissé de la marchandise contiennent:

(a) l'indication des points de départ et de destination;

(b) si les points de départ et de destination sont situés sur le territoire d'une même Haute Partie Contractante et qu'une ou plusieurs escales soient prévues sur le territoire d'un autre Etat, l'indication d'une de ces escales;

(c) la mention du poids de l'expédition.

Article 9

L'inobservation des dispositions des articles 5 à 8 n'affecte ni l'existence ni la validité du contrat de transport, qui n'en sera pas moins soumis aux règles de la présente Convention, y compris celles qui portent sur la limitation de responsabilité.

Article 10

(1) L'expéditeur est responsable de l'exactitude des indications et déclarations concernant la marchandise inscrites par lui ou en son nom dans la lettre de transport aérien,

ainsi que de celles fournies et faites par lui ou en son nom au transporteur en veu d'être insérées dans le récépissé de la marchandise ou pour insertion dans les données enregistrées par les autres moyens prévus à l'alinéa 2 de l'article 5.

(2) L'expéditeur assume la responsabilité de tout dommage subi par le transporteur ou par toute autre personne à l'égard de laquelle la responsabilité du transporteur est engagée, à raison des indications et déclarations irrégulières, inexactes ou incomplètes fournies et faites par lui ou en son nom.

(3) Sous réserve des dispositions des alinéas 1 et 2 du présent article, le transporteur assume la responsabilité de tout dommage subi par l'expéditeur ou par toute autre personne à l'égard de laquelle la responsabilité de l'expéditeur est engagée, à raison des indications et déclarations irrégulières, inexactes ou incomplètes insérées par lui ou en son nom dans le récépissé dfe la marchandise ou dans les données enregistrées par les autres moyens prévus à l'alinéa 2 de l'article 5.

Article 11

(1) La lettre de transport aérien et le récépissé de la marchandise font foi, jusqu'a preuve contraire, de la conclusion du contrat, de la réception de la marchandise et des conditions du transport qui y figurent.

(2) Les énonciations de la lettre de transport aérien et du récépissé de la marchandise, relatives au poids, aux dimensions et à l'emballage de la marchandise ainsi qu'au nombre des colis font foi jusqu'a preuve contraire; celles relatives à la quantité, au volume et à l'état de la marchandise ne font preuve contre le transporteur qu'autant que la vérification en a été faite par lui en présence de l'expéditeur, et constatée sur la lettre de transport aérien, ou qu'il s'agit d'énonciations relatives à l'état apparent de la marchandise.

Article 12

(1) L'expéditeur a le droit, sous la condition d'exécuter toutes les obligations résultant du contrat de transport, de disposer de la merchandise, soit en la retirant a l'aérodrome de départ ou de destination, soit en l'arrêtant en cours de route lors d'un atterrissage, soit en la faisant délivrer au lieu de destination ou en cours de route à une personne autre que le destinataire initialement désigné, soit en demandant son retour à l'aérodrome de départ, pour autant que l'exercice de ce droit ne porte préjudice ni au transporteur, ni aux autres expéditeurs et avec l'obligation de rembourser les frais qui en résultent.

(2) Dans le cas où l'exécution des ordres de l'expéditeur est impossible, le transporteur doit l'en aviser immédiatement.

(3) Si le transporteur se conforme aux ordres de disposition de l'expéditeur, sans exiger la production de l'exemplaire de la lettre de transport aérien ou du récépissé de la marchandise délivré a celui-ci, il sera responsable, sauf son recours contre l'expéditeur, du préjudice qui pourra être causé par ce fait à celui qui est régulièrement en possession de la lettre de transport aérien ou du récépissé de la marchandise.

(4) Le droit de l'expéditeur cesse au moment où celui du destinataire commence, conformément a l'article 13. Toutefois, si le destinataire refuse la marchandise, ou s'il ne peut être atteint, l'expéditeur reprend son droit de disposition.

Article 13

(1) Sauf lorsque l'expéditeur a exercé le droit qu'il tient de l'article 12, le destinataire a le droit, dès l'arrivée de la marchandise au point de destination, de demander au transporteur de lui livrer la marchandise contre le paiement du montant des créances et contre l'exécution des conditions de transport.

(2) Sauf stipulation contraire, le transporteur doit aviser le destinataire dès l'arrivée de la marchandise.

(3) Si la perte de la marchandise est reconnue par le transporteur ou si, à l'expiration d'un délai de sept jours après qu'elle aurait dû arriver, la marchandise n'est pas arrivée, le destinataire est autorisé à faire valoir vis-à-vis du transporteur les droits résultant du contrat de transport.

Article 14

L'expéditeur et le destinataire peuvent faire valoir tous les droits qui leur sont respectivement conférés par les articles 12 et 13, chacun en son propre nom, qu'il agisse dans son propre intérêt ou dans l'intérêt d'autrui, à condition d'exécuter les obligations que le contrat de transport impose.

Article 15

(1) Les articles 12, 13 et 14 ne portent aucun préjudice ni aux rapports de l'expéditeur et du destinataire entre eux, ni aux rapports des tiers dont les droits proviennent, soit de l'expéditeur, soit du destinataire.

(2) Toute clause dérogeant aux stipulations des articles 12, 13 et 14 doit être inscrite dans la lettre de transport aérien ou dans le récépissé de la marchandise.

Article 16

(1) L'expéditeur est tenu de fournir les renseignements et les documents qui, avant la remise de la marchandise au destinataire, sont nécessaires à l'accomplissement des formalités de douane, d'octroi ou de police. L'expéditeur est responsable envers le transporteur de tous dommages qui pourraient résulter de l'absence, de l'insuffisance ou de l'irregularité de ces renseignements et pièces, sauf le cas de faute de la part du transporteur ou de ses préposés.

(2) Le transporteur n'est pas tenu d'examiner si ces renseignements et documents sont exacts ou suffisants.

CHAPITRE III
RESPONSABILITE DU TRANSPORTEUR

Article 17

Le transporteur est responsable du dommage survenu en cas de mort, de blessure ou de toute autre lésion corporelle subie par un voyageur lorsque l'accident qui a causé le dommage s'est produit à bord de l'aéronef ou au cours de toutes opérations d'embarquement et de débarquement.

Article 18

(1) Le transporteur est responsable du dommage survenu en cas de destruction, perte ou avarie de bagages enregistrés lorsque l'événement qui a causé le dommage s'est produit pendant le transport aérien.

(2) Le transporteur est responsable du dommage survenu en cas de destruction, perte ou avarie de la marchandise par cela seul que le fait qui a causé le dommage s'est produit pendant le transport aérien.

(3) Toutefois, le transporteur n'est pas responsable s'il établit que la destruction, la perte ou l'avarie de la marchandise résulte uniquement de l'un ou de plusieurs des faits suivants:

(a) la nature ou le vice propre de la marchandise;
(b) l'emballage défectueux de la marchandise par une personne autre que le transporteur ou ses préposés;
(c) un fait de guerre ou un conflit armé;
(d) un acte de l'autorité publique accompli en relation avec l'entrée, la sortie ou le transit de la marchandise.

(4) Le transport aérien, au sens des alinéas précédents, comprend la période pendant laquelle les bagages ou marchandises se trouvent sous la garde du transporteur, que ce soit dans un aérodrome ou à bord d'un aéronef ou dans un lieu quelconque en cas d'atterrissage en dehors d'un aérodrome.

(5) La période du transport aérien ne couvre aucun transport terrestre, maritime ou fluvial effectué en dehors d'un aérodrome. Toutefois, lorsqu'un tel transport est effectué dans l'exécution du contrat de transport aérien en vue du chargement, de la livraison ou du transbordement, tout dommage est présumé, sauf preuve contraire, résulter d'un événement survenu pendant le transport aérien.

Article 19

Le transporteur est responsable du dommage résultant d'un retard dans le transpore aérien de voyageurs, bagages ou marchandises.

Article 20

Dans le transport de passagers et de bagages et un cas de dommage résultant d'un retard dans le transport de marchandises, le transporteur n'est pas responsable s'il prouve que lui et ses préposés ont pris toutes le mesures nécessaires pour éviter le dommage ou qu'il leur était impossible de les prendre.

Article 21

(1) Dans le transport de passagers et de bagages, dans le cas où le transporteur fait la preuve que la faute de la personne lésée a causé le dommage ou y a contribué, le tribunal pourra, conformément aux dispositions de sa propre loi, écarter ou atténuer la responsabilité du transporteur.

(2) Dans le transport de marchandises, le transporteur est exonéré, en tout ou en partie, de sa responsabilité dans la mesure où il prouve que la faute de la personne qui demande réparation ou de la personne dont elle tient ses droits a causé le dommage ou y a contribué.

Article 22

(1) Dans le transport des personnes, la responsabilité du transporteur relative à chaque passager est limité à la somme de 16.000 Droits de Tirage spéciaux. Dans le cas où, d'après la loi du tribunal saisi, l'indemnité peut être fixée sous forme de rente, le capital de la rente ne peut dépasser cette limite. Toutefois par une convention spéciale avec le transporteur, le passager pourra fixer une limite de responsabilité plus élevée.

(2)

(a) Dans le transport de bagages enregistrés, la responsabilité du transporteur est limitée a la somme de 17 Droits de Tirage spéciaux par kilogramme, sauf déclaration spéciale d'intérêt à la livraison faite par l'expéditeur au moment de la remise du colis au transporteur et moyennant le paiement d'une taxe supplémentaire, éventuelle. Dans ce cas, le transporteur sera tenu de payer jusqu'à concurrence de la somme déclarée, à moins qu'il ne prouve qu'elle est supérieure à l'intérêt réel de l'expéditeur à la livraison.

(b) Dans le transport de marchandises, la responsabilité du transporteur est limitée à la somme de 17 Droits de Tirage spéciaux par kilogramme, sauf déclaration spéciale d'intérêt à la livraison faite par l'expéditeur au moment de la remise du colis au transporteur et moyennant le paiement d'une taxe supplementaire, éventuelle. Dans ce cas, le transporteur sera tenu de payer jusqu' à concurrence de la somme déclarée, à moins qu'il ne prouve qu'elle est supérieure à l'intérêt réel de l'expéditeur à la livraison.

(c) En cas de perte, d'avarie ou de retard d'une partie des bagages enregistrés ou des marchandises, ou de tout objet qui y est contenu, seul le poids total du ou des colis dont il s'agit est pris en considération pour déterminer la limite de responsabilité du transporteur. Toutefois, lorsque la perte, l'avarie ou le retard d'une partie des bagages enregistrés ou des marchandises, ou d'un objet qui y est contenu, affecte la valeur d'autres colis couverts par le meme bulletin de bagages ou la même lettre de transport aérien, le poids total de ces colis doit être pris en considération pour déterminer la limite de responsabilité.

(3) En ce qui concerne les objets dont le passager conserve la garde, la responsabilité du transporteur est limitée a 332 Droits de Tirage spéciaux par passager.

(4) Les limites fixées par le présent article n'ont pas pour effet d'enlever au tribunal la faculté d'allouer en outre, conformément à sa loi, une somme correspondent à tout ou partie des dépens et autres frais du procès exposés par le demandeur. La disposition précédente ne s'applique pas lorsque le montant de l'indemnité allouée, non compris les dépens et autres frais de procès, ne dépasse pas la somme que le transporteur a offerte par écrit au demandeur dans un délai de six mois à dater du fait qui a causé le dommage ou avant l'introduction de l'instance si celle-ci est postérieure à ce délai.

(5) Les sommes indiquées en Droits de Tirage spéciaux dans le présent article sont considérées comme se rapporeant au Droit de Tirage spécial tel que défini par le Fonds

Monétaire International. La conversion de ces sommes en monnaies nationales s'effectuera en cas d'instance judiciaire suivant la valeur de ces monnaies en Droit de Tirage spécial à la date du jugement.

(6) Les sommes indiquées en Droits de Tirage spéciaux dans le présent article sont considérées comme se rapportant au Droit de Tirage spécial tel que défini par le Fonds monétaire international. La conversion de ces sommes en monnaies nationales s'effectuera en cas d'instance judiciaire suivant la valeur de ces monnaies en Droit de Tirage spécial à la date du jugement. La valeur, en Droit de Tirage spécial, d'une monnaie nationale d'une Haute Partie Contractante qui est membre du Fonds monétaire international, est calculée selon la méthode d'évaluation appliquée par le Fonds monétaire international à la date du jugement pour ses propres opérations et transactions. La valeur, en Droit de Tirage spécial, d'une monnaie nationale d'une Haute Partie Contractante qui n'est pas membre du Fonds monétaire international, est calculée de la façon déeterminée par cette Haute Partie Contractante.

Toutefois, les Etats qui ne sont pas membres du Fonds monétaire international et dont la législation ne permet pas d'appliquer les dispositions de l'alinéa 2(b) de l'article 22, peuvent au moment de la ratification ou de l'adhésion, ou à tout moment par la suite, déclarer que la limite de responsabilité du transporteur est fixée, dans les procédures judiciaires sur leur territoire, à la somme de deux cent cinquante unités monétaires par kilogramme, cette unité monétaire correspondant à soixante-cinq milligrammes et demi d'or au titre de neuf cents millièmes de fin. Cette somme peut être convertie dans la monnaie nationale concernée en chiffres ronds. La conversion de cette somme en monnaie nationale s'effectuera conformément à la législation de l'Etat en cause.

Article 23

(1) Toute clause tendant à exonérer le transporteur de sa responsabilité ou à établir une limite inférieure à celle qui est fixée dans la présente Convention est nulle et de nul effet, mais la nullité de cette clause n'entraîne pas la nullité du contrat qui reste soumis aux dispositions de la présente Convention.

(2) L'alinéa Ier du présent article ne s'applique pas aux clauses concernant la perte ou le dommage résultant de la nature ou du vice propre des marchandises transportées.

Article 24

(1) Dans le transport de passagers et de bagages, toute action en responsabilité, à quelque titre que ce soit, ne peut être exercée que dans les conditions et limites prévues par la présente Convention, sans préjudice de la détermination des personnes qui ont le droit d'agir et de leurs droits respectifs.

(2) Dans le transport de marchandises, toute action en réparation introduite, à quelque titre que ce soit, que ce soit en vertu de la présente Convention, en raison d'un contrat ou d'un acte illicite ou pour toute autre cause, ne peut être exercée que dans les conditions et limites de responsabilité prévues par la présente Convention, sans préjudice de la détermination des personnes qui ont le droit d'agir et de leurs droits respectifs. Ces limites de responsabilité constituent un maximum et sont infranchissables quelles que soient les circonstances qui sont à l'origine de la responsabilité.

Article 25

Dans le transport de passagers et de bagages, les limites de responsabilité prévues a l'article 22 ne s'appliquent pas s'il est prouvé que le dommage résulte d'un acte ou d'une omission du transporteur ou de ses préposés fait, soit avec l'intention de provoquer un dommage, soit témérairement et avec conscience qu'un dommage en résultera probablement, pour autant que, dans le cas d'un acte ou d'une omission de préposés, la preuve soit également apportée que ceux-ci ont agi dans l'exercise de leurs fonctions.

Article 25A

(1) Si une action ese intentée contre un préposé du transporteur à la suite d'un dommage visé par la présente Convention, ce préposé, s'il prouve qu'il a agi dans l'exercice de ses fonctions, pourra se prévaloir des limites de responsabilité que peut invoquer ce transporteur en vertu de l'article 22.

(2) Le montant total de la réparation qui, dans ce cas, peut être obtenu du transporteur et de ses préposés ne doit pas dépasser lesdites limites.

(3) Dans le transport de passagers et de bagages, les dispositions des alinéas 1 et 2 du présent article ne s'appliquent pas s'il est prouvé que le dommage résulte d'un acte ou d'une omission du préposé fait, soit avec l'intention de provoquer un dommage, soit témérairement et avec conscience qu'un dommage en résultera probablement.

Article 26

(1) La réception des bagages et marchandises sans protestation par le destinataire constituera présomption, sauf preuve contraire, que les marchandises ont été livrées en bon état et conformément au titre de transport.

(2) En cas d'avarie, le destinataire doit adresser au transporteur une protestation immédiatement après la découverte de l'avarie et, au plus tard, dans un délai de sept jours pour les bagages et de quatorze jours pour les marchandises à dater de leur réception. En cas de retard, la protestation devra être faite au plus tard dans les vingt et un jours à dater du jour où le bagage ou la marchandise auront été mis à sa disposition.

(3) Toute protestation doit être faite par réserve inscrite sur le titre de transport ou par un autre écrit expédié dans le délai prévu pour cette proteseation.

(4) A défaut de protestation dans les délais prévus, toutes actions contre le transporteur sont irrecevables, sauf le cas de fraude de celui-ci.

Article 27

En cas de décès du débiteur, l'action en responsabilité, dans les limites prévues par la présente Convention, s'exerce contre ses ayants droit.

Article 28

(1) L'action en responsabilité devra être portée, au choix du demandeur, dans le territoire d'une des Hautes Parties Contractantes, soit devant le tribunal du domicile du transporteur, du siège principal de son exploitation ou du lieu où il possède un établissement par le soin duquel le contrat a été conclu, soit devant le tribunal du lieu de destination.

(2) La procédura sera réglée par la loi du tribunal saisi.

Article 29

(1) L'action en responsabilité doit être intentée, sous peine de déchéance, dans le délai de deux ans à compter de l'arrivée à destination ou du jour où l'aéronef aurait dû arriver, ou de l'arrêt du transport.

(2) Le mode du calcul du délai est determiné par la loi du tribunal saisi.

Article 30

(1) Dans les cas de transport régis par la définition du troisième alinéa de l'article Ier, à exécuter par divers transporteurs successifs, chaque transporteur acceptant des voyageurs, des bagages ou des marchandises est soumis aux règlis par cette Convention, et est censé être une des parties contractantes du contrat de transport, pour autant que ce contrat ait trait à la partie du transport effectué sous son contrôle.

(2) Au cas d'un tel transport, le voyageur ou ses ayants droit ne pourront recourir que contre le transporteur ayant effectué le transport au cours duquel l'accident ou le retard s'est produit, sauf dans le cas où, par stipulation expresse, le premier transporteur aura assuré la responsabilité pour tout le voyage.

(3) S'il s'agit de bagages ou de marchandises, l'expéditeur aura recours contre le premier transporteur et le destinataire qui a le droit à la délivrance contre le dernier, et l'un et l'autre pourront, en outre, agir contre le transporteur ayant effectué le transport au cours duquel la destruction, la perte, l'avarie ou le retard se sont produits. Ces transporteurs seront solidairement responsables envers l'expéditeur et le destinataire.

Article 30A

La présente Convention ne préjuge en aucune manière la question de savoir si la personne tenue pour responsable en vertu de ses dispositions a ou non un recours contre toute autre personne.

CHAPITRE IV
DISPOSITIONS RELATIVES AUX TRANSPORTS COMBINÉS

Article 31

(1) Dans le cas de transports combinés effectués en partie par air et en partie par toute autre moyen de transport, les stipulations de la présente Convention ne s'appliquent qu'au transport aérien et si celui-ci répond aux conditions de l'article 1er.

(2) Rien dans la présente Convention n'empêche les parties, dans le cas de transports combinés d'insérer dans le titre de transport aérien des conditions relatives à d'autres modes de transport, à condition que les stipulations de la présente Convention soient respectées en ce qui concerne le transport par air.

CHAPITRE V
DISPOSITONS GÉNÉRALES ET FINALES

Article 32

Sont nulles toutes clauses du contrat de transport et toutes conventions particulières antérieures au dommage par lesquelles les parties dérogeraient aux règles de la présente Convention soit par une détermination de la loi applicable, soit par une modification des règles de compétence. Toutefois, dans le transport des marchandises, les clauses d'arbitrage sont admises, dans les limites de la présente Convention, lorsque l'arbitrage doit s'effectuer dans les lieux de compétence des tribunaux prévus a l'article 28, alinéa 1.

Article 33

Sous réserve des dispositions de l'alinéa 3 de l'article 5, rien dans la présente Convention ne peut empêcher un transporteur de refuser la conclusion d'un contrat de transport ou de formuler des règlements qui ne sont pas en contradiction avec les dispositions de la présente Convention.

Article 34

Les dispositions des articles 3 à 8 inclus relatives aux titres de transport ne sont pas applicables au transport effectué dans des circonstances extraordinaires en dehors de toute opération normale de l'exploitation aérienne.

Article 35

Lorsque dans la présente Convention il est question de jours, il s'agit de jours courants et non de jours ouvrables.

Article 36

La présente Convention est rédigée en français en un seul exemplaire qui restera déposé aux archives du Ministère des Affairs Etrangères de Pologne, et dont une copie certifiée conforme sera transmise par les soins du Gouvernement polonais au Gouvernement de chacune des Hautes Parties Contractantes.

Article 40A

(1) ——————

(2) Aux fins de la Convention, le mot territoire signifie non seulement le territoire métropolitain d'un Etat, mais aussi tous les territoires qu'il représente dans les relations extérieures.

PROTOCOL ADDITIONNEL

Ad Article 2

Les Hautes Parties Contractantes se réservent le droit de déclarer au moment de la ratification ou de l'adhésion que l'article 2, alinéa premier, de la présente Convention ne s'appliquera pas aux transports internationaux aériens effectués directement par l'Etat, ses colonies, protectorats, territoires sous mandat ou tout autre territoire sous sa souveraineté, sa suzeraineté ou son autorité.]

[4318]

NOTES

Inserted, as noted to Pt I, at **[4317]**.

Substituted by the Carriage by Air Acts (Implementation of the Montreal Convention 1999) Order 2002, SI 2002/263, art 2(1), (26), Sch 2.

CONVENTION ON THE CONTRACT FOR THE INTERNATIONAL CARRIAGE OF GOODS BY ROAD

(1956)

NOTES

The text of the following Convention appears as set out in the Carriage of Goods by Road Act 1965, Schedule.

CHAPTER I
SCOPE OF APPLICATION

Article 1

1. This Convention shall apply to every contract for the carriage of goods by road in vehicles for reward, when the place of taking over of the goods and the place designated for delivery, as specified in the contract, are situated in two different countries, of which at least one is a Contracting country, irrespective of the place of residence and the nationality of the parties.

2. For the purposes of this Convention, "vehicles" means motor vehicles, articulated vehicles, trailers and semi-trailers as defined in article 4 of the Convention on Road Traffic dated 19th September 1949.

3. This Convention shall apply also where carriage coming within its scope is carried out by States or by governmental institutions or organisations.

4. This Convention shall not apply—
   (a) to carriage performed under the terms of any international postal convention;
   (b) to funeral consignments;
   (c) to furniture removal.

5. The Contracting Parties agree not to vary any of the provisions of this Convention by special agreements between two or more of them, except to make it inapplicable to their frontier traffic or to authorise the use in transport operations entirely confined to their territory of consignment notes representing a title to the goods.

Article 2

1. Where the vehicle containing the goods is carried over part of the journey by sea, rail, inland waterways or air, and, except where the provisions of article 14 are applicable, the goods are not unloaded from the vehicle, this Convention shall nevertheless apply to the whole of the carriage. Provided that to the extent that it is proved that any loss, damage or delay in delivery of the goods which occurs during the carriage by the other means of transport was not caused by an act or omission of the carrier by road, but by some event which

could only have occurred in the course of and by reason of the carriage by that other means of transport, the liability of the carrier by road shall be determined not by this Convention but in the manner in which the liability of the carrier by the other means of transport would have been determined if a contract for the carriage of the goods alone had been made by the sender with the carrier by the other means of transport in accordance with the conditions prescribed by law for the carriage of goods by that means of transport. If, however, there are no such prescribed conditions, the liability of the carrier by road shall be determined by this Convention.

2. If the carrier by road is also himself the carrier by the other means of transport, his liability shall also be determined in accordance with the provisions of paragraph 1 of this article, but as if, in his capacities as carrier by road and as carrier by the other means of transport, he were two separate persons.

[4319]

NOTES

Article 1: it should be noted that the definitions set out in the Convention on Road Traffic dated 19th September 1949, art 4, are as follows—

"Motor vehicle" means any self-propelled vehicle normally used for the transport of persons or goods upon a road, other than vehicles running on rails or connected to electric conductors.

"Articulated vehicle" means any motor vehicle with a trailer having no front axle and so attached that part of the trailer is superimposed upon the motor vehicle and a substantial part of the weight of the trailer and of its load is borne by the motor vehicle. Such a trailer shall be called a "semi-trailer".

"Trailer" means any vehicle designed to be drawn by a motor vehicle.

CHAPTER II
PERSONS FOR WHOM THE CARRIER IS RESPONSIBLE

Article 3

For the purposes of this Convention the carrier shall be responsible for the acts and omissions of his agents and servants and of any other persons of whose services he makes use for the performance of the carriage, when such agents, servants or other persons are acting within the scope of their employment, as if such acts or omissions were his own.

[4320]

CHAPTER III
CONCLUSION AND PERFORMANCE OF THE CONTRACT OF CARRIAGE

Article 4

The contract of carriage shall be confirmed by the making out of a consignment note. The absence, irregularity or loss of the consignment note shall not affect the existence or the validity of the contract of carriage which shall remain subject to the provisions of this Convention.

Article 5

1. The consignment note shall be made out in three original copies signed by the sender and by the carrier. These signatures may be printed or replaced by the stamps of the sender and the carrier if the law of the country in which the consignment note has been made out so permits. The first copy shall be handed to the sender, the second shall accompany the goods and the third shall be retained by the carrier.

2. When the goods which are to be carried have to be loaded in different vehicles, or are of different kinds or are divided into different lots, the sender or the carrier shall have the right to require a separate consignment note to be made out for each vehicle used, or for each kind or lot of goods.

Article 6

1. The consignment note shall contain the following particulars—

(a) the date of the consignment note and the place at which it is made out;

(b) the name and address of the sender;
(c) the name and address of the carrier;
(d) the place and the date of taking over of the goods and the place designated for delivery;
(e) the name and address of the consignee;
(f) the description in common use of the nature of the goods and the method of packing, and, in the case of dangerous goods, their generally recognised description;
(g) the number of packages and their special marks and numbers;
(h) the gross weight of the goods or their quantity otherwise expressed;
(i) charges relating to the carriage (carriage charges, supplementary charges, customs duties and other charges incurred from the making of the contract to the time of delivery);
(j) the requisite instructions for Customs and other formalities;
(k) a statement that the carriage is subject, notwithstanding any clause to the contrary, to the provisions of this Convention.

2. Where applicable, the consignment note shall also contain the following particulars—
(a) a statement that transhipment is not allowed;
(b) the charges which the sender undertakes to pay;
(c) the amount of "cash on delivery" charges;
(d) a declaration of the value of the goods and the amount representing special interest in delivery;
(e) the sender's instructions to the carrier regarding insurance of the goods;
(f) the agreed time-limit within which the carriage is to be carried out;
(g) a list of the documents handed to the carrier.

3. The parties may enter in the consignment note any other particulars which they may deem useful.

Article 7

1. The sender shall be responsible for all expenses, loss and damage sustained by the carrier by reason of the inaccuracy or inadequacy of—
(a) the particulars specified in article 6, paragraph 1, (b), (d), (e), (f), (g), (h) and (j);
(b) the particulars specified in article 6, paragraph 2;
(c) any other particulars or instructions given by him to enable the consignment note to be made out or for the purpose of their being entered therein.

2. If, at the request of the sender, the carrier enters in the consignment note the particulars referred to in paragraph 1 of this article, he shall be deemed, unless the contrary is proved, to have done so on behalf of the sender.

3. If the consignment note does not contain the statement specified in article 6, paragraph 1(k), the carrier shall be liable for all expenses, loss and damage sustained through such omission by the person entitled to dispose of the goods.

Article 8

1. On taking over the goods, the carrier shall check—
(a) the accuracy of the statements in the consignment note as to the number of packages and their marks and numbers, and
(b) the apparent condition of the goods and their packaging.

2. Where the carrier has no reasonable means of checking the accuracy of the statements referred to in paragraph 1(a) of this article, he shall enter his reservations in the consignment note together with the grounds on which they are based. He shall likewise specify the grounds for any reservations which he makes with regard to the apparent condition of the goods and their packaging. Such reservations shall not bind the sender unless he has expressly agreed to be bound by them in the consignment note.

3. The sender shall be entitled to require the carrier to check the gross weight of the goods or their quantity otherwise expressed. He may also require the contents of the packages to be checked. The carrier shall be entitled to claim the cost of such checking. The result of the checks shall be entered in the consignment note.

Article 9

1. The consignment note shall be *prima facie* evidence of the making of the contract of carriage, the conditions of the contract and the receipt of the goods by the carrier.

2. If the consignment note contains no specific reservations by the carrier, it shall be presumed, unless the contrary is proved, that the goods and their packaging appeared to be in good condition when the carrier took them over and that the number of packages, their marks and numbers corresponded with the statements in the consignment note.

Article 10

The sender shall be liable to the carrier for damage to persons, equipment or other goods, and for any expenses due to defective packing of the goods, unless the defect was apparent or known to the carrier at the time when he took over the goods and he made no reservations concerning it.

Article 11

1. For the purposes of the Customs or other formalities which have to be completed before delivery of the goods, the sender shall attach the necessary documents to the consignment note or place them at the disposal of the carrier and shall furnish him with all the information which he requires.

2. The carrier shall not be under any duty to enquire into either the accuracy or the adequacy of such documents and information. The sender shall be liable to the carrier for any damage caused by the absence, inadequacy or irregularity of such documents and information, except in the case of some wrongful act or neglect on the part of the carrier.

3. The liability of the carrier for the consequences arising from the loss or incorrect use of the documents specified in and accompanying the consignment note or deposited with the carrier shall be that of an agent, provided that the compensation payable by the carrier shall not exceed that payable in the event of loss of the goods.

Article 12

1. The sender has the right to dispose of the goods, in particular by asking the carrier to stop the goods in transit, to change the place at which delivery is to take place or to deliver the goods to a consignee other than the consignee indicated in the consignment note.

2. This right shall cease to exist when the second copy of the consignment note is handed to the consignee or when the consignee exercises his right under article 13, paragraph 1; from that time onwards the carrier shall obey the orders of the consignee.

3. The consignee shall, however, have the right of disposal from the time when the consignment note is drawn up, if the sender makes an entry to that effect in the consignment note.

4. If in exercising his right of disposal the consignee has ordered the delivery of the goods to another person, that other person shall not be entitled to name other consignees.

5. The exercise of the right of disposal shall be subject to the following conditions—

(a) that the sender or, in the case referred to in paragraph 3 of this article, the consignee who wishes to exercise the right produces the first copy of the consignment note on which the new instructions to the carrier have been entered and indemnifies the carrier against all expenses, loss and damage involved in carrying out such instructions;

(b) that the carrying out of such instructions is possible at the time when the instructions reach the person who is to carry them out and does not either interfere with the normal working of the carrier's undertaking or prejudice the senders or consignees of other consignments;

(c) that the instructions do not result in a division of the consignment.

6. When, by reason of the provisions of paragraph 5(b) of this article, the carrier cannot carry out the instructions which he receives, he shall immediately notify the person who gave him such instructions.

7. A carrier who has not carried out the instructions given under the conditions provided for in this article, or who has carried them out without requiring the first copy of the consignment note to be produced, shall be liable to the person entitled to make a claim for any loss or damage caused thereby.

Article 13

1. After arrival of the goods at the place designated for delivery, the consignee shall be entitled to require the carrier to deliver to him, against a receipt, the second copy of the consignment note and the goods. If the loss of the goods is established or if the goods have not arrived after the expiry of the period provided for in article 19, the consignee shall be entitled to enforce in his own name against the carrier any rights arising from the contract of carriage.

2. The consignee who avails himself of the rights granted to him under paragraph 1 of this article shall pay the charges shown to be due on the consignment note, but in the event of dispute on this matter the carrier shall not be required to deliver the goods unless security has been furnished by the consignee.

Article 14

1. If for any reason it is or becomes impossible to carry out the contract in accordance with the terms laid down in the consignment note before the goods reach the place designated for delivery, the carrier shall ask for instructions from the person entitled to dispose of the goods in accordance with the provisions of article 12.

2. Nevertheless, if circumstances are such as to allow the carriage to be carried out under conditions differing from those laid down in the consignment note and if the carrier has been unable to obtain instructions in reasonable time from the person entitled to dispose of the goods in accordance with the provisions of article 12, he shall take such steps as seem to him to be in the best interests of the person entitled to dispose of the goods.

Article 15

1. Where circumstances prevent delivery of the goods after their arrival at the place designated for delivery, the carrier shall ask the sender for his instructions. If the consignee refuses the goods the sender shall be entitled to dispose of them without being obliged to produce the first copy of the consignment note.

2. Even if he has refused the goods, the consignee may nevertheless require delivery so long as the carrier has not received instructions to the contrary from the sender.

3. When circumstances preventing delivery of the goods arise after the consignee, in exercise of his rights under article 12, paragraph 3, has given an order for the goods to be delivered to another person, paragraphs 1 and 2 of this article shall apply as if the consignee were the sender and that other person were the consignee.

Article 16

1. The carrier shall be entitled to recover the cost of his request for instructions, and any expenses entailed in carrying out such instructions, unless such expenses were caused by the wrongful act or neglect of the carrier.

2. In the cases referred to in article 14, paragraph 1, and in article 15, the carrier may immediately unload the goods for account of the person entitled to dispose of them and thereupon the carriage shall be deemed to be at an end. The carrier shall then hold the goods on behalf of the person so entitled. He may however entrust them to a third party, and in that case he shall not be under any liability except for the exercise of reasonable care in the choice of such third party. The charges due under the consignment note and all other expenses shall remain chargeable against the goods.

3. The carrier may sell the goods, without awaiting instructions from the person entitled to dispose of them, if the goods are perishable or their condition warrants such a course, or when the storage expenses would be out of proportion to the value of the goods. He may also proceed to the sale of the goods in other cases if after the expiry of a reasonable period he has

not received from the person entitled to dispose of the goods instructions to the contrary which he may reasonably be required to carry out.

4. If the goods have been sold pursuant to this article, the proceeds of sale, after deduction of the expenses chargeable against the goods, shall be placed at the disposal of the person entitled to dispose of the goods. If these charges exceed the proceeds of sale, the carrier shall be entitled to the difference.

5. The procedure in the case of sale shall be determined by the law or custom of the place where the goods are situated. **[4321]**

CHAPTER IV
LIABILITY OF THE CARRIER

Article 17

1. The carrier shall be liable for the total or partial loss of the goods and for damage thereto occurring between the time when he takes over the goods and the time of delivery, as well as for any delay in delivery.

2. The carrier shall however be relieved of liability if the loss, damage or delay was caused by the wrongful act or neglect of the claimant, by the instructions of the claimant given otherwise than as the result of a wrongful act or neglect on the part of the carrier, by inherent vice of the goods or through circumstances which the carrier could not avoid and the consequences of which he was unable to prevent.

3. The carrier shall not be relieved of liability by reason of the defective condition of the vehicle used by him in order to perform the carriage, or by reason of the wrongful act or neglect of the person from whom he may have hired the vehicle or of the agents or servants of the latter.

4. Subject to article 18, paragraphs 2 to 5, the carrier shall be relieved of liability when the loss or damage arises from the special risks inherent in one or more of the following circumstances—

(a) use of open unsheeted vehicles, when their use has been expressly agreed and specified in the consignment note;
(b) the lack of, or defective condition of packing in the case of goods which, by their nature, are liable to wastage or to be damaged when not packed or when not properly packed;
(c) handling, loading, stowage or unloading of the goods by the sender, the consignee or persons acting on behalf of the sender or the consignee;
(d) the nature of certain kinds of goods which particularly exposes them to total or partial loss or to damage, especially through breakage, rust, decay, desiccation, leakage, normal wastage, or the action of moth or vermin;
(e) insufficiency or inadequacy of marks or numbers on the packages;
(f) the carriage of livestock.

5. Where under this article the carrier is not under any liability in respect of some of the factors causing the loss, damage or delay, he shall only be liable to the extent that those factors for which he is liable under this article have contributed to the loss, damage or delay.

Article 18

1. The burden of proving that loss, damage or delay was due to one of the causes specified in article 17, paragraph 2, shall rest upon the carrier.

2. When the carrier establishes that in the circumstances of the case, the loss or damage could be attributed to one or more of the special risks referred to in article 17, paragraph 4, it shall be presumed that it was so caused. The claimant shall however be entitled to prove that the loss or damage was not, in fact, attributable either wholly or partly to one of these risks.

3. This presumption shall not apply in the circumstances set out in article 17, paragraph 4(a), if there has been an abnormal shortage, or a loss of any package.

4. If the carriage is performed in vehicles specially equipped to protect the goods from the effects of heat, cold, variations in temperature or the humidity of the air, the carrier shall not be entitled to claim the benefit of article 17, paragraph 4(d), unless he proves that all steps

incumbent on him in the circumstances with respect to the choice, maintenance and use of such equipment were taken and that he complied with any special instructions issued to him.

5. The carrier shall not be entitled to claim the benefit of article 17, paragraph 4(f), unless he proves that all steps normally incumbent on him in the circumstances were taken and that he complied with any special instructions issued to him.

Article 19

Delay in delivery shall be said to occur when the goods have not been delivered within the agreed time-limit or when, failing an agreed time-limit, the actual duration of the carriage having regard to the circumstances of the case, and in particular, in the case of partial loads, the time required for making up a complete load in the normal way, exceeds the time it would be reasonable to allow a diligent carrier.

Article 20

1. The fact that goods have not been delivered within thirty days following the expiry of the agreed time-limit, or, if there is no agreed time-limit, within sixty days from the time when the carrier took over the goods, shall be conclusive evidence of the loss of the goods, and the person entitled to make a claim may thereupon treat them as lost.

2. The person so entitled may, on receipt of compensation for the missing goods, request in writing that he shall be notified immediately should the goods be recovered in the course of the year following the payment of compensation. He shall be given a written acknowledgement of such request.

3. Within the thirty days following receipt of such notification, the person entitled as aforesaid may require the goods to be delivered to him against payment of the charges shown to be due on the consignment note and also against refund of the compensation he received less any charges included therein but without prejudice to any claims to compensation for delay in delivery under article 23 and, where applicable, article 26.

4. In the absence of the request mentioned in paragraph 2 or of any instructions given within the period of thirty days specified in paragraph 3, or if the goods are not recovered until more than one year after the payment of compensation, the carrier shall be entitled to deal with them in accordance with the law of the place where the goods are situated.

Article 21

Should the goods have been delivered to the consignee without collection of the "cash on delivery" charge which should have been collected by the carrier under the terms of the contract of carriage, the carrier shall be liable to the sender for compensation not exceeding the amount of such charge without prejudice to his right of action against the consignee.

Article 22

1. When the sender hands goods of a dangerous nature to the carrier, he shall inform the carrier of the exact nature of the danger and indicate, if necessary, the precautions to be taken. If this information has not been entered in the consignment note, the burden of proving, by some other means, that the carrier knew the exact nature of the danger constituted by the carriage of the said goods shall rest upon the sender or the consignee.

2. Goods of a dangerous nature which, in the circumstances referred to in paragraph 1 of this article, the carrier did not know were dangerous, may, at any time or place, be unloaded, destroyed or rendered harmless by the carrier without compensation; further, the sender shall be liable for all expenses, loss or damage arising out of their handing over for carriage or of their carriage.

Article 23

1. When, under the provisions of this Convention, a carrier is liable for compensation in respect of total or partial loss of goods, such compensation shall be calculated by reference to the value of the goods at the place and time at which they were accepted for carriage.

2. The value of the goods shall be fixed according to the commodity exchange price or, if there is no such price, according to the current market price or, if there is no commodity exchange price or current market price, by reference to the normal value of goods of the same kind and quality.

[3. Compensation shall not, however, exceed 8.33 units of account per kilogram of gross weight short.]

4. In addition, the carriage charges, Customs duties and other charges incurred in respect of the carriage of the goods shall be refunded in full in case of total loss and in proportion to the loss sustained in case of partial loss, but no further damages shall be payable.

5. In the case of delay, if the claimant proves that damage has resulted therefrom the carrier shall pay compensation for such damage not exceeding the carriage charges.

6. Higher compensation may only be claimed where the value of the goods or a special interest in delivery has been declared in accordance with articles 24 and 26.

[7. The unit of account mentioned in this Convention is the Special Drawing Right as defined by the International Monetary Fund. The amount mentioned in paragraph 3 of this article shall be converted into the national currency of the State of the Court seised of the case on the basis of the value of that currency on the date of the judgment or the date agreed upon by the Parties.]

Article 24

The sender may, against payment of a surcharge to be agreed upon, declare in the consignment note a value for the goods exceeding the limit laid down in article 23, paragraph 3, and in that case the amount of the declared value shall be substituted for that limit.

Article 25

1. In case of damage, the carrier shall be liable for the amount by which the goods have diminished in value, calculated by reference to the value of the goods fixed in accordance with article 23, paragraphs 1, 2 and 4.

2. The compensation may not, however, exceed—

(a) if the whole consignment has been damaged the amount payable in the case of total loss;

(b) if part only of the consignment has been damaged, the amount payable in the case of loss of the part affected.

Article 26

1. The sender may, against payment of a surcharge to be agreed upon, fix the amount of a special interest in delivery in the case of loss or damage or of the agreed time-limit being exceeded, by entering such amount in the consignment note.

2. If a declaration of a special interest in delivery has been made, compensation for the additional loss or damage proved may be claimed, up to the total amount of the interest declared, independently of the compensation provided for in articles 23, 24 and 25.

Article 27

1. The claimant shall be entitled to claim interest on compensation payable. Such interest, calculated at five per centum per annum, shall accrue from the date on which the claim was sent in writing to the carrier or, if no such claim has been made, from the date on which legal proceedings were instituted.

2. When the amounts on which the calculation of the compensation is based are not expressed in the currency of the country in which payment is claimed, conversion shall be at the rate of exchange applicable on the day and at the place of payment of compensation.

Article 28

1. In cases where, under the law applicable, loss, damage or delay arising out of carriage under this Convention gives rise to an extra-contractual claim, the carrier may avail himself of the provisions of this Convention which exclude his liability or which fix or limit the compensation due.

2. In cases where the extra-contractual liability for loss, damage or delay of one of the persons for whom the carrier is responsible under the terms of article 3 is in issue, such person may also avail himself of the provisions of this Convention which exclude the liability of the carrier or which fix or limit the compensation due.

Article 29

1. The carrier shall not be entitled to avail himself of the provisions of this chapter which exclude or limit his liability or which shift the burden of proof if the damage was caused by his wilful misconduct or by such default on his part as, in accordance with the law of the court or tribunal seised of the case, is considered as equivalent to wilful misconduct.

2. The same provision shall apply if the wilful misconduct or default is committed by the agents or servants of the carrier or by any other persons of whose services he makes use for the performance of the carriage, when such agents, servants or other persons are acting within the scope of their employment. Furthermore, in such a case such agents, servants or other persons shall not be entitled to avail themselves, with regard to their personal liability, of the provisions of this chapter referred to in paragraph 1.

[4322]

NOTES

Art 23: para 3 substituted, and para 7 added, by the Carriage by Air and Road Act 1979, s 4(2).

CHAPTER V
CLAIMS AND ACTIONS

Article 30

1. If the consignee takes delivery of the goods without duly checking their condition with the carrier or without sending him reservations giving a general indication of the loss or damage, not later than the time of delivery in the case of apparent loss or damage and within seven days of delivery, Sundays and public holidays excepted, in the case of loss or damage which is not apparent, the fact of his taking delivery shall be *prima facie* evidence that he has received the goods in the condition described in the consignment note. In the case of loss or damage which is not apparent the reservations referred to shall be made in writing.

2. When the condition of the goods has been duly checked by the consignee and the carrier, evidence contradicting the result of this checking shall only be admissible in the case of loss or damage which is not apparent and provided that the consignee has duly sent reservations in writing to the carrier within seven days, Sundays and public holidays excepted, from the date of checking.

3. No compensation shall be payable for delay in delivery unless a reservation has been sent in writing to the carrier, within twenty-one days from the time that the goods were placed at the disposal of the consignee.

4. In calculating the time-limits provided for in this Article the date of delivery, or the date of checking, or the date when the goods were placed at the disposal of the consignee, as the case may be, shall not be included.

5. The carrier and the consignee shall give each other every reasonable facility for making the requisite investigations and checks.

Article 31

1. In legal proceedings arising out of carriage under this Convention, the plaintiff may bring an action in any court or tribunal of a contracting country designated by agreement between the parties and, in addition, in the courts or tribunals of a country within whose territory

(a) the defendant is ordinarily resident, or has his principal place of business, or the branch or agency through which the contract of carriage was made, or
(b) the place where the goods were taken over by the carrier or the place designated for delivery is situated,

and in no other courts or tribunals.

2. Where in respect of a claim referred to in paragraph 1 of this article an action is pending before a court or tribunal competent under that paragraph, or where in respect of such a claim a judgment has been entered by such a court or tribunal no new action shall be started between the same parties on the same grounds unless the judgment of the court or tribunal before which the first action was brought is not enforceable in the country in which the fresh proceedings are brought.

3. When a judgment entered by a court or tribunal of a contracting country in any such action as is referred to in paragraph 1 of this article has become enforceable in that country, it shall also become enforceable in each of the other contracting States, as soon as the formalities required in the country concerned have been complied with. The formalities shall not permit the merits of the case to be re-opened.

4. The provisions of paragraph 3 of this article shall apply to judgments after trial, judgments by default and settlements confirmed by an order of the court, but shall not apply to interim judgments or to awards of damages, in addition to costs against a plaintiff who wholly or partly fails in his action.

5. Security for costs shall not be required in proceedings arising out of carriage under this Convention from nationals of contracting countries resident or having their place of business in one of those countries.

Article 32

1. The period of limitation for an action arising out of carriage under this Convention shall be one year. Nevertheless, in the case of wilful misconduct, or such default as in accordance with the law of the court or tribunal seised of the case, is considered as equivalent to wilful misconduct, the period of limitation shall be three years. The period of limitation shall begin to run—

(a) in the case of partial loss, damage or delay in delivery, from the date of delivery;
(b) in the case of total loss, from the thirtieth day after the expiry of the agreed time-limit or where there is no agreed time-limit from the sixtieth day from the date on which the goods were taken over by the carrier;
(c) in all other cases, on the expiry of a period of three months after the making of the contract of carriage.

The day on which the period of limitation begins to run shall not be included in the period.

2. A written claim shall suspend the period of limitation until such date as the carrier rejects the claim by notification in writing and returns the documents attached thereto. If a part of the claim is admitted the period of limitation shall start to run again only in respect of that part of the claim still in dispute. The burden of proof of the receipt of the claim, or of the reply and of the return of the documents, shall rest with the party relying upon these facts. The running of the period of limitation shall not be suspended by further claims having the same object.

3. Subject to the provisions of paragraph 2 above, the extension of the period of limitation shall be governed by the law of the court or tribunal seised of the case. That law shall also govern the fresh accrual of rights of action.

4. A right of action which has become barred by lapse of time may not be exercised by way of counter-claim or set-off.

Article 33

The contract of carriage may contain a clause conferring competence on an arbitration tribunal if the clause conferring competence on the tribunal provides that the tribunal shall apply this Convention.

[4323]

CHAPTER VI
PROVISIONS RELATING TO CARRIAGE PERFORMED BY SUCCESSIVE CARRIERS

Article 34

If carriage governed by a single contract is performed by successive road carriers, each of them shall be responsible for the performance of the whole operation, the second carrier and each succeeding carrier becoming a party to the contract of carriage, under the terms of the consignment note, by reason of his acceptance of the goods and the consignment note.

Article 35

1. A carrier accepting the goods from a previous carrier shall give the latter a dated and signed receipt. He shall enter his name and address on the second copy of the consignment note. Where applicable, he shall enter on the second copy of the consignment note and on the receipt reservations of the kind provided for in article 8, paragraph 2.

2. The provisions of article 9 shall apply to the relations between successive carriers.

Article 36

Except in the case of a counter-claim or a set-off raised in an action concerning a claim based on the same contract of carriage, legal proceedings in respect of liability for loss, damage or delay may only be brought against the first carrier, the last carrier or the carrier who was performing that portion of the carriage during which the event causing the loss, damage or delay occurred; an action may be brought at the same time against several of these carriers.

Article 37

A carrier who has paid compensation in compliance with the provisions of this Convention, shall be entitled to recover such compensation, together with interest thereon and all costs and expenses incurred by reason of the claim, from the other carriers who have taken part in the carriage, subject to the following provisions—

(a) the carrier responsible for the loss or damage shall be solely liable for the compensation whether paid by himself or by another carrier;

(b) when the loss or damage has been caused by the action of two or more carriers, each of them shall pay an amount proportionate to his share of liability; should it be impossible to apportion the liability, each carrier shall be liable in proportion to the share of the payment for the carriage which is due to him;

(c) if it cannot be ascertained to which carriers liability is attributable for the loss or damage, the amount of the compensation shall be apportioned between all the carriers as laid down in (b) above.

Article 38

If one of the carriers is insolvent, the share of the compensation due from him and unpaid by him shall be divided among the other carriers in proportion to the share of the payment for the carriage due to them.

Article 39

1. No carrier against whom a claim is made under articles 37 and 38 shall be entitled to dispute the validity of the payment made by the carrier making the claim if the amount of the compensation was determined by judicial authority after the first mentioned carrier had been given due notice of the proceedings and afforded an opportunity of entering an appearance.

2. A carrier wishing to take proceedings to enforce his right of recovery may make his claim before the competent court or tribunal of the country in which one of the carriers concerned is ordinarily resident, or has his principal place of business or the branch or agency through which the contract of carriage was made. All the carriers concerned may be made defendants in the same action.

3. The provisions of article 31, paragraphs 3 and 4, shall apply to judgments entered in the proceedings referred to in articles 37 and 38.

4. The provisions of article 32 shall apply to claims between carriers. The period of limitation shall, however, begin to run either on the date of the final judicial decision fixing the amount of compensation payable under the provisions of this Convention, or, if there is no such judicial decision, from the actual date of payment.

Article 40

Carriers shall be free to agree among themselves on provisions other than those laid down in articles 37 and 38.

[4324]

CHAPTER VII
NULLITY OF STIPULATIONS CONTRARY TO THE CONVENTION

Article 41

1. Subject to the provisions of Article 40, any stipulation which would directly or indirectly derogate from the provisions of this Convention shall be null and void. The nullity of such a stipulation shall not involve the nullity of the other provisions of the contract.

2. In particular, a benefit of insurance in favour of the carrier or any other similar clause, or any clause shifting the burden of proof shall be null and void.

(*Chapter VIII relates to the coming into force of the Convention, the settlement of disputes between the High Contracting Parties and related matters.*)

PROTOCOL OF SIGNATURE

1. This Convention shall not apply to traffic between the United Kingdom of Great Britain and Northern Ireland and the Republic of Ireland.

[4325]

CONVENTION CONCERNING THE INTERNATIONAL CARRIAGE BY RAIL (COTIF)[1] [OFFICIAL TRANSLATION]

Berne, 9 May 1980
(consolidated version, December 1997)

NOTES

The United Kingdom's instrument of ratification was deposited on 10 May 1983 and the Convention entered into force for the United Kingdom on 1 May 1985.

This Convention is published as Cmnd 8535.

The original source of this convention is the Intergovernmental Organisation for International Carriage by Rail (OTIF). See http://www.otif.org.

See also Protocol of 3 June 1999 (the Protocol of Vilnius) for the modification of this Convention at **[4382]**.

THE CONTRACTING PARTIES,

MEETING in accordance with Article 69, § 1 of the International Convention concerning the Carriage of Goods by Rail (CIM) and of Article 64, § 1 of the International Convention concerning the Carriage of Passengers and Luggage by Rail (CIV) of 7 February 1970[2] and in accordance with Article 27 of the Additional Convention to the CIV of 26 February 1966 relating to the Liability of the Railway for Death of and Personal Injury to, Passengers,[3]

CONVINCED of the value of an international organisation

RECOGNISING the need to adapt the provisions of transport law to economic and technical requirements,

HAVE AGREED as follows—

NOTES

1 Previously published as Treaty Series No 52 (1993). This text incorporates amendments which have been accepted and were in force as at 1 November 1996. They were published as Treaty Series Nos 6–8 inclusive (1997) Cm 3530–3522.

2 Treaty Series No 41 (1975) Cmnd 5898.

3 Treaty Series No 20 (1973) Cmnd 5249.

TITLE I
GENERAL PROVISIONS

Article 1

Intergovernmental Organisation

§ 1. The Parties to this Convention shall constitute, as Member States, the Intergovernmental Organisation for International Carriage by Rail (OTIF), hereinafter referred to as "the Organisation".

The headquarters of the Organisation shall be at Berne.

§ 2. The Organisation shall have legal personality. It shall in particular have the capacity to enter into contracts, to acquire and dispose of movable and immovable assets and to be a party to legal proceedings.

The Organisation, members of its staff, experts called in by it and representatives of Member States shall enjoy such privileges and immunities as are necessary to discharge their duties, subject to the conditions laid down in the Protocol annexed to the Convention, of which the Protocol shall form an integral part.

Relations between the Organisation and the State in which it has its headquarters shall be regulated by a Headquarters Agreement.

§ 3. The working languages of the Organisation shall be French and German.

[4326]

Article 2

Aims of the Organisation

§ 1. The principal aim of the Organisation shall be to establish a uniform system of law applicable to the carriage of passengers, luggage and goods in international through traffic by rail between Member States, and to facilitate the application and development of this system.

§ 2. The system of law provided for in § 1 may also be applied to international through traffic using in addition to services on railway lines, land and sea services and inland waterways.

Other internal carriage performed under the responsibility of the railway, complementary to carriage by rail, shall be treated as carriage performed over a line, within the meaning of the preceding sub-paragraph.

[4327]

Article 3

CIV and CIM Uniform Rules

§ 1. Carriage in international through traffic shall be subject to—

— the "Uniform Rules concerning the Contract for International Carriage of Passengers and Luggage by Rail (CIV)", forming Appendix A to the Convention;

— the "Uniform Rules concerning the Contract for International Carriage of Goods by Rail (CIM)", forming Appendix B to the Convention.

§ 2. The lines or services referred to in Article 2, § 1, and § 2, first sub-paragraph, on which such carriage is undertaken, shall be included in two lists: a list of CIV lines and a list of CIM lines.

§ 3. The undertakings responsible for the services referred to in Article 2, § 2, first sub-paragraph, and included in the lists, shall have the same rights and obligations as those arising for railways under the CIV and CIM Uniform Rules, subject to such derogations as result from the operating conditions peculiar to each mode of transport, which shall be published in the same form as the tariffs.

Nevertheless, the rules as to liability may not be made the subject of derogations.

§ 4. The CIV and CIM Uniform Rules, including their Annexes, shall form an integral part of the Convention.

[4328]

Article 4

Definition of the expression "Convention"

In the following texts the expression "Convention" covers the Convention itself, the Protocol referred to in Article 1, § 2, second sub-paragraph, the Additional Mandate for the Auditing of Accounts, and Appendices A and B including their Annexes, referred to in Article 3, §§ 1 and 4.

[4329]

TITLE II
STRUCTURE AND FUNCTIONING

Article 5

Organs

The functioning of the Organisation shall be ensured by the following organs—

— General Assembly
— Administrative Committee
— Revision Committee
— Committee of Experts for the Carriage of Dangerous Goods
— Central Office for International Carriage by Rail (OCTI)

[4330]

Article 6

General Assembly

§ 1. The General Assembly shall be composed of representatives of the Member States.

§ 2. The General Assembly shall—

(a) establish its rules of procedure;
(b) determine the composition of the Administrative Committee in accordance with Article 7, § 1;
(c) issue directives concerning the work of the Administrative Committee and the Central Office;
(d) fix, for five-year periods, the maximum figure for the annual expenditure of the Organisation, or issue directives relating to the limitation of that expenditure;
(e) take decisions, in accordance with Article 19, § 2, on proposals to amend the Convention;
(f) take decisions on applications for accession submitted to the General Assembly in accordance with Article 23, § 2;
(g) take decisions on other questions placed on the agenda in accordance with § 3.

§ 3. The Central Office shall convene the General Assembly once every five years or at the request of one-third of the Member States, as well as in the cases provided for in Articles 19, § 2 and 23, § 2, and shall send the draft agenda to the Member States at least three months before the opening of the session.

§ 4. There shall be a quorum in the General Assembly when a majority of the Member States are represented there.

A Member State may arrange to be represented by another Member State; no State may however represent more than two other States.

§ 5. Decisions of the General Assembly shall be taken by a majority vote of the Member States represented at the time of the vote.

However, for the purpose of § 2, (d) and (e), in the latter case where there are proposals to amend the Convention itself or the Protocol, the majority shall be two-thirds.

§ 6. With the agreement of a majority of the Member States, the Central Office shall also invite non-Member States to attend sessions of the General Assembly in an advisory capacity.

With the agreement of a majority of the Member States the Central Office shall invite international organisations concerned with transport matters or with problems which have been placed on the agenda to attend sessions of the General Assembly in an advisory capacity.

§ 7. Before sessions of the General Assembly and as directed by the Administrative Committee, the Revision Committee shall be convened for preliminary consideration of the proposals referred to in Article 19, § 2.

[4331]

Article 7

Administrative Committee

§ 1. The Administrative Committee shall be composed of representatives of twelve Member States.

The Swiss Confederation shall have a permanent seat. Other States shall be appointed for five years. The composition of the Committee shall be determined for each five-year period, having regard in particular to an equitable geographical distribution of seats. No Member State may sit on the Committee for more than two consecutive periods.

If a vacancy occurs, the Committee shall appoint another Member State for the remainder of the period.

Each Member State with a seat on the Committee shall appoint one delegate; it may also appoint an alternate.

§ 2. The Committee shall—

(a) establish its rules of procedure and designate by a two-thirds majority the Member State which shall assume the Chairmanship for each five-year period;

(b) conclude the Headquarters Agreement;

(c) make regulations to govern the organisation and functioning of the Central Office and the conditions of service of its staff;

(d) appoint, taking account of the ability of the candidates and an equitable geographical distribution, the Director General, Deputy Director General, Counsellors and Assistant Counsellors of the Central Office. The Central Office shall inform the Member States in good time of any vacancy which may occur in these posts; the Swiss Government shall propose candidates for the posts of Director General and Deputy Director General;
the Director General and the Deputy Director General shall be appointed for a period of five years, renewable;

(e) exercise both administrative and financial control over the affairs of the Central Office;

(f) ensure the correct application by the Central Office of the Convention and of decisions taken by the other organs; it shall, if necessary, recommend measures to be taken to facilitate the application of the Convention and of the decisions;

(g) give reasoned opinions on questions which may affect the work of the Central Office and are submitted to the Committee by a Member State or by the Director General of the Central Office;

(h) approve the Central Office's annual programme of work;

(i) approve the annual budget of the Organisation, the annual report and the annual accounts;

(j) send to the Member States the annual report, the annual statement of accounts as well as of its decisions and recommendations;

(k) prepare and send to the Member States, at least two months before the opening of the session of the General Assembly which is to decide the Committee's composition, a report on its work and proposals as to how it should be reconstituted.

§ 3. Unless it decides otherwise, the Committee shall meet at the headquarters of the Organisation.

It shall hold two meetings each year; it shall also meet if the Chairman so decides or at the request of four of its Members.

The minutes of its meetings shall be sent to all Member States.

[4332]

Article 8

Committees

§ 1. The Revision Committee and the Committee of Experts on the Carriage of Dangerous Goods, hereinafter called the "Committee of Experts", shall be composed of representatives of the Member States.

The Director General of the Central Office or his representative shall attend the meetings in an advisory capacity.

§ 2. The Revision Committee shall—

(a) take decisions in accordance with article 19, § 3 on proposals to amend the Convention;

(b) consider in accordance with article 6 § 7 proposals submitted to the General Assembly.

The Committee of Experts shall—

take decisions in accordance with article 19, § 4 on proposals to amend the Convention.

§ 3. The Central Office shall convene the Committees either on its own initiative or at the request of five Member States, or in the case provided for in article 6, § 7, and shall send the draft agenda to the Member States at least two months before the opening of the meeting.

§ 4. There shall be a quorum in the Revision Committee when a majority of the Member States are represented there; there shall be a quorum in the Committee of Experts when one-third of the Member States are represented there.

A Member State may arrange to be represented by another Member State; no State may however represent more than two other States.

§ 5. Each Member State represented shall have one vote; voting shall take place by show of hands or, on request, by nominal vote.

A proposal shall be adopted if the number of votes in favour is—

(a) equal to at least one-third of the number of Member States represented at the time of the vote;

(b) greater than the number of votes against.

§ 6. With the agreement of a majority of the Member States the Central Office shall invite non-Member States, and international organisations having competence in transport matters or with problems which have been placed on the agenda, to attend meetings of the Committees in an advisory capacity. Under the same conditions, independent experts may be invited to meetings of the Committee of Experts.

§ 7. The Committees shall elect a Chairman and one or two Deputy Chairmen for each meeting.

§ 8. The proceedings shall be conducted in the working languagesThe substance of what is said during a meeting in one of the working languages shall be translated into the other; proposals and decisions shall be translated in full.

§ 9. The minutes shall summarise the proceedings. Proposals and decisions shall be reproduced in full. With regard to decisions, the French text shall prevail.

Copies of the minutes shall be distributed to Member States.

§ 10. The Committees may appoint working groups to deal with specific questions.

§ 11. The Committees may establish their own rules of procedure. **[4333]**

Article 9

Central Office

§ 1. The Central Office for International Carriage by Rail shall provide the Secretariat of the Organisation.

§ 2. The Central Office shall, in particular,

(a) carry out the duties entrusted to it by the other organs of the Organisation;

(b) examine proposals to amend the Convention, if necessary with the assistance of experts;

(c) convene the Committees;

(d) send to Member States, in due time, the documents necessary for the meetings of the various organs;
(e) maintain and publish the lists of lines provided for in article 3, § 2;
(f) receive communications from the Member States and from transport undertakings, and communicate them, where appropriate, to the other Member States and other transport undertakings;
(g) maintain and publish a card-index of legal precedents;
(h) publish a periodical bulletin;
(i) represent the Organisation in relations with other international organisations competent to deal with questions relevant to the aims of the Organisation;
(j) draw up the Organisation's draft annual budget and submit it to the Administrative Committee for approval;
(k) manage the financial affairs of the Organisation within the limits of the approved budget;
(l) endeavour, at the request of a Member State or transport undertaking, by using its good offices, to settle disputes between such States or undertakings arising from the interpretation or application of the Convention;
(m) give, at the request of the parties concerned—Member States, transport undertakings or users—an opinion on disputes arising from the interpretation or application of the Convention;
(n) collaborate in the settlement of disputes by arbitration in accordance with Title III;
(o) facilitate, as between transport undertakings, financial relations arising from international traffic and the recovery of outstanding debts.

§ 3. The periodical bulletin shall contain the information necessary for the application of the Convention, as well as studies, judgments and important information for the interpretation, application and development of railway transport law; it shall be published in the working languages.

[4334]

Article 10

List of lines or services

§ 1. Member States shall send to the Central Office notifications concerning the inclusion of lines or services in or deletion of lines or services from the lists provided for in Article 3, § 2.

In so far as they link Member States, the lines or services referred to in Article 2, § 2 shall only be included in the lists with the agreement of those States; for the deletion of such a line or service, notification by one of those States shall suffice.

The Central Office shall notify all the Member States of the inclusion or deletion of any line or service.

§ 2. A line or service shall become subject to the Convention one month after the date of notification of its inclusion.

§ 3. A line or service shall cease to be subject to the Convention one month after the date of notification of its deletion, except for traffic already in transit, which shall be carried to its destination.

[4335]

Article 11

Finances

§ 1. The expenditure of the Organisation shall be fixed for each financial year by the Administrative Committee on the basis of a proposal by the Central Office.

The expenditure of the Organisation shall be financed by the Member States in proportion to the length of the lines listed. However, services on sea routes and inland waterways shall count only in respect of one-half of the length of their routes; in the case of other lines or services operated under special conditions, the contribution may be reduced by up to one-half by agreement between the Government concerned and the Central Office, subject to the approval of the Administrative Committee.

§ 2. When sending its annual report and statement of accounts to the Member States, the Central Office shall invite them to pay their contributions towards the expenditure of the past financial year as soon as possible and not later than 31 December of the year in which the documents are sent out.

After that date, the amounts due shall bear interest at the rate of five per cent per annum.

If, two years after that date, a Member State has not paid its contribution, its right to vote shall be suspended until it has fulfilled its obligation to pay.

On expiry of a further period of two years, the General Assembly shall consider whether the attitude of that State should be regarded as a tacit denunciation of the Convention and, where necessary, shall determine the effective date thereof.

§ 3. Contributions that have fallen due shall remain payable in the cases of denunciation referred to in § 2 and in Article 25, and in cases of suspension of the right to vote.

§ 4. Sums not recovered shall as far as possible be made good out of the resources of the Organisation; they may be spread over four financial years. Any remaining deficit shall be debited in a special account to the other Member States, in so far as they were parties to the Convention during the period of non-payment; the debit shall be proportional to the length of their lines listed on the date on which the special account is opened.

§ 5. A State which has denounced the Convention may become a Member State again by accession, provided that it has paid the sum due.

§ 6. A charge shall be made by the Organisation to cover the special expenses arising from activities provided for in Article 9, § 2, (l) to (n); in the cases provided for in Article 9, § 2, (l) and (m), the charge shall be determined by the Administrative Committee on the basis of a proposal by the Central Office; in the case provided for in Article 9, § 2 (n), Article 15, § 2 shall apply.

§ 7. The auditing of accounts shall be carried out by the Swiss Government, according to the rules laid down in the Additional Mandate annexed to the Convention itself and, subject to any special directives of the Administrative Committee, in conformity with the provisions of the Financial and Accounting Regulations of the Organisation.

[4336]

TITLE III
ARBITRATION

Article 12

Competence

§ 1. Disputes between Member States arising from the interpretation or application of the Convention, as well as disputes between Member States and the Organisation arising from the interpretation or application of the Protocol on privileges and immunities may, at the request of one of the parties, be referred to an Arbitration Tribunal. The parties shall freely determine the composition of the Arbitration Tribunal and the arbitration procedure.

§ 2. Disputes

(a) between transport undertakings,
(b) between transport undertakings and users,
(c) between users,

arising from the application of the CIV Uniform Rules and the CIM Uniform Rules, if not settled amicably or brought before the ordinary tribunals may, by agreement between the parties concerned, be referred to an Arbitration Tribunal. Articles 13 to 16 shall apply to the composition of the Arbitration Tribunal and the arbitration procedure.

§ 3. Any State may, on signing the Convention or depositing its instrument of ratification, acceptance, approval or accession reserve the right not to apply all or part of the provisions of § 1 and § 2.

§ 4. Any State which has made a reservation in pursuance of § 3 may withdraw it at any time by informing the depositary Government. The withdrawal of the reservation shall take effect one month after the date on which the depositary Government notifies it to the States.

[4337]

Article 13

Agreement to refer to arbitration. Registry

The Parties shall conclude an agreement to refer to arbitration, which shall, in particular, specify—

(a) the subject matter of the dispute;
(b) the composition of the Tribunal and the agreed period for nomination of the arbitrator or arbitrators;
(c) the place where it is agreed that the Tribunal is to sit.

The agreement to refer to arbitration must be communicated to the Central Office which shall act as Registry.

[4338]

Article 14

Arbitrators

§ 1. A panel of arbitrators shall be established and kept up to date by the Central Office. Each Member State may nominate to the panel of arbitrators two of its nationals who are specialists in international transport law.

§ 2. The Arbitration Tribunal shall be composed of one, three or five arbitrators in accordance with the agreement to refer to arbitration.

The arbitrators shall be selected from persons who are on the panel referred to in 1. Nevertheless, if the agreement to refer to arbitration provides for five arbitrators, each of the parties may select one arbitrator who is not on the panel.

If the agreement to refer to arbitration provides for a sole arbitrator, he shall be selected by mutual agreement between the parties.

If the agreement to refer to arbitration provides for three or five arbitrators, each party shall select one or two arbitrators as the case may be; these, by mutual agreement, shall appoint the third or fifth arbitrator, who shall be President of the Arbitration Tribunal.

If the parties cannot agree on the selection of a sole arbitrator, or the selected arbitrators cannot agree on the appointment of a third or fifth arbitrator, the appointment shall be made by the Director-General of the Central Office.

§ 3. The sole arbitrator, or the third or fifth arbitrator, must be of a nationality other than that of either party, unless both are of the same nationality.

The intervention of a third party in the dispute shall not affect the composition of the Arbitration Tribunal.

[4339]

Article 15

Procedure. Costs

§ 1. The Arbitration Tribunal shall decide the procedure to be followed having regard in particular to the following provisions—

(a) it shall enquire into and determine cases on the basis of the evidence submitted by the parties, but will not be bound by their interpretations when it is called upon to decide a question of law;
(b) it may not award more than the claimant has claimed, nor anything of a different nature, nor may it award less than the defendant has acknowledged as due;
(c) the arbitration award, setting forth the reasons for the decision, shall be drawn up by the Arbitration Tribunal and notified to the parties by the Central Office;
(d) save where the mandatory provisions of the law of the place where the Arbitration Tribunal is sitting otherwise provide and subject to contrary agreement by the parties, the arbitration award shall be final.

§ 2. The fees of the arbitrators shall be determined by the Director-General of the Central Office.

The Tribunal shall determine in its award the amount of costs and expenses and shall decide how they and the fees of the arbitrators are to be apportioned between the parties.

[4340]

Article 16

Limitation. Enforcement

§ 1. The commencement of arbitration proceedings shall have the same effect, as regards the interruption of periods of limitation, as that attributed by the applicable provisions of substantive law to the institution of an action in the ordinary courts.

§ 2. The Arbitration Tribunal's award in relation to transport undertakings or users becomes enforceable in each of the Member States on completion of the formalities required in the State where enforcement is to take place. The merits of the case shall not be subject to review.

[4341]

TITLE IV
MISCELLANEOUS PROVISIONS

Article 17

Recovery of debts outstanding between transport undertakings

§ 1. Outstanding accounts in respect of transport operations subject to the Uniform Rules may be forwarded to the Central Office by the creditor transport undertaking for assistance in securing payment; to that end the Central Office shall formally call upon the debtor transport undertaking to pay the sum due or state the reasons for its refusal to pay.

§ 2. If the Central Office considers that the grounds for refusal are adequate, it shall advise the parties to have recourse either to the competent court or to the Arbitration Tribunal in accordance with Article 12, § 2.

§ 3. If the Central Office considers that the whole or part of the sum is properly due it may, after taking expert advice where appropriate, call upon the debtor transport undertaking to pay the whole or part of the debt to the Central Office; the sum so paid shall be retained until the competent court or the Arbitration Tribunal has given a final decision on the merits of the case.

§ 4. If within a fortnight the undertaking does not pay the sum fixed by the Central Office, the latter shall send a further formal notice and draw attention to the consequences of non-compliance.

§ 5. If no payment is received within two months after such further notice, the Central Office shall notify the Member State having jurisdiction over the undertaking, of the action taken and of the grounds therefor, inviting that Member State to take further action and in particular to consider whether the lines or services of that undertaking should remain on the list.

§ 6. If the Member State declares that, notwithstanding the failure to pay, it wishes the undertaking's lines or services to remain on the lists, or if it fails to reply to the Central Office communication within a period of six weeks, it shall be deemed to guarantee the settlement of all debts arising from transport operations subject to the Uniform Rules.

[4342]

Article 18

Judgments. Attachment. Security for costs

§ 1. Judgments pronounced by the competent court under the provisions of the Convention after trial or by default shall, when they have become enforceable under the law applied by that court, become enforceable in each of the other Member States on completion of the formalities required in the State where enforcement is to take place. The merits of the case shall not be subject to review.

This provision shall apply neither to judgments which are provisionally enforceable, nor to awards of damages in addition to costs against a plaintiff who fails in his action.

The first sub-paragraph shall apply equally to judicial settlements.

§ 2. Debts arising from a transport operation subject to the Uniform Rules, owed to one transport undertaking by another transport undertaking not under the jurisdiction of the same Member State, may only be attached under a judgment given by the judicial authority of the Member State which has jurisdiction over the undertaking entitled to payment of the debt sought to be attached.

§ 3. Rolling stock belonging to a railway, as well as all transport equipment belonging to that railway, such as containers, loading tackle and sheets may not be seized on any territory other than that of the Member State having jurisdiction over the owner railway, except under a judgment given by the judicial authority of that State.

Private owners' wagons, as well as all transport equipment contained in such wagons and belonging to the owner of the wagon, may not be seized on any territory other than that of the State in which the owner is domiciled, except under a judgment given by the judicial authority of that State.

§ 4. Security for costs shall not be required in proceedings founded on the provisions of the Convention.

[4343]

TITLE V
AMENDMENT OF THE CONVENTION

Article 19

Competence

§ 1. Member States shall send their proposals for amending the Convention to the Central Office, which shall immediately bring them to the notice of the other Member States.

§ 2. The General Assembly shall take decisions on proposals to amend provisions of the Convention not referred to in §§ 3 and 4.

The inclusion of a proposal for an amendment on the agenda for a session of the General Assembly must be supported by one-third of the Member States.

When seized of a proposal for an amendment the General Assembly may decide, by the majority required under article 6, § 5, that such proposal is closely linked with one or more provisions the amendment of which is within the competence of the Revision Committee in accordance with § 3. In that case the General Assembly is also empowered to take decisions on the amendment of such provision or provisions.

§ 3. Subject to decisions taken by the General Assembly in accordance with § 2, sub-paragraph 3, the Revision Committee shall take decisions on proposals to amend the provisions listed below—

(a) *Additional Mandate for the Auditing of Accounts*;

(b) *CIV Uniform Rules*—

- Articles 1, § 3, 4, § 2; 5 (except § 2), 6, 9 to 14, 15 (except 6), 16 to 21, 22, § 3; 23 to 25, 37, 43 (except §§ 2 and 4), 48, 49, 56 to 58 and 61;
- the amounts expressed in units of account in articles 30, 31, 38, 40 and 41, where the purpose of the amendment is to increase those amounts;

(c) *CIM Uniform Rules*—

- Articles 1, § 2; 3, §§ 2 to 5; 4, 5, 6 (except § 3), 7, 8, 11 to 13, 14 (except § 7), 15 to 17, 19 (except § 4), 20 (except § 3), 21 to 24, 25 (except § 3), 26 (except § 2), 27, 28 § 3 and 6; 29, 30 (except § 3), 31, 32 (except § 3), 33 (except § 5), 34, 38, 39, 41, 45, 46, 47 (except § 3), 48 (only in so far as it is a question of adaptation to international maritime transport law), 52, 53, 59 to 61, 64 and 65;
- the amount expressed in units of account in Article 40, where the purpose of the amendment is to increase that amount;
- Regulations concerning the International Haulage of Private Owners' Wagons by Rail (RIP), Annex II;
- Regulations concerning the International Carriage of Containers by Rail (RICo), Annex III;
- Regulations concerning the International Carriage of Express Parcels by Rail (RIEx), Annex IV.

§ 4. The Committee of Experts shall take decisions on proposals to amend the provisions of the Regulations concerning the International Carriage of Dangerous Goods by Rail (RID), Annex I to the CIM Uniform Rules.

[4344]

Article 20

Decisions of the General Assembly

§ 1. Amendments decided upon by the General Assembly shall be recorded in a Protocol signed by the representatives of the Member States. The Protocol shall be subject to ratification, acceptance or approval; instruments of ratification, acceptance or approval shall be deposited as soon as possible with the depositary Government.

§ 2. When the Protocol has been ratified, accepted or approved by more than two-thirds of the Member States, the decisions shall come into force on the expiry of a period of time determined by the General Assembly.

§ 3. As soon as the decisions enter into force, the application of the CIV and CIM Uniform Rules shall be suspended in respect of traffic with and between those Member States which, one month before the date fixed for such entry into force, have not yet deposited their instruments of ratification, acceptance or approval. Such suspension shall be notified to Member States by the Central Office; it shall end one month after the date of notification by the Central Office of the ratification, acceptance or approval of the said decisions by the States concerned.

Such suspension shall not apply to Member States which notify the Central Office that, without having deposited their instruments of ratification, acceptance or approval, they will apply the amendments decided upon by the General Assembly.

[4345]

Article 21

Decisions of the Committees

§ 1. Amendments decided upon by the Committees shall be notified to the Member States by the Central Office.

§ 2. Such decisions shall come into force for all Member States on the first day of the twelfth month following the month in which the Central Office notifies them to the Member States, unless one-third of the Member States have objected within four months from the date of such notification.

However, if a Member State lodges objections to a decision of the Revision Committee within the period of four months and denounces the Convention not later than two months before the date fixed for the entry into force of that decision, the latter shall only come into force at the time when the denunciation by the State concerned takes effect.

[4346]

TITLE VI
FINAL PROVISION

Article 22

Signature, ratification, acceptance and approval of the Convention

§ 1. The Convention shall remain open at Berne, with the Swiss Government, until 31 December 1980, for signature by the States which have been invited to the 8th Ordinary Revision Conference for the CIM and CIV Conventions.

§ 2. The Convention shall be subject to ratification, acceptance or approval; instruments of ratification, acceptance or approval shall be deposited with the Swiss Government, the Depositary Government.

[4347]

Article 23

Accession to the Convention

§ 1. Those States which have been invited to the 8th Ordinary Revision Conference for the CIM and CIV Conventions but have not signed the new Convention within the period specified in Article 22, § 1, may nevertheless signify their accession to the Convention before it comes into force. The instrument of accession shall be deposited with the Depositary Government.

§ 2. Any State wishing to accede to this Convention after it comes into force shall address its application to the Depositary Government together with a note on the situation of its rail transport undertakings from the standpoint of international traffic. The Depositary Government shall communicate them to the Member States and to the Central Office.

The application shall be deemed to be accepted six months after the aforesaid communication, unless five Member States lodge objections with the Depositary Government.

The Depositary Government shall inform the applicant State as well as the Member States and the Central Office accordingly. The new Member State shall comply with the provisions of Article 10 without delay.

In the event of an objection, the Depositary Government shall submit the application for accession to the General Assembly for decision.

Following the deposit of the instrument of accession, this shall take effect on the first day of the second month following the month during which the Central Office has notified the Member States of the list of lines and services of the new Member State.

§ 3. Any accession to the Convention may only relate to the Convention and amendments in force at that time.

[4348]

Article 24

Entry into force of the Convention

§ 1. When the instruments of ratification, acceptance, approval or accession have been deposited by fifteen States, the Depositary Government shall contact the Governments concerned with a view to reaching agreement on the entry into force of the Convention.[1]

§ 2. The entry into force of the Convention shall have the effect of abrogating the International Conventions concerning the Carriage of Goods by Rail (CIM) and the Carriage of Passengers and Luggage by Rail (CIV) of 7 February 1970 as well as the Additional Convention to the CIV relating to the Liability of the Railway for Death of and Personal Injury to Passengers of 26 February 1966.[2]

[4349]

NOTES

1. The Convention entered into force on 1 May 1985. A Protocol drawn up by the Diplomatic Conference convened with a view to bringing the Convention into force was signed on 17 February 1984.
2. CIM—Treaty Series No 40 (1975), Cmnd 5897. CIV—Treaty Series No 41 (1975), Cmnd 5898. Additional Convention to CIV—Treaty Series No 20 (1973), Cmnd 5249.

Article 25

Denunciation of the Convention

Any State which wishes to denounce the Convention shall inform the Depositary Government. The denunciation shall take effect on 31 December of the following year.

[4350]

Article 26

Functions of the Depositary Government

The Depositary Government shall inform the States which have been invited to the 8th Ordinary Revision Conference for the CIM and CIV Conventions, any other States which have acceded to the Convention, and the Central Office—

(a) of signatures to the Convention, of the deposit of instruments of ratification, acceptance, approval or accession and of notifications of denunciation;
(b) of the date on which the Convention is to enter into force pursuant to Article 24;
(c) of the deposit of instruments of ratification, acceptance or approval of the protocols referred to in Article 20.

[4351]

Article 27

Reservations to the Convention

Reservations to the Convention may only be made if there is provision for them in the convention.

[4352]

Article 28

Texts of the Convention

The Convention shall be concluded and signed in the French language.

The French text shall be accompanied by official translations in German, English, Arabic, Italian and Dutch.

The French text alone shall prevail. **[4353]**

IN WITNESS WHEREOF the undersigned, being duly authorised by their respective Governments, have signed this Convention.

DONE at Berne, this ninth day of May one thousand nine hundred and eighty, in a single original in the French language, which shall remain deposited in the archives of the Swiss Confederation. A certified copy shall be sent to each of the Member States.

ADDITIONAL MANDATE FOR THE AUDITING OF ACCOUNTS

1. The Auditor shall audit the accounts of the Organisation, including all the trust funds and special accounts, as he considers necessary in order to ensure—
   (a) that the financial statements are in conformity with the ledgers and accounts of the Organisation;
   (b) that the financial transactions which the statements account for have been carried out in conformity with the rules and regulations, budgetary provisions and other directives of the Organisation;
   (c) that securities and cash held at banks or in the cash box have either been audited by reference to certificates received directly from the depositories of the Organisation, or actually counted;
   (d) that the internal checks, including the internal audit of the accounts, are adequate;
   (e) that all assets and liabilities as well as all surpluses and deficits have been posted according to procedures that he considers satisfactory.

2. Only the Auditor shall be competent to accept in whole or in part certificates and supporting documents furnished by the Director General. If he considers it appropriate, he may undertake an examination and detailed audit of any accounting record relating either to financial transactions or to supplies and equipment.

3. The Auditor shall have unrestricted access, at any time, to all ledgers, accounts, accounting documents and other information which he considers needful.

4. The Auditor shall not be competent to reject such and such a heading of the accounts, but he shall immediately draw to the attention of the Director General any transaction of which the regularity or appropriateness appears to him to be questionable, so that the latter may take the requisite measures.

5. The Auditor shall present and sign a certificate in respect of the financial statements with the following wording: "I have examined the financial statements of the Organisation for the financial year which ended on 31 December .... My examination consisted of a general analysis of the accounting methods and the checking of the accounting records and other evidence which appeared to me to be necessary in the circumstances." That certificate shall indicate, according to the circumstances, that—
   (a) the financial statements satisfactorily reflect the financial position at the date of expiry of the period in question as well as the results of the transactions carried out during the period which ended on that date;
   (b) the financial statements have been drawn up in accordance with the accounting principles mentioned;
   (c) the financial principles have been applied in accordance with procedures which accord with those adopted during the previous financial year;
   (d) the financial transactions have been carried out in conformity with the rules and regulations, budgetary provisions and other directives of the Organisation.

6. In his report on the financial transactions, the Auditor shall mention—
   (a) the nature and extent of the audit which he has carried out;
   (b) factors connected with the completeness or correctness of the accounts, including as appropriate—
      1. information necessary for the correct interpretation and assessment of the accounts;
      2. any sum which ought to have been collected but which has not been passed to account;
      3. any sum which has been the subject of a regular or conditional expenditure

commitment and which has not been posted or which has not been taken into account in the financial statements;

4. expenditure in support of which no sufficient vouchers have been produced;
5. whether or not ledgers have been kept in good and due form. It is necessary to note cases where the material presentation of the financial statements diverges from accounting principles generally recognised and invariably applied;

(c) other matters to which the attention of the Administrative Committee should be drawn, for example—

1. cases of fraud or presumption of fraud;
2. wastage or irregular use of funds or other assets of the Organisation (even when the accounts relating to the transaction carried out were in order);
3. expenditure which could subsequently lead to considerable costs for the Organisation;
4. any defects, general or particular, in the system of checking the receipts and expenses or the supplies and equipment;
5. expenditure not in conformity with the intentions of the Administrative Committee, taking account of transfers duly authorised within the budget;
6. overstepping of appropriations, taking account of changes resulting from transfers duly authorised within the budget;
7. expenditure not in conformity with the authorisations which govern it;

(d) the correctness or incorrectness of the accounts relating to supplies and equipment, established from the inventory and the examination of the ledgers.

In addition, the report may mention transactions which have been posted in the course of an earlier financial year and about which new information has been obtained or transactions which are due to be carried out in the course of a later financial year and about which it seems desirable to inform the Administrative Committee in advance.

7. The Auditor shall on no account include criticisms in his report without first affording the Director General an adequate opportunity of giving an explanation.

8. The Auditor shall inform the Administrative Committee and the Director General of the findings made as a result of the audit. He may, in addition, submit any comments that he considers appropriate about the financial report to the Director General.

9. Where the Auditor has carried out a summary audit or has been unable to obtain adequate supporting documents, he shall mention the fact in his certificate and his report, specifying the reasons for his observations as well as the consequences which result therefrom for the financial position and the posted financial transactions.

[4354]–[4356]

NOTES

Table of signatures and ratifications appearing in Cmnd 8535 omitted. For current status of Convention, see http://www.otif.org.

PROTOCOL ON THE PRIVILEGES AND IMMUNITIES OF THE INTERGOVERNMENTAL ORGANISATION FOR INTERNATIONAL CARRIAGE BY RAIL (OTIF)

Article 1

§ 1. Within the scope of its official activities, the Organisation shall enjoy immunity from jurisdiction and execution save—

(a) to the extent that the Organisation shall have expressly waived such immunity in a particular case;

(b) in the case of a civil action for damages brought by a third party arising from an accident caused by a motor vehicle or other means of transport belonging to, or operated on behalf of, the Organisation, or in respect of a traffic offence involving such a means of transport;

(c) in the case of a counter-claim directly connected with proceedings initiated by the Organisation;

(d) in the case of attachment by court order, of the salary, wages and emoluments payable by the Organisation to a staff member.

§ 2. The property and assets of the Organisation, wherever situated, shall be immune from any form of requisition, confiscation, sequestration or any other form of seizure or distraint, except to the extent that this is rendered necessary as a temporary measure for the prevention of accidents involving motor vehicles belonging to or operated on behalf of the Organisation, or by enquiries in connection with such accidents.

However, if expropriation is necessary in the public interest, all the appropriate steps must be taken to avoid interference in the exercise by the Organisation of its activities and adequate prompt compensation must be paid in advance.

§ 3. In respect of the exercise of its official activities, the Organisation and its property and income shall be exempted from direct taxes by each Member State. Where purchase or services of substantial value and strictly necessary for the exercise of the official activities of the Organisation are made or used by the Organisation and where the price of such purchases or services includes taxes or duties, appropriate measures shall, whenever possible, be taken by the Member States to grant exemption from such taxes and duties or to reimburse the amount thereof.

No exemption shall be granted in respect of taxes or charges which are no more than payment for services rendered.

Goods imported or exported by the Organisation and strictly necessary for the exercise of its official activities, shall be exempt from all duties and charges levied on import or export.

No exemption shall be granted under this Article in respect of goods purchased or imported, or services provided, for the personal benefit of the staff members of the Organisation.

§ 4. Goods acquired or imported under § 3 may not be sold or given away, nor used otherwise than in accordance with the conditions laid down by the Member States which have granted the exemptions.

§ 5. The official activities of the Organisation referred to in this Protocol are those activities which correspond to the aims defined in Article 2 of the Convention.

Article 2

§ 1. The Organisation may receive and hold any kind of funds, currency, cash or securities; it may dispose of them freely for any purpose provided for in the Convention and hold accounts in any currency to the extent required to meet its obligations.

§ 2. For its official communications and the transmission of all its documents, the Organisation shall enjoy treatment no less favourable than that accorded by each Member State to other comparable international organisations.

Article 3

Representatives of Member States shall, while exercising their functions and during journeys made on official business, enjoy the following privileges and immunities in the territory of each Member State—

(a) immunity from jurisdiction, even after the termination of their mission, in respect of acts, including words spoken and written, done by them in the exercise of their functions; such immunity shall not apply, however, in the case of damage arising from an accident caused by a motor vehicle or other means of transport belonging to or driven by a representative of a State, nor in the case of a traffic offence involving such a means of transport;

(b) immunity from arrest and from detention pending trial, save when apprehended *flagrante delicto*;

(c) immunity from seizure of their personal luggage save when apprehended *flagrante delicto*;

(d) inviolability for all their official papers and documents;

(e) exemption for themselves and their spouses from all measures restricting entry and from all aliens' registration formalities;

(f) the same facilities regarding currency and exchange control as those accorded to representatives of foreign Governments on temporary official mission.

Article 4

The staff members of the Organisation shall, while exercising their functions, enjoy the following privileges and immunities in the territory of each Member State—

(a) immunity from jurisdiction in respect of acts, including words spoken and written, done by them in the exercise of their function, and within the limits of their prerogatives, even after they have left the service of the Organisation; such immunity shall not apply, however, in the case of damage arising from an accident caused by a motor vehicle or other means of transport belonging to or driven by a staff member of the Organisation, nor in the case of a traffic offence involving such a means of transport;

(b) inviolability for all their official papers and documents;

(c) the same facilities as regards exemption from measures restricting immigration and governing aliens' registration as are normally accorded to staff members of international organisations; members of their families forming part of their households shall enjoy the same facilities;

(d) exemption from national income tax, subject to the introduction for the benefit of the Organisation of an internal tax on salaries, wages and emoluments paid by the Organisation; nevertheless the Member States may take these salaries, wages and emoluments into account for the purpose of assessing the amount of tax to be charged on income from other sources; Member States shall not be obliged to apply this exemption from tax to payments, retirement pensions and survivor's pensions paid by the Organisation to its former staff members or their assigns;

(e) in respect of exchange control, the same privileges as are normally accorded to staff members of international organisations;

(f) in time of international crisis, the same repatriation facilities for themselves and the members of their families forming part of their households as are normally accorded to staff members of international organisations.

Article 5

Experts upon whose services the Organisation may call shall, while exercising their functions in relation to, or undertaking missions on behalf of, the Organisation, enjoy the following privileges and immunities to the extent that these are necessary for the exercise of their functions, including during journeys made in the exercise of their functions and in the course of such missions—

(a) immunity from jurisdiction in respect of acts, including words written and spoken, done by them in the exercise of their functions; such immunity shall not apply, however, in the case of damage arising from an accident caused by a motor vehicle or other means of transport belonging to or driven by an expert, nor in the case of a traffic offence involving such a means of transport; experts shall continue to enjoy such immunity even after they have ceased to exercise their functions in relation to the Organisation;

(b) inviolability for all their official papers and documents;

(c) the exchange control facilities necessary for the transfer of their remuneration;

(d) the same facilities, in respect of personal luggage, as are accorded to agents of foreign Government on temporary official mission.

Article 6

§ 1. The privileges and immunities provided for in this Protocol are instituted solely to ensure, in all circumstances, the unimpeded functioning of the Organisation and the complete independence of the persons to whom they are accorded. The competent authorities shall waive any immunity in all cases where retaining it might impede the course of justice and where it can be waived without prejudicing the achievement of the purpose for which it was accorded.

§ 2. The competent authorities for the purposes of § 1 shall be—

— the Member States, in respect of their representatives,

— the Administrative Committee, in respect of the Director General,

— the Director General, in respect of other staff members and of experts upon whose services the Organisation may call.

Article 7

§ 1. Nothing in this Protocol shall call into question the right of each Member State to take every necessary precaution in the interests of its public security.

§ 2. The Organisation shall co-operate at all times with the competent authorities of the Member States in order to facilitate the proper administration of justice, to ensure the observance of the laws and regulations of the Member States concerned and to prevent any abuse arising out of the privileges and immunities provided for in this Protocol.

Article 8

No Member State shall be obliged to accord the privileges and immunities referred to in this Protocol under

— Article 3, excluding item (d)
— Article 4, excluding items (a), (b) and (d)
— Article 5, excluding items (a) and (b)

to its own nationals or to persons who are permanent residents of that State.

Article 9

The Organisation may conclude with one or more Member States complementary agreements to give effect to the provisions of this Protocol as regards such Member State or Member States, and other agreements to ensure the efficient functioning of the Organisation.

[4357]

APPENDIX A TO THE CONVENTION CONCERNING INTERNATIONAL CARRIAGE BY RAIL (COTIF) OF 9 MAY 1980

UNIFORM RULES CONCERNING THE CONTRACT FOR INTERNATIONAL CARRIAGE OF PASSENGERS AND LUGGAGE BY RAIL (CIV)

TITLE I GENERAL PROVISIONS

Article 1

Scope

§ 1. Subject to the exceptions provided for in Articles 2, 3 and 33, the Uniform Rules shall apply to all carriage of passengers and luggage including motor vehicles, under international transport documents made out for a journey over the territories of at least two States and exclusively over lines or services included in the list provided for in Articles 3 and 10 of the Convention, as well as, in appropriate cases, to carriage treated as carriage over a line in accordance with Article 2, § 2, sub-paragraph 2 of the Convention.

The Uniform Rules shall also apply, as far as the liability of the railway in case of death of, or personal injury to, passengers is concerned, to persons accompanying a consignment whose carriage is effected in accordance with the Uniform Rules concerning the Contract for the International Carriage of Goods by Rail (CIM).

§ 2. The international tariffs shall determine the places between which international transport documents shall be issued.

§ 3. In the Uniform Rules, the term "station" covers: railway stations, ports used by shipping services and all other establishments of transport undertakings, open to the public for the execution of the contract of carriage.

Article 2

Exceptions from scope

§ 1. Carriage between stations of departure and destination situated in the territory of the same State, performed over the territory of another State only in transit, shall not be subject to the Uniform Rules—

(a) if the lines or services over which the transit occurs are exclusively operated by a railway of the State of departure; or

(b) if the States or railways concerned have agreed not to regard such carriage as international.

§ 2. Carriage between stations in two adjacent States and carriage between stations in two States involving transit through the territory of a third State shall, in cases where the lines or services over which the carriage is performed are exclusively operated by a railway of one of those three States and where there is nothing to the contrary in the laws and regulations of any of the said States, be governed by the internal traffic regulations applicable to that railway.

Article 3

Reservation concerning liability in case of death of, or personal injury to, passengers

§ 1. Each State may, at the time when it signs the Convention or deposits its instrument of ratification, acceptance, approval or accession reserve the right not to apply to passengers involved in accidents occurring in its territory the whole of the provisions concerning the liability of the railway in case of death of or personal injury to passengers, when such passengers are nationals of or have their usual place of residence in that State.

§ 2. Each State which has made the reservation mentioned above may withdraw it at any time by informing the Depositary Government. Withdrawal of the reservation shall take effect one month after the date on which the Swiss Government notifies Member States of it.

Article 4

Obligation to carry

§ 1. The railway shall be bound to undertake the carriage of any passengers and luggage subject to the terms of the Uniform Rules, provided that—

(a) the passenger complies with the Uniform Rules, the supplementary provisions and the international tariffs;

(b) carriage can be undertaken by the normal staff and transport resources which suffice to meet usual traffic requirements;

(c) carriage is not prevented by circumstances which the railway cannot avoid and which it is not in a position to remedy.

§ 2. When the competent authority decides that a service shall be discontinued or suspended totally or partially, such measures shall, without delay, be brought to the notice of the public and of the railways; the latter shall inform the railways of the other States of the measures with a view to their publication.

§ 3. Any contravention of this Article by the railway may constitute a cause of action for compensation for the loss or damage caused.

Article 5

Tariffs. Private agreements

§ 1. The international tariffs shall contain all the special conditions applicable to carriage, in particular the information necessary for calculating fares and other charges and, where necessary, the conditions for conversion of currencies.

The conditions of international tariffs may not derogate from the Uniform Rules unless the latter expressly so provide.

§ 2. The international tariffs shall be applied to all users on the same conditions.

§ 3. Railways may enter into private agreements for reduced fares or charges or other concessions, provided that comparable conditions are afforded to passengers in comparable circumstances.

Reductions in fares or charges or other concessions may be granted for the purpose of the railway or public services, or for charitable, educational or instructional purposes.

Publication of the measures taken under the first and second sub-paragraphs shall not be compulsory.

§ 4. The publication of international tariffs shall be compulsory only in those States whose railways are parties to such tariffs as railways of departure or destination. The tariffs and amendments thereto shall come into force on the date specified when they are published. Increases in fares or charges, and any other measures that have the effect of making the conditions of carriage prescribed in such tariffs more rigorous, shall come into force six days after their publication at the earliest.

Modifications to the fares and other charges provided for in the international tariffs made in order to take account of fluctuations in rates of exchange, as well as corrections of obvious errors, shall come into force on the day after their publication.

§ 5. At every station which is open for international traffic, the passenger should be able to acquaint himself with the international tariffs or with extracts therefrom showing the prices for international tickets on sale at that station and the corresponding registered luggage charges.

Article 6

Unit of account. Rate of exchange or of acceptance of foreign currency

§ 1. The unit of account referred to in the Uniform Rules shall be the Special Drawing Right as defined by the International Monetary Fund.

The value in Special Drawing Right of the national currency of a State which is a member of the International Monetary Fund shall be calculated in accordance with the method of valuation applied by the International Monetary Fund for its own operations and transactions.

§ 2. The value in Special Drawing Right of the national currency of a State which is not a member of the International Monetary Fund shall be calculated by the method determined by that State.

The calculation must express in the national currency a real value approximating as closely as possible to that which would result from the application of § 1.

§ 3. In the case of a State which is not a member of the International Monetary Fund and whose legislation does not permit the application of § 1 or § 2 above, the unit of account referred to in the Uniform Rules shall be deemed to be equal to three gold francs.

The gold franc is defined as 10/31 of a gramme of gold of millesimal fineness 900. The conversion of the gold franc must express in the national currency a real value approximating as closely as possible to that which would result from the application of § 1.

§ 4. Within three months after the entry into force of the Convention and each time that a change occurs in their method of calculation or in the value of their national currency in relation to the unit of account, States shall notify the Central Office of their method of calculation in accordance with § 2, or of the results of the conversion in accordance with § 3.

The Central Office shall notify the States of this information.

§ 5. The railway shall publish the rates at which—

(a) it converts sums expressed in foreign currencies but payable in domestic currency (rates of conversion);

(b) it accepts payment in foreign currencies (rates of acceptance).

Article 7

Supplementary provisions

§ 1. Two or more States or two or more railways may make supplementary provisions for the execution of the Uniform Rules. They may not derogate from the Uniform Rules unless the latter expressly so provide.

§ 2. The supplementary provisions shall be put into force and published in the manner required by the laws and regulations of each State. The Central Office shall be notified of the supplementary provisions and of their coming into force.

Article 8

National law

§ 1. In the absence of provisions in the Uniform Rules, supplementary provisions or international tariffs, national law shall apply.

§ 2. "National law" means the law of the State in which the person entitled asserts his rights, including the rules relating to conflict of laws.

§ 3. For the application of provisions relating to the liability of the railway in case of death of or personal injury to, passengers, national law shall be the law of the State on whose territory the accident to the passenger happened, including the rules relating to conflict of laws.

[4358]

TITLE II
THE CONTRACT OF CARRIAGE

CHAPTER I
CARRIAGE OF PASSENGERS

Article 9

Timetables and use of trains

§ 1. The railways shall bring the train timetables to the notice of the public in an appropriate manner.

§ 2. The timetables or the tariffs shall indicate restrictions on the use of certain trains or of certain classes of carriage.

Article 10

Refusal to carry. Acceptance subject to conditions

§ 1. The following persons shall not be permitted to travel or may be required to discontinue their journey—

(a) persons in an intoxicated condition or whose behaviour is improper or who infringe the provisions in force in individual States; such persons shall not be entitled to a refund of their fares or of any registered luggage charges they may have paid;

(b) persons who because of sickness or other cause appear likely to inconvenience other passengers, unless a whole compartment has been reserved for them or can be put at their disposal on payment therefor. However, persons who fall ill during a journey must be carried at least as far as the nearest station where they can be given the necessary attention; their fares shall be refunded in accordance with Article 25, subject to deduction of the amounts due for the distance travelled; where appropriate, the same shall apply to registered luggage charges.

§ 2. The carriage of persons suffering from infectious or contagious diseases shall be subject to international conventions and regulations or, failing that, to the laws and regulations of each State.

Article 11

Tickets

§ 1. Tickets issued for international carriage shall bear the initials CIV. As a transitional measure the mark Φ shall be permitted.

§ 2. The international tariffs or agreements between railways shall determine the form and content of tickets and the language and characters in which they are to be printed and made out.

§ 3. Save where the international tariffs otherwise provide, tickets must indicate—

(a) the stations of departure and destination;

(b) the route; if a choice of routes or modes of transport is permitted, that facility shall be stated;

(c) the category of train and class of carriage;

(d) the fare;

(e) the first day of validity;

(f) the period of validity.

§ 4. Covers containing sectional coupons issued under an international tariff shall be deemed to be a single ticket for the purposes of the Uniform Rules.

§ 5. Save where the international tariffs otherwise provide, tickets shall be transferable if they are not made out in the passenger's name and if the journey has not begun.

§ 6. The passenger must ensure, on receipt of the ticket, that it has been made out in accordance with his instructions.

§ 7. The period of validity of tickets and breaks of journey shall be governed by the international tariffs.

Article 12

Right to be carried. Passengers without valid tickets

§ 1. The passenger shall, from the start of his journey, be in possession of a valid ticket; he shall retain it throughout the journey and, if required, produce it to railway staff responsible for inspecting tickets and give it up at the end of the journey. The international tariffs may make provision for exceptions.

§ 2. Tickets which have been altered without authority are invalid and shall be withdrawn by the railway staff responsible for inspecting tickets.

§ 3. A passenger who cannot produce a valid ticket shall pay, in addition to the fare, a surcharge calculated according to the provisions of the railway requiring such payment.

§ 4. A passenger who refuses to pay the fare or the surcharge upon demand may be required to discontinue his journey. Such a passenger shall not be entitled to collect his registered luggage at any station other than the destination station.

Article 13

Reduced fares for children

§ 1. Children under five years of age for whom separate seats are not claimed shall be carried free without a ticket.

§ 2. Children of five or more years of age but under ten years of age, and children under five for whom separate seats are claimed, shall be carried at reduced fares. These shall not exceed one-half of the fare charged for adults, save for supplements charged for the use of certain trains or certain carriages, without prejudice to the rounding-up of amounts in accordance with the provisions applied by the railway issuing the ticket.

This reduction need not be made in the case of tickets issued at a rate below that of the normal single fare.

§ 3. However, the international tariffs may provide for different age limits from those laid down in §§ 1 and 2 provided that such age limits are not less than four years of age in respect of free travel under § 1, nor less than ten years of age in respect of reduced fares under § 2.

Article 14

Occupation of seats

§ 1. The occupation, allocation and reservation of seats in trains shall be governed by the provisions applied by the railway. For the carriage of motor vehicles, the railway may provide that the passengers shall remain in the motor vehicle during carriage.

§ 2. In accordance with the conditions laid down by the international tariffs, the passenger may occupy a seat of a higher class or travel on a train of a higher fare category than shown on the ticket, or may alter his route.

Article 15

Taking of hand luggage and animals into carriages

§ 1. The passenger may take with him into carriages, without extra charge, articles which can be handled easily (hand luggage).

Each passenger is entitled only to the space above and below his seat for his hand luggage, or another corresponding space where the carriages are of a special type, in particular, those containing a luggage area.

§ 2. The following shall not be taken into carriages—

(a) substances and articles which are not acceptable for carriage as luggage under Article 18(e), save where supplementary provisions or the tariffs otherwise provide;

(b) articles likely to annoy or inconvenience passengers or cause damage;

(c) articles which it is forbidden by the requirements of Customs or of other administrative authorities to take into carriages;

(d) live animals, save where the supplementary provisions or the tariffs otherwise provide.

§ 3. The international tariffs may prescribe the conditions under which articles taken into carriages contrary to §§ 1 and 2(b) shall nevertheless be carried as hand luggage or as registered luggage.

§ 4. The railway shall have the right to satisfy itself, in the presence of the passenger, with the nature of any articles taken into carriages, when there is good reason to suspect a contravention of § 2(a), (b) or (d). If it is not possible to identify the passenger who has taken with him the articles to be examined, the railway shall carry out the examination in the presence of two witnesses not connected with the railway.

§ 5. The passenger shall himself be responsible for the care of any articles and animals which he takes with him into the carriage, save when he cannot exercise such care because he is in a carriage of a special type referred to in § 1.

§ 6. The passenger shall be liable for all loss or damage caused by articles or animals which he has taken with him into the carriage unless he can prove that the loss or damage was caused by the fault of the railway or of a third party, or by circumstances which he could not avoid and the consequences of which he was unable to prevent.

This provision shall not affect any liability which may be incurred by the railway pursuant to Article 26.

Article 16

Missed connections. Cancellation of trains

§ 1. When a connection is missed owing to late running or when a train is cancelled for all or part of its route, and a passenger wishes to continue his journey, the railway shall convey him with his hand luggage and registered luggage, without extra charge and in so far as may be practicable, in a train proceeding towards the same destination station on the same line or by another line operated by the railways of the original route, so as to enable him to reach his destination with the least delay.

§ 2. The railway shall, where necessary, certify on the ticket that the connection has been missed or the train cancelled, extend the validity of the ticket so far as may be necessary and make it available by the new route, for a higher class or for a train of a higher fare category. Nevertheless, the tariffs or timetables may exclude the use of certain trains.

[4359]

CHAPTER II
CARRIAGE OF REGISTERED LUGGAGE

Article 17

Acceptable articles

§ 1. Articles appropriate for travel purposes, contained in trunks, baskets, suitcases, travelling bags and other similar receptacles, as well as the receptacles themselves, shall be accepted for carriage as registered luggage.

§ 2. The international tariffs may provide for the acceptance as registered luggage, on specified conditions, of animals and articles not mentioned in § 1, as well as of motor vehicles handed over for carriage with or without a trailer.

The conditions governing the carriage of motor vehicles shall specify in particular the conditions governing acceptance for carriage, registration, loading and carriage, the form and content of the transport document which must bear the initials CIV, the conditions governing unloading and delivery, as well as the obligations of the driver in respect of his vehicle and the loading and unloading of it.

Article 18

Unacceptable articles

The following shall not be accepted for carriage as registered luggage—

(a) articles the carriage of which is prohibited in any one of the territories in which the luggage would be carried;

(b) articles the carriage of which is a monopoly of the postal authorities in any one of the territories in which the luggage would be carried;

(c) goods intended for sale;

(d) bulky or excessively heavy articles;

(e) dangerous substances or articles, in particular loaded firearms, explosive or inflammable substances or articles, oxidising, toxic, radioactive, or corrosive substances, or substances that are repugnant or likely to cause infection; the international tariffs may provide for the acceptance as registered luggage, subject to conditions, of certain of these substances and articles.

Article 19

Registration and carriage of registered luggage

§ 1. Save where the international tariffs otherwise provide, luggage shall be registered only on production of tickets available at least as far as the destination of the luggage.

When the tariffs provide that luggage may be accepted for carriage without production of a ticket, the provisions of the Uniform Rules determining the rights and obligations of the passenger in respect of his registered luggage shall apply by analogy to the consignor of registered luggage.

§ 2. The railway reserves the right to forward the registered luggage by a different route from that taken by the passenger.

At the forwarding station, as well as at the junctions where the registered luggage must be transferred, the forwarding shall take place by the first appropriate train providing a regular service for registered luggage.

Luggage shall only be forwarded in the above-mentioned manner if the formalities required by Customs or other administrative authorities at departure or during the journey so permit.

§ 3. Save where the international tariffs otherwise provide, the carriage charges for registered luggage must be paid on registration.

§ 4. The tariffs or timetables may exclude or limit the carriage of registered luggage in certain trains or certain categories of trains or to or from certain stations.

§ 5. The formalities with regard to registration of luggage not governed by this article shall be determined by the provisions in force at the registering station.

Article 20

Luggage registration voucher

§ 1. A registration voucher shall be issued to the passenger at the time when the luggage is registered.

§ 2. Luggage registration vouchers issued for international traffic shall bear the initials **CIV**. As a transitional measure the mark **Φ** shall be permitted.

§ 3. The international tariffs or agreements between railways shall determine the form and content of luggage registration vouchers and the language and characters in which they are to be printed and made out.

§ 4. Save where the international tariffs otherwise provide, registration vouchers must indicate—

(a) the forwarding and destination stations;

(b) the route;

(c) the day and time on which the luggage is handed in for carriage;

(d) the number of passengers;

(e) the number of items of luggage and their mass [within the UK, analagous to *weight*];

(f) the carriage and other charges.

§ 5. The passenger must ensure, on receipt of the luggage registration voucher, that it has been made out in accordance with his instructions.

Article 21

Condition, packaging, packing and marking of registered luggage

§ 1. Items of registered luggage of which the condition or packaging is defective or which are inadequately packed or show obvious signs of damage may be refused by the railway. If they are nevertheless accepted, the railway may make an appropriate note on the luggage registration voucher. Acceptance by the passenger of a voucher bearing such a note shall be taken as evidence that the passenger has acknowledged its correctness.

§ 2. The passenger must indicate on each item of registered luggage in a clearly visible place, in a sufficiently durable, clear and indelible manner so as to avoid any possible confusion—

(a) his name and address,

(b) the station and country of destination.

Out-of-date details must be made illegible or removed by the passenger.

The railway may refuse to accept items which do not bear the prescribed details.

Article 22

Liability of the passenger. Verification. Surcharge

§ 1. The passenger shall be liable for all consequences of any failure to observe Articles 17, 18 and 21, § 2.

§ 2. When there is good reason to suspect a contravention, the railway shall have the right to verify that the contents of registered luggage comply with these provisions unless the laws or regulations of the State in which the examination would take place prohibit such verification. The passenger shall be invited to attend the verification. If he fails to attend or cannot be found, the verification shall be carried out in the presence of two witnesses not connected with the railway.

§ 3. If any contravention is established, the passenger must pay the costs arising from the verification.

In the event of any contravention of Articles 17 or 18, the railway may collect a surcharge as laid down in the international tariffs, as well as any difference in carriage charges and compensation for any loss or damage caused.

Article 23

Delivery

§ 1. Registered luggage shall be delivered on surrender of the luggage registration voucher and, where appropriate, on payment of the amounts chargeable against the consignment. The railway shall be entitled, but not obliged, to verify that the holder of the voucher is entitled to take delivery.

§ 2. It shall be equivalent to delivery to the holder of the voucher if, in accordance with the provisions in force at the station of delivery—

(a) the luggage has been handed over to the Customs or Octroi authorities at their premises or warehouses, when these are not subject to railway supervision;

(b) live animals have been handed over to third parties.

§ 3. The holder of the voucher may require delivery of the luggage at the office of the destination station as soon as sufficient time has elapsed, after the arrival of the train on which it was due to be carried, for it to be put at his disposal and, where appropriate, for the completion of any formalities required by Customs or other administrative authorities.

§ 4. Failing surrender of the voucher, the railway shall only be obliged to deliver the luggage to the person proving his right thereto; if the proof offered appears insufficient, the railway may require security to be given.

§ 5. Luggage shall be delivered at the station to which it has been registered. Nevertheless, if the holder of the voucher so requests in good time, if circumstances permit and if Customs requirements or the requirements of other administrative authorities are not thereby contravened, luggage may be handed back at the forwarding station or delivered at an intermediate station on surrender of the registration voucher and, if the tariffs so require, on production of the ticket.

§ 6. The holder of a voucher whose luggage has not been delivered in accordance with § 3 may require the date and time when he requested delivery to be endorsed on the voucher.

§ 7. If the person entitled so requires, the railway must carry out an examination of the registered luggage in his presence in order to establish any alleged damage. The person entitled may refuse to accept the luggage if the railway does not comply with his request.

§ 8. In all other respects delivery of luggage shall be in accordance with the provisions in force at the station of delivery.

[4360]

CHAPTER III
PROVISIONS APPLICABLE TO THE CARRIAGE OF BOTH PASSENGERS AND REGISTERED LUGGAGE

Article 24

Completion of administrative formalities

The passenger must comply with the requirements of Customs or other administrative authorities, both concerning his own person and any animals he takes with him and concerning the examination of his hand luggage and registered luggage. The passenger shall be present at such examinations save where otherwise provided by the laws or regulations of each State. The railway shall not be liable to the passenger for loss or damage arising from the passenger's disregard of these obligations.

Article 25

Refunds, repayments and additional payments

§ 1. Carriage charges shall be refunded wholly or in part, when—

(a) a ticket has not been used or has been only partially used;

(b) the ticket, owing to shortage of seats, has been used in a class or on a train of a lower fare category than shown on the ticket;

(c) luggage has been withdrawn at the forwarding station or delivered at an intermediate station.

§ 2. The international tariffs shall prescribe the documents and certificates which must be produced in support of a claim for refund, the amounts to be refunded and the charges to be deducted.

In specified cases, the tariffs may exclude refunds of carriage charges or make such refunds subject to certain conditions.

§ 3. No claim for a refund based on the preceding paragraphs or on Article 10, § 1(b) will be accepted unless made to the railway within six months. In the case of tickets the time allowed shall run from the day after the expiry of the period of validity and in the case of luggage registration vouchers from the date of issue.

§ 4. In case of incorrect application of a tariff, or of error made in the calculation or collection of the carriage and other charges, overcharges shall be repaid by the railway or undercharges paid to the railway only when they exceed *two* units of account per ticket or per luggage registration voucher.

§ 5. Overcharges or undercharges shall be calculated at the official rate of exchange for the day on which the carriage charges were collected. If the adjusting payment is made in a currency other than that in which the original charges were collected, the rate applicable shall be that for the day on which the adjusting payment is made.

§ 6. In all cases not provided for by this Article, and in the absence of agreements between railways, the provisions in force in the State of departure shall apply.

[4361]

TITLE III
LIABILITY

CHAPTER I
LIABILITY OF THE RAILWAY IN CASE OF DEATH OF, OR PERSONAL INJURY TO, PASSENGERS

Article 26

Basis of liability

§ 1. The railway shall be liable for the loss or damage resulting from the death of, personal injuries to, or any other bodily or mental harm to, a passenger, caused by an accident arising out of the operation of the railway and happening while the passenger is in, entering or alighting from railway vehicles.

The railway shall also be liable for the loss or damage resulting from the total or partial loss of, or damage to, any articles which the passenger, victim of such an accident, had on him or with him as hand luggage, including any animals.

§ 2. The railway shall be relieved of liability—

(a) if the accident has been caused by circumstances not connected with the operation of the railway and which the railway, in spite of having taken the care required in the particular circumstances of the case, could not avoid and the consequences of which it was unable to prevent;

(b) wholly or partly, to the extent that the accident is due to the passenger's fault or to behaviour on his part not in conformity with the normal conduct of passengers;

(c) if the accident is due to a third party's behaviour which the railway, in spite of having taken the care required in the particular circumstances of the case, could not avoid and the consequences of which it was unable to prevent; if the railway is not thereby relieved of liability, it shall be wholly liable up to the limits laid down in the Uniform Rules but without prejudice to any right of recourse which the railway may have against the third party.

§ 3. The Uniform Rules shall not affect any liability which may be incurred by the railway in cases not provided for in § 1.

§ 4. For the purposes of this chapter, the railway that is liable shall be that which, according to the list of lines or services provided for in Articles 3 and 10 of the Convention, operates the line on which the accident occurred. If, according to that list, there is joint operation of the line by two railways, each of them shall be liable.

Article 27

Damages in case of death

§ 1. In the case of the death of the passenger the damages shall include—

(a) any necessary costs following on the death, in particular those of transport of the body, burial and cremation;

(b) if death does not occur at once, the damages provided for in Article 28.

§ 2. If, through the death of the passenger, persons whom he had, or would have had in the future, a legal duty to maintain are deprived of their support, such persons shall also be indemnified for their loss. Rights of action for damages by persons whom the passenger was maintaining without being legally bound to do so shall be governed by national law.

Article 28

Damages in case of personal injury

In the case of personal injury or any other bodily or mental harm to the passenger the damages shall include—

(a) any necessary costs, in particular those of treatment and transport;

(b) compensation for financial loss due to total or partial incapacity to work, or to increased needs.

Article 29

Compensation for other injuries

National law shall determine whether and to what extent the railway shall pay damages for injuries other than that for which there is provision in Articles 27 and 28, in particular for mental or physical pain and suffering (pretium doloris) and for disfigurement.

Article 30

Form and limit of damages in case of death or personal injury

§ 1. The damages under Article 27, § 2 and Article 28(b) shall be awarded in the form of a lump sum. However, if national law permits payment of an annuity, damages shall be awarded in that form if so requested by the injured passenger or by the persons entitled referred to in Article 27, § 2.

§ 2. The amount of damages to be awarded under § 1 shall be determined in accordance with national law. However, for the purposes of the Uniform Rules, the upper limit per passenger shall be set at 70,000 units of account in the form of a lump sum or an annuity corresponding to that sum, where national law provides for an upper limit of less than that amount.

Article 31

Limit of damages in case of loss of or damage to articles

When the railway is liable under Article 26, § 1 sub-paragraph 2, it shall pay compensation up to the sum of 700 units of account per passenger.

Article 32

Prohibition on limiting liability

Any provisions of tariffs or of special agreements concluded between the railway and the passenger which purport to exempt the railway in advance, either wholly or partly, from liability in case of death of, or personal injury to, passengers, or which have the effect of reversing the burden of proof resting on the railway, or which set limits lower than those laid down in Articles 30 § 2 and 31, shall be null and void. Such nullity shall not, however, affect the validity of the contract of carriage.

Article 33

Carriage by more than one mode of transport

§ 1. Subject to § 2, the provisions relating to the liability of the railway in case of death of, or personal injury to, passengers shall not apply to loss or damage arising in the course of carriage by non-railway services, included in the list of lines or services referred to in Articles 3 and 10 of the Convention.

§ 2. However, where railway vehicles are carried by ferry, the provisions relating to the liability of the railway in case of death of, or personal injury to, passengers shall apply to loss or damage covered by Article 26, § 1, caused by an accident arising out of the operation of the railway and happening while the passenger is in, entering or alighting from the said vehicles.

For the purposes of the preceding sub-paragraph the "State on whose territory the accident to the passenger happened" means the State whose flag is flown by the ferry.

§ 3. When, because of exceptional circumstances, the railway finds itself obliged temporarily to suspend operations and itself carries the passengers or has them carried by another mode of transport, it shall be liable in accordance with the law relating to that mode of transport. Nevertheless, Article 18 of the Convention and Articles 8, 48–53 and 55 of the Uniform Rules shall remain applicable.

[4362]

CHAPTER II
LIABILITY OF THE RAILWAY IN RESPECT OF REGISTERED LUGGAGE

Article 34

Collective responsibility of railways

§ 1. The railway which has accepted luggage for carriage by issuing a luggage registration voucher shall be responsible for the carriage over the entire route up to delivery.

§ 2. Each succeeding railway, by the very act of taking over the registered luggage, shall become a party to the contract of carriage and shall assume the obligations arising therefrom without prejudice to the provisions of Article 51, § 3 relating to the railway of destination.

Article 35

Extent of liability

§ 1. The railway shall be liable for loss or damage resulting from the total or partial loss of, or damage to, registered luggage between the time of acceptance for carriage and the time of delivery as well as from delay in delivery.

§ 2. The railway shall be relieved of such liability if the loss, damage or delay in delivery was caused by a fault on the part of the passenger, by an order given by the passenger other than as a result of a fault on the part of the railway, by inherent vice of the registered luggage or by circumstances which the railway could not avoid and the consequences of which it was unable to prevent.

§ 3. The railway shall be relieved of such liability when the loss or damage arises from the special risks inherent in one or more of the following circumstances—

(a) the absence or inadequacy of packing;
(b) the special nature of the registered luggage;
(c) the despatch as registered luggage of articles not acceptable for carriage.

Article 36

Burden of proof

§ 1. The burden of proving that the loss, damage or delay in delivery was due to one of the causes specified in Article 35, § 2 shall rest upon the railway.

§ 2. When the railway establishes that, having regard to the circumstances of a particular case, the loss or damage could have arisen from one or more of the special risks referred to in Article 35, § 3, it shall be presumed that it did so arise. The person entitled shall, however, have the right to prove that the loss or damage was not attributable either wholly or partly to one of those risks.

Article 37

Presumption of loss of registered luggage

§ 1. The person entitled may, without being required to furnish further proof, consider an item of luggage as lost when it has not been delivered or placed at his disposal within fourteen days after a request for delivery has been made in accordance with Article 23, § 3.

§ 2. If an item of luggage deemed to have been lost is recovered within one year after the request for delivery, the railway shall notify the person entitled if his address is known or can be ascertained.

§ 3. Within thirty days after receipt of such notification, the person entitled may require the item of luggage to be delivered to him at any station on the route. In that case he must pay the charges in respect of carriage of the item from the forwarding station to the station where delivery is effected and shall refund the compensation received less any charges included therein. Nevertheless he shall retain his rights to claim compensation for delay in delivery under Article 40.

§ 4. If the item of luggage recovered has not been claimed within the period stated in § 3 or if it is recovered more than one year after the request for delivery, the railway shall dispose of it in accordance with the laws and regulations of the State having jurisdiction over the railway.

Article 38

Compensation for loss

§ 1. In case of total or partial loss of registered luggage, the railway shall pay, to the exclusion of all other damages—

(a) if the amount of the loss or damage suffered is established: compensation equal to that amount but not exceeding 40 units of account per kilogramme of gross mass missing or 600 units of account per item of luggage;

(b) if the amount of the loss or damage suffered is not established: liquidated damages of 10 units of account per kilogramme of gross mass missing or 150 units of account per item of luggage.

The method of compensation, by mass or by item of luggage, shall be determined by the international tariffs.

§ 2. The railway shall in addition refund carriage charges, Customs duties and other sums incurred in respect of carriage of the lost item of luggage.

Article 39

Compensation in case of damage

§ 1. In case of damage to registered luggage, the railway must pay compensation equivalent to the loss in value of the registered luggage, to the exclusion of all other damages.

§ 2. The compensation may not exceed—

(a) if all the luggage has lost value through damage, the amount which would have been payable in case of total loss;

(b) if only part of the luggage has lost value through damage, the amount which would have been payable had that part been lost.

Article 40

Compensation for delay in delivery

§ 1. In case of delay in delivery of registered luggage, the railway shall pay in respect of each whole period of twenty-four hours after delivery has been requested, but subject to a maximum of fourteen days—

(a) if the person entitled proves that loss or damage has been suffered thereby; compensation equal to the amount of the loss or damage, up to a maximum of 0.40 units of account per kilogramme of gross mass of the luggage or seven units of account per item of luggage, delivered late;

(b) if the person entitled does not prove that loss or damage has been suffered thereby; liquidated damages of 0.07 units of account per kilogramme of gross mass of the luggage or 140 units of account per item of luggage, delivered late.

The method of compensation, by mass or by item of luggage, shall be determined by the international tariffs.

§ 2. In case of total loss of luggage, the compensation provided for in § 1 shall not be payable in addition to that provided for in Article 38.

§ 3. In case of partial loss of luggage, the compensation provided for in § 1 shall be payable in respect of that part of the luggage which has not been lost.

§ 4. In case of damage to luggage not resulting from delay in delivery the compensation provided for in § 1 shall, where appropriate, be payable in addition to that provided for in Article 39.

§ 5. In no case shall the compensation payable under § 1 together with that payable under Articles 38 and 39 exceed the compensation which would be payable in the event of total loss of the luggage.

Article 41

Motor vehicles

§ 1. In case of delay in loading for a reason attributable to the railway or delay in delivery of a motor vehicle, the railway shall, if the person entitled proves that loss or damage has been suffered thereby, pay compensation the amount of which shall not exceed the charge for carriage of the vehicle.

§ 2. If, in case of delay in loading for a reason attributable to the railway the person entitled elects not to proceed with the contract of carriage, the carriage charges for carriage of the vehicle and of the passengers shall be refunded to him. In addition the person entitled may, if he proves that loss or damage has been suffered as a result of the delay, claim compensation not exceeding the charge for carriage of the vehicle.

§ 3. In case of total or partial loss of the vehicle, the compensation payable to the person entitled for the loss or damage proved shall be calculated on the usual value of the vehicle and may not exceed 8000 units of account.

§ 4. In respect of articles placed inside the vehicle, the railway shall be liable only for loss or damage caused by a fault on its part. The total compensation payable may not exceed 1000 units of account.

The railway shall be liable in respect of articles placed on the outside of the vehicle only in the case of wilful misconduct.

§ 5. A loaded or unloaded trailer shall be considered as a vehicle.

§ 6. The other provisions relating to liability in respect of registered luggage shall apply to the carriage of motor vehicles.

[4363]

CHAPTER III
COMMON PROVISIONS CONCERNING LIABILITY

Article 42

Loss of the right to invoke the limits of liability

The provisions of Articles 30, 31 and 38 to 41 of the Uniform Rules or those of national law, limiting compensation to a fixed amount, shall not apply if it is proved that the loss or damage resulted from an act or omission, on the part of the railway, done with intent to cause such loss or damage, or recklessly and with knowledge that such loss or damage will probably result.

Article 43

Conversion of, and interest on, compensation

§ 1. Where the calculation of compensation requires the conversion of sums expressed in foreign currencies, conversion shall be at the rate of exchange applicable on the day and at the place of payment of the compensation.

§ 2. The person entitled may claim interest on compensation payable, calculated at five per cent per annum, from the day of the claim referred to in Article 49 or, if no such claim has been made, from the day on which legal proceedings are instituted.

§ 3. However, in the case of compensation payable under Articles 27 and 28, interest shall accrue only from the day on which the events relevant to the assessment of the amount occurred, if that day is later than that of the claim or the day when legal proceedings were instituted.

§ 4. In the case of registered luggage, interest shall only be payable if the compensation exceeds eight units of account per luggage registration voucher.

§ 5. In the case of registered luggage, if the person entitled does not submit to the railway within a reasonable period allotted to him, the supporting documents required for the amount of the claim to be finally settled, no interest shall accrue between the expiry of the period laid down and the actual submission of such documents.

Article 44

Liability in case of nuclear incidents

The railway shall be relieved of liability under the Uniform Rules for loss or damage caused by a nuclear incident when the operator of a nuclear installation or another person who is substituted for him in liable for the loss or damage pursuant to a State's laws and regulations governing liability in the field of nuclear energy.

Article 45

Liability of the railway for its servants

§ 1. The railway shall be liable for its servants and for any other persons whom it employs to perform the carriage.

If however such servants and other persons, at the request of a passenger, render services which the railway itself is under no obligation to render, they shall be deemed to be acting on behalf of the passenger to whom the services are rendered.

Article 46

Other actions

In all cases to which the Uniform Rules apply, any action in respect of liability on any grounds whatsoever, may be brought against the railway only subject to the conditions and limitations laid down in those Rules. The same shall apply to any action brought against those servants and other persons for whom the railway is liable under Article 45.

Article 47

Special provisions

§ 1. Subject to Article 41, the liability of the railway in respect of loss or damage resulting from the late running or cancellation of a train or from a missed connection shall be determined by the laws and regulations of the State in which the incident occurred.

§ 2. Subject to Article 26, the railway shall not be liable in respect of articles and animals the care of which is the responsibility of the passenger under Article 15, § 5 or of articles which the passenger has on him, unless the loss or damage is caused by a fault on the part of the railway.

§ 3. The other Articles of Title III, and Title IV, shall not apply to the cases §§ 1 and 2.

[4364]

TITLE IV
ASSERTION OF RIGHTS

Article 48

Ascertainment of partial loss of, or damage to, registered luggage

§ 1. When partial loss of, or damage to, registered luggage is discovered or presumed by the railway or alleged by the person entitled, the railway must without delay, and if possible in the presence of the person entitled, draw up a report stating, according to the nature of the loss or damage, the condition of the registered luggage, its mass and, as far as possible, the extent of the loss or damage, its cause and the time of its occurrence.

A copy of the report must be supplied free of charge to the person entitled.

§ 2. Should the person entitled not accept the findings in the report, he may request that the condition and mass of the registered luggage and the cause and amount of the loss or damage be ascertained by an expert appointed either by the parties or by a court. The procedure to be followed shall be governed by the laws and regulations of the State in which such ascertainment takes place.

§ 3. In case of loss of an item of registered luggage, the person entitled must, to facilitate the enquiries to be made by the railway, give as accurate a description as possible of the missing item of luggage.

Article 49

Claims

§ 1. Claims relating to the liability of the railway in case of death of, or personal injury to, passengers shall be made in writing to one of the following railways—

(a) to the railway that is liable; if, in accordance with Article 26, § 4, two railways are liable, to one of them;

(b) to the railway of departure;

(c) to the railway of destination;

(d) to the railway of the passenger's domicile or of his usual place of residence, provided that the headquarters of that railway is on the territory of a Member State.

§ 2. Other claims relating to the contract of carriage shall be made in writing to the railway specified in Article 51, §§ 2 and 3.

On settlement of the claim, the railway may require the surrender of tickets or luggage registration vouchers.

§ 3. A claim may be made by persons who have the right to bring an action against the railway under Article 50.

§ 4. Tickets, luggage registration vouchers and other documents which the person entitled thinks fit to submit with the claim shall be produced either in the original or as copies, the copies to be duly authenticated if the railway so requires.

Article 50

Persons who may bring an action against the railway

An action may be brought against the railway by the person who produces the ticket or luggage registration voucher, as the case may be, or failing that, furnishes the proof of his right to sue.

Article 51

Railways against which an action may be brought

§ 1. An action based on the liability of the railway in case of death of, or personal injury to, passengers may only be brought against the railway that is liable within the meaning of Article 26, § 4. In the case of joint operation by two railways the person entitled may elect to sue either of them.

§2. An action for the recovery of a sum paid under the contract of carriage may be brought against the railway which has collected that sum or against the railway on whose behalf it was collected.

§3. Other actions arising from the contract of carriage may be brought against the railway of departure, the railway of destination or the railway on which the event giving rise to the proceedings occurred.

Such actions may be brought against the railway of destination even if it has not received the registered luggage.

§ 4. If the plaintiff can choose between several railways, his right to choose shall be extinguished as soon as he brings an action against any one of them.

§ 5. An action may be brought against a railway other than those specified in §§ 2 and 3 when instituted by way of counter-claim or by way of exception to the principal claim based on the same contract of carriage.

Article 52

Competence

§ 1. Actions based on the liability of the railway in case of death of, or personal injury to, passengers may only be instituted in the competent court of the State in whose territory the accident to the passenger happened unless otherwise provided in agreements between States or in acts of concession.

§ 2. Other actions brought under the Uniform Rules may only be instituted in the competent court of the State having jurisdiction over the defendant railway, unless otherwise provided in agreements between States or in acts of concession.

When a railway operates independent railway systems in different States, each system shall be regarded as a separate railway for the purposes of this paragraph.

Article 53

Extinction of right of action arising from liability in case of death of, or personal injury to, passengers

§ 1. Any right of action by the person entitled based on the liability of the railway in case of death of, or personal injury to, passengers shall be extinguished if notice of the accident to the passenger is not given by the person entitled, within six months of his becoming aware of the loss or damage, to one of the railways to which a claim may be made in accordance with Article 49, § 1.

Where the person entitled gives oral notice of the accident to the railway, the railway shall furnish him with an acknowledgement of such oral notice.

§ 2. Nevertheless, the right of action shall not be extinguished if—
(a) within the period of time specified in § 1 the person entitled has made a claim to one of the railways designated in Article 49, § 1;
(b) within the period of time specified in § 1 the railway that is liable, or one of the two railways if in accordance with Article 26, § 4 two railways are liable, has learned of the accident to the passenger in some other way;
(c) notice of the accident has been given, or has been given late, as a result of circumstances for which the person entitled is not responsible;
(d) the person entitled proves that the accident was caused by a fault of the railway.

Article 54

Extinction of right of action arising from the contract of carriage of registered luggage

§ 1. Acceptance of the luggage by the person entitled shall extinguish all rights of action against the railway arising from the contract of carriage in case of partial loss, damage or of delay in delivery.

§ 2. Nevertheless, the right of action shall not be extinguished—
(a) in the case of partial loss or of damage, if—
(i) the loss or damage was ascertained before the acceptance of the luggage in accordance with Article 48 by the person entitled;
(ii) the ascertainment which should have been carried out under Article 48 was omitted solely through the fault of the railway;
(b) in the case of loss or damage which is not apparent and is not ascertained until after acceptance of the luggage by the person entitled, provided that he—
(i) asks for ascertainment in accordance with Article 48 immediately after discovery of the loss or damage and not later than three days after the acceptance of the luggage;
(ii) and, in addition, proves that the loss or damage occurred between the time of acceptance for carriage and the time of delivery;
(c) in the case of delay in delivery, if the person entitled has, within twenty-one days, asserted his rights against one of the railways referred to in Article 51, § 3;

(d) if the person entitled furnishes proof that the loss or damage was caused by wilful misconduct or gross negligence on the part of the railway.

Article 55

Limitation of actions

§ 1. The period of limitation for actions for damages based on the liability of the railway in case of death of, or personal injury to, passengers shall be—

(a) in the case of a passenger, three years from the day after the accident;
(b) in the case of other persons entitled, three years from the day after the death of the passenger, subject to a maximum of five years from the day after the accident.

§ 2. The period of limitation for other actions arising from the contract of carriage shall be one year.

Nevertheless, the period of limitation shall be two years in the case of an action for loss or damage resulting from an act or omission done with intent to cause such loss or damage, or recklessly and with knowledge that such loss or damage would probably result.

§ 3. The period of limitation provided for in § 2 shall run—

(a) in actions for compensation for total loss, from the fourteenth day after the expiry of the period of time referred to in Article 23, § 3;
(b) in actions for compensation or partial loss, for damage or for delay in delivery, from the day when delivery took place;
(c) in actions for payment or refund of carriage charges, supplementary charges or surcharges, or for correction of charges in the event of a tariff being wrongly applied or of an error in calculation or collection: from the day of payment or, if payment has not been made, from the day when payment should have been made;
(d) in actions to recover additional duty demanded by Customs or other administrative authorities, from the day of the demand made by such authorities;
(e) in all other cases involving the carriage of passengers, from the day of expiry of validity of the ticket.

The day indicated for the commencement of the period of limitation shall not be included in the period.

§ 4. When a claim is presented to a railway in accordance with Article 49 together with the necessary supporting documents, the period of limitation shall be suspended until the day that the railway rejects the claim by notification in writing and returns the documents. If part of the claim is admitted, the period of limitation shall recommence in respect of that part of the claim still in dispute. The burden of proof of receipt of the claim or of the reply and of the return of the documents shall rest on the party who relies on those facts.

The period of limitation shall not be suspended by further claims having the same object.

§ 5. A right of action which has become time-barred may not be exercised by way of counterclaim or relied upon by way of exception.

§ 6. Subject to the foregoing provisions, the suspension and interruption of periods of limitation shall be governed by national law.

[4365]

TITLE V
RELATIONS BETWEEN RAILWAYS

Article 56

Settlement of accounts between railways

Any railway which has collected or ought to have collected carriage charges must pay to the railways concerned their respective shares of such charges.

Article 57

Recourse in case of loss or damage

§ 1. A railway which has paid compensation in accordance with the Uniform Rules, for total or partial loss of, or for damage to, registered luggage, has a right of recourse against the other railways which have taken part in the carriage, in accordance with the following provisions—

(a) the railway which has caused the loss or damage shall be solely liable for it;

(b) when the loss or damage has been caused by more than one railway, each shall be liable for the loss or damage it has caused: if such distinction cannot be made, the compensation shall be apportioned between those railways in accordance with (c);

(c) if it cannot be proved that the loss or damage has been caused by one or more railways in particular, the compensation shall be apportioned between all the railways which have taken part in the carriage, except those which can prove that the loss or damage was not caused on their lines; such apportionment shall be in proportion to the kilometric distances contained in the tariffs.

§ 2. In the case of the insolvency of any one of the railways, the unpaid share due from it shall be apportioned among all the other railways which have taken part in the carriage, in proportion to the kilometric distances contained in the tariffs.

Article 58

Recourse in case of delay in delivery

Article 57 shall apply where compensation is paid for delay in delivery. If the delay has been caused by more than one railway, the compensation shall be apportioned between such railways in proportion to the length of the delay occurring on their respective lines.

Article 59

Procedure for recourse

§ 1. The validity of the payment made by the railway exercising one of the rights of recourse under Articles 57 and 58 may not be disputed by the railway against which the right to recourse is exercised, when compensation has been determined by a court and when the latter railway, duly served with notice, has been afforded an opportunity to intervene in the proceedings. The court seized of the main proceedings shall determine what time shall be allowed for such notification and for intervention in the proceedings.

§ 2. A railway exercising its right of recourse must take proceedings by one and the same action against all the railways concerned, with which it has not reached a settlement, failing which it shall lose its right of recourse in the case of those against which it has not taken proceedings.

§ 3. The court shall give its decision in one and the same judgment on all recourse claims brought before it.

§ 4. The railways against which such action has been brought shall have no further right of recourse.

§ 5. Recourse proceedings may not be joined with proceedings for compensation taken by the person entitled on the basis of the contract of carriage.

Article 60

Competence for recourse claims

§ 1. The courts of the country in which the railway, against which the recourse claim has been made, has its headquarters shall have exclusive competence for all recourse claims.

§ 2. When the action is to be brought against several railways, the plaintiff railway shall be entitled to choose the court in which it will bring the proceedings from among those having competence under § 1.

Article 61

Agreements concerning recourse

By agreement, railways may derogate from the provisions concerning reciprocal rights of recourse set out in Title V, apart from that contained in Article 59, § 5.

[4366]

TITLE VI
EXCEPTIONAL PROVISIONS

Article 62

Derogations

The provisions of the Uniform Rules shall not prevail over those provisions which certain States are obliged to adopt, in traffic among themselves, in pursuance of certain Treaties such as the Treaties relating to the European Coal and Steel Community and the European Economic Community.

[4367]

SUPPLEMENTARY PROVISIONS* INTERPRETING THE UNIFORM RULES CONCERNING THE CONTRACT FOR INTERNATIONAL CARRIAGE OF PASSENGERS AND LUGGAGE BY RAIL (CIV), APPENDIX A TO COTIF, WHERE THE MANAGEMENT OF THE RAILWAY INFRASTRUCTURE IS SEPARATE FROM THE PROVISION OF THE TRANSPORT SERVICES BY THE RAILWAY UNDERTAKINGS

Whereas the Convention concerning international carriage by rail (COTIF) of 9 May 1980 is based on the principle that the railways are both managers of their infrastructure and providers of rail transport services, but that certain States are engaged in a process of separating these two activities,

Whereas the uniformity of the law achieved by COTIF constitutes an important element of legal certainty both for the users and for the carriers which facilitates international through carriage by rail in Europe and beyond,

Whereas it is, therefore, desireable that international carriage by rail should continue to be subject to COTIF,

Whereas COTIF does not presuppose that more than one railway undertaking carries out an operation of international carriage by rail as the contractual partner of the customer,

Conscious, however, that in such cases certain provisions of CIV can be redundant to the extent that they assume that several railways participate successively as carriers in the execution of an operation of international carriage by rail under a single contract,

Conscious that a revision of COTIF is necessary and urgent but that it requires considerable work, the representatives of the Member States of OTIF met from 22 to 26 November 1993 in Berne and prepared, by virtue of Article 7 of CIV, the following supplementary provisions and recommend to the Member States that they should come into force on 1 January 1995—

1. When rail lines are included in accordance with Article 2 § 1 of COTIF, it is sufficient that the organisation which manages the infrastructure should be included in the list of CIV lines.

2. There is only "operation" in the sense of Article 2 §§ 1 and 2 of CIV when "the railway" in question is at the same time the manager of the infrastructure and the provider of the rail carriage services.

3. With the exception of Article 2 of CIV, the term "railway" or "that which, according to the list of lines or services provided for in Articles 3 and 10 of the Convention, operates the line" (Article 26 § 4 of CIV), is considered to mean the provider of the rail carriage services on the CIV lines.

4. Where only one undertaking carries out an international rail carriage operation, the authorisations granted to CIV to adopt derogating regulations, either in the tariffs, or by agreement, should be understood to mean the provider of rail carriage services can enter into corresponding contractual agreements, in particular under Articles 5 §3, 17 § 2, 19 § 4 and 25 § 2 of CIV.

5. These supplementary provisions shall come into force and be published in accordance with the laws and regulations of each Member State. The supplementary provisions and their coming into force shall be communicated to the Central Office which shall advise all the other Member States of them immediately.

[4368]

NOTES

* The Supplementary Provisions were adopted by an ad-hoc committee of OTIF Member States (including United Kingdom) which met from 22–26 November 1993.

APPENDIX B TO THE CONVENTION CONCERNING INTERNATIONAL CARRIAGE BY RAIL (COTIF) OF 9 MAY 1980

UNIFORM RULES CONCERNING THE CONTRACT FOR INTERNATIONAL CARRIAGE OF GOODS BY RAIL (CIM)

TITLE I
GENERAL PROVISIONS

Article 1

Scope

§ 1. Subject to the exceptions provided for in Article 2, the Uniform Rules shall apply to all consignments of goods for carriage under a through consignment note made out for a route over the territories of at least two States and exclusively over lines or services included in the list provided for in Articles 3 and 10 of the Convention, as well as, where appropriate, to carriage treated as carriage over a line in accordance with Article 2, § 2, second sub-paragraph of the Convention.

§ 2. In the Uniform Rules the expression "station" covers: railway stations, ports used by shipping services and all other establishments of transport undertakings, open to the public for the execution of the contract of carriage.

Article 2

Exceptions from scope

§ 1. Consignments between sending and destination stations situated in the territory of the same State, which pass through the territory of another State only in transit, shall not be subject to the Uniform Rules—

(a) if the lines or services over which the transit occurs are exclusively operated by a railway of the State of departure; or

(b) if the States or the railways concerned have agreed not to regard such consignments as international.

§ 2. Consignments between stations in two adjacent States and between stations in two States in transit through the territory of a third State shall, if the lines over which the consignments are carried are exclusively operated by a railway of one of those three States, be subject to the internal traffic regulations applicable to that railway if the sender, by using the appropriate consignment note, so elects and where there is nothing to the contrary in the laws and regulations of any of the States concerned.

Article 3

Obligation to carry

§ 1. The railway shall be bound to undertake all carriage of any goods in complete wagon-loads, subject to the terms of the Uniform Rules, provided that—

(a) the sender complies with the Uniform Rules and supplementary provisions and the tariffs;

(b) carriage can be undertaken by the normal staff and transport resources which suffice to meet usual traffic requirements;

(c) carriage is not prevented by circumstances which the railway cannot avoid and which it is not in a position to remedy.

§ 2. The railway shall not be obliged to accept goods of which the loading, transshipment or unloading requires the use of special facilities unless the stations concerned have such facilities at their disposal.

§ 3. The railway shall only be obliged to accept goods the carriage of which can take place without delay; the provisions in force at the forwarding station shall determine the circumstances in which goods not complying with that condition must be temporarily stored.

§ 4. When the competent authority decides that—

(a) a service shall be discontinued or suspended totally or partially,

(b) certain consignments shall be refused or accepted only subject to conditions,

(c) certain goods will be accepted for transport in priority, these measures shall, without delay, be brought to the notice of the public and the railways; the latter shall inform the railways of the other States with a view to their publication.

§ 5. The railways may, by joint agreement, concentrate goods traffic between certain places on specified frontier points and transit countries.

These measures shall be notified to the Central Office. They shall be entered by the railways in special lists, published in the manner laid down for international tariffs, and shall come into force one month after the date of notification to the Central Office.

§ 6. Any contravention of this Article by the railway may constitute a cause of action for compensation for loss or damage caused.

Article 4

Articles not acceptable for carriage

The following shall not be accepted for carriage—

(a) articles the carriage of which is prohibited in any one of the territories in which the articles would be carried;
(b) articles the carriage of which is a monopoly of the postal authorities in any one of the territories in which the articles would be carried;
(c) articles which, by reason of their dimensions, their mass,[1] or their packaging, are not suitable for the carriage proposed, having regard to the installations or rolling stock of any one of the railways which would be used;
(d) substances and articles which are not acceptable for carriage under the Regulations concerning the international carriage of dangerous goods by rail (RID), Annex 1 to the Uniform Rules, subject to the exceptions provided for in Article 5, § 2.

NOTES

[1] Mass, for the purpose of the Convention within the UK, should be analagous to *weight.*

Article 5

Articles acceptable for carriage subject to conditions

§ 1. The following shall be acceptable for carriage subject to conditions—

(a) substances and articles acceptable for carriage subject to the conditions laid down in the RID or in the agreements and tariff clauses provided for in § 2;
(b) funeral consignments, railway rolling stock running on its own wheels, live animals and consignments the carriage of which presents special difficulties by reason of their dimensions, their mass or their packaging: subject to the conditions laid down in the supplementary provisions; these may derogate from the Uniform Rules.

Live animals must be accompanied by an attendant provided by the consignor. Nevertheless an attendant shall not be required when the international tariffs permit or when the railways participating in the carriage so permit at the consignor's request; in such cases, unless there is an agreement to the contrary, the railway shall not be liable for any loss or damage resulting from any risk which the attendant was intended to avert.

§ 2. Two or more States, by agreement, or two or more railways, by tariff clauses, may jointly determine the conditions with which certain substances or articles not acceptable for carriage under the RID must comply if they are nevertheless to be accepted.

States or railways may, in the same manner, make the conditions for acceptance laid down in the RID less rigorous.

Such agreements and tariff clauses must be published and notified to the Central Office which will bring them to the notice of the States.

Article 6

Tariffs. Private agreements

§ 1. Carriage charges, whether or not calculated separately for different sections of the route, and supplementary charges shall be calculated in accordance with the tariffs which are legally in force and duly published in each State and which are applicable at the time when the contract of carriage is made.

§ 2. The tariffs must indicate all the special conditions applicable to the carriage, in particular the information necessary for calculating carriage and supplementary charges and, where appropriate, the conditions governing the conversion of currencies.

The conditions of the tariffs may not derogate from the Uniform Rules unless the latter expressly so provide.

§ 3. The tariffs must be applied to all users on the same conditions.

§ 4. Railways may enter into private agreements for reduced charges or other concessions, provided that comparable conditions are granted to users in comparable circumstances.

Reductions in charges or other concessions may be granted for the purpose of railway or public services, or for charitable purposes.

Publication of the measures taken under the first and second sub-paragraphs shall not be compulsory.

§ 5. International tariffs may be declared compulsorily applicable in international traffic to the exclusion of the internal tariffs.

The application of an international tariff may be made conditional on there being an express request for it in the consignment note.

§ 6. The tariffs and amendments to the tariffs shall be regarded as duly published from the time when the railway makes all the details thereof available to the users.

The publication of international tariffs shall be compulsory only in those States whose railways are parties to such tariffs as railways of departure or destination.

§ 7. Increases in international tariff charges and any other provisions which would have the effect of making the conditions of carriage laid down by such tariffs more rigorous shall not come into force until at least fifteen days after their publication, except in the following cases—

(a) if an international tariff makes provision for the extension of an internal tariff to cover the whole route, the periods for publication of such internal tariff shall be applicable;

(b) if increases in the charges contained in an international tariff follow a general increase in the charges contained in the internal tariffs of a participating railway, they shall come into force on the day after their publication, on condition that the adjustment of the international tariff charges caused by such general increase has been announced at least fifteen days in advance; nevertheless, such announcement may not be made prior to the publication of the increase in the internal tariff charges in question;

(c) if the carriage and supplementary charges provided for in the international tariffs have to be modified to take account of fluctuations in rates of exchange or if obvious errors have to be corrected, such adjustments and corrections shall come into force on the day after their publication.

§ 8. In States where there is no obligation to publish certain tariffs or to apply them to all users under the same conditions, the provisions of this Article, to the extent that they contain such an obligation, shall not be binding.

§ 9. The railways may not charge any amount over and above the carriage and supplementary charges laid down in the tariffs other than the amounts disbursed by them. Such amounts shall be duly noted and entered separately in the consignment note, together with any relevant supporting information. When this information is provided in documents attached to the consignment note and if the corresponding amounts are to be paid by the consignor, the documents shall not be delivered to the consignee with the consignment note, but shall be forwarded to the consignor with the account of charges referred to in Article 15, § 7.

Article 7

Unit of Account. Rate of exchange or of acceptance of foreign currency

§ 1. The unit of account referred to in the Uniform Rules shall be the Special Drawing Right as defined by the International Monetary Fund.

The value in Special Drawing Right of the national currency of a State which is a Member of the International Monetary Fund shall be calculated in accordance with the method of valuation applied by the International Monetary Fund for its own operations and transactions.

§ 2. The value in Special Drawing Right of the national currency of a State which is not a member of the International Monetary Fund shall be calculated by the method determined by that State.

The calculation must express in the national currency a real value approximating as closely as possible to that which would result from the application of § 1.

§ 3. In the case of a State which is not a member of the International Monetary Fund and whose legislation does not permit the application of § 1 or § 2 above, the unit of account referred to in the Uniform Rules shall be deemed to be equal to three gold francs.

The gold franc is defined as 10/31 of a gramme of gold of millesimal fineness 900.

The conversion of the gold franc must express in the national currency a real value approximating as closely as possible to that which would result from the application of § 1.

§ 4. Within three months after the entry into force of the Convention and each time that a change occurs in their method of calculation or in the value of their national currency in relation to the unit of account, States shall notify the Central Office of their method of calculation in accordance with § 2, or of the results of the conversion in accordance with § 3.

The Central Office shall notify the States of this information.

§ 5. The railway shall publish the rates at which—

(a) it converts sums expressed in foreign currencies but payable in domestic currency (rates of conversion);

(b) it accepts payment in foreign currencies (rates of acceptance).

Article 8

Special provisions for certain types of transport

§ 1. In the case of the haulage of privately owned wagons, special provisions are laid down in the Regulations concerning the international haulage of private owners' wagons by rail (RIP), Annex II to the Uniform Rules.

§ 2. In the case of the carriage of containers, special provisions are laid down in the Regulations concerning the international carriage of containers by rail (RICo), Annex III to the Uniform Rules.

§ 3. In the case of express parcels traffic, railways may, by tariff clauses, agree on special provisions in accordance with the Regulations concerning the international carriage of express parcels by rail (RIEx), Annex IV to the Uniform Rules.

§ 4. Two or more States, by special agreement, or two or more railways by supplementary provisions or by tariff clauses, may agree on terms derogating from the Uniform Rules for the following types of consignments—

(a) consignments under cover of a negotiable document;

(b) consignments to be delivered only against return of the duplicate of the consignment note;

(c) consignments of newspapers;

(d) consignments intended for fairs or exhibitions;

(e) consignments of loading tackle and of equipment for protection of goods in transit against heat or cold;

(f) consignments over all or part of the route under cover of consignment notes which are not used for charging and billing;

(g) consignments sent under cover of an instrument suitable for automatic data transmission.

Article 9

Supplementary provisions

§ 1. Two or more States or two or more railways may make supplementary provisions for the execution of the Uniform Rules. They may not derogate from the Uniform Rules unless the latter expressly so provide.

§ 2. The supplementary provisions shall be put into force and published in the manner required by the laws and regulations of each State. The Central Office shall be notified of the supplementary provisions and of their coming into force.

PART V

Article 10

National law

§ 1. In the absence of provisions in the Uniform Rules, supplementary provisions or international tariffs, national law shall apply.

§ 2. "National law" means the law of the State in which the person entitled asserts his rights, including the rules relating to conflict of laws.

[4369]

TITLE II
MAKING AND EXECUTION OF THE CONTRACT OF CARRIAGE

Article 11

Making of the contract of carriage

§ 1. The contract of carriage shall come into existence as soon as the forwarding railway has accepted the goods for carriage together with the consignment note. Acceptance is established by the application to the consignment note and, where appropriate, to each additional sheet, of the stamp of the forwarding station, or accounting machine entry, showing the date of acceptance.

§ 2. The procedure laid down in § 1 must be carried out immediately after all the goods to which the consignment note relates have been handed over for carriage and where the provisions in force at the forwarding station so require such charges as the consignor has undertaken to pay have been paid or a security deposited in accordance with Article 15, § 7.

§ 3. When the stamp has been affixed or the accounting machine entry has been made, the consignment note shall be evidence of the making and content of the contract.

§ 4. Nevertheless, when the loading of the goods is the duty of the consignor in accordance with tariffs or agreements existing between him and the railway, and provided that such agreements are authorised at the forwarding station, the particulars in the consignment note relating to the mass of the goods or to the number of packages shall only be evidence against the railway when that weight or number of packages has been verified by the railway and certified in the consignment note. If necessary these particulars may be proved by other means.

If it is obvious that there is no actual deficiency corresponding to the discrepancy between the mass or number of packages and the particulars in the consignment note, the latter shall not be evidence against the railway. This shall apply in particular when the wagon is handed over to the consignee with the original seals intact.

§ 5. The railway shall certify receipt of the goods and the date of acceptance for carriage by affixing the date stamp to or making the accounting machine entry on the duplicate of the consignment note before returning the duplicate to the consignor.

The duplicate shall not have effect as the consignment note accompanying the goods, nor as a bill of lading.

Article 12

Consignment note

§ 1. The consignor shall present a consignment note duly completed.

A separate consignment note shall be made out for each consignment. One and the same consignment note may not relate to more than a single wagon load. The supplementary provisions may derogate from these rules.

§ 2. The railways shall prescribe a standard form of consignment note, which must include a duplicate for the consignor.

In the case of certain traffic, notably between adjacent countries, the railways may prescribe, in the tariffs, the use of a simplified form of consignment note.

In the case of certain traffic with countries which have not acceded to this Convention, tariffs may provide for recourse to a special procedure.

§ 3. The consignment note must be printed in two or where necessary in three languages, at least one of which shall be one of the working languages of the Organisation.

International tariffs may determine the language in which the particulars to be filled in by the consignor in the consignment note shall be entered. In the absence of such provisions, they must be entered in one of the official languages of the State of departure and a translation in one of the working languages of the Organisation must be added unless the particulars have been entered in one of those languages.

The particulars entered by the consignor in the consignment note shall be in Roman lettering, save where the supplementary provisions or international tariffs otherwise provide.

Article 13

Wording of the Consignment Note

§ 1. The consignment note must contain—

(a) the name of the destination station;

(b) the name and address of the consignee; only one individual or legal person shall be shown as consignee;

(c) the description of the goods;

(d) the mass, or failing that, comparable information in accordance with the provisions in force at the forwarding station;

(e) the number of packages and a description of the packing in the case of consignments in less than wagon loads, and in the case of complete wagon loads comprising one or more packages, forwarded by rail-sea and requiring to be trans-shipped;

(f) the number of the wagon and also, for privately-owned wagons, the tare, in the case of goods where the loading is the duty of the consignor;

(g) a detailed list of the documents which are required by Customs or other administrative authorities and are attached to the consignment note or shown as held at the disposal of the railway at a named station or at an office of the Customs or of any other authority;

(h) the name and address of the consignor; only one individual or legal person shall be shown as the consignor; if the provisions in force at the forwarding station so require, the consignor shall add to his name and address his written, printed or stamped signature.

The provisions in force at the forwarding station shall determine the meanings of the terms "wagon load" and "less than wagon load" for the whole of the route.

§ 2. The consignment note must, where appropriate, contain all the other particulars provided for in the Uniform Rules. It shall not contain other particulars unless they are required or allowed by the laws and regulations of a State, the supplementary provisions or the tariffs, and are not contrary to the Uniform Rules.

§ 3. Nevertheless, the consignor may insert in the consignment note in the space set apart for the purpose, but as information for the consignee, remarks relating to the consignment, without involving the railway in any obligation or liability.

§ 4. The consignment note shall not be replaced by other documents or supplemented by documents other than those prescribed or allowed by the Uniform Rules, the supplementary provisions or the tariffs.

Article 14

Route and tariffs applicable

§ 1. The consignor may stipulate in the consignment note the route to be followed, indicating it by reference to frontier points or frontier stations and where appropriate, to transit stations between railways. He may only stipulate frontier points and frontier stations which are open to traffic between the forwarding and destination places concerned.

§ 2. The following shall be regarded as routeing instructions—

(a) designation of stations where formalities required by Customs or other administrative authorities are to be carried out, and of stations where special care is to be given to the goods (attention to animals, re-icing etc);

(b) designation of the tariffs to be applied, if this is sufficient to determine the stations between which the tariffs requested are to be applied;

(c) instructions as to the payment of the whole or a part of the charges up to X (X indicating by name the point at which the tariffs of adjacent countries are applied).

§ 3. Except in the cases specified in Article 3, §§ 4 and 5 and Article 33, § 1 the railway may not carry the goods by a route other than that stipulated by the consignor unless both—

(a) the formalities required by Customs or other administrative authorities, as well as the special care to be given to the goods, will in any event be carried out at the stations indicated by the consignor; and

(b) the charges and the transit periods will not be greater than the charges and transit periods calculated according to the route stipulated by the consignor.

Sub-paragraph (a) shall not apply to consignments in less than wagon loads if one of the participating railways is unable to adhere to the route chosen by the consignor by virtue of the routeing instructions arising from its arrangements for the international carriage of consignments in less than wagon loads.

§ 4. Subject to the provisions of § 3, the charges and transit periods shall be calculated according to the route stipulated by the consignor or, in the absence of any such indication, according to the route chosen by the railway.

§ 5. The consignor may stipulate in the consignment note which tariffs are to be applied. The railway must apply such tariffs if the conditions laid down for their application have been fulfilled.

§ 6. If the instructions given by the consignor are not sufficient to indicate the route or tariffs to be applied, or if any of those instructions are inconsistent with one another, the railway shall choose the route or tariffs which appear to it to be the most advantageous to the consignor.

§ 7. The railway shall not be liable for any loss or damage suffered as a result of the choice made in accordance with § 6, except in the case of wilful misconduct or gross negligence.

Article 15

Payment of charges

§ 1. The charges (carriage charges, supplementary charges, Customs duties and other charges incurred from the time of acceptance for carriage to the time of delivery) shall be paid by the consignor or the consignee in accordance with the following provisions.

In applying these provisions, charges which, according to the applicable tariff, must be added to the standard rates or special rates when calculating the carriage charges, shall be deemed to be carriage charges.

§ 2. A consignor who undertakes to pay a part or all of the charges shall indicate this on the consignment note by using one of the following phrases—

(a)

(i) "carriage charges paid", if he undertakes to pay carriage charges only;

(ii) "carriage charges paid including …", if he undertakes to pay charges additional to those for carriage, he shall give an exact description of those charges; additional indications, which may relate only to the supplementary charges or other charges incurred from the time of acceptance for carriage until the time of delivery as well as to sums collected either by Customs or other administrative authorities shall not result in any division of the total amount of any one category of charges (for example, the total amount of Customs duties and of other amounts payable to Customs, value added tax being regarded as a separate category);

(iii) "carriage charges paid to X" (X indicating by name the point at which the tariffs of adjacent countries are applied), if he undertakes to pay carriage charges to X;

(iv) "carriage charges paid to X including …" (X indicating by name the point at which the tariffs of adjacent countries are applied), if he undertakes to pay charges additional to those for carriage to X, but excluding all charges relating to the subsequent country or railway; the provisions of (ii) shall apply analogously;

(b) "all charges paid", if he undertakes to pay all charges (carriage charges, supplementary charges, Customs duties and other charges);

(c) "charges paid not exceeding …", if he undertakes to pay a fixed sum; save where the tariffs otherwise provide, this sum shall be expressed in the currency of the country of departure.

Supplementary and other charges which, according to the provisions in force at the forwarding station, are to be calculated for the whole of the route concerned, and the charge for interest in delivery laid down in Article 16, § 2, shall always be paid in full by the consignor in the case of payment of the charges in accordance with (a)(iv).

§ 3. The International tariffs may, as regards payment of charges, prescribe the exclusive use of certain phrases set out in § 2 of this Article or the use of other phrases.

§ 4. The charges which the consignor has not undertaken to pay shall be deemed to be payable by the consignee. Nevertheless, such charges shall be payable by the consignor if the consignee has not taken possession of the consignment note nor asserted his rights under Article 28, § 4, nor modified the contract of carriage in accordance with Article 31.

§ 5. Supplementary charges, such as charges for demurrage and standage warehousing and weighing, which arise from an act attributable to the consignee or from a request which he has made, and shall always be paid to him.

§ 6. The forwarding railway may require the consignor to prepay the charges in the case of goods which in its opinion are liable to undergo rapid deterioration or which, by reason of their low value or their nature, do not provide sufficient cover for such charges.

§ 7. If the amount of the charges which the consignor undertakes to pay cannot be ascertained exactly at the time the goods are handed over for carriage, such charges shall be entered in a charges note and a settlement of accounts shall be made with the consignor not later than thirty days after the expiry of the transit period. The railway may require as security a deposit approximating to the amount of such charges, for which a receipt shall be given. A detailed account of charges drawn up from the particulars in the charges note shall be delivered to the consignor in return for the receipt.

§ 8. The forwarding station shall specify, in the consignment note and in the duplicate, the charges which have been prepaid, unless the provisions in force at the forwarding station provide that those charges are only to be specified in the duplicate. In the case provided for in § 7 of this Article these charges are not to be specified either in the consignment note or in the duplicate.

Article 16

Interest in delivery

§ 1. Any consignment may be the subject of a declaration of interest in delivery. The amount declared shall be shown in figures in the consignment note in the currency of the country of departure, in another currency determined by the tariffs or in units of account.

§ 2. The charge for interest in delivery shall be calculated for the whole of the route concerned, in accordance with the tariffs of the forwarding railway.

Article 17

Cash on delivery and disbursements

§ 1. The consignor may make the goods subject to a cash on delivery payment not exceeding their value at the time of acceptance at the forwarding station. The amount of such cash on delivery payment shall be expressed in the currency of the country of departure; the tariffs may provide for exceptions.

§ 2. The railway shall not be obliged to pay over any amount representing a cash on delivery payment unless the amount in question has been paid by the consignee. That amount shall be placed at the consignor's disposal within thirty days of payment by the consignee; interest at five per cent per annum shall be payable from the date of the expiry of that period.

§ 3. If the goods have been delivered, wholly or in part, to the consignee without prior collection of the amount of the cash on delivery payment, the railway shall pay the consignor the amount of any loss or damage sustained up to the total amount of the cash on delivery payment without prejudice to any right of recovery from the consignee.

§ 4. Cash on delivery consignments shall be subject to a collection fee laid down in the tariffs; such fee shall be payable notwithstanding cancellation or reduction of the amount of the cash on delivery payment by modification of the contract of carriage in accordance with Article 30, § 1.

§ 5. Disbursements shall only be allowed if made in accordance with the provisions in force at the forwarding station.

§ 6. The amounts of the cash on delivery payment and of disbursements shall be entered in figures on the consignment note.

Article 18

Responsibility for particulars furnished in the consignment note

The consignor shall be responsible for the correctness of the particulars inserted by, or for, him, in the consignment note. He shall bear all the consequences in the event of those particulars being irregular, incorrect, incomplete, or entered elsewhere than in the allotted space.

Article 19

Condition, packing and marking of goods

§ 1. When the railway accepts for carriage goods showing obvious signs of damage, it may require the condition of such goods to be indicated in the consignment note.

§ 2. When the nature of the goods is such as to require packing, the consignor shall pack them in such a way as to protect them from total or partial loss and from damage in transit and to avoid risk of injury or damage to persons, equipment or other goods.

Moreover the packing shall comply with the provisions in force at the forwarding station.

§ 3. If the consignor has not complied with the provisions of § 2, the railway may either refuse the goods or require the sender to acknowledge in the consignment note the absence of packing or the defective condition of the packing, with an exact description thereof.

§ 4. The consignor shall be liable for all the consequences of the absence of packing or defective condition of packing and shall in particular make good any loss or damage suffered by the railway from this cause. In the absence of any particulars in the consignment note, the burden of proof of such absence of packing or defective condition of the packing shall rest upon the railway.

§ 5. The supplementary provisions or the tariffs shall regulate the marking of packages by the consignor.

Article 20

Handing over of goods for carriage and loading of goods

§ 1. The handing over of goods for carriage shall be governed by the provisions in force at the forwarding station.

§ 2. Loading shall be the duty of the railway or the consignor according to the provisions in force at the forwarding station, unless otherwise provided in the Uniform Rules or unless the consignment note includes a reference to a special agreement between the consignor and the railway.

When the loading is the responsibility of the consignor, he shall comply with the load limit. If different load limits are in force on the lines traversed, the lowest load limit shall be applicable to the whole route. The provisions laying down load limits shall be published in the same manner as tariffs. If the consignor so requests, the railway shall inform him of the permitted load limit.

§ 3. The consignor shall be liable for all the consequences of defective loading carried out by him and shall, in particular, make good any loss or damage suffered by the railway through this cause. Nevertheless Article 15 shall apply to the payment of costs arising from the reloading of goods in the event of defective loading. The burden of proof of defective loading shall rest upon the railway.

§ 4. Unless otherwise provided in the Uniform Rules, goods shall be carried in covered wagons, open wagons, sheeted open wagons or specially equipped wagons according to the international tariffs. If there are no international tariffs, or if they do not contain any provisions on the subject, the provisions in force at the forwarding station shall apply throughout the whole of the route.

§ 5. The affixing of seals to wagons shall be governed by the provisions in force at the forwarding station.

The consignor shall indicate in the consignment note the number and description of the seals affixed to the wagons by him.

Article 21

Verification

§ 1. The railway shall always have the right to verify that the consignment corresponds with the particulars furnished in the consignment note by the consignor and that the provisions relating to the carriage of goods accepted subject to conditions have been complied with.

§ 2. If the contents of the consignment are examined for this purpose, the consignor or the consignee, according to whether the verification takes place at the forwarding station or the destination station, shall be invited to be present. Should the interested party not attend, or should the verification take place in transit, it shall be carried out in the presence of two witnesses not connected with the railway, unless the laws or regulations of the State where the verification takes place provide otherwise. The railway may not however carry out the verification in transit unless compelled to do so by operational necessities or by the requirements of the Customs or of other administrative authorities.

§ 3. The result of the verification of the particulars in the consignment note shall be entered therein. If verification takes place at the forwarding station, the result shall also be recorded in the duplicate of the consignment note if it is held by the railway.

If the consignment does not correspond with the particulars in the consignment note or if the provisions relating to the carriage of goods accepted subject to conditions have not been complied with, the costs of the verification shall be charged against the goods, unless paid at the time.

Article 22

Ascertainment of weight and number of packages

§ 1. The provisions in force in each State shall determine the circumstances in which the railway must ascertain the mass of the goods or the number of packages and the actual tare of the wagons.

The railway shall enter in the consignment note the results ascertained.

§ 2. If weighing by the railway, after the contract of carriage has been made, reveals a difference, the mass ascertained by the forwarding station or, failing that, the mass declared by the consignor, shall still be the basis for calculating the carriage charges—

(a) if the difference is manifestly due to the nature of the goods or to atmospheric conditions; or

(b) the weighing takes place on a weighbridge and does not reveal a difference exceeding two per cent of the mass ascertained by the forwarding station or failing that, of that declared by the consignor.

Article 23

Overloading

§1. When overloading of a wagon is established by the forwarding station or by an intermediate station, the excess load may be removed from the wagon even if no surcharge is payable. Where necessary the consignor or, if the contract of carriage has been modified in accordance with Article 31, the consignee shall be asked without delay to give instructions concerning the excess load.

§ 2. Without prejudice to the payment of surcharges under Article 24, the excess load shall be charged for the distance covered in accordance with the carriage charges applicable to the main load. If the excess load is unloaded, the charge for unloading shall be determined by the tariffs of the railway which carries out the unloading.

If the person entitled directs that the excess load be forwarded to the same destination station as the main load or to another destination station, or directs that it be returned to the forwarding station, the excess load shall be treated as a separate consignment.

Article 24

Surcharges

§ 1. Without prejudice to the railway's entitlement to the difference in carriage charges and to compensation for any possible loss or damage, the railway may impose—

(a) a surcharge equal to one unit of account per kilogramme of gross mass of the whole package;

(i) in the case of irregular, incorrect or incomplete description of substances and articles not acceptable for carriage under the RID;

(ii) in the case of irregular, incorrect or incomplete description of substances and articles which under the RID are acceptable for carriage subject to conditions, or in the case of failure to observe such conditions.

The supplementary provisions may provide for other methods of calculating the surcharge, in particular a fixed surcharge for empty private owners' wagons.

(b) a surcharge equal to five units of account per 100 kilogrammes of mass in excess of the load limit, where the wagon has been loaded by the consignor.

§ 2. The surcharges shall be charged against the goods irrespective of the place where the facts giving rise to the surcharges were established.

§ 3. The amount of the surcharges and the reason for imposing them must be entered in the consignment note.

§ 4. The supplementary provisions shall specify the case in which no surcharge is due.

Article 25

Documents for completion of administrative formalities. Customs seals

§1. The consignor must attach to the consignment note the documents necessary for the completion of formalities required by Customs or other administrative authorities before delivery of the goods. Such documents shall relate only to goods which are the subject of one and the same consignment note, unless otherwise provided by the requirements of Customs or of other administrative authorities or by the tariffs.

However, when these documents are not attached to the consignment note or if they are to be provided by the consignee, the consignor shall indicate in the consignment note the station, the Customs office or the office of any other authority where the respective documents will be made available to the railway and where the formalities must be completed. If the consignor will himself be present or be represented by an agent when the formalities required by Customs or other administrative authorities are carried out, it will suffice for the documents to be produced at the time when those formalities are carried out.

§ 2. The railway shall not be obliged to check whether the documents furnished are sufficient and correct.

§ 3. The consignor shall be liable to the railway for any loss or damage resulting from the absence or insufficiency of or any irregularity in such documents, save in the case of fault by the railway.

The railway shall, where it is at fault, be liable for any consequences arising from the loss, non-use or misuse of the documents referred to in the consignment note and accompanying it or deposited with the railway; nevertheless any compensation shall not exceed that payable in the event of loss of the goods.

§ 4. The consignor must comply with the requirements of Customs or of other administrative authorities with respect to the packing and sheeting of the goods. If the consignor has not packed or sheeted the goods in accordance with those requirements the railway shall be entitled to do so; the resulting cost shall be charged against the goods.

§ 5. The railway may refuse consignments when the seals affixed by Customs or other administrative authorities are damaged or defective.

Article 26

Completion of Administrative Formalities

§ 1. In transit, the formalities required by Customs or other administrative authorities shall be completed by the railway. The railway may, however, delegate that duty to an agent.

§ 2. In completing such formalities, the railway shall be liable for any fault committed by itself or by its agent; nevertheless, any compensation shall not exceed that payable in the event of loss of the goods.

§ 3. The consignor, by so indicating in the consignment note, or the consignee by giving orders as provided for in Article 31, may ask—

(a) to be present himself or to be represented by an agent when such formalities are carried out, for the purpose of furnishing any information or explanations required;

(b) to complete such formalities himself or to have them completed by an agent, in so far as the laws and regulations of the State in which they are to be carried out so permit;

(c) to pay Customs duties and other charges, when he or his agent is present at or completes such formalities, in so far as the laws and regulations of the State in which they are carried out permit such payment.

Neither the consignor, nor the consignee who has the right of disposal, nor the agent of either may take possession of the goods.

§ 4. If, for the completion of the formalities, the consignor designated a station where the provisions in force do not permit of their completion, or if he has stipulated for the purpose any other procedure which cannot be followed, the railway shall act in the manner which appears to it to be the most favourable to the interests of the person entitled and shall inform the consignor of the measures taken.

If the consignor, by an entry in the consignment note, has undertaken to pay charges including Customs duty, the railway shall have the choice of completing Customs formalities either in transit or at the destination station.

§ 5. Subject to the exception provided for in the second sub-paragraph § 4, the consignee may complete Customs formalities at the destination station if that station has a Customs office and the consignment note requests Customs clearance on arrival, or, in the absence of such request, if the goods arrive under Customs control. The consignee may also complete these formalities at a destination station that has no Customs office if the national laws and regulations so permit or if the prior authority of the railway and the Customs authorities has been obtained. If the consignee exercises any of these rights, he shall pay in advance the amounts chargeable against the goods.

Nevertheless, the railway may proceed in accordance with § 4 if the consignee has not taken possession of the consignment note within the period fixed by the provisions in force at the destination station.

Article 27

Transit periods

§ 1. The transit periods shall be specified either by agreement between the railways participating in the carriage, or by the international tariffs applicable from the forwarding station to the destination station. For certain special types of traffic and on certain routes these periods may also be established on the basis of transport plans applicable between the railways concerned; in that case they must be included in international tariffs or special agreements which, where appropriate, may provide for derogations from §§ 3 to 9 below.

Such periods shall not in any case exceed those which would result from the application of the following paragraphs.

§ 2. In the absence of any indication in regard to the transit periods as provided for in § 1, and subject to the following paragraphs, the maximum transit periods shall be as follows—

(a) for wagon-load consignments:
period for despatch .... 12 hours;
period for carriage, for each 400 km or fraction thereof..... 24 hours;

(b) for less than wagon-load consignments:
period for despatch .... 24 hours;
period for carriage, for each 200 km or fraction thereof ..... 24 hours;

All these distances shall relate to the kilometric distances contained in the tariffs.

§ 3. The period for despatch shall be counted only once, irrespective of the number of systems traversed. The period for carriage shall be calculated on the total distance between the forwarding station and the destination station.

§ 4. The railway may fix additional transit periods of specified duration in the following cases—

(a) consignments handed in for carriage, or to be delivered, at places other than stations;

(b) consignments to be carried—

(i) by lines of different gauge;
(ii) by sea or inland navigable waterway;
(iii) by road if there is no rail link;

(c) consignments charged at reduced rates in accordance with special or exceptional internal tariffs;

(d) exceptional circumstances causing an exceptional increase in traffic or exceptional operating difficulties.

§ 5. The additional transit period provided for in § 4 (a) to (c) shall be shown in the tariffs or in the provisions duly published in each State.

Those provided for in § 4 (d) must be published and may not come into force before their publication.

§ 6. The transit period shall run from midnight next following acceptance of the goods for carriage.

§ 7. Except in the case of any fault by the railway, the transit period shall be extended by the duration of the period necessitated by—

(a) verification or ascertainment in accordance with Article 21 and Article 22, § 1, which reveals differences from the particulars shown in the consignment note;

(b) completion of the formalities required by Customs or other administrative authorities;

(c) modification of the contract of carriage under Article 30 or 31;

(d) special care to be given to the goods;

(e) the trans-shipment or reloading of any goods loaded defectively by the consignor;

(f) any interruption of traffic temporarily preventing the commencement or continuation of carriage.

The reason for and the duration of such extensions shall be entered in the consignment note. If necessary proof may be furnished by other means.

§ 8. The transit period shall be suspended on Sundays and statutory holidays. It shall be suspended on Saturdays when the provisions in force in any State provide for the suspension of domestic railway transit periods on those days.

§ 9. When the transit period ends after the time at which the destination station closes, the period shall be extended until two hours after the time at which the station next opens.

§10. The transit period is observed if, before its expiry—

(a) in cases where consignments are to be delivered at a station and notice of arrival must be given such notice is given and the goods are held at the disposal of the consignee;

(b) in cases where consignments are to be delivered at a station and notice of arrival need not be given, the goods are held at the disposal of the consignee;

(c) in the case of consignments which are to be delivered at places other than stations, the goods are placed at the disposal of the consignee.

Article 28

Delivery

§1. The railway shall hand over the consignment note and deliver the goods to the consignee at the destination station against a receipt and payment of the amounts chargeable to the consignee by the railway.

Acceptance of the consignment note obliges the consignee to pay to the railway the amounts chargeable to him.

§ 2. It shall be equivalent to delivery to the consignee if, in accordance with the provisions in force at the destination station—

(a) the goods have been handed over to Customs or *Octroi* authorities at their premises or warehouses, when these are not subject to railway supervision;

(b) the goods have been deposited for storage with the railway, with a forwarding agent or in a public warehouse.

§ 3. The provisions in force at the destination station or the terms of any agreements with the consignee shall determine whether the railway is entitled or obliged to hand over the goods to the consignee elsewhere than at the destination station, whether in a private siding, at his domicile or in a railway depot. If the railway hands over the goods, or arranges for them to be handed over in a private siding, at his domicile or in a depot, delivery shall be deemed to have been effected at the time when they are so handed over. Save where the railway and the user of a private siding have agreed otherwise, operations carried out by the railway on behalf of and under the instructions of that user shall not be covered by the contract of carriage.

§ 4. After the arrival of the goods at the destination station, the consignee may require the railway to hand over the consignment note and deliver the goods to him.

If the loss of the goods is established or if the goods have not arrived on the expiry of the period provided for in Article 39, § 1, the consignee may assert, in his own name, any rights against the railway which he may have acquired by reason of the contract of carriage.

§ 5. The person entitled may refuse to accept the goods, even when he has received the consignment note and paid the charges, so long as an examination for which he has asked in order to establish alleged loss or damage has not been made.

§ 6. In all other respects, delivery of goods shall be carried out in accordance with the provisions in force at the destination station.

Article 29

Correction of charges

§ 1. In case of incorrect application of a tariff or of error in the calculation or collection of charges, undercharges shall be paid or overcharges repaid.

Undercharges shall be paid and overcharges shall be repaid only if they exceed eight units of account per consignment note. The repayment shall be made as a matter of course.

§ 2. If the consignee has not taken possession of the consignment note the consignor shall be obliged to pay to the railway any amounts undercharged. When the consignment note has been accepted by the consignee or the contract of carriage modified in accordance with Article 31, the consignor shall be obliged to pay any undercharge only to the extent that it relates to the costs which he has undertaken to pay by an entry in the consignment note. Any balance of the undercharge shall be paid by the consignee.

§ 3. Sums due under this Article shall bear interest at five per cent per annum from the day of receipt of the demand for payment or from the day of the claim referred to in Article 53 or, if there has been no such demand or claim, from the day on which legal proceedings are instituted.

If, within a reasonable period allotted to him, the person entitled does not submit to the railway the supporting documents required for the amount of the claim to be finally settled, no interest shall accrue between the expiry of the period laid down and the actual submission of such documents.

[4370]

TITLE III
MODIFICATION OF THE CONTRACT OF CARRIAGE

Article 30

Modification by the consignor

§ 1. The consignor may modify the contract of carriage by giving subsequent orders—

(a) for the goods to be withdrawn at the forwarding station;
(b) for the goods to be stopped in transit;
(c) for delivery of the goods to be delayed;
(d) for the goods to be delivered to a person other than the consignee shown in the consignment note;
(e) for the goods to be delivered at a station other than the destination station shown in the consignment note;
(f) for the goods to be returned to the forwarding station;
(g) for the consignment to be made subject to a cash on delivery payment;
(h) for a cash on delivery payment to be increased, reduced or cancelled;
(i) for charges relating to a consignment which has not been prepaid to be debited to him, or for charges which he has undertaken to pay in accordance with Article 15, § 2 to be increased.

The tariffs of the following railway may provide that orders specified in (g) to (i) are not acceptable.

The supplementary provisions of the international tariffs in force between the railways participating in the carriage may provide for the acceptance of orders other than those listed above.

Orders must not in any event have the effect of splitting the consignment.

§ 2. Such orders shall be given by means of a declaration, in the form laid down by the railway.

The declaration shall be reproduced and signed by the consignor in the duplicate of the consignment note which shall be presented to the railway. The signature may be printed or replaced by the despatch stamp.

Any order given in a form other than that laid down shall be null and void.

§ 3. If the railway complies with the consignor's orders without requiring the production of the duplicate, where this has been sent to the consignee, the railway shall be liable to the consignee for any loss or damage caused thereby. Nevertheless, any compensation shall not exceed that payable in the event of loss of the goods.

§ 4. The consignor's right to modify the contract of carriage shall, notwithstanding that he is in possession of the duplicate of the consignment note, be extinguished in cases where the consignee—

(a) has taken possession of the consignment note;
(b) has accepted the goods;
(c) has asserted his rights in accordance with Article 28, § 4;
(d) is entitled, in accordance with Article 31, to give orders as soon as the consignment has entered the Customs territory of the country of destination.

From that time onwards, the railway shall comply with the orders and instructions of the consignee.

Article 31

Modification by the consignee

§ 1. When the consignor has not undertaken to pay the charges relating to carriage in the country of destination, and has not inserted in the consignment note the words "Consignee not authorised to give subsequent orders", the consignee may modify the contract of carriage by giving subsequent orders—

(a) for the goods to be stopped in transit;
(b) for delivery of the goods to be delayed;
(c) for the goods to be delivered in the country of destination to a person other than the consignee shown in the consignment note;
(d) for the goods to be delivered in the country of destination at a station other than the destination station shown in the consignment note, subject to contrary provisions in international tariffs;
(e) for formalities required by Customs or other administrative authorities to be carried out in accordance with Article 26, § 3.

The supplementary provisions or the international tariffs in force between the railways participating in the carriage may provide for the acceptance of orders other than those listed above.

Orders must not in any case have the effect of splitting the consignment.

The consignee's orders shall only be effective after the consignment has entered the Customs territory of the country of destination.

§ 2. Such orders shall be given by means of a declaration, in the form laid down by the railway.

Any order given in a form other than that laid down shall be null and void.

§ 3. The consignee's right to modify the contract of carriage shall be extinguished in cases where he has—

(a) taken possession of the consignment note;
(b) accepted the goods;
(c) asserted his rights in accordance with Article 28, § 4;
(d) designated a person in accordance with § 1(c) and that person has taken possession of the consignment note, accepted the goods or asserted his rights in accordance with Article 28, § 4.

§ 4. If the consignee has given instructions for delivery of the goods to another person, that person shall not be entitled to modify the contract of carriage.

Article 32

Execution of subsequent orders

§ 1. The railway may not refuse to execute orders given under Articles 30 or 31 or delay doing so save where—

(a) it is no longer possible to execute the orders by the time they reach the station responsible for doing so;

(b) compliance with the orders would interfere with normal railway operations;

(c) a change of destination station would contravene the laws and regulations of a State, and in particular the requirements of the Customs or of other administrative authorities;

(d) in the case of a change of destination station, the value of the goods will not, in the railway's view, cover all the charges which would be payable on the goods on arrival at the new destination, unless the amount of such charges is paid or guaranteed immediately.

The person who has given the orders shall be informed as soon as possible of any circumstances which prevent their execution.

If the railway is not in a position to foresee such circumstances, the person who has given the orders shall be liable for all the consequences of starting to execute them.

§ 2. The charges arising from the execution of an order, except those arising from any fault by the railway, shall be paid in accordance with Article 15.

§ 3. Subject to § 1, the railway shall, in the case of any fault on its part, be liable for the consequences of failure to execute an order or failure to execute it properly. Nevertheless, any compensation shall not exceed that payable in the event of loss of the goods.

Article 33

Circumstances preventing carriage

§ 1. When circumstances prevent the carriage of goods, the railway shall decide whether it is preferable to carry the goods as a matter of course by modifying the route or whether it is advisable in the consignor's interest to ask him for instructions and at the same time give him any relevant information available to the railway.

Save fault on its part, the railway may recover the carriage charges applicable to the route followed and shall be allowed the transit periods applicable to such route.

§ 2. If it is impossible to continue carrying the goods, the railway shall ask the consignor for instructions. It shall not be obliged to do so in the event of carriage being temporarily prevented as a result of measures taken in accordance with Article 3, § 4.

§ 3. The consignor may enter in the consignment note instructions to cover the event of circumstances preventing carriage.

If the railway considers that such instructions cannot be executed, it shall ask for fresh instructions.

§ 4. If the instructions of the consignor change the consignee or the destination station or are given at the station where the goods are being held, the consignor must enter them in the duplicate of the consignment note and present this to the railway.

§ 5. If the railway complies with the consignor's instructions without requiring the production of the duplicate, when this has been sent to the consignee, the railway shall be liable to the consignee for any loss or damage caused thereby. Nevertheless, any compensation shall not exceed that payable in the event of loss of the goods.

§ 6. If the consignor, on being notified of a circumstance preventing carriage, fails to give within a reasonable time instructions which can be executed, the railway shall take action in accordance with the provisions relating to circumstances preventing delivery, in force at the place where the goods have been held up.

If the goods have been sold, the proceeds of sale, less any amounts chargeable against the goods, shall be held at the disposal of the consignor. If the proceeds are less than those costs, the consignor shall pay the difference.

§ 7. When the circumstances preventing carriage cease to obtain before the arrival of instructions from the consignor, the goods shall be forwarded to their destination without waiting for such instructions: the consignor shall be notified to that effect as soon as possible .

§ 8. When the circumstances preventing carriage arise after the consignee has modified the contract of carriage in accordance with Article 31, the railway shall notify the consignee, §§ 1, 2, 6, 7 and 9 shall apply analogously.

§ 9. Save fault on its part, the railway may raise demurrage or standage charges if circumstances prevent carriage.

§ 10. Article 32 shall apply to carriage undertaken in accordance with Article 33.

Article 34

Circumstances preventing delivery

§ 1. When circumstances prevent delivery of the goods, the railway shall without delay notify the consignor to ask for his instructions.

§ 2. When the circumstances preventing delivery cease to obtain before arrival at the destination station of instructions from the consignor the goods shall be delivered to the consignee. The consignor shall be notified without delay.

§ 3. If the consignee refuses the goods, the consignor shall be entitled to give instructions even if he is unable to produce the duplicate of the consignment note.

§ 4. The consignor may also request, by an entry in the consignment note, that the goods be returned to him as a matter of course in the event of circumstances preventing delivery. Unless such request is made, his express consent is required.

§ 5. Except as otherwise provided for above, the railway responsible for delivery shall proceed in accordance with the provisions in force at the place of delivery.

If the goods have been sold, the proceeds of sale, less any costs chargeable against the goods, shall be held at the disposal of the consignor. If such proceeds are less than those costs, the consignor shall pay the difference.

§ 6. When the circumstances preventing delivery arise after the consignee has modified the contract of carriage in accordance with Article 31, the railway shall notify the consignee, §§ 1, 2 and 6 shall apply analogously.

§ 7. Article 32 shall apply to carriage undertaken in accordance with Article 34.

[4371]

TITLE IV
LIABILITY

Article 35

Collective responsibility of railways

§ 1. The railway which has accepted goods for carriage with the consignment note shall be responsible for the carriage over the entire route up to delivery.

§ 2. Each succeeding railway, by the very act of taking over the goods with the consignment note, shall become a party to the contract of carriage in accordance with the terms of that document and shall assume the obligations arising therefrom, without prejudice to the provisions of Article 55, § 3, relating to the railway of destination.

Article 36

Extent of liability

§ 1. The railway shall be liable for loss or damage resulting from the total or partial loss of, or damage to, the goods between the time of acceptance for carriage and the time of delivery and for the loss or damage resulting from the transit period being exceeded.

§ 2. The railway shall be relieved of such liability if the loss or damage or the exceeding of the transit period was caused by a fault on the part of the person entitled, by an order given by the person entitled other than as a result of a fault on the part of the railway, by inherent vice of the goods (decay, wastage, etc) or by circumstances which the railway could not avoid and the consequences of which it was unable to prevent.

§ 3. The railway shall be relieved of such liability when the loss or damage arises from the special risks inherent in one or more of the following circumstances—

(a) carriage in open wagons under the conditions applicable thereto or under an agreement made between the consignor and the railway and referred to in the consignment note;

(b) absence or inadequacy of packing in the case of goods which by their nature are liable to loss or damage when not packed or when not properly packed;

(c) loading operations carried out by the consignor or unloading operations carried out by the consignee under the provisions applicable thereto or under an agreement made between the consignor and the railway and referred to in the consignment note, or under an agreement between the consignee and the railway;

(d) defective loading, when loading has been carried out by the consignor under the provisions applicable thereto or under an agreement made between the consignor and the railway and referred to in the consignment note;

(e) completion by the consignor, the consignee or an agent of either, of the formalities required by Customs or other administrative authorities;

(f) the nature of certain goods which renders them inherently liable to total or partial loss or damage, especially through breakage, rust, interior and spontaneous decay, desiccation or wastage;

(g) irregular, incorrect or incomplete description of articles not acceptable for carriage or acceptable subject to conditions, or failure on the part of the consignor to observe the prescribed precautions in respect of articles acceptable subject to conditions;

(h) carriage of live animals;

(i) carriage which, under the provisions applicable or under an agreement made between the consignor and the railway and referred to in the consignment note, must be accompanied by an attendant, if the loss or damage results from any risk which the attendant was intended to avert.

Article 37

Burden of Proof

§ 1. The burden of proving that the loss, the damage or the exceeding of the transit period was due to one of the causes specified in Article 36, § 2 shall rest upon the railway.

§ 2. When the railway establishes that, having regard to the circumstances of a particular case, the loss or damage could have arisen from one or more of the special risks referred to in Article 36, § 3, it shall be presumed that it did so arise. The person entitled shall, however, have the right to prove that the loss or damage was not attributable either wholly or partly to one of those risks.

This presumption shall not apply in the case referred to in Article 36, § 3(a) if an abnormally large quantity has been lost or if a package has been lost.

Article 38

Presumption in case of reconsignment

§ 1. When a consignment despatched in accordance with the Uniform Rules has been reconsigned subject to the same Rules and partial loss or damage has been ascertained after the reconsignment, it shall be presumed that it occurred during the latest contract of carriage if the consignment remained in the care of the railway and was reconsigned in the same condition as it arrived at the station from which it was reconsigned.

§ 2. This presumption shall also apply when the contract of carriage prior to the reconsignment was not subject to the Uniform Rules, if the Rules would have applied in the case of a through consignment from the original forwarding station to the final destination station.

This presumption shall moreover apply when the contract of carriage prior to the reconsignment was subject to a comparable international convention on international through rail transport, and when this contains the same presumption of law in favour of consignments sent in accordance with the Uniform Rules.

Article 39

Presumption of loss of goods

§ 1. The person entitled may, without being required to furnish further proof, consider the goods lost when they have not been delivered to the consignee or are not being held at his disposal within thirty days after the expiry of the transit periods.

§ 2. The person entitled may, on receipt of compensation for the lost goods, make a written request to be notified without delay should the goods be recovered within one year after the payment of compensation. The railway shall give a written acknowledgement of such request.

§ 3. Within thirty days after receipt of such notification, the person entitled may require the goods to be delivered to him at any station on the route. In that case he shall pay the charges in respect of carriage from the forwarding station to the station where delivery is effected and shall refund the compensation received, less any costs which may have been included therein. Nevertheless he shall retain his rights to claim compensation for exceeding the transit period provided for in Article 43 and 46.

§ 4. In the absence of the request mentioned in 2 or of any instructions given within the period specified in § 3, or if the goods are recovered more than one year after the payment of compensation, the railway shall dispose of them in accordance with the laws and regulations of the State having jurisdiction over the railway.

Article 40

Compensation for loss

§ 1. In the event of total or partial loss of the goods the railway must pay, to the exclusion of all other damages, compensation calculated according to the commodity exchange quotation or, if there is no such quotation, according to the current market price, or if there is neither such quotation nor such price, according to the normal value of goods of the same kind and quality at the time and place at which the goods were accepted for carriage.

§ 2. Compensation shall not exceed 17 units of account per kilogramme of gross mass short.

§ 3. The railway shall in addition refund carriage charges, Customs duties and other amounts incurred in connection with carriage of the lost goods.

Article 41

Liability for wastage in transit

§ 1. In respect of goods which, by reason of their nature, are generally subject to wastage in transit by the sole fact of carriage, the railway shall only be liable to the extent that the wastage exceeds the following allowances, whatever the length of the route—

(a) two per cent of the mass for liquid goods or goods consigned in a moist condition;
(b) one per cent of the mass for dry goods.

§ 2. The limitation of liability provided for in § 1 may not be invoked if, having regard to the circumstances of a particular case, it is proved that the loss was not due to causes which would justify an allowance.

§ 3. Where several packages are carried under a single consignment note, the wastage in transit shall be calculated separately for each package if its mass on despatch is shown separately in the consignment note or can otherwise be ascertained.

§ 4. In the event of total loss of goods or in the case of loss of a package, no deduction for wastage in transit shall be made in calculating the compensation payable.

§ 5. This Article shall not derogate from Articles 36 and 37.

Article 42

Compensation for damage

§ 1. In case of damage to goods, the railway must pay compensation equivalent to the loss in value of the goods, to the exclusion of all other damages. The amount shall be calculated by applying to the value of the goods as defined in Article 40 the percentage of loss in value noted at the place of destination.

§ 2. The compensation may not exceed—

(a) if the whole consignment has lost value through damage, the amount which would have been payable in case of total loss;

(b) if only part of the consignment has lost value through damage, the amount which would have been payable had that part been lost.

§ 3 The railway shall in addition refund the amounts provided for in Article 40, § 3, in the proportion set out in § 1.

Article 43

Compensation for exceeding the transit period

§ 1. If loss or damage has resulted from the transit period being exceeded, the railway shall pay compensation not exceeding four times the carriage charges.

§ 2. In case of total loss of the goods, the compensation provided for in § 1 shall not be payable in addition to that provided for in Article 40.

§ 3. In case of partial loss of the goods, the compensation provided for in § 1 shall not exceed three times the carriage charges in respect of that part of the consignment which has not been lost.

§ 4. In case of damage to the goods, not resulting from the transit period being exceeded, the compensation provided for in § 1 shall, where appropriate, be payable in addition to that provided for in Article 42.

§ 5. In no case shall the total of compensation payable under § 1 together with that payable under Articles 40 and 42 exceed the compensation which would be payable in the event of total loss of the goods.

§ 6. The railway may provide, in international tariffs or in special agreements, for other forms of compensation than those provided for in § 1 when, in accordance with Article 27, § 1, the transit period has been established on the basis of transport plans.

If, in this case, the transit periods provided for in Article 27, § 2 are exceeded, the person entitled may demand either the compensation provided for in § 1 above or that determined by the international tariff or the special agreement applied.

Article 44

Loss of the right to invoke the limits of liability

The liability limits provided for in Articles 25, 26, 30, 32, 33, 40, 42, 43, 45 and 46 shall not apply if it is proved that the loss or damage resulted from an act or omission, on the part of the railway, done with intent to cause such loss or damage, or recklessly and with knowledge that such loss or damage will probably result.

Article 45

Limitation of compensation under certain tariffs

When the railway agrees to special conditions of carriage through special or exceptional tariffs, involving a reduction in the carriage charge calculated on the basis of the general tariffs, it may limit the amount of compensation payable to the person entitled in the case of exceeding of the transit period, provided that such limit is indicated in the tariff.

When the special conditions of carriage apply only to part of the route, the limit may only be invoked if the event giving rise to the compensation occurred on that part of the route.

Article 46

Compensation in case of interest in delivery

In case of a declaration of interest in delivery, further compensation for loss or damage proved may be claimed, in addition to the compensation provided for in Articles 40, 42, 43 and 45, up to the amount declared.

Article 47

Conversion of, and interest on, compensation

§ 1. When the calculation of the compensation requires the conversion of sums expressed in foreign currencies, conversion shall be at the rate of exchange applicable on the day and at the place of payment of compensation.

§ 2. The person entitled may claim interest on compensation payable, calculated at five per cent per annum, from the date of the claim referred to in Article 53 or, if no such claim has been made, from the day on which legal proceedings are instituted.

§ 3. Interest shall only be payable if the compensation exceeds eight units of account per consignment note.

§ 4. If, within a reasonable period allotted to him, the person entitled does not submit to the railway the supporting documents required for the amount of the claim to be finally settled, no interest shall accrue between the expiry of the period laid down and the actual submission of such documents.

Article 48

Liability in respect of rail-sea traffic

§ 1. In rail-sea transport by the services referred to in Article 2, § 2 of the Convention each State may, by requesting that a suitable note be included in the list of lines or services to which the Uniform Rules apply, indicate that the following ground for exemption from liability will apply in their entirety in addition to those provided for in Article 36.

The carrier may only avail himself of these grounds for exemption if he proves that the loss, damage or exceeding of the transit period occurred in the course of the sea journey between the time when the goods were loaded on board the ship and the time when they were discharged from the ship.

The grounds for exemption are as follows—

(a) act, neglect or default on the part of the master, a mariner, pilot or the carrier's servants in the navigation or management of the ship;

(b) unseaworthiness of the ship, if the carrier proves that the unseaworthiness is not attributable to lack of due diligence on his part to make the ship seaworthy, to ensure that it is properly manned, equipped and supplied or to make all parts of the ship in which the goods are loaded fit and safe for their reception, carriage and protection;

(c) fire, if the carrier proves that it was not caused by his act or fault, or that of the master, a mariner, pilot or the carrier's servants;

(d) perils, dangers and accidents of the sea or other navigable waters;

(e) saving or attempting to save life or property at sea;

(f) the loading of goods on the deck of the ship, if they are so loaded with the consent of the consignor given in the consignment note and are not in wagons.

The above grounds for exemption in no way affect the general obligations of the carrier and, in particular, his obligation to exercise due diligence to make the ship seaworthy, to ensure that it is properly manned, equipped and supplied and to make all parts of the ship in which the goods are loaded fit and safe for their reception, carriage and protection.

Even when the carrier can rely on the foregoing grounds for exemption, he shall nevertheless remain liable if the person entitled proves that the loss, damage or exceeding of the transit period is due to a fault of the carrier, the master, a mariner, pilot or the carrier's servants, fault other than provided for under (a).

§ 2. Where one and the same sea route is served by several undertakings included in the list referred to in Articles 3 and 10 of the Convention, the regime of liability applicable to that route shall be the same for all those undertakings.

In addition, where such undertakings have been included in the list at the request of several States, the adoption of this regime shall be the subject of prior agreement between those States.

§ 3. The measures taken under this Article shall be notified to the Central Office. They shall come into force at the earliest at the expiry of a period of thirty days from the date of the letter by which the Central Office notifies them to other States.

Consignments already in transit shall not be affected by such measures.

Article 49

Liability in case of nuclear incidents

The railway shall be relieved of liability under the Uniform Rules for loss or damage caused by a nuclear incident when the operator of a nuclear installation or another person who is substituted for him is liable for the loss or damage pursuant to a State's laws and regulations governing liability in the field of nuclear energy.

Article 50

Liability of the railway for its servants

The railway shall be liable for its servants and for any other persons whom it employs to perform the carriage.

If however such servants and other persons, at the request of an interested party, make out consignment notes, make translations or render other services which the railway itself is under no obligation to render, they shall be deemed to be acting on behalf of the person to whom the services are rendered.

Article 51

Other actions

In all cases to which the Uniform Rules apply, any action in respect of liability on any grounds whatsoever may be brought against the railway only subject to the conditions and limitations laid down in the Rules.

The same shall apply to any action brought against those servants and other persons for whom the railway is liable under Article 50.

[4372]

TITLE V
ASSERTION OF RIGHTS

Article 52

Ascertainment of partial loss or damage

§ 1. When partial loss of or damage to, goods is discovered or presumed by the railway or alleged by the person entitled, the railway must without delay, and if possible in the presence of the person entitled, draw up a report stating, according to the nature of the loss or damage, the condition of the goods, their mass and, as far as possible, the extent of the loss or damage, its cause and the time of its occurrence.

A copy of the report must be supplied free of charge to the person entitled.

§ 2. Should the person entitled not accept the findings in the report, he may request that the condition and mass of the goods and the cause and amount of the loss or damage be ascertained by an expert appointed either by the parties or by a court. The procedure to be followed shall be governed by the laws and regulations of the State in which such ascertainment takes place.

Article 53

Claims

§ 1. Claims relating to the contract of carriage shall be made in writing to the railway specified in Article 55.

§ 2. A claim may be made by persons who have the right to bring an action against the railway under Article 54.

§ 3. To make the claim, the consignor must produce the duplicate of the consignment note. Failing this, he must produce an authorisation from the consignee or furnish proof that the consignee has refused to accept the consignment.

To make the claim, the consignee must produce the consignment note if it has been handed over to him.

§ 4. The consignment note, the duplicate and any other documents which the person entitled thinks fit to submit with the claim shall be produced either in the original or as copies, the copies to be duly authenticated if the railway so requires.

On settlement of the claim, the railway may require the production, in the original form, of the consignment note, the duplicate or the cash on delivery voucher so that they may be endorsed to the effect that settlement has been made.

Article 54

Persons who may bring an action against the railway

§ 1. An action for the recovery of a sum paid under the contract of carriage may only be brought by the person who made the payment.

§ 2. An action in respect of the cash on-delivery payments provided for in Article 17 may only be brought by the consignor.

§ 3. Other actions arising from the contract of carriage may be brought—

(a) by the consignor, until such time as the consignee has—
   (i) taken possession of the consignment note,
   (ii) accepted the goods, or
   (iii) asserted his rights under Article 28, § 4, or Article 31;

(b) by the consignee, from the time when he has—
   (i) taken possession of the consignment note,
   (ii) accepted the goods,
   (iii) asserted his rights under Article 28, § 4, or
   (iv) asserted his rights under Article 31 provided that the right of action shall be extinguished from the time when the person designated by the consignee in accordance with Article 31, §1(c) has taken possession of the consignment note, accepted the goods, or asserted his rights under Article 28, § 4.

§ 4. In order to bring an action, the consignor must produce the duplicate of the consignment note. Failing this, in order to bring an action under § 3(a) he must produce an authorisation from the consignee or furnish proof that the consignee has refused to accept the consignment.

In order to bring an action, the consignee shall produce the consignment note if it has been handed over to him.

Article 55

Railways against which an action may be brought

§ 1. An action for the recovery of a sum paid under the contract of carriage may be brought against the railway which has collected that sum or against the railway on whose behalf it was collected.

§ 2. An action in respect of the cash on delivery payments provided for in Article 17 may only be brought against the forwarding railway.

§ 3. Other actions arising from the contract of carriage may be brought against the forwarding railway, the railway of destination or the railway on which the event giving rise to the proceedings occurred.

Such actions may be brought against the railway of destination even if it has received neither the goods nor the consignment note.

§ 4. If the plaintiff can choose between several railways, his right to choose shall be extinguished as soon as he brings an action against any one of them.

§ 5. An action may be brought against a railway other than those specified in §§ 1, 2 and 3 when instituted by way of counterclaim or by way of exception to the principal claim based on the same contract of carriage.

Article 56

Competence

Actions brought under the Uniform Rules may only be instituted in the competent court of the State having jurisdiction over the defendant railway, unless otherwise provided in agreements between States or in acts of concession.

When a railway operates independent railway systems in different States, each system shall be regarded as a separate railway for the purposes of this Article.

Article 57

Extinction of right of action against the railway

§ 1. Acceptance of the goods by the person entitled shall extinguish all rights of action against the railway arising from the contract of carriage in case of partial loss, damage or exceeding of the transit period.

§ 2. Nevertheless, the right of action shall not be extinguished—

(a) in the case of partial loss or of damage, if—

(i) the loss or damage was ascertained before the acceptance of the goods in accordance with Article 52 by the person entitled;

(ii) the ascertainment which should have been carried out under Article 52 was omitted solely through the fault of the railway;

(b) in the case of loss or damage which is not apparent and is not ascertained until after acceptance of the goods by the person entitled, provided that he—

(i) asks for ascertainment in accordance with Article 52 immediately after discovery of the loss or damage and not later than seven days after the acceptance of the goods;

(ii) and, in addition, proves that the loss or damage occurred between the time of acceptance for carriage and the time of delivery;

(c) in cases where the transit period has been exceeded, if the person entitled has, within sixty days, asserted his rights against one of the railways referred to in Article 55, § 3;

(d) if the person entitled furnishes proof that the loss or damage was caused by wilful misconduct or gross negligence on the part of the railway.

§ 3. If the goods have been recognised in accordance with Articles 38, § 1 rights of action in case of partial loss or of damage, arising from one of the previous contracts of carriage, shall be extinguished as if there had been only one contract of carriage.

Article 58

Limitation of actions

§ 1. The period of limitation for an action arising from the contract of carriage shall be one year.

Nevertheless, the period of limitation shall be two years in the case of an action—

(a) to recover a cash on delivery payment collected by the railway from the consignee;

(b) to recover the proceeds of a sale effected by the railway;

(c) for loss or damage resulting from an act or omission done with intent to cause such loss or damage, or recklessly and with knowledge that such loss or damage will probably result;

(d) arising from one of the contracts of carriage prior to the reconsignment in the case provided for in Article 38, § 1.

§ 2. The period of limitation shall run;

(a) in actions for compensation for total loss, from the thirtieth day after the expiry of the transit period;

(b) in actions for compensation for partial loss, for damage or for exceeding the transit period, from the day when delivery took place;

(c) in actions for payment or refund of carriage charges, supplementary charges, other charges or surcharges, or for correction of charges in case of a tariff being wrongly applied or of an error in calculation or collection—

(i) if payment has been made, from the day of payment;

(ii) if payment has not been made, from the day when the goods were accepted for carriage if payment is due from the consignor, or from the day when the consignee took possession of the consignment note if payment is due from him;

(iii) in the case of sums to be paid under a charges note, from the day on which the railway submits to the consignor the account of charges provided for in Article 15, § 7; if no such account has been submitted, the period in respect of sums due to the railway shall run from the thirtieth day following the expiry of the transit period;

(d) in an action by the railway for recovery of a sum which has been paid by the consignee instead of by the consignor or vice versa and which the railway is required to refund to the person entitled, from the day of the claim for a refund;

(e) in actions relating to cash on delivery as provided for in Article 17, from the thirtieth day following the expiry of the transit period;

(f) in actions to recover the proceeds of a sale, from the day of the sale;

(g) in actions to recover additional duty demanded by Customs or other administrative authorities, from the day of the demand made by such authorities;

(h) in all other cases, from the day when the right of action arises.

The day indicated for the commencement of the period of limitation shall not be included in the period.

§ 3. When a claim is presented to a railway in accordance with Article 53 together with the necessary supporting documents, the period of limitation shall be suspended until the day that the railway rejects the claim by notification in writing and returns the documents. If part of the claim is admitted, the period of limitation shall recommence in respect of that part of the claim still in dispute. The burden of proof of receipt of the claim or of the reply and of the return of the documents shall rest on the party who relies on those facts.

The period of limitation shall not be suspended by further claims having the same object.

§ 4. A right of action which has become time-barred may not be exercised by way of counter-claim or relied upon by way of exception.

§ 5. Subject to the foregoing provisions, the suspension and interruption of periods of limitation shall be governed by national law.

[4373]

TITLE VI
RELATIONS BETWEEN RAILWAYS

Article 59

Settlement of accounts between railways

§ 1. Any railway which has collected, either at the time of forwarding or on arrival, charges or other sums due under the contract of carriage must pay to the railways concerned their respective shares.

The methods of payment shall be settled by agreements between railways.

§ 2. The forwarding railway shall be liable for carriage and other charges which it has failed to collect when the consignor has undertaken to pay them in accordance with Article 15.

§ 3. Should the railway of destination deliver the goods without collecting charges or other sums due under the contract of carriage, it shall be liable for these amounts.

§ 4. Should one railway default in payment and such default be confirmed by the Central Office at the request of one of the creditor railways, the consequences thereof shall be borne by all the other railways which have taken part in the carriage in proportion to their shares of the carriage charges.

The right of recovery against the defaulting railway shall not be affected.

Article 60

Recourse in case of loss or damage

§ 1. A railway which has paid compensation in accordance with the Uniform Rules, for total or partial loss or for damage, has a right of recourse against the other railways which have taken part in the carriage in accordance with the following provisions—

(a) the railway which has caused the loss or damage shall be solely liable for it;

(b) when the loss or damage has been caused by more than one railway, each shall be liable for the loss or damage it has caused; if such distinction cannot be made, the compensation shall be apportioned between those railways in accordance with (c);

(c) if it cannot be proved that the loss or damage has been caused by one or more railways in particular, the compensation shall be apportioned between all the railways which have taken part in the carriage, except those which can prove that the loss or damage was not caused on their lines; such apportionment shall be in proportion to the kilometric distances contained in the tariffs.

§ 2. In the case of the insolvency of any one of the railways, the unpaid share due from it shall be apportioned among all the other railways which have taken part in the carriage, in proportion to the kilometric distances contained in the tariffs.

Article 61

Recourse in case of exceeding the transit period

§ 1. Article 60 shall apply where compensation is paid for exceeding the transit period. If this has been caused by more than one railway, the compensation shall be apportioned between such railways in proportion to the length of the delay occurring on their respective lines.

§ 2. The transit periods specified in Article 27 shall be apportioned in the following manner—

(a) where two railways have taken part in the carriage—
  (i) the period for despatch shall be divided equally;
  (ii) the period for transport shall be divided in proportion to the kilometric distances contained in the tariffs;

(b) where three or more railways have taken part in the carriage—
  (i) the period for despatch shall be divided equally between the forwarding railway and the railway of destination;
  (ii) the period for transport shall be divided between all the railways—
    — one-third in equal shares
    — the remaining two-thirds in proportion to the kilometric distances contained in the tariffs.

§ 3. Any additional periods to which a railway may be entitled shall be allocated to that railway.

§ 4. The interval between the time when the goods are handed over to the railway and commencement of the period for despatch shall be allocated exclusively to the forwarding railway.

§ 5. Such apportionment shall only apply if the total transit period has been exceeded.

Article 62

Procedure for recourse

§ 1. The validity of the payment made by the railway exercising one of the rights of recourse under Articles 60 and 61 may not be disputed by the railway against which the right of recourse is exercised, when compensation has been determined by a court and when the latter railway duly served with notice, has been afforded an opportunity to intervene in the proceedings. The court seized of the main proceedings shall determine what time shall be allowed for such notification and for intervention in the proceedings.

§ 2. A railway exercising its right of recourse must take proceedings by one and the same action against all the railways concerned with which it has not reached a settlement, failing which it shall lose its right of recourse in the case of those against which it has not taken proceedings.

§ 3. The court shall give its decision in one and the same judgment on all recourse claims brought before it.

§ 4. The railways against which such action has been brought shall have no further right of recourse.

§ 5. Recourse proceedings may not be joined with proceedings for compensation taken by the person entitled on the basis of the contract of carriage.

Article 63

Competence for recourse

§ 1. The courts of the country in which the railway against which the recourse claim has been made, has its headquarters shall have exclusive competence for all recourse claims.

§ 2. When the action is to be brought against several railways, the plaintiff railway shall be entitled to choose the court in which it will bring the proceedings from among those having competence under § 1.

Article 64

Agreements concerning recourse

By agreement, railways may derogate from the provisions concerning reciprocal rights of recourse set out in Title VI, apart from that contained in Article 62, § 5.

[4374]

PART V

TITLE VII
EXCEPTIONAL PROVISIONS

Article 65

Temporary derogations

§ 1. If the economic and financial position of any State is such as to cause serious difficulty in applying Title VI, two or more other States may, by agreements, derogate from Articles 15, 17 and 30 by determining, for traffic with the State in difficulty, that—

(a) consignments from each of them shall be forwarded charges paid by the consignor as far as the frontiers of the State in difficulty, but not beyond;
(b) consignments to destinations in each of them shall be forwarded charges paid by the consignor as far as the frontiers of the State in difficulty, but not beyond;
(c) consignments to or from the State in difficulty must not be made subject to any cash on delivery payment or disbursement, except up to specified amounts;
(d) the consignor may not modify the contract of carriage as far as concerns the country of destination, pre-payment of charges and cash on delivery payments.

§ 2. Under the conditions specified in § 1 and with the authorisation of their Governments, the railways which have dealings with the railway of the State in difficulty may agree upon a derogation from Articles 15, 17, 30 and 31 in the traffic exchanged between them and the railway of the State in difficulty.

Such a derogation shall be decided by a two thirds majority of the railways having dealings with the railway of the State in difficulty.

§ 3. Measures taken in accordance with §§ 1 and 2 shall be notified to the Central Office.

The measures set out in § 1 shall come into force at the earliest on the expiry of a period of eight days from the date of the letter by which the Central Office shall have notified such measures to the other States.

The measures set out in § 2 shall come into force at the earliest on the expiry of a period of two days from the date of their publication in the States concerned.

§ 4. Consignments already in transit shall not be affected by such measures.

§ 5. Notwithstanding the provisions of this Article, each State may take unilateral measures in accordance with Article 3, § 4, letter (b).

Article 66

Derogations

The provisions of the Uniform Rules shall not prevail over those provisions which certain States are obliged to adopt, in traffic among themselves, in pursuant of certain Treaties such as the Treaties relating to the European Coal and Steel Community and the European Economic Community.

[4375]

ANNEX I
(ARTICLES 4 AND 5)

REGULATIONS CONCERNING THE INTERNATIONAL CARRIAGE OF DANGEROUS GOODS BY RAIL (RID)

The text of this Annex shall be that drawn up by the Committee of Experts, in accordance with Article 69, § 4 of the International Convention concerning the Carriage of Goods by Rail (CIM) of 7 February 1970, for the International Regulations concerning the Carriage of Dangerous Goods by Rail (RID), Annex I to the CIM. The Committee of Experts shall also edit the text to bring it into line with the Convention concerning the International Carriage of Goods by Rail of 9 May 1980.

[4376]

ANNEX II
(ARTICLE 8, § 1)

REGULATIONS CONCERNING THE INTERNATIONAL HAULAGE OF PRIVATE OWNERS' WAGONS BY RAIL (RIP)

The text of this Annex shall be that drawn up by the Committee of Experts, in accordance with Article 69, § 4 of the International Convention concerning the Carriage of Goods by Rail

(CIM) of 7 February 1970, for the International Regulations concerning the Haulage of Private Owners' Wagons (RIP), Annex IV to the CIM. The Committee of Experts shall also edit the text to bring it into line with the Convention concerning the International Carriage of Goods by Rail of 9 May 1980.

The text of this Annex is so drawn up as follows.

Article 1

Purpose of the regulations

1. These regulations shall apply to all haulage of private owners' wagons, empty or loaded, accepted for international traffic in accordance with Article 2 of this annex and consigned under the conditions of the CIM Uniform Rules.

2. In the absence of specific provisions in these regulations, the other provisions of the Uniform Rules shall apply to the haulage referred to in paragraph 1 above.

Article 2

Acceptance of wagons for international traffic

To be accepted for international traffic, wagons shall be registered in the name of a private party (whether an individual, a firm or a corporate body) by a railway to whose lines the Uniform Rules apply and shall be marked by that railway with the distinguishing mark [P].

In these regulations the private party, whose name shall be marked on the wagon, is referred to as the "owner".

Article 3

Use of wagons

The consignor may only use the wagon for the carriage of goods for which it is designated in accordance with the contract of registration. The consignor shall be solely responsible for the consequences resulting from the failure to observe this provision.

Article 4

Special apparatus

If the wagon is equipped with special apparatus (refrigerating equipment, water tanks, machinery, etc), the consignor shall be responsible for the servicing of such equipment or for arranging for it to be serviced. This duty shall pass to the consignee as soon as he exercises his rights under article 28 or 31 of the Uniform Rules.

Article 5

Presenting of wagons for haulage

1. The right to present a wagon for haulage shall be vested in the owner.

Any other consignor of a wagon, whether it be empty or loaded, shall present at the forwarding station, at the same time as the consignment note, an authority granted by the owner, which may relate to several wagons.

Such authority shall not be required if the consignor is the consignee of the wagon on its last journey and if, before time when the new contract of carriage is made, the station has not received by letter, by telegram or by telex from the owner an order not to despatch the wagon or wagons without his authority.

2. In the absence of the owner's order to the contrary, the railway shall be entitled to return to its home station automatically at the owner's expense, and under cover of a consignment note made out in his name and with his address—

any wagon which arrives empty if its loading has not been started within 15 days from the time it became available;

any wagon which arrives loaded if it has not been reconsigned within 8 days from the time when its unloading was completed.

If the railway does not avail itself of this power it shall, on expiry of the foregoing periods, advise the owner of the whereabouts of the wagon; in which case the railway shall not be entitled to return the wagon until the end of the eighth day following the despatch of advice to the owner.

This paragraph shall not apply to wagons within the country of the railway which has registered them nor to wagons on private sidings.

3. A hirer whose name is marked on the wagon with the consent of the registering railway shall, for the purpose of this Article, be deemed to be the owner.

Article 6

Particulars in the consignment note

1. In addition to the particulars required by the Uniform Rules, the consignor shall enter the following in the consignment note—

(a) in the space provided for the description of the goods
in the case of an empty wagon, the words "empty wagon P";
in the case of a loaded wagon, the words "loaded in wagon P" after the description of the goods,

(b) the characteristics of the wagon in the space provided.

2. If the consignor of an empty wagon wishes to obtain a special guarantee of the transit period according to Article 14, he shall enter in the space in the consignment note provided for his declarations, the words "special guarantee of transit period".

Article 7

Interest in delivery

1. The delivery of empty wagons shall not be subject to declaration of interest.

2. In the case of a loaded wagon, the declaration of interest in delivery shall only apply to the goods carried therein.

Article 8

"Cash on delivery" charges and disbursements

1. Empty wagons shall not be subject to "cash on delivery" charges and disbursements.

2. Loaded wagons may not be subject to a "cash on delivery" exceeding the value of the goods loaded therein.

Article 9

Extension of transit period

1. In addition to the cases provided for under Article 27.7 of the Uniform Rules, the transit period shall also be extended for the duration of any delay caused by damage to the wagon, unless the railway is liable for such damage under Article 12.

2. When the goods loaded in a damaged wagon are trans-shipped into another wagon, the delay shall terminate, in respect of the goods, at the time when, after trans-shipment, they can again be forwarded.

Article 10

Verification of damage to wagons or loss of parts

1. When damage to a wagon or loss of parts is discovered or presumed by the railway, or alleged by the party concerned, the railway shall immediately draw up, in accordance with Article 52 of the Uniform Rules, a report stating the nature of the damage or loss and, so far as possible, its cause and the time of its occurrence.

Such report shall be sent without delay to the registering railway, which shall send a copy of it to the owner. In the case of a wagon on which the name of a hirer is marked with the consent of the registering railway, a copy of the report shall be sent direct to this hirer.

2. If the wagon is loaded, a separate report shall, where necessary, be drawn up in respect of the goods in accordance with Article 52 of the Uniform Rules.

Article 11

Damage to a wagon preventing continuation of haulage

1. If a wagon consigned empty is so damaged as to prevent the continuation of haulage or to render the wagon unfit to carry a load, the station where the damage is discovered shall without delay advise the consignor and the owner by telegram or by telex, indicating as far as possible the nature of the damage.

2. Any empty wagon which is withdrawn from service shall be put into a fit state to run by the railway, unless the damage is so serious that it has to be loaded onto another wagon.

In order to render the wagon fit to run, the railway may of its own accord carry out repairs up to a limit agreed in the contract of registration.

These provisions shall apply without prejudice to the question of liability.

3. If the railway carries out repairs in accordance with paragraph 2, and if such work is expected to take more than four days to complete, the railway shall request the consignor by telegram or by telex to advise whether, when the work has been completed, the contract of carriage is to be carried out or modified.

If no instructions have been received from the consignor before the completion of the work, the contract of carriage shall be pursued.

4. If the railway does not carry out the repairs of its own accord the station where the damage is discovered shall request the consignor's instructions by telegram or by telex, directly and without delay. If the consignor is not also the owner, a copy of this request shall be transmitted without delay to the owner by telegram or telex.

In the absence of instructions from the consignor within a period of eight days from the date of despatch of the telegram or telex message, the railway shall be entitled of its own accord, after having, if need be, put the wagon in a fit state to run, to return it to its home station under a consignment note made out in the name of and with the address of the owner.

The reasons for its return shall be stated in the consignment note after the words "empty wagon P".

5. If damage prevents the continuation of the forwarding of a wagon consigned loaded and unloading becomes necessary, this Article shall apply to the unloaded wagon.

If the wagon can be repaired without unloading, paragraphs 1, 2, 3, 6 and 7 of this Article shall apply.

6. The carriage and other charges which have accrued up to the station at which the wagon was stopped, the cost of notifying the consignor and the owner, as well as any charges for complying with the consignor's instructions or for returning the wagon to its home station shall be charged against the consignment.

7. The hirer whose name is marked on the wagon with the consent of the registering railway shall, for the purpose of this Article, be deemed to be the owner.

Article 12

Liability of the railway for loss or damage to the wagon or its parts
Liability of the owner for damage caused by the wagon

1. In the case of loss or damage to the wagon or forwarding its parts sustained between the time of acceptance for forwarding and the time of delivery, the railway shall be liable unless it proves that the loss of damage was not caused by fault on its part.

2. In the case of loss of the wagon, compensation shall be limited to the value of the wagon; the basis of the calculation shall be determined in the contract of registration.

In the case of damage, compensation shall be calculated in accordance with the provisions of the contract of registration.

3. In the case of loss or damage to removable parts, the railway shall only be liable if such parts are listed on both sides of the wagon. The railway shall not be liable for the loss of or damage to loose equipment.

4. Unless the claimant proves that the damage was caused by wrongful act or neglect of the railway, the railway shall only be liable

— for damage to receptacles made of pottery, glass, terracotta, etc, if the damage is connected with damage to the wagon itself for which the railway is liable under the foregoing provisions;
— for damage to receptacles with interior linings (enamel, ebonite, etc) if the receptacles show signs of external damage for which the railway is liable under the foregoing provisions.

5. The owner shall be deemed to be the consignor or the consignee, as the case may be, in respect of compensation for loss or damage to the wagon or its parts. Claims shall only be

made to the registering railway and legal proceedings shall only be instituted against that railway which shall be treated as if it were the railway liable.

6. Legal proceedings instituted by the railway against the owner for damage caused by the wagon during forwarding shall be governed by the contract of registration. Only the registering railway shall be entitled to assert the rights of other railways against the owner.

7. The period of limitation for legal proceedings instituted under paragraphs 1 to 6 shall be three years.

This period runs—

in the case of legal proceedings instituted by the owner against the railway under paragraphs 1 to 5, from the day on which the loss or damage to the wagon was established, taking account, where appropriate, of the provisions of paragraph 1 of Article 13;

in the case of legal proceedings instituted by the railway against the owner under paragraph 6, from the day on which the damage occurred.

Article 13

Presumption of loss of wagon

1. The person entitled may, without having to provide further proof, consider the wagon to be lost when it has not been delivered to the consignee nor put at his disposal within three months following the expiry of the transit period.

Such period shall be extended by the period during which the wagon is immobilised through any cause not attributable to the railway or through damage.

2. If a wagon which has been considered lost is recovered after compensation has been paid, the owner may require, within a period of six months from his receipt of notice to that effect from the railway of registration, that the wagon be returned to him free of charge at its home station against refund of the compensation.

Article 14

Compensation for exceeding the transit period

1. If the railway is responsible for exceeding the transit period for an empty or loaded wagon, it must pay the person entitled a sum of money by way of liquidated damages for each complete day, or fraction thereof, of delay, irrespective of any compensation which may be due for exceeding the transit period for goods loaded in the wagon.

Such sum shall be fixed at—

(a) 450 units of account for modern bogie wagons and for similar wagons, as defined in the contract of registration,

(b) 3 units of account for other wagons.

2. If the exceeding of the transit period is due to wilful misconduct or gross negligence on the part of the railway, the liquidated damages shall be at the rate of 9 units of account for the wagons referred to in paragraph 1(a) and at the rate of 650 units of account for the wagons referred to in paragraph 1(b).

3. The consignor of an empty wagon may request a special guarantee of the transit period. A charge of one unit of account per 100 kilometres or fraction thereof shall then be made, subject to a minimum of 10 units of account. The whole amount of such charges shall always be paid by the consignor when the charges are paid under the conditions laid down in Article 15(2)(a)(iv) of the Uniform Rules.

If the transit period is exceeded, the railway shall pay by way of liquidated damages the sum of 9 units of account per day for the wagons referred to in paragraph 1(a) and the sum of 650 units of account per day for the wagons referred to in paragraph 1(b), subject to a minimum of 20 units of account.

[4377]

ANNEX III
(ARTICLE 8, § 2)

REGULATIONS CONCERNING THE INTERNATIONAL CARRIAGE OF CONTAINERS BY RAIL (RICO)

The text of this Annex shall be that drawn up by the Committee of Experts, in accordance with Article 69, § 4 of the International Convention concerning the Carriage of Goods by Rail

(CIM) of 7 February 1970, for the International Regulations concerning the Carriage of Containers (RICo), Annex V to the CIM. The Committee of Experts shall also edit the text to bring it into line with the Convention concerning the International Carriage of Goods by Rail of 9 May 1980.

The text of this Annex is so drawn up as follows—

CHAPTER I
GENERAL PROVISIONS

Article 1

Purpose of the regulations

1. These regulations shall apply to containers which are tendered for carriage under the conditions of the CIM Uniform Rules.

These containers shall belong to a railway or to private owners (whether physical persons or other subjects of law) and, in the latter case, shall either be approved by the railway or shall comply with the international standards of construction applicable to large containers.

2. For the purpose of these regulations, the term "container" shall mean an article of transport equipment (container, tank, or other similar structure)

— of a permanent character and accordingly strong enough to be suitable for repeated use,
— specially designed to facilitate the carriage of goods, by one or more modes of transport, without the need for the contents to be trans-shipped,
— fitted with devices to facilitate ready handling and securing,
— having an internal volume of not less than one cubic metre and of a size not exceeding the dimensions prescribed by the railway.

The term "large containers" means containers with an internal volume of more than 3 cubic metres and a length of 6 metres (20 feet) and over.

The term "container" shall include the accessories and equipment of the container, appropriate for the type concerned, provided that such accessories are carried with the container. It shall not cover vehicles, accessories and equipment of vehicles, or conventional packaging.

Article 2

General provisions

1. Except as otherwise provided in the tariffs, the contents of a container can be the subject of only one contract of carriage.

2. In the absence of special provisions in these regulations, the other provisions of the Uniform Rules shall apply to the carriage of containers whether empty or loaded.

Article 3

Door-to-door carriage

In the case of containers to be collected by the railway at the consignor's premises, the contract of carriage shall be deemed to be made at the consignor's premises. In the case of containers to be delivered to the consignee's premises, the contract of carriage shall be deemed to be terminated at the consignee's premises.

CHAPTER II
RAILWAY-OWNED CONTAINERS

Article 4

Provision, return and charges

A charge may be made for the use of containers and the amount of such charge shall be fixed by the tariffs. Furthermore, the tariffs shall determine the conditions under which the containers will be made available, the period within which they are to be returned and the charges which shall be made for exceeding this period.

Article 5

Particulars in the consignment note

In addition to the particulars required by the Uniform Rules, the consignor shall enter in the consignment note, in the spaces provided for this purpose, the category of the container, its marks, its number, its tare in kilogrammes and, where appropriate, other characteristics of its structure.

The tare of containers shall not include the mass of special internal and removable fittings which are for the purpose of packing or securing.

Article 6

Handling and cleaning

The tariffs shall determine the conditions under which the operations of loading and unloading are carried out. "Loading" includes placing the container on a wagon and operations ancillary thereto, in particular the securing of the container.

The consignee shall be responsible for returning the container in a perfectly clean condition. If this has not been done, the railway shall be entitled to make a charge of which the amount shall be fixed by the tariffs.

Article 7

Re-use

Containers delivered loaded shall not be reused by consignees on further loads except with the consent of the railway which has so delivered them.

Article 8

Loss of and damage to containers

1. Any person accepting a container, empty or loaded, from the railway shall check the condition of the container at the time it is placed at his disposal; he shall be liable for all damage found to exist on return of the container to the railway which was not indicated when the container was put at his disposal, unless he proves that the damage existed at that time or resulted from circumstances which he could not avoid, and the consequences of which he was unable to prevent.

2. The consignor shall be liable for the loss of or damage to a container arising during the performance of the contract of carriage if it results from his actions or from those of persons acting on his behalf.

3. If the container is not returned within thirty days from the day following the day on which it was delivered to the consignor or consignee, the railway may deem it to be lost and demand payment of its value.

CHAPTER III
PRIVATELY-OWNED CONTAINERS

Article 9

Approval

Privately-owned containers may be approved by a railway to whose lines the Uniform Rules apply, if they comply with the conditions laid down for construction and marking. Approved containers, other than large containers, shall be provided by the railway with the distinguishing mark [P].

Article 10

Particulars in the consignment note

In addition to the particulars required by the Uniform Rules, the consignor shall enter in the consignment note, in the spaces provided for this purpose, the following particulars:

the category of the container, its number, its tare in kilogrammes, and, where appropriate, other characteristics of the container,

in the case of approved containers, the mark of the railway system which has issued the approval, and, except for large containers, the letter "P",
in the case of empty containers, as a description of goods, either the words "empty container" or the words "empty large container".

Article 11

"Cash on delivery" charges

Empty containers shall not be subject to "cash on delivery" charges.

Article 12

Special equipment

If containers are equipped with special apparatus (refrigerating equipment, water tanks, machinery, etc), the consignor shall be responsible for the servicing of such equipment or for arranging for it to be serviced. This duty shall pass to the consignee as soon as he exercises his rights under Article 28 or 31 of the Uniform Rules.

Article 13

Return of empty containers or re-use

After the delivery of the container, and in the absence of special arrangements, the railway shall not be bound to take any action to secure the return of the empty container or its re-use as a loaded container.

Article 14

Compensation for loss of or damage to the container

Compensation payable in accordance with Article 40 of the Uniform Rules for the loss of the container shall be calculated according to the value of the container.

Compensation payable in accordance with Article 42 of the Uniform Rules for damage to the container shall be calculated according to the cost of repair.

Article 15

Compensation for exceeding the transit period

If the transit period is exceeded, the railway may, apart from the provisions of the Uniform Rules, provide for the payment of special compensation to the owner or the hirer of the container by special agreement with him.

[4378]

ANNEX IV
(ARTICLE 8, § 3)

REGULATIONS CONCERNING THE INTERNATIONAL CARRIAGE OF EXPRESS PARCELS BY RAIL (RIEX)

§ 1. Only such goods as are carried in a specially rapid manner subject to the conditions of an international tariff shall be deemed to be express parcels.

The only goods acceptable as express parcels shall be those which can ordinarily be loaded into the luggage vans of passenger trains. The international tariffs may derogate from this rule.

§ 2. The articles referred to in Article 4 of the Uniform Rules shall not be accepted for carriage as express parcels. The substances and articles enumerated in the RID or those covered by agreements and tariff clauses drawn up in pursuance of Article 5, § 2 of the Uniform Rules shall not be accepted for carriage as express parcels unless that form of carriage is expressly provided for in the RID or such agreements or tariff clauses. The international tariffs shall determine whether other goods may also be treated as unacceptable for carriage or accepted subject to conditions.

§ 3. Express parcels may be handed over for carriage under cover of a document other than that prescribed in accordance with Article 12, § 2 of the Uniform Rules. The form to be used, and the particulars which must or may be inserted therein, shall be determined by the international tariffs. The document must contain the following information—

(a) the names of the forwarding and destination stations;
(b) the names and addresses of the consignor and of the consignee;
(c) the description of the goods;
(d) the number of parcels and a description of the packing;
(e) a detailed list of the documents required by Customs or other administrative authorities and attached to the consignment note.

§ 4. Express parcels shall be carried by rapid means within the periods prescribed in the international tariffs. The transit periods shall in all cases be less than the periods applicable by virtue of Article 27 of the Uniform Rules.

§ 5. The international tariffs may also provide for derogations from the Uniform Rules other than those specified above. There shall however be no derogation from Articles 35–38, 40–42, 44 and 47–58 of the Uniform Rules.

§ 6. Unless the above provisions and those of the international tariffs require otherwise, the Uniform Rules shall be applicable to the carriage of express parcels.

[4379]

SUPPLEMENTARY PROVISIONS* INTERPRETING THE UNIFORM RULES CONCERNING THE CONTRACT FOR INTERNATIONAL CARRIAGE OF GOODS BY RAIL (CIM), APPENDIX B TO COTIF, WHERE THE MANAGEMENT OF THE RAILWAY INFRASTRUCTURE IS SEPARATE FROM THE PROVISION OF THE TRANSPORT SERVICES BY THE RAILWAY UNDERTAKINGS

Whereas the Convention concerning international carriage by rail (COTIF) of 9 May 1980 is based on the principle that the railways are both managers of their infrastructure and providers of rail transport services, but that certain States are engaged in a process of separating these two activities,

Whereas the uniformity of the law achieved by COTIF constitutes an important element of legal certainty both for the users and for the carriers which facilitates international through carriage by rail in Europe and beyond,

Whereas it is, therefore, desireable that international carriage by rail should continue to be subject to COTIF,

Whereas COTIF does not presuppose that more than one railway undertaking carries out an operation of international carriage by rail as the contractual partner of the customer,

Conscious, however, that in such cases certain provisions of CIM can be redundant to the extent that they assume that several railways participate successively as carriers in the execution of an operation of international carriage by rail under a single contract,

Conscious that a revision of COTIF is necessary and urgent but that it requires considerable work, the representatives of the Member States of OTIF met from 22 to 26 November 1993 in Berne and prepared, by virtue of Article 9 of CIM, the following supplementary provisions and recommend to the Member States that they should come into force on 1 January 1995—

1. When rail lines are included in accordance with Article 2 § 1 of COTIF, it is sufficient that the organisation which manages the infrastructure should be included in the list of CIV lines.

2. There is only "operation" in the sense of Article 2 §§ 1 and 2 of CIM when "the railway" in question is at the same time the manager of the infrastructure and the provider of the rail carriage services.

3. With the exception of Articles 2 and 4, letter (c) of CIM, the term "railway" is considered to mean the provider of the rail carriage services on the CIV lines. In Article 4, letter (c) of CIM the idea of "railways to be used" also includes the managers of the infrastructure.

4. Articles 18, 19 § 4, 20 § 3 and 25 § 3 of CIM regulate the responsibility of the consignor only between the parties to the contract of carriage.

5. Where only one undertaking carries out an international rail carriage operation, the authorisations granted by CIM to adopt derogating regulations, either in the tariffs, or by

agreement, should be understood to mean the provider of rail carriage services can enter into corresponding contractual agreements, in particular under Articles 27, 30 and 31 of CIM.

6. The term "registering railway" in RIP means the body which has registered wagons intended to be used in international traffic, in accordance with the provisions in force.

7. The term "railway which certifies" in RICo is understood to mean the body which has approved containers intended to be used in international traffic, in accordance with the provisions in force.

8. These supplementary provisions shall come into force and be published in accordance with the laws and regulations of each Member State. The supplementary provisions and their coming into force shall be communicated to the Central Office which shall advise all the other Member States of them immediately. **[4380]**

NOTES

* The Supplementary Provisions were adopted by an ad-hoc committee of OTIF Member States (including United Kingdom) which met from 22–26 November 1993.

CONVENTION FOR THE UNIFICATION OF CERTAIN RULES FOR INTERNATIONAL CARRIAGE BY AIR

(1999)

NOTES

The text of the following Convention appears as set out in the Carriage by Air Act 1961, Sch 1B.

THE STATES PARTIES TO THIS CONVENTION

RECOGNIZING the significant contribution of the Convention for the Unification of Certain Rules Relating to International Carriage by Air signed in Warsaw on 12th October 1929, hereinafter referred to as the "Warsaw Convention", and other related instruments to the harmonization of private international air law;

RECOGNIZING the need to modernize and consolidate the Warsaw Convention and related instruments;

RECOGNIZING the importance of ensuring protection of the interests of consumers in international carriage by air and the need for equitable compensation based on the principle of restitution;

REAFFIRMING the desirability of an orderly development of international air transport operations and the smooth flow of passengers, baggage and cargo in accordance with the principles and objectives of the Convention on International Civil Aviation, done at Chicago on 7 December 1944;

CONVINCED that collective State action for further harmonization and codification of certain rules governing international carriage by air through a new Convention is the most adequate means of achieving an equitable balance of interests;

HAVE AGREED AS FOLLOWS:

CHAPTER I
GENERAL PROVISIONS

Article 1

Scope of Application

1. This Convention applies to all international carriage of persons, baggage or cargo performed by aircraft for reward. It applies equally to gratuitous carriage by aircraft performed by an air transport undertaking.

2. For the purposes of this Convention, the expression international carriage means any carriage in which, according to the agreement between the parties, the place of departure and the place of destination, whether or not there be a break in the carriage or a transhipment, are

situated either within the territories of two States Parties, or within the territory of a single State Party if there is an agreed stopping place within the territory of another State, even if that State is not a State Party. Carriage between two points within the territory of a single State Party without an agreed stopping place within the territory of another State is not international carriage for the purposes of this Convention.

3. Carriage to be performed by several successive carriers is deemed, for the purposes of this Convention, to be one undivided carriage if it has been regarded by the parties as a single operation, whether it had been agreed upon under the form of a single contract or of a series of contracts, and it does not lose its international character merely because one contract or a series of contracts is to be performed entirely within the territory of the same State.

4. This Convention applies also to carriage as set out in Chapter V, subject to the terms contained therein.

Article 2

Carriage Performed by State and Carriage of Postal Items

1. This Convention applies to carriage performed by the State or by legally constituted public bodies provided it falls within the conditions laid down in Article 1.

2. In the carriage of postal items, the carrier shall be liable only to the relevant postal administration in accordance with the rules applicable to the relationship between the carriers and the postal administrations.

3. Except as provided in paragraph 2 of this Article, the provisions of this Convention shall not apply to the carriage of postal items.

CHAPTER II
DOCUMENTATION AND DUTIES OF THE PARTIES RELATING TO THE CARRIAGE OF PASSENGERS, BAGGAGE AND CARGO

Article 3

Passengers and Baggage

1. In respect of carriage of passengers, an individual or collective document of carriage shall be delivered containing:
   (a) an indication of the places of departure and destination;
   (b) if the places of departure and destination are within the territory of a single State Party, one or more agreed stopping places being within the territory of another State, an indication of at least one such stopping place.

2. Any other means which preserves the information indicated in paragraph 1 may be substituted for the delivery of the document referred to in that paragraph. If any such other means is used, the carrier shall offer to deliver to the passenger a written statement of the information so preserved.

3. The carrier shall deliver to the passenger a baggage identification tag for each piece of checked baggage.

4. The passenger shall be given written notice to the effect that where this Convention is applicable it governs and may limit the liability of carriers in respect of death or injury and for destruction or loss of, or damage to, baggage, and for delay.

5. Non-compliance with the provisions of the foregoing paragraphs shall not affect the existence or the validity of the contract of carriage, which shall, nonetheless, be subject to the rules of this Convention including those relating to limitation of liability.

Article 4

Cargo

1. In respect of the carriage of cargo, an air waybill shall be delivered.

2. Any other means which preserves a record of the carriage to be performed may be substituted for the delivery of an air waybill. If such other means are used, the carrier shall, if so requested by the consignor, deliver to the consignor a cargo receipt permitting identification of the consignment and access to the information contained in the record preserved by such other means.

Article 5

Contents of Air Waybill or Cargo Receipt

The air waybill or the cargo receipt shall include:

(a) an indication of the places of departure and destination;

(b) if the places of departure and destination are within the territory of a single State Party, one or more agreed stopping places being within the territory of another State, an indication of at least one such stopping place; and

(c) an indication of the weight of the consignment.

Article 6

Document Relating to the Nature of the Cargo

The consignor may be required, if necessary to meet the formalities of customs, police and similar public authorities, to deliver a document indicating the nature of the cargo. This provision creates for the carrier no duty, obligation or liability resulting therefrom.

Article 7

Description of Air Waybill

1. The air waybill shall be made out by the consignor in three original parts.

2. The first part shall be marked "for the carrier"; it shall be signed by the consignor. The second part shall be marked "for the consignee"; it shall be signed by the consignor and by the carrier. The third part shall be signed by the carrier who shall hand it to the consignor after the cargo has been accepted.

3. The signature of the carrier and that of the consignor may be printed or stamped.

4. If, at the request of the consignor, the carrier makes out the air waybill, the carrier shall be deemed, subject to proof to the contrary, to have done so on behalf of the consignor.

Article 8

Documentation for Multiple Packages

When there is more than one package:

(a) the carrier of cargo has the right to require the consignor to make out separate air waybills;

(b) the consignor has the right to require the carrier to deliver separate cargo receipts when the other means referred to in paragraph 2 of Article 4 are used.

Article 9

Non-compliance with Documentary Requirements

Non-compliance with the provisions of Articles 4 to 8 shall not affect the existence or the validity of the contract of carriage, which shall, nonetheless, be subject to the rules of this Convention including those relating to limitation of liability.

Article 10

Responsibility for Particulars of Documentation

1. The consignor is responsible for the correctness of the particulars and statements relating to the cargo inserted by it or on its behalf in the air waybill or furnished by it or on its behalf to the carrier for insertion in the cargo receipt or for insertion in the record preserved by the other means referred to in paragraph 2 of Article 4. The foregoing shall also apply where the person acting on behalf of the consignor is also the agent of the carrier.

2. The consignor shall indemnify the carrier against all damage suffered by it, or by any other person to whom the carrier is liable, by reason of the irregularity, incorrectness or incompleteness of the particulars and statements furnished by the consignor or on its behalf.

3. Subject to the provisions of paragraphs 1 and 2 of this Article, the carrier shall indemnify the consignor against all damage suffered by it, or by any other person to whom the consignor is liable, by reason of the irregularity, incorrectness or incompleteness of the

particulars and statements inserted by the carrier or on its behalf in the cargo receipt or in the record preserved by the other means referred to in paragraph 2 of Article 4.

Article 11

Evidentiary Value of Documentation

1. The air waybill or the cargo receipt is prima facie evidence of the conclusion of the contract, of the acceptance of the cargo and of the conditions of carriage mentioned therein.

2. Any statements in the air waybill or the cargo receipt relating to the weight, dimensions and packing of the cargo, as well as those relating to the number of packages, are prima facie evidence of the facts stated; those relating to the quantity, volume and condition of the cargo do not constitute evidence against the carrier except so far as they both have been, and are stated in the air waybill or the cargo receipt to have been, checked by it in the presence of the consignor, or relate to the apparent condition of the cargo.

Article 12

Right of Disposition of Cargo

1. Subject to its liability to carry out all its obligations under the contract of carriage, the consignor has the right to dispose of the cargo by withdrawing it at the airport of departure or destination, or by stopping it in the course of the journey on any landing, or by calling for it to be delivered at the place of destination or in the course of the journey to a person other than the consignee originally designated, or by requiring it to be returned to the airport of departure. The consignor must not exercise this right of disposition in such a way as to prejudice the carrier or other consignors and must reimburse any expenses occasioned by the exercise of this right.

2. If it is impossible to carry out the instructions of the consignor, the carrier must so inform the consignor forthwith.

3. If the carrier carries out the instructions of the consignor for the disposition of the cargo without requiring the production of the part of the air waybill or the cargo receipt delivered to the latter, the carrier will be liable, without prejudice to its right of recovery from the consignor, for any damage which may be caused thereby to any person who is lawfully in possession of that part of the air waybill or the cargo receipt.

4. The right conferred on the consignor ceases at the moment when that of the consignee begins in accordance with Article 13. Nevertheless, if the consignee declines to accept the cargo, or cannot be communicated with, the consignor resumes its right of disposition.

Article 13

Delivery of the Cargo

1. Except when the consignor has exercised its right under Article 12, the consignee is entitled, on arrival of the cargo at the place of destination, to require the carrier to deliver the cargo to it, on payment of the charges due and on complying with the conditions of carriage.

2. Unless it is otherwise agreed, it is the duty of the carrier to give notice to the consignee as soon as the cargo arrives.

3. If the carrier admits the loss of the cargo, or if the cargo has not arrived at the expiration of seven days after the date on which it ought to have arrived, the consignee is entitled to enforce against the carrier the rights which flow from the contract of carriage.

Article 14

Enforcement of the Rights of Consignor and Consignee

The consignor and the consignee can respectively enforce all the rights given to them by Articles 12 and 13, each in its own name, whether it is acting in its own interest or in the interest of another, provided that it carries out the obligations imposed by the contract of carriage.

Articles 15

Relations of Consignor and Consignee or Mutual Relations of Third Parties

1. Articles 12, 13 and 14 do not affect either the relations of the consignor and the consignee with each other or the mutual relations of third parties whose rights are derived either from the consignor or from the consignee.

2. The provisions of Articles 12, 13 and 14 can only be varied by express provision in the air waybill or the cargo receipt.

Article 16

Formalities of Customs, Police or Other Public Authorities

1. The consignor must furnish such information and such documents as are necessary to meet the formalities of customs, police and any other public authorities before the cargo can be delivered to the consignee. The consignor is liable to the carrier for any damage occasioned by the absence, insufficiency or irregularity of any such information or documents, unless the damage is due to the fault of the carrier, its servants or agents.

2. The carrier is under no obligation to enquire into the correctness or sufficiency of such information or documents.

CHAPTER III
LIABILITY OF THE CARRIER AND EXTENT OF COMPENSATION FOR DAMAGE

Article 17

Death and Injury of Passengers—Damage to Baggage

1. The carrier is liable for damage sustained in case of death or bodily injury of a passenger upon condition only that the accident which caused the death or injury took place on board the aircraft or in the course of any of the operations of embarking or disembarking.

2. The carrier is liable for damage sustained in case of destruction or loss of, or of damage to, checked baggage upon condition only that the event which caused the destruction, loss or damage took place on board the aircraft or during any period within which the checked baggage was in the charge of the carrier. However, the carrier is not liable if and to the extent that the damage resulted from the inherent defect, quality or vice of the baggage. In the case of unchecked baggage, including personal items, the carrier is liable if the damage resulted from its fault or that of its servants or agents.

3. If the carrier admits the loss of the checked baggage, or if the checked baggage has not arrived at the expiration of twenty-one days after the date on which it ought to have arrived, the passenger is entitled to enforce against the carrier the rights which flow from the contract of carriage.

4. Unless otherwise specified, in this Convention the term "baggage" means both checked baggage and unchecked baggage.

Article 18

Damage to Cargo

1. The carrier is liable for damage sustained in the event of the destruction or loss of, or damage to, cargo upon condition only that the event which caused the damage so sustained took place during the carriage by air.

2. However, the carrier is not liable if and to the extent it proves that the destruction, or loss of, or damage to, the cargo resulted from one or more of the following:

(a) inherent defect, quality or vice of that cargo;

(b) defective packing of that cargo performed by a person other than the carrier or its servants or agents;

(c) an act of war or an armed conflict;

(d) an act of public authority carried out in connection with the entry, exit or transit of the cargo.

3. The carriage by air within the meaning of paragraph 1 of this Article comprises the period during which the cargo is in the charge of the carrier.

4. The period of the carriage by air does not extend to any carriage by land, by sea or by inland waterway performed outside an airport. If, however, such carriage takes place in the performance of a contract for carriage by air, for the purpose of loading, delivery or transhipment, any damage is presumed, subject to proof to the contrary, to have been the result of an event which took place during the carriage by air. If a carrier, without the consent of the consignor, substitutes carriage by another mode of transport for the whole or part of a

carriage intended by the agreement between the parties to be carriage by air, such carriage by another mode of transport is deemed to be within the period of carriage by air.

Article 19

Delay

The carrier is liable for damage occasioned by delay in the carriage by air of passengers, baggage or cargo. Nevertheless, the carrier shall not be liable for damage occasioned by delay if it proves that it and its servants and agents took all measures that could reasonably be required to avoid the damage or that it was impossible for it or them to take such measures.

Article 20

Exoneration

If the carrier proves that the damage was caused or contributed to by the negligence or other wrongful act or omission of the person claiming compensation, or the person from whom he or she derives his or her rights, the carrier shall be wholly or partly exonerated from its liability to the claimant to the extent that such negligence or wrongful act or omission caused or contributed to the damage. When by reason of death or injury of a passenger compensation is claimed by a person other than the passenger, the carrier shall likewise be wholly or partly exonerated from its liability to the extent that it proves that the damage was caused or contributed to by the negligence or other wrongful act or omission of that passenger. This Article applies to all the liability provisions in this Convention, including paragraph 1 of Article 21.

Article 21

Compensation in Case of Death or Injury of Passengers

1. For damages arising under paragraph 1 of Article 17 not exceeding 100,000 Special Drawing Rights for each passenger, the carrier shall not be able to exclude or limit its liability.

2. The carrier shall not be liable for damages arising under paragraph 1 of Article 17 to the extent that they exceed for each passenger 100,000 Special Drawing Rights if the carrier proves that:

(a) such damage was not due to the negligence or other wrongful act or omission of the carrier or its servants or agents; or

(b) such damage was solely due to the negligence or other wrongful act or omission of a third party.

Article 22

Limits of Liability in Relation to Delay, Baggage and Cargo

1. In the case of damage caused by delay as specified in Article 19 in the carriage of persons, the liability of the carrier for each passenger is limited to 4,150 Special Drawing Rights.

2. In the carriage of baggage, the liability of the carrier in the case of destruction, loss, damage or delay is limited to 1,000 Special Drawing Rights for each passenger unless the passenger has made, at the time when the checked baggage was handed over to the carrier, a special declaration of interest in delivery at destination and has paid a supplementary sum if the case so requires. In that case the carrier will be liable to pay a sum not exceeding the declared sum, unless it proves that the sum is greater than the passenger's actual interest in delivery at destination.

3. In the carriage of cargo, the liability of the carrier in the case of destruction, loss, damage or delay is limited to a sum of 17 Special Drawing Rights per kilogramme, unless the consignor has made, at the time when the package was handed over to the carrier, a special declaration of interest in delivery at destination and has paid a supplementary sum if the case so requires. In that case the carrier will be liable to pay a sum not exceeding the declared sum, unless it proves that the sum is greater than the consignor's actual interest in delivery at destination.

4. In the case of destruction, loss, damage or delay of part of the cargo, or of any object contained therein, the weight to be taken into consideration in determining the amount to which the carrier's liability is limited shall be only the total weight of the package or packages

concerned. Nevertheless, when the destruction, loss, damage or delay of a part of the cargo, or of an object contained therein, affects the value of other packages covered by the same air waybill, or the same receipt or, if they were not issued, by the same record preserved by the other means referred to in paragraph 2 of Article 4, the total weight of such package or packages shall also be taken into consideration in determining the limit of liability.

5. The foregoing provisions of paragraphs 1 and 2 of this Article shall not apply if it is proved that the damage resulted from an act or omission of the carrier, its servants or agents, done with intent to cause damage or recklessly and with knowledge that damage would probably result; provided that, in the case of such act or omission of a servant or agent, it is also proved that such servant or agent was acting within the scope of its employment.

6. The limits prescribed in Article 21 and in this Article shall not prevent the court from awarding, in accordance with its own law, in addition, the whole or part of the court costs and of the other expenses of the litigation incurred by the plaintiff, including interest. The foregoing provision shall not apply if the amount of the damages awarded, excluding court costs and other expenses of the litigation, does not exceed the sum which the carrier has offered in writing to the plaintiff within a period of six months from the date of the occurrence causing the damage, or before the commencement of the action, if that is later.

Article 23

Conversion of Monetary Units

1. The sums mentioned in terms of Special Drawing Right in this Convention shall be deemed to refer to the Special Drawing Right as defined by the International Monetary Fund. Conversion of the sums into national currencies shall, in case of judicial proceedings, be made according to the value of such currencies in terms of the Special Drawing Right at the date of the judgement. The value of a national currency, in terms of the Special Drawing Right, of a State Party which is a Member of the International Monetary Fund, shall be calculated in accordance with the method of valuation applied by the International Monetary Fund, in effect at the date of the judgement, for its operations and transactions. The value of a national currency, in terms of the Special Drawing Right, of a State Party which is not a Member of the International Monetary Fund, shall be calculated in a manner determined by that State.

2. Nevertheless, those States which are not Members of the International Monetary Fund and whose law does not permit the application of the provisions of paragraph 1 of this Article may, at the time of ratification or accession or at any time thereafter, declare that the limit of liability of the carrier prescribed in Article 21 is fixed at a sum of 1,500,000 monetary units per passenger in judicial proceedings in their territories; 62,500 monetary units per passenger with respect to paragraph 1 of Article 22; 15,000 monetary units per passenger with respect to paragraph 2 of Article 22; and 250 monetary units per kilogramme with respect to paragraph 3 of Article 22. This monetary unit corresponds to sixty-five and a half milligrammes of gold of millesimal fineness nine hundred. These sums may be converted into the national currency concerned in round figures. The conversion of these sums into national currency shall be made according to the law of the State concerned.

3. The calculation mentioned in the last sentence of paragraph 1 of this Article and the conversion method mentioned in paragraph 2 of this Article shall be made in such manner as to express in the national currency of the State Party as far as possible the same real value for the amounts in Articles 21 and 22 as would result from the application of the first three sentences of paragraph 1 of this Article. States Parties shall communicate to the depositary the manner of calculation pursuant to paragraph 1 of this Article, or the result of the conversion in paragraph 2 of this Article as the case may be, when depositing an instrument of ratification, acceptance, approval of or accession to this Convention and whenever there is a change in either.

Article 24

Review of Limits

1. Without prejudice to the provisions of Article 25 of this Convention and subject to paragraph 2 below, the limits of liability prescribed in Articles 21, 22 and 23 shall be reviewed by the Depositary at five-year intervals, the first such review to take place at the end of the fifth year following the date of entry into force of this Convention, or if the Convention does not enter into force within five years of the date it is first open for signature, within the first year of its entry into force, by reference to an inflation factor which corresponds to the accumulated rate of inflation since the previous revision or in the first instance since the date

of entry into force of the Convention. The measure of the rate of inflation to be used in determining the inflation factor shall be the weighted average of the annual rates of increase or decrease in the Consumer Price Indices of the States whose currencies comprise the Special Drawing Right mentioned in paragraph 1 of Article 23.

2. If the review referred to in the preceding paragraph concludes that the inflation factor has exceeded 10 per cent, the Depositary shall notify States Parties of a revision of the limits of liability. Any such revision shall become effective six months after its notification to the States Parties. If within three months after its notification to the States Parties a majority of the States Parties register their disapproval, the revision shall not become effective and the Depositary shall refer the matter to a meeting of the States Parties. The Depositary shall immediately notify all States Parties of the coming into force of any revision.

3. Notwithstanding paragraph 1 of this Article, the procedure referred to in paragraph 2 of this Article shall be applied at any time provided that one-third of the States Parties express a desire to that effect and upon condition that the inflation factor referred to in paragraph 1 has exceeded 30 per cent since the previous revision or since the date of entry into force of this Convention if there has been no previous revision. Subsequent reviews using the procedure described in paragraph 1 of this Article will take place at five-year intervals starting at the end of the fifth year following the date of the reviews under the present paragraph.

Article 25

Stipulation on Limits

A carrier may stipulate that the contract of carriage shall be subject to higher limits of liability than those provided for in this Convention or to no limits of liability whatsoever.

Article 26

Invalidity of Contractual Provisions

Any provision tending to relieve the carrier of liability or to fix a lower limit than that which is laid down in this Convention shall be null and void, but the nullity of any such provision does not involve the nullity of the whole contract, which shall remain subject to the provisions of this Convention.

Article 27

Freedom to Contract

Nothing contained in this Convention shall prevent the carrier from refusing to enter into any contract of carriage, from waiving any defences available under the Convention, or from laying down conditions which do not conflict with the provisions of this Convention.

Article 28

Advance Payments

In the case of aircraft accidents resulting in death or injury of passengers, the carrier shall, if required by its national law, make advance payments without delay to a natural person or persons who are entitled to claim compensation in order to meet the immediate economic needs of such persons. Such advance payments shall not constitute a recognition of liability and may be offset against any amounts subsequently paid as damages by the carrier.

Article 29

Basis of Claims

In the carriage of passengers, baggage and cargo, any action for damages, however founded, whether under this Convention or in contract or in tort or otherwise, can only be brought subject to the conditions and such limits of liability as are set out in this Convention without prejudice to the question as to who are the persons who have the right to bring suit and what are their respective rights. In any such action, punitive, exemplary or any other non-compensatory damages shall not be recoverable.

Article 30

Servants, Agents—Aggregation of Claims

1. If an action is brought against a servant or agent of the carrier arising out of damage to which the Convention relates, such servant or agent, if they prove that they acted within the

scope of their employment, shall be entitled to avail themselves of the conditions and limits of liability which the carrier itself is entitled to invoke under this Convention.

2. The aggregate of the amounts recoverable from the carrier, its servants and agents, in that case, shall not exceed the said limits.

3. Save in respect of the carriage of cargo, the provisions of paragraphs 1 and 2 of this Article shall not apply if it is proved that the damage resulted from an act or omission of the servant or agent done with intent to cause damage or recklessly and with knowledge that damage would probably result.

Article 31

Timely Notice of Complaints

1. Receipt by the person entitled to delivery of checked baggage or cargo without complaint is prima facie evidence that the same has been delivered in good condition and in accordance with the document of carriage or with the record preserved by the other means referred to in paragraph 2 of Article 3 and paragraph 2 of Article 4.

2. In the case of damage, the person entitled to delivery must complain to the carrier forthwith after the discovery of the damage, and, at the latest, within seven days from the date of receipt in the case of checked baggage and fourteen days from the date of receipt in the case of cargo. In the case of delay, the complaint must be made at the latest within twenty-one days from the date on which the baggage or cargo have been placed at his or her disposal.

3. Every complaint must be made in writing and given or dispatched within the times aforesaid.

4. If no complaint is made within the times aforesaid, no action shall lie against the carrier, save in the case of fraud on its part.

Article 32

Death of Person Liable

In the case of the death of the person liable, an action for damages lies in accordance with the terms of this Convention against those legally representing his or her estate.

Article 33

Jurisdiction

1. An action for damages must be brought, at the option of the plaintiff, in the territory of one of the States Parties, either before the court of the domicile of the carrier or of its principal place of business, or where it has a place of business through which the contract has been made or before the court at the place of destination.

2. In respect of damage resulting from the death or injury of a passenger, an action may be brought before one of the courts mentioned in paragraph 1 of this Article, or in the territory of a State Party in which at the time of the accident the passenger has his or her principal and permanent residence and to or from which the carrier operates services for the carriage of passengers by air, either on its own aircraft, or on another carrier's aircraft pursuant to a commercial agreement, and in which that carrier conducts its business of carriage of passengers by air from premises leased or owned by the carrier itself or by another carrier with which it has a commercial agreement.

3. For the purposes of paragraph 2,

(a) "commercial agreement" means an agreement, other than an agency agreement, made between carriers and relating to the provision of their joint services for carriage of passengers by air;

(b) "principal and permanent residence" means the one fixed and permanent abode of the passenger at the time of the accident. The nationality of the passenger shall not be the determining factor in this regard.

4. Questions of procedure shall be governed by the law of the court seised of the case.

Article 34

Arbitration

1. Subject to the provisions of this Article, the parties to the contract of carriage for cargo may stipulate that any dispute relating to the liability of the carrier under this Convention shall be settled by arbitration. Such agreement shall be in writing.

2. The arbitration proceedings shall, at the option of the claimant, take place within one of the jurisdictions referred to in Article 33.

3. The arbitrator or arbitration tribunal shall apply the provisions of this Convention.

4. The provisions of paragraphs 2 and 3 of this Article shall be deemed to be part of every arbitration clause or agreement, and any term of such clause or agreement which is inconsistent therewith shall be null and void.

Article 35

Limitation of Actions

1. The right to damages shall be extinguished if an action is not brought within a period of two years, reckoned from the date of arrival at the destination, or from the date on which the aircraft ought to have arrived, or from the date on which the carriage stopped.

2. The method of calculating that period shall be determined by the law of the court seised of the case.

Article 36

Successive Carriage

1. In the case of carriage to be performed by various successive carriers and falling within the definition set out in paragraph 3 of Article 1, each carrier which accepts passengers, baggage or cargo is subject to the rules set out in this Convention and is deemed to be one of the parties to the contract of carriage in so far as the contract deals with that part of the carriage which is performed under its supervision.

2. In the case of carriage of this nature, the passenger or any person entitled to compensation in respect of him or her can take action only against the carrier which performed the carriage during which the accident or the delay occurred, save in the case where, by express agreement, the first carrier has assumed liability for the whole journey.

3. As regards baggage or cargo, the passenger or consignor will have a right of action against the first carrier, and the passenger or consignee who is entitled to delivery will have a right of action against the last carrier, and further, each may take action against the carrier which performed the carriage during which the destruction, loss, damage or delay took place. These carriers will be jointly and severally liable to the passenger or to the consignor or consignee.

Article 37

Right of Recourse against Third Parties

Nothing in this Convention shall prejudice the question whether a person liable for damage in accordance with its provisions has a right of recourse against any other person.

CHAPTER IV
COMBINED CARRIAGE

Article 38

Combined Carriage

1. In the case of combined carriage performed partly by air and partly by any other mode of carriage, the provisions of this Convention shall, subject to paragraph 4 of Article 18, apply only to the carriage by air, provided that the carriage by air falls within the terms of Article 1.

2. Nothing in this Convention shall prevent the parties in the case of combined carriage from inserting in the document of air carriage conditions relating to other modes of carriage, provided that the provisions of this Convention are observed as regards the carriage by air.

CHAPTER V
CARRIAGE BY AIR PERFORMED BY A PERSON OTHER THAN THE CONTRACTING CARRIER

Article 39

Contracting Carrier—Actual Carrier

The provisions of this Chapter apply when a person (hereinafter referred to as "the contracting carrier") as a principal makes a contract governed by this Convention with a passenger or consignor or with a person acting on behalf of the passenger or consignor, and another person (hereinafter referred to as "the actual carrier") performs, by virtue of authority from the contracting carrier, the whole or part of the carriage, but is not with respect to such part a successive carrier within the meaning of this Convention. Such authority shall be presumed in the absence of proof to the contrary.

Article 40

Respective Liability of Contracting and Actual Carriers

If an actual carrier performs the whole or part of carriage which, according to the contract referred to in Article 39, is governed by this Convention, both the contracting carrier and the actual carrier shall, except as otherwise provided in this Chapter, be subject to the rules of this Convention, the former for the whole of the carriage contemplated in the contract, the latter solely for the carriage which it performs.

Article 41

Mutual Liability

1. The acts and omissions of the actual carrier and of its servants and agents acting within the scope of their employment shall, in relation to the carriage performed by the actual carrier, be deemed to be also those of the contracting carrier.

2. The acts and omissions of the contracting carrier and of its servants and agents acting within the scope of their employment shall, in relation to the carriage performed by the actual carrier, be deemed to be also those of the actual carrier. Nevertheless, no such act or omission shall subject the actual carrier to liability exceeding the amounts referred to in Articles 21, 22, 23 and 24. Any special agreement under which the contracting carrier assumes obligations not imposed by this Convention or any waiver of rights or defences conferred by this Convention or any special declaration of interest in delivery at destination contemplated in Article 22 shall not affect the actual carrier unless agreed to by it.

Article 42

Addressee of Complaints and Instructions

Any complaint to be made or instruction to be given under this Convention to the carrier shall have the same effect whether addressed to the contracting carrier or to the actual carrier. Nevertheless, instructions referred to in Article 12 shall only be effective if addressed to the contracting carrier.

Article 43

Servants and Agents

In relation to the carriage performed by the actual carrier, any servant or agent of that carrier or of the contracting carrier shall, if they prove that they acted within the scope of their employment, be entitled to avail themselves of the conditions and limits of liability which are applicable under this Convention to the carrier whose servant or agent they are, unless it is proved that they acted in a manner that prevents the limits of liability from being invoked in accordance with this Convention.

Article 44

Aggregation of Damages

In relation to the carriage performed by the actual carrier, the aggregate of the amounts recoverable from that carrier and the contracting carrier, and from their servants and agents acting within the scope of their employment, shall not exceed the highest amount which could be awarded against either the contracting carrier or the actual carrier under this Convention, but none of the persons mentioned shall be liable for a sum in excess of the limit applicable to that person.

Article 45

Addressee of Claims

In relation to the carriage performed by the actual carrier, an action for damages may be brought, at the option of the plaintiff, against that carrier or the contracting carrier, or against both together or separately. If the action is brought against only one of those carriers, that carrier shall have the right to require the other carrier to be joined in the proceedings, the procedure and effects being governed by the law of the court seised of the case.

Article 46

Additional Jurisdiction

Any action for damages contemplated in Article 45 must be brought, at the option of the plaintiff, in the territory of one of the States Parties, either before a court in which an action may be brought against the contracting carrier, as provided in Article 33, or before the court having jurisdiction at the place where the actual carrier has its domicile or its principal place of business.

Article 47

Invalidity of Contractual Provisions

Any contractual provision tending to relieve the contracting carrier or the actual carrier of liability under this Chapter or to fix a lower limit than that which is applicable according to this Chapter shall be null and void, but the nullity of any such provision does not involve the nullity of the whole contract, which shall remain subject to the provisions of this Chapter.

Article 48

Mutual Relations of Contracting and Actual Carriers

Except as provided in Article 45, nothing in this Chapter shall affect the rights and obligations of the carriers between themselves, including any right of recourse or indemnification.

CHAPTER VI
OTHER PROVISIONS

Article 49

Mandatory Application

Any clause contained in the contract of carriage and all special agreements entered into before the damage occurred by which the parties purport to infringe the rules laid down by this Convention, whether by deciding the law to be applied, or by altering the rules as to jurisdiction, shall be null and void.

Article 50

Insurance

States Parties shall require their carriers to maintain adequate insurance covering their liability under this Convention. A carrier may be required by the State Party into which it operates to furnish evidence that it maintains adequate insurance covering its liability under this Convention.

Article 51

Carriage Performed in Extraordinary Circumstances

The provisions of Articles 3 to 5, 7 and 8 relating to the documentation of carriage shall not apply in the case of carriage performed in extraordinary circumstances outside the normal scope of a carrier's business.

Article 52

Definition of Days

The expression "days" when used in this Convention means calendar days, not working days.

CHAPTER VII
FINAL CLAUSES

Article 53

Signature, Ratification and Entry into Force

1. …

2. … For the purpose of this Convention, a "Regional Economic Integration Organisation" means any organisation which is constituted by sovereign States of a given region which has competence in respect of certain matters governed by this Convention and has been duly authorized to sign and to ratify, accept, approve or accede to this Convention. A reference to a "State Party" or "States Parties" in this Convention, otherwise than in paragraph 2 of Article 1, paragraph 1(b) of Article 3, paragraph (b) of Article 5, Articles 23, 33, 46 and paragraph (b) of Article 57, applies equally to a Regional Economic Integration Organisation. For the purpose of Article 24, the references to "a majority of the States Parties" and "one-third of the States Parties" shall not apply to a Regional Economic Integration Organisation.

Article 55

Relationship with other Warsaw Convention Instruments

This Convention shall prevail over any rules which apply to international carriage by air:

1. between States Parties to this Convention by virtue of those States commonly being Party to:
   - (a) the Convention for the Unification of Certain Rules Relating to International Carriage by Air Signed at Warsaw on 12 October 1929 (hereinafter called the Warsaw Convention);
   - (b) the Protocol to Amend the Convention for the Unification of Certain Rules Relating to International Carriage by Air Signed at Warsaw on 12 October 1929, Done at The Hague on 28 September 1955 (hereinafter called The Hague Protocol);
   - (c) the Convention, Supplementary to the Warsaw Convention, for the Unification of Certain Rules Relating to International Carriage by Air Performed by a Person Other than the Contracting Carrier, signed at Guadalajara on 18 September 1961 (hereinafter called the Guadalajara Convention);
   - (d) the Protocol to Amend the Convention for the Unification of Certain Rules Relating to International Carriage by Air Signed at Warsaw on 12 October 1929 as Amended by the Protocol Done at The Hague on 28 September 1955 Signed at Guatemala City on 8 March 1971 (hereinafter called the Guatemala City Protocol);
   - (e) Additional Protocol Nos. 1 to 3 and Montreal Protocol No. 4 to amend the Warsaw Convention as amended by The Hague Protocol or the Warsaw Convention as amended by both The Hague Protocol and the Guatemala City Protocol Signed at Montreal on 25 September 1975 (hereinafter called the Montreal Protocols); or

2. within the territory of any single State Party to this Convention by virtue of that State being Party to one or more of the instruments referred to in sub-paragraphs (a) to (e) above.

Article 57

Reservations

No reservation may be made to this Convention except that a State Party may at any time declare by a notification addressed to the Depositary that this Convention shall not apply to:

- (a) international carriage by air performed and operated directly by that State Party for non-commercial purposes in respect to its functions and duties as a sovereign State; and/or
- (b) the carriage of persons, cargo and baggage for its military authorities on aircraft registered in or leased by that State Party, the whole capacity of which has been reserved by or on behalf of such authorities.

[*Paragraphs 53* (*save for part of paragraph* 2), *54 and 56 and the concluding words of the Convention are not reproduced. They deal with signature, ratification, coming into force, denunciation and territorial extent where a State has more than one system of law.*]

[4381]

NOTES

Inserted by the Carriage by Air Acts (Implementation of the Montreal Convention 1999) Order 2002, SI 2002/263, art 2(1), (25), Sch 1.

PROTOCOL OF 3 JUNE 1999 FOR THE MODIFICATION OF THE CONVENTION CONCERNING INTERNATIONAL CARRIAGE BY RAIL (COTIF) OF 9 MAY 1980

(Concluded Vilnius, 3 June 1999)

NOTES

This Protocol is published as Cm 4873.

The original source of this protocol is the Intergovernmental Organisation for International Carriage by Rail (OTIF). See http://www.otif.org.

The Convention concerning International Carriage by Rail of 9 May 1980 (COTIF) is set out at **[4326]**.

In application of Articles 6 and 19 § 2 of the Convention concerning International Carriage by Rail, signed at Berne on 9 May 1980, hereinafter called "COTIF 1980", the fifth General Assembly of the Intergovernmental Organisation for International Carriage by Rail (OTIF) was held at Vilnius from 26 May to 3 June 1999.

— Convinced of the necessity for and usefulness of an intergovernmental organisation which deals so far as possible with all aspects of international carriage by rail at the State level,

— considering that for this purpose, taking account of the application of COTIF 1980 by 39 States in Europe, Asia and Africa as well as by the railway undertakings in those States, OTIF is the most appropriate organisation,

— considering the necessity of developing COTIF 1980, in particular the CIV Uniform Rules and the CIM Uniform Rules, in order to adapt it to the present needs of international carriage by rail,

— considering that safety during the carriage of dangerous goods in international rail traffic demands the transformation of RID into a regime of public law, whose application no longer depends upon the conclusion of a contract of carriage subject to the CIM Uniform Rules,

— considering that the political, economic and juridical changes which have occurred in a large number of Member States since the signing of the Convention on 9 May 1980 should be the motive for establishing and for developing prescriptions which are uniform covering other fields of law which are important for international rail traffic,

— considering that the States should adopt, while taking into account special public interests, more efficacious measures to eliminate the obstacles which persist in the crossing of frontiers in international rail traffic,

— considering that, in the interest of international carriage by rail, it is important to bring up to date the international multilateral conventions and agreements which exist in the railway field and to integrate them, where appropriate, into the Convention,

the General Assembly has decided the following:

Article 1

New version of the Convention

COTIF 1980 shall be modified according to the version appearing in the Annex which forms an integral part of this Protocol.

[4382]

Article 2

Provisional Depositary

§ 1 The functions of the Depositary Government, provided for in Articles 22 to 26 of COTIF 1980, shall be performed by OTIF, as Provisional Depositary, from the opening for signature of this Protocol and until the date of its entry into force.

§ 2 The Provisional Depositary shall inform the Member States

(a) of signatures of this Protocol and of the deposit of instruments of ratification, acceptance, approval or accession,

(b) of the day on which this Protocol enters into force in application of its Article 4, and shall perform the other functions of Depositary such as are set forth in Part VII of the Vienna Convention on the Law of Treaties of 23 May 1969.

[4383]

Article 3

Signature. Ratification. Acceptance. Approval. Accession

§ 1 This Protocol shall remain open for signature by the Member States until 31 December 1999. The signing shall take place at Berne at the office of the Provisional Depositary.

§ 2 In accordance with Article 20 § 1 of COTIF 1980, this Protocol shall be subject to ratification, acceptance or approval. The instruments of ratification, acceptance or approval shall be deposited as soon as possible with the Provisional Depositary.

§ 3 The Member States which have not signed this Protocol within the period provided for in § 1, as well as States of which the application to accede to COTIF 1980 is deemed to have been accepted in accordance with its Article 23 § 2, may accede to this Protocol before its entry into force by depositing an instrument of accession with the Provisional Depositary.

§ 4 The accession of a State to COTIF 1980 in accordance with its Article 23, the application to accede having been made during the period between the opening of this Protocol for signature and its entry into force, shall be considered as an accession to COTIF 1980 as well as to the Convention in its new version which appears in the Annex to this Protocol.

[4384]

Article 4

Entry into force

§ 1 This Protocol shall enter into force on the first day of the third month following that during which the Provisional Depositary will have notified the Member States of the deposit of the instrument by which the conditions of Article 20 § 2 of COTIF 1980 are fulfilled. States which, at the time of the decision of the fifth General Assembly, were Member States and which are still such at the moment when the conditions for entry into force of this Protocol are satisfied, shall be considered as Member States within the meaning of the said Article 20 § 2.

§ 2 However, Article 3 shall be applicable from the opening for signature of this Protocol.

[4385]

Article 5

Declarations and reservations

Declarations and reservations, provided for in article 42 § 1 of the Convention in the version in the Annex to this Protocol, may be made or lodged at any time, even before the entry into force of this Protocol. They shall take effect at the time of entry into force of this Protocol.

[4386]

Article 6

Transitional provisions

§ 1 At the latest six months after the entry into force of this Protocol, the Secretary General of OTIF shall convene the General Assembly in order to

(a) designate the members of the Administrative Committee for the next period (Article 14 § 2, letter (b) of COTIF in the version in the Annex to this Protocol) and, if appropriate, to take decisions about the end of the mandate of the current Administrative Committee,

(b) fix, for a period of six years, the maximum amount that the expenditure of the Organisation may reach during each financial period (Article 14 § 2, letter (e) of COTIF in the version in the Annex to this Protocol), and

(c) proceed, if appropriate, to the election of the Secretary General (Article 14 § 2, letter (c) of COTIF in the version in the Annex to this Protocol).

§ 2 At the latest three months after the entry into force of this Protocol, the Secretary General of OTIF shall convene the Committee of Technical Experts.

§ 3 After the entry into force of this Protocol, the mandate of the Administrative Committee, determined in accordance with Article 6 § 2, letter (b) of COTIF 1980, shall terminate on the date fixed by the General Assembly which must coincide with the beginning of the mandate of the members and deputy members of the Administrative Committee designated by the General Assembly (Article 14 § 2, letter (b) of COTIF in the version in the Annex to this Protocol).

§ 4 The mandate of the Director General of the Central Office, in office at the time of entry into force of this Protocol, shall terminate on the expiration of the period for which he has been appointed in accordance with Article 7 § 2, letter (d) of COTIF 1980. He shall exercise, from the time of entry into force of this Protocol, the functions of Secretary General.

§ 5 Even after the entry into force of this Protocol, the relevant provisions of Articles 6, 7 and 11 of COTIF 1980 shall remain applicable with regard to

(a) the auditing of the accounts and the approval of the annual accounts of the Organisation,
(b) the fixing of the definitive contributions of the Member States to the expenses of the Organisation,
(c) the payment of contributions,
(d) the maximum amount that the expenditure of the Organisation may reach during a five-year period, fixed before the entry into force of this Protocol.

Letters (a) to (c) refer to the year during which this Protocol enters into force as well as to the year which precedes that year.

§ 6 The definitive contributions of the Member States due for the year during which this Protocol enters into force, shall be calculated on the basis of Article 11 § 1 of COTIF 1980.

§ 7 At the request of the Member State whose contribution calculated pursuant to Article 26 of the Convention in the version in the Annex to this Protocol is greater than that for the year 1999, the General Assembly may determine the contribution of that State for the three years which follow the year of entry into force of this Protocol, taking account of the following principles:

(a) the basis for the determination of the transitional contribution shall be the minimum contribution pursuant to Article 26 § 3 above referred to or the contribution due for the year 1999 if this is greater than the minimum contribution;
(b) the contribution shall be adapted progressively in three steps at most to arrive at the amount of the definitive contribution calculated pursuant to Article 26 above referred to.

This provision shall not apply to Member States which owe the minimum contribution which, in any event, shall remain due.

§ 8 Contracts of carriage of passengers or goods in international traffic between Member States, concluded pursuant to the CIV Uniform Rules 1980 or the CIM Uniform Rules 1980, shall remain subject to the Uniform Rules in force at the time of the conclusion of the contracts even after the entry into force of this Protocol.

§ 9 Mandatory provisions of the CUV Uniform Rules and of the CUI Uniform Rules shall apply to contracts concluded before the entry into force of this Protocol one year after its entry into force.

[4387]

Article 7

Texts of the Protocol

§ 1 This Protocol shall be concluded and signed in the English, French and German languages. In the case of divergence, the French text shall prevail.

§ 2 On a proposal by one of the Member States concerned, the Organisation shall publish official translations of this Protocol in other languages, if one of these languages is an official language in the territory of at least two Member States. These translations shall be prepared in cooperation with the competent services of the Member States concerned.

In witness whereof, the undersigned plenipotentiaries duly authorised by their respective Governments have signed this Protocol.

Done at Vilnius on 3 June 1999, in one original in each of the English, French and German languages; these originals shall remain deposited in the archives of OTIF. Certified copies shall be sent to each of the Member States.

[4388]

(Followed by the signatures)

State of the signatures, ratifications, acceptances, approvals, accessions and entry into force

Declarations and reservations

F. INTERNATIONAL CARRIAGE: SEA

INTERNATIONAL CONVENTION FOR THE UNIFICATION OF CERTAIN RULES OF LAW RELATING TO BILLS OF LADING ("HAGUE RULES"), AND PROTOCOL OF SIGNATURE

(Brussels, 25 August 1924)

NOTES

Please note that this is not taken from the official document. Belgium is the official depositary of the Treaty. The Treaties Division of the Belgian Government can be contacted at www.diplomatie.be/en/treaties.

The President of the German Republic, the President of the Argentine Republic, His Majesty the King of the Belgians, the President of the Republic of Chile, the President of the Republic of Cuba, His Majesty the King of Denmark and Iceland, His Majesty the King of Spain, the Head of the Estonian State, the President of the United States of America, the President of the Republic of Finland, the President of the French Republic, His Majesty the King of the United Kingdom of Great Britain and Ireland and of the British Dominions beyond the Seas, Emperor of India, His Most Supreme Highness the Governor of the Kingdom of Hungary, His Majesty the King of Italy, His Majesty the Emperor of Japan, the President of the Latvian Republic, the President of the Republic of Mexico, His Majesty the King of Norway, Her Majesty the Queen of the Netherlands, the President of the Republic of Peru, the President of the Polish Republic, the President of the Portuguese Republic, His Majesty the King of Romania, His Majesty the King of the Serbs, Croats and Slovenes, His Majesty the King of Sweden, and the President of the Republic of Uruguay,

HAVING RECOGNIZED the utility of fixing by agreement certain uniform rules of law relating to bills of lading,

HAVE DECIDED to conclude a convention with this object and have appointed the following Plenipotentiaries:

WHO, duly authorized thereto, have agreed as follows:

Article 1

In this Convention the following words are employed with the meanings set out below:

(a) "Carrier" includes the owner or the charterer who enters into a contract of carriage with a shipper.

(b) "Contract of carriage" applies only to contracts of carriage covered by a bill of lading or any similar document of title, in so far as such document relates to the carriage of goods by sea, including any bill of lading or any similar document as aforesaid issued under or pursuant to a charter party from the moment at which such bill of lading or similar document of title regulates the relations between a carrier and a holder of the same.

(c) "Goods" includes goods, wares, merchandise and articles of every kind whatsoever except live animals and cargo which by the contract of carriage in stated as being carried on deck and is so carried.

(d) "Ship" means any vessel used for the carriage of goods by sea.

(e) "Carriage of goods" covers the period from the time when the goods are loaded on to the time they are discharged from the ship.

[4389]

Article 2

Subject to the provisions of Article 6, under every contract of carriage of goods by sea the carrier, in relation to the loading, handling, stowage, carriage, custody, care and discharge of such goods, shall be subject to the responsibilities and liabilities, and entitled to the rights and immunities hereinafter set forth.

[4390]

Article 3

1. The carrier shall be bound before and at the beginning of the voyage to exercise due diligence to:

(a) Make the ship seaworthy.
(b) Properly man, equip and supply the ship.
(c) Make the holds, refrigerating and cool chambers, and all other parts of the ship in which goods are carried, fit and safe for their reception, carriage and preservation.

2. Subject to the provisions of Article 4, the carrier shall properly and carefully load, handle, stow, carry, keep, care for, and discharge the goods carried.

3. After receiving the goods into his charge the carrier or the master or agent of the carrier shall, on demand of the shipper, issue to the shipper a bill of lading showing among other things:

(a) The leading marks necessary for identification of the goods as the same are furnished in writing by the shipper before the loading of such goods starts, provided such marks are stamped or otherwise shown clearly upon the goods if uncovered, or on the cases or coverings in which such goods are contained, in such a manner as should ordinarily remain legible until the end of the voyage.
(b) Either the number of packages or pieces, or the quantity, or weight, as the case may be, as furnished in writing by the shipper.
(c) The apparent order and condition of the goods.

Provided that no carrier, master or agent of the carrier shall be bound to state or show in the bill of lading any marks, number, quantity, or weight which he has reasonable ground for suspecting not accurately to represent the goods actually received, or which he has had no reasonable means of checking.

4. Such a bill of lading shall be *prima facie* evidence of the receipt by the carrier of the goods as therein described in accordance with paragraph 3(a), (b) and (c).

5. The shipper shall be deemed to have guaranteed to the carrier the accuracy at the time of shipment of the marks, number, quantity and weight, as furnished by him, and the shipper shall indemnity the carrier against all loss, damages and expenses arising or resulting from inaccuracies in such particulars. The right of the carrier to such indemnity shall in no way limit his responsibility and liability under the contract of carriage to any person other than the shipper.

6. Unless notice of loss or damage and the general nature of such loss or damage be given in writing to the carrier or his agent at the port of discharge before or at the time of the removal of the goods into the custody of the person entitled to delivery thereof under the contract of carriage, or, if the loss or damage be not apparent, within three days, such removal shall be *prima facie* evidence of the delivery by the carrier of the goods as described in the bill of lading.

If the loss or damage is not apparent, the notice must be given within three days of the delivery of the goods.

The notice in writing need not be given if the state of the goods has, at the time of their receipt, been the subject of joint survey or inspection.

In any event the carrier and the ship shall be discharged from all liability in respect of loss or damage unless suit is brought within one year after delivery of the goods or the date when the goods should have been delivered.

In the case of any actual or apprehended loss or damage the carrier and the receiver shall give all reasonable facilities to each other for inspecting and tallying the goods.

7. After the goods are loaded the bill of lading to be issued by the carrier, master, or agent of the carrier, to the shipper shall, if the shipper so demands, be a "shipped" bill of lading, provided that if the shipper shall have previously taken up any document of title to such goods, he shall surrender the same as against the issue of the "shipped" bill of lading, but at the option of the carrier such document of title may be noted at the port of shipment by the carrier, master, or agent with the name or names of the ship or ships upon which the goods have been shipped and the date or dates of shipment, and when so noted, if it shows the particulars mentioned in paragraph 3 of Article 3, shall for the purpose of this Article be deemed to constitute a "shipped" bill of lading.

8. Any clause, covenant, or agreement in a contract of carriage relieving the carrier or the ship from liability for loss or damage to, or in connexion with, goods arising from negligence,

fault, or failure in the duties and obligations provided in this Article or lessening such liability otherwise than as provided in this Convention, shall be null and void and of no effect. A benefit of insurance in favour of the carrier or similar clause shall be deemed to be a clause relieving the carrier from liability.

[4391]

Article 4

1. Neither the carrier nor the ship shall be liable for loss or damage arising or resulting from unseaworthiness unless caused by want of due diligence on the part of the carrier to make the ship seaworthy and to secure that the ship is properly manned, equipped and supplied, and to make the holds, refrigerating and cool chambers and all other parts of the ship in which goods are carried fit and safe for their reception, carriage and preservation in accordance with the provisions of paragraph 1 of Article 3. Whenever loss or damage has resulted from unseaworthiness the burden of proving the exercise of due diligence shall be on the carrier or other person claiming exemption under this Article.

2. Neither the carrier nor the ship shall be responsible for loss or damage arising or resulting from:

(a) Act, neglect, or default of the master, mariner, pilot, or the servants of the carrier in the navigation or in the management of the ship.

(b) Fire, unless caused by the actual fault or privity of the carrier.

(c) Perils, dangers and accidents of the sea or other navigable waters.

(d) Act of God.

(e) Act of war.

(f) Act of public enemies.

(g) Arrest or restraint or princes, rulers or people, or seizure under legal process.

(h) Quarantine restrictions.

(i) Act or omission of the shipper or owner of the goods, his agent or representative.

(j) Strikes or lockouts or stoppage or restraint of labour from whatever cause, whether partial or general.

(k) Riots and civil commotions.

(l) Saving or attempting to save life or property at sea.

(m) Wastage in bulk or weight or any other loss or damage arising from inherent defect, quality or vice of the goods.

(n) Insufficiency of packing.

(o) Insufficiency or inadequacy of marks.

(p) Latent defects not discoverable by due diligence.

(q) Any other cause arising without the actual fault or privity of the carrier, or without the actual fault or neglect of the agents or servants of the carrier, but the burden of proof shall be on the person claiming the benefit of this exception to show that neither the actual fault or privity of the carrier nor the fault or neglect of the agents or servants of the carrier contributed to the loss or damage.

3. The shipper shall not be responsible for loss or damage sustained by the carrier or the ship arising or resulting from any cause without the act, fault or neglect of the shipper, his agents or his servants.

4. Any deviation in saving or attempting to save life or property at sea or any reasonable deviation shall not be deemed to be an infringement or breach of this Convention or of the contract of carriage, and the carrier shall not be liable for any loss or damage resulting therefrom.

5. Neither the carrier nor the ship shall in any event be or become liable for any loss or damage to or in connexion with goods in an amount exceeding 100 pounds sterling per package or unit, or the equivalent of that sum in other currency unless the nature and value of such goods have been declared by the shipper before shipment and inserted in the bill of lading.

This declaration if embodied in the bill of lading shall be *prima facie* evidence, but shall not be binding or conclusive on the carrier.

By agreement between the carrier, master or agent of the carrier and the shipper another maximum amount than that mentioned in this paragraph may be fixed, provided that such maximum shall not be less than the figure above named.

Neither the carrier nor the ship shall be responsible in any event for loss or damage to, or in connexion with, goods if the nature or value thereof has been knowingly misstated by the shipper in the bill of lading.

6. Goods of an inflammable, explosive or dangerous nature to the shipment whereof the carrier, master or agent of the carrier has not consented with knowledge of their nature and character, may at any time before discharge be landed at any place, or destroyed or rendered innocuous by the carrier without compensation and the shipper of such goods shall be liable for all damage and expenses directly or indirectly arising out of or resulting from such shipment. If any such goods shipped with such knowledge and consent shall become a danger to the ship or cargo, they may in like manner be landed at any place, or destroyed or rendered innocuous by the carrier without liability on the part of the carrier except to general average, if any.

[4392]

Article 5

A carrier shall be at liberty to surrender in whole or in part all or any of his rights and immunities or to increase any of his responsibilities and obligations under this Convention, provided such surrender or increase shall be embodied in the bill of lading issued to the shipper.

The provisions of this Convention shall not be applicable to charter parties, but if bills of lading are issued in the case of a ship under a charter party they shall comply with the terms of this Convention. Nothing in these rules shall be held to prevent the insertion in a bill of lading of any lawful provision regarding general average.

[4393]

Article 6

Notwithstanding the provisions of the preceding Articles, a carrier, master or agent of the carrier and a shipper shall in regard to any particular goods be at liberty to enter into any agreement in any terms as to the responsibility and liability of the carrier for such goods, and as to the rights and immunities of the carrier in respect of such goods, or his obligation as to seaworthiness, so far as this stipulation is not contrary to public policy, or the care or diligence of his servants or agents in regard to the loading, handling, stowage, carriage, custody, care and discharge of the goods carried by sea, provided that in this case no bill of lading has been or shall be issued and that the terms agreed shall be embodied in a receipt which shall be a non-negotiable document and shall be marked as such.

Any agreement so entered into shall have full legal effect.

Provided that this Article shall not apply to ordinary commercial shipments made in the ordinary course of trade, but only to other shipments where the character or condition of the property to be carried or the circumstances, terms and conditions under which the carriage is to be performed are such as reasonably to justify a special agreement.

[4394]

Article 7

Nothing herein contained shall prevent a carrier or a shipper from entering into any agreement, stipulation, condition, reservation or exemption as to the responsibility and liability of the carrier or the ship for the loss or damage to, or in connexion with, the custody and care and handling of goods prior to the loading on, and subsequent to, the discharge from the ship on which the goods are carried by sea.

[4395]

Article 8

The provisions of this Convention shall not affect the rights and obligations of the carrier under any statute for the time being in force relating to the limitation of the liability of owners of sea-going vessels.

[4396]

Article 9

The monetary units mentioned in this Convention are to be taken to be gold value.

Those contracting States in which the pound sterling is not a monetary unit reserve to themselves the right of translating the sums indicated in this Convention in terms of pound sterling into terms of their own monetary system in round figures.

The national laws may reserve to the debtor the right of discharging his debt in national currency according to the rate of exchange prevailing on the day of the arrival of the ship at the port of discharge of the goods concerned.

[4397]

Article 10

The provisions of this Convention shall apply to all bills of lading issued in any of the contracting States.

[4398]

Article 11

After an interval of not more than two years from the day on which the Convention is signed, the Belgian Government shall place itself in communication with the Governments of the High Contracting Parties which have declared themselves prepared to ratify the Convention, with a view to deciding whether it shall be put into force. The ratifications shall be deposited at Brussels at a date to be fixed by agreement among the said Governments. The first deposit of ratifications shall be recorded in a *procès-verbal* signed by the representatives of the Powers which take part therein and by the Belgian Minister of Foreign Affairs.

The subsequent deposit of ratifications shall be made by means of a written notification, addressed to the Belgian Government and accompanied by the instrument of ratification.

A duly certified copy of the *procès-verbal* relating to the first deposit of ratifications, of the notifications referred to in the previous paragraph, and also of the instruments of ratification accompanying them, shall be immediately sent by the Belgian Government through the diplomatic channel to the Powers who have signed this Convention or who have acceded to it. In the cases contemplated in the preceding paragraph, the said Government shall inform them at the same time of the date on which it received the notification.

[4399]

Article 12

Non-signatory States may accede to the present Convention whether or not they have been represented at the International Conference at Brussels.

A State which desires to accede shall notify its intention in writing to the Belgian Government, forwarding to it the document of accession, which shall be deposited in the archives of the said Government.

The Belgian Government shall immediately forward to all the States which have signed or acceded to the Convention a duly certified copy of the notification and of the act of accession, mentioning the date on which it received the notification.

[4400]

Article 13

The High Contracting Parties may at the time of signature, ratification or accession declare that their acceptance of the present Convention does not include any or all of the self-governing dominions, or of the colonies, overseas possessions, protectorates or territories under their sovereignty or authority, and they may subsequently accede separately on behalf of any self-governing dominion, colony, overseas possession, protectorate or territory excluded in their declaration. They may also denounce the Convention separately in accordance with its provisions in respect of any self-governing dominion, or any colony, overseas possession, protectorate or territory under their sovereignty or authority.

[4401]

Article 14

The present Convention shall take effect, in the case of the States which have taken part in the first deposit of ratifications, one year after the date of the protocol recording such deposit.

As respects the States which ratify subsequently or which accede, and also in cases in which the Convention is subsequently put into effect in accordance with Article 13, it shall take effect six months after the notifications specified in paragraph 2 of Article 11 and paragraph 2 of Article 12 have been received by the Belgian Government.

[4402]

Article 15

In the event of one of the contracting States wishing to denounce the present Convention, the denunciation shall be notified in writing to the Belgian Government, which shall immediately communicate a duly certified copy of the notification to all the other States, informing them of the date on which it was received.

The denunciation shall only operate in respect of the State which made the notification, and on the expiry of one year after the notification has reached the Belgian Government.

[4403]

Article 16

Any one of the contracting States shall have the right to call for a fresh conference with a view to considering possible amendments.

A State which would exercise this right should notify its intention to the other States through the Belgian Government, which would make arrangements for convening the Conference.

[4404]

DONE at Brussels, in a single copy, August 25th, 1924.

PROTOCOL OF SIGNATURE

At the time of signing the International Convention for the Unification of Certain Rules of Law relating to Bills of Lading the Plenipotentiaries whose signatures appear below have adopted this Protocol, which will have the same force and the same value as if its provisions were inserted in the text of the Convention to which it relates.

The High Contracting Parties may give effect to this Convention either by giving it the force of law or by including in their national legislation in a form appropriate to that legislation the rules adopted under this Convention.

They may reserve the right:

1. To prescribe that in the cases referred to in paragraph 2(c) to (p) of Article 4 the holder of a bill of lading shall be entitled to establish responsibility for loss or damage arising from the personal fault of the carrier or the fault of his servants which are not covered by paragraph (a).
2. To apply Article 6 in so far as the national coasting trade is concerned to all classes of goods without taking account of the restriction set out in the last paragraph of that Article.

[4405]

DONE at Brussels, in single copy, August 25th, 1924.

THE HAGUE RULES AS AMENDED BY THE BRUSSELS PROTOCOL 1968 ("HAGUE-VISBY RULES")

NOTES

The text of these Rules appears as set out in the Carriage of Goods by Sea Act 1971, Schedule.

ARTICLE I

In these Rules the following words are employed, with the meanings set out below:—

(a) "Carrier" includes the owner or the charterer who enters into a contract of carriage with a shipper.

(b) "Contract of carriage" applies only to contracts of carriage covered by a bill of lading or any similar document of title, in so far as such document relates to the carriage of goods by sea, including any bill of lading or any similar document as aforesaid issued under or pursuant to a charter party from the moment at which such bill of lading or similar document of title regulates the relations between a carrier and a holder of the same.

(c) "Goods" includes goods, wares, merchandise, and articles of every kind whatsoever except live animals and cargo which by the contract of carriage is stated as being carried on deck and is so carried.

(d) "Ship" means any vessel used for the carriage of goods by sea.

(e) "Carriage of goods" covers the period from the time when the goods are loaded on to the time they are discharged from the ship.

ARTICLE II

Subject to the provisions of Article VI, under every contract of carriage of goods by sea the carrier, in relation to the loading, handling, stowage, carriage, custody, care and discharge of such goods, shall be subject to the responsibilities and liabilities, and entitled to the rights and immunities hereinafter set forth.

ARTICLE III

1. The carrier shall be bound before and at the beginning of the voyage to exercise due diligence to—

(a) Make the ship seaworthy.

(b) Properly man, equip and supply the ship.

(c) Make the holds, refrigerating and cool chambers, and all other parts of the ship in which goods are carried, fit and safe for their reception, carriage and preservation.

2. Subject to the provisions of Article IV, the carrier shall properly and carefully load, handle, stow, carry, keep, care for, and discharge the goods carried.

3. After receiving the goods into his charge the carrier or the master or agent of the carrier shall, on demand of the shipper, issue to the shipper a bill of lading showing among other things—

(a) The leading marks necessary for identification of the goods as the same are furnished in writing by the shipper before the loading of such goods starts, provided such marks are stamped or otherwise shown clearly upon the goods if uncovered, or on the cases or coverings in which such goods are contained, in such a manner as should ordinarily remain legible until the end of the voyage.

(b) Either the number of packages or pieces, or the quantity, or weight, as the case may be, as furnished in writing by the shipper.

(c) The apparent order and condition of the goods.

Provided that no carrier, master or agent of the carrier shall be bound to state or show in the bill of lading any marks, number, quantity, or weight which he has reasonable ground for suspecting not accurately to represent the goods actually received, or which he has had no reasonable means of checking.

4. Such a bill of lading shall be prima facie evidence of the receipt by the carrier of the goods as therein described in accordance with paragraph 3(a), (b) and (c). However, proof to the contrary shall not be admissible when the bill of lading has been transferred to a third party acting in good faith.

5. The shipper shall be deemed to have guaranteed to the carrier the accuracy at the time of shipment of the marks, number, quantity and weight, as furnished by him, and the shipper shall indemnify the carrier against all loss, damages and expenses arising or resulting from inaccuracies in such particulars. The right of the carrier to such indemnity shall in no way limit his responsibility and liability under the contract of carriage to any person other than the shipper.

6. Unless notice of loss or damage and the general nature of such loss or damage be given in writing to the carrier or his agent at the port of discharge before or at the time of the removal of the goods into the custody of the person entitled to delivery thereof under the contract of carriage, or, if the loss or damage be not apparent, within three days, such removal shall be prima facie evidence of the delivery by the carrier of the goods as described in the bill of lading.

The notice in writing need not be given if the state of the goods has, at the time of their receipt, been the subject of joint survey or inspection.

Subject to paragraph 6*bis* the carrier and the ship shall in any event be discharged from all liability whatsoever in respect of the goods, unless suit is brought within one year of their delivery or of the date when they should have been delivered. This period may, however, be extended if the parties so agree after the cause of action has arisen.

In the case of any actual or apprehended loss or damage the carrier and the receiver shall give all reasonable facilities to each other for inspecting and tallying the goods.

6*bis*. An action for indemnity against a third person may be brought even after the expiration of the year provided for in the preceding paragraph if brought within the time allowed by the law of the Court seized of the case. However, the time allowed shall be not less than three months, commencing from the day when the person bringing such action for indemnity has settled the claim or has been served with process in the action against himself.

7. After the goods are loaded the bill of lading to be issued by the carrier, master, or agent of the carrier, to the shipper shall, if the shipper so demands, be a "shipped" bill of lading, provided that if the shipper shall have previously taken up any document of title to such goods, he shall surrender the same as against the issue of the "shipped" bill of lading, but at the option of the carrier such document of title may be noted at the port of shipment by the carrier, master, or agent with the name or names of the ship or ships upon which the goods have been shipped and the date or dates of shipment, and when so noted, if it shows the particulars mentioned in paragraph 3 of Article III, shall for the purpose of this article be deemed to constitute a "shipped" bill of lading.

8. Any clause, covenant, or agreement in a contract of carriage relieving the carrier or the ship from liability for loss or damage to, or in connection with, goods arising from negligence, fault, or failure in the duties and obligations provided in this article or lessening such liability otherwise than as provided in these Rules, shall be null and void and of no effect. A benefit of insurance in favour of the carrier or similar clause shall be deemed to be a clause relieving the carrier from liability.

ARTICLE IV

1. Neither the carrier nor the ship shall be liable for loss or damage arising or resulting from unseaworthiness unless caused by want of due diligence on the part of the carrier to make the ship seaworthy, and to secure that the ship is properly manned, equipped and supplied, and to make the holds, refrigerating and cool chambers and all other parts of the ship in which goods are carried fit and safe for their reception, carriage and preservation in accordance with the provisions of paragraph 1 of Article III. Whenever loss or damage has resulted from unseaworthiness the burden of proving the exercise of due diligence shall be on the carrier or other person claiming exemption under this article.

2. Neither the carrier nor the ship shall be responsible for loss or damage arising or resulting from—

(a) Act, neglect, or default of the master, mariner, pilot, or the servants of the carrier in the navigation or in the management of the ship.
(b) Fire, unless caused by the actual fault or privity of the carrier.
(c) Perils, dangers and accidents of the sea or other navigable waters.
(d) Act of God.
(e) Act of war.
(f) Act of public enemies.
(g) Arrest or restraint of princes, rulers or people, or seizure under legal process.
(h) Quarantine restrictions.
(i) Act or omission of the shipper or owner of the goods, his agent or representative.
(j) Strikes or lockouts or stoppage or restraint of labour from whatever cause, whether partial or general.
(k) Riots and civil commotions.
(l) Saving or attempting to save life or property at sea.
(m) Wastage in bulk or weight or any other loss or damage arising from inherent defect, quality or vice of the goods.
(n) Insufficiency of packing.
(o) Insufficiency or inadequacy of marks.
(p) Latent defects not discoverable by due diligence.
(q) Any other cause arising without the actual fault or privity of the carrier, or without the fault or neglect of the agents or servants of the carrier, but the burden of proof shall be on the person claiming the benefit of this exception to show that neither the actual fault or privity of the carrier nor the fault or neglect of the agents or servants of the carrier contributed to the loss or damage.

3. The shipper shall not be responsible for loss or damage sustained by the carrier or the ship arising or resulting from any cause without the act, fault or neglect of the shipper, his agents or his servants.

4. Any deviation in saving or attempting to save life or property at sea or any reasonable deviation shall not be deemed to be an infringement or breach of these Rules or of the contract of carriage, and the carrier shall not be liable for any loss or damage resulting therefrom.

5.

(a) Unless the nature and value of such goods have been declared by the shipper before shipment and inserted in the bill of lading, neither the carrier nor the ship shall in any event be or become liable for any loss or damage to or in connection with the goods in an amount exceeding [666.67 units of account] per package or unit or [2 units of account per kilogramme] of gross weight of the goods lost or damaged, whichever is the higher.

(b) The total amount recoverable shall be calculated by reference to the value of such goods at the place and time at which the goods are discharged from the ship in accordance with the contract or should have been so discharged.

The value of the goods shall be fixed according to the commodity exchange price, or, if there be no such price, according to the current market price, or, if there be no commodity exchange price or current market price, by reference to the normal value of goods of the same kind and quality.

(c) Where a container, pallet or similar article of transport is used to consolidate goods, the number of packages or units enumerated in the bill of lading as packed in such article of transport shall be deemed the number of packages or units for the purpose of this paragraph as far as these packages or units are concerned. Except as aforesaid such article of transport shall be considered the package or unit.

[(d) The unit of account mentioned in this Article is the special drawing right as defined by the International Monetary Fund. The amounts mentioned in sub-paragraph (a) of this paragraph shall be converted into national currency on the basis of the value of that currency on a date to be determined by the law of the Court seized of the case.]

(e) Neither the carrier nor the ship shall be entitled to the benefit of the limitation of liability provided for in this paragraph if it is proved that the damage resulted from an act or omission of the carrier done with intent to cause damage, or recklessly and with knowledge that damage would probably result.

(f) The declaration mentioned in sub-paragraph (a) of this paragraph, if embodied in the bill of lading, shall be prima facie evidence, but shall not be binding or conclusive on the carrier.

(g) By agreement between the carrier, master or agent of the carrier and the shipper other maximum amounts than those mentioned in sub-paragraph (a) of this paragraph may be fixed, provided that no maximum amount so fixed shall be less than the appropriate maximum mentioned in that sub-paragraph.

(h) Neither the carrier nor the ship shall be responsible in any event for loss or damage to, or in connection with, goods if the nature or value thereof has been knowingly mis-stated by the shipper in the bill of lading.

6. Goods of an inflammable, explosive or dangerous nature to the shipment whereof the carrier, master or agent of the carrier has not consented with knowledge of their nature and character, may at any time before discharge be landed at any place, or destroyed or rendered innocuous by the carrier without compensation and the shipper of such goods shall be liable for all damages and expenses directly or indirectly arising out of or resulting from such shipment. If any such goods shipped with such knowledge and consent shall become a danger to the ship or cargo, they may in like manner be landed at any place, or destroyed or rendered innocuous by the carrier without liability on the part of the carrier except to general average, if any.

ARTICLE IV BIS

1. The defences and limits of liability provided for in these Rules shall apply in any action against the carrier in respect of loss or damage to goods covered by a contract of carriage whether the action be founded in contract or in tort.

2. If such an action is brought against a servant or agent of the carrier (such servant or agent not being an independent contractor), such servant or agent shall be entitled to avail himself of the defences and limits of liability which the carrier is entitled to invoke under these Rules.

3. The aggregate of the amounts recoverable from the carrier, and such servants and agents, shall in no case exceed the limit provided for in these Rules.

4. Nevertheless, a servant or agent of the carrier shall not be entitled to avail himself of the provisions of this article, if it is proved that the damage resulted from an act or omission of the servant or agent done with intent to cause damage or recklessly and with knowledge that damage would probably result.

ARTICLE V

A carrier shall be at liberty to surrender in whole or in part all or any of his rights and immunities or to increase any of his responsibilities and obligations under these Rules, provided such surrender or increase shall be embodied in the bill of lading issued to the shipper. The provisions of these Rules shall not be applicable to charter parties, but if bills of lading are issued in the case of a ship under a charter party they shall comply with the terms of these Rules.

Nothing in these Rules shall be held to prevent the insertion in a bill of lading of any lawful provision regarding general average.

ARTICLE VI

Notwithstanding the provisions of the preceding articles, a carrier, master or agent of the carrier and a shipper shall in regard to any particular goods be at liberty to enter into any agreement in any terms as to the responsibility and liability of the carrier for such goods, and as to the rights and immunities of the carrier in respect of such goods, or his obligation as to seaworthiness, so far as this stipulation is not contrary to public policy, or the care or diligence of his servants or agents in regard to the loading, handling, stowage, carriage, custody, care and discharge of the goods carried by sea, provided that in this case no bill of lading has been or shall be issued and that the terms agreed shall be embodied in a receipt which shall be a non-negotiable document and shall be marked as such.

Any agreement so entered into shall have full legal effect.

Provided that this article shall not apply to ordinary commercial shipments made in the ordinary course of trade, but only to other shipments where the character or condition of the property to be carried or the circumstances, terms and conditions under which the carriage is to be performed are such as reasonably to justify a special agreement.

ARTICLE VII

Nothing herein contained shall prevent a carrier or a shipper from entering into any agreement, stipulation, condition, reservation or exemption as to the responsibility and liability of the carrier or the ship for the loss or damage to, or in connection with, the custody and care and handling of goods prior to the loading on, and subsequent to the discharge from, the ship on which the goods are carried by sea.

ARTICLE VIII

The provisions of these Rules shall not affect the rights and obligations of the carrier under any statute for the time being in force relating to the limitation of the liability of owners of sea-going vessels.

ARTICLE IX

These Rules shall not affect the provisions of any international Convention or national law governing liability for nuclear damage.

ARTICLE X

The provisions of these Rules shall apply to every bill of lading relating to the carriage of goods between ports in two different States if:

(a) the bill of lading is issued in a contracting State, or

(b) the carriage is from a port in a contracting State, or

(c) the contract contained in or evidenced by the bill of lading provides that these Rules or legislation of any State giving effect to them are to govern the contract,

whatever may be the nationality of the ship, the carrier, the shipper, the consignee, or any other interested person.

(The last two paragraphs of this article are not reproduced. They require contracting States to apply the Rules to bills of lading mentioned in the article and authorise them to apply the Rules to other bills of lading.)

(Articles 11 to 16 of the International Convention for the unification of certain rules of law relating to bills of lading signed at Brussels on 25th August 1924 are not reproduced. They deal with the coming into force of the Convention, procedure for ratification, accession and denunciation, and the right to call for a fresh conference to consider amendments to the Rules contained in the Convention.)

[4406]

NOTES

Words in italics in square brackets are as set out in the Queen's Printer's version of the Act.

Art IV: words in square brackets substituted by the Merchant Shipping Act 1981, s 2(3), (4). These amendments continue in force by virtue of the Merchant Shipping Act 1995, s 314(2), Sch 13, para 5(1), (5). By s 314(2) of, and Sch 13, para 5(1), (6) to, that Act, para 5(d) above continues to have effect as if the date there mentioned were the date of the judgment in question.

Modification: as to the modification of Art I, para (c) where a contract contained in or evidenced by a bill of lading or receipt within s 1(6) ante applies to deck cargo or live animals, see the Carriage of Goods by Sea Act 1971, s 1(7) at **[701]**.

Protocol signed at Brussels on 21 December 1979: by virtue of the Merchant Shipping Act 1995, s 314(2), Sch 13, para 45(1), (7), Art X continues to have effect as if references to a contracting State included references to a State that is a contracting State in respect of the Rules without the amendments made by the Protocol signed at Brussels on 21 December 1979 (as to which, see the Carriage of Goods by Sea Act 1971, s 1(1) and the note thereto at **[701]**) as well as to one that is a contracting State in respect of the Rules as so amended, and s 2 at **[702]** shall have effect accordingly.

UNITED NATIONS CONVENTION ON THE CARRIAGE OF GOODS BY SEA ("HAMBURG RULES")

(30 March 1978)

NOTES

STATUS OF THIS CONVENTION

The States Parties to this Convention,

Having recognised the desirability of determining by agreement certain rules relating to the carriage of goods by sea,

Have decided to conclude a Convention for this purpose and have thereto agreed as follows:

PART I
GENERAL PROVISIONS

Article 1

Definitions

In this Convention:

1. "Carrier" means any person by whom or in whose name a contract of carriage of goods by sea has been concluded with a shipper.

2. "Actual carrier" means any person to whom the performance of the carriage of the goods, or of part of the carriage, has been entrusted by the carrier, and includes any other person to whom such performance has been entrusted.

3. "Shipper" means any person by whom or in whose name or on whose behalf a contract of carriage of goods by sea has been concluded with a carrier, or any person by whom or in whose name or on whose behalf the goods are actually delivered to the carrier in relation to the contract of carriage by sea.

4. "Consignee" means the person entitled to take delivery of the goods.

PART V

5. "Goods" includes live animals; where the goods are consolidated in a container, pallet or similar Article of transport or where they are packed, "goods" includes such Article of transport or packaging if supplied by the shipper.

6. "Contract of carriage by sea" means any contract whereby the carrier undertakes against payment of freight to carry goods by sea from one port to another; however, a contract which involves carriage by sea and also carriage by some other means is deemed to be a contract of carriage by sea for the purposes of this Convention only in so far as it relates to the carriage by sea.

7. "Bill of lading" means a document which evidences a contract of carriage by sea and the taking over or loading of the goods by the carrier, and by which the carrier undertakes to deliver the goods against surrender of the document. A provision in the document that the goods are to be delivered to the order of a named person, or to order, or to bearer, constitutes such an undertaking.

8. "Writing" includes, inter alia, telegram and telex.

Article 2

Scope of application

1. The provisions of this Convention are applicable to all contracts of carriage by sea between two different States, if:

(a) The port of loading as provided for in the contract of carriage by sea is located in a Contracting State, or

(b) The port of discharge as provided for in the contract of carriage by sea is located in a Contracting State, or

(c) One of the optional ports of discharge provided for in the contract of carriage by sea is the actual port of discharge and such port is located in a Contracting State, or

(d) The bill of lading or other document evidencing the contract of carriage by sea is issued in a Contracting State, or

(e) The bill of lading or other document evidencing the contract of carriage by sea provides that the provisions of this Convention or the legislation of any State giving effect to them are to govern the contract.

2. The provisions of this Convention are applicable without regard to the nationality of the ship, the carrier, the actual carrier, the shipper, the consignee or any other interested person.

3. The provisions of this Convention are not applicable to charter-parties. However, where a bill of lading is issued pursuant to a charter-party, the provisions of the Convention apply to such a bill of lading if it governs the relation between the carrier and the holder of the bill of lading, not being the charterer.

4. If a contract provides for future carriage of goods in a series of shipments during an agreed period, the provisions of this Convention apply to each shipment. However, where a shipment is made under a charter-party, the provisions of paragraph 3 of this Article apply.

Article 3

Interpretation of the Convention

In the interpretation and application of the provisions of this Convention regard shall be had to its international character and to the need to promote uniformity.

[4407]

PART II
LIABILITY OF THE CARRIER

Article 4

Period of responsibility

1. The responsibility of the carrier for the goods under this Convention covers the period during which the carrier is in charge of the goods at the port of loading, during the carriage and at the port of discharge.

2. For the purpose of paragraph 1 of this Article, the carrier is deemed to be in charge of the goods

(a) From the time he has taken over the goods from:

(i) The shipper, or a person acting on his behalf; or

(ii) An authority or other third party to whom, pursuant to law or regulations applicable at the port of loading, the goods must be handed over for shipment;

(b) Until the time he has delivered the goods:

(i) By handing over the goods to the consignee; or

(ii) In cases where the consignee does not receive the goods from the carrier, by placing them at the disposal of the consignee in accordance with the contract or with the law or with the usage of the particular trade, applicable at the port of discharge, or

(iii) By handing over the goods to an authority or other third party to whom, pursuant to law or regulations applicable at the port of discharge, the goods must be handed over.

3. In paragraphs 1 and 2 of this Article, reference to the carrier or to the consignee means, in addition to the carrier or the consignee, the servants or agents, respectively of the carrier or the consignee.

Article 5

Basis of liability

1. The carrier is liable for loss resulting from loss of or damage to the goods, as well as from delay in delivery, if the occurrence which caused the loss, damage or delay took place while the goods were in his charge as defined in Article 4, unless the carrier proves that he, his servants or agents took all measures that could reasonably be required to avoid the occurrence and its consequences.

2. Delay in delivery occurs when the goods have not been delivered at the port of discharge provided for in the contract of carriage by sea within the time expressly agreed upon or, in the absence of such agreement, within the time which it would be reasonable to require of a diligent carrier, having regard to the circumstances of the case.

3. The person entitled to make a claim for the loss of goods may treat the goods as lost if they have not been delivered as required by article 4 within 60 consecutive days following the expiry of the time for delivery according to paragraph 2 of this Article.

4.—

(a) The carrier is liable

(i) For loss or damage to the goods or delay in delivery caused by fire, if the claimant proves that the fire arose from fault or neglect on the part of the carrier, his servants or agents;

(ii) For such loss, damage or delay in delivery which is proved by the claimant to have resulted from the fault or neglect of the carrier, his servants or agents, in taking all measures that could reasonably be required to put out the fire and avoid or mitigate its consequences.

(b) In case of fire on board the ship affecting the goods, if the claimant or the carrier so desires, a survey in accordance with shipment practices must be held into the cause and circumstances of the fire, and a copy of the surveyor's report shall be made available on demand to the carrier and the claimant.

5. With respect to live animals, the carrier is not liable for loss, damage or delay in delivery resulting from any special risks inherent in that kind of carriage. If the carrier proves that he has complied with any special instructions given to him by the shipper respecting the animals and that, in the circumstances of the case, the loss, damage or delay in delivery could be attributed to such risks, it is presumed that the loss, damage or delay in delivery was so caused, unless there is proof that all or a part of the loss, damage or delay in delivery resulted from fault or neglect on the part of the carrier, his servants or agents.

6. The carrier is not liable, except in general average, where loss, damage or delay in delivery resulted from measures to save life or from reasonable measures to save property at sea.

7. Where fault or neglect on the part of the carrier, his servants or agents combines with another cause to produce loss, damage or delay in delivery the carrier is liable only to the

extent that the loss, damage or delay in delivery is attributable to such fault or neglect, provided that the carrier proves the amount of the loss, damage or delay in delivery not attributable thereto.

Article 6

Limits of liability

1.—

(a) The liability of the carrier for loss resulting from loss of or damage to goods according to the provisions of Article 5 is limited to an amount equivalent to 835 units of account per package or other shipping unit or 2.5 units of account per kilogram of gross weight of the goods lost or damaged, whichever is the higher.

(b) The liability of the carrier for delay in delivery according to the provisions of Article 5 is limited to an amount equivalent to two and a half times the freight payable for the goods delayed, but no exceeding the total freight payable under the contract of carriage of goods by sea.

(c) In no case shall the aggregate liability of the carrier, under both subparagraphs (a) and (b) of this paragraph, exceed the limitation which would be established under subparagraph (a) of this paragraph for total loss of the goods with respect to which such liability was incurred.

2. For the purpose of calculating which amount is the higher in accordance with paragraph 1(a) of this Article, the following rules apply:

(a) Where a container, pallet or similar Article of transport is used to consolidate goods, the package or other shipping units enumerated in the bill of lading, if issued, or otherwise in any other document evidencing the contract of carriage by sea, as packed in such Article of transport are deemed packages or shipping units. Except as aforesaid the goods in such Article of transport are deemed one shipping unit.

(b) In cases where the Article of transport itself has been lost or damaged, that Article of transport, if not owned or otherwise supplied by the carrier, is considered one separate shipping unit.

3. Unit of account means the unit of account mentioned in Article 26.

4. By agreement between the carrier and the shipper, limits of liability exceeding those provided for in paragraph 1 may be fixed.

Article 7

Application to non-contractual claims

1. The defences and limits of liability provided for in this Convention apply in any action against the carrier in respect of loss or damage to the goods covered by the contract of carriage by sea, as well as of delay in delivery whether the action is founded in contract, in tort or otherwise.

2. If such action is brought against a servant or agent of the carrier, such servant or agent, if he proves that he acted within the scope of his employment, is entitled to avail himself of the defences and limits of liability which the carrier is entitled to invoke under this Convention.

3. Except as provided in Article 8, the aggregate of the amounts recoverable from the carrier and from any persons referred to in paragraph 2 of this Article shall not exceed the limits of liability provided for in this Convention.

Article 8

Loss of right to limit responsibility

1. The carrier is not entitled to the benefit of the limitation of liability provided for in Article 6 if it is proved that the loss, damage or delay in delivery resulted from an act or omission of the carrier done with the intent to cause such loss, damage or delay, or recklessly and with knowledge that such loss, damage or delay would probably result.

2. Notwithstanding the provisions of paragraph 2 of Article 7, a servant or agent of the carrier is not entitled to the benefit of the limitation of liability provided for in Article 6 if it is proved that the loss, damage or delay in delivery resulted from an act or omission of such

servant or agent, done with the intent to cause such loss, damage or delay, or recklessly and with knowledge that such loss, damage or delay would probably result.

Article 9

Deck cargo

1. The carrier is entitled to carry the goods on deck only if such carriage is in accordance with an agreement with the shipper or with the usage of the particular trade or is required by statutory rules or regulations.

2. If the carrier and the shipper have agreed that the goods shall or may be carried on deck, the carrier must insert in the bill of lading or other document evidencing the contract of carriage by sea a statement to that effect. In the absence of such statement the carrier has the burden of proving that an agreement for carriage on deck has been entered into; however, the carrier is not entitled to invoke such an agreement against a third party, including a consignee, who has acquired the bill of lading in good faith.

3. Where the goods have been carried on deck contrary to the provisions of paragraph 1 of this Article or where the carrier may not under paragraph 2 of this Article invoke an agreement for carriage on deck, the carrier, notwithstanding the provisions of paragraph 1 of article 5, is liable for loss of or damage to the goods, as well as for delay in delivery, resulting solely from the carriage on deck, and the extent of his liability is to be determined in accordance with the provisions of Article 6 or Article 8 of this Convention, as the case may be.

4. Carriage of goods on deck contrary to express agreement for carriage under deck is deemed to be an act or omission of the carrier within the meaning of Article 8.

Article 10

Liability of the carrier and actual carrier

1. Where the performance of the carriage or part thereof has been entrusted to an actual carrier, whether or not in pursuance of a liberty under the contract of carriage by sea to do so, the carrier nevertheless remains responsible for the entire carriage according to the provisions of this Convention. The carrier is responsible, in relation to the carriage performed by the actual carrier, for the acts and omissions of the actual carrier and of his servants and agents acting within the scope of their employment.

2. All the provisions of this Convention governing the responsibility of the carrier also apply to the responsibility of the actual carrier for the carriage performed by him. The provisions of paragraphs 2 and 3 of Article 7 and of paragraph 2 of Article 8 apply if an action is brought against a servant or agent of the actual carrier.

3. Any special agreement under which the carrier assumes obligations not imposed by this Convention or waives rights conferred by this Convention affects the actual carrier only if agreed to by him expressly and in writing. Whether or not the actual carrier has so agreed, the carrier nevertheless remains bound by the obligations or waivers resulting from such special agreement.

4. Where and to the extent that both the carrier and the actual carrier are liable, their liability is joint and several.

5. The aggregate of the amounts recoverable from the carrier, the actual carrier and their servants and agents shall not exceed the limits of liability provided for in this Convention.

6. Nothing in this Article shall prejudice any right of recourse as between the carrier and the actual carrier.

Article 11

Through carriage

1. Notwithstanding the provisions of paragraph 1 of Article 10, where a contract of carriage by sea provides explicitly that a specified part of the carriage covered by the said contract is to be performed by a named person other than the carrier, the contract may also provide that the carrier is not liable for loss, damage or delay in delivery caused by an occurrence which takes place while the goods are in the charge of the actual carrier during such part of the carriage. Nevertheless, any stipulation limiting or excluding such liability is

without effect if no judicial proceedings can be instituted against the actual carrier in a court competent under paragraph 1 or 2 of article 21. The burden of proving that any loss, damage or delay in delivery has been caused by such an occurrence rests upon the carrier.

2. The actual carrier is responsible in accordance with the provisions of paragraph 2 of Article 10 for loss, damage or delay in delivery caused by an occurrence which takes place while the goods are in his charge.

[4408]

PART III
LIABILITY OF THE SHIPPER

Article 12

General rule

The shipper is not liable for loss sustained by the carrier or the actual carrier, or for damage sustained by the ship, unless such loss or damage was caused by the fault or neglect of the shipper, his servants or agents. Nor is any servant or agent of the shipper liable for such loss or damage unless the loss or damage was caused by fault or neglect on his part.

Article 13

Special rules on dangerous goods

1. The shipper must mark or label in a suitable manner dangerous goods as dangerous.

2. Where the shipper hands over dangerous goods to the carrier or an actual carrier, as the case may be, the shipper must inform him of the dangerous character of the goods and, if necessary, of the precautions to be taken. If the shipper fails to do so and such carrier or actual carrier does not otherwise have knowledge of their dangerous character:
   (a) The shipper is liable to the carrier and any actual carrier for the loss resulting from the shipment of such goods, and
   (b) The goods may at any time be unloaded, destroyed or rendered innocuous, as the circumstances may require, without payment of compensation.

3. The provisions of paragraph 2 of this Article may not be invoked by any person if during the carriage he has taken the goods in his charge with knowledge of their dangerous character.

4. If, in cases where the provisions of paragraph 2, subparagraph (b), of this Article do not apply or may not be invoked, dangerous goods become an actual danger to life or property, they may be unloaded, destroyed or rendered innocuous, as the circumstances may require, without payment of compensation except where there is an obligation to contribute in general average or where the carrier is liable in accordance with the provisions of Article 5.

[4409]

PART IV
TRANSPORT DOCUMENTS

Article 14

Issue of bill of lading

1. When the carrier or the actual carrier takes the goods in his charge, the carrier must, on demand of the shipper, issue to the shipper a bill of lading.

2. The bill of lading may be signed by a person having authority from the carrier. A bill of lading signed by the master of the ship carrying the goods is deemed to have been signed on behalf of the carrier.

3. The signature on the bill of lading may be in handwriting, printed in facsimile, perforated, stamped, in symbols, or made by any other mechanical or electronic means, if no inconsistent with the law of the country where the bill of lading is issued.

Article 15

Contents of bill of lading

1. The bill of lading must include, inter alia, the following particulars:

(a) The general nature of the goods, the leading marks necessary for identification of the goods, an express statement, if applicable, as to the dangerous character of the goods, the number of packages or pieces, and the weight of the goods or their quantity otherwise expressed, all such particulars as furnished by the shipper;
(b) the apparent condition of the goods;
(c) the name and principal place of business of the carrier;
(d) the name of the shipper;
(e) the consignee if named by the shipper;
(f) the port of loading under the contract of carriage by sea and the date on which the goods were taken over by the carrier at the port of loading;
(g) the port of discharge under the contract of carriage by sea;
(h) the number of originals of the bill of lading, if more than one;
(i) the place of issuance of the bill of lading;
(j) the signature of the carrier or a person acting on his behalf;
(k) the freight to the extent payable by the consignee or other indication that freight is payable by him;
(l) the statement referred to in paragraph 3 of Article 23;
(m) the statement, if applicable, that the goods shall or may be carried on deck;
(n) the date or the period of delivery of the goods at the port of discharge if expressly agreed upon between the parties; and
(o) any increased limit or limits of liability where agreed in accordance with paragraph 4 of Article 6.

2. After the goods have been loaded on board, if the shipper so demands, the carrier must issue to the shipper a "shipped" bill of lading which, in addition to the particulars required under paragraph 1 of this Article, must state that the goods are on board a named ship or ships, and the date or dates of loading. If the carrier has previously issued to the shipper a bill of lading or other document of title with respect to any of such goods, on request of the carrier, the shipper must surrender such document in exchange for a "shipped" bill of lading. The carrier may amend any previously issued document in order to meet the shipper's demand for a "shipped" bill of lading if, as amended, such document includes all the information required to be contained in a "shipped" bill of lading.

3. The absence in the bill of lading of one or more particulars referred to in this Article does not affect the legal character of the document as a bill of lading provided that it nevertheless meets the requirements set out in paragraph 7 of Article 1.

Article 16

Bills of lading: reservations and evidentiary effect

1. If the bill of lading contains particulars concerning the general nature, leading marks, number of packages or pieces, weight or quantity of the goods which the carrier or other person issuing the bill of lading on his behalf knows or has reasonable grounds to suspect do not accurately represent the goods actually taken over or, where a "shipped" bill of lading is issued, loaded, or if he had no reasonable means of checking such particulars, the carrier or such other person must insert in the bill of lading a reservation specifying these inaccuracies, grounds of suspicion or the absence of reasonable means of checking.

2. If the carrier or other person issuing the bill of lading on his behalf fails to note on the bill of lading the apparent condition of the goods, he is deemed to have noted on the bill of lading that the goods were in apparent good condition.

3. Except for particulars in respect of which and to the extent to which a reservation permitted under paragraph 1 of this Article has been entered:
(a) The bill of lading is prima facie evidence of the taking over or, where a "shipped" bill of lading is issued, loading, by the carrier of the goods as described in the bill of lading; and
(b) Proof to the contrary by the carrier is not admissible if the bill of lading has been transferred to a third party, including a consignee, who in good faith has acted in reliance on the description of the goods therein.

4. A bill of lading which does not, as provided in paragraph 1, subparagraph (h) of Article 15, set forth the freight or otherwise indicate that freight is payable by the consignee or does not set forth demurrage incurred at the port of loading payable by the consignee, is prima facie evidence that no freight or such demurrage is payable by him. However, proof to

the contrary by the carrier is not admissible when the bill of lading has been transferred to a third party, including a consignee, who in good faith has acted in reliance on the absence in the bill of lading of any such indication.

Article 17

Guarantees by the shipper

1. The shipper is deemed to have guaranteed to the carrier the accuracy of particulars relating to the general nature of the goods, their marks, number, weight and quantity as furnished by him for insertion in the bill of lading. The shipper must indemnify the carrier against the loss resulting from inaccuracies in such particulars. The shipper remains liable even if the bill of lading has been transferred by him. The right of the carrier to such indemnity in no way limits his liability under the contract of carriage by sea to any person other than the shipper.

2. Any letter of guarantee or agreement by which the shipper undertakes to indemnify the carrier against loss resulting from the issuance of the bill of lading by the carrier, or by a person acting on his behalf, without entering a reservation relating to particulars furnished by the shipper for insertion in the bill of lading, or to the apparent condition of the goods, is void and of no effect as against any third party, including a consignee, to whom the bill of lading has been transferred.

3. Such letter of guarantee or agreement is valid as against the shipper unless the carrier or the person acting on his behalf, by omitting the reservation referred to in paragraph 2 of this Article, intends to defraud a third party, including a consignee, who acts in reliance on the description of the goods in the bill of lading. In the latter case, if the reservation omitted relates to particulars furnished by the shipper for insertion in the bill of lading, the carrier has no right of indemnity from the shipper pursuant to paragraph 1 of this Article.

4. In the case of intended fraud referred to in paragraph 3 of this article the carrier is liable, without the benefit of the limitation of liability provided for in this Convention, for the loss incurred by a third party, including a consignee, because he has acted in reliance on the description of the goods in the bill of lading.

Article 18

Documents other than bills of lading

Where a carrier issues a document other than a bill of lading to evidence the receipt of the goods to be carried, such a document is prima facie evidence of the conclusion of the contract of carriage by sea and the taking over by the carrier of the goods as therein described.

[4410]

PART V
CLAIMS AND ACTIONS

Article 19

Notice of loss, damage or delay

1. Unless notice of loss or damage, specifying the general nature of such loss or damage, is given in writing by the consignee to the carrier not later than the working day after the day when the goods were handed over to the consignee, such handing over is prima facie evidence of the delivery by the carrier of the goods as described in the document of transport or, if no such document has been issued, in good condition.

2. Where the loss or damage is not apparent, the provisions of paragraph 1 of this Article apply correspondingly if notice in writing is not given within 15 consecutive days after the day when the goods were handed over to the consignee.

3. If the state of the goods at the time they were handed over to the consignee has been the subject of a joint survey or inspection by the parties, notice in writing need not be given of loss or damage ascertained during such survey or inspection.

4. In the case of any actual or apprehended loss or damage the carrier and the consignee must give all reasonable facilities to each other for inspecting and tallying the goods.

5. No compensation shall be payable for loss resulting from delay in delivery unless a notice has been given in writing to the carrier within 60 consecutive days after the day when the goods were handed over to the consignee.

6. If the goods have been delivered by an actual carrier, any notice given under this Article to him shall have the same effect as if it had been given to the carrier, and any notice given to the carrier shall have effect as if given to such actual carrier.

7. Unless notice of loss or damage, specifying the general nature of the loss or damage, is given in writing by the carrier or actual carrier to the shipper not later than 90 consecutive days after the occurrence of such loss or damage or after the delivery of the goods in accordance with paragraph 2 of Article 4, whichever is later, the failure to give such notice is prima facie evidence that the carrier or the actual carrier has sustained no loss or damage due to the fault or neglect of the shipper, his servants or agents.

8. For the purpose of this Article, notice given to a person acting on the carrier's or the actual carriers' behalf, including the master or the officer in charge of the ship, or to a person acting on the shipper's behalf is deemed to have been given to the carrier, to the actual carrier or to the shipper, respectively.

Article 20

Limitation of actions

1. Any action relating to carriage of goods under this Convention is time-barred if judicial or arbitral proceedings have not been instituted within a period of two years.

2. The limitation period commences on the day on which the carrier has delivered the goods or part thereof or, in cases where no goods have been delivered, on the last day on which the goods should have been delivered.

3. The day on which the limitation period commences is not included in the period.

4. The person against whom a claim is made may at any time during the running of the limitation period extend that period by a declaration in writing to the claimant. This period may be further extended by another declaration or declarations.

5. An action for indemnity by a person held liable may be instituted even after the expiration of the limitation period provided for in the preceding paragraphs if instituted within the time allowed by the law of the State where proceedings are instituted. However, the time allowed shall not be less than 90 days commencing from the day when the person instituting such action for indemnity has settled the claim or has been served with process in the action against himself.

Article 21

Jurisdiction

1. In judicial proceedings relating to carriage of goods under this Convention the plaintiff, at his option, may institute an action in a court which, according to the law of the State where the court is situated, is competent and within the jurisdiction of which is situated one of the following places:

(a) The principal place of business or, in the absence thereof, the habitual residence of the defendant; or

(b) The place where the contract was made provided that the defendant has there a place of business, branch or agency through which the contract was made; or

(c) The port of loading or the port of discharge; or

(d) Any additional place designated for that purpose in the contract of carriage by sea.

2.—

(a) Notwithstanding the preceding provisions of this Article, an action may be instituted in the courts of any port or place in a Contracting State at which the carrying vessel or any other vessel of the same ownership may have been arrested in accordance with applicable rules of the law of that State and of international law. However, in such a case, at the petition of the defendant, the claimant must remove the action, at his choice, to one of the jurisdictions referred to in paragraph 1 of this Article for the determination of the claim, but before such removal the defendant must furnish security sufficient to ensure payment of any judgement that may subsequently be awarded to the claimant in the action.

(b) All questions relating to the sufficiency or otherwise of the security shall be determined by the court of the port or place of the arrest.

3. No judicial proceedings relating to carriage of goods under this Convention may be instituted in a place not specified in paragraph 1 or 2 of this Article. The provisions of this paragraph do not constitute an obstacle to the jurisdiction of the Contracting States for provisional or protective measures.

4.—

(a) Where an action has been instituted in a court competent under paragraph i or 2 of this Article or where judgement has been delivered by such a court, no new action may be started between the same parties on the same grounds unless the judgement of the court before which the first action instituted is not enforceable in the country in which the new proceedings are instituted.

(b) For the purpose of this Article the institution of measures with a view to obtaining enforcement of a judgement is not to be considered as the starting of a new action;

(c) For the purpose of this Article, the removal of an action to a different court within the same country, or to a court in another country, in accordance with paragraph 2(a) of this Article, is not to be considered as the starting of a new action.

5. Notwithstanding the provisions of the preceding paragraphs, an agreement made by the parties, after a claim under the contract of carriage by sea has arisen, which designates the place where the claimant may institute an action, is effective.

Article 22

Arbitration

1. Subject to the provisions of this Article, parties may provide by agreement evidenced in writing that any dispute that may arise relating to carriage of goods under this Convention shall be referred to arbitration.

2. Where a charter-party contains a provision that disputes arising thereunder shall be referred to arbitration and a bill of lading issued pursuant to the charter party does not contain a special annotation providing that such provision shall be binding upon the holder of the bill of lading, the carrier may not invoke such provision as against a holder having acquired the bill of lading in good faith.

3. The arbitration proceedings shall, at the option of the claimant, be instituted at one of the following places:

(a) A place in a State within whose territory is situated:

(i) The principal place of business of the defendant or, in the absence thereof, the habitual residence of the defendant; or

(ii) The place where the contract was made, provided that the defendant has there a place of business, branch or agency through which the contract was made; or

(iii) The port of loading or the port of discharge; or

(b) Any place designated for that purpose in the arbitration clause or agreement.

4. The arbitrator or arbitration tribunal shall apply the rules of this Convention.

5. The provisions of paragraph 3 and 4 of this Article are deemed to be part of every arbitration clause or agreement, and any term of such clause or agreement which is inconsistent therewith is null and void.

6. Nothing in this Article affects the validity of an agreement relating to arbitration made by the parties after the claim under the contract of carriage by sea has arisen.

[4411]

PART VI
SUPPLEMENTARY PROVISIONS

Article 23

Contractual stipulations

1. Any stipulation in a contract of carriage by sea, in a bill of lading, or in any other document evidencing the contract of carriage by sea is null and void to the extent that it derogates, directly or indirectly, from the provisions of this Convention. The nullity of such a stipulation does not affect the validity of the other provisions of the contract or document of which it forms a part. A clause assigning benefit of insurance of the goods in favour of the carrier, or any similar clause, is null and void.

2. Notwithstanding the provisions of paragraph 1 of this Article, a carrier may increase his responsibilities and obligations under this Convention.

3. Where a bill of lading or any other document evidencing the contract of carriage by sea is issued, it must contain a statement that the carriage is subject to the provisions of this Convention which nullify any stipulation derogating therefrom to the detriment of the shipper or the consignee.

4. Where the claimant in respect of the goods has incurred loss as a result of a stipulation which is null and void by virtue of the present Article, or as a result of the omission of the statement referred to in paragraph 3 of this Article, the carrier must pay compensation to the extent required in order to give the claimant compensation in accordance with the provisions of this Convention for any loss of or damage to the goods as well as for delay in delivery. The carrier must, in addition pay compensation for costs incurred by the claimant for the purpose of exercising his right, provided that costs incurred in the action where the foregoing provision is invoked are to be determined in accordance with the law of the State where proceedings are instituted.

Article 24

General average

1. Nothing in this Convention shall prevent the application of provisions in the contract of carriage by sea or national law regarding the adjustment of general average.

2. With the exception of Article 20, the provisions of this Convention relating to the liability of the carrier for loss of or damage to the goods also determine whether the consignee may refuse contribution in general average and the liability of the carrier to indemnify the consignee in respect of any such contribution made or any salvage paid.

Article 25

Other conventions

1. This Convention does not modify the rights or duties of the carrier, the actual carrier and their servants and agents, provided for in international conventions or national law relating to the limitation of liability of owners of seagoing ships.

2. The provisions of Articles 21 and 22 of this Convention do not prevent the application of the mandatory provisions of any other multilateral convention already in force at the date of this Convention relating to matters dealt with in the said Articles, provided that the dispute arises exclusively between parties having their principal place of business in States members of such other convention. However, this paragraph does not affect the application of paragraph 4 of Article 22 of this Convention.

3. No liability shall arise under the provisions of this Convention for damage caused by a nuclear incident if the operator of a nuclear installation is liable for such damage:

(a) Under either the Paris Convention of 29 July 1960 on Third Party Liability in the Field of Nuclear Energy as amended by the Additional Protocol of 28 January 1964 or the Vienna Convention of 21 May 1963 on Civil Liability for Nuclear Damage, or

(b) By virtue of national law governing the liability for such damage, provided that such law is in all respects as favourable to persons who may suffer damage as either the Paris or Vienna Conventions.

4. No liability that arise under the provisions of this Convention for any loss of or damage to or delay in delivery of luggage for which the carrier is responsible under any international convention or national law relating to the carriage of passengers and their luggage by sea.

5. Nothing contained in this Convention prevents a Contracting State from applying any other international convention which is already in force at the date of this Convention and which applies mandatorily to contracts of carriage of goods primarily by a mode of transport other than transport by sea. This provision also applies to any subsequent revision or amendment of such international convention.

Article 26

Unit of account

1. The unit of account referred to in Article 6 of this Convention is the Special Drawing Right as defined by the International Monetary Fund. The amounts mentioned in Article 6 are

to be converted into the national currency of a State according to the value of such currency at the date of judgement or the date agreed upon by the parties. The value of a national currency, in terms of the Special Drawing Right, of a Contracting State which is a member of the International Monetary Fund is to be calculated in accordance with the method of valuation applied by the International Monetary Fund in effect at the date in question for its operations and transactions. The value of a national currency in terms of the Special Drawing Right of a Contracting State which is not a member of the International Monetary Fund is to be calculated in a manner determined by that State.

2. Nevertheless, those States which are not members of the International Monetary Fund and whose law does not permit the application of the provisions of paragraph i of this Article may, at the time of signature, or at the time of ratification, acceptance, approval or accession or at any time thereafter, declare that the limits of liability provided for in this Convention to be applied in their territories shall be fixed as: 12,500 monetary units per package or other shipping unit or 37.5 monetary units per kilogram of gross weight of the goods.

3. The monetary unit referred to in paragraph 2 of this Article corresponds to sixty-five and a half milligrams of gold of millesimal fineness nine hundred. The conversion of the amounts referred to in paragraph 2 into the national currency is to be made according to the law of the State concerned.

4. The calculation mentioned in the last sentence of paragraph I and the conversion mentioned in paragraph 3 of this Article is to be made in such a manner as to express in the national currency of the Contracting State as far as possible the same real value for the amounts in Article 6 as is expressed there in units of account. Contracting States must communicate to the depositary the manner of calculation pursuant to paragraph 1 of this Article, or the result of the conversion mentioned in paragraph 3 of this Article, as the case may be, at the time of signature or when depositing their instruments of ratification, acceptance, approval or accession, or when availing themselves of the option provided for in paragraph 2 of this Article and whenever there is a change in the manner of such calculation or in the result of such conversion.

[4412]

PART VII
FINAL CLAUSES

Article 27

Depositary

The Secretary-General of the United Nations is hereby designated as the depositary of this Convention.

Article 28

Signature, ratification, acceptance, approval, accession

1. This Convention is open for signature by all States until 30 April 1979 at the Headquarters of the United Nations, New York.

2. This Convention is subject to ratification, acceptance or approval by the signatory States.

3. After 30 April 1979, this Convention will be open for accession by all States which are not signatory States.

4. Instruments of ratification, acceptance, approval and accession are to be deposited with the Secretary-General of the United Nations.

Article 29

Reservations

No reservations may be made to this Convention.

Article 30

Entry into force

1. This Convention enters into force on the first day of the month following the expiration of one year from the date of deposit of the 20th instrument of ratification, acceptance, approval or accession.

2. For each State which becomes a Contracting State to this Convention after the date of the deposit of the 20th instrument of ratification, acceptance, approval or accession, this Convention enters into force on the first day of the month following the expiration of one year after the deposit of the appropriate instrument on behalf of that State.

3. Each Contracting State shall apply the provisions of this Convention to contracts of carriage by sea concluded on or after the date of the entry into force of this Convention in respect of that State.

Article 31

Denunciation of other conventions

1. Upon becoming a Contracting State to this Convention, any State party to the International Convention for the Unification of Certain Rules relating to Bills of Lading signed at Brussels on 25 August 1924 (1924 Convention) must notify the Government of Belgium as the depositary of the 1924 Convention of its denunciation of the said Convention with a declaration that the denunciation is to take effect as from the date when this Convention enters into force in respect of that State.

2. Upon the entry into force of this Convention under paragraph 1 of article 30, the depositary of this Convention must notify the Government of Belgium as the depositary of the 1924 Convention of the date of such entry into force, and of the names of the Contracting States in respect of which the Convention has entered into force.

3. The provisions of paragraphs 1 and 2 of this Article apply correspondingly in respect of States parties to the Protocol signed on 23 February 1968 to amend the International Convention for the Unification of Certain Rules relating to Bills of Lading signed at Brussels on 25 August 1924.

4. Notwithstanding Article 2 of this Convention, for the purposes of paragraph 1 of this Article, a Contracting State may, if it deems it desirable, defer the denunciation of the 1924 Convention and of the 1924 Convention as modified by the 1968 Protocol for a maximum period of five years from the entry into force of this Convention. It will then notify the Government of Belgium of its intention. During this transitory period, it must apply to the Contracting States this Convention to the exclusion of any other one.

Article 32

Revision and amendment

1. At the request of not less than one-third of the Contracting States to this Convention, the depositary shall convene a conference of the Contracting States for revising or amending it.

2. Any instrument of ratification, acceptance, approval or accession deposited after the entry into force of an amendment to this Convention, is deemed to apply to the Convention as amended.

Article 33

Revision of the limitation amounts and unit of account or monetary unit

1. Notwithstanding the provisions of Article 32, a conference only for the purpose of altering the amount specified in Article 6 and paragraph 2 of Article 26, or of substituting either or both of the units defined in paragraphs 1 and 3 of Article 26 by other units is to be convened by the depositary in accordance with paragraph 2 of this article. An alteration of the amounts shall be made only because of a significant change in their real value.

2. A revision conference is to be convened by the depositary when not less than one-fourth of the Contracting States so request.

3. Any decision by the conference must be taken by a two-thirds majority of the participating States. The amendment is communicated by the depositary to all the Contracting States for acceptance and to all the States signatories of the Convention for information.

4. Any amendment adopted enters into force on the first day of the month following one year after its acceptance by two-thirds of the Contracting States. Acceptance is to be effected by the deposit of a formal instrument to that effect, with the depositary.

5. After entry into force of an amendment a Contracting State which has accepted the amendment is entitled to apply the Convention as amended in its relations with Contracting States which have not within six months after the adoption of the amendment notified the depositary that they are not bound by the amendment.

6. Any instrument of ratification, acceptance, approval or accession deposited after the entry into force of an amendment to this Convention, is deemed to apply to the Convention as amended.

Article 34

Denunciation

1. A Contracting State may denounce this Convention at any time by means of a notification in writing addressed to the depositary.

2. The denunciation takes effect on the first day of the month following the expiration of one year after the notification is received by the depositary. Where a longer period is specified in the notification, the denunciation takes effect upon the expiration of such longer period after the notification is received by the depositary.

Done at Hamburg, this thirty-first day of March one thousand nine hundred and seventy-eight, in a single original, of which the Arabic, Chinese, English, French, Russian and Spanish texts are equally authentic.

[4413]

In witness whereof the undersigned plenipotentiaries, being duly authorised by their respective Governments, have signed the present Convention.

[Signatures omitted from this version.]

G. STATE IMMUNITY

UNITED NATIONS CONVENTION ON JURISDICTIONAL IMMUNITIES OF STATES AND THEIR PROPERTY

(2004)

Adopted by the General Assembly of the United Nations on 2 December 2004. Not yet in force. See General Assembly resolution 59/38, annex, *Official Records of the General Assembly, Fifty-ninth Session, Supplement No 49* (A/59/49).

The United Kingdom has signed but has not yet ratified the Convention.

The States Parties to the present Convention,

CONSIDERING that the jurisdictional immunities of States and their property are generally accepted as a principle of customary international law,

HAVING IN MIND the principles of international law embodied in the Charter of the United Nations,

BELIEVING that an international convention on the jurisdictional immunities of States and their property would enhance the rule of law and legal certainty, particularly in dealings of States with natural or juridical persons, and would contribute to the codification and development of international law and the harmonization of practice in this area,

TAKING INTO ACCOUNT developments in State practice with regard to the jurisdictional immunities of States and their property,

AFFIRMING that the rules of customary international law continue to govern matters not regulated by the provisions of the present Convention,

HAVE AGREED as follows*:*

PART I
INTRODUCTION

Article 1
Scope of the present Convention

The present Convention applies to the immunity of a State and its property from the jurisdiction of the courts of another State.

[4414]

Article 2
Use of terms

1. For the purposes of the present Convention:
   (a) "court" means any organ of a State, however named, entitled to exercise judicial functions;
   (b) "State" means:
      (i) the State and its various organs of government;
      (ii) constituent units of a federal State or political subdivisions of the State, which are entitled to perform acts in the exercise of sovereign authority, and are acting in that capacity;
      (iii) agencies or instrumentalities of the State or other entities, to the extent that they are entitled to perform and are actually performing acts in the exercise of sovereign authority of the State;
      (iv) representatives of the State acting in that capacity;
   (c) "commercial transaction" means:
      (i) any commercial contract or transaction for the sale of goods or supply of services;

(ii) any contract for a loan or other transaction of a financial nature, including any obligation of guarantee or of indemnity in respect of any such loan or transaction;
(iii) any other contract or transaction of a commercial, industrial, trading or professional nature, but not including a contract of employment of persons.

2. In determining whether a contract or transaction is a "commercial transaction" under paragraph 1(c), reference should be made primarily to the nature of the contract or transaction, but its purpose should also be taken into account if the parties to the contract or transaction have so agreed, or if, in the practice of the State of the forum, that purpose is relevant to determining the non-commercial character of the contract or transaction.

3. The provisions of paragraphs 1 and 2 regarding the use of terms in the present Convention are without prejudice to the use of those terms or to the meanings which may be given to them in other international instruments or in the internal law of any State.
[4415]

Article 3
Privileges and immunities not affected by the present Convention

1. The present Convention is without prejudice to the privileges and immunities enjoyed by a State under international law in relation to the exercise of the functions of:
(a) its diplomatic missions, consular posts, special missions, missions to international organizations or delegations to organs of international organizations or to international conferences; and
(b) persons connected with them.

2. The present Convention is without prejudice to privileges and immunities accorded under international law to heads of State *ratione personae.*

3. The present Convention is without prejudice to the immunities enjoyed by a State under international law with respect to aircraft or space objects owned or operated by a State.
[4416]

Article 4
Non-retroactivity of the present Convention

Without prejudice to the application of any rules set forth in the present Convention to which jurisdictional immunities of States and their property are subject under international law independently of the present Convention, the present Convention shall not apply to any question of jurisdictional immunities of States or their property arising in a proceeding instituted against a State before a court of another State prior to the entry into force of the present Convention for the States concerned.
[4417]

PART II
GENERAL PRINCIPLES

Article 5
State immunity

A State enjoys immunity, in respect of itself and its property, from the jurisdiction of the courts of another State subject to the provisions of the present Convention.
[4418]

Article 6
Modalities for giving effect to State immunity

1. A State shall give effect to State immunity under article 5 by refraining from exercising jurisdiction in a proceeding before its courts against another State and to that end shall ensure that its courts determine on their own initiative that the immunity of that other State under article 5 is respected.

2. A proceeding before a court of a State shall be considered to have been instituted against another State if that other State:

(a) is named as a party to that proceeding; or

(b) is not named as a party to the proceeding but the proceeding in effect seeks to affect the property, rights, interests or activities of that other State.

[4419]

Article 7
Express consent to exercise of jurisdiction

1. A State cannot invoke immunity from jurisdiction in a proceeding before a court of another State with regard to a matter or case if it has expressly consented to the exercise of jurisdiction by the court with regard to the matter or case:

(a) by international agreement;

(b) in a written contract; or

(c) by a declaration before the court or by a written communication in a specific proceeding.

2. Agreement by a State for the application of the law of another State shall not be interpreted as consent to the exercise of jurisdiction by the courts of that other State.

[4420]

Article 8
Effect of participation in a proceeding before a court

1. A State cannot invoke immunity from jurisdiction in a proceeding before a court of another State if it has:

(a) itself instituted the proceeding; or

(b) intervened in the proceeding or taken any other step relating to the merits. However, if the State satisfies the court that it could not have acquired knowledge of facts on which a claim to immunity can be based until after it took such a step, it can claim immunity based on those facts, provided it does so at the earliest possible moment.

2. A State shall not be considered to have consented to the exercise of jurisdiction by a court of another State if it intervenes in a proceeding or takes any other step for the sole purpose of:

(a) invoking immunity; or

(b) asserting a right or interest in property at issue in the proceeding.

3. The appearance of a representative of a State before a court of another State as a witness shall not be interpreted as consent by the former State to the exercise of jurisdiction by the court.

4. Failure on the part of a State to enter an appearance in a proceeding before a court of another State shall not be interpreted as consent by the former State to the exercise of jurisdiction by the court.

[4421]

Article 9
Counterclaims

1. A State instituting a proceeding before a court of another State cannot invoke immunity from the jurisdiction of the court in respect of any counterclaim arising out of the same legal relationship or facts as the principal claim.

2. A State intervening to present a claim in a proceeding before a court of another State cannot invoke immunity from the jurisdiction of the court in respect of any counterclaim arising out of the same legal relationship or facts as the claim presented by the State.

3. A State making a counterclaim in a proceeding instituted against it before a court of another State cannot invoke immunity from the jurisdiction of the court in respect of the principal claim.

[4422]

PART III
PROCEEDINGS IN WHICH STATE IMMUNITY CANNOT BE INVOKED

Article 10
Commercial transactions

1. If a State engages in a commercial transaction with a foreign natural or juridical person and, by virtue of the applicable rules of private international law, differences relating to the commercial transaction fall within the jurisdiction of a court of another State, the State cannot invoke immunity from that jurisdiction in a proceeding arising out of that commercial transaction.

2. Paragraph 1 does not apply:
   (a) in the case of a commercial transaction between States; or
   (b) if the parties to the commercial transaction have expressly agreed otherwise.

3. Where a State enterprise or other entity established by a State which has an independent legal personality and is capable of:
   (a) suing or being sued; and
   (b) acquiring, owning or possessing and disposing of property, including property which that State has authorized it to operate or manage,

is involved in a proceeding which relates to a commercial transaction in which that entity is engaged, the immunity from jurisdiction enjoyed by that State shall not be affected.

[4423]

Article 11
Contracts of employment

1. Unless otherwise agreed between the States concerned, a State cannot invoke immunity from jurisdiction before a court of another State which is otherwise competent in a proceeding which relates to a contract of employment between the State and an individual for work performed or to be performed, in whole or in part, in the territory of that other State.

2. Paragraph 1 does not apply if:
   (a) the employee has been recruited to perform particular functions in the exercise of governmental authority;
   (b) the employee is:
      (i) a diplomatic agent, as defined in the Vienna Convention on Diplomatic Relations of 1961;
      (ii) a consular officer, as defined in the Vienna Convention on Consular Relations of 1963;
      (iii) a member of the diplomatic staff of a permanent mission to an international organization or of a special mission, or is recruited to represent a State at an international conference; or
      (iv) any other person enjoying diplomatic immunity;
   (c) the subject-matter of the proceeding is the recruitment, renewal of employment or reinstatement of an individual;
   (d) the subject-matter of the proceeding is the dismissal or termination of employment of an individual and, as determined by the head of State, the head of Government or the Minister for Foreign Affairs of the employer State, such a proceeding would interfere with the security interests of that State;
   (e) the employee is a national of the employer State at the time when the proceeding is instituted, unless this person has the permanent residence in the State of the forum; or
   (f) the employer State and the employee have otherwise agreed in writing, subject to any considerations of public policy conferring on the courts of the State of the forum exclusive jurisdiction by reason of the subject-matter of the proceeding.

[4424]

Article 12
Personal injuries and damage to property

Unless otherwise agreed between the States concerned, a State cannot invoke immunity from jurisdiction before a court of another State which is otherwise competent in a proceeding which relates to pecuniary compensation for death or injury to the person, or damage to or loss of tangible property, caused by an act or omission which is alleged to be attributable to the State, if the act or omission occurred in whole or in part in the territory of that other State and if the author of the act or omission was present in that territory at the time of the act or omission.

[4425]

Article 13
Ownership, possession and use of property

Unless otherwise agreed between the States concerned, a State cannot invoke immunity from jurisdiction before a court of another State which is otherwise competent in a proceeding which relates to the determination of:

(a) any right or interest of the State in, or its possession or use of, or any obligation of the State arising out of its interest in, or its possession or use of, immovable property situated in the State of the forum;
(b) any right or interest of the State in movable or immovable property arising by way of succession, gift or *bona vacantia*; or
(c) any right or interest of the State in the administration of property, such as trust property, the estate of a bankrupt or the property of a company in the event of its winding up.

[4426]

Article 14
Intellectual and industrial property

Unless otherwise agreed between the States concerned, a State cannot invoke immunity from jurisdiction before a court of another State which is otherwise competent in a proceeding which relates to:

(a) the determination of any right of the State in a patent, industrial design, trade name or business name, trademark, copyright or any other form of intellectual or industrial property which enjoys a measure of legal protection, even if provisional, in the State of the forum; or
(b) an alleged infringement by the State, in the territory of the State of the forum, of a right of the nature mentioned in subparagraph (a) which belongs to a third person and is protected in the State of the forum.

[4427]

Article 15
Participation in companies or other collective bodies

1. A State cannot invoke immunity from jurisdiction before a court of another State which is otherwise competent in a proceeding which relates to its participation in a company or other collective body, whether incorporated or unincorporated, being a proceeding concerning the relationship between the State and the body or the other participants therein, provided that the body:

(a) has participants other than States or international organizations; and
(b) is incorporated or constituted under the law of the State of the forum or has its seat or principal place of business in that State.

2. A State can, however, invoke immunity from jurisdiction in such a proceeding if the States concerned have so agreed or if the parties to the dispute have so provided by an agreement in writing or if the instrument establishing or regulating the body in question contains provisions to that effect.

[4428]

Article 16
Ships owned or operated by a State

1. Unless otherwise agreed between the States concerned, a State which owns or operates a ship cannot invoke immunity from jurisdiction before a court of another State which is otherwise competent in a proceeding which relates to the operation of that ship if, at the time the cause of action arose, the ship was used for other than government non-commercial purposes.

2. Paragraph 1 does not apply to warships, or naval auxiliaries, nor does it apply to other vessels owned or operated by a State and used, for the time being, only on government non-commercial service.

3. Unless otherwise agreed between the States concerned, a State cannot invoke immunity from jurisdiction before a court of another State which is otherwise competent in a proceeding which relates to the carriage of cargo on board a ship owned or operated by that State if, at the time the cause of action arose, the ship was used for other than government non-commercial purposes.

4. Paragraph 3 does not apply to any cargo carried on board the ships referred to in paragraph 2, nor does it apply to any cargo owned by a State and used or intended for use exclusively for government non-commercial purposes.

5. States may plead all measures of defence, prescription and limitation of liability which are available to private ships and cargoes and their owners.

6. If in a proceeding there arises a question relating to the government and non-commercial character of a ship owned or operated by a State or cargo owned by a State, a certificate signed by a diplomatic representative or other competent authority of that State and communicated to the court shall serve as evidence of the character of that ship or cargo.

[4429]

Article 17
Effect of an arbitration agreement

If a State enters into an agreement in writing with a foreign natural or juridical person to submit to arbitration differences relating to a commercial transaction, that State cannot invoke immunity from jurisdiction before a court of another State which is otherwise competent in a proceeding which relates to:

(a) the validity, interpretation or application of the arbitration agreement;
(b) the arbitration procedure; or
(c) the confirmation or the setting aside of the award,

unless the arbitration agreement otherwise provides.

[4430]

PART IV
STATE IMMUNITY FROM MEASURES OF CONSTRAINT IN CONNECTION WITH PROCEEDINGS BEFORE A COURT

Article 18
State immunity from pre-judgment measures of constraint

No pre-judgment measures of constraint, such as attachment or arrest, against property of a State may be taken in connection with a proceeding before a court of another State unless and except to the extent that:

(a) the State has expressly consented to the taking of such measures as indicated:
  (i) by international agreement;
  (ii) by an arbitration agreement or in a written contract; or
  (iii) by a declaration before the court or by a written communication after a dispute between the parties has arisen; or
(b) the State has allocated or earmarked property for the satisfaction of the claim which is the object of that proceeding.

[4431]

Article 19
State immunity from post-judgment measures of constraint

No post-judgment measures of constraint, such as attachment, arrest or execution, against property of a State may be taken in connection with a proceeding before a court of another State unless and except to the extent that:

(a) the State has expressly consented to the taking of such measures as indicated:
  (i) by international agreement;
  (ii) by an arbitration agreement or in a written contract; or
  (iii) by a declaration before the court or by a written communication after a dispute between the parties has arisen; or
(b) the State has allocated or earmarked property for the satisfaction of the claim which is the object of that proceeding; or

(c) it has been established that the property is specifically in use or intended for use by the State for other than government non-commercial purposes and is in the territory of the State of the forum, provided that post-judgment measures of constraint may only be taken against property that has a connection with the entity against which the proceeding was directed.

[4432]

Article 20
Effect of consent to jurisdiction to measures of constraint

Where consent to the measures of constraint is required under articles 18 and 19, consent to the exercise of jurisdiction under article 7 shall not imply consent to the taking of measures of constraint.

[4433]

Article 21
Specific categories of property

1. The following categories, in particular, of property of a State shall not be considered as property specifically in use or intended for use by the State for other than government non-commercial purposes under article 19, subparagraph (c):

(a) property, including any bank account, which is used or intended for use in the performance of the functions of the diplomatic mission of the State or its consular posts, special missions, missions to international organizations or delegations to organs of international organizations or to international conferences;

(b) property of a military character or used or intended for use in the performance of military functions;

(c) property of the central bank or other monetary authority of the State;

(d) property forming part of the cultural heritage of the State or part of its archives and not placed or intended to be placed on sale;

(e) property forming part of an exhibition of objects of scientific, cultural or historical interest and not placed or intended to be placed on sale.

2. Paragraph 1 is without prejudice to article 18 and article 19, subparagraphs (a) and (b).

[4434]

PART V
MISCELLANEOUS PROVISIONS

Article 22
Service of process

1. Service of process by writ or other document instituting a proceeding against a State shall be effected:

(a) in accordance with any applicable international convention binding on the State of the forum and the State concerned; or

(b) in accordance with any special arrangement for service between the claimant and the State concerned, if not precluded by the law of the State of the forum; or

(c) in the absence of such a convention or special arrangement:

(i) by transmission through diplomatic channels to the Ministry of Foreign Affairs of the State concerned; or

(ii) by any other means accepted by the State concerned, if not precluded by the law of the State of the forum.

2. Service of process referred to in paragraph 1(c)(i) is deemed to have been effected by receipt of the documents by the Ministry of Foreign Affairs.

3. These documents shall be accompanied, if necessary, by a translation into the official language, or one of the official languages, of the State concerned.

4. Any State that enters an appearance on the merits in a proceeding instituted against it may not thereafter assert that service of process did not comply with the provisions of paragraphs 1 and 3.

[4435]

Article 23
Default judgment

1. A default judgment shall not be rendered against a State unless the court has found that:

(a) the requirements laid down in article 22, paragraphs 1 and 3, have been complied with;

(b) a period of not less than four months has expired from the date on which the service of the writ or other document instituting a proceeding has been effected or deemed to have been effected in accordance with article 22, paragraphs 1 and 2; and

(c) the present Convention does not preclude it from exercising jurisdiction.

2. A copy of any default judgment rendered against a State, accompanied if necessary by a translation into the official language or one of the official languages of the State concerned, shall be transmitted to it through one of the means specified in article 22, paragraph 1, and in accordance with the provisions of that paragraph.

3. The time-limit for applying to have a default judgment set aside shall not be less than four months and shall begin to run from the date on which the copy of the judgment is received or is deemed to have been received by the State concerned. **[4436]**

Article 24
Privileges and immunities during court proceedings

1. Any failure or refusal by a State to comply with an order of a court of another State enjoining it to perform or refrain from performing a specific act or to produce any document or disclose any other information for the purposes of a proceeding shall entail no consequences other than those which may result from such conduct in relation to the merits of the case. In particular, no fine or penalty shall be imposed on the State by reason of such failure or refusal.

2. A State shall not be required to provide any security, bond or deposit, however described, to guarantee the payment of judicial costs or expenses in any proceeding to which it is a respondent party before a court of another State. **[4437]**

PART VI
FINAL CLAUSES

Article 25
Annex

The annex to the present Convention forms an integral part of the Convention. **[4438]**

Article 26
Other international agreements

Nothing in the present Convention shall affect the rights and obligations of States Parties under existing international agreements which relate to matters dealt with in the present Convention as between the parties to those agreements. **[4439]**

Article 27
Settlement of disputes

1. States Parties shall endeavour to settle disputes concerning the interpretation or application of the present Convention through negotiation.

2. Any dispute between two or more States Parties concerning the interpretation or application of the present Convention which cannot be settled through negotiation within six months shall, at the request of any of those States Parties, be submitted to arbitration. If, six months after the date of the request for arbitration, those States Parties are unable to agree on

the organization of the arbitration, any of those States Parties may refer the dispute to the International Court of Justice by request in accordance with the Statute of the Court.

3. Each State Party may, at the time of signature, ratification, acceptance or approval of, or accession to, the present Convention, declare that it does not consider itself bound by paragraph 2. The other States Parties shall not be bound by paragraph 2 with respect to any State Party which has made such a declaration.

4. Any State Party that has made a declaration in accordance with paragraph 3 may at any time withdraw that declaration by notification to the Secretary-General of the United Nations.

[4440]

Article 28
Signature

The present Convention shall be open for signature by all States until 17 January 2007, at United Nations Headquarters, New York.

[4441]

Article 29
Ratification, acceptance, approval or accession

1. The present Convention shall be subject to ratification, acceptance or approval.

2. The present Convention shall remain open for accession by any State.

3. The instruments of ratification, acceptance, approval or accession shall be deposited with the Secretary-General of the United Nations.

[4442]

Article 30
Entry into force

1. The present Convention shall enter into force on the thirtieth day following the date of deposit of the thirtieth instrument of ratification, acceptance, approval or accession with the Secretary-General of the United Nations.

2. For each State ratifying, accepting, approving or acceding to the present Convention after the deposit of the thirtieth instrument of ratification, acceptance, approval or accession, the Convention shall enter into force on the thirtieth day after the deposit by such State of its instrument of ratification, acceptance, approval or accession.

[4443]

Article 31
Denunciation

1. Any State Party may denounce the present Convention by written notification to the Secretary-General of the United Nations.

2. Denunciation shall take effect one year following the date on which notification is received by the Secretary-General of the United Nations. The present Convention shall, however, continue to apply to any question of jurisdictional immunities of States or their property arising in a proceeding instituted against a State before a court of another State prior to the date on which the denunciation takes effect for any of the States concerned.

3. The denunciation shall not in any way affect the duty of any State Party to fulfil any obligation embodied in the present Convention to which it would be subject under international law independently of the present Convention.

[4444]

Article 32
Depositary and notifications

1. The Secretary-General of the United Nations is designated the depositary of the present Convention.

2. As depositary of the present Convention, the Secretary-General of the United Nations shall inform all States of the following:

(a) signatures of the present Convention and the deposit of instruments of ratification, acceptance, approval or accession or notifications of denunciation, in accordance with articles 29 and 31;

(b) the date on which the present Convention will enter into force, in accordance with article 30;

(c) any acts, notifications or communications relating to the present Convention.

[4445]

Article 33
Authentic texts

The Arabic, Chinese, English, French, Russian and Spanish texts of the present Convention are equally authentic.

IN WITNESS WHEREOF, the undersigned, being duly authorized thereto by their respective Governments, have signed this Convention opened for signature at United Nations Headquarters in New York on 17 January 2005.

[4446]

ANNEX TO THE CONVENTION

Understandings with respect to certain provisions of the Convention

The present annex is for the purpose of setting out understandings relating to the provisions concerned.

With respect to article 10

The term “immunity” in article 10 is to be understood in the context of the present Convention as a whole.

Article 10, paragraph 3, does not prejudge the question of “piercing the corporate veil”, questions relating to a situation where a State entity has deliberately misrepresented its financial position or subsequently reduced its assets to avoid satisfying a claim, or other related issues.

With respect to article 11

The reference in article 11, paragraph 2(d), to the “security interests” of the employer State is intended primarily to address matters of national security and the security of diplomatic missions and consular posts.

Under article 41 of the 1961 Vienna Convention on Diplomatic Relations and article 55 of the 1963 Vienna Convention on Consular Relations, all persons referred to in those articles have the duty to respect the laws and regulations, including labour laws, of the host country. At the same time, under article 38 of the 1961 Vienna Convention on Diplomatic Relations and article 71 of the 1963 Vienna Convention on Consular Relations, the receiving State has a duty to exercise its jurisdiction in such a manner as not to interfere unduly with the performance of the functions of the mission or the consular post.

With respect to articles 13 and 14

The expression “determination” is used to refer not only to the ascertainment or verification of the existence of the rights protected, but also to the evaluation or assessment of the substance, including content, scope and extent, of such rights.

With respect to article 17

The expression “commercial transaction” includes investment matters.

With respect to article 19

The expression "entity" in subparagraph (c) means the State as an independent legal personality, a constituent unit of a federal State, a subdivision of a State, an agency or instrumentality of a State or other entity, which enjoys independent legal personality.

The words "property that has a connection with the entity" in subparagraph (c) are to be understood as broader than ownership or possession.

Article 19 does not prejudge the question of "piercing the corporate veil", questions relating to a situation where a State entity has deliberately misrepresented its financial position or subsequently reduced its assets to avoid satisfying a claim, or other related issues.

[4447]

H. CROSS-BORDER INSOLVENCY

UNCITRAL MODEL LAW ON CROSS-BORDER INSOLVENCY

(1997)

NOTES

The following text is the modified form of the UNCITRAL Model Law on Cross-Border Insolvency implemented in the UK by the Cross-Border Insolvency Regulations 2006, SI 2006/1030 at **[2733]** and set out in Sch 1 of those regs. For the original text of the Model Law and Guide to enactment, see http://www.uncitral.org/uncitral/en/uncitral_texts/insolvency/1997Model.html. For the UK's approach to implementation of the Model Law, see the report prepared by the Insolvency Service at http://www.insolvency.gov.uk/insolvencyprofessionandlegislation/con_doc_register/UNCITRALconsultationreponse.pdf and the Explanatory Memorandum to the Regulations at http://www.opsi.gov.uk/si/si2006/draft/em/uksidem_0110741587_en.pdf.

CHAPTER I
GENERAL PROVISIONS

Article 1
Scope of Application

1 This Law applies where—

(a) assistance is sought in Great Britain by a foreign court or a foreign representative in connection with a foreign proceeding; or

(b) assistance is sought in a foreign State in connection with a proceeding under British insolvency law; or

(c) a foreign proceeding and a proceeding under British insolvency law in respect of the same debtor are taking place concurrently; or

(d) creditors or other interested persons in a foreign State have an interest in requesting the commencement of, or participating in, a proceeding under British insolvency law.

2 This Law does not apply to a proceeding concerning—

(a) a company holding an appointment under Chapter 1 of Part 2 of the Water Industry Act 1991 (water and sewage undertakers) or a qualifying licensed water supplier within the meaning of section 23(6) of that Act (meaning and effect of special administration order);

(b) Scottish Water established under section 20 of the Water Industry (Scotland) Act 2002 (Scottish Water);

(c) a protected railway company within the meaning of section 59 of the Railways Act 1993 (railway administration order) (including that section as it has effect by virtue of section 19 of the Channel Tunnel Rail Link Act 1996 (administration));

(d) a licence company within the meaning of section 26 of the Transport Act 2000 (air traffic services);

(e) a public private partnership company within the meaning of section 210 of the Greater London Authority Act 1999 (public-private partnership agreement);

(f) a protected energy company within the meaning of section 154(5) of the Energy Act 2004 (energy administration orders);

(g) a building society within the meaning of section 119 of the Building Societies Act 1986 (interpretation);

(h) a UK credit institution or an EEA credit institution or any branch of either such institution as those expressions are defined by regulation 2 of the Credit Institutions (Reorganisation and Winding Up) Regulations 2004 (interpretation);

(i) a third country credit institution within the meaning of regulation 36 of the Credit Institutions (Reorganisation and Winding Up) Regulations 2004 (interpretation of this Part);

(j) a person who has permission under or by virtue of Parts 4 or 19 of the Financial Services and Markets Act 2000 to effect or carry out contracts of insurance;

(k) an EEA insurer within the meaning of regulation 2 of the Insurers (Reorganisation and Winding Up) Regulations 2004 (interpretation);

(l) a person (other than one included in paragraph 2(j)) pursuing the activity of reinsurance who has received authorisation for that activity from a competent authority within an EEA State; or

(m) any of the Concessionaires within the meaning of section 1 of the Channel Tunnel Act 1987.

3 In paragraph 2 of this article—

(a) in sub-paragraph (j) the reference to "contracts of insurance" must be construed in accordance with—

(i) section 22 of the Financial Services and Markets Act 2000 (classes of regulated activity and categories of investment);

(ii) any relevant order under that section; and

(iii) Schedule 2 to that Act (regulated activities);

(b) in sub-paragraph (l) "EEA State" means a State, other than the United Kingdom, which is a contracting party to the agreement on the European Economic Area signed at Oporto on 2 May 1992.

4 The court shall not grant any relief, or modify any relief already granted, or provide any co-operation or coordination, under or by virtue of any of the provisions of this Law if and to the extent that such relief or modified relief or cooperation or coordination would—

(a) be prohibited under or by virtue of—

(i) Part 7 of the Companies Act 1989;

(ii) Part 3 of the Financial Markets and Insolvency (Settlement Finality) Regulations 1999; or

(iii) Part 3 of the Financial Collateral Arrangements (No 2) Regulations 2003;

in the case of a proceeding under British insolvency law; or

(b) interfere with or be inconsistent with any rights of a collateral taker under Part 4 of the Financial Collateral Arrangements (No 2) Regulations 2003 which could be exercised in the case of such a proceeding.

5 Where a foreign proceeding regarding a debtor who is an insured in accordance with the provisions of the Third Parties (Rights against Insurers) Act 1930 is recognised under this Law, any stay and suspension referred to in article 20(1) and any relief granted by the court under article 19 or 21 shall not apply to or affect—

(a) any transfer of rights of the debtor under that Act; or

(b) any claim, action, cause or proceeding by a third party against an insurer under or in respect of rights of the debtor transferred under that Act.

6 Any suspension under this Law of the right to transfer, encumber or otherwise dispose of any of the debtor's assets—

(a) is subject to section 26 of the Land Registration Act 2002 where owner's powers are exercised in relation to a registered estate or registered charge;

(b) is subject to section 52 of the Land Registration Act 2002, where the powers referred to in that section are exercised by the proprietor of a registered charge; and

(c) in any other case, shall not bind a purchaser of a legal estate in good faith for money or money's worth unless the purchaser has express notice of the suspension.

7 In paragraph 6—

(a) "owner's powers" means the powers described in section 23 of the Land Registration Act 2002 and "registered charge" and "registered estate" have the same meaning as in section 132(1) of that Act; and

(b) "legal estate" and "purchaser" have the same meaning as in section 17 of the Land Charges Act 1972.

[4448]

Article 2
Definitions

For the purposes of this Law—

(a) "British insolvency law" means—

(i) in relation to England and Wales, provision extending to England and Wales and made by or under the Insolvency Act 1986 (with the exception of

Part 3 of that Act) or by or under that Act as extended or applied by or under any other enactment (excluding these Regulations); and

(ii) in relation to Scotland, provision extending to Scotland and made by or under the Insolvency Act 1986 (with the exception of Part 3 of that Act), the Bankruptcy (Scotland) Act 1985 or by or under those Acts as extended or applied by or under any other enactment (excluding these Regulations);

(b) "British insolvency officeholder" means—

(i) the official receiver within the meaning of section 399 of the Insolvency Act 1986 when acting as liquidator, provisional liquidator, trustee, interim receiver or nominee or supervisor of a voluntary arrangement;

(ii) a person acting as an insolvency practitioner within the meaning of section 388 of that Act but shall not include a person acting as an administrative receiver; and

(iii) the Accountant in Bankruptcy within the meaning of section 1 of the Bankruptcy (Scotland) Act 1985 when acting as interim or permanent trustee;

(c) "the court" except as otherwise provided in articles 14(4) and 23(6)(b), means in relation to any matter the court which in accordance with the provisions of article 4 of this Law has jurisdiction in relation to that matter;

(d) "the EC Insolvency Regulation" means Council Regulation (EC) No 1346/2000 of 29 May 2000 on Insolvency Proceedings;

(e) "establishment" means any place of operations where the debtor carries out a non-transitory economic activity with human means and assets or services;

(f) "foreign court" means a judicial or other authority competent to control or supervise a foreign proceeding;

(g) "foreign main proceeding" means a foreign proceeding taking place in the State where the debtor has the centre of its main interests;

(h) "foreign non-main proceeding" means a foreign proceeding, other than a foreign main proceeding, taking place in a State where the debtor has an establishment within the meaning of sub-paragraph (e) of this article;

(i) "foreign proceeding" means a collective judicial or administrative proceeding in a foreign State, including an interim proceeding, pursuant to a law relating to insolvency in which proceeding the assets and affairs of the debtor are subject to control or supervision by a foreign court, for the purpose of reorganisation or liquidation;

(j) "foreign representative" means a person or body, including one appointed on an interim basis, authorised in a foreign proceeding to administer the reorganisation or the liquidation of the debtor's assets or affairs or to act as a representative of the foreign proceeding;

(k) "hire-purchase agreement" includes a conditional sale agreement, a chattel leasing agreement and a retention of title agreement;

(l) "section 426 request" means a request for assistance in accordance with section 426 of the Insolvency Act 1986 made to a court in any part of the United Kingdom;

(m) "secured creditor" in relation to a debtor, means a creditor of the debtor who holds in respect of his debt a security over property of the debtor;

(n) "security" means—

(i) in relation to England and Wales, any mortgage, charge, lien or other security; and

(ii) in relation to Scotland, any security (whether heritable or moveable), any floating charge and any right of lien or preference and any right of retention (other than a right of compensation or set off);

(o) in the application of Articles 20 and 23 to Scotland, "an individual" means any debtor within the meaning of the Bankruptcy (Scotland) Act 1985;

(p) in the application of this Law to Scotland, references howsoever expressed to—

(i) "filing" an application or claim are to be construed as references to lodging an application or submitting a claim respectively;

(ii) "relief" and "standing" are to be construed as references to "remedy" and "title and interest" respectively; and

(iii) a "stay" are to be construed as references to restraint, except in relation to continuation of actions or proceedings when they shall be construed as a reference to sist; and

(q) references to the law of Great Britain include a reference to the law of either part of Great Britain (including its rules of private international law).

[4449]

Article 3
International Obligations of Great Britain Under the EC Insolvency Regulation

To the extent that this Law conflicts with an obligation of the United Kingdom under the EC Insolvency Regulation, the requirements of the EC Insolvency Regulation prevail.

[4450]

Article 4
Competent Court

1 The functions referred to in this Law relating to recognition of foreign proceedings and cooperation with foreign courts shall be performed by the High Court and assigned to the Chancery Division, as regards England and Wales and the Court of Session as regards Scotland.

2 Subject to paragraph 1 of this article, the court in either part of Great Britain shall have jurisdiction in relation to the functions referred to in that paragraph if—

(a) the debtor has—
  (i) a place of business; or
  (ii) in the case of an individual, a place of residence; or
  (iii) assets,

  situated in that part of Great Britain; or

(b) the court in that part of Great Britain considers for any other reason that it is the appropriate forum to consider the question or provide the assistance requested.

3 In considering whether it is the appropriate forum to hear an application for recognition of a foreign proceeding in relation to a debtor, the court shall take into account the location of any court in which a proceeding under British insolvency law is taking place in relation to the debtor and the likely location of any future proceedings under British insolvency law in relation to the debtor.

[4451]

Article 5
Authorisation of British Insolvency Officeholders to Act in a Foreign State

A British insolvency officeholder is authorised to act in a foreign State on behalf of a proceeding under British insolvency law, as permitted by the applicable foreign law.

[4452]

Article 6
Public Policy Exception

Nothing in this Law prevents the court from refusing to take an action governed by this Law if the action would be manifestly contrary to the public policy of Great Britain or any part of it.

[4453]

Article 7
Additional Assistance under other Laws

Nothing in this Law limits the power of a court or a British insolvency officeholder to provide additional assistance to a foreign representative under other laws of Great Britain.

[4454]

Article 8
Interpretation

In the interpretation of this Law, regard is to be had to its international origin and to the need to promote uniformity in its application and the observance of good faith.

[4455]

CHAPTER II
ACCESS OF FOREIGN REPRESENTATIVES AND CREDITORS TO COURTS IN GREAT BRITAIN

Article 9
Right of Direct Access

A foreign representative is entitled to apply directly to a court in Great Britain.

[4456]

Article 10
Limited Jurisdiction

The sole fact that an application pursuant to this Law is made to a court in Great Britain by a foreign representative does not subject the foreign representative or the foreign assets and affairs of the debtor to the jurisdiction of the courts of Great Britain or any part of it for any purpose other than the application.

[4457]

Article 11
Application by a Foreign Representative to Commence a Proceeding under British Insolvency Law

A foreign representative appointed in a foreign main proceeding or foreign non-main proceeding is entitled to apply to commence a proceeding under British insolvency law if the conditions for commencing such a proceeding are otherwise met.

[4458]

Article 12
Participation of a Foreign Representative in a Proceeding under British Insolvency Law

Upon recognition of a foreign proceeding, the foreign representative is entitled to participate in a proceeding regarding the debtor under British insolvency law.

[4459]

Article 13
Access of Foreign Creditors to a Proceeding under British Insolvency Law

1 Subject to paragraph 2 of this article, foreign creditors have the same rights regarding the commencement of, and participation in, a proceeding under British insolvency law as creditors in Great Britain.

2 Paragraph 1 of this article does not affect the ranking of claims in a proceeding under British insolvency law, except that the claim of a foreign creditor shall not be given a lower priority than that of general unsecured claims solely because the holder of such a claim is a foreign creditor.

3 A claim may not be challenged solely on the grounds that it is a claim by a foreign tax or social security authority but such a claim may be challenged—

(a) on the ground that it is in whole or in part a penalty, or

(b) on any other ground that a claim might be rejected in a proceeding under British insolvency law.

[4460]

Article 14
Notification to Foreign Creditors of a Proceeding under British Insolvency Law

1 Whenever under British insolvency law notification is to be given to creditors in Great Britain, such notification shall also be given to the known creditors that do not have addresses in Great Britain. The court may order that appropriate steps be taken with a view to notifying any creditor whose address is not yet known.

2 Such notification shall be made to the foreign creditors individually, unless—

(a) the court considers that under the circumstances some other form of notification would be more appropriate; or

(b) the notification to creditors in Great Britain is to be by advertisement only, in which case the notification to the known foreign creditors may be by advertisement in such foreign newspapers as the British insolvency officeholder considers most appropriate for ensuring that the content of the notification comes to the notice of the known foreign creditors.

3 When notification of a right to file a claim is to be given to foreign creditors, the notification shall—

(a) indicate a reasonable time period for filing claims and specify the place for their filing;

(b) indicate whether secured creditors need to file their secured claims; and

(c) contain any other information required to be included in such a notification to creditors pursuant to the law of Great Britain and the orders of the court.

4 In this article "the court" means the court which has jurisdiction in relation to the particular proceeding under British insolvency law under which notification is to be given to creditors.

[4461]

CHAPTER III
RECOGNITION OF A FOREIGN PROCEEDING AND RELIEF

Article 15
Application for Recognition of a Foreign Proceeding

1 A foreign representative may apply to the court for recognition of the foreign proceeding in which the foreign representative has been appointed.

2 An application for recognition shall be accompanied by—

(a) a certified copy of the decision commencing the foreign proceeding and appointing the foreign representative; or

(b) a certificate from the foreign court affirming the existence of the foreign proceeding and of the appointment of the foreign representative; or

(c) in the absence of evidence referred to in sub-paragraphs (a) and (b), any other evidence acceptable to the court of the existence of the foreign proceeding and of the appointment of the foreign representative.

3 An application for recognition shall also be accompanied by a statement identifying all foreign proceedings, proceedings under British insolvency law and section 426 requests in respect of the debtor that are known to the foreign representative.

4 The foreign representative shall provide the court with a translation into English of documents supplied in support of the application for recognition.

[4462]

Article 16
Presumptions Concerning Recognition

1 If the decision or certificate referred to in paragraph 2 of article 15 indicates that the foreign proceeding is a proceeding within the meaning of sub-paragraph (i) of article 2 and that the foreign representative is a person or body within the meaning of sub-paragraph (j) of article 2, the court is entitled to so presume.

2 The court is entitled to presume that documents submitted in support of the application for recognition are authentic, whether or not they have been legalised.

3 In the absence of proof to the contrary, the debtor's registered office, or habitual residence in the case of an individual, is presumed to be the centre of the debtor's main interests.

[4463]

Article 17
Decision to Recognise a Foreign Proceeding

1 Subject to article 6, a foreign proceeding shall be recognised if—

(a) it is a foreign proceeding within the meaning of sub-paragraph (i) of article 2;

(b) the foreign representative applying for recognition is a person or body within the meaning of sub-paragraph (j) of article 2;

(c) the application meets the requirements of paragraphs 2 and 3 of article 15; and

(d) the application has been submitted to the court referred to in article 4.

2 The foreign proceeding shall be recognised—

(a) as a foreign main proceeding if it is taking place in the State where the debtor has the centre of its main interests; or

(b) as a foreign non-main proceeding if the debtor has an establishment within the meaning of sub-paragraph (e) of article 2 in the foreign State.

3 An application for recognition of a foreign proceeding shall be decided upon at the earliest possible time.

4 The provisions of articles 15 to 16, this article and article 18 do not prevent modification or termination of recognition if it is shown that the grounds for granting it were fully or partially lacking or have fully or partially ceased to exist and in such a case, the court may, on the application of the foreign representative or a person affected by recognition, or of its own motion, modify or terminate recognition, either altogether or for a limited time, on such terms and conditions as the court thinks fit.

[4464]

Article 18
Subsequent Information

From the time of filing the application for recognition of the foreign proceeding, the foreign representative shall inform the court promptly of—

(a) any substantial change in the status of the recognised foreign proceeding or the status of the foreign representative's appointment; and

(b) any other foreign proceeding, proceeding under British insolvency law or section 426 request regarding the same debtor that becomes known to the foreign representative.

[4465]

Article 19
Relief that may be Granted upon Application for Recognition of a Foreign Proceeding

1 From the time of filing an application for recognition until the application is decided upon, the court may, at the request of the foreign representative, where relief is urgently needed to protect the assets of the debtor or the interests of the creditors, grant relief of a provisional nature, including—

(a) staying execution against the debtor's assets;

(b) entrusting the administration or realisation of all or part of the debtor's assets located in Great Britain to the foreign representative or another person designated by the court, in order to protect and preserve the value of assets that, by their nature or because of other circumstances, are perishable, susceptible to devaluation or otherwise in jeopardy; and

(c) any relief mentioned in paragraph 1(c), (d) or (g) of article 21.

2 Unless extended under paragraph 1(f) of article 21, the relief granted under this article terminates when the application for recognition is decided upon.

3 The court may refuse to grant relief under this article if such relief would interfere with the administration of a foreign main proceeding.

[4466]

Article 20
Effects of Recognition of a Foreign Main Proceeding

1 Upon recognition of a foreign proceeding that is a foreign main proceeding, subject to paragraph 2 of this article—

(a) commencement or continuation of individual actions or individual proceedings concerning the debtor's assets, rights, obligations or liabilities is stayed;
(b) execution against the debtor's assets is stayed; and
(c) the right to transfer, encumber or otherwise dispose of any assets of the debtor is suspended.

2 The stay and suspension referred to in paragraph 1 of this article shall be—

(a) the same in scope and effect as if the debtor, in the case of an individual, had been adjudged bankrupt under the Insolvency Act 1986 or had his estate sequestrated under the Bankruptcy (Scotland) Act 1985, or, in the case of a debtor other than an individual, had been made the subject of a winding-up order under the Insolvency Act 1986; and
(b) subject to the same powers of the court and the same prohibitions, limitations, exceptions and conditions as would apply under the law of Great Britain in such a case,

and the provisions of paragraph 1 of this article shall be interpreted accordingly.

3 Without prejudice to paragraph 2 of this article, the stay and suspension referred to in paragraph 1 of this article, in particular, does not affect any right—

(a) to take any steps to enforce security over the debtor's property;
(b) to take any steps to repossess goods in the debtor's possession under a hire-purchase agreement;
(c) exercisable under or by virtue of or in connection with the provisions referred to in article 1(4); or
(d) of a creditor to set off its claim against a claim of the debtor,

being a right which would have been exercisable if the debtor, in the case of an individual, had been adjudged bankrupt under the Insolvency Act 1986 or had his estate sequestrated under the Bankruptcy (Scotland) Act 1985, or, in the case of a debtor other than an individual, had been made the subject of a winding-up order under the Insolvency Act 1986.

4 Paragraph 1(a) of this article does not affect the right to—

(a) commence individual actions or proceedings to the extent necessary to preserve a claim against the debtor; or
(b) commence or continue any criminal proceedings or any action or proceedings by a person or body having regulatory, supervisory or investigative functions of a public nature, being an action or proceedings brought in the exercise of those functions.

5 Paragraph 1 of this article does not affect the right to request or otherwise initiate the commencement of a proceeding under British insolvency law or the right to file claims in such a proceeding.

6 In addition to and without prejudice to any powers of the court under or by virtue of paragraph 2 of this article, the court may, on the application of the foreign representative or a person affected by the stay and suspension referred to in paragraph 1 of this article, or of its own motion, modify or terminate such stay and suspension or any part of it, either altogether or for a limited time, on such terms and conditions as the court thinks fit.

[4467]

Article 21
Relief that may be Granted upon Recognition of a Foreign Proceeding

1 Upon recognition of a foreign proceeding, whether main or non-main, where necessary to protect the assets of the debtor or the interests of the creditors, the court may, at the request of the foreign representative, grant any appropriate relief, including—

(a) staying the commencement or continuation of individual actions or individual proceedings concerning the debtor's assets, rights, obligations or liabilities, to the extent they have not been stayed under paragraph 1(a) of article 20;

(b) staying execution against the debtor's assets to the extent it has not been stayed under paragraph 1(b) of article 20;

(c) suspending the right to transfer, encumber or otherwise dispose of any assets of the debtor to the extent this right has not been suspended under paragraph 1(c) of article 20;

(d) providing for the examination of witnesses, the taking of evidence or the delivery of information concerning the debtor's assets, affairs, rights, obligations or liabilities;

(e) entrusting the administration or realisation of all or part of the debtor's assets located in Great Britain to the foreign representative or another person designated by the court;

(f) extending relief granted under paragraph 1 of article 19; and

(g) granting any additional relief that may be available to a British insolvency officeholder under the law of Great Britain, including any relief provided under paragraph 43 of Schedule B1 to the Insolvency Act 1986.

2 Upon recognition of a foreign proceeding, whether main or non-main, the court may, at the request of the foreign representative, entrust the distribution of all or part of the debtor's assets located in Great Britain to the foreign representative or another person designated by the court, provided that the court is satisfied that the interests of creditors in Great Britain are adequately protected.

3 In granting relief under this article to a representative of a foreign non-main proceeding, the court must be satisfied that the relief relates to assets that, under the law of Great Britain, should be administered in the foreign non-main proceeding or concerns information required in that proceeding.

4 No stay under paragraph 1(a) of this article shall affect the right to commence or continue any criminal proceedings or any action or proceedings by a person or body having regulatory, supervisory or investigative functions of a public nature, being an action or proceedings brought in the exercise of those functions.

[4468]

Article 22

Protection of Creditors and other Interested Persons

1 In granting or denying relief under article 19 or 21, or in modifying or terminating relief under paragraph 3 of this article or paragraph 6 of article 20, the court must be satisfied that the interests of the creditors (including any secured creditors or parties to hire-purchase agreements) and other interested persons, including if appropriate the debtor, are adequately protected.

2 The court may subject relief granted under article 19 or 21 to conditions it considers appropriate, including the provision by the foreign representative of security or caution for the proper performance of his functions.

3 The court may, at the request of the foreign representative or a person affected by relief granted under article 19 or 21, or of its own motion, modify or terminate such relief.

[4469]

Article 23

Actions to Avoid Acts Detrimental to Creditors

1 Subject to paragraphs 6 and 9 of this article, upon recognition of a foreign proceeding, the foreign representative has standing to make an application to the court for an order under or in connection with sections 238, 239, 242, 243, 244, 245, 339, 340, 342A, 343, and 423 of the Insolvency Act 1986 and sections 34, 35, 36, 36A and 61 of the Bankruptcy (Scotland) Act 1985.

2 Where the foreign representative makes such an application ("an article 23 application"), the sections referred to in paragraph 1 of this article and sections 240, 241, 341, 342, 342B to 342F, 424 and 425 of the Insolvency Act 1986 and sections 36B and 36C of the Bankruptcy (Scotland) Act 1985 shall apply—

(a) whether or not the debtor, in the case of an individual, has been adjudged bankrupt or had his estate sequestrated, or, in the case of a debtor other than an individual, is being wound up or is in administration, under British insolvency law; and

(b) with the modifications set out in paragraph 3 of this article.

3 The modifications referred to in paragraph 2 of this article are as follows—

(a) for the purposes of sections 241(2A)(a) and 342(2A)(a) of the Insolvency Act 1986, a person has notice of the relevant proceedings if he has notice of the opening of the relevant foreign proceeding;

(b) for the purposes of sections 240(1) and 245(3) of that Act, the onset of insolvency shall be the date of the opening of the relevant foreign proceeding;

(c) the periods referred to in sections 244(2), 341(1)(a) to (c) and 343(2) of that Act shall be periods ending with the date of the opening of the relevant foreign proceeding;

(d) for the purposes of sections 242(3)(a), (3)(b) and 243(1) of that Act, the date on which the winding up of the company commences or it enters administration shall be the date of the opening of the relevant foreign proceeding; and

(e) for the purposes of sections 34(3)(a), (3)(b), 35(1)(c), 36(1)(a) and (1)(b) and 61(2) of the Bankruptcy (Scotland) Act 1985, the date of sequestration or granting of the trust deed shall be the date of the opening of the relevant foreign proceeding.

4 For the purposes of paragraph 3 of this article, the date of the opening of the foreign proceeding shall be determined in accordance with the law of the State in which the foreign proceeding is taking place, including any rule of law by virtue of which the foreign proceeding is deemed to have opened at an earlier time.

5 When the foreign proceeding is a foreign non-main proceeding, the court must be satisfied that the article 23 application relates to assets that, under the law of Great Britain, should be administered in the foreign non-main proceeding.

6 At any time when a proceeding under British insolvency law is taking place regarding the debtor—

(a) the foreign representative shall not make an article 23 application except with the permission of—
   (i) in the case of a proceeding under British insolvency law taking place in England and Wales, the High Court; or
   (ii) in the case of a proceeding under British insolvency law taking place in Scotland, the Court of Session; and

(b) references to "the court" in paragraphs 1, 5 and 7 of this article are references to the court in which that proceeding is taking place.

7 On making an order on an article 23 application, the court may give such directions regarding the distribution of any proceeds of the claim by the foreign representative, as it thinks fit to ensure that the interests of creditors in Great Britain are adequately protected.

8 Nothing in this article affects the right of a British insolvency officeholder to make an application under or in connection with any of the provisions referred to in paragraph 1 of this article.

9 Nothing in paragraph 1 of this article shall apply in respect of any preference given, floating charge created, alienation, assignment or relevant contributions (within the meaning of section 342A(5) of the Insolvency Act 1986) made or other transaction entered into before the date on which this Law comes into force.

[4470]

Article 24
Intervention by a Foreign Representative in Proceedings in Great Britain

Upon recognition of a foreign proceeding, the foreign representative may, provided the requirements of the law of Great Britain are met, intervene in any proceedings in which the debtor is a party.

[4471]

CHAPTER IV
COOPERATION WITH FOREIGN COURTS AND FOREIGN REPRESENTATIVES

Article 25
Cooperation and Direct Communication between a Court of Great Britain and Foreign Courts or Foreign Representatives

1 In matters referred to in paragraph 1 of article 1, the court may cooperate to the maximum extent possible with foreign courts or foreign representatives, either directly or through a British insolvency officeholder.

2 The court is entitled to communicate directly with, or to request information or assistance directly from, foreign courts or foreign representatives.

[4472]

Article 26
Cooperation and Direct Communication between the British Insolvency Officeholder and Foreign Courts or Foreign Representatives

1 In matters referred to in paragraph 1 of article 1, a British insolvency officeholder shall to the extent consistent with his other duties under the law of Great Britain, in the exercise of his functions and subject to the supervision of the court, cooperate to the maximum extent possible with foreign courts or foreign representatives.

2 The British insolvency officeholder is entitled, in the exercise of his functions and subject to the supervision of the court, to communicate directly with foreign courts or foreign representatives.

[4473]

Article 27
Forms of Cooperation

Cooperation referred to in articles 25 and 26 may be implemented by any appropriate means, including—

- (a) appointment of a person to act at the direction of the court;
- (b) communication of information by any means considered appropriate by the court;
- (c) coordination of the administration and supervision of the debtor's assets and affairs;
- (d) approval or implementation by courts of agreements concerning the coordination of proceedings;
- (e) coordination of concurrent proceedings regarding the same debtor.

[4474]

CHAPTER V
CONCURRENT PROCEEDINGS

Article 28
Commencement of a Proceeding Under British Insolvency Law after Recognition of a Foreign Main Proceeding

After recognition of a foreign main proceeding, the effects of a proceeding under British insolvency law in relation to the same debtor shall, insofar as the assets of that debtor are concerned, be restricted to assets that are located in Great Britain and, to the extent necessary to implement cooperation and coordination under articles 25, 26 and 27, to other assets of the debtor that, under the law of Great Britain, should be administered in that proceeding.

[4475]

Article 29
Coordination of a Proceeding Under British Insolvency Law and a Foreign Proceeding

Where a foreign proceeding and a proceeding under British insolvency law are taking place concurrently regarding the same debtor, the court may seek cooperation and coordination under articles 25, 26 and 27, and the following shall apply—

(a) when the proceeding in Great Britain is taking place at the time the application for recognition of the foreign proceeding is filed—
  (i) any relief granted under article 19 or 21 must be consistent with the proceeding in Great Britain; and
  (ii) if the foreign proceeding is recognised in Great Britain as a foreign main proceeding, article 20 does not apply;

(b) when the proceeding in Great Britain commences after the filing of the application for recognition of the foreign proceeding—
  (i) any relief in effect under article 19 or 21 shall be reviewed by the court and shall be modified or terminated if inconsistent with the proceeding in Great Britain;
  (ii) if the foreign proceeding is a foreign main proceeding, the stay and suspension referred to in paragraph 1 of article 20 shall be modified or terminated pursuant to paragraph 6 of article 20, if inconsistent with the proceeding in Great Britain; and
  (iii) any proceedings brought by the foreign representative by virtue of paragraph 1 of article 23 before the proceeding in Great Britain commenced shall be reviewed by the court and the court may give such directions as it thinks fit regarding the continuance of those proceedings; and

(c) in granting, extending or modifying relief granted to a representative of a foreign non-main proceeding, the court must be satisfied that the relief relates to assets that, under the law of Great Britain, should be administered in the foreign non-main proceeding or concerns information required in that proceeding.

[4476]

Article 30
Coordination of more than one Foreign Proceeding

In matters referred to in paragraph 1 of article 1, in respect of more than one foreign proceeding regarding the same debtor, the court may seek cooperation and coordination under articles 25, 26 and 27, and the following shall apply—

(a) any relief granted under article 19 or 21 to a representative of a foreign non-main proceeding after recognition of a foreign main proceeding must be consistent with the foreign main proceeding;

(b) if a foreign main proceeding is recognised after the filing of an application for recognition of a foreign non-main proceeding, any relief in effect under article 19 or 21 shall be reviewed by the court and shall be modified or terminated if inconsistent with the foreign main proceeding; and

(c) if, after recognition of a foreign non-main proceeding, another foreign non-main proceeding is recognised, the court shall grant, modify or terminate relief for the purpose of facilitating coordination of the proceedings.

[4477]

Article 31
Presumption of Insolvency Based on Recognition of a Foreign Main Proceeding

In the absence of evidence to the contrary, recognition of a foreign main proceeding is, for the purpose of commencing a proceeding under British insolvency law, proof that the debtor is unable to pay its debts or, in relation to Scotland, is apparently insolvent within the meaning given to those expressions under British insolvency law.

[4478]

Article 32
Rule of Payment in Concurrent Proceedings

Without prejudice to secured claims or rights in rem, a creditor who has received part payment in respect of its claim in a proceeding pursuant to a law relating to insolvency in a foreign State may not receive a payment for the same claim in a proceeding under British insolvency law regarding the same debtor, so long as the payment to the other creditors of the same class is proportionately less than the payment the creditor has already received.

[4479]

I. SERVICE AND EVIDENCE

CONVENTION ON THE SERVICE ABROAD OF JUDICIAL AND EXTRAJUDICIAL DOCUMENTS IN CIVIL OR COMMERCIAL MATTERS

(Concluded The Hague, 15 November 1965)

NOTES

The United Kingdom instrument of ratification was deposited on 17 November and the Convention entered into force on 10 February 1969.

The original source of this Convention is the Hague Conference on Private International Law Actes et documents de la Dixième session (1964), tome III, Notification. See the website of the Hague Conference at http://www.hcch.net.

For current status of this Convention, see Table 3 at **[4678]**.

The States signatory to the present Convention,

DESIRING to create appropriate means to ensure that judicial and extrajudicial documents to be served abroad shall be brought to the notice of the addressee in sufficient time,

DESIRING to improve the organisation of mutual judicial assistance for that purpose by simplifying and expediting the procedure,

HAVE RESOLVED to conclude a Convention to this effect and have agreed upon the following provisions—

Article 1

The present Convention shall apply in all cases, in civil or commercial matters, where there is occasion to transmit a judicial or extrajudicial document for service abroad.

This Convention shall not apply where the address of the person to be served with the document is not known.

[4480]

CHAPTER I
JUDICIAL DOCUMENTS

Article 2

Each Contracting State shall designate a Central Authority which will undertake to receive requests for service coming from other contracting States and to proceed in conformity with the provisions of articles 3 to 6.

Each State shall organise the Central Authority in conformity with its own law.

[4481]

Article 3

The authority or judicial officer competent under the law of the State in which the documents originate shall forward to the Central Authority of the State addressed a request conforming to the model annexed to the present Convention, without any requirement of legalisation or other equivalent formality.

The document to be served or a copy thereof shall be annexed to the request. The request and the document shall both be furnished in duplicate.

[4482]

Article 4

If the Central Authority considers that the request does not comply with the provisions of the present Convention it shall promptly inform the applicant and specify its objections to the request.

[4483]

Article 5

The Central Authority of the State addressed shall itself serve the document or shall arrange to have it served by an appropriate agency, either—

(a) by a method prescribed by its internal law for the service of documents in domestic actions upon persons who are within its territory, or

(b) by a particular method requested by the applicant, unless such a method is incompatible with the law of the State addressed.

Subject to sub-paragraph (b) of the first paragraph of this article, the document may always be served by delivery to an addressee who accepts it voluntarily.

If the document is to be served under the first paragraph above, the Central Authority may require the document to be written in, or translated into, the official language or one of the official languages of the State addressed.

That part of the request, in the form attached to the present Convention, which contains a summary of the document to be served, shall be served with the document.

[4484]

Article 6

The Central Authority of the State addressed or any authority which it may have designated for that purpose, shall complete a certificate in the form of the model annexed to the present Convention.

The certificate shall state that the document has been served and shall include the method, the place and the date of service and the person to whom the document was delivered. If the document has not been served, the certificate shall set out the reasons which have prevented service.

The applicant may require that a certificate not completed by a Central Authority or by a judicial authority shall be countersigned by one of these authorities.

The certificate shall be forwarded directly to the applicant.

[4485]

Article 7

The standard terms in the model annexed to the present Convention shall in all cases be written either in French or in English. They may also be written in the official language, or in one of the official languages, of the State in which the documents originate.

The corresponding blanks shall be completed either in the language of the State addressed or in French or in English.

[4486]

Article 8

Each contracting State shall be free to effect service of judicial documents upon persons abroad, without application of any compulsion, directly through its diplomatic or consular agents.

Any State may declare that it is opposed to such service within its territory, unless the document is to be served upon a national of the State in which the documents originate.

[4487]

Article 9

Each contracting State shall be free, in addition, to use consular channels to forward documents, for the purpose of service, to those authorities of another contracting State which are designated by the latter for this purpose.

Each contracting State may, if exceptional circumstances so require, use diplomatic channels for the same purpose.

[4488]

Article 10

Provided the State of destination does not object, the present Convention shall not interfere with—

(a) the freedom to send judicial documents, by postal channels, directly to persons abroad,

(b) the freedom of judicial officers, officials or other competent persons of the State of origin to effect service of judicial documents directly through the judicial officers, officials or other competent persons of the State of destination,

(c) the freedom of any person interested in a judicial proceeding to effect service of judicial documents directly through the judicial officers, officials or other competent persons of the State of destination.

[4489]

Article 11

The present Convention shall not prevent two or more contracting States from agreeing to permit, for the purpose of service of judicial documents, channels of transmission other than those provided for in the preceding articles and, in particular, direct communication between their respective authorities.

[4490]

Article 12

The service of judicial documents coming from a contracting State shall not give rise to any payment or reimbursement of taxes or costs for the services rendered by the State addressed.

The applicant shall pay or reimburse the costs occasioned by—

(a) the employment of a judicial officer or of a person competent under the law of the State of destination,

(b) the use of a particular method of service.

[4491]

Article 13

Where a request for service complies with the terms of the present Convention, the State addressed may refuse to comply therewith only if it deems that compliance would infringe its sovereignty or security.

It may not refuse to comply solely on the ground that, under its internal law, it claims exclusive jurisdiction over the subject-matter of the action or that its internal law would not permit the action upon which the application is based.

The Central Authority shall, in case of refusal, promptly inform the applicant and state the reasons for the refusal.

[4492]

Article 14

Difficulties which may arise in connection with the transmission of judicial documents for service shall be settled through diplomatic channels.

[4493]

Article 15

Where a writ of summons or an equivalent document had to be transmitted abroad for the purpose of service, under the provisions of the present Convention, and the defendant has not appeared, judgment shall not be given until it is established that—

(a) the document was served by a method prescribed by the internal law of the State addressed for the service of documents in domestic actions upon persons who are within its territory, or

(b) the document was actually delivered to the defendant or to his residence by another method provided for by this Convention,

and that in either of these cases the service or the delivery was effected in sufficient time to enable the defendant to defend.

Each contracting State shall be free to declare that the judge, notwithstanding the provisions of the first paragraph of this article, may give judgment even if no certificate of service or delivery has been received, if all the following conditions are fulfilled—

(a) the document was transmitted by one of the methods provided for in this Convention,

(b) a period of time of not less than six months, considered adequate by the judge in the particular case, has elapsed since the date of the transmission of the document,

(c) no certificate of any kind has been received, even though every reasonable effort has been made to obtain it through the competent authorities of the State addressed.

Notwithstanding the provisions of the preceding paragraphs the judge may order, in case of urgency, any provisional or protective measures.

[4494]

Article 16

When a writ of summons or an equivalent document had to be transmitted abroad for the purpose of service, under the provisions of the present Convention, and a judgment has been entered against a defendant who has not appeared, the judge shall have the power to relieve the defendant from the effects of the expiration of the time for appeal from the judgment if the following conditions are fulfilled—

(a) the defendant, without any fault on his part, did not have knowledge of the document in sufficient time to defend, or knowledge of the judgment in sufficient time to appeal, and

(b) the defendant has disclosed a prima facie defence to the action on the merits.

An application for relief may be filed only within a reasonable time after the defendant has knowledge of the judgment.

Each contracting State may declare that the application will not be entertained if it is filed after the expiration of a time to be stated in the declaration, but which shall in no case be less than one year following the date of the judgment.

This article shall not apply to judgments concerning status or capacity of persons.

[4495]

CHAPTER II
EXTRAJUDICIAL DOCUMENTS

Article 17

Extrajudicial documents emanating from authorities and judicial officers of a contracting State may be transmitted for the purpose of service in another contracting State by the methods and under the provisions of the present Convention.

[4496]

CHAPTER III
GENERAL CLAUSES

Article 18

Each Contracting State may designate other authorities in addition to the Central Authority and shall determine the extent of their competence.

The applicant shall, however, in all cases, have the right to address a request directly to the Central Authority.

Federal States shall be free to designate more than one Central Authority.

[4497]

Article 19

To the extent that the internal law of a contracting State permits methods of transmission, other than those provided for in the preceding articles, of documents coming from abroad, for service within its territory, the present Convention shall not affect such provisions.

[4498]

Article 20

The present Convention shall not prevent an agreement between any two or more contracting States to dispense with—

(a) the necessity for duplicate copies of transmitted documents as required by the second paragraph of article 3,

(b) the language requirements of the third paragraph of article 5 and article 7,

(c) the provisions of the fourth paragraph of article 5,

(d) the provisions of the second paragraph of article 12.

[4499]

Article 21

Each contracting State shall, at the time of the deposit of its instrument of ratification or accession, or at a later date, inform the Ministry of Foreign Affairs of the Netherlands of the following—

(a) the designation of authorities, pursuant to articles 2 and 18,

(b) the designation of the authority competent to complete the certificate pursuant to article 6,

(c) the designation of the authority competent to receive documents transmitted by consular channels, pursuant to article 9.

Each contracting State shall similarly inform the Ministry, where appropriate, of—

(a) opposition to the use of methods of transmission pursuant to articles 8 and 10,

(b) declarations pursuant to the second paragraph of article 15 and the third paragraph of article 16,

(c) all modifications of the above designations, oppositions and declarations.

[4500]

Article 22

Where Parties to the present Convention are also Parties to one or both of the Conventions on civil procedure signed at The Hague on 17th July 1905, and on 1st March 1954,[1] this Convention shall replace as between them articles 1 to 7 of the earlier Conventions.

[4501]

NOTES

[1] The United Kingdom is not a party to either of these Conventions.

Article 23

The present Convention shall not affect the application of article 23 of the Convention on civil procedure signed at The Hague on 17th July 1905, or of article 24 of the Convention on civil procedure signed at The Hague on 1st March 1954.

These articles shall, however, apply only if methods of communication, identical to those provided for in these Conventions, are used.

[4502]

Article 24

Supplementary agreements between parties to the Conventions of 1905 and 1954 shall be considered as equally applicable to the present Convention, unless the Parties have otherwise agreed.

[4503]

Article 25

Without prejudice to the provisions of articles 22 and 24, the present Convention shall not derogate from Conventions containing provisions on the matters governed by this Convention to which the contracting States are, or shall become, Parties.

[4504]

Article 26

The present Convention shall be open for signature by the States represented at the Tenth Session of the Hague Conference on Private International Law.

It shall be ratified, and the instruments of ratification shall be deposited with the Ministry of Foreign Affairs of the Netherlands.

[4505]

Article 27

The present Convention shall enter into force on the sixtieth day after the deposit of the third instrument of ratification referred to in the second paragraph of Article 26.[1]

The Convention shall enter into force for each signatory State which ratifies subsequently on the sixtieth day after the deposit of its instrument of ratification.

[4506]

NOTES

[1] The Convention entered into force on 19 February 1969.

Article 28

Any State not represented at the Tenth Session of the Hague Conference on Private International Law may accede to the present Convention after it has entered into force in accordance with the first paragraph of article 27. The instrument of accession shall be deposited with the Ministry of Foreign Affairs of the Netherlands.

The Convention shall enter into force for such a State in the absence of any objection from a State, which has ratified the Convention before such deposit, notified to the Ministry of Foreign Affairs of the Netherlands within a period of six months after the date on which the said Ministry has notified it of such accession.

In the absence of any such objection, the Convention shall enter into force for the acceding State on the first day of the month following the expiration of the last of the periods referred to in the preceding paragraph.

[4507]

Article 29

Any State may, at the time of signature, ratification or accession, declare that the present Convention shall extend to all the territories for the international relations of which it is responsible, or to one or more of them. Such a declaration shall take effect on the date of entry into force of the Convention for the State concerned.

At any time thereafter, such extensions shall be notified to the Ministry of Foreign Affairs of the Netherlands.

The Convention shall enter into force for the territories mentioned in such an extension on the sixtieth day after the notification referred to in the preceding paragraph.

[4508]

Article 30

The present Convention shall remain in force for five years from the date of its entry into force in accordance with the first paragraph of article 27, even for States which have ratified it or acceded to it subsequently.

If there has been no denunciation, it shall be renewed tacitly every five years.

Any denunciation shall be notified to the Ministry of Foreign Affairs of the Netherlands at least six months before the end of the five year period.

It may be limited to certain of the territories to which the Convention applies.

The denunciation shall have effect only as regards the State which has notified it. The Convention shall remain in force for the other contracting States.

[4509]

Article 31

The Ministry of Foreign Affairs of the Netherlands shall give notice to the States referred to in article 26, and to the States which have acceded in accordance with article 28, of the following—

(a) the signatures and ratifications referred to in article 26;
(b) the date on which the present Convention enters into force in accordance with the first paragraph of article 27;
(c) the accessions referred to in article 28 and the dates on which they take effect;
(d) the extensions referred to in article 29 and the dates on which they take effect;
(e) the designations, oppositions and declarations referred to in article 21;
(f) the denunciations referred to in the third paragraph of article 30.

[4510]

In witness whereof the undersigned, being duly authorised thereto, have signed the present Convention.

Done at The Hague, on the 15th day of November, 1965, in the English and French languages, both texts being equally authentic, in a single copy which shall be deposited in the archives of the Government of the Netherlands, and of which a certified copy shall be sent, through the diplomatic channel, to each of the States represented at the Tenth Session of the Hague Conference on Private International Law.

ANNEX TO THE CONVENTION

Forms

Request

For Service Abroad of Judicial or Extrajudicial Documents

Convention on the service abroad of judicial and extrajudicial documents in civil or commercial matters, signed at The Hague, ... 196 .

Identity and address of the applicant	Address of receiving authority

The undersigned applicant has the honour to transmit—in duplicate—the documents listed below and, in conformity with article 5 of the above-mentioned Convention, requests prompt service of one copy thereof on the addressee, ie,
(identity and address)
....
....

(a) in accordance with the provisions of sub-paragraph (a) of the first paragraph of article 5 of the Convention*.

(b) in accordance with the following particular method (sub-paragraph (b) of the first paragraph of article 5)*: ....
....
....

(c) by delivery to the addressee, if he accepts it voluntarily (second paragraph of article 5)*.

The authority is requested to return or to have returned to the applicant a copy of the documents—and of the annexes*—with a certificate as provided on the reverse side.

List of documents

.... Done at ...., the ....

.... Signature and/or stamp.

....

....

....

....

* Delete if inappropriate.

Reverse of the request

Certificate

The undersigned authority has the honour to certify, in conformity with article 6 of the Convention,

(1) that the document has been served*

— the (date)
....

— at (place, street, number)
....

....

— in one of the following methods authorised by article 5:

(a) in accordance with the provisions of sub-paragraph (a) of the first paragraph of article 5 of the Convention*.

(b) in accordance with the following particular method*:

....

....

(c) by delivery to the addressee, who accepted it voluntarily*.

The documents referred to in the request have been delivered to:

— (identity and description of person)

....

....

— relationship to the addressee (family, business or other):

....

(2) that the document has not been served, by reason of the following facts*:

....

....

....

In conformity with the second paragraph of article 12 of the Convention, the applicant is requested to pay or reimburse the expenses detailed in the attached statement*.

Annexes

Documents returned:

....

....

....

In appropriate cases, documents establishing the service:

....

....

Done at ...., the ....

Signature and/or stamp.

* Delete if inappropriate.

Summary of the Document to be Served

Convention on the service abroad of judicial and extrajudicial documents in civil or commercial matters, signed at The Hague, the .... 196 .

(article 5, fourth paragraph)

Name and address of the requesting authority:

....

....

Particulars of the parties*:

....

....

Judicial Document**

Nature and purpose of the document:

....

....

Nature and purpose of the proceedings and, where appropriate, the amount in dispute:

....

....

Date and place for entering appearance**:

....

....

Court which has given judgment**:

....

....

Date of judgment**:

....

Time limits stated in the document**:

....

....

Extra Judicial Document**

Nature and purpose of the document:

....

....
Time limits stated in the document**:
....
....

* If appropriate, identity and address of the person interested in the transmission of the document.

** Delete if inappropriate.

[4511]–[4512]

NOTES

For signatures and ratifications, see Table 2 at **[4677]**.

CONVENTION ON THE TAKING OF EVIDENCE ABROAD IN CIVIL OR COMMERCIAL MATTERS

(The Hague, 18 March 1970)

NOTES

The original source of this convention is the Hague Conference on Private International Law Actes et documents de la Onzième session (1968), Tome IV, Obtention des preuves. See the website of the Hague Conference at http://www.hcch.net.

For current status of this Convention, see Table 4 at **[4679]**.

The States signatory to the present Convention,

DESIRING to facilitate the transmission and execution of Letters of Request and to further the accommodation of the different methods which they use for this purpose,

DESIRING to improve mutual judicial co-operation in civil or commercial matters,

HAVE RESOLVED to conclude a Convention to this effect and have agreed upon the following provisions—

CHAPTER I
LETTERS OF REQUEST

Article 1

In civil or commercial matters a judicial authority of a Contracting State may, in accordance with the provisions of the law of that State, request the competent authority of another Contracting State, by means of a Letter of Request, to obtain evidence, or to perform some other judicial act.

A Letter shall not be used to obtain evidence which is not intended for use in judicial proceedings, commenced or contemplated.

The expression "other judicial act" does not cover the service of judicial documents or the issuance of any process by which judgments or orders are executed or enforced, or orders for provisional or protective measures.

[4513]

Article 2

A Contracting State shall designate a Central Authority which will undertake to receive Letters of Request coming from a judicial authority of another Contracting State and to transmit them to the authority competent to execute them. Each State shall organize the Central Authority in accordance with its own law.

Letters shall be sent to the Central Authority of the State of execution without being transmitted through any other authority of that State.

[4514]

Article 3

A Letter of Request shall specify—

(a) the authority requesting its execution and the authority requested to execute it, if known to the requesting authority;

(b) the names and addresses of the parties to the proceedings and their representatives, if any;

(c) the nature of the proceedings for which the evidence is required, giving all necessary information in regard thereto;

(d) the evidence to be obtained or other judicial act to be performed.

Where appropriate, the Letter shall specify, *inter alia*—

(e) the names and addresses of the persons to be examined;

(f) the questions to be put to the persons to be examined or a statement of the subject-matter about which they are to be examined;

(g) the documents or other property, real or personal, to be inspected;

(h) any requirement that the evidence is to be given on oath or affirmation, and any special form to be used;

(i) any special method or procedure to be followed under Article 9.

A Letter may also mention any information necessary for the application of Article 11.

No legalization or other like formality may be required.

[4515]

Article 4

A Letter of Request shall be in the language of the authority requested to execute it or be accompanied by a translation into that language.

Nevertheless, a Contracting State shall accept a Letter in either English or French, or a translation into one of these languages, unless it has made the reservation authorized by Article 33.

A Contracting State which has more than one official language and cannot, for reasons of internal law, accept Letters in one of these languages for the whole of its territory, shall, by declaration, specify the language in which the Letter or translation thereof shall be expressed for execution in the specified parts of its territory. In case of failure to comply with this declaration, without justifiable excuse, the costs of translation into the required language shall be borne by the State of origin.

A Contracting State may, by declaration, specify the language or languages other than those referred to in the preceding paragraphs, in which a Letter may be sent to its Central Authority.

Any translation accompanying a Letter shall be certified as correct, either by a diplomatic officer or consular agent or by a sworn translator or by any other person so authorized in either State.

[4516]

Article 5

If the Central Authority considers that the request does not comply with the provisions of the present Convention, it shall promptly inform the authority of the State of origin which transmitted the Letter of Request, specifying the objections to the Letter.

[4517]

Article 6

If the authority to whom a Letter of Request has been transmitted is not competent to execute it, the Letter shall be sent forthwith to the authority in the same State which is competent to execute it in accordance with the provisions of its own law.

[4518]

Article 7

The requesting authority shall, if it so desires, be informed of the time when, and the place where, the proceedings will take place, in order that the parties concerned, and their representatives, if any, may be present. This information shall be sent directly to the parties or their representatives when the authority of the State of origin so requests.

[4519]

Article 8

A Contracting State may declare that members of the judicial personnel of the requesting authority of another Contracting State may be present at the execution of a Letter of Request. Prior authorization by the competent authority designated by the declaring State may be required.

[4520]

Article 9

The judicial authority which executes a Letter of Request shall apply its own law as to the methods and procedures to be followed.

However, it will follow a request of the requesting authority that a special method or procedure be followed, unless this is incompatible with the internal law of the State of execution or is impossible of performance by reason of its internal practice and procedure or by reason of practical difficulties.

A Letter of Request shall be executed expeditiously.

[4521]

Article 10

In executing a Letter of Request the requested authority shall apply the appropriate measures of compulsion in the instances and to the same extent as are provided by its internal law for the execution of orders issued by the authorities of its own country or of requests made by parties in internal proceedings.

[4522]

Article 11

In the execution of a Letter of Request the person concerned may refuse to give evidence in so far as he has a privilege or duty to refuse to give the evidence—

(a) under the law of the State of execution; or

(b) under the law of the State of origin, and the privilege or duty has been specified in the Letter, or, at the instance of the requested authority, has been otherwise confirmed to that authority by the requesting authority.

A Contracting State may declare that, in addition, it will respect privileges and duties existing under the law of States other than the State of origin and the State of execution, to the extent specified in that declaration.

[4523]

Article 12

The execution of a Letter of Request may be refused only to the extent that—

(a) in the State of execution the execution of the Letter does not fall within the functions of the judiciary; or

(b) the State addressed considers that its sovereignty or security would be prejudiced thereby.

Execution may not be refused solely on the ground that under its internal law the State of execution claims exclusive jurisdiction over the subject-matter of the action or that its internal law would not admit a right of action on it.

[4524]

Article 13

The documents establishing the execution of the Letter of Request shall be sent by the requested authority to the requesting authority by the same channel which was used by the latter.

In every instance where the Letter is not executed in whole or in part, the requesting authority shall be informed immediately through the same channel and advised of the reasons.

[4525]

Article 14

The execution of the Letter of Request shall not give rise to any reimbursement of taxes or costs of any nature.

Nevertheless, the State of execution has the right to require the State of origin to reimburse the fees paid to experts and interpreters and the costs occasioned by the use of a special procedure requested by the State of origin under Article 9, paragraph 2.

The requested authority whose law obliges the parties themselves to secure evidence, and which is not able itself to execute the Letter, may, after having obtained the consent of the requesting authority, appoint a suitable person to do so. When seeking this consent the requested authority shall indicate the approximate costs which would result from this procedure. If the requesting authority gives its consent it shall reimburse any costs incurred; without such consent the requesting authority shall not be liable for the costs.

[4526]

CHAPTER II
TAKING OF EVIDENCE BY DIPLOMATIC OFFICERS, CONSULAR AGENTS AND COMMISSIONERS

Article 15

In a civil or commercial matter, a diplomatic officer or consular agent of a Contracting State may, in the territory of another Contracting State and within the area where he exercises his functions, take the evidence without compulsion of nationals of a State which he represents in aid of proceedings commenced in the courts of a State which he represents.

A Contracting State may declare that evidence may be taken by a diplomatic officer or consular agent only if permission to that effect is given upon application made by him or on his behalf to the appropriate authority designated by the declaring State.

[4527]

Article 16

A diplomatic officer or consular agent of a Contracting State may, in the territory of another Contracting State and within the area where he exercises his functions, also take the evidence, without compulsion, of nationals of the State in which he exercises his functions or of a third State, in aid of proceedings commenced in the courts of a State which he represents, if—

(a) a competent authority designated by the State in which he exercises his functions has given its permission either generally or in the particular case, and

(b) he complies with the conditions which the competent authority has specified in the permission.

A Contracting State may declare that evidence may be taken under this Article without its prior permission.

[4528]

Article 17

In a civil or commercial matter, a person duly appointed as a commissioner for the purpose may, without compulsion, take evidence in the territory of a Contracting State in aid of proceedings commenced in the courts of another Contracting State if—

(a) a competent authority designated by the State where the evidence is to be taken has given its permission either generally or in the particular case; and

(b) he complies with the conditions which the competent authority has specified in the permission.

A Contracting State may declare that evidence may be taken under this Article without its prior permission.

[4529]

Article 18

A Contracting State may declare that a diplomatic officer, consular agent or commissioner authorized to take evidence under Articles 15, 16 or 17, may apply to the competent authority designated by the declaring State for appropriate assistance to obtain the evidence by compulsion. The declaration may contain such conditions as the declaring State may see fit to impose.

If the authority grants the application it shall apply any measures of compulsion which are appropriate and are prescribed by its law for use in internal proceedings.

[4530]

Article 19

The competent authority, in giving the permission referred to in Articles 15, 16 or 17, or in granting the application referred to in Article 18, may lay down such conditions as it deems fit, *inter alia*, as to the time and place of the taking of the evidence. Similarly it may require that it be given reasonable advance notice of the time, date and place of the taking of the evidence; in such a case a representative of the authority shall be entitled to be present at the taking of the evidence.

[4531]

Article 20

In the taking of evidence under any Article of this Chapter persons concerned may be legally represented.

[4532]

Article 21

Where a diplomatic officer, consular agent or commissioner is authorized under Articles 15, 16 or 17 to take evidence—

(a) he may take all kinds of evidence which are not incompatible with the law of the State where the evidence is taken or contrary to any permission granted pursuant to the above Articles, and shall have power within such limits to administer an oath or take an affirmation;

(b) a request to a person to appear or to give evidence shall, unless the recipient is a national of the State where the action is pending, be drawn up in the language of the place where the evidence is taken or be accompanied by a translation into such language;

(c) the request shall inform the person that he may be legally represented and, in any State that has not filed a declaration under Article 18, shall also inform him that he is not compelled to appear or to give evidence;

(d) the evidence may be taken in the manner provided by the law applicable to the court in which the action is pending provided that such manner is not forbidden by the law of the State where the evidence is taken;

(e) a person requested to give evidence may invoke the privileges and duties to refuse to give the evidence contained in Article 11.

[4533]

Article 22

The fact that an attempt to take evidence under the procedure laid down in this Chapter has failed, owing to the refusal of a person to give evidence, shall not prevent an application being subsequently made to take the evidence in accordance with Chapter I.

[4534]

CHAPTER III
GENERAL CLAUSES

Article 23

A Contracting State may at the time of signature, ratification or accession, declare that it will not execute Letters of Request issued for the purpose of obtaining pre-trial discovery of documents as known in Common Law countries.

[4535]

Article 24

A Contracting State may designate other authorities in addition to the Central Authority and shall determine the extent of their competence. However, Letters of Request may in all cases be sent to the Central Authority.

Federal States shall be free to designate more than one Central Authority.

[4536]

Article 25

A Contracting State which has more than one legal system may designate the authorities of one of such systems, which shall have exclusive competence to execute Letters of Request pursuant to this Convention.

[4537]

Article 26

A Contracting State, if required to do so because of constitutional limitations, may request the reimbursement by the State of origin of fees and costs, in connection with the execution of Letters of Request, for the service of process necessary to compel the appearance of a person to give evidence, the costs of attendance of such persons, and the cost of any transcript of the evidence.

Where a State has made a request pursuant to the above paragraph, any other Contracting State may request from that State the reimbursement of similar fees and costs.

[4538]

Article 27

The provisions of the present Convention shall not prevent a Contracting State from—

(a) declaring that Letters of Request may be transmitted to its judicial authorities through channels other than those provided for in Article 2;

(b) permitting, by internal law or practice, any act provided for in this Convention to be performed upon less restrictive conditions;

(c) permitting, by internal law or practice, methods of taking evidence other than those provided for in this Convention.

[4539]

Article 28

The present Convention shall not prevent an agreement between any two or more Contracting States to derogate from—

(a) the provisions of Article 2 with respect to methods of transmitting Letters of Request;

(b) the provisions of Article 4 with respect to the languages which may be used;

(c) the provisions of Article 8 with respect to the presence of judicial personnel at the execution of Letters;

(d) the provisions of Article 11 with respect to the privileges and duties of witnesses to refuse to give evidence;

(e) the provisions of Article 13 with respect to the methods of returning executed Letters to the requesting authority;

(f) the provisions of Article 14 with respect to fees and costs;

(g) the provisions of Chapter II.

[4540]

Article 29

Between Parties to the present Convention who are also Parties to one or both of the Conventions on Civil Procedure signed at The Hague on the 17th of July 1905[1] and the 1st of March 1954,[2] this Convention shall replace Articles 8–16 of the earlier Conventions.

[4541]

NOTES

1 State Papers, vol 99, p 990.
2 United Nations Treaty Series No 4173, vol 286, p 265.

The United Kingdom is not a party to either of these Conventions.

Article 30

The present Convention shall not affect the application of Article 23 of the Convention of 1905, or of Article 24 of the Convention of 1954.

[4542]

Article 31

Supplementary Agreements between Parties to the Conventions of 1905 and 1954 shall be considered as equally applicable to the present Convention unless the Parties have otherwise agreed.

[4543]

Article 32

Without prejudice to the provisions of Articles 29 and 31, the present Convention shall not derogate from conventions containing provisions on the matters covered by this Convention to which the Contracting States are, or shall become Parties.

[4544]

Article 33

A State may, at the time of signature, ratification or accession exclude, in whole or in part, the application of the provisions of paragraph 2 of Article 4 and of Chapter II. No other reservation shall be permitted.

Each Contracting State may at any time withdraw a reservation it has made; the reservation shall cease to have effect on the sixtieth day after notification of the withdrawal.

When a State has made a reservation, any other State affected thereby may apply the same rule against the reserving State.

[4545]

Article 34

A State may at any time withdraw or modify a declaration.

[4546]

Article 35

A Contracting State shall, at the time of the deposit of its instrument of ratification or accession, or at a later date, inform the Ministry of Foreign Affairs of the Netherlands of the designation of authorities, pursuant to Articles 2, 8, 24 and 25.

A Contracting State shall likewise inform the Ministry, where appropriate, of the following—

(a) the designation of the authorities to whom notice must be given, whose permission may be required, and whose assistance may be invoked in the taking of evidence by diplomatic officers and consular agents, pursuant to Articles 15, 16 and 18 respectively;

(b) the designation of the authorities whose permission may be required in the taking of evidence by commissioners pursuant to Article 17 and of those who may grant the assistance provided for in Article 18;

(c) declarations pursuant to Articles 4, 8, 11, 15, 16, 17, 18, 23 and 27;

(d) any withdrawal or modification of the above designations and declarations;

(e) the withdrawal of any reservation.

[4547]

Article 36

Any difficulties which may arise between Contracting States in connection with the operation of this Convention shall be settled through diplomatic channels.

[4548]

Article 37

The present Convention shall be open for signature by the States represented at the Eleventh Session of the Hague Conference on Private International Law.

It shall be ratified, and the instruments of ratification shall be deposited with the Ministry of Foreign Affairs of the Netherlands.

[4549]

Article 38

The present Convention shall enter into force on the sixtieth day after the deposit of the third instrument of ratification referred to in the second paragraph of Article 37.[3]

The Convention shall enter into force for each signatory State which ratifies subsequently on the sixtieth day after the deposit of its instrument of ratification.

[4550]

NOTES

[3] The Convention entered into force on 7 October 1972.

Article 39

Any State not represented at the Eleventh Session of the Hague Conference on Private International Law which is a Member of this Conference or of the United Nations or of a specialized agency of that Organization, or a Party to the Statute of the International Court of Justice may accede to the present Convention after it has entered into force in accordance with the first paragraph of Article 38.

The instrument of accession shall be deposited with the Ministry of Foreign Affairs of the Netherlands.

The Convention shall enter into force for a State acceding to it on the sixtieth day after the deposit of its instrument of accession.

The accession will have effect only as regards the relations between the acceding State and such Contracting States as will have declared their acceptance of the accession. Such declaration shall be deposited at the Ministry of Foreign Affairs of the Netherlands; this Ministry shall forward, through diplomatic channels, a certified copy to each of the Contracting States.

The Convention will enter into force as between the acceding State and the State that has declared its acceptance of the accession on the sixtieth day after the deposit of the declaration of acceptance.

[4551]

Article 40

Any State may, at the time of signature, ratification or accession, declare that the present Convention shall extend to all the territories for the international relations of which it is responsible, or to one or more of them. Such a declaration shall take effect on the date of entry into force of the Convention for the State concerned.

At any time thereafter, such extensions shall be notified to the Ministry of Foreign Affairs of the Netherlands.

The Convention shall enter into force for the territories mentioned in such an extension on the sixtieth day after the notification indicated in the preceding paragraph.

[4552]

Article 41

The present Convention shall remain in force for five years from the date of its entry into force in accordance with the first paragraph of Article 38, even for States which have ratified it or acceded to it subsequently.

If there has been no denunciation, it shall be renewed tacitly every five years.

Any denunciation shall be notified to the Ministry of Foreign Affairs of the Netherlands at least six months before the end of the five year period.

It may be limited to certain of the territories to which the Convention applies.

The denunciation shall have effect only as regards the State which has notified it. The Convention shall remain in force for the other Contracting States.

[4553]

Article 42

The Ministry of Foreign Affairs of the Netherlands shall give notice to the States referred to in Article 37, and to the States which have acceded in accordance with Article 39, of the following—

(a) the signatures and ratifications referred to in Article 37;
(b) the date on which the present Convention enters into force in accordance with the first paragraph of Article 38;
(c) the accessions referred to in Article 39 and the dates on which they take effect;
(d) the extensions referred to in Article 40 and the dates on which they take effect;

(e) the designations, reservations and declarations referred to in Articles 33 and 35;
(f) the denunciations referred to in the third paragraph of Article 41.

In witness whereof the undersigned, being duly authorized thereto, have signed the present Convention.

Done at The Hague, on the 18th day of March 1970, in the English and French languages, both texts being equally authentic, in a single copy which shall be deposited in the archives of the Government of the Netherlands, and of which a certified copy shall be sent, through the diplomatic channel, to each of the States represented at the Eleventh Session of the Hague Conference on Private International Law.

[4554]–[4556]

NOTES

For signatures and ratifications, see Table 4 at **[4679]**.

J. OTHER

EUROPEAN CONVENTION FOR THE PROTECTION OF HUMAN RIGHTS AND FUNDAMENTAL FREEDOMS

NOTES

The text of the Convention and the Protocols appear as set out in the Human Rights Act 1998, Sch 1. See also the website of the Council of Europe (http://conventions.coe.int).

PART I
THE CONVENTION

RIGHTS AND FREEDOMS

Article 2
Right to life

1. Everyone's right to life shall be protected by law. No one shall be deprived of his life intentionally save in the execution of a sentence of a court following his conviction of a crime for which this penalty is provided by law.

2. Deprivation of life shall not be regarded as inflicted in contravention of this Article when it results from the use of force which is no more than absolutely necessary:

(a) in defence of any person from unlawful violence;
(b) in order to effect a lawful arrest or to prevent the escape of a person lawfully detained;
(c) in action lawfully taken for the purpose of quelling a riot or insurrection.

[4557]

Article 3
Prohibition of torture

No one shall be subjected to torture or to inhuman or degrading treatment or punishment.

[4558]

Article 4
Prohibition of slavery and forced labour

1. No one shall be held in slavery or servitude.

2. No one shall be required to perform forced or compulsory labour.

3. For the purpose of this Article the term "forced or compulsory labour" shall not include:

(a) any work required to be done in the ordinary course of detention imposed according to the provisions of Article 5 of this Convention or during conditional release from such detention;
(b) any service of a military character or, in case of conscientious objectors in countries where they are recognised, service exacted instead of compulsory military service;
(c) any service exacted in case of an emergency or calamity threatening the life or well-being of the community;
(d) any work or service which forms part of normal civic obligations.

[4559]

Article 5
Right to liberty and security

1. Everyone has the right to liberty and security of person. No one shall be deprived of his liberty save in the following cases and in accordance with a procedure prescribed by law:

(a) the lawful detention of a person after conviction by a competent court;

(b) the lawful arrest or detention of a person for non-compliance with the lawful order of a court or in order to secure the fulfilment of any obligation prescribed by law;

(c) the lawful arrest or detention of a person effected for the purpose of bringing him before the competent legal authority on reasonable suspicion of having committed an offence or when it is reasonably considered necessary to prevent his committing an offence or fleeing after having done so;

(d) the detention of a minor by lawful order for the purpose of educational supervision or his lawful detention for the purpose of bringing him before the competent legal authority;

(e) the lawful detention of persons for the prevention of the spreading of infectious diseases, of persons of unsound mind, alcoholics or drug addicts or vagrants;

(f) the lawful arrest or detention of a person to prevent his effecting an unauthorised entry into the country or of a person against whom action is being taken with a view to deportation or extradition.

2. Everyone who is arrested shall be informed promptly, in a language which he understands, of the reasons for his arrest and of any charge against him.

3. Everyone arrested or detained in accordance with the provisions of paragraph 1(c) of this Article shall be brought promptly before a judge or other officer authorised by law to exercise judicial power and shall be entitled to trial within a reasonable time or to release pending trial. Release may be conditioned by guarantees to appear for trial.

4. Everyone who is deprived of his liberty by arrest or detention shall be entitled to take proceedings by which the lawfulness of his detention shall be decided speedily by a court and his release ordered if the detention is not lawful.

5. Everyone who has been the victim of arrest or detention in contravention of the provisions of this Article shall have an enforceable right to compensation.

[4560]

Article 6
Right to a fair trial

1. In the determination of his civil rights and obligations or of any criminal charge against him, everyone is entitled to a fair and public hearing within a reasonable time by an independent and impartial tribunal established by law. Judgment shall be pronounced publicly but the press and public may be excluded from all or part of the trial in the interest of morals, public order or national security in a democratic society, where the interests of juveniles or the protection of the private life of the parties so require, or to the extent strictly necessary in the opinion of the court in special circumstances where publicity would prejudice the interests of justice.

2. Everyone charged with a criminal offence shall be presumed innocent until proved guilty according to law.

3. Everyone charged with a criminal offence has the following minimum rights:

(a) to be informed promptly, in a language which he understands and in detail, of the nature and cause of the accusation against him;

(b) to have adequate time and facilities for the preparation of his defence;

(c) to defend himself in person or through legal assistance of his own choosing or, if he has not sufficient means to pay for legal assistance, to be given it free when the interests of justice so require;

(d) to examine or have examined witnesses against him and to obtain the attendance and examination of witnesses on his behalf under the same conditions as witnesses against him;

(e) to have the free assistance of an interpreter if he cannot understand or speak the language used in court.

[4561]

Article 7
No punishment without law

1. No one shall be held guilty of any criminal offence on account of any act or omission which did not constitute a criminal offence under national or international law at the time when it was committed. Nor shall a heavier penalty be imposed than the one that was applicable at the time the criminal offence was committed.

2. This Article shall not prejudice the trial and punishment of any person for any act or omission which, at the time when it was committed, was criminal according to the general principles of law recognised by civilised nations.

[4562]

Article 8
Right to respect for private and family life

1. Everyone has the right to respect for his private and family life, his home and his correspondence.

2. There shall be no interference by a public authority with the exercise of this right except such as is in accordance with the law and is necessary in a democratic society in the interests of national security, public safety or the economic well-being of the country, for the prevention of disorder or crime, for the protection of health or morals, or for the protection of the rights and freedoms of others.

[4563]

Article 9
Freedom of thought, conscience and religion

1. Everyone has the right to freedom of thought, conscience and religion; this right includes freedom to change his religion or belief and freedom, either alone or in community with others and in public or private, to manifest his religion or belief, in worship, teaching, practice and observance.

2. Freedom to manifest one's religion or beliefs shall be subject only to such limitations as are prescribed by law and are necessary in a democratic society in the interests of public safety, for the protection of public order, health or morals, or for the protection of the rights and freedoms of others.

[4564]

Article 10
Freedom of expression

1. Everyone has the right to freedom of expression. This right shall include freedom to hold opinions and to receive and impart information and ideas without interference by public authority and regardless of frontiers. This Article shall not prevent States from requiring the licensing of broadcasting, television or cinema enterprises.

2. The exercise of these freedoms, since it carries with it duties and responsibilities, may be subject to such formalities, conditions, restrictions or penalties as are prescribed by law and are necessary in a democratic society, in the interests of national security, territorial integrity or public safety, for the prevention of disorder or crime, for the protection of health or morals, for the protection of the reputation or rights of others, for preventing the disclosure of information received in confidence, or for maintaining the authority and impartiality of the judiciary.

[4565]

Article 11
Freedom of assembly and association

1. Everyone has the right to freedom of peaceful assembly and to freedom of association with others, including the right to form and to join trade unions for the protection of his interests.

2. No restrictions shall be placed on the exercise of these rights other than such as are prescribed by law and are necessary in a democratic society in the interests of national security or public safety, for the prevention of disorder or crime, for the protection of health or morals or for the protection of the rights and freedoms of others. This Article shall not prevent the imposition of lawful restrictions on the exercise of these rights by members of the armed forces, of the police or of the administration of the State.

[4566]

Article 12
Right to marry

Men and women of marriageable age have the right to marry and to found a family, according to the national laws governing the exercise of this right.

[4567]

Article 14
Prohibition of discrimination

The enjoyment of the rights and freedoms set forth in this Convention shall be secured without discrimination on any ground such as sex, race, colour, language, religion, political or other opinion, national or social origin, association with a national minority, property, birth or other status.

[4568]

Article 16
Restrictions on political activity of aliens

Nothing in Articles 10, 11 and 14 shall be regarded as preventing the High Contracting Parties from imposing restrictions on the political activity of aliens.

[4569]

Article 17
Prohibition of abuse of rights

Nothing in this Convention may be interpreted as implying for any State, group or person any right to engage in any activity or perform any act aimed at the destruction of any of the rights and freedoms set forth herein or at their limitation to a greater extent than is provided for in the Convention.

[4570]

Article 18
Limitation on use of restrictions on rights

The restrictions permitted under this Convention to the said rights and freedoms shall not be applied for any purpose other than those for which they have been prescribed.

[4571]

PART II
THE FIRST PROTOCOL

Article 1
Protection of property

Every natural or legal person is entitled to the peaceful enjoyment of his possessions. No one shall be deprived of his possessions except in the public interest and subject to the conditions provided for by law and by the general principles of international law.

The preceding provisions shall not, however, in any way impair the right of a State to enforce such laws as it deems necessary to control the use of property in accordance with the general interest or to secure the payment of taxes or other contributions or penalties.

[4572]

Article 2
Right to education

No person shall be denied the right to education. In the exercise of any functions which it assumes in relation to education and to teaching, the State shall respect the right of parents to ensure such education and teaching in conformity with their own religious and philosophical convictions.

[4573]

Article 3
Right to free elections

The High Contracting Parties undertake to hold free elections at reasonable intervals by secret ballot, under conditions which will ensure the free expression of the opinion of the people in the choice of the legislature.

[4574]

[PART 3
ARTICLE 1 OF THE THIRTEENTH PROTOCOL

Abolition of the death penalty

The death penalty shall be abolished. No one shall be condemned to such penalty or executed.]

[4575]

NOTES

Commencement: 22 June 2004.

Substituted by the Human Rights Act 1998 (Amendment) Order 2004, SI 2004/1574, art 2(3).

VIENNA CONVENTION ON THE LAW OF TREATIES

(Vienna, 23 May 1969)

NOTES

The United Kingdom ratified the Convention on 25 June 1971, and the Convention entered into force on 27 January 1980: see Cmnd 7964; 115 UNTS 331.

THE STATES PARTIES TO THE PRESENT CONVENTION,

CONSIDERING the fundamental role of treaties in the history of international relations,

RECOGNIZING the ever-increasing importance of treaties as a source of international law and as a means of developing peaceful co-operation among nations, whatever their constitutional and social systems,

NOTING that the principles of free consent and of good faith and the *pacta sunt servanda* rule are universally recognized,

AFFIRMING that disputes concerning treaties, like other international disputes, should be settled by peaceful means and in conformity with the principles of justice and international law,

RECALLING the determination of the peoples of the United Nations to establish conditions under which justice and respect for the obligations arising from treaties can be maintained,

HAVING IN MIND the principles of international law embodied in the Charter of the United Nations, such as the principles of the equal rights and self-determination of peoples, of the sovereign equality and independence of all States, of non-interference in the domestic affairs of States, of the prohibition of the threat or use of force and of universal respect for, and observance of, human rights and fundamental freedoms for all,

BELIEVING that the codification and progressive development of the law of treaties achieved in the present Convention will promote the purposes of the United Nations set forth in the Charter, namely, the maintenance of international peace and security, the development of friendly relations and the achievement of co-operation among nations,

AFFIRMING that the rules of customary international law will continue to govern questions not regulated by the provisions of the present Convention,

HAVE AGREED AS FOLLOWS:—

PART I
INTRODUCTION

Article 1

Scope of the present Convention

[4576]

The present Convention applies to treaties between States.

Article 2

Use of terms

1. For the purposes of the present Convention:
   (a) "treaty" means an international agreement concluded between States in written form and governed by international law, whether embodied in a single instrument or in two or more related instruments and whatever its particular designation;
   (b) "ratification", "acceptance", "approval" and "accession" mean in each case the international act so named whereby a State establishes on the international plane its consent to be bound by a treaty;
   (c) "full powers" means a document emanating from the competent authority of a State designating a person or persons to represent the State for negotiating, adopting or authenticating the text of a treaty, for expressing the consent of the State to be bound by a treaty, or for accomplishing any other act with respect to a treaty;
   (d) "reservation" means a unilateral statement, however phrased or named, made by a State, when signing, ratifying, accepting, approving or acceding to a treaty, whereby it purports to exclude or to modify the legal effect of certain provisions of the treaty in their application to that State;
   (e) "negotiating State" means a State which took part in the drawing up and adoption of the text of the treaty;
   (f) "contracting State" means a State which has consented to be bound by the treaty, whether or not the treaty has entered into force;
   (g) "party" means a State which has consented to be bound by the treaty and for which the treaty is in force;
   (h) "third State" means a State not a party to the treaty;
   (i) "international organization" means an intergovernmental organization.

2. The provisions of paragraph 1 regarding the use of terms in the present Convention are without prejudice to the use of those terms or to the meanings which may be given to them in the internal law of any State.

[4577]

Article 3

International agreements not within the scope of the present Convention

The fact that the present Convention does not apply to international agreements concluded between the States and other subjects of international law or between such other subjects of international law, or to international agreements not in written form, shall not affect:
   (a) the legal force of such agreements;
   (b) the application to them of any of the rules set forth in the present Convention to which they would be subject under international law independently of the Convention;

(c) the application of the Convention to the relations of States as between themselves under international agreements to which other subjects of international law are also parties.

[4578]

Article 4

Non-retroactivity of the present Convention

Without prejudice to the application of any rules set forth in the present Convention to which treaties would be subject under international law independently of the Convention, the Convention applies only to treaties which are concluded by States after the entry into force of the present Convention with regard to such States.

[4579]

Article 5

Treaties constituting international organizations and treaties adopted within an international organization

The present Convention applies to any treaty which is the constituent instrument of an international organization and to any treaty adopted within an international organization without prejudice to any relevant rules of the organization.

[4580]

PART II
CONCLUSION AND ENTRY INTO FORCE OF TREATIES

SECTION 1
CONCLUSION OF TREATIES

Article 6

Capacity of States to conclude treaties

Every State possesses capacity to conclude treaties.

[4581]

Article 7

Full powers

1. A person is considered as representing a State for the purpose of adopting or authenticating the text of a treaty or for the purpose of expressing the consent of the State to be bound by a treaty if:

(a) he produces appropriate full powers; or
(b) it appears from the practice of the States concerned or from other circumstances that their intention was to consider that person as representing the State for such purposes and to dispense with full powers.

2. In virtue of their functions and without having to produce full powers, the following are considered as representing their State:

(a) Heads of State, Heads of Government and Ministers for Foreign Affairs, for the purpose of performing all acts relating to the conclusion of a treaty;
(b) heads of diplomatic missions, for the purpose of adopting the text of a treaty between the accrediting State and the State to which they are accredited;
(c) representatives accredited by States to an international conference or to an international organization or one of its organs, for the purpose of adopting the text of a treaty in that conference, organization or organ.

[4582]

Article 8

Subsequent confirmation of an act performed without authorization

An act relating to the conclusion of a treaty performed by a person who cannot be considered under article 7 as authorized to represent a State for that purpose is without legal effect unless afterwards confirmed by that State.

[4583]

Article 9

Adoption of the text

1. The adoption of the text of a treaty takes place by the consent of all the States participating in its drawing up except as provided in paragraph 2.

2. The adoption of the text of a treaty at an international conference takes place by the vote of two thirds of the States present and voting, unless by the same majority they shall decide to apply a different rule.

[4584]

Article 10

Authentication of the text

The text of a treaty is established as authentic and definitive:
- (a) by such procedures as may be provided for in the text or agreed upon by the States participating in its drawing up; or
- (b) failing such procedure, by the signature, signature *ad referendum* or initialling by the representatives of those States of the text of the treaty or of the Final Act of a conference incorporating the text.

[4585]

Article 11

Means of expressing consent to be bound by a treaty

The consent of a State to be bound by a treaty may be expressed by signature, exchange of instruments constituting a treaty, ratification, acceptance, approval or accession, or by any other means if so agreed.

[4586]

Article 12

Consent to be bound by a treaty expressed by signature

1. The consent of a State to be bound by a treaty is expressed by the signature of its representative when:
   - (a) the treaty provides that signature shall have that effect;
   - (b) it is otherwise established that the negotiating States were agreed that signature should have that effect; or
   - (c) the intention of the State to give that effect to the signature appears from the full powers of its representative or was expressed during the negotiation.

2. For the purposes of paragraph 1:
   - (a) the initialling of a text constitutes a signature of the treaty when it is established that the negotiating States so agreed;
   - (b) the signature *ad referendum* of a treaty by a representative, if confirmed by his State, constitutes a full signature of the treaty.

[4587]

Article 13

Consent to be bound by a treaty expressed by an exchange of instruments constituting a treaty

The consent of States to be bound by a treaty constituted by instruments exchanged between them is expressed by that exchange when;
- (a) the instruments provide that their exchange shall have that effect; or
- (b) it is otherwise established that those States were agreed that the exchange of instruments should have that effect.

[4588]

Article 14

Consent to be bound by a treaty expressed by ratification, acceptance or approval

1. The consent of a State to be bound by a treaty is expressed by ratification when:

(a) the treaty provides for such consent to be expressed by means of ratification;
(b) it is otherwise established that the negotiating States were agreed that ratification should be required;
(c) the representative of the State has signed the treaty subject to ratification; or
(d) the intention of the State to sign the treaty subject to ratification appears from the full powers of its representative or was expressed during the negotiation.

2. The consent of a State to be bound by a treaty is expressed by acceptance or approval under conditions similar to those which apply to ratification.

[4589]

Article 15

Consent to be bound by a treaty expressed by accession

The consent of a State to be bound by a treaty is expressed by accession when:
(a) the treaty provides that such consent may be expressed by that State by means of accession;
(b) it is otherwise established that the negotiating States were agreed that such consent may be expressed by that State by means of accession; or
(c) all the parties have subsequently agreed that such consent may be expressed by that State by means of accession.

[4590]

Article 16

Exchange or deposit of instruments of ratification, acceptance, approval or accession

Unless the treaty otherwise provides, instruments of ratification, acceptance, approval or accession establish the consent of a State to be bound by a treaty upon:
(a) their exchange between the contracting States;
(b) their deposit with the depositary; or
(c) their notification to the contracting States or to the depositary, if so agreed.

[4591]

Article 17

Consent to be bound by part of a treaty and choice of differing provisions

1. Without prejudice to articles 19 to 23, the consent of a State to be bound by part of a treaty is effective only if the treaty so permits or the other contracting States so agree.

2. The consent of a State to be bound by a treaty which permits a choice between differing provisions is effective only if it is made clear to which of the provisions the consent relates.

[4592]

Article 18

Obligation not to defeat the object and purpose of a treaty prior to its entry into force

A State is obliged to refrain from acts which would defeat the object and purpose of a treaty when:
(a) it has signed the treaty or has exchanged instruments constituting the treaty subject to ratification, acceptance or approval, until it shall have made its intention clear not to become a party to the treaty; or
(b) it has expressed its consent to be bound by the treaty, pending the entry into force of the treaty and provided that such entry into force is not unduly delayed.

[4593]

SECTION 2
RESERVATIONS

Article 19

Formulation of reservations

A State may, when signing, ratifying, accepting, approving or acceding to a treaty, formulate a reservation unless:

(a) the reservation is prohibited by the treaty;
(b) the treaty provides that only specified reservations, which do not include the reservation in question, may be made; or
(c) in cases not falling under sub-paragraphs (a) and (b), the reservation is incompatible with the object and purpose of the treaty.

[4594]

Article 20

Acceptance of and objection to reservations

1. A reservation expressly authorized by a treaty does not require any subsequent acceptance by the other contracting States unless the treaty so provides.

2. When it appears from the limited number of the negotiating States and the object and purpose of a treaty that the application of the treaty in its entirety between all the parties is an essential condition of the consent of each one to be bound by the treaty, a reservation requires acceptance by all the parties.

3. When a treaty is a constituent instrument of an international organization and unless it otherwise provides, a reservation requires the acceptance of the competent organ of that organization.

4. In cases not falling under the preceding paragraphs and unless the treaty otherwise provides:
(a) acceptance by another contracting State of a reservation constitutes the reserving State a party to the treaty in relation to that other State if or when the treaty is in force for those States;
(b) an objection by another contracting State to a reservation does not preclude the entry into force of the treaty as between the objecting and reserving States unless a contrary intention is definitely expressed by the objecting State;
(c) an act expressing a State's consent to be bound by the treaty and containing a reservation is effective as soon as at least one other contracting State has accepted the reservation.

5. For the purposes of paragraphs 2 and 4 and unless the treaty otherwise provides, a reservation is considered to have been accepted by a State if it shall have raised no objection to the reservation by the end of a period of twelve months after it was notified of the reservation or by the date on which it expressed its consent to be bound by the treaty, whichever is later.

[4595]

Article 21

Legal effects of reservations and of objections to reservations

1. A reservation established with regard to another party in accordance with articles 19, 20 and 23:
(a) modifies for the reserving State in its relations with that other party the provisions of the treaty to which the reservation relates to the extent of the reservation; and
(b) modifies those provisions to the same extent for that other party in its relations with the reserving State.

2. The reservation does not modify the provisions of the treaty for the other parties to the treaty *inter se*.

3. When a State objecting to a reservation has not opposed the entry into force of the treaty between itself and the reserving State, the provisions to which the reservation relates do not apply as between the two States to the extent of the reservation.

[4596]

Article 22

Withdrawal of reservations and of objections to reservations

1. Unless the treaty otherwise provides, a reservation may be withdrawn at any time and the consent of a State which has accepted the reservation is not required for its withdrawal.

2. Unless the treaty otherwise provides, an objection to a reservation may be withdrawn at any time.

3. Unless the treaty otherwise provides, or it is otherwise agreed:

(a) the withdrawal of a reservation becomes operative in relation to another contracting State only when notice of it has been received by that State;

(b) the withdrawal of an objection to a reservation becomes operative only when notice of it has been received by the State which formulated the reservation.

[4597]

Article 23

Procedure regarding reservations

1. A reservation, an express acceptance of a reservation and an objection to a reservation must be formulated in writing and communicated to the contracting States and other States entitled to become parties to the treaty.

2. If formulated when signing the treaty subject to ratification, acceptance or approval, a reservation must be formally confirmed by the reserving State when expressing its consent to be bound by the treaty. In such a case the reservation shall be considered as having been made on the date of its confirmation.

3. An express acceptance of, or an objection to, a reservation made previously to confirmation of the reservation does not itself require confirmation.

4. The withdrawal of a reservation or of an objection to a reservation must be formulated in writing.

[4598]

SECTION 3
ENTRY INTO FORCE AND PROVISIONAL
APPLICATION OF TREATIES

Article 24

Entry into force

1. A treaty enters into force in such manner and upon such date as it may provide or as the negotiating States may agree.

2. Failing any such provision or agreement, a treaty enters into force as soon as consent to be bound by the treaty has been established for all the negotiating States.

3. When the consent of a State to be bound by a treaty is established on a date after the treaty has come into force, the treaty enters into force for that State on that date, unless the treaty otherwise provides.

4. The provisions of a treaty regulating the authentication of its text, the establishment of the consent of States to be bound by the treaty, the manner or date of its entry into force, reservations, the functions of the depositary and other matters arising necessarily before the entry into force of the treaty apply from the time of the adoption of its text.

[4599]

Article 25

Provisional application

1. A treaty or a part of a treaty is applied provisionally pending its entry into force if:

(a) the treaty itself so provides; or

(b) the negotiating States have in some other manner so agreed.

2. Unless the treaty otherwise provides or the negotiating States have otherwise agreed, the provisional application of a treaty or a part of a treaty with respect to a State shall be terminated if that State notifies the other States between which the treaty is being applied provisionally of its intention not to become a party to the treaty.

[4600]

PART III
OBSERVANCE, APPLICATION AND INTERPRETATION OF TREATIES

SECTION 1
OBSERVANCE OF TREATIES

Article 26

Pacta sunt servanda

Every treaty in force is binding upon the parties to it and must be performed by them in good faith.

[4601]

Article 27

Internal law and observance of treaties

A party may not invoke the provisions of its internal law as justification for its failure to perform a treaty. This rule is without prejudice to article 46.

[4602]

SECTION 2
APPLICATION OF TREATIES

Article 28

Non-retroactivity of treaties

Unless a different intention appears from the treaty or is otherwise established, its provisions do not bind a party in relation to any act or fact which took place or any situation which ceased to exist before the date of the entry into force of the treaty with respect to that party.

[4603]

Article 29

Territorial scope of treaties

Unless a different intention appears from the treaty or is otherwise established, a treaty is binding upon each party in respect of its entire territory.

[4604]

Article 30

Application of successive treaties relating to the same subject-matter

1. Subject to article 103 of the Charter of the United Nations, the rights and obligations of States parties to successive treaties relating to the same subject-matter shall be determined in accordance with the following paragraphs.

2. When a treaty specifies that it is subject to, or that it is not to be considered as incompatible with, an earlier or later treaty, the provisions of that other treaty prevail.

3. When all the parties to the earlier treaty are parties also to the later treaty but the earlier treaty is not terminated or suspended in operation under article 59, the earlier treaty applies only to the extent that its provisions are compatible with those of the later treaty.

4. When the parties to the later treaty do not include all the parties to the earlier one:
   (a) as between States parties to both treaties the same rule applies as in paragraph 3;
   (b) as between a State party to both treaties and a State party to only one of the treaties, the treaty to which both States are parties governs their mutual rights and obligations.

5. Paragraph 4 is without prejudice to article 41, or to any question of the termination or suspension of the operation of a treaty under article 60 or to any question of responsibility which may arise for a State from the conclusion or application of a treaty the provisions of which are incompatible with its obligations towards another State under another treaty.

[4605]

SECTION 3
INTERPRETATION OF TREATIES

Article 31

General rule of interpretation

1. A treaty shall be interpreted in good faith in accordance with the ordinary meaning to be given to the terms of the treaty in their context and in the light of its object and purpose.

2. The context for the purpose of the interpretation of a treaty shall comprise, in addition to the text, including its preamble and annexes:
(a) any agreement relating to the treaty which was made between all the parties in connexion with the conclusion of the treaty;
(b) any instrument which was made by one or more parties in connexion with the conclusion of the treaty and accepted by the other parties as an instrument related to the treaty.

3. There shall be taken into account, together with the context:
(a) any subsequent agreement between the parties regarding the interpretation of the treaty or the application of its provisions;
(b) any subsequent practice in the application of the treaty which establishes the agreement of the parties regarding its interpretation;
(c) any relevant rules of international law applicable in the relations between the parties.

4. A special meaning shall be given to a term if it is established that the parties so intended.

[4606]

Article 32

Supplementary means of interpretation

Recourse may be had to supplementary means of interpretation, including the preparatory work of the treaty and the circumstances of its conclusion, in order to confirm the meaning resulting from the application of article 31, or to determine the meaning when the interpretation according to article 31:
(a) leaves the meaning ambiguous or obscure; or
(b) leads to a result which is manifestly absurd or unreasonable.

[4607]

Article 33

Interpretation of treaties authenticated in two or more languages

1. When a treaty has been authenticated in two or more languages, the text is equally authoritative in each language, unless the treaty provides or the parties agree that, in case of divergence, a particular text shall prevail.

2. A version of the treaty in a language other than one of those in which the text was authenticated shall be considered an authentic text only if the treaty so provides or the parties so agree.

3. The terms of the treaty are presumed to have the same meaning in each authentic text.

4. Except where a particular text prevails in accordance with paragraph 1, when a comparison of the authentic texts discloses a difference of meaning which the application of articles 31 and 32 does not remove, the meaning which best reconciles the texts, having regard to the object and purpose of the treaty, shall be adopted.

[4608]

SECTION 4
TREATIES AND THIRD STATES

Article 34

General rule regarding third States

A treaty does not create either obligations or rights for a third State without its consent.

[4609]

Article 35

Treaties providing for obligations for third States

An obligation arises for a third State from a provision of a treaty if the parties to the treaty intend the provision to be the means of establishing the obligation and the third State expressly accepts that obligation in writing.

[4610]

Article 36

Treaties providing for rights for third States

1. A right arises for a third State from a provision of a treaty if the parties to the treaty intend the provision to accord that right either to the third State, or to a group of States to which it belongs, or to all States, and the third State assents thereto. Its assent shall be presumed so long as the contrary is not indicated, unless the treaty otherwise provides.

2. A State exercising a right in accordance with paragraph 1 shall comply with the conditions for its exercise provided for in the treaty or established in conformity with the treaty.

[4611]

Article 37

Revocation or modification of obligations or rights of third States

1. When an obligation has arisen for a third State in conformity with article 35, the obligation may be revoked or modified only with the consent of the parties to the treaty and of the third State, unless it is established that they had otherwise agreed.

2. When a right has arisen for a third State in conformity with article 36, the right may not be revoked or modified by the parties if it is established that the right was intended not to be revocable or subject to modification without the consent of the third State.

[4612]

Article 38

Rules in a treaty becoming binding on third States through international custom

Nothing in articles 34 to 37 precludes a rule set forth in a treaty from becoming binding upon a third State as a customary rule of international law, recognized as such.

[4613]

PART IV
AMENDMENT AND MODIFICATION OF TREATIES

Article 39

General rule regarding the amendment of treaties

A treaty may be amended by agreement between the parties. The rules laid down in Part II apply to such an agreement except in so far as the treaty may otherwise provide.

[4614]

Article 40

Amendment of multilateral treaties

1 Unless the treaty otherwise provides, the amendment of multilateral treaties shall be governed by the following paragraphs.

2. Any proposal to amend a multilateral treaty as between all the parties must be notified to all the contracting States, each one of which shall have the right to take part in:

(a) the decision as to the action to be taken in regard to such proposal;
(b) the negotiation and conclusion of any agreement for the amendment of the treaty.

3. Every State entitled to become a party to the treaty shall also be entitled to become a party to the treaty as amended.

4. The amending agreement does not bind any State already a party to the treaty which does not become a party to the amending agreement; article 30, paragraph 4(b), applies in relation to such State.

5. Any State which becomes a party to the treaty after the entry into force of the amending agreement shall, failing an expression of a different intention by that State:

(a) be considered as a party to the treaty as amended; and

(b) be considered as a party to the unamended treaty in relation to any party to the treaty not bound by the amending agreement.

[4615]

Article 41

Agreements to modify multilateral treaties between certain of the parties only

1. Two or more of the parties to a multilateral treaty may conclude an agreement to modify the treaty as between themselves alone if:

(a) the possibility of such a modification is provided for by the treaty; or

(b) the modification in question is not prohibited by the treaty and:

  (i) does not affect the enjoyment by the other parties of their rights under the treaty or the performance of their obligations;

  (ii) does not relate to a provision, derogation from which is incompatible with the effective execution of the object and purpose of the treaty as a whole.

2. Unless in a case falling under paragraph 1(a) the treaty otherwise provides, the parties in question shall notify the other parties of their intention to conclude the agreement and of the modification to the treaty for which it provides.

[4616]

PART V
INVALIDITY, TERMINATION AND SUSPENSION OF THE OPERATION OF TREATIES

SECTION 1
GENERAL PROVISIONS

Article 42

Validity and continuance in force of treaties

1. The validity of a treaty or of the consent of a State to be bound by a treaty may be impeached only through the application of the present Convention.

2. The termination of a treaty, its denunciation or the withdrawal of a party, may take place only as a result of the application of the provisions of the treaty or of the present Convention. The same rule applies to suspension of the operation of a treaty.

[4617]

Article 43

Obligations imposed by international law independently of a treaty

The invalidity, termination or denunciation of a treaty, the withdrawal of a party from it, or the suspension of its operation, as a result of the application of the present Convention or of the provisions of the treaty, shall not in any way impair the duty of any State to fulfil any obligation embodied in the treaty to which it would be subject under international law independently of the treaty.

[4618]

Article 44

Separability of treaty provisions

1. A right of a party, provided for in a treaty or arising under article 56, to denounce, withdraw from or suspend the operation of the treaty may be exercised only with respect to the whole treaty unless the treaty otherwise provides or the parties otherwise agree.

2. A ground for invalidating, terminating, withdrawing from or suspending the operation of a treaty recognized in the present Convention may be invoked only with respect to the whole treaty except as provided in the following paragraphs or in article 60.

3. If the ground relates solely to particular clauses, it may be invoked only with respect to those clauses where:

   (a) the said clauses are separable from the remainder of the treaty with regard to their application;
   (b) it appears from the treaty or is otherwise established that acceptance of those clauses was not an essential basis of the consent of the other party or parties to be bound by the treaty as a whole; and
   (c) continued performance of the remainder of the treaty would not be unjust.

4. In cases falling under articles 49 and 50 the State entitled to invoke the fraud or corruption may do so with respect either to the whole treaty or, subject to paragraph 3, to the particular clauses alone.

5. In cases falling under articles 51, 52 and 53, no separation of the provisions of the treaty is permitted.

[4619]

Article 45

Loss of a right to invoke a ground for invalidating, terminating, withdrawing from or suspending the operation of a treaty

A State may no longer invoke a ground for invalidating, terminating, withdrawing from or suspending the operation of a treaty under articles 46 to 50 or articles 60 and 62 if, after becoming aware of the facts:

   (a) it shall have expressly agreed that the treaty is valid or remains in force or continues in operation, as the case may be; or
   (b) it must by reason of its conduct be considered as having acquiesced in the validity of the treaty or in its maintenance in force or in operation, as the case may be.

[4620]

SECTION 2
INVALIDITY OF TREATIES

Article 46

Provisions of internal law regarding competence to conclude treaties

1. A State may not invoke the fact that its consent to be bound by a treaty has been expressed in violation of a provision of its internal law regarding competence to conclude treaties as invalidating its consent unless that violation was manifest and concerned a rule of its internal law of fundamental importance.

2. A violation is manifest if it would be objectively evident to any State conducting itself in the matter in accordance with normal practice and in good faith.

[4621]

Article 47

Specific restrictions on authority to express the consent of a State

If the authority of a representative to express the consent of a State to be bound by a particular treaty has been made subject to a specific restriction, his omission to observe that restriction may not be invoked as invalidating the consent expressed by him unless the restriction was notified to the other negotiating States prior to his expressing such consent.

[4622]

Article 48

Error

1. A State may invoke an error in a treaty as invalidating its consent to be bound by the treaty if the error relates to a fact or situation which was assumed by that State to exist at the time when the treaty was concluded and formed an essential basis of its consent to be bound by the treaty.

2. Paragraph 1 shall not apply if the State in question contributed by its own conduct to the error or if the circumstances were such as to put that State on notice of a possible error.

3. An error relating only to the wording of the text of a treaty does not affect its validity; article 79 then applies.

[4623]

Article 49

Fraud

If a State has been induced to conclude a treaty by the fraudulent conduct of another negotiating State, the State may invoke the fraud as invalidating its consent to be bound by the treaty.

[4624]

Article 50

Corruption of a representative of a State

If the expression of a State's consent to be bound by a treaty has been procured through the corruption of its representative directly or indirectly by another negotiating State, the State may invoke such corruption as invalidating its consent to be bound by the treaty.

[4625]

Article 51

Coercion of a representative of a State

The expression of a State's consent to be bound by a treaty which has been procured by the coercion of its representative through acts or threats directed against him shall be without any legal effect.

[4626]

Article 52

Coercion of a State by the threat or use of force

A treaty is void if its conclusion has been procured by the threat or use of force in violation of the principles of international law embodied in the Charter of the United Nations

[4627]

Article 53

Treaties conflicting with a peremptory norm of general international law (*jus cogens*)

A treaty is void if, at the time of its conclusion, it conflicts with a peremptory norm of general international law. For the purposes of the present Convention, a peremptory norm of general international law is a norm accepted and recognized by the international community of States as a whole as a norm from which no derogation is permitted and which can be modified only by a subsequent norm of general international law having the same character.

[4628]

SECTION 3
TERMINATION AND SUSPENSION OF THE OPERATION OF TREATIES

Article 54

Termination of or withdrawal from a treaty under its provisions or by consent of the parties

The termination of a treaty or the withdrawal of a party may take place:

(a) in conformity with the provisions of the treaty; or
(b) at any time by consent of all the parties after consultation with the other contracting States.

[4629]

Article 55

Reduction of the parties to a multilateral treaty below the number necessary for its entry into force

Unless the treaty otherwise provides, a multilateral treaty does not terminate by reason only of the fact that the number of the parties falls below the number necessary for its entry into force.

[4630]

Article 56

Denunciation of or withdrawal from a treaty containing no provision regarding termination, denunciation or withdrawal

1. A treaty which contains no provision regarding its termination and which does not provide for denunciation or withdrawal is not subject to denunciation or withdrawal unless:
   (a) it is established that the parties intended to admit the possibility of denunciation or withdrawal; or
   (b) a right of denunciation or withdrawal may be implied by the nature of the treaty.

2. A party shall give not less than twelve months' notice of its intention to denounce or withdraw from a treaty under paragraph 1.

[4631]

Article 57

Suspension of the operation of a treaty under its provisions or by consent of the parties

The operation of a treaty in regard to all the parties or to a particular party may be suspended:
(a) in conformity with the provisions of the treaty; or
(b) at any time by consent of all the parties after consultation with the other contracting States.

[4632]

Article 58

Suspension of the operation of a multilateral treaty by agreement between certain of the parties only

1. Two or more parties to a multilateral treaty may conclude an agreement to suspend the operation of provisions of the treaty, temporarily and as between themselves alone, if:
   (a) the possibility of such a suspension is provided for by the treaty; or
   (b) the suspension in question is not prohibited by the treaty and:
      (i) does not affect the enjoyment by the other parties of their rights under the treaty or the performance of their obligations;
      (ii) is not incompatible with the object and purpose of the treaty.

2. Unless in a case falling under paragraph 1(a) the treaty otherwise provides, the parties in question shall notify the other parties of their intention to conclude the agreement and of those provisions of the treaty the operation of which they intend to suspend.

[4633]

Article 59

Termination or suspension of the operation of a treaty implied by conclusion of a later treaty

1. A treaty shall be considered as terminated if all the parties to it conclude a later treaty relating to the same subject-matter and:
   (a) it appears from the later treaty or is otherwise established that the parties intended that the matter should be governed by that treaty; or
   (b) the provisions of the later treaty are so far incompatible with those of the earlier one that the two treaties are not capable of being applied at the same time.

2. The earlier treaty shall be considered as only suspended in operation if it appears from the later treaty or is otherwise established that such was the intention of the parties.

[4634]

Article 60

Termination or suspension of the operation of a treaty as a consequence of its breach

1. A material breach of bilateral treaty by one of the parties entitles the other to invoke the breach as a ground for terminating the treaty or suspending its operation in whole or in part.

2. A material breach of a multilateral treaty by one of the parties entitles:
   (a) the other parties by unanimous agreement to suspend the operation of the treaty in whole or in part or to terminate it either:

(i) in the relations between themselves and the defaulting State, or
(ii) as between all the parties;

(b) a party specially affected by the breach to invoke it as a ground for suspending the operation of the treaty in whole or in part in the relations between itself and the defaulting State;

(c) any party other than the defaulting State to invoke the breach as a ground for suspending the operation of the treaty in whole or in part with respect to itself if the treaty is of such a character that a material breach of its provisions by one party radically changes the position of every party with respect to the further performance of its obligations under the treaty.

3. A material breach of a treaty, for the purposes of this article, consists in:

(a) a repudiation of the treaty not sanctioned by the present Convention; or
(b) the violation of a provision essential to the accomplishment of the object or purpose of the treaty.

4. The foregoing paragraphs are without prejudice to any provision in the treaty applicable in the event of a breach.

5. Paragraphs 1 to 3 do not apply to provisions relating to the protection of the human person contained in treaties of a humanitarian character, in particular to provisions prohibiting any form of reprisals against persons protected by such treaties.

[4635]

Article 61

Supervening impossibility of performance

1. A party may invoke the impossibility of performing a treaty as a ground for terminating or withdrawing from it if the impossibility results from the permanent disappearance or destruction of an object indispensable for the execution of the treaty. If the impossibility is temporary, it may be invoked only as a ground for suspending the operation of the treaty.

2. Impossibility of performance may not be invoked by a party as a ground for terminating, withdrawing from or suspending the operation of a treaty if the impossibility is the result of a breach by that party either of an obligation under the treaty or of any other international obligation owed to any other party to the treaty.

[4636]

Article 62

Fundamental change of circumstances

1. A fundamental change of circumstances which has occurred with regard to those existing at the time of the conclusion of a treaty, and which was not foreseen by the parties, may not be invoked as a ground for terminating or withdrawing from the treaty unless:

(a) the existence of those circumstances constituted an essential basis of the consent of the parties to be bound by the treaty; and
(b) the effect of the change is radically to transform the extent of obligations still to be performed under the treaty.

2. A fundamental change of circumstances may not be invoked as a ground for terminating or withdrawing from a treaty:

(a) if the treaty establishes a boundary; or
(b) if the fundamental change is the result of a breach by the party invoking it either of an obligation under the treaty or of any other international obligation owed to any other party to the treaty.

3. If, under the foregoing paragraphs, a party may invoke a fundamental change of circumstances as a ground for terminating or withdrawing from a treaty it may also invoke the change as a ground for suspending the operation of the treaty.

[4637]

Article 63

Severance of diplomatic or consular relations

The severance of diplomatic or consular relations between parties to a treaty does not affect the legal relations established between them by the treaty except in so far as the existence of diplomatic or consular relations is indispensable for the application of the treaty

[4638]

Article 64

Emergence of a new peremptory norm of general international law (*jus cogens*)

If a new peremptory norm of general international law emerges, any existing treaty which is in conflict with that norm becomes void and terminates.

[4639]

SECTION 4
PROCEDURE

Article 65

Procedure to be followed with respect to invalidity, termination, withdrawal from or suspension of the operation of a treaty

1. A party which, under the provisions of the present Convention, invokes either a defect in its consent to be bound by a treaty or a ground for impeaching the validity of a treaty, terminating it, withdrawing from it or suspending its operation, must notify the other parties of its claim. The notification shall indicate the measure proposed to be taken with respect to the treaty and the reasons therefor.

2. If, after the expiry of a period which, except in cases of special urgency, shall not be less than three months after the receipt of the notification, no party has raised any objection, the party making the notification may carry out in the manner provided in article 67 the measure which it has proposed.

3. If, however, objection has been raised by any other party, the parties shall seek a solution through the means indicated in Article 33 of the Charter of the United Nations.

4. Nothing in the foregoing paragraphs shall affect the rights or obligations of the parties under any provisions in force binding the parties with regard to the settlement of disputes.

5. Without prejudice to article 45, the fact that a State has not previously made the notification prescribed in paragraph 1 shall not prevent it from making such notification in answer to another party claiming performance of the treaty or alleging its violation.

[4640]

Article 66

Procedures for judicial settlement, arbitration and conciliation

If, under paragraph 3 of article 65, no solution has been reached within a period of twelve months following the date on which the objection was raised, the following procedures shall be followed:

(a) any one of the parties to a dispute concerning the application or the interpretation of article 53 or 64 may, by a written application, submit it to the International Court of Justice for a decision unless the parties by common consent agree to submit the dispute to arbitration;

(b) any one of the parties to a dispute concerning the application or the interpretation of any of the other articles in Part V of the present Convention may set in motion the procedure specified in the Annex to the Convention by submitting a request to that effect to the Secretary-General of the United Nations.

[4641]

Article 67

Instruments for declaring invalid, terminating, withdrawing from or suspending the operation of a treaty

1. The notification provided for under article 65, paragraph 1 must be made in writing.

2. Any act declaring invalid, terminating, withdrawing from or suspending the operation of a treaty pursuant to the provisions of the treaty or of paragraphs 2 or 3 of article 65 shall be carried out through an instrument communicated to the other parties. If the instrument is not signed by the Head of State, Head of Government or Minister for Foreign Affairs, the representative of the State communicating it may be called upon to produce full powers.

[4642]

Article 68

Revocation of notifications and instruments provided for in articles 65 and 67

A notification or instrument provided for in article 65 or 67 may be revoked at any time before it takes effect.

[4643]

SECTION 5
CONSEQUENCES OF THE INVALIDITY, TERMINATION OR SUSPENSION OF THE OPERATION OF A TREATY

Article 69

Consequences of the invalidity of a treaty

1. A treaty the invalidity of which is established under the present Convention is void. The provisions of a void treaty have no legal force.

2. If acts have nevertheless been performed in reliance on such a treaty:
   (a) each party may require any other party to establish as far as possible in their mutual relations the position that would have existed if the acts had not been performed;
   (b) acts performed in good faith before the invalidity was invoked are not rendered unlawful by reason only of the invalidity of the treaty.

3. In cases falling under articles 49, 50, 51 or 52, paragraph 2 does not apply with respect to the party to which the fraud, the act of corruption or the coercion is imputable.

4. In the case of the invalidity of a particular State's consent to be bound by a multilateral treaty, the foregoing rules apply in the relations between that State and the parties to the treaty.

[4644]

Article 70

Consequences of the termination of a treaty

1. Unless the treaty otherwise provides or the parties otherwise agree, the termination of a treaty under its provisions or in accordance with the present Convention:
   (a) releases the parties from any obligation further to perform the treaty;
   (b) does not affect any right, obligation or legal situation of the parties created through the execution of the treaty prior to its termination.

2. If a State denounces or withdraws from a multilateral treaty, paragraph 1 applies in the relations between that State and each of the other parties to the treaty from the date when such denunciation or withdrawal takes effect.

[4645]

Article 71

Consequences of the invalidity of a treaty which conflicts with a peremptory norm of general international law

1. In the case of a treaty which is void under article 53 the parties shall:
   (a) eliminate as far as possible the consequences of any act performed in reliance on any provision which conflicts with the peremptory norm of general international law; and
   (b) bring their mutual relations into conformity with the peremptory norm of general international law.

2. In the case of a treaty which becomes void and terminates under article 64, the termination of the treaty:
   (a) releases the parties from any obligation further to perform the treaty;
   (b) does not affect any right, obligation or legal situation of the parties created through the execution of the treaty prior to its termination; provided that those rights, obligations or situations may thereafter be maintained only to the extent that their maintenance is not in itself in conflict with the new peremptory norm of general international law.

[4646]

Article 72

Consequences of the suspension of the operation of a treaty

1. Unless the treaty otherwise provides or the parties otherwise agree, the suspension of the operation of a treaty under its provisions or in accordance with the present Convention:

(a) releases the parties between which the operation of the treaty is suspended from the obligation to perform the treaty in their mutual relations during the period of the suspension;

(b) does not otherwise affect the legal relations between the parties established by the treaty.

2. During the period of the suspension the parties shall refrain from acts tending to obstruct the resumption of the operation of the treaty.

[4647]

PART VI
MISCELLANEOUS PROVISIONS

Article 73

Cases of State succession, State responsibility and outbreak of hostilities

The provisions of the present Convention shall not prejudge any question that may arise in regard to a treaty from a succession of States or from the international responsibility of a State or from the outbreak of hostilities between States.

[4648]

Article 74

Diplomatic and consular relations and the conclusion of treaties

The severance or absence of diplomatic or consular relations between two or more States does not prevent the conclusion of treaties between those States. The conclusion of a treaty does not in itself affect the situation in regard to diplomatic or consular relations.

[4649]

Article 75

Case of an aggressor State

The provisions of the present Convention are without prejudice to any obligation in relation to a treaty which may arise for an aggressor State in consequence of measures taken in conformity with the Charter of the United Nations with reference to that State's aggression.

[4650]

PART VII
DEPOSITARIES, NOTIFICATIONS, CORRECTIONS AND REGISTRATION

Article 76

Depositaries of treaties

1. The designation of the depositary of a treaty may be made by the negotiating States, either in the treaty itself or in some other manner. The depositary may be one or more States, an international organization or the chief administrative officer of the organization.

2. The functions of the depositary of a treaty are international in character and the depositary is under an obligation to act impartially in their performance. In particular, the fact that a treaty has not entered into force between certain of the parties or that a difference has appeared between a State and a depositary with regard to the performance of the latter's functions shall not affect that obligation.

[4651]

Article 77

Functions of depositaries

1. The functions of a depositary, unless otherwise provided in the treaty or agreed by the contracting States, comprise in particular:

(a) keeping custody of the original text of the treaty and of any full powers delivered to the depositary;
(b) preparing certified copies of the original text and preparing any further text of the treaty in such additional languages as may be required by the treaty and transmitting them to the parties and to the States entitled to become parties to the treaty;
(c) receiving any signatures to the treaty and receiving and keeping custody of any instruments, notifications and communications relating to it;
(d) examining whether the signature or any instrument, notification or communication relating to the treaty is in due and proper form and, if need be, bringing the matter to the attention of the State in question;
(e) informing the parties and the States entitled to become parties to the treaty of acts, notifications and communications relating to the treaty;
(f) informing the States entitled to become parties to the treaty when the number of signatures or of instruments of ratification, acceptance, approval or accession required for the entry into force of the treaty has been received or deposited;
(g) registering the treaty with the Secretariat of the United Nations;
(h) performing the functions specified in other provisions of the present Convention.

2. In the event of any difference appearing between a State and the depositary as to the performance of the latter's functions, the depositary shall bring the question to the attention of the signatory States and the contracting States or, where appropriate, of the competent organ of the international organization concerned. **[4652]**

Article 78

Notifications and communications

Except as the treaty or the present Convention otherwise provide, any notification or communication to be made by any State under the present Convention shall:
(a) if there is no depositary, be transmitted direct to the States for which it is intended, or if there is a depositary, to the latter;
(b) be considered as having been made by the State in question only upon its receipt by the State to which it was transmitted or, as the case may be, upon its receipt by the depositary;
(c) if transmitted to a depositary, be considered as received by the State for which it was intended only when the latter State has been informed by the depositary in accordance with article 77, paragraph 1(e). **[4653]**

Article 79

Correction of errors in texts or in certified copies of treaties

1. Where, after the authentication of the text of a treaty, the signatory States and the contracting States are agreed that it contains an error, the error shall, unless they decide upon some other means of correction, be corrected:
(a) by having the appropriate correction made in the text and causing the correction to be initialled by duly authorized representatives;
(b) by executing or exchanging an instrument or instruments setting out the correction which it has been agreed to make; or
(c) by executing a corrected text of the whole treaty by the same procedure as in the case of the original text.

2. Where the treaty is one for which there is a depositary, the latter shall notify the signatory States and the contracting States of the error and of the proposal to correct it and shall specify an appropriate time-limit within which objection to the proposed correction may be raised. If, on the expiry of the time-limit:
(a) no objection has been raised, the depositary shall make and initial the correction in the text and shall execute a *procès-verbal* of the rectification of the text and communicate a copy of it to the parties and to the States entitled to become parties to the treaty;
(b) an objection has been raised, the depositary shall communicate the objection to the signatory States and to the contracting States.

3. The rules in paragraphs 1 and 2 apply also where the text has been authenticated in two or more languages and it appears that there is a lack of concordance which the signatory States and the contracting States agree should be corrected.

4. The corrected text replaces the defective text *ab initio*, unless the signatory States and the contracting States otherwise decide.

5. The correction of the text of a treaty that has been registered shall be notified to the Secretariat of the United Nations.

6. Where an error is discovered in a certified copy of a treaty, the depositary shall execute a *procès-verbal* specifying the rectification and communicate a copy of it to the signatory States and to the contracting States.

[4654]

Article 80

Registration and publication of treaties

1. Treaties shall, after their entry into force, be transmitted to the Secretariat of the United Nations for registration or filing and recording, as the case may be, and for publication.

2. The designation of a depositary shall constitute authorization for it to perform the acts specified in the preceding paragraph.

[4655]

PART VIII
FINAL PROVISIONS

Article 81

Signature

The present Convention shall be open for signature by all States Members of the United Nations or of any of the specialized agencies or of the International Atomic Energy Agency or parties to the Statute of the International Court of Justice, and by any other State invited by the General Assembly of the United Nations to become a party to the Convention, as follows: until 30 November 1969, at the Federal Ministry for Foreign Affairs of the Republic of Austria, and subsequently, until 30 April 1970, at United Nations Headquarters New York

[4656]

Article 82

Ratification

The present Convention is subject to ratification. The instruments of ratification shall be deposited with the Secretary-General of the United Nations.

[4657]

Article 83

Accession

The present Convention shall remain open for accession by any State belonging to any of the categories mentioned in article 81. The instruments of accession shall be deposited with the Secretary-General of the United Nations.

[4658]

Article 84

Entry into force

1. The present Convention shall enter into force on the thirtieth day following the date of deposit of the thirty-fifth instrument of ratification or accession.

2. For each State ratifying or acceding to the Convention after the deposit of the thirty-fifth instrument of ratification or accession, the Convention shall enter into force on the thirtieth day after deposit by such State of its instrument of ratification or accession.

[4659]

Article 85

Authentic texts

The original of the present Convention, of which the Chinese, English, French Russian and Spanish texts are equally authentic, shall be deposited with the Secretary-General of the United Nations.

IN WITNESS WHEREOF the undersigned Plenipotentiaries, being duly authorized thereto by their respective Governments, have signed the present Convention.

[4660]

DONE AT VIENNA, this twenty-third day of May, one thousand nine hundred and sixty-nine.

ANNEX

1. A list of conciliators consisting of qualified jurists shall be drawn up and maintained by the Secretary-General of the United Nations. To this end, every State which is a Member of the United Nations or a party to the present Convention shall be invited to nominate two conciliators, and the names of the persons so nominated shall constitute the list. The term of a conciliator, including that of any conciliator nominated to fill a casual vacancy, shall be five years and may be renewed. A conciliator whose term expires shall continue to fulfil any function for which he shall have been chosen under the following paragraph.

2. When a request has been made to the Secretary-General under article 66, the Secretary-General shall bring the dispute before a conciliation commission constituted as follows:

The State or States constituting one of the parties to the dispute shall appoint:

(a) one conciliator of the nationality of that State or of one of those States, who may or may not be chosen from the list referred to in paragraph 1; and

(b) one conciliator not of the nationality of that State or of any of those States, who shall be chosen from the list.

The State or States constituting the other party to the dispute shall appoint two conciliators in the same way. The four conciliators chosen by the parties shall be appointed within sixty days following the date on which the Secretary-General receives the request.

The four conciliators shall, within sixty days following the date of the last of their own appointments, appoint a fifth conciliator chosen from the list, who shall be chairman.

If the appointment of the chairman or of any of the other conciliators has not been made within the period prescribed above for such appointment, it shall be made by the Secretary-General within sixty days following the expiry of that period. The appointment of the chairman may be made by the Secretary-General either from the list or from the membership of the International Law Commission. Any of the periods within which appointments must be made may be extended by agreement between the parties to the dispute.

Any vacancy shall be filled in the manner prescribed for the initial appointment.

3. The Conciliation Commission shall decide its own procedure. The Commission, with the consent of the parties to the dispute, may invite any party to the treaty to submit to it its views orally or in writing. Decisions and recommendations of the Commission shall be made by a majority vote of the five members.

4. The Commission may draw the attention of the parties to the dispute to any measures which might facilitate an amicable settlement.

5. The Commission shall hear the parties, examine the claims and objections, and make proposals to the parties with a view to reaching an amicable settlement of the dispute.

6. The Commission shall report within twelve months of its constitution. Its report shall be deposited with the Secretary-General and transmitted to the parties to the dispute. The report of the Commission, including any conclusions stated therein regarding the facts or questions of law, shall not be binding upon the parties and it shall have no other character than that of recommendations submitted for the consideration of the parties in order to facilitate an amicable settlement of the dispute.

7. The Secretary-General shall provide the Commission with such assistance and facilities as it may require. The expenses of the Commission shall be borne by the United Nations.

[4661]

UNCITRAL MODEL LAW ON INTERNATIONAL COMMERCIAL CONCILIATION

(2002)

NOTES

The Model Law is reproduced with the kind permission of the United Nations. The original source of this Model Law is the United Nations Commission on International Trade Law. See http://www.uncitral.org.

RESOLUTION ADOPTED BY THE GENERAL ASSEMBLY [ON THE REPORT OF THE SIXTH COMMITTEE (A/57/562 AND CORR.1)]

57/18. MODEL LAW ON INTERNATIONAL COMMERCIAL CONCILIATION OF THE UNITED NATIONS COMMISSION ON INTERNATIONAL TRADE LAW

The General Assembly,

Recognizing the value for international trade of methods for settling commercial disputes in which the parties in dispute request a third person or persons to assist them in their attempt to settle the dispute amicably,

Noting that such dispute settlement methods, referred to by expressions such as conciliation and mediation and expressions of similar import, are increasingly used in international and domestic commercial practice as an alternative to litigation,

Considering that the use of such dispute settlement methods results in significant benefits, such as reducing the instances where a dispute leads to the termination of a commercial relationship, facilitating the administration of international transactions by commercial parties and producing savings in the administration of justice by States,

Convinced that the establishment of model legislation on these methods that is acceptable to States with different legal, social and economic systems would contribute to the development of harmonious international economic relations,

Noting with satisfaction the completion and adoption by the United Nations Commission on International Trade Law of the Model Law on International Commercial Conciliation,[1]

Believing that the Model Law will significantly assist States in enhancing their legislation governing the use of modern conciliation or mediation techniques and in formulating such legislation where none currently exists,

Noting that the preparation of the Model Law was the subject of due deliberation and extensive consultations with Governments and interested circles,

Convinced that the Model Law, together with the Conciliation Rules recommended by the General Assembly in its resolution 35/52 of 4 December 1980, contributes significantly to the establishment of a harmonized legal framework for the fair and efficient settlement of disputes arising in international commercial relations,

1. Expresses its appreciation to the United Nations Commission on International Trade Law for completing and adopting the Model Law on International Commercial Conciliation, the text of which is contained in the annex to the present resolution, and for preparing the Guide to Enactment and Use of the Model Law;

2. Requests the Secretary-General to make all efforts to ensure that the Model Law, together with its Guide to Enactment, becomes generally known and available;

3. Recommends that all States give due consideration to the enactment of the Model Law, in view of the desirability of uniformity of the law of dispute settlement procedures and the specific needs of international commercial conciliation practice.

52nd plenary meeting,

19 November 2002

NOTES

1 Official Records of the General Assembly, Fifty-seventh Session, Supplement No 17 (A/57/17), annex I.

PART ONE

Article 1

Scope of application and definitions

(1) This Law applies to international[1] commercial[2] conciliation.

(2) For the purposes of this Law, "conciliator" means a sole conciliator or two or more conciliators, as the case may be.

(3) For the purposes of this Law, "conciliation" means a process, whether referred to by the expression conciliation, mediation or an expression of similar import, whereby parties request a third person or persons ("the conciliator") to assist them in their attempt to reach an amicable settlement of their dispute arising out of or relating to a contractual or other legal relationship. The conciliator does not have the authority to impose upon the parties a solution to the dispute.

(4) A conciliation is international if:
- (a) The parties to an agreement to conciliate have, at the time of the conclusion of that agreement, their places of business in different States; or
- (b) The State in which the parties have their places of business is different from either:
  - (i) The State in which a substantial part of the obligations of the commercial relationship is to be performed; or
  - (ii) The State with which the subject matter of the dispute is most closely connected.

(5) For the purposes of this article:
- (a) If a party has more than one place of business, the place of business is that which has the closest relationship to the agreement to conciliate;
- (b) If a party does not have a place of business, reference is to be made to the party's habitual residence.

(6) This Law also applies to a commercial conciliation when the parties agree that the conciliation is international or agree to the applicability of this Law.

(7) The parties are free to agree to exclude the applicability of this Law.

(8) Subject to the provisions of paragraph (9) of this article, this Law applies irrespective of the basis upon which the conciliation is carried out, including agreement between the parties whether reached before or after a dispute has arisen, an obligation established by law, or a direction or suggestion of a court, arbitral tribunal or competent governmental entity.

(9) This Law does not apply to:
- (a) Cases where a judge or an arbitrator, in the course of judicial or arbitral proceedings, attempts to facilitate a settlement; and
- (b) [...]

[4662]

NOTES

1 States wishing to enact this Model Law to apply to domestic as well as international conciliation may wish to consider the following changes to the text:
— Delete the word "international" in paragraph 1 of article 1; and
— Delete paragraphs 4, 5 and 6 of article 1.

2 The term "commercial" should be given a wide interpretation so as to cover matters arising from all relationships of a commercial nature, whether contractual or not. Relationships of a commercial nature include, but are not limited to, the following transactions: any trade transaction for the supply or exchange of goods or services; distribution agreement; commercial representation or agency; factoring; leasing; construction of works; consulting; engineering; licensing; investment; financing; banking; insurance; exploitation agreement or concession; joint venture and other forms of industrial or business cooperation; carriage of goods or passengers by air, sea, rail or road.

Article 2

Interpretation

(1) In the interpretation of this Law, regard is to be had to its international origin and to the need to promote uniformity in its application and the observance of good faith.

(2) Questions concerning matters governed by this Law which are not expressly settled in it are to be settled in conformity with the general principles on which this Law is based.

[4663]

Article 3

Variation by agreement

Except for the provisions of article 2 and article 6, paragraph (3), the parties may agree to exclude or vary any of the provisions of this Law.

[4664]

Article 4

Commencement of conciliation proceedings[1]

(1) Conciliation proceedings in respect of a dispute that has arisen commence on the day on which the parties to that dispute agree to engage in conciliation proceedings.

(2) If a party that invited another party to conciliate does not receive an acceptance of the invitation within thirty days from the day on which the invitation was sent, or within such other period of time as specified in the invitation, the party may elect to treat this as a rejection of the invitation to conciliate.

[4665]

NOTES

1 The following text is suggested for States that might wish to adopt a provision on the suspension of the limitation period:

Article X

Suspension of limitation period

1. When the conciliation proceedings commence, the running of the limitation period regarding the claim that is the subject matter of the conciliation is suspended.

2. Where the conciliation proceedings have terminated without a settlement agreement, the limitation period resumes running from the time the conciliation ended without a settlement agreement.

Article 5

Number and appointment of conciliators

(1) There shall be one conciliator, unless the parties agree that there shall be two or more conciliators.

(2) The parties shall endeavour to reach agreement on a conciliator or conciliators, unless a different procedure for their appointment has been agreed upon.

(3) Parties may seek the assistance of an institution or person in connection with the appointment of conciliators. In particular:

(a) A party may request such an institution or person to recommend suitable persons to act as conciliator; or

(b) The parties may agree that the appointment of one or more conciliators be made directly by such an institution or person.

(4) In recommending or appointing individuals to act as conciliator, the institution or person shall have regard to such considerations as are likely to secure the appointment of an independent and impartial conciliator and, where appropriate, shall take into account the advisability of appointing a conciliator of a nationality other than the nationalities of the parties.

(5) When a person is approached in connection with his or her possible appointment as conciliator, he or she shall disclose any circumstances likely to give rise to justifiable doubts as to his or her impartiality or independence. A conciliator, from the time of his or her appointment and throughout the conciliation proceedings, shall without delay disclose any such circumstances to the parties unless they have already been informed of them by him or her.

[4666]

Article 6

Conduct of conciliation

(1) The parties are free to agree, by reference to a set of rules or otherwise, on the manner in which the conciliation is to be conducted.

(2) Failing agreement on the manner in which the conciliation is to be conducted, the conciliator may conduct the conciliation proceedings in such a manner as the conciliator considers appropriate, taking into account the circumstances of the case, any wishes that the parties may express and the need for a speedy settlement of the dispute.

(3) In any case, in conducting the proceedings, the conciliator shall seek to maintain fair treatment of the parties and, in so doing, shall take into account the circumstances of the case.

(4) The conciliator may, at any stage of the conciliation proceedings, make proposals for a settlement of the dispute.

[4667]

Article 7

Communication between conciliator and parties

The conciliator may meet or communicate with the parties together or with each of them separately.

[4668]

Article 8

Disclosure of information

When the conciliator receives information concerning the dispute from a party, the conciliator may disclose the substance of that information to any other party to the conciliation. However, when a party gives any information to the conciliator, subject to a specific condition that it be kept confidential, that information shall not be disclosed to any other party to the conciliation.

[4669]

Article 9

Confidentiality

Unless otherwise agreed by the parties, all information relating to the conciliation proceedings shall be kept confidential, except where disclosure is required under the law or for the purposes of implementation or enforcement of a settlement agreement.

[4670]

Article 10

Admissibility of evidence in other proceedings

(1) A party to the conciliation proceedings, the conciliator and any third person, including those involved in the administration of the conciliation proceedings, shall not in arbitral, judicial or similar proceedings rely on, introduce as evidence or give testimony or evidence regarding any of the following:

- (a) An invitation by a party to engage in conciliation proceedings or the fact that a party was willing to participate in conciliation proceedings;
- (b) Views expressed or suggestions made by a party in the conciliation in respect of a possible settlement of the dispute;
- (c) Statements or admissions made by a party in the course of the conciliation proceedings;
- (d) Proposals made by the conciliator;
- (e) The fact that a party had indicated its willingness to accept a proposal for settlement made by the conciliator;
- (f) A document prepared solely for purposes of the conciliation proceedings.

(2) Paragraph (1) of this article applies irrespective of the form of the information or evidence referred to therein.

(3) The disclosure of the information referred to in paragraph (1) of this article shall not be ordered by an arbitral tribunal, court or other competent governmental authority and, if

such information is offered as evidence in contravention of paragraph (1) of this article, that evidence shall be treated as inadmissible. Nevertheless, such information may be disclosed or admitted in evidence to the extent required under the law or for the purposes of implementation or enforcement of a settlement agreement.

(4) The provisions of paragraphs (1), (2) and (3) of this article apply whether or not the arbitral, judicial or similar proceedings relate to the dispute that is or was the subject matter of the conciliation proceedings.

(5) Subject to the limitations of paragraph (1) of this article, evidence that is otherwise admissible in arbitral or judicial or similar proceedings does not become inadmissible as a consequence of having been used in a conciliation.

[4671]

Article 11

Termination of conciliation proceedings

The conciliation proceedings are terminated:

(a) By the conclusion of a settlement agreement by the parties, on the date of the agreement;

(b) By a declaration of the conciliator, after consultation with the parties, to the effect that further efforts at conciliation are no longer justified, on the date of the declaration;

(c) By a declaration of the parties addressed to the conciliator to the effect that the conciliation proceedings are terminated, on the date of the declaration; or (d) By a declaration of a party to the other party or parties and the conciliator, if appointed, to the effect that the conciliation proceedings are terminated, on the date of the declaration.

(d) By a declaration of a party to the other party or parties and the conciliator, if appointed, to the effect that the conciliation proceedings are terminated, on the date of the declaration.

[4672]

Article 12

Conciliator acting as arbitrator

Unless otherwise agreed by the parties, the conciliator shall not act as an arbitrator in respect of a dispute that was or is the subject of the conciliation proceedings or in respect of another dispute that has arisen from the same contract or legal relationship or any related contract or legal relationship.

[4673]

Article 13

Resort to arbitral or judicial proceedings

Where the parties have agreed to conciliate and have expressly undertaken not to initiate during a specified period of time or until a specified event has occurred arbitral or judicial proceedings with respect to an existing or future dispute, such an undertaking shall be given effect by the arbitral tribunal or the court until the terms of the undertaking have been complied with, except to the extent necessary for a party, in its opinion, to preserve its rights. Initiation of such proceedings is not of itself to be regarded as a waiver of the agreement to conciliate or as a termination of the conciliation proceedings.

[4674]

Article 14

Enforceability of settlement agreement[1]

If the parties conclude an agreement settling a dispute, that settlement agreement is binding and enforceable … [*the enacting State may insert a description of the method of enforcing settlement agreements or refer to provisions governing such enforcement*].

[4675]

NOTES

1 When implementing the procedure for enforcement of settlement agreements, an enacting State may consider the possibility of such a procedure being mandatory.

(Part Two (Guide to Enactment and Use) outside the scope of this work.)

TABLES

TABLE 1
JURISDICTION AND FOREIGN JUDGMENTS

A. MEMBER STATES OF THE EUROPEAN COMMUNITY

Member State	Date in Force			
	Regulation 44/2001[1]	Brussels Convention (1989)[2]	Brussels Convention (1998)[3]	Lugano Convention[4]
Austria	1 March 2002	–	1 December 1998	1 September 1996
Belgium	1 March 2002	1 October 1997	–	1 October 1997
Cyprus	1 May 2004	–	–	–
Czech Republic	1 May 2004	–	–	–
Denmark	–	1 March 1996[5]	1 December 1998[6]	1 March 1996[7]
Estonia	1 May 2004	–	–	–
Finland	1 March 2002	–	1 April 1999	1 July 1993
France	1 March 2002	1 February 1991	1 August 2000	1 January 1992
Germany	1 March 2002	1 December 1994	1 January 1999	1 March 1995
Greece	1 March 2002	1 July 1992	1 October 1999	1 September 1997
Hungary	1 May 2004	–	–	–
Ireland	1 March 2002	1 December 1993	1 December 1999	1 December 1993
Italy	1 March 2002	1 May 1992	1 June 1999	1 December 1992
Latvia	1 May 2004	–	–	–
Lithuania	1 May 2004	–	–	–
Luxembourg	1 March 2002	1 February 1992	1 May 2000	1 February 1992
Malta	1 May 2004	–	–	–
Netherlands	1 March 2002	1 February 1992[8]	1 December 1998[9]	1 January 1992[10]
Poland	1 May 2004	–	–	1 February 2000
Portugal	1 March 2002	1 July 1992	1 October 1998	1 July 1992
Slovakia	1 March 2002	–	–	–
Slovenia	1 March 2002	–	–	–

Spain	1 March 2002	1 February 1991	1 April 1999	1 November 1994
Sweden	1 March 2002	–	1 January 1999	1 January 1993
United Kingdom	1 March 2002	1 December 1991[11]	1 January 2001[12]	1 May 1992[13]

B. NON-MEMBER STATES OF THE EUROPEAN COMMUNITY PARTY TO THE 1988 LUGANO CONVENTION

Contracting State	Date in Force
Iceland	1 December 1995
Norway	1 May 1993
Switzerland	1 January 2002

C. STATES TO WHICH THE FOREIGN JUDGMENTS (RECIPROCAL ENFORCEMENT) ACT 1993 HAS BEEN EXTENDED[14]

Australia
Austria *
Canada (excluding Quebec)
France *
Germany *
Guernsey
India
Isle of Man
Israel
Italy *
Jersey
Netherlands *
Norway *
Pakistan
Suriname
Tonga

D. STATES TO WHICH THE ADMINISTRATION OF JUSTICE ACT 1920, PART II HAS BEEN EXTENDED[15]

Anguilla	Malta *
Antigua and Barbuda	Mauritius
Bahamas	Montserrat
Barbados	[Newfoundland]
Belize	New Zealand

Bermuda	Nigeria
Botswana	Territory of Norfolk Island
British Indian Ocean Territory	Papua New Guinea
British Virgin Islands	St Christopher and Nevis
Cayman Islands	St Helena
Christmas Island	St Lucia
Cocos (Keeling) Islands	St Vincent and the Grenadines
Republic of Cyprus*	[Saskatchewan]
Dominica	Seychelles
Falkland Islands	Sierra Leone
Fiji	Singapore
The Gambia	Solomon Islands
Ghana	Sovereign Base Areas of Akrotiri and Dhekelia in Cyprus
Grenada	Sri Lanka
Guyana	Swaziland
[Hong Kong]	Tanzania
Jamaica	Trinidad and Tobago
Kenya	Turks and Caicos Islands
Kiribati	Tuvalu
Lesotho	Uganda
Malawi	Zambia
Malaysia	Zimbabwe

NOTES

1 Council Regulation 44/2001/EC on jurisdiction and the recognition and enforcement of judgments in civil and commercial matters, as amended, at **[3080]**. (Source: Council Regulation No 44/2001/EC, Art 76; Treaty concerning the accession of the Czech Republic, the Republic of Estonia, the Republic of Cyprus, the Republic of Latvia, the Republic of Lithuania, the Republic of Hungary, the Republic of Malta, the Republic of Poland, the Republic of Slovenia and the Slovak Republic to the European Union (2004), Art 2.1 and Act of Accession, Art 2.)

For the geographical scope of Council Regulation 44/2001/EC, see EC Treaty, Art 299 at **[3012]**. Council Regulation 44/2001/EC does not apply to Denmark (see Council Regulation 44/2001/EC, recital (21), Art 1.3 at **[3080]**).

2 The 1989 San Sebastian Convention on the Accession of the Kingdom of Spain and the Portuguese Republic to the 1968 Brussels Convention on jurisdiction and the enforcement of judgments in civil and commercial matters and the protocol on its interpretation by the Court of Justice, amending the Brussels Convention. (Source: EC Council Agreements Office database—http://www.consilium.europa.eu/cms3_applications/Applications/accords/search.asp?lang=EN&cmsid=297. Only the declarations relating to geographical scope are referred to here, and the database should be consulted for full details of the reservations, declarations and other communications by the Contracting States.)

The geographical scope of the 1968 Brussels Convention, as amended, is to be determined in accordance with principles of public international law. See, however, the commentary on the (now deleted) territorial application provisions (formerly Art 60) in the Schlosser Report on the 1978 Accession Convention at **[3047A]** and the Cruz, Real and Jenard Report on the 1989 (San Sebastian) Accession Convention at **[3052]**. See also the declarations footnoted below.

3 The 1998 (Brussels) Convention on the Accession of the Republic of Austria, the Republic of Finland and the Kingdom of Sweden to the 1968 Brussels Convention, amending the Brussels Convention. (Source: EC Council Agreements Office database—see footnote 2 above. Only the declarations relating to geographical scope are referred to here, and the database should be consulted for full details of the reservations, declarations and other communications by the Contracting States.)

For the geographical scope of the 1968 Brussels Convention, as amended, see footnote 2 above and the declarations footnoted below.

4 The 1988 Lugano Convention on jurisdiction and the recognition and enforcement of judgments in civil and commercial matters. (Source: Swiss Ministry of Justice website—http://

www.ofj.admin.ch/etc/medialib/data/wirtschaft/ipr.Par.0015.File.tmp/Ratifikationsliste-e.pdf. Only the declarations relating to geographical scope are referred to here, and the website should be consulted for full details of the reservations, declarations and other communications by the Contracting States.)

The geographical scope of the 1988 Lugano Convention is to be determined in accordance with principles of public international law. See, however, footnote 2 above and the commentary in the Jenard and Möller Report on the Lugano Convention at **[3070]**. See also the declarations footnoted below.

5 Declaration: "Until further notice, the Convention will not apply to the Faroe Islands or Greenland."

6 Declaration: "Until further decision, the Convention will not apply to the Faroe Islands or Greenland."

7 Declaration: "The Convention is not extended to the Faroe Islands or Greenland."

8 Declaration: "The Convention shall apply only to the Netherlands in Europe." Previously, the Netherlands had extended the 1968 Brussels Convention to Aruba with effect from 30 June 1986, but had declared the 1978 Accession Convention (Denmark, Ireland and UK) to apply only to the Kingdom in Europe. See also fn 9 below. The Convention has not been extended to the Netherlands Antilles.

9 Declaration: "The Convention also applies to Aruba." The Convention has not been extended to the Netherlands Antilles.

10 Declaration: "The Convention is applicable to the Kingdom in Europe."

11 By declaration dated 30 July 1998, the United Kingdom declared "that the Convention shall apply to Gibraltar being a territory for whose international relations the Government of the United Kingdom are responsible. Declare that the following provisions of the Convention shall be implemented in Gibraltar in the manner specified below: Article 3—the references with respect to the United Kingdom in the second paragraph to certain rules enabling the founding of jurisdiction shall apply mutatis mutandis to Gibraltar; Article 30—the reference to the United Kingdom in the second paragraph shall apply to Gibraltar also; Article 32—an application for enforcement of a judgment shall be submitted to the Supreme Court of Gibraltar, or in the case of a maintenance judgment to the Magistrates' Court on transmission by the Attorney General of Gibraltar; Article 37—an appeal against a decision authorising enforcement shall be lodged with the Supreme Court of Gibraltar, or in the case of a maintenance judgment with the Magistrates' Court on transmission by the Attorney General of Gibraltar; the judgment given on the appeal may be contested only by a single further appeal on a point of law to the Court of Appeal of Gibraltar, or in the case of a maintenance judgment to the Supreme Court of Gibraltar by way of case stated; Article 38—the reference to the United Kingdom in the second paragraph shall apply to Gibraltar also; Article 40—an applicant may appeal against the refusal of an application for enforcement to the Supreme Court of Gibraltar, or in the case of a maintenance judgment to the Magistrates' Court; Article 41—a judgment on an appeal provided for in Article 40 may be contested only by a single further appeal on a point of law to the Court of Appeal of Gibraltar, or in the case of a maintenance judgment to the Supreme Court of Gibraltar by way of case stated. By analogy with the provisions of Article 62 of the Convention the date on which the Convention shall come into effect for Gibraltar is 1 October, 1998 being the first day of the third month following the deposit of this Note." Spain objected to this extension of the Convention, but withdrew its objection with effect 25 July 2000. See further the Civil Jurisdiction and Judgments (Gibraltar) Order 1997, SI 1997/2602 at **[2140]**.

12 For the extension of the Convention to Gibraltar, see footnote 11 above.

13 By declaration dated 31 July 1998, the United Kingdom sought to extend the 1988 Lugano Convention to Gibraltar. Spain objected to this extension, but withdrew its objection by declaration dated 21 September 2000.

14 See notes to the 1933 Act, s 1 at **[16]** for a full list of the statutory instruments extending the Act. For the text of those statutory instruments, see **[2003]**–**[2129]**. Entries marked with an asterisk are also Member States of the EC, to which Council Regulation 44/2001/EC applies, or Contracting States to the 1988 Lugano Convention—see further note to statutory instruments under the 1933 Act, s 1 at **[16]**.

15 Source: Reciprocal Enforcement of Judgments (Administration of Justice Act 1920, Part II) (Consolidation) Order 1984, SI 1984/129 at **[2104]**. See notes to the 1984 Order at **[2107]** for the position of Hong Kong, Newfoundland and Saskatchewan (in square brackets in the list below). Entries marked with an asterisk are also Member States of the EC, to which Council Regulation 44/2001/EC applies—see further notes to the 1984 Order at **[2107]**.

[4676]

TABLE 2
INTERNATIONAL ARBITRATION

PARTIES TO THE 1958 NEW YORK CONVENTION ON THE RECOGNITION AND ENFORCEMENT OF ARBITRAL AWARDS[1]

Party	Entry into Force	Reciprocity Declaration[2]	Commercial Relationship Declaration[3]
Afghanistan	30 November 2004	x	x
Albania	27 June 2001		
Algeria	7 February 1989	x	x
Antigua and Barbuda	2 February 1989	x	x
Argentina[4]	14 March 1989	x	x
Armenia	29 December 1997		
Australia[5]	26 March 1975		
Austria	2 May 1961		
Azerbaijan	29 February 2000		
Bahrain[6]	6 April 1988	x	x
Bangladesh	6 May 1992		
Barbados	16 March 1993	x	x
Belarus	15 November 1960	See note[7]	
Belgium	18 August 1975	x	
Benin	16 May 1974		
Bolivia	28 April 1995		
Bosnia and Herzegovina[8]	1 September 1993	x	x
Botswana	20 December 1971	x[9]	x
Brazil	7 June 2002		
Brunei Darussalam	25 July 1996	x	
Bulgaria	10 October 1961	See note[10]	
Burkina Faso	23 March 1987		
Cambodia	5 January 1960		
Cameroon	19 February 1988		
Canada	12 May 1986		x[11]
Central African Republic	15 October 1962	x	x
Chile	4 September 1975		
China[12]	22 January 1987	x	x
Colombia	25 September 1979		
Costa Rica	26 October 1987		
Côte d'Ivoire	1 February 1991		
Croatia[13]	26 July 1993		
Cuba	30 December 1974	See note[14]	x
Cyprus	29 December 1980	x	x
Czech Republic[15]	30 September 1993		
Denmark[16]	22 December 1972		x

Djibouti	14 June 1983		
Dominica	28 October 1988		
Dominican Republic	11 April 2002		
Ecuador	3 January 1962	See note[17]	See note[17]
Egypt	9 March 1959		
El Salvador	26 February 1998		
Estonia	30 August 1993		
Finland	19 January 1962		
France[18]	26 June 1959	x	
Georgia	2 June 1994		
Germany	30 June 1961		
Ghana	9 April 1968		
Greece	16 July 1962	x	x
Guatemala	21 March 1984	x	x
Guinea	23 January 1991		
Haiti	5 December 1983		
Holy See	14 May 1975	x	x
Honduras	3 October 2000		
Hungary	5 March 1962	x	x
Iceland	24 January 2002		
India	13 July 1960	x	x
Indonesia	7 October 1981	x	x
Iran	15 October 2001	x	x
Ireland	12 May 1981	x	
Israel	5 January 1959		
Italy	31 January 1969		
Jamaica	10 July 2002	x	x
Japan	20 June 1961	x	
Jordan[19]	15 November 1979		
Kazakhstan	20 November 1995		
Kenya	10 February 1989	x	
Kuwait[20]	28 April 1978	x	
Kyrgyzstan	18 December 1996		
Lao People's Democratic Republic	17 June 1998		
Latvia	14 April 1992		
Lebanon	11 August 1998	x	
Lesotho	13 June 1989		
Liberia	16 September 2005		
Lithuania	14 March 1995	See note[21]	
Luxembourg	9 September 1983	x	
Madagascar	16 July 1962	x	x
Malaysia	5 November 1985	x	x
Mali	8 September 1994		
Malta	22 June 2000	x	

Mauritania	30 January 1997		
Mauritius[22]	19 June 1996	x	
Mexico	14 April 1971		
Monaco	2 June 1982	x	x
Mongolia	24 October 1994	x	x
Morocco	12 February 1959	x	
Mozambique	11 June 1998	See note[23]	
Nepal	4 March 1998	x	x
Netherlands[24]	24 April 1964	x	
New Zealand[25]	6 January 1983	x	
Nicaragua	24 September 2003	x	x
Niger	14 October 1964		
Nigeria	17 March 1970		
Norway[26]	14 March 1961	x	
Oman	25 February 1999		
Pakistan	14 July 2005	x	
Panama	10 October 1984		
Paraguay	8 October 1997		
Peru	7 July 1988		
Philippines	6 July 1967	x	x
Poland	3 October 1961	x	x
Portugal	18 October 1994	x	
Qatar	30 December 2002		
Republic of Korea	8 February 1973	x	x
Republic of Moldova	18 September 1998	x	
Romania	13 September 1961	See note[27]	x
Russian Federation	24 August 1960	See note[28]	
Saint Vincent and the Grenadines	12 September 2000	x	x
San Marino	17 May 1979		
Saudi Arabia	19 April 1994	x	
Senegal	17 October 1994		
Serbia and Montenegro[29]	12 March 2001	x	x
Singapore	21 August 1986	x	
Slovakia[30]	28 May 1993		
Slovenia[31]	6 July 1992	x	x
South Africa	3 May 1976		
Spain	12 May 1977		
Sri Lanka	9 April 1962		
Sweden	28 January 1972		
Switzerland	1 June 1965		
Syrian Arab Republic[32]	9 March 1959		
Thailand	21 December 1959		

The Former Yugoslav Republic of Macedonia[33]	10 March 1994		
Trinidad and Tobago	14 February 1966	x	x
Tunisia	17 July 1967	x	x
Turkey	2 July 1992		
Uganda	12 February 1992	x	
Ukraine	10 October 1960	See note[34]	
United Kingdom[35]	24 September 1975	x	
United Republic of Tanzania	13 October 1964	x	
United States of America[37]	30 September 1970	x	x
Uruguay	30 March 1983		
Uzbekistan	7 February 1996		
Venezuela	8 February 1995	x	x
Viet Nam[38]	12 September 1995	See note[39]	x
Zambia	14 March 2002		
Zimbabwe	29 September 1994		

NOTES

1 Source: United Nations website—see http://untreaty.un.org/ENGLISH/bible/englishinternetbible/partI/chapterXXII/treaty1.asp. This website should be consulted for the full text of any declaration, reservations and other communications by the participating States. A list of parties, with summary information, also appears on the UNCITRAL website at http://www.uncitral.org/uncitral/en/uncitral_texts/arbitration/NYConvention_status.html. For the text of the 1958 New York Convention, see **[4221]**.

2 "When signing, ratifying or acceding to this Convention, or notifying extension under article X hereof, any State may on the basis of reciprocity declare that it will apply the Convention to the recognition and enforcement of awards made only in the territory of another Contracting State." (Art I.3, first sentence.)

3 "[A State] may also declare that it will apply the Convention only to differences arising out of legal relationships, whether contractual or not, which are considered as commercial under the national law of the State making such declaration." (Art I.3, second sentence.)

4 On signature, Argentina declared that: "If other Contracting Party extends the application of the Convention to territories which fall within the sovereignty of the Argentine Republic, the rights of the Argentine Republic shall in no way be affected by that extension."

On ratification, Argentina also declared that: "The Convention will be interpreted in accordance with the principles and clauses of the National Constitution in force or those resulting from modification made by virtue of the Constitution". Germany objected to that declaration by a communication dated 29 December 1989.

5 Extends to all external territories for the international relations of which Australia is responsible, except Papua New Guinea.

6 Bahrain also declared that its accession to the Convention "shall in no way constitute recognition of Israel or be a cause for the establishment of any relations of any kind therewith". In response, Israel submitted "the said declaration cannot in any way affect whatever obligations are binding upon Jordan under international law or under particular conventions" (communication to the Secretary General dated 22 September 1988).

7 "The Byelorussion Soviet Socialist Republic will apply the provisions of this Convention in respect to arbitral awards made in the territories of non-contracting States only to the extent to which they grant reciprocal treatment."

8 As successor to the former Socialist Federal Republic of Yugoslavia.

9 The terms of the declaration by Botswana confirm that it will apply the Convention to awards from other Contracting States, but does not on its face exclude the possibility of applying the Convention to non-contracting State awards.

10 "Bulgaria will apply the Convention to recognition and enforcement of awards made in the territory of another contracting State. With regard to awards made in the territory of non-contracting States it will apply the Convention only to the extent that these States grant reciprocal treatment."

11 Declaration excludes Quebec.

12 Applies to the Hong Kong Special Administrative Region and the Macao Special Administrative Region with the same qualifications (see notification dated 20 June 1997 (Hong Kong SAR) and declaration dated 19 July 2005 (Macao SAR)).

13 As successor to the former Socialist Federal Republic of Yugoslavia.

14 "Cuba will apply the Convention to the recognition and enforcement of arbitral awards made in the territory of another Contracting State. With respect to arbitral awards made by other non-contracting States it will apply the Convention only in so far as those State grant reciprocal treatment as established by mutual agreement between the parties."

15 As successor to Czechoslovakia.

16 Extends to Faroe Islands and Greenland (see communications dated 12 November 1975 and 5 January 1978).

17 "Ecuador, on a basis of reciprocity, will apply the Convention to the recognition and enforcement of arbitral awards made in the territory of another Contracting State only if such awards have been made with respect to differences arising out of legal relationships which are regarded as commercial under Ecuadorian law." On its face, this appears to be a curious hybrid of the two possible declarations.

18 Extends to all territories of the French Republic.

19 On accession, Jordan declared that it "shall not be bound by any awards which are made by Israel or to which an Israeli is a party". In response, Israel submitted "the said declaration cannot in any way affect whatever obligations are binding upon Jordan under international law or under particular conventions" (communication to the Secretary General dated 23 July 1980).

20 Kuwait also declared that "the accession of the State of Kuwait to the [Convention] does not mean in any way recognition of Israel or entering with it into relations governed by the Convention …".

21 "[The Republic of Lithuania] will apply the provisions of the said Convention to the recognition of arbitral awards made in the territories of the non-contracting States, only on the basis of reciprocity."

22 Extends to all territories forming part of the Republic of Mauritius.

23 "The Republic of Mozambique reserves itself the right to enforce the provisions of the said Conventions on the base (*sic*) of reciprocity, where the arbitral awards have been pronounced in the territory of another Contracting State."

24 Extended to Netherlands Antilles and Surinam (entry into force 24 April 1964). Also applies to Aruba, which was part of the Netherlands Antilles until 1 January 1986.

25 Not extended for the time being to the Cook Islands and Niue.

26 "[The Government of Norway] will not apply the Convention to differences where the subject matter of the proceedings is immovable property situated in Norway, or a right in or to such property."

27 "The Romanian People's Republic will apply the Convention to the recognition and enforcement of awards made in the territory of another Contracting State. As regards awards made in the territory of certain non-contracting States, the Romanian People's Republic will apply the Convention only on the basis of reciprocity established by joint agreement between the parties."

28 "The Union of Soviet Socialist Republics will apply the provisions of this Convention in respect of arbitral awards made in the territories of non-contracting States only to the extent to which they grant reciprocal treatment."

29 As successor to the former Socialist Federal Republic of Yugoslavia.

30 As successor to Czechoslovakia.

31 As successor to the former Socialist Federal Republic of Yugoslavia.

32 Accession by the United Arab Republic.

33 As successor to the former Socialist Federal Republic of Yugoslavia.

34 "The Ukrainian Soviet Socialist Republic will apply the provisions of this Convention in respect of arbitral awards made in the territories of non-contracting States only to the extent to which they grant reciprocal treatment."

35 Extended to Gibraltar (entry into force 24 September 1975), the Isle of Man (22 February 1979), Bermuda (14 November 1979), Belize and Cayman Islands (26 November 1980), Guernsey (19 April 1985) and Jersey (28 May 2002). Also extended to Hong Kong, now under the sovereignty of China (see footnote 12 above).

36 Declaration made after accession on 5 May 1980 in respect of the United Kingdom, Gibraltar, Hong Kong and the Isle of Man. Like declarations were subsequently made upon extension of the Convention to Bermuda, Belize, Cayman Islands, Guernsey and Jersey.

37 Extends to all the territories for the international relations of which the United States of America is responsible.

38 On accession, Viet Nam also declared that: "Interpretation of the Convention before the Vietnamese Courts or competent authorities should be made in accordance with the Constitution and the law of Viet Nam."

39 "[The Socialist Republic of Viet Nam] considers the Convention to be applicable to the recognition and enforcement of arbitral awards made only in the territory of another Contracting State. With respect to arbitral awards made in the territories of non-contracting States, it will apply the Convention on the basis of reciprocity."

[4677]

TABLE 3
SERVICE OF PROCESS

A. MEMBER STATES OF THE EUROPEAN COMMUNITY—THE SERVICE REGULATION[1]

Member State	Derogation under Art 9, para 3[2]	Permits Service by Diplomatic or Consular Agents (Art 13)[3]	Permits Service by Post (Art 14)[4]	Permits Direct service (Art 15)[5]	Declaration under Art 19, para 2[6]	Declaration under Art 19, para 4[7]
Austria		Yes	Yes[8]	No	X	
Belgium	X[9]	No	Yes[10]	Yes	x	1 year
Cyprus		Yes	Yes[11]	Yes	See note[12]	See note[11]
Czech Republic		Yes[13]	Yes[14]	No	x	
Estonia		Yes	Yes[15]	No	x	1 year
Finland	x	Yes	Yes[16]	Yes		
France	x[17]	Yes	Yes[18]	Yes	x	1 year
Germany		No	Yes[19]	No	x	1 year
Greece		Yes	Yes[20]	Yes	See note[21]	3 years
Hungary	x[22]	Yes	Yes[23]	No	x	1 year
Ireland	x	Yes	Yes[24]	Yes[25]	x	See note[26]
Italy		No	Yes[27]	Yes		
Latvia		Yes	Yes	No		
Lithuania	x[28]	No	Yes[29]	No	x	1 year
Luxembourg		No	Yes[30]	Yes[31]	x	See note[32]
Malta	x[33]	No	Yes[34]	Yes	See note[35]	
Netherlands	x[36]	Yes	Yes[37]	No	x	1 year
Poland	x[38]	No	Yes[39]	No		1 year
Portugal	x[40]	Yes	Yes[41]	No		1 year
Slovakia		No	Yes[42]	No		
Slovenia	x[43]	No	Yes[44]	No		
Spain	x[45]	Yes	Yes[46]	Yes	x	1 year
Sweden	x[47]	Yes	Yes	Yes[48]		
United Kingdom	x[49]	Yes	Yes[50]	See note[51]	x	See note[52]

NOTES

1 Regulation 1348/2000/EC on the service in the Member States of judicial and extra-judicial documents in civil and commercial matters at **[3528]**. (Source: consolidated version of information communicated by Member States under Art 23 of the Regulation at **[3551]**, and see http://ec.europa.eu/justice_home/judicialatlascivil/html/pdf/vers_consolide_en_1348.pdf, which should be referred to for the full text of any communication by a Member State and for additional information concerning, for example, the identity of transmitting agencies and central bodies and

permitted languages.) Denmark is not bound by the Service Regulation, but has signed a separate agreement with the European Community (at **[3586]**), yet to come into force.

2 Art 9, para 3: "A Member State shall be authorised to derogate from the provisions of paragraphs 1 and 2 for a transitional period of five years, for appropriate reasons.

This transitional period may be renewed by a Member State at five-yearly intervals due to reasons related to its legal system. That Member State shall inform the Commission of the content of such a derogation and the circumstances of the case."

3 Art 13: "Service by diplomatic or consular agents

1. Each Member State shall be free to effect service of judicial documents on persons residing in another Member State, without application of any compulsion, directly through its diplomatic or consular agents.
2. Any Member State may make it known, in accordance with Article 23(1), that it is opposed to such service within its territory, unless the documents are to be served on nationals of the Member State in which the documents originate."

4 Art 14: "Service by post

1. Each Member State shall be free to effect service of judicial documents directly by post to persons residing in another Member State.
2. Any Member State may specify, in accordance with Article 23(1), the conditions under which it will accept service of judicial documents by post."

5 Art 15: "Direct service

1. This Regulation shall not interfere with the freedom of any person interested in a judicial proceeding to effect service of judicial documents directly through the judicial officers, officials or other competent persons of the Member State addressed.
2. Any Member State may make it known, in accordance with Article 23(1), that it is opposed to the service of judicial documents in its territory pursuant to paragraph 1."

6 Art 19, para 2: "Each Member State shall be free to make it known, in accordance with Article 23(1), that the judge, notwithstanding the provisions of paragraph 1, may give judgment even if no certificate of service or delivery has been received, if all the following conditions are fulfilled:

(a) the document was transmitted by one of the methods provided for in this Regulation;
(b) a period of time of not less than six months, considered adequate by the judge in the particular case, has elapsed since the date of the transmission of the document;
(c) no certificate of any kind has been received, even though every reasonable effort has been made to obtain it through the competent authorities or bodies of the Member State addressed."

7 Art 19, para 4 allows a Member State to make it known by communication, in accordance with Art 23(1), that an application to relieve the defendant from the effects of expiry of time to appeal against a default judgment will not be entertained if it is filed after the expiration of a time to be stated by it in that communication, but which shall in no case be less than one year following the date of the judgment.

8 Subject to conditions, see **[3575]**.

9 See text of derogation at **[3559]**.

10 Subject to conditions, see **[3559]**.

11 Registered post.

12 The text of Cyprus' declarations under Art 19 is as follows:

"— it would be possible at the Court's discretion, at the request of the applicant;
— one year, as provided by para 4 of this Article, since at present there exists no specific period for such relief and it is left at the discretion of the Court provided that it is sought within a reasonable time after the defendant has knowledge of the judgment".

13 Subject to conditions, see **[3560]**.

14 Subject to conditions, see **[3560]**.

15 Subject to conditions, see **[3562]**.

16 Subject to conditions, see **[3580]**.

17 Derogation from Art 9(2) only. See text of derogation at **[3565]**.

18 Subject to conditions, see **[3565]**.

19 Subject to conditions, see **[3561]**.

20 Subject to conditions, see **[3563]**.

21 "The courts in Greece, notwithstanding paragraph 1, are not bound to give judgment if all the conditions of paragraph 2 are met."

22 Derogation from Art 9(2) only.

23 Subject to conditions, see **[3572]**.

24 Subject to conditions, see **[3566]**.

25 "In relation to paragraph 2 of this Article, Ireland does not object to the possibility that any person interested in a judicial proceeding may effect service of judicial documents directly through a solicitor in Ireland."

26 "In relation to Article 19(4), it is for the court to satisfy itself that the application for relief has been filed within a reasonable time after the defendant had knowledge of the judgment."

27 Subject to conditions, see **[3567]**.

28 Derogation from Art 9(2) only. "In Lithuanian law there are no specific time limits for the service of documents."

29 Subject to conditions, see **[3570]**.

30 Subject to conditions, see **[3571]**.

31 Subject to conditions, see **[3571]**.

32 Luxembourg states that, under Art 19(4), an application for relief may be rejected if it is not filed within a reasonable time, to be assessed by the court, either from the time when the defendant has

knowledge of the judgment or from the time when the impossibility of taking action ended; applications may not be filed more than one year after the decision has been delivered.

33 Derogation from Art 9(2) only.

34 Subject to conditions, see **[3573]**.

35 It is not possible as proof of service is required. However if judgment is given against a person and that person has not in the first place been duly served with a writ of summons, within 3 months from the delivery of the judgment, he may proceed with a claim for a new trial.

36 See text of derogation at **[3574]**.

37 Subject to conditions, see **[3574]**.

38 Derogation from Art 9(2) only.

39 Subject to conditions, see **[3576]**.

40 Derogation from Art 9(2) only.

41 Subject to conditions, see **[3577]**.

42 Subject to conditions, see **[3579]**.

43 Derogation from Art 9(2) only.

44 Subject to conditions, see **[3578]**.

45 Derogation from Art 9(2) only.

46 Subject to conditions, see **[3564]**.

47 Derogation from Art 9(2) only.

48 "However, the Swedish authorities are not required to provide assistance in such cases."

49 See text of derogation at **[3582]**.

50 Subject to conditions, see **[3582]**.

51 Yes: Scotland and Gibraltar. No: England and Northern Ireland.

52 "Period of time after the judgment has been given within which an application for relief provided for by paragraph 4 may be entertained:

1. England, Wales and Northern Ireland: When considering setting aside a judgment in default, the court must have regard to whether the person seeking to set aside the judgment made an application to do so promptly.
2. Scotland: No later than the expiry of one year from the date of decree—this would be in line with the Hague Convention and is the period incorporated in Scotland's court rules.
3. Gibraltar: When considering setting aside a judgment in default, the court must have regard to whether the person seeking to set aside the judgment made an application to do so promptly."

B. PARTIES TO THE 1965 HAGUE CONVENTION ON THE SERVICE ABROAD OF JUDICIAL AND EXTRAJUDICIAL DOCUMENTS IN CIVIL OR COMMERCIAL MATTERS[1]

Party	Entry into Force	Declaration of Opposition to Art 8 Service[2]	Declaration of Opposition to Art 10 Service[3] (a)/(b)/(c)	Declaration under Art 15, 2nd Para[4]	Declaration under Art 16, 3rd Para[5]
Antigua and Barbuda[6]	1 November 1981.				
Argentina[7]	1 December 2001		(a) (b) (c)	See note[8]	
Bahamas	1 February 1998				
Barbados	1 October 1969				
Belarus	1 February 1998				
Belgium	18 January 1971	x		x	1 year
Botswana[9]	1 September 1969		(b) (c)	x	
Bulgaria[10]	1 August 2000	x	(a) (b) (c)	x	1 year
Canada[11]	1 May 1989			x	1 year[12]

China[13]	1 January 1992	x	(a) (b) (c)[14]	x[15]	1 year[16]
Croatia[17]	1 November 2006				
Cyprus	1 June 1983			x	1 year
Czech Republic[18]	23 September 1981	x		x	1 year
Denmark	1 October 1969		(c)	x	1 year
Egypt[19]	10 February 1969	x	(a) (b) (c)		
Estonia	1 October 1996		(c)	x	3 years
Finland[20]	10 November 1969		See note[21]		
France[22]	1 September 1972	x		x	1 year
Germany	26 June 1979			x	1 year
Greece[23]	18 September 1983	x	(a) (b) (c)	x	
Hungary[24]	1 April 2005	x	(a) (b) (c)	x	1 year
Ireland	4 June 1994		(b) (c)[25]	x	
Israel	13 October 1972		(b) (c)[26]		1 year
Italy	24 January 1982				
Japan	27 July 1970		(b) (c)	x	
Korea, Republic of	1 August 2000	x	(a) (b) (c)	x	
Kuwait	18 May 2002	x	(a) (b) (c)	See note[27]	See note[28]
Latvia	1 November 1995				
Lithuania	1 June 2001	x	(a) (b) (c)	x	1 year
Luxembourg[29]	1 September 1975	x		x	1 year
Malawi	1 December 1972				
Mexico[30]	1 June 2000	x[31]	(a) (b) (c)[32]	See note[33]	1 year
Netherlands[34]	2 January 1976			x	1 year
Norway	1 October 1969	x	(a) (b) (c)	x	3 years
Pakistan	1 August 1989			x	See note[35]
Poland	1 September 1996	x	(a) (b) (c)		
Portugal	25 February 1974	x		x	1 year

Romania	1 April 2004	x			1 year
Russian Federation[36]	1 December 2001	x	(a) (b) (c)	x	
Saint Vincent and the Grenadines[37]	27 October 1979				
San Marino	1 November 2002	x	(a) (b) (c)	x	
Seychelles	1 November 1980	x	(b) (c)	x	1 year
Slovakia[38]	1 June 1982	x	(a) (b) (c)	x	
Slovenia	1 June 2001				
Spain	3 August 1987			x	16 months
Sri Lanka	1 June 2001	x	(a) (c)	x	
Sweden[39]	1 October 1969		See note[40]		
Switzerland[41]	1 January 1995	x	(a) (b) (c)		
Turkey	28 April 1972	x	(a) (b) (c)	x	1 year
Ukraine	1 December 2001	x	(a) (b) (c)	x	1 year
United Kingdom[42 43]	1 February 1969		(b) (c)[44]	x	1 year[45]
United States of America[46]	10 February 1969				See note[47]
Venezuela[48]	1 July 1994	x	(a)	x	See note[49]

NOTES

1 Source: Hague Conference on private international law website—see http://www.hcch.net/index_en.php?act=conventions.status&cid=17. This website should be consulted for the full text of any declaration, reservations and other communications by the participating States (including details of the designated Central Authorities). For the text of the 1965 Hague Service Convention, see **[4480]**.

Note that Belgium, Cyprus, Czech Republic, Estonia, Finland, France, Germany, Greece, Hungary, Ireland, Italy, Latvia, Lithuania, Luxembourg, Netherlands, Poland, Portugal, Slovakia, Slovenia, Spain, Sweden and the UK, as Member States of the European Community, are bound by the provisions of the Service Regulation (see Table A above and **[3528]**) which, in accordance with Art 21.1 of that Regulation prevails over the 1965 Hague Convention. See also Council Decision 2005/794 on the signing of the agreement between the EC and Denmark on the service of judicial and extrajudicial documents in civil and commercial matters at **[3583]**. This agreement is not yet in force.

2 See Art 21(a) (2nd para). Art 8 concerns direct service through diplomatic or consular agents of the State of origin, and Art 8, 2nd para allows a State to oppose such service within its territory, save with respect to nationals of the State of origin.

3 See Art 21(a) (2nd para). Art 10(a) concerns service by postal channels. Art 10(b) concerns service by judicial officers, officials or other competent persons of the State of origin through the judicial officers, officials or other competent persons of the State of destination. Art 10(c) concerns service by persons interested in a judicial proceeding through the judicial officers, officials or other competent persons of the State of destination.

4 See Art 21(b) (2nd para). Art 15, 2nd para allows a State by declaration to liberalise the requirements for giving judgment in circumstances where the defendant has not appeared, subject to the satisfaction of certain conditions.

5 See Art 21(b) (2nd para). Art 16, 3rd para allows a State by declaration to limit the time period for applications for relief for the expiration of time for appeal against a judgment entered against a defendant who has not appeared.

6 Accession of United Kingdom, adopted by Antigua and Barbuda on independence. For declarations, see entry for United Kingdom.

7 In accordance with Art 5, 3rd para, a Spanish translation must accompany documents served under Art 5, 1st para.

8 Argentina declared that it accepts declarations under Art 15, 2nd para and Art 16, 3rd para, but did not appear itself to make such declarations.

9 Botswana made the following declaration on accession:

"The authorities designated will require all documents forwarded to them for service under the provisions of the Convention to be in triplicate and pursuant to the third paragraph of Article 5 of the Convention will require the documents to be written in, or translated into, the English language."

By a Note dated 8 October 1974 the Office of the President of the Republic of Botswana declared that the authorities designated by Botswana in terms of the Convention require henceforth all documents forwarded to them for service to be in duplicate.

10 Documents served under Art 5, 1st para must be written in, or accompanied by, a translation into the Bulgarian language, in accordance with Art 5, 3rd para.

11 Canada made the following declaration with respect to translation requirements under Art 5, 3rd para:

"For Alberta, British Columbia, Newfoundland, Nova Scotia, Prince Edward Island, Saskatchewan, all documents must be written in or translated into English.

For Ontario, Manitoba, the Northwest Territories and Nunavut, all documents must be written in or translated into English or French.

For New Brunswick and the Yukon, all documents must be written in or translated into English or French. The Central Authority of New Brunswick or the Yukon may reserve the right to require documents to be translated into English or French depending on the language understood by the addressee.

For Quebec, translation will be required in all cases where the recipient does not understand the language in which the document is written. All documents which commence actions must be translated. Summary translation of all other documents is acceptable if the recipient agrees. Translation is to be done into the French language; however, the Quebec Central Authority may, upon request, allow a translation in English at the condition that the recipient understands this language."

12 Save in exceptional cases determined by the rules of the court seized of the matter.

13 Applies to Hong Kong Special Administrative Region and also extended to Macao Special Administrative Region (see diplomatic notes dated 10 June 1997 and 10 December 1999). Documents served in the Macao SAR must be written in Chinese or Portuguese, or accompanied by a Chinese or Portuguese translation.

14 The following declaration applies to the Hong Kong SAR:

"With reference to the provisions of sub-paragraphs b and c of Article 10 of the Convention, documents for service through official channels will be accepted in the Hong Kong Special Administrative Region only by the Central Authority or other authority designated, and only from judicial, consular or diplomatic officers of other Contracting States."

This declaration makes no reference to the mode of service in Art 10(a).

No declaration with respect to the modes of service in Art 10 applicable with respect to the Macao SAR.

15 No additional declaration with respect to Art 15, 2nd para applies to the Hong Kong SAR. Such a declaration was made upon extension to the Macao SAR.

16 No additional declaration with respect to Art 16, 3rd para applies to the Hong Kong SAR. Such a declaration was made upon extension to the Macao SAR.

17 In accordance with Art 5, 3rd para, a translation into the Croatian language must accompany documents served under Art 5, 1st para.

18 As successor to Czechoslovakia.

19 Accession of United Arab Republic.

20 Finland made the following declaration with respect to translation requirements under Art 5, 3rd para:

"A translation is not required; however, if the addressee does not accept a document made out in a foreign language, service can only be effected if the document is translated into one of the official languages of Finland, i.e. Finnish or Swedish, or if the addressee must be deemed to understand the foreign language. Accordingly, f.ex. companies with international business relations must be deemed to understand English, German or French."

21 Finland also declared on accession that "Finnish authorities are not obliged to assist in serving documents transmitted by using any of the methods referred to in sub-paragraphs (b) and (c) of Art 10 of the Convention".

22 The Convention applies to the entire territory of the French Republic (see the Circular from the French Ministry of Justice dated 1 February 2006, which is accessible at http://www.entraide-civile-internationale.justice.gouv.fr).

23 Documents served under Art 5, 1st para must be written in, or accompanied by, a translation into Greek, in accordance with Art 5, 3rd para.

24 In accordance with Art 5, 3rd para, a Hungarian translation must accompany documents served under Art 5, 1st para.

25 Ireland stated that its declaration with respect to Art 10(b) and (c) "is not intended to preclude any person in another Contracting State who is interested in a judicial proceeding (including his lawyer) from effecting service in Ireland directly through a solicitor in Ireland".

26 "The State of Israel, in its quality as State of destination, will, in what concerns Article 10, paragraphs (b) and (c), of the Convention, effect the service of judicial documents only through

the Directorate of Courts, and only where an application for such service emanates from a judicial authority or from the diplomatic or consular representation of a Contracting State."

27 Kuwait purported to enter a reservation against Art 15, 2nd para. It is unclear whether that reservation was intended to take effect as a declaration that Kuwait intended to apply the provisions of that paragraph.

28 Kuwait declared on accession that "[t]he understanding of Paragraph 3 of Article 16 of the Convention, as for the time limit, mentioned in this paragraph, is the time fixed by the law of the trial judge or one year following the date of judgment which ever is longer."

29 Luxembourg declared on accession that "[w]hen foreign judicial documents are served, in connection with Articles 5(a) and 10(b) and (c), through the intermediary of a Luxembourg official, they must be drawn up in French or German or accompanied by a translation into one of those languages."

30 Documents served under Art 5, 1st para must be written in, or accompanied by, a translation into Spanish, in accordance with Art 5, 3rd para.

31 Even in the case of nationals of the State of origin, Mexico requires that "such a procedure does not contravene public law or violate individual guarantees".

32 "In relation to Article 10, the United Mexican States are opposed to the direct service of documents through diplomatic or consular agents to persons in Mexican territory according to the procedures described in sub-paragraphs (a), (b), and (c), unless the judicial authority exceptionally grants the simplification different from the national regulations and provided that such a procedure does not contravene public law or violate individual guarantees. The request must contain the description of the formalities whose application is required to effect service of the document."

33 "In relation to Article 15, second paragraph, the Government of Mexico does not recognise the faculty of the judicial authority to give judgment when the defendant has not appeared and there is no communication establishing that the document was served, or that documents originating outside the country were indeed delivered, according to sub-paragraphs (a) and (b) of the first paragraph."

34 Extended to Aruba (entry into force 27 July 1986).

35 "As regards Article 16, paragraph 3, of the Convention it is hereby declared that in case of ex-parte decisions, an application for setting it aside will not be entertained if it is filed after the expiration of the period of limitation prescribed by law of Pakistan."

36 Documents served under Art 5, 1st para must be written in, or accompanied by, a translation into the Russian language, in accordance with Art 5, 3rd para.

37 Accession of United Kingdom, adopted by St Vincent and the Grenadines on independence. For declarations, see entry for United Kingdom.

38 As successor to Czechoslovakia.

39 Documents served under Art 5, 1st para must be written in, or accompanied by, a translation into Swedish, in accordance with Art 5, 3rd para.

40 Sweden declared on accession that "Swedish authorities are not obliged to assist in serving documents transmitted by using any of the methods referred to in sub-paragraphs (b) and (c) of Art 10".

41 Switzerland declared on accession that:

"With regard to Article 1, Switzerland takes the view that the Convention applies exclusively to the Contracting States. In particular, it believes that documents which are effectively addressed to a person resident abroad cannot be served on a legal entity who is not authorized to receive them in the country in which they were drawn up without derogating from Articles 1 and 15, first paragraph, of the Convention."

Switzerland also made the following declaration with respect to translation requirements under Art 5, 3rd para:

"Switzerland declares that in cases where the addressee does not voluntarily accept a document, it cannot officially be served on him or her in accordance with Article 5, first paragraph, unless it is in the language of the authority addressed, i.e. in German, French or Italian, or accompanied by a translation into one of these languages, depending on the part of Switzerland in which the document is to be served."

42 Extended to Anguilla (entry into force 2 December 1982) and to Bermuda, Cayman Islands, Falkland Islands, Gibraltar, Guernsey, Isle of Man, Jersey, Montserrat, Pitcairn, St Helena, Turks and Caicos Islands and (British) Virgin Islands. Argentina has objected to the extension to the Falkland Islands (in each case entry into force 19 July 1970).

43 Documents served under Art 5, 1st para must be written in, or accompanied by, a translation into English, in accordance with Art 5, 3rd para.

44 "With reference to the provisions of paragraphs (b) and (c) of Article 10 of the Convention, documents for service through official channels will be accepted in the United Kingdom only by the central or additional authorities and only from judicial, consular or diplomatic officers of other Contracting States." By letter dated 11 September 1980, the UK confirmed that this declaration "does not preclude any person in another Contracting State who is interested in a judicial proceeding (including his lawyer) from effecting service in the United Kingdom 'directly' through a competent person other than a judicial officer or official, eg, a solicitor". A like declaration was made in respect of the territories referred to at footnote 42 above.

45 Scotland only. See, for the Court of Session, Rules of the Court of Session 1994, r 19.2(5) at **[1095]** and, for the Sheriff Court, Ordinary Cause Rules 1993, r 8.1(4A) at **[1020]**.

46 Extended on accession to Guam, Puerto Rico and the (American) Virgin Islands Subsequently extended to Commonwealth of the North Mariana Islands (entry into force 30 May 1994).

47 In accordance with the third paragraph of Article 16, the United States of America declared that "an application under Article 16 will not be entertained if it is filed (a) after the expiration of the

period within which the same may be filed under the procedural regulations of the court in which the judgment has been entered, or (b) after the expiration of one year following the date of the judgment, whichever is later".

48 Venezuela made the following declaration with respect to the translation requirements under Art 5, 3rd para:

"The Republic of Venezuela declares that notices and documents and other items annexed to the notices will be accepted only when they are properly translated into the Spanish language."

49 "The Republic of Venezuela declares that the request allowed by the third paragraph of this Article shall not be admissible if it is made after the expiration of the period specified in Venezuelan law."

[4678]

TABLE 4
EVIDENCE

PARTIES TO THE 1970 HAGUE CONVENTION ON THE TAKING OF EVIDENCE ABROAD IN CIVIL OR COMMERCIAL MATTERS[1]

Party	Entry into Force	Declaration Excluding Pre-Trial Discovery of Documents[2]	Reservation Excluding Art 4, 2nd para[3]	Declaration Allowing Presence of Judicial Personnel of Requesting State under Art 8[4]	Reservation (R) Excluding Chapter II[5] or Declaration (D) under Art 15, 16, 17 and/or 18
Argentina	1 July 1987	x	x		R—Ch. II
Australia[6]	22 December 1992	x		x[7]	D—Art 15
Barbados	4 May 1981				
Belarus	6 October 2001		x	x[8]	D—Arts 16, 17, 18
Bulgaria	22 January 2000	x	x	x[9]	R—Ch. II
China[10]	6 February 1998	See note[11]			R—Ch. II, except for Art 15
Hong Kong SAR[12]		x[13]	Not French		D—Art 16 —see note[14]
Cyprus	14 March 1983	x[15]	Not French	x	D—Art 18 —see note[16]
Czech Republic[17]	1 July 1976				D—Arts 16, 18
Denmark	7 October 1972	x[18]	Not French	x[19]	R—Art 17 D—Arts 15, 16
Estonia	2 April 1996			x[20]	See note[21]
Finland	6 June 1976	x[22]		x[23]	D—Arts 16, 17
France[24]	6 October 1974	x[25]		x	D—Arts 16, 17

Germany	26 June 1979	x	x	x[26]	R[27] D—Arts 16, 17
Greece	19 March 2005	x	See note[28]	x[29]	D—Arts 15, 16, 17[30]
Hungary	11 September 2004	x	x	x[31]	R—Art 16, 18 D—Art 15
Israel	17 September 1979			x	
Italy	21 August 1982	x		x[32]	D—Art 18
Kuwait	7 July 2002				
Latvia	27 May 1995				
Lithuania	1 October 2000	x		x[33]	D—Arts 16, 17
Luxembourg	24 September 1977	x		x	D—Arts 16, 17
Mexico	25 September 1989	x[34]	x		R—Arts 17, 18
Monaco	18 March 1986	x	x[35]		D—Arts 16, 17
Netherlands[36]	7 June 1981	x[37]		x[38]	D—Art 16, 17
Norway	7 October 1972	x[39]	Not French		D—Art 15
Poland	13 April 1996	x	x		R—Ch. II, except for Art 15
Portugal	11 May 1975	x	x		R—Ch. II, except for Art 15 D—Art 15
Romania	20 October 1973	x[40]		x[41]	R—Arts 16, 17, 18
Russian Federation	30 June 2001				
Seychelles	17 March 2004				
Singapore	26 December 1978				
Slovakia[42]	11 July 1976				D—Arts 16, 18
Slovenia	17 November 2000				
South Africa	6 September 1997	x	Not French	x[43]	R—Arts 15, 16 D—Art 17
Spain	21 July 1987	x		x[44]	D—Arts 16, 17[45]
Sri Lanka	30 October 2000	x	x[46]	x[47]	R—Ch. II

Sweden	1 July 1975	x[48]		x[49]	D—Art 15
Switzerland[50]	1 January 1995	x[51]	See note[52]	x[53]	D—Arts 15, 16, 17
Turkey	12 October 2004	x	x[54]		D—Arts 16, 17
Ukraine	1 April 2001	x	x[55]	x[56]	R—Ch. II, except Arts 15, 20, 21 and 22
United Kingdom[57]	14 September 1976	x[58]		x	D—Art 18
United States of America[59]	7 October 1972			x[60]	D—Arts 16, 17, 18
Venezuela	31 December 1993	x[61]	x[62]		R—Ch. II

NOTES

1 Source: Hague Conference on private international law website—see http://www.hcch.net/index_en.php?act=conventions.status&cid=82. This website should be consulted for the full text of any declaration, reservations and other communications by the participating States (including details of the designated competent authorities). For the text of the 1970 Hague Evidence Convention, see **[4513]**.

Note that Cyprus, Czech Republic, Estonia, Finland, France, Germany, Greece, Hungary, Italy, Latvia, Lithuania, Luxembourg, Netherlands, Poland, Portugal, Slovakia, Slovenia, Spain, Sweden and the UK, as Member States of the European Community, are bound by the provisions of the Evidence Regulation at **[3598]**, which, in accordance with Art 21.1 of that Regulation, prevails over the 1970 Hague Convention.

2 Art 23. Several Contracting States, in making declarations under Art 23 or by additional declaration, have confirmed their understanding that the expression "Letters of Request issued for the purpose of obtaining pre-trial discovery of documents" includes "any Letter of Request which requires a person:

a. to state what documents relevant to the proceedings to which the Letter of Request relates are, or have been, in his possession, custody or power; or

b. to produce any documents other than particular documents specified in the Letter of Request as being documents appearing to the requested court to be, or to be likely to be, in his possession, custody or power" (taken from declaration of United Kingdom).

3 Art 33, 1st para. Art 4, 2nd para otherwise requires Contracting States to accept a Letter of Request in either English or French.

4 Under Art 8, a State may declare that members of the judicial personnel of the requesting State may be present at the execution of a Letter of Request, but the declaring State may require that prior authorisation be obtained from its own designated competent authority.

5 Reservation: Art 33, 1st para; Declarations: Art 15, 2nd para; Art 16, 2nd para; Art 17, 2nd para; Art 18, 2nd para.

Chapter II (Arts 15 to 22) provides for the taking of evidence by diplomatic officers, consular agents and commissioners.

Art 33 allows a State to exclude the provisions of Chapter II in their entirety.

Art 15, 2nd para allows a State, by declaration, to require that permission from its competent authority be obtained for the taking of such evidence without compulsion from nationals of the State which the diplomatic officer etc represents, where such evidence is in aid of proceedings commenced in the courts of the latter State. In the absence of such declaration, permission is not required.

Art 16 allows a State, by declaration, to dispense with the requirement of permission from its competent authority for the taking of such evidence without compulsion from persons other than nationals of the State which the diplomatic officer etc represents, where such evidence is in aid of proceedings commenced in the courts of the latter State. In the absence of such declaration, permission is required. Alternatively, a declaration under Art 16 may designate the competent authority for the obtaining of permission under Art 16 and specify general conditions to which any permission will be subject (see, eg, the declaration of France).

Art 17 allows a State, by declaration, to dispense with the requirement of permission for the taking of such evidence without compulsion in aid of proceedings in another Contracting State. In the absence of such declaration, permission is required. Alternatively, a declaration under Art 17 may designate the competent authority for the obtaining of permission under Art 17 and specify general conditions to which any permission will be subject (see, eg, the declaration of France).

Art 18 allows a State to designate a competent authority for the purposes of, and place conditions upon, applications by diplomatic officers etc for assistance in obtaining evidence by compulsion in the circumstances contemplated by Arts 15–17.

The specific terms of reservations and declarations with respect to Arts 15–18 (available on the Hague Conference website—see footnote 1 above) should be carefully noted.

6 Extends to all territories for whose international relations Australia is responsible.

7 Subject to prior authorisation.

8 Subject to prior authorisation.

9 Subject to prior authorisation.

10 Applies to Hong Kong Special Administrative Region (see below) and extended to Macao Special Administrative Region.

11 China declared on accession that "in accordance with Article 23 of the Convention concerning the Letters of Request issued for the purpose of obtaining pre-trial discovery of documents as known in common law countries, only the request for obtaining discovery of the documents clearly enumerated in the Letters of Request and of direct and close connection with the subject matter of the litigation will be executed".

12 See diplomatic note dated 10 June 1997.

13 Declaration also clarifies understanding of expression "Letters of Request issued for the purpose of obtaining pre-trial discovery of documents" in the terms set out at footnote 2 above.

14 "With reference to the provisions of Article 16 of the Convention, the diplomatic officer or consular agent of the other Contracting State will not be permitted to take the evidence of nationals of the People's Republic of China or of a third State in the Hong Kong Special Administrative Region."

15 Declaration also clarifies understanding of expression "Letters of Request issued for the purpose of obtaining pre-trial discovery of documents" in the terms set out at footnote 2 above.

16 "In accordance with Article 18 the Republic of Cyprus declares that a diplomatic officer, consular agent or commissioner authorized to take evidence under Articles 15, 16 or 17 may apply to the competent authority for appropriate assistance to obtain such evidence by compulsion as prescribed by the law for internal proceedings, provided that the requesting Contracting State has made a declaration affording reciprocal facilities under Article 18."

17 As successor to Czechoslovakia.

18 See additional declaration dated 22 July 1980 confirming understanding of expression "Letters of Request issued for the purpose of obtaining pre-trial discovery of documents" in terms similar to those set out at footnote 2 above.

19 Subject to prior authorisation.

20 Subject to prior authorisation.

21 "On the basis of Article 23, the Republic of Estonia fulfills (*sic*) a requisition where the producing of the documents or its copy is requested if it corresponds to the following requirements:

(a) process has been launched;

(b) documents have been reasonably identified according to the dates, the contents or other information;

(c) circumstances have been indicated giving ground to presume that the documents are in the property, possession of the person or known to him."

22 Declaration also clarifies understanding of expression "Letters of Request issued for the purpose of obtaining pre-trial discovery of documents" in terms similar to those set out at footnote 2 above.

23 Subject to prior authorisation.

24 Extends to the entire territory of the French Republic

25 "The declaration made by the French Republic in accordance with Article 23 relating to Letters of Request issued for the purpose of obtaining pre-trial discovery of documents does not apply when the requested documents are enumerated limitatively in the Letter of Request and have a direct and precise link with the object of the procedure."

26 Subject to prior authorisation.

27 Excluding Chapter II with respect to German nationals only.

28 "Without prejudice to article 33 Greece declares that, in terms of the provision of article 4, para 2 of the Convention, letters of request must be submitted in Greek or accompanied by a translation into Greek."

29 Subject to prior authorisation.

30 The declaration requires that execution be carried out in accordance with Greek law.

31 Subject to prior authorisation.

32 Subject to prior authorisation.

33 Subject to prior authorisation.

34 "With reference to Article 23 of the Convention, the United Mexican States declares that according to Mexican law, it shall only be able to comply with letters of request issued for the purpose of obtaining the production and transcription of documents when the following requirements are met:

(a) that the judicial proceeding has been commenced;

(b) that the documents are reasonably identifiable as to date, subject and other relevant information and that the request specifies those facts and circumstances that lead the requesting party to reasonable believe that the requested documents are known to the person from whom they are requested or that they are in his possession or under his control or custody;

(c) that the direct relationship between the evidence or information sought and the pending proceeding be identified."

35 French original Letter of Request or translation required.

36 Extended to Aruba (entry into force 27 July 1986).

37 Declaration also clarifies understanding of expression "Letters of Request issued for the purpose of obtaining pre-trial discovery of documents" in terms similar to those set out at footnote 2 above.

38 Subject to prior authorisation.

39 See additional declaration dated 7 August 1980 confirming understanding of expression "Letters of Request issued for the purpose of obtaining pre-trial discovery of documents" in terms similar to those set out at footnote 2 above.

40 "In accordance with Article 23 of the Convention, Romania declares that it will execute Letters of Request issued for the purpose of obtaining pre-trial discovery of documents as known in Common Law countries, to the extent that this expression refers to providing evidence (inquest in futurum)."

41 After prior information of the competent authority.

42 As successor to Czechoslovakia.

43 Subject to prior authorisation.

44 Subject to prior authorisation.

45 Limited to evidence taken in the premises of the diplomatic or consular representation of the requesting State.

46 "For purposes of Article 4 of the Convention, the letter of request should be in the English language or if in French, accompanied by an English translation."

47 Subject to prior authorisation.

48 See additional declaration dated 11 July 1980 confirming understanding of expression "Letters of Request issued for the purpose of obtaining pre-trial discovery of documents" in terms similar to those set out at footnote 2 above.

49 Subject to prior authorisation.

50 On accession, Switzerland declared that:
"With regard to Article 1, Switzerland takes the view that the Convention applies exclusively to the Contracting States. Moreover, regarding the conclusions of the Special Commission which met in The Hague in April 1989, Switzerland believes that, whatever the opinion of the Contracting States on the exclusive application of the Convention, priority should in any event be given to the procedures provided for in the Convention regarding requests for the taking of evidence abroad."

51 "In accordance with Article 23, Switzerland declares that Letters of Request issued for the purpose of obtaining pre-trial discovery of documents will not be executed if:
(a) the request has no direct and necessary link with the proceedings in question; or
(b) a person is required to indicate what documents relating to the case are or were in his/her possession or keeping or at his/her disposal; or
(c) a person is required to produce documents other than those mentioned in the request for legal assistance, which are probably in his/her possession or keeping or at his/her disposal; or
(d) interests worthy of protection of the concerned persons are endangered."

52 "In accordance with Articles 33 and 35, Switzerland declares, with regard to Article 4, second and third paragraphs, that Letters of Request and any accompanying documents must be in the language of the authority requested to execute them, ie in German, French or Italian, or accompanied by a translation into one of these languages, depending on the part of Switzerland in which the documents are to be executed. The documents confirming execution will be drawn up in the official language of the requested authority."

53 Subject to prior authorisation.

54 "Letters of Request which are to be executed under Chapter I of the Convention, shall be in Turkish or be accompanied by a Turkish translation in compliance with Article 4, paragraphs 1 and 5."

55 "In accordance with Article 4 of the Convention, letters of request to be executed under Chapter I of the Convention must be in the Ukrainian language or be accompanied by a translation into the Ukrainian language."

56 Subject to confirmation by consent of the Ministry of Justice.

57 Extended to Sovereign Base Areas on the Island of Cyprus (entry into force 24 August 1979), Anguilla (1 September 1986), Cayman Islands (15 November 1980), Falkland Islands (25 January 1980), Gibraltar (20 January 1979), Guernsey (18 January 1986), Isle of Man (15 June 1980) and Jersey (7 March 1987).

58 Declaration also clarifies understanding of expression "Letters of Request issued for the purpose of obtaining pre-trial discovery of documents" in the terms set out at footnote 2 above.

59 Extended to Guam, Puerto Rico and (American) Virgin Islands (entry into force in each case 10 April 1973).

60 Subject to prior authorisation.

61 "The Republic of Venezuela declares that it will only execute Letters of Request dealing with the procedure known in common law countries as pre-trial discovery of documents when the following conditions apply:
(a) that proceedings have been instituted;
(b) that the documents requested to be exhibited or transcribed shall be reasonably identified as regards their date, contents or other relevant information;
(c) that any facts or circumstances giving the plaintiff reasonable cause to believe that the documents asked for are known to the person requested to produce them so that they are or were in the possession or under the control or in the custody of that person, shall be specified;

(d) that the connection between the evidence or information sought and the pending litigation be made quite clear."

62 "The Republic of Venezuela will accept Letters of Request and documents and other items annexed thereto only when these are properly translated into the Spanish language".

[4679]

Index